A
GENEVA
SERIES
COMMENTARY

PSALMS

PSALMS

A CRITICAL AND EXPOSITORY COMMENTARY
WITH DOCTRINAL AND PRACTICAL REMARKS

WILLIAM S. PLUMER, D.D., LL.D.

THE BANNER OF TRUTH TRUST

THE BANNER OF TRUTH TRUST
3 Murrayfield Road, Edinburgh EH12 6EL
P.O. Box 621, Carlisle, Pennsylvania 17013, U.S.A.

*

First published 1867
First Banner of Truth Trust edition 1975
Reprinted 1978
ISBN 0 85151 209 7

*

Printed by offset lithograpy by
T. & A. Constable Ltd
Edinburgh

Studies in the Book of Psalms.

INTRODUCTION.

1. The Wonderful Character of the Psalms.

THE Psalms are wonderful. They have been read, repeated, chanted, sung, studied, wept over, rejoiced in, expounded, loved and praised by God's people for thousands of years. The most ancient of these productions is now [1866] three thousand three hundred and twenty-six years old. The least ancient of them is two thousand four hundred and fifty-three years old. The difference in date between the most ancient and the most modern of them is eight hundred and seventy-three years. They were all written in Asia, so that we in this Western World can have no national pride respecting them. Yet pious people here and all over the earth have found and can find no compositions more suitable for delineating their devout emotions, and for expressing their pious sensibilities than those of inspired Psalmists. If to any man these songs are unsavory, the reason is found in the blindness and depravity of the human heart. Hengstenberg: "The Psalms are expressions of holy feeling, which can be understood by those only, who have become alive to such feeling."

Horne: "Composed upon particular occasions, yet designed for general use; delivered out as services for Israelites under the law, yet no less adapted to the circumstances of Christians under the Gospel, the Psalms present religion to us in the most engaging dress; communicating truths which philosophy could never investigate, in a style which poetry can never equal, while history is made the vehicle of prophecy, and creation lends all its charms to paint the glories of redemption. Calculated alike to profit and to please, they inform the understanding, elevate the affections, and entertain the imagination. Indited under the influence of Him to whom all hearts are known, and all events foreknown, they suit mankind in all situations, grateful as the manna which descended from above, and conformed itself to every palate. The fairest productions of human wit, after a few perusals, like gathered flowers, wither in our hands, and lose their fragrancy; but these unfading plants of paradise become, as we are accustomed to them, still more and more beautiful; their bloom appears to be daily heightened; fresh odors are emitted, and new sweets extracted from them. He who hath once tasted their excellences will desire to taste them yet again; and he who tastes them oftenest will relish them best."

Other things being equal, he who has the most heavenly mind, will be the most successful student of the Psalms. Carnal tempers are ill suited to spiritual truths. The blind cannot see afar off. No natural acuteness, no learning, no amount of examination will answer the purpose unless we are taught from heaven and thus made docile. The best qualification for studying any portion of God's word is the influence of the Holy Spirit abiding in us, warming our cold hearts, giving us humbleness of mind, and right affections. Augustine: " Form thy spirit by the affection of the Psalm. . . If the Psalm breathes the spirit of prayer, do you pray; if it is filled with groanings, groan also thyself; if it is gladsome, do thou rejoice also; if it encourages hope, then hope thou in God; if it calls to godly fear, then tremble thou before the divine majesty; for all things herein contained are mirrors to reflect our own real characters. . . Let the heart do what the words signify."

Cassian: " That we may enjoy this treasure, it is necessary that we say the Psalms with the same spirit with which they were composed, and accommodate them unto ourselves in the same manner as if every one of us had composed them, or as if the Psalmist had directed them purposely for our uses; not satisfying ourselves that they had their whole completion in or by the Prophet, but discerning every one of us our own parts still to be performed and acted over in the Psalmist's words, by exciting in ourselves the same affections which we discern to have been in David, or in others at that time, loving when he loves, fearing when he fears, hoping when he hopes, praising God when he praises, weeping for our own or others' sins when he weeps, begging what we want with the like spirit wherein his petitions are framed, loving our enemies when he shows love to his, praying for ours when he prays for his, having zeal for the glory of God when the Psalmist professes it, humbling ourselves when he is humbled, lifting up our spirit to heaven when he lifts up his, giving thanks for God's mercies when he doth, delighting and rejoicing in the beauty of the Messias, and of the Church his spouse, when he is delighted and rejoiceth; when he relates the wonderful works of God in the creation of the world, bringing his people out of Egypt, etc., admiring and glorifying God as he stands amazed and glorifies him; and when he mentions the punishments inflicted on rebellious sinners, and rewards and favors bestowed on the obedient, we likewise are to tremble when he trembles, and exult when he exults, and walk in the court of heaven, the sanctuary, as he walks, and wish to dwell in it as he wishes. Finally, where he as a master teaches, exhorts, reprehends, and directs the just man, each of us must suppose him speaking to him, and answer him in such due manner as the instruction of such a master exacts." That we may in some measure perform this vital substantial part of our task, " Let us at the beginning of the Psalm, beg of God that light and affection, and gust and savor, with which David was affected when he made it, and that with the affection and desire of obtaining what he felt." As well might men hope that improvements in agriculture would render unnecessary the rain of heaven, as that any advancement in Biblical science would make us independent of the grace and Spirit of God, imparting to us right tempers and right views.

2. TESTIMONY OF COMMENTATORS.

Many, who have written on the Psalms, have left their testimony to the pleasantness of their labors. They seem to have been walking through the green pastures and by the still waters. Thus Calvin: " If the reading of these COMMENTARIES confer as much benefit on the church of God as I myself have reaped advantage from the composition of them, I shall have no reason to regret that I have undertaken this work."

Horne: " And now, could the author flatter himself, that any one would take half the pleasure in reading the following exposition, which he hath taken in writing it, he would not fear the loss of his labor. The employment detached him from the bustle and hurry of life, the din of politics, and the noise of folly; vanity and vexation flew away for a season, care and disquietude came not near his dwelling. He arose fresh as the morning to his task; the silence of the night invited him to pursue it: and he can truly say, that food and rest were not preferred before it. Every Psalm improved infinitely on his acquaintance with it; and no one gave him uneasiness but the last; for then he grieved that his work was done. Happier hours than those which have been spent on these Songs of Sion, he never expects to see in this world. Very pleasantly did they pass, and moved swiftly along: for when thus engaged, he counted no time. They are gone, but have left a relish and a fragrance upon the mind, and the remembrance of them is sweet." Chalmers quotes this experience of Horne as "an actual specimen of heaven upon earth, as enjoyed for a season of devotional contemplation on the word of God."

Morison speaks of his labors in this department as "a delightful task," and says, "Should the benefit of perusing this exposition be equal to that which has attended the writing of it, it will not be consulted in vain. Truly it has proved a source of spiritual excitement to the author, for which he hopes ever to be grateful to the God of his life. It has tended to endear the retirements of the closet, and to discover beauties in the word of God, which never fell with equal interest upon his mind."

Hengstenberg: "However this work may be received, the author has found an ample recompense in itself, and hopes that he shall be able to look back upon it with pleasure, even in eternity."

During a Christian and ministerial life, neither short, uneventful, nor free from dark days and sharp sorrows, the author has freely mingled with the suffering people of God of various names and conditions, and has never been able to secure to himself, or administer to others full support and abounding consolation without a resort to the Psalms. Here was always something well suited to every stage of religious experience and to every kind and degree of affliction. He has therefore preached much on texts chosen from this part of Scripture. This has been specially true of his weekly lecture, which he has maintained wherever he has exercised his ministry. And although this work has been prepared in the midst of other and pressing duties, yet he has often been refreshed by writing or revising even a paragraph. "Thy statutes have been my songs in the house of my pilgrimage." "Thy testimonies have I taken as an heritage forever; for they are the rejoicing of my heart."

3. THE PSALMS EXCELLENT.

The testimonies in favor of the Book of Psalms are numerous and striking. Athanasius calls it "an epitome of the whole Scriptures." Basil says it is "the common treasure of all good precepts . . . the voice of the church . . . a compendium of all theology." Ambrose: "The law instructs, history informs, prophecy predicts, correction censures, and morals exhort. In the Book of Psalms you find the fruit of all these, as well as a remedy for the salvation of the soul. The Psalter deserves to be called, the praise of God, the glory of man, the voice of the church, and the most beneficial confession of faith." Augustine: "What is there that may not be learned in the Psalms?" Luther: "The Psalter is a little Bible, and the summary of the Old Testament. One verse of the Psalms is sufficient for the meditation of a day; and he, who at the end of the day finds himself fully possessed of its sense and spirit, may consider his time well spent." Cassiodorus: "The Book of Psalms is splendid, illuminated with brightness, solacing the wounded heart, like the honey-comb refreshing the inner man, speaking the language of hidden virtues, inclining the proud to humility, making kings poor in spirit, yet gently nourishing and animating the timid and the feeble." Gerhard: "The Psalter is a theatre, where God allows us to behold both himself and his works; a most pleasant green field, a vast garden, where we see all manner of flowers; a paradise, having the most delicious flowers and fruits; a great sea in which are hid costly pearls; a heavenly school, where we have God for our teacher; a compend of all Scripture; a mirror of divine grace, reflecting the lovely face of our heavenly Father; and the anatomy of our souls." Melancthon says the Book of Psalms is "the most elegant work extant in the world." Calvin: "I have been accustomed to call this book, I think not inappropriately, 'an anatomy of the soul;' for there is not an emotion of which any one can be conscious that is not here represented as in a mirror. Or rather, the Holy Spirit has here drawn to the life all the griefs, sorrows, fears, doubts, hopes, cares, perplexities, in short, all the distracting emotions with which the minds of men are wont to be agitated. . . . There is no other book in which are recorded so many deliverances, nor one in which the evidences and experiences of the fatherly providence and solicitude, which God exercises towards us, are celebrated with such splendor of diction, and yet with the strictest adherence to truth." Rivet, borrowing from one of the early Fathers, compares this book to Paradise, where grow all manner of fruits, and says that his object in his exposition is to show the beauty, and gather the fruit of this pleasant garden and place it before his readers. Hooker adopts and amplifies the language of Augustine on the subject. On his death-bed the learned Salmasius said, "O I have lost a world of time. If one year more were added to my life, it should be spent in reading David's Psalms and Paul's epistles." John Brent says, "You may rightly and fitly call the Psalter an epitome of the sacred books." Of these sacred songs John Milton says, "Not in their divine argument alone, but in the very critical art of composition, they may be easily made appear over all the kinds of lyric poesy to be incomparable." Sir Daniel K. Sandford: "In lyric flow and fire, in crushing force and majesty, that seems still to echo the awful sounds once heard beneath the thunder-clouds of Sinai, the poetry of the ancient Scriptures is the most superb that ever burned within the breast of man." Why should not such a book be studied from age to age? I marvel not that Jerome in his letter to Læta respecting the education of her grand-daughter, said, "Let her learn the Psalms." I am not surprised, when a pious, infirm friend, nearly eighty years old, writes to me saying, "I constantly read the Psalms, and often commit them to memory." Could a child of God on the verge of the grave have a more heavenly employment? Well does David Dickson speak of "this sweet-smelling bundle of Psalms." Dodd: "The Psalms are fitted to all persons and ages, to all manner of employments, and to all conditions and circumstances of life: but they have still one further excellence, that they contain a variety of striking prophecies concerning Christ and his church." Clarke: "I know nothing like the Book of Psalms: it contains all the lengths, breadths, depths, and heights of the Patriarchal, Mosaic, and Christian Dispensations. It is the most useful book in the Bible, and is every way worthy of the wisdom of God." Tholuck: "Piety, Jewish or Christian, if *genuine*, and not formal, has derived more nourishment from the Psalms than from any other source."

He cites beautiful testimonies to the same effect from the great statesman, Moser, from the classical Herder, and from the historian, John Mueller.

Mueller: "The Psalms teach one to prize a much tried life. . . David yields me every day the most delightful hour. There is nothing Greek, nothing Roman, nothing in the West, nor in the land towards midnight, to equal David, whom the God of Israel chose to praise him higher than the gods of the nations. The utterance of his mind sinks deep into the heart, and *never in my life, never have I thus seen God.*"

Herder: "The use of the Psalms became the blessing of humanity, not only on account of their *contents*, but also on account of their form. . . *For two thousand years have the Psalms frequently and differently been translated*, and still there are many new formations of their much embracing and rich manner possible. . . The Psalter is the hymn-book for all times."

Moser: "How much comfort, light, and strength have the Psalms imparted to my fainting soul. I often not only missed the way, but lost the very trace of it. I sat me down as if I had become petrified. One word from the Psalms was a sunbeam to me; like a lark I settled on the pinions of that eagle; carried by her, I scaled the rock, and beheld from that eminence the world, with its cares and mine, stretched out beneath me; I acquired to think, infer, mourn, pray, wait, hope, and speak in the spirit of David. I thank thee, O Lord, that thou hast humbled me. I acquired to know and understand the rights of God—his purposes of love and faithfulness to every man, but especially to myself—his mighty wisdom towards us his creatures in our present state of probation, as well as the blessedness, benefit, and necessity of sufferings for our cleansing, purification, and perfection. I learned to esteem myself happy in being permitted to endure suffering. I attained to a better knowledge of the wisdom and love of God, the truth of his word and assurance, the unalterable faithfulness of his promises, the riches of his mercy and long-suffering; of my own dependence, insufficiency, nothingness, and inability without him, of the wickedness and deceit of my heart, of the world, of men, and of the profound wisdom of God in the blending of evil with good. I became less in my own sight, more suffering and affectionate, more sparing and forgiving, more severe with myself, more lenient to others. I learned to trust God in all my ways and to renounce the claims of fame, honor, and comfort. It was nourishment to my soul to be enabled to say: 'Lord, let me possess but Thee.' I asked for no more aid in temporal concerns than his wisdom might find good for the best of my soul. I learned to become more contented in my desires, more moderate in my enjoyments. I was enabled with tears to express my gratitude for mercies, which formerly I counted not as blessings, but as my right and due. If my soul would keep holy-day, the Psalms became my temple and my altar. Next to the writings of the New Testament, they are now to me my dearest and most precious book—the golden mirror, the cyclopædia of the most blessed and fruitful knowledge and experience of my life; to thoroughly understand them will be the occupation of eternity, and our second life will form their commentary."

In his *Cours de Literature* the celebrated Lamartine, probably regarding the last four Psalms (the Hallelujah Hymns) as one whole (as Hengstenberg also does) thus speaks: "The last Psalm ends with a chorus to the praise of God, in which the poet calls on all people, all instruments of sacred music, all the elements, and all the stars to join. Sublime finale of that opera of sixty years sung by the shepherd, the hero, the king, and the old man! In this closing Psalm we see the almost inarticulate enthusiasm of the lyric poet; so rapidly do the words press to his lips, floating upwards towards God their source, like the smoke of a great fire of the soul wafted by the tempest! Here we see David, or rather the human heart itself with all its God-given notes of grief, joy, tears, and adoration—poetry sanctified to its highest expression; a vase of perfume broken on the step of the temple, and shedding abroad its odors from the heart of David to the heart of all humanity! Hebrew, Christian, or even Mohammedan, every religion, every complaint, every prayer has taken from this vase, shed on the heights of Jerusalem, wherewith to give forth their accents. The little shepherd has become the master of the sacred choir of the Universe. There is not a worship on earth which prays not with his words, or sings not with his voice. A chord of his harp is to be found in all choirs, resounding everywhere and forever in unison with the echoes of Horeb and Engedi! David is the psalmist of eternity; what a destiny—what a power hath poetry when inspired by God! As for myself, when my spirit is excited, or devotional, or sad, and seeks for an echo to its enthusiasm, its devotion, or its melancholy, I do not open Pindar, or Horace, or Hafiz, those purely Academic poets; neither do I find within myself murmurings to express my emotion. I open the Book of Psalms, and there I find words which seem to issue from the soul of the ages, and which penetrate even to the heart of all generations. Happy the bard who has thus become the eternal hymn, the personified prayer and complaint of all humanity! If we look back to that remote age when such songs resounded over the world; if we consider that, while the lyric poetry of all the most cultivated nations only sang of wine, love, blood, and the victories of coursers at the games of Elidus, we are seized with profound astonishment, at the mystic accents of the shepherd-prophet, who speaks to God the Creator as one friend to another, who understands and praises his great works, admires his justice, implores his mercy, and becomes, as it were, an anticipative echo of the evangelic poetry, speaking the soft words of Christ before his coming. Prophet or not, as he may be considered by Christian or skeptic, none can deny in the poet-king an inspiration granted to no other man. Read Greek or Latin poetry after a Psalm, and see how pale it looks."

4. PECULIARITIES OF THE PSALTER.

The Book of Psalms is very peculiar. It differs from all other parts of God's word. It contains *one hundred and fifty* distinct compositions. Of these, some consist of a very few short sentences. Others are quite extended. One has a *hundred and seventy-six* verses. In the Hebrew the Psalter contains *two thousand five hundred and seventeen* verses. The middle verse is in Ps. lxxviii. 36. Of these compositions, sometimes *seventy-four*, sometimes *seventy-three*, and commonly *seventy-two* are ascribed to David, "The man raised up on high, the anointed of the God of Jacob, and the sweet Psalmist of Israel." There never arose another Psalmist like him. Jerome: "Simonides, Pindar, and Alceus, among the Greeks; Horace, Catullus, and Serenus, among the Latins, were famous for their poetic writings; but in his lyrics David personates Christ, and with his ten-stringed psaltery celebrates his rising from the dead." Augustine: "David was a man eminently skilled in songs, being one who loved musical harmony, not to produce a carnal delight, but with the will of faith." The son of Sirach says of David: "In all his works he praised the Holy One most high with words of glory; with his whole heart he sung songs, and loved him that made him. He set singers also before the altar, that by their voices they might make sweet melody and daily sing praises in their songs. He beautified their feasts, and set in order the solemn times unto the end, that they might praise his holy name, and that the temple might sound from morning." Ecclus. xlvii. 8–10.

Several of the Fathers and some more modern writers make David the sole author of the Book of Psalms, but this is unquestionably a mistake.

Twelve of the Psalms are ascribed to Asaph, who seems to have been a man of exquisite sensibilities, much tempted, but remarkably delivered. He was cotemporary with David, and wrote his first Psalm about one thousand and twenty years before Christ. He is mentioned as a composer of Psalms in 2 Chron. xxix. 30, where he is also called a Seer. Two of the Psalms are ascribed to Solomon, the son of David, a great preacher, and the wisest of mere men. 1 Kings iv. 29–34. Only one Psalm is believed to have been written by Moses, (and Kennicott denies even that to him, though on insufficient grounds,) Moses, the man that spoke to God in the mountain till his face had an intolerable brightness. Although Angus claims that Ps. lxxxviii. is of the greatest antiquity, being written, he thinks, B. C. 1531, yet in this he is pretty certainly mistaken; and we may safely say that the 90th Psalm is the most ancient of all these songs. Scott dates it 1460, and Angus 1489 years B. C.

One Psalm is ascribed to Heman the Ezrahite, and *one* to Ethan the Ezrahite. Of these men we know that they were the sons of Mahol, that they had two eminent brothers, Chalcol and Darda, that they were cotemporary with Solomon, and that they were wise men, though surpassed by their monarch. Some think Ethan and Jeduthun the same; but that is doubtful. Some think Psalms lxxxviii. and lxxxix. were written by persons living before the time of David. But this cannot be proven. Compare 1 Kings iv. 31; 1 Chron. xv. 17, 19; xxv. 1; 2 Chron. xxxv. 15. That the Ethan and Heman mentioned in 1 Chron. ii. 6 cannot be the authors of Psalms lxxxviii. and lxxxix. is evident from the contents of Psalm lxxxix. which records things said and done long after their day. Of the remaining *sixty-one* Psalms the authorship is either wholly unknown or somewhat uncertain. Of these, *eleven* are ascribed to the sons of Korah as authors, or are addressed to them as musical performers; but learned men are not agreed on this point. It is almost certain that David wrote some of those ascribed to the sons of Korah. It would not profit the reader here to inquire at length into this matter, which will probably in several cases never be fully settled. To us the sense of the Psalm, if clearly ascertained, is the same, whoever may have been the writer. It is certain that David was the author of several to which his name is not prefixed. Thus the second Psalm is not on its face ascribed to David, yet in Acts iv. 25 we learn from infallible authority that it was composed by him. In substance the same may be said respecting the 95th Psalm, which in Heb. iv. 7 is expressly ascribed to David, though there is no statement to that effect in the Psalter. It is said in Ps. lxxii. 20: "The prayers of David the son of Jesse are ended." Whatever else that phrase may mean, it cannot teach that no portion of the Psalms subsequent to the 72d in our arrangement was written by David.

5. THE PSALMS INSPIRED.

The real author of the Psalms is the Holy Spirit. In other words, the penmen of these compositions were inspired of God. So Chrysostom: "How does it concern me whether David was the author of all the Psalms, or whether some of them were written by others since it is certainly known that they were all written by the inspiration of the Holy Spirit?" Williams: "The divine authority of the Book of Psalms has, we believe, never been controverted by those who admit the inspiration of any part of the Old Testament." David expressly claims inspiration for himself: "The Spirit of the Lord spake by me, and his word was in my tongue. The God of Israel said, the Rock of Israel spake to me." 2 Sam. xxiii. 2, 3. This clearly claims inspiration. David was certainly inspired. On the day of Pentecost, Peter did but declare the judgment of the Church and the mind of God, when he said, "This Scripture must needs have been fulfilled, which the Holy Ghost by the mouth of David spake," etc. Acts i. 16. And in Acts xiii. 29–37, Paul speaks of the Psalms in a way that he surely would not do if he did not regard them as the word of God. Our Saviour himself teaches that in the *hundred and tenth* Psalm David spoke "by the Holy Ghost," and that "David in spirit called him Lord." Matt. xxii. 43, and Mark xii. 36. In his last interview with his disciples, just before his ascension, our Lord puts Moses, the Prophets, and the Psalms on the same level, as containing unfailing truths. Luke xxiv. 44. Indeed, Christ and his apostles always treated the Psalms as the infallible word of God. Heb. iii. 7. They are quoted or referred to scores of times in the New Testament as of the highest authority in religion, as may be seen from the following

TABLE

OF VERSES OF THE PSALMS QUOTED IN THE NEW TESTAMENT.

Psalm.	Verse.	Quoted in	Psalm.	Verse.	Quoted in
II.	1, 2.	Acts iv. 25, 26.	V.	10.	Rom. iii. 13.
II.	7.	Acts xiii. 33.	VIII.	3.	Matt. xxi. 16.
II.	9.	Rev. ii. 27.	VIII.	5.	Heb. ii. 6.

Psalm.	Verse.	Quoted in	Psalm.	Verse.	Quoted in
VIII.	6.	1 Cor. xv. 27.	LXXVIII.	2.	Matt. xiii. 35.
X.	7.	Rom. iii. 14.	LXXVIII.	24.	John vi. 31.
XIV.	1.	Rom. iii. 10.	LXXXII.	6.	John x. 34.
XVI.	8.	Acts ii. 25.	LXXXIX.	20.	Acts xiii. 22.
XVIII.	50.	Rom. xv. 9.	XC.	1.	Matt. xxii. 44.
XIX.	5.	Rom. x. 18.	XCI.	11, 12.	Matt. iv. 6.
XXII.	2.	Matt. xxvii. 46.	XCIV.	11.	1 Cor. iii. 20.
XXII.	19.	Matt. xxvii. 35.	XCV.	7.	Heb. iii. 7.
XXII.	19.	John xix. 24.	XCVII.	7.	Heb. i. 6.
XXII.	23.	Heb. ii. 12.	XCVIII.	22.	Matt. xxi. 42.
XXIV.	1.	1 Cor. x. 26.	CII.	25.	Heb. i. 10.
XXXII.	1, 2.	Rom. iv. 7, 8.	CIV.	4.	Heb. i. 7.
XXXIV.	13.	1 Peter iii. 10.	CIX.	3.	John xv. 25.
XXXV.	19.	John xv. 25.	CIX.	8.	Acts i. 20.
XXXVI.	2.	Rom. iii. 18.	CX.	1.	Matt. xxii. 24.
XL.	7.	Heb. x. 5.	CX.	1.	Mark xii. 30.
XLI.	9.	John xiii. 18.	CX.	1.	Luke x. 27.
XLIV.	22.	Rom. viii. 36.	CX.	4.	Heb. v. 6.
XLV.	7, 8.	Heb. i. 8, 9.	CXII.	9.	2 Cor. ix. 9.
LI.	6.	Rom. iii. 4.	CXVI.	10.	2 Cor. iv. 13.
LXVIII.	19.	Eph. iv. 8.	CXVII.	1.	Rom. xv. 11.
LXIX.	10.	Rom. xv. 3.	CXVIII.	6.	Heb. xiii. 6.
LXIX.	10.	John ii. 17.	CXVIII.	22, 23.	Matt. xxi. 42.
LXIX.	10.	Rom. xi. 9, 10.	CXL.	4.	Rom. iii. 13.
LXIX.	26.	Acts i. 20.			

Some of the Jews deny to David the title of prophet; but in Acts ii. 30 Peter expressly calls him a prophet. In whatever sense the word prophet may be taken, it surely belongs to David. He was a great teacher. He predicted many great events. No man can consistently deny inspiration to the Psalms without denying it to all the Scriptures. If the Psalms are inspired it is easy to understand why they should be so powerful in their influence over the minds and hearts of men. They are a fire and a hammer. They are life and spirit.

6. DIFFICULTY OF UNDERSTANDING THE PSALMS.

If any ask, why should a divinely inspired and devotional book be so hard to be understood, and lead to so considerable diversity of interpretation? the answer has been given a thousand times: The human mind is very weak, and liable to many prejudices and to much darkness; and the things of God are very excellent and glorious. The fact that the book is highly devotional and experimental takes nothing from the difficulty; for the nearer we are to the throne, the more dazzling is its effulgence found to be; and the more deeply truth enters into our spirits, the less able do we feel ourselves to tell its relations and describe its beauties. The Psalms were written a long time ago, in an age and country very diverse from our own, and in a language so peculiar as to have now no parallel. In his preface to the book of Psalms with notes, the learned Creswell thus accounts for much of the difficulty: "The Hebrew is not only a *dead* language, but the oldest of all dead languages; it is, moreover, the language of a people that lived under institutions and in a climate very different from those of our own country, so that the idioms with which it abounds cannot but be strange to our habits of thinking, and our modes of speech; nor have we any book but the Bible itself to consult for an illustration of these phraseological peculiarities.

The paucity of the words also contained in that ancient tongue is such, that the same Hebrew term very often bears a great variety of significations, the connection of which with each other cannot always be satisfactorily ascertained: and, again, there are words, each of which is found but once in the whole volume of Scripture, so that their meanings can only be conjectured, either from their affinity to other words, or from the purport of the passage where they occur.

"The following are amongst the many grammatical Hebraisms which we meet with in the Book of Psalms. The *future* and *past* tenses are put almost indiscriminately, the one for the other, and the former of them is used occasionally to designate not that which *will* happen, but that which is *accustomed* to happen. The *infinitive* is put for every other mood, and also for nouns even in the accusative case. The *future* tense is sometimes expressed by a verb in the imperative mood. Two substantives are put instead of a substantive and an adjective; a substantive is frequently used adverbially; and the same substantive repeated denotes multitude. When the *negative* particle occurs in the first member of a sentence, it is sometimes to be understood, and must be supplied, in the following members. Hebrew sentences are also in other respects very often elliptical, broken and imperfect; and in the same sentence there is in many instances a change of person in the speaker, without any express intimation of it.

"From the peculiarities above mentioned, and especially from the different ways in which an ellipse may be supplied, it is plain that the text of Scripture must needs admit of a considerable latitude of interpretation; so that although none of its important doctrines, whether they relate to faith or morals, are thereby left doubtful, yet does it contain passages the exact meanings of which are more or less uncertain. The candid and pious reader, however, will with Augustine gladly acknowledge that all which he fully comprehends in the sacred volume is most excellent; whilst he looks with feelings of veneration upon that smaller portion of it which he less perfectly understands, but which the diligence and erudition of future times may, through divine aid, be enabled to elucidate."

This is the proper place to remark on those forms of expression in the Psalms, which taken according to the sound are imprecations of evil upon enemies. Respecting these the following remarks are offered to show that the inconsistency of such passages with the existence of genuine benevolence is merely apparent. True piety is ever the same. It teaches us to do good for evil, to bless and curse not. The Psalms themselves show that the law of love was understood by David as we now understand it. See Psalm vii. 4. True religion requires men, always did require men to supplicate blessings, such as repentance, forgiveness and salvation on our earthly foes.

To explain these imprecatory forms of speech some say that they are not expressive of the feelings of the writers as private persons, but that they are inspired by the Holy Ghost to say these things in the name of God, or of Christ. But God swears that he has no pleasure in the death of sinners; Christ when dying prayed for his murderers; and the Divine Spirit is the author of all holy love in man's heart. The representative of the Holy One must be like him.

Nor does it aid the matter to say that all these persons, against whom imprecations are uttered, are incorrigible foes of God and good men; for *first*, it cannot be shown that in all cases they were so; and, *secondly*, Jesus Christ wept over the city, which he knew to be hopelessly doomed to destruction. We must be like Christ. If a man is *known* to be incorrigibly wicked, we may not pray for him; but we may not ask God to hasten his perdition.

Others say that such imprecations are simple expressions of a strong sense of the justice of God in sending calamities and curses on the wicked. No doubt every sin deserves God's terrible and eternal displeasure, and all ought to say so. But personal ill-desert is not confined to those, who shall be lost. The righteous are not saved because they have not sinned, nor because they have sinned less than others, nor because they do not deserve perdition. Their salvation is wholly gratuitous. Every regenerate man has a strong sense of the justice of his own destruction, if God should finally cast him off. Yet no good man uses any form of imprecatory words, respecting himself. And he has no right to use such phrases merely to convey the idea that the thing is just. For there are other modes, well known to pious men, of doing the same thing. It would be just in God to damn the world, but in saying that, we may not seem to ask him to do it. On the contrary we should pray for all, who are in the land of the living, and have not sinned unto death, even while we confess that no man deserves anything but wrath. It should never be forgotten, however, that all such passages are based upon the fact that the punishment of the wicked will be perfectly just.

Many say that the verbs in the clauses under consideration might and should be rendered in the future.

Horne: "The offence taken at the supposed uncharitable and vindictive spirit of the imprecations, which occur in some of the Psalms, ceases immediately if we change the imperative for the future, and read, not 'let them be confounded,' etc., but, 'they shall be confounded,' etc., of which the Hebrew is equally capable. Such passages will then have no more difficulty in them than the other frequent predictions of divine vengeance in the writings of the prophets, or denunciations of it in the gospels intended to warn, to alarm, and to lead sinners to repentance, that they may fly from the wrath to come. This is Dr. Hammond's observation; who very properly remarks, at the same time, that in many places of this sort, as particularly in Ps. cix., (and the same may be said of Ps. lxix.,) it is reasonable to resolve, that Christ himself speaketh in the prophet; as being the person there principally concerned, and the completion most signal in many circumstances there mentioned; the succession especially of Matthias to the apostleship of Judas. It is true, that in the citation made by St. Peter from Ps. cix., in Acts i. 20, as also in that made by St. Paul from Ps. lxix., in Rom. xi. 9, the imperative form is preserved: 'Let his habitation be void,' etc. 'Let their table be made a snare,' etc. But it may be considered, that the apostles generally cited from the Greek of the LXX. version; and took it as they found it, making no alteration, when the passage, as it there stood, was sufficient to prove the main point which it was adduced to prove. If the imprecatory form be still contended for, all that can be meant by it, whether uttered by the prophet, by Messiah, or by ourselves, must be a solemn ratification of the just judgments of the Almighty against his impenitent enemies, like what we find ascribed to the blessed spirits in heaven, when such judgments were executed: Rev. xi. 17, 18; xvi. 5, 6, 7: See Merrick's Annotations on Ps. cix., and Witsii Miscellan. Sacr. lib. i., cap. 18, sect. 24. But, by the future rendering the verbs, every possible objection is precluded at once."

Scott: "The future tense is often used for the imperative, or the optative mood, in the Hebrew, which has not that precision, as to tenses and moods, which prevails in many other languages. But where the literal rendering contains simply a *prediction*, and changing the future for the imperative, or optative, implies an *imprecation*, or a *wish*, the literal version is frequently preferable. . . We must by no means desire and pray for the destruction of our enemies, but we may predict the ruin of God's enemies, who will fall by their own counsels, and in the multitude of their iniquities." If these seeming imprecations are mere predictions, the matter is relieved of all serious difficulty. This view is well supported by authority.

But the use of the future tense instead of the optative mood does not in all cases satisfy Scott, for he says, "Yet it cannot be denied that the form of imprecation is often used, implying that the impenitent enemies of God and Christ will perish, with the approbation of all holy creatures; and that the very prayers of believers for themselves and the Church will be answered in the destruction of their enemies." Others have expressed similar views.

Therefore some adopt and enlarge on the idea that "we may predict the ruin of God's enemies." Surely we may do that. We must do it in all fidelity and tenderness. The view then is that the form of expression in our English Bible in many places is an ordinary method of prophetically announcing both curses and blessings. An examination of many passages in the Psalms and in the prophets would confirm this view.

Either this or the next preceding mode of explaining the difficulty will to most candid persons be satisfactory. The latter is perhaps to be preferred.

Some, however, unite both, and so cover the whole ground. Cobbin: "Such passages admit of translation in the future, and are rather predictions than imprecations." Morison also says that Psalm v. 10, "and all similar passages in the Psalms, will bear to be translated in the future tense. For the want of observing this circumstance, many have been stumbled at the apparent want of benevolence on the part of David. These words are a distinct but awful prophecy of the judgments which await the enemies of Christ and his Church."

The sense of the Christian world so far coincides with the idea that these seeming imprecations were mere predictions, that, with very limited exceptions, persons professing the Christian name have never been led to use similar forms of expression in their devotions. Those who form the exception have commonly been men heated with the intense malignity of partizans in political or theological controversy.

It should also be stated that such is the pious, benevolent spirit of the Psalms, that any one using these forms of speech to express real imprecations, would shock a Christian community. Alexander: "Such expressions in the Psalms have never really excited or encouraged a spirit of revenge in any reader, and are no more fitted to have that effect than the act of a judge who condemns a criminal to death or of the officer who executes the sentence." God will surely, by his very nature, be led to destroy the incorrigibly wicked. Nothing is more certain. Such truth should be proclaimed. The belief of it is eminently salutary.

Let us then not be surprised at these difficulties in ascertaining the sense of the Psalmists; in doubtful cases let us propose our views with unfeigned modesty; let us make reasonable allowance for human infirmity; and especially let us implore the guidance of the Holy Spirit. He is that unction which teacheth us all things. No wit, nor learning, nor study can ever render his teachings unnecessary. Let us thank God that so much is clear and intelligible. Let us also often cry, "Teach me thy statutes;" "Open thou mine eyes, that I may behold wondrous things out of thy law." God is himself the great Teacher.

7. Various Versions. The English Good.

Various translations of the Psalms are before the public. Many of them have much merit and preserve much of the heavenly savor of the original. All of them may occasionally afford a good hint. Of those made into English none can compare with the authorized version. Many devout persons have by long use become attached to the translation found in the prayer-book of the church of England. This version bears date from A. D. 1539. Their preference for this shows how precious God's word is in *any* translation, which is much used; but no competent scholar would agree that our authorized version has any successful rival. That just referred to is far more a translation of the Septuagint than of the Hebrew text. The Commentator Scott, who well deserves the epithet *Judicious*, says, "The Prayer-book translation is in no respect comparable to the Bible translation." Nearly all the translations now claiming public attention may be profitably consulted. The older English versions from quaintness, if not from elegance, do often give the sense in a very striking way. The Polyglot Bibles may with great advantage be consulted by those whose scholarship is sufficient. The author thinks proper here to record his high estimate of the value of the English Bible now in common use. It seems to him that his brethren, who seek to bring it into disrepute, might be much better employed. He gives it as his deliberate judgment that he has never seen even one chapter done into English so well anywhere else. The learning of the men, who made it, was vast, sound, and unquestionable. In this respect their little fingers were thicker than the loins of the men, who decry their labors. The common people ought to be told that they have God's word in a better translation than that of the Septuagint, which was freely quoted by Christ and his apostles. Nothing is inspired but the original; yet those learned and modest men, who have suggested improvements in the rendering of any text, should receive all due honor, and not be looked upon with suspicion. The old mode of paraphrasing Scripture had more serious objections to it than that of suggesting a new rendering.

For these reasons no new translation is presented in this work. One absolutely new, and paying any decent regard to the Hebrew text, is quite impossible, although it may be fairly original with its author. Yet the various translations, where they can cast any light on the text, or where candor requires the statement of views opposed to the sense conveyed by the common version, are freely given.

8. How far are the Psalms Messianic?

The weightiest matter in controversy respecting the interpretation of the Psalms regards their application to Christ. How far are they Messianic? Has any portion of them a primary application to David or Solomon, and a secondary reference to Christ? Were these kings types of the Saviour? if so, how far may we go in regarding them as typical? In this matter there may have been rashness and folly on both sides. An unbridled fancy may find supposed analogies, where none were intended to be suggested. And a cold critical turn of mind may reject the most striking types. To say that nothing in the Old Testament is a type of Christ unless in the New Testament it is expressly declared to be so is as contrary to reason as to say that no prophecy of the Old Testament relates to Christ unless it is quoted as such in the New. The entire old dispensation was full of figures. So Paul teaches in Hebrews x. 1. On the other hand fanciful men will pervert anything. In explaining God's word we must exercise sobriety. The Scripture calls on men to use common sense. Lacking this, they will err whatever may be the rules of interpretation adopted by them. They must prove all things.

It has often been said that Cocceius carried the typical interpretation to an extreme, finding Christ everywhere. Both Christ and his apostles taught that the Old Testament was very full of Messiah and his kingdom. See Luke xxiv. 44 and Acts iii. 24. These passages are supported by Luke xxiv. 27; 2 Timothy iii. 15, and many others. If therefore Cocceius did find Christ "in all the prophets," inspired men did the same thousands of years ago. He may have erred in some of his views, but some examination of his work on the Psalms satisfies me that he is a far safer and sounder guide than any of his traducers. This great man wrote at a time when the world was far gone astray, and his attempt to recall mankind to the simple truths of Scripture provoked violent opposition, which covered his name with unmerited reproach. He laid down no rule of interpreting the Psalms more comprehensive than that of Horsley: "There is not a page of this Book of Psalms, in which the pious reader will not find his Saviour, if he read with a view of finding him." Henry: "In the Book of Psalms there is so much of CHRIST and his gospel, as well as of GOD and his law, that it has been called *the abstract or summary* of both Testaments. . . David was a type of Christ, who descended from him, not from Moses, because he came to take away sacrifice (the family of Moses was soon lost and extinct) but to establish and perpetuate joy and praise: for of the family of David in Christ there shall be no end."

The great key to the interpretation of the Psalms respecting David and Solomon is found in 2 Samuel vii. where God gives a clear promise that the seed of David should reign for ever. In no sense can that promise be made good except in Christ Jesus. Bishop Chandler very justly remarks that the Jews "must have understood David, their prince, to have been a figure of Messiah. They would not otherwise have made his Psalms a part of their daily worship, nor would David have delivered them to the church to be so employed, were it not to instruct and support them in the belief of this fundamental article. Was the Messias not concerned in the Psalms, it were absurd to celebrate twice a day, in their public devotions, the events of one man's life, who was deceased so long ago as to have no relation now to the Jews, and the circumstances of their affairs; or to transcribe whole passages from them into their prayers for the coming of Messiah."

Bellarmine says, that in some of the Psalms the coming, the kingdom, the miracles, the sufferings, the resurrection, the ascension of Christ are so manifestly foretold, that one rather seems to be reading an evangelist than a prophet. Gill says, that "the subject-matter of the Psalms is exceeding great and excellent; many of the Psalms respect the person, offices and grace of Christ; his sufferings and death, resurrection, ascension, and session at the right hand of God; and so are exceeding suitable to the gospel dispensation." Dr. J. A. Alexander: "The chain of Messianic promises, which for ages had been broken, or concealed beneath the prophetic ritual, was now renewed by the addition of a new link in the great Messianic promise made to David (2 Sam. vii.) of perpetual succession in his family."

In discussing the question "whether all the Psalms should be applied to Christ or not," Scott says, "No doubt every pious mind will allow that each of them immediately points to him in his person, character, and offices; or may be so applied as to lead the believer's thoughts to Him who is the centre of all acceptable religion."

Leighton: "There are many things in the Psalms and other parts of the Old Testament applied by the apostles to Christ, which, but for their authority, perhaps no one would have considered as referring to him."

We might therefore agree with Morison, that we "perceive no infallible guide but in the comments and appropriations of Christ and his apostles;" and yet with consistency we might with him say, "That many of the Psalms have a double sense attached to them cannot be fairly disputed." And there is much truth in the remark of Dr. Allix, that "although the sense of near fifty Psalms be fixed and settled by divine authors, yet Christ and his apostles did not undertake to quote all the Psalms they could quote, but only to give a key to their hearers, by which they might apply to the same subjects the Psalms of the same composure and expression."

Nothing heretofore said was designed to oppose the rule of interpretation laid down by Melancthon, that we must always seek the grammatical sense of Scripture; nor that laid down by Hooker: "I hold it for a most infallible rule in expositions of sacred Scripture, that where a literal construction will stand, the farthest from the letter is commonly the worst." Let us then in all cases admit the literal or primary sense of

Scripture. But this should not hinder us from also admitting in many cases the spiritual or secondary sense. A thing spoken of David may be literally true of him. Thus we have the primary sense. But David was a type of Christ, and what he says primarily of himself may have a secondary fulfilment in Christ, and so we get the spiritual sense. Without admitting thus much, how is it possible ever to apply the doctrine of types in persons to the antitype? When we have a figure, the first thing is to discover the foundation and sense of the figure; the next is to apply it to the matter in hand.

This is not giving unbridled license to the vagaries of men of no judgment. Vitringa was right when he condemned what has often passed under the name of spiritualizing: "I do not deny that many men of uninstructed faculties and of shallow judgment have, in almost every age of the Church, commended to persons like themselves, under the name of allegorical interpretations of Scripture, certain weak and stupid fancies, in which there is neither unction, judgment, nor spiritual discernment: and have sought for those mysteries of theirs which spring from a most frigid invention, either in improper places, or promiscuously in every place, without any discrimination of circumstances, without any foundation in allegory, or in verisimilitude of language: so that I do not wonder that it has occurred to many sensible persons to doubt, whether it would not be better to abandon this study altogether, to the skilful use of which experience teaches us the abilities of but very few are adequate, than to expose Holy Scripture to the senseless experiments of the unskilful, so as to cause great injury to itself, and to excite the applause of the profane." The truth is that nothing is of more importance to the interpreter of Scripture than good common sense. A foolish or fanciful man will misapply the best rules of exposition. In vain do we expect wisdom from those who lack sobriety.

Martin Bucer: "It would be worth a great deal to the Church, if, forsaking allegories, and other frivolous devices, which are not only empty, but derogate very much from the majesty of the doctrine of Christ, we would all simply and soberly prosecute that which our Lord intends to say to us."

Nor can we rightly apply to Christ the *penitential* Psalms, or represent him as asking *forgiveness*. In himself he was holy, harmless, undefiled, separate from sinners, perfectly innocent, having nothing to repent of. And if sin imputed to him was to him forgiven, then it was not atoned for by him. Indeed, forgiveness is non-imputation. Nor can we ever apply to Christ those parts of the Psalter which plead for the subduing of *corruptions*. He had no corruptions to subdue. Yet the remark of Hilary is of great weight: "The key of the Psalms is the faith of Christ."

9. NAME OF THE PSALTER.

The name of this collection of songs in the Hebrew is *Book of Praises*, or *Praise-songs*. This is given because praise is a striking characteristic of these compositions. In them God is greatly exalted and extolled both for what he is and for what he does. According to all the teachings of this book, the Lord is a great God and King, greatly to be feared and greatly to be praised. Let men study the *Book of Praises*. From the Greek Testament we get the titles, PSALMS, and BOOK OF PSALMS. These names are chosen by inspiration. The word Psalm denotes a composition intended to be sung in connection with an instrument of music. The first men among the Levites were those who led the singing. They did not, like the rest of their tribe, fulfil their course and then retire to the villages and rural districts of Judea, but they made the holy city their home. 1 Chron. ix. 33, 34. This work of praise was a great matter among the ancient people of God. The instruments used were chiefly psalteries, and harps, and cymbals, 1 Chron. xv. 16–22; also trumpets, 1 Chron. xvi. 4–6. In 1 Chron.

xvi. 42, we read of "musical instruments of God." Those who led this part of public worship were divided into twenty-four classes or choirs. 1 Chron. xxv. Perhaps devotional music was never carried to greater perfection, nor shall be in this world, than when the thousands of trained Levites united in singing the Psalms. The music used is entirely lost, though Rabbi Benjamin says that in his time there were at Bagdad some Jews who knew how to sing the songs as the singers did when the temple was standing. There doubtless were men who so pretended, but they could hardly have retained this knowledge to so late a period.

10. INSCRIPTIONS.

The titles of the several Psalms (Hengstenberg calls them *superscriptions;* others, *inscriptions*) are as old as the Psalms themselves, being always found in the Hebrew. They were doubtless put there by divine authority. Tholuck: "The titles of the Psalms did not originate with the compilers, but with those who first wrote them down, or in the authors themselves." God, who would have all things done decently and in order, deigned to give minute directions for arranging the temple service, and especially respecting the public praise offered to his heavenly majesty. See 2 Chron. xxix. 25. He who did these things, also directed these inscriptions to be put to the Psalms, not always to give us the doctrine or matter therein contained, but to set up a memorial respecting events through which the writer had passed, or to give some general idea of the theme, or to address the piece to certain performers. The import of some of these titles may not be intelligible to us, though they may have been very clear when given. Many of them greatly aid us in giving a lively view of the state of things, in which the writer uttered his song. Where remark is called for in explanation of given titles it will be offered at the proper place. It is surprising that Fry should have ventured to say, "These titles are destitute of authority, as the careful reader of the Psalms will soon remark; they are to be regarded merely as marginal glosses of the Jews, but poor guides to the interpretation of Scripture." Even Morison says, "The authority of the several inscriptions is, to say the least, somewhat doubtful." And the annotator of Calvin quotes Fry's remark with approbation. But Alexander has well observed that "in all Hebrew manuscripts they bear the same relation to the body of the Psalm, that the inscriptions in the prophets or in Paul's epistles bear to the substance of the composition." This shows the great rashness of those, who boldly set aside the Hebrew heading. Jerome: "The titles of the Psalms are the keys, opening the door to a right understanding of them." Bossuet: "There can be no reason for expunging them, since they are found in the text and all the versions, and have been thought worthy of explanation by Jewish as well as Christian commentators. It is true, there are many who take these titles in different senses; but I cannot find one ancient interpreter who doubts of their authority."

11. THE PSALMS ARE ONE BOOK.

The very first remark of Hilary in his Prologue to the Psalms is that "the Book of Psalms is one, not five." He here refers to the fact that some of the Jews divided the Psalms into five books, corresponding to the five books of Moses. It is not necessary here to dwell on this matter. It is sufficient to inform the reader that such a division was a mere human invention, deriving no authority from God, and not even founded on the nature of the contents of these wondrous songs. In Luke xx. 42 and in Acts i. 20, we read of "The Book of Psalms," but nowhere do we read of "The Books of Psalms," nor of the *first, second, third, fourth,* or *fifth* Book of Psalms.

12. Pairs of Psalms.

Some have asserted that in several instances the Psalms were in pairs. It may be so, but there is no proof of it contained in the text of Scripture. Nor would the reader be profited by a long inquiry into this matter. All truth is related, and is harmonious. In this sense, almost any one Psalm may well be put as the mate of more than one other Psalm. At least, there seems to be no reason from the contents of any two psalms, why a close affinity should be discovered between them, and not between either of them, and some other portions of these divine songs. The classification here spoken of is harmless, and if any think it is based in the nature of these compositions, such an opinion should give no offence. Alexander thinks that " we may trace not only pairs but trilogies and even more extensive systems of connected Psalms, each independent of the rest, and yet together forming beautiful and striking combinations." Any remark from such a source is entitled to respect.

13. Alphabetical Psalms.

A peculiarity of several Psalms is that they are *alphabetical*. That is "the successive sentences or paragraphs begin with the letters of the Hebrew alphabet in their order." Without extraordinary ingenuity this could not be made to appear in any translation. Thus it would not be easy to make the first eight verses of the 119th Psalm begin with the *first* letter of our alphabet, and the *second* eight verses begin with the second letter of our alphabet, and so on. Nor is it necessary that we should make such an attempt. The sense of Scripture is of infinite weight. But it is of no importance to us whether our translation should *in this respect* copy the original. The mind of the Spirit is what we should seek. The version which gives that is what we need.

14. Hebrew Poetry.

The reader need hardly be told that the Psalms are highly poetical, and that our knowledge of Hebrew Poetry is very limited. On all subjects of sacred criticism our utterances should be modest; but in relation to the poetical portions of God's word we should be doubly careful to say nothing rashly. At the same time we may very properly consult all sober writers on such subjects, and get the best lights within our reach. Nor can we judge of Hebrew odes by canons applicable to modern languages. "The poetry of the Psalms is formed, not like that of modern languages, by the response of answering syllables, but of answering thoughts."

15. Selah.

The word, *Selah*, is found nowhere in Scripture but in thirty-nine of the Psalms and in the 3d chapter of Habakkuk—in the Psalms seventy-four times and in Habakkuk thrice. Our translators have left it as they found it. Bishop Jebb has devoted great attention to this word, and has reached the following safe conclusions, viz: that the word is an integral part of the sacred text; that it does not mean " *amen," forever,*" " *mark this well,*" or " *nota bene;*" that it never occurs in the alphabetical Psalms, nor in the Songs of degrees, nor in any Psalm composed after the Captivity; that the prayer of Habakkuk was composed at a time when the Temple service had been restored to great grandeur; that nothing can be confidently spoken respecting the etymological meaning of this word; that the Septuagint renders the word invariably by *Diapsalma*, which marks a division of some kind; and that the word is put as a musical notation. Many will doubt whether this writer has fairly maintained another view which had been formerly given by Burkius in his Gnomon Psalmorum, that *Selah* is a mark of division, discriminating one moral portion of a Psalm from another.

Without discussing at length this theory, which has been presented with some plausibility, it may be said that it does not seem to suit every case. The only ground yet taken, and successfully maintained is that *Selah* is a simple direction to the musicians, the precise force of which is not known to us. The word is not found "in the later editions of the Vulgate, nor in the Syriac, nor in the Arabic translations," nor does the church of England use it in her Psalter. Yet it is very properly retained in our authorized version of the Scriptures. And if any should feel disposed to pronounce it let none be offended. It is undoubtedly a part of the holy writings given to us. Patrick: "And here I must note once for all, that it cannot be certainly known what is meant by the word SELAH, which we meet withal thrice in this (the 3d) short Psalm. The most probable opinion is that it was a note in musick. . . That musick being now lost, some interpreters have wholly omitted this word, *Selah*, as I shall also do." Calvin: "As the word *Selal*, from which *Selah* is derived, signifies to *lift up*, we incline to the opinion of those who think it denotes the lifting up of the voice in harmony in the exercise of singing." Venema thinks it calls for an elevation of the voice in singing the Psalm. Alting thinks it calls for a repetition of the words immediately preceding. The Chaldee renders it *forever*. It should be stated however that it is designed to fix the minds of the godly on the matter, which has just been spoken of in any given case, as well as to regulate the singing in such a manner as to make the music correspond to the words and the sentiment. Alexander also says, that Selah is "properly a musical term, but generally indicates a pause in the sense as well as the performance." A writer in the Bibliotheca Sacra says:

"Rabbi Kimchi regards it as a sign to elevate the voice. The authors of the Septuagint translation appear to have regarded it as a musical or rythmical note. Herder regarded it as indicating a change of note; Mathewson as a musical note, equivalent, perhaps, to the word *repeat*. According to Luther and others, it means *silence!* Gesenius explains it to mean, "Let the instruments play and the singers stop." Wocher regards it as equivalent to *sursum corda*—up, my soul! Sommer, after examining all the seventy-four passages in which the word occurs, recognizes in every case "an actual appeal or summons to Jehovah." They are calls for aid and prayers to be heard, expressed either with entire directness, or if not in the imperative, "Hear, Jehovah!" or Awake, Jehovah! and the like still earnest addresses to God that he would remember and hear, etc. The word itself he regards as indicating a blast of the trumpets by the priests. Selah, itself, he thinks an abridged expression, used for Higgaion Selah—Higgaion indicating the sound of the stringed instruments, and Selah a vigorous blast of trumpets."

16. THE WORDS RENDERED MAN.

In the Psalter there are three Hebrew words rendered man, Adam, Ish and Enosh. The first and third of these occur in our Hebrew Bible more than *five hundred* times each, and the second more than *fifteen hundred* times. Each of these words is found in the Law, the Prophets, and the poetic books of Scripture. They are in the Pentateuch and in books written after the captivity. *Adam* is first found in Gen. i. 26, 27. In the 2d chapter of Genesis it occurs twelve times, where it is sometimes rendered *man*, and sometimes given as the proper name of the first man.

Ish is first found in Gen. ii. 23, 24, where it is rendered *man*. Enosh is first found in the plural at the close of Gen. vi. 4, and is rendered *men* of renown. By far the most common rendering of each of these words is *man*, or, in the plural, *men*. Indeed the first (Adam) is never otherwise translated except in seven cases (Num. xxxi. 28, 30, 35, 40, 46; Pr. vi. 12; Jon. iv. 11,) where it is rendered *person* or *persons*. The second (Ish) is also rendered simply *man;* very often to conform to English idiom.

every man, every one, any man; sometimes *one, any* with a negative *none, no man;* sometimes *that man, he* or *him;* frequently *one* followed by the word *another,* sometimes *person,* or, in the plural, *persons;* sometimes, *another, each, a certain,* meaning man; a few times *one* followed by the word *other;* once or twice *each one, one man, every, either, the good-man, champion* (literally *middle-man*) *fellow, people,* applied to the male head of a family, often *husband;* once *eloquent* (literally *man* of words); a very few times *whoso, whosoever;* sometimes Canaanite, Egyptian, for *man* of Canaan, *man* of Egypt, *reprover* for *man* reproving, *stranger,* for *man* strange. It is but once rendered *male,* and then in application to brutes.

Enosh is but about thirty times rendered otherwise than *man,* or, in the plural, *men,* and then by such words as *they* or *them, certain, divers, some, persons, fellows, counsellors* for *men* of counsel, *archers* for *men* of bows, etc. These statements are made in view of a discussion of some importance respecting the import of these words. Some claim that at least at times each of these words is emphatic, and especially when preceded by the Hebrew word rendered *son,* or *sons.* Thus it is contended that in Ps. xlix. 2, where for *sons of Adam* our translators give the word *low,* and in Ps. lxii. 9, where they render the same words *men of low degree,* the original is emphatic; and yet in Ps. xlix. 12, 20 we read of *man* being in honor and of *man* that is in honor, and yet the word *Adam* is used in both these verses. It is also said to have the same meaning in Pr. viii. 4, where it is rendered literally *sons of man,* Adam. In Isa. ii. 9 the common version renders Adam, *mean man.* In like manner some contend that our translators render sons of Ish in Ps. iv. 2, *sons of men,* meaning great men; and certainly in Ps. xlix. 2 they render *sons of Ish* by the word *high,* and in Ps. lxii. 9 by *men of high degree,* and in Pr. viii. 4 the plural of *Ish* by simply *men;* but in Isa. ii. 9 the singular *Ish* by *great man.* The words *sons of Enosh* are never found in the Hebrew Bible, but *son of Enosh* occurs once, Ps. cxliv. 3. Yet it is contended that the word *Enosh* is itself sometimes emphatic as in Ps. viii. 4: ix. 19, 20, and in some other places. Indeed in Job iv. 17 it is rendered *mortal man.*

Patrick: " *The son of man* [Ben Adam] and *the sons of men* [Bene Ish] are phrases which often occur; which I have good ground to think belong in the Scripture language to *Princes;* and sometimes the *greatest of Princes.* So I have expounded that known place, Ps. lxxx. 17: *The man* [Ish] *of thy right hand, the son of man* [Ben Adam] *whom thou madest strong for thyself;* and Ps. iv. 2: *O ye sons of men* [Bene Ish], i. e., rulers of people; and Ps. viii. 4: *What is man* [Enosh] *that thou art mindful of him?* or *the son of man* [Ben Adam] (i. e., the greatest of men), *that thou visitest him?* Ps. clxvi. 3: *Put not your confidence in princes, nor in the son of man* [Ben Adam] (how great a prince, that is, soever he may be, though of never such dignity and power), *in whom there is no help.*

"And thus the counsellors of Saul are called the *sons of men* [Adam]. And so I understand these words in Isa. li. 12: *Who art thou that thou shouldest be afraid of a man* [Enosh] *that shall die, and of the* SON OF MAN [Ben Adam] (that is, a prince) *who shall be as grass?*" Having made some other statements, he adds: "As for *Ben Enosh,* which we also render *son of man,* (Ps. cxliv. 3,) it hath another signification; importing the wretchedness of any man's condition."

It is best here once for all to examine this theory of interpreting these terms. In Ps. iv. 2, we have *sons of men* [Bene Ish]. Some think this means strong and powerful men, or nobles, or persons of rank. Edwards renders it, *Ye great ones.* Calvin regards the title here given as "an ironical concession of what they claimed to themselves, by which he ridicules their presumption in esteeming themselves to be noble and wise, whereas it was only blind rage which impelled them to wicked enterprises." Hengstenberg asserts that the expression rendered *sons of men* is in many places unquestionably used in an emphatic sense." In proof he cites Ps. xlix. 2; lxii. 9; Pr. viii. 4. Let us look a little at Ps. viii. 4: *What is man* [Enosh], *that thou art mindful of him? and the son of man* [Ben Adam], *that thou visitest him?* Piscator and Edwards render Enosh *a mortal.* Calvin: "The Hebrew word, which we have rendered *man,* expresses the frailty of man, rather than any strength or power which he possesses." For *man* Venema reads *miserable man;* and Henry paraphrases it *sinful, weak, miserable man.* The words *son of man* [Ben Adam] are commented on in like manner. Ainsworth says, "As men are called *Enosh* for their doleful estate by sin, so are they called *Adam,* and *sons of Adam,* that is, earthy, to put them in mind of their original and end, who were made of *Adamah,* the earth, even of the dust, and to dust shall return again." Patrick regards the phrase *son of man* in this verse as equivalent to "*the greatest of men.*" Anderson quotes Pye Smith as reading the words thus: "What is man, that thou art mindful of him? Even the [noblest] son of man, that thou visitest him?" and as saying, "Our language has no single terms to mark the distinction expressed" by these two words; and adding, "I have endeavored to approach the idea by one insertion of an epithet."

Patrick thinks that his theory gives us the key to the right understanding of the phrase, *the son of man,* so often found in the New Testament. But that title is sufficiently explained by simply saying that it declares the entire humanity of our Lord. No further meaning is required, or has been commonly accepted.

It may seem almost presumption to express a doubt whether this theory is correct. Yet candor and truth are always worth more than they cost. The author has studied the matter with some care, and is not satisfied that any Psalmist ever used either of the words, Adam, Ish, or Enosh, in an emphatic sense, or as conveying the ideas contended for, or that the *primary* meaning of the words is ever to be insisted on in any part of these sacred songs.

Besides the views already presented at the beginning of this section, it is proper to say that the words and phrases under consideration occur with great frequency, and if ever used emphatically, and in the senses contended for, it is very rarely indeed; and there is nothing requiring us so to regard them anywhere. As the words Adam, Ish, and Enosh occur so often, no collection of instances is here presented for comparison. Such a labor would be tedious. It is also quite unnecessary. But let any one compare the texts where the expression *son of man* [Adam] is found. See Num. xxiii. 19; Job xxv. 6; xxxv. 8; Ps. lxxx. 17; cxlvi. 3; Ecc. i. 13; Jer. xlix. 18; l. 40; li. 43; scores of times in Ezekiel, as an appellation of that prophet; and Dan. viii. 17.

Let him go further and compare the cases where the words *sons of men* [Adam] are found: Ps. xxxi. 19; xxxiii. 13; lvii. 4; lviii. 1; cxlv. 12; Pr. viii. 31; Ecc. i. 13; ii. 3, 8; iii. 10, 18, 19; viii. 11; ix. 3, 12; Is. lii. 14; Jer. xxxii. 19; Dan. x. 16; Mic. v. 7; Joel i. 12.

The phrase *sons of man* [Adam] occurs in Ps. xlix. 2; Pr. viii. 4. Besides those previously cited, these are the only cases where either of these phrases occurs in all the Hebrew Scriptures.

The expression *son of man* [Ish] is never found. That of *sons of man* [Ish] is found but once, Psalm lxii. 9, where our version reads *men of high degree.* That of *sons of men* is in but two places, in Psalm iv. 2 where it is rendered literally, and in Psalm xlix. 2 *high.* It is evident that any theory built on so small an induction as this must have a very slender foundation, unless there is something in the context or connection defining the word, or making it necessary to give it such a translation.

We never find the expression *sons of man* or *sons of men,* where Enosh is used.

And we but once find *son of man* [Enosh] in Psalm cxliv. 3. It can hardly be esteemed wise to build any doctrine of language on this one expression.

That these three Hebrew words are used so as to make it impossible to tell from any fair literal translation what the original word is in all ordinary cases may easily be made to appear by looking over the English concordance for the words *man* and *men*, trying to form an opinion of what the original is, and then turning to the Hebrew. Where memory gives no clue, it will be found to be mere guess-work. Let any one try his powers on these verses where *man* occurs, Ps. i. 1; xxxii. 2; xxxix. 11; lv. 13; civ. 15; cxii. 1; and on these where *men* occurs, Jud. xx. 17; Ps. xvii. 4; lxxvi. 5; 1 Sam. xxv. 13; Ps. lxvi. 12; lxxxii. 7. He will often find it impossible to tell what the original is.

It is not at all here asserted that there is any impropriety in adverting at any time to the primary meaning of these or any other words of Scripture, if thereby the sense of any passage receives force. But it is simply denied that we have satisfactory evidence that these Hebrew words rendered *man* have an emphatic sense in the Psalms.

At the same time there is no impropriety in rendering two of these "men of low degree and men of high degree," because that phrase in English is equivalent to this, "men by whatever name called," or "men of all conditions."

17. AUTHORS CONSULTED.

It is not necessary here to give an extended list of authors consulted in preparing this work. Except in a very few instances due credit is formally given. Any exception to this remark is unintentional, or is found in those places where many writers without giving credit to each other say the same thing. In all branches of study there are things, which have become the common property of mankind. To quote would be mere pedantry, unless the very words of an author are copied. For instance, many things are said by every commentator on the first Psalm, because they obviously belong to the matter in hand, and not because they have been said by others at previous times.

Nearly a century ago Dodd stated that "the number of commentaries on the Book of Psalms was almost endless; above six hundred are enumerated, exclusive of those which have been written on the whole body of the Scriptures, and on particular Psalms." Since that time the number has been much increased.

18. OBJECT OF THIS WORK.

The great object of this work is the glory of God in the edification of his church. If it shall fail of practical usefulness and religious profit, it will gain no important end. The author has endeavored to embody all the most valuable suggestions of others together with his own reflections on this inspired book. And he begs his readers to remember that as it is in vain to light a candle to examine the sun-dial, so human wit will make no good progress in learning this or any other portion of God's word except as the Sun of Righteousness by his Holy Spirit shines upon the sacred page. All attempts to understand the spiritual import of God's word without divine teaching must ever prove failures. This fact and the reasons of it are clearly given in Scripture. Let every one, therefore, seek help from God in earnest fervent prayer. John Newton: "A few minutes of the Spirit's teaching will furnish us with more real useful knowledge, than toiling through whole folios of commentators and expositors, —they are useful in their places, and are not to be undervalued by those, who can perhaps in general do better without them; but it will be our wisdom to deal less with the streams, and be more close in applying to the fountainhead. The Scripture itself, and the Spirit of God are the best and the only sufficient expositors of Scripture. . . It is absurd to read or study the Scripture with any other view than to receive its doctrines, submit to its reproofs, and obey its precepts that we may be made wise unto salvation. All disquisitions and criticisms that stop short of this, that do not amend the heart as well as furnish the head, are empty and dangerous, at least to ourselves of whatever use they may be to others. An experience of this caused a learned critic and eminent commentator (Grotius) to confess towards the close of his life, 'Alas! I have wasted my life in much labor to no purpose.'" Luther: "We must not simply read or sing the Psalms, as if they did not concern us; but we must read and sing them for this purpose, that we may be improved by them, may have our faith strengthened, and our hearts comforted amid all sorts of necessities. For the Psalter is nothing else than a school and exercise for our heart and mind, to the end, that we may have our thoughts and inclinations turned into the same channel. So that he reads the Psalter without spirit, who reads it without faith and understanding."

19. Ignorance of some Languages quoted.

As the author is not acquainted with Ethiopic, Syriac and Arabic, and yet freely quotes them, he would state that he relies upon the Latin translation of those versions, found in Walton's Polyglot. In many cases too he finds those versions given in Latin or English by other commentators. So that he hopes the quotations will be found sufficiently accurate.

20. Why this Work was undertaken.

If any ask why this work was undertaken the answer is, 1. The word of God is not bound. It is open to all. 2. The author had a mind to it. He has never felt more disposed to any work. He has always found it best to pursue that kind of literary labor, for which he had a strong inclination. 3. He saw no way in which he could more fitly spend a portion of the afternoon of his life than in the special study of this incomparable collection of sacred poems. 4. Others, who had devoted considerable time to the Psalms, uniformly testified that they were thereby great gainers. The author felt his own poverty and wished to be enriched. Archibald Symson in his preface to his work on the seven penitential Psalms says he undertook it; " Because this ocean is not dryed up, and hee that commeth last may as well fill his bucket as hee that came first." Musculus on a like occasion said: "If the treasure of the holy Scriptures be such that it can be drawn so dry by the diligent searches of pious and learned men, as that nothing shall remain to exercise the studies of them that succeed them; if there be at any time such an effusion of God's Holy Spirit, that after that time it is in vain to labor in finding out its mind, in the holy Scriptures; if there have been in the church, after the prophets, Christ, and his Apostles, men of such perfect accomplishments, that to them was imparted such a universal fullness of divine knowledge, as to make their writings absolutely complete; so that we need do nothing, but night and day study them alone: then truly I refuse not the censure of folly, nay of madness, for attempting anything now in the holy Scriptures, after such absolute writers. But if that most rich fountain of the divine oracles be altogether inexhaustible; and no age can be assigned to which alone the grace of the Holy Spirit was confined; and there were never any doctors at any time in the church, after Christ, the apostles and prophets. of such esteem, that nothing is wanting in their writings, nothing can be rightly added to them; nothing is in them which can be rightly taken away, or changed for the better: then I do not see why we may not profitably travel in the same way that others have done; with hopes of adding more light to that which they have left us." 5. Many of the most valuable works on the Psalms are in Latin, or are very scarce and high-priced.   The endeavor here is to aid the reader with the best suggestions of writers inaccessible to most, as well as to make original remarks, critical, explanatory, doctrinal and practical.   6. Several learned and judicious persons, who heard of the contemplated design and have examined parts of it after it was commenced, greatly encouraged the author to go on with his undertaking.

21. Names of the Most High.

It will be satisfactory to the plain reader and will save time here to note that the names of the Almighty occurring in the Psalter are significant, and are briefly explained in this work:

On *Jehovah* LORD, see on Ps. i. 2.
On *Adonai Lord*, see on Ps. ii. 4.
On *Elohim God*, see on Ps. iii. 2.
On *El God*, see on Ps. v. 4.
On *Gel-yohn Most High*, see on Ps. vii. 17.
On *Eloah God*, see on Ps. xviii. 31.
On *Jah* LORD,
On *Shaddai The Almighty*,   } See introduction to Psalm lxviii.

22. Punctuation.

In punctuation the usual rules are observed, except where a single sentence or phrase is cited in the various renderings of a clause or of a verse, and the author's name is immediately prefixed.   In that case the quotation marks are not given; but then the words cited do not go beyond one sentence or verse.   In all other cases, the credit is given in the usual way.

PSALM I.

1 Blessed *is* the man that walketh not in the counsel of the ungodly, nor standeth in the way of sinners, nor sitteth in the seat of the scornful.

2 But his delight *is* in the law of the LORD; and in his law doth he meditate day and night.

3 And he shall be like a tree planted by the rivers of water, that bringeth forth his fruit in his season; his leaf also shall not wither; and whatsoever he doeth shall prosper.

4 The ungodly *are* not so: but *are* like the chaff which the wind driveth away.

5 Therefore the ungodly shall not stand in the judgment, nor sinners in the congregation of the righteous.

6 For the LORD knoweth the way of the righteous: but the way of the ungodly shall perish.

THE date of this Psalm is to be determined very much by its authorship.   Two opinions have chiefly prevailed.   One is that David wrote it.   If so, it was written more than a *thousand* years before Christ.   Those who hold David to have been the author, seem to be influenced by such considerations as the following.   It seems proper that the author of the major part of the Psalms should be the author of the Introduction to the book.   It is alleged that the style is that of David, or at least of his times.   It is also said that the Jews uniformly united the *first* and *second* Psalms into one, and that David is confessedly the author of the *second*, and, if so, of the *first* also.   Some say that in several copies of the New Testament, Acts xiii. 33, speaks of the *first* and not of the *second* Psalm, and that this shows David to have been the author of both the *first* and *second* in our arrangement. If these two are in fact but one Psalm, and if David wrote the *first* verse of the *second* Psalm, as we know he did, then none will deny that he wrote all that properly belongs to that composition.

The other opinion respecting the date of this Psalm is that it was written about *four hundred and fifty* years before Christ by Ezra, or by some one in his times, when he was arranging the canon of Scripture. The reasons given for this opinion are that such was the general belief for a long time, that it was peculiarly proper and very natural that the collector of the canon of Scripture, who also arranged the Psalms, should, after all the rest was written, prefix the *first* Psalm as a prologue to the book, and that there is nothing in the style of this Psalm rendering it improbable that Ezra was the author. Nevertheless the weight of opinion is in favor of David as the author. Williams: "We know nothing of Ezra as a poet."

This Psalm has no title. This is so remarkable, that some have contended that the first clause should be regarded as the inscription. But this view is not supported by the requisite proofs. The fact is that the Psalm needs no title, because it is so plain, and because it is itself a preface to all the great matters, which come after it. Basil says, "What the foundation is to a house, the keel to a ship, the heart to an animal, the same is this Psalm to the whole book. It is a preface to the Psalter." Athanasius and Theodoret give it this title, *Blessedness*. The Arabic has this title: "The beauty of piety and the hope of another state."

The sum of this Psalm is that the just and he alone is blessed. It incites us to the love of righteousness by presenting proper hopes. By pointing to the dreadful end of the wicked, it warns us to flee from all iniquity. It is a compend of all the Psalms, and indeed of all Scripture. In many of our Bibles the caption given is, "The happiness of the godly. The unhappiness of the ungodly." Let us consider each verse in order.

1. *Blessed* is *the man that walketh not in the counsel of the ungodly.* The word translated *blessed* is in the Hebrew plural, while the word rendered *man* is singular. Scholars are not agreed whether the plural form of the first word is used simply from a regard to the idiom of the original, or whether it announces the richness of the variety of blessings secured to the righteous. The latter view is perhaps preferable. It is well to give all the fulness of meaning, which the grammatical construction and the analogy of faith will allow. However tried and afflicted, every servant of God has vast treasures of good things in possession and in prospect. Both the Psalmist and the Saviour began their teachings with pronouncing blessedness to be the portion of God's people. The Chaldee and Arabic read the first clause thus, "A blessing on the man;" Piscator and Michaelis use this paraphrase, "Oh the right goings, happy progress, and good success of the man;" Morison says, "Oh the blessedness of this man;" Alexander would paraphrase it, "How completely happy is the man;" Mudge. Edwards, and Anderson render it, "Oh the blessednesses of the man." The catalogue of mercies secured to God's people is long.

We have next a negative description of the man, who is so blessed. *He walketh not in the counsel of the ungodly.* A man's walk is the course of his life. When the tenor of one's ways is like that of the wicked, he is wicked. Like Enoch, all the righteous walk with God. The *counsel* of the wicked is a term used to denote not merely his advice, but his aims, his maxims, his principles, his practices. In all these, saints and sinners are unlike. The righteous hates the thought of sin, and so walks not with the impious. It is next said that this blessed man *standeth not in the way of sinners.* He seeks no intimacy with them as his companions. If he mingles with them, they are a grief to him. And *he sitteth not in the seat of the scornful.* In Scripture, scorning expresses the indifference and hatred of the wicked towards divine things. They *contemn* God. Nor is anything more expressive of the deadly malice of the wicked towards the righteous than the *cruel mockings*, to which the latter are often exposed. The natural tendency of all sin is to lead to outbreaking and deadly despite towards all that is good. Proud and haughty scorner is the name of all, who long resist divine calls and mercies. Bradley: "And in the habitation of scorners hath not dwelt." If this is an improvement on our version, it is not obvious.

2. The second verse describes the character of the righteous by two positive qualities. One is that *his delight* is *in the law of the* LORD. Here first occurs in the Psalms that great, dreadful, and incommunicable name of God, *Jehovah.* In Scripture no other name is nearly so often given to the Most High. It is expressive of self-existence, independence, unchangeableness, and eternity. It is never given to any but the true God. Our translators, following the Septuagint, commonly rendered this word LORD, printing it in small capitals. In all cases it might have been as well simply to transfer the word to our language. *The law of Jehovah* here spoken of embraces the whole word of God then written. A part is put for the whole. The law was a prominent part of the revelation of God's will in the days of the Psalmist. A good man loves the decalogue, because it is the transcript of God's moral character. He also loves all the law of the dispensation under which he lives. He cavils not at divine institutions, though they may be ceremonial. Christ would be baptized, and thus fulfil all righteousness. His piety caused him to obey every institution of God, which was then in force. This view of this clause shows that Rom. vii. 14–25, cannot describe the exercises of an unregenerate person. He never *delights in the law of God after the inward man.* If this were possible, the righteous and the wicked would be alike, and regeneration would make no difference in one's character, and so would be of no value. It is also clear that those who set aside any part of God's word, bring their souls into jeopardy. Our Saviour's warnings on this subject are awful. Matt. v. 19; Rev. xxii. 19. Let no man *break one of the least commandments, or teach others to do so.* Neither let men despise the doctrines of God's word. The spiritual man loves and embraces them. He is not a child of God who delights not in the Holy Scriptures.

Another positive sign of a renewed man is that he *meditates in the law of the* LORD *day and night.* "As a man thinketh in his heart, so is he." Vain thoughts lodge in all ungodly men. But the righteous hate sinful imaginings. What the wicked would be ashamed to act or speak out, the righteous is ashamed to think or desire. Yet his mind is full of activity. He *meditates.* The power of reflection chiefly distinguishes a man from a brute. The habit of reflection chiefly distinguishes a wise man from a fool. Pious reflection on God's word greatly distinguishes a saint from a sinner. Without meditation grace never thrives, prayer is languid, praise dull, and religious duties unprofitable. Yet to flesh and blood without divine grace this is an impossible duty. It is easier to take a journey of a thousand miles than to spend an hour in close, devout, profitable thought on divine things. Like prayer, Luke xviii. 7, meditation is to be pursued *day and night,* not reluctantly, but joyously, not merely in God's house, or on the Lord's day, but whenever other duties do not forbid, "with such incessant study," says J. H. Michaelis, "that even when the act ceases, there is no abatement of the pious affection." Nor does the true child of God slight any part of divine truth. He loves it all. Bates says, "Habitual and delightful thoughts are the best discovery of our hearts and our spiritual state. Words and actions may be overruled and counterfeit for divers reasons, but thoughts are the invisible productions of the soul, and without fear or mask, without restraint or disguise, undissemblingly discover the disposition of the heart. Thoughts are the immediate offspring of the soul; and as the waters that immediately flow from the spring are strongest of the mineral, so the thoughts are most deeply tinctured with the affections. A saint is therefore described by his ' meditating in the law of God day and night,' which is the natural and necessary effect of his delight in it."

3. Such a man *shall be like a tree planted by the rivers of water.* In Scripture a river means any running stream of water. Ps. cxix. 136. Lam. iii. 48. It may be natural as in 2 Kings v. 12, Ecc. i. 7, or artificial as in Pr. xxi. 1, Deut. xi. 10. In hot Eastern countries trees flourish most by the side of water courses. When all around is burnt up with heat and drought, they are fresh and green. Alexander says, " The original words properly denote canals or channels, as customary means of arti- ficial irrigation. Hence the single tree is said to overhang more than one, because surrounded by them." The righteous is a tree *planted.* No man is by nature a friend of God, a tree of righteousness. The wild olive must be grafted before it will be fruitful. Rom. xi. 17–24. By nature we are all outcasts. It is grace that makes us *the planting of the* LORD. To be *planted* signifies also *permanency* of connection. The faith of a good man is not temporary, neither are any of his graces. He has taken root in a good place, and so his life is well maintained. " Those that be planted in the house of the LORD shall flourish in the courts of our God. They shall still bring forth fruit in old age; they shall be fat and flourishing; to show that the LORD is upright." So the righteous *bringeth forth his fruit in his season.* His blossoms are fair, but his mature fruit is better. It comes in the right time and is beautiful in its season. It has often been noticed in false professors that their acts and words are ill-timed, and that the high expectations sometimes raised by them are never realized. " 'Tis the brand of a hypocrite to have devotion come by fits, to seem like an angel one day, and live like an atheist the next." Calvin thinks that the phrase, *in his season,* chiefly points to the *maturity of the fruit produced.* Street renders the passage thus, " It bringeth forth all its produce to maturity."

His leaf also shall not wither. The appearance of such a tree corresponds to its fruit. Applied to a child of God, the leaf has commonly been supposed to represent his religious profession. He will not fall away in time of temptation and persecution. He cannot forsake Christ. To whom else shall he go? Lot will be a good man even in Sodom. As a tree thus planted " exhibits all the fragrance and all the beauty of perpetual spring," so shall it be with the just man. Bellarmine's note on this passage is, that " there are some trees, which produce leaves only, and do not even long retain these. There are others, which produce leaves and long retain them, but their fruit is either ripe too soon to be full grown, or it is not ripe when it ought to be. Others put forth fruit at the right time, and are always covered with foliage, but sadly fail in bringing fruit to maturity. There are others, which alone can be said to be perfect in kind. These have both leaves and fruit, always retain their foliage, and always yield their ripe fruit in its season. Such trees are [Mediterranean] Pines, Palm-trees, and Olive-trees, to which the Scripture often compares righteous men. In this place the prophet says that the righteous are like these trees. The apostle says that the right- eous are *rooted* and *grounded in love.* By a lasting friendship they are hard by the living fountain, whence they ever draw the nourishment of grace, and bring forth good works in the right time, and all things work together for their good, and they shall perpetually flourish in glory and honor."

And whatsoever he doeth shall prosper. Some have thought that there was a refer- ence here to the tree of life. Gen. ii. 9. Rev. xxii. 2. But such a construction seems forced. The sense is complete without it. The just is blessed in his body and in his soul, in his basket and in his store; he is in covenant with God, and abides under the shadow of the Almighty; and so he cannot be a vain thing, he cannot beat the air, he cannot conceive wind and bring forth vanity. He shall have good success. He shall make progress and "do exploits" in the matters already noticed. As a religious man his course shall be upward and onward. "He shall run and not be weary, he shall walk and not faint." For a time his path may seem covered with darkness, and he may seem to be under the frown of God. But in the Mount it shall be seen. Enlargement and deliverance shall come at the right time and in the right way. God will teach all his people to walk by faith; and so he for a while may hedge up their way. But wait his time. Let him explain his own dealings with his people; and in all cases it shall be seen that the end of the Lord is wise, and that he is very pitiful and of tender mercy. It is often asserted that the New Testament far less clearly than the Old promises temporal blessings to the righteous. But is this so? Most respectable writers admit that temporal blessings are included in the promise made in Ps. xxxvii. 11, "The meek shall inherit the earth." Yet our Lord renews this promise in his sermon on the Mount. Matt. v. 5. If we exclude temporal blessings, how can we interpret Mark x. 29, 30? "Verily I say unto you that there is no man, that hath left house or brethren, or sisters, or father, or mother, or wife, or children, or lands, for my sake, and the Gospel's, but he shall receive an hundred fold, now in this time, houses, and brethren, and sisters, and mothers, and children, and lands with persecutions; and in the world to come, eternal life." And *thirty-five* years after Christ's ascension, his blessed servant, Paul, tells us that "godliness is profitable unto all things, having promise of the life that now is, and of that which is to come." 1 Tim. iv. 8. What more could we ask? It is true that in the case of his people God subordinates temporal to spiritual blessings. This is right. No wise man would have it otherwise. This was always so. In spiritual affairs this *prosperity* is great. The labor of the believer is not in vain in the Lord. All good works, pious desires, holy purposes shall in the end be found seeds of immortal bliss.

4. *The ungodly* are *not so.* There is a difference in character and prospects between the righteous and the wicked. The latter are not really blessed in anything. To such Jehovah says, "I will curse your blessings." Mal. ii. 2. They walk in the counsel of the ungodly, stand in the way of sinners, sit in the seat of the scornful; their delight is not in the law of the LORD, neither do they meditate in God's word day and night; nor are they like a well watered tree, bringing forth seasonable fruit, and covered with green foliage; and whatsoever they do shall in the end work their shame and overthrow. A sad and utter defeat of all their plans awaits the ungodly. For they are *like the chaff which the wind driveth away.* The chaff is nothing compared to the wheat. It is light, and when the wheat is winnowed, the chaff is carried by the wind from the threshing floor. Sudden removal awaits the worthless chaff. This is a figure often found in Scripture. John Baptist says that Christ "will burn up the chaff with unquenchable fire." The worthlessness of sinners for any purpose but to be burned is fearfully argued by an inspired prophet. Ezek. xv. The wicked are a lie. They are vanity. They shall soon and terribly disappear. They shall be driven away in their wickedness. When they cry, Peace and safety, then sudden destruction cometh. Bloody and deceitful men do not live out half their days. If the enemies of God as a class were as long lived as his friends, the state of society would be well nigh intolerable. One pious man often outlives several generations of the violent, the dissipated, and the debauched. The death of many wicked men is appalling. The signals of distress held out by expiring nature show that all is lost. The wicked often boast in great swelling words what they will do; but the first breath of the divine displeasure makes them mourn sore like doves, yea, roar like bears. It is proof of dreadful blindness that the wicked do not see what the end will be. The sign of their coming defeat, the tokens of their approaching

perdition are many, clear and alarming. Their reluctance to a removal from earth will not delay their departure. The wind will *drive* them away. One said, "O doctor, I will give you my plantation, if you will save my life." Voltaire offered a great sum to his physician, if he would prolong his life for a few months. A great monarch once said, "A world of wealth for an inch of time." No wonder Balaam was unwilling to die the death of the ungodly. It requires no grace, but only a little thought and common sense to make any man anxious to avoid such an end, as is coming on all the ungodly.

5. The death of the wicked is but the beginning of their overthrow. After death is the last account. *The ungodly shall not stand in the judgment.* To *stand* is to maintain one's cause, to hold one's own, to be unhurt and unterrified. But in the last day the wicked will have no confidence, no comfort, no support. Edwards: "They will not carry their cause." They will cry to the rocks and to the mountains to hide them from the face of the Judge and from the wrath of the Lamb. There is no evidence that the judgment here spoken of is the tribunal of man. Clearly the reference is to the judgment of God. Horne: "The *judgment* here intended is evidently the last judgment; the congregation of the righteous is their assembly at the judgment-seat of Christ."

Nor shall sinners stand in the congregation of the righteous. Now the people of God are dispersed all over the world. But a day is coming when they shall be *congregated.* Then shall be made an eternal separation between God's friends and God's foes. The general assembly and church of the First-born gathered in heaven is and ever shall be composed of all the choice spirits of the universe. Into the temple not made with hands shall enter nothing that defileth, or that loveth and maketh a lie. In this life the holy and the unholy are often found together at the Lord's table. The tares and wheat grow together until the harvest. The sheep and goats herd together till the Chief Shepherd shall appear. It is a blessed fact respecting the heavenly state, that there the wicked cease from troubling and the weary are at rest.

6. The great difference between saints and sinners shall soon appear, for *the* LORD *knoweth the way of the righteous.* God has a perfect understanding of the real character of his people. His omniscience is their guaranty against their being at last confounded with the wicked. Charnock: "Without such a knowledge and discerning, men would not have their due; nay, a judgment just for the matter would be unjust in the manner, because unjustly passed, without an understanding of the merit of the cause. It is necessary, therefore, that the Supreme Judge of the world should not be thought to be blindfold when he distributes his rewards and punishments, and muffle his face when he passes his sentence. It is necessary to ascribe to him the knowledge of men's thoughts and intentions; the secret wills and aims; the hidden works of darkness in every man's conscience, because every man's work is to be measured by the will and inward frame. It is necessary that he should perpetually retain all those things in the indelible and plain records of his memory, that there may not be any work without a just proportion of what is due to it. This is the glory of God to discover the secrets of all hearts at last; as 1 Cor. iv. 5: *The Lord shall bring to light the hidden things of darkness, and will make manifest the counsels of all hearts, and then shall every man have praise of God.* This knowledge fits him to be a judge." The reason why the *ungodly shall not stand in judgment,* is because God knows their ways, which is implied in his *knowing the way of the righteous.* Hengstenberg: "The *knowing* here comprehends *blessing* in itself as its necessary consequence. If the way of the righteous, their lot, is known by God as the omniscient, it cannot but be blessed by him as the righteous." To *know* also signifies to *approve,* to *love,* to *deal mercifully with.* Amos iii. 2: Matt. vii. 23. Grotius renders it, *approveth.* Thus much the word often signi-

fies. No love of man is comparable to the amazing tenderness of God to all his people. He pities like a God. He approves the graces implanted by his own Spirit, he loves his chosen with an everlasting love, he deals mercifully with all who put their trust in him. Bradley would read it, "The Lord shall cause the way of the righteous to be known." This is no improvement.

But the way of the ungodly shall perish, because God knows his folly and hardness of heart. Every divine perfection makes certain the ruin of wicked men. Their natural life shall cease, and with it all their pomp, and pride, and power, and plans, and pleasures, and hopes, and boastings. The rebels shall not always seem to have it their way. A full end will be made of their triumphing. Their way *shall perish.* Nothing is more certain, nothing is more dreadful. Some say that they do not believe their Maker will ever become their enemy, but they ought to take his word on that point: "He that made them will not have mercy on them, and he that formed them will show them no favor." Is. xxvii. 11. All the wicked are doing work for repentance —either for saving repentance in time, or for fruitless regrets in hell. "What the fool does in the end, the wise man does in the beginning."

DOCTRINAL AND PRACTICAL REMARKS.

1. It has ever been and will ever be true that if men would be saved, they must forsake bad company, v. 1. He who goes with a multitude to do evil, shall go with a multitude to suffer punishment. "The companion of fools shall be destroyed." He who persistently *walks,* and *stands,* and *sits* with the ungodly, shall *lie down* with them in hopeless sorrow. Bishop Hall: "I have often wondered how the fishes can retain their fresh taste, and yet live in salt waters, since everything partakes of the nature of the place where it abides, and of that which is around it. So it is with evil company, for besides that it blemisheth our reputation, and makes us thought evil of though we be good, it also inclines us insensibly to ill, and works in us, if not an approbation, yet a less dislike to those sins to which our eyes and ears are thus continually inured. For this reason, by the grace of God I will ever shun it. I may have a bad acquaintance, but I will never have a wicked companion."

2. All preaching and writing, which uniformly fail to draw a vigorous line between the friends and foes of God, cannot much profit men's souls. A discriminating statement of the truths of God's word is eminently scriptural. So we learn from the first Psalm and from all the sacred writers. Let the difference between sin and holiness, saints and sinners never be denied, never be forgotten. Eternity alone will show how great it is.

3. Wicked men naturally grow worse and worse. They first *walk* in evil courses; then they *stand* in the way of sinners; at length they *sit* in the scorner's chair. Ruffin: "To walk in the counsel of the ungodly is to consent to their wicked plots. To stand in the way of sinners is to persevere in evil works. To sit in the seat of the scornful is to teach others the evil which one practises himself." No one all of a sudden becomes very vile. There are crises in the lives of the wicked, but the approach to them is gradual. The unregenerate are very blind. The scorner thinks he is very philosophic, and free from whims and prejudices; but he is the dupe of his passions, the servant of sin, and the slave of the devil. Who has ever seen a candid infidel? Scorning is an old artifice to keep conscience quiet. Hengstenberg: "Religious mockery is as old as the fall." Beware of it and of all that leads to it. When a man commences a downward course, there is no telling where he will stop. Grace may arrest him at any stage in this life. Death may suddenly terminate his earthly career. Left to himself his eternal undoing is certain. Even scoffing alarms

him not, for the further he goes, the blinder he is. All sin hardens the heart, stupefies the conscience, and shuts out the light of truth.

4. Let no man think himself safe, because others, who lead a similar life, are not alarmed at their condition, v. 1. There is often a peculiar stillness just before the earthquake. Probably the sun rose as fair on the morning of the overthrow of the cities of the plain as it ever had done. The ungodly all around us may be making merry at threatened judgments. But that will not avert them. The sneers of the ungodly prove wrath to be near at hand. Their "judgment now of a long time lingereth not, and their damnation slumbereth not." 2 Pet. ii. 3.

5. It is a great thing to have a heart for religion, and for spiritual truth, v. 2. To *delight* in divine things is as necessary as to see their importance, or to believe their reality. We must love as well as know. If we have spiritual discernment we will have our affections engaged. No man can really perceive beauty without being affected by it.

6. He, who would be truly blessed, must become a student of Scripture. There is no substitute for this. God's word is able to make men wise unto salvation. It is quick and powerful. Nothing so penetrates the heart of man. With a good man it has authority. Even devils know and to some extent feel its power. Matt. iv. 11.

7. Any religion which sets aside God's law, is spurious. It is not the religion of the Psalmist, v. 2. It is not the religion of Jesus Christ. Matt. v. 17, 18. It is not the religion of his apostles. Rom. iii. 31. Antinomianism is one of the worst forms of error. It makes Christ the minister of sin.

8. It is no wonder that the truly pious grow in purity. Their thoughts dwell on the most ennobling themes. They meditate on God's word, v. 2. This gives an amazing elevation to their characters. And the Sanctifier specially blesses revealed truth to the spiritual good of all the saints. By faith we lay hold of the promises, and God fulfils them. Great and glorious truths are well suited to refine our natures.

9. Though this is a wicked and suffering world, yet even here the righteous have real blessedness, vv. 1, 3, 6. It is not complete as it shall be after the resurrection, nor perfect as it shall be immediately after death; but it is solid, genuine, and enduring. It is from God. Their reliance is on him, who knows how to give graces and comforts in right measure and in due season. The frames of the righteous vary, but their state is stable. The saving gifts of God are without repentance. With the saints something is settled. Their peace is secured by an everlasting covenant. Their principles are made strong by divine grace. They are like Mount Zion which cannot be moved, but abideth for ever. Clarke: "The most momentous concern of man is the state he shall enter upon after this short and transitory life is ended; and in proportion as eternity is of greater importance than time, so ought men to be solicitous upon what grounds their expectations with regard to that durable state are built, and on what assurances their hopes or their fears stand." Even the wicked often admit that for the next world the righteous have chosen the good part, which shall not be taken from them. In this life things may often happen to the righteous hard to be borne. Cummings: "The man, who is born again, and seeks to be holy, as God is holy, is like the poor captive bird in the cage. The cage cannot kill the bird; the bird cannot free itself from the cage; it can only still wait, and persevere, and sing, and seek, and look till the hour of its freedom. Its perfect emancipation into brighter realms and better days draws near."

But those, who deny that piety affords delights even in this life, are ignorant of its nature. It presents the most glorious themes, inspires the most blessed hopes, and affords the most elevated employments. Nothing in the service of God's people is degrading. It teaches the soul to lean on the bosom of God. South: "The pleasure of the religious man is an easy and portable pleasure, such an one as he carries about in his bosom, without alarming either the eye or the envy of the world. A man putting all his pleasures into this one is like a traveller's putting all his goods into one jewel; the value is the same, and the convenience greater." If any ask, what are the foundations of the advantages of the righteous over the ungodly, it is easy to show some of them. First, the just man has *truth* on his side. His hopes and his cause are not based in falsehood, in error, in deception, in disguise, in fiction, in fancy. Truth will outlive all its opposites, though for a time it may fall in the streets. So that any wise man would accept a good title to an acre, rather than a spurious title to leagues of land, would rather be charged with a murder, of which he was innocent, than be guilty of a murder, of which he was unsuspected. A truthful claim to a penny is really worth more than a fictitious claim to a pound. The reason is that in the end the truth, even in this life, does commonly appear. In the next world it cannot be concealed. "For there is nothing hid, which shall not be manifested; neither was anything kept secret, but that it should come abroad." Mark iv. 22. "Some men's sins are open beforehand, going before to judgment: and some men they follow after. Likewise also the good works of some are manifest beforehand: and they that are otherwise cannot be hid." 1 Tim. v. 24, 25. Again, the righteous is on the side of *duty*. He honestly intends and endeavors to do what is right, because it is right and obligatory. In the main even here it is found that fidelity brings the best rewards. Neglect of duty sometimes brings apparent ease and profit. But who would not prefer Joseph's dutifulness to Ahithophel's treachery? When the master is on a long journey, the lazy and disobedient servants may think their faithful brethren needlessly careful; but in the day of reckoning saints and sinners will alike see that a life spent in God's service ends happily, while a wicked life leads to misery alone. Besides, the people of God have *justice* on their side; and the impression is both general and well-founded that nothing forms a more ample shield to any one than having the right on his side. And the saints know that "God is not unrighteous to forget their work and labor of love." Moreover God with all his attributes is on the side of the righteous. "And if God be for us, who can be against us?" That is inspired reasoning. It is also clear and level to the apprehension of the simple. Nor is this all. The righteous consults his best *interests*. He puts the soul above the body, eternity above time, and he is right. If his soul is refreshed, he remembers that man shall not live by bread alone, but by every word that proceedeth out of the mouth of God. If a blessed eternity is before him, he well judges that it matters little how much he may suffer in this world. Nothing is of such moment as an eternal well-being. Nor are the righteous at war with their own consciences, or best feelings. Jesus Christ has often called his friends to sacrifice ease, fame, earthly goods, old friendships, and even life itself. But blessed be his name he never asked any man to defile his conscience, nor to tarnish his honor by an act of meanness. If Eugene Beauharnais will retain the imperial favor of his step-father Napoleon, he must publicly unite in approving the dishonor put on his own mother. But the Almighty never called one of his servants to do a base thing. God always leaves the good conscience and good principles intact; yea, he greatly strengthens them. How then can the righteous but be blessed?

Luther: "It is the practice of all men to inquire after blessedness, and there is no man on earth, who does not wish that it might go well with him, and would not feel sorrow if it went ill with him. But he, who speaks in this Psalm with a voice from heaven, beats down and condemns everything, which the thoughts of men might cogitate and devise in the matter, and brings forth the only true description of blessedness, of which the whole world knows nothing, declaring that he only is blessed and prosperous, whose love and desire are directed to the law of the Lord. This is a short description, and, indeed, one that goes against all sense and reason, especially against the reason of the worldly-wise and the high-minded. As if he had said, Why are ye so much in seeking counsel? why are ye ever in vain devising unprofitable things? There is but one precious pearl, and he has found it, whose love and desire is towards the law of the Lord, and who separates himself from the ungodly—all succeeds well with him. But whosoever does not find this pearl, though he should seek with ever so much pains and labor the way to blessedness, he shall never find it." The prophet Isaiah speaks to the same effect. Chap. lv. 2, 3.

10. Seldom do men forsake a wicked life, until they are convinced of its misery. Accordingly the Scriptures honestly tell them of their wretchedness, vv. 4, 5, 6. The prodigal never came to himself till he began to feed swine. Virtue does not indeed consist in merely seeking happiness; but it is useful to us to see that pain follows sinful pleasure, and that a just God will not permit a course of wickedness to triumph over all goodness. Hell follows close on the heels of transgression. The rivers do not more naturally run into the sea, than does iniquity tend to ruin. On this point the word of God is clear and emphatic. Let wicked men know that they are poor and miserable. Rom. iii. 16; Rev. iii. 17.

11. The ungodly, however moral, or amiable, or confident of their good estate, are yet destitute of spiritual life, of God's favor, of holy tempers, of well-grounded hopes, vv. 4, 5, 6. The fact is they have much to weep over, and nothing to rejoice in. The list of their wants is appalling. Paul sums up their case in the lack of five things; they are without God, without Christ, without the church, without the covenant, without hope, Eph. ii. 12. Is not this enough to fill any thoughtful man with alarm? A human arm separated from the body, of which it is a member, cannot live. It must perish. So a soul, separated from God, must lose all resources of permanent happiness and in the end be filled with all misery. Even that which the wicked seem to have, shall presently be taken away; all their works and expectations shall be driven away like chaff.

12. The doctrine of eternal judgment is no novelty, v. 5. It was preached with awful solemnity to the sinners of the old world. Jude 14, 15. It is clearly taught in the first Psalm. "Ewald justly refers the words [of verse 5] to the progression of the divine righteousness, which is perpetually advancing, though not every moment visible. All manifestations of punitive righteousness are comprehended in it. 'For God will bring every work into judgment, with every secret thing, whether it be good or whether it be evil.' " Eccle. xii. 14. Let the wicked prepare to meet their God. There must be a judgment. God has said so. Justice requires it.

13. One of the most striking effects of the last judgment will be a perfect and eternal separation between the righteous and the wicked, v. 5. Thenceforth they can meet no more for ever. Here they often live together, protected by the same laws, inhabiting the same city, frequenting the same places of worship, of business and of recreation, members of the same family, or lying in the same bed; and yet when on the last day they shall part, their intercourse shall never be renewed, while eternity endures. The apparent confusion of things in this present state will all give way to a great and blessed clearing up and an eternal separation of the sheep from the goats.

14. What a blessed gathering of the righteous that shall be, when the doves shall all come to their windows, the sheep all be in the one fold far from the prowl of wild beasts, the children all be gathered to their Father's house with its many mansions, the exiles return to their own city in everlasting peace and with everlasting joy. The righteous have and shall have the opposite of the wicked, as is implied in v. 5. Nor is the rest of the righteous inconsistent with eternal activity, nor with the perfection

of the communion of saints. The Scriptures often represent heaven as a social state. The church on earth is a type of the church above. Let us not hopelessly mourn our departed brethren in Christ. They are in the city of God. "There are our treasures, changeless and shining treasures. Let us look hopefully. They are not lost, but gone before; lost only like stars of the morning that have faded into the light of a brighter heaven: lost to the earth, but not to us."

15. The miseries of the wicked will in part be social, v. 5. They shall not stand in the congregation of the righteous; but they shall mingle with all the vile and malignant of fallen angels and incorrigible men. Isa. xiv. 9–19. Their doom and woes will be dreadful. Christ "will burn up the chaff with unquenchable fire." Matt. iii. 12. To denote eternal and irretrievable ruin God has employed a variety of speech indicating insufferable anguish. *The way of the ungodly shall perish.* And all the woe of the wicked shall be the fruit of their own doings. They shall reap what they have sowed, and not something else. Their way leads to hell and no where else.

16. It should be a great business of our lives to examine ourselves, whether we are righteous or ungodly. To this end in part this whole Psalm is given us. An aversion to this duty is no good sign. We have all much cause for noting the words of Luther: "When Scripture speaks of the ungodly, take heed that thou thinkest not, as the ungodly ever do, as if it referred to Jews and heathens, or, perhaps also to other persons; but present thyself also before this word, as what respects and concerns also thee. For a right-hearted and gracious man is jealous of himself, and trembles before every word of God." The truth will come out. No man will make his case worse by honestly looking into it. Some have escaped a dreadful overthrow by finding out in time that they were self-deceived. Amyrald: "Although the providence of God, whose ways are sometimes unsearchable, does not always place so remarkable a distinction between the righteous and the wicked, still the future life shall so distinguish them, that no one shall be longer able to doubt, who they are that follow the path of true prosperity." Of all the follies of men none can be worse than that of hiding from themselves their true condition and character.

17. Let us learn the art of applying God's word to our own cases. Whoever thus employs this Psalm shall be much profited. It is a poor thing to hide the truth from our hearts by a mere regard to the letter of Scripture. Criticism, when cold, is as likely to mislead us as anything else. We must have divine illumination and spiritual unction, else all our learning will but make us the greater fools. Many a man's knowledge, because unsanctified, serves but as a torch to light him to hell. He trusts in himself that he is in no danger, because he studies the Scriptures with taste and judgment, but forgets that spiritual discernment is essential to salvation. McCheyne's method of applying Scripture was to turn each verse into a prayer.

18. The plain and clear teachings of Scripture are the weighty matters, claiming immediate and universal attention. He, who rightly heeds such truths as are taught in the first Psalm will find himself led along till he shall apprehend enough of God's will to be infallibly saved. The great mysteries of salvation are best understood by those, who rightly receive the simplest teachings of God's word, and so reduce them to practical use.

19. In all our study of God's word we must have faith. Heb. iv. 2. This grace of the Spirit is of the greatest importance. Without it we always go astray, live in darkness, and are made miserable by the stings inflicted by our own minds. "Nothing greater can be said of faith, than that it is the only thing, which can bid defiance to the accusations of conscience." This it does by beholding the Lamb of God, that taketh away the sin of the world. Christ Jesus is the only hope of perishing sinners.

PSALM II.

1 Why do the heathen rage, and the people imagine a vain thing?

2 The kings of the earth set themselves, and the rulers take counsel together, against the LORD, and against his anointed *saying*,

3 Let us break their bands asunder, and cast away their cords from us.

4 He that sitteth in the heavens shall laugh: the Lord shall have them in derision.

5 Then shall he speak unto them in his wrath, and vex them in his sore displeasure.

6 Yet have I set my king upon my holy hill of Zion.

7 I will declare the decree: the LORD hath said unto me, Thou *art* my Son; this day have I begotten thee.

8 Ask of me, and I shall give *thee* the heathen *for* thine inheritance, and the uttermost parts of the earth *for* thy possession.

9 Thou shalt break them with a rod of iron; thou shalt dash them in pieces like a potter's vessel.

10 Be wise now therefore, O ye kings: be instructed, ye judges of the earth.

11 Serve the LORD with fear, and rejoice with trembling.

12 Kiss the Son, lest he be angry, and ye perish *from* the way, when his wrath is kindled but a little.   Blessed *are* all they that put their trust in him.

INSPIRATION has determined that David was the author of this Psalm.   Acts iv. 25.   Knowing the authorship we are not very uncertain as to its probable date.   The most probable view is that it is now (1866) two thousand nine hundred and six years old.   That is, it was written ten hundred and forty years before Christ. Dodd thinks it certain that this Psalm was penned after the removal of the ark to Sion, because it expressly speaks of *the hill of God's holiness*.   It was not such till the ark there rested, ten hundred and forty-eight years before Christ.   Some think this Psalm was written ten hundred and forty-seven, B. C.

Like the first Psalm, this has no title, giving its theme, occasion, or author.   The reason may be that the matter is so plain as to require no formal announcement.   The great design of the Psalm is to foretell the hatred of men to the person and reign of Christ, the glories of Messiah, the triumphs of his kingdom, and the dreadful downfall of his foes, thus laying a proper ground for solemn exhortation to all men to yield themselves subjects of the Prince of life.   Henry: "As the foregoing Psalm was *moral,* and showed us our *duty,* so this is *evangelical,* and shows us our *Saviour.*" Alexander: "This is the first of those prophetic Psalms, in which the promise made to David, with respect to the Messiah (2 Sam. vii. 16, and 1 Chron. xvii. 11–14), is wrought into the lyrical devotions of the ancient church."   Here is a great and glorious prophecy respecting our Lord Jesus Christ.   Let us study it with earnestness, humility and reverence.

Rivet and others have noticed that the form of this Psalm is dramatic.   Alexander " Little as this Psalm may, at first sight, seem to resemble that before it, there is really a very strong affinity between them.   Even in form they are related to each other. The number of verses and of stanzas is just double in the second, which moreover begins, as the first ends, with a threatening, and ends, as the first begins, with a beatitude.   There is also a resemblance in their subject and contents.   The contrast indicated in the first is carried out and rendered more distinct in the second.   The first is in fact an introduction to the second, and the second to what follows."   All divine truth is nearly related.

From three sources we are led to regard this Psalm as highly Messianic.   1. This view was so obvious that the old Jewish interpreters uniformly admitted its application to Christ. Jarchi, who flourished in the 12th century, says: "Our doctors have expounded this Psalm of the Messiah; but that we may answer the heretics (Christians) it is expedient to interpret it of David's person, as the words sound." Cocceius: "The ancient Hebrews with the Chaldee beyond a doubt take this Psalm as respecting Christ. Even Abenezra confesses that, if it is applied to Christ, it is far more clear and free from difficulty than if applied to David or some other king." Other interpreters follow the same train of thought. Bellarmine: "This whole Psalm is a most manifest prophecy concerning the kingdom of Christ." Henry: "This Psalm, as the former, is very fitly prefixed to this book of devotions, because, as it is necessary to our acceptance with God, that we should be subject to the precepts of his law, so it is likewise, that we should be subject to the grace of his gospel, and come to him in the name of a Mediator." Pool expounds it of Christ, but does not deny that the reign of David was a type of the kingdom of Christ. Many others have expressed the same views. 2. The matter of this Psalm shows that it respects Messiah. There are in it things which no law of language allows us to apply to any but Christ. Such are expressions found in verses 7, 8, and 12: "Thou art my Son," "I will give thee the uttermost parts of the earth for thy possession," "Kiss the Son," etc. Hengstenberg justly lays great stress on the fact that "two names of the Messiah, which were current in the time of Christ—the name of Messias itself, the anointed—and the name, Son of God, applied by Nathaniel in his conversation with Christ, John i. 49, and also by the high-priest in Matt. xxvi. 63, owed their origin to this Psalm in its Messianic meaning." 3. We have various inspired expositions of this Psalm. All the apostles in Acts iv. 24–27, Paul in Acts xiii. 33, and in Heb. i. 5, 8, and v. 5, and John in Rev. ii. 27, xix. 15, have put the matter beyond all fair dispute. Fabritius fitly regards the last two reasons here given as "infallible arguments."

Still the question recurs, Is not David in this Psalm a type of Christ? or is the Psalm purely prophetic without a type? It is not well needlessly to make types. So it is best not to say that there is a type here. We can explain the grammatical construction of every clause, and clearly get the whole sense without supposing that David is here a type. If David had never existed and if some other prophet, as Samuel or Isaiah, had written this Psalm, its doctrines would have been precisely the same as they are now, without a shade of difference even in their force. Why then should we insist on regarding David as here set forth a type of Christ? Besides, it would be simply profane to apply to David some of the phrases here used. At the same time there is no objection to supposing that the imagery of this Psalm was drawn from events happening in the reign of David. The ancient games furnished forms of expression, and illustrations to the mind of Paul, but they were not types of what he taught. Although not fully concurring in this view, Rivet admits that "nearly all the orthodox take this Psalm as simply and immediately referring to Christ, and interpret it accordingly." Beveridge: "The whole Psalm is to be understood of Christ and of him only." Scott: "The occasion of this Psalm might be taken from David's advancement to the throne, and his expectation of triumphing over the opposition made to his authority both by disaffected Israelites and the surrounding nations, (Notes, 2 Sam. ii. 4–9 and v.,) but it is throughout an evident prophecy of Christ, and repeatedly quoted as such in the New Testament."

From what has been said of the contents of this Psalm the reader will not expect expressions of deep emotion. Elevation and majesty more become the topic treated by the prophet. In other places we shall find the most tender and pathetic expressions of feeling.

1. *Why do the heathen rage?* The Syriac reads, Wherefore are the nations agi-

tated? The Arabic: Why are peoples disturbed? Calvin: Why do the nations rise tumultuously? church of England: Why do the heathen so furiously rage together? Edwards: Why do the heathen tumultuously bandy together? Fry, regarding the tense of the original: Why have the heathen raged? Alexander: *Why do nations make a noise,* tumultuate, or rage? The old marginal rendering of the verb is, Tumultuously assemble. *Why* is equivalent to, for what purpose? to what end? for what cause? That is, these madmen act without cause. Hengstenberg: "The *why* is an expression of astonishment and horror at the equally foolish and impious attempt of the revolters." Cocceius: "The form of interrogation concerning the cause points out the absurdity of the commotion, for Christ came not to take away the kingdoms of the world, but to bestow the kingdom of heaven on the nations. Why, therefore, are they in such commotion? *And why do the people imagine a vain thing?* The Syriac: Why do peoples plan vanity? Pool properly renders the verb in this clause in the future tense. Opposition to Christ is both old and lasting. Men have raged, and men shall meditate a thing of nought as long as wickedness reigns in their hearts. Calvin renders it, Why do the peoples murmur in vain? Alexander: Why will peoples imagine vanity? Henry thinks the whole verse refers exclusively to the temper of the Jews towards Christ. Burder thinks it refers exclusively to the hostility of the Gentiles. But why confine the sense to so narrow limits? The hatred of all wicked men to Christ is of old and has long been notorious. It is not confined to any nation. When he was a stumbling-block to the Jews, he was foolishness to the Greeks. History is full of accounts of this enmity against Christ. Every government on earth has some anti-christian laws or usages. But we have an inspired interpretation, applying this verse to all sorts of unrenewed men. In a prayer, common to them all, the apostles quote this and the next succeeding verses, and immediately add, "For of a truth against thy holy child Jesus, whom thou hast anointed, both Herod and Pontius Pilate, with the Gentiles and the people of Israel, were gathered together." Acts iv. 27.

2. By *the kings of the earth* the Psalmist points out those who have supreme power in the government of the world; and by *the rulers,* the princes, or chief persons under kings, men in power, senators, governors, privy counsellors. All these meet and plot. There is tumult and rage among them. This is followed on the part of the great ones by meetings, consultations, unions, confederations, and fixed purposes of hostility. Calvin renders it, The kings of the earth have confederated, and the princes have assembled together; Fabritius: The kings of earth convene and the princes consult together; Waterland: The kings of the earth rise up, and the rulers assemble together; Edwards makes the whole of the second verse like the first interrogative; Chandler: The kings of the earth set themselves in opposition, and instigate each other; Hengstenberg: The kings of the earth set themselves and the rulers sit with one another [for the purposes of counsel;] Alexander, following the tense of the original: (Why will) the kings of earth set themselves? or the kings of earth will set themselves, and rulers consult together. The word rendered *assemble* is probably to be taken in a military sense, rendezvous, post, or muster. So thinks Edwards. They do all this against the Lord [Jehovah] and against his anointed [Messiah.] Their quarrel, and mustering of forces, and laying of plots is "against all religion in general, and the Christian religion in particular." They are averse to true natural religion and to true revealed religion. The enemies of God are of two classes. Some know what they are doing, and their whole behaviour is in despite and malice and against much light. Others sin ignorantly, in unbelief, not knowing what they do, even when they commit the foulest deeds. Luke xxiii. 24; Acts iii. 17; 1 Cor. ii. 8; 1 Tim. i. 13. While such ignorance saves one from the fixed doom of the unpardon-

able sin, it does by no means remove guilt. The ignorance is itself sinful. Paul never forgave himself for having murdered the saints. He always thought that he had hardly escaped damnation for his persecutions. Men may fully evince hostility contrary to their earnest protestations. The great mass of wicked men lose their souls without intending any such thing. It is also clear that Jehovah regards opposition to his Christ as opposition to himself. The reason is given in Scripture: "I and my Father are one." John x. 30. "The Father is in me, and I in him." John x. 38. "He that receiveth me receiveth him that sent me." Matt. x. 40. "He that hath seen me hath seen the Father." John xiv. 9. "All things that the Father hath are mine." John xvi. 15. "And all mine are thine, and thine are mine." John xvii. 10. "He that believeth on me, believeth not on me, but on him that sent me, and he that seeth me, seeth him that sent me." John xii. 44, 45. See also John xiv. 20 and xv. 23. So that Jehovah and Messiah are one—one in nature—one in counsel—one in government. Therefore none can war against the Son without contending against the Father. Nor can any approach the Father but by the Son. John xiv. 6. The title Messiah, Christ, Anointed, here given to the Son of God, is very proper. Christ was anointed to his burial, but not to his office of Mediator, by any costly ointment prepared after the art of the apothecary. The oil of gladness poured on him was the Holy Ghost. Ps. xlv. 7; Heb. i. 9. This anointing of Christ is much spoken of. Luke iii. 22; iv. 1, 14, 16–21. Christ received the Spirit not by measure. John iii. 34. The fulness of the Godhead dwelt in him bodily. Jesus was the anointed of God beyond all others, or, as the Psalmist elsewhere expresses it, above his fellows. Ps. xlv. 7. He is the only anointed Saviour. All the enemies of Jehovah and of his Anointed thus expressed their hostility:

3. *Let us break their bands asunder, and cast away their cords from us.* The bands and cords are those of Jehovah and of his Anointed. To be bound and to feel bound to the Father and to his Son cannot but distress the ungodly. Calvin: "All the enemies of Christ, when compelled to be subject to his authority, reckon it not less degrading than if the utmost disgrace were put upon them;" Alexander: "The form of the Hebrew verb in this verse may be expressive either of a proposition or of a fixed determination. *We will break their bands*, we are resolved to do it. . . *And we will cast*, or *let us cast away from us their cords*, twisted ropes, a stronger term than *bands*." The *authority* of Christ human wickedness greatly abhors. Had he taught the great principles of morality found in the Gospels, but done it as a pharisee or philosopher, merely proposing things, there had never been such an outcry against him. But he asserts his *right* to *rule* mankind, and so men rebel against him. The kingly office of our Saviour is cordially hated by the unrenewed. God says, "They will reverence my Son." They reply, "We will not have this man to reign over us." Horne: "Doctrines will be readily believed, if they involve in them no precepts; and the church may be tolerated by the world, if she will only give up her discipline." If one of the propositions of Euclid, instead of proving what it does, did with equal clearness prove that men ought to be subject to Christ, the wicked would claim to have found a flaw in the argument. The enmity of the human heart rises higher against Christ, his authority, and his salvation than against anything else. The old controversy between Cain and Abel respected the Saviour. The strife was continued throughout the patriarchal dispensation. Abraham saw Christ's day and rejoiced in it, but the great mass of his cotemporaries despised, and wondered, and perished. Before the exodus from Egypt the great cause of the contempt which covered the Israelites was "the reproach of Christ." They were despised for looking for a Deliverer. And when his birth was announced "Herod was troubled and all Jerusalem with him." The greatest test of character to which men were ever subjected, is Jesus Christ himself. Nothing so

manifests their real dispositions towards God. Well did Simeon say, "This child is set for the fall and rising again of many in Israel; and for a sign, which shall be spoken against, . . . that the thoughts of many hearts may be revealed." Luke ii. 34, 35. Soon and strangely did the Pharisees and Herodians take counsel, how they might destroy him. Mark iii. 6. In less than three years after the public ministry of our Lord commenced, his enemies compassed his death. How dreadful were the persecutions of the followers of Christ by Nero, who put Paul and many Christians to death; by Domitian, who banished John to Patmos, and practised many refined cruelties; by Trajan, who threw Ignatius to the wild beasts; by Commodus, Severus, Maximin, Decius, and Diocletian, and by the apostate Julian, who forbade the Christians to give their children the advantages of a liberal education, and by many others down even to our own times. Venema: "What insanity has possessed Jews and Gentiles, and what unaccountable rage moves them, that without reason or any hope of final success they should thus cruelly and violently oppose themselves to the true religion and to the propagation of the Gospel! On one side the people seditiously rush upon the Christians and with horrible clamors drag them to destruction. On the other hand kings and governors of provinces, and emperors, even the Cæsars, deliberately consult to destroy the church by the direst persecutions, laboring even to blot out the Christian name." Jews, Infidels, Mahommedans, Pagans, and nominally Christian powers and people have all in their turn poured out their cruel scorn against the friends of Christ. So it always has been, and so it always shall be till "the kingdoms of the world shall become the kingdoms of our Lord, and of his Christ, and he shall reign forever and ever." Rev. ii. 15.

4. But to put down the kingdom of Christ is impossible. All this rage and malice are to such an end impotent. The war is unequal. Rivet: "It is as if a fly should attack an elephant, or a man endeavor to snatch the sun from the firmament." Morison compares all this tumult to "the effort of an infant to stay the whirlwind, or the unavailing yell of the maniac to calm the raging of the sea." Henry: "The moon walks in brightness though the dogs bark at it." No marvel, then, that "*He that sitteth in the heavens shall laugh: the Lord shall have them in derision.*" There is not an agreement in different copies respecting the original word, here rendered, Lord. In the best editions of our English Bible, *Lord* is not put in capitals, as it would be if it was regarded as a translation of *Jehovah*. In the Hebrew Bibles now in common use, the original word, rendered Lord, is *Adonai*. Yet Street tells us that "Sixty manuscripts of Dr. Kennicott's collection, and twenty-five of De Rossi's, have *Jehovah* here. And Dimock says, "Sixty-six manuscripts have Jehovah." The annotator of Calvin increases the difficulty when he informs us that in the Hebrew Bibles to which he had access, the original is *Elohai*. If this is the true reading, then we have a name which is supposed by many to be peculiarly appropriate in designating the object of religious worship. If *Adonai* is the right word, then we have the Ruler of the world pointed out. This is a name given sometimes to magistrates. Though the latter is perhaps the reading to be preferred, yet either gives a good sense, and either is applicable to the Sovereign of the universe, who puts no trust in his servants, who charges his angels with folly, before whom the moon shineth not, and in whose sight the stars are not pure, the nations are as a drop of a bucket, and are counted as the small dust of the balance. All nations are before him as nothing; and they are counted to him less than nothing and vanity. He sitteth upon the circle of the earth, and the inhabitants thereof are as grasshoppers. But to whom does the word *Lord* refer? to the Father or to the Son? This cannot be determined by the original, as Jehovah, Adonai, and Elohai are alike proper to either the Father or the Son. The only ground for determining that it distinctly refers to the Son, is that the Psalmist had previously intro-

duced both persons and spoken of *their* bands and *their* cords, that both are subsequently spoken of, and that the parallelism would suggest that both be mentioned in this verse. But, on the other hand, only one person is mentioned in the next verse, and this verse belongs to the same strophe as that. Nor is it necessary always rigidly to keep up the distinction between the divine persons, where acts or works common to them are spoken of. Creation and the resurrection are both specially ascribed to each person of the divine nature, yet it is proper to say that the world was made and that the dead shall be raised by God without specifying any one person of the Trinity. On this verse Hilary quotes John v. 21–23, and adds that "the distinction of honor or dishonor towards the persons of the Father and Son is not carefully preserved; that true piety equally respects both, and that contempt of one is a wrong to the other. He who despises either despises both. Both are one in divinity and glory. In true religion, both are one in honor. So that those who rise up against the Lord rise up also against his Christ. And those who are laughed at by him who sitteth in the heavens, those also the Lord holds in derision."

To *laugh* and *have in derision* are forms of expression borrowed from human emotions and actions. To let us know the divine mind and determination, God is said to repent, to be angry, to be pitiful, because these phrases are understood by us, and so we get some idea of our Maker. But God is without passions. He weeps not. He laughs not. In Job xli. 29, it is said that "Leviathan laugheth at the shaking of a spear." No one is thus led to suppose that this sea-monster has any emotion corresponding to laughter among men, but as men in a state of safety, and sure of a victory over their adversaries, may and sometimes do laugh them to scorn, even when they are in the height of their power, so God derides the assaults of his foes. Henry: "Sinners' follies are the just sport of God's infinite wisdom and power; and those attempts of the kingdom of Satan, which in our eyes are formidable, in his are despicable."

The incorrigibly wicked shall pass away from earth "into shame and everlasting contempt." Nothing but its wickedness can equal the folly of sin.

5. This silent contempt of God for his foes and their plots shall continue until the time chosen by infinite wisdom for a display of his glorious justice. *Then*, when their iniquity shall be full, when all men shall have seen his long-suffering towards them, and when it shall appear that they did but harden themselves in pride engendered by his mercies, *Then shall he speak unto them in his wrath, and vex them in his sore displeasure.*" To *speak* unto them is to make known his will by his acts. In men, actions speak louder than words. God's doings are mighty. His acts are terrible. He made the heathen tremble by the mighty deeds he did for Israel. When God lets out his wrath, men are troubled, and even nature stands aghast. The very mountains melt at his presence, and the sea flees before him. Into the destruction of the wicked enters every element that can heighten their misery. It is *just*, and so they cannot blame any other being. Every mouth will be stopped. Every sinner will be speechless. It is *unnecessary*, and might have been avoided, if sin had not been loved. Nothing but iniquity makes the doom of the finally impenitent what it is. Every man would have been wiser, better, happier, more useful, if he had fled from the wrath to come. It is *complete*, involving soul and body. It is a total destruction. Then it is *hopeless*. On the darkness of that gloom, which envelops them, no star ever rises, no light ever breaks. And it comes with *surprise*. They were not looking for it. They did not intend it. They did not expect it. When they cry, Peace and safety, then it is just at hand. It is an *eternal* destruction. There is no end to it. There can be no bounds set to it. God will vex the wicked by turning all their plans upside down. The people, whom they cursed and tormented, shall yet be made to appear

blessed and enter into rest. The religion which the wicked opposed shall yet triumph. The Saviour, whom they despised, shall yet see all knees bowing before him, and shall yet hear all tongues confessing to him. Jehovah, against whom they consulted, will exalt his Son and glorify himself transcendently. Dimock reads the last clause of this verse, The Lord shall strike them with a panic.

6. God will treat the wicked as they deserve: *Yet have I set my king upon my holy hill of Zion.* The Septuagint, Arabic, and Vulgate: But I have been made King by Him on Zion, his holy hill. Thus Christ is made the speaker here. But this is taking too large liberty with the original. Instead of *yet,* Pool would read *for,* or *in the meantime.* Alexander prefers *and;* as if it read, *You* pursue your course and *I* mine. *You* rage and *I* set my King on Zion. For *set,* the margin correctly reads *anointed.* Christ was anointed that he might be King. Scott: "When the priests and rulers prevailed on Pilate to crucify their anointed King, they eventually forwarded his exaltation." Luther: "Who thought, when Christ suffered and the Jews triumphed, that God was laughing all the time?" God says, I have set *my* king on Zion. Christ is God's equal, God's fellow, God's Son, God's first-born, God's only-begotten, and is by him chosen and set up as King forever. Luther's note is, "I have appointed a King as most closely related to me." Hengstenberg much prefers this to the modern expositions. Christ is *set, anointed, constituted* King in Zion. The gifts and calling of God even to his people are without repentance. Surely then he will never permit his Son, his elect, in whom his soul delighteth, to be dethroned. This point is so well settled in God's word and in the faith of his people, that saints are not even tempted to believe that Christ has ceased or shall cease to occupy the mediatorial throne. God is not a man, that he should repent.

7. For he acts according to a fixed plan, a holy purpose, a *decree.* If God should change his plan, it must be either for the better or the worse. If it could be changed for the better, then it is not now perfect. This is contrary to Scripture. Deut. xxxii. 4; 2 Sam. xxii. 22, 31; Ps. xviii. 30. If he should change for the worse, then who could have confidence in him? But his counsel shall stand. It is of old. It is faithfulness and truth. He does not say, I will *form* the decree. It had been formed in the counsels of eternity. But Christ, who is that Prophet, the great Teacher of the church, says, *I will declare the decree, q. d.,* I will now make known and publish abroad God's free, sovereign, eternal purpose, and let my enemies know that his determination is fixed. He is the Lord, and changes not. The speaker in this verse is he, who has been set as King in Zion. *The Lord* [Jehovah] *hath said unto me, Thou* art *my Son.* The stability of Christ's kingdom, rendering certain the defeat of his enemies, rests on three things; 1. On the anointing and setting up of Christ as King, v. 6; 2. On the fixedness of God's purpose; 3. On the relation subsisting between Jehovah and Christ, *Thou art my Son.* What is the full import of this language? Angels are in one book thrice called "Sons of God." Job i. 6; ii. 1; xxxviii. 7. Adam is called "the Son of God," Luke iii. 38. Pious men are called "Sons of God," Gen. vi. 2; Rom. viii. 14; 1 John iii. 1. But Paul proves that in the highest sense the angels are never called sons. Heb. i. 5. "For unto which of the angels said he at any time, Thou art my Son, this day have I begotten thee?"

Others may be God's sons inasmuch as he made them, or by his Spirit renewed them, and by his grace adopted them; but Christ is God's Son by an essential and eternal Sonship. Christ has the same nature and attributes with the Father, and his relation to him is rightly expressed by the name *Son.* In this sense he is the only-begotten of the Father. In nature and in all things he has the pre-eminence over all others ever called sons of God. The filiation of Christ is ineffable and unparalleled. Gill: "Christ is the true, proper, natural, and eternal Son of God, and as such declared, owned, and acknowledged by Jehovah the Father." *This day have I begotten thee.* The opposition to the Sonship of Christ has been strange and very determined. Even good men have often been led to make erroneous concessions on the subject, while the enemies of the doctrine have displayed great ingenuity in endeavoring to sap this foundation of hope. Some have contended that the words of v. 7 refer to his incarnation. Though his coming in the flesh was not his Sonship, nor the means of attaining his Sonship, yet it was an illustrious proof of it, and is so referred to in Scripture. The angel, who visited Mary said, " The Holy Ghost shall come upon thee, and the power of the Highest shall overshadow thee : therefore also that holy thing, which shall be born of thee, shall be called the Son of God." Luke i. 35. Nor was his public entrance on his ministry the beginning, or the ground of his Sonship, though on that occasion God did publicly own him ; for " lo, a voice from heaven, saying, This is my beloved Son, in whom I am well pleased." Matt. iii. 17. The same happened at his transfiguration. Mark ix. 7. A modern author contends that in Rom. i. 4, *declared* means *constituted*. He labors to show that Christ was *constituted* the Son of God by his resurrection. But twice before Christ's death God publicly from heaven declared Christ to be his Son. And the word in Rom. i. 4, beyond all reasonable doubt is properly rendered *declared, defined, marked out, distinguished from all others.* Nor was any subsequent step in his exaltation his Sonship or the ground of it. For his Sonship is the ground of his exaltation. The inheritance follows Sonship ; not Sonship the inheritance. See next verse. Samson : " Nor was the Sonship constituted by his exaltation ; for the apostles conjointly apply the circumstances of this Psalm to the persecutions which Christ suffered prior to his resurrection (and therefore prior to his exaltation), beginning with the attempts of Herod to destroy him, and ending with his sufferings under Pilate. See Acts iv. 24–28. Nor may anything be inferred to the contrary from the use which Paul makes of Ps. ii. 7, in Acts xiii. 33, " God hath fulfilled the same unto us their children, in that he hath raised up Jesus again ; as it is also written in the second Psalm, Thou art my Son ; this day have I begotten thee ;" for a careful examination of the apostle's speech on that occasion will show that he used the passage to prove the fulfilment of the promise made to the fathers. Compare verses 23 and 32. And this was a promise not of Christ's resurrection ; but that he should be raised up as a Saviour to Israel. Our translators have there rendered the original word, " raised up *again,*" gratuitously ; for the meaning of the promise is, that God would *rear a Saviour* for Israel. In proof of this the apostle *afterwards* proceeds, in v. 34, to raise his resurrection as a separate point, and, to support it, quotes a passage altogether different but appropriate. When thus explained, Paul makes the same primary and special application of the second Psalm in Acts xiii. 33, which the other apostles do in Acts iv. 24–28, viz : to the period of the Son's incarnation ; and the passage quoted proves the Sonship of Christ not only in, but *previous* to his incarnation." Some have harped much on the words *this day* in this verse, as implying that Christ's Sonship was of recent date, and not eternal. But let us remember that the speaker in this verse is He, that inhabiteth eternity and says, " Before the day was I am he." Is. xliii. 13 and lvii. 15. With him one day is as a thousand years and a thousand years as a day. 2 Pet. iii. 8. Owen : " To-day, being spoken of God, of him who is eternal, to whom all time is so present as that nothing is properly yesterday, nor to-day, does not denote necessarily such a proportion of time, as is intimated. But it is expressive of an act eternally present, nor past, nor future." Alexander has set this matter in a clear light : " This profound sense of the passage is no more excluded by the phrase *this day*, implying something recent, than the universality of Christ's dominion is excluded by the local reference to Zion. The point of time, like the point of space, is the centre of an infinite circle.

Besides, the mere form of the declaration is a part of the dramatic scenery or costume, with which the truth is here invested. The ideas of a king, a coronation, a hereditary succession, are all drawn from human and temporal associations. *This day have I begotten thee* may be considered therefore as referring only to the coronation of Messiah, which is an ideal one. The essential meaning of the phrase *I have begotten thee* is simply this, *I am thy father.* The antithèsis is perfectly identical with that in 2 Sam. vii. 14, " I will be his father, and he shall be my son." Had the same form of expression been used here, *this day am I thy father,* no reader would have understood *this day* as limiting the mutual relation of the parties, however it might limit to a certain point of time the formal recognition of it. It must also be observed, that even if *this day* be referred to the inception of the filial relation, it is thrown indefinitely back by the form of reminiscence or narration in the first clause of the verse. *Jehovah said to me,* but when? If understood to mean from everlasting or eternity, the form of expression would be perfectly in keeping with the other figurative forms by which the Scriptures represent things really ineffable in human language." This view relieves the passage of the difficulty arising from the use of the term *to-day,* as stated by Venema, and makes all consistent throughout. Every other exposition of this verse arrays one inspired man against another.

8. The doctrine of the kingdom and sonship of Christ, is immediately followed by the doctrine of his priesthood, one branch of which office is intercession, and we are at once told of its prevalence with God. Here is Christ's "patent for his office of Advocate." True, the high priest under the law entered the holy of holies and interceded for the people. But here we have the doctrine of the pleading of our great high priest stated without a figure. If we can fairly build any doctrine on the intercession of Christ, we may be assured that there is no firmer pillar of truth. This secures the recovery of the regenerate from all their lapses. Luke xxii. 31, 32. Here is the ground of Christian steadfastness. Heb. iv. 14. This makes salvation certain to all believers. Heb. vii. 25. The intercession of Christ is always prevalent. John xi. 42. It secures the calling of the Gentiles, the success of missions, the final and complete triumph of the Gospel. Jehovah says to the Son, "*Ask of me, and I shall give* thee *the heathen* for *thine inheritance, and the uttermost parts of the earth for thy possession.*" The intercession of Christ is the hope of the world. John xvii. 20. Nothing can hinder the final triumph of the Gospel,

9. Because power is given to Christ to execute vengeance on irreconcilable opposers. The Father says to him, " *Thou shalt break them with a rod of iron; thou shalt dash them in pieces like a potter's vessel.*" The Septuagint, Syriac, and Arabic: *Thou shalt feed them with a rod of iron;* The Vulgate reads, *rule.* Those, who favor the change of rendering, suppose the language to be ironical. Many give *sceptre* instead of *rod.* The sceptre is the sign or badge of sovereign power. This belongs to Christ, and he will use that power to crush all finally impenitent foes. The figure of a *potter's vessel* probably refers not to the little value so much as to the frail nature of the opposers of Christ. The objections made to the clear statements of this verse seem to arise not from the words used, but from a dislike to the exercise of divine authority in the punishment of the wicked. In other words, it is the doctrine and not any want of force in the manner of announcing it, that has given offence. But from the first promise to the last threatening of Scripture the same is taught or implied. He, who shall bruise the serpent's head, will not endure forever the venom and contempt of the children of the wicked one. He will surely banish from his presence those who persistently refuse his friendship on earth. The wrath of the Lamb will be most terrible. To reject such love and mercy as are now offered, and to incur such

wrath as is now threatened, is the height of madness. All this is included in the decree declared in v. 7.

10. *Be wise now therefore, O ye kings: be instructed ye judges of the earth.* Instead of *be wise,* Hengstenberg has *act wisely.* For *be instructed,* Waterland has *be reformed;* Piscator, Be ye chastened (*i. e.,* submit to chastisement and profit by it); several others, Be ye corrected; church of England, following the Septuagint, Be learned; Alexander, Be warned, be admonished of your danger and duty. The great error of the wicked is a total disregard of all the safe principles by which wise men are governed. If in temporal affairs any man should act as foolishly, as in spiritual affairs all the wicked act, he would have curators appointed over his estate, and be deprived of the power of making legal contracts. The great call on all the enemies of God is to learn wisdom. Oh that they were wise unto salvation. "The fear of the Lord is the beginning of wisdom."

11. Then they would surely have those reverential sentiments, which invariably characterize true piety, and so would obey the call so solemnly and earnestly made, *Serve the* LORD *with fear and rejoice with trembling.* Though in these last three verses kings and rulers are by name addressed, yet it is as heads of the people, so that all are included in the call to obedience. In all acceptable *service* rendered to Jehovah several things must unite. It must be *sincere.* Without this God abhors all offerings, however decent or costly. A service known to be feigned is offensive to all right-minded men. Much more must it be so to God. In serving him we must confine ourselves to things which he has *commanded.* It is only when people draw near to God with their mouth, and honor him with their lips, but have removed their heart far from him, that their fear towards him is taught by the precepts of men. Is. xxix. 13. Christ says, Ye are my friends, if ye do whatsoever *I have commanded* you. John xv. 14. Nor may our religious service be reluctant; it must be *willingly* rendered. God hates a grudging giver. Love is the fulfilling of the law. If we love we will obey. Our service must also be *faithful.* We must not be double-minded. We cannot divide our hearts between God and the world. We cannot serve God and mammon. And we must serve God with *fear.* Our approaches to him must not be familiar, but reverent; not easy, but awful. God is indeed on a throne of grace, but that is no less glorious and suited to inspire reverence than a throne of judgment. It is a remarkable fact that all false and corrupt forms of religion either generate that fear which has torment—a servile fear—or degenerate into an irreverent presumption, leading men to come before God as the horse rusheth into the battle. Such do not keep their feet when they go to the house of God; but are less ready to hear than to offer the sacrifice of fools. We must also serve God with *joy.* "Thou meetest him that rejoiceth and worketh righteousness." Isa. lxiv. 5. A good master delights not in seeing his servants exhibiting dejection of spirit. Let kings and subjects, rulers and people all serve the Lord with fear and rejoice with trembling. None is so high as not to need the friendship of God; none so low as to be beneath the divine notice. Henry: "Even kings themselves, whom others serve and fear, must serve and fear God; there is the same infinite distance between them and God, that there is between the meanest of their subjects and him."

12. And the approved method of serving God is by Jesus Christ. He is the way, the truth, and the life; no man cometh unto the Father but by him. Therefore, *Kiss the Son, lest he be angry, and ye perish* from *the way, when his wrath is kindled but a little.* There is considerable diversity in the rendering of this verse. The Septuagint reads the first words thus, Lay hold of instruction; Chaldee, Receive the doctrine; Vulgate, Avail yourselves of the discipline. The difference arises from the original using a word, which in pure Hebrew means one thing, and in the Chaldee

dialect another. It may, however, be sufficient to advise the reader that after very full investigation the best scholars appear to adhere to the sense given in our common English translation, and render it, Kiss the Son. So Calvin, Jebb, Hengstenberg, and Alexander. Even the church of England departs from the Septuagint here and reads, Kiss the Son. Fry reads, Adore the Son. Here he gives the significance of the act, rather than the word to describe it. Kissing was an act of worship among idolators. See Job xxxi. 27; 1 Kings xix. 18; and Hos. xiii. 2. So God says, Cease to kiss the calves and the images of Baal and other false gods, and kiss my Son; serve idols no longer; serve the Son of God. We must honor the Son, even as we honor the Father. We must call Christ Lord. We must worship the Lamb. Rev. v. 12, 13. To kiss was also to profess loyalty and allegiance. See 1 Sam. x. 1. So to *kiss the Son* is the same as to submit to him, to accept him in all his offices, to yield our wills to his, and obey his laws, however made known to us. To *kiss* is also to express affection. We must love Christ, or terribly perish. 1 Cor. xvi. 22. If Christ is not precious to us, it is because we are unbelievers. 1 Pet. ii. 7. To *kiss* is also to declare reconciliation and to say that we are at peace. Jesus Christ is our peace. With him, and, through him, with his Father we are at one. Kiss the Son, lest he be angry, and *ye perish* from *the way*. Hare: *Perish instantly* or *on the spot;* Alexander: *Lose the way* or *perish by the way, i. e.,* before you reach your destination; Calvin regards the words "as a denunciation against the ungodly, by which they are warned that the wrath of God will cut them off when they think themselves to be only in the middle of their race;" Fry: "Lest ye be cut off in your course." This is probably the best sense, although several versions read, Lest ye perish from the righteous way. In Ps. i. 6 we read, "The way of the ungodly shall perish." Let us remember that we may perish, *when his wrath is kindled but a little.* Patrick: When his wrath breaks out suddenly, like an unquenchable fire; Calvin: When his wrath is kindled in a moment; Fry: For yet a little, and his anger will blaze forth; Jebb: When there is a kindling, *though* but a little, of his wrath; Horsley: For, within a little, shall his wrath blaze forth; Hengstenberg: For soon will his wrath be kindled. However long the wicked may seem to prosper, their ruin will swiftly overtake them. The conclusion of the whole matter is that all those, who rely on the Son of God, and accept him as their Saviour, and none others, are truly happy. *Blessed* are *all they that put their trust in him.* Or, Oh the blessedness, etc. We may not trust in men, ourselves or others. In particular men may never put confidence in their own works, in their own merits, in their own strength, but must take Christ Jesus as their wisdom, righteousness, sanctification and redemption, their Prophet, Priest and King, their all and in all. Life, death, judgment and eternity will prove all such men blessed. God pronounces them so. Fuller: "The command of God here given is of a *spiritual* nature, including unfeigned faith in the Messiah, and sincere obedience to his authority. To *kiss the Son* is to be reconciled to him, to embrace his word and ordinances, and bow to his sceptre. To *serve him with fear and rejoice with trembling* denote that they should not think meanly of him on the one hand, nor hypocritically cringe to him, from a mere apprehension of wrath, on the other; but sincerely embrace his government, and even *rejoice* that they had it to embrace. That which is here required of unbelievers is the very spirit which distinguishes believers, a holy fear of Christ's majesty, and an humble confidence in his mercy; taking his yoke upon them, and wearing it with delight."

DOCTRINAL AND PRACTICAL REMARKS.

1. This Psalm shows us the nature of sin. It is rebellion the most wicked and daring, against the only perfect law and law-giver in the universe. It is rage and

fury, vv. 1, 2, 3. If sin had its way, it would annihilate God's government. It seeks to dethrone him. This is true of all sin. It is true of unbelief towards Christ. Calvin: "Let it be held as a settled point, that all who do not submit themselves to the authority of Christ make war on God. Since it seems good to God to rule us by the hand of his own Son, those who refuse to obey Christ himself deny the authority of God, and it is in vain for them to profess otherwise. . . The Father will not be feared and worshipped but in the person of his Son." To attempt anything contrary is to attack the highest authority of the universe.

2. None can adequately express the folly of sin, v. 1. Truly sinners *imagine a vain thing.* Did any ever see or hear of one in whose heart God's Spirit was shedding the light of truth, and who did not pronounce all his past behaviour unreasonable? Did any dying sinner ever applaud a wicked life as proof of wisdom, or as the road to happiness?

3. Let us not be surprised at any developement of wickedness, v. 2. Strange as it may seem, even opposition to Jehovah and to his Christ is no new thing. Henry: "One would have expected that so great a blessing to this world as Christ's holy religion, should have been universally welcomed and embraced, and that every sheaf should have immediately bowed to that of Messiah, and all the crowns and sceptres on earth should have been laid at his feet; but it proves quite contrary."

4. The reasons, why wicked men oppose God and Christ, are first, they by nature have carnal minds, which are at enmity against God. Rom. viii. 7. Men naturally hate God and his Son. Being destitute of love to him, and the mind having an active nature, enmity is inevitable. Then men soon find that the restraints of divine law thwart their selfish schemes and sinful purposes, and so they oppose the Bible because the Bible opposes them, and reject God's authority because it is contrary to them, vv. 1, 2, 3. Dickson: "Though the law and ordinances of God be most holy, most equitable, most harmless, yea, also most profitable; yet the wicked esteem them, as they call them here, *bands and cords,* because they curb and cross their carnal wisdom and licentiousness of life." It is impossible that men without regeneration should love God. They are dead in trespasses and sins.

5. It is painful to contemplate the extent to which the governments of the world are to this day anti-Christian; and those, who conduct them often love to have it so. It was so of old, v. 2. There is no earthly government that has not laws, principles, or usages directly in the teeth of Christianity. All of them to some extent sanction the desecration of the fourth commandment. It has always been so. It is painful to a pious mind to dwell on such themes. Dickson: "The chief instruments that Satan stirreth up against Christ, to be heads and leaders to heathen and godless people in opposing and persecuting Christ's kingdom and church, are the magistrates, rulers, and statesmen, that he may color his malice with the shadow of authority and law." This is just what is described in this Psalm. *Kings and rulers* set themselves in array against religion.

6. Yet let not the righteous be afraid. It is easy for God to restrain his and their foes, vv. 4, 5, 6. His fit title is, "King of kings, and Lord of lords." He does what he pleases among the armies of heaven, and the inhabitants of the earth. Long before his incarnation Isaiah saw his glory, and spoke of him. Newton: "He is Lord over those that hate him. He rules them with a rod of iron, and so disposes their designs as to make them (though against their wills) the means and instruments of promoting his own purposes and glory. They are his unwilling servants even when they rage most against him. He has a bridle in their mouths to check and turn them at his pleasure. He can and often does control them, when they seem most secure of success, and always sets them bounds, which they cannot pass." All

his enemies shall be put under him. No ungodly foot shall be left on the necks of the righteous. For in the next place—

7. It is easy for God to destroy his foes, vv. 5, 9. One light stroke of his iron rod will break the potter's vessel. Yea, men are in their best earthly estate but potsherds. They are weak as water. He who spits against the wind spits in his own face. He who strives with his Maker makes certain his own ruin. Dickson: "The Lord hath his appointed time wherein he will arise, and vex the enemies of his church, partly by disappointing them of their hopes, and partly by inflicting sore plagues upon them; *then shall he vex them in his sore displeasure.*" So he has always done. Behold Pharaoh, his wise men, his hosts, and his horses plouting, and plunging, and sinking like lead in the Red sea. Here is the end of one of the greatest plots ever formed against God's chosen. Of thirty Roman Emperors, governors of provinces and others high in office, who distinguished themselves by their zeal and bitterness in persecuting the early Christians, one became speedily deranged after some atrocious cruelty, one was slain by his own son, one became blind, the eyes of one started out of his head, one was drowned, one was strangled, one died in a miserable captivity, one fell dead in a mnaner that will not bear recital, one died of so loathsome a disease that several of his physicians were put to death because they could not abide the stench that filled his room, two committed suicide, a third attempted it, but had to call for help to finish the work, five were assassinated by their own people or servants, five others died the most miserable and excruciating deaths, several of them having an untold complication of diseases, and eight were killed in battle or after being taken prisoners. Among these was Julian the apostate. In the days of his prosperity he is said to have pointed his dagger to heaven defying the Son of God, whom he commonly called the Galilean. But when he was wounded in battle, he saw that all was over with him, and he gathered up his clotted blood, and threw it into the air, exclaiming, "Thou hast conquered, O thou Galilean." Voltaire has told us of the agonies of Charles IX. of France, which drove the blood through the pores of the skin of that miserable monarch after his cruelties and treachery to the Huguenots.

8. The Scripture cannot be broken, vv. 6, 7, 8. God's counsel must stand. The promises are confirmed by an oath. The threatenings are executed before our eyes every day. The precepts are heavenly and eternal truth. The prophecies are but God's free, sovereign, eternal, and unchangeable purposes revealed to us. Heaven and earth may pass away, but every jot and tittle of Scripture shall be fulfilled, just as this second Psalm has had and is having its accomplishment.

9. The kingdom of Christ shall surely triumph, v. 8. Nothing can resist its progress. Events, seemingly the most adverse, have but accelerated its march to perfect victory. The death of the Saviour was the signal for the fall of Satan's kingdom. The persecutions at Jerusalem filled surrounding nations with the tidings and the heralds of salvation. J. M. Mason: "Messiah's throne is not one of those airy fabrics which are reared by vanity and overthrown by time; it is fixed of old; it is stable and cannot be shaken, for it is the throne of God. He who sitteth on it is the Omnipotent. Universal being is in his hand. Revolution, force, fear, as applied to his kingdom, are words without meaning. Rise up in rebellion if thou hast courage. Associate with thee the whole mass of infernal power. Begin with the ruin of whatever is fair and good on this little globe. Pass from hence to pluck the sun out of his place, and roll the volume of desolation through the starry world. What hast thou done unto him? It is the puny menace of a worm against him whose frown is perdition. *He that sitteth in the heavens shall laugh.*" A drop of his wrath makes life intolerable. A smile of his face makes heaven.

10. Prophecy, history, their own want of perfection, the example of Christ, and the enmity of the wicked, should all lead Christians to expect trials. Why should they not? If they are not tried otherwise, the conduct of wicked men will fill them with sorrow. No good man can witness such conduct as is described in vv. 1, 2, 3, or such judgments as are mentioned in vv. 4, 5, 9, without distress. *I beheld the transgressors and was grieved*, is a chapter in the history of all who love the Saviour. Or if for a time the enemies of God should seem to be still, corruption within will distress the pious. "Ever since man was driven from Paradise, he has been trying to find or make another," but he has never succeeded, and he never shall. There is a *need be* for all that comes on the righteous. "God doth not at any time put off his people, because he is not in a capacity to give; but doth many times put them off because they are not in a capacity to receive a mercy." Luther: "Every one who is a sound Christian, especially if he teaches the word of Christ, must suffer his Herod, his Pilate, his Jews and heathens, who rage against him, to speak much in vain, to lift themselves up and take counsel against him."

11. But let not the child of God be much moved by all his trials, however contrary to flesh and blood they may be. They can never affect his relations to God. He abideth faithful, vv. 6, 7. Nor can anything disturb his eternal tranquillity. Luther: "He who cares for us *sitteth in the heavens*, dwells quite secure, apart from all fear, and if we are involved in trouble and contention, he fixes his regard upon us; we move and fluctuate here and there, but he stands fast, and will order it so, that the righteous shall not continue forever in trouble. Ps. lv. 22. But all this proceeds so secretly that thou canst not well perceive it, thou shouldst then need to be in heaven thyself. Thou must suffer by land and sea, and among all creatures; thou must hope for no consolation in thy sufferings and troubles, till thou canst rise through faith and hope above all, and longest for Him who dwelleth in the heavens, then thou also dwellest in the heavens, but only in faith and hope."

12. The manhood of Messiah is generally held and believed. In former times some denied it. Were it in danger now, the pious would wonderfully rally to its defence. Nor ought errorists to marvel that the orthodox show like zeal in defending the doctrine of Christ's true and proper divinity. The Bible is full of it, vv. 1, 2, 3, 6, 7, as expounded by inspired men. It was to a God-man Mediator that all the regenerate committed their souls in the day of their espousals to Christ. J. M. Mason: "The doctrine of our Lord's divinity is not, as a *fact*, more interesting to our faith, than, as a *principle*, it is essential to our hope. If he were not the *true God*, he could not be *eternal life*. When pressed down by guilt and languishing for happiness, I look around for a deliverer such as my conscience and my heart and the word of God assure me I need, insult not my agony by directing me to a creature—to a man, a mere man like myself! A creature! a man! My Redeemer owns my *person*. My immortal spirit is his *property*. When I come to die, I must commit it into his hands. My soul! my infinitely precious soul committed to a mere man! become the property of a mere man! I would not thus intrust my *body* to the highest angel that burns in the temple above. It is only the Father of spirits that can have *property* in spirits, and be their refuge in the hour of transition from the present to the approaching world." If there is a title, attribute, or degree of honor ascribed to the Father, and proving his divinity, which is not also ascribed to the Son, the enemies of Christ's essential divinity have failed to point it out. The vital use of this doctrine is clearly taught in Scripture. "Who is he that overcometh the world, but he that believeth that Jesus is the Son of God?" 1 John v. 5.

13. Bishop Beveridge has a sermon on Ps. ii. 11, the object of which is to show "the obligations of superiors to promote religion." He has clearly made out his

argument, but when he comes to point out the way in which the duty is to be performed, he presents views quite at war with ideas entertained by pious people in our country, and by the great mass of Dissenters in England. Still he is right in insisting, and we must insist, that no man is exempt from the obligation to make known the salvation of the gospel, and to take up stumbling-blocks, and remove hindrances to the spread of truth. In this matter each one must use all the influence entrusted to him by God. Especially is he bound by a pious example to adorn the doctrine of God our Saviour.

14. It is greatly to be regretted that so many, in authority and out of it, not only refuse their aid in diffusing the gospel, but do much to hinder that good work. No one has told us how men can be more fearfully occupied than in opposing the spread of the knowledge of salvation, vv. 9, 12. Paul says of certain Jews of his day that they " are contrary to all men : forbidding us to speak to the Gentiles that they might be saved, to fill up their sins always : for the wrath is come upon them to the uttermost." 1 Thess. ii. 15, 16. Ye bitter enemies of the spread of the gospel, the tokens of perdition are now upon you. Your puny efforts to put down the work of God are powerless. J. M. Mason : " The missionary cause must ultimately succeed. It is the cause of God, and shall prevail. The days roll rapidly on, when the shout of the isles shall swell the thunder of the Continent ; when the Thames and the Danube, when the Tiber and the Rhine shall call upon Euphrates, the Ganges, and the Nile ; and the loud concert shall be joined by the Hudson, the Mississippi, and the Amazon, singing with one heart and one voice, Alleluiah ! Salvation ! The Lord God Omnipotent reigneth !"

15. It is also clear from this Psalm that men are fitly addressed in a pointed and particular way, v. 10. Not that the heralds of the cross are in promiscuous assemblies to hold up particular living persons before an audience. But God's word must be preached with discrimination. Every man ought to have his portion of meat in due season. Magistrates, senators, rich, poor, all must be rightly dealt with by the ministers. Men will not learn their duty or their sins by mere hints, and allusions, but only by an honest declaration, a fearless and tender announcement of the truth. God's servants must proclaim that " it is no disparagement to the greatest monarchs to be subject to Christ Jesus, to stand in awe of him, to submit themselves to him, and to promote his service to the extent of their power ; for the command to all, and to them in particular, is, *serve the Lord in fear.*"

16. There is a consanguinity between all the graces of the Christian, v. 11. His faith agrees with humility, and so is not presumptuous. His zeal is kind, gentle and benevolent, so it degenerates not into bigotry and rage. His penitence has hope in it and so it is free from despair. His fear has joy in it and so it does not bring distress. His joy has fear in it and so it does not pass into levity. Bates : " This fear of God qualifies our joy. If you abstract fear from joy, joy will become light and wanton ; and if you abstract joy from fear, fear then will become slavish." There is symmetry, and there is harmony in the Christian character. It is not a jumble, it is not a contradiction, it is one.

17. Men must trust as well as obey, and obey as well as trust. Piety without confidence in God is impossible, v. 12.

18. If in the work of redemption there is room for Christ's intercession, even after his exaltation, v. 8, surely it is no strange thing that Christians in this life of trial should find a resort to prayer necessary.

19. None, who hear the Gospel, can give any solid reason for perishing, v. 12. One question the wicked can never answer, Why will ye die? Their sin is that after their hardness and impenitent hearts they treasure up unto themselves wrath against the day of wrath, Rom. ii. 5. Everything is against them. O reader, be wise ; turn and

live. Newton: "My heart wishes you the possession of those principles which would support you in all the changes of life, and make your dying pillow comfortable. Are you unwilling to be happy? Or can you be happy too soon? Many persons are now looking upon you, who once were as you now are. And I doubt not, they are praying that you may be as they now are. Try to pray for yourself; our God is assuredly in the midst of us. His gracious ear is attentive to every supplicant. Seek him while he is to be found. Jesus died for sinners, and he has said, 'Him that cometh to me I will in no wise cast out.' He is likewise the author of that faith, by which alone you can come rightly to him. If you ask it of him, he will give it you; if you seek it, in the means of his appointment, you shall assuredly find. If you refuse this there remaineth no other sacrifice for sin. If you are not saved by faith in his blood, you are lost forever. O 'kiss the Son lest he be angry, and you perish from the way, if his wrath be kindled, yea, but a little. Blessed are all they that put their trust in him.'"

20. "Unspeakable must the wrath of God be, when it is kindled fully, since perdition may come upon the *kindling of it but a little*," v. 12.

21. "Remission of sin, delivery from wrath, communion with God, and life everlasting are the fruits of embracing Christ, of closing in covenant with Christ, and resting on Christ; for *blessed are all they that put their trust in him*," v. 12.

PSALM III.

A Psalm of David, when he fled from Absalom his son.

1 Lord, how are they increased that trouble me! many *are* they that rise up against me

2 Many *there be* which say of my soul, *There is* no help for him in God. Selah.

3 But thou, O Lord, *art* a shield for me; my glory, and the lifter up of mine head.

4 I cried unto the Lord with my voice, and he heard me out of his holy hill. Selah.

5 I laid me down and slept; I awaked; for the Lord sustained me.

6 I will not be afraid of ten thousands of people, that have set *themselves* against me round about.

7 Arise, O Lord; save me, O my God: for thou hast smitten all mine enemies *upon* the cheekbone; thou hast broken the teeth of the ungodly.

8 Salvation *belongeth* unto the Lord: thy blessing *is* upon thy people. Selah.

THIS is the first Psalm having a title. The word rendered *Psalm* is not from the word giving a name to the whole collection. That signifies *Praises;* this, *song*, or *Psalm*, to be used with music. It is a Psalm *of David*, or *to David*, pertaining to him. He is its author. The title determines both the author and the occasion of the composition. Thus it is certain that the Psalm was not composed earlier than ten hundred and twenty-one years before Christ. It may have been still later, as we shall see. The objections urged by some of the German commentators against the accuracy and authority of this title are of no validity. Those claiming the least notice are sufficiently refuted by Hengstenberg. That the Psalm suits the occasion of David's flight in Absalom's rebellion is clear from the historic account of that event in 2 Samuel xv. xvi. xvii. xviii. Sad must have been the hour when "David said unto all his servants that were with him at Jerusalem, Arise, and let us flee; for we shall not else escape from Absalom: make speed to depart, lest he overtake us suddenly, and bring evil upon us, and smite the city with the edge of the sword. And David went up by the ascent of Mount Olivet, and wept as he went up, and had his head covered, and he went barefoot: and all the people that was with him covered every man his head, and they went up, weeping as they went up." 2 Sam. xv. 14, 30. Never had Jerusalem witnessed such a scene. The sweet singer of Israel in the dress of a mourner is fleeing from his own capital to escape the sword of a rebellious son, is mocked at and stoned by the vilest of his subjects (2 Sam. xvi. 5–13). Soon Jerusalem is swarming with rebels, so that it is proposed by their wily statesman (2 Sam. xvi. 23) to send that very night an army of *twelve thousand* men in pursuit of the royal fugitive. 2 Sam. xvii. 1. The saddest thing in all this tumult and civil war was that it was the punishment sent by God, according to prophecy, on David for his sin in the matter of Uriah: "Behold I will raise up evil against thee out of thine own house." 2 Sam. xii. 11. And here it is already.

The title is, *A Psalm of David, when he fled from Absalom his son.* Does this teach that David actually wrote the Psalm in the midst of the confusion of his flight? or did he afterwards write it concerning his flight? We may supply a word or two so as to give either sense, for the title is clearly elliptical. Thus we may read, "A Psalm of David *written* when he fled," etc., or, "A Psalm of David concerning the time when he fled," etc. The latter is the more probable, as we may infer from the circumstances of the case, and from the internal evidence of this composition. Every clause will thus suit the events noticed and the time of writing. Thus the songs of Moses and Miriam were composed *after* the escape of Israel from the Egyptians. Exod. xv. So also we have the writing (a poem) of Hezekiah, King of Judah, when he had been sick, and was recovered of his sickness. Is. xxxviii. 9–20. It is not arrogance to dissent from those pious and learned men who think that this Psalm was actually composed in the time of flight. The view here taken seems so natural and so free from difficulties in considering the whole composition, that it is adopted with some confidence. Nor is it unsupported by respectable commentators. Luther: "It is not probable that David should have composed it at the time of his flight and distress. For the Holy Spirit will have a calm, happy, cheerful, select instrument, whether for preaching or for singing. In the conflict, also, man has not understanding, but becomes capable of this only after the conflict is over—reflects then aright upon what has occurred to him under it. Therefore it is most likely that David composed this Psalm long after, when he came to quiet reflection, and obtained an understanding of his life and history, which had variously happened to him." Hengstenberg: "It is very probable that the conception and birth of the Psalm were separated from each other—that David did not immediately express in manifold forms what he had personally received in those moments of pressing danger, that he only afterwards, and by degrees, coined for the Church the gold bestowed upon himself in such moments." Dodd, following Chandler: "When David was resettled on his throne, he penned this Psalm, to commemorate both his danger and his deliverance."

In all the Scriptures we first find the word *Selah* in this Psalm. See Introduction, § 15.

Wherever the word LORD is found in our version of this Psalm, it is a translation of the word *Jehovah.* See above on Ps. i. 2.

Some have endeavored to show a close unity of subject in this Psalm. No doubt all that is said was very pertinent to the occasion. But in times of deep trouble the mind studies not logical unity. It is more apt to give vent to its emotions in broken sentences, yet really pertinent. A world of thought passes before it. It would therefore be easy to show that much matter is omitted in his summary of this Psalm, when Hengstenberg says that it "falls quite naturally into four strophes, each consisting of two verses, the first of which describes the necessity, the second, the ground of hope, while the third discloses the hope itself, and the fourth contains the prayer prompted by the hope." The fifth and sixth verses say much more of the strength and effects of the hope than of the hope itself, as is obvious at a glance.

This learned man is much more happy in representing the state of David's mind as calm and confident of final victory and of a restoration of his kingdom, even in the height of the rebellion. The contents of the Psalm clearly show this. Every verse, from the third to the end, evinces a strong confidence. The passages relied on to prove that David was in great uncertainty are these: "The king said unto Zadok, Carry back the ark of God into the city: if I shall find favor in the eyes of the LORD, he will bring me again, and show me both it and his habitation: but if he thus say, I have no delight in thee; behold, here am I, let him do to me as seemeth good unto him." "It may be that the LORD will look on mine affliction, and that the LORD will requite me good for his cursing this day." 2 Sam. xv. 25, 26; and xvi. 12. But surely the apostle did not wish Christians to lose confidence in God when he exhorted them to say, "If the Lord will, we shall live, and do this, or that." Jas. iv. 15. Hengstenberg well says of the passages just quoted from Samuel, that they "by no means indicate a complete uncertainty, and are mainly to be regarded as a simple expression of the humility which scarcely ventures to declare, with perfect confidence, the still never extinguished hope of deliverance, because feeling itself to be utterly unworthy of it." No doubt David had such a sense of his weakness, as to cut off all expectation of doing anything by his own power. His view of his own sinfulness showed him the justice of God in sending these, and even worse afflictions. But all his acts and plans manifest the hope that prevailed. In the midst of his flight he confiscates the property of Mephibosheth, and gives it to Ziba. 2 Sam. xvi. 4. His calmness under the insults of Shimei evinces the same state of mind. 2 Sam. xvi. 5–13. His sending back to the city the ark of God, Zadok, Abiathar, and Hushai, manifests great composure and wisdom. 2 Sam. xv. 24–30; and 32–37. David also knew the worth of prayer, and now he tries its efficacy. "O LORD, I pray thee, turn the counsel of Ahithophel into foolishness." 2 Sam. xv. 31. The conduct of David and his people mentioned in 2 Sam. xvi. 14, shows anything but a timid or dispirited heart. His state of mind seems to have been much the same as that of Paul and his coadjutors. "We are troubled on every side, yet not distressed; we are perplexed, but not in despair; persecuted, but not forsaken; cast down, but not destroyed." 2 Cor. iv. 8, 9.

1. LORD, *how are they increased that trouble me! many* are *they that rise up against me.* The Arabic: O my LORD, wherefore are they multiplied, who make me sad?" etc. Calvin: O LORD, how are my oppressors multiplied! many rise up against me; Venema: Jehovah, how many and how great are my foes; Fry: O JEHOVAH, how many are mine adversaries! etc.; Hengstenberg: O LORD, how are mine enemies so many! etc.; Jebb: LORD, how many are they that trouble me, etc.; Alexander: O LORD, how many, or how multiplied, are my foes! many rising up against me. For his translation Venema argues from the original word, and in proof he refers to Job xxxii. 9 and Jer. xli. 1. If the original word means *great ones*, it can hardly mean *many* also, and then there need be no repetition in v. 1. But we may read it, How the great men are my enemies, and the many rise up against me. All classes joined in Absalom's rebellion, and this in formidable numbers. The revolt also gave a fair opportunity for all old grudges and secret animosities, which had been growing up in his kingdom, to manifest themselves against David. From some things said in the history of this affair it is clear that Absalom had an alarming majority of the people on his side. He had long been at work. When David fled he had six hundred men with him, and that very night it was proposed to send an army of twelve thousand in pursuit of him. Henry says, David "speaks of Absalom's faction as one amazed; and well he might,

that a people he had so many ways obliged, should almost generally rebel against him, and choose for their head such a foolish and giddy young man as Absalom was." He was not only giddy and foolish, but his moral character was very bad. He had filled the heart of his father with grief and of his brothers with terror by his treacherous and malicious fratricide. 2 Sam. xiii. 23–36.

2. This host of opposers did not keep silence but spoke insolently. They were full of contempt. *Many* there be *which say of my soul*, There is *no help for him in God. Selah*. The sense is that the soul, the feelings are involved in the saying; Chaldee, Septuagint, Ethiopic, Syriac, Arabic, Vulgate, Calvin, Jebb, and Hengstenberg: Many there be which say *to* my soul; Venema: Many utter the scoff against me, to my very face; Alexander: There are many saying, or, how many are there saying, to my soul, *i. e.*, so as to affect my heart, though really said of him, not directly addressed to him; Calvin: "The word *soul*, in my opinion, signifies the seat of the affections, . . . David meant to say that his heart was in a manner pierced by the mockery of his enemies." If many openly insulted David to his face we have no account of it in history, though we are told of the personal scoffs of Shimei. But the language of his foes was doubtless reported to him, and so our common version well conveys the sense of the original. Some suppose the words, *there is no help for him in God*, were the utterances of timid and despondent friends, not given in scorn but in unbelief. Doubtless there were not a few of this class of persons in the kingdom. They despaired of seeing David's cause successful. Indeed they considered him a ruined man. Nehemiah was annoyed with a set of men, who advised him to play the coward. Even beyond those engaged in active hostilities, these may have tempted David to despair, than which bold enterprises and a holy life have no worse foe. Despair is the perfection of unbelief. "'Tis the offspring of fear, of laziness and impatience." Whoever may have uttered the words *there is no help for him in God*, doubtless intended to say he was ruined forever, temporally and spiritually. The word rendered *help* means *salvation;* Chaldee: There is no redemption for him in God forever; Septuagint, Ethiopic, Syriac, Arabic, Vulgate, Fry, Jebb and Alexander: There is no salvation. There is hardly a sweeter thought of heaven than that there we shall be done with temptation. And of all temptations none are more dangerous than those which incline us to despair. Thus Saul and Judas fell forever. Luther supposes David to understand them as saying: "They not merely speak as if I were abandoned and trodden upon by all creatures, but as if God also would no longer help me, who, while he assists all things, sustains all, cares for all, for me alone of all things has no care, and ministers to me no support. Though every possible assault, the assaults of a whole world, and of all hell beside, were concentrated upon one head, it were still nothing to the thought, that God is thrusting at a man—for preservation from which Jeremiah tremblingly begs and prays, xvii. 17, 'Be not a terror unto me, O thou my Hope in the day of evil.'" For *in God* some would read *in his God*. This is the first place in the Psalms where we meet that name of God, ELOHIM. Next to Jehovah it is by far the most common name given to God. It occurs in the Hebrew Scriptures considerably more than *two thousand* times. In form it is plural, though it is construed with singular verbs. Some have asserted that it is found in the plural because it was borrowed from those who believed in many gods. Some say it is used only as a majestic mode of speech. But others suppose it is employed on account of the doctrine of plurality of persons in the Godhead. This is probably correct. It has plural pronouns referring to it. Gen. i. 26; iii. 22. Havernick regards it as having special reference to God as Creator. It expresses the excellence of the divine nature and authority.

3. But true courage is not easily disheartened. Divine grace can give us the victory

in the worst times. So David says, *But thou, O* LORD, *art a shield for me.* The Chaldee, Arabic, Calvin, Hengstenberg and Alexander have *And* at the beginning of the verse instead of *But.* Yet Calvin says, "The copulative *and* should be resolved into the disjunctive particle *but.*" Septuagint, Ethiopic and Vulgate: Thou art he, who undertakes for me; Syriac and Arabic: Thou art my helper. But this is paraphrase, not translation. The shield was a piece of defensive armor. It was often made very large so as to protect the whole body. The shield of Goliath was borne by another person. This was probably not unusual. Abimelech had his armor-bearer. David once filled that office to Saul. So far as we know, the shield would, more than any other piece of armor, require the help of another. When it was very large it was a complete defence. Hence the beauty of the figure, comparing God to a shield, used by Moses and adopted by David. And truly God is the very shield his people need. O how he hides them from evil, covers their head in the day of battle, and brings them off conquerors, yea, more than conquerors. All that can be understood by conservation, protection and defence is secured to us, when God becomes our shield. To every genuine child of grace, Jehovah says, "Fear not: I am thy shield, and thy exceeding great reward." Gen. xv. 1. That this is no misapplication of Scripture is clear from Rom. xv. 4. God is both willing and able to defend his people. Our version reads, Thou art a shield *for* me. Although this gives the general sense, yet the original word corresponds entirely with the English word *about.* And Jebb has, Thou art a shield *about* me. The Chaldee and Hengstenberg support this rendering. Alexander: A shield about me, or around me, *i. e.,* covering my whole body, not merely a part of it, as ordinary shields do.

David also says, Thou art *my glory, and the lifter up of mine head.* Some of the versions for *glory* give *honor.* But honor and glory are nearly the same thing. Perhaps glory is commonly the stronger word. God was his glory as he was the cause and author of all his honors, of all wherein he might glory. Venema well says there is nothing unusual in this sense of the phrase. Cobbin: " My glory, the author of my greatness." David's meaning is that God had defended and maintained his cause and all, wherein he might rejoice up to this time, and would not now desert him. *And the lifter up of mine head.* When shame, or dejection or languor come upon men, they bow the head. It falls of itself. Yet God would so be the glory of David that as Calvin expresses it, " he became so bold that he declares he would walk with unabashed brow." But mere freedom from shame is not all. Joy is included, as is evident from Luke xxi. 28, " When these things begin to come to pass, then look up, and lift up your heads: for your redemption draweth nigh." And with these come strength and courage. God was the author of all these. When he thus lifts up the head, who can bow it down?

4. All these blessings are connected with prayer, which has always been—a part of the religion of sinners. *I cried unto the* LORD *with my voice, and he heard me out of his holy hill. Selah.* The chief variations in rendering this verse respect the tense of the verbs, *cry* and *hear.* The Septuagint, Ethiopic, Syriac, Arabic, Vulgate, Calvin, and Jebb use the past tense as in our English Bible. Fry and Hengstenberg prefer the present tense, *I cry* and *he heareth.* Alexander has *cry* in the future and *hear* in the present. In the Hebrew both verbs are future. On these variations see Introduction, § 6. Whichsoever tense is employed the doctrine taught is the same. But if we use the past tense, we make David encourage himself from former experiences of the divine kindness. If we use the present, we make him speak of exercises and mercies now his own. If we employ the future, then we make him express his confidence in God for days to come. It seems proper that both verbs should be given in the same tense. How wonderful a means is prayer. The cry of a worm enters the ears of the

Lord of Sabaoth, and he sends deliverance. With God hearing is answering. Alexander: The second verb is not the usual verb to hear, but one especially appropriated to the gracious hearing or answering of prayer." By the Jews prayer was addressed to God in his holy temple, which was for many ages on Mount Zion. Several elevations noticed in Scripture possess great interest. Of these special notice is due to Nebo, which is called the mount of God; the mount of Olives, where our Saviour often was, and the mount of transfiguration, expressly called the holy mount by Peter 2 Epis. i. 18. But commonly by the holy mountain or hill is to be understood mount Zion, which God chose as a place that he would make glorious. To the Jews this above all others was God's hill of holiness. Here God manifested himself of old by Urim and Thummim, by Shechinah, by holy fire, by the spirit of prophecy, and in Gospel days by miraculous influences and the abundant effusion of the Holy Ghost.

5. Prayer is a good preparation for sleep. After David had *cried unto the* LORD, he says, *I laid me down and slept; I awaked; for the* LORD *sustained me.* The Chaldee, Septuagint, Ethiopic, Syriac, Vulgate, Calvin, and Jebb all here use the past tense for each verb. Fry employs the past tense for the first three verbs, but puts the last in the present, *sustaineth.* The Arabic puts the first three verbs in the past tense, but the last in the present thus, *for Jehovah is my helper.* Alexander uses the past tense in all but the last verb, which he renders in the future, *will sustain.* In this he follows the original. Hengstenberg puts all the verbs in the present tense. Venema would render it, I have been accustomed to lie down, and sleep, and awake, because Jehovah sustained me. Perhaps our English version is as good as any. Hengstenberg thinks this Psalm was an evening hymn. Alexander thinks that if any such distinctions are admissible or necessary, it may be regarded as a morning rather than an evening hymn. The fact is, it is fit for morning, noon, or night. The world is often amazed at the composure of God's people. But the marvel ceases when we know that God is with them, sustains them, *props them up,* as Chandler renders it, and that their confidence in his protection is strong and well-founded. The wicked are not so. They are in peril asleep or awake, 1 Sam. xxvi. 7–15. But to the righteous God saith, " When thou liest down, thou shalt not be afraid; yea, thou shalt lie down, and thy sleep shall be sweet." Pr. iii. 24. The same is promised in Lev. xxvi. 6, and in Ezek. xxxiv. 25.

The Italian proverb is, To serve and not to please, to expect a friend and have him fail to come, to lie in bed and not to sleep are three things bad enough to run a man mad. The great fountain of peace, tranquility and security is confidence in God. He will sustain his servants at all times. The preserving care of God over us when asleep is truly wonderful. Sleep is a striking emblem of death. Sometimes indeed men fall asleep and never awake in this world, but commonly they awake again. In the case of the righteous, no time is more apt to bring a deep sense of the divine goodness than their earliest waking moments. The opinion of some that verse 5 relates to the death and resurrection of Jesus Christ is fanciful, or, as Venema says, without any reason.

6. He whose mind was thus stayed on God might well dismiss tormenting fears. Accordingly he says, *I will not be afraid of ten thousands of people, that have set* themselves *against me round about.* There is no reason for supposing that special reference is here made to the proposal of Ahithophel to send twelve thousand men after David at the beginning of his flight. 2 Sam. xvii. 1. For we have no evidence that David was then informed of Ahithophel's counsel, nor were the twelve thousand sent. Hushai's counsel prevented them from marching. But the whole country was agitated, and David knew his enemies to be very numerous. The translations of this verse are considerably varied. Septuagint and Ethiopic: I will not be afraid of myriads encircling me, or rushing upon me in a circle; The Syriac fixes the num-

bers at ten thousand; The Arabic: I will not fear myriads of nations encompassing me, insurgent against me; The Vulgate: I will not be afraid of thousands, etc.; Jebb: I will not be afraid for ten thousands of the people, which round about have set themselves against me; Calvin: I will not be afraid of ten thousands of people who have set their camps against me on all sides; Muller: I will not be afraid of the many thousands, etc.; Fry: I fear not the multitudes of people that have beset me around; Hengstenberg: I will not be afraid of ten thousands of people which they have set against me round about; Alexander: I will not be afraid of myriads or multitudes of people whom they have set round about against me. The reason of some of these various renderings is that in Hebrew the numeral for ten thousand may signify that precise number, or a countless multitude. The same is true in Greek and in English. Our word *myriad*, derived from the Greek, if taken definitely, signifies ten thousand; if indefinitely, any vast number. For the Greek usage, see Acts xxi. 20, where our version gives thousands for the original myriads. Venema thinks the phrase has respect to the time when it was sung in Israel, David has slain his ten thousands. The enemies of David *set themselves, i. e.,* in hostile military array; they posted themselves. But all to no purpose. Numbers are nothing where God is. He is the LORD of hosts. Omnipotence as easily disposes of millions as of tens, or units. Strong confidence in Divine protection is therefore as wise as it is pious and comforting.

7. This trust naturally leads to hearty and renewed prayer. *Arise, O* LORD; *save me, O my God.* The word *arise* describes the act of one who has sat still for a while beholding what was going on. At last he resolves to be quiet no longer and comes to the rescue. So David asks Jehovah to interfere and settle this civil war. And he pleads his covenant relation to him, calling him *my God.* He asks him to *save,* to *help,* to *redeem,* to *rescue* him. To *make me safe* is a signification given in several old translations to the word *save.* David was thus encouraged to pray by reason of his past experience, or possibly by what he had heard of the defeat of Ahithophel's counsel. And so he says, *for thou hast smitten all mine enemies upon the cheek bone; thou hast broken the teeth of the ungodly.* To smite on the cheek bone and *break the teeth* is sorely to plague and effectually to disable. Chandler: "A wild beast is disabled from devouring its prey when its jaws are broken and its teeth dashed out." The figure is drawn from the hunting of wild and ferocious animals, which are rendered harmless when their jaws are broken, or their teeth mashed in. In many respects David's foes were like wild beasts, thirsting for his blood, fierce and merciless; but God had already put it out of their power to do real harm. Their evil dispositions were still manifest, but their ability was already as nothing. David had a pious confidence that God was against his treacherous enemies. Though the verbs rendered *hast smitten* and *hast broken* are in the past tense, yet Hengstenberg following Luther seems to prefer the present, *thou smitest* and *thou breakest.* So that he makes the Psalmist tell what God is doing at the time the Psalm was conceived. Whether this is a better sense or not, it is true as he says, quoting Ewald, that the preterite not unfrequently denotes a past, reaching down to the present. Though God holds all his enemies in derision, yet there seems to be no reason for supposing that the smiting spoken of in this verse respects blows on the face to express contempt, as Morison thinks. We do not smite wild beasts to show them an indignity, but to disable them, or, as Morison adds, to deprive them of the power of inflicting pain and misery.

8. Such deliverances as God vouchsafed to David called for thanksgiving. Therefore he says that he had not escaped by any created power or skill, but solely by the LORD, Jehovah. *Salvation* belongeth *unto the* LORD. Hengstenberg: Salvation is the

Lord's. Calvin considers the natural and obvious meaning to be simply this, that salvation or deliverance is in the hands of God only. Venema: Salvation belongs unto thee, Jehovah; Dodd: Salvation be unto the Lord, *i. e.*, let it be ascribed unto him. But he gives no reason for this rendering, although the sense thus given is pious and consistent with the analogy of Scriptural teaching. If this is the right rendering it makes the passage strongly eucharistic. Let God be adored. Let him be praised. Nor does David confine his thoughts to his own case alone, but remembers his people also. *Thy blessing is upon thy people.* In the Hebrew of the eighth verse we find no verb, *belongeth and is* having been supplied by the translators. Fry, Hengstenberg, and Alexander, therefore prefer to make the clause read, Thy blessing be upon thy people. If this is right, the last clause is intercessory. And if by *thy people* is to be understood those to whom David was king, the passage presents him as praying for mercies on his foes. But why may we not regard him as forgetting himself and asking for the Divine blessing on all the genuine servants of Jehovah, the true Israel of God? Calvin: "David affirms that deliverance was vouchsafed, not so much to him as an individual, as to the whole people, that the universal church, whose welfare depended on the safety and prosperity of his kingdom, might be preserved from destruction." The whole verse then has this import, God alone can save and deliver, and thus God gives his enriching blessing to all his people, his true church.

Doctrinal and Practical Remarks.

1. Every one has his own troubles. The king is as liable to the alternations of joy and sorrow as any of his subjects. Thus this whole Psalm teaches. At times David was probably the most afflicted man in Israel, v. 1. Perhaps too there is a much more equal distribution of happiness and misery than we are sometimes ready to admit. Before repining at our lot as peculiarly severe, let us look into the state of some around us, and we shall find a very reasonable demand for sympathy made on us both by those above us and by those below us in social position.

2. The best of parents may have the worst of children. David had his Absalom. This is not common, but it is possible. The effects of a pious education are often not manifest until the heart of parents is nearly broken by the wickedness of their offspring. In some cases indeed those who have had the best examples and instructions live and die in sin. Grace is not hereditary. God is a sovereign.

3. How foolish are they who rely for happiness on popular favor. Nothing is more fickle. David may long reign and do good, but when the rebellion comes, the masses turn against him, v. 1. It was always so. One while Israel says there is none like Moses. Very soon trouble comes; then they murmur against him. The very people, who one moment pronounce Paul a murderer pursued by divine vengeance, the next moment say he is a God. The very crowd who cry, Hosanna to the son of David, in three days clamor for his crucifixion. Popular breath is as fickle as the wind, and as light as vanity. The want of it is proof against no man's worth. The possession of it confirms no man's title to esteem.

4. Great crimes ordinarily cannot be concealed. It seems to be God's plan to bring to light foul deeds, even when committed by great and good men. Our saying is, Murder will out. God can summon so many witnesses that exposure may follow at any moment. The chattering of a nest of birds made one confess parricide. The distress of Joseph's brethren made them acknowledge their guilt concerning their brother. Absalom seems to have been David's favorite son. 2 Sam. xiii. 39. Yet he was the sharpest thorn that ever pierced the side of his father. Thus God brings out the evil deeds of David and punishes them before the sun. He knows how to make the iron enter into the soul of his erring people.

5. If you would know things perfectly, go to school to experience. How its lessons sober the mind, expel folly, and bring before us the things of salvation. In this Psalm David speaks as one who knew whereof he affirmed. He had been taught some painful lessons, but they had been amongst the most profitable of his whole life.

6. God may greatly afflict his chosen even after they have truly repented of their sins, v. 2. It was so with David here. The Lord often sees it good for us to have the past in sad remembrance. When he does thus try us, let us fall into the arms of him, who chastises us. Henry: "Perils and frights should drive us *to* God, not *from* him." As soon as David's trouble comes, he goes to God. Blessed words are these: "We are chastened of the Lord, that we should not be condemned with the world."

7. When affliction comes, let us seek for the cause. "Wherefore contendest thou with me?" Nor let us cease our search, till we make thorough work. And when we find the cause of our troubles, let us deeply repent before God. We never receive from God a stroke more than we both deserve and need either for our purification or usefulness. And we never repent too frequently or too humbly for our sins. They are more hateful than we have ever felt them to be. True repentance is not a fit; it is a habit.

8. But let God's servants beware of despair. Let them cling to him the more closely, the sharper their sorrows are. Despair may do a prodigious deed of valor; it never performed a great work of faith or of patience. Let every child of God often say to his soul, Hope thou in God. Let the saints never believe the tempter when he says, There is no help for them in God. Humble and obedient trust in God is always safe and wise, vv. 2, 3.

9. We never act more wisely than when we do right and rely on God for protection of our lives and persons, and for the defence of our good names. He is our *shield*, and defends us. He is our *glory*, and our honor is safe in his hands, v. 3. God is himself the hope of Israel.

10. How sad is the state of men, when God no longer helps them. What had David to rely on in this affliction but God alone? Nor was his trial as great as we are all subject to. It might have been more severe. And if, when the day of sadness comes, God shall refuse his aid, are we not undone? Why do not the wicked see that they are working their own ruin, just as Absalom was steadily progressing to his own overthrow?

11. We are always safe in following the line of God's will clearly made known to us either in his word or in his providence. David well knew how God had called him to the throne and would secure it to him, and so he sees how others are warring against the Almighty. Calvin: "If our enemies in persecuting us, rather fight against God than against us, let the consideration of their doing so be immediately followed by the confident persuasion of our safety under the protection of him, whose grace, which he has promised to us, they despise and trample under foot." "If the whole world should unite its voice to drive us to despair, God alone is to be obeyed, and hope of promised deliverance from God is always to be cherished," v. 3.

12. We readily abuse everything. Even our past experience of God's mercies may, through the hardness of our hearts, lead us to seek for no further attainments in knowledge and grace. On the other hand, some derive but little comfort from the most marvellous deliverances of former days. In each new trouble they behave as much like children as they did in their earliest trials. Here is error on both extremes. We ought not so to think of the past as to say that we have felt or learned enough; but when tried, we ought to plead with God his former kindnesses, and to encourage ourselves in the remembrance of them, v. 4.

13. Prayer is efficacious. Mortals never wield any other weapon so mighty, v. 4. Oh that we all had hearts to resort to God in strong crying, as we ought. Henry: "Care and grief do us good and no hurt, when they set us a praying, and engage us, not only to speak to God, but to cry to him as those that are in earnest."

14. The calming power of piety is wonderful, v. 5. Clarke: "He who knows that he has God for his protector, may go quietly and confidently to his bed, not fearing the violence of the fire, the edge of the sword, the designs of wicked men, nor the influence of evil spirits." There is living a man who has lain down at the root of a tree in Africa, with a tiger near him on one side, and a jackal on the other. To flee from them was impossible. He left them to watch each other, committed himself to God, fell asleep, and awaked the next morning, finding the sun risen and both the beasts of prey gone. Leave all with God and fear nothing. Henry: "True Christian fortitude consists more in a gracious security and serenity of mind, in patient bearing, and patient waiting, than in daring enterprises, sword in hand."

15. When God upholds one's "spirit, his person, and his cause," what is more reasonable than that he should be of good courage? v. 5.

16. The war of the wicked on the Church of God is utterly hopeless. The very prayers of the saints of all ages form around her a bulwark of impregnable strength, vv. 4, 7.

17. So sure is the final victory, that it may be celebrated before it is crowned, v. 7. Morison: "So delightful is that confidence which the spirit of believing prayer inspires, that the Psalmist speaks of victory over his enemies as if *actually* established."

18. However oppressed, despised, persecuted, forsaken, let the servants of God betake themselves to his mercy and rely on his grace, v. 8. The Lord has pleasure in such. We can in no way put so abundant honor on God as by magnifying his grace and relying on his love.

19. How small a thing fatally depresses the wicked. David in flight is confident. Ahithophel at court is in despair and hangs himself.

20. David was a pattern of suffering. He was also a type of Christ. But whether in this Psalm he was designed to be regarded as typical is not entirely clear. Dr. Gill urgently favors the typical character of David here. But many will not regard his statements as conclusive. There is a sense in which all Christ's people *suffer with him*, and in some things like him; but that does not make them types of their Redeemer. Nor is there any error taught by *alluding* to any portion of sacred history, and thence drawing light by comparisons or analogies to explain any other part, provided always that it be done with sound judgment and in good taste. Thus Scott, without here finding any type, simply says, "We shall cease to wonder at the troubles of the king of Israel, and almost cease to *think* of our own light afflictions, if we duly look unto Jesus, and contrast his glory and his grace with the contempt and cruelty with which he was treated. Having yielded himself to death, he sanctified the grave, and became the first-fruits of the resurrection; his head was then lifted up above his enemies, and thus he has opened the kingdom of heaven to all believers. His enemies therefore will surely be disappointed and perish; but his people may go down to the grave, as to their beds, in hope and comfort; for the same God watches over them in both, and they will at length awake to everlasting happiness." Alexander: "The expressions are so chosen as to make the Psalm appropriate to its main design, that of furnishing a vehicle of pious feeling to the Church at large and to its individual members in their own emergencies."

21. The strifes and perils of war are a striking though inadequate representation of the terrible contests and enemies that rage within the heart of God's suffering people in all their earthly rejoicings. How they are deceived, betrayed, opposed, wounded,

and brought nigh unto death by their sins and temptations, so that the best of them are scarcely saved. Luther: "This Psalm is profitable to us for comforting weak and straitened consciences, if we understand in a spiritual sense, by the enemies and teeth of the ungodly, the temptations of sin and the conscience of an ill-spent life. For there indeed is the heart of the sinner vexed, there alone is it weak and forsaken; and when men are not accustomed to lift their eyes above themselves, against the floods of sin, and know to make God their refuge against an evil conscience, there is great danger; and it is to be feared lest the evil spirits, who, in such a case, are ready to seize upon poor souls, may at last swallow them up, and lead them through distress into doubt."

22. How strangely the Christian's blessings come to him. His strength comes out of weakness, his fulness out of emptiness, his joy out of sorrow, his life out of death. Apollinarius calls the third Psalm a *mournful song*, and so it is; yet where will you find higher confidence expressed than in portions of this wailing composition?

23. This Psalm shows that in a very short act of devotion, even when the mind is much exercised on one thing, there may be a rich variety of imagery and of topic employed. In devotion logical connection is of far less importance than fervor, humility, faith and the spirit of submission and importunity.

PSALM IV.

To the chief Musician on Neginoth, A Psalm of David.

1 Hear me when I call, O God of my righteousness: thou hast enlarged me *when I was* in distress; have mercy upon me, and hear my prayer.

2 O ye sons of men, how long *will ye turn* my glory into shame? *how long* will ye love vanity, *and* seek after leasing? Selah.

3 But know that the LORD hath set apart him that is godly for himself: the LORD will hear when I call unto him.

4 Stand in awe, and sin not: commune with your own heart upon your bed, and be still. Selah.

5 Offer the sacrifices of righteousness, and put your trust in the LORD.

6 *There be* many that say, Who will shew us *any* good? LORD, lift thou up the light of thy countenance upon us.

7 Thou hast put gladness in my heart, more than in the time *that* their corn and their wine increased.

8 I will both lay me down in peace, and sleep: for thou, LORD, only makest me dwell in safety.

THE title of this Psalm has brought out a great diversity of views. The Septuagint, Ethiopic, Vulgate and Doway render it, Unto the end, in verses, a Psalm of David. The sense of the phrase, *Unto the end*, is supposed to be that this Psalm is to be sung always, perpetually, or very frequently, thus declaring this composition of great value and utility; or that it is to be sung in honor of Christ, who is *the end of the law*. This view rests for its authority solely on the Septuagint, the others merely copying from it. It derives no countenance from the Hebrew according to any understanding of the words, which we can reach. It is certainly true that in the Chaldee, as in the versions just quoted there is no intimation that it should read, To the chief musician. Jerome: Unto the conqueror; Horsley: To the giver of victory, meaning thereby, the Lord of hosts, the God of battles; Morison would read it, a Psalm of

David, dedicated to the God of victory, and to be performed on the stringed instruments of the sanctuary; but Calvin well says, " I do not approve of rendering the word, *conqueror;* for although it answers to the subject-matter of the present Psalm, yet it does not at all suit other places where we shall find the same Hebrew word used." The translators of the English Bible were probably correct in their rendering of the whole, addressing the Psalm to the leader of the music, on Neginoth, *i. e.* on the stringed instruments. Scott thinks that Neginoth may either mean the instruments with which the Psalm was to be sung, or the tune to which it was set, but he does not give us his reason for so thinking. The chief musician here was the overseer of the music. The word signifies any superintendent or foreman. It here designates the leader of the band, which used stringed instruments. Fifty-three of the Psalms and the third chapter of Habakkuk are inscribed to the chief musician. The musicians and singers were divided into classes. They all prophesied according to the order of the king. 1 Chron. xxv. 2. Some prophesied with the harp, to give thanks, and to praise the Lord, v. 3. Others lifted up the horn, v. 5. All of them were for song in the house of the Lord, and were instructed in the songs of the Lord, vv. 6, 7. The word *Neginoth* is found also in Habakkuk iii. 19, and is the general name for all stringed instruments. Addressing the Psalm to one of the leaders of public worship shows that it was for the whole church and not for one man. It is public property.

Hengstenberg thinks that "in Psalms iii., iv. we have a pair inseparably united by the inspired writer himself." But his argument in favor of this position will probably carry conviction to few minds. As close a resemblance may be discovered between Psalms widely separated from each other. Yet if any think they find evidence of such relationship between these compositions, such an opinion is quite harmless.

That this Psalm was designed as an evening hymn or prayer is a more probable opinion. Yet it is suitable for any part of the day. It was sung in the temple in day-light. All God's word is fit for meditation day or night, morning or evening.

Those who insist on its being regarded as an evening hymn generally, if not invariably, regard it as composed on the same occasion as Psalm iii. But this cannot be proved. Indeed it is hardly probable. It is true that much in this Psalm would suit the occasion of Absalom's rebellion. It is no less true that it would well suit a long period of persecution under Saul. Nor are other events in the life of David wanting to make such a Psalm appropriate. Lightfoot refers its origin to the affair of Sheba, 2 Sam. xx., and Venema to the destruction of Ziklag, 1 Sam. xxx. But all is rather conjectural. There is throughout the Psalm a remarkable "absence of personal and local allusions." The reasons for not regarding this as having its origin in the tumult excited by Absalom are that that sad event had been duly noticed in the third Psalm, that no hint to that effect is given in the title or contents of this, and that at least one phrase in it ill suits that time of trial, but is well adapted to David's history in the time of Saul. That phrase is, *How long will ye turn my glory into shame?* etc. Calvin: "*How long* (verse 2) indicates that he had a lengthened struggle." The rebellion of Absalom was soon put down. Yet Calvin says, If any should refer it to the revolt under Absalom let us not greatly contend about the matter. The sense may be much the same on either supposition. There is no evidence that nearly all the Psalms were written for any particular occasion, though some of them were. Hengstenberg: "How much the peculiar phraseology of the Psalms fits them for the general use of the church is easily perceived. Only glance for a moment at this Psalm. How much less edifying should it have been had David, in place of *glory*, which can be taken in the most extended sense, so that the very least can possess and lose it, put his *kingly* honor and supremacy; or in place of *vanity* and *lies*, under which every one can think, according to his situation, of that kind of calumny and deception, to which he may be peculiarly exposed, had substituted the foolish counsels of Absalom and his companions in particular!" The style of this and many other Psalms is such as to adapt it to almost every occasion of distress in the life of God's people. For remarks on the words *Selah* see Introduction, § 15.

1. *Hear me when I call, O God of my righteousness.* The Septuagint, Ethiopic, Syriac, Arabic and Vulgate put both verbs *hear* and *call*, in the past tense, so as to read *When I called, the God of my righteousness heard me.* But the Chaldee, our translators, Calvin, Venema, Jebb, Fry, Hengstenberg and Alexander correctly give us the present tense. To *hear* is graciously to hear, so to hear as to answer. *God of my righteousness*, expresses confidence in God as just and righteous. All admit thus much. The appeal is to God, the righteous Judge between David and his foes. We are always safe in asking God to do that which is consistent with his infinite, eternal and unchangeable rectitude. He is a God of holiness. He will not deny himself. In the sight of God we are all sinners, and so deserve no good thing from him. Yet we may be very much wronged and injured by the opinions, words and actions of men. In such case we may plead our integrity, and ask God to defend the right, because he is righteous. But the phrase *God of my righteousness* means more. It teaches that God is the author and source of my righteousness, both justifying and purifying. Some learned men decline to favor this sense, but it is held by others no less entitled to respect. The God of my life is the God, who gives and sustains my life. That is, he is its sole author. The God of my salvation is the author of my salvation. This is a better sense than my salvation—God. We might as well read, My life—God. Let us not fritter away the sense of Scripture. How strong the argument in this case is. Those who have received righteousness from God to justify and to sanctify them may very safely confide in God to save them from wicked foes. He, who has done the greater will surely do the less. It is strange enough to see some of our modern Protestant commentators higgling about this interpretation and then turn to Bellarmine and find him saying that *God of my righteousness* signifies God, from whom is all my righteousness, that is, by whose grace I am made just. Morison paraphrases it thus, "O God to whose distinguishing mercy I owe all that I possess or anticipate." In thus appealing to God the Psalmist strengthened himself by referring to his own past experience: *Thou hast enlarged me* when I was *in distress.* Luther and Hengstenberg read this verb in the present tense, but our translation is to be preferred on two accounts. 1. The argument is thus more complete. 2. The old versions invariably so render it. *Thou hast enlarged me.* To be in straits is to be in distress. To be set in a large place is to be made joyful by success or deliverance. The pressure is then removed and the soul walks at liberty. Often it is all the child of God can do to call to mind the former days, when God was with him, and to hope for better days to come. Those are blessed times, when it is manifest that God alone has been our deliverer. It is sweet to receive all at his hand. Thus one is encouraged to cry, *Have mercy upon me, and hear my prayer.* What God has done, he can do again. What he has wrought for one of his people, we may confidently ask him to do whenever we are in similar need. Instead of Have mercy upon me, Fry prefers, Be gracious unto me. This does not materially vary the sense. Mercy to sinners is grace, or unmerited kindness. Here is the sole ground of hope for the perishing. Morison: "It is sin that stands in the way of the answer of our prayers; but when sin is pardoned, and the sinner is accepted, then our prayers, in themselves feeble and imperfect, ascend as incense, and the lifting up of our hands as the evening sacrifice."

2. *O ye sons of men.* This translation is the same as the Septuagint, Ethiopic, Syriac, Arabic and Vulgate; Venema gives it simply, *Men;* De Wette takes the same view; but the Chaldee gives it *sons of man.* This is the literal rendering. For

remarks on the words, *sons of man,* see Introduction, § 16. It cannot perhaps be shown that any particular class of men is here exclusively addressed. But if the view expressed by Calvin, Patrick and others is correct, then the meaning of the Psalmist is, O ye, who think yourselves mighty and wise and great, who regard yourselves as model men, be ye ever so great, let me ask, *How long will ye turn my glory into shame?* The Italian reads, *Your chief men.* John Rogers' translation reads, O ye sonnes of men how long wyll ye blaspheme myne honor? The Bishop's Bible and church of England use the same words. The words, *will ye turn,* are not in the original, but are supplied by the translators. But the Septuagint, Ethiopic, and Vulgate render it, How long will ye be dull of heart? *i. e.* how long will ye have a heart like a stone, hard, and inclined to the earth, literally a heavy heart? It requires but a slight change in the Hebrew to make this rendering proper. Nor is this a bad sense, but very pertinent to the matter in hand. Still we have no right to alter the Hebrew text. It is best therefore to leave the words *glory* and *shame* and supply what may be necessary to give the sense. Morison renders it, How long shall my glory be for a shame? It has always been sufficient to awaken the deepest enmity of the wicked to find one of their race honored of God in a way counter to their inclinations. Abel's acceptance drew down Cain's indignation. David's success against the champion of the Philistines brought against him the jealousy and rage of Saul. The *glory* mentioned in this verse was, as some think, God himself. In proof they cite Psalm iii. 3, where David expressly calls Jehovah, My glory. Other parallel texts are also adduced. If this is the sense then the passage should read, How long will ye blaspheme God, who is my glory, or How long will ye esteem or speak of him, who is my highest honor, as though ye would make me ashamed of him? By a slight change of the Hebrew, Dimock proposes to read this clause thus, How long will ye be hardened in heart? He quotes Muis, Houbigant, and Lowth as approving this rendering. Although this gives a good sense, yet it is no better than that of the common version, and requires a change in the reading of the original.

Others think that by *glory* David refers to all the honor that God had bestowed on him, as a man, a king, or a prophet. His enemies did all they could to take it away and cover him with reproach. Wicked men hate stable and just governments, especially when so administered by pious men, as that God's fear is thereby promoted. Hengstenberg thinks the words *How long* might fitly be used at the very commencement of open hostilities under Absalom. Calvin with more reason supposes that reference is had to the perverse obstinacy of David's enemies, who were not stirred up against him merely by some sudden impulse, but that the stubborn purpose of injuring him was deeply fixed in their hearts. Yet David was confident. He knew who had given him the throne, granted him plenary inspiration, and made him a glorious type of the Saviour of the world. He therefore would not yield any of his claims. Indeed he dared not by cowardice and unbelief help on the work of God's enemies. He saw their impatience. He knew their folly, and boldly said, How long *will ye love vanity,* and *seek after leasing?* The entire career of David's enemies had no other foundation than their foolish conceits and settled malice. From first to last the whole opposition might, but for the wickedness and guilt of his foes, have been regarded as a farce. Their conduct might justly have been ridiculed. The *vanity* here mentioned points to the idle course they were pursuing. They were beating the air. They were in pursuit of a thing of no value. Their hopes would never be realized. The *leasing* spoken of is by some referred to the falsehoods with which opposition to David was uniformly conducted. Hengstenberg specially refers to 2 Sam. xv. 7, 8. It is a remarkable fact that many, who ordinarily pay some decent regard to truth, seem to feel quite at liberty to lie and slander in political affairs. Their ordinary defence is that the characters of public men are public property. But what right has any man to burn down the legislative and judicial halls of a country, or otherwise to damage them on the ground that they are public property? And are not the good names of useful public men of far more value than any public buildings? The terms *vanity* and *lies* are often found in Scripture. They designate the deceit, folly, corruption and certain overthrow of every bad cause. *Leasing* is an old Saxon word signifying false-hood. It was in some of the early translations of the Bible and was retained in the common version. Truly if the *vanity* and *leasing* of their foes could have ruined the cause of the righteous, not one of the servants of God would ever have held his own, or entered into rest. God never goes over to the side of deceit, folly and malice; therefore it always ultimately fails. A good cause and a good conscience always have infinite wisdom and power to help them forward. The more stupendous the fabric of falsehood and wickedness, the more terrible the crash, when it shall come tumbling down on those, who have reared it. Amazingly glorious will be the characters and illustrious the positions of the people of God, when the dust and smoke of calumny shall all be blown away, and their right and righteousness amply vindicated. Fry applies this whole Psalm to Christ, and makes him the speaker throughout. Whether this is or is not the correct view, yet his humiliation and his complete victory are an index and a pledge of the certain victory of all the saints over all their foes. None did ever trust in God and was confounded. The sure foundation, on which the final deliverance of God's people rests, is the fixed and gracious purpose of Jehovah, which is next brought forward.

3. *But know that the* LORD *hath set apart him that is godly for himself.* There is very considerable variety in the rendering of these words. For *set apart* Fry reads distinguished, and Horsley distinguished, or bestowed peculiar honor upon. The Septuagint, Ethiopic, Syriac, Arabic, Vulgate, Patrick, Gejerus, Moller, Ainsworth, Pool, and Gill, all favor the idea that the act of separation was wonderful, that the setting apart was such as to call for admiration. Concerning the persons separated three opinions have been advanced. The first is that set forth by Cocceius who supposes the church is meant, and that the separation here spoken of consists in taking the kingdom of God from the Jews and giving it to the Gentiles. But there is no satisfactory evidence that the church in her collective capacity is here spoken of. Yet it is remarkable how well the most of this Psalm suits the varied trials and experience of the whole body of believers. The history of one servant of God well written is in substance, though not in detail, the history of the whole church. The communion of saints extends to their sufferings and victories as well as to their sympathies and privileges. The second opinion is that the person thus separated is the Lord Jesus Christ, God's Elect, in whom his soul delighteth. Fry thinks that none but Jesus Christ the righteous can be considered as the speaker throughout this Psalm. No doubt Messiah is here foreshadowed. It is not necessary for any to contend that the whole sense and scope of the Psalm is exhausted in the literal David. He may be the subject of a Psalm, and yet what is fulfilled in him may be but a sample of what happens to the people of God in every age; yea, it may have a far more glorious fulfilment in the spiritual David, the great deliverer of God's people. And this is the third view which may be taken of this Psalm. It records the struggles and conflicts of God's anointed to the throne of Israel. But in so doing nothing hinders that it should disclose the higher matters pertaining to David's greater Son. The whole of the old dispensation was a shadow of Gospel times. Heb. x. 1. David is also a striking type of Christ, and often so declared to be. Very considerable scope is left for the exercise of a sober judgment on the question whether Christ is prefigured in any particular Psalm not expressly declared to be typical. Some may go further

than others and yet no fatal mistake be committed on either side. But the first thing is to ascertain the grammatical sense of the words. Then we may afterwards make any lawful use of them in their varied applications. It is said: *The LORD hath set apart.* These words point to a divine ordination. David was chosen of God to be king of all Israel. The narrative of the first disclosure of this choice is given in 1 Sam. xvi. 1–13. It was done in a very striking manner. God refused all the other sons of Jesse, saying to Samuel respecting Eliab, "Look not on his countenance or on the height of his stature; because I have refused him: for the LORD seeth not as man seeth; for man looketh on the outward appearance, but the Lord looketh on the heart." v. 7. To set apart implies more than mere election. It includes, in David's case, his anointing to his office by God's command, and the consequent presence and power of God's Spirit, v. 13, qualifying him for his office as the earthly head of the Theocracy. Thus God showed his sovereignty when "he chose David also his servant, and took him from the sheep-folds; from following the ewes great with young, he brought him to feed Jacob his people, and Israel his inheritance." Ps. lxxviii. 70, 71. For *godly* in this verse Calvin reads *merciful* or *bountiful.* David was "a man after God's own heart." It is expressly said by Samuel to Saul, "The LORD hath rent the kingdom of Israel from thee this day, and hath given it to a neighbor of thine, that is better than thou." 1 Sam. xv. 28. Venema: God chose David "as one whom he knew to be well affected both toward himself and toward men." The Arabic: The Lord hath marvellously chosen his elect; church of England: The Lord hath chosen to himself the man that is godly; For *godly*, Fry reads BELOVED, and applies it directly to Christ. Others would render it *beloved*, but apply it to David. The objection to this rendering is briefly stated by Calvin: "I meet with no examples of this signification of the word in Scripture." This first clause of v. 3 may be taken either as a reason why his enemies should desist from persecuting David, or as a reason why they should become godly. If the former is the right view, then he reminds them that they are engaged in a perilous undertaking, for they are fighting against God. His people are the apple of his eye. It is very dangerous to offend one of the least of God's children. But David would not merely warn them of peril. He would invite them to a new and better life. He virtually says, You have tried vanity and lies. All has failed. Come and I will show you a more excellent way. If you wish to be truly blessed here is the great secret. The LORD blesses the godly, the truly merciful. Come and get that blessing for yourselves. You shall never perish if God sets you apart to himself. He saves his people because they are his. Nor is this all, for the prayers of such are efficacious. *The Lord will hear when I call unto him.* Every child of God may say so. He has blessed promises, examples, and experiences all to that effect. This view of verse 3 is the more to be considered because it agrees with the essential benevolence of true piety, and because verse 2 is confessedly an exhortation or earnest remonstrance. Having shown the folly of sinners it is kind and proper for the prophet to call on them to seek true wisdom in embracing the service of God, and in securing the blessings vouchsafed to the godly, the merciful, the upright. Therefore,

4. *Stand in awe, and sin not.* This clause is not without difficulty. The Septuagint, Ethiopic, Syriac, Arabic and Vulgate all read, Be ye angry and sin not; John Rogers' translation: Be angrye, but sinne not. Nor does the difficulty end here. Paul quotes literally the Septuagint version, Be ye angry, and sin not. Eph. iv. 26; on the other hand the Chaldee has, Tremble and sin not; The Bishops' Bible, the Genevan translation and even the church of England agree with our version. Which then is the right rendering? The Lexicons and Concordances show that the verb rendered, *Stand in awe,* or *Be ye angry,* may signify any great agitation produced by fear, by anger,

or by grief. In proof Alexander quotes Isa. xxxii. 11; 2 Sam. xviii. 33; and Pr. xxix. 9. The Commentators are no better agreed than the Lexicons and Concordances. We must therefore look elsewhere. It may clear the question of some difficulty to inquire whether a man can be angry and not commit sin. The answer is that he may. Formerly the church of Rome in her catechisms put down anger among the deadly sins. But of late at least in some cases she substitutes some other word as malice or hatred, both of which are always sinful. The Scriptures clearly teach that anger is sinful in either of the following cases; when it is without a cause, Matt. v. 22; when it is unreasonable and bears no proportion to the offence given, Pr. xxvii. 4; when it is sudden and gives no time for reflection on our part, or for explanation on the part of others, Pr. xv. 18; xvi. 32; Jas. i. 19; or when it is long continued, and settles down into hatred or malice, Eph. iv. 26. It is possible to be angry, and not sin, to feel and express a righteous and reasonable displeasure at wickedness without malice against any one. In this sense Jesus Christ himself was angry, Mark iii. 5. Augustine and Luther both think the sense to be substantially this, Be angry, if you please, but go not so far as to let your anger become sinful. The doctrine thus taught is good; but where is the pertinence of introducing such words in this place? This exhortation in Eph. iv. 26 is quite to the point. But is it so in the verse under consideration? To avoid the obvious difficulties of the case, Hengstenberg insists that the phrase, Be angry and sin not, is substantially the same as, Sin not through anger. Though this is a proper sentiment, yet the exposition has not perhaps any parallel in Hebrew, and the paraphrase based upon it makes David consent to their wrongs against him except for the wickedness of them: "I would indeed permit your anger if the only effect were the injury which might thereby alight upon me, but since you cannot be angry without sinning, I must warn you to abstain from it;" Alexander: "*Rage and sin not*, i. e., do not sin by raging, as you have done, against me the Lord's anointed, and indirectly therefore against himself." Yet he admits that this construction is "not the most obvious or agreeable to usage." In this state of case the following suggestion is offered with diffidence, but as involving less difficulty than any other explanation. It is to render the words in this Psalm as our version does, Stand in awe and sin not. This is admitted to be a good rendering of the Hebrew. It also makes the exhortation very pertinent to the matter in hand. It is a call to sobriety, seriousness, solemnity, reflection, reverence, repentance. Then let it be noted that in Eph. iv. 26, Paul does not give the words, Be ye angry and sin not, as a formal quotation, but introduces them just as if they were his own. Henry seems to incline to the opinion that they are his own. Calvin thinks Paul may have no more than alluded to the sentiment. Even if he quotes these words, he was aware of the familiar use of the Septuagint version, and in quoting it, he was using words well known to at least some of his readers. He surely might with propriety introduce any words without formal notice of authorship, provided they were true and he approved them as pertinent. He elsewhere quotes heathen poets both with and without formal notice, Acts xvii. 28; and 1 Cor. xv. 33. He surely might without fault quote even an erroneous translation of a part of a Psalm, provided the sentiment borrowed was correct and expressed his precise idea. Inspired writers do at times certainly quote the mere words of older prophets, where they suit their turn, without a strict regard to the sense, in which they were originally used. Compare Hos. xi. 1; and Matt. ii. 15; also Ps. xix. 4; and Rom. x. 18. It is not necessary for us to understand Paul as endorsing the correctness of the Septuagint rendering of these words by employing them in his epistle. He merely found in a celebrated, but uninspired and often erroneous translation of the Old Testament words which precisely suited his argument or purpose, and he inserted them without preface or apology. Since writing the foregoing, the author has examined Hodge on Ephesians iv. 26. The comment there given is confirmatory of the interpretation here given. He says, "It is not necessary to assume that the apostle uses these words in the precise sense of the original text; for the New Testament writers often give the sense of an Old Testament passage with a modification of the words, or they use the same words with a modification of the sense. This is not properly a quotation; it is not cited as something the Psalmist said, but the words are used to express Paul's own idea. . . It is certain that all anger is not sinful." He says more to the same effect. M'Ghee thinks the right interpretation of Eph. iv. 26 is, that "there are circumstances in which you may be provoked to be angry, and can be angry without sin. . . There is a righteous anger, a just anger." If these views are admissible, we may render the clause, Stand in awe and sin not; Calvin: Tremble then, and sin not; Fry: Tremble ye, and sin not. Surely men, who love vanity and seek lies, may in the most solemn and earnest manner be called to trembling, like the Jailor, Acts xvi. 29; Isa. xxxiii. 14; Jer. xxxi. 19; Luke vi. 24–26; James v. 1–5. Nor are very outrageous sinners likely to be arrested and turn from their sins but in some way suited to produce violent commotion in their feelings. There was great excitement on the day of Pentecost. So it was prophesied there should be under the preaching of the Gospel. Zech. xii. 10–14. If these things are so, then preaching is not to be condemned, because it greatly alarms the wicked, and even agitates their whole nature, soul and body. In order further to warn and invite his enemies to repentance and holiness, David calls them to the secret duties of religion, and says, *Commune with your own heart upon your bed, and be still.* John Rogers' translation: Comen wyth youre awn hertes upon youre beddes, and remember youreselves; Bishops' Bible: Commune with your owne hart, and in your chamber, and be still; the Genevan translation: Examine your owne heart upon your bed, and be still. For *be still* Fry reads *reflect.* For Commune with your own heart Jebb reads, Speak to your own heart. Hengstenberg: Say it in your heart upon your bed; and Alexander: Say in your heart. There seems to be no good ground for misunderstanding the import of this clause. Its aim is to bring those addressed to calm, serious, silent reflection, and so to genuine repentance. The great difficulty with wrong-doers is that they will not consider. This is the complaint God often makes against them. Andrew Fuller has an admirable treatise on self-communion founded on this clause; Cobbin paraphrases it, Ask your conscience if you are doing right. If we would be wise we must not only commune with ourselves, but also *be still* or *be silent.* Silence is often a duty as well as a privilege. He who tells all he thinks may be a good prater, but he will make no progress in the heavenly life. His worship will be irreverent and unprofitable. His tree will bear no fruit upwards, because it takes not root downwards. But he that reflects long and silently feels strongly. While he muses the fire burns. The Chaldee paraphrases this clause: Say the prayer that is in your mouth, or say your prayer with your lips, and offer the petition that is in your heart, and pray upon your bed, and always remember the day of your death. He who would enjoy and profit by public worship must not neglect meditation, prayer, and self-examination. He who loves and practises these will be ready for all acts of public worship and will receive in a right spirit the command,

5. *Offer the sacrifices of righteousness. Sacrifices of righteousness* is a phrase found in the Pentateuch. Deut. xxxiii. 19. Some have supposed that the Psalmist was exhorting them not to imitate the hypocritical services of Absalom mentioned in 2 Sam. xv. 7, 8. No doubt he would warn them against all mockery of God. Moses did the same when he used the same phrase. But what are *sacrifices of righteousness?* Fry regards the phrase as equivalent to "the due sacrifices." Doubtless the due sacrifices were all sacrifices of righteousness, but does the phrase mean no more than

"the proper sacrifices appointed by the ceremonial law?" These were indeed means of grace to those who lived under the Mosaic Institute, and rightly observed them. They did all point to Christ as the end of the law for righteousness to them who believe. But a sacrifice of righteousness is not only something *due*, because commanded, but it is something offered in a right frame of mind, in humility, with godly fear, and with an eye of faith directed to Jesus Christ, the one great sacrifice for sins. Under the old dispensation the sacrifices were of two kinds, material and spiritual. The material consisted of thank-offerings dedicated to religion, and of sacrifices for atonement. The spiritual consisted in prayer, in praise, in alms-giving, in penitence, in an entire devotion to God's cause. Ps. cxli. 2; Ps. cvii. 22; Jer. xvii. 26; Ps. li. 17; Heb. xiii. 15, 16; Hos. vi. 6. This latter class of sacrifices belongs to all dispensations, is obligatory under the gospel, 1 Pet. ii. 5, and was always by God preferred above all others. Ps. l. 8–15. Venema: The sacrifices of righteousness are true spiritual sacrifices, the opposite of those which are external and typical. Isa. i. 11–17, and Mark xii. 33, 34; Chaldee: Subdue your lusts, and it shall be counted to you for a sacrifice of righteousness. Waterland reads *true sacrifices*, and in justification refers to Vitringa on Isaiah. The substance of the command then is, Worship God in the way of his appointment by making all the offerings required by the ceremonial dispensation under which you live and in the manner required, bringing nothing maimed, torn, lame, sick, mean, blemished, stolen, or obtained by fraud. Mal. i. 13, 14; Deut. xxiii. 18; and Isa. lxi. 8. Also offer to God all that spiritual service required by him as a part of true religion under all dispensations. Berleberg Bible: "Offer the sacrifices of righteousness, therefore must ye desist from your sin and anger, and fulfil your obligations. For otherwise your faith will be vain, and your whole service unprofitable, even though ye sacrifice ever so much. It is not enough to bring sacrifices; they must also be offered in a right way. Whosoever hates his brother can bring to the altar no acceptable gift. His very prayer is sin. The Lord hates the religious services which are connected with unrighteousness, enmity, injury to neighbors, and renunciation of dutiful obedience. A penitent and contrite heart is required to a right sacrifice, Ps. li. 17, and an humble and thankful faith, Ps. l. 14, 23, that one may present himself to God as a living sacrifice, and his members as instruments of righteousness. Rom. vi. 13, and xii. 1. That the great duty here enjoined is spiritual is further manifest from the parallel clause, *And put your trust in the* LORD. The Jehovah here spoken of is Jehovah-jireh (the LORD will provide) known to Abraham, Gen. xxii. 14; Jehovah-nissi (the Lord is my banner) known to that great prophet Moses, Ex. xvii. 15; Jehovah-shalom (the Lord send peace) known to Gideon, Judges vi. 24; Jehovah-tsidkenu (the Lord our righteousness) foretold by the weeping prophet, Jer. xxiii. 6, and xxxiii. 16; Jehovah-shammah (the Lord is there) of the eloquent Ezekiel, Ezk. xlviii. 35; and Jehovah-rophi, *the* LORD *that healeth thee*, Ex. xv. 26. This trust in Jehovah must exclude reliance on all other beings and resources. It must be in God alone. It must be cheerful and not reluctant, constant and not temporary, firm and not wavering, obedient and not self-willed, from the heart and not feigned. For *trust* some read *hope* in the Lord. Such piety and such trust will satisfy the soul and cause it to cease its eager quest after merely earthly good, as is the custom of the multitude; for,

6. There be *many that say, Who will shew us* any *good?* Morison: Who will show us good? Edwards: The world saith, etc. There were many such in David's days. There always have been many such. Centuries ago a writer enumerated two hundred and eighty-eight opinions of philosophers and founders of sects or schools respecting the chief good. The confusion of tongues reigns over the earth on this subject. The whole unbelieving world is on this matter a Babel. Nor are men becoming any wiser

as the world advances, except as revelation and God's Spirit give them understanding. The great mass of men are still gaping after they know not what. What shall we eat? what shall we drink? wherewithal shall we be clothed? how shall we rise in worldly honor? where is perfect, or even real happiness? are questions, which have lost none of their interest to the masses. The answers and modifications of answers are endless. But carnal men feed on husks. They spend their strength for naught. Such is the sense if the Psalmist is addressing the wicked, as he probably is. But some think he is addressing his desponding followers, who ask, Whence shall deliverance come to us? who will show us any good? our cause seems desperate, or at least very discouraging. It is amazing to what extent God's intrepid servants having a righteous cause are annoyed by the unbelief of those around them. Nehemiah had such pests. Henry Martyn tells us that he had in his employment a man, who was continually saying to him, It is of no use to teach your religion to Hindoos. There seems to be no good cause for the rendering of Boothroyd: Who will show kindness unto us? To both friends and foes David may pertinently disclose the secret of true happiness, which is the favor of Jehovah: LORD, *lift thou up the light of thy countenance upon us.* This is what we all need, and this is what we may through God's mercy all attain. The import of the prayer may be gathered from the opposite phrase, which represents God as *hiding his face, i. e.* withdrawing his favor, refusing his protection. To countenance any one is to stand by him, or express kindness towards him. To discountenance is to frown upon, discourage, or withdraw from a man or a measure. Some suppose the figure to be taken from the Shechinah, whose bright side was towards Israel at the Red sea, but the dark side towards the Egyptians, and whose radiance till the destruction of the first temple often gladdened the hearts of God's people. Morison: In the expression, " *the light of thy countenance,*" I have no doubt allusion is made to the bright symbol of Jehovah's presence, which stood on the mercy-seat between the cherubims of glory. The form of expression in the text is first found in Numbers vi. 25, 26, where it is made a part of the blessing pronounced on the people by the priests. The phrase *granting the light of the countenance* doubtless includes also the favorable aspects of Providence. The petition here presented by David, like the four last petitions in the Lord's prayer, is not for himself alone but also for others; Alexander: " *Upon us* extends the prayer to his companions in misfortune, or to all God's people, or to men in general, as if he had said, this is the only hope of our lost race. The plural form may indicate the expansive, comprehensive spirit of true piety." Several of the old versions put the verb in this clause in the indicative mood, so as to read, The light of thy countenance is sealed, or is extended, or shines upon us. Although the authorized version is preferable, yet either rendering shows the contrast between the state of God's friends and that of his enemies, and points out the true source of blessedness. Calvin gives this as the purport of the whole: " The greater number of men greedily seek after present pleasures and advantages; but I maintain that perfect felicity is only to be found in the favor of God." Great is God's mercy to his chosen. Rich is the inheritance of his poorest and most afflicted servants, whereof David and every experienced child of God can bear witness, and say,

7. *Thou hast put gladness in my heart, more than in the time* that *their corn and their wine increased.* Situations and conditions are happy or otherwise as God grants or denies his presence and blessing. Several of the ancient versions much vary the rendering of this verse. The Septuagint, Ethiopic, Syriac, Arabic and Vulgate put in *oil* as well as corn and wine.

The Septuagint, Ethiopic, and Vulgate read: Thou hast put gladness into my heart. They are multiplied by the increase of corn, of wine, and of oil; The Chaldee and Syriac make David to have gladness from the time that others had these good things, while the Arabic makes him simply to rejoice over these things whenever they are given. On this rendering Gill says, it is as if David had said concerning his enemies, "I never envied their prosperity, I always rejoiced when they had a good harvest, or vintage, and still do, and yet they have risen up and rebelled against me, and requited me evil for good." Jarchi, Abenezra and Kimchi all give this sense. Bellarmine admits that *oil* is not found in the Hebrew text, but says it may have originally been there and been dropped by mistake, or that the authors of the Septuagint may have added it by way of explication. He also observes that the Scripture usually speaks of corn, wine and oil in the same connection. But none of these reasons is valid. The first would have weight, if there was evidence that it was founded in truth. The rendering given by the Vulgate of the latter part of the verse admits of a good sense. Respecting it Bellarmine says, The prophet adds another argument, from which men may understand that God is the author of all good things, to wit, that it is he, who multiplies the products of the earth and all its fruits. He then cites the words of Paul in Acts xiv. 17. Let us not tamper with the Hebrew text. Instead of *Thou hast put*, Hengstenberg employs the present tense, *Thou givest;* Jebb: Thou hast given gladness to my heart; Alexander: Thou hast given gladness in my heart, not to my heart, but to me in my heart, *i. e.* a real, inward, heartfelt gladness; Grotius thus connects this with the preceding verse; "If thou, LORD, wilt lift the light of thy countenance upon us, thou wilt put a greater gladness in my heart, than is generally expressed at a plentiful harvest of corn, or a great increase of wine." One thus blessed and happy surely may be calm and quiet when all the world is up in arms and agitated with commotions, and may with good reason say,

8. *I will both lay me down in peace, and sleep: for thou,* LORD, *only makest me dwell in safety.* Calvin: "He concludes by stating that as he is protected by the power of God, he enjoys as much security and quiet as if he had been defended by all the garrisons on earth." Truly blessed is the man that is free from all those fears which have torment, from all those cares which corrode, from all those vexations which belong to men, whose hope is in the things of earth. Our English version well expresses the force of the first two verbs. The rendering of the Doway and of the versions which it follows is awkward: In peace in the self-same I will sleep, and I will rest; Hengstenberg gives the full sense when he says, In peace I will both or at the same time lay me down to sleep, and I shall go to sleep. The word rendered *both* is by many correctly rendered *at the same time*, or *at once*. The meaning is that being at peace with God, having benevolent feelings towards men, and possessing a mind quiet and undisturbed by evil passions, he would assume the posture of rest, and would not fail to be refreshed by sleep. The reason is that God is his protector. Our version makes the word rendered *only* or *alone* to qualify the word Jehovah. God alone efficiently protects us, whether he does it directly by himself, or by the ministry of angels, or by the instrumentality of men, or by the use of other means. Perhaps the meaning is that the Psalmist had despaired of aid from all creatures, that his reliance was solely on God, and that he found this exclusive trust the most consoling and quieting, the small number of his adherents being quite inadequate to do anything for his defence without special aid from God. But the Psalmist was most probably consoling himself by the word of God, and applying to himself a promise long before made to the church in her collective capacity. For the use of the word here rendered *alone* is in the sacred writings rather peculiar and striking. It occurs *eleven* times in the Hebrew Scriptures. It is once rendered *solitary*, Lam. i. 1; once, *solitarily*, Mic. vii. 14; once *desolate*, Isa. xxvii. 10; seven times, *alone*. This verse contains the only place where it is rendered, *only*. It first occurs in Lev. xiii. 46, where it is said, The

leper shall dwell *alone*. It next occurs in the prophecy of Balaam where he says of Israel, Lo, the people shall dwell *alone*, and shall not be reckoned among the nations. It next occurs in Deut. xxxii. 12, The LORD *alone* did lead him. But the passage, which was doubtless before the mind of the Psalmist is in Deut. xxxiii. 28, Israel then shall dwell in safety alone; the fountain of Jacob shall be upon a land of corn and wine, etc. Here we have corn and wine as in the verse under consideration, and we also have the very words, originally spoken of the whole church, applied by David to himself. If this is the sense here, then David intends to say, that although he is forsaken by the great mass of mankind, so that he is made to dwell almost alone, yet he dwells in safety, or he declares how completely and safely he is separated and delivered from his enemies and all by the good hand of God upon him. Hengstenberg proposes "a sort of double sense" to the word *alone*: Thou only, O LORD, makest me dwell alone and in safety. The objection to this is not that it teaches any error, but where is the rule of grammar for making a word, which occurs but once in a sentence, signify both *only* and *alone* and at the same time qualify two words remote from each other? In Lev. xxv. 18, 19 the promise to Israel of dwelling safely is twice repeated. Hengstenberg thus impressively concludes his commentary on this Psalm: "With right does the Psalmist appropriate to himself the promises which originally referred to Israel. What is true of the whole is true also of the individual, in whom the idea of the whole is become vividly realized; so that we may again ascend from the individual to the whole."

DOCTRINAL AND PRACTICAL REMARKS.

1. The praises of God in the sanctuary should be conducted with so much skill as to be edifying. The subject of church music is worthy of attention from God's people and ministers. The Gospel neither prescribes nor forbids any particular mode of conducting this part of worship, provided only it be decent and edifying. Whether there shall be a "chief musician," or a band of musicians in each congregation, God has not decided, but in all places we should edify the church with psalms and hymns and spiritual songs. The people should sing.

2. How simple are the remedies provided for God's people in all their diversified trials. Dickson: "Though there be many and diverse troubles of the godly, yet there is but one God to give comfort, and but one way to draw it from God; to wit, by prayer in faith: *hear me when I call*, v. 1."

3. The great foundation of Christian hope is in justification by the righteousness of God, which is the righteousness of Christ, v. 1. This opens access to God.

4. How blessed is the doctrine of the divine mercy. It is all our hope, v. 1.

5. What an advantage the tried servant of God has over the young convert, vv. 1, 7. No teacher so impresses his lessons on us, as experience. Were we not very unbelieving, all older Christians would long since have had boundless confidence in God. He has so often appeared for us that we should never distrust him again. Great deliverances should excite great gratitude and inspire great calmness in new trials.

6. Let no man be surprised at having bitter and inveterate enemies, v. 2. Even old friends often turn against the godly. Venema: "The esteem and favor of men is very deceitful and variable." Let us not revile our slanderers, but warn them and call them to repentance. Calvin: "While nothing is more painful to us than to be falsely condemned, and to endure at one and the same time, wrongful violence and slander; yet to be ill spoken of for doing well is an affliction, which daily befalls the saints. And it becomes them to be so exercised under it as to turn away from all the enticements of the world, and to depend wholly upon God alone." Our duty

is done when we see to it that evil reports respecting ourselves are false, or, if true, that we heartily repent of the matter of them.

7. Let those who live under good governments set an example of contentment, moderation and obedience to the laws, and not unite with brawlers in railing against rulers and laws, which secure to them all the blessings they may reasonably expect. He, who resists a lawful government, resists God. He, who rails at it, rails at him who established it, v. 2.

8. It is a small matter to be judged of man's judgment. Those who love vanity and lies, rather commend than condemn us by their censures, v. 2. We must make it our business by holy lives to prove their calumnies false.

9. The wicked know not what they do when they annoy and persecute God's servants, vv. 2, 3. Not only of widows in Israel but of all his people on earth God is the avenger. Dickson: "The cause of the world's despising piety in the persons of God's afflicted children is the gross ignorance of the precious privileges of the Lord's sincere servants."

10. The wicked are always practising deception on themselves. They are false to all their own best interests. All they do is against them. Every error involves others. Their great difficulty is they are sensual, having not the Spirit. Dickson: "Mere natural men cannot be made wise, neither by the word of God, nor by experience in their own or others' persons, to consider that things of this earth, as temporal riches, honor and pleasure, are nothing but vanity and deceiving lies, which promise something and pay nothing but vexation of spirit, because of guiltiness and misery following upon the abuse of them."

11. The people of God never act more wisely than when they trust and hope in him, even in the darkest times, vv. 3, 5. Reliance on God is as safe for us as it is honorable to him. Venema: "The highest excellence and glory of man is to enjoy the favor and grace of God; and to have a hope of being heard, when we cry to him." "In the midst of perils and evils nothing is more safe than to make God our refuge."

12. How happy all God's servants are, v. 3. They are set apart to God as vessels of honor, 1, by a free, eternal, holy, unchangeable choice in Christ Jesus; 2, by a powerful, internal, spiritual regeneration; 3, by a perfect, irrepealable justification; 4, by a kind, wise, watchful providence, ordering everything in their lot, and distinguishing them in this, that all things work together for their good, making their sorrows more blessed than are the joys of the wicked, and giving them the victory even in death; 5, such shall be openly and gloriously owned and set apart in the last day. They are set apart to God's service and honor and enjoyment here and hereafter. The service and enjoyment are both imperfect here. In the next world saints shall love and rejoice in perfection. With all their imperfections they are God's jewels, and shall at last be so owned, Mal. iii. 17. The highest enjoyment on earth is found in communion with God. Dickson: "The comfort of God's Spirit, and sense of man's reconciliation with God in Christ, is greater than any worldly joy can be, and is able to supply the want of riches, honors, and pleasures worldly, and to season, yea, to swallow up the sense of poverty, disgrace, and whatsoever other evil," v. 7.

13. True faith is never at a loss for arguments to strengthen itself. It reasons from God's righteousness, from his past favors, from one's present distress, from God's mercy, v. 1, from his purposes, from his providence, v. 3. Indeed faith always has some good plea to urge. It is the unbelieving who have nothing to urge.

14. Let us learn to judge righteous judgment. How often the wicked judge by outward appearances. With many success and prosperity are the test of a righteous cause. Outward calamities never prove any one out of God's favor, though many wicked men think otherwise.

15. The views respecting anger presented in the exposition of v. 4, show the great importance of not holding any rule of moral conduct, which is beyond or beside the Scriptures. Whenever men try to be holier than God's law, they fall into confusion.

16. True religion is ready to make sacrifices, v. 5. It brings its offerings with a willing mind and an unsparing hand. To the grudging and reluctant it may be said, You will never get to heaven at such a rate. Henry: "Serve God without any diffidence of him, or any fear of losing by him. Honor him by trusting in him only, and not in your own wealth, nor in an arm of flesh; trust in his providence, and lean not to your own understanding; trust in his grace, and go not about to establish your own righteousness or sufficiency." Never dole out a small pittance. Give him all you have and are and hope for.

17. To do our whole known duty, and then to feel that we deserve nothing good, and are but unprofitable servants, needing all God's mercy in Christ, is the height of earthly wisdom, v. 5.

18. There is no piety without trust in God, v. 5. If we have no confidence in him, how can we have piety? Great deliverances should inspire strong trust in God.

19. Trust is an element of faith, and we know that without faith it is impossible to please God. The heathen delighted in worshipping objects of sense but "we must worship an unseen God, and seek an unseen good. 2 Cor. iv. 18. We look with an eye of faith further than we can see with an eye of sense."

20. Let all beware of deluding themselves with a reliance on the future of this life as likely to afford more enjoyment than their experience of the past would lead them to expect, v. 6. Bickersteth: "The *young* expect to find it when grown up and their own masters. *Parents*, when their children are settled and provided for. The *merchant*, when wealth is acquired, and independence secured. The *laborer*, when his day's or week's toil is ended. The *ambitious*, in gaining power and reputation. The *covetous*, in gaining money to supply all his wants. The *lover of pleasure* in earthly enjoyment. The *sick*, in health. The *student*, in gaining knowledge. The *self-righteous*, Rom. x. 2, 3."

21. Great perils commonly precede great preferments. David found it so. The way to any great attainment is usually steep and rough. This is true in everything. It is especially true in moral attainments. Let not the children of God be discouraged through the greatness of their way. No strange thing has happened to them.

22. Those are the sweetest consolations which succeed sore and terrible conflicts and afflictions, vv. 6, 7.

23. In v. 7 there is an allusion to the happy life of the agriculturist. It was a great mercy when for his sins man was sentenced to hard labor, God permitted that labor commonly to be in the open air, under the light of the sun, and generally on each man's own premises. Of all the innocent temporary joys of earth, few exceed those of the farmer. No life is more independent.

24. God's people have no grief beyond the reach of divine control and comfort, v. 7. Morison: "O happy religion of the cross! Thou canst irradiate the darkest scene by the bright rays of celestial peace! Thy joys are unearthly and unfading! They fill up the soul, in which they dwell."

25. Nearly the whole of this Psalm shows the value of a good conscience. How could David have ever borne himself as he did but for being free from a condemning heart?

26. The state of God's people is never desperate. Moller: "Hope in God remains to them when stript of all human aid and protection."

27. The people of God unquestionably possess a very remarkable secret of turning

evil into good—something far more valuable than the fabled alchymist's stone, which was to turn everything into gold.

28. When God puts us at any post we need fear nothing. He, who called us, can sustain us. David found it so. Payson said, if God should call him to rule half a dozen worlds, it would be quite safe to go forward, and humbly do his best; but that he would not feel it safe to attempt unbidden to govern as many sheep.

29. If we would secure God's blessing we must plead his promises. The unbelieving are fitly classed with the abominable. Nor should we forget that a promise made to the whole body of believers is valid to secure the interests of each one, and that a promise made to any one believer is of force for the good of all other believers to the end of the world.

30. Let us use all proper efforts, and then not rely on means but on him, who has ordained them. David fled before his enemies, but he expected his safety in God, not in flight.

31. Self-examination is a duty of true religion under all dispensations. Were men not very insensible to the value of eternal things, they would be more engaged in this duty. No doubt, some " are afraid and unwilling to look into their hearts, lest they should be convinced and overargued by conscience of their woful condition. Home is too hot for them." But surely a wise man will deal honestly with himself before the day of final trial shall come. Every evening specially invites to this duty. Then silence reigns; the world is absent; sleep, the very image of death, summons us to think of eternal things, v. 8. Even some of the heathen practised a nightly review of their moral conduct during the day.

32. In writing on this Psalm the author has with high satisfaction read not a few expositions and treatises on this portion of Scripture. On the other hand he may say that he has never been more impressed with the danger of drivelling, or of trying to make little of Scripture than in reading some others. When a preacher or writer undertakes to make as little as possible out of any part of God's word, he has reason to fear that he has quite missed its import.

33. How pleasant it is to walk with God and to have his comforts poured into the soul for refreshment, vv. 6, 7. Bates: "Communion with God is the beginning of heaven, and differs from the fulness of joy that is in the divine presence above, only in the degree and manner of fruition. As the blushes of the morning are the same light with the glorious brightness of the sun at noon-day."

34. If the literal David was so safe and if he so completely triumphed, how puny is all the array against him, who is both the root and offspring of David. His rest is indeed glorious.

35. Just as either David's adherents or his foes were surely wrong on a great public question, so now either saints or sinners are sadly playing the fool. One or the other will surely be put down. If sinners are right, saints are of all men most miserable. If the saints are pleasing God, sinners are madmen.

PSALM V.

To the chief Musician upon Nehiloth, A Psalm of David.

1 Give ear to my words, O LORD; consider my meditation.

2 Hearken unto the voice of my cry, my King, and my God: for unto thee will I pray.

3 My voice shalt thou hear in the morning, O LORD; in the morning will I direct *my prayer* unto thee, and will look up.

4 For thou *art* not a God that hath pleasure in wickedness: neither shall evil dwell with thee.

5 The foolish shall not stand in thy sight: thou hatest all workers of iniquity.

6 Thou shalt destroy them that speak leasing: the LORD will abhor the bloody and deceitful man.

7 But as for me, I will come *into* thy house in the multitude of thy mercy; *and* in thy fear will I worship toward thy holy temple.

8 Lead me, O LORD, in thy righteousness because of mine enemies; make thy way straight before my face.

9 For *there is* no faithfulness in their mouth; their inward part *is* very wickedness; their throat *is* an open sepulchre; they flatter with their tongue.

10 Destroy thou them, O God; let them fall by their own counsels; cast them out in the multitude of their transgressions; for they have rebelled against thee.

11 But let all those that put their trust in thee rejoice: let them ever shout for joy, because thou defendest them: let them also that love thy name be joyful in thee.

12 For thou, LORD, wilt bless the righteous; with favour wilt thou compass him as *with* a shield.

FOR an explanation of the words, To the chief musician, in the title of this Psalm see above on Psalm iv. *Nehiloth* is explained in several ways. Some think it signifies *armies*. These would render the preceding word not *upon*, but *against*, so as to read, To the chief musician against the armies, *i. e.*, a hymn to be sung against the hostile bands that arose in the country or invaded it. This view rests upon very slender grounds. Indeed it is quite conjectural. The second renders *Nehiloth* by the word *heritages*. This supposes that David here calls the twelve tribes *the heritages*, and that this Psalm is a prayer for the nation of Israel. Although this view is sanctioned by the Septuagint, Ethiopic, Arabic, and Vulgate, yet it is not well supported by reasons. Even those who introduce the word *heritages* are not agreed as to the sense in which it is to be taken. Some think *Nehiloth* is the first word of some song, to the tune of which this Psalm is to be sung. So Abenezra, Luther, Hengstenberg and Alexander are inclined to the opinion that *Nehiloth* points to the subject of the Psalm as being *the lots* of the righteous and the wicked. Other views, hardly demanding a statement, have been set forth. But the more probable opinion is that Nehiloth signifies *wind instruments*, as Neginoth in the preceding Psalm signified *stringed instruments*. Venema, Gill, Morison, Cobbin, Dimock, Fry, and Clarke agree in this rendering. The flute, horn, pipe, cornet, hautboy and organ are all wind instruments. Patrick selects the organ as the instrument chiefly designed; Calvin: "I adopt the opinion of those who hold that it was either a musical instrument or a tune; but of what particular kind I consider it of little importance to ascertain." One great difficulty in settling the question is that *Nehiloth* occurs no where else in Scripture. This precludes a comparison and leaves us very much to conjecture. This inscription in the Syriac reads, "A prayer in the person of the church when she comes early in the morning to the house of the Lord." But this is interpretation, not translation. Yet the idea that this was a morning hymn is favored by respectable writers. For other matters relating to the title see above on Psalm iv.

As to the occasion or precise date of the Psalm there is considerable diversity. Some think it refers to the events respecting Sheba noticed in 2 Sam. xx. Others think it refers to the rebellion of Absalom. Others suppose it is a Psalm composed by David after his long troubles with Saul. In the absence of light to guide us in this matter, any opinion must be purely conjectural. The occasion, if there was any, of its writing is concealed from us. We are not bound to hold that David wrote all the Psalms to suit particular times and events. Horsley entitles this Psalm, " A prayer of Messiah, in the character of a priest, coming at an early hour to prepare the altar of burnt-offering for the morning sacrifice." His view of the whole Psalm corresponds with this idea. But it cannot be shown that the Messiah is primarily spoken of in this Psalm. The names of God in this Psalm are *Jehovah* LORD, *Elohim God* and *El God*. On the first two see on Ps. i. 2; iii. 2. The third is explained in v. 4.

1. *Give ear to my words,* O LORD. The appeal is directly to Jehovah. Open a prayer-book of the church of Rome and you will see the devotee first directing his cries to Paul and Peter and a long list of beings considered more approachable than the great I AM. But such worship derives no countenance from God's word. Inspired men teach us to come to God directly through Jesus Christ. It is worthy of notice that the Psalmist in this and in the next verse does not say what his prayer was. He knew that God saw his heart: " Thou understandest my thought afar off." God's omniscience is a source of great comfort to the pious. They know that he will do not only up to what they think, but exceeding abundantly above all they can think. Therefore they cry, *Consider my meditation.* The Chaldee, Syriac, and Hengstenberg also read *my meditation;* Alexander: *My thought;* Horne: *My dove-like mournings;* Waterland and Horsley: *My sighing;* Fry: *My rising thoughts;* the Septuagint, Ethiopic and Vulgate: *My cry;* Venema: *My earnest desire;* Gill: Understand *my moan;* Cocceius: *My breathing,* meaning the inmost desires of my heart. For *consider* some read *understand, perceive.* He asks God to *think upon* the things which now fill his own soul with *thought.* The Most High knows the language of a sigh. He has heard many a cry that was never sent forth. Blessed be his name he hears " the groanings which cannot be uttered." Rom. viii. 26, 27. Both Calvin and Hengstenberg properly notice that the last clause of the first verse and the first clause of the second verse are not a mere repetition of the first clause of the first verse. Calvin says that David divides his words " into two kinds, calling the one obscure or indistinct moanings, and the other loud crying." When Horne speaks of *dove-like mournings* he is not fanciful, but his reference is to Isaiah xxxviii. 14, where the same word is used. Blessed be God, who knows all the soul-troubles of his servants, and hides not his face from their inexpressible groanings, their unutterable sighs. God's people can often do no more than say to him, " I am shut up, I cannot come forth, I have no words, I am in distress, I know not what to pray for." As Luther said on a great public occasion, " I can do nothing else. God help me." What a blessed truth that God often regards us as praying in faith when we have said nothing. He acknowledged Moses' prayer when that prophet had not spoken a word. Ex. xiv. 15. God heard also the prayer of Hannah when " she spake in her heart; only her lips moved, but her voice was not heard." 1 Sam. i. 13. Yet ordinarily when the heart is duly inflamed with desire sooner or later words will be found, and the feelings find vent Therefore David says:

2. *Hearken unto the voice of my cry, my King, and my God.* Calvin says, David " expresses one thing in three different ways; and this repetition denotes the strength of his affection, and his long perseverance in prayer. For he was not so fond of many words as to employ different forms of expression, which had no meaning; but being

deeply engaged in prayer, he represented by these various expressions [give ear to my words—consider my meditation—hearken unto the voice of my cry] the variety of his complaints. It therefore signifies, that he prayed neither coldly nor only in few words, but that, according as the vehemence of his grief urged him, he was earnest in bewailing his calamities before God; and that since it did not immediately appear what would be their issue, he persevered in repeating the same complaints." The *cry* here is emphatic. It is a piercing utterance of the heart in articulate sounds. Waterland does not strengthen the force when for *cry* he reads *supplication*. The address to *My King and my God* is a taking hold of the covenant, claiming the protection of a subject of him, whose kingdom is over all, and the loving-kindness of him who is over all God blessed forever. True faith will expel despondency. It will give hope, and enable the child of sorrow to say, My *God and my King, for unto thee will I pray.* Gill: "This is the boldness, freedom of speech, which the Scriptures speak of, Heb. iv. 16 and x. 19, and the saints are allowed to use in prayer before God; when they may pour out their souls unto him, and freely tell him all their mind." What would suffering believers do without access to the throne of grace? But with a mercy-seat always accessible, what can they lack? No marvel that the saints, though diverse in many things, are alike in the reality of their attachment to closet duties and to public worship. David was not alone in saying,

3. *My voice shalt thou hear in the morning,* O LORD; *in the morning will I direct* my prayer *unto thee, and will look up.* He declares that he is determined to give himself to prayer, and that with heartiness. When one is very intent on doing his work well, and abundantly, he rises betimes and prosecutes it diligently. To seek God early is to seek him earnestly. The man, who gives his first waking thoughts to God, will not be indisposed to acts of devotion at later hours of the day. Some think that *in the morning* signifies every morning, so that David declares what should be the habit of his future life. If men expect to maintain habits of devotion, it will be well to form strong resolutions on the subject. A good purpose is a good thing. But some think the Psalmist in this verse rather expresses his wish than his determination. So Calvin: *Oh that thou wouldest hear my voice in the morning;* and Hengstenberg: *My voice mayest thou hear in the morning.* In their comment both express a preference for the optative form. A good man asks for a spirit of prayer. He begs that he may not be left to wander on without any right desires after God. Some think that the stress is to be laid on the word *hear,* and that the import of the whole is, Do not turn away from my prayer, when in the morning I cry to thee. Either mode of explanation gives a good sense, but the latter seems preferable. The chief objection arises from the fact that putting the first clause in the optative destroys the parallelism in the verse, for even Calvin and Hengstenberg admit that the latter clause is to be rendered in the future, *In the morning will I direct my prayer unto thee.* The Arabic reads, *In the* morning I will stand before thee; Syriac: I will appear to [or before] thee; Dimock: I will prepare for thee; Mudge, Horsley and Morison prefer: I will set everything in order before thee. The words *my prayer* are not in the Hebrew. The English reader may see that they are supplied by our translators as they are in Italics. But herein they follow the old Jewish commentators. The word rendered *direct,* or *set in order,* is the word used to express the arranging of the wood and shew-bread, etc., on the altar. See Gill and Hengstenberg on the place. David adds, *And I will look up; i. e.,* look up with confidence, as not ashamed. Some render it, I *will look out.* So Montanus, Michaelis, Piscator, Gill and others; Calvin: And I will keep watch; Owen: "It is diligently to look out after that which is coming towards us, and looking out after the accomplishment of our expectation. This is a part of our waiting for God;" Horsley: I will watch for thee. The imagery is taken from placing one

in a watch-tower to announce the approach of a returning messenger or any one else. This state of mind is elsewhere described by the prophets. Thus Habakkuk ii. 1, "I will stand upon my watch, and set me upon the tower, and will watch to see what he will say unto me;" and Micah vii. 7: "There I will look [or look out] unto the LORD; I will wait for the God of my salvation; my God will hear me." When we send a letter or a message asking a favor, we look out for an answer. This looking is an act of confidence, of reliance on the love and power of God. The suppliant would not be restless and impatient, though he would be eager to catch the first sign of coming relief, as the watchman is to catch the first ray of morning. Well may he wait and hope.

4. *For thou* art *not a God that hath pleasure in wickedness.* To him that has righteousness on his side, it is for an anchor of hope that God is righteous and abhors iniquity. The Lord not only has no pleasure in any wickedness, but he has great delight in all goodness. Morison says the negative form gives emphasis to the words used in this clause. The nature of God determines the course of providence. He will at length check wickedness. The word EL, here rendered God, signifies *strong* or *mighty* when used as an adjective, and *might* or *power* when used as an abstract term. It here means God, the mighty God, the Almighty. As a name of God standing alone it is chiefly, if not exclusively, found in the poetic parts of Scripture. It occurs about *two hundred and forty* times in the Hebrew Bible, and in a majority of cases refers to the true God. This God hates sin. "If all sin were punished here, men would despair of mercy, but if no sin were punished here, men would deny a providence." For *wickedness* Fry reads, *an ungodly man,* and Horsley, *a wicked person.* This does not change the doctrine taught. *Neither shall evil dwell with thee.* For *evil* Waterland and Fry read, The wicked; and Horsley, An evil one. Fenwick thinks the evil one, the devil, is intended; but that is a sense remote from the scope of the Psalm. To *dwell* is to sojourn, or to be entertained as a guest. Some have thought that the language is borrowed from the fact that strangers, who were determined to retain idolatry, were not permitted to *reside* in the land of Canaan, though they might pass through it. To the renewed soul it is a great comfort that in the next world neither evil itself nor wicked beings shall dwell with or near God's redeemed ones. For,

5. *The foolish shall not stand in thy sight.* Fry, Hengstenberg, and Alexander, for *foolish* read *proud;* Horne: *mad;* Ainsworth: *insane boasters;* Dimock: *the profane;* Cobbin: *the madly profane;* the Septuagint: *transgressors of the law;* several ancient versions, *bad;* others, *malignant;* John Rogers' translation reads, Soche as be cruell may not stande in thy syght. All sin is folly and madness. On this point all rational beings will at last come to the same conclusion. There will be no diversity of judgment on this matter in the last day. All sin is in its own nature malignant and mischievous. Its natural tendency is to ruin and wretchedness. It would produce far more misery on earth than it does, were it not for the restraints put upon it by the Lord. All sin is cruelty to one's soul, to one's race, to a bleeding Saviour. All sin is proud and insolent. It affects independence of God. It swells and struts. It exalts itself against God. It is fond of high looks and proud imaginations. It trades in self-conceit, self-deception and fearful presumption. All sin is utterly opposed to God. As fire and water resist each other, as light and darkness are utterly diverse, so God resists the proud. His nature is wholly opposed to it. He cannot cease to abhor it, without ceasing to be God. No creature has any adequate conception of the evil of sin. None but God comprehends it. Because it is so vile, those who love it *shall not stand* in God's sight. They shall not be owned as servants; they shall not be heard in their petitions; they shall not accomplish their designs; they shall *fall* before terri

ble judgments; they shall fall in the great day of trial. The overflowing scourge shall sweep them away. The reason is found in the divine purity. *Thou hatest all workers of iniquity.* Those do greatly slander God, who teach that he will punish sin only because it is opposed to his law or his will, and not because it is opposed to his infinite, eternal, unchangeable rectitude. So repugnant to God's nature is iniquity, that he would not save even his elect, except in a way that should fully and forever put away both the guilt and stain of sin, and bring all conceivable odium on transgression. God would not even spare his Son, when he stood in the place of sinners, lest he might seem to spare sin. Could he cease to hate it, he would cease to be worthy of love and confidence. Nor is it merely some forms of sin that God abhors, but he hates *all* workers of iniquity. Nor does he hate sin in general, as some men profess to do, but countenance it in detail. For,

6. *Thou shalt destroy them that speak leasing.* On leasing, see on Psalm iv. 2. It is a proof of the divine benevolence that in all the Scriptures God has set himself so terribly against falsehood. If the malignity of a sin may be learned from the temporal miseries it produces, then can nothing be more opposed to God than the various forms of untruth, known among men. Some are satisfied with an insincere practice of the true religion, while others content themselves with a sincere practice of a false religion. The religion of some is all a lie. The profession of others is hypocritical. Let those who indulge in any species of untruthfulness remember the dreadful examples made of Gehazi, Ananias and Sapphira. Let them read the many terrible woes denounced in Scripture against falsehood, noting even the dreadful sayings of the last chapter in the Bible, Rev. xxii. 15. Truly God's face is set against those who invent, retail, or willingly believe falsehood. The Psalmist here says God shall *destroy* such. The dreadfulness of the destruction threatened against these wicked men is elsewhere described. When God destroys the ruin is utter, the wrath is terrible. God also marks for punishment the murderer. *The Lord will abhor the bloody man;* Gill and Horsley render it: *The man of blood;* Calvin and Horne: *The blood-thirsty;* The Septuagint, Ethiopic, Vulgate, Anderson and Morison: *The man of bloods;* several ancient versions, The shedder of blood; for *man of blood,* Jebb suggests *man of bloodshed;* some think that the plural form, *bloods,* in the Hebrew, points to the fact that men who once shed innocent blood are commonly ready to do it again; others suppose it is merely the Hebrew idiom, expressing no more than *a bloody man;* Mudge and Dodd think that a man of blood is one "whose blood, for any capital crime, is due to justice; *on whom is blood,* or the debt of blood;" *i. e.,* he is a man who ought to be put to death. That God's anger burns terribly against every form of murder is certain. No sentence of human law is more accordant with the revealed will of God than this, that the murderer should be capitally punished. The Lord *abhors* such men. In most cases his providence so orders it that those guilty of blood are detected and punished in this world. In the world to come they must, without repentance, meet a dreadful doom. The LORD also abhors *the deceitful man,* or as Horsley renders it, *The man of guile;* Fry: *The man of fraud.* Men may attempt to practise fraud on God, may be full of guile in all their apparent devotions, may be hypocrites and so lose their souls. Or they may flatter, slander, backbite, cheat, or deceive their neighbors. In either case God's abhorrence is against them. If the only thing in the way of the deliverance of God's people is that it involves the destruction of the men of falsehood, of blood, of deceit and of fraud, God will not stand at that. He would destroy a world of sinners rather than permit one of his people to be finally overthrown. He is righteous. Therefore each of his people may say,

7. *But as for me, I will come into thy house in the multitude of thy mercy.* Commentators are not agreed whether the Psalmist here expresses a determination as to what

he will do, or merely a persuasion of what he shall be able to do. The form, *but as for me*, seems to make it parallel to Joshua xxiv. 15, where that pious man says: "As for me and my house we will serve the LORD." In this place it is clear that a purpose of the mind is expressed. Others think that David merely expresses a strong hope of what he shall through God's great mercy be able to accomplish, viz., that though now driven far from the tabernacle (the temple was not yet built) he should in due time be allowed to visit the place, where God gloriously manifested himself. Both senses are good, and both may be intended, so that he may be regarded as saying, "Though I am driven from my own house and from the house of God also, I am not in despair, nor is my purpose to serve the Lord at all shaken. This shall all be shown as soon as God through his abundant mercy opens the way for my return, as I am confidently expecting him to do. Then one of my first acts shall be a public, solemn acknowledgment that he is my Deliverer." This is the view Calvin seems to favor: "The primary object of David was to encourage himself in the assured hope of preservation by the mercy of God; but at the same time he shows that upon obtaining deliverance, he will be grateful to God for it, and keep it in remembrance." Morison holds the same view: "He expresses his conviction, that this exile will not be of long duration, and declares his determination to embrace the earliest opportunity of entering into the house of God." Yet in all this David was humble. He relied not on the number of his adherents, nor on his own merits or wisdom, but solely on the abundance of God's mercy. Men never rest upon anything so safely as on God's undeserved favor, his unmerited kindness. He delights to give grace to all that hope in his mercy. Nor does a pious reliance on God beget presumption or irreverence, for the Psalmist says, And *in thy fear will I worship toward thy holy temple*. All worship, which is destitute of godly fear is not accepted. Where there is no fear, there is no scriptural piety. The word rendered *worship*, might be translated, *bow down*. The posture of worship should be decent and reverent. Some suppose that the time for this reverent worship is the same as that mentioned in the first clause of the verse, viz.: the time of deliverance from his enemies, and so they make *toward thy holy temple* to signify "towards the holy of holies, the ark, the mercy-seat, the Shechinah, the cherubims of glory." The word *temple* may easily be shown to designate not only the house of God built by Solomon, or the holy of holies, but also the whole tabernacle. Some think David's meaning to be that as soon as deliverance should come, he would reverently worship in the court towards the holy place. But why may we not supply a word, and so get a yet better sense, and at the same time retain the natural use of the word *toward*, so as to read the clause thus, And *now* in thy fear will I worship toward thy holy temple? *q. d.*, I will not wait till the day of my full deliverance. I will now begin this blessed work, and as I cannot worship *in* thy house, I will worship toward it. This form, *I will*, is found in many cases where it expresses an action to be begun very soon, although not now begun. This bowing and worshiping *towards* the temple was practised by the Jews wherever they might be. 1 Kings viii. 35, 44; Dan. vi. 10. Venema and Gill think that by *thy holy temple* David points to *heaven*, itself. If so, it makes it the more proper to regard the last clause as declaring what the Psalmist would do even before his deliverance from persecuting foes. Instead of *toward* Fry reads *at*, but this is not sustained. Beginning his worship at once he prays:

8. *Lead me, O* LORD, *in thy righteousness, because of mine enemies*. What a prayer! how suitable to every member of the church militant! How fitting to the occasion are these words! Instead of *enemies*, Morison is inclined to read, *Lookers on*; Horsley reads, *Them that watch me*; and several, *My observers*. Every servant of God is a spectacle to angels and men. He is watched over by angels, and he is watched by

wicked men, who hope to see him commit some great error. Every good man knows something of the plague of his own heart, and knows it is not to be trusted. But at this time, besides his spiritual foes, David had many personal and perhaps national enemies, whose hatred was deadly. One error on his part might blight all his prospects. And so he says, *Lead me.* If God guide us, we shall be safe. If he forsake us, we shall all go astray. Divine conduct is the only sure preservative against superlative folly. *In thy righteousness* is another appeal to God to judge between him and his foes, and a prayer to God for preservation in the way of righteousness, which includes two things, the spirit of submission to God's method of saving sinners by imputed righteousness and of obedience to God's righteous precepts. If the words of Habakkuk ii. 4, *The just shall live by faith,* refer to the Gospel method of saving sinners, as Paul shows, by what rule can we properly exclude from the word righteousness in this place the idea of something beyond simply administrative justice? If the *leading* here spoken of is to end in David's standing accepted before God in his temple, then how can this be but through the merits of Christ? There is no righteousness but that of the Redeemer, in which any mere man since the fall could ever appear before God with acceptance. The ingenious, learned and pious men, who have labored to make it appear that we have here a mere appeal to the divine rectitude, have not made out their case. Even Calvin does not take the word *righteousness* in an evangelical sense, yet he is evidently dissatisfied with so narrow a view, and adds, " *The righteousness of God,* in this passage, as in many others, is to be understood of his faithfulness and mercy which he shows in defending and preserving his people." But God's saving mercy and faithfulness are bestowed on sinners through Christ alone. Hengstenberg: " The righteousness here spoken of is the property of God, according to which he 'gives to every one his own—befriends the pious, who confide in his promises, and destroys the ungodly." But that attribute of God, by which he is led to give to every one his own, would, without Christ's righteousness imputed to us, save none of us but would send us all to endless ruin. For *mine enemies* Jebb reads *thine enemies;* but this is evidently an error in his printer, or is brought in from some erroneous edition of the Hebrew text. The next clause reads, *Make thy way straight before my face.* Fry following the Syriac and Arabic connects the words *because of mine enemies* with this part of the verse. The vigilance of his enemies was good cause for offering both petitions, but there is no good reason for dividing the clauses otherwise than as in the English text. Fry also reads the clause, *Make plain my way before me;* and in his commentary Morison reads *my way before my face.* This reading is probably to be accounted for as that of Jebb just noticed. No reason is given for this change. It does not even follow the Septuagint, Ethiopic and Vulgate, which read, *Direct my way in thy sight.* This is a very good prayer. It implores divine omniscience both to guide and to search one's way. Still our version is right. By *thy way* is signified the way of God in providence and in grace. The way of God is the way that pleases God. David implores divine guidance and deliverance with special earnestness on account of the desperate wickedness of his enemies:

9. *For* there is *no faithfulness in their mouth.* Some regard David here as virtually saying, Help me, for I am better than these men. It is true that David was not in the wrong in his controversy with them. Yet such a construction of his prayer is not very pleasing. David would not indeed use weapons, which they allowed. But if we make him say that the cause of his urgency for the divine aid is the perfectly unscrupulous character of his enemies, we have a good sense in a logical connection without making the Psalmist in any measure commend himself. One of the horrible accompaniments of ordinary war is that it is "a temporary repeal of all the principles of virtue." It legalizes artifice, slaughter, and horrible cruelties. But the wicked repeal

the code of morals whenever it suits them. David's foes fearfully departed from all
the law of God. For *faithfulness* Fry reads *truth;* Horsley: *constancy;* Calvin paraphrases it, They speak nothing uprightly, or in sincerity; Horne says, The charge
brought against them is, that truth and fidelity were not to be found in their dealings
with God or each other. The ancient versions for *faithfulness*, read *truth, rectitude*, or
equity. Rectitude and equity perish with veracity. The history of David's life shows
that very few men ever suffered more from the utter want of candor and truth in his
foes. Saul's whole deportment was of this description. He made promises only to
show his utter faithlessness. Nor was the conduct of Absalom, of Ahithophel, or his
heathen foes characterized by sincerity. One of the earliest and most painful tokens
of depravity is a want of regard to truth. Ps. lviii. 3. Instead of *their mouth* the
church of England following the Hebrew reads *his mouth*; Hengstenberg: "The use
of the singular suffix at the first is to be explained by the entire mass of enemies being
represented by the Psalmist as one person, as a personified ungodliness;" Alexander:
"For there is nothing in his mouth, *i. e.*, the mouth of any one of them, or of all concentrated in one ideal person, *sure* or *certain, i. e.*, true." Elsewhere David brings out
the same truth in another form: "They bless with their mouth, but they curse inwardly." Ps. lxii. 4. Nor is this want of faithfulness surprising when their real characters
are considered, for *their inward part* is *very wickedness*. The word rendered *wickedness*
is plural, *wickednesses*. Gill says it "signifies woes, calamities, mischiefs;" Septuagint: Their heart is vain; Calvin: Inwardly they are full of iniquity; Dodd and
Mudge give this sense: Their inward part is all woful, execrable stuff or rottenness;
Fry: Within them is deep depravity. In a foot-note he asserts that the word translated *wickedness* means the innate depravity of the human heart. All sin is naturally
traced to the fountain of a fallen and corrupt nature. For *inward part* Gill would
read *inward thought*, and for authority appeals to the rendering given in Ps. xlix.
11 and lxiv. 6. The heart of an unregenerate man is always worse than his life.
Inward wickedness is the parent of all visible vices, crimes and iniquities. Matt. xv.
18, 19; Mark vii. 21, 22. Nor is a religious experience of any permanent value,
unless it leads us from actual sins to trace up our corruption to its source. The Arabic
renders this clause: Iniquity is in their hearts. If there was no sin in the heart,
beyond a question the life and the speech would be faultless. But because their heart
is all wrong, *Their throat is an open sepulchre*. From a corrupt heart comes a foul
mouth. Some have thought that the figure of the text was in substance this: that the
throat like a sepulchre was the receptacle of much corruption. But not that which
goeth into the mouth defileth a man; but that which cometh out of the mouth, this
defileth a man. Matt. xv. 11. This principle is by Christ himself expressly applied
to the matter of wickedness. Mark vii. 20–23. But as a sepulchre, where human
bodies are decaying, sends forth a foul air, both unpleasant and unwholesome; so men,
whose inward part is wickednesses, naturally and necessarily in their speech breathe out
corruption, filling society with misery and greatly dishonoring God by their evil communications, their filthy and foolish words, their dreadful slanders, detractions, railings, revilings, complainings, murmurings, quarrelings, tattlings, heresies, oaths, curses,
imprecations, blasphemies. Cocceius thinks this clause has reference to perniciousness
of doctrine. The tongue is a world of iniquity. The lips of the wicked utter all
devouring words. Horne: "Their throat was an open sepulchre, continually emitting,
in obscene and impious language, the noisome and infectious exhalations of a putrid
heart, entombed in a body of sin." This seems to be all that properly belongs to the
figure here. Yet the other sense given teaches no falsehood respecting human nature,
and is supported by eminent writers. Thus Calvin: "*Their throat is an open sepulchre*
as if he had said, They are all-devouring gulfs, denoting thereby their insatiable desire

of shedding blood." Gill: "The throat of wicked men may be compared to an open sepulchre for its voracity and insatiableness; the grave being one of those three or four things, which never has enough or is satisfied; . . . and so may be expressive of the desire of the wicked after sin, who drink up iniquity like water, and of their delight in it and their fulness of it, and yet still greedy, insatiable, and not to be satisfied;" Patrick speaks of the open mouth, gaping for the destruction of the innocent; Henry: "They are likewise bloody, for *their throat is an open sepulchre*, cruel as the grave, gaping to devour and to swallow up; insatiable as the grave, which never says, *It is enough.* Prov. xxx. 15, 16. . . . The grave is open to them all, and yet they are as open graves to one another;" Hodge: "*Their throat is an open sepulchre, i. e.*, from their throat issue words as offensive and pestiferous as the tainted breath of an open grave; or, what from the next clause may appear probable, Their throat is always open and ready to devour like the insatiable and insidious grave." He adds: *They flatter with their tongue.* The variation of the rendering of this verse where it is quoted in the New Testament is not important. It there reads: With their tongues they have used deceit. In all flattery there is deceit. "A man that flattereth his neighbor spreadeth a net for his feet," Prov. xxix. 5. This is a sin highly offensive to God. "The Lord shall cut off all flattering lips," Ps. xii. 3. But he, who flatters men, will either pray not at all, or but deceitfully. So his prayer will be sin, because it will be hypocrisy. Piscator, Gejerus and Hengstenberg render this clause, They make smooth their tongue; Geddes: Their tongue is smooth to flatter; Horsley: They set a polish with their tongue; Venema: "They pretend love to God and man, that they may the more easily impose on the credulous, and overwhelm them;" "Morison: "Every word they uttered seemed to be in falsehood. Nothing they said could be relied on. They spoke only to mislead and deceive." This and the next preceding clause are quoted by Paul, Rom. iii. 13, in proof of the doctrine of the depravity of the whole race, both Jew and Gentile. What one unrenewed man is as to God, the same in kind are all the unconverted. What one sinner does respecting divine things, all sinners in like circumstances will do. As each angel in heaven is a specimen of the innumerable company of those pure spirits, who worship around the throne, so that if we knew how one of them would feel and act we might know the character of all; so it is with the wicked of our own or of any other race. Each is a sample of the whole. Morison: "There has been a mournful uniformity in the character of the wicked in all ages; whether they have set themselves to persecute the church in her collective form, or the individuals, who have ranked under her banner;" Calvin: "Paul does not wrest these words from their genuine meaning when he applies them to all mankind, but asserts, with truth, that David showed in them what is the character of the whole human family by nature." Men of this description, living under the government of a just God, must be terribly exposed to ruin. Accordingly the next words are:

10. *Destroy thou them, O God.* The Septuagint, Ethiopic, Arabic, and Vulgate: Judge them; Syriac and Hengstenberg: Hold them guilty; Chaldee and Alexander: Condemn them; Cocceius: Count them guilty; Calvin: Cause them to err; Fry: Convict them; Patrick: Pronounce the sentence of condemnation against them; Michaelis: Pronounce them guilty; Scott: Deal with them as guilty; Luther: The word [rendered Destroy] properly signifies such a decision and judgment as would show and manifest what sort of neighbors they are, when their ungodly dispositions are disclosed, and every one is made known. The metaphorical sense of the verb rendered *destroy* sometimes is to *err*. This led Calvin to render it as he did. He also supposed this and the next clause to be connected, this asking for the cause of ruin, and the next for the ruin itself. But he is not supported by others, although he has

made some excellent practical remarks. The marginal reading is as good as any if we use the words in the old English sense. Make them guilty, *i. e.*, condemn them. Guilt, meaning just exposure or liability to punishment, is in a large number of cases connected with the word rendered *Destroy.* Desolation and destruction follow condemnation or ascertained guilt. This is the first sentence, found in the Psalms, of an imprecatory form. For the right mode of understanding such expressions see Introduction, § 6.

On this verse Horne remarks that such clauses are spoken "by way of prediction rather than of imprecation," and renders them all in the future. Is it not sufficient to say that we have here the prophetic form of denouncing evil against the wicked, as in the next verse we have a prophetic annunciation of the blessings which shall come on the righteous? The very plans of the wicked will in the end prove their overthrow. *Let them fall* (or they shall fall) *by their own counsels.* Just as Haman was hanged on the gallows he erected for another, so the wicked are continually falling by devices designed to overwhelm others. If God let a man have his own way he will soon be in hell. A withdrawal of restraint, of wisdom, and of mercy, will at once complete any one's ruin. Calvin renders the clause, Let them fall from their counsels, *i. e.*, he supposes David to be praying that their counsels might come to naught, their undertakings prove unsuccessful; Alexander: "They shall fall from their plans, *i. e.*, before they can accomplish them, or in consequence, by means of them;" Patrick paraphrases it, Let their own devices, whereby they seek to ruin me, destroy themselves; The Septuagint, Ethiopic, Chaldee, Syriac, and Arabic also read *from their counsels.* It is easy for God to bring to naught the counsels of the greatest schemers and plotters against the peace of his church and the glory of his Son. And it is as righteous for him to do so as it is easy. They deserve his displeasure. *Cast them out* (or thou wilt cast them out) *in the multitude of their transgressions.* The number of their iniquities would terribly affright men, if they had any just conception of the evil nature of sin itself. Then they would look upon their transgressions as innumerable as the sands on the sea-shore, or the stars of heaven. To be cast out in sin is to be a cast-away—refuse—reprobate silver. To those who rejected him Christ said, Ye shall die in your sins. To die in a far country, or in prison, or in delirium, or in lunacy, is in itself very undesirable; yet such deaths may open the gates of heaven. But to die in sin is the worst thing that can happen to any man. For sin is flagitious. It is rebellion against God. *For they have rebelled against thee.* Sin attacks God. It flies in his face. He is the object against which all sin is directed. It is his law which sin breaks, his will which sin opposes, his authority which sin tramples under foot, his mercy which sin rejects. Hengstenberg: "God would not be God, if he should suffer them to go unpunished;" Morison says the original "implies the opposition and resistance not only of open rebellion, but also of an unbelieving, cavilling, and disputatious spirit." In character, temper, and destiny the wicked are quite the opposite of the righteous. Accordingly David says:

11. *But let all those that put their trust in thee rejoice.* In this world those who have the least right to rejoice often seem to be the most merry; and those who have the greatest cause of joy often seem to be the most sad. But things shall not always stand thus. God will in due time put all right. The righteous who now walk by faith and take God at his word, though they walk in darkness and have no light, shall soon commence a new career—a career of uninterrupted and unending joy and triumph. Accordingly he says, *Let them ever shout for joy. Ever,* both here and hereafter. "Blessed are ye that weep now: for ye shall laugh." Luke vi. 21. Let them learn to rejoice in tribulation; let them make known their inward comforts and supports; let them make their boast in God; let them not keep silence when they should shout for

joy. For all this there is good cause. *Because thou defendest them.* Waterland: *Thou shalt overshadow them.* Who can harm those that are the apple of God's eye, are in the hollow of his hand, and abide under the shadow of the Almighty? It matters not who assaults when God defends. The hand of God as safely protects against a world in arms as against one little worm. Therefore, *Let them also that love thy name be joyful in thee.* To love God's name is to love him and all, by which he has made himself known. All the righteous have this love. All of them think upon God's name, cherish it, glory in it. To hear it lightly spoken of gives them pain. To hear it blasphemed shocks their sensibilities. But when it is honored, extolled, praised, they are happy. They delight in God's name, titles, attributes, works, word, worship, ordinances, and people. The saints joy in God, not in the creature. In the world they have tribulation; but in him they are joyful. Alexander renders all the clauses of this verse in the future tense thus: And all trusting in thee shall be glad; forever shall they shout for joy, and thou wilt cover over them; and in thee shall exult the lovers of thy name. This is both declarative and prophetic. It cannot fail. Some suppose that David is praying that God's people may rejoice on account of the deliverances shown to him. This may be so. But a righteous man wishes God's people to be happy even if he himself should see much sorrow. True piety is benevolent. Could it have its way the saints should never shed another bitter tear. But true piety is also humble, and knows its own ignorance and quarrels not with God for his needful chastisements. God's nature is the basis of all spiritual comforts. And so it is said:

12. *For thou,* Lord, *wilt bless the righteous.* Both in the Greek and Hebrew Scriptures the same words are used whether to express the act of the creature blessing God, or the act of God blessing the creature; and yet there is a great difference between these. When man blesses God, the utmost he can do is to make known his desires that God may be honored by himself and all others. But when God blesses one he not only speaks good concerning him, but that good is sure to be accomplished. Man's blessing is optative; God's, authoritative. Nor is there any exception to the blessedness secured to the righteous. They are all in covenant. They are all blessed, not equally, but savingly, eternally, ineffably. This it is God's wont to do. There is no exception. For *the righteous,* Fry, after Nebiensis, reads, The *Just One.* He says that it is to be understood personally of Christ. He cites Horsley as favoring this view: "The Psalmist, speaking with the highest assurance of the final deliverance and happy condition of the good, is driven, as it were, by the Spirit that inspired him, to a choice of words, fixing the blessing to a single Person, to him who is blessed over all, and the cause of blessing." It is true that all the blessings of believers come to them through Christ; but there is no more reason for making the word *righteous* specially refer to Christ in this place, than in scores of others. If it be said that it is in the singular here, so is it in many other places, where no one thinks of applying it specially to Christ. Yet it is true that God has blessed him, and given him joys above all others, and has made him the depository of the blessings which so enrich his people; as well as the channel, through which they flow. Still the promise is to each believer. Morison: "Innumerable are the ways, in which Jehovah can fulfil this gracious promise to his people." In their lot in life, in their basket and in their store, in their bodies and souls, in their frames of mind and general tempers, in their relations with the world, in their joys and in their sorrows, in life and in death, in time and in eternity, thou, Lord, canst bless, wilt bless, and shalt bless the just. So that *with favor wilt thou compass him as* with *a shield.* Though the general figure, expressive of protection, is the same as in Ps. iii. 3, where God is called a shield, yet the word there rendered shield is not the same used here, this being often rendered *buckler,* and

describing a piece of armor which was both offensive and defensive, having a solid case for protection, and surmounted by a spear or spears, against which, if any pressed, they were pierced. Horsley renders this last clause: "Like a shield of good will thou wilt stand guard around him." And truly "the good will of him that dwelt in the bush" is the hope of us all. It makes rich and adds no sorrow. Every good thing the righteous receive is of God's mere grace, and sovereign mercy. It is of *favor*, not of debt. The righteous deserve no good thing. Their righteousnesses are filthy rags. What they are and what they hope to be is all by the grace of God. This now and forever *encompasses, fortifies, crowns, adorns* them. It is their defence, their beauty, their chief glory. Dodd says the word rendered *shield* must mean some pointed weapon, as a *spear*. So that the clause should read, *Thou wilt encircle him with favor, as with a fence of spears,* as a prince is encircled with spears or spearmen. But this is forced. The word is never rendered spear, but always shield, buckler, or target. A shield embossed with spikes or spears seems to be the armor described. All over is the servant of God protected and altogether is he surrounded with loving-kindnesses.

DOCTRINAL AND PRACTICAL REMARKS.

1. In prayer it is well to resort to the aid of language to express our thoughts and petitions, v. 1. "Take with you words and turn to the Lord," Hos. xiv. 2. It is well to have definite conceptions of what we need.

2. If God gives us a heart to pray, he will give us a blessing in answer to our prayers, v. 1. All his names, all his offices, all his promises secure thus much. He hears our sighs; he knows their meaning; he can and will attend to our case.

3. Meditation and prayer are kindred duties, v. 1. Each leads to the other. They dwell together. Bates: "Meditation before prayer is like the tuning of an instrument and setting it for the harmony. Meditation before prayer doth mature our conceptions and exercise our desires." In Genesis xxiv. 63, our translators put the word *meditate* in the text, but in the margin they put the word *pray*. No man can devoutly meditate without praying, or devoutly pray without meditating.

4. If in prayer words should be wanting, and we should be conscious of no more than breathing, sighing, meditation, others have been in like straits, v. 1. Let us not then be discouraged. He who will not quench the smoking flax can hear a breath, as well as a cry, a moan as well as words, a meditation as well as a speech.

5. Idolatry must be very hateful to God. As the sovereign of an empire must set himself against those who would cut off his revenue; so Jehovah must abhor all those practices, which deprive him of the tribute of prayer and praise, supplication and thanksgiving, which are his due, v. 2. All sin is a wrong to God. That which hinders, or corrupts his worship is a direct affront, a daring robbery.

6. True prayer is never careless or listless. It is earnest. It is importunate. It thinks. It also cries, v. 2. Delay of the answer for a season but inflames its desires.

7. No wickedness should drive us from God's throne of grace. If our own sins rise up against us, let them impel us to plead for mercy. And we see David here urged on to prayer by the wickedness of those who sought his destruction. If the wicked curse, let us pray; if they lie, let us pray; if they flatter, let us pray; if they shed the blood of the saints, let us pray, vv. 1, 2, 3.

8. If we would have the LORD for our God, let us also take him for our King, v. 2. If we reject his laws, it is certain we reject his grace. If we refuse his yoke, we surely do not accept his mercy. If his sceptre is an offence to us, so is his plan of saving sinners by his blood. If Christ is made of God unto us righteousness, he is also made of God unto us sanctification.

9. It is well when we can plead with the Lord as *our* King and *our* God to bless

us, v. 2. He bids us do it. Nothing but our unbelief holds us back. If he calls us his sons, surely we may cry, Our Father. If he says, Ye are my people, we may say Our God. Thomas made progress when he cried, My Lord and my God.

10. True submission and obedience to God will not make us dull but lively in his service, v. 3. It will arouse the spirit of devotion, v. 2. True religion is not *quietism*, nor *stoicism*, nor *atheism*. It brings the soul into communion with God. It arouses all its activities. It gives wondrous energy. It stirs up thought at midnight. It begets habits of devotion. It goes not by fits and starts.

11. Every well spent day must be begun with God, v. 3. It is right he should have our first and best thoughts. Gill: "The morning is a proper time for prayer, both to return thanks for refreshing sleep and rest, for preservation from dangers by fire, by thieves and murderers, and for renewed mercies in the morning; as also to pray to God to keep from evil and dangers the day following; to give daily food, and to succeed in business and the employments of life; and for a continuation of every mercy, temporal and spiritual." What a wonderful example was that set us by our Lord: "In the morning, rising up a great while before day, he went out and departed into a solitary place, and there prayed." Mark i. 35. It is not to be supposed that this was a solitary instance. Luke vi. 12; xxi. 37. Is there a thriving Christian on earth, who gives his earliest thoughts to the world and only later ones to God?

12. Genuine prayer will be looking out for answers, v. 3. The presentation of the petition is important as it secures the blessing. Prayer lives in a watch-tower. The Oratory should be an observatory. Berleberg Bible: "One must keep on the watch, if one would receive anything from God, and wait with longing for the desired answer, also be constantly looking out for help, and giving heed to whatsoever the Lord may speak." Henry paraphrases thus, "I will look up; will look after my prayers, and *hear what God the* LORD *will speak*, Ps. lxxxv. 8, that, if he grant what I asked, I may be thankful; if he deny, I may be patient; if he defer I may continue to pray and wait, and may not faint." Gill says the phrase, *I will look up*, or *out*, is "expressive of hope, expectation, faith, confidence that an answer would be returned."

13. Wrong views of the character of God spoil all religion, v. 4. When man's hope is built on the idea that God is like his erring creatures, that he is not holy, just, or true, all his solemn services are worthless, and his prospects are dismal. God is inflexibly just. If he saves a sinner who believes, he will so do it as to condemn sin in the flesh. Impunity is unknown in God's government.

14. Because God is holy, all who love holiness shall triumph over all who love wickedness, v. 4. There is no bond of sympathy so strong and enduring as that, which results from similarity of moral character. God cannot but love his own image. He cannot but hate the image of the wicked one. Light and darkness may be so mingled as to produce a twilight, but God and wickedness can never dwell together. Charnock: "Holiness can no more approve of sin than it can commit it."

15. There must be something inconceivably monstrous in all impiety, else God would not so often put upon it the brand of folly, v. 5. Dickson: "Let wicked men seem never so wise politicians among men, yet they shall be found mad fools before God, selling heaven for trifles of earth, holding war with the Almighty, and running upon their own destruction in their self-pleasing dreams, to the loss of their life and estate, temporal and eternal." God's views of sin may be learned from such places as Hab. i. 13; Zech. viii. 17; Amos v. 21–23; Isa. i. 14; Jer. xliv. 4. Charnock: "Sin is the only primary object of God's displeasure." It cannot be shown that God hates anything but sin.

16. Persecutors, heretics, false teachers, deceivers, and haters of all goodness are no

novelty. Good men have always been hated, hunted, harassed by evil doers. Demas will forsake the church. Diotrephes will form parties. Absalom and his friends will seize on the temple. But the triumph of the wicked is short. If workers of iniquity abound, no new thing has happened, v. 5.

17. Because God is holy and man sinful, regeneration is necessary. God, and sinners who love iniquity, cannot dwell together, vv. 4, 5, 6. To expect happiness in heaven without a new nature is more foolish than any dream of madmen. Men may believe the world is flat or round, that it moves or stands still, and yet be virtuous, and happy, and on the road to heaven. But without a new heart no man can be saved. Christ justly expressed amazement that Nicodemus, a master in Israel, supposed to know the Old Testament Scriptures, should be ignorant of this doctrine.

18. There must be future retribution because God is holy, because men are not here dealt with according to their characters, because God has determined to destroy the wicked, and because that destruction comes not in this life, v. 6. This doctrine is implied in hundreds of texts, where it is not declared.

19. All hypocrisy is vain. Nothing is more idle, v. 6. We never can impose on the Almighty. Morison: "Let all workers of deceit, all hypocritical pretenders, whether in the intercourse of life or in the fellowship of the church, know that they are hateful in the divine sight; that their prayers will not be heard; that their offerings will not be accepted; that nothing short of repentance and deep contrition of spirit will be associated with the returning smile of divine mercy and compassion. Continuing in their present course of deceit and falsehood, they can expect to meet nothing but the wrath of an angry God." No wickedness on earth is more common than the various forms of deceit.

20. God is not the author of sin. He abhors it. Nothing is so repugnant to his nature, vv. 4, 5, 6. He permits sin, but he does not approve it. He overrules sin, but he hates it. He may sustain in being very wicked men while they commit sin, but he never works wickedness. To charge him with being the author of sin is blasphemy.

21. Honesty is the best policy. It commonly appears so in this life; invariably, in the next, v. 6. The perpetual toil and scuffle of the false man to make things stick together and to preserve appearances might warn him of worse trouble yet to come. Morison: "Let the sentiment of this verse teach the importance of candor, and benevolence, and sincerity in all the intercourses of life. How many there are who will meet you as friends, and give you the right hand of good brotherhood, while they are stabbing you in the dark, and whispering something, even in the ear of your familiar friend, which may lessen you in his esteem. And yet these very dastardly characters will not dare to breathe in your presence any other sentiments save those of kindness and respect. Let such men remember, that in the holy scriptures, *lying* and *murder* are the invariable companions of *deceit*, and *treachery*, and *circumvention*." When God utterly forsakes a man, he soon confounds all moral distinctions. To such a one black is white, bitter is sweet, evil is good. Many of the vices are cognate. They dwell together.

22. Neither in fact, nor in the esteem of good men is there any substitute for the public worship of God, v. 7. Take away from the pious of earth all the recollections, impressions, purposes, refreshments, encouragements, hopes, joys, and other graces, which owe their origin, or their vigor to the house of God, and what a change would be witnessed. It is a great mercy in God to give us public ordinances. They reprove, cheer, warn, reclaim, animate, strengthen all God's people.

23. The only hope of sinners is in mercy; nor will a little answer their purpose. They need a great deal, v. 7. Calvin says this verse teaches us "the general truth.

that it is only through the goodness of God that we have access to him; and that no man prays aright but he, who, having experienced his grace, believes and is fully persuaded that he will be merciful to him. The fear of God is at the same time added, in order to distinguish genuine and godly trust from the vain confidence of the flesh." God has taken peculiar pains to assure us of his mercy and grace. Reliance on these is of great use. Dickson: "The faith, which the godly have in the mercies of God, doth encourage them to follow his service; and in some cases doth give them hope to be loosed from the restraints which hinder them from enjoying the public ordinances." It is a great thing to be able to keep the eye fixed on God's great compassions.

24. No good man is offended because God is greatly to be feared, v. 7. The true fear of God has no torment in it. The righteous would on no account part with reverential feelings.

25. The greater our perils, the more should our prayers abound; the more enemies, the more supplications, v. 8. That is a wicked perversion of any event, which drives us from the mercy-seat.

26. It is right that we should pray to be kept in a plain way, and not be allowed to fall into darkness respecting either faith or practice, v. 8. Inscrutable points of doctrine, mysterious providences, and insoluble questions in casuistry are often occasions of terrible temptations. To ask for light on our path is therefore the same as praying not to be led into temptation. Satan loves to fish in muddy water. Mental confusion is unfriendly to the steady course of piety. Let us beg God to make crooked things straight. Dickson: "So much the more as the godly are sensible of their own blindness, and weakness, and readiness to go out of the right way, so much the more do they call for, and depend upon God's directing them."

27. The Scriptures speak one uniform and unmistakable language respecting the universal and dreadful depravity of man, v. 9. There was no stronger language used on this subject by David than we find in Genesis vi. 5. And when Paul would prove Jew and Gentile all lost he finds no more fitting testimony than in this Psalm. Rom. iii. 13. Compliments to unregenerate men respecting their goodness are as much out of place as praise of a corpse for its beauty. They are all dead. Morison: "There has been a mournful uniformity in the character of the wicked in all ages."

28. Dickson: "Among other motives to make the godly take heed of their carriage in time of trial, this is one; they have to do with a false world, and hollow-hearted men, who will make false pretences of what is not their intention, and will make promise of what they mind not to perform, and will give none but rotten and poisonable advice, gilded with false flattery, and all to deceive the godly and draw them into a snare," v. 9.

29. The ruin of the incorrigibly wicked is inevitable, v. 10. Everything is against them. God, with all his nature, plans and providence, the inherent weakness and wretchedness of their cause, the multitude of their offences, the heinous character of their rebellion, unite with all the teachings of Scripture and all the worship of God's people in making the overthrow of the impenitent beyond all doubt certain. God's people cannot thank him that no weapon formed against Zion shall prosper, nor pray, Thy kingdom come, nor adore God for one of his attributes, nor cry, God be merciful to me a sinner, nor repeat a prophecy concerning the final triumph of truth and righteousness, without pointing to great principles, all of which say, The ungodly shall perish.

30. But the righteous are safe, v. 11. All, that makes sure the ruin of the wicked, renders certain the victory of the righteous. God is with them, defends them, blesses them.

31. We ought to pray for God's people, v. 11.   They need our prayers.   They have a right to them on the score of brotherhood.   Henry: "Let us learn of David to pray, not for ourselves only, but for others; for all good people, for all that trust in God, and love his name, though not in everything of our mind, or in our interest. Let all that are entitled to God's promises have a share in our prayers.   Grace be with all them that love our Lord Jesus Christ in sincerity.   This is to concur with God."   What a model of tenderness and earnestness in intercession for others we have in Abraham.   Gen. xviii. 23–32.   Nor can any circumstances of personal affliction or distress excuse us from praying for all God's saints as we learn from the example of David recorded here and elsewhere.

32. Whoever denies that the true people of God have solid, strong and enduring joys shows that he is ignorant of the whole matter of spiritual religion, v. 11.   The most exultant anthems ever sung on this earth are the songs of God's people passing through the wilderness, the fire and the floods.

33. What a comfort the Scriptures are to all the children of God in sorrow.   How this whole Psalm has been read and wept over and rejoiced in by the saints for nearly three thousand years, and shall be till time shall be no longer.   The comfort of the Scriptures gives hope.   Rom. xv. 4.   Just as a man is taught and sanctified by the Spirit will such portions of truth rejoice his heart, and make him exult.

34. The whole Psalm shows that never in this life shall we get beyond the means of grace.   Nor is it best we should.   It is enough that we travel the road watered with the tears of the sweet singer of Israel, and use the means he used.   Yea, more, David's Lord in the days of his flesh poured out strong cryings and tears to God.   Let us follow Christ, and know the fellowship of his sufferings.

35. If our cause is good, let us not be uneasy about the issue.   In courts of human judicature we may have a good cause, a good judge, a good jury, good counsel and good witnesses, and yet we may often fail.   But he, who has a good cause in the court of heaven, shall not be cast.   So the whole Psalm teaches.

36. This Psalm shows that in essentials true religion is the same in all ages.   It has sorrows, but then it has joys; it has conflicts, but then it has victories; it has darkness, but then it has trust; it has foes, but it also has an infallible guide; it has perils, but it is surrounded with God's favor as with a shield.

37. The whole Psalm shows that salvation is of God.   The righteous would soon fall by the malice and machinations of their foes, if they had to manage their own cause.   But God holds them up, so that they fall not; he covers them, so that the enemy cannot get at them; he guides them, so that they miss not their way.

38. If this Psalm refers to Christ, of whom David was a type, then his victories are no less a source of joy to his people than were those of his servant David; nay, they are more so.

PSALM VI.

To the chief Musician on Neginoth upon Sheminith, A Psalm of David.

1 O LORD, rebuke me not in thine anger, neither chasten me in thy hot displeasure.

2 Have mercy upon me, O LORD ; for I *am* weak: O LORD, heal me ; for my bones are vexed.

3 My soul is also sore vexed: but thou, O LORD, how long ?

4 Return, O LORD, deliver my soul : oh save me for thy mercies' sake.

5 For in death *there is* no remembrance of thee: in the grave who shall give thee thanks?

6 I am weary with my groaning; all the night make I my bed to swim; I water my couch with my tears.

7 Mine eye is consumed because of grief; it waxeth old because of all mine enemies.

8 Depart from me, all ye workers of iniquity; for the LORD hath heard the voice of my weeping.

9 The LORD hath heard my supplication; the LORD will receive my prayer.

10 Let all mine enemies be ashamed and sore vexed: let them return *and* be ashamed suddenly.

THE reader is referred to the beginning of the Commentary on the third Psalm for remarks on the words, A Psalm of David, and to the *fourth* Psalm, whose title otherwise is precisely the same as we find here, except that in this Psalm we have the additional words *upon Sheminith*. This phrase is found in 1 Chron. xv. 21 where we are told of the appointment of certain singers to sound with harps on the Sheminith, " to excel." It is also found in the title of the *twelfth* Psalm precisely as it is here. Respecting the signification of *Sheminith* there exists considerable diversity. Fenwick renders it, *On the unction*, meaning the anointing of the Holy Spirit. But how this sense could be gotten from the word, *Sheminith*, or why any special unction should be claimed either for the words or the music of this song over others in the same collection does not appear. Bellarmine mentions an opinion, which he says is not to be slighted, viz.: that Sheminith points to the day of final judgment, which is to follow the six days of toil of this life and the seventh day of rest of souls, and then comes the *eighth* day, which is the end of the world. But the contents of the Psalm clearly show that the eternal judgment is not even once referred to unless it be very remotely, as in the preceding Psalm. Horsley renders it, *upon the superabundance*. But the difficulty is that it is only by some very remote and perhaps fanciful allusion that the idea of *superabundance* could in any way be connected with *Sheminith*. The literal rendering of *upon Sheminith* is *upon the eighth*. This is the marginal reading in the best editions of our English Bible wherever the word occurs. Some of the Jewish writers thought there was a reference to the *eighth* day, the day of circumcision. Gill says some ancient Christians referred it to the Lord's day, being the day after the seventh, or the Jewish Sabbath. Theodoret refers it to the eighth age, the millenium. But these three views are purely fanciful, receiving no support from the contents of the Psalm. Nor is there more support to the opinion that *the eighth* refers to a song of eight notes, to the tune of which this Psalm was sung. If for *the eighth* we read *the octave*, our minds instantly turn to something relating to music, and so this term seems to point to something pertaining to music in the public worship of God. Hengstenberg: " The correct explanation is given by those who take it for an indication of the tune." He cites no one as agreeing with him, nor does any one appear to take the same view as himself. Vatablus supposes it to be a tune in which the *octave note* prevails. Pool thinks Sheminith is " the shrillest or loftiest note;" while Gill cites some as thinking that it refers " to the eighth note, which was grave, and which we call the bass." Many others think it refers to an instrument, perhaps a harp of eight strings. This view is favored by the Chaldee, Jarchi, Kimchi, and Ben Melech; by Bellarmine, Waterland, Moller, Gill, Patrick, Morison, Cobbin, Fry, and Scott. Venema is in doubt whether it is an instrument of eight cords, or the lower octave tune that is designed; Calvin: " I do not know whether it would be correct to say it was a harp of eight strings. I am rather inclined to the opinion that it refers to the tune;" Alexander says Sheminith " corresponds exactly to our *octave;* but its precise application in the ancient music we have now no means of ascertaining." It may well be left to each one to form his own opinion in the case, and specially to commend care in rejecting the view maintained by the great mass of commentators, viz.: that a particular instrument is referred to. But no heresy is taught, nor spiritual truth rejected by holding any of the fore-cited explanations, though some of them are wild and unreasonable.

The authorship of this Psalm is properly ascribed to David. Of his having written it there is no cause of serious doubt. Seven of the Psalms have long been styled penitential. These are the 6th, 32d, 38th, 51st, 102d, 130th, and 143d. From this list some drop the 102d and insert the 25th. They have been called penitential not merely because they contain earnest supplications becoming sinners, but also confessions of sin and expressions of sorrow appropriate to a penitent. But the very same reasons would lead us to include at least three others under the same designation, viz.: the 25th, 69th, and 86th. Still there is no objection to calling this a penitential Psalm. But on what occasion it was written we cannot determine. There is a strong tendency in commentators to refer many of the sorrowful Psalms to David's penitence respecting the matter of Uriah. But David was a penitent before he incurred guilt in that affair. And both before and after that sad business his great trouble, as is that of every believer, was the plague of his own heart, the fountain of depravity within him. His whole life was a conflict with corruption. Paul had committed no recent outbreaking sin when he uttered that exceedingly bitter cry, " O wretched man that I am, who shall deliver me from the body of this death?" It was indwelling sin that distressed him.

Some have supposed that this Psalm has special reference to bodily disease, and for proof refer to vv. 2 and 5. Others think it has special reference to the terrible machinations and assaults of his enemies, and refer to vv. 7 and 10. Others suppose there is special reference to some spiritual troubles, vv. 3 and 4. The fact is that all these things may have borne him down at the same time. It has grown into a proverb that troubles never come alone. See how affliction brought on a sense of sin in Joseph's brethren. It is a great thing to learn to bow to the rod of correction in a temper becoming a sinner, who through grace has become a child of God. It is not probable that this Psalm was composed at the time of the affliction, but after it had passed away. Yet it doubtless contains the petitions offered during the anguish occasioned by the sore visitation. It also records the blessed issue of his troubles and his happy deliverance from them. In this Psalm the original of the word LORD is in each case *Jehovah*, on which see above on Ps. i. 2.

1. O LORD, *rebuke me not in thine anger, neither chasten me in thy hot displeasure.* The variations in rendering this verse are slight. For *hot displeasure*, some have proposed to read *wrath, indignation, glow* or *heat.* But in each case the sense is the same. The two clauses express the same idea—"Fury untempered with grace and insupportable wrath." Each contains a petition, the purport of which has not been always agreed upon. Some suppose that David here implores the removal of his afflictions. Others with more reason regard him as asking that his afflictions may be the chastisements of a son, not the punishments of a cast-away. Such suppose this petition to be the same in substance as that of the weeping prophet: "O LORD, *correct me, but with judgment; not in thine anger, lest thou bring me to nothing,*" Jer. x. 24. The same idea is expressed in Jer. xlvi. 28, "I will not make a full end of thee, but correct thee in measure; yet I will not leave thee wholly unpunished." This view therefore consists with the analogy of Scriptural teaching. Nor would a wise and good man under divine inspiration be ready to ask that he might be exempt from trial. But any man may without qualification humbly ask to be dealt with as a child, not as a rebel. Luther: "This he regards not, nay, he will readily suffer, that he be punished and chastened; but he begs that it might be done in mercy and goodness, not in anger and fury. . . Therefore the prophet teaches us here, that there are two rods of God, one of mercy and goodness, another of anger and fury;" Calvin gives this as the sense:

"O Lord, I confess that I deserve to be destroyed and brought to naught; but as I would be unable to endure the severity of thy wrath, deal not with me according to my deserts, but rather pardon my sins, by which I have provoked thine anger against me;" De Wette: "The sufferer prays not for a remission, but only for an alleviation of the calamity;" Patrick's paraphrase is: "O LORD, who delightest in mercy, moderate, I beseech thee, thy sharp correction; and do not proceed to inflict upon me the severest marks of thy displeasure;" Morison: "He does not deprecate the divine rebuke, for he remembers how awfully it had been provoked; but he entreats that Jehovah would not rebuke him in his anger, that he would not chasten him in his hot displeasure. He felt that a creature's weakness would not withstand the shock of incensed Omnipotence;" Henry: "He does not pray, Lord, rebuke me not; Lord, chasten me not; for, as many as God loves, he rebukes and chastens, as the father the son in whom he delights." This view is also taken by Venema, by Gill and, as Hengstenberg owns, by "most expositors." The wrath of God destroys, but his paternal love corrects, reclaims and saves. It is itself a mercy and he who receives it may well pray

2. *Have mercy upon me*, O LORD. How suitable to every condition in life is the cry for mercy. It is first an acknowledgment of the justice of all the evil that has befallen us. It is also a confession of our utter weakness and incapacity for relieving ourselves. It is next a confession of our faith in the power of God to give us succor if he will but undertake our cause. It is also a declaration that the divine compassions are so great that whatever our distress may be, we may safely rely on him. Such a prayer befits us, in health and in sickness, in life and in death. No more appropriate words ever fell from the lips of mortals. No man ever promotes his own comfort by denying the justice of the sufferings he is called to endure at the hand of God. Indeed a suspicion to the contrary will fill any mind with torture, and a conviction to the contrary will make any man outrageous. Listen to Cain: "My punishment is greater than I can bear." Listen to Quintilian on the death of his wife and children, especially the recent death of a promising son: "Who would not detest my insensibility, if I made any other use of my voice, than to vent complaints against the injustice of the gods, who made me survive all that was dearest to me? . . . There reigns a secret envy, jealous of our happiness, which pleases itself in nipping the bud of our hopes." Let sinners always feel and say that justice is against them, and that their hope for anything good is in the divine mercy. Let them continually admit that they deserve all sorts of afflictions, and if saved from them, it must be by the mere favor of God. Let them bring all their woes before him and cry for mercy, as did David, when he said, *for I am* weak. Hengstenberg reads, *for I am faint*, or *withered* ; Morison: *I am extremely weak*, or *I am languishing* ; Jebb: *very weak am I* ; Alexander: *drooping am I*. David here complains of bodily distress, though it may have arisen from mental anguish. Calvin says: "David calls himself weak, not because he was sick, but because he was cast down and broken by what had now befallen him." There is a very mysterious connection between our souls and our bodies. No man in great anguish of mind ever felt well in body, although he might have done so in an hour, if his mind had been put quite at ease. Morison: "The weakness or debility, of which David complains, seems to attach more immediately to the soul, and to the soul as enervated and wasted in its spiritual strength by sin." The reason he assigns is not valid: "This appears from the circumstance that the divine mercy is appealed to for relief. Mercy has relation to guilt and unworthiness, rather than to mere bodily malady and distemper." But is not every blessing a mercy to sinners? Especially is not our continued existence a great mercy? Lam. iii. 22. Have we not all forfeited our lives? Several commentators seem at a loss on this clause; and all from not

admitting that David's affliction was not one. He had enemies plotting against him; he had mental distress; he had bodily infirmity. All these at once pressed him hard. In this way every expression in the Psalm may be made clear, and even the commentators made generally to harmonize. The same remarks suit the next clause: O LORD, *heal me, for my bones are vexed.* For *vexed* Calvin reads *are afraid;* Hengstenberg: *Are terrified;* Fry and Alexander: *Are shaken.* Morison observes that by the bones Jewish expositors understand the body generally, but says, he can see no reason why the bones should not be spoken of literally. Calvin: "He attributes fear to his *bones,* not because they are endued with feeling, but because the vehemence of his grief was such that it affected his whole body. He does not speak of his flesh, which is the more tender and susceptible part of the corporeal system, but he mentions his bones, thereby intimating that the strongest parts of his frame were made to tremble for fear." The sense seems to be that his bodily distress was not slight, but deep, and incapable of being removed by any ordinary remedies. God alone could heal him. He therefore betook himself to the great physician. Luther: "Where the heart is troubled, the whole body is faint and broken." "A wounded spirit who can bear?" Alexander: "To regard the bodily distress as a mere figure for internal anguish would be wholly arbitrary and destructive of all sure interpretation. The physical effect here ascribed to moral causes is entirely natural and confirmed by all experience." This state of things was itself sad. But the sufferer adds:

3. *My soul is also sore vexed.* The Syriac and Hengstenberg read: *And my soul is greatly terrified;* most of the ancient versions and Morison: *My soul is exceedingly troubled;* Calvin: *My soul is greatly afraid;* Fry: *My soul is shaken exceedingly;* Alexander: *My soul is greatly agitated.* The verb rendered *vexed* in this place is the same rendered *vexed* in the preceding verse. There are no troubles like soul-troubles. Sin will mar anything. It will make any soul wretched. Morison: "It depresses its spiritual energies, quenches the ardors of devotion, darkens the prospect of faith and hope, produces slavish dread, creates an inaptitude to spiritual services and enjoyments, and acts, in all respects upon the mind of a believer, as fell disease does upon the body." Calvin very properly rejects the opinion, which here takes *soul* for *life.* It does not suit the scope of the passage. The soul of David was so distressed that time seemed long. This is very natural. Many have experienced this effect of pain, bodily and mental, in making the hours tedious. He cries out, *But thou, O LORD, how long?* The Chaldee: How long ere thou wilt refresh me? church of England: How long wilt thou punish me? Hengstenberg tells us that the words, O LORD, *how long?* were Calvin's motto, and that the most intense pain could not extort from him anything more expressive of desire for relief. They have been the words of many a great sufferer. The sentence is unfinished, but neither unmeaning nor unimpressive. The very ellipsis points to great distress, and is a piteous cry for relief. Dimock proposes to supply what is wanting thus: And how long wilt thou be angry, Jehovah? and refers to Ps. lxxix. 5 in support. But great grief is apt to utter broken sentences. Ejaculations are often abrupt and incomplete, yet nothing is more expressive. Highly finished periods do not beseem those, who are sorely afflicted. The sentence may be filled up many ways, and give a good sense thus: How long before thou wilt have mercy? how long shall my bones and my soul be thus vexed? how long wilt thou permit me to suffer as I do? how long before I shall be rescued? An afflicted saint familiar with Scripture, does not care to have all words supplied. Morison: "David seems like an individual choked with grief, and feels himself incapable of completing the sentence he had begun." He thus paraphrases the words, O LORD, *how long?* "How long wilt thou continue to hide thy face, to afflict my spirit, to chastise my body, to deny me the refreshing tokens of thy love, to shut thine ears against my complaints,

to leave me, the victim of grief, and the subject of torturing disease? How long, O Lord, shall this be the case? Shall not a day of mercy and deliverance at last dawn? Wilt thou not again look upon my pain, and forgive all my sins? Hast thou afflicted, and wilt thou not heal?" Calvin: "This elliptical form of expression serves to express more strongly the vehemence of grief, which not only holds the minds but also the tongues of men bound up, breaking and cutting short their speech in the middle of the sentence." Luther: "In all emotions of the heart, such as fear, love, hope, hatred, and the like, a state of suspense and delay is vexatious and difficult to be borne, as Solomon says in Prov. xiii. 12, 'Hope deferred maketh the heart sick.' But in troubles of this kind, delay is the most severe and insupportable pain." At such a time what a privilege is prayer! What a mercy to be allowed to pour out our tears and complaints to GOD, and to cry,

4. *Return, O* LORD, *deliver my soul.* God's essential presence is everywhere. This encourages his people to pray to him, knowing that he *can* hear them. But his gracious presence is often wanting to his people. One of the most grievous afflictions is the absence of God. In this alarming strain he threatens his people: "I will go and return to my place, till they acknowledge their offence, and seek my face: in their affliction they will seek me early." Hos. v. 15. When God hides his face his people are troubled. His return is regarded as a great mercy. The Arabic reads, Be propitious, O Lord. "When the humble and penitent soul is made conscious of the divine withdrawment, nothing will satisfy it but a sense of God's returning smile." If he comes, he will bring salvation, and so David cries, *deliver my soul.* He not only prayed for his life, but for his soul. If that is lost, all is lost. If that is safe, other things are of slight importance. Our worst foes are the enemies of our souls. They are our sins, our tempters and our tormentors. To deliver from these is the work of God alone. Yea, it is his sovereign work. If moved to it, it cannot be by anything seen in the creature. In bestowing any favor God is self-moved. Therefore David says, *Oh save me for thy mercies' sake.* The ancient versions, with Calvin, Jebb, Gill, Horne, and Alexander follow the original and read *mercy,* not *mercies.* Fry reads, *tenderness.* The word here rendered *mercy* occurs more than *two hundred* times in the Hebrew Bible and is rendered *favor, pity, kindness, mercy, goodness, loving-kindness, merciful-kindness.* So that beyond all question we here have a confession that hope of deliverance for a sinner in any distress is found in the unmerited compassions of God. Luther's paraphrase is: "Not for mine own services, which indeed are nothing, as is sufficiently and more than sufficiently proved by this terror at thy anger, and my trembling bones, and the sadness of my heart and soul. Therefore help me for thy mercies' sake, that thine honor and the glory of thy compassion may be forever connected with my deliverance." God takes great pains to inform his people in all ages that all their hope is in his sovereign favor and rich grace, and that it is not the merit or the misery of mortals, that moves him to show them pity, or extend deliverance. Ezek. xxxvi. 22, 32; Eph. ii. 4–9. It is well when we have faith to draw arguments from God in favor of our petitions. God's mercy gets great honor when it extends great favors to great sinners. We may safely plead with God to do that which will be an honor to his attributes. In this verse David pleads for God's mercy's sake; in the next he urges an argument drawn from the silence of the grave.

5. *For in death* there is *no remembrance of thee; in the grave who shall give thee thanks?* John Rogers and the Bishops' Bible both render the first clause thus: "For in death no man remembreth the;" in this they follow some of the ancient versions, which read, "In death there is no one remembering thee." The doctrine of this verse may be the same as that of Ps. xxx. 9; lxxxviii. 10; cxv. 17, 18: and

Isa. xxxviii. 18. This last reads, "The grave cannot praise thee, death cannot celebrate thee." Two senses have been given to this fifth verse. The first is that in this world true religion, in which God's honor is deeply involved, is kept alive by means of the testimony of his friends. God says to such, Ye are my witnesses. If the witnesses are dead, they can testify no more. One of the chief ways of honoring God on earth is by speaking his praise. "Whoso offereth praise glorifieth me." Ps. l. 23. The same doctrine is taught in Heb. xiii. 15. The voice of the dead is never heard any more on all the earth praising God. This is a good sense, consistent with other portions of revealed truth, and given by Calvin, Patrick, Gill, and Alexander. The other sense supposes that David had a fearful discovery of his sin and misery, and felt that if God pursued him in wrath he must soon drop into hell, being utterly consumed by divine terrors, bereft of hope, and left among those miserable outcasts, who on earth forget God, and who in the future world have no pleasure in ever remembering him. The *death* here spoken of then is the death of the soul—eternal death. If this view is correct, then we must read the last clause, as Jebb does, In hell who shall give thanks to thee? The original word here rendered *grave* occurs in the Hebrew Scriptures *sixty-five* times. Thirty-two times it is rendered *grave*, thirty times *hell*, and three times *pit*. Sometimes it cannot signify anything but hell as we now understand that word. See Ps. ix. 17. Strange to say, even the Doway Bible here reads *hell*. The church of England reads *the pit*. Henry's paraphrase is, "Lord, send me not to that dreadful place where there is no devout remembrance of thee, nor any thanks given to thee." Labored criticisms on the words used to designate the separate state of souls departed seem not to have been profitable, owing perhaps to the fact that too much of the material for them has been taken from the mythology of the heathen, or that they have been written to establish some preconceived theory. In the two clauses of this verse *death* and *the grave* are parallel, and the question of the second clause is in general import equivalent to the negation of the first. The word rendered *give thanks* is of frequent occurrence and is otherwise rendered *praise*, *thank, confess*. The Septuagint, Ethiopic, Syriac, and Vulgate read *confess*. The foregoing interpretations are entirely consistent with each other. Both are admissible. If either of them is true, then this passage cannot be brought to prove that between death and the resurrection men's souls are unconscious. Such a view derives no countenance from Scripture, but is opposed to many of its clear teachings. Nor does this verse teach that death is an eternal sleep. We know that it is not. Old Testament believers knew it was not. Jude 14, 15; Ex. iii. 6; Matt. xxii. 32; Mark xii. 27; Luke xx. 38; 2 Sam. xii. 23. One thus exercised must be sorely troubled. No wonder he says:

6. *I am weary with my groaning.* The pains, the sins, the enemies of David had so long filled him with groanings that he was wearied with them. He knew the sharp pains of bodily disease, the sorest afflictions of life, the saddest disappointments and failures, terrible temptations, inherent and outbreaking sins, the hidings of God's face, the pangs of deep conviction, and fears full of torment. He groaned till he was weary, and begged God to show him mercy. Was not this a case, in which divine mercy would be greatly honored by extending help before it became worse? *All the night make I my bed to swim.* Calvin: I soak my couch; Jebb: I wash every night my bed; Fry and Hengstenberg: Every night I make my bed to swim. Of course this language is exaggerated; but it is a lawful use of the hyperbole. He does not say in this clause how he made his bed to swim. It may have been in good part by those dreadful sweats, which break out on persons suffering from mental anguish while in bed whether awake or asleep. This is the view of Venema and Patrick. But the more common opinion is that his bed swam with the tears he shed. *Every night* is a

better rendering than *all the night*. The Septuagint, Ethiopic, Arabic, Vulgate and Alexander, following the original, put the verb *make* in this clause and the verb *water* in the next in the future tense. Alexander thus connects the clauses: "I am weary in my groaning . . . and unless I am relieved, I shall (still as hitherto) make my bed swim every night, my couch with tears I shall dissolve, or make to flow." The meaning is that his grief will never cure itself, and that if God shall not interpose, his sorrows will utterly waste and exhaust him. Indeed they had already made sad work with him; for he says,

7. *Mine eye is consumed because of grief.* For *consumed*, some read *withered, sunken, blasted, dimmed, become dull, fretted, worn away.* Poets have sung of the effects of grief on the eye.

> His eye-balls in their hollow sockets sink.—DRYDEN.

> Sunk was that eye
> Of sovereignty; and on the emaciate cheek
> Had penitence and anguish deeply drawn
> Their furrows premature, etc.—SOUTHEY.

There is great force in that phrase, He wept his eyes out. For *eye* Morison reads *countenance;* John Rogers' Translation: My countenance is changed for very inwarde grefe; Bishops' Bible: My beautie is gone for verie trouble; Genevan Translation: Mine eye is dimmed for despite. Hengstenberg thinks the word rendered *eye* never occurs in the sense of *face.* But in this is he not mistaken? In 2 Kings ix. 30, it is rendered *face*, and cannot mean the *eye.* And in Num. xi. 7, it is twice rendered *color.* And why may it not mean the same here? My color or complexion is consumed because of grief, etc., would give a good sense. For *grief*, Calvin, Hengstenberg and Alexander read *vexation;* Gill and many others, *indignation.* But whether it is his own indignation at the outrageous wrongs done him, or the indignation of God towards him for his sins is not agreed. The latter is the better sense. My beauty is wasted, my color is consumed by thy indignation, etc. He adds, respecting his eye, or countenance, *It waxeth old because of all mine enemies.* The marks of premature old age are often brought on by bodily disease, by mental distress, and by the vexatious behaviour of wicked men. Pain, or spiritual distress, or oppressive cares, will make their mark on the eye, on the whole countenance. In this case a premature old age showed that, unless mercy interposed, death would soon follow. Morison: "By his own inward griefs, the afflictions of his body, and the cruel persecutions of his enemies, he felt the encroachments of a premature old age; and beheld in the languid eye, and in the sunken cheek, and in the pallid countenance, the appearances of a dissolution rapidly approaching." But with the saints the darkest hour is just before day. Therefore in a very altered strain David begins the next verse.

8. *Depart from me, all ye workers of iniquity. Iniquity* the same as in Ps. v. 5; also, *vanity* as in Ps. x. 7; also, *mischief* as in Ps. lv. 10; also *sorrow*, in Ps. xc. 10. Fry here has *vanity.* Those who work iniquity, always work mischief, vanity and sorrow. He, who would avoid these, must shun that. And so David says to all who work iniquity, *depart from me*, thus declaring that he will not be of their company. This is the sense most naturally suggested by the words themselves. But the subsequent context shows the language to be that of defiance and triumph. He orders them off with all their menaces and taunts and disheartening speeches. He says, I will listen to you no longer; I will be distressed by you no more; you have tormented me long enough; I am myself again; take yourselves off; *for the* LORD *hath heard the voice of my weeping.* By what sign David knew that his prayer was heard we are not told. Some favorable change in the aspect of public affairs, some check

to corruption, some succor from temptation, some sweet sense of God's love, some improvement in health, one or all of these may have united with an increase of faith to persuade him that the worst was over, and that deliverance was sure and near at hand. This Psalm may have been composed some time after the sore trials mentioned in preceding verses. If it was, then the clause under consideration may express David's gratitude after deliverance had been fully and openly secured to him. Yet he would on no account forget by whom he was saved. When prayer is answered and we are rescued, let us give God the glory. He often comes suddenly to the confusion of his enemies and the rescue of his chosen. Amyrald: "Those violent commotions, in which after the most bitter and dolorous lamentations and testimonies concerning human weakness, faith suddenly regains the ascendant, and through the offered hope of deliverance, sheds light and serenity over the mind, are very common in the Psalms." He might have added that they still abound in Christian experience. Weeping may endure for a night, but joy cometh in the morning. Mercies, obtained by weeping and prayer, are well suited to give courage. They are like armor won in battle and hung up as trophies to show what can be done.

> The Lord can clear the darkest skies,
>   Can give us day for night,
> Make drops of sacred sorrow rise,
>   To rivers of delight.

The voice of my weeping is the same as my loud weeping. There are many sorrows, which we cannot tell to men. There are others, which overwhelm us and strike us dumb. But it is well when God enables us to roll all our burdens over on him; and permits us to weep and plead before him. The voice of weeping was not confined to eastern saints. It is heard by God wherever his suffering people dwell. David insists that his deliverance was by God's gracious answer to his strong crying and tears, and so he says,

9. *The* LORD *hath heard my supplication.* This is but another form of repeating what he had said in the last clause. But the next expression has given rise to some difficulty. *The* LORD *will receive my prayer.* If the idea in the mind of the Psalmist was of the future, then it is the expression of a confident assurance, supported by past experience, that God will never refuse to hear his prayer. This would convey a proper and weighty idea, consistent with Scripture and with Christian experience. The future tense is preferred by our translators, and by Jebb and others, who follow the Hebrew. Alexander: "The combination of the past and future represents the acceptance as complete and final, as already begun and certain to continue." All the ancient versions and Calvin employ the past tense—*hath received*, thus making this clause re-affirm the substance of the two previous clauses. But Fry and Hengstenberg think it best to employ the present tense—*receiveth or receives.* Thus the Psalmist asserts that he is now receiving evidence of a gracious acceptance. Either rendering teaches truth, but the present tense is perhaps preferable to the past, and the future to the present. Because his prayer was heard, he says:

10. *Let all mine enemies be ashamed and sore vexed.* For *sore vexed*, Calvin reads *greatly confounded;* Hengstenberg: *terrified;* Fry: *greatly terrified.* There is the same variety in the rendering here as in some other cases. Our English version and some others use the imperative form of all the verbs in this verse, making the several clauses imprecatory. If read thus, see commentary on Ps. v. 10. Fry uses the present tense of the indicative mood, and reads, *All mine enemies are confounded.* etc. But the church of England, Gill, Jebb, Hengstenberg and Alexander prefer the future, making the whole a prediction, *All mine enemies shall be ashamed*, etc.

This reading is on all accounts to be preferred. Meantime we have here a strong confirmation of the fact that those parts of the Psalms, which look like asking God to send evil on one's enemies are but prophetic and infallible declarations that the evil will come. See Introduction, § 6. And so they shall *return* and *be ashamed suddenly.* Some of the older commentators as well as some more modern, instead of *return* read *again,* thus; they shall be again ashamed. But this is no improvement on the common version. The sense is, They shall return from their pursuit of David, and shall be ashamed *suddenly.* It is easy for God in a moment to put to confusion all our enemies. The overthrow of the wicked commonly takes them by surprise. No faithful warnings, no clear prophecies can prepare the minds of unbelievers for dreadful coming events. Hengstenberg thinks that the *returning* of the Lord in v. 4, and the returning (or flight) of the enemies in v. 10, stand related to each other as cause and effect.

DOCTRINAL AND PRACTICAL REMARKS.

1. With believers when things get to the worst then they get better. To them darkness is the harbinger of light; grief, of gladness; humility, of exaltation; death, of life. The whole Psalm teaches thus.

2. Let men beware how they harden themselves in sin by pleading the falls of David. If they resemble him only in sinfulness, they will miserably perish. Unless like him they repent, they are undone forever. And this repentance must be speedy, for as Augustine says, " Though after this life repentance be perpetual, it is in vain."

3. It is better to weep now when God will hear than hereafter when mercy shall be clean gone forever. To us sinners sorrow must come. The wise prefer to mourn when mourning for sin shall be followed by peace and joy.

4. No small part of spiritual wisdom consists in knowing how to behave under severe and complicated trials. Some melt away under them and lose all heart and courage. This is one extreme, and very dangerous. Others harden the heart and act as if God was not chastising them. Hengstenberg: " That supposed greatness of soul which considers suffering as a plaything, upon which one should throw himself with manly courage, is not to be met with on the territory of Scripture; upon that everywhere appear faint, weak, and dissolving hearts, finding their strength and consolation only in God. This circumstance arises from more than one cause. 1. Suffering has quite another aspect to the members of God's church than to the world. While the latter regard it only as the effect of accident, which one should meet with manly courage, the pious man recognizes in every trial the visitation of an angry God, a chastisement for his sins. This is to him the real sting of the suffering, from which it derives its power to pierce into marrow and bone. ' Rightly to feel sin,' says Luther, ' is the torture of all tortures.' . . To make light of tribulations is all one, in the reckoning of Scripture, with making light of God. 2. The tenderer the heart the deeper the pain. Living piety makes the heart soft and tender, and refines all its sensibilities, and, consequently, takes away the power of resistance, which the world possesses, from the roughness of its heart. Many sources of pain are opened up in the Christian, which are closed in the ungodly. Love is much more deeply wounded by hatred, than hatred itself; righteousness sees wickedness in quite a different light from what wickedness itself does; a soft heart has goods to lose which a hard one never possessed. 3. The pious man has a friend in heaven, and on that account has no reason to be violently overcome by his sorrow. He permits the floods of this quietly to pass over him, gives nature its free, spontaneous course, knowing well that beside the natural principle there is another also existing in him, which always unfolds its energy the more, the more that the former has its

rights reserved to it—that according to the depths of the pain, is the height of the joy which is derived from God—that every one is consoled after the measure in which he has borne suffering—that the meat never comes but from the eater, and honey from the terrible. On the contrary, whosoever lives in the world without God, he perceives that for him all is lost when he is lost himself. He girds himself up, gnashes at his pain, does violence to nature, seeks thereby to divert himself, and to gain from nature on the one side what it abstracts from him on the other, and thus he succeeds in obtaining the mastery over his pain, so long as God pleases. 4. The pious man has no reason to prevent himself and others from seeing into his heart. His strength is in God, and so he can lay open his weakness. The ungodly, on the other hand, consider it as a reproach to look upon themselves in their weakness, and to be looked upon by others in it. Even when smarting with pain inwardly, he feigns freedom from it, so long as he can."

5. How different is all this from the miserable shifts to which ungodly men are driven. In their extremity dreadful sullenness and remorse, alternate bluster and fainting, boasting and cowering mark their state. Shortly before his death, Byron said: "Shall I sue for mercy?" Pausing a considerable time, he made this desperate answer to his own question: "Come, come, no weakness; let's be a man to the last." That miserable pupil of Voltaire, the pedantic king Frederick II. of Prussia, had lived to feed his ambition, and after remarkable successes was compelled to say: "It is unhappy that all who suffer must flatly contradict Zeno, as there is none but will confess pain to be a great evil. It is noble to raise one's self above the disagreeable accidents to which we are exposed, and a moderate stoicism is the only means of consolation for the unfortunate. But whenever the stone, the gout, or the bull of Phalaris mix in the scene, the frightful shrieks which escape from the sufferers, leave no doubt that pain is a real evil. . . When a misfortune presses us, which merely affects our person, self-love makes a point of honor to withstand vigorously this misfortune: but the moment we suffer an injury which is forever irreparable, there is nothing left for us in Pandora's box which can bring us consolation, besides, perhaps, for a man of my advanced years, the strong conviction that I must soon be with those who have gone before me, (i. e., in the land of nothingness.) The heart is conscious of a wound, the Stoic freely confesses; I should feel no pain, but I do feel it against my will, it consumes, it lacerates me; an internal feeling overcomes my strength, and extorts from me complaints and fruitless groans."

6. This Psalm shows us what extreme and terrible sufferings of conscience may come upon a good man after sad departures from God. It is thought by some that the convictions and distresses of the real children of God, when aroused to a sense of their backsliding and guilt, far surpass the anguish of the same persons at the time of their first conversion. No doubt this is often so. Let the people of God flee from sin as from hell. It will bring the pains of hell into their consciences. Spiritual distress and spiritual conflicts are the worst trials on earth.

7. But whatever our afflictions may be, let us betake ourselves to God, v. 1. The child, that falls into the bosom of parental faithfulness, shortens the stroke and breaks the force of the rod, which is lifted in chastisement. Morison: "Whether we contemplate the maladies of the soul, or those of the body, we are equally compelled to turn to Jehovah as the great Physician." The sooner we learn this lesson, the better for us. The very name, Jehovah, rightly understood must encourage all to pour their tale of sorrow into his ear.

8. In all our afflictions it is our duty promptly to inquire, Wherefore contendest thou with me? And it is always safe to take it for granted that a sufficient cause may be found in our corruptions and iniquities, v. 1. Calvin: "Those persons are

very unsuitably exercised under their afflictions who do not immediately take a near and steady view of their sins, in order thereby to produce the conviction that they have deserved the wrath of God. And yet we see how thoughtless and insensible almost all men are on this subject; for while they cry out that they are afflicted and miserable, scarcely one among a hundred looks to the hand which strikes. From whatever quarter, therefore, our afflictions come, let us learn to turn our thoughts instantly to God, and to acknowledge him as the Judge who summons us as guilty before his tribunal, since we, of our own accord, do not anticipate his judgment."

9. Amazing is God's kindness in not punishing his people as they deserve, v. 1. This is their only hope. This is a sufficient hope. "Fear thou not, O Jacob my servant, saith the LORD: for I will make a full end of all the nations whither I have driven thee: but I will not make a full end of thee, but correct thee in measure; yet I will not leave thee wholly unpunished," Jer. xlvi. 28. Jehovah will discriminate between saints and sinners. He will not punish them alike, Gen. xviii. 25.

10. If blessings are delayed, let us continue in prayer. It is never wise nor safe to cease calling on God, however sad our state. Dickson: "No delay of comfort, no sense of sin, no fear of God's utter displeasure can be a reason to the believer to cease from prayer, and dealing with God for grace: for the prophet is *weary*, but giveth not over."

11. Prayer and praise should go together, vv. 1–5. The Assembly's Annotations: "God having revealed, that the most acceptable service men can render him is to call on him in trouble, and after deliverance to glorify him, those holy men of old, being in danger of death, could fix on no better consideration than this of God's glory, by which to press the plea of their prayers for life and prosperity." All *ten* of the lepers were glad to be healed, yet but *one* returned to give glory to God. Many a man prays for recovery from sickness, and, when it comes, he returns no thanks.

12. The only hope of sinful men for any good thing is in the mere mercy of God, vv. 2, 4. Moller: "To the pious the grace of God is the only light of life. As soon as God gives any sign of his wrath, they not only grow pale, but are well nigh plunged into the darkness of death; but as soon as they behold him reconciled and propitious, their life is restored." Calvin: "Men will never find a remedy for their miseries until, forgetting their own merits, by trusting to which they only deceive themselves, they have learned to betake themselves to the free mercy of God." If men would always forsake their own righteousness, and look to Christ alone, all would be safe. Human merits can help none into heaven. And human demerits can shut out of heaven none who flee to Christ and take him for their righteousness.

13. How reasonable it is that we should pray and labor for that cheerfulness of mind, without which life is a burden, and devotion a source of distress. Calvin: "It is only the goodness of God sensibly experienced by us, which opens our mouth to celebrate his praise; and whenever, therefore, joy and gladness are taken away, praises also must cease."

14. He, who knows us better than we know ourselves, often sees fit to send on us severe bodily pain, that we may draw nigh to him, v. 2. It is a great secret to know how to be sick, and to profit by sickness. Dickson: "The LORD can make the strongest and most insensible parts of a man's body, sensible of his wrath, when he pleaseth to touch him; for here David's bones are vexed." Many a man's soul has been saved by the destruction of his body with wasting disease. Muis: "As often as we are visited with sickness, or any other suffering, we should, after the example of David, call our sins to remembrance, and flee to God's compassion: not like the ungodly, who derive their evil, as well as their good, everywhere else than from God, and hence are never led, either by the one to repentance, or by the other to gratitude.

Sickness or calamity is not to be estimated according to the mind of the flesh, but of the Spirit; and we must reflect that if God afflicts us, he deals towards us as sons, that he may chasten and improve us."

15. In all our distresses, bodily and mental, we should avoid a spirit of petulance and impatience. It is dreadful to be left to find fault with God, to charge him foolishly. Such a course provokes the Almighty, hardens the heart, and sooner or later gives great power to the conscience to torment us. We may cry: "O LORD, how long?" v. 3. Calvin: "God, in his compassion towards us, permits us to pray to him to succor us; but when we have freely complained of his long delay, that our prayers or sorrow, on this account, may not pass beyond bounds, we must submit our case entirely to his will, and not wish him to make greater haste than shall seem good to him."

16. What mighty motives to activity and fidelity in our Master's work are furnished in the brevity of our lives and in the silence of the tomb, v. 5. See Ecc. ix. 10; John ix. 4. It is said that as men grow old they become covetous. This may be so. But if we should find them covetous of time, instead of money, it would be a proof of advancing wisdom. Even Paul and Whitefield and Brainerd and Nevins are no longer allowed to say one word for God in this world. O ye ministers, preach away! O ye Christians, pray on!

17. The end of life is to glorify God, v. 5. If we fail here, we fail utterly. Let us honor him with all our faculties of body and mind.

18. After reading accounts of such sufferings as are described in this Psalm we ought not to make much ado over any light afflictions, which may come on us. If better men suffered more than we, and without a murmur, we ought to take heed lest we displease God by our complaints under any trials. There was true virtue in that saying of the church, "I will bear the indignation of the Lord," etc., Mic. vii. 9.

19. Dreadful must sin be in its very nature, when even in this life and on a pardoned man it produces such effects as are described in this Psalm. Moller: "Sorrow proceeding from a sense of the Divine wrath exceeds all others."

20. Very terrible sufferings on account of particular sins may come on even good men. It was so with David. It was so with Jacob. It was so with some of the early Christians. 1 Cor. xi. 30. God loves his people too well to let them wander on in sin, and drop into hell for the want of a little needful and wholesome severity. 1 Cor. xi. 32.

21. Nothing enables a good man to defy the malice and power of his enemies, like an assurance that his prayers are heard and answered, v. 8. God's grace and power are infinite. Faith in him will dispel any sadness. Dickson: "The Lord can shortly change the cheer of an humble supplicant, and raise a soul trembling for fear of wrath, to a triumphing over all sorts of adversaries, and over all temptations to sin arising from them." The presence of divine grace expels all foes, or disarms them of their dreaded power. The Berleberg Bible on the words, Depart from me, etc., says: "Depart from me ye false tormenting accusations, ye rage and fury of menacing spirits and powers, that terrify me to death, and have shut up my blessed life as in the abyss of hell; ye are the real evil-doers, whom my external foes merely represent."

22. If God hears our prayers once, it should encourage us to hope that he will hear us again, v. 9.

23. How highly we should prize the privilege of communion with God. It is our life and our joy. Morison: "Those, who have once known the unspeakable enjoyment of communion with a reconciled God, cannot long endure the sensible withdrawment of divine mercy. They have breathed an element out of which they cannot long exist; they have stood with their Redeemer on the mount of transfiguration, and they are ready to exclaim, 'Lord, it is good to be here.' Nor must it be forgotten that

the divine return to any backsliding soul is its true deliverance. As the rising sun scatters the darkness of night, so when God returns to his people, in smiling mercy. he scatters the dark forebodings of unbelief, and liberates their souls from the bondage of sin."

24. If sin has such power to bring anguish in this world, what will it not do here-after, when it shall be *finished?* Jas. i. 15; Luke xxiii. 31; Jer. xii. 5.

25. It is right and profitable often to say that our deliverances are from God, and when our prayers are answered, to celebrate God's mercies. David twice or thrice tells how God had heard him, vv. 8, 9.

26. Is there wanted in our day anything so much as a fervent spirit of prayer? Morison: "Where are those mighty meltings of heart which took place in days of old, when our forefathers were deprived of liberty, and sought shelter 'in the mountains, and caves, and dens of the earth?' It may be said, indeed, that this is the age of *action;* but how worthless and unacceptable will that action be which is not fostered and urged on by 'the spirit of grace and supplications?'"

27. As what is promised to one believer is also promised to all, so that which is denounced against one enemy of God, is alike denounced against all of like character. The result of the conflict between David and his foes is a sample of what shall fall out in every like case. Let the righteous rejoice. Let sinners tremble.

28. Let us never fall into the error of the wicked, who have long and always delighted in deriding the suffering people of God, and especially in making light of their pious grief for sin. Dickson: "The insulting of enemies over the godly when the Lord's hand is heavy upon them, because it reflecteth upon religion and upon God's glory, is a main ingredient in the sorrow of the godly," v. 7. There is a great difference between "encouraging the exercise of a salutary repentance," and provoking feelings of "unmitigated despair."

29. How apt God is to punish in kind. David's enemies pursued him till he was sore vexed. In the end they were sore vexed themselves, vv. 3, 10. Compare Judges i. 5–8; 2 Sam. xxii. 27; Ps. xviii. 26; cix. 17, 18; Matt. v. 7; Jas. ii. 13.

30. All is well that ends well. Horne: "Many of the mournful Psalms end in this [triumphant] manner, to instruct the believer, that he is continually to look forward, and solace himself with beholding that day, when his warfare shall be accomplished; when sin and sorrow shall be no more; when sudden and everlasting confusion shall cover the enemies of righteousness; when the sackcloth of the penitent shall be ex-changed for a robe of glory, and every tear become a sparkling gem in his crown: when to sighs and groans shall succeed the songs of heaven, set to angelic harps, and faith shall be resolved into the vision of the Almighty."

PSALM VII.

Shiggaion of David, which he sang unto the LORD, *concerning the words of Cush the Benjamite.*

1 O LORD my God, in thee do I put my trust: save me from all them that persecute me, and deliver me:

2 Lest he tear my soul like a lion, rending *it* in pieces, while *there is* none to deliver.

3 O LORD my God, if I have done this; if there be iniquity in my hands;

4 If I have rewarded evil unto him that was at peace with me; (yea, I have delivered him that without cause is mine enemy ;)

5 Let the enemy persecute my soul, and take *it;* yea, let him tread down my life upon the earth, and lay mine honour in the dust. Selah.

6 Arise, O Lord, in thine anger, lift up thyself because of the rage of mine enemies: and awake for me *to* the judgment *that* thou hast commanded.

7 So shall the congregation of the people compass thee about: for their sakes therefore return thou on high.

8 The Lord shall judge the people: judge me, O Lord, according to my righteousness, and according to mine integrity *that is* in me.

9 Oh let the wickedness of the wicked come to an end; but establish the just: for the righteous God trieth the hearts and reins.

10 My defence *is* of God, which saveth the upright in heart.

11 God judgeth the righteous, and God is angry *with the wicked* every day.

12. If he turn not, he will whet his sword; he hath bent his bow, and made it ready.

13 He hath also prepared for him the instruments of death; he ordaineth his arrows against the persecutors.

14 Behold, he travaileth with iniquity, and hath conceived mischief, and brought forth falsehood.

15 He made a pit, and digged it, and is fallen into the ditch *which* he made.

16 His mischief shall return upon his own head, and his violent dealing shall come down upon his own pate.

17 I will praise the Lord according to his righteousness: and will sing praise to the name of the Lord most high.

THE title of this Psalm has occasioned considerable difficulty. The word *Shiggaion* occurs nowhere else, though the plural form of it, Shigionoth, is found in the *first* verse of the *third* chapter of Habakkuk. Any signification given to the word in one place ought to suit the other, unless some cause for a difference can be shown. The word from which Shiggaion is derived is often found in the Bible; and any sense not fairly drawn from it must be very doubtful in its application here. On these and like grounds it is safe to reject the following renderings; *plaintive song,* by the Arabic; *elegiac,* by Cobbin; *care,* by Cocceius; *ignorance,* by Bellarmine; *innocence,* by Luther; *interpretation,* by the Chaldee; *psalm,* by the Septuagint; *song,* by the Syriac; *delight, joy* and *pleasure,* by some of the Rabbies. Nor is there any evidence that Shiggaion was the first word of a song, the tune of which was to be used in singing this Psalm. No such song is produced. There seems to be no doubt that it is the name of a song; for it is said David *sang* it. This may mean either that he *composed* it, or that he recited it to some tune. Shiggaion means *a wandering.* Four explanations are offered. One is that this composition was to be sung to a *wandering* tune, *i. e.* a tune full of variations of tone, time and style of execution. The second is, that this is a Psalm of various metre. The third is, that David was singing of his own wandering, but whether it refers to his uncertain dwelling in the wilderness, or to some *error,* or moral wandering, is not agreed. The fourth is that David is singing of the wanderings, or errors of others in their treatment of him. Hengstenberg favors this fourth view. But this explanation does not suit the word in Habakkuk. Neither does the third. Calvin, Venema and Scott embrace the first view, and not without cause, though Calvin with characteristic good sense adds, " I do not contend about a matter of so small importance."

The next inquiry is, Who is meant by *Cush?* The eldest son of Ham bore that name; but the difficulty arises from the fact that no such person is spoken of in history as cotemporary with David. Some have thought that by Cush was meant Hushai, who dissuaded Absalom from following the counsel of Ahithophel. 2 Sam. xvii. 5–15. This view was maintained by Athanasius. The objections to it are that Hushai and Cush are quite different words, not only in our translation but also in the Hebrew; and that there is no evidence that Hushai was a Benjamite. He is called the Archite, and Archi was a city of Manasseh beyond Jordan. Besides, Hushai spoke no calumny against David, as Cush seems clearly to have done, v. 3. Others have supposed that by Cush was meant Shimei, who was indeed a Benjamite, and reviled David. But the words Cush and Shimei are wholly dissimilar; and there is no reason for supposing that Shimei ever bore the proper name of Cush. Others take Cush to be Saul himself. He was indeed a Benjamite, and he was the son of Cis, or Kish; but he was not Cis himself. Those, who maintain this view derive some countenance from the Chaldee, which thus renders this title: "The interpretation of an ode of David, which he sang before the Lord, when he delivered a poem upon the death of Saul, the Son of Cis, who was of the tribe of Benjamin." Those who hold that the word *Cush* signifies an Ethiopian should not forget that *Cush* designates Ethiopia, and *Cushi*, an Ethiopian. Hengstenberg says, some "Consider the name Cush as symbolical, and suppose David to have applied the epithet to his enemy on account of his dark malice, as being too inveterate to admit of a change for the better." He refers to "almost all the Jewish expositors" in confirmation of his views. He also cites Luther, who reads *Moor* for Cush, and who says; "He calls him Moor, on account of his unabashed wickedness, as one incapable of anything good or righteous. Just as we commonly call a lying and wicked fellow *black*. Hence the language of the poet:

He is black, O Roman; be thou ware of him.—*Horace.*

As we also call him *fair*, who deals with people in an honest and upright manner,—who has a heart that is free of envy. Therefore it is said, David has entirely left out his proper name, and given him a name in accordance with his perverse heart and ways." Hengstenberg favors this view, and cites Jer. xiii. 23 and Amos ix. 7, and says that as Saul was the son of Kish, David plays upon the name of his father. Venema cites the same line from Horace, and the same passages in the prophets as appropriate, if the word *Cush* is to be taken figuratively. Cocceius understands by Cush, "Saul, who as an Ethiopian changes not his skin, so was he impenitent, stubborn and malicious." Others have taken substantially the same views. Perhaps, however, most men will feel little satisfied with such an explanation. Calvin: "The opinion of some that Saul is here spoken of under a fictitious name is not supported by any argument of sufficient weight. . . In my opinion he here expresses by his proper name, and without a figure, a wicked accuser, who had excited hatred against him by falsely charging him with some crime." This view is every way natural, and is embraced by Patrick. In Acts xx. 35, Paul quotes words spoken by Christ though not recorded by any evangelist. And Paul in 2 Tim. iii. 8, gives us the cognomen of two celebrated magicians of Egypt, whose names are not found in any part of the Old Testament. A large part of David's life was spent in turmoil. He may have had hundreds and thousands of mischievous and bitter foes, whose names are not given even once in any part of Scripture. We should expect as much. Inspiration gives but a short sketch of the sayings and doings of the antitype of David, Jesus Christ. John xxi. 25. It takes but an hour or two to read everything written in Bible history respecting David. When this Psalm was written and first sung, Cush and his slanders may have been well known to devout and intelligent Israelites. For reasons similar to those mentioned in commenting on preceding Psalms it is supposed that this Psalm was not actually written, though its leading thoughts may have come up, at the time when David was sore pressed by his enemies. Before he closes, he raises the song of victory and thanksgiving. Some, however, have supposed that he did this because by faith he anticipated complete deliverance. The names of the Creator found in this Psalm are *Jehovah* LORD, *Elohim God, El God,* and *Gel-yohn Most High.* On the first three see above on Ps. i. 2; iii. 2; v. 4. On the last see below on v. 17. David is unquestionably the author of this Psalm, but at what time he wrote it, we know not. Some have fixed the date at the year B. C. 1058.

1. O LORD *my God, in thee do I put my trust.* This is the first instance in the Psalms where David addresses the Almighty by the united names Jehovah and my God. No more suitable words can be placed at the beginning of any act of prayer or praise. These names show the ground of the confidence afterwards expressed. They "denote at once supreme reverence and the most endearing confidence. They convey a recognition of God's infinite perfections, and of his covenanted and gracious relations." Fry renders the first clause, *I have taken shelter in thee;* Jebb: *In thee do I seek refuge.* Our translators hardly ever vary in rendering this verb *trust.* Once they give, *hath hope,* Pr. xiv. 32; once *make my refuge,* Ps. lvii. 1. The marginal readings more frequently vary. Calvin and Hengstenberg use the present tense. But the ancient versions follow the original, and use the past tense, *I have trusted,* or I *have hoped.* Alexander gives the full force when he reads, "*I have trusted,* and do still trust;" that is, David here describes a continuous act. Calvin: "David does not boast of a confidence which he constantly entertained in his afflictions. And this is a genuine and undoubted proof of our faith, when, being visited with adversity, we yet persevere in cherishing and exercising hope in God. From this passage we also learn that the gate of mercy is shut against our prayers, if the key of faith do not open it for us. Nor does he use superfluous language when he calls Jehovah *his own God;* for by setting this as a bulwark before him, he beats back the waves of temptations, that they may not overwhelm his faith." Nothing is more certain than the all-sufficiency of God. Nothing has greater power than that. Nothing is more sure than its sustaining energy to every one who relies on God alone. He may with boldness say: *Save me from all them that persecute me, and deliver me.* Persecutors have various methods of wearing out the saints. Sometimes they try flames, and wild beasts, and racks, and gibbets, and the sword, and dungeons. Again they employ expatriation, confiscation of goods, civil disabilities. But a universal weapon against the friends of truth is the tongue. By scorn, by railing, by mocking, by misrepresentation, by slander the people of God are wronged, distressed, cast down. Horne: "To a tender and ingenuous spirit the 'persecution' of the tongue is worse than that of the sword, and with more difficulty submitted to; as indeed a good name is more precious than bodily life. Believers in every age have been persecuted in this way; and the king of saints often mentions it as one of the bitterest ingredients in his cup of sorrows. Faith and prayer are the arms with which this formidable temptation must be encountered, and may be overcome." Slanders are often uttered in order to afford a pretext for violent measures against men's persons and lives. For this cause charges of conspiracy against the government are often falsely made, as against Nehemiah, Jeremiah, Christ and Paul, and here against David. But God can *save* and *deliver;* and if we rely on him, he will surely do it, although our enemies may be very numerous, as David's were, for he speaks of *all* his persecutors. Sometimes a multitude of enemies assail us at once, but they are led on by one man, who has power and malice, which make him very dangerous to us. This seems to have been the case here, for next we read:

2. *Lest he tear my soul like a lion, rending* it *in pieces, while* there is *none to deliver.* The Arabic reads, *Lest they take away my soul,* but this is unsupported by any text or authority. This verse more than any other seems to point to Saul in the plenitude of his royal power as the most formidable enemy David had. For "the king's wrath is as the roaring of a lion;" and "the fear of a king is as the roaring of a lion;" Pr. xix. 12; xx. 2. But even "the king's heart is in the hands of the Lord;" and he can turn it as easily as the gardener turns the rivulets of water in the little

channels made for the purposes of irrigation, Pr. xxi. 1. How easily God can do this, even in the case of Saul, we see in 1 Sam. xxiii. 27, 28. But it is not certain that Saul is here pointed out. There may have been some other powerful adversary, whose name is not given us. Or Cush himself may have been the terrible as well as the slanderous foe. But Hengstenberg thinks that the one person mentioned in this verse is a *personification*, represented by Saul. If so, the idea is not materially varied. The image of a terrible wild beast tearing a lamb or a sheep in pieces had been familiar to David from his boyhood. 1 Sam. xvii. 34–36. Indeed the figure was natural and just. See also 2 Tim. iv. 17. It is also used by Peter (1 Epis. v. 8,) in reference to the great adversary of our souls. To *tear the soul*, is to destroy the life and kill the person of a man. From the enemies of his people there is no pledge of deliverance, but in God only. He can give succor. Henry: "It is the glory of God to help the helpless."

3. *O* Lord *my God, if I have done this* [which is alleged against me—if I have conspired against the life of the king—or been guilty as charged;] *if there be iniquity in my hands* in the affair as charged by Cush, so that my enemies have just cause for their hostility to me. [This verse and the next find their application in v. 5.]

4. *If I have rewarded evil unto him that was at peace with me.* Alexander: *If I have repaid my friend evil;* Fry: *If I have made returns of evil;* Castalio: *If I have returned evil for evil;* Waterland: *If I have repaid evil to him, who dealt ill with me;* Dimock gives a similar rendering; Patrick: *If I have injured him when he was kind to me;* Edwards: *If I have done evil to my friend.* The import of the passage is that of a solemn protestation that he had not been guilty of base ingratitude in the case charged by Cush, whatever it may have been. He adds, (*Yea, I have delivered him that without cause is mine enemy.*) This is the more literal, but not the more common rendering. None of the ancient translations put this in parenthesis, nor does any other now at hand except our common English version and the Psalter of the church of England. The Septuagint, Ethiopic, Arabic, and Vulgate: Let me deservedly fall empty before mine enemies, thus making this the beginning of the woe invoked in case of guilt. The objection is that the original will not bear out such a rendering. The Chaldee: If I have afflicted those who have in vain brought me into straits. The sense is good and pertinent, but where was it found? The Syriac: If I have oppressed my enemies without cause; Fry: If I have spoiled those that without cause are mine adversaries; Hammond and Hengstenberg also prefer *spoiled*. Waterland uses *despoiled*. But I find not that the verb is ever in this form elsewhere in our version rendered *spoiled*. Calvin: *If I have not delivered*, etc. But he admits that the word *not* has to be supplied. The simplest mode of meeting the difficulty is that adopted in our English version. Then the verb has the rendering given it everywhere else in this form, *i. e., deliver;* no negative is required; the sense is good; and the Psalmist declares his benevolence to those who were without cause hostile to him. *Good for evil* has always been the doctrine of good men. Certainly it was with David. Twice he had Saul completely in his power, first, at En-gedi, then in the trench, but he would not hurt a hair of his head, nor suffer any one else to injure him. Doubtless he would treat any other foe with true Scriptural benevolence. 1 Sam. xxiv. xxvi. The sense then is, If I am the guilty man they say I am, yea, if I am not benevolent even to my worst foes, then

5. *Let the enemy persecute my soul, and take* it; *yea, let him tread down my life upon the earth, and lay mine honour in the dust. Selah.* See remarks on Selah in the Introduction, § 15. The import of the whole seems to be this: If Cush can make good his accusations, then let the worst come on me, that my enemies desire—let the

enemy take my life—cut short my existence—and *lay mine honor in the dust*. The word here rendered *honor* is the same, that in Psalms xxx. 12, lvii. 8, cviii. 1 is rendered *glory*, and in those cases clearly means the *tongue*. If this is the meaning here, then he says, Let my tongue lie silent in death. This is very pertinent and apposite. But the word is often and properly rendered *honor* as in Num. xxiv. 11; 1 Kings iii. 13; 1 Chron. xxix. 12, 28; Ps. lxvi. 2; cxii. 9. So that David as much as says, *let infamy cover me and let my memory rot if I am the man I am said to be.* This is an extension of the woes mentioned in the preceding clauses. By *honor* Hengstenberg after Muis and others understand the soul, the noblest part of man's nature. But he does not make the matter clear. He is probably wrong. He does not even notice the difficulties of such an exposition. When circumstances demand it, and the truth is on our side, we may in the most solemn manner protest our innocence, 2 Cor. i. 23; Phil. i. 8. Yea, we may properly declare ourselves ready to undergo punishment, if it can be shown that we deserve it, Acts xxv. 11. Such forms of asseveration should be kept for solemn and weighty occasions. A serious assault upon our characters is always felt by good men to be an overwhelming calamity if we cannot be rescued by legitimate means of defence. For *persecute* and *take* Jebb reads *pursue* and *overtake*, and he says these words keep up the image of a wild beast introduced in v. 2. What a bulwark the upright find in conscious integrity. What boldness it gives David in prayer. Therefore he says,

6. *Arise, O* Lord, *in thine anger.* Our cause does not speed well merely because it is in the main just, but when the righteous Lord, who loveth righteousness, undertakes it for us. To him we must come in humility at all times. Against him we have sinned grievously, and should he make use of our enemies to scourge us, at his hands we deserve it all. The Berleberg Bible shows the relation between this and the preceding verses thus: "But, because my conscience acquits me of such things, and testifies that I am innocent in that respect, therefore I seek thy protection, and call upon thy righteousness, which is wont to defend the guiltless." There is considerable variety in rendering the next clause of this verse. Our version reads: *Lift up thyself because of the rage of mine enemies*; the Septuagint, Ethiopic and Vulgate: Be thou exalted in the borders of mine enemies; Chaldee: Lift up [thyself] in fury upon my oppressors; Arabic: Lift up thyself upon the necks of mine enemies; Syriac, nearly the same; Calvin: Lift up thyself against the rage of mine enemies. It is generally agreed that the contrast is between the anger of God and the rage of David's foes. Fry changes the pointing and reads the first two clauses thus: Arise, Jehovah: in thine indignation lift up thyself against the raging of mine adversaries. This effectually brings the anger of God to oppose the wrath of man. Calvin and Hengstenberg put the very shortest pause between *anger* and *lift up;* but Hengstenberg reads *with*, not *against.* Alexander reads *in* or *amidst.* If the anger of God is invoked to oppose the rage of David's enemies, *against* gives the sense as well as any other word. Calvin: "David here sets the anger of God in apposition to the rage of his enemies; and when we are in similar circumstances we should act in the same manner. When the ungodly are inflamed against us, and cast forth their rage and fury to destroy us, we ought humbly to beseech God to be inflamed also on his side; in other words, to show in truth that he has no less zeal and power to preserve us, than they have inclination to destroy us." The next clause reads: *And awake for me* to *the judgment* that *thou hast commanded.* For *commanded* Calvin and Street read *ordained.* This, however, does not materially vary the sense. The judgment here referred to is not the final decision of men's destinies in the last day, but that vindication of David, which he had a right to expect from him, who had called him to be king over Israel, from him whose nature was wholly righteous.

The Judge of all the earth will do right. On that point there can be no doubt. Though for awhile he may keep still as one that sleepeth, yet in due time he will *awake,* and do the work of retribution. And when God should do that work then says David,

7. *So shall the congregation of the people compass thee about: for their sakes, therefore, return thou on high.* Allowing that David refers to Saul, Scott's comment on this and the preceding verse is very judicious: "David was assured that the Lord intended to cut off Saul. This was the 'judgment which he had commanded,' and for which David prayed, not only on his own account, but for the sake of the people. Saul's tyranny and neglect of his duty as king of Israel had crushed and scattered the Israelites: and his persecution and impiety had driven them from the ordinances and worship of God, and seduced them into many crimes. The Psalmist therefore prayed that the righteous Judge would ascend his exalted tribunal, exert his omnipotent authority, and by some visible interposition check the progress of impiety, and give encouragement to his servants; that they might be again collected in his courts, and unite in his holy worship." Some extend the scope of this verse beyond the Israelites, and read *peoples* or *nations* for *people,* and the Hebrew word is plural. No doubt the ill effects of Saul's administration were felt in surrounding nations, as were afterwards the happy effects of the reigns of David and of Solomon. But the word rendered *congregation* here is the same that is so rendered in Ps. i. 5; lxxiv. 2, and very often elsewhere. It generally refers to the people of Israel, and so seems to restrict the sense to the application given by Scott, although it is sometimes applied to other assemblies. Of those, who extend the term so as to include Gentile nations, Calvin takes the clearest and most concise view: "Lord, when thou shalt have put me in a peaceable possession of the kingdom, this will not only be a benefit conferred on me personally, but it will be a lesson common to many nations, teaching them to acknowledge thy just judgment, so that they shall turn their eyes to thy judgment-seat." The call on God to *return on high* is a petition that he would as Judge of the earth resume the seat, out of which by a bold figure he is now said to be for a season. Kimchi: "When God seems to take no notice of the transgressions of men, it is as if he descended from the place of his power, and from his judgment-seat; but when he visits and judges their iniquities, he seems to elevate himself on high, or to return to his judgment-seat." The words rendered *for their sakes* are by Calvin, who here follows some old versions, rendered *on account of this, i. e.* the benefit of the divine judgment to many nations. Horsley, Fry and Hengstenberg read *over it,* and Alexander *above it,* i. e. *the congregation.* The passage is confessedly difficult. A careful consideration of what has been offered has not afforded satisfactory evidence that our translation can be improved. It agrees with Luther and Jebb. Often a solemn procession was formed and marched around the temple or the altar. This is distinctly alluded to in Ps. xxvi. 6. To *compass about* God or his altar was therefore to offer solemn religious worship. The worshippers also gathered around the altar. David was confident his prayer should be answered and so he says:

8. *The* LORD *shall judge the people.* Fry and others, following the original, render the last word plural, *nations, i. e.,* all nations. The assertion is that God is Judge of all the earth, and shall assuredly prove this to be so. Of this David had a full persuasion. Calvin properly remarks that the verb SHALL JUDGE in the future denotes here a continued act. As God thus determines controversies between the righteous and the wicked, David asks that his case may be now taken up and tried: *Judge me, O* LORD, *according to my righteousness, and according to mine integrity* that is *in me.* God is not oppressed with the care and judgment of the nations. To ask him to execute judgment in a given case is to beseech him to do what he is always doing on a much

larger scale. He who governs the world can surely govern one man. He who judges all nations will not despise the case of one sufferer. He who does the greater will surely do the less. The appeal to his own innocence is confined to the matter respecting which David had been slandered. It has nothing to do with his standing in the sight of God as a sinful man. Before God none more earnestly cried for mercy: "Enter not into judgment with thy servant: for in thy sight shall no man living be justified." Ps. cxliii. 2.

9. *Oh let the wickedness of the wicked come to an end.* For *wickedness* Calvin reads *malice* and Alexander *badness.* There never was a regenerate man that did not heartily offer that prayer. There never was a renewed soul that was not sorely grieved by the wickedness of his times. Hypocrites may make an idle lament over the degeneracy of their age, but God's real people enter into such grief with heartfelt sincerity. Some men spend all their sighs about the wickedness of others, forgetting their own sins. But the child of God hates and laments all sin, because it dishonors God. His own sins dreadfully distress him. So do the transgressions of others. When wickedness is rampant the righteous fear and tremble and utter strong cries against it. • The best English Bibles use *Oh* in this case, not as an exclamation, like *O,* but optative. This is the precise idea of the original. The word *wicked* is plural. A pious man laments not merely those sinful acts which personally annoy him and his friends; he deplores all sin and would have it cease everywhere. There is no reason for rendering the clause, *Let the wickedness of the wicked consume them,* as some have suggested. David also prays, *but establish the just* [man.] Some of the old versions read, *Direct the just.* The word may be so rendered, but *establish* is a more common and in most cases a better rendering. God establishes the just man in part by properly directing him. The singular being used here probably shows the special reference to David, yet the truth asserted is universal. And God can be at no loss to tell who is the just and who are the wicked; *for the righteous God trieth the hearts and reins.* Among the Hebrews the kidneys (or reins) no less than the heart were often spoken of as the seat of pain and pleasure, joy and grief, knowledge and thought. So to cover all the theories in the popular mind, all the words that would aid in conveying an idea of God's omniscience are employed. We have a like reference to popular belief respecting the constitution of man in 1 Thess. v. 23. In such cases there is no sanction of popular theories. The Bible teaches not philosophy. The import of the clause is that God knows all the thoughts, motives, secrets, uprightness or wickedness of men, and so can easily mete out justice to every soul. Fry renders it, And let the righteous God try the hearts and reins; Hengstenberg: And the trier of the heart and reins art thou, O righteous God. This last makes the address direct to God throughout. But in the Psalms there is manifested a remarkable facility in changing from the second to the third person. The doctrine taught by each of these modes of translation is the same. To such a God David gladly appeals.

10. *My defence* is *of God, which saveth the upright in heart.* The word rendered *defence* here is in Ps. iii. 3, and in a dozen other places in the Psalms rendered *shield,* sometimes *buckler,* and sometimes *defence.* For *in God* some read *with God,* or *upon God;* but our version gives the sense. If our cause is good, then the divine rectitude is a comfort to us, for a righteous God hates iniquity. Yea, he *saves, delivers, gives the victory* to the upright in heart. The word rendered *upright* is in our translation of the Psalms uniformly rendered *upright* or *right.* In other parts of Scripture it is once rendered *just,* Pr. xxix. 10, and sometimes *righteous,* Num. xxiii. 10; Job xxiii. 7; Pr. ii. 7; iii. 32. It is several times rendered *straight,* Jer. xxxi. 9; Ezek. i. 7, 23. Alexander regards *straight-forward* or *sincere* as synonymous. The heart of a regene-

rate man is the best part about him. He is not deceitful. He intends and aims to do better than he does. And so,

11. *God judgeth the righteous, and God is angry* with the wicked *every day.* The words ELOHIM and EL are both found in this verse. See on Ps. iii. 2; v. 4. There is no good ground for the rendering of the Septuagint and some other old versions, *God is a Judge just, strong, and long-suffering,* nor for the interrogative form of the last clause in the Vulgate, *Is he angry every day?* John Rogers' translation is, *God is a ryghteous Judge, and God is ever threatenynge,* and Ainsworth reads, God angrily threateneth every day. Though the words *with the wicked* are not in the Hebrew, yet the contrast is between the righteous and the wicked, and the wicked are surely here spoken of. Because the wicked are always wicked and because God is always holy, therefore his relation to them is ever one of opposition, of threatening, of anger. No holy creature could delight in a God who was not displeased with wickedness. *Every day* is equivalent to *all the time, unceasingly.* Charnock: "Uninterruptedly in the nature of his anger, though not in the effect of it." It is true that sentence against an evil work is not always executed speedily; but God's purpose is inflexible, and there is never a day when one blessed with spiritual discernment may not see infallible tokens of God's anger, at least against such forms of wickedness as are atrocious and notorious. But delay is not connivance. That the word *wicked* is properly supplied here is evident from the next verse:

12. *If he turn not, he will whet his sword.* The word here rendered *turn* is also found in Ps. xxii. 27. All the ends of the world shall remember and *turn* unto the LORD; and in Ps. li. 13, Sinners shall be *converted* unto thee. The doctrine of conversion is no new doctrine. Because the wicked is wicked, he must turn or perish. He is a wise man who counts the long-suffering of God salvation. God commonly gives space for repentance, but then *he limiteth a day.* To *whet his sword* is to make ready to execute vengeance. The sword was the weapon used in beheading or slaying. The figure is an old one, Deut. xxxii. 41. If God shall punish, his inflictions will be terrible. Moreover, *he hath bent his bow.* The bow often used in war was the cross-bow, which was bent by putting the foot on the middle and then pulling the string, and so the word rendered *bent* is literally *trodden* on. See Deut. i. 36; Josh. xiv. 9; Isa. lxiii. 3. This is an image like the last taken from the habits of warriors. The work of destroying the wicked will not require any special preparation. Every sinner on earth is continually ready to drop into hell. Hengstenberg: "It is a remarkable instance of Divine foresight, but such as often occurs in history, that in the death of Saul the bow and the sword both actually had their share. Saul was hit by the archers, and sore pressed, so that he despaired of his life. 'Then said he to his armor-bearer, Draw thy sword, and thrust me through therewith, lest these uncircumcised come and thrust me through, and abuse me: but his armor-bearer would not; for he was sore afraid. Therefore Saul took a sword, and fell upon it.'" 1 Sam. xxxi. 3, 4.

13. *He hath also prepared for him the instruments of death.* The first pronoun *He* refers to God, who as a man of war was about to meet his foes. The second pronoun *Him* has perplexed commentators. Calvin reads *it,* meaning the bow; God hath prepared for it [his bow] the instruments of death. Fry thinks the meaning is that God has prepared for himself—for his own use—the instruments of death. But Alexander reads, *At him* [the *wicked* enemy] *he has aimed,* or directed, the instruments of death. Fry in this case is to be preferred to Calvin. Either Fry or Alexander gives the full sense; though the latter is the more ingenious. If his view is correct then as he says, "This is still another step in advance. The weapons are not only ready for him, but aimed at him." And so *he ordaineth his arrows against the persecutors.* For *persecutors* some would read

burning or *hot* ones, supposing that persecutors burn with wrath and envy. The word does not occur often, but *pursue* or *persecute* is not an unusual rendering. It occurs but once more in the Psalms (x. 2) and is there rendered *persecute*. But some following the Arabic and Syriac join the word to arrows. Hengstenberg reads, He makes his arrows burning, and Alexander, His arrows to (be) burning he will make: thus referring to the fiery darts or arrows thrown into beleaguered cities. Fry also reads *swift arrows*, but says in a note that it may be, "flaming arrows." Waterland reads, He will make his arrows to pursue. Perhaps most minds will rest satisfied with our English version. The sense given by it seems to have been more generally accepted than any other.

Morison: "The figure, which represents Jehovah as having bent his bow and made it ready, is awfully descriptive of the exposed situation of every sinner until he returns to the Shepherd and Bishop of souls. The whole system of nature and providence is ready, at the bidding of the Almighty to inflict the blow that shall hurl him to perdition. The archer of divine vengeance stands, as it were, with bended bow, and the next arrow that he discharges may pierce, with everlasting anguish, the soul that now glides on securely in the career of thoughtlessness and crime."

Bates: "This description of God's righteous displeasure is more powerful to shoot through the conscience of hardened sinners than the bare threatening that justice will surely punish them."

Luther, speaking of the bold figure of verses 12 and 13, says, "The prophet takes a lesson from a coarse human similitude, in order that he might inspire terror into the ungodly. For he speaks against stupid and hardened people, who would not apprehend the reality of a divine judgment, of which he had just spoken; but they might possibly be brought to consider this by greater earnestness on the part of man. Now the prophet is not satisfied with thinking of the sword, but he adds thereto the bow; even this does not satisfy him, but he describes how it is already stretched, and aim is taken, and the arrows are applied to it, as here follows. So hard, stiff-necked, and unabashed are the ungodly, that however many threatenings may be urged against them, they will still remain unmoved. But in these words he forcibly describes how God's anger presses hard upon the ungodly, though they will never understand this until they actually experience it. It is also to be remarked here, that we have had so frightful a threatening and indignation against the ungodly in no Psalm before this; neither has the Spirit of God attacked them with so many words. Then in the following verses, he also recounts their plans and purposes, shows how these shall not be in vain, but shall return again upon their own head. So that it clearly and manifestly appears to all those who suffer wrong and reproach, as a matter of consolation that God hates such revilers and slanderers above all other characters."

14. *Behold, he travaileth with iniquity.* The pains taken by wicked men to do evil are often worthy of a better cause. They sleep not except they do some mischief. They toil hard in the service of a cruel master. They *travail*. This is true of every man, that fears not God. It is specially true of every persecutor. He *hath conceived mischief, and brought forth falsehood.* Alexander gives all the verbs of this verse in the future and says, "The meaning seems to be that while bringing his malignant schemes to maturity, he will unconsciously conceive and bring forth ruin to himself." A parallel passage is found in Job xv. 35. Luther renders it, Behold, he has evil in his heart, with misfortune he is pregnant, but he will bring forth a failure; Fry: Behold he is in travail with iniquity; but though mischief is conceived, disappointment is brought forth. The church of England, following the Septuagint and Vulgate, renders it, He travaileth with mischief; he hath conceived sorrow and brought forth ungodliness; Hengstenberg: Behold, he travails with mischief, and is big with misery,

and brings forth falsehood. The wicked shall find all their plans frustrated, and all their hopes disappointed. What a miserable show both Saul and Absalom made at the winding up of their plots against David. So doubtless did Cush if he was a third person. The sinner here spoken of was restless and busy, and so

15. *He made a pit, and digged it*, i. e., he made a pit by digging it. Pits are made to catch wild beasts or thieves or enemies, who prowl about. They are dug so deep that either man or beast falling into them cannot leap out. The mouth of the pit is covered over with boughs of trees, or straw so that it is not perceived. Cush and those who favored his views pursued David like a wild beast; they used open assault; they hunted him; they at length resorted to artifice. But all was in vain. They fell into their own pit. Sternhold and Hopkins have given a version of this and the next verse, which has attracted attention.

> He digs a ditch and delves it deep,
>   In hope to hurt his brother;
> But he shall fall into the pit
>   That he digged up for other.
> Thus wrong returneth to the hurt
>   Of him in whom it bred;
> And all the mischief that he wrought,
>   Shall fall upon his head.

Speaking of the burning fury of the ungodly, as here represented, Luther says, "So active and diligent are they to have the pit dug, and the hole prepared. They try everything, they explore everything, and not satisfied that they have dug a pit, they clear it out and make it deep, as deep as they possibly can, that they may destroy and subvert the innocent." *And is fallen into the ditch* which *he made.* Hengstenberg renders it the pit *which he makes.* He says: "We must not expound: into the pit *which he has made.* The wicked man is still occupied with the pit, still working at it, when he falls into it. The punishment overtakes him in the midst of his guilty career."

The teaching of the 14th and 15th verses is repeated in the 16th. *His mischief shall return upon his own head.* For *mischief*, Calvin reads *wickedness;* church of England, *travail.* The original word often occurs in the Hebrew Bible. In our English version it is but once rendered *wickedness*, Job iv. 8, and once *perverseness*, Num. xxiii. 21. It is also rendered *pain, travail, trouble, sorrow, misery, grievance, grievousness;* more commonly, *mischief* and *labor.* But does not Hengstenberg use too sweeping language when he says this word always denotes the evil one suffers, not that which one *inflicts?* See Num. xxiii. 21; Job iv. 8; xv. 35; Ps. xciv. 20; cxl. 9; Pr. xxiv. 2. This return of mischief will be dreadful. It will come with crushing force. *And his violent dealing shall come down upon his own pate.* The word rendered *violent dealing* is never so translated elsewhere. Very generally, it is given simply as *violence*, sometimes *cruelty, damage, wrong, injustice.* The meaning is that the whole final effects of the measures taken against David were felt by his enemies, as a righteous retribution. For *pate*, Calvin's translator reads *crown.* The sense is the same. The result of the whole is,

17. *I will praise the* LORD *according to his righteousness: and will sing praise to the name of the* LORD *most high.* Hengstenberg: "*The righteousness and the praise shall correspond.*" God's righteousness is boundless, so shall be his honors. The truly devout do not willingly limit their praises of the LORD. This is the first place in the Psalms where we find Jehovah called the *Most High.* We first meet with the word thus rendered in Gen. xiv. 18. It occurs several times in the Pentateuch, and often in later books. It is found more than *twenty* times in the Psalms. God is the Most

High in his glorious elevation of nature, of counsel, and of government. There is none like him. There is none with him. There is none beside him. He is not only in all and through all; but he is above all and over all God blessed forever.

DOCTRINAL AND PRACTICAL REMARKS.

1. It is right to turn every event of life into an occasion of devotion. What could be less suited directly to arouse pious emotions than the sayings and doings of Cush? Yet thereupon David falls to praying and singing in a way to comfort himself and animate the church in all coming ages.

2. In devotion it is well to use the various Scriptural names and titles of God, vv. 1, 3, 11, 17. They are all suited to strengthen our faith. We ought not, however, to use them as mere expletives, nor with such frequency as shows a want of reverence.

3. Moller: "Even under the most grievous calumnies, by means of which men seek to destroy our good name and life itself, we should retain that choice moderation and equanimity, exemplified by David and by other saints."

4. It is a great blessing to have so much faith as to be able sincerely to say, *My God*, v. 1. He who can thus plead, virtually declares as Henry says, "Thou art my God, and, therefore, whither else should I go but to thee? Thou art my God, and therefore my shield; (Gen. xv. 1) my God, and therefore I am one of thy servants, who may expect to be protected;" Calvin: "This is a genuine and undoubted proof of our faith, when, being visited with adversity, we, notwithstanding, persevere in cherishing and exercising hope in God. . . The gate of mercy is shut against our prayers if the key of faith do not open it for us;" Morison: "In darkest seasons faith looks upon God as a sure refuge and defence, as ever near to God's afflicted servants in the hour of their greatest extremity."

5. Persecution is no novelty, v. 1. It began with Cain. It was taken up by evil men in subsequent ages, including Cush, and Pilate and thousands of others. The church of Rome binds all her bishops by oath to persecute as they have power. Persecution will last, while the wicked rage and are permitted to show their malice. All persecutors are so far alike that they hate holiness in God and man, especially in man, because they see it.

6. Salvation and deliverance from the least, as from the greatest enemies is to be sought and expected from God only, v. 1.

7. The opposition of carnal men to truth and piety is fierce, cruel and deadly, v. 2. Aroused, they are like wild beasts. Dickson: "If God do not interpose himself, for defence of his unjustly slandered servants, there is nothing to be expected from wicked enemies enraged, but merciless beastly cruelty."

8. No human power could have saved the church from utter extinction long since, vv. 1, 2. Moller: "The perils of the church are more and greater than can be comprehended in any statement. Like Daniel, she dwells among lions. Always and everywhere the roaring lion and ravening wolves lie in wait for the pious. But calling on God brings us to a safe refuge;" Morison: "Satan is an *accuser*, an *adversary*, a *liar* and the *father of lies*, the *old serpent*, the *prince of the power of the air*, the *God of this world*, the *prince of darkness*, the *spirit that now worketh in the children of disobedience*, and none can withstand him effectually, but in the *armor* of God, on the right hand and on the left." But our Saviour is Almighty. That settles the question.

9. It is every way right that we should submit ourselves to the government of God, as the righteous Judge of all the earth, vv. 3–5.

10. Humility does not require of us to acknowledge the truth of false charges brought against us. What humility demands is a judgment of ourselves, not below the truth, nor above it, but according to it, vv. 3–5.

11. Moller: "Against wicked rumors we ought to be content to oppose the single judgment of God." Some controversies will not be settled till the last day.

12. Conscious innocence is a wonderful shield, vv. 3–5. The righteous is as bold as a lion. For uprightness there is no substitute. This is our brazen wall, as one of the poets calls it. This is the fountain of delight to all the saints. "Our rejoicing is this, the testimony of our conscience;" 2 Cor. i. 12. Dickson: "Though innocence cannot exempt a man from being unjustly slandered, yet it will furnish him with a good conscience, and much boldness in the particular before God."

13. The doctrine of doing good for evil and of loving enemies is as old as true piety. It was practised by David. Dickson: "The more a man doth render good for evil, the more confidence shall he have when he cometh to God; for innocence served David for this good use, that he delivered Saul, who without cause was his enemy;" v. 4. Horne: "Happy he, who can reflect that he has been a benefactor to his persecutors;" Calvin: "When any one not only does not retaliate injuries received, but strives to overcome evil with good, he exhibits a genuine specimen of heaven-born virtue, thus demonstrating that he is one of the sons of God, for such a gentleness proceeds only from the spirit of adoption;" Luther: "Let this also be remarked that David here manifests an evangelical degree of righteousness. For to recompense evil with evil, the flesh and old Adam think to be right and proper. But it was forbidden even in the law of Moses, as evil was to be inflicted only by the magistrate, consequently not of one's own malice and authority." That the law of Sinai required good will and good for evil, we know from the sermon on the mount, Matt. v. 43–48, and from these sayings; "Love is the fulfilling of the law;" and "Love worketh no ill to his neighbor." That David practised on this principle is admitted by Saul himself: "If a man find his enemy, will he let him go well away? Wherefore the Lord reward thee good for that thou hast done unto me this day." 1 Sam. xxiv. 19.

14. Good men are not mistaken in putting honor above life, v. 5. Death was in David's esteem an evil, but the laying of one's honor in the dust was greater. Blessed be God's name, though he sometimes calls for life, he never requires us to sacrifice honor. It is a doctrine of the deceiver that the greatest calamity is the loss of natural life. Job ii. 4. We may easily love life too much. Our integrity cannot be preserved too carefully; our lives may.

15. The rage of the wicked shall surely be checked. If thoughts of God's mercy will not stop them, a sense of his wrath shall overwhelm them, v. 6. If the wicked can kindle dreadful fires, God can kindle hotter and greater burnings. If the wicked can send heavy woes and curses, God can send heavier. Dickson: "When our enemies are desperately malicious, and nothing can mitigate their fury; let the consideration of God's justice mitigate our passion: *for he will arise in anger against them.*"

16. It is a blessed thing when we know that our prayers concur with the divine plan. This made David earnest, v. 6. This aroused Daniel, chap. ix. 1–27. This is the soul of prayer. For "this is the confidence that we have in him, that, if we ask anything according to his will, he heareth us." 1 John v. 14. Let us chiefly pray for those things God commands us to ask for. In other things, let us always confess that we know not what is best, and ask God to choose for us.

17. Before God's judgment comes it may seem long; but when it shall have come, saint and sinner shall say that it lingered not, v. 6.

18. God's dealings with the wicked are useful. "The Lord is known by the judgment which he executeth." Ps. ix. 16. "When thy judgments are in the earth, the inhabitants of the world will learn righteousness." Is. xxvi. 9. Bad as the

world is, it would be unspeakably worse, were it not that God holds it in check by the severity of his dealings with some, whom he sets up as beacons; yea, by the checks he gives to all.

19. We may plead with God for his church's sake, v. 7. See also Isa. lxiii. 17. This does not imply that there is merit in the church. Merit is in Christ alone. But God loves Zion, and therefore we may ask him to do that, which will advance the cause he has set his heart upon.

20. We may therefore plead with God not to yield his government, nor even to seem to do so, v. 8. The world is most at peace when good laws human and divine are uniformly enforced.

21.   Though in a given contest with man we may be wholly innocent, and may so say before heaven and earth, vv. 3, 4, 5, 8; yet we must be careful not to plead that as before God we are without sin, or even that we are not heinous sinners.

22. We may rest assured that wickedness will be finally and utterly overthrown. God has said it. His people desire it, v. 9. Charnock: "God may be reconciled to the sinner, not to the sin."

23. The stability of the saint is as great as the instability of the sinner, v. 9. Whatever makes for one of these makes for the other also.

24. Let us often dwell on the divine omniscience, v. 9. If the fact that God tries the heart and reins is no comfort to us, it must be because we do not understand it, or love it as we should. The vilified and slandered of earth have been able to comfort themselves with this truth. "The clouds of calumny which have settled over the pious, have compelled them the oftener to submit their hearts and reins to the examination of the all-seeing eye."

25. As all the graces of the Christian are allied, so all the duties of religion are helpful to each other. Meditation helps prayer, vv. 9, 10.

26. It is on the common truths of religion we must chiefly rely to stir us up, and support us, vv. 9–11. That which is recondite is seldom of much service. Men are not saved by metaphysics, nor by truths hard to be understood by the docile, but by simple and plain truths.

27. Those, who are not upright in heart, sincere in their love, honest with God and man, have no right to expect to be heard and saved, v. 10. Scott: "We cannot stand before him (who tries the heart and reins) even according to his new covenant of mercy, 'without simplicity and godly sincerity,' and conscientious integrity in our habitual conduct."

28. Let not the wicked think that God's forbearance is connivance at sin, v. 11 God is really and terribly angry with the wicked all the time. Henry: "As his mercies are new every morning toward his people, so his anger is new every morning against the wicked."

29. The doctrine of a change of heart and life is inwoven into all the Scriptures, v. 12. Repentance or perdition, conversion or ruin are the alternatives presented in God's word. No wonder Christ expressed surprise that a Nicodemus should be ignorant of this doctrine. It is taught in all the Old Testament.

30. When God shall choose, he can easily destroy his foes. His weapons and instruments are all ready, vv. 12, 13.

31. God's wrath against persecutors burns with dreadful intensity. Scott: "Persecutors must expect his severest vengeance. . . The persecuted servants of God will be celebrating his praises, and rejoicing in his favor, while their persecutors are cast into the pit of destruction, and enduring the wrath of their righteous Judge, and all their subtle projects will concur in bringing about this final event." Henry: "Of all sinners, persecutors are set up as the fairest marks of divine wrath; against them

more than any other God has ordained his arrows. They set God at defiance, but cannot set themselves out of the reach of his judgments." Morison: "It is both our wisdom and our safety to leave all our persecutors and slanderers in the hands of our Almighty deliverer. He can 'restrain their wrath, and make the remainder thereof to praise him.' Or he can change their cruel purpose, and awaken in their bosoms feelings of gentleness and benevolence."

32. The very misery of the wicked should convince them of their sin and folly. They have travail, but the result is vanity. They project, and the result is failure. Nothing satisfies. All the time the stones, which the wicked are throwing into the air, are falling on themselves. Saul was killed by the Philistines whom he wished to employ to kill David. "And the Jews, who excited the Romans to crucify Christ, were awfully destroyed by the Romans, and numbers of them crucified." Henry: "The sinner takes a great deal of pains to ruin himself, more pains to damn his soul than, if directed aright, would save it." If the wicked were not blind, they would see all this. Even here their bad passions, counsels and lies hurt them more than others, vv. 15, 16. Luther: This is the incomprehensible nature of the divine judgment, that God catches the wicked with their own plots and counsels and leads them into the destruction, which they had themselves devised." If these things are so in this life, where nothing is finished, what may we not expect in the next?

33. In the darkest hours it is well to praise God, v. 17. Job did so. So did Paul and Silas in the jail at Philippi. If we are God's servants, we can always praise God for what he is, for what he has done for others, for much that he has done for us, for what we expect him to do for us. We should often give thanks for anticipated victories. We should praise him for our keenest afflictions. Aristotle tells us of a bird that sings sweetly, yet always lives among thorns.

34. After a deliverance not to give hearty thanks is monstrous. Good manners require us to praise our Deliverer. Chrysostom: "Let us praise the Lord perpetually; let us never cease to give thanks in all things, both by our words, and by our deeds. For this is our sacrifice; this is our oblation; this is the best liturgy, or divine service; resembling the angelical manner of living. If we continue thus singing hymns to him, we shall finish this life inoffensively, and enjoy those good things also which are to come."

35. Many verses of this Psalm show that the truths of religion, which are often the least dwelt on are the most useful. God's perfections and government are a great study. Let us often recur to them and other foundation truths.

36. Dickson: "The fruit of faith joined with a good conscience is access to God in prayer, confidence, peace and tranquility of mind, mitigation of trouble, protection and deliverance, as the prophet's experience here doth prove."

37. The old, the safe, the only way to the kingdom of heaven is through much tribulation.

38. Scott: "Let us under all our trials look unto the Saviour. He alone was perfect in righteousness, yet none was ever reviled, slandered, and hated as he was. He lived and died doing good to his enemies, and praying for them." We never err in looking to Jesus for example, or precept, or strength, or wisdom, or righteousness.

PSALM VIII.

To the chief Musician upon Gittith, A Psalm of David.

1 O LORD our Lord, how excellent *is* thy name in all the earth! who hast set thy glory above the heavens.

2 Out of the mouth of babes and sucklings hast thou ordained strength because of thine enemies, that thou mightest still the enemy and the avenger.

3 When I consider thy heavens, the work of thy fingers, the moon and the stars, which thou hast ordained;

4 What is man, that thou art mindful of him? and the son of man, that thou visitest him?

5 For thou hast made him a little lower than the angels, and hast crowned him with glory and honor.

6 Thou madest him to have dominion over the works of thy hands; thou hast put all *things* under his feet:

7 All sheep and oxen, yea, and the beasts of the field;

8 The fowl of the air, and the fish of the sea, *and whatsoever* passeth through the paths of the seas.

9 O LORD our Lord, how excellent *is* thy name in all the earth!

IT requires no lengthened argument to prove that David is the author of this Psalm. The title says it is his. The only occasion of doubt on the subject has been found in Heb. ii. 6, where Paul, quoting a part of the Psalm, mentions not David, but simply says, "One in a certain place testifies." But surely this cannot create any rational doubt. Similar modes of quotation are common, because natural.

There is no special importance attached to the inquiry, at what period of his life David wrote this Psalm. It does not appear that in it he celebrates any particular event in his own history.

Upon the words, *To the chief musician,* see on the title of Ps. iv. The word *Gittith,* has occasioned considerable discussion. Some regard this Psalm as one of triumph, sung to God, the author of a great victory obtained over some haughty enemy, as Goliath of Gath, or the Gittite. This view is taken by Hammond and Patrick. It is also favored by Edwards.

This method of explaining *Gittith* seems to be effectually set aside by its recurrence in the titles of Psalms lxxxi. and lxxxiv., where neither of these modes of solution would be at all admissible. Neither of these last-named Psalms can possibly be supposed to have any reference to Goliath, the Gittite.

The word *Gath* in Hebrew signifies a *wine-press.* See Jud. vi. 11; Lam. i. 15; Joel iii. 13. In the plural we have in Neh. xiii. 15, *Gittoth,* very nearly the same as *Gittith.* From this some have supposed that this was a song to be sung "*concerning the wine-presses.*" This view is taken by Theodoret, Ainsworth, Horsley, and Clarke. The Septuagint, Ethiopic, Vulgate: *For the wine-presses;* Doway: *For the presses;* but it has a note stating *Gittith* is supposed to be a musical instrument. Bellarmine says he cannot doubt that the Hebrew word should be the same as is found in Neh. xiii. 15. But he is the blind follower of the Septuagint and Vulgate. He also says, it is hard to divine what is designed. Others, who favor the rendering of the Septuagint, suppose that the reference is to a style of music, common at the vintage. But all these views will probably appear to most readers as strained.

Others think that Gittith means an instrument from Gath. Mudge says, it is "in all probability the *Gath-instrument,* as we say the *Cremona fiddle,* the *German Flute;* Alexander: "As David once resided in Gath, and had afterwards much intercourse with the inhabitants, the word may naturally here denote an instrument there invented or in use, or an air or style of performance, borrowed from that city;' Calvin: "Whether *Gittith* signifies a musical instrument or some particular tune, or the beginning of some famous and well-known song, I do not take upon me to determine. . . Of these three opinions, it is not of much importance which is adopted;" Venema thinks that *Gittith* clearly points to the air or melody to be used in singing this Psalm; The Chaldee: "A Psalm of David to be sung upon the harp that came from Gath;" Hengstenberg thinks it should be rendered, Upon the harp of Gath, or in the Gathic style; Rivet says it is uncertain what Gittith signifies; Fry says, that on this point, "nothing is known for certain. The most probable conjecture refers it to the tune or music;" Scott: "Gittith is perhaps the name of some tune, which David had learned when in Gath, or from the Gittites, and to which this and two other Psalms were set." Sebastian Schmidt, having noticed some of the most plausible of the foregoing opinions, says that he had rather give no account of the matter than one so full of uncertainty. Piscator says the point is of little moment. The other opinions respecting Gittith are probably not deserving of consideration. At least one of the other Psalms *upon Gittith* was composed by Asaph; so that whatever is meant thereby was not confined to David. Hengstenberg: "It is worthy of remark, that all the three Psalms distinguished by this name are of a joyful, thanksgiving character." Yet an examination of them shows that this remark needs some qualification.

There is not an agreement among commentators whether this Psalm is to be interpreted by reference to any historical event. Mudge says " it is evident enough from v. 2, that it was occasioned by some particular incident; either a remarkable deliverance from wild beasts, or something of that kind, perhaps granted to a child." Edwards agrees with Mudge in the general opinion, but suggests the victory over Goliath as the event celebrated, " or some other surprising conquest effected by very weak forces, whom the Psalmist may, in a poetical manner, call *babes* and *sucklings*." Patrick paraphrases it throughout as a celebration of the victory gained over Goliath by David. Hengstenberg thinks this Psalm " needs no historical exposition and bears none." It is a great error to suppose that every devotional composition in the Scriptures had its origin in some stirring incident. Perhaps we commonly err in attempting by conjecture to fix on some event in history, as the key of the interpretation of any Psalm.

Scott fixes the date of this Psalm at 1050 B. C.

In the Hebrew the *first* word of the *first* and of the *eighth* verses is Jehovah.

Although this Psalm is thrice quoted in the New Testament (Matt. xxi. 16; Heb. ii. 6–9; 1 Cor. xv. 27); yet there has been more than usual diversity in the views taken of its scope and design. Without noticing all the opinions presented on this subject, it is safe and proper to say that the obvious sense of the words grammatically construed must give us the primary meaning, and then that any authorized or sober use of a secondary import may properly be received.

Hengstenberg says the theme of this Psalm is, " *The greatness of God in the greatness of man*." Elsewhere he speaks of this Psalm as a devotional composition on the first chapter of Genesis. This is probably the correct view of the primary sense of the words. But the Syriac scholiast says, " The eighth Psalm is concerning Christ our Redeemer;" Luther says, " This is a prophecy concerning Christ—concerning his passion, his resurrection, and his dominion over all creatures;" Rivet also says, " It is certain that here the Psalmist had respect to the Messias, who was to come." So uniformly has the more pious and sober part of the Christian world regarded this as a highly Messianic Psalm that an assertion to the contrary rather shocks the godly than awakens their doubts. These suggestions concerning the purport of the Psalm have led many to take the ground, that both the foregoing views are correct, the one primary, the other secondary, the one literal, the other typical. Pool would apply it to man in general and to the man Christ Jesus in particular, to God's glory as manifested in creation and providence, but especially in redemption. He says the Psalmist first admires the excellent glory of God in heaven and earth, but most of all sings the love of God, by which he hath so wondrously exalted vile man. He adds that without doubt this Psalm is a prophecy respecting Christ. Alexander: "We have here a description of the dignity of human nature, as it was at first, and as it is to be restored in Christ, to whom the descriptive terms may be applied, without forced or fanciful accommodation on the one hand, and without denying the primary generic import of the composition on the other;" Morison: "While we may here be reminded of the first Adam and his posterity, and of the eminent rank and dominion of man over all the creatures of God upon this terrestrial globe; we shall yet, in a more striking manner, be reminded of Him, who, as 'the second Adam, the Lord from heaven,' has been placed, in glorious majesty, at the head of that new creation, which, consisting of redeemed and sanctified men, shall reflect the lustre of his matchless beauty and excellence through all eternity." Many others present substantially the same views.

The Psalm opens with an outburst of strong emotion, showing that the mind was already full of matter. The apparent abruptness of the beginning is quite in keeping with the genius of true poetry and true devotion.

Venema favors the opinion that this Psalm was composed at night, when David was watching the flock, notes the fact that the sun is not here mentioned among the heavenly bodies, and adds that the contemplation of the heavens under these circumstances was well suited to stir up such meditations. Hengstenberg rejects this view, but does not give very strong reasons. The probability is that the Psalm was an evening meditation, not composed during David's pastoral life, but afterwards. Yet the thoughts naturally suggested by gazing at the heavens during his early life were doubtless familiar to him, when he actually wrote this song.

1. *O* LORD *our Lord.* John Rogers' Translation, the Bishops' Bible and the church of England read, *O* LORD *our governor.* The Septuagint renders both these names of God by the word which in the New Testament is always rendered Lord. The latter word *Lord* is derived from a verb, which would justify us in rendering it as above, *governor, judge, supporter.* The Chaldee renders it *preceptor.* In our English version it is almost invariably rendered *Lord.* O Jehovah, our Ruler, *How excellent is thy name in all the earth!* For *excellent* some would read *glorious,* as the Syriac; *admirable,* as the Septuagint, Ethiopic, Vulgate and Arabic; *adorable,* as Fry; *wonderful,* as Calvin. Others suggest *great, illustrious, magnificent, renowned, powerful.* Our English Bible renders it elsewhere sometimes *excellent,* Ps. xvi. 3, lxxvi. 4; *glorious,* Is. xxxiii. 21; *famous,* Ps. cxxxvi. 18; Ezek. xxxii. 18; *mighty,* Zech. xi. 2; applied to ships, *gallant,* Is. xxxiii. 21; to flocks, *principal,* Jer. xxv. 34, 36; applied to men, *noble,* Jud. v. 13; *goodly,* Ezek. xvii. 8; *worthy,* Nah. ii. 5.

The name of God is that by which he is known. "Thou hast magnified thy word above all thy name," Ps. cxxxviii. 2, *i. e.,* above all whereby thou hast made thyself known. Alexander regards *manifested excellence* as synonymous with *name* in this case; Calvin: "The *name* of God is here to be understood of the knowledge of the character and perfections of God, in so far as he makes himself known to us." The form of announcing this glory of God is a clear confession of weakness and ignorance in man. In contemplating the Divine glory often the most and the best we can do is to cry out, How excellent! how wonderful! It is a mark of a *wise* man to know the limits of human knowledge, and of a *devout* man to adore where he cannot further inquire. Some ignorance is better than some knowledge. Paul was wiser in saying, O the depth of the riches, etc., Rom. xi. 33, than if he had claimed to know all about it. So here David gives us his idea by telling us that his theme is above any words he can command. There is some diversity in rendering the rest of the verse. Our translation is, *who hast set thy glory above the heavens.* Fry: Thy glory that is set forth above the heavens; Edwards: Thou who settest thy majesty above the heavens; Calvin: To set thy glory above the heavens! The French translation quoted by Anderson: Because thou hast set, etc.; and the marginal reading of the same is, Who hast set, or even to set; Hengstenberg: Who hast crowned the heavens with thy majesty. The old versions show a like diversity. The Septuagint, Ethiopic and Vulgate read, For thy magificence is elevated above the heavens; Syriac after *magnificence* adds the words [of thy splendor;] Arabic: That thou shouldest give thy name above the heavens. The Chaldee is very nearly if not quite the same with our common version. The foregoing variations are not material improvements on the English version. The word *glory* is elsewhere rendered *beauty, comeliness,* more frequently *majesty, honor,* yet oftener *glory.* Our translation doubtless gives the sense. Hengstenberg's rendering is perhaps the next best. The Jews spoke of three heavens; *first* the atmosphere, and so we read of the fowls of heaven; *secondly* the starry heavens, see Ps. xix. 1; and the heaven of heavens, or the third heavens, where God peculiarly manifests himself. Neither one nor all of these can contain him. His glory is above them all; and yet his glory is on them all. The starry heavens are covered with the proofs of his majesty. So great is God's glory in this respect that the young and feeble-minded find themselves absorbed in contemplations on these works of God.

2. *Out of the mouth of babes and sucklings hast thou ordained strength because of thine enemies, that thou mightest still the enemy and the avenger.* In every generation God has received and shall receive great honors from children, youth and simple-minded people, in their admiration of his works and in their wonderful questions and observations respecting his nature and works. Ofttimes the excellency of a principle is shown in its application to new and unexpected cases. Jesus Christ quoted this verse to show that praise to God proceeding from the lips of the young and the simple was no new thing, that if they wondered and praised God for the glories spread abroad in the heavens, they might very reasonably be expected to be moved to speak his honors when he should be filling the land with his miracles of love and with his words of grace and truth, Matt. xxi. 14–16. Our Saviour delighted to dwell on such truths as this, that the kingdom of heaven was open to the little ones, to babes, Matt. xi. 25, 26; Luke x. 21; xviii. 17. Instead of *ordained strength* the Septuagint version reads *perfected praise,* and Christ quotes this paraphrase rather than the literal original. This shows that it is lawful to make a free use of a version, even if it be not perfect, as indeed no work of uninspired man can be. Although the word rendered *strength* occurs more than *ninety* times in the Hebrew Scriptures, yet in our English Bible it is nowhere rendered *praise.* Except in Ecc. viii. 1, where it is rendered *boldness,* it is invariably translated, *might, power, strength,* or turned into the adjective corresponding to these words. So obviously is this rendering correct that even the church of England, which very much follows the Septuagint, departs from it here and reads *ordained* strength. The word rendered *ordained* is commonly translated *founded.* Some would read *constituted, appointed,* or *decreed. Appointed* gives the sense. Some have tried to show that it was merely in babes as works created by God that he got praise. But this makes no provision for the phrase *out of the mouths.* It may relieve some minds to state that Hebrew mothers seem to have nursed their children much longer than is now customary in

Europe or America. Hengstenberg says they suckled their children till the third year. Hannah did not wean her son till he was old enough to appear before the LORD and to abide in the temple and to worship the LORD there, though it is still said of him, he was young, 1 Sam. i. 22, 24, 28. The enemies of the truth have a wretched cause, when it can be shaken and subverted by the mouths of babes and sucklings. Hengstenberg: "God obtains the victory over his rebellious subjects, by means of children, in so far as it is through their conscious or unconscious praise of his glory, as that is manifested in the splendor of creation, especially of the starry firmament, that he puts to shame the hardihood of the deniers of his being or his perfections." Even Koester quoted by Hengstenberg admits that in the word which we render *strength* "there is contained a pointed irony, indicating that the lisping of infants forms a sort of tower of defence against the violent assaults of the disowners of God, which is perfectly sufficient." To *still* is to *silence,* or *confound.* Calvin prefers *put to flight.* The verb rendered *still* is in other forms rendered *rest* or *rested,* Gen. ii. 2, 3 and many other places. Some would read *cause to cease.* Our translation often has it so, Neh. iv. 11; Isa. xiii. 11; Ezek. vii. 24. *Enemy* and *avenger* are names here given to the wicked. They are not too strong. Mortal hatred against God and holiness belong to the unregenerate heart of man. Fry for *avenger* reads *accuser;* Ainsworth, Horsley and Morison, *self-tormentor;* Edwards and Hengstenberg read *revengeful.* This better corresponds with the true import, than the word *avenger* in its modern sense. The spite and malice of the human heart against God are dreadful. They are without a cause. They are inveterate. They are invincible except by divine grace. That the wicked bear malice against God is manifest in many ways. If they do not hate God, how can we account for the extent to which a large part of mankind have long been ignorant of Jehovah? At two periods, once in the family of Adam, and once in the family of Noah, the knowledge of God has been in the possession of every member of the human family; yet the great mass of men have rejected the true religion, and taken up with idolatry. In no way can this loss of divine knowledge be accounted for except by a strange aversion. Paul tells the secret. Men did not "like to retain God in their knowledge." This is a clear and the only satisfactory explanation. The enmity of men against God is also manifest by the way in which God's name is treated. It is continually profaned and blasphemed, even by millions, who know the third commandment, and the terrible doom of him, who violates it. There are more hard speeches uttered on this earth against God than against any thousand wicked men or any thousand fallen angels. Men would not curse and contemn God as they do, if they did not cordially hate him. See too how they reject and despise his laws. They break them every day openly, wilfully, insultingly. "The carnal mind is enmity against God; it is not subject to his law, neither indeed can be," Rom. viii. 7. If men did not hate God, they would not hate his people as they have always done. From the first generation of men to this hour, the blood of the saints has been crying to heaven. Millions on millions have died cruel deaths for no other reason than that they were followers of the Lamb. Besides, the Bible expressly says that unregenerate men hate God, and all goodness; that they hate him without a cause; that they hate him continually. Nor is this all. When God was manifest in the flesh and filled the world with miracles of mercy, he was persecuted, denied, rejected, derided, and crucified. They who hated the Son hated the Father also. The wicked are enemies of God by wicked works, and revengeful against all who take sides with him. Yet often have they been stilled by men and means apparently contemptible. "God hath chosen the foolish things of the world to confound the wise; and the weak things of the world to confound the things which were mighty; and base things of the world, and things which are despised, yea, and things, which are not, to bring to naught things that are." Many a time has the unlettered confessor confounded the philosopher, the plain man put to silence the prating of the learned, the child silenced the bold infidel. See church history. See what Sabbath-schools have done. Calvin: "Babes and sucklings are the invincible champions of God, who, when it comes to the conflict, can easily scatter and discomfit the whole host of the wicked despisers of God, and those who have abandoned themselves to impiety." God loves to stain the pride of all glory and show that man is a worm.

3. *When I consider thy heavens, the work of thy fingers, the moon and the stars, which thou hast ordained.* As in all curious workmanship men use the fingers, so in condescension to our capacities God is said to have made the heavens by his *fingers*, though he is without bodily parts. Such a mode of speech is no more liable to mislead than any other form of figurative language. To *ordained*, Calvin prefers *arranged;* Fry, *disposed;* Edwards, *established;* Alexander, *fixed;* Hengstenberg, *founded.* Although the word here rendered *consider* is used many hundreds of times simply in the sense of *see, look, behold;* yet it has other meanings, as to *regard,* Ps. lxvi. 18, and it is also very properly several times rendered *consider* as in Ps. ix. 13; xxxi. 7; Ecc. iv. 4, 15. It is here in the future, that is the form of expressing a habit, *q. d.,* when I am accustomed to consider the heavens, etc. A view of the firmament by night seems to have begotten at once the most elevated conceptions and the most devout affections. Astronomy is a sublime science. It always was so. It carries our contemplations far out into the boundless fields of space, and shows us creation. But theology is a still sublimer science. It takes the honest inquirer far beyond the remotest star up to God. The one shows us nature; the other, nature's author; the former, creation; the latter, the Creator. There is nothing in any of the heavenly bodies, which renders them objects in any way fit to receive worship. It is evident to any one that they are not intelligent, nor independent. He, who worships them must be as truly sottish as he who worships a brute. All idolatry is stupid, though not all equally indecent. But a devout admiration of the works of God is promotive of true piety. The heavens bear no marks of self-existence. The Psalmist very properly calls them *God's heavens.* His kingdom ruleth over all. He fills immensity. The number of the stars is known to be immense. Though our earth is more than *ninety-five* millions of miles from the sun, yet the planet Neptune is more than thirty-one times further. No man would be able in one hundred and sixty-five years to count the miles between the sun and that distant world, whose year is equal to 164 of ours. But the nearest fixed star is many thousands of times further from our sun than any of the known planets. And the number of the fixed stars is countless. Six thousand men busily counting for a whole day, from morning till night, could not raise their aggregate total as high as the number of the smallest-sized stars. There are known to be at least 300,000,000 of them. The probability is that these are but as a drop of the bucket, or as the small dust of the balance compared with the whole. Our sun is more than a million times larger than our earth. And there may be worlds a million times larger than the sun. If on the day that Adam and Eve were created, a messenger had been started from the Sun to announce to the inhabitants of Neptune the creation of man on earth, and if he had travelled day and night at the rate of fifty miles an hour in a straight line, he would not yet have reached his destination nor delivered his message. The Lord is a great God. Infants praise him. The heavens declare his name to be great above that of all others. It is *excellent* in all the earth. It is excellent in every respect. The next verse finishes the sentence here begun:

4. *What is man, that thou art mindful of him? and the son of man that thou visitest*

him? For remarks on the words rendered *man*, and *son of man*, see Introduction, § 16. Whether the views there suggested by Piscator, Venema, and others be correct or not, Calvin well observes that "the prophet teaches that God's wonderful goodness is displayed the more brightly in that so glorious a Creator, whose majesty shines resplendently in the heavens, graciously condescends to adorn a creature, so miserable and vile as man is, with the greatest glory, and to enrich him with numberless blessings." However considered man had an humble origin. He was of the earth, earthy. In some respects he is inferior to other creatures. He is not so long-lived, so strong, so active, or in his gait so elegant as some beasts, over whom at creation God gave him perfect dominion, and over whom to some extent he still has authority.

The word rendered *visitest* is of frequent occurrence, being found in twenty-eight of the thirty-nine books of the Old Testament. It is used in a good sense in Gen. xxi. 1; l. 24, 25; Ruth i. 6; 1 Sam. ii. 21; Ps. lxv. 9; lxxx. 14; in a bad sense in Ex. xx. 5; xxxii. 34; Job xxxv. 15; Ps. lxxxix. 32, and in many other places. Indeed it is often in our English Bible rendered *punish*. So that if the context did not give another sense we might paraphrase it thus, Man is so feeble, so frail, and compared with God, so insignificant that it fills me with wonder that thou regardest him in any way, either to govern or to judge, to bless or to curse him. I marvel that thou leavest him not as an atom too small to be accounted of at all. The pious John Newton tells us that at one stage of his religious experience he was greatly distressed, not with a fear of being punished for his sins so much as with an apprehension that God would entirely overlook him. The poet Pollok has described a very similar feeling in one understood to be himself. But the whole Psalm shows that David is speaking of the kindly *visits*, the merciful regards of God. Calvin paraphrases the words thus: "This is a marvellous thing, that God thinks upon men, and remembers them continually." If we take *visitest* in a good sense, then the force of the whole is much heightened. If to notice at all is condescension, to notice favorably is amazing loving-kindness.

5. For *thou hast made him a little lower than the angels.* The chief difficulties in this clause relate to the words *little* and *angels*. According to our version man even here is in degree but *little* lower than the angels. But is this so? Is there not a vast difference between them both in attainment and in position? In the next world, indeed, there is an important sense, in which the righteous shall be *equal unto the angels*, Luke xx. 36. But now it is far otherwise. To meet this difficulty many have proposed to read *for a little while.* Our translators have set the example in Job xxiv. 24; Ps xxxvii. 10; Hag. ii. 6. This rendering is also admissible in the corresponding Greek in Heb. ii. 7. The word is so used in Luke xxii. 58, and in Acts v. 34. The word equally applies to time, space, or degree. The context must decide to which it refers. In case of doubt we may choose that which gives the best sense. It will be found in this case safest to read *for a little while.* The church of England avoids the difficulty by wholly omitting the word *little. Thou madest him lower,* etc. Rivet, Moller, Cocceius, Venema, Fabritius, S. Schmidt, Dodd, Morison and Fry all read, *for a little while.* John Rogers' translation reads, *for a season.* The word rendered *angels* is the same that in Genesis i. 1, and in thousands of other cases is rendered *God.* It is plural. The Genevan translation reads, Thou hast made him a little lower than God. Calvin does the same and says, "I explain the words of David as meaning the same thing as if he had said, that the condition of men is nothing less than a divine and celestial state." But earth never was heaven, or comparable to it. Scott: "Adam, even when created in the image of God was *infinitely* beneath his Maker." There is no greater

gulf than that, which separates the created and uncreated, the finite and infinite, man and God.   Fry reads, For a little while lower than the gods, and he undertakes to prove that the proper application of the term is never in Scripture made to any being less than the Most High and that it is applied to angels or demons only in respect of their having become objects of worship to idolatrous men.   But this view is hardly tenable.   The inspired writers would surely not sanction an improper application of any name ever given to God.   The Septuagint renders the word *angels* here, in Ps. xcvii. 7, quoted by Paul in Heb. i. 6, and in Ps. cxxxviii. 1.   This rendering is followed by the Chaldee, Ethiopic, Arabic, Syriac, Vulgate, by numerous Jewish interpreters, by Rivet, Edwards and others.   When we find the Apostle in Hebrews using *angels* we may safely follow him, though it is not claimed that the inspired writers in quoting Scripture invariably paid further regard to the Hebrew than to give the sense so far as fell in with their argument. Angels are very exalted creatures. Man is inferior to nothing that God has made except the angels.   God has done great things for him.   Thou *hast crowned him with glory and honor.*   The great mass of translations in different languages commonly cited use the word, *crowned,* or a precisely corresponding word.   But some have suggested *encircled, decorated.*   Our English version prefers to render it *crowned,* Ps. lxv. 11, or *compassed.* Ps. v. 12.   The nouns rendered *glory* and *honor* are in our English version both translated by the word *glory* and both by the word *honor.*   The latter is also rendered *majesty,* and Fry prefers so to read here.   Alexander: "These nouns are elsewhere put together to express royal dignity." Ps. xxi. 5; xlv. 3.   Calvin thinks that by the language of this verse the Psalmist "intends the distinguished endowments which clearly manifest that men were formed after the image of God, and created to the hope of a blessed and immortal life.   The reason with which they are endued, and by which they can distinguish between good and evil; the principle of religion, which is planted in them; their intercourse with each other, which is preserved from being broken up by certain sacred bonds; the regard to what is becoming, and the sense of shame which guilt awakens in them, as well as their continuing to be governed by laws; all these things are clear indications of pre-eminent and celestial wisdom.   Not without good reason therefore does David exclaim that mankind are adorned with glory and honor."

6. *Thou madest him to have dominion over the works of thy hands.*   This seems to be a devout rehearsal of the truths taught in Gen. i. 26, 28; ix. 2, and often alluded to in the sacred writings down to near the close of the canon of Scripture. James iii. 7. *Thou hast put all* things *under his feet,* i. e., thou hast placed them in subjection to him.   This subjection was at creation perfect.   By the fall it has been impaired. Still it is not destroyed.   Calvin: "What David here relates belongs properly to the beginning of the creation, when man's nature was perfect."

The 3, 4 and 5 verses of this Psalm are quoted at length in Heb. ii. 6–8, and applied to Christ.   This has given rise to a considerable diversity of views.   Calvin goes so far as to express the opinion that "what the apostle says in Heb. ii. 6–8 concerning the abasement of Christ for a short time is not intended by him as an explanation of Ps. viii. 5–7; but, for the purpose of enriching and illustrating the subject on which he is discoursing, he introduces and accommodates to it what had been spoken in a different sense."   But is not this going too far?   In all the early part of the epistle to the Hebrews the apostle is conducting an argument respecting the priesthood of Christ, and if there is loose reasoning, the mind of the church would be much disturbed.   Samson speaks more advisedly when he says, "It requires but little stretch of faith to believe that a passage which so easily admits of the application here made, is so applied, not *by accommodation* merely, but in consistency with its proper original meaning."   Let us not attempt to weaken the apostle's argument.   That is impregnable. Yet we may with Hengstenberg say that by the quotation in Heb. ii. 6–8 we are not "necessitated to refer the Psalm, in its primary and proper sense, to Christ. Although David, in the first instance, speaks of the human race generally, the writer of the epistle might still justly refer what is said to Christ, in its highest and fullest sense. For while the glory of human nature, as here delineated, has been so deteriorated through the fall, that it is to be seen only in small fragments, and what is here said is to be referred to the idea rather than the reality, it appears anew in Christ in full splendor. The writer of the epistle describes the glory obtained for humanity in Christ over the things of creation, whereby it is to be raised above the angels." If these views of interpretation are correct, they are alike applicable to the quotation and use of the 6th verse of this Psalm in 1 Cor. xv. 27. Still the question recurs, where is the great grace to man in the humiliation and exaltation of Christ? Is not Christ divine? The answer is, *first*, Christ had two natures. One was divine. By this he was equal with the Father, and was infinitely removed from us. His other nature was human and as such had in itself no more claim to authority than that of any other sinless human being. But he was God's elect. To him was this honor given that his human nature should be assumed into an eternal and ineffable union with the divine. This is the most amazing exercise of God's love and sovereignty on record. Augustine: "The highest illustration of predestination and grace is in the Saviour himself, the man Christ Jesus, who has acquired this character in his human nature, without any previous merit either of works or of faith;" and Calvin: "What was bestowed upon Christ's human nature was a free gift, nay, more, the fact that a mortal man, and the son of Adam, is the only Son of God, and the Lord of glory, and the head of angels, affords a bright illustration of the mercy of God." Thus human nature, in this one instance, is exalted. But *secondly*, Jesus Christ was a public person, a representative of all our race, whose existence beyond this life shall be either desirable or tolerable. In his exaltation and glory they all partake. The higher he rises the greater their glory. *They* reign by sitting on *his* throne. To man here is love beyond a parallel—beyond all names of tenderness.

7. God gives to man here, even in his fallen estate, some tokens and remnants of power. He has therefore put under him *all sheep and oxen, yea, and the beasts of the field*. Morison thinks that by the last phrase the Psalmist exclusively designates those animals, which are not domesticated. But an examination of the passages, where it is found, will probably lead to the opinion that his language is too strong. The Scriptures expressly speak of WILD *beasts of the field*, when they wish them to be exclusively regarded. Ps. l. 11; lxxx. 13. See also Isa. xiii. 21, 22; xxxiv. 14; Jer. l. 39. The phrase seems to denote all beasts wild and tame. Man's impaired though real dominion over cattle, and flocks, and the whole race of brute beasts enables him to live in some peace and comfort. But the passage has a far higher application than this, even to the dominion given to Christ over all sorts and conditions of men. His people are his *sheep*, John x. 1–16. His ministers are called *oxen*, 1 Cor. ix. 9, 10. And the prophet employs the boldest figures drawn from the animal kingdom to represent the subjection of all classes of men to the authority of Christ, Isa xi. 6–9; lx. 6, 7. Nor does the matter of dominion stop here.

8. God has also given him power to some extent over *the fowl of the air, and the fish of the sea*, and whatsoever *passeth through the paths of the seas*. Broken as man's power is, and liable as he is to be made the prey of wild beasts, of the birds of heaven, of the sea-monsters, yet to a remarkable extent he still has dominion over them. The food, and clothing, and ornament, and treasure he daily obtains from the regions noticed in this verse are worth many millions of money. Horne thus applies verses 7, 8 to Christ and his kingdom: "The souls of the faithful, lowly and harmless, are

the sheep of his pasture; those who, like oxen, are strong to labor in the church, and who, by expounding the word of life, tread out the corn for the nourishment of the people, own him for their kind and beneficent Master; nay, tempers fierce and untractable as the wild beasts of the desert, are yet subject to his will; spirits of the angelic kind, that, like the bird of the air, traverse freely the superior region, move at his command: and those evil ones, whose habitation is in the deep abyss even to the great Leviathan himself; all, all are put under the feet of King Messiah." It is sufficient to maintain that the terms employed in these verses are designed to be very comprehensive. But to give this verse in connection with the preceding the higher application to Christ, it is not necessary to become fanciful and insist that each of the terms corresponds to some one thing in the spiritual world, though the ravens are subject to Christ and at his bidding fed the prophet, and the angels who fly through the midst of heaven are his ministers to do his pleasure, and the devils, the spirits of the bottomless abyss, are subject to him. The kingdom of Christ has as its willing subjects all holy intelligences, and has subsidized all, whether friendly or hostile, that can in any wise affect its progress. Such thoughts may well fill the pious mind with adoring exclamations.

9. *O* LORD *our Lord, how excellent* is *thy name in all the earth.* This verse is like the first. There seems to be no variation of design or of application. It is a devout repetition of words of adoration.

DOCTRINAL AND PRACTICAL REMARKS.

1. We must not give up the truths of natural religion, v. 1. We must maintain them and insist on them. They are as clear as they are necessary. They are declared *in all the earth.*

2. God's names and titles are to be reverently and adoringly used, repeated, celebrated and extolled, v. 1.

3. To plead our covenant relation with God as our God is a duty enforced by the constant example of the pious, v. 1.

4. God's mercies of every kind are to be duly noticed. Moller: "Among the wonderful bounties of God conferred on man, the chief are these two, viz.: the creation of all men in Adam, and the restoration of the elect in Christ."

5. Dickson: "The godly are not always borne down with trouble; sometimes they have liberty to go and delight themselves in beholding God's glory and goodness towards themselves."

6. Morison: "What a reverential view does it convey to us of the spirit of prophecy when we contemplate it as surmounting the imperfection of an obscure dispensation, as penetrating into the hidden mysteries of future ages and generations, and as giving forth to the church, as in historic narrative, an announcement of facts, which could be known only to the ominiscient research of the Infinite mind."

7. In all our plans of usefulness let children hold their proper place. Nothing ever awakened the hatred of Christ's enemies more than the praises of children, because they knew the power of such an example. Scott: "The new-born infant is such a display of God's power, skill, and goodness, as unanswerably confutes the cavils of atheism. Even little children have been taught so to love and serve him that their praises and confessions have baffled and silenced the rage and malice of persecutors." We should therefore labor to promote early piety. He who is old enough to hate God and break his commandments, is old enough to love him and walk in the way of his testimonies. Piscator: "Those who deny the providence of God are confuted by the support and preservation of sucking children and of those in the tender age, commonly given to play. Consider Christ's saying in Matt. xviii. 10."

8. One reason why God makes so much use of plain, humble, and feeble instruments, is that he would let all men see that the excellency of the power is of him and not of man. He will have all the glory.

9. The reason why men must be born again, is because they are wicked, *enemies*, and *revengeful*, v. 2.

10. The wicked have a very bad cause and as feeble as it is wicked. They sometimes cry out that a fox running on the walls of Zion will shake them down. But little David is a match for their greatest giants. Yea, babes and sucklings have often confounded them, v. 2.

11. While we reverently study God's word let us not slight his works, but *consider* them, v. 3. Everything that God has made or has done may teach us some lesson. Sin will pervert anything, even the noblest truths and sciences, but wisdom will grow wiser thereby.

12. The stability of the heavenly bodies and of the universe is well suited to beget confidence in God. This is one great use of such studies. Isa. xl. 26.

13. And if the use of the telescope in the blazing universe above us should at any time lead us to doubt God's care of us, let us seize the microscope and see his wondrous care of the myriads of creatures beneath us, and surely our reason must be satisfied, and by God's blessing our faith must be strengthened.

14. And let all God's works and mercies humble us, v. 4. This is their proper effect on every rational creature. Scott: "What are we but mean, guilty, polluted, ungrateful, rebellious, and apostate creatures?" Our place is in the dust. And let us not fear to take a low place. Our origin, our wickedness, our feebleness all put us there. If we shall ever rise, it must be by lying down; if we are ever exalted, it must be by self-abasement.

15. How blessed is the truth that our Saviour can no more be brought low *for the suffering of death*, vv. 5, 6, compared with Heb. ii. 6–9. His work is done, his conflict is over, his temptations are ended. Just so shall it in due time be with all his chosen ones.

16. The great power God has given to man over the brute creation should be exercised mercifully. Cruelty to dumb creatures dreadfully hardens the heart, and must be provoking to God. "A righteous man regardeth the life of his beast; but the tender mercies of the wicked are cruel." Pr. xii. 10. Compare Deut. xxii. 6.

17. The church will stand. Christ has it by covenant of old, v. 6.

18. How great is our Immanuel. He is the second Adam, the Lord from heaven. He rules the universe, vv. 5–9.

19. What revelations are effected by redemption. The whole of man's happy state lost by sin is recovered and restored by faith in the incarnation and mediation of Jesus Christ.

20. That is a happy train of thought which begins and ends in devout and hearty adoration, vv. 1, 8.

21. As oft as we behold the heavens, let us meditate on God and praise him for what he is and does; and especially let our views of creative power and providential care lead us to the higher theme of salvation by Christ.

22. It is marvellous that men who have no heart to praise God here should expect to be admitted to heaven to praise him there. Dying will not make any man fond of celestial music or employments.

23. When Christ's work shall all be done, all his enemies be put down, and all his redeemed brought home, then it will be confessed that the greatest movement ever made respected man's recovery, the greatest kingdom ever set up was the kingdom which is not of this world, the greatest conqueror ever known was the Captain of our

salvation. Now indeed nothing is finished. In fact oftentimes all seems *tohu vau bohu*, "without form and void." Calvin: "Paul reasons in this manner, If all things are subdued to Christ, nothing ought to stand in opposition to his people. But we see death still exercising his tyranny against them. It follows then that there remains the hope of a better state than the present." But when the top-stone is put on the church, and its glory revealed, none will say that Zion is not glorious, nor that her Head is not the chiefest among ten thousand.

PSALM IX.

To the chief Musician upon Muth-labben, A Psalm of David.

1 I will praise *thee*, O LORD, with my whole heart; I will shew forth all thy marvellous works.

2 I will be glad and rejoice in thee: I will sing praise to thy name, O thou Most High.

3 When mine enemies are turned back, they shall fall and perish at thy presence.

4 For thou hast maintained my right and my cause; thou satest in the throne judging right.

5 Thou hast rebuked the heathen, thou hast destroyed the wicked, thou hast put out their name for ever and ever.

6 O thou enemy, destructions are come to a perpetual end: and thou hast destroyed cities; their memorial is perished with them.

7 But the LORD shall endure for ever: he hath prepared his throne for judgment.

8 And he shall judge the world in righteousness, he shall minister judgment to the people in uprightness.

9 The LORD also will be a refuge for the oppressed, a refuge in times of trouble.

10 And they that know thy name will put their trust in thee: for thou, LORD, hast not forsaken them that seek thee.

11 Sing praises to the LORD, which dwelleth in Zion: declare among the people his doings.

12 When he maketh inquisition for blood, he remembereth them: he forgetteth not the cry of the humble.

13 Have mercy upon me, O LORD; consider my trouble *which I suffer* of them that hate me, thou that liftest me up from the gates of death:

14 That I may shew forth all thy praise in the gates of the daughter of Zion: I will rejoice in thy salvation.

15 The heathen are sunk down in the pit *that* they made: in the net which they hid is their own foot taken.

16 The LORD is known *by* the judgment *which* he executeth: the wicked is snared in the work of his own hands. Higgaion. Selah.

17 The wicked shall be turned into hell, *and* all the nations that forget God.

18 For the needy shall not always be forgotten: the expectation of the poor shall *not* perish for ever.

19 Arise, O LORD; let not man prevail: let the heathen be judged in thy sight.

20 Put them in fear, O LORD: *that* the nations may know themselves *to be but* men. Selah.

FOR remarks on the words, *To the chief musician*, see on Ps. 4th at the beginning. There is much diversity of opinion, as to the right explanation of *upon muth-lab-ben*. The word *muth* taken by itself means *death*, and *labben* may mean *white, fair*, or *for a son*. This is all that is certainly known on the subject. All the rest is conjecture, with various degrees of probability, but no one view is to be received without some doubt. Some interpret it of *the death* of Saul. But in this there is nothing plausible. Others think it refers to *the death* of David's *son*, Absalom. But David's feelings and behaviour on that mournful occasion were very diverse from the tenor of this Psalm, 2 Sam. xviii. 33. Others suppose that *Labben* was the name of some great captain, who commanded forces hostile to David and to Israel, and that this Psalm celebrates deliverance from him after his *death*. It is not pretended that any such name is found in the catalogues of names of the hostile cotemporaries of David. The whole is a sheer conjecture as to the name, though it is not a wild conjecture. The contents of the Psalm show indeed that David's enemies had been signally defeated once or oftener. Some have supposed that this Psalm celebrates the victory gained by the death of Goliath. Some, who take this view, hold that *Labben* is a fictitious name given to the giant. Calvin mentions some, who so held. Patrick has warmly embraced the view that Goliath is intended, but not under a fictitious name. He says, " I mention, Goliath, because, among the various opinions about *muth-labben*, I find none so probable as theirs, who think it hath some relation to him : to whom there are three ways of applying those Hebrew words. All of them by *Almuth* understand to be meant *upon the death*. And then *Labben*, some think, signifies *the Son*, that is, a great man, as I have expounded in my preface to this work. Others render it *the White;* that is an illustrious, noble person, or one famous in arms, as Goliath was. Others render it *intermediate;* which agrees also to that champion, who came out and stood *between* the two armies, and defied Israel, 1 Sam. xvii. 4 and onward." The whole of the remarks here offered on *labben* are so strained that perhaps no one will feel disposed to follow the venerable author. It is, however, due to him to say that the Chaldee has it, "To praise upon the death of the man, who went out between the camps." Some have thought it related to the death of the Son of man on Calvary ; but the contents of the Psalm show this to be pretty certainly a mistake. Bythner quotes Arias Montanus as inverting the letters and reading, *nabal;* and Hengstenberg says, " The true mode of explanation was hit upon by Grotius, who supposed that *labben*, or *Laban* was put by a transposition of letters for *Nabal*, and that the superscription marks the object of the Psalm. But he erred in this that he took *Nabal* as a proper name, *upon the dying of Nabal*—a subject to which the Psalm could not possibly refer—instead of : *upon the dying of a fool*. This error being rectified, the superscription accords precisely with the contents, the destruction of the fool (comp. Ps. xiv. 1) is actually the subject of the Psalm." The number, who will be persuaded that the inspired writer was here giving us an anagram, will probably be very small. Others would read it, *For the hidden things of the son*. This is the rendering of the Septuagint, Ethiopic and Vulgate. The Arabic is much the same, *Concerning the mysteries of the son*, but it adds, *with respect to the glory of Christ, and his resurrection and kingdom, and the destruction of all the disobedient*. Houbigant reads, The mysteries of the Son. Theodoret applies it to Christ's victory over death, by submitting to death, which was a hidden thing. The remaining opinions interpret *muth-labben* of either the tune, the music, or the instrument to be used in singing the Psalm. Ainsworth and others think it may signify the note, which is called counter-tenor. Fry mentions some, who hold that it relates to some unknown regulations for the music. Mudge thinks the two words *upon* and *muth* should be read as one, which he regards as " the beginning of a celebrated composition, to which, perhaps, a particular kind of instrument was appropriated, or at least a particular tune ; to which this Psalm is directed to be sung." Calvin thinks it more probable that *muth-labben* was the beginning of some well known song, to the tune of which this Psalm was composed. The remaining view is that it signifies the musical instrument to be used in singing this Psalm. Calvin says some held this opinion. Such unite the words *upon* and *Muth*, and read *alamoth*, which word is found in the title of Ps. xlvi. They also think that *Ben* in *labben* is the name of the chief musician, who with his family and companions were appointed to sing with psalteries on alamoth. 1 Chron. xv. 18, 20. The reader will probably be ready to say that none of the views presented are sustained by satisfactory evidence or authority. It is even so. Venema and Edwards admit the difficulty to be beyond their powers of solution.

The subject of the Psalm will be best learned by an examination of each verse. Jerome, Ainsworth and Gill all apply it to Anti-Christ. But the Psalm seems to record past victories rather than to predict future triumphs. The Psalm will be found a mixed devotional composition, containing praises, expressions of confidence in God, and supplications for mercies considerably mixed together.

That David was the author of this Psalm we have no reason to doubt. The inscription gives it to him.

We cannot fix the date of this Psalm. Scott puts it at ten hundred and twenty-one years, and Clarke about ten hundred and forty-two years before Christ. It was written after the ark was carried to Mount Zion, as is evident from vv. 11, 14. In his Introduction Clarke expresses the opinion that this Psalm was sung by David on bringing the ark from the house of Obed-edom. But God could not be said to have "dwelt in Zion," nor to have been "praised in the gates of the daughter of Zion" till the ark was brought to that hill. It is useless to attempt to interpret this Psalm by any historical incident. The life of David was full of conflicts and troubles, out of which he was, however, mercifully delivered. This song would therefore suit almost any period of his reign. And as David was identified with the people of Israel, the Psalm is evidently composed in the name of the chosen nation, the visible church. Calvin: "It is a mistake to limit to one victory this thanksgiving, in which David intended to comprehend many deliverances." Luther: "The Prophet here speaks in his own person, and in that of all the saints also, who are afflicted for the sake of the word of God."

The names of the Almighty found in this Psalm are *Jehovah* LORD, and *Gel-yohn Most High*, on which respectively see above on Ps. i. 2; vii. 17.

1. *I will praise* thee, O LORD, *with my whole heart*. The Septuagint for *praise* uses a word, which is in the New Testament frequently rendered *confess*, as in Matt. iii. 6; Mark i. 5. But it is also translated by the verb *thank* as in Matt. xi. 25; Luke x. 21. Sometimes it means to *own* or *acknowledge* as a friend, and sometimes to covenant or *promise* as in Luke xxii. 6. Sometimes it seems to include all the acts of religious worship, even when rendered *confess* as in Rom. xiv. 11; xv. 9. So that the Vulgate, which uses the word *confess*, may be followed without great error, if we take that word in its old and fullest sense. Yet *thankfulness* is here the prominent idea in the word. Worshippers are divided into three classes. There are those whose whole service is sheer and gross hypocrisy. How many are of this description no mortal can tell. We may hope that where God's word is freely and abundantly preached, the number is comparatively small. A second class is made up of those, who would shudder at wilful hypocrisy, but they serve God with a *divided heart*. There is reason to fear that in the purest churches there are many such. The third class of worshippers consists of those, who bring *the whole heart* into God's service. This is a form of expression often used in Scripture. It declares the sincerity and earnestness of the worshipper. It is the opposite of *feigned*. Jer. iii. 10. It does not imply absolute perfection in the service offered. In the same spirit David says, *I will shew forth all thy marvellous works*. For *shew forth* Edwards and Alexander read *recount*; Calvin and Fry, *tell of*; church of England *speak of*; Clarke, *number out or reckon up*; Morison, *publish abroad, openly declare*. Instead of *marvellous works*, Jebb reads *marvels*; Hengstenberg and Alexander, *wonders*. The word is rendered in our English Bible, *wonders, marvels, miracles, wondrous works, wondrous things*. The honor, which God has received by the wonders he has wrought on the earth is very great. Christians

are not wise when they yield an iota of the argument in favor of the true religion drawn from miracles. What a profound impression was made on nearly all the nations of the world by the stupendous displays of the power of God in the days of Moses! The reason of the hostility of wicked men to the doctrine of miracles is found in the fact that if miracles are true, the ungodly are utterly undone. Until the modern Deistical controversy, by a miracle was meant any wonderful display of divine power, whether the laws of nature were suspended or not. Of late it implies a suspension of those laws. To *thank* God, and devoutly speak of the *wonders* he has wrought at any time or for any purpose is a great part of piety and a great nourisher of holy affections.

2. *I will be glad and rejoice in thee.* For *rejoice* Calvin, Morison and Fry read *exult;* Alexander, *triumph.* In our common version in Ps. xxv. 2, it is rendered *triumph,* everywhere else, *rejoice* or be *joyful.* Venema paraphrases the words thus, *I will rejoice even to exultation.* It is our duty not only to *submit* to God, but to be happy not only in his word and his government, but in himself, in his nature and perfections. Communion with God has ever been a precious doctrine in the church of God. *I will sing praise to thy name, O thou Most High.* For *sing praise* Jebb reads *make a psalm.* The word is commonly rendered *sing praise, sing praises,* or simply *sing;* but in 1 Chron. xvi. 9 and Ps. cv. 2 it is rendered in our common version *sing psalms.* Calvin and Edwards read, *I will celebrate in* [or with] *songs thy name;* Horsley and Fry read *I will chant;* Calvin, *celebrate in songs;* Venema and Edwards, *celebrate with songs;* Alexander, *praise* or *celebrate in song.* God's *name* is that by which he is known. Alexander thinks it equivalent to *manifested excellence.* If men ever worship God aright, they must *purpose* to do it.

3. *When mine enemies are turned back, they shall fall and perish at thy presence.* The verbs *fall* and *perish* are in the future, but this does not exclude the past. It expresses what is *habitually* done. Hengstenberg: "The use of the future is to be explained from the lively nature of the representation." See Introduction to this work, § 6. When his enemies are forced to retreat they fall into great confusion, are terrified, adopt foolish, and reject wise measures for their preservation. Or from their past defeat, he argues to what shall be their dismay. The beginning of defeat to the wicked is a sign that, without repentance, a terrible overthrow is coming, Esther vi. 13. The word rendered *fall,* is in Ps. xxvii. 2; Isa. viii. 15, and many other places translated *stumble;* though it is as often perhaps rendered *fall;* and sometimes, *be overthrown.* Hammond: "It refers to those that either faint in a march or are wounded in a battle, or especially that in flight meet with galling traps in their way, and so are galled and lamed, rendered unable to go forward, and so fall, and become liable to all the chances of pursuits, and as here are overtaken and perish in the fall." One of the strongest marks of wisdom is simply to know whence our help comes. If our enemies fall or flee, it is at *God's presence.* He can alarm the most resolute, take away natural courage, put a dreadful sound in men's ears, and fight terribly, though invisibly, against his foes. Some, however, change the pointing and so alter the relation of these clauses. Thus Fry:

> Verse 2.   I will rejoice and exult in thee;
> I will chant thy name, O Most High;
>
> Verse 3.   Because my enemies are turned back:
> They fall; they perish at thy presence.

Edwards points in very much the same way. Alexander thinks the third verse may either be connected with what goes before, or it may begin a new sentence. If it belongs to the preceding, then Fry and Edwards are right in reading *because* instead of *when*. For remarks on the name, *Most High*, see Ps. vii. 17. "God is in the loftiest and most exalted pre-eminence, and sovereignty over the whole creation; and in essence and glory, surpassing all comprehension."

4. *For thou hast maintained my right and my cause; thou satest in the throne judging right.* The word rendered *hast maintained*, is in Gen. i. 31, ii. 2, and in *hundreds* of cases translated *hast made*. It is also frequently rendered *hast done*, and sometimes *hast wrought, shewed, executed, fulfilled, granted*. Edwards: *hast asserted*. Fry: *hast done me justice and right*. Hengstenberg: *hast made my judgment and right*. The work done was judicial. The Judge of all the earth took up the matter. The *right* must be mighty, when God is on the side of the wronged. The last clause is rendered by Calvin, Thou satest upon the throne a righteous judge; Hengstenberg: Thou satest on the throne as righteous judge; Edwards: Thou satest upon thy throne judging righteously. The sense is given by either, or by our version. As kings, when about to try a cause in a solemn manner, sat down on their thrones, so God had in good earnest taken up the cause of David and decided against his enemies.

5. *Thou hast rebuked the heathen.* *Rebuked* in our Bible commonly so rendered, sometimes *reproved*. Here the *rebuke* was the pronouncing and execution of the judicial sentence, formed by God sitting as judge, as noticed in v. 4. The word here rendered *heathen*, is plural, and in that form occurs *five* times in this Psalm, vv. 5, 15, 17, 19, 20. In vv. 17, 20, it is translated *nations*. It is very often rendered *Gentiles*. The list of the names of the people, who often conspired against God's people is long and shows the most singular alliances and combinations. See Gen. xv. 19–21; Deut. vii. 1; 2 Kings xxiv. 2; Ezra iv. 7–10; Ps. lxxxiii. 2–8. But numerous as the enemies of God's church have ever been, he has always overpowered them. What is the stubble to the fire? So it is added, *Thou hast destroyed the wicked*. The word rendered *wicked* here is in the first Psalm rendered *ungodly*, and in this Psalm three times, *wicked*, vv. 5, 16, 17. It is in the singular, and may mean that these hostile nations were leagued as *one* man, or as Alexander suggests, we may read *many a wicked enemy*. The word rendered *destroyed* is in another form in vv. 3, 18, of this Psalm rendered *perish*. When transitive, it is the usual word for *destroy;* when intransitive, for *perish*. The destruction of the wicked is *perdition*. And so, *Thou hast put out their name for ever and ever*. Calvin, Edwards, and Fry read, *blotted out*. Hengstenberg: "Thou hast so completely extirpated them that their memory has perished with them." The phrase rendered *forever and ever* is very strong and emphatic. Clarke: "He who contends it means only *a limited time*, let him tell us *where* the Hivites, Perizzites, Jebusites, etc., now dwell, and *when* it is likely they are to be restored to Canaan?"

6. *O thou enemy, destructions are come to a perpetual end; and thou hast destroyed cities; their memorial is perished with them.* There is much diversity in rendering this verse. Boothroyd: Desolations have utterly consumed the enemy; thou didst destroy their cities; their remembrance is lost; Edwards: As for the enemy, they are utterly destroyed; they are become everlasting desolations, for their cities hast thou erased; the memory of them, as well as themselves, is perished; Mudge: As for the enemy, they are quite destroyed; everlasting desolations; their cities thou hast extirpated; their memory, as well as themselves, is annihilated; Fry: Desolations have consumed the enemy forever: the cities thou hast destroyed, their memory is perished with them; Jebb: O thou enemy, *thy* swords are come to a perpetual end: and cities thou hast brought to ruin: their memorial is destroyed with them; Horne reads the first clause, The destructions of the enemy are completed to the utmost, meaning that the

work of their ruin as enemies is forever finished; Venema: The enemies are consumed by destructions forever: and thou hast destroyed the foes: their memory is perished with them; Clarke: The enemy is desolated forever: for thou hast destroyed their cities, and their memory is perished with them; Hengstenberg: The enemy, finished are the destructions forever, and thou hast destroyed cities, their memorial is perished with them; Alexander: The enemy, *or* as to the enemy, finished are (his) ruins forever: and their cities hast thou destroyed: gone is their very memory; Morison: Devastations have utterly consumed the enemy; and their cities which thou hast destroyed, their very names have perished with them. In a note he supports this translation by a reference to the Hebrew and Latin Bible of Montanus, by the renderings of Horne and Horsley, and by that of Bishop Lowth in Merrick's Annotations. Green renders the first clause, The desolations of the enemy are ceased forever. Dimock supposes we may perhaps read, The houses of the enemy are desolations forever. The marginal rendering of this verse, which Scott prefers, is, The destructions of the enemy are come to a perpetual end: and their cities hast thou destroyed, etc. The first difficulty regards the word *enemy*. Is he here addressed, or is he spoken of? Perhaps the latter is correct. The weight of modern authority is on that side. The word, *thou*, in that case is simply continued from the preceding verse, and refers to God. The next difficult word is that variously rendered *destructions, desolations, ruins, swords*. The first three renderings are substantially the same. The last has for its support the Septuagint, Ethiopic, Vulgate. The Arabic also reads *arms*. A very slight variation in the Hebrew would allow us to read either *swords* or *desolations*. Perhaps the latter is here to be preferred. The rendering of Edwards probably conveys as accurate an idea as we can get in so few words. The interpretations of this passage are as various as the renderings. Calvin has thus summed up several of the leading views: "Some read this sixth verse interrogatively . . . as if David, addressing his discourse to his enemies, asked whether they had completed their work of devastation, even as they had resolved to destroy everything; for the first verb signifies sometimes *to complete*, and sometimes *to put an end to anything*. And if we here take it in this sense, David, in the language of sarcasm or irony, rebukes the foolish confidence of his enemies. Others, reading the verse without any interrogation, make the irony still more evident, and think that David describes, in vv. 6, 7, 8, a twofold state of matters; that, in the first place (v. 6) he introduces his enemies persecuting him with savage violence, and persevering with determined obstinacy in their cruelty, so that it seemed to be their fixed purpose never to desist until the kingdom of David should be utterly destroyed; and that, in the second place (vv. 7, 8) he represents God as seated on his judgment-seat directly over against them, to repress their outrageous attempts. If this sense is admitted, the first word of the *seventh* verse must read *but*, not *and*, thus: Thou, O enemy, didst seek after nothing except slaughter and the destruction of cities; but, at length, God has shown that he sits in heaven on his throne as judge, to put into proper order the things, which are in confusion on the earth. According to others, David gives thanks to God, because, when the ungodly were fully determined to spread universal ruin around them, he put an end to their devastations. Others understand the words in a more restricted sense, as meaning that the desolations of the ungodly were completed, because God, in his just judgment, had made to fall upon their own heads the calamities and ruin which they had devised against David. According to others, David, in the sixth verse, complains that God had, for a long time, silently suffered the miserable devastation of his people, so that the ungodly, being left unchecked, wasted and destroyed all things according to their pleasure; and, in the seventh verse, they think he subjoins for his consolation that God, notwithstanding, presides over human affairs." But if the sixth verse speaks *of* the enemy and not *to* him, then none of these views are so good as that suggested by the rendering of Edwards, of Fry, or of Alexander. Hengstenberg says that the three verbs in this sixth verse "stand in exact parallelism. Now, if the affairs of the enemy are described by the last two, as going to perdition, the same explanation must be held also to be the only correct one in regard to the first." He also thinks there is here a reference to Ex. xvii. 14; Deut. xxv. 19; Num. xxiv. 20, where we find these expressions, "I will utterly put out the remembrance of Amalek from under heaven;" "thou shalt blot out the remembrance of Amalek from under heaven;" "Amalek was the first of the nations; but his latter end shall be that he perish forever." It is a great and universal principle of God's government, that "the memory of the wicked shall rot." This verse therefore may be regarded as having a sense complete in itself without any reference to succeeding verses. It is a blessed truth that though the enemies of God pass away and perish, yet Jehovah is unchangeable.

7. *But the* LORD *shall endure forever.* The word here rendered *endure* is in verse 11, and very often elsewhere rendered by the verb *dwell;* but in verse 4 of this Psalm as also in Ps. i. 1; ii. 4 and in many places it is rendered by some form of the verb *sit;* Calvin and Fry: *sitteth;* Alexander: *will sit.* It probably has reference to his *sitting* in his throne as noticed in v. 4. Hengstenberg is so confident of this that he reads, The LORD is enthroned forever. This is pretty certainly the correct view. It derives support from the preceding context, the imagery here filling the writer's mind, the use of the word in v. 4, and the parallelism in the next clause. *He hath prepared his throne for judgment.* Men, who live in opposition to God, have a great dislike to the doctrine of divine and eternal judgment. Yet its importance and the very hostility of the human mind render it proper that it should often be repeated. So we had it in Ps. i. 5, and now here also. Nor is it obscurely revealed. We have it still more clearly in the next verse.

8. *And he shall judge the world in righteousness.* Even Paul in his great address on Mars' hill a thousand years after could find no better words, in which to teach the Athenians the doctrine of the judgment-day than the Septuagint rendering of this clause. Calvin: "The pronoun, *He,* is of 'great weight.'" It is as if he had said, *He himself,* or *He exclusively* shall judge the world. The same is again repeated, *He shall minister judgment to the people in uprightness.* The word *people* is plural, *peoples,* or *nations.* The word *uprightness* is plural. Job: "He is excellent in power and in judgment, and in plenty of justice:" chap. xxxvii. 23. In Ps. xcviii. 9; xcix. 4, it is rendered *equity.* The words here used are different from those in the preceding clause. Edwards: He administers judgment to the nations in equity. Fry gives the same except he puts *justice* for *judgment.* Nor is this doctrine at all unwelcome to the righteous. Nay, it is their hope; for,

9. *The* LORD *also will be a refuge for the oppressed.* The word here rendered *refuge* is in the margin here and elsewhere rendered *an high place.* It occurs twice in this verse, and thirteen times elsewhere. It is variously rendered *defence, refuge, high tower, high fort, place of defence;* and in Jer. xlviii. 1 it is left as a proper name. The idea seems to be that of a fortification of great natural strength, where an enemy cannot come, or even get a sight of those, whom he would destroy. Venema: "David is the first, so far as I have noticed, who by this term calls God, a high place." He first uses it in 2 Sam. xxii. 3, where it is rendered *my high tower.* David often experienced safety in such places, when fleeing from Saul. For *will be* Fry reads *was;* the Arabic, Septuagint, Ethiopic and Vulgate also use the past tense; Edwards: *is.* But the Chaldee and Syriac agree with our version, which is to be preferred. The word rendered

oppressed is found also in Ps. x. 18; lxxiv. 21 and in Prov. xxvi. 28. In the latter case it is rendered *afflicted;* in the others, *oppressed.* The Septuagint, Ethiopic, Vulgate, Arabic and Syriac read *poor* instead of *oppressed.* For the LORD the Chaldee reads *the word of the Lord.* This gives a good sense, but cannot be admitted because it narrows down the broad truth of the text to *one* thing, and because it does not agree with the Hebrew text; yet it is but a paraphrase. The truth is repeated in the next clause. The LORD will be *a refuge in times of trouble.* Morison: "In their greatest *straits,* God's people shall find themselves garrisoned by omnipotent love." One of the excellencies of true religion is that it is a source of the greatest consolation, when consolation is most needed, viz., *in times of trouble,* or, as Alexander reads, *in times of distress,* or, as Edwards, *at critical times of distress,* or, as Calvin, *in seasonable times in distress.* He makes the seasonableness of the protection and aid prominent in the exposition. The word rendered *trouble* is also rendered *anguish, tribulation, adversity, affliction* and *distress;* our translators evidently regarding either of these words a fit rendering. Nor is God a *high place* inaccessible to his saints. So the Psalmist adds:

10. *And they that know thy name will put their trust in thee.* The word rendered *trust* is very generally so rendered, or *hope,* or *put confidence.* In this Book it is first found in Ps. iv. 5, and next here. The word here rendered *name* is the same as was found in Ps. v. 11; vii. 17; viii. 1. Calvin: "His name means his character, so far as he has been pleased to make it known to us." To know God's name is to have his excellence revealed in our hearts by his Spirit, so that we apprehend his nature, and have a spiritual discernment of his beauty and glory. It is impossible truly to see beauty without loving it. It is impossible to have essentially right views of God without delighting in him. So that there is a broad difference between the saving knowledge of God, and those dreamy speculations of him, which float in the minds of the unrenewed. Right apprehensions of God's character will inspire *confidence* in him. And the more men thus know of him, the more will they *trust in him: for thou,* LORD, *hast not forsaken them that seek thee.* It is a great and delightful truth that in the annals of redemption not one case has been found, where God deserted to the ruinous power of sins or enemies any soul, that had fled to him for refuge. One well authenticated case of that kind would destroy all confidence in the divine character and government. To *seek God* is put for the whole of religion, which consists in seeking to know him, to be like him, to possess his favor and his protection, to serve and obey him, to have communion with him, and finally to be with him in glory. Men must seek him intelligently, not superstitiously; diligently, not carelessly; humbly, not proudly; with all the heart, not hypocritically; in the name of Christ, and not relying on any merits but those of the Redeemer. Such truths as God here reveals, authorizing our confidence in him, may well animate us with joy. Therefore it is said,

11. *Sing praises to the* LORD, *which dwelleth in Zion.* To speak of God as *dwelling in Zion* proves this Psalm to have been written after the removal of the tabernacle to that holy hill, and not at the slaying of Goliath, nor at any time previous to the removal of the ark from the residence of Obed-edom. The call upon men to sing praises is a declaration that not merely one man, but that all men were bound to magnify the name of the Lord for such mercies as are here recorded. No man has a heart truly to praise God, but when he also wishes all others to do it. Nor is secret praise for public mercies enough. We must sing a song or psalm, or, as Jebb reads it, " make a psalm," to God on such occasions. We must not only tell a few friends, but spread abroad the fame of Jehovah. Therefore it is added, " *Declare among the people his doings.*" The word rendered *people* is here plural. It is sometimes rendered *folk, nation, nations,* but most commonly *people.* It is not the same word that is found in v. 8. Here it clearly refers to surrounding nations. Calvin, Edwards, Jebb, Fry,

and Alexander have *nations*. The things to be declared were God's *doings*. Elsewhere this word is rendered in a good sense *works, deeds, acts, actions;* in a bad sense *works, inventions*. Ps. xiv. 1; xcix. 8. Morison: "By the doings of God, we may understand either the mighty acts of his providence, or his revealed designs and purposes concerning his church and her enemies;" Calvin: "The meaning is that his doings are not published or celebrated as they deserve, unless the whole world is filled with the renown of them. To proclaim God's doings among the nations was indeed, as it were, to sing to the deaf; but by this manner of speaking David intended to show that the territory of Judea was too narrow to contain the infinite greatness of Jehovah's praises." His mighty acts in Egypt, in the settlement of David, and in subduing his enemies are proper matters of praise in all lands and ages, because they were illustrious, and because what God did then he will, if necessary, do again. He does not work miracles now. His providence may, however, be as truly marvellous as if he did. There must be some very serious and alarming malady in the souls of men to make it necessary for inspiration so often to call on us to praise God, which is one of the most obvious and ought to be one of the most pleasant duties in the life of a good man.

12. *When he maketh inquisition for blood, he remembereth them: he forgetteth not the cry of the humble.* This verse has occasioned much perplexity. Various renderings have been proposed. Calvin: For in requiring blood he hath remembered it; he hath not forgotten the cry of the afflicted; Edwards: For he that maketh inquisition after blood remembereth them; he forgets not the cry of the afflicted; Fry: He hath required blood, he hath taken account of it, he hath not disregarded the cry of the afflicted; Hengstenberg: For the avenger of blood is remembered by him, he forgetteth not the cry of the afflicted; Alexander: For seeking blood, *or* as an inquisitor of blood, he has remembered it, *i. e., the blood;* he has not forgotten the cry of the distressed. The interpretations of these verses are also very diverse. Scott: "God sometimes indeed permitted his servants to be tried by persecution; but there would be a season of inquisition for blood, when the prayers of the humble would be remembered and completely answered;" Horsley gives this paraphrase: "When God requireth the innocent blood of Jesus at the hands of the Jews, his murderers, he will not forget the peoples; but will manifest himself to them, mindful of the original promises. When the Jews are cut off the Gentiles shall be grafted in;" Patrick's paraphrase is: "Though God may seem to wink for a time at the cruelty of violent men, yet he will call them at last to a strict account for all the innocent blood they have shed, and for their unjust and unmerciful usage of meek and humble persons, whose cry he never forgets (though he doth not presently answer it) but takes a fit time to be avenged of their oppressors." Many other views might be quoted. The first clause of the verse is, *When he maketh inquisition for blood.* All agree that *he* refers to Jehovah. *To make inquisition for blood* is to *require blood.* Under all dispensations God has declared his abhorrence of bloody crimes. The first persecutor was a murderer. To him God said, "Thy brother's blood crieth unto me from the ground." To Noah he said, "Surely your blood of your lives will I require." The word rendered *make inquisition* is in Gen. ix. 5, and often elsewhere rendered *require.* It is the same word that in the 10th verse of this Psalm is rendered *seek.* It is often so rendered, as also by the words *inquire, search for,* etc. The meaning then is that God will see that innocent blood is rightly avenged. The Hebrew word for blood is plural here as often elsewhere. See Ps. v. 6, and comment on it. When God requires, searches or makes inquisition for blood, it is said, *he remembereth them* or *it.* If we read *it* we refer to *blood.* As the noun in Hebrew is plural, *bloods,* so is the pronoun *them.* If in following the English idiom we make the *noun* singular, we must make the *pro-*

noun singular also, if we believe it refers to *blood*. But it is evident our translators and many others regarded the pronoun as referring to *persons*, not to *bloods*, or murders. But what persons are intended, the enemies of all goodness, or the humble mentioned in the last clause? The word rendered *remembereth* is used in the Bible both in a good and bad sense. God may *remember* men to bless them, or to punish them. So that we can get no light from that quarter. If *them* refers to the enemies of God's people, we should have to go back several verses to find the noun of which *them* is the substitute. If *them* refers to God's friends, we can find its noun in v. 10, or in the last word of v. 12. There are difficulties in each of these modes of explanation. Hengstenberg thinks the parallelism is best preserved by giving this sense, " God remembers blood, he forgets not the cry of the afflicted." But the parallelism in many places, as in vv. 4, 11, 14, 17, 19, of this very Psalm would suggest the contrary. It is evident, however, to any candid mind that the method of reading the verse adopted by Calvin and others who follow him is far the most free from difficulties. Mudge and Edwards suppose *them* refers to the last word *humble*, or afflicted. And Calvin admits that the *pronoun* often precedes the noun in Hebrew. Whichever of these modes of explanation is adopted, the doctrine of the verse is not altered. If God requires blood he of course remembers it, and the man who shed it and the man who was slain ; and in particular *he forgetteth not the cry of the humble*, or, as some read it *the afflicted*, or *the poor*, or *the meek*. The word is fitly rendered either way. Such views of God must encourage a pious persecuted man to pray. Therefore the Psalmist earnestly addresses himself to God.

13. *Have mercy upon me*, O LORD. The marginal reading is, *Be gracious unto me*. In our version it is rendered by such phrases as those already given, and by *Have pity, Show favor*. The human heart is distressingly inclined to despair of the mercy of God, and when it has no hope toward God, its ruin is complete. It is a great thing for a poor soul to be able so far to confide as to pray in hope of being heard. And we make a right use of past deliverances when we employ them to arouse us humbly to beg for yet other mercies. Luther : " In the same way do all feel and speak, who have already overcome some tribulation and misfortune, and are once more oppressed, tormented and plagued. They cry and beg that they may be delivered." The Psalmist repeats his cry for mercy, saying, *Consider my trouble*, which I suffer *of them that hate me*. The word rendered *consider* is in our version often so given, for more frequently *see*, sometimes *mark*, sometimes *behold, look upon, have respect to*. It is a great matter when we can get the Judge of all the earth to *mark* our cause, to *look upon* our *trouble*, to *have respect* to our *affliction*. The word rendered *trouble* is more than *thirty* times in our version rendered *affliction*, and but two or three times *trouble*. But our translators use these and several other words as synonymous. The words, *which I suffer*, are not in the original, but are properly supplied, as all admit. Even the Doway Bible has them. This affliction came to David from *them that hated him*. Of these there were not a few. They often far outnumbered his friends ; so that his case would have been hopeless, if he could not have pleaded with Jehovah, as *thou that liftest me up from the gates of death*. The word rendered *death* is *Muth*, not *Sheol*, as some expositions would lead one to suppose. *Sheol* is never in our version rendered *death*. The word rendered *gates* is the same as is found in v. 14, and is commonly so translated. The *gates of death* is a phrase found elsewhere. See Ps. cvii. 18. It denotes great peril, as if we were to enter the grave. The figure in the mind of the writer was probably that of a prison with *gates* and *bars*. The same figure is in Scripture applied to the state of the dead. Job xvii. 16; Is. xxxviii. 10. It is hardly probable that David had the figure of a fortified city in his mind. He says thou *liftest*. He refers not merely to what God would do, or was now doing,

but what he was in the habit of doing, or had often done. Calvin: God is accustomed not only to succor his servants, and to deliver them from their calamities by ordinary means, but also to bring them from the grave, even after all hope of life is cut off." Such deliverances from death, whether threatened by violence or by pestilence, should be received by us with the utmost humility and the liveliest gratitude, and should be by us improved as occasions for glorifying God. So David thought:

14. *That I may shew forth all thy praise in the gates of the daughter of Zion.* Public mercies call for public praise, and great mercies for great thanksgivings. If those who experience gracious interpositions shall keep silence, how can God be honored any more by the righteous, than by the wicked? We may all say as Bishop Hall, " O my God, I am justly ashamed to think what favors I have received from thee, and what poor returns I have made to thee! Truly, Lord, I must needs say, thou hast thought nothing either in earth or in heaven too good for me. . . O thou who hast been so bountiful in heaping thy rich mercies upon me, vouchsafe to me yet one gift more: give me grace and power to improve all the gifts to the glory of the Giver." *Shew forth,* in this verse is the same word as is found in the beginning of this Psalm. See on second clause of the first verse. To show forth *all* God's praise is to enter largely into the work. An occasional *God I thank thee* is no fit return for a perpetual stream of rich benefits. This work of public praise was to be conducted in the most public place in Jerusalem, here called the daughter of Zion. Cities are in Scripture often spoken of as young women, delicate ladies, or venerable matrons. Ps. xlv. 12; Isa. xxiii. 10, 12; Gal. iv. 26. So Jerusalem was beautiful for situation, the joy of the whole earth. Hengstenberg is very confident that *in the gates* means simply *within* and no more. There is no evidence as some have asserted that Jerusalem was called the daughter of Zion, because that city was built round about that holy hill, nor because Jerusalem derived its chief importance from the religious solemnities celebrated on Mount Zion. Some praise God in a manner decent for its solemnity, but gloomy in its temper. This was not David's mind. "*I will rejoice in thy salvation.* Blessed is he, who loves to praise and give thanks. Mudge, Edwards, and others regard vv. 13, 14, as containing the *cry of the afflicted,* mentioned in v. 12, and so Edwards put them in marks of quotation. But there is no evidence that these verses are words put into the lips of another. They are an appropriate part of this devotional composition. God's *salvation* is the deliverance God secures to believers and accomplishes in them. The word rendered *rejoice* is always in our version as translated, or *be glad,* or *be joyful.* And while God's people are shouting deliverance, his enemies are gnawing their tongues for anguish; for,

15. *The heathen are sunk down in the pit* that *they made.* For an explanation of the figure here employed, see above on Ps. vii. 15. The particular event or events here referred to are concealed, perhaps designedly, from our view. The wicked are always meeting such overthrows. Hengstenberg thinks the prophet here speaks of an " *ideal* past," but we have as good and as true a sense by making it a historical past. Some, yea, many of Israel's and of David's foes had actually fallen. Instead of *the* pit Alexander prefers *a* pit, and in the next clause *a* net. For David adds, *In the net, which they hid is their own foot taken.* The persons here spoken of are the same as before, *the heathen,* or *the nations,* see comment on v. 5. It is impossible to tell which is most detestable, the malice or the deceit of the enemies of God. The best of them is a brier: the most upright is sharper than a thorn hedge. They have the cunning and venom of the serpent, the fierceness of wild beasts, the malice of fallen angels. They love to dig pits and spread nets. But cunning is not wisdom. Every device of the wicked, like the cannon of a captured fort, may be turned to

the destruction of those whom it was designed to defend. Nothing is too hard for God. He taketh the wise in their craftiness. And so,

16. *The* LORD *is known* by *the judgment,* which *he executeth.* Even a child is known by his doings. Wise and foolish kings thus reveal their characters. Let God be known in the same way; by the worlds he has made; by the providence he exercises over them; by the laws he has given them; by the mercy he has revealed to sinners; and *by the judgment, which he executeth,* both for the righteous and against the wicked. So well is God's character known in this way that at times the wicked have the most fearful apprehensions of coming wrath. The whole ungodly world in Christian, Mohammedan and Pagan lands may in a moment be brought into the deepest distress by the terrors of God. For although when they knew God, they glorified him not as God, yet this very failure to do known duty is the greatest element of weakness in the cause and character of the wicked. Their counsels are so narrow compared with omniscience that they fall by the very means devised for their safety; and so *the wicked is snared in the work of his own hands.* *The wicked,* singular, each and every incorrigible sinner, is thus snared. There is more than one sense, in which every sinner is his own destroyer. The figure of being *snared* is as old as the days of Moses. Deut. xii. 30. This verse concludes with the words: *Higgaion. Selah.* For remarks on Selah see Introduction, § 15. The word Higgaion occurs here for the first time. It is also found in Ps. xix. 14, where it is rendered *meditation;* in Ps. xcii. 3, where it is translated *a solemn sound;* and in Lam. iii. 62, where we read *device.* In Ps. xix. 14, and in Lam. iii. 62, it clearly means *meditation, a musing,* or *thought.* Junius, Amesius, Henry and Scott, hold that the two words here are equivalent to *a thing to be meditated on with the greatest attention.* Edwards thinks Higgaion a term relating to the music. Morison inclines to the opinion that it was intended to mark with emphasis the sentiment of the Psalm. Calvin is of the same mind. Bythner says the word means a discourse, a meditation, a murmur, a sound, and thinks the import of the two words here much the same as that given by Junius, etc. Hengstenberg thinks it may be rendered *a musing* in every case, even in Ps. xcii. 3. He thinks the word here calls for reflection. The Doway Bible neither gives the word, nor any translation, or interpretation of it; though in his Explanation of the Psalms Bellarmine admits that it is in the Hebrew, and says, it signifies that the judgments of God afore-mentioned are to be assiduously and continually thought of. If the word signifies anything beyond a musical notation, the import of which is not now understood, there is no better explanation given of it than that of the old commentators first quoted. Clarke says it means, " Meditate on this."

17. *The wicked shall be turned into hell,* and *all the nations that forget God.* The *wicked* here are the same as mentioned in the preceding verse. The word is here plural. In the first Psalm and elsewhere it is rendered *the ungodly.* *The wicked,* universally and indiscriminately, *shall be turned into hell.* But what does this mean? There is nothing in the verb *shall be turned* that necessarily signifies evil. Some say the meaning is that the wicked shall all die and go into the *grave.* But that is as true of the *righteous* as of the wicked. The Hebrew word (Sheol) is in our version according to its connexion rendered *grave, pit, hell.* In this case it must be *hell,* else nothing happens to God's enemies but what comes on his friends also. It may be well to cite attention to a few places where it must mean *hell.* In Ps. cxxxix. 8, it is the opposite of heaven: "If I ascend up into heaven, thou art there; if I make my bed in hell, behold thou art there." In Pr. v. 5; vii. 27, it is said of the vile woman that *her steps take hold on hell,* and that *her house is the way to hell.* Does this mean no more than that those who visit her will die? In Pr. xv. 24: "The way of life is above to the wise, that he may depart from hell beneath." A good man, here called wise, does

not escape the grave, but he does escape hell.   In Isa. xiv. 9, it is said to Belshazzar, "Hell from beneath is moved for thee to meet thee at thy coming, it stirreth up the dead for thee," etc.   Now the *grave* never received Belshazzar.   He never was buried. In v. 19 it is said, Thou art cast out of thy grave as an abominable branch, etc.   The word here rendered grave is not Sheol, but the word which in Ps. v. 9 is rendered *sepulchre,* and in Ps. lxxxviii. 5, 11 the *grave.*   Besides the grave is silent.   In Isa. xiv. 10–20 hell is spoken of as a place abounding in taunts and derisions.   Something more than the *grave* must be meant in all these places.   Horne says, " All wickedness came originally with the wicked one from hell : thither it will be again remitted, and they who hold on its side must accompany it on its return to that place of torment, there to be shut up forever ;" Clarke says the full rendering is, The wicked shall be turned " headlong into hell, down into hell.   The original is very emphatic ;" Scott : " The future condemnation of the wicked seems to be intended ; for as all men go down to the *grave,* the word, rendered *hell,* must in this connexion have a more awful meaning ;" Henry speaks here of Sheol as "a state of everlasting misery and torment ; a pit of destruction, in which the wicked and all their comforts will be cast forever." Nor shall any of the incorrigibly wicked escape this dreadful doom.   The word *and* is nòt in the original.   It would have been better omitted here, so that we might read, The wicked shall be turned into hell, all nations that forget God.   Numbers on the side of the wicked shall not save them.   If whole nations forget God, whole nations shall perish.   How mild these words, yet how terrible their import, if we consider the sin here spoken of—*forgetfulness of God.*   Henry: "Forgetfulness of God is the cause of all the wickedness of the wicked."   To *forget God,* or *the Lord,* occurs very often in Scripture and is descriptive of irreligion.   It is not confined as Venema seems to think to those who " tread all law and righteousness beneath their feet, and manifest that they have thrown off all regard to God, the Judge of the world, and the avenger of crime."   That forgetfulness of God naturally leads to the worst open sins, and does actually lead many into the greatest excesses is true.   The same may be said of unbelief.   But both these are spiritual sins.   They may both be practised while there is a decent exterior.   Let the reader examine Deut. viii. 14 ; Ps. cvi. 21 ; Isa. xvii. 10 ; Jer. iii. 21, and parallel passages, and he will see that forgetfulness of God is not necessarily and in all cases accompanied with the most profligate morals.   It is a sin of the heart, the seat of depravity.

18. *For the needy shall not always be forgotten.*   That is, by a well-known figure of speech he says, they shall never be forgotten.   We have a like figure in 1 Pet. iv. 3. There seems to be an allusion to the preceding verse. *q. d.,* if the wicked, even nations of them, forget God, yet it is a glorious truth, publish it abroad, that God shall not always seem to have forgotten the needy.   The word, *For,* if that is the correct translation, gives the reason, why the wicked shall be turned into hell.   But the word is elsewhere rendered *surely, certainly, truly, assuredly, doubtless.*   See Gen. xxix. 32 ; Ex. iii. 12 ; Josh. ii. 24 ; 1 Kings i. 13 ; Isa. lxiii. 16.   Either of these words would here give a very good sense.   The word rendered, *for,* is also sometimes translated *when, while, whereas,* Gen. iv. 12 ; Deut. xix. 6 : Gen. xxxi. 37.   If this is the rendering we may read the two verses thus : The wicked shall be turned into hell, all nations that forget God ; while (or whereas) the needy shall not be always forgotten.   And because they are not forgotten, they shall not be ruined.   *The expectation of the poor shall* not *perish forever.*   The word *not* is properly supplied from the preceding clause, or we may read this hemistich as a question, Shall the expectation of the poor perish forever ?   A strong mode of asserting, it shall not.   The word rendered *needy* is always in our version rendered *poor* or *needy,* except once when it is translated *beggar.*   This is the first place in the Psalms, where it occurs.   The word rendered *poor* in the last clause is

the same that occurred in v. 12., and is there rendered *humble*, or in the margin *afflicted*. It is elsewhere in our version translated *meek, lowly*. Ps. xxv. 9; Pr. iii. 34. In both clauses the persons spoken of are the pious sufferers. Their full deliverance may be lawfully prayed for, as David does in the next verse.

19. *Arise, O* LORD; *let not man prevail.* Some here render *man* by adding a word such as *frail*, or *mortal*. On that point see Introduction, § 16. The *prevailing* of man is the carrying of his counsels and measures against the laws of God and the principles of righteousness. God is invoked to *arise* to his throne, and put down this monstrous state of things where a worm seems to *be strong*, as the word *prevail* might read, against omnipotence. And so *let the heathen be judged in thy sight.* The *heathen*, or *nations* here are the same spoken of in the whole Psalm. They had long vexed the people of God. The prayer is that God as Judge would decide against their cruel and unrighteous course. But the verb *judge* is often taken in a good sense. See Ps. lxxii. 4; Ecc. iii. 17; Isa. i. 17, and many other places. In this very Psalm, v. 4, the corresponding noun commonly rendered *judgment* is translated *right*. See also Ps. lxxii. 1; Isa. xxxii. 1; xlii. 1, 3, 4, and many other places. So that the prayer, *Let the heathen be judged* might perhaps signify, *Let them be brought under the power of truth and righteousness.* The serious difficulty to this view arises from the fact that the phrase *in thy sight*, and the whole preceding structure of the Psalm refer to God sitting as a Judge, and not to his becoming the author of salvation to the wicked. The only reason for supposing the word *Judge* to be here as in some other cases used in a good sense is the fact that the next verse has been so interpreted by some. In our version it reads:

20. *Put them in fear, O* LORD that *the nations may know themselves* to be but *men.* John Rogers' translation: *O Lord, set a scolemaster over them, that the heithen maye knowe themselves to be but men.* Coverdale: *O Lorde, set a scolemaster over them.* Fenwick renders it thus:

> Let them a guide and teacher have, O Lord!
> Their helpless state make thou the nations know.

Moller: *Set a teacher over them*, but he thinks *teacher* means one who chastises, as Cyrus was the teacher of Belshazzar. He says it cannot signify that the Holy Spirit was to be their teacher. Piscator mentions this view and expresses no dissent from it; Horsley: *O Lord*, place a teacher among them. Brent uses a Latin translation, which reads, Place a teacher over them; The Septuagint, Ethiopic, Syriac, Vulgate and Doway all read, Put a law-giver over them; Morison: Place a teacher or law-giver over them; The Arabic: Appoint a teacher of the law over them; Bellarmine thinks it a prophecy respecting Constantine and other Christian Emperors, who were afterwards set over the nations. Scott first gives the sense as indicated by our translation and adds, "The original word, rendered *fear*, by varying a vowel point, means a *Teacher*; and in this sense the prayer is for their instruction and conversion. Bythner allows it may read, Instruct them. Having given the view suggested by the English version, as specially applied to Anti-Christian powers, Gill says, "Or these words are a prayer for the conversion of many among the nations, and may be rendered *put, O Lord, fear in them;* that is, the true grace of fear, *that the nations may know* themselves, their sin and guilt and danger, and know God in Christ, and Christ, and the way of salvation by him; for at the word *know* should be a stop, concluding a proposition, since the accent *Athnach* is there; and then follows another, *they are men, Selah:* destitute of the fear and grace of God, are capable of it, but cannot give it to themselves. Some notice that the word rendered *fear* sometimes means a *razor*, and refer to Judg. xiii. 5; Isa. vii. 20. Calvin, Cocceius, Patrick, Edwards, Fry, Hengstenberg and Alexander reject the foregoing interpretations, and suppose that our version gives the true idea, taking the word *fear* in the sense of dread. They are probably correct. Calvin: "The scope of the passage requires that we should understand it of fear or dread; and this is the opinion of all sound expositors." There is nothing malevolent in this prayer. It is a mercy to any man so far to be put in fear as to make him know that he is but a man, a frail, dying, feeble creature. Calvin says that David's "language is as if he had said, Lord, since it is their ignorance of themselves, which hurries them into their rage against me, make them actually to experience that their strength is not equal to their infatuated presumption, and after they are disappointed of their vain hopes, let them lie abashed and confounded with shame. It may often happen that those, who are convinced of their own weakness do not yet reform; but much is gained when their ungodly presumption is exposed to mockery and scorn before the world, that it may appear how ridiculous was the confidence which they presumed to place in their own strength. With respect to the chosen of God, they ought to profit under his chastisements after another manner. It becomes them to be humbled under a sense of their own weakness, and willingly to divest themselves of all vain confidence and presumption. And this will be the case, if they remember that they are but men."

For the sense of *Selah* see Introduction, § 15.

DOCTRINAL AND PRACTICAL REMARKS.

1. What a great teacher is experience! How it enriches the soul with knowledge and with confidence. The Christian's strength is acquired in exercising himself unto godliness. Of this truth, this whole Psalm is proof.

2. The first great element of true religion is godly sincerity. When we begin to worship and do other duties *with our whole heart*, we begin to live, v. 1. Without this all our doings are *dead works*, offensive to God.

3. Hengstenberg: "A *spirit of thankfulness* is one of the marks by which the family of God is distinguished from the world. He who cannot from the heart give *thanks* shall *beg* in vain. The *receiver* raises himself more easily to the hope of future kindnesses, when he throws himself back on the remembrance of former benefits derived from the giver. The foundation of despair is always ingratitude," v. 1.

4. It is no less a duty than a privilege to recount God's wonders, v. 1. What a great advantage in this respect is possessed by old Christians, who have seen many marvellous tokens of God's love to his chosen. He, who has been in the wars, is commonly listened to with interest.

5. One good work or purpose naturally leads to another. If the people will heartily praise God, they will soon have something to tell of his wonderful works, v. 1.

6. In true religion nothing will satisfy but God himself, v. 2. Dickson: "Not any benefit or gift received of God, but God himself, and his free favor is matter of the believer's joy." Calvin remarks that David means to say "that he finds in God a full and overflowing abundance of joy, so that he is not under the necessity of seeking even the smallest drop in any other quarter."

7. We should find out the most fitting way of making known God's praises, vv. 2, 11, 14, and not tire in that good work. Horne: "He, who, with the spirit and the understanding, as well as with the voice, 'sings praise to thy name, O Most High,' is employed as the angels are, and experiences a foretaste of the delight they feel." Let us learn to sing with grace in our hearts, making melody to the Lord, praising him for existence, for his many temporal gifts, and passing to the higher themes of redemption and glory.

8. We need never fear that God will be dethroned, or overreached, or defeated.

He is the Most High, v. 2. His natural no less than his moral perfections put him beyond the reach of all malice, earthly and infernal.

9. How easily the wicked are discomfited. Their flight is a rout, v. 3. Their ruin comes like an armed man. Saints and sinners commonly both die a natural death, but any wise man had rather die the death of the Christian a thousand times than the death of the sinner once.

10. God's presence will confound any foe, v. 3. Nor should we make much of the means, but only of the Author of our deliverances from dismayed enemies. Dickson: "The way of giving God the glory in every action, and in special of our victories over our enemies, is to acknowledge him to be the chief worker thereof, and the creatures to be but instruments, by whom he turneth the enemy back."

11. The side God is on is sure to conquer, v. 4. No other reason of victory need be assigned. This covers the whole ground.

12. Past defeats should forewarn the wicked of the sad disasters and inevitable destruction, that must speedily come on them, v. 4. Since the world began, they have never carried a point. Even the death of Christ was the most dreadful blow ever given to the empire of darkness. And before they leave the shores of time the great mass of them confess that sin is a lie and the world a cheat. Who ever heard "the people of the world speak well of it at parting?"

13. At earthly tribunals a good cause is not enough to ensure success; but God is always with the right, v. 4. He judges righteous judgment. Three things should make our confidence in God perfect—"God is ever the same, and his throne remains unshaken—his administration of the affairs of the world is one of strict justice—he is still his people's refuge, and still the hearer of prayer."

14. The men, the cities, the nations, that have perished, might well warn every man inclined to revolt against God to beware, v. 5. The fall of every rebel is God's advertisement that none can transgress with impunity. The persecutors and persecuting powers of earth, when found irreclaimable, have always had a dreadful overthrow. Nations, inflamed by ambition, lusting for conquest, and regardless of right, have always sooner or later met a terrible doom. Clarke solemnly warns "all the nations of the earth, who, to enlarge their territory, increase their wealth, or extend their commerce, have made destructive wars. For the blood, which such nations have shed, their blood shall be shed."

15. The wicked and the righteous are every way opposite, v. 6. If one is right, the other must be wrong; if one pleases God, the other must be continually provoking the heavenly majesty; if one is saved, the other must be damned. The converse is true. If one is wrong, the other is right; if one shall be damned, the other must be saved. God cannot love both. He must love him, whose moral character is like that of his Maker.

16. Amidst all the changing scenes of earth and men, how glorious is the truth that God *endures* and *reigns* forever, v. 7. In human governments one dies and another succeeds. But he, who alone hath immortality, is on the throne of the universe. If on earth we have a good chief magistrate, we know not that he will live a day, nor have we any certainty that his successor will not be a foolish or bad man.

17. Because God cannot deny himself, he must preside over all human affairs. He cannot vacate the throne of judgment any more than he can cease to exist. Dickson: "Courts of justice among men are not always ready to hear plaintiffs; but the Lord holdeth court continually; the taking in of no man's complaint is delayed so much as one hour, though thousands should come at once, all of them with sundry petitions." Morison: "Delightful is it to feel, that the reign of evil will not be everlasting; that

however long it may be permitted tó exist, it shall, at last, cease; nor is it less reviving to know, that the reign of peace, and truth, and righteousness, shall be everlasting."

18. The day of judgment will be a great revealer, v. 8.   It cannot be otherwise.

19. How vain is a religion of forms.   How idle it is to attempt to hide ourselves in ordinances and ceremonies, seeing Jehovah himself is the refuge of his saints, v. 9.

20. God can easily put his people beyond the reach of their mightiest foes.   He is their *high place*, v. 9.

21. The true knowledge of God promotes quietude.   Henry: "The better God is known, the more he is trusted."

22. What everlasting pillars of truth are set up through all the Scriptures for the comfort of the saints, v. 10.   See also Heb. xiii. 5.   Every such doctrine and promise is as durable as the throne of God.

23. The duty of publishing all the truth, that shall be honorable to God and advance his kingdom, is no novelty, v. 11.   The Old Testament reveals many of the principles on which the missionary enterprise rests.   And in this work we have great encouragement; for, as Dickson says, "The acts of the Lord for his people are so stamped with the impression of his divinity, that they are able to purchase glory to God even among the nations that are without the church, and to draw them to him, and so it is not a needless, fruitless, or hopeless work *to declare his doings among the nations*."

24. Let men be warned against all murder and against all malice, which leads to murder, v. 12. Scott: "The blood of many martyrs has been shed, and their persecutors have supposed that no inquisition would be made for it: but from time to time the Lord anticipates that day when 'the earth shall disclose her blood, and shall no more cover her slain.'   He is ever mindful of the cry of the humble."

25. Let not those persecuted for righteousness fear lest they shall be overlooked or forgotten by God, v. 12.

26. An humble, fervent prayer is never lost, v. 12.   Chrysostom: "Prayer is a haven to the shipwrecked man, an anchor to them that are sinking in the waves, a staff to the limbs that totter, a mine of jewels to the poor, a healer of diseases, and a guardian of health.   Prayer at once secures the continuance of our blessings, and dissipates the clouds of our calamities.   O blessed prayer! thou art the unwearied conqueror of human woes, the firm foundation of human happiness, the source of ever-enduring joy, the mother of philosophy.   The man who can pray truly, though languishing in extremest indigence, is richer than all beside; whilst the wretch who never bowed the knee, though proudly sitting as monarch of all nations, is of all men most destitute."   Never give up prayer.

27. How harmonious is the character of a good man.   He is called humble, v. 12, and yet the very same word may be rendered by other words and there will be no error taught.   He is *meek*, he is *afflicted*, he is *lowly*.   One evil passion may expel another so as completely to take its place, but the graces of the Christian all dwell together in unity.

28. The old way of coming to God, stripped of self-righteousness, is the best, the only way.   The holiest mere man that ever lived had great need to cry for mercy, v. 13.

29. Great notice should be taken of the marvellous escapes from death which we experience, v. 13.   God lifts us up from the gates of that dark prison.   I know a man who was puny all his childhood, and in youth had so little health that it was often said, he will soon be in his grave.   Almost invariably he was attacked with every prevailing malignant disease until he was thirty years old.   Once in his early childhood he was within a few yards of a huge, ravenous bear.   Soon after he was felled

to the ground by a terrible blow from an axe, unintentionally inflicted on his face. Once he fell from a great height, and barely escaped death. Once he was so nearly drowned that his life was saved only by his crawling to shore on the bottom of the river. Once it seemed impossible but that he should be pitched headlong down a precipitous bank, towards which he and his wagon were borne by a powerful and uncontrollable team. He has been in a storm at sea under the command of a drunken captain, who soon afterwards lost his vessel in a gentle breeze in broad daylight inside the capes. Repeatedly has the most furious personal violence been threatened him. Often has he been in the power of drunken drivers, who had not sense enough to guide the gentlest team. Yet after more than a half century of such narrow escapes he still lives to recount God's mercies. Ought he not to do it with glowing love? And yet perhaps half his cotemporaries might narrate things no less strange.

30. Till God undertakes our cause we must despair. But with his aid we may shout on the field of battle before a gun is fired, or a sword drawn, v. 14.

31. Clarke: "There is nothing that a wicked man does that is not against his own interest. He is continually doing himself harm, and takes more pains to destroy his soul than the righteous man does to get his saved unto eternal life," vv. 15, 16.

32. How dreadful must be the doom of the wicked, v. 17. By whatever sound law of language we interpret the words of Scripture respecting their doom, we must tremble when we think of their passing out of time into eternity. Morison says that the *seventeenth* verse of this Psalm undoubtedly contains "a threatening of punishment in an unseen state of existence; and establishes the position that a future state of rewards and punishments was not unknown to the ancient Jewish church. Whatever difficulties may arise as to the critical meaning of the word *hell*, two things perhaps will be admitted; first, that it is here introduced as a threatening; and second, that it is intended to describe a fate peculiar to the wicked. If it be a threatening, it cannot be the peaceful repose of the grave; and if it be intended to represent the ignominy of the wicked, it must, of course, involve conscious existence; and if so, the hell spoken of can be neither more nor less than that prison of darkness, in which the spirits of the lost are reserved till the judgment of the great day."

33. Let the distressed people of God know that the day of their deliverance is at hand, v. 18. Their time is coming; and a blessed time it shall be. Mal. iii. 16–18.

34. However far the wicked may go, they shall establish nothing. God will arise, and their plans will be dissipated like the morning mist, v. 19.

35. Every decision that God has ever made, or ever shall make, has been or shall be against the wicked, v. 19.

36. What a blessing it would be if men but knew enough of themselves to abate their extravagant folly, and still more to give them some genuine modesty. Augustine says that "all man's humility consists in a knowledge of himself." But alas, "Sin doth so beset' ignorant and graceless people, that they forget that they are mortal, and that God is their judge."

37. This whole Psalm shows that the church is not likely to be called to endure more than she has already triumphed over.

38. Will not each reader lay to heart these great and awful truths? Surely we all have an interest in securing salvation. But when shall it once be? Chalmers says, "Faith is the starting post of obedience; but what I want is, that you start immediately—that you wait not for more light to spiritualize your obedience; but that you work for more light, by yielding a present obedience up to the present light which you profess—that you stir up all the gift which is now in you; and this is the way to have the gift enlarged, that whatever your hand findeth to do in the way of service to God, you now do it with all your might. And the very fruit of doing it

because of his authority, is that you will at length do it because of your own renovated taste.   As you persevere in the labors of his service, you will grow in the likeness of his character.   The graces of holiness will both brighten and multiply upon you.   These will be your treasures, and treasures for heaven, too,—the delights of which mainly consist in the affections, and feelings, and congenial employments of the new creature."   Surely if men have any reason or sense left, they will use them to urge their flight from the wrath to come.

PSALM X.

1 Why standest thou afar off, O LORD? *why* hidest thou *thyself* in times of trouble?

2 The wicked in *his* pride doth persecute the poor: let them be taken in the devices that they have imagined.

3 For the wicked boasteth of his heart's desire, and blesseth the covetous, *whom* the LORD abhorreth.

4 The wicked, through the pride of his countenance, will not seek *after God:* God *is* not in all his thoughts.

5 His ways are always grievous; thy judgments *are* far above out of his sight: *as for* all his enemies, he puffeth at them.

6 He hath said in his heart, I shall not be moved: for *I shall* never *be* in adversity.

7. His mouth is full of cursing and deceit and fraud: under his tongue *is* mischief and vanity.

8 He sitteth in the lurking places of the villages: in the secret places doth he murder the innocent: his eyes are privily set against the poor.

9 He lieth in wait secretly as a lion in his den: he lieth in wait to catch the poor: he doth catch the poor, when he draweth him into his net.

10 He croucheth, *and* humbleth himself, that the poor may fall by his strong ones.

11 He hath said in his heart, God hath forgotten: he hideth his face; he will never see *it.*

12 Arise, O LORD; O God, lift up thine hand: forget not the humble.

13 Wherefore doth the wicked contemn God? he hath said in his heart, Thou wilt not require *it.*

14 Thou hast seen *it;* for thou beholdest mischief and spite, to require *it* with thy hand: the poor committeth himself unto thee; thou art the helper of the fatherless.

15 Break thou the arm of the wicked and the evil *man:* seek out his wickedness *till* thou find none.

16 The LORD *is* King for ever and ever: the heathen are perished out of his land.

17. LORD, thou hast heard the desire of the humble: thou wilt prepare their heart, thou wilt cause thine ear to hear:

18 To judge the fatherless and the oppressed, that the man of the earth may no more oppress.

IN the Septuagint this Psalm is merged into the ninth so as with it to form one Psalm, and so as to change all the numbers by one on to the 114th Psalm, into which the 115th is also merged.   To complete the number of *one hundred and fifty* the Septuagint divides our 116th Psalm into two and our 147th into two also, so that in the Septuagint, Ps. x., corresponds to our Ps. xi., and so on.   Only the *first* NINE and the *last* THREE Psalms correspond in number in all the Bibles.   The Vulgate and Doway follow the Septuagint.   We follow the Hebrew original.   The Vulgate and Doway admit that the union of Psalms ix. and x. in one is not according to the Hebrew.   The reason for uniting the two may probably be found in the similarity of topics and in the modes of treating them.   But this reason would as much apply to many other Psalms confessedly distinct.   It is also probable that the absence of any title invited to this union.   Even Venema joins it with the ninth.   No one claims any original caption for it.

Many have expressed the opinion that this Psalm referred to particular times and events. Some have supposed that it respected Saul's persecution of David. No solid reason is given for this. It certainly derives very little strength from the contents of the Psalm. Piscator thinks it relates to domestic enemies. Others apply it to the invasion of Canaan by the hordes of Philistines. This receives *some* countenance from the contents, but very few will think the amount of evidence sufficient. Mudge and Edwards think "that this Psalm was penned when the Assyrians made inroads under Hezekiah." Some have thought it was written during the Babylonish captivity. Morison: "It is not, by any means, an improbable conjecture that the envious and persecuting conduct of Sanballat and his associates occasioned its composition by some unknown bard of Israel." Clarke also: "It was probably made in reference to *Sanballat* and the other enemies of the Jews." Some contend that it refers to the dreadful persecutions under Antiochus Epiphanes and the times of the Maccabees. See Venema on the place. Luther, Bugenhagius, Cocceius, Tillius, Gill and Fry think it refers to Antichrist. Luther and Gill insist on this view. The Syriac version has this caption: "Of the attack of the enemy on Adam and his race, and how Christ shall put down his arrogance." Horsley regards this Psalm as a general account of the oppression of the righteous by apostate spirits, atheists, and idolaters. He seems to have followed Patrick, who says this Psalm "is a most lively description of the insolency of wicked atheistical men, when they have power and are in authority." Slade thinks it "describes the character of some wicked and cruel enemy, or enemies, who persecuted David and the church in his day; and, no doubt, was intended to describe the enemies of Christ and his church." Calvin regards this Psalm as a complaint "that fraud, extortion, cruelty, violence, and all kinds of injustice prevailed everywhere in the world." Although Scott is inclined to the opinion that this Psalm was composed with reference to the persecutions of David and other good men during the reign of Saul, yet he makes this very just remark: "Several of the Psalms seem intentionally to have been written in general terms, that they might serve to direct the devotions of the church in persecution, and those of every believer in his personal troubles and afflictions." Hengstenberg is strongly in favor of its *general* character: "No trace is anywhere to be found of an individual reference." This is probably the correct view. The fact of so great diversity among good men who would give it a historic origin or interpretation rather tends to confirm this opinion. The Psalm suits the pious of very different countries and ages. Surely sinners in power often show very much the same dispositions towards God's people.

Those who hold that this Psalm was written after David's time do not of course regard him as the author. But Calvin, Venema, Amesius, Henry, Scott, Hitzig, Hengstenberg and Alexander very properly ascribe it to the "sweet Psalmist of Israel." It is found in the midst of Psalms, confessedly Davidic in authorship. Hengstenberg notices the fact that the words rendered *in times of trouble* in the first verse are found nowhere else but in Ps. ix. 9, which was written by David.

The names of the Almighty occurring in this Psalm are *Jehovah* LORD, *Elohim God* and *El God*, on which see above on Ps. i. 2; iii. 2; v. 4.

Of course the date of this Psalm is put down according to the views of different writers respecting its authorship and the events it notices. Clarke thinks it was written B. C. 445, and Scott B. C. 1058. Cocceius: "This Psalm is indeed not difficult in its matter or sense; but some difficulty arises from the changeable manner of its construction and from the ambiguity of some words found in it."

1. *Why standest thou afar off*, O LORD? The verb in this clause is generally given in the present tense in modern versions. The original is in the future; so also is the Chaldee. Septuagint, Syriac, Arabic and Vulgate use the preterite. Alexander says

the futures here and in the next clause imply the present with a prospect of continuance. The expostulation is reverent and not unusual. A like form was employed by the Saviour on the cross. It is based on the belief that God sees what is going on, has power to give relief, is a righteous God, and will finally do justice. Why then does he seem to be an indifferent spectator and withhold aid when it is so much needed? The question is repeated in other words: Why *hidest thou* thyself *in times of trouble?* The *why* is brought forward from the first clause and *thyself* is also supplied. All the old versions make both clauses of the verse interrogative. Some moderns drop the *why* and read *Dost thou hide*, etc. So Montanus and Ainsworth. But Venema drops the form of question in this clause; so also does Alexander, both of them reading, Thou wilt hide, etc.; Jebb: Thou hidest, etc.; Hengstenberg: Thou coverest, etc. These various renderings do not materially affect the sense. Either gives an idea weighty and solemn, but the parallelism is best preserved by retaining the interrogative form. The expostulation is thus strengthened. On the phrase *in times of trouble*, see above on Ps. ix. 9.

2. *The wicked in* his *pride doth persecute the poor.* There seems to be no good ground for including this verse, as Edwards does, in the same sentence with the first, and rendering it, During the insolence of the wicked, whilst he persecutes, etc. The word *wicked* here is the same that is so rendered in Ps. vii. 9; ix. 5; in Ps. i. 1, 4, 5, 6 and iii. 7 it is rendered *ungodly*. The word rendered *pride* is in Ps. lxviii. 34 and in Deut. xxxiii. 26, 29 translated *excellency*. This has led some to think the word here refers to the *elevated position*, occupied by persecutors, and employed to oppress the righteous. Yet the word is commonly rendered *pride*, and so most think it should be translated here. The *poor* of this verse are *the humble* of Ps. ix. 12 and *the poor* of Ps. ix. 18. The word *persecute* some would read *is inflamed or burneth*. Some of the old translations as well as some critics so read. Although the word may be so rendered yet it is given *pursued, hotly pursued, chased*, Gen. xxxi. 36; Lam. iv. 19; 1 Sam. xvii. 53. In Ps. vii. 13 the participle is rendered *persecutors*. Our version is probably the best. The wicked are often "exceeding mad," hot with rage, against the afflicted people of God. The next clause reads, *Let them be taken in the devices that they have imagined.* Edwards: *And they are taken in the plots that they have devised.* The word here rendered *devices* is in v. 4 *thoughts*. It may be taken in either a good or bad sense. Here it is evidently in a bad sense. Fry and Horsley render it "subtleties." Horsley: "I choose this ambiguous word; being in doubt whether the petition against the wicked be that they may be ruined by their own stratagems against the righteous, or that they may be the dupes of their own atheistical speculations upon moral and religious subjects." This goes on the supposition that the *wicked* are caught in their own traps. If so, the idea is the same as is presented in Ps. vii. 14–16; ix. 15, 16. Horne and Morison seem inclined to favor the reading, They shall be taken, etc. This is better than that of our version. But none of these seem to give the true sense. It is not probable that the Psalmist here offers a petition. He does that towards the close of the Psalm. He is now stating his case. The Septuagint and Vulgate read, They are caught in the counsels which they have plotted. Venema, Gill, Fry, Hengstenberg and Alexander favor the interpretation, That the poor are caught in the devices of the wicked. This makes the words harmonize with the context. If this view be followed, the best sense is obtained by reading, They [the poor] are caught in the counsels which they [the wicked] have plotted.

3. *For the wicked boasteth of his heart's desire.* This rendering closely follows the Chaldee. The Septuagint and Vulgate: The sinner is praised in the desires of his soul; Syriac and Arabic: The ungodly glories in the lusts of his soul; Secker and Horsley: The wicked is mad upon the desire of his soul; Hengstenberg: The wicked

extols the desire of his soul. The word rendered *boasteth* is also very often rendered *praise*, sometimes *glory, commend, celebrate*. The sense is that the wicked here spoken of has ceased to be ashamed of his vileness, but openly speaks of it in a commendatory strain. Clarke: "This shows the excess of a depraved and embruted spirit. He, who can boast of his iniquity, is in the broad road to ruin. Should such a one repent, and turn to God, it will be equal to any miracle." Hengstenberg: "When the wicked ventures to laud in public the shameful lusts of his heart, as what need not shun the light, this is the highest degree of depravity, and betokens, at the same time, how secure he has become in consequence of his impunity, how sad the condition of the poor, how much occasion there is for such to fear, how necessary it hence is for God to interfere, and what reason there was for the *why* in the first verse." He, who has thus far departed from God, goes further, *and blesseth the covetous*, whom *the* LORD *abhorreth*. Mudge and Edwards read, And the greedy of gain blesseth himself; the marginal reading is, The covetous blesseth himself, he abhorreth the LORD. Fry: He adoreth gain, despising Jehovah; Calvin: The violent man blesseth himself; he despiseth Jehovah; Hengstenberg: Whosoever makes gain blesses, despises God; Alexander: And winning blesses, despises Jehovah. The last two authors regard this clause as parallel to Zech. xi. 3, 4, 5. If this is the correct view, then *blesses* has God for its object, and the man, who is filled with unlawful gains, is represented as attempting to sanctify, or at least to sanction his iniquities by blessing God for his unrighteous possessions; and in so doing he despises God, contemns his moral character, as if he would make him a partaker of his evil deeds. But our version gives a good sense, and has long been approved by pious scholars. The original fairly allows it. When a wicked man is quite vile and secure in his own sins, the next thing is to practise that gratuitous kind of iniquity, which consists in having pleasure in the sins of others. Rom. i. 32. The reader may see that the word *whom* is not in the Hebrew. If any change is made in the reading it would perhaps be best to follow Calvin in this last clause: The violent man blesseth himself; he despiseth Jehovah. But there seems to be no good reason for using *violent* instead of *covetous*. That the wicked bless the vile, who are successful, is evident from Ps. xlix. 16–18.

4. As a natural consequence of despising the LORD, the ungodly fall into general irreligion: *The wicked, through the pride of his countenance, will not seek* after God. Here and in the Chaldee, the words *after God* are supplied. Kimchi: "To seek God or to seek after God is a common phrase to designate the whole of religion." Dimock and Jebb read *seek God*. A wicked man's devices, and boastings, and pleasure in evil doers are tokens of a ruinous pride, which excludes all honest desires after the knowledge, favor, image, service and fellowship of God. Ainsworth: The wicked inquireth not into the height of his [God's] anger; Fry: The wicked in the pride of his anger inquireth not. In the Psalms as elsewhere *anger* is the more common rendering of the word which we here render *countenance*. But the English translation in this case is to be preferred. Bad tempers are the basis of all the cruelty, persecutions and irreligion of evil men. Calvin would read, The wicked, etc. inquireth not; Edwards: He will make no inquiry. Calvin thinks that supplying any noun improperly limits the signification: "David simply means, that the ungodly, without examination, permit themselves to do anything, or do not distinguish between what is lawful and unlawful because their own lust is their law, yea, rather, as if superior to all laws, they fancy it is lawful for them to do whatever they please. The beginning of well-doing in a man's life is inquiry. . . The exercise of inquiry proceeds from humility, when we assign to God, as is reasonable, the place of Judge and Ruler over us;" but Hengstenberg, following Venema, who had followed Dieu, would read it: The wicked, in his pride (says) he (God) searches, or perceives not. The Hebrew verb

in this sentence is that found in Ps. ix. 10, 12, rendered *seek* and *make inquisition;* and in vv. 13, 14 of this Psalm, rendered *require* and *seek out.* So that this makes the wicked deny a providence. In accordance with this view, Venema says of these men, "Their counsels and projects were such, that in their very nature they involved the denial of God, and if an inference might be drawn from these concerning the faith of those who entertain them, we should conclude them to be deniers of God." Either of these interpretations gives us a weighty doctrine consistent with truth elsewhere clearly revealed. Yet that which leaves the text very much as it is in our common version, will probably be found, on full investigation, the most satisfactory. The natural tendency of every error is to downright atheism. This ungodly man was ready for any gross opinion, and so it is added, *God is not in all his thoughts.* The *is* is here properly supplied. The literal rendering of the Hebrew is, No God, all his thoughts. The Septuagint and Vulgate read, God is not before his face; Arabic: God is not before him; Syriac: Nor is God in all his thoughts; Edwards: He will make no inquiry; There is no God, are all his wicked thoughts; Waterland: All his thoughts are without God; Jebb: There is no God, are all his thoughts; Brent: All his thoughts tend to this, that there is no God; the margin: All his thoughts are, There is no God; Mudge: No God is all his wicked politics; Horsley: No God is the whole of his philosophy; Hengstenberg: God is not, are all his purposes; *q. d.,* his purposes are a continued practical denial of God; Alexander: He will not require, there is no God—are all his thoughts; Fry: "There is no God," is all his thought. For *thoughts* Ainsworth reads "presumptuous cogitations." Chaldee: He says in his heart that all his thoughts are not manifest to God. It will be remembered that the word rendered *thoughts* is in v. 2 translated *devices.* To say that God is not in all his *devices,* that is, that he lives, and plans, and feels, and thinks as if he were persuaded that there is no God is as good a sense and as consistent with the text and context as any other.

5. *His ways are always grievous.* The Septuagint: His ways are always profane; Arabic: He defiles his ways; John Rogers' translation: His wayes are allwaye filthye; Genevan translation: His wayes alway prosper; Schroeder: His ways are crooked; Calvin, Venema and Hengstenberg: His ways are always prosperous; Horsley and Fry: His ways are ever confident; Alexander: His ways are firm in all time; Bernard's Bible: His ways are always secure; Edwards: His ways are impious at all times. For *grievous* Edwards reads *perverse;* Slade, *offensive* and *hurtful.* These renderings are of three classes; one asserts his ways to be *sinful,* wicked, profane, defiled, filthy, crooked, impious, perverse; the second represents them as *successful,* prosperous, firm, confident, secure; *i. e.,* he has no fears and no reverses; the third is that his ways are *sorrowful,* grievous, painful, vexatious, to himself at least, and perhaps to others also. The difficulty in the case arises from this, that all these explanations are in accordance with facts often existing in the lives of the wicked, and with the teachings of Scripture respecting them; and from the further fact that the original will bear various renderings, the translations differing according to the derivation of one word. A forcible reason for preferring the Genevan translation in this case is that it best suits the context. The Psalmist is expostulating with God on the existing state of things, and he brings in the persecutions, artifices, boastings, pride, and atheism of the wicked; and to crown all, he adds that this man is prosperous. Moreover he is as stupid as he is vile; for *thy judgments* are *far above out of his sight.* The mind of such a man is debased, "the thoughts are otherwise occupied, the taste is perverted, the conscience is seared, the judgment itself is bewildered; nothing, in short, pertaining to the spiritual world can be seen in its true character." God's judgments, whether by that term we understand the decisions of his word, his

usual and righteous sway over the events of life, or the terrific displays of his anger sometimes made against atrocious rebels, are quite beyond the apprehension of such a besotted man, quite out of his sight. He is blind and cannot see afar off. This is the most obvious sense. But Hengstenberg thinks it has regard to his exemption from afflictions—"thy righteous chastisements are so far removed from him, that they never reach him." If this is the correct view, this clause is no advance on the last, but only a repetition. Alexander thinks this "clause describes him as untouched or unaffected by God's providential judgments." When a man ceases to fear God, he soon learns not to regard men, Luke xviii. 2, 4. So here: As for *all his enemies, he puffeth at them.* The Septuagint, Vulgate and Arabic read, He lords it over them; Chaldee: He is wrathful towards them; Ainsworth thinks it means that he *defies* them; Syriac: He despises them; Patrick's paraphrase: He contemns them all and values them not a straw; Clarke: "He whistles at them; insults God, and despises men. He overthrows them with his *breath;* he has only to give orders and they are destroyed;" Hengstenberg: He blows at them, *i. e.,* he drives them away with little trouble, he has only to breathe and they vanish. This clause describes him, says Alexander, "as easily ridding himself of all his human adversaries." Venema, however, properly suggests that this language refers to his own estimate of what he can do. Using the plural instead of the singular respecting the wicked, Calvin gives this explanation of the whole verse: "As they enjoy a continued course of prosperity, they dream that God is bound or plighted to them; and hence they put his judgments far from them; and if any man oppose them, they are confident they can immediately put him down, or dash him to pieces with a puff or breath."

So confident is he that,

6. *He hath said in his heart, I shall not be moved: for* I shall *never* be *in adversity.* The first negative here is very strong, *q. d.,* I shall not *from age to age,* I shall not *generation upon generation,* I shall not in all coming ages, I shall *never, no never* be moved. Edwards employs simply *never.* Hengstenberg says, The meaning is: Misfortune shall never overtake me. Horne gives the spirit of the passage: "Prosperity begets presumption, and he who has been long accustomed to see his designs succeed, begins to think it impossible they should ever do otherwise. The long-suffering of God, instead of leading such an one to repentance, only hardens him in his iniquity. Because sentence against an evil work is not executed speedily, he thinks it will not be executed at all. He vaunteth himself, therefore, like the proud Chaldean monarch, in the Babylon which he hath erected, and fondly pronounceth it to be immortal. Such, it is too evident, are often the vain imaginations of triumphant wickedness." The word rendered *adversity* in the last clause is used to express both natural evil, and moral evil. Here it evidently means *natural* evil. In this sense it is also translated *evil, wretchedness, hurt, trouble, affliction.* This vain man says, he shall never see these things. So strong and so strange are these delusions of wicked men, that some have thought we have here an ideal personage. But it is not necessary to frame such a device. Many a wicked man thinks all this, see Isaiah xxviii. 15. That is he says it *in his heart,* in his wish, in his desire, and often he believes this horrid lie. He does not stop to think soberly or honestly, for

7. *His mouth is full of cursing and deceit and fraud; under his tongue* is *mischief and vanity.* The word here rendered *cursing,* is elsewhere *oath, swearing,* Jer. xxiii. 10; *curse,* Job xxxi. 30; *execration,* Jer. xlii. 18; Calvin adds, *perjury;* the word *deceit* is plural, *deceits,* and is elsewhere *subtilty, treachery;* the word *fraud* is in our version always rendered so, or *deceit.* Calvin gives it *malice;* Fry, *injury;* Hengstenberg, *oppression.* For *mischief* the church of England reads *ungodliness;* Hengstenberg, *sorrow;* Alexander, *trouble;* in our version it is elsewhere rendered *perverseness, sorrow,*

wickedness, trouble, mischief, misery, travail, grievousness, iniquity, etc. The word *vanity* is in our version elsewhere rendered *iniquity* (the rendering also of Calvin, Edwards, Jebb and Alexander) *mischief* (used also by Hengstenberg) *affliction, wickedness,* etc. Surely when the ruling power of a country was in the hands of a man or men ready to do such deeds, it was high time for the righteous to call on God, and it was time for him to work. Some think that the imagery of this verse is partly drawn from serpents, which carry their poison in their mouths, under their tongue. It may be so, Ps. cxl. 3. But it is probable that it refers to the sweet morsel under the tongue, Job xx. 12. Such vileness of character will show itself; and so, "From words the description proceeds to actions."

8. *He sitteth in the lurking-places of the villages: in the secret places doth he murder the innocent: his eyes are privily set against the poor.* All the verbs in this verse are in Hebrew in the future, and are so given by Calvin and Alexander. Calvin says he leaves these verbs in the future, "because they imply a continued act, and also because this Hebrew idiom has extended even to other languages." Many have been perplexed with this and the two following verses by regarding them as a literal description of the wicked previously noticed, whereas they contain the language of bold comparison; *q. d.,* he is like the lurking, cruel, sneaking felon. Thieves have long had their dens; murderers, their caves; and robbers, their plots. Striking parallel passages are in Job xxiv. 14–17; Ps. lvi. 6; Pr. i. 11, 12. John Rogers' translation is, He sytteth lurkyng in the gardens; the Bishops' Bible: He sitteth lurking in the thievish corners of the streetes; Horsley gives the whole verse thus, "He sitteth in ambush in the villages in secret places; he murdereth the innocent; his eyes are ever watching for the helpless." In a note he expresses a preference for another form of rendering the first clause: "He sitteth prowling about the farm-houses." He adds, "The image is that of a beast of prey of the lesser order, a fox or a wolf, lying upon the watch about the farm-yard in the evening." Perhaps no other commentator agrees with Horsley in this view. The assassin, murderer and robber seem to be in the writer's mind. Scott applies it to Saul's bloody and deceitful conduct; Clark, to the insidious behaviour of Sanballat and his companions. But it cannot be shown that the Psalm has a special reference to any particular person. The word rendered *villages* is often found. In the singular it generally signifies an enclosure or *court* as of the temple, or tabernacle, of a prison, or of a king's house. In the plural it is rendered *courts* in Ps. lxv. 4; lxxxiv. 2, 10. It is also rendered *towns,* and in many cases *villages.* In our version it is never rendered *palace* or *palaces.* Yet upon the supposition that it may be so translated is based the remark of Gill that "the allusion is not to mean thieves and robbers, but to persons of note and figure. Hence the Septuagint, the Vulgate, Arabic and Ethiopic versions render it, *he sitteth in lurking-places with the rich;* and may be fitly applied to the pope and his cardinals." But there is no proof that this Psalm is prophetic of events under the gospel further than that what wicked persecutors are in one age they will in like circumstances be in all ages. All the enemies of God's people, when unrestrained, display the worst tempers. If intrigue, deceit, oppression, iniquity, blood-thirstiness and violence could have exterminated the church of God, there would not have been left of it a vestige. The word rendered *poor* in the last clause is found in this Psalm, vv. 8, 10, 14, and nowhere else. The rendering in our version is uniform. In many other places *poor* is equivalent to *humble;* here, to *afflicted.* Alexander uses the word *sufferer.* Calvin reads the last clause, His eyes will take their aim, etc., and adds that *their eyes are bent or leering,* by a similitude borrowed from the practice of dart-shooters, who take aim with leering, or half-shut eyes, etc. Mant uses the phrase *peering eyes,* and assigns the same reason as given

by Calvin above. But the simile drawn from the felons of those ancient times did not cover the whole ground. Therefore it is said,

9. *He lieth in wait secretly, as a lion in his den: he lieth in wait to catch the poor: he doth catch the poor, when he draweth him into his net.* For *den* Gesenius and Horsley read *lair*. In Jer. xxv. 38, it is *covert*. The word twice rendered *poor* in this verse is not the same found in v. 8, but that found in vv. 2, 12 in the latter case rendered *humble*. It is also rendered *humble* in Ps. ix. 12 and *poor* in Ps. ix. 18. In this verse the comparison is changed from that of an assassin and murderer to that of a lion and then again to that of a hunter. Calvin and Alexander also very properly retain the futures in this verse, and for the reason given under the last. Violence, cunning and cruelty are the ideas here involved. There has never been an honest, candid, kind, gentle, tender-hearted persecutor of God's servants. *Net*, the same as in Ps. ix. 15.

10. *He croucheth,* and *humbleth himself, that the poor may fall by his strong ones.* There is much diversity in the rendering of this clause. The Septuagint, Ethiopic, Arabic and Vulgate: He will crouch and fall when he shall have power over (or overcome) the poor; Syriac: He shall lie low and fall, and in his bones *are* or *shall be* grief and pangs; Ainsworth: He [the lion] falleth with his strong paws on the troop of poor; Brent: He smites, he humbles, and violently casts down the poor; Edwards: The feeble are borne down, and fall by his superior strength; Calvin: He will crouch low, and cast himself down, and then shall an army of the afflicted fall by his strengths, or by his strong members; Fry: He croucheth, he stoopeth, and falleth down. The wretched are in his snares; church of England: He falleth down and humbleth himself, that the congregation of the poor may fall into the hands of his captains; Amesius: He lessens himself, he bends himself, he falls down flat in all his limbs as if they had no strength; Jebb: And the destitute fall by his strong ones; Hengstenberg: Crushed, he [the poor man] sinks down; and the poor falls through his strong ones; Alexander: And bruised he will sink; and by his strong ones fall the sufferers. The margin for *croucheth* reads *breaketh himself*. The following explanations are offered. The word rendered *poor* is here plural. It is a long word and some think it is composed of two words, the first of which means company, army, congregation, troop. Scholars of former times held this view more than those who have written in the present century. The teaching is precisely the same whether we say *the afflicted generally,* or *the company of the afflicted.* The word *strong* is also a plural adjective, and has no noun following it. Some think the figure of a lion is not kept up here, but suppose the wicked is spoken of as a persecutor in power and so they add *ones,* meaning *men* and *captains.* Others suppose he is here spoken of as a hunter and so they read *snares,* meaning *strong* snares. This gives us precisely the same idea of the enemy, on the whole, as if we suppose with many that the figure of a lion is to be preserved in the whole verse. In that case we read *strong parts, limbs, bones, jaws, paws, members, teeth.* The Assembly's Annotations gives *teeth* or *paws.* This explanation is probably to be preferred. It is harmonious throughout; it is drawn from the context; it is consistent with the habits of the lion; it suits the meaning of the words. Buffon says, "When the lion leaps upon his prey he gives a spring of ten or fifteen feet, falls on it, seizes it with his fore paws, tears it with his claws, and afterwards devours it with his teeth." Cumming gives quite the same account of the habits of this animal. Indeed they are notorious. If this view is correct then the sense is that the wicked imitates the lion in crouching, lying low, not showing himself, seeming even careless about his prey, but at the moment when without trouble he has his victims in his power, he pounces upon the harmless and defenceless, and they are overcome at once. If any more satisfac-

tory exposition has been furnished let it be adopted. The simile of a lion is here dropped, and the wicked is next spoken of as an infidel or atheist, as in vv. 2–7.

11. *He hath said in his heart, God hath forgotten : he hideth his face ; he will never see it.* For the import of the first clause see comment on v. 6. Although all the Hebrew verbs here are in the preterite, yet our translation probably gives the sense of the whole by employing the past, present and future. See Introduction, § 6. The word rendered *never* would literally be *not forever, not to eternity.* The sense is that the wicked denies that God has a providence over the world, that he remembers, sees, or has his face turned towards human affairs, or holds men accountable to him. They deny his moral government. That the wicked rise to this awful height of presumption is elsewhere declared, Isa. xxix. 15. God's delay to punish sinners is not pardon of their sins ; it is not even connivance, though they often think it is. Such dreadful atheism makes the case urgent, and so David says :

12. *Arise,* O LORD ; *i. e.,* arise to thy throne of judgment. See Ps. ix. 19. Try and decide this cause. *O God, lift up thine hand.* For the name here given to God, see Ps. v. 4. He is invoked not only to give a decision, but also to execute it. The hand is lifted up for various purposes. Here it seems to be equivalent to *address thyself to this matter. Forget not the humble.* The reference is clearly to v. 11. The same verb is used in both places. For remarks on *humble* see Ps. ix. 12. The import of the prayer is, Show all men that these thy enemies are mistaken in saying that thou hast forgotten the cause between thy people and their persecutors.

13. *Wherefore doth the wicked contemn God? he hath said in his heart, Thou wilt not require* it. The phrase *in his heart* is here found for the third time in this Psalm. See above on v. 6. For *contemn* many read *despise.* But in Hebrew it is the past tense, *hath despised, hath contemned ; i. e.,* why has the wicked been allowed so long to despise or contemn God? The word here rendered *doth contemn* is in v. 3 *abhorred.* The church of England reads, Wherefore should the wicked blaspheme God, while he doth say in his heart, Tush, thou God carest not for it? This verb is rendered by *provoke, abhor, blaspheme, contemn, despise.* Besides the two places in this Psalm, see Ps. cvii. 11 ; Pr. i. 30 ; Nu. xvi. 30 ; Ps. lxxiv. 18. Why should the wicked do either or all of these things? He who does one of them will do them all. The Scripture word *blaspheme* does not necessarily imply scornful railing, but only evil speaking of any description. The oldest translations terminate the interrogation with the first clause, but Amesius, Edwards, Jebb, Fry, Hengstenberg and Alexander continue it to the end of the verse. The word here rendered *require* is found also in Ps. ix. 10, 12, and in vv. 4, 15 of this Psalm. See comment on Ps. ix. 12. Edwards' translation gives the sense, Why should the wicked despise God? Why should he say in his heart, Thou wilt make no inquisition?

14. *Thou hast seen* it; *for thou beholdest mischief and spite to requite* it *with thy hand.* That is, Thou, who seest all things, hast seen all this wrong of which I complain; although the wicked say the contrary, v. 11. Nor art thou indifferent to mischief and spite. Edwards has *mischief* and *injustice;* church of England, *ungodliness* and *wrong;* Calvin, *mischief* and *vexation;* Hengstenberg, *suffering* and *anger;* Alexander, *trouble* and *persecution;* Doway, *labor* and *sorrow.* The word rendered *mischief* is the same that is so rendered in Ps. vii. 14, 16; in Ps. xxv. 18, *pain;* in Ps. lv. 10, *sorrow;* in Ps. lxxiii. 5, *trouble;* in Ps. xc. 10, *labor;* in Prov. xxxi. 7, *misery.* The word rendered *spite* is in Ps. vi. 7, rendered *grief;* in Ps. lxxxv. 4, *anger;* in Prov. xii. 16, *wrath;* in Eccle. vii. 3, *sorrow;* in 1 Kings xxi. 22, *provocation.* God sees and marks all these things whether we are the objects or the subjects of them. In particular he never fails to mark for retribution all the unwept and unforsaken cruelties and wrongs manifested to his people. The Chaldee reads, It is known (or clear) unto thee, that thou wilt send upon the wicked

sorrow and wrath; thou lookest to render a good reward to the righteous. The word rendered *requite* here is in Ps. i. 3, *bring forth;* in Ps. ii. 8, *give;* in Ps. iv. 7, *put;* in Ps. viii. 1, *set.* Elsewhere it means to *deliver,* to *grant,* etc. To *give* what is due is the sense here. Thus confidence in God's moral character is maintained. And so *the poor committeth himself unto thee; thou art the helper of the fatherless.* The word *poor* is the same as in vv. 8, 10, found in this Psalm only. The word rendered *fatherless* is never in our version translated otherwise, yet it often has the sense of friendless, forlorn, comfortless. So we have a variety of versions of these clauses all good, though some are excellent. The Septuagint and Vulgate: The poor is left to thee, and to the orphan thou wilt be a helper; Arabic: In thee the poor is comforted; thou art the help of the orphan; Syriac: To thee the poor commits himself, and thou art the helper of the orphan; Chaldee: In thee the poor shall hope; thou wilt sustain the orphan; Calvin: Upon thee shall the poor leave [himself and his concerns]; thou shalt be a helper to the fatherless; church of England: The poor committeth himself unto thee; for thou art the helper of the friendless; Edwards: The feeble leaveth himself to thee; for thou art the helper of the friendless; Amesius: He, who is wanting in strength, commits himself to thy faithfulness, and thou art the helper of the orphan boy; Venema: To thee each sorrowful one leaves it, thou hast been the helper of the fatherless; Brent: On thee the poor is cast; to the orphan thou art a helper; Jebb: To thee the destitute committeth himself: The fatherless, *it is* Thou *who* art indeed his helper; Fry: Upon thee the wretched casteth himself: thou hast been the helper of the destitute; Hengstenberg: The poor surrenders to thee. The orphan, thou art the helper; Alexander: Upon thee the sufferer will leave [his burden]. An orphan thou hast been helping. Not one of these renderings teaches error. We have here a delightful illustration of the harmony of God's people in their views of practical truth, and of the rich and varied fulness of the promises of God.

15. *Break thou the arm of the wicked and the evil* man: *seek out his wickedness* till *thou find none.* To *break the arm* is utterly to destroy the power. Our version agrees with the ancient versions. For *evil* Edwards reads *flagitious;* church of England, *malicious;* Alexander, *bad.* Fry reads this clause, The arm of the wicked is broken; thus making the pious sufferer rejoice in a deliverance fully secured by relief already experienced, or by faith distinctly foreseen. The word *man* is supplied in our version. The word rendered *evil* may be either an adjective or a noun. As the latter it is found in Ps. v. 4; vii. 4, 9; x. 6. Commonly in the Psalms it points to a person. This has led some to terminate the first clause with the word *wicked.* Hengstenberg reads the last clause—*and the evil, seek out his wickedness, find them not.* The sense he gathers is, Thou mayest seek his wickedness, and not find it. That is, it will be utterly overthrown and, as it were, annihilated; Houbigant: Seek out for his iniquity, that it may not prevail; Fry: Thou mayest search for the wicked, thou canst not find him; Dimock: Thou shalt seek the wicked, but shalt not find him. But the word rendered *seek* is the same as is found in Ps. ix. 10, 12; x. 4, 13. Some think it has the same meaning here as in v. 13, *require;* Houbigant has it *require his iniquity.* And so they understand the Psalmist as asking God so to subvert and bring to naught this wickedness that not a trace of it shall be left even where it seemed most rampant. This view is confirmed by the next verse. Clarke paraphrases it, Continue to judge and punish transgressors, till not one is to be found. For the form of imprecation here used, see Introduction, § 6.

16. *The* Lord *is King for ever and ever.* The Septuagint, Ethiopic, Arabic and Vulgate read this clause in the future; The Lord shall be king, or shall reign forever. The verb is here supplied. See comment on Psalm ix. 5. Scott says, The original words rendered *for ever and ever* appear "always strictly to denote eternity." All comfort would at once fail God's people, if there was a shadow of doubt thrown over

the stability and eternity of the divine government. In proof of the truth of the two preceding clauses a great and notorious fact is called up: *The heathen are perished out of his land;* Fry reads, *from off his earth, i. e.,* God's earth, God's land; either the whole earth, or that part of it, which they once inhabited. The word is the same so often rendered *earth* in the early part of Genesis. It is also rendered *land, country, ground.* Hitherto in the Psalms it has been rendered *earth.* Ps. ii. 2, 8, 10; viii. 1, 9. The *heathen* here are called by the same Hebrew name as in Ps. ii. 1, 8; ix. 5, 15, 17, 19, 20.

17. LORD, *thou hast heard the desire of the humble.* It is often said God hears the prayers and cries of his people. In Ps. v. 1, he is asked to hear a *meditation.* Here it is said he has heard a *desire.* Right desires are in God's esteem good prayers. In v. 3, the wicked is said to boast of his heart's desire; but the righteous was too humble to boast; he longed; he had his *desire;* God heard it—the same word is used in both verses. The *humble* are the *needy,* the *meek,* the *afflicted,* the *poor.* The same word as in Ps. ix. 12, 18; x. 12, is rendered *humble* and *poor.* This clause may teach that God has been in the habit of hearing the desire of the meek, or that he has done so in this particular case. The latter is probably what is here intended. If so, then the sense may be that God has done so, either in the anticipations of a strong faith, or in the terrible overthrow already visited on the enemy. There was good cause for the favorable regard shown to the wishes of the righteous. *Thou wilt prepare their heart, i. e.* God by his Holy Spirit has always given his people right dispositions before him, and he always will do it. The mercy here spoken of is never to be discontinued, Rom. viii. 26. Of course God will honor and answer the desires put into the hearts of his people by the Comforter. This is the more obvious sense of the passage, and is adopted by Henry, Scott, and others. Clarke says, "See the economy of the grace of God; 1. God *prepares* the *heart;* 2. *suggests the prayer;* 3. *Hears* what is prayed; 4. *Answers* the petition. He who has got a cry in his heart after God, may rest assured that that cry proceeded from a Divine preparation, and that an answer will soon arrive. No man ever had a cry in his heart after salvation but from God. He, who continues to cry, shall infallibly be heard." The most common rendering of this and some other forms of the verb of this clause is to *prepare* or *make ready.* See Gen. xliii. 25; 1 Chron. xv. 1; Ps lxv. 9; Pr. xxx. 25. Yet good scholars have suggested other renderings. Some instead of *prepare* read *direct.* This is much the same as *prepare.* If God directs our hearts, that is the very preparation we need in prayer and in all duties. This rendering of the word is elsewhere sometimes found in our version. Fry, reads *strengthenest,* but in none of its forms is the verb ever so translated in our English Bible. Boothroyd, Horsley and Jebb, prefer *establish.* This is frequently the meaning of the word, and it is so rendered by our translators. Ps. lxxxix. 2, 4; 2 Chron. xvii. 5. With this substantially agrees the rendering of Hengstenberg, Make firm; and of Alexander, Settle (or confirm.) Yet how does God establish the hearts of his people but by giving them grace, which leads them to cry mightily to him for help, and then granting them strength? Perhaps most will prefer our common version. For, *Thou wilt cause thine ear to hear.* Calvin: "The meaning of this clause is, that it is not in vain that God directs the hearts of his people, and leads them in obedience to his command, to look to Himself, and to call upon him in hope and patience,— it is not in vain, because his ears are never shut against their groanings. Thus the mutual harmony between two religious exercises is here commended. God does not suffer the faith of his servants to fail, nor does he suffer them to desist from praying; but he keeps them near him by faith and prayer, until it actually appears that their hope has been neither vain nor ineffectual."

18. This verse is connected with the preceding. God will hear cries and grant desires offered to him, *to judge the fatherless and the oppressed.* The *fatherless,* the same word *and* of the same import as in v. 14. *Oppressed,* the same as in Ps. ix. 9, found four times, thrice rendered *oppressed,* once in Pr. xxvi. 28, *afflicted.* The word *judge* is the same as in previous Psalms. The meaning is that God will decide in favor of the defenceless and the wronged. And he will do this, *that the man of the earth may no more oppress.* There is benevolence in all God does. His government is amiable. So far as it is respected and honored, his creatures are happy. Indeed the only perfectly joyful society in the universe is one, where there is never an infraction of any law of God. But some men will not learn by words. Examples must be put before them. Such is "the man of the earth," a phrase found no where else, but like *men of the world,* found in Ps. xvii. 14, although in the Hebrew the two phrases have not a word in common. The man of the earth is earthy, terrestrial, in his aims, hopes and desires. The men of the world have their portion in this life. They may become persecutors and oppressors at any moment. Compare these verses. For *oppress* some read *out-brave, withstand, terrify.* Mudge gives this paraphrase: "*This worthless mortal,* how much soever *a man of earth,* cherished with all its favors, and supported with all its strength, *shall no longer be able to terrify the people of Jehovah, the God of heaven.*"

Doctrinal and Practical Remarks.

1. It is no new thing for God to seem for a while to leave his people to the power of their enemies, v. 1. This ought not to cast them down. God's servants of former days endured all this, and yet came off conquerors.

2. There is not in all the militant church of Christ a case of wrong suffered, or of persecution endured so bad as to render it doubtful whether we should at once bring it before God, v. 1. "Good people would be undone, if they had not a God to go to, a God to trust in, and a future bliss to hope for." Cast all your care on him, for he careth for you. It is God's office, work and personal delight to help the feeble and defend the injured.

3. However sore may be the trials of his saints, God never finally, nor totally forsakes them. True, as Henry says, "God's withdrawings are very grievous to his people at any time, but especially in times of trouble." But God's time of coming to the rescue is often the nearest, when we think it furthest off. "Man's extremity is God's opportunity." Amesius draws this as the first lesson from this Psalm, that "in their straits pious men chiefly complain of the absence of God; because they have found that in all that concerns them, God and his providence are chiefly to be regarded, because the absence of God is cause of the greatest consternation to all creatures, and because the presence of God brings adequate consolation against all evils."

4. The abuse of God's patience and mercy by each successive generation of his enemies does not seem to vary in the least particular. The cavils, and scoffs, and arts of the wicked, when they dare indulge them, have a tedious uniformity. The language of the wicked found in this Psalm has been repeated in every succeeding age. See other Psalms, the prophets, the evangelists, the last chapter of second Peter, and church history generally.

5. Persecution is no new thing, v. 2. When God's people have much of the Spirit of Christ, and when Christ's enemies have the power, the blood of the martyrs will flow. But blessed be God, it is better to suffer wrong than to do wrong. The temper of the wicked cares not for righteousness if they can have their way. Their pride will carry them on. Henry: "Tyranny, both in State and Church, owes its original

to pride;" Horne: "Inconceivable is that malignant fury, with which a conceited infidel persecutes an humble believer, though that believer hath no otherwise offended him than by being such." Were there any mercy in the hearts of persecutors, the harmlessness and the helplessness of God's people would awaken their compassions. But they are relentless. Truly it is a great mercy to be kept out of the power of the wicked. No wonder God is aroused by the violence done to his saints.

6. Nor is it any new thing for the wicked to glory in their shame, v. 3. They have long been foaming it out.

7. But let men beware how they attempt to sanction their wickedness by pleading that God gives them power, v. 3; Isa. x. 12–15.

8. One of the most dangerous things man can do is to bless wicked men, to put bitter for sweet and light for darkness, v. 3. He, whose commendations are for the vilest, is utterly ruined.

9. Will men ever learn the evil of covetousness? It is the root of all evil. It is condemned in the moral law, in the Psalms, in the prophets, in the gospels, in the epistles, by conscience, by common sense, by the voice of mankind, by many dreadful examples made of men, who were greedy of gain. The covetous man abhorreth the Lord, and the Lord abhorreth him, v. 3. It is no more possible for a man to be saved without hating covetousness, than for him to be saved without hating lying or murder.

10. Pride is a sin of like description, vv. 3, 4. It turns all blessings into curses. It makes men shameless. It is denounced by all, renounced by few. One is proud of his humble origin, another of his noble birth, one of his fine clothing, another of his rough garments, one of his virtues, another of his vices. There is no ascertainable difference in the destructive tendency of the different kinds of pride, Pr. xvi. 18; xxix. 23.

11. One of Amesius' lessons drawn from this Psalm is that "In nothing does the impiety of the proud overleap all bounds more than in this that they are accustomed to praise themselves and those who resemble them in wickedness," v. 3; Deut. xxix. 19, 20, 21.

12. A sufficient cause of the irreligion of all wicked men is found in their bad passions, vv. 3, 4. What crowds of men, like King Saul, have convictions, and sometimes express them with seriousness and tenderness, but are hurried away into sin by their self-will, malice, worldliness, ambition, or jealousy.

13. And how can men be expected to come to a saving knowledge of divine things, when they will not seek to be informed? v. 4. No honest inquirer after truth has ever perished. The personal history of every infidel gives the clue to his skepticism. It is a fact that the history of the world has not yet told us of one calm, praying, unprejudiced rejecter of Gospel doctrine and Gospel mercy.

14. If sin had its way, it would both dethrone and annihilate God, v. 4. As far as it can, it acts and feels and thinks as if he existed not.

15. We should not be surprised at finding the sinner vile, v. 5. Security in sin is an infallible token of impiety, no less than gross outbreakings. All transgressions are the fruit of an unregenerate heart. It ought to confound us, if an evil tree brought forth good fruit.

16. Nor should we be surprised to find the ways of sinners grievous even to themselves, v. 5. The wicked always were and always must be like the troubled sea.

17. Nor should the prosperity of the wicked amaze us, v. 5. They get nothing worth having in eternity. They get all their good things in this life.

18. It is no new thing for sinful men to lack spiritual discernment, v. 5. They are so blinded by sin, so in love with delusion, that, without a supernatural change, they cannot perceive any beauty even in holiness.

19. "If thou seest the perversion of the poor and violent perverting of judgment and justice in a province, marvel not at the matter," v. 5.   It was so in Solomon's day; it has always been so; but God will yet put all right.

20.   Though wicked men do sometimes rise to wondrous heights of power, yet their arrogance commonly rises still higher, v. 5.

21. The incorrigibly wicked could not continue in the secure commission of his sins but for some strange delusions, some remarkable rejection of evidence, some wonderful capacity of false reasoning, v. 6.   A living man may as wisely say, I shall never die, as a prosperous man say, I shall never be in adversity, or as a sinner say, I shall not lose my soul.

22. None will be more surprised than the wicked themselves at the depth and suddenness of their fall.   This is unavoidable, if they remain in unbelief.   An angel from heaven could not open their eyes to see their coming doom, if they have no willingness to know the truth, vv. 6, 7.

23. There is a consanguinity between all sins.   Compare v. 6 with several preceding and succeeding verses.   Pride, cruelty, cunning, boasting, lust, covetousness, false peace, want of docility, practical atheism, spiritual blindness, contempt, cursing, deceit, fraud, mischief and vanity are a frightful sisterhood.

24. The apostle James told us no new thing when he depicted (chap. iii. vv. 2–13) the dreadful evils of a wicked tongue, v. 7.   Death and life are in its power.   There is no greater wickedness than that, which breaks out in words.

25. It is amazing what mean artifices are resorted to by the best of the opposers of God's truth and people, even by people commonly fair in other matters, vv. 7, 8.

26. The fawning, crouching, sycophantic part often played by the cruel and wicked can deceive none but the simple and inexperienced, v. 10.

27. The Scripture account of the folly of sin, is fully sustained by the defences which it sets up.   No maniac ever reasoned more illogically than the unbeliever, vv. 6–11.

28. It is very safe for those, who have a good cause, to petition the infallible judge to proceed at once to decide the controversy between them and their enemies, v. 12. Calvin: "This verse contains the useful doctrine, that the more the ungodly harden themselves, through their slothful ignorance, and endeavor to persuade themselves that God takes no concern about men and their affairs, and will not punish the wickedness which they commit, the more should we endeavor to be persuaded of the contrary; yea, rather their ungodliness ought to incite us vigorously to repel the doubts, which they not only admit, but studiously frame for themselves."

29. When men see the lengths to which sin leads the ungodly, v. 13, is it unreasonable to suppose that every sinner would be appalled and scream out in horror, if at the beginning of any course of folly the end should be clearly seen by him?

30. The divine omniscience is as comforting to saints as it is terrible to sinners, v. 14.

31. The divine vengeance, which seems so slow to do its work, will not tarry.   Its approach is more swift than is thought by many.   It lingereth not; it slumbereth not, v. 14.

32. When we consider what a friend the poor and the orphan have in God, it is not wonderful that they rise from the dunghill and sit among princes.   Their very hardships are a good school for them.   Their very helplessness makes them fit objects of divine compassion.   Let all such remember God's readiness to help them, v. 14. Divine power can crush any number of foes to save its friends.

33. The destruction of the wicked will be utter, v. 15.   God will leave them neither root nor branch.

34. If we did not read history like atheists, we must learn some awful and salutary

lessons, v. 16. Where are all the ancient empires and emperors? Where are the nations that forgot God? Dickson: "Earthly kings cannot live still to help their friends, followers, or flatterers, or to persecute and molest God's church: but Christ is the Lord and King forever and ever to defend his people, and punish his foes."

35. If we are sure we have good desires, we should be encouraged to hope for their fulfilment, v. 17.

36. It is as really a mercy as it is a revealed truth that we are dependent on God for everything, even for one right thought or feeling. If he did not prepare our hearts, they would never be fit for any part of his service, v. 17.

37. It is not possible that scriptural prayer should not be heard and answered, v. 17. It must be so because God is God.

38. It is a great mercy that God judges in the earth, v. 18. The Lord reigneth, let the earth rejoice.

39. In all ages wickedness is much the same. The most learned men are not agreed whether this Psalm best suits Saul and his courtiers, Antiochus Epiphanes, Belshazzar, Sanballat and his coadjutors, or the Pope and his myrmidons. The fact is that the temper and arts of the haters of God's church are so much alike in disposition, that as they have opportunity, they act very much alike.

40. The Assembly's Annotations says, "This whole Psalm may serve for an ample confutation of the error of those, who make the worldly success of great undertakers an argument of the goodness of their cause; as also for the consolation and confirmation of those, who suffer though it be much and long."

41. It is unquestionably wise to serve God. The last account will bring all right. Here there is darkness about some things. But saints and sinners will in the last day have the same judgment respecting the folly of sin and the wisdom of piety.

42. Cobbin: "Our ground of glorying in God is that he is just. He tries the righteous as gold is tried in the furnace, but he punishes the wicked. The one is corrected, the other is destroyed. Both may suffer; but the one for his present and eternal good, the other as the prelude to everlasting ruin." "Cecil was pacing to and fro in the Botanic Garden at Oxford, when he observed a fine specimen of the pomegranate almost cut through the stem. On asking the gardener the reason, he got an answer which explained the wounds of his own bleeding spirit. 'Sir, this tree used to shoot so strong, that it bore nothing but leaves. I was, therefore, obliged to cut it in this manner, and when it was almost cut through, then it began to bear plenty of fruit.' Ye suffering members of Christ, be thankful for every sorrow which weakens a lust or strengthens a grace. Though it should be a cut to the heart, be thankful for every sin and idol shorn away. Be thankful for whatever makes your conscience more tender, your thoughts more spiritual, and your character more consistent. Be thankful that it was the pruning-knife and not the weeding-hook which you felt: for if you suffer in Christ, you suffer with him; and if with him you suffer, with him you shall also reign."

43. What an awful lesson this Psalm teaches to tyrants, tyrant monarchs, tyrant judges, tyrant executive officers, tyrant landlords, tyrant husbands, tyrant masters, tyrant creditors, tyrant teachers. O how the down-trodden of earth will yet rise up, and clank their chains, and show their scars, and call to mind their cries for mercy when all were in vain.

44. To the weary, tempted, persecuted follower of Christ, how sweet the rest of heaven will be. Scott: "From heaven alone will all sin and temptation be excluded: no Canaanite shall find entrance there; no lust shall then remain in the heart of any inhabitant; no imperfection will be known; but all shall be complete in love, purity, and joy."

PSALM XI.

To the chief Musician, *A Psalm* of David.

1 IN the LORD put I my trust: how say ye to my soul, Flee *as* a bird to your mountain?

2 For, lo, the wicked bend *their* bow, they make ready their arrow upon the string, that they may privily shoot at the upright in heart.

3 If the foundations be destroyed, what can the righteous do?

4 The LORD *is* in his holy temple, the LORD'S throne *is* in heaven: his eyes behold, his eyelids try the children of men.

5 The LORD trieth the righteous: but the wicked and him that loveth violence his soul hateth.

6 Upon the wicked he shall rain snares, fire and brimstone, and a horrible tempest: *this shall be* the portion of their cup.

7 For the righteous LORD loveth righteousness; his countenance doth behold the upright.

FOR remarks on the caption, see on Psalm iv. The words *A Psalm* are not found in the Hebrew, but are properly supplied in the Septuagint, and other versions ancient and modern, including the English. There is no good reason for doubting that David was the author of this ode.

Commentators have frequently expressed the opinion that David here describes some part of his troubled life during the reign of Saul. Theodoret thus held. This view is favored by Calvin, Moller, Fabritius, Patrick, Edwards, Henry, Gill, Dodd, Scott and Morison. Hengstenberg thinks quite differently: "How little color the Psalm affords for a personal construction is evident from this, that among those, who take that view, it is a subject of perpetual controversy, whether it refers to the times of Saul or of Absalom." To this it may be replied that such controversy does not disprove its reference to either time, or even to both, so far as they were alike. But nothing is gained by fixing on a given time or event to suit a Psalm, if it has as much fitness to many other conditions of its author, or of the just man, whom he personifies. It is entirely probable that much of the language is suggested by occurrences in the eventful life of David. Rosenmuller: "The occasion of this Psalm is wholly uncertain, but we may reckon it, with *De Wette,* among those, which, in the name of the people, implore divine aid against barbarous enemies." Yet this view is not sustained by the contents. Brent's first remark is, "This Psalm is not a prayer, but a confession of faith, against calumniators;" Amesius; "The scope of David in this Psalm is openly to declare that consolation, which he possessed, and which he studied more and more to enjoy, in opposition to all those temptations, which assailed him on every side." Hengstenberg quotes with approbation Claus, saying, "Confidence in the Lord and his protection, even against the *huge* force of the wicked, is the one subject of this Psalm." Throughout the Psalm the original for LORD is *Jehovah.* See on Ps. i. 2. Some have thought that this Psalm was put next the *tenth* on account of a general similarity of contents, and especially of a resemblance between Ps. x. 8; Ps. xi. 2. But no such reason seems to have governed in making the arrangement, else many other changes would have been made, differing from the present order.

1. *In the Lord put I my trust; how say ye to my soul, Flee as a bird to your mountain?*

The first verb in this verse is the same as is found in Ps. ii. 12; v. 11; vii. 1. Our version always gives it *trust,* or *put trust in,* except in Ps. lvii. 1, where it is rendered *make my refuge,* and in Pr. xiv. 32, where we read, *hath hope.* Many Latin versions read *confide in.* Trust in God is a vital matter in religion. It is at the foundation of all rational piety. The Chaldee has: In the word of the Lord do I hope; Ains worth: In Jehovah do I hope for safety. Commentators are not agreed as to the persons addressed by the pronoun *ye*. Luther says that they are "erroneous and fanatical spirits, who draw away men . . . characters having the peculiar mark of hypocrites,—that they arrogantly, proudly, and with high looks despise and deride the truly godly;" Slade supposes that "David's friends recommended him to fly;" Patrick thinks "David's friends" were here his tempters; Morison calls them "his short-sighted and misjudging friends;" Alexander speaks of them as "timid and desponding friends rather than taunting and exulting enemies;" Scott supposes "timid friends" to be addressed; Gill holds the same view; so also does Clarke; but Hengstenberg regards the tempters here as "godless enemies;" Amesius also speaks of the language as that of "adversaries." If they were friends, they were very much like Job's wife. Cowardice is always dangerous. Nothing is so rash. It is commonly criminal, proceeding from unbelief. Any advice to desert a post of duty is unwise and wicked. On the words *to my soul*, see comment on the same expression in the Hebrew in Ps. iii. 2. What they said distressed him, wounded his feelings. The advice given him was, *Flee as a bird to your mountain*. The word rendered *bird* is commonly so rendered, but in Ps. viii. 8; cxlviii. 10, and some other cases, it is rendered *fowl;* and in Ps. lxxxiv. 3; cii. 7 it is rendered *sparrow*. Morison: "The words which denote the names of most animals in the Hebrew admit of application to the individual or the species." Some have thought this clause proverbial, but if so, the evidence seems not to have been afforded. It is clear that Pr. xxvii. 8, relied on by some, does not prove it. There is some diversity in the rendering also. Hammond: "The Hebrew reads, 'To your mountain, a sparrow;' all the ancient interpreters, uniformly, 'to your mountain as a sparrow;' and so possibly the reading anciently was. However, if it be, 'fly, sparrow, to your mountain,' the sense will be the same;" Horsley: Flee, sparrows, to your hill; Alexander: Flee (to) your mountain (as) a bird. But none of these variations materially alter the sense. We get the same idea whether we read *bird* or *sparrow*, and whether we suppose David is called a bird and bid to flee, or whether he is told to flee as a bird. In each case we have the same general idea. But instead of reading, Flee *to* your mountain, some would read *from* your mountain, meaning Zion, or the hill country of Judea, or some particular hiding-place. The first who suggested this rendering were certain Jewish expositors. Gill names Kimchi and Ben Melech, and Morison speaks of "many of the Jewish writers" as taking this view; and adds, "It must be admitted that the word [rendered *flee*] does signify more the act of passing *from* than that of fleeing *to*." This remark is hardly borne out by the use of the word. But some have proposed to read *in* or *through* the mountain. If the word rendered *flee* is to determine the preposition following, this would be as good as either of the others, if not better. The participle is in Gen. iv. 12, 14 rendered *vagabond*. If they said to him, Go, wander in the mountain, having no certain place of resort, then we have the whole sense contended for by Calvin, though he reads *into*, and not *in* or *through*. He says that "men advised David to leave his country, and retire into some place of exile, where he might be concealed, inasmuch as there remained for him no hope of life, unless he should relinquish the kingdom, which had been promised to him." Calvin: "I do not, however, think that any particular mountain is pointed out, but that David was sent away to the desert rocks, wherever chance might lead him." *To, into, in,* or *through*, gives a better sense than *from*. But the pronoun *your* and the verb *flee* are in Hebrew plural. So this counsel given is not merely to David, but to all his associates, all, who made common cause with him. The church of England version is therefore not good: How say ye to my soul that she should flee as a bird unto the hill? Instead of *as a bird*, Brent reads *swiftly*. Our translators never so render the word. No doubt swiftness is implied in the flight, so also are danger, fearfulness and helplessness.

2. *For, lo, the wicked bend* their *bow, they make ready their arrow upon the string, that they may privily shoot at the upright in heart.* The translations of this verse vary. Edwards: For behold the wicked bend the bow, they fix their arrows upon the string to shoot in the dark at the upright in heart; Fry: For, lo! the wicked bend their bow; they have fixed their arrow upon the string; to shoot secretly at the upright in heart; Jebb: For behold, the ungodly bend the bow; they make ready their arrow upon the string, to shoot at them in darkness, *even* at the upright in heart; Calvin: Surely, behold! the ungodly shall bend their bow, they have fixed their arrows upon the string, to shoot secretly at the upright in heart; church of England: For lo, the ungodly bend their bow, and make ready their arrows within the quiver, that they may privily shoot at them which are true of heart; Hengstenberg: For, lo! the wicked bend the bow, place their arrow upon the string, to shoot in the dark at the upright. The word rendered *string* is in our version never translated *quiver*, and ought in no case to be. For *quiver* two other and very different words are found in the Hebrew. Gen. xxvii. 3; Ps. cxxvii. 5. The bending of the bow here is to be explained as in Ps. vii. 12. The word rendered *arrow* is in the singular. The tenses of the verbs in our version will be found as good as in any other translation. See Introduction, § 6. But are the words of this verse spoken by those who advised David to flee, or by David himself? The former opinion is embraced by Boothroyd, Edwards, Gill, Horne, Slade, Scott, Clarke, Morison, Hengstenberg and Alexander. But Calvin thinks that David "here continues his account of the trying circumstances in which he was placed. His design is not only to place before our view the dangers with which he was surrounded, but to show us that he was even exposed to death itself. He therefore says, that wherever he might hide himself, it was impossible for him to escape the hands of his enemies." This view is probably to be preferred. If so, then in the first verse David tells us what others said, and in this informs us of the actual state of things. Everywhere the enemies of David and his associates were surrounded by foes already armed and prepared in the most stealthy manner to shoot at the *upright in heart*, the men of rectitude. Vitringa: "It is implied in the idea of rectitude, that there is some canon, rule, or common measure, according to which judgment may be given in regard to all spiritual operations. What is conformed to this standard is morally straight, as that is also called in architecture, which is done according to the line or plummet." God's people, so far as they are sanctified, are not crooked, but *straight, straightforward, upright*. The same word is found in Ps. vii. 10, and in the 7th verse of this Psalm.

3. *If the foundations be destroyed, what can the righteous do?* There is great diversity in the renderings of this verse. Septuagint: They have destroyed the things which thou hast prepared: but what has the righteous done? Chaldee: For if the foundations be destroyed, why does the righteous work good? Arabic: They have destroyed that which thou hast prepared: but what has the innocent done? Boothroyd: When the foundations of justice are subverted, what can even a righteous man do? Calvin: Truly, the foundations are destroyed: what hath the righteous One done? Edwards: When the foundations are pulled up, what has the righteous man to do? church of England: For the foundations will be cast down; and what hath the righteous done? Amesius: When the foundations themselves are destroyed, what shall the just man do? Jebb: For the foundations will be cast down: the righteous, what can he do? Fry: For the foundations are overthrown: what has the Just One done? Hengstenberg: For the foundations are destroyed: the righteous, what does he do? Alexander: For the pillars (or foundations) will be (are about to be) destroyed;

what has the righteous done, *i. e.*, accomplished? The word rendered *foundations* is also in Isa. xix. 10, where it is translated *purposes* in the text, but in the margin *foundations*. By *foundations* Jerome understands *laws*. But this is not defining the word, but interpreting it. Some Jewish writers suppose the reference to be to the counsels, plots and snares of wicked men, which are broken and overthrown by the Lord, and not by men, for what can the righteous do in a matter of so cunning and extensive devices? Some apply it to the destruction of the priests of Nob. 1 Sam. xxii. The other opinions are that the word should be rendered *pillars* or *foundations*. Figuratively *pillars* may signify *princes* or *nobles*. But the more common impression is that David is speaking of the foundations *of justice* as Boothroyd and others. Alexander: "The pillars or foundations are those of social order or society itself;" Clarke: "They have utterly destroyed the foundations of truth and equity;" Venema: "The foundations are destroyed in communities remarkably corrupt, in which the laws of right and equity are wantonly trodden under foot." Hengstenberg regards the clause as descriptive of a general state of moral dissolution, which deprived the righteous of any footing, subverting the basis of society, which is the supremacy of justice and righteousness." This is pretty certainly the correct view. The verb *be destroyed* is in Hebrew *future*. The idea is that this dreadful disorder now exists and is likely to continue. If so, *what can the righteous do?* Some put this in the past tense, literally rendering the Hebrew, What has the righteous done? They understand the question to be in substance, What has the righteous effected to hinder this dreadful state of things? But the obvious sense gathered from our version is very good, *i. e.*, This state of things continuing, what can a righteous man accomplish? The grammar will admit of this rendering. There is no evidence that for *righteous man* we should read Just One, meaning Messias. Calvin understands the question, What hath the righteous done? as equivalent to, what evil hath he done? But this is pretty certainly a misapprehension of the sense. The Psalmist thus distressed looks around for relief. Nor is his faith without an object.

4. *The* LORD *is in his holy temple.* This doubtless should read, *The* LORD *is in the palace of his holiness.* The word here rendered *temple* is repeatedly rendered *palace*, plural *palaces.* 2 Kings xx. 18; Ps. xlv. 8, 15; cxliv. 12; Pr. xxx. 28; Is. xiii. 22, and many other places. It is true that the name of *temple* is given to the tabernacle before David was born, 1 Sam. i. 9; iii. 3, so that no argument can be drawn from that source. But the connection shows that David is here speaking of God as a Judge and King, governed by righteousness, sitting in heaven, not presenting himself in the Shechinah of the tabernacle. See Comment on Ps. v. 7. Calvin renders this clause, Jehovah is in the palace of his holiness; Alexander: Jehovah (is) in his palace (or temple) of holiness; Fry: Jehovah is in his holy habitation; Venema and Patrick also use *palace*. That David here refers to heaven, the true sanctuary of which the temple was but a figure, is evident from the next clause, where he says expressly, *The* LORD's *throne is in heaven; q. d.*, On earth at present all is confusion, one can obtain no justice or equity, but I do not trust in man, but in him whose kingdom ruleth over all, ever dealing in righteousness, ever lifted up above the power of malice, and never relinquishing his rights as Governor and Judge of all. Calvin: "There is in these words an implied contrast between heaven and earth; for if David's attention had been fixed on the state of things in this world, as they appeared to the eye of sense and reason, he would have seen no prospect of deliverance from his present perilous circumstances. But this was not David's exercise; on the contrary, when in the world all justice lies trodden under foot, and faithfulness has perished, he reflects that God sits in heaven perfect and unchanged, from whom it became him to look for the restoration of order from this state of miserable confusion.

He does not simply say that God dwells in heaven; but that he reigns there, as it were, in a royal palace, and has his throne of judgment there." Such is David's confidence in the existence and efficiency of the providence of Jehovah that he immediately adds: *His eyes behold, his eyelids try the children of men.* God is an earnest spectator of all that passes even in states of the wildest confusion. His book of remembrance is continually recording all that occurs whether good or bad. There is no authority for adding, as the Septuagint and Fry, after *behold* the words "the poor one," or "the afflicted one." The verb rendered *behold* is found also in v. 7. There is no better translation of it than that of our version. The verb rendered *try* is found also in v. 5. It is often rendered by the verb *prove*, Ps. xvii. 3; lxvi. 10; lxxxi. 7. In Ps. xxvi. 2 it is rendered *examine.* *Eyelids* is parallel to *eyes* in the preceding clause. *The children of men*, literally, *the sons of Adam.* See Introduction, § 16. Patrick's paraphrase of this verse is striking. He makes David say to those who tempted him and to all these sad disorders, "My answer is, that the world is not governed by chance, nor can men carry things just as they please: but the LORD into whose holy palace no unjust counsels can possibly enter, and whose throne is infinitely above that of the highest king on earth: He, I say, is the supreme and most righteous Ruler of all affairs; and no mischief can be so secretly contrived, no wicked design so artificially dissembled, but it lies open before his eyes, and he sees through it: nor need he take any pains to discover it; for at the first glance, as we speak, he perfectly discovers how all men are inclined, and looks to the very bottom of their hearts." So grateful is this view of the Divine government that David dwells on it in the next verse.

5. *The* LORD *trieth the righteous.* God *proves, examines* his people. See v. 4. For *trieth* Edwards uses *explores.* The word rendered *righteous* is the same as in Ps. i. 5, 6; v. 12; vii. 9. In Hebrew the verb *try* here and in v. 4 is in the future, thus declaring that God does this thing and will continue to do it. There is no danger that he will ever cease to do it. Some think that this clause ought to be extended so as to include the word *wicked*, and so as to read, *The* LORD *trieth the righteous and the wicked.* This is favored by the Septuagint, Vulgate, Ethiopic, Arabic, and by Ainsworth, Brent, Edwards and Fry. Alexander also regards this division as admissible. On the other hand the Chaldee and Syriac with Calvin, Amesius and Hengstenberg retain the division of our version. There seems to be no good reason for adopting the suggestion of some so as to read, The righteous Jehovah trieth, *i. e.*, God proceeds as a righteous Judge. This is indeed true, but is not the truth here taught. If we adopt the pointing suggested above, then the last clause reads, *And him that loveth violence his soul hateth.* For *loveth* Edwards gives *delighteth;* Calvin and Fry, *approveth.* The cruelty, rage and pride of violence are utterly repugnant to the divine nature. Luther says this clause "is spoken emphatically, in that the prophet does not simply say that God hates, but *his soul hates*, thereby declaring that God hates the wicked in a high degree, and with his whole heart." In our version hardly any word has so uniform a rendering as the last verb in this verse. When given as a verb it is uniformly translated *hate.* Not fire is so opposed to water as the nature of God to sin. To him it is a horrible thing. Consequently,

6. *Upon the wicked he shall rain snares, fire and brimstone, and a horrible tempest:* this shall be *the portion of their cup.* In this verse the word *snares* has occasioned considerable discussion. Hare and Edwards think it does not belong to the Hebrew text, and ought to be stricken out. They object that it injures the metre. But the Psalms have never been shown to be metrical in the original. They further object that this word injures the sense. But this will be easily answered. Edwards indeed

translates it, putting it in *Italics*. But he thinks that if any word be used, it should be another word than the one commonly found in the Hebrew Bible, and so reads *hot cinders*. Brent also reads *hot cinders*. The word rendered *coals* in Pr. xxvi. 21; Isa. xliv. 12; liv. 16, very much resembles the word here rendered *snares*. But it is not the same. The word rendered *snares* is found in the singular or plural in the Psalms *nine* times, and in our version is uniformly translated. In some other parts of Scripture our version uses the word *gin* as a fit rendering, but a *gin* is a *snare*. Jebb regards the word much as Edwards does, and connects it with the next word and reads the whole, He shall rain upon the ungodly coals of fire, and brimstone, and a wind of horror; Boothroyd: On the wicked he raineth flakes of sulphureous fire, a horrible tempest is the portion of their cup; Waterland: Upon the wicked he shall rain snares: Fire and brimstone and a tempestuous wind shall be the portion of their cup; Horsley: Upon the impious he shall rain glowing embers: Fire and brimstone, and a tempestuous blast, is the portion of their cup; Fry: He will rain upon the wicked lightning, fire, and sulphur; and the hot "wind of the desert," shall be the portion of their cup. Amesius reads, *burning coals;* the margin, *quick burning coals;* Lowth prefers *live coals* or *hot burning coals*. He says, " This is certainly more agreeable to the context than *snares*. Michaelis and others say that the Arabians call *lightnings, snares, i. e., fiery ropes*. The verb rendered *shall rain* expresses a great abundance of anything good or bad descending from above. Thus it is applied to the descent of manna and of quails in the wilderness. Ex. xvi. 4; Ps lxxviii. 24, 27. So also it is applied to the descent of hail, Ex. ix. 23. In Gen. xix. 24 it is used to show how Sodom and Gomorrah were destroyed by fire and brimstone, viz.: by a copious descent of those destructive elements. That the wicked are to be caught in *snares* is frequently asserted in Scripture. In Job xviii. 9; Ps. lxix. 22; Pr. vii. 23; xxii. 5; Ecc. ix. 12; Is. viii. 14; xxiv. 17, 18; Jer. xlviii. 43, 44 the same word is used as is found in the text, showing how familiar to inspired writers was the idea of the destruction of the wicked by *snares*. And even where the same word is not used, the same idea is often presented in other words as in Ps. vii. 15; ix. 15, 16; Is. viii. 15; xxviii. 13. So that destruction by snares is not, without better cause than has yet been shown, to be rejected from this place. Hengstenberg: " While the wicked believe that they have the righteous in their snares, and are now able, with little difficulty, to destroy them, suddenly a whole load of snares is sent down upon them from heaven, and after all flight is cut off for them, they are smitten by the overpowering judgment of God." Calvin: " The Psalmist, with much beauty and propriety, puts *snares* before fire and brimstone. We see that the ungodly, while God spares them, fear nothing, but give themselves ample scope in their wayward courses, like horses let loose in an open field; and then if they see any adversity impending over them, they devise for themselves ways of escape: in short, they continually mock God as if they could not be caught, unless he first entangle and hold them fast in his snares. God, therefore, begins his vengeance by snares, shutting up against the wicked every way of escape; and when he has them entangled and bound, he thunders upon them dreadfully and horribly, like as he consumed Sodom and the neighboring cities with fire from heaven." No doubt the figure of fire and brimstone is taken from the overthrow of the cities of the plain. *An horrible tempest* shall also beat on the wicked. The word rendered *horrible* is found also in Ps. cxix. 53 where we read *horror* and in Lam. v. 10 where we read *terrible*. Bythner thinks it signifies a sudden tempest that burns and scorches as it goes. It is literally a *wind of horrors* or of *terrors*. Some commentators think the figure is drawn from the wind, which the Arabs call Smum, Samum, or Samoom, as it is variously spelled. But this wind never blows in Palestine, and would hardly be here mentioned. Hengstenberg: " The only well-grounded exposition is *strong wrath.*" Edwards reads it *stormy tempests;* Alexander, *raging wind,* literally *wind* or (*blast of furies;*) church of England, *storm and tempest;* Calvin, *a storm of whirlwinds.* The last phrase, *the portion of their cup,* is probably originally taken from the custom of putting into the cup of each guest the portion designed for him at feasts. It is a common figure of Scripture denoting the allotments of providence. It is often taken in a bad sense. Ps. lxxv. 8; Isa. li. 17; Ezek. xxiii. 32–34; Matt. xx. 22, 23; xxvi. 39; Luke xxii. 42. The prominent ideas presented in the whole verse are the abundance, the suddenness, the terribleness, the destructiveness and the irresistible violence of the calamities, which shall at last come on the wicked, however appearances may for a long time be to the contrary. Morison: "All these terrific images are but sensible, and therefore defective representations of invisible and spiritual realities. The most fearful objects, with which the human eye or the human imagination is familiar, can furnish no just [adequate?] representation of that scene of horror and dismay upon which the wicked enter at death. Enough, however, is revealed of it, to awaken salutary fear, and to cause every man to tremble lest he should come into this place of torment." Nor is the punishment of the wicked, nor the treatment of the righteous capricious. God acts as he does because he is what he is. And so it is said,

7. *For the righteous* LORD *loveth righteousness; his countenance doth behold the upright.* For *doth behold,* Calvin reads *approveth.* Edwards reads the whole verse, For Jehovah is righteous; he loveth upright actions; his countenance beholds with pleasure that which is just; Hengstenberg: For righteous is the Lord, he loves righteousness, his countenance beholds the upright; Alexander: For righteous (is) Jehovah; righteousness he loves; the upright (man) shall his face behold. Instead of *the upright,* the church of England reads *the thing which is just.* The sense given by each of these renderings is good and scriptural. None of them is any improvement on our English version, which is concise, and well corresponds to the original. There is no good reason for reading with Dimock, Jehovah will justify him that loveth righteousness, etc. The word *behold* is the same that is so rendered in v. 4. There it is said *his eyes behold,* here *his countenance doth behold, i. e.,* the aspect of his countenance is friendly towards the upright. In the former part of the Psalm David had argued from God's office as King and Judge that he would be against the wicked. Here he argues from the divine nature that he will favor the righteous. Calvin appropriately says, "It is a strained interpretation to view the last clause as meaning that the upright shall behold the face of God." The reason why such a rendering has been thought of is that the verb is singular, and the word upright is singular, while the word *countenance* is plural. But it is not inconsistent with Hebrew usage to have a singular verb and a plural nominative. See Introduction, § 6. This is especially the case, where the doctrine of the Trinity may be supposed to be brought to view, as here. The aspect of every person in the Godhead is unitedly benignant towards God's people.

DOCTRINAL AND PRACTICAL REMARKS.

1. Faith in God is necessary under all dispensations and in all situations. It is impossible to proceed a step in the right way without it, v. 1.

2. There is always ground of hope to one who trusts in God. All is not lost, that is brought into jeopardy. While God lives and reigns, there is hope for a good cause and for a good man. We may boldly challenge all who would drive us to despair, v. 1.

3. He, who purposes to do his duty, must make up his mind to know no man

after the flesh, and to listen to no counsel however kindly it may seem to be given, if it conflicts with the known will of God, v. 1.

4. How extreme is the folly of sin. Nothing seems more justifiable in the eyes of carnal men than flight in time of peril. Yet we must often cry out, How say ye, etc., v. 1.

5. It is always wise to stand in our lot, v. 1. The post of duty is a high tower. Henry: "That which grieved David in this matter, was, not that to flee would savor of cowardice, and ill become a soldier, but that it would savor of unbelief, and would ill become a saint, who had so often said, *In the Lord put I my trust.*" Calvin: "This verse teaches us, that however much the world may hate and persecute us, we ought nevertheless to continue steadfast at our post, that we may not deprive ourselves of a right to lay claim to the promises of God, or that these may not slip away from us, and that however much and however long we may be harassed, we ought always to continue firm and unwavering in the faith of our having the call of God."

6. In maintaining an unwavering profession and steadfastness we must carefully avoid all influence from the wisdom of the flesh, v. 1. Men, who are Christians, may yet be carnal to a sad degree, 1 Cor. iii. 1. When they are so their advice often is much the same as that given by ungodly men.

7. Good men should not be surprised at any amount of wickedness they shall witness. Bad men have always been very bad, v. 2. The wicked always shall do wickedly. It is in their hearts. Every generation has its Cain, its Ahithophel, its Sanballat, its Judas, its Demas, its false brethren, its dogs, its unprincipled cowards and brutal tyrants.

8. There is a nice adaptation between the proceedings and purposes of evil men. Stealthy acts befit stealthy plans, v. 2. Many a sinner shoots privily, who has too much shame to enable him to attack openly. Deeds of darkness befit the children of darkness.

9. It is important that we often ask ourselves, Are we upright? v. 1. If we are, we are also downright, outright, straight, straightforward. Crooked ways belong not to godliness. When we find ourselves inclined to an uncandid course, we may know all is not right.

10. It is always necessary to adhere to first principles, v. 3. This is as important in religion as in anything else. Henry: "If you destroy the foundations, if you take good people from off their hope in God, if you can persuade them that their religion is a cheat and a jest, and can banter them out of that, you ruin them, and break their hearts indeed, and make them of all men the most miserable." With care and examination adopt first principles. When adopted, stick to them.

11. In temptations, which lead us to deny first truths in religion, there is one advantage, viz., we see at once that we must hold fast our integrity, or give up conscience, peace of mind, principle, God and salvation. It is a great point when we are able to see the bearings of our conflicts. If the foundations shall fail, all is lost, v. 3.

12. What an inestimable blessing is a good government, established and conducted on true, just and uniform principles. If those, who complain of ordinary burdens in a good government, were placed even for a short time under the terrors of misrule or anarchy, they would find a state of things, which would probably make them thankful for a return to any form of regular and free government, v. 3.

13. But if we are placed by God in states of social and civil life, wholly unsettled, let us remember that others before us have seen all order subverted, all justice denied, v. 3. Through God they have outlived such a state and come to better days; and

so may we. A Roman would not despair of the republic. A Christian should hope well of all affairs in the government of God. Horne: "All is not over, while there is a man left to reprove error, and bear testimony to the truth; and a man, who does it with becoming spirit, may stop a prince, or senate, when in full career, and recover the day. . . No place on earth is out of the reach of care and trouble. Temptations are everywhere; and so is the grace of God."

14. We see what would be the state of things if infidels had the sway. All virtue and with it all justice and all order would perish. Every foundation would be destroyed. Morison: "Such men are wont to boast of liberty; but wo to the righteous of the land when left to their tender mercies! Those, who have impiously shaken off their allegiance to the Almighty, cannot be supposed to treat with much deference his humble and devoted servants. The liberty, of which infidels talk so much, is but an exhibition of that selfishness, above which their system can never elevate them, and it only requires that the same selfishness should dictate a line of persecution, for them instantly to adopt it. In the absence of all principle they are necessarily driven wherever passion, or prejudice, or interest may impel them."

15. However wild confusion may reign around us, and the true ends of government be forgotten, yet it may well make the hearts of the righteous to rejoice that God is not, and cannot be dethroned, v. 4. All other sceptres shall be broken and all other crowns fall to the ground, but the pious shall ever shout, Alleluiah, for the Lord God omnipotent reigneth.

16. The more wholly the springs of earthly comfort go dry, the more should we come to the wells of salvation, and with delight draw thence all needed refreshments, v. 4. Calvin: "Being destitute of human aid, David betakes himself to the providence of God. It is a signal proof of faith to borrow light from heaven to guide us to the hope of salvation, when we are surrounded in this world with darkness on every side. All men acknowledge that the world is governed by the providence of God; but when there comes some sad confusion of things, which disturbs their ease and involves them in difficulty, there are few who retain in their minds the firm persuasion of this truth." Yet that is the very time, when faith is most needed and may be most illustrious.

17. How consolatory to the humble soul is the doctrine of God's omniscience, v. 4. If one such is ashamed of his own imperfections and shortcomings he can appeal to God for his sincerity. If men misunderstand and misconstrue his best actions and designs, he is sure that Jehovah approves them. If he feels that wicked counsels are more than a match for his penetration, he has an almighty Friend, who fathoms all wicked devices. Henry: "God not only sees men, but he sees through them, not only knows all they say and do, but knows what they think, what they design, and how they really stand affected, whatever they pretend. We may know what men *seem* to be, but he knows what they *are*, as the refiner knows what the value of the gold is, when he has tried it."

18. It should make men solemn to know that God searches and tries them, v. 5. Many make in words very solemn appeals to their Maker, but in their hearts they are light and vain. The heart-searcher has no pleasure in fools. He trifles with none. He will not be trifled with by any.

19. Wicked men have no more right to believe that God will favor their evil doings than that he will change; for his whole moral nature is set against the workers of iniquity, v. 5. Calvin: "God hates those who are set upon the infliction of injuries, and upon doing mischief. As he has ordained mutual intercourse between men, so he would have us maintain it inviolable. In order, therefore, to preserve this his own sacred and appointed order, he must be the enemy of the wicked, who

wrong and are troublesome to others." Society is God's ordinance. All that tends to its subversion God will punish.

20. Because God is what he is, it is impossible that the righteous and the wicked should forever fare alike, much less that the wicked should always have the righteous in his power, and be able to torment him, v. 5.

21. If God does try the righteous, it is for their good; and so there is a vast difference between the sufferings of saints and of sinners, not in the degree, so much as in the design, end and effects, v. 5. Morison: "We here perceive the unspeakable difference between fatherly chastisements and the infliction of God's displeasure on his enemies. The one is for correction, the other is for punishment; the one is an expression of covenanted regard, the other is an intimation of righteous displeasure and approaching judgment; the one is the rebuke of a father, justly offended; the other is the uplifted rod of a judge, who will, ere long, smite down all his foes."

22. The calamities, that shall overtake the wicked, are inconceivably dreadful, v. 6. The Bible beyond all books is sober, and even in its boldest figures gives no exaggerated view of the future misery of wicked men, who die impenitent. How intolerable must the wrath of God be, when it is expressed by such terrific words as are used in this Psalm and elsewhere in the Bible. I marvel not that great and good men, who have proclaimed salvation in a loud and earnest manner, have commonly spoken on the loss of a soul in subdued tones and with many tears. But there is nothing to excuse silence on so awful a matter, Ezek. iii. 18; xxxiii. 7, 8. Damnation is more dreadful than it has ever been represented.

23. Henry: "Though honest good people may be run down, and trampled upon, yet God does and will own them, and favor them, and smile upon them, and that is the reason why God will severely reckon with persecutors and oppressors, because those whom they oppress and persecute are dear to him; so that, whosoever toucheth them, toucheth the apple of his eye," v. 7.

24. This whole Psalm teaches us that if tempted, we must not comply, but resist the devil, and he shall flee from us.

25. Nor can we read such Psalms without seeing that there is a difference betwixt saints and sinners, those that serve God and those that serve him not.

26. All the evils, which in this life come on the ungodly, are but the beginning of their sorrows, but the righteous has all his evil things before he reaches eternity.

27. One thing should greatly cheer the saints in their approaches to God, viz: that it is now known not only that he reigns, but that he reigns by one, Jesus Christ. God is surely on his throne. He is as surely in Christ Jesus.

28. Morison closes his comments on this Psalm thus: "Impenitent sinner! read this Psalm, and mark your approaching doom! To flatter yourself with the hope of escape is vain. The elements of omnipotent wrath are all prepared, and the tempests which will hurl you to perdition will speedily begin to blow. Already the moral heavens are covered with threatening clouds, and the lightning's flash is seen playing around your devoted head, the gulf from beneath is yawning wide to receive you; but one more stage in impenitence, and you are undone forever; the Judge stands at the door, the last call to repentance is about to be addressed to you, the knell of judgment shall speedily be heard, and through the gloomy shade of death you shall pass into a region where the wrath of God shall be the everlasting portion of your cup. Hasten then, O sinner, to the cross of Christ. He who died on that cross welcomes you, after all your impenitence he welcomes you. Your hard and flinty heart he can soften and change. Your sins of crimson dye he can pardon and remove; but forget not that the day of your merciful visitation hastens to a close, and that the insulted compassion of a dying Saviour will realize a fearful vindication in the ceaseless torments it will produce."

PSALM XII.

To the chief Musician upon Sheminith, A Psalm of David.

1 Help, LORD; for the godly man ceaseth; for the faithful fail from among the children of men.

2 They speak vanity every one with his neighbor: *with* flattering lips *and* with a double heart do they speak.

3 The LORD shall cut off all flattering lips, *and* the tongue that speaketh proud things:

4 Who have said, With our tongue will we prevail; our lips *are* our own: who *is* lord over us?

5 For the oppression of the poor, for the sighing of the needy, now will I arise, saith the LORD; I will set *him* in safety *from him that* puffeth at him.

6 The words of the LORD *are* pure words: *as* silver tried in a furnace of earth, purified seven times.

7 Thou shalt keep them, O LORD, thou shalt preserve them from this generation for ever.

8 The wicked walk on every side, when the vilest men are exalted.

FOR an explanation of the title see above on Psalms iv. and vi. at the beginning. There is no good cause for doubting that David wrote this Psalm.

Many attempts have been made to fix a time and place for the composition of this Psalm, but without success. Hengstenberg quotes Geier as rightly describing this Psalm when he says it contains "the common complaint of the church of all times." Many a period of David's history and of the history of every good man is here set forth. But it cannot be shown to have any more distinct fulfilment in the times of Doeg and the Ziphites, or of Absalom than in the days of the Babylonish captivity or of Antiochus Epiphanes. Rampant wickedness has always shown itself in the manner here described.

Two words, used as names of God, are found in this Psalm—*Jehovah* LORD and *Adonai Lord*, on which see above on Ps. i. 2; ii. 4.

1. *Help*, LORD; *for the godly man ceaseth; for the faithful fail from among the children of men.* By far the most common rendering of the first verb in this verse is *save;* after that *deliver, preserve, avenge, rescue, help.* The same word in the same form is found in 2 Sam. xiv. 4; 2 Kings vi. 26, and is rendered *help.* It is found in Ps. iii. 7; vi. 4; vii. 1, and is rendered *save.* The Septuagint, Vulgate, Ethiopic, Arabic read, Save *me;* church of England, Help *me.* But the Syriac and Chaldee simply, *Save.* Luther well says, "It sounds more impressive, when one says, Deliver, or give help, than to say, deliver me. As one therefore says in our language, under circumstances of great distress, or approaching death: Help, thou compassionate God, crying aloud with the utmost vehemence, and using no prefatory words upon the danger in hand; so does the prophet, as one inflamed with zeal on account of the oppressed state of God's people, cry out without any prefatory words, and implore in the most impressive manner, the help of God." The language of strong emotion is commonly abrupt and elliptical, but not therefore the less intelligible, or impressive. The word *help* does not call for merely *some* aid, but for full and effectual deliverance. The reason assigned comes next, *for the godly man ceaseth; for the faithful fail from among the children of men.* There is considerable diversity in rendering these words. The Septuagint: For the holy (man) has left, and truths have become few among the children of men; Vulgate: For the holy (man) has failed; for truths are diminished from among the children of men; the Ethiopic follows the Septuagint; Arabic: For the just (man) has failed, and truth is diminished among the sons of men; Syriac: For the virtuous has failed, and fidelity is wanting in the earth; Chaldee: For the righteous are consumed; for the faithful

fail from among the sons of men; Calvin: For the merciful man hath failed, and the faithful are wasted away from among the children of men; Amesius: For the benefi- cent (man) is wanting, for the truthful have failed from among the sons of men; Brent: For the man that does good is rare; and few are the sincere among the sons of men; Edwards: For the good man is no more; for the faithful are not to be found among the sons of men; Fry, (applying the Psalm to Gospel times): For the Beloved hath failed, for the faithful have expired among the children of men; church of England: For there is not one godly man left: for the faithful are min- ished from among the children of men; Jebb: For there is a ceasing of the godly: for there is a minishing of the faithful among the children of men; Alexander: For the merciful (or the object of divine mercy) ceaseth, for the faithful fail from (among) the sons of men. The word rendered *godly* is (in the plural) most fre- quently rendered *saints;* (in the singular) sometimes *holy;* thrice, *Holy one;* some- times *merciful;* once, *good;* in Ps. iv. 3; xxxii. 6, *godly.* No better rendering can be given to the second adjective than *faithful* or *truthful.* The verbs rendered *cease* and *fail* are in the preterite in the Hebrew, showing that the state of things here described was not merely beginning to exist, but even now was a sad reality. These words, descriptive of the dreadful state of society, are not to be taken as denying that there were some good men left, as the faithful band, who adhered to David, and others; but as asserting that good men were already scarce, making the call on God to be urgent. Micah vii. 2, is a parallel passage. Patrick well speaks of this part of the Psalm as "a sad complaint of the corrupt manners of that age, in which it was hard to find an honest plain-dealing man, in whom one might confide." *Children of men,* literally *sons of Adam.* Lacking holiness and truth, the mass of the people were ready for any enormity, and so he says,

2. *They speak vanity every one with his neighbour.* For *vanity* the Septuagint, Vul- gate and Ethiopic have *vain things;* Chaldee, *a lie;* Syriac, Mudge, Edwards and Fry, *falsehood;* Luther, *profitless things;* Calvin, *deceit.* In our English version the word is more commonly rendered *vanity,* or *in vain,* as twice in the third com- mandment, Ex. xx. 7; but sometimes it is translated by *false, lying,* etc. Ainsworth has it *false vanity,* or *vain falsehood;* Alexander translates it "*vanity, i. e.,* falsehood;" Hengstenberg suggests that the word *neighbour* in this case points to a very intimate relationship. It may be so, but it is the same word found once in the 9th and three times in the 10th commandments. It is the word used in Lev. xix. 18, which Jesus Christ has explained, Luke x. 29–37. It is indeed sometimes rendered *friend, fellow, companion, brother.* Deut. xxiv. 10; Jud. vii. 13; 1 Sam. xiv. 20; 2 Sam. xvi. 17; 1 Chron. xxvii. 33. But it is also often rendered by the simple word *another.* Gen. xi. 3, 7; xv. 10; 2 Kings vii. 9. In the Psalms it is always rendered by one of these words, *neighbour, friend,* or *companion.* Ps. xv. 3; xxxv. 15; cxxii. 8. The parallel clause is With *flattering lips* and *with a double heart do they speak.* Edwards: They speak with smooth tongues and double hearts; Jebb: With a lip of flatteries, with a double heart they speak; Horsley has *smooth lips,* and explains that they are "not smooth with flattery, but with glossing lies, with ensnaring eloquence, and specious arguments in support of the wretched cause which they espouse." Flattering lips are *smooth lips, slippery lips.* Literally it would read *a lip of flatteries, of blandish- ments, of smoothnesses.* The word rendered *lip* is often translated by *language* or *speech,* as in Gen. xi. 1, 6, 7, 9; Ps. lxxxi. 5; Pr. xvii. 7. The phrase *with a double heart* is in the Hebrew literally *with a heart and a heart.* This form is retained in the Septuagint, Ethiopic, Syriac, several Latin, and some of the French versions. This is a form of speech unknown among us. The sense according to English idiom is given in the text of our version. The English word, *duplicity,* seems to convey the precise idea.

That is, these men thought one thing, and spoke another; they said one thing to one man, and a different thing to another; they did not speak the truth in their hearts. Ps. xv. 2.   The phrase is found nowhere else but in 1 Chron. xii. 33, where as here it is rendered *a double heart*. Hengstenberg seems to think it much the same as that of a "double-minded man," in Jas. i. 8.   Yet he gives weight to the explanation of Venema: "With a double mind, the one which they express, and another which they conceal, the former bland and open, the other impious and malignant;" and of Umbreit, "That is that they have one for themselves, and another for their friends." The phrase is probably parallel to that of "divers weights" and "divers measures," in Deut. xxv. 13, 14, which literally would be *a weight and a weight* (or a stone and a stone,) and *a measure and a measure* (an ephah and *an ephah*.)   Clarke: "They seem to have two hearts; *one* to speak fair words, and the *other* to invent mischief." This state of things should not last always; for,

3. *The* Lord *shall cut off all flattering lips.*   Edwards: May the Lord cut off all smooth lips; Jebb: The Lord shall cut off all lips of flattery; Calvin: Let Jehovah cut off all flattering lips; church of England: *The* Lord shall root out all deceitful lips; Fry: Jehovah will cut off all flattering lips; Hengstenberg: The Lord cut off all flattering lips; Alexander: May Jehovah destroy all lips of smoothness, *i. e.*, flattering lips.   The form of the verb is here best rendered in the future and is so given in a majority of cases in our common version, *The Lord shall cut off.   Flattering lips*, the same words in the Hebrew as in the preceding verse, except that *lips* is plural. *To cut off* is by far the most frequent rendering of the verb, though it is sometimes given *cut down*, etc.   The meaning is that God will in wrath remove these sinners from their earthly possessions, and that he will separate them from the congregation of the blessed.   Excision from the congregation of the holy shall come on flatterers. Nor is this all.   God shall also cut off *the tongue that speaketh proud things.*   The word rendered *proud* occurs about *thirty* times in the Psalms, and is in every other case translated *great*.   Here and in Ps. lxxi. 19, it is plural and in the latter case it is rendered *great things*.   This rendering is favored by the Chaldee, Septuagint, Vulgate, Ethiopic, Syriac, Calvin, Jebb, Hengstenberg and Alexander.   The same word is found in Jer. xlv. 5 and is translated *great things*.   Hengstenberg renders it, The tongue that speaks big; Morison gives the sense when he says "proud boasters" are pointed out—"those who talk big, who speak great things;" Hengstenberg regards these phrases as designating the same class of persons as those mentioned in Isa. xxviii. 15, who say, "We have made lies our refuge, and under falsehood have we hid ourselves."   When men flatter, lie and slander, they are on the road to hell; when they boast of their skill in these things and rely on them to bring them through, they are ready to drop into hell.

4. *Who have said, With our tongue will we prevail.*   Hengstenberg: Through our tongue we are strong; Alexander: By our tongues will we do mightily; Edwards: We are masters of our tongues; Horsley: We will flay the man with our tongue; Calvin: We will be strengthened by our tongues; several ancient versions: We will magnify our tongue.   None of these renderings give the sense more clearly than our translation; though several cast light on it.   This clause is one of those *proud things* mentioned in the preceding verse.   Shocking as is the wickedness thus bursting forth, it is but an expression of the depravity common to men.   Only hundreds may say it, yet millions think it.   The forms of speech, on which wicked men rely, are slander, flattery, boasting, scorning, lying, misrepresentation of every kind.   But all such boasting is evil.   It cannot stand because the truth is not its basis.   Men may affect but can never effect independence of God.   These same rebels say, *Our lips* are *our own*.   Calvin: Our lips are in our own power; Brent: Our speech is in our own

hand; church of England: We are they that ought to speak; Alexander: Our lips are with us, meaning either that they are our own, at our disposal, or, they are on our side; Fry: Our lips for us; Edwards, Jebb, and the Doway agree with the authorized version. Morison gives the sense: "We may utter what we please. We have skill, power, and liberty to speak. . . They think and speak as if their lips were their own, by absolute right. In the utterance of imprecations, falsehood, impurity, and irreligion, they have no feeling that they are strictly accountable. Their lips they consider as their inalienable property, and they uniformly employ them in the service of a depraved heart." And so they add, *Who is lord over us?* This form of irreligious speech seems to be peculiarly congenial to depraved minds. It expresses in the form of a challenge the atheism of the heart. The sense is, Who is so our master, as to hinder us from saying and doing what we please? Fry: Who shall be our master? But such cruelty and wickedness cannot last always. The triumphing of the wicked is short. Accordingly we next read,

5. *For the oppression of the poor, for the sighing of the needy, now will I arise saith the* LORD; *I will set* him *in safety* from him that *puffeth at him. For* means *because of, on account of.* The word rendered *poor* is found in Ps. ix. 12 and is there rendered *humble.* That rendered *needy* is found in Ps. ix. 18. See on those verses. This whole verse is quite variously rendered. Calvin: Because of the spoiling (or oppression) of the needy, because of the groaning of the poor, I will now arise, Jehovah will say; I will set in safety him whom he snareth, *i. e.,* him for whom the wicked lay snares; Edwards: For the oppression of the afflicted, for the groaning of the needy, I will now arise, saith Jehovah; I will set him, whom he would ensnare, in safety; Horsley thinks "cruel treatment of the helpless" would be better than "oppression of the poor," and instead of "sighing of the needy," he prefers "outcry of the poor;" church of England: Now for the comfortless troubles' sake of the needy: and because of the deep sighing of the poor; I will up, saith the Lord, and will help every one from him that swelleth against him, and will set him at rest; Hengstenberg: Because of the desolation of the poor, because of the sighing of the needy, now will I arise, saith the Lord; place will I in safety him who sighs after it: Alexander: From the desolation of the wretched, from the sighing of the poor, now will I arise, shall Jehovah say, I will place him in safety that shall pant after it; Fry has the last clause: I will set him in safety from him that panteth after him, understanding a panting like a savage beast, with eager desire to devour his prey; Houbigant: I will procure them safety, that they may breathe. Instead of *puffeth at him,* the Italian reads, *speaketh boldly against him;* Chaldee: I will ordain redemption to my people, but against the wicked I will testify evil. For the meaning of the word, *arise,* see above on Ps. iii. 7; vii. 6; ix. 19; x. 12, where the same verb is used, though in a different tense. God sees the wrongs and hears the sighs of his people, however needy, poor, humble and afflicted, and will in due time arise to judge and avenge them, seems to be the sum of what is meant in the first part of the verse. The verb rendered, *saith* in the original is in the future, but so it is in many other cases, where it is rendered in the present and even in the past tense. Ps. xi. 1; xli. 5; lv. 6; lxxvii. 10; Isa. i. 11; xxxviii. 21. The sum of what is promised in the second clause is rest, deliverance, salvation from proud, insidious, taunting foes. All this is made sure by the promise of God to all the humble and needy, who long for repose in the bosom of God. No marvel that such promises are very precious to the saints. They praise them, saying:

6. *The words of the* LORD *are pure words.* The word rendered *pure* is translated *clean* in Ps. xix. 9; li. 10, and in many other places, and *pure* in Hab. i. 13; Mal. i. 11. It often occurs in connection with the word gold, and is then always rendered *pure, i. e.,* free from alloy. The reference here seems to be, not to gold, but to another

precious metal, for it is added that God's words are as *silver tried in a furnace of earth, purified seven times.* God's words are pure from all error, all mistake, all equivocation, all deception, all encouragement to sin, all weakness. They are more replete with meaning, with faithfulness, with grace than the best minds and the strongest faith have ever conceived or alleged. There is something amazing in the power of God's word. It differs from all other writings. Some confine the sense of this clause to the words of God spoken in the preceding verse. Although they are included in this statement, the proposition here laid down respecting God's words is a universal truth. There is considerable diversity in rendering a part of this verse. Calvin and Amesius: Silver melted in an excellent crucible of earth; Edwards: Like silver refined in an earthen vessel; Jebb: Silver tried in the furnace from the earth; church of England: Even as the silver, which from the earth is tried; Fry: Silver refined from the crucible; Horsley: Silver assayed in a crucible of earth; Alexander: Silver purged in a furnace of earth. The intelligent reader will probably find his confidence in the common version strengthened by these renderings. But Hengstenberg would have it that David here says God's words are purified silver of a lord of the earth; and he has a long comment to show that this is the only correct rendering. But his argument will hardly satisfy many. Still it must be admitted that this clause is not without difficulties on account of the unusual collocation of words. Venema, besides his own learned exposition, gives a note from a learned friend, showing that great difficulties attend the philology of the clause. The number *seven* was among the Jews a number of perfection. *Seven times purified* is the same as *perfectly purified.* Notwithstanding the difficulties in some of the words, yet the general sense is remarkably clear. Even the Doway Bible does not lead us astray in the practical truth taught: The words of the Lord are pure words: as silver tried by the fire, purged from the earth, refined seven times. God's words are full of consolation as well as of purity.

7. *Thou shalt keep them, O* LORD, *thou shalt preserve them from this generation forever.* The persons referred to by the pronouns of this verse are those mentioned in verse 5. These pronouns, because they designate the same persons, are properly both given in the plural, *them,* though in the Hebrew the latter is singular, *him.* But Hammond thinks *them* refers to the words of the Lord mentioned in the preceding verse, and *him* to the just man, and so he would read, Thou, O LORD, shalt keep, or perform, those words; thou shalt preserve the just man from this generation forever. The word rendered *keep* is applied to keeping covenant, keeping truth, as well as keeping one in safety, or preserving one. It has probably as great a variety of signification as our English word, *keep.* The idea is well given in the English version. Some have supposed that by putting *him* in the second instance there is a reference to the small number of the pious, but such things belong to the idiom of the language, and it is not wise to strain things in this way. For *him,* Edwards has *each one of them;* Chaldee: Thou wilt preserve just (men), thou wilt guard them. The Septuagint, Vulgate, Ethiopic, Arabic and Fry have *us* instead of *them.* This reading rests on the authority of one manuscript, an insufficient support. By *this generation* is meant *this sort of men,* viz., those described in vv. 2, 3, 4. Calvin says, that from this expression "we learn that the world, at that time, was so corrupt, that David, by way of reproach, puts them all, as it were, into one bundle. Moreover it is of importance to remember that he does not here speak of foreign nations, but of the Israelites, God's chosen people." The wicked shall not have power either to corrupt and debauch, or to destroy and exterminate the saints. *Forever* is a correct rendering. Hengstenberg: It always means eternity. See above on Ps. ix. 5, 7. Blessed be God, by and by the wicked shall cease from troubling and the weary shall be at rest. Though the wicked shall not be annihilated, they shall be outcasts and deprived of power to torment the saints.

8. *The wicked walk on every side, when the vilest men are exalted.*   Perhaps no verse of Scripture has been more variously rendered than this.   Hare acknowledges that he does not understand it.   John Rogers' translation: And why? when vanyte and ydlenes getteth the overhande among the chyldren of men, all are full of the ungodly; Bishops' Bible: The ungodly walke on every syde: when they are exalted, the children of men are put in rebuke; the Genevan translation: The wicked walke on every side: when they are exalted it is a shame for the sonnes of men; Doway, following the Septuagint, Vulgate, and Ethiopic: The wicked walk round about; according to thy highness, thou hast multiplied the children of men.   Other old translations are also variant.   Calvin: The ungodly walk on every side; when they are exalted, there is reproach to the children of men; Edwards: The wicked walk up and down on every side; as thou art high exalted, thou art become contemptible to the sons of men; church of England: The ungodly walk on every side: when they are exalted, the children of men are put to rebuke; Brent renders it as our English, except that he reads *vain* for *vilest;* Clarke: The wicked walk on every side, as villany gains ground among the sons of Adam.   As Hengstenberg's views are quite peculiar, his translation is given together with so much of his comment as may convey his full idea: "*The wicked walk round about,* they have compassed the righteous on all hands, so that without God's help deliverance is impossible.   Comp. Ps. iii. 6.   *As elevation is depression to the sons of men, i. e.,* although now the righteous are overborne by the wicked, yet their distress is to be regarded in the light of prosperity, because God forsakes not his own, but will rightly recompense them for the sufferings they have endured."   Perhaps the general verdict will be that our common version is better than any of these, and that among those, which materially vary from it, one is hardly to be preferred to another.   Clarke: "Were we to take this in its obvious sense it would signify that at that time wickedness was the way to preferment, and good men the objects of persecution."   There seems to be no good reason for Patrick's paraphrase: It "will make the wicked not know which way to turn themselves; but be ready to burst with anger and vexation, when they see these poor men, whom they contemned and vilified, not only preserved, but exalted by thy favor to dignity and honor."

Doctrinal and Practical Remarks.

1. It is no new thing for the church to be small.   In the old world it was reduced to the family of Noah.   In the days of Elijah there were in all the kingdom but seven thousand, who did not bow the knee to Baal.   In the days of David the godly ceased, grew scarce, v. 1.   Jacob has commonly been small.   Once the cry was, The world against Athanasius, and Athanasius against the world.   Christ's people are a little flock.   The strength of the church consists not in the number of her visible members, but in the almightiness of her Head.

2. If the church is small, let us pray for her enlargement, v. 1.   No matter of prayer is more pleasing to God.   True followers of God are the light of the world and the salt of the earth.   "The Lord make his people a hundred times so many more as they be."

3. One of the ways in which good men become scarce, is by death.   Some think there is a reference to such an event in v. 1.   It is right to lament the death of good men.   How sadly does Isaiah say, "The righteous perisheth, and no man layeth it to heart: and merciful men are taken away, none considering that the righteous is taken away from the evil to come," Is. lvii. 1.   The children of Israel wept for Moses in the plains of Moab thirty days, Deut. xxxiv. 8.   So devout men carried Stephen to his burial and made great lamentation over him, Acts viii. 2.

4. In all our troubles, in particular in our sadness respecting the low state of reli-

gion, let us rely on none but God. *Help*, LORD, v. 1. Desertion of our post of duty
is no good sign in any man. Go where we will, we shall never be beyond the reach
of trouble. Slade: "Temptations are everywhere, and so is the grace of God." The
sooner we go to God with our cares the better for us.

5. So marvellously is society bound together that if one member rejoices, and is
saved, or suffers, errs, and perishes, others are thereby deeply affected, v. 1. Every
human being adds something to the vice or virtue, to the happiness or misery of his
generation. For good cause there is mourning or shouting at the death of every human being. None of us liveth to himself.

6. Unchecked depravity manifests itself with great uniformity. One by one faithful, godly, honest, candid men disappear from the community; as when clouds arise
in the night star after star is covered till not a ray of light comes down to cheer the
traveller, v. 1.

7. The church of God has never been perfect. In this world spots and wrinkles
and blemishes are ever found on her. Calvin: "David does not here accuse strangers
or foreigners, but informs us that this deluge of iniquity prevailed in the church of
God. Let the faithful, therefore, in our day, not be unduly discouraged at the melancholy sight of a very corrupt and confused state of the world." No new thing has
happened. People who glorify past ages as all purer than the present, must forget
the church in the days of the prophets and apostles. Every generation has had much
to deplore. Horne: "The universal depravity of Jew and Gentile caused the church,
of old, to pray earnestly for the first advent of Christ; and a like depravity among
those who call themselves Christians, may induce her to pray no less earnestly for his
appearance the second time unto salvation."

8. Wherever sin is dominant, it is sure to manifest itself in vanity, falsehood, flattery and deceit, v. 1. In other words as society forsakes God, it becomes hollow;
hollowness requires deception to disguise its baseness; and so instead of hearty good
wishes we hear idle compliments; instead of serious profitable discourse we have froth
and vanity. The manner in which God everywhere condemns these sins, shows their
utter contrariety to holiness. Henry: "The devil's image complete is a complication
of malice and falsehood."

9. Some sins imply others. He that will steal will also lie. He who blasphemes
God will live without prayer. Horne: "When men cease to be faithful to their God,
he who expects to find them so to each other will be much disappointed," vv. 1, 2.

10. Nothing so deforms the church of God as disingenuous, hypocritical members,
v. 2. Morison: "Honest-hearted worldlings, who shrink not from the avowal of their
proper characters, are innocent members of the community, compared with those who
wound character and feeling under the hallowed garb of friendship, formed and fostered in the sanctuary of God."

11. Dickson: "Vain talk, cozening speeches, flattering words are unbeseeming
honest men, and argue in so far as men affect them, ungodliness, unfaithfulness, and
deceitfulness in man," v. 2.

12. Truth and kindness are elements of society so essential, that their absence will
induce general wretchedness among all thinking men, v. 2. Morison: "It is a mournful thing when those who are brethren cannot confide in each other. It is still more
mournful when deceit and falsehood are resorted to, in order to impart a coloring and
a complexion to events, which they would not otherwise wear."

13. Horne: "They who take pleasure in deceiving others, will at the last find themselves most of all deceived, when the sun of truth, by the brightness of his rising,
shall at once detect and consume hypocrisy," v. 3.

14. Calvin: "Certainly falsehood and calumnies are more deadly than swords and

all other kinds of weapons," v. 3. "Life and death are in the power of the tongue," is a divine decision.

15. No set of men are more vain than boasters—those whose talk is big, v. 3. "He that boasteth himself of a false gift is as clouds and wind without rain." One reason why men should not tell all the good they know of themselves, is that such are apt, for lack of something veracious, to tell something quite beyond the truth.

16. The temporal judgments, which often befall the wicked, are forerunners of worse things to come. They who in wrath are cut off here (v. 3) are cut off from the life everlasting.

17. How dismal are the prospects of the wicked. All their hopes rest on the most monstrous errors, such as that God does not care what they do, and that their tongues are omnipotent, v. 4. Because for awhile they can make a lie pass for a truth, they hope to do so always, but they shall be sorely disappointed. A day is coming when eloquence will all be vain. There may be as much eloquence in hell as in heaven. The wicked now say all religion is vain superstition, that true philosophy is about to gain the ascendancy, and that the world will soon be better by reason of a new era in thought, but they are mistaken. All their brightest hopes shall fail them.

18. None but *wicked* men would dare to deny their perfect accountability, saying, *Our lips are our own*, v. 4. "By thy words thou shalt be justified, and by thy words thou shalt be condemned."

19. The denial of God's ownership of us does not in the least impair its perfection, any more than a denial that he created us would change the fact in that case, v. 4. God is our Master, our Owner, our Lord. To deny this may prove us atheists, but it cannot weaken his claims to our hearty and cheerful obedience.

20. Dickson: "From the faults of the wicked, v. 4, we must learn three contrary lessons; to wit: 1. That nothing which we have is our own. But, 2. Whatsoever is given to us of God is for service to be done to him. 3. That whatsoever we do, or say, we have a Lord over us to whom we must be answerable when he calleth us to account."

21. Blood and tears both have voices. They cry louder and are heard farther than thunder, v. 5. They travel even to the throne of God, though shed in some secret place on earth.

22. When God undertakes our cause deliverance must come, salvation cannot be far off, v. 5. The wicked may puff and blow, may exert their fury and their power, but God is a munition of rocks. And when God delivers it is with a strong arm. He did not enable the Israelites to outrun the Egyptians; he utterly destroyed the latter. To the Jews in Babylon he not merely sent deliverance from Belshazzar; he sent them to rebuild their city and temple. Calvin: "To the unjustly oppressed God promises an entire restitution."

23. How excellent is holy Scripture. It is pure from all tendency to sin. It countenances no iniquity, unrighteousness, or crime. It denounces all error, deceit, falsehood. *The words of the Lord are pure words*, etc. Henry: "This expression denotes (1.) The sincerity of God's word; everything is really as it is there represented, and not otherwise; it does not jest with us, nor impose upon us, nor has it any other design toward us than to do us good. (2.) The preciousness of God's word; it is of great intrinsic value, like silver refined to the highest degree; it has nothing in it to depreciate it. (3.) The many proofs that have been given of its power and truth; it has been often tried, all the saints in all ages have trusted it, and so tried it, and it never deceived them, or frustrated their expectations; but they have all set to their seal that God's word is true." Their experience and their faith well agree. To add to the truth of Scripture is superstition; to take from it is sacrilege. Morison: "O Chris-

tian! bind God's word to your very heart. Read it with care, study it with diligence, pray over its hallowed contents with fervor and importunity. Ask the teaching of the divine Spirit, that you may understand and obey its pure dictates, and only quit the study of it with existence itself." The promises are all confirmed with an oath.

24. Therefore what Christians need is not less trial, or lighter affliction, but stronger and simpler faith. There are but few men who impiously deny the truth of Scripture. But Calvin well observes that "those, who while lying in the shade and living at their ease, liberally extol by their praises the truth of God's word, when they come to struggle with adversity in good earnest, although they may not venture openly to pour forth blasphemies against God, often charge him with not keeping his word. Whenever he delays his assistance we call in question his fidelity to his promises and murmur just as if he had deceived us. There is no truth which is more generally received among men than that God is true; but there are few who frankly give him credit for this when they are in adversity."

25. When God is our keeper and preserver, all enemies are vain, v. 7. The chaff cannot contend with the whirlwind, nor the feather with the burning fiery furnace; neither can sinful worms war against the Almighty. Neither the multitude of God's enemies, nor the fewness of his friends at all affects the certainty of deliverance to the righteous. A bundle of wheat is worth more than ten thousand fields of tares. God's people are not saved by their own wisdom, strength, righteousness, or numbers. Some eminent Christian men have enumerated hundreds of instances, in which God marvellously rescued them from imminent perils. God never deserts his people so that their enemies can compass their ruin.

26. Civil and political broils and commotions are no novelty, v. 8. Those, which occur in modern times are often as nothing, compared with the agitations and turmoils of David's day.

27. It is clearly a right as well as a duty to pray for our rulers, that they may be wise, good, useful and happy men. Such rulers are the richest blessings, 2 Sam. xxiii. 4.

28. What a vast difference there is in all things between saints and sinners. Their hopes and fears, joys and griefs, tastes and aversions, ends and aims all differ. The state of things described in this Psalm greatly afflicted David, but to the unprincipled wicked it was a time of great rejoicing. The same is seen now. The sinners of our day complain of bad crops, decay of trade, heavy taxes, low wages, war and pestilence. In their esteem these and such like things make bad times. But the practical judgment of the pious is that times are bad when God is dishonored, Christ rejected, the Spirit resisted, the gospel despised, or, as Henry has it, "when there is a general decay of piety and honesty among men; . . . when dissimulation and flattery have corrupted and debauched all conversation; . . . when the enemies of God, of religion and of religious people are impudent and daring, and threaten to run down all that is just and sacred; . . . when the poor and needy are oppressed, and abused, and puffed at; . . . and when wickedness abounds and goes bare-faced, under the protection and countenance of those in authority, then the times are very bad."

29. To the righteous the darkest night is followed by the bright morning. There is hope always left for the humble. Slade: "However the wicked may prevail, their triumph is but short; as Jesus said to his enemies who came to take him, 'This is your hour, and the power of darkness.'" Sadness shall one day take her eternal flight from the redeemed. "The LORD shall be thine everlasting light, and the days of thy mourning shall be ended," Isa. lx. 20. "From the uttermost part of the earth have we heard songs, *even* glory to the righteous," Isa. xxiv. 16.

30. There is a day coming, when peace and righteousness shall greatly prevail, when the church of God shall receive as much favor from earthly potentates, as in former ages she received disfavor, when kings shall be her nursing fathers, and queens her nursing mothers, and "earth shall keep jubilee a thousand years."

PSALM XIII.

To the chief Musician, A Psalm of David.

1 How long wilt thou forget me, O LORD? for ever? how long wilt thou hide thy face from me?

2 How long shall I take counsel in my soul, *having* sorrow in my heart daily? how long shall mine enemy be exalted over me?

3 Consider *and* hear me, O LORD my God: lighten mine eyes, lest I sleep the *sleep of* death;

4 Lest mine enemy say, I have prevailed against him; *and* those that trouble me rejoice when I am moved.

5 But I have trusted in thy mercy; my heart shall rejoice in thy salvation.

6 I will sing unto the LORD, because he hath dealt bountifully with me.

FOR remarks on the title, see above on title of Ps. iv.

Theodoret thought this Psalm was written by David, not during his troubles with Saul, but during the rebellion of Absalom. For this opinion he assigns this reason, "that the trouble which Saul gave him was before his great sin, and so he was full of confidence; but that of Absalom was after it, and this made him cry out in this doleful manner." Patrick and Scott favor this view. Morison argues in favor of it. He says it " seems by no means void of support. There is a pensiveness of feeling evinced in its different parts, exceedingly characteristic of the state of mind, which the repentant monarch must have cherished on that mournful occasion. When he fled from Saul, his heart was not bowed down by the remembrance of 'presumptuous sins;' but when he hastened from the face of Absalom, the cloud of outward sorrow was but a faint emblem of that more than midnight darkness, which brooded over his soul." Although many have thought there was a tincture of sadness in the Psalms written by David after his fall beyond that found in his earlier compositions, yet it is not manifest that this Psalm is any more sad than others which were confessedly written to commemorate events occurring in the days of Saul.

Clarke says this Psalm " is supposed to have been written during the Captivity; and to contain the prayers and supplications of the distressed Israelites, worn out with long and oppressive bondage." But against this view, we have the authority of the title, which expressly ascribes it to David; we have also the whole structure of the Psalm. Hengstenberg: "The situation [of the author] is that of one, who, through lengthened persecutions and continued withdrawal of divine help, has been brought to the limits of despair, and is plunged in deadly sorrow. This particular state of mind may be recognized in the four times repeated question, *how long?*"

Luther: " This is a prayer full of the sighings and groanings of an afflicted heart in the hour of darkness, and almost overwhelmed, under that darkness, with the extreme of grief and sorrow, and driven to the greatest strait of mind." He understands it of every pious man, who was persecuted as David was. The Arabic has this title: " In this Psalm mention is made of the insolence of his enemies, with a prophecy concerning the presence of Christ."

Scott dates this Psalm B. C. 1057; Clarke B. C. 540. The names of the Most High in this Psalm are *Jehovah* LORD and *Elohim God,* on which see respectively on Ps. i. 2; iii. 2.

1. *How long wilt thou forget me, O* LORD? *for ever? How long wilt thou hide thy face from me?* The Septuagint, Vulgate, Ethiopic, Chaldee, Syriac, Calvin, Fabritius, church of England, Brent, Fry, Hengstenberg and Alexander, make but one question closing with *for ever.* Venema without good reason drops *for ever,* out of his translation; Piscator and Amesius read: How long O Lord? Wilt thou forget me for ever? Edwards and Jebb give the pointing as in our English version. This is perhaps to be preferred. Instead of *for ever,* Hengstenberg reads *continually;* and he says the original word "marks the uninterruptedness, and consequently the entireness of the forgetting. The Psalmist's darkness was enlightened by no ray of divine favor, his misery had no lucid intervals." Yet he subsequently expresses doubt whether this is the correct view. In Pr. xxi. 28, the same word is rendered *constantly.* Yet this is the only instance. It is commonly translated *alway, for ever,* and with a negative *never,* literally *not for ever.* Used as an adjective it is also translated *perpetual.* Fry has *still,* and Houbigant *utterly,* instead of *for ever.* Luther and Gesenius prefer *entirely.* The same view is taken by Muis: "Thou showest thyself to me such as if thou hadst entirely forgotten me." In our version the word is never rendered *still, utterly,* or *entirely,* nor is there any instance, except this verse and Pr. xxi. 28, where it is known that any one contends for such a meaning. Alexander thinks both words may be preserved in the same sentence, sense and reason crying out *for ever?* but faith, *how long?* But all these difficulties are avoided by adopting the punctuation of the English Bible, or that of Piscator and Amesius. The words *how long?* are found four times in this and the next verses. Some have thought that this was on account of the fourfold captivity of Israel, viz. the Babylonish, the Median, the Grecian, and the Roman, so making this Psalm an enigmatical prophecy. But this is an unsafe way of interpreting God's word. Luther speaks much more to the purpose. "In Hebrew the word *how long* is four times repeated without alteration; instead of which, however, the Latin Translator has substituted another word at the third repetition, because he wished to make some variation. But we would rather preserve the simplicity of the Hebrew dialect, because by the fourfold use of the same word, it seeks to express the affection of the prophet, and the impressiveness of which is weakened by the change adopted by the Latin interpreter." Morison: "The words, *how long,* express the utmost distress, and the most earnest cry for deliverance." Calvin: "The words, *how long, for ever?* are a defective form of expression; but they are much more emphatic than if he had put the question according to the usual mode of speaking, *Why for so long a time?* By speaking thus, he gives us to understand, that for the purpose of cherishing his hope, and encouraging himself in the exercise of patience, he extended his view to a distance, and that, therefore, he does not complain of a calamity of a few days' duration, as the effeminate and the cowardly are wont to do, who see only what is before their feet, and immediately succumb at the first assault." As to forget God is a form of expression denoting wickedness in us, so for God to *forget* us is for him to withhold his needed aid, Ps. ix. 12, 18; x. 12. To *hide the face* is to refuse to look into an affair so. as to grant relief, Ps. x. 11, or to withhold smiles of approbation. The Chaldee has it, "How long wilt thou hide the glory of thy face from me?" Morison: "The hiding of Jehovah's face is an expression borrowed, in all probability, from the sensible manifestations of the divine presence in the tabernacle." Horne: "While God permits his servants to continue under affliction, he is said, after the manner of men, to have 'forgotten, and hid his face from' them."

2. *How long shall I take counsel in my soul*, having *sorrow in my heart daily?* The *how long* is the same as before. This part of the verse is variously rendered. Hare renders the first part thus: How long shall I have vexation in my soul? Boothroyd: How long shall I be distressed in mind? Indeed all the part of the verse quoted above is given with some variety. Edwards: How long shall I grieve in my soul, and have sorrow in my heart? Calvin: How long shall I take counsel in my soul? and have sorrow in my heart daily? Jebb: How long shall I take counsel in my soul, with sorrow in my heart daily? church of England: How long shall I seek counsel in my soul, and be so vexed in my heart? Fry: How long shall I lay up anxiety in my soul, sorrow in my heart all the day? Alexander: *Till when,* how long, *shall I place* (or *lay up*) *counsels,* plans, *in my soul, grief in my heart by day?* Morison says, The Alexandrine Septuagint reads the last clause afore given: How long shall I have grief day and night? Boothroyd: How long [shall I] be all day grieved in heart? The word rendered *counsel* is in the original plural, *counsels.* It occurs nearly *ninety* times, is once rendered *advice,* once *advisement,* twice *purpose,* in all other cases *counsel,* or where united with another noun *counsellor, i. e., man of counsel.* Morison: "It is evidently the act of painful rumination that is here described." Luther: "When the unhappy man finds that God feels towards him in the manner described, it then happens to him as follows:—That is, his heart is as a raging sea, in which all sorts of counsels move up and down; he tries on all hands to find a hole through which he can make his escape; he thinks on various plans, and still is utterly at a loss what to advise. . . As soon as the face of God is turned away from us, presently follow consternation, distraction, darkness in the understanding and uncertainty of counsel, so that we grope, as it were, in midnight, and seek everywhere how we may find escape." Alexander: "*By day* is elsewhere put in opposition to *by night,* as for instance in Ps. i. 2 above. Here it may possibly mean *all day,* but more probably it means *every day, daily,* as in Ezek. xxx. 16." The last clause of this verse is, *How long shall mine enemy be exalted over me?* Calvin and Jebb's rendering of this is identical with our version; church of England: How long shall mine enemies triumph over me? Edwards: How long shall my enemy exalt himself against me? Hengstenberg: How long shall my enemy exalt himself over me? Alexander: Till when shall my enemy be high above me? To be *high* or *exalted* is to be successful, to be beyond the reach of effectual opposition. The word here rendered *enemy,* occurs some hundreds of times, and is always rendered *enemy,* in the plural *enemies,* except once, where it is *foes.* It may point to any foe, visible or invisible, human or diabolical.

3. *Consider* and *hear me, O* LORD *my God; lighten mine eyes, lest I sleep the* sleep of *death.* This verse is variously rendered. Calvin: Behold [or look upon me,] answer me, O Jehovah my God; enlighten mine eyes lest I sleep in death; Edwards: Look upon me; answer me, Jehovah my God; enlighten my eyes, lest I sleep the sleep of death; Alexander: Look, hear me, Jehovah, my God, lighten my eyes, lest I sleep the death. The verb rendered *consider* does not occur more than *seventy* times in the Hebrew Bible. It is commonly rendered *look, behold, see,* but it is sometimes rendered *consider,* sometimes *regard, have respect.* Ps. cxix. 6; Lam. v. 1; Hab. i. 5. The word here seems to signify, *Consider favorably.* The verb rendered *hear* is found in Ps. iii. 4. It is more commonly rendered *answer.* That is the sense here. The meaning is, kindly regard and answer me. Everywhere else this form of the verb *lighten* is rendered, *cause to shine,* or *make to shine.* Ps. xxxi. 16; lxxx. 3, 19; cxix. 135; Dan. ix. 17. Perhaps it would be better to retain that form here, Cause mine eyes to shine, *i. e.,* to have that peculiar lustre, which evinces health, gladness and confidence. The Chaldee has it: "Enlighten mine eyes in thy law, lest I sin, and sleep with them which are guilty of death." But no such spiritual sense is

naturally suggested by the words. All these petitions seem naturally to arise out of the sad state of things described in the former verses. To *consider* is the opposite of *forgetting* to *answer*, of *hiding the face*; and to *enlighten* is the very mercy needed by one who has been perplexed and filled with distrust and sorrow. Calvin and Hengstenberg explain the *enlightening of the eyes* by a reference to the effect the honey had on Jonathan's eyes, 1 Sam. xiv. 27, 29. Hengstenberg also thinks that to *sleep the sleep of death* is a phrase like that in Jer. li. 39, 57. Luther: "When the Lord lifts upon us the light of his countenance, and turns his face towards us, listening to our cry, then are our eyes again enlightened, and we have no difficulty in obtaining counsel." The third verse does not produce a pause in the sense as is seen from the beginning of the next verse.

4. *Lest mine enemy say, I have prevailed against him.* The *enemy* here is the same mentioned, v. 2. Whether Saul, or Satan, or any other particular person is intended, the scorn and contempt he manifested were terrible to David. Cruel mockings either from men or devils are not easily borne. That is a very bitter cry in Ps. cxxiii. 3, 4: "We are exceedingly filled with contempt. Our soul is exceedingly filled with the scorning of those that are at ease, and with the contempt of the proud." No trial has a keener edge than the insults and exultations of enemies. Where they are clearly the enemies of God, their derisions terribly pierce the righteous. But as they greatly dishonor God, we may appeal to him not to permit his name to be evil spoken of through the audacious success and open triumph of ungodly enemies. But David had many foes, to none of whom he desired triumph in their evil course. And so he prays for mercy and deliverance, assigning this reason, lest *those that trouble me rejoice when I am moved.* The wicked are greatly emboldened by success, even though it be but temporary. Calvin reads it, *And [lest] those who afflict me rejoice if I should fall;* Edwards: And [lest] my enemies exult, when I am fallen; church of England: For if I be cast down, they that trouble me will rejoice at it; Fry: My adversaries rejoice because I am moved; Alexander: And [lest] my adversaries shout when I am shaken, or because I shall be shaken; Doway: They that trouble me will rejoice when I am moved. The last verb in this clause is commonly rendered as here, or *be removed;* yet in Ps. lxxxii. 5 it is rendered *are out of course.* In Ps. xlvi. 5, and Isa. liv. 10, it is applied to the convulsions of nature; in Deut. xxxii. 35 it is rendered *slide,* and in Ps. xvii. 5 *slip.* The *moving* here spoken of may regard either the dismay, the defeat, the death, or the spiritual discomfiture of David. Any failure, which would give occasion of exultation to the enemy, was here prayed against. After *moved* the Chaldee adds *from thy ways.*

5. *But I have trusted in thy mercy.* Calvin and Hengstenberg: I trust in thy goodness; Edwards and Jebb: But as for me, in thy mercy I trust; Fry:·But I, I have trusted in thy tenderness; church of England: But my trust is in thy mercy; Alexander: And I in thy mercy have trusted. The past tense, *have trusted,* agrees with the original, and gives the fullest and best sense. Trust in God's mercy was an old habit of mind with David, and was still kept up. It should never forsake him. Such a one may well say, *My heart shall rejoice in thy salvation.* Morison: "The word rendered *rejoice* involves in it the idea of ardent exultation corresponding to the great salvation." There is no better assurance of final victory than that drawn from the grace which enables us to trust in the divine mercy in the darkest hours. The church of England reads: My heart is joyful; Hengstenberg and Fry also use the present tense, *rejoices;* Calvin, Edwards and Jebb use the future, *shall* or *will;* Alexander: Let my heart exult in thy salvation. *Salvation* in every Scriptural sense of the term has long been owned by the church of God to be exclusively from the Lord. In him alone is safety and protection. Even deliverance from temporal ills can be wrought

by none except God be with him. How much more then is spiritual deliverance, the salvation of the soul, the work of God. He alone devised the wondrous plan. He alone executed it by his Son. He alone applies it by his Holy Spirit. But every effectual deliverance is from Jehovah. One thing is very noticeable in God's dealings with his people;—his interpositions are so arranged as to show that relief comes from him alone. He interposes, when all other helpers fail. If we adopt the rendering, Let my heart exult in thy salvation, then the prayer is that all other trust may be excluded, and all disposition to fix any time for his rescue be laid aside.

6. *I will sing unto the* LORD, *because he hath dealt bountifully with me.* The order of this Psalm is natural and beautiful. In vv. 1, 2, David four times cries out, How long? In v. 3, he begins earnestly to pray for help. In v. 4, he uses that argument so often prevalent with God to vindicate his name and that of his chosen against the wicked. Thus pleading, he increases in faith. Thus believing, he rejoices in God. Thus rejoicing, he breaks forth into songs of praise. Alexander prefers another form of gradation: " First a fact is stated: 'I have trusted in thy mercy;' then a desire is expressed: 'let my heart rejoice in thy salvation;' then a fixed purpose is announced: 'I will sing unto Jehovah.'" The verb rendered *dealt bountifully* is rendered in the same way in Ps. cxvi. 7; cxix. 17; cxlii. 7. Elsewhere it is rendered by the verb *rewarded.* Parkhurst contends for that sense here, applying the Psalm to Messiah. The word *recompense* is also used to translate it, 2 Sam. xix. 36; Joel iii. 4. In Pr. xi. 17, the participle from it is rendered *doeth good.* Amesius here renders it, *hath done me good.* Our version cannot be improved. It agrees with Luther, Hengstenberg and many others. But God's favors should awaken gratitude, and gratitude demands a song for its expression ; and so David says, *I will sing unto the* LORD. A good resolution is a capital thing. If any man ever glorifies God in thought, word, or deed, it must be consequent upon a solemn, humble, deliberate purpose to do so. Edwards reads: I will sing to Jehovah for having been gracious to me; church of England: I will sing of the Lord because he hath dealt so lovingly with me. In the Septuagint and the versions which follow it, this clause is added to the end of the verse: I will make a Psalm (or sing) *to the name of the Lord most high.* But these words are not found in the Hebrew text. Jebb and Merrick follow Lowth in supposing that they ought to be added in order to complete the usual form of Hebrew poetry. In the Septuagint the clause added is precisely the same as the last clause of Ps. 7, which see.

DOCTRINAL AND PRACTICAL REMARKS.

1. **Dark days are to the people of God no new thing,** vv. 1, 2. David saw such times. All the saints have seen them. Dickson: "Trouble outward and inward, of body and spirit, fightings without, and terrors within, vexations from heaven and earth, from God deserting and men pursuing may fall upon a child of God." No temptation befalls good men now but such as has always been common to the saints.

2. **No darkness is so dreadful as spiritual darkness,** v. 1. Job's misery reached its height when he said, "O that I knew where I might find him. . . Behold, I go forward, but he is not there; and backward, but I cannot perceive him: on the left hand, where he doth work, but I cannot behold him: he hideth himself on the right hand, that I cannot see him." Luther says that David here "paints this most pungent and bitter grief of mind, in the most graphic words, as one that feels he has to do with a God alienated from him, hostile, unappeasable, inexorable, and forever angry. For here hope itself despairs, and despair hopes notwithstanding, and there only lives the unutterable groaning with which the Holy Spirit intercedes in us,

Rom. viii. 26, who moved upon the darkness which covered the waters, as is said at the beginning of Genesis. This no one understands who has not tasted it."

3. When God delays his visits of relief, he has wise reasons for his conduct. God's time of deliverance is commonly further off than man's ignorance esteems best, vv. 1, 2. Yet it is often nearer than man's unbelief allows him to hope. The reason is, God is wiser and greater than man.

4. To cry out under the hidings of God's countenance is not sinful. Even the man without sin cried, "My God, my God, why hast thou forsaken me?" Let us imitate his lowliness and his faith. We must guard our souls against the great error of inferring refusal from postponement of deliverance. We must give God his time.

5. Because God's people love him above all else, therefore the thought of final and total rejection is intolerable, v. 1. They can bear anything but this. They will die, if they behold not his face in peace and in righteousness.

6. All repetition in prayer is not forbidden, but only vain repetition, vv. 1, 2. Four times does David cry out, *How long?*

7. It is well for us often to ask ourselves in the midst of trials, Will this thing much affect me a month, or a year hence? what will I think of it in a dying hour? in eternity will I regard it as of any moment? Calvin says that by crying out, *How long? forever?* David "teaches us to stretch our view as far as possible into the future, that our present grief may not entirely deprive us of hope."

8. Yet what poor creatures the greatest and best men are, if forsaken of God! vv. 1, 2. How bitter is the cry of the soul, unsustained by God. Henry: "Nothing is more killing to a soul than the want of God's favor, nothing more reviving than the return of it. . . Long afflictions try our patience and often tire it. It is a common temptation, when trouble lasts long, to think it will last always; despondency then turns into despair, and those that have long been without joy, begin, at last, to be without hope."

9. Calvin: "It is the peculiar office of God to repress the audacity and insolence of the wicked, as often as they glory in their wickedness." Therefore let us at all times carry our cause to him as David did, vv. 1, 2, 3. God's character forbids that he should abandon the righteous to the power and derision of his and their enemies. *That be far from thee, O Lord.*

10. There must be a great deal of dross in even good men to make daily and long-continued sorrow necessary to their sanctification, vv. 1, 2.

11. Let none be surprised that the haughty wicked often have for a time considerable success, and carry things with a high hand. It has long been so, v. 2. Their time of defeat and disaster is coming.

12. How marvellous it is that God should often permit his people to be for a time under the power of cruel, tyrannical husbands, parents, masters and rulers, v. 2. Daniel and his pious cotemporaries must live under those capricious Chaldean monarchs. Abigail lives with a husband, who is such a son of Belial that a man cannot speak a word to him. Such is the school, where the saints are often disciplined for usefulness and even for glory. Intolerable hardship leads to bliss and victory.

13. If faith had no victories and comforts, it would quite despond, v. 3. Blessed be the name of God, he never leaves himself without witness, nor permits his people to be tempted beyond what they are able to bear.

14. That is good for us, which leads us to pray, v. 3. It is better to be praying in the whale's belly than asleep in the ship. How prayer here helps David. "God's mercy supported his faith; his faith in God's mercy filled his heart with joy in his salvation; his joy in God's salvation would fill his heart with songs of praise."

Henry: "It is some ease to a troubled spirit to give vent to its griefs, especially to give vent to them at the throne of grace, where we are sure to find one, who is afflicted in the afflictions of his people, and is troubled with the feeling of their infirmities."

15. We cannot too often plead our covenant relation to God, v. 3. How uniformly do the saints cry, O Lord my God. Let them never disuse so excellent a practice. It is a great nourisher of the soul. If men will not *consider* our cause, God will.

16. Nothing so cheers the heart and lightens the eyes as the gracious presence of God, v. 3. It is the life of the soul.

17. How dreadful is the malice of the wicked. They often rejoice when God's people suffer in character, or person, or plans, v. 4. The hatred, which rejoices at calamities on the good, will surely be requited, Pr. xvii. 5. How much does wickedness on earth resemble that of the world of woe! How justly and inevitably hell follows unpardoned, unrepented sin!

18. How essential at every stage of the Christian life is faith, v. 5. Calvin: "It is not in a human way, or from natural feelings, we recognize in our misery that God cares for us, but by faith we apprehend his invisible providence. So David, as far as he could gather from the actual state of things, seemed to himself to be deserted by God. Still, however, having previously enjoyed the light of faith, he penetrated, with the eye of his mind, into the hidden grace of God; else how should he have directed his groans and desires to him?"

19. To the believing sinner or sufferer how sweet is mercy, v. 5. He lives by it. He hopes in it. He prefers it to all other sources of joy. He is never more blessed than when he thinks of no other resource.

20. However long the time of suffering to the righteous, it shall not last always, but be soon followed by a time of joy, v. 5. Tholuck: "A great number of our own [German] hymns were composed in the gloomy days of the thirty years' war." All God's people should here begin the work of praise, and so tune their souls to immortal songs.

21. No change is so great or so sudden that God will not effect it for his people, if it is for their good. David begins his song in sadness, but he ends it in joy.

22. The salvation which succeeds warfare, temptation and sorrow, will be wonderful, v. 5. The rest of Canaan was a delightful successor to the weary journey of the wilderness.

23. The trials and victories of the saints of all ages are so uniform that the same complaints and songs suit successive generations of God's people. This Psalm is as applicable to believers in this as in any preceding age.

PSALM XIV.

To the chief Musician, *A Psalm* of David.

1 THE fool hath said in his heart, *There is* no God. They are corrupt, they have done abominable works, *there is* none that doeth good.

2 The LORD looked down from heaven upon the children of men, to see if there were any that did understand, *and* seek God.

3. They are all gone aside, they are *all* together become filthy: *there is* none that doeth good, no, not one.

4 Have all the workers of iniquity no knowledge? who eat up my people *as* they eat bread, and call not upon the LORD.

5 There were they in great fear: for God *is* in the generation of the righteous.

6 Ye have shamed the counsel of the poor, because the LORD *is* his refuge.

7 Oh that the salvation of Israel *were come* out of Zion! when the LORD bringeth back the captivity of his people, Jacob shall rejoice, *and* Israel shall be glad.

THE title has not the word *Psalm* in it, but it is properly supplied in our English Bible. Calvin and Hengstenberg propose to read the title thus: To the chief musician of David. This is a literal rendering of all that is in the Hebrew title. But Alexander agrees with the sense of the English version, and renders it: To the chief musician, by David. This is probably correct.

In either case the inscription indicates the date of the Psalm, *i. e.*, some period in David's life. That he is its author is made sufficiently to appear by Hengstenberg, although Edwards, Rosenmuller and others employ a very confident tone of denial, arguing especially from the *seventh* verse. But there is no evidence that the language of that verse is in its true intent more applicable to times hundreds of years after David than during his life. Good men always longed for the coming salvation.

The attempt of some to apply this general description of evil men to the heathen, and not to human nature generally, is an awkward failure. For *first* the descriptions elsewhere given of man quite correspond with the statements here made; and *secondly*, the inspired apostle quotes this Psalm in proof that both Jews and Gentiles are all under sin, Rom. iii. 9, 12. Not only are the heathen sinners; all men are sinners also.

The resemblance of this Psalm to Ps. liii. has been often noticed. It is not certain, though it is probable this is the older composition. Venema well says that between these Psalms there is "no variation, which does not provide a sense excellent in both Psalms, and suited to the scope." The strain of the liii. is more elevated in some points than this. Venema properly adds that "the style of this Psalm is plain, easy and simple." The whole composition is well adapted to the use of the church in all ages.

In this Psalm we have *Jehovah* LORD and *Elohim* GOD, on which see above on Ps. i. 2; iii. 2.

1. *The fool hath said in his heart*, There is *no God*. *The fool* here spoken of is the sinner. Diodati says the fool is "the sensual and profane man, not enlightened with the lively light of God's Spirit: who, through the malice of his heart, puts out as far as in him lieth the natural lights of knowledge, and of conscience, concerning God, his providence, law and judgment, that he may run headlong to all manner of evil." Morison: "The Hebrew word, rendered *fool*, is derived from a verb, which signifies to fade and wither, as the falling leaves of autumn; and which connects with this primary signification, as applied to persons, the idea of moral decay and worthlessness. As a verbal it seems to denote not only an individual foolish and vaporing, but one who is very depraved and ungodly. It is worthy of notice that the corresponding word in Arabic signifies an atheist, an unbeliever." For *fool* Fry reads *wretch*, and in a note explains the word as signifying "a fallen, decayed, vile, contemptible, or foolish wretch:" Calvin: "As the Hebrew word, translated *fool*, signifies not only a fool, but also a perverse, vile and contemptible person, it would not have been unsuitable to have translated it so in this place; yet I am content to follow the more generally received interpretation, which is, that all profane persons, who have cast off all fear of God, and abandoned themselves to iniquity, are convicted of madness." The meaning is not that in their own eyes, nor in the eyes of worldly men they are fools; but that they **are** so in the eyes of God and of sound reason, and the result will show it. The word

rendered *fool* is in Isa. xxxii. 5, 6, rendered *the vile person;* but elsewhere it is in our version invariably rendered as here *fool* or *foolish.* The corresponding noun is in the English text rendered *folly, villany, so vile* a thing, and in the margin *wickedness.* Gen. xxxiv. 7; Isa. xxxii. 6; Jer. xxix. 23; Josh. vii. 15; Jud. xix. 24. There is no evidence that the word *fool* designates merely open libertines and profane persons; much less is it confined to the heathen.

The fool *hath said.* Edwards reads *saith;* Luther and Hengstenberg, *speaks;* the Syriac also uses the present tense, *says.* But in the Hebrew the verb is in the preterite, *hath said.* Alexander: " The preterites [of this verse] include the present, but suggest the additional idea that the truth here asserted is the result of all previous experience and observation." There seems to be no ground for a play on the word *said,* such as Lord Bacon supposes, in opposition to *thought. In his heart.* By this term Fry understands " secretly." Chillingworth: He is " both a resolute, secret atheist, and withal wise enough to keep his folly to himself;" Alexander: " To himself. if not to others;" Morison: " The word signifying *heart* has reference, as used among the Hebrews, more to the *intellect* than the feeling. It seems here to refer to the evil thoughts and surmises of a depraved and atheistical mind." On the other hand Hengstenberg thinks " the discourse here is not of the atheism of the understanding, but of the atheism of the heart." The word rendered *heart* is found more than *five hundred* times in the Hebrew Bible. It is used in Gen. vi. 5, 6, twice in Gen. viii. 21. It is often used in Exodus where the hardening of Pharaoh's *heart* is mentioned. See also Ps. iv. 7; ix. 1, and many other places. In moral judgments the *heart* has great power. " The *wish* is father to the thought." There is *no God.* The words *there is* are supplied by the translators. Morison and Alexander argue that the translators correctly supply, *There is.* Perhaps they are right. The same is done in the last clause of the verse, where all admit its propriety. Yet some learned men have supposed that it was best to omit *There is,* and read, " *No God, i. e.,* Let there be no God—I wish there was no God." However this may be we know there are these kinds of atheists: 1. Those who wish that there was no God. They are atheists in desire. Henry: " The fool cannot satisfy himself that there is no God, but he wishes there were none, and pleases himself with the fancy that it is possible there may be none; he cannot be *sure* there is one, and therefore he is willing to *think there is none.*" Could the wicked have it their way there would be no God. They hate him and do not like to retain him in their knowledge. 2. We have practical atheists. Chillingworth: " They live as if there were no God, having no respect at all to him in all their projects, and therefore, indeed, and in God's esteem, become formally, and in strict propriety of speech, very atheists. In heart and life many are and act very much as if there was no God. Luther: " The fool speaks there is no God, not with the mouth, gesture, appearance, and other external signs, for in such respects he often boasts before the lovers of God that he knows God—but in *heart,* that is, in his inward sentiments. These in the ungodly are deluded, and thence presently follows blindness of understanding, so that he can neither think rightly of God, nor speak, nor direct his conduct properly. Accordingly, those alone have God who do not believe in God with hypocritical faith. All besides are fools, and say in their hearts: there is no God." 3. There are speculative atheists whose foolish heart is so darkened, whose conscience is so defiled, and whose minds are so alienated from the life of God through the ignorance that is in them, that they prevailingly doubt or in word deny that there is a God. There have been such persons. They have shown great zeal for their opinions, and even a readiness to die for them. 4. But many who admit the divine existence deny the divine government and providence. How it can evince wisdom or do good to admit that there is a God, who yet does nothing, sees nothing, cares nothing, regards nothing, punishes nothing, rewards nothing, has never been shown. Many suppose that this is the class of atheists here referred to. *First*, there are such persons described in this book, Ps. xciv. 7. *Secondly*, the word used here is not *Jehovah* but *Elohim*. They do not say there is no self-existent, independent, eternal, unchangeable being, but "there is no Elohim, no Judge or Governor of the world, no Providence presiding over the affairs of men." The Chaldee paraphrases it, There is no (power or) government of God in the earth. It very naturally follows respecting such, *They are corrupt*. The Chaldee reads, They corrupt their works; Edwards: They corrupt themselves; Alexander: They have done corruptly. From any and every kind of atheism flows a corruption so horrible that nothing on earth can be worse. Atheists not only become corrupt after embracing their huge error, but their corruption made them atheists. The verb here used is in the preterite. It is sometimes rendered *marred*, frequently *corrupted*, more frequently *destroyed*. The wicked have marred themselves, broken themselves, destroyed themselves by their corruption. *They have done abominable works*. Edwards: They commit abominable actions; Mudge: They are abominable in their frolics; Jebb: They are abominable in their doings; Horsley: They are abominable in their profligacy; Fry: They have done abominable deeds; Hengstenberg: They are abominable in their actions; Calvin: They have done abominable works; church of England: They are become abominable in their doings; Alexander: They have done abominably (in) deed (or act;) Doway: They are become abominable in their ways; Syriac: They are become corrupt in their artful devices. Each of these gives a good sense, though some are rather too free translations. There is *none that doeth good;* Septuagint: There is none that doeth good, no, not one; Edwards: There is not one that doeth good; Alexander: There is none doing good. The most literal rendering is, There is not (any) that doeth good. The works of sinners are themselves sinful. Their ploughing is sin, Pr. xxi. 4. Their sacrifice is an abomination, Pr. xv. 8. Even their solemn meeting is iniquity, Is. i. 13. Wicked men may do that which is right for the matter of it, but their motives are all wrong. They do nothing that God esteems a good work, for he looks at the heart. "Love is the fulfilling of the law," and they have no love. "Without faith it is impossible to please God," and they are swayed by unbelief. Sin mars and ruins all the works of the wicked.

2. *The* LORD *looked down from heaven upon the children of men to see if there were any that did understand* and *seek God*. Edwards and Hengstenberg put the first verb in the present tense, *looks* or *looketh*. But not without cause, Calvin, Fry, Jebb and Alexander agree with the English version in using the past tense, *looked*. The last of these writers well says however that "the force of the preterite is the same as in the preceding verse." The tense used denotes here a continuous act. From the beginning God has done this thing, Gen. vi. 12; xi. 5; xviii. 21. There is an all-seeing eye, and it has always been inspecting human affairs. While men rave against God, that very God upholds them in existence, or banishes them to hell. In this verse "the infallible judgment and scrutiny of God" determine the universal corruption of human nature. Man's depravity is a doctrine, not of human invention or of sourness of mind. It is the clear teaching of him, who loves purity, and has searched the earth with the scrutiny of omniscience, and found all men very far gone in sin. This depravity manifests itself chiefly in two ways, blindness and aversion to God. Men neither *understand*, nor do they *seek God*. If their minds were not darkened they would see the beauty of divine things, and then they would love them. And if men loved and so sought divine things, they would soon perceive something, yea, much of their beauty. We cannot see beauty without loving it, and we cannot feel a lively and pleasing interest in anything without being in such a

state as readily to embrace true perceptions respecting it. The participle here rendered *understand* is elsewhere rendered *wise, prudent, expert, skilful,* Dan. xii. 10; Amos v. 13; Jer. l. 9; Dan. i. 4; it is also rendered to *teach, to behave wisely,* 2 Chron. xxx. 22; 1 Sam. xviii. 14, 15. Other forms of the word are rendered by the verbs *to consider, to prosper, to instruct, to be instructed, to have good success, to deal prudently,* Job xxxiv. 27; Jer. x. 21; xx. 11; xxiii. 5; Neh. ix. 20; Pr. xxi. 11; Josh. i. 8; Isa. lii. 13. In their soul's affairs the wicked are neither wise, nor prudent, nor expert, nor skilful, nor do they behave wisely, nor teach correctly, nor are they well instructed, nor do they duly consider, nor do they deal prudently, nor have they good success, nor do they prosper. They are all silly. There is not one element of wisdom in all their behaviour concerning duty and salvation. The remark of Hengstenberg that the word rendered *understand* is " always used of the conduct, to *act prudently,*" does not appear to be well founded. The word rendered *seek* is often so translated, as in Ps. ix. 10; xxii. 26; and many other places. It is also rendered to *inquire,* Deut. xiii. 14; to *search,* Jer. xxix. 13; to *regard,* Job iii. 4; to *care for,* Deut. xi. 12; Ps. cxlii. 4. The wicked are very vile. They neither regard God, nor care for him, nor inquire after him, nor search for him, nor seek him. The correlative verb in some cases is to *find.* True wisdom consists in seeking and finding God. The next verse contains God's decision respecting man's character.

3. *They are all gone aside.* Chaldee: They are all turned backward; Arabic: They have all gone astray at once; The Doway agrees with the authorized version; Edwards; They are all gone out of the right way; Calvin: Every one of them has gone aside; Fry: They are all gone astray; church of England: They are all gone out of the way; Jebb: They are all gone aside together; Hengstenberg: All are gone away; Alexander: The whole has apostatized. Venema reads this whole verse as if it was a continuation of the inquiry begun in the previous verse. But for this there appears to be no good reason. Calvin: "Some translate the verb rendered, *gone aside, to stink,* as if the reading were, *Every one of them emits an offensive odor,* that it may correspond in meaning with the verb in the next clause, which in Hebrew signifies *to become putrid* or *rotten.* But there is no necessity for explaining the two words in the same way, as if the same thing were repeated twice." Ainsworth: *The all,* that is, *the whole universal multitude is departed;* All in general, and every one in particular. It is added: *They are* all *together become filthy.* The word *all* is supplied from the preceding clause, these here spoken of being the same as those there mentioned. The word rendered *filthy* is found but three times in the Hebrew Bible, is in each case rendered the same way, and in each case applied to man. Ps. liii. 3; Job xv. 16. For *filthy* Edwards, Fry, Hengstenberg, and the Arabic use *corrupt;* Calvin: *putrid* or *rotten;* the Septuagint, Vulgate and Doway, *unprofitable;* Alexander: Together they have putrefied; Morison: The allusion, perhaps, is to an animal substance in a state of dreadful decay. In whatever else mankind may differ, in this they are agreed, that they have deeply revolted against God, and are become offensive. They are *together,* or in like manner become filthy. There is union, agreement, verisimilitude here. He adds: There is *none that doeth good, no, not one.* In the Hebrew, the Septuagint, and the Vulgate, this clause is precisely like the last clause of the first verse, which see. How the variation in the English was brought about is not certain. In some editions of the Septuagint the words, *No, not one,* are wanting. In the common editions of that version they are found both here and in the first verse. Some contend that later editors inserted them in the text of the Septuagint bringing them from Rom. iii. 12. But this is hardly probable. The Septuagint Interpreters gave what they regarded as the sense of the author, and Paul approves of this as the true meaning of the Psalmist, and so adopts it. There

is no sufficient ground for believing that Paul misquoted the Greek version. The church of England here inserts several verses from Rom. iii. but quite without authority. They are not found in the Hebrew, nor even in the Syriac, or Chaldee, though they are in the Septuagint.

4. *Have all the workers of iniquity no knowledge?* Many unregenerate men make great proficiency in science, in literature, in the arts of war and peace, of government and civilization; but in religious matters they are left to themselves, and "an archangel left to himself would be a fool." In religious matters, in his soul's affairs, every wicked man sets at defiance every maxim of sound wisdom, every dictate of divine knowledge. Sin is as great a madness as it is a wickedness. Edwards renders this clause, Do not any of the workers of iniquity observe? church of England: Have they no knowledge, that they are all such workers of iniquity? The chief reference in this clause is thought by some to be to the great self-ignorance of the wicked. They know not their own sinfulness, or guilt, or misery, or ruin. *Who eat up my people.* Horsley and Morison connect these words with the first clause of the verse, and make a full pause in the sense at the word people. They then read the residue of the verse: *They eat bread, and call not upon the name of the Lord.* The word *as*, in our version, has nothing in the original to correspond to it. This reading also gives a good sense. The great mass of the wicked are slaves to sense and lust and appetite. They know nothing but what they know naturally as brute beasts. They are fond of the good things of this life; but they are averse to prayer and praise. They call not upon the Lord. This may be the teaching of the place; but it has not been the common understanding of the passage. None of the ancient versions so read the verse. Most moderns approve the sense given in our version. The cruelty of the wicked is well expressed by their eating up the saints, both here and in Ps. xxvii. 2; Mic. iii. 3. *Eat*, often so rendered, also to *consume*, to *devour*. *Eat* is the best word here. Luther: "Those eat the people, who draw only profit from them, and who do not employ their station for the glory of God, and the salvation of those over whom they are placed." Persecutors eat up the church when they vex, torment, and murder the saints.

5. *There were they in great fear.* Literally, *There they feared a fear.* So Jebb. Calvin: There they did tremble with fear. Our version gives the true sense. There seems to be no good reason for the rendering given by Fry: Tremble with fear. The word is never so rendered in our version, although in Job iv. 14 a kindred word *shake* is used. But the verb is in the preterite, just as several other verbs in this Psalm. The best sense is obtained from the common version. The Septuagint, Vulgate, Arabic, Ethiopic and church of England add the words, *Where no fear was.* These words are brought here from Ps. liii. 5; but they are not in the Hebrew, Chaldee, or Syriac of this Psalm. The wicked have their fears so roused at times as to make earth like hell. One cried, "O hell! if thou canst cover me, take me." Another: "O the insufferable pangs of hell and damnation." Many of the profane and blasphemous speeches of ungodly sinners are signs of the fearful strife in their minds. The late school-boy whistles as he passes by the grave-yard. One great fact troubles the wicked. They have not the favor of God themselves, and they fear. For *God* [Elohim] is *in the generation of the righteous.* Chaldee: For the word of God is in the generation of the just. But the original justifies no such limitation of the sense. God himself is so remarkably with his people that the heathen have been struck with it, Esther vi. 13. The sense of *in* Calvin thinks is *with* or *for.* John Wesley, dying, said: "The best of all is, God is with us." In this world sinners are often overwhelmed and brought to repentance by a full conviction that God is with his people, 1 Cor. xiv. 25.

6. *Ye have shamed the counsel of the poor because the* LORD *is his refuge.* The word rendered *counsel* is always so translated, or by the words *advice, advisement, purpose,*

Ps. i. 1; xiii. 2. The *poor* is the *suffering*, the *afflicted*, in the singular. In Ps. ix. 12 the word is rendered *humble*. See comment on that place. The word rendered *shamed* is often rendered *confounded*. The wicked often fill the hearts of God's people with grief, shame and confusion by opposing and defeating all their wise and benevolent plans and counsels for the glory of God and the good of men, even for the salvation of their opposers and contemners. The verb in Hebrew is in the future. And so Alexander reads: The plan of the sufferer ye will shame; Edwards makes it a question: Will ye laugh at the resolution of the afflicted because Jehovah is his refuge? Venema also makes a question of the first clause: Will ye shame the counsel of the afflicted and poor? Mudge: Will ye now shame or laugh at the poor oppressed people for making God their refuge? But I find no ancient and few modern versions using the interrogative form. There seems to be no propriety in translating the first clause as Horsley: The counsel of the helpless man shall put them to shame. If our version is correct, then the sense is that the very piety of the afflicted provokes the contempt of the wicked, as we know it often does, Ps. xxii. 8; Matt. xxvii. 43. Some have thought the language ironical: You may confound the plan of the righteous if you can. But this is hardly authorized. Instead of *because*, Diodati proposes to read *but*, and this is authorized by our translation of Gen. xvii. 15. This gives a good sense. The wicked may laugh at the *poor*, the sufferer, as they please, but Jehovah is his refuge. He is as safe when the world blasphemes as when it utters its idle praises. Boothroyd also has it, But Jehovah will be his refuge. Hardly any word is more variously rendered than that translated *because*. *Refuge*, elsewhere *twice* translated *shelter*, Job xxiv. 8; Ps. lxi. 3; and twice *hope*, Jer. xvii. 17; Joel iii. 16; in all other places *refuge*.

7. *Oh that the salvation of Israel* were come *out of Zion!* There is great diversity in rendering this clause. Most of the ancient versions read, Who shall give out of Zion deliverance to Israel? Chaldee: "Who shall bring forth out of Zion the redemption of Israel? Calvin: Who shall give salvation to Israel out of Zion? Montanus: Who will give from Zion the salvation of Israel? Edwards: Oh that the deliverance of Israel might be granted from Zion; Boothroyd: O that some would give from Zion the salvation of Israel; Jebb: Who will give from Sion salvation to Israel? Fry: O that the salvation of Israel were given out of Zion! Hengstenberg says it is literally, Who will give from Zion the deliverance of Israel? Yet he does not reject the sense given by the English version, which is as good as any. Fabritius and Alexander say that the phrase *who will give* is an idiomatic optative in Hebrew. All the pious associations of the Israelites were with Zion as the capital of the theocracy, the city of their solemnities, and the prophetic source of deliverance, Rom. xi. 26. The salvation sought is for the church and is deliverance from the wickedness and wicked men above described; and that these foolish people may have a better mind, and no longer deny God, or providence, but piously confess both. *When the* LORD *bringeth back the captivity of his people, Jacob shall rejoice*, and *Israel shall be glad*. Calvin agrees with our version except that for *bringeth* he reads *shall have brought*. The word rendered *bringeth back* has very varied significations. It is found in precisely the same form in Ps. liii. 6; cxxvi. 1. Often elsewhere it is found in connection with *captivity*. See Job xlii. 10; Jer. xxix. 14; Eze. xvi. 53. In Ps. xxiii. 3 it is *restoreth*. It is often rendered *turn*, *return*. Edwards has it, When Jehovah restoreth his captive people, Jacob will exult, Israel will be glad. But this rendering is based on the supposition that this Psalm was written during the Babylonish captivity, which is a mistake. Edwards is followed by Fry. Hengstenberg connects the whole verse and reads, Oh that the salvation of Israel were come out of Zion, and the Lord returned to the imprisonment of his people! Then let Jacob rejoice and Israel be glad; Alexander: Who will give out of

Zion salvation to Israel, in Jehovah's returning the captivity of his people? Let Jacob exult, let Israel joy. The chief difficulty arises from the phrase, *bringing back the captivity*. Whoever will examine all the places where it (or in the original the same phrase *turn again the captivity*) occurs, will at once see that it has no reference to literal imprisonment, or bondage. Job was never sent to prison, nor was he ever sold into captivity. To *turn* or bring back captivity is to set free from any great evil or distress. And so when God gives his people deliverance there is joy, and the greater the deliverance, the greater the joy. Jacob [infirmity] shall rejoice. Israel [a prevailing prince] shall be glad. These names are given to the whole church. When she is *weak* she is *strong*. There seems to be no good reason for supposing as Calmet and Patrick, that Jacob means Judah, and Israel the ten tribes. Ainsworth: "Jacob is a name that noteth infirmity; for he strove for the birth-right, but obtained it not, when he took his brother by the heel in the womb, and thereupon was called Jacob. But *Israel* is a name of *power* and *principality;* for after he had wrestled with the angel, behaved himself princely, wept, prayed, and prevailed, his name was changed from *Jacob* to *Israel*, as a *prince* or *prevailer* with God." Alexander: "*Let Jacob exult, let Israel joy.* . . . This is both an exhortation and a wish, but the latter is the prominent idea, as the parallelism of the clauses show."

Doctrinal and Practical Remarks.

1. The leading truths of natural religion are so clear that it is folly to deny them, v. 1. Rom. i. 19, 20.

2. The boast of philosophy and wisdom, so often made by sinners, is all vain, v. 1 Fabritius: "Impiety has its birth in folly, that is, in ignorance of God;" Dickson: "Every man, so long as he lieth unrenewed and unreconciled unto God, is in effect nothing but a madman, running to his own destruction in losing his soul and eternal life, even when he seems most to gain the world;" Calvin: "There is no stupidity more brutish than forgetfulness of God."

3. No utterances are decisive of character but the utterances of the heart, v. 1. Words are cheap; but what a man *says in his heart* shows whether he is a wise man or a fool, a saint or a sinner. The seat of all goodness and of all wickedness in man is his heart.

4. While wicked words disprove all claims to piety, right words cannot establish a character for godliness, if in actions we deny God, v. 1. The life must be holy as well as the profession.

5. As all error has its rise in the practical atheism of the heart, so all error naturally leads to open and avowed atheism in belief, v. 1. To one who is fairly started in a career of false doctrine, there is no guaranty that he will stop short of the disbelief of the divine existence. Horne: "Infidelity is the beginning of sin, folly the foundation of infidelity, and the heart the seat of both."

6. It is no novelty to see men avowing the most horrible opinions and indulging the vilest practices, even mocking at sacred things. Calvin: "David does not here bring against his enemies the charge of common foolishness, but rather inveighs against the folly and insane hardihood of those whom the world accounts eminent for their wisdom. We commonly see that those, who, in the estimation both of themselves and of others, highly excel in sagacity and wisdom, employ their cunning in laying snares, and exercise their ingenuity in despising and mocking God."

7. The doctrine of the universal depravity of man is and always has been true, since the fall of Adam. It is asserted in all the Scriptures, vv. 1, 2, 3, 4. See many parallel passages, also Jer. v. 1; Matt. xv. 19; Rom. i., ii., iii. Luther: "See how many redundant words he uses, that he may comprehend all men in the charge, and

except none. First, he says *all*, afterwards once and again, that there is not so much as one;" Calvin: "All of us, when we are born, bring with us from our mother's womb this folly and filthiness manifested in the whole life, which David here describes, and we continue such until God makes us new creatures by his mysterious grace."

8. It is a great advantage in learning human nature from the Bible that we there find the results of divine, omniscient and infallible scrutiny, v. 2. Dickson: "God is the only right judge of regeneration and unregeneration, and the only true searcher of the heart."

9. The reason, why hearts and motives are properly brought into view in deciding our real characters in God's esteem, is that God's kingdom is not only over us but within us. If the heart is wrong, all is wrong, vv. 2, 3.

10. The human understanding no less than the human heart needs renewal, v. 2. It is marvellous that any should have denied this. The Scriptures make it clear. Eph. i. 17, 18; iv. 18; Ps. cxix. 18; 1 Cor. ii. 14, 15. If men saw the real beauty and excellence of divine things they would seek them.

11. If the Scriptural designations of things should determine our views, then we cannot have too terrible conceptions of moral evil, vv. 1, 2, 3, 4. It is folly, corruption, abomination, lack of understanding, refusal to seek God, apostasy, going astray, filthiness, iniquity. Those who commit evil are sinners, rebels, unjust, wicked, enemies of God, fools, haters of God, accursed.

12. The agreement of the unrenewed in sinning against God is perfect, v. 3. They are all *together* become filthy. In stature, in complexion, in intellect, in disposition, and even in the outward acts of sin there is diversity; but in hardness of heart, which is the core of depravity, in unbelief and rebellion all sinners are agreed.

13. In the treatment of divine things the wicked show that they are destitute of every principle of sound knowledge, v. 4. The workers of iniquity have *no* knowledge of God or of themselves, of truth, duty, privilege, or obligation. Luther: " Will they then not once perceive that they are such people, as occasion sorrow to themselves? There is not one sound principle of conduct entering into the behaviour of the enemies of God and of his church." Calvin: " The effect of the habit of sinning is, that men grow hardened in their sins, and discern nothing, as if they were enveloped in thick darkness."

14. The greediness, with which sinners devour the saints is amazing, v. 4. They eat them as bread. They make nothing of injuring the church of God. Dickson: " The nature of all unrenewed men is to bear deadly enmity against those that are really God's people, and delight to undo the godly, as contemners of all that live not as they do."

15. A sufficient cause for the spirit of persecution in sinners against the godly is found in the prayerless lives they lead, v. 4. They so lightly esteem Jehovah as not to call upon him, and so they naturally hate those, whose example condemns their irreligion.

16. Wicked men may rage and blaspheme, may boast and be confident; but they will all prove themselves the veriest cowards at last, v. 5. Not one of them will have boldness in the day of judgment. They cannot fortify even here against fears the most idle, yet the most terrible. Lev. xxvi. 17, 36; Pr. xxviii. 1; 1 Thess. v. 3. Often are they a terror to themselves and their friends. Jer. xx. 4. Dickson: " The near conjunction which God hath with the godly is the reason of the greatness of the sin of persecuting them for godliness; for here it is given as a reason why there they were in fear." Morison: "When least anticipating any sorrowful reverse, and when least prepared to meet it, the wicked are often thrown into a state of consternation as alarming as it is unexpected. Either the dispensation itself is very awful, or their minds,

being full of guilty recollections, are an easy prey to the first onset of alarming events. The courage of which ungodly men not unfrequently boast, in general forsakes them in the hour of sudden overwhelming calamity. With a heart all corroded with care, and all distracted with bitter anguish and remorse, they are but ill prepared for a transition from sensual ease and pleasure, to a prospect all gloomy and terrific."

17. Men may now laugh at the divine protection of the saints; but when all God's mercies to his people shall appear, the wicked themselves will pronounce them blessed, v. 6.

18. No such refuge is found as God himself, v. 6.

19. What remarkable words are found in all the Scriptures respecting God's people. This Psalm is the third, in which we find the word *salvation*, v. 7. Ps. iii. 8; ix. 14. There is no sweeter word than this! It is a word of constant recurrence in the worship of the temple not made with hands.

20. Our dependence on God is complete and absolute. We are always in captivity until he sets us free, v. 7.

21. God's saving interpositions occasion unfeigned joy in the true church of all names and ages, v. 7.

22. The minds of the prophets are full of the great theme of salvation, and often turn to it with apparent abruptness, v. 7. That the salvation spoken of in the last verse is that of which Christ is the author has been held by many. Diodati applies it to David, but especially to the great Saviour of the world, of whom David was only a type, to gain everlasting salvation for his church. Hengstenberg: "The wish here expressed found its highest fulfilment in Christ, and this is also to reach its highest stage of developement in the future, when the triumphant church shall take the place of the militant. Till then we shall have occasion enough to make the wish of the pious Psalmist our own." This application to Christ seems to be supported by such passages as Luke i. 68–74; iv. 18. Gill: "The Jews refer this to the times of the Messiah." He is clear and decided in doing so himself. Morison: "To whatever extent this prayer might apply to existing outward calamities, it seems, beyond all reasonable doubt, to have had an ultimate reference to the coming of Messiah, and to the mighty achievements of his spiritual reign." Cobbin: "Oh that Christ the Saviour of Israel were come out of Zion." Horne not only applies this verse to the salvation from the captivity under sin and death, but like Hengstenberg regards its most glorious fulfilment as yet future: "How doth the whole church, at this time, languish for the consummation of her felicity, looking, even until her eyes fail, for that glorious day of final redemption, when every believing heart shall exult, and all the sons of God shall shout aloud for joy." Henry, Scott and Clarke also refer the last verse to the coming of Christ.

23. Venema: "This whole Psalm may very well be applied to all times, when the church is afflicted and her hope derided by the ungodly, and is most admirably adapted to confirm the hope of the pious, and to prevent despairing thoughts."

PSALM XV.

A Psalm of David.

1 LORD, who shall abide in thy tabernacle? who shall dwell in thy holy hill?

2 He that walketh uprightly, and worketh righteousness, and speaketh the truth in his heart.

3 *He that* backbiteth not with his tongue, nor doeth evil to his neighbour, nor taketh up a reproach against his neighbour.

4 In whose eyes a vile person is contemned; but he honoureth them that fear the LORD. *He that* sweareth to *his own* hurt, and changeth not.

5 *He that* putteth not out his money to usury, nor taketh reward against the innocent. He that doeth these *things* shall never be moved.

THE title is the same with the first part of the title of Psalm iii. remarks on which see. No name of God but *Jehovah* LORD is found in this Psalm. See above on Psalm i. 2.

It seems very fitting that this Psalm should immediately follow the fourteenth. That delineates the character of the sinner; this shows us the character of the saint; that, of the bad man; this, of the good. From the resemblance of this Psalm to the twenty-fourth some have supposed that it was written on the occasion of the removal of the ark to Mount Zion. This may be so, but the evidence is not conclusive. It is certain however that David is the author of it, for the title ascribes it to him. Some think that the use of the word tabernacle as applied to the resting place of the ark shows that it could not have been written later than the reign of David, or the beginning of that of Solomon. After that period it is alleged that the word *tabernacle* is used, if at all, not more than once in application to the abode of the ark of God, and then figuratively, or as a designation of the holy city. Lam. ii. 4. After that time the *temple* is spoken of, or some term employed that avoids the word tabernacle. Nor could it have been written earlier than the time of David, for he removed the ark to Mount Zion.

Tholuck thinks this Psalm is quoted in Isa. xxxiii. 14–16. If so, it can have no historic reference to the Babylonish captivity.

1. LORD, *who shall abide in thy tabernacle? who shall dwell in thy holy hill?* Calvin: O Jehovah, who shall dwell in thy tabernacle? Who shall rest in the mountain of thy holiness? In this he very nearly agrees with the Septuagint, Vulgate, Syriac, Ethiopic and church of England. Edwards: Jehovah, who shall sojourn in thy tabernacle? Who shall lodge upon thy holy mountain? Jebb: LORD, who shall sojourn in thy tabernacle? Who shall dwell in the hill of thy holiness? Fry: Jehovah! who shall abide in thy tabernacle? Who shall dwell on thy holy hill? Other translations generally agree with some of the foregoing. There has been much said to show that one of the verbs in this verse has more respect to permanency of abode than the other. If this were so, it would not support the theories that have been based upon this interpretation. Each clause of the verse evidently has the same general import, and so the parallelism is here preserved. But there is a discrepancy among critics, as to which is the stronger word. Fry thinks the first verb refers to perpetual residence, and for proof refers to Ps. lxi. 4. Clarke and Jebb maintain (the former at some length) that the first verb implies a brief abode, and that the latter work regards a long continued residence. That the latter verb has necessarily no reference to permanent abode is evident from Gen. xxii. 5; Ex. xxiv. 14; Nu. xxii. 19. Mount Zion was a type of the Gospel Church, and Jerusalem was a type of the heavenly abode of the redeemed. And so the questions of this verse inquire, Who shall be an acceptable

worshipper of God on earth, and so be prepared to worship God in the temple not made with hands? Diodati: " Who shall be a true member of thy church, never to be cast out of it? and who shall enter into thine everlasting tabernacles of glory?" The tabernacle in David's time on Mount Zion was a new one prepared by that royal prophet, and not that which had been used in the wilderness which remained at Gibeon. The holy hill, or mountain of holiness, is Mount Zion in Jerusalem. See above on Ps. iii. 4. The Chaldee reads: The mount of the house of thy holiness; Tholuck:"The fundamental thought of Psalm xv. is this: *He only who shows his piety not only in God's public worship, but in his life, is worthy of the prerogative of dwelling in the house of God.* As it is the object of this Psalm to show the indissoluble connection between the adoration of God in the temple and its evidences in life, it cannot seem strange that it insists upon our duties towards man." Who then is accepted of God in his worship on earth, and so has the essentials of a character fitting him for heaven? This question is of the greatest weight and the most solemn moment. It is answered in vv. 2, 4 positively, and in vv. 3, 5 negatively.

2. This verse has in it three clauses responding to v. 1. Perhaps each of them, and certainly the first, relates to the habit of the life. It is, *He that walketh uprightly.* Chaldee: He that walketh in perfection; Septuagint, Vulgate, Arabic, Syriac, Ethiopic and Doway: He that walketh without blemish [or spot.] The Septuagint in translating the word rendered *uprightly* uses the word, which in Eph. i. 4 is rendered *without blame;* in Eph. v. 27, *without blemish;* in Heb. ix. 14, *without spot;* in Rev. xiv. 15, *without fault;* in Jude 24, *faultless;* and in Col. i. 22, *unblamable.* Calvin and Venema: He who walketh in integrity; Edwards: He who walketh with integrity; church of England: Even he that leadeth an uncorrupt life; Fry: He that walketh in sincerity; Hengstenberg: He who walks blamelessly; Alexander: Walking perfect. The accepted worshipper is as the Scriptures use these terms perfect, blameless, sincere, uncorrupt, a man of integrity, faultless, unblamable, upright, etc. The word rendered *uprightly* is in the Old Testament applied to lambs to be offered in sacrifice, which were to be without blemish. In Ps. cxix. 1 it is rendered *undefiled.* A servant of God must keep himself unspotted from the world. The good man's heart is the best part about him. He loves holiness. He hates sin. Indwelling sin and outbreaking sin greatly annoy and distress him. He hates vain thoughts. He loves God's law. If he could have his wish he never would sin again. He abhors iniquity. He despises the crooked ways of carnal men. He is honest with God, with men, with himself. Deceit is no part of a gracious character. The second clause of the description is, *and worketh righteousness.* All the ancient versions render this clause the same way. The Doway Bible here as commonly elsewhere uses *justice* for *righteousness.* Calvin, Edwards, Jebb and Fry: Doeth righteousness; Alexander: Doing right. In the English Bible the word is commonly rendered *righteousness,* a few times *justice, right.* No child of God is a worker of iniquity. It is his habit to do justly. *And speaketh the truth in his heart.* There is a remarkable agreement in ancient versions with our English Bible in rendering this clause; though Venema, Edwards, Fry and the church of England read *from the heart.* Calvin well says: " *To speak in the heart* is a strong figurative expression, but it expresses more forcibly David's meaning than if he had said *from the heart.* It denotes such agreement and harmony between the heart and tongue as that the speech is, as it were, a vivid representation of the hidden affection or feeling within." The first clause of this verse requires rectitude or sincerity in the largest sense; the second, honesty and justice; the third, truth, or a correspondence between the signs of language or gesture, and one's real thoughts. Alexander thinks the last phrase, *in his heart,* qualifies both *working righteousness* and *speaking truth.*

3. The next verse describes this same man negatively. He that *backbiteth not with his tongue.* Chaldee: Does not practise detraction with his tongue; Septuagint and most of the versions which follow it: Who hath not used deceit in his tongue; Syriac: Neither is he crafty in his tongue; Arabic: And he does not deceive any one with his tongue; Calvin: He that slandereth not with his tongue; Edwards: That detracteth not with his tongue; Jebb: He backbiteth not with his tongue; Fry: Who hath no slander on his tongue; Hengstenberg: He slanders not with his tongue; Alexander: (Who) hath not slandered with his tongue. The word *backbiting* is found but twice in our translation of the Old Testament, viz.: here and in Pr. xxv. 23. But in the latter case the word is not the same as here, but a word meaning *covert* or *secret,* or *hiding.* The word here rendered *backbiteth* is but once so translated, and once, *slandered,* 2 Sam. xix. 27. It is commonly in our version rendered by the verb *spy,* and the participle by the noun *spies.* The verb means literally *to go, to walk.* And as slanderers are restless bodies and go about, spying out other peoples' affairs and spreading injurious or false reports, the word came to designate the act of backbiting. Hengstenberg thinks there is an allusion to Lev. xix. 16. He is probably correct.

The next thing said of this good man is, *Nor doeth evil to his neighbour.* Chaldee. Nor brings evil on his neighbour; Septuagint, Vulgate, and Ethiopic: Nor has done evil to his neighbour; Arabic, Syriac and Venema: Nor doth he evil to his neighbour; Calvin: Nor doeth evil to his companion; Edwards: Doth no evil to his friend; Jebb: He doeth not to his neighbour evil; Fry: Who hath done no evil to his friend; Hengstenberg: He does not evil to his friend; Alexander: (Who) hath not done his neighbour harm. The word rendered *evil* is elsewhere commonly so translated in our English Bible, and frequently *wickedness, bad,* [as opposite of good,] *hurt, harm, ill, sorrow, mischief, wrong, displeasure, affliction, adversity, trouble, calamity.* The word rendered *neighbour* is commonly so found in our version, also sometimes *friend, fellow, companion.* See above on Ps. xii. 2. *Neighbour* is the best rendering if we follow Christ's explanation of that word, Luke x. 29–37. A good man will not of choice do anything to harm, wrong, or needlessly displease, trouble, or afflict any human being. Calvin well explains the word *companion* and *neighbour* found in his rendering of this verse, as designating "all men, to whom we are bound by the ties of humanity and a common nature." One, who thus far does well, will be safe in other respects, and so it is added, *Nor taketh up a reproach against his neighbour.* The word rendered *take up* is elsewhere translated *bear, spare, accept, stir up, suffer, respect, exalt, contain, raise, regard, bring, help,* and often *lift up. Reproach,* always so rendered in the Psalter but once, where it is *rebuke.* In Dan. xii. 2 it is *shame.* It is found in Ps. xxii. 6; xxxi. 11; xxxix. 8. A good man is not willingly even the repository of evil rumors against any of his kind. The word here well rendered *neighbour* is not the same as in the preceding clause. It is often applied to those who are *near* of kin. *Neighbour* is a good translation. It points out any one, with whom we have the intercourse of life. Though the words here are so few and clear, yet this clause has occasioned considerable difficulty and is quite diversely rendered. Gill explains it that this good man "does not himself raise any scandalous report on his neighbour, nor will he bear to hear one from another, much less will he spread one; nor will he suffer one to lie upon his neighbour, but will do all he can to vindicate him, and clear his character." This is very good, if our translation is to be preferred. But other renderings are suggested. Chaldee: Does not sustain or support a reproach, etc.; Calvin: Nor raiseth up a calumnious report, etc.; Alexander: And a scandal hath not taken up against his neighbour. Hengstenberg thinks the best rendering is, Who does not take up, or raise a reproach against his neighbour. Edwards, following Mudge, thinks this rendering the best: Nor throweth a disgrace

upon his neighbour, viz.: by dishonoring his wife or daughter. He says, "I understand it so for two reasons, one that the common translation comes too near the
meaning of the first clause of this verse; the other that otherwise something very
essential to a good man, and which is usually made part of his character (see Ezek.
xviii.) would be omitted." The great objection to this view is that we have no right
to make such a specification without some authority. It is purely conjectural. Some
think the verb in this clause may signify to *originate* or *invent*, to *make up* slanderous
stories without cause. But Calvin well says that "here is also rebuked the vice
of undue credulity, which, when any evil reports are spread against our neighbours,
leads us either eagerly to listen to them, or at least to receive them without sufficient
reason; whereas we ought rather to use all means to suppress and trample them
under foot. When any one is the bearer of invented falsehoods, those who reject
them leave them, as it were, to fall to the ground; while, on the contrary, those who
propagate and publish them from one person to another are, by an expressive form
of speech, said to raise them up."

4. This verse resumes the positive account of a gracious character, and in three
clauses continues the delineation. *In whose eyes a vile person is contemned.* There is
quite a variation in rendering this passage. Chaldee: Who is despised and worthless in his own eyes; church of England: He that sitteth not by himself but is
lowly in his own eyes; Jebb: He is contemned in his own eyes, he is abased. Such
a rendering destroys the antithesis between this and the next clause. Yet the sense
is good. The righteous often abhors himself and blushes and is ashamed to look
up on account of his vileness. Septuagint: In his eyes a malignant person is *set at
naught*, as the same Greek verb is rendered in Mark ix. 12. Several translations
follow this. The Syriac is peculiar: In his eyes a provoking man is despised. But
the Hebrew word is never rendered in our version in the sense of one, who excites
another to anger. Calvin: In his eyes the offcast [reprobate, wicked, vile, abomi-
nable] is despised; Edwards: That despise a worthless person; Fry: The reprobate
is despised in his eyes. The word we render a *vile person* may, according to Bythner
and others, be rendered *rejected, despised, reprobate.* Our version of Jer. vi. 30, uses
reprobate; and our translation of several other places would justify us in using *cast
away.* The word designates one who is justly *cast off, rejected, abhorred.* Hengstenberg: In his eyes the rejected is despised; Alexander: Despised in his eyes (is) a
reprobate. Morison supposes the vile person here spoken of to be "an ungodly,
profane, contemptible individual, whose very intercourses carry pollution and death
along with them. Such a man the expectant of glory rejects; he will have no unnecessary fellowship with him; for his good and the good of others, he stands at a
distance from him; and never ventures to come near to him, save with the hope of
benefitting his perishing soul." Wealth, rank, wit, learning, power and beauty can
never hinder a good man from despising such a castaway. Memorable instances of
good men despising reprobates we have in Mordecai's behaviour towards Haman,
Elisha's, towards Ahab, and Daniel's, towards Belshazzar, Esth. iii. 2; 2 Kings iii.
14; Dan. v. 17, and onward. The same is illustrated in Bunyan's treatment of
Charles II. It is proper to say that the feeling of the righteous towards the wicked
is not that proud, haughty, malignant contempt, which marks the behaviour of the
wicked towards the children of God. It is just, true, benevolent. It is the abhorrence of his character, not of his person.

Such a man will have other good traits of character; therefore it is said, *But he
honoureth them that fear the* LORD. The word here rendered *honoureth* is in many
places in our version rendered *glorify*, Ps. l. 15, 23; lxxxvi. 9, 12. *Glorify* is used
in many of the ancient and in the Doway versions. But the word *glorify* in Eng-

lish commonly denotes the honor the righteous give to God, or the honor God gives to his people. The highest kind of honor demanded by the nature of the case is here intended, Ex. xiv. 4, 17; Nu. xxii. 17; 1 Sam. ii. 30. The church of England has it, And maketh much of them that fear the LORD. Habitually to do this requires a higher character than belongs to man by nature. Calvin: "As those who fear God are often, as it were, the filth and the offscouring of all things in the estimation of the world, so it frequently happens that those who show them favor and sympathy, excite against themselves everywhere the hatred of the world. The greater part of mankind, therefore, refuse the friendship of good men, and leave them to be despised, which cannot be done without grievous and heinous injury to God." The house of God ignores the factitious distinctions set up by human society and exalts the distinctions owned by God, James ii. 1–7. He who goes thus far, will do whatever else is required by integrity. Therefore it is added, He that *sweareth to* his own *hurt*, and *changeth not*. Hammond: "LXX., instead of *to hurt*, seem to have read *to his fellow*, and so the Syriac, Latin, Arabic and Ethiopic." The Hebrew words for *hurt* and *fellow* are very much alike. It also gives a good sense to read, *He sweareth to his neighbours, and changeth not*, or as the Syriac has it, *lies not*, deceives not. But Anderson well observes that our English version, which gives the ordinary reading, "sets forth the moral integrity of the good man in a still more striking light, by describing him as performing his oath in the face of the greatest temptations to break it, when the performance of it may prove detrimental to his own interests; and this is no mean trial of a man's virtue." Alexander justly thinks there is a reference to Lev. v. 4; "if a soul swear to do evil or to do good," *i. e.*, whether to his own advantage or the contrary, or as Hengstenberg has it "for hurt, or for benefit." That is, the oath is binding, however we may regard it as affecting our interests. Hengstenberg: "When he happens to have made a promise or oath, which tends to his hurt, he still most religiously fulfils it." Luther: "I believe that what the prophet here says of keeping an oath is to be understood also of every sort of promise. For its object is to inculcate truth and fidelity among men. But it makes special mention of the oath, because, in a pre-eminent way, good faith is thereby kept or broken."

5. The last verse completes the description of the character of the righteous by giving two additional points in a negative form. First, He that *putteth not out his money to usury*. The word rendered *money* is everywhere else in the Psalms, and most commonly in the other scriptures, rendered *silver*. It occurs very often. There is hardly a point of morals, concerning which the people of the Nineteenth Century have more need of instruction, than that contained in this clause. Many trading men are evidently living in ignorance or error respecting usury. The original word here rendered *usury* is derived from a verb that is commonly translated to *bite*, as a serpent, Gen. xlix. 17; Num. xxi. 6, 8, 9; Pr. xxiii. 32; Ecc. x. 8; Jer. viii. 17; Am. v. 19; ix. 3; Mic. iii. 5; Hab. ii. 7. Morison well says, this is "a striking emblem of a greedy, griping usurer, who grinds the faces of the poor and distressed." By a figurative use of the word it expresses in Deut. xxiii. 19, 20 the act of *lending upon usury*. Whoever wishes to see all the passages where the word here rendered *usury* is found in the Hebrew Scriptures, may examine Ex. xxii. 25; Lev. xxv. 36, 37; Deut. xxiii. 19; Pr. xxviii. 8; Ezek. xviii. 8, 13, 17; xxii. 12. The word has one uniform rendering throughout our English version. In the Doway Bible it is also invariably rendered *usury*. A verb of the same root is twice found in Jer. xv. 10, and is rendered *lent on usury*. In Ex. xxii. 25 it is translated *as an usurer*. In Isa. xxiv. 2 it is rendered *as with the taker of usury*. But as lenders and creditors in corrupt states of the Jewish nation often became usurers, so the form of the verb under consideration came to sig-

nify to lend, Deut. xv. 2; xxiv. 10, 11, then a *creditor*, 2 Kings iv. 1; Isa. l. 1; then to *exact*, Neh. v. 7, 10, 11. And as usury is often accompanied with extortion, our translators render the verb in Ps. cix. 11 *the extortioner*, though another word for extortioner is employed by Isa. xvi. 4. The word *extortion* found in Ezek. xxii. 12 is also of a different derivation. The foregoing passages are all that are found in the Hebrew Scriptures bearing on the subject. Perhaps as to the origin, force and uniform usage of words, there never was a clearer case of exposition than that of this clause prohibiting usury. And none of these views are repealed or modified in the New Testament.

The word *usurer* is not found in the New Testament, and the word *usury* but twice, Matt. xxv. 27; Luke xix. 23. The allusion in these cases shows that usury was still in the estimation of the people a practice peculiar to "hard men."

One who has the preceding principles of morality will be proof against bribery, and so it is added, *Nor taketh reward against the innocent.* Our version often renders the word as here *innocent*, also *guiltless, clear, blameless. Reward* is also rendered *gift, bribe, present.* A good man, called to sit in judgment in any matter, because he knows his own weakness, is not willing to receive a gift, knowing its power to lead one astray. "The king by judgment establisheth the land: but he that receiveth gifts overthroweth it," Pr. xxix. 4. Of all social evils not one is worse than the perversion of law, justice and equity. The corruptions attending such a state of things are countless and frightful. The spirit of extorting money from even poor prisoners, and from weak and injured parties, has polluted the fountains of justice in all ages, Ex. xxiii. 8; Deut. xvi. 19; xxvii. 25; Acts xxiv. 26. When law is administered by favor, the poor are sold for a pair of shoes. But when the balance of justice is held by an impartial hand, the humblest has his rights secured. Such a man as is described in this Psalm shall be blessed. *He that doeth these* things *shall never be moved.* In his holy, innocent life, he has the evidence that he is a child of God. He shall never in God's esteem be separated from the congregation of accepted worshippers. Sometimes the word rendered *moved* is translated *fallen in decay, shaken, slip, slide, removed*, etc. A man of the foregoing character shall never so fall into decay, as not to flourish in eternal youth, never be so shaken as to lose his steadfastness, never so slip as not to recover himself, never so slide as to rise no more, never be removed from the Mount Zion above. Instead of *never*, we might read *not forever.* Eternity itself shall see no ruin, no overthrow, come on this man. Slade: "He shall hold on his way towards heaven, unmoved by temptation, and arrive there in safety. . . He shall not be moved, to eternity."

Doctrinal and Practical Remarks.

1. Because God is God, therefore he alone can determine what will and what will not please him in his worshippers. His decision is infallible, and so we should resort to him, v. 1.

2. We cannot too often or too solemnly inquire, What is a true profession of the true religion? v. 1. There is no more important question.

3. He is not fit for the church on earth, who is not fit for the church in glory. He who is accepted of God here, is accepted there, v. 1. Tholuck: "Only those shall share in the communion of the kingdom of glory, who were no strangers to it on earth."

4. The tenor of one's life is his *walk*, and must determine his character, v. 2. A river may run in various directions, but its course is in the main to its mouth, else it would not empty itself.

5. Religion without morality is monstrous. It has no countenance in Scripture,

vv. 2–5. Justification is by faith *sole*, but not *solitary*. True faith purifies the heart, works by love, and overcomes the world. Cobbin: "No man can be a true member of the church of God who is a stranger to moral righteousness."

6. Without holiness no man shall see the Lord, v. 2. Sincerity, uprightness, integrity are essentials of a gracious character. Dickson: "The sincere endeavor of universal obedience in a man's conversation is a fruit and evidence of true faith, and a mark of a true member of the church invisible;" Luther: "Not on this account, because thou art a holy monk; not on this account, because thou prayest much, because thou dost miracles, because thou teachest admirably, because thou art dignified with the title of Father, nor, finally, because of any particular work, except righteousness, shalt thou dwell upon the holy hill of God;" Henry: "I know no religion but sincerity," John i. 47; 2 Cor. i. 12; Calvin: "No doubt, God adopted Abraham freely, but, at the same time, he stipulated with him that he should live a holy and upright life, and this is the general rule of the covenant which God has, from the beginning, made with his church. . . If we really wish to be reckoned among the number of the children of God, the Holy Ghost teaches us, that we must show ourselves to be such by a holy and an upright life."

7. The great pillar of the morality which God teaches is *justice*, v. 2. Without this charity is a fraud, a monstrous lie. Morison: "A professing servant of God, without common honesty, is surely a fearful anomaly."

8. Another of the great pillars of a sound morality is truth, v. 2. Nothing more marks an heir of perdition, a child of the devil, than lying. John viii. 44. Morison: "In the intercourse of society, truth is an essential quality to the peace, honor, and ornament of life. Nothing can proceed comfortably without it, in the church or in the world. It is a kind of element which must pervade all things. True piety, therefore, must include it, as a constituent part of the renewed heart. In the heart it must have its seat, or in the life and conversation it will never be exhibited." The doom of liars is most fearful, Rev. xxi. 8, 27; xxii. 15.

9. If the aggravation of sin may be determined by the shame and misery it causes here, few sins will be more terribly punished in eternity than that of evil-speaking, call it backbiting, slander, detraction, or by any other name. The good man hates it cordially, v. 3. Saurin: "Slander is a vice that strikes a double blow, wounding him that commits it, and him against whom it is committed." Sir Walter Raleigh: "If the divines do rightly infer from the sixth commandment, *Thou shalt not kill*—scandalizing one's neighbor with false and malicious reports, whereby I vex his spirit, and consequently impair his health, is a degree of murder." Tillotson: "A good word is an easy obligation; but not to speak ill requires only our silence, which costs us nothing." Beveridge: "I am resolved by the grace of God, to speak of other men's sins only before their faces, and of their virtues only behind their backs." Henry: "The citizen of Zion knows the worth of a good name, and therefore he backbites not, defames no man, speaks evil of no man, makes not others' faults the subject of his common talk, much less of his sport and ridicule, nor speaks of them with pleasure, nor at all but for edification; he makes the best of everybody and the worst of nobody." Dickson: "A fruit of faith is conscience-making of what a man speaketh." Calvin: "David sets down calumny and detraction as the first point of injustice by which our neighbors are injured. If a good name is a treasure, more precious than all the riches of the world, (Prov. xxii. 1,) no greater injury can be inflicted upon men than to wound their reputation. . . It cannot be doubted that the design of the Holy Spirit is to condemn all false and wicked accusations." A heathen once said, "A slanderer is the most terrible of wild beasts."

10. The law of love to our neighbor has always been binding, v. 3.   Men always were bound to love others as themselves.

11 Tale-hearing is one of the worst vices.   No good man will allow it, v. 3.   The Rev. Charles Simeon of blessed memory said, "The longer I live, the more I feel the importance of adhering to the following rules, which I have laid down for myself in relation to such matters:

1st. To hear as little as possible what is to the prejudice of others.

2d. To believe nothing of the kind until I am absolutely forced to it.

3d. Never to drink into the spirit of one who circulates an ill report.

4th. Always to moderate, as far as I can, the unkindness which is expressed towards others.

5th. Always to believe that if the other side were heard, a very different account would be given of the matter."   William Penn said: "Believe nothing against another, but on good authority; nor report what may hurt another, unless it be a greater hurt to another to conceal it."

What a wonderful example in this point we have in our blessed Saviour.   It seems to have been universally understood that he abhorred all backbiting.   "The north wind driveth away rain: so *doth* an angry countenance a backbiting tongue."   Pr. xxv. 23.   Morison: "That man must have a black heart, if it were dissected, who would not exert himself to stay the desolating progress of an evil report.   If he knew himself, or felt the glow of genuine benevolence, he would shrink with horror from the crime of standing sentinel upon his brother, ready to seize on him and drag him to punishment, on the discovery of the slightest offence."   The author would here record his serious belief that a full half of all the misery he has witnessed, in the course of a life neither short, nor unattended with fair opportunities of observation, was caused by a sinful abuse of the power of speech, and that more than half the misery thus caused would have been avoided, if all in the community who had no part in originating them had at once done their duty, and frowned on evil reports.   James iii. 2–10.

12. As a good man does not and cannot feel alike towards saints and sinners, so his conduct towards men must vary according to his conception of their character, v. 4.   Dickson: "A fruit of faith is the low estimation of any worldly excellency wherewith a wicked man can be busked, . . . but where he seeth one that feareth God, he esteemeth highly of him in his heart."   Morison: "Genuine piety will ever struggle to breathe its own healthful element.   It will draw heart to heart.   It will seek its own appropriate companionship.   Wherever it sees the image of God, it will honor that image.   However lowly may be the outward garb, it will be sufficient to proclaim in its hearing—'This is a child of God.'"   When indeed we find wicked men in power, we must honor them in their office, submit cheerfully to all their lawful requirements, and pray for them; but we cannot be expected to love or revere those *persons*, who are odious and vile.   Calvin: "Paul teaches us, (Eph. v. 11,) that it is a species of fellowship with the unfruitful works of darkness when we do not reprove them."   Isa. v. 20.

13. The law respecting promises and oaths is that the inconvenience of fulfilling them does not in the least dissolve their obligation, v. 4.   If we have rashly bound ourselves to any lawful act, our solemn and faithful performance of our engagements may not only cure our hastiness of spirit, but it will evince our strength of principle.   Calvin: "The faithful will rather submit to suffer loss than break their word.   When a man keeps his promises, in so far as he sees it to be for his own advantage, there is in this no argument to prove his uprightness and faithfulness."   Every lawful promise, covenant and oath must be kept, unless we are released not by constraint, but willingly by the party, to whom we are bound.   Unlawful engagements of every kind are to be

repented of and broken. But let men beware lest they pronounce that unlawful, which is merely contrary to their wishes or self-interest.

14. This Psalm casts light upon the practice of usury, which is so prevalent in this nineteenth century, v. 5. Where the usury given or received is greater than the law of the land allows, the sin is against all those divine precepts, which require obedience to every ordinance of man, that is not wicked, Rom. xiii. 1–5; 1 Pet. ii. 13. Every good man is a good citizen, and keeps the laws. When the receiving of usury damages the poor and needy, it is manifestly condemned, though the amount may be no greater than the laws of the land allow. Nor is there anywhere in Scripture a hint to the contrary of these principles, even though money be borrowed or lent for the purposes of commerce. Indeed the violation of these principles is sufficient to bring about those alternate expansions and contractions, which for a long time have been afflicting the commercial world. It is true that a return to sound practice on this subject will not be compassed by one man. But the truth is mighty. And the truth on this subject is as potent as on any other matter. On such a subject let others speak. Calvin, speaking of the first clause of the fifth verse, says: "With respect to this clause, as David seems to condemn all kinds of usury in general, and without exception, the very name has been everywhere held in detestation. But crafty men have invented specious names under which to conceal the vice; and thinking by this artifice to escape, they have plundered with greater excess than if they openly and avowedly lent on usury. God, however, will not be dealt with and imposed upon by sophistry and false pretences. He looks upon the thing as it really is. There is no worse species of usury than an unjust way of making bargains, where equity is disregarded on both sides. Let us then remember that all bargains in which the one party unrighteously strives to make gain by the loss of the other party, whatever name may be given to them, are here condemned. . . I would, above all things, counsel my readers to beware of ingeniously contriving deceitful pretexts, by which to take advantage of their fellow-men, and let them not imagine that anything can be lawful to them which is grievous and hurtful to others.

"With respect to usury, it is scarcely possible to find in the world a usurer who is not at the same time an extortioner, and addicted to unlawful and dishonorable gain. Accordingly Cato of old justly placed the practice of usury and the killing of men in the same rank of criminality, for the object of this class of people is to suck the blood of other men. It is also a very strange and shameful thing, that, while all other men obtain the means of their subsistence with much toil . . . money mongers should sit at their ease, and receive tribute from the labor of all other people."

Morison: " 'He that putteth not out his money to usury.' By the spirit of a subtle philosophy, the entire force of this precept, or rather declaration, may be done away with. It may be urged that money, like every other commodity, is a species of property, and that a man has the right to make the best of it. In this mode of putting the argument there may be a speciousness to deceive weak minds, and quiet consciences which greatly need the application of such a balm; but can a man who really fears God, and is acting under the direction of his principles, suffer himself to take advantage of a distressed neighbor, because he happens to have more than he, at any given time, of this particular commodity of money? The law of God, whatever may be the avaricious feeling of the human heart, says, No; the principle of true benevolence says, No; the honor of the Christian profession says, No. And let philosophy, and infidelity, and covetousness have all the happiness, which can be the result of setting at naught considerations which, if uniformly acted upon, would turn this wilderness of sin and death into the paradise of God."

The foregoing views are so clear, so sound, so Scriptural, that they cannot be refuted.

15. The dreadful corruption sometimes manifested in courts is no novelty, v. 5; Eccle. v. 8. Yet the doom of corrupt judges and jurors, dying without repentance, will be dreadful, Isa. v. 23, 24.

16. While everything else is fickle, God's people are stable, v. 5. Gibraltar, the Himalayas and the Apalachian range shall melt like wax, but God's people shall not be moved, to eternity.

17. This whole Psalm shows us that hypocrisy is no novelty. It was always necessary to distinguish between the genuine and spurious convert. False professors can do wonders for awhile, but they cannot perseveringly keep the law of God. Luther: "This Psalm strikes against the lovers of outward show. For the Jews boasted themselves over all other people, on the two grounds that they alone were the seed of the Fathers, and alone possessed the law of God." Calvin: "If we really wish to be reckoned among the number of the children of God, the Holy Ghost teaches us that we must show ourselves to be such by a holy and upright life; for it is not enough to serve God by outward ceremonies, unless we also live uprightly and without doing wrong to our neighbors."

18. The grace of God is absolutely necessary to enable poor, fallen man to maintain, through all temptations, the morality required by the law of God, even as expounded in this short Psalm. Morison: "How unlike this picture to the shuffling, mean, and ungenerous conduct of many who only bear the Christian name to disgrace it! In so far as they are bound by human laws, you may calculate on their honor and integrity; but if you leave anything to the native impulse of their principles, alas! alas! you will be fatally deceived! They are a compound of selfishness, injustice, and worldly policy; and a more hideous compound cannot be contemplated."

19. This Psalm is specially clear as to the character of true and accepted worshippers. Calvin: "Access to God lies open to none but his pure worshippers." Morison: "It cannot be too strongly impressed upon the minds of men that principles merely professed, however excellent, which do not sanctify the heart and mould the character, cannot be acceptable with God."

20. In the delineation of the character of an approved citizen of Zion the second table of the law alone is referred to in this Psalm. The same is true in many other parts of Scripture. The reason is that if we love not our brother, whom we have seen, it is idle to pretend to love God whom we have not seen.

21. This Psalm and parallel passages furnish an excellent standard by which to examine ourselves.

PSALM XVI.

Michtam of David.

1 Preserve me, O God: for in thee do I put my trust.

2 *O my soul*, thou hast said unto the LORD, Thou *art* my Lord: my goodness *extendeth* not to thee,

3 *But* to the saints that *are* in the earth, and *to* the excellent, in whom *is* all my delight.

4 Their sorrows shall be multiplied *that* hasten *after* another *god:* their drink offering of blood will I not offer, nor take up their names into my lips.

5 The LORD *is* the portion of mine inheritance and of my cup: thou maintainest my lot.

6 The lines are fallen unto me in pleasant *places;* yea, I have a goodly heritage.

7 I will bless the LORD, who hath given me counsel: my reins also instruct me in the night seasons.

8 I have set the LORD always before me: because *he is* at my right hand, I shall not be moved

9 Therefore my heart is glad, and my glory rejoiceth: my flesh also shall rest in hope.

10 For thou wilt not leave my soul in hell; neither wilt thou suffer thine Holy One to see corruption.

11 Thou wilt shew me the path of life: in thy presence *is* fulness of joy; at thy right hand *there are* pleasures for evermore.

THAT David is the author of this Psalm is declared by the title, by Peter on the day of Pentecost, Acts ii. 25, and by Paul, Acts xiii. 35–37.

The word *Michtam* found in the title is also in the titles of five other Psalms, lvi., lvii., lviii., lix., lx. Perhaps no word has occasioned greater diversity of opinion. Kimchi thinks it is the name of a musical instrument. Jarchi supposes it refers to the tune to be sung. Calvin inclines to this opinion. Some regard it as derived from a word which signifies to *cut,* to *engrave,* denoting, as Anderson says, "that the Psalm is fit to be engraven on a valuable and durable pillar." This is the view taken by Theodoret. Chaldee: *A right engraving* (or *a straight sculpture,* as some;) Septuagint: *An inscription on a pillar;* Vulgate: An inscription of a title to David himself. The Syriac is still different: Of David. The election of the church and the resurrection of Christ; the Arabic has the same with the addition, A writing concerning the covenant; Edwards following Mudge thinks it may designate *a Psalm to be written in gold letters to teach.* Many have thought that *Michtam* is derived from a word which signifies gold and that it is intended to designate this as a *golden Psalm,* that is a composition very precious, a writing exceedingly excellent. This view is favored by Boothroyd, Amesius, Luther, Gill, Dimock, Patrick, Diodati, Ainsworth, Morison, Cobbin, Henry, Scott, Clarke and many others. Greater weight of authority can be adduced for this than for any other opinion. But Houbigant renders *Michtam* by the Latin *arcanum, a secret.* Hengstenberg is of the same mind, A secret— *a song with* a deep import; Alexander takes the same view and thinks it "signifies a mystery or secret. . . It probably indicates the depth of doctrinal and spiritual import in these sacred compositions." Mant seems to favor the union of two of the foregoing views: " *As a sepulchral inscription,* it might have been written on our Redeemer's tomb; *as a triumphal monument,* it might have been sung by him in the region of departed spirits; and in either, or in any sense, it may well be considered as a *golden* composition, as *apples of gold in a net-work of silver,* invaluable in its subject, most pleasing in its structure." Those who favor the explanation drawn from *gold* quote many titles of eastern and ancient productions, as the golden verses of Pythagoras, etc. But there seems to be no good reason for giving any pre-eminence to the *six* Psalms having *Michtam,* so as to call them *Golden* above all others.

After this array of great names it may seem almost rash to prefer another opinion. It is that *Michtam* here is the same as *Michtab,* found in Isa. xxxviii. 9 and several other times in Scripture. The best scholars assert that the letters by which this variation would be produced, are often interchanged. If this is the true view, then Michtam here simply means *A writing.* This would militate against the view of Hengstenberg that David is fond of enigmatical designations in the titles, yet even Hengstenberg admits that very probably David just changed a letter and thus " transformed a word from a very common meaning into a similar one of deeper signification." *Michtam of David* is then probably *A writing of David.*

That this is a Messianic Psalm is shown by Peter, Acts ii. 25–36, and by Paul, Acts xiii. 35–37. Some have insisted that everything in this Psalm refers exclusively to Christ. That there is no need of so construing this excellent song is shown, perhaps sufficiently, in the Introduction, § 8. Even Cocceius says: "Many, as well ancients as moderns, suppose that Christ is the speaker in this Psalm. But I think David speaks in the whole Psalm. I suppose the mode of applying it to Christ and to David is best explained in Acts ii. 29, 30."

At what period in the life of David this Psalm was written we have no means of determining.

The names of the Almighty in this Psalm are *El God, Jehovah* LORD, and *Adonai Lord*, on which respectively see above on Ps. v. 4; i. 2; ii. 4.

1. *Preserve me, O God:* Chaldee, Septuagint and Calvin: Keep (or guard) me, O God. The same verb is rendered also by such words as *observe, mark, take heed to, wait for, regard, save.* Horsley: "The Hebrew word expresses the actions of those who watch over another's safety, as of guards attending their king, or a shepherd keeping his flock." The more full the sense, the better in this case. Alexander: "The prayer, *preserve me,* implies actual suffering or imminent danger." The word here rendered *God* is not *Elohim,* but *El.* The reason why he thus boldly asks to be guarded and saved is his confidence in God, which he now exercises, but which is no new thing with him. *For in thee do I put my trust.* In the Hebrew it is, *In thee I have trusted,* yet implying continued action. In the Chaldee it is, *I have depended on thy word.* This paraphrase often puts God's *word* for *himself.* This prayer was in substance suitable for David and for Christ, who in the days of his flesh offered up prayers and supplications with strong crying and tears unto him that was able to save him from death.

2. O my soul, *thou hast said unto the* LORD, *Thou* art *my Lord.* The words, *O my soul,* are not in the Hebrew. Our translators have followed the Chaldee and supplied them. This is better than with the Septuagint, Vulgate, Ethiopic, Syriac, Arabic, Edwards and Fry, to read, *I have said,* although some MSS. so have it. Calvin, Hengstenberg, Tholuck, Alexander, church of England and others give their weight in favor of our version. What the soul said was, *Unto Jehovah.* Reliance on him is well founded; and obedience to him is most reasonable. Whoso is wise, let him say to Jehovah, Thou art my Lord. The word is *Adonai.* The last clause of the verse is full of difficulty: *My goodness extendeth not to thee.* Chaldee: My good is given only by thee; Syriac: My goodness is of thee; Septuagint, Vulgate, Ethiopic, and Doway: Thou hast no need of my goods; Arabic: Thou hast no need of my good works; John Rogers' translation: My goodes are no thinge unto the; Bishops' Bible: My goodes are nothing unto thee; Genevan translation and Calvin: My well-doing extendeth not to thee; Edwards following Mudge: My good things are not suited to thee; Jebb: My goodness is nothing unto thee; Fry: The benefit of my services is not to thee; Venema: My goodness is nothing above thee; Hengstenberg: My salvation is not without thee; Alexander: My goodness (is) not besides thee (or beyond thee); Amesius: Thou wilt not lay up my goodness with thee; Horsley: Thou art my good,—not beside thee; Boothroyd: No good have I but from thee; Kennicott: My goodness is not without thee; Clarke: My bounty is not to thee; Houbigant and Lowth: I have no goodness without thee. None of these renderings teach any dangerous doctrine. The word, which we read *goodness,* is also rendered *good, prosperity, wealth, welfare, good deeds, pleasure, kindness.* Of all these senses that of *kindness* seems to be the best in 2 Sam. ii. 6; 2 Kings xxv. 28, *kindly;* in 2 Chron. vi. 41; Ps. xxi. 3; xxiii. 6, the word means *kindness,* though rendered *goodness;* see also Ps. lxv. 11; lxviii. 10. In Hos. xiv. 2 it is rendered *graciously, i. e., in kindness.* Whether these words relate to David in person or as a type of Christ, this gives a good sense—*My kindness is not to thee,* as its object. God is independent, sovereign, beyond want. We cannot profit the Almighty, J b xxii. 2, 3; xxxv. 7, 8;

Luke xvii. 10. Compassion towards God is impossible. To him we can manifest no grace. We can never give him but of his own, 1 Chron. xxix. 14. All we can pay him is his just due. He needs no help, no pity, no kindness. Even Christ did not become incarnate and die, to show kindness to God, but to exhibit to sinners the kindness of God and of his Son. If we take the word *goodness* in the sense of *merit*, the clause would be true of David as a man, but not of Christ, whose infinitely precious righteousness is before God, and is by him esteemed of great worth, meritorious beyond all bounds. Other explanations are offered, but that given seems to be preferable to all others.

3. But *to the saints that* are *in the earth.* That is, my goodness or kindness is to, upon, or towards the people of God on earth. This is true of David the type, and of Christ the anti-type. All good men love God's saints. Jesus loves them. He gave himself for them. Good men wish well to all, but especially to those who wear the image of God. Jesus Christ came not into the world to condemn the world, but he laid down his life for his sheep. His kindness and grace, as well as the brotherly love of his people, are pre-eminently to the saints that are in the earth, *and to the excellent.* For the signification of the word *excellent*, see Ps. viii. 1, 9. For solid worth, for upright dispositions, for exalted aims, all of which will stand the test of the last day, God's people are the choice ones of the race, the flower of the world, the *élite* of the universe. *In whom* is *all my delight.* Both Christ and his people have complacency in the righteous. Their kindness is towards them. Their delight is in them, 1 John iv. 7 ; Prov. viii. 27–31. The word rendered *delight* is also translated *desire, pleasure, purpose.* Their desire is in them. Their pleasure is in them. Their purpose of heart is toward them. It is fixed in that direction.

4. *Their sorrows shall be multiplied* that *hasten* after *another* god. This verse has led some to suppose this Psalm was written by David during his residence among the Philistines. But a devout and intelligent mind may know and be deeply affected with the miseries of the heathen without having ever resided among them, and of course after having seen them and removed from them. The sixth verse would greatly discourage the idea that David was now among any heathen people. All do not render these words in the same way. Chaldee : They multiply their idols, and then hasten that they may offer gifts ; Septuagint, Vulgate, Ethiopic and Doway : Their infirmities were multiplied : afterwards they made haste ; Arabic : Their sorrows were multiplied, and then they made haste ; Syriac : The worst sorrows were swiftly multiplied to them ; Amesius : They multiply their sorrows, who endow another ; Calvin : Their sorrows shall be multiplied who offer to a stranger that is, to a strange God—another than the true God ; Edwards : Their pains will increase who bribe another God ; Jebb and Fry agree with our English Bible ; Hengstenberg : Many are the sorrows of those, who purchase of another [god ;] Alexander : Many (or multiplied) shall be their sorrows—another they have purchased. Many understand *god* after *another*. Prof. Stuart, after *another* puts *way*, but the prophet had previously said nothing of a *way*, though he had of a God and a Lord, vv. 1, 2. The same remark applies to the supposition of Gill and Clarke that we may read *another Messiah*. The authorized version probably gives the true sense of the whole clause. Though idols are vanities and vexations, yet *sorrows* is the best word here. One reason why the early Christians, who had been converted from idolatry, prized the Christian religion so highly was that it saved them from so much temporal misery and was such a fountain of happiness even in this life. Some of them express themselves much as we should expect the damned to do, if they were now saved from hell. They had known by a horrible experience the truth of this clause. For *hasten after*, our translators authorize in the margin, *give gifts to*, but I

do not find the word so rendered in the text of the common version except in Ex.
xxii. 16; where we have *endow*, and no where else than here in the margin. *Their
drink-offerings of blood will I not offer, nor take up their names into my lips.* This
rendering gives the whole sense. Hengstenberg well remarks that the words *their*
before *drink-offerings* and *names* are referred by many expositors to " the idolaters, and by some again to the idols. The admissibility of the latter exposition
cannot be denied." Calvin holds this view; Hengstenberg also thinks there is a
reference to Ex. xxiii. 13; as there is also in Hos. ii. 17. He adds: " *The drink-
offerings of blood* are understood by various expositors literally; but in this reference
to a particular heathenish custom, . . . the connection is not attended to . . . One
must rather, with a comparison of Isa. lxiii. 3, explain thus the drink-offerings of
blood: drink-offerings, which are as much objects of abhorrence as if they consisted,
not of wine, which externally they were, but literally of blood. The expression *of
blood*, was the more natural as wine is named the blood of grapes in Gen. xlix. 11;
Deut. xxxii. 14; Drink-offerings outwardly of the blood of grapes, inwardly of the
blood of men." The real saints of whom David was one, much more Christ himself,
abhorred idolatry in every shape and form. The gods of the heathen are no gods.
They are vanities and lies. They that serve them are like unto them.

5. *The* Lord *is the portion of mine inheritance and of my cup.* The language of
this verse and of the next is evidently borrowed from the partition of the land of
Canaan, giving to each man his *inheritance* or *heritage* or *portion by lot*, and bounding
it by *lines*. In that division the whole land was distributed by *lot, i. e.*, by casting
lot, but no share was given to the priests and Levites. Jehovah was their portion,
the lot of their inheritance. So, here David says his portion was in God. The same
is elsewhere asserted by David, Ps. cxix. 57; and by Asaph, Ps. lxxiii. 26. There is
a remarkable agreement in the ancient versions in rendering this clause. Horsley's
reading varies from the common: Jehovah, my measured portion, and my cup, art
thou; Alexander gives it very succinctly: Jehovah (is) my allotted portion, and my
cup. And as these words were true of David, so are they of David's greater Son.
His portion both of suffering and reward was given him by Jehovah, Matt. xxvi. 39,
42; Isa. xlix. 5–12; Heb. xii. 1, 2. It is added: *Thou maintainest my lot.* The verb
in the original, is in the future, not that the act was not now performing, but he was
confident it would be continued to the end. The Chaldee and Jebb have it in the
future; Venema: Thou wilt make my lot ample; Alexander: Thou wilt enlarge
my lot; Hengstenberg: Thou makest my lot glorious; Edwards: Thou art he that
upholdeth my lot. For *maintainest* several read *sustainest*. It is the word applied
to the act of *staying up* the hands of Moses, Ex. xvii. 12. It is often rendered by
retain. There seems to be nothing to justify the rendering of the Septuagint, Vulgate, Ethiopic, Syriac: It is thou that wilt restore my inheritance to me.

6. *The lines are fallen unto me in pleasant* places; *yea, I have a goodly heritage.*
David seems to have had great delight in his portion in Canaan. Even the water
of his own city seemed to him better than that of any other place, 2 Sam. xxiii. 15;
1 Chron. xi. 17. But his portion of land in Israel was hardly more than a memento
of his real and great inheritance, which was God himself. So also Christ Jesus,
though Maker of all worlds and Lord of all, yet gloried not in any temporal or
worldly possessions. In the midst of all things justly his own, he yet lived in poverty,
chiefly dependent, during his public ministry, on charity even for the necessaries of
life. Yet the Lord will " divide him a portion with the great." Isa. liii. 10–12. His
heritage excels that of all men and of all angels, Heb. i. 5–13.

7. *I will bless the* Lord, *who hath given me counsel.* The ancient versions are quite
agreed in the sense of this passage. The moderns vary it somewhat. Church

of England: I will thank the LORD for giving me warning; Calvin: I will magnify Jehovah, who giveth me counsel; Fry: I bless Jehovah, who hath disclosed to me his counsels. The English version can hardly be improved. David was led by God to adopt that counsel and those views, which betoken coming salvation. Calvin's view is excellent: "David confesses that it was entirely owing to the pure grace of God that he had come to possess so great a good, and that he had been made a partaker of it by faith. . . Let us know that both these things proceed from the free liberality of God; first, his being our inheritance, and next our coming to the possession of him by faith." It was the Spirit resting on the man Christ Jesus, that made him also so wise and wonderful in counsel, Isa. xi. 1–5; lxi. 1–3; Luke iv. 18–20. *My reins also instruct me in the night-seasons.* For the signification and use of the word *reins* see Ps. vii. 9. Walford: "The reins or kidneys are used to signify the interior faculties; and the divine speaker observes, that in seasons of solitude, his thoughts were instinctively employed in contemplating the heavenly discoveries that were communicated to him." In Tyndale's Bible it is: My reins also have chastened me in the night; Alexander: Also by night have my reins prompted me. The word rendered *night* or *night-season* is in the plural, and points to the habit of mind both of David and of Christ. Indeed in all ages pious men have chosen the night as a time peculiarly favorable to deep reflection and devout exercises of every kind. The eighth and nineteenth Psalms seem to have been in good part the result of meditation at night. How our Saviour retired from all the noisy and busy scenes to solitary places and places for prayer, and there spent the night in the highest acts of personal communion with God the gospel declares, Luke vi. 12; xxi. 37.

The four remaining verses, with the exception of the last clause of the last verse, are quoted from the Septuagint literally by Peter on the day of Pentecost, and are commented on by him as follows:

"Ye men of Israel, hear these words; Jesus of Nazareth, a man approved of God among you by miracles, and wonders, and signs, which God did by him in the midst of you, as ye yourselves also know: Him, being delivered by the determinate counsel and foreknowledge of God, ye have taken, and by wicked hands have crucified and slain: Whom God hath raised up, having loosed the pains of death; because it was not possible that he should be holden of it. For David speaketh concerning him,

"'I foresaw the Lord always before my face, for he is on my right hand, that I should not be moved: Therefore did my heart rejoice, and my tongue was glad; moreover, also, my flesh shall rest in hope: Because thou wilt not leave my soul in hell, neither wilt thou suffer thine Holy One to see corruption. Thou hast made known to me the ways of life; thou shalt make me full of joy with thy countenance.'

"Men and brethren, let me freely speak unto you of the patriarch David, that he is both dead and buried, and his sepulchre is with us unto this day. Therefore being a prophet, and knowing that God had sworn with an oath to him that of the fruit of his loins, according to the flesh, he would raise up Christ to sit on his throne; he seeing this before, spake of the resurrection of Christ, that his *soul was not left in hell, neither his flesh did see corruption.*

"This Jesus has God raised up, whereof we are all witnesses. Therefore being by the right hand of God exalted, and having received of the Father the promise of the Holy Ghost, he hath shed forth this, which ye now see and hear. For David is not ascended into the heavens: but he saith himself, *The* LORD *said unto my Lord, Sit thou on my right hand, until I make thy foes thy footstool.* Therefore let all the house of Israel know assuredly, that God hath made that same Jesus, whom ye crucified, both Lord and Christ," Acts ii. 22–36.

Any interpretation of these four verses of the Psalm, which is inconsistent with

Peter's inspired remarks upon them, is of course erroneous, and must be given up. Let us briefly consider each verse.

8. *I have set the* LORD *always before me.* There is no evidence that David was pious from his birth, much less that his love and obedience, even after his regeneration, were without fault. Yet this expression seems to be equivalent to a claim of spotless perfection. If so, it cannot belong to any but the Son of man. The rendering of the authorized version is certainly more literal than that of the Septuagint quoted by Peter in Acts. Calvin: I have set Jehovah continually before me; Amesius: I propose to myself Jehovah always; Edwards: I set Jehovah always before me; Jebb: I have set the Lord before me continually; Fry: I have set Jehovah ever before me; church of England: I have set God always before me; Hengstenberg: I set the Lord always before me; Alexander: I have set Jehovah before me always. The act here spoken of is one of pious regard to God's nature and will, as they are made known by himself. To eye God in everything is a mark of a holy life. If this clause be taken in such a modified sense as makes it declare sincerity and integrity of character, yet admitting want of absolute perfection, then indeed it might apply to David. But Peter's aim on the day of Pentecost was to prove that the passage quoted by him had no application whatever to David. This is conclusive. In this and the following verses we have an instance of transition from one subject to another like it or suggested by it. The destruction of Jerusalem was so terrible that in its horrors it resembled the last great day. So Christ naturally passes from an account of the one to the other, and it is not always easy to say where the one subject is wholly dropped, and the other first taken up. This difficulty is removed in the present instance by Peter's sermon. Christ's piety was perfect. In it infinite purity saw no blemish. It is added, *Because* he is *at my right hand, I shall not be moved.* The foregoing reasonings would apply this clause also to Christ. The Chaldee reads: Because his majesty [or Shechinah] rests upon me, I shall not be moved. The other ancient versions retain very much the sense of ours. Jehovah was at the right hand of Christ "to counsel and instruct, to help, protect, and defend." The power and wisdom of God secured and shall ever secure to Christ a certain victory. He shall *not be moved.* The word is the same that is so rendered in Ps. x. 6; xiii. 4; xv. 5, which see. The mediatorial purpose, work, throne and glory are as stable as the nature of God, Isa. xlii. 4; l. 5–9.

9. *Therefore my heart is glad, and my glory rejoiceth.* Most of the life of the Redeemer on earth was marked with tears and sorrows. Yet even here there was an hour when he rejoiced in spirit, Luke x. 21. And in his greatest sufferings there was a secret perception of good things to come. "The joy set before him" made the cross as nothing. He despised the shame, Heb. xii. 2. And when the heart is glad, the "glory" of a man, that is, his tongue rejoiceth. When the fire burns within, then soon the mouth will be open. For *glory* Peter uses *tongue,* quoting the Septuagint. In the Psalms the word more than once has this sense, see xxx. 12; lvii. 8; cviii. 1. For *glory* Calvin reads *tongue,* Edwards and Fry *soul.* Hengstenberg and Alexander interpret it of the *soul.* The word is that commonly rendered *glory* or *honor.* Anderson is confident it here means the *tongue. My flesh also shall rest in hope, i. e.,* in hope of a speedy and glorious resurrection as is explained in the next verse.

10. *For* [meaning *because*] *thou wilt not leave my soul in hell; neither wilt thou suffer thine Holy One to see corruption.* John Rogers' Translation: For why? thou shalt not leave my soule in hell, nether shalt thou suffre thy saincte to see corrupcyon; Genevan Translation: For thou wilt not leave my soule in the grave: neither wilt thou suffer thine holy one to see corruption; Calvin: For thou wilt not leave my soul

in the grave; neither wilt thou make thy Holy One to see the pit; Edwards: For thou wilt not leave my soul to the grave; thou wilt not suffer thy favored one to see corruption; Fry: For thou wilt not leave my soul in the abode of the dead, nor suffer thy beloved to see corruption: Alexander: For thou wilt not leave my soul to Hell; thou wilt not give thy Holy One to see corruption; Hengstenberg is still different: Thou wilt not leave my soul to hell, nor give up thy holy ones to see corruption; Venema also has the plural *thy pious ones* in the text, and in brackets the singular; Jebb says it " is plural among the received copies of the Jews; but Dr. Kennicott remarks that it is in the singular number in six editions of the printed Talmud. In one hundred and eighty copies of Kennicott, in the LXX., and Syriac it is singular." So is it also in the Arabic, Ethiopic and Vulgate. Peter quotes it in the singular, and his argument requires that it be applied to *one* not to many. Paul quotes it the same way in Acts xiii. 35–37. In explanation of the difficulties of the case it may be remarked that the word rendered *soul*, though it often has that signification, yet by no means necessarily requires that rendering in all cases. Horne thinks it means *his animal frame*. In Gen i. 20, 30, and often elsewhere it is translated *life*. In Gen. i. 21, 24; ii. 19, and elsewhere it is rendered *creature*. In Gen. xxiii. 8 it is *mind*. In many cases it signifies *persons*. Gen. xxxvi. 6; xlvi. 15, 18, 22, 25, 26; Ex. i. 5, etc. In Lev. xix. 28; xxi. 1; xxii. 4, and elsewhere it is rendered *the dead*. In Nu. ix. 6, 7, 10 it is rendered *dead body*. In this Psalm it seems to mean no more than *dead body*. Then it may read, Thou wilt not leave my dead body in the grave. This is all that the parallelism of the verse requires. It is all that the word rendered soul makes *necessary*. It is all that Peter drew from it on the day of Pentecost. For remarks on the word rendered *hell*, see on Ps. vi. 5; ix. 17. Its most common signification is *the grave, the pit*. To *suffer thine Holy One* is literally to *give thine Holy One*. See the same form of expression in Gen. xx. 6; xxxi. 7; Ex. iii. 19, and often elsewhere, where it is rendered *suffer* or *let*. To *see corruption* is to *become corrupt*, to *rot*; as to *see death* is to *die*. Ps. lxxxix. 48; Luke ii. 26. Christ's body was *dead*, but it never was dissolved. The word rendered *corruption* is rendered *ditch*, Ps. vii. 15; *pit*, Ps. ix. 15; *destruction*, Ps. lv. 23; the *grave*, Job xxxiii. 22; and *corruption* here, Ps. xlix. 9; Jon. ii. 6. The sense here is clearly *corruption* or *destruction*. Peter and Paul both approve this sense, as Luke informs us in the Acts of the Apostles.

11. *Thou wilt shew me the path of life.* The Chaldee and Alexander: Thou wilt teach me the way of life; Syriac; Thou wilt show me the way of life; Calvin: Thou wilt make me to know the path of life; Edwards has the same as our version; Hengstenberg: Thou wilt make known to me the way of life; Fry: Thou makest known to me the path of life. The word rendered *life* is in the plural. This may denote the excellence and richness of the life of the risen Saviour. Some think it may allude to the fact that Christ's resurrection secures the resurrection and eternal life of all his people. This is a truth whether taught here or not. Christ's resurrection was to be permanent, not followed by mortality, but by his walking in the path of life—life without end. *In thy presence* is *fulness of joy*. The Septuagint: Thou shalt make me full of joy with thy countenance. Christ's resurrection was followed by his ascension, and his ascension by his session at the right hand of God. There his joy is perfect. There he is exalted. There he is glorified. *At thy right hand* there are *pleasures for evermore*. This clause is not quoted by Peter on the day of Pentecost. It was not essential to his purpose. What those pleasures are no mortal can comprehend, but they are such as forever ravish the pure spirits around the throne. They satisfy the God-man, Christ Jesus for all his toils and sorrows.

DOCTRINAL AND PRACTICAL REMARKS.

1. Anything is good for us, if it leads us to hearty, believing prayer, v. 1.

2. It is a wonder that more men do not sink into despair, so many are sore pressed, and yet so few know the way to the mercy-seat, v. 1.

3. If the Lord Jesus Christ in his humiliation, for the support and encouragement of his human nature, so constantly and earnestly betook himself to prayer, how vain are those poor sinful men, who think they can do without it, v. 1. It is impossible that any mere man on earth should live in holiness and peace without constant help from God.

4. Wonderfully and reasonably God demands our trust and confidence at every step. We can do nothing aright without faith, v. 1. Calvin: "Our safety both in life and in death depends entirely upon our being under the protection of God."

5. True faith naturally leads to prayer, v. 1. Luther: "See here how trust calls upon the Lord. How can he call upon the Lord, who has not confided in him? Confidence and believing trust are reckoned among those things that regard God as gracious according to his compassion, and through which he will make us perpetually blessed."

6. True religion is matter of experience. He, who is in the enjoyment of it, can appeal to his own consciousness, and address his own soul, v. 2. This was true of Christ and of every good man that ever lived. Dickson: "The first solid evidence of the sincerity of saving faith is the testimony of the conscience, bearing witness to a man that he hath laid hold on the covenant of grace, and hath chosen God for his protector and master, and that he is resolved to depend upon God, and serve him."

7. It is of the essence of true piety always and devoutly to acknowledge God's right of dominion over us. We should often say to him, Thou art my Lord, v. 2. Thus pious men have always done. Thus Christ acknowledged himself a servant. We are not our own property. We are not our own masters.

8. The doctrine that after our best obedience we are still unprofitable servants is no novelty. It was taught of old, v. 2. Calvin: "Let men strive ever so much to lay themselves out for God, yet they can bring no advantage to him, Our goodness extendeth not to him, not only because, having in himself alone an all-sufficiency, he stands in need of nothing, but also because we are empty and destitute of all good things, and have nothing wherewith to show ourselves liberal towards him." Scott: "Even the perfect righteousness of the Saviour can add nothing to the *essential* glory and happiness of the Father; but it is the meritorious cause of the acceptance and sanctification, and eternal felicity of his people, in whom *alone* of Adam's race he greatly delights."

9. And so Christ's benevolence was to the sinner and not to the Sovereign sinned against, v. 3. The same truth is taught in John iii. 16; xvii. 19. And as Christ set us an example of pity and kindness to feeble, prejudiced, sinful men, so we must walk in his footsteps. Calvin: "As our good deeds cannot extend to him, God substitutes the saints in his place, and towards them we are to exercise our charity."

10. The friendship of the pious is well bestowed on the saints, for they are the *excellent* of the earth, v. 3. One of great purity of character and close discernment will indeed see many blemishes in the best of mere men; still believers are the salt of the earth. As a class they are so superior to mere worldlings that a true child of God finds them to be as gold compared with dross. Diodati: They are "the true, free, and noble children of God, heirs of his kingdom, and transformed into his image from glory to glory." Hengstenberg: "The saints are the chosen ones, those

whom God has taken out of the territory of the profane world, and raised to the standing of his people. Of this elevation in dignity, an elevation in sentiment is certainly the consequence." The love of Christ to his people was first that of good will. He pitied them and redeemed them. It is next that of delight in their characters, not as perfect, but as sincere and upright. Christ loves his own image wherever he sees it.

11. True benevolence would certainly demand the universal diffusion of the saving knowledge of God, because the wretchedness of all, who embrace false religions, is so great, v. 4. *Their sorrows are multiplied.* Alexander: "In the word translated *their sorrows* there seems to be an allusion to a very similar form, which would mean *their idols,* as if to suggest that false gods are mere troubles and vexations."

12. Yet how strongly and strangely are men bent to falsehood, and, even to the grossest form of it, idolatry. The heathen are mad upon their idols. The wicked hasten after another God, v. 4. Human nature is foolish, perverse and depraved. This is the only way of accounting for human folly in matters of religion. Morison: "The tendency of apostate human nature to run into idolatrous practices is one of its most marked features. Every people on the face of the earth has displayed this tendency; and there is no instance upon record in which the work of *self-deliverance* has been effected." The idolatry of the heart towards anything that God has made will be followed by like misery.

13. Let us never under any circumstance do anything to countenance any form of false worship, v. 4. The last clause of that verse finds its parallel in Ex. xxiii. 13.

14. God himself is the portion of all the souls that trust in him, v. 5. In many things the righteous is wise. He puts truth before error, eternity before time, saints before sinners, the spirit before the flesh; but the height of his sagacity is in preferring God's will to his own, God's favor to that of all creatures, and God himself to the universe beside.

14. Nor is the believer an intruder, nor a usurper in his claims to the love and blessing of God. He has it by *inheritance,* v. 5, not the less certain or binding because he has it through his co-heir, Jesus Christ. He has it by gift from God, the very title by which we hold our existence. Yea, better, it is bought with the blood of Christ.

15. If by the *cup* the prophet means, as some think, temporal blessings, then God's people shall never lack bread or water. If that is not intended then something better is, and so the temporal comes with the spiritual, v. 5.

16. Reliance on God will never disappoint our hopes. He will carry us through and *maintain our* lot, v. 5.

17. Even in this life the just are happy. They have a *goodly heritage,* v. 6. It must be different with their enemies. Rivet: "The way to blessedness is wholly unknown to the natural man. True blessedness consists in beholding the face of God." This is done by faith here, by vision in glory. God's people have good things now, and better coming.

18. How reasonable therefore is the duty of praising and *blessing the Lord,* v. 7. Let us abound in this heavenly employment.

19. All wise men make God's *counsel* their guide, v. 7. Why should they not? He makes no mistakes. All his counsels are of old faithfulness and truth. He is the infallible counsellor. Some think the word *Jehovah* in this verse points to Christ. Whether it does or not, other Scriptures style him the "Wonderful, COUNSELLOR, The mighty God, The everlasting Father, The Prince of Peace."

20. Strike out of the religious character and history of God's people all their heart-searchings, thoughts, prayers, praises and meditations *in the night season,* and what a hideous gap would appear, v. 7.

21 True piety will uniformly evince itself by so setting the Lord before us as "to keep all our senses bound and captive, that they may not run out and go astray after any other object," v. 8. In Christ Jesus piety was perfect, and so he never lost sight of God's will and law and glory, even when the light and comfort of God's countenance were withheld. To be like Christ in any measure is grace; to be like him in perfection is glory.

22. Horne: "The method taken by Christ as man to support himself in time of trouble and persevere unto the end, was to maintain a constant actual sense of the presence of Jehovah, whom when he thus saw standing at his right hand, ready, at the appointed hour, to succor and deliver him, he then feared not the powers of earth and hell combined for his destruction," v. 8.

23. God's protection and support of David, or Christ, or any one else is enough. Such shall *not be moved*, v. 8.

24. No death is comfortable without, and none is miserable with the hopes and supports of true religion, v. 9. When the *flesh rests in hope* death is disarmed. Is. lvii. 2. This was true of Christ, and it is true of all his people. Henry: "Dying Christians, as well as a dying Christ, may cheerfully put off the body in a believing expectation of a joyful resurrection;" Morison: "Blessed Redeemer! Thou hast perfumed the noisome grave by thy temporary abode in its dreary mansions; from a prison thou hast changed it into a scene of hope; thou hast made it the resting-place of weary pilgrims; and all the members of thy mystical body can look on it as the gate of heaven."

25. It would have been a great thing for plain pious souls if they had never been troubled by curious questions of human invention respecting the abode of souls separated from their bodies in connection with this *tenth* verse and similar Scriptures. The whole difficulty seems to have had a close connection with that clause of the Apostles' Creed, which says of Christ, "*He descended into hell.*" Pearson: "It appears that the first intention of putting these words into the creed was only to express the burial of our Saviour, or the descent of his body into the grave." Had the matter rested here it would have been comparatively harmless. The words in the creed seem to be built on the tenth verse of this Psalm. Calvin says that "both the Greek and Latin Fathers have strained these words to a meaning different from that of exempting the life of Christ from the dominion of the grave, referring them to the bringing back of the soul of Christ from hell." Morison: "The word *hell*, according to the present usage of our language, always denotes the place of torment; but the original word, rendered *hell* in our Bibles, often signifies the darkness and covering of the grave; and that it does so here is obvious from the inspired comment of the Apostle Peter in Acts ii. 27." Usher says that the word which in this Psalm is rendered hell signifies, "when spoken of the body, the grave; when of the soul, that state in which the soul is without the body, whether *Paradise* or *Hell*, properly so called."

26. The question, Was Christ's body incorruptible? has often been discussed in connection with verse 10. Nor does there seem to be any need of dismissing the question with alarm or abhorrence. It is admitted that Christ's whole person was undefiled by either original or actual sin; that he was impeccable; that he fully satisfied in our stead the demands of the law; that the union of the divine and human natures of our Saviour was neither dissolved nor suspended by the separation of his soul and body in death; and that the Father had promised that his body should not be corrupted. How was it possible then that it should see corruption? Dickson: "The body of Christ not only was to rise from the dead, but also could not so much as putrefy in the grave."

27. This Psalm incontestably requires the resurrection of Christ, vv. 9–11. The New Testament abundantly declares the fact. This article of faith is from its nature

and from the admission of inspired writers fundamental in Christianity. Rom. i. 4; iv. 25; 1 Cor. xv. 12–19.

28. And as Christ arose, so shall his people. His resurrection makes theirs certain, 1 Cor. xv. 20–22. Christ is the head; his people are the members. As the Head arose, the members cannot perish. Horne: "Through this thy beloved Son and our Saviour, thou shalt show us likewise, O Lord, the path of life; thou shalt justify our souls by thy grace now, and raise our bodies by thy power at the last day; when earthly sorrow shall terminate in heavenly joy, and momentary pain shall be rewarded with everlasting felicity." Isa. xxvi. 19.

29. After humility comes honor, vv. 10, 11. It was so with Christ. It shall be so with his people. Everything in its order. Morison: "The glorified Saviour did not take possession of the heavenly inheritance in his own name merely. He entered into his rest as a public person, and all the members of his body, the church, shall share with him the perfection of the bliss which he now enjoys."

30. What a place heaven must be, both relatively as compared with earth, and absolutely in itself! Here all is without form and void, dark and imperfect, vain and fleeting. There all is so perfect, so glorious, so permanent that nothing is wanting, and even inspired writers seem at a loss for words to convey some idea of the eternal bliss. *Fulness of joy, pleasures, in thy presence, at thy right hand, for evermore!* v. 11. Who can comprehend these terms? Morison: "What a magnificent thought is the idea of a world all pure, all triumphant!" Henry: "Those who live piously, with God in their eye, may die comfortably, with heaven in their eye."

31. Cobbin: "Exalted devotion brings the soul into contact with the mind of God."

PSALM XVII.

A Prayer of David.

1 HEAR the right, O LORD, attend unto my cry; give ear unto my prayer, *that goeth* not out of feigned lips.

2 Let my sentence come forth from thy presence; let thine eyes behold the things that are equal.

3 Thou hast proved mine heart; thou hast visited *me* in the night; thou hast tried me, *and* shalt find nothing: I am purposed *that* my mouth shall not transgress.

4 Concerning the works of men, by the word of thy lips I have kept *me from* the paths of the destroyer.

5 Hold up my goings in thy paths, *that* my footsteps slip not.

6 I have called upon thee, for thou wilt hear me, O God: incline thine ear unto me, *and* hear my speech.

7 Shew thy marvellous loving-kindness, O thou that savest by thy right hand them which put their trust *in thee* from those that rise up *against them.*

8 Keep me as the apple of the eye; hide me under the shadow of thy wings,

9 From the wicked that oppress me, *from* my deadly enemies, *who* compass me about.

10 They are inclosed in their own fat: with their mouth they speak proudly.

11 They have now compassed us in our steps: they have set their eyes bowing down to the earth;

12 Like as a lion *that* is greedy of his prey, and as it were a young lion lurking in secret places.

13 Arise, O LORD, disappoint him, cast him down: deliver my soul from the wicked, *which is* thy sword:

14 From men *which are* thy hand, O Lord, from men of the world, *which have* their portion in *this* life, and whose belly thou fillest with thy hid *treasure:* they are full of children, and leave the rest of their *substance* to their babes.

15 As for me, I will behold thy face in righteousness: I shall be satisfied, when I awake, with thy likeness.

THE word rendered *prayer* in the title occurs frequently in the Scriptures, and is in our version always so translated. Ps. iv. 1; vi. 9. There are four other Psalms, which have the word *prayer* in the title, viz., lxxxvi., xc., cii., cxlii. It is also found as a caption to Habakkuk iii. 1. As the words *a prayer of Habakkuk* simply point out that prophet as the author, not as the subject of the prayer, so with this Psalm. It is a prayer belonging to David as its author. The Syriac has it, "Written by David, a prayer." Whether his own case is or is not brought forward is not determined by the title. Alexander: "This Psalm is called a prayer because petition is its burden, its characteristic feature, its essential element." The same remark applies to the other Psalms which have *prayer* in the title.

There is nothing in this Psalm to determine the occasion, on which it was written. Several learned men have suggested particular events in the history of David, as furnishing the occasion of this pious *prayer*. According to their various views, men suppose this Psalm has reference to events recorded in 1 Sam. xx., xxiv., xxvi., xxvii. But all this is conjecture. There is indeed considerable reason for the opinion, held by many, that the conduct of Saul and his adherents is distinctly referred to, at least so far as to suggest some of the forms of expression. The fact is that the Psalm is well adapted to express the pious sentiments of David on many occasions during and after the time of Saul.

Some think this Psalm has so peculiar a resemblance to Ps. xvi. that the two may be regarded as a pair. Venema: "Such is the agreement between this Psalm and the preceding, that I am almost ready to regard them as one Psalm." Hengstenberg: "This Psalm has many coincidences with Ps. xvi. which are so important that they give color to the idea of both Psalms having been united by the author into one pair." Others no less respectable have made similar observations. The more this subject of *pairs* in the Psalms is examined, the more uncertain will it probably appear. That, which in one place is relied on to establish it, in other cases entirely fails, or manifestly opposes the idea. Still the theory is harmless. Hengstenberg goes so far in this matter as to attempt to show a connection between this Psalm and the *seventh*. Nor is he content with that. He insists on a connection between vv. 1–5 of this Psalm and vv. 20–27 of Psalm xviii. The utmost that is well established on this point is that all truth is connected, and that many truths are quite similar, and expressed in quite similar words not only by the same writer, but by different inspired penmen. See Introduction, § 12.

This Psalm has long been exceedingly precious to the afflicted people of God. Perhaps no portion of this collection of *Praises* has been more sung by the saints of God for hundreds of years than the various versions of this *Prayer*. The contents give it a prominent place in the experience of God's people. And although it is nowhere in the New Testament declared to refer to Messiah, yet there is not in it an expression, which might not have been fitly used by Christ Jesus, when on earth. Indeed, the title in the Arabic is, "A prayer in the person of a perfect man, and of Christ himself, and of every one that is redeemed by him." That class of interpreters, therefore, who feel constrained to apply to Christ everything in the Psalms, which can possibly bear that construction, find no difficulty here. A long list of interpreters from Jerome to Fry maintain this view. Perhaps the safer mode is to notice how these things were fulfilled in Christ, and also in his people. Alexander thus begins his notice of this

Psalm: "A SUFFERER, in imminent danger, professes his sincere conformity to God's will, and invokes his protection." There is no safe rule of interpretation, which will allow us to *confine* the application of this Psalm to Christ. He was tempted in all points as his people, and his experience of sorrow and trial gives both light and encouragement to all, who walk in his footsteps.

The names of the Most High in this Psalm are *Jehovah* LORD and *El God*, on which see above on Ps. i. 2; v. 4.

1. *Hear the right*, O LORD. The Vulgate, Ethiopic, Arabic and Doway: Hear O Lord, my justice, or my righteousness. Calvin: Hear my righteousness; Edwards: Hear what is right; Jebb: Hear, O LORD, righteousness; Fry: Hear my just cause; Hengstenberg: Hear righteousness; Alexander: Hear, Oh Jehovah, the right. All these substantially agree with our English version. So also do Venema, Diodati, Ainsworth, Amesius and Tholuck. But the Septuagint: Hear, O Lord of my righteousness; Syriac: Hear, O righteous Lord. This rendering is preferred by Boothroyd, Houbigant, Waterland, Horne and Clarke. Jerome, Aquila and Horsley favor the following: Hear the just one. The reader will observe great authority in favor of the common version. There is a special fitness in this rendering, as the whole weight of the petition urged is made to rest on the *righteousness* of the cause which is pleaded. *To hear* is to give ear, to answer and help. See on Ps. iv. 1. *Right*, in the Hebrew the same as in Ps. iv. 1, 5; vii. 8, is rendered *righteousness*; in Ps. ix. 4, *right*; in Ps. xxxv. 27, *righteous cause*; in Ps. lxxxiv. 14, *justice*. *Attend unto my cry*. The word rendered *attend* is often rendered *hearken*, Ps. v. 2; 1 Sam. xv. 22; Job xiii. 6; Dan. ix. 19; Mic. i. 2; in Job xxxiii. 31, *mark well*; in Jer. xviii. 18, *give heed*; in Pr. i. 24, *regard*; often *attend*. The meaning is very uniform. The word rendered *cry* has not previously occurred in the Psalms, though it occurs frequently hereafter. It always signifies earnest speech or expression, whether joyful or sad. In 1 Kings xxii. 36, it is *proclamation*; in Ps. xlii. 4, *joy*; in Ps. xlvii. 1, *triumph*; in Ps. cv. 43, *gladness*; in Ps. cxxvi. 2, *singing*; in Pr. xi. 10, *shouting*. In Ps. lxi. 1, it is used in the same sense as here—that of an earnest lifting up of the voice, a heartfelt call on God for help and relief. Calvin explains it as "earnest prayer," denoting "vehement, intense earnestness of soul." And so the Psalmist adds, *Give ear unto my prayer*, that goeth *not out of feigned lips*. *Prayer*, the same as that found in the title. The word rendered *give ear* has no other meaning, though in one case it is translated *give good heed*, Ecc. xii. 9; sometimes *hearken* and sometimes *hear*. *Feigned lips*, literally, *lips, not of deceit*. The same word is found in Ps. v. 6; x. 7, and signifies *craft, subtilty, guile*. "We must be *honest* with God. He abhors a lie in worship no less than in trade. The language of this verse cannot be that of a wicked man, for although even irreligious persons may often be able justly to boast of having a good cause; yet as they do not acknowledge that the world is governed by the providence of God, they content themselves with enjoying the approbation of their own conscience, as they speak, and, gnawing the bit, bear the injuries which are done to them rather obstinately than steadfastly, seeking for consolation neither in faith, nor in prayer. But the faithful not only depend upon the goodness of their cause; they also commit it to God that he may defend and maintain it." The verse therefore may be applied to David as a just man, having truth and equity on his side, being innocent of the wrongs, whereof he is accused. Or the prayer may suit a representative person, who is righteous and guileless. It is a delightful truth that the imputation of Christ's merits for our justifying righteousness before God is always accompanied by the bestowment of integrity and uprightness of character. Many, however, contend, and not without plausibility, that the verse has special reference to Christ. Amyrald: "In the exposition of this

Psalm, and of some others, the left eye must be fixed on David, that the right may be kept intent on Christ." Fry: "Christ is the suppliant; but, as usual in these Psalms, he prays as the Head and Surety of his body, the church, making their cause his own. He pleads his righteousness in their behalf."

2. *Let my sentence come forth from thy presence.* Calvin: Let my judgment [judgment in my favor] come forth from the presence of thy countenance; Edwards thinks our version cannot be improved; Jebb: From thy presence let judgment come forth; Fry: From thee let my sentence come forth; Dathe: I pray thee to be the judge of my cause; Hengstenberg: Let my right go forth from thee; Alexander: From before thee my judgment shall come forth. Horsley thinks the meaning well expressed thus: Be thou, O Jehovah, my *judge* in thine own person. In the original and in the Chaldee the verb is in the future. The language is that of petition and confidence united. When a decision is given on the throne of judgment, the next thing is its promulgation and execution. The Psalmist asks God that the right may be publicly and before all vindicated. *Let thine eyes behold the things that are equal.* This is the very office of a judge. To do this finally and infallibly is the prerogative of God alone. Calvin: Let thine eyes look upon mine uprightness; Ainsworth: Let thine eyes view righteousnesses; Edwards: Let thine eyes look upon equity; Jebb adopts the common version; Fry: Let thine eyes regard with equity; Hengstenberg: Let thine eyes behold uprightness; Alexander: Thine eyes shall behold equities; Septuagint: Let mine eyes (or mine eyes shall) behold equal things. The sense of the verse is well given by Diodati: "Give thou the sentence, according to mine innocency, well known unto thee, make it appear and defend it by the effect." The word rendered *the things that are equal* is plural. It may designate all causes that are just, or it may indicate that in this case the right is all on one side and is perfect. Ainsworth: My most righteous cause. One can hardly fail to see how wonderfully this expresses the thoughts of Christ, Is. xlix. 4; "Surely my judgment is with the LORD, and my work with my God." Often did he say much the same. He "committed himself to him that judgeth righteously." 1 Pet. ii. 23.

3. *Thou hast proved mine heart.* Chaldee, Septuagint, Vulgate, Arabic, Ethiopic, Doway, Calvin and Jebb render the clause as our version; Syriac and Edwards: Thou hast explored me; Hengstenberg: Thou provest my heart; Alexander: Thou hast tried my heart; the church of England unites this and the next clause: Thou hast proved and visited mine heart in the night-season; Morison: "The word rendered *thou hast proved* imports more properly the act of strict examination and search, with a view to discovery." The word is variously rendered *try, prove, examine,* and once *tempt,* Mal. iii. 15. It is used to express the trying of gold, Zech. xiii. 9. We have the same word in Ps. xi. 4, 5. Any examination had, or proof made by *omniscience* cannot fail to be thorough, impartial, conclusive. The whole of this verse is a solemn and reverent appeal to God, asserting the prophet's truth and sincerity. God knew that he was no hypocrite. Luther: "He had prayed, that the Lord would regard his righteousness; now he declares what sort of confidence he had to rest on in begging this." The way in which God had proved him is next stated: *Thou hast visited me in the night.* To the wicked night is the great time for evil thoughts and plans, Job xxiv. 13–17. Night is the time when business, company and the whole structure of society leave the heart the most unrestrained. To know a man's habitual thoughts at night is to know the complexion of his whole character. Yea, in those lone and solemn hours, when one's thoughts so fearfully accuse, or so clearly excuse him, God knew how sincere were all the professions of his servant. *Thou hast tried me.* Chaldee and Syriac: Thou hast examined me; Calvin: Thou hast examined it [mine heart]; Septuagint, Vulgate, Ethiopic and

Arabic: Thou hast tried me by fire; Geddes: Thou hast smelted me; Hengstenberg: *Thou* purgest me; Alexander: Thou hast assayed me. Elsewhere the verb is rendered *try, refine, melt, purge away,* and, in the form of a noun, *refiner, founder, goldsmith.* Morison: "It denotes primarily the act of melting, or fusing metals." If the figure here is that drawn from melting in order to try metals, then we extend it to the next phrase, And *shalt find nothing.* For *nothing* Ainsworth prefers *no dross,* or *deceit;* Chaldee, *no corruption;* Syriac, *no iniquity;* Septuagint, Vulgate, and Ethiopic: In me iniquity was not found; Arabic: Thou didst not find in me wickedness; Calvin: Thou shalt find nothing; Edwards: Thou canst find no wicked design in me; Fry: Thou couldest find nothing; Hengstenberg: Thou findest not; Alexander: Thou wilt not find; church of England: And thou shalt find no wickedness in me. If this expression is true of David in regard to Saul and his adherents, it is true in a much higher sense of Christ, who said, "The prince of this world cometh, and hath nothing in me." An upright man will show his rectitude by his speech: *"I am purposed* that *my mouth shall not transgress.* This is confessedly a very difficult passage. Calvin: My thoughts shall not pass beyond my mouth; Jebb: I am purposed that there shall not be transgression in my mouth; Hengstenberg: My thought oversteps not my mouth; church of England: For I am utterly purposed that my mouth shall not offend; Alexander: My mouth shall not exceed my thought. Nor does the difficulty stop here. The Septuagint, Vulgate, Ethiopic, Syriac, Arabic, Doway, Edwards and Fry connect this clause with the next in one verse. The Doway, following the Septuagint, etc., renders it: That my mouth may not speak the works of men; Edwards: My mouth transgresses not because of the works of men; Fry: No thoughts pass from my mouth according to the deeds of men. The Chaldee is still more difficult: I have thought evil, it hath not passed my mouth. All these renderings need not here be considered at length. Diodati gives his apprehensions of the sense in this paraphrase: "My words are all true, loyal, and correspondent to the inward thoughts of my heart." David probably designed to say that not only was his heart pure from the wickedness imputed to him, but he had said nothing and should say nothing to the contrary of all he had thus professed. Scott: "He had avoided every disrespectful word concerning Saul, the Lord's anointed." If any can find a better construction, let it be accepted. If the words be regarded as spoken by Messias, they are a declaration of his sinless speech. No guile was found in his mouth. This view leaves the next verse to begin as in our version:

4. *Concerning the works of men, by the word of thy lips I have kept* me from *the paths of the destroyer. Concerning* means *respecting, touching, as relates to,* q. d., if we speak of the works of men. The word for *men* is Adam, which means not only the first man, but his descendants, who have his likeness. David had spoken of his heart and then of his tongue. He now speaks of his acts, and says respecting these he has kept himself from the paths of the destroyer by the word which God had spoken. The warning, cleansing effect of God's word is often mentioned in Scripture, Ps. xix. 11; John xv. 3. The word rendered *kept* is the same as in Ps. xvi. 1 is translated *preserve,* the same found in v. 8 of this Psalm. It is well rendered here. Edwards renders it *shunned. Destroyer,* by John Rogers rendered *murtherer;* by Genevan translation, *cruell man;* by Edwards, *oppressive;* by Calvin, *violent;* by Hengstenberg, *transgressor.* It comes from a word, which would be used to signify the breaking down of the walls of a city. There is no better rendering than *destroyer.* To shun the paths of the destroyer is to avoid the life and work of a destroyer. This David did during all his troubles with Saul. This David's greater Son did also, see Luke ix. 56; John iii. 17. The other views of this passage are so poorly supported that it is hardly necessary now to consider them.

5. David knew his own weakness. He had not kept himself from wicked ways by his own power and virtue. And so he prays: *Hold up my goings in thy paths*, that *my footsteps slip not*. This might be the sense, if the verse applied to David alone. Calvin, Jebb and the church of England give the sense of the common version. These have authority on their side. But another rendering is justly preferred by many. Edwards: I have kept my steps steady in thy paths; my feet have not deviated; Hengstenberg: My steps hold fast by thy paths, my feet slide not; Alexander: My steps have laid hold of thy paths, my feet have not swerved. If this is the correct rendering, the verse contains a renewed profession of innocence. Fry says it is "the most positive assertion of unsinning obedience that can well be imagined." Alexander: "The common version violates the context by converting the first clause into a prayer, which would here be out of place." Even if David personally, or as an example of God's suffering people, is alone referred to, this latter is the better view.

6. *I have called upon thee; for thou wilt hear me, O God.* Some versions, modern as well as ancient, greatly weaken the force of this passage by giving the tenses different from the common version, which follows the Hebrew. The preterite is first used as expressive of an action continued to this time. The future is employed to express the *hope* that uniformly sustained and encouraged him in prayer. The Chaldee, Calvin, Venema, Jebb, church of England and Alexander give the tenses as in our version. Edwards varies: I call upon thee, because thou usest to hear me; Fry: I have called upon thee: for thou dost answer me. Men in despair never pray. Hope in God's mercy is essential to any hearty calling on God. The experience of God's people in this matter has great power over them. They have proved God and found him faithful. Therefore they come boldly and cry: *Incline thine ear unto me*, and hear *my speech*. Luther well says that this verse in its scope "comprehends in itself the past as well as the future. The meaning of it appears to be this: I have confidence that my words shall not be in vain, since I know how, according to thy grace, thou art wont to hear me. Hence the compassion of God is celebrated, which consists in this, that he hears when we cry. This moves us, and is the reason why we can presume to call." Christ was heard in that he feared, when he uttered strong crying and tears in the days of his flesh.

7. *Shew thy marvellous loving-kindness, O thou that savest by thy right hand them which put their trust* in thee *from those that rise up* against them. The verb first found in this verse is elsewhere rendered *sever, set apart, separate, put a difference, wonderfully make*. Our translators put in the word *marvellous* in order to convey the full idea. But it is made to qualify *loving-kindness*, and not the verb *shew*. *Wonderfully shew thy loving-kindness* would be more literal. Calvin: Make marvellous thy mercies; Edwards: Exert thy goodness in a wonderful manner; Jebb: Show the marvels of thy mercies; Hengstenberg: Single out thy loving-kindnesses; Morison: Make great thy mercies; Alexander: Distinguish thy mercies. The noun is in the plural. He asks God to make a remarkable display, an illustrious exhibition of his mercies for his deliverance. The word rendered *loving-kindness* is commonly rendered *mercy*, Ps. v. 7; vi. 4; xiii. 5, and *twenty-six* times in Ps. cxxxvi. It is also rendered *good deeds*, Neh. xiii. 14; *goodness*, Neh. xxxii. 32; often *kindness*, Jon. iv. 2; sometimes *pity*, Job vi. 14; *merciful kindness*, Ps. cxvii. 2. Such an exercise of *mercy* was called for in David's circumstances to save him in a clear and decided way. *The right hand* is a phrase often occurring in the Scriptures, and more frequently in the Psalms than in any other book. In this and in several other places it seems to refer to the strong power of God. The remainder of the verse has no serious difficulty. The ellipses are well supplied in our version.

8. *Keep me as the apple of the eye. The apple of the eye* is the rendering of a phrase

found also in Deut. xxxii. 10; Pr. vii. 2. It is literally *the little man, the daughter* or *the black of the eye*—the part which reflects the image of a man when he looks into it. The word rendered *apple* is elsewhere *obscure, black.* Prov. vii. 9; xx. 20. No part of our frame is more constantly, instinctively, or carefully guarded than the apple of the eye. The least danger threatened, or injury inflicted rouses all our powers of defence. The word rendered *keep* is the same as that rendered *preserve* Ps. xvi. 1, which see. The same prayer is, according to our version, expressed in other words: *Hide me under the shadow of thy wings.* This rendering is sustained by the Septuagint, Vulgate, Ethiopic, Syriac, Arabic, church of England, Calvin, Venema, Amesius, Edwards, Fry, Jebb, and Hengstenberg. But Ainsworth and Alexander prefer the literal rendering in the future, *in the shadow of thy wings thou wilt hide me.* Ainsworth: "It is the property of the Hebrew tongue often to set down a prayer in this form, especially in the end of a sentence, as noting some assurance to have the request fulfilled." In proof he cites Ps. x. 17; lix. 1; lxiv. 1; and several places in Job. Alexander: "What he asks in one clause he expresses his assured hope of obtaining in the other." He supposes Deut. xxxii. 10 referred to in the first clause, and Deut. xxxii. 11 in the second. Matt. xxiii. 37 is thought by many to be a carrying out of the figure in the last clause. Dodd and others think the reference is to the wings of the cherubim, which overshadowed the mercy-seat. Ps. lvii. 1 is quoted in proof. This is not decisive. The defence secured was to be

9. *From the wicked that oppress me,* from *my deadly enemies* who *compass me about.* Tholuck probably gives the main ideas of this verse: "David states that his persecutors are most determinately set upon his destruction, that they try to stop every means of escape." Yet the diversity of rendering is considerable. Calvin: From the face of the ungodly, who go about to destroy me: and of mine enemies, who besiege [or encompass] me; Edwards: From the wicked that ravage me; from my mortal enemies who encompass me; Venema: In the presence of the wicked, who rise up against me, my enemies, who with a haughty spirit have surrounded me; Amesius: On account of the wicked, who waste me; my mortal enemies who surround me; Jebb: From the presence of the ungodly that waste me: mine enemies my soul do surround; Fry: From the face of the wicked who have assailed me—my enemies who have encompassed me; Ainsworth reads, Because of the wicked, etc.; church of England: From the ungodly that trouble me; mine enemies compass me round about to take away my soul; Hengstenberg: From the wicked, who disperse me, mine enemies, who against the soul compass me about; Alexander: From the face of the wicked who have wasted me; mine enemies to the soul will surround me. *From the face of the wicked* is the best rendering of the first clause. The word rendered *oppress* is to waste, *lay waste, destroy, spoil.* The latter is by far the most frequent rendering. It is never rendered *oppress* but in this place. The *wicked* of the first clause are the *enemies* of the last. Mudge, Kennicott and Clarke regard the imagery of the latter part of this verse and of the next two verses, as taken from huntsmen, who surround a large tract of forest, and drive their game to the centre, where they are caught, or killed. This excludes the idea of a close siege, and gives that of a hot pursuit on all sides in a chase. *Compass* is the most common rendering of the verb in this clause. The same word is found in Job xix. 6. God hath *compassed* me with his net. In Ps. xxii. 16 we have the same word: The assembly of the wicked have *inclosed* me. *Deadly enemies* are those who seek the life, and will be satisfied with nothing till it is destroyed. Alexander, speaking of the last clause of this verse, says: "The future form suggests that the danger, which the first clause had described as past, was still present and likely to continue." Those who refer this

Psalm to Christ as the anti-type of David, find no difficulty in the application of this verse.

10. *They are inclosed in their own fat.* John Rogers' translation: Whych mantyne thyr awne welthynesse wyth oppressyon. The other old English versions generally agree with that in common use. Chaldee: Their wealth is multiplied; Vulgate and Doway, following the Septuagint: They have shut up their fat. By *fat* the Doway says *bowels of compassion* are signified. But this is mere assertion, not founded on any imagery familiar to Hebrews. The fact is that in man no part has less sensibility than the *fat*. That word never expresses tenderness. With our version substantially agree Calvin, Jebb, Alexander and others. But Houbigant, Lowth, Kennicott, Edwards, Horsley, Fry and Clarke read, They have inclosed me in their net. The great objection to this reading is: "It receives no support from ancient versions or manuscripts." The transposition of one letter in the original would however justify it. This is one of the most respectable of modern emendations, and makes the clause fall in with the imagery of vv. 9, 11, if that is drawn from hunting. But the common version gives an excellent sense, and coincides with a figure familiar to the inspired writers. Deut. xxxii. 15; Job xv. 27; Ps. lxxiii. 7; cxix. 70. David's condition was that of consuming sorrow; that of his enemies consisted with the utmost insensibility fostered by arrogance and presumption. Their speech corresponds with their state and so, *With their mouth they speak proudly.* Both ancient and modern versions remarkably coincide with the above rendering. It is always true that out of the abundance of the heart the mouth speaketh. The proud will speak proudly. The word rendered *proudly* (literally *in pride*) is in Ps. lxxxix. 9 *raging:* Thou rulest the *raging* of the sea. How the wicked raged against David and Christ is well known to all who read the Scriptures.

11. *They have now compassed us in our steps.* *Compassed*, not the same word as in v. 9, but the same as that in Gen. ii. 11, 13; 2 Kings vi. 15; viii. 21. In Ps. xlviii. 12 it is *walk about.* The hunters having driven their prey together, and thinking it secure *walk about*, and with confidence contemplate their easy victory. The Septuagint, Ethiopic, Arabic, Syriac, Vulgate, Doway, Calvin, Venema, Edwards and Hengstenberg follow the Hebrew text, and read *me*, not *us*, though the Masora and many agree with our version. The sense is the same in either case. The way the wicked hated David and David's Lord is a specimen of their malice against all good men. The *look* of the wicked over their prey has been noticed in every time of persecution, and so it is added, *They have set their eyes bowing down to the earth.* Kimchi thinks the sense is, They have their eyes on the earth, to spread nets for our feet; Arabic and Syriac render it so as to give this sense, They have set their eyes that they may strike me to the earth, or prostrate me on the earth; Calvin: They have fixed their eyes to cast down to the earth; Edwards: They fix their eyes upon me, stooping down to the earth; Venema: In the most secret manner they set their eyes on the earth to spy; Jebb: Their eyes they have set, turning down to the earth; Fry: They fix their eyes to cast us on the ground; Horne: They have set or fixed their eyes upon us to lay us prostrate upon the earth; Hengstenberg: They direct their eyes to turn aside in the land; Alexander: Their eyes they will set to go astray in the land. In this verse as in the preceding the first verb is in the preterite; the second, in the future, showing that dangers were still imminent, and that no door of escape was open to sight. These senses have been gathered: *first*, these pursuers had a demure and innocent (though hypocritical) look; *secondly*, they were as hunters watching the footsteps of their prey; *thirdly*, their eyes were intent on the persecuted to bring them low; *fourthly*, their eyes were set on wickedness, and so they went more and more astray; *fifthly*, they act like a beast, with eyes intent, crouching to spring on its prey.

The *fourth* of these views is the best sustained by the usage of the words; but the *fifth* best agrees with the scope and subsequent context:

12. *Like as a lion* that *is greedy of his prey, and as it were a young lion lurking in secret places.* There is very slight variation in the rendering of these words, some being more full than others, but all preserving the same imagery. The *young lion* is not the whelp in the lair, but the grown young lion that hunts his own meat, the strongest lion. Persecutors are terrible wild beasts. The figure is natural and forcible, Ps. x. 8–10. Paul is supposed to call Nero a lion, 2 Tim. iv. 17. In such straits, surrounded by enemies, the help of man is vain, and hope is clean gone, unless God will appear. So the prayer is:

13. *Arise, O* LORD, *disappoint him, cast him down. Arise,* commonly so rendered. See Ps. iii. 7; vii. 6; x. 12. *Disappoint him,* literally *prevent his face, i. e.,* step in before him, hinder him from compassing his designs. Hengstenberg has it, Surprise him. The word is in our version almost uniformly *prevent, go before, come before,* Ps. xviii. 5; lxxxix. 14; Mic. vi. 6. *Cast him down,* is rendered *bend him* by the Chaldee, Cocceius, Venema and Street; *lay him prostrate on the ground* by Calvin; *bring him down* by Edwards; *make him bow* by Alexander; *bring him to his knees* by the Septuagint. This last rendering cannot be improved. By humbling their enemies, God often saves his chosen from their cruel power. And so David adds: *Deliver my soul from the wicked.* The word *deliver* is rendered with great uniformity in our version, Ps. xxxi. 1; lxxi. 4; lxxxii. 4. Once it is *Cause me to escape,* Ps. lxxi. 2. *The wicked,* the same as *the ungodly* of Ps. i. The prayer is for complete deliverance from present dangers and enemies. Our version reads, *Deliver my soul from the wicked,* which is *thy sword.* With this rendering agree the Septuagint, Arabic, Ethiopic, Vulgate, church of England, Patrick and Scott. The Chaldee, however, has it, *from the wicked, who deserves to be slain with the sword;* Syriac: *From the wicked and from the sword;* Calvin: *From the ungodly man by thy sword.* With Calvin agree Venema, Amesius, Houbigant, Boothroyd, Dathe, Edwards, Jebb, Fry, Horne, Horsley, Hengstenberg and Alexander. Those who agree with our common version cite Isa. x. 5, where the Assyrian is called *the rod of God's anger.* In either case we have a good sense. That of our version has long been precious to many of God's people. Perhaps it is to be preferred. The wicked are God's sword, whether this verse declares it or not, and without repentance they shall perish by his sword, the instrument of executing his dreadful anger. The Psalmist continues his prayer for deliverance

14. *From men,* which are *thy hand,* O LORD. There is much the same diversity here as in the preceding clause, Calvin and others reading, *From men by thy hand.* The remarks on the last clause of v. 13 are here fairly applicable. The principle which governs the reading in that phrase must prevail here also, though a few have capriciously varied the translation. The common English rendering of this verse is generally so excellent that it will be hard to find a better. Although the original is confessedly difficult, and many changes have been suggested, where is the sense, required by the context and the grammatical construction, given more clearly than in our version? This makes the word *sword,* v. 13, to be in apposition with *the wicked,* and the word *hand* to be in apposition with *men,* meaning the same as the *sword* and *the wicked* of v. 13. Then there is a further description of the persons intended when he continues to ask for deliverance *from men of the world;* Calvin: Men who are of long duration, [who are from an age]; Edwards: Men, I say, of the earth; church of England: The men I say, and from the evil world; Venema: The partners, I say, of a fortunate age; Ainsworth: Mortal men of the transitory world; Street: The mortals of this age; Horne: Mortals of the transitory world; Clarke: Mortal men of time; Dathe: Men who are prosperous; Hengstenberg: The men of continuance.

The word rendered *world* may signify duration, age, time, world, or the things of the world, Job xi. 17 ; Ps. xxxix. 5 ; xlix. 1 ; lxxxix. 47. Our common version can be sustained. The changes suggested are not improvements. We need deliverance from the principles, examples and power of the men of the world, Which have *their portion in* this *life.* Calvin : Whose portion is in life ; Venema, Amesius, Edwards and Fry agree with our version ; Geddes : Whose portion in life is permanent ; Alexander : Their portion is in (this) life. Persecutors are often full of wealth. They have their good things before they reach eternity. They have the means of indulging their appetites. And so it is added of them, *And whose belly thou fillest with thy hid* treasure. The word *treasure* is not in the original. Instead of it Calvin reads *Goods ;* Syriac, Arabic, Venema, Edwards and Hengstenberg, *Treasures ;* Fry, *Good things ;* Alexander, *Hoard,* corresponding to the Chaldee ; Septuagint, Vulgate and Ethiopic, *Hidden things ;* Doway, *Hidden stores ;* Diodati, *Temporal things ;* Amesius and Jebb have *Treasure.* In the Hebrew the word rendered *hidden* is singular. The common version is good. Such men are often at the head of large families. *They are full of children.* The Chaldee, Syriac, Arabic, Vulgate : Their children are filled ; Calvin : Their children are full of them [the goods]. In this view concur Venema, Amesius, Tholuck, Edwards and Fry. But Luther, Pool, Jebb, Hengstenberg and Alexander give the sense of our version. Either is good. That of Calvin and others makes some variation in the meaning of the last word of the next clause : *And leave the rest of their* substance *to their babes.* If we read, *Their children are filled,* then the *babes* are the children's children of the *men of the world,* and so with Tholuck we say their " fulness of earthly goods is so great that not only is there enough for their children, but even a portion left for their grandchildren." The wealth of many godless men reaches to the third generation. This gives a fuller meaning than that suggested by the common version, and is well supported by authority.

15. *As for me I will behold thy face in righteousness.* Scarcely any clause of the Psalms is more uniformly rendered. *I* and *in righteousness* come together, *i. e.,* I in a justified state and with a sanctified nature, I in righteousness shall behold thy face. This will be better than all the boasted wealth and pleasure and children of the wicked. The most persecuted and down-trodden servant of the Lord shall yet with all the tokens of a divine acceptance see God. This will produce blessedness indeed : *I shall be satisfied, when I awake, with thy likeness.* The verb *shall be satisfied* is the same as that found in v. 14, and there rendered *are full.* It is in the future in both cases, implying continuance. It is evidently used here to contrast the blessedness of the righteous with the fulness of the wicked. The word rendered *likeness* is also rendered *image, similitude,* Job iv. 16 ; Num. xii. 8, where it is promised to Moses, " The similitude of the LORD shall he behold." The sight of God is either by faith on earth, or by vision in heaven. Beholding as by a glass darkly the glory of the Lord on earth is a pledge of beholding his glory in the visions of immortality. I shall be satisfied with thy likeness, *when I awake* either every morning, and find myself with God, enjoying his favor and friendship, and so beholding him in his works of providence and grace ; or as when one awakes from sleep, the emblem of death, I shall be delivered from these impending evils, and shall thus be assured of thy love ; or above all, when I awake from my last sleep of death and in the glories of a resurrection state I shall see God face to face, then my discoveries of him shall bring everlasting satisfaction to my soul. For *likeness* some would substitute *glory, presence,* but the word means *bright manifestation, visible appearance.* Hengstenberg prefers *form.* But to give a good sense to us, *form* must be much varied from ordinary usage. Owen : " It is Christ alone, who is the *likeness* and image. When we awake in the other world with our minds purified and rectified, the beholding of him shall be always

satisfying to us. There will be then no satiety, no weariness, no indispositions; but the mind being made perfect in all its faculties, powers and operations, with respect unto its utmost end, which is the enjoyment of God, is satisfied in the beholding of him forever."

DOCTRINAL AND PRACTICAL REMARKS.

1. This Psalm, like many others, shows that all our devotions of a metrical or musical character need not, as some have asserted, be of the nature of praise and thanksgiving. We may sing of anything that belongs to a devotional frame of mind, though there be not a word of direct praise in it.

2. Justice in the character of any ruler, and especially in the Ruler of the universe, is an amiable attribute. Give any man the *right* in a controversy, which God is to decide, and he can have his cause in no better hands. He confidently cries, *Hear the right,* v. 1.

3. Because God is righteous, a good cause is sure finally to triumph, v. 1.

4. It is a great mistake, commonly committed by carnal men, to glory in the justice of their cause; and yet never to carry it before the tribunal of him, who alone executeth justice and judgment in the earth.

5. Cobbin: "Happy is he who can appeal to God for the integrity of his heart and actions. True devotion in prayer, an upright conscience, guarded words and temper, cautious and holy walking; these will allow of reflection, and afford sweet solace to the mind in the time of trouble."

6. A blessed privilege is prayer. Without it, what could the righteous do? The very goodness of his cause makes David bold in prayer, v. 1. Verse 9 proves that "the greater the terror, with which we are stricken by the cruelty of our enemies, the more ought we to be quickened in prayer." If we are wrong, we need forgiveness; if we are right, we still need protection. If we are prosperous, we should beg for caution and moderation; if we are afflicted, we should ask for support, sanctification and timely relief, v. 1.

7. Acceptable prayer must be fervent. Cold prayers are hypocritical. The repetition of David's prayer and his use of the word *cry* show how vehement were his desires, and how earnest his supplications, v. 1. All repetition in prayer is not *vain.*

8. Nor do we need refined speech in prayer. David's language is simple, v. 1. Calvin: "When we present ourselves before God, let us learn that it is not to be done with the ornaments of an artificial eloquence, for the finest rhetoric and the best grace, which we can have before him, is pure simplicity."

9. Prayer, and all acts of religious worship, demand sincerity, v. 1. Feigned lips are God's abhorrence. Compare Ps. lxvi. 18; John ix. 31. Luther: "We see how everywhere zeal and hatred break forth against hypocrisy, which the saints avoid with great horror."

10. It is not unusual for God to delay for a season the execution of justice, even in behalf of his people, v. 2. Delay is not refusal. He will come at the best time. "Shall not God avenge his own elect, which cry day and night unto him, though he bear long with them? I tell you, that he will avenge them speedily." Therefore "men ought always to pray and not to faint."

11. In the endurance of wrong and sorrow, we can do nothing better than to leave our cause with God, v. 2. Our afflictions are great miseries when they lead us from God, and not to God.

12. The whole of the divine character is approved by the righteous, and is a source of joy to him. David rejoices in the divine omniscience, v. 3. That attribute, if understood, terrifies the ungodly; but it gives great peace to the pious. Every good

man begs for an examination by the all-searching eye. It is true that hypocrites may often appeal to the Searcher of hearts even when they are wrong; but they do it insincerely and profanely. If they really thought God was about to let men see them as he sees them, they would be filled with dismay.

13. That, which makes our trials too strong for us is our weakness. Were we all right, the more we were proved and tried, the more would our integrity appear, v. 3. "Every man is tempted, when he is drawn away of his own lust and enticed." One may kindle a great fire on the ice, yet the river will not be burned up. But a spark will explode a magazine of gunpowder.

14. A good resolution is one of the means of preserving us. No man will be free from sins of *heart*, of tongue, or of life, unless he is *purposed* to avoid iniquity, v. 3.

15. Especially have all good men found it hard to keep clear of sins of the tongue, v. 3. "If any man offend not in word, the same is a perfect man, and able also to bridle the whole body. . . The tongue is a fire, a world of iniquity. . . It sets on fire the course of nature, and it is set on fire of hell. . . The tongue can no man tame; it is an unruly evil, full of deadly poison."

16. Although in carnal contests one wrong generally provokes another; yet it never justifies it, v. 4. If ever personal vengeance could have been right, it was when Saul, the king, was persecuting David for his great public services. When Saul was in his power, David hurt not a hair of his head, but kept himself *from the paths of the destroyer.* "Vengeance is mine; I will repay, saith the Lord." "Dearly beloved, avenge not yourselves, but rather give place unto wrath." "The wrath of man worketh not the righteousness of God"—never did help a good cause.

17. Past supports and deliverances should make us humble and watchful, v. 5. If our weakness is our strength, as Paul teaches, surely our strength may become our weakness. Calvin: "Certainly the more any one excels in grace, the more ought he to be afraid of falling; for it is the usual policy of Satan to endeavor, even from the virtue and strength which God has given us, to produce in us carnal confidence, which may induce carelessness."

18. How often must our resort be to prayer, vv. 5–9. Often we can do nothing but pray, never can we do anything better, than to call upon God.

19. A blessed principle is confidence in God. Some lightly esteem it. The belief that his prayer would be heard kept David at the mercy-seat, crying for help, v. 6. Luther: "See how quickly affection makes an excellent orator. He recommends to God his cause in the most favorable light, he seeks to put himself on good terms with him, he makes complaint against his adversaries, he tries to have these made hateful, and this he does in very few and urgent words. But he does so, not as if these were necessary for God, in order that he might be prevailed on, but for the sake of faith. For the more vigorous and fervent our faith is, the more always does God work through it."

20. It is dreadful for a poor tempted or persecuted soul to lose sight of the divine mercy. Let him hope in God's marvellous loving-kindness, v. 7. Dickson: "The believer must hold his eye in times of dangers and straits especially upon God's good-will and kindness, as a counter-balance to all the malice of men." Great deliverances will never cease till the last of the redeemed reaches the rest above. Every successive saint is a wonder unto many.

21. Great difficulties arising from human perversity and malice are no novelty, v. 7. It is remarkable, too, that often the most gentle and the most tender spirits are thrown out on the most tempestuous seas. David and Jeremiah through all their youth showed unusual peaceableness of disposition, yet God made them men of contention, despite all their predilections. Yet it is one of the greatest blessings and

ought to be sought by prayer that we may lead quiet and peaceable lives in all godliness and honesty.

22. Every inspired prayer contains a promise of good to the righteous. So the petitions of v. 8, are fulfilled in all the saints. Dickson: "The care God hath of his poor children that depend upon him is unspeakable; and the tender love he beareth unto them no one similitude can express. . . God's care of them is comparable to man's care of *the apple of his eye;* God's love to them is comparable to the love of the bird-mother toward her young ones, whom she warmeth, and *hideth under the shadow of her wings."* God's people are safe. Nothing can harm them.

23. The imagery of evil is all exhausted in giving an account of the character and conduct of bad men. They are fat and proud, boasting and vaporing, v. 9. They are cunning hunters, fetching a compass. They are spies on God's people. They are lions and young lions, vv. 11, 12. Christ called Herod a fox. They are deadly enemies. Their hostility, if their hearts remain unchanged, will never cease. They are full of malice. Scott: "David's persecutors were prosperous, self-indulgent and luxurious; and thus they grew arrogant, impious, unfeeling and presumptuous." Persecutors of all ages are much alike.

24. God's people are as much under his care in time of siege, or when surrounded by foes, as at any other time, v. 11. At such seasons the most feeble child of God may sing: "The LORD is my light and my salvation; whom shall I fear? the Lord is the strength of my life; of whom shall I be afraid? When the wicked, even mine enemies and my foes came upon me to eat up my flesh, they stumbled and fell. Though an host should encamp against me, my heart shall not fear; though war should rise against me in this will I be confident." Beza mentions as many as six hundred remarkable deliverances wrought for him in the troublous days, in which he lived.

25. Wicked men are always wicked. Wickedness is their trade, their nature. The lion no more loves flesh and blood than do the wicked love sin, v. 12. Nor are they ever satisfied. They sin on.

26. When to the saints the peril is extreme, the deliverance is at hand, v. 13. "When danger is most nigh, God is more nigh." Nothing is easier than for God to bring to naught human devisings.

27. In afflictions it is a great thing to be able to acknowledge God as the author of our distresses, even though he employs men as instruments, vv. 13, 14. This was the support of the man of Uz, Job i. 20, 21. This quieted David in his sorrowful departure from Jerusalem in time of Absalom's rebellion, 2 Sam. xvi. 5–12. In like manner Eli received the dreadful tidings of the approaching death of his wicked sons: "It is the Lord," 1 Sam. iii. 18. He, who in affliction dwells much on second causes will have sorrow on sorrow. The wickedest men are but God's *rod,* and *hand,* and *sword.* They can do nothing except it be given them of God, John xix. 11. The ungodly are merely scourges.

28. Doleful is the case of the wicked. They have their portion in this life, v. 14. Their riches may leave them in a moment. The power of enjoying earthly things may go as soon. They may leave much to their descendants, but they cannot tell whether they will be wise men or fools, prudent or spendthrifts. Dodd: "We should look with pity at the bargain which men of the world have made for themselves, and tremble more at what they are to suffer hereafter, than be troubled for what they for the present enjoy. When we see men languishing in fevers and dropsies, we do not envy them the pleasure they have enjoyed in former riots and excesses; and when we see men wasted and faint in consumptions, or wore away by more noisome diseases, we do not envy them the pleasure of their former lusts and license."

29. The way to heaven is rough. Yet two things greatly support the saints. One is that they have many comforts and cordials by the way. Sometimes they have a blessed vision of God, v. 15. They walk with him and he shows them his covenant. The other is, they have a heaven to go to, and of that they have a blessed assurance in God's word, and a sure hope in their souls. Tholuck: "Wondrously enlightened by the Holy Ghost, David speaks with a clearness, which seems possible to Christian minds only, of the glories of heaven, where the struggle with sin shall be changed into perfect *righteousness*, faith into *face-to-face vision*, satiation with the divided goods of this life into *satiation with the one perfect good*, which renders everything besides unnecessary." How such a ray from the throne above pierces the darkness of this world!

PSALM XVIII.

To the chief Musician, *A Psalm* of David, the servant of the LORD, who spake unto the LORD the words of this song in the day *that* the LORD delivered him from the hand of all his enemies, and from the hand of Saul: And he said,

1 I will love thee, O LORD, my strength.

2 The LORD *is* my rock, and my fortress, and my deliverer; my God, my strength, in whom I will trust; my buckler, and the horn of my salvation, *and* my high tower.

3 I will call upon the LORD, *who is worthy* to be praised: so shall I be saved from mine enemies.

4 The sorrows of death compassed me, and the floods of ungodly men made me afraid.

5 The sorrows of hell compassed me about: the snares of death prevented me.

6 In my distress I called upon the LORD, and cried unto my God: he heard my voice out of his temple, and my cry came before him, *even* into his ears.

7 Then the earth shook and trembled; the foundations also of the hills moved and were shaken, because he was wroth.

8 There went up a smoke out of his nostrils, and fire out of his mouth devoured: coals were kindled by it.

9 He bowed the heavens also, and came down: and darkness *was* under his feet.

10 And he rode upon a cherub, and did fly: yea, he did fly upon the wings of the wind.

11 He made darkness his secret place; his pavilion round about him *were* dark waters *and* thick clouds of the skies.

12 At the brightness *that was* before him his thick clouds passed, hail *stones* and coals of fire.

13 The LORD also thundered in the heavens, and the Highest gave his voice; hail *stones* and coals of fire.

14 Yea, he sent out his arrows, and scattered them; and he shot out lightnings, and discomfited them.

15 Then the channels of waters were seen, and the foundations of the world were discovered at thy rebuke, O LORD, at the blast of the breath of thy nostrils.

16 He sent from above, he took me, he drew me out of many waters.

17 He delivered me from my strong enemy, and from them which hated me: for they were too strong for me.

18 They prevented me in the day of my calamity: but the LORD was my stay.

19 He brought me forth also into a large place; he delivered me, because he delighted in me.

20 The LORD rewarded me according to my righteousness; according to the cleanness of my hands hath he recompensed me.

21 For I have kept the ways of the LORD, and have not wickedly departed from my God.

22 For all his judgments *were* before me, and I did not put away his statutes from me.

23 I was also upright before him, and I kept myself from mine iniquity.

24 Therefore hath the LORD recompensed me according to my righteousness, according to the cleanness of my hands in his eyesight.

25 With the merciful thou wilt shew thyself merciful; with an upright man thou wilt shew thyself upright;

26 With the pure thou wilt shew thyself pure; and with the froward thou wilt shew thyself froward.

27 For thou wilt save the afflicted people; but wilt bring down high looks.

28 For thou wilt light my candle: the LORD my God will enlighten my darkness.

29 For by thee I have run through a troop; and by my God have I leaped over a wall.

30 *As for* God, his way *is* perfect: the word of the LORD is tried: he *is* a buckler to all those that trust in him.

31 For who *is* God save the LORD? or who *is* a rock save our God?

32 *It is* God that girdeth me with strength, and maketh my way perfect.

33 He maketh my feet like hinds' *feet*, and setteth me upon my high places.

34 He teacheth my hands to war, so that a bow of steel is broken by mine arms.

35 Thou hast also given me the shield of thy salvation: and thy right hand hath holden me up, and thy gentleness hath made me great.

36 Thou hast enlarged my steps under me, that my feet did not slip.

37 I have pursued mine enemies, and overtaken them: neither did I turn again till they were consumed.

38 I have wounded them that they were not able to rise: they are fallen under my feet.

39 For thou hast girded me with strength unto the battle: thou hast subdued under me those that rose up against me.

40 Thou hast also given me the necks of mine enemies; that I might destroy them that hate me.

41 They cried, but *there was* none to save *them: even* unto the LORD, but he answered them not.

42 Then did I beat them small as the dust before the wind: I did cast them out as the dirt in the streets.

43 Thou hast delivered me from the strivings of the people; *and* thou hast made me the head of the heathen: a people *whom* I have not known shall serve me.

44 As soon as they hear of me, they shall obey me; the strangers shall submit themselves unto me.

45 The strangers shall fade away, and be afraid out of their close places.

46 The LORD liveth; and blessed *be* my rock; and let the God of my salvation be exalted.

47 *It is* God that avengeth me, and subdueth the people unto me.

48 He delivereth me from mine enemies: yea, thou liftest me up above those that rise up against me: thou hast delivered me from the violent man.

49 Therefore will I give thanks unto thee, O LORD, among the heathen, and sing praises unto thy name.

50 Great deliverance giveth he to his king; and sheweth mercy to his anointed, to David, and to his seed for evermore.

DAVID wrote this Psalm. See title, verses 43–50, and 2 Sam. xxii. where we have the whole with some variations. Tholuck regards the form of this song in the *tenth* book of Scripture as the original. Hengstenberg and Alexander think this the first conception.

No point of doctrine or of duty is affected by taking either view. The assertion that the variations between the two editions of this Psalm are owing to carelessness in transcription is wholly inadmissible. Much less can we admit with Tholuck that the form in Samuel owes its origin to verbal tradition.

The names of the Almighty in this Psalm are *Jehovah* LORD, *Elohim God, El God, Eloah God* and *Gel-yohn Highest*, on which respectively see above on Ps. i. 2; iii. 2; v. 4, and below on v. 31; Ps. vii. 17.

This Psalm was composed late in the life of David, after he had obtained rest from all his enemies, among whom Saul was very prominent. Hengstenberg well calls it, "a great hallelujah, with which David retired from the theatre of life. . . In it the Psalmist thanks God, not for any single deliverance, but has throughout, before his eyes, a great whole of gracious administrations, an entire life rich with the experiences of the loving-kindness of God."

No Psalm affords a superior sample of the power and comprehensiveness of Hebrew poetry. Morison says, "In the most celebrated specimens of classic elegance and sublimity it has no equal."

Is this Psalm Messianic? For general views on this subject see Introduction, § 8. David doubtless speaks throughout of himself primarily, but then he is a type of Christ, and so the language has a secondary reference. Some able writers apply the whole Psalm to Christ. Kennicott speaks of it as containing "the Messiah's sublime thanksgivings," and says that "from New Testament quotations it is perfectly obvious that this Psalm breathes a prophetic spirit, and alludes to the Messiah; yet it is equally certain that its primary reference is to the literal David." Horne applies the whole "to the sufferings, resurrection, righteousness and conquests of Christ, to the destruction of the Jews, and conversion of the Gentiles." Calvin speaks more safely when he says that in this Psalm David "shows that his reign was an image and type of the kingdom of Christ, to teach and assure the faithful that Christ, in spite of the whole world, and of all the resistance which it can make, will, by the stupendous and incomprehensible power of the Father, be always victorious." Alexander says that the application of the promises "not merely to David as an individual, but to his posterity forever, thus including Christ, shows the whole composition to be one of those Messianic Psalms, in which he is the principal subject of the prophecy, though not the only one, nor even the one nearest to the eye of the observer." Morison goes so far as in the title to translate the word *David*, which signifies *The Beloved*. Also the word Saul (Sheol) he translates *Hell*. In this he agrees with Montanus and Horsley. Without adopting any extreme line of remark, it may be observed that sound commentators are unusually agreed in admitting that this Psalm has its highest fulfilment in Christ, the Son of David. They could hardly have admitted less, for it is twice quoted by Paul in application to Christ, Rom. xv. 9; Heb. ii. 13.

On the first clause, *To the chief musician*, see on title of Ps. iv. The words *a Psalm* in the title are properly supplied by our translators. The phrase, *The servant of the Lord* is not found in the title as given in 2 Sam. xxii. Neither is the phrase, *To the chief musician*. The reason is obvious. These phrases belong to poetry, not to history. The phrase, *The servant of the Lord* is also found in the title of Psalm xxxvi. Tholuck: "The term 'servant of God' is used either of any pious man, anxious to make the commandments of God the rule of his life, or of those who are called to specific services of God." In the former sense David calls himself "the servant of God," Ps. xix. 11, 13; 2 Sam. vii. 26; xix. 20; in the latter he is so called by others, Ps. lxxix. 3, 20. The apostles use the same language, Tit. i. 1; Jas. i. 1. The title is pretty uniformly rendered in ancient versions, except in the Syriac, which reads: *Of David* [a song.] *A giving* of thanks: and *concerning the ascension of Christ;* or as some have it, *A thanksgiving upon the ascension of Christ.* But this is interpretation, not translation. On vv. 28–32 Calvin says: "As to the tenses of the verbs, we would inform our readers once for all, that in this Psalm David uses the past and the future tenses indifferently, not only because he comprehends different histories, but also because he presents to himself the things of which he speaks as if they were still taking place before his eyes, and, at the same time, describes a continued course of the grace of God towards him."

1. *I will love thee*, O LORD, *my strength.* All the ancient versions except the Arabic put the verb *love* in the future. So do the great body of the best scholars. The original requires it. The love thus expressed has already begun and shall not fail. The word is nowhere rendered *love* except here. In Ps. ciii. 13 it describes the tender *pity* of a father. It seldom expresses human affections, but often divine *pity, mercy,*

compassion. Calvin: I will affectionately love thee; Bythner: I will vehemently love thee; Venema: I will most tenderly love thee; Piscator, Amesius and Clarke: From my inmost bowels I will love thee; Ainsworth: I will dearly love thee; Patrick: I love thee with the most passionate and ardent affection; Street: I love thee exceedingly; Edwards: I dearly love thee; Fry: Much do I love thee; Pool: I will love thee most affectionately, and with my whole soul; Horne: With all the yearnings of affection I will love thee; Hengstenberg: Heartily do I love thee; Barker: I will dearly—heartily, with my inmost affections—love thee. The verb expresses more than mere friendship, even hearty, tender, constraining love; Cocceius says it "is to love with the strongest and deepest affections of the heart, with the moving of all the bowels." The word rendered *my strength* is very expressive; Ainsworth: My firm strength. God is strength to his people in every sense, in which they can need strength. He supports them and gives them courage, success and establishment. This is easily accounted for because also,

2. *The* LORD *is my rock, and my fortress, and my deliverer.* The word rendered my *rock* is translated with much uniformity, yet it is once rendered *strong-hold.* The meaning is that the Lord is to his people for all the purposes of defence like those natural and impregnable hiding-places, where one man may repel the assault of a thousand, and two put ten thousand to flight. Such are often mentioned in Scripture, especially in the history of David. Palestine abounded in such places. God is called the *stone of Israel,* Gen. xlix. 24. He is first called the *Rock* and the Rock of salvation in Deut. xxxii. 4, 15. After this the title is often given. In the Psalms it first occurs here; afterwards in Ps. xxxi. 3; xlii. 9, etc. It is true the word rendered *stone* in Gen. xlix. 24 is wholly different from that rendered *rock* in Deut. xxxii. 4, 15, and neither of these is the same as that used in this verse. But in the second clause of this verse we have the very word used in Deut. xxxii. although our version renders it *strength.* The generic idea running through all these three words in application to God is solidity, strength, unchangeableness. *Rock* and *strength* in this verse have the additional idea of fitness for a hiding-place. In Isa. xxxiii. 16 we have the munitions of *rocks,* where the same word here rendered *rock* is found. The next title given is that of *fortress.* The word occurs more than *twenty* times in the Hebrew Bible and is most commonly rendered *fortress, fort, hold, strong place, strong-hold, defence.* 2 Sam. v. 7, 9, 17; Job xxxix. 18; Ps. xxxi. 2; lxxi. 3. God is also a *deliverer.* The verb corresponding to the participle here found is used in Ps. xvii. 13 and also in v. 43 of this Psalm. There is no better rendering than *deliverer,* meaning one who *causes us to escape,* or who *carries us away safely.* See Ps. lxxi. 2; Isa. v. 29. David adds: Thou art *my God, my strength, in whom I will trust.* The word *God* is *El,* rendered by Aquila, *My strong One.* See on Ps. v. 4. *Strength,* the same that in Deut. xxxii. 4, 15 is rendered *Rock.* The Septuagint, Syriac, Arabic, Ethiopic, Vulgate and Doway instead of *strength* give *helper;* church of England, *might;* Hengstenberg, *strong-hold;* Calvin, Venema, Amesius, Edwards, Jebb, Fry and Alexander, *rock.* In Scripture God often has this title. *Strength* here is not the same as in v. 1. In such a God and rock it is safe and wise to *trust,* to confide. David says God is also *my buckler, and the horn of my salvation,* and *my high tower. Buckler* here is *shield* in Ps. iii. 3, which see. In Ps. vii. 10 it is *defence.* The figure of the *horn* is borrowed from those animals whose horns are their protection. Luke i. 69. *High tower,* in Hebrew one word, in Ps. ix. 9 twice rendered *refuge,* also in Ps. xlvi. 7, 11; xlviii. 3. In Ps. cxliv. 2 as here it is *high tower,* and in Isa. xxv. 12 *high fort.* It expresses a place wholly impregnable and inaccessible by human means, if the assailants are at all opposed.

3. *I will call upon the* LORD, *who is worthy to be praised.* The words *who is worthy*

are not in the original. The Chaldee: In a hymn I pour out my prayers before the Lord; Septuagint, Ethiopic, Vulgate and Doway: Praising I will call upon the Lord; Syriac: I will call on the Lord; Arabic and Luther: I will praise the Lord, and I will call upon him; Calvin and Amesius: I will call upon the praised Jehovah; Venema: Let him be praised, I have called on Jehovah; Edwards: Praised be Jehovah; I will call upon Jehovah; Jebb: With praise will I call upon God; Fry: I call upon Jehovah, the theme of my praise; Street: Singing praise, I invoke Jehovah; Hengstenberg: As on the glorious one, I will call upon the Lord; Alexander: To be praised I will call Jehovah. The sense is nowhere better given than in the common version. Alexander says, the word which we render *worthy to be praised*, "is a standing epithet of Jehovah in the lyrical style of the Old Testament." Ainsworth: *Praised, that is, glorious, excellent, praiseworthy.* It describes Jehovah, and not the state of the worshipper. Whoso comes to God as he should will not call in vain: *So shall I be saved from mine enemies.* The right kind of prayer is the most potent instrumentality known on earth. Every approach to God should be with adoring views and with thanksgiving, Job i. 21; Phil. iv. 6. No enemy, no number of enemies can resist Jehovah. If God be for us, who can be against us?

4. *The sorrows of death compassed me.* *Sorrows*, elsewhere *lines, cords, bands, ropes, pangs, portions,* and in the singular *lot, company, destruction.* The same word occurs in the next verse. It is generally though not uniformly rendered as here. The general sense is the same whether we read *cords, sorrows,* or *pangs,* only the figure is different. Calvin and others prefer *cords.* This represents death as a giant or conqueror binding his victim or as a hunter capturing his prey. *Sorrows* covers the whole case, including all the distresses that beset him. The Chaldee: "Trouble surrounded me as of a woman who sitteth in the birth, and hath no strength to bring forth; and she is in danger of death." *And the floods of ungodly men made me afraid.* *Floods* point to the number and violence of the enemies. The Hebrew word for *ungodly men* is *Belial,* a word long used to designate evil men, Deut. xiii. 13. It signifies worthlessness, wickedness, destruction, and. so by ellipse bad men, *i. e.,* men of a worthless, wicked, or destructive character. Morison: "The term Belial expresses whatever is malevolent in purpose, or cruel and ungodly in action;" Gesenius would read: Floods of destruction. The Septuagint has it, Torrents of iniquity, meaning iniquity as acted out by wicked men. The verb in this clause is in the future, David in imagination conceiving himself as not yet fully delivered.

5. *The sorrows of hell compassed me about.* On the word *sorrows* see the preceding verse. The verb *compassed* is first used in Josh. vi. 3, 7. It there describes the act of surrounding a city to destroy it. It is also found in Ps. vii. 7; xvii. 11. It is not the same word as that rendered *compassed* in v. 4, which is always so rendered, but is not often used and almost without exception in poetical compositions. The word rendered hell is *sheol.* See above on Ps. vi. 5; ix. 17; xvi. 10. He adds: *The snares of death prevented me.* *Snares* also rendered *gins, traps,* not before found in the Psalms, though several times hereafter,.also several times in the Pentateuch. *Prevented,* found in Ps. xvii. 13. It recurs in v. 18. In our version it commonly signifies *prevent, meet, go before, come before.* The Chaldee has it *beset;* Arabic, *caught;* church of England and Jebb, *overtook;* Edwards and Hengstenberg, *surprised;* Amesius, *met;* Venema, *rushed upon;* Fry, *encompassed;* Alexander, *encountered.* The sense of vv. 4, 5 is that he had been in extreme peril, that his enemies were mighty, many and cunning, and had done their work so skilfully as to beget just and distressing fears. The work of ruin was nearly accomplished. What then?

6. *In my distress I called upon the* LORD, *and cried unto my God.* The variation in the rendering here is chiefly in the tense of the verb. The preterite of our version is

supported by the Septuagint, Ethiopic, Syriac, Arabic, Vulgate, Doway, Calvin, Venema and Fry. But the Chaldee, Amesius and Hengstenberg use the present tense *call* and *cry;* the church of England and Alexander render literally, and use the future, *will call* [or invoke] and *will cry.* This last is to be preferred, if the right view was given of v. 4, *i. e.,* that David is here poetically speaking of himself as still in the midst of his perils. *Distress,* in Ps. ix. 9, trouble. *Called,* the same as in Ps. iv. 1, 3; in Ps. iii. 4 it is *cried. Cried,* uniformly *cried, cried out, cried aloud, shouted.* It expresses vehemence. Nor was his cry in vain. *He heard my voice out of his temple, and my cry came before him,* even *into his ears.* The tenses of the verbs here are the same as in the first clause of the verse. The variations of the rendering are the same. The *hearing* of prayer is no new thing. God delights to hear *cries,* which come to him "out of the depths." *Temple,* the same as in Ps. v. 7, on which see. It may point either to the tabernacle where the ark abode, or to heaven itself. The latter gives the higher sense. The earthly temple was a type of the heavenly. The more exalted God is, the greater is his condescension, and the more glorious his power in saving his afflicted.

From the beginning of v. 7 to the end of v. 15 may be found some of the boldest and sublimest imagery known even in the poetry of the Hebrews.

Some indeed have supposed that David here describes certain astounding exhibitions of divine power in his own behalf, but Calvin correctly says that "David does not relate this as a piece of history, or as what had actually taken place, but he employs these similitudes for the purpose of removing all doubt, and for the greater confirmation of faith as to the power and providence of God." The imagery employed is well suited to the purpose the prophet had in view. That is, he declares that God as manifestly delivered him as if he had wrought these great effects in nature.

7. *Then the earth shook and trembled. The earth,* as in Gen. i. 1, commonly so rendered. There is a remarkable resemblance between the Hebrew words rendered *shook* and *trembled.* To preserve it, or give some idea of it, Jebb and Alexander read, *did shake and quake. The foundations also of the hills moved and were shaken, because he was wroth.* The word rendered *hills* is in Gen. vii. 20; Ps. xlvi. 2, and in many other places rendered *mountains.* Our English Bible does not regard the modern distinction between hill and mountain. In Deut. xxxii. 22 we first meet with the phrase, *foundations of the mountains,* or *hills.* Instead of *he was wroth,* Jebb reads *wrath was with him.* God's power can easily convulse the whole frame of nature.

8. *There went up a smoke out of his nostrils, and fire out of his mouth devoured.* Calvin: "David compares the mists and vapors which darken the air to the thick smoke which a man sends forth from his nostrils when he is angry." Some have thought that the reference was to furious beasts, whose breath is like smoke, especially when excited. A still better basis of the figure in the first two clauses is perhaps found in Ex. xix. 18: "And Mount Sinai was altogether on a smoke, because the LORD descended upon it in fire." *Coals were kindled by it, i. e.,* by the fire out of his mouth. The most prodigious effects are produced by the divine anger.

9. *He bowed the heavens also, and came down: and darkness was under his feet.* Luther: "When there is a clear heaven the clouds are high; but when a storm comes one feels as if it pushed against the roof;" Calvin: "When dense vapors occupy the middle of the air, the clouds seem to us to come down and to lie upon our heads;" Alexander: "The scene seems here to be transferred from heaven to earth." For *bowed.* Fry has *lowered;* for *darkness,* the Chaldee has *a dark cloud;* Calvin, *thick darkness;* Ainsworth, *gloomy darknesse,* myrke; Alexander, *gloom.* Our version renders the same word *thick darkness* in eight instances, Ex. xx. 21; Deut. iv. 11; v. 22; 1 Kings viii. 12; 2 Chron. vi. 1; Job xxxviii. 9; Joel ii. 2; Zeph. i. 15. It is

not the usual word for darkness. It occurs in the Bible *fifteen* times. The whole imagery is well explained by Ex. xix. 16, and Deut. v. 22. This mode of manifesting himself fills God's friends with awful though salutary fear, Heb. xii. 21; but it strikes terror and dismay into his foes. Michaelis: "That the wicked might not perceive his serene countenance, but only the terrible signs of his severe anger, and of his punishment."

10. *And he rode upon a cherub, and did fly.* The Chaldee, Septuagint, Ethiopic, Syriac, Arabic, Vulgate and Doway put *cherub* in the plural, *cherubim.* The word is supposed by some to be derived from a Syriac word signifying that which is great, strong, powerful. We first read of cherubim in Gen. iii. 24. Diodati and Ainsworth by Cherubim understand *Angels.* This name is given to the two figures that stood over the mercy-seat, Ex. xxv. 18–20. Ainsworth supposes that in 1 Chron. xxviii. 18, *Cherubim* are called a *chariot.* The fullest account we have of cherubim is in Ezek. x. These heavenly beings are creatures, full of life, possessed of great swiftness and strength and courage. The sound of their wings was as the voice of the Almighty God when he speaketh. Some have suggested that the word may signify a *guard* or *keeper,* others, a *courser of the sky,* others, a *minister.* The cherubim which stood over the mercy-seat were figures between which the Shechinah rested, and so God is often said to dwell between the cherubim. They are the lively, swift, courageous, watchful ministers of Jehovah. They are the swift chariots of God. *Yea, he did fly upon the wings of the wind.* Maimonides says it was the *cherub* that *did fly.* But see Ps. civ. 3. The change of one letter in the Hebrew verb would make this clause read as it does in 2 Sam. xxii. 11: *He was seen upon the wings of the wind.* Representing God as moving in a swift cloud is not unusual in Scripture, Isa. xix. 1. Several critics notice with pleasure the remarkable version of Sternhold and Hopkins:

> "On cherub and on cherubim
> Full royally he rode;
> And on the wings of mighty winds
> Came flying all abroad."

11. *He made darkness his secret place; his pavilion round about him* were *dark waters* and *thick clouds of the skies.* The Chaldee has: "He placed his majesty in the darkness, and his glory was encompassed with clouds as a pavilion; and he made the rain of kindness to descend on his people, and mighty waters from the agitation of the clouds to fall upon the wicked from the height of the world." For *secret place* Edwards and Waterland have *covert;* Street:

> He made darkness his covering,
> That which compassed him, his pavilion,
> Watery darkness in clouds of the sky.

The idea is the same as that presented in the preceding verse; Alexander: "The two nouns in the last clause both mean clouds, but the second is used only in the plural, and seems properly to designate the whole body of vapors constituting the visible heavens or sky." *Thick clouds* occurs again in v. 12. It is sometimes rendered simply *cloud,* or *clouds,* as in Ps. civ. 3; Isa. lx. 8. A *pavilion* is a *tent,* or *tabernacle,* or *booth.*

12. *At the brightness* that was *before him his thick clouds passed, hail* stones *and coals of fire. Brightness,* commonly so translated, but sometimes *shining, clear shining, light;* Edwards: At the splendor before him, his thick clouds dispersed, and hail, and coals of fire; Fry: By the glare of the lightning his clouds were unfolded, they dropped down the hail, with balls of fire; Alexander: From the blaze before him

his clouds passed—hail and coals of fire. Verse 11 presented God as withdrawn from view and hidden in thick darkness. Here he lets us see his power in the lightning. Luther: "It is a description of lightning. When he pleases, he rends the clouds asunder, and darts forth a flash such as the clouds cannot restrain; it breaks through just as if there were no clouds there... The whole heaven, as it were, opens when there is lightning." A frequent effect of lightning is cold and hail. So we have the heavens in a blaze, and at the same time dropping down ice. God has often plagued his foes with hail-stones and fire, Ex. ix. 24, 25; Josh. x. 11; Ps. lxxviii. 47, 48; cv. 32; Hag. ii. 17.

13. *The* LORD *also thundered in the heavens.* Thunder is the report of lightning. Though God employs natural causes in the production of storms, yet he produces them. In the next clause it is added, *And the Highest gave his voice.* The thunder is God's voice, 1 Sam. vii. 10; Job xxxvii. 5; xl. 9; Ps. civ. 7. On *Most High* see on Ps. vii. 17. Thunder is followed by *hail* stones *and coals of fire.* More lightning produced more hail, and as the storm continued, the lightning shot forth its fiery balls in every direction. This is expressed in other words:

14. *Yea, he sent out his arrows and scattered them; and he shot out lightnings, and discomfited them.* The *arrows* and the *lightnings* in this verse are the same. Lightnings are God's arrows. The Chaldee, Septuagint, Syriac, Arabic, Ethiopic, Vulgate, Doway, Calvin and Fry: Multiplied his lightnings; Jebb: His lightnings he showered; Clarke: He shot out lightnings; Alexander: He shot forth his lightnings; Edwards: He darted lightnings; Street: He darted many lightnings; Hengstenberg: He sent out much lightning; Venema: He scattered his lightnings more thickly; Clarke thinks that the very sound of the Hebrew words corresponds with the crash and terror of a fearful storm. The same has often been noticed in other languages in the words used for thunder and lightning. The effect of God's arrows or lightnings was to *scatter* and *discomfit* David's foes. Calvin: "The import of his words is, Whosoever does not acknowledge that I have been preserved by the hand of God, may as well deny that it is God who thunders from heaven, and abolish his power which is manifested in the whole order of nature, and especially in those wonderful changes which we see taking place in the atmosphere."

15. *Then the channels of waters were seen, and the foundations of the world were discovered at thy rebuke, O* LORD, *at the blast of the breath of thy nostrils.* There is considerable uniformity in rendering this verse, except that for *channels,* Calvin has *sources;* Edwards, *streams;* Fry, *depths;* the Septuagint, those who follow it and Venema, *fountains;* Hengstenberg, *brooks.* But Amesius, Jebb and Alexander agree with our version. Calvin and Morison suppose there is an allusion to the miracle at the Red sea: *q. d.,* God as certainly and manifestly delivered me as he did Israel escaping from the Egyptians, when he laid bare the channels of the sea, and exposed the foundations of the world. This seems to be a better interpretation, than that which supposes the Psalmist to represent himself as buried in deep waters, as in Ps. cxliv. 7, where he prays, Deliver me out of great waters. And yet this latter view is well supported by the context immediately succeeding.

16. *He sent from above, he took me, he drew me out of many waters.* It is not said precisely how God sent from heaven, whether merely by the awful agencies of storm, and thunder, and lightning, or by the ministry of angels. The latter well coincides with inspired teachings, Heb. i. 14. He *sent* by whom he would. Pool: "He sent angels or assistance otherwise." He *took.* God's grasp cannot be broken. None can pluck his chosen out of his hand. The verb *drew out,* evidently alludes to Moses, which signifies, *drawn out of the water,* Ex. ii. 10; Ainsworth: The word is used no where else. In Scripture *waters* signify *troubles,* or *people.* The ancient versions, to-

gether with Calvin, Venema, Fabritius and Edwards, use the past tense in the verbs here as in our version; Amesius, Brent, Hengstenberg and Fry prefer the present; while Jebb and Alexander follow the original, and give the future. See Introduction, § 6. Doubtless the acts described by these futures were in fact past at the time this Psalm was composed.

17. *He delivered me from my strong enemy, and from them which hated me: for they were too strong for me.* The remarks respecting tense in the preceding verse apply here also, the original of the first verb being in the future. *Delivered,* the same verb (though in a different tense) as that found in the title and in v. 48. David's enemies were neither few, nor weak, nor mild. They had malice and power. Clarke thinks that David here specially refers to the facts stated in 2 Sam. xxi. 16, 17. But David was often marvellously delivered. Patrick's paraphrase is: "He delivered me first from that mighty giant *Goliath,* and then from *Saul,* whose power I was not able to withstand; and afterwards from the *Philistines* and *Syrians,* and many other nations, whose forces were far superior unto mine, and whose hatred instigated them to do all they could to destroy me."

18. *They prevented me in the day of my calamity: but the Lord was my stay.* *Prevented,* the same as in v. 5, but here it is in the future. See Ps. xvii. 13, where it is rendered *disappoint.* *Calamity* always so rendered, or *destruction.* Alexander prefers a more literal rendering: *They will encounter me in the day of my calamity, and Jehovah has been for a stay to me.* He supposes that David anticipates new assaults and encourages himself by past experiences. But the great mass of commentators agree with our version. Even Jebb puts the first verb in the past tense. Several refer to 1 Sam. xxiii. xxiv. as containing the history here specially referred to. Walford: "They set their faces against me in the day of my calamity." *Stay* is always so rendered in our version. The word means *prop, support.* Chaldee: The word of the Lord was my stay.

19. *He brought me forth also into a large place.* To be in a narrow place, in a tight place, in a strait is a figure common to many languages, and expresses great distress. To be brought out into a large, *wide,* or spacious place is to have deliverance, to be rescued, so as to have freedom and safety, and be exempt from perplexity; see Ps. xxxi. 8. *He delivered me, because he delighted in me.* *Delivered,* elsewhere *loosed, drew out,* in this form always rendered by the verb *deliver.* In Hebrew it is in the future. Alexander prefers that rendering, as in our version in Ps. l. 15; xci. 15. Fry translates it in the present, *delivereth,* as in our version of Ps. xxxiv. 7. Probably a majority of versions agree with ours in preferring the past. *Because he delighted in me,* by some rendered *he loved me, had a good will to me, was inclined to me, was well pleased with me.* God has a complacential love to all who walk uprightly.

20. *The* LORD *rewarded me according to my righteousness; according to the cleanness of my hands hath he recompensed me.* It is common to consider this and the four following verses together. They do certainly relate to the same matter. Some have thought that such language could in no sense be applied to any who has lived on earth since the fall, except the man Christ Jesus. But surely God will "hear the right" even between man and man. "Righteousness and judgment are the habitation of his throne." Several ancient versions and Alexander follow the original and put both verbs in the future; Syriac, Fry and Hengstenberg use the present tense; but the large majority agree with our version. *Rewarded,* in Ps. xiii. 6; cxvi. 7· in the preterite rendered *hath dealt bountifully.* The uprightness of God's servants is the *occasion* of great blessings. The *cause* is found in his infinite excellence. *Recompensed,* elsewhere rendered *returned, rewarded, requited, brought back, restored.*

The principle involved here is the same so fully asserted in vv. 25, 26, and in Gal. vi. 7, 8.

21. *For I have kept the ways of the* LORD, *and have not wickedly departed from my God.* Good men are as slow to confess sins of which they are not guilty, as they are ready to acknowledge their real faults. David's enemies accused him of "rebellion and treason, plunder and robbery, sedition, cruelty and many flagitious actions." Of all these charges he declares himself innocent. God had put him in the way of rising to the throne, and he left his cause with God without taking any wicked measures to effect the result. The last verb employed in this verse denotes "not one fall only, but a revolt or defection, which utterly removes and alienates man from God." A fall is not an apostasy.

22. *For all his judgments* were *before me, and I did not put away his statutes from me.* In this place, as in Ps. xix. 9, and sometimes elsewhere, by *judgments* is to be understood *authoritative decisions.* To make the word here signify *punishments*, or *alarming events* of providence gives a poor sense. By *statutes* we are to understand the precepts of the whole law of God under which David lived. David devoutly studied, and habitually lived by the only infallible rule, and so proves his righteousness and the cleanness of his hands. There seems to be no sufficient reason for making *judgments* refer to the second table of the law, and *statutes* to the first.

23. *I was also upright before him, and I kept myself from mine iniquity.* Calvin: " All the verbs in this verse are put by David in the future tense, *I will be upright*, etc., because he does not speak confidently of one act only, or of a good work performed by fits and starts, but of steady perseverance in an upright course." For the signification of *upright*, see on Ps. xv. 2. To be upright *before God*, or *with God* is not merely to be *sincere* in his sight, but *undefiled* in his way. It is not the phrase found in Ex. xx. 3, and rendered *before me, before my face.* David was sorely tempted and vexed. Saul had been in his power; but he refrained from taking his own cause into his own hands. He resisted all inducements to do wrong to his enemies.

24. *Therefore hath the Lord recompensed me according to my righteousness, according to the cleanness of my hands in his eyesight. Recompensed, righteousness* and *cleanness of hands*, the same as in v. 20. This is a repetition, after argument, of what was there stated to be true, but was not yet proven. All this particular history prepares the way for the general proposition laid down in several forms in the next verse, viz.: that God deals with men very much after the manner of their own acts.

25. *With the merciful thou wilt shew thyself merciful. Merciful*, elsewhere rendered *holy*, Ps. lxxxvi. 2; *godly*, Ps. iv. 3; and in the plural *saints*, Ps. xxx. 4. Hengstenberg: Toward the pious thou art pious; Alexander: With the gracious thou wilt show thyself gracious; Edwards: With the beneficent man thou behavest thyself beneficently; Venema, almost the same; Fry: With the tender thou wilt show thyself tender; Septuagint, Vulgate and Doway: With the holy thou wilt be holy; Syriac: With the pure thou wilt be pure; Arabic: With the innocent thou wilt be innocent. Though in our version some of these words are never given as a correct rendering of the original, yet all the above propositions are true. The doctrine taught is often asserted in Scripture, Matt. v. 7. The converse is also true, James ii. 13. The same principle extends to the three succeeding clauses. *With an upright man thou wilt shew thyself upright.* Septuagint, Ethiopic, Vulgate and Doway: With the innocent man thou wilt be innocent; Arabic: With the honest thou wilt be honest; Syriac: With the simple thou wilt deal in simplicity; Venema: To the man of integrity thou art accustomed to show thyself uncorrupted; Jebb: With the man of perfectness thou wilt be perfect; Alexander: With the perfect man thou wilt show thyself perfect; Fry: With the perfect man thou showest thy perfections; or, With the plain,

honest, simple man, thou dealest with simplicity; or, With the man that was perfectly or wholly with thee, thou wilt show thyself to be wholly with him. For the various shades of meaning given in our version to *upright*, see on Ps. xv. 2.

26. *With the pure thou wilt shew thyself pure.* Septuagint, Ethiopic, Arabic, Syriac, Vulgate and Doway: With the elect thou wilt be elect; Jebb: With the clean thou wilt be clean; Fry: With the true thou showest thyself true; Pool: "*Purity* is often put for *sincerity*." The same principle extends to the wicked. *And with the froward thou wilt shew thyself froward.* In 2 Sam. xxii. 27, it is, With the froward thou wilt show thyself unsavory. The word first rendered *froward* is always so rendered, or it is translated *perverse* or *crooked*. Most of the ancient versions, Calvin, Edwards and Hengstenberg prefer *perverse;* Fry: With the politic thou showest thy policy; or, With the crooked thou showest thyself to be *tortuous;* Jebb: With the froward thou wilt wrestle; Alexander: With the crooked thou wilt show thyself perverse, Judges i. 7. Any course of divine justice will bring certain, righteous and amazing ruin on the incorrigibly wicked. When Jehovah shall arise, they will find that he is to them a more terrible enemy than the most *perverse* of all their earthly foes, though he swerve not from perfect truth and rectitude. It could not be otherwise.

27. *For thou wilt save the afflicted people. Afflicted,* elsewhere rendered *meek, poor, humble, lowly.* It is God's nature and plan to grant deliverance to them that are poor, meek, lowly. His past deeds show what he will ever do. In effecting such deliverances the wicked must often perish, and so it is added: *But* [thou] *wilt bring down high looks.* God resisteth the proud. He hates pride in any. He will correct it in his people and punish it in his foes. He will bring down high looks. He that exalteth himself, whether saint or sinner, shall be abased; but he that humbleth himself shall be exalted.

28. *For thou wilt light my candle.* From the earliest ages darkness has been the emblem of distress and perplexity, and light the emblem of comfort, of knowledge of the right way, and of the favor of God. A *candle* [or lamp] gives light; so several times in Job as here also it is used to express the above blessings. In 2 Sam. xxii. 29 it is, *For thou art my lamp.* God is a light to his people, when he causes light to arise unto them in darkness. *The* LORD *my God will enlighten my darkness.* The truth taught is the same as in the first clause, though it is differently expressed.

29. *For by thee I have run through a troop; and by my God I have leaped over a wall.* Of the events here noticed we know nothing beyond the simple statement here and in 2 Sam. xxii. 30, unless the latter clause refers to 2 Sam. v. 7. This boasting is not idle. It is *in God,* 1 Cor. xv. 10; 2 Cor. xii. 9, 10; Phil. iv. 13. Luther: "In confidence on thee I am terrified at no assault, contend against all kinds of enemies, leap over walls, and whatever else is opposed to me; that is, I who in myself am weak shall be invincible in thee." *In God* is better than *by God.* To *leap over a wall* may have been to escape a foe, or to capture a fortress. The Chaldee: By the word of my God I shall subdue fortified towns; Hammond: By my God I have taken a fort. In the Hebrew the verbs are in the future.

30. As for *God his way is perfect. God, El* as in Ps. v. 4. God's way is perfectly just, perfectly wise, perfectly holy, perfectly good, perfectly sure to prevail, perfectly honorable to himself, perfectly safe to his people. It sometimes looks dark or doubtful, because we see not the end. When that comes all is right. *Perfect,* also rendered in our version *upright,* Ps. xv. 2; vv. 23, 25. *The word of the* LORD *is tried.* Tried, some render it *fire-tried, purified, most pure, refined, free from dregs.* Some suppose there is special reference to God's *word* of *promise.* But all his word has been thoroughly tried ten thousand times, and always like pure gold was none the worse for the severity of the trial. It never has failed, though tried in times both of peace

and of peril, by old and by young, for comfort, support, guidance, deliverance and glory. See REMARKS on Ps. xii. 6. *He is a buckler to all those that trust in him.* *Buckler,* the same in v. 2. In v. 35, and in Ps. iii. 3, it is *shield;* in Ps. vii. 10, *defence.*

31. *For who is God save the* LORD? Here first in the Psalms occurs the name *Eloah,* rendered *God.* It occurs more than *fifty* times in the Scriptures, but only *four* times in the Psalms. It is the singular of Elohim. Many have supposed that this name specially refers to God as an object of religious worship. That idea may well be prominent in this place. He adds: *Or who is a rock save our God?* On God considered as *a rock,* see on v. 2.

32. It is *God that girdeth me with strength, and maketh my way perfect.* *God El.* See on Ps. v. 4. Both here and in v. 30, Alexander instead of *God* has *Almighty.* We need no stronger girdle. *Almightiness* can protect any man in any circumstances. David delights in often stating that his deliverances were from God. From the same source comes the blessing that our *way* is *perfect.* *Perfect,* the same in Hebrew as in v. 30, on which see. Without God nothing is strong, nothing holy, nothing finished, nothing successful, nothing perfect.

33. *He maketh my feet like hinds'* feet. The *hind* or female deer, is wonderfully active and nimble, can leap a great distance, and run with great swiftness, and though naturally timid, yet, when excited to contend, is a formidable enemy, fighting with the fore feet. The reference here is to the swiftness of this animal. Hengstenberg: "In the Egyptian paintings, the hind is the image of fleetness." The swiftness here claimed by David was not used merely for flight, but also for attack, 2 Sam. ii. 18; 1 Chron. xii. 8; Hab. iii. 19. God who does these things does more. He *setteth me upon my high places.* *High places* always so rendered except once, where it is *heights.* This word not only designates generally all eminences as hills and mountains, but it points out particularly high positions, that are made strong by nature or art, the fastnesses of a country, the strong-holds of a land. David here asserts that he is quite beyond the reach of his foes.

34. *He teacheth my hands to war, so that a bow of steel is broken by mine arms.* According to Scripture everything skilfully done in the arts of peace or war is ascribed to divine teaching, Gen. x. 9; Ex. xxxi. 2–5; Ps. cxliv. 1. The word rendered *steel* occurs ten times, and is thrice rendered *steel* and seven times *brass.* Clarke: "A bow of *steel* is out of the question. In the days of David it is not likely that the method of making *steel* was known. The method of making *brass* out of *copper* was known at a very early period of the world; and the ancients had the art of *hardening* it, so as to work it into the most efficient swords." Is not this learned author probably mistaken? Our translators are not apt to impute to the ancients a knowledge which they did not have. They thrice give us the word *steel.* The art of converting iron into steel is as well understood far in the interior of Africa as at Sheffield. Brass has very little elasticity in it and would be of little use in making bows. And while the ancients could indeed make brass, yet where is the evidence that they could make it equal to steel? It is admitted that they could give to copper a temper equal to that of a Damascus blade. But the proof that they could do the same with brass is not before the public. The Septuagint, Vulgate, Ethiopic, Arabic and Syriac read: Thou hast placed or strengthened my arms like a brazen bow; Horsley follows this; Chaldee: Thou hast given me my arms as a bow of steel; Calvin and Amesius prefer *steel;* Venema, Edwards, Jebb, Fry, Hengstenberg and Alexander prefer *brass;* Ainsworth is satisfied with either *brass* or *steel;* Pool's paraphrase is: "My strength is sufficient, not only to bend a *bow of steel,* but to break it;" Diodati: "This seems to be understood of David's admirable strength, 1 Sam. xvii. 35." Street has it: "Making mine arms of the stiffness of brass." To bend a strong bow without the aid of

the feet required great strength. But to break it required prodigious muscular power. The rendering and sense of our version are probably to be preferred.

35. *Thou hast also given me the shield of thy salvation.* On the word *shield* see v. 30. God's protection is unfailing. His shield always secures deliverance. It is none the less sure because bestowed on those who deserve no good thing. It is *given* to his people. *And thy right hand hath holden me up.* Omnipotence can make a worm as strong as an angel, and none, who are upheld by God's right hand, can fall. *And thy gentleness hath made me great.* The word rendered *gentleness* is elsewhere translated *humility, meekness,* Pr. xv. 33; Zeph. ii. 3. Calvin reads *thy clemency;* Venema, *thy all-sufficiency;* Edwards, *thy answering me;* Street, *thy kindness;* Fry, *thy aid* or help; Horsley, *thy humiliation;* Hengstenberg, *thy lowliness;* Cobbin and Alexander, *thy condescension.* The Septuagint reads, *Thy discipline has corrected me.* If Christ, who was meek and lowly, was so perfectly like the Father, that he who had seen the Lord had seen the Father, then Jehovah is meek and lowly, lenient, gentle and condescending. Just such God proves himself to be in all his word, by all his dispensations to his chosen. It is this patience, forbearance, clemency and condescension of God, that make great and good men all that they are. Otherwise they would be ruined.

36. *Thou hast enlarged my steps under me, that my feet did not slip.* The leading idea has been several times expressed. The form of it is often found in Scripture. Gen. ix. 27; Isa liv. 2. "Enlargement and deliverance" properly go together, v. 19; Esth. iv. 14. The enlarging of the steps, or place of standing gave a firmness and courage which nothing could shake. His feet *slipped not;* Calvin: *staggered not.* David had often clambered among the precipitous cliffs of Judea, where he had but small foot-hold, a fit emblem of the peril he was in. But now he has a plain, open path, and his standing is secure. Hengstenberg, instead of *feet did not slip,* reads *ankles fail not;* this is no improvement.

37. *I have pursued mine enemies and overtaken them: neither did I turn again till they were consumed.* For a long time it seemed as if David could never sit on the throne of Israel, yet how utterly and how suddenly his enemies lost their power, and how perfect was his victory. Some prefer the future in this and the next verse in accordance with the original, thinking it gives a better sense, *i. e.,* expresses confidence for the future drawn from past experiences. This may be so, but the sense in our version is good. David not only gained a victory, but it was complete.

38. *I have wounded them that they were not able to rise; they are fallen under my feet.* For *wounded* Calvin has *afflicted* or *smitten;* Hengstenberg, *dash in pieces;* Edwards, *crush them* to pieces. They were effectually and utterly disabled and disarmed; yea, as enemies they were extinct. He wished them no lower. Like the mire of the street, they were under his feet. The reason for such perfect success is next given:

39. *For thou hast girded me with strength unto the battle,* [or war]. Venema: Thou hast girded me with warlike courage. David would arrogate to himself nothing. All his strength and success were of God. On this he insists also in the next clause: *Thou hast subdued under me those that rose up against me.* For *subdued* Calvin has *bowed down;* Edwards, *bringest down. Cast down* gives the exact idea.

40. *Thou hast also given me the necks of mine enemies; that I might destroy them that hate me.* When God fights against men, what can they do? There is some doubt whether *neck* or *back* is the best rendering. The original word is rendered both ways. See Ex. xxiii. 27; Is. xlviii. 4. The import is clear. David had his enemies completely in his power, even to their destruction. They were routed and so turned the *backs;* he could take their lives and so had their *necks.*

41. *They cried, but* there was *none to save* them: even *unto the* LORD, *but he answered them not.* Hengstenberg's rendering is very concise: They cry, but there is no helper,

to the Lord, but he does not hear them. Some suppose they cried first to idols, and, not succeeding, they cried to Jehovah. But the structure of the sentence and the history of the opposition to David's accession to the throne do not *require* such a view. Men may maintain any form of worship to the true God, and may pray very earnestly, yet so long as they are warring against God's counsels and righteousness they cry in vain. God cannot, will not deny himself. Denial of such petitions preferred to him is wholly consistent with the tenor of Scripture, Prov. i. 24–28; Is. lxv. 12–15; Jer. vii. 13–16; Zech. vii. 13.

42. *Then did I beat them small as the dust before the wind; I did cast them out as the dirt in the streets.* John Rogers' translation: I wyll beate them as small as the dust claye in the winde, I wyll cast them out as the claye in the stretes; Bishop's Bible: I will beat them as small as the dust before the winde: I will cast them out as the clay in the streetes; Genevan translation: Then I did beate them as small as the dust before the winde: I did tread them flat as the clay in the streetes. Hengstenberg thinks the sense of the first clause is, Their crushing is only a sort of pastime to me; and of the second, I have as little respect for them, I use as little ceremony with them as with the offscourings which one treads upon. Perhaps it would be better to employ the future in rendering the verbs of this verse, as do many ancient and modern translations. Like several other verses of this Psalm this never had its complete fulfilment in David. It points to Christ.

43. *Thou hast delivered me from the strivings of the people; and thou hast made me the head of the heathen: a people* whom *I have not known shall serve me.* This verse cannot have its complete fulfilment except in Christ. The best sense is probably obtained by rendering all the verbs in the future, thus expressing confidence gathered from promises and past successes. "The people" here spoken of are his own people, the people of Israel, in whose contentions he would often have perished but for God's timely and merciful interpositions. Before David's accession to the throne his country had been greatly harassed and oppressed; but on becoming king, he destroyed the power of the adjacent nations, making many of them tributary. So great was David's success that some, quite remote from Judea, felt and acknowledged his power. See 2 Sam. viii. throughout, as explanatory of the latter clauses of this verse. Verses 9–12 specially explain the last clause.

44. *As soon as they hear of me, they shall obey me.* The fame of David's successes, like that of other great captains, saved him many a battle. Nothing in the form of human influence is more potent than the *prestige* of great conquerors. One has it, "As soon as the fame of my name reaches their ears, they shall obey me." *The strangers shall submit themselves unto me.* There is an evident allusion here to Deut. xxxiii. 29, "Thine enemies shall be found liars (shall feign) unto thee." See also Ps. lxvi. 3; lxxxi. 15, where the same word is used. Abenezra, followed by Munster and Edwards, explains these words: "They who before gloried and boasted of their great courage and valor, and of their future victory over me, as they vainly promised themselves, are found to be *liars*, when they submit to me; or, they *lie to me.*" Mudge, followed by many others: "They *fawn, sneak* and *disguise* the real sentiments of the heart, profess a most profound respect and submission, though at the same time within they retain their enmity." Calvin: "They shall be humbled after a slavish manner." Hengstenberg thinks it expresses "an external and constrained obedience," so that "the fear awakened overcame the strongest aversion." For *the strangers* Calvin has *the children of strangers*; Hengstenberg, *the sons of the stranger*; Edwards, *the sons of the foreigners*; Alexander, *the sons of outland.* The same phrase is found at the beginning of verse

45. *The strangers shall fade away. Fade away* in Ps. i. 3; xxxvii. 2, *wither*; in

Isa. i. 30; Jer. viii. 13; Ezek. xlvii. 12, *fade.* Sometimes it is rendered *act foolishly, come to naught, be lightly esteemed,* Pr. xxx. 32; Job xiv. 18; Deut. xxxii. 15. The meaning is, They shall lose their power before David, as a plant in a dry place withers before a scorching sun. *And be afraid out of their close places.* Calvin: Tremble out of their places of concealment; Edwards: Tremble in their strong-holds; Fry: Delivered themselves up from their strong-holds; Alexander: Tremble out of their enclosures; Horne: They shall come trembling from their strong-holds, as places not able to protect them, therefore they shall sue for peace. A fortress is no defence when God weakens the hearts and hands of those who hold it. The cause of all this success to David, and of failure to his foes is next given, vv. 46–50.

46. *The* LORD *liveth.* Jehovah is not dead, as the gods of the heathen are. No. He has life in himself. He alone hath independent immortality. No marvel then that he only doeth wonders. There seems to be no good reason for the rendering preferred though not insisted on by Calvin, *Let Jehovah live.* Nor does there seem to be any intended allusion to the form of the Hebrew oath, *As the Lord liveth.* David is accounting for his victories. He adds, *And blessed* be *my rock. Rock,* see on v. 2, where the same word occurs. Calvin renders it *strength,* meaning thereby him who gives strength. The word *blessed* here is not the same as in Ps. i. 1. It does not mean, Let God be happy, but, Let him be praised. The verb is the same used in Ps. lxvi. 8; lxviii. 26; xcvi. 2, where it is rendered *bless.* He adds, *And let the God of my salvation be exalted.* Hengstenberg, following the German fondness for compound words, prefers *My salvation-God.* This is not idiomatic English. Alexander says the phrase designates God, of whom it is one essential character that he is a Saviour. The original is striking. To exalt God is to extol him, to praise his name, to ascribe to him the excellence and wonders, which are his due, and so to make him *high,* not in himself, but in the esteem of his creatures. Like his nature his works are full of marvellous loving-kindness.

47. It is *God that avengeth me. God,* original *El.* The Mighty, the Almighty, God who is might. To *avenge* is to *do justice* in behalf of one. This commonly implies terrible retribution on the wrong-doer. God, who had given David a throne, in coming to which he was greatly wronged, was now doing him ample justice by the overthrow of his enemies. This was manifestly the work of God and none other. *And subdueth the people unto me. The people,* plural, *peoples.* It includes all the nations, who had annoyed him. The same word in the singular is found in Ps. iii. 6. Jehovah is the God of battles. He lifts up one and puts down another.

48. *He delivereth me from mine enemies. Delivereth,* in v. 2 rendered *deliverer.* Another form of the same verb is found in v. 43, *hast delivered. Enemies,* the same word is found in the title and vv. 3, 37 and 40 of this Psalm. *Yea, thou liftest me up above those that rise up against me. Liftest up,* the same verb in v. 46 is *be exalted.* To *lift up, to exalt,* and *to lift up the head* or *the horn* indicate success, victory. As when one is ashamed or languid, the head droops, so when he is strong, courageous, or flushed with victory he holds up his head. Yea, God's deliverance to David was such that his whole person was quite beyond the power of his foes. *Thou hast delivered me from the violent man. Hast delivered,* the same word as that so rendered in the title; it is sometimes rendered *preserved, saved, rescued,* Gen. xxxii. 30; 2 Sam. xix. 9; 1 Sam. xxx. 18. It implies that danger had been imminent, and that deliverance was not in the course of nature. It points to help from without. *Violent man,* literally, *man of violence,* elsewhere rendered *oppressor,* Pr. iii. 31. See Ps. vii. 16.

49. *Therefore will I give thanks unto thee,* O LORD, *among the heathen.* Calvin: " The meaning is, O Lord, I will not only give thee thanks in the assembly of thy people, according to the ritual which thou hast appointed in thy law, but thy praises

shall extend to a greater distance, even as thy grace towards me is worthy of being recounted through the whole world." *Heathen,* the same word found in v. 43, and in Ps. ii. 1, 8, which see. *And* [I will] *sing praises unto thy name.* Alexander: "The verb in the last clause means to praise by music." Ainsworth: "This sense is applied in Rom. xv. 9 to the calling of the Gentiles unto the faith of Christ, and praise unto God *therefor.* By which we are taught that of *Christ* and *his* kingdom this Psalm is chiefly intended."

50. *Great deliverance giveth he to his king.* David was God's king in opposition to Saul, whom God had rejected. The will of God in this matter was well made known by God's sending Samuel to anoint David, when yet a lad. This is referred to in the next clause; *And* [he] *sheweth mercy to his anointed.* The whole ceremony of the anointing is stated in 1 Sam. xvi. 1–13. He next states that the *anointed* is *David.* No good man could doubt that David was called of God to reign. This mercy is not only to David, but also *to his seed for evermore.* Here again we clearly find the reference to 2 Sam. vii. 16. In this verse we are compelled to look beyond David and Solomon to Christ.

DOCTRINAL AND PRACTICAL REMARKS.

1. Both the title and body of this Psalm suggest that a very fit employment of old age is the recounting of God's mercies received through life. We should go far back. At the writing of this song Saul had been dead for a long time, perhaps thirty years; yet David speaks as if his death were of recent occurrence. Neither our sins nor God's mercies ought ever to grow out of date.

2. However long the strife of God's people may last, it will at length have a close. God will finally deliver from *all enemies.*

3. All the Scriptures call for ardent love to God. We cannot delight in him too much, v. 1; Deut. vi. 5; x. 12; xi. 1; xiii. 22; xix. 9; xxx. 6; Mark xii. 30, 33; Luke x. 27. Love to man is often inordinate; love to God, never. Luther: "Our sweet and joyful affection ought to impel us with great force to those to whom we owe it, when we have been delivered from huge evil and misfortune."

4. How very feeble we are! Like the conies our strength is in the *rock.* We can do nothing as of ourselves; yet God is a sufficient protection, support and deliverer, v. 2. Morison: "How sweet is our belief of God's moral government of the world, when we are enabled to feel that some of its most striking agencies have been made to bear on our own particular condition." Calvin: "Those whom God intends to succor and defend are not only safe against one kind of dangers, but are as it were surrounded by impregnable ramparts on all sides, so that, should a thousand deaths be presented to their view, they ought not to be afraid even at this formidable array," John xix. 11.

5. Necessary is belief in the stability and unchangeableness of the divine nature and counsels, v. 2. No name nor title of God fairly interpreted implies the contrary. Nearly all of them fairly assert it. He is our *rock, fortress, God,* etc.

6. How condescending is God, to present himself before us as in this Psalm, particularly in v. 2; Calvin: "Let us learn to apply to our own use those titles which are here ascribed to God, and to apply them as an antidote against all the perplexities and distresses, which may assail us." Cobbin: "*A believing view of God's greatness and power will cause us to exult in him.* Whatever is strong in art, may be heaped together as emblems of the believer's God, who is his rock, fortress, buckler, high-tower. Whatever is grand in nature only reflects his greatness and majesty."

7. There is in Scripture hardly any limit to the commendations of prayer, v. 3. Here we have example to arouse us. Here as elsewhere prayer and praise are also

united, Phil. iv. 6; Col. iv. 2; 1 Tim. ii. 1. Many a prayer is hindered because while it supplicates blessings, it fails to adore God for what he is and to thank him for what he has already done. Morison: "What honor has been put upon prayer and praise in every age! They have been as a mystic ladder between heaven and earth, upon which the angels of mercy have been ascending and descending." Luther: "One cannot believe what a powerful assistance such praise of God is in pressing danger. For the moment thou wilt begin to praise God, the evil also will begin to abate, the consoled heart will grow, and then will follow the calling upon God with confidence."

8. To what great straits even good men are often brought, vv. 4, 5. The sorrows of death and of hell, the floods of ungodly men and the snares of death surround and beset them. In this way they are disciplined and made courageous. Good soldiers are not made in parlors. The fearful strife of the battle-field is necessary to show who is calm and valorous. It is no small mercy that God lets us triumph in many a conflict before the last great battle is fought.

9. Hordes of the sons of Belial are no novelty, v. 4. Although they are finally put down, they have long made good men afraid. It is not without cause that discerning people have a peculiar dread of suffering sent by the hand of the wicked, 2 Sam. xxiv. 14. The cruel taunts and horrid brutality of the wicked give a fearfulness to temporal misery, which it could never otherwise acquire.

10. However frightful our conflicts, it is well to review them when past, vv. 4, 5. The greater our just apprehensions of danger, when instant, the higher will be our estimate of divine wisdom, power and mercy in our rescue. Bunyan never forgot Bedford jail. He loved to think of the mercies he had there received, and of the deliverance God had granted him from its bars and gloom.

11. Many portions of Scripture enjoin earnestness in prayer, v. 6. *Calling upon the Lord* may denote any religious service offered to Jehovah, though not excluding prayer. But *crying* to him denotes *earnest supplication*. We may as well not pray at all, as offer our petitions in a lifeless manner. Every sacrifice was consumed with fire. Calvin: "No calamities however great and oppressive may hinder us from praying, or create an aversion to it."

12. Such prayer is wondrously efficacious, v. 6. Nothing is more so. Dickson: "No strait is such but God can deliver out of it, no case is so desperate as to make prayer needless or useless." Morison: "All nature pays homage to the spirit of prayer, by becoming the willing, active deliverer of him, who pours out his complaint before that gracious Being, who is nature's Sovereign, and who can summon all her most mysterious agencies to the defence of his chosen people." Jonah: "Out of the belly of hell cried I, and thou heardest my voice."

13. As it is a bad sign after a deliverance to strive to make little of it, so it is a good sign to strive to magnify every mercy granted us, vv. 7–15.

14. No folly can be greater than that of fighting against God, v. 7. When he is wroth, all nature stands aghast. Solid mountains and the earth itself tremble like a leaf.

15. When God chooses, his judgments are as terrific as they are ever represented to be, v. 8.

16. All attempts to comprehend God must ever prove failures. The very darkness, with which he surrounds himself, is but an emblem of the impenetrable obscurity, in which he forever abides, vv. 9, 11. Owen: "God hath ends of surprisal, hardening, and destruction towards some, for which they must be left unto their own spirits, and led into many snares and by-paths, for their trial, and the exercise of others, which could not be accomplished, did he not come in the clouds, and were not darkness his

pavilion and his secret place; on this account is that cry of men of profane and hardened spirits, Isa. v. 19."

17. When God comes to punish his foes and rescue his people, nothing has ever surprised his friends or his foes more than the admirable swiftness, with which he moves and acts, v. 10. He flies on the wings of the wind.

18. God is at no loss for agents to effect any purpose. Whenever he will he commands the cherubim, v. 10. The universe is not a howling wilderness. It is well peopled with living creatures.

19. Nor does Jehovah ever lack means to execute his wrath or display his delivering power, vv. 12–15. Thick clouds, hail-stones, balls of fire, lightnings, stormy wind, all things in nature are tributary to the purposes of God, and at a moment will execute his will.

20. It must ever be utterly impossible for men to arrive at a settled conclusion that there is no God. The phenomena of nature often so grand and terrific must themselves invest with uncertainty so monstrous a proposition, if in no other way at least in this, by raising the question whether the cause that produces so great effects might not do things that would satisfy the most incredulous that there is a First Cause, a Being whose existence is uncaused? He who can do what is said in vv. 12–15 to have been done might do anything, might to the most skeptical prove his own existence.

21. How marvellous the displays of God's power in producing from the same cloud the most vivid lightnings and a shower of balls of ice, v. 12. Surely if things so contrary may be evolved from a wild storm-cloud, we ought not to be surprised at very variant results proceeding from the moral government of God.

22. It is a clear duty of piety to recognize God in nature, vv. 13, 14. He thunders. His voice shakes heaven and earth. Let us learn to read his will in his works as well as in his words. Calvin: "The import of the words is, Whoever does not acknowledge that I have been preserved by the hand of God, may as well deny that it is God who thunders from heaven, and abolish his power which is manifested in the whole order of nature, and especially in those wonderful changes which we see taking place in the atmosphere."

23. God works without labor, vv. 14, 15. His word is followed by the most amazing results. His will is the law of universal nature. To him nothing is hard, nothing difficult, nothing impossible, nothing wearisome.

24. It is a glorious truth that God would, if necessary, change the whole course of nature to save one of his children, vv. 15, 16. He will shake the pillars of heaven, and make the earth to reel like a drunken man, so as to deliver one poor man from his foes.

25. Seldom do troubles come alone, and as seldom are God's deliverances from one trouble only, v. 16. Often does God draw his loved ones *out of many waters*. He can save from a world of troubles as easily as from one. Nor does our inability to help ourselves make the displays of God's power less but more illustrious. Whether he saves by means, or without means, or contrary to means, he is still our deliverer.

26. With amazing interest does an experience of personal distress invest every portion of Scripture, especially that which records the trials and deliverances of eminent servants of God, v. 17. Any afflicted, persecuted friend of God, understanding the scope of this Psalm, must be greatly encouraged by its teachings.

27. The escapes of God's people from bodily death, from worldly ruin and from spiritual overthrow are all worthy of deep reflection and religious celebration, v. 17.

28. How busy are our foes, v. 18. They never rest. They always oppose us. It is marvellous that they do not sometimes accomplish the ruin of a good man. But they never do, for

29. God is on his side. *The Lord was my stay*, v. 18. If God puts underneath us the everlasting arms we shall surely be holden up.

30. When God undertakes our cause he delivers like a God. It is no partial rescue that he effects, v. 19. He brings his chosen *into a large place*. When he restores peace and joy to Jacob's family the reconciliation between the hostile members is perfect. When he heals the lame man he walks and leaps and praises God. When he undertakes to put David on the throne all the kingdom of Israel may oppose, but cannot hinder the design.

31. If God is dear to his people, v. 1, so are his people dear to him, v. 19. *He delights in them.* They are as the apple of his eye. Before all worlds God's eternal Son thought with delight on the souls he should redeem, Pr. viii. 31.

32. It is a glorious truth that infinite rectitude will forever reign in all God's ways and decisions, v. 20. If in our conflicts with men we are right and innocent, all will in the end be as we could wish. Many a time slander covers us with the foulest ignominy, as it did David. But God showed his innocence, and abundantly "freed him from the slanders of ingratitude, rebellion, treachery against his father-in-law, and his prince." Calvin: "God will never fail us, provided we follow our calling, keep ourselves within the limits it prescribes, and undertake nothing without the command or warrant of God."

33. Who can duly estimate the unspeakable value of a good conscience? v. 21. Without it David could not possibly have passed through all his trials with composure and confidence. Nothing but uprightness and a pure conscience could ever present that sublime spectacle, recorded in 1 Sam. xxvi. 21–25. This was but a sample of what often occurred. As "no man ever offended his own conscience, but first or last it was revenged upon him for it;" so no man ever kept a good conscience, but that in his hour of trial it gave him wondrous support.

34. True piety renders universal obedience to the preceptive will of God, v. 22; Ps. cxix. 6; Rom. vii. 22; 1 John v. 3. The obedience of God's servants on earth may be imperfect, but it is not hypocritical. It falls short of the law, but not intentionally. They love holiness.

35. So that real piety will bear divine scrutiny, v. 23. God often judges his people more favorably than they judge themselves, Job i. 8; xlii. 6, 7. True piety implores the examination of omniscient purity, Ps. cxxxix. 23, 24; John xxi. 15–17. Blessed be God, he knoweth them that are his, and can see a grain of wheat in a bushel of chaff.

36. It is lawful for good men to defend their good name, when it is wickedly assailed, v. 24. To do this both with meekness and firmness is no easy task. Let us never take our cause out of the hands of God. In this David, and much more he, of whom David was but a type, set us a good example, 1 Pet. ii. 23.

37. The great principles of retribution are the same from age to age, vv. 25, 26. Compare Lev. xxvi. 21–24. God's government is so perfect, so comprehensive, that it is impossible for man to violate any of its great laws without sooner or later meeting consequences the most painful, making him feel that his pains are the fruit of his own folly and wantonness. When it is said that with the froward God will show himself froward, the meaning is that the result will be as if it were so. Pool: "Man's perverseness is moral and sinful, but God's perverseness is judicial and penal."

38. God's hatred of pride is right, v. 27. Calvin: "The more the ungodly indulge in gratifying their own inclinations, without any fear of danger, and the more proudly they despise the afflicted poor who are under their feet, so much nearer are they to destruction."

39. Light and comfort, manifestly received from God, are great blessings, v. 28. The gift has its value chiefly from the giver. Calvin: "It is certain that we will

never have the comfort of seeing our adversities brought to an end, unless God disperse the darkness which envelops us, and restore to us the light of joy."

40. However many and great may have been our exploits, let them all be referred directly to God, vv. 29–34. From him we have all our strength, agility, courage, wisdom, success. To think and feel otherwise is to practise atheism. Calvin: "Strength and skill in war proceed only from a secret virtue communicated by God." Prodigies of valor and strength can be performed when God stands by any man. Horne: "Vain is every effort, by whomsoever it is made, against the counsels of omnipotence."

41. There is never a post so difficult, a trial so severe, a night so dark, a duty so hard, but that it is as wise as it is obligatory to trust the Lord, v. 30.

42. Nor should we ever forget that God's word, though tried so long, and by so many, in every condition of life, has never failed in one instance, v. 30. Could such a case be found our joy would be at an end. Morison: "The accumulated experience of the whole church of God has but served to demonstrate, that gold seven times purified is not more genuine or unmixed, than is that word of the living God, which has been the guide, the spiritual nourishment, and the divine support of the children of God in every age."

43. Nor is there any helper, or defence like God, who is *power*, is *almighty*, vv. 30, 31. All claims to divinity by any other are idle. The gods of the heathen are vanities.

44. It is easy to carry out our plans, and effect our purposes, when God girds us with strength, v. 32. Then the worm Jacob threshes the mountains, and beats them small, and makes the hills as chaff.

45. To be beyond the reach of enemies is as great a mercy as to be saved in the midst of foes, v. 33.

46. A good man may sometimes clearly see that his steps have been ordered by the Lord; yea, and upheld by him often in the most singular manner, v. 35. In our perils for our own temporal advantage it may not be our duty to risk much. But in the cause of God it may be right to risk all. Luther: "It proceeds from the divine loveliness and grace, if we are held up and honored, not from our designing and undertaking; so that the whole glory remains with God." His succors are seasonable; his condescension infinite. *Thy gentleness hath made me great.*

47. It is marvellous that failures are not more frequent. How easy it is to *slip*, v. 36. The righteous are scarcely saved.

48. The righteous may confidently expect an *utter* routing of all their foes at last, vv. 37–42. Calvin: "As the victories secured to David involve a security of similar victories to us, it follows that there is here promised us an impregnable defence against all the efforts of Satan, all the machinations of sin, and all the temptations of the flesh."

49. Let God have the praise of all our victories, vv. 39, 40, 41, 43, 48. Let God be exalted, and man abased.

50. Even prayer will not save a bad cause, v. 41. Could anything, rightly considered be more alarming to sinners!

51. The disesteem, into which workers of iniquity are often brought on earth, points to something far worse hereafter, v. 42. If in a state of imperfect retribution so dreadful ills came on the wicked here, what must be the shame and everlasting contempt, which shall befall them when God's hand fully takes hold on vengeance!

52. Many worldly victories and perhaps all spiritual victories reach much further than it is at first supposed, vv. 43, 44. When the wicked begin to fall, they generally plunge on from depth to depth till their ruin is complete. In the mean time the righteous rise higher and higher, Esther vi. 13.

53. When he shall so will, it will be easy for Christ to subdue the earth to himself, v. 44. Missions shall surely succeed. The brightness of Immanuel's rising shall scatter all his foes. He can cut short the work in righteousness.

54. Opposition always gives way as of no account, when God comes down to settle contests, v. 45. When he would fully give the kingdom to David, his old enemy king Saul falls on his own sword, and ends his days. When he would break the neck of the persecution against the Jewish converts, he brings Saul of Tarsus to his knees as in a moment.

55. Admit the existence of Jehovah, and all other religious truth naturally follows, ver. 46. It may require statement and even argument; but it is still a logical deduction from the first great truth.

56. Nor is there any fear that we shall ever by word or deed exalt God too much. Let us praise him at all times, v. 46. In the darkest days of the Reformation, Luther said, "Come, let us sing the 46th Psalm, and let them do their worst."

57. How sweet is peace after war, especially when it is plainly and clearly God's blessing, v. 47. When he giveth peace, who shall cause trouble?

58. Even when our trials are brought upon us by means of men, it is best to leave all in God's hands, v. 48. He can deliver us from violent and unreasonable men also, and he alone can effectually give relief.

59. Even personal benefits often call for the most public praises of God, v. 49. This is true of many inferior gifts as well as of salvation.

60. Morison: "We may learn from this Psalm, that the best of men, that such even as are after God's own heart, may be greatly overwhelmed with the sorrows, afflictions and persecutions of life. Such was David's condition; but he sought and found relief at a throne of grace; and so will every one who honors God in this exercise."

61. Much of the Old Testament points to Christ! Many passages of the prophets can bear no full interpretation, unless applied to our Saviour. This is true of portions of this Psalm. The last verse is a striking illustration of this remark. See Acts iii. 18, 24; Rom. xv. 9; Heb. ii. 13. Clarke says, this last word of this Psalm, "shows that another *David* is meant, with another kind of *posterity*, and another sort of *kingdom*. From *the family of David* came the *man Christ Jesus*. His *posterity* are *genuine Christians;* his *kingdom*, in which they are *subjects*, is *spiritual*. This *government* shall last through all time, and extend through eternity; for that is the kingdom of glory in which Jesus Christ reigns on the throne of his Father, and in which his followers shall reign with him forever and ever."

PSALM XIX.

To the chief Musician, A Psalm of David.

1 THE heavens declare the glory of God; and the firmament sheweth his handywork.

2 Day unto day uttereth speech, and night unto night sheweth knowledge.

3 *There is* no speech nor language, *where* their voice is not heard.

4 Their line is gone out through all the earth, and their words to the end of the world. In them hath he set a tabernacle for the sun,

5 Which *is* as a bridegroom coming out of his chamber, *and* rejoiceth as a strong man to run a race.

6 His going forth *is* from the end of the heaven, and his circuit unto the ends of it: and there is nothing hid from the heat thereof.

7 The law of the LORD *is* perfect, converting the soul: the testimony of the LORD *is* sure, making wise the simple.

8 The statutes of the LORD *are* right, rejoicing the heart: the commandment of the LORD *is* pure, enlightening the eyes.

9 The fear of the LORD *is* clean, enduring for ever: the judgments of the LORD *are* true *and* righteous altogether.

10 More to be desired *are they* than gold, yea, than much fine gold: sweeter also than honey and the honeycomb.

11 Moreover by them is thy servant warned: *and* in keeping of them *there is* great reward.

12 Who can understand *his* errors? cleanse thou me from secret *faults.*

13 Keep back thy servant also from presumptuous *sins;* let them not have dominion over me: then shall I be upright, and I shall be innocent from the great transgression.

14 Let the words of my mouth, and the meditation of my heart, be acceptable in thy sight, O LORD, my strength, and my redeemer.

WE have had the same words in titles. See on Ps. iii., iv. Cobbin puts this song next in time after Ps. xii.; Scott, eighteen years later; while Rosenmuller says: "When this Psalm was composed, cannot be shown with any probability."

Strangely enough Clarke says: "It is not very clear that this Psalm was written by David." The title expressly gives it to him. Nor is there either internal or historic evidence to the contrary. Hengstenberg: "Of the Davidic authorship of this Psalm there can be no doubt."

The names of the Most High here found are *El God* and *Jehovah* LORD, on which see respectively on Ps. v. 4; i. 2.

Henry's first remarks on this Psalm are: "There are two excellent books which the great God has published for the instruction and edification of the children of men. this Psalm treats of them both, and recommends them both to our diligent study. I The book of the creatures, in which we may easily read the power and Godhead of the Creator. II. The book of the Scriptures, which makes known to us the will of God concerning our duty." Rivet divides the Psalm into three parts; the first giving us lessons from nature, which is common to all men; the second pointing us to the oracles of God deposited with his church; and the third treating of experimental religion, or the internal, efficacious and saving grace of God, administered by the Spirit. Alexander: "The doctrinal sum of the whole composition is, that the same God who reared the frame of nature is the giver of a law, and that this law is in all respects worthy of its author." Scott: "This Psalm seems especially to have been intended to prove, that the idolatry and irreligion of mankind were wholly inexcusable." Mudge: "The author in this Psalm, as in many other places, considers the works of nature, and the words of revelation, as both of them laws of the same hand, and standing firmly by the same authority; both highly perfect in their kind, and containing great matter of instruction, one for the whole world, the other for his favored people, and himself particularly." Geddes: "No poem ever contained a finer argument against atheism, nor one better expressed." Sherlock: "When a king stands before the altar, we may well expect a regal sacrifice."

1. *The heavens declare the glory of God. Heavens,* as in Gen. i. 1. The term embraces all the known creation except the earth. *Declare,* the same word is often rendered *speak, tell, show forth.* It signifies to narrate, preach, or proclaim. -Jebb and Alexander: The heavens are telling the glory of God. The form of the Hebrew implies that the heavens are continually declaring God's *glory,* that is, his *honor,* as it is rendered in Ps. vii. 5; iii. 3; iv. 2. *And the firmament sheweth his handywork.* For *firmament* the Chaldee, Calvin, Edwards, Venema, Amesius, Bythner and Mant read *expanse.* The same word is often used in Gen. i. The Hebrew gives no countenance

to the Greek philosophy indicated by the word *firmament*. God's *handywork* is the work of his hand, nothing more.

Each clause of this verse teaches the same truth, and each contains a bold personification.

How much can we know of God from his works alone? Here David says that we learn God's *glory* and see that he has been at *work*. Paul says that from God's works of creation we learn "his eternal power and Godhead." From his works we may learn his existence, goodness, wisdom, power, sincerity, and providence. Beyond this it is hardly safe, surely it is not necessary to any end of religious doctrine to assert anything.

In selecting the heavens, David does not deny that the earth teaches the same lessons; but he selects a striking and excellent part of creation, which a man must be blind not to see. Calvin: "When a man, from beholding and contemplating the heavens, has been brought to acknowledge God, he will learn also to reflect upon and to admire his wisdom and power as displayed on the face of the earth, not only in general, but even in the minutest plants." Hengstenberg tells us that "when C. Niebuhr, many years after his return from the East, lay in bed under the blindness and exhaustion of old age, 'the glittering splendor of the nocturnal Asiatic sky, on which he had so often gazed, imaged itself to him in the hours of stillness, or its lofty vault and azure by day, and in this he found the sweetest enjoyment.'" Returning from Egypt through the Mediterranean, Napoleon heard his officers avowing atheism. Pointing to the stars he said, Who made all these? and atheism had no answer. Early in June, 1858, at Lewisburg, Va., some two thousand feet above the level of the sea, the atmosphere was in the best condition for seeing. The heavens were so brilliant that I do not think I can forget the splendid vision while memory does her office. Bright stars and numerous nebulæ overwhelmed my imagination. Had a man never before beheld such a sight, it seems impossible but that he must have confessed a God. So stupendous and glorious is the blazing universe above and around us that one of our poets has said,

An undevout astronomer is mad.

Cicero: "What can be so plain and so clear as when we behold the heavens and view the heavenly bodies, that we should conclude there is some deity of a most excellent mind by whom these things are governed?"

2. *Day unto day uttereth speech, and night unto night sheweth knowledge.* Edwards; Day succeeding day uttereth instruction, and night after night discovereth knowledge; Fry: Day after day language is poured forth, and night after night knowledge is communicated; Venema expresses the force of the first verb by adding the words *in a perpetual stream*. The verbs are in the future, and so intimate that day and night shall continue to teach these lessons. Calvin gives an excellent summary of the respectable opinions concerning this verse: "*First*, No day passes in which God does not show some signal evidence of his power: *Secondly*, Every succeeding day contributes something new in proof of the existence and perfections of God: *Thirdly*, The days and nights talk together, and reason concerning the glory of the Creator." This last preserves the personification. It is certain that there is but one Being in the universe who could make so wondrous and glorious a display as that which we behold any day, or any night. A day or a night without clouds is perhaps most impressive to contemplative minds. But the alternations of day and night, and the exact recurrence of the same annual phenomena at a distance of three hundred and sixty-five days demonstrate beyond all reasonable doubt the existence and power of God.

3. There is *no speech nor language* where *their voice is not heard*. The *voice* is that

of *the heavens* and of *the firmament.* So the context shows. There are good reasons for adhering to the sense suggested by the authorized version. It is sustained by the ancient versions and by the old English translations generally, also by others. If this is correct, then the import of the verse is that however diverse human languages and tongues may be, and however unintelligible the speech of one people may be to another, yet the mute, inarticulate but clear language of the heavens above us is that there is a glorious Creator, a *strong God,* as *El* signifies. Yet quite a number of able writers take another view. Waterland: They have neither speech nor words: without these is their voice heard; Boothroyd: No speech, no language, nor is their voice heard; Jebb: There is no speech, and there is no language; it is not heard, their voice; Amesius; There is no speech, nor are there words to them; and without these their voice is understood; Fry: There is no speech, there are no words; no voice is heard among them; Hengstenberg: There is not speech and there are not words, their voice is not heard: Alexander: There is no speech, and there are no words; not at all is their voice heard. The margin supports this rendering. So also do Clarke and Scott. The sense then would be that, " The traces of God's glory are so strongly impressed on the heavens that they need no speech to make him known as their Creator, but as dumb heralds of the divine greatness publish abroad his glorious existence." Either view gives a good sense.

4. *Their line is gone out through all the earth, and their words to the end of the world.* *Line* is the only rendering anywhere in the English version. In Isa. xxviii. 10 it evidently points to a line of legible writing. So in this place Calvin reads *writing* instead of *line.* Then the sense is " that the glory of God is written and imprinted in the heavens, as in an open volume which all men may read." Instead of *line* Fry reads *call;* Jebb, *voice;* Septuagint and Vulgate, *sound.* Paul quotes the Septuagint in Rom. x. 18. But he may have employed the passage merely because it conveyed the idea he wished to express, and without sanctioning the translation as the best as he did, Ps. iv. 4. Bellarmine thinks the Hebrew text was corrupted by some transcriber after the time of Jerome, and with Glassius and others prefers to add a letter so as to read, *their voice.* Calvin: " The apostle designed to say that God, from ancient times, had manifested his glory to the Gentiles, and that this was a prelude to the more ample instruction which was one day to be published to them." *Their* and *them* refer to the *heavens* and the *firmament.* *In them hath he set* [pitched, placed, made] *a tabernacle* [pavilion or tent] *for the sun.* The plain meaning is that the place of the sun is in the heavens, but the poetic figure is that, like an oriental dignitary, the sun in the skies has his pavilion.

5. *Which is as a bridegroom coming out of his chamber.* This imagery is borrowed from eastern marriages; the forms of which are still to some extent preserved. Bridegrooms put on their best apparel, assumed the most joyous manners and were attended by the best retinue possible in their circumstances. There is no good reason for the rendering which makes the *tabernacle* to be the abode of God, and the place of it the *sun.* A sun-rise at sea, or on a prairie, or on a mountain often surpasses all human powers of description. In October, A. D., 1838, a number of us stood on the top of the Blue Ridge at Rockfish Gap in Virginia, just after the sun had risen. Dense fogs covered the valleys, but left exposed to the sun the tops of the high hills for perhaps forty miles eastward. Our great elevation by means of the reflected rays of the sun, discovered to us below a sea of glory all studded with beautiful islets. It was a view of a like scene at the same spot that led a great but eccentric orator and statesman to say to his servant: " Johnny, if you ever see a man who says, There is no God, tell him he is a fool." The sun is also compared to a giant courser—And *rejoiceth as*

a strong man to run a race. In his Seasons Thomson has this figure, but in an enfeebled form:

> But yonder comes the glorious king of day,
> Rejoicing in the east.

A king may be very feeble and faltering, but a strong man rejoicing in his race none can mistake. *Strong man,* in 1 Sam. xvii. 51 rendered *champion;* commonly *mighty man,* Gen. vi. 4; Josh. i. 14; Ps. xxxiii. 16; lii. 1; sometimes *valiant man,* Cant. iii. 7. Nothing could better express a high conception of the grandeur of the motions of the sun than that of a powerful racer, exulting in his vigor. Homer speaks of "the unwearied sun."

6. *His going forth is from the end of the heaven, and his circuit unto the ends of it: and there is nothing hid from the heat thereof.* This language is popular, not scientific. Calvin: "David proposes to us three things to be considered in the sun—the splendor and excellency of his form—the swiftness with which he runs his course—and the astonishing power of his heat." On the first see vv. 4, 5; on the second, vv. 5, 6; on the third, v. 6. Both the light and heat of the sun are necessary to animal and vegetable life. The number, vigor and beauty of plants are much affected by the quantity of light and heat. Professor Wildenow says: "In Spitzbergen there are 30 plants; in Lapland 534; in Iceland 553; in Sweden 1299; in the Marquisate of Brandenburg 2000; in Piedmont 2800; on the coast of Coromandel nearly 4000; as many in the island of Jamaica; in Madagascar above 5000." Similar remarks might be made in regard to the animal kingdom. Without the light and heat of the sun this world would be dreary in the extreme. With all his power during long summers many mountains even in warm climates are covered with perpetual snow and ice. Even in Virginia there is in Hampshire County a mountain on the north side of which ice may be found any day of the year. Some have thought that the heat is here spoken of as if it were an enemy pursuing us. Calvin "understands it of the violent heat which scorches men, plants and trees." But Edwards more nearly gives us the clue to a right interpretation when he translates: Nothing is hid from his enlivening heat; Boothroyd: nothing is deprived of his heat. That the *beneficial* effects of the sun are here spoken of is required by the following verses. Wonderful and excellent as are the heavens, and especially the sun, yet David has something of still higher excellence to celebrate. Alexander: "The God, whose glory is thus shown forth by the material creation, is the author of a spiritual law, which the Psalmist now describes in the next three verses, by six characteristic names, six qualifying epithets, and six moral effects produced by it."

7. *The law of the* LORD *is perfect, converting the soul.* Dimock: "The expressions in this, and the following verses, showing the superior influence of the *law* upon the *soul* to that of the *sun* upon the *earth,* are very beautiful." *Law,* very commonly so rendered; in the margin, *doctrine.* Ainsworth: "It implies both *doctrine* and an orderly disposition of the same." We had the word in Ps. i. 2. It is a general name given to Scripture, of which the law is an important part. Besides, all Scripture is a rule, a precept—profitable for doctrine, for reproof, for correction, for instruction in righteousness. But it is the *law of Jehovah* that has this power. Rules of life invented by serious men among the heathen and in Christian lands may have produced a civil discipline, and so may have profited for this life. But they were much mixed with error. Nor had they saving power. They were not *perfect,* as is the law of God "in doctrine, in precept, in promise, in threatening." Nor did they *convert the soul.* He who knew them all and lived accordingly, had not yet the key of knowledge, but was blind, and foolish, and far from the right way. His soul was not thereby restored from its wanderings, its errors, its sins, its sicknesses, its death. Nor was it converted

to truth, to righteousness, to life, to God. There is no good reason for limiting the meaning of the word, *converting*, to anything short of a saving change of heart. God's word is not the agent but only the instrument in the renewal of the soul. It is a *fit* instrument, and as such is greatly honored of God. He has exalted it above all his name. Although every restoration is not strictly a conversion, yet every *conversion* is a *restoration*. The word here rendered *converting* is of the same root as that which in Ps. xxiii. 3 is rendered *restore;* in Ps. lxxxv. 1, *hast brought back;* in Ps. xiv. 7, *bringeth back;* in Ps. lxxxv. 4, *turn* us; in Ezek. xiv. 6, *repent*, and often *turn ye*. For *converting*, Hengstenberg reads *quickens*. We have another name given to God's word in this verse: *The testimony of the* LORD *is sure, making wise the simple.* *Testimony*, not before found in the Psalms, but the same which occurs so often in the pentateuch, in Ps. cxix., and elsewhere. In his word God appears as a witness for truth and righteousness. His testimony is his word. It is *sure*, that is reliable, durable, faithful, trustworthy, standing fast, to be believed. *Sure*, in Hebrew a participle of the verb, from which the adverb *amen* is formed. There is no doubt about a thing, if God once says it. His testimony *makes wise the simple*. Many translations, including John Rogers', Calvin, Vulgate, etc., for *simple* read *babes*, or *little ones*. Ezekiel (xlv. 20) once uses the word rendered *simple* in the precise form found here. With this exception, it is found only in the writings of David and his son, Solomon. The latter always uses it in a bad sense, as indicating a vicious character; but his father David uses it in a good sense, pointing out those who indeed need instruction, but are willing to receive it. The rendering is unvarying, except in Pr. ix. 6, *foolish*. The testimony of God in his word relates in chief part to things which we never could have known, had he not spoken. It is suited to make wise, not only for the true and excellent matter it contains, but because it is clear, teaches the best lessons in the simplest manner, is precisely adapted to man's weakness and wickedness, being the testimony of him who knows all hearts. The fact that it does make wise the simple is manifest in the case of every pious student of the Bible. In the life of such men as Bunyan, its power is illustrious. It is also shown in its vast influence over nations.

8. *The statutes of the* LORD *are right, rejoicing the heart.* Calvin: "The word rendered *statutes* is by some restricted to ceremonies, but improperly, in my judgment: for I find that it is everywhere taken for ordinances and edicts. In Ps. ciii. 18; cxi. 7, the same word is rendered *commandments;* in Ps. cxix. it is always rendered *precepts;* here only *statutes*. But the sense is the same. These statutes are *right, i. e., upright, righteous, in equity*. They rejoice the heart of all right-minded persons. No good man counts any commandment of God grievous, even though it enjoins new and difficult duties, or forbids customary sins. Of course all other parts of revealed truth make glad the saints of God. He who loves the precepts will love the promises and the doctrines." *The commandment of the Lord* is *pure, enlightening the eyes.* The word rendered *commandment* is not before found in the Psalms. It occurs frequently in Deuteronomy, in Ps. cxix., and in several other books of Scripture. Hengstenberg: "The name here given to the law is one that prescribes what one has to do." It points to the whole law. Paul also uses the singular even where he speaks of the decalogue, Rom. vii. 8–12. The commandment is *pure*. It is free from injustice, error, sin. The Septuagint has it, *clear, radiant, bright*. The doctrines of Scripture show us what we must believe; the precepts, what we must do; the threatenings, what we must shun; the promises, what we must hope for; and so far as these are necessary to our salvation they are wonderfully clear. Instead of *pure*, Hammond has *for food;* and his paraphrase is "God's commands are our spiritual food." There is no error taught by this rendering. Yet the change is not required, nor is it supported by sufficient reasons. This pure, clear commandment *enlightens the eyes.* It removes a thou-

sand misconceptions, prejudices and follies which like fog and darkness obscure our perceptions. It shows us the real nature of the things of which it treats, the greatest things in the world. Calvin: "Understanding is the most excellent endowment of the soul." Illumination, knowledge and wisdom are names often given to the whole of religion, because they are so excellent a part of it.

9. *The fear of the* LORD *is clean, enduring for ever.* The word rendered *fear* is given in our version with great uniformity. Only in Ps. lv. 5 it is *fearfulness.* Once or twice it is rendered as an adjective *afraid,* or *dreadful.* Once does the Scripture say, The fear of the LORD is the beginning of knowledge; twice, The fear of the LORD is the beginning of wisdom; and once, The fear of the LORD, that is wisdom. God complains of some that their fear toward him is taught by the precepts of men. In this case the fear of Jehovah, the effect, is put for the word of God, the cause, which teaches us to fear him. The word is elsewhere so used. Ps. xxxiv. 11; Pr. ii. 5. Diodati: "The rule, of his fear and of all true religion contained in his word." Calvin: "It is taken in an active sense for the doctrine which prescribes to us the manner in which we ought to fear God." Rivet and Cobbin take the same view. Hengstenberg: "The fear of the Lord here marks the instruction afforded by God for fearing him." This fear of God is *clean;* Edwards, *uncorrupt;* Fry, *pure;* Doway, *holy;* Ethiopic and Arabic, *chaste.* Our version follows the Chaldee, Syriac and many others. No man perfectly following God's word will ever be defiled. It leads to no corrupt thoughts, emotions, words or deeds. Particularly does it maintain a pure worship. This fear of the Lord *endureth for ever.* Amesius, Fry and Alexander: *standing forever;* Hengstenberg: *continues for ever.* In Ps. cxix. 91 it is *continue;* in Ps. xxxiii. 9, *stood fast;* in Ps. cii. 26; cxi. 3, 10, *endure.* Jesus Christ neither abolished nor changed the law. Nay, the final conflagration shall not relax the bond, which binds us to purity, reverence, holiness in heart and worship. "This is the treasure of everlasting happiness." The rest of the verse reads: *The judgments of the* LORD *are true* and *righteous altogether.* By *judgments* Diodati understands the statutes and ordinances by which God judgeth man, and according to which men ought likewise to frame their conscience. Alexander: "*Judgments* are properly judicial decisions, but here as in Ps. xviii. 22 are put for all God's requisitions." The same word is often found in the Hebrew Scriptures, but occurs with great frequency in Deuteronomy, in Ps. cxix., in Isaiah and Ezekiel. It is given in our version with much uniformity, *judgments.* Pool: "The judgments of the Lord are his laws, frequently called his judgments, because they are the declarations of his righteous will, and as it were his legal and judicial sentence, by which he expects that men should govern themselves, and by which he will judge them at the last day." God's decisions in his word are *true.* For *true* Calvin, Venema, Amesius, Edwards, Hengstenberg and Alexander following the original read *truth.* The word is the same as in Ps. xv. 2; xxv. 5; cxlvi. 6, the common word for truth. *Thy word is truth*—truth without any mixture of error, fiction, falsehood, deceit. Moreover God's judgments are *righteous.* Vulgate and Doway: *justified in themselves;* Calvin: *justified together;* Venema: *together just;* Amesius: *alike just;* Ainsworth: *just together,* that is, *all of them together,* and *each of them* apart, is *just,* or *justified;* Edwards: full of righteousness all together. Hammond paraphrases it thus: "They are in themselves most just and equitable, fittest to be done by us, if they were not commanded, nor should ever be rewarded in us." *Altogether,* the same rendered *together* in Ps. ii. 2; xiv. 3; in Ps. iv. 8, *both;* in Ps. xxxiii. 16, *alike;* in Ps. lxxiv. 6, *at once;* in Ps. cxli. 10 *withal.*

10. *More to be desired* are they *than gold, yea, than much fine gold.* The things here said to be *more to be desired* are God's *judgments,* embracing his law, testimony,

statutes, commandment and the precepts concerning his fear. All parts of God's word are of the highest value, above gold, yea, much fine gold. The word rendered *fine gold* occurs *nine* times in Scripture, and is always so rendered except once (Ps. xxi. 3) where it is *pure gold*. It is first found in Job xxviii. 17. The Septuagint sometimes as here renders it "*a precious stone;*" in Ps. cxix. 127, *a topaz*. According to Hesychius *topaz* is derived from *paz*, which is the Hebrew word here rendered *fine gold*. Calvin: "The sense is, that we do not esteem the law as it deserves, if we do not prefer it to all the riches of the world." It is a great matter to have our practical judgments of divine things correct. But men may loudly praise God's word as the fountain of history, of sublime composition, of instruction on the weightiest matters, yea, as divinely inspired; and yet they may have no relish for its truths, and so be unable to add concerning God's decisions that they are *sweeter also than honey and the honeycomb.* Calvin, Ainsworth, Street, Venema, Edwards, Fry, Jebb and Alexander would read *sweeter than honey, and the dropping of* [the combs or] *the honeycombs.* Amesius in his translation speaks of the *unboiled* or *unheated honey.* The first word rendered *honey* signifies honey of any kind; the last signifies the pure honey, as it dripped down without any pressure or heating, which could injure flavor and quality. So to the taste of David and all right-minded men God's word is a precious feast. The same is declared in Ps. cxix. 103. Hear Job also: "I have esteemed the words of his mouth more than my necessary food," chap. xxiii. 12; Jeremiah: "Thy words were found, and I did eat them; and thy word was unto me the joy and rejoicing of my heart," chap. xv. 16. No estimate of God's word will avail unless we have a taste, a relish, a zest for its holiest requirements.

11. *Moreover by them is thy servant warned.* For *warned*, Calvin, following the Chaldee, has *made circumspect;* Edwards: *admonished;* Ainsworth and Pool: *clearly admonished;* Boothroyd: *instructed;* Clarke: *fully instructed;* Street, Hengstenberg and Alexander: *enlightened;* church of England: *taught;* the Ethiopic, Arabic, Vulgate and Doway all follow the Septuagint and read: *For thy servant keepeth them.* But our version is preferable. In this clause David simply tells what had been up to this time the practical influence of God's word on his life. In the next clause he tells of the success attending such a course. *In keeping of them there is great reward.* Alexander: "*Reward* is here used not to signify a recompense earned in strict justice, but a gratuity bestowed." There are rewards of grace as well as of debt. The latter are inferior to the former. Though God's people do not serve him with a mercenary spirit, yet they do not forget the end reached by the obedient, Heb. xi. 26; Matt. vi. 4, 6; 1 Tim. iv. 8. Patrick's paraphrase is: "I say nothing but what I have tried: for by following the admonitions of thy holy laws, both in my private and my public capacity, thy servant is become thus illustrious: and in their observance there is not only much satisfaction at present, but a far greater reward in the conclusion." Yet no good man, with any tolerable degree of knowledge of himself, can be ignorant of the fact that he comes far short of the absolute perfection required by God's word, especially by the law, and so David exclaims:

12. *Who can understand* his *errors?* By *errors* Ainsworth understands *unadvised errors,* or *ignorant faults,* unwitting and inconsiderate sins. Alexander: "The word translated *errors* is akin to one sometimes used in the law to denote sins of inadvertence, error, or infirmity, as distinguished from deliberate, wilful and high-handed sins such as are deprecated in the next verse. See Lev. iv. 2, 27; Num. xv. 27." Many other passages might also have been cited. Yet the same verb seems in other places to have in general the signification of *sinful error,* see Isa. xxviii. 7; (where it occurs thrice,) 1 Sam. xxvi. 21; and elsewhere. This led Calvin to say that "all the sins to the commission of which men give themselves loose reins, not being duly

sensible of the evil that is in them, and being deceived by the allurements of the flesh, are justly included under the Hebrew word here used by David, which signi· fies *faults* or *ignorances*. Pool also says, "*his errors* are either, 1. His sins of ignor· ance, of which the word is used, Lev. iv. 2, 22, 27; Ecc. v. 6; or rather, 2. His sins in general, (which afterwards he divides into *secret* and *presumptuous sins*) or all de- viations from God's law, which are thus called, 1 Sam. xxvi. 21; Ps. cxix. 67, 118; Heb. ix. 7; Jas. v. 20." This view is the safest, gives the fullest sense, and coin- cides with the analogy of faith. It is as true of sins committed against light as of sins of ignorance chargeable to any man, that he knows neither their number, mag- nitude, guilt, depravity, nor the mischief they are likely to effect. David next prays, *Cleanse thou me from secret* faults. The word *faults* is supplied by the trans- lators. Horsley has *disguises, concealments, dissimulations*. The word *secret* is in v. 6, rendered *hid*. The common rendering of the verb from which this participle is derived is to hide, Ps. xiii. 1; xvii. 8. Our faults may be hidden from our neigh- bors, and from ourselves, but not from God. To him all things are naked and opened. The sum of this petition is, Cleanse me from those sins which may be un- known to my neighbors, or which are unknown to myself. The primary and promi- nent idea suggested to the Hebrew mind by the word *cleanse*, is that of *remission, holding guiltless*, or *guiltless, clearing, setting free from punishment, acquitting*. Num. v. 31; Jud. xv. 3; Num. xiv. 18; Pr. xi. 21; Nah. i. 3. Schmidt says: "It is a judicial term and means acquittal;" Calvin: "The word *cleanse* is to be referred not to the blessing of regeneration, but. to free forgiveness; Amesius; *Absolve me;* Hengstenberg: *Acquit me*. He adds that the word rendered *cleanse*, "always signi- fies to *declare* innocent, to acquit." Alexander for *cleanse* reads *clear*. But as in both the Old and New Testaments justification and sanctification are declared to be inseparable, Ps. xxxii. 1, 2; Rom. viii. 1; and as it is common to take an important part for the whole, so we are not to understand David as saying that he desired *mere* remission without purification. Pool therefore well says: "*Cleanse thou me;* both by justification, or the·pardon of my sins, through the blood of thy Son, which is to be shed for me; and by sanctification through thy Holy Spirit, co-working in and with thy word, to the further renovation of my heart and life; for these are the two ways of *cleansing* sinners most frequently mentioned both in the Old and New Tes- tament; though the first may seem to be principally, if not only intended, because he speaks of his past sins which could be cleansed no other way but by remission." God may also cleanse us by leading us not into temptation, by restraining us from sin. Edwards: *Keep me clean from secret faults;* Fry: *From concealed ones do thou keep me clear*. Prevention is better than cure. It is better not to sin than to sin, and repent. It is a sad thing to be always repenting of the sins we have committed, and repeating the sins of which we have repented.

13. *Keep back thy servant also from presumptuous* sins. Here is prayer for restraining and supporting grace. The Septuagint, Vulgate and Ethiopic for *presumptuous sins* read *strangers;* Doway: From my secret sins cleanse me, O Lord; and from those of others spare thy servant; Chaldee: Set thy servant free from the proud; Syriac: From iniquity restrain thy servant; Venema: Withhold thy servant from the proud: Amesius: Withdraw thy servant from the contumacious; Fry: From presumption, etc.; Horsley: From evil spirits, etc. The context is speaking of *sins*, not of *persons*. When the word rendered *presumptuous* is found without a noun we have no right to supply *men* or *spirits*, if we can as well use the word found in·the preceding verse, which is *errors, faults, sins*. Calvin: "By *presumptuous sins* he means known and evident transgressions, accompanied with proud contempt and obstinacy." Hammond understands "known deliberate sins, which have not the alleviation of ignorance or

weakness, but are committed against express knowledge of duty, and after mature consideration." The word is in our version rendered either *presumptuous* or *proud*, Ps. lxxxvi. 14; and the corresponding noun *pride* or *presumption*, Deut. xvii. 12; xviii. 22; Pr. xi. 2; Obad. 3. Such sin is always based in arrogance and contempt of God. It is the fruit of an imperious lust. It is not the result of mere surprise. In its nature it is daring. *Keep back*, also rendered *withhold, hold back, hinder, spare, reserve*, and in the margin *restrain*. *Let them not have dominion over me*. *Dominion* is *prevailing power*. The Canaanites lived in Judea even after the times of Joshua, and they greatly annoyed the Israelites, but they were not the lords of the land. In Ps. viii. 6 to *have dominion* expresses man's supremacy over inferior animals. The participle is often rendered *ruler*, Gen. xlv. 8; Jud. xv. 11; Ps. cv. 20, 21; Pr. xxviii. 15. The import of the prayer is, Let not any presumptuous sin have the mastery over me. Hengstenberg: "Presumptuous sins are here personified as tyrants who strive to bring the servant of God into unbecoming subjection to them. That the Lord alone can keep from this servitude, discovers the depth of human corruption." Thus saved from outbreaking sins he adds: *Then shall I be upright.* *Upright*, as in Ps. xviii. 25; elsewhere *perfect, finished*, Job xxii. 3; Josh. iv. 10. Absolute perfection is found in no mere man on earth, 1 Kings viii. 46; Ecc. vii. 20. Comparative perfection or uprightness belongs to sincerity, and is found in the consistent holy life of every child of God. Such a man may add: *And I shall be innocent from the great transgression.* *Be innocent*, elsewhere *be clear, be guiltless, be blameless, be cleansed, be cleared*, the same root as *cleanse* in v. 12. From *the great transgression;* Chaldee: From *great sin;* Calvin: From *much wickedness;* Edwards: From *heinous transgressions;* Venema: From *much defection;* Amesius: From *great defection;* Hengstenberg: From *great iniquity;* Alexander: From *much transgression.* Doubtless the best sense is he shall be free "from innumerable sins, which usually follow the commission of one presumptuous sin." There seems to be no good reason for inserting *the* before *great;* nor for rendering it, as Fry, *the great rebellion;* nor as Horsley, *the great apostasy.* Morison thinks it refers to "the easily besetting sin of a man's constitution and temperament;" but this cannot be shown to be always the worst kind of transgression.

14. *Let the words of my mouth, and the meditation of my heart be acceptable in thy sight*, O LORD, *my strength and my redeemer.* The Chaldee, Syriac, church of England, Calvin, Venema, Amesius, Edwards, Pool, Horne, Henry, Scott, Clarke, Jebb and Hengstenberg agree with our version in making this a prayer, Let, etc. But the Septuagint, Arabic, Ethiopic, Vulgate, Doway, Fry and others closely follow the original, and read it in the future: *Then shall be acceptable*, etc. The pious student of Scripture gets an excellent sense from either reading. Each coincides with truth and experience. If the future form is to be adopted then we have an inspired declaration that the words and even the thoughts of such a man as is previously described are pleasing to God. But if we follow the common version, which is perhaps the best, then the Psalmist prays that God would not merely free him from sins *secret* and *presumptuous*, but that he would make his speech to be pure, kind, godly, edifying, and his thoughts chaste, devout, holy, heavenly. There seems to be no good reason for supposing that the *words* and *meditation* are merely those contained in this Psalm, and none else, as some have thought. *Be acceptable*, elsewhere be to the pleasure, to the good pleasure, to the good-will, to the favor, to the delight, to the acceptance. Two grounds of confidence in this petition are expressed. 1. The LORD is his *Strength*, or Rock. See Ps. xviii. 2. Clarke thinks the word equivalent to *Fountain* or *Origin.* He gives no reason for this rendering, nor is the word ever so translated in our common version. There it is rendered Rock, Strength, Beauty, mighty One,

mighty God. David's confidence was in God's ability to do all he needed and all he asked. 2. The LORD is his Redeemer—literally, *The one that redeems me;* or, My kinsman, whose right and office it is to redeem. An old Psalter reads it, My Helper and my Buyer. We are bought with a price, a great price, a price far above our value. Well may every believer say: "In the Lord" Jesus "have I righteousness and strength."

DOCTRINAL AND PRACTICAL REMARKS.

1. The distinction between natural and revealed religion is just. Truth requires it. The Scriptures admit it, vv. 1–11.

2. All unperverted knowledge is useful. Everything God has made and everything God has spoken, with all the relations and uses of each, may teach us some valuable lesson, vv. 1–11.

3. If man had never sinned, if he were laboring under no blindness of mind, nor hardness of heart, the teachings of natural religion are so clear and so impressive that they would assuredly awaken pious wonder and devout praise to the Maker of all things, vv. 1–4. His works *declare, preach, show, publish* his existence all the time and in every place. Tholuck: "Though all the preachers on earth should grow silent, and every human mouth cease from publishing the glory of God, the heavens above will never cease to declare and proclaim his majesty." The smallest piece of granite or of old red sandstone, the least shell or insect as truly requires a Creator as the heavens above us. Morison: "It is impossible to direct even a cursory glance to the greater and lesser lights which rule by day and night, without being compelled to think with reverential awe of that incomprehensible Being who kindles up all their fires, directs all their courses, and impresses upon them all laws, which contribute alike to the order, beauty and happiness of the universe." Well did the apostle say that all men, even the heathen, are *without excuse.* Even *one* day or *one* night proves that there is a God, as there is but one being that could cause either. Everett: "I had occasion, a few weeks since, to take the early train from Providence to Boston; and for this purpose rose at two o'clock in the morning. Everything around was wrapt in darkness and hushed in silence, broken only by what seemed at that hour the unearthly clank and rush of the train. It was a mild, serene, midsummer's night— the sky was without a cloud—the winds were whist. The moon, then in the last quarter, had just risen, and the stars shone with a spectral lustre but little affected by her presence. Jupiter, two hours high, was the herald of the day; the Pleiades just above the horizon shed their sweet influence in the east; Lyra sparkled near the zenith; Andromeda veiled her newly-discovered glories from the naked eye in the South; the steady pointers far beneath the pole looked meekly up from the depths of the north to their sovereign.

"Such was the glorious spectacle as I entered the train. As we proceeded, the timid approach of twilight became more perceptible; the intense blue of the sky began to soften; the smaller stars, like little children went first to rest; the sister-beams of the Pleiades soon melted together; but the bright constellations of the west and north remained unchanged. Steadily the wondrous transfiguration went on. Hands of angels hidden from mortal eyes shifted the scenery of the heavens; the glories of night dissolved into the glories of the dawn. The blue sky now turned more softly gray; the great watch-stars shut up their holy eyes; the east began to kindle. Faint streaks of purple soon blushed along the sky; the whole celestial concave was filled with the inflowing tides of the morning light, which came pouring down from above in one great ocean of radiance; till at length as we reached the Blue Hills, a flash of purple fire blazed out from above the horizon, and turned the dewy tear-drops of flower and leaf into rubies and diamonds.   In a few seconds, the everlasting gates of the morning were thrown wide open, and the lord of day, arrayed in glories too severe for the gaze of man, began his state. . .

" I am filled with amazement, when I am told that in this enlightened age, and in the heart of the Christian world, there are persons who can witness this daily manifestation of the power and wisdom of the Creator, and yet say in their hearts, 'there is no God.' "

Morison : " The bridegroom's ornaments, and the giant's power are but faint images of the sun's mild splendor, and his swift penetrating light.   All nature rejoices at his approach ; the sweet melody of wood and grove hails his rising ; before his face the shadows of night flee away ; wild beasts of the forest hasten to their retreats ; and light, and cheerfulness, and happy industry revisit the habitations of men."   Indeed one bright sun should forever silence all cavillings respecting the fundamental truths of natural religion.   " Where is your God? show him to me," said a proud heathen monarch to a devout Jew.   " I cannot show you my God, but come with me and I will show you one of his messengers."   Taking him to the open air he pointed to the unclouded sun, and said, " Look at that."   " I cannot, it pains my eyes," said the monarch.   " Then," said the Jew, " how couldst thou look on the face of him, at whose rebuke the pillars of heaven tremble?"

4. A poor, puny creature is man! Compared with God he is as nothing.   All nature and all revelation teach him that he is a mite, a worm, a vanity.   He looks up and sees the sky as a molten looking-glass, Job xxxvii. 18, reflecting the image of God ; but all nations of men are so much like the grasshoppers that their image is not once seen, except they look downward.   Everything above us speaks of the greatness of God not of man.

5. Some good pieces have been written on the poetry of Scripture and on the indebtedness of elegant literature to the Bible.   Much more remains to be told.   Let some one lay out his strength on the subject.   The imagery of the sun in vv. 4, 5, is but a specimen of what is meant.

6. Thankful should we poor gentiles be that to us God always gave the lessons of natural religion as clearly as to others, that in so doing there was a prophetic pledge that he would finally give us clearer light, and that that light, even the Sun of righteousness, has arisen on the nations.   When God suffered all nations to walk in their own ways, he nevertheless left not himself without witness, Acts xiv. 16, 17, thus proving to them all the time that he was as good and would be as gracious as Revelation said he should be to the blinded aliens from the commonwealth of Israel.

7. Glorious as the sun is, compared with other creatures, it is yet infinite condescension in God to make the sun an emblem of himself to us poor ignorant mortals, Ps. lxxxiv. 11.

8. Great as are man's natural endowments, and clear as are the lessons taught by God's works, yet history and observation alike prove that a revelation was necessary.   The world by wisdom never did know God.   Having forsaken him, every step men take in any system of mythology or philosophy leads them farther from the truth.   The Bible was a needed blessing.   " If God is seen in his works, he is much more seen in his word."

9. The rule of faith and practice given in Scripture is perfect, v. 7.   It is perfect in wisdom, in truth, in equity.   In it nothing is lacking, nothing redundant, nothing vexatious, nothing capricious.   We need all it teaches us ; and it teaches us all we need to learn.   When one examines the collected wise sayings of the heathen, the impression is necessarily made, that in the truths relating to a right belief and a right life the best of them were mere children.   And when one searches the word of God,

he does not wonder that under its teachings the simple grow wise, and the immoral become pure. The rules, the encouragements, the directions, the incentives are perfect. They all have adequate clearness, authority and majesty. Even the promises are august; the threatenings, salutary and awful.

10. In the hand of God's Spirit Scripture has all the power necessary to control the strongest inclinations of human nature. It converts the soul, v. 7. Nor is this energy confined to a few cases. It renovates millions. Nor is it adapted to change the hearts of none but the moderately wicked. No demon ever enters the soul, but that it can be made to say, Paul I know, and Jesus I know.

11. It is infinite condescension in the God of truth personally to become a witness, and give us his testimony, v. 7. Nothing short of this would have met our case; but our weakness and low estate had put us far beneath the glory of Jehovah, and our sins had exposed us to his righteous displeasure. In salvation everything is of mercy.

11. But God gives his testimony not only to the heads of society, the dignitaries of earth, but to the humblest souls, v. 7. He loves to instruct the feeblest, who has a teachable disposition. Renunciation of our own wisdom, and child-like simplicity are essential to success in the study of God's word, 1 Cor. iii. 18.

12. Good men delight in the law of God and intend to keep it, v. 8. He who loves God must love his law, for it is a transcript of his character.

13. True piety has its sorrows, weeping over sins and short-comings; but it has its joys also, v. 8. These are unspeakable and full of glory. A good conscience is the best treasure ever held, the best pleasure ever tasted, the best honor ever conferred. To a sinner it comes through atoning blood: but it never co-exists with a slighting of God's statutes.

14. Although many systems of false religion do contain some truth; yet it is the peculiar glory of Scripture that it contains *pure* truth, and no error, v. 8. It is always safe to receive what God has spoken.

15. God's word contains all necessary truth. It so *enlightens the eyes* that they need no further illumination, v. 8. He who should know the true sense of all that God has revealed would be unspeakably the wisest mere man that ever lived. To be wise unto salvation is the highest feat of sagacity.

16. The religion of the Bible differs from all false religions by the purity it requires and promotes. *The fear of the Lord is clean*, v. 9. All other religions agree in leaving sin and corruption to riot in the soul. They crop out even in their worship.

17. The more true religion is tried, the more it is found unto praise; for it has in it indestructible excellence. It endureth forever, v. 9. While all that is false, base and selfish shall be forever put down; the true, the noble, the benevolent shall *stand*, eternally stand. The foundation of all stability is truth and righteousness.

18. Every part of Scripture condemns will-worship and human inventions in the house of God, v. 9. God's *fear* and *judgments* have a very different basis from man's precepts.

19. Everywhere in Scripture *right, rectitude, holiness* have the pre-eminence, v. 9. No inspired writer ever expresses a doubt concerning the final triumph of a principle or of a cause, if it is righteous.

20. The renewal of man's fallen nature by the word and Spirit of God is a reality. Conversion is not a dream, vv. 8, 10. Luther: "This is a great wonder of the Holy Spirit and of the judgments of the Most High, that they change everything, rendering that most acceptable, which was before distasteful. For what do men seek more eagerly than riches and pleasures? and yet the spirit has far greater delight in

the law of God, than the flesh can have in its goods and pleasures." Every generation contains *some* men who do prove that they are born of God.

21. How vain are great riches compared with God's word, v. 10. They are fleeting, disturbing, inferior even to many earthly good things. But the divine word enriches the soul of man. "It is able to bring to him an everlasting kingdom." Wealth can heal no wounded spirit, cheer no sinking soul, give hope to no desponding mind, defend against none of the worst ills of life, point no weary traveller to the way of rest, give no assurance of happiness beyond the grave. God's word can do all these things, and a thousand times more.

22. No marvel then that to a pious soul, God's word has an incomparable sweetness, v. 10. The divine life within us is full of comforts and supports, pleasant beyond anything the world ever tastes.

23. In a teacher or witness, experience is a good quality, v. 11. By experience God's children know how blessed is his service, and they speak what they know. The wicked know not what they say, when they rail at religion.

24. From the doctrine of gracious rewards taught us in v. 11, let us like Paul make this very weighty inference: "Therefore, my beloved brethren, be ye steadfast, unmovable, always abounding in the work of the Lord, forasmuch as ye know that your labour is not in vain in the Lord." Those were blessed words spoken to Abraham: "I am thy exceeding great reward." Well may such words arouse and animate any man to do his best in God's cause. Yet every good man will sympathize with Hooker, of New England, who, when told that he was going to receive his reward, said, "I am going to receive mercy."

25. How useful for humiliation is the whole law of God! v. 12. It shows mortals their defects and enormities in such a way that the very best men have cried out bitterly under a sense of their manifold corruptions.

26. There is great folly in claiming to be without fault, v. 12. Modern perfectionism gets no countenance from Scripture. Calvin: "The more diligently any one examines himself, the more readily will he acknowledge with David, that if God should discover our secret faults, there would be found in us an abyss of sins so great as to have neither bottom nor shore."

27. If our sanctification goes no further than we can see our own faults, and so particularly renounce each one, we shall never be saved, v. 12. Blessed be God, he sees all our sins, and if he loves us, he will not leave us under their power.

28. How important is prayer, especially such prayer as David offers in vv. 12, 13. If we ever get beyond prayer, we shall either be fit for heaven or for hell.

29. Although it is of great importance, on many accounts, that we should have a high degree of self-knowledge, yet observation unites with inspiration in teaching that it is exceedingly difficult of attainment. Very few men know themselves, and especially their own defects. It would seem that the mind of man, like his eye, was originally made rather to look out on the works of God than on itself. It is only by a reflex act that we get a knowledge of the size, color, or appearance of our eyes, or of the powers, tempers and exercises of our minds. Mental philosophy makes slow progress. Sin also blinds the mind, so that though men have eyes they see not. Self-love has become inordinate, so that in civil and criminal suits no man is allowed to be his own judge; yet in matters of self-knowledge each man is judge, jury, witness, prosecutor and advocate. Self-inspection is to most men irksome. Sin riots in carelessness. Nor is this all. Good and bad in character often seem very much alike. Saul and Judas appeared to repent much as Peter. Ahab's humility looked like that of David. Herod's reformation appeared to go almost as far as was required. Systems of education in which concealment has a large place also help to rivet upon us

the chains of self-ignorance. When a man has learned to deceive others, he has learned still more effectually to deceive himself. In fact, our very familiarity with our own faults hides their deformity from us. How many men mistake their talents and their manners, thinking the latter agreeable when they are highly offensive, and the former shining when they are hardly up to a tedious mediocrity. Good men deplore their want of self-knowledge; and bad men evince it in many ways. Hazael considered himself insulted when the prophet predicted his career of crime, yet he did all the wickedness foretold of him. In some cases even the conscience of men is perverted so that they believe their worst crimes to be virtues. No marvel then that men's judgment of themselves should often be erroneous.

30. Sins of ignorance are yet sins, and need forgiveness as well as others, v. 12. Henry: "The best of men have reason to suspect themselves guilty of many secret faults, and to pray to God to cleanse them from that guilt, and not to lay it to their charge; for even our sins of infirmity and inadvertency, and our secret sins would be our ruin, if God should deal with us according to the desert of them. Even secret faults are defiling, and render us unfit for communion with God; but when they are pardoned, we are cleansed from them," 1 John i. 7. Beware of secret sins.

31. Some sins are worse than others. All sins are criminal, but some are presumptuous, v. 13. "These we should particularly lament, against these we should particularly pray."

32. Even regenerate men may commit great sins, enormous crimes. Left to themselves they are as weak as water, vv. 12, 13. Rivet: "Inasmuch as David, who here calls himself the servant of God, and who was truly such, confesses his need of divine restraint so that he may not boldly and impudently break the law of God, and fall into transgressions, it is clear that no one should so far presume on his own virtue or strength, as to regard himself beyond the possibility of the worst falls, as Paul also teaches, 1 Cor. x. 12;" Morison: "One secret sin, unsubdued, may plunge the soul into perdition; but open, glaring, and presumptuous transgression may lead at once to the double 'shipwreck of faith and a good conscience,' and may render the subject of it an equal outcast from earth and heaven. It will not do in the face of such imminent dangers as this, to indulge the fearful, and, I had almost said infernal, casuistry, how far a man may be plunged into the gulf of sin and yet be recovered?"

33. If sin has dominion over us, we are its servants and not the servants of God, v. 13; Rom. vi. 16.

34. Though some sins are less than others, yet the tendency of all sin is to ruin; and the least sins often lead to the worst; and a great sin often leads to many lesser sins, vv. 12, 13.

35. Constantly and in all things we need divine grace, v. 14. Dickson: "As pardoning grace, and preventing grace, and restraining grace must be prayed for; so also powerful, sanctifying, or enabling grace, both for inward and outward service; yea, and grace accepting the service when it is offered, must be sought for by prayer to God."

36. Sherlock: "The best of men have their failings, and an honest Christian may be a weak one: but weak as he may be, the goodness and sincerity of his heart will entitle him to put up the petition of v. 14, which no hypocrite or cunning deceiver can ever make use of."

37. Everywhere as here the Scriptures call our serious attention to the words of our mouth, v. 14. Let men take heed to their tongues.

38. Yet out of the heart are the issues of life. As a man thinketh in his heart so is he, v. 14. If our thoughts are not such as to please God, we may be sure our lives are not holy.

39. Gloriously is Christ the end of the law, meeting its demands, satisfying its

claims, bringing in everlasting righteousness. All depends on him, who is our strength and our Redeemer, v. 14.   Dickson: "As all our prayers, and all our holy endeavors, and abilities to serve God must be furnished unto us by our Redeemer, who is Jesus Christ: so also every other grace, and the acceptance of our persons and services must come through him."

40. Sherlock: "The piety of this Psalm is so natural, and yet so exalted; so easy to be understood, so adapted to move the affections, that it is hardly possible to read it with any attention, without feeling something of the same spirit by which it was indited."

PSALM XX.

To the chief Musician, A Psalm of David.

1 THE LORD hear thee in the day of trouble; the name of the God of Jacob defend thee;

2 Send thee help from the sanctuary, and strengthen thee out of Zion;

3 Remember all thy offerings, and accept thy burnt sacrifice; Selah.

4 Grant thee according to thine own heart, and fulfil all thy counsel.

5 We will rejoice in thy salvation, and in the name of our God we will set up *our* banners: the LORD fulfil all thy petitions.

6 Now know I that the LORD saveth his anointed; he will hear him from his holy heaven with the saving strength of his right hand.

7 Some *trust* in chariots, and some in horses: but we will remember the name of the LORD our God.

8 They are brought down and fallen: but we are risen, and stand upright.

9 Save, LORD: let the king hear us when we call.

FOR an explanation of the title see on titles of Psalms iii. iv.   That David wrote this Psalm is generally agreed.   Those who think differently give no sufficient reason for their views.   On this matter the title is decisive.   Scott dates it B. C. 1037; Clarke, B. C. 1036.   This is conjectural rather than historical.   There is nothing, by which the particular year of its composition can be ascertained.   It is supposed by both these writers to be of the same date with Psalm xxi.   Patrick, Pool, Dodd, Scott, Clarke and others, following the Syriac, think it probable (from v. 7) that it was composed by David to be used in prayer for his success in his great expedition against the Ammonites and Syrians, who came with vast numbers of horses and chariots to fight with him, 2 Sam. x. 6, 8; 1 Chron. xix. 7.   Arama supposes it to have been composed on the occasion of David's great victory over the Philistines.   Luther: "It seems to me as if David had composed this Psalm, that it might serve as a devout and pious battle-cry, whereby he might admonish himself and the people, and draw them to prayer;" Calvin: "The design of the Holy Spirit, in my judgment, was to deliver to the church a common form of prayer, which, as we may gather from the words, was to be used whenever she was threatened with any danger.   God commands his people, in general, to pray for kings, but there was a special reason, and one which did not apply to any other kingdom, why prayer was to be made in behalf of this kingdom; for it was only by the hand of David and his seed that God had determined to govern and maintain his people.   It is particularly to be noticed, that under the figure of this temporal kingdom, there was described a government far more excellent, on which the whole joy and felicity of the church depended.   The object, therefore, which David had expressly in view, was to exhort all the children of God to cherish such a holy solicitude about the kingdom of Christ, as would stir them up to continual prayer in its behalf." This view is perhaps to be preferred; though the Chaldee explicitly applies the whole to Messiah, the king; Abenezra says some interpret it of Messiah; and Ainsworth says, The whole Psalm is a prophecy of Christ's sufferings, and his deliverances out of them, for which the church with him triumpheth. Horne also applies it all directly to Christ. Yet the view of Calvin is more natural, consistent throughout and no less evangelical and heavenly in its doctrines.

This Psalm can be well interpreted without making it a dialogue as Mudge, Morison, Clarke and Tholuck have done.

The names of the Almighty here found are *Jehovah* LORD and *Elohim God*, on which see above on Ps. i. 2; iii. 2.

The verbs *hear, defend*, etc., in the Hebrew are in the future. See Introduction, § 6. Jebb prefers the future; Fry, the present tense. But the Chaldee, Septuagint, Ethiopic, Syriac, Vulgate, Doway, Calvin, church of England, Edwards, Amesius, Venema, Hammond, Ainsworth, Diodati, Patrick, Pool, Henry, Scott, Hengstenberg, Alexander and others properly prefer the optative form, as in the English text.

1. *The* LORD *hear thee in the day of trouble. Hear*, commonly rendered *answer*. It means so to hear as to answer, as in Ps. iii. 4; iv. 1 and often. For *trouble* the Doway, following the Vulgate, has *tribulation*. The same Hebrew word is found in Ps. ix. 9; x. 1. It is elsewhere rendered *affliction, distress, adversity, anguish. The name of the God of Jacob defend thee.* The *name* of God is here put for God himself. This is often done in Scripture, Deut. xxviii. 58; Neh. ix. 5; Ps. xliv. 8, 20; Pr. xviii. 10. God's essence is hid from us; his name is that by which he is known to us. The prayer is that all whereby we know God may *defend* the king. God remarkably defended Jacob in great perils. This may be the reason why his name is here introduced. Jacob is also a name of God's church. Jehovah is the God of all Israel, and keeps his people as the apple of his eye. The sense is perhaps this: *May he who is the God of the whole church defend thee. Defend*, set thee up, set thee on high, exalt thee, make thee safe, Is. ix. 11; Ps. lxix. 29; Job xxxvi. 22; Pr. xxix. 25. Hengstenberg thinks *defend* here is to transfer to a high and secure place. Waterland and Houbigant read, *Raise thee up.*

2. *Send thee help from the sanctuary.* For *sanctuary*, Jebb and Fry read *the holy place;* Calvin, Venema, and Alexander follow the Chaldee and Syriac, and read *his sanctuary.* Help was said to come from the abode of the ark, 1 Kings viii. 29–49. The holy place, the sanctuary was pre-eminently God's earthly residence. *Send*, commonly so rendered. *Help*, always so rendered. The appeal is to God's covenant, of which the prescribed worship of the temple was a sign and memorial. *And strengthen thee out of Zion. Strengthen*, so rendered in Ps. xli. 3; civ. 15, elsewhere *uphold, establish, refresh*, several times *comfort*, Pr. xx. 28; Ps. xciv. 18; Isa. ix. 7; 1 Kings xiii. 7; Jud. xix. 5, 8. Calvin: "As God, by appointing mount Zion to be the place where the faithful should continually worship him, had joined the kingdom and priesthood together, David, in putting into the lips of the people a prayer for help out of Zion doubtless had an eye to this sacred bond of union. Hence I conjecture that this Psalm was composed by David in his old age, and about the close of his life."

3. *Remember all thy offerings. Remember*, commonly so rendered; sometimes *think upon, be mindful of, record, recount, make mention of.* The word may be taken either in a good or bad sense, the connection determining, Hos. vii. 2; Neh. vi. 14. Here it is evidently in a good sense; Remember for good. *Offerings;* Ainsworth and Edwards: *oblations;* Venema, Jebb, Amesius and Alexander: *gifts;* Hengstenberg:

meat-offerings. The same word is found in Gen. iv. 3–5. Elsewhere in that book it is always rendered *present*, Gen. xxxii. xxxiii. In Exodus, Leviticus and Numbers it is almost without exception rendered *meat-offering*. It is the name of a *gift* to God or to man, Is. xxxix. 1; Hos. x. 6; Ps. xl. 6. Here it clearly points to the *meat-offering*, which was consumed by fire on the altar, and was offered with oil and incense for a *memorial*, Lev. ii. 1–3. The prayer proceeds: *And accept thy burnt sacrifice.* *Accept*, *turn to ashes, consume* with fire, that is, express acceptance by causing fire from heaven to consume the sacrifice. The same word is often rendered to *make fat*, Pr. xi. 25; xiii. 4; xxviii. 25; Is. xxxiv. 7. The margin allows this reading here. Hengstenberg: " The word signifies to make fat and then to declare fat, good, to accept with satisfaction." Our version gives the sense. *Burnt sacrifice;* the old versions use *whole burnt-offering.* The sense of both clauses of this verse is a prayer for the public and divine acceptance of the king in each act of solemn prescribed worship. On *Selah* see Introduction, § 15.

4. *Grant thee according to thine own heart, and fulfil all thy counsel.* *Heart* and *counsel* in the usual sense. *Counsel* as in Ps. i. 1. Calvin: " As it would be absurd to ask God to grant foolish and wicked desires, it is to be regarded as certain, that there is here described a king who was neither given to ambition, nor inflamed with avarice, nor actuated by whatever the unruly passions might suggest, but wholly intent on the charge which was committed, and entirely devoted to the advancement of the public good; so that he asks nothing but what the Holy Spirit dictated to him, and what God, by his own mouth, commanded him to ask."

5. *We will rejoice in thy salvation.* Hengstenberg, Alexander and others continue the optative form, May we rejoice, etc. The original bears this construction. Calvin has, That we may rejoice, etc., thus stating the effect of granting former petitions. But many versions besides that in common use suggest a better sense by making the petitioners here express joy through confidence in the *salvation*, or *safety*, or *deliverance* of their king in the great enterprize which he had on hand. Any one of these renderings is good. Each shows the same pious state of mind. The first is perhaps to be preferred. *And in the name of our God we will set up our banners.* The same remarks as on the preceding clause apply to the construction here. *To set up banners* is to display ensigns of victory, to hold up signals of triumph already effected or confidently expected. Horsley: " The sense is, We will take the field against our enemies, in full reliance upon God's assistance." For *set up banners* Street following the Septuagint reads *grow great.* Conquerors displayed many *ensigns* and *trophies,* thus declaring the greatness of their achievements. *The* LORD *fulfil all thy petitions.* Our version, church of England and others here return to the optative form. *Fulfil, i. e.,* grant to the full extent all thy *petitions.* In Ps. xxxvii. 4 the same word is rendered *desires* of thine heart.

6. *Now know I that the* LORD *saveth his anointed.* Clarke supposes the speaker here to be the high-priest, after the victim was consumed. Morison thinks it is David himself, or his great antitype. Fry supposes Christ himself is the speaker. But the weight of opinion is against these views. There is no necessity for supposing a new speaker here. In the Psalms a change in number and person is common. Alexander: " The change to the first person singular does not indicate a different speaker, but merely puts what follows into the mouth of each individual believer or of the whole body viewed as an ideal person." The Hebrew rendered *saveth* is literally *hath saved;* thus expressing high confidence that the thing will as surely be done as if it had already been accomplished. *I know;* I have an assurance without doubt. *His anointed,* literally *Messiah.* David was God's *anointed,* but Jesus of Nazareth was the Messiah, the Christ, the anointed in a much higher sense than all who came before

him, or shall come after him. He received the oil of gladness. He had the Spirit without measure. The next clause has the future form of the verb. *He will hear from his holy heaven with the saving strength of his right hand.* Calvin: He will hear from the heavens of his sanctuary, in the mightiness of the salvation of his right hand; church of England: And will hear him from his holy heaven, even with the wholesome strength of his right hand; Mudge: He will answer him from his holy heavens; with the victorious prowess of his right arm; Edwards: He will answer him from the holy heavens with the victorious strength of his right hand; Houbigant: He will hear him from his holy heavens: the salvation of his right hand will be most powerful; Ainsworth: He answereth him out of the heavens of his holiness, with powers the salvation of his right hand; Fry: He answereth from his holy heavens—in mighty deeds is the victory of his right hand; Hengstenberg: He hears from his holy heaven, through his right hand salutary exploits. Diodati thinks the last clause equivalent to these words, *with miracles and glorious effects of his power.* Horsley's exposition is: "In all situations of power and strength, whatever a man's natural means of deliverance may be, his preservation must be the work of God's right hand." The idea of the last clause of the text is elsewhere in Scripture expressed more clearly, as in Ps. cxviii. 16, the right hand of the LORD is exalted; the right hand of the LORD doeth valiantly. See also Ps. lxxxix. 13; Ex. xv. 6. The right hand is the emblem of strength and prowess.

7. *Some* trust *in chariots, and some in horses: but we will remember the name of the* LORD *our God.* Lowth:

> These in chariots, and those in horses;
> But we in the name of Jehovah our God will be strong.

The word *trust* is not found in the Hebrew anywhere in this Psalm, nor is it supplied by any of the ancient versions. The *substance* of what is taught is no doubt given by our version and by Calvin in the French, both using *trust.* Fry has *boast.* The correct rule in all such cases is to supply the verb from the immediate context, if that will make good sense. In this verse we have such a verb, *remember,* for the significations of which see on v. 3. We may adopt any one of the significations there given, and supply it here, and the sense will be good. Thus we may read: Some *think upon* chariots, and some upon horses, but we will *think upon* the name of the Lord our God; or, Some *make mention* of chariots, and some of horses, but we will *make mention* of the Lord our God. As the verb in another form is used in v. 3 it is probably repeated here with design; *q. d.,* As God remembers the offerings of our anointed king, we will remember his name. For he is *the* LORD *our God;* ours by a gracious, glorious covenant.

8. *They are brought down and fallen;* i. e., those who trust in chariots and those who trust in horses are *brought down;* Calvin, Edwards and Jebb, *bowed down;* Fry, *bent down;* Alexander, *bowed;* Hengstenberg, *stoop.* The Hebrew in some forms expresses the *couching* of a beast, Num. xxiv. 9. In Judges v. 27 it is thrice applied to Sisera. Sometimes it expresses *kneeling,* 1 Kings viii. 54. In 2 Kings ix. 24 it is *sunk down.* *Are fallen;* the verb is often followed by the phrase, *by the sword.* It here signifies *complete overthrow* and *powerlessness* to do further harm. Not so those who remember the name of the Lord. They say: *But we are risen and stand upright,* as men neither discomfited, nor disheartened. Calvin: *Are risen and are erect;* Edwards: *Rise and stand firm;* Hengstenberg: *Rise and stand upright.* The verbs in this verse are all in the preterite. Alexander: "Here, as in v. 6, the past tense expresses the certainty of the event, or rather the confidence with which it is expected.—The last verb occurs only here in this form, which is properly reflexive, and may be explained to mean, *We have straightened ourselves up.*"

9. *Save,* LORD; *let the king hear us when we call.* Calvin, Amesius, Hengstenberg and Alexander give the same punctuation as in our version. But there is great diversity both in pointing and in translating the verse. Venema: Jehovah has saved the king; he will hear us in the day when we shall call; Street:

> Jehovah hath saved the king,
> He answereth us always, when we invoke him;

Edwards: Jehovah save the king, and hear us when we call upon thee; Houbigant: May Jehovah save the king, and hear us, when we call; Jebb: O LORD, save the king: hear us in the day when we call; Fry: O Jehovah, give the victory to the king: he heareth us in the day of our calling; Ainsworth: Jehovah, save thou the king, he answers us in the day we call; Waterland: Lord save the king: he will hear us when we call; Horsley: Jehovah hath saved the king, and will hear us when we call; Septuagint, Arabic, Ethiopic, Vulgate, Doway: *O Lord,* save the king: and hear us in the day that we shall call upon thee; church of England: Save, LORD; and hear us, O King of heaven, when we call upon thee; Hammond: Lord, save the king. He will hear us in the day of our calling; Chaldee: O Lord, redeem us; O mighty King, receive our prayer in the day of our invocation; Syriac: The Lord shall deliver us, and our king shall hear us. It must be confessed that there is great difficulty in this passage, not in finding a good sense, but in knowing the mind of the Spirit. The Hebrew would indicate a pause at the words *save* LORD; but the pointing is not infallible, and Pool asserts, perhaps he proves, that the pause in the sense does not invariably attend similar pointing. Some think that by *king,* the King of kings is spoken of. If so, then our version is right. Others suppose *Christ* alone is intended by the *king;* and that he is supplicated. Others think that by *king,* David is pointed out. If so, the Septuagint rendering is to be preferred. It is surely unusual to mingle in the same song and even in the same verse prayers to Jehovah and requests to any creature, though he be a type of Christ. Perhaps it is best to read the whole thus: *Jehovah, save the king,* meaning *David,* both as a leader of Israel and a type of Christ; and then to give the last clause in the future: *He* [the Lord] *will hear us when we call.* This requires a change from the second to the third person, but that is very common. Alexander: "By taking the last verb as a future proper the Psalm may be made to close with a confident anticipation of God's blessing." The words *save* and *hear* in this verse evidently allude to v. 6. Patrick thus paraphrases it: "Let it be unto us, O LORD, according to our desires, and our hopes: preserve our king; and in the day when we cry unto thee for help, make our armies victorious." Clarke thinks the easiest way of making all plain is to paraphrase it thus: "*Lord, save David, and David will save us.* If thou preserve *him,* he will be thy minister for good to us." These views of Patrick and Clarke are inserted rather out of respect to their authors than from confidence in their correctness.

DOCTRINAL AND PRACTICAL REMARKS.

1. God's word invests the persons and acts of lawful rulers with a high dignity, teaching all, whom they govern, to pray for them, vv. 1–5; compare 1 Tim. ii. 1–3. Jeremiah called his prince "the breath of our nostrils, the anointed of the LORD, under whose shadow we shall live among the heathen," Lam. iv. 20. Abuse of lawful magistrates is no part of true piety.

2. The greatest men, even mighty kings, are subject to sorrow, and need the prayers of others, and the help of God.

3. When our troubles are so great and grievous as to lead us directly to God, we

often get a safe deliverance from them, or a sanctified use of them much sooner than when they are lighter or less sharp.

4. None but a foolish and wicked man would make light of the prayers of the humblest people in his behalf. Henry: "Even great and good men, and those that know well how to pray for themselves, must not despise, but earnestly desire the prayers of others for them, even those that are their inferiors in all respects." David composed this Psalm that the people might pray for him.

5. Cobbin: "*A praying nation is not disregarded in heaven.* In some way or other they shall see an answer to their prayers, and shall be able to rejoice in God's salvation."

6. In all trouble, personal, domestic, or national, prayer is the best resort of high and low. On earth no man is so afflicted, or forsaken, or beset by the wicked, that God cannot save him, and no man is so great as not to need help from on high. Henry: "David, though a man of business, a man of war, was constant to his devotions; though he had prophets, and priests, and many good people among his subjects to pray for him, he did not think that excused him from praying for himself."

7. The church has experience of the power, pity, care and faithfulness of her God and friend. He is the God of Jacob, v. 1. He will treat every believer as faithfully and defend him as effectually as he did the patriarch Jacob in his eventful life. God will not, cannot forsake his people, because they are his, and because it would be contrary to all his past dealings with them, and a disregard of all his relations to them. The *name*—the perfections, and the providence of Jehovah, shall defend those, whose cause God espouses.

8. The relations of God to his people are by a gracious compact. Of that covenant Zion, the sanctuary, and all the accepted worship in it were signs, v. 2. Help from the sanctuary is federal.

9. When in anything we get help in God's appointed way, it is not only sweet in itself, but a pledge of farther good, v. 2. Help from Zion and the sanctuary has in all ages been uniform and of like excellent nature.

10. How admirable is the condescension of God, making himself known in Zion, and the sanctuary as he has, v. 2. If he is to reveal himself at all, how could he do it more seasonably, more graciously, more instructively, or in a more captivating way than he has done in his law and gospel, his word and worship?

11. Accepted worship is an amazing mercy. No wonder it is greatly desired by good men, v. 3. It is an infallible token of all truly good things here and hereafter.

12. It is an inestimable blessing to have good rulers, for the granting of whose wishes and fulfilling of whose plans we can heartily pray, v. 3.

13. True religion and accepted worship are always substantially the same. Luther: "As in the new law, there are other persons, other matters, other times, other places, so are there also other sacrifices; though still there remain one faith and one spirit; the external only has changed, the internal remains the same."

14. As the pious Jew had his thank-offerings, so he had his bloody sacrifices for atonement, v. 3. In like manner sinners, in the midst of their thanks and praises, must not forget that now, as in the days of Abel or Aaron, without the shedding of blood, even the precious blood of Christ, there is no remission.

15. God certainly and gloriously concurs with good wishes, good counsels, pious prayers, vv. 4, 5. His whole nature and purposes lead him precisely in that direction. Henry: "Those, who make it their business to glorify God, may expect that God will, one way or other, gratify them; and they who walk in his counsel may promise themselves that he will fulfil theirs."

16. The more we have prayed for a deliverance, and the more manifestly it is from God, the greater is our joy, v. 5.

17. When we set up our banners, engage in any necessary contest or conflict, personal or national, or give expression to the joys of victory, it ought always to be *in the name of our God*, v. 5. David went forth against Goliath in the name of the Lord of hosts, and so he slew him, 1 Sam. xvii. 45–51. All issues are with God. We have no more right to make war like atheists, than we have to live without God in the world in times of peace.

18. Those, who are sharers in the church's afflictions shall also be partakers of her glorious victories, vv. 1–5.

19. Dickson: "A believer may be sure that he hath his request granted, when he hath prayed according to God's will; in special when he prayeth for the safety of the church and kingdom of Christ. '*I know that the Lord saveth his anointed*,'" v. 6.

20. As neglect of prayer makes faith weak, so lively prayer greatly strengthens our reliance on God's word, vv. 1–6.

21. Often in Scripture is salvation made to appear in close union with the *anointed* of the Lord, v. 6. If the deliverance is temporal in the kingdom of David, yet it must be by him whom God anointed for that end. Much more is eternal salvation by the great *Anointed*, CHRIST, THE MESSIAH.

22. Everywhere in Scripture the law has a shadow of good things to come, even the sanctuary being a type of heaven itself, vv. 2, 6. Compare Heb. viii. ix. Calvin: "Under the visible sanctuary, which was made with hands, there is set forth the fatherly goodness of God, and his familiarity with his people; while, under the heavenly sanctuary, which was not made with hands, there is shown his infinite power, dominion and majesty."

23. Vain is the confidence of all wickedness. In war, chariots, horses, navies, numbers, discipline, former successes are relied on; but the battle is not to the strong. "Providence favors the strong battalions" may sound well in a worldling's ear; but neither providence nor the Bible so teaches. In peace riches, friends, ships, farms, stocks are relied upon, yet they can neither help nor save. Let him that glorieth glory in the Lord, v. 7.

24. Very different are the effects of religious truth on different minds, v. 7. God's servants think on his name with delight; but the wicked with aversion. The saints know that the worst which comes is right, because sent by God; but this reconciles no wicked man to sad events. The pious think on God in prosperity; but at that time the wicked despise him. The righteous fear God and cling to him; the wicked fear him and are driven from his presence by terror. They remember God and are troubled.

25. The righteous put nothing with God to form the basis of their joy and trust. He alone is enough. They need neither help, nor guidance, nor wisdom, nor strength, nor righteousness but in him alone, v. 7.

26. In its power over human nature the faith of God's elect is the most wonderful principle known. It walks in darkness, has no light, and yet trusts in the Lord. It endures as seeing him, who is invisible. It anticipates victories when appearances are all against it, v. 7. Dickson: "That which terrifieth the believer in the first assault of a temptation, before he go to his refuge, is contemned by the believer when he looks to the Lord, his true defence."

27. This is not marvellous, for a change in the positions and states of saints and sinners must come, vv. 7, 8. God's word makes it sure. The righteous sees it coming; the wicked does not.

28. As often as the grasp of true faith is weakened or slackened, it must and will renew its hold on the covenant and perfections of God, v. 9.

29. The atheism of nations respecting God's dealings with them is commonly much more striking in their latter than in their early history—in their fulness and prosperity, than in their weakness and besetments. This Psalm would hardly be acceptable to a whole people, on whom wealth and victory had long exerted their usually corrupting influence.

30. The bearing of this whole Psalm on the great ANOINTED and his kingdom is generally and piously admitted by the best commentators. Scott: "In answer to the hopes and prayers of the Old Testament church, the anointed King of God's people came in the appointed season: he was heard in the day of his trouble; his sacrifice was accepted; his intercessions have prevailed; his kingdom has been set up; and we are called to partake of its blessings." Morison: "The desire of Messiah's heart, in the salvation of millions of perishing sinners, was granted to him, and all his counsels, purposes, and plans have succeeded, and shall ultimately triumph over all the opposition of earth and hell. . . Nor shall one petition for himself or his church fall to the ground ineffectual. All shall be heard, all shall be answered; and each member of the redeemed family shall share his inalienable part in the intercession of his Lord." Calvin: "Since Christ our King, being an everlasting priest, never ceases to make intercession with God, the whole body of the church should unite in prayer with him; and farther, we can have no hope of being heard except he go before us, and conduct us to God."

31. In the great conflict between Christ and the dragon the issue is not doubtful. A battle may seem to be lost, but the war must end in the triumph of truth, in the reign of righteousness, in the crowning of Messiah. Luther: "How should God not hear when his kingdom, his interest, his honor are in danger?"

32. Really good wishes are good things, and should be expressed in words and deeds. The whole Psalm thus teaches. "Christian sympathy is a great branch of Christian duty. There may be a great deal of obliging kindness in that which costs us little."

PSALM XXI.

To the Chief Musician, A Psalm of David.

1 THE king shall joy in thy strength, O LORD; and in thy salvation how greatly shall he rejoice!

2 Thou hast given him his heart's desire, and hast not withholden the request of his lips. Selah.

3 For thou preventest him with the blessings of goodness: thou settest a crown of pure gold on his head.

4 He asked life of thee, *and* thou gavest *it* him, *even* length of days for ever and ever.

5 His glory *is* great in thy salvation: honour and majesty hast thou laid upon him.

6 For thou hast made him most blessed for ever: thou hast made him exceeding glad with thy countenance.

7 For the king trusteth in the LORD, and through the mercy of the Most High he shall not be moved.

8 Thine hand shall find out all thine enemies: thy right hand shall find out those that hate thee.

9 Thou shalt make them as a fiery oven in the time of thine anger: the LORD shall swallow them up in his wrath, and the fire shall devour them.

10 Their fruit shalt thou destroy from the earth, and their seed from among the children of men.

11 For they intended evil against thee: they imagine a mischievous device, *which* they are not able *to perform*.

12 Therefore shalt thou make them turn their back, *when* thou shalt make ready *thine arrows* upon thy strings against the face of them.

13 Be thou exalted, LORD, in thine own strength: *so* will we sing and praise thy power.

FOR an explanation of the title see on Psalms iii. iv.

But few of the Psalms, without testimony from other parts of Scripture, are more clearly of Davidic authorship than this. There is no good reason for doubting that he wrote it. Clarke and Scott both give to it the same date as to Psalm xx.; Clarke B. C. 1036, and Scott B. C. 1037. The precise date is not known.

The application of this Psalm is not confined to any particular occasion. Theodoret singularly supposes it to have been written on occasion of the sickness and recovery of king Hezekiah. There is no evidence to support this opinion. Delaney and Tholuck think it was composed by David in the height of his joy and in the spirit of thanksgiving after the conquest of Rabbah, and the victory over the Ammonites, 2 Sam. xii. 26–31. This opinion, though less improbable than the foregoing, needs confirmation. Mudge thinks the Psalm of the same kind as Ps. xx. Calvin says its subject is almost the same. Some have thought that this Psalm relates to the fulfilment of the prayer in that. Alexander thinks neither the structure nor contents would justify this view. He says these two songs " are rather parallel than consecutive, the principal difference being this, that while the twentieth Psalm relates to the specific case of assistance and success in war, the twenty-first has reference to the whole circle of divine gifts bestowed upon the Lord's Anointed."

The most important matter relates to its aspect towards Christ. The Chaldee and several Jewish interpreters apply it to Messiah. On this point Calvin is very decided: " Above all, it was the design of the Holy Spirit here to direct the minds of the faithful to Christ, who was the end and perfection of this kingdom [of David], and to teach the whole people that they could not be saved except under the head which God himself had appointed over them." Ainsworth is no less disposed to give it a distinct and direct reference to Christ. With him agree Horne, Horsley, Fry and others. On the Messianic character of the Psalm see Introduction, § 8, and the preceding Psalm. The church of England uses it on Ascension day.

The names of the Almighty here found are *Jehovah* LORD and *Gel-yohn Most High*, on which see above on Ps. i. 2 ; vii. 17.

This Psalm is not dramatic; though some have thought differently, and introduce several speakers. That would not necessarily vary the practical truths taught.

1. *The king shall joy in thy strength, O* LORD. *The king*; Chaldee has *King Messiah*; Street, *a king*; others, *the king*, i. e., David, the king of Israel, the type of Christ. *Shall joy*; some read, *will joy*, elsewhere, *be glad*, or *rejoice*, Ps. v. 11 ; ix. 2 ; xiv. 7 ; xvi. 9. The king shall be glad *in thy strength*; i. e., says Diodati, in the effects of thy sovereign power, which thou hast unfolded for his deliverance, victory, preservation and exaltation. *Strength*, the same word as in Ps. viii. 2, elsewhere rendered as here, also *might, power*. It never signifies *authority*. The prophet here celebrates the divine *efficiency*. *And in thy salvation how greatly shall he rejoice !* *Salvation*, sometimes *help*, or *deliverance*, more commonly, *salvation*, Ps. iii. 2, 8 ; xiii. 5 ; xiv. 7 ; xviii. 50. *Greatly*; elsewhere *exceedingly, mightily, diligently, especially, loudly, very much*, Gen. vii. 19 ; Deut. vi. 3 ; Ps. xxxi. 11 ; cxix. 4, 107 ; Nah. ii. 1. Ains-

worth prefers *vehemently*. *Rejoice;* like the first verb, it is rendered not only as here commonly, but *be glad, be joyful*. Amesius, Edwards, Fry and Alexander prefer *exult;* Hammond: *Rejoice and triumph exceedingly;* Venema: *Is carried to the highest exultation.* Both the verbs in this verse are in the future. Alexander says this shows "that the gift has not yet been consummated, without excluding the idea of it as begun already."

2. *Thou hast given him his heart's desire. Hast given, appointed, ordained, made, delivered, sent.* It was purely the act of God. *And hast not withholden the request of his lips.* Calvin, Edwards, Jebb and Fry also read *request;* Ainsworth, *earnest request;* Doway, *will;* Hengstenberg, *desire;* Alexander, *quest.* Hengstenberg: "The silent wish and the spoken prayer stand in contrast;" Luther: "The arrangement is certainly fine here, namely, that the prayer of the heart must go before, without which the prayer of the lips is an unprofitable howling." For remarks on *Selah* see Introduction, § 15.

3. *For thou preventest him with the blessings of goodness.* The Septuagint, Ethiopic, Arabic, Syriac, Vulgate, Doway, Diodati, Edwards and Pool render the verb in the past tense; Chaldee, Calvin, church of England, Venema, Jebb and Alexander in the future; Amesius, Ainsworth, Fry and Hengstenberg in the present. In Hebrew both the verbs of this verse are in the future. The most common rendering of the first verb is by the word *prevent*, which is literal and which in the early stages of English literature signified the same as the Latin *prævenio, go before* or *come before*, not hinder. Fry has *meetest;* Hengstenberg, *surprisest.* See Ps. xvii. 13; xviii. 5. *With the blessings of goodness;* Ainsworth, church of England and Alexander do not differ from the common version; Calvin, Amesius and Venema: With the blessings of good; Vulgate and others which follow it: With blessings of sweetness; Arabic: With the best blessings; Syriac: With the best blessing; Edwards: With the choicest blessings; Fry and Hengstenberg: With the blessings of prosperity. The word rendered *goodness* is found in Ps. iv. 6; xiv. 1, 3; xvi. 2. Castalio renders the clause: *Thou hast bestowed most eminent favors on him.* Calvin: "The king shall want nothing which is requisite to make his life in every respect happy, since God of his own good pleasure will anticipate his wishes and enrich him with an abundance of all good things." Diodati: Thou hast prevented him with thy graces and benefits, which thou hast bestowed upon him of thine own free will." *Thou settest a crown of pure gold on his head.* For remarks on the word rendered *pure gold*, see Ps. xix. 10. This is the clause which led Patrick, Morison and Clark to suppose that the *crown* alluded to is that mentioned in 2 Sam. xii. 30; 1 Chron. xx. 2. But this gives a very low sense. David was hardly so weak as to be tickled with a flashing gewgaw taken from the head of an idolatrous enemy; nor would he be apt to mention it in devout song. The lowest admissible sense is that the crown is the emblem of royal majesty; and so the meaning would be that God had, even when he was thinking of no such blessing, given him a kingdom. But as Patrick well says, "Truly there are some things in this Psalm which are more literally fulfilled in CHRIST than in David;" so it is with ease that we refer this expression, through David, to his seed, Christ. Of him language of the same import had been used in Ps. ii. 6; viii. 5. The same imagery is found carried forward into the latest prophecy, Rev. xiv. 14; xix. 12, 16, where it is applied to the glorified person of our Redeemer. Hengstenberg: "The setting on of the crown marks the bestowment of dominion. David was crowned, as it were, anew,—or even for the first time, for the earlier crowning did not come, in this respect, into consideration,—when he received that great promise of the everlasting supremacy of his offspring," 2 Sam. vii. "That respect could not be had to David's first crowning, or to the conferring on him of the kingly office in general, is shown by the following con-

text, which is to be regarded as a farther enlargement of the words before us." Scott: "The passage, in its fullest import, can only be accomplished in Christ himself." Calvin and others express themselves much to the same effect. Gill: "This crown being of *pure gold* denotes the purity, glory, solidity, and perpetuity of his kingdom."

4. *He asked life of thee*, and *thou gavest* it *him*, even *length of days for ever and ever*. The Septuagint, Ethiopic, Syriac, Arabic, Vulgate and Doway: He asked life of thee: and thou hast given him length of days forever and ever; Calvin: He asked life from thee, and thou hast given him length of days forever and ever; church of England: He asked life of thee, and thou gavest him a long life, even forever and ever; Ainsworth: Life he asked of thee, thou gavest *it* him; length of days ever and aye; Venema: Life he asked of thee, and thou gavest *it* him; thou wilt give him long life to everlasting; Amesius: Life he asked of thee, thou gavest *it* him, even length of days forever and everlastingly; Jebb: Life he asked of thee: Thou gavest him length of days for ever and ever; Fry: He asked of thee life— thou gavest it him; Lengthening of days forever and ever. Edwards: He asked life of thee; thou hast given him length of days forever and ever; Hengstenberg: He asked of thee life, thou gavest him long life forever and ever; Alexander: Life he asked of thee, thou hast given (it) to him, length of days, perpetuity and eternity. Both the verbs in this verse are in the same form. The rendering, *asked*, and *gavest*, is the best. Horsley for *life* reads *immortality*, and for *length of days, the whole extent of infinite duration*, but this is not translation. The Chaldee has it, *Eternal life* he asked, etc.; and Diodati says that the phrase, *length of days*, "is to be referred to eternal life, which David had assurance of by God's Spirit, besides temporal blessings, Matt. xix. 29; 1 Tim. iv. 8; Eph. iii. 20. Or else to the continuance of his kingdom in his posterity until the coming of Christ, who should change it into an everlasting kingdom, 2 Sam. vii. 19." The *life* David is here said to have *asked* for was not eternal life, a blessed immortality; this would have made his prayer and the blessing secured in no wise different from that of any other pious man; but the *life* he asked was his natural life, which for a long time was in hourly peril, hunted by Saul and his men like a partridge on the mountains. This *life* he *asked* might not be taken away, and he had his wish, and a great deal more. He lived to a good old age, died in peace, was succeeded in the throne by his own posterity while the polity of the Jewish people lasted, and then God gave him a Son, who was at once the root and the offspring of David, and who has *perpetuity* and *eternity* in his kingdom. And as David's life was in danger, so often was the life of Jesus, the great stem of Jesse, but it was preserved in the midst of more deadly enemies than ever beset any other man, until his hour was come, when he breathed out his spirit into the hands of his Father, who speedily gave him a nobler life, so that he dieth no more, death hath no more dominion over him, behold he is alive for evermore, Rom. vi. 9; Rev. i. 18; Heb. v. 7; vii. 25. The highest contrast in this verse is between the natural life of David in peril and the everlasting kingdom of his Son, as promised in 2 Sam. vii. 13, 16; Ps. lxxxix. 4, and as now possessed by him in heaven. Alexander: "The last words of the verse are often used adverbially to mean *for ever and ever*, but as they are both nouns, it is best to put them here in apposition with the same part of speech which immediately precedes." See above on Ps. ix. 5.

5. *His glory is great in thy salvation.* There is great uniformity in rendering this clause both in ancient and modern versions. Fry varies it thus: His glory is great in the victory thou givest. But in our version the word is never anywhere rendered *victory*, usually *salvation*, a very few times *deliverance, help*. We have the same word in Ps. iii. 8; xx. 5. *Glory*, commonly so rendered, sometimes *honor*. The verb in this clause must be supplied. Alexander prefers to give it in the future,

shall be. The sense of the passage is that the great honor of David was, and the high glory of Immanuel should be manifestly through the power of God, and not by the wit of man. So the people devoutly confess. The next clause is of like import: *Honour and majesty hast thou laid upon him.* The variations in the rendering here are not very important. For *honour* and *majesty* Calvin has *splendour* and *beauty.* The first of these words is found in Ps. viii. 1, where it is rendered *glory;* the second, in Ps. viii. 5, where it is rendered *honour.* Both words are frequently rendered *majesty;* the latter sometimes *comeliness* as in Isa. liii. 2. The sense is that by whatever words dignity, majesty and excellence are expressed, they are all manifest in the throne of David, and shall be far more illustrious in that of his glorious offspring, Christ, the Son of God.

6. *For thou hast made him most blessed for ever.* Edwards follows our version. The Septuagint, Ethiopic and Arabic read, Thou wilt give to him a blessing, etc.; Chaldee, Syriac, Vulgate and Doway: Thou wilt give him to be a blessing, etc.; Calvin, Fabritius and Horne: Thou hast set him to be blessings forever; Venema: Thou wilt set him to be blessings forever; Amesius: Thou hast appointed to him blessings for ever; Ainsworth: Thou hast set him to be blessings for perpetual aye; Fry: Thou hast decreed him blessings forever; Jebb: Thou set on him blessings forever; church of England: Thou shalt give him everlasting felicity; Clarke: Thou hast set him for blessings forever; Hengstenberg: Thou settest him for blessing forever; Alexander: Thou wilt make him a blessing to eternity. Indeed it seems hardly possible to examine the verse with critical care without reaching the conclusion that our version is not so good as that given by several just cited. The verb rendered *hast made* is the same that is rendered *settest* in v. 3, though in the Hebrew in both these cases it is in the future. If the primary reference is to David and through him to Christ, which is perhaps the best interpretation, then the verb is best put in the past tense; but if it is a direct prophecy respecting Christ, then it is best to follow the original exactly. If it should be rendered *set him to be blessings,* then it is a declaration that he is set or shall be set to be the instrument or source of manifold blessings to others. In this case there is probably a reference to Gen. xii. 2. Some think the sense is that he is *set* as an example, showing how greatly God can bless one, and leading others to pray that they may be as highly favored. This is Calvin's view: "The king, abounding in all kinds of good things, was an illustrious pattern of the liberality of God." Yet it must be admitted that our version gives a good sense, and is not without support from parallel passages, which are rendered in the same way and with confessed propriety, as Pool shows. Hengstenberg: "The plural points to the rich fatness of the blessing." *Thou hast made him exceeding glad with thy countenance.* The Arabic, Syriac, Calvin, Ainsworth, Fabritius, Amesius, Edwards and Fry here use the past tense; Hengstenberg, the present; Chaldee, Septuagint, Ethiopic, Vulgate, Doway, church of England, Venema, Jebb and Alexander, the future. The remarks on the tense in the first clause of this verse are applicable here. This gladness was imparted by God's countenance, see on Ps. iv. 6; xi. 7.

7. *For the king trusteth in the* LORD. The way of accounting for the preceding blessings is to point to their all sufficient cause, Jehovah, and to show that he, on whom the blessings came, was in communion with God by the exercise of pious confidence united with hope. See on Ps. iv. 5. It is added, *And through the mercy of the Most High he shall not be moved.* For the force of the word *mercy* see Ps. v. 7; xvii. 7. It signifies *favor, goodness, loving-kindness.* On *Most High,* see Ps. vii. 17. *He shall not be moved;* Venema: *Shall not waver.* He shall not be moved from his purpose, from his throne, from his honors, from his victories and successes, from the love and favor of Jehovah. The Chaldee reads it: *King Messiah trusteth in Jehovah.*

8. *Thine hand shall find out all thine enemies: thy right hand shall find out those that hate thee.* There seems to be no good cause for varying the rendering of these two clauses as is done by the Chaldee, Septuagint, Vulgate, Doway and church of England. In the Hebrew the verbs are the same, and both in the future. By far the most common rendering of these verbs is *find*, sometimes *find out*, then *get hold upon.* Edwards in each case has *will reach;* Fry, *reacheth.* Alexander: "If any difference of meaning was intended, it is probably not greater than that between *find* and *find out* in English." In Num. xi. 22 our version has *suffice.* Calvin says some "explain the verse as if it had been said, Thy hand shall be able for all thine enemies, thy right hand shall find out those that hate thee. Thus the sentence will ascend by degrees,—Thy hand shall be able to withstand, thy right hand shall lay hold upon thy enemies, so that they shall not escape destruction." Horsley favors this view: Thine hand shall be successful. There is no error taught by such a reading, but it is hardly supported. The reader will notice that the third person of v. 7 is here changed to the second person. Does not this verse receive its complete and highest fulfilment in Christ alone, who is maintained in his kingdom by all the perfections of God?

9. *Thou shalt make them as a fiery oven in the time of thy anger.* The ancient versions are quite harmonious in rendering this clause very much as we have it above. Some moderns vary considerably. Calvin, Venema, Rogers, Horsley and Walford: Thou shalt put [or place] them as it were into [or in] a furnace of fire. The verb is often rendered *put*, frequently *set*, sometimes *appoint, lay, make.* The word rendered *oven* is either *oven* or *furnace.* It occurs *fifteen* times in the Hebrew, and is four times rendered *furnace;* in all other cases *oven.* Both these images are employed in Scripture to represent the doom of God's foes. Horsley thinks this passage " describes the smoke of the Messiah's enemies perishing by fire, ascending like the smoke of a furnace." In the Apocalypse John says of the wicked: "The smoke of their torment ascendeth up forever and ever." Mant: "How awfully grand is that description of the ruins of the cities of the plain, as the prospect struck on Abraham's eye on the fatal morning of their destruction: 'And he looked toward Sodom and Gomorrah, and toward all the land of the plain, and beheld, and lo! the smoke of the country went up as the smoke of a furnace.'" But the word here rendered *oven* is not that rendered *furnace* in Gen. xix. 28; but it is the word rendered *oven* in Mal. iv. 1. Pool thinks that the sense is that as "wood, when cast into an oven, is quickly consumed," so God will destroy his foes. Hengstenberg: "Thou wilt put them in such a condition that they shall be as if they were in a fiery oven." This shall be done *in the time of thine anger.* Surely the ultimate reference here must be to the *Lamb* and to the great day of *his* wrath. It is at once added: *The* LORD *shall swallow them up in his wrath. Swallow up*, the word used of the whale *swallowing up* Jonah, Jon. i. 17; of Aaron's rod *swallowing up* those of the magicians, Ex. vii. 12; of the dragon, Jer. li. 34. It intimates a total destruction, Ps. lvi. 1, 2, so that there is nothing of them left. *And the fire shall devour them.* Calvin: "It does not seem to me to be out of place to suppose, that in this clause, there is denounced against the enemies of Christ a destruction like that which God in old time sent upon Sodom and Gomorrah." Destruction as by fire is a just and frequent method of representing the overthrow of the wicked.

10. *Their fruit shalt thou destroy from the earth. Fruit;* Chaldee, *children;* Edwards, *descendants;* Fabritius and Clarke, *posterity.* Other versions commonly cited in this work give *fruit.* Speaking of children as *fruit* is very old, Gen. xxx. 2; Deut. vii. 13; xxviii. 4; Ps. cxxvii. 3; cxxxii. 11; Isa. xiii. 18; Lam. ii. 20; Hos. ix. 16; Mic. vi 7. So that the Psalmist here teaches the same truth as in the next clause: *And* [thou shalt destroy] *their seed from among the children of men.* For awful

instances of the destruction of the children of the wicked see Josh. vii. 23–26; Isa. xiv. 21, 22. That God will so deal with men he fully declares, Ex. xx. 5; xxxiv. 7; Num. xiv. 18; Deut. v. 9. In accomplishing this work God may employ Joshua or Cyrus, as we have seen, or David and his anti-type, Messiah, as in this verse.

11. *For they intended evil against thee.* Intended evil; Edwards, *laid out mischief;* Alexander, *stretched out evil.* The meaning is they were intent upon doing mischief, and thought they had made all necessary arrangements to effect his ruin. The imagery is by some thought to be taken from weavers, who warp their yarn, or from archers, who bend their bows. Perhaps the latter is the better. *They imagined a mischievous device.* Calvin: They have devised a stratagem; Edwards: They have contrived a plot; Ainsworth: They have thought a crafty purpose; Fry: They formed a plan; Hengstenberg: They conceived designs; Alexander: They devised a plot. But it was a *device,* which *they are not able* to perform. If this world could be made as the wicked would have it, if they could bring to pass all the evil that is in their hearts, earth would soon differ but little from hell; but they are often as impotent as they are base and malignant. They are always so, when God sees best to restrain them. How true is this verse of the literal David and of Messiah also.

12. *Therefore shalt thou make them turn their back,* when *thou shalt make ready* thine arrows *upon thy strings against the face of them.* The general import of this verse is no doubt given by our version, but the difficulty is in construing the Hebrew, so as fairly to get this sense. Perhaps the word *when* supplied in our version might as well be omitted, and the verse be left as vv. 8, 9, 10, in two distinct clauses. The first clause has several classes of renderings, which may here be noticed. The first substantially agrees with our version. The church of England and Jebb have it, Thou shalt put them to flight; Alexander: For thou shalt make them turn their back. The second is that suggested by the word *shoulder,* as given in the margin of our version. Some would read it, Thou wilt make them turn their *shoulder.* The Hebrew word is commonly in our version rendered *shoulder.* Here as in 1 Sam. ix. 2, where the same word is found, the sense, whether you read *back* or *shoulder,* is the same, equivalent to *put to flight.* But Hengstenberg renders it: For thou wilt make them for shoulder, which he paraphrases thus: Thou wilt transplant them into a condition, that they shall be altogether shoulder, thou wilt chase them in flight. Moller and Brent: Thou wilt make them a shoulder. This may be interpreted as Hengstenberg does his version; The Chaldee: Thou hast set them to thy people one shoulder. Hammond thinks this "signifies sure and uniform slaughter." The third rendering is that of Piscator and Calmet, Thou wilt place them as a heap of earth. The sense is either they shall be as the grave, where the earth is heaped up, or they shall be no more regarded than a heap of earth. The fourth construction is that of several Jewish writers, Thou wilt thrust them into a corner. They contend that the word rendered *back* sometimes signifies a corner. A fifth mode of translation is that of Mudge and Edwards, approved by Dodd and others: Thou wilt make them as Shechem; the original word rendered *back* being *Shechem.* They contend that the phrase is proverbial, and in proof refer to Ps. lx. 6; cviii. 7. The sense, they say, is, Thou shalt subdue them, and portion them out, as formerly the two brothers did Shechem. The sixth rendering is that of Calvin, Venema, Ainsworth, Castellio, Diodati, Pool, Horne and others: Thou wilt set them as a butt. Fry varies a little: Thou dost set them as a target; Horsley: Truly, thou shalt make them a butt for thine arrows. In support they refer to Job vii. 20; xvi. 12; Lam. iii. 12, where the same idea is brought forward. This is perhaps the best rendering. A *shoulder* seems in some way to have come in figurative language to signify a *target,* perhaps as a retreating foe's shoulders were mere targets to the archers. This rendering is favored by

the last clause: When *thou shalt*, or, *Thou shalt make ready* thine arrows *upon thy strings against the face of them*. The imagery seems clearly taken from archery. In explanation of its use here see Ps. vii. 12, 13.

13. *Be thou exalted*, LORD, *in thine own strength*. This rendering agrees with the Chaldee, Septuagint, Ethiopic, Arabic, Syriac, Vulgate, Doway, church of England, Amesius, Piscator, Calmet, Fabritius, Ainsworth, Pool, Brent, Edwards and Jebb. But others vary. Calvin: Raise thyself, O Jehovah, in thy strength; Venema: Thou art high [or mayest thou be high,] Jehovah, in thy strength; Fry: Arise, O Jehovah, in thy strength; Hengstenberg: Praise to thee, O Lord, for thy strength; Alexander: Be high, Jehovah, in thy strength. Calvin, Henry, Scott and Fry regard this clause as a prayer, while Venema and Hengstenberg look upon it as praise. Scott: " This conclusion greatly resembles the first petitions, and closing doxology of the Lord's prayer." Fry: " The prayer of the redeemed of Christ must ever be agreeable with the closing verses of this Psalm: Hallowed be thy name, thy kingdom come, thy will be done in earth as it is in heaven.—So let all thine enemies perish, O Lord: but let them that love HIM be as the sun when he goeth forth in his might." But the parallelism is best preserved by making both clauses of the verse expressive of praise. Hengstenberg's paraphrase of the first member is : " Be exalted in our consciousness, *i. e.*, praise to thee." Alexander: " *Be high*, exalted, both in thyself and in the praises of thy people." The *power* of God both in settling David and Messiah in their respective kingdoms is very illustrious. The Psalmist adds: So *will we sing and praise thy power*. Calvin's rendering is more full: Then we will sing, and celebrate in psalms thy power; Jebb: We will sing, and make a psalm to thy power; Fry: We will sing and chant thy might; Edwards: Let us sing and celebrate thy power. Alexander says the last verb always means to *celebrate* by music. In 1 Chron. xvi. 9, it is rendered *sing psalms;* in Ps. vii. 17; ix. 2, 11; xviii. 49, and many other places it is *sing praise* or *sing praises*.

DOCTRINAL AND PRACTICAL REMARKS.

1. Happy is that people, whose chief magistrate and all whose officers fear God, and joy in his strength, and in his salvation, v. 1. Such blessings are rare, but in a truly pious and patriotic mind they awaken high joy.

2. All effectual deliverances are from God, v. 1. If he saves, we may well defy all foes.

3. There are many reasons why God's people delight in his interpositions and rejoice in his salvation, v. 1. One is that he rescues so effectually. All foes are seen to be harmless. Another is that the deliverance was effected by so unexpected means. Another is that it came in the very nick of time. Nothing could be more seasonable. "God is never a moment too late with his mercies, but he sometimes comes just at the last moment."

4. The Scriptures do not repress or discourage the *highest* religious emotions. We have divine authority for *rejoicing greatly* and for being *exceeding glad*, vv. 1, 6. We may rejoice with joy unspeakable and full of glory. So fear may rise so high that rottenness will enter into our bones, and love be stronger than death, and faith know that its Redeemer liveth. Those, who are truly converted, ought to have *more* religion. The present prevailing type of piety is too low.

5. In prayer the *heart's desire* and the *request of the lips* must agree, v. 2. God can never be pleased with an idle form. There is no substitute for sincerity. The cattle on a thousand hills are as nothing without the heart.

6. When the heart and lips unite in seeking things agreeable to God's will, we may confidently expect speedy answers and great mercies, v. 2. A full record

of gracious answers to prayer would comprise nearly the whole of the history of believers.

7. If God is good to us, we ought to be ready to say so, v. 2. Henry: "God's gracious returns of prayer do, in a special manner, require our humble returns of praise."

8. A large portion of our blessings is given us before our asking or seeking, v. 3. Existence, reason, intellect, a birth in a Christian land, the calling of our nation to the knowledge of Christ, and Christ himself, with many other things, are unsought bestowed on men, as was David's right to the throne on him. No one ever asked for a Saviour till God of his own motion promised "the seed of the woman." God is always *preventing* men *with the blessings of his goodness.* Henry: "When God's blessings come sooner, and prove richer, than we imagine; when they are given before we prayed for them, before we were ready for them, nay, when we feared the contrary; then it may be truly said that he prevented us with them."

9. God is a sovereign over sovereigns, v. 3. He gives crowns and he takes them away. He is King of kings. The mightiest potentate on earth is a worm, a rod, a sword, a curse or a blessing in God's hand, as he is sent in mercy or in wrath.

10. Christ's crown and kingdom shall never be taken from him, vv. 3, 4. He is God's elect to all the ends and offices of a glorious and perpetual mediatorship. His human nature did not aspire to union with the divine; but the divine nature in amazing condescension sought union with the human. Christ is no usurper. He has right and title to all the glories of his everlasting and infinite possessions. Calvin: "The doctrine of the everlasting duration of the kingdom of Christ is, therefore, here established, seeing he was not placed upon the throne by the suffrages of men, but by God, who, from heaven, set the royal crown upon his head with his own hand."

11. It is lawful to pray for the continuance of life, v. 4. David did it. Hezekiah did it. Christ did it. We may pray earnestly for such a blessing; yet we must pray submissively, always adding as did our Lord, Nevertheless, not my will but thine be done, O Father. Life is not an absolute good. It is not a good of itself, as pardon and renewal and glory are. It is only a good when God makes it so. For several reasons and on several occasions we may greatly desire life. One is when wicked attempts are made to take it away, as in the case of David. Another is when we are in the midst of our days, and our departure out of the world would frustrate some important purpose, as the education of our children, or the accomplishment of some great design for the public good. The love of life, if not inordinate, is neither unnatural, a weakness, nor a sin.

12. God often gives more than we ask, v. 4. David asked for life and got majesty, and honor, and glory. The same is strikingly illustrated in Solomon, 2 Chron. i. 10–12, and in the case of every truly pious man, Mat. vi. 33. Nevins prayed for years that he might write *one* tract. Who can tell the good he has done with his pen? Heaven will be more blessed, the crown of righteousness brighter, the weight of glory heavier, the rest of heaven sweeter, than any mortal ever dared to hope or was able to conceive.

13. Full of Christ are the minds of the prophets! Easily they pass from all other subjects to the person and kingdom of Messiah, from the types to the anti-type, vv. 3, 4. To them no theme seems so welcome as that of "Him who is to come." To true piety it is pleasant to find the Saviour everywhere spoken of. Well did Jesus on his way to Emmaus begin at Moses and all the prophets, and expound to his disciples in all the Scriptures the things concerning himself, Luke xxiv. 27; see also Acts iii. 24. Surely the Old Testament contains much more of Christ than some admit. Parts of this Psalm can never receive any but a flat and meager interpretation, unless they are

applied to Christ, yet it is never once quoted for any purpose in the New Testament, though it may perhaps be once or twice alluded to, as in Heb. ii. 9; xii. 2.

14. The more manifestly our deliverances are from God, the greater may be our glorying, v. 5. Dickson: " Nothing can make men more glorious, even before the world, than God's owning them before the world, and putting respect upon them." No small part of the glory of the redeemed in the day of judgment will arise from the fact that God and Christ will then *publicly* treat them as friends.

15. It is a joy to believers that they never can be in a worse condition than some who have gone before them, and who have been rescued, delivered, glorified, vv. 4, 5. See David hardly escaping the jaws of death for years, yea, see Christ crowned with thorns, disowned with every mark of malice and ignominy, tried, condemned, crucified, dead and buried. Yet God saved them from all at last. Believer, thou canst never be lower than some good men, who have gone before thee, never so burdened and afflicted as was thy Redeemer. Yet he is alive for evermore, yea, he is over all blessed forever.

16. There is no point of honor so high that God cannot, if he choose, raise us to it, v. 5. He takes the poor from the dunghill and sets him among princes. He takes David from the sheep-cote and puts him on the most dazzling throne on earth. Jesus receives from God the Father glory and honor, and from the sepulchre of Joseph he ascends to the throne of the universe. Let no virtuous, pious soul fear anything. God is on its side.

17. What a glorious person is the Lord Jesus Christ! v. 5. All honor, majesty, glory, comeliness centre in him. He is THE WONDERFUL.

18. All history, all experience, all observation, unite with all inspired writings in saying that out of evil comes good; out of weakness, strength; out of sorrow, joy; out of trouble, glory. The whole history of David and of Messiah, as brought out in this Psalm, shows this.

19. When God begins truly to bless, it is commonly the signal for a long series of amazing mercies, v. 6. Dickson: " God will never make an end of blessing whom he will bless."

20. Men may gauge the dimensions of most blessings which are purely temporal, but who can tell the value of any mercy which possesses the attribute of eternity? vv. 4, 6.

21. The plaudits of millions may soon be followed with an eternal overthrow; but the favoring providences, the comforting communion, and the inestimable blessings expressed by God's *countenance*, shall appear more and more valuable, the longer duration lasts, the more thoroughly fair tests are applied, and the more fully causes have their course, v. 6.

22. Jehovah is himself an all-sufficient good, v. 7. He who has God for his God, needs no more. Calvin: " The world turns round as it were upon a wheel, by which it comes to pass, that those who were raised to the very top are precipitated to the bottom in a moment; but it is here promised, that the kingdom of Judah, and the kingdom of Christ, of which it is a type, will be exempted from such vicissitude. Let us remember, that those only who have the firmness and stability here promised, who betake themselves to the bosom of God by an assured faith, and relying upon his mercy, commit themselves to his protection."

23. As in the divine plan the kingdom of David was inwoven with that of Messiah, so is the inheritance of every believer with that of his Redeemer. God could not break covenant with his people without breaking covenant with his Son. The saints are heirs of God and joint-heirs with Jesus Christ. They are one in him. Because he lives they shall live also, v. 7. Compare Ps. cxxv. 1.

24. The wicked of all ages are alike. They are the *enemies* and *haters* of good men. of Christ and of God, v. 8. The sentence, "his enemies shall lick the dust," is perfectly righteous and wholly necessary. There never was so unreasonable and wicked aversion as that which turns sinners away from God, his Christ, his people and his laws, Rom. viii. 7. All this hatred is "without a cause." Nothing can justify it.

25. The Lord will so govern the world as shall finally, infallibly and universally lead to the detection, arrest and punishment of his foes, v. 8. Even in this life they seldom wholly escape. But full and final exposure and retribution are reserved for another world. The open blasphemer, the cunning hypocrite, the profane and the unbelieving moralist shall find that there is a God who judgeth in the earth, Mark iv. 22; Luke viii. 17. There is no worse logic than that which from divine forbearance infers impunity. The defeat and overthrow of the enemies of the literal David were mere shadowings forth of what shall befall the haters of Messiah. Rocks and mountains cannot hide from the wrath of the Lamb.

26. It is right that a time of mercy abused should be followed by a *time of anger*, v. 9. The day of judgment cannot possibly be postponed. The day is appointed. To none more than to those who scoff at sacred things will it seem to come with awful speed and suddenness.

27. The doom of the wicked will be exceedingly terrible, v. 9. The history of the Jews "from the siege and sack of Jerusalem to this day, awfully warns every one, not to entail misery on his descendants, and bring destruction on himself, by opposing the Redeemer's kingdom, or neglecting his salvation. The discoveries however which will be made, and the vengeance which will be executed, at the day of judgment, on every enemy of Christ, will form the most tremendous comment on this Psalm."

28. As in an *oven* every combustible thing helps to destroy and consume everything like itself, so does one wicked man help to destroy others, though like the brand in the oven he finally perishes himself, v. 9.

29. Why do not the wicked believe the dreadful things here threatened against them? Is there not an unaccountable mystery in their slumbers? They have fair warnings in Scripture, v. 9 and in many events, and in many states of their own minds. Morison: "In ten thousand ways God can and does still terrify his incorrigible foes. He blights their schemes of ambition and pride; he withers their prospects in life; he cuts down the desire of their eyes; he dries up the stream of their comfort; he makes their beauty consume like the moth; and withal he sends awful terrors into their conscience, making them pine away under the touch of his anger, and causing their very hearts within them to "*burn like a fiery oven*." There are infallible signs of a coming storm. Why do not men discern them?

30. The coming destruction of the wicked will be total. It will *swallow them up*. It will *devour them*, v. 9. It will leave them neither root nor branch. It will leave them no peace, no joy, no hope, no comfort, no recreation, no amusement, no means of escape, no means of grace, no gospel, no heart to pray, no room for prayer, no Saviour, no Comforter, no God. Even their souls will be lost.

31. There must be something to mortals inconceivably dreadful and malignant in the nature of sin to make its dire consequences reach so far, even to all a man's works, and labors, yea, and even to his posterity, v. 10. Dickson: "After the Lord's vengeance is come upon the enemies of Christ's kingdom, his curse shall follow the works of their hands, and upon whatsoever they sought to make themselves happy by in their life: and his vengeance shall follow upon their posterity, till he have rooted out their memorial from among men." Calvin: "It is a doctrine common enough in Scripture, that God not only inflicts punishment upon the first originators of wickedness, but makes it even to overflow into the bosom of their children," Isa lxv. 6. 7.

All that forsake the Lord shall be ashamed; and they that depart from him shall be written in the earth, Jer. xvii. 13.

32. No man can do his duty to his offspring, nor give a good account of himself or of them in the last day, unless he is at heart a friend and servant of God. Without love to God how can he bring up his children in the nurture and admonition of the Lord? And yet "there is a blessing attending the religious training of families, which extendeth itself often to many generations; but there is also an equally general curse attendant upon the unhappy neglect of family religion. Impiety seems in many families to be a sort of entail upon the wretched descendants."

33. Endless are the *devices* of wicked men, v. 11. Craft and cunning and artifice seem to be the necessary fruit of depravity. Sin is in its nature tortuous and guileful. It is essentially a lie. It is wonderful that the righteous escape the snares spread and the pits dug for them. But the wicked *are not able to perform* the half of the *evil they intend.*

34. Wicked as may be the lives of ungodly men, their intentions are still worse, v. 11. Their hearts are the worst part about them. This is not all. The worse they are, the better they often think themselves to be. Even when they persecute the innocent, they do it under some false charge or pretext.

35. Bold, daring and impudent as the wicked may be now, in the end they will all prove cowards and *turn the back,* v. 12.

36. Nothing is more vain than the war waged by the wicked. He, who attempts to face the arrows of the Almighty will but prove himself a monument of folly.

37. The salvation of the church or of any of her members is not by power inherent in the creature, but only by the *strength* of Jehovah, v. 13.

38. It is a mark of true piety to have and evince a good will to Zion and her head, to wish well to the people and kingdom of Messiah, v. 13.

39. Good cause of continual praise and thanksgiving have all the people of God, v. 13. There is not an hour, a state, a condition, a sorrow, a temptation, or a pang, but that God's children still have far more reason for joy than for grief. If they can say no more they can shout and sing, The Lord God omnipotent reigneth: Jesus lives: All things work together for good to them that love God.

40. Christ is the wonderful! On earth he was a pattern of all virtues, of all goodness, of all excellence. In him still dwells all fulness of grace and truth. But his sorrows are all ended. He is now of a long time full of ineffable joy. Indeed his joy is made the measure and sum of heavenly bliss. "Enter thou into the joy of thy Lord." Matt. xxv. 21. Scott: "If David rejoiced greatly in the honor conferred on him, as king of Israel; what is the joy of our Redeemer in his exaltation to the mediatorial throne, and in the salvation of his people! And if Israel, from love to David and his auspicious government, rejoiced, and praised God for him, how great should be our joy to behold by faith our Brother and Friend thus glorified, and our praises for all the blessings we may expect from him."

PSALM XXII.

To the chief Musician upon Aijeleth Shahar, A Psalm of David.

1 MY God, my God, why hast thou forsaken me? *why art thou so* far from helping me, *and from* the words of my roaring?

2 O my God, I cry in the day-time, but thou hearest not; and in the night season, and am not silent.

3 But thou *art* holy, *O thou* that inhabitest the praises of Israel.

4 Our fathers trusted in thee: they trusted, and thou didst deliver them.

5 They cried unto thee, and were delivered: they trusted in thee, and were not confounded.

6 But I *am* a worm, and no man; a reproach of men, and despised of the people.

7 All they that see me laugh me to scorn: they shoot out the lip, they shake the head, *saying,*

8 He trusted on the LORD *that* he would deliver him: let him deliver him, seeing he delighted in him.

9 But thou *art* he that took me out of the womb: thou didst make me hope *when I was* upon my mother's breasts.

10 I was cast upon thee from the womb: thou *art* my God from my mother's belly.

11 Be not far from me; for trouble *is* near; for *there is* none to help.

12 Many bulls have compassed me: strong *bulls* of Bashan have beset me round.

13 They gaped upon me *with* their mouths, *as* a ravening and a roaring lion.

14 I am poured out like water, and all my bones are out of joint: my heart is like wax; it is melted in the midst of my bowels.

15 My strength is dried up like a potsherd; and my tongue cleaveth to my jaws; and thou hast brought me into the dust of death.

16 For dogs have compassed me: the assembly of the wicked have inclosed me: they pierced my hands and my feet.

17 I may tell all my bones: they look *and* stare upon me.

18 They part my garments among them, and cast lots upon my vesture.

19 But be not thou far from me, O LORD: O my strength, haste thee to help me.

20 Deliver my soul from the sword; my darling from the power of the dog.

21 Save me from the lion's mouth: for thou hast heard me from the horns of the unicorns.

22 I will declare thy name unto my brethren: in the midst of the congregation will I praise thee.

23 Ye that fear the LORD, praise him; all ye the seed of Jacob, glorify him; and fear him, all ye the seed of Israel.

24 For he hath not despised nor abhorred the affliction of the afflicted: neither hath he hid his face from him; but when he cried unto him, he heard.

25 My praise *shall be* of thee in the great congregation: I will pay my vows before them that fear him.

26 The meek shall eat and be satisfied: they shall praise the LORD that seek him: your heart shall live for ever.

27 All the ends of the world shall remember and turn unto the LORD: and all the kindreds of the nations shall worship before thee.

28 For the kingdom *is* the LORD's: and he *is* the governor among the nations.

29 All *they that be* fat upon earth shall eat and worship: all they that go down to the dust shall bow before him: and none can keep alive his own soul.

30 A seed shall serve him; it shall be accounted to the Lord for a generation.

31 They shall come, and shall declare his righteousness unto a people that shall be born, that he hath done *this.*

THIS Psalm may be called THE GOSPEL ACCORDING TO DAVID. For an explanation of the words, *To the Chief Musician,* and *A Psalm of David,* see above on titles of Psalm iii., iv. The remainder of the title, *Upon Aijeleth Shahar,* occurs in no other Psalm. *Aijeleth* is not found in the Hebrew Bible except here and in Prov. v. 19; Jer. xiv. 5, where it is rendered *hind*. *Shahar* is in Gen. xix. 15; Ps. cxxxix. 9; Cant. vi. 10, and frequently rendered *morning;* in Job xxxviii. 12, *day-spring*. Instead of *Upon Aijeleth Shahar*, the margin has it, *Upon the hind of the morning*. So also Calvin, Fabritius, Rivet, Moller, Pool, Hammond and Alexander. Ainsworth: Concerning the Hind of the morning; Hengstenberg: On the hind of the morning-twilight; Mudge and Edwards: To the morning-hind. Those who give these renderings are not agreed as to the import of the phrase. Calvin: "I think it highly probable that it was the beginning of some common song; nor do I see how the inscription bears any relation to the subject-matter of the Psalm." Pool thinks it is given "to note that the person here designed was like a *hind*, comely and meek, and every way lovely, but withal persecuted by wicked men, and that oftentimes is *in the morning*, when she comes out of her lurking and lodging-place, and when the hunters used to go abroad to their work. Or this was the title of some musical instrument, or tune, or song, which was usually sung in the morning." Ainsworth thinks it "means *Christ*, who as a *hind* was by Jews and Gentiles, the *dogs*, v. 7, hunted and worried in the morning, John xviii. 28, and also rose from death early in the morning, John xx. 1, when God had made his feet like hinds' feet, and set him on his high places, Ps. xviii. 33." Hengstenberg: "It will be very readily admitted that the *hind* is a very appropriate emblem of the suffering and persecuted righteous man who meets us in this Psalm. . . That the *hind* may be a figurative expression significant of suffering innocence is put beyond a doubt by the fact, that the wicked and the persecutors in this Psalm, *whose peculiar physiognomy is marked by emblems drawn from the brute creation*, are designated by the terms *dogs, lions, bulls*," etc. Alexander: "The *hind* may be a poetical figure for persecuted innocence, and the *morning*, or rather *dawn* for deliverance after long distress;" Hammond: "The title, belonging primarily to David in time of his persecution, very fitly also belongs to Christ at his crucifixion." Instead of the foregoing, Piscator and Amesius read, At [or To] the early morning. There seems to be nothing sufficient to bear out this rendering. Jebb does not translate it, but says, "What is there to hinder us from supposing that *Aijeleth* may mean a harp of *Aijilon*," though he says he is "utterly unable to assign any probable meaning to the epithet *Shahar*." Horsley renders it, "Concerning the interposition of the darkness." It is not easy to see how such a rendering was reached, even if the Psalm be allowed to refer to "THE HOUR OF DARKNESS." Fry thinks it probable that it "refers to some direction concerning the music or tune." Chaldee: "For the strong oblation, perpetual to the morning;" or, For the mighty continual morning sacrifice. The whole caption of the Syriac is: A Psalm "of David, when he was mocked by his persecutors. Also concerning the passion of Christ, and the calling of the Gentiles;" Arabic: "Spoken by him when he had subdued his enemies. Also a prophecy respecting the crucifixion." But the Septuagint, Ethiopic, Vulgate, Symmachus, Bellarmine, Calmet and the Doway read, For the morning protection, or, For the help of the morning; Street: An earnest petition for aid. From the resemblance of the word *Aijeleth* to another Hebrew word, Fenwick would render it *strength*, and so read *The strength of the morning*. He thinks it relates to Christ as the bright and morning star, the day-spring from on high. Luke i. 78; Rev. xxii. 16. The various plausible opinions reached by different writers may be thus summed up.

1. The words in question are by some supposed to designate the choir, who should sing the piece. Such would read the whole title thus: "A Psalm of David, addressed to the music-master, who presides over the band called the Morning Hind." So Calmet and others.

2. Some suppose these words designate a piece of music, well known in the service

of the tabernacle by the name of *Aijeleth Shahar*. This view is favored by Abenezra, Gesenius and Calvin. Pool does not wholly reject it.

3. Others think *Aijeleth Shahar* is the name of a musical instrument. This view is favored by Jarchi and Kimchi. "And Leo Mutinens, an Israelite of great learning, goes so far as to say that *Aijeleth Shahar* was the particular musical instrument which the mourning women used on account of distress which was sudden, not known till it came, as a man does not think of the morning till he sees it." This view is favored by Jebb.

4. Others think the title contains the subject-matter of the Psalm. See names already cited and the various opinions expressed favoring this view.

The sympathies of the pious naturally incline them to favor the last view especially if the Psalm is applied in any distinct manner to Christ. But Harmer and Clarke have showed at some length that it is customary in the East to give pleasing titles to odes without the slightest regard to their subject-matter. After the fullest investigation the author has been able to make, he inclines to the opinion that no key to the interpretation of the Psalm can be obtained from the title, that either of the foregoing views is harmless, that the whole subject is likely to remain involved in uncertainty, and that it is probable that *Aijeleth Shahar* in some way relates to the *music*. Calvin, speaking of the views differing from his own, says: "I find no solidity in these subtleties." Clarke says: "To me many seem to have spent their time uselessly in the investigation of such subjects;" Calmet: "Many titles of the Psalms are covered up in great darkness. This one is beset with peculiar difficulties. Interpreters speak as if they were divining, and nothing at all uniform or settled is found in their views."

A question of much more importance is, "*Of whom speaketh the prophet this? of himself, or some other man?*" The sense and import of the whole depend on our answer to this question. The devices of interpretation have been very numerous. Jahn applies this Psalm to Hezekiah; Hitzig, to Jeremiah; some Jews, to Esther and her people in captivity, she being their head; other Jews, among whom is Rabbi David, to the present humiliating condition of the Jewish church, which though formerly famous, shining like a star, or the brightness of the morning, now lies forsaken and in obscurity; and some Jews and Christians, to the true Israel of God of all ages. It would hardly edify the reader to enter into a formal refutation of these opinions. It is as clear as words can make it that the Psalm speaks, not of bodies of people, but of an individual sufferer. Hezekiah and Jeremiah lived long after this Psalm was composed; and many of the things expressly stated in this Psalm never happened to either of them. Some others think that this Psalm refers to the personal history of David, and was all therein fulfilled. What part of his life is specially referred to is not agreed on. Some suppose it was his persecutions under Saul, especially as stated in 1 Sam. xxiii. 25, 26. Others think it refers to the perils into which he was brought in the rebellion of Absalom. Some, who hold this view, do not deny that in the higher sense some parts of the Psalm have their fulfilment in Christ. But many of the things here mentioned never at any time happened to David. There are three other views, either of which may substantially admit the application of the Psalm to Christ, but which nevertheless are not all equally good. The first is that of Hengstenberg: "While all existing interpretations are thus encumbered with serious difficulties, we make our escape at once, and completely from the region of embarrassment and constraint, if we consider the Psalm as referring to *the ideal person of the Righteous One*—a character which is introduced more frequently throughout the Psalms than any other, so that nothing but ignorance can object to this interpretation that it is an arbitrary one." So also Alexander: "The immediate speaker in the Psalm is an ideal person, the righteous servant of Jehovah, but his words may, to a certain extent, be appropriated by any suffering believer, and by the whole suffering church, as they have been in all ages." There are serious objections to this mode of expounding the Psalm. 1. It is confessedly novel. It was never heard of till the time of Hengstenberg, as himself informs us. 2. It is quite unnecessary. Every part of the Psalms can be well explained without it. This has been done for thousands of years. 3. It is a dangerous invention, very liable to abuse. In the hands of so evangelical, judicious and learned men as those just quoted it may be harmless. But when adopted by sound men it will probably soon be resorted to by those of an opposite character, and with a little ingenuity be applied to the wresting of many Scriptures. 4. It is a bad sign that instead of good strong arguments in its favor Hengstenberg uses such words as these: "Nothing but ignorance can object to this interpretation." It is proper to state distinctly that Alexander says this Psalm "is so framed as to be applied without violence to any case belonging to the class described, yet so that it was fully verified only in Christ, the head and representative of the class in question." Hengstenberg also says: "Every previous fulfilment pointed forward to a perfect one yet to come. By those in whom hope in the Messiah was in all circumstances a living one, this could be expected only in him. . . As the glory of God will be in proportion to the salvation vouchsafed, it must be in the time of the Messiah that this will for the first time appear in all its extent and depth, as here described." So that the result of this modern German invention is not *necessarily* against the most thoroughly evangelical views of the Psalm.

Another mode of explanation is that adopted in this work in regard to some of the previous Psalms, commonly called the *Typical-Messianic* plan. It supposes David to be here a type of the Messiah, and that things are said which cannot but very remotely, if at all, have any truth in application to the type, but are fully true of the antitype alone, yet that so much is literally true of the type as fitly to make him a figure of him that was to come. This is the view of Calvin, Melancthon, Fabritius, Calmet, Amyrald, Diodati, Rivet, Venema, Edwards, Dickson, Patrick and Hammond. That the reader may see the precise grounds of these authors, let us hear some of them: Calvin: "David sets before us, in his own person, a type of Christ, who he knew by the Spirit of prophecy behooved to be abased in marvellous and unusual ways previous to his exaltation by the Father." Calmet: "By occasion of his own griefs and sorrows David has here described the passion, death, burial and resurrection of Messiah, the calling of the Gentiles, and the rise of the church. This is his first and chief object. If he does now and then speak of himself, he does so only as he is a figure of Jesus Christ; but in many places David himself is entirely lost sight of." Fabritius: "Although we cannot doubt that David composed this Psalm from a consideration of his own most grievous afflictions, and so in some sense this composition suits him personally; yet it is also certain that it has respect to something beyond his own person, and that being led on by the Spirit of prophecy, even at the very time when he was writing this Psalm, he spread out before God his complaints and prayers, his whole mind and thought were carried by the Holy Spirit from a view and sense of his present griefs and calamities to a prophecy respecting the passion, death, resurrection, glory and spread of the kingdom of Christ, of whom he was not ignorant that he himself was a type." Venema: "Weighty reasons demand that the Psalm be applied both to David and to the Messiah, so that no course is left but to unite both as the subject of the Psalm, David *directly* and in a primary sense, Messiah *indirectly* and in the more inward sense."

The last mode of explication is that of applying the Psalm directly, entirely and exclusively to Christ. This view was taken by many in the primitive church, by

Ainsworth, Piscator, Amesius, Calovius, Bellarmine, Fenwick, Gill, Henry, Horne, Horsley, Scott, Stevenson and others.   Justin Martyr: "The whole Psalm is spoken of Christ."   Tertullian says it contains an account of "the whole passion of Christ." Theodoret: "The testimony of all the evangelists, and of the apostle Paul, and the words of the Psalm itself most clearly evince that whatsoever things are spoken in it are to be expounded of our Lord Christ."   He says Christians should not doubt or question this view.   Indeed when a celebrated critic, Theodore of Mopsuesta, denied that this Psalm had its literal fulfilment in Christ, he was condemned by the second council of Constantinople, which was the fifth general council.   Ainsworth: "Christ speaketh this Psalm to God his Father;"   Piscator: "This Psalm is *prophetical*.   For it contains a prophecy of the sufferings and death of Christ, as also of his resurrection and spiritual kingdom.   But this prophecy is by that figure of speech called personification, so that Christ himself is introduced as speaking, and even as hanging on the cross;"   Gill: "It is plain that a single person is spoken of throughout; and he is manifestly distinguished from others, from his brethren, from the congregation, from the seed of Jacob and Israel, vv. 22, 23, and indeed, no other than the Messiah can be meant: and of this there ought to be no doubt with Christians;"   Henry: "The Spirit of Christ, which was in the prophets, testifies in this Psalm, as clearly and fully as anywhere else in all the Old Testament, *the sufferings of Christ and the glory that should follow;* (1 Pet. i. 11) of him, no doubt, David here speaks, and not of himself, or any other man;"   Scott: "No reasonable doubt can be made, that our Lord should be considered as the speaker, throughout this whole prophetical Psalm. It may even be questioned, whether David had any reference to his own case in it; as everything is applicable to Christ, and most things utterly inapplicable to David;" Horsley: "It seems to be the best account that can be given of this Psalm, to say that the Psalmist personates the Messiah in the garden; first, oppressed with the foresight of the circumstances of his sufferings; then comforted with the assurance of exaltation."   Indeed Hengstenberg himself says: "The view which has always obtained throughout the Christian church, is that, which refers the Psalm directly and exclusively to *Christ*.   The author by no means regrets that he adopted this view in his Christology.   It was the easiest and most natural of those, which were then before the world, to which his attention was more immediately directed."

These remarks from several authors sufficiently explain what is meant by saying that the Psalm applies entirely, directly and exclusively to Christ.   If any ask how he *speaks* here, the answer is, by David personating Christ.   This has been already stated.   It is also given by Amesius: "The subject of this Psalm is nothing else than a prayer presented to God by David, representing the person of Christ."

In confirmation of this latter view the following reasons are assigned.   1. The ancient Jews did not deny that this Psalm referred to the Messiah, just as they admitted that Gen. xlix. 10 and Isa. liii. 2–12 applied to him.   Their device of turning it at all from him dates since the establishment of the Christian religion. 2. With the ancient Jews agree the primitive Christians.   It would be surprising, if the whole church for hundreds of years both before and after the coming of Christ was mistaken about so important a prophecy as this.   3. Let any man give his reasons for applying Isaiah liii. 2–12 directly and exclusively to Christ, and he will find that a parity of reasoning will go far to make the same disposition of the whole of this Psalm.   4. Parts of this Psalm can, in no way but by a very meager interpretation, be applied to any but Christ.   5. There is no part of the Psalm that may not be applied to Messiah.   6. The scope of the whole composition requires this. 7. Many parts of it are expressly applied to Christ in the New Testament, Matt. xxvii. 46; Mark xv. 34.   In the same chapter of Matthew, v. 35, and in John xix.

24 the evangelists show that v. 18 of this Psalm was fulfilled at the crucifixion. Matthew also tells that v. 8 of this Psalm contains the very words of taunt and bitterness used by Christ's murderers, Matt. xxvii. 43. The whole history of the crucifixion shows the fulfilment of that clause in v. 16. *They pierced my hands and my feet.* Now crucifixion was not a Jewish but a Roman punishment. Paul in Heb. ii. 12 arguing on the humanity and sufferings of Christ expressly applies to him the whole of v. 22. Immediately on his resurrection Christ calls the disciples "my brethren," Matt. xxviii. 10; John xx. 17, 'n fulfilment of the twenty-second verse of this Psalm. Indeed it would be hard to frame any argument proving any prophecy directly and exclusively Messianic, if this is not so.

But some may ask, Have individual believers no interest in this Psalm? May they never adopt any of these words as their own? The answer is that any child of God may properly adopt any of the language of this Psalm that suits his case; just as any follower of Christ may properly use any petition offered by Christ when on earth, if it expresses his own holy desires, such as, "Father forgive them, they know not what they do;" "O my Father, if it be possible, let this cup pass from me: nevertheless, not as I will, but as thou wilt;" "Father, into thy hands I commend my spirit." Nor is this all. Believers have communion with Christ in his sufferings, so that Paul is very bold and says, "The sufferings of Christ abound in us," 2 Cor. i. 5. Indeed we have the best authority for praying that we may "know Christ and the power of his resurrection, and the fellowship of his sufferings." As God delivered Christ, so will he save all his people. Jesus says, "Because I live, ye shall live also." Death itself shall not hold the redeemed but till the appointed time, for, "them that sleep in Jesus will God bring with him."

There is no reason for doubting that David is the author of this Psalm. The few, who have held or hinted a contrary opinion, have stated nothing that was even plausible in support of their novelty.

Scott dates this Psalm B. C. 1060, and Clarke, B. C. 1058.

There is no good reason for supposing that any particular event in the life of David caused the writing of this ode.

The names of the Most High found in this Psalm are *El God, Eloah God, Jehovah* LORD, and *Adonai Lord*, on which respectively see on Ps. v. 4; xviii. 31; i. 2; ii. 4.

1. *My God, my God, why hast thou forsaken me? My God*, Hebrew *El*. The Septuagint, Ethiopic, Arabic, Vulgate and Doway, after *my God*, have *look upon me*. This is without authority. The whole of this clause was repeated by Christ on the cross (Matt. xxvii. 46; Mark xv. 34); only that for the Hebrew verb he used a word in the Syro-Chaldaic, which was then commonly spoken; but both Matthew and Mark in explaining the cry of our Saviour use the verb here employed by the Septuagint, rendered *hast forsaken*. Instead of *hast forsaken* Venema and Street read *hast deserted*. According to the modern theological use of words this is the better rendering, though in our version it is never given *desert*, but commonly *leave, leave off, leave destitute, fail, forsake*, Gen. xxiv. 27; xxxix. 12; Ruth ii. 20; Ps. ix. 10; xxxviii. 10. The sense seems to be, Why hast thou *failed* me? *left* me *destitute*. Christ was innocent and holy, kept the law and perfectly pleased his Father, yet when he took the place of sinners, assumed their guilt and bore their punishment, then the wicked of earth and hell were let loose upon him, his friends hid as it were their faces from him, and even his Father left him without succor from the tormentors, and worse than all without his own comfortable presence. He felt the dreadful sting of sin, the sword of justice, the fire of wrath. Christ is often called a *mysterious sufferer*, and so he was. In his sorrows were manifested love so amazing, condescension so unparalleled, holiness so spotless, justice so inflexible, wisdom so boundless that without the explana-

tions of Scripture we could know nothing satisfactory on the subject. Dreadful as were our Lord's sufferings he felt no remorse, for he was innocent, and no despair, for he still pleaded his covenant with the Father, saying, *My God, my God.* Faith may be very vigorous, when comfort is all gone. The misery of the man of Uz was at its height when he said, Though he slay me, yet will I trust in him, Job xiii. 15. There is no better evidence of piety than that given by him, who fears God and obeys his voice, while he walks in darkness and has no light. No man more than such a one has a good warrant for trusting in the Lord, Is. l. 10. God never made a more important communication to Abraham respecting the nation that should descend from him than when "a horror of great darkness had fallen upon him," Gen. xv. 12–16. When the sun goes down the stars appear. When God hides his face, faith looks to the promises, the oath, the covenant. It is evident, therefore, that there are two ways in which God may forsake or desert a creature. One consists in a total and final withdrawal of all his mercies; the other, in a withdrawal of his animating, soul-cheering presence, which, however it may express his punitive displeasure at the time, shall be followed by marvellous mercies. There are also two very different modes of asking the question, *Why hast thou forsaken me?* One is a bold defiant mode of declaring all one's sufferings unjust. This Christ never did. The other is an humble, submissive, believing mode of addressing our cries and complaints to God. Christ knew that he was the substitute for sinners and that he was suffering for others. But his human nature was ready to sink under the load of our sins, and under the hidings of his Father's face, and he encouraged himself in this pious and natural way. The complaint expresses the same state of pious distress, of which we read in Matt. xxvi. 39, 42. He adds: Why art thou so *far from helping me,* and from *the words of my roaring?* Our translators have here supplied several words. The Chaldee: Far from my redemption are the words of my crying, *i. e.,* my words of crying do not bring deliverance. The rendering of the Septuagint, Ethiopic, Vulgate and Doway is quite inadmissible: Far from my salvation are the words of my sins. The authors of the Doway feel that some explanation is called for and therefore give this note: " *The words of my sins.* That is, the sins of the world, which I have taken upon myself, cry out against me, and are the cause of all my sufferings." Though this note quite relieves the shock, which such a rendering is fitted to give, yet the construction is forced. Still worse if possible is the rendering of the Syriac: Thou hast put my salvation far from me on account of the words of my follies. Equally bad is the Arabic: Thou art far removed from my salvation on account of the language of my foolishness. The word rendered *roaring* in our version never signifies *fault, sin, folly,* or *foolishness.* In our version it is uniformly rendered *roaring.* The language seems to be borrowed from the roar of the lion, Jud. xiv. 5; Isa. v. 29; Jer. ii. 15; Hos. xi. 10; Amos iii. 4; Zeph. iii. 3; Ps. xxii. 13. Mant: "It is often applied to the deep groaning of men in sickness." Calvin: Why art thou far from my help, and from the words of my roaring? Hare and Lowth: Why art thou so far from my cry, from the words of my roaring? Quite a number, among whom are Amesius, Ainsworth, Edwards, Street, Jebb, Hengstenberg and Alexander read the whole verse in one sentence, and as one continued question, thus avoiding the repetition of *Why?* But our English version gives the full sense, preserves the parallelism in the verse, and is to be preferred.

2. *O my God, I cry in the day-time, but thou hearest not; and in the night season, and am not silent.* *My God,* as in the preceding verse, see on Ps. v. 4. *Cry,* the same as in Ps. iii. 4; xviii. 3; and often *call.* Either rendering is approved. *Day* and *night,* equivalent to *continually* and *earnestly.* Christ led a remarkable life of prayer, Matt. xxvi. 39, 42, 44; Mark i. 35; xiv. 35, 39; Luke iii. 21; v. 16; vi.

12; ix. 18, 29; xi. 1; xxii. 32, 41; Heb. v. 7. But no prayer of faith ever seemed for a season to be less answered than that of Christ. The blessing sought may not come in the time or manner most agreeable to flesh and blood, and it may seem as if our prayer was not heard at all. The phrase, *am not silent*, is perhaps not so well rendered in our version. Still worse is that of the Septuagint, Ethiopic, Vulgate, Doway: *It shall not be reputed folly in me.* But the Chaldee has it, There is no silence to me. This is followed by the Margin of our version, by Calvin, Amesius, Piscator, Ainsworth, Rivet, Pool and Alexander. The sense as given by Calvin is that the sufferer experienced no comfort or solace, nothing which could impart tranquillity. The parallelism requires that it correspond to *hearest not* in the first member of the verse. Waterland, Street, Hammond and Fry: *I have no rest;* Jebb: *There is no rest to me;* Edwards: *I have no respite from my misery;* Horsley: *No relief is given me;* Syriac: *Thou attendest not to me;* Arabic: *Thou hast not heard me;* Hengstenberg: *I am not silenced;* which he says, "is exactly parallel to *thou answerest not,*" as he renders the verb in the first clause. Dreadful were the agonies of Christ. Never was there such praying. Never was there so great apparent cause for discouragement in prayer. Yet the Father heard him always.

3. *But thou* art *holy,* O thou *that inhabitest the praises of Israel.* The Septuagint and kindred versions: But thou dwellest in the holy place, the praise of Israel; church of England: And thou continuest holy, O thou worship of Israel; Arabic: And yet thou dwellest in the holy places, O thou glory of Israel; Syriac: And thou, O holy one, art also sitting [as King on his throne] in Israel thy glory; Venema: For thou art holy, inhabiting the splendid praises of Israel; Amesius and Piscator: But thou art holy, continuing, the perfect praise of Israel; Ainsworth: Thou art holy, sitting, the praises of Israel; Edwards: Yet thou art the holy one that dwellest amongst the praises of Israel; Pool: But thou abidest holy, O thou who art the praises of Israel; Jebb: But thou continuest holy, thou that art the praise of Israel; Fry: Yet thou sittest in the sanctuary, the praise of Israel; Horsley: Yet thou, inhabiting holiness, art (the theme of) Israel's praise; Boothroyd: But thou inhabitest the sanctuary, amidst the praises of Israel; Hengstenberg: And thou art holy, sitting enthroned on Israel's praise; Calvin: Yet thou art holy, who inhabitest the praises of Israel; Alexander; And thou (art) holy inhabiting the praises of Israel. Street makes vv. 5, 6 a part of some well-known song of praise, quoted into this Psalm, and reads:

> But, O thou that inhabitest the sanctuary,
> The songs of Israel are,—
> " In thee our fathers trusted," etc.

But in this he seems not to be supported by reason, or authority. The best sense and that well sustained every way is that of our version, Calvin, Edwards, Hengstenberg and Alexander. The word rendered *inhabit* occurs in the sense of *sit* in Ps. i. 1; ii. 4; xxix. 10; cx. 1; *dwell* in Ps. ix. 11; xxiii. 6; ci. 7; cxxxii. 14; *abide, endure,* in Ps. ix. 7; lxi. 7. The participle in the plural is commonly rendered *inhabitants.* *Praises,* uniformly rendered. The conception is that the holy God, as king sits enthroned in the midst of the praises of Israel. Thus explained the whole verse may express either Christ's amazement at innocence suffering as he did under the government of a *just* and *holy* God; or, it is a strengthening of himself by reflecting that as God is *holy,* so in the end all will come right. There is no objection to including both of these ideas. The same general view may be taken of the force of the next verse:

4. *Our fathers trusted in thee: they trusted, and thou didst deliver them.* *Trusted,*

found twice in this verse and once in the next, commonly so rendered, also *hoped*, *put confidence*. The same word occurs in Ps. iv. 5; ix. 10; xiii. 5; and in v. 9 of this Psalm. The praises of Israel were specially rendered to God for the deliverances he had wrought for their fathers. They never ceased to celebrate the wonders shown in the days of Moses and Aaron, of Joshua, of Samuel and of David. It is a great thing for any people to have a famous history. No nation could recount such prodigies of salvation as the Jews. Messiah here looks to the history of God's servants for long ages before him, and expresses *first* his amazement that he should be the only righteous one, who seemed quite deserted of God, and *secondly* his determination to adhere to God in pious confidence, because it was not possible that Jehovah would deny himself, and *finally* depart from the course of his administration established for ages. *Deliver*, the same as in v. 8. See also Ps. xvii. 13; xviii. 2, 48.

5. *They cried unto thee, and were delivered.* The faith of the fathers was not inoperative. It made them pray with the utmost earnestness. They *cried* unto God, and *escaped*, as the word is better and more commonly rendered. Calvin: "It is not without good reason that David has put the word *cried* in the middle between these words, *They trusted in thee, they trusted*, in the fourth verse, and these words, *They trusted in thee*, in the fifth verse." *They trusted in thee, and were not confounded.* *Confounded*, "continually used in Scripture for the disappointment and frustration of the hopes." Our version in a majority of cases, and many scholars often use *ashamed*.

6. *But I* am *a worm, and no man.* Chaldee: I am a weak worm. Christ here speaks, not of his nature, nor of his real character, but of his condition, and of the esteem in which he was held. That this is so is clear from the next clause: [I am] *a reproach of men, and despised of the people.* The whole verse has a strict parallel in Isa. liii. 3; and both verses may be alluded to in Matt. ii. 23, "He shall be called a Nazarene;" that is, he shall be despised, contemned and reproached, as were the inhabitants of Nazareth. Christ was lightly esteemed, not merely by a few, but by *men* in the masses, by the *people*. His rejection by the Jews as a people was both *national* and *individual*. "He came to his own, and his own received him not."

7. *All they that see me laugh me to scorn;* i. e., *deride me, mock me.* In Ps. ii. 4 the same is rendered *have in derision.* The Hebrew is in the future indicating that the *scorning* shall last to the end of our Saviour's life, as it did. His enemies were never more *derisive* than when his agonies were the greatest. Horsley: All who see me insult me with derision; Ainsworth: All that see me do scoff at me. *They shoot out the lip, they shake the head.* "To protrude the lower lip is, in the East, considered a very strong indication of contempt. Its employment is chiefly confined to the lower orders." Something of the same is manifest in the usages of all countries. When pity is called for, derision gives a sorry answer, yea, it is as iron entering the soul. The art of deriding is one of the most cruel. Gaping, shaking the head, putting out the lip and protruding the tongue are old arts of mockery, Job xvi. 4, 10; Ps. xxxv. 21; xliv. 14; Isa. lvii. 4. This verse and the next are applied to Christ in Matt. xxvii. 39, 43. See also Mark xv. 29; Luke xxiii. 35, 36. Some ancient and many modern translations unite in representing the next verse as containing the taunting *words* of those, who in this verse are said to mock by *gestures*. Here is their speech:

8. *He trusted on the* Lord *that he would deliver him: let him deliver him, seeing he delighted in him.* *He trusted*, literally *he rolled on the Lord;* margin: *He rolled himself on the Lord;* Calvin: He has committed his cause unto Jehovah, or devolved his cause upon Jehovah; Edwards: He resteth upon Jehovah; Hengstenberg: Devolve upon the Lord; Alexander: "The literal meaning of the first clause is: *roll to* (or *on*) *Jehovah*, which would be unintelligible but for the parallel expressions in Ps. xxxvii. 5, *roll thy way upon Jehovah*, and in Prov. xvi. 3, *roll thy work* upon Jehovah'

See also 1 Pet. v. 7.   At the cross the wicked said that Christ had at all times professed a reliance on God alone; and Christ claimed that he was the object of his
Father's complacential love.

9. *But thou art he that took me out of the womb.*   The Chaldee, Septuagint, Ethiopic,
Vulgate and Doway give substantially the rendering of our version: Thou hast drawn,
or, Thou art he that hast drawn me out of my mother's womb; Syriac: Thou art
my trust from the womb; Calvin: Surely thou didst draw me forth from the womb;
Gesenius: Thou drewest me from my mother's womb; Horsley: Thou hast been my
bringer-up from the womb.   The common version is as good as any.   There is a very
weighty and important sense, in which God is the author of the existence and birth
of every man; but much more was he the Father of the human nature of Christ,
who by the miraculous power of the Holy Ghost was begotten in the womb of the
virgin Mary.   The argument is this: Thou didst great things for me in giving me
existence and birth; how can I despair of help from thee now, as thou art righteous,
and hast declared thyself well pleased in me?   Yea, more, *Thou didst make me hope*
when I was *upon my mother's breasts.*   Margin: Thou didst keep me in safety.   He
who has often ordained strength out of the mouths of babes and sucklings, and who
caused John Baptist before his birth to leap for joy in prospect of the birth of Christ,
doubtless gave to Christ a wonderful infancy and childhood and remarkable religious
exercises.   Even at the breast, the infant Saviour was not without joyous expectations
of the love and care of his heavenly Father.   To the holy *child*, as well as to the
man Christ Jesus the Father "gave not the Spirit by measure," John iii. 34; see Luke
ii. 40.   For valuable thoughts on the work of the Holy Spirit on the human nature
of Christ, see John Owen's Works, Vol. II., p. 188.   Clarke: "Thou hast made me;
and hast guided and defended me from my earliest infancy."

10. *I was cast upon thee from the womb.*   There is a sense, in which every pious man
looks back with wonder at the helplessness of his early life, and at the mercies which
attended it.   But Jesus Christ was in infancy very poor and peculiarly hated.   The
wise men brought from a great distance gifts; gold and frankincense, and myrrh,
which sustained Joseph and Mary and the child in the flight into Egypt.   At his
birth Herod was troubled and all Jerusalem with him.   Never were such cruel plots
laid against the life of any other child.   Yet God frustrated them.   Christ's whole
life was spent in imminent peril from wicked conspirators.   Yet God kept him safe.
Edwards: Upon thee I have been thrown ever since I was born; Horsley: I was cast
upon thy lap from the birth.   There seems to be no good reason for the rendering of
Dathe: To thee I have been committed from the womb.   The figure of this clause
seems to be borrowed from the act of receiving a child at birth, Ruth iv. 16.   This
clause is beautifully paraphrased by Hengstenberg: "Thou didst receive me, when I
was helpless, under thy mild protection; I fell as it were into thy lap, which was
stretched out to receive me at my birth; and from having been fostered and cared for
by thee I retained my life; whereas, otherwise, I would most assuredly have been the
prey of death."   *Thou art my God from my mother's belly.*   The plea of this clause is
of a covenant relation existing from the earliest infancy.   The doctrine of this clause
and of the context is clearly taught in Isa. xlix. 1.   Scott: "Christ was not only the
peculiar care of Providence from his birth; but from his earliest infancy he exercised
the most perfect faith, hope and love towards his God and Father."

11. *Be not far from me.*   Septuagint: Stand not aloof from me; Vulgate and Doway:
Depart not from me; Dathe: Desert me not; Horsley: Withdraw not thyself from
me.   The great mass of scholars do not essentially vary from our common version.
Christ prayed that his Father might not stand aloof from him.   The same form of the
verb is found in v. 19, also in Ps. xxxv. 22; xxxviii. 21; lxxi. 12.   The urgency of

the prayer for God's presence is next stated: *For trouble is near.* The word rendered *yor* should not be *when* as some have suggested. Its signification in this and the next clause is clearly *because.* So it is commonly rendered. *Trouble,* the same as in Ps. ix. 9; x. 1; xx. 1. Never was there such trouble on earth as that foreseen and endured by Christ, Luke xii. 50. A reason for urgency in desiring God's presence is: *For* there is *none to help.* The margin: For there is not a helper. The sympathy of Christ's disciples would have been most welcome to him. Yet they "all forsook him and fled." True, they could have given him no effectual *help,* but they might have wept and prayed with him. He trod the wine-press alone, and of the people none were found with him. Never was a soul so beset with troubles. It was "exceeding sorrowful even unto death." His troubles and enemies were terrific.

12. *Many bulls have compassed me: strong* bulls *of Bashan have beset me around.* Morison: "The bull is the fit image of strength, fierceness, pride and cruelty; and the bulls of Bashan, as inhabiting a rich and fertile country on the opposite side of Jordan, would be the appropriate emblems of these qualities in their highest degree. Bashan was a rich mountainous district, the very place to breed the wild ox to perfection, Deut. xxxii. 14. J. Brown of Haddington: "Wicked men, chiefly rulers or warriors, are called *bulls,* and *bulls of Bashan,* to denote their prosperity, strength, untractableness and mischievous violence and fierceness." See Ps. lxviii. 30. The Chaldee: People like many bulls, the great bulls of Bashan surrounded me; Horsley: Huge bulls surround me: strong (bulls) of Bashan form a ring about me. The Saviour meek, unoffending, unresisting, was in the midst of foes of great strength, fierceness and fury. Like bulls they tossed him on their horns or trampled him down in their rage. The English word, *bully,* has its origin in the habits of fierce bulls. Christ's foes had the evil and alarming qualities not only of bulls, but also of lions.

13. *They gaped upon me* with *their mouths, as a ravening and roaring lion.* The lion chiefly roars when he is seeking his prey, or when he has it in his power and is about to devour it, Ps. civ. 21; Amos iii. 4. Scott: "A helpless infant, or a harmless lamb, surrounded by furious bulls and hungry lions, aptly represented the Saviour encompassed by his insulting and bloody persecutors." Christ's trouble was not merely or chiefly outward. "The sufferings of his soul were the soul of his sufferings." He says:

14. *I am poured out like water, and all my bones are out of joint: my heart is like wax; it is melted in the midst of my bowels.* Clarke: "The images of this verse are strongly descriptive of a person in the deepest distress; whose strength, courage, hope and expectation of succor and relief had entirely failed." Perhaps there never were words better chosen to describe a "soul sorrowful even unto death." The versions are remarkably agreed in rendering the first clause as we have it in English. Edwards: I am dissolved like water; Horsley: Like water I have lost my firmness; Fenwick: As water spilt, and poured out, I seem. Hengstenberg regards Ps. lviii. 8; 1 Sam. vii. 6; 2 Sam. xiv. 14 as parallel passages. Enemies without and distress within, the rage of men and the wrath of God took away Christ's strength. For *out of joint* the margin has *sundered.* Boothroyd and Street, following the Arabic: All my bones are dissolved; Chaldee, Septuagint, Syriac, Ethiopic, Vulgate and Doway: My bones are scattered; Calvin: All my bones are disjointed; Ainsworth: All my bones dispart themselves; Horsley: All my bones are starting asunder; Fry: All my bones are rent asunder; Hengstenberg: All my bones are separated; Alexander: All my bones are parted. The phrase denotes not only "complete powerlessness and exhaustion," but dreadful torment, as if one were on the rack. David's distress of mind is compared to broken bones, Ps. li. 8. Bones out of joint are often more painful. The next clauses teach the same thing: *My heart is melted like wax; it is*

melted in the midst of my bowels. Luther: "Those, who have good hope and are cheerful, are said to have a fresh, strong, confident, stout, good heart, which stands immovable like a hard rock. And thus, also, on the other hand, those who are cast down and terrified, are said to have a soft and feeble heart, which dissolves and melts like wax." The melting of wax is a figure often found in Scripture and for various purposes, Ps. lxviii. 2; xcvii. 5. None but he, who bore these dreadful sufferings, knew the full import of these dreadful words.

15. *My strength is dried up like a potsherd.* The word here rendered *potsherd* occurs *sixteen* times in the Hebrew Bible. The plural of it is once rendered *stones;* it is twice rendered *sherd* or *sherds;* it is *five* times rendered as here, *potsherd;* in all other cases it is connected with another word, as vessel, bottle or pitcher, and is rendered *earthen* or *of earth.* Earthen vessels were made thoroughly dry and burned in a kiln. The sense is that his strength was as effectually consumed as the moisture of an earthen vessel subjected to the process of drying and burning. *Moisture* is elsewhere used to express that state, which is connected with health and joyousness. Ps. xxxii. 4. *And my tongue cleaveth to my jaws.* One of the Latin poets describes the effect of mental agitation on the mouth and throat in words, which one might think borrowed from this place. Luther: "It is incredible how this inward anguish, and terror, and dismay withers and dries up completely and suddenly the whole moisture of all the parts of the body, and makes them weak and good for nothing, especially the moisture of the tongue, with which we chiefly feel this thirst and drought;" Calvin: "We know that excessive grief not only consumes the vital spirits, but also dries up almost all the moisture which is in our bodies." Hengstenberg for *my jaws* has *the roof of my mouth.* Quenchless thirst is often a forerunner of death, and so it is added: *And thou hast brought me into the dust of death.* Hengstenberg: "The *dust of death* is the dust which has reference to death, that is, the dust of the grave." The Hebrew verb is in the future, which is the form preferred by the church of England, Jebb and Alexander. Some also render it in the present, as Amesius, Fry and Hengstenberg. The majority of versions agree with the common English. The sense of the passage seems to be, "Thou hast already brought me to the brink of the grave."

16. *For dogs have compassed me.* Previously Christ's foes were likened to bulls and lions; now to dogs. In his Metaphors Keach gives six particulars in which wicked men are compared to bulls, eight in which they are like lions, and sixteen in which they resemble dogs. Wicked men are spoken of as dogs in the last chapter of the New Testament. The allusion to dogs would be more striking to any one who had travelled in Syria than to those who know the dog only as a domestic animal. We are at once told who the dogs are: *The assembly of the wicked have inclosed me.* The Chaldee: The wicked, who are like to many dogs, have surrounded me. *Assembly* in Ps. i. 5; vii. 7, and commonly rendered *congregation.* The reference seems to be to the show of a trial gotten up against Christ. Nor did his foes merely rave and make a noise like dogs: *They pierced my hands and my feet.* Concerning these words there is considerable difficulty. Those who wish to make a very extended examination will consult others. The difficulty has perhaps been needlessly exaggerated. For there is uncommon agreement in the ancient versions. The Septuagint, Syriac, Arabic, Ethiopic, Vulgate, Calvin, Amesius, church of England, Houbigant, the Complutensian Polyglot, Jebb, Fry, Tholuck and Alexander agree in the rendering of our common version. Nor is it necessary with Jebb to suppose a falsification of the text by the Jews, the text and the marginal reading of the Hebrew varying so very little that any transcriber might easily have made the mistake that has produced the difficulty. Edwards: They make deep wounds in my hands and

my legs; Mudge: "The image is of a man encompassed by dogs, and extending his arms to keep them off, but they come about him and fix their teeth and claws in his arms and legs, as they could not reach his body." The word rendered *feet* is often found and in our version is never rendered *legs* except in 1 Sam. xvii. 6; Chaldee: They bite like a lion my hands and my feet. Though these words are never quoted in the New Testament as descriptive of the manner of Christ's death, yet they do well state the act of fastening him to the cross; and *piercing* is a form of representing his sufferings at the hand of man well known to the writers of both Testaments, Zech. xii. 10; John xix. 34; Rev. i. 7. Scott well says that there seems scarcely the shadow of a doubt that our version is correct. See John Owen on the "Integrity and Purity of the Hebrew and Greek Text," vol. iv. pp. 466–67.

17. *I may tell all my bones: they look* and *stare upon me.* Theodoret: "When he was extended, and his limbs distorted on the cross, it would be easy for a spectator to *tell all his bones.*" For *I may tell*, some prefer, *I will tell, I could tell*, or *I tell*. Perhaps the last is the best, corresponding in tense with *look* and *stare*. Diodati: " *They look*, feeding their eyes and passions with my misery, as with a pleasant spectacle," Matt. xxvii. 36; Luke xxiii. 35. Edwards: They stare and feast their eyes upon me; Hengstenberg: They enjoy themselves in looking at one disfigured to a skeleton.

18. *They part my garments among them and cast lots upon my vesture.* Surely these words have their fulfilment nowhere but in the events recorded in the Gospels, Matt. xxvii. 35; Mark xv. 24; Luke xxiii. 34; John xix. 23, 24. Nothing like this ever happened to David or to any other worthy of Scripture. Luther: "I hold that the soldiers did not divide the clothes from need, or for gain, but in the way of jest, and for the purpose of enjoying a laugh, and as a sign that it was now all over with this Christ, that he was utterly ruined, destroyed, extirpated, and never more to be heard of." This may be so, but the impression seems to have been that the soldiers divided his raiment for gain. In the time of the *reign of terror* in France a small spot of ground by the guillotine was rented out for mountebanks to make their gains. Here at the foot of the cross a lottery is opened to dispose of the raiment of one not yet dead.

19. *But be not thou far from me,* O LORD. The sufferer on Calvary never forgot his covenant relation to God. To *be far from* one is to refuse aid. The petition is for assistance: *O my strength, haste thee to help me.* God is our refuge and strength a very present help in trouble. Hengstenberg: "The expression *make haste to help me*, refers us back to the eleventh verse, *there is none to help.*

20. *Deliver my soul from the sword; my darling from the power of the dog.* The Chaldee: Set free my soul from those, who kill with the sword; the spirit of my body from the power of the dog; Septuagint: Rescue my soul from the sword; my only-begotten from the power of the dog; Vulgate, Ethiopic and Doway: Deliver, O God. my soul from the sword; my only one from the hand of the dog; Calvin, Venema, Amesius, Waterland, Houbigant, Mudge, Jebb and others for *darling* read *only one*, and in a note Calvin explains it thus, "Namely, my life, which is alone;" Ainsworth: Rid my soul from the sword, my lonely *soul* from the hand of the dog; Street: Protect my life from the sword, my solitary state from the hand of dogs; Boothroyd: Deliver my life from the sword, my dear life from the power of the dog; Edwards: Rescue my life from the sword; my soul from the paws of the dog; Horsley: Deliver my soul from the sword, my UNITED ONE from the power of the dog. That the substance of the passage is a prayer for life is not doubtful. Luther: "He wishes to say my soul is alone and forsaken by every body, there is no one who inquires after it, cares for it, or comforts it." Calvin: "If it is asked how this can be applied to Christ, whom the Father did not deliver from death, I answer, in one word, that he was more

mightily delivered than if God had prevented him from falling a victim to death, even as it is a much greater deliverance to rise again from the dead than to be healed of a grievous malady."

21. *Save me from the lion's mouth.* This prayer, like that of the preceding verse, is for deliverance and life. The figure of the lion is here continued from v. 13. *For thou hast heard me from the horns of the unicorns.* Two points in this clause claim notice. The first relates to the tense. The Hebrew is preterite. So is the rendering of the Chaldee, church of England, Venema, Ainsworth, Fry, Horsley and Alexander. But Calvin, Amesius, Edwards and Jebb read, Hear me; Hengstenberg, Thou hearest me. If the preterite is preferred, then he is so confident of final triumph that he speaks of it as already gained, or he is encouraging himself from his past experience, or he is announcing that his victory is already begun. Horsley takes the latter view and reads the whole verse: "Save me from the mouth of the lion, and from the horns of the unicorns. Thou hast answered me." It is generally admitted that the remaining verses of this Psalm contain the language of one, whose prayer has been heard. If the victory is not announced in the words, *Thou hast heard me;* they at least form the clause of transition from a depressed to an exultant state. The other point of difficulty is in the word rendered *unicorns.* There are two large creatures which have but one horn each. One is the monodon, a species of whale; the other is a land animal, the rhinoceros. So that the unicorn is not a fabulous animal. If to either of the foregoing reference is here had, it is doubtless to the latter. The Chaldee Septuagint and Vulgate read, *unicorn.* Edwards thinks the reference is to the one-horned cloven-footed wild-goat, called the *Oryx.* Venema, Hengstenberg and others think the *bubalus,* the buffalo, or wild ox is meant. Others think the reference is to a species of antelope. If the reader is curious in this matter, he can consult the Lexicons and Carpenter's "Scripture natural history." Neither the monodon, nor rhinoceros could have been known to the Hebrews except by report or by their travelling into distant lands. The same may be said of the one-horned deer of Africa. Roberts says that it is still a prayer in the East, Save me from the horns of the *kandam.* But this animal is unknown to those, who use the prayer. *Unicorn,* found *nine* times in the Hebrew Bible, and always rendered as here. See Nu. xxiii. 22; xxiv. 8; Deut. xxxiii. 17; Job xxxix. 9, 10; Ps. xxix. 6; xcii. 10; Isa. xxxiv. 7. The old Psalter, quoted by Clarke says: "The unicorn es ane of the prudest best that es, so that he wil dye for dedeyn if he be haldyn agayne his wil." The passages of Scripture where the word occurs show the animals here spoken of to be very strong, wild, fierce and gregarious. The sufferer of this passage was as if surrounded by them and saved from their horns. Luther: "The rage of the furious devil is so great, that the prophet does not consider it enough to have represented it by a sharp sword, but introduces further, for the same purpose, the tearings of raging, furious dogs, the mouth of the greedy and hungry lion, which stands already open, and is ready to devour, and the dreadfully fierce wrath of the raging terrible unicorn."

22. *I will declare thy name unto my brethren: in the midst of the congregation will I praise thee.* Scott: "The whole Psalm is allowed to be highly poetical; but this transition is peculiarly beautiful. For here the scene at once changes and brightens. The Saviour turns his eyes from his sufferings to the glory which followed: and, anticipating the extensive and permanently blessed effects of his passion and exaltation, he breaks forth into exulting predictions and praises at the prospect." In this view many concur. Paul applies this whole verse to Christ in proof of his humanity, Heb. ii. 12. Soon after he rose from the dead, our Lord said: "Go to my brethren." Christ is so the brother of all men that he has human nature. But in the highest sense none except genuine believers are his brethren, Luke viii. 21. To *declare God's*

name is to make it known, to publish abroad his mighty deeds which illustrate his perfections. And to praise him *in the midst of the congregation* is to show forth his glory in the most public and solemn manner. *Congregation*, not the same word as in Ps. i. 5; elsewhere *multitude, assembly, company.* It awakens painful surprise to find respectable commentators attempting to explain this verse without even an allusion to the inspired exposition given by Paul in Heb. ii. 12.

23. *Ye that fear the Lord, praise him.* Christ's *brethren* of the preceding verse are the *Lord-fearers* of this. Dathe, Lowth, Street, Boothroyd and others regard this verse and the next as containing the song promised in v. 22. But a pious declaration of intention to praise God is itself praise. This whole verse contains an earnest summons to others to unite in acts of devout gratitude and adoration. This also is praise to God. The designation of pious men as those that *fear the* LORD is very common. See on Ps. ii. 11. *All ye the seed of Jacob, glorify him; and fear him, all ye the seed of Israel.* *Jacob* and *Israel* are terms sufficiently comprehensive of those who are God's willing servants. The three verbs, *praise, glorify* and *fear,* well describe the nature and effects of living piety in the soul. Vital godliness will never turn away from such commands; particularly will it not be offended at any call to work out its salvation with fear and trembling.

24. *For he hath not despised nor abhorred the affliction of the afflicted; neither hath he hid his face from him; but when he cried unto him, he heard.* This is ground enough for all the righteous to praise the Lord, especially when we remember that the *afflicted* One here spoken of was the blessed Son of God. Every step in Christ's exaltation fills the hearts of the pious with joy and praise. His success is the pledge of their victory. His resurrection makes sure the redemption of their bodies. If God heard Christ when he was bearing the sin of the world, he will not deny his intercessions in heaven. And if when sin was imputed to his Son, God did so *afflict* him, let all men *fear,* lest sin be found charged to them in their last account.

25. *My praise* shall be *of thee in the great congregation; I will pay my vows before them that fear him.* *Congregation*, as in v. 22. The two places express the same idea. In this verse we first find in the Psalms the word *vows*, which has a uniform rendering. There is great beauty and completeness in the exposition of Hengstenberg: "It was customary, in circumstances of great distress, to make *vows*, which were wont to consist of a promise to offer a certain number of *sacrifices*. After deliverance had been obtained, it was customary to invite to the feast, connected therewith, the widow, the orphan and the poor, and to make them sharers of the joy. In such cases the enjoyment throughout was not merely of a sensual kind; the guests enjoyed at the same time the friendship of the master of the feast. The soul of the feast was admission into the community of thanks and praise. And hence, in the passage before us, when the gratitude of the delivered sufferer expresses itself under the emblem of paying a vow—the usual expression of gratitude—it is exceedingly natural that others should be invited to share in the blessing and thanksgiving, under the *image* of a great *sacrificial feast* given by him, in which all that fear God take part." This view is borne out by the next verse:

26. *The meek shall eat and be satisfied.* *Meek*, elsewhere rendered also *poor, humble, lowly.* See Ps. ix. 12, 18; x. 12, 17. The eating is at the feast where the vow was paid. It was to *satisfaction.* No guest was neglected. Each was *filled* or *satisfied.* The humble find the Gospel-feast sufficient to meet all their wants. Such are both joyful and grateful. *They shall praise the* LORD *that seek him.* On the words *seek him,* see on Ps. ix. 10. All who seek him shall praise him, because they find a *satisfying* blessing. To such it is said, *Your heart shall live forever;* shall live in peace and joy, in purity and love, in rest and confidence. Eternal life is begun on earth. This

blessedness shall last and increase forever.   To be spiritually-minded is life and peace. To be perfectly pure and perfectly redeemed will be heaven—the life above.

27. *All the ends of the world shall remember and turn unto the* LORD.   *The ends of the world, i. e.,* the remotest and least known of all the nations; in Ps. ii. 8, rendered *the uttermost parts of the earth.   All* these belong to Christ.   *All* shall yet own their Lord.   This they shall do by *remembering* him, his commandments, wonders, judgments, word and righteousness, so evincing true piety, Num. xv. 39; Neh. iv. 14; ix. 17; Ps. lxxi. 16; cxix. 15; Josh. i. 13; Jon. ii. 7; Ecc. xii. 1.   If men's characters are ever improved, it must be by divine grace disposing and enabling them rightly to use their faculties.   Hengstenberg well says that the word here rendered *remember* "very frequently signifies to ponder, to lay to heart."   The same is true of the English word *remember.*   Fry has *reflect.*   The *turning unto the Lord* implies a forsaking of all others.   This is the more obvious as the nations here spoken of were for ages mad upon their false worship.   *And all the kindreds of the nations shall worship before thee.* Edwards: And all the families of the heathen will worship before thee; Calvin: And all the tribes of the Gentiles shall prostrate themselves before his face; the Chaldee, Septuagint, Syriac, Vulgate and Ethiopic: And all the families of the Gentiles shall worship in his presence.   To *prostrate* is literal.   That was often the posture in eastern worship.   The wide range of the effects of Christ's death has not yet been conceived. The certainty of the glorious results is complete.   The reason is given.

28. *For the kingdom is the* LORD'S.   Patrick: "The Lord is the Sovereign of the whole world."   He has all authority.   He can put down all rule.   He is able to subdue all things to himself.   He has mercy for the Gentiles.   *And he is the governor among the nations.*   Calvin renders the whole verse: For the kingdom is Jehovah's, that he may be the governor among the nations; Edwards: For Jehovah is supreme monarch of the world; and he reigneth over the heathen.   The exaltation of Christ began in his resurrection and shall go on till the whole earth owns her king.   The calling of the Gentiles began in mercy, and shall be completed in their *fulness* being brought in.   All without exception must own him.   So it is said:

29. *All they that be fat upon earth shall eat and worship: all they that go down to the dust shall bow before him.*   The figure of a votive feast is here resumed.   The blessings of the Gospel are often represented as the provisions of a feast.   Isa. xxv. 6; Luke xiv. 16–24.   This feast is for rich and poor.   The *fat* and they *that go down to the dust,* are all invited and shall come.   Hengstenberg: "It is a feast at which all earthly distinctions are removed, because here all guests are poor, and God is rich for all."   *If those that go down to the dust* refers to v. 15, as some think, then it is parallel to the next clause, *And none can keep alive his own soul.*   Then the meaning is that the feast was for the *fat* ones who yet were ready to perish, and " who could not deliver themselves from that death, into which they had fallen."   They should all alike be welcome to the blessings of the great Deliverer.

30. *A seed shall serve him.*   In Isa. liii. 10 we have the same word *seed:*   He shall see *his* seed.   Calvin: Their seed shall serve him; Edwards: Their descendants will serve him; Septuagint, Vulgate and Fry: My seed shall serve him; Hengstenberg and Alexander: Posterity shall serve him.   Those, who read *their seed,* understand the seed of the Gentiles.   Those, who read *my seed,* explain it by saying all believers are the sons of God.   Those who understand the seed to be *Christ's* are sustained by Hebrews ii. 13.   It is a blessed fact that Christ has a people from age to age.   This seed shall not be disowned.   *It shall be accounted to the Lord for a generation.*   Both God and man shall repute and regard the seed of Christ in subsequent times as the true people of God, the *generation* of the upright.   Diodati: "Others shall be enrolled to the Lord in all ages."   Calvin: " As the name *Jehovah,* which is expressive

of God's essence, is not here used as it is a little before, but the word *Adonai* [rendered Lord,] I do not disapprove of the opinion of those who think that Christ is here expressly invested with authority over the church that he may register all who shall give in their names as on the side of God his Father." Hengstenberg prefers another rendering: It shall be told of the Lord to the generation. That is the present generation shall tell it to the next. This is not good; for the next verse brings out that truth:

31. *They shall come, and shall declare his righteousness unto a people that shall be born, that he hath done this.* The ancient versions exceedingly vary in rendering this verse. But the modern translations are more agreed, and come nearer our common version. Calvin: They shall come and shall declare his righteousness to a people that shall be born, because he hath done it; Edwards: And they will declare to the people which shall be born the righteousness which he hath executed; Fry: They shall come, who shall declare his righteousness to a people that shall be born, whom he hath prepared; Boothroyd: To the next generation they shall declare his righteousness; to a people that shall be born, what he hath done; Horsley:

> They shall come and declare his righteousness;
> To a people that shall be born, what he hath done:

Hengstenberg: They shall come and make known his righteousness to the people which then have been born, that he has done it. The passage predicts that the knowledge of Christ and God's righteousness in and by him shall be made known to people as yet unborn. The phrase *that he hath done this* well conveys the force of the original, and refers to what he *hath done* as recorded in this Psalm, *i. e.*, he has exalted Christ after all his sufferings and humiliation.

Doctrinal and Practical Remarks.

1. It is right that the followers of an afflicted Saviour should know the fellowship of his sufferings and be made conformable unto his death. They all need instruction and discipline; and they are sure to get both. "God had on earth one Son without sin; but never a son without affliction." "All Christians have been taught in one school; all have known the power of affliction in some of its forms." Ponder Heb. xii. 3.

2. Of all the forms of affliction to the pious soul none is more dreadful than the hiding of God's countenance, v. 1. In the case of Christ "this desertion was a judicial act on the part of God towards sin." In the case of his people it is for their purification, or to make them bright patterns of suffering affliction. In all cases, "spiritual desertions are the saint's sorest afflictions." He can stand anything better than the loss of comfortable communion with God. A minister near death and in darkness said to a brother, "What is to be thought of one who has long preached Christ to others, and in death has not the comforting presence of God?" The other replied, "What think you of the dreadful darkness and desertion of a Saviour dying?" This remark brought peace.

3. Great perturbation may consist with eminent piety. Christ's soul was agitated until that dreadful distress indicated by *roaring*, was upon him, v. 1.

4. If sin, when imputed to a voluntary and innocent sufferer, may produce such unparalleled sorrow as is described in this Psalm, what will be the portion of the man, who dies in sin, and has neither conscious innocence, nor the assurance of speedy deliverance, nor the soul-cheering presence of God to support him? Luke xxiii. 31. "No man knows the exceeding sinfulness of sin, but he who learns it at the cross of Christ."

5. Sense and faith are very diverse. Sense may cry, *Why hast thou forsaken me?* while faith cries, *My God, my God.* It is "possible, that when deserted by the great God, man can still address him in the language of affiance."

6. There is but one method of satisfactorily explaining the awful scenes of the crucifixion. Stevenson: "That was the judgment-day of the Saviour of the world. At the tribunals of men he was condemned—under their sentence he was executed: and while his body hung in torture on the cross, he was arraigned in spirit before the bar of God, under the imputation of human guilt. The court of heaven, as it were, descended to Mount Calvary. . . These awful words, 'Let the law take its course,' are uttered by the eternal Judge." This explanation alone is sufficient. With his stripes we are healed. By his chastisement we have peace. By his death we live. Otherwise we never can defend the character of God concerning the humiliation of Christ. He never permitted a holy angel to suffer even the slightest indignity.

7. When sore pressed, our resort must be to earnest prayer and strong crying to God, v. 2. Calvin: "The true rule of praying is this, that he who seems to have beaten the air to no purpose, or to have lost his labor in praying for a long time, should not, on that account, leave off, or desist from that duty."

8. Dickson: "Were temptations ever so black, faith will not hearken to an ill word spoken against God, but will justify God always," v. 3. This is much wiser than to plunge into reasonings too deep for us. Often is silence eminent wisdom. Trust is better than logic. Let us never charge God foolishly, as we shall surely do, if we attempt to solve all the mysteries of providence.

9. It is often well to look at the days of old and see God's former wonders, v. 4. This will cause us to encourage ourselves in the Lord our God.

10. Under the government of God there has never been a final or utter failure of a righteous cause, v. 5. Such a thing is impossible. God's whole nature, government, word and oath forbid it. All who have trusted were, *in due time, in the best time,* delivered.

11. The case of believers can never be worse in the eyes of men, than was that of Christ on the cross. He was regarded and treated as a *worm,* and *no man,* v. 6. Low as believers may sink, their Saviour sank lower.

12. If we are subjected to derision and scorn for righteousness' sake, the same befell our Saviour, v. 7. If we fare no worse than he, why should we complain? Morison: "How incomprehensible to mortals was that patience which the incarnate Messiah exercised towards those, who poured all the impotence of a creature's derision upon him! How infinitely worthy of the divine Being the proposed results of a dispensation which involved such ignominy and abasement to the spotless Redeemer!" Reproach broke the Saviour's heart, Ps. lxix. 20.

13. Let us learn to roll our burdens on the Lord. He can sustain us, v. 8. The heavier the load, the greater our need of God's supporting hand. Stevenson: "Grievous indeed it is to have our words distorted to falsehood, converted into jest, retorted against ourselves, and blazed abroad to our discredit. Christ endured this fourfold contradiction." But God carried him through it all to glory ineffable.

14. He, who made us, can take care of us, v. 9. He, who gave us life, can support it. "Is not the life more than meat, and the body than raiment?" Matt. vi. 25. Every pious man may say to God: Thou gavest me my earthly existence, and, so long as it is for thy glory and my good, thou wilt maintain it.

15. Early piety is possible, v. 9. Had our first parents not sinned, all their posterity would have loved and served God from their earliest existence. It requires no more intellect to love God than to hate him, to please than to displease him, to obey than to disobey him. Is it not true that many seem rather to thank God that he has

hid heavenly things from babes, and has revealed them unto the wise and prudent, than to unite with the Saviour in his joy over the opposing truth, Luke x. 21? Let us believingly pray that God would make our children *hope* in him; even when they are babes and sucklings.

16. In every one's early history is much that is interesting. One says that any man's biography well written would be to him one of the most interesting books. Were we not practical atheists, we should all adopt the language of v. 10. Many can put a peculiarly tender meaning on the saying, "I was cast upon thee from the womb." John Brown of Haddington: "I was left a poor orphan, and had nothing to depend on but the providence of God;—and I must say, that the Lord has been the Father of the fatherless, and the orphan's stay;" Calvin: "If it were not that ingratitude had blinded our eyes, every birth would fill us with amazement, and every preservation of a child in its tender infancy, exposed as it is, even at its very entrance into the world, to death in a hundred forms."

17. When God is with us all is well. His gracious presence is the sum of all needed good things, v. 11. Clarke: "A present God is a present blessing."

18. The less help and the less prospect of help from man, the more should we hope from God, v. 11.

19. We can never have fiercer, more cruel, or more brutal enemies than had our blessed Lord, vv. 12, 13. Stevenson: "Mockery accompanied the Saviour from the garden of Gethsemane till he expired on Calvary. Judas set the example with his insidious kiss. The men, that apprehended him, mocked him. The officers at the several courts mocked him. The chief priests, scribes and pharisees mocked him. The high-priest, Caiaphas, mocked him. The servants of his house and others surrounded the Saviour, and mocked him. They smote him with their staves, and with the palms of their hands—they did spit in his face—they plucked off the hair—they blindfolded him; then they did buffet him with their fists, saying, 'Prophesy unto us, thou Christ, who is he that smote thee?' Matt. xxvi. 68. Herod and his men of war mocked him, and set him at naught—arraying him in a gorgeous robe, they sent him away as a laughing-stock to the place whence he was brought. Pilate regarded him as a weak, inoffensive creature, and, jestingly asking him, 'What is truth?' brought him forth, saying, 'Behold the man,' and sent him to crucifixion with this mock title, 'The King of the Jews.' The Roman soldiers mocked him with a perfect mockery. They acted it to the very life. They procured a crown—it was of thorns: royal garments—they were a cast-off purple vest, and a scarlet robe: a sceptre—it was a reed. They paid him homage as a king—it was mock-kneeling, laughter and derision. They lavished their honors upon him. Their salutation was a scoff, 'Hail, king of the Jews!' Their gifts were not gold but strokes—not frankincense, but spitting—not myrrh, but mockery. . . Imagine this dreadful scene. Behold this motley multitude of rich and poor, of Jews and Gentiles. Some stand in groups and gaze. Some recline at ease and stare. Others move about in restless gratification at the event. There is a look of satisfaction on every countenance. None are silent. The velocity of speech seems tardy. The theme is far too great for one member to utter. Every lip, and head, and finger is now a tongue. The rough soldiers, too, are busied in their way. The work of blood is over. Refreshment has become necessary. Their usual beverage of vinegar and water is supplied to them. As they severally are satisfied, they approach the cross, hold some forth to the Saviour, and bid him drink as they withdraw it." O child of God! thy enemies can never be worse than were those of thy Saviour! Be still.

20. Christ's pains were of body and mind, and both dreadful, v. 14. Calvin: "Being a real man, he was truly subject to the infirmities of our flesh, only without

the taint of sin. The perfect purity of his nature did not extinguish the human affections; it only regulated them, that they might not become sinful through excess." And although not a bone of him was broken, yet all his bones were out of joint. The theory of crucifixion was death by nervous distress.

21. Grief can waste us away and bring us to death, v. 15. There is such a thing as breaking the heart. What a mercy to be able to sing

Ten thousand thousand precious gifts
My daily thanks employ;
Nor is the least a cheerful heart,
That tastes those gifts with joy.

And if cheerfulness be denied us, it is a great blessing to be quiet and patient. Calvin: "In Christ these two things were wonderfully conjoined, namely, terror, proceeding from a sense of the curse of God; and patience, arising from faith, which tranquillized all the mental emotions, so that they continued in complete and willing subjection to the authority of God."

22. Wicked men are as base as the Scriptures represent them. They are dogs, v. 16. They are unfit for the society of heaven. "Without are dogs," Rev. xxii. 15. They will not always have it in their power to bark at and devour the saints.

23. Left to themselves, wicked men will stop at nothing. They murdered Jesus Christ, v. 16. Were he on earth attacking men's sins and vices as of old, he would, unless miraculously preserved, be put to death in less than three months. Unregenerate human nature is not a whit improved.

24. Can any fallen creature be worse than man? Were there ever perpetrated by devils in hell such horrible crimes as have been committed by men on earth? vv. 16, 17. If so, what? by whom? when?

25. There is not in all the range of history besides Christ another person in whom was fulfilled the prediction in v. 18. It alone might well settle the interpretation of this Psalm and the Messiahship of Jesus. Christ's seamless vesture was not left by him to any friend. His murderers got that. "Perhaps it was the cherished gift of some pious disciple. Tradition says it was his mother's present." But he gave it to no one. Papists have sometimes claimed to have it. This they cannot prove. If they have it they got it not from him, but from his murderers.

26. In our trials effectual help can come from God only. The sooner and more directly we go to him, the wiser we are, and the more closely do we follow the example of Christ, v. 19.

27. The humiliation of Christ was unspeakable. He was given to "the power of the dog," the basest of all wicked beings; and to the sword—the flaming, two-edged, glittering sword of eternal justice, v. 20; Zech. xiii. 7.

28. Let us wait God's time and method of relief. Dickson: "Christ was no less delivered from dogs, lions, unicorns, his persecuting enemies, by his resurrection after death, than if he had been taken out of their hands, when they came to apprehend him in the garden; yea, this delivery out of the grave was a far greater delivery than if he had not been slain at all; for then he had delivered himself only, and not us."

29. The believer can be in no circumstances too dark for prayer. His Saviour was once in greater darkness and sorrow, and he then set us the example of prayer, intending that we should follow it, vv. 19–21; 1 Pet. ii. 21. "He that will not be satisfied without the blessing shall be satisfied with it. Ask and you shall have. . . The simplest prayer is a sublime mystery. The feeble voice of a child influences God."

30. The proper use of deliverances already received is to awaken gratitude for the past, and give encouragement for the future, v. 21. When David was about to meet the giant of Gath he called to mind his victory over the lion and the bear.

Our Saviour's heart was encouraged by remembering what God had done for him in former times.

31. Wonderful is Christ's condescension to his people, even the humblest of them. He is not ashamed to *call them brethren*, v. 22. Oftentimes they are rude, ignorant, poor, and through life they labor under prejudices and errors, and have many faults and defects of character, yet the Saviour owns the weakest of them, even when they are disowned by their censorious brethren. If Christ calls us brethren, it is a small matter to be judged of man's judgment.

32. As Christ's humiliation was public, so is his exaltation, v. 22. Every step in his glorious progress is fitly open. He was seen of angels. He who wore the crown of thorns is worthy to be in the midst of the throne of God; he who had a reed put into his hand is fit to wield the sceptre of universal dominion; he who wore the robes of mock royalty is rightly owned to be God over all, blessed forever.

33. In his great sufferings the human nature of our Lord was sustained *first*, by his divine nature; else the stroke had been more than he could have borne; and *secondly*, by the blessed vision of success, "the joy that was set before him," the crown he should wear forever when in the midst of his redeemed he should celebrate his victories, v. 22. Morison: "It is impossible for finite minds to comprehend the extent of blessedness which he felt when atonement was made, when justice was satisfied, when Satan was vanquished, when the prophetic testimony concerning his death and resurrection was fulfilled."

34. In Christ's joy at the progress of his kingdom and glory all that fear the Lord participate and give thanks, v. 23.

35. True piety glorifies God, v. 23. This distinguishes it from all that is spurious.

36. True piety fears God, v. 23. "To fear the Lord is a lesson with which every disciple must be familiar. It is the first in the school of Christ. Every pupil must learn it. Happy is he who knows it by heart."

37. When will men learn the value and efficacy of prayer? v. 24. There has never in any age or nation been one case in which God has despised or abhorred the affliction of true believers, nor refused to hear them when they cried.

38. We have Christ's authority in favor of public praise, v. 25. Compare Ps. xl. 9, 10. Public mercies demand public acknowledgements. When secret worship is made a hindrance, and not a help to public devotions, it is sadly defective in some important respect.

39. Vows, as acts of solemn worship, are lawful, v. 25. The word of God gives us many instances from the days of Jacob down to apostolic times.

40. The provisions of the Gospel are ample, v. 26. They fully meet all the demands of the meek of the earth. To all others they are distasteful and so are rejected.

41. It is unspeakably to the honor of religion that every one who has with all the heart sought the Lord, has found abundant matter of joy and thanksgiving, v. 26.

42. The eternal consequences of true religion must be brought into the estimate, if we would decide aright the question of the wisdom of serving God and of the folly of a life of sin, v. 26.

43. The universal spread of the Gospel is clearly revealed, vv. 27–31. The thing is certain, for the mouth of the Lord hath spoken it. One clear prophecy on any point pledges the divine perfections to bring it to pass. But where much is said on a subject it shows that God regards the matter as of great importance, and would have us fully assured and often reminded of its accomplishment. Blessed be God: The Gospel of the kingdom shall be preached among all nations. The prayers of saints, the intercession of Christ, the reward secured to the Redeemer, God's promise and oath all require that the whole earth be converted unto God.

44. Wicked as this world is, God governs it. He has never resigned his authority over any people, v. 28. A blessed truth is this. He can at any time so display his power, justice and grace as to subdue the proudest people, fill the most self-righteous with alarm, and bring the most guilty to hope in his mercy. "Is he the God of the Jews only? is he not also of the Gentiles? yes, of the Gentiles also: seeing it is one God, which shall justify the circumcision by faith, and the uncircumcision through faith." "For there is no difference between the Jew and the Greek: for the same Lord over all is rich unto all that call upon him. For whosoever shall call upon the name of the Lord shall be saved." "His kingdom ruleth over all." "The earth is the Lord's, and the fulness thereof."

45. Very glorious is the free, indiscriminate offer of the Gospel, v. 29.

> While grace is offered to the prince,
> The poor may take their share;
> No mortal has a just pretence
> To perish in despair.

Dickson: "Kings, rulers and magistrates shall have no cause of jealousy from Christ's kingdom, and his governing over nations; for so many of them as shall embrace Jesus Christ, not only may brook their places, honors, riches, and all lawful benefits, wherein their fatness and worldly welfare seem to consist; but also shall be made partakers of the Lord's house, which shall so satisfy their souls, as they shall count his gospel their choice cheer, and shall bless God for his consolations." No man is so *fat* as not to need the bread of heaven; none is so poor as not to be welcome to the feast of fat things provided in the Gospel.

46. The preservation of the church in all ages is truly wonderful. Christ has always had a seed to serve him, v. 30. His enemies often have things outwardly much their own way, but even then his "hidden ones" are not few. When Elijah thought he was the only true worshipper of God left in all Israel, Jehovah said that he had *seven thousand* men who had not bowed the knee to Baal. Calvin: "The perpetuity of the church is here abundantly proved, and in very clear terms: not that it always flourishes or continues in the same uniform course through successive ages, but because God, unwilling that his name should be extinguished in the world, will always raise up some sincerely to devote themselves to his service."

47. To the best interests of men for both worlds nothing is more important than the publication of God's *righteousness*. The weight of this matter increases continually as the earth is more and more filled with people and stirred by commerce, v. 31.

48. Utterly vain are all the hopes of the wicked. So this Psalm abundantly declares. If ever earth and hell united in a plot dark, cunning and malignant above all others, it was that of compassing the death of the Son of man; yet out of that very event arise the greatest good to men, the greatest reward to Christ, and the greatest glory to God. The triumph of the wicked is short.

49. We live in exciting times. While sad tidings often make our ears to tingle, yet the tide of redemption is rolling on. The kingdom of God is surely coming. "Does not every fresh messenger from the heathen world bear to our ears the tidings of some new victory of our all-conquering Redeemer? Is not nation after nation beginning to feel the reviving influence of the Gospel of peace?" During the present generation, whole tribes of people have been led to forsake idols, and turn to Jehovah as the only living and true God. If the changes for the better, which have been going on for thirty years, shall continue and be proportionably accelerated for a hundred years longer, the Gospel will be well nigh universally diffused.

50. In this Psalm and in many other portions of Scripture we have a more sure word of prophecy, whereunto we do well to take heed as unto a light that shineth in a dark place, until the day dawn, and the day-star arise in our hearts.

PSALM XXIII.

A Psalm of David.

1 THE LORD *is* my shepherd; I shall not want.

2 He maketh me to lie down in green pastures: he leadeth me beside the still waters.

3 He restoreth my soul: he leadeth me in the paths of righteousness for his name's sake.

4 Yea, though I walk through the valley of the shadow of death, I will fear no evil: for thou *art* with me; thy rod and thy staff they comfort me.

5 Thou preparest a table before me in the presence of mine enemies: thou anointest my head with oil; my cup runneth over.

6 Surely goodness and mercy shall follow me all the days of my life: and I will dwell in the house of the LORD for ever.

SCOTT dates this Psalm B. C. 1057; Clarke, after the captivity. He assigns no reason. As a composition this ode contains nothing to indicate such an origin. The general impression is doubtless correct, that the Psalm was writen by David. The title says so. Many think this was one of the earliest compositions of David. The habits of his early life would furnish all the imagery of the first part of the Psalm. David was eminently fitted to write a devout pastoral. There is not a word in it that would indicate another authorship. On the title see on Ps. iii.

It is probable no *six* consecutive verses of Scripture are more frequently committed to memory than those of this Psalm. Morison: "It is impossible for language to express the extent and variety of spiritual consolation, which this incomparable ode has been the means of imparting. It has been felt to be the common property of that mystic flock that hear and know the voice of the Shepherd. In the depth of their sorrows, they have sung it, in the hope of deliverance; and when the candle of the Lord has shone round about them, they have been compelled to adopt it as the most natural expression of those sentiments of gratitude and praise which have struggled for suitable·utterance. There is a sweet tenderness in all the allusions of the Psalm, which will ever endear it to hearts that have felt the softening touch of divine grace; and there is, moreover, a character of moral beauty and loveliness belonging to it, which must leave the compositions of uninspired men at an almost infinite distance." Lowth: "What can be conceived sweeter or finer than this representation of God as a Shepherd?"

It is of some importance to determine whether this Psalm is to be applied to God the Father, or to God the Son. From Ps. xxviii. 9; lxxvii. 20; lxxx. 1, some have argued that God the Father is held forth as a Shepherd, and that here he is specially to be regarded. To this it is answered that the same titles, as Saviour, Father and Redeemer, are given to both the first and the second persons of the Godhead; and nothing forbids that the title *Shepherd* should have a like application. That the Psalm has a special reference to the Lord Jesus Christ seems to be very clear. J. M. Mason: "There is no difficulty in ascertaining the person here intended; for the description agrees to no other than our Lord Jesus Christ, who is at once JEHOVAH and the SHEPHERD *promised to the fathers.* He has ever delighted in this character, which, from the beginning, has supported the faith of the church, and animated her worship. The testimony which Jacob, with his dying breath has left to the Shepherd of Israel, she has perpetuated and improved." The passages of Scripture commonly cited on this subject are Gen. xlix. 24; Isa. xl. 11; Ezek. xxxiv. 23; xxxvii. 24; Zech. xiii. 7; John x. 11, 14; Heb. xiii. 20; 1 Pet. ii. 25; v. 4. The preceding

Psalm told us how the "Good Shepherd laid down his life for the sheep." This tells us how he lives to care for his flock. Scott: "As Christ is 'the good,' 'the great,' 'the *chief* Shepherd;' we cannot doubt that he is JEHOVAH, and is specially intended." Morison: "That this Psalm contains in it a prophetic reference to Him, who is 'the chief Shepherd,' and who 'gave his life for the sheep,' can only be doubted by those who would deprive the composition of one of its essential charms." Stevenson: "Jesus of Nazareth is the Messiah-Shepherd, the Jehovah-Shepherd." The only name of God in this Psalm is *Jehovah* LORD, on which see on Ps. i. 2.

1. *The* LORD *is my shepherd.* The Chaldee: "The Lord fed his people in the wilderness; Septuagint, Syriac, Arabic, Ethiopic and Ainsworth: The Lord feeds me; Vulgate and Doway: The Lord ruleth me. But the Doway has a note, stating that "in Hebrew" the reading is "The Lord is my shepherd, viz., to feed, guide, and govern me." The word rendered *shepherd* is a participle of the verb rendered *feed, keep,* etc., often rendered *shepherd.* The great body of scholars agree with the common version. Hengstenberg: "Of all the figures that are applied to God in the Old Testament, that of a shepherd is the most beautiful." This was probably the general impression of all the servants of God in the East. Oriental nations commonly called their good rulers and kings Shepherds. Only "every shepherd is an abomination unto the Egyptians," Gen. xlvi. 34. Speaking of God as a Shepherd Luther says: "The other names sound somewhat too gloriously and majestically, and bring, as it were, an awe and fear with them, when we hear them uttered. This is the case when the Scriptures call God our Lord, King, Creator. This, however, is not the case with the sweet word *shepherd.* It brings to the godly, when they read it or hear it, as it were a confidence, a consolation, or security like the word *father.*" The ground of the confidence expressed by David was that the Lord was not only *a* shepherd, but he says he is *my* shepherd. *I shall not want.* The Chaldee paraphrases this to suit its rendering of the first clause: They lacked nothing; Septuagint, Ethiopic, Vulgate and Doway: I shall want nothing; Syriac and Arabic: He will not suffer me to want anything; Ainsworth: I shall not lack; Amesius: I cannot be in want; Fry: I have no want; Hengstenberg: I want for nothing. But the rendering of our version in the future, *shall not want,* agrees with the original, is most commonly adopted, and includes the present also, *q. d.,* I shall neither now, nor at any future time want. Luther: "I shall assuredly want nothing. I shall eat and drink, and have abundance of clothes, food, protection, peace, and necessaries of every kind, which contribute to the support of life." Alexander: "Spiritual gifts are neither excluded, nor exclusively intended. No nice distinction between these and temporal advantages is here made for us and none need be made by us." The Scriptures sometimes catalogue the blessings of God's people, Matt. v. 3–12; 1 Cor. iii. 21–23; Gal. v. 22, 23. All these are secured to Christ's people. Other Scriptures say: "No good thing will he withhold from them that walk uprightly;" "All things work together for good to them that love God;" "My grace is sufficient for thee," Ps. lxxxiv. 11; Rom. viii. 28; 2 Cor. xii. 9. How can the saints want? The Lord will give them every good thing, "every good cross, every good comfort," every needed chastisement, every needed supply, all timely lessons, all good deliverances.

2. *He maketh me to lie down in green pastures.* The Chaldee: In a dry place he makes me to rest in the pleasantness of grass; Vulgate, Ethiopic and Doway: He hath set me in a place of pasture; Syriac: Upon the pastures of strength he shall make me to dwell; church of England: He shall feed me in a green pasture; Street: In pleasant places full of grass he maketh me repose; Fry: In green pastures he letteth me lie down; Jebb: In pastures of tender grass he shall make me lie down; Ainsworth: In folds of budding grass he maketh me lie down; Hengstenberg: He

layeth me down on the green meadows; Alexander: In pastures of verdure he will make me lie down. The Hebrew is future, and includes the present. The reference is clearly to the custom of leading flocks to repose at noon. See Cant. i. 7; Ezek. xxxiv. 15. *He leadeth me beside the still waters.* Septuagint: He hath led me by the water of quietness; Ethiopic, Vulgate and Doway: He hath brought me up on the water of refreshment; church of England: He shall lead me forth beside the waters of comfort; Calvin: He leadeth me to gently flowing waters: Venema: He shall supply to me drink near the waters of reposings; Street: Unto waters *inviting to* rest he gently leadeth me; Boothroyd: By gently flowing streams he leadeth me; Fry: Unto the waters of resting places he gently conducteth me; Ainsworth: He easily leadeth me by the waters of rests; Jebb: By waters of quietness he shall lead me; Edwards: He leads me to soft-flowing streams; Hengstenberg: He tendeth me by the waters of rest; Alexander: By waters of rest he will lead me. The verb is in the future here also. Calvin, Pool, Gill and Edwards think the quietness refers to the waters themselves. But sheep are not afraid of cascades or swift currents. Street's rendering is literal—*waters of rests*—i. e., the waters near which the flock finds ample repose. There is here no parallelism to Isaiah viii. 6, "the waters of Shiloah that go softly." Hengstenberg: "The plural indicates that the rest imparted is of a manifold kind, and respects not one gift, but a whole train of gifts." There can be no more lovely imagery than that here presented. It would be so in any country; but when we remember that it refers to a land that had a thirsty soil and but two rainy seasons in the year, it is very pleasing. Both clauses of the verse relate to the same thing— *repose,* or *rest,* or *peace.* God's people have a three-fold peace—peace with God, peace with their own consciences, and peace in their own affections. They are not hateful and hating one another. For innocence they are doves. Their consciences do not condemn them, neither does God. The first verse of this Psalm contains the main proposition, of which the second, third and fourth verses are an elucidation. Very strikingly does the second verse "depict the condition of believers. The world around them is a land of deserts and of drought, which yields nothing to *satisfy the longing soul.* Sooner shall the body be nourished by whirlwinds and the dust, than the spirit with things of mere time and sense." But with Christ for a Shepherd we have rest far above that when Joshua enfeoffed Israel in Canaan. Nor is our Saviour's care confined to the more rugged and vigorous. While "he shall feed his flock like a shepherd: he shall gather the lambs with his arm, and carry them in his bosom, and shall gently lead those that are with young," Isa. xl. 11. The more tender, helpless, or burdened any of the flock may be, the greater will be his compassion. He comforts the feeble-minded, and commands all his people to do the same, 1 Thess. v. 14. "He giveth power to the faint; and to them that have no might he increaseth strength," Isa. xl. 29–31.

3. *He restoreth my soul.* This rendering is sustained by the Genevan translation, Calvin and Edwards. The Septuagint, Syriac, Ethiopic, Vulgate and Doway: He hath converted my soul; church of England and Bishops' Bible: He shall convert my soul; Venema: He shall refresh my soul; Amesius: He maketh my soul quiet; Ainsworth: He returneth my soul; John Rogers' Translation: He quickeneth my soul; Pool: He bringeth back my soul; Waterland and Mudge: He refresheth my soul; Jebb: My soul he shall restore; Fry: He reneweth my strength; Hengstenberg: He revives my soul; Alexander: "To restore the soul here, as in Ps. xix. 7, is to vivify or quicken the exhausted spirit." Morison thinks that the form of the verb "denotes the act of *animating* or *invigorating,* in circumstances where life has been nearly extinct, or strength has been greatly exhausted. The idea of restoration to a forsaken path is, I think, here combined with that of recovered strength to walk

in it." A careful examination will show that the word is used in the broadest sense of *restoring*. In Isa. lviii. 12 we have the participle rendered, The *restorer* of paths to dwell in. Often is the word rendered *bring back*, or *bring again*, when it cannot signify merely to recover from faintness or weariness. See Isa. xlix. 5; Jer. l. 19; Ezek. xxxix. 27. This is the more natural construction also as sheep are exceedingly inclined to wander off into dangerous places. Restoration from wandering seems to have been by far the most common idea attached to this clause. It is however a blessed truth that God has in his gospel cordials for the fainting and correctives for the straying. Mason: "Sheep are prone to wander; and the farther they proceed, the more are they bewildered, and the more unlikely to return. Alas! the resemblance is too exact. . . Christians, although *renewed in the spirit of their mind*, carry about with them in the remnant of corruption a principle of *departure from the living God*. Take away, or suspend the influence of his grace, and the work is done: the most enlightened and tried believer goes astray the next moment. . . How far the regenerated may go it is not for us to conjecture, and it would be madness to try. That they shall not finally perish is one of the plainest promises of the Bible. But between the circumspection of grace and the damnation of hell there is ample room for sinning and for chastisement. . . Lost attainment, forfeited joy, withering graces, barrenness, leanness, lameness, and a long train of kindred miseries follow the steps of disobedience." In *restoring* his people Christ chooses his own time and method. But the process includes these things, a conviction of sin and folly in departing from God, Pr. xiv. 4; deep and heartfelt self-reproach and sorrow; a longing for renewed communion with God, Job xxiii. 3, 4; occasional fears of final desertion, Jer. xv. 18; and great distress of soul from a sense of sin, Jer. ii. 17–19. The pangs of restoration to God often exceed those of a first conversion. The penitent humbles himself under God's mighty hand, and is as a weaned child. At length help comes and hope revives. Jesus becomes a horn of salvation in the house of his servant David; that we should be saved from our enemies and from the hand of all that hate us; "that we, being delivered out of the hand of our enemies, might serve him without fear, in holiness and righteousness before him all the days of our life." Thus he gives "knowledge of salvation unto his people, by the remission of their sins, through the tender mercy of our God; whereby the day-spring from on high hath visited us, to give light to them that sit in darkness and in the shadow of death, to guide our feet into the way of peace." Thus "the good Shepherd *restores peace to his mourners*. For he leads them, by faith, to a renewed application of his blood for pardon: and he pardons most freely. *I am pacified*, saith he, *I am pacified towards thee for all that thou hast done*. This, O this melts the heart. Such patience! such compassion! such forgiveness! All the springs of contrition are opened at once; *Rivers of waters run down their eyes;* they throw away with disgust the idols which they had laid in their bosom, and *turning their feet unto the divine testimonies*, say, *Behold, we come unto thee, for thou art the Lord our God*. They now regain the *fellowship of their Saviour's death*, and *crucify the flesh with the affections and lusts*." To a soul thus exercised Christ in all his offices is precious. This restoration is often so marvellous to him, who is the subject of it, that he takes it for a first conversion. It is followed by the happiest effects: *He leadeth me in the paths of righteousness for his name's sake*. The Chaldee, John Rogers' and Genevan translations, Calvin, Amesius, Dathe, Ainsworth, Edwards and Fry prefer the present tense, *leadeth*. Septuagint, Syriac, Arabic, Ethiopic, Vulgate and Doway prefer the past, *hath led;* church of England, Bishops' Bible, Venema, Jebb and Alexander prefer *will lead*. In Ps. lxxiii. 24; Isa. lvii. 18, the same form of this verb is given—*shalt guide, will lead*. But elsewhere our version often renders it in the past or present. Divine guidance to believers is essential. Walford and some others, instead of " paths of righteousness" prefer " straight paths"—" such as are direct and easy." The reason assigned is that our version presents " an incongruous mixture of physical and moral figures." But is not this a mistake? Are not the physical and moral beautifully united in the preceding clause and indeed in the whole Psalm? As to sheep in Judea or any other hill country finding the " direct" to be the " easy" way, it was frequently just the reverse. The shepherd often led them about in a winding way that was to them safe and convenient. As the shepherd guides his flock in ways that he thinks best, so God guides his chosen in ways that he approves. Hengstenberg is confident that the word rendered *righteousness* " never stands in a physical sense for straightness: it always means righteousness. And this signification could only be considered as unsuitable from assuming the false position, that the Psalmist everywhere must use expressions that are borrowed from the relations connected with the figure which he is, for the time, employing in illustration of spiritual matters." The word does never in Scripture actually mean physical straightness. See all the passages where it occurs. To be led in the paths of righteousness may denote: 1, Guidance in ways of uprightness or justice towards men; 2, Guidance in the ways of righteousness or holiness towards God; 3, Guidance in those ways of providence which God's rectitude would lead him to select for his servant. God's righteousness makes him faithful to his saints. Montanus reads *tracks of righteousness*, or *well marked ways of righteousness*; Morison: Jesus " leadeth the sheep of his pasture into the right way; he causes them to choose the paths of holiness which they had forsaken; he strengthens them against the power of sin; he draws them to himself with the cords of love; he makes the most self-denying duties pleasurable; and enables them to derive lessons of humility, and caution, and watchfulness, and self-denial, and prayer, from their past failures."

This divine conduct to the people of God is not for their sakes, but *for his name's sake*. Our names are worthless. Our merits are naught. God is self-moved. "I, even I, am he that blotteth out thy transgressions for mine own sake, and will not remember thy sins," Isa. xliii. 25. Compare Isa. xlviii. 9, 11; Ezek. xxxii. 22. That which moves God to save his people is found in him, not in them. This should be known and remembered *first*, because it is true; *secondly,* because it is greatly to the glory of divine grace to select undeserving objects; and *thirdly,* because if God found in himself cause for beginning our salvation, and if he never changes, then shall he find in himself cause for crowning with glory the work of salvation begun in us. If he loved and pitied us when enemies, much more he will love and save us when friends. Steir: "Not for any merit of mine, but out of free grace;" Pool: "Not for any worth in me, but merely for the demonstration and glory of his justice, and faithfulness, and goodness;" Diodati: "Without having regard to any merit of mine, nor to my faults and unworthiness, but to make use of his goodness, and fulfil the truth of his promises;" Calvin: "Certainly his choosing us to be his sheep, and his performing towards us all the offices of a Shepherd, is a blessing which proceeds entirely from his free and sovereign goodness." Unmerited grace will finish what it began.

4. *Yea, though I walk through the valley of the shadow of death, I will fear no evil: for thou art with me; thy rod and thy staff they comfort me.* What are we to understand by *the valley of the shadow of death?* Bunyan has used this phrase, not as pointing to death, but to a time of great sadness, darkness and trial. His acquaintance with Scripture imagery and his almost inimitable use of it are generally confessed. He is sustained by many. Owen: "As death is the worst of evils, and comprehensive of them all, so the shadow of death is the most dismal and dark representation of those evils to the soul, and the valley of that shadow the most dreadful bottom and depth of that representation." J. M. Mason says *the valley of the shadow of death*

"does not signify *dying:* for it is not the valley of *death,* but of the *shadow* of death, and the shadow of an object cannot be the same thing with the object itself. The psalmist speaks of *walking* through this valley: which is a Scriptural term for a habit of action, or a course of suffering. But death is neither the one nor the other; but is a *single* event. . . The valley of the shadow of death is a scene of great and uncommon distress—of such trials as overpower the soul; throw it into amazement; break its purposes; fill it with alarm and horror like that which invades trembling nature at the approach of the 'king of terrors.'" Calvin, Venema, Patrick, Dodd, Dickson and Tholuck favor the same view. Ainsworth says this phrase "denoteth *imminent danger,* Jer. ii. 6; *sore affliction,* Ps. xliv. 19; cvii. 10–14; *fear and terror,* Job xxiv. 17; and *dreadful darkness,* Job x. 21, 22." Diodati paraphrases it: "Though I were in the terrors and dangers of present death;" Alexander: "*Death-shade* is a strong poetical expression for the profoundest darkness." Edwards speaks of "a vale overspread with a deadly shade." Yet many pious writers of good judgment suppose *death* itself is intended. Thus Scott: "Between that part of the flock which is on earth, and that which is gone to heaven, death lies, like a deep valley, that must be passed in going from the one to the other." Henry inclines to the same view. So also do Gill, Horne and Fry. It must be confessed that this latter is the popular view. How often is this verse repeated by dying saints. The writer has long noticed that many eminent ministers in the pulpit and in their devotional writings use the phrase in this sense.

But why may we not unite these views? Pains, which long continued would produce death, are called the pains of death. Paul says he was *in deaths oft,* because he suffered things which commonly lead to death. The phrase, *ways of death,* includes the misery of a wicked life here and hereafter, Prov. xiv. 12; xvi. 25. The darkness in our way through life is often a fit emblem of the gloom of a dying hour. It is probable that by *shadow of death* we are several times to understand all that is dark in life and in death. Once it seems clearly to point to death itself, being used interchangeably with that word, Job xxxviii. 17. Stevenson: "The 'valley of the shadow of death' is a remarkable phrase. It is peculiar to the Holy Scriptures, and to oriental literature. It is used to represent those horrible trials, those extreme difficulties and dangers, which darken the lot of humanity. Its import in this Psalm is not however to be limited to the troubles and sufferings of active life. The Psalmist neither excludes nor overlooks these; but he rises above and beyond them all. He reaches a climax of asseveration—'Yea, though I walk'—which comprehends every conceivable trial, and especially the last and severest to which our nature is exposed. Death is the principal object in the Psalmist's view. He has now reached the last point in his beautiful similitude; and the introduction of this comprehensive sentiment imparts a finish and completeness to the whole picture which he has so graphically delineated."

When *walking* refers to a man's behaviour, it indicates the course of his life. But when the subject is of a different nature, it has not necessarily any such import. We have the verb here rendered *walk* in these verses: David *went* to Jerusalem; Solomon *went* to the high place; Rehoboam *went* to Shechem, 1 Chron. xi. 4; 2 Chron. i. 3; x. 1. In Ps. xxxix. 13 we have the same verb in reference to death itself—"before I go [walk] hence, and be no more." One walks *through* the valley. The saints often pass through it in a short time. If *walking* be here taken to indicate the course of life, then David says that though much of his life should be spent in a darkness so dreadful as to remind him of the near approach of death, he would not be alarmed: *I will fear no evil.* Calvin: "As a sheep, when it wanders up and down through a dark valley, is preserved safe from the attacks of wild beasts and from harm in other ways, by the presence of the shepherd alone, so David now declares that as often as he shall be exposed to any danger, he will have sufficient defence and protection in being under the pastoral care of God. . . Now, since God, in the person of his only begotten Son, has exhibited himself to us as our Shepherd, much more clearly than he did in old time to the fathers who lived under the law, we do not render sufficient honor to his protecting care if we do not lift up our eyes to behold it, and keeping them fixed upon it, tread all fears and terrors under our feet." Our Shepherd walked through this valley in the days of his flesh. He entered the grave itself. He knows how necessary to our support is the divine presence, in our trials and in our dying agonies. If his people can look up and say to him, *Thou art with me*, they cannot yield to fear. Hengstenberg: *I dare fear no evil. Thy rod and thy staff they comfort me.* The *rod* was for guidance and defence, and the *staff*, for support. It was a crook and was put under the body of the sheep to *stay* it in slippery or miry places. Daniel Webster in his last hours, found no words more fit to express the support needed by a dying man than "thy rod and thy staff." Here as in previous clauses the verb is in the future, *will comfort.*

With the fourth verse the figure of a shepherd is dropped. Then that of a kind and rich host, exercising a large hospitality, is introduced. The imagery is drawn from the customs of oriental nations.

5. *Thou preparest a table before me in the presence of mine enemies.* Boothroyd and Street would attach the words, *in the presence of mine enemies,* to the next clause. For this change there is no good reason, nor is it favored by many. For *preparest* Calvin, Jebb and Alexander prefer the future, *shalt prepare.* For *enemies* Calvin reads *persecutors;* Ainsworth, *distressors;* church of England, *them that trouble me;* Septuagint, *those that afflict me;* Alexander, *adversaries.* To *prepare a table* was to *make ready a feast.* It was to do more than to give a loaf of bread to a weary pilgrim. It was to detain one as a guest and set before him the best of everything that could under the circumstances be had. The object was to give excellent food, solid refreshment. Stevenson is quite confident that the imagery of this verse is drawn from David's entertainment at the court of Saul; "David had experienced a remarkable and sudden elevation. The youthful shepherd had become a valiant warrior—and the attendant of a fold had now become an inhabitant of a court! His splendid victory over Goliath, his wide-spread fame as the deliverer of his country, his exalted honors as the favorite of the king, excited the envy and hatred of many. He knew that some of Saul's servants regarded him as their rival, and entertained towards him no friendly sentiments. The king himself, however, was still his friend; nor had his mind as yet experienced any unfavorable change." It seems a pity to spoil so beautiful an exposition. But whoever will read the history of David after slaying the giant of Gath will see that in some strange unaccountable way this excellent author has fallen into a total mistake. The eighteenth chapter of 1 Samuel is itself perfectly conclusive against his view. Saul's servants and subjects were David's warm friends, when the king himself was seeking the life of the champion of Israel. At Saul's house David was never a favorite of the king. It is surprising that even Tholuck says: "The first portion of David's stay at the court of Saul seems the most likely."

Some of the good things, with which the Saviour entertains and blesses his saints have been mentioned on verse 1. Others are stated in many Scriptures. He, who gives his life for our *ransom*, his body for our *meat*, and his blood for our *drink*, will surely give us all we need, Rom. viii. 32: John vi. 55. This feast was to be given *in the presence of mine enemies*, that is, *in spite of them and with their knowledge.* Alexander: "They are forced to witness my enjoyment without being able to disturb it." In this world the saints are never out of sight of foes, who would kill them if they could. Every sinner is at heart like Cain, though mercifully most of them are under restraint from education, law, conscience, or the common operations of God's Spirit. Wicked as the world is, there is a just and general impression, that in the last day, a little genuine piety, approved of God, will amount to more than all worldly power, wealth, honors and pleasures. And in this life the most wicked sometimes make singular acknowledgments of the value of true religion, Num. xxiii. 10; Esther vi. 13.

Not only is the feast in all the largeness of eastern hospitality; but the usual sign of welcome, of gladness and of honor is also given: *Thou anointest my head with oil.* There is nothing to warrant the reading of the Chaldee: Thou hast anointed with the anointing oil the head of my priests. The Chaldee, Septuagint, Syriac, Arabic, Ethiopic, Vulgate, Doway, church of England, Jebb, Fry and Alexander follow the original and use the past tense—*hast anointed;* Calvin has it, *wilt anoint.* Many agree with the common version—*anointest.* The verb rendered *anointest* is another form of the verb rendered *accept* in Ps. xx. 3. It is found only in these two places in the Psalms. Ainsworth gives the usual rendering of the word in other places and reads: *Thou makest fat my head with oil.* See Prov. xi. 25; xiii. 4; xxviii. 25; Isa. xxxiv. 6, 7. When men were sad they covered themselves with dust and ashes. When joyous they washed and anointed themselves, Job ii. 12; xlii. 6; 2 Sam. xii. 20. Men never anointed themselves in token of grief, Ps. xlv. 7. The anointing of guests was also to show them honor, and to declare their welcome. Capt. J. Wilson: "I once had this ceremony performed on myself in the house of a great and rich Indian, in the presence of a large company. The gentleman of the house poured upon my head, my hands and arms, a delightful odoriferous perfume. He then put a golden cup into my hands, and poured wine into it till it ran over; assuring me at the same time, that it was a great pleasure to him to receive me, and that I should find a rich supply in his house." The clause probably means: "Thou treatest me like a well-accepted guest at the table which thou hast prepared for me." The oils at feasts were aromatic, and diffused sweet odors. The custom of anointing the head was common, Ps. xcii. 10; Am. vi. 6; Matt. vi. 17; Luke vii. 38, 46. It created joy, Ps. civ. 15; Eccle. ix. 8; Isa. lxi. 3. Hengstenberg: "The oil, which is the symbolical expression of joy, is one of the necessary accompaniments of a festive and joyful entertainment." But viands and anointing oil were not alone, and so he adds: *My cup runneth over.* There is no good reason for the rendering of several versions followed by the Doway: My chalice which inebriateth *me,* how goodly is it. The church of England and Fry have it: My cup shall be full; Calvin, Edwards and Hengstenberg: My cup overflows; Jebb: My cup shall overflow; Alexander: My cup is overflowing. The cup handed at feasts was designed to cheer the guests. The Lord can give gladness in the darkest hour. We are not straitened in him.

6. *Surely goodness and mercy shall follow me all the days of my life.* The verbs of this verse are best rendered in the future. The weight of authority is in that direction, though a few prefer the present tense. It is a great attainment when God's people are persuaded of his "admirable freeness and readiness to do good to his people." Several versions made in the last three centuries read: *Only* for *surely.* But though authorized by the lexicons, and giving a good sense, they are not generally followed. The Septuagint, Ethiopic, Vulgate and Doway erroneously omit *goodness.* Morison suggests that *goodness* may relate to providential or temporal blessings; and *mercy* may more immediately express those spiritual blessings which essentially involve the act of showing mercy to persons as guilty. But this distinction is not uniformly preserved in the English version. *Goodness,* as in Ps. xvi. 2; lxviii. 10. *Mercy,* commonly a richer word than *goodness* often rendered *mercy,* as in each verse of Ps. cxxxvi.; *loving-kindness* in Ps. li. 1. For *goodness* the church of England reads *loving-kindness:* Hammond, *bounty.* For *mercy* Fry has *tenderness;* Edwards, *favor;* Hammond,

superabundant mercy; Hengstenberg, *love.* David's persuasion was that goodness and mercy *should follow* him. His enemies had *followed* him, perhaps were now *following* him, and might *follow* him again with relentless enmity; but these things did not move him, while he knew that goodness and mercy should *follow* him. The ground of this agreeable persuasion was the promise of God, his experience of the love and care of his Shepherd, and the condescension and bountifulness of Him, who had spread the feast and made the son of Jesse a welcome, though undeserving guest. His bright hopes embraced, says he, *all the days of my life.* This rendering is literal and is generally adopted. So blessed an experience, so comforting persuasions could not naturally stop here. They must arouse the soul to other thoughts: *And I will dwell in the house of the* LORD *for ever.* To the true Israel the *house of God* was from early times an emblem of the house not made with hands. Jesus said, " In my Father's *house* are many mansions." Those, who heard him, doubtless understood him as speaking of heaven. So that the last clause of this verse points not only to great blessings arising from communion with God on earth; but to the still higher, richer enjoyments of those, who worship in the sanctuary above. Diodati: " I shall dwell in his church in this world, and in the everlasting kingdom of heaven afterwards." Scott: " It is the desire, expectation, and determination [of his people] to seek their happiness in the service of God here; and they hope to enjoy his love, without enemy or interruption, for length of days, even forever in heaven hereafter. *For ever,* literally *unto length of days.* So the margin, the ancient versions, Calvin and Alexander. Jebb has *end of days;* Horsley and Fry, *unto eternity,* church of England, Edwards and Hengstenberg, *for ever;* in Ps. xciii. 5, *for ever.*

DOCTRINAL AND PRACTICAL REMARKS.

1. God is most loving. In condescension to our weakness he calls himself a *Shepherd,* that he may persuade us of his care and pity, v. 1. None but he, who dwells with the humble and contrite ones, would allow such titles to be given him.

2. This Psalm celebrates a time of prosperity. Then may we be sure that God's bounties of every kind are real blessings when they incline us to devout and thankful acknowledgments; and when they strengthen our purposes of holy obedience; otherwise they carry a curse with them. Blessed is he who " knows how to abound." He shall know " how to be abased," " to be hungry," and " to suffer need."

3. The Bible was not written to teach logic, yet finer specimens of strong reasoning can nowhere be found than in the sacred volume. Verse one is a specimen: " The Lord is my Shepherd; I shall not want." There are many like it: " Fear not, for I have redeemed thee;" " Because I live, ye shall live also;" " If God be for us, who can be against us?" " If children, then heirs;" " If, when we were enemies, we were reconciled to God by the death of his Son; much more, being reconciled, we shall be saved by his life;" " He that spared not his own Son, but delivered him up for us all, how shall he not with him also freely give us all things?"

4. If you would be happy, set your hope in God alone, v. 1. David did not say, Because I am renowned, have lands of my own and a royal revenue beside, and also because " *the* LORD is my Shepherd; I shall not want." The last was enough. It was all that was worth mentioning. We need nothing but what we find in God. We but weaken our faith by relying on appearances and creatures.

5. This Psalm, like most others celebrating personal experience, teaches the excellence of an appropriating faith, which can say, *My* Shepherd, v. 1. If divine promises are to help us, we must embrace them. The faith which can truly say, *My* Shepherd! *My* Lord! *My* God! *My* Rock! turns prophecies into history, promises into deliver-

ances, sorrows into joys, prisons into palaces, perils into victories, death into life. Nothing else can do so much.

6. As we need much in this life and more in the next, that which can keep us from *want* is precisely what ought to be the object of our quest, v. 1. He who has not the LORD for his Shepherd, may seek and obtain everything catalogued by the wise of earth, and he is still a poor creature. Riches take wings and fly away. The greatest heroes often die unwept. The greatest favorites of the mighty are often the first to feel the weight of their displeasure. Nothing created or liable to change can do us permanent good.

7. The richest man in a city may be the poorest; for if he has not his Shepherd's favor and care he lacks the most necessary thing. And the poorest man in a city is often the richest; for *first*, he thinks he has enough, and so is content; *secondly*, his eternal life is in the hands of Christ; *thirdly*, he has the sympathy of his Shepherd, who knows by experience what poverty is. Stevenson: "Our blessed Saviour's life on earth has honored and adorned the poor man's lot. Jesus of Nazareth was always poor, yet he never wanted. He lived on the providence of his heavenly Father, and never, in a single instance, did he perform a miracle to relieve his hunger." *Fourthly*, the eternal interests of the pious poor man are all secured. "The world loves *its* own, and God loves *his* own." He will provide. Earthly parents may die at any time, but the Christian's Father never dies.

8. So that the believer must be happy, v. 1. It cannot be otherwise unless second causes can thwart the great First cause, unless weakness can hinder omnipotence, unless folly can subvert wisdom. God is the believer's portion. Christ is his elect Saviour. The Holy Spirit is his Comforter. The world is his. Heaven is his. Nothing rests on a surer basis than his permanent happiness.

9. Some pious souls are troubled because they cannot at all times, or often use in its joyous import the language of this Psalm. Such should remember that David, though he lived long, never wrote but one twenty-third Psalm. Some of his odes do indeed express as lively a faith as this, and faith can walk in darkness. But where else do we find a whole Psalm expressive of personal confidence, joy and triumph from beginning to end? God's people have their seasons of darkness and their times of rejoicing. Luther: "The prophet has not at all times been so happy; he has not been able at all times to sing as he does here."

10. The saints cannot but find refreshment in the word and ordinances of God. These constitute the *green pastures* of the flock, v. 2. If you would know why the words of God are so nourishing and excellent to the souls of his people, read Psalms xix. cxix. They "rejoice at his word, as one that findeth great spoil." In like manner God's worship in all its parts builds up believers in faith, comfort and holiness; so that generally they esteem one day in the courts of the Lord better than a thousand.

11. As it is the habit of sheep, reposing at noon after feeding on the green pastures, to ruminate their food, so many pious writers, from v. 2 take occasion to urge the duty of devout meditation.

12. Some suppose that in v. 2, where *waters* are spoken of, the Holy Spirit is referred to. Though many may doubt this, yet in other parts of Scripture that allusion is clearly made. Indeed in John vii. 37, it is formally stated. The quietness and refreshments which the souls of believers enjoy, come from that blessed source. When he speaks peace, who can give trouble?

13. The doctrine of *restoring the soul*, v. 3, or of converting it to God, should in a world like ours excite gratitude at the mercy of God, which makes such a blessing possible and actual. What is clearer than that the lost must be recovered or perish, that those who are rushing headlong to ruin must be stopped, and their course

changed or they cannot see life? Conversion is an old doctrine. He, who practically rejects it, is undone.

14. But even after a first sound conversion to God, the soul may err like a lost sheep, and so need to be restored again. To Christians this is a mournful but a very practical subject. Solemn heart-searchings should be made in all the churches that every man may learn how his case stands with God. Am I a backslider in life or in heart? is never an idle question.

15. Everywhere in the Scriptures holiness is made essential to salvation, v. 3. He who dreams that he can enter heaven without purity of heart and righteousness of life, and dies in that delusion, will awake to shame and everlasting contempt.

16. One essential element of holiness is total self-renunciation, and an acknowledgement that we are nothing at all. God is everything, v. 3. What he does for us he does *for his name's sake*. Nothing can more oppose God than to cry with the Pharisee, "God, I thank thee that I am not as other men are;" or with Priestley, "Repentance and a good life are of themselves sufficient to recommend us to the divine favor;" or with Mrs. Barbauld, "When will Christians permit themselves to believe that the same conduct, which gains them the approbation of good men here, will secure the favor of heaven hereafter?" Will men never cease to make God to serve with their sins, and to weary him with their iniquities? Isa. xliii. 24.

17. Seasons of great joy should be made sober by remembering the days of darkness, which will come. When we ride upon our high places we should not forget *the valley of the shadow of death*, v. 4. "From troubles of some kind there is no exemption in the present state." Commonly the longer we live the sorer are our trials. At all times of distress, let us trust God and *fear no evil*, never be afraid with any amazement, never anticipate evils which may not come upon us, never magnify the trials we endure, never rely with confidence on human devices for deliverance, never deplore what is unavoidable, never hew out cisterns which can hold no water, always put the best construction on God's procedure, always expect that more light will remove much of our perplexity, always remember that if God should cease to be a mysterious being, he would cease to be God; and that a government without acts inexplicable to mortals, cannot be divine.

18. Solemn and even awful as is the subject of death, the fear of it can be quite overcome, v. 4. Compare Heb. ii. 15. Christ can conquer every foe, and drive away every fear, and cause his people to shout and sing of victory even in the agonies of dissolution. Henry: "Here is one word which sounds terrible; it is death, . . . but there are four words which lessen the terror. 1. It is but the *shadow* of death, there is no substantial evil in it; the shadow of a serpent will not sting, nor the shadow of a sword kill. 2. It is the *valley* of the shadow, deep indeed, and dark, and dirty; but the valleys are fruitful, and so is death itself fruitful of comforts to God's people. 3. It is but a *walk* in this valley, a gentle pleasant walk: the wicked are chased out of the world, and their souls are required; but the saints take a walk to another world as cheerfully as they take their leave of this. 4. It is a walk *through* it; they shall not be lost in it, but get safe to the mountain of spices on the other side of it."

19. Christ must be a wonderful person that his presence should produce so amazing effects. His birth troubled Herod and all Jerusalem with him, because they were wicked; but it gave joy in heaven. His presence greatly troubled the Gadarenes; but it calmed the troubled sea. His grasp is death; his frown is hell; his grace is salvation; his smile is heaven. "The Lamb is the light thereof." Truly this is the Son of God.

20. The blessings which Jesus pours on his people are rich and varied, v. 5. He

is the Master of the house of God. He alone is fit to rule there. His kindness is unbounded. His condescension is amazing. His resources are infinite. O blessed be the God and Father of our Lord Jesus Christ, who hath blessed us with all spiritual blessings in heavenly places in Christ. He makes us a feast of fat things. So costly provisions were never heard of before. He invites the maimed, the halt and the blind; but he cures all their maladies. He calls the poor and the outcast; but he clothes them with the garments of salvation. All the choice spirits of the universe shall be at the marriage supper of the Lamb. He loves his saints. He often shows them a token for good. He anoints their heads with oil. Their cup runneth over.

21. The anointing of v. 5, clearly points to the effusion of the Holy Ghost. When he is poured out, the whole character is changed. Every grace of the Christian is savory like the oil, compounded after the art of the apothecary, and poured upon the head of Aaron, when he became high priest, Ps. cxxxiii. 1, 2.

22. The cup that runneth over, v. 5, has special reference to divine consolations. Wine cheers the heart of man. Much more does the gracious presence of God's Spirit enliven and animate the soul of the believer. It makes him hope against hope. It lifts him up above the world. It takes away the bitterness of death. It gives boldness in the greatest perils. The day of judgment shall not terrify the saints, 1 John iv. 17.

23. Past experience of God's favor has its due effect upon us, when it leads us humbly and firmly to rely on his goodness and mercy for days to come, v. 6. The wicked often have a vain confidence for the future. It is not set in God. But the righteous know whom they have believed. They have tried him, and found him unfailing.

24. Love to God's house, accompanied by a desire and purpose to maintain with it a permanent connection, belongs to true piety, v. 6. It was not peculiar to David to say, "One thing have I desired of the Lord, that will I seek after; that I may dwell in the house of the Lord all the days of my life, to behold the beauty of the Lord and to inquire in his temple," Ps. xxvii. 4. The reason is given in Ps. xxxvi. 8–10; lxxxiv. 4–11.

25. Christian worship gains an important end when by it we are made heavenly-minded, and our contemplations and affections are lifted to glorious things at God's right hand, v. 6. The attractions of that world are great, and always increasing. Why think we so little of our eternal home?

26. The want of faith renders nugatory even the most precious portions of Scripture. This Psalm is often admired as a poetic composition by men to whom its divine teachings have no more saving power than the ode of a heathen poet.

27. The distinction between saints and sinners is not idle, or modal, or formal. It is true, real, necessary. It is made by God himself. There is a difference between him, who is led by the good Shepherd, and him, who is led captive by the devil at his will; between him, who feeds in the *green pastures,* and him, who feeds on vanity. Oh that men saw this difference as they ought. Oh that in all preaching it were more carefully observed and made prominent.

28. Sinner! Will you be saved? You are wandering on the dark mountains. Will you not take the Lord as your Shepherd? Your wants are many and are constantly increasing. Will you not turn? Oh that you would. You are lost, *lost,* LOST! Your state is dismal but not hopeless, forlorn but not desperate. Hear the voice of Jesus: "I am the good Shepherd: the good Shepherd giveth his life for the sheep." "I am the door: by me if any man enter in, he shall be saved, and shall go in and out and find pasture," John x. 9, 11. You are lost, but Christ's errand into this world was to *seek and to save that which is lost.* The door is now open, but it will soon

be shut. Mercy is now offered; but mercy slighted will inconceivably enhance your damnation.

29. What a Saviour is Jesus! He is matchless. Lavington: "Blessed Jesus! how infinitely hast thou outdone the best shepherd that ever existed! Many have been remarkable for looking diligently to the state of their flocks, providing for them suitable pasture, taking care that none of them go astray, and defending them against the beasts of prey to which they were exposed; but when did any one lay down his life for his sheep? Yet this has been done by our compassionate Shepherd." He deserves all our love.

> Had I ten thousand thousand tongues,
> Not one should silent be;
> Had I ten thousand thousand hearts,
> I'd give them all to thee.

PSALM XXIV.

A Psalm of David.

1 The earth is the LORD'S, and the fulness thereof; the world, and they that dwell therein.

2 For he hath founded it upon the seas, and established it upon the floods.

3 Who shall ascend into the hill of the LORD? or who shall stand in his holy place?

4 He that hath clean hands, and a pure heart; who hath not lifted up his soul unto vanity, nor sworn deceitfully.

5 He shall receive the blessing from the LORD, and righteousness from the God of his salvation.

6 This is the generation of them that seek him, that seek thy face, O Jacob. Selah.

7 Lift up your heads, O ye gates; and be ye lifted up, ye everlasting doors; and the King of glory shall come in.

8 Who is this King of glory? The LORD strong and mighty, the LORD mighty in battle.

9 Lift up your heads, O ye gates; even lift them up, ye everlasting doors; and the King of glory shall come in.

10 Who is this King of glory? The LORD of hosts, he is the King of glory. Selah.

ON the title see on title of Psalm iii.

It seems to be pretty well agreed that this ode was composed 1042 or 1043 B. C. The proof of the Davidic authorship is strong and is generally acknowledged. Cocceius, Amesius, Williams, Hammond, Horsley and Fry regard this Psalm as a dialogue. This opinion gives no advantage in interpreting it, and is justly rejected by a large majority of Commentators.

Many give it a historic origin, though there is no general agreement what that was. Diodati supposes it has special reference to the removal of the ark, as mentioned in 2 Sam. vi; 2 Chron. iii. See also 1 Chron. xv. xvi. This view is followed by Patrick, Delany and Bishop Lowth; strongly maintained by Hengstenberg, and favored by Alexander. The most serious objection to it is that in 1 Chron. xvi. 8–36, there is given us at length the Psalm sung on that occasion. It consists of *twenty-eight* verses; this, of but *ten*. It no more resembles this than any other joyful sacred ode of comprehensive adoration and gratitude. It may be said that Psalms xv. and xxiv. were also sung on that occasion. This can neither be proven nor disproven. Others think this Psalm was composed by David to be sung at the dedication of the temple, which he knew by prophecy should be built by Solomon. But in the account we have of the dedication of that wonderful house it is not hinted that this Psalm or any part of it was used. Mudge takes another view: "This seems to be a song of triumph; returning victorious from the war, they are supposed ascending up to the temple, as the Romans did to the capitol, and there replacing in it the ark with great pomp." Others are of the same mind. Against this Hengstenberg argues with spirit, though not conclusively. The Septuagint adds to the title these words "*of the first day of the week,*" signifying that this Psalm was sung on the day succeeding the Sabbath. The Jewish doctors expressly say this was actually done, as Ainsworth has shown. Williams quotes from Bruce's travels an account of a ceremony observed in the reception of the king of Ethiopia, which he supposes may have had its origin in this Psalm, or in some Eastern custom, even more ancient than this sacred song. Could it be shown that ancient orientals had such a usage, it might give us a knowledge of the origin of some of the imagery of the Psalm; but it is hardly safe to follow such a conjecture.

This Psalm contains a blessed prophecy respecting Christ and the glory of his kingdom. Any language in it borrowed from the ascent of Mount Zion at any time, or from any Eastern usage, had but an allusion to things seen, which were types of things yet to come in the setting up of Christ's kingdom on earth, and in his glorious ascension to heaven, *first*, forty days after his own resurrection, and *secondly*, after he shall have gathered all his chosen to himself in the last day. There were no gates to the acropolis of Mount Zion; nor were there any *everlasting* doors to the tabernacle or to the temple. The former was made of curtains that perished, as did also the doors of the latter. And it is confidently said that the doors of the temple opened as do our doors, and not by being lifted up. That the Typical-Messianic view is not unwarranted has been the opinion of many. Cocceius says the theme of this Psalm is "the spiritual kingdom of God;" Henry: "This Psalm is concerning the kingdom of Jesus Christ;" Nicholson: "The subject of this Psalm is Christ, called the king of glory;" Scott: "This Psalm is supposed to have been written and sung, with some others, when David removed the ark to Jerusalem; and perhaps it might also be used when the ark was carried into Solomon's temple. But the ascension of Christ into heaven seems to have been sublimely prefigured under these typical events." Horsley: "Messiah is certainly the Jehovah of this Psalm;" Fry: "The ascension of our great High Priest into the courts of the Zion, which is above, is very evidently the subject of this Psalm." "Hengstenberg: "The coming of the Lord of glory, the high demands upon his people proceeding from this, the absolute necessity to prepare worthily for his arrival form the subject matter of this Psalm." Alexander: "The sanctuary of the old economy, both in its permanent and temporary forms, was intended to symbolize the doctrine of God's special presence and residence among his people; and as this was realized in the advent of Christ, the Psalm before us has a permanent interest and use, and in a certain sense may be described as Messianic."

The reader will notice the resemblance between this and the *fifteenth* Psalm. Yet they are independent compositions, probably introduced into the temple service about the same time. Hengstenberg thinks this the older composition. Alexander thinks they were "composed for use on a similar if not the same occasion." Scott dates them the same year.

The names of the Most High in this Psalm are *Jehovah* LORD and *Elohim God,* on which see on Ps. i. 2; iii. 2.

1. *The earth is the Lord's.* This clause contains the truth on which the rest of the Psalm is founded. The message is to the inhabitants of earth, and the first thing said to them is, The very earth on which you walk is Jehovah's, not yours.

Here God has rights of ownership and rights of sovereignty, undeniable and inalienable. He is proprietor to the exclusion of all others. Satan is the God of this world in no other sense than as a usurper, supported by the wicked, who are his children. The gods of the heathen are vanities and lies. They can neither see, nor save, nor hear, nor help. They and the devil have no rights here. The earth is the Lord's, *and the fulness thereof.* Chaldee: And the creatures thereof; Arabic: In its entireness; Amesius and Hengstenberg: And that which fills it; Edwards: And all that it contains; Fry: And all that is therein; church of England: And all that therein is; Ainsworth: And the plentie thereof; Horsley: And its whole furniture; Pool: "All the creatures, and especially the inhabitants wherewith it is replenished." Calvin: "Under the word *fulness* all the riches with which the earth is adorned are comprehended." 1 Cor. x. 26. If there was in the world one man, or one creature, or one atom, over which God was not sovereign, it would be impossible to foretell the evil and confusion that might follow. *The world, and they that dwell therein,* also belong to Jehovah. Morison: "The *world* is the poetic substitute for earth, and generally denotes the inhabited earth." Hengstenberg and Alexander regard it as denoting the productive or fruit-bearing portion of the earth. The same word is found in Ps. ix. 8; xviii. 15; xxxiii. 8; l. 12; lxxvii. 18; lxxxix. 11. Call the world by what name you will, the Lord is its sole and sovereign proprietor. This truth is next proven:

2. *For he hath founded it upon the seas, and established it upon the floods.* For *established* the Septuagint, Ethiopic, Vulgate, Doway and church of England read *prepared.* Hengstenberg: For he has founded it above the seas, and made it fast above the floods. The language is popular, not philosophical. It speaks of things as they appear. *Founded* and *established* are words that point out the stability of the order of things witnessed on earth, marking the presence of an almighty, all-wise and unchangeable Jehovah. God's right to the earth is based on his having created it, and given it all its laws, products and blessings.

3. *Who shall ascend into the hill of the* LORD? Chaldee: Who shall ascend into the mountain of the house of the sanctuary of the Lord? Septuagint and kindred versions: Who shall ascend into the mountain of the Lord? Calvin: Who shall ascend unto the hill of Jehovah? Venema, Amesius, Edwards and Ainsworth: Who shall ascend into the mountain of Jehovah? Hengstenberg: Who shall ascend the hill of the Lord? Alexander: Who shall go up into the mountain of Jehovah? The hill or mountain was Zion where God's worship was so long, so splendidly and so edifyingly celebrated. *Or who shall stand in his holy place? i. e.,* in Jehovah's holy place? The import of both questions in this verse is the same: Who shall truly and acceptably worship God in his earthly courts, and so at last be admitted to heaven itself? Alexander: "The verb in the last clause does not simply mean to *stand,* but to *stand fast,* to maintain one's ground," Ps. i. 5. Many enter the house of God and the church of God, and soon fall away. Others without any saving change of heart maintain their visible good standing for a long time, some even till life ends, but in eternity they awake to shame and everlasting contempt. God told them beforehand what sort of worshipper he would accept:

4. *He that hath clean hands and a pure heart.* Chaldee, Septuagint, Ethiopic, Vulgate, Doway and Venema: The innocent of hands and clean of heart; Ainsworth: The clean in hands, and pure in heart; Amesius: The innocent in hands and pure in mind; Street, Jebb, Fry and Alexander: The clean of hands, and pure of heart; Calvin: He who is clean of hands and pure of heart. In Scripture language he has clean hands who has not defiled them with blood, or violence, or bribery, or fraud, or unjust gain, or wrong doing of any kind towards God or man, the hands being the instruments of action,

But the hands are governed by the *heart,* so that must be *pure.* " As a man thinketh in his heart so is he." None but the pure in heart shall see God, Matt. v. 8. Men judge of the heart by acts, but God judges acts by the heart, and the heart by itself. A *pure heart* shows itself chiefly in two ways: by hatred of guile, hypocrisy, vain thoughts, vile affections, sins of every kind; and by love to truth, purity, holiness, uprightness, God and all his excellence. He who meets the foregoing description is also one *who hath not lifted up his soul unto vanity. Vanity* so rendered also in Ps. xii. 2; xli. 6; cxix. 37 and often. Though idols are *vanities,* yet a man may lift up his soul to vanity without open idolatry. Many things besides idols are a *vanity,* a *lie,* as the word is elsewhere rendered. All their lives some walk in a vain show. But the godly prefers truth to any form of delusion, seriousness and even sorrow to levity and trifling. Such a man can be trusted. *Nor* [hath he] *sworn deceitfully.* Our version is literal. Chaldee: Hath not sworn to a falsehood to the condemnation of his own soul. Other ancient versions generally agree with ours, some adding without cause, *to his neighbor. Sworn deceitfully,* Edwards renders: Sworn with deceitful intentions; Fry: Hath not sworn to a falsehood; Hengstenberg: Nor swears deceitfully; Alexander: Has not sworn to fraud; Street: Doth not swear with intention to deceive; Ainsworth: Doth not swear to deceit. One may swear deceitfully to his Maker as well as to his fellow-mortal. Vows to God are of the same solemn nature with oaths, Ps. cxix. 106. Some regard this clause as parallel to the last clause of Ps. xv. 4, and so it is to some extent; but this covers more ground than that. Perhaps no verse of holy Scripture in so few words more clearly delineates the character of a real saint. Such a man shall be saved; for,

5. *He shall receive the blessing from the* LORD, *and righteousness from the God of his salvation. The blessing* is better than *a blessing,* or *blessing.* For *righteousness* the Septuagint and kindred versions have *mercy.* The word occurs more than *thirty* times in the Psalms, and is uniformly rendered *righteousness.* Elsewhere it is sometimes rendered *justice, right,* but never *mercy.* For *righteousness* Edwards reads *a gracious reward.* Pool favors this sense " as the *work* is often put for the reward of it," Job vii. 2; Ps. cxix. 20. But this is a limitation of an idea intended to be far more comprehensive. The good man *shall receive the blessing, i. e.,* every good and perfect gift, temporal and spiritual, pleasing and disciplinary—*the blessing* which maketh rich and addeth no sorrow, including grace and glory, all of earth that is worth having, and all of heaven that his capacities can embrace. He shall in the end have *justice* done to his motives, his character, his heavenly aims. He shall receive such an elevation of personal character as shall make him equal to the angels, and in his measure like unto God himself. Jehovah shall evince his perfect approval of his character by many infallible signs. Yea, the Lord shall make him an eternal partaker of that perfect and spotless righteousness which was wrought out by Christ, which is the sole ground of our acceptance with God, and gives a right to the tree of life, Rev. xxii. 14. We have the best authority for saying that *righteousness* had this last meaning at least as early as the days of Abraham, Gen. xv. 6; Rom. iv. 22, 23; Gal. iii. 6. Why are men so averse to finding in God's word the doctrine of a gratuitous salvation by imputed righteousness? The phrase—*the God of his salvation*—points to something far beyond mere *justice,* as that term is commonly understood. There is always a race of such justified and upright men on earth, and so it is added,

6. *This* is *the generation of them that seek him.* Calvin: " By the demonstrative pronoun *this,* the Psalmist erases from the catalogue of the servants of God, all counterfeit Israelites, who, trusting only to their circumcision and the sacrifices of beasts, have no concern about offering themselves to God; and yet, at the same time, they rashly thrust themselves into the church." *Generation,* the same as in Ps. xiv. 5;

xxii. 30. To *seek Jehovah* is to be truly and habitually devoted to his fear and service. The phrase comprehends the whole of religion. See on Ps. ix. 10. This is the race that seek Jehovah, *that seek thy face, O Jacob.* This clause has perplexed many. The leading views are these. Some read, That seek thy face in Jacob. That is, they seek out the true church and desire by faith a union with her, because God is with her. There is little to support this, although it gives not a bad sense. Others suppose there is an unusual ellipsis here, and for *O Jacob* read *O God of Jacob.* The reasons for this rendering are these: 1. In two of Kennicott's Manuscripts this is the reading of the Hebrew text. 2. The Septuagint, Ethiopic, Syriac, Arabic, Vulgate, Doway, Horne and others all have it *God of Jacob.* 3. This gives a good sense. The change of person from the third to the second is quite common in Hebrew poetry. The great objection to reading *God of Jacob* is that the Hebrew text of collated MSS. does not sufficiently authorize it. Others read, That seek thy face *as Jacob, i. e.,* very earnestly, and importunately *as Jacob,* so as to prevail. This is not much urged. Nor can much be said in its favor. Hengstenberg renders it: This is the generation which reverences him, who seek thy face, are Jacob. This is not very intelligible. But in his exposition he regards it as asserting, " that only those who are earnest in their pursuit after holiness, according to the good pleasure of God, are the true posterity of Jacob, and form the people of the covenant, who are under grace. The others, notwithstanding their descent from Jacob, belong not to Jacob, but are heathen, and thus children of wrath." Alexander's translation is lucid: This is the generation seeking him: the seekers of thy face (are) Jacob, *i. e.,* the true Jacob, the true Israel. Perhaps the best rendering is that of Ainsworth: This is the generation of them that inquire for him, of them that seek thy face, of Jacob. Thus *of Jacob* has the same import as the two preceding phrases. This translation is every way allowable, and avoids the necessity of supposing any ellipse. The parallelism is thus fully preserved. The sense then is, This is the generation, the true progeny of Jacob, the body of true Israelites, the congregation of worshippers who shall be accepted in the holy hill, John i. 47 ; Rom. ix. 6. The distinction between true and false Israelites is maintained in all the Scriptures. On *Selah* see Introduction, § 15.

7. *Lift up your heads, O ye gates.* Septuagint, Ethiopic, Arabic, Vulgate and Doway: Lift up your gates, O ye princes; John Rogers: Open your gates, O ye princes. The objections to this rendering are serious. They need not be given in detail. The grammatical difficulty is insurmountable. With the English version substantially agree the Syriac, Calvin, church of England, Bishops' Bible, Genevan Translation, Venema, Amesius, Ainsworth, Edwards, Jebb, Fry, Hengstenberg, Alexander and others. Chaldee: Ye gates of the house of the sanctuary, lift up your heads. The common version is correct. *And be ye lifted up, ye everlasting doors.* The renderings of this verse are quite uniform. At least the variations are unimportant. The object of opening the gates and doors is to this end: *And the King of glory shall come in.* It seems almost impossible to give to this verse an interpretation that should confine its import to any scene ever enacted in Judea. Hengstenberg: " The gates of the newly built temple could not possibly be called everlasting gates." If so, they could hardly be so called when not in existence, and when they lasted so short a time, Isa. lxiii. 18. We are compelled to seek a higher sense than any that should confine it to the removal of the ark. The language of the prophet rises far above the solemn scenes witnessed on earth, and at once passes to the things shadowed forth by the ark, the tabernacle and temple, all of which were figures of Christ and of heaven. The removal of the ark to Mount Zion was a faint shadow of the ascension of Christ, the King of glory, to receive whom the heavens opened their everlasting gates. Scott " This may represent the Saviour at his ascension, demanding by his attendant angels

admission into heaven, as Man and Mediator; yet at the same time as 'the King of glory,' and the LORD strong and mighty;" Morison: "And what was the bright cloud which shone resplendently from off the mercy-seat, from between the cherubim of glory, but an anticipated exhibition of that 'mystery of godliness, God manifest in the flesh?' He emphatically is 'the King and Lord of glory,' whose triumphant ascension to the portals of the celestial sanctuary was hailed by the shout of myriads of angelic bands, who gladly threw open 'the everlasting doors' to the glorified human nature of the Son of God, and saw him with rapture sit down, in everlasting majesty, 'on the right hand of power;'" Fry: "King, or Lord of Glory, is an undoubted title of Messiah."

8. *Who is this King of glory?* If the gates of the celestial city are to be opened to him, if the everlasting doors of the temple not made with hands are to be lifted up, that one, who has never in his present form reigned there before, may enter in triumph, it is natural to inquire, For whom are claimed such exalted honors? The answer is, *The* LORD [Jehovah] *strong and mighty, the* LORD *mighty in battle.* The honors here ascribed to Christ are no greater than those given him in Isa. vi. 1–5; ix. 6, 7, and in many other places. He is Jehovah. He is mighty. He is almighty. He is the Lord of lords and the King of kings, Rev. i. 8; xix. 16. He is *mighty in battle.* He is the Captain of our salvation. He is invincible. Who ever hardened himself against Christ and prospered?

9. *Lift up your heads, O ye gates; even lift* them *up, ye everlasting doors; and the King of glory shall come in.* The language varies very slightly from that of v. 7. The repetition of it expresses fixedness of purpose, and the consciousness of possessing authority to require the thing to be done.

10. *Who is this King of glory?* This is not a vain repetition of the question in v. 8. It is as if the psalmist had said, I have said something of him. Would any know more of him? Does any ask further of his glory? I will declare it. I have already said that on earth his power is resistless. I will further state that he is *The* LORD *of hosts, he* is *the King of glory.* He is the Jehovah of armies. He has authority over all the heavenly hosts. So the Scriptures assert, Matt. xxviii. 18; Eph. i. 21; iii. 10; Col. i. 16; ii. 10. The Lord of Sabaoth is a glorious title. It is retained in two cases in the New Testament, Rom. ix. 29; James v. 4. On *Selah* see Introduction, § 15.

DOCTRINAL AND PRACTICAL REMARKS.

1. God is sole Creator of the universe and its inhabitants, v. 1. This pillar of truth must stand unshaken or all our religion becomes heathenish, Acts xvii. 24–26.

2. The Lord made all things, not for the glory and honor of any race of creatures, much less of any particular tribe, or order of men, but for himself, v. 1. "Of him, and to him, and through him, are all things; to whom be glory for ever. Amen." Rom. xi. 36.

3. The scope of the opening of the Psalm seems to be the same as that of Deut. x. 14–16. "Behold the heaven and the heaven of heavens is the LORD's thy God, the earth also, with all that therein is. Only the LORD had a delight of thy fathers to love them, and he chose their seed after them, even you above all people, as it is this day. Circumcise therefore the foreskin of your hearts, and be no more stiff-necked." Peculiar distinctions and privileges, whether national or personal, impose peculiar obligations. God's sovereignty is a precious and a profitable doctrine. It gladdens the pious heart, Matt. xi. 25, 26. It humbles the soul. God chose not the Jewish nation because they were descended from a race of pious ancestors, Josh. xxiv. 2. Of this he often reminds them. Christians are by nature as vile as others.

4. If God is universal Creator and Preserver, his worship ought to be universal. And it would be, if men were not wicked. His tender mercies are over all his works. Towards him all hearts should be tender and obedient.

5. Instead of its being a very surprising thing that the world was once deluged with water, the wonder rather is that it is not always so. Instead of this it is firmly *founded upon the seas and established upon the floods*, v. 2. Yet the water is far lighter than the dry land. The only reason why the earth is not deluged all the time is given by God to the man of Uz, Job xxxviii. 8–11.

6. Cobbin: *"The pious mind views all things in God, and God in all things,"* vv. 1, 2. This is right. If men were not without God in the world, they would all do so. Devout thoughts of the Creator are as elevating as they are just.

7. While there is nothing in natural science to convert the soul, yet when men's hearts are renewed by the Holy Ghost, they do find much food for devout adoration in all God's works, vv. 1, 2. Cobbin: *"Those who duly contemplate the works of God will worship him.* Such men as Sir Isaac Newton and Linnæus could not be infidels; the one saw his God in the splendor of the heavens; the other, even in the thorny heath, decked with its yellow flowers: he saw, and adored."

8. God's proprietary title is perfect; being built on his creative and providential control of all things, vv. 1, 2. Consequently sin is an attempt to take away God's rights. It is fraud, theft, robbery, impudence, rebellion against God. Sin is the worst thing that God or man ever contemplated, Isa. i. 2; Jer. ii. 12.

9. Truth has vast bearings and logical connections. From the words of verse 1, *The earth is the Lord's, and the fulness thereof*, Paul infers *first*, It is in itself lawful to eat any wholesome food; *secondly*, We ought not by eating anything to tempt our neighbor to do wrong, for we can eat other things as well; *thirdly*, Whether we eat or drink or whatsoever we do, we must do all to the glory of God, for he owns all, 1 Cor. x. 25–31.

10. Men, who make their philosophy a fountain of atheism, are as much out of the way in their science as in their religion. We all may properly speak of the laws of nature; but if by them we mean more than the fixed principles on which God governs nature, or the uniform methods of the divine procedure, we are atheists; for Jehovah has founded and established and maintains the whole course of nature. From him it has all its stability, v. 2. Providence as loudly proclaims a presiding, as creation does an originating Deity.

11. Often do the Scriptures present the question of the nature of true religion, v. 3. No weightier matter can claim human attention. J. Edwards: "There is no question of greater importance to mankind, and that it more concerns every individual person to be well resolved in, than this: *What are the distinguishing qualifications of those that are in favor with God, and entitled to his eternal rewards?* Or, which comes to the same thing, *What is the nature of true religion, and wherein lie the distinguishing notes of that virtue which is acceptable in the sight of God?"* It is a great mercy that God's word speaks so frequently and so clearly on the subject.

12. There always has been, there now is, and till time shall end there always shall be a church on earth, v. 3. Wherever God has recorded his name, has heard prayer, has been worshipped in spirit and in truth, there he has had a *holy place*, whether on a *hill*, or in the valley. It has always been true that where two or three were met in God's name, they have had his blessing. Yea, one man of fervent prayer has found a barren spot in a desert to be none other than the house of God and the gate of heaven.

13. Outward membership in the visible church is not itself saving, nor is it an infallible sign of one's being in a saving state, v. 3. It is always pertinent and proper

to note the difference in the two classes that compose the church, some having the form of godliness but denying its power, others cleaving to the Lord with purpose of heart, and perhaps caring but little for the ceremonies of religion.

14. One of the master-pieces of Satanic craft has been to effect a divorce between morality and religion, while God's plan is to join them inseparably together, vv. 3, 4. Nor does our great enemy seem to have any marked preference for religion without morality over morality without religion. Why should he? Morality without religion is but a smooth way of descending to hell. Religion without morality is monstrous. Williams: "Neither painted hypocrites, nor self-righteous Pharisees, nor mere formal professors; but the true worshippers only of the true God will Jehovah admit to reside with him." A wicked life destroys all hope of salvation arising from any boasted experience, or the most flaming profession. Judgment, mercy and faith are weighty matters of the law, Matt. xxiii. 23. If professed piety makes men no better, what is it worth? Clean hands and a pure heart must accompany any valid profession of religion. Spotless outward behaviour without real sanctity of internal character proves no man to be on his way to glory.

15. Our English word *vanity* as used by our best classics points to a foolish desire to be esteemed above one's real merits. It also signifies an idle display, a vain ostentation, a petty pride. Sometimes it describes a tripping levity contrary to reasonable sobriety of mind. Again it points to falsehood, deceit. In all these senses of the word, vanity is sinful—is condemned in Scripture. Each kind shows a great lack of understanding, leads to self-deception, is unfriendly to truth, is without holidays, makes men sooner or later appear foolish, is very common, is very difficult of cure; and is always odious to right-minded people. Indeed none seem to dislike vanity in others more than the vain themselves. An accepted worshipper must not *lift up his soul unto vanity* of any kind, v. 4.

16. The Scriptures throw a sacredness around promises, contracts, covenants, vows and oaths, v. 4. To society this is a great mercy. When truth is fallen in the streets, iniquity riots. Perhaps no one thing adds so much to the personal happiness of men as truth-telling, and nothing adds more to the sum of human misery than lying. It is a misery to him who speaks it, to him who hears it, and to him of whom it is spoken. It destroys all self-respect and subverts all confidence. It is especially painful to witness the laxity of men's moral sentiments respecting oaths—oaths in the halls of justice, in bills in chancery, in custom-houses, and oaths of office. He, who *swears deceitfully*, will find no admission to the assembly of the spirits of just men made perfect.

17. Without holiness no man shall see the Lord, vv. 4, 5. Where purity is lacking, all else is useless. Heaven is not a harbor for rogues, nor a hive for drones, nor a dormitory for sluggards, nor a kennel for dogs.

18. No higher praise can be given to any than this: "Behold an Israelite indeed in whom is no guile." Nor can a fouler blot be put on any character than by a just charge of deceit, treachery, unfaithfulness. God abhors the latter as much as he approves the former. He cares not for our attendance on ordinances, if the heart is not in the matter. Luther: "It is not he who sings so well or so many Psalms, nor he who fasts and watches so many days, nor he who divides his own among the poor, nor he who preaches to others, nor he who lives quietly, kindly and friendly; nor, in fine, is it he who knows all sciences and languages, nor he who works all virtuous and all good works that ever any man spoke or read of, but it is he alone, who is pure within and without."

19. The blessed man is he whom the Lord blesses, and no other, v. 5.

20. When in his holiness God secures to his persecuted ones justice, to his faithful

ones a rich reward, to his chosen ones an abundance of the gift of *righteousness*, how can they suffer want? v. 5.

21. All men are not utterly base and unprincipled; there is *a generation that seek God*, v. 6. Those, who say there is no genuine piety in the world, are as wide of the mark as those, who say that all professors have true godliness. Wheat is not tares; nor are tares wheat. Sheep are not goats, even if goats mingle with them. In the divine mind the line that separates saints and sinners, genuine and spurious professors, is as broad as the earth.

22. And as God knows who are his, so by his *blessing* he will in due time make them known to others, saying that they are Jacob, the true Israel, v. 6. "The good works of some are manifest beforehand: and they that are otherwise cannot be hid." 1 Tim. v. 25.

23. There are great events and great sights before all the saints, vv. 7, 9. There is no danger that after this life the just will lack a divine entertainment. The removal of the ark to mount Zion was a dull affair compared with Christ's ascension to heaven; and his ascension to heaven as seen from earth was as nothing, compared with his second coming, although this shall be *in like manner*. Nor shall the *final* judgment present the last grand spectacle that shall be witnessed by the redeemed. It will be but the beginning of unceasing wonders.

24. Christ Jesus is in the midst of worshipping assemblies. The king of glory comes in, vv. 7, 9. In all places where I record my name, I will come unto thee, and I will bless thee, Ex. xx. 24. Compare Matt. xviii. 20. From age to age Christ is gracious to the penitent, who tremble at his word, and call on his name.

25. Christ must be received, v. 7. This is indispensable. Not to welcome him is to reject him. Not to open the heart to him is to bar it against him. Dickson: "The way to make men true converts, true believers, true saints and inheritors of heaven, is to receive Christ heartily, and honorably to cast up doors in hearty consent of faith and love, like triumphant arches, for welcoming so glorious a conqueror to be their guest." We must with full consent receive Christ, Rev. iii. 20.

26. Hitherto men have known Christ chiefly in a lowly condition, but he is the King of glory, vv. 7-10. He was so even in his humiliation. At times his glory shined forth illustriously as in his miracles, John ii. 1-11; in his transfiguration, Matt. xvii. 1-7; in his resurrection, Acts ii. 24; and in his ascension to glory, Acts i. 9-11. He offered no more blessed petition for his chosen than that they should be with him and behold his glory, John xvii. 24. That vision will be heaven, Rev. xiv. 1.

27. So glorious a person is fit to be a King, yea, King of kings and Lord of lords. He is Lord of all, God over all, blessed forever, vv. 7-10. Let us own him. Let us rejoice and be glad in him. His human nature has its exaltation by reason of its union with his divine nature. He is *Jehovah of hosts*, v. 10. Because he is God, it is no marvel that "by him were all things created, that are in heaven, and that are in earth, visible and invisible, whether they be thrones or dominions, or principalities or powers: all things were created by him, and for him: and he is before all things, and by him all things consist," Col. i. 16, 17.

28. Great comfort and joy have all the saints in the glorious scheme of redemption! Barker: "The strength of our salvation consists in this, that our Redeemer and Intercessor is the Lord of Hosts. Every other work shall be destroyed, but the work of redemption is for ever." "Lift up your eyes to the heavens, and look upon the earth beneath; for the heavens shall vanish away like smoke, and the earth shall wax old like a garment, and they that dwell therein shall die in like manner; but my salvation shall be for ever, and my righteousness shall not be abolished," Isa. li. 6.

PSALM XXV.

A Psalm of David.

1 Unto thee, O Lord, do I lift up my soul.

2 O my God, I trust in thee: let me not be ashamed, let not mine enemies triumph over me.

3 Yea, let none that wait on thee be ashamed: let them be ashamed which transgress without cause.

4 Shew me thy ways, O Lord; teach me thy paths.

5 Lead me in thy truth, and teach me: for thou *art* the God of my salvation; on thee do I wait all the day.

6 Remember, O Lord, thy tender mercies and thy loving-kindnesses; for they *have been* ever of old.

7 Remember not the sins of my youth, nor my transgressions: according to thy mercy remember thou me for thy goodness' sake, O Lord.

8 Good and upright *is* the Lord: therefore will he teach sinners in the way.

9 The meek will he guide in judgment: and the meek will he teach his way.

10 All the paths of the Lord *are* mercy and truth unto such as keep his covenant and his testimonies.

11 For thy name's sake, O Lord, pardon mine iniquity; for it *is* great.

12 What man *is* he that feareth the Lord? him shall he teach in the way *that* he shall choose.

13 His soul shall dwell at ease; and his seed shall inherit the earth.

14 The secret of the Lord *is* with them that fear him; and he will shew them his covenant.

15 Mine eyes *are* ever toward the Lord; for he shall pluck my feet out of the net.

16 Turn thee unto me, and have mercy upon me; for I *am* desolate and afflicted.

17 The troubles of my heart are enlarged: *oh* bring thou me out of my distresses.

18 Look upon mine affliction and my pain; and forgive all my sins.

19 Consider mine enemies; for they are many; and they hate me with cruel hatred.

20 Oh keep my soul, and deliver me: let me not be ashamed; for I put my trust in thee.

21 Let integrity and uprightness preserve me; for I wait on thee.

22 Redeem Israel, O God, out of all his troubles.

FOR remarks on the title see on title of Psalm xi. Scott dates this Psalm B. C. 1021; Clarke, 443 years later. Of course the latter denies the Davidic authorship of this ode. But his error on this point is probably owing to his mistaken and extreme disregard of titles. The great mass of sober writers for good cause admit that David is the author. Among these may be named Calvin, Venema, Amesius, Ainsworth, Calmet, Edwards, Pool, Patrick, Gill, Henry, Scott, Williams, Morison, Hengstenberg, Tholuck, Bouchier.

Patrick, Gill, Scott, Morison and others suppose this Psalm was written upon occasion of Absalom's rebellion. Tholuck refers it to the latter part of Saul's reign. Neither of these opinions can be proven or disproven. We gain nothing by assigning a given occasion to each Psalm. Clarke refers this " to the case of the captives of Babylon, who complain of oppression from their enemies." This learned man is as much inclined to find the occasion of the Psalms in that captivity, as Patrick, in the rebellion of Absalom.

This is an alphabetical Psalm. See Introduction, § 13. The other six alphabetical Psalms are the xxxiv. xxxvii. cxi. cxii. cxix. cxlv. This has twenty-two stanzas, corresponding to the number of Hebrew letters. But the alphabetic arrangement is not perfect. Irregularities are found in vv. 2, 5, 18, 22. It is not necessary with Clarke to impute such variations to the *carelessness* of transcribers. We should rather expect them to be guided by their alphabet to rectify an error. It is not peculiar to this Psalm to have the regular order of the alphabet broken. Why the alphabetical arrangement was ever adopted we know not. Kimchi admits the Jews knew not the reason. Some moderns have spoken lightly of this as a poetic conceit; but there is nothing to justify such a remark. It is not so difficult or so artistic as rhyme, and yet when well used that is not despicable. The opinions which have been set forth respecting the design of the alphabetical form of composition, are these: Some say it was to enable one the easier to remember the Psalm in its order, if committed to memory. Others think it an index to matter specially weighty. Alexander thinks the "arrangement is peculiar to those Psalms, in which a single theme or idea is repeated under various forms, and, as it were, in a series of aphorisms." Whether any of these views will be found satisfactory to the reader or not, it must be admitted that they have not antiquity to sustain them. The fact is that the alphabetic arrangement is simply the bestowment of an extraordinary degree of art, which is lawful and in itself is pleasing to the reader.

The names of the Almighty found in this Psalm are *Jehovah* LORD and *Elohim God*, on which see on Ps. i. 2; iii. 2.

1. *Unto thee*, O LORD, *do I lift up my soul.* Chaldee: Before thee, Lord, will I lift up my soul *in prayer.* The church of England, Venema, Amesius and Alexander also prefer the future, *will lift.* But the Septuagint, Ethiopic, Arabic, Syriac, Vulgate and Doway employ the past tense, *have lifted.* Edwards, Jebb and others prefer the present, *I lift.* Fry: On thee, Jehovah, my God, I fix my heart; Hengstenberg: To thee, O Lord, I draw my soul. Either of the tenses gives the sense according to the true principles of Hebrew Grammar. The Hebrew is future, *will lift.* Calvin: "By the future tense David denotes a continued act." See Introduction, § 6. The words *draw* and *fix* are not better than *lift.* In the ancient Hebrew worship the posture was that of standing, lifting up the hands and the eyes and the voice towards heaven, Ps. lxiii. 4; cxxi. 1; Isa. xxiv. 14; Lam. iii. 41. In all these cases the same form of the same verb is used as in the clause under consideration. Compare Luke xviii. 13. From this posture is probably derived the form of expression here; *q. d.,* I will not merely lift up my hands and my eyes; I will also lift up my soul, my heart to thee; I will address my sincere prayers and make known my hearty desires, expecting an answer in peace. Alexander: "All agree that the essential idea is that of confident desire."

2. *O my God, I trust in thee.* *Trust,* elsewhere *hope, put confidence,* in the future, *will trust.* He had formerly relied on God, he did so still, and he was fully purposed to continue to do so. Thus in hope he prays, *Let me not be ashamed.* For *ashamed* the Chaldee, Syriac, Arabic, church of England and Fry have *confounded.* In the common version it is often so rendered. Jebb: I shall not be ashamed. The common version is better and is generally approved. To *be ashamed* is to be stunned, confounded, overwhelmed, like men surprised by finding themselves completely in the power of their enemies, or covered with disgrace. He begs for deliverance from so great a calamity, basing his prayer on the dreadful nature of the evil which threatened him, viz.: the scorn and cruelty of the wicked. And so he adds, *Let not mine enemies triumph over me.* The scorn and triumph of the wicked are to the righteous as cruel and tempting as to God they are dishonoring.

3. *Yea, let none that wait on thee be ashamed.* *Wait;* the same word found in vv. 5, 21. It signifies waiting with expectation. Ainsworth: *Earnestly expect.* It is often rendered *look,* Job xxx. 26; Isa. viii. 17; Jer. xiii. 16. It implies hope as well as patience. Scott: "The term *wait* implies a simple, dependent, expecting, attentive state of heart, which leads to frequency and perseverance in the use of proper means, notwithstanding delays and discouragements, with a determined rejection of all other

confidences, and all inconsistent measures." Several ancient versions, Calvin, Jebb, Hengstenberg, Alexander and others put the last verb in the future. But the rendering of the common version is no less pertinent to the matter in hand. The sense is so far the same that both renderings alike declare it is a principle in God's government that his confiding ones shall not be disappointed, though others may. *Let them be ashamed which transgress without cause.* Chaldee: Robbers and vain persons shall be ashamed; Septuagint, Ethiopic, Vulgate and Doway: Let them be confounded that act unjust things without cause; Arabic: Let those who are wicked in their vanity be confounded; Syriac: They that are wicked in their vanity shall be confounded; Calvin: They shall be ashamed that deal falsely without cause: Venema: The perfidious in their emptiness shall be confounded with shame; Amesius: Let those who deal falsely without a cause be ashamed; Ainsworth: They shall be abashed that unfaithfully transgresse in vaine; Waterland: Let them be ashamed who deal perfidiously in vain; church of England: Such as transgress without a cause shall be put to confusion; Edwards: Let those be ashamed that act basely towards me without reason; Jebb: They shall be ashamed who transgress without cause; Horsley: Let the revolters to vanity be brought to shame; Fry: Let the vain apostates be confounded; Hengstenberg: Those shall be put to shame who act perfidiously without cause; Alexander: Ashamed shall be the traitors without cause; Tholuck: Let them be ashamed that wickedly despise thee. Hammond says the word rendered *without cause* "signifies any *falseness, perfidiousness, violation of oath or league;* and not simply any kind of *transgression,* but those of *lying* or *falseness.*" *Without cause* means without *justifying* cause. Diodati: "By mere and wilful malice, no way merited nor provoked through any offence of mine." The wickedness complained of was wanton. Sin and uprightness shall not be treated alike under God's government.

4. *Shew me thy ways,* O LORD. The ancient versions substantially agree with this. Calvin: O Jehovah, make me to know thy ways; Venema: O Jehovah, make thy ways known to me; Amesius: Cause that I may walk by thy truth. God's *ways* are either the orderings of his providence, or the paths of obedience pointed out by him. It is right for us to commit our whole way to God, to beg him to do all for us, and to enable us to live to him. We are not fit to govern ourselves. We are not able to find the right ways of God in which we should walk. The prayer is renewed: *Teach me thy paths; q. d.,* Teach me to understand what I may know of thy providential dealings and instruct me in "the straight ways in which thy pious and faithful servant should walk." Hengstenberg admits that by "the ways and paths of the Lord" expositors generally understand "that manner of life which is well pleasing to him," but thinks that in this case "the ways of God are the ways of *deliverance* which he makes known to his own, that they may walk in them." The terms used and the context allow us to include both senses.

5. *Lead me in thy truth, and teach me.* The Chaldee: Lead me in thy righteousness and teach me; Arabic: Direct me to thy justice, and teach me; Syriac: Rule me in thy truth and teach me; Septuagint, Ethiopic, Vulgate and Doway: Direct me in thy truth, and teach me. Some think the sense is, Lead me to see thy veracity, cause me to experience thy faithfulness. Others think it is, Lead me to understand and embrace thy truth. No state of mind is more friendly to the success of our tempters than that of mental confusion, in which we see not distinctly the boundaries between truth and error, right and wrong. It is therefore a great matter to be preserved in God's truth, and to receive instruction from heaven. Our necessities urge us to cry for divine guidance; and our relation to God and his covenant engagements with us authorize us so to plead. Accordingly David gives this reason for his prayer: *For thou art the God of my salvation.* As God alone is the author of salvation, to whom

should we go for any effectual aid but unto him? And as he undertakes the case of all the poor and needy who look to him, so we may plead his promise with the strongest confidence. This is specially true when we find that we do not habitually or allowedly depart from him, but can say: *On thee do I wait all the day.* The original is in the preterite. This is followed by the Septuagint, Ethiopic, Syriac, Arabic, Vulgate, Doway, church of England, Calvin, Venema and Alexander. But Amesius, Ainsworth, Edwards, Jebb and Hengstenberg agree with the common version. In each case the doctrine is the same. If we use the past tense, it denotes a habit well established; if the present, it shows the existing state of mind resulting from previous devout exercises. These things seem fairly implied in waiting; expectation of good, confidence in the divine character, and a readiness to obey the divine will. The more prominent idea is that of indulging strong hope in God. The verb is of the same root as the word *wait* in v. 3. *All the day* means *continually.* The Arabic reads, *I have served thee all my days.*

6. *Remember, O Lord, thy tender mercies and thy loving-kindness; for they* have been *ever of old.* There is no better rendering of this verse. Our translators seem to have been remarkably happy in the selection of English words and phrases to represent the divine benevolence towards man. The word rendered *tender mercies* is elsewhere, *pity, mercy, bowels, compassions.* That rendered *loving-kindnesses* elsewhere *mercy, kindness, goodness, pity, favor.* The verse contains a petition and an argument. The petition is that God would call to mind those glorious attributes of his nature, pity, love, compassion, mercy, and not allow wickedness longer even to *seem* to triumph over innocence. The reason urged is that an opposite course would be out of character with God. *Of old* he had been known as *loving* and *tender.* God cannot deny himself. He cannot be merciful to the righteous to-day, and show the same regard to their foes to-morrow. Alexander: "*Ever of old* is less exact and expressive than the literal translation *from eternity,* to which there is less objection here, as the words relate not merely to God's acts but to his attributes."

7. *Remember not the sins of my youth nor my transgressions.* The Septuagint, Ethiopic, Vulgate and Doway: The sins of my youth and my ignorances do not remember; Arabic: Remember not the sins of my youth and of my folly; Syriac: The follies of my youth remember not against me; church of England: O remember not the sins and offences of my youth. The first noun is in our version almost invariably rendered *sin*, or *sin-offering,* and precisely corresponds to the Greek word so translated. The second is commonly rendered as here, sometimes *trespass*, a few times *sin.* Though there is *folly* in all sin, yet neither of these words is in the English version ever so rendered. Undoubtedly the clause contains a confession of sin and a petition for forgiveness. This confession is of the right kind. It is particular. It mentions not only all transgressions, but it specifies the sins of youth, thus going back to the beginning of life, and confessing that not merely of late but of a long time God had just cause for sending on him all his present sore calamities, and would have been righteous had he sent even worse. The remark of Luther on this place, though quoted with approbation by Hengstenberg, is certainly harsh and unwarranted: "Youth is not fit for virtue, or for anything that is good, because the blood is still too young and fresh, it cannot govern itself, or think of anything that is useful or good." He speaks more correctly when he says: "If any one will allow a youth to grow up, and do as he likes, he will become quite a devil before one is aware of what he is doing." Youthful lusts have a fearful power. But the grace of God is stronger. Nor are we ever in greater straits than when God makes us to possess the iniquities of our youth, Job xiii. 26. The forgiveness of sins is not to be sought or expected otherwise than through God's boundless grace. David adds: *According to thy mercy remember thou me for thy*

goodness' sake, O Lord. Mercy, same as *loving-kindness, pity, favor,* etc. See *tender mercies,* v. 6. On the word *goodness* see on Ps. iv. 6; xvi. 2. God's mercy is rich, free, infinite, unchanging. This is the very kind of favor needed by sinners in all their straits. This mercy must not only have its rise in God, but the cause of its exercise must be not in any goodness in us, but only in God. With him *goodness* is an unfailing attribute. If God ever exercises an act of perfect sovereignty, it is when of his mere good pleasure he receives into his favor a sinner of Adam's race, and thus covenants to care for him through life and forever.

8. *Good and upright is the* Lord. There is no good reason for rendering *good* by *sweet,* as the Vulgate and others do. The attributes of God are the foundation of all true religion. They are sufficient to that great end. The pious soul resorts continually to them. Its reasoning is, If God is good and I am in covenant with him, nothing truly evil can come upon me; and if he is upright, his rectitude will in like manner be my shield. Indeed his perfections direct all his goings forth. *Therefore will he teach sinners in the way.* All the conversions in the world proceed from the glorious perfections and purposes of God. And the guidance of poor souls converted, yet but partially sanctified, shows the amazing love and goodness of our adorable Lord. Calvin: "To attribute to God an uprightness which he may exercise only towards the worthy and the meritorious is a cold view of his character, and of little advantage to sinners, and yet the world commonly apprehends that God is good in no other sense." No mortal has so high and adoring views of the boundless benevolence and beneficence of Jehovah as his glorious nature would justify. On the other hand we cannot too carefully guard against the conception that God can ever act contrary to his holiness and infinite purity. His mercy is not indifference to the moral qualities of men or of their actions. It is always so manifested as to show that he is essentially just and pure, and abhors iniquity.

9. *The meek will he guide in judgment.* The *meek,* elsewhere called *the poor, the afflicted, the humble, the lowly.* See Ps. ix. 12, 18. All God's servants are *poor* in spirit, *afflicted* by some means, or in some way, especially by their sins, *humble* on account of past transgressions and present infirmities, *lowly* in mind and heart. Such are in a temper to be guided. And God will guide them in *judgment,* in their decisions of important affairs, especially those which relate to the soul; and in the exercise and practice of all justice or righteousness of life. Or the language may apply to God, and then the sense is that God will *in righteousness* guide the feet, the life, the important decisions of his people. These senses do not destroy but establish each other. They are all good. And the doctrine is weighty. It is repeated: *And the meek will he teach his way.* *Meek,* the same word so rendered in the beginning of this verse. The sense is, God will teach the lowly the way that it pleases him for us to walk in, or he will teach us the way, which his wise providence and government have marked out for us. There seems to be no good reason for putting the verbs of this verse in the present tense as some do.

10. *All the paths of the* Lord *are mercy and truth unto such as keep his covenant and his testimonies.* The paths of Jehovah are those, which he approves for us to walk in, Isa. ii. 3; Mic. iv. 2; or they are those in which he walks himself, Ps. cxliii. 3; Prov. ii. 20. There is no objection to either interpretation. If the former is preferred, then the meaning is that every rule which God approves for his people to walk by, is in the end found to be *mercy,* conducive to their best good; and *truth,* free from those falsehoods, which delude and deceive the wicked. If the latter interpretation is chosen, then the meaning is that in the end no good man will question either the love or the faithfulness of God, as he reviews the paths in which providence has led him. God's true people *keep* his covenant. The same verb is in verse 21, rendered *preserve.* It is

the word commonly rendered *keep*, Ps. cxix. 22, 33, 34, 56, 69, 100, 115, 129, 145. To keep God's *covenant* is to be faithful to our engagements to be the Lord's. To keep his *testimonies* is to walk honestly and holily in the commandments and ordinances of Jehovah. This service must be sincere and hearty. If it is so, God will accept it. Hengstenberg: "*Sins of infirmity* cannot deprive a man of interest in the promises of the covenant."

11. *For thy name's sake, O* Lord, *pardon mine iniquity; for it is great.* Whatever good is done to sinners must proceed from some procuring cause outside of themselves. There is nothing in them to merit esteem. See on Ps. xxiii. 3. The tense of the verb here is variously given. The Septuagint, Ethiopic, Vulgate, Doway, Venema, Amesius, Ainsworth, Hengstenberg and Alexander follow the Hebrew, and give the future. But the Chaldee, Syriac, Arabic, church of England, Calvin, Edwards and Jebb render as in the common version. Calvin: "The letter, which is equivalent to *and*, has often the force of changing the tense in the Hebrew verbs, so that the future tense is often taken in the sense of the optative." The word rendered *pardon* is of special significance. Ainsworth gives it *mercifully pardon*. It is first used by Moses in a case of great offence, Ex. xxxiv. 9. It signifies *to pardon upon pacification*, or *of grace and mercy*. Paul interprets it as being merciful, propitious or appeased, Heb. viii. 12. The same verb is found but once more in the Psalms, where in another form it is rendered *forgiveth*, Ps. ciii. 3. God is therefore asked graciously and to the end of complete pacification to blot out the sin, not because it is small or trivial, but because *it is great*. Diodati: "The expiation of that iniquity must be a work of thine infinite mercy, whereunto thou art chiefliest moved, when thou seest the greatest misery and necessity, and the offender grieving most for it." Great sins demand great displays of grace, and great displays of grace are wondrously to the glory of God. David therefore says that his is a case calling for just such mercy as can be found in God only, and such as will forever illustrate the glory of the divine attributes. *Great*, often rendered *many*, sometimes *much, mighty, a multitude*, and *manifold*. The last word every way accords with the original and with the English idiom. It weakens the force of the passage to read as some, *although it is great*. Neither does the Hebrew easily bear such a rendering. Such a gloss would probably not have been offered, "except either out of dislike to the doctrine implied in our version, or a fear of its being perverted." But God can defend his own honor better than we. Let him be heard. Hengstenberg: "His iniquity is so great that he must be irremediably lost, if God were to deal with him according to his works."

12. *What man is he that feareth the* Lord? The sense is the same as if he had said, Show me a man that fears Jehovah; or, Wherever a man is found that fears Jehovah; or, Find a God-fearing man wherever you can. The idiom of the Hebrew hardly seems to bear the construction of some that the interrogative form implies that the fear of God is very rare. For the import of *fearing the Lord*, see Ps. ii. 11; xv. 4; xix. 9. Of the man who thus piously fears Jehovah, whatever his rank or condition, the following things are true. First of all: *Him shall he teach in the way* that *he shall choose*. Some make God to *choose* the way. No doubt God appoints the paths of his people. But the sense probably is that God guides the just in his choice. He shall guide him in judgment, and teach him his duty and privileges, and show him how wise and good and perfect are the acts of providence respecting him; and how seasonable and gracious is God's way of delivering him, even when escape seemed almost hopeless. Yet in all these leadings of Jehovah there shall be no violence done to the will, nor is any miracle necessary. But the good man shall exercise his own entire freedom of will, and at each successive stage of his progress *choose* the very way, in which God would have him walk. Sinners saved by grace

are *drawn* but not dragged; they are *made willing*, not borne reluctantly along. They are made to choose and glory in things and ways, to which they once had the strongest repugnance. Courses of life and sufferings, which it once seemed impossible to contemplate without horror or dismay, are at length welcomed and *chosen* by the child of grace, 2 Cor. xii. 9, 10. This is the crowning glory of true religion. It overcomes the strongest national, personal and religious prejudices; it controls the mightiest passions and inclinations of men. Saul of Tarsus *chose* to blaspheme; but Paul *chose* to pray. Saul of Tarsus *chose* to persecute; but Paul the apostle *chose* to be persecuted. John Calvin and John Knox, even after conversion, both had an extreme unwillingness to preach the gospel; yet to no men was the pulpit for a long time more like a throne. There they reigned as kings. There they loved to herald forth mercy. Nor is this all the mercy made sure to the man who fears Jehovah.

13. *His soul shall dwell at ease.* The English phrase to *dwell at ease*, or *be at ease*, has a good or bad sense according to the connection. Here it is taken in a good sense. In Amos vi. 1 it is in a bad sense. But the word rendered *ease* is not here the same as there. Here it is the word rendered *good* in Ps. iv. 6; xiv. 1, 3; and *goodness* in Ps. xvi. 2; xxi. 3; xxiii. 6. To *dwell* is to *lodge*. The margin: *His soul shall lodge in goodness.* The connection of the God-fearer with *goodness* and all blessings is not like that of a man strolling along by goodly habitations; but of one who is at home in them. The *goodness* is not his personal quality, but his rich portion. The Septuagint well renders it *good things. His soul*, that is, he himself *shall dwell at ease.* Horsley: His soul shall rest in bliss; Street: He shall continue in prosperity. Nor is the blessing exhausted on *him*, for it is added, *And his seed shall inherit the earth.* Chaldee: And his children by a hereditary title shall enter into possession of the land. The Syriac is nearly as strong. The verb rendered *inherit* signifies to *possess*, but especially to *possess by inheritance*, as the Israelites did the promised land. As Canaan was the promised land, and as a holy life led to quiet and thrift, so to *dwell in the land* came to signify the possession of all good things, Ex. xx. 12; Matt. v. 5. The extent, to which under God we are indebted to a pious ancestry, is understood by few. Let men know that their conduct will have a vast bearing for good or evil on those who shall come after them. *Land* is perhaps a better rendering than *earth*, as the figure is probably not drawn from all the earth, but from the land of Israel. More than all this:

14. *The secret of the Lord is with them that fear him.* The Septuagint and imitating versions have it: The Lord is a stay to them that fear him; Arabic: The Lord is the courage of them that fear him. For *secret* Calvin and Street prefer *counsel;* Hengstenberg and Alexander, *friendship.* But the church of England, Venema, Amesius, Edwards, Jebb, Fry and many others have *secret.* In our English version the word is never rendered *friendship*, often *secret*, Gen. xlix. 6; Job. xv. 8; xxix. 4; Pr. iii. 32; Am. iii. 7; and several times *counsel*, Ps. lv. 14; Pr. xv. 22; Jer. xviii. 18, 23. Either gives a good sense. Both are true. If we read *counsel*, then the meaning is that God's plans and purposes are not against but for his people, not far from them, but with them; and so they must succeed; for the counsel of the Lord it shall stand. Street: "The counsel of Jehovah is in favor of them that fear him." If we read *secret*, then we have all God's people taught according to the revelation of the mystery, which was kept secret since the world began. So that they have a saving knowledge of the mystery of God and of Christ. Christ is revealed unto them. And a thousand things, which to the world are enigmas and paradoxes, are to them glorious truths, full of light and full of comfort. They have intimate communion with God. They trust and glory in him. Nor is their confidence

misplaced, nor shall their love be unrequited, for it is added: *And he will shew them his covenant.* His *covenant* some say is his *secret.* No doubt the two agree. But covenant is the stronger word, as it contains the idea of compact, stipulation, promise and full provision for every exigency. God will show to his people the great amplitude, the excellent arrangement, and the absolute certainty of his covenant. They shall see these things both in the word and in the providence of God. There is no good reason for limiting the sense to the outward display of God's fidelity, mercy and power.

15. *Mine eyes* are *ever toward the* LORD. This clause seems to have very much the same import as that of *waiting on the Lord,* v. 3. There is great uniformity in the rendering of this verse. For *ever* Calvin, Ainsworth, Jebb and Fry have *continually;* Hengstenberg and Alexander, *always.* Edwards: My eyes are ever directed to Jehovah. In trouble, especially in that which is the immediate fruit of sin, the sooner we wholly despair of all help from any but God, the better. Nor shall any expectation directed to the Lord ever be disappointed. David had good reason for looking to God: *For he shall pluck my feet out of the net.* Edwards: For he it is that must bring my feet out of the net; Jebb: For it is he who shall pluck from the net my feet. *Pluck out,* in v. 17, *bring out;* in Ps. xxxi. 4, *pull out.* God's deliverances are opportune, surprising, irresistible. For an explanation of the use of *nets,* etc., see on Ps. ix. 15; x. 9. The cunning craftiness and the deadly enmity of the wicked are well expressed by the term *net.* Those who spread nets did it for *destruction.* They had no mercy. Horne: "An unfortunate dove, whose feet are taken in the snare of the fowler, is a fine emblem of the soul, entangled in the cares and pleasures of the world; from which she desires, through the power of grace, to fly away, and to be at rest, with her glorified Redeemer."

16. *Turn thee unto me.* The Chaldee and many versions: Look thou upon me. Calvin: Have respect unto me. In Lev. xxvi. 9; 1 Kings viii. 28; 2 Chr. vi. 19; the same word is rendered *have respect.* In Isa. xlv. 22; Ps. cxix. 132, and often it is rendered *look.* It is here used in a good sense. He adds: *And have mercy upon me, i. e.,* Deal graciously with me, show me favor, have pity upon me. We have the same word in Job xix. 21; Ps. iv. 1; xxxi. 9; li. 1. David declares his solemn belief that his case calls for divine aid, and that none but God can help him. He adds: *For I* am *desolate and afflicted. Desolate,* literally *one, lonely, only, solitary,* then *desolate.* See Gen. xxii. 2; Zech. xii. 10. When feminine it is rendered *my darling,* Ps. xxii. 20; xxxv. 17. The Septuagint has it *only begotten.* But *desolate* is better. *Afflicted, poor, humble, lowly, needy.* See Ps. ix. 12, 18; Pr. iii. 34; xxxi. 20. David represents his case as one of the very class that God delighted to undertake; one, in which it would greatly honor God to give relief; one quite beyond the aid of any and of all others.

17. *The troubles of my heart are enlarged.* No affliction comes alone. Whoever has one distress has others. In this case things past, present and future, sins, former friends and old enemies were all against him. *Troubles,* as in Ps. ix. 9; x. 1; xx. 1; xxii. 11. For *enlarged* some read *multiplied,* which is no improvement. David says his case is urgent, the waters have risen high, and help must be sought from Jehovah. He adds: Oh *bring thou me out of my distresses.* Saving the sinful and the sorrowful, who look to him, is the very work of God. He delights in it. He does it easily and effectually. To *bring out* is in v. 15, to *pluck out. Distresses* always so rendered in our version in the plural; in the singular sometimes *anguish.* Lowth reads the verse thus:

> Set at large the sorrowful contractions of my heart,
> And bring me out of my difficulties.

18. *Look upou mine affliction and my pain. Look upon, see, behold, perceive, regard, consider. Affliction*, always so rendered in our version except in three cases. See Ps. ix. 13, where it is *trouble. Pain*, elsewhere *sorrow, trouble, labor, travail, grievance, mischief, misery*, a few times *perverseness, wickedness, iniquity.* Nu. xxiii. 21 ; Job iv. 8 ; Hab. i. 13. It is evidently not to be taken here in the sense of moral evil. He would desire God to avert his face from all his transgressions. The next words are : *And forgive all my sins.* No solid foundation can ever be laid for settled peace, so long as sin remains unpardoned. In one unforgiven transgression there is a sting so keen, so envenomed as to destroy all abiding happiness. Contrite souls know this, and so never give over crying for mercy, till they are assured of God's love. Sin pardoned, our other troubles and our foes may yet be many and mighty, but they cannot bring on us eternal destruction. Yet they may be far too strong for us, and so we must look to God and cry :—

19. *Consider mine enemies. Consider*, in v. 18, *look upon.* To two things in his enemies David specially implored the divine inspection ; 1, their number, *for they are many ;* 2, their dreadful malice, *they hate me with cruel* [violent, unrighteous, implacable] *hatred.* Scott, who refers this Psalm to the occasion of Absalom's rebellion, says, David "was aware, that even his own son, and his bosom-counsellor, and a large part of the nation thirsted for his blood : and would decline no violence, treachery, or cruelty, to destroy him : so that his life could be preserved only by the same divine power and mercy in which he trusted for the salvation of his own soul." Dying in the peaceable possession of the throne seemed to be a necessary pledge of the fulfilment of the great promise made to David, 2 Sam. vii. Accordingly he desires safety for other causes beside the natural love of life.

20. *Oh keep my soul, and deliver me. Keep ;* the same word in Ps. xvi. 1, and elsewhere is rendered *preserve.* See also Ps. xvii. 8. Some use a military term, *guard.* Our life and all our interests, our souls and all their vast affairs can in no way be preserved, but by the exercise of God's glorious perfections. Forsaken of him we shall be dismayed. So he prays : *Let me not be ashamed. Ashamed*, as in vv. 2, 3. In this life the righteous often blush for their sins and follies. But the issue will be well. Their shame will in eternity be all gone. Even here they may confidently plead to be saved from disaster and confusion, because God's honor is involved : *For I put my trust in thee.* When one cannot save those, who confide in him, he cannot be a God. And were it credible that God cared not for his friends, all true religion would soon perish from the earth.

21. *Let integrity and uprightness preserve me.* The Chaldee : Perfection and uprightness shall preserve me ; Septuagint, Ethiopic, Syriac, Vulgate, and Doway : The innocent and the upright have adhered to me ; Arabic : The innocent and the upright have followed me ; Venema : Integrity and uprightness shall preserve me ; Hengstenberg : Blamelessness and uprightness shall preserve me ; Alexander : Integrity and rectitude shall preserve me. But Calvin, Diodati, Amesius, Ainsworth, Pool, Edwards, Jebb and others have the optative, Let, etc. Some would make the Psalmist pray that the *perfection* and *uprightness* of God may preserve him. But he is rather asking that his own *integrity* and *uprightness* may keep him. There are two senses, in which this may occur. 1. "Let these virtues always keep me from doing evil, and never depart from me." This sense is admitted by Diodati and others. It is a wise prayer, based on self-knowledge. 2. The more common exposition is, Let my cause be tried and rest on its righteousness, and on my fairness and uprightness in this whole business : Calvin : "David prays that he may be preserved from all mischief, on the ground that he had conducted himself inoffensively towards others, and had abstained from all deceit and violence." Scott : "In the sight of God,

David pleaded guilty of great and many sins, but he had acted an upright part towards his unnatural son, and treacherous subjects." Pool and others hold this view. It is perhaps the best every way. The reason given is: *For I wait on thee; q. d.,* I am thy servant, I look to thee, I confide in thee as taking sides with the upright. Boothroyd: For in thee do I hope. Whoever has suffered all the trials of David and has a benevolent heart desires that God's church may escape from her enemies and find full deliverance. Therefore he prays:

22. *Redeem Israel, O God, out of all his troubles.* Alexander: " This verse forms no part of the alphabetical series, but begins with the same letter as v. 16. Like the first verse it consists of a single clause, as if the two together were designed to constitute one sentence." There seems to be no good reason for supposing with Mudge that. " this is a detached sentence, in which the author shows his zeal for his country, and that it was the usual close of many of their sacred songs ;" nor with Rosenmuller that it was added at a later period. Nothing was more fitting than that David, who had prayed much for himself, should enlarge his petitions and ask God for blessings on his people: *q. d.,* Save, not me only, but the whole nation, now rent, torn, distracted with feuds and civil war. Send peace, send prosperity. Settle our difficulties, for no power or sagacity of man can give effectual aid. Unless thou undertake for us our case is helpless. Calvin thinks this clause clearly shows that the allusion is to Saul and his associates who cruelly treated the church. But Israel has always had many troubles, and the prayer was always seasonable.

DOCTRINAL AND PRACTICAL REMARKS.

1. The teaching of Scripture respecting prayer is uniform. It must be to Jehovah ; it must be sincere, v. 1. Slade: " In vain will our voices be lifted up in prayer, unless our souls be lifted up to God." Henry: " Prayer is the ascent of the soul to God ; God must be eyed and the soul employed. *Up with your hearts* was anciently used as a call to devotion." Times of great peril should be times of great prayer. Nor can the mind of any be too steadfastly set on God alone.

2. The greater our trouble, the greater should be our trust, v. 2. Dangers should drive us to seek divine aid. Henry: " If we make our confidence in God our stay, it shall not be our shame; and if we triumph in him, our enemies shall not triumph over us, as they would, if we should now sink under our fears."

3. The principle of shame in our nature is not without its use. Sinners would often be more wicked, saints would often be less holy, but that a keen sense of shame restrains the former or arouses the latter. Nothing has more power to torment us, v. 2. In the wicked it will last forever, Dan. xii. 2. Nor is there in all Scripture any negative promise of more precious import than that God's people shall never come into contempt or be ashamed.

4. It is both a privilege and a duty to pray that the wicked may not triumph over the righteous, v. 2. Such a state of things would argue a total subversion of the divine government. The hope of the wicked shall surely perish. The throne of God's grace is against them. The universe is against them. All nature has groaned under the weight of them ; and all nature shall fight against them.

5. To *wait* on God is a duty often insisted on in Scripture, vv. 3, 5. The frequency, with which it is mentioned, shows the high value set on it by God. Yet it is an unfashionable duty, mentioned far less frequently in private conversation and in pulpit discourses than in the word of God. Great promises are made to this duty; and great rewards shall follow it. " Even the youths shall faint and be weary, and the young men shall utterly fall: but they that wait upon the LORD shall renew their

strength; they shall mount up with wings as eagles; they shall run and not be weary; and they shall walk, and not faint," Isa. xl. 30, 31.

6. It heightened the wickedness of David's foes that he had never wronged them, v. 3. So it is a fearful aggravation attending all sin *against God* that it is wanton, *without cause*, and therefore without excuse.

7. It is a great mercy to be allowed to understand God's will, both as revealed in Scripture, and as made known in providence. No less than four times does David beg to be enlightened on this subject, vv. 4, 5. One of the greatest trials is perplexity. Commonly Satan has a great advantage over us when he can make us seriously doubt respecting truth or duty. Clearness of mind is a great blessing. God alone can give it, v. 12.

8. A clear discovery of any of God's attributes, especially of his veracity, goodness, righteousness and mercy, is a high attainment, vv. 5, 6, 8, 10. He, who studies not and loves not the divine perfections, cannot plead with God, or be joyful in him, as does he, who delights himself in the Almighty. God's attributes are fountains of joy to pious souls. To love and embrace all revealed truth, and especially that which relates to the divine nature and will is of the essence of true piety.

9. If God should do for us all else, and not teach us his will and his ways, he would not be *the God of our salvation*, v. 5. We are blind and cannot see afar off. We know nothing as we ought to know it until we are taught from heaven. Blessed be the Lord, he is continually making good the promise: " I will bring the blind by a way that they knew not; I will lead them in paths that they have not known; I will make darkness light before them, and crooked things straight. These things will I do unto them, and not forsake them," Isa. xlii. 16.

10. It is not enough to begin a right course. We must continue in well-doing, v. 5. Perseverance in duty is the only infallible mark to ourselves and the world that we are born of God. Nothing can be a substitute for this.

11. From what God by his acts has shown himself to be we may well argue what he will do hereafter, v. 6. Nor should any appearances to the contrary make us waver respecting either the wisdom or the constancy of the divine compassion. Dickson : " Though the course of kindness and mercy seem to be interrupted by afflic-tion and temporal desertion, and to be forgotten on God's part; yet faith must make use of experiences, and read them over unto God out of the register of a sanctified memory."

12. Arguments drawn from God's character in favor of our cause are far more likely to prevail than those drawn from our own character, v. 6. Calvin: " He who derives everything from the fountain of the divine mercy alone finds nothing in him-self entitled to recompense in the sight of God."

13. Afflictions often possess remarkable power to remind us of our sins, vv. 7, 18. When Joseph's brethren were in the greatest straits then they cried, " We are verily guilty concerning our brother." When the son of the widow of Zarephath died she said to Elijah, " Art thou come unto me to call my sin to remembrance?" Dickson : " Sore troubles will waken up the conscience of sin afresh, and call to mind forgiven and buried sin." Nothing can meet these terrible memories of wickedness but a new application of the blood of Jesus and a sweet sense of God's mercy in Christ. A religious experience that has all joys and no pangs in it is good for nothing. We should rather seek to reprove ourselves for our old sins, yea, for all our sins, than to forget them. Anything is good for us, if it humbles us and leads us to the mercy-seat. In these respects nothing has a happier effect than a solemn review of our past deficiencies. Henry: " Our youthful faults and follies should be matter of our repent-ance and humiliation long after, because time does not wear out the guilt of sin.

Old people should mourn for the sinful mirth, and be in pain for the sinful pleasures of their youth." Blessed is the old man who has grace penitently to weep at the sins of his early days.

14. Sweet is the doctrine of forgiveness! In mercy God has clearly and abundantly revealed his forgiving love to all who have his word, vv. 7, 18. The doctrine of forgiveness is as weighty as it is clear. Calvin: "It is true, in general, that men pray in a wrong way and in vain, unless they begin by seeking the forgiveness of their sins. There is no hope of obtaining any favor from God unless he is reconciled to us." Let us plead with God for his name's sake, not for our own. We are sinners, and the tears and even the blood of a sinner can never wash away guilt.

15. David's youth seems to have been spent in more freedom from open transgression than is common, yet his view of his early life was just. No man can answer for one of a thousand of his offences during any year of his rational just accountability. One may soon become a monster, if God's grace be wanting.

16. It is an unspeakable mercy to be brought in our early years to love and serve God, and to keep his commandments. Many harrowing recollections and tormenting reflections are thus avoided, v. 7. Temptation is thus deprived of many of its most envenomed shafts. Surely as the latter day glory approaches, the young, even little children, will be found turning to the Lord, and imbued with his Holy Spirit.

17. But for these and all other blessings we are wholly dependent on the divine *mercy*, v. 7. This has always been the doctrine of God's real people. They know that they are sinners saved by grace. To deny that would be monstrous.

18. "*Seasons of danger are seasons for meditation*, v. 8. . . The humble soul shall find mercy. He that fears the Lord shall 'unravel those dispensations' which perplex others. His meditation shall be sweet, and inspire confidence in the interposition of his God. His meditations will give energy to his prayers, and urge their repetition." It is not amiss to reason and soliloquize in prayer, if we follow the Scriptural pattern, v. 8.

19. God is the sole author of conversion, pardon and salvation, vv. 8, 9. The old doctrine of *preventing grace* is as true as it is consolatory. God's grace must *go before* all acts of man in order to his salvation. The difference between saints and sinners is not natural, but supernatural; not by blood or birth, but by the adoption and grace of God.

20. The essence of the *meekness* required in God's word is found in that chastened state of the soul which results from the teaching of the Holy Ghost, v. 9. A view of personal ill-desert makes one *humble*. A sense of one's vileness deeply *afflicts* him. So that he is quiet, submissive, leaving all in the hands of God. True meekness not only tames the ferocity, but it checks the impetuosity of men. It is essential to true piety. It would not be a miracle, but a contradiction for God to guide the proud, the self-conceited into all truth. If any would learn he must be docile. The wayward err because they are wayward. To guide ourselves is impossible. Unless taught of God we must live and die in profound ignorance of the most necessary things.

21. To the righteous are pledged God's mercy and truth, v. 10. The former secures to them the pardon of sin and the loving favor of God in all things and at all times. The latter makes sure to them every doctrine, and every promise of God. It no less secures the overthrow of the wicked, without which the victory of the righteous would not be complete. And on whichsoever side are God's truth and mercy, on the same side are all his adorable attributes. Calvin: "We have no reason to believe that God will fail us if we persevere in his covenant." Dickson: "Whosoever hold fast the covenant of grace and make conscience of obeying God's word they may be

sure that all their troubles and variety of exercise are nothing but God's way to make them partake of his promises."

22. But if we would know that God is with us we must be faithful to his covenant and keep his testimonies, v. 10. No ceremonies, professions, raptures or revelations did ever, can ever take the place of sincere, hearty, unquestioning obedience to all God's known will.

23. Self-righteous hopes are as delusive as they are preposterous, v. 11. Many texts show the same thing. No man has any Gospel to preach, any good news to herald forth in this world, unless on a divine warrant he can show that there is hope for the lost, mercy for the rebellious, and that the greatness of our sins does not debar us from humbly casting ourselves at the feet of God in the hope of salvation through a divine Redeemer.

24. There is a general and correct impression that when a subject is often introduced by the sacred penmen, it is in God's esteem of great and pressing moment. Judging by this rule *the fear of the Lord* is of the highest importance, vv. 12, 14.

25. Man needs no direction and guidance beyond what is clearly promised in the covenant, v. 12. The straits of the Christian are often great. He knows nothing. He can do nothing. He cannot of himself even pray aright. His will is naturally corrupt. But God can help him through all his trials, and give him the victory over all his enemies.

26. Glorious is the portion of the righteous, v. 13. Every fit form of expression is employed to give us some idea of it; and it far surpasses all that has ever been conceived of it.

27. Rich and precious are the benefits of a pious ancestry. If anything could turn our natural affection to account in the cause of virtue, it would seem to be such promises as the Bible contains concerning the seed of the righteous, v. 13. If you would be blessed, and have your children blessed also, fear God.

28. It is in vain to fight against God's *counsel,* v. 14. Nothing can change it. Nothing can defeat it. It is wiser and stronger than man.

29. If in v. 14 we understand *secret,* not *counsel,* then how vain is the pretence of the Romish church in withholding from the common people the word of God, when his *secret is with them that fear him,* and when he has expressly said that "things which are revealed belong unto us and to our children for ever."

30. If men, who think themselves wise because they succeed in worldly schemes knew as much as the plain, simple-hearted Christian, that is, if they were in the *secret of the Lord,* they would neither think, nor feel, nor speak, nor act as they now do, v. 14. They are deplorably ignorant of the main point of wisdom.

31. The state of the godly has in it all the stability which can be derived from a *covenant,* the covenant of God, ordered in all things and sure, v. 14.

32. None can look too steadfastly and confidingly to God, v. 15. We never honor him more, nor please him better than when in trouble and darkness we still trust him and believe that he will do all things well.

33. God, and none but God, can save us, v. 15. Our enemies are so crafty, their snares so cunningly spread, their malice so terrible, that we should soon perish but for God's seasonable and mighty aid.

34. However dark our prospects and strong our fears, let us continue in prayer, v. 16. It cannot hurt us. That is a great point made sure. It may be the means of a speedy and blessed deliverance. If not, it will in due time bring a still richer blessing.

35. The more lowly and lonely our state, the more earnestly should we commit it to God, for the more glorious will it be for him to interpose, v. 16.

36. Let no good man be surprised that his affliction is great, and to him of an unaccountable character. It has always been so with God's people, v. 17. The road to heaven is soaked with the tears and blood of the saints.

37. Blessed be God, we are not required to be silent before him, when trouble comes, vv. 17, 18. We may not complain of God, but we may complain to God. With submission to his holy will we may earnestly cry for help and deliverance.

38. It is a great matter to have God so far engaged on our side as that he will look on our affliction and consider our case, vv. 18, 19.

39. All our safety is in God alone, v. 20. In him we may rejoice and be exceeding glad always.

40. No cause is strong without justice and truth, and no cause is weak that has integrity and uprightness in it, v. 21. Sin is worse than misery. Prayers for a wicked cause are an offence to God. Dickson: " Integrity of life, or a good behaviour after prayer, is as needful as before it."

41. The church of God is always so much distressed, that we may well pray that she be delivered out of all her troubles, v. 22. She is in the wilderness. She has a great fight of afflictions. But her friends remember her at the throne of grace. In the end she shall have all the glory which the blood and righteousness and intercession of her head and husband can secure to her.

PSALM XXVI.

A *Psalm* of David.

1 Judge me, O LORD; for I have walked in mine integrity: I have trusted also in the LORD; *therefore* I shall not slide.

2 Examine me, O LORD, and prove me; try my reins and my heart.

3 For thy loving-kindness *is* before mine eyes: and I have walked in thy truth.

4 I have not sat with vain persons, neither will I go in with dissemblers.

5 I have hated the congregation of evil doers; and will not sit with the wicked.

6 I will wash mine hands in innocency: so will I compass thine altar, O LORD:

7 That I may publish with the voice of thanksgiving, and tell of all thy wondrous works.

8 LORD, I have loved the habitation of thy house, and the place where thine honour dwelleth.

9 Gather not my soul with sinners, nor my life with bloody men:

10 In whose hands *is* mischief, and their right hand is full of bribes.

11 But as for me, I will walk in mine integrity: redeem me, and be merciful unto me.

12 My foot standeth in an even place: in the congregations will I bless the LORD.

THAT this Psalm was written by David is clear. The title ascribes it to him. There is not a phrase in it which he might not with evident propriety have employed. It certainly has a close affinity with other odes composed by him, especially with the twenty-fifth. Calvin: "This Psalm, for the most part, is similar to the preceding." Even Clarke admits that David may have written it, although with Calmet he is more disposed to refer it to the captivity. He dates it 578 years before Christ; Scott, 480 years earlier or B. C. 1058.

The opinions respecting the occasion of its composition are very variant and are mere conjectures, without evidence, though some of them are less improbable than others. Hengstenberg: "All attempts to find out an individual application for our

Psalm, or to mark out any historical circumstances, with which it may be connected, have utterly failed." On *Jehovah* LORD (the only name of God used in it) see on Ps. i. 2.

On the title see on titles of Psalms iii. iv.

1. *Judge me, O* LORD. In the rendering of this clause there is great uniformity. The sense is well given by Hengstenberg: "Interpose to give me justice, deliver me from a condition in which, if it were to be regarded as permanent, it would be unrighteous to suffer me to remain." The same prayer is found in Ps. vii. 8; xxxv. 24; xliii. 1. The word rendered *judge* is, in Ps. lxxxii. 3, rendered *defend*. The meaning is, Judge effectually, judge so as to *defend* me. Hammond has it, Plead for me, or defend me; Waterland: Plead for me; Green: Vindicate me; Castellio: Take my part; Pool: Plead my cause, or, Give sentence for me; Horsley: Give sentence for me; Fry: Pass sentence on me. None of these are improvements on the common rendering. The best of them is: Give sentence for me. The reasons of his prayer are next given. *First*, he urges his personal innocence of the crimes alleged against him and the uprightness of his conduct towards those who are his bitter foes: *For I have walked in mine integrity*. *Integrity* is from the same word so rendered in Ps. vii. 8; xxv. 21. It is sometimes rendered *uprightness*. The Chaldee, *Perfection;* Septuagint, Vulgate, Ethiopic, *Innocence;* Arabic, *Humility, simplicity, perfection.* He declares that the whole tenor of his life [indicated by *walked*] towards them had been blameless. *Secondly*, he says: *I have trusted also in the* LORD. He asserts that he had kept a good conscience, and not made man, or any but Jehovah his hope or confidence. He had resorted to no wicked or doubtful expedient. He had made God his trust. Pool: "I have committed my cause and affairs to thee, as to a just Judge and merciful Father, and my hope and trust is fixed upon thee alone; therefore thou wilt not deceive my trust, but wilt uphold me against all mine enemies." Hengstenberg: "*To walk in integrity* has reference to the commandments of the *second* table, and *to trust in the Lord* to those of the *first*." He adds: Therefore *I shall not slide*. The word *therefore* is properly supplied by our translators. For *slide* the Septuagint has *be unstable;* Ethiopic and Syriac, *be moved;* Vulgate, *be weak;* Arabic, *fear;* church of England and Edwards, *fall;* Venema and Amesius, *waver;* Fry, *be shaken;* Ainsworth, *stagger;* Alexander, *swerve;* Hammond suggests also *trip, totter, be inconstant.* The Chaldee and Hengstenberg have *slide.* The sense may be, I shall not fall from my hope, I shall be found firm and stable in my course and in my adherence to the Lord. Calvin unites all the clauses: Because I have walked in mine integrity, and trusted in Jehovah, I shall not be moved. In his uprightness and reliance on God he is confident and so he begs the scrutiny of the Lord into his cause and character.

2. *Examine me, O* LORD, *and prove me; try my reins and my heart.* The verbs of this verse, *examine, prove* and *try* are by many used interchangeably. They all have the same import. *Examine*, in Ps. xi. 4, 5, rendered *try;* in Ps. xvii. 3, *prove. Prove*, commonly so rendered, also *try, tempt.* The last verb *try* is by some rendered *cleanse, purify, melt, burn, assay.* It expresses the trial of metals by fire, Ps. xii. 6; xvii. 3. On *reins* or kidneys, see above on Ps. vii. 9; xvi. 7. David desired that the Lord would search him through and through. Knowing his innocence in the matters charged, he asked that God would prove it and manifest it.

3. *For thy lovingkindness is before mine eyes.* The rendering of this clause is quite uniform, only that some have *love, mercy* or *pity* for *lovingkindness.* The meaning is that he remembers God's kindness in the past, he dwells on it in his present thoughts, and he hopes in it for days to come. The foundation of his piety was laid in just views of God's character; and as in the divine dispensations towards his people generally and towards David in particular there was a delightful superabounding of *pity*,

mercy, loving-kindness, so in all his thoughts David dwells much on that aspect of the character of God. The effect was most happy: *And I have walked in thy truth.* Alexander: "The verb translated *walked* is an intensive form of that used in verse 1." Diodati thus paraphrases the whole verse: "Mine eye of faith hath been always upon thy favor, and I have sincerely obeyed the truth of thy word, which I have taken for a light and rule of my conscience, which otherwise may err and deceive me." There does not seem to be good cause for connecting this verse in the same sentence with the next. In so doing the sense is good, but the third verse is complete in itself.

4. *I have not sat with vain persons.* For *vain persons* the Vulgate has *council of vanity;* Syriac, *malignant;* Edwards, *men of falsehood;* Ainsworth, *mortal men of false vanity;* Horsley, *wretched sons of vanity;* Hengstenberg and Alexander, *men of falsehood.* The language points to men who build their hopes on falsehood. Every untruth is a vanity. The verb is in the preterite. The wicked may be *before us,* Ps. xxxix. 1. We may in a sense be compelled to mingle with evil men, or else leave the world, 1 Cor. v. 10. But no good man will choose such as his associates. The companion of fools shall be destroyed. David had not willingly mingled with such. He had not sought bad company. This course of purity had commended itself to him. It had given him courage and comfort. Since he had tried it, he was more than ever purposed to adhere to it; and so he says: *Neither will I go in with dissemblers.* As has been my practice, so shall be my future life. For *dissemblers* some read *wicked, workers of iniquity, ungodly, infamous;* but a better sense is given by *deceitful, hypocrites, those that hide themselves, those who seek concealment.* The Chaldee: I will not go in with those that hide themselves to do evil. Wickedness is uncandid, and loves concealment, while truth and righteousness are open and seek scrutiny, Job xxiv. 13–17; John iii. 20, 21. None will deny that the candid man has far fewer troubles with his own conduct than the tortuous and deceitful. The righteous shun the wicked both for the *sin* and for the *misery* that are in their ways.

5. *I have hated the congregation of evil doers. Congregation,* body or assembly. For *evil doers* some read *malignant, wicked, transgressors, villanous men.* Morison says the original "denotes individuals of malignant, discontented and revengeful minds." *And* [I] *will not sit with the wicked.* That is, he would not sit to advise and consult with men of this character. Their principles and his were wholly opposed. Hengstenberg: "The import is, 'I take no part in the assemblies for the ruin of others;'" Alexander: "The change of tense is anything rather than unmeaning. 'I have not sat with them in time past, and I will not go with them in time to come.' The form of expression is borrowed from Gen. xlix. 6." All nations agree that men are known by the company they choose.

6. *I will wash my hands in innocency.* Of these words the renderings are various, though they substantially agree. The rendering cannot be improved. Washing was one of the rites of purification to the priesthood, Ex. xxix. 4; xxx. 19–21; xl. 12; Lev. xvi. 4, 24; xvii. 15, 16; xxii. 6. It was also a becoming preparation for solemn worship. It was an act symbolical of purity. As religion was corrupted, men began to lay the greatest stress on the mere act. In the Yad Tephillah we are told: "The hands are to be washed before prayers." And Aristeas says: "It is the custom for all the Jews to wash their hands as often as they pray to God." It was a saying among them: "Whosoever despiseth the washing of hands is worthy to be excommunicated; he comes to poverty, and will be extirpated out of the world." Another was this: "Whosoever has his seat in the land of Israel, and eats his common food in cleanness, and speaks the holy language, and recites his phylacteries morning and evening, let him be confident that he shall obtain the life of the world to come." The Jews tell us that one of their number, R. Aquiba, being in prison, and not having

water enough to drink and to wash his hands also, chose to do the latter, saying, "It is better to die of thirst than transgress the tradition of the elders." Maimonides says: "Of old the religious did eat their common food in cleanness, and took care to avoid all uncleanness all their days, and they were called Pharisees." All this was the invention of men and not the commandment of God. Cleanliness is one of the decencies of divine worship, but it is itself no part of true devotion. Yet that which is symbolized by it, viz., personal holiness, is a grand requisite in all acceptable worship. "If I regard iniquity in my heart, the Lord will not hear me." "When ye make many prayers, I will not hear; your hands are full of blood; wash you, make you clean," Ps. lxvi. 18; Isa. i. 15, 16. The sense therefore is that David would worship God *in rectitude and moral purity.* Some, however, think that the *washing in innocency* has reference to the custom of *protesting one's innocence* by washing the hands with water. This was practised by Pilate, Matt. xxvii. 24. The usage seems to have been well understood. Indeed it is found in the law of Moses as an ordinance, Deut. xxi. 1–9. And it must be confessed that this view gives a good sense, and well agrees with the scope and context. Perhaps the two interpretations may be united so as to teach that David would, not hypocritically, but sincerely, as in the sight of God, truly and successfully protest his innocence. There is some contrariety in the renderings as to the tense of the verb *wash.* The Hebrew is future. That indeed does not itself show that the common version is the best. See Introduction, § 6. The verbs of the two verses next preceding are in the preterite; but that does not determine that this shall be so. Indeed there is a fitness in the change of tense just at this point. The rendering of the English Bible is the best. There seems to be no reason for using the *present* tense. David was resolved to maintain a blameless character, and in his uprightness to worship God. *So will I compass thine altar, O* LORD. To *compass* may signify to *lay hold of,* or to *march around* in procession, or to *unite with others in standing around.* Perhaps the last is best. The second gives also a good sense. For although usually none but the priests went in procession around the altar, yet on the seventh day of the feast of tabernacles, the people solemnly marched seven times around the altar as a memorial of the fall of Jericho. The verb here rendered *compass,* in the same form is found in Ps. vii. 7. In Gen. xxxvii. 7, in another form it is rendered *stood round about.* The meaning of the Psalmist in the whole verse seems to be: I will solemnly and truly profess my uprightness, and I will render thee the sincere and holy worship prescribed in thy word. Such a character and such conduct eminently become all who approach the great King, and are the best foundation for solid usefulness:

7. *That I may publish with the voice of thanksgiving, and tell of all thy wondrous works.* God is honored when the righteous praise, and thank him and speak forth his marvellous deeds. The Hebrew does not sustain the rendering of some of the old versions, *That I may hear the voice of thy praise;* though it might warrant this, *That I may cause to be heard the voice of thanksgiving.* The same verb in the same form is found in 2 Chron. v. 13; Isa. lviii. 4. But to *make to be heard* is the same as to *publish.* Fry well renders it, To cause the sound of thy praise to be heard; Hengstenberg, That I may cause the voice of praise to be heard. The clause, says Alexander, "admits of several constructions: 1. To publish thanksgivings with the voice. 2. To publish with a thankful voice, without expressing what. 3. To publish and recount all thy wondrous works with a voice of thanksgiving." As the pious never want *wondrous* things in God's character and providence to celebrate, so God ought never to want friends and followers to utter his praise. *Thanksgiving,* in the English version almost uniformly rendered *thanks, thank offering, thanksgiving,* or *praise.* Twice only is it rendered *confession,* Josh. vii. 19; Ezra x. 11. But in these cases it is

probable that a part of worship is put for the whole. *Wondrous works*, literally *things done wonderfully*.

8. LORD, *I have loved the habitation of thy house, and the place where thine honour dwelleth*. Chaldee: I have loved the habitation of the house of thy holiness, and the place of the *tabernacle* of thy glory; Septuagint, Ethiopic and Vulgate: I have loved the beauty of thy house, and the place of the tabernacle of thy glory; Syriac: I have loved the service of thy house, and the place of the habitation of thy glory. Venema, Amesius, Edwards, Green and Ainsworth put the verb in the present tense, *I love;* but the majority of translators properly follow the orignal, *I have loved*, an act continued to this time. The verb expresses the affection of Abraham to Isaac, Gen. xxii. 2. In Ps. xi. 7 it expresses God's love of holiness. Surely the author of such a sentiment was spiritually-minded and loved communion with God. The pious soul delights in God however manifested, whether in works of creation or providence, in word or ordinances, in the tabernacle, or in the temple, or under the simpler worship of the Gospel dispensation.

9. *Gather not my soul with sinners.* The Chaldee gives the same rendering. The Septuagint, Ethiopic and Vulgate: Destroy not with the ungodly my soul; church of England: O shut not up my soul with the sinners; Edwards and Alexander: Take not away my soul with sinners. Diodati's paraphrase is: "Do not enfold me in the same ruin and curse" with sinners; Patrick's: "I hope thou wilt not let me suffer with those from whose society I have always separated myself." In many places the word rendered *gather* signifies *assemble*. In Ps. lxxxv. 3; Isa. iv. 1; Jer. xvi. 5, it is translated *take away*. For this reason it is used for *death*. In 1 Sam. xv. 6, it is *destroy;* in Isa. lvii. 1, *taken away;* in Ezek. xxxiv. 29, *be consumed*. The clause is a petition against being left to the companionship and doom of wicked men. *Nor* [gather] *my life with bloody men*. The prayer is of the same import as that in the preceding clause. David desired that no portion of his *existence*, neither the general course of his temporal life, nor its solemn close, nor his existence beyond the grave might be in common with the wicked. The reasons for such a prayer are found in all the differences of the characters, pursuits, preferences, habits, aims, ends and destinies of saints and sinners. They do not think alike, feel alike, speak alike, act alike, live alike, die alike, or fare alike. David wished to be remembered, cared for, and *gathered*, but not with sinners. For the sense of the phrase *bloody men*, or *men of bloods*, see on Ps. v. 6. In the next verse we have a further account of these *bloody men*.

10. *In whose hands is mischief.* For *mischief* the Chaldee has *the counsel of wickedness;* Septuagint, Ethiopic, Vulgate, Doway, *iniquities;* Arabic, *wrongs;* Syriac, *fraud;* Calvin, *maliciousness;* Venema and Amesius, *wickedness;* Edwards, *plotted mischief;* Fry, *an evil design;* Hengstenberg and Alexander, *crime*. *Men of blood* are always criminals, who deserve severe punishment from human law and from the divine judge. To live with them is torment to a pious soul. To spend an eternity with them is damnation. *And their right hand is full of bribes*. The word rendered *bribes* is in the singular, but is properly rendered plural from its connection with *full*, thus conforming to the English idiom. Literally it would be a *gift*. It is rendered *gifts* by the church of England; *gifts of corruption* by Amesius and Piscator; *bribery* by Fry and Hengstenberg; *a bribe* by Alexander. In our common version it is rendered a *gift, reward, present, bribery* and *bribes*, Ex. xxiii. 8; Deut. x. 17; 1 Kings xv. 19; Job xv. 34; 1 Sam. viii. 3. The sense of the word is well given in Ps. xv. 5; as "taking a *reward* against the innocent." Nothing more effectually blinds the eyes, perverts the judgment, and vitiates the character than bribery. It poisons the very fountain of justice and is practised only by unprincipled men. The Scripture

rule on this subject is correct. It forbids persons who are to act as judges, jurors, umpires or arbitrators even to receive a *present*. From bloody and deceitful men, who practised bloodshed and bribery, David desired to be separated both in this life and the next. His inclinations led him in a different direction.

11. *But as for me, I will walk in mine integrity. Integrity*, elsewhere *simplicity, perfection*. See Ps. vii. 8; xxv. 21. In other versions it is rendered *innocence, gentleness, perfectness, perfection*. It seems to embrace the idea of *entireness* of virtuous behaviour, thus securing symmetry of character and universality of obedience. It cannot therefore be better rendered than it is in the English text. This sense is made clearer and stronger by the verb *will walk*, indicating the course of the life, the uniform habit of the man. Such a life David was *resolved* to lead. He says, *I will*. The words, *But as for me*, exhibit his purpose in contrast to the wicked mentioned in the two verses next preceding. See Josh. xxiv. 15. One, thus honest with man and faithful with God, may confidently pray: *Redeem me, and be merciful unto me. Redeem*, elsewhere sometimes *deliver, rescue*, but most commonly as here. The same verb in the same form is found in Ps. xxv. 22. Redemption was commonly by a price, or at great risk. God saves the soul by a great sacrifice, but he is so strong, so wise and so good that he runs no risk. He saves with a mighty hand and abundant mercy. In the case of all sinners any *deliverance* is a *mercy*. The greater the deliverance, the greater the undeserved kindness. The prophet does not say, Redeem me and be *just* unto me. His plea is all of mercy. *Be merciful unto me; i. e.*, be gracious to me, be favorable unto me, have mercy upon me, have pity upon me. See Ex. xxxiii. 19; Jud. xxi. 22; Ps. iv. 1; li. 1; Pr. xix. 17. If David justified himself against the malicious slanders of his enemies, he did not plead that he was beyond the need of Jehovah's mercy and grace.

12. *My foot standeth in an even place.* He, that walketh uprightly, walketh surely. Sooner or later the Lord sends deliverance. It is not unusual to close the saddest Psalms with an expression of lively confidence that all will be right: yea, so firmly is this pious hope settled that even before relief actually comes, it is spoken of as past or present. The verb in this clause is put in the preterite by the Chaldee, Septuagint, Vulgate, Arabic, Syriac, Doway and Calvin, who follow the Hebrew. But the majority of scholars prefer the present, *standeth*. See Introduction, § 6. Alexander reads "*stands*, or *has* (at last) *stood*." By an *even place* the oldest versions generally understand *rectitude;* the Vulgate and Doway, *direct way;* Calvin, *uprightness;* church of England, *right;* Ainsworth, *in righteousness;* Waterland, *the court.* Some think the reference is to those words in v. 1, *I shall not slide.* When he said these words in v. 1, he expressed a hope or a prayer. Now he is assured that he stands firm. Diodati: "By faith I do already hold myself victorious over mine enemies, freed from all dangers and difficulties, and settled in secure happiness." Such a state of mind is fitly followed by the declaration: *In the congregations will I bless the* LORD. Chaldee: In the congregation of the just will I bless the Lord; Septuagint and Venema: In the assemblies will I bless the Lord; Vulgate and Doway: In the churches I will bless thee, O Lord; Ainsworth: In the churches I will bless Jehovah; Hengstenberg: In the assemblies will I praise the Lord. The verb rendered *will bless* is found in Ps. v. 12; xvi. 7. Even private benefits often call for public thanksgiving. But public mercies, wherein God delivers our lives and souls from deadly enemies and great perils, always summon us to bless him *in the congregations*.

DOCTRINAL AND PRACTICAL REMARKS.

1. To be misjudged and calumniated is the lot of all good men, v. 1. Neither

David, nor our Saviour escaped this trial. Sometimes these slanders are so many, so terrible, so distressing, that with all our energies we can do no more than patiently bear our sorrows, and quietly look to God for defence.

2. In many cases the wronged and persecuted have no more precious privilege than to refer their whole case to him, who is Judge of all, v. 1. When they can do this with a conscience void of offence towards God and man, they need not be afraid with any amazement. Cobbin: "*A good cause, a good conscience, and a good deportment are good grounds of appeal to God.* They are not meritorious grounds, but they are evidential grounds."

3. It is always wise to be more afraid of sin than of temporal evil, of doing wrong than of suffering wrong. Nothing hurts us till our souls are hurt. If we do right, we may boldly defy the universe of malignant creatures to do us real harm, v. 1. He, who renders evil for evil, withdraws his case from the chancery of heaven, and provokes the God of peace to rise up against him. Any comfortable appeal to God is entirely destroyed and any successful appeal to God is effectually hindered by our wilful wrong-doing.

4. It is instructive to see how often in Scripture our duties to man are appealed to as the test of sincerity, v. 1. Mere morality is not saving; but religion without morality is an abomination to God and to good men. When we walk in *integrity*, then we may hope that our *trust in God* is not a sheer pretence. No zeal, no devotion, no orthodoxy, no professions can prove him a servant of God, whose observance of the last six commandments is lax, or doubtful.

5. It is not wrong for good men, when slandered, to protest their innocence and defend their character, v. 1. This should be done humbly and mildly; but it may be done firmly and confidently. Job: "Till I die I will not remove my integrity from me." It is no mark of a virtuous character to be indifferent to reproach. And yet in many cases silence is best, Matt. xxvii. 12, 14; Mark xiv. 61; xv. 3, 5; Luke xxiii. 9. There is a time to be silent. There is also a time to speak.

6. If we would have the comforts of religion we must maintain *habits* of piety, v. 1. When David says, *I have trusted also in the Lord*, he does not refer to some occasional act, but to the tenor of his life. Fits of pious emotions save no man.

7. Although the duties of the second table of the law are often and justly insisted on as evidences of piety, yet when not accompanied by those of the first, they give no encouragement to hope for God's favor. He, who properly regards man, must also fear God. He, who is uncorrupt in morals, must also *trust in the Lord*, v. 1. Hengstenberg: "Trust in God is the *fountain* of integrity. Whoever places his hope in God need not seek to advance his worldly interests by violating his duty towards his neighbor: he waits for everything *from above*, and is, at the same time, always determined that he will not be deprived of the favor of his heavenly Father through violating his commandments."

8. Stability of morals is looked for in vain, where piety is wanting; and piety is vain and hypocritical, where uprightness of life is wanting, v. 1. Justification and sanctification are never separated, Ps. xxxii. 1, 2; Rom. viii. 1. To be just to man and to rob God as clearly establishes a bad character as to be pious towards God, and dishonest towards men.

9. The difference between saints and sinners extends not only to their views respecting Christ and the Holy Ghost, the law and the gospel, but also to the foundations of religious truth. Not only the moral but the natural attributes of God, which are by the wicked contemplated with aversion, are, to the righteous objects of love and joy, v. 2. By the wicked even the omniscience of God is hated. The Osage Indian spoke the sentiments of the carnal heart: "I do not like this God of the white people. I

hate him ; for he is always looking at me. I would shoot him, if I could see him."
This was not the feeling of the renewed heart of David. God's omniscience was his
comfort. He appealed to it humbly but gladly for the scrutiny of his character.
One of the most marked conversions the author ever witnessed was that of a lady,
who in the evening felt a dreadful opposition to God's knowing all that was in her
heart, and in the morning was rejoicing in that very truth, Ps. cxxxix. 23, 24.

10. It would be better for us, if we should think more of God's loving-kindness,
and more frequently celebrate it. It should ever be *before our eyes* as a theme of contemplation, and on our lips as a theme of praise, v. 3. The heart is best won to God
by the mild aspects of the divine character. "It is the pitifulness of the divine
bosom, which awakens confidence in the afflicted and sorrowing heart." Nothing more
revives our faith. Nothing more animates our zeal and our obedience.

11. Not isolated acts, but the course of one's life must determine character. Unless
we *walk in God's truth*, we are not his servants, v. 3. Henry: "Those only may
expect the benefit of God's loving-kindness, that live up to his truths, and his laws
that are grounded upon them. Some understand it of his conforming himself to
God's example in truth and faithfulness, as well as in goodness and loving-kindness.
Those certainly walk well, that are followers of God as dear children."

12. One of the greatest mysteries in human nature is the slowness of men to learn
that no good is likely to come to those who love and frequent evil company ; while
blessings of the greatest value seem naturally to fall on those, who shun the society of
the vicious and love that of the godly, v. 4. Morison: "In the present state of society
we cannot always avoid civil intercourse with some of the worst of men ; but he who
sits with the wicked, and finds delight in their unholy conversation, proves himself to
be an enemy of God, and a destroyer of his own soul."

13. Guile and dissembling belong to evil courses, v. 4. David's example teaches
that "though innocency may seem to make the godly a prey to their enemy, yet it
will promote their cause more before God, and give greater contentment to the conscience than witty wicked plotting against witty and wicked enemies."

14. The sagacity of God's people is truly wonderful. That kind of instinct, which
preserves them from associations with the crafty and the wicked, can only proceed
from a spiritual discernment. Calvin: "Their prudence is altogether different from
that of the flesh. Under the guidance and government of the Holy Spirit, they take
every necessary precaution against snares, but in such a manner as not to practise any
craftiness." The friendship of the world is enmity with God.

15. A good purpose is a good thing, vv. 6, 11, 12. He, who has it not, never
accomplishes great and desirable ends. "Without a purpose life is vain and vague."
If you would take heaven by storm, you must resolve to do it.

16. There is hope of a man and of a cause so long as God gives a heart to *compass
his altar* and *love the habitation of his house*, vv. 6, 8. A heart to pray and praise, to
adore God and confess sin is never given in vain. God's glory and our weakness, his
nature and our sorrows, his mercy and the gratitude due him demand our highest and
holiest worship. If pious prophets, apostles, judges, lawgivers and kings felt the worship of God to be so important, what vanity it is in us to decline it, or be indifferent
to it!

17. There was never a dispensation of God to men that did not distinguish between
true and false worship, between humble worshippers and vain hypocrites. Insincerity
was as offensive to God before as since the coming of Christ. The example of David,
as here set forth, deserves both to be studied and copied. There was probably
never more Antinomianism in the world than in this very age. It is indigenous to
the human heart. It is not expelled by all the checks given it. It perverts every

truth. He, who lives wickedly cannot worship acceptably. Morison: "It is a fearful thing to approach God's ordinances with a heart cherishing its own evil desires. The inveterate love of one sin will render abortive every attempt to serve a God of spotless purity."

18. It is a great mistake of some that they confine their praises to occasions of prosperity and joyfulness. This is not God's arrangement. This was not David's plan, vv. 7, 12. Paul and Silas prayed and sang praises in the prison at Philippi. Let us bless and praise the Lord at all times, because at all times we have cause for so doing.

19. Marvels worthy of celebration are never wanting to the grateful believer, v. 7. At the time referred to in this Psalm David's circumstances were very trying, yet in the history and prospects of himself and of God's people he found abundant cause for telling the *wondrous works* of the Lord.

20. Dickson: "The Lord hath a harvest and a gleaning time set, for cutting down and binding together, in the fellowship of judgments, God's enemies, who have followed the same course of sinning; for here we are given to understand that God will *gather their souls*, and so will let none escape," v. 9.

21. The farther the wicked progress in their career towards the final judgment, the more manifest will it be that saints and sinners are wholly diverse. In tastes, in principles, in habits, in desires, in aims, in prospects, in destiny there can be no greater diversity. Heaven and hell are not more unlike. The *gathering* time will make this clear. So that among all the profane and daring rebels, who during their earthly life have defied and blasphemed God, there will not be one, whose soul will not be filled with horror at the thought of receiving the portion of the wicked. No marvel then that the righteous, who by faith sees what is coming, and who abhors iniquity, desires never to be united with the congregation of evil doers. Scott: "Having loved the courts of the Lord, and every place and company, where his praises were displayed, and his glorious truth discoursed on; he would dread above all things the final doom of wicked men. A few hours with the covetous, malicious and deceitful are very painful: eternity in such company would be hell to him. This antipathy gives just confidence that his soul shall never be gathered with them, and animates him still to walk in his integrity, and to cry for mercy and complete redemption."

22. Prayers against being gathered with the wicked are not out of place in the case of the best men on earth. If God should deal with the most pious according to their personal deserts, who could stand? No man could account for one of a thousand of his offences. It is ever wise to cry, Enter not into judgment with thy servant.

23. The difference between the destinies of God's friends and foes will be no greater than that which their present characters call for. Clarke: "As I have never loved their company, nor followed their practice, let not my eternal lot be cast with them! I neither love them nor their ways:—may I never be doomed to spend an eternity with them."

24. There must be something dreadful in sin. The Bible exhausts the vocabulary to show its dreadful nature. At one time it is mischief, v. 10. At another it is sin, iniquity, transgression, rebellion, idolatry, harlotry, an evil and a bitter thing, a horrible thing. No man ever dreaded or hated sin excessively.

25. Whoever is engaged in administering justice should put and keep himself beyond the slightest suspicion of partiality, v. 10. In all matters, in this particularly, men should so behave that their good shall not be evil spoken of. The ermine of justice should be unstained. It is horrible to think of living in a country where this is not the case.

26. The whole plan of God respecting duty and salvation is to individualize our

race. Religion is a personal matter. Men must learn to stand faithful among the faithless. Every one of us must give account of himself to God. So that every one must determine for himself. "As for me," v. 11, *q. d.*, Let others do as they will, I will do right. To go with the multitude is one thing. To follow the Lord is another. Men are not saved in troops. One is taken and another is left.

27. Blessed is he who can truly say, *I have walked in mine integrity;* and from a blessed experience of the peace, wisdom and pleasure of such a course, is by God's grace enabled to say, I will walk in mine integrity, vv. 1, 11. Death is not an evil to be compared with the loss of integrity.

28. Whether we seek temporal or spiritual good things, redemption from earthly ills or from the wrath to come, we should never forget that nothing good is to be expected by us poor sinners, except from the mere grace, favor and mercy of God, v. 11.

29. All is well that ends well, v. 12. He who can conclude the review of any scene in his life as David closes this Psalm, may shout and give thanks for all that has happened to him. Morison: "It is a source of unspeakable enjoyment, even here, to unite in the congregations of the saints, and to give utterance to the grateful feelings of a redeemed heart; but what will it be to mingle in the raptures of the skies, to feel the gratitude 'of just men made perfect,' to swell the anthem of heavenly harmony, to lift up our voices with ten thousand times ten thousands, and thousands of thousands, all of whom have washed their robes and made them white in the blood of the Lamb!" Nor is this all. It is a tribute due to God, and a service due to our tempted and suffering brethren "that every one should publicly celebrate his experience of the grace of God, as an example to others to confide in him."

30. From the strength of the protestations of *integrity* and *innocence* here found, some have thought that this Psalm must have its fulfilment in Christ alone, and could not be at all applied to David. Fry's first remark is that "a Psalm, commencing with a demand for justice at the tribunal of the Almighty, must necessarily belong to our righteous Advocate." Amyrald uses language nearly as strong. But Horne clears the matter sufficiently when he says that "we have here an appeal to God in behalf of injured innocence. . . A trial of this sort might be desired by David, and may be desired by men, like him, conscious of their integrity, as to the particular crimes charged upon them by the malice of their enemies. Christ alone could ask such a trial at large, as being equally free from every kind and degree of sin, and certain of receiving additional lustre from the increasing heat of the furnace." No doubt David, in his struggles for his crown and in the opposition of wicked men, was a type of Christ, and an example of all believers, who should come after him. But under the charges brought against him, he would not do otherwise, if he spoke at all, than maintain his innocence. "False humility is really a lie, and cannot be acceptable to a God of truth."

PSALM XXVII.

A Psalm of David.

1 The LORD *is* my light and my salvation; whom shall I fear? the LORD *is* the strength of my life; of whom shall I be afraid?

2 When the wicked, *even* mine enemies and my foes, came upon me to eat up my flesh, they stumbled and fell.

3 Though a host should encamp against me, my heart shall not fear: though war should rise against me, in this *will* I *be* confident.

4 One *thing* have I desired of the LORD, that will I seek after; that I may dwell in the house of the LORD all the days of my life, to behold the beauty of the LORD, and to inquire in his temple.

5 For in the time of trouble he shall hide me in his pavilion: in the secret of his tabernacle shall he hide me; he shall set me up upon a rock.

6 And now shall mine head be lifted up above mine enemies round about me: therefore will I offer in his tabernacle sacrifices of joy; I will sing, yea, I will sing praises unto the LORD.

7 Hear, O LORD, *when* I cry with my voice: have mercy also upon me, and answer me.

8 *When thou saidst*, Seek ye my face; my heart said unto thee, Thy face, LORD, will I seek.

9 Hide not thy face *far* from me; put not thy servant away in anger: thou hast been my help; leave me not, neither forsake me, O God of my salvation.

10 When my father and my mother forsake me, then the LORD will take me up.

11 Teach me thy way, O LORD, and lead me in a plain path, because of mine enemies.

12 Deliver me not over unto the will of mine enemies: for false witnesses are risen up against me, and such as breathe out cruelty.

13 *I had fainted*, unless I had believed to see the goodness of the LORD in the land of the living.

14 Wait on the LORD: be of good courage, and he shall strengthen thine heart: wait, I say, on the LORD.

EXCEPT as to the relation between Psalms xxv. xxvi. the remarks on the Davidic authorship of the Psalm next preceding apply with force to this.

Hengstenberg: "All attempts to find out any particular event in the life of David, to which the Psalm may more especially be referred, have failed." This remark is fully sustained by a consideration of the variety of opinions presented by judicious writers, and often by the same writer. Patrick mentions three opinions as entitled to respect: 1. That it relates to Saul's persecutions of David; 2. That it relates to the time when David had to fly from Absalom; 3. That it refers to the time, "when, in fight with the Philistines, he had engaged himself so far among the enemies that he was in danger of being killed by a giant, if Abishai had not seasonably stepped in and relieved him." On this last occasion David was old and infirm. He was as brave as ever, but had neither the agility nor strength of youth. The people were so concerned at nearly losing their king and captain that they came and swore to him, saying, *Thou shalt go no more out with us to battle, that thou quench not the light of Israel*, 2 Sam. xxi. 17. Patrick admits that it is "not easy to resolve" the matter. Scott prefers the first of the foregoing opinions, but speaks with respect of those which refer it to later times. The terms of this ode are too general to enable us to fix on any one occasion of distress as causing it to be written.

Scott dates it B. C. 1059; Clarke, B. C. 578. If it was written during the urgency of distress it shows how strong was the prophet's faith to enable him to give thanks, as if the deliverance had been already wrought. Even if written after succor had reached him, it still embodies the sentiments which actuated him during his trial, although there may be more prominence given to his joyous sentiments in composing the ode than actually existed in his mind while the affliction lasted. It is not necessary to suppose with Calvin that the thanksgivings which David mingles with his desires and meditations, show that the Psalm was composed after his deliverance. Many a shout goes up from the field of battle.

On the title see on titles of Psalms iii. xi. There is neither reason nor authority for the addition made to the title by the Syriac: "On account of an infirmity which fell upon him;" nor of that of the Septuagint, Ethiopic, Vulgate and Doway: "A Psalm of David *before he was anointed*." David was thrice anointed, 1 Sam. xvi. 13; 2 Sam. ii. 4; 2 Sam. v. 3; so that if the addition were allowed it would still leave the matter very vague, as it would not determine which anointing was referred to.

The names of the Most High in this Psalm are *Jehovah* LORD and *Elohim God*, on which see on Ps. i. 2; iii. 2. On *God of my salvation* see on Ps. xviii. 46.

1. *The Lord is my light.* This Psalm relates to a season of darkness, when probably the faith and courage of some respecting David's success were much shaken by means of the fierceness, taunts and power of his enemies. The fears of his friends were probably not concealed from him. To silence them and to encourage himself he declares his resources to be in Jehovah: *The Lord is my light.* Light is the emblem of joy. The word is uniformly rendered. See on Ps. iv. 6. Light is sown for the righteous, Ps. xcvii. 11. Unto the upright there ariseth light in the darkness, Ps. cxii. 4. Jehovah is an unfailing source of joy. He has all resources. David says he is my light *and my salvation.* *Salvation,* thrice rendered *safety,* in all other cases *salvation.* It implies all needed deliverance. Jehovah, as he sees best, saves through trouble, out of trouble, or from trouble altogether. In the end he will do the last. Because he can and will so deliver, any one of his chosen may in the time of greatest trial say, *Whom shall I fear?* Neither spiritual nor military heroes do exploits through cowardice. Courage is a necessary virtue. In Jehovah is the best possible foundation for unflinching intrepidity. It is added: *The* LORD *is the strength of my life.* The word rendered *strength* has not before occurred in the Psalms. It is however in Ps. xxviii. 8, and frequently thereafter. It is variously rendered *rock, fort, fortress, strong-hold,* and more commonly *strength.* Once we read of the God *of forces,* the word being plural, Dan. xi. 38. So Jehovah was David's safe and impregnable refuge. So sure was he of this that he repeats the question: *Of whom shall I be afraid?* One Almighty is mightier than all mighties. Appearances may be quite against one, but if God be for him who can be against him? Calvin: "Weighing, as it were, in scales the whole power of earth and hell, David accounts it all lighter than a feather, and considers God alone as far outweighing it all." David has faith to appropriate all God's nature to his defence, and so he speaks of God as *my* light, *my* salvation, and the strength of *my* life. Hengstenberg: "If he only remain an inmate in the house of God, in possession of the favor of God, he is hid; for God protects his own."

2. *When the wicked,* even *mine enemies and my foes, came upon me to eat up my flesh, they stumbled and fell.* *Wicked, evil-doers* in Ps. xxvi. 5; those who *do hurt,* Jer. xxv. 6; those who *do harm,* 1 Sam. xxvi. 21; those who *afflict,* Ps. xliv. 2; those who *do mischief,* Pr. iv. 16; those who *vex* others, Num. xx. 15. *Enemies,* commonly so rendered, or *adversaries,* those *who give trouble,* or those *who give anguish. Foes,* in Ps. iii. 7; vi. 10; and always rendered as here or *enemies.* The wicked will as certainly do wickedly as that they are the enemies of God and the foes of good men. They thought David would hardly be a meal for them. So they came upon him, or *drew near* to him, to *eat up his flesh,* to make a full end of him; but they found unexpected difficulties. They *stumbled,* elsewhere *fell, fell down, fell backward, failed, were cast down, were overthrown. Stumbled* is a good and common rendering. *And* they *fell* or *died,* Gen. xxv. 18; or *perished,* Ex. xix. 21. In Jud. v. 27 it occurs thrice and signifies *died* though rendered *fell,* or *fell down.* See Ps. x. 10; xx. 8. An assault on a God-protected man is fatal to the assailant. There is no good reason for rendering any of the verbs in this verse in the future, as Castellio: "If they invade me—they shall stumble and fall." Nor is there any more reason for rendering them in the present tense, as do Piscator, Amesius, Edwards, Green and Hengstenberg. In the original the verbs are in the preterite; and we get the best sense by allowing David in great apparent peril to call to mind what God had done on former occasions; or, after the peril is over, to celebrate the deliverance. Calvin prefers the former explanation. From this time the Psalmist sees no just cause for doubting that he should have the help of God in any extremity:

3. *Though an host should encamp against me, my heart shall not fear.* An *host,* a band,

a *company*, a *camp*, an *army* in the field, a host numerous, actually armed for war, and trained to violence, is generally esteemed formidable. But though such an host should *pitch their tents, encamp*, array themselves against him, his heart should not fear. If not before, yet now came deliverance, which David joyfully celebrated: "By my God I have run through a troop." No combining and drilling of human forces ever prevails against *the God of forces*, Dan. xi. 38. Embattled legions are in God's esteem but as grasshoppers. Providence often fights against the strongest party, Eccle. ix. 11. He adds: *Though war should rise against me, in this* will *I* be *confident*. *War* refers to actual war, fighting. *Battle* would perhaps be a better rendering here. There is no reason for putting the last phrase, *In this* will *I* be *confident*, in connection with the next verse. It fairly belongs here. The sense of the clause is complete in itself: Though battle be arrayed against me, yet in this alarming and terrible state of things, I will be confident, *sure, secure*, Prov. xi. 15; Jud. xviii. 27. Although David was thus undaunted in the midst of perils, yet his heart was not in war. In the hairbreadth escapes of the fight he had no pleasure. Nor had he any delight in scenes of carnage, though he and his friends should be victors; "for every battle of the warrior is with confused noise, and garments rolled in blood." To such scenes he greatly preferred the quiet of peace, when he could be about the tabernacle and the holy city.

4. *One* thing *have I desired of the* Lord, *that will I seek after*. The meaning is, "I have desired one thing preëminently, I have desired it so much that in comparison I have desired nothing else. And I have sought it religiously, devoutly, by prayer, of the Lord; and I will never cease to desire it." This one thing, which he so earnestly sought for himself is thus expressed: *That I may dwell in the house of the* Lord *all the days of my life*. Three principal interpretations are given to this clause, each of them having a good sense. One is that the priests lodged at or in the house of the Lord, and David is here speaking of the desirableness of their life beyond that of a king in war. On this interpretation the pious Henry says: "Disdainfully as some look upon God's ministers, one of the greatest and best kings, that ever was, would gladly have taken his lot, have taken his lodging among them." No doubt David highly esteemed the priest's office; but as the head of the nation under the theocracy, as a prophet, as the sweet singer of Israel and as a type of Christ, he occupied a place in the house of God higher than that of any of the ordinary priests. Besides, the priests did not actually dwell in the temple. This could hardly have been his meaning, certainly not the whole of it. The second supposes that David here expresses his desire to have the peace of the realm restored, that he, as had been his wont, might piously and daily frequent the house of God, and unite in its solemnities. This may have been all that was intended. It is as much as most commentators get from it. And pious souls have always greatly loved the house and public worship of God. But the phrase, *house of the Lord*, at least sometimes has a much wider scope than that of any visible structure on earth. See Ps. xxiii. 6. Therefore, a third exposition is given. This makes the dwelling in God's house to be spiritual; and to be equivalent to having Jehovah for light and salvation. In this way we get the best sense to the phrase, *One* thing *have I desired*. This certainly signifies more than the mere privilege of being a visible worshipper in the tabernacle, which David knew was soon to be followed by a glorious temple. But why may not these views be united, and we regard the Psalmist as desiring to live in that state of peace, which would allow him to frequent the house of God, there to worship in the beauty of holiness, and thus have a pledge of the protection, guidance, and blessing of Jehovah here and hereafter? Two chief objects he had in view in this desire. One was, *To behold the beauty of the* Lord. To *behold* is not only to *perceive*, but to *enjoy*. For *behold* some read *contemplate, meditate upon*.

But so to *perceive* as to *enjoy* is a better signification, and is often found in the Old Testament, and in the corresponding Greek verb in the New Testament. For the *beauty* of the Lord, others read the *pleasure*, the *delight*, the *gracious countenance*, the *fair beauty*, the *loveliness*, the *desirableness*, the *pleasantness*, the *cheering countenance*, the *amiable* and *glorious majesty*, the *excellence* and *sweetness*, the *infinite* and *transcendant amiableness* of the Lord. Venema: "The beauty of the Lord here denotes whatever in the Lord is sweet, pleasant and salutary to the sinner, and therefore his excellencies of goodness and grace together with all their signs and effects." So to see as to enjoy the whole of God's character as revealed in Scripture is given to none but regenerate souls. They only have spiritual discernment, 1 Cor. ii. 14. Yet though they see them supernaturally, they do it not miraculously. They enjoy these things by the Holy Spirit's blessing on the word and ordinances of God. The other object David had in view in dwelling in God's house is thus expressed, *And to inquire in his temple.* There seems to be no good reason for rendering the verb here *contemplate*, or *visit*, or *meditate*, as some have proposed. To *search*, to *make inquiry*, to *seek early*, *i. e.*, *diligently*, is the real force of the original. *In his temple*, in his *palace*. See Ps. v. 7. Alexander: "Properly palace, the earthly residence of the great King, and therefore equally appropriate to the temple and the tabernacle." The word is rendered *palace* in 1 Kings xxi. 1; Ps. xlv. 8; and elsewhere.

5. *For in the time of trouble he shall hide me in his pavilion.* Pavilion, also rendered in our common version, *booth*, *tabernacle*, *tent*, *cottage*, *covert.* The sense evidently is that as a booth is a place of shelter from the sun, or as a tent is a *covert* from inclement weather; so Jehovah shall effectually hide his people in his *pavilion* when *trouble*, *mischief*, *harm*, *wickedness*, *adversity*, *affliction*, any *evil*, natural or moral shall threaten them. *In the secret of his tabernacle shall he hide me.* Often when all human solace and support failed him, David had found both in God as revealed in his tabernacle. He had thus learned to trust for days to come, and he felt assured of protection. Yea, his confidence was not that he should be barely hidden, but quite beyond the reach of his foes: *He shall set me up upon a rock; i. e.*, upon one of those high and impregnable natural fortresses, which were found in Judea; see Ps. xviii. 2; xxxi. 4; xix. 14. In these elevations one man was equal to the task of repelling many. The swords, spears, arrows and slung stones of foes reached him not. In the Hebrew the verbs of this verse are in the future. The rendering of the common version should be retained, though Hengstenberg, following several ancient versions, employs the preterite. Yet even he admits the future to be best in the next verse.

6. *And now shall mine head be lifted up above mine enemies round about.* God protects effectually. The more acquaintance the saints have with him, the more are they persuaded of his excellence as a hiding-place. A soul saved by him may look down in defiance at his haughtiest and mightiest foes. The cony in the rock is safe from the thousand hounds yelping at it. *Round about*, more commonly so rendered; frequently, *on every side.* There is no propriety in rendering the phrase, *I have made a circuit*, or *I have gone round*, as several ancient versions have done, thus connecting it with the next clause. The Syriac comes nearer the sense when it reads, And now my head is lifted up above my enemies, *who surrounded me.* Such deliverances would call for suitable acts of devotion: *Therefore will I offer in his tabernacle sacrifices of joy.* Chaldee: And I will sacrifice in his tabernacle acceptable sacrifices; Septuagint, Ethiopic, Arabic, Vulgate and Doway: I have offered up in his tabernacle a sacrifice of jubilation; Syriac: I will sacrifice in his tabernacle the sacrifices of praise; church of England: Therefore will I offer in his dwelling an oblation, with great gladness; Venema: And I will sacrifice in his tent the victims of a joyful outcry; Amesius:

That I may sacrifice in his tent the sacrifices with the sound of trumpets; Ainsworth: And I will sacrifice in his tent sacrifices of shouting; Edwards: And I shall offer in his tabernacle sacrifices of thanksgiving; Fry: And I sacrifice at his tabernacle sacrifices of triumph; Hengstenberg: And I will offer in his tabernacles offerings of joy; Alexander: And I will sacrifice in his tabernacle sacrifices of joyful noise. *Joy*, in Ps. xxxiii. 3, *a loud noise;* in Ps. xlvii. 5, *a shout;* in Ps. lxxxix. 15, *the joyful sound.* Hammond: "*Sacrifices of jubilation* are those of the solemn feasts, attended not only with the harmony and music of the Levites, but the hosannas and acclamations of the people. Hence Jeremy compares the military clamors of the victorious Chaldeans in the temple to those that were formerly made there in the day of a solemn feast, Lam. ii. 7. *They have made a noise in the house of the Lord, as in a day of a solemn feast.*" The psalmist adds: *I will sing, yea, I will sing praises unto the* LORD. The first verb is in our version almost uniformly rendered *sing*, as in Ps. xiii. 6; xxi. 13. The second is frequently rendered as here, Ps. vii. 17; ix. 2; also *sing, sing praise*, and once *sing Psalms*, 1 Chron. xvi. 9. Several ancient versions give *recite a Psalm;* others, *make a Psalm.* The prophet says that he will do all in his power to exalt God by speech and music.

7. *Hear, O* LORD, *when I cry with my voice.* The confident and exultant tone is here dropped, and the language of earnest desire and hearty prayer is adopted. *Cry,* so rendered in Ps. iii. 4; lxvi. 17; cxix. 145; cxxx. 1; often *call*, as in Ps. xiv. 4; xvii. 6; often *proclaim*, Is. lxi. 1, 2; Joel iii. 9. The phrase, *with my voice*, shows that the prayer was vocal and not merely in the heart. *Have mercy also upon me, and answer me. Have mercy*, as in Ps. iv. 1; xxvi. 11.

8. When thou saidst, *Seek ye my face; my heart said unto thee, Thy face*, LORD, *will I seek.* With this verse our translators have taken unusual, though not unwarrantable liberties. It is not possible to give the sense in English, unless something is supplied. This is proven by the attempt and failure of many. Castellio thus paraphrases it: "I thus think in my mind, that thou wouldst have thy face sought; thy face, Lord, I seek." With this substantially agrees Patrick's paraphrase. Indeed the best sense is fairly reached by our version, and those which in the main agree with it. To seek God's face is to come before him with requests and petitions, such as the following:

9. *Hide not thy face far from me.* The word *far* is unnecessarily supplied by our translators. To *hide the face* is to refuse as a judge to hear the cause, and give relief. The form of speech is borrowed from the preceding verse. Another request is, *Put not thy servant away in anger.* This translation is good. Calvin's is as good: Cast not away thy servant in thy wrath; so also is that of Edwards: Turn not off thy servant in anger. Horsley prefers that of the Septuagint and Vulgate: Turn not away in anger from thy servant. The reasoning of the Psalmist seems to be: My sins are many: God might in righteous indignation cast me off: But he is merciful and in him do I trust. And until he does *put me away*, I am under his guardianship and protection, and so I am safe. To pray thus he is emboldened by his past experience of God's love and mercy: *Thou hast been my help:* q. d., I remember the affair of the bear, the fight with the lion, and the death of Goliath, in all of which cases thou alone didst save me, and so I know whom I am addressing, and am bold to plead thy care and help again. He urges his plea in other like words: *Leave me not, neither forsake me, O God of my salvation.* For *forsake* Calvin reads *forsake utterly;* others suggest slight changes; but none of them give a better sense, nor are they more true to the original. Because of their connection with blessed promises, the English verbs here used have become very precious to the saints, Josh. i. 5; 1 Sam. xii. 22; 1 Kings viii. 57; Heb. xiii. 5. The last text is as wonderful a promise

as the Bible contains. In our Psalm, the language is that of prayer. Every in-spired prayer is a promise.

10. *When my father and my mother forsake me, then the Lord will take me up.* *For sake*, the same as in the preceding verse, but here in the preterite. The second verb is in the future. The renderings of this verse are considerably diverse, yet the import of the passage is not doubtful. For *take up* the Chaldee and Ainsworth read *gather;* Edwards, *take in.* The Syriac, church of England and Hengstenberg have the last verb in the present tense; Septuagint, Ethiopic, Arabic, Vulgate and Jebb, in the preterite; Chaldee, Calvin, Amesius and Alexander, in the future. Instead of *When* Ainsworth and Edwards have *Though.* In Ex. xiii. 17 it is *although.* Did David's father and mother ever forsake him? The last account we have of them, they still adhered to him and his cause, 1 Sam. xxii. 3, 4. To meet this difficulty several things have been said. 1, The verb rendered *forsake* as well describes the separation by death as by wilful desertion, Psalm xlix. 10; Jer. xlix. 11. 2, Some suppose the case to be merely supposititious. This requires the sentence to begin with *although,* and the verb to be rendered *should forsake.* 3, Some have supposed that David often and actually fell under the displeasure of his parents, as he did, at least on one occasion, under that of a brother, 1 Sam. xvii. 28. But there is no proof that David ever incurred the disapprobation of his parents. Sharp as were his trials, there is no evidence that they lacked confidence in his wisdom, integrity or ultimate success. It is remarkable that Hengstenberg, who favors the view suggested by the third remark, finds no trace of evidence in the history of Jesse or David, but rests the whole weight of the assertion on the proverb, "The unfortunate may lay their account with contempt;" on the experience of Job, when for his calamities friends and wife forsook him; on an expression used by another Psalmist, Ps. lxxxviii. 8; and on the general principles of human nature. But Jesse and his wife are in Scripture held up as models of piety. They are always mentioned with respect or with commendation. They doubtless believed God's hand was in all their troubles, and that their son was divinely called to these sore trials, perhaps as a preparation for reigning over a great nation. 4. Another explanation is that father and mother here represent near and dear friends, who often die, and who often voluntarily withdraw their confidence and esteem. This is admitted by Hengstenberg. This and the first remark fully meet the difficulty. 5. Calvin makes the forsaking yet future, but that is hardly justified by the original. *The Lord will take me up.* It is not without cause that Edwards prefers *take in.* Hengstenberg: "*The Lord takes me up,* like one who takes a weary wanderer or a fugitive, who has lost his way, into his house, and treats him kindly." The same verb is used in Josh. xx. 4; Judges xix. 15. The same idea is conveyed in v. 5. Our Saviour laid great stress on hospitality, Matt. xxv. 35, 43. So did his Apostles, Rom. xii. 13; 1 Tim. iii. 2; Tit. i. 8; 1 Pet. iv. 9.

11. *Teach me thy way, O* LORD. The Chaldee, Syriac, church of England, Calvin, Venema, Amesius and many others quite agree with the common version. Septuagint, Ethiopic, Vulgate and Doway: Set me, O Lord, a law in thy way; Fry: Instruct me, Jehovah, concerning thy way; Alexander: Guide me, Jehovah, (in) thy way. There are but two admissible senses. One is that David prays to be preserved from sin; the other is that he asks to be guided in the ways of God's choosing to a happy issue. There is no objection to uniting them both, and to understand him as asking to be kept from sin, and so guided to a full deliverance. *And lead me in a plain path.* For *plain* the ancient versions and many modern translations read *right;* Edwards and Hengstenberg, *even;* Alexander, *level.* Crooked ways are to be avoided because they are wicked; rough ways, because they are uncomfortable; and dark ways, because

they are perilous.   Praying against sinful ways so as to be guided in safe ways exhausts the meaning.   For these petitions he gives an urgent reason : *Because of mine enemies.*   As if he had said, Because my enemies are many, deceitful, malignant, watching for my halting, and seeking my life.

12. *Deliver me not over unto the will of mine enemies.   Enemies,* by some *tormentors,* by some *distressers,* by others *observers* or *spies.*   It is a dreadful thing to be, even for a season, in the power of bad men, especially when their passions are excited, and they are ready to deal out cruelties.   The wicked do often make portions of this world very much like hell.   Their temper and malice show that they are of their father the devil, and his works will they do.   A special reason is given for urging the prayer : *For false witnesses are risen up against me.*   Who can stand before false testimony? How it pierces the soul with anguish !   It is the most intolerable species of murder. It kills by torture.   When it extends to judicial oaths it shows the worst possible state of society.   Where false witnesses are found there also are *Such as breathe out cruelty.*   There is a doubt among scholars whether this clause should be read in the singular or plural.   Our rendering is supported by some translations and able scholars; while a large majority would read, " He that breathes out cruelties."   Without some knowledge of Hebrew the discussion could hardly be understood.   Nor is the sense materially varied ; for often does one of a class stand for many like himself.   This clause reminds one of Saul of Tarsus, who *breathed out threatenings and slaughter.* Such language describes one whose thoughts and purposes are all bent in one direction, and who is eager upon his evil design.   His breath stinks of blood.

13. I had fainted, *unless I had believed to see the goodness of the* LORD *in the land of the living.   I had fainted* is supplied by our translators, and some think needlessly. None of the ancient versions have it. · Yet it seems to have been commonly understood that something was to be here supplied, legibly or mentally.   So Calvin (in the French version) supplies, *I should have perished ;* church of England, I should utterly have fainted; Amesius, They would have borne me away by force; Edwards, I should sink under my trouble.   Another very respectable class of scholars decline to supply anything, yet admit that the sense is imperfect without something understood.   Thus Ainsworth: Except I had believed to see the goodness of Jehovah in the land of the living; Calvin (in his commentary), Jebb, Hammond, Clarke, Hengstenberg and Alexander virtually agree to this rendering.   Hammond: "In the Hebrew there is an aposiopesis, a figure of elegance, purposely breaking off in the midst of the speech; yet so as every man can foresee what kind of conclusion should follow, if he did not purposely divert to the contrary."   This figure of speech is common, and belongs to the language of promise or threatening, and specially suits subjects of an awful character.   This virtually agrees with our version, because it admits that some such clause is to be supplied, at least in the mind of the reader.   It leaves the Hebrew text unaltered, and it gives a good sense, and that with much beauty and force.   *The land of the living* is a phrase that has caused some doubt.   The Chaldee: The land of eternal life; Septuagint, Ethiopic, Vulgate, Syriac, Doway, church of England, Ainsworth, Edwards, Jebb, Fry and others agree with the English version.   The Arabic and Alexander read *in the land of life.*   As David is speaking of temporal distresses and persecutions, it is perhaps best to read *land of the living,* meaning thereby the opposite of land of the *dead.*

14. *Wait on the* LORD.   Some have thought David here turns from himself, and addresses others, calling on them to do their duty and leave results with God.   But the words are most fitly addressed, not to others, but to himself.   Horsley, however, regards this whole verse as containing the words of an oracular voice.   But it is as well to regard the Psalmist as addressing himself, or his soul, as he often does.   The

exhortation of the whole verse is a seasonable check to the language of alarm, begun to be uttered in the preceding verse. *Waiting on the Lord* is not only being ready to serve him, but also patiently looking for him, and confidently expecting him. So far from supposing its trials over, it rather looks for new ones. The Chaldee: Confide in the Lord; Vulgate, Venema, Amesius and Fry: Expect the Lord; several versions: Hope in the Lord; church of England: O tarry thou the Lord's leisure; Alexander: Wait thou for Jehovah. This waiting was to be in cheerfulness, not in sullenness: *Be of good courage, and he shall strengthen thine heart.* The Chaldee: Be inflexible and strengthen thy heart; Septuagint, Ethiopic and Vulgate: Act manfully, and let thy heart be strengthened; church of England: Be strong, and he shall comfort thy heart. The great mass of translators agree in the main with the common version. Hengstenberg and Alexander read the latter clause, And may he strengthen thy heart. This form of the first verb is in our version most commonly rendered, *Be strong,* or *Be of good courage;* once or twice, *Be sure, Be courageous.* The second verb is well rendered *strengthen,* meaning the same as *confirm, establish, fortify.* Those who would be strong and courageous must exercise the strength and courage which they have, and not wickedly yield to despondency. Nor let any forget that a time of trial, so far from relaxing the bonds of obligation, does rather call for increased attention to our duties, and so the Psalmist again exhorts himself to stand in his lot, and hope for better days: *Wait, I say, on the Lord.* In the Hebrew as in the English we have the very same words as those found in the beginning of the verse: *Wait on the Lord.* There is nothing but the conjunction, which we commonly render, *and,* in the Hebrew, to correspond with the words, *I say.* Though the Hebrew may not be literally so rendered, yet the English idiom justifies our translation.

DOCTRINAL AND PRACTICAL REMARKS.

1. Jehovah is himself the infinite good, the portion of his saints, their all and in all, their light and joy, their safety and deliverance, their strength and refuge, v. 1. Were our faith as strong as it should be, nothing could fill us with dismay or terror. Because God changes not, the state of his people is never desperate.

2. One of the best ways to dispel doubts and fears is to summon to our aid the very strongest doctrines and highest truths of religion, v. 1. Weak doctrines will not be a match for powerful temptations.

3. No confidence is so well placed as confidence in God; no joy is like that which he gives; no deliverances are so manifestly glorious as those he works; life is never so sweet as when felt to be the renewed gift of God, v. 1.

4. Courage is both a duty of man, and a gift of God, v. 1. We should sharply reprove ourselves for all disheartening timidity. If we duly fear God, all tormenting fear is idle. There is no cause for it. There is no getting on without intrepidity. We must be heroic, or we must perish.

5. It is an unspeakable privilege to be in covenant with God, so as to be able to say of him, He is *my* light, *my* salvation, and the strength of *my* life, v. 1. An impersonal God is hardly more full of vagueness, than is a God to whom we sustain no personal or federal relations.

6. There was great wisdom in the prayer of John Wesley: "Lord, if I must contend, let it not be with thy people." When we have for foes and enemies those who hate good men, we have at least this consolation, that God is not on their side, and therefore it is essentially weak, v. 2.

7. The hatred of the wicked to the righteous is deadly. They would eat up their flesh, v. 2. It was so from the beginning. It has been so always. O how they have slaughtered the people of God!

8. The way the wicked fail is terrible. If they had any wisdom at all, the deluge, the fall of Sodom and Gomorrah, the overthrow of Pharaoh and his hosts, or any one of their great defeats would have fully satisfied them that their war on God, his truth, and his saints was hopeless folly. Since the world began, the end of every battle they have fought against God and his people has been this, *they stumbled and fell*, v. 2. ' The temporary success of the wicked is only an introduction to their deeper disgrace and misery."

9. As it is easy to abuse, so it is possible rightly to use past experiences and deliverances. In this David sets us a good example, vv. 2, 9. He who has delivered can deliver. He who made the world can do anything. He who has been our help and light and safety and strength is everlasting and unfailing.

10. God can as easily defeat a world in arms against one of his chosen, as he can bring to naught the counsel and the rage of one man, v. 3. To him a *host* is as one man; and all nations are as grasshoppers. If we would have much comfort we must study God's attributes and acquaint ourselves with him. He, who hopes for no more, than appearances lead him to expect, will be a poor creature; while he, who hopes against hope, will be a pillar.

11. When the worst comes to the righteous, then things grow better. The *host* encamps, the *battle* rages, then comes the decision, and the result is that the righteous are calm and confident, and so victorious, v. 3.

12. Dickson: "It is a mean to strengthen faith, to resolve by the grace of God to put faith in act, in whatsoever difficulty, and in a manner to lay hands on ourselves, to hold up this shield against whatsoever fiery darts, albeit possibly when it cometh to push of pike, we be not found so strong as we are stout," v. 3.

13. Calvin: "Then does faith bring forth its fruit in due season, when we remain firm and fearless in the midst of dangers," v. 3.

14. It proves no man wrong to have war made against him, v. 3. The best causes and the best men often meet with the fiercest opposition.

15. God's visible worship ever has been and ever must be a source of continual joy to the right-minded, v. 4. There is no evidence that this will cease to be the case in a future world. We know it will not. See the book of Revelation. God's ordinances of worship are all edifying. Surely those, who hope to spend their eternity in the praises of God, ought to get their harps in tune to his service before they leave this world.

16. When we have a good thought or desire, we must not yield it up to temptation, but hold on to it and cherish it, v. 4. When some one admired Leighton's library, he said: "One devout thought is worth more than it all." He was right.

17. Sometimes men have spoken slightingly of the love of gratitude to God, and sometimes of the love of complacency in God. The Bible does neither. As elsewhere it commends the former, Ps. cxvi. 1; so here it does the latter, v. 4. The great error of the wicked respecting Christ is that when they see him there is in their eyes no beauty that they should desire him. He, who cares not to behold the *beauty* of the Lord, is a poor blinded sinner.

18. A sense of ignorance lies at the foundation of all solid improvement in learning. Only those, who manifest a docile spirit are in any mood to learn, or to *inquire in God's temple*, v. 4.

19. The safety of God's people in this life does not consist in exemption from troubles and perils; but in the care and protection of him, who hides them in his pavilion, and in his tabernacle, and sets them upon a rock, v. 5.

20. While gravity and solemnity become the house of God, yet we should, even at the most trying times, conduct our worship in cheerfulness, yea, in joyfulness, v. 6.

Grimace and superstition are never pleasing to God nor to right-minded men. Henry: " Whatever is the matter of our joy ought to be matter of our praise. And when we attend upon God in holy ordinances, we ought to be much in joy and praises." *" Thanks be to God who always causeth us to triumph."*

21. The saints shall not only be saved; they shall be saved manifestly and abundantly. Their heads shall be lifted up above all their enemies, v. 6. It shall be no secret that God's people are delivered. Even here God often brings them out with a strong arm and a mighty hand. And where for good cause he tries them long, he often removes from their own minds all doubt of their perfect victory. Dickson: " The Lord can give a believer assurance of what he would have, and make him so clear of the possession of the promise, as if it were in his hand." " Happy are they, whose faith and hope are as vigorous as the security is valid."

22. All mercies call for gratitude; and some, though personal, demand public and joyful acknowledgment, and even exultation, v. 6.

23. It is impossible to explain God's word according to any sound rules of interpretation, so as to condemn the use of joyful, solemn music in his public worship, v. 6. On this point the New Testament is as clear as the Old, 1 Cor. xiv. 15; Eph. v. 19; Col. iii. 16; James v. 13. God's worship should not be wholly silent and inaudible.

24. Prayer and praise are both duties. Worship is as much God's due as anything can be, vv. 6, 7. If he deserves not the highest acts of adoration, he deserves nothing. He, who piously seeks God's face, obeys a very binding and a very gracious command, v. 8. He may rest assured that he shall lack neither mercy nor protection, nor instruction, nor redemption, nor salvation—eternal life. Of such inestimable price is God's favor that the righteous would gladly forego all blessings in comparison of it.

26. Divine desertion is fatal to any cause. The righteous know this, and so are very urgent in praying against so great a calamity, v. 9. Nothing worse can happen to any man than to be left to himself. To be wholly and finally and eternally forsaken of God is hell.

27. One of the best exercises of a devout mind is converting promises into prayers. God says "I will never leave thee, nor forsake thee." Let us continually pray, " Leave me not, neither forsake me." We may also rest assured that everything, for which we find warrant to pray, is to believers made sure in the oath of the covenant. God never stirs up a soul to cry, " Leave me not, neither forsake me," without saying, " I will never leave thee nor forsake thee." All that is promised is rightly prayed for; all that is rightly prayed for is surely promised, v. 9.

28. No desertion of friends, however dear, should make us despair, v. 10. At one time almost everybody was against David, yet he triumphed. Devils and wicked men were against Christ; one disciple betrayed him, another denied him, and all forsook him; even his Father drew against him the dreadful sword of inflexible justice, and buried it deep in his holy soul; yet none ever triumphed as he triumphed. From his resurrection to this day has been one unbroken series of victories. So it shall be till he hath put all things under him. " God is a surer and better Friend than our earthly parents are, or can be."

29. No man can too highly prize or too diligently seek or too closely follow divine guidance and conduct, v. 11.

30. We must see that we do right things in a right way, and that our good be not evil spoken of. Dickson: " There is danger of desertion, or of God's leaving us to the will of our enemies, if we carry not a good cause in a lawful, holy and tender way," v. 11.

31. If we have enemies, so had others before us, vv. 2, 11, 12. Some men seem to have a fondness for speaking much of their enemies. This may arise from a vanity which delights in the conspicuity thus obtained, or from a desire to secure sympathy, or from a heart full of distress at being beset by haters and opposers. Yet when our enemies are many and violent and cruel, it is often a relief to speak of them. It is not given to man to be great, or useful, or influential, without incurring the malice of the ignoble. There is a large class of men who suspect and often hate all who excel them. Which of the prophets or apostles lived without bitter enemies? Christ himself was hated without a cause. Let no good man be surprised at finding men hating him.

32. We should often and gratefully acknowledge the goodness of God, which keeps us out of the power of the wicked, v. 12. When men are not only wicked but when their wickedness takes the form of tyranny, then to be in their power makes an earthly existence to cease to be desirable. Cruelty and oppression are sometimes worse than strangling and death.

33. Those, who are disposed to apologize for the wicked as being but moderately vile, would do well to study the delineations of their characters as given in the Bible. There, their very *breath* is said to be cruel and murderous, v. 12.

34. A lively hope and strong faith are good things, v. 13. O it is good for a man that he both hope and quietly wait for the salvation of God. Morison: " What a light in darkness is confidence in God's paternal care !"

35. Those, who exercise the grace they have, shall have more grace, v. 14. To him that hath shall be given. Calvin: " As David was conscious of his weakness, and knew that his faith was the great means of preserving him safe, he seasonably strengthens himself for the future. Under the word *waiting*, too, he puts himself in mind of new trials, and sets before his eyes the cross which he must bear."

36. As we have opportunity we should to the comfort of the saints and the glory of God speak of our marvellous and narrow escapes, v. 13. It mightily emboldens the saints to hear one of their number just out of the furnace give such an exhortation as that in v. 14.

37. Dickson : " Albeit the Lord let the trouble lie on, and strong temptations to increase, and grief of heart to grow, yet must we still wait: for at the due time the outgate shall come," v. 14.

38. Be of good courage, all ye saints : Wait, I say, on the Lord.

PSALM XXVIII.

A *Psalm* of David.

1 Unto thee will I cry, O LORD my rock; be not silent to me: lest, *if* thou be silent to me, I become like them that go down into the pit.

2 Hear the voice of my supplications, when I cry unto thee, when I lift up my hands toward thy holy oracle.

3 Draw me not away with the wicked, and with the workers of iniquity, which speak peace to their neighbours, but mischief *is* in their hearts.

4 Give them according to their deeds, and according to the wickedness of their endeavours: give them after the work of their hands; render to them their desert.

5 Because they regard not the works of the LORD, nor the operation of his hands, he shall destroy them, and not build them up.

6 Blessed *be* the LORD, because he hath heard the voice of my supplications.

7 The LORD *is* my strength and my shield; my heart trusted in him, and I am helped: therefore my heart greatly rejoiceth; and with my song will I praise him.

8 The LORD *is* their strength, and he *is* the saving strength of his anointed.

9 Save thy people, and bless thine inheritance: feed them also, and lift them up for ever.

THERE is no good reason for doubting that David wrote this Psalm. For an explanation of the title see on Psalms iii. xi. The Vulgate and Doway give the title: A Psalm for David himself; Chaldee: To David; Septuagint: Of David; Ethiopic: Of David himself; Arabic: A prayer and a prophecy; Syriac: Of David, a supplication and a prayer; also that we should implore help.

The occasion of the writing of this Psalm, if there was any, is not apparent. Calvin, after Theodoret: "It is probable that he speaks of his persecutions by Saul;" Morison: "It is highly probable that this Psalm was composed on the same occasion with the former;" Hengstenberg: "The contents throughout apply very well to David during the time of Absalom's rebellion;" Dodd: "This, as well as the foregoing, is supposed to have been written by David towards the latter end of his reign;" Gill: "It might be made by David when he was persecuted by Saul, or when delivered from him, or at least when he had faith and hope that he should be delivered;" Scott: "It is not agreed, whether it was written during David's persecutions from Saul, or at a later period;" Clarke: "It belongs most probably to the times of the captivity, though some have referred it to David in his persecutions." Edwards justly says: "The particular occasion is uncertain." Scott dates it B. C. 1059; Clarke, B. C. 578. Alexander: "The collocation of the Psalm is clearly not fortuitous, but founded on its close resemblance to the one before it." Hengstenberg, however, thinks that this Psalm and the twenty-ninth make up one pair. Here we have new proof of the great uncertainty in the doctrine of pairs.

The only name of God in this Psalm is *Jehovah* LORD, on which see on Ps. i. 2.

One class of commentators make this ode exclusively Messianic. Fry: "These are still the supplications of our great High-Priest." Horne is no less decided in applying it to Christ alone and exclusively. Others seem to drop all idea of Christ from their interpretations. The truth probably is that the Psalm details the experience of the literal David, but also presents him as a type of the great Anointed, who was to come; and so we may regard it as *Typical-Messianic*. David is as certainly spoken of as *anointed* of God as was the great promised Deliverer. The mere occurrence of that word determines nothing as to its application.

This Psalm is not in form dramatic.

1. *Unto thee will I cry, O LORD my rock.* *Will cry*, the same verb as in Ps. xxvii. 7. The Chaldee, Amesius, Ainsworth, Fabritius, Edwards, Fry and Hengstenberg use the present, *cry*; Septuagint, Ethiopic, Arabic and Syriac the preterite, *have cried*; Venema, *I am used to cry*; Vulgate, Doway, church of England, Calvin and Jebb follow the Hebrew as does our version, *will cry*; Alexander, *will call*. *My rock.* Some versions separate this word from the first clause, and make it the beginning of the second, but this is not best. The Hebrew for *rock* is the same as in Deut. xxxii. 4, 15, 18, 30; Ps. xviii. 31, 46. See on Ps. xviii. 2; xix. 14, where it is rendered *strength*. *Be not silent to me.* Arabic: Neglect me not; Calvin: Hold not thy peace from me; Edwards: Be not regardless of me; Boothroyd: Be not thou deaf to my prayer; Dathe: I am unwilling that thou shouldest be absent from me; Alexander: Be not silent from me. The same verb in the same form is elsewhere rendered, Hold not thy peace, Ps. xxxix. 12; lxxxiii. 1; cix. 1. The prayer is that God would no longer keep silence, but speak out to the joy of his servant and to the confusion of his enemies. *Lest if thou be silent to me, I become like them that go down into the pit; i. e.,*

die and go into the grave. The prominent idea is that of utter helplessness and ruin unless prompt and sensible aid come from God. Calvin: "It is as if he had said, I am nothing if thou leavest me; if thou succorest me not I perish." One begins to be in a good way when, with a heart to pray, he learns that he is nothing.

2. *Hear the voice of my supplications.* The rendering of this clause could not well be different. For *supplications* the church of England has *humble petitions.* The word means earnest pleas for undeserved favor. *When I cry unto thee.* This verb is almost invariably rendered *cry.* It here denotes audible, earnest pleading with God. *When I lift up my hands toward thy holy oracle. Oracle,* uniformly rendered. It occurs more than a *dozen* times. The ancient versions all give it temple; church of England, mercy-seat; Calvin, sanctuary; Venema and Amesius, most holy place. The reference is to Ex. xxv. 22: "I will meet with thee, and I will commune with thee from above the mercy-seat, from between the two cherubims, which are upon the ark of the testimony." See Num. vii. 89; 1 Kings vi. 19. The mercy-seat pre-figured Christ, who is the Word of God, the revealer of God, and the propitiation, John i. 1; xiv. 9; Rom. iii. 25; 1 John ii. 2. As in prayer we now by faith look to Christ, so the pious of old with their natural eyes looked to the *oracle,* the *mercy-seat. Lifting up the hands* was a common gesture in prayer, Ps. xliv. 20; lxiii. 4; lxxxviii. 9; cxli. 2; cxliii. 6.

3. *Draw me not away with the wicked.* Arabic: Snatch not away my soul with sin-ners; Syriac: Number me not with the ungodly; Hammond: Seize not on me with the wicked. The English is supported by the Chaldee, Septuagint and Vulgate and by most modern translations. Fry thinks the allusion is to a shepherd selecting out a portion of his flock. The same verb is applied to that matter in Ex. xii. 21. But the word *draw* is applied to *drawing* a bow, *drawing* in a yoke, *drawing* into a net, etc. The meaning is, Let not my life and portion be with *the wicked,* described as *the workers of iniquity,* a class of men well known in sacred writings, as given over to wickedness. See Ps. v. 5; vi. 8; xiv. 4. These are men *which speak peace to their neighbors, but mischief* is *in their hearts.* Every one of them is a fox, a serpent, a deceiver, a dissembler, an impostor, a pretender. Where is the worker of iniquity, who does not use guile, fraud, cunning, trick, artifice, intrigue, feigned words, smooth speeches? Nothing is more offensive to a pure mind than double dealing.

4. *Give them according to their deeds, and according to the wickedness of their endea-vours: give them after the work of their hands; render to them their desert.* The verbs are in the imperative. See Introduction, § 6. For *endeavours* some read *inventions* as in Ps. cvi. 39; in all other cases it is *works,* or *doings.* It is right men should reap what they have sowed, and not something else. God would not be adorable, nor his government amiable were it otherwise. It is just, certain and published abroad that the incorrigibly wicked shall be condignly and terribly punished. The wicked are in a doleful condition, for so long as they are bent on sinning, they have the prayers of good men against them perpetually.

5. *Because they regard not the works of the* LORD, *nor the operation of his hands, he shall destroy them, and not build them up.* This is a foretelling that cannot fail. A God-inspired prayer is as sure of an answer as a God-inspired prediction is of fulfil-ment. It made the case of these men more dreadful, that they despised divine judg-ments. Providences, however benignant or terrible, did not affect them. They were far gone in sin, Jer. v. 3.

6. *Blessed* be the LORD, *because he hath heard the voice of my supplications. Blessed,* see on Ps. v. 12; xviii. 46. The meaning is, Let him be proclaimed *blessed.* Let blessings be pronounced on him. He does not say how much he would have the Lord blessed. He is not afraid of excess in that matter. The reader will observe the con-

nection between this and the second verse. There something is sought in prayer. Here the same thing is said to have been secured; thus fulfilling the promise: "And it shall come to pass that . . . while they are speaking, I will hear," Isa. lxv. 24. When we offer spiritual and hearty prayer, we know that deliverance or something better is not far distant.

7. *The* LORD *is my strength and my shield. Strength,* as in Ps. viii. 2; xxi. 1, 13. Some versions use *helper. Shield,* sometimes *buckler,* the same as in Ps. iii. 3; vii. 10; xviii. 2; xxx. 35. Some versions have *protector.* That is good paraphrase, *My heart trusted in him and I am helped.* As in the preceding verse, so here he tells how promptly the desired aid was given. Those mercies of God which seem most seasona ble cause the greatest gladness. He adds: *Therefore my heart greatly rejoiceth, and with my song will I praise him.* Alexander: "*My heart* is twice used in this sentence to express the deep and cordial nature of the exercises, which he is describing. The same heart that trusted now rejoices."

8. *The* LORD *is their strength. Strength,* as in v. 7. But to what does the word *their* refer. Calvin says to David's armies. But he had said nothing of armies. Some ancient versions borrow the word *people* from the next verse, and read, *The Lord is the strength of his people.* This is better. This Psalm has throughout respect to David as the head of the nation. *And he* is *the saving strength of his anointed.* To him Jehovah is *saving strength,* literally strength of *salvations,* implying completeness and perfection of deliverance. David was God's *anointed* to the kingdom, yet he must make his way to the actual possession of it through great perils and troubles. When one is satisfied of the lawfulness of his calling, this may animate him to hold fast his best hopes even in the darkest hours.

9. *Save thy people and bless thine inheritance: feed them also, and lift them up for ever.* In all ages God's people are his inheritance. Four things are here sought for them; 1. Deliverance and safety in the amplest sense of these terms; 2. Benediction, which, when it comes from God, is effectual; 3. Government and nourishment, such as good shepherds give their sheep; 4. Elevation above all foes, fears and perils to the possession of the most excellent inheritance and glory. All these are eternal, *forever.* The blessings of a temporal character sought under these terms are small compared with the spiritual good things thus desired.

DOCTRINAL AND PRACTICAL REMARKS.

1. Luther: "We may use the Psalm against tyrants and fanatical spirits; for in this way are tyrants and persecutors of the word wont to pretend peace in word, yet secretly plan counsels of slaughter and murder all the while."

2. Jehovah alone is the proper object of prayer, v. 1. He alone can always hear, help, see and save.

3. To a distressed soul nothing is so suitable as prayer, v. 1. What is here taught by example is in the New Testament taught by precept, Jas. v. 13.

4. Dickson: "A soul in great straits is not able to suspend and want comfort long; it must have. some comfortable answer, because of what God is to it by covenant," vv. 1, 2.

5. Does it not clearly prove prayer efficacious, that the practice is kept up and commended by the pious of each successive generation? Would this be done, if they had not power with God? If he never answered, would they always call on him? The superstitious and pharisaical pray for other reasons, one to feed a blind, fanatical zeal, the other to be seen of men. But the intelligent and devout ask, that they may receive a divine blessing.

6. It is as needful to believe prayer to be efficacious as it is to pray, v. 1. Any

philosophy, or dogma, teaching us to doubt the efficacy of prayer is as hurtful as it is untrue.

7. When we pray aright we will be concerned to get an answer in peace, v. 1. Whoever leaves his prayer, as the ostrich leaves her egg in the sand, and cares no more for it, does not pray at all. When Elijah prayed for rain, he sent his servant to "look toward the sea," to see if it was coming. Scott: "While others are troubling their fellow-creatures with unavailing complaints; believers should, under distresses, cry the more earnestly to 'the Rock of their salvation:' and they should not rest till they have received some satisfactory token that their prayers are heard; for if the Lord could refuse to answer them, their case would resemble that of those who have perished in their sins, to whose agonizing cries no gracious answer will be made forever." Men can be in no worse state than to be where prayer is not heard.

8. It is no hindrance, but a help to have a sense of utter personal helplessness, v. 1. Boasted ability does nothing, while humility, relying on infinite strength, does wonders.

9. Prayer must be earnest and vehement. Every sacrifice was offered with fire. We must *cry* to the Lord, v. 1. We must pray with groanings that cannot be uttered. Heartless petitions avail not. We must use the *voice* of *supplications,* v. 2. David "was so stricken with anxiety and fear, that he prayed not coldly, but with burning vehement desire, like those who, under the pressure of grief, vehemently cry out."

10. The Scriptures attach no importance to posture or gesture in prayer, v. 2. One lifts up his hands and eyes to heaven. Another does not so much as lift up his eyes to heaven. Hezekiah turns his face to the wall, and Isaac walks in the fields. It is not the attitude or gestures of the body that please God. In public prayer our postures should be reverent. We are at liberty to stand or kneel as may be most convenient. If one posture is found more favorable to devotion than another, that should be adopted.

11. As the ancient *oracle* was a type of Christ, to which devout worshippers looked, so must we look to our Saviour alone. Let it be our unceasing joy that Jesus has "gone, not into the earthly places made by hands, which were only the figures of the true; but into heaven itself, there to appear in the presence of God for us." Glorious Redeemer! Gracious Intercessor! Kind Saviour! We owe thee all.

12. In all ages the pious have been afraid of being numbered and punished with the wicked, v. 3. To them nothing is more alarming or repulsive. In Ps. xxvi. we had the prayer, *Gather not my soul with sinners.* Here we have it, *Draw me not away with the wicked.* To this state of mind many blessings are secured. One is well stated by Henry: "Those that are careful not to partake with sinners in their sins, have reason to hope that they shall not partake with them in their plagues," Rev. xviii. 4.

13. Candor is an essential quality in a good character. The want of it vitiates everything, and marks a man as belonging to the class of evil doers, v. 3. There is a good sense in which "an honest man is the noblest work of God" on earth—a man who does to others as he would have others do to him; a man whc gives his Maker the praise, honor, service and homage which are his due; a man who would die before he would knowingly rob God or defraud man; a man who would rather be imposed on a thousand times than do one act of injustice. Such a man, in gold or in rags, in prison or in state, is the noblest specimen of all God's works on earth.

14. Many as are the infirmities of the righteous, they do not make a trade of sin; they are not *workers of iniquity,* v. 3. The Bible method of determining character is brief, but clear and decisive: "He that doeth righteousness is righteous; he that committeth sin is of the devil."

15. Truly the wicked are making sad work for themselves, v. 4. If there is not a speedy and powerful change in their characters, there is neither man nor angel who

can adequately describe or conceive the misery and horror of their doom. As the sins of Korah, Absalom, Belshazzar, Judas and Herod naturally produced the dreadful ends of these men, so shall all unrepented sin, however secret or popular, infallibly bring its subjects to a doom frightful to contemplate, and the more frightful the more it is contemplated.

16. God is just. God is righteous, v. 4. "He practises the *jus talionis* according to his own righteousness. Justice reverberates: the unrighteous blow which I aim at another recoils, according to the moral government of the world, back upon myself."

17. Retribution shall be not only for what men shall have actually accomplished, but for what they shall have *endeavored* to effect, v. 4.

18. When neither favoring events of providence, nor God's terrible judgments duly affect men, damnation is at the door, v. 5. Let every honest man ask himself: Under providences do I behave as sinners behave?

19. If the wicked in a Gospel land are not converted from their sins to God, it will not be for want of many events suited to make them regard the operations of God's hands and the intimations of his will, especially as they are set forth in his blessed word, v. 5.

20. Every believer has abundant cause for *blessing* and *praising* God, vv. 6, 7. When he thinks of all God has been, is, and ever shall be to him, of all that God has done, is doing, and ever shall be doing for him, of the ills he has escaped, and the good things he is authorized to hope for, how can his laudings of the Almighty be excessive?

21. The life of every good man should abound in *joy* and *rejoicing*. In the past, in the present, in the future, in God, in his ways, in ten thousand things are proper and abundant themes of gladsomeness. This should not show itself in the "frantic mirth" and wild revelry so agreeable to sinners; but in the holy gladness of chastened and trustful minds.

22. However sad the case and dark the mind of the genuine believer may at any time be, better days are coming; compare vv. 1, 2, 7, 8. The longest night has its morning dawn. Morison: "The scene of sorrow and persecution shall be exchanged for the bright shining of a day alike cloudless and serene. The wailings of penitence shall be succeeded by the sweet consciousness of forgiving mercy; the sorrowing of affliction shall usher in a long day of joy and prosperity; and the cry of oppressed innocence shall bring down upon some guilty head the ministers of divine wrath."

23. What God is to one saint he is to all saints, vv. 7, 8. This shall never cease to be so. This affords abundant cause of being glad whenever it goes well with others. Henry: "The saints rejoice in their friends' comforts as well as their own; for as we have not the less benefit from the light of the sun, so neither from the light of God's countenance, for others' sharing therein; for we are sure there is enough for all, and enough for each. This is our communion with all saints, that God is their strength and ours; Christ, their Lord and ours," 1 Cor. i. 2.

24. If men, who seem at a loss for language in prayer, would carefully study the Scriptures, and store their minds with the words of the Holy Ghost, they would soon have a delightful copiousness and comprehensiveness in their petitions, v. 9.

25. So great are the privileges and so abundant the blessings of God's saints that a complete schedule of them would contain no small part of the entire word of God, v. 9. Christian, as you can, make an inventory of your mercies and blessings, and so be prepared to give thanks.

26. Ought not all rulers to pray for their people? David prayed for his, v. 9.

27. In praying for his subjects David also prayed for Zion, v. 9. Let us imitate so good an example. "Pray for the peace of Jerusalem."

28. Henry: "Those and those only, whom God feeds **and rules**, who are willing to be taught, and guided, and governed by him, shall be saved, and blessed, and lifted up forever."

29. As David, a type of Christ, was delivered and so was able to bless his friends, who had stuck to him in adversity; so Christ having overcome all his enemies, is able to bless forever his friends, who have followed him through good report and through evil report. Yea, as he overcame, so shall we. As he has sat down on his throne, so shall we. Here we may have howlings; in heaven, we shall have hallelujahs.

30. How diverse the tastes, fears, hopes and minds of saints and sinners. No wicked man allows his mind to dwell on the words *for ever* without pain; while to the Christian *eternity* never seems too long for him to speak his Maker's praise, enjoy his Saviour's love, and drink at the fountains of unfailing bliss.

PSALM XXIX.

A Psalm of David.

1 Give unto the LORD, O ye mighty, give unto the LORD glory and strength.

2 Give unto the LORD the glory due unto his name; worship the LORD in the beauty of holiness.

3 The voice of the LORD *is* upon the waters: the God of glory thundereth: the LORD *is* upon many waters.

4 The voice of the LORD *is* powerful; the voice of the LORD *is* full of majesty.

5 The voice of the LORD breaketh the cedars; yea, the LORD breaketh the cedars of Lebanon.

6 He maketh them also to skip like a calf; Lebanon and Sirion like a young unicorn.

7 The voice of the LORD divideth the flames of fire.

8 The voice of the LORD shaketh the wilderness; the LORD shaketh the wilderness of Kadesh.

9 The voice of the LORD maketh the hinds to calve, and discovereth the forests: and in his temple doth every one speak of *his* glory.

10 The LORD sitteth upon the flood; yea, the LORD sitteth King for ever.

11 The LORD will give strength unto his people; the LORD will bless his people with peace.

ON the title see on title of Psalm iii.

The Vulgate and Doway add to the title these words: *At the finishing of the tabernacle*, meaning, no doubt, the new tabernacle, which David built for the ark and the other signs of God's presence, 2 Sam. vi. 17. This addition seems to have no higher authority than the conjecture of Jerome and Augustine. The Arabic reads: *A prophecy concerning the incarnation, the ark and the tabernacle.* There is nothing to support this, except that Kimchi refers this Psalm to the times of Messiah. Nor is there anything to support the reading of the Syriac: *Concerning the oblation.* The Septuagint and Ethiopic add to the common title these words: *At the going out of the tabernacle, i. e.*, of the feast of tabernacles or booths. In Lev. xxiii. 36; Num. xxix. 35, the Septuagint renders the Hebrew word (which we translate *assembly*) *a going out, an exit, or exodus.* This was on the eighth day of the feast; and Maimonides says "that every day of the days of that feast they said a peculiar song for the addition of the day; and on the first of the working days of the solemn feast they said Psalm xxix." This addition to the title had therefore the usage of the Jews, but is of no other authority. It never was in the Hebrew text.

That David wrote this Psalm is asserted in the title and is generally admitted.

Scott dates it B. C. 1040; Clarke, B. C. 1019. David died 1014 years before Christ, so according to Clarke this Psalm was written but five years before his death; according to Scott, twenty-six. Expositors have spoken confidently, yet diversely as to the occasion of this Psalm. Clarke: "It was probably written to commemorate the abundant rain which fell in the days of David, after the heavens had been shut up for three years, 2 Sam. xxi. 1–10;" Patrick: "This Psalm seems to have been composed by David after some extraordinary great thunder, lightning and rain: (whereby it is probable) God had so discomfited his enemies, and put their forces into such disorder, that he easily got the victory over them." With him agrees Dodd, who cites attention to the history given in 2 Sam. viii. in illustration. Pool favors the same view; and Morison mentions it with respect. Mudge is decidedly of the same opinion.

After his return from Palestine McCheyne gave to Dr. James Hamilton of London an interpretation of this Psalm, drawn from the natural scenery and the course of storms in the mountains of that land. Dr. Hamilton has given it to the world. And in the Works of McCheyne, vol. I. pp. 260–264 we have McCheyne's own statement of the whole matter. He says that in this Psalm "the strength of Jehovah is celebrated; and the exemplification of it is evidently taken from a thunder-storm in Lebanon." Whatever may be thought of the correctness of this view, none can read either of these writers without being struck with the exceedingly great beauty of the illustrations offered, and of the exquisite taste displayed in the method of presenting it. It is accessible to all, and need not be here transcribed.

But Hengstenberg says: "There is no ground for the idea that the Psalm was occasioned by the sight of a thunder-storm. 'The freshness of the painting, the vigorous conceptions, and the rapid transition of the whole' will give rise to this view only when low ideas are entertained of the power of poetry;" Alexander: "The superficial notion that this Psalm is merely a description of a thunder-storm, or of Jehovah as the God of thunder, may be corrected by observing that the last verse gives the key-note to the whole composition."

Calvin's view is still different: "David, that he may humble all men before God, from the highest to the lowest, celebrates his terrible power in the various wonders of nature, which he affirms are not less fitted to arouse us to give glory to God, than if he were to assert his empire and majesty with his own voice. After he has struck fear into the proud, who are reluctant to yield, and addressed an exhortation to them accompanied by a gentle reproof, he sweetly invites the faithful voluntarily to fear the Lord."

Between these conflicting views the reader must judge for himself. Perhaps he may reject them all. Why may not verses 1, 2, as well set forth the aim of the author as verses 10, 11?

The names of the Most High in this Psalm are *Jehovah* LORD and *El God*, on which see on Ps. i. 2; v. 4.

1. *Give unto the* LORD, *O ye mighty.* This rendering is substantially and fully supported by Calvin, Venema, Amesius, Ainsworth, Edwards, Jebb, Fry, Anderson, Hengstenberg and Alexander: only Ainsworth has, *sons of the mighties;* and Edwards, *ye great ones.* By the *mighty* the Chaldee, Hengstenberg and Alexander understand *angels;* several others, *great men, princes.* Doubtless the command is to all creatures, who bear the awful name of gods, Ps. lxxxii. 6; John x. 34; or of mighty ones, Ps. lxxxix. 7; Ezek. xxxii. 21. There is no reason for confining it to angels. The call is to *give, yield, render, ascribe* something to God. The Septuagint and kindred versions have rams, or the offspring of rams. This requires but a slight change in the original. But there is nothing to support it. The next clause states

what is to be ascribed to God: *Give unto the* LORD *glory and strength.* The Septuagint, Ethiopic, Syriac, Vulgate and Doway read *glory* and *honor;* Arabic, *glory* and *veneration;* church of England, *worship* and *strength;* Amesius, *glory* and *praise;* Fry, *glory* and *power;* Alexander, *honor* and *strength.* The Chaldee, Calvin, Venema, Ainsworth, Edwards and Jebb support the English. *Glory,* so rendered in Ps. iii. 3; iv. 2; viii. 5; and *honor* in Ps. vii. 5; xxvi. 8. The second word is in the common version always rendered *strength* or *power,* Ps. viii. 2; xxi. 1; lix. 16; lxiii. 2. The import of the verse is well given by Clarke: "Ascribe all excellence and might to him;" and by Diodati: "Let there be no greatness nor height in the world, that doth not humble itself before the great and terrible God."

2. *Give unto the Lord the glory due unto his name.* Literally it is *the glory of his name.* The sense is *glory worthy of his name, glory belonging to his name.* The common version is good. The *name* of God is all that by which he has made himself known. See Ps. v. 11; vii. 17; viii. 1. The repetition of the same word *Give* three times shows the urgency of the duty enjoined. The meaning of the preceding verse and of this clause is further evinced by the next clause: *Worship the Lord in the beauty of holiness.* The Chaldee: Worship before the Lord in the beauty of holiness; Septuagint, Ethiopic, Vulgate: Worship the Lord in his holy court; Arabic: Worship the Lord in his holy habitation; Syriac: Worship the Lord in the court of his holiness; church of England: Worship the Lord with holy worship; Calvin: Worship before Jehovah in the brightness of his sanctuary; Venema: Worship Jehovah in the glorious beauty of holiness; Amesius: Bow yourselves down, thus manifesting honor to Jehovah in the beauty of holiness; Ainsworth: Bow down yourselves to Jehovah, in the comely honor of the sanctuary; Edwards: Prostrate yourselves before Jehovah in the magnificent sanctuary; Street and Fry: Worship Jehovah with holy reverence; Hengstenberg: Adore the Lord in holy attire: Alexander: Bow to Jehovah in beauty of holiness. The verb rendered worship is the same that in the second commandment and often elsewhere is rendered *bow down,* Ex. xx. 5; Deut. v. 9; Ps. xcv. 6. It is sometimes rendered *do obeisance,* Ex. xviii. 7; 2 Sam. i. 2; xv. 5. When applied to God, the Doway generally renders it *adore.* In our version the more common rendering is *worship.* That religious worship is here intended is certain. Besides the various renderings of the last phrase already noticed, Boothroyd offers two readings both of which differ from our version: *In holy splendor,* or *With holy reverence;* Green, *In his beautiful sanctuary;* Horsley, *In the pomp of holiness.* Neither of these, nor any of those previously noticed is any improvement on the English version. We have the same phrase *beauty of holiness* elsewhere, 1 Chron. xvi. 29; Ps. xcvi. 9. See also 2 Chron. xx. 21. The margin of our version reads *In his glorious sanctuary.* The great ones of earth are never more properly employed than in humbling themselves before God, and in adoring his excellent majesty. One of the best specimens of such worship we have in Dan. iv. 34–37. The great sin of rulers is forgetfulness of God, and a refusal to give him the glory, which is his due. These lead to all their worst errors and crimes.

3. *The voice of the* LORD *is upon the waters. The voice of the Lord* frequently in this Psalm seems to mean *thunder,* at least in its connection with lightning and the usual accompaniments of storm. The very next clause of this verse seems so to explain it. In several parts of Scripture the phrase has this sense, Job xxxvii. 4, 5; xl. 9; Ps. xviii. 13; Isa. xxx. 30. *The waters* are not merely or chiefly the rivers and seas, but also the clouds, which are full of waters; and so we read of "the waters which are above the firmament," Gen. i. 7. See also Job xxxvi. 28; Ps. xviii. 11; lxxvii. 17; Jer. x. 13. God's voice *is* or *was* high in the heavens, even above the clouds. The effect of all the sublimities of a thunder storm on the human mind,

especially when it has been very bold in error and wickedness, has been long and much spoken of: Ex. ix. 27–29.   Calvin and Henry both refer to the celebrated ode of Horace, which speaks of the effect of thunder and lightning on men.   God's voice may be heard in all nature.   But the mass of men seem not to stand in awe of him till he speaks in thunder.   Then Volney is on his knees like other guilty sinners, pleading for mercy.   The Psalmist tells us what his meaning is.   *The God of glory* [the glorious God] *thundereth.*   Philosophize as we may respecting these amazing natural phenomena, they are wondrous and awful exhibitions of the power and majesty of God himself, *the God of glory.*   Modern science divests a storm of none of its terrors.   *The* LORD *is upon many waters.*   In the storm there is a presiding God, and he is Jehovah.   Calvin: " The very figures which he uses, sufficiently declare that David's design was to subdue by fear the obstinacy which yields not willingly otherwise.   Thrice he repeats that God's voice is heard in great and violent tempests, and in the subsequent verse he adds, that it is full of power and majesty."

4. *The voice of the* LORD *is powerful.*   Several ancient and some modern versions for *powerful* read in [or with] power and strength ; others, very powerful ; church of England, mighty in operation ; Hengstenberg, power ; Ainsworth, with able power. None of these are better than the common version.   David adds: *The voice of the* LORD *is full of majesty.*   The Chaldee, Calvin and Amesius, for *full of majesty* have, in beauty : Septuagint, Ethiopic, Vulgate and Doway, in magnificence ; Arabic, with a vast glittering brightness ; Syriac, with glory ; church of England, a glorious voice ; Venema, very magnificent ; Edwards, majestic ; Hengstenberg, majesty.   The last Hebrew noun is in Ps. viii. 5, rendered *honor ;* in Ps. xxi. 5, *majesty.*   So terrible is thunder that many great beasts on land, and even some sea-monsters are said to be still, as if in awe of their Maker's voice.

5. *The voice of the* LORD *breaketh the cedars.*   Like the moderns, the ancients did not in common parlance nicely distinguish between thunder and lightning.   *Thunder-struck* is still a good word in our language, although we all know that it is the lightning which strikes, thunder being mere sound.   The power of lightning is simply and absolutely inconceivable ; " enormous cedars are shivered and scattered by it in a moment."   No substance known to us is in strength a match for it.   Yet it is not an independent agent.   It is the *voice,* the *messenger* of Jehovah, and so he adds : *Yea, the* LORD *breaketh the cedars of Lebanon.*   For ages men have heard of the majestic cedars of the ancient and fertile mountain of Lebanon which may still be seen.   For their natural history see Bible Dictionaries.

6. *He maketh them also to skip like a calf ; Lebanon and Sirion like a young unicorn.* Some refer *them* to the cedars of Lebanon just mentioned ; but others regard *them* as used by anticipation for Lebanon and Sirion.   This seems to accord with Scripture, usage, Ps. cxiv. 4, 6.   Some of the best commentators give this sense.   Calvin: He maketh Lebanon to skip like a calf, and Sirion like a young unicorn ; Green :

> He maketh Lebanon to skip like a calf,
> And Sirion like a young unicorn.

Edwards: He made Lebanon to skip like a calf, and Sirion like a young oryx. Others favor the same reading.   Perhaps it is better than the common version.   Still better is that of Amesius: The voice of the Lord causes that Lebanon and Sirion leap as a calf, as a young unicorn.   The language is that of bold hyperbole.   It seems as if the mountains were tossed with the tempest.   The Septuagint is not good: He shall beat them small.   Like Alps, Lebanon signifies white ; its top being covered with snow at all seasons.   It was famous in the literature of Judea.   Sirion is the Sidonian name of Shenir or Hermon, sometimes also called Sion, Deut. iii. 8, 9 ; Cant. iv. 8 ; Josh. xiii. 11 ; Ps. cxxxiii. 3.   *Unicorn,* see on Ps. xxii. 21.

7. *The voice of the* LORD *divideth the flames of fire.* For *divideth* it is best to read *striketh* or *striketh out.* God's voice strikes terrible flames from the clouds. Calvin: "This is done when the vapors, being struck, as it were, with his hammer, burst forth into lightnings and thunderbolts." Horsley: The voice of the Lord striketh out the forked flame of fire. This is better than Hengstenberg's: The voice of the Lord heweth with flame of fire.

8. *The voice of the* LORD *shaketh the wilderness; the* LORD *shaketh the wilderness of Kadesh. Shaketh,* puts into anguish, makes to travail. The verse speaks of but one wilderness, that of Kadesh, or Kedesh. From its geographical position McCheyne thinks Kadesh-Naphtali is meant. See Josh. xx. 7; xxi. 32. It was one of the cities of refuge. There was also a Kadesh in the tribe of Issachar, 1 Chron. vi. 72. There was also Kadesh some twenty miles from Hebron on the border of the wilderness of Paran. Moses speaks of it as in the "uttermost border of Edom," Num. xx. 16. Lightfoot thinks Miriam died there. From this place Moses sent spies into Caaaan. Beyond this place south and east lay the great wilderness of Zin, over which tempests swept with terrible power. This was probably the tract of country referred to in this verse. If by the *voice of the Lord* we understand his power, as some do, we may include not only tempests but also earthquakes which have long been the terror of Syria. That at Aleppo in 1822 is still remembered.

9. *The voice of the* LORD *maketh the hinds to calve.* This rendering agrees with the Chaldee and with the Genevan translation. Syriac: The voice of the Lord which shaketh the boughs. This is poor. Lowth, Secker, Dimock, Green, Horsley and Fry: The voice of the Lord maketh the oaks to tremble. To this there are three objections: 1. It requires a change of the Hebrew text, which ought to be received as correct, if the manuscripts agree. 2. It omits all reference to the effect of storms and convulsions on the denizens of the forest. 3. It presents a specimen of the art of sinking. The oaks of Palestine are small compared with the cedars of Lebanon. We therefore confidently recur to *hinds.* Septuagint, Ethiopic and Vulgate: The voice of the Lord prepareth [or which prepareth] the stags; John Rogers' translation: The voyce of the Lorde moveth the hyndes; Edwards: The voice of Jehovah terrified the hinds; Bishops' Bible: The voyce of the Lord maketh the hinds to bring forth yong. This and the common version are virtually sustained by Calvin, Amesius, Dathe, Clarke, Jebb, Hengstenberg and Alexander. Ainsworth: The voice of the Lord maketh the hinds tremblingly to travail. These expositions are given: 1. That as hinds bring forth their young with great difficulty (see Job xxxix. 1, 3,) the fright of the storm aids them in calving. 2. That the agitation produced by the storm sometimes makes them cast out their young prematurely. This falls in with the figurative language of the context. 3. That God's power, expressed by his voice, causes those changes, by which the forest is kept full of inhabitants. 4. The verb in this verse is the same as *shaketh* in v. 8; *i. e.*, putteth in pain, terrifieth. This agrees with the scope of the Psalm. *And discovereth* [strippeth, maketh bare] *the forests.* This may be done either by stripping the leaves and branches from the trees, or by destroying the animals, or by driving them to their dens, and leaving the forest without living inhabitants. Chaldee: The animals flee to the wood. *And in his temple doth every one speak of his glory.* Four explanations are given: 1. While storms are thus raging in Lebanon and in the wilderness, a very different scene is witnessed in the temple at Jerusalem. There every one is crying, Glory. 2. The whole frame of nature is the temple or palace of God and all his works proclaim his glory. This is a bold and beautiful conception, though rather western than oriental. 3. By *his temple* some understand the church of God. Calvin: "God's voice fills the whole world and spreads itself to its farthest limits; but the prophet declares that his glory is

celebrated only in his church, because God not only speaks intelligibly and distinctly there, but also there gently allures the faithful to himself." The church of God is preëminently his temple, Eph. ii. 21. There, says Gill, the saints "dwell and speak of the glory of God, of his divine perfections, and of his works of creation and pro vidence; and of the glory of the person of Christ, and salvation by him; and of the glorious work of grace begun in their souls by the blessed Spirit." 4. Others think that the temple is the temple not made with hands, even heaven itself, where all that are truly good and great, the sons of God, thrones and powers, dominions and princi- palities, even every one of the blessed inhabitants of that better world praise the Lord. So the Chaldee: And in his sanctuary which is above all his ministers sing glory before him. If but one of these views be accepted, perhaps it should be the third. But neither of them necessarily excludes allusion to the others. The lower may point to the higher; and the higher imply the lower. Hengstenberg's rendering is beautiful and literal: And in his temple everything says, Glory.

10. *The* LORD *sitteth upon the flood.* The word rendered *flood* is found only here and about a *dozen* times in Genesis. In every place but this it certainly points to the Noachic deluge. It is not safe to apply it to anything else. The Hebrew verb is in the preterite, *sat.* It is so rendered by the Chaldee, Edwards, Hengstenberg, Ains- worth and Alexander. Venema has *presided over.* The prophet here reminds all great ones that the Lord whom they are called to fear and serve, is the awful God, who presided over the deluge, and who of course manages the lesser commotions of the elements, clouds, lightnings, thunders, winds, torrents of waters and earthquakes. In the deluge, Jehovah showed his power to destroy his foes, and to save alive his friends. The apostle of the circumcision refers to the deluge for the same purpose, 2 Pet. iii. 5, 6. *Yea, the* LORD *sitteth King forever.* Chaldee: He sat also upon the seat of mercy, and delivered Noah, and reigneth over his sons forever; Septuagint and kindred ver- sions: The Lord shall sit King forever; Alexander thus paraphrases the verse: "The God, whose voice now produces these effects, is the God who sat enthroned upon the deluge, and this same God is still reigning over nature and the elements, and will be able to control them forever."

11. *The* LORD *will give strength unto his people; the* LORD *will bless his people with peace.* Chaldee: The Lord gave a law to his people; the Lord will bless his people with peace. For *strength* the Syriac has *courage.* By strength is to be understood all that is necessary to sustain life. To give *peace* is to make existence happy and desira- ble. To *bless with peace* is the strongest kind of phrase indicating the divine favor. This reminds one of the blessing pronounced by Aaron and his sons, Num. vi. 24–26.

DOCTRINAL AND PRACTICAL REMARKS.

1. Right affections will find matter of adoration and praise in all the works of God, in all the aspects of nature. If "an undevout astronomer is mad," so is an undevout meteorologist, or geologist, or sailor, or warrior, or artisan, or husbandman. God is everywhere. His wonders are everywhere. All but the blind or perverse see and worship.

2. No creature, however exalted, is too high to acknowledge his absolute depen- dence on God for all that has given him either honor or power, *glory* or *strength*, v. 1. *What hast thou that thou hast not received?* is the universal and awful challenge.

3. Dickson: "Of all men, princes should be most careful to glorify God, and yet it is most rare to see them humble themselves before him." To this duty they are loudly called by the multitude of their blessings, and the solemnity of their account. "To whom much is given, of him shall much be required." But earthly potentates are

greatly tempted by their high station, by the flatteries of courtiers, and by the corruptions of the natural heart, which rejects God's easy reign.

4. Nor is there any danger that man or angel in the worship of God will exceed due bounds in ardor, humility or reverence, v. 1. Absolutely all perfection should be ascribed to him, who made us. Right worship is founded on the divine nature. To God belong *glory* and *strength*, every excellence in an infinite degree.

5. It is as right that God should have all his dues as that men or angels should have theirs, v. 2. To deny God's rights is most dangerous; nor should we pay him merely a part and not the whole of what he claims. He is infinitely amiable, and so should be unspeakably loved; he is infinitely powerful and majestic, and so is entitled to the most awful reverence.

6. We have made but little progress in religion till we see that there is a transcendant beauty in holiness, v. 2. There is no beauty like that, because it is the beauty of the Lord, and makes us like him. The superiority of angels over devils consists preëminently in the purity of the former and the corruption of the latter. Let our worship be to God, to God alone, offered just as commanded, and full of humility, simplicity, reverence and confidence.

7. God should be recognized in all the works of his hands, both in creation and providence, in the greatest and in the least things, in the uniform and in the unusual course of nature, in the *waters* above the earth and under the earth, in the calm and in the storm, when he *thundereth*, v. 3.

8. It is very marvellous that all sinners do not foresee and bewail the terrors that shall overtake them. If the thunder of God's power moves them so mightily here, can they hope to be unshaken in the day of wrath? v. 3. Experience shows that none are more easily overwhelmed with terror than those poor deluded souls, who commonly in the land of peace affect the greatest contempt of God and of heavenly things.

9. If men were governed by right affections and right reason, the standing works of creation, the clear, calm sky, the gentle zephyr would as truly and profitably impress them as the most terrific exhibitions of omnipotence in tempests and earthquakes. It is proof that unregenerate men are dreadfully depraved that they seldom wake up to a lively sense of the divine existence, except when some sad reverse, or awful accident, or terrific phenomenon startles them. "The thunder or the eclipse will move more than the making of heaven and earth."

10. It is fit that mercy should speak in notes of love and tenderness, while it is as fit that the revelations of wrath should be in tones of terror, v. 3. "If men will not listen to the still small voice of God's love, they shall be compelled to hear him in accents of thunder."

11. The evidences of the resistless power of God furnished in nature, particularly in the violent agitations of the earth and air, should satisfy every man that nothing will be easier than to accomplish the most terrible works of vengeance ever threatened, vv. 4–9. When God thundered, the emperor Caligula used to go and hide himself under his bed; and when God shall utter his last thunders, sinners will call to the rocks and the mountains, Fall on us and hide us from the wrath of the Lamb. God can easily bring about all the terrors of the last day.

12. He who commands the lightning, can rule anything, v. 7. It is a glorious truth both of natural and revealed religion, that nothing is too hard for God. Omnipotence is never balked.

13. If God's *voice* in nature is so powerful, we should naturally expect that his *word* in revelation would be mighty. And it is a fire and a hammer to break in pieces the flinty rock. Scott: "The voice of the divine law, if duly attended to, would fill the consciences of sinners with more terror and amazement than all the convulsions in

nature; and the effects of the word of God, when attended by the operations of his Holy Spirit, are far greater upon the souls of men than that of thunder in the material world. By its energy the stoutest are made to tremble, the proudest are abased, the secrets of the heart are detected, sinners are converted; and the savage, the sensual, and the unclean become harmless, gentle and pure, resembling doves and lambs," Heb. iv. 12.

14. Great dread of thunder and lightning does not always prove one worse than his neighbors. Tornadoes, earthquakes and shattered nerves are not subject either to reason or piety. In many cases education has much to do with our agitations in times of terrible tempest. Yet pious people may safely remember that he who rides upon the storm and manages the seas, is their reconciled God and their heavenly Father. He will do all things well. "The children need not fear their Father's voice when he speaks in anger to his enemies." Let the saints never be afraid with any amazement.

15. No part of the earth, its centre or circumference, is hidden from God, or uncared for by him. The "great and terrible wilderness" is his, and is as much the abode of his essential presence as any part of creation, v. 8. To gracious souls the howling wilderness or barren islet has often been like heaven on earth, Gen. xxviii. 17; Rev. i. 9, 10.

16. The analogy between nature and revelation and between God's natural and moral government, should long since have satisfied mankind that everything threatening evil to those who incur the penalty of the divine laws, shall surely come to pass, vv. 5–8. It is monstrous that men should so study second causes as to forget him who is the sole Author of universal nature.

17. If man has a heart to learn, he can never be in want of a teacher. All nature has lessons for him, vv. 3–9. Some are startling, more are quiet and gentle. The best lessons are often given in the gentlest tones. Wo to him who sees, and hears, and feels, and cares for nothing of all that occurs around him.

18. Yet God's most glorious utterances are in, by, through and to his church, with her worship, doctrines and discipline, v. 9. So teach the Scriptures expressly, Eph. iii. 10.

19. We have the highest authority for the highest acts of worship, even adoration and praise, v. 9. To this very end the church was constituted.

20. The wicked of almost every age have found peculiar delight in deriding the judgments of God, especially in the *deluge;* but there is awful evidence that over that great event in our world God presided, v. 10. Nor can men ever set aside the terrors of that catastrophe except by terribly playing the fool.

21. God's government is fixed. It cannot be subverted, v. 10. Empires rise and decline, fall or vanish away, but his kingdom changes not. Others are sometimes strong and sometimes weak; but his possesses all vigor and might, world without end. It endures forever. It includes all duration and all worlds. Even the waste of waters, on which are seen no footprints of man or angel, proclaims there is a God, who *sitteth King forever.*

22. It is by God and by God alone that we live. All our strength is from him, v. 11. This is true of the natural life of all; it is delightfully true of the spiritual life of the saints. Arnd: "This is glorious consolation against the contempt and persecutions of poor Christians, the little flock, which has no outward protection in the world, no outward strength. But the Holy Ghost imparts consolation, and says, the world shall not give strength and power to the church, but the Lord; as King Hezekiah comforted himself when he said, 'With them is an arm of flesh, but with us is the Lord of hosts;' and John, 'He who is in us is greater than he who is in the world.'"

23. The reconciliation between God and his people is perfect. The consequence is necessarily *peace*, v. 11. And peace with God cannot fail to be followed by salvation. "Being justified by faith, we have peace with God through our Lord Jesus Christ." "Great peace have they that love thy law; and nothing shall offend them."

PSALM XXX.

A Psalm *and* Song *at* the dedication of the house of David.

1 I will extol thee, O LORD; for thou hast lifted me up, and hast not made my foes to rejoice over me.

2 O LORD my God, I cried unto thee, and thou hast healed me.

3 O LORD, thou hast brought up my soul from the grave: thou hast kept me alive, that I should not go down to the pit.

4 Sing unto the LORD, O ye saints of his, and give thanks at the remembrance of his holiness.

5 For his anger *endureth but* a moment; in his favour *is* life: weeping may endure for a night, but joy *cometh* in the morning.

6 And in my prosperity I said, I shall never be moved.

7 LORD, by thy favour thou hast made my mountain to stand strong: thou didst hide thy face, *and* I was troubled.

8 I cried to thee, O LORD; and unto the LORD I made supplication.

9 What profit *is there* in my blood, when I go down to the pit? Shall the dust praise thee? shall it declare thy truth?

10 Hear, O LORD, and have mercy upon me: LORD, be thou my helper.

11 Thou hast turned for me my mourning into dancing: thou hast put off my sackcloth, and girded me with gladness;

12 To the end that *my* glory may sing praise to thee, and not be silent. O LORD my God, I will give thanks unto thee for ever.

THE views respecting the design and occasion of this ode are these: 1. That it was written long after the time of David, for the dedication of the second temple, and was used on that occasion. This conjecture is set aside by the title. 2. That it was prophetically prepared for the dedication of the first temple. This cannot be proven, nor is it probable. 3. Calvin, Diodati, Grotius, Patrick and Gill think it was written after the death of Absalom, and David's return to his palace, 2 Sam. xx. 3. Morison quite rejects this opinion. 4. Some think it was made to celebrate recovery from some dangerous illness. So Mudge and Horne. To confine it to this is contrary to the title. 5. Theodoret and Horsley make the Psalm mystical; the former regarding the *house* as that reared by Messiah, and maintaining that it treats of the restoration of human nature by the resurrection of Jesus Christ from the dead; the latter referring the whole to the days of Messiah and the spiritual condition of the church. He esteems "the sickness, that of the soul, in consequence of the fall; the recovery, that of the soul by redemption." 6. Bellarmine, Chandler, Bouchier, Williams and others think this Psalm was used at the dedication of David's own palace, built by the liberality and artizans of Hiram, 2 Sam. v. 11; 1 Chron. xiv. 1. This well agrees with the common rendering of the title and with the pious usages of the Jews, Deut. xx. 5. It is much less objectionable than either of the preceding. It was while dwelling in this house that David expressed the pious sentiments found in 2 Sam. vii. 2. 7. The best view is that this Psalm was composed for the dedication of the altar in the threshing floor of Araunah, or Ornan on Mount Moriah, the site of the temple, 2 Sam. xxiv. 18–25; 1 Chron. xxi. 18–30. David expressly calls it *the house of the* LORD *God*, 1 Chron. xxii. 1. An edifice is not necessary to the being of a *house* of God, Gen. xxviii. 22. The old tabernacle was now in Gibeon, and could neither be visited nor be brought to Zion, 1 Chron. xxi. 29, 30. This service at the threshing floor God accepted by the usual token—fire from heaven. This view well suits the contents of the Psalm. It is approved by Venema, Calmet, Dathe, Clarke, Morison, Tholuck, Hengstenberg and Alexander. It requires a different rendering of the title. But this can be made without any difficulty. Alexander's rendering is: A Psalm. A Song of Dedication (for) the House. By David. Tholuck's is better: A Psalm *and* Song of David *at* the dedication of the Temple. Hammond admits that *the house* points to the sanctuary, although he prefers the view next preceding. The Chaldee refers it to *the dedication of the house of the* sanctuary. If this is correct, it cuts off those previously stated, also all belief that it relates to the persecutions of Saul, etc. Nor does the title refer to the *tune* but to the *occasion* of the Psalm. For numbering the people God sent the pestilence, and it swept away many, till at the intercession of David and his elders, God bade the angel of death sheathe his sword. On the spot, where mercy was revealed. David reared the altar. The title therefore aids us in interpreting the Psalm. Hengstenberg: "This Psalm affords a very remarkable proof of the correctness and originality of the titles."

Some of these poems bear the name, *A Psalm;* some, *A Song;* some, *A Psalm* and *Song,* or *Psalm-Song;* and some, *A Song* and *Psalm,* or *Song-Psalm.* Diodati thinks that the double name implies that both voice and instruments were to be employed when the ode was used in the temple service; that when we have *Psalm-song,* the instruments preceded the voice; when *Song-Psalm,* the voice had precedence. But this is conjecture, or at best vague tradition. Luther: "This is a remarkable Psalm and truly Davidical." David's authorship is generally admitted. Scott dates it B. C. 1021; Clarke, 1017. It was written in David's old age. In style it is very terse and elegant, abounding in lofty sentiments of devotion. The names of the Most High here found are *Jehovah* LORD and *Elohim God,* on which see on Ps. i. 2; iii. 2.

1. *I will extol thee, O* LORD. *Extol,* often elsewhere *exalt*, Ex. xv. 2; Ps. cxviii. 28; Isa. xxv. 1. It is equivalent to highly praise. Horsley reads, *Hast brought me low;* but the verb never means to *depress.* In Ex. ii. 16, 19, it is applied to drawing water. God had brought him out of a horrible pit. Rogers: Thou hast drawn me up as it were out of a dungeon. *And hast not made my foes to rejoice over me.* Their malignant hopes perished. This verse is an introduction to the whole Psalm. It celebrates deliverance from sore calamity pressing, and worse impending. David's use of the pronoun *I* and *me* does not discourage the idea that he refers to the sin of numbering the people, the consequent plague, and the merciful deliverance from it; for he distinctly said: "Lo, I have sinned, I have done wickedly; but these sheep what have they done," 2 Sam. xxiv. 17. The wicked always rejoiced when David erred or fell into any trouble, 2 Sam. xii. 14.

2. *O* LORD *my God, I cried unto thee, and thou hast healed me. Cried,* the word used by Jonah to describe his distress and earnestness in prayer when in the fish's belly, Jonah ii. 2. See also Ps. xviii. 6; xxii. 24. We know how earnest and humble was David's prayer for the removal of the plague, when he and the elders of Israel besought God to show mercy, 1 Chron. xxi. 16, 17. Tholuck: "The words 'to heal' and 'to build' are used in the Old Testament to denote any kind of healing. David tottered when his kingdom tottered." *Healing* is applied to converting a wicked heart, Isa. vi. 10; to repairing breaches, Ps. lx. 2; to recovering men from religious declen-

sion, Jer. iii. 22; to comforting the sorrowful, Ps. cxlvii. 3; to making whole a broken vessel, Jer. xix. 11. Calvin: "It may properly enough mean here any deliverance." Preservations and deliverances are none the less pleasing and powerful, when they are manifestly from God, as in this case. David had seen the angel of the LORD standing between the earth and the heaven, having a drawn sword in his hand, stretched out over Jerusalem; and from the lips of the same angel by the mouth of Gad he had received a message of mercy from the Lord, 1 Chron. xxi. 16, 18. None but God had brought deliverance to him and to Israel. Although David did not die, yet his life was threatened:

3. *O* LORD, *thou hast brought up my soul from the grave.* Grave elsewhere *pit, hell,* and often *grave,* Ps. vi. 5; ix. 17; xvi. 10; Job xvii. 16. Our translation agrees well with the ancient versions. Amesius: Jehovah, thou hast brought my soul out of the sepulchre; Fry: Thou hast brought up my soul from the abode of the dead; Horne: Thou hast brought up my animal frame from the grave; Green: Thou didst bring up my life, O Lord, from the grave. The next phrase is of like import: *Thou hast kept me alive, that I should not go down to the pit.* The Chaldee: Thou hast strengthened me, that I might not descend into the pit. Others read, Thou hast brought me to life, Thou didst recover me, Thou hast quickened me, etc. On the word *pit* see on Ps. vii. 15; xxviii. 1. It is sometimes rendered a *well,* a *cistern,* a *dungeon,* but oftener a *pit.* John Rogers' translation thus gives the whole verse: Thou Lord hast brought my soul out of hell: thou hast kept my life, whereas they go down to the pytte; Bishops' Bible: Thou Lorde hast brought my soul out of hell: thou hast kept my life from them that go down into the pit; Genevan translation: O Lord, thou hast brought up my soule out of the grave: thou hast revived mee from them that go downe into the pit. Calvin: "David reckoned that he could not sufficiently express in words the magnitude of the favor which God had conferred upon him, unless he compared the darkness of that period to the grave and the pit." By a sense of his sin and folly, by an apprehension of the terrible justice of God, by an overwhelming depression of mind at the loss of so many of his people, and perhaps by feeling the symptoms of the terrible pestilence in his own body he had for a time been led to account himself as a dead man. But God was better than his fears.

4. *Sing unto the* LORD, *O ye saints of his.* Sing, often rendered *sing praises,* Ps. vii. 17; ix. 2, 11; sometimes used in connection with the words *psaltery* and *harp;* and commonly supposed to refer to singing with the accompaniment of musical instruments. Some render it, Sing a Psalm; others, Play; others, Make music. The call on the *pious, godly, merciful* or *saints* is to unite in the most solemn and joyful manner to praise and exalt God. Nor should the worship be mere adoration. An amazing mercy had been received, and gratitude was called for. So it is added: *And give thanks at the remembrance of his holiness.* The Chaldee and Venema: Celebrate the remembrance of his holiness; Septuagint, Ethiopic, Arabic, Syriac and Vulgate: Declare [or acknowledge] the remembrance of his holiness; Amesius: Speak much to the memory of his holiness; Edwards: Give thanks to his holy name; Alexander: Give thanks to the memory of his holiness. The sense doubtless is, *Confess,* celebrate, speak, utter praise in honor of his holiness. Holiness is the sum of the moral excellence of God's character, and is the sheet-anchor of the hopes of the righteous. It secures them the final victory in every case. Monuments and *memorials* should everywhere be erected to the praise and glory of God's infinite rectitude. By that he governs the world. Moved by that holiness, which is as kind as it is just, Jehovah had averted the plague, and now let him be duly praised.

5. *For his anger* endureth but *a moment; in his favour* is *life: weeping may endure for a night, but joy* cometh *in the morning.* Perhaps there are not in all the Scriptures

a dozen verses more remarkable for pith and brevity than this. Let the reader omit the words supplied by our translators, and he will see the force of this remark. Doway: For wrath is in his indignation; and life in his *good* will. In the evening weeping shall have place, and in the morning gladness; Edwards: For his anger is but for a moment; in his favor is life; sorrow may last out the evening, but joy cometh in the morning; Jebb: For there is *but* a moment in his anger: Life is in his favor: Through the night endureth weeping, but in the morning there is singing; Green: For his anger is only for a moment; but his favor is for life. Sorrow may continue for an evening; but joy cometh before morning. The common version gives the sense in idiomatic English. Hengstenberg: "In the second half of the verse, WEEPING is personified and represented by the figure of a wanderer, who leaves in the morning the lodging, into which he had entered the preceding evening. After him another guest arrives, viz., JOY." Of course the only persons of whom this verse is always true are the *saints*, the *meek* of the preceding verse. The verse is striking even according to the common interpretation; but it is even more striking, if, as some suppose, the plague lasted less than *twenty-four* hours. For the sin of proudly counting his subjects, God gave David a choice of three evils; 1. Seven years of famine; 2. Three months of war; or, 3. Three days of pestilence. He chose the latter. The work of death began. But it did not last three days. It endured but a part of a calendar day. In our version of 2 Sam. xxiv. 15 it reads, "So the Lord sent a pestilence upon Israel from the morning even to the time appointed." But Hengstenberg is confident that instead of "to the time appointed" it should read "till the time of meeting," and that by this we are to understand "the evening religious assembly" or "the time of the evening sacrifice," 1 Kings xviii. 29, 36; 2 Kings xvi. 15. This is ingenious and probably correct. It allows room for the efficacy of David's intercessory prayer and the gracious answer to it as given in the history. The word *appointed* though often so rendered is often given *congregation, feast, assembly, solemn feast, solemn assembly, set time, solemnities.* The plague had hardly broken out till God said to the destroying angel: "It is enough: stay now thine hand." Truly God's anger endureth but a moment; in his favor [or good will] is life: weeping may endure [abide or lodge] for a night; but joy cometh [arriveth or succeedeth] in the morning. Having celebrated the great mercy received he proceeds to state the *secure* and *vain* condition of his mind before his affliction.

6. *And in my prosperity I said, I shall never be moved.* For *prosperity* the Chaldee has *boldness* or *security*; Septuagint, *success*; Vulgate, *abundance*; Arabic, *time of my riches*; Syriac and Amesius, *tranquillity*; Venema, *serene prosperity*; Ainsworth, *false quietness*; Fry, *peace*; Hengstenberg and Alexander, *security*. The best rendering is *ease, security, carelessness*, induced by success. The carnal mind naturally and easily perverts even a little prosperity to the engendering of pride and self-sufficiency, forgetfulness of God and practical atheism. The mere taking of a census is not wicked, as is evident from the Scripture itself, Ex. xxx. 12; neither is the beholding of a city, nor the making of a speech, nor the opening of a cabinet; but the doing of any of these things out of vain glory is very offensive to God, Isa. xxxix. 1–7; Dan. iv. 29–33; Acts xii. 21–23. Buddæus: "The thing itself shows that David, in the whole matter, was actuated by pride and vain glory." Even Joab saw the folly David was about to commit and faithfully warned him against it, 2 Sam. xxiv. 3. The pestilence was an awful rebuke, and the shortness of its continuance a great mercy.

7. LORD, *by thy favour thou hast made my mountain to stand strong. Favour*, so rendered in v. 5; elsewhere *will, good-will, voluntary will, pleasure, good pleasure.* All that is great, good, wise, holy, or stable, is so by the sovereign will of God alone. *Mountain* seems to point to the kingly power and authority of David. Diodati: " *My*

kingdom, whose chief seat was mount Zion;" Pool: "Thou hast so firmly settled me in my kingdom; which he calls his *mountain*, partly because kingdoms are usually called mountains in prophetical writings, Ps. xlvi. 3, 4; Isa. ii. 2; Jer. li. 25; Dan. ii. 34, 35, 44, 45; and partly with respect to mount Zion." There seems to be no good reason for reading *beauty* instead of *mountain*, as do the Septuagint, Ethiopic, Arabic, Vulgate and Doway; nor for the rendering of Edwards: "By thy favor thou hast given a settled firmness to my bloom;" nor for the rendering of Houbigant, Mudge and Green, who read, "Thou by thy favor hadst given such firmness to my health." Ainsworth's rendering is striking: "Jehovah, in thy favorable acceptation thou hast settled strength to my mountain." There is a question whether this clause is connected with what he said in v. 6 before the pestilence, or whether he spoke it after his affliction. On this expositors are divided. Many, among them Venema, Patrick, Chandler, Henry, Pool, Fry, Scott, Morison and Tholuck, favor this first view. Scott says: "While David ascribed his great prosperity, and the firm establishment of his authority to the faithfulness, power and love of God; he seems to have given way to unwarranted confidence, and to have remitted his vigilance and activity, and probably the fervency of his devotion." But Hengstenberg clearly takes the other view, and supposes this clause to have been uttered as expressive of David's mind after the affliction was over. He thus paraphrases the clause: "I have learned by painful experience that the power of my kingdom had its root in thy favor." This view is the most simple and natural. Experience instructed him: *Thou didst hide thy face, and I was troubled.* To *hide the face* is to *be displeased.* Applied to God, it denotes the withholding of those mercies, which comfort us, and the letting loose of those calamities, which overwhelm us. *Troubled* is the rendering of a very strong word. Alexander: "*I was confounded*, agitated, terrified, perplexed." The affliction in this case was *public, national, swift* and *terrible.* No wonder it drove David to prayer.

8. *I cried to thee*, O LORD. *Cried*, elsewhere *called*, Ps. xlii. 7; cxlv. 18, but often *cried*, Isa. xxi. 8; xl. 2, 6. It expresses heartiness and earnestness. The next clause is parallel. *And unto the Lord I made supplication.* This verb is sometimes rendered *besought, intreated*, and often *made supplication.* It describes the *cry* for *mercy*, the plea of *gracious dealing.* The Syriac, church of England, Calvin, Amesius, Ainsworth, Jebb, Fry and Hengstenberg read the verbs of this verse according to our version in the past tense. The Arabic and Edwards put them in the present. But the Chaldee, Septuagint, Ethiopic, Vulgate, Doway, Luther, Venema and Alexander follow the Hebrew, and read in the future. On this subject see Introduction, § 6. If we understand the words, *and I said*, as prefacing this verse, then the sense is much the same as if we use the past tense. Great weight is due to the remark of Alexander: "The translation of the futures as past tenses is a license, which could only be justified by extreme exegetical necessity." Some have thought that necessity existed here. Perhaps it does. Calvin: "This is the chief advantage of afflictions, that while they make us sensible of our wretchedness, they stimulate us again to supplicate the favor of God." The change from the second to the third person in the use of the word *Jehovah* is remarkable, though there are instances of changes as great.

9. *What profit* is there *in my blood, when I go down to the pit?* For *pit* the Chaldee reads *the place of the sepulchre;* the Septuagint, Ethiopic, Syriac, Vulgate, Doway, Ainsworth and Alexander, *corruption;* Hengstenberg, *the grave;* others generally *pit.* See Ps. vii. 15, where it is rendered *ditch.* In Ps. xvi. 10, it is rendered *corruption.* In Ps. lv. 23, ciii. 4, it is *destruction.* The impossibility of the dead rendering any service to God on earth is clearly stated in Scripture, Ecc. ix. 10. And it is employed more than once as an argument for the sparing of the life of God's servants, Isa.

xxxviii. 16–19; Ps. vi. 5; lxxxviii. 10–12.   The same thing is repeated in other words: *Shall the dust praise thee?*   *Dust*, the body after it ceases to be animated, when it has mouldered to dust.   Yet again does he urge the plea: *Shall it* [the dust] *declare thy truth?* q. d., "Shall my cold and dead remains be to thy enemies any proof of thy faithfulness, thy truth as a covenant-keeping God? My death will afford new grounds of exultation to all who hate thee and me; and I shall never again on earth be allowed to speak one word to thy praise."   These considerations were much strengthened by David's peculiar relations to the theocracy and the throne of Israel, God having promised to establish him and his seed in it.   That David was not actuated by any mere terror of dying, nor by a natural love of life, is certain, for he freely offered to die, if his death would arrest the progress of the pestilence, 2 Sam. xxiv. 17.

10. *Hear, O LORD, and have mercy upon me.*   This is still a continuance of his prayer. It was a cry for *mercy, pity, favor, gracious dealing.* Not only had David sinned in numbering the people, but he ruled a guilty nation whose iniquities were not forgotten before God, as is evident from 2 Sam. xxiv. 1, 2.   They had been both ungrateful and rebellious.   In many ways they had offended God.   The arresting of the terrible plague would therefore be an act of pure, undeserved mercy both to David and to Israel, though David speaks of it as though it were pity to himself alone.   LORD, *be thou my helper.*   The Septuagint and some kindred versions read, *The Lord became my helper.*   But the Chaldee, Syriac, Calvin, church of England, Venema, Amesius, Ainsworth, Edwards, Jebb, Fry, Hengstenberg and Alexander make each clause of the verse a petition.   This is best.

11. *Thou hast turned for me my mourning into dancing.*   Here begin the words of triumph.   The word rendered *mourning* expresses any great and violent grief, elsewhere rendered *wailing, lamentation,* not elsewhere in the Psalms.   See Gen. l. 10; Est. iv. 3; Jer. vi. 26; xlviii. 38.   *Dancing,* always so rendered in the text of the common version.   It expresses a high degree of joy, corresponding with the degree of grief formerly felt.   The whole account of the staying of the plague, and the effect of that happy cessation of pestilence, would fully justify the strength of the language here employed, 2 Sam. xxiv. 18–25; 1 Chron. xxi. 18–27.   Araunah himself was greatly moved by this providence, and offered David every facility for a joyful sacrifice.   True, this man of heathen descent may have become a real and an open convert to the true religion; but of this we have no assurance.   Great public mercies sometimes deeply affect even unregenerate men.   David adds: *Thou hast put off my sackcloth, and girded me with gladness.*   The idea is the same as in the preceding clause. The language is borrowed not only from the general custom of the Israelites and other ancient nations in covering themselves, when sad, with sackcloth, but from the fact that David and the elders of Israel had, during the plague, literally been clothed in sackcloth, 1 Chron. xxi. 16.   Hengstenberg: "Sackcloth is a hair garment, which mourners put on: it was, as it were, *the robe of penitence.*"   How great was the change produced, as in a moment, by the mercy of God.   He interposed in love, and *gladness* followed.   Though the plague probably lasted considerably less than an entire day, yet it had already swept away *seventy thousand* men.   Had it raged the entire three days, as David had been led to expect, and with the increased violence which pestilence is apt to acquire by the panic created in the public mind, its devastations must have been terrible.   From so overwhelming a judgment David and Israel were delivered, and the sacrifice offered was that of grateful, joyful hearts.   Such a mercy was not to be uninfluential.   David says it was

12. *To the end that my glory may sing praise to thee and not be silent.*   *Glory,* for the general signification of the word see Ps. iii. 3; iv. 2; vii. 5; viii. 5; and for its particular signification here, see Psalm xvi. 9.   By *glory* we should understand *tongue.*

So Ainsworth and many; though for *my glory* the Chaldee has The honorable of the world; church of England, Every good man; Jebb, My Spirit; Edwards, Fry and Hengstenberg, My soul; Alexander, Everything glorious. But most prefer the common interpretation, Tongue. Calvin: "As David adds immediately after, *I will celebrate thy praise forever*, the context demands that he should particularly speak of his own duty in this place." The last phrase is, O Lord *my God, I will give thanks unto thee forever.* The verb here is the same rendered in v. 4 *give thanks;* in v. 9, *praise.* Hengstenberg: "The *forever* indicates that the Psalmist will set no limits to the praise of God."

DOCTRINAL AND PRACTICAL REMARKS.

1. Even in this world of sorrow no small part of our fit work is praise, vv. 1, 12. As long as life lasts, especially in the case of the righteous, mercies greatly abound. Much more will they be called to praise in heaven, Isa. liv. 7, 8. Let us extol him here with heart and voice, for life and all its blessings; then may we hope to spend our eternity in his blissful presence and service. If God exalts us, let us exalt him. If he humbles us without destroying us, let us count it a great mercy, and give thanks. "All the vicissitudes of our earthly existence are subject to his sovereign disposal." They could not be in better hands.

2. In state, spirits and hopes the best men are liable to great depression, v. 1. The condition of the believer in covenant with God is one of safety, not of security. Though his enemies shall not finally prevail, yet they often and dreadfully annoy him.

3. Because the wicked hate the righteous, they rejoice over them as often as they see them sad and dejected, v. 1. "Ye are not of the world, therefore the world hateth you."

4. The whole Psalm shows how dreadful is sin in those who rule or represent the nation. It brings down terrible chastisements. The reason why national sins are so sorely punished in this world, is that nations, *as such*, will not be judged in the next world. Their existence will then have ceased. In the final judgment individuals alone will undergo the examination of God.

5. There is no getting on without prayer, v. 2. We may be saved without learning or great sagacity, but not without prayer. Cobbin: "In God's own time and way he can deliver us when we call upon him for help. In this fluctuating state our joys are nearly allied to our sorrows, our prosperity to adversity, and our seasons of sacred joy to those of deep depression. But who ever besieged the mercy-seat in vain?"

6. When God heals and helps, the work is done to purpose, v. 2. None can resist him. He needs no assistance.

7. The preservation of human life is so great a work as to be always and easily referable to God alone, v. 3. No positive act on his part is necessary to terminate it. His simple and total withdrawal would cause us instantly to perish.

> That life which thou hast made thy care,
> Lord, I devote to thee.

Surely we ought to give all to God. The dangers seen and unseen, which we are constantly encountering, at once overcome us, if God leaves us for a moment. If we have never been in the perils of war or of famine, yet who of us has always been beyond the reach of pestilence.

8. He, who heartily loves God and sincerely praises him, wishes all others to do the same, v. 4. The reasons are 1, true religion is benevolent; 2, God is infinitely excellent and glorious, and so worthy of boundless honor and devotion. Dickson: "Dwelling a while upon the consideration of mercies shown unto us bringeth with it rejoicing in God, and a singing disposition, whereunto when we are once wakened and warned, we will think

that one mouth to praise God is too little, as here we see in David, who not only praiseth God himself, but also setteth all the saints on work to the same purpose, saying, *sing to the Lord, all ye saints of his.*"

9. Yet it is idle to ask any but *saints* to join in so spiritual an exercise, v. 4. However much wicked men may love good gifts, they always hate the Giver of all good things. Many of them do not even thank him for existence. Voltaire put it in print: "I wish I had never been born." Thousands to this day despise his "unspeakable gift," Jesus Christ. If God got no honor except what the wicked give him, his praise would soon cease to be heard and his name cease to be reverently pronounced on earth.

10. God's holiness is as amiable as it is spotless. Because it is infinite, it is to be trusted and rejoiced in. It is ever just cause of thankfulness, v. 4. Has our religion such a temper as to enable us to adore and glory in the holiness of God?

11. Though to the wicked the night of death is followed by a night of endless despair, yet to the righteous the longest and darkest night has its morning of joy, v. 5. Sharp as are the trials of the saints, they are but short. Great is the mercy to us that God is slow to anger and that his anger endureth but *a moment.* If he delighted in punishing, who could stand before him? While the Scriptures assure us that God's anger is short, they as clearly teach us, that his mercy endureth for ever. Oh that the saints would study God's character. Wonderful love, mercy and purity shine in it all. His name is the glory of the universe.

12. Inspired writers carefully maintain the distinction between saint and sinner. This Psalm sets it forth wonderfully. Hengstenberg: "The divine judgments are *annihilating* in their character to the *ungodly:* in their case joy never follows weeping." On the other hand the very afflictions of God's people promote their eternal well-being.

13. Though prosperity may come to a good man, yet it is never without peril. Even David was not strong enough to withstand its power, v. 6. Because of our sinfulness its natural tendency is to harden the heart and draw away the affections from duty and from God. This is often declared in Scripture. Sometimes the language of Inspiration is very striking. See especially Deut. viii. 10–18; xxxii. 15; Pr. i. 32; Ezek. xvi. 49, 50; Hos. xiii. 6. We are sadly wrong when we pervert God's blessings to the encouragement of carnal security. When the sun shines, why should we say, There will never be a storm or a cloud?

14. If we have success, surely we ought to refer it to God, v. 7. Without him there is neither strength, nor wisdom, nor joy, nor speed, nor stability.

15. In God is our life. If he hides his face we cannot but be *troubled,* v. 7.

16. Anything is good for us that puts us to praying earnestly, v. 8.

17. It is very lawful in prayer to fill our mouths with arguments drawn either from the glory of God, or our own weakness and necessities, v. 9. Surely then we may plead the merits of the great Redeemer. "Faith in God is very argumentative."

18. Let none suppose that it is wicked to die, or to offer to die, if we can thereby promote the good of our race, the cause of truth, or the glory of God. The right way is to leave the time and manner of our departure to the sovereign disposal of God.

19. God's people ought not to object to leaving this world for a better. Death is no enemy to a believer, 1 Cor. iii. 22. The union between Christ and his people is not dissolved by death. They sleep in Jesus. It is not to death that a good man persistently objects, but to a death that will bring dishonor on God. Scott: "We should entreat the Lord that we may not close our lives under his frown, in a way dishonorable to his name, or unprofitable to our brethren."

20. What we want is mercy, v. 10. Not a good thing do we deserve. All we need must flow to us through undeserved kindness and great pity, or we shall never get any good.

21. If we obtain help of God, we need no other aid, v. 10. He is sufficient. He alone is all-sufficient.

22. It is not wicked to be very sad, to mourn and put on sackcloth, v. 11. It is not sinful to shed tears and heave sighs. Jesus wept. His soul was sorrowful even unto death. There is a time to weep, and a time to mourn, Ecc. iii. 4. Dickson: " It becometh the child of God to weep when he is beaten, and to humble himself in the exercise of prayer and fasting." One of the worst signs is to be scourged and refuse to be humbled.

22. It is not wicked to be very glad, v. 11. There is a time to laugh, Ecc. iii. 4. We may rejoice with joy unspeakable and full of glory. Blessed be God, his plan is not to make stocks and stones of us, but to make us exceedingly joyful.

23. Our best faculties of body and mind, those which constitute our *glory* above the beasts, belong to God, v. 12. Never is speech better employed than in commending Christ, glorifying God, praising the Holy Spirit, uttering all the memory of God's loving-kindness.

PSALM XXXI.

To the chief Musician, A Psalm of David.

1 IN thee, O LORD, do I put my trust; let me never be ashamed: deliver me in thy righteousness.

2 Bow down thine ear to me; deliver me speedily: be thou my strong rock, for a house of defence to save me.

3 For thou *art* my rock and my fortress; therefore for thy name's sake lead me, and guide me.

4 Pull me out of the net that they have laid privily for me: for thou *art* my strength.

5 Into thine hand I commit my spirit: thou hast redeemed me, O LORD God of truth.

6 I have hated them that regard lying vanities: but I trust in the LORD.

7 I will be glad and rejoice in thy mercy: for thou hast considered my trouble; thou hast known my soul in adversities;

8 And hast not shut me up into the hand of the enemy: thou hast set my feet in a large room.

9 Have mercy upon me, O LORD, for I am in trouble: mine eye is consumed with grief, *yea,* my soul and my belly.

10 For my life is spent with grief, and my years with sighing: my strength faileth because of mine iniquity, and my bones are consumed.

11 I was a reproach among all mine enemies, but especially among my neighbors, and a fear to mine acquaintance: they that did see me without fled from me.

12 I am forgotten as a dead man out of mind: I am like a broken vessel.

13 For I have heard the slander of many: fear *was* on every side: while they took counsel together against me, they devised to take away my life.

14 But I trusted in thee, O LORD: I said, Thou *art* my God.

15 My times *are* in thy hand: deliver me from the hand of mine enemies, and from them that persecute me.

16 Make thy face to shine upon thy servant: save me for thy mercies' sake.

17 Let me not be ashamed, O LORD; for I have called upon thee: let the wicked be ashamed, *and* let them be silent in the grave.

18 Let the lying lips be put to silence; which speak grievous things proudly and contemptuously against the righteous.

19 *Oh* how great *is* thy goodness, which thou hast laid up for them that fear thee; *which* thou hast wrought for them that trust in thee before the sons of men.

20 Thou shalt hide them in the secret of thy presence from the pride of man: thou shalt keep them secretly in a pavilion from the strife of tongues.

21 Blessed *be* the LORD: for he hath shewed me his marvellous kindness in a strong city.

22 For I said in my haste, I am cut off from before thine eyes: nevertheless thou heardest the voice of my supplications when I cried unto thee.

23 Oh love the LORD, all ye his saints: *for* the LORD preserveth the faithful, and plentifully rewardeth the proud doer.

24 Be of good courage, and he shall strengthen your heart, all ye that hope in the LORD.

ON the title see on titles of Psalms iii. iv. There is no good reason for the opinion of Mudge and Edwards that Jeremiah wrote this ode. Verse 13 is quoted by the weeping prophet, Jer. xx. 10. So verse 5 is quoted by Christ, Luke xxiii. 46. But these things in no way impair the Davidic authorship. The title gives it to him. Ingenuity and learning have failed to find for it any historic occasion. Theodoret refers it to the rebellion of Absalom; Kimchi, Patrick and others, to the time when David was sore pressed by Saul after he had escaped from Keilah, and was in the wilderness of Maon, 1 Sam. xxiii. 13–26; Arama, to the time when David was in Keilah, 1 Sam. xxiii. 1–12. Hengstenberg: "Several abortive attempts have been made to find out a *particular historical occasion* for the Psalm." It represents, as Cocceius has well remarked, "the perpetual conflict, which believers and the church have to maintain in this world, and the deliverance and victory by which that conflict is sure to be followed."

Critics have often noticed the exceeding simplicity of the language of the whole composition. Everything involved is avoided. This is thought by some peculiarly to belong to those Psalms, which do not refer to individual sufferings, so much as they describe sufferings common to all God's people. Perhaps there is some force in the suggestion. Scott dates this Psalm B. C. 1060; Clarke, B. C. 1062. The names of the Most High here found are *Jehovah* LORD, *El God* and *Elohim God*, on which respectively see on Ps. i. 2; v. 4; iii. 2.

1. *In thee, O* LORD, *do I put my trust.* The verb is that usually so rendered, or hope, or have hoped. But Venema reads placed my protection; Amesius, betake myself; Ainsworth, hope for safety; Jebb, have taken refuge; Fry, have taken shelter. See on Ps. vii. 1; xi. 1; xvi. 1; xxv. 20. The Hebrew is in the preterite. This signifies that the act is continued until now. Though we may not fix on any one event of David's life as being here specially noticed; yet it is clear that the Psalm relates to a state of peril, perhaps of many perils. In this condition an avowal of strong confidence in God is eminently proper. "What time I am afraid I will trust in the Lord." This is the best method of quelling his anxieties, of enabling him to behave as he ought. He also states his trust as a ground of argument with God: *Let me never be ashamed. Never*, literally *not for ever, not to eternity. Ashamed*, also *confounded.* See on Ps. vi. 10; xxv. 2, 3. The shame and confusion are such as arise from defeat and overthrow. *Deliver me in thy righteousness.* "God displays his righteousness in performing his promise to his servants." It is a *righteous* thing with God both to save his people and destroy his foes, 2 Thess. i. 6, 7. That justice, which governs the world and which will preside at the last day, is a glorious and lovely attribute. It is every way consistent with all else that is adorable in the character of God. Righteousness is certainly more than faithfulness, but without the latter, the former could not exist. The righteousness was God's, not David's.

2. *Bow down thine ear to me.* The Arabic unites this and the next clause and ren-

ders them : Speedily give me a hearing. The language of the whole verse is that of genuine and strong emotion. To *incline the ear* is to show a readiness to listen to even a whisper. *Deliver me speedily.* The case was urgent. The danger was imminent. A true apprehension of real peril seeks immediate relief; and a true faith seeks that deliverance from God alone. He adds: *Be thou my strong rock, for a house of defence to save me.* There is considerable variety in rendering this clause. For rock and defence some read munition and fortress, protector and refuge, helper and refuge, strong rock and strong fortress. All these give the same sense. However the words may be rendered, there is no doubt that the imagery is borrowed from a place by nature very strong, and by art rendered impregnable. Such a defence we all need and should all seek.

3. *For thou* art *my rock and my fortress.* The words rendered *rock* in this verse and the preceding are not the same. Both are found in Ps. xviii. 2; the former rendered *strength*, the latter *rock*. See on that place. The word rendered *fortress* is the same as that rendered *defence* in v. 2. This clause therefore asserts that God *is* to the psalmist what in verse 2, he prayed God *would be* to him. We never have ill-success in our approaches to God, when we can truly plead a covenant relation with him. David adds: *Therefore for thy name's sake lead me and guide me.* Instead of *guide*, the Chaldee, Septuagint, Vulgate, Ethiopic and Arabic read *nourish.* On the phrase *for thy name's sake* see on Ps. xxiii. 3. Alexander: "The futures in this second clause suggest the idea of necessity, and might perhaps be correctly rendered by the use of our auxiliary *must.*"

4. *Pull me out of the net that they have laid privily for me.* On the use of *nets* see on Ps. ix. 15. The wicked are sometimes permitted to lay snares from which nothing but infinite wisdom and power can rescue the righteous. So God's servants often feel and look to him alone. *For thou* art *my strength.* Strength, as in Ps. xxvii. 1. We have the same word in verse 2, rendered as an adjective, *strong* rock, literally rock of *strength.* Good cause have all the righteous for going to God; first, he can save them, secondly, none else can.

5. *Into thine hand I commit my spirit.* For *commit* many versions read *commend.* This does not materially change the sense. Our Lord used the Septuagint rendering, *commend*, Luke xxiii. 46. Alexander: "The verb means to entrust or deposit anything of value." This is the precise and final form, in which we find the idea in Scripture, 2 Tim. i. 12. Every believer, living or dying, may use these words. Our Lord Jesus greatly loved all Scripture. And many things in this ode were very well suited to express his thoughts. But he did not quote all this verse: *Thou hast redeemed me, O LORD God of truth.* This clause "more properly relates to the type than to the antitype," for although the verb is sometimes rendered *deliver*, yet it is far more commonly *redeem*, and properly signifies deliverance by redemption, Ex. xiii. 13; Lev. xxvii. 27; Num. xviii. 15. *God of truth* was a very fitting title in this case. It reminded David of the faithfulness of his defender, and it contained an unanswerable argument with God to continue his mercies. In his plea with God David was also able to present his own uprightness and honesty of character:

6. *I have hated them that regard lying vanities.* There seems to be nothing to justify the change in the rendering of this clause adopted by the Septuagint and kindred versions: *Thou hast hated*, etc. The sense is good, but not so good as that given by our version. The Chaldee is quite against it. Hengstenberg: "The sense does not suit the connection, and Ps. xvi. 4; xxvi. 5 are in favor of the first person." The hatred here spoken of is that of displacency, not of malevolence. We have the same word in the same sense in Ps. v. 5; xi. 5; cxxxix. 22. The form of the verb here points to a habit of the life long since formed and continued until now. *Regard,*

elsewhere rendered *keep, observe, take heed to.* The care and attention manifested by the wicked to different forms of sin and folly are great. They guard them as if they were treasure. They observe the maxims of wickedness as the righteous do the ordinances of God. They take heed to evil as if it were good. They *regard lying vanities.* For *lying vanities* various versions read vanities, vanities to no purpose, vanities of falsehood, vanities of vain falsehood, vainest vanities, idolatrous vanities, vanities of worship. Alexander: "The words here combined are highly contemptuous, denoting *vanities of nothingness,* or *nothings of nonentity.*" Doubtless idols and idol worship are chiefly intended. In Scripture idols are often called *vanities.* Paul says *an idol* is *nothing in the world,* 1 Cor. viii. 4. Idol worship, however splendid, is the merest farce, a mockery of God and of man, fit matter of divine ridicule; see Ps. cxv.; Isa. xliv. No marvel David hated the whole system of false worship. His confidence was in no creature, and so he adds, *But I trust in the* LORD. *Trust,* it here denotes the repose of the soul on Jehovah.

7. *I will be glad and rejoice in thy mercy.* There is great uniformity in rendering this clause, only for the first verb some prefer *triumph,* or *exult.* The more the true religion is tried, the more is it found to be a fountain of joy. Unfeigned confidence in God will surely in the end bring gladness and exultation. The divine *mercy* is perfectly reliable. It meets all the wants of every humble soul. Past mercies lay the foundation for the expectation of greater mercies yet to come. Experience of the divine kindness is a marvellous nourisher of gladness. *For thou hast considered my trouble.* When God takes in hand any grievance, he does not give partial relief and lay the matter aside. He *considers* the whole case. The proper remedy necessarily flows from the divine nature. How often are we ready in darkness to say, " My way is hid from the LORD, and my judgment is passed over from my God." But this is the language of sinful unbelief. It is well when we can say as David here, *Thou hast known my soul in 'adversities.* God *notices* all that happens to the righteous. He is ignorant of none of their distresses. Some regard the first clause of this verse as an anticipation of deliverance yet to come, and thus throw great animation into the verse; but the sense is as good and the construction more natural to make the *triumph* and *gladness* be in view of infallible tokens of relief already vouchsafed.

8. *And hast not shut me up into the hand of the enemy.* Often had David's enemies almost grasped him. It has always been true that the righteous were *scarcely saved.* Yet they *were* saved. There was always a *way of escape.* If all others are shut, God opens a passage to the skies. God does not long leave his chosen in straits. *Thou hast set my feet in a large room.* Where the Spirit of the Lord is, there is liberty. The worst chains are the bonds of iniquity and the fetters of a fiery condemnation. These taken away, and God's favor secured, nor men nor angels can hedge us up, or hinder our progress Zionward.

9. *Have mercy upon me, O* LORD, *for I am in trouble. Have mercy,* as in Ps. iv. 1 ; vi. 2 ; ix. 13 ; xxv. 16 ; li. 1. The *mercy* sought is *favor, grace,* unmerited kindness, not a debt due him, but a gratuity. For *trouble* some read *affliction, distress.* Hengstenberg : I am hard pressed. In trouble we often feel our need of mercy more than in prosperity. He adds : *Mine eye is consumed with grief,* yea, *my soul and my belly.* Hengstenberg urges that the *grief* is vexation, dejection. Calvin renders it anger, and needlessly thinks it signifies sinful anger. This is not supported by the text or context. Grief is enough to waste and consume the eye, giving it a sunken appearance, to take away the appetite, the courage, the whole strength. The bodily effects produced by mental distress, when long continued and violent, are marked and uniform. Life itself is often taken by this means. Many die of a broken heart.

10. *For my life is spent with grief, and my years with sighing. Spent, i. e., wasted,*

consumed. Hengstenberg: "The sense is, 'My constant pain, my continual sighing, wear me out before the time, end my life, shorten my years.'" It is always a solemn thing to die; but to feel that life is waning and wasting merely through the wickedness and perversity of men clothes the whole matter with sadness. It is terrible to see ourselves killed inch by inch through the depravity of others. Sad indeed is our lot when the business of each day is weeping and sighing. David adds: *My strength faileth because of mine iniquity, and my bones are consumed.* The chief doubt respecting this passage arises from the word rendered *iniquity.* In favor of our version is the Chaldee, Ainsworth, church of England, Jebb and Alexander. Hengstenberg has Guilt; Castellio, This punishment; Horsley, My punishment; Amesius, Punishment of sin; Venema, Writhing; Calvin and Fry, Sorrow; Mudge, Edwards, Green and Rogers, Affliction. The word occurs very often and is commonly rendered iniquity, sometimes fault, punishment. It is best to give it here the usual signification. David had an abiding sense of his own sinfulness. He often confessed it. Though he did not deserve at the hands of men the cruel treatment he received from them, and so often pleads his righteousness, yet he had learned that the wicked were God's sword, and admitted that he deserved all that came upon him. Sin is the real cause of all our suffering. In the true sense of that term in Scripture, David was righteous. Yet he was not in himself free from all iniquity. He often smarted for his sins. Tholuck: "The sting of conscience had blended with the external causes of misery." *Strength* and *bones* are aptly spoken of as failing together.

11. *For I was a reproach among all mine enemies, but especially among my neighbors.* To be a jest, a reproach is the severest kind of trial, to which man can subject us. The enemies of the Lord's anointed king started all sorts of evil reports against him. The more they lied against him, the more they hated him. So terrible was the popular outcry that even David's former *neighbors* and friends to a sad extent became his despisers in proportion as they had once esteemed him. He was not only a derision but also a terror to his former friends. *And a fear to mine acquaintance.* They were afraid to be seen with him, or to be suspected of intimacy or even sympathy with him. They considered his cause ruined, his prospects dismal. They thought God had forsaken him, and so it was easy to persecute and take him. How far this was carried is next declared: *They that did see me without fled from me. Without i. e.,* abroad, in the *streets,* or in the *fields.* If any man has ever seen former and esteemed friends evidently avoiding him, he will know what the prophet here means. Yea, he had been so long and painfully separated from his usual places of resort, that to many he was as if dead:

12. *I am forgotten as a dead man out of mind.* Calvin: I am forgotten as one dead; Fry: I was given up as one that is dead; Boothroyd: I am disregarded as one dead; Hengstenberg: I am forgotten in the heart like a dead man; Alexander: I was forgotten as a dead man out of mind. The verb is in the preterite, but shows that for some time he had been, and still was *forgotten.* The present tense best suits the English idiom. There is no difference between being forgotten *in the heart* and forgotten *out of mind.* He adds: *I am like a broken vessel.* Anderson: "Utterly neglected as being worthless;" Berleberg Bible: "A broken vessel, which is good for nothing, which can be made no use of, cannot be made whole again, for which no one cares and the fragments of which are thrown away." In subsequent Scriptures we often find the same figure.

13. *For I have heard the slander of many.* For *slander of many,* John Rogers' translation and the Bishops' Bible read blasphemy of the multitude; Genevan translation, the railing of great men. It means evil report, defamation. In this verse *for* seems to refer back to verse 9, where he pleads for mercy, and begins to assign reasons, and

continues to do so through this verse. The word is not elsewhere found in the Psalms, and but a few times in any place. Its signification is uniform. *Many, the many, a multitude, the multitude.* The enemies of David were many and powerful. The object of *slander* in cases like this is twofold, first, to gratify a wicked, fiendish spirit of lying and malice; and secondly, to withdraw sympathy from the sufferer by persuading the masses that he is an evil man. *Fear* was *on every side.* That is, fear has been and still is on every side. The Hebrew is very brief and forcible. Every path seemed beset with danger. No rational prospect of deliverance presented itself. The persecutors could be satisfied with nothing but the extremest measures: *While they took counsel together against me, they devised to take away my life.* All envy, slander and malice naturally lead to murder. These men were bent on shedding David's blood. Tholuck: "A man exiled by his king, who would with royal favor reward those who betrayed him (1 Sam. xxii. 7, 8; xxiii. 21,) could not but become the reproach of those, whose houses he used to frequent. Nor does the fear of his kindred seem strange, since their connection with him (especially at a time when enmity towards an individual became transferred upon all his family) was no doubt fraught with danger to them. We read indeed that David, in order to secure the safety of his parents, deemed it necessary to remove them to the land of the Moabites. (1 Sam. xxii. 3.) It was even true that his nearest relatives and friends had forgotten him like a dead man: he could no longer meet with Jonathan, and probably saw his relatives during his decennial flight on that occasion only when he met them in the cave of Adullam. (1 Sam. xxii. 1.) That cave was near Bethlehem, the town of David's tribe, and he seems afterwards not to have been so near the capital. . . No secret nook or corner of the country was too remote to prevent infuriated Saul from attempting the seizure of the fugitive."

14. *But I trusted in thee, O* Lord. *Trusted*, the same verb in the same form as in verse 6, where it is given in the present tense. Nothing was left to David but confidence in God. This was enough; *I said, Thou* art *my God.* The covenant relation may always be pleaded. Entire reliance on God did never fail any soul. The fiercer the storm, the more does the anchor sure and steadfast show its value. The darker the night, the more blessed is the light of one bright star.

15. *My times* are *in thy hand.* Chaldee: In thy hand are the times of my redemption; Septuagint and Vulgate: In thy hands are my lots; Arabic: In thy hands is my inheritance; Syriac: In thy hands are the times; Jebb: In thy hand is my time; Edwards: My critical times are in thy hands; Calvin: "The import of the language is, Lord, it is thy prerogative, and thou alone hast the power to dispose of both my life and death. Nor does he use the plural, *times*, in my opinion without reason; but rather to mark the variety of casualties, by which the life of man is usually harassed." The whole of life, with all that threatens it, with all that continues it, is in the hand of the wise, good, powerful, perfect ruler of all things. This lays a good foundation for the prayer: *Deliver me from the hand of mine enemies, and from them that persecute me.* His enemies sought his life. They hunted him like a wild beast. But it was all in vain. His *times* were not in the hand of Saul, or of any finite creature.

16. *Make thy face to shine upon thy servant.* Making the face to *shine* is a very ancient form of expressing the manifest presence of God and his lively comforts to his people, Num. vi. 25. We had the same figure in Ps. iv. 6. When God's face shines on any one, his grace is marvellously manifest to him. Such lively comforts and hopes as are thus imparted are all the fruit, not of man's desert, but of God's mere favor; and so David prays: *Save me for thy mercies' sake. Mercies, loving-kindnesses.* In God, not in man, must be found the cause of every deliverance, even to the best saints.

17. *Let me not be ashamed, O* LORD. *Ashamed,* as in v. 1. It occurs again in this verse. The argument used here is: *For I have called upon thee.* The argument used in v. 1 is: *In thee do I put my trust.* These are not diverse. He, who trusts, will pray. He, who prays aright, must confide. That trust, which leads to calling on God, and that prayer, which is offered in faith, cannot fail. They must bring help to the righteous. They must as surely bring a downfall to their incorrigible foes: *Let the wicked be ashamed.* For an explanation of the imprecatory form, found here and in verse 18, see Introduction, § 6. And *let them be silent in the grave.* Grave, as in Ps. vi. 5; in ix. 17, *hell.* Death puts it beyond the power of the wicked to harass the people of God any more. Their craft and malice and blasphemies are powerless when their earthly career is closed.

18. *Let the lying lips be put to silence.* Surely God will bring to naught every falsehood and all who love it. To ask him to do so is but to ask him to exercise the glorious holiness of his nature. The liars here spoken of did not satisfy themselves with inventing harmless fables for their own diversion, but rage and malice were in their words: *Which speak grievous things proudly and contemptuously against the righteous. Grievous things, opprobrious things, iniquity, a hard word, a hard and mean thing,* so some. The margin has it, *a hard thing.* Others prefer an adverb, *hardly, cruelly, recklessly, insolently.* All these are true, but the marginal reading is perhaps the best. The speeches of the wicked are often very galling to the righteous. And then they utter their falsehoods in *pride* and *contempt.* The present scorn and haughtiness of the wicked will only be equalled by their final shame and confusion. The meanness, cowardice and deceitfulness of their real characters will burst forth at last. The war against God's saints must and shall be put down. It is too wicked to be allowed to last forever.

19. Oh *how great is thy goodness which thou hast laid up for them that fear thee.* Here seems to be a very sudden transition. But it is justified. The prophet had gained a sight of the dreadful end of the wicked, which must be the signal for the glorious triumph of the righteous. The fitness of the bold language here used arises from the fact that David either foresaw deliverance coming, or had already experienced it. The latter is the more probable opinion. This part of the Psalm, if not all of it, was probably composed when David saw the schemes of his persecutors disappointed, God's promise to him respecting his authority fulfilled, and his enemies either dead, or fled, or quite in his power. The goodness here referred to seems to be God's providential goodness in this life—a sure token indeed of greater goodness yet to come; but yet a great thing in itself. Several things commonly heighten the displays of God's providential goodness to his saints: 1. Its principal acts are usually very unexpected. At such a time as men look not for him Jehovah appears. 2. It is very seasonable. A day or an hour sooner or later would have quite changed the aspect of the whole event. 3. God's operations are commonly noiseless. He comes not with observation. God made a world with less noise than man makes a coffin. 4. When God manifests his providential goodness he does it effectually. The enemies are all gone; the victory is complete. Not an Egyptian was left alive at the Red sea. 5. If means and instruments are used they are so inadequate, so unexpected that our wonder is greatly increased. Ahithophel's suicide breaks the neck of Absalom's rebellion. 6. God's providential goodness to the righteous is by covenant and according to a fixed plan. He always designed to lift up David's head above all his enemies round about. His goodness is *laid up, hidden, reserved,* or *treasured up* for the saints. It is hidden in God's purpose. It is hidden as treasure of great value. It is laid up as a portion, an inheritance that none but they shall have. Yet God's tender mercies are over all his works, and he " maketh his sun to rise on the evil and

on the good." But to his saints God's goodness is unmixed, unfailing. It does great things for them because they *fear* him. On the *fear of God*, see on Ps. ii. 11. This goodness is not only *laid up* for the righteous, but at proper times it is manifested for them : Which *thou hast wrought for them that trust in thee before the sons of men !* It is chiefly known to be laid up, because on fit occasions it is *wrought* for the saints, described here as those that *trust in* God. For the nature of this *trust*, see on Ps. vii. 1. *Before the sons of men* refers to the *trust* publicly expressed, or to the *goodness* publicly displayed. The latter gives the better sense. Genuine trust in God, however secret, shall not be publicly disappointed. Friend and foe shall see that God is righteous and faithful.

20. *Thou shalt hide them in the secret of thy presence from the pride of man.* Instead of pride various versions have wrath, disturbance, strife, trouble, provoking, insults, association, leagues. God's *face* or *presence* in this place points, not so much to the sanctuary, as to the aspects of his providence. His presence shields his friends, but confounds his foes, Ex. xiv. 20. *Thou shalt keep them secretly in a pavilion from the strife of tongues.* For strife some have broils, contradiction, contention, quarrel. The English text gives the sense as well as any other. A *pavilion* or tent was a hiding-place for men and things, sheltering the former from the heats of .summer and the cold blasts of all seasons, hiding the latter from the sight and cupidity of men. The saints are made quite safe. Arnd: " This our beloved God does secretly, so that no human eyes may or can see, and the ungodly do not know that a believer is, in God, and in the presence of God, so well protected, that no reproach or contempt, and no quarrelsome tongues can do him any harm." If good men could be ruined by reproaches, and slanders, and plots of violence, and strifes of tongues, not one of them would ever reach heaven. But none of these things can harm them, because they are hidden in God.

21. *Blessed* be *the* LORD. See on Ps. v. 12 ; xviii. 46 ; xxviii. 6. *For he hath shewed me his marvellous kindness in a strong city.* Arnd : " The strong city is God himself, and his powerful and gracious protection, in which we are even more secure than in a strong city." Calvin suggests that we read, *as in a strong city.* There is no valid objection to this. It doubtless gives the true sense. Walford : " The particle of similitude is wanting in Hebrew, as is not uncommon. The intention of the Psalmist is evidently to describe by a metaphor his signal deliverance as if he had been guarded by invincible fortifications."

22. *For I said in my haste, I am cut off from before thine eyes.* Chaldee : But when I sought a place to fly to I said, I am cut off from the presence of thy glory ; Septuagint, Vulgate and Ethiopic : But I said in the high excitement [*or* excess] of my mind ; I am cast away from before thy eyes ; Arabic : I said in my senselessness, Have I fallen away from the sight of thy eyes ? Syriac : I said in my haste, I have perished from the sight of thine eyes ; Calvin : I said in my perturbation, I am cast out of thy sight ; Edwards : For I said in my consternation, I am banished from the sight of thine eyes ; Hengstenberg : And I said in my rapid flight, I am torn away from thine eyes. The chief doubt is whether we should read *haste, flight, fear,* or *terror. Trepidation,* which expresses haste arising from fear, is perhaps as good a rendering as any other. It is clear that David here deplores a weakness and confesses a sin. He had allowed his mind to become sinfully despondent respecting a cause in which he had God's word. But this sad temptation did not finally prevail : *Nevertheless thou heardest the voice of my supplications when I cried unto thee.* If God required perfect faith before he answered a prayer, all our petitions would be rejected. But he regards our cry, even when we serve him, in much weakness and in many temptations.

23. *Oh love the Lord, all ye his saints.* Love to God is generally said to embrace— 1. Love to him for what he has done for us, Ps. cxvi. 1. So here also we have an expression of the love of *gratitude.* 2. Love of *complacency,* which *delights* in God and loves him for what he is. There can be no piety in man or angel without this love. It is much spoken of in Scripture, Ps. xxxvii. 4; Ps. xlii. 2. We must take pleasure in the Almighty. 3. Love of *benevolence,* which bears good will to the kingdom of God, wishes him honored, and is pleased when he is glorified. We are called on to *love* God in each of these senses. For *the* LORD *preserveth the faithful, and plentifully rewardeth the proud doer.* By his government God shows his adorable and lovely nature. He ought to be loved for all he is and for all he does. His character would not be perfect, of course it would not be wholly lovely, if he either failed to preserve the faithful, or put down the proud. For *The* LORD *preserveth the faithful,* we might read, The *Lord keepeth faith,* viz., *with his saints.* This is the settled judgment of every believer. On the other hand some admit that in this life to the wicked there is some recompense, but they say, Where is the proportion between crime and punishment? The answer is, that in the end, punishment shall be condign. In due time God will *plentifully, abundantly, in the highest degree,* send a just recompense on the proud. The inference from all the foregoing is a timely exhortation to all the saints, or *meek,* or *gracious ones;*

24. *Be of good courage, i. e.,* quit you like men, be ye steadfast, be ye established, or be ye strong. The command carries with it the promise of help to all who obey. *And he shall strengthen your heart.* He who will exercise the grace he has, shall have more grace. Every victory won in faith shall prepare the way for another conflict, which shall also have a happy issue. Alexander: "Be strong in purpose and desire, and he will make you strong in fact." Nor is it one class only of God's servants that need such exhortation. The address is to all: *All ye that hope in the Lord.* All true piety, however feeble, has some *hope,* some confidence in *Jehovah.* All who have thus set their hope in God, will accept in meekness these exhortations.

DOCTRINAL AND PRACTICAL REMARKS.

1. Great honor is brought to God by the trust which his people repose in him in the darkest hours, v. 1. This is a reason why they should diligently study to be hopeful and confident in God at all times.

2. Genuine trust in God is in him *alone.* It mingles not human helps and friendships with the divine. It is silent as the grave respecting all resources but the infinite, eternal and unchangeable One, v. 1.

3. Genuine trust may always be pleaded as a reason why God should grant our prayers, v. 1. He never awakens hope or inspires confidence to disappoint them. That be far from him.

4. The righteous have many good and no bad prospects for *eternity,* v. 1. They shall *never* be ashamed. All the good things they receive here are but pledges of better things to come; while the evil they receive here is all the evil that shall ever befall them.

5. Every attribute of God demands and secures the salvation of believers. They were sinners, and so deserved ill. But because they are in covenant with God, even his righteousness requires their full deliverance, v. 1. Compare 1 John i. 9. Dickson: "As the Lord sendeth, in his wisdom, trouble after trouble upon a believer, so he sendeth, in his justice and faithfulness, promised delivery after delivery."

6. It is a great mercy that God hears prayer. We may confidently ask him to hear our prayers, condescendingly *bowing his ear to us,* v. 2. Arnd: "O God, thou hearest what is offered in such a soft voice that thou hearest my sigh! Ah! keep not at such

a distance from me! I have no temporal defence; no place of strength and safety; be thou my castle and strong-hold."

7. When men are greatly in earnest and their hearts truly engaged, they desire the *speedy* assistance of God, v. 2. A pious soul in darkness asks that the darkness may now be dispelled. He who rightly wishes deliverance from sin, asks that he may now be saved.

8. It is well to despair of all created help, to renounce all trust in ourselves or other creatures. David had no hope but in God alone, vv. 1, 2.

9. God can fully and effectually defend and save. He is a *strong rock*, a *place of munitions*, a *rock* and a *fortress*, vv. 2, 3. Trust in him cannot be vain. The thing is impossible. His nature forbids it. No truth is more sure or clear.

10. If merely a creature's honor, the credit of ministers, or the glory of angels were involved, man's salvation would indeed be uncertain. But every step involves the honor of God. We plead for *his name's sake*, v. 3. If God should begin and not continue, or if he should carry on but not complete the work, all would admit that it was for some reason that must bring reproach on the Almighty. This can never be. God was self-moved to undertake man's salvation. His glorious name makes it certain the top-stone shall be laid in glory.

11. Divine guidance cannot be too earnestly and constantly sought, v. 3. Left to ourselves, we make fatal mistakes. If man could be his own guide, why could he not be his own Saviour? It is therefore right to submit the whole understanding to the teaching of God and the heart to the purification of the Holy Ghost.

12. The history of God's people unites with Scripture in showing that the righteous are *scarcely saved*. Many a time are their feet in the *net*, and none but God can *pull* them out, v. 4. In this matter their success in no wise depends on native genius, or force of character, but on the purpose and grace of God. Dickson: "Though the godly be both weak and simple-witted, yet they have a wise and strong God to call upon, who is able to break the snare, and set his own free."

13. The more the Scripture is studied and the more we learn by experience, the clearer will it appear that God's almightiness is a truth necessary to Christian peace and joy, v. 4. There has lately passed from this earth one, whose memory is embalmed in the hearts of thousands, REV. JAMES WADDELL ALEXANDER, D. D. Among his many contributions to piety none deserves a higher place than his work entitled "CONSOLATION." None of its chapters is more full of blessed truth than the fourth, entitled, "THE OMNIPOTENCE OF GOD A GROUND OF ENLARGED CHRISTIAN EXPECTATION."

14. It is a privilege of believers at all times to commit and commend their spirits to God, v. 5. It is delightful specially to do so in a dying hour. So did our Saviour. Dying Stephen, Rev. James Waddell, D. D., the celebrated blind preacher of Virginia, Mrs. Sarah B. Judson and many others, when dying, cried, "Lord Jesus, receive my spirit." On the way to the stake Huss frequently said: "Into thy hands I commend my spirit; thou hast redeemed me, my Lord Jesus, God of truth." Luther dying thrice said: "Into thy hands I commit my spirit." John Janeway's last words were: "Come, Lord Jesus, come quickly." John Frederic Oberlin: "Lord Jesus, take me speedily; nevertheless, *thy* will be done." Calvin: "Whoever relies not on the providence of God, so as to commit his life to its faithful guardianship, has not learned aright what it is to live."

15. How precious is redemption! All the saints love to speak of it, and glorify its author, v. 5. No marvel that inspired pens never weary of this theme, and often break forth in songs of praise respecting it, even without formal notice.

16. If men are not grieved when they behold the transgressors, they are not saints,

v. 6. When Paul saw the city of Athens terribly sunk in idolatry, his spirit was stirred in him. He, who without sorrow and aversion can behold the wickedness of the wicked, has a heart very unlike the heart of God.

17. There is no reasonable way of accounting for idolatry, except on the supposition that men are terribly blinded, perverted and debased by sin. The whole system of idol-worship and of magic, necromancy, auguries and divinations, is such a mass of *lying vanities*, that none but a depraved mind could for a moment receive it.

18. Real mercies never lose their use to a pious mind, v. 7. Long after their reception we may call them to mind. Jacob did so when dying, Gen. xlviii. 16. He, who has no heart to think of past mercies, can hardly plead in any right way for new blessings. Sometimes the only light left us is the light of the promises, increased by the light of a blessed experience.

19. It is obligatory on us to maintain and cultivate joy and gladness in God's service, v. 7. It would bring an indelible stigma on religion if all its professors showed by their deportment that they served a hard master, who sent them a warfare at their own charges, and left them in such sadness as to make their lives bitter. Blessed be his name, he giveth songs in the night. "Thou meetest him that rejoiceth and worketh righteousness."

20. God *knows* our souls in affliction, v. 7. He weighs well our cause. He always *looks to* his saints, especially when they are bathed in tears, or are buffeting the waves of adversity. He *considers* all our *trouble*. Blessed be his name for that.

21. "Troubles seldom come alone." David's were multiplied. Read the list, vv. 7–13. How heavy the load—how hard it pressed. When sorrows begin to come, blesssed is he, who is prepared for the worst.

22. If it were possible for God, even for a short time, to take sides with the wicked against the righteous, it would destroy all religion in the world. But he never, even for an hour, *shuts up* a good man *into the hand of the enemy*, v. 8.

23. When God gives enlargement, who can put us in straits? v. 8.

24. Let all good men keep alive the knowledge and memory of the divine mercy, v. 9. In it is the life of men. The dying saint and the living Christian have no other resort. Dr. McLaren of Scotland dying said: "I am gathering together all my sermons and all my prayers, all my good deeds and all my evil deeds, and am throwing them overboard, determined to swim to glory on the plank of free grace." Let us never hold a doubtful doctrine on this vital point.

25. The worst sting of any trial is sin, v. 10. This gives our griefs their dreadful poignancy. Dickson: "The conscience of sin joined with trouble is a load above a burden, and able to break a man's strength more than any trouble." The reason is that sin is the bitterest and most accursed thing, the most venomous and deadly poison, the most killing and horrible evil in the universe. Nothing, nothing can compare with it. Though a man seems all gay and blithe, yet if sin be upon him he pines away and dies.

26. If the existence and contemplation of sin produce such effects here, what must they bring on the soul in the next world, where retribution will be perfect?

27. If we experience sharp trials at the hand of man, so did David, v. 11; so did Christ. If we fare no worse than the Master and his great type, we may call ourselves happy. Oftentimes the bitterest ingredient in our cup is the part former friends are allowed to act. This too entered into the trials of David and of Christ.

28. When almost all men either contemn or despair of a good cause, it is an illustrious act of faith not to give it up. In this case David hoped against hope. He followed the promise, not appearances. That which made the faith of the penitent thief most remarkable was that he steadily looked to the Sun of righteousness,

though he was under an eclipse ; believed on a Saviour, who was deserted by his own disciples, dying in ignominy, and confessing that he was forsaken of God. No marvel that such an instance of faith has been celebrated ever since and shall be to the end of the world.

29. Neither the *multitude* of our foes nor their *slanders,* nor their *counsels,* nor their *murderous devisings,* nor anything else can destroy us, or dismay us, if God be with us, v. 13.

30. Confidence in *Jehovah* as *our God* shall never, no never, no never be disappointed, v. 14. There is a sentence in one of the Apocryphal books of the Old Testament, which once gave poor Bunyan great relief. He thought it was in the Bible. He was mistaken in that, but not in supposing that it embodied a Scripture truth: " Look at the generations of old and see ; did ever any trust in the Lord, and was confounded ? or did any abide in his fear, and was forsaken ? or whom did he ever despise, that called upon him ?" Ecclus. ii. 10.

31. How comforting is the Scripture doctrine of providence, v. 15. We might as well believe there is no God, as believe that he neither sees, nor hears, nor cares, nor acts in human affairs. If we trust his government, all shall be well, and none will more surely, loudly or joyfully say so, than those, who in this life meet the saddest reverses.

32. Persecution is no novelty, v. 15. The spirit of it has raged from the days of Cain and will continue till the last sinner is converted. The offence of the cross will never cease till all flesh shall see the salvation of God.

33. When the sun shines, we do not need candles, and when we have the light of God's countenance, it matters but little, whether men smile or frown, praise or blame, bless or curse, v. 16.

34. *Shame,* defeat, overthrow, *silence* and confusion are surely coming, but not to the righteous, v. 17.

35. It will be unspeakable bliss to live in such a country as heaven, where *lying lips* are never opened, where *grievous things* are never spoken, where *pride* and *contempt* are unknown, v. 18.

36. He, who has God for his God, " possesses God, with all his treasures of grace, with all his goodness, and love, and friendship," v. 19. God withholds nothing from those, who withhold nothing from him.

37. It is an unspeakable blessing to be allowed to lead a quiet and peaceable life, even though it be in troublous times, when the world is all in an uproar. This can never be done but by that peace which is God's peculiar gift. He *hides* his chosen *in the secret of his presence,* in a *pavilion,* v. 20. Dickson : " How great peace of conscience before God, and comfort in the Holy Ghost, the Lord can give a believer when he hath to do with proud, open persecutors, and privily whispering slanderers, it is a secret and hid mystery to the worldly man !" Calvin : " The power of divine providence alone suffices to ward off every species of evil." In Bedford jail Bunyan was quietly stealing away to heaven, while his detestable prince, with his minions and myrmidons, was tossed on the sea of vanity.

38. He, that will see, may see wonders of mercy wrought for those, who love and fear God, v. 21.

39. Dickson : " There may be in a soul at one time both grief oppressing and hope upholding ; both darkness of trouble and the light of faith ; both desperate doubting and strong gripping of God's truth and goodness ; both a pointing and a fighting ; a seeming yielding in the fight and yet a striving of faith against all opposition ; both a foolish haste and a stayedness of faith," v. 22.

40. Distrust of God's goodness, love and mercy is a sin to be confessed, v. 22. Sincerely confessed, we will guard against it with much vigilance.

41. Love to God is an old doctrine, v. 23. It is as clearly taught in the Pentateuch as in the Gospels, in the Psalms as in the Epistles.

42. No faithful soul ever perishes. The reason is God reigns and *preserves* it, v. 23.

43. The recompense to the incorrigibly wicked will be soon enough and terrible enough, without our making ourselves busy to do them evil, v. 23.

44. Let all the servants of God be of good courage. Let no cowardly behaviour ever mark their conduct, v. 24. He, that fights their battles, is the Almighty. " If God be for us, who can be against us ?"

45. This Psalm shows that David was in many respects a type of Christ. Let us study the figure, as well as him who was pre-figured.

PSALM XXXII.

A Psalm of David, Maschil.

1 BLESSED *is he whose* transgression *is* forgiven, *whose* sin *is* covered.

2 Blessed *is* the man unto whom the LORD imputeth not iniquity, and in whose spirit *there is* no guile.

3 When I kept silence, my bones waxed old through my roaring all the day long.

4 For day and night thy hand was heavy upon me: my moisture is turned into the drought of summer. Selah.

5 I acknowledged my sin unto thee, and mine iniquity have I not hid. I said, I will confess my transgressions unto the LORD; and thou forgavest the iniquity of my sin. Selah.

6 For this shall every one that is godly pray unto thee in a time when thou mayest be found: surely in the floods of great waters they shall not come nigh unto him.

7 Thou *art* my hiding place; thou shalt preserve me from trouble; thou shalt compass me about with songs of deliverance. Selah.

8 I will instruct thee and teach thee in the way which thou shalt go: I will guide thee with mine eye.

9 Be ye not as the horse, *or* as the mule, *which* have no understanding: whose mouth must be held in with bit and bridle, lest they come near unto thee.

10 Many sorrows *shall be* to the wicked: but he that trusteth in the LORD, mercy shall compass him about.

11 Be glad in the LORD, and rejoice, ye righteous: and shout for joy, all *ye that are* upright in heart.

ON the title see on Psalms iii. xi. The word *Maschil* is here first found in the title of a Psalm. Subsequently it occurs in Psalms xlii. xliv. xlv. lii. liii. liv. lv. lxxiv. lxxviii. lxxxviii. lxxxix. cxlii. Of the thirteen, having this title, at least six were written by David, viz. xxxii. lii. liii. liv. lv. cxlii. Some Jewish writers say that *Maschil* is prefixed to no Psalms but such as were dictated by an interpreter; others, that all Psalms thus marked were explained by an interpreter; others, that *Maschil* is the name of a musical instrument used when the Psalm was sung; others, that *Maschil* was the first word of a song, to the tune of which the Psalm was to be sung. In support of these views, or any of them there appears no solid reason. Yet a few respectable writers favor the last.

There is no reason for regarding Christ as the speaker in this Psalm. *Maschil* is no doubt derived from a verb found in verse 8, which signifies to *instruct, be wise, consider, understand.* By the Chaldee, *Maschil* is rendered *a good·understanding,* by the Septuagint, Ethiopic and Vulgate, *knowledge, intelligence, understanding.* In the Hebrew title, it is a participle, which by Musculus, Montanus, Vatablus and Munster is rendered, teaching; by Gejerus, giving information; by Calvin, giving instruction; by Venema, hastening. Amesius gives the whole title, A didactic ode of David; Ainsworth, An instructing Psalm of David; Pool thinks *Maschil* the same as Instructor; Dodd, David's Instruction; Jebb says, its obvious meaning is, A wise direction, a moral lesson, a didactic composition; Fabritius, Piscator and Junius call it, A didactic ode; the marginal reading and Symson, A Psalm of David, *giving instruction;* Boothroyd, An instructive Psalm of David; Hengstenberg, A Didactic Poem; Williams, An instructing or didactic Psalm; Alexander, An instructive or didactic Psalm; Tholuck, A Psalm of David giving instruction. Authority is clearly in favor of *Instruction.* Yet some Psalms bearing this inscription are no more *instructive* than some, which have a different inscription, or no inscription. All admit this to be one of the penitential Psalms. See introductory remarks on Ps. vi. That David wrote it is claimed in the title, asserted in Rom. iv. 6, and generally admitted.

Scott and Clarke agree in giving the same date, B. C. 1034, though Clarke thinks it somewhat older than Psalm li., while Scott and Tholuck suppose it later. In this opinion they are probably correct. When David wrote the li. God had not *restored to him the joy of his salvation.* In this it is evident he was enjoying a sweet sense of God's favor. This composition clearly refers to the great error of David's life. The Scriptures declare his very great rectitude of character and conduct with that one exception, 1 Kings xv. 5. The matter of Uriah was the only one in which David seems to have showed a reluctance to acknowledge the truth. The contents of the Psalm quite agree with this view. Hengstenberg: "Most commentators suppose that David composed this Psalm when he obtained forgiveness from God after his adultery with Bathsheba, and the death of Uriah, to which that sin led. The correctness of this view can scarcely be called in question."

Many difficulties have been urged against the evangelical view of this composition; but each of them seems to be based in ignorance of the nature of true experimental religion. A minute consideration of them all would not be profitable. Some of them may be noticed hereafter. The only name of God used in the Psalm is *Jehovah,* on which see on Ps. i. 2. On *Selah* see Introduction, § 15.

1. *Blessed* is he whose *transgression* is *forgiven. Blessed,* as in Ps. i. 1, on which see. O the blessednesses—a rich variety of happinesses. *Transgression,* elsewhere *sin, rebellion, trespass,* but commonly as here. The Septuagint has it in the plural, *transgressions. Forgiven,* in verse 5 in another form *forgavest,* literally, *lifted up, borne away.* If this is so, the language must have been well understood by a pious Jew, who annually saw the service of the scape-goat solemnly performed; one goat being slain and the other led away to a land uninhabited. Whose *sin* is *covered.* All the ancient versions, except the Chaldee, read *sins* not sin. *Sin,* so commonly; once *sin-offering;* cognate to the word so often rendered *sin* and *sin-offering.* The Septuagint uses the word commonly rendered *sin* in the New Testament. *Covered,* the same as is in verse 5 rendered *hid.* This is the verb used in Deut. xxiii. 13, from which Usher supposes the figure of *covering sin* is derived. Yet in Ex. xv. 10, it is applied to Pharaoh and his hosts who were *covered* in the Red sea. It is also applied to the act of filial piety performed by the sons of Noah, when they *covered* his nakedness, Gen. ix. 23. In fact the word seems to be used to describe any act of effectual hiding.

2. *Blessed* is *the man unto whom the* Lord *imputeth not iniquity. Blessed,* the same word as in verse 1. The Chaldee has *son of man,* and puts the verb in the future *will*

not impute; as do also the Septuagint, Ethiopic, Syriac, Venema, Jebb and Alexander. The Arabic and Vulgate use the preterite. Calvin, Amesius, Ainsworth, Edwards, Piscator, Fabritius and Hengstenberg have the present, *imputeth.* The Hebrew is future; but see Introduction, § 6. Our version gives the sense. The word rendered *impute* first denotes the *reckoning, counting,* or imputing to men that which is supposed to be properly their own. Thus in Gen. xxxviii. 15; 1 Sam. i. 13; 2 Sam. xix. 19; "When he saw her he *thought* her to be an harlot;" "Eli *thought* that she had been drunken;" "Let not my Lord *impute* iniquity unto me." The word is used in the same sense in Lev. xvii. 4; Neh. xiii. 13; and elsewhere. It has this proper signification here. Then it signifies that there is reckoned, counted, imputed to one something, which did not belong to him previous to such reckoning or imputation. So it is used in Num. xviii. 27, "And this your heave-offering shall be *reckoned* unto you, as though it were the corn of the threshing-floor, and as the fulness of the wine-press." See also Lam. iv. 2, and many other places. In the first case we regard and treat persons according to what they personally are; in the second, according to what they relatively are. To impute sin in the first sense "is to charge guilt upon the guilty in a judicial way, with a view to his being punished for it." To impute sin in the second sense is to hold one liable in law for the acts of his representative. The doctrine of the Old and New Testaments on this point is the same. Thus Paul prayed that the sin of those who had deserted him, might not be laid to their charge, 2 Tim. iv. 16. Here we have the word in its first sense. And in Phil. 18, we have it in its second sense: "If he hath wronged thee, or oweth thee aught, put that on my account." In all these cases the Hebrew and Greek words are those we render *impute.* God may and does charge upon the guilty their own sins; he may and does impute to Adam's posterity the sin of their federal head; he did impute to Christ the sins of his people; and he may and does impute to believers the righteousness of Christ. In all these cases the Scripture is clear and the testimony and teaching of orthodox Christians is almost unvarying. The clause under consideration speaks of the *non-imputation* of sin. To *impute iniquity* is to charge iniquity in condemnation, and to act accordingly. *Not to impute* sin is just the opposite. It is to remit the offence, pardon, forgive, absolve the sinner, cast his sins behind the back so as not to see them, bury them in the sea, remove them out of sight, blot them out, so that they rise not in judgment to condemn one. He, who receives such a favor receives another of great price, viz., purity of heart: *And in whose spirit* there is *no guile.* Septuagint: In whose mouth there is no guile. In Scripture *guile* is a name often given to sin. The reason is that sin is always *deceitful,* a *falsehood,* a *lie.* There is no *honest* sinning. If a transgressor is candid to men, he yet deceives himself, robs his own soul, robs God, lies to the Almighty and defrauds his Maker; or, in attempting to climb up some other way than through Christ, he is a thief and a robber. One must be regenerated before he can be "an Israelite in whom there is no guile." Clarke: In these two verses "*four* evils are mentioned: 1. *Transgression;* 2. *Sin;* 3. *Iniquity;* 4. *Guile.* The *first* signifies *passing over a boundary; doing what is prohibited.* The *second* signifies the *missing of a mark,* not doing what was commanded; but is often taken to express *sinfulness;* or sin in the nature, producing transgression in the life. The *third* signifies *what is turned out of its course* or *situation;*—anything *morally distorted* or *perverted. Iniquity,* what is contrary to *equity* or justice. The *fourth* signifies *fraud, deceit, guile,* etc. To remove these evils, *three* acts are mentioned:—*Forgiving, covering,* and *not imputing.* 1. TRANSGRESSION must be *forgiven,* borne away, *i. e.,* by a vicarious sacrifice; for *bearing away sin* always implies this. 2. SIN must be *covered,* hidden from the sight. It is odious and abominable, and must be put out of sight. 3. INIQUITY, what is *perverse* or *disturbed,* must not be *imputed,* must *not* be *reckoned to his account.* 4. GUILE must be annihilated from the soul." In Rom. iv. 6–10 we have an inspired interpretation of the first three clauses of vv. 1, 2: "Even as David also describeth the blessedness of the man unto whom God imputeth righteousness without works, *saying*, [Paul quotes the Septuagint] Blessed are they whose iniquities are forgiven, and whose sins are covered. Blessed is the man to whom the Lord will not impute sin. *Cometh* this blessedness then upon the circumcision *only*, or upon the uncircumcision also? For we say that faith was reckoned to Abraham for righteousness. How was it then reckoned? when he was in circumcision, or in uncircumcision? Not in circumcision but in uncircumcision." These words taken in their connection clearly show: 1. That the forgiveness of sin and the justification of the believer are never separated; that the non-imputation of sin is always accompanied by the *imputation of righteousness without works*, which is *Christ's righteousness*. 2. Under every dispensation the method of justification is the same whether Abraham, David or a believer under the Gospel is concerned. 3. Justification in the full sense of the term, including both pardon and acceptance, lies at the foundation of all real *blessedness* to man. 4. Man, sinner as he is, may be received, regarded and treated as if he were righteous. 5. In justification, rites and ceremonies, even though they be instituted by God, do not effect our justification. Abraham was justified before his circumcision.

Having stated the blessedness of justification, David proceeds to narrate his own behaviour and experience respecting the commission and confession of sin.

3. *When I kept silence, my bones waxed old through my roaring all the day long.* For *waxed old*, others have *wasted, wasted away, wore away, consumed, decayed.* For roaring Boothroyd has *pangs;* others, *crying. Kept silence, i. e.*, before God, or refrained from due confession. Diodati: "When I have not disburdened my conscience by a sincere confession of my sins to God, and have not with prayer sought the true means to obtain grace;" see v. 5. Some think that for eighteen months, all agree that for several months after David's first great wrong to Uriah he made even to God no full ingenuous confession of his sin. The child, which was the fruit of adultery, was born before Nathan visited David, 2 Sam. xi. 27; xii. 14. David had too much conscience to live easily under the burden of such sins; but as yet he had too little humility to confess the whole truth. He *kept silence*, but he was filled with tumults and perturbations. He had conscience of sin, which he believed to be unpardoned; but he was not roused to cry for forgiveness. Remorse was gnawing at his vitals. His spirits ran low by means of his disquietness. His sin was from the first fearfully aggravated, and David was too enlightened not to have painful apprehensions. Yet he stood out against all these. Doubtless he saw that when his people should by his own acknowledgment regard him as an adulterer and a murderer, it would naturally and terribly weaken the attachment of the pious to a dynasty headed by so great an offender. A thousand courses of false reasoning were doubtless suggested to him. Yet this concealment did not bring relief. Sins never grow out of date. There is no statute of limitation for crimes either at God's bar, or at the bar of conscience. And so his *bones waxed old*, wasted away, grew weak. His health threatened to fail him quite. Appetite failed. He forgot to take food. God held his eyes waking. Dry, profitless grief was drinking up his blood and spirits. His disquietness was terrible. It was like the roaring of a hunting lion, or of a ranging bear, or of a wild bull caught in a net. *Roaring*, almost uniformly used in Scripture to describe the roaring of *lions* hunting their prey, or figuratively of terrible warriors whose near approach strikes terror like the roar of a lion, or lastly the distress of a soul greatly disquieted, Job iii. 24; iv. 10; Ps. xxii. 1; Isa. v. 29; Ezek. xix. 7; Zech. xi. 3. There seems to be no warrant for Patrick's opinion that the allusion is to a *wounded* lion. This grief was *all the day long, continually*, or

every day. Such distress had its judicial cause in his sins, but its effectual cause in divine providence and the power of God's Spirit:

4. *For day and night thy hand was heavy upon me.* Chaldee: For day and night thy stroke grew heavier upon me. The other ancient versions mainly agree with the English. Nor do the modern versions materially vary. God's *hand* was manifested in withholding wonted comforts of mind, and in letting loose an angry conscience. Such a state of things might well produce the most distressing effects. *My moisture is turned into the drought of summer.* *Moisture,* life-blood, vital moisture, freshness. Grief, especially such as that begotten by remorse, or by a sense of being forsaken of God, has always been noted for drying up the juices of the animal system, Ps. xxii. 15. *The drought of summer* was a strong figure in Judea, where there were but two rainy seasons in the year, and the summer was long, and hot, and dry. Respecting the summer of Palestine, Dr. Russell says: "From the end of May, if not sooner, not so much as one refreshing shower falls, and scarce a friendly cloud appears to shelter from the excessive heat of the sun till about the middle of September; the verdure of spring fades before the middle of May; and before the end of that month the whole country puts on so parched and barren an aspect, that one would scarce think it capable of producing anything, there being but very few plants which have vigor enough to resist the extreme heat." The *drought of summer* is therefore a very strong expression. There is nothing in the Hebrew to warrant the form of some ancient versions: I am turned in my anguish, whilst the thorn is fastened.

5. *I acknowledged my sin unto thee, and mine iniquity have I not hid.* The Arabic puts the first of these verbs in the present, and the second in the preterite. Fry puts both in the present. The Septuagint, Syriac, Ethiopic and Vulgate put both in the past tense. Amesius puts both in the future. The Chaldee, Venema, Jebb and Alexander follow the Hebrew and put the first verb in the future, and the second in the preterite. Those who think we have no right to anticipate *I said,* may well regard the common version as probably the best. But we have a right to supply *I said* at the beginning of the verse and then the Hebrew tenses should be followed. *Acknowledged,* literally *caused to know.* One ingenuous acknowledgment goes farther to secure peace of mind than all false disguises. When we know that we deal honestly with God and with our own consciences, we may safely hope that Jehovah will deal mercifully with us through Jesus Christ. *Sin,* nearly the same word and of the same signification as that so rendered in v. 1. *Hid,* in v. 1, *covered.* *Iniquity,* so rendered in v. 1. All this acknowledgement was made in accordance with a purpose. *I said, I will confess my transgressions unto the* LORD. *Confess,* it includes confession of sin and solemn worship and adoration with thanksgiving, 1 Kings viii. 33, 35; 2 Chron. vi. 24, 26; Ps. xxx. 12; Isa. xii. 1. *And thou forgavest the iniquity of my sin.* *Forgavest, iniquity, sin,* as in previous clauses. Chaldee: Thou didst remit the impiety of my sin forever; Arabic: Thou forgavest to me the iniquity of my heart; Syriac: Thou remittest to me all my sins; Vulgate and Doway: Thou hast forgiven the wickedness of my sin; Edwards: And so thou forgavest my heinous sin; Alexander: And thou didst take away the guilt of my sin.

6. *For this shall every one that is godly pray unto thee in a time when thou mayest be found.* In lieu of the last clause several propose such words as these, acceptable time, seasonable time, time of finding, right time for finding.

For this evidently refers to what went before, viz., David's success in confession and prayer as recorded in v. 5. *Godly,* the same word is elsewhere rendered *holy, merciful, good,* in the plural often *saints,* Deut. xxxiii. 8; 2 Sam. xxii. 26; Mic. vii. 2; Ps. xxx. 4; xxxi. 23. *Pray,* so rendered in Ps. v. 2; lxxii. 15. *Mayest be found,* points to prayer *seasonably* offered, viz.: in the day of grace. Nor shall his prayer be unavailing: *Surely in the floods of great waters they shall not come nigh unto him.* From the time of the deluge *floods* of *great waters* fitly described overwhelming calamities. When they abound, the devout child of God shall have a high rock and shall be untouched. This interpretation agrees with the context, is natural, and is supported by the analogy of Scripture teaching. There is no good cause for searching out a recondite meaning when this is so obvious, and so well sustained. On him, whose sins are pardoned, overwhelming calamities shall have no power. The reason is given:

7. *Thou* art *my hiding place.* No calamities sweeping over the land, no fierceness and lawlessness of men can reach him, whose refuge is Jehovah. The punctuation of the next two clauses varies considerably. *Thou shalt preserve me from trouble; thou shalt compass me about with songs of deliverance.* Chaldee: Thou shalt preserve me from tribulation, with songs of redemption thou shalt encompass me; Syriac: Thou, preserve me, and from my enemies free me, encompass me with glory and salvation. With the common version virtually agree the church of England, Calvin, Venema, Amesius, Ainsworth, Jebb and Alexander. A few, as Edwards and Hengstenberg, prefer the present tense. There is no good reason for materially varying from the common version, which is fully sustained by the Hebrew. *Shalt preserve,* see on Ps. xii. 7; xxv. 10, 21. *Trouble,* it is specially such as comes from the conduct of enemies. Sometimes in the singular it is rendered *enemy, adversary:* and often in the plural *enemies, adversaries.* See on Ps. iii. 1; iv. 1. *Compass, surround, come round about,* sometimes in a good and sometimes in a bad sense. We had it in Ps. xvii. 11; xviii. 5; xxii. 12, 16. It here expresses the *abundance* and the *perfection* of the deliverance wrought. Scott: "The Psalmist daily received so many mercies, which he celebrated with the songs of deliverance, that he was wholly compassed about with them."

8. *I will instruct thee and teach thee in the way which thou shalt go: I will guide thee with mine eye.* The speaker in this place, some think, is God, who in response to the strong faith and joyful hope previously expressed gives this assurance. The Chaldee is striking: I will give thee understanding and will teach thee: in the way in which thou shalt walk I will counsel thee, and I will set mine eye upon thee for good. This is indeed paraphrase; but it is very good; we have none better. The first verb *instruct* closely corresponds with *Maschil* in the title of the Psalm and evidently alludes to it. The whole verse is a promise of divine guidance. That the eighth verse contains the words of God is the opinion of Ainsworth, Morison, Fry, Horsley and Clarke. Tholuck regards it as an oracular utterance like that of Ps. xl. 4. Horne regards the Redeemer as the speaker. Scott and Pool allow that either God or David may be the speaker, yet Pool evidently inclines to the latter view. But Calvin, Diodati, Patrick, Dodd, Mudge, Henry, Slade, Hengstenberg, Alexander and others think David is certainly the speaker here. The objection urged to making God the speaker is that it quite breaks the connection and allows the introduction of another, when David himself is desirous of giving instruction from his own experience. It must be admitted that there is force in the statement. Yet many undeniable instances might be found where the connection is, without any notice, interrupted by the introduction of another speaker. If the phrase *guide thee with mine eye* be understood as meaning no more than guiding by counsel drawn from experience and exercised with watchfulness, then is there nothing in v. 8, which may not be attributed to David. Hengstenberg regards Ps. li. 13, as parallel to this verse. Those, who thus expound this verse, regard the rest of the Psalm as pointing out the way in which David would

warn us to go. But the remaining verses give the same lessons whether we regard God or David as the speaker. The first lesson respects docility:

9. *Be ye not as the horse*, or *as the mule*, which *have no understanding*. Ancient and modern versions are usually agreed in giving the sense of these words: Be not stubborn, untractable. Show that you have mind, and know things beyond the brutes. The residue of the verse has caused much diversity: *Whose mouth must be held in with bit and bridle, lest they come near unto thee.* It is generally agreed that the bit and bridle, or curb and rein, are for controlling these animals. To this many add the idea of ornament. But what is the meaning of *Lest they come near unto thee?* Calvin has, Lest they kick against thee; Horsley: Be ye not like a horse or a mule which no man can govern with a bridle; but the muzzle must compress his jaws, that he fall not upon thee. The original is elliptical and obscure. The last clause is literally, Not to come to thee, or There is not a coming to thee. Hammond's remarks are just and forcible: "Our English, that renders *lest they come near unto thee*, supposeth, without reason, that the use of the bridle is to keep the horse and mule from doing violence to thee, as if they were bears and tigers, and the like ravenous beasts. The true use is quite the contrary, to make them come to thee, or go, or turn the way that thou wouldest have them; and their not doing so is the effect of their obstinacy and want of managery; and that is it wherein we are forbidden to be like them." Having called them to docility and a right temper, he gives the lessons promised:

10. *Many sorrows* shall be *to the wicked*. In the Hebrew the verb is wanting. Many sorrows always have been, now are, and ever shall be to them. Calvin and Jebb have *shall be*. The Chaldee, Arabic, Syriac, church of England, Venema, Amesius, Ainsworth, Edwards, Fry, Hengstenberg and Alexander supply a verb in the present tense, *are*, or *remain*. For *sorrows* in some versions we find *plagues, pains, galling pains, wounds*. The word is here found first in the Psalter. It is also in Ps. xxxviii. 17; lxix. 26; Jer. li. 8. *Wicked*, in Ps. i. and often *ungodly*. Such shall have sorrows: *But he that trusteth in the* LORD, *mercy shall compass him about.* *Trusteth*, as in Ps. iv. 5; ix. 10; xxii. 4. *Mercy*, rendered *goodness, kindness, loving-kindness*, Ps. v. 7; vi. 4; xxxi. 7, 16, 21. The aim of the verse is a double contrast *first*, between *men*, one *wicked*, the other *confiding in Jehovah*; secondly, between the *portions* of such, one having *many sorrows*, the other having *mercy compassing* him. The mercy of the Lord puts a wall of fire around the righteous, a cloud of goodness over him, a bow of promise before him. The God of mercy is his God. Very fittingly does the Psalm close with the exhortation:

11. *Be glad in the* LORD *and rejoice, ye righteous; and shout for joy, all* ye that are *upright in heart*. We have here three verbs expressive of holy mirth. *Be glad, rejoice, shout* for joy. They are rendered be glad, exult, glory; rejoice, exult, sing for joy. They express the varied emotions and manifestations of joy, the calmest and the most exultant. The command thus to rejoice is given to the *righteous* and to the *upright in heart*. We had the first of these terms in Ps. i. 5, 6; the second, in Ps. vii. 10. They include the two chief characteristics of good men, who are *just*, justified, righteous, and *upright*, honest, sincere, earnest, holy in heart. *All* the saints have cause for these rejoicings.

DOCTRINAL AND PRACTICAL REMARKS.

1. To deny our sinfulness is to deny our need of pardon, and to cut off all hope of salvation and of eternal happiness. Blessedness does not begin till pardon is received, v. 1, and an offer of pardon to the innocent is an insult.

2. Though the Bible is a sober book, it uses a variety of terms and phrases respecting sin, all of which are improper unless sin is a dreadful evil. In Ex. xxxiv. 7,

we have *iniquity, transgression* and *sin.* Here we have the same and in addition *guile*, vv. 1, 2. Elsewhere other names and phrases mark it as *rebellion, revolt, wickedness,* a *horrible thing, folly, madness,* a *lie, contempt of God, vileness, desperation.* It discards all the principles of reason. It defies all the attributes of God. Left to itself it is incorrigible. It is blind to all that is glorious and terrible. It counts ruin a trifle, and puts the creature before the Creator. It makes its victims esteem God such an one as themselves. It forgets the infinite holiness of him, in whose eyes the heavens are not pure and the stars are not clean. God's indignation strikes no just and lasting terror into the stupid souls of wicked men, myriads of whom suppose the wrath of heaven may be averted by rites, the fires of hell extinguished by tears, and peace secured by self-inflicted tortures. Oh that all would " learn, 1, That sin draweth on a debt which no man can satisfy, such a debt as a man must perish, if it be not *forgiven.* 2. That sin is a filthiness which neither God can behold, without abominating the sinner, nor the guilty conscience can look upon without horror except it *be covered.* 3. That sin draweth on a guiltiness which may draw men to damnation if it shall be *imputed.* 4. That there is no justification of a sinner before God by his good works."

3. With the Lord is mercy and with him is plenteous redemption. To the Lord our God belong mercies and *forgivenesses.* It is his glory and his delight to *forgive transgressions, cover sin,* and not *impute iniquity,* vv. 1, 2. He still gives knowledge of salvation unto his people, Luke i. 77. He has exalted his Son a Prince and a Saviour to grant repentance and remission of sins unto Israel, Acts v. 31. Salvation is possible. To believers it is certain.

4. God's salvation is not partial. He not only pardons, he accepts as righteous. He does *not impute iniquity,* he does *impute righteousness without works,* vv. 1, 2 ; Rom. iv. 6–8. He not only saves from wrath, but he gives *a right* to the tree of life. The question is not between Christ's righteousness and our own, for we have none. All our righteousnesses are as filthy rags. The question for our sinful race is merely between Christ's righteousness and damnation. Without his merits, we perish. Nor can we have his righteousness otherwise than by its being set to our account. It is not imparted. It is imputed. We are invested with it. It is our linen white and clean. It is our glorious wedding garment.

5. Justification and sanctification are distinguishable but not separable. Where one exists, the other is not wanting. Where sin is *forgiven, guile* is banished, vv. 1, 2. Compare Rom. viii. 1. He, who believes that one may have God's favor and not his image also, that one may be under the smiles of heaven while he loves sin, and that God has no sentence of wrath against one who loves deceit, is already undone. Nothing but a miracle of mercy, opening his eyes, removing his deceptions, and converting his soul to God, will save him from a rueful eternity.

6. Of all the forms of sin none is more congenial with its nature than *guile, deceit, falsehood,* a *lie,* v. 2. Yet to deceive God is impossible ; to deceive our fellow-men can do us no permanent good ; and to deceive ourselves will ruin us. Berleberg Bible: " As children imagine that they are not seen, when they put their hands upon their eyes, and cover them so that they themselves see no one, in like manner, men act with equal folly, in supposing that their sins and crimes, when concealed from themselves, are also concealed from the all-seeing eye of God."

7. None have more need of thorough experience in religion than those, who would teach others, vv. 1–4.

8. Vital piety has a deadly foe in carnal security. It hinders all the good we might otherwise gain. It makes sinners and hypocrites cry, Peace and Safety, when destruction is at the door. It causes the truly pious to settle on their lees, and rest

satisfied when their state is deplorable.   Men may have some conscience of sin and yet deal treacherously with themselves and with God.   Those, who think themselves well, seek no remedies.

9. Nor is carnal security less a foe to solid peace.   It strengthens delusions, which in the end only heighten misery.   Even in their progress they commonly torment. Calvin: "It often happens that those are tortured with the sharpest grief, who gnaw the bit, and inwardly devour their sorrow, and keep it enclosed, and shut up within, without discovering it, although afterwards they are seized as with sudden madness, and the force of their grief bursts forth with the greater impetus the longer it has been restrained."   Arnd: "Melancholy arising from Sin consumes away the body, reduces it to a wretched condition, and gives rise to a secret weeping at heart, so that there is constantly a howling."

10. The distinction between the judicial and fatherly forgiveness of God is sound and Scriptural.   Immediately upon David's saying to Nathan, "I have sinned against the Lord; Nathan said unto David, The Lord also hath put away thy sin." Yet after this David wrote Psalm li. and had the experience here described in v. 3–5.   Tholuck: "The prophet pronounced forgiveness; but it was a different thing for David to appropriate and rejoice in it before the Lord."

11. Sin is a dreadful entanglement.   One sin leads to another, evil begetting evil without end, unless the grace of God steps in to break the fearful succession.   David looked—lusted—committed adultery—resorted to artifice—stained his soul with innocent blood—for a long time virtually justified himself—grew obstinate and irritable and would soon have plunged into ruin, had not the love of God sought and humbled him.

12. The sorrows of unpardoned sin may at any moment become intolerable, wasting our health and sinking us into despondency and even despair, vv. 3, 4.   No fire burns like the wrath of God dropped into a guilty conscience.   No hurts are so fearful as those of a spirit wounded by transgression.

13. The Scriptural doctrine of confession of sin is of great importance and holds a prominent place in both Testaments, vv. 3–5.   The confession here mentioned is not *auricular to a priest*, so much extolled by Romanists; nor that mutual confession of infirmities commended by an Apostle, James v. 16; nor acknowledgments of wrongs done to a brother, Luke xvii. 3, 4; but that confession which is due to God alone as Lord of conscience and final Judge.   On this the Scriptures of the Old and New Testaments are clear and harmonious, Pr. xxviii. 13; 1 John i. 8–10.   All godly confession of sin is full, ingenuous, humble, penitent.   Henry: "Those, that would have the comfort of the pardon of their sins, must take shame to themselves by a penitent confession of them."   That such confession is necessary is clear, 1, from the command of God; 2, from the example of good men; 3, from the nature of the case, no man being ready to forsake sin, until he is prepared to confess it; and no man being in a mood to acknowledge the mercy of pardon for a sin, whose heinousness he is not ready to admit.

14. The excellency of confession consists not in any merit that is in it as some vainly dream, but as it is an act demanded by the simple truth in the case, and as it makes God's gracious pardon a welcome gift.   The connection between confession and pardon is close and intimate.   We cannot love and cherish God's enemies, and love and fear him at the same time.   God is more ready to forgive sin than we are to forsake it, or confess it, v. 5.

15. To everything there is a season.   Especially is there a time to turn to the Lord by confession and prayer.   The wise call upon God when there is a possibility

of finding him, v. 6. Isa. lv. 6. There will be praying at the judgment day and in hell, but it will be too late. God will not then hear.

16. If we have had an experience of God's methods of dealing with souls, we should first profit by it ourselves, and then modestly let it be known that others may avoid our errors, and avail themselves of the encouragements afforded by our success at the mercy-seat, v. 6. One right act may have a very wide scope. Praying people are safe in times of the most overwhelming calamities. The floods of great waters shall not come nigh unto them.

17. Dickson: "Experience of God's mercies bygone should fasten resolution to make use of faith hereafter in all troubles. After one trouble the godly should prepare for another, after one delivery expect another," v. 7.

18. Whether God or his servants invite us to be instructed, we should attend unto the things which are spoken for our learning, v. 8.

19. Henry: "Those are best able to teach others the grace of God, who have themselves had the experience of it; and those who are themselves taught of God, ought to *tell* others *what he has done for their souls*," v. 8.

20. In any pursuit in life the right temper is of great importance; but in receiving instruction a wrong temper is fatal. He, whose only resemblance to the horse consists in his restifness, and he, who resembles the mule only in his obstinacy, will make no progress in learning the lessons of salvation. Submission, docility, quietness are essential. Sin has no worse effect on man's character than in gendering that dreadful perverseness, which precludes amendment.

21. Our headlong and headstrong dispositions will in some way meet a terrible check. Berleberg Bible: "If we do not consent to serve God *willingly*, we *must* serve him in the long run whether we will or not. He, who runs away from God's willing service, falls into his compulsory service. On this account the wise Stoic prayed, 'Lead me, O God, the way which thou hast chosen: and if I *will* not, nothing is better than that I be compelled.' Recourse is not had to bit and bridle, unless we will not become wise by gentler means. God employs these for the purpose of delivering us from destroying ourselves."

22. The miseries of the unconverted are inconceivably dreadful. Over them depravity reigns; guilt loads their souls with its fiery chains; ignorance blinds their minds; and they have no might to do good. God, the stars and all nature will yet fight against the impenitent. Many sorrows shall be to the wicked, v. 10. The connection between sin and misery is closer than that between soul and body—it is inseparable. Though the wicked exalt himself as the eagle, and though he set his nest among the stars, thence will God bring him down. Sinners have to bear all their troubles alone. They know not God. They have no access to the mercy-seat. The only remedy for human woe is found in Christ. Because sinners reject him, they have nothing but wretchedness left them. The righteous get good out of all the evil that befalls them; but the wicked so pervert everything as to get evil out of all the good sent them.

23. Both Testaments rightly make it the duty of God's servants to be filled with holy joy, even in times of trial, bereavement and tribulation, v. 10. They have good cause of exultation. Mercy compasses them about.

24. If the righteous may so rejoice even to exultation, while they are yet in the vale of sorrow and on the battle-field of life, what will not their rejoicings be when the war shall be ended, and God himself shall come forth to bless them?

25. Even in this life real blessedness is possible, vv. 1, 11. It is all laid in the pardon of sin, and in a free justification. If guilt makes men cowards, pardon and acceptance make them intrepid. If guilt poisons every cup of joy, justification

sweetens every cup of anguish. If guilt makes death the king of terrors, an interest in Christ makes the believer shout, "Death is swallowed up in victory." If guilt shall make the wicked in the last day cry to the rocks and to the mountains to fall on them and cover them from the face of him that sitteth on the throne and from the wrath of the Lamb, the *right*, which believers have to the tree of life, shall give them boldness in the day of judgment. The sinner saved by grace has all things and abounds, because he has Christ for his sacrifice and Christ for his righteousness. Bouchier: "The criminal may be pardoned; but he is returned into a scorning world with a tainted name and a ruined character. He is released from the temporal penalty of his guilt to seek shelter and subsistence where he may, compelled almost to return to the former associates of his sin, as the only beings who will admit him into their brotherhood without a sneer or a reproach. No friendly voice is by his side to instruct and teach him in the way he should go, no eye looks kindly on him to guide and direct him." Worse than all he has no peace within, no change of heart. Left to himself he is as vile as ever he was. But the sinner, who has fled to Jesus, finds all he needs; grace, friends, a home, eternal oblivion of his past crimes, and assurance of everlasting victory over all his foes. O how amazing is the Gospel Plan.

26. And now, dear reader, will you accept the pardon offered, the salvation provided? Now is your time. If out of Christ, this may be your last call to salvation. Why will you die? How can you escape if you neglect so great salvation? What will you say, when God shall punish you? Will you confess your sin, accept Christ and be saved? WILL YOU?

PSALM XXXIII.

1 Rejoice in the LORD, O ye righteous: *for* praise is comely to the upright.

2 Praise the LORD with harp: sing unto him with the psaltery *and* an instrument of ten strings.

3 Sing unto him a new song; play skilfully with a loud noise.

4 For the word of the LORD *is* right; and all his works *are done* in truth.

5 He loveth righteousness and judgment: the earth is full of the goodness of the LORD.

6 By the word of the LORD were the heavens made; and all the host of them by the breath of his mouth.

7 He gathereth the waters of the sea together as a heap: he layeth up the depth in storehouses.

8 Let all the earth fear the LORD: let all the inhabitants of the world stand in awe of him.

9 For he spake, and it was *done;* he commanded, and it stood fast.

10 The LORD bringeth the counsel of the heathen to nought: he maketh the devices of the people of none effect.

11 The counsel of the LORD standeth for ever, the thoughts of his heart to all generations.

12 Blessed *is* the nation whose God *is* the LORD; *and* the people *whom* he hath chosen for his own inheritance.

13 The LORD looketh from heaven; he beholdeth all the sons of men.

14 From the place of his habitation he looketh upon all the inhabitants of the earth.

15 He fashioneth their hearts alike; he considereth all their works.

16 There is no king saved by the multitude of a host: a mighty man is not delivered by much strength.

17 A horse *is* a vain thing for safety; neither shall he deliver *any* by his great strength.

18 Behold, the eye of the LORD *is* upon them that fear him, upon them that hope in his mercy·

19 To deliver their soul from death, and to keep them alive in famine.

20 Our soul waiteth for the LORD: he *is* our help and our shield.

21 For our heart shall rejoice in him, because we have trusted in his holy name.

22 Let thy mercy, O LORD, be upon us, according as we hope in thee.

IN the Hebrew this Psalm has no title. The inscriptions given it by several of the ancient versions are without authority. "In eight of Kennicott's MSS. this Psalm is written as part of the preceding." Venema says: "I have joined these two Psalms together because the latter is not only subordinate to the former, but because, as Lyra testifies, some suppose that they are to be taken as one. This is plain partly in the want of a title in Ps. xxxiii. and partly from the obvious connection of the last verse of Ps. xxxii. with the subject of this ode." Yet the last verse of Ps. xxxii. is to it a very fit termination; and the first clause of v. 1 is as fit a heading to Ps. xxxiii. But few agree with Venema, and we shall not spend more time on the matter. We have already considered Psalms i. ii. and x. neither of which has a title.

The Septuagint, Arabic, Ethiopic and Vulgate ascribe this Psalm to David. So also do the great mass of learned men. This may be correct. There is nothing in the style to forbid the supposition. The writer was but the penman of the Holy Ghost.

Commentators have not agreed on the occasion on which the Psalm was written. It contains no marks pointing out any such. The Psalm was well suited to many periods of the ancient church. From vv. 7, 9, 10, 15, 16, 18, Dodd thinks it was probably composed by David to celebrate the deliverance of Israel at the Red sea, and God's conduct of his people through the wilderness. Perhaps more unite in supposing that it celebrates the wisdom, power and goodness of God in creation and providence than in any other one view. The names of the Most High in this song are *Jehovah* LORD and *Elohim God*, on which see on Ps. i. 2; iii. 2. Scott dates it B. C. 1034; Clarke gives no date. Amyrald: "The style is pleasing, flowing, measured, without any poetical digressions or figures, at least of such a kind as to occasion any difficulty."

1. *Rejoice in the Lord, O ye righteous.* The translations of this clause vary only in the strength of the word used for *rejoice*, as sing praises before the Lord, praise him, leap for joy, exult. Alexander: "The Hebrew verb, according to the etymologists, originally means to dance for joy, and is therefore a very strong expression for the liveliest exultation." The summons is to the *righteous*, the *just*. The reason for thus rejoicing is: For *praise is comely for the upright.* Pious exultation, publicly expressed, with gratitude for mercies, *becomes* good men. If the upright refuse to praise the Lord, who shall extol him? *Comely*, seemly, desirable, beautiful. Calvin: "The real meaning is that there is no exercise in which they can be better employed." Praise is often commanded; to it amazing mercies summon all the saints; it is a great privilege, refreshing the heart, reviving the spirit and exciting others to the same blessed service. All the upright have countless reasons for praising God.

2. *Praise the Lord with harp: sing unto him with the psaltery* and *an instrument of ten strings.* The first verb is the same noticed in Ps. xxxii. 5, and there and elsewhere rendered *confess.* When we acknowledge God's mercies, we oblige ourselves to the work of thanksgiving. The second verb *sing* is often rendered *sing praises.* We met it in Ps. vii. 17; ix. 2; xviii. 49. It occurs often. The first name here given to a musical instrument is uniformly rendered *harp;* the second, when it designates a musical instrument, is always rendered *psaltery,* except in few cases where it is *viol;* the third, when used on this subject is always rendered as here an instrument of ten strings. See Ps. xcii. 3; cxliv. 9. The *and* is not in the Hebrew, and some make the passage speak of but two instruments, the *psaltery* being of *ten strings* as they suppose. So Venema, Hammond, Edwards, Jebb, Hengstenberg and Alexander. But others fitly agree with our version; as Calvin, Ainsworth, Amesius. For *psaltery* some read *lute* or *lyre.* But the names of musical instruments in the Bible are the torment of translators and scholiasts. We do not certainly know the shape, size, or

power of any of them; though it is *generally* supposed that all those mentioned in this verse were *stringed* instruments.

3. *Sing unto him a new song.* This clause could hardly be rendered otherwise, if a decent respect should be paid to the Hebrew and the English. The verb *sing* and the noun *song* in both languages have the same origin. The only peculiarity in the clause arises from the word *new.* What does it mean? Some think the prophet says his themes are not sufficiently celebrated in any sacred ode of his time, and so he calls the *just* and the *upright* to unite in a song, with which they were not as yet familiar. Calvin regards *new* as equivalent to *rare* and *choice.* "It is no common song, therefore, which he exhorts them to sing, but a song corresponding to the magnificence of the subject." Hengstenberg: "A *new* song is a song which springs up from the heart." Compare Ps. xxxiii. 3; xcvi. 1; xcviii. 1; Rev. v. 9. The glory of God is new every morning. New mercies demand new praises. *Play skilfully with a loud noise.* Chaldee: Behave beautifully by singing in a joyful shout; church of England: Sing praises lustily unto him with a good courage; Calvin: Sing loudly with joyfulness; Venema: Play elegantly well with a loud noise; Amesius: Play in the best style with a loud noise; Edwards: Play skilfully, and sing with exalted voices; Hengstenberg: Play skilfully with shouts of joy; Alexander: "The import of the clause is substantially the same as that of the first: Render a strong and striking testimony to the praise and honor of God."

4. *For the word of the Lord is right.* Calvin supposes the term *word* here signifies *counsel* or *ordinance.* Alexander: "The *word* here meant is the word of promise;" Hengstenberg: "The Psalmist speaks of God's *truth* and *faithfulness;*" Pool makes it comprehend "all God's counsels and commands;" Gill, "the revealed word of God;" Tholuck, "God's promises." If there was any conceivable sense, in which the word of the Lord was not *right,* holy, just, good, wise, true and pure, our hope would perish. He who will not execute his threatenings, cannot be relied on to fulfil his promises. We cannot trust God in any respect, unless we can trust him in all respects. It does not diminish the force of the passage to make it express a universal truth. As is God's word, so are his doings. *And all his works* are done *in truth,* i. e., in sincerity, in faithfulness, with uniformity and stability. Jehovah's ways are not fickle, or changeable. We know what we are doing when we rely on him. In creation and providence are not found gins, and snares, and traps to catch the honest. Luther: "What the Lord has spoken, that he holds for certain. We cannot argue for a revelation, nor against the wiles of the devil, unless we believe God to be true." Even Balaam's Theology taught him, "God is not a man that he should lie, nor the son of man that he should repent: hath he said, and shall he not do it? or hath he spoken and shall he not make it good?" Num. xxiii. 19.

5. *He loveth righteousness and judgment.* God is one in essence and excellence. His character is a perfect whole. The Chaldee and Syriac quite agree with the English, but the Septuagint, Ethiopic, Arabic and Vulgate read, He loveth mercy and judgment. The first of these nouns never means *mercy,* but always *right, justice* or *righteousness.* Our version is supported by the church of England, Calvin, Venema, Amesius, Ainsworth, Edwards, Jebb, Fry, Hengstenberg and Alexander. For *judgment* some read *justice.* The extent, to which Jehovah carries his love of righteousness and judgment, is that he has never done a wrong, and never taken sides with a wrong doer. Jehovah could not cease to love righteousness and judgment without ceasing to be. Nor is the divine character and conduct marked by mere uprightness and purity. *The earth is full of the goodness of the Lord.* The *earth,* the same word generally so rendered. *Goodness,* in vv. 18, 22; Ps. v. 7; vi. 4; xxxii. 10, *mercy;* in Ps. xvii. 7, *loving-kindness.* In creation all things show God's *goodness,* his benevolence, and

moral excellence. In providence his *goodness, loving-kindness* and *mercy* appear. In redemption they shine forth illustriously. Creation and providence are here specially referred to. There is not a little sprinkling of the divine *goodness* in the world. The *earth* is *full* of it.

6. *By the word of the* LORD *were the heavens made; and all the host of them by the breath of his mouth.* Instead of *breath*, the Chaldee, Septuagint, Ethiopic, Arabic, Syriac, Vulgate, Calvin, Doway and Ainsworth have *spirit*. The *Word* of God is a name expressly given to Christ, John i. 1. Many suppose that the doctrine of the divine personality of the Son and Spirit of God is here taught. Scott: "Most of the ancient expositors, by the Word of the LORD, and the breath, or spirit of his mouth, understand the Son of God, the personal Word, and the Holy Spirit, as proceeding from the Father and the Son." It is as certain as inspiration can make it that the Son of God did create all things, John i. 3; Heb. i. 2. It is no less certain that the Holy Spirit is Creator, Gen. i. 2; Job xxvi. 13. So that those referred to by Scott teach no error, but that which is clearly supported by God's truth. The *heavens* is a name given to the universal frame of nature, the great part of which is above and around us. The *host of heaven* points to the sun, moon and stars, and to the angels.

7. *He gathereth the waters of the sea together as a heap.* For *gathereth* some read *gathered.* Perhaps this is better. The clause refers to the work of God stated in Gen. i. 9, 10, and continued in providence, Job xxxviii. 8–11; Jer. v. 22. *Heap* is the best rendering. See Ex. xiv. 22; xv. 8; Ps. lxxviii. 13. The notable thing to which our attention is called is that at the creation and ever since the water, which is the very emblem of instability (Gen. xlix. 4), God has gathered into seas and large bodies and keeps it there with such uniformity, as to make safe an abode even on the sea-shore. All this is the more wonderful as the seas are on the outside of a ball moving with a rapidity more than *two thousand times* greater than the ordinary speed attained on our best railroads. Nay, more, Jehovah puts away the waters in secret places: *He layeth up the depth in store-houses.* Some read in the cellars of the abysses; others, in treasures or treasuries. There are vast caverns in the earth filled with water, in Scripture called the fountains of the great deep, Gen. vii. 11. David tells us of the *paths of the sea;* and a remarkable scientific book of modern times begins thus: "There are rivers in the sea."

8. *Let all the earth fear the* LORD. He, who built and upholds the world, is surely a being of awful majesty and infinite glory. His worship must be reverential. His favor must be ineffable bliss. His wrath must be inconceivably dreadful. Worms may trifle with worms. But God is to be greatly feared and had in reverence. All the earth was made by him. His supporting hand withdrawn, all nature would fall headlong. There is good reason for fearing him. *Let all the inhabitants of the world stand in awe of him.* If the human mind can stand in awe at any time, or for any cause, it should be at thoughts of God, or in beholding the amazing displays of his adorable nature. *World*, parallel to *earth* in the first clause.

9. *For he spake, and it was* done; *he commanded, and it stood fast.* See on verse 6. It would be better to omit the word *done.* In sublimity of style this verse is nearly parallel to the words of Moses, Gen. i. 3, noted by Longinus and other critics as furnishing a very striking specimen of the sublime in writing.

10. *The* LORD *bringeth the counsel of the heathen to nought.* Some render the verb *dissipates.* Even as the sun scatters the mist, so when God sets himself against any plan, or *counsel*, of the wicked, there is presently nothing of it left. Calvin and Jebb have *scattereth;* Edwards, *hath baffled;* Alexander, *has annulled.* *Heathen*, also rendered *nations, Gentiles.* The ease, with which God annuls the counsels of men, is illustrated in the history of every age. The cackling of geese once defeated a wise plan for

destroying an empire. The First Cause of all things, holds all second causes in his hand, and can subvert any plot in a moment, and by means and instruments esteemed the most contemptible. *He maketh the devices of the people of none effect. Devices, inventions, thoughts. People,* in the plural number, *peoples,* parallel to *heathen,* in the preceding clause. *He maketh of none effect, breaketh, discourageth, disalloweth* the thoughts of the people. Under his rule nothing wicked can stand. The Septuagint, Ethiopic, Arabic and Vulgate add a clause to this verse, " and frustrates the counsels of princes." But this is not in the Hebrew, Chaldee, or Syriac. It is doubtless mere paraphrase.

11. *The counsel of the* LORD *standeth forever, the thoughts of his heart to all genera-tions. Standeth,* literally *shall stand.* Here *counsel* and *thoughts* precisely correspond to *counsel* and *devices* in v. 10. Many causes make human plans and purposes feeble and uncertain; infinite perfections make God's plans and counsels immovable and infallible. Because he is God, and all his enemies worms, he shall establish all his *thoughts. For ever,* to eternity.

12. *Blessed* is *the nation whose God* is *the* LORD. Blessed, as in Ps. i. 1; xxxii. 1. Such a nation shall be protected, guided, defended, have peace, prosperity, success, stability. If God is with a people, their cause is safe. He repeats: And [blessed is] *the people* whom *he hath chosen for his own inheritance.* Both clauses refer to the Jewish people, who alone at that time were as a nation acquainted with the true God, and in covenant with him. But it was to the pious portion of the nation that the richest blessings came. The church is here clearly spoken of. The truth asserted is of universal application.

13. *The* LORD *looketh from heaven; he beholdeth all the sons of men.*

14. *From the place of his habitation he looketh upon all the inhabitants of the earth.* All the ancient versions, together with Calvin, Jebb, Fry and Alexander put all these verbs in the preterite. Ainsworth, Venema, Amesius, Edwards and Hengstenberg with the English use the present tense. In both verses this seems best to suit the scope of the argument. The theme of the Psalmist is God's universal and particular providence over human affairs. This providence the wicked often deny, Ps. x. 11. But here we are told God does *see, look, behold all the sons of men, all the inhabitants of the earth.* Not one is above his ken, beneath his notice, or beyond his grasp. He looks not as an idle spectator, but as a Judge and Governor, *from the place of his habitation,* or as Calvin, *from the dwelling-place of his throne.* Compare Pr. xv. 3; Ecc. xii. 14.

15. *He fashioneth their hearts alike.* In rendering this clause there is some diversity. Jebb closely adheres to the English. He fashioned alike their hearts. Amesius most closely follows the Hebrew and probably gives the sense: He is equally the former of their heart. God is the maker of all hearts and turns them as he will. God's providence embraces the free acts of rational creatures. *He considereth all their works.* The Syriac has *considereth;* the other ancient versions, Calvin, Jebb and Fry, *under-standeth;* Venema, *distinctly understandeth;* Edwards, *observeth;* Boothroyd, *inspecteth;* Hengstenberg, *marketh.* Ainsworth: He discreetly attendeth unto all their works. Jehovah knows, searches, weighs, considers all that men think, say or do. " Nothing in the circumstances of any of his creatures can remove them from the penetrating search of that eye which is as a flame of fire."

16. *There is no king saved by the multitude of a host.* In doctrine the passage is of the same import as that in Ps. xliv. 5–8. It has historic illustration in 1 Sam. xiv. 4–23; 1 Kings xx. 20, 21; 2 Chron. xiv. 9–17. Modern history is full of remarkable instances showing the same truth. The reason, why numbers count nothing as against God and his providence, is that all creatures, if left to themselves, are foolish and

powerless. There is no proportion between all finite force and skill on the one hand, and infinite wisdom and energy on the other. Even when a cause is good and its friends are successful, they are so by the blessing of the Lord. It is added: *A mighty man is not delivered by much strength.* For *mighty man* many read *giant*. *Strength* as in Ps. xxii. 15; xxxi. 10; also rendered *force, might, power.* Even good men are not saved by inherent strength, independently of God. But human power arrayed against God's plans and authority is like stubble before the flame. The strongest man is no more than the weakest; the mightiest army, if arrayed against Omnipotence, is no more than a squad.

17. *A horse is a vain thing for safety; neither shall he deliver any by his great strength.* Syriac: Deceitful is the safety of a horse, nor by the abundance of his strength shall he rescue his rider. The English closely adheres to the Hebrew, except that for *vain thing*, the original has *a lie*. The truth here taught is repeated in Pr. xxi. 31.

18. *Behold, the eye of the* LORD *is upon them that fear him, upon them that hope in his mercy; i. e.,* God's eye is upon them for good. He *looks* to them; he *has respect* to them, Isa. lxvi. 2; Gen. iv. 5, 6. He watches them day and night. Calvin: "A doubt might creep into the minds of the weak, whether God would extend this protection to every individual; but when the psalmist introduces him as keeping watch and ward, as it were, over the safety of the faithful, there is no reason why any one of them should tremble, or hesitate with himself a moment longer, since it is certain that God is present with him to assist him, provided he remain quietly under his providence." The objects of this tender care are described as both *fearing* and *hoping.* Upon such the eye of God is constantly set:

19. *To deliver their soul from death, and to keep them alive in famine.* "In him we live and move and have our being." Compare Acts xiv. 17. It is only through the mercy of God that earth is not covered with perpetual sterility, and stripped of all its inhabitants. But such is the divine goodness that in the greatest exigencies God's people may safely trust in him. He will either keep them alive by miracle as he did some of old, or by ordinary means as he commonly does, or he will take them to himself, thus at once setting them free from all troubles. God's goodness in time of scarcity has been wonderfully illustrated many a time, especially in days of persecution. See the histories of those times and the lives of martyrs and confessors. The result of all this teaching and experience is most happy.

20. *Our soul waiteth for the* LORD. *Waiting* on God implies a quiet and submissive spirit, a conscientious discharge of known duty, heartiness and earnestness of soul in expecting deliverance at the right time and in the right way. Sometimes it points to the pious believing expectation of a coming Messiah, Isa. xxv. 9; Luke ii. 25. Again it refers to his coming to effect any needed deliverance, Isa. viii. 17; Lam. iii. 26. Impatience is an enemy to waiting, Ps. xl. 1. Living in sin shows that we have no proper regard to God. Not to expect is to despise or despair. *Waiting* is one of the exercises of that *fear* and *hope,* mentioned in v. 19. The next clause shows that *waiting* is not a hopeless duty. *He* is *our help and our shield.* *Help,* as in Ps. xx. 2; in Ps. cxv. 9, 10, 11, as here, it is united with *shield.* On the shield and its use see Ps. iii. 3.

21. *For our heart shall rejoice in him, because we have trusted in his holy name.* Experience confirms everything taught in God's word; and all the trust of the pious leads to joy, giving them irrefragable proof of the truth of the religious system which they have embraced.

22. *Let thy mercy, O* LORD, *be upon us, according as we hope in thee.* Alexander: "The claim in reality amounts to a petition that as God had given the desire he

would fulfil it." Great faith brings great mercies; great hope shall issue in great deliverances.

DOCTRINAL AND PRACTICAL REMARKS.

1. *Rejoicing* in God must be a principal duty of pious men, v. 1; Ps. xxxii. 11; etc. Joy in the Lord is one of the bonds between the old and new dispensations, one of the bonds between the church militant and the church triumphant.

2. True joy in God has fit expression in devout praise, v. 1. "Is any merry, let him sing Psalms." Dickson: "There is no exercise more becoming the godly, than praising of God, whether we look to the object of the praise, which is God; or whether we look to their obligation above all people in the world; *for praise is comely to the upright.* And there is no exercise whereunto we have more need to be stirred up, than to praise; such is our dulness, and such is the excellency and necessity of the work."

3. The praises offered to God should be of the most spirited kind, v. 2. We should stir ourselves up to take hold on him. Henry: "Here is a good rule for this duty: 'Do it skilfully, and with a loud noise; let it have the bent both of head and heart; let it be done intelligently, and with a clear head; affectionately, and with a warm heart.'"

4. The second and third verses of this Psalm bring directly before us the subject of instrumental music. A few things are here offered on the propriety of now employing such music in public worship.

a. It is entirely certain that the primitive Christians did not use any instruments of music in their public worship. This is plain from the teachings of Justin Martyr, Chrysostom and Theodoret. On Psalms cxliii. cxlix. Chrysostom, and on our Psalm v. 2, Theodoret give decisive testimony. It is collected in Bingham, Vol. II. pp. 494, 495. Chrysostom says "it was only permitted to the Jews as sacrifice was, for the heaviness and grossness of their souls. God condescended to their weakness, because they were lately drawn off from idols; but now instead of organs, we may use our own bodies to praise him withal."

b. It is certain that organs were not introduced into Christian churches anywhere till at least as late as the middle of the thirteenth century. Thomas Aquinas says expressly, "Our church does not use musical instruments, as harps and psalteries, to praise God withal that she may not seem to Judaize." Both Protestants and Romanists admit this testimony to be decisive as to the fact that instruments were not used as late as the time of the great Schoolman, A. D. 1250.

c. It is quite clear from Scripture that instruments of music were used before the days of Moses to express the joyful feelings of the heart, Job xxx. 31.

d. Few will deny the lawfulness of using instruments of music in private to raise the joyous emotions of the soul, even in devotion. Such a view would generally be regarded as extreme.

e. The introduction of instruments of music in aid of sacred song is not a provision of the law of Moses. This came in the days of David. It was no essential part of the ceremonial institute of the great prophet who wrote the pentateuch.

f. In discussing and settling this question it will not aid in finding the truth to lose our tempers and employ harsh and extravagant language, as is too often done.

g. Those who decline or refuse the use of instrumental music themselves, ought not to judge their brethren who think it profitable. "Who art thou that judgest another man's servant?"

h. Brethren who wish to have instrumental music, ought not to use their liberty maliciously. It is not right to make a schism in the body of Christ on such points.

i. Those who insist on the sinfulness of employing these aids are in all fairness bound to produce at least one clear text, or adduce a fair and plain inference from some passage of Scripture, sustaining their views.

j. If instruments are used in public worship, it ought to be only as aids to congregational singing. Where they discourage this, they are an intolerable offence. "Light and silly voluntaries, long and unmeaning interludes between the stanzas, loud accompaniment, fancy *stop*, and see-saw *swell*-playing, and other things similar," should be wholly discountenanced.

k. In very high latitudes the Moravians found the organ of great use in aiding the people in keeping their voices from sinking to a low key.

l. It will probably interest the reader to see the views of two eminent worthies on this subject. Calvin: "It is evident that the Psalmist here expresses the vehement and ardent affection which the faithful ought to have in praising God, when he enjoins musical instruments to be employed for this purpose. He would have nothing omitted by believers which tends to animate the minds and feelings of men in singing God's praises. The name of God, no doubt, can, properly speaking, be celebrated only by the articulate voice; but it is not without reason that David adds to this those aids by which believers were wont to stimulate themselves the more to this exercise; especially considering that he was speaking to God's ancient people. There is a distinction, however, to be observed here, that we may not indiscriminately consider as applicable to ourselves everything which was formerly enjoined upon the Jews. I have no doubt that playing upon cymbals, touching the harp and the viol, and all that kind of music which is so frequently mentioned in the Psalms, was a part of the education; that is to say, the puerile instruction of the law: I speak of the stated service of the temple. For even now, if believers choose to cheer themselves with musical instruments, they should, I think, make it their object not to dissever their cheerfulness from the praises of God. But when they frequent their sacred assemblies, musical instruments in celebrating the praises of God would be no more suitable than the burning of incense, the lighting up of lamps, and the restoration of the other shadows of the Law. The Papists, therefore, have foolishly borrowed this, as well as many other things from the Jews. Men who are fond of outward pomp may delight in that noise; but the simplicity which God recommends to us by the apostle is far more pleasing to him. Paul allows us to bless God in the public assembly of the saints only in a known tongue, 1 Cor. xiv. 16. The voice of man, although not understood by the generality, assuredly excels all inanimate instruments of music; and yet we see what St. Paul determines concerning speaking in an unknown tongue. What shall we then say of chanting, which fills the ears with nothing but an empty sound? Does any one object that music is very useful for awakening the minds of men and moving their hearts? I own it; but we should always take care that no corruption creep in, which might both defile the pure worship of God and involve men in superstition. Moreover, since the Holy Spirit expressly warns us of this danger by the mouth of Paul, to proceed beyond what we are there warranted by him, is not only, I must say, unadvised zeal, but wicked and perverse obstinacy."

It is probable the views of Calvin are as strong, and as strongly expressed as any person on that side of the question would desire. On the other side Richard Baxter, in his Christian Directory, Works, vol. v., pp. 499–501, thus delivers himself: "Quest. cxxvii., *Is church-music by organs or such instruments lawful?*

Answer. I know that in the persecuted and poorer times of the church, none such were used (when they had not temples, nor always a fixed meeting place.) And that the author of the *Quest. et Resp.* in Justin Martyr speaketh against it. And I grant, 1. That as it is in the power of weak, diseased Christians, to make many things unlawful to their brethren lest we be hurtful to them, and to deprive us of much, not only of our liberties but our helps, so in abundance of congregations, church-music is made unlawful by accident, through their mistake. For it is unlawful (cæteris paribus) by an unnecessary thing to occasion divisions in the churches; but where one part judgeth church-music unlawful, for another part to use it, would occasion divisions in the churches, and drive away the other part. Therefore I would wish church-music to be nowhere set up, but where the congregation can accord in the use of it; or at least where they will not divide thereupon. 2. And I think it unlawful to use such strains of music as are light, or as the congregation cannot easily be brought to understand; much more on purpose to commit the whole work of singing to the choristers, and exclude the congregation. I am not willing to join in such a church where I shall be shut out of this noble work of praise. 3. But plain intelligible church-music, which occasioneth not divisions, but the church agreeth in, for my part I never doubted to be lawful. For, 1. God set it up long after Moses' ceremonial Law, by David, Solomon, etc.

2. It is not an instituted ceremony merely, but a natural help to the mind's alacrity: and it is a duty and not a sin to use the helps of nature and lawful art, though not to institute sacraments, etc., of our own. As it is lawful to use the comfortable helps of spectacles in reading the Bible, so is it of music to exhilarate the soul towards God.

3. Jesus Christ joined with the Jews that used it, and never spake a word against it.

4. No Scripture forbiddeth it, therefore it is not unlawful.

5. Nothing can be against it, that I know of, but what is said against tunes and melody of voice. For whereas they say that it is a human invention; so are our tunes (and metre, and versions.) Yea, it is not a human invention; as the last psalm and many others show, which call us to praise the Lord with instruments of music.

And whereas it is said to be a carnal kind of pleasure, they may say as much of a melodious, harmonious concert of voices, which is more excellent music than any instruments.

And whereas some say that they find it do them harm, so others say of melodious singing: but as wise men say they find it do them good. And why should the experience of some prejudiced self-conceited person, or of a half-man that knoweth not what melody is, be set against the experience of all others, and deprive them of all such helps and mercies, as these people say they find no benefit by.

And as some deride church-music by many scornful names, so others do by singing (as some congregations near me testify, who these many years have forsaken it, and will not endure it: but their pastor is fain to unite them, by the constant and total omission of singing psalms.) It is a great wrong that some do to ignorant Christians, by putting such whimsies and scruples into their heads, which as soon as they enter, turn that to a scorn, and snare, and trouble, which might be a real help and comfort to them, as it is to others."

m. The author knows not how better to close remarks on this subject than by quoting with entire approbation a sentence or two from Morison: "Never let it be forgotten, that no sounds of the most exquisite harmony, whether proceeding from human voices, or from harp of sweetest sound, can be acceptable with Jehovah, if the music of a redeemed heart does not give tone and emphasis to the song of praise. It is infallibly certain that there can be no religion in mere sounds of any description, unless the worshipper sings with grace in his heart, making melody unto the Lord."

5. We may rest assured that whatever affects the joyful solemnity of God's worship is not unimportant, v. 3.

6. A broad foundation for pious confidence is laid in the truth and excellence of

God's word, v. 4. If one precept, promise, doctrine, threatening, or prediction of God could fail, then indeed we would be undone. But that can never be.

7. The uniformity, stability and righteousness of providence in administering human affairs, and especially in carrying out the principles of Holy Scripture in all things to which they apply are truly admirable, v. 4. All the events of providence " make up a harmony of well-ruled concords and discords."

8. In all earthly affairs change is the order of things. The winds, the tides, the seasons, the face of nature, and even friends change, but in all our calculations we may rely on the immutable holiness, justice and goodness of God, v. 5. The Judge of all the earth will do right. He never errs, never wrongs a creature, never is unkind.

9. Creation and providence, stars and seas, the heavens and the laws of matter all publish the claim of Jehovah to supreme and holy worship, vv. 6, 7. If the Creator and Governor of the world is not to be adored, religious worship can never be regarded as proper. If it is not due to him who made and keeps us, who feeds and clothes us, it is due to none.

10. Sentiments of profound reverence for God should be felt by all men, if they even consulted nature alone, vv. 8, 9. "His omnipotence, manifested in framing and settling the world at a word, should move men to fear him."

11. No weapon formed against Zion shall prosper, v. 10. If plans and plots, counsels and devices, the most cunning and the most cruel, could have injured the church of God, there had not been left even a small remnant. Long, long ago the enemy hoped to make a full end of the worship and service of God on earth; but he has failed, and shall ever fail.

12. God's counsels and thoughts being all infinitely holy, just and good, could not be changed but for the worse, and all his perfections forbid any change whatever. All is right, when God plans it. All is sure to come to pass because he has planned it. The more they are tried, the firmer will God's word and counsels be found to be. He, whose hope of success rests on a failure of the divine purpose, will meet a dreadful overthrow. "God has promised nothing but what he has determined to perform."

13. Righteousness exalteth a nation, v. 12. When people heartily enter on a course of piety, they initiate a process of mental and social improvement, which must elevate them far above anything they ever before attained.

14. It is a rich mercy that God makes the first motion towards the salvation of men! If any people are his inheritance, it is because he has chosen them, v. 12. The doctrine of the New Testament is the same. "Ye have not chosen me, but I have chosen you."

15. In all the vast extent of creation, nothing is hid from the observation of the Almighty, vv. 13, 14. If anything could escape his notice, or elude his grasp, that might be fatal to his plans and to the salvation of his people. Unless he controls all causes, that one, which he does not control, may do untold mischief.

16. He, that made the hearts of all men, cannot but know them, and understand all their operations, v. 15. This proves that he is God, that he can fully save his people from their sins, and that the wicked shall not gain an advantage over God's people.

17. All the names and forms of strength and power belonging to creatures are nothing without God, vv. 16, 17. Four of these are here specified, a king, a host, a giant and a horse. Where the word of a king is, there is power, Ecc. viii. 4. But when God does not support it, or wars against it, it is as powerless as the chattering of a swallow. The mightiest monarch can do nothing except it be given him of God,

John xix. 11. David often acknowledges that God made him all he was. Neither is an army a protection if God be against it. The very greatness of a host has often been its ruin. God, who made the stars fight against Sisera, can easily defeat any military preparations. Without lifting a finger he can send an angel and in one night he shall destroy the greatest army that ever invaded a country. A giant has many a time done great things. But let not the mighty man glory in his might, Jer. ix. 23. Giants shall die like men. God has given to the horse strength, and clothed his neck with thunder. The glory of his nostrils is terrible. He paweth in the valley and rejoiceth in his strength. He goeth on to meet the armed men. He mocketh at fear, and is not affrighted. He smelleth the battle afar off. Yet he is nothing without God. He may as soon carry his rider into danger as out of it.

18. No man ever acts with true wisdom till he fears God, and hopes in his mercy, v. 18.

19. A good man may be sure of natural life as long as it is best for him to have it, and when it is taken away, he may confidently expect a better life in a better world, v. 19. Compare Isa. xxxiii. 16; xli. 17, 18; 1 Tim. iv. 8.

20. Is not *waiting* upon the Lord a duty too little insisted on in our day? v. 20. The author does not remember that he ever heard more than one or two public discourses respecting this excellent exercise.

21. There is a beautiful proportion in the character of truly pious men. Where there is genuine trust, there is gracious fear, and where these are, there is also holy joy, vv. 18, 21.

22. The cry for *mercy* ever becomes us, till we get our crown, v. 22. It is never out of place. Even in closing a triumphant song it is proper.

PSALM XXXIV.

A Psalm of David, when he changed his behaviour before Abimelech; who drove him away, and he departed.

1 I will bless the LORD at all times: his praise *shall* continually *be* in my mouth.

2 My soul shall make her boast in the LORD: the humble shall hear *thereof*, and be glad.

3 Oh magnify the LORD with me, and let us exalt his name together.

4 I sought the LORD, and he heard me, and delivered me from all my fears.

5 They looked unto him, and were lightened: and their faces were not ashamed.

6 This poor man cried, and the LORD heard *him*, and saved him out of all his troubles.

7 The angel of the LORD encampeth round about them that fear him, and delivereth them.

8 Oh taste and see that the LORD *is* good: blessed *is* the man *that* trusteth in him.

9 Oh fear the LORD, ye his saints: for *there is* no want to them that fear him.

10 The young lions do lack, and suffer hunger: but they that seek the LORD shall not want any good *thing*.

11 Come, ye children, hearken unto me: I will teach you the fear of the LORD.

12 What man *is he that* desireth life, *and* loveth *many* days, that he may see good?

13 Keep thy tongue from evil, and thy lips from speaking guile.

14 Depart from evil, and do good; seek peace, and pursue it.

15 The eyes of the LORD *are* upon the righteous, and his ears *are open* unto their cry.

16 The face of the LORD *is* against them that do evil, to cut off the remembrance of them from the earth.

17 *The righteous* cry, and the LORD heareth, and delivereth them out of all their troubles.

18 The LORD *is* nigh unto them that are of a broken heart; and saveth such as be of a contrite spirit.

19 Many *are* the afflictions of the righteous: but the LORD delivereth him out of them all.

20 He keepeth all his bones: not one of them is broken.

21 Evil shall slay the wicked: and they that hate the righteous shall be desolate.

22 The LORD redeemeth the soul of his servants: and none of them that trust in him shall be desolate.

ON the title see on titles of Psalms iii. xi. We know the historic occasion of this ode. See title and 1 Sam. xxi. 10–15; xxii. 1, 2. The name of the king before whom David appeared was Achish. His title was Abimelech, which means my Father the King. It occurs often in Scripture. Like Pharaoh and Cæsar, it was worn by a succession of princes. The Syriac and Theodoret strangely confound Abimelech with Ahimelech the priest mentioned in 1 Sam. xxi. 1–8. For *behaviour* in the title some read *sense,* some *intellect,* some *countenance.* Luther has *behaviour.* That gives the sense. Beyond reasonable doubt David is the author of this Psalm. This is an alphabetical poem. See Introduction, § 13, and on Ps. xxv. The alphabetical arrangement is not perfect, the sixth letter being omitted, and the seventeenth beginning vv. 16, 22.

The morality of David's conduct before Achish is matter of dispute. Did he sin in feigning madness? On this question some judicious commentators give no opinion. Those who justify stratagem in war would approve of this device. Those, who believe that under all circumstances truth and candor are obligatory, would condemn his conduct. Calvin speaks safely when he says: "Although God sometimes delivers his people, while at the same time they err in choosing the means, or even fall into sin in adopting them, yet there is nothing inconsistent in this. The deliverance was the work of God, but the intermediate sin, which is on no account to be excused, ought to be ascribed to David." Some have even thought that this Psalm gives evidences of compunction for this artifice. But this is doubtful. The object of the ode is to celebrate the divine goodness, and to awaken just sentiments in his own mind, and in the minds of others. The whole structure of the Psalm would lead us to suppose that it was composed after David was quite out of peril. Some have thought he wrote it in the cave of Adullam. While this cannot be proved, it is not a wild conjecture, 1 Sam. xxii. 1, 2.

That the occasion of this Psalm fully justified the high strains it employs is manifest from the great peril, in which the history shows David to have been, and from the very remarkable prayer, which David offered on that occasion, as we have it in Ps. lvi. Jebb: "The characteristic word of this Psalm is Jehovah," on which see on Ps. i. 2. Clarke dates it B. C. 1062; Scott B. C. 1061.

1. *I will bless the* LORD *at all times. Bless,* as in Ps. v. 12, which see. *At all times;* some read, in all time; some, at every time. The meaning is, in every condition, prosperous or adverse; "in every posture of my affairs." He repeats: *His praise* shall *continually be in my mouth. Continually,* always, ever.

2. *My soul shall make her boast in the* LORD. Calvin: "The term *soul* in this place signifies not the vital spirit, but the seat of the affections." The *boasting* of a good man, when approved of God, is a high degree of exultant enjoyment of good in possession, united with a persuasion of bright and glorious prospects. Were this boasting in one's own strength or holiness, nothing could be more vain; but when it is *in the Lord,* nothing is more ennobling or commendable. It is also a great encouragement to others: *The humble shall hear* thereof *and be glad.* For *the humble* Luther has *the miserable;* many, *the meek;* and many, *the humble.* See on Ps. ix. 12, 18. It is applied to Moses, Num. xii. 3. A word closely resembling this is rendered *humbled,* in

Ps. xxxv. 13. The *meek* of the earth must take courage at what they see done for their *poor* brethren. Being *humble*, they know they deserve no good thing. They are grateful for mercies, which the world lightly esteems; and they are hopeful and glad when they see great things done for the *lowly*. Even a faint-hearted Israelite might have waxed bold when he saw the three young men walking loose in the fiery furnace; or when he met them afterwards, and found not a hair of their head singed, nor their coats changed, nor the smell of fire passed on them. Peter was not more affected with his miraculous deliverance from prison than were his brethren, Acts xii. 11, 16.

3. *Oh magnify the* LORD *with me. Magnify, make great, lift up.* For many good reasons every true worshipper desires others to unite with him in adoring and praising Jehovah. God is so excellent, his mercies are so marvellous, the work of praise is so enlivening, and any praise rendered by one falls so far short of what God deserves, that if a good man could, he would enlist the universe of creatures in aid of the worship he offers. From the peculiar construction of this clause in the Hebrew some think that the word *name* in the next clause should be here *understood*. If so, the sense will not be varied. David repeats his call on others: *And let us exalt his name together.* United, religious worship, celebrating the praises of Jehovah, is that, to which all are here cited.

4. *I sought the* LORD, *and he heard me, and delivered me from all my fears.* Here is the great event which caused the vows and challenges of the preceding verses. He *sought the Lord* by prayer and in faith. His *fears* were great. He had killed Goliath, the great champion of the very king before whom he now stood a helpless stranger, fugitive and prisoner. The Philistines remembered the deed, and no doubt accused David to their prince. To sense and reason all looked dark. In that sad hour David's mind was turned to God, and he gained his cause. The Lord, in whose hands is the king's heart, made Abimelech indifferent respecting his prisoner; nay, he *drove him away;* and so the royal sufferer was permitted to go to a stronghold, and meet his whole family and his friends. God can save by few or by many, from the jaws of lions, or the swords of kings. The more pressing the calamity, the more earnest should be our applications to the throne of grace:

5. *They looked unto him, and were lightened: and their faces were not ashamed.* The Chaldee agrees with our version. But all the other ancient versions put the first and second verbs in the imperative and the last in the future: Come ye to him [or look to him] and be enlightened: and your faces shall not be confounded. Calvin puts all the verbs in the future; the church of England, all in the preterite; Edwards, all in the imperative; Fry: Look unto him and be ye gladdened, and your faces shall not be made ashamed; Horsley: Look towards him, and thou shalt be enlightened; and your faces shall never be ashamed; Hengstenberg: They look at him and are brightened, and their countenance is not ashamed. There is considerable difficulty in getting at the precise sense of this verse. Jehovah is spoken of in each of the preceding verses, and so by *him* the great mass of sober commentators understand God. But unless we admit that this is a dramatic Psalm, we must admit that David is spoken of in the next verse in the third person singular, as *this poor man* and *him.* Yet there would be a good sense, if we supposed the *humble* to *have looked,* or to *be looking* at David's deliverance, and thus getting assurance that they should not be ashamed. There is doubt respecting the best rendering of the verbs as to tense. But the authorized version is most conformed to the original, and the verse may well be understood as declaring that David's deliverance was not peculiar to himself, but that whenever the *humble looked* unto God, they were *lightened,* and were not left to shame. The first two verbs in Hebrew are in the past; the last is in the future. We might read the whole: They looked unto him and were light-

ened, *i. e.*, were cheered as by light. Nor shall their past experience deceive them and their faces shall not be ashamed.

6. *This poor man cried, and the* LORD *heard* him, *and saved him out of all his troubles.* Poor, rendered *humble* in Ps. ix. 12; *afflicted* in Ps. xviii. 27; *lowly* in Pr. iii. 34; *needy* in Pr. xxxi. 20. The prayer offered by this poor man was earnest and fervent. He *cried.* His cry brought down the blessing. He was saved out of all his *troubles, distresses, tribulations, adversities, anguishes,* see Ps. ix. 9; xxii. 11. Calvin and others think David in this verse introduces all the godly as pointing to him and speaking of him. This is not necessary to the understanding of the passage; nor is it favored by many. The safest rule respecting the introduction of the dramatic form is not to resort to it unless the sense requires it. The inspired writers often introduce themselves in the third person. Of this there are many instances in the writings of Moses. See also Ps. cxxxii. 1; Hos. i. 2; John xxi. 24; 2 Cor. xii. 2, 4. In vv. 1–4 the psalmist speaks of himself; in v. 5, of God's people generally; in v. 6, of himself; in v. 7, he returns to general views.

7. *The angel of the* LORD *encampeth round about them that fear him, and delivereth them.* Three views have been held respecting *the angel of the Lord.* 1. Many think it means any heavenly messenger sent to protect the righteous, or fight against their foes. 2. Others think that by *angel* in the singular, we are to understand angels. The word rendered *encampeth* resembles Mahanaim, *armies;* see Gen. xxxii. 1, 2. In Hebrew the singular is often put for the plural—one for the species. 3. Others think that by the angel of the Lord we are here and often elsewhere to understand the Redeemer, Gen. xlviii. 16; Ex. xxiii. 20, 23; xxxii. 34; Judges xiii. 15–22; Mal. iii. 1. See Hengstenberg's Christology. This sense does not forbid us to suppose him to be attended by the heavenly host. He is "The captain of the Lord's host," and "All the host of heaven stands by him on his right hand and on his left," Josh. v. 14; 1 Kings xxii. 19; Heb. i. 6, 7. The special ministry of angels is to them that *fear Jehovah,* or to "them, who shall be heirs of salvation." The angel *delivereth them,* however many their foes, however great their own weakness, however feeble their hopes, however alarming their case.

8. *Oh taste and see that the* LORD *is good.* To *taste* is to make proof by experience. To *see* is either to gain the result of such *tasting,* or it is to *enjoy.* The word *see* has both significations. The former seems to be the more appropriate here, and is equivalent to *knowing certainly.* *Blessed* is *the man* that *trusteth in him.* Blessed, as in Ps. i. 1; xxxii. 1. *Trusteth,* rendered elsewhere putteth trust, hath hope, maketh a refuge. Edwards renders it: O try, and be sensible of the goodness of Jehovah: how happy the man, who trusteth in him.

9. *Oh fear the* LORD, *ye his saints.* Fear, as in v. 7; Ps. xv. 4; xxii. 23; xxxiii. 18. *Saints, holy ones.* There is nothing more unfriendly to true piety than its degenerating into irreverence and familiarity with God. Fear gone, all solemnity vanishes, and love becomes fondness. The command is clear. An encouraging reason is given: *For* there is *no want to them that fear him.* There is nothing *wanting* in the symmetry of their characters, in the supply of their temporal necessities, in furnishing them against the machinations of the wicked One, in the day of conflict, in the hour of death. For such persons an ample provision is made in all respects and for all duration Among all the redeemed in glory there is not one who looks back and sees that on earth there was any mistake in the divine conduct towards him. God doeth all things well.

10. *The young lions do lack, and suffer hunger.* The Septuagint, Syriac, Arabic, Ethiopic, Vulgate, Luther and Houbigant instead of *lions,* or young *lions,* read *the rich.* John Rogers' translation is much the same: The ryche shall want and suffre hunger, but they which seke the Lord, shall want no maner of thynge, that is good.

While Ainsworth gives *lions* in the text he yet says: "Hereby may be meant the rich and mighty of the world, whom God often bringeth to miserie." Rapacious and cruel men are in Scripture often compared to lions, 1 Chron. xi. 22; Ps. xxxv. 17; Jer. ii. 15; Neh. ii. 11–13; 2 Tim. iv. 17. Hengstenberg thinks that the connection and the word rendered *lack*, which is literally "reduced to poverty," require us by *lions* to understand powerful and violent men. Alexander: "The sentiment then is, that while the most powerful and least scrupulous of men may be reduced to want, the people of God shall be abundantly and constantly provided for." But the Chaldee, church of England, Calvin and Amesius retain in the text *lions*. In either way we get a good sense. *Young lions* are not those, which cannot hunt their prey, or are feeble. This is clear from Ps. lviii. 6, where we read of "the great teeth of the young lions," and from other places, Job iv. 10; Ps. xvii. 12; Mic. v. 8. The argument is, that those, who like young lions rely on their strength and rapacity, shall suffer because God is against them. *But they that seek the* Lord *shall not want any good* thing. *Seek the* Lord, a phrase, like the *fear* of the Lord, denoting the whole of religion, as in v. 4; Ps. ix. 10; xiv. 2. Calvin: "If it is objected, that the good and the virtuous are not always exempted from penury, I answer, that the hand of God is stretched out to succor them in due season, when they are reduced to the greatest straits, and know not to what side to turn, so that the issue always shows that we seek not in vain from him whatever is necessary to the sustenance of life." Sanctified poverty, sanctified afflictions of every kind are not real evils, but truly *good* things.

11. *Come, ye children.* Most of the versions have *children;* Edwards has *young men;* Ainsworth, Hengstenberg and Alexander have *sons.* In our version it is *sons*, Ps. iv. 2; xxxi. 19; and *children* in Ps. xi. 4; xii. 1. The address is to *young people*, whatever their age. *Hearken unto me.* Heedlessness is a great sin among youth. They are slow to *hear, listen, weigh, ponder, consider.* Folly is often bound up in their hearts. They must be warned, exhorted, commanded to *pay attention* to the lessons which so much concern them. They ought to hearken. It is a great matter, it is their life. *I will teach you the fear of the* Lord. If this be taken as the point to which all the residue of the Psalm refers, then David here proposes to show them, 1. What it is to fear the Lord; 2, What are the proper fruits of godly fear; 3, What are the motives to fear God. The first appeal is to the natural desire for happiness:

12. *What man* is he that *desireth life*, and *loveth* many *days, that he may see good?* The sense is not varied by some of the ancient versions, rendering the last clause, Who loveth to see good days? The sinner is himself the greatest loser by his crimes; and the saint the greatest gainer by his holiness. The cause of piety would labor under a sad disadvantage, if in the long run the saint fared no better than the wicked. The love of happiness being natural and universal, and having some influence over all men, who are not desperate, an appeal to it for the purpose of securing attention is not out of place. True, piety has a higher motive, and virtue a higher spring than anything ending in personal advantage. But that does not impair the strength of the consideration here presented. On the temporal benefits of true piety see on Ps. i. 3. The first direction for *seeing good*, or *good days* is:

13. *Keep thy tongue from evil, and thy lips from speaking guile. Keep, hold back, restrain, vigilantly guard, preserve.* The same word is applied to *keeping* the commandments, *keeping* covenant, *keeping* the law, *keeping* the heart. This ought to be easy work; but sin has made it very difficult, and, without divine grace, impossible, Jas. iii. 2–10. Yet we may not on that account be excused from our duty, Jas. i. 26. The ways in which men sin with the tongue are many. Laurentius says there are as many

sins of the tongue as there are letters in the alphabet. Richard Baxter has catalogued thirty. The best expositions of the decalogue mention even more. Speaking becomes sinful when it is hasty, rash, continual, unseasonable, excessive, clamorous, senseless, unchaste, indelicate, impure, filthy, prevaricating, quibbling, deceitful, lying, slanderous, tattling, babbling, backbiting, detractive, reproachful, opprobrious, flattering, seductive, betraying confidence, revealing secrets, awakening groundless suspicions, talebearing, news-carrying, railing, reviling, boastful, scornful, desperate, murmuring, foolish, egotistical, vain, proud, malignant, bitter, resentful, cursing, profane, or blasphemous. "The tongue is a world of iniquity." Sins of the tongue lead to horrors of conscience, loss of peace of mind and loss of appetite; to broils, quarrels and bitter contentions; to fightings, stabbings, shootings and murders. Perhaps no form of sin more terribly destroys personal, domestic, social and public peace and prosperity. "The tongue is a fire." It burns all who abuse it. It burns them up. Dreadful plagues befall it here and hereafter, Ps. lii. 5; cxx. 4. The two forms of sinful speaking noticed in the verse are *evil* and *guile.* The latter word is elsewhere in our version rendered *deceit, subtlety, treachery, craft,* and several times *guile. Evil,* elsewhere, *mischief, wickedness, wrong.* Hengstenberg: "In giving the details of the fear of God, the duties toward our neighbor are, according to David's usual way, dwelt upon with particular care, because there hypocrisy, which is so ready to appropriate to itself promises with which it has nothing to do, finds least scope for its exercise." Guard your lips, but do more:

14. *Depart from evil and do good. Evil,* as in vv. 13, 16. *Evil* and *good* are here used as in common parlance. This mode of pointing out our duty is very fitting: "Cease to do evil; learn to do well," Isa. i. 16, 17. While our direct duty to God is not ignored, our duty to man is the chief matter involved in this verse and the preceding. *Seek peace and pursue it. Peace,* that is the things which make for peace, for the quiet and order of men, of families, of neighborhoods, and of nations. Peace is a great blessing, and, where principle is not sacrificed, it is never purchased at too great a cost, Rom. xii. 18; Heb. xii. 14. The great means of seeking and promoting peace are uprightness, kindness, forbearance, forgiveness, gentleness, quietness. We are at liberty, in some cases we are bound, to sacrifice our own rights for the sake of peace. We are to *pursue* peace, if she seems to flee from us, until the further pursuit would involve faithlessness or an evil conscience; then we must stop. It is not *possible* to *live peaceably* with some men. They love strife. Without formal quotation, verses 12, 13, 15, 16 of this Psalm are inwoven into 1 Peter iii. 10–12. The duties of vv. 13, 14 are enforced thus:

15. *The eyes of the* LORD *are upon the righteous.* That is, his providence is over them for good; to notice their wrongs and distresses; to mark their wants and desires; to supply their lack and necessities; to give them restraining and sustaining grace; and to crown their lives with goodness, and their conflicts with victory. *And his ears are open unto their cry.* The righteous are often in great straits, but they know how to cry unto the Lord, and his ears are never closed to their entreaties. He never fails to regard the voice of earnest, humble, believing prayer. This is their happy lot. It is far different with the wicked.

16. *The face of the Lord is against them that do evil, to cut off the remembrance of them from the earth. Face,* the Hebrew word occurs very often and is commonly so rendered. It is also rendered *countenance, mouth, presence, anger.* The last seems to give the best sense, and is fully justified by the rendering of the same word in Ps. xxi. 9; Lam. iv. 16. Yet God's *mouth,* that is, all he speaks, is against the wicked. And his *presence,* although it may accompany the wicked, is *to cut off the remembrance of them from the earth,* to extirpate them utterly. See on Ps. ix. 5, 6. No

man on earth hopes or desires to spend his eternity with thieves, liars, burglars, murderers, tyrants, oppressors, persecutors and blasphemers who died in their sins. Who now cares for Cyrus, Alexander, Cæsar or Charlemagne? Their names, though still repeated on earth, have no sweet odors. No man reveres their memory, fears their power, or would give a farthing to be of their lineage. Whereas there are millions on earth who think of Abel, Enoch, Abraham, Isaac, Jacob, David, Hannah, Anna, Mary, John, Peter and Paul, and hope soon to see them in glory and be joined to their assembly.

17. The righteous *cry, and the* LORD *heareth, and delivereth them out of all their troubles.* That which in v. 6 is recorded of David is here asserted to be true of all the servants of God. Our translators have supplied *the righteous,* because *they* are evidently here spoken of. Some suppose the word so rendered has been lost from the Hebrew text. But of this there is no considerable proof. Others propose to make v. 16 parenthetical. But this is not necessary. In seeking for an antecedent to a pronoun or for a nominative to a verb, it is very common to go back until the reading will make good sense. That this verse speaks of the righteous is so clear that the Chaldee, Septuagint, Arabic, Syriac, Ethiopic and Vulgate all supply that word. The next verse speaks of the same persons as *penitents:*

18. *The* LORD *is nigh unto them that are of a broken heart; and saveth such as be of a contrite spirit.* Both clauses describe the same character, and the same state of mind. *Broken,* as in Ps. li. 17; Isa. lxi. 1. *Contrite,* as in Ps. li. 17; Isa. lvii. 15. It means bruised, crushed, smitten, humbled. He who has a *broken heart* and a *contrite spirit* is heartily sorry for having offended God, violated his law, and grieved his Spirit. He makes a full surrender. He has no hope in himself. He sees that he is self-destroyed. God has smitten him, conscience has smitten him, the law has slain him. If God does not save him he sees he is ruined forever. But the LORD *is nigh unto* such. He *binds up the broken-hearted.* He *sets at liberty them that are bruised.* He will not *break the bruised reed.* He *revives the spirit of the contrite ones.* To the poor in spirit he gives the kingdom of heaven.

19. *Many* are *the afflictions of the righteous. Afflictions,* the plural of the word rendered *evil* in other verses of this Psalm. Taken in the sense of *evil suffered,* it is rendered *hurt, harm, sorrow, mischief, wretchedness, wrong, adversity, trouble, calamity, misery.* The word seems specially to point to such evils as are brought on us by the wickedness of men. The Septuagint, Ethiopic and Vulgate have *tribulations;* Syriac and Arabic, *calamities.* The sources of *afflictions* to the righteous man are, 1. Himself. Gladly would he have no longer need to cry, O wretched man that I am! He is grieved at his own coldness, unbelief, ingratitude, and the ease with which he yields to temptation. All his sins afflict him. 2. The righteous beholds the transgressors and is grieved. Rivers of water run down his eyes because men keep not God's law. Not only the pride, the slanders, the scorn, the cruelty of the wicked against himself, but all their known sins afflict him. 3. Then because the righteous man is not perfect here, his heavenly Father afflicts him in mind, body and estate. Moreover, God often afflicts him that by example he may illustrate the power of sustaining grace. His trials are multiplied, his afflictions many. But they are not permitted to destroy him, or depress him above measure. Left to himself, they would sink him into the lowest depths, *but the* LORD *delivereth him out of them all. Delivereth,* the same verb as in vv. 4, 17; Ps. xxxiii. 16, 17. This deliverance is effectual, seasonable, well ordered. This verse explains, limits and relieves from misconstruction the doctrine of v. 18.

20. *He keepeth all his bones: not one of them is broken.* Hutchinson adduces this verse as proof that the whole Psalm refers to Messiah. His canon is that a sentence in any Psalm, clearly applicable to Christ, determines the whole composition to

refer to him. An attempt to carry out such a rule would show its absurdity. Yet this verse is expressly applied to Christ in the New Testament, John xix. 31–37. It has its most glorious fulfilment in him. In his case there was no limit to its fullest import. But it was fulfilled in David also, and it is fulfilled in all believers so far that not a bone of them is "broken without God's wise and merciful appointment." His care of his chosen is most tender and loving. The hairs of their heads are all numbered. Not one falleth to the ground without their Father. He giveth his angels charge concerning them. It is estimated that one generation of men converted to God in early life outlives two generations of godless, violent, treacherous men. The Scriptures intimate as much, Ps. lv. 23.

21. *Evil shall slay the wicked.* *Evil*, as in vv. 13, 14, 16, and in v. 20, in the plural, *afflictions.* The renderings are various. Chaldee and Arabic: The death of the ungodly is evil; Septuagint, Ethiopic and Vulgate: The death of sinners is very evil; Syriac: Evil [or malice] shall slay the wicked; church of England: Misfortune shall slay the wicked; Calvin and Genevan translation: Malice shall slay the wicked; Venema: To the bad evil shall bring death; Amesius: Affliction has power over the wicked in death; Edwards: Calamity will destroy the wicked; Jebb: Evil shall slay the ungodly; Hengstenberg: Misfortune slays the wicked. John Rogers' translation: But mysfortune shall slaye the ungodly. Pool thinks the evil is " either, 1. The evil of sin. His own wickedness, though designed against others, shall destroy himself. Or, 2. The evil of misery. When the afflictions of good men shall have a happy issue, theirs shall end in their total and final destruction." If the word be rendered *affliction*, then the contrast is between the *righteous* of v. 19, who survive *many afflictions*, while one affliction often kills the wicked; or *misery* at last kills him. But there is clearly a reference to the righteous retribution, which shall at last and with certainty bring on the wicked the fruit of his own doings: *And they that hate the righteous shall be desolate.* For *desolate* the Syriac has *fail;* Arabic, *perish;* Edwards, *doomed to perish;* Hengstenberg, *become guilty;* Chaldee, *be condemned;* Ainsworth, *be condemned as guiltie;* Fry, *be held guilty;* Septuagint, Ethiopic, Vulgate, John Rogers' Translation, Jebb, Alexander and margin, *be guilty.* The verb is in the future. All who hate the righteous shall be held and treated as guilty persons. The law will condemn them. Tholuck: "Guilt shall not leave the wicked, for it cannot be forgiven until it be confessed, repented of, and covered by faith." The consequence of unpardoned *guilt* is horrible *desolation.*

22. *The* LORD *redeemeth the soul of his servants.* The ancient versions all put the verb in the future, *shall redeem* or *shall preserve.* But the church of England, Calvin, Venema, Amesius, Ainsworth, Edwards, Jebb, Fry, Hengstenberg and Alexander have it in the present, agreeing with our version. The Hebrew word is a participle, *redeeming.* In our version the verb is rendered *rescue, deliver, ransom, redeem.* Jehovah delivers now, and shall always deliver; he redeems by the blood of his Son; he ransoms by the great price paid on Calvary; he rescues from every impending evil; he saves eternally. *And none of them that trust in him shall be desolate. Trust,* the same as in v. 8. *Shall be desolate,* precisely the same as in v. 21, only here it is preceded by the negative. There is nothing to warrant Fry in placing v. 22 betweer vv. 5, 6.

DOCTRINAL AND PRACTICAL REMARKS.

1. Truth, candor, honesty cannot be too highly esteemed. They are essential in a gracious character. Henry: "We cannot justify David in his dissimulation. It ill became an honest man to feign himself what he was not, and a man of honor to feign himself to be a fool and a madman. If, in sport, we mimic those who have not so good

an understanding as we think we have, we forget that God might have made their case ours."

2. There is on earth and in heaven no nobler work than praise. It is angelic. We ought to be much in it *at all times*, v. 1; "in pain, sickness, poverty, persecution, and even in the agonies of death." We should praise him *continually*, because *continual* blessings, not one of which is deserved, are descending upon us; and because some mercies conferred on us are so great that we ought often to make mention of them. Special mercies demand special praises. Tholuck: "Every day of a pious man's life is marked with the monuments and tokens of the mercy of God, so that he has every day to sing a new song." Calvin: "If by one benefit alone God lays us under obligation to himself all our life, so that we may never lawfully cease from setting forth his praises, how much more when he heaps upon us innumerable benefits?"

3. It is lawful and agreeable to the example of wise men to form good purposes, v. 1.

4. It is very proper to call to mind past mercies, when present trials press us sore and to sing in days of darkness, v. 1. It is a sad error to rely on past mercies so as to seek no new ones. But it is no less a sin to be so eager after new mercies as to slight or forget old ones.

5. Religious joy cannot be too high. We may *exult* and *make our boast* in God, v. 2. He that glorieth, let him glory in the Lord, and let him glory in the Lord as much as he pleases.

6. It profits our brethren and honors God for us truthfully to narrate his gracious dealings with his people. Therefore we should mention the loving-kindness of the Lord that others may *hear thereof* and *be glad*, v. 2. But we should not cast pearls before swine. "Only humble souls sensible of their own weakness are the people who reap benefit by God's mercies bestowed on others."

7. The unity of divine worship, which is founded on the unity of the divine nature, is best maintained when with our *souls* and all our affections we heartily invite all God's servants to join with us in our highest acts of devotion, vv. 2, 3. He, who has cheered us, can cheer others; and he, who has saved us, can save any one, however great his sins, or afflictions.

8. Dickson: "The fear of what is like to be should not hinder prayer; for the fears of the godly are not certain prophecies; for God can deliver out of them all," v. 4.

9. The old and tried method of obtaining deliverance from our fears by seeking the Lord in the way of prayer and a good conscience is far safer and more successful than any *finesse* men may adopt. David says nothing in praise of the latter, but often commends the former, v. 4.

10. God's grace and kindness to one of his servants has a mighty effect on others, so that they *look* and *brighten up* and their *faces are not ashamed,* v. 5. Not an example of mercy to one saint was ever lost upon others, who feared God, and knew of the deliverance vouchsafed to their brother.

11. The substance of one good man's experience in grace and providence so closely resembles that of all the saints as to make it of easy application and of excellent use to their cases.

12. The best way to profit by God's wonders showed to any of the worthies of old is not unduly to magnify their gifts and excellencies, so as quite to put them out of sight of us poor creatures, but to admit, as they themselves did, that they were *poor*, v. 6. Yea, the best of them said they were poor and, miserable and blind and naked.

13. A religion, which would exclude prayer, would be contrary not only to nature,

but to the oft-repeated precepts and examples of Scripture, vv. 4, 5, 6, 17. Dickson: "The Lord putteth the godly to trouble, and by trouble putteth them to their prayers, and delays answer till the need be great, and then they cry to the Lord, and he giveth evidence of his hearing, and sendeth deliverance."

14. Every example of a believer in distress rescued from trouble, is a warrant to all other souls, who are cast down and self-renouncing to lay fast hold of the covenant. Even if verse 6 does not positively decide who *this poor man* was, any humble soul may fill the blank with his own name. To him that believeth all things are possible. Morison: "O how bright with mercy will be the records of that world, where shall be seen inscribed, in the book of providence, all the salvation that God has wrought for his ransomed church."

15. It is very important to entertain correct and lively views concerning the ministry of angels, v. 7. Much is said on this subject in God's word, 2 Kings vi. 15–17; Ps. xci. 11; Luke xvi. 22. However great the number and power of our enemies, these heavenly messengers are more numerous and more mighty. There is an innumerable company of them, and they excel in strength.

> "Millions of spiritual creatures walk the earth,
> Unseen, both when we sleep, and when we wake."

16. How dare any teach that the fear of God is not an essential part of true piety, when it is so often spoken of as if it were the whole of godliness? vv. 7, 9, 11.

17. Nothing better prepares us to call on others to serve God in all his ways than a blessed experience of his grace and mercy in our own souls and lives, v. 8. He, who has *tasted* and *seen*, is fittest to call on others to *taste* and *see*. The blind never call on their fellows to admire a rainbow. The deaf never urge others to listen to music. Tholuck: "Heaven and earth are replete with the goodness of God. We omit to open our mouths and eyes, on which account the Psalmist desires us to *taste* and *see*."

18. Dickson: "All that the believer can attain to in this life of spiritual consolation, whether by faith or experience, sweetened with lively comforts of the Holy Ghost, is but a *taste* in comparison of what is to be had hereafter, and yet that *taste*, O how sweet, a joy unspeakable, and full of glory is it!" v. 8.

19. It is a duty of all, who have found mercy, to call on others to seek the Lord, embrace the Redeemer, and set their seal to the covenant, v. 8; John i. 42, 45; Rev. xxii. 17.

20. *Reliance* or trust is an essential ingredient in faith, v. 8. Without this, faith is as a fable. No more seasonable prayer is ever offered in distress than this: "Lord, increase our faith." Calvin: "Our own unbelief is the only impediment which prevents God from satisfying us largely and bountifully with abundance of all good things."

21. Everything in Scripture makes clear the necessity of inward purity, personal holiness in all the servants of God. In other places they are called by many names of endearment and of tenderness; but often as here they are called *saints*, v. 9. The church of Rome enrols the names of dead men and women in the calendar for various days in the year and calls them saints' days. But Moses, and David, and Solomon, and Daniel, and Paul speak of all God's children as his saints. So let it be. They are called to be saints.

22. The provision made for all that fear God is very rich. There is *no want* to them; *i. e.*, they *want no good* thing. This is ever true of them, vv. 9, 10. Calvin: "Sooner shall the lions perish with hunger and want, than God will disappoint of their necessary food the righteous and sincere, who, content with his blessing alone, seek their food only at his hand." Tholuck: "We shall feel no want though we be

in want." The covenant extends the promised aid of God much further than to mere bodily and temporal wants, embracing the whole catalogue of benefits, 1 Cor. iii. 21, 22; Rom. viii. 32; Matt. v. 3–12.

23. He, who relies on his native power and vigor, his talents or his political influence, and especially if want of virtue shall unite with temptation to lead him to rapacity and wrong, shall sooner or later find that like the *young lions*, he has quite failed of a needed supply, v. 10.

24. Teachers ought to be kind, and address their pupils as if they were their *children* or *sons*, v. 11. Oh that all teachers knew the meaning of this: "Learn of me; for I am meek and lowly in heart." The tone of severity and the language of harshness ill become instructors.

25. We ought to condescend to men of low estate, to youth and children, and to persons of feeble understanding, v. 11. The old seldom remember what they are taught. The middle aged are often too busy to listen to their teachers. But the young, even the very young, may hear, and learn, and remember, and live. Henry: "Though a man of war, and anointed to be king, David did not think it below him to teach children; though now he had his head so full of cares, and his hands of business, yet he could find heart and time to give good counsel to young people."

26. The young are specially bound to set their hearts to learn, particularly when older people propose to give them the lessons of experience and wisdom on the most weighty matters, v. 11. "David was a famous musician, a statesman, a soldier; but he does not say to the children, 'I will teach you to play on the harp, or to handle the sword or spear, or to draw the bow, or, I will teach you the maxims of state policy;' but I will teach you *the fear of the Lord*, which is better than all the arts and sciences, better than all burnt-offerings and sacrifices." If teachers would do great good, let them select weighty topics, use plain words, and speak in a kind manner.

27. The young, no less than others, should be taught that all is not gold that glitters, all is not piety that passes under that name. The nature and evidences of true piety should be clearly stated to all, and to none more than to beginners, vv. 12–15.

28. No marvel the righteous never regret the choice they have made, nor utterly forsake the way of God, for all their experience is on the side of God, of truth, and righteousness, v. 12. The godly life of the righteous here shall be followed by one infinitely glorious hereafter.

29. Cannot something be done in family government, in social and ecclesiastical arrangements, in private and public teaching, to arrest the dire evils arising from the wicked abuses of the power of speech? v. 13. Parents consider! Neighbors consider! Pastors consider! Wise men consider! Earth is sometimes so much like hell as to make one doubt whether on the whole existence here is desirable.

30. A truly virtuous and pious character has both negative and positive good traits. It *departs from evil;* it *does good,* v. 14.

31. No philosopher, moralist or prophet has ever put too high a positive value on the inestimable blessing of being permitted and enabled to lead a quiet and peaceable life in all godliness and honesty, v. 14. Oh that all men loved peace and hated strife, 1 Cor. xiii. 4–7; 2 Cor. xiii. 11. If Christians, we serve the God of peace. But one thing on earth is worse than a life of contention; that is a life of wickedness. Yet if we are forced to contend, God will not condemn us, but will sustain us. Calvin: "David means that in our own personal affairs we should be meek and condescending, and endeavor, as far as in us lies, to maintain peace, though its maintenance should prove to us a source of much trouble and inconvenience."

32. The providence of God, which we should devoutly study, has two aspects. One smiles on the righteous; the other frowns on the wicked, vv. 15, 16; Ex. xiv. 19, 20.

33. We have Scriptural authority for esteeming a good name above riches; but what a delusion the wicked are under when they pursue *fame* as a great good. The memory of the wicked shall rot. God will cut off their remembrance from the earth, v. 16. A youth passing a bank of sand, with his staff wrote the word "Fame." Returning from school on the evening of the same day, he saw that already the winds had driven the sands over it and covered it up. In later life he referred to it as having taught him a good lesson, and led him to desire above all things to have his name written in the book of life.

34. The apostle Peter makes a practical use of vv. 12–16, which has not yet been formally noticed. He says the truths here taught should moderate our grief and calm our minds, making us compassionate, pitiful, courteous, giving blessing for cursing, etc., 1 Pet. iii. 8–12. Very fairly do they teach as much, and some of them point to the highest sanctions.

35. Ever since man became a sinner, true religion has had in it the element of *penitence*, v. 18; Ps. li. 17; Isa. lvii. 15. Let us often inquire whether we have this penitence. It is far different from remorse. It is a great error of some that they so little cultivate a penitent state of mind.

36. The Christian religion is the only form of doctrine on earth that candidly admits the full extent of human wo; and at the same time makes adequate provision for the support of the pious sufferer, and for his full and final deliverance from all that can harass the mind, v. 19. "Through much tribulation we must enter into the kingdom of God." Tholuck: "Were the pious freed from every trouble and affliction, motives to piety would become impure, faith would grow faint, prayer cease, and carnal security abound." Afflictions are proofs of love. "Stripes are the marks of sonship." All our troubles are as nothing compared with what we deserve, with what the righteous of other days have suffered, with what our Saviour suffered, with the grace granted to sustain us, or with the everlasting bliss that awaits us. So thought Paul, 2 Cor. iv. 17. Luther: "Although the bones and members of the saints are, above all others, cruelly scattered and broken, burnt in the fire, and left to rot in the graves; yet, even though they be thus sown in ignominy, they shall be raised in glory: they shall be quickened again with all their limbs and bodies; and all their bones shall be restored; and the just shall shine like the sun in the kingdom of their Father."

37. Even in this life the deliverances of God's people are often amazing, v. 19. Witness that of the prophet in 2 Kings vi. 18–23. Behold the mercies showed to Peter in prison, when about to be beheaded, Acts xii. 3–11. "It is recorded of that holy man Bernard Gilpin, called the Apostle of the North, that in the time of the Marian persecutions, he was apprehended by Bonner's messengers and carried off to London—and to the stake. 'But mark,' says his biographer, 'mark the providence of God!' In his way to London he broke his leg, which stopped for a time his journey. The persons in whose custody he was, took occasion to retort upon him a remark he had frequently made, 'that nothing happens to us but what is intended for our good,' and asked him whether he thought the breaking of his leg was so intended, to which he meekly answered, he made no doubt it was: and so it proved in the strictest sense, for before he was able to travel, Queen Mary died, and he was set at liberty."

38. While we cannot make this whole Psalm Messianic, yet it is delightful to see what a welcome theme the coming Saviour is to all the prophets, and how without the least formal notice they introduce him into their sacred compositions as here, v. 20.

39. There is no telling what evil shall bring to a miserable end the career of a sinner. It may be the sword of an enemy or of himself, the sting of conscience or of a bee, an evil *natural* or an evil *moral*, v. 21. Sin is always the procuring cause of death. It is sometimes the very means of terminating a wicked life.

40. If the only sin charged to the wicked in a gospel land were their enmity to good men, their destruction would be most just and terrible, v. 21.

41. It is always a safe rule for determining the final destiny of the sinner that it shall be in all respects the opposite of that of the saint. One shall be desolate. The other shall not be desolate, vv. 21, 22. One shall be condemned. The other shall not come into condemnation. One shall be held *guilty*. The other shall be held *righteous*. God is *against* the one. God is *with* the other.

42. The redemption of God's people shall at last be complete. God has undertaken that work, v. 22. He never puts his hands to the plough and looks back. The Lord is of one mind, and none can turn him.

43. Fearful desolation is based in guilt, vv. 21, 22. Sin is damning so as nothing else is. We are not hurt till our souls are hurt. Henry: "No man is desolate, but he whom God has forsaken, nor is any man undone till he is in hell."

PSALM XXXV.

A Psalm of David.

1 Plead *my cause*, O LORD, with them that strive with me: fight against them that fight against me.

2 Take hold of shield and buckler, and stand up for mine help.

3 Draw out also the spear, and stop *the way* against them that persecute me: say unto my soul, I *am* thy salvation.

4 Let them be confounded and put to shame that seek after my soul: let them be turned back and brought to confusion that devise my hurt.

5 Let them be as chaff before the wind: and let the angel of the LORD chase *them*.

6 Let their way be dark and slippery: and let the angel of the LORD persecute them.

7 For without cause have they hid for me their net *in* a pit, *which* without cause they have digged for my soul.

8 Let destruction come upon him at unawares; and let his net that he hath hid catch himself: into that very destruction let him fall.

9 And my soul shall be joyful in the LORD: it shall rejoice in his salvation.

10 All my bones shall say, LORD, who *is* like unto thee, which deliverest the poor from him that is too strong for him, yea, the poor and the needy from him that spoileth him?

11 False witnesses did rise up; they laid to my charge *things* that I knew not.

12 They rewarded me evil for good *to* the spoiling of my soul.

13 But as for me, when they were sick, my clothing *was* sackcloth: I humbled my soul with fasting; and my prayer returned into mine own bosom.

14 I behaved myself as though *he had been* my friend *or* brother: I bowed down heavily, as one that mourneth *for his* mother.

15 But in mine adversity they rejoiced, and gathered themselves together: *yea*, the abjects gathered themselves together against me, and I knew *it* not; they did tear *me*, and ceased not:

16 With hypocritical mockers in feasts, they gnashed upon me with their teeth.

17 Lord, how long wilt thou look on? rescue my soul from their destructions, my darling from the lions.

18 I will give thee thanks in the great congregation: I will praise thee among much people.

19 Let not them that are mine enemies wrongfully rejoice over me: *neither* let them wink with the eye that hate me without a cause.

20 For they speak not peace: but they devise deceitful matters against *them that are* quiet in the land.

21 Yea, they opened their mouth wide against me, *and* said, Aha, aha, our eye hath seen *it*.

22 *This* thou hast seen, O LORD: keep not silence: O Lord, be not far from me.

23 Stir up thyself, and awake to my judgment, *even* unto my cause, my God and my Lord.

24 Judge me, O LORD my God, according to thy righteousness; and let them not rejoice over me.

25 Let them not say in their hearts, Ah, so would we have it: let them not say, We have swallowed him up.

26 Let them be ashamed and brought to confusion together that rejoice at mine hurt: let them be clothed with shame and dishonour that magnify *themselves* against me.

27 Let them shout for joy, and be glad, that favour my righteous cause: yea, let them say continually, Let the LORD be magnified, which hath pleasure in the prosperity of his servant.

28 And my tongue shall speak of thy righteousness *and* of thy praise all the day long.

ON the title see on titles of Psalms iii. xi. David is the author of this ode. Both Scott and Clarke date it B. C. 1061. If it had a historic occasion, it is probably that mentioned in 1 Sam. xxiv. 9–15, where David uses the very ideas with which he begins this Psalm: "The Lord therefore be judge, and judge between me and thee, and see, and plead my cause, and deliver me out of thine hand." But the same language was as well suited to any one of many occasions. The Syriac suggests that it was written on occasion of the attack of the Idumeans. The Arabic says it is a prophecy concerning the incarnation, and concerning those things which the people did to Jeremiah. Our Saviour quoted a part of v. 19, in application to himself, John xv. 25. Of course those, who adopt Hutchinson's rule noticed in Ps. xxxiv. 20, regard this as wholly Messianic. Fry: "This Psalm is evidently a prayer of the Mediator." It is admitted that David was in many respects a type of Christ. Men hated them both without a cause. While Hutchinson's rule is justly rejected, there seems to be no safe method of interpreting this poem without making David in much of it a figure of the suffering and triumphing Redeemer. So say Scott, Morison, Bouchier, Cobbin and others. In this Psalm we have three names of the Most High: *Jehovah* LORD, *Adonai Lord* and *Elohim God*, on which respectively see on Ps. i. 2; ii. 4; iii. 2.

1. *Plead* my cause, *O* LORD, *with them that strive with me.* In several versions, as in the Hebrew, the words rendered *plead* and *strive* are forms of the same verb and of precisely the same signification. Morison: "The word rendered *plead*, denotes the act of contending, as a barrister would contend for his client in a court of justice." Alexander: "The original verb is one specifically used to denote judicial contest." The word rendered *my cause* is not in the first verse, but is properly supplied from verse 23, where it is found. It is a word kindred to *plead*. The object of the Psalmist is to commit his *cause* to God as *Advocate, Judge, Avenger.* He adds: *Fight against them that fight against me.* Here too the verbs are forms of the same root in the Hebrew, Chaldee and many others besides the English. *Fight, eat, devour*, Ps. cxli. 4; Prov. iv. 17; xxiii. 1, 6; Deut. xxxii. 24. David's enemies proposed to eat him up. His prayer is that the Lord would be on his side and do all that his case required, especially in view of the false accusations and deadly persecutions of his enemies.

2. *Take hold of shield and buckler.* Septuagint, Ethiopic, Arabic, Syriac and Vulgate: Take hold of arms and shield; church of England: Lay hand upon the shield and buckler; Chaldee and many others virtually agree with the English. He prays, Make ready for immediate and decisive action. The battle is now raging. Thy powerful aid is now required. For some account of the armor called *shield*, see on Ps. iii. 3; vii. 10; of that called *buckler*, see on Ps. v. 12. *And stand up for mine help.* This was just what David needed. The above armor was for protection and defence.

3. *Draw out also the spear.* *Spear*, a weapon of assault, always in our version so rendered, or *javelin*; but several ancient versions here have *sword*. The verb here found, when used in connection with sword, signifies to *unsheath.* In connection with *spear*, it may signify to *bring forth* from any place of deposit. *And stop* the way

against them that persecute me. The language describes the act of a host coming to the rescue of their comrades, when about to be overpowered. He asks that Jehovah would arrest the further progress of his persecutors by opposing them himself. Hengstenberg: Set a barrier against my persecutors. *Say unto my soul, I* am *thy salvation.* *Unto my soul, i. e.,* unto my heart and affections. See on Ps. iii. 2. *I am thy salvation,* the cause and author of thy deliverance.

4. *Let them be confounded and put to shame that seek after my soul.* This and several other verses of this Psalm contain forms of speech, on the right construction of which see Introduction, § 6. In this instance the language is used respecting the incorrigible foes of God, whose final success must impair confidence in the divine righteousness and faithfulness. Either God's friends or foes must be defeated. The contest was for life. Enemies were deadly. *Confounded,* as in Ps. vi. 10; xxii. 5; xxv. 2, 3, 20; xxxi. 1, 17. We have not before had the word rendered *put to shame;* but it occurs hereafter several times, and is also rendered *blush, ashamed, confounded, put to confusion.* Confusion and shame would necessarily follow the defeat of their devices. *Let them be turned back and brought to confusion that devise my hurt. Turned back, repulsed, driven back,* Ps. xl. 14; or *fail through weakness of resolution,* as in many places it imports. *Shame* and *confusion* are remarkably united in signification. *Brought to confusion,* also rendered *shamed, put to shame.* All the verbs of this verse in Hebrew are in the future. Hammond is strongly in favor of so rendering them. Fry prefers the present. But the Chaldee, Septuagint, Ethiopic, Arabic, Syriac, Vulgate, Doway, church of England, Calvin, Venema, Amesius, Ainsworth, Edwards, Jebb, Hengstenberg and Alexander accord with our version. And the form of the verbs in the next two verses, which continue the discourse here begun, would argue for the optative form throughout.

5. *Let them be as chaff before the wind. Chaff,* in our version so uniformly. We had the same figure in Ps. i. 4. It is often found. Many versions have *chaff;* but the Septuagint, Ethiopic, Syriac, Arabic, Vulgate, church of England and Jebb read *dust.* The method of winnowing grain in Judea made the figure of chaff intelligible and striking. *And let the angel of the* LORD *chase them.* On *the angel of the* LORD, see on Ps. xxxiv. 7. The language is very terrible. *Chase,* in our version elsewhere, *thrust at, overthrow, cast out, cast down, drive.* The original is a participle which Alexander renders *smiting.* Hengstenberg thinks it means to *thrust* or *knock down.* Men are undone when God lets loose his destroying angel among them. This makes a full end of their nefarious purposes.

6. *Let their way be dark and slippery.* For *dark* and *slippery* the Chaldee has darkness and mist; Septuagint, Ethiopic, Vulgate and Calvin, darkness and slipperiness; Arabic, sliding and dark; Syriac, obscure and slipperinesses. It adds strength to the expression that in Hebrew the words are nouns. The *way* is that on which they retreat. The imagery is not essentially different from that of Jer. xiii. 16; *stumbling on the dark mountains. And let the angel of the* LORD *persecute them.* A slippery way, a dark night and a swift and mighty destroyer in pursuit are the terrible images presented in the verse. In defending the righteous angels must often discomfit and even destroy their foes. God may send wicked angels to do the work of destruction; but there is no evidence that *the angel of the* LORD ever means a devil.

7. *For without cause have they hid for me their net* in a pit, which *without cause they have digged for my soul.* On *pits* and nets see on Ps. ix. 15. Compare also Ps. x. 9; xxv. 15; xxxi. 4. If our version is correct, it would seem that the *net* was sometimes hidden *in* the *pit,* and the two devices were united. David's foes never once dealt honestly and fairly with him. This was one reason why he had a right to ex-

pect God to be on his side. The Lord loves truth, candor, fairness. The other reason, why David hoped and prayed for the help of the Lord, was that the opposition to him was causeless and unreasonable. He had done nothing to provoke their murderous wrath. In killing Goliath, he had saved Saul and his army from contempt, if not from destruction. He had been anointed by Samuel, but God had sent the prophet after him. He had not aspired to the throne. In no case had David wronged Saul or his associates. Yet they sought his *soul*, *i. e.*, his life. Such wickedness must have an end.

8. *Let destruction come upon him at unawares*. *Destruction*, in Pr. i. 27, and elsewhere, *desolation*. Calvin has *confusion*, or *ruin*. At *unawares*: margin, which he knoweth not; literally, [which] he shall not know. No wicked man is ever prepared for overthrow. Its suddenness is a part of its dreadfulness, Pr. i. 27 ; Isa. xlvii. 11 ; 1 Thess. v. 3. *And let his net that he hath hid catch himself : into that very destruction let him fall*. *Come, catch* and *fall* are in the Hebrew all in the future. Sinners deceive none so much as themselves. They sow the seeds of all their own miseries. They plant all the thorns that pierce them. They weave and spread all the nets, which catch them. Look at Haman, Judas and all whose history is fully given. The ruin of sinners has in it appalling elements.

9. *And my soul shall be joyful in the* LORD. On *be joyful* see on Ps. ix. 14 ; xiii. 4, 5. There is no better rendering. Fry weakens the force of the clause in its connection by putting the verb in the present tense. We are joyful in the Lord not only when we are pleased with his whole character, but also with his relations to us. David's rejoicing was hearty. It engaged the affections of his *soul*. *It shall rejoice in his salvation*, *i. e.*, in the deliverance he has effected or shall effect for me. David knew nothing of the baseness of ascribing to fortune, to his own wit, or to any creature the safety secured to him by God. Some put the verb in the optative ; but is not David rather declaring that when deliverance shall come, it will not be wasted on an ingrate ? This more clearly seems to be the sense, when we look at verse

10. *All my bones shall say*, LORD, *who is like unto thee, which deliverest the poor from him that is too strong for him, yea, the poor and the needy from him that spoileth him*. Hengstenberg : " The *bones* denote the innermost nature." Alexander : " The bones, the frame, the person, are here put for the whole man." Morison : " As the bones are the strongest parts of the human frame, the Psalmist here, in anticipation of deliverance, proposes to serve and glorify God with all his strength." Calvin and Scott use similar language. Paul puts the *body* for the entire nature, Rom. xii. 1. In this verse the word *poor* occurs twice. See on Ps. ix. 12, 18 ; x. 12, 17 ; xxii. 26. Ainsworth renders it *poor, afflicted* ; Alexander, *sufferer*. *Needy*, elsewhere rendered *poor* ; once *beggar*, 1 Sam. ii. 8. The first of these words commonly designates those who are poor in spirit ; the latter, those who are poor in estate. For such a one God works deliverance from him that is too *strong*, or *mighty*, or *hard* for him ; even from *him that spoileth*, strippeth, or preyeth upon him. The interrogative form of this verse contains a challenge.

11. *False witnesses did rise up*. The word rendered *false* is a noun, which is elsewhere rendered *violence, wrong, cruelty, injustice*. We met it in Ps. vii. 16 ; xxvii. 12. It points to the *fierce* and *injurious* character of the witnesses, which rose up. The word occurs more than *fifty* times in the Hebrew Bible and is not elsewhere rendered *false*. The Chaldee, Septuagint, Ethiopic and Vulgate read *unjust* ; Calvin, *violent* ; Hengstenberg, *malicious* ; Ainsworth, *witnesses of cruel wrong*. David adds : *They laid to my charge things that I knew not*. The word, rendered *laid to charge*, might be rendered *asked, desired, inquired, requested, required, demanded*. The mode of examining persons charged with crime by proposing to them interrogatories is

probably alluded to. So that the common version gives the true sense. The Chaldee: They ask me *things*, which I knew not. This is closely or virtually followed by the Septuagint, Ethiopic, Arabic, Syriac, Vulgate, Ainsworth, Jebb, Hengstenberg and Alexander. They question me of things that I knew not. In contests between saints and sinners, the wicked act as if they thought that the multiplication of charges was equal to their proof. If anything could establish the feebleness of the cause of the wicked, it is that the whole kingdom of Satan is built on wrong, violence and falsehood.

12. *They rewarded me evil for good.* Saul confessed that this was so, 1 Sam. xxiv. 17. *Rewarded, rendered, repaid, requited, recompensed.* The Hebrew, Arabic, Syriac and Jebb have the verb in the future; Calvin, Venema, Amesius, Edwards, Fry and Alexander, in the present; Chaldee, Septuagint and kindred versions, Ainsworth and Hengstenberg, in the preterite. David's foes were unscrupulous. They were ready, says he, for the *spoiling of my soul*, which either means the taking of his life, or the loss, destruction, discomfort, bereavement of his soul. In Isa. xlvii. 8, 9, the word is rendered *loss* of children. Diodati; "The Hebrew signifieth a privation of all help, comfort, joy and assistance."

13. *But as for me, when they were sick, my clothing* was *sackcloth.* Sackcloth was the usual covering of those who were deeply afflicted. It was never put on for trifles. The death of a son, the death of a great man, a dreadful dearth, or some sad event furnished the occasion of wearing sackcloth, Gen. xxxvii. 34; 2 Sam. iii. 31; Joel i. 13. David showed his love for those who were now his foes by having put on the ensigns of grief when they had been seriously sick. Yea, more he says, *I humbled my soul with fasting.* Sackcloth and *fasting* were fitly united, Dan. ix. 3. In these ways men *humbled* and chastened their souls. To fasting he added intercession: *And my prayer returned into mine own bosom.* A large number of translations have the verb in the preterite as here. Others have it *shall return*, or *shall be turned.* What is it for a prayer to return to the bosom of the suppliant? Some think the phrase equivalent to praying *continually*, as if the petition, being offered from the heart, at once returned to the heart, and was again offered. Although this gives a good sense, it is not the true sense. Others think that it means that his prayer returned to him without effect on those who slighted and despised it. But this cannot be the sense. His prayer was heard. They did recover. Their sickness was healed. Hengstenberg thinks we get the true conception by considering the posture of Elias in prayer, 1 Kings xviii. 42. "He who prays with his head down, appears to bring the prayer back, as it were, to the bosom from which it proceeded." Boothroyd: "When the Orientals pray seriously in grief they hide their face in their bosom: and to this custom the Psalmist here alludes. Rabbi Levi, Dathe and others explain it in like manner." If the verb *return* be read in the future then it may express a hope or a prophecy that good shall yet come to him from those pure and benevolent prayers. Perhaps a still better sense is had by putting the verb into the imperative, Let my prayer return into my own bosom, *q. d.*, I am so sure that I heartily wished them well, that I now say, Let my prayer return on me. If I wished them any ill, let that ill come on me; but if I wished them good, let that good come to me. This accords with the import of the phrase, recompensing *into the bosom* found elsewhere, Ps. lxxix. 12; Isa. lxv. 6, 7; Jer. xxxii. 18; Luke vi. 38.

14. *I behaved myself as though* he had been *my friend* or *brother.* The supplied words are well chosen. But the rendering needlessly changes the plural to the singular. If it read: I behaved myself as though my friend *or* brother *were sick*, this difficulty would be avoided, and the sense be preserved. Several versions coincide with the English. For *behaved*, some prefer went, went on, went along; Chaldee, walked.

Our version surely gives the sense. *I bowed down heavily, as one that mourneth* for his *mother.* Our version is sustained by the Chaldee, Calvin, Venema, Amesius, Edwards, Ainsworth, Jebb, Fry, Hengstenberg and Alexander. To sackcloth some added dust and ashes. He mourned *heavily* or greatly. In the afflictions of those who were now his enemies, David gave all the usual signs of strong grief.

15. *But in mine adversity they rejoiced, and gathered themselves together.* The *noun* may be rendered either *adversity* or *halting.* If *halting,* yet it is admitted to be used figuratively, and in the sense of *adversity.* Sometimes the anguish of a sufferer melts even the hard-hearted. It was not so with David's foes. Yea, *the abjects gathered themselves together against me.* *Abjects* variously rendered *beaten, smitten, stricken, ungodly, evil men, scourges, rabble, revilers, smiters, base, vile* or *wicked persons, cripples;* and yet those, who thus vary the rendering, seem generally to understand the same as is taught by our version. The *beaten, stricken,* or *smitten* were those who had been publicly punished, or who had merited such ignominy. *Evil, ungodly, base* or *wicked* are all interpretations having the same bearing. *Rabble,* the lowest class of men. *Revilers,* who *smite* with the tongue. Alexander: "When I limped, cripples mocked at me; *i. e.,* those who were themselves contemptible, treated me with contempt." No word is better than *abjects.* Patrick has "The very scum of the people." David adds: *And I knew* it *not.* Some have it, *Whom I knew not.* If this is right, it points to the obscure character of some who had risen up against him. The man of Uz had like trials, Job xxx. 1–10. If we follow the common version, the sense is that these people had carried on their assaults on David's character and interests in a clandestine manner. *They did tear me,* or *rend,* or *cut, i. e.,* with their calumnies and slanders. *And ceased not.* Hengstenberg: *And are not silent;* Alexander: *And were not silent.* The Hebrew is in the preterite. According to other renderings of the same verb in our version, we might read *rested not, did not forbear, were not still, held not their peace.*

16. *With hypocritical mockers in feasts, they gnashed upon me with their teeth.* Perhaps very few passages are more idiomatic or have been more variously rendered. Chaldee: With scornful and derisive words of flattery, they gnashed with their teeth against me; Calvin: "Among perfidious jesters at feasts, they gnash upon me with their teeth; Ainsworth: With hypocrites, scoffers for a cake of bread, gnashing their teeth against me; church of England: With the flatterers were busy mockers, who gnashed upon me with their teeth; Hengstenberg: The vile, who mock for bread, gnash against me with their teeth; Alexander: With worthless mockers for bread—gnashing with their teeth. *Hypocritical,* in our version always so rendered or *hypocrite.* Others render it *profane, vile, worthless, flatterers.* Hammond thinks that from the Hebrew word comes our English word *knave. Mockers in feasts,* are mockers for bread, *cake-mockers,* who make sport for a living, or to curry favor with rich ungodly men, who were willing to have them at their table, if they would play the buffoon at the expense of David and his cause. Patrick calls them *trencher-buffoons.* A modern infidel says that "ridicule is the test of truth;" another, that "a *bon-mot* is better than an argument." A profane jest is much more congenial to a wicked mind than any serious attempt at reasoning. This derision is full of deadly malice. *They gnash their teeth,* thus exhibiting their rage. Their behaviour, like that of wild beasts around the fold or the barnyard, shows what they would do if they were within.

17. *Lord, how long wilt thou look on? i. e.,* how long wilt thou see these things and not give deliverance? Some versions have it, When wilt thou see? *i. e.,* take up my case and consider it? or, When wilt thou look upon me? Though the general sense thus gained is the same as that given in the common version, yet the English version is more true to the Hebrew. Common trials make weak faith soon cry out, How long? But great trials will make even strong faith do the same. *Rescue my soul from their*

destructions, my darling from the lions. For *destructions,* some read *tumults, desolations, ruins.* The deliverance sought is from the complete destruction, which these bitter foes were plotting. *Darling,* see on Ps. xxii. 20. *Lions,* men as *fierce* as lions, having no more mercy than lions. Such a rescue as is here sought would not be ungratefully forgotten :

18. *I will give thee thanks in the great congregation. Congregation,* as in Ps. xxii. 22, 25. The sense is that thanks should be given in the most public manner, calling on the assembly of God's true worshippers to unite in it. *I will praise thee among much people. Much people,* the *great congregation* of the first clause. For *much* some have *mighty.* In our version the word is everywhere else rendered *strong* or *mighty ;* but an assembly is often mighty in numbers and in the range of its interests, when its inherent power is small.

19. *Let not them that are mine enemies wrongfully rejoice over me. Enemies,* usually so rendered, see Ps. iii. 7 ; vi. 10 ; xvii. 9. *Wrongfully,* some prefer *with falsity, falsely, lying, without cause,* or *deceitfully ;* often in our version *wrongfully,* Ps. xxxviii. 19 ; lxix. 4 ; cxix. 86. The rejoicing here noticed is that of merciless and relentless foes, who would exult at his downfall. Neither *let them wink with the eye that hate me without a cause.* Diodati : "[*Wink*] a gesture of a malicious scoffer." Alexander : "Winking is here referred to as a gesture of mutual congratulation among accomplices in guilt." See Pr. vi. 13 ; x. 10. He prays that his foes may have no cause to exult over him. The last clause of this verse is quoted in application to Christ, John xv. 25 ; and the language of this and some preceding verses remarkably coincides with portions of Psalm xxii. David is led first to speak of himself, and is then " carried beyond himself by the spirit of prophecy to use language applicable to far more important transactions."

20. *For they speak not peace.* Without reason the Septuagint and kindred versions have, They indeed spoke peaceable things. The Chaldee and Syriac agree with our version. David says his foes are persistent in their enmity ; they have no idea of abating their ferocity ; in their consultations they never propose to let him alone. Strange is human malignity, directed against the saints. It never tires. Even to propose peace to persecutors often makes them increasingly violent, Ps. cxx. 7. By incorrigibleness they make it certain and necessary that either themselves or God's people shall be prostrated. When such an issue is made, it is easy to tell who will fall and who will triumph. They not only decline all terms of reconciliation, *but they devise deceitful matters against* them that are *quiet in the land.* This is well rendered. The variations from it are unimportant or erroneous. The people of God are quiet and love peace, Gen. xiii. 7–9 ; Jas. iii. 18. The wicked love disturbance. They scatter arrows, firebrands and death :

21. *Yea, they opened their mouth wide against me,* as brawlers and persons of lawless speech are in the habit of doing ; and *said, Aha, aha, our eye hath seen* it. There is considerable difficulty in rendering idiomatically the derisive and exultant exclamations of one language into another. The word *aha* expresses the scorn of one who thought his triumph was or soon would be complete. The Septuagint and kindred versions render it, Well done, well done ; church of England, Fie on thee, fie on thee ; Hengstenberg, There, there. We have the same in Job xxxix. 25, Ha, ha. Alexander : "It seems to be a natural expression of joyful surprise." So they add, *we have seen it, i. e.,* we see his cause already begin to fail ; or we are so sure that it will fail that we may say we see it.

22. *This thou hast seen, O* LORD. It is for a joy to the righteous, that Jehovah is a spectator of every contest, and has perfect knowledge of the behaviour of each of the contestants. Nor is he an uninterested beholder of the strife between Cain and

Abel. If there is a right, God takes sides with that. The contrast is between God's sight of David's state and the sight his enemies had of him. The wicked *see* and God *sees;* but O how differently. David has warrant to pray: *Keep not silence, i. e.,* speak out as a Judge and settle this conflict; bring forth my righteousness, as the noon-day; let the events of thy providence soon determine who is right. *O* LORD, *be not far from me.* See Ps. xxii. 11, 19; xxxviii. 21; lxxi. 12, where we have just the same. The meaning is that as one, who is afar off can give no prompt and effectual aid, he beseeches God to draw nigh and give decisive help.

23. *Stir up thyself, and awake to my judgment. Stir up,* often so, also often *awake,* Ps. vii. 6; xliv. 23; Cant. iv. 16; Isa. li. 9. *Awake,* commonly so rendered, once *arise. To my judgment, i. e.,* so as to give a decision in my favor. This is further explained thus: Even *unto my cause, my God and my Lord.* In verse 1, David had prayed: *Plead* my cause. That is virtually what he asks here, but in another form. It is as if he had said: Take up my cause, address thyself to my cause, I am sure what thy decision will be, if thou shalt but attend to it. He continues:

24. *Judge me, O* LORD, *my God, according to thy righteousness.* A good cause, once heard and decided in the court of heaven, always triumphs. If Jehovah settles a case, he who has the right will never complain of the decision, for it is always in *righteousness, justice, right. And let them not rejoice* [exult or triumph] *over me.* It is a great trial to be afflicted. But in adversity insults from God's enemies are among the very sorest temptations.

25. *Let them not say in their hearts* [much less with their lips] *Ah, so we would have it.* Patrick: "Let them have no occasion to think within themselves they shall prevail; saying to their souls, So now all goes well; cheer up, we shall have our desires." *Let them not say, We have swallowed him up.* To *swallow up* is utterly to *destroy,* to *devour.* The more bold and voracious they were, the more does the Psalmist plead that they may be defeated, not merely for his own safety, but in illustration of the rectitude of God's government.

26. *Let them be ashamed and brought to confusion together that rejoice at mine hurt.* In v. 4 of this Psalm the first word of this verse is rendered, Let them be confounded. *Brought to confusion,* the same so rendered in v. 4. The malignity of these men appeared in this, that they *rejoiced* at the *hurt* of one who deserved well at their hands. *Hurt,* as in v. 4; in v. 12, *evil. Let them be clothed with shame and dishonor that magnify* themselves *against me.* Chaldee: Who are magnified above me; Septuagint, Ethiopic and Vulgate: Who speak great things against me; Arabic: Who make great their speech against me; Syriac: Who lift themselves up against me; church of England: That boast themselves against me; Ainsworth: That magnify against me; Venema: Who have turned themselves against me. But Calvin, Amesius, Edwards, Jebb, Fry and Hengstenberg agree with the common version. His foes should be *clothed, dressed, covered, arrayed,* apparelled with shame and disgrace. The verbs of this verse, which in English are in the imperative, are in Hebrew in the future.

27. *Let them shout for joy, and be glad, that favor my righteous cause.* The first verb is in our version rendered *shout, sing, cry out, rejoice, triumph;* the second, *rejoice, be joyful, make merry, be glad. Favor, desire, delight in.* Just below in this same verse it is rendered *hath pleasure in.* These verbs and the two verbs next following are all in the future. *Yea, let them say continually, Let the* LORD *be magnified, which hath pleasure in the prosperity of his servant. Magnified,* the same verb as in v. 26, but in a different form. *Prosperity,* in v. 20 and commonly *peace.* In Isa. ix. 6 we have Prince of *Peace,* where the same word is used.

28. *And my tongue shall speak of thy righteousness* and *of thy praise all the day long. Speak of, utter, declare, talk of.* God's *righteousness* is his rectitude, or *justice.*

Deliverance effected by the Lord would be worthy of *praise all the day long*, or continually.

DOCTRINAL AND PRACTICAL REMARKS.

1. The Lord is the Advocate of his people. He *pleads* their cause, v. 1. Its merits will be made to appear. Here a defence is often denied them. When allowed, it is often feeble. But the infinite Advocate will bring forth their righteousness as the light, and their judgment as the noonday. There will be a final and perfect eclaircissement of all human affairs, contests and disputes.

2. It may well reconcile us to trials involving our good name, our legal rights, and even our lives to read this Psalm. David was a "holy man, alike eminent for his beneficence and inoffensiveness towards all men, and, by his courtesy and meekness, had merited, both in public and private, the esteem and favor of all;" yet he was maligned, hated, vilified; yea, he was hunted like a wild beast. His good name was torn all to pieces.

3. The Lord is Judge, vv. 1, 24. He is the Judge of all the earth. He is known by the judgments which he executeth. To the pious it is and ever shall be for a joy that there is a tribunal above all the assizes of earth, Ecc. v. 8. A large part of the findings of courts and the sentences of judges on earth will be reversed in the last day.

4. The Lord is a man of war. When necessary he grasps not only the shield and buckler, but also the spear, and goes forth conquering and to conquer, vv. 1–3. Blessed be his name, he fights the battles of the saints. None can resist him. He is the only being in the universe who can do as well with few as with many, with feeble as with mighty instruments.

5. It is a great comfort to have a lively sense of God's favor, when he speaks to *our souls*, v. 3. We ought to be thankful for the promises, for faith to trust the promises, and still more for a lively sense of their sweetness. If assurance were more sought, it would be oftener found.

6. We may well leave foes in God's hand. He will arrest their mad career, *stopping their way*, v. 3. He can do this in a thousand ways. Even Saul of Tarsus was arrested, when he least thought of it.

7. When God says, *I am thy salvation*, it is folly to look further, v. 3. We ought never to ascribe to creatures what belongs to God in our successes.

8. The defeat and overthrow of the finally and incorrigibly wicked will be inconceivably dreadful, vv. 4, 5, 6. No tongue can describe it. Eye has not seen it, ear has not heard it, heart has not conceived it. Their doom will be perfectly just, fearfully distressing, and absolutely total. When they shall begin to slide their way will be so slippery that they will never stop. It will be from darkness into the blackness of darkness. Nor will their destruction be difficult. It is easy for the wind to carry off the *chaff* and the *dust* from the threshing-floor.

9. Not only do angels fight for the saints, but they fight against the wicked, vv. 5, 6. Whatever provision men may make against visible foes, they can do nothing against these invisible warriors who *chase* and *persecute* those that fight against God's people. If men will war against God, they must expect his angels to war against them. If they would have the angels on their side, let them come over to God's side.

10. There is nothing in the principles or practices of true piety to justify the rage of the wicked against the sons of God. Their hatred is without cause, vv. 7, 19.

11. If others practise the arts of deception, let us set an example of candor and simplicity, v. 7. The more deceitful others are, the more careful should we be to

avoid all appearance of artifice. If uprightness and fairness cannot save our cause or credit, they will at least save our conscience, and that is better.

12. With all their cunning the wicked are great fools, v. 7. They are willingly ignorant of some things, without which they cannot act wisely. The king of Syria could not understand how all his plots against Israel failed, 2 Kings vi. 8–12 Dickson: "Though the enemies of the godly do plot secret devices against them, yet not so secret but God can give warning of it, and make it an errand for the godly to pray to him to disappoint the plot."

13. It is for a wonder that the wicked do not confidentially expect an overthrow, when they know there is no fairness in their contest with truth and righteousness. Take from them their nets and pits, their lies and scoffs, and what have they left? v. 7. If they believed the cause of the righteous no better than their own, they would leap for joy. Neither with David, nor with Christ had they at any time a reasonable prospect of success.

14. Sinners are so blind and stupid as to be caught in their own snares, v. 8. In this respect one generation is no wiser than that which went before. Calvin: "It never for a moment occurs to them as at all possible that their stratagems and craft, their wicked practices, and all the snares which they lay for the good and the simple, turn to the destruction of themselves who have devised them."

15. Wondrous is that providence, which brings on the wicked punishment in kind, v. 8. They sought the ruin of another; and they ruined themselves. Morison: "It not unfrequently happens, that when a man is preparing sorrows for his fellow-creatures, he is only, in reality, framing a weapon for his own chastisement, and whetting the edge of those miseries which shall afflict his own soul!"

16. When the wicked perish, there is shouting, v. 9. The wicked, who felt the iron heel of tyranny, are glad to be rid of such a curse. And the righteous adore him, who has put an end to the cruelties of their oppressors.

17. It is a blessed comfort and support to the righteous that they really need nothing, but that it will be for the divine glory to supply it; so that in a most important and encouraging sense their cause is God's cause, and so must succeed, v. 9.

18. How miserable must be the state of the man, who cannot rejoice in all the deliverances God works for those who trust in him, v. 9.

19. Our whole nature should be enlisted on the Lord's side, v. 10. God righteously claims heart, soul, mind and strength; and the truly pious cheerfully give him all. Their *bones* praise him. Calvin: "Men, in general, praise God in such a manner that he scarcely obtains the tenth part of his due."

20. When God works, he does marvellous things. His deliverances are wonderful. There is none like him in counsel, in deeds and mighty acts, and in glorious excellence, v. 10.

21. As all God's merciful interpositions demand humble and thankful acknowledgment, so the prospect of coming deliverances may well bring from us the humble promise of the highest services, when the rescue shall have been vouchsafed to us. Dickson: "It is a sort of engaging God to deliver, when the heart of the believer engageth itself to glorify God after the delivery."

22. In Jehovah the poor and needy have a protector, who is more than a match for all their oppressors and tormentors, v. 10. He is the Friend of the friendless; the Father of the fatherless; the hope of the despondent; the strength of the weak. It is his office and his delight to take up neglected causes and raise up those that are bowed down.

23. Let none be sore distressed because false witnesses rise up against him, v. 11. Compare Matt. v. 11, 12. It is a sort of compliment to a good man to be slandered.

His enemies must speak evil against him *falsely* or not at all.   He is then in the line of safe precedents.   Blessed is he, who can, like the Master, say to accusers, Which of you convinceth me of sin? John viii. 46.   The prince of this world had nothing in Christ.   His foes had a deal of trouble in getting witnesses, who could tell a tolerably coherent story against him. Matt. xxvi. 59, 60.   Even then the wicked, vacillating judge, who sat in his case, was compelled by his conscience repeatedly to say to his accusers: I find no fault in him, Luke xxiii. 4; John xviii. 38; xix. 4, 6.

24. In the time of evil report and of false accusation, it is an unspeakable blessing to have a good conscience, v. 11.

25. Tholuck: "Oppression and violence are never more painful than when they proceed from those who have experienced the proofs of our love," v. 12. Ps. lv. 12.

26. Nothing more clearly proves the dreadful wickedness of ungodly men than their reversal of every great law of God. One is, Render good for evil; but they reward evil for good, v. 12.

27. Fasting was a proper mode of humiliation under the law, v. 13. Moses prescribed no stated fast except that on the great day of atonement, Lev. xxiii. 27–32. But God's people were left each man to judge for himself when fasting was called for by special personal or public calamities; except that now and then by an inspired prophet men were called to this duty.   It is not certain, though it is probable that the patriarchs fasted.   Under the Gospel the law of fasting fixes no time for this duty.   It leaves it wholly to the judgment of God's people from age to age. Probably no religious duty has been more perverted both in ancient and modern times. Isa. lviii. 3–12; Matt. vi. 16–18.   Fasts are of two kinds, *total* and *partial*. In the former we abstain from *all food;* in the latter from *pleasant* food.   Under the gospel fasting is lawful, Luke v. 35; Acts xiii. 2, 3.

28. Praying for enemies and seeking their good was a duty, and among the best men a practice under the law as it is under the gospel, vv. 13, 14.   Christ commanded and did the same.   Great numbers of the martyrs prayed for their murderers.   Christ gave no new law for loving enemies; he simply rescued the old law from perversion and neglect.   David and Christ thus prayed.   "The type was amiable, the anti-type divine."   Hearty prayer for wicked foes, earnestly asking on them the blessings we seek for ourselves, is good evidence of a new heart.

29. Without any piety in the world, how much would earth resemble hell, vv. 15, 16.

30. Divine delays prove divine forbearance, and, if they answer no other end, this alone may justify them, v. 17.   Compare 2 Pet. iii. 9, 15.

31. It is admitted that public mercies call for public thanks; but in some cases even personal mercies call for public thanks, v. 18.   Our religion should not be ostentatious, but it ought not to be clandestine.

32. To ask that the wicked may not prevail against us and insult us is to beseech God to exercise his glorious attributes in a manner suited to beget godly fear and firm confidence, v. 19.

33. When we consider the fondness of wicked men for strife and contention, it is a wonder that the world is as quiet as it is, v. 20.

34. There are no new arts employed by wicked men against God's saints and ministers.   The favorite resort of every age is contempt. This is very old, vv. 21, 25.

35. Meanness and wickedness walk arm in arm.   Nothing is baser than insulting an innocent man fallen under reproach.   Yet David's foes did this, v. 21.

36. It is a great mercy that God knows the whole state of every case, and watches the progress of every wrong inflicted on those, who trust in his name, v. 22.

37. Dickson: "The hardest condition that can befall a believer, is a tolerable case and condition, if God draw near to his soul," v. 22.

38. With submission to God we may urgently ask him no longer to delay his appearance for our relief, vv. 22, 23.

39. The last resort of the saints in all their trials is the righteousness of God, v. 24. This never fails them.

40. The hearts of wicked men make all their wars against God and godliness to be deadly. They would *swallow up* and *devour* the saints, if they could, v. 25. In eighteen centuries they have put to death fifty millions of them.

41. The more the wicked magnify themselves against the saints, the greater in the end will be their shame and confusion, v. 26.

42. The righteous have cause for all their joys. God himself sustains them in their highest exultations, v. 27. They are not glad in a thing of nought, when they rejoice in the Lord. It is not idle vaunting to boast in God.

43. It is no less the purpose than the hope of all the saints to spend their whole future existence in praising and extolling God, v. 28.

44. As God saved David from the hand of all his foes, so shall he save all his chosen from their sins and adversaries. He who put David on the throne of Israel and Jesus on the throne in glory, will assuredly exalt all his people to an everlasting kingdom.

PSALM XXXVI.

To the chief Musician, *A Psalm* of David the servant of the LORD.

1 The transgression of the wicked saith within my heart, *that there is* no fear of God before his eyes.

2 For he flattereth himself in his own eyes, until his iniquity be found to be hateful.

3 The words of his mouth *are* iniquity and deceit: he hath left off to be wise, *and* to do good.

4 He deviseth mischief upon his bed; he setteth himself in a way *that is* not good; he abhorreth not evil.

5 Thy mercy, O LORD, *is* in the heavens; *and* thy faithfulness *reacheth* unto the clouds.

6 Thy righteousness *is* like the great mountains; thy judgments *are* a great deep: O LORD, thou preservest man and beast.

7 How excellent *is* thy loving-kindness, O God! therefore the children of men put their trust under the shadow of thy wings.

8 They shall be abundantly satisfied with the fatness of thy house; and thou shalt make them drink of the river of thy pleasures.

9 For with thee *is* the fountain of life: in thy light shall we see light.

10 Oh continue thy loving-kindness unto them that know thee; and thy righteousness to the upright in heart.

11 Let not the foot of pride come against me, and let not the hand of the wicked remove me.

12 There are the workers of iniquity fallen: they are cast down, and shall not be able to rise.

THE several clauses of the title are explained in titles of Psalms iii. iv. xi. xviii. The words, *the servant of the* LORD, are by some regarded as a claim of speaking by God's authority. Others think it is a setting of God's authority directly over against the wicked speeches of the ungodly here noticed. This would be a sufficient reason; but the same is not done in Ps. xiv. liii. where the profane are represented as boldly uttering vile sentiments. David is the author of this Psalm. A few have expressed a counter opinion, but without good cause. We cannot determine whether it had any historic occasion. The Syriac and Arabic refer it to some period in the Sauline persecutions. Scott dates it B. C., 1062; Clarke thinks it was written during the Babylonish captivity. It is a composition of rare excellence. Luther: "This is a Psalm containing a very necessary doctrine;" Tholuck: "It is a lofty Psalm of supplication;" Clarke: "It is one of the finest Psalms in the whole collection." Others bear like testimony. In it we find these names of the Most High, *Jehovah* Lord and *Elohim God*, on which see on Ps. i. 2; iii. 2. On *El*, see v. 6.

1. *The transgression of the wicked saith within my heart, that there is no fear of God before his eyes.* Musculus: "This verse is obscure and variously rendered." The classes of various renderings of the first clause are such as these: Montanus: The oracle of wickedness, to the ungodly, is in the inmost of his heart; Boothroyd: The oracle of transgression, to the wicked, is within,—even his own heart; Lowth: The wicked man, according to the wickedness in his heart, saith, There is no fear of God before mine eyes. This requires a change of the Hebrew text. Many versions, so far as intelligible, coincide with the sense gained from our version. Some think that *saith* points to oracular authority. *Transgression*, also sin, trespass. *Wicked;* in Ps. i. ungodly; often as here. *Within my heart, i. e.*, in my inward part, as in Ps. v. 9; or to my inward thought, as in Ps. xlix. 11. Perhaps the first clause means: "The trespass of the ungodly, as clearly as the oracles of God, makes known to me in my heart so as to affect me." This gives a good sense, agrees with the context, has no unanswerable objection to it and requires but a legitimate use of personification. The latter clause is, with the exception of Lowth, uniformly rendered. These views coincide with those of the mass of commentators. See Calvin, Pool, Henry, Scott and others. Diodati: "Through the experience I have of his wicked life, I do discover and conclude within myself that he hath forsaken all manner of piety and fear of God;" Alexander: "Depravity itself bore witness against the wicked, in the Psalmist's mind, that there was no fear of God before his eyes." "Not having the fear of God before his eyes," has become inwoven into proceedings in criminal courts. When a man has no fear of God, he is prepared for any crime.

2. *For he flattereth himself in his own eyes, until his iniquity be found to be hateful.* In rendering this verse, there are many variations, most of which claim no attention. The following are given; Montanus: For he has smoothed over in his own eyes, with respect to the finding out of his iniquity to hate it; Ainsworth: For he flattereth himself in his own eyes, to find his iniquity which he ought to hate; Edwards: Though he smootheth over his iniquity to himself in his own eyes, yet it must at last be found out and make him detestable; Green: But though he flattereth himself in his own sight, his iniquity must be found out and make him odious. To flatter [or smooth over as to] himself is better than to read, flatter God, as Tholuck does. No rendering is better than our version. That the verbs of the last clause may be taken as passive many assert. For examples see Josh. ii. 5; Esther vi. 6; Ps. xxxii. 9; li. 6. Is his iniquity hateful to *himself*, or to his *neighbors?* The latter best accords with the preceding clause and with fact. Many a vile man is self-complacent long after his sins have made him odious to all around him. This is the view of Calvin and others. Scott: "The wicked man not only disguises his crimes or intentions from others; but, through the excess of self-love, he becomes his own flatterer, calls his vices by soft names or mistakes them for virtues; and deems his conduct justifiable, perhaps meritorious, when in fact it is a hateful compound of impiety, injustice and malevolence, and will very soon be proved to be so." How rarely do we find, even in the cells of convicts, a man who regards his sentence just, or himself vile. Martin

Bucer: "As the wicked have no regard for God, so they exceedingly please and flatter themselves."

3. *The words of his mouth* are *iniquity and deceit.* *Iniquity*, as in Ps. v. 5; vi. 8 also rendered vanity, wickedness, sorrow, affliction; in verse 4, mischief. *Deceit*, as in Ps. v. 6; x. 7; in Ps. xxxiv. 13, guile; in Gen. xxvii. 35, subtilty. It is not surprising that he adds concerning such a man: *He hath left off to be wise*, and *to do good* Chaldee: He hath ceased to understand, (so) that he might do good; Syriac: Nor does he wish to do good; Alexander: He has ceased to act wisely, to act well. Each of these renderings speaks a truth, but none of them is better than the authorized version.

4. *He deviseth mischief upon his bed.* *Mischief*, in verse 3, iniquity. The good man on his bed *meditates* on God and good things; the wicked, on things of vanity and impiety. Compare Ps. xciv. 11; Gen. vi. 5. A wicked man carries with him a wicked heart, even to bed, yea, to the sanctuary. The result is: *He setteth himself in a way* that is *not good.* *Setteth*, Chaldee, remaineth; Arabic, stood; Alexander, will take his stand. He, who allowedly lives in one known sin, is on the high way to all iniquity. Sin is in its nature stubborn, wilful, perverse. So that, *He abhorreth not evil.* *Abhorreth*, refuseth, rejecteth, despiseth, contemneth, Job xlii. 6; Ps. xv. 4; lxxviii. 59. There is no stronger Hebrew verb for expressing aversion. The wicked neither dreads nor detests iniquity. How then should he avoid it? It is always courting him, pressing upon him, seducing him. Bad as he is, he is constantly growing worse, Jer. ix. 3; 2 Tim. iii. 13.

5. *Thy mercy, O* LORD, is *in the heavens.* *Mercy*, as in Ps. v. 7; xvii. 7. *In the heavens, i. e.*, exalted, excellent, rising high, abundant, very great. And as God has goodness, loving-kindness, mercy as one of his infinite perfections, so has he unfailing fidelity to all his promises: and *thy faithfulness reacheth unto the clouds.* The Hebrew noun is elsewhere once rendered *faith*, Hab. ii. 4; once *stability*, Isa. xxxiii. 6; frequently, *truth*, Ps. lxxxix. 49; xcvi. 13; xcviii. 3; but most commonly *faithfulness.* God's veracity cannot fail. It knows no limits, Lam. iii. 23. It rises high, *reaching to the clouds*, which are quite beyond our grasp. His *faithfulness* is infinite. Arnd: "In all tribulations, let them be ever so high, so deep, so broad and long, God's truth and grace are still greater and higher." The transition in this and subsequent verses from the subject of vv. 1–4 is very happy. *There* the prophet had given the unscrupulous, self-conceited, deceitful, cruel, unrighteous character of the wicked; *here* he holds up to our faith the glorious character of God:

6. *Thy righteousness* is *like the great mountains.* *Righteousness*, as in Ps. v. 8; xi. 7; xxiv. 5. Septuagint, Ethiopic, Arabic, Vulgate: Thy righteousness is as the mountains of God. This is followed by Calvin, Venema, Marloratus, Ainsworth, Brent, Fabritius, Jebb, Tholuck, Hengstenberg and Alexander. The Syriac has it: Thy righteousness is as the mountains, O God. For *great* Fry has *mighty;* Chaldee and church of England, *strong;* Piscator and Edwards agree with our version. This diversity arises from the fact that the word rendered *great* is *El*, in many places rendered *God.* This does not indeed vary the sense. It is a Hebrew form of expression. The *mountains of God* are *great mountains.* We have the same word applied to a *river*, in Ps. lxv. 9; to *cedars*, in Ps. lxxx. 10; to *trees*, in Ps. civ. 16. In Psalms lxv. civ. our version follows the Hebrew; but in Ps. lxxx. 10 we have *goodly.* Our version misleads no one, because it gives the meaning and is therefore in the best sense a *translation.* There are two senses in which God's righteousness resembles the mighty mountains; first, in stability, secondly, in height or vastness, Ps. lxxi. 19. It shall endure forever. It is infinite. The next clause fitly follows: *Thy judgments are a great deep.* Parallel to this is Rom. xi. 33, "How unsearchable are his judgments."

Judgments, see on Ps. x. 5; xix. 9; God's decisions, whether given in his word or in providence. Here the reference seems to be to his ways in providence. Chaldee: Thy judgments are deep like a great abyss. Lowth reads a vast abyss; Ainsworth, a great depth; Hengstenberg, a great flood; Tholuck, like great seas. Immeasurableness, infinitude seems to be the primary idea intended. From this naturally follows their incomprehensibleness, and so their mysteriousness. All God's decisions have a scope far beyond our perception. They flow from eternal *righteousness*. They are final and unimpeachable, because they are good and are the judgments of God. O LORD, *thou preservest man and beast*. God's righteous ways in providence produce all the happiness there is on earth, among brutes or men. Each living thing is an unanswerable proof of the goodness of providence. Beasts and birds are often mentioned as sharing the providential goodness of God. The argument is that if God takes care of them, much more will he provide for men. And if he is kind to *all* men, even very kind to them, much more will he be unspeakably gracious to the righteous, who put their trust in him.

7. *How excellent* is *thy lovingkindness, O God!* *Lovingkindness*, so also in v. 10; in v. 5, *mercy*. *Excellent*, in Ps. xlv. 9, *honorable*; in Ps. cxvi. 15, *precious*. *Therefore the children of men put their trust under the shadow of thy wings.* For *therefore* some have *but;* some, *and;* and some omit it altogether; but the best have *therefore*, or *accordingly*. This most perfectly shows the connection. *Children of men;* Chaldee, *Men;* many versions, *Sons of men;* Venema and Ainsworth, *Sons of* Adam; Alexander, *Sons of man*. The imagery here presented, the *shadow of wings*, is either drawn from the wings of the cherubim overshadowing the ark of the covenant, or from the wings of a fowl protecting her young. The former view seems to have been taken by the Chaldee, and is favored by many modern translations. Many others, no less respectable, adopt the latter view. The verse (Deut. xxxii. 11) adduced by Bishop Hare, does not refer to the *protection* of young eagles in the nest, but to training them to fly, after the nest is broken up. The passages generally supposed to be parallel are Ps. xvii. 8; lvii. 1; lxi. 4; lxiii. 7; xci. 1. All of these may be interpreted either way. But Ps. xci. 4, and Matt. xxiii. 37, clearly point to the latter mode of exposition. All the confidence reposed by the humble of earth in the Almighty, is justified by his manifested excellence—his *precious lovingkindness*.

8. *They shall be abundantly satisfied with the fatness of thy house.* For *abundantly satisfied*, some suggest *inebriated, plenteously moistened, watered, drenched*. But none of these are good. Some read *drink, be refreshed, be most richly filled, be satiated*. These are good, but not better than the common version. The figure points to guests entertained at a feast in God's house. *Fatness* abounded in feasts, Job xxxvi. 16; Ps. lxiii. 5; Isa. lv. 2; Jer. xxxi. 14. We ought not to limit the significancy of this promise to any one class of blessings. Clearly both the words and the analogy of faith embrace all good things, temporal and eternal. The parallelism is preserved in the next clause: *And thou shalt make them drink of the river of thy pleasures.* *Pleasures;* also rendered delights. Clarke, Anderson, Hengstenberg and Alexander think the Hebrew points to Gen. ii. 10. The word rendered pleasures is the plural of *Eden*. The abundance of excellent things secured to the righteous is often taught by the figure of a river, Ps. xlvi. 4; Zech. xiv. 8; John iv. 10; Rev. xxii. 1. God will bring his people to the river, and cause them to drink, and they shall thirst no more. All this he can easily do.

9. *For with thee* is *the fountain of life*. The *fatness* and *river of pleasures* of the preceding verse are here explained by the word *life*, which points to the sum of bliss and of all good things. Calvin: " There is not a drop of life to be found without God." Compare Acts xvii. 28; Rom. vi. 23. Life and light agree: *In thy light*

shall we see light. Chaldee: In the brightness of thy glory shall we see light. The common version is literal. Alexander: "It is only by the light of God's countenance that man can see any good. It is only in God's favor that he can be happy. The only bliss attainable or desirable is that which is bestowed by God and resides in him." We are by nature blinded, benighted, lost in darkness, yea, we are *darkness* itself, so that while "the light shineth in darkness, the darkness comprehendeth it not." John i. 5; Eph. v. 8; 1 Pet. ii. 9. There are no richer promises than those found in Isa. lx. 20; Rev. xxii. 5; and they both respect *light.* He who relishes God's blessings, desires that they may last:

10. *Oh continue thy lovingkindness unto them that know thee. Lovingkindness,* as in vv. 5, 7. Those that *know God* are the truly pious, *the knowledge of God* being an essential part of real godliness. *Continue,* elsewhere *draw out, prolong,* Ex. xii. 21; Ps. lxxxv. 5; Isa. xiii. 22; Ezek. xii. 25, 28. Hengstenberg: "With God there is never a new beginning, but only a continuation; if he continues to act as he has done, he helps us." David and all the saints knew and confessed that they should need *goodness, mercy, lovingkindness* to the end of life. We shall need it at the day of judgment, 2 Tim. i. 18. He adds; *And* [prolong] *thy righteousness to the upright in heart. Righteousness,* as in v. 6. See also Ps. v. 8. The *upright* are the same as those who savingly *know God.* See on Ps. vii. 10. God's servants are in heart *honest, sincere, truthful.* They are not deceivers. Calvin: "The light of faith must necessarily dispose us to uprightness of heart."

11. *Let not the foot of pride come against me.* Trials brought on us by insolent men are among the severest of a good man's life. He has no heart to return insolence for insolence. He sees and abhors the injustice dealt out to him. A good man may well ask to be saved from such a trial. The next clause is parallel: *And let not the hand of the wicked remove me.* In the former clause we have the *foot,* and in in this the *hand* for the person. The prophet is praying against being in the power of bad men. The transition from the plural in preceding verses to the singular in this shows that the Psalm relates to matters common to all good men. He asks that the wicked may not *remove* him, *i. e.,* not be able to *make* him a *wanderer.* In Gen. iv. 12, 14, the participle is rendered *vagabond.* Montanus: "He shall not cause me to wander;" Alexander: "The last verb is causative and strictly means to put to flight, cause to wander, or send into exile."

12. *There are the workers of iniquity fallen.* His prayer was hardly offered till it was answered, or till he was assured it should be answered. He saw the foot of pride and the hand of violence approaching, and cried for deliverance; and lo! they are already fallen. The first word, rendered *there,* justifies this construction. Mudge: "It represents strongly before the eye the downfall of the wicked. Upon the *very* spot where they practise their treachery, they receive their downfall." *Iniquity,* as in vv. 3, 4. The unregenerate are always the *workers of iniquity.* When the wicked fall, they are undone. *They are cast down, and shall not be able to rise,* Ps. xviii. 38. It is far different with the righteous, Ps. xxxvii. 24; Pr. xxiv. 16; Micah vii. 8.

Doctrinal and Practical Remarks.

1. Wicked men are very blind and foolish, else they would learn their own characters from their own lives. Discerning people see through them. Their character is no secret, v. 1. Those, who hypocritically profess religion, are not exceptions. "You know a servant in the present day by the livery he wears; and so. if you see a sinner doing Satan's works, and hear him using Satan's language, and going here and there at Satan's bidding," you know that he is Satan's servant, 1 John iii. 8.

2. It is a great mercy when God so shows us the wickedness of others as to let us see the odiousness of their sins and the danger of their course, v. 1. Tholuck: "There are moments in our life, when the dimness and mystery of the course of the world suddenly dissolve, and the world, seen in the light of faith, assumes a new appearance."

3. *Total depravity* is not too strong a term to describe human wickedness. The sinner has no *fear of God*, v. 1. Where that is wanting, how can there be any piety? And if there is no piety, there must be total want of right affections, and that is the very essence of depravity.

4. Professors of religion may judge of their state by ascertaining whether they do truly fear God, and how much they fear him. If they have no fear, they have no grace. If their fear is very imperfect, so is their whole Christian character.

5. Self-flattery and self-deception seem to be born with sin; and, if not resisted, will certainly prove our ruin, v. 2. Not a word of ingenuous confession escaped the lips of either Adam or Eve, when called to account. The very men, who were plotting the death of Christ, said, "Who goeth about to kill thee?" Compare Isa. xxviii. 15.

6. The progress of sin is very fearful, v. 2. Conscience, peace, hope, character, self-respect, health all go by a "*paulatim* process," until the poor soul is ready for ruin; and even then God sometimes seems to arrest the natural course of things for a short season, till at last some slight event terminates the earthly career, and the soul drops into the lake of fire.

7. We cannot too often or too earnestly ask God to make us honest with ourselves, that we may not by self-flattery fall into the condemnation of the wicked, v. 2.

8. It is possible to sin so boldly and atrociously as to become detestable, v. 2. Even vile and wicked men are often struck with horror at some crimes. To the wicked all sin will ere long appear more mischievous and ruinous, than to good men it now appears.

9. While the righteous cannot too tenderly pity, nor too earnestly pray for poor sinful men, they cannot too profoundly abhor their ways and characters, v. 2. If even a sinner may see the odiousness of some transgressions, surely those, who are born from above, ought to hate all sin, wherever seen, and ought to hate it intensely, Ps. cxxxix. 21, 22.

10. We ought always to be alarmed when we find ourselves pleading for wickedness, or excusing it in ourselves or others, v. 3.

11. If nothing else evinced the character of bad men, their speech proves their hearts evil, v. 3. Reader, would you know by what rule your destiny will at last be determined, read Matt. xii. 37.

12. A great part of the sin of men consists in omission, "in leaving off to be wise and to do good," v. 3. Compare Dan. v. 23. "Lord, forgive my sins of omission." Not only are sins of omission *sins*, but they are the high way to all sins.

13. Diligence in doing evil is a mark of deep depravity, v. 4.

14. When all the sinful desires, vain thoughts, evil words and wicked deeds of men shall be made known, angels and men will confess the justice of the sentence, which shuts the sinner out of paradise. The *mischief* he has *devised upon his bed* would itself justify damnation, v. 4. Compare Ecc. xii. 14. Morison: "Could the nightly thoughts and practices of the wicked be laid open to the eye of man, as they are to the eye of God, what a scene of moral guilt and pollution would they disclose!"

15. The contrast between saints and sinners is great, vv. 1–4. Modest and retiring as a good man may be, his deportment says to those, who have spiritual discernment, The fear of God is before his eyes. Instead of flattering himself, he judges himself, condemns himself, abhors himself and repents in dust and ashes. The law of kind-

ness and of truth is in his mouth. He seeks and finds wisdom from above. He does good as he has opportunity. The cause he understands not he seeks out. He is firm as a rock, when he knows he is right. He abhors evil. In all these respects the saint and sinner radically differ.

16. Sinners have *set* themselves to do evil, v. 4. They are always doing it. They sleep not except they have done some mischief. Even dying sinners seem commonly to prefer to be lost rather than to obey the Gospel.

17. He that does not *abhor evil* is in a bad way. Yet where is the unrenewed man, that can even persuade himself that he has a strong dislike to everything forbidden or condemned in God's word?

18. With pleasure does the devout mind turn away from the contemplation of the vile character of the *wicked* as here delineated, to that of the glorious character of God, in vv. 5–9! The sublimest tracks of thought ever pursued, and those yielding the richest harvest of comfort and edification, are found in the existence, attributes, providence, worship and glories of Jehovah. Here we have themes at once awful and pleasing, dreadful and refreshing.

19. In our thoughts, prayers and preaching we may safely follow the Scriptures and give a delightful prominence to the *mercy*, the *lovingkindness* of the Lord, speaking of that *first* and *most frequently*, vv. 5, 7, 10. God will not show mercy at the expense of justice; but God is love, and has infinite delight in exercising his loving nature, and in filling heaven with its monuments, and he has sworn that he has no pleasure in the death of sinners.

20. God is also *faithful*, v. 5. His faithfulness is unto all generations. It is great, *unto the clouds*. Therefore the laws of nature are stable; an humble sinner never perished; and a believer in extremity is as safe as one in no unusual peril.

21. Nor let us forget that *justice*, as it is amiable in any ruler, is peculiarly so in the Governor of the universe, v. 6. In him it has infinite scope. It is like the great mountains. There is an ample field for the exercise of God's righteousness, respecting his people.

22. Nor should we avert our attention from God's *judgments*, though they are often incomprehensible, v. 6. They furnish much food for pious contemplation, and they are "stupendous and unfathomable as the waters of the great deep." The Noachic Deluge and the destruction of the cities of the plain were two of the most terrific of God's judgments. Evidences of the former are found on every mountain. Of the latter the Dead Sea stands an irrefragable proof. What two events in history have been more useful to keep the world in awe, to remind Christians that the Lord is God, and to assure all the saints that when the worst comes on the wicked, God makes a difference between those, who serve him, and those, who serve him not? He, who is rightly affected with God's terrible judgments, will revere all his *decisions*.

23. God's providence embraces absolutely all things, v. 6. *Man* and *beast*, all causes and effects, all creatures celestial, terrestrial and infernal, all events, all things are controlled by the Almighty.

24. We shall never be able to find terms by which to express all God's love to his people, v. 7. Some ignorance is better than some knowledge. I had rather hear the exclamation, How excellent! than the cry, I know it all.

25. The more we trust in God, the more evidence we have that we rightly esteem his *excellent* character, v. 7.

26. If a man would let his soul delight itself in fatness, if he would drink and thirst no more, let him embrace the truth and covenant of God. Then he shall have food indeed; and he shall drink of the river of God's pleasures, v. 8. Compare Jer. xxxi. 25. Making souls and satisfying them are prerogatives of God.

27. There can never be a failure of good things to those whom God loves, for "with him is the fountain of life," v. 9. If the *fountain* is with him, the streams can never be cut off from those who are in his bosom. Is not that clear? All other good is but a drop. With God is the ocean.

28. Clarke: "No man can illuminate his own soul: all understanding must come from heaven," v. 9.

29. If God will go on with the saints as he has begun, all will be well. They can ask no more, v. 10. He has already given them his Son, his Spirit, himself, his word, his oath, and his covenant established on the best of promises. He will finish his work on the scale on which he began it.

30. *Knowledge* and *uprightness* are essential properties of a gracious character, v. 10. One is as important as the other. "Ye worship ye know not what" is a sentence fatal to any hopes of salvation. And a *crooked* way did never point to a new heart.

31. It is a great mercy to have exemption from the scorn, cruelty and violence of the proud and wicked! v. 11. If those who are now often murmuring with their lot, were but for a few weeks subjected to the tyranny of Saul and Doeg, or to the ingratitude and baseness of Absalom, or to the refined cruelties of Charles II., or to the brutality and vengeance of Jeffries and Claverhouse, how would their views be altered.

32. Dickson: "It is the Lord only who can divert proud persecutors, that they hurt not his children; and it is the Lord only who can keep his children in the course of faith and obedience, when the wicked employ their power against them," v. 11.

33. The overthrow of the wicked will be beyond expression fearful. They will never recover, they will never begin to recover, they will never hope to recover from their dreadful fall, v. 12. Tholuck: "The present prosperity of the wicked can only be regarded as a term of the long-suffering of God, which gives them the opportunity, by repentance, to escape the final judgment of God." And if they should not count that long-suffering salvation, who can conceive the horrors of their state?

34. The church is safe, vv. 5–12.

PSALM XXXVII.

A Psalm of David.

1 Fret not thyself because of evil doers, neither be thou envious against the workers of iniquity.

2 For they shall soon be cut down like the grass, and wither as the green herb.

3 Trust in the LORD, and do good; *so* shalt thou dwell in the land, and verily thou shalt be fed.

4 Delight thyself also in the LORD; and he shall give thee the desires of thine heart.

5 Commit thy way unto the LORD; trust also in him; and he shall bring *it* to pass.

6 And he shall bring forth thy righteousness as the light, and thy judgment as the noonday.

7 Rest in the LORD, and wait patiently for him: fret not thyself because of him who prospereth in his way, because of the man who bringeth wicked devices to pass.

8 Cease from anger, and forsake wrath: fret not thyself in any wise to do evil.

9 For evil doers shall be cut off: but those that wait upon the LORD, they shall inherit the earth.

10 For yet a little while, and the wicked *shall* not *be:* yea, thou shalt diligently consider his place, and it *shall* not *be.*

11 But the meek shall inherit the earth; and shall delight themselves in the abundance of peace.

12 The wicked plotteth against the just, and gnasheth upon him with his teeth.

13 The Lord shall laugh at him: for he seeth that his day is coming.

14 The wicked have drawn out the sword, and have bent their bow, to cast down the poor and needy, *and* to slay such as be of upright conversation.

15 Their sword shall enter into their own heart, and their bows shall be broken.

16 A little that a righteous man hath *is* better than the riches of many wicked.

17 For the arms of the wicked shall be broken: but the LORD upholdeth the righteous.

18 The LORD knoweth the days of the upright: and their inheritance shall be for ever.

19 They shall not be ashamed in the evil time: and in the days of famine they shall be satisfied.

20 But the wicked shall perish, and the enemies of the LORD *shall be* as the fat of lambs: they shall consume; into smoke shall they consume away.

21 The wicked borroweth, and payeth not again: but the righteous sheweth mercy, and giveth.

22 For *such as be* blessed of him shall inherit the earth; and *they that be* cursed of him shall be cut off.

23 The steps of a *good* man are ordered by the LORD: and he delighteth in his way.

24 Though he fall, he shall not be utterly cast down: for the LORD upholdeth *him with* his hand.

25 I have been young, and *now* am old; yet have I not seen the righteous forsaken, nor his seed begging bread.

26 *He is* ever merciful, and lendeth; and his seed *is* blessed.

27 Depart from evil, and do good; and dwell for evermore.

28 For the LORD loveth judgment, and forsaketh not his saints; they are preserved for ever: but the seed of the wicked shall be cut off.

29 The righteous shall inherit the land, and dwell therein for ever.

30 The mouth of the righteous speaketh wisdom, and his tongue talketh of judgment.

31 The law of his God *is* in his heart; none of his steps shall slide.

32 The wicked watcheth the righteous, and seeketh to slay him.

33 The LORD will not leave him in his hand, nor condemn him when he is judged.

34 Wait on the LORD, and keep his way, and he shall exalt thee to inherit the land: when the wicked are cut off, thou shalt see *it*.

35 I have seen the wicked in great power, and spreading himself like a green bay tree.

36 Yet he passed away, and, lo, he *was* not: yea, I sought him, but he could not be found.

37 Mark the perfect *man*, and behold the upright: for the end of *that* man *is* peace.

38 But the transgressors shall be destroyed together: the end of the wicked shall be cut off.

39 But the salvation of the righteous *is* of the LORD: *he is* their strength in the time of trouble.

40 And the LORD shall help them, and deliver them: he shall deliver them from the wicked, and save them, because they trust in him.

IT is remarkable that the title of this long and precious Psalm should in the Hebrew consist of a single word, the name of its author. See on titles of Psalms iii. xi. This is the third alphabetical Psalm. But the alphabetical arrangement is irregular, and even imperfect. The *sixteenth* letter of the alphabet is wholly omitted. One letter has three verses assigned to it. Three letters have but one verse each. The rest have two verses each. On this subject see Introduction, § 13, and on Ps. xxv. There is nothing to justify a belief that David did not compose this Psalm. The title is conclusive. Hengstenberg: "The reasons, which have been brought against the Davidic origin of this Psalm, are of no weight." The most prominent theme of this and of Psalms xlix. lxxiii. seems to be the mysteriousness of providence in allowing to the wicked so much apparent prosperity. The Psalm abounds in proverbial wisdom. It is full of weighty doctrine expressed in few and well-chosen words. Horne: "The Psalm is rather a collection of divine aphorisms on the same subject, than a continued and connected discourse." Hengstenberg says it is an "unquestionable fact, that the Psalm forms the basis of a series of declarations in the Proverbs of Solomon." However this may be, it is full of "many excellent cautions and counsels." Delaney supposes this ode written for the comfort of Mephibosheth under the calumny of Ziba. Alexander: "The whole Psalm seems to have reference to David's own experience in the case of Saul, Nabal, Absalom, Ahithophel, and others." This is very much the view of Luther and Hengstenberg. Dodd: "This Psalm was made by David in his old age." Scott dates it B. C. 1017, three years before David's death. It excels in giving us line upon line. A good rule for instructing the young, the feeble, or the tempted is, A little at a time and often repeated. Things of the same import are here said again and again, yet with a pleasing diversity of expression. Amyrald compares the sentences of this Psalm to "so many precious stones or pearls strung together upon one thread to form a necklace." Luther: "The sum of this Psalm is,—Suffer; that is, learn patience. Every evil must be overcome by bearing it with patience. Cast thy cares upon the Lord. Do not murmur; be not angry; wish no ill to the wicked. Leave the management and government of all to God: he is a righteous Judge." Few will agree with Horsley, that "the Messiah, if not exclusively, is yet principally the subject of this Psalm." See Introduction, § 8. We have here three names of the Most High, *Jehovah* LORD, *Adonai* Lord and *Elohim* God, on which see on Ps. i. 2; ii. 4; iii. 2.

1. *Fret not thyself because of evildoers.* The Chaldee: Be not moved against the malicious so that thou become like them; Piscator and Fabritius: Be not inflamed with anger because of evil-doers; Marloratus: Be not troubled on account of the malicious; Edwards: Be not inflamed with indignation against evil-doers; Hengstenberg: Inflame not thyself against the miscreants. In the authorized version the verb is never rendered, *Fret thyself*, except in one form, and then only here, in vv. 1, 7, 8, and in Prov. xxiv. 19, probably copied hence. A very good rendering would be, *Be not incensed, Be not displeased,* Isa. xli. 11; xlv. 24; 1 Chron. xiii. 11; Hab. iii. 8. The sins but not the prosperity of bad men should grieve the righteous. The subject of remark is the estate, not the character of evildoers. Grieving at their success naturally leads to other evil feelings: *Neither be thou envious against the workers of iniquity.* The Chaldee: Neither be thou envious against the workers of iniquity that thou mayest be joined with them. Most other versions very much coincide with the English. Fretting leads to hatred, and envy to malice; and these sinful feelings indulged make men evildoers. The tendency of bad passions to make us like the worst of men is often declared, v. 8; Prov. iii. 31; xiv. 17; xxii. 24, 25; xxix. 22. The great preservative against all envy and malice is the fear of the Lord, Prov. xxiii. 17. This first verse is a very strong proof of the divine origin of the Psalm. None but inspired writers insist on purity of heart. The evil tendency of fretting at the perverseness of bad men is well illustrated in the case of David respecting Nabal, as recorded in 1 Sam. xxv. 4–38.

2. *For they shall soon be cut down like the grass, and wither as the green herb.* Often and admirably in Scripture is the frail nature of man compared to growing herbs, 2 Kings xix. 26; Ps. xc. 5; xcii. 7; ciii. 15; Isa. xxxvii. 27; xl. 6, 7; Jas. i. 10; 1 Pet. i. 24. Ten days after David turned aside from slaying Nabal, that miserable man died. Just as a great number of good men were about to be martyred, bloody Mary went to her account. Arnd: "When grass has stood its time, it will be cut down. So, when the ungodly have accomplished their end by their prosperity, God sends one against them, who cuts them off; as may be seen in Saul and Ahab, who, as soon as they were ripe, were swept away, by an enemy sent on purpose by God. And when the flowers and green herbs have stood and bloomed their time, they fall of themselves and wither away. So is it with all the ungodly amid their temporal prosperity. And then they are such flowers, as, when once fallen, revive no more, but forever corrupt and waste, and blossom not again. Ah! why should we then be filled with anger at them, and begrudge them their short-lived good? We should rather pity their blindness." For *cut down* Alexander reads *mown*. *Wither,* as in Ps. i. 3, most commonly *fade,* as in Ps. xviii. 45; Isa. xl. 7, 8. None ever envied the temporal greatness of one, who, he knew, would be a dead man in one hour.

3. *Trust in the* LORD, *and do good.* Chaldee: Confide in the word of the Lord and do good; Syriac: Hope in God, and do good. Other renderings very nearly agree with the common version. *Trust,* as in Ps. iv. 5; ix. 10; in Ps. xxii. 9, *hope.*

For *do good* the church of England has *be doing good*. This is better, signifying that life should consist of continued acts of beneficence to man and of piety towards God. The call upon these tempted souls to exercise faith in God was most seasonable. Without this confidence in God the great mass of men will ever trust in uncertain riches, or in something as worthless. True faith acts well its part. It delights to *do good*. So *shalt thou dwell in the land, and verily thou shalt be fed*. Perhaps the following renderings may aid the reader : Calvin and Jebb : Dwell in the land, and be fed in truth ; Brent : Dwell in the land, and seek sustenance honestly ; Venema : Dwell in the land and nourish constancy ; Edwards : So shalt thou dwell in the land and live securely ; Tholuck : Dwell in the land, and be honest ; Hengstenberg : Inhabit the land, and feed on faithfulness. In Hebrew the verbs are in the imperative. But see Introduction, § 6. Here the future is best, especially in the last verb. *Verily*, a noun rendered *faithfully* in 2 Kings xii. 15 ; xxii. 7 ; 2 Chron. xxxiv. 12 ; once, *truly* in Pr. xii. 22. Either of these renderings gives a good sense. Alexander thinks the chief emphasis of the last clause "lies in representing the veracity of God, or the certain fulfilment of his promise, as the very food by which the believer is sustained, and his hope nourished." Others seem no less confident that yet other interpretations are sound. But none of them are safer or better than that suggested by the common version. Perhaps the most plausible view different from that is that which supposes that the people are here exhorted to abide in their own land, and not become dispersed among surrounding nations, inasmuch as God would at home supply their necessary wants. By *the land* we are probably not to understand *the earth*, as Fry does ; but *the land* of Canaan, which " was considered as the sum of earthly and the type of heavenly felicity : to be provided for in the Lord's land, and there to dwell under his protection, near his ordinances, and among his people, was all that the genuine Israelite could desire."

4. *Delight thyself also in the* LORD. Syriac : Hope in the Lord. Other versions, ancient and modern, remarkably concur in giving the sense gathered from the English text. *Delight*, as in v. 11 ; Job xxvii. 10 ; Isa. lv. 2. Take refined pleasure, or, Let your most exquisite delight be in the existence, names, titles, attributes, works, providence, word and ordinances of God. There is an absurdity in calling on men to be delighted with vanities. But when Jehovah is presented as the sea of love and enjoyment, we may well ask the weary to bathe and be refreshed. Whoso thus delights himself in the Lord will have holy wishes, pleasing to the Most High : *And he* [Jehovah] *shall give thee the desires of thine heart*. *Desires; requests, petitions, demands, counsels, askings*. The most enlarged and noble longings of pious hearts have been fulfilled. Moses had a great desire to see God's glory ; and the Lord showed him as much as he could bear. Solomon had a quenchless thirst after knowledge and wisdom, and Jehovah made him the wisest of mere men. The reigning desires of eminently pious people are that they may glorify God on earth, grow in knowledge and grace, holiness and usefulness, comfort and courage ; and in heaven enjoy God, have rest and glory, complete salvation and endless felicity. All these things shall be given them, Ps. x. 17 ; xxi. 2 ; cxlv. 19. We shall have the petitions that we ask of him, 1 John v. 15 ; Ps. xx. 5.

5. *Commit thy way unto the* LORD. Syriac : Direct thy way before the Lord; the other ancient versions give to the verb the sense of discover, disclose, reveal, or manifest ; Ainsworth : Turn confidently thy way upon Jehovah. But Calvin, Piscator, Fabritius, Venema, Amesius, Brent, Gesenius, Hammond, Hengstenberg and Alexander all prefer rendering it, Roll [or devolve] on Jehovah thy way [or ways.] See on Ps. xxii. 8. The verb is often rendered *roll* as in Gen. xxix. 3, 8; Josh. v. 9; x. 18 ; 1 Sam. xiv. 33 ; Isa. ix. 5. Several other versions agree with the English text

and have *Commit,* etc.   In Pr. xvi. 3: Commit thy works unto the Lord; literally Roll thy works on Jehovah.   Our *ways* are our *works, enterprises, undertakings.* Diodati: "Thy businesses, actions, and all the passages and chances of thy life." The first clause of the verse is explained by the second: *Trust also in him. Trust,* as in v. 3.   *And he shall bring* it *to pass.*   If God favor an enterprise, it will not fail. If he build the house, it will stand.   The error against which we are here warned is reliance on our own strength or wisdom.   The encouragement here given to renounce all self-confidence and to look to God alone, is that he will graciously undertake our case, bear our burdens, and accomplish for us that which we could never bring to pass. David had a beautiful illustration of the truth here urged, in his coming into full and peaceable possession of the throne.

6. *And he shall bring forth thy righteousness as the light, and thy judgment as the noonday.*   This has special reference to the calumnies and misrepresentations under which good men often suffer, especially when carrying on any work for God's glory. It was well illustrated in the history of Nehemiah in rebuilding the holy city.   Calvin's paraphrase is: "We may be often grievously oppressed, and God may not seem to approve our innocence, yet this vicissitude should no more disturb our minds than the darkness of the night which covers the earth; for then the expectation of the light of day sustains our hopes."   Patrick thinks the illustration is drawn from murky weather followed by clear shining: "If thou shouldst be accused as a man of evil designs; let not that trouble thee neither: for though thy fame may be obscured for a time by calumnies and slanders, as the sun is by mists and clouds; yet as that scatters them all at last, so shall thy integrity appear, and shine as bright as the sun at noonday."   In the end all the righteous will be satisfied with the vindication of their characters, and the reward of their deeds.   Hengstenberg cites Job xi. 17; Isa. lviii. 8; Mic. vii. 9, as illustrating the nature of the blessing promised in the *light* and the *noonday.*

7. *Rest in the* LORD.   The verb is that from which our word *dumb* is probably derived.   Many read, Be silent, be still, hold still, acquiesce.   It is in various forms rendered *rest, cease, stand still, tarry, wait, be still, forbear, hold one's peace, keep silence, be silent, quiet one's self,* Josh. x. 12, 13.   We have a good illustration in Lev. x. 3. Two of Aaron's sons, being ministers of the sanctuary, were for their sins by God's judgment terribly destroyed, And Aaron *held his peace.*   The sins forbidden in this clause are murmuring, complaining, and charging God foolishly.   Men may be silent through sulkiness and stubbornness.   But what is here required is *in the* LORD, in Jehovah, by reason of faith and trust in him and from love to him.   *And wait patiently for him.*   No better rendering has been proposed.   We are warned against hastiness of spirit, and exhorted to cheerful standing in our lot, calmly expecting deliverance at the right time, God's time.   *Fret not thyself because of him who prospereth in his way, because of the man who bringeth wicked devices to pass.   Fret,* see on v. 1.   *Wicked devices;* in Ps. x. 2, 4, *devices, thoughts;* in Ps. xxi. 11, *mischievous device.*   Calvin has *Wickedness;* church of England, *Evil counsels;* Alexander, *Plots.*   Well did David heed this rule.   Often was Saul in his power, yet he would not hurt him, but left his whole cause with God, expecting him to send deliverance.

8. *Cease from anger.*   Other renderings substantially coincide; only some for *anger* have *wrath.*   The common version sometimes elsewhere has wrath, Ps. ii. 5.   See also Ps. vi. 1; xxx. 5.   *And forsake wrath.   Wrath,* also rendered *rage, fury, hot displeasure;* applied to the venom of serpents, it is rendered *poison.   Fret not thyself in any wise to do evil.   Fret,* as in vv. 1, 7.   We cannot indulge any kind or degree of *fretful, angry* or *wrathful* feeling at the prosperity of the wicked without *doing evil.*

Such indulgence, just so far as it goes, makes us like them, and of them. Luther: "And what avails such rage. It makes the matter no better, nay, only sinks you deeper in the ditch. Thou hast prevented God, so that thou hast lost his grace and favor, and art become like evildoers, and wilt perish with them."

9. *For evildoers shall be cut off.* Evildoers, as in v. 1. *Cut off,* in another form so rendered in vv. 28, 38. See also Ps. xii. 3; xxxiv. 16. There is no better rendering. It is a terrible form of describing the ruin of the enemies of God. Calvin: "He intimates that they shall flourish fresh and green till the time of their destruction shall arrive." *But those that wait upon the* LORD, *they shall inherit the earth.* *Wait,* from the same verb as in Ps. xxv. 3, 5. It signifies *waiting for God, tarrying* at our post till he appears. *The earth* in vv. 3, 29, 34, *land;* in vv. 11, 22, *earth.* Those who here render it *land,* refer it to the land of Canaan, which was regarded as the best of all lands, and a type and pledge of better things in the world to come. We need not limit the sense. Calvin: "He means that they shall live in such a manner as that the blessing of God shall follow them, even to the grave." The same blessing was pledged anew by Christ, Matt. v. 5.

10. *For yet a little while, and the wicked shall not be.* The verb is properly supplied. For *shall not be,* the church of England reads *shall be clean gone.* Now for a time things look dark, and providences are mysterious. But let the saints wait even *a little while,* and God will show that he is righteous by bringing to an end the prosperity of the wicked. *Yea, thou shalt diligently consider his place, and it shall not be.* Possibly it should read, *and he shall not be.* But the common version gives a very good sense. The very land he occupied as a home, and the title to which was unimpeachable, is no longer *his place.* It has passed into other hands. Nothing of all he had on earth is his. He is as poor as the most miserable abject that subsisted on alms. The rich and the poor lie down together.

11. *But the meek shall inherit the earth.* Meek, poor, humble, lowly, as in Ps. ix. 12, 18. *Inherit the earth;* see on vv. 3, 8. The humble all live as long as is most for their good. As a class they vastly outlive the wicked. Then too they have God's blessing always abiding upon them: *And* [they] *shall delight themselves in the abundance of peace.* While the world is in an uproar concerning things that are vain and fleeting, the meek are quietly passing through earth to heaven. Their bosoms are not rent with angry passions. They have peace of conscience and peace with God. All this is but the prelude to the perfect rest and peace above, where the wicked cease from troubling, where providence will never frown, where ineffable smiles from the Redeemer's face satisfy the longings of every mind; see v. 37. *Peace,* commonly so rendered, also *welfare, health, prosperity,* Gen. xliii. 27; 2 Sam. xx. 9; Ps. xxxv. 27; lxxiii. 3.

12. *The wicked plotteth against the just.* The opposition of the wicked towards the righteous is far too systematic, uniform and cunning to pass for accidental or unpremeditated. It is all *plotted, thought out, devised* and *purposed.* Were the conduct of the wicked without plan, it would sometimes happen to be on the side of righteousness. The wicked goes further, *and gnasheth upon him with his teeth.* Gnasheth, always so rendered, see on Ps. xxxv. 16. But his craft shall be defeated; and his malice shall be in vain.

13. *The Lord shall laugh at him.* Duly considered, no words of Scripture should make a more awful impression. When men act so vilely that the infinitely loving and merciful God shall have them in derision, can their case be worse? See on Ps. ii. 4. *For he seeth that his day is coming;* i. e., God sees that the day for punishing the wicked is coming. Ainsworth: "Day is often used for the time of punishment." In proof he cites Job xviii. 20; Ps. cxxxvii. 7; Isa. ix. 4; Jer. xii. 3; Hos. i. 11.

How soon the day of wrath will be here God sees; and by faith God's servants see the same.

14. *The wicked have drawn out the sword, and have bent their bow.* That is, they have made every hostile preparation. *Drawn out*, literally *opened*, or *loosed, i. e.*, from its scabbard. *Bent*, for the force of this word see on Ps. vii. 12; xi. 2. The *bow* was a cross-bow, and it was bent by putting one foot upon the middle and then drawing back the string. All this was done, not for show, or parade; but *to cast down the poor and needy.* The ruin of the good man is seriously intended. The wickedness of the hostility of the ungodly is greatly heightened by the character of those, against whom they war, viz: the *poor, afflicted, lowly, humble*, see Ps. ix. 12, 18. His war is also against the *needy*, also rendered *poor, beggar.* See Ps. ix. 18; xxxv. 10. The lowliness and afflictions of good men, one would think, might awaken the relentings of their enemies. And *to slay such as be of upright conversation.* *Conversation*, conduct, behaviour, life. Alexander has *way*, "a common figure for the course of life." *Slay*, or kill, applied to the slaughtering of *sheep*, or *oxen*, or of any *beasts* for food, not for sacrifice; or to the destruction of human beings in war and by violence. But divine justice, divine honor and divine faithfulness forbid that such wicked persecutions of innocent men should last long, or pass unpunished.

15. *Their sword shall enter into their own heart; and their bows shall be broken.* These are the weapons mentioned in v. 14. Now they are rendered powerless by being broken and by destroying those who wielded them. It is a marvel that the wicked continue to indulge the hope of ever having any valuable successes. In due time everything is against them. Especially do their own weapons and devices destroy them. If all this is so, then it is clear that

16. *A little that a righteous man hath is better than the riches of many wicked.* Church of England: A small thing that the righteous hath is better than great riches of the ungodly. *Many*, rendered *great* in Ps. xix. 11, 13; xxxi. 19; xxxvi. 6, and often. *Riches*, the original is that from which our word *mammon* is supposed to be derived. Ainsworth has it, "plenteous mammon." This verse some think has its parallel in Pr. xv. 16; and nearly its parallel in Pr. xvi. 8. *Riches*, sometimes rendered *tumult, noise*, 1 Sam. iv. 14; xiv. 19; 2 Sam. xviii. 29; Am. v. 23. Hence some think there is reference to the turmoil attending large possessions. In some cases this may be; but the word is used to express a multitude of anything, as of *rain*, etc. Clarke: "This is a solid *maxim.* Whatever a good man has, has God's blessing in it; even the *blessings* of the wicked are *cursed.*"

17. *For the arms of the wicked shall be broken.* To break the arms is to render helpless and to put into anguish: "I will cause the sword to fall out of his hand. . . He shall groan before him with the groanings of a deadly wounded man." Ezek. xxx. 22, 24. We had the same form of speech in Ps. x. 15. See also Job xxii. 9; 1 Sam. ii. 31. While the wicked are thus left in a state most grievous to them, it is far different with the people of God: *But the* LORD *upholdeth the righteous.* *Upholdeth*, as in v. 24 and often, elsewhere sustaineth, beareth up; Edwards and Fry, supporteth; but these give the same sense. The righteous are in themselves as weak as water. But the Lord sustains his servants, girding them with omnipotence, so that they wax valiant in fight and never utterly fall, for God holds them up. They are mighty through God.

18. *The* LORD *knoweth the days of the upright.* Ainsworth: Jehovah knoweth the days of perfect men; Edwards: Jehovah watches over the days of the upright; Fry: Jehovah ordaineth the days of the upright; Hengstenberg: The Lord knows the days of the pious. *Knoweth*, see on Ps. i. 6. The good providence of God orders all the affairs of his saints during their whole life. He sees their trials and sorrows. He

knows how much aid and grace they need, and has vast storehouses of mercy at his command. It is added: *And their inheritance shall be for ever.* This clearly points to " an inheritance incorruptible, and undefiled, and that fadeth not away, reserved in heaven." In heaven are no vicissitudes. To those, who believe, all this is sure. *Upright,* elsewhere *undefiled, complete, perfect, without blemish.* See on Ps. xv. 2.

19. *They shall not be ashamed in the evil time.* *Ashamed,* see Ps. vi. 10; xxxv. 4, 26. The *evil time* is the time of *calamity* or *adversity,* when the wicked are confounded. All along God's people expected their religion to stand them in stead when the day of trial should come, and they were not disappointed. Their afflictions were as great as those of the wicked; often they were greater; but then their supports were transcendent, and that made the difference. *And in the days of famine they shall be satisfied.* They know that God doeth all things well; that he makes no mistakes; that man liveth not by bread alone, but by every word that proceedeth out of the mouth of God; that if they have but little, God's blessing is on that; and that they shall have as much food and everything else as infinite wisdom, boundless mercy and everlasting faithfulness shall judge to be on the whole best. So they shall be *filled* with comfort and peace; see Ps. xvii. 15; Isa. xxxiii. 16. God's goodness to the *poor* saints has been celebrated in the church in all ages.

20. *But the wicked shall perish, and the enemies of the* LORD shall be *as the fat of lambs: they shall consume, into smoke shall they consume away.* Although most of this verse is variously rendered, yet every translation points to utter destruction. John Rogers' translation: And when the enemyes of the Lorde are in their floures, they shall consume, yee even as the smoke shall they consume away. For *fat* Calvin has preciousness; Ainsworth, precious fat; Hengstenberg, joy. Tholuck for fat of lambs has "the pride of the pastures." When the fat of the sacrifice was burned, its smoke soon vanished away, and nothing was left. This does not represent a more complete extinction than that described in v. 10. The figure of this clause was very striking to a Jew. The English version gives the *sense* as well as any other. The *fat,* because used in burnt offerings, was properly called the *preciousness,* or best part of the victim.

21. *The wicked borroweth, and payeth not again.* *Borroweth,* properly so rendered here, though another form of the same word is *lendeth* in v. 26. It properly signifies an act of mutual dealing, either *borrowing* or *lending* according to its form and connection; see Deut. xxviii. 12, 44; Isa. xxiv. 2; Pr. xix. 17. One of the blessings promised to the obedient Israelites was that they should be able to lend, and should not need to borrow, Deut. xv. 6; xxviii. 12; and one of the curses denounced on them, if they should prove refractory, was that they should be forced to borrow and not be able to lend, Deut. xxviii. 44. The vices of the wicked, his impiety, his extravagance at length bring him to want. Perhaps he turns rogue and does not pay when he can. The humiliation, to which he is subjected, is extreme. At length he falls so low that he is neither able nor willing to meet his engagements. Far different is it with the good man: *But the righteous sheweth mercy and giveth.* He has a *compassionate* nature, and God so far gratifies his benevolent heart as to afford him the means of *giving.* He may have but little to give. But he gives it with a good will. One reason why we should be diligent in an honest calling, and earnestly pray for a divine blessing on our labors, is that we may have something to give to the needy, Eph. iv. 28.

22. *For* such as be *blessed of him shall inherit the earth,* see on vv. 3, 11. *And* they that be *cursed of him shall be cut off,* see on v. 9; also vv. 28, 38, where we have the same verb in another form. *Blessed* and *cursed;* no words are more opposite.

Ainsworth and some others read *his blessed ones*, and *his cursed ones;* but our version is better because it gives in our idiom the true sense of the original.

23. *The steps of a* good *man are ordered by the* LORD: *and he delighteth in his way.* The word *good* is supplied because it is supposed to give the true mind of the Spirit. Those, who would reject it both from the text and from the interpretation, maintain that the first clause contains a general proposition, like those in Pr. xvi. 9; xx. 24; Jer. x. 23; Acts xvii. 28. Against this some urge that the word rendered *man* virtually signifies a *good man.* It is not *Adam, Ish* nor *Enosh,* but another word, which at times is doubtless emphatic, as in 2 Sam. xxiii. 1; Job xxxiv. 7; Lam. iii. 1; Zech. xiii. 7. Jebb contends that it "always signifies some excellence of mind or body, among the more ancient Hebrew writers." For "good man" Ainsworth reads "the man;" Edwards, "the upright." Doubtless the word is indeed sometimes but not always emphatic. The last clause of the verse surely describes the same man, whether by it we understand that the man delights in the Lord's way, or, as is preferable, that the Lord delights in the man's way. Green connects the clauses more closely than our version: The steps of a man are firmly fixed by the Lord, when he delighteth in his way. Instead of *ordered* we have the authority of the common version in other places for reading, if we choose, *prepared, fastened, set fast, directed, confirmed, fashioned, fixed, established.* In all these respects God's agency in the affairs of the upright can be relied on; because he approves the *way,* the *life,* the *course* of his people and delights in it, Ps. i. 6. Calvin: "As God sees that the faithful act conscientiously, and do not turn aside from the way which he has appointed, he blesses their efforts."

24. *Though he fall, he shall not be utterly cast down.* Some versions, varying from this, are striking. Septuagint, Ethiopic and Vulgate: When he shall fall, he shall not be dashed in pieces; church of England: Though he fall, he shall not be cast away; Ainsworth: When he shall fall, he shall not be cast off; Edwards: Though he fall, he will not be left on the ground; Hengstenberg: If he falls, he will not be laid prostrate. The last verb is that used by the erring prophet, when he says, *Cast* me *forth* into the sea, Jon. i. 12. Alexander: "The contrast of a mere fall and a permanent prostration is intended to express that between occasional misfortune and utter ruin." Clarke: "Neither the *Text* nor any of the versions intimate that a *falling into sin* is meant, but a falling into *trouble, difficulty,*" etc. Calvin says nearly the same, and thinks 2 Cor. iv. 9 parallel. The reason why a saint is not utterly prostrated is thus given: *For the Lord upholdeth* him with *his hand.* Luther's paraphrase is just: "Let it be so, that the righteous falls; he still cannot remain lying thus and be cast away; he must be up again though all the world doubts of it. For God catches him by the hand, and raises him again."

25. *I have been young, and* now *am old, yet have I not seen the righteous forsaken, nor his seed begging bread.* The proposed alterations in the rendering are not good, unless the following, in Morison, be such: I have been young and *now* am old; yet have I not seen the righteous forsaken; nor his seed *forsaken, though* begging bread. Most of the difficulties attending this passage have probably arisen from overlooking the fact that David here asserts no universal proposition, but simply gives the result of his long observation. In his Commentary on the place Clarke gives a like testimony. I have heard the late Dr. Leonard Woods say, that he never saw but one exception. This shows that such cases are rare, and that the general plan of God is to preserve his people and their virtuous posterity from abject want. Yet Lazarus was a beggar, and may have been the child of pious parents. But at last he went from famishing want to Abraham's bosom. There are in Scripture many *general* principles stated, which are not universally true, though they are commonly so, and

the exceptions to them are rare. The rendering quoted from Morison is very natural and quite relieves the whole passage of serious difficulty, as it admits that cases may arise where poverty and disease will compel some virtuous people to ask for bread, but even then they are not forsaken by God. If anything beyond the prophet's own observation and the implied general principle of God's government be insisted on as here taught, we must supply before the word *forsaken* some such word as *wholly, finally,* or *utterly.* Words are to be known by their connections, and this word *forsaken* is near the word *cast down* which our translators thought had the force of *utterly cast down.*

26. He is *ever merciful and lendeth. Merciful,* in v. 21, the same participle is rendered *sheweth mercy;* elsewhere *hath pity,* or *hath mercy. Lendeth,* see above, on v. 21. He is of a kindly disposition, and God gives him the ability to oblige others, and he does it. Nor is he any loser thereby, Ps. xli. 2, 3; Pr. xi. 25. Nor are his children the poorer for all this pious alms-giving: *And his seed is blessed.* It is a great mercy to be descended from such a man. His good name is to his posterity a better inheritance than great riches. Many wish them well for their father's sake. His example was of great service in forming their principles and habits. Moreover, God's blessing rests on the worldly estate left by such a man, and nothing but a wicked rejection of their father's God will deprive offspring of great mercies. Ainsworth: And his seed are in the blessing; Edwards: And his seed is a blessing; Calvin: And his seed is for blessing; Alexander: And his seed (is) for a blessing. The last author thinks the form of expression is borrowed from Gen. xii. 2. *Ever* is a better translation than *all the day.* The latter is literal, the former gives the sense.

27. *Depart from evil and do good.* See Ps. xxxiv. 14, where precisely the same words are found. *Do good,* see on v. 3. *And dwell for evermore, i. e.,* Thou shalt *to eternity* have the blessings typified by a residence in the land of Canaan. See vv. 3, 9, 11, 18, 22. All this is sure and cannot fail,

28. *For the* LORD *loveth judgment, i. e.,* he loveth justice in exercise. He loves to make and execute righteous decisions; and these are always in the end for the support and salvation of good men. See v. 6. See on the same phrase in Ps. xxxiii. 5. *And forsaketh not his saints. Forsaketh,* see on v. 25. *Saints,* frequently so rendered, also *holy, godly, good,* Ps. iv. 3; lxxxvi. 2; Mic. vii. 2. Here a better rendering perhaps is *merciful,* 2 Sam. xxii. 26; Jer. iii. 12. See on Ps. xviii. 25. *They are preserved for ever. Preserved, kept.* See on Ps. xii. 7; xvi. 1. God's people are surrounded by walls of fire, by a heavenly host, by the infinite care of God. They are *kept* as the apple of God's eye, Ps. xvii. 8. The verb in Hebrew is in the past tense. *But the seed of the wicked shall be cut off. Cut off,* as in vv. 9, 22, 38. The frequent repetition of this threatening here, in the pentateuch and in the later prophets is impressive. Berleberg Bible: " If such perdition does not always meet the bodily eye or sense, still everything is only contributing to their deeper ruin. For the destruction of their poor souls is certainly much more dreadful before God." There is another alarming thought in this clause, viz., that though God may suspend his punishments for a long time, even so that a guilty man may seem quite to escape them, yet his children after him will feel the curse and plague of his transgressions. This is clearly a doctrine of the Scriptures, Num. xiv. 18; Ex. xx. 5; Deut. v. 9. Achan "perished not alone." Ahab was hardly dead till his offspring were killed by the myrmidons he had trained to cruelty and murder. Belshazzar had hardly passed to his long account, when the cry was heard, " Prepare slaughter for his children." Compare Isa. xiv. 20.

29. *The righteous shall inherit the land, and dwell therein for ever.* See on vv. 3, 9, 11, 18, 22, 27. They shall ever continue in possession of those good things typified by an inheritance in Canaan; those good things, of which God's temporal blessings

are but pledges and earnests. Having described the blessedness of the good man, the prophet next describes his character in three particulars.

30. *The mouth of the righteous speaketh wisdom, and his tongue talketh of judgment.* Good discourse, including a sacred regard to truth, justice, charity, purity and piety, is an essential characteristic of a righteous man. *Wisdom*, a word rendered with remarkable uniformity. It is in Scripture used to express the great gift of God to Solomon, 1 Kings ii. iii. iv. v. vii. x. xi. It often occurs in the writings of Solomon. We have not before met it in the Psalms. Its primary meaning seems to have been *skill*, or *cunning*, in the sense of that old English word. But it sometimes signifies sound and extensive learning. It often denotes moral excellence, piety. Here it points to that knowledge of sacred things, which is derived from God's word, from the indwelling of his Spirit, and from a blessed religious experience. Cruden's paraphrase is, "When the discourses of other men are either wicked or vain, his are pious and profitable; they flow from, and are so many evidences of WISDOM, and have a tendency to make others spiritually wise." By *judgment* in this verse we may understand the knowledge and discernment of right and wrong, of good and evil, in morals and religion, including justice and equity to man, and God's kind and holy government of the world.

31. *The law of his God* is *in his heart.* Often in Scripture does a like phrase describe unfeigned piety. See on Ps. i. 2. Writing or putting the law in the heart is an Old Testament mode of pointing to regeneration, Jer. xxxi. 33. The language of this clause expresses love to God's law. The affections go out towards it. From this love necessarily flows prompt, cheerful, humble and universal obedience. He who thus loves the law is stable and steadfast. *None of his steps shall slide.* Other versions for *slide* have totter, stagger, slip, be moved, be supplanted, falter. Alexander: His steps shall not swerve [or waver] *from the straight path.* Thus shall the righteous hold on his way, and he that hath clean hands wax stronger and stronger. In these particulars all hypocrites and self-deceivers are deficient; and the outbreaking sinner has no claims whatever to such characteristics. On the contrary, his words are wrong; his heart is wrong; his life is wrong.

32. *The wicked watcheth the righteous, and seeketh to slay him.* Watcheth, to be taken here in a bad sense, that of spying, watching with jealousy, envy or hatred. Hengstenberg renders it *lurks for.* The wicked is at heart a murderer. All he wants is a good opportunity, a promise of impunity, and a plausible pretext to kill the righteous; for God, who knows his heart, says he *seeketh to slay him.* No sinner ever loved a saint. To do that is infallible evidence of conversion, 1 John iii. 14. But, except so far as God permits, the malice of the wicked against the pious is impotent.

33. *The* LORD *will not leave him in his hand.* The good man seems often to be in the power of the wicked; but he is not left there. God will deliver him as he did David from Saul, or Peter from Herod: or, if no other way of escape from the malice of enemies shall be provided, God will open the gates of paradise, and take his ransomed home to glory as he did Stephen and all the martyrs. God will not desert a good man to his foes, *Nor condemn him when he is judged.* Compare Rom. viii. 1, 33, 34. The prophet may here refer to the final judgment. The wicked may grow to such effrontery as in the next world to demand the condemnation of those whom they hated here. It gives an inferior but a good sense to suppose the prophet to be here representing God as the actual though invisible Judge of the earth, listening to the accusations of the wicked, and the complaints and pleas of the righteous, and refusing to condemn the innocent. The idea of God as actual and supreme Judge of the whole earth is very ancient, Gen. xviii. 25. In judging between those women, who were disputing about the child, for a time Solomon seemed to be equally indifferent to both.

But in the end he secured all the rights of the loving mother. So for a season God may keep silence; but in due time his hand will take hold on judgment. See on v. 6.

34. *Wait on the* LORD. See on v. 9. *And keep his way. Keep*, in v. 37 *mark*, elsewhere *preserve*. See on Ps. xii. 7; xvi. 1. God's *way* is the path he marks out to us in his word and providence. *Tarry for* God, expect him, do your duty even in the humblest condition and state, *And he shall exalt thee to inherit the land.* See on vv. 3, 9, 12, 18, 22, 27, 29. *When the wicked are cut off, thou shalt see* it. *Cut off*, as in vv. 9, 22, 28, 38. In this life or the next his people shall know that Jehovah is just and righteous altogether.

35. *I have seen the wicked in great power, and spreading himself like a green bay tree.*

36. *Yet he passed away, and, lo, he* was *not: yea, I sought him, but he could not be found.* The word here rendered *in great power*, is by the Chaldee, Marloratus and Fabritius rendered *strong;* by the Septuagint and kindred versions, *highly exalted;* by Musculus, *great and terrible;* by Ainsworth, *daunting terrible;* by Green, *formidable to all around him;* by Bythner, *formidable;* by Hengstenberg, *insolent;* by Venema, *violent;* by Calvin, Edwards, Jebb and Alexander, *terrible.* A wicked man in power is *terrible.* The bay-tree is the laurel of the Mediterranean. It is an ever-green. Crowns for victors were made of it. It is celebrated of old. Calvin, church of England, Fry and others read *bay-tree.* The old Saxon, the French and Ainsworth, *green self-growing laurel;* Marloratus, *green laurel.* But Bythner says he knows no reason for rendering it *laurel.* And Anderson quotes the illustrated commentary: "For the reading of *bay-tree*, we are not aware of any authority, except the very feeble one which is offered by some of the older of the more modern versions in Great Britain and on the Continent." The Septuagint, Arabic, Ethiopic, Vulgate, Doway, Houbigant, Boothroyd and Geddes read, *As the cedars of Lebanon;* Hengstenberg, *Like a tree green and deep rooted;* Chaldee, Jerome, Bucer, Piscator, Fabritius, Diodati, Bythner, Venema, Amesius, Mudge, Gesenius, Waterland and Alexander give *indigenous* or *native*, meaning perhaps, as Green expresses it, *a flourishing tree in its native soil. He passed away*, in v. 36. With our version agree Calvin, Fabritius, Piscator, Marloratus, Edwards, Hengstenberg and Alexander. But the Septuagint, Ethiopic, Syriac, Vulgate, church of England, Houbigant, Green, Jebb and Fry all read, *I passed by.* The common version is best sustained by the text. Hengstenberg: "Undoubtedly in this verse David had the image of Saul swimming before his eyes." Clarke: "Does not this refer to Nebuchadnezzar and to the vision he had of the great tree, which was in the midst of the earth, the head of which reached up to heaven? Dan. iv. 10." But 1. David never prophesied of that Babylonish monarch, though he certainly wrote this Psalm; 2. The *stump* of *that* tree was left, and it rose again, but *this* tree was never found again. Scott speaks more safely: "Thus Saul, Doeg and Ahithophel. in David's time had flourished, and thus they had vanished."

37. *Mark the perfect* man, *and behold the upright. Mark*, observe, take heed. See on v. 34; Ps. xvi. 1; xvii. 8. *Perfect* and *upright* explain each other. They are synonymous. *Perfect*, in Gen. xxv. 27, *plain;* in Prov. xxix. 10, *upright;* in Cant. v. 2; vi. 9, *undefiled. Upright* also *righteous*; see on Ps. vii. 10. *For the end of* that *man is peace.* A saint has God's blessing on him in life and in death, and you may see it, if you will. The obvious sense is the best. Saints and sinners at the last fare very differently. The righteous has *peace;*

38. *But the transgressors shall be destroyed together. Transgressors* and *destroyed*, well rendered. *Together*, as in Ps. ii. 2; xiv. 3. See on Ps. xxxiii. 15. Those who have sinned in common shall perish in common. *Korah and his company fared alike. The end of the wicked shall be cut off.* Jebb: The end of the wicked is that they are cut off. This gives a good sense. But the common version is as good. The wicked

are *driven away*, their end is *cut off*. They are never prepared for their last, great, solemn change. Their end is not peaceful, nor desirable.

39. *But the salvation of the righteous* is *of the* LORD. Their safety and deliverance are from the Lord, and so are marked, decisive, complete; not partial, nor doubtful. Calvin: "The sum of the whole is, that whatever may happen, the righteous shall be saved, because they are in the hand of God, and can never be forgotten by him." He is their *strength in the time of trouble. Strength, rock, strong rock, fortress, strong-hold.* See on Ps. xxvii. 1; xxviii. 8; xxxi. 3. *Trouble,* rendered *distress, anguish, adversity, tribulation, affliction.* See on Ps. ix. 9. Well does the prophet add:

40. *And the Lord shall help them, and deliver them.* He shall help them as much as they need. He shall so help them as finally to deliver them from all evils and from all enemies. *He shall deliver them from the wicked, and save them.* He shall save them completely and finally. He shall do this, for by his nature and by his word he is bound to do it; *Because they trust in him.* God cannot deny himself, and so he cannot but save all who have at his bidding confided in him.

DOCTRINAL AND PRACTICAL REMARKS.

1. We should never deny that God's providence is mysterious. Not only do mercies and judgments often seem to fall without discrimination on saints and sinners; but many a time the wicked seem to have much prosperity, while the righteous are greatly afflicted. Let us not deny the facts; but let us not be perplexed by them. All will be clear in due time.

2. We cannot too carefully watch against the insidious attacks of evil tempers. Even a little indulgence in irritability will torment us and displease God. We may not even *fret.* So earnest is the prophet on this point that he thrice warns us, vv. 1, 7, 8. Bouchier: "We do not perhaps lay much stress on fretfulness as evil: we look upon it more as an unhappy temper of mind, bringing indeed its own punishment with it, but involving no vast amount of evil. . . Yet fretfulness, unchecked and allowed to have its way undisturbed, will eventually undermine and corrode all that is valuable and estimable and lovely in the character." Fretting leads to

3. *Envy,* v. 1. When one becomes emulous of the prosperity of others, and sickens at their success, then he is nigh unto ruin. There is no worse passion than envy. It is foolish and cruel. All prosperous sinners are like oxen fattening for the slaughter.

4. The prosperity of the wicked affords no just cause for the least disquiet. However great, it is short-lived and is just cause of pity, not of alarm or ill-will, vv. 2, 9, 10, 13, 20, 34, 35, 36, 38. We brought nothing into this world and it is certain we can carry nothing out. Morison: "Both the name and the place of the wicked shall be blotted out and forgotten. Yet a little while and he is gone; his vain pomp and glory are levelled in the dust; and a future generation shall search in vain for the place of his abode: he shall have no memorial but such as his crime and infamy have procured for him."

5. It is impossible to live well or die well, to profit by God's word or providences, unless we *trust in the Lord,* vv. 3, 5.

6. Negative virtue is not enough; we must *do good,* vv. 3, 27. He who regards his condition safe, because he does not lie, or steal, or murder, or practise any of the vices, and yet has not grace to perfect holiness and work out his salvation with fear and trembling, is deceived.

7. Great as are the trials of God's people, their temporal wants are supplied, and oftentimes in a marvellous manner, v. 3. After all his afflictions, who in the main passes through this world in a more quiet and desirable way than the child of God?

8. True religion calls into lively exercise the highest and most refined affections of

our nature, and presents suitable objects for them to settle upon. We may well and wholly delight ourselves in the Lord and in the fulness of his blessings, vv. 4, 8. Nor is such piety unrequited. Morison: "When we learn greatly to delight in the Lord, he will grant unto us the desire of our souls. The heart that delights in God will learn to relish and approve all his appointments; for he that prays from the heart, 'Thy will be done,' can never fail to realize the blessing he implores." God gratifies the desires of the saints, for he has awakened them, and he approves them.

9. True piety relies on God, and *rolls its burden on the Lord*, v. 5. What could we do without such a resource? They who rely most are the best and the happiest Christians.

10. He who makes God his refuge, has a right to expect that his lawful undertakings will be finally crowned with more than ordinary success, although for a time things may look dark, v. 5.

11. It is always safe to leave a good cause and our good name in the hands of God, v. 6. Henry: "If we take care to keep a good conscience, we may leave it to God to take care of our good name." Reproach is terrible. It broke the heart of the Son of man. But the just shall at last be delivered from it. Morison: "By ten thousand agencies God can extricate his servants from unmerited contempt and can bring forth their integrity as the morning light."

12. True repose is had only when our hearts are hushed on the bosom of Jehovah and *rest in him*, v. 7. The right place for the brood in time of cold or storm is under the wings of the hen. The right place for the lambs in chilly weather is the shepherd's bosom.

13. Nicolson thus sums up the duties taught in vv. 3–8. "Desert not thy station. Enjoy quietly what thou hast at present. Be pleased with God's way. Labor in an honest vocation, and leave the rest to him. Acquiesce in his will and in the dispensations of his providence; wait patiently for him. His time is best."

14. Patient waiting on God must be a very important duty, and one to which we are but little inclined; it is so often enjoined in Scripture, vv. 7, 9, 34.

15. Fretting and envy naturally lead to the display of the worst passions, even outrageous *anger*, and terrible *wrath*, against which we cannot be too guarded, v. 8.

16. The portion of God's people is an inheritance, vv. 9, 11, 22, 27, 29, 34. Their great interests shall never be disturbed, v. 18. Because they are sons, they are heirs. Because they are heirs of God, their inheritance shall be everlasting.

17. The plots and rage of the wicked are sure signs that their cause is bad, and must come to nought under the government of a just God, vv. 12, 14, 32. God has set his face against all wicked devices.

18. Consequently every thing, which the wicked do, does and must turn against them, v. 15. The nature of all sin is to recoil on its author.

19. The overthrow of the wicked must be inconceivably dreadful, else inspiration would not use so alarming language respecting it, v. 13. Can a more fearful representation be made than that the infinitely loving Jehovah shall laugh at the miseries of his guilty foes? O sinner! Stop and think! Stop and think!

20. That, which conclusively determines the character and destiny of the righteous is their pious walk, their holy living, their *upright conversation*, v. 14. Nothing can set aside the evidence of a holy life. It is better than a revelation from heaven.

21. Dickson: "When the wicked are most near to do a mischief, then is a mischief most near unto them; *their sword shall enter into their own heart*," v. 15.

22. Let the humble pious be content, v. 16. If they have not much, they have more than they deserve; they have as much as infinite love sees best for them; they have no account to give of what never was under their control; and they have God's blessing on what is theirs.

23. However for a time the wicked may seem to wax strong, yet their helplessness, when God forsakes them or fights against them, is utter. More pitiable objects have never been. Their *arms are broken,* v. 17.

24. The successes and conquests of God's people depend upon the nature and will of God; and so they cannot fail, vv. 17, 24. There is an adequate cause for all the good that happens to the righteous.

25. God's approval and blessing will make any life happy and any course desirable, v. 18. Wonderfully does he order, choose, arrange and moderate our trials; and deliver us from them. Most seasonably and tenderly does he reveal our mercies to us.

26. Rightly considered the peace and happiness of God's people in times of trial, when all others are overpowered, show the unspeakable excellence of their principles, and give us good ground of confidence in their final and eternal triumph, v. 19.

27. It is as certain as God's word can make it that, sore as are the afflictions of the saints, yet the great harvest of misery is among sinners, v. 20.

28. The pious and benevolent affections of the righteous have room for exercise even here, v. 21. Hereafter they shall have enlargement: for all that is truly good in man's estate will grow better.

29. Dickson: "The blessing of God on the godly maketh the odds betwixt them and the wicked, for it is to them as good as the inheritance of the whole earth; but God's curse rooteth the wicked man out of the earth," v. 22.

30. The kind providence of God over the righteous is to them ample protection against all that could do them real harm, v. 23. The arrangements, which God makes, will all come out right in the end.

31. The reverses of the saints are temporary, v. 24.

32. Let old people make it their business to tell what they have seen of God's wonders in providence and in grace, v. 25. They cannot be better employed than in thus commending the loving-kindness of the Lord to the rising generation.

33. Good men are never hard-hearted and cruel, v. 26. Whatever they may have been before conversion, the grace of God makes the lion the fit companion of the lamb, and the bear, of the calf. Saul of Tarsus, renewed, was as tender as a nurse.

34. One of the best inheritances parents can lay up for their children is in deeds of alms and of liberality, v. 26. Horne: "So far is charity from impoverishing, that what is given away, like vapors emitted by the earth, returns in showers of blessings into the bosom of the person who gave it; and his offspring is not the worse, but infinitely the better for it."

35. A broad and enduring foundation of quietness and assurance is laid, for all right-minded persons, in the spotless and infinitely excellent character of God, v. 28. All hopes based on anything contrary to this must fail us at last.

36. Dickson: "The Lord may well exercise his children with trouble, yet he will not withdraw himself from them in trouble, but will stay with them and bear them company, and save them to the uttermost," v. 28.

37. If men have not the due fear of God, yet they might reasonably be restrained from many courses of wickedness by remembering the sad effects of transgression upon their posterity, v. 28.

38. No staid behaviour, no secret emotions, no sanctimoniousness of character can prove any man to be a child of God, if his speech is loose, foolish, vain, slanderous or wicked, v. 30. See Matt. xii. 37.

39. True religion has its seat in the heart. Genuine purity is internal, v. 31.

40. True religion is steadfast, v. 31. The fickle and unstable have no part in the inheritance of the saints.

41. Whenever men find themselves resorting to sly and cunning behaviour, they may rest assured that they are already in the territory of the wicked one, v. 32.

42. It is certain that the final judgment is approaching, v. 33. It is as certain that all the redeemed will be well pleased with the awards of the last day.

43. The path of duty, however steep and thorny, always terminates in the land of peace and blessedness, v. 34.

44. Death and what is beyond it will show who is wise and who is a fool, vv. 37, 38.

45. It is for a rejoicing to the righteous that their salvation and all that leads to it, and all the steps and parts of it are of the Lord, v. 39. The debt, the infinite debt of love they owe is to him, whom they shall ever love to adore.

46. Dickson: "So long as God is pleased to let righteous men's trouble continue, he will now and then comfort them, and enable them to bear their trouble when comfort is suspended."

47. Scott: "It is of vast importance to understand the present and future condition of the righteous and the wicked, that we may know what to choose and to expect."

48. Luther: "O shame on our faithlessness, mistrust, and vile unbelief, that we do not believe such rich, powerful, consolatory declarations of God, and take up so readily with little grounds of offence, whenever we but hear the wicked speeches of the ungodly. Help, O God, that we may once attain to the right faith. Amen."

PSALM XXXVIII.

A Psalm of David, to bring to remembrance.

1 O LORD, rebuke me not in thy wrath: neither chasten me in thy hot displeasure.

2 For thine arrows stick fast in me, and thy hand presseth me sore.

3 *There is* no soundness in my flesh because of thine anger; neither *is there any* rest in my bones because of my sin.

4 For mine iniquities are gone over mine head: as a heavy burden they are too heavy for me.

5 My wounds stink *and* are corrupt because of my foolishness.

6 I am troubled; I am bowed down greatly; I go mourning all the day long.

7 For my loins are filled with a loathsome *disease:* and *there is* no soundness in my flesh.

8 I am feeble and sore broken: I have roared by reason of the disquietness of my heart.

9 Lord, all my desire *is* before thee; and my groaning is not hid from thee.

10 My heart panteth, my strength faileth me: as for the light of mine eyes, it also is gone from me.

11 My lovers and my friends stand aloof from my sore; and my kinsmen stand afar off.

12 They also that seek after my life lay snares *for me;* and they that seek my hurt speak mischievous things, and imagine deceits all the day long.

13 But I, as a deaf *man,* heard not; and *I was* as a dumb man *that* openeth not his mouth.

14 Thus I was as a man that heareth not, and in whose mouth *are* no reproofs.

15 For in thee, O LORD, do I hope: thou wilt hear, O Lord my God.

16 For I said, *Hear me,* lest *otherwise* they should rejoice over me: when my foot slippeth, they magnify *themselves* against me.

17 For I *am* ready to halt, and my sorrow *is* continually before me.

18 For I will declare mine iniquity; I will be sorry for my sin.

19 But mine enemies *are* lively, *and* they are strong: and they that hate me wrongfully are multiplied.

20 They also that render evil for good are mine adversaries; because I follow *the thing that* good *is.*

21 Forsake me not, O LORD: O my God, be not far from me.

22 Make haste to help me, O Lord my salvation.

THE title correctly ascribes this Psalm to David. The contents well agree with this. We know nothing of the particular circumstances under which it was written, except that its author was in deep distress. Hengstenberg: "Of any particular occasion there is found no trace in the Psalm." Some have thought otherwise; but they have not well sustained their opinions. The title has claimed considerable attention. On the first part see on title of Ps. iii. The latter part occurs nowhere but here and in Psalm lxx. The Hebrew is well rendered in our version, though there is no objection to the renderings of others: *For remembrance; To commemorate; To call to mind; To remind.* But who is to *be reminded?* Hengstenberg: "The person who is to be put in remembrance, by the Psalm, is not, as is generally supposed, the Psalmist himself, or the whole church, but God, who seemed to have forgotten the Psalmist." With him agrees Alexander. Calvin: "The title indicates that David composed this Psalm as a memorial for himself, as well as others, lest he should too soon forget the chastisement by which God had afflicted him." Morison is of the opinion that "this Psalm was composed by David as a memorial of the deep sorrow of mind, when his spirit was burdened with the remembrance of some grievous offence against God." May it not have been as a remembrancer to God, and also a memorial to himself? It is not likely that any part of the title has reference to the *music* with which the Psalm was to be sung. The ancient versions, without authority, add much to the title. There is nothing in the Psalm respecting the *Sabbath.* Nor is there apparently either *thanksgiving* or *prophecy.* Nor has the Psalm any peculiar adaptedness to David's circumstances before *Achish.* Yet it may be "for a good memorial to Israel." It also contains a good "form of confession for us."

This is commonly counted as the third of the seven Psalms called *penitential,* see observations on Psalm vi. Anderson notes the "curious fact, that when Galileo was sentenced to be confined in the dungeons of the Inquisition for an indefinite period, for having maintained the Copernican system, he was enjoined to repeat as a penance these seven penitential Psalms every week for three years; by which it was doubtless intended to extort some sort of confession from him of his guilt, and an acknowledgment of the justice of his sentence."

A question, affecting the interpretation of several verses of this Psalm, is, Whether any part of David's affliction here mentioned was bodily disease? Some are confident that he several times speaks of such affliction, particularly in vv. 3, 5, 7. While we have no historical account of David's suffering from disease, yet we have no right to suppose that he was always exempt from it. But we have no reason for supposing as some that David ever had leprosy. It is also true that some of the language used would fitly describe bodily disease; but, figuratively used, it as fitly describes mental distresses. It is probably to be so taken. Tholuck: "It appears from Genesis iv. 23; Isa. i. 5, 6; liii. 5, that *disease, wounds,* and *sores* were used to denote every kind of suffering and pain." In this Psalm we have three names of the Almighty: *Jehovah* LORD, *Adonai Lord* and *Elohim God,* on which see on Ps. i. 2; ii. 4; iii. 2.

1. *O* LORD, *rebuke me not in thy wrath: neither chasten me in thy hot displeasure.* In our version we have these very words in Ps. vi. 1. In the Hebrew, though the resemblance between the two verses is close, the words are not wholly identical. Yet this bears the same interpretation as that. For his urgent prayer he assigns his reason in verse

2. *For thine arrows stick fast in me.* For *stick fast in me* some read *fall furiously on me; are fastened in me; go down in me; are entered deep into me; press sore on me; are sunk into me.* None of these better gives the sense than our version; although it might be more literal to read *have entered deep into me.* As *arrows* were used in war, and, when shot from powerful bows, were very tormenting and destructive, so

they were fit emblems of God's chastisements. The figure is ancient, Job vi. 4; Deut. xxxii. 23. It is applicable to any sharp distress inflicted by God. Scott: "Acute pains, anguish of spirit, and sharp sufferings of any kind are spoken of under the figure of barbed arrows, which fasten and rankle in the flesh, and cannot be extracted without the most exquisite torture." *And thy hand presseth me sore.* Chaldee: And the wound of thy hand remains upon me; Arabic: And the deeds of thy hand have been hard upon me; Calvin and Venema: And thy hand has come down upon me. This clause is parallel to the first. Alexander: "The verbs of the two clauses are active and passive forms from the same root." It is both an affliction and a comfort to a good man to see the hand of God in all his troubles—an affliction, inasmuch as it shows us how vile we must be to need such sore corrections from the loving One:—a comfort, because we may be assured that mercy shall order everything. Blessed are they who "turn unto him that smiteth them, and seek the LORD of hosts," Isa. ix. 13.

3. There is *no soundness in my flesh because of thine anger.* For *soundness* in other versions we find health, rest, wholeness, sound place, salvation. His afflictions had reached a measure beyond his strength. He was perfectly miserable. God's *anger* was crushing him. *Neither* is there any *rest in my bones because of my sin, q. d.,* I feel in my entire nature the terrible effects of thy displeasure against my sins.

4. *For mine iniquities are gone over mine head. Are gone over,* the same verb in the same form as in Ps. xlii. 7. It expresses the multitude and greatness of his sins in his present apprehension of them, and in the evils he was suffering for them. On him billows were rolling and torrents were pouring. *As an heavy burden they are too heavy for me.* His sense of his sins was sinking him down. His sufferings for his sins were crushing him like a heavy load beyond his strength.

5. *My wounds stink,* and *are corrupt because of my foolishness.* All sin is foolishness; the greater the sin, the greater the madness; and sooner or later the boldest shall confess their want of wisdom in transgressing. This folly however is such that it in no wise abates aught of their guilt. Sin and folly are in the Bible convertible terms. He, that sows to the flesh, shall of the flesh reap corruption. If the thousandth part of the natural fruit of wickedness should appear, there is not a sinner in the world, who would not cry for deliverance.

6. *I am troubled.* The Chaldee, Calvin and Fry: I am bent; Septuagint, Ethiopic and Vulgate: I am become miserable; Arabic: I am afflicted; Syriac: I feared greatly; Ainsworth: I am crooked; Edwards: I am greatly distorted and hurt; Venema, Amesius and Jebb: I am distorted; Morison: I am withered; Hammond: I was bowed down; Hengstenberg: I am beside myself; Alexander: I have writhed. The margin has *wearied.* Hengstenberg thinks the phrase equivalent to: ' I am crazy;' but 'I writhed in agony,' better expresses the sense. *I am bowed down greatly.* Pain of body tends to draw the extremities together. This may be the basis of the figure. In times of great distress the ancient Hebrews often sat down on the ground with their heads covered and bowed between their knees. The allusion may be to this. The sense is, I am greatly distressed and abased. *I go mourning all the day long.* The literal for *mourning* would be *black;* but our version properly gives the sense, not only here, but in Job xxx. 28; Ps. xlii. 9; xliii. 2. The *black,* however, in ancient mourning was not in the color of the apparel, but in dust and ashes, the unwashed state of the sad one. *All the day long,* equivalent to *continually.*

7. *For my loins are filled with a loathsome* disease. The variations in the rendering are putting for *loins,* heels, reins, flanks, mind. *Loins* is best; also for *loathsome disease,* tremor, burning, vileness, parching, inflammations. The Chaldee has illu-

sions. Some think this clause determines that bodily disease had certainly seized on David. Yet even they do or might admit that the chief reference is to the soul, defiled by sin, which is an old, hereditary, perpetual, universal, complicated, loathsome, mortal, and, so far as all human means are concerned, an incurable disease. He adds : *And* there is *no soundness in my flesh.* On same words see on v. 3. His case was most pitiable and deplorable, calling for divine interposition. He had become vile in his own esteem, and all for his sin.

8. *I am feeble and sore broken.* *Feeble*, faint, weakened, afflicted, disquieted, humbled. So some. *Sore broken*, exceedingly humbled, exceedingly out of heart, sore smitten, sunk to the last degree, exceedingly bruised. So some. In Ps. li. 17, *contrite;* several times,*broken.* David was like a man full of *bruises.* He was exceedingly out of heart. *I have roared by reason of the disquietness of my heart.* The verb here used occurs more than *twenty* times in the Hebrew Bible, and in the common version is always rendered *roar.* See on Ps. xxii. 1, 13. It expresses the loudest and strongest cry of distress, coming from the *disquietness, tumult, murmur, groaning, roaring* of his heart. His anguish was not of his bodily frame, but of his *heart.* Calvin : " The uncontrollable emotions of his heart forced him to cry out."

9. *Lord, all my desire* is *before thee ; and my groaning is not hid from thee.* The appeal is to God's omniscience. This cuts off the necessity of multiplying words ; it gives relief to a pious mind to rest in the assurance of divine notice ; and it implies a confidence that God will hear the *groaning*, and grant the *desire* of his servant. Alexander paraphrases the verse thus : " Thou knowest, O Lord, what I ask and what I need, the depth of my necessities and the intensity of my desires." The Psalmist does not as yet see any answer to his prayer, or any sign of coming relief, yet he leaves all with God.

10. *My heart panteth.* Ainsworth, Jebb and Alexander also have panteth. Others use such words as throbs, is troubled, flutters, is in a violent agitation. The verb describes a depressed state of mind, full of anxiety. Distress affected both body and mind : *My strength faileth me.* Several ancient and many modern versions follow the Hebrew, and give the verb in the past tense, my strength has left me, or has failed me. Perhaps this is best, signifying that his ability to do anything was quite gone. *As for the light of mine eyes, it also* is *gone from me.* The Chaldee reads and punctuates the verse thus : My strength has failed me, and the light of my eyes : And even they themselves [my eyes] are not with me. This follows the Hebrew literally, and is probably the best mode of dividing and rendering the clauses. Many in the main agree with the Chaldee ; others with the English. We have seen in Ps. vi. 8, how sorrow sinks the eyes. But the loss of the light complained of, doubtless meant more than a partial or threatened loss of vision. It was a general failure of comfort.

11. *My lovers and my friends stand aloof from my sore ; and my kinsmen stand afar off.* The Chaldee : My friends and my neighbors stood opposite to my wound ; and my near relatives stood far away ; Calvin : My friends and my companions stand away from my sore ; and my kinsfolk stand afar off ; Ainsworth : My lovers and my nearest friends stand from before my stroke, and my neighbors stand afar off ; Horsley : My friends and my companions come into my presence, and stop short, and the nearest of my kindred stand aloof ; Hengstenberg : My lovers and my friends stand over against my stroke, and my neighbors stand afar off. Hammond thinks the behaviour of David's friends is like that described in Luke x. 31, 32. By *sore, stroke, wound,* grief, trouble, or plague, is doubtless to be understood David's present *affliction*, whatever it may have been. *Standing aloof* implies a knowledge of his *distress* with a lack of proper affection for him, or of tender sympathy with him under the belief that God was against him.

12. *They also that seek after my life lay snares* for me. The enemies of truth and righteousness have never been fair and candid. The hatred, which the wicked bear to the righteous is deadly. They *seek after his life.* They *lay snares.* The Chaldee, church of England, Calvin, Ainsworth, Amesius, Edwards, Jebb, Fry, Hengstenberg and Alexander agree with the English version. *And they that seek my hurt speak mischievous things.* Instead of *mischievous things,* the Chaldee has a *lie;* Syriac, *falsehood;* Calvin, *treachery;* Ainsworth, *woful evils;* Venema, *enormous things;* Amesius, *grievous things;* Edwards, *nothing but what is corrupt;* Hengstenberg, *mischief;* Alexander, *mischiefs.* Lying, slandering and misrepresentation constitute a part of warfare carried on by the wicked in all ages. *And* [they] *imagine deceits all the day long.* The imagination of the wicked is racked to find out some new method of opposing righteousness. This is done, not once in a long time, not occasionally, but incessantly —*all the day long.* The human mind has never been under so high excitement as in opposing God's plans and people and Son. On this and the preceding verse Calvin says: "The purport of what is stated is, that while his friends cowardly sit still and will do nothing to aid him, his enemies vigorously bestir themselves, and seek by every means to destroy him." Surely if God shall ever give help, here is a fit occasion for so doing.

13. *But I, as a deaf* man, *heard not;* I was *as a dumb man* that *openeth not his mouth.* Two things often unite to make the suffering child of God behave like a deaf mute. One is the unreasonableness and violence of enemies, by which he is overwhelmed, seeing no possible good resulting from an attempt to gain a hearing from them. The other is that God most surely and speedily undertakes the cause of those, who quietly and patiently leave all in his hands. The scope of the verse shows that on the score of urgency and meekness David's case loudly called for divine interposition.

14. *Thus I was as a man that heareth not, and in whose mouth* are *no reproofs.* The prominence, given to the duty of pious silence in these two verses, is by no means unsustained in other parts of God's word, Lev. x. 3; Ps. xxxix. 1, 2; Isa. liii. 7; Matt. xxvi. 62, 63; John xix. 9. For *reproofs* some read *answers,* or *replies,* or *disproofs,* or *confutations,* or *retorts.* Either of these words is better than reproofs.

15. *For in thee, O* LORD, *do I hope: thou wilt hear, O* LORD, *my God.* The confidence here expressed was founded in the character of God, and might well induce the Psalmist to be quiet and to leave his cause in hands that could not fail to manage all things well. In the usual Hebrew text of this verse we have the three names of God, Jehovah, Adonai and Elohim. But Clarke and Anderson both say that in one hundred and two of Kennicott's and De Rosse's MSS. the original of the second word rendered *Lord* is not *Adonai* but *Jehovah.* An error in the text is possible, but not probable. No doctrine, or duty, or encouragement is affected by reading it either way.

16. *For I said,* Hear me, *lest* otherwise *they should rejoice over me: when my foot slippeth, they magnify* themselves *against me.* It is clear that something is to be here supplied. The words thrown in by our translators are natural. Hengstenberg suggests these: *It is matter of concern,* or, *It is to be feared;* Ainsworth, *It is to be feared.* He correctly says the original is *an unperfect speech through passion.* The language of powerful emotion is apt to be broken and elliptical. The plea is that God would not by forsaking him deliver him to the taunts and insults of his foes. Anticipating a failure they gave a shout, and *magnified themselves against* him. He further urges his plea by stating that his case was critical, that he could not without some relief hold out much longer.

17. *For I* am *ready to halt.* The Chaldee: I am ready to die; Horsley: Truly I am ready to make a false step; Hengstenberg: For I am given over to suffering.

The English version is followed by many, and itself closely follows the Hebrew. There is no better rendering than *ready to halt*. It gives a poor sense to refer the matter to bodily lameness. We have other places to sustain us in the figurative use of *halting*. Indeed in Ps. xxxv. 15, the word here rendered *halting* is rendered *adversity*. See Jer. xx. 10. The parallel clause quite corresponds to this explanation: *And my sorrow is continually before me*. The meaning is that his mind constantly dwelt on his affliction.

18. *For I will declare mine iniquity, I will be sorry for my sin*. That which made David's griefs so great was sin. This is *the* sting of all afflictions. *Confession* of sin and *sorrow* for it are clearly called for in the case of all transgression. Nothing could be more proper. There is often a strange power in affliction to remind us of our ill deserts. While David was thus crushed by sorrow and by a sense of sin, it was far otherwise with his foes.

19. *But mine enemies* are *lively*, and *they are strong: and they that hate me are multiplied*. *Many, strong* and *lively* enemies arrayed against *one feeble, sorrowing* man, forsaken by all, who might be expected to cleave to him! This is the picture of woe.

20. *They also that render evil for good are mine adversaries; because I follow* the thing that *good* is. The depravity here described is but a little removed from the very last stages of corruption. If men are quite given over to hating others for their goodness, a few more steps in the downward road will land them in hell. To do good for evil is common among saints. To do good for good is common among publicans. But to do evil for good is the mark of a devil. Calvin: "It must be admitted, that those are froward and wicked in the extreme, nay, even of a devilish disposition, who hold uprightness in such abhorrence that they deliberately make war upon those who follow after it."

21. *Forsake me not, O Lord: O my God be not far from me*. This is a very appropriate prayer for one in great trouble. It is in substance used several times, and uniformly when some distress was imminent, Ps. x. 1; xxii. 1; xxxv. 22. "A present God is all our strength."

22. *Make haste to help me, O Lord my salvation*. Pressing dangers demand speedy assistance. It is clear that David was not in despair, or he would not have used the last word in the Psalm. Calvin considers the last two verses together, and says that in them, "David briefly states the chief point which he desired, and the sum of his whole prayer; namely, that whereas he was forsaken of men, and grievously afflicted, God would receive him and raise him up again."

Doctrinal and Practical Remarks.

1. The title, which sets forth the design of this Psalm, points to the propriety of setting up solemn memorials of the trying scenes through which we have passed. Hezekiah did so, Isa. xxxviii. Jeremiah forgot not his affliction and his misery, Lam. iii. 20.

2. Calvin: David "was also mindful of his own high calling; for, as he was appointed master and teacher over the whole church, it was necessary that whatever he had learned in particular by divine teaching should be made known, and appropriated to the use of all, that all might profit thereby."

3. Or if it is God that is to be *reminded* by the Psalm, then in prayer we are God's remembrancers, and we are continually to bring to his notice our wants, and sorrows, and the help we need.

4. We should not think strange concerning the fiery trial which is to try us. Dickson: "It is consistent with God's fatherly love, and our sonship, to taste of fatherly wrath against our sins," v. 1.

5. Yet any man may well deprecate the divine wrath, v. 1. God's hot displeasure is terrible. Whoever has felt it will wish never to feel it again. One drop of the divine anger falling into the conscience of man makes him turn pale and tremble and die away.

6. If troubles come, we may well plead that they be made as light as possible, and that they be tempered with mercy, and not sent in vengeance, v. 1. We may well ask God to remember that we are dust. Our spirits would soon fail before his fierce anger.

7. If God's chastisements of his people make them cry out as they often do (see vv. 2, 3, 5, 6, 7, 8, 10;) what must be the doom of sinners when God's hand shall take hold of vengeance? This kind of reasoning is often and properly resorted to by inspired men, Luke xxiii. 31; 1 Pet. iv. 17, 18.

8. That which chiefly embitters affliction, and gives it its dreadful sting, is sin, v. 3. Yet a just sense of our ill desert is necessary to make us submissive in our trials. Calvin: "If we would render to God the praise which is due to him, let us learn by the example of David to connect our sins with his wrath." This view, by its very justness, would overwhelm us, if we had no hope in a Redeemer, if we could flee to no atoning blood. When suffering is intolerable, a sense of its righteousness but increases our anguish. But in Christ there is hope for the guiltiest.

9. In many things our estimates are extravagant; but we never over-estimate the evil of sin, v. 4. It is as corrupting as it is damning. It covers the soul with plague-spots, with the leprosy, Isa. i. 5, 6.

10. A very little of the natural fruit of our evil doings would show us the folly and madness of transgression, v. 5. Every prison, every gibbet, every pillory, and the varied and multiplied miseries of the vicious are but signs of what is coming. In the next world a villany, which on earth was every way successful, will appear to be as foolish as the crime that was promptly detected and condignly punished.

11. When God frowns and lets loose his messengers of wrath, the stoutest heart is full of anguish and terror. Those who make a mock at sin will yet find themselves roaring by reason of the disquietness of their hearts, v. 8. Here the wicked are often able by self-flattery, by the aid of mirthful company, by strong drink and by a wilful blindness, greatly to smother their torments of conscience and quiet their apprehensions. But this cannot last always.

12. To him who is upright with God, it is an unspeakable comfort that the Almighty knows his whole case, understands all his sorrows and desires, and perceives what relief and support are best, v. 9.

13. Hengstenberg: "The ninth verse has for all sufferers the import of an impressive admonition, not to seek help from God for pretended or imaginary sufferings, and in their complaints not to go beyond the measure which the occasion itself warrants. The help of God, the omniscient, directs itself, not according to the greatness of the lamentation, but according to the greatness of the suffering."

14. He who knows not how to seek relief in prayer, is destitute of one of the most important secrets ever made known to man; for "it is not wrestling with trouble within ourselves, nor venting our grief as natural men, which can give us ease, but pouring out our heart before the Lord, which must do it. *All my desire is before thee.*"

15. It is no new thing for good men to see their old friends and near relatives withdrawing their sympathy and support from them, vv. 10, 11. The leaves cling close enough while they can draw sap and nourishment from the tree and its branches; but when the frosts of adversity come, they soon fall off.

16. If we find men deceitful, we may know that, however righteous our cause may be, they will upon any strong temptation turn against us; and we may be as sure that

when men are without cause our enemies, we may never expect fair dealing at their hands. No hatred is harder to overcome than that which is based in a wrong done to another, v. 12.

17. Good men should not be in the slightest degree moved by finding *false* charges brought against them, v. 12. Tholuck: "We are entitled to hope for the aid of the Lord, according as the accusations of our adversaries are unfounded, and every attempt of remonstrating against their obduracy and cunning is useless, and according as the sufferer (as does David) absolutely commits the justice of his cause to God as his best Advocate."

18. We may carry the worst possible case of distress to God, and confidently tell it all to him, v. 12. Calvin: "If we are altogether destitute of human aid and assistance, if our friends fail us in the time of need, and if others seek our ruin, and breathe out nothing but destruction against us, let us remember that it is not in vain for us to lay these things in prayer before God, whose province it is to succor those who are in misery, to take under his protection those who are perfidiously forsaken and betrayed, to restrain the wicked, and not only to withstand their violence, but also to anticipate their deceitful counsels and to frustrate their designs."

19. Silence is sometimes right, vv. 13, 14. He that reproves a scorner gets to himself a blot. He that gives that which is holy unto the dogs, may expect them to turn again and rend him. The more his victims answered him, the more Jeffreys raved. It is no small part of wisdom to know when to speak and when to be silent. Tholuck: "Experience confirms it, that if we have to deal with any crafty and embittered foes, resigned suffering is more likely to benefit than a zealous apprehension of our good cause."

20. In this dark world where sorrow so abounds, there is no substitute for trust and hope in God, v. 15. Sometimes providences are adverse, friends become cold and even unkind, enemies plot our ruin, then our feet well nigh slip. In a thousand cases what can we do but look to God?

21. It is not wrong for us to wish to do right and to be sustained in our course that we may avoid the insults and reproaches of wicked men, v. 16. Calvin: "It is indeed true, that there is nothing which wounds those of an ingenuous disposition of mind more than when wicked and ungodly men recompense them in a manner so dishonorable and unjust; but when they reflect upon this consolatory consideration, that God is no less offended with such ingratitude than those to whom the injury is done, they have no reason to be troubled beyond measure."

22. One of our best protections against any sin or failure is the candid confession of our own weakness and liability to err, v. 17.

23. We may boldly come and tell God all our sorrows, v. 17. This is true not only of all our great afflictions, but of our minor grievances. When John the Baptist was beheaded, his disciples came and "told Jesus."

24. Good resolutions are good things, v. 18. When kept, they lead to the highest attainments men ever make.

25. We cannot too often or too humbly confess to God and bewail our sins, v. 18. On this subject the error lies in reluctance, not in freedom; in restraint, not in excess.

26. It is a marvel that any man escapes ruin, the dangers which beset even the best being many and terrible, v. 19. None but God could have brought David, through all his troubles, to the throne of Israel. None but God could take a poor tempted soul, through all its trials, to the kingdom of heaven.

27. The necessity for punishing sin and dealing with the wicked in the way of eternal damnation will at last be as clear as their doom will be righteous, v. 20 They could not be saved, because they perverted everything. They even *rendered evil for good* both to God and man.

28. Let us cry to God, come what will, vv. 21, 22. Appearances may be all against us, but God can change appearances. Dickson: "We must not limit the Lord to give us comfort and deliverance when we think we have greatest need of it, but must leave our prayer at his feet."

29. At last all Israel shall be saved, for *Jehovah* is *salvation* to every soul that trusts in him, v. 22. "The bond of the covenant is able to bear the weight of the believer's heaviest burden."

PSALM XXXIX.

To the chief Musician, *even* to Jeduthun, A Psalm of David.

1 I said, I will take heed to my ways, that I sin not with my tongue: I will keep my mouth with a bridle, while the wicked is before me.

2 I was dumb with silence, I held my peace, *even* from good; and my sorrow was stirred.

3 My heart was hot within me; while I was musing the fire burned: *then* spake I with my tongue,

4 LORD, make me to know mine end, and the measure of my days, what it *is;* *that* I may know how frail I *am.*

5 Behold, thou hast made my days *as* a handbreadth; and mine age *is* as nothing before thee: verily every man at his best state *is* altogether vanity. Selah.

6 Surely every man walketh in a vain shew: surely they are disquieted in vain: he heapeth up *riches,* and knoweth not who shall gather them.

7 And now, Lord, what wait I for? my hope *is* in thee.

8 Deliver me from all my transgressions: make me not the reproach of the foolish.

9 I was dumb, I opened not my mouth; because thou didst *it.*

10 Remove thy stroke away from me: I am consumed by the blow of thine hand.

11 When thou with rebukes dost correct man for iniquity, thou makest his beauty to consume away like a moth: surely every man *is* vanity. Selah.

12 Hear my prayer, O LORD, and give ear unto my cry; hold not thy peace at my tears: for I *am* a stranger with thee, *and* a sojourner, as all my fathers *were.*

13 Oh spare me, that I may recover strength, before I go hence, and be no more.

*T*O the chief *Musician,* and *A Psalm of David* are phrases explained on titles of Psalms iii. iv. Respecting Jeduthun, or, as the Hebrew has it, Jedithun, we know but little. There is no evidence that he is the same as Ethan. The name occurs several times in the historic books of Scripture, 1 Chron. xvi. 38, 41, 42; xxv. 1, 3, 6; 2 Chron. v. 12; xxix. 14; Neh. xi. 17. It is also in the title of Psalm lxxvii. The name, which signifies *one who gives praise,* was most appropriate to a leader of a band of trained singers and players on instruments. The descendants of this man are noticed long after the death of David. There is not the slightest evidence that *Jeduthun* points to the tune or the instrument used in singing this song. David wrote this Psalm. So says the title. There is nothing to set aside this opinion. It is held by the great mass of commentators. Theodoret and some others suppose it was written on occasion of Absalom's rebellion. But it as well suits many another trying time in David's life. Good and sound men are not agreed on the question, Does David in this Psalm express sinful impatience? Calvin, Diodati, Pool, Henry, Gill, Scott, Tholuck, Hengstenberg and Alexander think he does. In this opinion they are all decided, but not all equally strong. On the other hand Luther, Patrick, Mudge, Edwards, Clarke, Morison, Slade and others see nothing rash or impatient in any part of this poem. And the church of England has actually adopted vv. 4–13 into her burial service. That the latter is the correct view is nearly certain. 1. Every verse and clause admit of a good sense without any straining of the signification of words. 2. The great mass of pious people almost uniformly regard this Psalm as containing language fit to be used by us in our devotions. Commonly that is the true sense of God's word, which in a fair translation is conveyed to the minds of plain pious persons. Versions of this Psalm are sung throughout the Christian world without a suspicion on the part of the worshippers that they are rehearsing sentiments of impatience and wickedness. 3. An examination of the passages referred to in the margin will show that the clauses deemed objectionable have their parallels in Scriptures not suspected of impiety. 4. It is but sheer justice to any writer to give such a construction to his language as will afford a good sense, if this can be done without violating any of the laws of language. This is very clear in all moral writings, where the whole scope of the author is evidently to promote piety towards God. Morison numbers this among the penitential Psalms; but it is not generally so considered. In it are two names of God, *Jehovah* LORD and *Adonai Lord*, on which see on Ps. i. 2; ii. 4. On *Selah*, see Introduction, § 15.

1. *I said, I will take heed to my ways, that I sin not with my tongue.* The first word expresses a settled purpose. Pool: I fully resolved; Venema: I firmly resolved and prescribed to myself this law. *Take heed*, i. e., *guard, watch, keep. Ways*, the course of the life. *Sin not with my tongue.* In no way are men more apt to sin. In nothing is it more difficult to avoid sinning. "If any man offend not in word, the same is a perfect man, and able also to bridle the whole body. . . The tongue can no man tame," Jas. iii. 3, 8. Many so sin with the tongue that in eternity they will wish that they had been born dumb, yea, that they had never been born at all. *I will keep my mouth with a bridle, while the wicked is before me. Keep*, rendered take heed to in the first clause. The *bridle* was for *restraint* and *guidance.* Here the latter is the main idea. Because the *bridle* of old times was more like a muzzle or halter than the *bridle* now in use, some would here read muzzle. But the muzzle was also used to restrain animals from feeding; so that the common rendering here is best. The Septuagint, Ethiopic, Vulgate and Arabic have it *set a watch* or *set a guard*, instead of *keep with a bridle. While the wicked is before me.* David's silence seems to have been entire at such times. Before the wicked he did not accuse his foes, nor vindicate himself, nor render railing for railing, nor express his perplexities respecting providence, nor even utter his pious sentiments. His practice and instruction may have led Solomon to give the rule which we find in Prov. ix. 7, 8.

2. *I was dumb with silence;* i. e., he was as silent as if he could not speak at all; or as if he were a dumb man. Ainsworth: I was dumb with stillness; Hengstenberg: I grew dumb; Calvin: I was dumb in silence. *I held my peace, even from good.* The Chaldee: From the words of the law. Hengstenberg's rendering is not good: I was silent, not for good. He thinks the sense is that keeping silence did him harm. Edwards gives the true sense: I refrained from speaking what was good. Yet consciousness of having not sinned with the mouth nor charged God foolishly does not hinder grief. *And my sorrow was stirred.* Septuagint: My grief was renewed; Edwards: My pain was irritated. We ought not to speak unless we can say something good. But if our strength is small, our best resolutions will fail under the weight of increasing woes. A deep sense of our weakness, watchfulness over ourselves and reliance on God alone constitute the sum of our wisdom. But though bound to a wise silence before men, we may always pour out our cries to God. Nay, the greater our sorrow the more need of prayer to him, who made the world.

3. *My heart was hot within me.* David's state of mind was one of deep excitement. *Was hot,* the same verb is rendered *waxed warm* in 2 Kings iv. 34, and *have heat* in Eccle. iv. 11. David here says he had ardent emotions, burning thoughts. The Chaldee: My heart boiled within my body; Septuagint and Edwards: My heart grew hot within me. This phrase is explained by the next: *While I was musing the fire burned.* There is no more reason for supposing that the words *was hot* and *burned* describe a sinful state of mind than that the disciples at Emmaus are confessing their criminality when they say: "Did not our hearts burn within us, while he talked with us by the way?" These words express earnest thought attended with strong emotion. Piety often makes exquisite feeling silent for a season. But at length utterance is gained: Then *spake I with my tongue.* What he said is found in the following verses.

4. LORD, *make me to know mine end, and the measure of my days, what it is; that I may know how frail I* am. We have the parallel in Ps. xc. 12. The last clause is variously given. Chaldee: That I may know when I shall fail from the world; Calvin: That I may understand how long I may live; margin: That I may know what time I have here; church of England: That I may be certified how long I have to live. For *frail,* others read *brief,* short lived, etc. He prays, not that God would make a revelation to him of the time of his approaching death, but that he would give him such a just estimate of his frailty that he might be a better and wiser man. Poets have long sung of the brevity of life. Euripides speaks of the "little work of life;" Homer, of "men living a little while and then coming to an end;" and Horace, "Be mindful of how short a life thou art." It is mentioned as a proof of wisdom in the father of Alexander the great, that he required himself to be aroused every morning with the cry: "Philip, thou art mortal."

5. *Behold, thou hast made my days* as *an hand breadth.* Instead of *an hand breadth,* the Chaldee has *swift;* Arabic, *short;* Vulgate and Doway, *measurable.* The hand breadth or span of the ancients was the breadth of the four fingers, and not of the extended thumb also. So Hesychius followed by Diodati, Ainsworth and Hammond. *And mine age is as nothing before thee. Before thee,* in thy sight. See Ps. lxxviii. 12. For *age,* Ainsworth has worldly time; Jebb, short life; Fry, time. Hengstenberg: My life is as non-existence before thee. By many figures, the Bible teaches the brevity of life. *Verily every man at his best state is altogether vanity.* Arabic: Yea, whatever pertains to a living man is vain; Syriac: All men tarry but as a vapor; Horsley: Also everything is vanity;—even every man with all his pride; Chaldee: Moreover all things are counted as nothing, but all the righteous shall live in life eternal. If the whole life and end of man are earthly, then he is nothing but vanity. On *vanity,* see on Ps. xxxi. 6. Parallel passages are 1 Cor. vii. 31; James iv. 14.

6. *Surely every man walketh in a vain shew.* For *vain shew,* the Septuagint, Ethiopic, Arabic, Syriac, Vulgate, Montanus, Piscator, Cocceius, Ainsworth, Venema, Amesius, Hengstenberg and Alexander have *image;* church of England, *vain shadow;* Jebb, *shadow;* Edwards, *phantom.* The interpretations given to the word are such as these: a false resemblance, a wandering shadow, an imaginary life, an ideal scene, a delusion. Dathe renders it, Surely every man pursues a shadow. When in the Bristol election, his competitor died, Burke said, "What shadows we are, and what shadows we pursue." *Surely they are disquieted in vain.* See men compassing land and sea; toiling and travelling day and night; their hurried gait and anxious look showing that they are ill at ease; but all is in vain. Now and then one rises high, but sits down on some peak to shiver in bleak loneliness. If he gains wealth, his abundance will not suffer him to sleep. All is vanity. *He heapeth up* riches, *and knoweth not who shall gather them.* The thief, the swindler, the extortioner may

catch all. His heirs may be fools or spendthrifts. The ocean may ingulf, or the fire consume all that he has made. To look to men and to things which perish is folly. In this cheerless state of things, have we no duty to perform? Is there no hope?

7. *And now,* LORD, *what wait I for?* Many render the Hebrew literally: What have I been expecting? It is the language of surrender of all hope of real good from sources so delusive. Yet he does not sink into despair, as Ahithophel did; but at once addresses himself to the Lord: *My hope* is *in thee.* Hengstenberg errs in making David in this verse complain of God. *Now* has much force, *q. d.*,"I will no longer take sad views; I will encourage myself in the Lord my God; I will seek for happiness only in his love and service, expecting assistance as my necessities require."

8. *Deliver me from all my transgressions.* For *deliver,* other versions have *free, set free, rescue;* and for *transgressions,* wickedness, iniquities, failings, offences, trespasses. In sin are both guilt and pollution, liability to punishment and defilement. From both of these, good men seek deliverance, though forgiveness is here the prominent idea. *Deliver,* as in Ps. vii. 1; xxii. 20. The word *all* is not to be overlooked. If *one* sin remains unpardoned, or in possession of the dominion of the soul, salvation is not possible. *Make me not the reproach of the foolish.* Chaldee: Put not the reproach of the fool upon me; Syriac: Do not make me a reproach to foolish men; Hengstenberg: Let me not be a mockery to the fool. By *fool* Calvin understands *the idle and debauched,* a contemptible man, one who is utterly worthless and base; Diodati, *the worldly man;* Alexander, *the impious unbeliever;* Clarke, *the godless and profane;* Pool and Scott, *the wicked.* All agree that the *fool* is a *bad* man. To be the reproach of such is justly esteemed one of the greatest afflictions, Ps. xliv. 13, 14; lxxix. 4. Let me not fall into the hand of man.

9. *I was dumb; I opened not my mouth; because thou didst it.* See on vv. 1, 2; Ps. xxxviii. 13, 14. The quietness of an afflicted believer under the stroke of God is a duty taught in many ways, Lev. x. 3; 2 Sam. xvi. 10; Job i. 22; xl. 4, 5; Ps. cxxxi. 2. Murmuring is a great sin. But to pray is not to find fault. On this clause is founded that excellent treatise, "The Mute Christian." No man prays more frequently or fervently than he who is *thus* dumb.

10. *Remove thy stroke away from me.* For *stroke* several ancient versions read *scourge* or *scourges.* Several moderns prefer *plague.* This does not materially vary the meaning. David is pointing to the chastisement he was undergoing. He begs for its removal, confessing his weakness: *I am consumed by the blow of thine hand.* For *consumed,* some read fainted, failed, or wasted away. The meaning is, I am fast failing; help me before I sink.

11. *When thou with rebukes dost correct man for iniquity, thou makest his beauty to consume away like a moth.* The Chaldee: By chastisement for sin man is corrected: and his body is dissolved like a moth broken asunder. Several versions for *moth* read *spider,* referring to the history of that creature as destroying itself by spinning its web and laying its eggs and so disappearing. The church of England has it, Like as it were a moth fretting a garment; Ainsworth: Thou makest that which is to be desired of his, to melt away as a moth; Walford: Thou destroyest his goodliness as a moth destroyeth a garment; Hengstenberg: Thou dost consume, as by a moth, what he loves. Very few think that the Chaldee gives the correct view. Nearly all think that the reference is to the silent and secret destruction carried on in cloths by the moth; see Job xiii. 28; Isa. l. 9; Hos. v. 12. Calvin: "At first view the comparison of God to a moth may seem absurd; for what relation is there, it may be said, between a small moth-worm and the infinite majesty of God? I answer, That David

has with much propriety made use of this simile, that we may know that although God does not openly thunder from heaven against the reprobate, yet his secret curse ceases not to consume them away, just as the moth, though unperceived, wastes by its secret gnawing a piece of cloth or wood." But see Job iv. 19, where the moth itself seems to be the emblem of frailty. So it may be here. Either way we get a good sense. *Surely every man is vanity. Selah.* Chaldee: Truly every man is always nothing; Septuagint, Ethiopic and Vulgate: Surely every man is disquieted in vain; Syriac: And all men are as a vapor; Hengstenberg: Only vanity are all men. See on v. 5. It is impossible too often to remind men of their frailty.

12. *Hear my prayer,* O LORD, *i. e.,* so hear as to answer. *And give ear unto my cry.* When a good judge *gives ear,* he who has a good cause and can state it is safe. The *cry* is the earnest prayer, proceeding from a distressed heart. *Hold not thy peace at my tears.* To a manner earnest in its tones, he added weeping in prayer. If he had not said a word God, who knows the meaning of a sigh, understands also the language of a tear. He then casts himself upon the Lord in language which has not previously occurred in the Psalms. *For I am a stranger with thee,* and *a sojourner, as all my fathers were.* God who was the author of the law of Moses, had repeatedly enjoined kindness to strangers, Ex. xxii. 21; Lev. xix. 10, 33. Surely an appeal to the author of such a law cannot be in vain. The last clause probably refers to such acknowledgments as were made by Abraham and Jacob, Gen. xxiii. 4; xlvii. 9. But the words have a higher bearing. Cruden thinks *stranger* in this place is "one who uses this world as if he used it not, who does not think himself at home in this world, but has his mind and eye fixed on his country which is above." Paul gives the true exposition of such words: "They confessed that they were strangers and pilgrims on the earth. For they that say such things declare plainly that they seek a country. . . They desire a better country, even an heavenly: wherefore God is not ashamed to be called their God." Compare 1 Chron. xxix. 15; Ps. cxix. 19. Tholuck: "Man traverses life like a pilgrim and a stranger, making but a short stay."

13. *Oh spare me that I may recover strength, before I go hence and be no more.* Hengstenberg notices the fact that "all the words of this closing verse occur in different places in the book of Job," Job vii. 8, 19, 21; x. 20, 21; xiv. 6. His inference that the author of that book lived as late as the author of this Psalm does not logically follow. The renderings of the first verb are very various: Stay me, stay from me, let me alone, forgive me, set me free, give me some respite, look away from me. Those who prefer the last form understand the Psalmist as asking God to avert his angry face. Our version agrees with the Arabic literally, and with several translations substantially. Instead of "recover strength," some prefer "be revived," "be refreshed," "refresh myself," "recover myself." Our version retains the idea, not the exact form, which would be "that I may be invigorated." The last words in the Hebrew are very brief and striking, literally, "Before I go [or walk] and be not."

DOCTRINAL AND PRACTICAL REMARKS.

1. Though some do vainly put a good resolution for a good deed, and do make it only to break it, and when broken do vainly make another just as worthless; yet he who expects to do right, must resolve to do right, v. 1.

2. As one of the most difficult duties is rightly to manage our speech, wise men of every age have been much concerned to govern their tongues with care, vv. 1, 2, 9. Calvin: "There is nothing more slippery or loose than the tongue." Quarles: "If thou desire to be held wise, be so wise as to hold thy tongue."

3. Excellent rules for governing our speech are found in many books. Read them. See the proverbs of Solomon and the best versions of this Psalm.

4. There are many circumstances in which we may wisely be silent, v. 2.   Morison: "There are seasons when a good man must be blind to what he sees, deaf to what he hears, and dumb when temptation to speak is peculiarly strong."   Towards God we should always be silent, unless we can say something to his honor, Jer. xx. 9; Lam. iii. 39.   Towards man we should be silent when our speaking will not promote peace, or truth, or justice, or piety, or edification.   Calvin: "David might have encountered the ungodly with a good defence of his own innocence, but he rather preferred to forego the prosecution of his righteous cause than indulge in any intemperate sorrow."

5. It is not wicked to be sad, v. 2.   He, who laughs when he should weep, or is glad when he should be grieved, is at least a fool.

6. Extended reflection on any of the great matters relating to God's government of the world will awaken strong emotion.   If our thoughts and hearts are right, the more we are aroused, the more will we be inclined to carry our cause before the Lord, v. 3.

7. Of all the petitions we ask of God none is more appropriate than begging for knowledge and instruction, not only as to God's glorious nature, will, ways and works; but also on our own destiny, responsibility, privileges and duties, and particularly our own sin, misery and frailty, v. 3.

8. Human life is a trifle.   Nothing is more fleeting.   If in this world man attains the highest ends of his existence, it is not possible to vindicate the divine government, vv. 3, 4, 5, 6, 11.   When one of the greatest men died, an eloquent survivor said: "A pebble has fallen into a vast lake.   The surface is somewhat rippled; but soon all will be smooth as ever."   A large part of human wisdom consists in knowing and remembering that we are but shadows passing over the plain: and that the highest pursuits, which prepare us not for a better world are far below the desires of any good man.   Paul mentions it as a great truth that in many ways concerned Christians: "The time is short," 1 Cor. vii. 29.   When things are alike fleeting, uncertain, and filling us with care, surely we ought to grasp them with neither fondness nor eagerness.   Because life is short "no sufferer needs to anticipate centuries of misery in this vain world.   Because life is so short, those, who would save themselves and bless their generation, must be up and doing."

9. One of the most profitable ways of studying human life is to contrast it with the eternal ages of him who made the world.   This David perhaps does in v. 5.   "Mine age is as nothing before thee."   Moses does this much more at length in the *ninetieth* Psalm, vv. 1–10.

10. In the darkest times that visit us, the great source of hope, and joy, and success still remains to all, who have any true piety, v. 7.   God never dies, never retires behind clouds so dark that faith and hope and love cannot apprehend him.

11. Morison: "Of all the burdens which press upon a believer, sin is the heaviest," v. 8.   The reason is that in its nature it is the greatest of all evils.   So God has pronounced.   So the renewed soul perceives.   Whatever shows us the evil of sin is good for us.   On that subject the best saints have the clearest views.

12. It is wise to seek relief from all our distresses by beginning with earnest cries for pardon and purification, v. 8.

13. It is perfectly right to ask exemption from the derisions of ungodly men, v. 8.   Scorn is more than most men can bear without loss of temper or of comfort.   It is horrible to have dogs turned loose on us.

14. Because our strength is small, it is wise, with submission to the sovereign will of God, to ask that any of our sufferings may be assuaged, any of our afflictions be made light, v. 10.   We must indeed close all such prayers with the sentence, "Thy will be done."   Still we may beseech the Lord thrice, seven times, very often and very

earnestly, and if the thorn in the flesh be not taken away, we shall at least have grace to bear it, and that is better than freedom from sorrow.

15. Henry: " When we are under the correcting hand of God, our eye must be to God himself, and not to any other, for relief. He only that inflicts the stroke can remove it." Were this truth remembered, how much sin and misery would be avoided! When Israel sinned and chastisement came in the shape of war, instead of returning to God by repentance, in their unbelief they sent to Egypt or Assyria for horsemen. How much we resemble them in this folly.

16. God's stroke is terrible. It will consume any who are not mercifully spared and sustained, vv. 10, 11. It is not anywhere of record that man or angel has hardened himself against God and prospered.

17. In v. 12, David virtually asks for the same thing three times. In other Psalms he begs for the same blessing over and over again. True earnestness is importunate, though it is not wordy.

18. It is a blessed thing to be a pilgrim on any terms. Scott: " The Christian's sorrows are all sanctified; the gracious Lord will wipe away his tears, and answer all his prayers: he cannot but feel his afflictions; yet as a stranger and a pilgrim on earth, he hopes for a better and more enduring habitation in heaven, where his heart and his treasure are already. He expects weariness and ill-treatment by the way: but his stay here will not be long; and, walking with God by faith, he goes forward on his journey, undiverted from his course, and not much cast down by the ill accommodation or difficulties with which he meets." In heaven

> There is no sorrow, nor any sighing,
> Nor any sinning, nor any dying.

19. Cobbin: " There is nothing wrong in desiring to be spared that we may do God's work on earth, and be better prepared by his grace to enjoy the substantial and never-failing blessings of glory." " Let my soul live, and it shall praise thee." It is a sad thing to die, when our hearts are not in a state of nearness to God. " A good man would not wish to meet his Judge in a state of spiritual declension." Who would not desire to lay up some good provision for passing over Jordan? A parent may lawfully pray to live till the character of his offspring is formed. There is also something exceedingly mournful in dying in the midst of one's days. So thought Hezekiah. And it is truly grievous to be called away before the great enterprise of a man's life is accomplished; as if David had died before he was peaceably settled in the throne, or Solomon when the temple was yet unfinished. What made Moses' death so sad was *first*, that it was for a special sin, and *secondly*, he had not led the Israelites into the promised land—he had not finished what he began.

20. View death as we may, it is a solemn event. To him who dies daily it has no terrors. Some, like Paul, find themselves in a strait betwixt two, not knowing whether to abide here, or to depart and be with Christ, which is far better. To such dying is not alarming. But to the guilty, the worldly-minded, the backslider, and the lukewarm death is naturally terrible. Some one asked Leighton if he had been to hear a sermon. He answered: " I met a sermon, for I met a corpse; and rightly and profitably are funeral rites performed when the living lay it to heart." Bouchier: " The best preparation for our own funeral is to meditate seriously and prayerfully over another's grave, and take home with us the solemn truths it enforces."

PSALM XL.

To the chief Musician, A Psalm of David.

1 I waited patiently for the LORD; and he inclined unto me, and heard my cry.

2 He brought me up also out of a horrible pit, out of the miry clay, and set my feet upon a rock, *and* established my goings.

3 And he hath put a new song in my mouth, *even* praise unto our God: many shall see *it*, and fear, and shall trust in the LORD.

4 Blessed *is* that man that maketh the LORD his trust, and respecteth not the proud, nor such as turn aside to lies.

5 Many, O LORD my God, *are* thy wonderful works *which* thou hast done, and thy thoughts *which are* to us-ward: they cannot be reckoned up in order unto thee: *if* I would declare and speak *of them*, they are more than can be numbered.

6 Sacrifice and offering thou didst not desire; mine ears hast thou opened: burnt offering and sin offering hast thou not required.

7 Then said I, Lo, I come: in the volume of the book *it is* written of me,

8 I delight to do thy will, O my God: yea, thy law *is* within my heart.

9 I have preached righteousness in the great congregation: lo, I have not refrained my lips, O LORD, thou knowest.

10 I have not hid thy righteousness within my heart; I have declared thy faithfulness and thy salvation: I have not concealed thy lovingkindness and thy truth from the great congregation.

11 Withhold not thou thy tender mercies from me, O LORD: let thy lovingkindness and thy truth continually preserve me.

12 For innumerable evils have compassed me about: mine iniquities have taken hold upon me, so that I am not able to look up; they are more than the hairs of mine head: therefore my heart faileth me.

13 Be pleased, O LORD, to deliver me: O LORD, make haste to help me.

14 Let them be ashamed and confounded together that seek after my soul to destroy it; let them be driven backward and put to shame that wish me evil.

15 Let them be desolate for a reward of their shame that say unto me, Aha, aha.

16 Let all those that seek thee rejoice and be glad in thee: let such as love thy salvation say continually, The LORD be magnified.

17 But I *am* poor and needy; *yet* the Lord thinketh upon me: thou *art* my help and my deliverer; make no tarrying, O my God.

ON the title see on titles of Psalms iii. iv. The Arabic says it *treats of the church:* Syriac: A Psalm of David according to the letter: when Shemaiah brought the names of those who minister in the house of the Lord. In a spiritual sense, it is a thanksgiving to God by his worshippers and church. The supposed reference is to the history recorded in 1 Chron. xxiv. 6. These additions to the title are purely conjectural. In the Hebrew the word *David* is placed before the word *Psalm;* whereas in previous Psalms it is just the reverse. But this transposition signifies nothing, though some have attached importance to it. Ainsworth would read it, *A Psalm concerning David*, and by David would understand Christ, referring to Jer. xxx. 9; Ezek. xxxiv. 23; xxxvii. 24; Hos. iii. 5. But this is surely attaching too much importance to a transposition of words, which does not at all affect the sense, any more than when in English we say, *David's Psalms* instead of *The Psalms of David*. That David wrote this Psalm is clear. Hengstenberg: "Scarcely even the semblance of an argument has been brought against David's being the author;" Clarke: "I am satisfied the Psalm was composed by David."

In interpreting this Psalm, the great question is, What is its relation to Christ? For general observations on this subject see Introduction, § 8, and preliminary remarks on Psalms xvi. xxii. If the views there given are sound, the judicious reader will easily see how we should interpret this composition. These things are clear:

1. Unquestionably this Psalm contains a prophecy of the Messiah. This is unanswerably established by Hengstenberg in his Christology, Vol. I.; and by almost innumerable authors ancient and modern, especially commentators on the Psalms and on the Epistle to the Hebrews. Sampson: "To the reverent believer in inspiration the sufficient proof is that an inspired author has ascribed the words of the Psalm to Christ."

2. There is not sufficient evidence that the whole Psalm, like Psalm xxii. is a prophecy, applying directly, solely and exclusively to Christ. Those, who maintain that it is, find themselves beset with difficulties on all hands, forcing them to interpretations that seem fanciful, and shocking to the feelings of the pious, maintaining that verse 12 contains the words of our Lord Jesus Christ. It is very freely admitted that the word there rendered *iniquities* may mean *punishments, calamities, sufferings* on account of sin; but ancient and modern translations are so uniform in rendering it *iniquities, sins, wickednesses*, that it looks like a mere device of interpretation to resort to such an explanation. The Scripture is careful not to call the sins, for which Messiah suffered, *his*, but always *ours:* "He was wounded for *our* transgressions; he was bruised for *our* iniquities; the chastisement of *our* peace was upon him; the LORD hath laid on *him* the iniquity of *us* all," Isa. liii. 5, 6.

3. It is not necessary to find or establish formal divisions in this Psalm, as some have done, in order to ascertain what was personal to David, and what pertained to Messiah. Kennicott divides it "into three distinct parts, the *first* ending with the fifth verse, the *second* with the first word of the twelfth verse, and the third reaching to the close of the Psalm." Other partitions have been suggested; but none so plausible as this; yet even this is plainly capricious.

4. This Psalm is best interpreted by classing it under the head of *Typical-Messianic*. This supposes David, the speaker, to be a type of Christ, and yet to utter things, which cannot but remotely, if at all, have a just application to the type, but are only or fully true of the antitype; yet that so much is literally true of the type as fitly to make him a figure of him that was to come. This mode of expounding other portions of Scripture is common with the best commentators. See on Ps. xvi. Morison: "I can never read this Psalm without some doubts whether it is altogether, in every part, prophetic." A large number of sound expositors agree with him. Even Cocceius admits that part of the words may be applied to Christ and part not so applied without any impropriety. Scott: "In this Psalm, David seems to have intended to speak of his own case; but the Holy Spirit led him to use language, which in its full meaning can be applied to none but the Lord Jesus himself." Clarke: "The *sixth, seventh,* and *eighth* verses contain a remarkable prophecy of the incarnation and sacrificial offering of Jesus Christ." With slight variations the last five verses of this Psalm compose Psalm lxx. Such repetitions are not unusual in the Scriptures. In this Psalm we have *Jehovah* LORD and *Elohim God*, on which see on Ps. i. 2; iii. 2.

1. *I waited patiently for the* LORD. In the Hebrew and nearly all the ancient versions, the first word is doubled: *Waiting, I waited; Expecting, I expected; Hoping, I hoped.* Ainsworth: "This doubling notes earnestness, constancy, patience." Our Lord used a like phrase: "With desire have I desired to eat this passover." Only in Luke xxii. 15 *desire* is a noun and *desired* a verb; whereas in this Psalm both words are verbs. Alexander thinks the repetition "is perhaps exclusive of all other means. 'I simply waited; I did nothing but wait.'" This form of expression probably had its origin with the Hebrews; but we find examples in the Greek Classics. We had the same verb in Ps. xxv. 3, 5, 21; xxxix. 7. It is commonly rendered *wait*, or *look*, in the sense of *expect*. Such pious behaviour could not be unrequited. Berleberg

Bible: "If we only wait in patience upon God, he will presently manifest himself." *And he inclined unto me, and heard my cry.* For *inclined* some read *bended, bowed, was attentive.* Either gives the true sense. The more a judge is interested in a suitor, the more he leans forward and listens to him. The Lord *heard,* i. e., so as to answer.

2. *He brought me up also out of a horrible pit.* For *horrible pit* the margin has *pit of noise.* This is literal and is approved by the Chaldee, Montanus, Musculus, Piscator, Cocceius, Jebb and Alexander. The Septuagint, Ethiopic and Vulgate read *pit of misery;* Syriac, *pit of woe;* Arabic, *pit of perdition;* Calvin and Fry, *roaring pit;* Edwards, *dreadful pit;* Horsley, *void pit;* Hammond, *a resounding pit;* Ainsworth, *the pit of sounding calamity;* Hengstenberg, *the roaring deep.* The prophet designs to say that his condition had been like that of one in a pit or pool, where by some cause the waters, being greatly agitated, resounded from deep and horrible caverns. In this sad plight was he, when God *brought him up,* or drew him out, or rescued him. The pit did not contain clear waters, and God rescued him *out of the miry clay.* Chaldee, *mire of filth;* Syriac and Arabic, *mud of corruption;* Septuagint, Ethiopic and Vulgate, *the filth of dregs;* Ainsworth, *the mire of mud;* Edwards, *deep clay;* Fry, *overwhelming mire;* Hengstenberg, *the mud;* Amesius, *the filthy mud.* The condition, from which he had been rescued, was one every way horrible. Such imagery as this was borrowed from what was actually known in countries familiar to the inspired writers. *And set my feet upon a rock.* The *rock* is a favorite emblem of inspired writers, see Ps. xix. 14; xxvii. 5. Here it is in contrast with *miry clay.* And *established my goings.* For *established* the Arabic, Septuagint, Ethiopic and Vulgate read *directed;* church of England and Jebb, *ordered;* Ainsworth, *ordered steadily;* Edwards, *secured;* Alexander, *fixed;* Ainsworth, *set fast.* *Established* is best.

3. *And he hath put a new song in my mouth,* even *praise unto our God. Song,* commonly so rendered; found in the title of Ps. xxx. *Praise,* in Hebrew the same, from which the book of *Psalms,* or *Praises,* takes its name. In the common version it is uniformly rendered *praise,* in the plural *praises.* The word *new* points to the novel occasion on which David was called to praise. Alexander supposes the terms used to be equivalent to *fresh praise.* Calvin: "He uses the word *new* in the sense of exquisite, not ordinary." A song is the consummation of a deliverance or victory. Such mercy and compassion could not be without effect: *Many shall see* it, *and fear, and shall trust in the Lord.* Remarkable displays of God's power and wisdom in providence, even though they be very merciful to those for whom they are made, seem to have a great effect in producing a salutary awe in the minds of men, Ps. cxxx. 4; Isa. xli. 5; Acts ii. 43. This may be merely a fear producing restraint, or it may be a godly fear. *Fear,* it expresses any kind of dread, pious or natural. It often points to a gracious state of mind. We have the same phrase in Ps. lii. 6. The *fear* here spoken of was holy; it brought forth good fruits. It led men to *trust in the Lord.* There seems to be no reason for connecting this verse and the next by supplying the word *saying.*

4. *Blessed* is *that man that maketh the* LORD *his trust.* On the first word see on Ps. i. 1; literally, *O the blessednesses.* The blessings, coming on him who trusts in the Lord, are multiform, countless, endless, immeasurable. A good man trusts in the Lord, *And respecteth not the proud. Respecteth,* looketh or turneth to; in Ps. xxv. 16, *Turn thee* unto me. Our version gives the sense. Hengstenberg: "To turn one's self to any one is as much as to take up with his side, to go over to his party, to espouse his principles." To *respect* in the sense of this verse is the opposite of *contemn* in Ps. xv. 4. *The proud* are the *insolent,* or *violent;* here only. The pious man respecteth not these, *Nor such as turn aside to lies.* By *lies* we may understand not only falsehoods, but also idols, which are lying vanities; earthly things, which

disappoint all who trust in them; men, who as a rock of confidence are a lie; or any fatal delusion or mistake respecting our religious hopes or views, especially perhaps such as spring from self-conceit. The Syriac has *lying speech;* Arabic, *lying fables;* Septuagint, *lying madnesses.*

5. *Many, O* LORD *my God,* are *thy wonderful works* which *thou hast done, and thy thoughts* which are *to us-ward: they cannot be reckoned up in order unto thee:* if *I would declare and speak* of them, *they are more than can be numbered.* The Chaldee has the first clause thus: Many signs hast thou given, O Lord our God. Several other versions: Many admirable things hast thou done. *Many,* also *great,* see Ps. iii. 1; xix. 13; xxv. 11. *Wonderful works, wonders, marvels, miracles, marvellous works, wondrous works, wondrous things, great wonders.* See on Ps. ix. 1. There is nothing gained by separating *many* and *wonderful works.* For *reckoned up in order* Hammond prefers *I cannot set in order,* meaning *I cannot recount,* or *enumerate.* The Septuagint reads: There is none, that shall be likened unto thee; Hengstenberg: Nothing is to be compared to thee. The word does sometimes refer to *comparing, likening,* but even then we should include the idea of *arranging* or *setting in order* for the purpose of *comparison.* The common version is best. The last clause is variously given. Calvin: They are more than can be told; Hengstenberg: They are not to be numbered. All teach the same thing. There is nothing to justify us in exclusively applying the term *wonderful works* to the signs and wonders wrought by the hand of Moses and Aaron in Egypt, at the Red sea and in the wilderness; nor in exclusively applying the term *thoughts* to God's secret decrees on the one hand, or to his revealed will on the other. We should not causelessly limit Scriptural terms.

In the next three verses the Psalmist uses language, all of which is eminently applicable to Christ, and a part of which is applicable to none else. It is so applied by Paul in Heb. x. 5–9. When men are not inspired, we may subject all they say to free and fair criticism without any blame. But when men, moved by the Holy Ghost, announce heavenly doctrines, or expound the sacred writings, it is wicked to cavil. To the pious soul it is a source of unspeakable consolation to find a divinely authorized exposition of this Scripture. Paul quotes the Septuagint version, with slight alterations. For the purpose, which he had in view, the Septuagint rendering was as good as any. It had the advantage of being familiarly known. The great point, on which the Apostle was laying out his strength, was that all the sacrifices and offerings in preceding ages, were powerless, while Christ's offering was truly efficacious.

6. *Sacrifice and offering thou didst not desire.* Sacrifice the same as in Ps. iv. 5; xxvii. 6. In Gen. xxxi. 54 where the text reads, "Jacob offered sacrifice," the margin has it, he "killed beasts." It denotes bloody offerings, in which the life of the animal was taken. *Offering,* in Gen. iv. 4, 5. We had it in Ps. xx. 3. In the law it is commonly rendered *meat-offering,* which was an oblation not of *flesh,* as the English word *meat* leads some to suppose, but of flour, or corn and wine and oil, etc. The same word is often rendered, *gift, present.* The fact that God does not desire such *sacrifice* and *offering* is declared in Ps. l. 8; li. 16; 1 Sam. xv. 22; Isa. i. 11; Hos. vi. 6. The only sins, for which such sacrificial offerings seem to have been appointed under the law, were: 1, sins of ignorance; 2, sins against man, admitting of restitution; 3, sins against the precepts of the ceremonial law. But for murder, ungodliness, malice, hardness of heart, pride, unbelief, all classes of spiritual sins the law of Moses appointed no sacrifice. Even where God had positively ordained oblations, he preferred piety and mercy to them. They never had efficacy in removing the guilt of sin. They merely typified the sacrifice of Christ. They were shadows and not the very image of good things. As God did not rest in them, so neither did his true worship-

pers. In comparison of either piety or mercy they were as nothing, Compared with the finished work of Christ, God utterly rejected them, Isa. lxvi. 3. *Mine ears hast thou opened.* *Opened,* margin *digged.* This is literal. In Ps. vii. 15, *He made* [or digged] *a pit;* in Ps. xxii. 16, *pierced;* often *digged,* see Gen. xxvi. 25; Ps. lvii. 6; cxix. 85. We have similar language in Isa. l. 5: "The LORD God hath opened mine ear." This is immediately explained by the clauses: "And I was not rebellious, neither turned away back." In Job xxxvi. 10 we have a similar phrase: "He openeth also their ear to discipline." Doubtless there is an allusion, as many think, to Ex. xxi. 5, 6. See also Deut. xv. 16, 17. Jesus Christ took upon him the form of a servant. He was not rebellious. He did and he suffered all God's will. He was God's servant so as none else ever was. He voluntarily humbled himself to more service and to greater suffering than any other. Several versions render it, "Thou hast pierced or bored through my ears." The chief difficulty arises from the Septuagint version, which has: *A body hast thou prepared me.* One mode of solving this difficulty is by supposing that the text of the Septuagint has been altered. Hammond has an extended note summing up the chief points of evidence to show that this has probably been done. The Vulgate has *ears* not *body.* The ancient scholiasts, Eusebius Cæsariensis in the Catena of the Greek Fathers and their exposition of this place as set out by Corderius furnish the grounds, on which Hammond relies. But this can hardly be deemed satisfactory. The text of the copies of the Septuagint is very harmonious. Those who think it has been altered, make Paul himself the first to read *body* instead of *ears,* and suggest that the Septuagint text was altered to correspond with Paul's version. But this was hardly the case. The variation in the rendering was aside from Paul's main argument, and he had no motive for changing the text. As he found it, it was quite to his purpose. Sampson thinks the meaning of the phrase is: "Thou hast given me the form and the spirit of a servant." And Alexander paraphrases the whole verse thus: "Thou hast not required ceremonial services, but obedience, and hast pierced my ear, as a sign that I will hear thee and obey thee forever." However the authors of the Septuagint may have been led to render the clause as they did, their translation and the original do so far agree as to teach quite the same thing, viz.: that by the ordinance of God Christ solemnly became the servant of God. This is sufficient. Hengstenberg: "The thought is not altered by the Septuagint translation." *Burnt offering and sin offering hast thou not required.* This is a repetition of the assertion in the first clause in terms different from the former, but denoting the want of efficacy in expiatory offerings for sin. Clarke: "It is remarkable that all the offerings and sacrifices which were of an atoning or cleansing nature, offered under the law, are here enumerated by the Psalmist and the apostle, to show that *none* of them, nor *all* of them, could take away sin; and that the grand sacrifice of Christ was that alone which could do it."

7. *Then said I, Lo, I come.* This clause is prophetical of two things: 1. The coming of Christ in the flesh and as the Saviour: 2. The readiness with which he came to his work. This last is more explicitly declared in the next verse. It is a fundamental truth that Christ came willingly, suffered willingly, and died willingly. Let pious souls remember this. *In the volume of the book* it is *written of me.* Some make this clause parenthetical. Perhaps they do so, because Paul does it. But that can hardly justify us inasmuch as he quoted the words for one purpose, which has been already stated, and not that he might expound each clause. He quoted all that bore on the point he was arguing. *Volume,* from a word which signifies *to roll.* The *roll* was anciently the invariable form of books among the Jews, until the days of our Saviour, Luke iv. 17. Even to this day they sometimes use that form. Often there were two rollers of wood near to each other. As one turned to unfold the law,

the other received it. But oftentimes the parchment having received its form was not attached to wood. When the Septuagint uses *head* instead of *volume*, it employs a word which Suidas shows meant *roll*. *Roll* occurs often in Jeremiah, several times in Ezekiel, and once or twice in Zechariah, and is always rendered *roll*, except in Ps. xl. 7. *Book*, commonly so rendered; sometimes *bill, letter, scroll*. It is not very different from our word *Scripture* or *writing*. For *it is written of me*, some prefer *it is prescribed to me*. All this seems to rest very much on the supposition that these verses chiefly refer to David, and that the *volume of the book* is the pentateuch, and that the part specially referred to is Deut. xvii. where the duty of rulers is prescribed. But surely something more is taught. Even if it could be shown that the *volume of the book* meant the pentateuch, Christ is predicted there, John v. 46, 47. If the Old Testament generally is meant by *the volume of the book*, then Christ says: "Search the Scriptures; for in them ye think ye have eternal life: and they are they which testify of me," John v. 39. In either of these ways we get a good sense, amply sustained by Scripture, Luke xxiv. 27; Acts iii. 18, 21, 24; xxvi. 22. There is therefore no necessity for supposing with Hammond that the *Volume of the book* refers to "the bill or roll of contract betwixt God the Father and the Son, wherein is supposed to be written the agreement preparatory to that great work of Christ's incarnation." This does indeed teach no erroneous doctrine; but all we know of the covenant of Redemption is revealed in Scripture. It is often referred to in the Old Testament, see Ps. ii.; cx.; Isa. xlix. So that still we are brought back to the old Testament Scriptures as *the volume of the book* referred to in this verse. To this view some object that little, if any of the Old Testament besides the pentateuch was written when this Psalm was composed, and so all or the chief parts of the Old Testament cannot be embraced. But this is sufficiently answered by stating that as verses 6–8 of this Psalm contain an undoubted "prophecy concerning Messiah, it may be carried down to that period in the Redeemer's history, in which the prophetic testimony concerning him was complete; and moreover, it may be observed, that the Apostle, in illustrating and applying this very prophecy, fixes the period of its reference to the time when Messiah 'cometh into the world,' (Heb. x. 5;) at which time Moses, the Prophets, and the Psalms were all complete, and were collected into one uniform record." See Morison on this place, and McLean on Heb. x. 5–7.

8. *I delight to do thy will, O my God.* Christ's obedience to God's will in all things was perfect. His life was a wonderful illustration of the truth: "Love is the fulfilling of the law." The Father wholly approved of Christ's undertaking, and *called* him to it, Heb. v. 4, 5. He announced in an audible voice from heaven that he was well-pleased in Christ. By raising him from the dead and setting him at his own right hand, he showed his continued and immeasurable approval of all that the Son had done and suffered. None could do anything with more *delight* than Christ evinced in fulfilling the whole will of God. Not a flaw has man, or angel, or omniscience ever found in his character and obedience. *Yea, thy law* is *within my heart.* Such language denotes a prompt, cheerful, hearty spirit of obedience to the entire known will of God, Jer. xxxi. 33; Heb. viii. 10; Ps. i. 2. But there is no objection to giving to *the will of God* a more extended signification. Sampson: "The special will of God here is that by which he desires the salvation of his people through an adequate satisfaction to the divine law. Upon this condition alone can he will their salvation. Hence he rejects the offerings of bulls and goats, and demands that of Christ, as alone sufficient to the exigencies of the case." This language is not too strong. Paul's use of this prophecy fully justifies it, Heb. x. 10.

9. *I have preached righteousness in the great congregation. Preached*, announced,

proclaimed, published, spread the tidings of. The *righteousness* is the righteousness of God, as we learn from the next verse. The *great congregation* points to great publicity. If this verse and the next have any fulfilment in David, it was in his making the most open and grateful mention of the Lord's dealings with him, in solemn and thankful acts of worship in the temple and before all Israel. But it is impossible to compare the declaration here made with that in Ps. xxii. 22, without seeing that there is a remarkable similarity between these Scriptures. There is no violence done in regarding verses 9, 10 of this Psalm as applicable to Christ. The intent of the three preceding verses has been determined by inspiration. These two may well be applied to the same glorious person. It is admitted that there is no natural pause in the sense till the beginning of verse 11. *Lo, I have not refrained my lips,* O LORD, *thou knowest.* No one could so truly say this as Christ himself. As he used no sinful words, so he indulged no sinful silence. He always spoke when he ought, and always said what he ought. Christ was incomparably the greatest preacher this world ever saw.

10. *I have not hid thy righteousness within my heart; I have declared thy faithfulness and thy salvation: I have not concealed thy lovingkindness and thy truth from the great congregation.* This verse is very much an amplification of the preceding. It treats of the same matter in the same forms, both negatively and positively. Five things are here said to have been published and made known. 1. *God's righteousness, rectitude, equity, or justice* in all things. This is the great pillar of God's government. So long as God is just, there is hope for those who have a good cause. 2. *God's faithfulness,* the word has the same root as *Amen;* it signifies *stability, truth, fidelity* to engagements. 3. *God's lovingkindness,* or *mercy, favor, kindness, goodness, merciful kindness.* See on Ps. xvii. 7. 4. *God's Truth,* including his *sincerity* and *veracity.* See on Ps. xv. 2. 5. *God's salvation.* To those, who trust his righteousness, faithfulness, lovingkindness and truth, salvation is sure to come, bringing with it full redemption. Hengstenberg: "It may seem, on a superficial observation, as if David used here too many words. But they will judge quite otherwise, who understand the natural coldness of the human heart, its lukewarmness in the praise of God, its forgetfulness and unthankfulness, and the inclination of the lazy mouth to silence." We need all God has promised. If these verses refer to Christ, then we see how all the attributes of God are pledged to build up his throne, establish his kingdom, and make him see his seed, and satisfy him with ample reward for all his fidelity and eminent services in vindicating the divine honor in all he said and did, speaking for God as none else ever did. At the close of these verses we find a transition from praise to prayer. Our Saviour did indeed pray, but it has been shown in the introduction to this Psalm that he could not have fitly used *some* of the petitions of this Psalm. It is not necessary that we should apply any part of the remainder of the Psalm to Christ. All the petitions suit the case of David.

11. *Withhold not thou thy tender mercies from me, O* LORD. The doctrine of the divine attributes and government laid down in the preceding verse is here used for personal support and encouragement. *Tender mercies,* in the Hebrew one word, often so rendered, also *mercies, compassions, bowels. Let thy lovingkindness and thy truth continually preserve me. Lovingkindness* and *Truth* as in v. 10. Our version makes the whole verse a prayer; but the original has it in the future, and so some render it.

12. *For innumerable evils have compassed me about. Evils,* either *natural* or *moral,* either *sins* or *afflictions.* The Hebrew original, like our word *evil,* does not determine which class of *evil* is intended. This is left to the connection. See on Psalm v. 4; vii. 4, 9; x. 6; xv. 3. The next clause shows which class of *evils* is spoken of: *Mine iniquities have taken hold upon me, so that I am not able to look up. Not to be*

able to look up is to be ashamed, filled with self-reproach and remorse. Our Saviour never had either remorse or despair. He could not have had either, simply because he was pure and innocent. Nor did he bear the sins of *himself;* for first, he had no sins, and then, he *bare the sin of* MANY, not of *one.* Our iniquities take hold of us when we have a terrible sense of God's just displeasure against them, and when we see their guilt, their multitude and their aggravations. For *taken hold upon* many prefer *overtaken.* Whoever has a just view of one of his sins commonly sees that his offences are countless: *They are more than the hairs of mine head.* Christ truly convinced the woman of Samaria of *one* sin, and she went away and said, " Come, see a man that hath told me *all* things that ever I did." *Therefore my heart faileth me.* Clearly these words apply to the type and not to the antitype. Psalm lxx. is nearly the same as the residue of this, and no one applies that to Christ.

13. *Be pleased, O* LORD, *to deliver me. Be pleased,* not before found in the Psalms. The same word is rendered *Delight, take pleasure.* It is a petition that God would *set his heart* on rescuing his servant. *Deliver,* as in Ps. vii. 1; xxii. 20. *O* LORD, *make haste to help me.* The case was urgent. The crisis had arrived.

14. *Let them be ashamed and confounded together that seek after my soul to destroy it; let them be driven backward and put to shame that wish me evil.* See on Ps. xxxv. 4, 26. Alexander: " Strictly speaking, this is not so much the expression of a wish as of a confident expectation." See Introduction, § 6.

15. *Let them be desolate for a reward of their shame that say unto me, Aha, aha.* On *Aha* see on Ps. xxxv. 21, 25. *Desolate,* a dreadful word, expressive of a complete overthrow, sometimes rendered *astonished,* as at a fearful catastrophe.

16. *Let all those that seek thee rejoice and be glad in thee.* The relevancy of the petitions of this verse, as of the three preceding, is this, that when God finally and fully decides for the righteous and against the wicked, he acts out his own excellent and unchangeable nature. So that a deliverance now wrought for David, a representative of a class, would give joy to many. *Let such as love thy salvation say continually, The* LORD *be magnified.* The deliverance wrought for David has made millions glad. They have cried out, Great is the Lord, or, Let the Lord be great, *i. e.,* in the eyes of all his creatures.

17. *But I* am *poor and needy. Poor,* see on Ps. ix. 12, 18. *Needy,* see on Ps. ix. 18; xii. 5; *q. d.,* I am in a low condition, I am afflicted, I bear my trials in a meek and humble way, I am just in that state in which divine interposition will be honorable to God. Yet *the* LORD *thinketh upon me.* This declares his confidence that his prayer is heard, and his judgment not passed over. The Chaldee: God meditates good for me; other versions: The Lord careth for me; Alexander: The Lord will think of me. The phrase is one of hope and confidence. *Thou* art *my help and my deliverer.* He was satisfied that his prayer would be fully answered. *Make no tarrying, O my God.* The deliverance was not yet fully achieved. Speedy aid was what his case required. Arnd: " Thou art my help in heaven, because I have no helper and deliverer on earth. Therefore delay not. I know thou wilt choose the right time and not neglect me." The old English Psalter: " Let us not be so long under distress and misery that we lose our patience and our love to Thee."

DOCTRINAL AND PRACTICAL REMARKS.

1. Patient waiting is a very difficult duty, but it is essential to Christian character and comfort, v. 1. It belongs to true piety under all dispensations. " Faith is not thoroughly tried except by long endurance."

2. There is a remarkable similarity in the accounts of the experiences of God's people from age to age. The whole account given in vv. 1–3 of David's deliverance

would well suit any great deliverance wrought in behalf of himself or of any other saint, whether from temporal or spiritual distress, whether from awful convictions, or religious depression. The real author of the Scriptures must have known all things, else he could not have cast so great variety of mental exercise into so few and brief moulds of words.

3. Many of the trials of God's people are truly dismal and horrible. A *pit of noise* and *miry clay* are apt images to represent the evils they endure, v. 2. Distress, perplexity, a terrible and protracted warfare with sin and hell are the lot of the saints. Adams of Wintringham: "I found myself a sinner at three-score and ten, and I find myself a sinner still at four-score."

4. Deliverances are generally such as to show that none but God could have wrought them, v. 2. The pit was too deep for a created arm to reach to its bottom. The load was too heavy for created strength to bear. God will have, because he deserves to have all the glory of man's salvation.

5. The greater the trial, the greater is the deliverance, and the more joyous and loud should be the song which we sing to the praise and glory of God, v. 3. To praise God for redemption only as we do for a cup of water is shocking. Dickson: "It is a part of our duty to glorify God after every mercy, and in a special manner when the mercy is very notable."

6. The reason why wicked men do not become wise, is not that no truth is set before them, that no examples are placed before them, or that no wonders are wrought in their sight. All who open their eyes do *see*, and *fear*, and *trust*, v. 3. God always instructs such as love the truth. Nature, providences, Scripture, all point to God, to truth and to duty.

7. No mortal can tell half the blessedness of a truly good man, v. 4. Some pious and able men have spent a long time in stating the privileges and advantages of godliness. Nor has their work been useless or unimportant. But none of them has had complete success. The best enumeration that man can make must end with etc., etc., etc.

8. As true piety does not turn to the wicked with complacency, so its expectations of help and succor are not at all from that quarter, v. 4.

9. What an ennobling theme of meditation and praise have we in God's providences! v. 5. From what miseries has he delivered us! How amazing have been our escapes! How gracious have been the answers to our prayers! How pleasant have been our friends! How few and feeble have been our enemies! How abundant have been the means provided for our sustenance, our refreshment, and our entertainment! "Great are the works of the Lord, sought out of all them that have pleasure therein."

10. Not only are God's works in themselves admirable, but also as they disclose his plans, his counsels, his *thoughts*, v. 5. *These* we learn both from Scripture and providence. God does what he will, and so we know his *mind*. He says what he will do, and so we learn his thoughts. The thoughts and plans of God are in many respects amazing. They comprehend all worlds, all agents, all objects, all subjects, all causes, all effects. They provide for all contingencies. They all favor piety. They all frown on sin. They are friendly to the poor, the humble, the stranger, the forsaken. They are true, and holy, and righteous altogether.

11. Creation and providence are noble themes of study and of worship; but redemption is still greater, vv. 6–8. Morison: "The wonders of the great salvation shall engage the counsels and fill up the praises of eternity; but the works and thoughts of Jehovah to our fallen race, especially as displayed in Christ Jesus the Son of his love, shall far exceed all finite powers of calculation, and shall be forever telling, yet untold."

12. Another matter illustrated by vv. 6–8 is the fact that Christ and his redemption are ever welcome themes to the prophets. They take it for granted that these subjects will be grateful to their pious readers. Often they give no notice, and ask no permission to introduce Messiah, his work, his sufferings and his recompense. "The testimony of Jesus is the spirit of prophecy."

13. How effectually everything in salvation is arranged to secure glory to God. The Father devised the scheme; the Son executed it; the Spirit applies it. All men, who receive it, renounce all personal merit and all boasting, They unitedly sing, "Glory to God in the highest!" The *plan* is God's *will*. Christ *does* that will. Long since God revealed the plan. Long since it was *finished*. All works and sufferings of man are as nothing compared with this great device. Even the most costly *gifts* and *sacrifices* are wholly rejected, vv. 6–8.

14. When will the world learn that forms and ceremonies, though ordained by God, are wholly inefficacious for salvation? v. 6. Baptism and the Lord's Supper can do no more good than sacrifices and circumcision did of old. To despise any ordinance of God is certainly sin; but to put an ordinance in the place of hearty piety towards God is to despise God himself; and to put any ordinance in the place of Christ is to become a thief and a robber.

15. If any ask our reason for receiving Jesus of Nazareth as the Messiah, we point to "the volume of the book" of God, and there find that Messiah was to be, to do and to suffer just what Jesus was, and did, and suffered, and that no other person, who has ever appeared on this earth bore those prophetic marks, v. 7.

16. It is to the joy of all pious hearts as it is to the glory of God that Christ's obedience was perfect in all respects, v. 8. It lacked nothing. It was divinely accepted. Neither has the most enlightened conscience ever found it insufficient.

17. God desires truth in the inward parts. In his eye all true holiness flows from an internal principle. Henry: "When the law of God is written in our hearts, our duty will be our delight." Then also it will be the delight of God, v. 8.

18. There is a universal obligation to make known the glorious attributes of God, proclaiming them in all proper ways, and never concealing the truth which he has made known, vv. 9, 10. Tholuck: "Though the wonders of divine mercy cannot be numbered, should we not count as many as we are able?" Let us recount the mercy of the Lord forever. "The more faithful preachers are to declare the gospel to the salvation of souls, the more confidence and comfort shall the testimony of their conscience afford to them in the day of their trouble, when they come before God."

19. After our best services we have as much need to plead for *tender mercies* as ever before, v. 11. Our prayer to our dying day must be, "Forgive us our debts."

20. Though our views of sin may through life be inadequate, yet we have no reason for believing that our sanctification will progress rapidly, or ever be perfected without our experiencing a deep sense of personal vileness and ill-desert, v. 12. A perfect view of his iniquities would sink any man in despair, unless he had far clearer apprehensions of God's mercy in Christ than are attained by the majority of converted men. Let us ask for such a sense of our sins, as we can bear, and as will make the cross of Christ most dear to us. Dickson: "Nothing can so empty a man, and lay him low, and fill him with confusion of face, as his sin pursuing him." Whatever thus abases him is useful to him.

21. In all our straits and trials effectual help must come from God only, v. 13.

22. The higher the wicked rise, and the more they seem to prosper, the more disastrous will be their overthrow, v. 14.

23. The dreariness of the final state of the foes of God is indescribable. It is *desolation*, v. 15. There shall be left to them *nothing* to be glad of.

24. The joyfulness of saints is a great fact established by history and authorized by all God's word and arrangements, v. 16. Their bliss shall increase forever.

25. God's people greatly prefer that all their deliverances, all their salvation should come from God alone, v. 16. There is no other Saviour. They do not desire another. They refuse all others.

26. This Psalm, like many others, illustrates the rule that before honor is humility. God's plan is that service should precede reward, and trial go before the crown.

27. In like manner we see how honor always comes after humility. Our low estate is not despised by God. He as readily goes to a hovel as to a palace. He has powerful leanings to the poor and sorrowful. Nor will he make any *tarrying*, when the right time for their deliverance comes, v. 17.

PSALM XLI.

To the chief Musician, A Psalm of David.

1 Blessed *is* he that considereth the poor: the Lord will deliver him in time of trouble.

2 The Lord will preserve him, and keep him alive; *and* he shall be blessed upon the earth: and thou wilt not deliver him unto the will of his enemies.

3 The Lord will strengthen him upon the bed of languishing: thou wilt make all his bed in his sickness.

4 I said, Lord, be merciful unto me: heal my soul; for I have sinned against thee.

5 Mine enemies speak evil of me, When shall he die, and his name perish?

6 And if he come to see *me*, he speaketh vanity: his heart gathereth iniquity to itself; *when he* goeth abroad, he telleth *it*.

7 All that hate me whisper together against me: against me do they devise my hurt.

8 An evil disease, *say they*, cleaveth fast unto him: and *now* that he lieth he shall rise up no more.

9 Yea, mine own familiar friend, in whom I trusted, which did eat of my bread, hath lifted up *his* heel against me.

10 But thou, O Lord, be merciful unto me, and raise me up, that I may requite them.

11 By this I know that thou favorest me, because mine enemy doth not triumph over me.

12 And as for me, thou upholdest me in mine integrity, and settest me before thy face for ever.

13 Blessed *be* the Lord God of Israel from everlasting, and to everlasting. Amen, and Amen.

ON the title see on titles of Psalms iii. iv. Some make Psalms xl. and xli. a pair; but see Introduction, § 12. As the Jews divided the Psalter into books, this was the last of the first book; see Introduction, § 11. The title and general consent make David the author of this ode. If it had a historic occasion, we know not what it was. The Syriac title reads: "A Psalm of David when he appointed overseers to take care of the poor." Patrick, Dodd, Scott and others think it finds its occasion in David's sickness and in the rebellion of Absalom. But we can prove none of these things; though the latter conjecture is plausible. Unless we certainly know the occasion, it is not safe to lay much stress on it. The scope of the poem is of much more importance. The Arabic title says it is "a prophecy concerning the incarnation, and also concerning the salutation of Judas." Horsley: "In this Psalm Messiah is the speaker." Fry: "The *poor* is none other than the same holy sufferer, whose sorrows and injuries have been all along the subject of these Psalms." Horne: "The prophet is speaking of the person of the Messiah." But the confession of personal sin *in* v. 4 is fatal to the theory that Christ is the speaker throughout the Psalm. The safest mode of interpretation is that called Typical-Messianic. See remarks on Ps. xl. Calvin: "Certainly we ought to understand that, although David speaks of himself in this psalm, yet he speaks not as a common and private person, but as one who represented the person of Christ, inasmuch as he was, as it were, the example after which the whole Church should be conformed—a point well entitled to our attention, in order that each of us may prepare himself for the same condition. It was necessary that what was begun in David should be fully accomplished in Christ; and, therefore, it must of necessity come to pass, that the same thing should be fulfilled in each of his members, namely, that they should not only suffer from external violence and force, but also from internal foes, ever ready to betray them, even as Paul declares that the Church shall be assailed, not only by "fightings without," but also by "fears within." Scott dates this Psalm B. C. 1021; Clarke, B. C. 1033; while Tholuck thinks it was written during the reign of Saul. The names of the Most High here found are *Jehovah* LORD and *Elohim God*, on which see on Ps. i. 2; iii. 2.

1. *Blessed is he that considereth the poor. Blessed*, as in Ps. i. 1; xxxii. 1; O the *blessednesses.* *Considereth the poor;* Chaldee: Attendeth to the distressed affairs of the poor so as to pity them; Arabic: Is kind to the poor; Calvin: Judgeth wisely of the poor! Ainsworth: Prudently attendeth unto the poor weakling; Fry: Rightly considereth the afflicted; Hengstenberg: Acts wisely towards the poor; Ainsworth thinks the word rendered *considereth* "implies both a skilful minding or judging, and a carriage according in word and deed." Scott: "This clause is generally understood to refer to the considerate, active, and liberal kindness, shown to the poor and afflicted, from genuine faith and love." Diodati: "It consists as well in judging soberly and charitably, of the hidden causes of their affliction, as in words and acts of humanity and mercy." The purely benevolent man shall not be unrequited. *The* LORD *will deliver him in time of trouble. Deliver; save, preserve, cause to escape.* Calvin has comfort. *Trouble; evil, affliction, mischief, wrong.* See on Ps. v. 4; vii. 4, 9. God allows his people to see *trouble*, but he saves them from the *evil of affliction.* They have learned the art of rejoicing in tribulation. But the wicked faint when they are rebuked. Some have thought that the word *him* refers to the *poor;* others, to him that *considereth the poor.* Both senses are good. The latter pretty certainly gives the meaning of the prophet. The same is true in vv. 2, 3.

2. *The* LORD *will preserve him and keep him alive.* These verbs are in the future. Some of the ancient versions, but for no good cause, put them in the optative. The best scholars follow the Hebrew. The connection is thus kept up. *Preserve,* keep, guard; see on Ps. xii. 7; xvi. 1. To *keep alive* is to cause to live, to save alive, to *quicken,* to *recover from sickness.* There is no objection to making the clause include the promise of a resurrection and of a happy life beyond. Good things given in covenant love here are pledges of better things to come. And *he shall be blessed upon the earth.* Godliness has promise of both worlds. Calvin regards this clause and the preceding as of like import, and says the prophet "does not in the least exclude by these expressions the hope of a better life after death." For *blessed*, Calvin and Fry prefer *prosper*, and Alexander, *be prospered.* The Hebrew is commonly rendered *blessed*, though it seems primarily to signify *led, guided,* and afterwards *relieved,* and finally *blessed* in general. See Pr. xxiii. 19; Isa. i. 17; ix. 16. God will lead, guide, relieve such a man. *And thou wilt not deliver him unto the will of his enemies.* They *will,* they wish and seek his ruin temporal and eternal; they love to make him appear ridiculous, contemptible, odious and vicious. The wicked shout when they see the righteous stumble. The verb is by many rendered in the optative, *Do not thou give him up;* but this is not good.

3. *The* LORD *will strengthen him upon the bed of languishing. Strengthen;* pri-

marily *prop, stay, uphold*, then *sustain, strengthen*. The Chaldee: The word of God will aid him in his life; Calvin: The Lord will support him on the bed of sorrow; Jebb: The Lord will preserve him upon the couch of languishing; Green: When he languisheth upon his bed, the Lord shall support him. The renderings quite agree in all but the tense. The future is best. The next clause fully maintains the parallelism. *Thou wilt make all his bed in his sickness.* Septuagint, Vulgate, Ethiopic and Doway: Thou hast turned all his couch in his sickness; Calvin and Ainsworth: Thou hast turned all his bed in his sickness; Green: Thou shalt make his whole bed *easy* during his sickness; Fry: Thou hast changed all his bed in his suffering. Some have thought that the meaning was that in sickness God would change (that is exchange) the bed for something else. But the more common and obvious view is better. It represents God as exercising the office of a nurse, smoothing the pillow and making the bed of his sick and distressed servants.

4. *I said,* LORD, *be merciful unto me.* To any soul rightly affected with a sense of sin the cry for mercy is natural. Good men in this life never get beyond the prayer of the publican, Luke xviii. 13. The former verses of this Psalm seem to declare a doctrine coincident with the experience David is about to recite, a sorrowful experience in which he had conflicts and trials. He begins with earnest crying for mercy and help. If we get rid of any affliction, it must be through *mercy.* Justice would rivet upon us every sorrow that ever befalls us. *Heal my soul.* The worst of all troubles are soul-troubles. *For I have sinned against thee.* Saul and Judas each said: "I have sinned;" but David says: "I have sinned against thee." Compare 2 Sam. xii. 13; Ps. li. 4. We never get right views of the nature of sin, till we see that it is *against Jehovah.* The enormity of every offence is to be determined in part by the character of him against whom it is perpetrated. A sense of sin deeply affected the Psalmist. He seems to have connected his distress with his transgression, and he "expects that as soon as he had obtained forgiveness, he would also obtain relief from his affliction."

5. *Mine enemies speak evil of me. Evil* may be *ill, mischief, sorrow,* and then *speak* has the sense of *predict* or *imprecate;* or evil may be *wickedness* or *malice,* and then to *speak* is to *utter.* The wicked hate the righteous in a deadly manner. The proof is that they say: *When shall he die, and his name perish?* The form of question here is optative and not interrogatory. There are many instances of this form of speech, Ps. xlii. 2; ci. 2. The wicked desire the utter overthrow of the righteous, and at times they seem confidently to expect it. They forget that a just man falleth seven times, and riseth up again. Even when the wicked witness the temporal death of the saints, they but see a mysterious method of raising them to glory. The hope that the *name* of the righteous shall *perish* is quite idle; the righteous shall be had in everlasting remembrance.

6. *And if he come to see me, he speaketh vanity.* Enemies are either open or secret. Open enemies were mentioned in the preceding verse. *Here* we have a hypocrite visiting David in his sickness. A more difficult duty is seldom before us than when hypocritical men call on us in our sickness. Such men are both more detestable and more dangerous than overt enemies. The change of number from plural to singular is not unusual and does not vary the sense. Some read *one of them* for *he;* but this is not necessary. *His heart gathereth iniquity to itself, i. e.,* He is "collecting materials for calumnious reports;" and is framing them together ready for use, or, he is "devising some deceitful and malicious purpose," some real *iniquity,* and in due time he will bring it out. Fry has it, *He surmiseth evil.* One of the greatest afflictions of good men is that they are not judged fairly, nor have their motives rightly construed. *Evil surmisings* are among the most mischievous acts of human wickedness. They soon

burst forth in slanderous words and uncharitable deeds. When *he goeth abroad, he telleth it.* Pent up malice will break out in some form, sooner or later.

7. *All that hate me whisper together against me.* Conspiracy and falsehood are ap propriately represented in all good writings as first *muttered.* The *whisperer* of the Bible is one of the worst characters, Prov. xvi. 28; Rom. i. 29; 2 Cor. xii. 20. The Hebrew is here very idiomatic: *Together against me they whisper,* all my *haters.* The action is first declared, then the actors, then their unanimity. *Against me do they devise my hurt.* *Hurt* is *evil, damage.* When one man sets himself to manufacture falsehoods, and to invent modes of injuring another, he sometimes accomplishes much; but when a number of the ill-disposed put their heads together, they can do a deal of mischief, especially if they are so far sunk in sin as to go to praying over their wickedness.

8. *An evil disease,* say they, *cleaveth fast unto him.* *Evil disease,* literally, a word of Belial. For *word* we have the authority of the Chaldee, Syriac, Septuagint, Vulgate, Montanus, Musculus, Cocceius, Gejerus, Venema, Bythner, Gill, Hammond, Alexander and others. Belial signifies nothingness, worthlessness, or destruction. A man of Belial is a worthless or wicked man. If we read *word,* then the meaning is, some foul or terrible reproach, some hellish crime, is fastened on him, so that his char- acter is ruined. This is the easiest mode of explanation, and agrees with the next clause: *And* now *that he lieth he shall rise up no more.* "The calumniator may destroy and ruin, as well as the pestilence." Slanderers often foolishly think that they have forever prostrated the just. Others understand by *evil disease,* some 'devilish thing, something which cannot be accounted for in a natural way.' That we may read *thing* is beyond dispute, Ps. ci. 3. Either interpretation is pertinent. The first is preferable.

9. *Yea, mine own familiar friend in whom I trusted, which did eat of my bread, hath lifted up* his *heel against me.* *Mine own familiar friend,* literally the man of my peace. Oriental notions of hospitality were utterly opposed to treachery in host or guest. To *eat of one's bread* did also sometimes signify an honorable dependence, to forget which could not but have been an act of basest ingratitude. This verse is *partly* quoted by Christ in application to Judas, John xiii. 18. But he neither calls Judas *the man of my peace,* nor does he say, *I trusted in him.* Our Saviour never in his heart confided in Judas, but knew that he was a devil, John vi. 70. But Judas did hold an honora- ble post in Christ's family and did eat of his bread. The verse is primarily fulfilled in the treatment David received at the hand of Ahithophel or such men; but David is so far the type of Christ that these words had also a fulfilment in our Saviour. To *lift up the heel* is to kick as the horse or ass does against his master. Instead of *hath lifted up his heel against me,* Mudge and Green read *hath shown great treachery towards me.*

10. *But thou, O LORD, be merciful unto me, and raise me up, that I may requite them.* The form of the mercy here desired was such entire recovery from his distressed con- dition as to be able to bring to an account his bitter foes. A restoration short of this would be but a sad continuance of his affliction. To the innocent and the injured it is a blessed day when God lifts up their heads above all their enemies round about. In all contests, where either the righteous or the wicked must from the nature of the case triumph, it is right for all good men to desire the total defeat of the cruel and malignant. Nor do the Scriptures, which forbid all malice, prohibit public persons in authority from executing vengeance. If this verse, as some think, relates to Christ, it is his intercession for his own glorious reward, in which he should make a show of his enemies openly, triumphing over them in his cross, and receiving from God the Father glory and honor.

11. *By this I know that thou favorest me, because mine enemy doth not triumph over*

me. The general truth of this verse is illustrated in the history of every good man. The foot of David sometimes well nigh slipped, but the Lord held him up. The wicked can go no further than Jehovah pleases. They never gain the final victory. If the Saviour is through his type, David, still the speaker here, then how marvellously did he always defeat his great adversary. The prince of darkness never had such a blow struck against his kingdom as on Mount Calvary. Alexander: "The last verb means properly to shout or make a noise as a sign of exultation, more especially in war." See 1 Sam. xvii. 20.

12. *And as for me, thou upholdest me in mine integrity, and settest me before thy face forever. Integrity,* the same word is also rendered *uprightness,* Job iv. 6; Pr. xxviii. 6. It is also rendered *simplicity,* 2 Sam. xv. 11. The Septuagint and Hengstenberg have *blamelessness;* Syriac, Vulgate and Ethiopic, *innocence;* Jebb, *perfectness;* Fry, *perfection;* Calvin, *integrity* or *soundness.* The most common rendering is *integrity.* God's people are *upright, simple, sound, men of integrity.* That absolute perfection is not claimed by David is clear from v. 4. Even the measure of *uprightness* attained by him was the fruit of divine grace. Thou upholdest [*literally,* thou hast upheld] me in mine integrity. In one place David prays for the blessing which he here says he had received: Hold thou me up, and I shall be safe, Ps. cxix. 117. *To set before the face* denotes approval and blessing. The perpetuity of the mercy here recorded is expressed both by the future form of the verb and by the word *forever.* This verse has an unlimited fulfilment in Messiah.

13. *Blessed* be *the Lord God of Israel from everlasting, and to everlasting.* This doxology is well placed here whether we regard it as merely the conclusion of this Psalm, or as also the close of what the Jews call the first book of Psalms. Morison: "Similar additions have been made to the other divisions of the books of the Psalter." The terms of the doxology are plain and well understood. *Blessed,* as in Ps. v. 12; xviii. 46. "In the triumphant song of eternity angels and men shall unite; so that from age to age, from generation to generation, and from eternity to eternity, the Lord's name shall be praised." *Amen, and Amen.* Amen means *sure, firm,* then *true, faithful.* The Septuagint and Vulgate render it, *So let it be.* The Arabic erroneously substitutes a single *Alleluiah* for the double *Amen.* At the beginning of a sentence Amen is a solemn mode of asseveration, Matthew xviii. 3; John iii. 3. At the close of a sentence, it expresses a wish that what has been said may be found true, and a confidence that it shall come to pass. It is twice applied to God in one verse, and is there rendered *truth,* Isa. lxv. 16. It is one of the titles of Christ, Rev. iii. 14.

DOCTRINAL AND PRACTICAL REMARKS.

1. The union between Christ and believers is so close that even prophets in describing the conflicts and victories of the saved often describe those of the Saviour himself and *vice versâ.* We suffer with him; and he was tempted in all points like as we are. Commentators, even the best, are often in doubt whether a prophet is speaking of himself, or of some other man. This commonly produces no harmful perplexity. Christ and his people are one.

2. Wicked as the world is, charitable judgments concerning all humble and patient sufferers are not only most conducive to personal happiness, but are actually nearest the truth. God's blessing is on those, who *rightly consider* the cases of affliction known to them, v. 1. Harsh judgments concerning our fellow-men are common and grievous sins.

3. Although we may fitly judge ourselves with a severity, which would ill become us in judging others, yet it is a blessed thing to be able to hold fast a well-grounded

confidence of our interest in Christ, and to take cheerful views of our own case, when we are *poor*, or *sick*, or *afflicted*, or *forsaken*, v. 1.

4. Wherever we go, we may expect to meet with those, who need our compassion. This is implied in v. 1. It is declared elsewhere, " Ye have the poor always with you."

5. Right thoughts will produce right actions. He that *properly considereth* the poor will be sure to open the hand, and secure the blessings of charity; and they are many—even *blessednesses*, v. 1. Henry: " Liberality to the poor is the surest and safest way of thriving; such as practise it may be sure of seasonable and effectual relief from God." We know who it is that said: " Inasmuch as ye have done it unto one of the least of these my brethren, ye did it unto me;" and, " It is more blessed to give than to receive." Morison: " We cannot bless others without being blessed ourselves."

6. But in all our acts of supposed charity let us carefully scrutinize our motives. There is reason to fear many have no genuine, Christian principle in kind deeds towards men. Prodigality is not beneficence.

7. The penitent poor and he, who cares for such, shall alike have *deliverance in time of trouble*, v. 1.

8. Yea, the righteous shall also be *preserved* and *kept alive*, v. 2. The narrow escapes of almost any good man, if well written, would form a wonderful chapter, if not a volume. Such deliverances as are wrought for the saints are themselves good, and pledges of good things yet to come.

9. The benevolent and beneficent man shall have many temporal good things: *He shall be blessed on the earth*, v. 2. Compare Ps. xxxvii. 16; Pr. x. 22. Dickson: " None of the godly man's afflictions shall hinder or take away his begun blessedness, even in this world."

10. Much as Satan and wicked men resemble ravenous wild beasts, greedy for their prey, and surely as they think they have secured it, yet they shall not in a single case get the soul that makes God his refuge. God *will not deliver him unto the will of his enemies*, v. 2.

11. We may all reasonably calculate on being both sick and sad. We ought to prepare for such trials. They are needful for our sanctification. When they shall come, we shall need strength and help. Henry: " God has not promised that his people shall never be sick, nor that they shall not lie languishing, nor that their sickness shall not be unto death; but he has promised to enable them to bear their affliction with patience, and cheerfully to wait the issue." We shall then need *strengthening* and *soothing*, v. 3, which none but God can give. " When he giveth quietness who can make trouble?" Job xxxiv. 29. " I am calm, because I am in the hands of a calm God," said Mrs. Hewitt.

12. Sickness of soul is the worst disease, v. 4. Scott: " Nothing is so distressing to the contrite believer, as a sense of the divine displeasure, guilt on his conscience, and the prevalence of sin in his heart: pain and sickness will remind him to pray especially for pardoning mercy, and for the healing of his soul, which is wounded and diseased, because he has sinned against the Lord."

13. Let us continue our cry for mercy however long our trials may last, or however great our prosperity may be, v. 4. We always need God's gracious compassion. Blessed is he, who feels this truth. Anything is good for us, if it makes us loathe ourselves, and penitently sue for mercy. Let affliction in its worst forms assail us, if it but make our consciences tender, abase us for past follies, and show us the hideous nature of sin and the preciousness of redemption.

14. The tongue is a world of iniquity, v. 5. Evil speaking is no new thing.

15. If the wicked had their way in this world, they would not leave a remnant

of the pious, nor a vestige of goodness, v. 5. Utter destruction and misery would be in their ways. The hatred of Cain to Abel was the type of all malice against the church.

16. Impudent hypocrisy and foul double-dealing have antiquity on their side, v. 6. Insincerity is always odious, but peculiarly so, when it comes with its grimaces to the sanctuary, and with its whines of pretended sympathy to the house of mourning and affliction. Beware of men. There must be a *hell* as well as a *heaven*. A just God will not put sincere Christians and vile hypocrites into the same company.

17. No man knows the falsehoods whispered, or the plots muttered against him, v. 7. But God knows all wicked devices. He can defeat the counsel of Ahithophel, and rebut the slanders of many. Our safety is in his omniscience, as well as in his omnipotence and boundless mercy.

18. If ill will and ill words could have destroyed the church, long since she would have been rased to the foundations, v. 8. Compare Ps. cxxiv. 1–5; Isa. i. 9; Rom. ix. 29. But the Lord loves the gates of Zion more than all the tents of Jacob.

19. The spirit of prophecy is the testimony of Jesus, v. 9. Everywhere in Moses, in the Psalms, and in all the prophets even as many as have spoken, we find hints, allusions, types, or direct predictions of Christ. The more calumnious and murderous our foes, the closer should we cling to his doctrine, his example and his person. He, who would pass to glory without the hatred, contempt and ingratitude of the wicked, cannot know the fellowship of our Lord's sufferings, Phil. iii. 10. If friends turn to foes, let us turn the more to him, who commendeth his love to us in that while we were yet enemies he died for us.

20. It has often happened that a man's foes were they of his own house. It was so with David. It was so with Christ, v. 9. If the wicked should now act differently we should suspect the truth of revelation.

21. It is marvellous that the wicked are not alarmed at the thought that every step they take in sin is contrary to the prayers of saints, v. 10. The cause which cannot succeed, except by God's refusal to hear the prayer of faith offered by his whole church every day, must be absolutely desperate and forlorn.

22. Let us commit our cause to him that judgeth righteously, fully purposing to do all that is right, and leaving results with him, v. 10. Dickson: "Every believer may be assured of this, that what injuries are done to Christ in his person, Christ shall requite his persecutors."

23. We ought therefore to pray earnestly, and we may pray in hope that the wicked may not triumph, but be effectually put down, v. 10.

24. There are always some tokens for good to the righteous, v. 11. If they are troubled on every side, yet they are not distressed; if they are perplexed, yet they are not in despair; if they are persecuted, yet they are not forsaken; if they are cast down, yet they are not destroyed; if they are sorrowful, yet they rejoice in tribulation; if the rod of the wicked falls, yet it does not rest on the lot of the righteous; if their feet well nigh slip, yet the Lord holds them up; if their enemies do get the foot of pride on their necks, yet they cannot quite stamp them into dust. And then when they begin to rise, let Haman and all like him look out! Esth. vi. 13.

25. God's people are a generation of *upright* men. They are *simple*. They are *honest*, not deceitful, not double-tongued, not knavish. They are men of *integrity*. They would rather be right and be thought wrong, than be wrong and be thought right. Yet a good man does not covet reproach, but esteems a good name above great riches.

26. Even in this world, in the long run, innocence under a cloud is better than iniquity in its gaudiest glitter. Dickson: "Uprightness is a special means to bring a man through difficulties, and whatsoever infirmities the believer be subject unto, he

shall not want comfort, if he keep conscience of integrity, uprightness and sincerity. This is the Psalmist's rejoicing," v. 12.   It was Paul's also, 2 Cor. i. 12.

27. If any of us have *integrity*, real excellence of character, it is all owing to God's mercy and grace to us, *upholding* us in it, v. 2.   It is a demand of common honesty for us to say so.

28. God loves his own image and approves his own workmanship, v. 12.   Alexander: "As man sets God before him as an object of trust, so God sets man before him as an object of protection."

29. The worship of God by doxology is very ancient, v. 13.   It seems to have been among the earliest methods of devotion, Gen. ix. 26; xiv. 20; xxiv. 27; Ex. xviii. 10. The New Testament gives us a rich variety of doxology.   This kind of worship greatly abounds in the temple above.

30. Let us learn to say *amen* to every suitable doxology, thanksgiving, prayer, confession and adoration.   An audible *amen* is no indecency in the house of God, if seasonably and reverently made.   But we should always say it in our hearts.   Pool: "The doubling of the word shows the fervency of his spirit in this work of praising God."

PSALM XLII.

To the chief Musician, Maschil, for the sons of Korah.

1 As the hart panteth after the water-brooks, so panteth my soul after thee, O God.

2 My soul thirsteth for God, for the living God: when shall I come and appear before God?

3 My tears have been my meat day and night, while they continually say unto me, Where *is* thy God?

4 When I remember these *things*, I pour out my soul in me: for I had gone with the multitude, I went with them to the house of God, with the voice of joy and praise, with a multitude that kept holyday.

5 Why art thou cast down, O my soul? and *why* art thou disquieted in me? hope thou in God: for I shall yet praise him *for* the help of his countenance.

6 O my God, my soul is cast down within me: therefore will I remember thee from the land of Jordan, and of the Hermonites, from the hill Mizar.

7 Deep calleth unto deep at the noise of thy waterspouts: all thy waves and thy billows are gone over me.

8 *Yet* the LORD will command his lovingkindness in the daytime, and in the night his song *shall be* with me, *and* my prayer unto the God of my life.

9 I will say unto God my rock, Why hast thou forgotten me? why go I mourning because of the oppression of the enemy?

10 *As* with a sword in my bones, mine enemies reproach me; while they say daily unto me, Where *is* thy God?

11 Why art thou cast down, O my soul? and why art thou disquieted within me? hope thou in God: for I shall yet praise him, *who is* the health of my countenance, and my God.

ON *To the chief Musician* see on title of Psalm iv.   On *Maschil*, Instruction, see on title of Psalm xxxii.   The rest of the title is not clear.   Some regard *the sons of Korah* as the authors.   Such supply in the title *A Psalm*, as we do in title of Psalms xi. xiv.   It is also true that instead of *for* we may read *of* as in title of Psalm iii. and often.   Against the authorship of the sons of Korah, it may be stated 1, that in no Psalm whose origin we know, are two or more persons united in the authorship.   2, Ps. lxxxviii. is also said to be "for the sons of Korah," and yet it is added that it is *Maschil*, or an Instruction "of Heman the Ezrahite." Nor does it weaken this statement though we should admit that Heman was probably one of the sons of Korah. 3. There is reason for regarding David as the author. It is written as of one man, and not as of many. It says, *I*, *mine*, *me*, and not *we*, *our*, *us* as in Ps. cxxxvii. where the afflictions of a people are described. It well suits the case of David in his long exile from Jerusalem in the days of Saul. As the Psalms were designed for the temple, it is not probable that the private experience of any obscure person would be made the theme of public worship. The geographical position of David in his exile corresponds with that noted in v. 6, *i. e.*, it was in the land of Jordan and of Hermon. Hengstenberg, however, thinks David's experience is the subject of the Psalm and that one of the sons of Korah was its author, and sang it "as from the soul of David." With him agrees Tholuck. But we have no right to say that *one* man composed it, if the title ascribes it to several. Besides, as Alexander says, "It is a much more obvious supposition that David himself wrote it to express his own feelings at a particular juncture of his history." 4. The great weight of authority is on the side of the Davidic authorship. So the Syriac, Rabbi Moses, Calvin, Bellarmine, Gussetius, Piscator, Fabritius, Cocceius, Patrick, Gill, Dodd, Jebb, Hammond, Morison, Horne, Scott and Alexander. Add to this that Ps. xliii. is commonly admitted to have been written by the author of this, and that the Septuagint, Vulgate, Ethiopic and Syriac all give David as the author of that Psalm.

If David wrote it, or even if he is the subject of it, to what period in his life does it refer? Several incline to the notion that it points to the time of Absalom's rebellion. But it as well suits the time when Saul drove David from the sanctuary. Moreover, the rebellion of Absalom was of too short continuance to make the language of this Psalm so appropriate to that occasion as to David's former exile. But who were the sons of Korah? These opinions have more or less prevailed. One is that they sprang from some one of that name in the days of David. Mudge and others think the sons of Korah were a society of musicians, founded or presided over by Korah. Others think that the sons of Korah were the surviving descendants of that miserable man who, together with two hundred and fifty of his adherents, who were princes, perished, when "the earth opened her mouth, and swallowed them up together with Korah." In Num. xxvi. 11 we read: "Notwithstanding the children of Korah died not." They had taken the warning given, and had departed from the tents of those wicked men, Num. xvi. 24, 26. It must be admitted that the name *Korah*, and the patronymic *Korahite* are found in the Scriptures in a way that creates considerable doubt respecting the particular man from whom the Korahites are named. See 1 Chron. i. 35; ii. 43; vi. 22, 54; ix. 19; xxvi. 1; 2 Chron. xx. 19. Yet the more common belief is that they descended from him who perished for his gainsaying. This view is taken by Ainsworth with entire confidence, by Gill and others. Korah, who perished, was a Levite. Whatever may have been their origin, it is clear *the sons of Korah* were " a Levitical family of singers." Nothing then could be more appropriate than the dedication of a sacred song to these very people. Samuel the prophet was of this family. Some have thought that this Psalm and the forty-third form a pair; and some have even united them into one composition. In as many as thirty manuscripts, the Hebrew copyists have transcribed them as if they were but one composition. But in other MSS. they are divided. Their being placed near together may be owing to mere accident. Alexander thinks that the next Psalm was actually written as an appendix or continuation of this. See Introduction, § 12. Morison: "It does not appear that any regular order has been preserved in the disposal of the various materials of this BOOK. They seem rather to have been inserted as they presented themselves to the attention of the collectors." This is the *first* Psalm in what the Jews called the Second

Book of Praises. But that division was a human invention. See Introduction, § 11. Scott dates it B. C. 1021. In it we have three names of the Most High, *Jehovah* LORD, *El God* and *Elohim God*, on which see on Ps. i. 2; v. 4; iii. 2. The Psalms inscribed to the sons of Korah have been thought remarkable for the frequent use of *Elohim*.

The *scope* of this Psalm is not always agreed upon. The Syriac says this is "a Psalm of David sung when he was an exile, and desired to return to Jerusalem." The Arabic calls it "a prayer for the Jews who had fallen," or backslidden. Luther and Hengstenberg think the best insight is gained by duly regarding God as sometimes hiding his face and then clearly revealing himself in mercy as a light and deliverer.

1. *As the hart panteth after the water-brooks, so panteth my soul after thee, O God.* The public worship of God as ordained in his sanctuary was to pious Jews the liveliest representation of spiritual good things. Even when they were in distant countries they prayed towards their holy temple. David, now in exile, breaks forth into intense longings for communion with God. Some have expounded this verse and the next as if all the Psalmist desired was to revisit the tabernacle. But truly pious men were never satisfied with the ordinances of God without the God of ordinances. Alexander: "The first noun is masculine, but the verb feminine; so that we may either read *hart* or *hind*." The Septuagint, by using the feminine article, pronounces for *hind*. The other ancient versions have it *hart* or *stag*. *Panteth*, or *brayeth*, as in the margin and some others, or *desireth*, as the Septuagint. In Joel i. 20, *cry*. The hind is said to be more thirsty than the hart. But either of them hunted over the hills or plains of Judea was an exceedingly fit emblem of a soul intensely longing for some absent good. *Water-brooks*, fountains of waters, streams of waters, or springs of waters. See on Ps. xviii. 15. In the sanctuary everything reminded the devout worshipper of God.

2. *My soul thirsteth for God, for the living God: when shall I come and appear before God?* The first and last word here rendered God is *Elohim;* the second, *El.* The verb is the same as in the preceding verse. The repetition of the declaration shows the intensity of the desire. No doubt the pious Jew thought much of the tabernacle, the shew bread, the altar, the sacrifices, the visible glory and other things pertaining to the temple. But the God of Jacob, who made a Bethel in a desert, could always make any place the gate of heaven. Evidently more is here meant than a mere longing for the privilege of public worship. Piety, which has its seat in the soul, consists much in communion with God, not in rites and forms. Hengstenberg: "The longing of the Psalmist is described as directed towards God himself, not towards the place of his worship." True piety engages the affections. It awakens the longings of the soul. Because the best men are very imperfect and have but low actual attainments, true piety in this life consists very much in desires after holiness. The knowledge of God, his favor, his image, his soul-cheering presence and the hopeful prospect of dwelling forever with him are objects of sufficient worth and excellence to draw out the heart of the best and greatest of men. What a wondrous revelation of these we have in the person, work and sufferings of Christ! "He that hath seen me, hath seen the Father." Scott: "David longed and mourned after the courts of God: but still more for the living God himself; for his presence, and favor, and those pleasures which he had enjoyed in communion with him." *The living God*, not dead as mere idols are, Ps. cvi. 28; 1 Thess. i. 9; or living, in the sense of active, powerful, Ps. xxxviii. 19; Heb. x. 31; or living, as a fountain, Jer. xvii. 13. This longing for God was increased by the taunts of the ungodly.

3. *My tears have been my meat day and night, while they continually say unto me, Where is thy God?* They who can do nothing but shed tears, commonly must shed those tears alone. Mankind are so busy, each one with his own affairs, the human

heart has so little genuine philanthropy in it, and overtures of sympathy have been so often met with ingratitude, that sadness is commonly left solitary. Oftentimes human wickedness makes things worse than ever. It charges the subjects of distress with hypocrisy and wickedness. Or, it declares the sufferer's case to be hopeless. *Where is thy God? q. d.,* God has deserted you; you may as well give up all hope. By saying that *tears were* his *meat* [or bread] *day and night,* he declares that he had lost his appetite for his food, and found no relief but in continual weeping. See Ps. lxxx. 5. The taunt, *Where is thy God?* has obvious reference to strong confidence formerly and publicly professed. It denies God's covenant relation and faithfulness to David. Steir: "Although the railers may not incessantly cause such things to be heard, yet the oppressed soul continually hears their raillery clanging in itself."

4. *When I remember these* things, *I pour out my soul in me.* These verbs are by Venema, Marloratus, Hengstenberg and Alexander rendered in the future; by the Syriac, Arabic, Septuagint, Vulgate and Ethiopic, in the preterite; but Calvin, church of England, Vatablus, Piscator, Amesius, Ainsworth, Fabritius, Mudge, Green, Waterland, Edwards, Jebb, Horsley, Fry and Tholuck agree with our common version. This makes as good sense as we gain in any other way. For *things* Boothroyd and Edwards read *times.* This does not vary the sense. *These things* are those mentioned in the context—his former privileges, his present banishment from God, his want of comfortable communion with God, and the remembrance of his present condition compared with what it had been. For *I pour out my soul in me;* Chaldee: *I will pour out upon me the thoughts of my soul;* Syriac: *My soul was troubled;* Ainsworth: *I pour out upon me my soul.* The sense of the phrase is well expressed by the Syriac though our version is more literal. *For I had gone with the multitude, I went with them to the house of God, with the voice of joy and praise, with a multitude that kept holy day.* The *memory* of this greatly troubled him. The variations in the renderings of this part of the verse are considerable. But they either greatly disregard the Hebrew text; or they so overstrain the matter as hardly to merit an extended notice; or they do *substantially* justify the common version. For *I had gone* some read *marched.* The procession that ascended Mount Zion to the temple was very solemn, orderly, and imposing. Hengstenberg: "The use of music in the processions is clear," 2 Sam. vi. 5. Solemn dancing was not unknown at such times, 2 Sam. vi. 14. Thoughts on these scenes so depressed David, that he would have quite despaired, but that God enabled him to adminster timely reproof and exhortation to his own soul:

5. *Why art thou cast down, O my soul? and* why *art thou disquieted in me?* His *dejection* and *disquiet* were great. Present appearances were against any hope of a change for the better; enemies were rancorous; his condition was sad and forlorn; but the covenant and its promises stood firm. *Hope thou in God, i. e., confide in God, trust in God.* Jebb and Alexander: *Wait thou for God;* Ainsworth: *Wait hopefully for God;* Green and Fry: *Wait patiently for God.* For so doing the Psalmist had cause: *For I shall yet praise him* for *the help of his countenance.* To faith the darkest night has a star of hope. Adverse providences may be followed by happy results. *Praise,* as in Ps. ix. 1; xxx. 4. The *countenance* or *face* was a term well understood among the Hebrews from the days of Aaron, Num. vi. 25, 26; see above on Ps. iv. 6. By *the help* literally *helps, supports, salvations* of God's countenance every conflict is at last decided in favor of the righteous. Calvin: "*The countenance of God* is taken for the manifestation of his favor." Even the *hope* of it keeps us from despair while the billows roll high.

6. *O my God, my soul is cast down within me. Cast down,* as in v. 5. In both verses the form is reflexive, *q. d., My soul casts itself down. Within me,* literally *upon me. Therefore will I remember thee from the land of Jordan, and of the Hermon-*

ites, from the hill Mizar. Two views may be taken of this passage. One is that David would remember God in order to cheer up his own soul. This is favored by the tense of the verb *remember* in the Hebrew. The common version and many others give this construction. The other is that thoughts of God troubled David. Those, who thus understand it instead of *therefore*, read *when, because,* or *for that,* and instead of *will remember,* have *remember.* The Hebrew *future* may be taken for the *present* where it is clearly required by the sense. See Introduction, § 6. Thus Calvin: O my God, my soul is cast down, when I remember thee. Ainsworth has much the same. But the common rendering is to be preferred. The geographical positions pointed out in this verse demand some notice. *From the land of Jordan;* some think it designates the region lying on both sides of the Jordan. This seems the more obvious view. Others think it denotes only the region beyond Jordan as one goes down from Jerusalem. So Calvin. Others suppose it has special reference to the region at the head waters of the Jordan. So Diodati. Others, among them Hengstenberg, think that the *land of Jordan* must be taken in connection with the next phrase, *and of the Hermonites,* and that these two designate generally the Transjordanic region. Pool takes all the phrases referring to geography not to designate a particular locality, but all the places and parts of the land, to which David might be driven. This gives a good sense and is accompanied with fewer difficulties than most of the others. But what are we to understand by the land of the Hermonites? The original word is plural of Hermon—*Hermonim.* The word in this form occurs no where else. It pretty certainly designates not a people, but a range of mountains, *the Hermons,* because there were several high points in the range to which this name was given, as we say the Alps, Alleghenies. The singular, *Hermon,* designates chiefly the Southern portion of Anti-Libanus. If a large mountainous region is designated by the *Hermons,* then we have the reason given for David's remembering God, viz. his remoteness from the sanctuary and his perils in that wild district. *Mizar* means *little.* The Chaldee understands Mount Sinai. But Piscator, church of England, Mudge and others understand some little hill in Hermon. Dodd: "Hermon probably rose in more eminences than one, and therefore is expressed plurally, one of them perhaps smaller than the rest is called here *Mizar,* the little one." The Septuagint, Arabic, Syriac, Vulgate, Ethiopic, Ainsworth, Amesius, Horsley, Tholuck and Hengstenberg all render it, *from the little mountain.* Ainsworth thinks that the singular may be here put for the plural; and that the author of the Psalm may refer to the Southern mountains, which compared with Hermon, were small. Lighfoot thinks Mizar is the same as Zoar, "near the extreme part of Jordan, close to the salt sea." There is no doubt that by these phrases conjointly the Psalmist would designate the general route of his wanderings. Pool thinks all these geographical terms equivalent to this: "From all the places and parts of the land to which I shall be driven." The passages supposed to refer to the same locality as Hermon, are Num. xxxiv. 7; Deut. iii. 8; Ps. lxxxix. 12.

7. *Deep calleth unto deep at the noise of thy waterspouts.* John Rogers' Translation: One depe calleth another wyth the voyce of thy whystles; Genevan: One deepe calleth another deepe by the noyse of thy water spoutes; church of England: One deep calleth another, because of the noise of thy water-pipes. *Deep,* often rendered *abyss.* The representation is that of one ready to perish in the sea, when it is agitated by high winds, and when water-spouts add to the peril. Some think the whole imagery of the verse is probably taken from the Noachic flood. However this may be, miseries multiplying upon us have long been compared to a tempestuous sea with angry and heavy clouds passing over it. The great home of water-spouts is Cape Horn and the adjacent waters; but Shaw saw them at three points on

the coast of Syria. They at times visit all tropical and temperate latitudes. Anderson: "A water-spout is a large tube or cylinder formed of clouds, by means of the electric fluid, the base being uppermost, and the point let down perpendicularly from the clouds. It has a particular kind of *circular motion* at the point; and being hollow within attracts vast quantities of water; which it frequently pours down in torrents on the earth or the sea." It is a great terror to seamen. If one empties itself on a ship she is gone. *All thy waves and thy billows are gone over me.* He was in a sea of troubles. For *waves* and *billows* some read *breakers* and *floods.* Both terms point to huge masses of agitated waters. There could be no fitter mode than that here adopted, of describing great troubles, some from men here below, and some direct from God. Yet great as were his sorrows and temptations, he was not in despair.

8. Yet *the* Lord *will command his lovingkindness in the daytime, and in the night his song* shall be *with me,* and *my prayer unto the God of my life.* It is well when hope puts on her helmet, and mirth sings her song, and faith at the same time offers up her prayer. *Command* is a word of authority. *Lovingkindness, kindness, mercy, goodness, favor;* see on Ps. v. 7; xvii. 7. The Lord's *song* is the song of thanksgiving. The *God of my life* is the God who gave and preserves my life. The *prayer* is not that of sadness but of cheerfulness of heart. The Arabic, Edwards and Hengstenberg put the verb *command* in the present tense; Vulgate, church of England, Boothroyd and Hammond, in the preterite; Fry has the optative form. Our version and many others of high authority properly follow the original. God's servant, in the darkest state of his affairs, still relied on Jehovah, thankfully praising him and devoutly praying to him.

9. *I will say unto God my rock.* The word here rendered *God* is *El. Rock,* as in Ps. xviii. 2. *Why hast thou forgotten me? Remembering* denotes care, support, reward; so *forgetting* denotes neglect, forsaking, consigning to misery, Judges xvi. 28; 1 Sam. i. 11; Neh. xiii. 14; Luke xxiii. 42; Gen. xl. 23; Judges iii. 7; Ps. lxxvii. 9; cvi. 21. It seemed as if God had deserted David's cause. But the prophet filled his mouth with arguments. He humbly expostulated against the Lord's desertion of him and his cause. Prayer may have great vehemence and strong argument in it. *Why go I mourning because of the oppression of the enemy? Mourning, i. e., squalid, with garments covered with dust and ashes,* as was the manner of mourners, see on Ps. xxxv. 14. The *weight* of the evil brought on us by adversaries is sometimes all but intolerable. It greatly *oppresses* us. Yet the righteous may earnestly plead with God for the removal of so great a calamity. His honor and their purity demand it, Ps. cxxv. 3.

10. As *with a sword in my bones, mine enemies reproach me: while they say daily unto me,* Where is *thy God?* The *taunt* and *derision* of the question in this verse are the same as in v. 3. David says they were like a sword in his bones. For *sword* the margin and Chaldee read *killing;* Hengstenberg and Alexander, *murder;* Ainsworth, *murdering weapon;* in Ezek. xxi. 22, the same word is rendered *slaughter.* It describes excruciating pain.

11. *Why art thou cast down, O my soul? and why art thou disquieted within me? hope thou in God: for I shall yet praise him.* Thus far the verse is quite as the beginning of v. 5. It is added, Who is *the health of my countenance, and my God.* The variation of this clause from the corresponding clause in v. 5 is that here we have *my countenance* for *his countenance.* This ought to appear in any version. There is no reason for correcting the text. It is right already. Such changes are natural and beautiful. *Health,* in v. 5, help; see Ps. iii. 2, 8; most commonly *salvation,* then *help, welfare, deliverance, health, saving health;* here and in v. 5 plural.

The health of my countenance is he, who graciously looks on me and gives me bold-ness when otherwise I should sink into despair. Alexander: "*And my God* is not an unmeaning or gratuitous addition, but has reference to the taunting question in the preceding verse, *Where is thy God?*"

DOCTRINAL AND PRACTICAL REMARKS.

1. Love to God's house is of the essence of true piety. It always has been so, v. 1. There is no piety without a devotional spirit; and that spirit is always gratified in the assemblies of the saints. Even the memory of hours spent in the delights of public worship is cheering to one deprived of the ordinances.

2. Dickson: "It is not a bare formal use of the ordinances, but communion with God himself, which the lively believer seeketh after, in the use of public ordinances," v. 1.

3. Ought not those, who leave the churches of our old settlements, to see to it that some provision be made for edifying public worship in the places where they settle? Ought not those, who go into voluntary exile from God's worship, to suspect that all is not right? Can it be safe for them, of their own accord, to do what it so grieved David to be compelled to do? v. 1.

4. It would greatly promote true religion, if all God's people would put a just estimate on the privileges of public worship, vv. 1, 2. Henry: "Sometimes God teaches us effectually to know the worth of mercies by the want of them, and whets our appetite for the means of grace, by cutting us short in those means."

5. True religion consists much more in longing desires for more grace and know-ledge, than in being satisfied with that, which we have attained, vv. 1, 2. Com-pare Matt. v. 6. The Saviour represents the desires of the pious, after holiness both by *hunger* and *thirst*; David by *thirst* only. Thirst is said to be more tormenting than hunger.

6. It is a blessed thing to be able to mourn an absent God and to desire his soul-cheering presence, v. 2. It is better to weep and cry for lost spiritual privileges and comforts with a relish even for their memory, than it is to be at ease in the fulness of earthly comforts. Godly mourning is better than carnal rejoicing.

7. True religion is ever the same and always produces similar effects on character, v. 2.

8. As the ordinances, without God's blessing, do not satisfy a believer, so also the most precious seasons of devotion on earth do awaken in him heavenly-mindedness, and great longings to participate in the worship of the temple not made with hands, vv. 1, 2. There sin never mars delight. There the face of Jesus in his glory shines on every redeemed soul. There floods of glory and salvation fill the soul with ineffable delight.

9. It is no new thing for good men to be filled with anguish and to pour out tears day and night, v. 3. The happiest may soon be plunged into the deepest distress. Wicked men, fallen angels, God's providences, dismal fears, loss of courage, banish-ment from home and a thousand frightful forms of ill may all be against us.

10. It is a favorite device of the great adversary and his minions to attempt in various ways to drive believers to despondency and even to despair, v. 3. If they cannot destroy, they are determined to torment God's people.

11. Taunts are no novelty. The greatest and best of men need not be surprised at them. Reproach is a *sword*, vv. 3, 10. Calvin: "Whenever the ungodly triumph over us in our miseries, and spitefully taunt us, saying that God is against us, let us never forget that it is Satan who moves them to speak in this manner to overthrow our faith." Let the wicked spit their spite, but let us be steadfast with God.

12. Appearances of help are often wanting when succor is at hand, vv. 3, 10. The

darkest hour in the history of man's redemption was just before the resurrection of Christ.

13. Even if the memory of past joys has some tendency to deepen present distress, yet it is best not to forget them, for he, who once filled our mouth with praise, can bring back the days when the candle of the Lord shined upon us, v. 4.

14. When tempted to despond, we must rally and exhort ourselves by a consideration of the truths suited to our cases, vv. 5, 11. Dejection is not the offspring of piety. We must have faith and hope in God, or we must lose our cause.

15. It is a great mercy that we may tell God all our sorrows and griefs, v. 6. He has an ear to hear and a heart to feel for all our woes.

16. No situation in life, no anguish of mind, no cares or duties can justify us in forgetting God, v. 6. We must call him to mind, though nothing but our wants and sorrows in a howling wilderness remind us of him.

17. Let none be surprised at the violence of temptations, v. 7. They often come in like a flood. Onset succeeds onset, until we are ready to yield. But the only thing that ever lost a believer the victory was cowardice.

18. Let all prepare for the worst. We may well expect sorrow upon sorrow. In David's case *deep called unto deep*. One unclean spirit often brings seven others with him.

19. All our hope is in the lovingkindness of the Lord, v. 8. We need no other ground of peace and joy.

20. We may lawfully be very earnest and urgent with God for his gracious interposition, v. 9. It is eminently fit for God to undertake cases which without divine assistance are hopeless.

21. The loss of God's gracious presence and of the light of his countenance constitutes the greatest grief of pious souls, v. 4.

22. Some rely wholly on past experience without inquiring how it is now with them. Others forget all God has done for them as soon as new troubles rise. Let us avoid both these errors. Tholuck: "Those who are rich in past experience possess in it an eminence from which they may also enjoy genial prospects of the future.

23. However evils may press upon us now, if we are saints, good days are coming; and if we are saints and have good times now, still better are coming, vv. 5, 11. Redemption draweth nigh. We shall soon be forever with the Lord.

24. In every extremity let believers plead their covenant relation with God, saying, Thou art my God, v. 11. This will sustain them when all else fails. Often this is all they can do. Dickson: "Although the Lord, for a time, shall neither remove the outward affliction nor inwardly give comfort, yet faith will sustain itself by the covenant, and lay its whole weight upon it."

25. This Psalm shows that of old, as in modern times, the saints had groanings which cannot be uttered.

26. To all true Christians "the house of the Lord is where the word of God, and the promise of grace are preached;" where Christ is held up as the hope of glory, and a heaven of sinless holiness promised to the faithful.

PSALM XLIII.

1 Judge me, O God, and plead my cause against an ungodly nation: oh deliver me from the deceitful and unjust man.

2 For thou *art* the God of my strength: why dost thou cast me off? why go I mourning because of the oppression of the enemy?

3 Oh send out thy light and thy truth: let them lead me; let them bring me unto thy holy hill, and to thy tabernacles.

4 Then will I go unto the altar of God, unto God my exceeding joy: yea, upon the harp will I praise thee, O God my God.

5 Why art thou cast down, O my soul? and why art thou disquieted within me? hope in God for I shall yet praise him, *who is* the health of my countenance, and my God.

IN Hebrew this Psalm has no title. Syriac: *A Psalm* of David when Jonathan informed him that Saul desired to slay him, and a prayer of the prophet. He also speaks lightly of the Jews; Arabic: A prayer for the Jews who had backslidden; Septuagint: A Psalm of David. All these are unwarranted. Kennicott, Lowth, Horne, Mudge, Edwards, Horsley, Tholuck, Cobbin and others make it a part of Ps. xlii. Williams: "The Jewish choristers having, on some occasion, found the anthem too long, have divided it for their own conveniency, (no uncommon thing among choristers;) and being once divided, it was ignorantly supposed, it ought to be so divided." But this is a sweeping statement, with little to support it. Psalms xlii. and xliii. when united, contain fewer verses and less matter than many which the choir sang. Besides, the church of God has never so carelessly regarded her sacred writings as to allow such liberties. The want of a title proves not that this belongs to Ps. xlii. The reasons against uniting these two Psalms are given at length by Hengstenberg and Alexander. The authorship is pretty certainly the same as that of the xlii. Of the date we know nothing certainly. Scott gives it as B. C. 1021. In it we have two names of Jehovah, *Elohim God* and *El God*, on which see on Ps. iii. 2; v. 4.

1. *Judge me, O God.* Chaldee: Judge me, O God, with the judgment of truth; Syriac: Judge my judgment, O God. We had the same verb in Ps. vii. 8; xxvi. 1; Ps. lxxxii. 3, *defend.* Fry: Give me justice, O God. *And plead my cause;* the same verb as in Ps. xxxv. 1, which see. Syriac: Undertake my defence; Arabic: Relieve me; Ainsworth: Plead my plea; Fry: Sustain my cause; Hengstenberg: Plead my quarrel; literally, Strive my strife, contend my contention. If we vary from the common version, we can get nothing better than, Conduct my controversy. The Septuagint, Calvin, Ainsworth and others have a pause after *cause.* But the Syriac, Arabic, Vulgate and others without any pause immediately add the clause, which we render *against an ungodly nation.* Chaldee, *against an unjust race;* Syriac, *against a merciless people;* Vulgate, *a nation that is not holy;* Calvin, *a cruel nation;* Mudge, *an ungenerous people;* Jebb, *a people without mercy.* The mass of the people showed unkindness to David whenever his life was sought. Of all foes none are more to be dreaded than a people unjustly excited against a great and good man, especially, one who has rendered eminent public services. Some of his foes were particularized: *Oh deliver me from the deceitful and unjust man.* This description so well suits the case of Ahithophel that some hence conclude that this Psalm *certainly* refers to Absalom's rebellion, in which that fox was the cunning adviser. But no wicked plot was ever conducted with candor and justice. It may describe any bitter, crafty foe. He, who designs or perpetrates a wrong against a good man, must either be very miserable, or must harden himself in crime by deliberate deceit.

2. *For thou* art *the God of my strength.* This is also rendered *my God and my strength,* also *God my strength. Strength,* also rock, fort, fortress, Judges vi. 26; Dan. ii. 19; Jer. xvi. 19. The most common rendering is strength; see on Ps. xxvii. 1. *Why dost thou cast me off?* Chaldee: Why hast thou forsaken me? Syriac: Why hast thou forgotten me? Arabic: Why hast thou driven me away? Calvin: Why art thou estranged from me? In the Hebrew the verb is in the preterite, but it expresses the act as continued to present time. He is deploring his exile from the house and public worship of God. *Why go I mourning because of the oppression of the enemy?* see on Ps. xlii. 9.

3. *Oh send out thy light and thy truth. Darkness* represents distress and danger; *light,* relief and deliverance. Here the light sought is that of the divine countenance, the favorable aspect of providence; see on Ps. iv. 6. *Truth* is the truth promised to David, involving the divine faithfulness. The Syriac reads thy *faithfulness;* the Arabic, thy *equity.* To *send out* or *send forth* light and truth is to bring them to bear on the case. *Let them lead me.* God can make darkness light and crooked things straight. His faithfulness never lets go its hold on believers. *Let them bring me unto thy holy hill, and to thy tabernacles.* Alexander: "The mention of the tabernacle and the holy hill shows that the Psalm is neither earlier nor later than the times of David and Solomon, before whom there was no holy hill, and after whom there was no tabernacle." *Tabernacles,* in the plural, may be thus explained: 1. There were different parts of the great tent, as we learn from many Scriptures. Paul fully explains this matter in Heb. ix. 1–8. So that the one tabernacle may be spoken of in the plural. 2. In David's time there were two *tabernacles* where God was duly ·worshipped, one in Mount Zion, as many Scriptures show; the other at Gibeon as we learn from 1 Chron. xvi. 37–39. So that in two ways we may justify the use of the plural.

4. *Then will I go unto the altar of God. God,* Hebrew, *Elohim.* Here is the vow, made in distress, as vows commonly are. It is a solemn pledge and engagement that he would make offerings to God before all Israel. Some regard these words as the expression of a hope that he shall be able to do these things. This may be so; but the other is the better explanation. *Unto God my exceeding joy. God,* Hebrew, *El.* Chaldee: My God, from whom is the joy of my exultation; margin, Jebb and Alexander: To God the gladness of my joy; church of England: Even unto the God of my joy and gladness. In his existence, personality, attributes, providence, word and salvation God is the source of unspeakable joy. *Yea, upon the harp will I praise thee, O God, my God. Harp,* see on Ps. xxxiii. 2. Praise is comely, even in times of distress, and the purpose to render it is always becoming. The covenant relation expressed in the words *God, my God,* was the foundation of perpetual confidence to David.

5. *Why art thou cast down, O my soul? and why art thou disquieted within me? hope in God: for I shall yet praise him,* who is *the health of my countenance, and my God.* See on Ps. xlii. 11. Tholuck: "Having committed his cause to the Lord, he succeeds for the last time in appeasing his troubled soul."

DOCTRINAL AND PRACTICAL REMARKS.

1. It is an unspeakable comfort to be able to ask God to *judge* us, v. 1. His judgment is true, impartial, not after appearances, but after the heart. He who can with a good conscience commit his way to God, has nothing to fear.

2. For where our cause is good, our Judge becomes our Advocate and *pleads our cause,* v. 1. When the Lord is on our side, it cannot go ill with us. He knows all truth. He is a Counsellor.

3. No public service, no piety, no benevolence, no humility can exempt God's servants from ill will and wrong doing in this wicked world. David had his foes, v. 1. Christ had his murderers.

4. The enemies of God's servants are often so many, so cruel, so cunning and so powerful, that it is a marvel they do not eat them up. Less grace, less aid than God affords would not meet their case.

5. As the righteous cannot practise the deceit and injustice, nor use the weapons employed against them, the only resource left them is to enlist God, v. 1.

6. The confidence which the righteous repose in God is not misplaced. He is the God of their *strength*, v. 2.

7. It is wise and profitable to inquire into the cause of our afflictions. *Why dost thou cast me off?* v. 2. A failure so to do leaves us without profit from our sorest trials.

8. One of the direst forms of affliction is the *oppression of the wicked*, v. 2. Man is cruel.

9. In the darkest hour on earth we may pray, we ought to pray, v. 3. We may always ask for light, truth, guidance, and comfort from the word of God.

10. Cobbin: "In some way or other we may expect that earnest prayer will meet with a gracious answer, v. 3. The faith of the Psalmist saw the successful end of his prayer, and transported him at once to the sacred altar. Such holy and ardent desires as he expressed will be sure to obtain an audience in heaven."

11. He who has no love for the house of God has no piety, v. 3. Henry: "Those whom God leads, he leads to his holy hill, and to his tabernacles; those therefore who pretend to be led by the Spirit, and yet turn their backs upon instituted ordinances, certainly deceive themselves."

12. It is optional with us whether in our affliction we will engage to do something we are not commanded to do. Even distress does not oblige us to vow. But when the vow is made, it must be kept, v. 4; Ecc. v. 5.

13. As under the law no fitter place for a sinner could be found than the *altar* of God where atonement was made by bloody offerings, so under the gospel the first thing every sinner should seek is the expiation of sin by the blood of Christ, v. 4. He is our Altar, Sacrifice, Lamb, Righteousness. Live in sight of the Cross.

14. God himself is the source of ineffable joy to all holy creatures, v. 4. Slade: "The faithful servant of God is always either delighting in him, or mourning after him." Heaven will chiefly consist in the enjoyment of God.

15. Seeing we have God for our *exceeding joy*, surely we ought never to be disheartened, nor faint by the way, v. 4. If outward things look dark, let us look to the throne of God. There all is radiant with glory.

16. On instrumental music in the worship of God, see REMARK No. 4, on Ps. xxxiii.

17. If seasons of terrible depression come, no strange thing has happened to us. The same came to the author of this Psalm. A horror of great darkness once fell on Abraham himself, Gen. xv. 12.

18. If temptation is sore, if afflictions multiply, if enemies are many and powerful, let us hold fast and firm God and his truth, v. 5. The more terrible the storm, the more necessary is the anchor, Heb. vi. 19. *Hope in God.*

PSALM XLIV.

To the chief Musician for the sons of Korah, Maschil.

1 We have heard with our ears, O God, our fathers have told us, *what* work thou didst in their days, in the times of old.

2 *How* thou didst drive out the heathen with thy hand, and plantedst them; *how* thou didst afflict the people, and cast them out.

3 For they got not the land in possession by their own sword, neither did their own arm save them: but thy right hand, and thine arm, and the light of thy countenance, because thou hadst a favour unto them.

4 Thou art my King, O God: command deliverances for Jacob.

5 Through thee will we push down our enemies: through thy name will we tread them under that rise up against us.

6 For I will not trust in my bow, neither shall my sword save me.

7 But thou hast saved us from our enemies, and hast put them to shame that hated us.

8 In God we boast all the day long, and praise thy name for ever. Selah.

9 But thou hast cast off, and put us to shame; and goest not forth with our armies.

10 Thou makest us to turn back from the enemy: and they which hate us spoil for themselves.

11 Thou hast given us like sheep *appointed* for meat; and hast scattered us among the heathen.

12 Thou sellest thy people for nought, and dost not increase *thy wealth* by their price.

13 Thou makest us a reproach to our neighbours, a scorn and a derision to them that are round about us.

14 Thou makest us a byword among the heathen, a shaking of the head among the people.

15 My confusion *is* continually before me, and the shame of my face hath covered me,

16 For the voice of him that reproacheth and blasphemeth; by reason of the enemy and avenger.

17 All this is come upon us; yet have we not forgotten thee, neither have we dealt falsely in thy covenant.

18. Our heart is not turned back, neither have our steps declined from thy way;

19 Though thou hast sore broken us in the place of dragons, and covered us with the shadow of death.

20 If we have forgotten the name of our God, or stretched out our hands to a strange god;

21 Shall not God search this out? for he knoweth the secrets of the heart.

22 Yea, for thy sake are we killed all the day long; we are counted as sheep for the slaughter.

23 Awake, why sleepest thou, O Lord? arise, cast *us* not off for ever.

24 Wherefore hidest thou thy face, *and* forgettest our affliction and our oppression?

25 For our soul is bowed down to the dust: our belly cleaveth unto the earth.

26 Arise for our help, and redeem us for thy mercies' sake.

THE several parts of the title are explained on titles of Ps. iv. xxxii. xlii. The date and authorship are wholly uncertain. The Syriac says that it was sung by the people and Moses at Horeb. Calvin and Clarke regard it as probably belonging to the times of the captivity. Patrick and Edwards suppose it was written by Hezekiah. Geddes thinks it was written during the persecutions of Antiochus Epiphanes; while Scott conjectures that David was the author, and that it was written for the use of the church in all ages. Tholuck thinks it probably belongs to the time when Jehoiachin and thirty-two nobles were carried into captivity. There is nothing to justify us in dating it as early as the time of Moses. We do not find the chapters relied on, 2 Chron. xxix. xxxi; 2 Kings xviii. 13, 17; Isa. xxxvi. 1, sufficient evidence to date it in the times of Hezekiah. If we compare verses 17–22, with Dan. ix. 3–18, we can hardly refer it to the captivity. Geddes relies on 1 Maccabees i. ii., and supposes Matthias was the author. But we have no evidence that the canon of Scripture was enlarged at that time by the addition of a chapter or a song. The reign of Jehoiachin lasted but a few months, nor did the character of his people then correspond with the teachings of vv. 17–22. The most probable opinion is that it was written by David or one of his cotemporaries. To this there is no unanswerable objection. Many so hold. Theodoret and others make David speak prophetically of Antiochus Epiphanes, "who first hated and persecuted the Israelites on account of their religion," but who could not seduce them to idolatry. Paul quotes v. 22, as applicable to Gospel times, Rom. viii. 36. Calvin: "It is to be observed that the state of the church such as it was to be after the appearance of Christ is here described. Paul did not understand this Psalm as a description of the state of the church in one age only, but warns us that Christians are appointed to the same afflictions." But there is no good reason for denying that it describes a state of things existing in the lifetime of David, when there were much piety and prosperity, and yet some very painful events. Hengstenberg gives it the same historic occasion as that of Ps. lx. See 1 Kings xi. 15, 16; 2 Sam. viii. 14; 1 Chron. xviii. 12, 13; Ps. lx. cviii. Alexander thinks it cannot have a later date than the times of David. Any defeat to the arms of Israel produced the greatest public distress. See Josh. vii. 6. Any disaster in war to that remarkable people, owing to their peculiar relations to Jehovah, argued that he was angry with them. There is nothing gained by dividing the Psalm into various portions and making it dramatic. Its scope is pretty clear to the attentive reader. In it we find two names of Jehovah, *Elohim God* and *Adonai Lord;* on which see on Ps. iii. 2; ii. 4.

1. *We have heard with our ears, O God, our fathers have told us,* what *work thou didst in their days, in the times of old.* What we have heard with our ears is contrasted with what we now see. The former triumphant state of Israel made their present depressed condition the more sad, and furnishes an argument from what God had done to what he is desired to do. The *work* was the conquest of Canaan, or the marvellous delivery of the people in generations gone. We have a parallel to this verse in Judg. vi. 13. There is no need of confining, as some do, the historic reference of the verse to any one period of ancient history previous to the date of the Psalm.

2. How *thou didst drive out the heathen with thy hand, and plantedst them;* how *thou didst afflict the people, and cast them out.* Many versions give the sense better than the English, owing to the indefinite nature of the pronoun *them.* Syriac: Thy hand destroyed the peoples, but those thou didst plant; thou didst trouble kingdoms, but those thou didst establish. Beyond reasonable doubt the word *them* or *those,* in both clauses refers to the Israelites, though our translators do not seem so to have understood the latter clause. *Heathen,* see on Ps. ii. 1, 8; ix. 5, 15, 17, 19, 20. *People,* see on Ps. ii. 1. *Cast out* has the sense of expelling in Gen. iii. 23; Isa. l. 1; in numerous places it signifies to multiply, propagate, cause to flourish, extend or stretch out, Ex. ix. 15; Num. xxi. 6; Ps. xviii. 14; lvii. 3; lxxviii. 25; lxxx. 11; Prov. vi. 14; Ezek. xvii. 7. Here it pretty certainly signifies to increase or cause to flourish as a branch. Diodati says, it is "a term borrowed from vines and other plants which do bud and spread abroad after they are planted and have taken root." Geddes: "The whole metaphor is taken from the vine or some other luxuriant tree." Edwards: "Thou madest them like young trees shoot forth their roots and branches." In the first clause we have God's people spoken of as *planted;* in this, as *made to flourish, to increase.* The Hebrew has it, *Thou, thy hand.* If this doubling has any signification, it is that beyond a doubt the work of conquering Canaan, and of establishing the Israelites in it, was the work of God alone. So the pious Jews did always confess.

3. *For they got not the land in possession by their own sword, neither did their own arm save them: but thy right hand, and thine arm, and the light of thy countenance, because thou hadst a favor unto them.* Tholuck: "Israel had to fight for the possession of the land of Canaan. But faith knows that the strength in man is not his, but the

Lord's, who has created heaven and earth. The Psalmist therefore confesses that it was the hand of God which brought those mighty feats to pass." Ecc. ix. 11. It is true the Israelites as they came out of Egypt and as they entered Canaan were very numerous; but their foes were far more so. The seed of Jacob in Egypt was trained to agriculture, brick-making and servile occupations, and not at all to the use of arms; while many of their foes learned war from their youth. Every victory they gained was clearly not by numbers, by discipline, by skill or by prowess; but by the Lord alone. Yea, his *right hand*, his *arm*, that is his skill and power, and the *light* of his *countenance*, the favoring aspects of his providence, gave them all they gained. Nor did Jehovah thus fight for them for any merit in any of them but because he had *a favor unto them;* literally, because thou *didst like* them, *didst take pleasure in* them, *accept* them, *delight in* them, 1 Chron. xxviii. 4; Ps. cii. 14; cxix. 108; lxii. 4. God's love to Israel was free, unmerited and amazing, and he gave them a land for which they did not labor, and cities which they built not, and vineyards and olive-yards which they planted not, Josh. xxiv. 13. In some cases neither sword nor bow were used; but hornets were the instruments of conquest, Josh. xxiv. 12. Since the fall of Adam all good things in the lot of any mere man are undeserved kindnesses.

4. *Thou art my King, O God.* Septuagint, Vulgate, Ethiopic and some modern versions read: Thou art thyself my king and my God, or, Thou art he, my king and my God. Walford: "The speaker throughout the Psalm is the church, which accounts for the use of both the singular and plural numbers in different parts." The change of person has here the significancy of converting history into argument, and of making a plea, from what God had done of old to his chosen people, in behalf of David and of every other true Israelite. *Command deliverances for Jacob.* Syriac and Arabic: Who hast commanded salvation for Jacob; Edwards: [My God] that commandeth the victories of Jacob. Amesius, Piscator, Fabritius, Calvin, Ainsworth, Jebb, Hengstenberg and Alexander agree with the English version. The language is that of *authority*, which *kings* have. It is of frequent use. *Jacob*, i. e., the chosen nation, descended from him.

5. *Through thee will we push down our enemies. Enemies*, see v. 7, and on Ps. xxvii. 2. *Push down*, rendered *gore*, Ex. xxi. 28, 31. It means to push as *with a horn.* Clarke: "Literally, 'We will toss them in the air with our horn,' a metaphor taken from an ox or bull tossing the dogs into the air, which attack him;" Anderson: "The allusion is to the pushing, striking or butting of oxen and other animals with their horns, and means *to vanquish*, or *subdue*," Deut. xxxiii. 17; 1 Kings xxii. 11; Dan. viii. 4. The form of the verb expresses confidence of victory; and the power by which that is done is none else than that of God, *through thee* or *in thee*, i. e., in union with thee. *Through thy name will we tread them under that rise up against us. Tread under*; Chaldee, *bring into subjection*; Arabic, *taunt* or *defy*; Septuagint, Ethiopic, Vulgate and Doway, *contemn*; Alexander, *trample*; in Pr. xxvii. 7, *loatheth*; most commonly *tread down.* The imagery is drawn from the habits of animals, when furiously trampling that which they hate, or from the habits of both men and beasts in treading on that, which they do not regard. *Them that rise up against us*, a participle, one word. Syriac, *our enemies*; Hengstenberg, *our adversaries*; Alexander, *our assailants.* This victory over enemies was in *God's name*, i. e., by his strength, direction and authority. The confidence here expressed is strong, drawn from the historic facts stated in vv. 1–3, and from God's promises.

6. *For I will not trust in my bow, neither shall my sword save me.* Syriac: Not in our bows, nor in our arms do we trust that they may set us free. In v. 3 past deliverances are wholly ascribed to God, so here reliance for future victories is solely on him. Alexander's paraphrase is just and beautiful: "What was true of my

fathers is equally true of me. As they did not prevail by their own strength, neither can I hope to prevail by mine."

7. *But thou hast saved us from our enemies, and hast put them to shame that hated us.* **But**, better read, *because*. So the word commonly means; thus we get the best sense, and best preserve the connection. *Hast saved*, literally, *hast caused to save. Enemies*, adversaries, *those that trouble us;* see on v. 5; it is also in v. 10. To *put to shame* is to *rout, discomfit, bring into felt contempt;* see on Ps. vi. 10; xxii. 5; xxv. 2. The verse assigns a reason for the purpose expressed in v. 6.

8. *In God we boast all the day long;* i. e., continually. Hengstenberg reads, God we extol continually; Hammond and others, We have praised God; Edwards, In God we glory all day long, *q. d.,* It is not ourselves, it is God alone, to whom all honor and glory are due for making our nation what it has been. *And praise thy name forever.* Chaldee: Thy name will we confess forever and ever; Syriac: We will confess to thy name forever; Arabic: We will give thanks to thy name forever; Edwards: We will celebrate thy name forever; Alexander: Thy name unto eternity will we acknowledge. *Selah.* See Introduction, § 15.

9. *But thou hast cast off and put us to shame. Cast off*, as in v. 23; Ps. xliii. 2; Lam. iii. 17, *remove one to a distance. Put to shame*, the same verb as in Ps. xxxv. 5; xl. 14; commonly rendered, as here, but sometimes blush, confound, and in one form to be reproached. The Jews had a peculiar sense of shame at being vanquished. They could not retreat with a grace, 2 Sam. xix. 3. The law of their warfare required success. Alexander: Thou hast rejected and disgraced us; Calvin: Thou hast abhorred us and put us to shame; Edwards: Thou hast deserted us and put us to shame. *But, yet,* or *and yet. And goest not forth with our armies.* See Joshua vii. 7, 8; 2 Sam. v. 24. Jehovah was the commander and the ally of the armies of Israel. He was the LORD of hosts. But when Israel sinned, he forsook them and was turned to fight against them. Then they always failed.

10. *Thou makest us to turn back from the enemy.* The reason why even a slight defeat so affected the Jews was that for long centuries they had properly regarded it as a sign of a curse resting on them, Josh. vii. 12. How heavy was the loss at this time we know not. The death of about "thirty-six men" at Ai filled the camp of Israel with sore dismay, and made even Joshua say: "Would to God we had been content, and dwelt on the other side Jordan," Josh. vii. 5, 7. The defeat at this time may have been no more disastrous. Flight was followed by plundering: *And they which hate us spoil for themselves.* Edwards: Those that hate us plunder us. This rendering takes no notice of *for themselves*, which teaches "that their enemies destroyed them at their pleasure and without any resistance, as their prey." Alexander: "*Spoiled for themselves*, not merely for their own advantage, but at their own will and discretion."

11. *Thou hast given us like sheep* appointed *for meat.* Calvin: Thou hast given us as sheep for food; church of England: Thou lettest us be eaten up like sheep; Hengstenberg: Thou makest us like sheep for slaughter. When our English translation was made *meat* was equivalent to *food, flesh* then being used as *meat* is in this century. The exceedingly dreadful nature of ancient war, especially as conducted by heathen nations, appears from all its annals. Even now every battle of the warrior is with confused noise, and garments rolled in blood. But then no mercy was commonly shown to the conquered. This clause and one in v. 22 declare the helplessness of the sufferers and the low estimate in which their lives were held. They were slaughtered like sheep. *And* [*thou*] *hast scattered us among the heathen.* It was a national calamity to Israel to see one of the chosen people carried into captivity by the heathen. The bondage was hard, commonly for life, and often attended by the most appalling

circumstances. Calvin: "A dispersion among the heathen was to the Israelites a hundred times more grievous than death."

12. *Thou sellest thy people for nought.* The argument is that delivering over the Israelites to these sad calamities had been no advantage to the cause of true religion among surrounding nations. The inspired writer does not say that Israel had not so sinned as to merit severe rebukes; but that the heathen rather despised than revered Jehovah for the troubles sent on Judea. The next clause is of like import: *And [thou] dost not increase thy wealth by their price.* Arabic: Thou hast diminished the multitude of their number; Calvin: Thou hast not increased the price of them; Edwards: Thou art not enriched by the sale of them; Hengstenberg: Thou receivest nothing for it. So far as these vary from the sense of the English version, they are not improvements. Anderson says it is "as if they had said, Thou hast sold us to our enemies at whatever price they would give; like a person who sells things that are useless at any price, not so much for the sake of gain as to get quit of what he considers of no value and burdensome." Hammond's paraphrase is: "We are thus sadly handled, without the comfort of bringing in any honor to thee by our calamities; since thy church among us is defaced, and no other people taken instead of us, by whom thy name may be glorified." Hengstenberg properly regards Jer. xv. 13 as parallel.

13. *Thou makest us a reproach to our neighbours.* *Reproach*, well and almost invariably so rendered; here used in the concrete, as are also the nouns following: *A scorn and a derision to them that are round about us.* For *scorn* and *derision*, Ainsworth has scoff and scorn; Alexander, scoff and jest. *Make us*, literally *set us*, or *place us.*

14. *Thou makest us a byword among the heathen.* *Makest*, i. e., *placest*, or *settest.* For *byword* Hengstenberg has *similitude;* Syriac and Amesius, *fable;* Septuagint and Ainsworth, *parable;* Chaldee, Arabic, Venema, Edwards and Fry, *proverb.* The common version gives the sense. The sense is clear, viz., that the Israelites were both contemned and detested, "so that their very name was bandied about everywhere in proverbial allusions, as a term of reproach;" see Deut. xxviii. 37, where the same word is rendred *proverb.* The Israelites were also by God made *a shaking of the head among the people,* i. e., an object at which men derisively shook their heads. Tholuck: "The shaking of the head denotes here, as in Psalm xxii. 7, derisive joy." By the *heathen* and the *people* we are to understand surrounding and even somewhat distant nations. Roman literature contains evidences of the execration in which the Jews were held even in Italy.

15. *My confusion is continually before me.* Calvin: My reproach is daily before me; Venema: Daily my disgrace is before me. *All the day*, continually. *Confusion*, elsewhere *reproach, shame, dishonor.* *Before me*, in my presence, i. e., so presented before me that I cannot avoid perceiving it. *And the shame of my face hath covered me.* *Shame*, commonly so rendered; once, *a shameful thing*, and sometimes *confusion.* *Covered, concealed, clothed, hid,* as with a veil, or garment. When a good man's clothing is shame, his distress is extreme. Incessant insolence and scorn produce the saddest effects on men's minds and spirits. One of the ingredients of infernal misery is "everlasting contempt."

16. *For the voice of him that reproacheth and blasphemeth.* *Him that reproacheth*, a participle having the same root as the noun *reproach* in v. 13. It sometimes means *defy*, i. e., with reproaches. Alexander renders it *slander.* *Him that blasphemeth*, a participle. The verb is in our version always rendered as here, except in Num. xv. 30. See 2 Kings xix. 6, 22; Isa. xxxvii. 6, 23; Ezek. xx. 27. In both the Old and New Testaments *blasphemy* is reviling, *reproachful speech*, whether it be spoken of God

or of man.   All this was *by reason of the enemy and avenger.*   The *avenger* corresponds to *him that blasphemeth;* and the *enemy* to *him that reproacheth* in the former clause. Calvin: "*Avenger,* a term which, among the Hebrews, denotes barbarity and cruelty, accompanied with pride."   See Ps. viii. 2.

17. *All this is come upon us.   All,* i. e., what had been said from the beginning of v. 9.   *Yet have we not forgotten thee.*   To forget God is to fall into general irreligion. This clause is the beginning of a plea alleging the general fidelity of the nation to their covenant engagements.   *Neither have we dealt falsely in thy covenant.*   Pool paraphrases these clauses: "Although we cannot excuse ourselves from many other sins for which thou hast justly punished us, yet this we must say for ourselves, that through thy grace we have kept ourselves from apostasy and idolatry, notwithstanding all the examples and provocations, rewards proposed and promised, or punishments threatened to induce us thereunto; which we hope thou wilt graciously consider, and not suffer us to be tempted above what we are able to bear."   Though good men are imperfect, they are not hypocrites.

18. *Our heart is not turned back, neither have our steps declined from thy way.   Declined,* swerved, deviated.   *Way,* the path of duty.   David's reign was remarkable for the absence of idol-worship, and for the general attachment of the people to the service of Jehovah.

19. *Though thou hast sore broken us in the place of dragons.   Sore broken,* by most ancient versions rendered *sunk, humbled, abased;* Calvin, *wasted;* Ainsworth, Fry and Alexander, *crushed;* Edwards, *afflicted;* Jebb, *shattered;* Hengstenberg, *bruised;* in Ps. x. 10, *croucheth.*   Perhaps we might here read: Thou makest us to lie down.   *The place of dragons;* Syriac, *a miserable place;* Arabic, *a place of torment;* Septuagint, *a place of slaughter;* Vulgate, *a place of affliction;* Edwards, *the place of serpents;* Hengstenberg and Tholuck, *the place of jackals.*   Hengstenberg: "The jackals appear often as inhabitants of waste and desert places."   He refers to Isa. xiii. 22; xxxiv. 13; xliii. 20; Jer. ix. 11, in proof.   But in all these places and wherever it occurs, the authors of the English translation never rendered it *jackal,* but always *dragons,* except once in the text it is *whale;* but in the margin even there they read *dragon.*   Alexander: "*Dragons* may here be understood as meaning wild beasts or lonely animals in general."   Aquila: In a desert place where great serpents are found; Hare: In desert places among wild beast and serpents; Edwards: In a wild desolate place, where were serpents, and other noxious animals.   Mant refers it to the wilderness, and quotes Shaw as authority to prove the great number of serpents in the wilderness of Sin. But Calvin says: "The word which others translate *dragons,* I would rather render *whales.*"   Williams: "In the place of sea-monsters, perhaps crocodiles."   Of course such suppose the allusion is to a shipwreck.   But that is not clear.   *Dragons* seems to be nearly equivalent to our word *monsters.*   The condition of God's afflicted ones as here described is clearly one most unpleasant and perilous.   Clarke paraphrases: "Thou hast delivered us into the hands of a fierce, cruel and murderous people." *And* [thou hast] *covered us with the shadow of death.   Covered,* as in v. 15; Ps. xxxii. 1, 5.   There is no better rendering.   On *shadow of death,* see on Ps. xxiii. 4.

20. *If we have forgotten the name of our God, or stretched out our hands to a strange god.   Forgotten,* as in vv. 17, 24.   The name of God is that by which he is known. To *stretch out the hands* to God is to offer him worship, Ps. cxli. 2.   If we have done these things,

21. *Shall not God search this out?*   This is one of many instances of the strongest affirmations by an interrogative form of speech.   Hengstenberg renders it: Would not God require it?   *Search,* as in Ps. cxxxix. 1, 23.   Because God is omniscient he must *search.   For he knoweth the secrets of the heart.   Knoweth,* see on Ps. i. 6.   There

is no higher proof of divinity than a knowledge of the secrets of men's hearts. Hengstenberg and some others regard vv. 20, 21, as containing the formula of an oath. But we have a better sense without regarding it as an oath.

22. *Yea, for thy sake are we killed all the day long; we are counted as sheep for the slaughter.* This verse shows the extreme and constant sufferings of God's people, even at a time when they had not displeased him by any recent or visible defection. It is pertinent to the scope of the Psalm. It does not deny that good may be brought out of our afflictions, nor that it is not better to suffer for well-doing than for evil-doing; nor that it is not better to suffer in God's cause than our own. But it is an appeal for mercy on the grounds of freedom from covenant-breaking with God, and of the great cruelty of persecutors, who insulted Jehovah by murdering his people. These words have a sad fulfilment, whenever God's people fall under persecution; see Rom. viii. 36. *Sheep for the slaughter,* see on v. 11.

23. *Awake, why sleepest thou, O* LORD? God is sometimes spoken of *as if* he had the form, the affections, or the weakness of a man; here as if he had fallen asleep. The call on him is to act like a resistless avenger awaking out of sleep, and finding his premises invaded, and his children cruelly treated. *Arise, cast us not off forever.* For *arise* some read *awake, wake up. Cast off,* see on v. 9. *Forever* points out the long continuance of the invasion and persecution.

24. *Wherefore hidest thou thy face?* See on Ps. x. 11; xiii. 1; *q. d.,* Why dost thou withhold the favorable aspects of thy providence? And [why] *forgettest* [thou] *our affliction and our oppression? Forgettest,* see on vv. 17, 20; *i. e.,* Why dost thou treat us as though thou hadst forgotten? The *affliction* and *oppression* have been described.

25. *For our soul is bowed down to the dust: our belly cleaveth unto the earth, i. e.,* we are greatly distressed and broken. Hengstenberg: "We are as to body and soul smitten and thrown down, glued as it were to the ground, so that we cannot raise ourselves up." It is as if the psalmist had said, The curse denounced against the serpent (see Gen. iii. 14) has fallen on us; we are sunk to the earth; and, left to ourselves as we are now, we shall rise no more; we have no heart even to make an effort to help ourselves.

26. *Arise for our help. Arise,* in v. 5, *rise up. Help,* always so rendered. *And redeem us for thy mercies' sake.* So familiar was the idea of deliverance by *redemption* that even an escape from temporal calamities was sought in prayer by such petitions as this. The Hebrew word for *mercies'* is in the singular, and so it should read *for thy mercy's sake.* God's mercy is the ground and measure of all the good we receive.

DOCTRINAL AND PRACTICAL REMARKS.

1. The knowledge of the true religion is greatly kept alive and extended by older persons telling their juniors what God has done in former times, v. 1. Tholuck: "It was the admirable occupation of old men in Israel to immortalize the works of the Lord in the nation, that the remembrance might in a continuous chain go from century to century," Ex. x. 2; Ps. lxxviii. 3–6. "While the songs of other nations sing of the heroism of their ancestors, the songs of Israel celebrate the works of *God.*"

2. Every important part of church history illustrates the excellence of the doctrine of the unity of the true church and of the communion of saints. No child of God rejoiceth or weepeth, liveth or dieth to himself. God's people have not to this day ceased to celebrate the passage through the Red sea, or over Jordan. Why should they? "Whatsoever things were written aforetime were written for our learning, that we through patience and comfort of the Scriptures might have hope."

3. Striking providences in the history of every Christian nation are eminently proper subjects of meditation and of recital to the rising generation, v. 2. Henry: "It is a debt which every age owes to posterity to keep an account of God's works of wonder, and to transmit the knowledge of them to the next generation."

4. We ought diligently to study God's mercies to others in times past; for though the memory of them may cast us down, if we presently experience no deliverance, yet a mind rightly guided by faith will be led to say, He, who helped others, will in his time help me; and so hope and courage will both be revived. "God's old works have new use in all ages." So Gideon reasoned: "Where be all his miracles, which our fathers told us of?" Judges vi. 13.

5. It is a mercy that in nearly all important events of the life of man, or in the history of a nation, God's hand is so clear, that nothing but impiety can cherish atheistic thoughts, or ascribe to human might or wisdom the results effected by God, v. 3. We are weak as water; and commonly God lets us see and feel our impotence before he sends relief. At least "faith knows that the strength of man is not his, but God's."

6. The reason, why one succeeds better than another, and one nation outshines another, is that God *favors* one more than another. Divine mercy makes the difference. God is a sovereign. This doctrine is very old, Deut. vii. 7, 8.

7. A time of trouble is no time to deny or forget the Lord. Then, if ever, we should avouch him to be our God and our King, v. 4. Dickson: "Trouble maketh faith thirsty, and teacheth the believer to make use of his right and interest." "Relations between God and his people stand constantly in adversity, as well as in prosperity."

8. It often happens that our state is so perplexed, and our affairs so entangled, that we need not merely a deliverance, but *deliverances;* not merely salvation, but *salvations,* v. 4. All this is graciously promised.

9. When God *commands* deliverance, it shall surely come. "Where the word of the king is, there is power." He made the world by his word. He commanded and it stood fast. Nothing costs God labor. He has all power, all causes, all means, all agents, all results under his control.

10. God helping us, we can do anything, overcome any enemies, resist any assaults, vanquish any legions; for it is God that breaks the shield, the sword and the battle, v. 5. Every genuine child of God achieves victories more worthy of celebration than that of David over the lion, the bear and the giant.

11. Means must be used but not relied on, v. 6. Not to use them is to despise God's ordinance; but to trust in them is to despise God himself. Man must sow and water; God gives the increase. Man is to bend his bow and sharpen his sword in the day of battle, and use both with his utmost skill; and then trust God as if he were unarmed.

12. Sooner or later *shame* will overtake the wicked, v. 7. It cannot be otherwise. Mercy may long defer the fatal hour; but it will come at last, yea, come soon to all the impenitent.

13. Very exulting language and behaviour are not unbecoming to the righteous, if they are produced solely by God's acts and directed only to his glory, v. 8. Nor should mere change of circumstances, from pleasant to painful, hinder us from making our boast in God. We should always suspect our own tempers, when they do not lead us to this duty.

14. Good men may be brought into great straits; yea, the best of men into the greatest straits, v. 9. There is imperfection enough in every man living to justify Jehovah in chastening him. All the vessels of mercy need scouring; all the children

of God are the better for correction. The best churches are much marred with imperfection. He, whose they are, may wisely purge them in the furnace of affliction. Churches, nations and armies may in the main be right, yet so far wrong as to need rebuke, defeat, disaster for their own good.

15. If trouble befalls men, churches or nations, they may rest assured there is a cause for it. "How should one chase a thousand, and two put ten thousand to flight, except their Rock had sold them, and the LORD had shut them up," Deut. xxxii. 30.

16. The horrors of war in all ages are unspeakable, involving *flight, pillage, captivity* and *death*, vv. 10, 11. If for our many sins we must be punished, let it not be by war or by famine, where men's malignant passions will be at work, but by pestilence. Oh let us fall into the hands of the Lord.

17. When the character of her foes is remembered, the church should expect no mercy from them, v. 11. Their cry has ever been, Rase it, rase it, even to the foundations thereof, Ps. cxxxvii. 7. They have no pity.

18. Perhaps there was seldom a time when the Israelites had not cause to believe that some of their nation were in captivity. This should have taught them humility and dependence on God, with pity to the captives, v. 12. And there is seldom a time when some of the human race are not in a miserable captivity. This should greatly affect us. We should often remember the prisoner, and ask God to hear his sighing.

19. Let us often pray that we may not be tried with the taunts and derision of mankind, vv. 13, 14. That test is too severe for most men.

20. If we have great grief for a long time, even when we have in the main done right, let us not be surprised. It has been so before, vv. 15, 19.

21. When men are fairly started in a course of wickedness, and especially of persecution, it may be expected that, if left to themselves, they will stop at nothing, v. 16.

22. When by our sufferings or the reproaches heaped upon us men get the impression that we are suffering for some great sin, we may humbly, modestly and firmly defend our characters, vv. 17, 18. If we can truly deny the charge of backsliding and covenant-breaking, we may certainly do so.

23. Whatever befalls us, let us hold fast the profession of the true religion, and never swerve from the worship and service of Jehovah. A knowledge that we have done so will afford us relief and solace, when all without looks dark, v. 20.

24. Let all that do wickedly be sure that their sin will find them out, vv. 20, 21. The nature of man and the nature of sin render it probable, but the nature of God makes it certain that what is done in a corner shall be proclaimed on the house-top.

25. Be much concerned respecting the state of your heart. If that is right, all is right; if that is wrong, all is wrong. It is only man that judgeth by the appearance.

26. Persecution is the common lot of God's people, v. 22. Calvin: "Lest the severity of the cross should dismay us, let us always have present to our view this condition of the church, that as we are adopted in Christ, we are appointed to the slaughter." Dickson: "It is a mercy to us, that when God might punish us for our sins, he maketh our correction honorable, and our troubles to be for a good cause: *for thy sake are we killed*." Reader, are you at heart a martyr? Would you stand *fire* for Christ?

27. We ought at all times, and especially in distress, to resort to a throne of grace, and by earnest prayer, by strong crying and by filling our mouth with arguments beg of God to undertake our cause, vv. 23–26. But let us at such time be especially guarded against self-righteousness and vain-glory. We are poor, and miserable, and blind, and naked, and sinful.

28. Let us often and with delight dwell on the glorious theme of *Redemption*, v. 26. Let us not forget to mention it in our prosperity. In adversity let us remember that

the worst would have come on us forever, but for redemption. "Redemption is precious."

29. Grace! grace! grace! has ever been the song of the church and ever shall be, v. 26. All we have and hope for is for his *mercy's* sake. This is best for us, while it is most honorable to God.

PSALM XLV.

To the chief Musician upon Shoshannim, for the sons of Korah, Maschil, A Song of loves.

1 My heart is inditing a good matter: I speak of the things which I have made touching the king: my tongue *is* the pen of a ready writer.

2 Thou art fairer than the children of men: grace is poured into thy lips: therefore God hath blessed thee for ever.

3 Gird thy sword upon *thy* thigh, O *most* mighty, with thy glory and thy majesty.

4 And in thy majesty ride prosperously, because of truth and meekness *and* righteousness; and thy right hand shall teach thee terrible things.

5 Thine arrows *are* sharp in the heart of the king's enemies; *whereby* the people fall under thee.

6 Thy throne, O God, *is* for ever and ever: the sceptre of thy kingdom *is* a right sceptre.

7 Thou lovest righteousness, and hatest wickedness: therefore God, thy God, hath anointed thee with the oil of gladness above thy fellows.

8 All thy garments *smell* of myrrh, and aloes, *and* cassia, out of the ivory palaces, whereby they have made thee glad.

9 Kings' daughters *were* among thy honourable women: upon thy right hand did stand the queen in gold of Ophir.

10 Hearken, O daughter, and consider, and incline thine ear; forget also thine own people, and thy father's house;

11 So shall the king greatly desire thy beauty: for he *is* thy Lord; and worship thou him.

12 And the daughter of Tyre *shall be there* with a gift; *even* the rich among the people shall entreat thy favour.

13 The king's daughter *is* all glorious within: her clothing *is* of wrought gold.

14 She shall be brought unto the king in raiment of needle-work: the virgins her companions that follow her shall be brought unto thee.

15 With gladness and rejoicing shall they be brought: they shall enter into the king's palace.

16 Instead of thy fathers shall be thy children, whom thou mayest make princes in all the earth.

17 I will make thy name to be remembered in all generations: therefore shall the people praise thee for ever and ever.

ON several phrases of the title, see on titles of Ps. iv. xxxii. xlii. *Upon Shoshannim;* it may be stated, 1. We have it in the singular *Shushan* with *eduth* annexed in the title of Ps. lx.; *Shoshannim* in the title of Ps. lix.; and *Shoshannim-eduth* in the title of Ps. lxxx. We find it in no other title. 2. Formerly many referred its use to the *six-stringed* instruments; but now it is generally agreed that *Shoshannim* signifies *lilies,* and *Eduth,* testimony. The compound is *Lilies of testimony.* 3. *Upon* may point to a theme, an instrument, or a tune. If it refers to a tune, or an instrument, it was to one called Lilies. Those who think it refers to a theme suppose that the daughters or virgins mentioned in the Psalm are called *lilies;* those flowers being fit emblems of female beauty. This view is best supported. There is no evidence that this Psalm is modelled after some other, although it bears a remarkable resemblance to the Song of Solomon. If *lilies* refers to females, so probably does *loves,* which doubtless means *loved ones,* as *love* in the Canticles means a *loved one.* The date and authorship are uncertain. A quite common opinion fixes it in the days of Solomon, and ascribes its authorship to the sons of Korah. But see Introduction, § 4, and on title of Ps. xlii. There is no insuperable objection to the opinion that David wrote it. He was a prophet; he wrote Ps. lxxii., which is a prediction respecting Solomon as a type of Christ. No supposition is attended with so few difficulties. Much of the imagery is drawn from the marriage of an eastern prince, and the whole is in honor of him. If Solomon is here spoken of, still the Psalm is Messianic. So think the soundest expositors. Luther: "This is a prophecy concerning the gospel and kingdom of Christ;" Hengstenberg: "Nearly all the older Christian expositors understand it of the Messiah;" Alexander: "The allegorical or Messianic sense is given by the oldest interpreters, both Jewish and Christian;" Morison: "There is not, perhaps, in the entire book of Psalms a more direct or sublime prediction of Christ and the church than the one embodied in this beautiful ode. To a mind that is spiritual, it will ever suggest thoughts of loftiest devotion;" Scott: "It is entirely a prophecy of Christ, and is quoted as such by the apostle," Heb. i. 8, 9. The Chaldee and Arabic interpret it of Christ. Except on the belief of its allegorical and Messianic sense it never could have had a place in the canon of the Old Testament. It is in the usual form addressed to the leader of the public praises of Israel. It is *an Instruction*, a Didactic Psalm. The relation of Jehovah to his church is often represented by that of marriage. As early as the time of Moses, unfaithfulness to Jehovah was branded with the infamy due to a faithless wife, Ex. xxxiv. 15, 16; Lev. xvii. 7; xx. 5, 6; Num. xiv. 33; Deut. xxxi. 16. And after the time of David to the close of the canon of the New Testament the inspired writers evince a familiarity with the same idea of a marriage relation. See Isa. liv. 5; lxii. 4, 5; Jer. iii. 1; Ezek. xvi.; xxiii.; often in Hosea; Matt. ix. 15; John iii. 20; Rom. vii. 4; 2 Cor. xi. 2; Eph. v. 27, 32; Rev. xix. 7; xxi. 2; xxii. 17. So that Venema speaks well when he says, "No other can possibly be thought of here than Messiah or Solomon." He and others state the two modes in which it is applied to Christ, either remotely under the figure of Solomon, or directly and immediately as a mere prophecy. Either method secures substantial accuracy. But the latter is to be preferred, with the understanding that much of the imagery is borrowed from the nuptials and palace of Solomon. Many things in this song could have had no fulfilment in any mere man. "Behold, a greater than Solomon is here." In this Psalm we have *Elohim God* and *Adonai Lord*, on which see on Ps. iii. 2; ii. 4. Clarke dates it B. C. 1008; Scott, B. C. 1020.

1. *My heart is inditing a good matter.* Chaldee: My heart hath cast forth a good discourse; Calvin: My heart is boiling over with a good matter; Boothroyd: My heart teemeth with excellent matter; Edwards: My heart is full of a good thing; Tholuck: My heart welleth forth a fair song. The sense is: My heart has well thought over and is now full of a good matter. Probably the primary meaning of the verb is to seethe over a fire. His heart was warmed with his subject. *I speak of the things which I have made touching the king.* Chaldee and Syriac: I will speak my works to the king; Calvin: I shall speak of the works which I have made concerning the king; Amesius: I will speak my poems concerning the king; Edwards: I will speak what I have made upon the king; Hammond: My composures will I deliver [or recite] to the king; Tholuck: I say: I will sing touching the king. These words are hardly an exclamation, for they are preceded and followed by a narrative clause. The aim of v. 1 is to give notice of what is about to be done, as in Isa. v. 1. Our version would give the precise sense by putting the participle in the future *will speak*. Many versions do so. *My tongue is the pen of a ready writer.* Syriac and Arabic: My tongue *is* the pen of a skilful writer; Doway: My tongue *is* the pen of a scrivener that writeth swiftly; Calvin: My tongue is as the pen of a swift writer; Edwards: My tongue is

like the pen of a learned scribe. The clause doubtless claims inspiration. Holy men spake and wrote as they were moved by the Holy Ghost. Scott: "The tongue was guided by the Spirit of God, as entirely as the pen is by the hand of a ready writer, to express promptly and fully the mind of the Spirit, and nothing more;" Fry: "I conceive that the subserviency of the human faculties to the Spirit of inspiration is alluded to under the figure of a pen in the hand of a ready and expert writer." There seems to be no good reason for changing the phrase from a declaration into an invocation: Let my tongue be as the pen of a ready writer. The prophets claim, but do not invoke the guidance of the Spirit in their compositions. The whole verse tells how the writer's mind is imbued with the subject of Messiah, and how fully he is purposed to speak his praises.

2. *Thou art fairer than the children of men.* Chaldee: Thy beauty, O King Messiah, is above that of the sons of men; Mudge: Thou art wonderfully fair beyond the sons of men; Alexander: Beautiful, beautiful art thou above the sons of men. This clause determines that the ode cannot have its fulfilment in Solomon. He was indeed very wise; but for piety, purity, unbending integrity, holiness of heart and righteousness of life he had many superiors. In moral worth Noah, Daniel and Job certainly far outshined him, Ezek. xiv. 14, 20. But every word is true respecting Christ. He is above all, before all, over all. Diodati: "Thou art excellent and perfect in all manner of virtue, and such dost thou appear to be to thy church," Isa. xxxiii. 17; Cant. v. 10, 16. Alexander: "On any supposition but the Messianic one, this verse is unintelligible." *Grace is poured into thy lips.* The key to the right interpretation of this clause is given us by two evangelists. "And all bare him witness, and wondered at the gracious words which proceeded out of his mouth," Luke iv. 22; "The Word was made flesh and dwelt among us, full of grace and truth;" and "Grace and truth came by Jesus Christ," John i. 14, 17; Compare John vii. 46; Matt. vii. 28, 29; Horne: "His word instructed the ignorant, resolved the doubtful, comforted the mourners, reclaimed the wicked, silenced his adversaries, healed diseases, controlled the elements, and raised the dead." Many translations agree precisely with the English text. There is difficulty attending the supposition that 1 Kings x. 8, is parallel to this. Christ's words are still mighty. *Therefore God hath blessed thee forever.* There is much uniformity in rendering the clause; except that for *therefore* some read *because.* If *therefore* is preferred, then the sense is God has blessed our King forever because he well executed his prophetical office; if *because* then the sense is that Christ executed his office well, owing to the fact that God had given him a permanent blessing. Both are true and scriptural ideas. Compare Isa. lxi. 1–3; Phil. ii. 5–10.

3. *Gird thy sword upon thy thigh, O* most *mighty, with thy glory and thy majesty.* The word *most* is put in by the translators for interpretation. It is not in the Hebrew. *Mighty,* in Ps. xix. 5, *a strong man;* in Job xvi. 14, *giant;* in Isa. x. 21, applied to Jehovah, *mighty* God; in Isa. ix. 6, it is certainly applied to Messiah. This verse cannot be applied to Solomon, but only to Christ. He wholly pursued the arts of peace, and was no warrior. For *mighty* Mudge, Edwards and Hengstenberg read Hero; Horsley, Warrior. It is quite according to inspired usage to speak of Christ's word as a sword, Eph. vi. 17; Heb. iv. 12; Rev. ii. 12, 16. With this he goes forth to subdue the earth to himself. To gird on the sword is to prepare for battle, 1 Sam. xxv. 13. Because Messiah was *mighty* and *blessed for ever*, his warlike undertakings would surely be successful. *Glory* and *majesty* would attend him. Both these words express high royal state and even divine grandeur, Ps. xxi. 5; xlvi. 6. Christ goes forth conquering and to conquer.

4. *And in thy majesty ride prosperously, because of truth and meekness and righteous-*

ness. Clarke: "These words cannot be spoken of Solomon: they are true only of Christ." The warlike figure of the preceding verse is here retained. Kings often went into battle in chariots, and as the enemy was routed they pressed forward triumphantly. But their conquest was with weapons of death, and amidst the slaughtered corpses and dying groans of their enemies. But the victories of Messias are those of *truth,*—his word, of *meekness,*—the meekness of Christ, and of *righteousness,*—the glorious rectitude of God, his glorious method of justifying sinners, and the unbending integrity of his people, whose righteousness exceeds that of the Scribes and Pharisees Some other renderings may interest the reader; Calvin: And in thy majesty do thou prosper: ride forth upon the word of truth, and meekness, and righteousness; Edwards: Ride on prosperously in the cause of truth, righteousness, and humanity, Green: Ride on successfully in the cause of truth, righteousness and meekness; Boothroyd: And in thy majesty ride prosperously on, in the cause of truth, meekness and righteousness. The clause may mean that Christ's riding prosperously is in the cause of truth, meekness and righteousness. *And thy right hand shall teach thee terrible things.* Chaldee: And the Lord shall teach thee to work fearful things with thy right hand; Green: And let thy right hand direct thee *to do* formidable things; Horsley: For thy own right hand shall show thee wonders; Hengstenberg: And thy right hand will teach thee terribleness. The sense is that his right hand should guide him to do things terrible to his foes. Nothing fills men's hearts with greater fear than the rapid spread of the truth, humility and righteousness of the Gospel, Acts ii. 43. Compare Ps. xl. 3.

5. *Thine arrows* are *sharp in the heart of the king's enemies;* whereby *the people fall under thee.* No arrows pierce so deep as the arrows of truth. They produce the most pungent convictions, pricking men in the heart, making them cry aloud for mercy, Acts ii. 37; xvi. 29; 1 Cor. xiv. 24, 25. There are two ways in which the wicked *fall* before Christ; one is to ask and receive mercy; the other is to sink under the weight of his wrath. If men despise his grace, they shall be crushed by his power, Isa. viii. 14, 15; Luke ii. 34. He is "a king, against whom there is no rising up." All his incorrigible foes must perish, for he is God:

6. *Thy throne, O God,* is *forever and ever.* This verse and the next are quoted entire by Paul in Heb. i. 8, 9, for the purpose of establishing the divinity of Jesus Christ. We may rely with infallible certainty upon the interpretation there given. The rendering of this clause in all the ancient versions is the same as that of the English. It is a groundless conceit that the name *God* is applied to Messiah here not in his divine nature, but in his mediatorial character only. The true and proper divinity of Christ is plainly and beyond all question here asserted. The clause refers to him who is by John called *the true God* and by Isaiah *the mighty God.* It cannot without violence be applied to Solomon. His *throne,* either as held by himself or his carnal offspring, was not *for ever and ever,* or to *eternity and perpetuity.* Strenuous efforts have been made to turn aside this passage from its obvious and inspired interpretation. But Hengstenberg well says that the non-Messianic expositors have not been able to bring forward anything grammatically tenable. *The sceptre of thy kingdom is a right sceptre.* Arabic and Hengstenberg: A sceptre of equity is the sceptre of thy kingdom; Calvin: The sceptre of thy kingdom is the sceptre of equity; Tholuck: The sceptre of thy kingdom *is* a sceptre of justice; Alexander: A sceptre of rectitude (is) the sceptre of thy kingdom. This clause can be applied without stint or qualification to Messiah; but only in a limited sense to Solomon, who at times very far departed from *rectitude.* Solomon often erred; Messiah never, never, never.

7. *Thou lovest righteousness, and hatest wickedness.* Here our version has *lovest, hatest;* in the New Testament it follows the Hebrew and Septuagint, *hast loved, hast*

hated. This clause is applicable to Solomon in a very limited sense only; to Christ without restriction. *Therefore God, thy God, hath anointed thee with the oil of gladness above thy fellows.* Messiah was "that holy thing" at his birth. He was by nature, not by a process of sanctification, "holy, harmless, undefiled, and separate from sinners." He never offended his Father, but pleased him well. Therefore above all the kings of earth, his *fellow* princes, has his joy arisen, and it shall be perpetual and augmenting forever. Christ had the anointing of the Holy Ghost without measure. Hence some have thought perhaps correctly that the direct reference here was to the Spirit. The allusion is based on the custom of anointing honored guests at feasts. See on Ps. xxiii. 5. All this coincides with Paul's teachings in Phil. ii. 8–11. Scott happily blends both ideas: " God the Father, as ' his God,' in respect of his human nature and mediatorial offices, has given him the Holy Spirit, without measure, that, being thus anointed to be our Prophet, Priest and King, he might have the pre-eminency in the gladdening gifts and graces of the Holy Spirit, the Comforter; and from his fulness might communicate them to his *fellows*, his brethren in human nature." The anointing oil of the ancients was compounded after the art of the apothecary, Ex. xxx. 25, there being added to it costly aromatics:

8. *All thy garments* smell *of myrrh, and aloes,* and *cassia, out of the ivory palaces, whereby they have made thee glad.* Our version of these words gives the sense and agrees with the Syriac, although there is in the Hebrew no verb corresponding to *smell.* Here are a few of the various renderings. Chaldee: All thy vestments are perfumed with the tender myrrh, the lign-aloes and the cassia. From palaces which are built of *Armenian* ivory they shall gladden thee; Edwards: All thy garments gladden thee with the odors of myrrh, aloes and cassia out of the ivory cabinets; Green: All thy garments out of the ivory wardrobes, *perfumed* with myrrh, aloes, and cassia, delight thee *with their fragrance.* *Myrrh,* mentioned in the directions given for making the " oil of holy ointment" in Ex. xxx. 23–25. See also Est. ii. 12; Pr. vii. 17; Cant. i. 13; iii. 6; iv. 6, 14; v. 1, 5, 13. *Aloes* are mentioned in three other places in the Old Testament, sometimes in the masculine as in Num. xxiv. 6, [rendered lign-aloes;] Pr. vii. 17; in Cant. iv. 14, as here in the feminine. In several parts of Asia there is a shrub, or tree called aloes, seldom growing higher than eight or ten feet. The wood and the resin gathered from it are very aromatic. The Egyptians used it in embalming. Nicodemus brought a hundred pounds of myrrh and aloes to embalm the sacred body of Jesus. Cassia was an ingredient of the holy oil mentioned above. It was a part of the merchandize of Tyre, Ezek. xxvii. 19. It was a bark, somewhat like cinnamon but not of so fine a flavor, though highly esteemed.

The garments of eastern princes were very costly, Luke vii. 25. The richest were worn only on great occasions. King's raiment was often kept in *wardrobes,* or *cabinets,* as some prefer, rather than *palaces.* These were often costly and ornamented with *ivory.* Or the *ivory palaces* may have been the abodes of kings or of rich men about whose residences was much work made of ivory. Ahab had such a palace, 1 Kings xxii. 39; Amos iii. 15 speaks of "houses of ivory." The best sense of the phrase—*From which they rejoice thee*—is had by making *they* refer to the *kings' daughters* mentioned in the next verse. Indeed some versions put no pause after *glad,* and make kings' daughters the nominative of the last verb in v. 8, though this is unnecessary.

9. *Kings' daughters* were *among thy honourable women.* Among the early converts to Christ, "honorable women" are expressly mentioned, Acts xvii. 12. And some lovely specimens of piety have been found in palaces. "Not many noble," still some such are called. *Upon thy right hand did stand the queen in gold of Ophir.* Four opinions more or less obtain as to the geographical position of Ophir. 1. Some place it in southern Arabia; 2. Others think it was in south Africa; 3. Josephus places it

in the peninsula of Malacca; 4. Others suppose it designates India generally. The controversy is not likely to be settled. What we can learn of it may be found in 1 Kings ix. 26–28; x. 11, 22; xxii. 48; 2 Chron. viii. 18; ix. 10. The "gold of Ophir" was celebrated as early as the days of the man of Uz, Job xxii. 24; xxviii. 16. It was of the best quality. The queen was arrayed in it, *i. e.*, her ornaments were made of it, or it was inwoven in her attire. Scott: "By 'the queen,' the collective body of believers seems to be intended, who, clothed in the righteousness of Christ, enriched by his bounty, and adorned by the graces of his Spirit, adhered to him in singleness of affection and fidelity, and are admitted to the most endeared union and communion." *Queen*, wife, spouse, consort; but the wife of the king is queen. The stability of the relation between Christ and his spouse is not feebly intimated in the word rendered *stand*. The right hand is the place of highest honor; see 1 Kings ii. 19.

10. *Hearken, O daughter, and consider, and incline thine ear.* These words summon the bride to seriousness, thoughtfulness, and attention to a weighty charge: *Forget also thine own people, and thy father's house.* As a wife should give up all that is dearest to her, and forsake even father and mother, and cleave to her husband, so the church is called on to put a comparatively low estimate on everything that has been most dear to her, and cleave unto Christ. She must come out from the world, its follies, iniquities and idolatries.

11. *So shall the King greatly desire thy beauty.* Serving Christ in simplicity and godly sincerity, with purity and fidelity, is the way to please him. "The righteous Lord loveth righteousness." The whole tenor of Scripture shows the necessity of personal holiness. Wo to him that makes Christ the minister of sin, and from his grace infers that we may live in uncleanness. Christ is to be obeyed and worshipped. *For he is thy Lord.* Others have had dominion over us; but to Christ only may we yield implicit and supreme obedience. He is Lord of all to the glory of God the Father and to the comfort of all his saints. *And worship thou him. Worship*, in Ex. xx. 5 and often, *bow down;* and often as here, Ps. xxix. 2; xcvi. 9; xcvii. 7. Even in his humiliation Jesus Christ never refused humble and adoring worship. He receives the worship of angels and saints in glory, Rev. v. 9–14.

12. *And the daughter of Tyre* shall be there *with a gift.* Chaldee: The inhabitants of the city Tyre shall come with a gift. A city is often called *daughter.* The Arabic erroneously has daughters of Tyre. Hengstenberg and others blend this clause with the next, so as to give this sense: The daughter of Tyre, even the rich among the people, shall implore thee with gifts. Perhaps there is no good objection to this construction. Tyre was the commercial metropolis of the world. She also had great wealth. She is fitly named as the most famous of Gentile cities, and as leading the way in bringing riches, honor and glory, and laying them at the feet of Jesus. If the two clauses are not blended we have in the second an extension of the main thought of the first: Even *the rich among the people shall entreat thy favour.* This rendering is clear and good.

13. *The king's daughter is all glorious within. King's daughter* here is the same as *queen* in v. 9. *Within* is by the best expositors referred to her position *within doors*, in the interior of the palace, whence she had not yet come forth. Boothroyd: All glorious is the queen in her apartment. *Her clothing is of wrought gold, i. e.,* gold inwoven into her clothing. Her attire is suitably and richly adorned with gold Boothroyd: Her robe is embroidered with gold.

14. *She shall be brought unto the king in raiment of needlework.* Fry: In a robe of embroidery is she conducted to the king; Hengstenberg: In variously wrought garments she is brought to the king; Alexander: With variegated clothes shall she

be conducted [or, escorted in procession] to the king. Without overstraining any figure here found, it is with pleasure that the devout mind discovers the admirable fitness of such terms, as we have in vv. 13, 14, to express the Scriptural doctrine of the glorious righteousness with which believers in Christ are adorned. The allusion no doubt is to the custom of going forth to meet the bridegroom, as we at once read: *The virgins her companions that follow her shall be brought unto thee.*

15. *With gladness and rejoicing* shall *they* be brought: *they shall enter into the king's palace.* The eastern mode of celebrating marriage, here alluded to, was in vogue in our Saviour's day; and indeed is still observed in some places. As the friend of the bridegroom rejoiced in the bridegroom's voice and happiness; so did the virgins rejoice in the gladness and honors of the bride. All nations have agreed that a marriage should be regarded as an occasion of joy. The marriage of kings and princes is fitly attended both with joy and magnificence.

16. *Instead of thy fathers shall be thy children, whom thou mayest make princes in all the earth.* The Hebrew text shows that the queen is not here addressed, but the king, who is spoken of in v. 1, and directly addressed in vv. 2–9. To him is promised a seed to serve him, a seed, who should be great indeed. They should be *princes*, and prevail with God. God's people are *kings* and *priests* even upon earth, Rev. i. 5, 6. Calvin: "It is easy to gather that this prophecy is spoken expressly concerning Christ; for so far were the sons of Solomon from having a kingdom of such an extent, as to divide it into provinces among them, that his first successor retained only a portion of his kingdom." The sons of God on earth are not made lords over God's heritage. They have no dominion over the faith of men. But in prayer, in a pious life and in holding forth the truth of God they exert a prodigious power over men. Christ's religion has marvellously revolutionized the opinions and practices of mankind.

17. *I will make thy name to be remembered in all generations.* Several versions and interpreters prefer to render thus: They (meaning *thy sons*) in perpetual succession shall make thy name to be remembered." This indeed gives a good sense. Christ's people are his witnesses to the ends of the earth. But the safer way is to make the Father the speaker here, and then the promise is parallel to Isa. liii. 10, 11. Or, the author of the Psalm is the speaker and by the Spirit of prophecy foretells the happy use that would be made of this ode in all coming generations. *Therefore shall the people praise thee for ever and ever.* This settles the question of the everlasting duration of Christ's kingly office and of the glorious reward secured to him. Not only shall unborn generations yet praise him on the earth, but all glorified spirits shall forever praise him in the house not made with hands, eternal in the heavens.

DOCTRINAL AND PRACTICAL REMARKS.

1. It is a blessed thing to be a friend of the Lord Jesus Christ. All his people are his *loves*, or *loved ones*. His love is stronger than death. It never grows cold. It never changes. It makes persons happy, families blessed, churches joyful and nations glorious.

2. Let nothing unsettle our faith in the divine inspiration of the Scriptures. They assert it. They claim it, v. 1; and often elsewhere. Henry: "We call the prophets the *penmen* of Scripture, whereas they were but the *pen*."

3. When the heart is full and warm, the tongue will not be silent, v. 1. It is a sad thing to be possessed of a dumb devil. It is a blessed thing both to have good thoughts, and when they have duly affected us, to utter them.

4. In religion everything turns on our views of Christ, v. 2. What do we think of him? Is he in our esteem incomparable? Do we regard him as "fairer than the children of men?" Is he, or is he not the chiefest among ten thousand and alto-

gether lovely? If thou lovest him not, if thou admirest him not, if thou wouldst not on a fair trial die for him, thou art none of his, Luke xiv. 26, 27, 33.

5. None can decide in which of his offices the Lord Jesus Christ is the most glorious, or most precious. He does all his work to the admiration of saints and angels and the entire good pleasure of his Father. *Grace is poured into his lips,* v. 2. His testimonies are wonderful, Ps. cxix. 129. His doctrines are pure truth. His commands are all right. The very officers sent by the priests and Pharisees to arrest him were rendered powerless by his words, and returned without him, saying, Never man spake as this man, John vii. 46. He is the great subject and the author of holy Scripture, Rev. xix. 10; 1 Pet. i. 11.

6. He, who fully and rightly believes that God is just and true, ought to regard Jesus Christ as sent of God, for God *has blessed him for ever,* v. 2. And yet it is mournfully certain that many reject him. No man can call him Lord except by the Holy Ghost. Oh that all would receive him. Then should they have power to become the sons of God, John i. 12.

7. There are no victories like those of truth, v. 3. No triumphs compare with those of God's word; all its conquests are benevolent and full of peace in the end.

8. Christ's kingdom being righteousness, and peace, and joy in the Holy Ghost, is not advanced by carnal weapons. Therefore God employs only such as are spiritual, v. 4. The cause of truth is not to be promoted by a lie. Fierceness will not teach men to be meek. The wrath of man worketh not the righteousness of God. It is a doctrine of none but the worst of men that we may do evil for the purpose of doing good.

9. There is much in Christ's kingdom that is *terrible* to wicked men. It is remarkable that even the threatenings and judgments of Zion's King often do not seem to strike so deep terror into their hearts, as do the displays of his love and mercy. The conversion, more than the sudden death of a notorious sinner, has often alarmed the secure.

10. And as Christ's *sword,* so his *arrows* make conquests for him and subdue his foes, v. 5. Morison: "By the two methods of judgment and mercy the Messiah deals with the children of men: his arrows either pierce the heart and humble it to receive his great salvation, or they smite the guilty opposer in the dust, and leave him the instructive monument of divine wrath."

11. On the first clause of v. 6, Dr. John M. Mason has given to the world the best discourse he ever preached. Should this remark lead the reader to procure and examine that sermon, he will be repaid. It is entitled "Messiah's Throne."

12. Whatever mistakes men have fallen into respecting Christ and his kingdom, none is wider of the truth than that he will at any time or in any way forget or fail to do justice, equity, righteousness. Justice and judgment are the habitation of his throne. His very *sceptre* is *rectitude,* v. 6. He *loves righteousness* so that he gave his soul to death rather than attempt to take sinners to heaven over the down-trodden government of God. He *hates wickedness* so that nothing that *defileth,* or *loveth a lie* shall ever enter the holy city, v. 7.

13. How kind and condescending is Christ towards humble believers. Here they are "his fellows." In Ps. xxii. 22, they are his "brethren." In John xv. 15, he calls them "friends." In other places he calls them "children," "heirs," "sheep," "lambs." O kind Redeemer, win us to thyself. Persuade and enable us to love thee more.

14. Christ's exaltation is in just proportion to his former humiliation; his joy, to his former grief; his riches, to his earthly poverty. Because none ever served or suffered as he, none reigns or rejoices as he. In all things he has the pre-eminence.

He is the first-born of every creature, v. 7. Clarke: "None was ever by the will of God constituted *prophet, priest,* and *king,* but Messias himself." His name is as ointment poured forth. His very raiment is full of sweet odors, v. 8.

15. Persons of high birth and rank may be saved, vv. 9, 12. There is much danger that such will be hardened in pride and wholly forget God. But in all ages there have been some pious persons of high social position in the church of God.

16. The Lord Jesus loves the church. She is near and dear to him, and honorable in his sight. She is *at his right hand,* v. 9. Nothing is so precious in his sight. He died for her.

17. Nothing is more proper than that we should renounce all for Christ, v. 10. It is easy to love the best earthly and temporal things excessively; but it is impossible to love Christ too much.

18. Jesus Christ loves entire consecration to his service; he considers it *beauty,* and much *desires* it, v. 10. The way to be rich is to become poor. The way to have much communion with the Saviour is to care for nothing so much as his love. No bridegroom ever rejoiced over his bride, or loved her as Jesus loves his spouse, in her purity and integrity.

19. If Christ is the Husband, he also is the *Lord* of his church, v. 11. He must be obeyed promptly, uniformly, universally, cheerfully, lovingly.

20. If the worship which we are commanded to render to Jesus Christ (v. 11) does not establish his divinity, how can any man establish the divinity of the Father or his claim to religious homage?

21. Dickson: "When the church honoreth Christ he will honor her, and make the noble and the potent in the world submit themselves to her, and seek communion with her," v. 12. Luther: "Hold thy bridegroom in honor, and thou shalt be in honor among all people, for he is so very powerful."

22. As prophets foretold the calling of the Gentiles, we ought like the early Christians to make much of that great event, v. 12. Compare Ps. lxxii. 8–11; Isa. lx. 4–17: Acts xi. 18; Rom. xv. 10–16. Since the resurrection of Christ the calling of the Gentiles has been the most important event that has occurred.

23. Christ's people are wonderfully adorned by the spotless robe of righteousness which they wear, and by the personal holiness wrought in them by the Holy Spirit, vv. 11, 13, 14. Compare Rev. iii. 18; xix. 8.

24. Every pure person shall be saved, vv. 14, 15. Every man who can enter into the holy delight of heaven shall go to that happy place. None shall be shut out of paradise to whom it would be a paradise.

25. True religion has joys both here and hereafter, v. 15. They are spiritual. They shall last and increase for ever.

26. Christ's glories are not from his progenitors, but from his progeny; not from his ancestors, but from his children, v. 16.

27. The glories of Christ's kingdom on earth shall increase more and more, v. 16. Much as the princes of this world despise it, it is a kingdom of *princes.* It shall yet fill the whole earth. Christ shall be *remembered* and *praised* by numbers far exceeding all that have ever yet followed him.

28. Much good may be done by composing even one of the songs of Zion. David foresaw that this Psalm would be used to the end of time, v. 17. A good paragraph or hymn written now may refresh the saints even through the Millennium. Bishop Heber's missionary hymn has done more to advance religion and make known the name of the author than the two volumes of his literary remains beside.

PSALM XLVI.

To the chief Musician for the sons of Korah, a Song upon Alamoth.

1 GOD *is* our refuge and strength, a very present help in trouble.

2 Therefore will not we fear, though the earth be removed, and though the mountains be carried into the midst of the sea;

3 *Though* the waters thereof roar *and* be troubled, *though* the mountains shake with the swelling thereof. Selah.

4 *There is* a river, the streams whereof shall make glad the city of God, the holy *place* of the tabernacles of the Most High.

5 God *is* in the midst of her; she shall not be moved: God shall help her, *and that* right early.

6 The heathen raged, the kingdoms were moved: he uttered his voice, the earth melted.

7 The LORD of hosts *is* with us; the God of Jacob *is* our refuge. Selah.

8 Come, behold the works of the LORD, what desolations he hath made in the earth.

9 He maketh wars to cease unto the end of the earth; he breaketh the bow, and cutteth the spear in sunder; he burneth the chariot in the fire.

10 Be still, and know that I *am* God: I will be exalted among the heathen, I will be exalted in the earth.

11 The LORD of hosts *is* with us; the God of Jacob *is* our refuge. Selah.

ON all the title except the last two words, see on titles of Psalms iv. xxx. xlii. xlv. *Upon Alamoth* occurs also in 1 Chron. xv. 20, where we read that certain persons "were appointed to sound with Psalteries on Alamoth." *Alam* signifies secret or hidden. It is so rendered by the Septuagint, Arabic and Vulgate. The Chaldee explains it of Korah being *hidden* [or swallowed up]. The Arabic calls it a prophecy concerning the secrets of the Son; Horsley: Concerning mysteries. This explanation is not satisfactory to many. Alamoth is rendered *virgins* in Cant. i. 3, 6, 8. Some would here read virginals or virgin tunes. A majority refer it to the tune or the instrument. So Calvin, Ainsworth, Patrick, Morison and others. Tholuck: To the tune of the virgins; Hengstenberg: After the virgin manner; Alexander thinks it denotes soprano or treble voices. It probably in some way refers to the music. The date and authorship of this ode are both uncertain. The Syriac, Patrick and Dodd ascribe it to David; Rosenmuller thinks it was written on occasion of the great victory of Jehoshaphat, noticed in 2 Chron. xx. Patrick thinks it celebrates some of the great victories gained by David and mentioned in 2 Sam. viii. Dodd and Henry are of the same opinion. Gill regards it as a prophecy of the church in gospel times, and as applicable to any state of confusion and distress among the nations. Calmet puts it much later, and thinks it refers to the convulsions which shook the Persian Empire after the death of Cambyses. Venema and some others refer it to the times of the Assyrian troubles, and make Isaiah the author. Calvin, Scott, Tholuck, Hengstenberg and Alexander refer it to the times of Hezekiah when Sennacherib's great army perished in a night. The stirring events of David's time would allow us to ascribe it to him. Scott dates it B. C. 710; Clarke B. C. 519. This was Luther's favorite Psalm. His famous hymn, written on his way to the Diet at Worms, beginning

A strong fortress is our God,

is very much taken from it. In the darkest times he used to say, "Come, let us sing the 46th Psalm, and let them do their worst." He says, "We sing this Psalm to the praise of God, because God is with us, and powerfully and miraculously preserves and defends his church and his word, against all fanatical spirits, against the gates of hell, against the implacable hatred of the devil, and against all the assaults of the world, the flesh and sin." Arnd: "This is a fine consolatory Psalm, wherein God's marvellous working is praised, as he protects his little flock of believers, and preserves them through such great necessities of war and persecutions, that it might seem as if the world was going to wreck." Anderson: It contains "rather the language of faith under threatened difficulties, than of triumph over vanquished foes." In it we have three names of the Almighty, *Jehovah* LORD, *Elohim God* and *Gel-yohn Most High*, on which see on Ps. i. 2; iii. 2; vii. 17. On *Selah* see Introduction, § 15.

1. *God* is *our refuge and strength.* This is an abrupt but exalted opening, *q. d.,* Others may rely on armies or on created things, but to us God alone is a refuge and strength. *Refuge,* as in Ps. xiv. 6; commonly so rendered; sometimes *shelter, trust, hope,* Ps. lxi. 3; lxxiii. 28; Jer. xvii. 17; Joel iii. 16. *Strength,* as in Ps. viii. 2; xxviii. 7, and often; in Hab. iii. 4, *power.* It may mean either the depository or the source of power. All our strength is in him. All our strength is from him. He is *a very present help in trouble.* The first clause announced a general proposition, this gives a particular under it. It is rendered variously. Chaldee: He shall be eminently found a help in affliction; Arabic: And our helper in times of tribulation, thou hast stood by us in all time; Ainsworth: A help in distresses we shall find very great; Clarke: He is found an exceeding, or superlative help in difficulties; Hengstenberg: A help in necessities is he found most truly. For *present* Pool prefers *sufficient;* Edwards, *immediate. Help,* as in Ps. xxvii. 9; xxxv. 2. *Trouble,* as in Ps. ix. 9; plural here—*troubles, adversities, tribulations, distresses, afflictions.* The truth of this verse is fulfilled to the saints of all ages.

2. *Therefore will not we fear, though the earth be removed, and though the mountains be carried into the midst of the sea.* The pronoun *we* relates to such as truly receive the truth of v. 1. Alexander: "The simple idea expressed by these strong figures is, in the midst of the most violent changes and commotions." *Though the earth be removed* is by some rendered *Though the earth be turned upside down.* The *fear* here spoken of is the fear of dismay, or of amazement, freedom from which is not the same as insensibility, but results from the confidence of faith. The heart of Mordecai is firm in the darkest day he ever saw, Esther iv. 14. *Mountains* are apt figures of the most stable states, or political constitutions.

3. Though *the waters thereof roar* and *be troubled,* though *the mountains shake with the swelling thereof. Selah.* This is an extension of the confident declaration begun in the preceding verse. Agitated *waters* are scriptural emblems for popular commotions. *Mountains* here also represent things supposed to be the most settled and stable. Some think the reference is specially to "secular rulers" long established in authority. Mountains do also represent strong natural defences. The righteous will not yield to disastrous fear, though the nations are convulsed with terrible excitements, and all the apparent safeguards of society are gone; no, not even when there is upon the earth distress of nations, with perplexity, and wicked men's hearts fail them for fear, and for looking after those things which are coming. Morison: "The earth thrown into a state of wild confusion, the mountains hurled into the mighty deep, the sea tossed into a tempest, and the everlasting hills drifting on its foaming billows, are the vivid images by which the divine judgments on wicked and persecuting nations are described in the language of the prophets."

4. There is *a river, the streams whereof shall make glad the city of God, the holy* place *of the tabernacles of the Most High.* The ancient versions and most modern translations are not so good as the common English. Edwards thinks the stream is the holy place. Calvin, Diodati, Green and others think the imagery is drawn from the small streams, which watered Jerusalem. By *stream* Watts understands Scripture; Henry, God's word and ordinances; Scott, the graces and consolations of the Holy

Spirit; Morison, the overflowing stream of divine mercy, which gladdens the saints. Hengstenberg interprets it of the stream of "the blessings of the kingdom of God," and cites, after Ainsworth, Gen. ii. 10; Ps. xxxvi. 8; John iv. 14; Ezek. xlvii.; Zech. xiv. 8; Rev. xxii. 1, in proof of his position. Alexander: "The mention of *streams* in the plural indicates variety and fulness of divine favor." At Smyrna the Scottish mission found a street watered by a river, occupying the place of the causeway, with trees overhanging it on each side, and securing refreshment to the inhabitants at all hours. In passages like this it is best to give to a word or phrase the fullest and richest meaning its usage, the context and the analogy of faith will allow. The streams of spiritual blessings flowing from God through Jesus Christ, by the Holy Ghost, make glad the city of God continually. Jerusalem was the type of the true church of all ages.

5. *God is in the midst of her.* Chaldee: The majesty of God is in the midst of her. God, with all his nature and perfections, is on the side of his church. Such a form of expression indicates gracious and powerful presence, Deut. xxiii. 14; Isa. xii. 6. *She shall not be moved.* All her history shows that the presence of God is sufficient to give stability to his church in any circumstances. *God shall help her.* The verb *help* here is of the same origin and import as the noun *help* in v. 1. It signifies the kind and measure of assistance required. It shall also be timely and seasonable. And that *right early.* Margin: When the morning appeareth; Calvin and Jebb: At the dawn of the morning; Fry: At early dawn; Green: Before the morning appears; Hengstenberg: At the break of morning. The sense is clearly: At the peep of day, *i. e.*, as Pool has it, "speedily, after a short night of affliction, compare Ps. xxx. 5; and seasonably, when the danger is greatest, and the enemies prepare to make the assault; which is commonly done in the morning." Diodati had given the same explanation and refers to Ex. xiv. 24, 27; 2 Chron. xx. 20, as illustrating the passage. Some give the additional idea that the help comes *very early* before the enemy could make the assault. Alexander: "The terms of this verse become still more significant and striking, if we suppose a specific reference to the night in which Sennacherib's host was smitten, and the sight which was disclosed at break of day," Isa. xxxvii. 36; xvii. 14.

6. *The heathen raged, the kingdoms were moved.* Church of England: The heathen make much ado. *Heathen,* nations, Gentiles, see on Ps. ii. 1. *Raged,* were *troubled,* were disquieted; in v. 3, in the future *roar.* By the *kingdoms* we are to understand all the surrounding hostile nations, whose kings sought the destruction of the Jews. *Were moved,* the preterite of the verb in v. 5, rendered *shall be moved.* Hengstenberg, *shake;* see on Ps. x. 6. Edwards renders the two clauses: The nations made an uproar; kingdoms were in a commotion. At length the right time came for God to step forth. *He uttered his voice, the earth melted.* The Chaldee refers all this to the giving of the law. But there is nothing to point us to Sinai. There is hardly any where a better specimen of condensed thought and rapid description than in this verse. The Hebrew is even more terse than the English. When Jehovah speaks, all nature stands aghast at the sound of his voice.

7. *The* LORD *of hosts is with us, the God of Jacob is our refuge. Selah.* LORD *of hosts* or *Jehovah of armies,* as in Ps. xxiv. 10. In Rom. ix. 29; Jam. v. 4, the common version gives us the Hebrew word here used for hosts—*Sabaoth.* On the title *God of Jacob,* see on Ps. xx. 1. By his natural attribute of omnipresence God is everywhere, but when he makes bare his arm, the saints triumph. There is great propriety in referring to the *God of Jacob* as a refuge. He protected that patriarch in a remarkable manner. *Refuge,* not the same as in v. 1, but the same as in v. 11; see on Ps. ix. 9; elsewhere *high tower, high fort, high place, defence.*

8. *Come, behold the works of the* LORD, *what desolations he hath made in the earth.* Chaldee: Walk about, see the works of God who hath made desolations among the ungodly of the earth; Arabic: Come to see the works of God, the miracles which he has done upon the earth; Calvin: Come ye, consider the works of Jehovah, what desolations he hath made in the earth; church of England: O come hither, and behold the works of the Lord, what destruction he hath brought upon the earth. For *desolations* some read *devastations.* If the reference is to the destruction of Sennacherib's army, the *desolations* were indeed frightful, though none fought against his hosts but the angel of the Lord, 2 Kings xix. 35; Isa. xxxvii. 36.

9. *He maketh wars to cease unto the end of the earth; he breaketh the bow, and cutteth the spear in sunder; he burneth the chariot in the fire.* Calvin: He maketh battles to cease even to the end of the earth; Edwards: He has destroyed the whole apparatus of war throughout the country; Mudge and Dodd: He hath destroyed the artillery of war, to the end of the earth, or the land; Hengstenberg: Who silences wars to the ends of the earth. The rendering of the common version justly represents the extent of the peace procured—the end of the earth; church of England: All the world. *Chariot,* the Syriac, church of England, Calvin, Ainsworth, Edwards, Jebb, Fry and Alexander follow the Hebrew plural, *chariots.* The primary idea in the word is *round.* The Chaldee, Arabic, Septuagint, Vulgate, Ethiopic, Doway and Hammond have *shield* or *shields,* which indeed may well be put with the bow and the spear. It is admitted that a very different word is used when *chariots of war* are mentioned; see Ps. xx. 7; lxxvi. 6. The best exposition is probably given by Anderson: "There is probably here an allusion to the ancient custom of collecting the arms and armor of the vanquished into a heap, and setting it on fire. The image is employed to express complete victory," Josh. xi. 6; 2 Sam. viii. 4; Ezek. xxxix. 8–10. This was "also a Roman custom." See Æneid, book viii., line 560. "A medal struck by Vespasian, the Roman emperor, to commemorate the termination of his wars both in Italy and through all parts of the world, represents the goddess of Peace holding an olive branch with one hand, and in the other a lighted torch, with which she sets fire to a heap of armor."

10. *Be still, and know that I am God. Be still,* be quiet, stand off, leave off, forbear. Some make Ps. iv. 4 parallel. Strong restraint upon their passions is necessary, if men would learn anything to purpose, and especially if they would know that the Lord is God. *I will be exalted among the heathen, I will be exalted in the earth.* Jehovah has ever and in all lands been doing things which evinced his eternal power and godhead. His name was of old a terror to millions that rebelled against him. *Heathen,* as in v. 6. Even to the Gentiles God is known by the judgments which he executes. They are here warned "that if they proceed to act like madmen, God's power is not enclosed within the narrow limits of Judea, and that it will be no difficult matter for him to stretch forth his arm afar to the Gentiles."

11. *The* LORD *of hosts is with us; the God of Jacob is our refuge. Selah.* In v. 7 we have the very same words both in Hebrew and English.

DOCTRINAL AND PRACTICAL REMARKS.

1. In seeking comfort and protection go to God himself, v. 1. All his attributes, all his titles, all his promises show that he is wise and loving. The practice of the saints in all ages has been not to rest in any means or creature; but in God only.

2. It is specially wise to seek to God in the day of adversity—*in trouble,* v. 1. One great end of affliction is to cause us to return unto the Most High. The greater our distress, the more we need him. Experience is a great school for Christians. Without it they would be babes all their days. It works hope, and hope maketh not ashamed.

3 When God's people are weak, they are strong; when they are poor, they are rich; when they are brought low, they are raised high; when they are greatly afflicted, they are greatly comforted, because God is an *exceedingly great help* in trouble, v. 1.

4. The more the saint is tried the more will his confidence in God be seen to be well founded, vv. 1, 2, 3. Scott: "If our faith were as strong as our security is good, we need fear no combination of enemies, no revolutions in kingdoms, and no convulsions in nature; but, in the most tremendous dangers, might triumph in the fullest assurance of security and victory." Calvin: "Our faith is really and truly tested only when we are brought into very severe conflicts, and when even hell itself seems opened to swallow us up." The nature, throne and covenant of God being unchangeable, his children need not trouble themselves much with the things about which the children of darkness are eager. All nature may dissolve, but that does not affect the stability of the divine government and protection.

5. The resources of God's people are found in the perpetual stream of blessings which flow from his wisdom and mercy through Jesus Christ, v. 4. The glorious Lord is unto us a place of broad rivers and streams. Henry: "The spiritual comforts which are conveyed to the saints by soft and silent whispers, and which come without observation, are sufficient to balance the most loud and noisy threatenings of an angry and malicious world."

6. God's presence with his church secures her stability and her timely succor, v. 5. Calvin: "If we desire to be protected by the hand of God, we must be concerned above all things that he may dwell amongst us; for all hope of safety depends on his presence alone;" Dickson: "God's presence among his people will not exempt them from trouble, but from perdition in trouble; he will not exempt the bush from burning, but from being consumed."

7. The church is safe, v. 5. She cannot be overthrown. Her walls are salvation.

8. No real harm can befall any child of God walking in the path of duty. To such sooner or later enlargement and deliverance will come. God will send timely supplies, v. 5. Seasonable blessings are double blessings.

9. It is no new thing for the world to be in commotion; but God can put down violent agitations anywhere, v. 6. De Wette: "Jehovah commands quiet, and man obeys."

10. The resources of the Almighty are infinite. He is the Lord of hosts, v. 7. He commands and the stars fight his battles. He sends legions of angels where he will, and one angel destroys in one night an army of *one hundred and eighty-five thousand* men. All plagues and storms and earthquakes, all causes and all effects, are under his control.

11. All the truth and mercy shown to saints of old will be shown to God's people to the end of time. There is no change in the character of Jehovah. He is still the God of Jacob, v. 7. He is, forever, the refuge of his afflicted ones. Never was anything more futile than the war against the Lamb.

12. God's past mercies clearly show that no weapon formed against Zion shall prosper, and that rather than let his church perish he will fill the earth with desolations, v. 8.

13. Dickson: "Long preparations for war, arms and ammunition, which have been made with great labor and expense against his church, the Lord can soon give a short account of them, and make them useless when he pleaseth," vv. 8, 9.

14. Let all men, before engaging in acts of national hostility, well weigh the evils of war. It brings fearful *desolations*, v. 8. Before its instruments of destruction a land may be as the garden of Éden, but behind them a desolate wilderness, and nothing shall escape them, Isa. xiii. 6–10. Henry: "War is a tragedy which commonly

destroys the stage it is acted on." Let men who delight in the cruelties of war remember that their day is coming, Isa. x. 12–19.

15. A right estimate of the evils of war may teach us the true value of the blessings of peace, v. 9. Oh that all men would study the things that make for peace. The God of heaven is the God of peace.

16. Let modesty, quietness and docility mark all our behaviour as in the sight of God. Let all hearts *be still,* and *know that Jehovah is God,* v. 10. Horne: "Let our rebellious passions hear this divine edict, tremble, and obey."

17. Let us study with care the nature, the word and the will of God. Especially let us know that he is God, v. 10. Let us "understand that he is the Fountain of power, wisdom, justice, goodness, and truth."

18. There is hope for the heathen, not in their innocence, not in their virtues, not in their ignorance; but in the mercy of God, in the covenant of redemption, and in the prophecies respecting them, v. 10.

19. Verses 7, 11 remind us of the dying words of John Wesley: "The best of all is, God is with us." Slade: "Through life and death let this be our answer to every trouble, and every enemy, and every danger, and every fear, 'The LORD of hosts is with us, the God of Jacob is our refuge;'" Dickson: "The strength of the church stands in renouncing her own and fleeing unto God's strength;" Arnd: "If only our support does not depart from us, we may say, as Joshua and Caleb did of the heathen, Fear ye not, they are as bread to us, for their support has departed from them."

PSALM XLVII.

To the chief Musician, A Psalm for the sons of Korah.

1 Oh clap your hands, all ye people; shout unto God with the voice of triumph.
2 For the LORD most high *is* terrible; *he is* a great King over all the earth.
3 He shall subdue the people under us, and the nations under our feet.
4 He shall choose our inheritance for us, the excellency of Jacob whom he loved. Selah.
5 God is gone up with a shout, the LORD with the sound of a trumpet.
6 Sing praises to God, sing praises: sing praises unto our King, sing praises.
7 For God *is* the King of all the earth: sing ye praises with understanding.
8 God reigneth over the heathen: God sitteth upon the throne of his holiness.
9 The princes of the people are gathered together, *even* the people of the God of Abraham: for the shields of the earth *belong* unto God: he is greatly exalted.

ON the title see on titles of Psalms iii. iv. xlii. Scott dates this ode B. C. 1042; Clarke, B. C. 519. Calvin: "Perhaps it was composed by David." Abenezra and Kimchi refer it to the times of Messiah. Luther: "This is a prophecy concerning Christ." Gill thinks it foretells Christ's ascension to heaven and the consequent spread of the Gospel. Diodati, Patrick, Pool, Henry, Dodd, Morison and Scott make it Messianic. Some think it pairs with Ps. xlvi.; some with Ps. xlviii. See Introduction, § 12. A few, but with little support, think it was composed when the temple was dedicated. Hengstenberg and Alexander refer it to the victory of Jehoshaphat, 2 Chron. xx. Whether any historic occasion suggested its imagery we know not. We have here *Elohim God, Jehovah* LORD and *Gel-yohn Most High,* on which see on Psalms i. 2; iii. 2; vii. 17. The latter, v. 2, is rendered as an adjective.

1. *Oh clap your hands all ye people. People,* in the plural, *peoples.* Here it is used

to call both Jews and Gentiles—all nations.   To *clap the hands* is sometimes a sign of derision, as in Job xxvii. 23; Lam. ii. 15; Nah. iii. 19; Ezek. xxv. 6.   Here and in other places it expresses becoming joyfulness, 2 Kings xi. 12; Ps. xcviii. 8; Isa. lv. 12. Some think that clapping the hands also expresses *approbation;* but great joyfulness is certainly the main thing signified, when no derision is expressed.   *Shout unto God with the voice of triumph.*   Ainsworth: Shout *triumphantly* unto God with voice of shrilling; church of England: O sing unto God with the voice of melody; Edwards: Shout to God with triumphant voices; Hengstenberg: Shout to God with jubilee-voice.   *Triumph,* in the common version often rendered *singing;* also *rejoicing, crying,* once, *shouting,* Prov. xi. 10.   It signifies any loud and earnest cry, whether of gladness or of distress is determined by the connection.   The language of much of this Psalm may be borrowed from the victories of the Israelites over their enemies; but surely the eye of the prophet is fixed on something greater than any carnal conquests.   The great occasion of gladness is the ascension of Messiah to heaven and the consequent spread of the Gospel and reign of righteousness over the nations.

2. *For the* LORD *most high is terrible; he is a great King over all the earth.*   Calvin follows some ancient versions and has: For Jehovah is high, terrible, and a great King over all the earth; Green: For Jehovah, the Most High, is to be feared, he is the great King over all the earth; Hengstenberg: For the Lord, the Most High, is terrible, a great King over all the earth.   *Terrible,* a participle, commonly so rendered, or *dreadful, fearful, to be feared, to be had in reverence,* and in Ps. cxi. 9, *reverend.* Calvin: "This language is applicable only to the kingdom of Christ, who is called a high and terrible King."   Our Saviour is as greatly to be feared as he is worthy to be loved.   The love, which does not submit and obey, is spurious.   He is *King over all the earth,* universal Monarch and Sovereign.   Therefore,

3. *He shall subdue the people under us, and the nations under our feet.*   For *subdue* Calvin has *set in order;* Mudge, *destroy.*   The Hebrew verb is in the future.   Though many prophecies are delivered in the past tense, yet the future is always appropriate to a prediction.   *Subdue,* in its other forms commonly rendered *speak;* so here it may signify to *subdue* by speech, that is by a preached Gospel.   Pool, referring to Isa. v. 15; Mic. ii. 12, gives to *subdue* the sense of *lead* like *sheep,* or *bring into the fold,* and adds: "He seems to speak of such a subjugation of them, as was for the good of the people subdued, because this is matter of rejoicing to them, v. 1."   This is true of all who bow and take the yoke of Christ.

4. *He shall choose our inheritance for us, the excellency of Jacob whom he loved.*   Calvin: He hath chosen our inheritance for us, the glory of Jacob whom he loved; Ainsworth: He hath chosen for us our inheritance, the high excellency of Jacob, whom he loveth.   The *excellency* here spoken of is the *inheritance* of the first clause.   Some give the verb in the present, some in the preterite, and some, following the Hebrew, in the future.   The last is best here, if we regard the verse as a prophecy.   But Diodati prefers the preterite and thus paraphrases it: "He hath by his free election given us an excellent inheritance chosen out above all other, wherein consists all our glory; namely, the kingdom of heaven."   *Selah,* see Introduction, § 15.

5. *God is gone up with a shout, the* LORD *with the sound of a trumpet.*   This verse is the key to the right understanding of the whole Psalm.   There is no better rendering. For *shout* some have *triumph, jubilee.*   It denotes joy uttered in a hilarious voice. Calvin thinks there is here an allusion to the ancient ceremony, when the sound of trumpets was wont to be used in solemn assemblies.   Yet he says: "At the same time, the sacred writer, under that shadowy ceremony, doubtless intended to lead us to consider another kind of going up more triumphant—that of Christ when he 'ascended up far above all heavens,' (Eph. iv. 10) and obtained the empire of the world, and

armed with his celestial power, subdued all pride and loftiness." Diodati: "Spiritually and chiefly this verse ought to be referred to Christ's ascension into heaven."
The mass of interpreters give it this direction, either as the sole, or as the mystical
sense. The narrrative of our Lord's ascension in the New Testament is very brief.
But that it was the most august of all joyous events yet witnessed on earth we cannot
doubt. In his Gospel Luke says it was celebrated with great gladness, chap. xxiv.
50–53. Clarke: "The *shout* may refer to the exultation of the evangelists and apostles in preaching Christ crucified, buried, risen from the dead, and ascended to heaven."
Although there is no mention of a *trumpet* at Christ's ascension, yet the angels said he
should return as he left the world, and we know that his second coming will be with
the sounding of the trumpet, 1 Cor. xv. 52; 1 Thess. iv. 16. The whole scene of
Christ's ascension and the consequent reception of the Gospel were joyful events. He
led captivity captive and received gifts for men, even for the rebellious, Ps. lxviii. 18.

6. *Sing praises to God, sing praises; sing praises unto our King, sing praises.* As
in the English, so in the Hebrew we have the same verb four times repeated, sing, sing
Psalms, or sing praises. *Our King,* who has gone up, is *God.* The Lord Jesus is
divine, is truly the Son of God, is equal with God, is God. How praises were sung,
see Luke xxiv. 50–53. How they have been sung ever since, even in prisons and at
the stake, church history testifies. How closely the singing of praises is connected with
a lively state of piety, revivals of religion have always shown. No duty is more urgent.

7. *For God* is *the king of all the earth.* So Jesus claimed for himself, John v. 22;
Matt. xxviii. 18; Rev. i. 5; see also Rom. ix. 5 and many parallel places. He, who
rules as universal monarch, is to be worshipped. *Sing ye praises with understanding.*
Arabic: Sing to him with understanding; Septuagint and Ethiopic: Sing intelligently;
Vulgate and Doway: Sing ye wisely; Jerome: Sing learnedly; Amesius: Sing a didactic
Psalm; Green: Sing praise most skilfully; Clarke: Sing an instructive song; *i. e.,*
"Let *sense* and *sound* go together. Let your *hearts* and your *heads* go with your
voices;" Hengstenberg: Sing a song with edification. On *Maschil* here rendered *with
understanding,* see on title of Ps. xxxii. Then is God truly, rightly worshipped when
we sing with the spirit and with the understanding also, 1 Cor. xiv. 15. Such praises
are very proper:

8. *God reigneth over the heathen.* Calvin: He hath obtained the kingdom over the
heathen. *Heathen* as in Ps. xlvi. 6, 10. *Reigneth,* the verb uniformly expresses kingly
authority in exercise. He, who governs the Gentiles, sends them all the blessings
they have, and calls them to a knowledge of his great salvation, is worthy to be
lauded, for he does no wrong. *God sitteth upon the throne of his holiness.* Christ's
throne is holy because its decisions are those of spotless rectitude. *Sitting* here
expresses the readiness of the Judge of all the earth to hear causes and redress
wrongs.

9. *The princes of the people are gathered together,* even *the people of the God of
Abraham.* Calvin's rendering puts a new face on these words: The princes of the
peoples are assembled together to the people of the God of Abraham. The *princes*
here named are not the heads of tribes among the Israelites, but those among the Gentiles. Instead of *even* in the English version we may read *and, as, with,* or *to.* Alexander
prefers *as;* Calvin, Edwards, Jebb and Hengstenberg *to;* Mudge and Fry prefer *with.*
Even as would give the whole sense. The most distinguished and noble of the Gentiles
shall come and worship God *even as* the pious Jews. The reward of Messias was very
anciently expressed by a *gathering* of the people to him, Gen. xlix. 10. The same is
taught in later times, Isa. xi. 10. *The God of Abraham* is he, who is as faithful to
all his servants as he was to Abraham. This work shall surely be accomplished, *For
the shields of the earth* belong *unto God.* We had the word *shield* in Ps. iii. 3; vii. 10;

xviii. 2. Here the sense is that *protection* in every case, *protections*, are from God; or, that the *princes* of the nations, who are their *shields* and guardians, do yet belong to Jehovah. In Hos. iv. 18 the word is rendered *rulers*. All agents, all causes, all instruments, all means are God's, and so *He is greatly exalted.* He, who rules the world, can have no superior. He is Lord of angels; he is Lord of all.

DOCTRINAL AND PRACTICAL REMARKS.

1. Neither the prophecies, nor the Gospel confine the blessings of Christ's kingdom to the Jews, or to any one tribe of men, but extend them to *all peoples*, v. 1. Luke ii. 28–32; Rom. xi. 11, 13.

2. Those are greatly mistaken, who think the religion of Christ furnishes no cause of joy to those, who truly embrace it, v. 1. See REMARKS on Ps. ii. 11. In fact the blessings of the Gospel awaken the strongest and most pleasing emotions of the human heart, and shall yet fill the whole earth with incredible joy. Even of old the saints had cause of exulting and rapturous delight in the Lord and his ways. This is much greater under the Gospel. It shall be yet more unspeakably increased in heaven.

3. When religious affections are lively and controlling, they will often produce effects on men's bodily actions, quite unintelligible to mere formalists, v. 1. Henry: "Such expressions of pious and devout affections as to some may seem indecent and imprudent ought not to be hastily censured or condemned, much less ridiculed, because, if they come from an upright heart, God will accept the strength of the affection, and excuse the weakness of the expressions of it."

4. Yet we should never forget that godly fear is a part of all true worship, v. 2. Jehovah is the great and dreadful God, Deut. vii. 21; x. 17; Neh. i. 5; iv. 14; ix. 32; Isa. viii. 13. See REMARKS on Ps. ii. 11.

5. The kingly office of Christ is justly celebrated in the Scriptures, vv. 2, 7. It ought to possess a prominent place in our teachings and in our thoughts. He, who does not take Christ as his king, does not truly receive him as his prophet or priest. It is no intrusion upon the rights of others that Christ should establish his worship and kingdom in every nation; for he is King of kings and Lord of lords.

6. It is certain that the Gospel shall take effect and exert controlling power over the nations of the earth. Prophecy requires this, v. 3. The covenant of redemption requires it, Isa. xlix. 4–12. The covenant of grace requires it, Isa. lx. 1–22. Christ's death requires it, Isa. liii. 11, 12; Heb. xii. 2. Christ's intercession makes it sure, Ps. ii. 8. It cannot be that the earth shall not be full of the knowledge of the Lord as the waters cover the sea.

7. It is better for God to choose our inheritance for us than it is for us to choose it for ourselves, v. 4. It is better for us to have a sorrowful lot of God's choosing than a joyful portion of our own choosing. An affliction at God's hands is better than a joy of our own creation.

8. Excellent as are the earthly good things, bestowed on the saints, they are as nothing compared with heavenly blessings. Canaan in Syria was a dungeon compared to the Canaan above. The inheritance of the tribes of Israel was a mean and sorry thing compared to the inheritance which is incorruptible, undefiled, and that fadeth not away, reserved in heaven for all who are kept by the power of God, through faith unto salvation, ready to be revealed in the last time.

9. Christ's exaltation is taught in the Old Testament as well as in the New; and is as necessary to be believed as his humiliation, v. 5. Morison: "How glorious the tidings to the church, that her victorious Lord has gone up with a shout, to take possession of the heavenly inheritance in her behalf, and to assume the sceptre of universal empire." With majesty and glory shall he come again, Eph. iv. 8–10.

10. Our disinclination to spiritual duties must be very great to make it necessary so often to summon us to their performance, vv. 6, 7. Four times in one verse we are called on to *sing praises*. In the Hebrew there are six words in the verse, and four of them we render, *Sing praises*. In the next verse the call is repeated. God sees that we need line upon line. Yet praise is a heavenly duty. It will be the employment of the redeemed for ever and ever. Sinners saved by grace should abound in this duty. Luther: "Christ's kingdom is not one of that kind that stands in the power of arms, but in the word of praise, and in the singing of thanksgivings." Clarke: "Feel your obligation to God;—express it in thanksgiving;—be thankful;—be eternally thankful to God your king."

11. Because superstition is a great foe to true religion and offensive to God, our worship should always be *with understanding*, v. 7. This is also the doctrine of the New Testament. So Christ taught the woman of Samaria, John iv. So Paul taught his converts, 1 Cor. xiv. 7–19. We should sing *instructive Psalms*, offer intelligent and intelligible prayers, and *rightly divide* the word of God.

12. The Divinity of the Lord Jesus Christ is interwoven with all the prophecies respecting him, vv. 7, 8. To deny that he is equal with the Father is to rob him of his glory. Dickson: "He is eternally God, and no man reasonably or with understanding can praise him as the Redeemer, and Perfecter of what is spoken of him in Scripture, except he acknowledge him to be God; therefore is Christ *eight* times in this Psalm called God, besides ascribing unto him works proper to God only; and twice he is called by the incommunicable name Jehovah, LORD;" and in v. 2, he is called *most high*, or *highest*. His divinity is supreme.

13. All nations are now under the providential government of Christ, and all nations shall yet be willingly subject to him as Lord of all, v. 8. Morison: "The prophets are accustomed to speak of things future as if they actually existed, and hence Jehovah is presented to our view as swaying the sceptre of his authority and love over the heathen." Ever since God had a church of redeemed sinners on earth, the future of her destiny has been brighter than her past history. It will be so forever.

14. The Judge of all the earth will do right. The King of heaven can do no wrong, because rectitude is the basis of his throne, v. 8. It is an inexpressible comfort to the upright to know that He, into whose hands as Judge and King they have committed their eternal all, cannot fail to do that, which is spotlessly pure!

15. The riches and glory of the Gentiles shall be brought to Christ, v. 9.

16. It is not idle for believers to appeal to Jehovah as the God of Abraham, because to all believers God is the same as he was to Abraham, in faithfulness, love and mercy, v. 9. We are too apt to look on Abraham rather as a Jew than as a Gentile, and to forget that the covenant was made with him while he was yet an uncircumcised Gentile, Rom. iv. 9–13. Hengstenberg: "The designation of God as the God of Abraham, points, as appears, to the promise of blessing on all peoples."

17. Calvin: "All who would be reckoned among the children of God, ought to seek to have a place in the Church, and to join themselves to it, that they may maintain fraternal unity with all the godly." They should be gathered to the people of the God of Abraham, v. 9.

18. Let us never forget that all our protection is from the Lord and from none other. The *shields* are all his, v. 9.

19. God is supreme. He is over all. He is greatly exalted, v. 9. Clarke: "Great as secular rulers are, God is greater, and is above all; King of kings, and Lord of lords: and the hearts of kings and governors are in his hand; and he turns tnem whithersoever he pleases."

PSALM XLVIII.

A Song *and* Psalm for the sons of Korah.

1 GREAT *is* the LORD, and greatly to be praised in the city of our God, *in* the mountain of his holiness.

2 Beautiful for situation, the joy of the whole earth, *is* mount Zion, *on* the sides of the north, the city of the great King.

3 God is known in her palaces for a refuge.

4 For, lo, the kings were assembled, they passed by together.

5 They saw *it, and* so they marvelled; they were troubled, *and* hasted away.

6 Fear took hold upon them there, *and* pain, as of a woman in travail.

7 Thou breakest the ships of Tarshish with an east wind.

8 As we have heard, so have we seen in the city of the LORD of hosts, in the city of our God: God will establish it for ever.   Selah.

9 We have thought of thy lovingkindness, O God, in the midst of thy temple.

10 According to thy name, O God, so *is* thy praise unto the ends of the earth: thy right hand is full of righteousness.

11 Let mount Zion rejoice, let the daughters of Judah be glad, because of thy judgments.

12 Walk about Zion, and go round about her: tell the towers thereof.

13 Mark ye well her bulwarks, consider her palaces; that ye may tell *it* to the generation following.

14 For this God *is* our God for ever and ever: he will be our guide *even* unto death.

ON the title see on titles of Psalms xxviii. xxx. xlii.   Luther takes it for granted that David wrote this Psalm: "David is here celebrating the truth of God." Calvin is as confident that it is of later date: "It is easy to gather from the subject matter of the Psalm that it was composed after the death of David." Junius and Tremellius and Dodd are of opinion that it may be as old as the time of the sweet singer of Israel.   Ainsworth, Mudge, Dathe, Pool, Clarke, Hengstenberg and several others think it was written at a later day.   Clarke puts it after the captivity. Of those who give it a later date some find its historic occasion in 2 Chron. xx.; others, in the deliverance under Hezekiah, recorded in 2 Kings xviii. xix.   All these views are merely conjectural.   Henry speaks as wisely as any one when he says: "For aught I know, it might be penned by David, upon occasion of some eminent victory obtained in his time; yet not so calculated for that, but that it might serve any other the like occasion in after times."   Scott dates it B. C. 892; Clarke, B. C. 519.   In it we have *Jehovah* LORD and *Elohim* God, on which see on Ps. i. 2; iii. 2. On *Selah* see Introduction, § 15.   The whole Psalm, as applied to the gospel church, has a pleasing fulfilment from generation to generation.

1. *Great is the Lord, and greatly to be praised.*   For *greatly* Ainsworth has vehemently; church of England, highly; Chaldee, Vulgate, Doway, Jebb, Hengstenberg and Alexander, *exceedingly.*   In Ps. xxi. 1 the same word is rendered *greatly;* in Ps. xxxi. 11, *especially;* in Ps. xlvi. 1, *very;* in Ps. cxix. 4, *diligently.*   *Greatly* is not cognate to the *great* in this clause.   On two accounts God is greatly to be praised.   The first is the boundless excellence of his nature.   *Great is the Lord.*   The other is the amazing excellence of his acts—celebrated in the body of the Psalm.   *Praised,* as with Psalms.   The verb is of the same root as that from which the book of Psalms or *Praises* takes its name.   The Lord is greatly to be praised *in the city of our God,* in *the mountain of his holiness, i. e.,* in Jerusalem, and especially in the temple worship on Mount Zion.   On *mountain of his holiness,* see on Ps. ii. 6.   From Jerusalem and Zion in Judea our minds easily pass to the church of God on earth and then in heaven, where God is greatly to be praised.   See on Ps. xlvi. 4.

2. *Beautiful for situation, the joy of the whole earth,* is *mount Zion,* on *the sides of the north, the city of the great King.* Instead of *Beautiful for situation,* Horsley and others read, *Beautiful in extension, i. e.,* in the prospect which it presents to the eye; Hengstenberg: Beautiful by its elevation; Tholuck: A beautiful hill. But none of these is better than the common version. As seen from a distance Jerusalem was rather a city on a plateau than a high elevation as it seemed to the traveller who came in sight of it. For *the whole earth* some read *all the land, i. e.,* of Judea. If this is right, all will admit the perfect propriety of the language. A great part of human happiness on earth has in some way resulted from the existence of a church, of which Jerusalem was a type. Zion was in the southern part of Jerusalem. The part lying north is probably noticed to complete the account of the whole; or, some think the reference is to the *north side* of Mount Zion, where the temple stood. Whatever is the precise idea intended we cannot doubt that the language is drawn from a sight of *the city of the great King.* Jerusalem was the seat of the theocracy.

3. *God is known in her palaces for a refuge. Palaces,* the word occurs again in v. 13, and in Ps. cxxii. 7; not elsewhere in the Psalms. It might well be rendered *fortresses,* or *castles.* Green has *fortifications;* Mudge and Fry, *towers. Refuge,* see on Ps. ix. 9; elsewhere also rendered *high tower, high fort, defence. God is known* by his word, his oath, his covenant, and the history of his dealings with his people, individually and as a body; *known* in all the church, wherever his word is preached, and the Spirit of his grace poured out; *known* in all the high places of Zion as a *refuge,* a *refuge* to the poor and needy, the helpless and the perishing, who look to him for mercy and protection. His saints must not trust in fortresses, castles, palaces; but in God alone.

4. *For, lo, the kings were assembled, they passed by together.* Those who suppose this Psalm has special reference to the events recorded in 2 Chron. xx., or in 2 Kings xviii. xix., regard this and the next two verses as decisive in their favor. But from the first settlement in Canaan the nation of Israel often had kings and princes leagued against the people of Jehovah. The narrative of Ps. lxxxiii. is but a specimen of what often occurred. David himself was often conspired against. *Were assembled,* we are not told where, but at a point agreed upon, perhaps not far from Jerusalem. *Passed by,* either in their march upon Jerusalem, or in their making observations from the heights surrounding it, or they "*passed away*" from the city without accomplishing their designs. Fry: They passed away at once.

5. *They saw it, and so they marvelled; they were troubled,* and *hasted away.* Some regard this as an amplification of the fourth verse. If it is, it shows how the enemies were discomfited. A *sight* of the holy city filled them with *wonder,* and *trouble,* and they *hasted away.* Calvin: They saw, so they marvelled; they were frightened, they fled precipitately; Green: They no sooner looked, but were dismayed; they were routed, and fled away in confusion; Alexander: "The whole verse is descriptive of a panic leading to a disorderly retreat or flight." The verse is a fine specimen of rapid description.

6. *Fear took hold upon them there,* and *pain, as of a woman in travail.* Nothing is more unaccountable than panic. No man, no body of men can adequately guard against such terror. He who made the ears, can easily make them to tingle. He who holds the winds in his fist, can easily make them whisper alarm, or roar dismay. This is specially to be expected when men so act as to have their own consciences against them, Job xv. 21. But God can at any time so forsake men as that they shall be unmanned, and play the fool exceedingly, Lev. xxvi. 36. Men have fought bravely several battles and then played the coward. *A woman in travail* denotes the suddenness and the power of the fear which seized them.

7. *Thou breakest the ships of Tarshish with an east wind.* Anderson: "In the preceding verse the Psalmist had compared the terror which seized upon these combined powers with the pangs of a woman in travail; and here he compares it to the trembling which seized upon mariners when the fury of the east wind, which shattered in pieces the largest and strongest vessels, as the ships of Tarshish probably then were, was let loose upon them." For *east wind* the Chaldee has *a strong east wind from the presence of the Lord;* the Syriac, Arabic, Vulgate and Doway, *a vehement wind;* Septuagint, *a violent wind;* Mant says, "Such a wind is well known to the modern mariner by the name of *Levanter.*" Some suppose that "Euroclydon," in Acts xxvii. 14, is the same wind. The east wind of Syria and the Mediterranean has been famous in all ages. It parched up everything. It was very destructive. See Gen. xli. 6; Ex. xiv. 21; Job xxvii. 21; Isa. xxvii. 8; Jer. xviii. 17; Ezek. xix. 12; xxvii. 26; Jonah iv. 8. *Tarshish,* sometimes, designated a given place. This was probably a city near the site of the present *Cadiz* in the south of Spain. A *ship of Tarshish* was a ship that traded at Tarshish, or Tartessus. Afterwards any ship, intended for a long sea voyage, seems to have borne the name of this city, because like a ship of Tarshish it was large and strong. Thus Solomon fitted out ships on the Red Sea, which were called ships of Tarshish, probably, not because they sailed around Africa to Spain, nor because they sailed to a place called Tarshish in India, but because they were great ships, and sailed to far distant lands. Some assert that *Tarshish* signifies *Ocean,* or *Ocean-sea.* If so, a ship of Tarshish is merely a ship of the sea.

8. *As we have heard, so have we seen in the city of the* LORD *of hosts, in the city of our God.* History and experience are two great teachers. They well agree in giving the same lessons. What they had heard of God's doings at other times and places, they now witnessed before their eyes. The *city* here spoken of was Jerusalem, the type of the church of the living God. *The* LORD *of hosts* is he who commands the stars and they obey him, to whom the angels of heaven yield a swift obedience, and who decides every battle between conflicting hosts. *God will establish it for ever.* Some put the verb in the preterite, and some in the present tense; but we get the best sense by following the original, *will establish.* God will establish it against all foes, all perils, all machinations. Alexander: "As Jerusalem is here regarded not as a mere town, but as the seat of the theocracy, the earthly residence of God, the promise is still valid, in its strongest sense, with respect to the church, of which the ancient Zion was the constituted type and local centre."

9. *We have thought of thy lovingkindness, O God, in the midst of thy temple.* Arabic: O God, we have known thy mercy in the midst of thy people; Septuagint: We expected thy mercy in the midst of thy people; Vulgate and Doway: We have received thy mercy, O God, in the midst of thy temple; Ainsworth: We have quietly waited thy mercy, O God, in midst of thy palace. Hammond observes that this verb carries with it the "signification of *quiet, rest, silence, patient expecting, thinking, considering,* and must be determined to any of these senses by the context." He prefers here the sense of *expecting,* or *patient waiting.* The rendering *temple* by *people* is evidently an error in transcription, where one letter would make the difference. The thoughts and hopes of pious men in all ages have been wondrously stirred up in the worship of God.

10. *According to thy name, O God, so is thy praise unto the ends of the earth.* God's name is that by which he is known. And so we have here the assertion that where men have the true knowledge of Jehovah, there he is correspondingly praised. This is the most obvious sense. Calvin: "The Psalmist intended to show that wherever the fame of the name of God may be spread, men will know that he is worthy of the highest praise." With him agree Pool, Morison and Clarke. *Thy right hand is full*

of righteousness. See Job xxxvii. 23. The God of heaven does no wrong, and he plentifully rewardeth the proud doer.

11. *Let mount Zion rejoice, let the daughters of Judah be glad, because of thy judgments.* Green renders the verbs of this verse in the preterite; Edwards, Fry and Hengstenberg prefer the present; Calvin, Venema and Alexander follow the Hebrew closely and give the future; but the ancient versions, the church of England, Piscator, Fabritius, Amesius, Ainsworth, Boothroyd and Jebb agree with the English text. The term *daughters of Judah* may designate either the female portion of the Jewish people, who often figured in the exultations as also in the lamentations of the nation, Ex. xv. 20; 2 Chron. xxxv. 25; or, it may designate the cities or smaller towns which were dependent on Jerusalem; see Josh. xv. 45, 47. The latter view is preferred by Calvin, Diodati, Ainsworth and many others. The *joy* and *gladness* was to be *because of thy judgments.* *Thy judgments,* glorious decisions, and in this case the display of God's power and wrath against the wicked and in defence of his people. Several ancient versions and some modern translations close the verse with *O Lord,* but the Hebrew text does not allow it.

12. *Walk about Zion, and go round about her; tell the towers thereof.* The word rendered *towers* has not before occurred in the Psalms. It is almost uniformly rendered as here in the English version. In 1 Chron. xxvii. 25 it is rendered *castles.* In Gen. xi. 4, 5 in the singular, it designates the *tower* of Babel. It is the name for a strong fortification built by the skill and labor of man, and so not natural. The survey of Zion here called for was for the purpose of ascertaining the strength of that fortified hill.

13. *Mark ye well her bulwarks, consider her palaces.* *Bulwarks,* literally bulwark, are the rampart, the outer wall of a fortified town. Commonly there was a trench (sometimes filled with water) connected with it to render the wall more inaccessible. The word occurs again in Ps. cxxii. 7; and so does the word *palaces,* uniformly so rendered, except in Prov. xviii. 19, where it is *castle.* Perhaps *castles* might be a fit rendering here. It denotes strong and costly edifices. The renderings of verse 12 and of the first part of this verse are quite various, but in the end amount very much to the same thing. For *consider,* Tholuck has *roam through.* The common version gives the sense as well as any other, though the last verb does no doubt signify to *separate, count,* then to *consider* or *admire.* But there was no such prodigious strength of fortification at Jerusalem as to challenge peculiar admiration. We are compelled to seek a higher sense than we get from the literal Mount Zion. This we have in the church of God. Whatever the fortifications of Jerusalem were, they have all long since perished; but "the things signified by them shall remain for ever." If there is a historic reference in this Psalm then there may be a fitness in pointing to Jerusalem yet unhurt by the vaunting foe, now wholly discomfited; but the spiritual import of the passage is chiefly to be regarded, *that ye may tell* it *to the generations following.* No material structures at Jerusalem were ever worthy of so lasting recital as is here required; even if that city was once truly magnificent.

14. *For this God* is *our God for ever and ever.* The words are plain. The covenant relation of God to his people is for a standing joy to the righteous. His nature does not change. His relation to believers is *ever* the same. Therefore: *He will be our guide* even *unto death,* literally, He will lead us [or direct] us. *Even unto death, i. e.,* as long as we live; and not as some have it, *over death* or *at death,* though he will surely do these things also.

There seems to be no good reason for supposing with Hare and some others that the words *unto death* belong to the title of Psalm xlix. Nor is there any evidence as some think that the *first* verse of this Psalm belongs to Psalm xlvii.

DOCTRINAL AND PRACTICAL REMARKS.

1. Great thoughts of God are very becoming, because they are just and true, v. 1. They are very important, 1, to give us right views of our sinfulness and weakness, and 2, to elevate our conceptions in all our attempts to worship him.

2. It is not possible for us to praise God too much or in strains too exalted, for he is to be praised *exceedingly*, v. 1. God's nature demands no less. "None on earth render him due honor, except the citizens of the heavenly Jerusalem, who worship him in the mountain of his holiness, as their God and Saviour." And even their songs are poor compared with those which are sung in the temple not made with hands.

3. God's presence makes any place notable and desirable, v. 2. It makes a stone in the wilderness a Bethel. It makes Jerusalem the most famous city in the world. The birth of Jesus made Bethlehem, and his residence made Nazareth famous to all coming time. But all these were otherwise poor places, and the latter of them was even infamous.

4. What the holy city was to all Judea, the church of God is or shall be to the whole world—a joy and a rejoicing, v. 2. Dickson: "The church is the joy of the whole earth by holding out to all the light of saving doctrine, and showing the authority, power, wisdom, and grace of Christ."

5. Such joy is truly blessed, but all else is short-lived and unsatisfying. Calvin: "If the joy which men experience and cherish is without God, the issue of their joy at length will be destruction, and their laughter will be turned into the gnashing of teeth."

6. Christ's kingly authority is never to be forgotten or slighted. He is a "Great King," v. 2. Blessed are all they, who bow to his sceptre. But woe to him that rebels.

7. If God demands a service, he makes more than an adequate return; if he is our King, he is also a refuge, v. 3. "The great founder of the church is also her protector and defender." Palaces, towers, redoubts and bulwarks were not the defence of Israel, but God himself.

8. Neither the multitude nor the greatness of the church's foes need alarm her friends. Men can do nothing but play the fool and the coward, if God be against them, vv. 4, 5, 6. "As the east wind shatters the ships of Tarshish, so the divine power strikes terror and astonishment" into the hearts of sinners. All the imaginations that fill the minds of the foes of God and of truth will vanish like the mist of morning. The record of a people against whom God is fighting is very brief. Montgomery beautifully versifies a part of this ode:

> "At the sight of her splendor the kings of the earth
>   Grew pale with amazement and dread;
> Fear seized them like pangs of a premature birth;
>   They came, they beheld her, and fled.
> Thou brakest the ships from the sea-circled clime,
>   When the storm of thy jealousy lowers:
> As our fathers have told of thy deeds in their time,
>   So, Lord, have we witnessed in ours."

Dickson: "Such, as come to bring trouble to God's church, come to catch trouble to themselves."

9. In his nature and in his works and ways God is always equal to the best reports we have heard of him, v. 8. He always acts like himself. He never denies himself. Morison: "Nor shall the Lord of hosts leave himself without witness in any age of the church. The history of the past shall be but the model of the future; and every

successive generation of the saints shall prove the faithfulness and unchangeable conduct of him, who has promised to establish and build up Zion forever."

10. As worship is itself a delight to the pious, so the memory of seasons spent in the house of God is precious to the saints. They love to call them to mind, v. 9. Abraham probably never forgot Moriah; nor Jacob, Bethel.

11. If God were truly known and loved by all, then would all unceasingly praise him, v. 10. To all who know and love him the glorious Lord will be a sure defence. Of course he must be praised, and extolled, and become very high. If this Psalm has reference to the events noticed in 2 Chron. xx. then verse 29 of that chapter probably casts light on the kind of *praise* here spoken of.

12. We need never fear that God will act out of character. As there is a delightful harmony in the divine nature, so is there a glorious consistency in the divine conduct, v. 10. Henry: "In the great things that God has done, and is doing, for his church, it is good to take notice of the fulfilling of the Scriptures."

13. We cannot in any song or service dismiss the idea of God's infinite justice. His right hand is full of righteousness, v. 10. Compare Job xxxvii. 23. The divine clemency is worthy to be eternally celebrated, yet no more so than the awful rectitude of the divine character, which is the sure foundation of settled comfort in the church.

14. The Lord is known by the judgments which he executes. His enemies hate and tremble at his glorious deeds; but his people rejoice and adore, when Jehovah comes forth to enforce the decisions which he has made, Rev. xviii. 20. Dickson: "It becometh all men to be glad to see God glorify himself in deciding controversies equitably."

15. The church of God is impregnable, indestructible, vv. 8, 11, 12. Slade: "The church of Israel was preserved in the midst of her enemies, and why? 'God was well known in her palaces for a sure refuge.' The church of Christ has also been preserved in the midst of her enemies; and for the same reason." So shall it be till time shall be no longer, and all Israel shall be saved.

16. A reason why people when young and vigorous should study God's word and the history of his dealings with his church is, that they may have something instructive and profitable to talk about to the next generation, v. 13. All should publish the glory of God.

17. It is both fitting and obligatory to plead the covenant relation between God and us. It has always been done by pious men. What would become of poor afflicted believers, if they could not use such language as that in Isa. xxv. 9?

18. How precious is the doctrine of the unchangeableness of God. Because he is ever the same, we may infer safety and protection from mercies shown to like persons in ancient times, and may assure all that shall come after us that as God has been kind to us so will he be to them, if they will trust and obey him.

19. If we had nothing but prosperity and tokens of God's pleasure here, we should not care for a better world than this; and if we had no mercies here, we should hope for none hereafter. Tholuck: "Faith in a blissful eternity awakes most vividly when the mercy of God powerfully shines upon our temporal existence."

20. We feel the want of no blessing more than that of sufficient guidance; and we should appreciate such a favor very highly and have adoring gratitude for it. It is made sure to the meek. Dickson: "God will guide them whose God he is, when they seek his counsel out of desire to follow it, and he will not lay down the conducting and governing of those who have committed themselves unto him, but will guide them constantly all the days of their life."

21. Luther: "*We* sing this Psalm, because God is pleased to preserve his church

and gospel against the roaring and hatred of kings and princes; who cease not from attacking them by violence and craft with all their might : and yet, they shall perish and be confounded, and covered with shame, while the gospel shall remain as it was before, unhurt and unhindered."

PSALM XLIX.

To the chief Musician, A Psalm for the sons of Korah.

1 Hear this, all *ye* people; give ear, all *ye* inhabitants of the world:

2 Both low and high, rich and poor, together.

3 My mouth shall speak of wisdom; and the meditation of my heart *shall be* of understanding.

4 I will incline mine ear to a parable: I will open my dark saying upon the harp.

5 Wherefore should I fear in the days of evil, *when* the iniquity of my heels shall compass me about?

6 They that trust in their wealth, and boast themselves in the multitude of their riches;

7 None *of them* can by any means redeem his brother, nor give to God a ransom for him:

8 (For the redemption of their soul *is* precious, and it ceaseth for ever:)

9 That he should still live for ever, *and* not see corruption.

10 For he seeth *that* wise men die, likewise the fool and the brutish person perish, and leave their wealth to others.

11 Their inward thought *is, that* their houses *shall continue* for ever, *and* their dwelling places to all generations; they call *their* lands after their own names.

12 Nevertheless man *being* in honour abideth not: he is like the beasts *that* perish.

13 This their way *is* their folly: yet their posterity approve their sayings. Selah.

14 Like sheep they are laid in the grave; death shall feed on them; and the upright shall have dominion over them in the morning; and their beauty shall consume in the grave from their dwelling.

15 But God will redeem my soul from the power of the grave: for he shall receive me. Selah.

16 Be not thou afraid when one is made rich, when the glory of his house is increased;

17 For when he dieth he shall carry nothing away: his glory shall not descend after him.

18 Though while he lived he blessed his soul: and *men* will praise thee, when thou doest well to thyself:

19 He shall go to the generation of his fathers; they shall never see light.

20 Man *that is* in honour, and understandeth not, is like the beasts *that* perish.

ON the title see on titles of Psalms iii. iv. xlii. The style of the original is confessedly obscure. The date cannot be fixed. Scott supposes it may have been written B. C. 1034. Alexander: "The inscription *to the sons of Korah* is consistent with any date from the time of David to that of Ezra." The authorship is uncertain. It is not wild to ascribe it to David; some have thought Solomon wrote it. On the authorship of the sons of Korah, see on title of Ps. xlii. On *Selah* see Introduction, § 15. The only name of God in this Psalm is *Elohim;* see on Ps. iii. 2. The design of this ode is variously conceived. Henry: "This Psalm is a sermon. In most of the Psalms we have the penman praying or praising. Here we have him preaching. . . The scope and design of this discourse is to convince the men of this world of their sin and folly in setting their hearts upon the things of this world, and so to persuade them to seek the things of a better world; as also to comfort the people of God, in reference to their own troubles, and the grief that arises from the prosperity of the wicked." Dodd: "It seems to be a meditation on the vanity of riches, and the usual haughtiness of those who possess them." Luther:

"This is a Psalm that instructs us unto faith, and teaches us to trust in God against that great god of this world, who is called Mammon." The Psalms, which most nearly resemble this in scope and design, are xxxvii. xxxix. lxxiii.

1. *Hear this, all* ye *people; give ear, all* ye *inhabitants of the world. People,* in the plural, *peoples,* all nations. The latter clause of the verse is parallel—*inhabitants of the world. World,* in Ps. lxxxix. 47, *time;* in Job xi. 17 ; in Ps. xxxix. 5, *age;* then by a transition well known in Greek and English the world where such duration is spent. The claim is for the marked attention of all mankind.

2. *Both low and high, rich and poor, together,* literally *both sons of Adam, and sons of men,* meaning mankind by whatever name called. See Introduction, § 16. The Chaldee has it, sons of old Adam, and sons of Jacob, equivalent to Jews and Gentiles. God's word nowhere denies that men's relations to each other are different; but their relations to God are all so far the same that they are all his servants, alike bound to hear and obey his word, alike accountable to him, liable at any moment to be summoned to his bar and to be judged in righteousness by him. Let all flesh give ear to the word of the Lord.

3. *My mouth shall speak of wisdom.* This is a reason why all should give the earnest heed and close attention claimed in vv. 1 and 2. *Wisdom,* plural *wisdoms,* denoting richness of wisdom. What is about to be uttered is of great weight. The language is not boastful, but arousing; it is modest, for it is simply true. *And the meditation of my heart shall be of understanding,* literally *understandings;* Ainsworth, *prudencies;* Edwards, *matters of understanding.*

4. *I will incline mine ear to a parable: I will open my dark saying upon the harp. Parable,* in a bad sense, byword, taunting speech, Ps. xliv. 14; Isa. xiv. 4; in a good sense, *parable, proverb,* a sententious saying, a weighty doctrine, constructed with ingenuity. For *dark saying,* many read enigma, riddle; Edwards, weighty doctrine; Horsley, mysterious doctrine; Fry, song; others, problem, proposition. To *incline the ear,* some think, is to sit in the posture of one about to play on the harp; it more naturally signifies the giving of earnest heed, Ps. lxxviii. 1. To *open* is to begin. Merrick unites these two senses: "I will myself give attention to the instructive parables of revelation, and I will propound them in this ode to others." Pool also: "I will hearken what God by his Spirit speaks to me, and that and nothing else will I now speak to you, and therefore it is well worth your hearing."

5. *Wherefore should I fear in the days of evil,* when *the iniquity of my heels shall compass me about?* This is very obscure. These words cannot mean that unpardoned sin is not good cause of fear. These solutions are offered. 1. The Chaldee for *when* has *unless when.* This arbitrarily supplies a most important word. 2. For *iniquity* Dimock has affliction; Houbigant, trouble; so that they understand not sin but natural evil. 3. For *iniquity* the Syriac and Arabic have enemies; Hengstenberg, treaders-down; Alexander, oppressors. 4. Others read the iniquity of those who lie in wait for me, or who are at my heels, or who supplant me, or who plot against me. So Dimock, Dodd, Glassius and Horsley. Horne: "Why should I give way to fear and despondency, in the time of calamity, when the wickedness of my wealthy and powerful adversaries compasses me about, to supplant and overthrow me. This is the best solution.

6. *They that trust in their wealth, and boast themselves in the multitude of their riches.* This is a description of a class of wicked men, found in the world in all ages. A good man may be rich, but he does not trust in gold. He is confident in God, not in the multitude of his possessions. But all wicked men, living in a state of carnal security, and having riches, do trust in them, love them, and virtually say to them, Ye are our gods. The folly of such vain trust is gross and manifest. Riches, even vast

riches may leave us in a day as they did Job. They profit not in the day of wrath. They multiply our cares and sorrows, especially when public calamity stalks abroad, or when death approaches. Neither can they aid our friends to the extent some vainly suppose. Men may own millions, but

7. *None* of them *can by any means redeem his brother, nor give to God a ransom for him.* Like his poor neighbor the rich is powerless, when he would prolong life, his own or his brother's, by means of earthly possessions. It is even more vain to offer gold as a *ransom, atonement* or *expiation* for the guilty soul, our own or a brother's. Surely no man should make much of that, which can in no way help in saving the soul, nor in prolonging life on earth. Death laughs at bags of gold. The justice of God holding fast the sinner scorns the richest bribe.

8. (*For the redemption of their soul* is *precious, and it ceaseth forever.*) *Precious*, also rendered *costly, excellent,* 1 Kings v. 17; vii. 9–11; once, precious because rare, 1 Sam. iii. 1. We were not redeemed with corruptible things, as silver and gold; but with the precious blood of Christ, as of a lamb without blemish and without spot. It cost God nothing to make the world. He spake and it was done. But to redeem it required the incarnation, sufferings and death of Jesus Christ. Scott: "The ancient fathers referred the verse to Christ, in this sense, 'No man can redeem his brother, he alone excepted, who is also God.'" *And it ceaseth forever.* Clarke: "This is very obscure." A good sense is given by Henry: "Life, when it is going, cannot be arrested, and when it is gone, it cannot be recalled." A higher sense is given by Hammond: "The redemption of the soul shall be precious, shall be high-prized, it shall cost very dear; but, being once wrought, it shall never need to be repeated," Heb. ix. 25, 26; x. 12. Or the phrase may signify that the *ransom,* which men vainly suppose can be effected by riches, never did avail and never can. Pool: "The soul's redemption is never to be accomplished by any mere man." It has no existence eternally. Either of these is better than that of Hengstenberg: And precious is the ransom of their souls, and he must put it off forever. The next verse should be read in connection with v. 7.

9. *That he should still live forever,* and *not see corruption.* The immortality of man on earth, or the blessed immortality of man beyond this life are alike beyond the price any mere man can pay. Man's life and his eternal life are solely and wholly at the disposal of God. We must feel this. Bossuet quotes a Jewish interpreter as understanding these verses "of the King Messiah, who, having died for the redemption of his brethren, afterwards liveth forever."

10. *For he seeth* that *wise men die, likewise the fool and the brutish person perish, and leave their wealth to others. He seeth,* i. e., any man may see, every man should see it. Mudge: It is evident; Slade: It is seen; it is indisputably so. *Wise men die.* Alas! alas! how the strong rods are broken. Even if a wise ruler or counsellor is found, how short is his life, how soon he passes away! Nor does death spare *the fool,* the poor wicked sinner, nor *the brutish person,* the man who has no spiritual discernment, though neither of these classes is prepared to undergo the awful examination of God. One of England's greatest monarchs dying said: "A world of wealth for an inch of time." But the offer was not accepted. The rich *leave their wealth to others,* whether to wise or foolish heirs they know not, but the heirs will find the fortune as vain and unsatisfying, as those who accumulated it.

11. *Their inward thought* is, that *their houses* shall continue *forever.* This is confessedly a verse very difficult of translation. None better than the above has been given. For *that* some read *how.* But this is not good. These rich wicked men could not act more atheistically if they had never heard that there was a God. They also think that *their dwelling places* shall continue *to all generations,* literally *to generation*

and generation. One of the hardest things is to make a wealthy sinner consent to be a pilgrim and a stranger upon earth. Septuagint: And their sepulchres are their houses forever; Chaldee, Syriac, Arabic, Vulgate, Edwards, Fry and others also read *sepulchres.* Calvin calls this interpretation *ingenious,* and a satirising of those who think to perpetuate their memory after death by rearing mausoleums. Still he prefers the sense given in the common version. *Houses* may mean *families,* or *descendants,* but here it seems to mean *habitations. They call* their *lands after their own names.* This does not declare that men leave their names on their tombs as some think; but that they give their own names to their landed estates, a custom still common in some places.

12. *Nevertheless man* being *in honor abideth not.* All those dreams of permanency described in the preceding verse vanish in actual life. However great or honorable man may become, he has no *continuance.* Nothing is fixed. *Abideth,* literally lodgeth, tarrieth as for a night, in the future shall abide. Hengstenberg: *But man remains not in honor.* Earthly existence is fleeting. Several versions, ancient and modern, for shall not abide, read shall not understand. The change of a single letter in the Hebrew would cause the mistake, for such it doubtless is. The Hebrew text, the Chaldee and the mass of authority sustain the common version. *He is like the beasts that perish.* If the present is the whole life of man, as the prevailing sentiments and conduct of the wicked would indicate, then how is man better than a brute? Calvin: " It is true that there is a great difference, as far as the soul is concerned, between man and the brute creation; but the Psalmist speaks of things as they appear in this world, and in this respect he was warranted to say of the ungodly that they die as the beasts. His subject does not lead him to speak of the world to come."

13. *This their way* is *their folly. Folly,* elsewhere rendered *hope, confidence.* Their very *hope* is *folly.* That in which they trust is foolishness. For *folly* the Septuagint has *scandal,* signifying *offence* or *stumbling-block. Yet their posterity approve their sayings.* For *posterity* some read *imitators;* and the word does sometimes signify a *follower.* But to say that an imitator approves that which he follows is a truism. On the other hand to say that posterity approve the principles of progenitors, especially when they have been wrong, is to declare that like begets like; and there is hardly a more solemn truth. Ainsworth: And their posterity like well of their mouth; Fry: Yet those that come after them delight in their maxims.

14. *Like sheep they are laid in the grave; death shall feed on them; and the upright shall have dominion over them in the morning; and their beauty shall consume in the grave from their dwelling.* This verse is variously rendered. Chaldee: They adjudge the just to death like sheep; and slay them; and wear out the just and those who revere the law, and smite the upright. Therefore their bodies shall grow old in hell, because they stretched forth their hand and destroyed the house of the habitation of his majesty; John Rogers' Translation: They lye in the hell like shepe, death shall dnawe upon them, and the ryghtuous shall have dominacyon of them in the mornynge by tymes: their strength shall consume, and hell shall be their dwellynge; Edwards: They are laid in the region of the dead like sheep; death feedeth on them; and the righteous will have dominion over them in the morning; their form will moulder away; the grave is their habitation. The foregoing are samples of the variety of renderings. The general import of the verse is given by all; but the precise signification of some words and the precise sense of some clauses are not agreed upon. *Like sheep they are laid in the grave.* Kennicott: Like cattle do they advance to the grave; Alexander: Like a flock to the grave they drive [or are driven.] *Like sheep,* without thought, heedlessly, not knowing where they are going. *Death shall feed on them.* Calvin: Death shall feed them; Venema: Death shall act as their shepherd;

Tholuck: Death is their shepherd [or driver,] *i. e.*, Death gathers them into his fold, and guides them as he will. His control over them shall be perfect. *Have dominion, rule*, as those who are vastly superior, and so triumph over. *In the morning, very soon*, very early, or early, Ps. ci. 8. The triumph of the wicked is short. Or *morning* signifies the time of judgment and decision, as courts tried causes *in the morning.* So Dathe. Or it signifies the time of the resurrection, which follows death. So many. This interpretation is to be preferred. The last clause is clear except the phrase *from their dwelling*, which is probably better read by uniting it with a part of what goes before, and so reading, hell their dwelling.

15. *But God will redeem my soul from the power of the grave: for he shall receive me. Selah.* That is, my life shall not be prematurely cut off, whatever perils may menace it; and, when I shall die, it will be in a firm faith in a blessed resurrection, which shall forever put away the dishonor, weakness and corruption of natural death. Calvin: "The prophet did not consider that the ground of his hope for a better resurrection was to be found in himself, but in the gratuitous adoption of God who had taken him into his favor." The *redemption* of this verse is doubtless in contrast of that in vv. 7, 8. The doctrine of the first part of the Psalm the prophet now applies in a practical way, either to himself, or to his learner.

16. *Be not thou afraid when one is made rich.* *Be not afraid*, suffer not thy mind to be filled with apprehensions, neither for thyself, nor for the public, neither for the State, nor for the church. As one's power is commonly increased with his wealth, fears are apt to arise respecting ill-disposed rich men. But we need not fear. For, 1, God governs the world; 2, the most wicked and powerful can do nothing except it be given him of God; 3, riches often destroy the energy the wicked would otherwise have, and leave them effeminate and feeble; 4, their riches may leave them any moment; 5, they may be called out of time without notice, or preparation. If riches serve to make a show, it is a vain show. Be not afraid, *When the glory of his house is increased.* *Glory*, the splendor of wealth, the applause of the ungodly, the admiration of fools are the glory of riches. *House*, the same as in v. 11, meaning here their *family*, or *household*. Riches held by others should awaken neither envy nor alarm.

17. *For when he dieth he shall carry nothing away.* The passage is parallel to Job i. 21; 1 Tim. vi. 7. The wicked will soon die. His possessions are soon scattered. *His glory shall not descend after him.* His very name shall *rot*. His power on earth shall be as nothing, so soon as he is dead; and in the next world, that which was his glory here shall be his everlasting shame. Nothing shall be more certain than the confusion and contempt which shall fall on every wicked man, however rich,

18. *Though while he lived he blessed his soul, i. e.*, called and counted himself a happy man, thought well of himself, put himself quite above many around him, and thought more of his own dog or horse than of his neighbour's soul or child. *And* men *will praise thee when thou doest well to thyself.* Ainsworth: They will confess thee when thou doest good to thyself, *i. e.*, own thee as a friend; Skinner: Yea, though men praise thee when thou indulgest thyself, *i. e.*, flatterers will praise thee when thou indulgest in unrestrained luxury; Fry: But he shall praise thee because thou hast done well for thyself. Hammond thinks it means, "Thou shalt be praised for doing that which may tend really and eternally to thy good, and not for applauding thy present felicity." The former is the more obvious construction, though either gives a good sense.

19. *He shall go to the generation of his fathers, i. e.*, He shall pass into the invisible world, where his forefathers or exemplars in sin are gone. Calvin has it: He shall come but to the age of his fathers; meaning as they at length passed away, so shall he. Either sense is good. *They shall never see light.* Everlasting darkness! O who

can fathom the woe here threatened. *Light*; Horsley: "That light, which emphatically deserves the name—that light, of which created light is but a faint image; the light of God's glory. He shall have no share in the beatific vision."

20. *Man that is in honor, and understandeth not, is like the beasts that perish.* This is very much like v. 12. This has made some think that there was an error in the text of v. 12; but it is very common to make two sentences much alike, yet leaving a slight difference between them. In v. 12 wicked men are compared to beasts, as to their mortality; in v. 20 to brutes, on account of their want of understanding. Compare Isa. i. 3; Jer. viii. 7.

DOCTRINAL AND PRACTICAL REMARKS.

1. Nothing is more just than the claim made on us to give close and earnest attention to divine things, v. 1. It is not a vain thing, it is our life. The ears and the hearts of men must be circumcised. "A prepared and sanctified ear is necessary for heavenly doctrine."

2. Before God all human distinctions and gradations are as nothing, v. 2. The difference between the greatest and the least of men is but the difference between two worms, two atoms. The highest of men is as truly bound to humble himself before God as the lowest. Rulers, sometimes in Scripture called gods, shall die like men.

3. Religious teachers should speak *wisdom, much wisdom,* v. 3; even the wisdom of God, 1 Cor. ii. 6, 7. God hath abounded towards us in all wisdom, and we ought to abound towards others in the same. In order to this, teachers must be students. Calvin: "Wisdom is not the growth of human genius. It must be sought from above, and it is impossible that any should speak with the propriety and knowledge necessary for the edification of the church, who has not, in the first place, been taught at the feet of the Lord."

4. There is a rich and excellent variety of matter and manner of teaching. At one time we have a *parable*, then a *dark saying*, v. 4; at one time a great doctrine, then an epic poem, then a psalm, then an exhortation. The preacher should be wise, and seek out and set in order many proverbs and excellent sentences. A good teacher must be a good student. He should be ingenious in stating and enforcing the lessons of heavenly wisdom, and endeavor by clearness, by meekness, by self-denial, by prudence and by courage, to bring home to men's hearts all the word of the Lord. He should *meditate* on what he teaches and try to feel it. "That which ministers speak from their own hearts is most likely to reach the hearts of their hearers."

5. The mysterious aspect of divine truth (v. 4) is chiefly owing to the sublimity of its nature and to the blindness of the human mind. To those who have spiritual discernment, the parables and proverbs, so far from being a hindrance, are a help to understand and treasure up the things of God. To a mind blinded by prejudice and sin nothing is clear, nothing is pleasing, unless it be something low and carnal.

6. Do right, and trust in God. Fear God, and then fear nothing else, v. 5. The Lord reigns over all, in wisdom, justice, mercy and power. The eulogy pronounced on John Knox was short but well-deserved: "There lies he who never feared the face of man."

7. Let no servant of God be surprised at finding himself surrounded by supplanters and oppressors, v. 5. Treachery seems to be a part of all opposition to godliness. Cruelty certainly is.

8. It is better to be a poor man and trust in God, and have him for a portion, than to be a rich man and worship mammon, v. 6. Of the former class not one fails of heaven; of the latter, not one enters heaven.

9. One way in which riches corrupt men and destroy their souls, is by engendering

the spirit of vain *boasting*, v. 6. Than this, hardly anything more blinds the mind, or hardens the heart. Men who have wealth are always in danger of pride and self-conceit; and the consequence is that self-denial and self-loathing are far from them, without which there is no salvation.

10. If riches are capable of many good uses, as the Bible admits; so in a multitude of cases they are utterly powerless, v. 7. They cannot buy talent, or any excellence of mind or heart. They cannot give a good constitution, nor prolong life for a day. They rather increase than diminish fears. "The abundance of the rich will not suffer him to sleep." They cannot quiet an uneasy conscience. They cannot cool a fever, or drive away a chill. They cannot soothe a pain in the head, or an ache in the heart. Towards one's salvation they can contribute nothing whatever. Nor can they aid our kin or our friends more than they can ourselves. Tholuck: "A rich man may buy much with his money, goods of every kind, pleasures, honors, but he cannot buy eternal life." The tenure, by which all earthly good is held is very frail. They who trust in wealth, shall find that they had no foresight. Foolish as is this love of riches, it is very prevalent, Jer. vi. 13. Many think the account given of the rich fool in Luke xii. 19–21, and of the rich man in Luke xvi. 19–31, illustrated by this Psalm. However this may be, we should heed the words of Christ in the same Gospel, Luke vi. 24, 25.

11. Such views of the vanity of wealth may be profitably contrasted with the blessings of sanctified poverty, Luke vi. 20, 21. Morison: "There is one limit, at least, to the tyrannous usurpation of wicked powers, and that limit is the grave; a destiny from which wealth cannot redeem, and power cannot rescue." One of the best things written by John Newton was "On the advantages of a state of poverty."

12. If "redemption is precious," those who are made partakers of its benefits ought constantly to celebrate its wonders, v. 8. Its costliness was greater than that of all things else. All the prices ever paid for other good things are as nothing compared with the price of redemption. No wonder that it has already contributed more to the glory of God and the elevation of man than all things else. It is the mystery of mysteries; the theme of the highest and sweetest songs sung in heaven.

13. The only immortality, which is worth having, is that which is made blessed by redemption, v. 9. Oh that each of us may attain unto it. An immortal existence without the salvation of the Gospel would be but perpetual torment.

14. Scripture and reason unite in claiming attention to the subject of death, v. 10. Even some of the heathen have acknowledged the wisdom of reflecting on that last, great, solemn change. One of the Latin poets says: "It is death, which forces us to confess how worthless the bodies of men are." If men would duly meditate on death, surely they would not be so wild and extravagant as they are. But the mere contemplation of death will neither make it easy nor safe to die. The death of Christ alone rightly viewed and believed can make our death comfortable and truly blessed. Henry: "The children of God, though ever so poor, are in this truly happy, above the most prosperous of the children of this world, that they are well-guarded against the terrors of death, and the judgment to come."

15. All earthly things are fleeting and vain, v. 11. He who dreams of stability in any worldly matter, is a fool. Horne: "Various are the contrivances of vain men, to have their names written on earth, and to procure after their deaths, an imaginary immortality, for themselves and their families, in the memory and conversation of posterity; which is not often obtained; and, if obtained, is of no value; when, with less trouble, they might have had their names written in heaven, and have secured to themselves a blessed immortality, in the glorious kingdom of their Redeemer."

16. If all other things on earth were stable and enduring, yet man himself abides

not, and so he cannot regard himself as permanent possessor of any earthly thing, v. 12.

17. It requires the grace of God to make a man wiser and better than his ungodly ancestors. A sinner lives and flourishes, and vanishes away; and his children if left to themselves follow in his track, and do as he did, v. 13. The example and dreadful end of sinners will never sufficiently warn their offspring from following in their footsteps.

18. Why does not the fearful rapidity with which men die put us all to thinking? v. 14. If the earth contains *eight hundred million* souls, and we allow *thirty* years to a generation, then every year more than *twenty-six millions* of souls pass into eternity. This is largely upwards of *two millions* for every month, more than *seventy-four thousand* for every day, more than *three thousand* for every hour, more than *fifty* for every minute.

19. In the midst of the death and misery, which stalk abroad over all the earth, it is delightful to know that reliance on God for salvation shall never be disappointed, v. 15. God is true and cannot deceive. Henry: "The believing hopes of the soul's redemption from the grave, and reception to glory, are the great support and joy of the children of God in a dying hour." Morison: "It is the doctrines of a resurrection and of a future judgment, which send preëminent lustre upon all the apparent inequalities of life." If believers' pains are sharp, they are not long; and if they are long, they are not sharp. It is a poor thing to have wealth, and honor, and ease follow us to the grave, and then mercy forsake us forever; but it is a blessed thing to live poor, and die poor, and then enter into eternal glory.

20. We need not fear the rising fortunes of ungodly men, v. 16. The butterfly with all its gaudiness will not live half so long as the poor caterpillar, whom it seems to despise; see on Ps. xxxvii. 35, 36.

21. If anything could settle the question of the folly of man's mind, we should suppose it would be the necessity of reminding us that when we die we can carry none of our possessions with us, v. 17.

22. All other flattery would be harmless, if we did not flatter ourselves, v. 18.

23. It would do us good often to sit down and think how universally and swiftly the nations, and conquerors, and tyrants, and persecutors of former times have passed away, v. 19. Compare Job iii. 17–19.

24. However we may interpret the language of inspiration respecting the recompense of the wicked in a future world, candor compels us to admit that its import is fearful, v. 19. Some deceive themselves with the thought that the threatening language of Scripture is figurative; but, if the figures are justly used, then the import is even more terrific than if plain language were employed.

25. Will men never learn? will they never *understand?* v. 20. Never, never, till God's Holy Spirit illuminates the poor benighted soul. Clarke: "The rich and honorable man, who has no spiritual understanding, is a *beast* in the sight of God." If the great principles of righteousness and religion were an occult science, how could they be more effectually hidden from the unregenerate than they now are? Horne: "At the call of Folly, what multitudes are always ready to assemble! But Wisdom, eternal and essential Wisdom, crieth without; she lifteth up her voice in the streets, and who is at leisure to attend her heavenly lectures?" Tholuck: "Divine wisdom only rises above the destiny of beasts."

26. Let men in these gospel times know their day, and be wise. Slade: "If the people, in the psalmist's day, were so foolish for looking to earthly things alone, what must we be, now that the blessed Jesus, by the glorious truth of his gospel, and

his rising again from the grave, has plainly assured us of a resurrection and a life to come!"

27. In the end it shall infallibly be seen that he who serves God is the only wise man. "Let prosperous sinners be afraid for themselves, but let not even suffering saints be afraid of them."

28. What shall it profit a man, if he gain the whole world and lose his own soul?

PSALM L.

A Psalm of Asaph.

1 The mighty God, *even* the LORD, hath spoken, and called the earth from the rising of the sun unto the going down thereof.

2 Out of Zion, the perfection of beauty, God hath shined.

3 Our God shall come, and shall not keep silence: a fire shall devour before him, and it shall be very tempestuous round about him.

4 He shall call to the heavens from above, and to the earth, that he may judge his people.

5 Gather my saints together unto me; those that have made a covenant with me by sacrifice.

6 And the heavens shall declare his righteousness: for God *is* judge himself. Selah.

7 Hear, O my people, and I will speak; O Israel, and I will testify against thee: I *am* God, *even* thy God.

8 I will not reprove thee for thy sacrifices or thy burnt offerings, *to have been* continually before me.

9 I will take no bullock out of thy house, *nor* he goats out of thy folds:

10 For every beast of the forest *is* mine, *and* the cattle upon a thousand hills.

11 I know all the fowls of the mountains: and the wild beasts of the field *are* mine.

12 If I were hungry, I would not tell thee: for the world *is* mine, and the fulness thereof.

13 Will I eat the flesh of bulls, or drink the blood of goats?

14 Offer unto God thanksgiving; and pay thy vows unto the Most High:

15 And call upon me in the day of trouble: I will deliver thee, and thou shalt glorify me.

16 But unto the wicked God saith, What hast thou to do to declare my statutes, or *that* thou shouldest take my covenant in thy mouth?

17 Seeing thou hatest instruction, and castest my words behind thee.

18 When thou sawest a thief, then thou consentedst with him, and hast been partaker with adulterers.

19 Thou givest thy mouth to evil, and thy tongue frameth deceit.

20 Thou sittest *and* speakest against thy brother; thou slanderest thine own mother's son.

21 These *things* hast thou done, and I kept silence; thou thoughtest that I was altogether *such a one* as thyself: *but* I will reprove thee, and set *them* in order before thine eyes.

22 Now consider this, ye that forget God, lest I tear *you* in pieces, and *there be* none to deliver.

23 Whoso offereth praise glorifieth me: and to him that ordereth *his* conversation *aright* will I shew the salvation of God.

THE authorship of this Psalm is not uncertain. See title; Introduction, § 4, 1 Chron. vi. 39; xv. 17, 19; xxv. 1, 2; Neh. xii. 46. Scott dates it B. C. 1035; many, fifteen years later. It suited any state of the church during David's reign. Some think Asaph's style less polished and flowing than that of his monarch; but he always awakens the sympathies of God's afflicted people in his inspired utterances. The tincture of sadness pervading them well agrees with the experience of many. Concerning the scope of this Psalm, there is some diversity, arising perhaps from an attempt to discover a strict unity of design in it. It treats of the nature of true religion, what it requires of us towards God and man, how it forbids hypocrisy and formality in worship; it shows us how exalted and pure is God, and points us to his awful judgments against sinners. In it we find five names of the Almighty, *El God*, *Eloah God*, *Elohim God*, *Jehovah* LORD and *Gel-yohn Most High*, on which see respectively on Ps. xviii. 3; v. 4; iii. 2; i. 2; vii. 17.

1. *The mighty God*, even *the* LORD. Chaldee: The mighty One, the God Jehovah. Many others: The God of gods, Jehovah; Venema and Schmidt: God, God, Jehovah; Horsley: The omnipotent God, Jehovah; Amesius: The mighty God, God Jehovah; Hengstenberg: God, the Almighty, the Lord; Alexander: The Almighty, God, Jehovah. See the same form of speech in Josh. xxii. 22, rendered, The LORD God of gods. This awful God *hath spoken, and called the earth from the rising of the sun unto the going down thereof.* The summons is to all the inhabitants of the earth, those that were near and those afar off. The occasion of this call is the solemn trial of his people. As in the last day, so here God lays open the character of his dealings with his professed people, and the manner in which they had requited him. Compare Deut. xxx. 19; Isa. i. 2.

2. *Out of Zion, the perfection of beauty, God hath shined.* The call is not from Mount Sinai with its blackness and thunderings; but from Mount Zion, the most favored spot on earth, and to a pious Jew, "the perfection of beauty." No place equalled Zion. This is the more common interpretation, and is sustained by Ps. xlviii. 2; yet the Septuagint, Luther and others put "perfection of beauty," in apposition with God. The doctrine is good, but is the excellence of God's character intended to be taught by that phrase? *Shined*, as in Deut. xxxiii. 2, " *He shined forth* from mount Paran." In Ps. lxxx. 1, in the imperative it is, *Shine forth;* and in Ps. xciv. 1, *Show thyself*, margin, *Shine forth.* When God chooses, he can easily display intolerable brightness.

3. *Our God shall come, and shall not keep silence.* The God, who shall come, is in covenant with those, who fitly call him *our God. Shall come;* Alexander: " *He is coming*, as if the sound of his voice and the light of his glory had preceded his actual appearance." *To keep silence* is to show forbearance and to withhold deserved punishment. Tholuck: "The long-suffering of God has long been silent, he will now make it known that his long-suffering was not indifference, but mercy." *A fire shall devour before him, and it shall be very tempestuous round about him.* The imagery is doubtless drawn from the appearances and manifestations at mount Sinai, Ex. xix. 16, 18; Heb. xii. 18–21. If with several old Jewish interpreters we refer this Psalm to the day of Judgment, these terms used have an awful significance. But God is himself a consuming fire, whenever he deals with men otherwise than in amazing mercy, Deut. iv. 24; Isa. xxx. 33; xxxiii. 14; Heb. xii. 29.

4. *He shall call to the heavens from above, and to the earth, that he may judge his people.* Clarke: The first six verses of this Psalm seem to contain a description of the *great judgment:* to any minor consideration or fact it seems impossible, with any propriety, to restrain it." It is not necessary to give it this exclusive reference; but its terms naturally carry the mind from looking through any other scrutiny of men's characters to the investigations of the last day, when the *heavens above*, and the *earth beneath* shall be alike brought before the tribunal of God. False professors are tried in this Psalm. The same class were severely dealt with by the prophets, and afterwards by John the Baptist, Hos. vi. 5; Matt. iii. 10–12. The Saviour himself introduced such clearness and discrimination into his teachings, that the formalists and hypocrites of his time "could not abide the day of his coming." But the last great day will, more than any before it, yea, will perfectly separate the wheat from the chaff.

5. *Gather my saints together unto me; those that have made a covenant with me by sac-*

rifice. Chaldee: Gather to me my saints, who have struck my covenant, and confirmed my law, and been diligent in prayer, which is like an oblation; Arabic: Be
ye gathered to him, O ye saints of his, who place his covenant above sacrifices; Luther: Gather me mine holy ones, that regard the covenant more than offering;
Amesius: Gather to me those whom I have been pursuing with kindness, and who
have struck covenant with me by sacrifice; Matthew's Bible: Gather my saints together unto me, those that set more by the covenant than by any offering; Hengstenberg: "Gather to me my saints who close with my covenant on sacrifice." Hengstenberg puts the verse in quotation marks, as being the address of God. Doubtless
he is the speaker. *Saints,* holy, godly, merciful, Deut. xxxiii. 8; 2 Sam. xxii. 26;
Ps. iv. 3; Mic. vii. 2. It may be taken ironically, and then they are spoken of as
what they ought to be, or what they profess to be; or it may be taken as a just
epithet, and then they are gathered together for protection and blessing. Some have
regarded this verse as the call to the first resurrection, when the reapers, the angels,
shall gather all the wheat into the garners. If the reference is directly to the Jewish nation as God's professed people, then the allusion to a covenant is naturally
drawn from Ex. xxiv. 3–8; Josh. xxiv. 14–28. A covenant was often made by slaying a victim, sprinkling its blood and burning its fat on the altar, cutting the animal into two parts, and the parties passing between them. All God's people make
a covenant with him through the sacrifice of his Son.

6. *And the heavens shall declare his righteousness.* In some other places the *heavens*
means the *angels.* Perhaps it does so here. The angels will be Christ's attendants
and assessors. If angels are not here referred to, then the sense of the clause is that
from *the heavens,* or in the most public and illustrious manner, God will *declare,* or
make known his righteousness in all things, especially in his sentence against a hypocritical people. It will fill heaven with eternal gladness that in the annals of the universe
there is not found one record or case of a decision given by God contrary to infinite
rectitude. It could not be otherwise, *for God is judge himself.* As "the Father
judgeth no man, but hath committed all judgment to the Son;" this verse clearly
points to Immanuel.

7. *Hear, O my people, and I will speak; O Israel, and I will testify against thee: I
am God, even thy God.* The rendering is better than any offered in its place. By
speaking and *testifying* he refers to the solemn charge and admonition he would give
them and to the announcement of the principles on which the final judgment will be
conducted. He insists upon his name and character, as being well known to them in
their history in centuries gone by. He had been their friend, and guide, and benefactor, and deliverer, and law-giver. He also gave assurance that he had not yet cast
them off. Alexander: "I will testify against thee, that I am thy God, although I am
not so regarded or so treated."

8. *I will not reprove thee for thy sacrifices, or thy burnt-offerings,* to have been *continually before me.* Tholuck: "It is so deeply impressed on the heart of man that his
life should be a continuous worship, that he seeks to calm his conscience by outward
offerings and works of obedience at least. But they can neither calm the conscience
nor satisfy God." God often takes the will for the deed, but never the deed for the
will. Hearty piety towards God and genuine kindness towards men always were, and
from God's nature ever must be preferred to any attention to the ritual of religion.
See Isa. i. 11–15; Mark xii. 28–34. The words, *to have been,* supplied by our translators, do not aid. Patrick gives the sense: "I have no complaint to make about the
matter of sacrifices: thy burnt-offerings, I acknowledge, never fail to be brought both
morning and evening to my altar; and I see how busy thou art in that employment."
Alexander: "I do not charge thee with withholding the material offerings to which I

am entitled, for in truth they are ever before me." *Sacrifices*, strictly speaking, were offerings of animals in which the life was destroyed. In *burnt-offerings* a bullock, a male lamb, or a kid, or, in cases of great poverty, a turtle-dove, or pigeon, was offered.

9. *I will take no bullock out of thy house*, nor *he goats out of thy folds*. *Bullock*, the word determines only the sex, but not the size or age of the animal. The oxen of the Jews were bulls. In modern Jewish books of devotion the word *steer* is uniformly used instead of *bullock*. In this place Calvin has *calf*. Three views are taken of this verse. 1. "The time is coming when I will take no bullock or he-goat from you or from any people, but I will require only spiritual sacrifices." This is very good doctrine; but there is nothing corresponding to the words *the time is coming*, except as indicated by the future form of the verb, *will take*. 2. The Jews had begun to conceive of God as requiring animals in sacrifice to meet some demand of his nature. To this gross conception the verse is regarded as a denial. 3. Some think it is as if God had said, "I will not accept these animals *from you* in your present wicked state of mind, as though your sacrifice was pleasing to me: I cannot do it: you are putting forms in the place of substance." The second view best corresponds with the subsequent context.

10. *For every beast of the forest* is *mine*, and *the cattle upon a thousand hills*. The interpretation given by the Chaldee is striking, though not supported: For mine is every beast of the wood, and I have prepared for the just in the garden of delights clean animals, and the wild ox feeding daily on a thousand mountains. Hengstenberg: "If God *needed* the sacrifices, he would not require to seek them of men, as his whole creation stands at his command." The scope of this verse is the same as that of vv. 11, 12.

11. *I know all the fowls of the mountains*. *I know*, I make, govern and feed. At God's bidding they would flock to him from all quarters. Even vultures obey his voice, 1 Kings xvii. 4, 6. Omniscience implies omnipotence and universal providence. *And the wild beasts of the field* are *mine*. Calvin: The wild beasts of the field are at my command; Edwards: The wild beasts of the field are at my call; Hengstenberg: And what moves upon the field is known to me. There is nothing but wild imagination in support of the Chaldee: And the cock of the wood, whose feet stand on the earth, and whose head touches heaven, sings before me.

12. *If I were hungry, I would not tell thee*. Patrick: "If I were hungry, I would not come to acquaint thee with it, that thou mightest provide me food." *For the world is mine and the fulness thereof*. God's resources are not confined to Judea. They are found all over the earth. *The fulness of the world* embraces everything here below.

13. *Will I eat the flesh of bulls, or drink the blood of goats?* *Bulls*, see Ps. xxii. 12, rendered *strong*. It is applied to *men*, or *horses*, or *angels*. But here the sense confines it to the strongest kind of clean animals, fit for sacrifice, and these were bulls. *Goats*, in v. 9 *he goats*. Martin: "The fire, which descended from heaven upon the sacrifices, was considered mystically as the mouth of God, which devoured the flesh of the victims; and it was on that account that God had expressly forbidden to consume them by fire obtained elsewhere, because this *strange fire*, not being that which descended from heaven, could not be regarded mystically as the mouth of God." Perhaps some had become so gross in their notions as to suppose that Jehovah had some physical necessity for food and drink. If so, he here reproves their folly in doubting his spirituality and independence.

14. *Offer unto God thanksgiving*. Chaldee: Repress vile concupiscence, and before God it shall be counted as the sacrifice of confession. This is a poor conceit. *Thanksgiving*, also elsewhere praise, thanks, confession, sacrifice of praise. The sense here requires thanksgiving, not thank-offering, which much resembled a *sin-offering*, Lev. vii. 2–13. We

have the same word rendered *praise* in v. 23. God is not enjoining more bloody but spiritual sacrifices. *And pay thy vows unto the Most High.* The word rendered *vows* occurs in the singular and plural about *sixty* times. In our version it is uniformly rendered. But in a few cases it means a *votive offering*, Lev. vii. 16; Num. xxix. 39. The law of such offerings is given in Lev. xxii. 18–24. Clarke thinks that the call here is to pay *vow-offerings;* but a vow might relate to a life of holiness, to some particular act of benevolence, to anything proper to be done by a servant of God, and did not exclusively relate to *sacrifices*, Gen. xxviii. 20–22; xxxi. 13. Vows are made and paid by pious people under the gospel. They will be a part of worship to the end of the world. In general, vows are engagements to be the Lord's, Ps. lvi. 12; but in particular a vow is a solemn voluntary engagement to do something, which we were not bound to do until we made the promise, see Pr. xx. 25; Ecc. v. 4, 5.

15. *And call upon me in the day of trouble: I will deliver thee, and thou shalt glorify me.* The rendering of this verse is very excellent in all respects. *And* is not a mere continuation of the discourse, but closely connects this verse and the preceding. Thanksgiving, paying vows and calling on God are to be united. To *call on the Lord* sometimes is put for the whole of religious worship. Its specific meaning is best expressed by *prayer.* Here the prominent idea is that of supplication. All this service is to be hearty, and spiritual. Then with it shall be connected success, *I will deliver thee;* and also new cause of gratitude: *And thou shalt glorify me.* Alexander: "Thou shalt have occasion to renew thy praises and thanksgivings for new benefits received."

16. *But unto the wicked God saith, What hast thou to do to declare my statutes, or that thou shouldest take my covenant in thy mouth?* *The wicked*, in general any *wicked* person, or particularly the kind of *wicked* man just described—a heartless hypocrite. This and following verses find an extended parallel in Rom. ii. 17–24. The Scriptures everywhere insist that pure motives and real sincerity are essential to the right worship of God. In vain does man expect his Maker to accept *bulls, lambs* and *goats*, instead of faith, justice, mercy and the love of God. To *declare* God's statutes is to publish them, teach them to others, either officially or unofficially. To *take* God's *covenant* is to converse upon sacred things, profess the true religion, and claim to be of the number of God's people.

17. *Seeing thou hatest instruction.* Chaldee: When thou hatest the correction of the wise; Syriac, Arabic, Septuagint, Ethiopic and Vulgate: Thou hast hated my discipline; Calvin: Also thou hatest correction; Edwards: Since thou hatest reproof. The charge against this teacher is that he does not himself do the known will of God. *And castedst my words behind thee.* This describes contempt towards the clear teachings of God's oracles. All such men made void the law by their myths and glosses.

18. *When thou sawest a thief, then thou consentedst with him, and hast been partaker with adulterers.* It would be monstrous indeed that so willing and greedy a violator of the 7th and 8th commandments should bear the office of teacher of the decalogue, and publish to others rules of life which in practice he himself utterly rejected. He forgot also the 9th commandment.

19. *Thou givest thy mouth to evil, and thy tongue frameth deceit.*

20. *Thou sittest* and *speakest against thy brother; thou slanderest thine own mother's son.* The first clause of v. 19 describes the general habit of the tongue. The second shows how evil-speaking grows on men. Verse 20 shows that lying and slander finally stop at nothing. They attack even a *brother*, not only the son of the same father, but also of the same *mother.* Compare Ps. lxix. 8. The following renderings are striking: Vulgate: Thy mouth hath abounded with wickedness, and thy tongue framed deceits. Horsley: Thy mouth hath been fruitful in mischief, and thy tongue frameth deceit. Thou sittest and speakest against thy brother, against the son of thy mother

thou pourest out abuse. *Sitting* may denote 1, the act of a judge; 2, the place, as in public; 3, the habit of life, Ps. i. 1. The last is best here.

21. *These* things *hast thou done, and I kept silence. Kept silence*, as in v. 3. God's long-suffering is terribly perverted. *Thou thoughtest that I was altogether* such a one *as thyself.* Instead of counting the long-suffering of God salvation, men infer from it that God is weak, or that he is irresolute in punishing sin. The great mass of ungodly men, and especially false professors, do by their acts declare that in their esteem God is insignificant. Such wickedness must in due time be noticed: But *I will reprove thee, and set* them *in order before thine eyes. Reprove, call to account,* the opposite of *keeping silence.* Judgment may be delayed a long time, but is never indefinitely postponed. At last men's evil deeds are arrayed not only before their Judge, but before themselves. A clear sight of his sins would overwhelm any man with dismay. Calvin: "The Psalmist warns them that ere long they will be dragged into the light, and that those sins which they would have hidden from the eyes of God would be set in all their enormity before their view." That conviction, which God can easily produce, will make any soul miserable.

22. *Now consider this, ye that forget God, lest I tear* you *in pieces, and* there be *none to deliver.* For *tear in pieces,* Calvin has *seize upon you;* church of England, *pluck you away;* Alexander, *rend you.* The verb expresses destruction by a strong and fierce animal, Gen. xxxvii. 33; xliv. 28; Ps. vii. 2; compared with Hos. v. 14. God's wrath is terrible. Oh that men would *consider.* To our race it is a reproach that but here and there one is *thoughtful. Consider,* often so, elsewhere *understand, perceive, discern, regard.*

23. *Whoso offereth praise glorifieth me. Praise,* in v. 14 rendered *thanksgiving.* God is honored when he receives the praise which is his due. And no man gives God his own who does not often give him thanks. Alexander: "It is really a promise that he whose offerings are genuine expressions of thanksgiving shall have cause or occasion to praise God for his mercies." *And to him that ordereth* his *conversation* aright *will I shew the salvation of God.* There are both diversity and difficulty in rendering this clause. Beza and Amesius: Him who regulates his conduct I will cause to enjoy the salvation of God; Edwards: To him that is upright in his way I will show the salvation of God. With these virtually agree Calvin, Ainsworth, church of England, Jebb and others. *Conversation, i. e.,* conduct, life, *behaviour, way.* The sense is the same whether we read, *Will I show salvation,* or *He shall see salvation.* In either case the meaning is, *He shall experience salvation. The salvation of God* is either a *great* salvation, so some; or it is a salvation of which God is undeniably the author. Both are true.

DOCTRINAL AND PRACTICAL REMARKS.

1. A message from God claims prompt, solemn and universal attention, v. 1. Nothing can be more dangerous than to despise it. It would have been folly in Naaman to slight the saying of the little captive maid that served his wife. David would have acted foolishly had he disregarded the counsel of his friend Jonathan. But the infinitude of God's whole nature makes it madness to slight any call coming from him.

2. It unspeakably concerns *all* men to know what God *has spoken,* v. 1. His word is very pure and very weighty. A man may be ignorant of all learning, of all arts, of all philosophy; but if he does not know what God speaks to him, he is undone.

3. Zion is the perfection of beauty, v. 2. "The true visible church, where God's ordinances are set up as he hath appointed, where his word is purely preached, is the most beautiful thing under heaven." The word of the Lord goes forth from Jerusalem, Isa. ii. 3; Mic. iv. 2. The little good that is in the world is by means of the

church.   Saints keep alive piety on earth, John vii. 38 ; Ps. lxvii. 1, 2.   But for the righteous, sinners would all drop into hell, Matt. xxiv. 22 ; Mark xiii. 20.   He who does not admire the light of the moon, will hardly have his attention arrested by the glories of the sun.   He who does not love the church, does not love him who bought the church.

4. Because God's vengeance against wickedness does not instantly break forth and destroy evil doers, they say he is not angry with them, v. 3.   But they are sadly mistaken, Ps. vii. 11 ; Ecc. viii. 11.   Strange that reasonable beings should give no earnest heed to the most weighty matters, except as they are forced to think of them by awful visitations.

5. The longer God delays punishment, the more terrible will it be when it comes, v. 3.   God waited a *hundred and twenty* years with the old world ; but when the deluge came, it swept all away.   Its scenes of horror were more dreadful than imagination has ever conceived.

6. Any reckoning of God with man is solemn, and of all the accounts we shall give to God, the last will be the most so, v. 4.   We need not perplex ourselves to know how God will raise the dead.   He who called us into being can easily *call* us to his bar.   God spake to men from Eden as a Creator ; from Sinai as a Law-giver ; from Zion as a Redeemer.   In due time he will speak to the congregated universe as a Judge.   In that day the greater the blessings and privileges abused, the heavier will be the doom, Lam. ii. 15.   Oh that men would listen to the voice of mercy before the day of wrath comes.   It is only true Christians who shall " have boldness in the day of judgment," 1 John iv. 17.

7. All the teachings of Scripture respecting righteous men are kind, v. 5.   God calls them " *my saints,*" " my sheep," " my friends," " my sons and daughters."   He says many kind things of them and to them.   He loves to have them near him.   He will finally gather them all into his own house.

8. As of old the best covenants were made by sacrifice, so the great covenant, securing life to the soul of a believer, is made by the sacrifice of Christ, of which all others were at best mere types, v. 5.

9. God's justice, though now for a time to blind mortals it seems obscured, shall at last be illustrious.   The *heavens shall declare* it, v. 6.   Two things in providence often perplex us.   1. Frequently good and evil seem to come alike to all, Ecc. ix. 2.   2. The righteous are often greatly afflicted, while the wicked prosper.   But give God time.   Let him to time add eternity, and all will seem to be right, Luke xvi. 25.

10. It is a blessed thing that there can be no mistake in the decisions of the last day.   Christ, who shall give the award, knows what is in man, knows all things, John ii. 25 ; xxi. 17.   Infinite knowledge and infinite rectitude alike render a wrong decision impossible, v. 6.

11. It should greatly humble good men to find that as often as divine wisdom pronounces on the character of the visible church, it finds something, often much to censure, v. 7.   Compare Rev. ii. 4, 14, 20 ; iii. 2, 15.

12. To the observance of any ritual, even one divinely prescribed, God has never attached any importance compared with that belonging to true piety, consisting of love and mercy, truth and justice, fidelity and humility, simplicity and godly sincerity, vv. 8–11.   Compare 1 Sam. xv. 22 ; Ecc. v. 1 ; Mic. vi. 6, 7, 8 ; Isa. lviii. 1, 2 ; lxvi. 3 ; Hos. vi. 6 ; Matt. ix. 13 ; xii. 7.   Why will men deceive themselves with the opposite belief?   Morison : " God will not accept an outward for a spiritual homage, the mere carcass of religion for its living fires on the altar of the heart."

13. As we cannot offer to God anything that is not already his gift to us, how vain is the hope of some that they can do or suffer anything that will *deserve* heaven at

God's hand! vv. 9–12. When we have given God all we have and are, we have simply given him his own. And when we have kept all the commandments, we have merely done our duty, and no more, 1 Chron. xxix. 14; Luke xvii. 10.

14. Those figures of speech (anthropomorphy and anthropopathy), by which we represent God as having the form or the affections of man, are not sinful, for they are used by inspired men. But they are liable to be abused, and so we should guard men against overstraining them, vv. 12, 13. Are our conceptions of God more pure than those of "the carnal Israelites who conceived that a fat sacrifice was as acceptable to God as a fat dinner was to themselves?"

15. Because God is the self-existent Jehovah, he is necessarily an independent being, vv. 10–12; Isa. lxvi. 1, 2. We depend on him for all things; he depends on us for nothing. He was as happy before as since creation showed forth his glory, and sang his praises, Job xxxv. 6–8.

16. We are always deceiving ourselves, when we forget that God's service is spiritual, vv. 14, 15. This was as true, if not so abundantly declared, under former dispensations as now.

17. In all our worship *praise* ought to be prominent, v. 14. Calvin: "Could we suppose men to come into the world in the full exercise of reason and judgment, their first act of spiritual sacrifice should be that of thanksgiving." If the public worship of the nineteenth century is out of proportion generally, it is probably in allowing the matter of praise too little space. In secret worship has thanksgiving its share?

18. It is not wrong to make *vows*, v. 14. We should not make them rashly. We should not vow to do any wicked or impossible thing. But we may vow.

19. Under all dispensations *prayer* has been a duty, v. 15. It is a branch of natural religion. It is often inculcated in the Bible. It is a fit exercise for all times. It is of special propriety *in the day of trouble*, though he, who prays only when in affliction, has reason to suspect his sincerity, Job xxvii. 10. A sense of want, though there be no special affliction resting on us, is essential to the sincerity of any supplication; and as long as we are in the flesh we have many wants. Anything is good for us, if it leads us to the throne of grace.

20. Prayer is a fit exercise for a sinful and dependent creature, and in its nature it is suited to our case. But the great blessing connected with it is that God hears and answers it, v. 15.

21. Mere profession even of the true religion, though it be decent and to the eye of man consistent, is not only vain but is offensive to God; but when a religious profession does not restrain us from overt wickedness, it is not only hateful to God, but an abomination to all right-minded men, v. 16.

22. This is preëminently so in regard to an unconverted ministry. No character is more odious to God than that of a prating, preaching hypocrite. God speaks of such as with astonishment and abhorrence, v. 16.

23. "Consistency is a jewel;" and the want of it is a blur and a blot, v. 16. A corpse in a state of dissolution is not the less offensive because it may be covered with flowers.

24. One of the surest signs of swift destruction coming on a man is hatred of reproof, of warning, of counsel, of good doctrine and of timely admonition; and when this amounts to a scornful rejection of God's word, then the case is indeed fearful, v. 17.

25. All false professors are upon close examination found to be defective in the duties required by the second table of the law, vv. 18–20. Arnd: "Such a person was Ahab, who could appear so pious, but when Elias rebukes him, he curses and persecutes the prophets to death." "Those, who trust to a righteousness of their own,

are too generally wanting in those very qualities to which they attribute such extraordinary effects."

26. Sins of the tongue terribly grow on a man, and when the spirit of slander fairly gets possession of one, it balks at nothing, vv. 19, 20.

27. It is of the Lord's mercies that we are not consumed, v. 21.

28. The real character of God is fundamental in a system of truth. Wrong ideas of him are as mischievous in their effect on man as anything can possibly be, v. 21.

29. We may be sure that our sins will find us out, v. 21. They may seem to be laid quietly away; but we know not the moment when the Lord will cause them to spring upon us and seize us as armed men.

30. Ought not more to be said in the pulpit and in religious writings against the sin of *forgetting God?* v. 22. It is often mentioned in the Bible. It is a very heinous offence. Henry: "Forgetfulness of God is at the bottom of all the wickedness of the wicked."

31. It is a fearful thing to fall into the hands of the living God, v. 22. What is the full import of *tearing in pieces* none can know till he enters upon a rueful eternity.

32. In joy and in sorrow, sick and well, at home and abroad, let us abound in *praise*, v. 23. The circumstances of Paul and Silas in jail, were very distressing, and so they *prayed.* Many blessings and mercies remained to them, and so they *sang praises.*

33. But true praise is always connected with a holy life. We must also *order our conversation aright*, v. 23. Without personal holiness no man shall see the Lord. He, who would be truly holy, must take God's word for his rule of living, God's Son for his Saviour, God's Spirit for his guide, comforter and sanctifier, God's people for his chosen companions, God's glory for the aim and object of his life, God's love as the great animating principle of his conduct.

34. Whatever we do in religion, let it be done as of sincerity, as of God, in the sight of God. This whole Psalm warns us against hypocrisy. If our hearts are cold or lukewarm, let us, in our approaches to the throne of grace, freely so confess. Let us be unaffected in modesty, humility, sorrow for sin, zeal and everything good.

35. This Psalm calls for close self-examination, and it furnishes excellent hints for aiding us in that important duty. It calls special attention to the practical duties of life, and invites us to investigate that subject. Reader, Are you ready for the scrutiny of God?

PSALM LI.

To the chief Musician, A Psalm of David, when Nathan the prophet came unto him, after he had gone in to Bath-sheba.

1 Have mercy upon me, O God, according to thy lovingkindness: according unto the multitude of thy tender mercies blot out my transgressions.

2 Wash me thoroughly from mine iniquity, and cleanse me from my sin.

3 For I acknowledge my transgressions: and my sin *is* ever before me.

4 Against thee, thee only, have I sinned, and done *this* evil in thy sight: that thou mightest be justified when thou speakest, *and* be clear when thou judgest.

5 Behold, I was shapen in iniquity; and in sin did my mother conceive me.

6 Behold, thou desirest truth in the inward parts: and in the hidden *part* thou shalt make me to know wisdom.

7 Purge me with hyssop, and I shall be clean: wash me, and I shall be whiter than snow.

8 Make me to hear joy and gladness; *that* the bones *which* thou hast broken may rejoice.

9 Hide thy face from my sins, and blot out all mine iniquities.

10 Create in me a clean heart, O God; and renew a right spirit within me.

11 Cast me not away from thy presence; and take not thy Holy Spirit from me.

12 Restore unto me the joy of thy salvation; and uphold me *with thy* free Spirit.

13 *Then* will I teach transgressors thy ways; and sinners shall be converted unto thee.

14 Deliver me from bloodguiltiness, O God, thou God of my salvation; *and* my tongue shall sing aloud of thy righteousness.

15 O Lord, open thou my lips; and my mouth shall shew forth thy praise.

16 For thou desirest not sacrifice; else would I give *it:* thou delightest not in burnt offering.

17 The sacrifices of God *are* a broken spirit: a broken and a contrite heart, O God, thou wilt not despise.

18 Do good in thy good pleasure unto Zion: build thou the walls of Jerusalem.

19 Then shalt thou be pleased with the sacrifices of righteousness, with burnt offering and whole burnt offering: then shall they offer bullocks upon thine altar.

ALL agree that this is a penitential Psalm. The title makes David the author. In this concur all the ancient versions, Luther, Calvin, Diodati, Piscator, Fabritius, Ainsworth, Venema, Amesius, Symson, Edwards, Jebb, Dathe, Patrick, Morison, Henry, Horne, Scott, Hengstenberg, Tholuck and Alexander. One is surprised to find Kennicott, Horsley, Mudge, Clarke, Fry, De Wette and Hitzig denying the Davidic authorship, and on grounds wholly insufficient. The historic occasion of this ode is found in 2 Sam. xi. xii. This Psalm and the xxxii. refer to the same painful matters. In that David tells of his misery before repentance, and of his happiness after confession. In this, he states more fully his exercises under the influence of godly sorrow. On the first part of the title, see on titles of Psalms iii. iv. *After he had gone in to Bathsheba* embraces the time of David's avowed marriage with her, Judges xv. 1. Bathsheba [or Bathshuah] was the daughter of Eliam, or of Ammiel, see 2 Sam. xi. 3; 1 Chron. iii. 5. Her husband Uriah, the Hittite, held the rank of captain, and was a faithful subject and soldier. His death was a great wrong. Hengstenberg: "We swim in mid-air so long as we do not perceive the reference to the discourse of Nathan." In gifts and in station, Nathan was David's inferior. But he was the right man to bring his king to repentance.

This Psalm is often and fitly called THE SINNER'S GUIDE. In some of its versions, it often helps the returning sinner. Athanasius recommends to some Christians, to whom he was writing, to repeat it when they awake at night. All evangelical churches are familiar with it. Luther: "There is no other Psalm which is oftener sung or prayed in the church." Scott and others date it B. C. 1034. In it we have these names of the Most High, *Eloah God, Elohim God* and *Adonai Lord,* on which see on Ps. xviii. 31; iii. 2; ii. 4. This is the first Psalm in which we have the word *Spirit,* used in application to the Holy Ghost.

1. *Have mercy upon me, O God. Mercy,* equivalent to undeserved favor. It always implies pity to the miserable; commonly, grace to the guilty. Here both ideas are embraced, see Judges xxi. 22; Job xix. 21; Ps. xli. 4; cxix. 29; Isa. xxxiii. 2. Without mercy in God, we should all be undone. "His power would destroy us, his wisdom confound us, his justice condemn us, his majesty affright us, but by his mercy all these turn to our good." Pool paraphrases this clause: "Pity, and help, and answer me, in the desires I am now spreading before thee;" Clarke: "Without mercy I am totally, finally ruined and undone." He wanted mercy. *According to thy lovingkindness.* It was all to be found in God's nature. *Loving-kindness,* elsewhere mercy, kindness, merciful kindness. He asks for a large measure of grace: *According unto the multitude of thy tender mercies, blot out my transgressions.*

Multitude, abundance, plenty, greatness. *Tender mercies*, one word, *compassions*, *bowels*, also *mercies*. Alexander: "It is a term expressive of the warmest and tenderest affections." Some fitly note a gradation of increasing strength in the words *mercy*, *lovingkindness*, and *tender mercies*. *Blot out*, cancel, obliterate as one did when he turned the smooth end of his writing instrument and passed it over the tablet of wax, on which an account was charged. *Transgressions*, plural, *sins*, *trespasses*. Discontent, ingratitude, covetousness, hardness of heart, selfishness, pride, worldliness, unbelief, adultery and murder were all chargeable to David in the matter of Uriah. A clear sight of one sin is sure to show us others, John iv. 29.

2. *Wash me thoroughly from my iniquity, and cleanse me from my sin.* *Wash thoroughly*, literally, multiply to wash, as in Isa. lv. 7, *abundantly pardon* is multiply to pardon; equivalent to "Wash me again and again." *Iniquity, wrong, injury, unrighteousness*, sometimes *perverseness* or *wickedness*. *Sin*, commonly so rendered; sometimes, sin-offering. *Cleanse*, to make clean or to pronounce clean. Both these verbs refer rather to justification than to sanctification, though both ideas must be retained. Pardon and purification are never separated. Either by itself would not satisfy a good man. Nathan had said, "The Lord hath put away thy sin; that thou shalt not die," 2 Sam. xii. 13. This did not quiet his mind. Adultery and murder were both punishable with death. There was no magistrate higher in office than David, and so there was no man authorized to put him to death. Not even the Sanhedrim could arraign and punish kings, although the Talmudists say they could. But they never did. God himself by a direct judgment would have inflicted the penalty had he not graciously remitted the just sentence of temporal death. No doubt the pardon included the remission of the penalty of eternal death; for it would have been a small matter to have had his life spared, if his soul were damned. How then does David still pray for pardon? Some have thought he was asking not for judicial pardon, but for fatherly forgiveness. No doubt he did desire God to afford him his paternal smiles and the tokens of his love. But a mere assertion of our free pardon made by one of God's ministers however high in office and gifts, never satisfies a penitent soul. Calvin: "Although God, through the promise of forgiveness, freely invites us to peace, we are still to lay to heart our guilt, that deeper pain may penetrate our hearts. Hence it comes to pass, that with the small measure of our faith, we cannot at once take in the entire fulness of the divine grace, which has been brought unto us." Those, whom God forgives, do not readily forgive themselves; and a true hope of pardon desires assurance of that blessing. It is one thing to have a promise. It is another thing to be able to appropriate that promise.

3. *For I acknowledge my transgressions.* *Transgressions*, the same word as in v. 1. For *acknowledge* the Septuagint, Vulgate, Calvin, Venema, Alexander and others read *know;* Syriac, *have known;* but a declaration that we *know* our trespasses is an *acknowledgment* of them. The verb however is in the future, *will know*, thus declaring that he expected to retain a deep sense of his sin, as long as he should live. *And my sin is ever before me.* If the verb supplied here shall follow the tense of the parallel clause, it would be, my sin shall ever be before me, q. d., I have now and I expect always to have a painful sense of my miserable misconduct. I am justly condemned. Luther: "That little word *for* must be so understood as not to imply that his sins must be forgiven him because he had confessed them; for sin is always sin, and deserving of punishment, whether it is confessed or not; still confession of sin is of importance on this account that God will be gracious to no one, but to those who confess their sin; while to those who do not confess their sin, he will show no favor;" see on Ps. xxxii. 3–5.

4. *Against thee, thee only, have I sinned, and done* this *evil in thy sight.* This clause

is much urged against the Davidic authorship of this Psalm. It is said that David's sins were against Bathsheba, Uriah and those who perished with him; and that he could not truly say that he had sinned against God *only.* Clarke: His sins were "public, grievous, and against society at large, as well as against the peace, honor, comfort, and *life* of an innocent, brave and patriotic man." This is the objection. Sufficient answers can be given. 1. God alone was above David in the kingdom. To God alone was he legally responsible for his acts. 2. All sin is against God in this sense that it is his law that is broken, his authority that is despised, his government that is set at naught. Bishop Hall: "It is thy prohibition, O God, that can make a sin. I have sinned against men, but it is thy law that I have violated, in that is my offence." We never see sin aright until we see it as against God. Pharaoh and Balaam, Saul and Judas each said, *I have sinned,* Ex. ix. 27; Num. xxii. 34; 1 Sam. xv. 30; Matt. xxvii. 4; but the returning prodigal said: I have sinned *against heaven* and before thee; and David: Against thee, thee only have I sinned. 3. If David sinned not "against God only" in an absolute sense, yet comparatively his offence was against God only. That, which made his sin peculiarly and preëminently heinous, and grievous, and burdensome to his conscience, was that it offended God, brought dishonor on religion, and exhibited against the Most High the vilest ingratitude. So that it is not necessary to resort to the turn of thought given by the Chaldee: Before thee only have I sinned, though in a sense that was true also, "Thou didst it secretly," 2 Sam. xii. 12. David had so sinned, and so saw his sin that he felt it to be just in God to pass that heavy sentence in 2 Sam. xii. 10–14. Yea more: *That thou mightest be justified when thou speakest, and be clear when thou judgest.* God's throne would have been spotless in pronouncing the sentence of everlasting banishment from his presence. All men ought to acknowledge that their damnation would be just. All penitent men do so confess. The quotation of the Septuagint version of this verse, found in Rom. iii. 4, if rightly translated, does not give a sense materially different from that which we have gathered here. *Speaking* and *judging* are parallel terms, signifying the *pronouncing of a sentence.* *Clear*, might be rendered *clean*, or *quit, i. e.,* justified or victorious in the contest with David, *overcome* being the word used in Rom. iii. 4.

5. *Behold, I was shapen in iniquity; and in sin did my mother conceive me.* That the doctrine of original and universal depravity was taught from the first is clear from Gen. v. 3; vi. 5; viii. 21; Job xiv. 4; xv. 14; xxv. 4. That David embraced it is clear from his writings, v. 5; Ps. lviii. 3. David is not excusing but condemning himself. There is no blot on the character of his father Jesse. By the Holy Ghost he twice informs us of the piety of his mother, Ps. lxxxvi. 16; cxvi. 16. To say that David is here merely publishing the sins of one or both of his parents is trifling with sacred things. Even the Council of Trent, Bellarmine and Bossuet maintain the doctrine of hereditary depravity. The doctrine is taught in the symbols of all the purest churches in the world, and by all the best commentators. Commonly all, who hold the orthodox doctrine on this subject, cite this verse in proof. It is very pertinent. David is humbling himself and repenting before God. In doing so, he renounces all merit, confesses his actual sins, and then traces them up to their fruitful source, "*birth-sin*," as the church of England styles it. Calvin: "David here refers to original sin with the view of aggravating his guilt, acknowledging that he had not contracted this or that sin for the first time lately, but had been born into the world with the seed of every iniquity."

6. *Behold, thou desirest truth in the inward parts.* *Desirest, hast desired, hast required.* God has always done so, and does so still. *Truth*, as in Ps. xv. 2. *Inward parts;* Chaldee, reins; Edwards, inmost parts; not the word rendered reins in Ps. vii. 9; but parts *overspread* as with fat. *And in the hidden part thou shalt make me to know*

wisdom. In Hebrew the verb is in the future. It is best so rendered, as expressive of hope. Some read, Do thou teach. This also gives a good sense and is admissible. *Wisdom,* equivalent to true and intelligent piety, variously expressed in the Bible, as *understanding, a good understanding.*

7. *Purge me with hyssop, and I shall be clean. Purge,* in the future, *shalt purge;* but the common version is good. Chaldee: Thou wilt sprinkle me as the priest, which sprinkleth the unclean with the purifying waters, with hyssop, with the ashes of an heifer, and I shall be clean. *Hyssop,* a plant included in the studies of Solomon, 1 Kings iv. 33; the same word in Hebrew, Greek, Latin and English. It was used in sprinkling the blood of the passover lamb, Ex. xii. 22; it was also used in the ceremony of admitting the healed leper to the privileges of the congregation, Lev. xiv. 4, 6, 49, 51, 52; also in making the waters of purification, Num. xix. 6, 18. It is not certain to which of the above ceremonial uses David refers in this verse. He may have them all in view. But there is no objection to the supposition that he distinctly had before his mind the cleansing of the leper, *i. e.,* the pronouncing of him clean. This is probable, not only from the fitness of the thing itself, but also from the allusion to this ceremony in the word *cleanse* in Lev. xiv. 2. Morrison: "The word, rendered *purge me,* should be translated, *Do thou purge me from sin.*" Clarke has it: " *Thou shalt make a sin-offering for me.*" The law had a shadow of good things to come, and men taught of God understood much of its great import even before Christ came. *Wash me, and I shall be whiter than snow. Wash,* as in v. 2. *Whiter than snow.* We have the same figure in Isa. i. 18. Some cite 1 Cor. vi. 11 as parallel.

8. *Make me to hear joy and gladness;* that *the bones* which *thou hast broken may rejoice.* A broken bone gives great and constant pain. For a moment the mind may be diverted from it, or sleep may supervene and a man may forget his pain; but as soon as one is fully awake, or his mind released from that which had called it away, it reverts to the old pain. Where many bones are broken the condition is truly deplorable. David says he knows neither joy nor gladness, nor shall he till God shall undertake for him. Calvin and Symson think the use of the word *hear* points to the comfort which David sought from *hearing the word of God.*

9. *Hide thy face from my sins.* When we wish no longer to think of an object, we avert our faces. So David desires that God would no longer behold his sins. To *hide the face* is to refuse to see, equivalent to justify, Num. xxiii. 21. *And blot out all mine iniquities. Blot out,* see on v. 1. *Iniquities,* the plural of the same word in v. 2. He asks not merely for the remission of one sin, of a few sins, of many sins, but of *all* sins. One unpardoned sin is fatal to peace and salvation. The verbs of this verse are in the imperative.

10. *Create in me a clean heart, O God. Create,* as in Gen. i. 1. Its use shows that David was not asking to have his nature *improved,* but *renewed;* not *amended,* but *created anew.* Much of the preceding part of the Psalm contains prayer for remission of sins. This verse brings out clearly what had been implied in vv. 2, 7, viz., his desire for sanctification, a thorough renovation of nature. We cannot find words better suited to express a desire after holiness. The sense of total want, and total dependence, accompanied by a reliance on God alone for grace and purification, is well expressed. The work of renewal must be inward, in the *heart;* it must be thorough, amounting to a *creation.* It is mighty. If there is any greater exercise of power than that which brought all things out of nothing, it is that which brings a clean thing out of an unclean, or makes a saint out of a sinner. *And renew a right spirit within me. Spirit,* the word commonly so rendered. *Right,* elsewhere fixed, established, ready, perfect. Mudge has firmly stayed; Venema and Ainsworth, firm;

Trench and Skinner, steadfast. *Within me*, literally in the midst of me; Chaldee, in my innermost parts.

11. *Cast me not away from thy presence.* He admits that such banishment from God would be just. The loss of the light of God's countenance, and of comfortable communion with him is truly dreadful. The apprehension of so dreadful an evil fills the renewed soul with the deepest sadness. No prayers are more fervent than those offered by good men against such a doom. *And take not thy Holy Spirit from me.* No name of the third person of the Trinity is so often found in Scripture as that of the Holy Spirit, or Spirit of holiness. He is a *Spirit.* He is *holy* in his nature, and in his works. He is the author of holy Scripture and of all holiness in the heart of man. If he leaves us we are undone. All our offerings without the Holy Ghost are an offence to God. All our efforts to reach the haven of eternal rest without the heavenly Sanctifier and Comforter are unavailing. No mental and moral culture secures the growth of right principles and affections without his efficiency. For no blessing is a good man more earnest in supplication than for the indwelling of the Holy Ghost.

12. *Restore unto me the joy of thy salvation.* There are real joys in salvation. He who has once experienced them does not lightly esteem them, or easily forget them. Yet a good man may by sin lose much of the comforts of religion. When he does so, and is made sensible of it, he is very miserable until they are restored. *And uphold me* with thy *free Spirit.* Syriac: And thy glorious Spirit shall sustain me; Arabic: And with a powerful spirit establish me; Vulgate and Doway: And strengthen me with a perfect spirit; Venema: And thy free Spirit shall sustain me; Dimock: Let a *free* spirit sustain me; *i. e.,* Let me not be enslaved, as I have been, by my sinful passions; Jebb: And with the spirit of freedom uphold me; Boothroyd: And let a free spirit sustain me; Hengstenberg: And with a joyful spirit do thou support me. In this Psalm, Spirit is used in application to David's temper and to the third person of the Trinity. If it here refers to the Holy Spirit, it is very plain, gives a good sense, and agrees with the analogy of faith. This is the view of many. Fry renders it: And let thy bountiful Spirit support me. He thinks *bountiful* might be "spontaneously flowing," and supposes it has its explanation in John iv. 14; vii. 38. The best commentators generally regard the Spirit of God as here spoken of. In Rom. viii. 2, 15; 2 Cor. iii. 17; Gal. iv. 6, 7, we get light as to the freedom of the Spirit. In our version *free* is elsewhere willing, liberal; in the plural, princes, Ps. xlvii. 9. If any choose to understand free of David's temper, the sense is not so good, still a king may well pray for a *liberal* and *princely* spirit.

13. Then *will I teach transgressors thy ways; and sinners shall be converted unto thee.* *Then* is supplied the better to preserve the connection. We must have God's Spirit, and be sustained by the joys of religion, if we would be apt, diligent and successful in leading others to repentance. *Thy ways*, that is, thy will, law and gospel, revealed for our salvation, thy way of holiness, thy way of saving sinners, thy way of recovering backsliders.

14. *Deliver me from blood guiltiness, O God, thou God of my salvation.* *Deliver*, generally so rendered; see on Ps. vii. 1; xxii. 20. *Blood guiltiness*, literally *bloods;* see on Ps. v. 6. The prayer is for deliverance from the guilt of innocent blood already shed, and preservation from shedding innocent blood hereafter. In his prayer he looks to God alone, even the God who had saved him hitherto, and had promised to save him hereafter. And *my tongue shall sing aloud of thy righteousness.* Great mercies call for great songs. *Sing aloud*, the word used to express the joy of angels at creation, Job xxxviii. 7; often as here, also *shout, shout for joy, rejoice, cry out.* Calvin: Sing aloud with joy; Hengstenberg, Joyfully extol; Alexander, Celebrate. It always expresses vehemence, and if of pleasant emotions, exultation. *Thy righteousness*, "not that of

the law," says Diodati, "which condemneth irremissibly; but that of the gospel, which maintains the promises of grace, and according to them doth grant pardon, Rom. iii. 26." Or it refers, some think, to his readiness always to proclaim God's righteousness in all he had threatened against David and his family.

15. *O Lord, open thou my lips,* "which are shut with shame, and grief, and horror." Nothing so effectually closes the mouth as a just sense of our sins, Matt. xxii. 12; Rom. iii. 18. The future form of the Hebrew verb expresses hopeful expectation. *And my lips shall shew forth thy praise.* Luther: "If we have through faith in Christ received the righteousness and grace of God, we can do no greater work than speak and declare the truth of Christ." A soul released from guilt, and wrath, and shame, cannot but publish in some fit way the goodness of God displayed towards it. *Shew forth,* elsewhere *tell, utter, report, declare.* Compare Ps. l. 14, 23.

16. *For thou desirest not sacrifice; else I would give* it: *thou delightest not in burnt offering.* Besides the general doctrine taught in Ps. l. that sacrifices cannot put away sin from the soul, and are of no value compared with the spiritual duties of religion; it is here also stated that for such crimes as David had been guilty of no sacrifice was appointed in the law. God ordained no bleeding victims for murder, or adultery, or for any of the sins of heart that led to these. In such a case he did not *desire,* would not accept a burnt offering.

17. *The sacrifices of God are a broken spirit: a broken and a contrite heart, O God, thou wilt not despise.* The *sacrifices of God, great sacrifices;* as the *trees of God* are *the great trees,* and the *river of God,* the *great river.* *Sacrifices,* in the plural, q. d., A broken spirit is worth more than all other sacrifices. The phrase also includes the idea that they are such as God has appointed, and such as will please him. *Broken,* the same in both cases in this verse. See on Ps. xxxiv. 18. *Contrite;* in v. 8, another form of the word is rendered *hast broken;* in Ps. xxxviii 8, *sore broken.* The prominent idea seems to be *bruised* or *crushed.* That, which breaks the heart, is God's word, Jer. xxiii. 29. There is no better rendering than *contrite,* which primarily signifies *broken small* as by *braying.* *Wilt not despise,* by a common figure of speech much more is implied than is said. It means that a broken and contrite heart is a delight to God. See Ps. xxxiv. 18; cii. 17; cxlvii. 3; Isa. lvii. 15; lxi. 1; lxvi. 1, 2; Luke vii. 36–50. On this blessed truth the mind of David finds repose.

18. *Do good in thy good pleasure unto Zion.* The church should pray for kings, 1 Tim. ii. 1, 2; but kings should pray for the church, according to David's example. "No man can truly pray for himself, unless he pray for the church also." "Prayer hath more power than armor." Gill thinks that the *good pleasure* of God here mentioned may refer either to the time of his good pleasure, the Gospel dispensation, or to the cause and source of God's blessings to the church, viz., his sovereign good will. *Zion* is the church. *Build thou the walls of Jerusalem.* *Jerusalem* is a name for the church, parallel to Zion. It is needless to defend the Davidic authorship of this Psalm from the alleged inconsistency of David praying that the walls of the holy city might be built. By his sin he had weakened the cause of religion. He asks God to repair the breaches which his own misconduct had made. Scott: "David feared lest his guilt should render him as an *Achan* in the congregation of Israel; and therefore he concluded his penitential prayer, with entreating God to protect and prosper Zion." He had given great occasion to the enemy to speak reproachfully; had done much damage to religion, and had brought a curse on his own house, 2 Sam. xii. 10–14. While acknowledging the justice of God's severity against himself and his family, he prays that the holy city may be protected and made strong, and especially that the church may not be weakened by his fall. God is answering his prayer to this day. That this Psalm was not written when by exile it was impossible to offer

sacrifices is evident from v. 16, where David says he would make such offering, not if it were possible, but if God desired it.

19. *Then shalt thou be pleased with the sacrifices of righteousness, with burnt offering and whole burnt offering.* The meaning is that when God shall build up Jerusalem, and cause true religion to flourish, then all its outward expressions, divinely appointed, will be pleasing to him, because they will be the fruit of piety and not a substitute for it; they will be sincere, hearty and pure, not formal and so offensive to God. The sacrifices then will be those of *righteousness*, (see on Ps. v. 4) not of deceit, and hypocrisy; such as prayer, praise, penitence, doing good to the poor and afflicted, as well as *burnt offering*, or *burnt sacrifice*. *Whole burnt offering* is the translation of " a single Hebrew word, meaning a sacrifice entirely consumed upon the altar." Alexander: " It does not describe something wholly distinct from the burnt-offering, but the burnt-offering itself considered as a complete and unreserved oblation. See 1 Sam. vii. 9." See also Rom. xii. 1. *Then shall they offer bullocks upon thine altar. Bullocks* were the largest and most costly sacrifices. When religion flourishes in the hearts of God's people, they do not meanly count the cost of any service they render to him.

Doctrinal and Practical Remarks.

1. Nathan's fearlessness and faithfulness in reproving sin in David instructs all, who are called to the like painful duty, that they should go straight forward, and trust in God. Who knows but that the faithful reprover may save a soul from death, and hide a multitude of sins? Our inferior gifts and station cannot justify us in suffering sin upon our brother, though he be our monarch. And let not great men despise their humble friends, who tell them of their sins.

2. Such fidelity is made specially necessary by the amazing stupidity of conscience that we observe even in good men, when they have sadly departed from God. How could David so long remain quiet? Sin awfully blinds the mind and hardens the heart. To be at ease, to cry peace, to have no fears does not prove any man innocent.

3. When a sin, though secretly committed at last becomes public, our confession of it and our sorrow for it should not be merely expressed to one or two, but before all. The king is no exception.

4. This Psalm gives us much insight into the nature of sin. It is a missing of the mark. It is *transgression*. It is rebellion. It is *iniquity*. It is *evil*, and only *evil*. It covers us with guilt and shame and filthiness. It is folly, the opposite of *wisdom*. It is a lie, the opposite of *truth*. It unmans a man. Left to itself it *crushes* him who indulges it. It covers the soul with a pall of the deepest sadness. It separates between God and his creature. One sin naturally leads to another. It shuts the mouth. It opens hell. It debases the best mental gifts. Like a foul disease it is hereditary, loathsome and a reproach; it banishes from the best society, even that of heaven, it makes men dull and heavy, it cannot be cured by any finite power or human means. Even a heathen once said: " If I knew that the gods would pardon me, and men would not see me, yet I would not sin, because of the vileness of sin." And God hates it. To him it is " horrible," " abominable." Nothing worse does inspiration say of sin than that it is " exceeding sinful." If we think lightly of sin, we shall not be much concerned to be rid of its guilt or defilement, nor be very watchful against its assaults, nor very thankful for supposed deliverance from its curse or its power.

5. This Psalm also gives us refreshing views of God's grace. It tells us of *mercy*, of mercy to a great sinner, of *loving-kindness*, of the *multitude of God's tender mercies*, of his *blotting out transgressions*, of his *thoroughly washing* a man that confessed he was very vile. These are the very mercies sinners need, worth more than all temporal good things. They are the foundation of a blissful eternity. Well is it that

our God is merciful, long-suffering, slow to anger, and ready to forgive. With him mercy is original, infinite, everlasting. As we sin daily, we must daily pray, *Forgive us our debts*. It is natural for poor afflicted souls to cry for mercy, and it is a glorious truth that God's mercy endureth forever. When we remember to how many sinners God shows mercy, how heinous and numerous their sins are, and how rich are the undeserved blessings he bestows on them, surely we may say, his mercy is great. All this mercy is free, without money, without price, without merit on the part of men. It is wondrously rich and efficacious.

6. Without the pardon of sin all other things would not be blessings to us. It is the first thing David seeks, v. 1. He asks for it over and over again, vv. 7, 9. In Ps. ciii. it is the first mercy catalogued. Sinners need nothing more than pardon. Why are not all men crying for pardon?

7. In this Psalm as often in other Scriptures justification and sanctification are not confounded, but united, vv. 1, 2, 6–17. Whose sins are blotted out, he is also washed and made clean. Whose sins are purged with hyssop sprinkling the blood of the Lamb of God, he has a *clean heart* and a *right spirit* put within him. It is the error of some that they seek knowledge but not holiness, hope of pardon and acceptance, but not the image and spirit of Christ.

8. We do but deceive and torment ourselves when we refuse to confess to God our sins whatever they may be, v. 3. If God should pardon and accept us while we refuse to acknowledge our transgressions, we should be proud in proportion to our assurance of salvation. God's plan is to humble us, so as to make it every way safe to receive us into his favor. Scott: "While sinners conceal or palliate their sins, they are out of the way of mercy: but when they humbly and ingenuously plead guilty, and unreservedly confess their crimes, they may even plead that confession as a reason why they should be spared: for this yields the point in contest; namely, that the Lord might justly punish, and that salvation must be all of grace."

9. Real and genuine conviction of sin is not transient. "My sin is *ever* before me," v. 3.

10. The worst thing in every sin is that it is *against God*, v. 4. When just *human* laws are broken, the *divine* law is much more violated. All sin is against him, who is infinite, eternal and unchangeable in his being, wisdom, power, holiness, justice, goodness and truth.

11. The doctrine of original sin is both true and practical. It is taught in the holy Scriptures. It has its place in a genuine religious experience, v. 5. We must maintain it, however it may be derided and reviled. Luther: "In this Psalm we have it clearly expressed, that sin is a great and innate evil, and an awful depravation and corruption of nature, in all the powers both of soul and body." Calvin: "David confesses that he brought nothing but sin with him into the world, and that his nature was entirely depraved." Horne: "A creature begotten by a sinner, and formed in the womb of a sinner cannot be without that taint, which is hereditary to every son and daughter of Adam and Eve." Hengstenberg: "That Adam's fall is the fall of the human family is implied in the *punishment*, which affects not the individual, but the entire race." Symson: "What is the reason that a young fox newly whelped doth not slay a lamb? Is it not because it lacketh strength, and is not come to that maturity to execute its inclination, which is naturally cruel? So are infants naturally inclined to sin; and therefore so soon as they can think anything, speak or do anything, it is evil, as daily experience teacheth."

12. It is vain to attempt to impose upon God by a maintenance of decent appearances, v. 6. God's law will relax nothing on account of our sinfulness. There is no innocent way of becoming or continuing vile and hypocritical. It is wicked to be a

sinner by nature or practice. We may speak of doing as well as we can, and of being sincere; but mere natural sincerity in God's service, without a change of nature, is heartless hypocrisy.

13. Prayer should have hope in it, v. 6. Petitions offered in despair are desperate folly. If we dare not hope that God will hear us, he will not hear us. If we would be saved by his mercy, we must honor him with our confidence.

14. True *wisdom* is from above. If we ever attain it, it must be by God *making us to know it,* v. 6. Symson: "This age hath heard many lessons, and God hath manifested his whole will unto them; but because they obey them not, their knowledge shall augment their pains. God must be our great Doctor and Teacher. We must be *Theodoctai,* taught of God. Neither nature, learning, experience, practice, nor age can teach us wisdom," Jas. i. 5, 6.

15. As under the law there was no remission without blood, so neither is there under the Gospel; only the blood sprinkled with the bunch of hyssop was that of a beast or bird, whereas we are cleansed only by the blood of Jesus, v. 7. The type admitted the worshipper to a place in the public congregation. The antitype admits the worshipper into the favor of God, and finally into heaven itself. The blood of a lamb brought ceremonial purification; much more has the blood of Jesus all-sufficient efficacy, Heb. ix. 13, 14.

16. Salvation by Christ is perfect in all respects. The vile, guilty, polluted soul, on embracing Christ, and being washed in his blood, and renewed by his Spirit, is made *whiter than snow,* v. 7.

17. If a truly awakened and convinced sinner ever finds joy and gladness, it must be by the cross and Spirit of Christ, as we are made acquainted with them by God himself, v. 8. Compare also vv. 7, 10, 11, 12.

18. Well may a real child of God hope and pray for joy and gladness, v. 8. Some commentators think that the sad fall, which caused David to write this Psalm, had a chastening effect on him all the latter part of his life, and caused a tincture of sadness to appear in his subsequent compositions; yet there is abundant proof that if he was sorrowful, he also rejoiced. Symson: "As a Christian is the most sorrowful man in the world, so there is none more glad than he. For the cause of his joy is greatest: in respect his misery was greatest, his delivery greatest, therefore his joy greatest: from death and hell is he freed, to life in heaven is he brought. What can make men more glad than this, if we believe?"

19. Genuine conviction of sin is not *slight,* v. 8. It gives pains like to *broken bones.* Tholuck: "The point which every sinner must reach, who would realize the forgiveness of his sins, is that he feels himself condemned by his conscience without being accused of men, and that he cannot but acknowledge the justice of the condemning sentence of God." Arnd: "What these *bones broken* are, no one can tell, but he who feels, in great temptations, the wrath of God, the curse of the law, the sting of death which is sin, and the power of sin which is the law. Then one experiences what the office and strength of the law is."

20. Because that which is born of the flesh is flesh, and only that which is born of the Spirit is spirit, therefore regeneration, called also a resurrection, a translation, a passing from death unto life, a new creation, and in v. 10 a *creation,* is the only hope of fallen man. I greatly marvel at the mercy of this great change: but I have long since ceased to marvel at its necessity. How else can the love of sin be cured? How else can the love of God be shed abroad within us?

21. He, who rests satisfied with a fitful religion, and has no stability of character, does but deceive himself. A *right* spirit is a *fixed* spirit, v. 10.

22 It is an amazing mercy not to be forsaken of God, and we should earnestly

pray against a doom so dreadful, v. 11. His favor is life and his loving-kindness is better than life. Forsaken by him, nothing goes right. Horne: "Rejection from the *presence* and desertion by the *Spirit* of God is the most deplorable and irremediable effect of sin; but it is one, that in general perhaps is the least considered and regarded of all others."

23. Whoever has felt the joy of God's salvation knows by experience that it is both real and unspeakable. God alone can give it at the first, and God alone can restore it when lost, v. 12.

24. Let not humble souls be cast down with overmuch sorrow, because their joys do not always abound. Life is a checker work. Summer and winter alternate. We all have our ups and downs. After Paul's abundant revelations came the thorn in the flesh, the messenger of Satan. "After a Christian hath mourned he will rejoice. He, who never sorrowed for sin, will never rejoice for grace. He that never grieved for the affliction of Joseph, will never rejoice for the consolation of Israel."

25. Let us not be high-minded, but fear. The whole of life is a test of the strength of our principles. Some seasons are peculiarly so. David, Samson and Peter were all strong in the Lord, stronger perhaps than thou art, gentle reader; but being left to themselves, how they fell and lost their comforts. "I never saw any who presumed above others of their own strength, but they have proved the weakest soldiers, who by Thrasonical confidence in their wisdom, holiness, constancy, and other of their virtues, bragged above their neighbors, yea, contemned them, but in the end they prove cowards presuming in pride, and falling with shame."

26. True penitents honestly promise and engage to render obedience and service, as God shall help them and fit them to do so, v. 13. When Peter should be converted, he was to strengthen his brethren, Luke xxii. 32.

27. Clear and remarkable conversions, especially of great sinners, are in many ways well suited to bring about other conversions, v. 13. Compare Matt. xxi. 32; 1 Tim. i. 16.

28. As "there is no enemy like an offended conscience, no anguish like self-reproach, no war so fierce as that which a man wages with himself," so of all the burdens arising from crimes against man, none seems to be so intolerable as that from *blood-guiltiness*, v. 14. Juvenal says: "Seldom do tyrants die an unbloody death." Even when they are not killed by violence, conscience kills them, as in the case of Charles IX. of France, when by its horrors it drove the blood through his skin.

29. Pardoned sinners should both engage and endeavor to proclaim the sovereign mercy of God, and with the loudest praises, v. 14. Henry: "Penitents should be preachers;" Luther: "If we have, through faith in Christ, received the righteousness and grace of God, we can do no greater work than speak and declare the truth of Christ;" Symson: "There shall be a natural song, which we shall sing forever, even the song of Moses the servant of God. Let us therefore begin on earth and learn our gamut here." Let us specially *sing* of him, who is the *Lord our righteousness*, and who is faithful and just to forgive us our sins, if we confess and forsake them.

30. The dreadful state of a convicted and unpardoned sinner is well set forth by the sealed lips of David in v. 15. Suppose God should fully show a man his sins and all their aggravations, and then leave him in that state forever, would it not be of itself hell?

31. Dickson: "Howsoever proud spirits think that they can do anything they please in God's service, yet an humbled soul under exercise knoweth that it is God who giveth both to will and to do of his good pleasure; such a man knoweth that the habit of grace is a gift, and the bringing of the habit into exercise is another

gift; he knoweth that when one hath gotten grace to will to praise God, he must have grace to put this will to act effectually," v. 15.

32. We should sincerely profess our willingness to do or suffer anything in our power, if it be to the glory of God, and according to his will, v. 16.

33. No man can prove that God is better pleased with innocence in an angel than he is with penitence in a sinner, v. 17.

34. In joy and in sorrow, repenting or rejoicing, in public and in private, let us pray for Zion, v. 18. She is dear to God. She is dear to his saints.

35. When true religion flourishes, and Zion is a praise among men, then God is pleased with all the appointed services of his house, v. 19. They may be plain and simple, they may be neither costly nor showy; but Jehovah smiles upon them, and blesses them.

36. Let us always give God the best of everything, v. 19.

37. The whole Psalm calls God's people to give the most earnest heed to the things of religion, lest at any time they should let them slip. "The best of men need to be warned against the worst of sins."

38. If you would know the nature of true repentance, study this Psalm. It is full of wisdom and sound doctrine.

39. Will not the impenitent reader be persuaded to follow the example of David, and cry for mercy? Let him come to God humbly and penitently, casting himself at the feet of sovereign mercy. O dying man! confess your guilt, bewail your transgressions, forsake your sins, beg for the application of the blood of Christ! God is merciful. You need no more mercy than he is fully willing to bestow. If your faults are many, he will give you double for all your sins. He will abundantly pardon. His mercy reaches to the heavens. He never cast away any that came to him through Christ Jesus.

PSALM LII.

To the chief Musician, Maschil, *A Psalm* of David, when Doeg the Edomite came and told Saul, and said unto him, David is come to the house of Ahimelech.

1 Why boastest thou thyself in mischief, O mighty man? the goodness of God *endureth* continually.

2 Thy tongue deviseth mischiefs; like a sharp razor, working deceitfully.

3 Thou lovest evil more than good; *and* lying rather than to speak righteousness. Selah.

4 Thou lovest all devouring words, O *thou* deceitful tongue.

5 God shall likewise destroy thee for ever, he shall take thee away, and pluck thee out of *thy* dwellingplace, and root thee out of the land of the living. Selah.

6 The righteous also shall see, and fear, and shall laugh at him:

7 Lo, *this is* the man *that* made not God his strength; but trusted in the abundance of his riches, *and* strengthened himself in his wickedness.

8 But I *am* like a green olive tree in the house of God: I trust in the mercy of God for ever and ever.

9 I will praise thee for ever, because thou hast done *it:* and I will wait on thy name; for *it is* good before thy saints.

ON the first three clauses of the title see on titles of Psalms iii. iv. xi. xxxii. The rest of the title refers to a piece of history fully recorded in 1 Sam. xxi. 1–9; xxii. 6–23. The common opinion is that throughout the Psalm David has Doeg in his mind. But some think that Edomite is too inconsiderable a person, and so they make Saul the prominent character in the Psalm. But in the cruel affair of slaying the priests and all the inhabitants of a town, none can tell whether Doeg or Saul was the most atrocious offender. Walford: "If we are confounded by the savage ferocity of a prince who could order the execution of eighty-five persons of most venerable station for a crime which existed alone in his disturbed imagination, we shall feel disposed to execrate the ruthless villain who could imbrue his hands in the blood of so many innocent victims; and we shall be ready to draw the conclusion, that both Saul and Doeg were prompted to this deed of atrocious cruelty, not merely by their hatred of David, but by a malevolence, almost without a parallel, against the ministers of religion; and which rendered conspicuous their contempt and hatred of God himself." So far as the baseness of their conduct is considered, the Psalm might have chief reference to either Saul or Doeg. Nor can we think of the wickedness of one of these evil men in this matter without at the same time seeing that like thoughts would suit the other. Still the common view is perhaps the best, viz., that David speaks particularly of Doeg in this Psalm. The narrative in 1 Samuel certainly so inclines the reader. Clarke: "All the versions agree in this title except the Syriac, which speaks of it as a Psalm directed against vice in general, with a prediction of the destruction of evil." There is no doubt that David wrote it. Clarke dates it B. C. 1062; Scott, B. C. 1061. The names of the Most High here found are *El God* and *Elohim God*, on which see on Ps. v. 4; iii. 2. On Selah see Introduction, § 15.

1. *Why boastest thou thyself in mischief, O mighty man?* *Boastest*, in the future, why wilt thou boast? *Mischief*; Syriac, *malice*; Ainsworth, Jebb, Fry and Alexander, *evil*. For *mighty man*, church of England has *tyrant*. After his horrid butchery, Doeg spoke and acted as though he had done a brave thing. No other man in Saul's camp dared to perpetrate the atrocity. Diodati thus paraphrases: "Why dost thou triumph in thy wickedness and cruelty, which thou findest to be favored and recompensed by Saul?" The question contains the language of defiance to an insolent foe. *The goodness of God endureth continually.* *Continually, daily, all the day*; Hengstenberg has *forever*. Persecutions do not annihilate God's kindness to his people. For a time malice may run riot; but at last God will appear for his saints. Indeed they constantly experience his mercies, even when murderers are let loose upon them.

2. *Thy tongue deviseth mischiefs; like a sharp razor, working deceitfully.* The *tongue* is said to *devise, think,* or *contrive* mischiefs, because when they are so devised the tongue utters them, the tongue being an essential instrument of boasting, slandering, reviling and other evil speaking. The razor works most keenly and effectually when it is sharpest and makes least noise. So "the words of a talebearer are as wounds, and go down into the innermost parts of the belly." And reproach is like "a sword in the bones," Ps. xviii. 8; Ps. xlii. 10. Pool: "*Like a sharp razor, working deceitfully;* wherewith a man pretending to shave off the hair doth suddenly and unexpectedly cut the throat. So Doeg pretended only to vindicate himself from the imputation of disloyalty, 1 Sam. xxii. 8, but really intended to expose the priests, who were friends to David, to the king's fury and cruelty."

3. *Thou lovest evil more than good.* No man equally loves good and evil. It is a natural impossibility, as it is for a man to serve two masters. The reason is that good and evil are directly opposed. There are no neutral moral characters. No man can love evil to a certain extent, and good to the same extent. The meaning of the clause therefore is, Thou art given over to evil, to work iniquity with greediness. Here the delight was in producing *misery* to others. And [thou lovest] *lying more than to speak righteousness.* Doeg had inflamed the irritable spirit of Saul by perverting the facts in regard to David's visit to Nob. He had *lied* respecting the conduct of Ahimelech.

Perversion of facts is often the most cruel method of falsehood and of subverting *right*.

4. *Thou lovest all devouring words, O* thou *deceitful tongue*. Evil words are well said to be *devouring*. They are as a madman casting firebrands, arrows, and death, Pr. xxvi. 18; Gal. v. 15. Doeg was a man who took pleasure in all words and deeds that seemed to give him advantage with a cruel prince, however much misery fell upon the innocent victims of his malice. *Deceitful tongue*, literally *tongue of deceit*, or *tongue of guile*. The *tongue* here is put for the man, as it had been a chief instrument of the mischief he had wrought.

5. *God shall likewise destroy thee forever*. There is remarkable agreement in the different translations in rendering this verb *destroy*, or *utterly destroy; though the same verb in the common version is elsewhere also rendered *break down, throw down, pull down, cast down, beat down, overthrow*, applied to demolishing *altars, houses*, or *towers*. The *destruction* threatened is complete. It is also *perpetual, i. e., forever*. There are three ways of explaining this threat, 1. David was inspired to utter woes against Doeg unless he should repent. We have the rule in Jer. xviii. 7, 8. It was acted on in the case of Nineveh. 2. David uttered views gathered from the general course of Providence. He had seen how bloody and deceitful men came to an early and violent death, (Ps. xxxvii. 11; lv. 23;) and he inferred it could not be that Doeg would prove an exception. 3. David speaking by the Holy Ghost, predicts the dreadful ruin of this man as an event awfully certain and now inevitable, as Christ did that of "the son of perdition." Henceforth he was a doomed man. This is not the only case noticed in the Old Testament, in which God showed one of his servants that he would certainly destroy a given wicked man, 2 Chron. xxv. 16. This last mode of explaining the language is, perhaps, to be preferred. The same remarks are applicable to the remaining clauses of this verse. *He shall take thee away*. Chaldee, *scatter thee;* Arabic, Septuagint, Ethiopic, Vulgate, Doway, Fry, *pluck thee out;* Ainsworth, *pull thee away;* Edwards, *snatch thee away*. As a *coal* removed from the hearth and left to itself, dies out, so should it be with Doeg. *And* [he shall] *pluck thee out of thy dwellingplace*. *Pluck* implies violence, in Prov. ii. 22, it is *root out*. "The wicked is driven away in his wickedness," Prov. xiv. 32. The Hebrew of *dwelling-place* is *tent* or *tabernacle*, and does not determine whether it was a private abode, or that in which God was worshipped. The original has nothing corresponding to *thy*. The Syriac, Arabic, Vulgate, Calvin, church of England, Edwards, Jebb and Alexander supply *thy*. But the Chaldee, Septuagint, Fabritius, Piscator, Ainsworth, Hammond, Venema, Amesius, Fry and others read simply *the tabernacle*. The Chaldee is very explicit: *He shall cause thee to depart from inhabiting in the place of the Shechinah*. Abenezra, Patrick and Henry expound it of the place where the ark was. If this latter view is correct, then the clause is equivalent to the greater excommunication, which, according to Hammond and others, delivered up the guilty man to the hands of God, to be cut off, himself and his posterity. If this is so, it throws light on the last clause of the verse: *And root thee out of the land of the living*. Such is the interpretation given of this clause by all the ancient versions, and by others. His posterity should perish with him, as did that of Achan. Doeg had pretended to worship God and had no doubt reaped advantages from the worship of Jehovah (1 Sam. xxi. 7); but he and his posterity should be alike cut off from these forever, and so fall under the terrible judgments of God. Horne: "Wonderful is the force of the verbs in the original of this verse. They convey to us the four ideas of 'laying prostrate,' 'dissolving as by fire,' 'sweeping away as with a besom,' and 'totally extirpating root and branch,' as a tree eradicated from the spot on which it grew."

6. *The righteous also shall see, and fear, and shall laugh at him*. We have a full

account of the end of Saul, but none of the end of Doeg. Yet we may rest assured that all that is here predicted came to pass; and when it did, it was observed by good men, and the sight increased their godly fear, as it always does, Isa. xxvi. 9. But while they feared God, they held this wicked man in derision. His name, like that of Cain, or Judas Iscariot, is never given to children. If ever mentioned, it is only as a synonyme for deceit, cruelty, and officious lying. What the righteous, as they saw his end, thought and said is now told us:

7. *Lo*, this is *the man* that *made not God his strength; but trusted in the abundance of his riches*, and *strengthened himself in his wickedness*. The verbs in Hebrew are in the future, signifying the perverseness and stubbornness of the sinner to the last of his life. The common version gives the sense, and is as good as any other. Doeg "trusted and feared Saul more than God, and was willing to purchase Saul's favor with God's displeasure." We know not the amount of Doeg's wealth. It probably was very considerable. He was 'the chiefest of Saul's herdsmen.' Doubtless he found his office profitable. And his slaughter of the helpless priests, women and children was probably rewarded by Saul with considerable gains. Perhaps he may have had great possessions for a man of his birth and prospects. And he trusted in uncertain riches. And the more he prospered the greater was his *wickedness*. The goodness of God did not lead him to repentance. Alexander: "The word translated *wickedness* is the singular of that translated *mischiefs* in v. 2 above. It seems to signify particularly an inclination to malicious mischief." For wickedness the marginal reading is *substance*. So also in Pr. x. 3. Perhaps it should read so here.

8. *But I* am *like a green olivetree in the house of God*. For *green* several versions read *fruit-bearing*, but this is interpretation, not translation. *Flourishing* is better. So the word is sometimes rendered, Ps. xcii. 14. The olive, in a healthy state, is perpetually covered with leaves, and from the time it is small to its latest healthy age it bears good fruit, and with its *fatness honors God and man*, Judg. ix. 9. It also lives to a great age, some say two thousand years. Henry thus paraphrases the clause: "This mighty man is plucked up by the roots; but *I am like a green olive-tree*, planted and rooted, fixed and flourishing; he is turned out of God's dwelling-place, but I am established in it, not *detained*, as Doeg, by anything but the abundant satisfaction I meet with there." So *excellent* is the olive-tree that in Scripture it is made an emblem of the visible church of our Lord Jesus Christ, Rom. xi. 17. *I trust in the mercy of God for ever and ever*, q. d., I have no confidence for my sustenance or deliverance at any part of my existence, present or future, but God alone; not that I deserve his aid, but I trust in his *mercy*, his *goodness*, his *favor*, his *kindness, loving-kindness*, his *merciful kindness*.

9. *I will praise thee for ever, because thou hast done* it; *i. e.*, because thou hast made this difference between the righteous and the wicked, between Doeg and me. *And I will wait on thy name, wait* in all the ways of thy appointment, public and private, in social and in secret worship, trusting in thy power, justice, mercy, and faithfulness, and so shall I renew my strength, Isa. xl. 31. *For it is good before thy saints*. Either God's name is *good*, or it is *good* to wait on him. The latter is the better. *Before, in the sight of, in the presence of*. *Saints, holy, godly, merciful* ones.

DOCTRINAL AND PRACTICAL REMARKS.

1. To have the best acts of our lives misrepresented, and to be belied and betrayed is no new thing. There is a Doeg in almost every large community. We ought so to think, and act accordingly. Human nature, unrestrained by divine grace, is no better in modern than in ancient times.

2. One of the most decisive evidences of reprobacy is to glory in our shame, v. 1.

Slade: "It is bad enough to imagine and to do mischief; but far worse to boast of it."

3. Doeg was a poor creature. He thought himself a *mighty man*, a giant, a hero. He killed, under the protection of the king's guards, eighty-five priests with their linen ephods on them, and a town full of unarmed and helpless men, women and sucklings. This was his prowess. There was not another man in all Saul's army mean enough to do the base deed even when commanded. No doubt Doeg thought he was very brave, yea, valorous. He was not the last man that gloried in a thing of naught.

4. The present seeming success of base conduct does not in the slightest degree change its character or its doom, v. 1. Calvin: "Any triumph, which may be obtained by violence, treachery, or other unjustifiable means, is short-lived." Let all men remember that.

5. In the darkest times God's benignity to his saints is unfailing, v. 1. Dickson: "So long as God's unchangeable kindness endureth, the wicked have no cause to exult over the godly, nor have the godly cause to faint or be discouraged." If we have God for our friend, it matters not who is our foe.

6. If sinners are bold and boastful, let not the righteous be timid and sneaking, but fearlessly charge home on the ungodly their atrocious crimes, and warn them of impending judgments, vv. 1–7. It is not only lawful but often obligatory, "even in very trying circumstances, supported by the elevating influence of faith, to inveigh against" the conduct of mean and unprincipled men in all positions in life, especially when they seem to be in the full tide of success. Our denunciations may strengthen ourselves, encourage our brethren, and warn men of weak virtue, who otherwise might become base informers, or miserable persecutors, or fall into some dreadful practices. Had David yielded to dismay when Doeg rose to high royal favor, he would probably not have had a handful of followers left. Indeed the bloody death of the innocent priests must have made many persons afraid to show any favor whatever to David and his cause. That was no time for playing the dastard.

7. Truthful records of human nature, left to act itself out in unrestrained freedom, will always show that the tongue has been an instrument of much evil, vv. 2–4. See on Ps. x. 7. Slade: "A false and deceitful tongue is dangerous and dreadful, cutting like a razor, devouring like a sword," James iii. 2–10. Words, as God knows them, are a sure index of the character.

8. There is a sense, in which the atrocious character of the wrongs we receive from wicked men may give us comfort, v. 2. God is righteous, and never really takes sides with wickedness against equity and truth. So when our enemies are clearly and wholly and solely in the wrong, we may rest assured God will in the end be favorable to us. There is always hope in our cause, if we are right, "and it is plain that the farther our enemies proceed in the practice of iniquity, they proportionally provoke the anger of the Lord," and make him to be their enemy. If Haman had merely felt some dislike to the Jews, he might have lived out all his days. But when he contrived their slaughter, he was a doomed man.

9. How smoothly and plausibly a deceitful man can talk. Doeg 'pretended only to vindicate himself from the charge of disloyalty, in making known to the king the transactions at Nob; but the whole affair shows that he intended evil against Ahimelech and the priests, because they were the friends of David, and the enemies of Saul's oppression.' Every generation has like hypocritical pretenders to patriotism and public spirit and zeal for government, when the fact is that revenge and love of plunder and the spirit of murder do actuate them.

10. There is a great deal of lying in the world, consisting of caricaturing, of suppressing parts of the truth, of narrating things out of their connection and of gar-

bling statements. Dickson: "It is no advantage to a malicious calumniator, to pretend that he told nothing but the truth, and told no more than what he saw; for it is true that David came to the house of Ahimelech," as Doeg said. Yet the conspiracy against Saul implied in what Doeg said, and in his manner of saying it, was all a wicked fabrication; and so he is justly charged with all the consequences that followed his officious informing of Saul.

11. Hypocrites are often very fond of the house of God, even when they are about to commit some great sin. Perhaps they hope to consecrate their vices. Doeg, even when detained in the house of God, had his naughty wicked heart with him, and was even then preparing to belie the ministers of God. One of the vilest characters mentioned in the Bible was after her way very pious, Pr. vii. 14, 15.

12. The smooth, adroit manner of executing a wicked device neither hides nor abates its wickedness. Murder with a *sharp razor* is as wicked as murder with a meat-axe or a bludgeon, v. 2. A lie very ingeniously framed and rehearsed in an oily manner is as great a sin and in the end will be seen to be as great a folly as the most bungling attempt at deception.

13. Dickson: "When a man speaketh no more of a tale of his neighbor, but what may serve to the man's hurt and prejudice, and keepeth up the relation of that part of the tale which might clear the man's innocence, or might give a right construction of his actions; albeit that part of the tale told be true, if all the rest of the tale had been told with it, yet being told alone as if it were the full history, *it is evil, it is false lying*. It is a murdering and devouring speech, and full of deceit, and argueth the speaker to be such a one as Doeg was."

14. Wicked men have a real love of sin, vv. 3, 4. This is the secret of all their abominations. But for this they might easily be amended by instruction and example. Henry: "It is bad to speak devouring words, but it is worse to love them, either in others or in ourselves."

15. Guile is an ingredient of every form of sin known, v. 4. It is so in hell. Satan is the father of lies. It enters into self-deception, into self-ignorance, into all cozening, all pride, all vanity, all pretences, all transgressions. There never was a thoroughly candid, upright opposer of God's truth, or Gospel.

16. The ruin of the incorrigibly wicked will be complete and utter, v. 5. His overthrow is self-procured. "As any wicked man is instrumental for bringing temporal destruction on the godly, so is he instrumental in drawing everlasting destruction upon himself from God's hand."

17. Yet wicked men are seldom made wiser by the destruction of their companions. The gambler has been known to make a card-table of the coffin of his dead brother. It is not promised that despisers shall grow wise. Nothing opens the eyes of those who will not see, Pr. xxvii. 22. Calvin: "The wicked are incapable of profiting by the judgments of God, being blind to the plainest manifestations which he has made of himself in his works."

18. But *the righteous* can *see*, grow wise, and have a salutary *fear* increased by beholding the end of the wicked, v. 6. Indeed to good men everything does good. God's severity inspires them with dread. Even his forgiveness begets godly fear. And so they are carried along. Every event of providence is the stroke of the sculptor's chisel. It tends to bring out the hidden beauties of the unsightly block on which it falls.

19. The exultation, which a righteous man may indulge at the defeat of the wicked, is not a malignant joy that calamity has overtaken any human being. This is forbidden, even in the Old Testament, Job xxxi. 29; Pr. xxiv. 17. David was filled with grief at the miserable end of Saul, 2 Sam. i. 17–27. Alexander: "The

sense of the absurdity of sin must be strongest in the purest minds, and cannot therefore be incompatible with pity, the rather as it is ascribed to God himself, Ps. ii. 4." Calvin: "I need not say that the destruction of Doeg could only communicate comfort to David's mind, in the way of convincing him that God was the avenging judge of human cruelty, and leading him to infer that as God had punished his wrongs, so he would advance him to renewed prosperity."

20. The end of every sinner teaches us some good lesson, which we ought carefully to ponder, v. 7. It is not possible for us to have too vivid a sense of the folly of living and dying an enemy to God. The end of every unbeliever may teach us much wisdom. Scott: "The believer foresees that God will cast down, sweep away, eradicate and extirpate from the earth, and destroy forever in hell those who do not make him their strength, but idolize their wealth and prosperity, and who encourage themselves in wickedness: and no criminals will perish with greater exultation to the righteous than hardened persecutors. Their success is like the luxuriant growth of some poisonous plant, which it is a public service to destroy."

21. If Christians would grow, they must be planted in the house of the Lord, which is his garden, his vineyard. There they shall prosper. Tholuck: "It is the eternal assurance of faith, which no appearance can baffle, that he who has cast his root in God, shall flourish in the house of God—i. e., in communion with him. Those who do not see it in time shall assuredly see it in eternity. He shall flourish and prosper like the favored olive-tree, which yields much fruit without almost any culture, and its leaves fade not even in winter," Jer. xi. 16.

22. But if the child of God would make progress in the divine life, he must walk by faith, not by sight. He must *trust*, even when things look darkest, v. 8. Compare Isa. l. 10; 1 Pet. i. 13.

23. Some mercies call for everlasting songs, v. 9. Such are the benefits received by all the true children of God; but some of these are so marked, so seasonable, and so unexpected, that a grateful heart will naturally give them prominence. Nor is one expression of thanks for such mercy enough, even if it be sincere. Calvin: "There is no religious duty, in which it does not become us to manifest a spirit of perseverance; but we need to be especially enjoined to it in the duty of thanksgiving, disposed as we are so speedily to forget our mercies, and occasionally to imagine that the gratitude of a few days is a sufficient tribute for benefits, which deserve to be kept in everlasting remembrance."

24. Let all believers learn and practise the duty of *waiting on God*, not only in the forms of religion, but in the temper and habit of their own minds. It is an excellent duty, and when *patiently* performed, it gives an excellence to the character not easily acquired, v. 9.

25. The judgment of saints is that God's service is good, v. 9. On this point there are no dissensions among God's real children.

PSALM LIII.

To the chief Musician upon Mahalath, Maschil, *A Psalm* of David.

1 The fool hath said in his heart, *There is* no God. Corrupt are they, and have done abominable iniquity: *there is* none that doeth good.

2 God looked down from heaven upon the children of men, to see if there were *any* that did understand, that did seek God.

3 Every one of them is gone back: they are altogether become filthy; *there is* none that doeth good, no, not one.

4 Have the workers of iniquity no knowledge? who eat up my people *as* they eat bread: they have not called upon God.

5 There were they in great fear, *where* no fear was: for God hath scattered the bones of him that encampeth *against* thee: thou hast put *them* to shame, because God hath despised them.

6 Oh that the salvation of Israel *were come* out of Zion! When God bringeth back the captivity of his people, Jacob shall rejoice, *and* Israel shall be glad.

THIS Psalm is so much like Ps. xiv. that Calvin, Horne, Tholuck and Hengstenberg have no separate comment on it. The differences are very slight. The probability is that David himself made them. Alexander: "The variations are such as render the expressions stronger, bolder, and in one or two cases more obscure and difficult." In Ps. xiv. *Jehovah Lord* frequently occurs. Here we have only *Elohim God,* on which see on Ps. iii. 2. On the title, see on Ps. iii. iv. xi. xxxii. *Upon Mahalath* is a part of the title which has not previously occurred. It is found also in Ps. lxxxviii. Abenezra and Mudge suppose it refers to the tune; Jarchi, Diodati, Hammond, Pool, Patrick and Edwards, to the instruments to be used in singing this Psalm. Ainsworth thinks Mahalath may be rendered either instrument or infirmity. The Tigurine version renders it diseases; Gill spiritualizes the word and understands it of the disease of sin and the weakness following it. Alexander also regards it as 'an enigmatical enunciation of the subject of the Psalm,' and by *disease* understands 'the spiritual malady with which all mankind are affected, and which is really the theme or subject of the composition.' The interpretation of Gill and Alexander is perhaps the most plausible. The Syriac gives a caption that fixes the *date* of the Psalm to Ahithophel's advice to Absalom to pursue and destroy David and his band. Indeed it makes that wily statesman the subject of the Psalm.

1. *The fool hath said in his heart,* There is *no God.* See on Ps. xiv. 1. *For fool* the Syriac has *unrighteous,* and Fry *wretch. Corrupt are they, and have done abominable iniquity.* This is just the same as in Ps. xiv. except that *here* we have *iniquity* for *deeds* in the former ode. There is *none that doeth good;* as in Ps. xiv. 1.

2. *God looked down from heaven upon the children of men, to see if there were* any *that did understand, that did seek God.* This presents a very bold figure—*God looking down to scrutinize.* The result of the investigation is:

3. *Every one of them is gone back.* Chaldee: All have gone back; Syriac: All have wandered away; Arabic: All have erred together; Septuagint and Vulgate: All have gone aside; Fry: They are all gone astray. The corresponding clause in the former ode differs not in sense, though the verb is slightly different in signification; *They are all gone aside.* See on Ps. xiv. 3. The next clause is: *They are altogether become filthy.* In Hebrew the same in both Psalms. *Altogether* is better than *all together; together,* signifying *alike,* or *at once,* is better than either. For *are become filthy* the Syriac has *are polluted;* the Septuagint and Vulgate, *are become unprofitable;* Morison, *have become rotten and putrid;* Alexander, *have putrified.* The corruption is total and perfect. There is *none that doeth good, no, not one,* as in Ps. xiv. which see.

4. *Have the workers of iniquity no knowledge?* Alexander: "This has been noticed by some critics as the only case in which the language of the fourteenth Psalm is stronger than the parallel expression of the fifty-third." *Who eat up my people as they eat bread: they have not called upon God.*

5. *There were they in great fear, where no fear was.* The last four words are an addition to the words of Psalm xiv. When men cease to fear God, they become subject to many fears, some guilty, some superstitious, all tormenting. A conscience defiled with the blood of God's people must have dreadful fears and apprehensions.

even when no evil is at hand. The language of the original is peculiarly Hebrew: *They have feared a fear. For God hath scattered the bones of him that encampeth* against *thee.* Some, who suppose this Psalm to have been altered after the days of David, regard this clause as having been written to suit the state of things after the destruction of Sennacherib's army. But it suits as well any defeat of beleaguering foes. Instead of *him that encampeth against thee,* Alexander has *thy besieger.* The Hebrew word is a participle in the singular, yet here it clearly denotes a body of enemies. To *scatter the bones* is to slay and leave the carcasses on the field, where they are torn apart. Scott: "The army of Absalom, which encamped against David, was easily routed; numbers fell in the forests; and, being left unburied, their bones were scattered." *Thou hast put* them *to shame,* because God hath despised *them.* The side God is against cannot prevail. Verse 6 of Ps. xiv. is wholly omitted here.

6. *Oh that the salvation of Israel were come out of Zion ! When God bringeth back the captivity of his people, Jacob shall rejoice, and Israel shall be glad.* Here we have in the Hebrew *salvations* for *salvation* in the corresponding verse of Psalm xiv. The church of England renders the first and second clauses both in the optative: Oh that, etc. It is clear from this verse that this Psalm was not made or altered to suit the Babylonish captivity; for instead of deliverance then coming *out of Zion,* the Hill of Zion was itself in the hands of enemies. If the reference of the whole Psalm is to the ruined spiritual condition of man, then the deliverance is also spiritual, and this is to be through the church as the depository of the truth, and the light of the world, Isa. ii. 3; Mic. iv. 2; John vii. 38; Acts i. 8.

Doctrinal and Practical Remarks.

1. Human sinfulness is often asserted in Scripture. Wise men believe it.

2. All sin is folly, v. 1. But some forms of it are so egregious that we hardly know how to characterize them. All allowed sin is virtual atheism or leads to it. Is not he a fool who thinks he can elude the scrutiny of omniscience, escape from the grasp of omnipotence, or succeed in setting aside the decisions of inflexible justice?

3. The fountain of all actual sin is *in the heart,* v. 1. If men were not wrong there, things would be easily put right, Matt. xv. 18. Whoever says he has by nature a good heart is a traitor to himself.

4. A great point would be gained if men could be brought to confess and bewail the *vileness* of their natures. They are *corrupt, filthy, abominable,* vv. 1, 3. There is no corruption so odious as moral corruption, no filthiness like the filthiness of sin.

5. Evil men are not only guilty of sins of commission, having done abominable iniquity, but they are guilty of many sins of omission. In fact they have never done one holy act, v. 3. They may be moral, decent, amiable, they may belong to the church; but *there is none that doeth good, no, not one.*

6. To deny our sinfulness is to deny that God knows all things and speaks the truth; for he has investigated the matter fully and given sentence in the case, vv. 2, 3.

7. Wilful ignorance will not excuse the guilty soul. Men often act as if they had no knowledge, and even in Christian countries some men seem to know little or nothing. But it is their own fault. They might know better. They ought to know better.

8. "There is an irreconcilable enmity between the seed of the woman and the seed of the serpent," John xv. 18; 1 John iii. 13. The hatred of sinners to saints stops at nothing till God arrests it. Like wild beasts the wicked devour the flock of God, v. 4.

9. While hypocrites, to be seen of men, may retain some of the forms of religion, yet ordinarily even they do not persevere in them; and persecutors are commonly a prayerless crew, v. 4.

10. Often the wicked here make a great ado about their courage, and some of them

possess much natural bravery and daring; but every unregenerate man is a coward so soon as God lets loose his conscience upon him, or delivers him over to alarming providences, v. 5. This shall be specially true of those who in the day of their power and prosperity seemed very courageous.

11. If men who are ashamed of Christ and his gospel would but reflect on God's word, they would see a discomfiture approaching of a nature so appalling, that surely they would not attach to the finger of scorn pointed at them by man such importance as to brave the derision of the Almighty, v. 5.

12. How glorious is deliverance by Christ. It is *salvation*, yea, it is *salvations*, v. 6. Luther: "This Psalm at the close gives a prophetic declaration concerning the gospel and the kingdom of Christ."

PSALM LIV.

To the chief Musician on Neginoth, Maschil, *A Psalm* of David, when the Ziphim came and said to Saul, Doth not David hide himself with us?

1 Save me, O God, by thy name, and judge me by thy strength.

2 Hear my prayer, O God; give ear to the words of my mouth.

3 For strangers are risen up against me, and oppressors seek after my soul: they have not set God before them. Selah.

4 Behold, God *is* mine helper: the Lord *is* with them that uphold my soul.

5 He shall reward evil unto mine enemies: cut them off in thy truth.

6 I will freely sacrifice unto thee: I will praise thy name, O LORD; for *it is* good.

7 For he hath delivered me out of all trouble: and mine eye hath seen *his desire* upon mine enemies.

WE have two accounts of Saul being informed by the people of Ziph as to David's retreat; one in 1 Sam. xxiii. 14–28; the other in 1 Sam. xxvi. 1–25. It is not certain in which of these we are to find the historic occasion of this Psalm, although most commentators incline to the opinion that it was the first. If this is so, then David probably wrote it at En-gedi, 1 Sam. xxiii. 29; if it refers to the last, then at Gath, 1 Sam. xxvii. 1–4. In his flight from Saul David went to the southern part of the Holy Land, and took refuge in the mountains near to Ziph. No sooner do the Ziphim (or Ziphites) learn that he is there, than messengers are started to inform Saul. The persecutor, intent on his prey, loses no time in marching an army to the mountain, where David is and attempts to cut off his retreat. Just as he thinks he is about to secure the victim of his envy, he hears that the Philistines have invaded his country, and with haste he leaves that district, and marches to the protection of his kingdom. Thus David escapes and goes to En-gedi. On the title see on title of Ps. iv. xi. xxxii. Here any believer may find fit words to express his desires in times of temptation, perplexity or persecution. The church of England seems to have regarded David in this Psalm as a type of Christ, appointing it for Good Friday. Scott dates it B. C. 1060; Clarke, B. C. 1061. The names of the Most High in it are *Elohim God* and *Jehovah* LORD, on which see on Ps. iii. 2; i. 2. On *Selah* see Introduction, § 15. The authorship of the Psalm is undisputedly Davidic.

1. *Save me, O God, by thy name. Save*, also *help, deliver, preserve*. See on Ps. iii. 7; xii. 1; xxii. 21. Calvin: "Surrounded as David was by hostile troops, and hemmed in on every side by apparently inevitable destruction, we cannot but admire the rare

and heroical intrepidity, which he displayed in committing himself by prayer, to the Almighty." David knew that infinite wisdom and power are never in straits. True and lively faith has peculiar delight in looking to Jehovah, when all is dark, and none but he can save. *By thy name,* may mean by *thyself;* or, by *all those perfections and acts whereby thou hast made thyself known.* From the parallel clause next following, David would seem to have specially in his eye the *ability* of God to deliver. Pool thinks we might read *for thy name, i. e., for thy own glory. For* sometimes has the signification *for the sake of.* In this case none but God could save, and it would be greatly to his honor, if he should save. *And judge me by thy strength. Judge,* most frequently so rendered, also *plead, plead the cause, minister judgment.* As no other resource seems left, he casts all his reliance on the *strength* of God. The Hebrew verb in this clause is in the future. This expresses confidence that the prayer will be heard, not only now, but hereafter.

2. *Hear my prayer, O God.* The prophet now returns to the imperative form, *hear;* but the Chaldee has it in the future, *The Lord will hear. Prayer,* always so rendered. David was sure that he should not pray in vain, for he was asking for no more than God had promised. *Give ear to the words of my mouth, i. e.,* the words of prayer that I have uttered.

3. *For strangers are risen up against me.* For *strangers* the Chaldee has *the proud.* Venema and Mudge admit that we may so render it. The change of a single letter would produce the variation. The Ziphites were David's countrymen, but instead of acting as Ahimelech and Abigail, they acted as *aliens* or *barbarians.* They had the spirit of foreigners. *And oppressors seek after my soul.* Alexander: "The original expression implies the possession of power and its lawless exercise. For *oppressors* the ancient versions read *the mighty;* Calvin, *the terrible ones;* Ainsworth, *daunting tyrants;* Amesius and Hengstenberg, *the violent;* Edwards, *the oppressive.* By *strangers* Clarke understands the Ziphites; by *oppressors,* Saul, his courtiers and his army. To *seek after the soul* is to attempt to destroy the life. The enemies of David were an ungodly company: *They have not set God before them.* When men do not fear God, they will not long regard men, especially one in adversity and persecuted. Not to *set God before the eyes* is to be generally irreligious, to live so as to please the carnal nature, to despise the authority of heaven.

4. *Behold, God is mine helper,* literally, *is helping me.* See Ps. x. 14; xxii. 11; xxx. 10. David had some true friends; but from them he expects no effectual relief. With an emphatic note of attention he says: *Behold, God is my helper. The* LORD is *with them that uphold my soul.* David's friends and comforts were the gift of God. His friends *upheld, sustained, supported* him with their presence, their sympathy, their counsel, and their readiness to risk all for him.

5. *He shall reward evil unto mine enemies.* Some prefer *the evil,* meaning the very evil they had intended for him, *i. e., death.* If so, the passage is parallel to Ps. vii. 16. The verb is in the imperative. Yet our version gives the sense. Alexander: "The imperative in this case is only a stronger form of prediction." See Introduction, § 6. *Cut them off in thy truth.* For *truth* the Arabic has *justice.* Although all God's threatenings are made in righteousness, yet the reference here seems to be to the veracity of God in promising to raise David to the throne, and in threatening to bring about the overthrow of all his unreasonable foes.

6. *I will freely sacrifice unto thee. Freely,* commonly rendered *free-will-offerings,* or *free offerings.* Perhaps the sense here is, Free-will-offerings will I sacrifice. It is also rendered *willing, willingly, freely,* 2 Chron. xxxv. 8; Ps. cx. 3; Hos. xiv. 4. In either way we get a good sense. Calvin: "David engages to sacrifice freely, and in another manner than the hypocrite, whose religion is the offspring of servility and constraint."

To sacrifices he would add thanksgiving: *I will praise thy name, O* LORD; *for* it is *good.* It is *good* in the eyes of God and of all his saints to praise him, Ps. lii. 9. Up to this point we probably have the very words, or the substance of the language used by David in the mountains of Ziph. The next and last verse is by some supposed to have been added after immediate danger was over. Or the past tense of verse 7 may indicate, that David was so confident of his deliverance, that he spoke of it as already accomplished.

7. *For he hath delivered me out of all trouble. Trouble, distress, adversity, affliction, tribulation, anguish.* Unless we regard the clause as prophetic, *anguish* is the better word here, as David could hardly be said to be free from *affliction* or *adversity*, while he was yet an exile. *And mine eye hath seen* his desire *upon mine enemies.* Those, who favor this rendering and supply *his desire*, regard themselves as supported by such passages as Ps. xci. 8; xxxvii. 34; Mal. i. 5. But Calvin, Horne, and others have it: *Mine eye hath looked upon mine enemies.* If this is right, it is a declaration that although his enemies were almost upon him, yet he had seen them marching away. No doubt David beheld this retreat with joy. As at the time he probably knew not the motive of his persecutors' retreat, it must have been very marvellous in his eyes; and not less so when he duly reflected upon the cause of the sudden change in Saul's movements.

DOCTRINAL AND PRACTICAL REMARKS.

1. We cannot get rid of bad men by moving. David found the wicked at Ziph; Edwards, at Stockbridge. Such things will beget sadness, but we ought not to be overwhelmed with grief when God subjects us to them. We should especially try to find out what duties our new position requires, and faithfully perform them.

2. Marked trials and great deliverances claim special notice and long continued remembrance. If we are not able to commemorate them in song, we must at least treasure up the memory of them in our hearts and speak of them to our friends.

3. It is no new thing to be betrayed. David and Christ and many others so suffered. The world is no better than it was.

4. Dickson: "Mighty men will readily find more friends in an evil cause, than the godly find in a good one." The reason is that an evil cause mortifies no vile affection and requires no self-denial.

5. Whatever makes us feel our entire dependence on God is good for us. David could not have had the blessed experience of this Psalm if Saul and his myrmidons had not sought his life.

6. "The name of the Lord is a strong tower; the righteous runneth into it, and is safe," Prov. xviii. 10. Solomon may have learned this blessed truth from the many mercies shown to his father in times of great peril.

7. In the nature of God and in his regard for his own glory, we have abundant cause of joyful confidence in his holy, wise and powerful providence, v. 1.

8. We have a right to be greatly encouraged in prayer, when we know that we are asking for things agreeable to God's will, things that he has taught us to pray for, things that he has promised to grant us when we do pray for them. God had secured to David by covenant all he here seeks, v. 1. We should be very careful not to offer a selfish, malignant or covetous prayer. Calvin: "In asking the divine protection it is indispensably prerequisite we should be convinced of the goodness of our cause, as it would argue the greatest profanity in any to expect that God should patronize iniquity," James iv. 1–3.

9. Berleberg Bible: "We should learn from the example of David, that even in the greatest danger we should resort to no forbidden means, nor grow faint, but

should call upon the name of God, and commit to him all our concerns as to the Supreme Judge." Compare 1 Sam. xxvi. 8–12. We should never have recourse to doubtful expedients, much less to confessedly wicked measures.

10. The certainty of future events does not render useless prayer or other means for bringing them about. David had God's word and oath that he should survive Saul and come to the kingdom. He believed God, and yet here he prays for deliverance, as if he had no such assurance. God revealed to Paul that not a man of his company should perish; yet the sailors must abide in the ship, or they could not be saved. He who has ordained the end has also appointed the means.

11. In prayer it is lawful and helpful to use words, as David here teaches us, v. 2. Compare Hosea xiv. 2. Mental prayer may be as acceptable as audible prayer; but words often help us to fix our thoughts.

12. It is sad when those of our own nation, tribe or family turn against us, v. 3. "Is it not a grief unto death, when a companion and friend is turned to an enemy?" Ecclus. xxxvii. 2. Slade: "Our nearest relations may prove more unkind than strangers; those, who ought to protect us, may become our oppressors; fellow Christians, in name, may slander and revile and injure us, more than even unbelievers do;" Dickson: "False countrymen, false brethren, false friends, false alliance are those of whom men may expect least in their need."

13. Of two opposing classes, one of whom set the Lord always before them, and the other have not God in all their thoughts, we need not doubt which God will help in the end, v. 3. The wicked may balk at nothing, they may be numerous and confident; but that will not settle the question, for 'the less hope there be of man's mercy, the more hope is there of God's help; the more unkind and cruel men be, the more may the Lord's kindness and comfort be expected.'

14. Hearty prayer is a great refreshment, v. 4. David comes forth from it strong. Yea, in the midst of it he cries, Behold, God is my helper. Arnd: "This is a fruit of prayer and of the Holy Spirit, that the heart is comforted and rejoiced after prayer."

15. We need no helper but God, and we do always need his aid and his arm, v. 4. If any professed believer thinks himself safe, or strong, or wise, or happy without God, he is in an awful condition. Calvin: "David was a fugitive among the dens of the earth, and even there in hazard of his life. How then could he speak of God as being near to him? He was pressed down to the very mouth of the grave; and how could he recognize the gracious presence of God? He was trembling in the momentary expectation of being destroyed; and how is it possible that he can triumph in the certain hope that divine help will presently be extended to him?" Behold the power of faith. It hopes against hope.

16. It is a great comfort to us to see God sustaining our sustainers, befriending our friends, giving skill to our advocates, and strength to our defenders, v. 4. God will ever take part with those who take part with his meek and sorrowful ones.

17. It shall be ill with the wicked. God will send *evil* unto them. And their doom will be just. It will be their *reward*, their proper recompense, v. 5.

18. How can sinners hope to succeed in their wicked plans, when they do not humbly pray for their own success, and when the prayers of the saints are always against them? v. 5.

19. All God's perfections are fully set against the wicked. His mercy and power are never on one side, and his *truth* on the other. There is a blessed harmony of the divine attributes in all his counsels and works.

20. Though we are not called after mercies received to bring incense and fatlings and fire, and make an offering on an altar of stone, yet it is our duty and privilege

to present freely our spiritual sacrifices on all fit occasions, and there are many such, v. 6.

21. The history of David's escape from Saul, when it seemed as if the persecutor was sure of his victim, shows us that God can save his people as well without a miracle as with it. The retreat of Saul is a wonderful illustration of the truth of Pr. xxi. 1. Ordinary means are as effective as extraordinary, if only the Lord imparts power to them.

22. Great will be the joy of complete and final deliverance from pains, perils and tribulations, v. 7.

PSALM LV.

To the chief Musician on Neginoth, Maschil, *A Psalm* of David.

1 Give ear to my prayer, O God; and hide not thyself from my supplication.

2 Attend unto me, and hear me: I mourn in my complaint, and make a noise;

3 Because of the voice of the enemy, because of the oppression of the wicked: for they cast iniquity upon me, and in wrath they hate me.

4 My heart is sore pained within me: and the terrors of death are fallen upon me.

5 Fearfulness and trembling are come upon me, and horror hath overwhelmed me.

6 And I said, Oh that I had wings like a dove! *for then* would I fly away, and be at rest.

7 Lo, *then* would I wander far off, *and* remain in the wilderness. Selah.

8 I would hasten my escape from the windy storm *and* tempest.

9 Destroy, O LORD, *and* divide their tongues: for I have seen violence and strife in the city.

10 Day and night they go about it upon the walls thereof: mischief also and sorrow *are* in the midst of it.

11 Wickedness *is* in the midst thereof: deceit and guile depart not from her streets.

12 For *it was* not an enemy *that* reproached me; then I could have borne *it:* neither *was it* he that hated me *that* did magnify *himself* against me; then I would have hid myself from him:

13 But *it was* thou, a man mine equal, my guide, and mine acquaintance.

14 We took sweet counsel together, *and* walked unto the house of God in company.

15 Let death seize upon them, *and* let them go down quick into hell: for wickedness *is* in their dwellings, *and* among them.

16 As for me, I will call upon God; and the LORD shall save me.

17 Evening, morning, and at noon, will I pray, and cry aloud; and he shall hear my voice.

18 He hath delivered my soul in peace from the battle *that was* against me: for there were many with me.

19 God shall hear, and afflict them, even he that abideth of old. Selah. Because they have no changes, therefore they fear not God.

20 He hath put forth his hands against such as be at peace with him: he hath broken his covenant.

21 *The words* of his mouth were smoother than butter, but war *was* in his heart: his words were softer than oil, yet *were* they drawn swords.

22 Cast thy burden upon the LORD, and he shall sustain thee: he shall never suffer the righteous to be moved.

23 But thou, O God, shalt bring them down into the pit of destruction: bloody and deceitful men shall not live out half their days; but I will trust in thee.

ON the title see on titles of Psalms iii. iv. xi. xxxii. liv. The Syriac says it was written by "David when he was lamenting the death of his son Absalom; and that it contains a prophecy concerning those who were cruel and violent against Christ." The Davidic authorship is generally admitted. The Chaldee, Syriac, Diodati, Ainsworth, Hammond, Gill, Dickson, Mudge, Edwards, Morison, Scott, Clarke and Tholuck find its historic occasion in the rebellion of Absalom; Calvin and Moller, in the Sauline persecution. But there is no general agreement as to the particular event calling it forth. It is evident that it was written in circumstances of distress from persecution. Hengstenberg: "Against the supposition of a particular occasion, it is enough to awaken in us misgivings, that those who maintain that, cannot agree among themselves respecting it;" Alexander: "Although there seem to be allusions to the writer's own experience, in the times both of Saul and Absalom, the whole description can be applied exclusively to neither." Scott dates it B. C. 1021; Clarke, B. C. 1023. In it we have four names of the Most High, *El God, Adonai Lord, Jehovah* LORD and *Elohim God,* on which respectively see on Ps. v. 4; ii. 4; i. 2; iii. 2. On *Selah* see Introduction, § 15.

1. *Give ear to my prayer, O God. Give ear,* as in Ps. v. 1; xvii. 1. *Prayer,* as in Ps. iv. 1; liv. 2, uniformly rendered. It may point to intercession for others, or supplication for one's self. *And hide not thyself from my supplication.* Alexander: "To hide one's self is an expression used in the law to describe the act of wilfully withholding aid from one who needs it," Deut. xxii. 1, 4. Compare Isa. lviii. 7. *Supplication,* a plea for unmerited kindness.

2. *Attend unto me, and hear me: I mourn in my complaint and make a noise.* The Hebrew is very concise and emphatic. The first and second verbs are in the imperative; the third and fourth, in the future. This is followed by the Chaldee, Calvin, Venema and Alexander. But most of the ancient versions, Ainsworth, Amesius, Edwards, Jebb, Fry and others, use the form of our version. Horsley paraphrases thus: Attend unto me, and hear me: I am dejected in my meditation, and am in a violent tumultuous agitation, as the waves of the sea; Green: While in my complaint I weep and cry aloud, attend unto me and answer me; Hengstenberg: Attend to me and hear me, I give free course to my sorrow and will cry aloud. Chandler regards the last phrase as expressive of the *greatest consternation.* This Psalm is a *meditation,* a *prayer* and a *complaint* made to God. The prophet immediately tells us that he thus speaks,

3. *Because of the voice of the enemy, because of the oppression of the wicked.* The *oppression* here spoken of is the *persecution,* the *sore pressing* of the enemy. Calvin renders it *affliction;* Ainsworth, *vexation. For they cast iniquity upon me.* The Chaldee: For they will direct a lie against me; Syriac: For they have stretched out snares for me; Arabic: For they have turned aside after me with fury; church of England: For they are minded to do me some mischief; Edwards: For they are plotting iniquity against me; Horsley: For they slide iniquity upon me, *i. e.,* by oblique and artful insinuations they asperse my character. Pool: "The sense is, either, 1. They make me the great object of their wicked, and injurious, and mischievous practices; or, 2. They lay many crimes to my charge falsely." Was ever one of these things done, and not the other? May not both be meant? *And in wrath they hate me, i. e.,* their hatred is violent and unrestrained. Ainsworth: *In anger they spitefully hate me.*

4. *My heart is sore pained within me.* The Chaldee: My heart trembled within me; church of England: My heart is disquieted within me; Edwards: My heart throbbeth within me; Fry: My heart is in travail within me; Alexander: My heart writhes in the midst of me. The phrase expresses violent mental distress. So the parallel clause: *And the terrors of death are fallen upon me.* The *terrors of death* are those awful sensations which, coming on men, make them feel as if they could not live, Mark xiv. 33, 34.

5. *Fearfulness and trembling are come upon me, and horror hath overwhelmed* [margin *covered*] *me.* We must remember that verses 2–5 were uttered by him, who long before had fought with a lion and a bear and the champion of the Philistines, and

with undaunted courage had conquered them all. He was no chicken-hearted man. But now foes without and fears within were too many for him. No man knows how he will behave in any severe trial, until it is over. We are wholly dependent on God for constancy of mind.

6. *And I said, Oh that I had wings, like a dove;* literally, *So that I said, Who will give me a wing like a dove.* "Doves have no gall, feed on pure food, are mild, harmless, beautiful, fruitful, defenceless, hated by ravenous birds, chaste to their mates, and much given to mourning if they lose them." The dove is gentle, never contends, never defends itself, is often pursued, but seldom captured, being able to save itself by its amazing speed of flight and by finding strong hiding-places in the rock. Some of the stories respecting its powers of flight are fabulous; but we know that no bird of prey possesses such speed, and the Scriptures tell us of its hiding in holes, Jer. xlviii. 28. David says he has the desire for the quiet and security which the dove has. Though he has not the power of securing tranquillity he wishes he had; For then, says he, *would I fly away and be at rest.*

7. *Lo, then would I wander far off.* Ainsworth: Lo, I would make far off *my* wandering flight. The dejected state of David's mind may be judged of, when we see him thus expressing his desire to be a fugitive, rather than longer contend with his foes, although God's word secured to him the kingdom. That he does not contemplate a mere temporary flight is evident from the parallel clause: And *remain in the wilderness.* For *remain* the Chaldee and Arabic have *dwell;* Syriac and Calvin, *repose.* *Wilderness* does not necessarily imply an *arid desert,* for we read of the *pastures of the wilderness,* and the *pleasant places of the wilderness.* Hengstenberg: "The wilderness in v. 7 stands opposed to human society." How many have felt as David here expresses himself, Pr. xxi. 19; Jer. ix. 2.

8. *I would hasten my escape from the windy storm* and *tempest. Doves* fly to their *windows* or *holes* as the storm rises; so would David from this tempest of human passions. Calvin renders it: I will hasten a deliverance for me, from the wind raised by the whirlwind, understanding thereby "a violent wind, such as compels the traveller to fly and seek shelter in the nearest dwelling." *Tempest,* also rendered whirlwind, Jer. xxiii. 19; xxv. 32; xxx. 23; Ps. lxxxiii. 15; Amos i. 14; Jon. i. 4, 12. Troubles of a distressing kind are well and often represented by *storms.* Such keen and pressing calamity drove the royal psalmist to the mercy-seat. He was compelled to invoke divine interposition.

9. *Destroy, O Lord,* and *divide their tongues. Destroy,* commonly swallow up. Some think the reference is to the end of Korah and his company. Some think the text originally read, *Divide, O Lord, divide.* There are cases of such reduplication; but it is conjecture alone that would put it here. The Psalmist supplicates God to bring upon them such confusion of counsel, and such disruption of league, as would make them powerless for evil. Some think the sense is given by reading, *destroy by dividing them.* Many suppose there is a reference to the confusion of tongues at Babel, Gen. xi. 7. Some, who give to the Psalm a historic occasion in Absalom's rebellion, suppose the prayer is like that in 2 Sam. xv. 31, *O LORD, I pray thee, turn the counsel of Ahithophel into foolishness.* On the form of the verb see Introduction, § 6. *For I have seen violence and strife in the city.* Some think this refers to the city of Keilah, where for a season David dwelt, 1 Sam. xxiii.; and some, to the city of Gibeah, where Saul for a while had his forces. More probably he refers to *Jerusalem,* which was in great confusion both in Absalom's rebellion and often in Saul's time also, he being absent seeking to destroy one of his best subjects, when he should have been at home suppressing violence, and punishing wrong-doers. Pool: "This circumstance is noted as an aggravation of their wickedness, that it was committed in

that city, where the throne and seat of public justice was settled; and where God was in a special manner present and worshipped; and where they had great opportunities, both for the knowledge and practice of their several duties."

10. *Day and night they go about it upon the walls thereof; mischief also and sorrow are in the midst of it.* *They* may refer to the enemies generally; but Calvin, Mant and Anderson think *violence* and *sorrow* are personified. *Mischief*, in v. 3 and often, rendered *iniquity;* also *sorrow, vanity, affliction,* a few times *mischief.* *Sorrow* also rendered *perverseness, wickedness, mischief, labor, sorrow, trouble, pain, travail, grievousness.* Thus in one clause we have two words showing the connection between sin and misery, the very names, by which they are known, being interchangeable. If *violence* and *strife* hold the walls, and *mischief* and *sorrow* reign in the heart of the city, how corrupt and wretched the whole mass must be. As was Jerusalem, so was the land. If religion, justice, truth, and good morals were there held in disesteem, the whole land felt the consequences.

11. *Wickedness is in the midst thereof.* *Wickedness*, in the plural, *wickednesses;* sometimes *mischief, mischievous things, calamities, perverse things;* another instance of the same word being applied to moral and natural evil. *Deceit and guile depart not from her streets.* *Deceit* and *guile, i. e.,* all *craft, fraud, subtilty.* These vices reigned in the *streets,* the public places, where trade was conducted and justice administered.

12. *For* it was *not an enemy* that *reproached me; then I could have borne* it. There are four methods of explaining the use of the singular in this and the two next verses. 1. Some think the reference is directly to Ahithophel. 2. Others make the person an ideal character. 3. Others think there is a change from the singular to the plural, but that the eye is still to be kept on those previously spoken of. 4. Others think that in vv. 12–14 the prophet considers one case of atrocious hypocrisy and treachery, but does not intend to point out the man, so that we could name him. Either of these may be correct. The last has fewest difficulties. *I could have borne it* may mean I could have borne it with comparative ease. This is the more common view. But Calvin thinks the meaning is, 'I could then have *met it,* as one meets and parries off a blow, which is aimed at him. Against a known foe we are on our watch, but the unsuspected stroke of a friend takes us by surprise.' The usual signification of the verb is to *bear, lift,* or *carry.* Calvin's method of explaining it makes this clause more nearly parallel to the next. *Neither* was it *he that hated me* that *did magnify* himself *against me; then I would have hid myself from him;* and so avoided any ill consequence from his malice.

13. *But* it was *thou, a man mine equal, my guide and mine acquaintance.* The Chaldee: And thou Ahithophel, a man like me, the teacher who taught me, and made known to me wisdom; Calvin: But it was thou, a man of mine own order, my leader and mine acquaintance; Edwards: But it is thou, a man whom I valued as my own self, my guide and acquaintance; Green: But it is thou, the man whom I took for my guide and my friend; Horsley: But thou, a man, put upon a level with myself, my confidant, and my familiar friend. From such a one injury must have been very keenly felt. Were friendships sacred and never disgraced by treachery, some might doubt the depravity of man. But as things are, there is no room for incredulity.

14. *We took sweet counsel together,* and *walked unto the house of God in company.* Calvin: " We sweetly exchanged our most secret thoughts; we walked into the house of God in company; Edwards: We joined together sweetly in secret consultation; we walked to the house of God amidst the crowd; Green: We sweetly communicated our secrets in private, and in public we walked to the house of God. The common version gives the sense, *took sweet counsel together.* *In company,* the Hebrew signifies a *crowd* or *multitude,* such as went in procession up the hill of Zion

15. *Let death seize upon them*, and *let them go down quick into hell.* By *them* we are to understand not only the *equal* and *guide* of v. 13, but all the persecutors noticed in the former part of the Psalm. On the imprecatory form see Introduction, § 6. The whole force of the Hebrew is given by Fry: *Desolations are upon them. They go down alive into the abode of the dead;* or by Horsley: *Death shall take them away; they shall go down quick into hell. Desolations* (are) *upon them! They shall go down to Sheol alive. Quick, alive, living* not *quickly* or *speedily.* Does not the prophet here allude to the dreadful end of Korah, Dathan and Abiram, and declare that the awful judgments, which swept them from the earth, would be just in this case also? *For wickedness* is *in their dwellings,* and *among them. Wickedness,* literally *wickednesses,* or *mischiefs. Among them, in them,* Alexander, *in their heart.*

16. *As for me, I will call upon God; and the* LORD *shall save me. As for me, I,* literally *I,* emphatic and contrastive; *q. d.,* 'As they and I differ in the courses of our lives, so shall we in our ends.' Calvin: "He does not content himself with saying that he will pray, for many do this in a perfunctory manner, and soon become wearied with the exercise; but he resolves to display both assiduity and vehemency:"

17. *Evening, and morning, and at noon, will I pray, and cry aloud; and he shall hear my voice. Pray, meditate, talk, complain.* The connection determines the precise meaning. Here it clearly should be rendered *pray.* There is no contrariety in these significations, for prayer should be *meditated,* then *uttered,* and as we are full of sins and sorrows we should *complain* to God, and supplicate his blessing, and that is *praying;* see v. 2; Ps. lxxvii. 3, 12; cxix. 27, 148. "To pray frequently is to pray fervently." David prayed thrice a day, and was in great earnest, he *cried aloud* or *roared.* David's praying was no dull formality. Nor was it unavailing.

18. *He hath delivered my soul in peace from the battle* that was *against me. Soul,* in this case *life.* Calvin reads *into peace*—'a strong expression, signifying the danger to which he had been exposed, and the almost miraculous manner in which he had been delivered from it.' David uses the past tense, *hath delivered,* either as expressing his entire confidence that his prayer should result in deliverance; or the Psalm was composed after the danger was over and the deliverance effected. The latter is perhaps more probable, for speaking of the contest as over, he adds: *For there were many with me.* To this phrase two constructions are given. One is that many *had been fighting with, i. e., against him.* This view is favored by Calvin, Pool, Fry, Walford, Hengstenberg and Alexander. The deliverance was great because in the *battle* or *war* his enemies had been numerous. The other construction is that he intends to say that God, his angels and many pious Israelites were on his side. This view is admitted by Calvin to be a 'comfortable truth' and is strongly embraced by Mant, Horsley and others. Green renders it: *For he is on my side against multitudes.* The doctrine of the ministry of angels was well understood and heartily embraced by pious people in Old Testament times, 2 Kings vi. 16, 17; Ps. xxxiv. 7. Ainsworth and Gill admit either interpretation.

19. *God shall hear and afflict them, even he that abideth of old.* John Rogers' translation of the whole verse is: Yee even God that endureth for ever, shall heare me, and brynge them downe. Selah. For they will not turn: and why? they feare not God. *God shall hear,* either, 1. The *complaint* and the *prayer* that David offers in this Psalm; or, 2. The cry uttered by the reproaches and wickedness of his persecutors. The first is the view of Calvin, Patrick, the church of England, Edwards, Green, Horne, Scott and Tholuck. But Hengstenberg and Alexander are quite in favor of the second view. Alexander: "As God has heard me in mercy, so will he hear them in wrath. As he has answered my prayer in the way described above, v. 19, so will he answer them in the way described below, v. 24." Pool and Gill admit either view,

as sufficiently correct. The first mode of interpretation has the least serious difficulties, is the most natural, and is most generally received. *Afflict* also rendered *answer*. The English version is well supported, and gives the sense. For *of old* the Chaldee has *from the beginning;* Cocceius and Chandler, *from everlasting;* Green, *eternally;* Ainsworth, *from antiquity;* Durell, *from eternity.* In Hab. i. 12, the same word is rendered *from everlasting;* often *of old.* *Because they have no changes, therefore they fear not God.* *Changes,* the word does not of itself determine the nature of the change, whether it is of *character* or of *condition.* This has given rise to two interpretations; one suggested by the Chaldee: "Wicked men, who change not their evil course, and fear not the face of God, shall perish." So Diodati understands it *of changes of repentance and conversion.* This view is also favored by Dathe, Gesenius and Horne. The other is that the change refers to *condition;* Green: They experience no change *of fortune,* and *therefore* will not fear God; Fry: Because they have no vicissitudes, therefore they fear not God; Chandler paraphrases it: "They are prosperous, and have no reverse of fortune, think of none, and fear none; and so fear not God." Patrick: "Having prospered hitherto in their villany, there is not one of them that repents; but they all pertinaciously persist in their rebellion, without any fear of the divine vengeance." So many others. This interpretation is obvious, is generally received, agrees with other Scriptures (Prov. i. 32; Jer. xlviii. 11) and with our observation of the effect of prosperity on the wicked. Other modes of explaining these words have been suggested but they are too recondite and overstrained.

20. *He hath put forth his hands against such as be at peace with him: he hath broken his covenant.* This is a further account of the wicked enemies of David. To describe one was to describe all. They regarded not friendships, and they were *truce-breakers.* *Broken,* literally *profaned, i. e.,* acted as if a covenant was not binding. Oppression is also commonly accompanied by deceit.

21. The words *of his mouth were smoother than butter, but war* was *in his heart: his words were softer than oil, yet* were *they drawn swords.* Smooth and *oily words* are not kind and gentle, but deceitful and feigned. So cruel words are well likened to sharp weapons for wounding. Compare Ps. xxviii. 3; lvii. 4; lxii. 4; lxiv. 3; Pr. v. 3, 4, xii. 18. Such figures are common to many languages. *War,* in v. 8, *battle.* The first clause has been strikingly rendered: *Their mouth is butter, and their heart is war.*

22. *Cast thy burden upon the* LORD. For *burden* the margin and Calvin have *gift;* Chaldee, *hope;* Syriac, Arabic, Septuagint, Ethiopic, Vulgate, Doway, *care;* Ainsworth, *careful burden;* Edwards, *lot;* Jebb, *allotment, portion;* Hengstenberg, *salvation;* Tholuck, *burden.* Hammond: "The Hebrews generally render it *burden.*" Diodati: " *Thy burden,* viz., Thy cares, travails, and businesses which trouble thee." The great weight of authority is in favor of the common version. An apostle quotes the Septuagint version as being sufficiently correct for his purpose, 1 Pet. v. 7, *casting all your care upon him,* the word *care* having the sense of *solicitude.* Cast thy burden on Jehovah, *and he shall sustain thee.* The ancient versions, church of England and Fry: He shall nourish thee; Calvin and Venema, He shall feed thee; Edwards, He will support thee; Hengstenberg, He shall take care of thee. Peter does not quote the Septuagint corresponding to this clause, but uses his own words: *He careth for you.* Then follows the assurance that God's *care* or *support* shall be effectual in all coming duration: *He shall never suffer the righteous to be moved.* *Be moved,* as in Ps. x. 6; xv. 5; xvi. 8; in Ps. cxxv. 1, *be removed.* Alexander: " It is the word so often used to signify the violent disturbance of a person in the midst of his prosperity." Some of the various renderings may show the richness of the promise. The Chaldee: He will not give over the just to perpetual want; Syriac: He will not suffer his just ones to be continually vexed; Calvin: He shall not suffer the righteous always to stagger;

Venema: He shall not permit the righteous to be bowed down for ever; Edwards: He will not suffer the righteous to be harassed forever. The negation is literally *not for ever*.

23. *But thou, O God, shalt bring them down into the pit of destruction.* *Them*, viz., David's maligners and persecutors. *Pit*, any deep excavation in the earth, as very often a *well*, thence a *pit*, thence figuratively, *ruin*, Pr. v. 15; xxiii. 27; Ps. lxix. 15; *Destruction*, as in Ps. ciii. 4; in Ps. xvi. 10; xlix. 9; Jon. ii. 6 *corruption*. The most common rendering is *pit*. The Chaldee reads, *the deep Gehenna*. The meaning is that in due time God will bring the life and days of these wicked men to a miserable end. He adds, *Bloody and deceitful men shall not live out half their days. Bloody and deceitful men*, literally *men of bloods and deceit;* see on Ps. v. 6. Compare Ps. xxvi. 9. It is not important to learn whether the prophet here speaks of his persecutors alone, or of all men of like character; for these words are in every age fulfilled in an appalling manner. Besides, " the life of the wicked, however long it may be protracted, is agitated by so many fears and disquietudes that it scarcely merits the name, and may be said to be death rather than life. Nay, that life is worse than death which is spent under the curse of God, and under the accusations of a conscience which torments its victim more than the most barbarous executioner." *Shall not live out half their days* gives the sense of the text, and is idiomatic English. The Septuagint, Vulgate and margin of the common version give it literally, *shall not halve their days*. *But I will trust in thee*, q. d., ' I leave all in God's hands. He can and will in due time put down my foes and give me full deliverance. I give him his own time to do his own wonders of severity and of mercy.' Often is the prediction of premature death seen to be fulfilled in history. To possess the empire Phocas put to death all the sons of Mauritius, the emperor, and then slew him; but this Phocas was pursued by his son-in-law, Priscus, who cut off his ears and feet and then killed him. Blood has a terrible power to bring down vengeance, 2 Sam. xxi. 1.

DOCTRINAL AND PRACTICAL REMARKS.

1. When we are rightly disposed, and guided by God's Spirit, we may get an *instruction* from the most distressing events in our history.

2. We shall never be done weeping and praying till we are done with earth, and have passed to the enjoyment of God, v. 1. 'Disappointments and losses, the unkindness of friends and the malice of enemies, the weaknesses both of the body and of the soul' will prolong our night of weeping and of wrestling with the Angel of mercy till eternal day bursts upon us, and fills us with its glories.

3. When God seems to hide himself from believers and their supplications, they should regard it as a trial of faith and perseverance, and not as a discouragement to prayer, v. 1.

4. True faith and earnestness are not satisfied with any form or amount of prayer, until they secure an answer, v. 2.

5. If our distress be very great, so that we even *make a noise*, let us still pray on, v. 2.

6. It proves nothing against religious feeling that it is attended by sensible effects on the body, v. 2. David *mourned* or 'was bathed in tears;' 'was in the greatest consternation.' It is a mercy that sometimes we can obtain relief by outward expressions of grief.

7. In all ages and under all circumstances unrenewed men are substantially alike, show the same hostility to holiness, and resort to the same *clamor* and *harsh measures* for distressing the saints, v. 3. The controversy concerning right and wrong, truth and error, has not materially changed its character since the days of Cain and Abel.

8. It seems to be a principle of Satan's kingdom that a lie is as as good as the truth, if it answers a present purpose, v. 3. God's people ought not to be surprised or dejected if they find all manner of evil spoken of them falsely for Christ's sake.

9. Wicked men prescribe no bounds to their malice. They allow it to become 'wrath,' v. 3. Malignancy knows no law.

10. Oftentimes 'our greatest comfort under persecution is conscious rectitude.' The very fact that we do not deserve ill-treatment is a pledge that a righteous God will vindicate our cause.

11. There are several reasons why truly pious men should be *sore pained*, v. 4. God loves them and so afflicts them. The world and the devil hate them and so trouble them. They are very jealous of themselves, and so they continually prove and humble themselves. Religion refines their sensibilities, and so they are more distressed at a vain thought than ungodly men are at a naughty deed.

12. One reason, why God lets loose upon us *the terrors of death* long before our departure out of this world, is probably to prepare us for death itself, v. 4. It would be almost a miracle for us to learn to despise pain, if we never felt it.

13. Painful and even terrible experiences are not peculiar to any one child of God, v. 5. Nor should we be surprised to find our natural fortitude failing us in the hour of severe trial. Calvin: "We are all good soldiers so long as things go well with us, but when brought to close combat, our weakness is soon apparent;" Dickson: "It is not a thing inconsistent with godliness to be much moved with fear in time of danger; natural affections are not taken away in conversion, but sanctified and moderated."

14. It seems to be natural for men to think that they would be happier and even more virtuous, if they were in perfect solitude, than they can be surrounded by imperfect and sinful men, vv. 6–8. But the experiments, which have been made, seem to prove the contrary. Yet it is a dreadful thing to be so situated that we cannot be retired when we choose. Henry: "Gracious souls wish to retire from the hurry and bustle of this world, that they may sweetly enjoy God and themselves; and, if there be any true peace on this side heaven, it is they that enjoy it in those retirements."

15. He is a wise man, who knows when to flee and when to stand his ground. So soon as any trouble rises, some are in David's mood, vv. 6–8. Compare Matt. x. 23; xxiv. 16; Neh. vi. 11. He, who acts from timidity, almost uniformly regrets his conduct. We should not be governed by ill-grounded apprehensions. And if a man chooses to run risks, and prefers death rather than flight, no one will blame him for his courage.

16. What shall we think of men who, to be rid of trouble and vexation, wish to leave the world? Slade: "Sometimes the burden is so heavy and the prospect so dark, that we would rather leave the world at once, and fly away, and be at rest." But any wish based in selfishness and pusillanimity ought not to be indulged. Jonah was subject to such feelings, and yet they are evidently not recorded to his credit, Jon. iv. 3, 4, 9.

17. It is easy for God to defeat all the plans and plots of the wicked. He often does it by giving them over to distracted counsels, v. 9. The greatest conspiracy ever formed against God was at Babel, and he soon made a BABEL of it. Calvin: "It is thus that to this day he weakens the enemies of the church, and splits them into factions, through the force of mutual animosities, rivalries, and disagreements in opinion."

18. The most powerful weapon ever used in this world against cruel and unreasonable men is prayer, v. 9.

19. Troubles and discords in the church are no new thing. They were known even

under the Theocracy, v. 9. Scott: "With anguish of heart the believer often perceives violence and discord in the congregations where the gospel of peace is preached and professed; by which the common cause is weakened, the truth disgraced, and far more mischief done than by all the fury of persecutors."

20. If the connection between sin and misery is so close on earth, where retribution is barely begun, what must it not be in the next world, where it is finished? v. 10.

21. Very soon and certainly wickedness against God turns to fraud and wrong-doing against man! v. 11.

22. That which to virtuous minds makes treachery so abhorrent, is that it always involves ingratitude and essential meanness of character, vv. 12–14. Calvin: "We are taught by the Spirit to reverence all the natural ties which bind us together in society. Besides the common and universal one of humanity, there are others of a more sacred kind, by which we should feel ourselves attached to men in proportion as they are more nearly connected with us than others, by neighborhood, by relationship, or by professional calling, the more as we know that such connections are not the result of chance, but of providential design and arrangement."

23. False and hollow as are some professions of friendship, there are others of an opposite kind. Isabella Graham and Mrs. Christy were true to each other. The elder Edwards, dying, said, "Give my kindest love to my dear wife, and tell her that the uncommon union which has so long subsisted between us has been of such a nature as, I trust, is spiritual, and therefore will continue forever." But 'we must not wonder, if we be sadly deceived in some that have made great pretensions to those two sacred things, religion and friendship.'

24. When we see wickedness in men's houses, we may be sure it is in their hearts, v. 15. Some are so vile that 'wherever they set down their feet, they leave traces of their wickedness, and defile all places with their impurities.'

25. We must resolutely *continue* instant in prayer, v. 16. Horne: "Prayer is the believer's universal medicine for all the disorders of the soul within, and his invincible shield against every enemy that can attack him from without."

26. But we must pray in hope, vv. 16, 17, 19. Prayer without expectation of receiving a blessing is like salt without savor.

27. And we must pray earnestly, v. 17. When beggars ask alms, they sometimes plead that they want but little, that they have seldom, if ever asked aid, and that they do not expect to do so again for a long time to come. But all such pleas are an insult to God, when we seek his blessing.

28. There is certainly an advantage in having set times for prayer, v. 17. Like David the great prophet in Chaldea also prayed three times a day, Dan. vi. 10. When modern discovery searched out Pitcairn's island, the people, from one little Bible, had been instructed to observe a season of prayer thrice a day. If our poor frail bodies need refreshment from food three times a day, who, that knows his own weakness, will say that we need not as frequent refreshment for our poor frail spirits?

29. We need not fear the number of our foes, v. 18. There is no king saved by the multitude of an host. God's government is not managed by majorities.

30. God's people have many on their side, v. 18. Compare 2 Kings vi. 16; 1 John iv. 4. If it were necessary to save one of his people, God would send twelve legions of angels at any time to do the work.

31. The study of each of the divine attributes is in its place proper and useful. Here the Psalmist mentions God's perpetuity, v. 19. Many promises and mercies are by that divine perfection made sure to us! Because God is eternal he is unchangeable, and therefore his government is unchangeable, and therefore all he did for saints of old he will, if it be necessary, do for saints now and hereafter.

32. If God should grant us prosperity, let us be vigilant lest we fall into that state denoted in Scripture by being *at ease*, and by good writers by being in *carnal security*, v. 19.   To grow worse under benefits is not uncommon, but it is a dark sign.

33. Have we spoken or acted unkindly to any?   Are we true to our friendships? Have we always kept our word?   Are our present morals blameless on these points? Such inquiries are not idle, v. 20.

34. Though candor may not be in vogue, yet both God and good men must ever abhor all kinds of insincerity, v. 21.   Horne: "Of this complexion are the cant of hypocrites, the charity of bigots and fanatics, the benevolence of atheists, the professions of the world, the allurements of the flesh, and the temptations of Satan, when he thinks proper to appear in the character of an angel of light."   Luther: "Virulent, outside-show hypocrites distress the hearts of those that fear God in a manner that is beyond description."

35. One class of deceivers, peculiarly dangerous to the young and inexperienced consists of flatterers, v. 21.   They are mean, servile, selfish, malignant to a degree almost inconceivable, till you find them out.

36. So long as we have a God to go to, what more do we need? v. 22.   Rivers of sorrow may roll over us, and mountains of care rest upon us, but if we cast all on God, he will sustain us.   "When shall we trust Christ to govern the world which he has redeemed?"

37. A sight of the end of the wicked would at once remove all envy from the mind of a wise man, v. 23.

38. The triumph of the wicked is short, v. 23.

39. Whatever comes, let us practise the duties of piety, and especially let us exercise holy trust in God, which is at the foundation of every stable Christian character, v. 23.

Psalm LVI.

To the chief Musician upon Jonath-elem-rechokim, Michtam of David, when the Philistines took him in Gath.

1 Be merciful unto me, O God, for man would swallow me up: he fighting daily oppresseth me.

2 Mine enemies would daily swallow *me* up: for *they be* many that fight against me, O thou Most High.

3 What time I am afraid, I will trust in thee.

4 In God I will praise his word, in God I have put my trust; I will not fear what flesh can do unto me.

5 Every day they wrest my words: all their thoughts *are* against me for evil.

6 They gather themselves together, they hide themselves, they mark my steps, when they wait for my soul.

7 Shall they escape by iniquity? in *thine* anger cast down the people, O God.

8 Thou tellest my wanderings: put thou my tears into thy bottle: *are they* not in thy book?

9 When I cry *unto thee*, then shall mine enemies turn back: this I know; for God *is* for me.

10 In God will I praise *his* word: in the LORD will I praise *his* word.

11 In God have I put my trust: I will not be afraid what man can do unto me.

12 Thy vows *are* upon me, O God: I will render praises unto thee.

13 For thou hast delivered my soul from death: *wilt* not *thou deliver* my feet from falling, that I may walk before God in the light of the living?

ON parts of the title see on titles of Psalms iv. xvi. xxxiv.   *When the Philistines took him in Gath* doubtless refers to the scrap of history in 1 Sam. xxi. 10–15. If so, the historic occasion of this Psalm is the same as that of Ps. xxxiv.   That part of the title now calling for explanation is *Upon Jonath-elem-rechokim*—Upon the dove of silence (in places) afar off; Calvin: Upon the silent dove in distant places. The variations from this are unimportant, or are attempts at interpretation.

There are three principal opinions respecting the meaning of this part of the title: 1. That it refers to the instrument used in performing the Psalm. So Jebb and others. 2. That these words point to the musical notes which were to be used in singing this Psalm. So Bochart, Fry, Mudge, Edwards; 3. The more probable and better supported view is that the title is mystical, or enigmatical. So several of the ancient versions, Calvin, Ainsworth, Horsley, Tholuck, Alexander and others. Scott: "David had been harmless as a dove, in the midst of Saul's persecutions; he was silent and patient under oppression; he was now driven, like a timorous dove, to a distance from his home and from the ordinances of God; and when exposed to extreme danger from the Philistines, set on perhaps by the relations of Goliath, he bore all patiently and attempted no revenge." Hammond has an extended note to show that David was in no danger among the Philistines; but this is so contrary to the almost uniform impression made by reading the narrative that it requires no formal refutation. Beyond a doubt David wrote this Psalm. Scott dates it B. C. 1061; Clarke, B. C. 1062. In it we have two names of the Creator, *Elohim God* and *Jehovah* LORD, on which see on Ps. iii. 2; i. 2. *Most High* will be noticed in its place.

1. *Be merciful unto me, O God;* in Ps. li. 1, rendered *Have mercy upon me, O God.* The urgency of this case is next expressed: *For man would swallow me up.* The ancient versions read, hath trodden me under foot; church of England, goeth about to devour me. Others suggest hunts, persecutes, gapes after, pants after; in Job vii. 2, the same verb is, *earnestly desireth.* It denotes the insatiable rage, with which they assailed him. On *Enosh* here rendered *man* see Introduction, § 16. It points to his foes, Jews and Philistines. *He fighting daily oppresseth me. Fighting,* see on Ps. xxxv. 1. *Oppresseth, crusheth.* The hostility to David was deadly all round. Saul sought his life. The Philistines were full of wrath against the man, that had killed their champion.

2. *Mine enemies would daily swallow me up. Daily* and *would swallow,* the same as in v. 1. The change from the singular to the plural is quite common. For *enemies* the margin would allow us to read *observers,* meaning those who kept a sharp and unfriendly eye upon him. *For* they be *many that fight against me. Fight,* as in Ps. xxxv. 1. Except a handful of true friends, it seemed as if the world was against the son of Jesse. *O thou Most High.* The Hebrew is not that rendered *Most High* in Ps. vii. 17, nor in our version is it ever rendered *Most High* in any other place, although found in the Hebrew Bible more than *fifty* times. There are but two other places where it is applied, as an epithet, to God; Ps. xcii. 8; Mic. vi. 6. It is commonly rendered *from above, on high, high places, high;* once *loftily,* Ps. lxxiii. 8. So Anderson would render it here. Dathe, Berlin, Gesenius and Hengstenberg render it *Proudly;* The Arabic, Septuagint, Venema, Amesius, Piscator, Horsley, Clarke, Scott, Fry and Jebb, *from on high;* Mudge, *with a high hand;* Chandler, *in high places,* or *stations;* Edwards, *at great advantage;* Tholuck, *insolently.* The common version agrees with the Chaldee, Calvin, Ainsworth, Aquila, Horne and Alexander. The probable meaning is they 'fight against me from the high places of authority, both in Jerusalem and in Gath,' q. d., My enemies are in power.

3. *What time I am afraid, I will trust in thee.* Some vary the tense of both clauses, but the mass of translations virtually agree with the common version. A pious man confides in God's existence, perfections, providence and word. On these he relies surely and steadfastly. *Will trust,* the same verb as in Ps. iv. 5, and in the same form as in Ps. ix. 10. David was no braggart. He did not deny that fear

sometimes invaded his mind. At such times his piety showed him the refuge—holy trust.

4. *In God I will praise his word. In God, i. e.,* either 1. *By, with,* or *through,* his help and favor; in Ps. lx. 12, it is rendered *through* God; or, 2. *Emphatically in God,* and not in another, or, 3. In God I will boast (as to) his word. We need divine assistance even in praise. In God David saw much to praise, but at this time he praises his word, all the truth he has spoken, perhaps with a special reference to his word of promise and prophecy respecting David's accession to the throne. Things now looked dark, but the word of God was unchanged and unchangeable. *In God I have put my trust.* The verb is in the preterite, expressing a habit of his life. *I will not fear what flesh can do unto me.* We know what is to be the result when the omnipotent God is on one side and impotent man on the other. We have parallel texts in v. 11; Ps. xxvii. 1; cxviii. 6; Isa. xxxi. 3; Heb. xiii. 6. David's confidence was wholly in God, and not at all in man.

5. *Every day they wrest my words. Wrest,* pervert, torture, distort. Hammond thinks the meaning is, they made my words detestable; church of England for *wrest* has *mistake.* It is easy by the change of a word, or by tone or gesture to make men utter things which they abhor. In this evil art some have made great proficiency. Such foes have no friendly mind. *All their thoughts* are *against me for evil.* Edwards: They think of nothing else but to do me mischief; church of England: All that they imagine is to do me evil; Jebb: Against me all their imaginings are for evil. Nor were David's enemies idle:

6. *They gather themselves together.* Not merely one or two foes but a large number of wicked men opposed him, and they met and consulted. *They hide themselves, i. e.,* They practise secret and uncandid arts towards me that they may find out my plans and acts, and that they may conceal their own intentions and snares. *They mark my steps.* Calvin: They watch my heels. The sense is either that they dog his steps to do him evil, or that they watch for his stumbling. Alexander gives a third interpretation and thinks the Hebrew word has probably the same sense as in Ps. xlix. 5, on which see. *When they wait for my soul, i. e.,* wait to destroy my life. 'Nothing would satisfy them but his death.'

7. *Shall they escape by iniquity?* Some drop the interrogative form. Some for *iniquity* read *vanity, mischief.* The meaning pretty certainly is that so far as they have succeeded it has been by wicked means, or, so far as they hope for success it is wholly by unrighteous measures. *In thine anger cast down the people, O God. People,* in the plural *peoples*—all who had united to destroy David. On the imprecatory form of this clause see Introduction, § 6.

8. *Thou tellest my wanderings. Tellest,* countest, takest account of, payest attention to. The clause is a grateful recognition of God's kindness up to this hour, and implies confidence that it will be continued. *Put thou my tears into thy bottle, i. e.,* Remember all my tears and sorrows. Valuable liquors the Jews put into a bottle, Josh. ix. 13; Judg. iv. 19; 1 Sam. xvi. 20; Matt. ix. 17. So David here asks that God will remember and treat as precious the tears [literally tear] he has shed. Some indeed suppose that there is a reference to the *lachrymaries* used by the Greeks and Romans. These were little urns, capable of being closed, and were often deposited full of tears with the bodies of lamented relatives; but we know not that this custom was in vogue among the ancient Jews. *Are they not in thy book?* Here as in many other cases the interrogation has the force of strong assertion. A *book* was for remembrance or registry. He, who numbers the hairs of our heads will not overlook our *wanderings* in exile, nor forget our *tears.*

9. *When I cry unto thee, then shall mine enemies turn back. Turn back,* see on Ps.

vi. 10, where the same verb is rendered *return*. David often beheld marked deliverances. Shame and defeat are implied in this *turning back*. Their retreat should begin when David should pray earnestly against them. *This I know, i. e.,* I know that my enemies shall flee when I cry to the Lord. *For God* is *for me, i. e.,* so as to be *against* them. Other interpretations are given to the latter part of this verse, but none is so good as this.

10. *In God will I praise* his *word; in the* Lord *will I praise* his *word*. See on v. 4. David was walking not by appearances, but by the light of the promises and doctrines of the Bible. To these we must often resort and reassure our confidence.

11. *In God have I put my trust: I will not be afraid what man can do unto me.* See on v. 4. As often as we are tempted, we must again and again profess and confirm our hope and confidence in Jehovah.

12. *Thy vows* are *upon me, O God.* On *vows* see on Ps. xxii. 25; l. 14. David here acknowledges that he was firmly bound to the service of God by solemn religious engagements. Many of these vows were probably made in the anguish of his soul in the time of great affliction. One of them no doubt was that he would make a suitable return of gratitude. *I will render praises unto thee.* How well David kept these vows is proven by the *Book of Praises,* the larger part of which he wrote. Calvin thinks his vow includes also sacrifices. No doubt that is correct, as the ancient worship was celebrated with such offerings. But even this hearty praise was better than bullocks, Ps. l. 14, 23.

13. *For thou hast delivered my soul from death;* 'either, thou hast often saved my life; or, thou hast on some one recent occasion done so; or, I am so sure that my life shall be spared by God, that I speak of it as already accomplished.' Perhaps the latter is the point here intended. Wilt *not* thou deliver *my feet from falling, that I may walk before God in the light of the living?* The *falling* is either *in death* or *into sin.* The former is certainly included. *Walk* points out the course of life. Alexander: "*To walk before God* is to live in the enjoyment of his favor and protection." The *light of the living* is the opposite of the darkness of the grave, or of the dead. The last clause may be taken either as a prayer, or as a declaration of strong confidence that it would be done.

Doctrinal and Practical Remarks.

1. Blessed is he, who is so much like a *silent dove* that he can appropriate to himself the encouragements of this sacred ode. At home or *in distant places* he may make his boast in God.

2. As long as we live, and in every variety of situation we have need of *mercy,* v. 1. If we need pardon, we must hope for it through *mercy;* if we seek protection against men and devils, it must all come through *mercy.*

3. The war of the wicked against the godly is deadly, vv. 1, 6. Even wild beasts seldom if ever prey upon their own kind; but a furious man is viler than they. All persecutors are alike actuated by relentless rage.

4. Contests, especially with fierce and wicked men, are very uncongenial to good men, v. 1. Yet sometimes there is no escaping from them. In that case we must cry to God to support us.

5. The hostility of the wicked against the righteous seems never to rest, v. 2. One would think that even enmity itself would sometimes grow weary. But nothing but divine grace can take it away.

6. The multitude of foes who rise up against us is often very surprising, v. 2. The wicked rely greatly on numbers. The loud yelp of one hound commonly brings the pack.

7. Good men are not wholly free from occasional fears, v. 3. Some of these are salutary and lead to precaution. But even those which have torment in them may gain temporary possession of a pious mind. Calvin: "Fear and hope may seem opposite and incompatible affections, yet it is proved by observation, that the latter never comes into full exercise unless there exists some measure of the former." It is therefore not uncommon for good men to have a painful sense of their own weakness, and need of help from God. Oftentimes 'faith grows valiant in fight. Albeit it begins like a coward, and staggers in the first conflict, it grows stout and triumphant.'

8. There is a vast difference between saints and sinners. The wicked would swallow up the righteous, v. 2. The righteous would not willingly harm a human being. The wicked are *oppressors*. The righteous love to lighten grievous burdens. The wicked have fears that end in despair. The righteous hath hope in the darkest hour, vv. 1, 3. Arnd: "This is the way of all enemies, who, confiding in human strength, in external force and earthly might, are full of pride and insolence; but they who commit themselves to God's grace are humble, confide in God, boast themselves not, for they know that everything depends on God's grace, in which all believers are included, are secure against the rage and swelling of the enemies, overcome at last by patience, and see their high minded adversaries overthrown."

9. There is no comfort without trust, vv. 3, 4, 11. If we lean not on God, we are as without God. A staff not used gives no support.

10. It is idle to indulge engrossing fears of puny mortals, vv. 4, 11. They are *flesh*, and all flesh is grass. We never act more unwisely than when we succumb to apprehensions arising from *man's* wisdom or power. Until our foes can cope with the Almighty, can 'confront omnipotence,' or 'check the stream of the divine benignity,' or 'oppose the artillery of the skies,' a righteous man, having a righteous cause, has no ground of alarm. Henry: "As we must not trust to an arm of flesh, when it is engaged for us, so we must not be afraid of an arm of flesh, when it is stretched out against us." Morison: "The fear of God is the great antidote against the fear of man."

11. Let God's people ever cling to his word and praise it, vv. 4, 10. Its promises and doctrines contain all we need to hold us up in the darkest hours. This was David's reliance, into whose mouth Luther puts these words: "I will glory in the word of God: for I have a command, a declaration and a promise in my favor." Arnd: "As Saul and the potentates of the world boast of their hosts of war, their thousands of men, and their munitions, I will glory in God's word and promise."

12. If we have not the deliverance, yet if we have the promise of it, let us be calm and undisturbed, v. 4.

13. He must be weak and ignorant, who thinks some strange thing has happened, when his words are grossly perverted, v. 5. It has always been so. Christ himself was subject to this grievance.

14. The human mind without grace is a nest of wickedness swarming with *thoughts* of *evil*, v. 5. Compare Gen. vi. 5; viii. 21; Ps. v. 9; Matt. xv. 19.

15. If the secrecy of the plottings of the wicked was complete, concealing them from God himself, they would have a great and decisive advantage, for they are uncandid and full of chicanery. But Jehovah sees them when *they hide themselves*. If the saints do not know the evil designed against them, their heavenly Father does; and so it all comes to nought, v. 6. A just man in a just cause, finding his enemies countless, united, powerful, spiteful, cruel and crafty, may still be confident. Henry: "None are raised so high, or settled so firmly, but the justice of God can bring them down, both from their dignities, and from their confidences."

16. It is all in vain to hope that sin will in a single case end well, v. 7. This would require that Jehovah should change or be dethroned.

17. Because God leads us to a place and keeps us there for a season, that is no evidence that he will not call us to yet other places, and bless and preserve us there also, v. 8. Some commentators number as many as *twelve* different *removals* made by David. Scott: "The Lord graciously notes and orders the *removals* of his people: while they keep in the path of duty, they cannot be driven from his gracious presence; and their tears of godly sorrow and those which are extorted by persecution, or sympathy with the sufferings of others, will be reserved to be jewels in their crown of glory." Dickson: "God hath so great compassion on his servants in trouble that he reckoneth even the steps of their wanderings and pilgrimage." Blessed be his holy name forever and ever; and let every creature say, Amen, Ps. cxlvi. 9.

18. God will not be unmindful of our tears and sorrows. O no! He puts them in his bottle, v. 8. He registers them in his book. Trials will bring tears. "But," says Arnd, "here lies a powerful consolation, that God gathers up such tears, and puts them into his bottle, just as one would pour precious wine into a flagon, so precious and dear are such tears before God, and God lays them up as a treasure in the heavens; and if we think that all such tears are lost, lo! God hath preserved them for us a treasure in the heavens, with which we shall be richly consoled in that day, Ps. cxxvi. 5." Calvin: "We may surely believe, that if God bestows such honor upon the tears of his saints, he must number every drop of their blood. Tyrants may burn their flesh and their bones, but the blood remains to cry aloud for vengeance; and intervening ages can never erase what has been written in the register of God's remembrance."

19. God is *for* the righteous, and they ought to *know* it, v. 9. Who then can be against them? What more do they need? He is infinite, eternal, unchangeable. 'Faith is not a fallible conjecture.'

20. Who can tell the power of prayer, indited by the Holy Spirit and offered in true faith? v. 9. It secures Omnipotence on its side. Morison: "How vain and fruitless then to contend with the prayers of the faithful, when all Heaven's resources are, as it were, at their command! How many judgments have they both averted and inflicted!"

21. Calvin: "When exposed to the opposition of assailants formidable for strength, or policy, or any worldly advantages, let us learn with David to set God in opposition to them, and we shall be speedily able to view the mightiest of them without dismay," v. 11.

22. Whatever the nature of our religious *vows*, if they be but lawful, let us fulfil them heartily and cheerfully, v. 12. Clarke: "Reader, what hast *thou vowed* to God? To renounce the devil and all his works, the pomps and vanities of this wicked world, and all the sinful desires of the flesh; to keep God's holy word and commandments, and to walk before him all the days of thy life. These things hast *thou* vowed; and these *vows* are *upon thee*. Wilt thou *pay* them?" Dickson: "An honest heart is no less desirous to perform the duty of praise after delivery, than he was ready to make his vow and his promise before his delivery."

23. Whatever our case may be, let us always render *praises*, v. 12. They are always due to God. Continual mercies call for continual thanksgivings, and 'singular deliverances call for singular expressions of gratitude and praise.'

24. A past deliverance should not be allowed to grow out of date; but should be frequently mentioned both for the strengthening of faith in ourselves and others, and for the glory of our great Deliverer, v. 13.

25. "Those that think they stand must take heed lest they fall, because the best stand no longer than God is pleased to uphold them," v. 13.

26. A desire for the continuance of life is natural, and is not necessarily nor always wicked, v. 13.

27. This **Psalm** teaches us that in times of freedom from bloody persecutions the saints should give thanks accordingly. It is a great mercy not to be called to resist unto blood.

PSALM LVII.

To the chief Musician, Al-taschith, Michtam of David, when he fled from Saul in the cave.

1 Be merciful unto me, O God, be merciful unto me, for my soul trusteth in thee: yea, in the shadow of thy wings will I make my refuge, until *these* calamities be overpast.

2 I will cry unto God most high; unto God that performeth *all things* for me.

3 He shall send from heaven, and save me *from* the reproach of him that would swallow me up. Selah. God shall send forth his mercy and his truth.

4 My soul *is* among lions: *and* I lie *even among* them that are set on fire, *even* the sons of men, whose teeth *are* spears and arrows, and their tongue a sharp sword.

5 Be thou exalted, O God, above the heavens; *let* thy glory *be* above all the earth.

6 They have prepared a net for my steps; my soul is bowed down: they have digged a pit before me, into the midst whereof they are fallen *themselves*. Selah.

7 My heart is fixed, O God, my heart is fixed: I will sing and give praise.

8 Awake up, my glory; awake, psaltery and harp: I *myself* will awake early.

9 I will praise thee, O Lord, among the people: I will sing unto thee among the nations.

10 For thy mercy *is* great unto the heavens, and thy truth unto the clouds.

11 Be thou exalted, O God, above the heavens: *let* thy glory *be* above all the earth.

ON parts of the title see on titles of Psalms iv. xvi. *When he fled from Saul in the cave* may be understood as referring either, 1, to David's hiding himself in the cave of Adullam, 1 Sam. xxii. 1–5; 2 Sam. xxiii. 13, 14; 2, to his residence in the cave of En-gedi, 1 Sam. xxiii. 29; xxiv. 1–22; 3, generally to his life in the caves of his country. The contents of the Psalm would suit either view. Nor can we decide which is historically correct, nor would it do us any good, if we could. Patrick, Dodd, Gill, Morison, Horne, Clarke and Tholuck favor the second view; Hengstenberg and Alexander the third. The cxlii. Psalm was "A prayer of David when he was in the cave." We have not before met with *Al-taschith*. It subsequently occurs in the titles of Psalms lviii. lix. lxxv. It is generally agreed that it means *Destroy not*. The opinions respecting its signification are various. Dimock thinks it 'denotes an instrument of *nine* strings.' Abenezra and Edwards regard it as referring to the *music* to be used in singing the Psalm. Hammond, Patrick, Dodd, Clarke and Morison suppose it means *Destroy him not*, viz.: Saul. This very language is used by David to Abishai in 1 Sam. xxvi. 9. Morison: "The words, *Al-taschith*, therefore may be intended to show that this sacred ode was composed on that memorable occasion when David was restrained, by an unseen hand, from inflicting any injury upon his cruel adversary, when he might easily have effected his destruction, and when all the external circumstances were such as to have tempted the commission of the unhappy deed." But the Chaldee, Cocceius, Gill, Scott, Hengstenberg and Alexander suppose it means, *Destroy me not*. Cocceius: 'These words David, no doubt, in his great distress, constantly repeated, and afterwards, when he composed this Psalm, committed them to the church and to believers of all ages, that they might make use of them in times of opposition and persecution." It is not an unimportant fact that this explanation suits all the Psalms where *Al-taschith* occurs.

Many mark resemblances between this and Ps. lvi. Some of them appear in the common version. The authorship of this is undoubtedly Davidic. Scott dates it B. C. 1060, and Clarke B. C. 1061. In it we have four names of the Creator: *Elohim God, El God, Gel-yohn Most High* and *Adonai Lord*, on which respectively see on Ps. iii. 2; v. 4; vii. 17; ii. 4. On *Selah* see Introduction, § 15.

1. *Be merciful unto me, O God, be merciful unto me;* as in Ps. li. 1; lvi. 1. The reduplication of the prayer shows the great straits to which David was now reduced, and the great vehemence of his mind in seeking deliverance. *For my soul trusteth in thee.* Chaldee: For in thy word my soul hath hoped; Ainsworth: For in thee my soul hopeth for safety; Venema: For in thee my soul has had a protector; Amesius: For to thee my soul hath betaken herself; Alexander: For in thee has my soul sought refuge. The verb is quite the same as in Ps. vii. 1; xi. 1; xvi. 1. When we have at God's bidding committed our case to him, we may plead his honor for our protection. *Yea, in the shadow of thy wings will I make my refuge.* Ainsworth renders the verb will I hope for safety; church of England, shall be my refuge; Venema, will I have a protector; Hengstenberg, I confide; Alexander, will I seek refuge; literally, will I trust; in this verse rendered *trust.* The figure of *wings* is borrowed from those of the cherubim over the mercy-seat, or of a fowl protecting her young. The latter is best. *Until* these *calamities be overpast. Calamities,* elsewhere rendered *mischiefs, perverse things, mischievous things,* also in the singular, *iniquity, wickedness, naughtiness,* see Ps. v. 9; lv. 11. The *calamities* of David at this time were the fruit of the *wickedness* of other people, and are therefore well expressed by a word that means both *calamity* and *iniquity.* Calvin renders it *wickedness* in this place.

2. *I will cry unto God most high.* Even David, God's prophet, and the sweet singer of Israel, at times had no resource but the promises and prayer. Although *most high* is here used as an adjective, and not put in capitals, yet it is the same word used in Deut. xxxii. 8; Ps. vii. 17; ix. 2; xviii. 13. David repeats that he will cry, *Unto God that performeth* all things *for me.* Calvin understands the clause as equivalent to ' God who carries forward to perfection the work which he has begun.' Horsley renders it, ' God, who will bring things to a conclusion for me.' Pool understands it as signifying that ' God *perfects,* or *finishes* all that he has promised.' *El God,* by Amesius rendered *the mighty God;* by Alexander, *the Almighty.*

3. *He shall send from heaven and save me.* Chaldee: Sends *his angel.* Jehovah sends angels, commands, energy, all that is necessary to work deliverance. He will send help from heaven and *save me, i. e.,* rescue me from the power and craft of my foes, from the *calamities* now passing over me, the *wickednesses* now pressing me. Saul shall not have my life. From *the reproach of him that would swallow me up.* This clause is variously rendered. The word *from* is supplied by our translators. Chaldee: He shall save me, *covering with eternal disgrace him that was treading me down;* Arabic: And made those, who were trampling upon me, a reproach; Septuagint and Vulgate: He gave to reproach them that trod upon me; Ainsworth: He hath put to reproach him that would swallow me up; Hare: He will expose him to shame who would devour me; the margin has: He reproacheth him that would swallow me up. This is certainly better than the English text. Hammond throws the weight of his name against the common rendering. The sense may be, 1. My enemy uses opprobrious language; or, 2. God is now delivering (or shall deliver) my foe to reproach. *Swallow up,* see on Ps. lvi. 1, 2. God shall *send forth his mercy and his truth. Mercy,* often so rendered, also *loving-kindness,* Ps. xvii. 7; *kindness,* Ps. xxxi. 21; *goodness,* Ps. xxxiii. 5; *merciful kindness,* Ps. cxvii. 2. *Truth,* almost invariably so rendered, embracing the ideas of stability, uprightness, faithfulness. On fit occasions God displays both mercy and

truth to the joy of his people, to the confusion of his enemies, to the glory of his name. Clarke: "Mercy and truth are personified;" Morison: "By a beautiful figure of speech, the divine mercy and faithfulness are here represented as messengers ever ready to be dispatched from heaven to execute redemption for the church."

4. *My soul is among lions.* Chaldee: My soul burns as if in the midst of flames; Arabic, Septuagint, Ethiopic, Vulgate and Doway: And he hath delivered my soul from the midst of the young lions; Amesius: I am among fierce lions; Kennicott and Clarke: My soul dwells in parched places. Of these renderings some are mere interpretations; others depend on a misapprehension of the root of the word rendered *lions.* The common version is best and is well sustained by authority. And *I lie even among* them *that are set on fire.* For *them that are set on fire* the Chaldee has coals; Ainsworth, inflamers; Amesius and Green, incendiaries; Edwards, all on fire; Boothroyd, all burning with rage. The verb, in the future, is best rendered in the present. See Introduction, § 6. It is pretty clear that David intends to say that he is among men of a fiery, fierce spirit, filled with hatred and violence, and exercising their malice towards him in many ways. These are described as *The sons of men,* literally the sons of Adam; *Whose teeth* are *spears and arrows, and their tongue a sharp sword.* Horne: "The fiercest of beasts, the most devouring of elements, and the sharpest of military weapons, are here selected to represent the power and fury of David's enemies." Calvin: "David encountered no heavier trial than the false and calumnious charges which were levelled against him by his enemies."

5. *Be thou exalted, O God, above the heavens; let thy glory be above all the earth.* This verse looks like an abrupt and illogical change of subject. But pious minds in the midst of their greatest sufferings turn with alacrity from themselves to God. Thus our Lord Jesus in his agony cried, Father, glorify thy name, John xii. 28. So here the type of Christ forgets his discomforts or cheerfully submits to them, asking that thereby the Lord may be honored. God's exaltation and glory are and ought to be *supreme,* above all his works, *above the heavens, above all the earth.* This verse is a pious ejaculation. The next verse resumes the thread of discourse.

6. *They have prepared a net for my steps.* Nets were for catching fishes, birds, or wild animals. Here and often the word points to the snares and artifices of wicked and crafty men, whereby they would inveigle men into sin, folly, or ruin, Ps. ix. 15; x. 9; cxl. 5; Mic. vii. 2. Indirection and deceit are essential elements in schemes of wickedness. Living in this state of things was very afflicting to David. *My soul is bowed down. Bowed down,* as in Ps. cxlv. 14; cxlvi. 8. *They have digged a pit before me into the midst whereof they are fallen* themselves. *Pit,* as in Ps. cxix. 85; Jer. xviii. 22. We have the same idea in Ps. ix. 15.

7. *My heart is fixed, O God, my heart is fixed. Fixed,* margin *prepared;* Ps. xxxviii. 17, ready; Ps. li. 10, right. *Established* gives the meaning; see on Ps. li. 10. Although David was in great distress, yet his mind was settled as to his principles. He was *fixed* in his determination to cleave to the Lord with purpose of heart, to stand in his lot, to adopt no unlawful means of relief, to trust God in the darkest hour, and to be thankful and joyous in God's worship. *I will sing and give praise.* The latter verb may be rendered *Sing Psalms* or *sing praises;* see on Ps. vii. 17; ix. 11. Heartless or even languid praise is an offence to God.

8. *Awake up my glory.* Our natural powers are dull and sluggish in God's praises, and so they must be aroused by self-exhortation. *My glory, i. e.,* my tongue. By articulate speech hardly less than by reason is man distinguished above all the other inhabitants of earth. What would soon be the state of the world were all its inhabitants now struck dumb, and their muteness made perpetual? David would employ not only his tongue, but instruments of music: *Awake, psaltery and harp;* see on Ps.

xxxiii. 2. *I* myself *will awake early, q. d.,* With all my powers, and at early dawn I will enter on this work. Hammond, Geddes, Secker, Street, Fry, Hengstenberg and Alexander would render it, 'I will awaken the morning,' or 'I will call up the dawn.' This is highly poetical. Anderson here cites Ovid and Milton.

9. *I will praise thee, O* LORD, *among the people. Praise,* give thanks. *People,* plural *peoples,* or *nations* as in Ps. vii. 8. The next clause is parallel: *I will sing unto thee among the nations. Sing,* or *sing praises,* or *sing Psalms. Nations,* rendered *people* in Ps. ii. 1. In Rom. xv. 9, Paul directly applies these words to the kingdom of Christ in its relations to the Gentiles.

10. *For thy mercy is great unto the heavens, and thy truth unto the clouds. Mercy* and *Truth,* as in v. 3. God's attributes are not limited. It is wicked to teach that they can be bounded. The *heavens* and the *clouds* are the most elevated objects that strike the sense, and so are fit to be employed to teach us the exceedingly exalted nature of God, and especially his *mercy* and his *truth* to sinners, who seek refuge under the shadow of his wings; see on Ps. xxxvi. 5.

11. *Be thou exalted, O God, above the heavens: let thy glory be above all the earth.* In the Hebrew as in English this verse is precisely the same as v. 5. It were idolatry and degrading superstition to use towards any creature the Psalms, and hymns and spiritual songs, which we are bound to use in the service of God.

DOCTRINAL AND PRACTICAL REMARKS.

1. Pious men have often found some set words in prayer very suitable to themselves. David's mind, if we understand the title, often led him to cry, *Destroy me not.*

2. While life lasts we shall never be done crying for *mercy,* v. 1. Whether it be famine, pestilence or war, whether it be foes without, or fears within, whether it be at sea or on land, whether it be in sickness or health, in life or in death, our great need is *mercy.* Yea, we shall need it at the day of Judgment, 2 Tim. i. 18. Nothing but mercy can protect us from human malice or diabolical rage, from personal vindictiveness or legal injustice, from sin in life, from despair in death, or from hell in eternity. When man hates us, let us seek the love of God; when man reproaches us, let us seek the honor that comes from God only; when man is cruel, let us seek God's lovingkindness. A good daily prayer, a good motto for every tempted, troubled soul would be Al-Taschith.

3. The Scriptures are harmonious in declaring the relations of believers to God to be of the most precious and substantial nature. He first approaches us and proposes his covenant. By the grace of his Spirit we *trust in him,* make *him our refuge,* and thus set to our seal that he is true, and in so doing he comes to be on our side. Henceforth we may plead his gracious engagement with the utmost freedom and earnestness, v. 1. "Where faith in trouble fleeth unto God it cannot but speed." Jer. xiv. 21.

4. How condescending is God to compare himself to a fowl tender of her young, v. 1. Calvin: "There are seasons when we are permitted to enjoy the calm sunshine of prosperity; but there is not a day of our lives in which we may not suddenly be overtaken by storms of affliction, and it is necessary we should be persuaded that God will cover us with his wings."

5. There is no getting on without *trust,* confidence in God, v. 1. The want of it annihilates our comforts.

6. Every generation has its *calamities,* v. 1. Of these none are harder to be borne than those, which come to us through the *wickedness* of man. God himself is our only sure refuge. Compare Isa. xxvi. 20, 21.

7. If we would have our prayers answered, they must not be dull. We must *cry unto God,* v. 2. If anything is worth asking for, it is worth asking for in good

earnest. 'Elias prayed earnestly.' Without some measure of earnestness prayer is solemn mockery.

8. Our past experience of God's mercies should encourage us to come to him with boldness. If he has *performed all things* for us hitherto, let us not doubt his mercy at any time hereafter, v. 2. He changes not, but fulfils his engagements.

9. Henry: "In everything that befalls us, we ought to see, and own the hand of God; whatever is done, is of his *performing*, in it his counsel is accomplished, and the Scripture is fulfilled," v. 2.

10. Like his attributes, God's resources are infinite. He has many on earth, of which we wot not. And he has all heaven beside. And if heaven and earth were all gone, he has himself. It is always safe to expect him to save by raising up instruments and messengers here below, or by *sending them from heaven*, v. 3. Dickson: "If ordinary means fail, faith assureth itself of God's working wonders for perfecting his promises."

11. It is no new thing for good men to have barbarous foes, who would, if they could, *swallow them up*, v. 3. Compare Pr. xxx. 14.

12. No reasonable man can doubt the awful depravity of the wicked. Could inspiration have used more decided or forcible language than it has? It says they are fierce, cruel, savage as *lions;* that they are violent, blind and heedless of all claims for tenderness as *fire* itself; that the very powers which God has given them for nourishing themselves, *their teeth*, are used to devour their neighbors, even their best friends; and that their *tongue*, man's glory, has become, not an instrument of blessing God and man, but *a sharp sword* to make men bleed, to fill them with pain, and to kill them, v. 4. Such tormentors are quite like their father the devil. His works they are constantly doing. Compare Mic. iii. 5; Gal. v. 15; Hab. i. 13; Ps. lii. 4. The destructive power of evil speaking alone is frightful.

13. Well may good men shut their mouths in uncomplaining silence, seeing their sufferings fall far below those of David, v. 4. If we fare as well as the man after God's own heart, we should never murmur. "The horrors of a lion's den, the burning of a fiery furnace, and the cruel onset of war are the striking images by which David here describes the peril and wretchedness of his present condition."

14. However desperate our own affairs may seem to be, even when we are beset by lies, taunts, calumnies, reproaches, cruel mockings, threats, betrayers and betrayals, rage and wrath, let us chiefly care for the glory of God, vv. 5, 11. If he is exalted, it is well for us to be humbled; if he is glorified, it matters not if we be esteemed the off-scouring of all things. "Father, glorify thy name."

15. Let not God's people in their war with wickedness resort to the devices used by their enemies. O no! The weapons of our warfare are not carnal. We may not use net for net, nor dig pit for pit, v. 6. The sins of man work not the righteousness of God. Religion has no need of unhallowed tempers for her promotion. When men serve God as if the devil was in them they bring great reproach on his blessed name.

16. Good men may be cast down, v. 6. It is not wicked to be sad. Even the Saviour of the world was greatly dejected during most of his life, and unusually so near the time of his death. It is enough to make any good man 'droop and hang the head' to find that even when he has been blameless, he is suspected and maligned. It was always so.

17. Punishment in kind is common even in this world. Men commonly fall into their own pits, v. 6. The Greek proverb is: "Evil advice often becomes most ruinous to the evil adviser;" the Roman, "There is no law more just than that which condemns a man to death by the instrument which he has invented to take away the

life of others." Guillotine, who invented the instrument, which bears his name, was executed by the guillotine.

18. One of the darkest signs in some professors of religion is want of stability. Their hearts are not *fixed*, v. 7. Their principles are not established. They are not settled. This may be owing to ignorance of Scripture doctrine, to natural levity of mind, to evil habits long indulged, to the weakness or want of grace. In every case, instability is a bad sign. Professor of religion, art thou a reed shaken with the wind, a wave of the sea tossed to and fro?

19. It should alarm the wicked that they are contending with a people, who sing and shout on the battle-field, v. 7. Yea, they never sing louder than when most distressed and afflicted. Whether the saints conquer or are conquered, they still sing on. Blessed be God for that. Let sinners tremble at contending with men of a spirit so heavenly.

20. In the whole work of praising and serving God let us use *all* our powers of body and soul, our tongues, our hands, our voices, our every faculty, v. 8. And let us begin our work *early;* not forgetting that "the little word *early* is not to be understood merely of the morning season, but of great diligence, activity, desire and love in the praising of God."

21. Instrumental music in the public worship of God is lawful, v. 8. See REMARKS on Ps. xxxiii. 2.

22. We should not only praise God in secret, but also in the most public manner and before all peoples and nations, if we have opportunity, v. 9. Dickson: "We seriously mind the praise of God when, according to our place, we labor to make others also know God, as we know him."

23. We constantly need the guidance of the Holy Spirit in the study of the Scriptures, that we may get their true scope and meaning. The prophets largely spoke of the Gentiles coming in, v. 9. Yet how slow were even the primitive Christians to believe that the Gospel was for any one beyond Judea!

24. God's perfections, in particular his *mercy* and his *truth* make him the fit object of all religious worship, v. 10. To refrain from his worship, when he is duly known and loved, is impossible.

25. As verse 9 is actually quoted in the New Testament as applicable to Gospel times, and as David was in many respects a type of Christ, there is nothing forced or strained in regarding this Psalm as *Typical-Messianic.* If David was victorious, much more shall Christ be. If David put down all his foes, much more shall Christ subdue all things to himself.

PSALM LVIII.

To the chief Musician, Al-taschith, Michtam of David.

1 Do ye indeed speak righteousness, O congregation? do ye judge uprightly, O ye sons of men?

2 Yea, in heart ye work wickedness; ye weigh the violence of your hands in the earth.

3 The wicked are estranged from the womb: they go astray as soon as they be born, speaking lies.

4 Their poison *is* like the poison of a serpent: *they are* like the deaf adder *that* stoppeth her ear;

5 Which will not hearken to the voice of charmers, charming never so wisely.

6 Break their teeth, O God, in their mouth: break out the great teeth of the young lions, O

7 Let them melt away as waters *which* run continually: *when* he bendeth *his bow to shoot* his arrows, let them be as cut in pieces.

8 As a snail *which* melteth, let *every one of them* pass away: *like* the untimely birth of a woman, *that* they may not see the sun.

9 Before your pots can feel the thorns, he shall take them away as with a whirlwind, both living, and in *his* wrath.

10 The righteous shall rejoice when he seeth the vengeance: he shall wash his feet in the blood of the wicked.

11 So that a man shall say, Verily *there is* a reward for the righteous: verily he is a God that judgeth in the earth.

ALL the phrases of the title are explained on titles of Psalms iv. xvi. lvii. The authorship of David is undoubted. This Psalm has no known historic occasion, although its contents show that it refers to a time of bitter persecution. Scott and Clarke both date it B. C. 1061. In it we find *Jehovah* LORD and *Elohim God*, on which see on Ps. i. 2; iii. 2.

1. *Do ye indeed speak righteousness, O congregation? do ye judge uprightly, O ye sons of men?* Chaldee: Does it indeed seem to you that ye speak justice when ye [who are or ought to be] just ones are silent in the time of strife? Judge the sons of men in uprightness; Amesius: Do ye truly speak justice, O band? do ye judge the things, which are right, ye sons of men? Edwards: Do ye really pronounce righteous sentence? and do ye judge equitably, ye sons of men? Horsley: Are ye in earnest, O faction, when ye talk of righteousness, do ye give sentence uprightly, O ye sons of men? Hengstenberg: Are ye then indeed dumb, that ye will not speak what is righteous, and judge what is upright, ye children of men? For *righteousness*, Waterland has *truth*. For *congregation* we may read Band, Company, Assembly, Council, literally a *sheaf*. Patrick supposes it designates Saul's *Privy Council*. In the Hebrew Bible it nowhere else means assembly. This has led many to think the word should be rendered *dumb* or *silent*. If we drop or vary the Masoretic points, this may well be the reading. The change of a letter would then also give us *princes* or *judges*. In this case the sense is given by Alexander in his paraphrase: "Can it be? is it possible? are you really silent, you whose very office is to speak for God, and against the sins of men? See Deut. i. 16, 17." Taking the clauses according to the common version, we may regard them as a bold and unqualified denial of the justice of the accusations against him. David honors these men by calling them an *assembly* or *council;* but he also calls them *sons of man*, either to remind them of their frailty and accountability, or, to let them know that even here their real characters are understood and they are not *sons of God*.

2. *Yea, in heart ye work wickedness.* All the time they were sitting as solemn and dignified judges, they were meditating wrong and injury. Their very station should have warned them against injustice, but they intentionally used their position to *work wickedness. Ye weigh* [or ponder] *the violence of your hands in the earth.* What they did, they did deliberately, with malice prepense. *Violence*, often so rendered, also *wrong, cruelty, injustice, damage, violent dealing*, Ps. vii. 16; xxvii. 12. It further aggravated their crimes that they did all this injustice *in the land* of Israel, where were excellent statutes and ordinances of justice, and where God had presented many and urgent motives to uprightness in all, especially in judges.

3. *The wicked are estranged from the womb.* For estranged some have alienated, aliens, froward, wicked, strangers to pity. The clause asserts native hereditary depravity. Compare Isa. lxviii. 8; Eph. ii. 3. Ainsworth: "This noteth man's natural corruption;" Pool: "The sense is, No wonder they act so unrighteously, for their very natures and principles are corrupt from their birth; they are the wicked offspring of

sinful parents." *They go astray so soon as they be born, speaking lies. Estrangement from God* is very naturally attended by signs of wickedness towards man, and especially by want of truthfulness. What parent's heart has not ached at infallible evidence of a tendency to falsehood in his offspring? It requires the best precepts and examples, enforced by the highest authority and the most steadfast government to save children and youth from growing up to be arrant liars.

4. *Their poison* is *like the poison of a serpent.* *Poison*, elsewhere rendered also *rage, wrath, fury, anger;* see on Ps. vi. 1, where it is rendered *hot displeasure.* Here it means venom. The poison of serpents is a 'fiery liquor,' which is soon spread through the system. It is a fit emblem of the deadly malice of violent men. I have seen a man thrown by it in a few minutes into a raging fever, and into dreadful pain. In this verse there may be an allusion also to the *old serpent,* Rev. xx. 2. These violent men resembled one species of serpent in another respect: They are *like the deaf adder* that *stoppeth her ear.* Some have alleged that the stories respecting some kinds of serpents being unaffected by sounds are fabulous. This can hardly be so. The belief is too widely spread in countries where serpents abound. The species here spoken of is the *asp.* The word here rendered *adder* occurs six times in the Bible, and is always rendered *asp* except here and in Ps. xci. 13; and even then the margin gives *asp.* Other words are rendered *adder* in Gen. xlix. 17; Ps. cxl. 3; Pr. xxiii. 32. There was no remedy for the poison of the asp. Its bite was fatal in a few minutes. Some modern travellers say that this species of serpent is still found in countries east of the Mediterranean.

5. *Which will not hearken to the voice of charmers, charming never so wisely.* Charmers of serpents are still common in India and Egypt. That they possess power over venomous reptiles so as to make them harmless cannot be denied, for they often exhibit themselves and their serpents. Compare Eccle. x. 11; Jer. viii. 17. But over the asp these men are said to have had no power. The reason given by some is that asps are entirely deaf; by others that though they have hearing, yet to the *murmuring* noise made by charmers they close their ears; and by others that they are so venomous that the charmer has no power over them at any time. Which of these is true in natural history the author has no means of determining. The latter is most probable. The import of the passage is that David's enemies were obstinately deaf to all tender appeals, to all the demands of justice, to the dictates of nationality and of conscience. Such a transaction as that recorded in 1 Sam. xxiv. 4–20 ought forever to have terminated the Sauline persecutions. They were not provoked even by imprudence, much less by any crime.

6. *Break their teeth, O God, in their mouth.* On *breaking the teeth,* see on Ps. iii. 7. The allusion is to rendering beasts of prey powerless by breaking their teeth. This is a very old figure among sacred writers, Job iv. 10. *Break out the great teeth of the young lions, O* LORD. On young lions see on Ps. xvii. 12; xxxiv. 10. A friend, who has spent a quarter of a century in South Africa, informs me that the old lion becomes toothless and clumsy, and has great difficulty in securing his prey, or in eating it, as he has first to tear it to pieces with his claws. Compare Job iv. 11. The prayer of David is that his enemies, though strong and active, may be rendered powerless for mischief and cruelty against him. On the imprecatory form see Introduction, § 6.

7. *Let them melt away as waters* which *run continually.* The verbs are in the future. The modern signification of the word *melt* renders it not so good here as *flow* or *pass away.* The same form of the verb is in Job vii. 5 rendered *become loathsome.* Calvin: Let them flow away like waters, let them depart; church of England: Let them fall away like water that runneth apace; Green: Let them waste away like water which runneth continually; Chaldee (interpreting): Let them melt away in their sins like

water, let them flow away from themselves; Septuagint, Ethiopic, Vulgate and Doway: They shall come to nothing, like water running down. When *he bendeth* his bow to shoot *his arrows let them be as cut in pieces.* On the mode of bending the bow see on Ps. vii. 13; xi. 2; xxxvii. 14. The reader will notice that in the common version much is supplied by the translators. Rogers: "I am persuaded that some word, the name of something with which the wicked, perishing under the divine vengeance, were compared, is lost in the Hebrew." The chief difficulty is in determining what are the antecedents of *he* and *them.* The Chaldee, Syriac, Arabic, Septuagint, Ethiopic, Doway, Jarchi, Venema, Edwards, Horsley, Green and Fry regard *he* as referring to God, and *them* to the enemies of David. On the other hand Calvin has: Let them bend their bow, and let their arrows be as broken. In the interpretation thus indicated Amesius, Patrick, Mudge and Hengstenberg concur. Ainsworth, Gill and Alexander mention both with respect, but express no preference for either. As it is very common in Hebrew to pass from the plural to the singular and for *them* read *him,* there is evidently less difficulty in admitting it to be the wicked who bends his bow; q. d., 'When the wicked bends his bow to shoot the righteous, when he devises mischief against him, shoots out bitter words, and desires to destroy his good name and even his life, let it be as if the string of his bow and his arrows were cut in pieces; let all his wicked designs, words and actions be without effect.'

8. *As a snail* which *melteth,* let every one of them *pass away.* The word rendered *snail* is found nowhere else in the Hebrew Bible, another word, probably signifying a kind of *lizard,* being so rendered in Lev. xi. 30, the only other place where the word *snail* is found in our English Bible. Instead of *As a snail,* the Syriac, Arabic, Septuagint, Ethiopic, Vulgate, Doway, Horsley and Fry read *Like wax.* But the Chaldee fairly allows the English translation, and it has been adopted by nearly all modern interpreters. The word *melteth* is very expressive in application to the *snail,* which smears its track wherever it goes, and if it continues to move in the open air is soon wasted away. Like *the untimely birth of a woman,* that *they may not see the sun.* Compare Job iii. 16. Calvin: "If we consider the length of time to which in their vain confidence they expected their lives to extend, they may be said to pass out of this world before they have well begun to live." Alexander gives it another turn: "So far from living too long, as I feared, they seem scarcely to have lived at all."

9. *Before your pots can feel the thorns, he shall take them away as with a whirlwind, both living, and in* his *wrath.* Anderson: "This verse has been deemed one of the most difficult passages in the Psalter, and has greatly perplexed commentators." Yet the perplexity has not regarded its import, but the method of explaining its figurative language. In attempting to understand it, let us remember that the burning of thorns under a pot is a frequent figure of Scripture; see Ps. cxviii. 12; Ecc. vii. 6. The manifest object of these passages is to teach us how soon the wicked and their merriment pass away. To this day on the routes of eastern travel the chief fuel in many places is found in the thorns and briars, the furze and stick-weeds that grow in those regions. These burn with great intensity, but their blaze is soon over, for they have very little substance. So the prophet here predicts that 'the prosperous rage of his foes would soon be extinct,' and that they should be removed even sooner than a fire of thorns would make a pot to boil; yea, that they should be *taken away as with a whirlwind.* This is another allusion well understood in the east; see Pr. i. 27; x. 25; Hosea xiii. 3. So we have two figures here, both striking, not mixed, but closely following each other. Then if we refer *living* and *in wrath* to God, we have a good sense. The *living* God *in* his *wrath* shall take them away. This leaves the particle *as,* or *so,* or *thus,* or *when,* or *as it were* unexplained. May we not however thus render the whole? 'Before your pot can be heated with a fire

of thorns, even as by a whirlwind, so the living *God*, even as in his wrath, shall take them away.' Grotius gives much the same: Before your pots can perceive *or* feel the thorns, so likewise shall the anger of God snatch you away, as it were in a whirlwind. Tholuck: "As the tempest of the desert tears away the half-burnt thorns ere the pots can feel their flame."

10. *The righteous shall rejoice when he seeth the vengeance. Vengeance, i. e.*, righteous retribution, vindicating God's government from the charge of not seeing or caring for what is done on earth, setting David free from their malice, and putting it out of their 'power to do further mischief. Compare Ps. lii. 6; lxiv. 10; cvii. 42; Pr. xi. 10. *He shall wash his feet in the blood of the wicked.* The allusion is to the battle where the enemy leaves the ground covered with gore, so that when the victor comes he bathes or moistens his feet in blood. The victory of the righteous over the wicked shall in the end be perfect, complete, entire; see Ps. lxviii. 23; Isa. lxiii. 3; Rev. xiv. 20. It spoils the figure to put *hands* for feet in this place, as the Syriac, Arabic, Septuagint, Ethiopic, Vulgate and Doway have done.

11. *So that a man* [*i. e.*, any man, every man] *shall say, Verily* there is *a reward for the righteous.* The word rendered *reward* occurs more than *one hundred* times, and is in all other cases rendered *fruit*, or in the plural, *fruits.* Even here the margin has *fruit.* But it often signifies *reward* in the highest sense, as in Pr. i. 31; Mic. vii. 13. *Reward*, like *fruit*, may signify *deserved recompense* or *appropriate consequence.* Here it is used in the latter sense. And every man shall say, *Verily he is a God that judgeth in the earth.* To *judge* is to make laws, to rule, and to enforce decisions, as well as to preside in trials and pronounce sentence. *In the earth;* not merely in heaven as some profanely allege, but in this world and in this life Jehovah reigns.

DOCTRINAL AND PRACTICAL REMARKS.

1. "In all ages wickedness has borne the same leading characteristics." A truthful description of human sinfulness in David's time suits our age, vv. 1–4. *Men* may be changed by divine grace; but *man* is unchanged.

2. Uprightness and justice are essential qualities in any good character, and in every government, v. 1. No smooth exterior, no profession of honor and of piety, no deeds of charity can be accepted as substitutes. In rulers want of purity is monstrous. Scott: "Injustice established by law, and decreed by judges, is more malignant than any other." Solomon knew no greater vanity and vexation than when he "saw under the sun the place of judgment, that wickedness was there." Compare Ecc. v. 8.

3. Though our conduct in the presence of our rulers should be humble and meek; yet it need not be mean and servile. Nay, we may lawfully and manfully appeal to them when they are prejudiced or violent, and ask for our rights and not a mockery of justice, vv. 1, 2. So did David. So did Christ. So did Paul. Scott: "We may very properly appeal to the consciences of such iniquitous judges, whether indeed they speak righteously, and decide uprightly?" We may say, "Is this the justice you pretend to administer? Is this the countenance which an honest man, and an honest cause may expect from you? Remember you are mortal and dying, and that you stand upon the same level, before God, with the meanest of those you trample upon, and must yourselves be called to an account and judged."

4. A grand support is a good conscience. With it David could challenge his persecutors, though they were in power, vv. 1, 2. Calvin: "Although the whole world be set against the people of God they need not fear, so long as they are supported by a sense of their integrity, to challenge kings and their counsellors, and the promiscuous mob of the people. Should the whole world refuse to hear us, we must

learn, by the example of David, to rest satisfied with the testimony of a good conscience, and with appealing to the tribunal of God."

5. When men *weigh* and ponder and meditate their schemes of wickedness, that they may lay deep plots, and provide against all contingencies likely to result in failure, then they are on the highway to the deepest corruption, the deepest infamy, and the heaviest doom, v. 2.

6. Native depravity is taught in all the Scriptures, not as an excuse for a wicked life, but as the cause of it, v. 3. David says it involved him in his great crime, Ps. li. 5. He here says it was the cause of the wickedness perpetrated against him, v. 3. Calvin: "We all come into the world stained with sin, possessed, as Adam's posterity, of a nature essentially depraved, and incapable, in ourselves, of aiming at anything which is good; but there is a secret restraint upon most men, which prevents them from going all lengths in iniquity." Scott: "When we behold the effects of natural depravity in the atrocious crimes of others, we should be humbled by recollecting that the principles of them all are in our hearts also." Hengstenberg: "That the inborn depravity is quite general, extending to the whole family of man appears from Gen. viii. 21; Ps. li. 5; Job xiv. 4." Morison: "The death and sufferings of infants sufficiently demonstrate the existence of original sin." Slade: "While we mourn over the wickedness and the crimes of ungodly men, let us be humbly thankful that it hath pleased our merciful Lord to 'make us differ' from them. We were born with the same corrupt nature as they, inclined ' to go astray and speak lies,' and commit all manner of sin." Dickson: "Men's wicked actions prove the wickedness of their natures."

7. The enmity of the seed of the bond woman to the seed of the free woman is deadly. It is like the poison of a serpent, v. 4. If God prevent not, it kills.

8. When one is made to feel the malice of sinners, as it is sometimes let loose, he will not find the terms of Scripture too strong to express his sense of their virulence, v. 4. *Poison* of serpents will seem to him mild language.

9. None are so deaf as those who will not hear, vv. 4, 5. This is the ruinous art of sinners, who have the Gospel and continue in sin. They have ears but do not hear. This was the cause of the horrible murder of Stephen, Acts vii. 57, 58.

10. The doom of incorrigible sinners will be as just as it will be dreadful; because they *refuse* to hear, or feel, or obey the loudest, sweetest calls that even mercy sends forth, vv. 4, 5. If they know not the right, it is because they love not truth.

11. O slanderer! quit thy nefarious and atrocious business. Thy fangs are more deadly than those of the asp, vv. 4, 5. Verily thou art worse than the most evil beasts. God does not hate asps, but he hates thy practices.

12. However affluent and mighty the wicked may now be, God can at any moment make them entirely powerless, v. 6. And he will probably do it much sooner than any one expects.

13. David's faith led him confidently to pray for the defeat of the schemes of his foes, and as confidently to predict their overthrow, vv. 6–9. He did this when they were in full possession of power and of the resources of the land, with a fair prospect of continuance. Yet he prayed that all this might come to nothing, and he predicted it should come to nothing, and to nothing it came. If our cause is just, let us confide in God, even in the darkest hour.

14. It is as easy for God to scatter all our foes, as it is for him to dissipate the mists of the morning, or to maintain the law, by which heaps of water separate from each other, seeking their own level, and thus entirely losing their power, v. 7.

15. As compared with one another men may be and often are very respectable; but as compared with God they are as nothing, v. 7. If the sinner draws his bow, God

can easily cut his arrows in pieces. If he heaps up wealth, God can blow upon it, and it vanishes. In his most assiduous labors he is often as a partridge that sitteth upon eggs and hatcheth them not. Luther: "The enemies of God and truth plan, plot and breathe out dreadful things; but like a mighty flame, where there is no more fuel left to feed it, their fury ends in nothing." Calvin: "Let us not cease to pray, even after the arrows of our enemies have been fitted to the string, and destruction might seem inevitable."

16. After all their vaporing and vaunting, the wicked are alike *snails* and *abortions*, v. 8. Compare Eccle. viii. 12, 13.

17. The destruction of the wicked is awfully sudden, as by a *whirlwind*, v. 9. Compare Prov. xxix. 1; 1 Thess. v. 3. This is righteous. It could not be otherwise. They would not be warned. Morison: "In the midst of their oppressive and impious career the tokens of divine judgment may overtake them, in a moment, in the twinkling of an eye." Clarke: "From the time that the fire of God's wrath is kindled about you, it will be but as a moment before ye be entirely consumed by it." Dickson: "Howsoever the ungodly hope to procure for themselves good cheer by their works of iniquity, and rejoice awhile in their hopes, yet before they find any ripe satisfaction by their ill deeds, suddenly they are destroyed."

18. The victory of the righteous over all who oppose their salvation will be so perfect, that it is now one of the greatest exercises of faith simply to believe that the sons of God shall wet their feet with the blood of all their foes, v. 10. The victory of David over Saul, of Elijah over Ahab, of the martyrs over the persecuting emperors was complete without their lifting a finger.

19. It is impossible for good men to refrain from rejoicing at the defeat of the malicious schemes of ungodly men, even though it involves the ruin of many, v. 10. Compare Ex. xiii. Isa. xiv. But this rejoicing must not spring from malice, nor from gratified impatience. It must be that God is honored, innocence vindicated, wickedness put down, and the cause of truth rendered triumphant.

20. However things may seem to be here, in the end all will be so well with the righteous that he himself *shall rejoice* in it, v. 10. Compare Isa. iii. 10. No man serves God for nought.

21. God has a government on earth, v. 11. "If no sin were punished here, we might be tempted to think there was no God, or that he was not just. And if all sin were adequately punished how could we believe in the divine mercy?"

22. A great end of judgments is attained when God is glorified and sinners are brought to confess his righteousness and authority, v. 11. Compare Isa. xxvi. 9.

23. O ye righteous, lift up the head. Give thanks at the remembrance of God's holiness, mercy and providence. Your redemption draweth nigh. Rejoice and be exceeding glad, for great is your reward in heaven. The more you are rubbed by affliction here, the brighter you will shine hereafter.

24. And, O sinner, wilt not thou think on thy ways? Because they are sinful, they are dark, dangerous and dismal. They lead to hell. They lead no where else. O! it is a fearful thing to fall into the hands of the living God. "All nature cannot furnish images adequately to represent the dreadful doom that awaits you, if you die in your sins." Oh that you were wise!

PSALM LIX.

To the chief Musician, Al-taschith, Michtam of David; when Saul sent, and they watched the house to kill him.

1 Deliver me from mine enemies, O my God: defend me from them that rise up against me.

2 Deliver me from the workers of iniquity, and save me from bloody men.

3 For, lo, they lie in wait for my soul: the mighty are gathered against me; not *for* my transgression, nor *for* my sin, O LORD.

4 They run and prepare themselves without *my* fault: awake to help me, and behold.

5 Thou therefore, O LORD God of hosts, the God of Israel, awake to visit all the heathen: be not merciful to any wicked transgressors. Selah.

6 They return at evening: they make a noise like a dog, and go round about the city.

7 Behold, they belch out with their mouth: swords *are* in their lips: for who, *say they*, doth hear?

8 But thou, O LORD, shalt laugh at them; thou shalt have all the heathen in derision.

9 *Because of* his strength will I wait upon thee: for God *is* my defence.

10 The God of my mercy shall prevent me: God shall let me see *my desire* upon mine enemies.

11 Slay them not, lest my people forget: scatter them by thy power; and bring them down, O Lord our shield.

12 *For* the sin of their mouth *and* the words of their lips let them even be taken in their pride: and for cursing and lying *which* they speak.

13 Consume *them* in wrath, consume *them*, that they *may* not *be:* and let them know that God ruleth in Jacob unto the ends of the earth. Selah.

14 And at evening let them return; *and* let them make a noise like a dog, and go round about the city.

15 Let them wander up and down for meat, and grudge if they be not satisfied.

16 But I will sing of thy power; yea, I will sing aloud of thy mercy in the morning: for thou hast been my defence and refuge in the day of my trouble.

17 Unto thee, O my strength, will I sing: for God *is* my defence, *and* the God of my mercy.

ON several clauses of the title see on titles of Psalms iv. xvi. lvii. *When Saul sent, and they watched the house to kill him* doubtless refers to that interesting scrap of history (which see) in 1 Sam. xix. 11–18, especially v. 11. Doubtless this tells its historic occasion, and David is its author, though Clarke thinks not so. Scott dates it B. C. 1061; Clarke, B. C. 445. The names of the Most High in it are *Elohim God, Jehovah* LORD and *Adonai Lord*, on which see on Ps. iii. 2; i. 2; ii. 4. On *Selah* see Introduction, § 15.

1. *Deliver me from mine enemies, O my God. Deliver*, as in Ps. vii. 1; xxii. 20. *Enemies*, uniformly so rendered, Ps. iii. 7; vi. 10; l. 9. *Defend me from them that rise up against me. Defend*, in the future, *thou wilt defend*. It expresses the strong confidence David had in his escape. Yet the language of petition is not excluded. The same form of the verb is elsewhere rendered *defend*, Ps. xx. 1; *set on high*, Ps. lxix. 29; xci. 14; cvii. 41; *set up*, Isa. ix. 11. Horne renders it *exalt*. It signifies to *set up* so as to render *safe*. *Them that rise up*, we had the same participle in Ps. xvii. 7. Alexander renders it *insurgents* or assailants.

2. *Deliver me from the workers of iniquity. Deliver*, as in v. 1. *Workers of iniquity*, as in Ps. v. 5; vi. 8. It describes those, who make a trade of sin, particularly of injustice. *And save me from bloody men*, literally *men of bloods*. See on Ps. v. 6. Compare Ps. xxvi. 9; lv. 23. David was now so situated that none but God could save him. The city was surrounded by Saul's troops; David's house was besieged by Saul's bloody guards, who *watched* him with murderous purpose. Saul was determined to have him sick or well, dead or alive. The two verses make known his

desire, and the peril of his situation arising from the hatred and violence of his assailants, and from their unprincipled and murderous characters.

3. *For, lo, they lie in wait for my soul. Lie in wait*, elsewhere *lie in ambush. Soul* here evidently signifies *life*. They had surrounded David's house, but not openly. They supposed he could not go out without their seeing him. *The mighty are gathered against me. Mighty*, also rendered *strong, fierce, rough*, Ps. xviii. 17; Gen. xlix. 7; Pr. xviii. 23. The plea is from their *power*, guile, numbers and *cruel* wrath. He had not provoked their violence. He was hunted, *not for my transgression, nor for my sin*, O LORD. The basest deceivers and the worst criminals are so much in the habit of making solemn protestations of innocence, that an assertion of our freedom from criminality has with many very little weight. Yet to the innocent it is an unspeakable consolation to be able to deny every charge; and before God in prayer the argument of injured innocence has prodigious power. It was to the Lord David was making his protestation of innocence. The whole power of such a plea depends on its being *true*. If *false*, it brings down wrath. In denying *transgression*, he emphatically denies that form of it, which implies *revolt*. Saul himself knew David had committed no crime, 1 Sam. xviii. 12–17; xix. 1–7.

4. *They run and prepare themselves without my fault. Run* expresses activity and energy, Gen. xviii. 7; Ps. cxix. 32; Cant. i. 4. Alexander says both verbs are 'military terms.' So they sometimes are; but the cases cited above express no more than activity and diligence. *Prepare*, see on Ps. lvii. 7, where its participle is rendered *fixed*. It here signifies to *set* things *in order*, or *make arrangements. Without my fault*, a new assertion of freedom from crime and from blame. *Fault*, commonly *iniquity*. Innocence cannot condemn itself; cannot but lay its claim on a fit occasion to protection. *Awake to help me, and behold*. For a time wickedness had seemed to reign. David now calls on God to *awake*, to *stir himself up* to attend to his condition, to *behold* or *see* the real state of the case, and so to *help, literally* to *meet* him, evidently in a friendly way.

5. *Thou, therefore, O LORD God of hosts, the God of Israel, awake to visit all the heathen*. Some have alleged that this accumulation of divine names proved this Psalm to be later than the time of David. But one acquainted with Jewish history and theology to the time of Samuel might fitly use all these names. That David did such things is historically certain from 2 Sam. vii. 18–29, especially in v. 27. Gejerus: "The names contain the reasons for the divine help being immediately extended to him." Compare Pr. xviii. 10. *Awake*, not the same word so rendered in v. 4, but *awake* as out of sleep. Thus in Ps. xliv. 23, "Why sleepest thou, O Lord? *Arise*," or *awake*. Though the word *visit* is sometimes taken in a good sense, yet it far more frequently signifies to *punish* or *do judgment* on the guilty, Isa. xiii. 11; Jer. ix. 25; li. 52. *The heathen*, in the plural *nations*, or *Gentiles*. The use of this word has led some to doubt whether the Psalm could refer to the Sauline persecution. But it is sufficient to justify its use under the circumstances to state that Saul had *heathen* among his prominent men, as Doeg the Idumean; that the entire persecution was unworthy any prince, who professed the true religion, and was in its inception and entire prosecution *heathenish* in principle and manner; that it was an oft-repeated lesson that numerous and powerful as were the Gentiles, yet they were in the grasp of the Almighty, who threshed them in his anger; and much more would he punish a people who knew his laws and rebelled against them. God is the judge of all the earth. Tholuck: "At the judgment of the heathen, the judgment of *heathenish-minded Israel* will not fail to take place, for God is *good to that Israel only that are of a clean heart*, Ps. lxxiii. 1." Calvin thinks that in speaking of *all the heathen* or nations, it is probable David may have been struggling with a temptation with which

he was severely assailed, connected with the number of his enemies, for these did not consist merely of three or four abandoned individuals. They formed a great multitude, and he rises above them all by reflecting that God claims it as his prerogative, not only to reduce a few refractory persons to submission, but also to punish the wickedness of the whole world." Hengstenberg: "That the Psalmist especially places God here before his eyes as the judge of all the heathen, so that he might be no more disturbed by the great number and might of his enemies, is manifest from the *eighth* verse." David often spoke of the number of his foes as very great, Ps. xxvii. 3; cxviii. 10–12. *Be not merciful to any wicked transgressors.* Ainsworth: Be not thou gracious to any that unfaithfully work iniquity; Edwards: Show no favor to any perfidious workers of iniquity; Green: Show no favors to any who practise idolatry; Horne: Thou wilt not be merciful to any wicked transgressors. The verb is in the future; often rendered *be gracious*, Amos v. 15; Mal. i. 9; the same as the first word in Psalm li. The Hebrew *all* is best rendered *any* to suit English idiom. *Transgressors*, a participle describing persons who *transgress* in a *treacherous* manner. On the imprecatory form see Introduction, § 6.

6. *They return at evening.* Ordinary laborers quit work in the evening. Although David's foes were not idle during the day, yet like dogs, which infest oriental cities, they renewed with great eagerness their pursuit of him at night when honest men commonly went to sleep. *They make a noise like a dog, and go round about the city.* See on Ps. xxii. 16. The terrible hunger of the undomesticated dog of the east led him to howl and prowl about cities and to run furiously in every direction for something to eat; so David's foes felt such insatiable raven for their prey that they acted more like fierce brute beasts than like human beings. They were actuated by a blind fury as were the dogs at night. The verbs of this verse are in the future; but the English is perhaps right in giving them in the present.

7. *Behold, they belch out with their mouth.* Belch out; Calvin, *prate;* Edwards, *speak without reserve;* Alexander, *pour out.* See Ps. xix. 3; cxlv. 7; Pr. i. 23; xv. 2; Ecc. x. 1. It was not necessary to say what they uttered, because such men speak curses, lies, reproaches, predictions of evil. The Chaldee supplies *sharp words. Swords are in their lips.* See on Ps. lv. 21; lvii. 4. Their speech is thus lawless and cruel, because they fear not God. *For who*, say they, *doth hear?* Our version makes this question to proceed from the persecutors. This gives the best sense. The sentiment is precisely the same as that often expressed by the wicked, Ps. x. 11; xciv. 7.

8. *But thou, O* LORD, *shalt laugh at them; thou shalt have all the heathen in derision. Heathen;* see on v. 5. On the divine derision of the foolish schemes of the wicked, see on Ps. ii. 4; xxxvii. 13. Calvin: "When the wicked have perfected their schemes to the uttermost, God can, without any effort, and, as it were in sport, dissipate them all."

9. Because of *his strength will I wait upon thee.* This clause is very obscure. The following are the different constructions put upon it. For *his* strength some read *my* strength. Then we may read, I will keep my strength to thee. So the Chaldee, Septuagint, Ethiopic, Vulgate, Doway, Anglo-Saxon, Clarke, an old English Psalter, Edwards, Jebb, Fry, Green, Mudge and Horsley. The sense then is: *I will repose my strength on thee.* But Mudge, Horsley and Green make strength a title of God, O my strength. The church of England gives another sense: My strength will I ascribe unto thee. Reading *my* strength requires a change in the Hebrew text, which is authorized by only fourteen of Kennicott's and De Rossi's MSS. Others suppose that by *his strength* is meant *God's strength.* This of course demands a change of the person of the pronoun from *his* to *thee* in a very short clause. Such transitions may be found, but they rather surprise us when they occur, and we ought not to suppose them to exist, where they do not. The third mode of explanation is that by *his strength*

we are to understand the strength of Saul, or of the embodied enemy. Then the sense is, 'On account of the power of my foe I look to Jehovah.' This is a good sense, though it requires a change of number in the pronoun from that of v. 8. Yet that is not infrequent. This is the sense our translators seem to have gathered from the place. So Calvin: His strength is with thee, I will wait. So Bishop Hall: "The more strong and the more malicious Saul is, the more will I look to thee." The prophet gives the best reason in the world for his conduct: *For God* is *my defence, refuge, high tower*, or *high fort; see* on Ps. ix. 9; xviii. 2; xlvi. 7.

10. *The God of my mercy shall prevent me.* *Prevent*, see on Ps. xvii. 13; xviii. 18; here it signifies *go before*, in the way of guidance and protection. *Mercy*, in Ps. li. 1 rendered *lovingkindness.* *God shall let me see* my desire *upon mine enemies.* The Chaldee: God will show to me his vengeance against my oppressors; Waterland: God shall make me look upon my enemies; Green: God shall let me look in the face of those who lie in wait for me; see on Ps. liv. 7. *Enemies*, not as in v. 1, but as in Ps. v. 8, meaning unfriendly *observers.*

11. *Slay them not, lest my people forget.* The sense seems to be, Do not suddenly or utterly destroy them, but so bring about thy gracious ends, by marked providences weakening their dangerous power, that it shall make a profound impression on my people, and they shall not soon or easily *forget* it. Compare 2 Sam. iii. 29. *Scatter them by thy power.* Break the head of their strength, dissolve the bonds that hold them closely together, and make them wanderers. The same verb in another form in v. 15 is rendered, Let them wander up and down. In Gen. iv. 12 the participle is rendered a *fugitive.* *And bring them down, O Lord our shield.* *Shield*, see on Ps. iii. 3; vii. 10; xviii. 2.

12. For *the sin of their mouth* and *the words of their lips let them even be taken in their pride.* Hammond thinks the meaning is, '*Every word of their lips* is *the sin of their mouth*, so many words, so many sins.' So Hengstenberg: 'They sin as often as they speak.' *Taken, caught, holden.* It is the verb that is used for capturing a city. *In their pride, i. e.*, while they are indulging their haughty tempers and insolent speeches. *And for cursing and lying* which *they speak.* Calvin: "He means that their mouth was continually filled with horrid imprecations, and that they were wholly addicted to deceit and calumniating." Instead of *for*, some read *with*, and some *from;* but it points out the cause of their being *taken.* *Cursing*, rendered *swearing*, Jer. xxiii. 10; an *oath*, Deut. xxix. 12; *execration*, Jer. xlii. 18.

13. *Consume* them *in wrath, consume* them, *that they* may *not* be. *Consume, waste; utterly destroy, finish, make an end of.* This is not contrary to the prayer of v. 11. He prays not that their lives may be taken away, but that their combination and conspiracy may be *brought to an end;* that they may *not be*, as they now are a powerful band of evil doers, having every apparent advantage on their side. Patrick: "Let them waste away by degrees in their dispersions, till there be none of them found." *And let them know that God ruleth in Jacob unto the ends of the earth.* *Them* refers to men in general, and is in sense connected with the last words of the clause, *q. d.*, Let men to the ends of the earth know. It was a great point gained when mankind were convinced of the power and providence of the true God, Ex. ix. 16; Jos. iv. 24; 1 Sam. xvii. 46; 1 Kings viii. 43; Isa. lii. 10; Dan. vi. 26, 27. *Jacob*, here, as often elsewhere, a term designating the church of God.

14. *And at evening let them return.* The verb is in the future, the prophetic form. The same verb in v. 6 is also in Hebrew in the future, but is probably rightly put in the present in English. See Introduction, § 6. If this is correct then the meaning is, As they delighted to play the dog in howling and fierceness at night, so let them act out the part of the dog in their being outcasts. *And let them make a noise like a*

dog, a noise expressive of distress and disappointment. They once howled for the innocent as prey. Let them now howl and whine like the dog, who failed to secure any prey. *And* [let them] *go round about the city.* To this day in the cities of the east dogs live at large. They roam about, especially at night, in quest of food which they may seize.

15. *Let them wander up and down for meat. Wander*, the future of the verb rendered *scatter* in v. 11 ; *i. e.*, let them lead (or they shall lead) the life of vagrants, often perplexed and distressed even for *food. And* [let them] *grudge, if they be not satisfied. Grudge, murmur*, or *tarry all night*, viz., in the street, *i. e.*, let no one pity them ; if they hunger, let them hunger and howl. On the imprecatory form see Introduction, § 6.

16. *But I will sing of thy power. Sing*, always so rendered. It expresses a gladsome exercise, Ps. xiii. 6. *Power*, commonly rendered *strength*, sometimes *might*. See on Ps. viii. 2. *Yea, I will sing aloud of thy mercy in the morning. Sing aloud, shout, shout for joy*, see Ps. v. 11. *Mercy*, as in vv. 10, 16. *Power and lovingkindness*, guided by wisdom, can effect for us the greatest deliverances, and when so exercised for us, are proper themes of the devoutest thanksgiving. *In the morning*, see on Ps. v. 3. Some think that *In the morning* has a relation to Saul's servants watching for David in the morning to kill him, 1 Sam. xix. 11. *For thou hast been my defence and refuge in the day of my trouble. Defence*, as in v. 9. *Refuge, a way of flight* or *a place to flee to*, Jer. xvi. 19 ; xxv. 35. *Trouble, strait, distress, vexation, affliction*, particularly such as arises from *enemies ;* see on Ps. ix. 9 ; x. 1.

17. *Unto thee, O my strength, will I sing.* Calvin : My strength is with thee, I will sing Psalms ; Fry : O my strength, thou art the theme of my song. The common version gives the true meaning. *Sing*, not the same as either of the words so rendered in v. 16, but another found in Ps. ix. 11 ; lvii. 7. *For God is my defence* and *the God of my mercy. Defence*, as in verse 16. *God of my mercy* as in v. 10, meaning God who is the source and author of mercy to me, in English idiom, *My merciful God.*

DOCTRINAL AND PRACTICAL REMARKS.

1. The spirit of persecution is awfully wicked. It overrides all barriers, forgets all public services, contemns all private worth. Innocence seems only to provoke it. It is as fierce against a son-in-law as against a stranger. It balks not at murder. The great mass of persecutors are doomed men.

2. Whatever means we may adopt for our preservation, and however successful they may be, God is the sole author of deliverance, and we ought to pray, and praise, and preach accordingly. Michal used a device, but God was the Saviour of David. So he felt at the beginning, and so he felt at the end of his troubles.

3. We shall find it necessary to cry for help and deliverance as long as we have enemies ; and we shall probably have enemies as long as we live, v. 1. Even if God restrains persecutors, he may leave us to be harassed by our adversary the devil. So that we must cry to God as long as we live. " Prayer is our best weapon against our enemies, the best of all means, and the first of all to be used." No power but that which is invoked in prayer is a match for our foes.

4. We should be very careful not to furnish either cause or occasion to right-minded men to be unfriendly to us ; but we should not be dismayed, if, with all prudence and innocence on our part, adversaries should still arise, even in the visible church of God. The temper and character of wicked men are such as to bring about a result so painful, v. 2.

5. The more vicious and depraved our foes may be, if our cause is surely right, the more confident may we be that God will amply protect us. We may in truth plead

the barbarity and unreasonableness of wicked men as a reason why God should not help them, but succor us, v. 2.

6. When we find men practising the arts of chicanery and guile, *lying in wait* and not dealing frankly, it is wise to be on our guard against them, and put no confidence in them, but betake ourselves wholly to the Lord, v. 3. "When power and subtilty combine against the righteous, where can they look but to the throne of heaven?" And this we may do in perfect confidence; for Jehovah 'has taken the church, with all her believing members, under his powerful support.'

7. When our foes are *mighty*, let us think of David, how God remembered him and all his afflictions, and saved him from the power of one of the most terrible leagues and conspiracies ever formed, v. 3.

8. If we are innocent, unmerited suffering can do us no real harm. It is sin, not sorrow that inflicts mortal wounds. "When we suffer for well-doing, we are conformed to our Redeemer, and have an evidence of our acceptance with God. We should indeed greatly fear suffering as 'evil doers, or busy-bodies in other men's matters;' but we ought not to be either afraid or ashamed of the hatred of the workers of iniquity."

9. While we have a right boldly to assert our innocence in a given matter, if we can do so in truth, and while it is an unspeakable comfort to be able to do so with a clear conscience; yet in doing so we ought strictly to confine ourselves to the matter in hand, and not deny that we are sinners by nature and practice against God our Maker, v. 3. Morison: "The consciousness of integrity as it respects our fellow-men will in no way tend to diminish in a mind divinely illuminated the sense of manifold transgressions against God."

10. The zeal and diligence of the wicked in the cause of unrighteousness might well reprove the languor and tardiness of saints in the work of faith and labor of love, v. 4. In the church of God nothing is the source of more mischief than the want of true zeal and liveliness. It is only when 'many run to and fro' that 'knowledge shall be increased.'

11. Dickson: "The Lord will let the plot go on, and the danger of the godly grow, as if he minded not to take notice of it, that he may first put his children to prayer, and then appear in the fit time: *awake to help me, and behold,*" v. 4.

12. When once we get Jehovah with all his glorious names, titles and attributes secured to our cause, we are safe, come what will, v. 5. It is a special part of wisdom to bring to mind such excellent things in God's character and government as are best suited under the circumstances to strengthen our confidence, and awaken our joyful hopes.

13. Those who live and act like *heathen* should remember that unless they repent the doom of such *wicked transgressors* awaits them, v. 5. "Counterfeit professors and professed pagans are in effect all one before God."

14. That sin is most degrading and sinners dreadfully debased are shown by the fact that inspiration itself has used the strongest language and the most forcible metaphors to impress these ideas upon us. Here the wicked are compared to *dogs*, v. 6. The Scriptures often do the same, Ps. xxii. 16, 20; Matt. vii. 6; Phil. iii. 2; Rev. xxii. 15. Other Scriptures compare them to *swine*, to the *ass*, to the silly *dove*. Oh that men saw their real character. If they did, surely they could not live as they do.

15. When men *pour out* torrents of abuse, of reproaches, of calumnies, of harsh and severe censures and judgments, and persist in such courses, you may know that they have so far lost all sense of shame, and all fear of God as virtually to deny providence and to be practical atheists, v. 7. Sinning hardens the heart, sears the

conscience, blinds the mind, perverts the affections and distorts nature itself until he, who was once the joy of his mother, is a monster of depravity.

16. God's people may always and confidently expect enlargement and deliverance, however dark their present prospects may be; for he counts as nothing all the cunning, power and malice arrayed against them, v. 8.   True, the wicked think not so.   "No sooner," says Calvin, "does God connive at their proceedings, than their pride and insolence take occasion to manifest themselves: for they forget that even when he seems to have suspended operation, he needs but nod, and his judgments shall be executed."

17. If our foe is strong, God is stronger, and we should make him our defence, v. 9. We need no more.

18. Trusting in God, we have a right to anticipate good and not evil, v. 10.   To God no set of circumstances creates a crisis, an emergency, or an exigency.   He is eternally and infinitely calm.

19. God will surely make the incorrigible enemies of his people a gazing-stock to all his saints, v. 10.   They, who have such delight in beholding the miseries and mortification of others, are but preparing to receive shame and everlasting contempt from all right-minded men, as well as undying reproaches and recriminations from their companions in sin.

20. It is lawful for us to ask God so to order his providence and execute judgment respecting the wicked as to strengthen the faith and all the graces of his own people, v. 11.   Calvin: "We are apt to think, when God has not annihilated our enemies at once, that they have escaped out of his hands altogether; and we look upon it as properly no punishment that they should be gradually and slowly destroyed."

21. And let the wicked remember that all sparing is not in the end a mercy.   It may be in wrath, v. 11.   Some apparent preservations are really but reservations.

22. God can break the power of leagues against his saints, without slaying the conspirators, by simply *scattering* them as he did at Babel, or at the court of Saul, v. 11.   It is a great mercy when in his providence he defeats wicked men, who have wily counsels, by introducing confusion and perplexity.

23. How can the righteous perish or suffer real damage when God is *his* God, v. 1; his *shield*, v. 11; his *refuge* and *defence*, vv. 16, 17?   What more can he want?

24. If there is a God and he has a government, it is impossible to doubt that he will have dealings of terrible severity with impenitent men, who have uttered lies and curses, reproaches and calumnies, taunts and boastings against the innocent and against the truth, v. 12.   If such die unpardoned and unrenewed, and are eternally left with their vile propensities, and denied the means of gratifying them, their damnation will be truly dreadful.   Henry: "There is a great deal of malignity in tongue-sins, more than is commonly thought of."

25. However long God may spare his enemies, not for their sakes but to show forth his own long-suffering, yet if they prove incorrigible, they shall surely and totally perish and be consumed.   The prayers of God's people and the prophecies of his servants make all this certain, v. 13.

26. God loves his church and rules in and over her with a perfect government, whatever seemings there may be to the contrary, v. 13.   He loved and ruled her when she used to be called *Jacob*, Israel, Zion, Jerusalem.   He loves her still.   He will love her to the end.   She is Christ's body.

27. By comparing vv. 6, 14, 15, we learn how terribly God sometimes punishes men in the way in which they have chosen to sin.   David's foes chose to act like dogs, and God left them to act out to the bitter end the characters they had chosen to assume.   Horne: "The punishment inflicted on the wicked often carries the mark

of their crime;" Dickson: "It is suitable to God's justice and no strange thing to see such as have been messengers, servants, officers of persecuting powers, or searchers out of the godly as beadles, or blood-hounds, made beggars, vagabonds, and miserable spectacles of God's wrath before they die, roving to and fro like hungry and master-less dogs."

28. Let us call on our souls after every great deliverance and often to *sing, shout,* and *sing Psalms* to the Lord. Our last victory shall be our greatest. "How glorious will be that morning when the united anthems of redeemed millions shall proclaim the eternal victory of the church."

29. As long as we live let us make frequent and pious mention of the mercy of God, and of *the God of our mercy,* v. 17.

30. The minds of many, perhaps most evangelical commentators, seem to have been turned, especially by considering the curses foretold in this Psalm, to the case of the poor Jews, who have long and wickedly rejected Messias and brought on themselves terrible plagues and woes. Reader, do you pray for the descendants of Abraham?

PSALM LX.

To the chief Musician upon Shushan-eduth, Michtam of David, to teach; when he strove with Aram-naharaim and with Aram-zobah, when Joab returned, and smote of Edom in the valley of salt twelve thousand.

1 O God, thou hast cast us off, thou hast scattered us, thou hast been displeased ; oh turn thy-self to us again.

2 Thou hast made the earth to tremble ; thou hast broken it : heal the breaches thereof ; for it shaketh.

3 Thou hast shewed thy people hard things : thou hast made us to drink the wine of aston-ishment.

4 Thou hast given a banner to them that fear thee, that it may be displayed because of the truth. Selah.

5 That thy beloved may be delivered ; save *with* thy right hand, and hear me.

6 God hath spoken in his holiness : I will rejoice : I will divide Shechem, and mete out the valley of Succoth.

7 Gilead *is* mine, and Manasseh *is* mine ; Ephraim also *is* the strength of mine head ; Judah *is* my lawgiver ;

8 Moab *is* my washpot ; over Edom will I cast out my shoe : Philistia, triumph thou because of me.

9 Who will bring me *into* the strong city ? who will lead me into Edom ?

10 *Wilt* not thou, O God, *which* hadst cast us off ? and *thou,* O God, *which* didst not go out with our armies ?

11 Give us help from trouble : for vain *is* the help of man.

12 Through God we shall do valiantly : for he *it is that* shall tread down our enemies.

ON several parts of the title see on titles of Psalms iv. xvi. xlv. lvii. Hengsten-berg and Alexander think that *Upon Shushan-eduth* here refers to the *law of God as found in the books of Moses.* Proof is sought in 2 Kings xi. 12 ; Deut. xxxi. 19. The enigmatical titles are, however, very difficult of explication, and perhaps the reader will not be satisfied with this view. This is the last of the six Psalms having *Michtam* in the title. *To teach* has not before occurred in a title. The original word sig nifies both to *teach* and to *learn,* though in this form always rendered *teach.* It probably has much the same import as *Maschil,* to give *Instruction.* The historic occasion of the Psalm is next given, *When he strove with Aram-naharaim and with Aram-zobah, when Joab returned, and smote of Edom in the valley of salt twelve thousand. Strove* is well rendered. It does not signify *conquered* or *gained a victory*. The result was favorable to Israel but this word simply announces a *conflict*, a *battle*. *Aram* designates Syria; and *Naharaim*, Mesopotamia. Calvin renders it, *With the Syrians of Mesopotamia*. Naharaim is literally the two rivers; *i. e.*, Tigris and Euphrates, between which lay a large country inhabited by men descended of ancient Syrians. In Gen. xxiv. 10; Deut. xxiii. 4; Jud. iii. 8, the word Naharaim is rendered *Mesopotamia*. *Aram-zobah* designates that part of *Syria*, to which Syria of Mesopotamia was tributary, and which at that time was ruled over by Rehob. Clarke thinks it the same as Celosyria. It is not supposed that this *title* mentions all the successes of David's army, but only some of the early and principal victories. Sacred history explicitly states his victory over the Syrians of Damascus also, which was much nearer to Jerusalem than either of the countries named. We have next an allusion to the victory over the Edomites in the valley of salt. All the record we have of these events is in 2 Sam. viii. x.; 1 Chron. xviii. To David as head of the nation, to Joab as the highest officer in the army, and to Abishai as head of one of the divisions of the army under Joab, these victories are variously ascribed according to the view the writer had in his mind. The present name of the *Valley of salt* is probably *El-Ghor*. It lies a few miles south of the Dead Sea. It is very desolate. It is on the borders of the ancient Idumea. The valley of salt was subsequently famous for another victory over the Edomites by the forces of Amaziah, 2 Kings xiv. 7. The historic record mentions *eighteen thousand* slain, and here but *twelve thousand*. The greater of course includes the less. The discrepancy may be explained by supposing that the *title* contains the numbers slain by one division of the army, or that the *twelve thousand* were slain in the battle, and the residue in the flight. Or an error may have crept into the text. Every scholar admits that there is sometimes serious difficulty in settling the numbers of the Old Testament. In this place Calvin has *two and twenty thousand*, the common version *twelve thousand*, while the original is *two ten thousand*, which taken in one way would mean *twenty thousand, i. e., two tens of thousands*. Hammond refers the numbers slain to different battles and so avoids the difficulty.

There was much confusion and trouble in the kingdom during the latter part of Saul's life, and the early part of David's reign. Doubtless defeat was sometimes experienced by David's forces. The heathen nations had become very fierce and cruel. This may account for the sad and depressed tone of the first verses. There remained enemies unsubdued, as well as intestine troubles unsettled even after the victories here alluded to. If this is so, there is no need of adopting the conjecture of Hare, Secker and others that the first three verses belong to Ps. lxxxv.

There is no room for serious doubt that David wrote this Psalm about B. C. 1040, as Scott dates it, although Clarke puts it 500 years later. The only name of the Lord used in this Psalm is *Elohim God*, on which see on Ps. iii. 2. On *Selah* see Introduction, § 15.

1. *O God thou hast cast us off*. The Chaldee: Thou hast left us; Syriac: Thou hast forgotten us; Edwards: Thou hast forsaken us; Other ancient versions, Calvin, Amesius, Jebb, Hengstenberg and Alexander agree with the English text. *Cast off*, see Ps. xliii. 2; xliv. 9. The complaint is that the nation was treated as if God had rejected it. *Thou hast scattered us*. Margin and many others, *broken us; hast broken*; in Ps. lxxx. 12; lxxxix. 40, *broken down*. Mudge: Thou hast made a breach upon us. The latter part of Saul's administration was full of disaster to the nation, nor did David's accession at once bring relief. The people were not all

of a sudden united on him, and the heathen were very daring and troublesome. *Thou hast been displeased.* The sins of Saul had been countenanced or connived at by a great body of the people. Irreligion had grown apace and God was angry with the people, and made them feel his judgments. But he is a God of mercy: *Oh turn thyself to us again.* Chaldee: Turn to us again in thy glory; Edwards: Bring us to life again; Jebb: Oh return to us. In Ps. xxiii. 3, the verb is rendered *restoreth.* In the *title* of this Psalm it is simply *returned.* In this clause it is in the future, expressing desire and expectation.

2. *Thou hast made the earth to tremble.* *Earth* probably the *land* of Israel. *Tremble*, shake or quake; see on Ps. xviii. 7; xlvi. 3. *Thou hast broken it;* Septuagint and Vulgate: Hast troubled it; Jebb: Hast rent it asunder; Alexander: Hast riven it. David is not speaking of an earthquake and of fissures made in the earth, but by the metaphor of an earthquake and its ordinary effects he describes the rent and torn condition of his nation. Saul had brought the nation to the verge of ruin. *Heal the breaches thereof; for it shaketh.* So critical was the state of the nation that it tottered to its fall. To *heal its breaches* would be to restore it to its former vigor. Compare 2 Chron. vii. 14. None but God could give effectual relief. Hence the application to the throne of grace.

3. *Thou hast showed thy people hard things*, very uniformly rendered. The divine severity is truly dreadful. When Jehovah's wrath is kindled but a little we perish. *Thou hast made us to drink the wine of astonishment.* See on Ps. xi. 6. *Astonishment;* in Isaiah li. 17, 22, the same word is rendered *trembling.* Examine Job xxi. 20; Ps. lxxv. 8; Jer. viii. 14; xxv. 15, 28; xlix. 12; li. 57; Ezek. xxiii. 32–34; Rev. xiv. 10. The Chaldee has *wine of malediction;* Septuagint, Ethiopic, Vulgate, Doway, *wine of sorrow;* Waterland, *a myrrhate draft;* Edwards, *an intoxicating liquor;* Anderson, *wine of trembling.* Respecting this metaphor one view is that it is taken from any ordinary fermented wine that will intoxicate; a second, that it is taken from wine drugged so as to stupefy but not to kill; the third, that it is taken from wine drugged with poison, intended to kill. Of these opinions the first is the least probable; and the second more probable than the third. The people were astonished, stupefied by the awful judgments of God. They had neither heart nor power to do anything effectual. Sorrow had filled their hearts. Such a state of things continuing would soon waste away any people. But

4. *Thou hast given a banner to them that fear thee.* *Banner*, the word occurs about twenty times; applied to a ship it means her *sail;* applied to Korah and his company, *a sign, i. e.,* a signal warning to others, Nu. xxvi. 10; in Nu. xxi. 8, 9, a *pole;* in all other cases, *banner, ensign,* or *standard.* What was the *banner* God had given them? In Ex. xvii. 15, we have Jehovah *Nissi,* the Lord *my banner.* It would make good sense to say that the Lord had given himself, and so had become the banner of his people. But the next clause gives us an interpretation which we are bound to adopt: *That it may be displayed because of the truth.* The *banner* then is the *truth,* the truth of God, which had been much obscured in the reign of Saul, but was now to be *lifted up* in the pious care of David for the sound instruction of the people and for the pure worship of God. In David's accession to the throne itself there was a remarkable display of the truth of God's promise. It was a pledge that God would yet unite and succor his people.

5. *That thy beloved may be delivered, save with thy right hand, and hear me.* It would make good sense to connect the first clause of this verse with the preceding verse, and so some do. But it seems better to make the whole verse a prayer. The *beloved* are the same as *those that fear God* in v. 4. David asks that they may be delivered from their personal and national miseries, from their discouraged and dis-

heartening views, and especially from all their foes, and that in a marked manner, by *God's right hand*, denoting a powerful deliverance.

6. *God has spoken in his holiness.* 'God has spoken and his holiness forever precludes the possibility of his failing to fulfil his word: I rely on his *truth* as in v. 4; I rely on his infinite rectitude, his *holiness*.' Some think that David regarded God as bound by an oath. And God's word is as good as his oath. Compare Am. iv. 2. God may have spoken, 1. By oracle when David, on some occasion not recorded, consulted it, and so *in his holiness* may mean as it often does *in his sanctuary*, or *in his holy place*. This is not well supported; yet the Chaldee, Septuagint, Vulgate, Doway, Mudge, Street, Secker, Dimock and Morison adopt it. 2. The reference may be to the specific promise made to David through Nathan; see 2 Sam. vii. 10–17 and 1 Chron. xvii. 9–15. 3. The promises and prophecies relied on may be those made to the fathers, and often repeated, Gen. xii. 1–3; xv. 7–21; Josh. i. 6 and xii.–xvii. The pronoun *I* which occurs so often in this and in subsequent verses designates either the Jewish nation, or David himself as the head of that people. The latter is the better interpretation. David is the author of the Psalm, but composes it for public use. Resting on God's word he breaks forth by saying: *I will rejoice; I will triumph*, or, *I will exult*. Instead of a mournful dirge, he breaks forth into joy. Pool: "Therefore I will turn my prayers into praises and rejoicings for what God has already done, and, as I am assured, will further do, on my behalf." He then tells us how he will claim, and conquer, or portion out the land: *I will divide Shechem, and mete out the valley of Succoth.* Shechem and Succoth were both famous in history. The reason for mentioning them here is not certainly known. Some suppose that they had been strongly enlisted for the house of Saul, and were much opposed to David; and that he here says they shall not form an exception to his kingly sway. Shechem was west, and Succoth east of the Jordan. By naming them both some think he asserts by synecdoche that he will divide the *whole land*, on both sides of the river. *Divide*, in Num. xxvi. 53, 55, 56 in the passive form, and in Josh. xiii. 7; xviii. 5, 10 in the active. *Mete out*, commonly rendered *measure*. It occurs very often in Ezekiel xl.–xlvii. as well as in the books of Moses.

7. *Gilead is mine.* Gilead, sometimes taken for the large tract of country east of the Jordan and included in the land of Israel, Deut. xxxiv. 1; sometimes only that fine fertile mountainous region lying east of the Jordan and held in considerable part by the tribe of Gad, which was very warlike, as was predicted by Jacob and Moses, Gen. xlix. 19; Deut. xxxiii. 21. This is the country here intended. Mount Gilead is a mountain about nine or ten miles long. There was also a city called Gilead. But the land held by Gad is pretty certainly pointed out here. *Manasseh is mine.* Manasseh, the eldest son of Joseph had descendants enough to constitute a full tribe. They settled in nearly equal numbers on each side of the Jordan. To them belonged much if not all of that fine grazing country, Bashan. Though not equal to Ephraim, yet this was a powerful tribe, Gen. xlviii. 15–22; xlix. 22–26; Deut. xxxiii. 13–17. *Ephraim also is the strength of mine head*, corresponding to the predictions just cited respecting the two sons of Joseph. The *strength of the head* was for *pushing*, and so this place corresponds to the predictions in Gen. xlviii. 19; Deut. xxxiii. 17. Yet this tribe did not always play the man, Ps. lxxviii. 9–11. The tract of land held by it was large, central and very productive. Samaria was in the territory of Ephraim, and was the capital of the ten tribes. *Judah is my lawgiver*, or *governor*. We have the same expression in Ps. cviii. 8. The allusion to Gen. xlix. 10 is clear. "No government could stand, which was not resident in Judah," says Calvin. That which most strikingly distinguishes several clauses of this verse from the prophecies in Genesis

and Deuteronomy is first their brevity, and then David as head of the nation claiming them as his own.

8. *Moab is my washpot.* Eastern hospitality and eastern customs required that for refreshment the feet of guests and others should be washed. This was done by menials, 1 Sam. xxv. 4. Our Saviour could perform no act more likely to impress a lesson of humility than by washing his disciples' feet. Gataker, LeClerc and Anderson refer to the father of profane history as giving an anecdote of Amasis, who expressed the meanness of his own origin by comparing himself to a pot for washing the feet in. The meaning of the Psalmist is that he would reduce or had reduced Moab to a very low condition of servitude, and this he certainly did, 2 Sam. viii. 2; 1 Chron. xviii. 1, 2. Clarke: "The Moabites shall be reduced to the *meanest* slavery." *Over Edom will I cast out my shoe.* Edom or Idumea was inhabited by the descendants of Esau. They bore an old grudge against the Israelites. Often it broke out into hostilities. But David says he would reduce them to subjection. The form of expression which he uses has been variously explained. Some think it means he will put his foot on the neck of his enemies, as eastern conquerors used to do; some, that he says he will cast his shoe to them, as his slaves, that they may clean it; and some, that he speaks of Edom as a mean place to be used for inferior purposes, as a place where a man casts his shoes. All services rendered to the feet, as washing them, or removing the shoes, were humble, Matt. iii. 11; Mark i. 7; Luke iii. 16; Acts xiii. 25. Hence the force of such words as we find in 1 Tim. v. 10. David completely subjected the Edomites, 2 Sam. viii. 14; 1 Chron. xviii. 13. Clarke: "I will subject the Edomites to the meanest offices." *Philistia, triumph thou because of me.* Church of England: Philistia, be thou glad of me; Calvin: Palestina, triumph over me; in Ps. cviii. 9, Over Philistia will I triumph. Taking the words as they stand we may regard them as ironical, or as expressing a feigned or abject though reluctant submission, as in Ps. xviii. 44; or as stating that Philistia must receive him with shouts as subjects welcome a prince. The second mode of explanation is attended with fewest difficulties.

9. *Who will bring me into the strong city? Who will lead me into Edom?* Whoever will look into the travels of Stevens in the East, cannot doubt that the *strong city* here spoken of is Petra, by nature and art so fortified as, according to the ancient modes of warfare, to seem to defy the assault of great armies, if there were even but comparatively few within it to defend it. See Obad. vv. 3, 4. Some think however that the reference is to the fenced cities of Edom generally. Others think David has in his eye Rabbah, the great city of the Moabites; but in this verse he seems to be speaking of Edom, and not of Moab. By these questions, he admits that no mortal power is adequate to the task:

10. Wilt *not thou, O God,* which *hadst cast us off?* and thou, *O God,* which *didst not go out with our armies?* This refers to the periods of disaster alluded to in the opening of the Psalm. But God had changed the tide of victory, and David appeals to him to finish the work of subjecting all the hostile nations, and to give to Israel the whole of Canaan.

11. *Give us help from trouble.* Lord, to whom shall we go but unto thee? Thine is the kingdom, the power, the wisdom and the mercy we all need. *Help,* always so rendered, as in Ps. xxvii. 9; xxxv. 2; xlvi. 1. *Trouble,* as in Ps. iii. 1; iv. 1; lix. 16. It is specially suited to express trouble arising from foes. Indeed in the plural it is often rendered *foes, adversaries,* or *enemies. For vain is the help of man.* The particle rendered *for* is literally *and;* but in sentences like this the best scholars think they convey the force of the original by using *for. Help,* not the same Hebrew word as in the first clause of this verse, but a word commonly rendered *salvation, safety, victory, deliverance,* a few times *help,* Ps. xxxiii. 17; li. 14. The nation had been trying to do

without God, and they wrought only misery and mischief for themselves. Their wisest plans and greatest efforts were nugatory. God does not help man to govern the world; he governs the world. "Such confidences as are not derived from God are worthless and vain."

12. *Through God we shall do valiantly.* Hengstenberg regards this clause as a virtual quotation from Balaam's prophecy, Num. xxiv. 18, where he says, "Israel shall do valiantly." Perhaps it may be, but two ordinary words in a clause are hardly sufficient to establish a quotation. *For he* it is that *shall tread down our enemies.* As in the preceding verse, *for* is instead of *and.* *Tread down,* as in Ps. xliv. 5. It is the act of one who *loathes* an object, and so treads it under foot. In Pr. xxvii. 7 the same form of the verb is rendered *loatheth.* *Enemies, troublers, adversaries.* Clarke: "Through thee *alone* shall we do valiantly; Thou *alone* canst tread down our enemies, and to thee *alone* we look for conquest."

DOCTRINAL AND PRACTICAL REMARKS.

1. Sin is dreadful. It has filled hearts, and houses, and nations, and our world with woe. Scott: "The anger of God against sin is the sole cause of all misery, personal or public, in families, churches and nations, which has been, is, or shall be endured, in time or to eternity," v. 1.

2. Among the worst temporal consequences of sinning against God are dreadful public calamities, loss of public confidence, misrule in many forms, anarchy, confusion, wars, famines, pestilences, men's hearts failing them for fear, injury, oppression, violence, vv. 1–3.

3. It is much to the credit of any man, after long and fearful contests, wrongfully waged against him or his cause, wholly to forgive and forget all personal injury, and mourn over public calamities, and pray and labor for the public good, vv. 1–3. "It is the glory of a man to pass over a transgression."

4. It is well when our distresses, personal or national, lead us to a throne of grace, and make prayer our frequent business, vv. 1, 2.

5. Let good men commit their country to God. David's country was perhaps reduced to a lower point of depression than it is easy for us to conceive, and he carried the case to God, vv. 1, 2. Let us do the same. There is hope of peace when we look to the God of peace.

6. If God should send on each man and nation the judgments which they deserve, every one would soon be drinking the *wine of astonishment,* v. 3.

7. If we see *hard things,* let us remember that our sins call for them, that they are perhaps necessary for our growth in grace, and that good men such as David saw the same, v. 3. David's Greater Son saw still harder things than any of his people.

8. If we have been in affliction, and prosperity begins to return, let us not forget our chastisements, but remember them for our own good and for God's glory, vv. 1–3. Such an exercise promotes both humility and hope, Lam. iii. 19, 20, 21.

9. Those who fear God have sources of encouragement that the world knows not of, v. 4. They have a banner, for which they would die. Under it they can never perish; see on Ps. xxv. 14.

10. If the banner of God's truth and covenant are so glorious in their effects on those who know and love the gospel, why should it not be displayed in every valley and on every mountain-top, and sinners of every nation and tongue under heaven be led to embrace Jesus Christ and his salvation? Compare Isa. xi. 10.

11. It is perfectly safe for the righteous always to fight under the banner of *truth,* because the truth is always for them and not for their enemies, v. 4.

12. Though the world thinks not so, yet it is abundantly clear that those who fear God are his *beloved* ones, vv. 4, 5.

13. In none of our distresses is it safe or wise or right for us to call in and rely on power not omnipotent, v. 5. God's *right hand* is full of strength.

14. Because God is holy he cannot speak a word that is not true, and because he is holy he will fulfil all he has promised and all he has threatened, v. 6.

15. Whatever success and advantage a Christian may gain, yet his great reliance for final victory is not on what he sees, or feels, or does, but on God's blessed word, v. 6. *God hath spoken . . . I will rejoice.*

16. The conquest of surrounding hostile nations to David's government was a type of the blessed reign of Messias, who shall yet be Lord of every land and nation to the glory of God the Father, vv. 6–8. He must rule over all the earth, for the mouth of the Lord hath spoken it.

17. The conquest and subjugation of Moab, Edom and Philistia by David, acting under a special direction of God, who would punish those nations for their sins, can never warrant wars of conquest and of cruelty waged by men, who have no such revelation from heaven. By the gospel all tyranny and cruelty are forbidden. Let invading conquerors remember that.

18. It is not conclusive evidence that we are not called to undertake a given work or perform a certain duty, because it is very difficult, or even impossible for us to succeed without special help from God, vv. 9, 10. If God calls David to take Petra, he shall take Petra.

19. God undertaking for us, we can do anything, v. 10. Only let us look to him alone.

20. Whatever our *trouble* may be, let us look to God for help, v. 11. When we think we can carry our own burden, it is always too heavy for us.

21. Never trust in man. His help is vain, v. 11. Cursed is he that trusteth in man, and maketh flesh his arm. This is a universal sin.

22. Let us expect an answer to our supplications. Henry: "David prays in hope His prayer is, *Give us help from trouble,* v. 11. Even in the day of their triumph, they see themselves in trouble, because still in war, which is troublesome even to the prevailing side."

23. However feeble we may be in numbers, in strength, in resources, yet through God we can do valiantly, v. 12.

24. Jehovah treads down many and mighty as easily as few and feeble foes, v. 12.

25. Let us be doubly careful that we do not at any time ascribe to creatures the honor due to God alone, v. 12. Dickson: "Praise of the valor and gallantry of victorious soldiers must not separate betwixt God and the victor: but whatsoever God doth in us or by us, must be no less wholly ascribed unto God, than if he had done all the work without us; for, both the valor of the instrument, and the victory are the works of the Lord."

26. Tholuck: "The course of life alternates between the heights and depths. Such was the experience of David, as here recorded." Let us not hope to cross the sea of life without storms.

PSALM LXI.

To the chief Musician upon Neginah, *A Psalm* of David.

1 Hear my cry, O God; attend unto my prayer.

2 From the end of the earth will I cry unto thee, when my heart is overwhelmed: lead me to the rock *that* is higher than I.

3 For thou hast been a shelter for me, *and* a strong tower from the enemy.

4 I will abide in thy tabernacle for ever: I will trust in the covert of thy wings. Selah.

5 For thou, O God, hast heard my vows: thou hast given *me* the heritage of those that fear thy name.

6 Thou wilt prolong the king's life: *and* his years as many generations.

7 He shall abide before God for ever: oh prepare mercy and truth, *which* may preserve him.

8 So will I sing praise unto thy name for ever, that I may daily perform my vows.

ON the title see on titles of Psalms iv. xi. *Neginah* is the singular of *Neginoth,* literally, Upon a stringed instrument. Calvin, Morison and more than thirty MSS have the plural. David wrote this Psalm; 1. The title ascribes it to him; 2 The contents throughout suit David. Scott dates it B. C. 1021; Clarke, B. C. 536. Commentators are not agreed as to its historic occasion. The Syriac says it was written " by David, when Jonathan made known to him the determination of Saul who was devising David's death. But spiritually it intimates a prayer with the giving of thanks." Tholuck gives the title thus: " A PSALM of David, sung at Mahanaim, beyond Jordan on the borders of Palestine, when he fled from before Absalom." The historic record referred to by Tholuck and others who take the same view is found in 2 Sam. 8th chapter. Dimock and Anderson both say: " It is generally agreed that this Psalm refers to 2 Sam. xvii. 22, 24." The phrase, *from the ends of the earth* indicates that it was written in exile. The historic occasion of this Psalm is probably much the same as that of Ps. iii. This conjecture is more probable than that of the Syriac, or that of Mudge, who thinks it was written on the same occasion with Ps. lx. The Psalm has a public use derived from the typical character of David. Hengstenberg: " Even in our day the Psalm has its complete use, inasmuch as the promises in 2 Sam. vii. have undoubtedly their complete fulfilment in Christ." The only name of the Most High here used is *Elohim God,* on which see on Ps. iii. 2. On *Selah* see Introduction, § 15.

1. *Hear my cry, O God. Hear,* as in Ps. iv. 1; xvii. 1; xxviii. 2. *Cry,* as in Ps. xvii. 1 and often. Here it clearly means earnest supplication. *Attend unto my prayer. Attend,* also *hearken, give heed,* as in Ps. v. 2; lxxxvi. 6; cxlii. 6; Pr. xvii. 4. *Prayer,* invariably so rendered, Ps. iv. 1; lv. 1. The intent of both clauses is to secure the gracious notice of God to his petitions; and as he was urgent and vehement he uses strong language, and in different words twice asks for the same thing.

2. *From the end of the earth will I cry unto thee, when my heart is overwhelmed. Cry,* not from the same root as *cry* in v. 1, but from the same as *cried* in Ps. iii. 4; Ps. xviii. once rendered *call,* once *cry,* vv. 3, 6. For *earth* it is better to read *land,* meaning the land of Israel, to a remote part of which David had now been driven, perhaps by Absalom's rebellion; see on Ps. xxxvii. 3, 9. In Mahanaim David found refuge during the early part of Absalom's rebellion. Although it seems to have been a place of some note, yet it was in the tribe of Gad, Josh. xxi. 38, and was remote from Jerusalem. It had been the centre of Ishbosheth's kingdom, 2 Sam. ii. 8. To David, who had been used to the delights of the daily public worship of God in Jerusalem it must have been a dreary place, so that his *heart was overwhelmed.*

The Chaldee and Syriac read, *in the anxiety of my heart;* Septuagint, Ethiopic, Vulgate and Doway, *when my heart was in anguish;* church of England, *when my heart is in heaviness;* Edwards, *now when my heart is sinking.* We can never be so remote from the usual scenes and places of public worship as to excuse us from devotion. *Lead me to the rock* that *is higher than I.* It is a poor and low sense, and ill suited to the circumstances under which the Psalm was written to make *rock* here mean the city of Petra, as Mudge does. On the general use and import of the word *rock,* see on Ps. xviii. 2, where it is rendered *strength.* God is the rock of all his saints. Scott: "The divine mercy, support and protection formed the rock on which he desired to rest his soul, out of the reach of the tempestuous waves, which dashed and raged below." Hengstenberg: "The Psalmist grounds his prayer not only on what God *has been,* but on what he *always is* to him." To be able to avail ourselves of God's protection, we must be *led,* guided and lifted up by him, for he is high, beyond our reach; nay, without special grace we cannot find or know him at all, Job xxiii. 3, 8, 9. With this verse and the next compare Ps. xviii. 2; lxii. 2.

3. *For thou hast been a shelter for me. Shelter,* in Ps. xiv. 6; xlvi. 1, *refuge;* in Jer. xvii. 17; Joel iii. 16, *hope.* David is encouraging himself by his past experience. Perhaps too he refers to all his past history. Why should he not? It was all marvellous. And [thou hast been] *a strong tower,* [Heb. tower of strength] *from the enemy. Tower,* see on Ps. xlviii. 12. *Strength,* as in Ps. viii. 2, David is trying to lay hold on God. To this end he calls to mind former deliverances. "Nothing doth more strengthen our faith, than the remembrance of God's succor in times past."

4. *I will abide in thy tabernacle for ever. Abide, sojourn, dwell, be an inhabitant.* It expresses more than an occasional or temporary connection with God's worship. *Tabernacle,* as in Ps. xv. 1; xix. 4; xxvii. 5, 6; not applied to the temple; this Psalm was written before the temple was built. *I will,* or *shall,* expressing either a purpose or a hope, perhaps both. *For ever* expresses as great a duration as is predicable of his existence, *first,* in this world, equivalent to *as long as I live; secondly,* as God's house on earth was always a type of heaven there is doubtless a reference to the pleasing hope and solemn purpose he had of spending his *eternity* (literally *eternities*) in heaven; see on Ps. xxiii. 6. *I will trust in the covert of thy wings.* Some think the allusion is to the wings of the cherubim over the mercy-seat; but the cherubim were in the holy of holies, which was entered by the high-priest only, and not even by the king. The allusion pretty certainly is to the feathered dam covering her young. See on Ps. xvii. 8. Compare Ps. xxxvi. 7; lvii. 1; lxiii. 7; xci. 4. The confidence of a soul abiding under the protection of God is a firm *trust.* Calvin is confident that this verse is expressive of David's sentiments *after* he had returned from his exile; but there is no objection to the admission that it is the language of his heart, so soon as he was able to recover from the painful surprise of his banishment.

5. *For thou, O God, hast heard my vows.* No sincere act of divinely appointed worship ever escapes the favorable notice of God. *Hast heard,* that is so as to respond favorably; see on Ps. iv. 1. *Vows,* see on Ps. xxii. 25; l. 14; lvi. 12. *Thou hast given me the heritage of those that fear thy name. Hast given,* freely granted. *Heritage,* inheritance, or possession. It means either the *land* of Israel, which was the heritage of Israel, and over which David was to rule; or, as David was a true worshipper of God, he should have such an inheritance as God has promised to all who fear him; or, as David was a type of Christ, this clause may have a reference to the great promise and prophecy in 2 Sam. vii. 12–17; 1 Chron. xvii. 11–14. These words were the polar star of David's life and destiny. He seems seldom to have forgotten them. If the reference is to the typical character of David, then God had granted him a great honor, viz., to rule a people who should give a name to his church forever, and

in a way that made him a type of his great descendant, who should eternally be a king. These several views are not inconsistent with each other, and may be united. Some succeeding verses require that we do not lose sight of the last.

6. *Thou wilt prolong the king's life.* *King* in the third person is often used by David as a designation of him, Ps. xx. 9 ; xxi. 1, 7. He also uses it of Christ, Ps. ii. 6 ; xlv. 1 ; xiv. 14. It was not he personally, but he in his posterity, Messias, that was to be so enduring. The promise finds its parallel and enlargement in Isa. liii. 10–12. The Hebrew literally is, *Days upon the days of the king thou wilt add.* The *king* must be the root and the offspring of Jesse, Jesus the Son of God. The words have no ample fulfilment in the person of David. Neither has the next clause : And *his years as many generations*, literally, *His years* (shall be) *as generation and generation, i. e., generation upon generation.* We are forced by every fair rule of interpretation to say that this whole verse has no adequate fulfilment without including Messias. Calvin : " There can be no doubt that the series of years, and even ages, of which he speaks, extends prospectively to the coming of Christ." In this evangelical commentators generally agree.

7. *He shall abide before God for ever.* *He,* that is *the king* before mentioned. David actually reigned over even Judah hardly forty years. But this king is the Son of man mentioned by the prophet, Dan. vii. 13, 14. Instead of *abide,* some very well read *sit,* as expressive of dignity and permanence. *Before God,* says Hengstenberg, " is under the protecting guardianship of God's grace ; compare 2 Sam. vii. 29." *Oh prepare mercy and truth,* which *may preserve him.* This reminds one of Ps. lxxii. 15, " Prayer also shall be made for him continually." The Prayer is for the *king.* Alexander thinks mercy and truth are personified as in Ps. xl. 11 ; lvii. 3. Perhaps they are, but we get as good a sense by taking them without a figure. *Prepare,* often so rendered, also *appoint.* *Preserve,* as in Ps. xi. 7 ; xxv. 21 ; often rendered *keep,* as in Deut. xxxii. 10.

8. *So will I sing praise unto thy name for ever, that I may daily perform my vows.* *Sing praise,* as in Ps. vii. 17 ; lvii. 7 ; rendered also *sing, sing praises,* and by some *sing Psalms ;* from the same root as the word rendered *Psalm* in many of the titles. To *sing praise* was to express gratitude in solemn devotions. David was a pattern in this duty. He had promised no less in his *vows,* and he was determined to *perform* them.

DOCTRINAL AND PRACTICAL REMARKS.

1. It is a sad mistake with some to offer prayers and then care no more for them It is not the prayer but the answer to it that brings the blessing. David looked out and pleaded for that, v. 1.

2. However unfriendly our situation may be to the maintenance of habits of devotion, yet we must not give up our intercourse with God even from the ends of the earth. David from Mahanaim, Daniel from Babylon, the sailor from the mast-head, the prisoner from his cell, the sinner in his guilt and wretchedness must all call on God, v. 2. Morison : " There is no scene of exile from which the humble suppliant may not look to the rock that is higher than he." Henry : " That which separates us from other comforts should drive us so much the nearer to God, the Fountain of all comfort." If we cannot go to a house of worship, God himself has promised to be to us for *a little sanctuary,* Ezek. xi. 16.

3. If real saints have such a longing for God's appointed public worship, what shall be thought of professing Christians, who voluntarily exile themselves from the privileges of God's house under an evangelical ministry ? v. 2.

4. If we should always pray, how much more should we do so when deeply afflicted, v. 2. Scott : " When cares, fears, sorrows, or temptations, like a wild deluge, overwhelm our hearts, our cries unto God should be more fervent than ever." The greater the need, the louder should be the cry for help.

5. Stoicism is no part of a pious character. True religion refines the sensibilities, and so of necessity the child of grace feels poignantly griefs that affect others but little, v. 2. Sorrow brings weeping and "weeping must quicken praying, not deaden it."

6. It is a sad mistake to be driven from devotion, public or private, by the very causes that ought to make the throne of grace more precious than ever. Not so with David, v. 2. Slade: "Some unwise people plead their trials, at home and in the world, as a reason why they cannot attend to spiritual duties. This shows a very unchristian state of mind and heart."

7. If ever we are safe, or happy, or blessed, it must be by finding a Rock that is higher than we; and if we are but led thither, all shall be well, v. 2. To attain such heights of bliss and safety, we must have divine aid and guidance. Scott: "We should therefore pray fervently for the Holy Spirit of promise, that we may by his gracious teaching and assistance 'believe to the saving of our souls.'"

8. The protection which every believer has found in God is truly wonderful, v. 3. The *shelter* is ample and the *tower* strong. No *enemy* can reach him.

9. A fair trial of God's love and care would surely determine any wise man to be for him and not for another, vv. 3, 4. Scott: "As genuine experience is acquired, encouragement will abound."

10. In true religion nothing compares with the favor and service of God, v. 4. No griefs for outward afflictions were so pungent as those which took from David the enjoyments of God's house. "He accounts it a higher pleasure to lie as a suppliant before the altar, than to sit upon the throne of a king."

11. If the tabernacle and service of God on earth are so dear to the saints, how unspeakable must be the glories and joys of the upper temple, Heb. ix. 8, 9, 24. Heaven will not come short of any pious expectation ever entertained of it.

12. On the general doctrine of *vows*, vv. 5, 8, see REMARKS on Ps. xxii. 25; l. 14; lvi. 12. With God a vow never comes to be out of date. Tholuck: "David promises never more to forget that he owes these blessings neither to his own sagacity and valor, nor to blind fate, but that he will forever sing praises to the name of the Lord, and that his whole life shall be the payment of the vows which he made in the hour of need."

13. Very different is the portion of the sinner from the heritage of those that fear the Lord, v. 5. The joys, passions and hopes of the wicked are transient, delusive, unsatisfactory; the prospects and expectations of the righteous endure forever and brighten every day. Even their sorrows are blessed, being sent in covenant love.

14. If David had the honor of being according to the flesh the ancestor of Christ and of receiving promises of the glory of that descendant's kingdom; believers now are no less endearingly related to the same blessed and exalted personage. Compare Matt. xii. 48–50. Dickson: "The inheritance of the chief of God's servants, and of the meanest and weakest of them, is one."

15. Some are afraid of being singular, or of being esteemed so; but if we ever reach heaven, it will not be without divine grace making us differ from others, v. 5. The saints are peculiar in their belief, principles, practice, destiny.

16. As Christ's kingdom is permanent and abiding, so of course are all the blessings secured to believers, vv. 6, 7. Compare Luke i. 32, 33. Blessed be God.

17. Great as our wants and necessities may be, they cannot exceed the measure of the *mercy* and *truth* secured in the covenant of redemption to Christ himself and through him to all believers, v. 7.

18. Dickson: "The best retreat, that can be made, after wrestling and victory over troubles, are prayer and praises, according to David's example," vv. 7, 8. Henry: "Praising God, and paying our vows to him must be our constant daily work."

PSALM LXII.

To the chief Musician, to Jeduthun, A Psalm of David.

1 Truly my soul waiteth upon God: from him *cometh* my salvation.

2 He only *is* my rock and my salvation; *he is* my defence; I shall not be greatly moved.

3 How long will ye imagine mischief against a man? ye shall be slain all of you: as a bowing wall *shall ye be, and as* a tottering fence.

4 They only consult to cast *him* down from his excellency: they delight in lies: they bless with their mouth, but they curse inwardly. Selah.

5 My soul, wait thou only upon God; for my expectation *is* from him.

6 He only *is* my rock and my salvation: *he is* my defence; I shall not be moved.

7 In God *is* my salvation and my glory: the rock of my strength, *and* my refuge, *is* in God.

8 Trust in him at all times; ye people, pour out your heart before him: God *is* a refuge for us. Selah.

9 Surely men of low degree *are* vanity, *and* men of high degree *are* a lie: to be laid in the balance, they *are* altogether *lighter* than vanity.

10 Trust not in oppression, and become not vain in robbery: if riches increase, set not your heart *upon* them.

11 God hath spoken once; twice have I heard this; that power *belongeth* unto God.

12 Also unto thee, O Lord, *belongeth* mercy: for thou renderest to every man according to his work.

ON the title see on titles of Psalms iii. iv. xxxix. A marked peculiarity of this Psalm is the frequent recurrence of one word rendered in the English text *truly*, *only* and *surely*. Some have made this very significant. But it is probably not of any importance further than that it was a fit word in each place to give the author's precise meaning. That David wrote the Psalm is generally admitted. Even Clarke expresses no doubt about it. It seems to be commonly agreed that it was composed on the occasion of Absalom's rebellion. Amyrald: "There is. in it throughout not one single word (and this is a rare occurrence) in which the prophet expresses *fear* or *dejection*, and there is also no *prayer* in it, although, on other occasions, when in danger, he never omits to pray." In it we have these names of the Most High, *Elohim God* and *Adonai Lord*, on which see on Ps. iii. 2; ii. 4. Hengstenberg: "The reason why Elohim is used throughout is because the Psalmist is speaking of God in opposition to everything of an earthly and human nature." On *Selah* see Introduction, § 15. Alexander seems confident that the theme or burden of the Psalm is a contrast between God and man, as objects of confidence. Scott dates it B. C. 1060; Clarke, B. C. 1023. Of course Scott does not favor the idea that it relates to Absalom's rebellion. In this Clarke is probably nearer the truth.

1. *Truly my soul waiteth upon God.* *Truly*, the original is found *six* times in this Psalm, *once* rendered *truly*, once, *surely*, and *four* times, *only*. It will make good sense to render it *surely* or *truly* throughout, and so some do, as Venema, Jebb. This is often its meaning. Yet it also has the signification of *only, merely*. Piscator, Amesius, Hengstenberg and Alexander render it *only* in every case in this Psalm. Calvin has it *nevertheless* or *yet*. Others vary the rendering as is done in the English version, or according to each one's judgment. No important point is gained by the adoption of either rendering. Yet if a preference is given to any exclusively, perhaps it is best to read *only*. *Waiteth*, better rendered (is) *in silence*. The corresponding *verb* is in Ps. iv. 4 rendered, *Be still;* in Ps. xxx. 12, *Be silent;* in Ps. xxxvii. 7, *Rest*. It is found in v. 5 of this Psalm. Reading it (is) *in silence*, the whole clause may be rendered, *Unto God only is my soul silent.* Margin: My soul keepeth silence unto God.

This is the rendering of many, *q. d.*, I bow in silence to every word and act of the Almighty. Clarke: "He has a right to lay on me what he pleases; what he lays on me is much less than I deserve, therefore, am I *dumb* before God;" Pool: "My soul silently, quietly and patiently looks up to God for deliverance, and that in his time and way, without murmuring or despair, or using indirect or sinful practices." He did this to God *only*. To man, however wise or great, he answered, and argued, or remonstrated, as the case might be, but not to God. Anderson: "Doubtless the Psalmist intended to say that his soul was quiet, submissive, and subject; the rebellious affections being tamed and subdued." To God and to God only he implicitly yielded control of everything. *From him* cometh *my salvation, q. d.*, If he cannot save me, none else can. *Salvation*, sometimes rendered *help*, but commonly *salvation;* see on Ps. iii. 2, 8.

2. *He only* is *my rock and my salvation. Rock*, see on Ps. xviii. 2; lxi. 2. It is the word used by Moses in Deut. xxxii. 4, 15. *Salvation*, as in v. 1. This clause asserts both David's creed and his purpose. He believes he has no other; his resolution is to reject all other aid and safety. He is *my defence, high tower, high fort*, or *refuge;* see on Ps. ix. 9; xviii. 2; lix. 9, 17. Compare Ps. cxliv. 2; Isa. xxv. 12. *I shall not be greatly moved.* Chaldee: I shall not be moved in the day of great affliction; Arabic: So that I shall never be moved; Septuagint, Ethiopic, Vulgate and Doway: I shall be moved no more; Ainsworth and Venema: I shall not be moved much; Hengstenberg: I shall not be much shaken; Pool: "Though I may be shaken, I shall not be overthrown;" Clarke: "I may be *shaken*, but cannot be *cast down*." In Ps. xvii. 5; xxxviii. 16, other forms of the same verb are rendered *slip;* but see on Ps. x. 6; xlvi. 5.

3. *How long will ye imagine mischief against a man?* The rendering is very various. Venema: How long will ye throw yourselves (violently) upon a man? Edwards: How long will ye thrust yourselves against a man? Hengstenberg: How long do you rage all of you like a storm let loose against a man? The difficulty arises in good part from the fact that the verb rendered *imagine mischief* is found here only, and that a kindred word in the Arabic has been a chief guide to the meaning. Although we may be in doubt respecting the precise signification of the word, yet we can be at no loss concerning the import of the passage, which is a remonstrance against his enemies for pursuing him with evil devices, evil speeches, violence and rage. He warns them: *Ye shall be slain all of you.* This rendering is substantially supported by Calvin, Ainsworth, Venema, Amesius, Piscator and Jebb; but the ancient versions, also Fabritius, Edwards, Fry, Hengstenberg and Alexander, give the verb an active sense, Will ye murder *him* all of you? or, Ye would all of you murder; or, Ye all go about as manslayers. If we take it in the former sense, then the last clauses are well rendered in the English version: *As a bowing wall* shall ye be, and as *a tottering fence*. But if we take the verb in the active sense, then the meaning is, *Will ye murder* (or *ye murder*) the man who is *as a bowing wall and a tottering fence?* The decisive reason for following the common version is the general spirit of the Psalm, which is not supplicatory, or deprecatory, but bold and confident. In his weakness David did compare himself to a *partridge*, and even to a *flea*, 1 Sam. xxiv. 14; xxvi. 20. But he was then in a low tone of feeling, and had Saul and the mass of the kingdom against him. This Psalm is anything but dispirited and timid. He predicts that his enemies shall be slain, fall down and be as a bowing wall and a tottering fence, *i. e.*, be as nothing to hinder David's return to Jerusalem and to his throne. So it soon came to pass. *Tottering, thrust down, struck*, or *overthrown.* See on Ps. xxxvi. 12. Compare also Ps. cxl. 4; Isa. xxx. 13.

4. *They only consult to cast* him *down from his excellency. Consult, purpose, advise,*

counsel. One thought is uppermost in their minds, and it has assumed the form of a regular plan. The Hebrew verb is in the preterite. *Cast down,* also *drive, drive out, thrust away, chase. Excellency, dignity, elevation, exaltation.* The meaning is that their one deliberate plan was to hinder David from attaining the great hopes and realizing the proper ends of the royal dignity. For this purpose, *They delight in lies.* The war against David and against Christ has always been carried on by falsehood. Men have relished these untruths. The verb is in the future *will delight,* like, *accept, enjoy, take pleasure in, have a favor to. They bless with their mouth, but they curse inwardly. Inwardly;* margin, *in their inward parts.* Parallel passages are Ps. xii. 2 ; xxviii. 3 ; lv. 21 ; see also Jer. ix. 8.

5. *My soul, wait thou only upon God.* Here we have the same words as in the first clause of v. 1, except 1, that here *soul* is spoken to, as is David's wont, Ps. xlii. 5, 11 ; xliii. 5 ; 2, here we have the verb *be silent* or *wait* in the imperative mood ; see on v. 1. The meaning is, Bow to the sovereign will of God ; in silence submit to him, hoping in his mercy, and not despairing of his aid, but being subject to him in a spirit of patience. Good reason had David thus to exhort his soul : *For my expectation* is *from him. Expectation,* as in Ps. ix. 18 and elsewhere ; often *hope,* once *the thing that I long for,* Job vi. 8 ; vii. 6.

6. *He only* is *my rock and my salvation ;* he is *my defence : I shall not be moved.* This verse is exactly like v. 2, except that *greatly* in v. 2 is here omitted. This shows a growth of confidence. There he said he should not be moved *greatly ;* here he says he shall not be moved at all.

7. *In God* is *my salvation and my glory. Salvation,* always so rendered or *safety,* see on Ps. xii. 5 ; li. 12. *My glory,* as in Ps. iii. 3. *The rock of my strength. Rock,* as in vv. 2, 6. *Rock of my strength* is equivalent to the rock where I find my strength, or my strong rock. And *my refuge* is *in God. Refuge,* in Ps. lxi. 3, *shelter.*

8. *Trust in him at all times. Trust,* as in Ps. iv. 5, also rendered *hope. Ye people, pour out your heart before him. People,* in the singular, meaning the Jewish nation. We *pour out our hearts before God,* when we tell him all that is in our hearts, whether it be our burdens, our griefs, our shame and penitence, or our joy and gladness. In distress we sometimes resign ourselves to despondency or despair when we ought to be praying in hope of an early deliverance. *God* is *a refuge for us. Refuge,* as in v. 7.

9. *Surely men of low degree are vanity, and men of high degree are a lie.* Chaldee : Wherefore the sons of men are nothing, and the sons of a man are a lie ; Arabic : All the sons of men pass away as a shadow, and those who are laid in the balances are liars ; John Rogers' translation : As for men, they are but vayne, men are dysceatful ; Calvin : Nevertheless, the sons of Adam are vanity, and the children of men a lie ; Ainsworth : Surely the sons of base men are vanity, the sons of noble men are a lie ; Edwards : Men of low rank are vanity ; those of an elevated station are a mere nothing. On the use of the words *Adam* and *Ish,* here rendered *men,* see Introduction, § 16. None of the ancient versions justify us in making any such distinction as is conveyed in the English version, or by Ainsworth and Edwards. Clarke's interpretation is pleasing but fanciful : "*Adam* was the name of the first man when formed out of the *earth ; Ish* was his name when united to his wife, and they became one flesh. *Before,* he was the *incomplete* man ; *after,* he was the *complete* man : for it seems, in the sight of God, it requires the male and female to make one *complete human being.*" The sum of what is taught by this clause is that men by whatever name called are vain, fleeting, of little force, and disappoint our expectations, as a lie, if credited, would do. Nay, more. *To be laid in the balance, they* are *altogether* lighter *than vanity. Altogether* is here used in its old sense of *conjunctly.*

The word *together* is better. Put all men together in the scales, and they *go up*, or as we say *fly up*. They are lighter than vanity. A Hebrew could not have used stronger language to express his conception of the utter nothingness of our miserable race. The pertinence of this verse is to establish the great truths, that God only is worthy of reliance, that he only is a refuge.

10. *Trust not in oppression, and become not vain in robbery.* "An inheritance may be gotten hastily at the beginning; but the end thereof shall not be blessed." A resort to immoral or doubtful expedients for escaping poverty and other ills of life will in the end benefit no man. *Oppression*, not before found in the Psalms, most commonly so rendered, once *extortion*, and in the margin *fraud* and *deceit.* *Robbery*, not before found in the Psalms. *Oppression* here is obtaining possession of other men's property by fraud; *robbery* obtains that which is not its own by *violence*. All unjust modes of accumulation bring a curse. *If riches increase, set not your heart* upon them. This lesson is often taught, Ps. lii. 7; Luke xii. 15; 1 Tim. vi. 17. Even when the increase is lawful, we must guard against the love of riches or the undue care of their growth or preservation.

11. *God hath spoken once; twice have I heard this, that power* belongeth *unto God. Power, strength, might*, as in Ps. viii. 2; xxviii. 7. There is no need of explaining this as if David had two separate revelations from God. The words are best taken in the popular sense, that God had repeatedly impressed upon his mind the lesson, as in Job xxxiii. 14. This impression had been made not merely by God's word, but perhaps especially by his providence. The English text agrees with the Chaldee, Syriac, church of England, Calvin, Amesius, Ainsworth, Piscator, Fabritius, Pool, Jebb, Fry and Tholuck. But another rendering is favored by many: *God has spoken once* or *one word, yea, there are two which I have heard.* This is sanctioned by the Arabic, Septuagint, Vulgate, Ethiopic, Gill, Horne, Clarke, Morison, Hengstenberg and Alexander. Venema and Scott approve either way of rendering. For *twice* Edwards has *oftentimes;* and no doubt that is the *meaning*, if we read the word as an adverbial numeral. But if we read: *Two things have I heard*, then we must not close this verse with a period, but connect it with the next. The first thing he heard was concerning God's omnipotence. The other of the two things is now mentioned:

12. *Also unto thee, O Lord*, belongeth *mercy. Mercy*, as in Ps. v. 7; in Ps. li. 1, *lovingkindness.* Some think the publication of these perfections of God here intended was chiefly made at Sinai, others in all revelation. But the phrase, *God hath spoken once, yea, twice*, principally teaches the certainty of the thing; see Tillotson's Sermon on this passage. *For thou renderest to every man according to his work.* Instead of *for*, the Syriac and Arabic read *and;* Alexander, *but;* Fry, *truly;* Calvin, *certainly.* The renderings of Fry and Calvin are sanctioned by the English translators in some other places, Gen. xxix. 32; Ex. iii. 12; 1 Kings i. 13; Isa. lxiii. 16, where we have *surely, certainly, assuredly, doubtless.* Some are offended that in the rewards of the last day *God will render to every man according to his works.* But the doctrine is often asserted in Scripture, Prov. xxiv. 12, 29; Jer. xxxii. 19; Ezek. vii. 27; Matt. xvi. 27; Rom. ii. 6; 1 Cor. iii. 8; Eph. vi. 8; 1 Pet. i. 17; Rev. xxii. 12. What is more fair than that a man's life and character should furnish the rule of the divine distribution? See on Ps. xviii. 25, 26. If our works are wicked, we shall be lost; if they are good, we shall be saved, yet not for any *merit* that is in them, but only for Christ's sake.

DOCTRINAL AND PRACTICAL REMARKS.

1. While true religion is not *exclusive*, in the sense of denying admission to any humble soul to the privileges of the Gospel, it is always *exclusive*, in the sense of deny-

ing to any but God *only* the supreme homage of the heart, vv. 1, 2, 5, 6, 9. True piety finds and pronounces God all-sufficient. The proffer of another is an offence to the believer as it is to God himself.

2. *Silence*, unmurmuring submission to the divine will, and patient *waiting* on God are better than all the pragmatical efforts of any man to help himself, vv. 1, 5. God, the author of our trials, never errs. "Christ would not be delivered from his sufferings by any other means than those which the Father ordained." Let us walk as he walked. No doubt David had a sharp conflict with his own heart. He was a very spirited man; but by God's grace he obtained the victory over his own will.

3. It is marvellous grace in God by his word, Spirit and providence to make so clear to all teachable spirits the essential matters of religion; in particular that salvation is wholly of him. The rescue of Israel at the Red sea; the escape of David in the Sauline persecution and in Absalom's rebellion and the conversion of every sinner may well make every man cry, *From him cometh my salvation*, v. 1.

4. What time we are afraid and our enemies fierce, let us in imitation of David call to mind the appropriate titles of the Almighty our *Rock*, our *Salvation*, our *Defence*, our *Glory*, the *Rock of our strength*, our *Refuge*, vv. 2, 6, 7, 8. These words fall far short of the excellent truths they represent. Still when we can thus address God, "we may draw the animating conclusion that we shall not be shaken or cast down by anything that the malice or wickedness of men can effect." Believers are led to rely more and more upon God, the more they prove him, and experience his grace, and the more they study and understand the covenant of his love with its exceeding great and precious promises. Though a true Christian may be worsted in a battle, yet he always in the end comes off conqueror, and more than conqueror through him that loved him.

5. If God is for us, we *shall not be greatly moved*, v. 2. Nay, we *shall not be moved* at all, v. 6, in any way that will do us real damage. Dickson: "As a man resolveth to believe and follow the course of sound faith, so he may assure himself of establishment and victory over all temptations, notwithstanding his own weakness."

6. It is no new thing, and, if God is with us, it is no ruinous thing, to have many and mighty foes banded together against us, employing all the arts of deceit and all the rage of malice for our destruction. Scott: "However blamelessly the believer may conduct himself, he must expect a measure of the same enmity, with which the world treated his Saviour; when every device was framed, every deceit used, and every slander propagated, to 'cast him down from his excellency.' But the doom of David's persecutors, and of the crucifiers of Christ, may be expected by all, who endeavor to tempt his people to sin, or to vilify their characters." Nothing can be more vain than the constant and amazing efforts of ungodly men to harm the followers of the Lamb, vv. 3, 4. There is no infatuation like that of an unregenerate man, a foe of God and of all goodness.

7. The awful doom of incorrigible sinners, and in particular of persecutors, is made certain in two ways. 1. The mouth of the Lord hath spoken it: "Ye shall be slain all of you." 2. Their proclivities, even now, show their destiny: they are 'as a bowing wall and as a tottering fence,' v. 3. The strongest of the wicked are but feeble. Every fair trial evinces their weakness and the badness of their cause, Isa. xxx. 13; Jer. xii. 5.

8. So futile are all *counsels* and devices against God and righteousness, that it is a marvel that the wicked do not cease to *consult*, v. 4. If directed against truth and God's people, one plan is as foolish as another, for each one shall come to nought. Wisdom is not wisdom, if it is employed against the Almighty.

9. How can any expect that the God of truth will allow men to succeed, who 'delight in lies?' All the laws of his moral government must be reversed before such

could be the case. If there is anything that God hates, it is deceit. He has set the whole might of his omnipotence against it.

10. It is a great comfort that God is our only *hope*, and *trust*, and *expectation*, vv. 5, 6, 8. When we find him, we need seek no further. He is all-sufficient. The more he is tried, the more he is found to be the very friend we need.

11. If God has dealt well with us, and made his candle to shine upon us, and made us to triumph, when our foes were many, our fears strong, and our discouragements great, then we ought to show forth his praises, and summon all whom we can influence to unite with us in such a course of piety and devotion as will secure to them the same blessings, v. 8. Dickson: "The duty of comforted and victorious believers is to communicate the fruit of their experience, for strengthening their brethren, and edification of others."

12. In all acts of devotion, in particular in prayer and supplication, we should give earnest heed to the matter of engaging our affections in the work, so that we shall truly *pour out our hearts before God*, v. 8. There is no substitute for godly sincerity. "God is not mocked."

13. Are our enemies lively, our burdens heavy, our temptations terrible? then surely our resort should be to God in prayer, v. 8. Even when our trials are light we must still look to God. I have known a man to behave well under a terrible trial, who lost his temper and behaved badly under a very slight provocation. In the former case he went to the throne of grace; in the latter, he attempted to walk alone.

14. There are many ways of drawing us from God and from duty, many snares spread for our feet, many ways of falling into idolatry. There are dangers at home and dangers abroad, dangers in prosperity, and dangers in adversity. David names some in vv. 9, 10, but they are mere samples. Remember this is a wicked, dangerous world.

15. Let every one beware of reliance on man, v. 9. He is often indisposed, and still oftener unable to minister the slightest relief, Ps. cxviii. 8, 9. The very best and greatest man is a poor creature. Luther: "Many are to be found, who trust in the favor of kings and princes; and on that account they are puffed up with pride and insolence, and oppress others with the more confidence; and especially if they see their wall bowing and giving way; that is, if they see a man declining in his affairs, who was once in prosperity, or if they see him not protected by wealth and influence against injury: such an one as this, they endeavor to overthrow wholly; and to that end, ingratiate themselves with the powerful, and wind themselves into the affections of those, on whom they depend, as on a propitious deity. But such see not how fallacious is the favor of man, and how variable and uncertain are their wills, nor will they believe it to be vain, until they find it out by experience and are brought to lament their error." To do us real good in important matters men are wanting in will and power, in candor and fidelity, or in energy and promptness. All, all that is under the power of sin is nought, nought, nought.

16. Apparent and even long-continued success is no evidence that our course of life is either right, safe, or pleasing to God, v. 8. He, who makes his prosperity the test of his virtue, has no better evidence of his uprightness than had many of the most atrocious wrong-doers, who have cursed the earth.

17. Let good men be very careful what means they employ to promote their own advancement, or effect their own deliverance. Sin is worse than poverty, reproach and the most depressed condition of our affairs. *Oppression* and *robbery*, like all other sins, will in the end do us no good. "When in affliction, turn whithersoever you like, if you turn not to God, you will find no rest." Sin is worse than all other evils. It makes earth like hell, and it makes hell what it is.

18. Trust not in wealth, however acquired, or secured, v. 10. Nothing is more uncertain, deceitful, or unsatisfying. Scott: "*Reliance* on increasing riches, however obtained, is idolatry, and totally inconsistent with the life of faith." Arnd: "Riches are like a stream, which soon flows to a person, and may also soon flow away, so that where one had first to pass with a boat, he may in a short while be able to cross by a step, and by and by to walk over with dry feet." Compare Job xx. 15; Ps. xxxvii 16; xxxix. 6; lii. 7; Pr. xi. 4, 28; xxiii. 5; Matt. xiii. 22; Mark x. 23.

19. Great truths often taught in Scripture and enforced in providence, respecting the character and government of God ought to make a deep and lasting impression on our minds and hearts, v. 11.

20. When God thus speaks to saint or sinner, he changes not, v. 11. If God says a thing once, it is true; if he says it often, it shows that in his kindness he would often remind us of it. 'The word of God is a decree, steadfast and irreversible.' The Scripture cannot be broken, John x. 35. The promises and the threatenings will all be kept.

21. It is a great thing to have the mind clear and the faith settled respecting the *Power of God*, v. 11. If we think anything is too hard for him, half our troubles, and those the heaviest we will try to bear without his aid. It was therefore a great revelation that the Lord made to the patriarch: "I am the Almighty God," Gen. xvii. 1. Since his ascension to glory the Saviour has taught us no more weighty truth than his almightiness, Rev. i. 8. "All the powers of all the creatures are derived from God, depend upon him, and are used by him as he pleases," John xix. 11.

22. Nor is it less important that our views of the *mercy* of God be clear and settled, v. 12. This was among the earliest and clearest revelations God made of himself, Ex. xxxiv. 5–7. In a religion of sinners the absence of mercy would be like the absence of light in a world where the inhabitants depended entirely on vision for ability to do anything.

23. But it is very important that our views of God's *power* and *mercy* should harmonize, vv. 11, 12. Dickson: "To induce a soul to trust in God only, it is necessary, that it so look to his power, as it looks to his mercy, and lay hold on both: faith hath need of both, as of two wings, to carry it up to God above all vain enticements, and terrors, and temptations." God has power to save, and a kindness inclining him to save.

24. Whatever misgivings may arise in our minds respecting the justice of the divine conduct in the unfinished affairs of this life, all our doubts will be at once and forever removed when God shall wind up this dispensation in the decisions of the last day, and *render to every man according to his work*, v. 12. "No service done to God shall go unrewarded, nor any affront given him go unpunished, unless it be repented of."

25. The character of God is a perfect and glorious whole. He has power to crush the heaven-daring and to raise the poor from the dunghill. He has mercy that condescends to the vilest, takes a favorable notice of the poorest pious services, and forgives innumerable sins. He has justice that forever bars the gates of heaven against the wicked, and as certainly bars the gates of hell against the righteous, vv. 11, 12. He has wisdom that never erred, that cannot err; faithfulness that reaches to the heavens in height and to all generations in duration; holiness that is glorious, and every conceivable perfection. Oh study God's character. Study it all.

26. Is God inflexibly, eternally and unchangeably just, then, if we are innocent, or our cause is good, we may know assuredly that he will, in due time, redress our wrongs, and relieve our sufferings. But we cannot plead his justice in any matter, where we are even partially in the wrong. Let appeals to the divine justice be never made without great reverence and after great heart-searchings.

PSALM LXIII.

A Psalm of David, when he was in the wilderness of Judah.

1 O God, thou *art* my God; early will I seek thee: my soul thirsteth for thee, my flesh longeth for thee in a dry and thirsty land, where no water is;

2 To see thy power and thy glory, so *as* I have seen thee in the sanctuary.

3 Because thy lovingkindness *is* better than life, my lips shall praise thee.

4 Thus will I bless thee while I live: I will lift up my hands in thy name:

5 My soul shall be satisfied as *with* marrow and fatness; and my mouth shall praise *thee* with joyful lips:

6 When I remember thee upon my bed, *and* meditate on thee in the *night* watches.

7 Because thou hast been my help, therefore in the shadow of thy wings will I rejoice.

8 My soul followeth hard after thee: thy right hand upholdeth me.

9 But those *that* seek my soul, to destroy *it*, shall go into the lower parts of the earth.

10 They shall fall by thy sword: they shall be a portion for foxes.

11 But the king shall rejoice in God; every one that sweareth by him shall glory: but the mouth of them that speak lies shall be stopped.

ON *A Psalm of David* see on title of Ps. iii.   On *When he was in the wilderness of Judah* opinions are divided, some thinking this Psalm was written in the Sauline persecution; others, in the rebellion of Absalom.   During both these periods David was often in the wild parts of Judah.   Those, who hold that the Psalm refers to the Sauline persecution, point us to 1 Sam. xxii. 5; xxiii. 14, 25; xxiv. 1; Josh. xv. 55, 62, and assert that the forest of Hareth, and the wilderness of Ziph, Maon, and Engedi were all in the tribe of Judah.   But those who contend that the title points to the rebellion of Absalom also cite 2 Sam. xv. 23, 28; xvi. 2, 14; xvii. 16, 29 in proof that the title refers to this latter period.   The common impression is that the reference is to that region mentioned in Matt. iii. 1; iv. 1, as *the wilderness*, or *the wilderness of Judea*.   We have some light from other quarters, perhaps enough to guide us.   David never calls himself *king* during the life of Saul.   After that event he uses the title freely.   Yet in v. 11 of this Psalm he speaks of himself as "*the king*."   Calvin, however, thinks that it was great magnanimity in David to call himself king, at a time when he was not and had not been in actual possession of the kingdom, but relied upon the divine promise alone for his authority.   This can hardly be regarded as satisfactory.   David acknowledged Saul's kingly authority till that persecutor died.   David was very far from arrogating either titles or prerogatives.   There is also a striking correspondence between the description of the situation of David and his friends in v. 1 of this Psalm, and the account given of them in 2 Sam. xvi. 2, 14, in fleeing from Absalom.   Hengstenberg also urges that this stands in close connection with such Psalms as confessedly relate to the affair of Absalom.   He cites Psalms iii. iv. xlii. lxi. and adds: "Modern criticism ought to be somewhat distrustful of itself, as the fact is evident, that, in general, only those Psalms are related to each other, which are announced by the titles to belong to each other."   But few commentators, as Patrick, Slade and Alexander agree with Hengstenberg in referring this Psalm to the time of Absalom.   Gill and Morison are not clear whether it refers to the time of Saul or of Absalom.   The great mass of commentators, as Theodoret, Luther, Diodati, Ainsworth, Venema, Pool, Henry, Chandler, Scott, Clarke and Dickson agree with Calvin in supposing it to have been written in the time of Saul.   The forms of title prefixed to four of the ancient versions, also Hilary, Jerome, Augustine and Bellarmine for *Judah* in the title read Idumea.   But there is no warrant for this, nor for the Syriac in saying, it relates to David's interview with "the king of Moab when he said, My father and mother fled to thee from the face of Saul; and I also take refuge with thee. The Davidic authorship is generally admitted though Calmet thinks it is a prayer by the captives in Babylon. Scott dates it B. C. 1060; Clarke, B. C. 1061. In it we have *Elohim God* and *Eli my God*, on which see on Ps. iii. 2; v. 4; xviii. 2. This ode has been greatly praised by many, much read and esteemed by more.

1. *O God, thou* art *my God. My God* includes the two ideas of omnipotence and covenant relation, q. d., O God, thou art *mighty, almighty*, the Governor of the world, and thou hast promised to be my friend and helper. Thy word has been pledged to me. I now plead the fulfilment of all thou hast promised. *Early will I seek thee;* in its participial and infinitive form rendered *diligently seek*, Pr. vii. 15; xi. 27. A man, who begins his labor *early*, is supposed to be *diligent* and *in earnest*. It is authorized to retain *early* here, Pr. xiii. 24; see also Pr. i. 28; viii. 17. The corresponding *noun* always signifies *morning*. David was in great earnest because he was in great straits, and had hope in God alone. *My soul thirsteth for thee, my flesh longeth for thee in a dry and thirsty land, where no water is. My soul* and *my flesh, i. e.,* my whole nature. David's condition in the wilderness was very trying. He was poor, destitute, forsaken, persecuted, deprived of the privileges of God's public worship, and having but small personal religious enjoyment. Indeed if this Psalm refers to the rebellion of Absalom, David knew his present sufferings were brought on by his former sins, 2 Sam. xii. 9–12, and so he must have been greatly overwhelmed. His outward condition is well set forth in 2 Sam. xvi. 14; xvii. 2, 29. Now he seeks God as his Father, greatly desiring the light of his countenance, and as his Deliverer from pressing and sore distress. No doubt the great want felt by David was the soul-cheering presence of the Lord. Hengstenberg: "A king who could not get even a drink of water to quench his thirst! all human fountains of consolation and happiness were dried up to the Psalmist. But he thirsts all the more earnestly after the divine fountain which still remained open to him. It is by this that he is known as a child of God." His wish was

2. *To see thy power and thy glory, so as I have seen thee in the sanctuary.* He specifies no instances of religious enjoyment in the sanctuary. It was not necessary. He had had frequent refreshment in God's worship, when his soul had had blessed discoveries of the divine power and majesty. In spiritual communion with God David had long found his chief enjoyment. He loved to think of such seasons. To *see* God is to enjoy him, Ps. xxvii. 13; xxxiv. 8, 12; xlix. 19; Matt. v. 8; John iii. 36. Some explain *glory*, as referring to the ark of the covenant, but that was kept in the holy of holies, and David did not see it in the sanctuary.

3. *Because thy lovingkindness* is *better than life, my lips shall praise thee. Lovingkindness*, as in Ps. li. 1. It is better not to exist than to exist without God's favor. It is better to die enjoying his lovingkindness than to live without it. *Life*, some think, means prosperity. It probably never has that signification in Hebrew. There is nothing gained by separating this clause from the words *My lips shall praise thee. Praise, commend, glory* or *triumph*, Ecc. viii. 15; 1 Chron. xvi. 35; Ps. cvi. 47.

4. *Thus will I bless thee while I live. Bless*, as in Ps. v. 12; xvi. 7. It is the word of benediction. *Thus* refers to the manner of exalting God, which he had previously stated. The clause contains a vow that while life lasted he would publish the honor of God as he had been doing. *I will lift up my hands in thy name.* Mant: "The practice of lifting up the hands in prayer towards heaven, the supposed residence of the object to which prayer is addressed, was anciently used, both by believers, as appears from various passages of the Old Testament, and by the heathen, agreeably to numerous instances in the classical writers." This is true not only of prayer

regarded as supplication, but of any act of religious worship, adoration or praise, Ps. cxxxiv. 2. In this place to lift up hands is to *praise* and *bless* and *extol* God.

5. *My soul shall be satisfied as* with *marrow and fatness; and my mouth shall praise thee with joyful lips.* It is an expression of hope of better days and of a purpose to give to God the praise of a favorable change. Scott: "The Psalmist waited for the pleasure of communion with God, with more ardent desire than any epicure ever anticipated the enjoyment of sensual pleasure." The clause points to a *luxurious banquet,* here used for a large measure of all the blessings now wanted by David, but which he hoped to obtain. All this David says, not because he sees clearly how it is to be brought about, but because he trusts in the living God, however dark present appearances.

6. *When I remember thee upon my bed* and *meditate on thee in the* night *watches.* Chaldee: If I shall remember thee upon my bed, in the watches I will meditate in thy word; Arabic: I remembered thee upon my bed, and in the early morning thou art the subject of my thought; Calvin: I shall surely remember thee upon my couch, I will meditate upon thee in the night watches; Alexander: When I remember thee upon my bed, in the night watches I will meditate upon thee. Perhaps the reader will not err in preferring the common version. In the time of David the Hebrews divided the night into three watches of equal length. After the subjugation of the Jews by the Romans they adopted the division of four watches of equal length. *Meditate,* see on Ps. i. 2.

7. *Because thou hast been my help, therefore in the shadow of thy wings will I rejoice. Help,* as in Ps. xxvii. 9; xxxv. 2; in the plural once rendered *helpers.* If anything could win the confidence of an ingenuous soul to God, it would be such a history and experience as David had in his eventful life, full of perils and deliverances. They led him to rest in God. On the figure of the last clause see on Ps. xvii. 8; xxxvi. 7; lvii. 1; lxi. 4. This rest in God was not reluctant or despondent. It made him *shout for joy* as the verb is rendered in Ps. v. 11.

8. *My soul followeth hard after thee.* The verb is in the past tense, but expresses what had long been and still was the habit of David's heart; commonly rendered cleaveth, or sticketh, Gen. ii. 24; xxxiv. 3; Josh. xxiii. 8; Ps. cxix. 31. Hengstenberg: "Cleaves to him, like a bur to a coat;" Clarke: "My soul cleaves, or is glued after thee;" Waterland: "My soul hath kept close—hath adhered to thee." The common version is good. It is the same in several other places, as 1 Sam. xiv. 22; 2 Sam. i. 6; 1 Chron. x. 2. It expresses the exceeding eagerness and intentness of David after a close walk with God. But he should not have had any mercy left, nor should he have been alive but for the good hand of God upon him: *Thy right hand upholdeth me. Right,* equivalent to *strong* and perhaps *friendly.* In reviewing his history, yea, in looking at his present circumstances David felt that God alone, *stayed, held up,* or *maintained* him, as the verb is rendered in Ps. xvi. 5; xvii. 5.

9. *But those* that *seek my soul, to destroy* it, *shall go into the lower parts of the earth.* The war on David both by Saul and by his own rebellious son was fierce, cruel, deadly. His foes cared not what should become of him, if they could but be rid of him. But they brought on themselves the ruin which they sought for him. Alexander with confidence renders the first clause: And they to (their) ruin are seeking my soul, and in proof refers to Ps. xxxv. 8. *Lower parts of the earth,* the *pit,* the *grave* are always thought of as down *'under ground.'* The prediction is that the earth should soon cover them. Some think there is a reference to the earth opening and swallowing them alive as it did Korah and his company, Num. xvi. 31–34. But David's enemies did not so perish, as we know from history. Indeed the very next verse tells the manner of their death, and their want of burial.

10. *They shall fall by the sword: they shall be a portion for foxes.* How Absalom

and his followers perished is recorded in 2 Sam. xviii. 16–17. None of them seem to have had burial. Even Absalom himself was thrown into a pit, and a great heap of stones was laid upon him. *Foxes*, in our version always so rendered, though Hengstenberg renders it *jackals*.

11. *But the king shall rejoice in God.* In the fall of Absalom the king, his father, had deep sorrow, 2 Sam. xviii. 33; xix. 1–7. But in God he could rejoice and be glad. That lesson was deeply impressed upon him by the awful judgments of God on his foes. Nor should the king alone rejoice in God. *Every one that sweareth by him shall glory.* By him, *i. e.*, by the king, see Gen. xlii. 15; 2 Sam. xv. 21. Indeed some kind of oath seems to have been taken in regard to persons of less consideration than a king, 1 Sam. i. 26; xx. 3. Or, the particle may be rendered *to* and not *by*, and then the meaning is that every one that sweareth allegiance *to* him should glory. But others think that the swearing is by *God*, and that here as in other places solemn swearing is put by synecdoche for the whole of worship, see Isa. xix. 18; xlv. 23; lxv. 16; Rom. xiv. 11. The prediction is that such should in the end *glory*, or *boast*, or *praise*. *But the mouth of them that speak lies shall be stopped*, *i. e.*, they shall not in the end *glory*, or *boast*, or *praise*. Their falsehoods shall at last cover them with confusion. Every mouth shall be stopped, and all the world shall become guilty before God. Of the unprofitable servant it is said, "And he was speechless." For an example of the confusion and humiliation of a slanderer and reviler even in this life, see 2 Sam. xix. 19, 20.

DOCTRINAL AND PRACTICAL REMARKS.

1. It is no new thing for a good man to be driven to the wilderness, and deprived of the comfort of the society of God's people and the enjoyment of God's ordinances. It so happened to David, and to many of the best men that ever lived, Heb. xi. 37, 38. Some think prophecy teaches that God's saints shall yet be sorely persecuted.

2. We should always approach God, not only as God, glorious and almighty, but as our God, v. 1. He keepeth covenant. Arnd: "Just as the magnet has lost all its power when it does not quickly turn to the north, so faith has lost all its power and is dead, when it does not without delay turn to God, and say, O my beloved God;" Tholuck: "The power of prayer consists in the knowledge that God is *our* God;" Cobbin: "There is nothing in this world to satisfy the desires of a heavenly-minded man." Even ordinances, though often the means of refreshment, are power-less without God's own gracious presence.

3. This is a reason why the saints of all ages have so uniformly found it good to give their *earliest* thoughts to sacred things, v. 1. Was there ever a truly devout man, whose devotions uniformly began not till hours after he had been awake? Horne: "The Christian dedicates to God 'the sweet hour of prime;' he opens the eyes of his understanding, together with those of his body, and awakes each morning to righteousness."

4. While resolutions made in reliance on human strength yield to temptation, yet it is well for us to strengthen ourselves by a good purpose. *Early will I seek thee*, v. 1. It is a great thing fully to have made up our minds. To many a temptation it is a fit answer: *I have said I will*, or *I have said I will not*, Ps. xxvii. 8; xxx. 1.

5. The preciousness of access to God and of a covenant relation to him is sure to be sensibly felt by the real child of God in times of distress and deprivation, v. 1. Commonly the greater the trial, the more eagerly does the pious mind turn to Jehovah and rely upon him. To offer to satisfy such a soul with the things of time is to offer ashes to one dying of thirst. "Gracious souls look down upon the world with a holy disdain, and look up to God with a holy desire."

6. A great benefit of religious instruction is found in the *impression* received from it, and a great blessing connected with God's spiritual worship is found in the pleasant memories it allows us to carry through life, v. 2. Calvin: "It is noticeable of ignorant and superstitious persons, that they seem full of zeal and fervor so long as they come in contact with the ceremonies of religion, while their seriousness evaporates immediately upon these being withdrawn. David, on the contrary, when these were removed, continued to retain them in his recollection, and rise, through their assistance, to fervent aspirations to God."

7. If men are surprised at the conduct of consistent Christians, their wonder would cease if they saw things with the same eyes as God's people do, v. 2. The saints have some just *sight* of eternal things. They have *seen* God's power and glory.

8. God's people give up much, but they gain more. Sometimes they yield up life itself, and get eternal life. Even here the Lord satisfies them as with marrow and fatness, vv. 3, 5. Tholuck: "Life is valueless without the divine mercy." There is not an exercise of the renewed soul, that does not promote the sum of its happiness; and there is not a want of a penitent soul that is not met in the Gospel and promises of God.

9. That these things are so is established by universal Christian experience and by the unanimous suffrages of God's children. Why then, O why will not sinners turn from transgression, secure a crown of life and be forever saved?

10. Whatever be our circumstances let us not forget that our duty continually calls us to bless and praise the Lord with joyful lips, vv. 3, 4, 5.

11. Genuine devotion is something that affects the heart. It has in it the fire of love. It moves the affections, v. 5. Scott: "Can any candid man read this Psalm, and then speak of true devotion as merely *intellectual*, a *dispassionate* exercise of the understanding, without any warm emotions or affections of the heart? Weighed in the balance of such phlegmatic Christians, the man after God's own heart must be numbered among enthusiasts; for, though his devotion was most rational, it certainly was most fervent and enraptured; and in fact the more rational on that very account."

12. Such is the nature of true religion and the power of divine grace, that it gets good out of all evil, and turns even a sleepless night to some valuable account, v. 6. Blessed is the man, who has learned the art of not wasting precious hours in the night-watches, although he may be denied the repose, which his weary nature demands!

13. Some men sadly err by living on from month to month in barrenness and darkness relying entirely on exercises and experiences of former days; but those also err, who in the day of their trial never recur to what God has done for them in former straits, v. 7. We should often call to mind the years of the right hand of the Most High, when the candle of the Lord shone upon us. This will cheer us, 'when we see the wicked wallowing and rioting in the abundance of the things of this world, while we ourselves are left to pine under the want of them.'

14. In *following hard after God*, our great aim should be to be intent upon knowing him, serving and pleasing him, being accepted of him, being made like unto him, longing for his fellowship and the light of his countenance, and seeking to be forever with him, v. 8.

15. There is no hope that any man will be able to behave wisely, to keep his good resolutions, or even to seek salvation, except as he is inclined and strengthened thereunto by God, *who upholdeth him*, v. 8. The best of us is as a rag. But with help from on high we can do wonders, Heb. xi. 33–38. Arnd: "God holds heaven and earth with his hand, he will therefore be able both to hold up and to bear such a little atom of dust as thou art."

16. Though we may not have the gift of prophecy respecting the end of our adver-

saries, as David had of his, yet we may know as assuredly as did he or any prophet, that wicked and relentless haters and persecutors of God's people shall certainly come to an end no less dreadful than that, which overtook the miserable men that sought to destroy David, v. 9. Horne: "Their habitation must be in the 'pit;' their punishment, the flaming 'sword' of almighty vengeance; and their companions, those crafty and malicious ones, who, having contributed to seduce, will help to torment them."

17. If outwardly and to all human appearance the end of one of God's people should resemble that of David's foes, and he should fall by the sword, and his bones be scattered on the earth's surface, as in v. 10; yet there is this for their joy that they sleep in Jesus, that their dust is precious in his eyes, and that their Redeemer lives, and will bring them with him in glory.

18. The greatest men are best employed in gladly adoring and serving God, v. 11. The king can do nothing beyond that in dignity and nobleness.

19. But the enjoyments of religion, even the highest of them are not reserved for crowned heads. They are also for every true worshipper. So that the poor pious peasant, artisan, exile, beggar or prisoner shall at last *glory* as much as any other, v. 11. "Christ's second coming will be the everlasting triumph of all his faithful friends and followers, who may now therefore triumph in the believing hopes of it."

20. The overthrow of the wicked will at last be with dreadful confusion, v. 11.

21. How blessed is the believer. At home, abroad, surrounded by friends, menaced by foes, in his own abode, in exile, he has peace with God through our Lord Jesus Christ; "his soul hangeth upon him, as its chief, its only good. With God he sleeps, and with God he awakes, with God he lives, and with God he hopes to die." He will soon be in glory singing the song of Moses and the Lamb.

PSALM LXIV.

To the chief Musician, A Psalm of David.

1 Hear my voice, O God, in my prayer: preserve my life from fear of the enemy.

2 Hide me from the secret counsel of the wicked; from the insurrection of the workers of iniquity:

3 Who whet their tongue like a sword, *and* bend *their bows to shoot* their arrows, *even* bitter words:

4 That they may shoot in secret at the perfect: suddenly do they shoot at him, and fear not.

5 They encourage themselves *in* an evil matter: they commune of laying snares privily; they say, Who shall see them?

6 They search out iniquities; they accomplish a diligent search: both the inward *thought* of every one *of them,* and the heart, *is* deep.

7 But God shall shoot at them *with* an arrow; suddenly shall they be wounded.

8 So they shall make their own tongue to fall upon themselves: all that see them shall flee away.

9 And all men shall fear, and shall declare the work of God; for they shall wisely consider of his doing.

10 The righteous shall be glad in the LORD, and shall trust in him; and all the upright in heart shall glory.

ON the title see on titles of Psalms iii. iv. xi. That David wrote this Psalm is admitted by all the ancient versions, by Calvin, Diodati, Ainsworth, Patrick, Pool Dimock, Gill, Dodd, Henry, Scott, Edwards, Jebb, Morison, Hengstenberg, Tholuck, Alexander. Calmet, followed by Clarke, however, thinks it a complaint of tne captives of Babylon. We cannot assign to it a historic occasion, although one or two of the ancient versions attempt to do so. The amount of *evil speaking* noticed in it points to a time of dreadful tumult. There is nothing gained, but something lost, by seeking special occasions for Psalms that describe David's conflicts during a considerable part of his life. Scott dates the Psalm B. C. 1060; Clarke, about B. C. 568. The names of the Almighty in this Psalm are *Elohim God* and *Jehovah* LORD; on which see on Ps. iii. 2; i. 2.

1. *Hear my voice, O God, in my prayer. Hear*, as in Ps. iv. 1; xvii. 1; lxi. 1. *Prayer*, elsewhere rendered *complaint, meditation, communication*. See on Ps. lv. 2, where it is *complaint*. Vulgate: Hear, O God, my prayer, when I entreat; Green: Hear my prayer, O God, when I pour out my complaint; Horsley: Hear my voice, O God, in my secret prayer. But there is no evidence that the word signifies private, as distinct from public prayer. This Psalm was directed to the leader of the prayers which were set to music. There is an intimate connection between *prayer* and meditation when rightly performed. *Preserve my life from fear of the enemy. Preserve*, as in Ps. xii. 7; xxv. 21; lxi. 7; more frequently *keep*; in the future, *wilt keep*. This form expresses confidence that the prayer would be answered. *Fear* is here used either for the tormenting passion of fear, or for the cause of fear as in Ps. liii. 5, *i. e.*, Preserve me from cowardice and unmanly behaviour and my life from danger, or from that which might reasonably create alarm. His life was now in peril.

2. *Hide me from the secret counsel of the wicked. Secret counsel*, in the Hebrew one word; in Ps. xxv. 14, *secret*; in Ps. lv. 14, *counsel. From the insurrection of the workers of iniquity. Insurrection*, an *assembling, a multitude, a crowd, a tumultuous body of men*. See on the cognate verb in Ps. ii. 1, rendered *rage*, and on the word rendered *company* in Ps. lv. 14. *Workers of iniquity*, see on Ps. v. 5; and compare Ps. vi. 8; lix. 2. The two clauses of the verse describe the two kinds of hostility shown to David, *plotting* and *violent rage of wicked men*. Clarke: "*Workers of iniquity* are those who make *sin* their *labor*, their daily employment. It was their *occupation* and *trade*." The verb is in the future *wilt hide*, thus expressing hope that the *complaint* would be heard, the *prayer* answered.

3. *Who whet their tongue like a sword*. He who has been subjected to the taunts, revilings, slanders and lying machinations of a large number of men will see the force of this terrible clause. Comparing words to swords is frequent in the Psalms, Ps. lv. 21; lvii. 4; lix. 7. When words are made as sharp as possible by wit and malice, they have a frightful keenness of penetration. *Whet*, in the Hebrew *whetted*, or *have whetted*, implying that they have done it for some time, and are doing it still. And *bend* their bows to shoot *their arrows*, even *bitter words*. The common version supplies a great deal. The verb in Hebrew is *have bent*. This is not the only case where we have *bending arrows* in the Hebrew for *bending bows to shoot arrows;* see Ps. lviii. 7. On the mode of bending the [cross] bow, see on Ps. vii. 12. Literally it would be *have trodden their arrows, bitter words*. In Hebrew the last noun is singular, *word, speech*. The Chaldee has it, They have smeared their arrows with a grievous and deadly poison. And no poison rankles like grievous words. The same word here translated *bitter* is rendered *bitterness* in 1 Sam. xv. 32; 2 Sam. ii. 26; and *bitter* in Pr. v. 4; Ecc. vii. 26.

4. *That they may shoot in secret at the perfect*. The more mischief a slanderer does and the more stealthily he does it, the more does he rejoice in the evil he has wrought. *Perfect*, in the third person singular,—meaning David. On *perfect* see on Ps. xxxvii. 37. It designates a man of *integrity, simplicity, sincerity*, as the corresponding noun is rendered. The Syriac and Hengstenberg render it *innocent;* Edwards, *upright*. In the great troubles with Saul, David was not in the least to be blamed. Saul him-

self publicly so confessed. 1 Sam. xxvi. 21–25. The less ground of hatred they had, the higher their envy rose. *Suddenly do they shoot at him, and fear not.* Hengstenberg: "Suddenly" is "while he is thinking there is no harm." The same word occurs in v. 7. It has uniformly the same signification. Both the verbs are in the future, *will shoot* and *will not fear. Fear not, i. e.,* fear not God, fear not anything that wise and good men fear.

5. *They encourage themselves* in *an evil matter.* The verb is in the future, *encourage,* elsewhere *strengthen, make strong,* still better here *harden,* as the same verb is oftentimes rendered in reference to Pharaoh, Ex. iv. 21; ix. 12. So also in Josh. xi. 20. To be of good courage in wickedness must harden the heart. Indeed boldness in wrong-doing can only be acquired by a dreadful process of deadening the sensibilities. *They commune of laying snares privily,* or of *hiding snares. Commune, tell, declare, speak,* or *show forth,* what snares they have hid, are now hiding, or intend to hide. See on Ps. ii. 7; ix. 1; xliv. 1. The verb *commune* is in the future, showing an expected continuance of the same evil course. *They say, Who shall see them?* *Them* may refer either to the *snares,* or to these persons spreading them. The question either declares their belief in the consummate artifices they were employing, or it expresses their practical atheism in denying that even Jehovah took account of their nefarious schemes. The latter is probably the right view; if so, the clause is parallel to Ps. x. 11; xii. 4; lxxiii. 11; Job xxii. 13.

6. *They search out iniquities,* or *wickednesses,* or *unrighteousness, i. e.,* methods of accomplishing their wicked purposes. And they rack their brain to find out something more nefarious and fatal than ever, and so *They accomplish a diligent search.* There is much diversity in rendering this clause. Our version is not literal, but it fairly gives the sense. *Both the inward* thought *of every one* of them, *and the heart is deep. Deep,* the word is used in the sense of profound, or unsearchable as in Job xi. 8; xii. 22; Pr. xx. 5; it is also used in a bad sense, as dangerous, entangling, ruinous, Pr. xxii. 14; xxiii. 27; Eze. xxiii. 32. Here it may include both ideas, *inscrutable,* and *ruinous. Inward thought,* in Ps. v. 9, *inward part;* in Ps. cix. 18, *bowels;* in Ps. xlix. 11, *inward thought;* in Ps. li. 10, *within me.*

7. *But God shall shoot at them,* with *an arrow; suddenly shall they be wounded.* The structure, the leading ideas and to some extent the very words are evidently borrowed from vv. 3, 4, especially from v. 4. Alexander: "By an abrupt but beautiful transition he describes the tables as completely turned upon the enemy." Thinking to destroy others, they are destroyed themselves. *Suddenly shooting an arrow* at the upright man, God *suddenly shoots an arrow* at them; and the wound is incurable. Hengstenberg's rendering of the verse is very forcible: There God shoots at them with a sudden arrow; there are THEIR wounds.

8. *So shall they make their own tongue to fall upon themselves.* Calvin: "The poison concocted in their secret counsels, and which they revealed with their tongues would prove to have a deadly effect upon themselves." No man can injure others as much by his wicked speeches as he injures himself, because by sin he provokes God to fight against him, and *his* resources are infinite. However much foresight the wicked may have, it is all borrowed, and God will never lend them enough to subvert his designs, nor to bring real or incurable evil on one of his people. Parallel passages are found in Ps. vii. 14–16; ix. 16; x. 2; xxxv. 8; xciv. 23; cxli. 10. This shall be so marvellously done that, *All that see them shall flee away.* God's judgments are often frightful even to spectators. It was so when he made the violence and slanders and wickedness of Saul to return on his own pate: "And when the men of Israel that were on the other side of the valley, and they that were on the other side Jordan saw that the men of Israel fled, and that Saul and his sons

were dead, they forsook the cities and fled : and the Philistines came and dwelt in them." 1 Sam. xxxi. 7 ; 1 Chron. x. 7. Parallel passages are found in Num. xvi. 34 ; Ps. xl. 3 ; liii. 5. When God chooses, he can easily make the wicked a terror to themselves and to all their friends.

9 *And all men shall fear, and shall declare the work of God,* i. e., all classes of men, cotemporary or in later times, who see or hear of these judgments, which are as instructive to us as to the subjects of Saul and of David, shall be inspired with a wholesome dread of offending the divine majesty, and shall tell of the 'admirable work of divine power, and wisdom, and faithfulness,' and justice by which the wicked are put down and the righteous exalted, Saul and his false courtiers slain and David enthroned. This wonderful history instructs millions of men every week : *For they shall wisely consider of his doing.* Such amazing acts of providence are so clearly the *doing* of God and are withal so instructive that they can hardly fail to impress their lessons on men so as to bring them to *consideration,* and to *wisdom.*

10. *The righteous shall be glad in the* LORD. They shall see that these are his doings, that they are worthy of him, and so they *are glad,* or *rejoice* in Jehovah, in his existence, perfections, government, word and ordinances. Or, the word *righteous* being in the singular may mean the same as *perfect* in v. 4, and so this may refer to David. The more extended is perhaps the better view, the change of number being common. *And shall trust in him. Trust,* as in Ps. vii. 1 ; lvii. 1, always rendered *trust,* or *put trust. And all the upright in heart shall glory,* or *make their boast.* The same form of the same verb is found in Ps. xxxiv. 2 ; lii. 1. Compare Ps. lxiii. 10.

DOCTRINAL AND PRACTICAL REMARKS.

1. In all our troubles, whether beset by 'the unceasing and infinite malice of the devil, the perfidy of men, or the ingratitude of the world,' it is best to carry our cause immediately to God in prayer, v. 1.

2. When men are so outrageous and behave so ill as to fill us with fear, we may mention their very depravity as a plea before God ; for, if we are right, 'the more cruel and unjust the conduct of our enemies may be, we have proportionally the better ground to believe that God will interpose in our behalf.' Horne : " A victory gained by the fear of God over the fear of man is a necessary step, and a happy prelude, to a full and final triumph over every enemy of our salvation."

3. David had often virtually offered the same petitions contained here, but on a renewal of his afflictions, he has recourse to the same prayers, but in varied forms of expression.

4. Good men may be in danger, the best of men in the greatest danger, so as to fill them with fear, v. 1. David had a united kingdom against him. It is a wonder that he escaped.

5. Yet God can preserve us in the midst of the direst hazards. Neither in purpose nor in resources is God ever wanting to his faithful children. "The danger cannot be so great, that in it help may not be had from God."

6. No man knows what plots may now be laid against his person, or name, or life, and it is not necessary that he should, for his defence is not in himself but in another, v. 2. 'God can so overrule and outwit the devices of our enemies,' that they shall either adopt foolish measures, or he will defeat their wise counsels. He can do either. He has often done both.

7. "Children that are corrupters" is one of the odious titles earned by the wicked. They band and *counsel* together in *secret,* and then openly *rise up* against men better than themselves, v. 2. Sinners egg each other on in their wicked courses. It has always been so.

8. If we must have foes, it is better they should be strangers than kindred, and enemies of God than doers of his will, v. 2.

9. It is better to have all manner of evil spoken against us falsely than truly; yea. it is better to be reproached for conscientious adherence to duty than to be praised for dereliction of duty. Of all the things laid to David's charge he was innocent, and so the charges did him no real damage, although maliciously aimed at his destruction, v. 3.

10. If David, the modest, humble man, who in difficult circumstances acted so wisely, and was withal the man after God's own heart, was permitted to be so traduced that probably no mere man was ever more vilified than he, vv. 3, 4, surely we, who fall so far short of his attainments in everything good ought not to be surprised if we suffer sadly in the same way. Yea, against the spotless Son of God the tongues of men were more envenomed than ever against his type and progenitor, David. "Would to God it had never been since employed against him and his disciples, or by his disciples against each other."

11. The ingenuity of man has been wonderfully tasked and exercised in two things, inventing destructive weapons of war, and devising various methods of ruining men by wicked words. The list of the former is found in military writings. But the various forms of evil speaking can hardly be catalogued. Evil speakers have arrows, sharp, barbed, dipped in poison. They have 'swords, flaming swords, two-edged swords, drawn swords, drawn in anger, with which they cut, and wound, and kill the good name of their neighbor.' Sins of the tongue are commonly very cruel. When slander is secret, as it commonly is, you cannot defend yourself from its assaults. Its canons are infernal. One of them is, If a lie will do better than the truth, tell a lie. Another is, Heap on reproach; some of it will stick.

12. The reason why wicked men are so bad is that they do not fear what they ought to fear, and especially they do not fear God, v. 4.

13. Let every one beware of hardening his heart in sin. This he may do by refusing to think; by indulging in sin after pondering the wickedness he is about to perpetrate; but chiefly by *encouraging* himself in the way of transgressors, saying, 'All will be well,' when God says the contrary, v. 5.

14. Men ought to suspect their own motives, and the righteousness of their cause, when they find themselves about to employ the arts of chicanery and *commune of laying snares privily*, v. 5. Tortuousness and indirection have a consanguinity with meanness and crime. Horne: "Sin doth not often appear abroad without a veil; and the more atrocious the sin, the more specious the pretence which is to cover it. Envy and malice crucified the Son of God; but, during the course of the proceedings against him you hear only of zeal for the law, and loyalty to Cæsar."

15. The denial of providence is often virtually made; and in its effects on the heart is every way as unhappy as the denial of a God, v. 5. If God does not *see* or hear, how can he help or save? or who will trust him?

16. Why will the wicked dig into hell? Why will they torture their brain for that which, without repentance, will damn them forever? v. 6. Henry: "Half the pains that many take to damn their souls would serve to save them."

17. Because sinners are in their plots and combinations too *deep* and inscrutable for us, therefore we must hand them over to God, that he may put a hook in their nose, restrain them from doing us harm, and guide their actions so as to bring glory to his name. The poor man must fall by the hand of his enemy unless there be higher than the highest of mortals.

18. Who ever saw a blind man that refused to be led to a place of safety when he was told that frightened horses were galloping towards him, or that a terrible storm

was rising? Yet sinners are blinder and are utterly perverse. Every good man on earth sees the bow of the Almighty made ready and the arrow about to pierce the rash and heaven-daring sinner, and he gives him warning, but, without divine grace, it is all in vain.

19. The retribution that will overtake the incorrigibly wicked will be condign, terrible, sudden and richly deserved, vv. 7, 8. "Where desperate malice is seen, there sudden mischief may be foreseen." Calvin: "God is ever watching, as it were, the opportunity of converting the stratagems of the wicked into means just as completely effective of their destruction, as if they had intentionally employed them for that end." O why will not sinners repent and live?

20. It was not merely of old that wicked men fled from their companions who had fallen under God's judgments. I have seen more than one wicked man forsaken by his boon companions when the hand of God touched him, and made him feel the beginnings of dire retribution.

21. It is well when the divine judgments are abroad in the earth, if men learn righteousness, and *fear*, and *declare the work of God*, v. 9.

22. If men would think aright, it is impossible they should continue as foolish as they are. Oh that they would *wisely consider*, v. 9. Compare Deut. xxxii. 29.

23. Because the righteous rejoice *in the* LORD, their joy shall continue forever, v. 10. He is the fountain of living waters. He is a well-spring of salvation to all who look to him.

24. Christian *joy* and *trust* go well together, v. 10. One strengthens the other. Joy without trust would soon pass away for want of vigor and solidity. Trust without joy would be a sullen exercise. But the two united can carry the soul through midnight darkness without tremor.

25. Tholuck: "God does not exercise his judgments for the gratification of our passions or revenge, but with the sublime and holy design to instruct us that his hand pierces the doings of man, and that the works of men, even of the ungodly, must serve him as instruments for the accomplishment of his own purposes; that the righteous may ever rejoice in being under the jurisdiction of such a Lord; and lastly, that the community of believers should render to him the praises which he is worthy to receive. We must, therefore, be on our guard, lest in rejoicing at the downfall of the ungodly by the hand of God, we dim the sacred flame by unholy feelings," vv. 9, 10. Compare Pr. xxiv. 17, 18.

26. What an unspeakable blessing it is to be allowed to lead a quiet and peaceable life in all godliness and honesty, free from the tempests which have tossed the barks of so many good men, of whom David was but a sample. But let us not forget that a calm which puts us to sleep may be more fatal than a storm which keeps us wide awake. David was in more danger when he was attracted by the beauty of Bathsheba, than when Saul was pursuing him in the wilderness.

27. It seems impossible for the pious mind to dwell long on this Psalm without a growing impression that there is in it a reference to Christ and his persecutors. In remarking on vv. 7–10, Morison says: "In the fearful retribution here described, how much is there to remind us of the fate of that nation who filled up the measure of their iniquity by crucifying the Lord of Glory."

PSALM LXV.

To the chief Musician, A Psalm *and* Song of David.

1 Praise waiteth for thee, O God, in Zion: and unto thee shall the vow be performed.

2 O thou that hearest prayer, unto thee shall all flesh come.

3 Iniquities prevail against me: *as for* our transgressions, thou shalt purge them away.

4 Blessed *is the man whom* thou choosest, and causest to approach *unto thee, that* he may dwell in thy courts: we shall be satisfied with the goodness of thy house, *even* of thy holy temple.

5 *By* terrible things in righteousness wilt thou answer us, O God of our salvation; *who art the* confidence of all the ends of the earth, and of them that are afar off *upon* the sea:

6 Which by his strength setteth fast the mountains; *being* girded with power:

7 Which stilleth the noise of the seas, the noise of their waves, and the tumult of the people.

8 They also that dwell in the uttermost parts are afraid at thy tokens: thou makest the outgoings of the morning and evening to rejoice.

9 Thou visitest the earth, and waterest it: thou greatly enrichest it with the river of God, *which* is full of water: thou preparest them corn, when thou hast so provided for it.

10 Thou waterest the ridges thereof abundantly, thou settlest the furrows thereof: thou makest it soft with showers, thou blessest the springing thereof.

11 Thou crownest the year with thy goodness; and thy paths drop fatness.

12 They drop *upon* the pastures of the wilderness: and the little hills rejoice on every side.

13 The pastures are clothed with flocks; the valleys also are covered over with corn; they shout for joy, they also sing.

ON the title see on titles of Psalms iii. iv. xxx. Though a few have given it a later authorship yet the title, Chàldee, Syriac, Arabic, Septuagint, Ethiopic and the great mass of modern interpreters ascribe it to David. Without cause the Vulgate ascribes it to Jeremiah and Ezekiel. To these the Complutensian adds Haggai. The Doway has a note admitting that the Hebrew does not give Jeremiah and Ezekiel, but citing the authority of the Septuagint. Yet Clarke says it is not in the "best copies of the Septuagint." Nor is it in any copy of the Septuagint now at hand. Those who maintain for it a historic occasion are of many minds. The Syriac says it was composed on the removal of the ark to Zion. The Arabic refers it to the transmigration of the people to Babylon. Mudge thinks it was "composed by a person just come to Jerusalem from some very distant parts, where, upon his prayers and vows, he had been signally delivered from the fury of the sea, and uproar of the natives; which leads him into a general acknowledgment of the divine Providence, which extended itself to the end of the earth." Some make it a thanksgiving for rain after drought and refer to 2 Sam. xxi. Some think it was composed for the feast of tabernacles, and some for the passover, or for spring. It was evidently composed when some mercy had awakened the spirit of gratitude, and the mind was led to take an extended view of God's goodness. This is often the case. Luther: "It is the custom of the prophets, when they speak of the mercies and gifts of God of one kind, to speak also of others, especially of his grace." Morison: "I cannot help thinking that the Psalm, in addition to its primary reference, contains in it some distant prophetic allusion to the blessings of redemption, the conversion of the Gentiles, and the glory and felicity of the Gospel church." Scott dates it B. C. 1017; Clarke, about B. C. 520. On *Elohim God,* the only name of the Most High in it, see on Ps. iii. 2.

1. *Praise waiteth for thee, O God, in Zion.* *Waiteth,* as in Ps. lxii. 1. Chaldee: Before thee praise is reputed as silence. The other ancient versions: Praise becomes thee, befits thee, is agreeable to thee. Hammond thinks the exact sense is: To thee belong silence and praise. Boothroyd: "Praise waiteth as a servant, whose duty it is

to do what thou commandest." Others also personify *praise*, and think that *waiting* points to servants watching in silence the signs of their master's will. If we understand it without a personification, the meaning is that at all times in God's church there is found matter of praise and a heart for the work. This praise should not be babbling, but reverential, not tumultuous but chastened. The chief place of praise in Judea was Zion; but now it is the church of God, wherever found. Luther: "Whoever now believes in Christ, and acknowledges him, gives thanks to the true God, in the true Zion." *And unto thee shall the vow be performed.* The Arabic and Vulgate, without cause, add to this clause the words, *in Jerusalem.* On the *vow* see on Ps. xxii. 25; l. 14; lvi. 12; lxi. 5, 8. As long as the world shall stand there will be constantly occurring new causes of gratitude, best expressed in acts of solemn worship.

2. *O thou that hearest prayer, unto thee shall all flesh come.* Surely this points to the calling of the Gentiles, for the Jewish people are never in Scripture once called *all flesh.* To *hear* prayer is to *answer* it. *Prayer*, as in Ps. iv. 1 and title of Ps. xvii. That which shall surely cause all flesh to go to God will be a sense of want and of dependence, awakened by the power of God's word and Spirit.

3. *Iniquities prevail against me.* The renderings and interpretations are chiefly of two classes. The ancient versions and many moderns have *words of iniquities*, or *iniquitous actions*, meaning those of other people. Others understand his own iniquities. This is probably correct. The words do not seem to refer to indwelling corruption, but to the accusing power of sin, provoking the anger of God. This agrees with the next clause. Diodati: "We were overcome with evils and calamities, which we had drawn upon ourselves by reason of our sins." Pool: "*Iniquities prevail against me; i. e.*, they are a burden too heavy for me, as he complains, Ps. xxxviii. 4. They are so many and great, that for them thou mightest justly reject my prayers, and destroy my person." The clause is parallel to Isa. lix. 2. But David is not left in despair: As for *our transgressions, thou shalt purge them away. Purge, forgive, cleanse, put off*, but far the most frequently *make atonement*, or *make reconciliation*, literally cover; see Ps. lxxviii. 38; Jer. xviii. 23; Num. xxxv. 33; Isa. xlvii. 11. In the last four books of Moses it is more than fifty times rendered *make* or *made atonement.* Bishop Hall: "O God, our iniquities stand in the way of thy mercies, and prevail strongly against all the endeavors of my reformation: but, do thou both mercifully forgive, and powerfully remedy our offences."

4. *Blessed* is the man, whom *thou choosest, and causest to approach* unto thee, that *he may dwell in thy courts.* Very elliptical, but the ellipsis in each case easily supplied. *Blessed*, as in Ps. i. 1; xxxii. 1, *happy*, literally, O the blessednesses of the man. *Choosest*, in the future *wilt choose*, quite uniformly rendered; see Deut. iv. 37; xii. 5, 11, 14, 18, 21, 26; Ps. xxv. 12; xlvii. 4. *Causest to approach*, in the future, *shalt bring near. Dwell*, very uniformly rendered, see on Ps. xv. 1. *Courts*, as in Ps. lxxxiv. 2, 10. *We shall be satisfied with the goodness of thy house, even of thy holy temple. Satisfied, filled, satiated*, see on Ps. xvii. 15. Compare Ps. lxiii. 5. *Goodness*, also rendered *pleasure, good*, see on Ps. iv. 6; xiv. 1; xvi. 2. *Temple*, a name given to the tabernacle as well as to the more solid structure built by Solomon, Ps. v. 7; xviii. 6; xxvii. 4. The transition from *he* to *we* is quite in accordance with Hebrew usage. It is a jejune interpretation of this passage, that supposes it to refer merely to the outward participation of divine worship. We must include also the blessings which are apprehended by faith.

5. By *terrible things in righteousness wilt thou answer us.* Calvin, Ainsworth, Piscator, Fabritius, Amesius, Hengstenberg and Alexander do not supply *by*, but read, *terrible things.* Understanding the verse according to the sense thus conveyed, we see how God answered the prayers of his friends in the *terrible things* brought on

the Egyptians, the Canaanites, the Philistines, the Syrians, the Babylonians, and on the Jews and the Gentiles who resisted early Christianity. God often defends his chosen people by *terribly* punishing their foes. This is the best interpretation, the prevailing signification of the participle being *terrible, fearful, dreadful,* and not *wonderful,* as some would render it; see Gen. xxviii. 17; Ex. xv. 11; Ps. xlv. 4; Isa. lxiv. 3; in Ps. lxiv. 4, 9, one form of the verb is rendered *fear, shall fear,* and in v. 8 of this Psalm it is rendered *are afraid.* God's judgments are terrible not only to the wicked on whom they fall, but to spectators, sinners and saints. Yet the righteous do not fear so as to despair, but they rather trust the Lord, for these terrible things are never sent but *in righteousness.* The address is to the Most High: *O God of our salvation,* who art *the confidence of all the ends of the earth, and of them that are afar off* upon *the sea.* The God *of our salvation* is God the author of our salvation. He is also a fit object of the *confidence, trust, hope* of men, however remote from Mount Zion, not only in distant parts of the holy land, but in the corners of the world, yea, upon the sea. The Chaldee renders the last clause, And of the islands of the sea which are remote from the continent. God is not only worthy of *hope* and *trust,* but he is so exclusively; and he shall yet be confided in by the most distant people. Hengstenberg: "God is called the confidence of all the ends of the earth, in reference to what he is *actually in himself,* not in reference to his being *acknowledged as such.*" Compare Isa. xlii. 4. Calvin: "It follows that the grace of God was to be extended to the Gentiles." Great is this God,

6. *Which by his strength setteth fast the mountains.* It is probable that by *mountains* here we are also to understand *kingdoms* or *empires,* Ps. xlvi. 3; Jer. li. 25. God is the Father of nations, as well as the Maker of the world, Ps. xxii. 28. The obvious reference however is primarily to the fabric of creation. The reader may have been familiar with mountain scenery from infancy. If so, he can doubtless remember many times in his life, even when very young, that he thus gained high conceptions of the power of God. Or if he never saw a great mountain, until he was adult, he can easily recall the profound impressions the sight made upon him. The imagery is therefore well chosen, as it shows the *strength* of the Creator. Being *girded with power.* *Strength* and *power,* though quite different words in Hebrew, are interchangeably rendered *strength, might, power.* Here they both refer to the almightiness of God.

7. *Which stilleth the noise of the seas, the noise of their waves.* By God's power the mountains were steadfast. The ocean also, often lashed into fury, and exhibiting amazing violence, was a continual proof of the constant superintendence and controlling providence of God. Jehovah manages it exclusively and literally. But vast agitated waters are in Scripture an emblem of nations in commotion, and so he adds that God stilleth *the tumult of the people. People,* in the plural *peoples,* or *nations.* Figures drawn from great waters are found in Ps. xlvi. 2, 3; xciii. 3, 4; Isa. xvii. 12, 13. The doctrine here taught is the same as that in Ps. lxxvi. 10.

8. *They also that dwell in the uttermost parts are afraid at thy tokens. Uttermost parts,* *i. e.,* of the earth, as is explained in v. 5, where we have the masculine of the word here found in the feminine. *Are afraid,* from the same root as the participle rendered *terrible* in v. 5. God's wonders declaring his eternal power and Godhead are everywhere—within us, above us, beneath us, around us. Some of the *tokens* he displays in blighting vegetation, in lightning, in tempest, in earthquake are enough to strike terror into the heart of the rudest savage. But the reference here is more immediately to the effect exerted on people dwelling far from the scene of national tumults, by the amazing providence of God over public commotions. If there were sufficient material for writing a history of all the effects of such an event as the destruction of Sennacherib's army on distant nations, we should all be astonished at its revela-

tions. The prophet now proceeds to state that the effect of God's dealings with the people should not be merely to inspire *terror*, but also to an equal extent gladness. *Thou makest the outgoings of the morning and evening to rejoice.* John Rogers' translation: Thou makes both the mornyng and evenying starres to prayse thee. The *outgoings of the morning* is a phrase meaning the east, the point from which the morning comes; and the outgoings of the evening, the west, where we behold the setting sun, followed by the evening. The phrase embraces the world, from the rising of the sun to the going down of the same. The extensive region thus described is of course put for the people in it. The meaning then is, Thou makest the inhabitants of the world from east to west rejoice at the amazing displays of thy power over nature and nations; see Isa. xli. 5. The prophet is celebrating God's power and goodness in "dispelling the storms of the counsels of war, slaughter and bloodshed. For war is nothing less than a horrible storm and tempest, which hurls into confusion all things divine and human." But the prophet now leaves this subject and passes to themes most pleasing to the pious husbandman.

9. *Thou visitest the earth, and waterest it.* The verbs are in the preterite. Calvin: "They denote action continually going forward, and may therefore be rendered in the present tense." Science has never revealed the half that the smile of God does to fertilize the earth. If he would but remove the curse from it, it would again be as Eden for fruitfulness, Gen. iii. 17–19. One of the ways, in which he blesses it is by *watering* it. In many countries the rains are frequent, and fall as they are needed. In others they are gathered in reservoirs and distributed by artificial rivulets over immense plateaus. In some cases the tide is with unspeakable advantage turned in on vast meadows and grain fields. In yet others, streams overflow their banks bringing down from higher regions large deposits of fertilizing mud, and soaking the earth that it does not become parched again for months. This was the case with many ancient rivers as well as the Nile, Ecc. xi. 1; Isa. xxxii. 20. In Isa. xxiii. 3, *Sihor* means Nile. *Thou greatly enrichest it* [the earth] *with the river of God, which is full of water.* So that there is an abundant supply of water for all purposes, in particular for agriculture, which is here specially noticed. For *river* the Syriac and Arabic have *rivers.* Horsley: "God is he who filleth the rivulets with water." The objection to this mode of explaining the phrase, *the river of God*, is that it demands an unwarranted change of the Hebrew text. Others by *the river of God* understand the Jordan, which ran through the holy land, and which like the Nile overflowed its banks and enriched its low grounds. But is Jordan ever once called the river of God? Others by *river of God* understand Siloah, or Shiloah, whose *waters go softly*, Isa. viii. 6, and flow "hard by the altar of God." Calvin thinks this river is held in contrast with the Nile and that there is an allusion to Deut. xi. 10–12. But is Siloah ever in Scripture called the river of God? Others suppose the *river of God* to be a *great river*, according to the Hebraism explained in Ps. xxxvi. 6. This is legitimate. But *river* in Scripture sometimes means an *abundance*, a *full supply*, as in Ps. xxxvi. 8, on which see. Anderson: "The treasures of water which descend from the clouds may, with great poetical beauty, be termed the river of God. He collects them there by the wonderful process of evaporation, and he pours them down. They are entirely in his hand, and absolutely beyond the control of man. 'The keys of the clouds,' say the Jews, 'are peculiarly kept in God's hand, as the keys of life and resurrection.'" Possibly this is the best explanation. It well agrees with Scripture teaching and known facts. See Lev. xxvi. 4; Deut. xi. 14; Job v. 10; xxxviii. 28; Joel ii. 23. Hengstenberg's rendering is: The fountain of God has plenty of water. Alexander gives yet another view: " *The river of God*, as opposed to earthly streams. However these may fail, the divine resources are exhaust-

less." *Thou preparest them corn, when thou hast so provided for it.* Calvin: "This means, that the reason of that abundance with which the earth teems, is its having been expressly formed by God in his fatherly care of the great household of mankind, to supply the wants of his children." If after *formed* he had added [and by rain prepared] the sense would have been complete.

10. *Thou waterest the ridges thereof abundantly.* *Ridges*, everywhere else rendered *furrows*. It means the uneven surfaces produced by plowing. Perhaps *furrows*, meaning the depressions in plowed ground would be the better rendering here, and *ridges*, of the corresponding word in the next clause. *Thou settlest the furrows thereof.* The rain dissolves the hard clods and smooths the uneven surfaces. *Thou makest it soft with showers.* There is no substitute for moisture in softening the earth for the growth of plants; and there is no method of diffusing moisture so good as when it drops as the rain and distils as the dew. *Thou blessest the springing thereof.* *Springing, branch, budding,* or *growth.* *Thereof*, *i. e.*, of the earth, where earth is put for the things which grow in it. Luther: "Thou art the right Master-cultivator, who cultivates the land much more and much better than the farmer does. He does nothing more to it than break up the ground, and plough, and sow, and then lets it lie. But God must be always attending to it with rain and heat, and must do everything to make it grow and prosper, while the farmer lies at home and sleeps."

11. *Thou crownest the year with thy goodness.* The translation perfectly expresses the idea of the original, although the verb is in the preterite *hast crowned.* But see on the first clause of v. 9. Luther: "In the spring, there first appear the blossoms; and then, shortly after, the strawberries and cherries; and then, ere long, plums, apples, and berries of various juice and virtue; (to say nothing about the perpetual verdure of the herbs which flourishes all the while, and is continually revived with fresh supplies of dew.) To these we are to add, the infinite variety of herbs and odors. And then, at the time of harvest, our barns are filled with wheat, rye, barley, and corn, and grain of every kind. In the autumn, our presses overflow with wine of an infinite variety of taste and fragrance, and our vats are filled to the brim. Thus the Lord fills the whole revolution of the year, and every part of it, with his overflowing and infinite goodness." *And thy paths drop fatness.* *Paths, goings,* or *ways,* Pr. v. 6, 21. Wherever God goes in mercy, there is fertility, so that a piece of hitherto barren land visited by him has the smell of a field, which the Lord hath greatly blessed. *Fatness,* always so rendered, see Ps. xxxvi. 8; lxiii. 5. It seems here specially to refer to productiveness, and so this is parallel to the first clause. This remarkable effect of God's goings is seen everywhere, even in uncultivated lands.

12. *They* [thy goings] *drop* [fatness] upon *the pastures of the wilderness.* These *pastures* were unplowed and generally broken parts of the country, to which flocks and herds were driven at certain seasons of the year for grazing. There they were herded and guarded with care. Though the hand of man had done nothing to make them fertile, yet God had greatly beautified them by a delightful freshness. *And the little hills rejoice on every side.* Literally, *The hills are girded with joy;* see margin. *Hills* abounded in the uncultivated lands, where the pastures of the wilderness were. And by God's blessing on them making them fruitful, they are said to have a girdle, not of such ornaments as men and women wore in oriental countries but, of *gladness,* or *rejoicing,* as if for a joyous dance.

13. *The pastures are clothed with flocks.* Church of England: The folds shall be full of sheep; Meibomius: The flocks clothe the mountains; Delaney: The fields have clothed themselves with cattle; Hengstenberg: The flocks are clothed with lambs. The common version is sustained wholly or substantially by Calvin, Ainsworth, Pisca-

tor, Fabritius, Venema, Amesius, Mudge, Green, Edwards, Jebb, Fry, Hammond, Tholuck and Alexander. This clause relates to the unplowed ground; the next, to cultivated land: *The valleys also are covered with corn.* *Corn,* all grains which grow in ears, and which are used for making bread. *They* [the valleys] *shout for joy.* *Shout,* a very exultant word, sometimes rendered *triumph,* or *make a joyful noise,* used to describe the joy of angels at the creation, the loud cries of Israel in battle, the joy of the pious at the removal of the ark; Josh. vi. 5; 1 Sam. iv. 5; Job xxxviii. 7; Ps. xli. 11. *They* [the valleys] *also sing.* This verb and the last are both in the future. The latter is the weaker word, but this is not the only case in Hebrew poetry where the stronger word goes before. The last *five* verses of this Psalm contain as beautiful poetry as perhaps was ever written, even by the pen of inspiration.

DOCTRINAL AND PRACTICAL REMARKS.

1. Take from God the sincere and intelligent praise, which he receives in Zion, and what has he left? v. 1. The wicked will not exalt his name. They love his gifts, but contemn the giver.

2. The praise offered to God should be reverent. It may be loud but not clamorous, v. 1. It may be with thundering hallelujahs as it is in heaven, when it is the expression of the fulness of the heart, but even then it should be with solemn awe. "The LORD is in his holy temple: let all the earth keep silence before him," Hab. ii. 20. Compare Isa. lx. 15; Heb. xii. 22–29.

3. Although all the parts of appointed worship are to be duly performed, and well agree with each other, yet they are not all obligatory at the same time. One entire act of devotion may consist of praise, v. 1.

4. Vows, consisting of engagements to serve God in the ordinary way of revealed duty, or in a way lawful but not binding except through our promise, are a part of true worship, v. 1. See REMARKS on Ps. xxii. 25; l. 14; lvi. 12; lxi. 5, 8.

5. Of all we know of God, nothing should more cheer us than this, *Thou that hearest prayer,* v. 2. Whatever God might be in himself, if he were deaf to our cries, we should be forever undone. Calvin: "The answer of our prayers is secured by the fact, that in rejecting them God would in a certain sense deny his own nature." Dickson: "The hearing and granting of prayer are the Lord's property, and his usual practice, and his pleasure, and his nature, and his glory."

6. The conversion of the heathen nations ought not to have awakened surprise or opposition among the Jews; for their own Scriptures predict that glorious event, v. 2. We poor sinners of the Gentiles should never cease to admire and adore the grace that thus enriches us.

7. In all worship a deep sense of personal unworthiness becomes us, v. 3. Henry: "Our sins reach to the heavens, iniquities prevail against us, and appear so numerous, so heinous, that, when they are set in order before us, we are full of confusion, and ready to fall into despair. They prevail so against us, that we cannot pretend to balance them with any righteousness of our own; so that when we appear before God, our own consciences accuse us, and we have no replication to make." Compare Ps. xxxviii. 4; xl. 12. Calvin: "God will not be entreated of us, unless we humbly supplicate the pardon of our sins." Tholuck: "Every prayer should begin with the confession that our lips are unclean." Morison: "It is the sense of sin which drives us to the cross."

8. But mere convictions of guilt will save no one. We must exercise hope and confidence in God that he will put away our sins, v. 3. This is the stay of the soul. The number and aggravation of our offences need not hinder this boldnes. God's word amply warrants even the chief of sinners to come and plead for mercy.

9. Many, many are the blessings of those who are chosen and called of God, and made true worshippers, v. 4. Sometimes we have enumerations of such blessings; see Ps. ciii.; Rom. v. 1–11; 1 Cor. iii. 21–23; but even these are imperfect. There is a telling in God's mercies, and we shall be telling them forever.

10. The doctrine of a divine election of sinners to the blessings of salvation is as certainly taught in the Old Testament as in the New, v. 4. It is greatly to be regretted that a truth, which has often caused the hearts of God's servants to break forth into thanksgivings, should have been rejected by some and by others received with suspicion. Compare v. 4; Matt. xi. 25, 26; Luke x. 21; Eph. i. 3–6. Our eternal salvation depends on our election, John vi. 37, 44. This choice of God is most free, none of our works constraining him thereto, Rom. ix. 11–13. The proof of our election is always and only to be found in a holy life.

11. The true friends and worshippers of God are not tossed from vanity to vanity, but are *satisfied* with the goodness of his house, v. 4. The glorious things of God do *fill* and *satiate* the soul, Jer. xxxi. 25.

12. True religion always was experimental, v. 4. Morison: "How useless are ordinances, if we have no communion with God in observing them. Without experience in religion everything else must be vain and fruitless."

13. It is vain to expect all summer and no winter, all sunshine and no cloud, all pleasant and no *terrible* things, v. 5. No vigorous character was ever formed under mere blandishments and indulgences. There is need for the severe as well as for the mild. Calvin: "It is in no common, or ordinary manner that God has preserved his church, but with terrible majesty. It is well that this should be known, and the people of God taught to sustain their hopes in the most apparently desperate exigencies."

14. Remoteness from any supposed centre of the religious, or political world does not place a man beyond the pale of God's providential care and blessing, v. 5. He fills the heart of the poor heathen with food and gladness. He sends his Gospel to the islands of the sea and to us Americans, inhabiting a land not known to the civilized world till nearly *fifteen hundred* years after the birth of Christ. Hengstenberg: "The mercies of God are coextensive with human need." Luther: "One may run over the wide world, even to its utmost extremity, yet thou, O Lord, art the only foundation on which the trust of man's heart can stand and remain." Let men and nations beware how they treat Christ and his Gospel, Matt. xiii. 17; Luke x. 24; xii. 48.

15. The stupendous works of God are of excellent use in furnishing us with conceptions and images of the strength and power of the Creator, v. 6. If God had never done anything requiring omnipotence, we should certainly doubt whether he had that infinite perfection; but who can look at the mountains, the ocean, or the starry heavens, and be skeptical?

16. Dickson: "There is nothing so turbulent, and raging, and reasonless in the whole world, which God doth not rule and bridle, and make quiet as he pleaseth: *he stilleth the noise of the seas, the noise of their waves,*" v. 7. Bishop Hall: "The sea brooked not me, nor I the sea, an unquiet element made only for wonder and use, not for pleasure." Yet in what element do more creatures sport and rejoice?

17. In like manner God stills the tumult of the people, v. 7. The terrible commotions resulting from seditions, persecutions, tyranny, insurrection and civil war are uncontrollable by any but the hand of omnipotence. The Lord can hush all nature and all nations as in a moment. We do not think enough, or make enough of the power of God. We are too much like that lord in Samaria, 2 Kings vii. 2.

18. If men did not dislike the knowledge of God, it would be impossible to account

for the present deplorable ignorance of the divine character among mankind; for God gives *tokens in the uttermost parts* of the world, infallible *signs* of his eternal power and Godhead, v. 8. Calvin: "It would seem as if the more perspicacity men have in observing second causes in nature, they will rest in them the more determinedly, instead of ascending by them to God."

19. Miserable as this world is, every human bosom has sometimes been glad. But whatever rejoicing earth in all her length and breath has ever witnessed, had God for its author, v. 8.

20. The goodness of God is wondrously manifest in nature, and nothing in nature more than in water, v. 9. There are billions of tons of this great element. The great reservoirs of it are salted, so as to keep it perfectly pure, yet not so much salted as to destroy the life of innumerable tribes of living things. Into these great reservoirs all the rivers pour their floods. Thence by evaporation all lands are provided with supplies of the purest, sweetest water falling from the clouds. Thus the face of nature is refreshed, and the surplus of water, percolated through various earths, sands and minerals, is kept cool and sweet for drink, or impregnated with medicinal properties, that heal tens of thousands. To man water is a great necessity. It is an ingredient of every human body. When cold it is a tonic; when warm, a laxative; when hot, a stimulant. It is one of the best emetics. It has no equal as a purifier. Arnd: "When a *visit* is made by rich and affectionate friends, they do not come empty, but bring with them a blessing, a good gift, to testify their favor. . . So when in time of drought God gives a gracious fertilizing shower, it is as if he paid us a *visit*, and brought along with him a great blessing, that we may mark his love and his goodness."

21. But in Scripture water is an emblem of the Holy Ghost in his abundant, refreshing and purifying influences, and so verse 9 has been by many understood to point to the effusion of the blessed Spirit. Scott: "The rising of 'the Sun of Righteousness,' and the pouring out of the Holy Spirit, that 'River of God,' full of the waters of life and salvation, render the hearts of sinners, which before were hard, barren and worthless, fruitful in every good work; and change the face of nations far more than the sun and rain do the face of nature." Morison: "I know not but this imagery may have been introduced by the Spirit of God for the purpose of picturing to our minds the wonderful character of the moral transformation, which takes place in the hearts of men, when showers of divine influence are poured down from heaven, when the wilderness and solitary place are made to rejoice and blossom as the rose." Compare Isa. xxxii. 15; xxxv. 7; xliv. 3–6.

22. The census of any thrifty agricultural people, respecting the products of their labor in the fruits of the earth, will fill any devout mind with wonder and with gratitude, v. 10. Yet the earth has long been under a curse. But a time is coming when she shall yield her increase, and when a teeming population shall in all lands be supplied with the fruits that God shall cause to grow. The future of this world, agriculturally, socially, civilly, politically and religiously, is far brighter than any part of its history, since the first pair forsook the path of duty.

23. It is well for us to dwell upon the wondrous beauties of the seasons and the blessings they bring with them. If we did it with any right views and feelings, surely we should find our reflections profitable, vv. 9–13.

24. Those happy persons, to whom God has appointed the innocent pleasures of rural life, and whom he has exempted from the weariness of study, the anxieties of trade and the frightful scenes familiar to military men, ought to be not only contented, but devoutly thankful, vv. 9–13.

PSALM LXVI.

To the chief Musician, A Song *or* Psalm.

1 Make a joyful noise unto God, all ye lands:

2 Sing forth the honour of his name: make his praise glorious.

3 Say unto God, How terrible *art thou in* thy works! through the greatness of thy power shall thine enemies submit themselves unto thee.

4 All the earth shall worship thee, and shall sing unto thee; they shall sing *to* thy name. Selah.

5 Come and see the works of God: *he is* terrible *in his* doing toward the children of men.

6 He turned the sea into dry *land:* they went through the flood on foot: there did we rejoice in him.

7 He ruleth by his power for ever; his eyes behold the nations: let not the rebellious exalt themselves. Selah.

8 Oh bless our God, ye people, and make the voice of his praise to be heard:

9 Which holdeth our soul in life, and suffereth not our feet to be moved.

10 For thou, O God, hast proved us: thou hast tried us, as silver is tried.

11 Thou broughtest us into the net; thou laidest affliction upon our loins.

12 Thou hast caused men to ride over our heads; we went through fire and through water: but thou broughtest us out into a wealthy *place.*

13 I will go into thy house with burnt offerings: I will pay thee my vows,

14 Which my lips have uttered, and my mouth hath spoken, when I was in trouble.

15 I will offer unto thee burnt sacrifices of fatlings, with the incense of rams: I will offer bullocks with goats. Selah.

16 Come *and* hear, all ye that fear God, and I will declare what he hath done for my soul.

17 I cried unto him with my mouth, and he was extolled with my tongue.

18 If I regard iniquity in my heart, the Lord will not hear *me:*

19 *But* verily God hath heard *me;* he hath attended to the voice of my prayer.

20 Blessed *be* God, which hath not turned away my prayer, nor his mercy from me.

ALL parts of the title are explained on titles of Psalms iii. iv. xxx. The authorship cannot be certainly determined. The Arabic and some others ascribe it to David. To this there is no unanswerable objection. Some think it was written by some cotemporary of the royal singer, unknown to us. Quite a number give it a much later date. "Venema refers it to the reign of Hezekiah, and supposes it to celebrate the deliverance which was effected by the destruction of Sennacherib's army. Rudinger is of opinion that it celebrates the opening of the second temple, after the return from Babylon." Clarke dates it about B. C. 520 years; Scott, B. C. 1023. Both date and authorship are uncertain. Many notice some resemblance to Ps. xlvi. We have here two names of the Almighty, *Elohim God* and *Adonai Lord,* on which see on Ps. iii. 2; ii. 4. On *Selah* see Introduction, § 15.

1. *Make a joyful noise unto God, all ye lands. Make a joyful noise,* in the Hebrew one word, rendered as here in Ps. lxxxi. 1; xcviii. 4, 6; c. 1; very often *shout,* as in Ps. xlvii. 1; *shout for joy,* as in Ps. lxv. 13; *triumph,* as in Ps. lx. 8. It expresses exultant gladsome emotions. Edwards: Sing with exalted voices to God; Alexander: "The verb is plural in its form, which shows that *earth* has a collective sense." Our translators therefore did right in rendering it, *all ye lands;* they might have read, Ye dwellers in *the whole earth.*

2. *Sing forth the honor of his name.* The various renderings give the same sense as the common version: Sing praises to the glory of his name; Sing Psalms to the glory of his name; Sing the honor of his name; Celebrate the glory of his name. *Make his praise glorious.* Chaldee: Order the glory of his praise; Syriac: Sing to the honor of his praise; Calvin: Make glorious his praise; Edwards: Give him the glory

of his praise. Abenezra supposes the sense to be, Let it be your glory to praise him. So also Patrick: Place your principal glory in this, that you have the honor to sing his praises. But Calvin is perhaps right when he says the sense is that we highly exalt his praises that they may be glorious.

3. *Say unto God, How terrible* art thou in *thy works.* The Chaldee, Syriac, Arabic, Septuagint, Ethiopic, Vulgate, Doway, Ainsworth, Edwards, Fry and Alexander make *terrible* agree with *works.* How fearful are thy doings. But the church of England, Calvin, Piscator, Fabritius, Venema, Amesius, Jebb and Hengstenberg, guided by the proper rendering of v. 5 below, sustain the common version and supply the words *art thou in.* *Terrible,* the same as in Ps. lxv. 5, on which see. It is also rendered *fearful, dreadful.* It occurs again in v. 5. God has often stricken the hearts of his foes with terror. See history. He built up the Jewish nation by showing *great terrors,* Deut. iv. 34; xxxiv. 12. *Through the greatness of thy power shall thine enemies submit themselves unto thee.* *Submit themselves,* see on Ps. xviii. 44. The margin reads *lie,* or *yield a feigned obedience.* God's foes should at least profess submission to him, because they should be persuaded of *the greatness of his power.*

4. *All the earth shall worship thee.* *All the earth,* as in v. 1. *Worship, do obeisance, do reverence, bow down,* or *worship,* 2 Sam. i. 2; ix. 6; Ex. xx. 5; Ps. v. 7. The Romish Church is very anxious to give it in the second commandment the sense of *adore,* and so she often renders it as here and in many places. But even the Doway Bible sometimes has *worship,* as in 2 Sam. ix. 6; Gen. xxvii. 29; and *bow down,* as in Gen. xxvii. 29; xxxiii. 3; xxxvii. 7. The word is used to express *bowing down* as an act either of civil or religious worship. *And* [all the earth] *shall sing unto thee.* *Sing,* as in v. 2. *They shall sing* to *thy name.* *Sing,* as in the preceding clause. God's *name* here means *himself,* as revealed to us.

5. *Come and see the works of God.* *Works,* as in Ps. xlvi. 8. The invitation is not merely to take a sight of God's works, but to *consider* or *regard* them as the word is also rendered, v. 18; Ps. xxxi. 7; Ecc. xi. 4. He is *terrible* in his *doing toward the children of men.* *Terrible,* as in v. 3. *Doing, action, work, deed,* 1 Sam. ii. 3; Ps. ix. 11; xiv. 1. *Sons of men, sons of Adam,* see Introduction, § 16. God's acts of providence are well suited to fill all minds with dread. To his foes his fear is a torment, while to his friends it is a strong confidence, Isa. viii. 14, 15; 1 John iv. 18; Pr. xiv. 26. Compare Ps. xl. 5. The *doing* of God might be devoutly *considered* in the plagues of Egypt, in the overthrow of Pharaoh, in the fall of Jericho, in the destruction of the Canaanites, in short, in all history. One of these events is immediately mentioned:

6. *He turned the sea into dry* land. If Pharaoh and his hosts had possessed any real sagacity, they would not have assayed to follow the Israelites. They knew that the sea was made to stand on heaps for the chosen people, and not at all for their persecutors. But they were blind, mad, incorrigible. On they pressed, and the power, which stayed the waves for Israel, withdrew; the waters found their level, and the persecutors sank like a stone. *They went through the flood on foot.* *Flood,* almost uniformly rendered *river,* as in Gen. ii. 10; Ps. xlvi. 4; lxxii. 8. If here it is *river,* it refers to the crossing of Jordan, which was also miraculously effected and was every way an event suited to impress the mind of any one, Josh. iii. These escapes of Israel and the destruction of their foes were so marked that it could not but awaken gladness in pious minds: *There did we rejoice in him.* The particular form of rejoicing, caused by the rescue of Israel and the overthrow of their foes at the Red sea is given at length in the exultant song of Moses and Miriam, Ex. xv. 1–21; one of the most elevated compositions in the Hebrew language. The passage of the Red sea might well have led each one to say:

7. *He ruleth by his power for ever.* The divine government is conducted, not by the permission, assistance, or sufferance of men or angels; but by God's own inherent and resistless energy. It shall be so *to eternity. His eyes behold the nations.* Pool: "He sees all their secret and subtle devices, and can and will defeat them, when he sees fit." Alexander: "The divine inspection here described implies that man can no more evade God's power than resist it." God's *providence* is as truly and as constantly over the wicked as over the righteous, though for a different end. *Let not the rebellious exalt themselves,* i. e., Let them not act, as if God had them not in his power, and would not hold them to a strict account. Compare Isa. xiv. 13–15; Obad. 4.

8. *Oh bless our God, ye people, and make the voice of his praise to be heard. Bless,* as in Ps. v. 12. As all *people,* all *nations,* receive the divine mercies, and all have good cause to *bless* him, they should speak openly of his works and publish his praise. If the nations had not been shockingly depraved, they would long since have been won to the faith, and obedience, and worship of Jehovah by the wonders he has showed. He is evidently God,

9. *Which holdeth our soul in life.* The nation of Israel was evidently kept and continued in existence against the fixed and malicious purposes of surrounding nations, not by its own inherent strength, but by the power of Jehovah. Often did it seem as if destruction was at the door, but God averted such strokes as would have wiped them out of existence. *And suffereth not our feet to be moved,* i. e., so as to be rooted out as a nation. Many a deliverance wrought for Israel, for the Gospel church, and for individual Christians has been like life from the dead. Perhaps it is this verse more than any other which led some of the ancient interpreters to entitle this *A Psalm of the Resurrection.*

10. *For thou, O God, hast proved us: thou hast tried us, as silver is tried.* Instead of *For* we might better read *Yet,* or *Though,* as some suggest. *Proved,* as in Ps. xvii. 3; in Ps. vii. 9, *try;* in Ps. xxvi. 2, *examine.* It implies *thorough searching, close scrutiny. Tried,* as in Ps. xvii. 3. It signifies *melting, refining,* or *founding* when applied to precious metals. To *try as silver* is to test severely, see on Ps. xii. 6. Though God had brought his chosen people to great eminence, yet it had been by such trials, as no other nation had endured. Alexander: "The general idea here is that of affliction, as a means both of trial and purgation, and is carried out in the following verses."

11. *Thou broughtest us into the net. Net,* sometimes rendered *fort, fortress, hold, strong place;* also *snare, net,* Ezek. xii. 13; xvii. 20. *Net* is the word here. They were not caught in some artifice of enemies, but God himself had allowed their affairs to become complicated and themselves perplexed. *Thou laidest affliction upon our loins. Affliction,* here only. There is great diversity in the rendering, chain, tribulation, affliction, straitness, sore pressure, heavy load. A *heavy burden* is perhaps the best rendering, as the word is here evidently used figuratively in connection with the loins. The probable reference is to the general course of severe discipline by which God had trained Israel.

12. *Thou hast caused men to ride over our heads.* Anderson: "*To ride over* signifies to insult or tyrannize over. Or the image may be taken from the trampling of warhorses in the day of battle." Clarke: "Thou hast permitted us to fall under the dominion of our enemies; who have treated us as broken infantry are when the cavalry dashes among their disordered ranks, treading all under the horses' feet." Pool thinks it means to "ride upon our shoulders. By thy permission they have used us like slaves, yea, like beasts to carry their persons or burdens. Compare Isa. li. 23." *We went through fire and through water.* Anderson: "Fire and water, the one of which elements consumes, while the other suffocates, is a proverbial expression, signifying extreme danger and complicated calamities." See Num. xxxi. 23; Ps. xxxii. 6;

lxix. 2; Isa. xliii. 2; Ezek. xv. 7; xxx. 8. Thus far the verse had a remarkable fulfilment in the sufferings of the Israelites in Egypt. Yet they were not left there to groan and perish. *But thou broughtest us out to a wealthy place.* The last word occurs seldom. In various translations we have it, refreshment, wide place, rest, fruitful place, affluence, abundance, place of ease. There was a wonderful difference between living as bondmen in Egypt and as proprietors in Judea. The consideration of such mercies affected the heart of the Psalmist:

13. *I will go into thy house with burnt offerings.* *House* does not necessarily signify *the temple* properly so called. The name is given to the *tabernacle,* Ex. xxiii. 19; Josh. ix. 23; Judg. xviii. 31; xix. 18. On burnt offerings see Ps. l. 8. The Psalmist makes an engagement in good faith and with an honest heart to pay the public worship of the dispensation under which he lived. *I will pay thee my vows.* Vows, see on Ps. xxii. 25; l. 14; lvi. 12; lxi. 5, 8; lxv. 1. These *vows* seem to have been of things, which became obligatory because they were promised. He says of them,

14. *Which my lips have uttered, and my mouth hath spoken, when I was in trouble.* Clarke: "This is generally the time when good resolutions are formed, and vows made:—but how often are these forgotten when affliction and calamity are removed." Compare Jer. xxii. 23.

15. *I will offer unto thee burnt sacrifices of fatlings, with the incense of rams, I will offer bullocks with goats.* In this verse are mentioned all the kinds of four-footed creatures that were appointed to be offered in sacrifice under the law. This shows that the Psalmist had made very comprehensive vows, and felt called upon to exercise unusual gratitude. The sense is well given by Scott: "I will liberally provide for every part of the service at the tabernacle;" by Clarke: "Thou shalt have the best of the herd and of the fold;" and by Patrick: "I will not come empty into thy house; so I will not bring thee a niggardly present; but offer sacrifices of all sorts, and the best and choicest of every kind." Scott well says, 'The incense of rams' conveys no clear meaning; and he proposes an amended translation: "I will offer unto thee the burnt-sacrifices of fatlings, even rams, with incense; I will offer bullocks and goats." Horsley renders the verse thus: "Offerings of fatlings I will offer unto thee, with incense; I will sacrifice rams, bullocks, and full-grown goats." That *incense* should not be connected with *rams* is admitted by the Chaldee, Arabic, Ethiopic, Ainsworth, Piscator, Fabritius, Amesius, Edwards and Fry.

16. *Come* and *hear, all ye that fear God, and I will declare what he hath done for my soul.* All the Scriptures are for public use; but the wicked neither understand nor relish the lively oracles, nor the experiences of God's children. So the Psalmist asks not the scoffing world, but those who *fear God*, to listen to his song. God's children make an attentive audience.

17. *I cried unto him with my mouth, and he was extolled with my tongue.* *I cried,* in my danger and distress; I prayed with great fervor and earnestness; and even then I forgot not to adore and exalt God. I knew that if he chose, he could save me. I had no hope in any other, and I solemnly said so. I remember my trying circumstances. I magnify his mercy. When rescued, I gave him thanks. Patrick: "The ardent prayers, which I made unto him, in a very low condition, are now turned into the highest praises of his powerful goodness." Calvin: "The term *extol* intimates, that we cannot honor God more in our worship than by looking upwards to him for deliverance."

18. *If I regard iniquity in my heart, the Lord will not hear* me. Clarke: "*If I have seen iniquity in my heart*—if I have known it was there, and *encouraged* it; if I *pretended* to be what I *was not;* if I *loved iniquity,* while I *professed to pray* and be *sorry* for *my sin:—the Lord Adonai,* my Prop, Stay, and Supporter, would not have

heard; and I should have been left without *help* or *support.*" *Regard*, see on v. 5, where it is rendered *see.*

19. But *verily God hath heard* me. The issue showed that God approved the Psalmist's character and conduct. Sometimes the divine vindication is so marked that none can deny that the Lord has done it. *He hath attended to the voice of my prayer. Attended*, rendered *attend* in Ps. xvii. 1; lv. 2; lxi. 1, and *hearken* in Ps. v. 2.

20. *Blessed* be *God, which hath not turned away my prayer, nor his mercy from me. Blessed*, from the same root as *bless* in v. 8. God's mercy is the cause of our deliverance from unjust and violent men, whom we have not wronged; for though we have not sinned against them, we have sinned against God.

Doctrinal and Practical Remarks.

1. To those, who wholly reject vocal music from God's worship, a considerable part of Scripture must appear strange, vv. 1, 2, 8.

2. No nation or tribe is so degraded or wretched that it has not abundant cause for showing forth the glory of God, and uttering his praise, v. 1. Morison: "As Jehovah is entitled to the universal and undivided homage of all the dwellers upon earth, the Psalmist here calls upon all lands to shout joyfully before him, to chant the glory of his name, and to celebrate the praise of his infinite perfections."

3. We should do all in our power to make the worship of God not only decent, solemn, and impressive, but *glorious*, v. 2. We should never seek to set forth God's praises moderately, but in the highest strains and most animated manner. Scott: "Nothing but human depravity prevents this reasonable employment from being as universal on earth as in heaven."

4. Take from the Bible its awful doctrines, and from providence its *terrible* acts, and the whole system, under which God has placed us, would be emasculated, vv. 3, 5. "Much of religion lies in a reverence for the Divine Providence."

5. Neither God nor religion are responsible for the *feigned submission*, the real hypocrisy of many in the world, v. 3. Were they wise, or docile, or ingenuous, the truths and judgments, which make them hypocrites, would make them the honest and sincere followers of the Lamb.

6. How glorious will be the day when the fulness of the Gentiles shall be brought in, and all the earth shall serve Jehovah and his Christ. This worship shall not be feigned, but shall abound in hearty singing, v. 4. Calvin: "Praise is the best of all sacrifices, and the true evidence of godliness." One of the richest sources of joy to believers is the anticipation of the time when all flesh shall see the salvation of God.

7. It should be a considerable part of our business in this life earnestly to call men's attention to the wonderful *works* and *terrible doings* of the Almighty, v. 5. This is the prescribed duty of parents, of teachers and of preachers of the gospel, yea, of all men as they have opportunity.

8. All God's doings are worthy of pious notice and remembrance; but some of his acts deservedly make such an impression on a man, a nation, or a generation, that they may well be mentioned till time shall end, yea, some of them while eternity endures. Such was the history of one day's transactions at the Red sea. Such was the march across the Jordan, v. 6. But 'in redemption by the death of Christ, and the glories which followed that grand event, we have far more surprising and affecting subjects to contemplate, than Israel's deliverance from Egyptian bondage.' The conversion of a man's soul and his safe and happy death in Christ will be themes of rejoicing forever. Hengstenberg: "God's guidance of his people is a constant drying up of the sea and of the Jordan, and the joy over his mighty deeds is always receiving new materials."

9. God's kingdom is from everlasting to everlasting. *He ruleth by his power for ever,* v. 7. Whoever will duly consider the nature and history, the perils and escapes of his own life, will not want evidence of the constant care of a sleepless and almighty providence.

10. Let the potsherd strive with the potsherds of the earth, but wo to him that striveth with his Maker. *Let not the rebellious exalt themselves,* v. 7. No man ever hardened himself against God and prospered.

11. Whoever can truly say *Our God* will not rest satisfied without calling on all around him to *bless God,* v. 8. A regenerated child of God correctly judges that his own private estimate of the divine blessings is not enough, but that he should heartily endeavor to make others partakers of the true knowledge and worship of the Most High.

12. Both persons and nations should acknowledge that their life in its beginning and in its continuance is wholly from God, v. 9. And surely he, who depends on another for life, is wholly dependent. Oh that men would humble themselves under the mighty hand of God, and own that their existence, and all their privileges, civil, social and religious come from above. As God supports natural life, so does he spiritual life; and so all believers in Christ are wondrously safe.

13. The whole of life is a test, a trial of what is in us, so arranged by God himself, and it is of great importance that we so regard it, v. 10. Nothing is more quieting to the pious soul than to remember, *It is the Lord.* Compare Job i. 21; Amos iii. 6.

14. Many of the tests to which God subjects his people are painful, vv. 11, 12. Sometimes captivity, hard bondage, cruel oppression, fire and water, heat and cold, are sent to prove them. Sometimes their trials are wholly unknown to the world. We ought to be specially thankful, if we are saved from tyranny, from persecution for conscience' sake, from all that class of trials, which bring upon us the fiendish passions of men. When men are let loose *to ride over our heads,* we are indeed in a sad case.

15. However long and sharp the trials of God's people may be, they shall have a happy issue out of them, and a blessed enlargement, which none but God can give, v. 12. O yes, the trial of their faith, being more precious than of gold that perisheth, though it be tried with fire, shall be found unto praise, and honor, and glory, at the appearing of Jesus Christ, 1 Pet. i. 7. Compare Isa. i. 25; xlviii. 10; Zech. xiii. 9. Arnd: "The pious martyr Babylas said, when he was led to death: 'Be now joyous, O my soul, God is doing good to thee.'"

16. It is right for persons of every rank and condition to observe all the ordinances appointed by God in the dispensation under which they live, vv. 13, 15. Especially should we feel and confess that we are miserable sinners, and so must ever come with a deep sense of unworthiness, and with a lively faith in the great sacrifice of the one Mediator.

17. My soul, remember the vows and promises thou hast made to God in the day of sorrow. Hast thou paid them? vv. 13, 14. Or hast thou passed thy word to thy Maker and been found a liar? O how is this? Of nothing must a more awful account be given than of broken vows.

18. If it is praiseworthy to tell of outward deliverances and to invite others to listen to a narrative of God's mercies in that behalf; surely it cannot be wrong to state clearly, modestly and thankfully God's dealings with our souls. It is one proof of the low state of piety in this century that there is so little solemn and profitable conversation among professors of religion concerning the work of God in their own hearts. Scott: "Besides the general example of gratitude for our mercies, which

we publicly exhibit; we should more particularly declare to those who fear God, what he has done for our souls, and how he has heard and answered our prayers: *they* alone are capable of understanding our experience, and they will be edified and encouraged by it, and will join with us in prayer and praise, and this will turn to our mutual comfort, and to the glory of God." Morison: "It is an excellent sign of the power of religion in the heart, when it pants for opportunity of bearing testimony to the faithfulness and mercy of Jehovah in the dispensations of his providence and grace." Henry: "God's people should communicate their experiences to each other; we should take all occasion to tell one another of the great and kind things, which God has done for us, especially for our souls." Tholuck: "The experience of every individual pious man is the common possession of all."

19. True prayer is earnest; it *cries* unto God, v. 17. Length is no substitute for fervor in our devotions.

20. It cannot be denied that there is much praying in the world; but it must be admitted that much of it fails to bring the blessing. Why is this? An answer may be found in v. 18. We ask that we may consume it upon our lusts, our pride, our ambition, our ease, our sloth, our vanity, our worldliness. Horne: "The prayer which is *heard* is the prayer of the penitent, heartily grieved and wearied with sin, hating and longing to be delivered from it." Slade: "There must be no double dealing with Jehovah." John ix. 31. Calvin: "Integrity of heart is indispensable." Henry: "If I have favorable thoughts of iniquity, if I love it, indulge it, allow myself in it, if I treat it as a friend, and bid it welcome, make provision for it, and am loath to part with it, if I roll it under my tongue as a sweet morsel, though it be but a heart-sin that is thus countenanced and made much of, if I delight in it after the inward man, God will not hear my prayer."

21. The comfort of answered prayers is very great, vv. 19, 20. Indeed it constitutes the substance of the Christian's support. We may use it as we will and when we will. Scott: "The feeblest petition of the repenting sinner, coming from a broken heart, will by no means be despised." God may turn his ears from prattling prayers, or preaching prayers, but never from penitent, believing prayers.

22. If prayer is answered, if blessings descend, we should never forget that it is all of *mercy*, v. 20. Calvin: "It is entirely of his free grace that God is propitious, and that our prayers are not wholly ineffectual." Henry: "What we win by prayer, we must wear with praise."

PSALM LXVII.

To the chief Musician on Neginoth, A Psalm *or* Song.

1 God be merciful unto us, and bless us; *and* cause his face to shine upon us; Selah.

2 That thy way may be known upon earth, thy saving health among all nations.

3 Let the people praise thee, O God; let all the people praise thee.

4 Oh let the nations be glad and sing for joy: for thou shalt judge the people righteously, and govern the nations upon earth. Selah.

5 Let the people praise thee, O God; let all the people praise thee.

6 *Then* shall the earth yield her increase; *and* God, *even* our own God, shall bless us.

7 God shall bless us; and all the ends of the earth shall fear him.

ON the title see on titles of Psalms iii. iv. xxx. That David wrote this ode is admitted by the Arabic, Septuagint, Ethiopic and Vulgate, and is esteemed probable by Luther, Patrick, Dodd, Scott, Morison and Hengstenberg. The Syriac and Abenezra say its author is unknown. The silence of many commentators on this matter shows that their minds are not clear. Of course it has no known historic occasion. The Syriac says "the people sang it when they brought David over the river Jordan," after the suppression of Absalom's rebellion. That occasion is described in 2 Sam. xix. 11–43. But I find no support for this opinion. The Syriac has better foundation for saying that "to us it intimates a prophecy in it concerning the calling of the Gentiles and the preaching of the apostles, and also concerning the judgments of the Lord." Horsley thinks it is "a hymn for the feast of the tabernacles, prophetic of a general conversion of the world to the worship of God." Patrick thinks it probable it was used in blessing the people, after bringing the ark to Jerusalem. But the contents of the Psalm are our sole guide in this matter, and they fix no occasion for its special use. Scott dates it B. C. 1023; Clarke, about B. C. 520. The only name of the Most High in it is *Elohim God*, on which see on Ps. iii. 2. On *Selah* see Introduction, § 15.

1. *God be merciful unto us, and bless us; and cause his face to shine upon us.* This is the substance of the form of benediction (with a change of person in the pronoun) used by the priests under the law, Num. vi. 24–26. Tholuck: "The *shining* countenance of God on his people is a *gracious* one, the lustre of which refreshes the hearts, and pours blessings on all the ways of the people." *Be merciful*, in Ps. li. 1, *Have mercy*. *Bless*, as in Ps. v. 12; lxvi. 8. For the sense of *causing his face to shine*, see on Ps. iv. 6; xxxi. 16. The Hebrew verbs both here and in Num. vi. are in the future, though perhaps well rendered in the imperative; yet if we use the future, they contain a promise of a blessing yet to come. *Us* has no doubt a primary reference to the godly among the Israelites. To them as to us all blessings come through *mercy* and *grace*. Rich and numerous were the blessings that God promised to Israel, as may be seen in Deut. xxviii. 1–14, which may be regarded as an '*expansion*' of Num. vi. 24–26.

2. *That thy way may be known upon earth, thy saving health among all nations.* God's *way* is his covenant, says Calvin; his procedure, says Hengstenberg; his mode of dealing with his people, says Alexander; the 'way' to eternal life, says Horne. Clarke explains it as equivalent to "Thy will, thy gracious designs towards the children of men,—Thy way of reconciling them to thyself,—of justifying the ungodly, and sanctifying the unholy. . . God's *way* is God's *religion*." The more evangelical the explanation of the first clause, the better it tallies with the second, which is parallel. Our version has *saving health*. But the word occurs more than *seventy* times in the Hebrew Bible and in more than *fifty* instances it is rendered *salvation*, sometimes *help*, *welfare*, *deliverance*, twice *health*, Ps. xlii. 5, 11, here only, *saving health*. See on Ps. xlii. 11. *Saving health* seems to have been inserted from an old translation in use in the days of King James.

3. *Let the people praise thee, O God; let all the people praise thee.* *People* in both cases plural, *nations*. *Praise*, the same verb in both clauses, rendered *give thanks* in Ps. vi. 5; in Ps. xxxii. 5, *confess*. The verb is in the future in both instances, *shall praise*, but well enough rendered in the imperative. Both are forms of prediction. See Introduction, § 6. It clearly foretells the time when the Gentiles shall have the light of the Gospel.

4. *Oh let the nations be glad and sing for joy*; or, The nations shall be glad and shout for joy. Verses 3, 5 in precisely the same words call on all nations to give thanks. Verse 4 assigns a reason for so doing. God shall make them *glad* and give them cause for *shouting*. The calling of the Gentiles to a participation of the blessings of the Gospel was to them life from the dead. It opened to them boundless fields of glad thought and emotion. It showed them, contrary to their former appre-

hensions, that the world was not governed by chance, nor by demoniacal hatred, but equitably: *For thou shalt judge the people righteously, and govern the nations upon earth.* The rule of Christ over the nations is righteous altogether. The glory of any government depends on its righteousness. The Scriptures give us all needed assurance on this point, and make it the foundation of rejoicing, Ps. xcvi. 10–13; xcvii. 1, 2; xcviii. 8, 9; Isa. xi. 3–10. This righteousness is marvellously displayed in all the provisions of the Gospel. *People*, plural *peoples*, see on Ps. ii. 1. *Nations*, as in v. 3.

5. *Let the people praise thee, O God; let all the people praise thee.* In Hebrew and English this is a literal copy of v. 3. It is repeated because it calls attention to a great and neglected duty, because in v. 4, abundant cause is assigned for performing it, and because God would teach us that his *salvation* would awaken *thanksgiving.* No man can read the writings of early Christians converted from heathenism without seeing that they felt themselves almost as marvellously rescued, as if they had been brought out of hell itself.

6. Then *shall the earth yield her increase.* The verb is in the preterite, *has yielded.* So confident is the prophet that he speaks of it as already accomplished. It points us to a time foretold when abundance and praise shall mark the world for a long time together. Temporal and spiritual blessings shall yet abound, the earth shall yet yield her increase of food and her harvest of souls and her revenue of praise, Ezek. xxxiv. 27; Ps. lxxxv. 12. And *God, even our own God shall bless us. Bless us* temporally, spiritually, eternally, in all respects. *Bless* as in v. 1, and with allusion to it. He repeats:

7. *God shall bless us.* There is no doubt of it. *And all the ends of the earth shall fear him.* God's goodness to his people leads his enemies to wish to be his friends. Calvin: "Every benefit, which God bestowed upon his ancient people, was, as it were, a light held out before the eyes of the world, to attract the attention of the nations to him."

DOCTRINAL AND PRACTICAL REMARKS.

1. While it is lawful for us to pray for ourselves individually, it is also consonant with the nature of true piety to join others with ourselves in supplicating blessings: God be merciful unto *us*, v. 1, etc.

2. We shall have need to pray for *mercy* as long as we live, v. 1. No child of God can go to a communion table, or leave this world with more fitting words on his lips than these: "God be merciful unto me a sinner." We need mercy at every step. We shall need it to the last.

3. Mercy shall flow to those who rightly pray for it, v. 1. Believing prayer never asks more than is promised. A heart to pray is a pledge that the blessing shall come.

4. Without God's blessing we are nothing, vv. 1, 6, 7. Why are we so careless to secure it? Henry: "God's speaking well to us amounts to his doing well for us."

5. What a poor thing is the soul of man separated from God, and how necessary to its well-being is its communion with its Maker, v. 1. Without his love we die; without a sense of it we wither. Henry: "We need desire no more to make us happy, than to have God's face shine upon us, to have God love us, and let us know that he loves us."

6. There is a connection between the blessings that descend on Christians, and the salvation of others, who are yet in their sins. This seems to be taught in the obvious connection between vv. 1, 2, and vv. 6, 7. See REMARKS on Ps. li. 12, 13. Compare John vii. 38. Scott: "When the Lord shines upon his people, and fills them with light, purity, and consolation, it exceedingly tends to spread the knowledge

of his salvation." No out-pouring of God's Spirit on his people is without good to others.

7. "The world is ignorant of true religion, till God by his own instruments reveals it." This ignorance is none the less dangerous, because it is wilful and by human power incurable.

8. If *praise* and thanksgiving have been made by God tests of genuine piety, vv. 3–5, then it is to be feared that there is not much piety in the world. Ten lepers were healed. Only one returned to give glory to God. The world is full of murmurers and complainers. How few abound in hearty thankful praise.

9. The Gospel was designed to be and it is great cause of joy to men, v. 4. How could it be otherwise? Clarke: "The great work which is performed by it is in destroying the power, pardoning the guilt, cleansing from the infection of all sin ; and filling the soul with holiness, with the mind that was in Christ." Such a religion must conduce to human happiness. It is for a lamentation that so few of the nations of the earth have yet heard that Gospel, but the work is going on and shall go on yet faster.

10. Let God's people openly and uniformly acknowledge and vindicate the divine *righteousness* in all respects and at all times, v. 4. This is not asking much, but we cannot do less than this without gross sin.

11. We do greatly misrepresent the Jewish religion, when we speak of it as excluding any humble penitent soul from its blessings. Where will any find more fervent prayers for the conversion of the Gentiles than in this very Psalm? vv. 3–5.

12. It would greatly add to the comfort of pious souls to remember that God reigns in all nature, and that he and he only can make the earth to give her increase, v. 6. He controls second causes, being himself the First Cause.

13. How richly God blesses his own people they know and testify, vv. 6, 7. God never had one faithful servant, who was not an honest and a willing witness of the riches of grace poured upon every believing soul.

14. True piety is never separate from the fear of God, v. 7.

15. Surely good times are coming. So the prophecies declare ; so the prayers of saints for centuries lead us to expect. Horne: "Hasten, O hasten the dawning of that happy day, when congregations of converted Gentiles shall everywhere lift up their voices, and perhaps in the words of this very Psalm sing to thy praise and glory, thou blessed Lord."

16. The conversion of the Jews is a most desirable, and will be a most important event. When God *blesses* them with his salvation, then *the ends of the earth shall* soon *fear him,* v. 7. Paul argues in the same way, Rom. xi. 12.

PSALM LXVIII.

To the chief Musician, A Psalm *or* Song of David.

1 Let God arise, let his enemies be scattered: let them also that hate him flee before him.

2 As smoke is driven away, *so* drive *them* away: as wax melteth before the fire, *so* let the wicked perish at the presence of God.

3 But let the righteous be glad; let them rejoice before God: yea, let them exceedingly rejoice.

4 Sing unto God, sing praises to his name: extol him that rideth upon the heavens by his name JAH, and rejoice before him.

5 A father of the fatherless, and a judge of the widows, *is* God in his holy habitation.

6 God setteth the solitary in families: he bringeth out those which are bound with cnains: but the rebellious dwell in a dry *land.*

7 O God, when thou wentest forth before thy people, when thou didst march through the wilderness. Selah:

8 The earth shook, the heavens also dropped at the presence of God: *even* Sinai itself *was moved* at the presence of God, the God of Israel.

9 Thou, O God, didst send a plentiful rain, whereby thou didst confirm thine inheritance, when it was weary.

10 Thy congregation hath dwelt therein: thou, O God, hast prepared of thy goodness for the poor.

11 The Lord gave the word: great *was* the company of those that published *it.*

12 Kings of armies did flee apace: and she that tarried at home divided the spoil.

13 Though ye have lain among the pots, *yet shall ye be as* the wings of a dove covered with silver, and her feathers with yellow gold.

14 When the Almighty scattered kings in it, it was *white* as snow in Salmon.

15 The hill of God *is as* the hill of Bashan; a high hill *as* the hill of Bashan.

16 Why leap ye, ye high hills? *this is* the hill *which* God desireth to dwell in; yea, the LORD will dwell *in it* for ever.

17 The chariots of God *are* twenty thousand, *even* thousands of angels: the Lord *is* among them, *as in* Sinai, in the holy *place.*

18 Thou hast ascended on high, thou hast led captivity captive: thou hast received gifts for men; yea, *for* the rebellious also, that the LORD God might dwell *among them.*

19 Blessed *be* the Lord, *who* daily loadeth us *with benefits, even* the God of our salvation. Selah.

20 *He that is* our God *is* the God of salvation; and unto GOD the Lord *belong* the issues from death.

21 But God shall wound the head of his enemies, *and* the hairy scalp of such a one as goeth on still in his trespasses.

22 The Lord said, I will bring again from Bashan, I will bring *my people* again from the depths of the sea:

23 That thy foot may be dipped in the blood of *thine* enemies, *and* the tongue of thy dogs in the same.

24 They have seen thy goings, O God; *even* the goings of my God, my King, in the sanctuary.

25 The singers went before, the players on instruments *followed* after; among *them were* the damsels playing with timbrels.

26 Bless ye God in the congregations, *even* the Lord, from the fountain of Israel.

27 There *is* little Benjamin *with* their ruler, the princes of Judah *and* their council, the princes of Zebulun, *and* the princes of Naphtali.

28 Thy God hath commanded thy strength: strengthen, O God, that which thou hast wrought for us.

29 Because of thy temple at Jerusalem shall kings bring presents unto thee.

30 Rebuke the company of spearmen, the multitude of the bulls, with the calves of the people, *till every one* submit himself with pieces of silver: scatter thou the people *that* delight in war.

31 Princes shall come out of Egypt: Ethiopia shall soon stretch out her hands unto God.

32 Sing unto God, ye kingdoms of the earth; oh sing praises unto the Lord; Selah:

33 To him that rideth upon the heavens of heavens, *which were* of old; lo, he doth send out his voice, *and that* a mighty voice.

34 Ascribe ye strength unto God: his excellency *is* over Israel, and his strength *is* in the clouds.

35 O God, *thou art* terrible out of thy holy places: the God of Israel *is* he that giveth strength and power unto *his* people. Blessed *be* God.

ON the several parts of the title see on titles of Ps. iii. iv. xxx. The authorship is ascribed to David by the Hebrew, Chaldee, Syriac, Arabic, Septuagint, Ethiopic, Vulgate, Calvin, Ainsworth, Horne, Henry, Pool, Clarke, Patrick, Tholuck and Hengstenberg. Its historic occasion is not certain. Some think David is here celebrating victories in general gained over the enemies of his country. But this assigns to it no time. Some think it was written on occasion of the victories recorded in 1 Chron. xix. 6–19; 2 Sam. xii. 26–31. Others fix it to the time of removing the ark of God either from Kirjath-Jearim or from the house of Obed-Edom. Which of these conjectures is most probable, the reader must judge for himself. The Psalm confessedly abounds in beauties, excellencies and difficulties. Amyrald: "There are in it poetic descriptions, bold metaphors, frequent apostrophes, magnificent personifications, and words which are of rare occurrence, and well selected, and therefore not easily understood." Muis styles it "the torture of critics and the reproach of commentators." Pages might be filled with like confessions. Hengstenberg and Alexander think there is a close connection between this and Ps. xviii.

This Psalm certainly contains Gospel truths. Luther: "It is a signal prophecy concerning Christ." Horne applies it to Christ throughout. Vitringa says it refers to "the ascension of Christ into heaven and his sitting at the right hand of the Father, and the effects thereof." The Syriac styles it "a prophecy concerning the dispensation of Christ and the calling of the Gentiles to faith." Pool: "By the spirit of prophecy David looked through and beyond the present actions and types unto the great mysteries of Christ's resurrection and ascension into heaven, and of the special privileges of the Christian church, and of the calling of the Gentiles unto God." Anderson: "As every thing under that dispensation was typical or prophetical, it is very natural to regard the triumphant manner in which the ark ascended the holy mountain, as an emblem of the far more triumphant ascension of the Lord Jesus Christ to the highest heavens." Paul explicitly quotes and applies to Christ a portion of this Psalm, Eph. iv. 8–13. Scott dates it B. C. 1045; Clarke, about B. C. 1042. Hengstenberg quotes with approbation Boettcher as saying: "It belongs assuredly to the most remote age of Hebrew poetry;" and Hitzig: "The poem may be pronounced with confidence to be as remarkable for its antiquity as for its originality." The names of the Most High in this Psalm are *Elohim God, El God, Jehovah* LORD *Adonai Lord*, on which respectively see on Ps. iii. 2; v. 4; i. 2; ii. 4. We have here, for the first time in the Psalms, *Shaddai the Almighty*. It is found in Genesis, Exodus, Leviticus, Job, Isaiah, Ezekiel and Joel; in all the Scriptures not quite *fifty* times. It is uniformly rendered. It occurs again in Ps. xci. 1. It asserts the all-sufficiency of God. We have also twice in this Psalm God's name, *Jah*, which is the poetic form of *Jehovah*, and of the same signification. It does not occur often, and is chiefly found compounded with the verb *Hallelu, praise ye, Jah the Lord*. We have had no other Psalm in which so many of the names of God are used. On *Selah* see Introduction, § 15.

1. *Let God arise, let his enemies be scattered: let them also that hate him flee before him.* The whole verse is but a slight variation of the words used by Moses "when the ark set forward." "*Rise up*, LORD, and let thine enemies be scattered; and let them that hate thee flee before thee." The four verbs are the same here and in Num. x. 35. Following the Hebrew many versions read: God shall arise; his enemies shall be scattered; and they who hate him shall flee before him. But see Introduction, § 6. Calvin and others, perhaps with reason, regard the first verse as a *preface* of the whole Psalm, as containing the subject of the whole. Tholuck: "It is indeed a theme which in ever new variations is being repeated at different epochs in the history of the kingdom of God, until the final judgment shall absorb and complete all the preceding judgments of God." God is always *arising*, and scattering his foes. He does so in every generation. In Num. x. 35 the name of the Supreme Being used is *Jehovah* LORD; here it is *Elohim God*. But both names are used separately and conjointly in the first two chapters of Genesis; and to an intelligent pious Jew this signified no more than it does to an intelligent pious Christian.

2. *As smoke is driven away*, so drive them *away; as wax melteth before the fire, so let the wicked perish at the presence of God.* Luther: "Two beautiful emblems, smoke and

wax; the smoke disappears before the wind; the wax before the fire. It is most contemptuous to compare, to smoke and wax, such mighty enemies who think they can combat heaven and earth." *Smoke*, as a figure of evanescence is employed in Ps. xxxvii. 20; cii. 3. Wax as an emblem of dissolution is found in Ps. xxii. 14; xcvii. 5. *Perish*, in Hebrew the same and in the same form as in Judges v. 31, where Deborah sings: *So let all thine enemies perish*, O LORD. The verbs *drive away* and *perish* are both in the future. Read either way, it is a sure word of prophecy. Deborah added, But let them that love him be as the sun when he goeth forth in his might; so David says:

3. *But let the righteous be glad; let them rejoice before God: yea, let them exceedingly rejoice.* *Righteous*, in the plural, showing that they are all included, however many there may be of them. The verbs here also are in the future. *Be glad*, in Ps. v. 11 rejoice. *Rejoice*, as in Ps. ix. 2. Hengstenberg renders it *shout for joy;* Alexander, *triumph*. *Exceedingly rejoice*, margin (literally) *rejoice with gladness;* Hengstenberg, *exult for gladness*. The verbs of this verse are in contrast with those of v. 2.

4. *Sing unto God, sing praises to his name.* The first verb here is cognate to the word *Song*, and the second to the word *Psalm* in the title. The *first* verb is the same as in Ps. xiii. 6; lxv. 13; the *second*, as in Ps. vii. 17; ix. 11; lxi. 8; and is by many rendered *sing Psalms*. *Extol him that rideth upon the heavens by his name JAH, and rejoice before him.* This rendering is substantially supported by the Chaldee, Calvin, John Rogers' translation, Bishops' Bible, Genevan translation, church of England and Jebb. Horsley: Cast-up-a-way for him that is riding through the wilderness; in JAH is his name, therefore exult before him. This is in the leading parts substantially supported by several of the ancient versions, also by Jerome, Venema, Ainsworth, Chandler, Waterland, Tholuck, Hengstenberg and Alexander. *Extol,* in Ex. ix. 17; Pr. iv. 8, the same Hebrew word is rendered *exalt*. But in Isa. lvii. 14; lxii. 10, it is rendered *cast up*, meaning to *make smooth* or *plain* a way. Diodati: "The terms are taken from what is used to be done at the triumphal coming in of kings, whom they used to meet, and make plain and mend the ways by which they are to come, if they be broken, or ragged, or stopped; so here is meant the preparation for the bringing in of the ark: but especially the spiritual preparations for Christ's coming, and reception in the world; which is a wilderness, void of all goodness, justice, and life; which preparations were made by his prophets, and especially by John the Baptist, Isa. xl. 3; Mal. iii. 1; Matt. iii. 3." Hengstenberg admits that the manner of *preparing the way* was by *songs of praise;* and this is *extolling* him. As to reading *wilderness* or *deserts* instead of *heavens*, it is surely no improvement, and Hammond, supported by Buxtorf, has shown satisfactorily that the word in the plural, as it is here, may signify *heavens;* yet it is but candid to admit that Calvin reads *upon the clouds*, and that the word is nowhere else rendered *heavens*, but always *plain, desert, wilderness, champaign*. The Chaldee has it the *ninth heaven*. Others have it the *seventh heaven*. But these are human additions. *By his name Jah* is better than *in Jah is his name*, and signifies that he comes in his own appropriate name and character as the self-existent, independent, eternal and unchangeable Jehovah. As reasons for *rejoicing before him* we have the matters contained in vv. 1–3; also in vv. 5, 6.

5. *A father of the fatherless, and a judge of the widows* is God *in his holy habitation.* *Fatherless*, often joined with *stranger* and oftener with *widow*. Sometimes the stranger, fatherless and widow are all named together, Deut. xxiv. 19–21; Ps. cxlvi. 9. These terms always describe those, who are in a helpless or forlorn condition. Although the religion of the Jews cast the shield of its mighty protection over widows and orphans, yet such were the corrupt opinions of surrounding nations in regard to the

weak, and such is the evil propensity of men to take advantage of those who cannot defend themselves, that even in Jewry *widows* and *orphans* were words expressive of a very low condition. Calvin: "There can be no doubt that orphans and widows are named to indicate in general all such as the world are disposed to overlook as unworthy of their regard. Generally we distribute our attentions where we expect some return. We give the preference to rank and splendor, and despise or neglect the poor." In this we are not like God. Hengstenberg: "*Orphans* and *widows* are expressions designed to individualize the *miserable*." *Father* and *Judge* seem to bear the general sense of defender, protector, vindicator; the first best expresses the pity and tenderness of God; the latter, his authority and ability to protect. *His holy habitation* may mean either *heaven*, where God sits as a Judge forever; or the *tabernacle*, where by laws and statutes, by Urim and Thummim, and by judgments as the head of the government he made himself known.

6. *God setteth the solitary in families.* These senses are suggested. 1. God makes those of like temper to dwell in a house; 2. God gives the solitary a home; 3. Hammond, followed by many scholars for solitary reads destitute, and gets this sense: God relieves the destitute so that he may abide at home and not seek abroad. Boothroyd: God maketh outcasts to dwell at home; Patrick: God provides for those who are utterly destitute, and settles them in comfortable habitations; Hengstenberg: God makes the solitary to dwell in houses. By *solitary* he understands *miserable*, and the blessing they receive consists in being *brought under roof and shelter*. 4. Horsley: God is bringing home his chosen ones, meaning from the Babylonish captivity. 5. Others refer the passage to the settlement in their own homes in Canaan of those, who had been bereft of friends in Egypt, or in the wilderness. 6. The Chaldee, Syriac, Calvin, Piscator, Fabritius, Amesius, the Genevan translation and Jebb sustain the reading of the English text. Clarke: "Is not the meaning, God is the author of marriage; and children, the legal fruit of it, are an inheritance from him?" Pool: "Such as were single and solitary he blesseth with a wife and children, as he did Abraham. *Houses* are often put for posterity, Exod. i. 21; Ruth iv. 11; 2 Sam. vii. 11." There is no better sense. *He bringeth out those which are bound with chains.* The release of prisoners is a favorite figure of inspired writers, Ps. cii. 20; cxlvi. 7; Isa. xlii. 7; xlix. 9; Zech. ix. 11, 12. Some refer this language to the release of Joseph from prison; some, to the deliverance of Israel from Egypt; some, to the rescue of the destitute from want and poverty; and some to the changes mercifully brought about in giving a people a good instead of a bad government. All desirable changes among men or nations are the fruit of God's mercy and power. But such language has a wider reach and points to the rescue of God's penitent people from wrath, guilt, gross darkness, fatal error, the dominion of sin, and the slavery of vile lusts and appetites; and bringing them forth to the liberty of the children of God. *But the rebellious dwell in a dry land. But, only, surely,* or *truly;* see on Ps. lxii. 1. By the rebellious, the Chaldee understands the Egyptians, who were reluctant to dismiss the Israelites. But the subsequent context shows that it has a wide application. Indeed Israel, when rebelling, found the words awfully true. They are of universal application, and are parallel to Ps. xxxii. 10; Pr. ix. 12; Isa. iii. 11; Ezek. xviii. 4. To *dwell in a dry place* is to lack comforts and refreshments, and so to be miserable.

7. *O God, when thou wentest forth before thy people, when thou didst march through the wilderness; Selah:*

8. *The earth shook, the heavens also dropped at the presence of God; even Sinai itself was moved at the presence of God, the God of Israel.* These verses are a simple rehearsal of the great historic fact that God led his people forth from Egypt and

through the wilderness. The remarkable effects produced on the natural world are recorded in Ex. xix. 16–20. Nor was this a solitary case, Judg. v. 4, 5. Instead of *Sinai itself*, some read *this Sinai;* some connect the pronoun with God, *this God;* and some *this* (was at) *Sinai.* In favor of *this God* we have Isa. xxv. 9. There are objections to referring *dropped* to the *manna.* It is never used in that connection, but another word, *rained*, Ex. xvi. 4; Ps. lxxviii. 24. Nor does it probably refer to the plague of thunder and hail and rain in Egypt, Ex. ix. 22–34. After *dropped* the Chaldee supplies *dew.* May we not by *dropped* understand *lowered?* Yet as these verses are clearly borrowed from Judg. v. 4, we may supply *rain* or *water.* This agrees with verse

9. *Thou, O God, didst send a plentiful rain, whereby thou didst confirm thine inheritance, when it was weary.* God's *inheritance* was either the land of Canaan, made over to the Israelites as an inheritance, or it was the body of pious Israelites themselves. The next verse favors the first view. The *weariness* seems to refer to the people, but it may imply the thirstiness of the soil of Judea until it was watered from heaven. Nothing but miraculous interpositions saved the Israelites from fainting and perishing in the wilderness. Instead of *plentiful rain* the Chaldee has *vivifying dews*, and *spontaneous rains;* Ainsworth, *a rain of liberalities;* Venema, *a shower of abundances;* Mudge and Edwards, *blessings;* Hengstenberg, *a rain of gifts;* Alexander, *a rain of free gifts.* Among the blessings granted to the Israelites in the wilderness were manna, quails, and water in great abundance. To *confirm* here means to *strengthen*, inducing a state the opposite of *being weary.*

10. *Thy congregation hath dwelt therein,* i. e., in the promised land, which was *the inheritance* of the Israelites. *Thou, O God, hast prepared of thy goodness for the poor.* Canaan was the gift of God to the people escaped from bondage. So are all the blessings God bestows on his children who are *poor, afflicted, humble, lowly;* see on Ps. ix. 12; xviii. 27. *Goodness*, in Ps. iv. 6; xiv. 1, 3, *good;* in Ps. xvi. 2, *goodness.*

11. *The Lord gave the word: great was the company of those that published it. Gave* in the future, but see Introduction, § 6. In the rest of the verse the allusion is clearly to the song of Deborah, already noticed. *Those that published it*, one word, a participle in the feminine. Women took part in shouting the triumphs of armies, Ex. xv. 20; Judg. xi. 34; 1 Sam. xviii. 6. It is only remotely that this verse can allude to the giving of the law. It may refer to the preaching of the Gospel in the same way as Ps. xix. 4 is made to do in Rom. x. 18.

12. *Kings of armies did flee apace; and she that tarried at home divided the spoil.* The verbs in Hebrew are in the future, but are doubtless well rendered in the preterite. The Scriptures mention *great kings* and *famous kings* and *mighty kings*, who fled before Israel, or were slain by their hosts, Ps. cxxxv. 10, 11; cxxxvi. 17–20; Josh. viii. 2; Judg. i. 6, 7; iv. 24, and many other places. On dividing the spoil of their enemies, see Num. xxxi. 26–54; Josh. xxii. 8; 1 Sam. xxx. 24. Some of the accounts of ancient spoil seem almost fabulous.

13. *Though ye have lain* [in many editions lien] *among the pots, yet shall ye be as the wings of a dove covered with silver, and her feathers with yellow gold.* Lowth: "I am not at all satisfied with any explication I have ever met with of these verses, either as to sense or construction, and I must give them up as unintelligible to me." But is not this the import of the passage, Though in former times in Egypt, in the wilderness, and in camp your condition has been depressed, yet there shall be a great change and ye shall be beautified? *Pots* here only; in Ezek. xl. 43, rendered *hooks.* Others render it end-irons, hearth-stones, trivets, tripods; many, pots. In either case it refers to a low and sorrowful condition. Some think it refers to the kilns of Egypt. The plumage of some species of pigeons or doves is changeable according to the light

in which it is seen, and in any good light is as rich in color as silver or gold. Patrick: "Though you have endured great hardships in *Egypt*, where you looked not like valiant soldiers, but rather like vile scullions besmutted among kettles and pots, you shall hereafter appear most beautiful and splendid, and the wings of your armies shall shine like those of a dove when they glister as if they were covered with silver and gold." Alexander: "The beautiful allusion to the colors of a dove's plumage seems intended to suggest the idea of a peaceful and splendid prosperity." Henry: "From a low and despised condition they had been advanced to splendor and prosperity." Many give a like exposition. Many practical writers, especially in the seventeenth century, applied this verse to the fallen state of God's people by nature, and to their backslidings after conversion, followed by the excellences of redemption, sanctification and glory. Dr. Gill thinks this is the best use of all. Those, who have thus regarded the passage, are so many and so respectable, that it is not wise to scorn them.

14. *When the Almighty scattered kings in it, it was* white *as snow in Salmon.* Diodati: "After all these victories obtained against the enemies of the church, the land, which before seemed horrid through war and desolation, Ps. lxxiv. 20, became beautiful, and flourishing in justice, peace, and blessings, even as the hill of Salmon, being shady and dark of its own nature, and as the Hebrew name imports, becometh white when the snow is fallen upon it. Concerning this hill see Judg. ix. 48." Alexander: "The change from war to peace is likened to the dazzling whiteness of snow in the midst of blackness or darkness." *Salmon* signifies *shade.* Snow is just the reverse of darkness.

15. *The hill of God* is as *the hill of Bashan; a high hill* as *the hill of Bashan.* On the country called *Bashan,* see on Ps. xxii. 12. The mountain of Bashan was renowned for its size, beauty and fertility; but Mount Zion was its equal, not in these respects, but in being the chosen spot where Jehovah revealed himself in so glorious a manner. By a figure well understood more is meant than is expressed as in 1 Pet. iv. 3. The meaning is, Mount Zion is far better than Bashan. In Isa. ii. 2, it is said *the mountain of the Lord's house* shall be established *in the top of the mountains, and shall be exalted above the hills.* This is a plain and obvious sense, approved by many; among later writers, by Pool and Hengstenberg. Others understand that the meaning is that Bashan is a great mountain, in Hebrew phrase, a mount of God, displaying the vastness of God's creative power. This may be warranted; see on Ps. xxxvi. 6; lxv. 9. Compare Ps. civ. 16. Horsley: A hill of God is the hill of Bashan. A hill of lofty brows is the hill of Bashan. But this is not so good as that already suggested.

16. *Why leap ye, ye high hills?* Hammond: "The word rendered *leap ye* occurs here only, and is by guess rendered to *leap.*" Chandler has it, Why look ye askance? *i. e.,* why are ye jealous? Aquila and Jerome, Why contend ye? Clarke: Why envy ye? Pool well paraphrases it: "Why do ye triumph and boast of your height, and look upon poor Zion with scorn and contempt, as an obscure and inconsiderable hill, if compared with you?" *Leaping* would point to scornful exultation expressed by vaulting. This is *the hill,* which *God desireth to dwell in, yea, the* LORD *will dwell* in it *forever.* The Most High is here revealed by his two names *Elohim* and *Jehovah.* He chose Zion, and not the greatest mountain on earth. He made it great by his choice. To this day the greatest ranges and highest peaks of mountains are as nothing for celebrity compared with Mount Zion.

17. *The chariots of God* are *twenty thousand,* even *thousands of angels.* The enemies of Israel often tried to make themselves formidable by chariots, Ex. xiv. 7; Judg. iv. 3; 1 Sam. xiii. 5; 2 Sam. viii. 4; x. 18. Here David opposes to them the chariots of God. The fullest representation made of this matter is found in 2 Kings vi. 17. But

such ideas were familiar to the minds of pious men of old. There is some doubt as to the rendering of the numbers in this verse. The Hebrew and Clarke read two myriads of thousands doubled; John Rogers' translation, many thousande tymes a thousande; Calvin and Genevan translation, twenty thousand thousand; Horsley, twenty thousand thousand of thousand. The difficulty respecting Hebrew numbers has been previously explained; see on title of Ps. lx. *Myriad* may mean *ten thousand,* or be used indefinitely for a vast multitude, Ps. iii. 6. There is a still further difficulty. It is evident that the authors of the English version and many others regarded the word rendered *angels* as included in the Hebrew text, for they do not mark it as supplied, and yet there is no word corresponding to it except the word rendered *double.* That word occurs nowhere else, and modern authorities will not allow us in any case to render it *angels;* for it is literally thousands of *repetition, i. e.,* thousands *repeated.* Jude 14 would allow us to read *holy myriads* there; and the theology of the Jews would allow us to supply angels here. But it is evident that the authors of the common version thought they had on this subject some light, of which we know nothing. Compare Deut. xx. 1–4; Ps. xx. 7. The law was given from Sinai by the ministration of angels, Gal. iii. 19; Heb. ii. 2. Jewish writers give as a confident tradition that there were *seventy thousand* angels at the giving of the law. There may have been many more. The Bible does not fix the number. But the latter part of this verse seems to allude to that transaction: *The* LORD is *among them* as in *Sinai, in the holy* place. This is supposed to be elliptical, and might be read, The Lord (*Adonai*) is among them (the chariots or angels) as in Sinai, so also in the holy place (or Zion) at this time. Alexander: "Under the law, Sinai was renewed in Zion. Under the Gospel, Zion superseded Sinai."

18. *Thou hast ascended on high, thou hast led captivity captive: thou hast received gifts for men; yea, for the rebellious also, that the* LORD *God might dwell* among them. With unspeakable delight does the pious mind here find Messiah, and in the New Testament an inspired exposition of the whole verse, Eph. iv. 8–16. The passage no doubt has its primary application to God as a conqueror for Israel. God having engaged in the conflict won the day and ascended to his seat or throne either on Mount Zion or in heaven. He *led captivity captive,* a phrase occurring first in the song of Deborah, Judg. v. 12, and signifying that he had taken many captives, or that he had put away cause of fear that his people should be subject to captivity. The *gifts* were the *spoils* of the enemy, and they were designed for the *stubborn,* the *refractory,* or *rebellious* Israelites, that a sense of God's kindness might win them to himself. But all this is low, compared with the high and ultimate sense of the passage as expounded by Paul in application to Christ, who has ascended up far above all heavens, who turned the captivity of his people, who bound their enemies Satan, sin and death, who received great gifts, especially of the Holy Ghost, for men, Acts ii. 4, 33; and who bestows his gifts on *rebellious man.* Thus the LORD God (*Jah Elohim*) Immanuel, *God with us,* dwells among sinners.

19. *Blessed be the* LORD, who *daily loadeth us* with benefits, even *the God of our salvation. Blessed,* see on Ps. v. 12; xviii. 46. *Daily,* literally *day by day,* meaning *continually. Loadeth,* this verb may be taken either in a good or bad sense; here manifestly in a good sense. The LORD *God* of this verse is *Adonai El.*

20. He that is *our God* is *the God of salvation. God,* in each case in this verse is *El. Salvation,* in the plural, *salvations,* see on Ps. iii. 2, 8. Chaldee: Our God is strength and redemption. *And unto God the* LORD belong *the issues from death.* Why the name of the Most High is thus rendered in this verse does not appear. The Hebrew is *Jehovah Adonai,* Jehovah the Ruler, commonly LORD *Lord.* Calvin has it *the Lord Jehovah;* Alexander, *Jehovah the Lord.* The sense of the clause is that on

God we depend for our escapes, deliverances, or goings forth from death. Death is not a monarch, but a servant of God. Calvin: "Death may threaten us in ever so many forms, yet God can easily devise the necessary means of preservation."

21. *But God shall wound the head of his enemies,* and *the hairy scalp of such a one as goeth on still in his trespasses.* *But,* rendered *truly* in Ps. lxii. 1; in this place by Calvin *surely;* see on Ps. lxii. 1. To *wound the head and hairy scalp* is to kill; elsewhere *smite, smite through, strike through, pierce,* Num. xxiv. 8, 17; Job xxvi. 12; Ps. cx. 5. It expresses the infliction of a deadly blow. God will send utter destruction on such as persist in *trespasses.* His people's enemies are his enemies. Alexander: "The hairy scalp is merely a poetical equivalent to *head.*"

22. *The Lord [Adonai] said, I will bring again from Bashan, I will bring* my people *again from the depths of the sea.* Three explanations are offered. One is that God here reminds his people of having delivered them from Og, king of Bashan and his hosts, and of having brought them through the Red sea, that thus he may teach them anew the lesson of their dependence. This is the view of Calvin. Another is that God here assures his people that though their case should become sad, even as if they were in terror of the power of Og, king of Bashan, and in the perils of the Red sea, yet he would safely bring them through all their troubles as he had done their fathers. This view is favored by Patrick, Gill, Pool, Henry, Horne, Scott, Anderson. A third supposes that God is not in v. 22 speaking of his people at all, but of his *enemies,* and is telling them that though they should climb to the heights of the great mountains, or hide in the sea yet he would thence bring them forth to punishment. The historic Scripture explaining the allusion to Bashan is Num. xxi. 33–35. The passage of the Red sea is recorded in Ex. xiv. This last view is confidently held by Tholuck, Hengstenberg and Alexander. In favor of it it may be stated that *my people* is supplied outright, not being even taken from the context, whereas *enemies* are expressly named in vv. 21, 23. A passage supposed by some to be quite parallel to this is found in Amos ix. 2, 3. On the other hand we have the judgment of a long line of very judicious commentators in favor of the *second* view stated. Besides some suppose that the phrase *The* LORD *said* at the beginning of v. 22 refers to 2 Sam. iii. 18, where Abner says, *The* LORD *hath spoken.* In that place we find expressly *my people.*

23. *That thy foot may be dipped in the blood of* thine *enemies, and the tongue of thy dogs in the same.* The first clause is parallel to the last clause of Ps. lviii. 10. For *dipped* the margin has *red.* The meaning is that the true Israel should gain as complete a victory as a conqueror does when pursuing his retreating foes, he dips his feet in the blood of the slain. We know the fondness of the dog for blood, and are furnished in sacred history with an illustration, 1 Kings xxii. 38. If these verses continue the discourse begun in v. 18, then they point to the resurrection and ascension of Christ, the spread of the Gospel, the downfall of paganism, the striking dumb of heathen oracles and the perfect victory of Messiah over his enemies.

24. *They have seen thy goings, O God; even the goings of my God, my King, in the sanctuary.* If the imagery is drawn from the return of the ark to Jerusalem after successful wars, then we may give to *they* a very extended signification, and include all who had seen the wonders wrought by Jehovah—the same Jehovah who had long shown his glory *in the sanctuary,* and who was David's *God* and *King.* David points away from himself and invites the people to adore *God.* The Lord is God and King, and a man of war heading his armies in battle and in their triumphant return.

25. *The singers went before, the players on instruments* followed *after.* The order of the procession here noted is, says Hengstenberg, "because, in intellectual true religion, the Word takes everywhere the first place." *Among* them were *the damsels playing with timbrels.* The instrument known to moderns, most nearly resembling the ancient

timbrel, is the *tambourine*. Hengstenberg calls it the 'hand-kettle-drum.' It was struck with the fingers. It was the same with the tabret, Gen. xxxi. 27 ; Ex. xv. 20 ; 1 Sam. x. 5 ; Nah. ii. 7. In joyful processions for victories females bore a part, Ex. xv. 20 ; 1 Sam. xviii. 6, 7.

26. *Bless ye God in the congregations*, even *the Lord, from the fountain of Israel*. The margin renders the last phrase, Ye that are of the fountain of Israel, meaning all the people of the stock of Israel. Compare Deut. xxxiii. 28 ; Isa. xlviii. 1. The *congregations* are the *assemblies* of God's people. *Bless*, the usual word for *benediction*. In further describing the procession he says :

27. *There is little Benjamin* with *their ruler*. Benjamin signifies a *son of days*, meaning that he was the son of Jacob's old age, Gen. xliv. 20. For *little* the Septuagint has *the younger*. The tribe of Benjamin was never very numerous ; and after the loss of so many of their people on account of the crime of the men of Gibeah, it was very small, Judges xix. xx. xxi. Yet this Benjamin furnished a *Ruler*, King Saul. Himself at first modestly declined the kingdom on the ground that his tribe was so inconsiderable, 1 Sam. ix. 21. The only objection to supposing Saul to be alluded to is that it would have been unseasonable to call to mind his reign, which had in it so many crimes and disasters. To this it is replied, *first*, Saul had done great things for the good of his country, 1 Sam. xiv. 47, 48 ; *secondly*, so far from ignoring the good Saul had done, David made sincere and tender lamentation for him after his death, 2 Sam. i. 17–27. [There are] *the princes of Judah* and *their council*. Some read *the princes of Judah in their assembly*. David was of the tribe of Judah, and the prophecies going before had long marked out that as a *ruling* tribe, holding *assemblies* or *councils* for the government of the nation, Gen. xlix. 8–10 ; Deut. xxxiii. 7. The *princes* of any people were the heads of tribes or of families. Moreover [there were] *the princes of Zebulon*, and *the princes of Naphtali*. Benjamin and Judah were near to the holy city. Zebulon and Naphtali were very remote from it. Benjamin and Judah were two of the most Southern tribes ; Zebulon and Naphtali were two of the most Northern. They were also remarkable for their prowess, Judges v. 18, and for their learning, Gen. xlix. 21 ; Judges v. 14. This enumeration is equivalent to saying, All the tribes of Israel, small and great, near and remote, are there. Other explanations are offered, but none so good as this. It is noticeable, and has often been remarked, that the four tribes here named are conspicuous in New Testament history. Our Saviour began his ministry in Zebulon and Naphtali, and called most of his apostles from those tribes. Our Lord himself sprang out of Judah. Several of his apostles were of the same tribe. Paul was of the tribe of Benjamin, Matt. iv. 12–22; Heb. vii. 14; Phil. iii. 5. If the prophet is still continuing his reference to gospel times, the naming of these tribes has a special significancy.

28. *Thy God hath commanded thy strength*. The people Israel are here addressed. *Commanded*, a word of frequent occurrence. It expresses *authority*. *Strength*, that kind of *might* which wins the battle and gives stability to kingdoms. *Strengthen, O God, that which thou hast wrought for us*. *Strengthen*, cognate of the noun *strength* in the same verse. The prayer is for stability to Israel in all the varied interests of the nation, especially in the settlement of the land, and in freedom from the fear of surrounding nations ; see Isa. xxvi. 12.

29. *Because of thy temple at Jerusalem shall kings bring presents unto thee*. The common version is abundantly sustained. The *temple* may mean either the tabernacle, or the more durable structure built by Solomon ; see on Ps. v. 7 ; lxv. 4. Here it pretty certainly points to the tabernacle. *Presents*, found here only, and in Ps. lxxvi. 11 ; Isa. xviii. 7 ; but the bringing of gifts as an act of worship to the true God is often mentioned, 2 Chron. xxxii. 23 ; Ps. lxxii. 10, 11 ; Isa. lx. 3–11 ; Matt. ii. 11.

30. *Rebuke the company of spearmen.* This is a clause not easily rendered or interpreted. In favor of the common version are Calvin, church of England, Bishops' Bible, Genevan translation, Piscator, Amesius and Hammond. But the margin, all the ancient versions, John Rogers' translation, Fabritius, Edwards, Jebb, Boothroyd, Horne, Mudge, Green, Horsley, Fry, Tholuck, Hengstenberg and Alexander prefer, Rebuke the beasts of the reeds. Some explain that rendering to mean, Destroy our enemies, which are like the destructive beasts, the lion, crocodile and hippopotamus, that live among the reeds, Isa. xxxv. 7; Jer. xlix. 19; l. 44; Zech. xi. 3. But spears and other missiles were often made of reeds, and the word *company* is plural, so that *company of the spear* is perhaps the best rendering. Yet great respect is due to the learning of those who take a different view. That the image of terrible beasts may have been before the prophet's mind appears from the next clause: [Rebuke] *the multitude of the bulls with the calves of the people.* On *bulls* as persecutors, see on Ps. xxii. 12. Compare Isa. xxxiv. 7; Jer. l. 11. Others think *bulls* and *calves* are here introduced solely as objects of worship in Egypt, and that God is invoked to destroy the Egyptian *worship,* as in the first clause he was asked to destroy the Egyptian *power* represented by the beasts of the reed. Referring the whole verse thus to the Egyptian *power* and *worship* gives a good sense. The prophet asks God to go on conquering, Till every one *submit himself with pieces of silver,* i. e., either bring the tribute money or (which is better) bring the *presents* mentioned in v. 29, and humbly own that Jehovah is God alone. *Scatter thou the people* that *delight in war.* The Hebrew is in prophetic style, *he has scattered,* i. e., he surely will scatter. Pool well explains the phrase *delighting in war* as referring to those " that without any necessity or provocation, and merely out of a love to mischief and spoil, make war."

31. *Princes shall come out of Egypt,* i. e., they shall come bringing the presents and submitting themselves. On the word *princes,* (literally *fat ones*) see on Ps. xxii. 29. This clause favors the application of the first part of v. 30 to Egypt. This prominence is properly given to Egypt because that was in David's day a powerful kingdom and very hostile to the true religion, and the scope of the prophecy is that people remote, mighty and hitherto much opposed to the worship of Jehovah shall adore him. In like manner a people even more remote, no less hostile to the true religion, and yet covering a much larger district, and even more powerful, *Cush,* shall do as Egypt. *Ethiopia shall soon stretch out her hands unto God.* The Hebrew is very strong: Cush will hasten to extend her hands to God, or more literally will cause her hands to run out to God. We need not determine whether this *stretching out of the hands* is in supplication, or in the offering of presents. The two always go together. How great was the Ethiopia of Scripture appears from passages in more than one of the subsequent prophets. See Concordance. The land here described lay beyond Egypt and around the upper part of it. One of the first converts to Christianity from among the heathen was a great man of Ethiopia, Acts viii. 26–39.

32. *Sing unto God, ye kingdoms of the earth; O sing praises unto the* LORD. On the two verbs see on v. 4, where they both occur. Sing praises

33. *To him that rideth upon the heavens of heavens,* which were *of old.* The heavens *of heavens* are the third heavens, the highest heavens, the abode of the peculiar presence and glory of Jehovah. In v. 4 we have a similar phrase but quite another word rendered *heavens.* The *riding* is that of majesty and triumph. There is no place so glorious but that God is the glory of it, so bright but that he is the light thereof. He has supreme, perpetual and universal dominion. The heavens, and especially the heaven of heavens, are fit similitudes to represent antiquity. They were *of old.* Lo, *he doth send out his voice,* and that *a mighty voice.* Either God commands the thunder, or speaks in the thunder; see on Ps. xxix. 3, 4.

34. *Ascribe ye strength unto God.* *Strength*, as in Ps. viii. 2; often rendered *power.* It occurs *five* times in this Psalm, *twice* in this verse. *His excellency* is *over Israel, and his strength* is *in the clouds.* Some put the words *over Israel* at the close of the first clause, but, though admissible, this is no improvement. *Excellency*, so rendered, or *highness*, when referring to God. *In the clouds*, exalted above all earthly powers.

35. *O God*, thou art *terrible out of thy holy places.* *Terrible*, as in Ps. xlv. 4; xlvii. 2; lxv. 5; lxvi. 3, 5. It is the participle of the verb rendered *fear*, and *be afraid* in Ps. iii. 6; xxiii. 4. *Holy places, sanctuaries*, not often in the plural. Calvin: "The plural number is used because the tabernacle was divided into three parts." Wherever God has a sanctuary, or holy place, his word and worship are suited to beget awe. *The God of Israel* is *he that giveth strength and power unto* his *people. Strength*, as in v. 34. *Power*, in the plural *powers*, also rendered *strength.* Whoever has power, or might, or strength of any kind, has it from God, the God of Israel. *Blessed* be *God.* The usual form of *blessing* the *Elohim.*

DOCTRINAL AND PRACTICAL REMARKS.

1. In prayer, praise, confession, adoration or supplication we can often find excellent patterns in the holy Scriptures, as David does in the words of Moses and Deborah, quoted in this Psalm, vv. 1, 2. One reason why we should study God's word and commit large portions of it to memory is that we may have the best language for devotion.

2. It is vain to deny that unrenewed men are the *enemies of God*, v. 1. They are so spoken of in all the Scriptures.

3. When God arises, all opposers are *scattered* and *flee* away, v. 1. All the combined powers of earth and hell are dissolved and dissipated before him. He may endure with much long-suffering the vessels of wrath; but he will at last arise. Luther: "When the Jews thought that they had gained the victory, now that Christ was laid in the grave, God awakes and calls Christ from the dead. Then the tables are turned: the disciples assemble, the Jews divide, some to grace who believe, others to wrath who are destroyed by the Romans."

4. The destruction of the wicked is easy and very natural, v. 2. It is like the passing away of smoke, or the melting of wax. They may make a great show, they may bluster, they may appear ever so formidable, but they shall *perish.* Calvin: "God needs no array of preparation in overthrowing his enemies. He can dissipate them with a breath."

5. When men boast of their strength and courage, their freedom from fear and their undaunted spirit, and say nothing can unman them, they have not been in the awful presence of God and know not how even they would shrink, and melt away, and perish there, vv. 1, 8, 9.

6. The Scriptures justly maintain a strong and fearful contrast between both the character and the destiny of the wicked and the righteous. They are not alike. They do not think, feel, or fare alike, vv. 2, 3. Heaven and hell are appropriate places for the reception of their respective inhabitants.

7. As it is a privilege, so it is a duty to *be glad*, to *rejoice*, yea, *exceedingly* to *rejoice*, v. 3. He, who knows and loves and receives little, may rejoice little. But surely he, who has experienced the saving grace of God, ought not to be tame and torpid in his exultations. If we duly rejoiced in God, we should not so often seek a portion here below. When the heart is full of joy in God, the trifles and vanities of time lose their enchantments.

8. Our joy should be solemn as well as lively, and should take a devotional turn, v. 4. "Is any merry? let him sing Psalms." There is not an hour, a condition, an

event, but in some respects calls for praise. We have God, his perfections, his works, his word; we have Christ and his benefits; we have the Sabbath and its hallowed influences; we have food, raiment, shelter and friends. What have we not? If we are Christians, all things are ours. As we cannot rejoice in the Lord too much, so we cannot *extol* him too highly.

9. We mightily wrong God, when we take from him the honor, which he well deserves, for his care, and love, and pity to widows and orphans, strangers and prisoners, the neglected and injured, the crushed and destitute of earth, vv. 5, 6. How much is God honored, when the widow says, 'I trusted in God and was not forsaken;' when the orphan says, 'I was cast on the Lord from the womb and was not left to want;' when the stranger says, 'I was among a people whose speech I knew not, but God raised me up friends;' when the prisoner says, 'I was bound in affliction and iron, but Jehovah was a light unto me.' Scott: "God's condescension is equal to his majesty: he always patronises the afflicted and oppressed; and poor sinners, helpless and exposed more than any destitute orphans, are readily admitted among his sons and daughters, and share all the blessings of that high relation." Arnd: "Great potentates in the world respect the noblest and the richest in the land, the men who may adorn their court and strengthen their authority. But the highest glory of God is to compassionate the miserable." Never did God so manifest his glorious pity and condescension, as when his Son became incarnate, married our nature, and died for his helpless yet malignant foes.

10. Very few have a just estimate of the blessings of the family state, or are adequately thankful for them, v. 6. Let us often sing our song of praise on account of them. Many good treatises have been written on this subject; but it is not exhausted. How many precious thoughts are at once presented by the very mention of *husband, wife, father, mother, brother, sister, daughter, son.* When for his sins God drove man out of paradise, he allowed him to carry with him two of its most precious institutions, marriage and the Sabbath. No good man is ready to say which of these is the greatest blessing.

11. The wretchedness of a sinful state is dreadful. Verily the rebellious dwell in a *dry* land, v. 6. Who ever had comfort in pride, or lies, or fraud, or violence? "The wages of sin is death." Henry: "The best land will be a dry land to those that by their rebellion have forfeited the blessing of God, which is the juice and fatness of all our enjoyments."

12. We may feel very easy about going into great trials, even such as passing through a *wilderness*, if only God be with us, v. 7. He never brings his people into difficulties, but to bring them out again. He never forsakes his loved ones. With his chosen, Christ is ever present.

13. Such grand and awful displays of the divine majesty as were made at Mount Sinai ought not to be forgotten, but frequently mentioned, v. 8.

14. All our valuable supplies are from above, v. 9. Compare Ps. lxxviii. 24, 27; Jas. i. 17. The food of the Israelites was supplied as they needed it, to try and to humble them, Deut. viii. 16. But far richer blessings come on the Gospel church. We have Christ the true bread that came down from heaven, and the Holy Spirit, who is poured out in floods on thirsty souls. We have the antitypes, the substance, the consummation, the glory. We are bound for the heavenly Canaan.

15. It is a grand excellence of true religion that it suits the *poor*, the *afflicted*, the *humble*, v. 10. To such it is real *goodness*. No unpardoned, unconverted sinner ever dreamed of such blessings and refreshments as every renewed soul experiences.

16. When God speaks the word, the contest is decided, vv. 11, 12; Ecc. ix. 11. God is judge of all. Without him no man, nor thing can stand; with him the feeble

is as David, and weak things have power. Calvin: "The mightiest preparations, which the enemies of the Church may make for its destruction, shall be overthrown." All the victories of Israel's armies under David are small and mean, compared with the glorious spiritual victories of the Church under the great Captain of salvation. There are no trophies like souls redeemed from sin, and death, and hell. Arnd: "Is it not a valuable spoil, that so many thousands of men have been converted from heathenism, among whom have been so many glorious teachers and lights of the church, such as Justin, Augustine, Ambrose, not to speak of the innumerable martyrs, brought out of heathenism, and put to death because of their attachment to the Christian faith?"

17. The depth from which, and the height to which God raises those on whom he sets his love, must both be brought into the estimate, if we would judge aright of the divine mercy, v. 13. We go from the *pots*. We become as *doves*. We escape hell. We rise to heaven.

18. What a blessing is peace! The prophet compares it to the snow that made Salmon to glisten, v. 14. Dickson: "As a dark, dusky mountain, whereupon groweth no green thing but black heath, is made white, when covered with snow; so is a disgraced, shamed, impoverished, enslaved land made glorious again by a merciful manner of delivery manifesting the Lord's kind respects unto it."

19. No exaltation is like that, which comes from a connection with God and his religion, vv. 15, 16. Mount Sinai, Mount Zion and Mount Calvary are the three most famous mountains on earth, yea, they are and ever will be much spoken of in heaven; yet thousands of peaks and ranges are in themselves more striking and more worthy of note. The reason is that from one, the law was given, on another, was the temple, on the third, sin was expiated.

20. We need not fear that God cannot defend us at all times and in all cases. He has the power. He has the will. He has the resources. He has the agents. He is the Lord of hosts. His armies are numerous and mighty. He has "an innumerable company of angels." And *the Lord is among them.*

21. Of all the acts and scenes of earth none are so important, none so well worthy of celebration as those connected with the birth, life, death, resurrection and ascension of Christ, v. 18. This theme the prophets often introduce without notice. On this subject they never tire. By bloodshedding Christ redeemed us. By rising from the dead and ascending to heaven we have assurance of his power to save us. Truly the Sabbath, which commemorates Christ's resurrection, ought never to be a fast-day. It is true that "Christ did not enter into his glory without a battle going before, and that with strong and many enemies: and in his fighting he carried the victory, and after his victory he triumphed, first in the cross and then in his ascension, over sin, Satan, the world, hell, the grave and all." Let us never lose sight of Christ.

22. It should never be forgotten, and it should greatly heighten our estimate of Christ's love, that he showed his kindness to his foes—even *the rebellious*, v. 18. Compare John xv. 13; Rom. v. 8, 10; 1 Pet. iii. 18; 1 John iii. 16.

23. Our praises and thanksgivings should keep pace with the mercies we receive. If God loads us with *daily benefits*, why should we not *daily* shout and sing of his love? v. 19.

24. If we are in the right, we have God on our side; and if we have God on our side, we need fear nothing; for he is the *God of salvations*, of all kinds and varieties of deliverances for his people, vv. 19, 20. Let us walk by faith, not by sight. God has ten thousand ways, unseen and unthought of by us, to save us from trouble and from death. "When Jehovah takes the field, deadly is the battle to his enemies," and glorious is the victory to his friends.

25. It is a fearful thing to fall into the hands of the living God, v. 21.   Surely the Lord would not use such terrific language as he does respecting the doom of sinners, if it were not inconceivably dreadful.   Nothing can protect persistent and obstinate offenders from the sword of Divine Justice.   Compare Amos ix. 3, 4; Obad. 4.

26. Nothing in nature, respecting God's friends or foes, is beyond his control, v. 22. Bashan and the ocean are alike in the hollow of his hand and exposed to his view.

27. Whatever appearances there may be to the contrary for a season, yet in all cases ultimately God will make his church triumphantly victorious, to the eternal shame of her enemies, v. 23.

28. If any wish to read providence so as to understand it, let them go to the sanctuary, v. 24.   God's *goings* are incomprehensible without the light of the lamp of his house, his blessed word.   Compare Ps. lxxiii. 16, 17.   As the Shechinah dwelt in the Sanctuary, so does God in answer to the prayers of his people there display his glory, and thence come forth to bless and save his chosen.

29. Our religion should be social and lively, v. 25.   Even our most solemn acts of worship should not be gloomy or doleful.   And in this joyful service let all unite. Dickson: "Where all receive a benefit, it becometh all the people publicly and solemnly, and with their best expression, as God appointeth, to praise God, and in his worship to see that all things be done orderly."   On instrumental music, see REMARKS on Ps. xxxiii. 2.

30. Though formalists and hypocrites abuse public worship to the neglect of secret devotion, yet public worship is binding, v. 26.   All God's people know it to be edifying and comfortable.   It is to the pious a great means of promoting the observance of closet duties.

31. In the great work of glorifying God, and maintaining his worship, no tribe, or family, or person is so exalted or obscure, so learned or ignorant, as to be excused from the blessed service, v. 27.

32. We may safely and confidently pray for all that God has commanded or promised, v. 28.   We need no other warrant than his word for presenting any petition before him.

33. Two things we ought never to forget.   One is that if we have succeeded in our enterprises, on the battle-field, in agriculture, in trade, in preaching God's word, in anything, it was because God *commanded* our *strength*, and gave us success.   The other is that for the future we are as dependent on divine succor as if we had no experience of the divine kindness in days past, v. 28.   Not in our wit or wisdom, not in our experience or ability, not in great captains nor heavy battalions, not in the patronage of kings and governments, not in funds or estates, but in the Lord Jehovah is all our hope and all our salvation.

34. God gets his chief honor on earth, from having amongst us an organized church, a people publicly united in his service, as in the *temple*, still more in the gospel church, v. 29.   She is the light of the world, the salt of the earth, the depository of the truth, the witness for God and Christ, the conservator of good morals, good manners and true religion.

35. There is no army that God cannot rebuke, no armada that he cannot bring to nothing, v. 30.   Men may have the best arms, but all will be in vain without God's assistance.   Men may be trained to war till they are as fierce as *bulls* of Bashan, and they may be such a *multitude* that no man can count them, yet in a moment God can make them destroy each other, and tread each other down as the mire of the streets. Let us not be afraid though an host should encamp against us.   Calvin: "In comparing their enemies to the beasts mentioned in v. 30, and taking notice that they delighted in war, it was no doubt David's intention to influence the minds of the people

of God to the contrary dispositions of clemency and mercy, as being that frame of spirit in the exercise of which they might expect to receive the divine assistance. The more violently their enemies raged, and the more lawless their attempts might prove, they had only the more reason to expect the interposition of God, who humbles the proud and the mighty ones of this world."

36. It is clear from verse 30 and many passages of Scripture that the love of war, with its scenes of carnage, forms no part of a gracious character. Hatred, and wrath, and strife, and clamor are never pleasant to a child of God. Henry: "David had himself been a man of war, but could appeal to God, that he never delighted in war and bloodshed for its own sake; as for those that did, and would not agree to the fairest terms of peace, he does not doubt but God would scatter them. Those are lost to all the sacred principles of humanity, as well as Christianity, that can delight in war, and take pleasure in contention; let them expect that, sooner or later, they shall have enough of it, Isa. xxxiii. 1; Rev. xiii. 10." Scott: "May the Lord speedily so strengthen his cause upon earth, that all the proud, idolatrous and oppressive,—all that delight in war, or maintain opposition to his church, may be scattered and brought down; that all kings and nations may share the blessings of his Gospel, and sing praises to his name." Amen and amen.

37. Ever since the propagation of the true religion, and especially since the promulgation of Christianity remarkable changes have been going on in the world, and marvels of mercy have been displayed. For a long time there were powerful and flourishing churches in Egypt and Ethiopia, v. 31. There shall be again. There are now thousands of Christians on earth, who were born idolaters, and some of them cannibals. Divine grace has lost none of its saving energy.

38. All flesh should and shall praise God. Mighty kingdoms are no exception, v. 32. Pure Christianity shall yet wonderfully and widely prevail on the earth. God has promised it and he will surely bring it to pass. When this shall be, rests with him; but it shall surely be. When that event shall take place, the worship of false gods will utterly cease.

39. Let us never forget that God is exalted, v. 33. Nothing more infallibly marks worship as base than lack of profound reverence for the divine majesty. The Lord rideth upon the heavens. We are worms crawling upon earth.

40. God is strong; God alone is strong; God is so strong that he cannot be resisted, v. 34. Ascribe to him strength as ye do to nothing else. Angels have strength, but it is all derived and limited. He is the author of life and all our mercies.

41. God is majestic. He is highly exalted. His excellency is over Israel, v. 34. None is high as God is high.

42. God is holy. His presence makes a place holy, v. 34. Without him nothing is holy. His holiness is a consuming fire. Henry: "No attribute of God is more dreadful to sinners than his holiness." And no attribute of God is more rejoiced in by unfallen angels and redeemed men than his holiness.

43. It has often been found that to none is God more terrible than to those, who in their health and prosperity affected to be incapable of fear, v. 35. This will appear in the most signal manner in the last day.

44. If we have any strength or success, let us never forget that it is all from God, v. 35. It is only he that makes strong the arms of the hands of his people. Scott: "While all unite in ascribing power and dominion unto him, may all experience strength communicated from him, enabling them to resist temptation, and to overcome every enemy of his salvation." What God is and has, he is and has for his people's good.

45. Blessed be God, v. 35. "If all be from him, let all be to him."

PSALM LXIX.

To the chief Musician upon Shoshannim, *A Psalm* of David.

1 Save me, O God; for the waters are come in unto *my* soul.

2 I sink in deep mire, where *there is* no standing: I am come into deep waters, where the floods overflow me.

3 I am weary of my crying: my throat is dried: mine eyes fail while I wait for my God.

4 They that hate me without a cause are more than the hairs of mine head: they that would destroy me, *being* mine enemies wrongfully, are mighty: then I restored *that* which I took not away.

5 O God, thou knowest my foolishness; and my sins are not hid from thee.

6 Let not them that wait on thee, O Lord GOD of hosts, be ashamed for my sake: let not those that seek thee be confounded for my sake, O God of Israel.

7 Because for thy sake I have borne reproach; shame hath covered my face.

8 I am become a stranger unto my brethren, and an alien unto my mother's children.

9 For the zeal of thine house hath eaten me up; and the reproaches of them that reproached thee are fallen upon me.

10 When I wept, *and chastened* my soul with fasting, that was to my reproach.

11 I made sackcloth also my garment; and I became a proverb to them.

12 They that sit in the gate speak against me; and I *was* the song of the drunkards.

13 But as for me, my prayer *is* unto thee, O LORD, *in* an acceptable time: O God, in the multitude of thy mercy hear me, in the truth of thy salvation.

14 Deliver me out of the mire, and let me not sink: let me be delivered from them that hate me, and out of the deep waters.

15 Let not the waterflood overflow me, neither let the deep swallow me up, and let not the pit shut her mouth upon me.

16 Hear me, O LORD; for thy lovingkindness *is* good: turn unto me according to the multitude of thy tender mercies.

17 And hide not thy face from thy servant; for I am in trouble: hear me speedily.

18 Draw nigh unto my soul, *and* redeem it: deliver me because of mine enemies.

19 Thou hast known my reproach, and my shame, and my dishonour: mine adversaries *are* all before thee.

20 Reproach hath broken my heart; and I am full of heaviness: and I looked *for some* to take pity, but *there was* none; and for comforters, but I found none.

21 They gave me also gall for my meat; and in my thirst they gave me vinegar to drink.

22 Let their table become a snare before them: and *that which should have been* for *their* welfare, *let it become* a trap.

23 Let their eyes be darkened, that they see not; and make their loins continually to shake.

24 Pour out thine indignation upon them, and let thy wrathful anger take hold of them.

25 Let their habitation be desolate; *and* let none dwell in their tents.

26 For they persecute *him* whom thou hast smitten; and they talk to the grief of those whom thou hast wounded.

27 Add iniquity unto their iniquity: and let them not come into thy righteousness.

28 Let them be blotted out of the book of the living, and not be written with the righteous.

29 But I *am* poor and sorrowful: let thy salvation, O God, set me up on high.

30 I will praise the name of God with a song, and will magnify him with thanksgiving.

31 *This* also shall please the LORD better than an ox *or* bullock that hath horns and hoofs.

32 The humble shall see *this, and* be glad: and your heart shall live that seek God.

33 For the LORD heareth the poor, and despiseth not his prisoners.

34 Let the heaven and earth praise him, the seas, and everything that moveth therein.

35 For God will save Zion, and will build the cities of Judah, that they may dwell there, and have it in possession.

36 The seed also of his servant shall inherit it: and they that love his name shall dwell therein.

ON the title see on titles of Psalms iii. iv. xi. xlv. That David wrote this Psalm is admitted by the title and the great mass of commentators, and is declared by

Paul, Rom. xi. 9. It is idle to spend time in answering men who claim for it a much later origin. It is in vain to seek for it a historic occasion. It is very decidedly Messianic. The only question is, whether it is directly and fully prophetic or Typical-Messianic. There is no valid objection to the admission that in some parts David, as a sufferer, speaks as a type of Christ, and that in others he rises to the height of un-qualified prediction respecting Messiah. Verse 4 is cited in John xv. 25; v. 9, in John ii. 17; Rom. xv. 3; v. 21, in Matt. xxvii. 34, 48; Mark xv. 23; John xix. 28, 29; vv. 22, 23, in Rom. xi. 9, 10; and v. 25, in Acts i. 16, 20. Sound commentators generally admit that it has its fulfilment in Christ. Theodoret: "It is a prediction of the sufferings of Christ, and the final destruction of the Jews on that account." Cal-vin: "David wrote this inspired ode, not so much in his own name, as in the name of the whole church of whose head he was an eminent type." Vitringa: "It is admitted among Christians, that in the *sixty-ninth* Psalm Christ, and Christ as a sufferer, is to be placed before our eyes. We add, that it refers to Christ crucified as the Evangelists Matthew, Mark and John apply it." Fabritius: "In this Psalm David is a figure of Christ." Alexander: "The only individual in whom the traits meet is Christ." Hodge: "This Psalm is so frequently quoted and applied to Christ in the New Testa-ment, that it must be considered as directly prophetical." Similar remarks might be cited from Gill, Anderson, Scott and others. Calvin's first remark on this Psalm is: "There is a close resemblance between this and the xxii. Psalm." Many others have observed the likeness. This is a composition of great beauty and poetic excellence. Scott dates it B. C. 1021. The names of the Most High in it are *Elohim God, Ado-nai Lord* and *Jehovah* LORD, on which respectively see on Ps. iii. 2; ii. 4; i. 2.

1. *Save me, O God; for the waters are come in unto* my *soul. Waters*, a favorite emblem of Scripture for overwhelming distress; see on Ps. xlii. 7. Compare Ps. lxxiii. 10; lxxxviii. 7. As David was not a faint-hearted, but a truly heroic man, we may conceive how heavy must have been the pressure of his load of grief to make him cry so bitterly. If we apply these words to Christ, who had neither remorse nor despair, and was incapable of either, what a conception they give us of the dreadful load of human hatred, diabolical malice and divine wrath which he bore. The type and antitype each felt that his case was beyond any effectual aid from man; hence the cry: *Save, help, rescue, deliver* me. See on Ps. iii. 7; xii. 1. Gill: "The petitioner is Christ; not as a divine person, as such he is blessed forever, and stands in no need of help and assistance; but as man, and in distressed and suffering circumstances." That Jesus felt the deepest distress and offered the humblest and most earnest prayers is sufficiently declared in Scripture, Matt. xxvi. 39; John xii. 27; Heb. v. 7. The *great* troubles of David and of Christ were in the *soul* or heart. Hengstenberg: "When one is covered over with water, the water comes into his soul."

2. *I sink in deep mire where* there is *no standing. Mire*, here only and in Ps. xl. 2, where it is rendered *miry*. The figure is of turbid waters in a river or sea, probably the latter. *Deep*, rendered *depths* in Ps. lxviii. 22; Mic. vii. 19; in Zech. x. 11 *deeps;* literally mire of the *deep*. The sea, when troubled, often casts up mire and dirt, Is. lvii. 20. When one finds himself in such thick waters, and can reach no *bottom*, get no *footing*, nothing *solid* to stand upon, it is all over with him, unless he can get help from another. *I am come into deep waters, where the floods overflow me. Deep waters,* as in v. 14. *Deep*, a noun, commonly rendered *depths*, Ps. cxxx. 1; Isa. li. 10; Ezek. xxvii. 34. Here the *overflowing* is distinctly expressed. The verbs *sink* and *come* in Hebrew are in the preterite. The trial had lasted some time and was not yet over. The language expresses the wild confusion arising from great distress. Horne: "The divine displeasure, like a stormy tempest, was let loose upon him; the sins of the

world as deep mire enclosed and detained him; whilst all the waters of affliction went over his head and penetrated to his vitals."

3. *I am weary of my crying.* With crying would better give the sense. It does not mean that he was tired of earnest prayer; but that he had prayed so long, so earnestly and under such distress of mind that his nature was exhausted. Although he had found no relief, yet he persevered. What else could he do? *My throat is dried.* Calvin gives the sense, My throat is become hoarse with crying. *Throat,* also rendered *neck* or *mouth,* Isa. iii. 16; Ezek. xvi. 11; Ps. cxlix. 6. *Mine eyes fail while I wait for my God.* When we long watch for a messenger whom we expect by a given road, and he does not come into view, the eyes become weary. Cresswell: "The metaphor is taken from the pain occasioned to the eyes when they are long and intently fixed upon the same point." *Fail,* elsewhere *faint, are consumed.* It is applied to the *eyes,* to the *flesh,* to the *heart,* to the *soul,* to the *spirit,* to the *life,* Ps. xxxi. 10; lxxiii. 26; lxxxiv. 2; cxix. 81, 82, 123; cxliii. 7; Jer. xiv. 6; Lam. ii. 11. Calvin: "Although his bodily senses failed him, the vigor of his faith was by no means extinguished." *While I wait for my God.* Painters have endeavored to give us a conception of Christ's wan and agonized countenance in the garden and on the cross; and sometimes they have made us shudder; but none of them have ever succeeded in doing justice to the subject. There never was such *thirst* as Christ had; no eyes ever failed as his; because none ever bore such wrath as he bore, Ps. xxii. 14, 15; Zech. xiii. 7.

4. *They that hate me without a cause are more than the hairs of mine head.* This clause is applied to himself by our Saviour, John xv. 23–25. There is a like clause in Ps. xxxv. 19, on which see. David had foes; Christ had more. For an explanation of the phrase *more than the hairs of mine head,* see on Ps. xl. 12. It is equivalent to *innumerable. They that would destroy me,* being *mine enemies wrongfully, are mighty.* He had said his foes were *many.* Here he says they are *mighty.* There was no doing anything with them. They pursued their course out of *hatred,* and their hatred was *without a cause,* and so was itself *wrongful.* A discerning man is always sorry when one without provocation does him a wrong; for he is sure the thing will not stop there. Conscious guilt will beget hatred towards the injured, and thus another wrong will follow. Poor human nature without God's Spirit decides thus: "I have injured a man, therefore I hate him." Whoever knew a man to do one deliberate injury and there stop, unless by divine grace he became penitent? If I have wronged a man I can apologize, or ask pardon, or make restitution; but how can I deal with a man, to whom I owe no apology, who is malignant and obstinate? David often for himself declares truly that he had done nothing to merit at the hands of men the treatment he received, Ps. xxxv. 7, 19; xxxviii. 19, 20. It is better to suffer undeservedly, than deservedly, 1 Pet. ii. 19–21; iv. 13–16. But we ought to see to it that we lie not, when we protest our innocence. *Enemies wrongfully;* Calvin renders it *lying adversaries;* and Hengstenberg, *lying enemies.* They fabricated grounds of their own hatred, and on these they endeavored to induce others to hate him. This was true of David's foes. It was much more true of Christ's enemies. *Then I restored that which I took not away.* The meaning is, 'I have been treated as if I were a cheat, a thief, or a robber, when I am wholly innocent. I have wronged no man.' Patrick: "I have been so far from provoking their malice, that I am content, rather than quarrel with them, to part with my own right; and make satisfaction for a wrong that I never did them." The verse is parallel to Ps. xxxv. 11. David had sad experience of false accusations, 2 Sam. xvi. 8. The particular matter here referred to is not stated. Walford: "There is an apparent impropriety in the language of this clause, though the sense is perfectly clear. It is a proverbial expression, to mark

the injustice and extortion of the enemies that are referred to, who compelled the speaker, without any right, to yield up his goods to persons to whom he was not indebted." We all know how often our Saviour was wrongfully accused. Some apply this passage directly to him. Diodati: "I am guiltless, though I am used as if I were guilty. It is spoken of Christ, meaning that he who was just suffered for us men, who were unjust, Isa. liii. 4–6; 1 Pet. iii. 18." Gill: "Christ satisfied justice he had never injured, though others had; he fulfilled a law and bore the penalty of it, which he never broke; he made satisfaction for sins he never committed; and brought in a righteousness he had not taken away; and provided a better inheritance than was lost by Adam." Scott: "Then did the Lord Jesus make restitution for our *robbery*, and satisfaction for our crimes, and restored to the divine law that honor which he had not taken away. David indeed was hated wrongfully, and in many things receded from his right: but the whole and especially the concluding words were far more emphatically verified in Christ." Horsley says, the meaning is, "I have been accountable for the crimes of others." Anderson: "This pre-eminently applies to Christ, who was perfectly holy, but who, by bearing the punishment due to the guilt of man, made satisfaction to divine justice for sins, which he never committed, and restored those blessings which he never took away." Others might be quoted to the same effect.

5. *O God, thou knowest my foolishness; and my sins are not hid from thee.* We get no light on this passage by the various renderings. Nor is there any reason for taking *foolishness* in the sense of *simplicity* of character. The original is never used in a good sense. Tholuck, Hengstenberg and Alexander regard these words as David's confession of sin before God. This is simple and natural. Tholuck: "It is one of the wiles of Satan, that man, when persecuted with unmerited reproaches, becomes more prone to delude himself as to his real guilt. Not so David. He ignores righteousness before the Lord, though he may courageously show his face to man." One, who may be free from all the charges man brings against him, may for good cause deeply abase himself before God. Calvin, Diodati, Piscator, Patrick, Boothroyd and Morison, regard the words as a simple appeal to omniscience for his innocence. This is not very natural or good. But hear Calvin: "As a means of preserving himself from succumbing under the perverse judgments of men, David appeals to God as the judge of his cause; and possessing as he did the approving testimony of a good conscience, he regards in a great measure with indifference the unjust estimate which men might form of his character." Diodati: "Thou knowest whether I be guilty of those faults which are laid to me or no." Those, who take the clause as a protestation of innocence, are not agreed whether Christ or David only is to be regarded as the speaker. Calvin and Patrick apply it to David only. But Morison applies it to Christ. Augustine, Gill, Horne, Horsley and Fry regard Christ as the speaker, and suppose that he is stating his sufferings for the sins and follies of men, made his by imputation. Horsley: "The Messiah here may speak of the follies and crimes of men, for which he had made himself answerable as his own." The strongest Scripture language supporting this interpretation is Isa. liii. 4–6; 2 Cor. v. 21. There is great room for doubt whether this view is correct. The Scriptures never speak of Christ as suffering for *his* sins, but always for *our* sins. See preliminary observation No. 2, on Ps. xl. Scott: "Perhaps it should be explained as the language of the type, rather than of the antitype." Like Ps. xl. this whole Psalm cannot be fairly made a simple and direct prophecy respecting Christ. Patrick's paraphrase is: "O God, the righteous Judge, I make my appeal to thee, who knowest the very worst of me: and protest, that whatsoever my mistakes or my wil-

ful sins have been, which cannot escape thy sight, I never did them [my enemies] any injury, nor give them cause to persecute me."

6. *Let not them that wait on thee, O Lord* GOD *of hosts, be ashamed for my sake: let not those that seek thee be confounded for my sake, O God of Israel.* The appeal is to the self-existent, independent, eternal and unchangeable Ruler of the universe, who is a God of might, has all resources, and hears prayer. Compare Ps. xxv. 3. *Ashamed* and *confounded*, see on Ps. vi. 10; xxii. 5; xxv. 3; xxxv. 4; xl. 14. It is lawful to appeal to God to preserve his honor untarnished in the eyes of good men. "Do not disgrace the throne of thy glory," Jer. xiv. 21. Compare Ex. xxxii. 11, 12; Num. xiv. 13–16. Such argument is never powerless. To good people, who *wait on him*, and *seek him* God will never give cause to distrust him, or to question his faithfulness. We may at a glance see how fatal to Christian hope it would have been for God in one clear case to have given the ultimate victory to sin and sinners. Sure hope and pious confidence would have given up the ghost, if David had perished in the Sauline persecutions; or if Christ had continued under the power of death.

7. *Because for thy sake I have borne reproach; shame hath covered my face.* The two clauses are parallel, and give the reason for the prayer in v. 6. It was not on his own account but on God's account that he endured shame. He professed belief in God's promises, and for that was despised. This was true of David. It was true of Christ! Isa. l. 6. For avowing fealty to God, and confidence in the fulfilment of all he had promised they were both persecuted with deadly malice. Calvin: "Reproach is more bitter to an honorable man, than to suffer a hundred deaths. For many will be found ready to suffer death, who cannot bear reproach."

8. *I am become a stranger unto my brethren, and an alien unto my mother's children.* By *brethren* we may understand any blood relations; by *mother's children* those most endeared to us; see on Ps. l. 20. The anguish of being disowned by those, whose friendship ought to have been reliable, cannot be easily estimated. Compare Ps. xxvii. 10; xxxviii. 11. How much of such anguish Jesus bore may be learned from Isa. liii. 3; John i. 11; vii. 5; viii. 48, and parallel passages.

9. *For the zeal of thine house hath eaten me up.* See a like clause in Ps. cxix. 139. *Zeal*, often so rendered, Isa. xxxvii. 32; lix. 17; more commonly *jealousy*, Ps. lxxix. 5; Isa. xlii. 13; Ezek. xxxvi. 5; Zech. i. 14; viii. 2. The true application is given in John ii. 14–17. No doubt David had a genuine and burning though imperfect zeal for the church; but our Saviour's zeal did eat him up. *And the reproaches of them that reproach thee are fallen upon me.* This is by infallible authority applied to Christ, Rom. xv. 3. Hodge: "Such was my zeal for thee, that the reproaches cast on thee I felt as if directed against myself." It is impossible to dishonor God without dishonoring his Son, John x. 30; xiv. 11; xvi. 15. The unity of Christ and of the Father is perfect. Patrick's paraphrase is, "I could not endure the blasphemies which I heard against thee, but they moved my indignation as much as if they had been against myself." The *noun* and *verb* rendered *reproach* are cognate. The noun is rendered with entire uniformity; see on Ps. xv. 3. The verb is in the Psalms uniformly rendered; in other books sometimes *rail* or *defy*, 2 Chron. xxxii. 17; 2 Sam. xxiii. 9. It expresses contumely, scorn, reviling. If David was grieved with blasphemies against God (2 Sam. xii. 14;) Christ much more.

10. *When I wept* and chastened *my soul with fasting, that was to my reproach.* For I wept and chastened my soul, the Syriac and Arabic have I humbled my soul with fasting; Calvin: And I wept, my soul fasted; Ainsworth: And I wept, with fasting *afflicted* my soul; Fry: I wept away my soul in fasting; Green: When I humble myself with fasting; Alexander: And I wept (away) my soul *or wept myself away*, in fasting. The sense is, When I wept, and, as an act of humiliation of my soul, fasted;

see on Ps. xxxv. 13. Weeping and fasting go together, 2 Sam. xii. 16–22. It is sad indeed when even acts of piety and humiliation are ground of new *reproaches*. When everything a man does is perverted by his foes, he is in great temptation, and none but God can sustain him. How Christ's enemies perverted even his most benevolent deeds, as well as his acts of piety all the gospels declare.

11. *I made sackcloth also my garment.* The three chief outward tokens of grief common among the Israelites were weeping, fasting and covering the person with coarse cloth, to which some added dust and ashes; see on Ps. xxx. 11; xxxv. 13. To him that is afflicted pity should be shown; but when David and Christ were most afflicted even for the sins and calamities of men, they had no sympathy from the wicked, but were for a derision. *And I became a proverb to* them. *Proverb, parable, similitude,* in a bad sense a *taunting speech,* as in the margin in Isa. xiv. 4, or *by-word,* as in Ps. xliv. 14.

12. *They that sit in the gate speak against me.* Those, *who sit in the gate,* are judges, Job xxix. 7–17; Deut. xxv. 7; Josh. xx. 4; Ruth iv. 1, 2; 1 Kings xxii. 10; Lam. v. 14. *The gates* of cities were the places of judgment. Calvin: "Had David been molested only by vulgar buffoons and the refuse of the people, it would have been more easily endured; for it is not surprising when mean persons, who have no regard to what is becoming and honorable, degrade themselves by indulging in defamation without shame. But when the very judges, forgetful of what is demanded by the dignity of their office, abandon themselves to the same audacious conduct, the iniquity and baseness of it are greatly aggravated." The judicial proceedings against Jesus Christ were a disgrace to human nature. All have not so explained these words. Rosen-müller: " *They that sit in the gate*—vain and idle persons who spent their time there, where there used to be a confluence of people." Tholuck: "They sit in the gates where idlers assemble." Cresswell: " *They that sit in the gate; i. e.,* the elders. The expression may, however, be put for the crowd assembled there to hear the decisions of the magistrates." Alexander: "It seems more natural to make the sitters in the gate mean simply those frequenting public places." This is answered by Calvin: "Although men of every rank and condition assembled at the gates, yet none but the judges and counsellors *sat* there." In Deut. xxv. 7, the Chaldee interprets *gate* to mean the gate of the house of judgment; and in Ruth iv. 1, to mean the *gate* of the house of Judgment of Sanhedrim. *And I was the song of the drunkards.* Some think this clause points to those, who had wealth and were able to purchase costly liquors. But the more correct opinion is that it designates the dregs of society, who had been degraded by drunkenness, and kindred vices. Patrick explains it "of the idle and dissolute companions, who, in their drunken meetings, make abusive songs and libels on me;" Tholuck, of the "inns where drunkards meet, (Job xxx. 9), gossiping and singing away the conscientious scruples, which the sight of a man, who weeps over the sins of the race, might possibly have aroused." The margin, more literal than the text, for *drunkards* has *drinkers of strong drink.* Chrysostom says the peculiar liquor here named was made of the juice of the palm-tree. The word occurs more than *twenty* times in the Hebrew Scriptures, and is invariably rendered *strong drink* except in this place, and in Num. xxviii. 7, *strong wine.* The Hebrew is that from which the Greeks and Latins took their word *Sicera,* which Ainsworth defines as embracing *all manner of strong drink except wine.* In Scripture this strong drink is carefully distinguished from wine, Lev. x. 9; Num. vi. 3; Deut. xiv. 26; Judg. xiii. 4, 7, 14; Pr. xx. 1; Mic. ii. 11. There is no evidence that the mean and drugged intoxicating liquors of the east were beyond the reach of the poor. How ribaldry prevailed amongst high and low against the Lord of glory during his sojourn on earth we all know, Matt. xi.

19; LUKE vii. 34. While the wicked were thus raging and insulting, he, whom they hated and reviled, was very differently occupied:

13. *But as for me, my prayer is unto thee, O* LORD, *in an acceptable time.* Almost the only resource left the persecuted and innocent sufferer is his access to the throne of the heavenly grace. Tyrants cannot close that fountain of refreshment. *Prayer,* always so rendered; see on Ps. iv. 1; vi. 9. The time *acceptable* is the time *of God's good pleasure,* the time of *favor,* the time of his *good will.* If we would pray so as to be heard and answered, we must pray at such time as God appoints, not when it is too late, not when life is ended. So some understand it. Others connect it with the next clause, and make the speaker refer the time of answer to God's sovereign will. So that it would read: *In the time that pleases thee hear me.* The sense is good. The English text is best. *O God, in the multitude of thy mercy hear me, in the truth of thy salvation. Hear,* i. e., answer, give what is sought. This he asked of the *multitude, abundance, greatness,* or *plenty* of God's *mercy, goodness, kindness, merciful kindness,* or *lovingkindness.* He also asked for these blessings *in the truth of God's salvation. Truth,* the opposite of fiction, faithlessness, deception, falsehood. The truth *of God's salvation* is the truth which he has provided and promised to secure *salvation* to such as trust in him, Isa. xlix. 8; lv. 6; lxi. 2; 2 Cor. vi. 2. *Salvation* of the same root as *save* in v. 1.

14. *Deliver me out of the mire, and let me not sink. Mire,* not the same as in v. 2, but *dirt* in Ps. xviii. 42, and *clay* in Ps. xl. 2. It is rendered *dirt* in Isa. lvii. 20; *clay* in Isa. xli. 25; and five or six times *mire,* as in Mic. vii. 10; Zech. ix. 3; x. 5. In vv. 14, 15, there is no doubt a reviving of the figurative language of vv. 1, 2. *Deliver,* as in Ps. vii. 1. *Let me be delivered from them that hate me, and out of the deep waters.* All the terms have been explained in previous verses. This clause gives the true sense of that next preceding.

15. *Let not the waterflood overflow me, neither let the deep swallow me up. Overflow,* as in v. 2. *Swallow,* as in Ps. xxi. 9, and commonly; in Ps. lv. 9, *destroy. Deep,* as in v. 2. *And let not the pit shut her mouth upon me.* Calvin: "Let not the great multitude and weight of my afflictions overwhelm me, and let not sorrow swallow me up." Tholuck: "David prays that the one vista of the bright heavens above might not be stopped, that the pit might not shut its mouth over him."

16. *Hear me, O* LORD, *for thy lovingkindness is good. Hear,* as in vv. 13, 17. *Lovingkindness,* in v. 13, *mercy. Good,* pleasant, rich, precious. *Turn unto me according to the multitude of thy tender mercies. Turn,* elsewhere *have respect, look, regard.* Averting the face expresses displeasure or neglect; so *looking* to one expresses favorable regard. See on Ps. xxv. 16; xl. 4. *Multitude of tender mercies,* see on Ps. li. 1. The distress expressed in the petitions of this verse is very great.

17. *Hide not thy face from thy servant.* See on Ps. xiii. 1; xxvii. 9. The *hidden face* of God deeply distresses the soul, whether it relates to the aspects of providence, or to sensible communion with him. *For I am in trouble. Trouble,* as in Ps. iii. 1; iv. 1. *Hear me speedily. Hear,* as in vv. 13, 16. *Speedily,* hastily, suddenly, shortly, swiftly. Margin: *Make haste to hear me.*

18. *Draw nigh unto my soul, and redeem it.* To the eye of sense, judging from appearances, it seemed as if God had withdrawn to a distance and left the sufferer to the power of his foes. Hence the earnest request that he would *come near* unto his soul and *deliver* it, for it was in great peril. As long as we may lawfully call on God, and can exercise faith, our affairs are not desperate. *Deliver me because of mine enemies.* The enemies had brought things to a state, from which none but God could deliver. It was therefore a fitting occasion for the display of his justice, power and

grace. Or it means that if God would deliver him, it would teach a lasting lesson of wisdom to his enemies. Hengstenberg regards Ps. xiii. 4 as parallel.

19. *Thou hast known my reproach, and my shame, and my dishonour.* If the passage is spoken of David, we know what contumely was heaped upon him in the time of Saul and of the rebellion. If it is spoken of Christ, we have parallel passages in Ps. xxii. 6, 7; Isa. liii. 3; Heb. xii. 2. *Reproach* and *shame,* commonly so rendered. *Dishonor,* more frequently rendered *shame, reproach, confusion. Mine adversaries are all before thee, i. e.,* their number, power and malice, with all their devices, are known to thee, *q. d.,* 'Nothing in my case in any of its relations is hidden from the all-seeing eye, although for the present he seems to leave me to the power of my enemies.' Calvin: "Lord, thou knowest how, like a poor sheep, I am surrounded by thousands of wolves." Alexander: "The conviction that God knows all involves a persuasion that he will do justice to both parties." Hengstenberg: "It is a great consolation in unmerited sufferings, when reflections on the omniscience of God take full possession of the soul." The verse doubtless has its principal fulfilment in Christ, and, together with several verses following, is best interpreted by those portions of the Gospels, which narrate his sufferings near the close of life.

20. *Reproach hath broken my heart.* Upon this expression a modern writer has founded a theory respecting the physical causes of the death of Christ, viz., that he died of a broken heart, *i. e.,* that grief and pain burst his heart. But all this is set aside by the fact that Jesus Christ did not die of exhaustion, but by a voluntary surrender of his life. Just before expiring he cried with a loud, strong voice, and then dismissed his own soul. The passages of Scripture establishing this position are sufficient, Matt. xxvii. 50; Mark xv. 37; Luke xxiii. 46; John x. 11, 18; xix. 30. Although the phrase *yielded up the ghost* or *gave up the ghost* occurs often in our English Bible, yet neither in the Septuagint, nor in the Greek Testament is there found such a phrase applied to any mere man as that used by Matthew or that used by John respecting Christ. Mark and Luke, rendered literally, say, *He expired;* John, *he delivered up the spirit;* and Matthew, *he dismissed the spirit.* It is unaccountable that our version should have rendered these and like phrases in the Hebrew all in the same words, so that Sapphira is made to leave the world even as Christ. Doddridge well says that Christ's words in John x. 18, the language of Matthew, and the *strong cry* which so much impressed the centurion show that Jesus "died by the *voluntary act* of his own mind, according to the *power received from the Father,* and in a way peculiar to himself, by which *he alone,* of all men that ever existed, could have continued alive, even in the greatest tortures, as long as he pleased, or have retired from the body whenever he thought fit." Jesus died like *the Prince of life.* Reproach may become an intolerable burden. To Christ's pure and holy mind the vile accusations against him were in the highest degree afflicting and grievous. A *broken heart* is in Scripture a figure for great and violent anguish of mind, Ps. li. 17. *And I am full of heaviness.* In the Hebrew the whole phrase is expressed by one word variously rendered; I am afflicted; I am quite dejected; I faint with sickness; *I am sick.* Tholuck: "The reproach, which had broken his heart, also crushed his body." *And I looked* for some *to take pity, but* there was *none; and for comforters, but I found none. Looked, tarried, waited. Take pity, be sorry, bemoan. Comforters,* a participle often so rendered. Horne: "In the extremity of his passion, Christ was left alone, without a comforter, a friend, or an attendant; while all that were round about him studied to infuse every bitter and acrimonious ingredient into his cup of sorrow." Even his apostles 'could not watch with him one hour.' He was betrayed by one, denied by another, forsaken by all. He trod the wine-press alone, and of the people there was

none with him. Christ's death was *solitary.* Even his Father hid his face from him. David was never so forsaken by all.

21. *They gave me also gall for my meat; and in my thirst they gave me vinegar to drink.* Meat, food, nourishment, here only. *Thirst,* always so rendered. Taken literally we know of nothing in the life of David corresponding to these words. If we take them figuratively, we know his foes dealt out to him the *bitterness* or *sourness* of malice. But these words find a literal fulfilment in Christ, as we learn from infallible authority, Matt. xxvii. 34, 48; Mark xv. 23. There were two, if not three, periods in the agony of our Lord when some liquid was offered him. First they offered him *vinegar* (always so rendered) mingled with *gall* (a word found only in Matt. xxvii. 34; Acts viii. 23.) In the second they gave him simply *vinegar,* (the same word is used as before) but there is no mention of any addition to it, Matt. xxvii. 48. In the third they gave him *wine,* the word always so rendered in the New Testament, Matt. ix. 17; John ii. 3, 9, 10; 1 Tim. v. 23, mingled with *myrrh,* a name applied to an aromatic balsam. It is impossible to reconcile all the accounts thus given in the gospels with the idea that drink was offered to the dying Saviour but once. The *vinegar* may have been that in common use among the Roman soldiers. The *wine* and *myrrh* may have been good wine spiced. Both of these may have been suited to alleviate suffering. But the *vinegar mingled with gall* was certainly offered in derision or despite. In this Psalm it is noticed in sad complaint, and not as an act of kindness. One evangelist expressly says that once drink was offered in mockery, Luke xxiii. 36. Because the Scripture cannot be broken, the potion was actually given in any other temper than that of love. The word rendered *gall* occurs eleven times in the Hebrew Bible. It is eight times rendered *gall,* once *poison,* once *venom,* and once *hemlock.* This *gall* is not that on the liver of animals, but that which *grows on a root* or plant, Deut. xxix. 18. In the judgment of our translators it was a poisonous herb, probably a powerful narcotic. See marginal rendering of Deut. xxix. 18; xxxii. 33; Job xx. 16; Hos. x. 4. *Vinegar,* uniformly rendered. It occurs but a few times. Christ's enemies treated him cruelly, and his outward sufferings were but a fit emblem of the *bitterness* of his soul.

22. *Let their table become a snare unto them: and* that which should have been *for* their *welfare,* let it become *a trap.* This verse is clearly connected with the next three, so that the right use of *one* being ascertained, we know the application of the others. Christ applied to his scornful countrymen the twenty-fifth verse, and this goes with it. Paul makes the same application of this verse and the next, Rom. xi. 9, 10; so that we have the key to the right exposition. In the Hebrew of vv. 22–25 the future and the imperative are both used, though our version employs only the imperative. See Introduction, § 6. Whatever the form of the verb, it is clearly the language of prediction. Augustine: "These things are not said by way of wishing, but, under the form of wishing, by way of prophecy." Christ prayed *for,* not *against* his murderers, Luke xxiii. 34. The prediction in the first clause is that their table, their most ordinary and necessary enjoyments shall lose their pleasantness and involve them in trouble, as a snare does the animal caught in it. If the common version of the last clause of this verse is correct, then the Hebrew is very elliptical. The Chaldee renders it: And let their sacrifices be for an offence. Hammond thinks this gives the true sense, understanding by *sacrifices, victims,* or *peace-offerings.* Edwards: And [let] their sumptuous feasts prove a trap to them; Hengstenberg renders it: And [let] their peace [be] their fall; Alexander: And to those secure, *thinking themselves safe,* (let it be for or become) a trap. *Welfare,* in the plural, welfares, prosperities. In the singular the word is commonly rendered *peace.* *Snare,* sometimes *gin.* *Trap,* uniformly rendered.

23. *Let their eyes be darkened, that they see not.* This verse is quoted by Paul in

application to the Jews, who rejected the gospel, Rom. xi. 10. Parallels are found in Isa. vi. 9, 10; John xii. 39, 40; 2 Cor. iii. 14. The darkening is spiritual. Those who have fought against Christ and his church, have always been void of understanding. There is no wise way of doing a foolish thing. The longer the Jews reject Messiah, the grosser is the darkness surrounding them. *And make their loins continually to shake.* Paul quotes the Septuagint literally: *And bow down their back always.* The strength of man and beast is very much in the loins. Whoever is weak in the back is fit for no hard service. Alexander: " *And their loins do thou cause to bend,* give way, or swerve, *i. e.,* paralyze their strength." To take strength from the loins is to render one helpless.

24. *Pour out thine indignation upon them, and let thy wrathful anger take hold of them. Indignation,* often so rendered, also *anger, rage. Anger,* often so rendered, also *wrath. Wrathful,* in Hebrew a noun, rendered *fierceness, wrath, fierce wrath, sore displeasure,* used as an adjective, *fierce.* The whole verse is a prediction of the sorest punishments from the hand of Jehovah.

25. *Let their habitation be desolate.* This clause is quoted by Christ in his lament over Jerusalem, and applied to the Jewish nation, showing its prophetical character, Matt. xxiii. 37, 38. It is also quoted by Peter and applied to Judas Iscariot, Acts i. 16–20. He speaks of it as a prophecy: "This Scripture must needs be fulfilled." These things show that the common form of prediction is no just cause of offence. No doubt it foretells the awful doom of all those who malignantly reject the gospel and despise the person of the Mediator. The Jews and Judas were representative men, and as such the clause is applied to them. *And let none dwell in their tents.* This is a repetition of the prediction of the first clause, and refers to the loss of their own land by the unbelieving Jews, and, together with the first, predicts the evils that should fall on the posterity of such as wilfully and finally reject Christ and the authority of God, Ex. xx. 5; Isa. xiv. 20, 21.

26. *For they persecute* him *whom thou hast smitten; and they talk to the grief of those whom thou hast wounded.* The course they pursued was inhuman, and utterly opposite to the law of kindness, Job vi. 14; xix. 21. There is much difficulty in making application of this passage to any given period in the life of David. But it is easy to apply it to Christ, for " we did esteem him stricken, *smitten of God,* and afflicted. He was *wounded* for our transgressions," Isa. liii. 4, 5; Zech. xiii. 6, 7. When the Shepherd was smitten, the sheep were scattered. The cruelty shown to Christ was as a sword piercing the soul of his mother and of every pious spectator. The *talk* of these persons was harsh and scornful. Horsley renders: " And [they] have added to the anguish of those who are wounded of thee."

27. *Add iniquity unto their iniquity.* The ancient versions do all sustain this rendering; so do Calvin, Hengstenberg, Alexander and others. Green and Edwards: Let them commit iniquity upon iniquity; church of England: Let them fall from one wickedness to another; Ainsworth: Add sin unto their sin, *i. e., Give them over to a reprobate mind.* Clarke thinks it means, " Treat their *perverseness* with *perverseness:*—act in thy judgments as *crookedly* towards them, as they dealt *crookedly* towards thee. They shall get, in the way of punishment, what they have dealt out in the way of oppression." Horsley: Give them punishment upon punishment. The word rendered *iniquity* occurs in the Hebrew Bible nearly *ninety* times. In a majority of cases it denotes moral evil; but also the fruit of sin, *vanity, affliction, mourning, sorrow.* If by it we understand *sorrow,* or *affliction,* then the sense is that God will surely *multiply* their sorrows and mournings. But does not God sometimes punish one iniquity by leaving a man to commit another? Muis: "God is used to punish sins with new sins." Hammond has shown that the word rendered *add* does not necessarily

mean more than *permit;* and we know God does suffer the wicked to do wickedly. Calvin thinks the sense is, Let their wickedness increase more and more. Bossuet says that by deserting the wicked, and by suffering them, though not by acting upon them, God lets them add sin to sin. That God may in wrath give men over to a reprobate mind is expressly taught, Ps. cix. 6–20; Rom. i. 28; 2 Thess. ii. 11, 12. Tholuck: "It is the curse of sin to beget new sin." *And let them not come into thy righteousness.* Horsley: Admit them not to thy justification; Diodati: "Let them have no share of that righteousness which thou shalt manifest in thy gospel, in grace and justification of sinners;" Alexander: "The *righteousness* of God is that which he bestows by the judicial act of justification, including pardon." Calvin thinks this clause of v. 27 cuts off all hope and declares the absence of all desire of amendment of life, of repentance unto salvation. Where there is no justification, there is surely no sanctification.

28. *Let them be blotted out of the book of the living, and not be written with the righteous.* The figure of a *book* containing the names of those whom God accepts is very old, Ex. xxxii. 32, 33. It was familiar to inspired writers. See concordances. Three different customs are brought in to explain its use. Dodd: "The allusion seems to have been taken from the custom of generals and commanders of armies who, upon the desertion or death of a soldier, strike him out of the muster-roll;" Mant: "This phrase alludes to the custom of well ordered cities, which kept registers, containing all the names of the citizens. Out of these registers the names of apostates, fugitives, and criminals were erased, as also those of the deceased: whence the expression 'blotting' or 'erasing names from the book of life.'" Hammond thinks it refers to the ancient custom of keeping "a register of names of those who live in any kingdom. Thus, Luke ii. 1, we have the *enrolling* (in our version *taxing*) of all in the emperor's dominions: and accordingly the word here rendered *book* is ordinarily taken for a *catalogue;* and the *catalogue of the living* is the number of those that are alive at any time." It matters little which of these customs gave rise to the figure of the text, although that of Mant is perhaps the most striking. The *book of the living* here is the same as the *book of life* in the New Testament. To *be blotted out of this book* is the same thing as not to *be written with the righteous.* The clauses are parallel. The meaning of the verse therefore is that these bitter and incorrigible persecutors of innocence shall not be regarded or treated as the righteous. From this figure some of the ablest commentators draw the doctrine of the divine decrees. But God's decrees are eternal and unchangeable. There are no blots in the book of God's holy, everlasting and immutable purposes. As many as are ordained to eternal life believe, Acts xiii. 48; and he that believeth shall be saved.

29. *But I* am *poor and sorrowful, i. e.,* I am not one of these vile and violent men. I am *poor, i. e., afflicted, humble, lowly,* and *sorrowful, sad, sore, grieving, pained, q. d.,* I am too much borne down with the hugeness of my sorrows to feel and act as my enemies seem quite at liberty to do. *Let thy salvation, O God, set me up on high.* Calvin: *Thy salvation shall exalt me.* If the verse refers to Christ, it shows how he foresaw his own resurrection from the dead, his ascension to heaven and his glorious session at the right hand of God. As it finds its fulfilment in every believer, it shows him how he should bear his sorrows and how he "should depart out of the world, joyfully relinquishing its goods, patiently bearing its evils, and confidently expecting a resurrection to glory."

30. *I will praise the name of God with a song, and will magnify him with thanksgiving.* All Christ's life even on earth was not made up of sorrow and anguish alone. There was an hour when he rejoiced in spirit, Luke x. 21. But all his life from his resurrection is a new life. He sorrows no more forever. Horne: "Here as in the

xxii. and many other Psalms, the scene changes from sorrow to joy; from a state of suffering to one of triumph: from the passion to the resurrection;" or, these words may express the purpose of his soul to celebrate the name of God in confident assurance that deliverance would come, though it was still distant.   Foreseeing it, he magnifies the Lord with thanksgiving.

31. This *also shall please the* LORD *better than an ox* or *bullock that hath horns and hoofs.* This verse is parallel to Ps. l. 13, 14, 23, on which see.

32. *The humble shall see* this, and *be glad.* There is no more effectual way of consoling *afflicted, humble* souls than by God's Spirit leading them rightly to view the deliverances which he has wrought for others; see on Ps. xl. 3. *And your heart shall live that seek God.* To *live* in this case is much the same as to *be glad,* 1 Thess. iii. 8. Or it expresses the spiritual and eternal life, which God secures to all who *seek him,* and have the exercises of the renewed soul, Ps. xxii. 26. On *seeking God,* see on Ps. ix. 10; x. 4; xiv. 2.

33. *For the* LORD *heareth the poor.   Heareth, i. e.,* is already answering, according to that in Isa. lxv. 24. *Poor,* plural, often rendered *needy,* expressing poverty of spirit, humbleness of mind. The proposition is universal, embracing all in every place who are of this temper. *And despiseth not his prisoners.* The *Lord's prisoners* are such as go to prison for his sake and in his cause, or they are such as he has bound in affliction and iron, vv. 7, 26; Ps. cvii. 10; or they are souls under the power and guilt of sin, on whom he has yet set his love. Deliverance to the humble and afflicted is often represented by the rescue of captives, Isa. lxi. 1; Ps. lxviii. 6. Jehovah hears even the sighing of the prisoners, Ps. lxxix. 11. He does not *despise* them, *i. e.,* he lovingly notices and attends to them. How gloriously was this fulfilled in the release of our great Surety, whom God has set at liberty, and highly exalted at his own right hand. "He rose for our justification."

34. *Let the heaven and earth praise him, the seas, and every thing that moveth therein.* This is an animated demand, for universal praise. Horne: "The mercies of God in Christ are such, that they cannot worthily be praised by anything less than an universal chorus of the whole old and new creation." *Praise,* in the future, a prediction rather than a prayer.

35. *For God will save Sion.* In saving an individual believer God gives a pledge that he will save every other believer. In exalting his Son from the deepest humiliation he gave the most blessed assurance that he will save his whole church. By reason of her, blessings shall come on all connected with her: *And* [God] *will build the cities of Judah; that they* [the *poor,* the *humble,* the *prisoners* of vv. 32, 33,] *may dwell there, and have it in possession.* They have the *blessing,* which is the most opposite to the *curse* denounced in v. 25.

36. *The seed also of his servants shall inherit it; and they that love his name shall dwell therein.* To *inherit* a portion in the promised land was a proof of God's faithfulness to the natural seed of Abraham, and where it was enjoyed with thankfulness and in faith, it was a token and pledge of God's favor for the life to come, Ps. xxv. 13; xxxvii. 29. Calvin: "Although that land was given to the chosen people to be possessed until the advent of Christ, we should remember that it was a type of the heavenly inheritance, and that, therefore, what is here written concerning the protection of the church, has received a more true and substantial fulfilment in our day."

DOCTRINAL AND PRACTICAL REMARKS.

1. The very best of men may be in extreme danger. That is a good reason for looking to God, and hoping in his mercy, v. 1.

2. Let us not forget that we have for an example of suffering affliction not only the

prophets, but Messias himself, vv. 1, 2. What more do we need for pattern, for encouragement, for showing us how God works deliverance? None of us have sufferings peculiar to ourselves. No temptation has befallen us but such as is common to men. Let us neither faint, nor rebel, 'neither be soured by discontent, nor sink into despair,' Heb. xii. 3.

3. When our affairs seem to be at the worst, that is a fit time for God to undertake for us, vv. 1, 2.

4. Answers to earnest, hearty, believing prayer may, for wise and holy purposes be long delayed, v. 3. The Father answered the Son in the best time and in the best way; but not till reproach had broken his heart, not till his followers were nonplused with his sufferings and humiliation, not till he had lain in the sepulchre of Joseph.

5. Calvin: "When we reflect that David has spoken, as it were, out of the mouth of Christ, and, as it were, out of the mouth of all true saints who are the members of Christ, we ought not to think that any strange thing happens to us, if at any time we are so overwhelmed with death as to be unable to discern the slightest hope of life," v. 3.

6. Let us distinguish between pusillanimity and the manly cry of distress, v. 3. Let us bear in patience all we can bear, acknowledging the righteousness of God in all that comes upon us. Tholuck: "The piteous complaints of the prophet begin not with the first stroke of the rod, as effeminate minds are wont to do; but the hero of the battle-field, who had slain his ten thousands, is equally a hero in endurance."

7. If we have *many, mighty, wanton, unreasonable* enemies, so had others before us, v. 4. Let us in the name of the Lord defy all the hosts of hell. Let us remember too, that none of us suffers to himself. Tholuck: "The church is one body—You cannot touch a toe without affecting the whole body, 1 Cor. xii. 26. If our sufferings are useful to others, we should not murmur; for we shall not lose our reward." Dickson: "He that is most just may be troubled and hated without a cause, and may be dealt with as a thief."

8. It is better to suffer wrong than to do wrong, v. 4. Slander cannot destroy us, any more than it destroyed David or Christ. Calvin: "If, after we have done all in our power to make men form a favorable opinion respecting us, they misconstrue and pervert every good word which we utter, and every good action which we perform, we ought to maintain such greatness of mind as boldly to despise the world and all false accusers, resting contented with the judgment of God, and with that alone." 1 Cor. iv. 5. Several commentators here cite the case of Socrates, who, when his wife visited him in prison, and grieved at his suffering without a cause, asked, "*Would you rather see me suffer as guilty?*"

9. It should greatly humble us that among the most illustrious types of our Saviour, which are found among men, there was so much imperfection, foolishness and iniquity, that they properly confessed and bewailed them before God, v. 5.

10. We may boldly and confidently plead with God not to confound or put to shame any of his true and humble servants, v. 6.

11. We may well be calm under suffering, yea, glory in it, when it is for God's sake, for his cause, his truth, or his people, v. 7. Dickson: "When one of God's children is persecuted for righteousness, all the rest are waiting to see the event, and it would be a great dash to them to see the righteous lie under, or a good cause lie long oppressed."

12. To live retired, without acquaintance and without friends, is the fancy of a few; but to those, with whom friendship is a sacred thing full of enjoyment, the withdrawal of the confidence and sympathy of those, whom we had enrolled as friends, is truly dreadful, v. 8. Such has ever been matter of bitter complaint among good men. Let such

mind two things: " 1. In affliction for God's cause friends will more readily forsake a sufferer, than in his affliction for a civil cause: 2. The power of religion in the godly is stronger than the bonds of blood with their kinsmen, and it will make them cleave to God, when their kindred cast them off."

13. To be without zeal in religion makes duties irksome, shows that the love of God is not shed abroad within us, and proves that we are not like Christ, v. 9. A religion without zeal chills its possessor and all around him. If zeal had always been pure and benevolent, it would not have been held in so much disesteem by some.

14. Let us make common cause with God, even when his interests are most depressed, v. 9. " Even Christ pleased not himself; but, as it is written, The reproaches of them that reproached thee are fallen on me," Rom. xv. 3. We cannot be more hated or worse treated for adhering to God's cause in the day of rebuke and blasphemy than was our blessed Lord. It is a good sign when we are no less affected by injuries done to God's name and truth and people than by wrongs done to ourselves.

15. If our religion and religious actions expose us to shame, our experience is neither novel nor alarming, vv. 9, 10, 11. Those, who do not weep for their own sins can hardly be expected to understand the feelings of those, who weep for sin in themselves and others too.

16. In nothing are all classes of wicked men so united as in opposing the cause of God, v. 12. Pilate and Herod had a serious rupture, but the events attending the trial and crucifixion quite made them friends. In religion wicked magistrates and wicked rabble see eye to eye and feel heart to heart.

17. In the worst case that we can be in, let us hold fast the privilege of prayer, v. 13. Of this none can deprive us. Men may silence our defence at the public tribunals; but they cannot cut us off from supplication to God. For resisting the derisions of the proud and foolish there is nothing like prayer.

18. There is a time *accepted*, acceptable to God, a time fit for our respective duties, v. 13. God will not bless the farmer, who plants corn in mid-winter, nor the man, who defers prayer till life is gone, Isa. lv. 6.

19. All our hope is not merely in the fact that God is merciful, but that his mercy abounds, vv. 13, 16. In God we find " mercy, a multitude of mercies, all kinds of mercy, inexhaustible mercy, mercy enough for all, enough for each."

20. Our prayers are most likely to be suitable when the matter of them is drawn from the circumstances in which God's providence has placed us, vv. 1, 2, 14, 15.

20. We may fitly urge our sore troubles as a reason why God should speedily attend to our cry, and help us. When afflictions press hard, we may press hard our suit before God.

21. If we shall be saved from any foe, fear, or peril, it must be by God alone, v. 18. Blessed is he, who constantly so believes and acts accordingly.

22. If Christians were well informed and wise they would greatly comfort themselves with the remembrance of God's omniscience, v. 19. Often it is the chief source of consolation to them. Tholuck: " It is one of the most potent consolations that the earthly struggles of the pious are as it were performed on a stage while the Eternal with his angels and the host of perfected saints are the spectators."

23. It is worth while to suffer much, as did David and Christ, if through the divine mercy we may be brought to breathe their spirit and love the prayers they offered, and rejoice in the perfections of God as they did.

24. It is no new thing to have a heart broken with grief, v. 2. The Saviour knows all about such sorrow. He is touched with the feeling of our infirmity. However great our distresses, they do not equal his.

25. One of the infallible evidences of a foul depravity in man is that comforters

are scarce on earth, v. 20. Henry: "We cannot expect too little from men, miserable comforters are they all; nor can we expect too much from God, for he is the Father of mercy and the God of all comfort and consolation."

26. It no less establishes the truth of our fallen state that tormentors are plenty in this world, v. 21. Some seem to have nothing else to do. But let not God's people be cast down on that account. "As all the sufferings of the saints are but shadows of the sufferings of Christ, so are they all mitigated and sanctified in the sufferings of Christ." We are walking in Christ's footsteps, and have his blessing, and that is enough.

27. Does not the example of our Saviour in refusing the narcotic and stupefying drugs offered him on the cross instruct us to avoid, as far as we can, even in a dying hour, those drinks, which would becloud our reason or our senses?

28. Blessings are blessings only while God makes them so, v. 22. When he says, I will curse your blessings, (Mal. ii. 2,) our case is sad indeed. Calvin: "As things which naturally and of themselves are hurtful become the means of furthering our welfare when we are in favor with God; so, when his anger is kindled against us, all those things which have a native tendency to produce our happiness, are cursed, and become so many causes of our destruction."

29. Spiritual blindness is an awful curse, v. 23. If there is any greater, what is it? Morison: "Judicial blindness is heaven's frequent punishment for abused privileges."

30. The bodily weakness and trembling brought on by sin are but signs of the elements of weakness inherent in transgression, v. 23. When the joints of Belshazzar's loins were loosed and his knees smote together, it was an index to the more fearful falling to pieces of all his powers of manliness, courage, and self-control.

31. There is no way of reconciling the language of Scripture with candor unless we admit that it is an awful thing to fall into the hands of the living God, v. 24. Tholuck: "Patient endurance in the heat of tribulation, and the forgiveness of our neighbor's offences are *our* duties, while it is the office of *God* to distribute justice among the obdurate."

32. The effects of God's judgments on men for their sins are often seen on their posterity for generations, so that their house after them is left *desolate*, v. 25. How such a curse has come on the murderers and rejecters of Christ the world has seen for eighteen hundred years. 'And in a sense equally awful and impressive may we regard the doom of all who reject Messiah, and despise the great salvation.'

33. It is extremely perilous to insult and injure the afflicted, v. 26. Perhaps few things are more wicked and deserving of punishment. If the wicked had any wisdom, when they see God's people afflicted, instead of deriding them, they would say, If God thus grieves, when he is chastening his children, what will he not do, when he takes hold on vengeance to punish his enemies? Luke xxiii. 31. Henry: "Those that are of a wounded spirit, under trouble and fear about their spiritual state, ought to be very tenderly dealt with, and care must be taken not to *talk to their grief, and not to make the heart of the righteous sad*, Zech. i. 15." Dickson: "Whatsoever may be the reason of the Lord's smiting and wounding his own children, yet their wicked enemies have no just reason to malign them, or to trouble them, and therefore their troubling them is persecution."

34. Nothing more dreadful can befall a man than to be left to sin more and more, to wax worse and worse, to add iniquity to iniquity, v. 27. Greediness and success in sinning are the foulest plague-spots that appear in this life.

35. When men are left without restraint and without interruption to sin, they have

a right to believe that they are hopelessly cut off from justification, from God's right-eousness, from Jehovah's plan of pardoning and accepting sinners, v. 27.

36. A wicked man may die such a death as to show that he is doomed to worse sufferings in the world to come; but whether this *appear* or not, the death of every sinner is the end of hope concerning him for ever, v. 28.

37. All the Scriptures unite in teaching that our salvation and eternal life depend on God and on God alone, v. 29. To a good man this is cause of joy; to the proud and rebellious, of fear and alarm.

38. If Christ's people are poor and sorrowful, their Master was so before them, v. 29. And as Christ was finally and gloriously delivered, so shall his people be. Everything that makes sure the woes of God's enemies makes sure the bliss of his saints.

39. None is so poor, so sunk down in sorrow or reproach, that God cannot save him, v. 29. Nor does the pious sufferer desire deliverance except on God's terms, and in his time and way.

40. Let us render praise and thanksgiving both in the prospect of mercies expected, and for mercies already received, vv. 30, 31. As there was never a man too humble or too penitent for sin, so never was there one too thankful for God's favors. Calvin: "There cannot be a more powerful incitement to thanksgiving than the certain conviction that this religious service is highly pleasing to God; even as the only recompense which he requires for all the benefits, which he lavishes upon us, that we honor and praise his name."

41. The deliverances wrought by God for his poor suffering people, and especially the glorious exaltation of his Son work the happiest effects on the *humble* of every generation, who seek God, v. 32. The history of God's dealings with his people of all past ages is the best possible commentary on all those exceeding great and precious promises, with which the Scriptures abound.

42. Circumstances of distress and of outward depression, so far from causing God to lose interest in his people, or to *despise* them, rather call forth his tender care and great compassion, v. 33. *Prisoners* are as dear to him as princes. Morison: "From the threefold bondage of sin, death and hell, he will finally rescue all his faithful servants, and will enable them to shout victory through the blood of the Lamb."

43. God's ways and character deserve great honor. The whole universe should unite in one chorus of hallelujah, v. 34.

44. Let what will come, the church is safe, because Jehovah makes her so, v. 35. Jerusalem, the type, has been trodden down of the Gentiles. But believers are receiving 'a kingdom which cannot be moved.'

45. All that is connected with Zion is so far blessed. The cities of Judah were far more honored and favored than the cities of Egypt or of Arabia, v. 35.

46. If the earthly Canaan was so much blessed, how wondrous must be the heavenly Canaan, where are gathered or gathering all that *love the name of God*, all that are themselves lovely in God's esteem.

47. How refreshing and encouraging it is to read and study such a Psalm as this. It is like conversing familiarly with one of the martyrs in the midst of his sufferings. Or it is as if one had heard Christ's words to his sorrowful disciples near the close of his life.

49. Christian, art thou wantonly, cruelly, slanderously treated? Remember how thy Saviour was hated without a cause, 'rejected, reviled, persecuted; condemned, buffeted, tortured; betrayed, denied, forsaken; nailed to the cross, mocked' of men and forsaken by his Father. Think of Christ's sufferings till you forget your own.

50. Scott: "It behooves us carefully to examine, whether the things which pertain to the Lord Jesus form as important a part of our religion, as they do of the holy

Scriptures; and whether our judgment, experience and affections are, as it were, imbued with them, as the word of God is in all its parts."

PSALM LXX.

To the chief Musician, *A Psalm* of David, to bring to remembrance.

1 *Make haste*, O God, to deliver me; make haste to help me, O LORD.

2 Let them be ashamed and confounded that seek after my soul: let them be turned backward, and put to confusion, that desire my hurt.

3 Let them be turned back for a reward of their shame that say, Aha, aha.

4 Let all those that seek thee rejoice and be glad in thee: and let such as love thy salvation say continually, Let God be magnified.

5 But I *am* poor and needy; make haste unto me, O God: thou *art* my help and my deliverer; O LORD, make no tarrying.

ON the title see on titles of Psalms iii. iv. xi. xxxviii. With slight variations this ode is found at the close of Ps. xl. Of the literary history of the two pieces we know nothing, though some indulge in conjectures. This bears to Ps. xl. the same relation that Ps. liii. does to Ps. xiv. Some have thought this was a kind of appendix to Ps. lxix. and a sort of preface to Ps. lxxi. The supposition is harmless perhaps, but it is unsupported, and nothing is gained thereby. Whoever wrote Psalm xl. wrote this also. The titles ascribe both to David. Psalm xl. has been shown to be *Typical-Messianic*. This may lawfully be so esteemed also, as Gill and others think. Yet it has by some been supposed to be in this form to 'suggest general hints for prayer, to pious persons, under very afflictive circumstances.' Clarke and Scott both fix the date about 1023 years before Christ. The names of the Most High here found are *Elohim God* and *Jehovah* LORD, on which see on Ps. iii. 2; i. 2. Many commentators refer the reader solely to their exposition of Ps. xl.; but as there is some variation a few words are offered.

1. Make haste, *O God, to deliver me; make haste to help me,* O LORD. The variations between this and Ps. xl. 13, are a substitution of *Elohim* in the first clause for *Jehovah,* and *Make haste* for *Be pleased.* The case required speed. It seemed as if the crisis had come.

2. *Let them be ashamed and confounded that seek after my soul: let them be turned backward, and put to confusion, that desire my hurt.* The form is rather prediction than imprecation. See Introduction, § 6. This verse and Ps. xl. 14 are just the same except that here we have not the words *together* and *to destroy it. Turned back* and *Driven back* are different renderings of the same verb. For the meaning of *ashamed* and *confounded,* see on Ps. xxxv. 4, 26.

3. *Let them be turned back for a reward of their shame that say, Aha, aha.* In this verse we have *turned back* for *desolate* in Ps. xl. 15, and *to me* is here omitted. But *turned back* here is not the same so rendered in v. 2, but a word which might be rendered either *be converted* or *be requited.* The latter probably gives the sense. On *Aha,* see on Ps. xxxv. 21, 25. It is a note of derision. The general import of the verse is the same as of Ps. xl. 15.

4. *Let all those that seek thee rejoice and be glad in thee; and let such as love thy salvation say continually, Let God be magnified.* The very same words are found in Ps. xl. 16, except that here the second clause begins with *and.*

5. *But I* am *poor and needy.* See on Ps. xl. 17, where we have precisely the same words. *Make haste unto me, O God.* In Ps. xl. 17, we have *Adonai Lord* instead of *Elohim God* in this place. *Thou* art *my help and my deliverer,* just as in Ps. xl. 17. O LORD, *make no tarrying,* as in Ps. xl. 17, except that here we have *Jehovah* LORD, instead of *Elohim God* in the prior Psalm. This verse also omits the pregnant phrase found in Ps. xl. 17: *The* LORD *thinketh upon me.*

DOCTRINAL AND PRACTICAL REMARKS.

1. The greater our need, the greater should be our urgency in making known our requests unto God. "Prayer is a swift messenger, which in the twinkling of an eye can go and return with an answer from heaven." Sometimes God delays his answers that he may raise our estimate of his mercies and increase our longings after them.

2. A deliverance is doubly valuable, when it comes in the very nick of time, v. 1. We may confidently ask for those things which are needful for us. "Give us day by day our daily bread."

3. None but God can give effectual aid in any distress; but sometimes it is so evident that none but he can help, that we easily withdraw confidence from all creatures. It is a mercy to be able to do so, even in the greatest straits.

4. There is no weapon more commonly used against good men, than scorn and derision. The aim of the ungodly is to cover them with shame and so make them odious. In this they often think they succeed. It will therefore be but retributive justice if shame and confusion shall come on all such, v. 2. Other Scriptures are no less decisive, Dan. xii. 2. It is enough to settle forever the character of sin, that whosoever commits it will assuredly and deeply regret it; and, if he dies without genuine repentance, he will regret it eternally.

5. It is good evidence of the coming doom of ungodly men that they are now malevolent, and *desire the hurt* of God's people, v. 2. Wickedness towards the righteous knows no limits, except as God bounds it. It seeks the life 'to destroy it; the mind to disturb' it; the heart to entice it; and the soul to sink it to despair. It often pours out its venom in the foulest imprecations.

6. Taunts are no new thing and ought not to disturb our equanimity, v. 3. They are harmless, and have been proved to be so in a thousand cases.

7. To seek God is a part of true religion, v. 4. He, whose longings and inquiries go not out after the knowledge, favor, image, service and enjoyment of God, has no piety that will abide the test of truth, the scrutiny of omniscience.

8. Dickson: "Whatsoever be our own hard condition at any time, we should seek the welfare and prosperity of the rest of God's children, and it is the property of each of the godly in their trouble, to wish all the rest to be partakers of the blessedness which their own souls seek after, but not to be like to them in trouble or bonds," v. 4.

9. There is joy, there is gladness in salvation, v. 4. They, who assert the contrary, do slander God and his cause.

10. Pious men had rather not be delivered at all from earthly trials than be delivered at the cost of God's honor. Their desire is that he may *be magnified,* v. 4. If that cannot be done, they will lie still and suffer on. Paul and Silas would not sneak out of the jail at Philippi.

11. A desire to glorify and magnify Jehovah belongs to true religion, v. 4.

12. If we are poor and needy, sad and afflicted, so have others been before us; and if our trials make us meek and lowly, we cannot have too many of them, as long as we may come and tell God the worst of our case, v. 5.

13. The poorer and more afflicted we are, the more need is there that we abound

in prayer and supplication, v. 5. Henry: "Poverty and necessity are very good pleas in prayer to a God of infinite mercy."

14. Scott: "No worldly possessions or distinctions can prevent the humbled sinner from feeling himself to be poor and needy; hence his entire dependence upon a merciful God, and his fervent supplications to him."

PSALM LXXI.

1 In thee, O LORD, do I put my trust: let me never be put to confusion.

2 Deliver me in thy righteousness, and cause me to escape: incline thine ear unto me, and save me.

3 Be thou my strong habitation, whereunto I may continually resort: thou hast given commandment to save me; for thou *art* my rock and my fortress.

4 Deliver me, O my God, out of the hand of the wicked, out of the hand of the unrighteous and cruel man.

5 For thou *art* my hope, O Lord GOD: *thou art* my trust from my youth.

6 By thee have I been holden up from the womb: thou art he that took me out of my mother's bowels: my praise *shall be* continually of thee.

7 I am as a wonder unto many; but thou *art* my strong refuge.

8 Let my mouth be filled *with* thy praise *and with* thy honour all the day.

9 Cast me not off in the time of old age; forsake me not when my strength faileth.

10 For mine enemies speak against me; and they that lay wait for my soul take counsel together,

11 Saying, God hath forsaken him: persecute and take him; for *there is* none to deliver *him*.

12 O God, be not far from me: O my God, make haste for my help.

13 Let them be confounded *and* consumed that are adversaries to my soul; let them be covered *with* reproach and dishonour that seek my hurt.

14 But I will hope continually, and will yet praise thee more and more.

15 My mouth shall shew forth thy righteousness *and* thy salvation all the day; for I know not the numbers *thereof.*

16 I will go in the strength of the Lord GOD: I will make mention of thy righteousness, *even* of thine only.

17 O God, thou hast taught me from my youth: and hitherto have I declared thy wondrous works.

18 Now also when I am old and grayheaded, O God, forsake me not; until I have shewed thy strength unto *this* generation, *and* thy power to every one *that* is to come.

19 Thy righteousness also, O God, *is* very high, who hast done great things: O God, who *is* like unto thee!

20 *Thou,* which hast shewed me great and sore troubles, shalt quicken me again, and shalt bring me up again from the depths of the earth.

21 Thou shalt increase my greatness, and comfort me on every side.

22 I will also praise thee with the psaltery, *even* thy truth, O my God: unto thee will I sing with the harp, O thou Holy One of Israel.

23 My lips shall greatly rejoice when I sing unto thee; and my soul, which thou hast redeemed.

24 My tongue also shall talk of thy righteousness all the day long: for they are confounded, for they are brought unto shame, that seek my hurt.

LIKE the *first* this Psalm has no title. It required none. That David wrote it is generally admitted. A review of his life near its close probably suggested its chief topics. Hengstenberg: "There may be truth in the assumption that David here comforts the suffering righteous man in his old age with that same comfort wherewith he himself had been comforted in his old age." Clarke dates it about B.

C. 1023 ; Scott, B. C. 1021. We have in it three names of the Almighty, *Jehovah* LORD, *Elohim God* and *Adonai Lord*, on which see Ps. i. 2 ; iii. 2 ; ii. 4.

Verses 1–3 are, with slight variations, found in Ps. xxxi. 1–3. They are not here transcribed, and the reader is referred to the comment and REMARKS on the previous ode. Verse 1 in both places is the same. Verse 2 is slightly varied, here dropping the urgent word *speedily* and duplicating the plea for deliverance. The imagery of v. 3 is the same in both pieces. To give *commandment to save* reveals a purpose and a promise of salvation, Ps. xliv. 4. On verses 1–3, Tholuck says, "The old man, cast down by the visitations of providence, appears before his God. He is supported by the promise of the Lord, that those who trust in him shall never be put to confusion, and by his faith, confirmed by the experience of his whole life, that the Lord is indeed a rock and a fortress."

4. *Deliver me, O my God, out of the hand of the wicked, out of the hand of the unrighteous and cruel man.* *Deliver me,* in v. 2, *cause me to escape;* in Ps. xxxi. 2, and elsewhere as here. The enemy, whom he dreaded and from whose power he sought safety, is described 1, as *wicked, ungodly, one that does wrong,* Ex. ii. 13 ; Ps. i. 4 ; Ps. vii. 9 ; 2, as *unrighteous, unjust, iniquitous;* and 3, as *cruel,* literally *leavened violent, malicious,* or perhaps *abandoned.* We say *bitter persecutors* and so describe the same character. Though God can sustain his people in any trials, yet the temptation brought on us by leaving us in the hands of bad men is peculiarly dreadful to the righteous, 2 Sam. xxiv. 14. By using the singular *man,* he does not intimate a fear of one only. His resort is to God alone.

5. *For thou art my hope, O Lord* GOD : *thou art my trust from my youth.* *Adonai Elohim* here mentioned is a fit object of *hope* and *trust, expectation* and *confidence.* Tholuck : "He has clung to faith and hope throughout the entire period of his existence." David relied on God when he was a mere lad, 1 Sam. xvii. 37. Nay, he now acknowledges that God took care of him before he knew his Preserver.

6. *By thee have I been holden up from the womb.* The care of God over little children by their parents, by his angels, and by his direct exercise of power, is astonishing. If we saw no other proof of God's providence, his care of little children ought to remove all skepticism on the subject. See on Ps. xxii. 9, 10. But David goes back still further : *Thou art he that took me out of my mother's bowels.* The wonder is that any one is ever born, or born alive. To many the womb is the grave. Birth is 'a great and wonderful, though a common and neglected work of God's power and goodness.' "Blessed be God that ever I was born," said Halyburton. *My praise* shall be *continually of thee.* Such tokens of divine regard as he had received in his formation, birth and protection demanded that his lips should be opened in praise. He declares his purpose never to cease to speak to the honor of his Creator and Preserver. Alexander : "In thee is my praise always; it originates, revolves, and ends in thee."

7. *I am as a wonder unto many.* *Wonder,* often so rendered, also *sign, miracle.* Several ancient versions and not a few moderns render it *prodigy.* Diodati explains it that men 'have been afraid of me, because that such strange accidents and afflictions have befallen me ; and have scorned, and had me in abomination by reason of my extreme miseries.' Calvin, Ainsworth, Green, Horsley, French and Skinner, Alexander and others give it the same explanation. But the word rendered *wonder* may as well be taken in a good sense. So the Arabic has it: I am become the admiration of many. Anderson : "Others suppose that the word rendered *wonder,* implies that the great and many dangers to which he had been exposed, and the extraordinary deliverances from them which he had experienced, marked him out as an object of wonder, so that men looked upon him as if he were exempted from the

common lot of mankind, as if he possessed a charmed life, and were invulnerable to all assaults." The translators of the English Bible evidently had the first view; for they rendered the particle in the next clause *but;* yet its far more common rendering is *and,* which if used here would have the sense of *for,* and so some do give it. *But thou art my strong refuge. Refuge* as in Ps. xiv. 6; xlvi. 1, also rendered *shelter,* and figuratively *hope,* meaning object of hope. *Strong,* in Hebrew not an adjective but a noun, and we may read *refuge* and *strength.*

8. *Let my mouth be filled* with *thy praise* and with *thy honor all the day long.* The Hebrew verb is in the future. Many think that is the better rendering here. This duty of praise was most agreeable to David. He was fully purposed to engage in it. Yet he felt his dependence on God for grace to do anything aright, and so it gives a good sense to make it a prayer as in the common version. *Honor,* a word in Hebrew, that we have not before had in the Psalms, often rendered as here, also *beauty, glory, majesty.* Here it seems clearly to mean *declarative glory.* To praise God he desires and resolves shall be his work *all the day, i. e.,* continually. An ingrate has no praises for God in the day of adversity; but the true child of God praises him in the darkest night. He at least says, God is holy and righteous, and adores him for his perfections. He also thanks him for mercies past, and for mercies left.

9. *Cast me not off in the time of old age.* Parallel passages are found in Ps. xcii. 13–15; Isa. xlvi. 3, 4. To *cast off* is to *cast away,* or *reject* as valueless or offensive. *Forsake me not when my strength faileth. Forsake,* often *leave.* It expresses the desertion of the feeble or helpless by such as might give aid. When his servant grew sick and feeble, that Amalekite went away and *left* him, 1 Sam. xxx. 13. But God never so treats his servants. David had given to God the dew of his youth, and the vigor of his manhood, and God had given him infallible tokens of divine acceptance. He might, therefore, confidently plead that he might not be neglected when he most needed God's help, seeing that he had grown old in his service. Such a plea, when true, God never despised.

10. *For mine enemies speak against me. Enemies,* always so rendered. For *speak against,* several read *speak of me;* Alexander: *have said (so) to me, i. e.,* have told me that God would forsake me, or had forsaken me. These enemies had spoken wrongfully, and David declares their speeches slanders against God, and desires Jehovah so to prove. *And they that lay wait for my soul take counsel together.* The foes of David were never fair, but sly and cunning, *laying wait,* literally watching, but in a bad sense. They were also deadly. They lay wait for the *soul,* or the *life.*

11. *Saying, God hath forsaken him: persecute and take him; for* there is *none to deliver* him. *Hath forsaken,* the preterite of the same verb found in v. 9. *Pursue* is better than *persecute* here; and *catch* is the sense of *take.* The wicked often say that things are or will be thus or so, because thus and so would they have them. Even the basest men, engaged in the most atrocious schemes for wronging and injuring others, often persuade themselves that Providence has put no obstacle in the way, but has even called them to their nefarious deeds. So great a support does the human mind receive from a persuasion of the divine sanction, that the wicked often assert that God approves when he abhors their whole procedure. If this Psalm was written during Absalom's rebellion, as some think, there is in this verse probably an allusion to the words of Ahithophel in 2 Sam. xvii. 1, 2.

12. *O God, be not far from me; O my God, make haste for my help.* The same forms of petition are found in Ps. xxii. 11, 19; xxxv. 22; xxxviii. 21, 22; lxx. 1. It has always been an artifice of the wicked to allege that God is against his people, else he would not allow them to be brought into such straits. "It was therefore," says Calvin, "an evidence of heroic fortitude on the part of David, thus to rise superior

to their perverse judgments, and, in the face of them all, to assure himself that God would be gracious to him, and to betake himself familiarly to him."

13. *Let them be confounded* and *consumed that are adversaries to my soul: let them be covered* with *reproach and dishonor that seek my hurt.* The import of these two clauses is just the same. *Confounded*, often also rendered *ashamed;* see on Ps. vi. 10; xxv. 2, 3; xxxv. 4. *Consumed,* also rendered *waxed old*, as a garment, signifying useless through age. *Covered, arrayed*, as with a garment, or *filled*, as a pool with rain, 1 Sam. xxviii. 14; Isa. lix. 17; Jer. xliii. 12; Ps. lxxxiv. 6. *Reproach*, commonly so rendered, once *shame* and twice *rebuke*. *Dishonor*, also rendered *shame, reproach, confusion*. All the verbs of this verse in Hebrew are in the future; and are so rendered by many. Scott: "There is no reason to think, that David had recorded one *prayer* in the Psalms, which St. Paul would in similar circumstances have scrupled."

14. *But I will hope continually.* The very perfections of God, which made him foresee and foretell the doom of his enemies, caused him to *hope, wait, trust.* All God's nature inspires *confidence* and so quietness of mind, if we and our cause are right. *Continually*, also rendered *always*, sometimes *daily.* And [I] *will yet praise thee more and more.* Some read: *I will add to all thy praise;* others: *I will add* this *to thy praise;* others: *I shall be added to thy praise.* Horsley adopts the last and thinks the sense is: Thy mercies to me will furnish the servants of God with a new topic of thy praise and thanksgiving. Alexander prefers the first and thinks the sense is: To all thy praise which I have uttered hitherto, I will continue still to add. The common version gives the exact sense, though it is not so literal as the first of those suggested. Patrick: "That shall be the subject of my songs, to publish thy mercy and truth in judging righteously between me and my enemies: this shall be my continual employment; though I shall never be able to tell the least part of that mercy, which will appear in my deliverance from such formidable enemies." Scott: "Because thy benefits towards me are innumerable, I cannot but continually meditate on them, and rehearse them."

15. *My mouth shall shew forth thy righteousness* and *thy salvation all the day.* It was his purpose to do it now, in confident expectation of deliverance from his persecutors; and to do it yet more hereafter when God's *righteousness*, or justice should be manifested in his deliverance. This he would do *all the day*, or continually, for there was no danger of running into excess: *For I know not the numbers thereof. Numbers*, in the plural. Alexander: "*I know not numbers* to express them;" church of England: I know no end thereof. The Chaldee, Syriac and a great weight of authority are in favor of the English version. Hammond thinks there is singular elegance in this passage. The verb *show forth* and the word *numbers* are cognate.

16. *I will go in the strength of the Lord* GOD. *Go*, a verb of frequent occurrence, rendered *go, go in, come, come in, enter in.* Some suppose it refers to *going into* the tabernacle, but it is applied to any *going.* It may express the tenor of the life. *Strength*, plural *strengths*, that is, abundance of strength. Some of the ancient versions read, I will enter into the strength, meaning, I will avail myself of his strength. *Lord Jehovah* is better than *Lord* GOD. *I will make mention of thy righteousness*, even *of thine only.* Here as in verse 15, *righteousness* embraces all that is comprehended in *faithfulness*, based upon infinite rectitude. *Make mention*, or *record*, the usual rendering; in other forms commonly *remember*. Here literally: *I will cause to remember.* After our deliverances no righteousness, faithfulness, wisdom, mercy, or power is worthy of religious mention, but those of God *only.*

17. *O God, thou hast taught me from my youth.* Divine teaching has been the joy of God's people in all ages. A heart to praise is as needful as a theme for praise. To our shame we often have the occasion without the disposition. In David's case the

teaching had been effectual: *And hitherto have I declared thy wondrous works.* *Declared* them willingly, joyfully, thankfully, to thy honor. The verb is in the future, *shall declare.* Some make it a vow, or the expression of a purpose respecting time to come. In that case *hitherto* should belong to the first clause, and *I will declare* [show or tell] *thy wondrous works* to the last. The objection to this is that it destroys the connection with what follows. That the grammar is not against the common version is clear. Hengstenberg has it: *Hitherto have I made known thy wonders.*

18. *Now also, when I am old and grayheaded, O God, forsake me not.* *Forsake,* as in v. 9. *Old and grayheaded,* literally *unto old age and gray hairs.* Such mercy he desired of the Lord, *Until I have shewed thy strength unto* this *generation,* and *thy power to every one* that *is to come.* *Strength,* literally *arm,* that being in man the chief instrument of exercising strength for deliverance; also rendered *power.* Chaldee: *The strength of thy arm.* *Power,* also rendered *might, strength, mastery.* *Generation* and *every one that is to come,* many think, are in apposition. Some think the latter is the more comprehensive. Our translators evidently thought so. *Shewed* does not signify *furnished an instance of,* but *declared* as in v. 17. The blessing here sought is manifestly great, if we reflect on the feebleness of the aged, and their absolute dependence on God. If God forsakes us all past experiences are nothing.

19. *Thy righteousness also, O God, is very high, who hast done great things.* As in vv. 15, 16, *righteousness* includes not only the essential rectitude and inflexible justice of God, but also his faithfulness in the fulfilment of all his promises, and in the exercise of all his attributes for the defence of his chosen. In this as in every other sense God's righteousness is *very high, i. e.,* 'it is in itself very sublime, or it is in the eyes of those who consider thy dealings with me very exalted, glorious or illustrious.' Elsewhere he says: "Thy righteousness is like the great mountains," which are very grand and elevated objects. Chaldee: *To the high heavens;* Hengstenberg: *Stretches to heaven.* The English version gives the whole sense. *O God, who* is *like unto thee?* Compare Ps. xxxv. 10; lxxxvi. 8; lxxxix. 6, 8; Ex. viii. 10; ix. 14; xv. 11; Deut. iii. 24; xxxiii. 26; 2 Sam. vii. 22; 1 Chron. xvii. 20. God is incomparable.

20. Thou, *which hast shewed me great and sore troubles, shalt quicken me again, and shalt bring me up again from the depths of the earth.* *Troubles* are often spoken of as *depths, deep places,* the sorrowful as *dead* men, and relief from trouble as a restoring to life, Ps. lxxxviii. 6; cxxxviii. 7. So we may understand this verse. The only objection to this explanation is that the word rendered *depths* commonly means the *sea.* This is true, especially in the singular form, but we also read of "the seas, and all *deep places,*" where we have the same word as here, Ps. cxxxv. 6. Such bold figures derive great force from the doctrine of the resurrection. Indeed they have little or no fitness where it is not known and believed. Like other ancient worthies, David was by it greatly sustained. Without that last great deliverance—"a better resurrection"—"the resurrection of the just"—all minor deliverances were as nothing.

21. *Thou shalt increase my greatness, and comfort me on every side.* The expected deliverance was to be followed by enlargement and increased blessings. To those in covenant with God one mercy is the forerunner of another. The resurrection itself will be followed by ineffable glories. Ainsworth properly regards *greatness* as signifying *magnificence, majesty, honor.* Christ himself suffered and then entered into his glory. Instead of *comfort me on every side,* the Hebrew is: *Thou shalt compass, thou shalt comfort me.* Some would read: *Thou shalt turn, thou shalt comfort me,* meaning *thou shalt comfort me again;* and the verb does bear this rendering, but the former is perhaps the better view.

22. *I will also praise thee with the psaltery, even thy truth, O my God.* *Psaltery,* see on Ps. xxxiii. 2; lvii. 8. *Truth,* the general word for divine veracity, is here used

as synonymous with faithfulness. God is to be adored for all his attributes. He is particularly to be praised for keeping covenant. *Unto thee will I sing with the harp. O thou Holy One of Israel. Harp*, see on Ps. xxxiii. 2; xliii. 4. *Holy One of Israei* is a title given to Jehovah not less than *thirty* times in the Scriptures; more than *twenty* times in Isaiah alone. It is most honorable. He possesses all and infinite perfections. No other god is, holy.

23. *My lips shall greatly rejoice when I sing unto thee; and my soul, which thou hast redeemed.* Horsley: *My lips shall move briskly, when I sing unto thee, and my souι shall rejoice, which thou hast redeemed.* Praising God is a delightful privilege, but a miserable task—the drudgery of hypocrites.

24. *My tongue also shall talk of thy righteousness all the day long. Talk of*, literally *meditate*, then *utter. Righteousness*, as in vv. 2, 15, 16, 19. *For they are confounded, for they are brought unto shame, that seek my hurt.* Here we have the fulfilment of the prediction uttered in v. 13. He was so confident of triumph, that he sang of it before it came. To his mind, it was as if judgment had been already executed.

Doctrinal and Practical Remarks.

1. Without *settled confidence* in God, we cannot enter into rest, v. 1.

2. Scott: "It is very honorable to God, that his word encourages sinners to plead their confidence in him, as a reason why he should save and help them," v. 1.

3. Dickson: "As long as a child of God liveth in the world, he must look for new afflictions, as here the experience of the Psalmist tossed in his old age warneth us," v. 1.

4. Henry: "They that are at home in God, that live a life of communion with him, and confidence in him, that continually resort unto him by faith and prayer, having their eyes ever toward him, may promise themselves a strong habitation in him, such as will never fall of itself, nor can ever be broken through by any invading power," vv. 1–3.

5. God is the best, the only safe refuge in the day of trial, v. 3.

6. It is a great mercy, one highly to be prized, one earnestly to be prayed for, that we may be delivered from wicked, unrighteous, cruel and unreasonable men, v. 4; 2 Thess. iii. 2. Wild beasts are not more dangerous, and are never so refined in their cruelty.

7. None but God can effectually deliver us from any threatened evil, and particularly from those terrific combinations of ungodly men, which are often formed against his cause and servants, v. 4. Dickson: "It is a great advantage to be a confederate with God, when we have to deal with his enemies and ours in any debate."

8. If in contests with men we see our cause is bad, let us abandon it, and ask God to forgive us for having engaged in it; but if we know that the matter for which we contend is weighty as well as just, let us not fear the issue, nor hesitate to bring our complaints before Jehovah.

9. When men are *ungodly*, they are so far ready to be *cruel*, v. 4. Compare Luke xviii. 2, 4. Every sin has its kindred vices. Ungodliness implies all.

10. A solid foundation for wisdom and confidence is found in a life-long experience of the divine guidance and mercy, v. 5. Such an experience gives a hope that maketh not ashamed. It is a great thing to be habituated from early life to trust in the Lord, and hope in his mercy. Happy are they who seek the Saviour early. Slade: "Should they be cut off, as many are, when young, they will be removed from this troublesome world, to a land of perfect peace and perfect beauty; transplanted, as flowers in the bud, to bloom and ripen in paradise. And should they live to be old, their gray hairs will be honorable; and they will be blessed with solid comfort

and satisfaction in looking back upon the years, in which they have walked with God, through the grace of his Holy Spirit."

11. Very few days of man's appointing are more fitly observed in a serious, religious way, than the anniversary of one's birth, which was a wonder second only to the new birth. Rich is the mercy therein displayed. But for this our "very birth would be an entrance into a thousand deaths."

12. It is a pious custom, adopted by all good men, often and solemnly to review the events of providence in their own lives and histories, v. 6. In this matter we should follow the wise and pious. If we thought more on such matters, we should oftener sing 'songs in the night.'

13. If ungodly men *wonder* at the righteous now for their peculiar principles, and sometimes for their singular sufferings, they will *wonder* still more at the victories which they shall accomplish, and the glory that shall be revealed in them. Let not the saints therefore be cast down because they find that they are made gazing-stocks, v. 7. Christ himself was "a sign everywhere spoken against." His Apostles were reputed the off-scouring of all things. All this did not in the end diminish their happiness. God was their *refuge*, and he is as willing to be ours.

14. It is right to form a solemn purpose to praise God abundantly, and to offer fervent prayer that we may be able to keep our engagements, v. 8.

15. The aged believer with his long experience, has a solid ground of confidence and assurance in approaching God, v. 9. In his infinite mercy Jehovah does not reject a truly broken heart, offered him by the aged sinner, 2 Chron. xxxiii. 13. But how hard it is for inveterate sinners to approach God with any boldness! Slade: "It is a sad thing to be looking for religion in old age, when we ought to be enjoying the comforts of it—to be sowing when we ought to be reaping." Tholuck: "If God did help us in the time of our youth and manhood, when our strength aided us to overcome many difficulties, how much more will *his* strength deliver us when ours is gone, especially when the wicked challenge his mighty arm."

16. If God should forsake us at any stage of our existence we should be undone. But there is peculiar dreariness attending an old age unsupported by the grace and power of God. And there is a peculiar sweetness attending pious old age. God is not offended at decrepitude. Scott: "As old age approaches, our strength in many respects will fail us: but God will not cast off his gray-headed servants, when they are no longer capable of laboring as they have done. And his people should imitate his example, in their kindness towards such as have spent their health and strength in their service." Henry: "He that was our Help from our birth ought to be our Hope from our youth. If we received so much mercy from God before we were capable of doing him any service, we should lose no time when we are capable."

17. So long as we live and serve God we may expect to have enemies, who will do what they can to injure us, especially with their tongues, v. 10.

18. No man knows what plottings may be going on for his destruction, v. 10. Yet they are powerless, if God does not allow them to gain head.

19. Egregiously do the wicked err in their judgments of spiritual things, and in particular of the designs of God in his providential dealings with his people, v. 11. Calvin: "Measuring the favor of God only by what is the present condition of men, they conceive that all whom he suffers to be afflicted are despised, forsaken, and cast off by him." How different from this is God's exposition of his own government. "As many as I love I rebuke and chasten." Horne: "They who saw David ascending Mount Olivet in tears, when Absalom had driven him from Jerusalem, and they who beheld Jesus led forth out of the same Jerusalem, to be crucified on Mount Calvary, were tempted to regard both the one and the other, as finally deserted by

God." Let us not be blind through unbelief, nor talk to the grief of those whom God has wounded, Ps. lxix. 26.

20. The more pressing and violent our foes, the more urgent may we be with God to appear for us, vv. 11, 12.

21. The doom of the wicked is coming. Their woes will soon be upon them, and they will be dreadful, yea, intolerable, v. 13.

22. As good men, however cast down, are never quite in despair, so they have a right to hope always, v. 14. God's word and providence both justify such confidence. True faith looks not so much at appearances as at what God has said and done to his people.

23. The longer we live and the more we know and experience, the more should we abound in praise to God, v. 14.

24. A sense of our ignorance and insufficiency, and of the inadequacy of our services should not deter us from honestly and heartily endeavoring to do our whole duty, v. 15. Let us know what we can, and do what we know.

25. All our strength in living, in serving God, and in suffering for him, is in and from the Lord, and should be so declared by all, by the aged in particular, v. 16. Tholuck : "To praise the righteousness and goodness of the Lord is the proper employment of old age." He, who fights without God, will but beat the air.

26. God's righteousness and all his perfections throw all our attributes quite into the shade, so as to be unworthy of notice, v. 16. God is God alone. No glory, no power, no love, no wisdom, no holiness, no justice, no mercy in comparison of his are worthy to be *mentioned*.

27. Divine teaching is both necessary and sufficient to bring us to think and speak well of God and his marvellous doings, v. 17. Indeed we can do no duty without the help of divine grace.

28. Consistent piety, exhibited through youth and manhood may be pleaded in the day of darkness and sorrow as a reason why God should not forsake us ; because it is most agreeable to his nature to remember old friendships, vv. 17, 18. Calvin : "His reasoning is, Since thou, O God, hast from the commencement of my existence given me such abundant proofs of thy goodness, wilt thou not stretch forth thy hand to succor me, when now thou seest me decaying through the influence of old age?"

29. Aged saints have some great advantages in speaking for God and religion ; and they ought not to keep silent, but utter the memory of all his goodness, and show forth his praise all the day long, v. 18. Tholuck : "Are there better preachers of the works of God to be found than hoary parents in the circle of their children, or grand-parents in that of their grand-children ?"

30. It is to God's unspeakable and everlasting glory that much as he has done, filling the earth with the fame of his deeds, he has yet done all things in righteousness, v. 19. One act of unrighteousness or unfaithfulness on his part would forever destroy pious confidence. It is therefore for a perpetual joy to the church on earth and the church in heaven that the Judge of all the earth doeth right, and can do no wrong. There is no more glorious song sung in heaven or earth than those found in Deut. xxxii. 4; Rev. xvi. 5, 7.

31. God is incomparable, v. 19. Were it not so, it would be impossible to see how his character could be a fountain of joy, or we find repose on his bosom. We dare not wholly trust the best men, or the chief angels. But we can trust an infinite God.

32. There are no depths of earthly woe, from which the arm and mercy of God cannot rescue his suffering children, v. 20. David found it so. Calvin : "We must be brought down even to the gates of death before God can be seen to be our deliverer."

33 Henry: "Sometimes God makes his people's troubles contribute to the increase of their greatness, and their sun shines the brighter for having been under a cloud," v. 20.

34. It is no small part of heavenly wisdom in times of trial to seize upon the strong doctrines of Scripture for our consolation, such as those of the universal providence of God and the resurrection, vv. 20, 21.

35. Whatever may befall believers here, it is certain that their career in the next world will be brighter and brighter for ever, v. 21. Dickson: "As no trouble cometh alone, but multitudes of troubles joined together, when the Lord will humble and try a man; so no comfort cometh single or alone, when the Lord will change the man's exercise, but a multitude of comforts joined together: *Thou wilt comfort me on every side.*"

36. On the use of musical instruments in God's worship, see REMARKS on Ps. xxxiii. 2, 3.

37. Wherever God has a people, there praise and joy should abound, vv. 22–24. Tholuck: "We think it a lovely sight to see an old man spend his days in singing the praise of God with trembling lips to the notes of the harp. And there is no more beauteous sight to God—and the notes of the harp sound up to the highest heaven." Morison: "The motives of gratitude and triumph under the New Testament are augmented a thousand-fold; and the consecration of both heart and life should be in proportion to the benefits enjoyed."

38. To aged saints this Psalm furnishes an excellent form of prayer. Let them often employ it. Cobbin: "At all periods of life there is a necessity for prayer, but it is most urgent in old age. When the heart and flesh fail, who can be our strength but God? When worse enemies than Ahithophel conspire against our peace, whither can we flee but unto God as our rock and fortress? When the earth is receding beneath our feet, God alone can be our hope and trust."

39. We cannot preach to the aged without preaching to the young. This Psalm offers fit occasion to say to the young, Behold the wisdom of early piety. Youth may be your only period of life. If you do not improve that, you may be forever undone. But if you live to old age, you will need all the consolations arising from the fact that you early gave your hearts to God. "Oh come to God, ye young people, without delay; or you may never come at all. The world will tempt and court you; but believe it not; it is a wicked flatterer, full of deceit, promising pleasure but ending in ruin," Matt. vi. 33.

PSALM LXXII.

A *Psalm* for Solomon.

1 Give the king thy judgments, O God, and thy righteousness unto the king's son.

2 He shall judge thy people with righteousness, and thy poor with judgment.

3 The mountains shall bring peace to the people, and the little hills, by righteousness.

4 He shall judge the poor of the people, he shall save the children of the needy, and shall break in pieces the oppressor.

5 They shall fear thee as long as the sun and moon endure, throughout all generations.

6 He shall come down like rain upon the mown grass: as showers *that* water the earth.

7 In his days shall the righteous flourish; and abundance of peace so long as the moon endureth.

8 He shall have dominion also from sea to sea, and from the river unto the ends of the earth.

9 They that dwell in the wilderness shall bow before him ; and his enemies shall lick the dust.

10 The kings of Tarshish and of the isles shall bring presents: the kings of Sheba and Seba shall offer gifts.

11 Yea, all kings shall fall down before him : all nations shall serve him.

12 For he shall deliver the needy when he crieth; the poor also, and *him* that hath no helper.

13 He shall spare the poor and needy, and shall save the souls of the needy.

14 He shall redeem their soul from deceit and violence: and precious shall their blood be in his sight.

15 And he shall live, and to him shall be given of the gold of Sheba: prayer also shall be made for him continually ; *and* daily shall he be praised.

16 There shall be a handful of corn in the earth upon the top of the mountains; the fruit thereof shall shake like Lebanon: and *they* of the city shall flourish like grass of the earth.

17 His name shall endure for ever: his name shall be continued as long as the sun: and *men* shall be blessed in him : all nations shall call him blessed.

18 Blessed *be* the LORD God, the God of Israel, who only doeth wondrous things.

19 And blessed *be* his glorious name for ever: and let the whole earth be filled *with* his glory. Amen, and Amen.

20 The prayers of David the son of Jesse are ended.

ON supplying *A Psalm* in the title, see on title of Ps. xi. Scott and Clarke date this ode B. C. 1015. The names of the Most High in it are *Elohim God* and *Jehovah* LORD, on which see on Ps. iii. 2; i. 2. *For Solomon,* or *To Solomon* in the title is better than *Of Solomon.* Some very respectable writers have conjectured that Solomon wrote it, or at least reduced it to poetical measure. But several ancient versions, also Diodati, Ainsworth, Calmet, Patrick, Henry, Clarke, Horne, Pool, Morison and Dickson correctly ascribe it to David. The last verse is decisive. Theodoret regarded Messiah and his reign as its only theme; but that is an extreme view. Solomon is certainly spoken of, though chiefly as a type of Christ. The Psalm is therefore *Typical-Messianic.* This view is attended with comparatively few difficulties. Calmet well states the case: "Transported with joy and gratitude at the crowning of Solomon, David addressed this Psalm to God, in which he prays him to pour out his blessings on the young king and upon the people. He then, rapt in a divine enthusiasm, ascends to a higher subject, and sings the glory of the Messiah, and the magnificence of his reign. So that in this Psalm we may see a great number of expressions, which cannot relate to Solomon, unless in a hyperbolical and figurative sense: but applied to Christ, they are literally and rigorously exact." Pool: "That David, or at least the Holy Ghost, who dictated this Psalm, did look beyond Solomon, and unto the Messiah, of whom Solomon was an illustrious and unquestionable type, seems manifest from divers passages of this Psalm, which do not agree to Solomon, nor to any other king but the Messiah, and from the confession of the Jewish doctors themselves, who so understand it." Horne and others present similar views. See Isa. xxxii. 1–7; Luke i. 32, 33 ; John v. 22, 23.

1. *Give the king thy judgments, O God, and thy righteousness unto the king's son.* Solomon was both *king* and *the king's son.* This honor pertained neither to David nor Saul, both of whom were the sons of obscure men. David prays and predicts that to his *son, the king,* Solomon, God would grant *judgments* and *justice,* by which we are not so much to understand *decisions in his favor,* when he was in *the right,* as grace and wisdom to give decisions pleasing to God and consistent with justice. "Thus his reign would be an apt resemblance, as it was an evident type, of the kingdom of Messiah." Alexander: "The judicial power, under the theocracy, was exercised in God's name, and by his representatives; see Deut. i. 17; Pr. viii. 15; 2 Chron. xix. 6." Very aptly does Solomon, whose name signifies *peaceable,* or *perfect,* and the entrance on whose work was marked by consummate wisdom, typify King Messiah, who was the root and offspring of David, Isa. ix. 7 ; xi. 3, 4.

2. *He shall judge thy people with righteousness, and thy poor with judgment.* *Righteousness* and *judgment*, as in v. 1. The Septuagint, Ethiopic, Vulgate and Doway put the verb *judge* in the infinitive, and the Syriac, Arabic, church of England and Ainsworth connect it with v. 1, so as to give the same sense as if it were in the infinitive; but the Chaldee, Calvin, Venema, Tremellius and Junius, Piscator, Fabritius, Jebb, Hengstenberg and Alexander follow the Hebrew and render it in the future, without any particle connecting it with v. 1. Morison thinks there is an obvious connection between the petition of v. 1 and the prediction of v. 2, between the gifts supplicated and the character to be ultimately sustained, and so he commends the rendering of the church of England, of Green and others, who begin v. 2 with the word *Then.* But if v. 1 is as truly a prediction as v. 2, it is not necessary to preserve such connection. *People* may either designate the Jewish *nation*, over whom Solomon reigned, or the whole body of God's redeemed, the church, of which the tribes of Israel were a figure. The latter view best corresponds with the designations afterwards given of God's servants, as the *poor, humble, lowly, afflicted.*

3. *The mountains shall bring peace to the people, and the little hills, by righteousness.* We shall get the same general idea from this verse, whether by *mountains* and *hills* we understand all parts of the land, or regard them as figurative designations of kingdoms or governments. The proper effect of good government is *peace*, a word used in Scripture to include not merely *quiet*, but the blessings of plenty, prosperity and general happiness. Morison: "The word is often used to denote all manner of prosperity." All this is produced *in* or *by righteousness*, i. e., by a government conducted on right principles. The same is taught elsewhere, 2 Sam. xxiii. 3, 4. The blessings of good government are very great; see 1 Kings iii. 28. The blessings of Messiah's reign are greater than those of all other governments. They are unspeakable, inconceivable. Compare Isa. lxiv. 4; 1 Cor. ii. 9; Eph. iii. 8. The word *peace* in the first clause is to be repeated in the second, as *in righteousness* in the second belongs also to the first.

4. *He shall judge the poor of the people.* *Poor*, as in v. 3. *Judge*, often used in the sense of *govern* with protection, also *avenge* so as to vindicate, Judg. xvi. 31; 1 Sam. iv. 18; 2 Sam. xviii. 19, 31. *He shall save the children of the needy.* *Judgment* results in *salvation*. By the *needy*, elsewhere often rendered *poor*, we are to understand the *poor* of the preceding clause, either under Solomon such as from poverty were thought to be unable to contend with the rich and powerful, or under Messiah *the poor in spirit.* And [he] *shall break in pieces the oppressor.* *Break*, also rendered *bruise, crush, humble, destroy*, Isa. liii. 10; Lam. iii. 34; Jer. xliv. 10; Job vi. 9. *Oppressor*, the participle of the verb rendered *oppress, defraud, do wrong, do violence.* The meaning is he will effectually suppress wrong and outrage. How wisely Solomon did this is seen in the first act of his royal life. How much more effectually Messiah does it by his conquering grace is shown by the sanctifying power of his word and Spirit.

5. *They shall fear thee as long as the sun and moon endure, throughout all generations.* Here we rise quite above Solomon to the great antitype under whose reign men shall be truly pious. *Thee* refers to God, who is addressed in v. 1. *As long as the sun*, literally *with the sun*, i. e., parallel with his career, as long as the sun is with them. *And moon*, literally *before the moon*, i. e., as long as the moon shines. These expressions are explained by the last clause *generation of generations* or *throughout all generations.* Solomon reigned not more than forty years. Under his descendants instead of holding its own his kingdom lost much. Neither did piety flourish greatly. So that this verse must relate to the perpetuity and glory of Christ's kingdom.

6. *He shall come down like rain upon the mown grass: as showers that water the earth.* Solomon's reign was just, peaceful and eminently suited to revive all the interests of his nation, for "every man dwelt safely under his vine and fig-tree, from Dan even to

Beersheba, all the days of Solomon," 1 Kings iv. 25. In this it was a fit though feeble type of the beneficent reign of Messiah, under whose authority all the spiritual and eternal interests of believers are eminently prospered. The way in which this is done is most refreshing, even like rain upon meadows newly mowed, where the roots and tufts of grass, which have long been shaded, are now exposed to a scorching sun. In a parched region, as Judea was for many months of the year, a *pouring shower* was a very fit emblem of the refreshment of Messiah's dominion. Patrick: " He shall not endeavor to be formidable to them like a tyrant; whose government imitates the thunder, storms and tempests: but condescend most graciously to the meanest, and rule them in so soft and gentle a manner, as shall make his authority no less acceptable and beneficial, than the rain is to the after-grass, or dripping showers, which fall in the summer heat, to refresh the parched earth.' If such was the reign of Solomon, how much more glorious and excellent is the dominion of Christ, who by his blessed Gospel, and the saving influences of his Spirit pours light, life, peace and joy into the hearts of men otherwise the most wretched and afflicted.

7. *In his days shall the righteous flourish. Flourish, grow, bud, spring, blossom. Flourish* gives the sense, expressing the benign effects accompanying the Gospel. This clause was but feebly fulfilled in Solomon's time. Though the word righteous here and in many other places is singular, yet it includes all the just. *And abundance of peace so long as the moon endureth,* [or *till* there be *no moon.*] *Abundance*, elsewhere *much, great, manifold, sufficient.* Though Christianity has not yet gained sufficient influence to expel national contests from among men, yet finally it shall cause men to 'learn war no more.' Just so far as it is truly embraced, it extinguishes the lust of power and the fires of contention, and gives peace of conscience and peace with God. Jesus, in a far higher sense than any other, is the Prince of peace. Under him concord *flourishes.*

8. *He shall have dominion also from sea to sea, and from the river unto the ends of the earth.* The passages of Scripture, showing the correct understanding of these words so far as Solomon's dominion is concerned, are Gen. xv. 18; Ex. xxiii. 31; Deut. i. 7; xi. 24; Josh. i. 3, 4. These contain the *promises.* Those which declare the historic verity are 1 Kings iv. 21, 24; 2 Chron. ix. 26; Ezra iv. 20. Scott: " The queen of Sheba came to Jerusalem with munificent presents, and all the kings round about brought tribute or gifts to him. Yet this faintly shadowed forth the Redeemer's kingdom." This verse has and is to have its most glorious fulfilment in the setting up of Christ's kingdom in all the world. Phrases, like this, "From Dan to Beersheba," or like those in this verse, seem soon to become proverbial, and denote the whole region or territory under consideration; see Am. viii. 12; Mic. vii. 12; Zech. ix. 10. Hengstenberg: " The dominion of this king extends from any one sea to any other sea, and from any river even to the ends of the earth,—it is a kingdom of boundless extent." That this is the right view of these words is clear from the expansion and interpretation they receive in the following verses.

9. *They that dwell in the wilderness shall bow before him. Wilderness* here does not seem to refer at all to any particular locality, as the wilderness of Judea, of Shur, of Paran, or of Sin, but in general to all wild, or *desert* parts of the world. *They that dwell in the wilderness* is in Hebrew all expressed by one short noun *Ziim.* In Isa. xiii. 21; xxxiv. 14; Jer. l. 39, it is rendered *wild beasts of the desert.* Here it means the wild, fierce and roaming tribes of men. *Shall bow,* not the verb rendered *bow down* in the second commandment, Ex. xx. 5, and *fall down* in v. 11, also often *worship;* but one rendered *couch, bring low, cast down, subdue,* Num. xxiv. 9; Jud. xi. 35; Ps. xvii. 13; xviii. 39. The next clause shows that complete mastery is designed. *And his enemies shall lick the dust. Enemies,* as in Ps. iii. 7, and often. *Lick,* also ren-

dered *lick up;* see 1 Kings xviii. 38; Num. xxii. 4; Mic. vii. 17. Perhaps the phrase, *lick the dust,* had its origin in the form of curse pronounced on the serpent, Gen. iii. 14. Clarke thinks it denotes 'abject vassalage;' Hengstenberg, 'reverence and submission.'

10. *The kings of Tarshish and of the isles shall bring presents.* On *Tarshish* see on Ps. xlviii. 7. *Isles,* places reached by navigation. *Presents* were tokens of good will, feigned or sincere. *The kings of Sheba and Seba shall offer gifts.* *Sheba* and *Seba* are first used in Scripture as the names of men, Gen. x. 7, 28. They afterwards were used to designate places. Alexander: "The distant south is represented by *Sheba,* a province of Arabia Felix; and *Seba,* now commonly supposed to be Meroe, a part of ancient Ethiopia, both famous for their wealth and commerce." It is candid to say that much difficulty attends the geography of these places. But the import of the whole verse as indicating the reception of Messiah by distant nations is undoubted. There is also an evident prophecy of the visit of the queen of the South to Solomon, 1 Kings x. 1–10; 2 Chron. ix. 1–9; Matt. xii. 42; Luke xi. 31. The prophet waxes more bold:

11. *Yea, all kings shall fall down before him; all nations shall serve him.* This verse may be admitted to have had such a fulfilment in Solomon as to make him a remarkable type of Christ, 1 Kings iv. 20, 21; x. 23–25. But surely it is not torturing the passage to say that its complete and glorious fulfilment can be found in Christ only, and not in him as yet, for he is still waiting till his enemies become his footstool. Scott: "No doubt the millenium is here foretold." The *falling down* and *serving* here are the very words, which in the second commandment are rendered *bow down* and *serve.* That we are here to understand religious homage and obedience, is evident from the extent of the homage and service predicted.

12. *For he shall deliver the needy when he crieth.* *Deliver,* as in Ps. vii. 1, 2; xxii. 20. *Needy,* as in v. 4. *Crieth,* an earnest word as in Ps. xviii. 6, 41. *He shall deliver the poor also, and* him *that hath no helper.* *Poor,* as in vv. 2, 4. "Woe to him that is alone." In his distress he has no *helper,* or none *helping* him, Ps. x. 14.

13. *He shall spare the poor and needy, and shall save the souls of the needy.* *Poor,* not as that in vv. 2, 4, 12, but in Ps. xli. 1; in the margin sometimes rendered *weak,* or *sick.* *Needy,* as in vv. 4, 12. The word rendered *spare* is also rendered *regard, pity, have pity.* This verse as well as verses 12, 14 far more fitly "express the spiritual blessings of Christ's kingdom, than any temporal effects of the very best government on earth." Indeed Solomon never saved men's *souls,* though he saved their *lives,* when others were seeking to destroy them. Compare Job xxix. 12.

14. *He shall redeem their soul from deceit and violence.* *Redeem,* commonly so rendered, sometimes, *do the part of a kinsman,* and sometimes, *avenge.* The participle is rendered *avenger,* or *revenger of blood.* The nearest of kin was to *redeem* and also, if necessary, to *avenge. Deceit, fraud, violence, injustice, wrong, cruelty. And precious shall their blood be in his sight.* So far as Solomon is here alluded to, the meaning is that "he will not be prodigal of the lives of his subjects, casting them away merely to gratify his own revenge, or covetousness, or insatiable desire of enlarging his empire, as earthly kings commonly do, but, like a true father of his people, will tenderly preserve them." Solomon wasted neither blood nor treasure in insane wars. But the passage applies to Christ also. He will not suffer the blood of his saints to be shed for nothing. If persecuted even unto death, he will avenge it. It shall cry to him from the ground and from underneath the altar, Gen. iv. 10; 1 Sam. xxvi. 21; 2 Kings i. 13; Ps. cxvi. 15; Rev. vi. 9, 10.

15. *And he shall live, and to him shall be given of the gold of Sheba: prayer also shall be made for him continually; and daily shall he be praised.* There is a difference

among interpreters respecting this verse, some thinking that throughout the verse *the king* (Solomon, or Christ) is spoken of; others, that the *needy man* or *poor man* is spoken of. In favor of the former view, we have Calvin, Luther, Diodati, Ainsworth, Venema, Piscator, Pool, Morison, Nicolson, Patrick, Dickson and Scott. Indeed so united have been the views of interpreters that often they do not hint at another exposition. Gill, however, gives both views, seeming to prefer the latter. Tholuck, Hengstenberg and Alexander are decidedly in favor of the latter, although Alexander says that the former gives "a good sense in itself and appropriate to the context." There is not much reason to doubt that the former is correct, and that the English version gives the meaning of the prophet. Solomon's happy reign ended with his natural life. Jesus, our king, was dead, but is alive forevermore. Because he lives, his people live also, John xiv. 19. Tribute of gold was brought from afar to Solomon, 1 Kings x. 2; 2 Chron. ix. 1, 13, 14. Gold was also brought as a present to Christ, Matt. ii. 11. But as gold is precious, so the meaning is that the most excellent offerings should be made to him. Prayer is not to be made for the happiness and well-being of the person of Christ, since his exaltation; but we express our good-will to him by prayer for the spread and stability of his kingdom and glory, Ps. xviii. 4; Matt. vi. 10, and parallel passages. The church of England reads: Prayer shall be made *unto him;* the Septuagint: Prayer shall be made *concerning* him. Praise and blessing were fitly offered to Christ when on earth, and are fitly offered to him in glory, Matt. xxi. 9; Mark xi. 9; Luke xiii. 35; Rev. v. 12, 13.

16. *There shall be a handful of corn in the earth upon the top of the mountains; the fruit thereof shall shake like Lebanon: and they of the city shall flourish like grass of the earth.* The word translated *handful* may also be rendered *heap,* or *abundance,* and is so rendered by the Syriac, John Rogers, the Bishops' Bible, church of England, Edwards, Green, Rosenmüller, Tholuck and Hengstenberg. But the Genevan translation, Calvin, Diodati, Ainsworth, Amesius, Meibomius, Tremellius and Junius, Piscator, Secker, Nicolson, Patrick, Pool, Henry, Horne, Jebb, Clarke, Scott and Alexander give their weight in favor of the common version. The other renderings, such as *firmament,* do not seem to be entitled to much thought. The difficulty arises from the fact that the word rendered *handful* is found nowhere else in the Hebrew Bible, and is of doubtful derivation. The English text has antiquity and the analogy of other Scriptures to support it, Matt. xiii. 31; Mark iv. 31; Luke xvii. 6. The corn here referred to is Christ, who speaks of himself as a corn of wheat, John xii. 24. Gill says that Christ is compared to wheat "for its choiceness and purity, and for its usefulness for food; and he may be compared to a handful of it, because of the little account he was made of here on earth, and the little that was expected of him; and on account of the small beginnings of his kingdom, which came not with observation." He also quotes R. Obadiah Gaon as giving the same interpretation: "Messiah shall be at first as an handful of corn; but afterwards a multitude of disciples shall grow as the grass." Some think the figure is made stronger by supposing that the *mountains* here mentioned are dry and barren places. Others imagine they are mentioned because they are conspicuous objects. The things concerning Jesus Christ were not done in a corner, Acts xxvi. 26. *Lebanon* is supposed to mean *the trees of Lebanon.* The wonders of salvation by Jesus Christ are grand indeed. Lebanon has nothing so glorious, although its majestic cedars and firs *wave* to and rro, or *shake* under strong winds. Alexander: "*From the city* seems to mean from Jerusalem or Zion, as the centre of Messiah's kingdom and his royal residence, out of which this productive influence was to go forth," Isa. ii. 3; Mic. iv. 2.

17. *His name shall endure for ever.* Surely "a greater than Solomon is here."

For although he reigned longer than many a king, and his fame is still great, yet it is Jesus Christ that has a name above every name, which shall last and even increase to *everlasting*, or *perpetually*, as the original signifies. *His name shall be continued as long as the sun*, literally *before the sun*, or *in the presence of the sun*. Nor should he be a curse to men: *And* men *shall be blessed in him*. Thus should be fulfilled the predictions recorded of old, Gen. xii. 3; xviii. 18; xxii. 18; xxviii. 14. The form of expression here found was used in later times, Jer. iv. 2. A more literal rendering would be: And in him shall they bless themselves, or call themselves blessed. *All nations shall call him blessed*. In the preceding clause *blessed* is equivalent to *receiving a benediction*, as in Ps. v. 12; in this it is equivalent to *very happy*, as in Ps. i. 1.

18. *Blessed* be the LORD *God, the God of Israel, who only doeth wondrous things. Blessed, i. e., praised*. It is a doxology. *Jehovah God* was the God of the man and of the people called Israel. The history of his dealings with them showed how marvellous were his works. There was none like him. Scott: "God alone has done most wonderful things, in blessing the nations by Jesus Christ; and he will do wonderful things." They will all result in the exaltation of his Son."

19. *And blessed* be *his glorious name for ever. Blessed, praised, receiving* benediction as in v. 18. *For ever*, as in v. 17. *His glorious name*, literally *his name of glory*. A parallel is found in Neh. ix. 5. *And let the whole earth be filled* with *his glory*. The verb is in the future, *shall be filled*. The prophet was confident of the event. A parallel is found in Num. xiv. 21. The prophet closes the verse with the solemn words, *Amen, and Amen*. On this phrase see on Ps. xli. 13. The Septuagint: *So let it be, So let it be*. The repetition is significant.

20. *The prayers of David the son of Jesse are ended*. This may mean either: 1, that this is the last Psalm, which David ever composed, being written after Solomon was actually king, and but a short time before David's death; 2, that this was the last composition he wrote which belonged to the class called *prayers;* 3, that David having foretold and *prayed* for the kingdom of Solomon, and for the glory of Messiah, he felt as if he had no more to ask for; 4, that this is the last Psalm which David himself arrranged for public worship, the rest being collected by Hezekiah and, after him, by Ezra; or, 5, that this is the end of the second book of Psalms, according to the Jewish method of dividing the Psalter. The Syriac interprets it to favor this last view. Yet it cannot be shown that the book of Psalms was at so early a day divided into *five* books by the Jews themselves. See Introduction, § 11. The Arabic wholly omits this verse and closes with *Alleluiah*. The reader will not forget Montgomery's beautiful hymn founded on this Psalm:

"Hail to the Lord's anointed."

DOCTRINAL AND PRACTICAL REMARKS.

1. There can be no more fit employment for the aged than prayer, v. 1. Compare Luke ii. 37. Parents, stricken in years, ought to pray much for their children, especially if called to posts of difficulty in Church or State. They should earnestly supplicate God's blessing in the way of divine guidance and support. No man is fit for any office without endowments from God. Blessed is he who by God's Spirit is prepared for his work. Scott: "Pious parents will be the more earnest in prayer for their children, in proportion to the importance of those stations which they are likely to occupy." Good men will not forget posterity.

2. We are specially bound to pray for our rulers, whether they are our kin or others, v. 1. Compare 1 Tim. ii. 1–3. Dr. R. Anderson: "All who desire the success of missions should make continual 'supplications, prayers, intercessions, and giving of thanks,' 'for kings and for all that are in authority,' that missionaries, in the

several countries where they labor, 'may lead a quiet and peaceable life, in all godliness and honesty.'" We ought to pray for others besides those under whose government we live—even all rulers.

3. The best thing we can ask for children or rulers is that they may be governed by God's *decisions,* and controlled by his word, v. 1.

4. Good government is a great blessing, whatever be its form, vv. 2, 3. Perhaps the worst settled government on earth is not so bad as anarchy. But how blessed is the reign of Messiah, Isa. xxxii. 17, 18. Indeed inspired poets and prophets have exhausted all the beauties of language in foretelling the blessedness of Christ's kingdom. It has every excellence. It is conducted by *righteous* rulers and laws, v. 2. It protects and provides for those who cannot take care of themselves, v. 3. It is stable as the mountains. No wrong-doer can resist it, v. 4. Christ rules his subjects not by tyranny and cruelty, not by racks and whips, but by godly *fear,* v. 5. However low may be the condition of Christ's people at a given time, yet they shall be revived and made to flourish. Nor is Christ's kingdom composed of abjects and wretches, but of souls *righteous* in the eye of the law, and in heart also, v. 7. His kingdom is also *peace,* as well as righteousness and joy in the Holy Ghost, v. 7. It is *catholic,* embracing all lands, bringing salvation to savage and polished nations, to kings, peasants and paupers, the most exalted and the most down-trodden, vv. 8–13. "The man that hath nothing within him or without him to commend him to Christ, to assist, help, relieve, or comfort him in heaven or earth, is not despised by Christ." Christ deals gently with his people, and rescues them, not permitting tempters and tyrants to destroy or harm them, highly valuing their lives, v. 14. Christ's kingdom shall be everlasting, vv. 7, 15, 17. The glory and excellency of the nations shall be brought into it. It shall be maintained not by arms and craft, but by acts of devotion, especially by prayer and praise, v. 15. Christ has no reluctant subjects. All his people are willing in the day of his power. Nor does his kingdom come with observation, nor is it dependent on appearances, v. 16. Though temporal princes may not aspire to universal empire, nor to be like Christ in some things, yet ought they to imitate him in their care of the poor, and needy, and defenceless, in seeking to be beloved and justly praised as well as revered, and in putting down oppression and wrong-doing.

5. There is hope for the heathen in the promises and prophecies of God's word, vv. 8–11. Tholuck: "The most *uncivilized,* the most *distant,* and most *opulent* nations shall pay their homage to him."

6. It shall be for an everlasting joy that Christ shall die no more, but is forever beyond the reach of the insults of the wicked, and the power of evil. *He shall live,* v. 15.

7. As prophecy foretells, so also duty requires that the best of everything shall be given to the service and for the honor of Christ, v. 15. To offer him the lame, and the torn, and the mean, and the blemished is to imitate the Jewish Church in her most corrupt days.

8. In this Psalm we have ample instruction on the matter of offering religious worship to Christ. The fit object of prayer and praise must be divine, v. 15. Compare Acts vii. 59, 60.

9. It is our wisdom to conform all our plans to the method of God, which is to bring great results from causes by carnal men esteemed contemptible, v. 16. It is only fools who despise the day of small things.

10. The perpetuity and enlargement of Christ's kingdom are fair arguments for his divinity, vv. 15, 17. So thought Napoleon, when he compared the work of great earthly conquerors with the work of Christ. For these temporal monarchs, when

dead a hundred years, no man was willing to die. But Jesus has millions of followers in every age, who would not hesitate to lay down their lives for his cause and honor.

11. Eternity will be required to show to angels and men the greatness of the *blessing*, which Christ is to his ransomed ones. None are more ready than they to say they cannot fathom the depths, nor measure the height of his love and mercy.

12. Benediction shall forever and ever be heaped upon him, who has brought salvation to men, v. 17. Are we now doing our part in this work?

13. It were to be wished that God's people and ministers were better acquainted with the doxologies of Scripture, and did more abound in the use of them, vv. 18, 19.

14. As Christ shall live and reign, be known, loved and adored eternally, let us take his yoke upon us, for it is light; let us receive him as the Lord our righteousness; let us richly partake of his Spirit; let us follow his footsteps; let us be kind to his people and cast in our lot with them; let us not live to ourselves, but to him that bought us with his blood; let us glory in his cross; let us not be offended in him, nor ashamed of him or his word; let us live and die in his service and to his glory.

Psalm LXXIII.

A Psalm of Asaph.

1 Truly God *is* good to Israel, *even* to such as are of a clean heart.

2 But as for me, my feet were almost gone; my steps had well nigh slipped.

3 For I was envious at the foolish, *when* I saw the prosperity of the wicked.

4 For *there are* no bands in their death: but their strength *is* firm.

5 They *are* not in trouble *as other* men; neither are they plagued like *other* men.

6 Therefore pride compasseth them about as a chain; violence covereth them *as* a garment.

7 Their eyes stand out with fatness: they have more than heart could wish.

8 They are corrupt, and speak wickedly *concerning* oppression: they speak loftily.

9 They set their mouth against the heavens, and their tongue walketh through the earth.

10 Therefore his people return hither: and waters of a full *cup* are wrung out to them.

11 And they say, How doth God know? and is there knowledge in the Most High?

12 Behold, these *are* the ungodly, who prosper in the world; they increase *in* riches.

13 Verily I have cleansed my heart *in* vain, and washed my hands in innocency.

14 For all the day long have I been plagued, and chastened every morning.

15 If I say, I will speak thus; behold, I should offend *against* the generation of thy children.

16 When I thought to know this, it *was* too painful for me;

17 Until I went into the sanctuary of God; *then* understood I their end.

18 Surely thou didst set them in slippery places: thou castedst them down into destruction.

19 How are they *brought* into desolation, as in a moment! they are utterly consumed with terrors.

20 As a dream when *one* awaketh; *so,* O Lord, when thou awakest, thou shalt despise their image.

21 Thus my heart was grieved, and I was pricked in my reins.

22 So foolish *was* I, and ignorant: I was *as* a beast before thee.

23 Nevertheless I *am* continually with thee: thou hast holden *me* by my right hand.

24 Thou shalt guide me with thy counsel, and afterward receive me *to* glory.

25 Whom have I in heaven *but thee?* and *there is* none upon earth *that* I desire besides thee.

26 My flesh and my heart faileth: *but* God *is* the strength of my heart, and my portion for ever.

27 For, lo, they that are far from thee shall perish: thou hast destroyed all them that go a whoring from thee.

28 But *it is* good for me to draw near to God: I have put my trust in the Lord God, that I may declare all thy works.

PSALMS l. lxxiii.—lxxxiii. were written by Asaph. See Introduction, § 4, and on title of Ps. l. Alexander: "There is not the slightest ground for doubting the correctness of the title, which ascribes the Psalm to Asaph." If 2 Chron. xxix. 30 proves there were two Asaphs, as some maintain, it also proves there were two Davids, Psalmists. Scott dates it B. C. 1020; Patrick, Jebb, Rosenmüller and Clarke give it a later date, some as late as the captivity. In this ode are five names of the Creator; *Elohim God, El God, Gel-yohn Most High, Adonai Lord* and *Jehovah* LORD, on which respectively see on Ps. iii. 2; v. 4; vii. 17; ii. 4; i. 2. Hengstenberg thinks it is nearly related to Psalms xxxvii. xlix. Luther: "This is a Psalm, that instructs us against that great offence and stumbling-block concerning which all the prophets have complained: namely, that the wicked flourish in the world, enjoy prosperity, and increase in abundance, while the godly suffer cold and hunger, and are afflicted, and spit upon, and despised, and condemned; and that God seems to be against his friends and to neglect them, and to regard, support and give success to his enemies. This offence has existed, and has exercised and vexed the godly from the very beginning of the church." The modern Jews put this and the sixteen compositions next following into what they call *the third book* of Psalms. But see Introduction, § 11.

1. *Truly God is good to Israel, even to such as are of a clean heart. Truly*, see on Ps. lxii. 1. The Septuagint and the versions, which follow it, read, *How good is God;* Calvin and others: *Yet God is good;* Hengstenberg and others: *Only good is God,* meaning that God is *always* good. Alexander thinks this verse is "the theme of the whole Psalm." *Israel* is explained in the last clause of the verse as designating *such as are of a clean heart.* Scott: "The same distinction between an Israelite by nation, and the true Israelite, which is often made in the New Testament, is here explicitly established." Compare Matt. v. 8; John i. 47–51; Rom. ii. 25–29. Hengstenberg: "The distinction which the Psalmist makes among the Israelites themselves, at the very beginning of the Psalm, goes directly against those, who consider the Psalm as having a national reference." *Good*, sometimes rendered *goodness*, Ps. lxviii. 10; cvii. 9. God is *goodness* itself, Matt. xix. 17. Calvin: "The Psalmist does not ascend into the chair to dispute after the manner of the Philosophers, and to deliver his discourse in a style of studied oratory; but, as if he had escaped from hell, he proclaims with a loud voice, and with impassioned feeling, that he had obtained the victory."

2. *But as for me, my feet were almost gone; my steps had well nigh slipped. As for me*, well rendered. There is a fitness in making it emphatic. The man, who makes the profession in v. 1, is the very one, who had endured the most distressing temptations to an opposite belief—temptations which were within a *very little* of casting him into the gulf of atheism, leading him to deny providence, and thus ruining him forever. *Gone, turned aside, gone down, declined, wrested, perverted. Slipped,* literally *poured out*, like water flowing in any channel open to it. We met the same word in Ps. xxii. 14. It expresses extreme sadness and dejection. The cause of this dreadful depression was that he was tempted to give up first truths of religion.

3. *For I was envious at the foolish, when I saw the prosperity of the wicked. Envious*, elsewhere also rendered *zealous*, and *jealous*. We had it in Ps. xxxvii. 1. It may signify either that he felt the risings of sinful envy towards the wicked themselves, or that he was jealous of God's love to him, when he saw Jehovah showering outward blessings on his open enemies. The latter is the more probable. But he may have been tempted in both ways. *Foolish*, literally *boasters*, those who think and say that they are something when they are nothing. The Chaldee renders it *scoffers;* Syriac, *the unjust;* Arabic, *the lawless;* Boothroyd, *the madly profane;* Ainsworth and Fry, *the vain-glorious;* Hengstenberg, *the haughty;* Alexander, *the proud. Prosperity*, literally *peace*, and so the fruits of peace. Sometimes the enemies of God

have no sad changes for a long time. The *foolish* of the first clause are the same as the *wicked, the ungodly* of the last; see on Ps. i. 1. *Saw,* in the future *shall see.* What Asaph saw he expected to continue to see. He had long noticed this, and perceived no signs of a change.

4. *For there are no bands in their death. Bands,* found only here and in Isa. lviii. 6. It has occasioned much difficulty. Le Clerc: *They have no pains when they die.* Hammond has an unusually long note upon it. His conclusion is that we may read, *There are no pangs in their death,* meaning they die with ease; or, *There are no heavy burdens bound on them in their death,* meaning no hard sufferings; or, *There are no sentences of death,* from courts or diseases, *upon them;* or, *There are no conspiracies for their deaths,* meaning no persons bound by agreement to destroy them. The idea of band, or tie, in some form is to be preserved in the translation. Chaldee: *They are not terrified nor troubled on account of the day of their death.* They think not much of dying before death comes. And when they do die, it is often not with that distress, or even that concern, which one would expect. Jebb: *They are in no terror of death.* Diodati: " They do sweetly pass over their natural course of life, and are not violently drawn to an untimely death, through sickness or other chances." Clarke's note is very good: " Many of the godly have sore conflicts at their death. Their enemy then thrusts sore at them that they may fall; or that their confidence in their God may be shaken: but of this the ungodly know nothing. Satan will not molest *them;* he is sure of his prey; they are entangled, and cannot now break their nets: their consciences are seared, they have no sense of guilt. If they think at all of another world, they presume on that mercy which they never sought, and of which they have no distinct notion. Perhaps, ' they die without a sigh or a groan; and thus go off as quiet as a lamb'—to the slaughter." *But their strength is firm, fat, rank, plenteous.* Chaldee: *Their heart is fat and brave;* Ainsworth: *Lusty is their strength;* Edwards: *But [they] are lusty and strong;* Fry: *Their strength is perfect and firm;* Mudge: *But they are plump and strong;* Green: *But [they] are vigorous and strong.*

5. *They are not in trouble* as other *men; neither are they plagued like* other *men. Trouble,* a noun elsewhere also rendered *toil, labor, sorrow, misery, pain, travail, grievousness. Plagued,* elsewhere also rendered *smitten, stricken,* literally *touched.* The corresponding noun is commonly rendered the plague. It is so more than *fifty* times in Leviticus. See also Gen. xii. 17; Ex. xi. 1. The prophet throughout this account speaks not of wicked men *universally,* but tells what *often* happens to them. Nor does he speak so much of the reality as of appearances in their case. The verb is in the future, signifying that appearances are that they *will not be plagued* at any time of life like other men; their exemption from trouble seems to last a long time.

6. *Therefore pride compasseth them about as a chain. Pride, swelling, haughtiness.* Chains of gold were used for ornament, and some think also as badges of office. Compare Gen. xli. 42; Cant. i. 10; iv. 9; Ezek. xvi. 11; Dan. v. 7, 16, 29. *Violence covereth them as a garment.* The Chaldee divides and renders the verse differently : Therefore pride compasseth them about: the crown which they put on their head is from their rapine. But the common rendering is better. To be *clothed* or *covered* with any sin or vice shows the great lengths men have gone in evil. Calvin: "David meant to comprehend, in one word, the whole attire of the person."

7. *Their eyes stand out with fatness.* Chaldee: Their countenance is changed by fatness. Scott: "Their looks discovered their excessive sensuality and voluptuousness." No doubt the common version gives the sense. Morison: "They are conspicuous for the grossness of their sensuality." *They have more than heart could wish.* There is diversity in rendering this clause. Church of England: They do even what they lust;

Ainsworth and Venema: They pass the imaginations of the heart; Amesius: The thoughts of their heart exceed all proper bounds; Edwards: They are prosperous beyond the imagination of their hearts; Clarke: They surpass the thoughts of their heart. The object of the prophet is not so much to tell how wicked they are, but to let us see how prosperous they appear to be. If the common version does not give the meaning, it comes very near it. Perhaps the exact sense is, They have more than they expected. They have more than a *right* heart could wish.

8. *They are corrupt.* I can find no reason for this rendering. The verb of which the above is a translation is that from which lexicographers derive our English word, *mock.* Jerome: They have scoffed; Calvin: They become insolent; Fry: They speak jestingly of evil, literally, they joke and talk; Abu Walid, quoted in Hammond: They prate foolishly in their speech; Hengstenberg: They scoff; Alexander: They mock. Pretty certainly the sense is, *They are deriders. And* [they] *speak wickedly* concerning *oppression.* They by speech suggest, favor and argue for *oppression, extortion, cruelty. They speak loftily,* or *from on high,* as if they were some great ones. Clarke: "They vindicate excessive acts of government; they push justice to its rigor. They neither show equity, lenity, nor mercy: they are cruel, and they vindicate their proceedings."

9. *They set their mouth against the heavens.* The ancient versions quite agree with the English in rendering this clause. So also do Calvin, Venema, Ainsworth, Tremellius and Junius, Piscator, Edwards, Pool and others. The sense then seems to be that the prosperous wicked speak impudently and profanely against God's name, word, worship, providence, Gospel and people; they pour contempt on all serious piety, they make light of eternal things. They blaspheme. But the church of England has it: For they stretch forth their mouth unto the heaven; Fry: They set their mouths in the heavens. This rendering is favored by Jebb and others. Alexander: "They speak as if they thought themselves superior beings, their mouth in heaven." This view of the passage is not so good as the first. It makes it virtually a repetition of the last preceding clause, and so there is no progress in the description. *And their tongue walketh through the earth.* They say they are licensed characters. They have no bridle on their tongues. They roam at large like wild beasts. They say what they will and of whom they will. Henry: "They take liberty to abuse all that come in their way. No man's greatness or goodness can secure him from the scourge of the virulent tongue; they take a pride and pleasure in bantering all mankind." They are traducers. They are full of reproaches and of bitterness. Such a state of society fills good men with the deepest distress.

10. *Therefore his people return hither; and waters of a full cup are wrung out to them.* Chaldee: Therefore they are turned against the people of God, that they may slay them, and smite them with mauls, so that they may shed tears. In Hebrew poetry *waters* rather point to *adversity* than prosperity. In the second clause *them* refers to God's people, not to the wicked. *Return,* as in Mal. iii. 18. It is probably to be taken for an act of the mind, particularly of *reflection.* So Diodati interprets it as *returning to these thoughts.* Ainsworth: "By *waters of a full cup* are meant *abundance of tears.*" God's people are often filled with sorrow, when they look at the afflictions of the righteous and the success of the wicked. Against temptations arising from such a source David warns us in Ps. xxxvii. Into this very matter the weeping prophet inquires, Jer. xii. 1. False reasonings on this subject involved Job's three friends in their serious errors. Scott: "The verse is in the future, and it seems most natural to explain it, as the Psalmist's apprehension, that the prosperity of daring sinners would eventually prove an invincible temptation, and a great source of sorrow to believers." Alexander thinks the most natural interpretation is "that which under-

stands the sense to be, that God still suffers or requires his people to survey the painful spectacle and drain the bitter draught presented by the undisturbed prosperity of wicked men." No commentator has better expressed the spirit of the passage than Henry: "Because the wicked are so very daring, therefore his people return hither; they are at the same pause, the same plunge, that I am at; they know not what to say to it, any more than I do, and the rather, because waters of a full cup are wrung out to them; they are not only made to drink, and to drink deep of the bitter cup of affliction, but to drink all; care is taken that they lose not a drop of that unpleasant potion, the waters are wrung out unto them, that they may have the dregs of the cup. They pour out abundance of tears when they hear wicked people blaspheme God and speak profanely." Ps. cxix. 136.

11. *And they say, How doth God know? and is there knowledge in the Most High?* The church of England has it: Tush, say they, how should God perceive it? is there knowledge in the Most High? Prosperity unsanctified soon leads to practical atheism; see on Ps. x. 11. It is the language, not of good men, but of the wicked. So says the next verse:

12. *Behold, these* are *the ungodly, who prosper in the world; they increase* in *riches.* *Ungodly*, in v. 3 *wicked*. The prosperity which the wicked have is only *in the world*, or this *age*. The word rendered *who prosper*, is an adjective, *the prosperous*, and is, perhaps, to be regarded as nominative to the verb rendered *increase*. *Riches*, also rendered *wealth, substance, strength, power, valor*. It may signify that these men were to all appearance growing in wealth, numbers, and influence, so as to carry everything their own way.

13. *Verily I have cleansed my heart* in *vain, and washed my hands in innocency.* Both clauses describe the man who serves God; one expressing the uprightness of his motives; the other, of his life. *In vain* qualifies both clauses. *Verily*, see on v. 1, and on Ps. lxii. 1. *Innocency*, always so rendered when it refers to moral character, equivalent to blamelessness. The state of the Psalmist's mind was this: If these foolish, wicked, ungodly men are allowed to enjoy such quiet and prosperity under the government of God for a long time, what am I to think of the laws of providence? As yet, my own abhorrence of wickedness and freedom from iniquity appear to produce no advantage, but, on the contrary, unhappy results. Calvin: "Truly I have labored in vain to obtain and preserve a pure heart and clean hands, seeing continued afflictions await me, and, so to speak, are on the watch to meet me at break of day. Such a condition surely shows that there is no reward for innocence before God, else he would certainly deal somewhat more compassionately towards those who serve him."

14. *For all the day long have I been plagued, and chastened every morning.* *Plagued*, as in v. 5. *Chastened*, the Hebrew word is a noun elsewhere rendered *chastisement, rebuke, reproof, correction*. Alexander: "While they, though wicked, still increase in wealth, and seem secure forever, I, who have faithfully endeavored to avoid sin and to do the will of God, am subjected, every day and all day, to privation and distress."

15. *If I say, I will speak thus; behold, I should offend* against *the generation of thy children.* Diodati: "That is, I do God's church a great deal of injury, which hath always been under afflictions, if I think or say, that all her piety hath been without hope, or her hope without effect." For *offend*, Ainsworth has *unfaithfully wrong;* Edwards, *betray;* Fry, *wrong;* Horsley, *be a traitor to;* Green, *be false to;* Hammond, *deal perfidiously with*. We do a great wrong to believers, and a special harm to weak Christians, when we tell our foolish and wicked thoughts. Hengstenberg: "What had gone before was a soliloquy. Those who fear God never let their inward doubts become known abroad. They do not repair with them to the streets, where ignorant people would make them the occasion of open ungodliness; but they take them to the

sanctuary of God; and give expression to their doubts, like the Psalmist, when they can, at the same time, make known their victory." *The generation of God's children* here are the same as *the generation of the righteous*, Ps. xiv. 5; *the generation of them that seek God*, Ps. xxiv. 6; *the generation of the upright*, Ps. cxii. 2. Hammond: " The word generation often signifies a set or sort of men." The generation of God's people includes all who love and fear God, profess his religion, maintain his worship, obey his laws and trust his grace.

16. *When I thought to know this it* was *too painful for me*. There are no subjects more inscrutable than the nature and providence of God. No creature can comprehend either. Such knowledge is high. We cannot attain unto it. For *painful* Boothroyd has difficult; Green, hard; Horsley, perplexing. The word rendered *too painful* is a noun, elsewhere in this Psalm rendered *trouble;* see on v. 5. It is a *travail*, a *grievousness* to even good men to see a course of events which no mortal can explain, and which, without revelation, must confound us. Calvin: " Whoever, in applying himself to the examination of God's judgments, expects to become acquainted with them by his natural understanding, will be disappointed, and will find that he is engaged in a task at once painful and profitless; and, therefore, it is indispensably necessary to rise higher, and to seek illumination from heaven." But the Psalmist is not in despair. This verse contains not a finished sentence, q. d., I was for a while confounded,

17. *Until I went into the sanctuary of God. Sanctuary*, so rendered by many; in Ps. lxviii. 35, *holy places*. Horsley thinks it means, " Until I entered into the secret grounds of God's dealings with mankind." Cresswell thinks the meaning is, " Until I entered into the grounds of God's dealings with men, as explained by the sacred writings, which are laid up in the place dedicated to his worship." Luther: " Until I hear or read the word, and find what God saith concerning the ungodly; and until I look into the histories and behold the judgments of God, which have been since the foundation of the world." God's word was kept in the sanctuary, it was there illustrated in public worship, and explained by the priests, whose lips kept knowledge, and were commanded to expound it, Mal. ii. 7. In the sanctuary too for many centuries God spake by Urim and Thummim, though we have no evidence that in this matter Asaph sought answer by oracle. God's word is wonderful and makes all plain: Then *understood I their end*. The Bible brings this life and the next, time and eternity, human conduct and the last judgment, the sinner's career and the sinner's *end* into view at once. This makes a vast difference. Indeed it affords a perfect clearing up of doubt, and quite removes perplexity on this hard point of providence. In God's house he learned that the lot of the wicked was not desirable.

18. *Surely thou didst set them in slippery places*. In Moses' last great sermon we have the same idea : " Their feet shall slide in due time," Deut. xxxii. 35; compare Ps. xxxv. 6. In Job xxvii. 7, 8; Ps. xc. 5, the same doctrine is taught, though in different language. Many parallel passages are found in the sacred writings given to the church before or during the time of Asaph. *Surely*, by some rendered *only*, as in v. 1; Ps. lxii. 1. *Slippery places*, literally *slipperinesses*, or *smoothnesses*. *Set*, in v. 28 and often rendered *put*. Here in Hebrew it is in the future, *wilt set*. See Introduction, § 6. The common version doubtless gives the sense. *Thou castedst them down into destruction. Castedst*, literally *hast caused them to fall. Destruction*, plural *destructions*, only here and in Ps. lxxiv. 3, where we read *desolations*. The latter rendering is followed by many. Their fearful elevation makes their fall the more dreadful. " When the wicked spring as the grass, and when all the workers of iniquity do flourish; it is that they shall be destroyed for ever." The ox is fattened for the slaughter.

19. *How are they* brought *into desolation as in a moment! Desolation*, often ren-

dered *astonishment,* Deut. xxviii. 37; Jer. xxv. 9; Ezek. xxiii. 33. They drink the wine of astonishment. Yea, *They are consumed with terrors.* There are no greater cowards than the greatest blusterers. None finally suffer more with *terrors* than those who appear to be commonly most free from apprehension. Nor can such tell at what moment they may be seized with the most terrible fears, and never be able to shake them off, no, not while eternity endures. Nor will God himself then help or save or pity them, Isa. xxvii. 11; Jer. xiii. 14. Compare Zech. vii. 11–13. Yea, more:

20. *As a dream when* one *awaketh; so, O Lord, when thou awakest, thou shalt despise their image.* Chaldee: As a dream *vanishes* from a man, when he awakes; so, O Lord, in the day of great judgment when they shall be raised from their sepulchres, thou wilt in wrath despise their image. *Image,* always so rendered except in Ps. xxxix. 6, where it is *vain shew.* Horsley would so render it here: Like the dream of a man beginning to wake publicly, O Lord, thou renderest their vain show contemptible. Green has it: As a dream, when they awake, *vanisheth away,* so shalt thou, O Lord, when thou rousest *them* up, make their imaginary *happiness* to disappear. Diodati's paraphrase is good: " When these vain shadows of the world shall be past, in which thy providence seemeth to sleep, when thou shalt bring forth everything into the light of thy judgment, thou shalt make it appear that their prosperity hath been but a false illusion: and thou shalt change this worldly lustre into everlasting ignominy."

21. *Thus my heart was grieved.* Syriac: My heart was troubled; Calvin and Edwards: My heart was in a ferment; Fry: My heart has been vexed. *And I was pricked in my reins.* Calvin and Hengstenberg: I was pierced in my reins; Edwards: I felt acute pains in my reins. *Reins,* see on Ps. vii. 9; compare Ps. xvi. 7; xxvi. 2. Alexander: " The verbs are properly reflexives, my heart exacerbates itself, I pierce myself, and are perhaps intended to describe his sufferings as the fruit of his own sin and folly."

22. *So foolish* was *I, and ignorant.* Chaldee: I am a fool, who know not; Arabic: I am vile and ignorant; Jebb: I myself was brutish and did not know; Alexander: I (am) brutish and know not (the true state of the case.) *Brutish* is better than *foolish. I was* as *a beast before thee. Beast,* Hebrew, *Behemoth,* either such a monster as is described in Job xl. 15, or in the plural *cattle* in general; see Ps. viii. 7; l. 10; any *beast* whatever. This verse and the preceding Clarke paraphrases: " The different views which I got of this subject quite confounded me: I was equally astonished at their sudden overthrow, and my own ignorance. I felt as if I were a *beast* in stupidity. I permitted my mind to be wholly occupied with *sensible things,* like the beasts that perish, and did not look into a future state; nor did I consider, nor submit to the wise designs of an unerring Providence." Compare Ps. xlix. 10; xcii. 6; xciv. 8; Pr. xxx. 2.

23. *Nevertheless I* am *continually with thee: thou hast holden me by my right hand.* The two clauses teach the constant care and support of divine providence towards him, notwithstanding his great errors and brutish ignorance. " The Lord knoweth how to deliver the godly out of temptations," 2 Pet. ii. 9. By faith we have hold on God; but our grip is often feeble. Our great safety lies in this that God holds us with an omnipotent grasp, and never entirely lets us go. The deliverance was as remarkable as the danger had been great. His mind was now satisfied that a holy, wise and powerful God was his friend, guide, and support. This was attended with confidence for the future:

24. *Thou shalt guide me with thy counsel, and afterward receive me to glory.* Of difficult verses perhaps none is better translated than this. *Counsel,* applied either to God's *word,* or to his *plan. Glory* doubtless includes eternal blessedness, and all that leads to it. See on Ps. iii. 3; viii. 5. Calvin: " It comprehends the whole course of

our happiness from the commencement, which is seen here upon earth, even to the consummation which we expect to realize in heaven."

25. *Whom have I in heaven* but thee? *and* there is *none upon earth* that *I desire besides thee.* The words supplied in the English text doubtless give the sense. Edwards: Whom have I in heaven but thee? and there is nothing upon earth I love equally with thee; Clarke: Who is there to me in the heavens? And with thee I have desired nothing in the earth; Green: Whom have I in heaven *but thee ?* And on earth I delight in none besides thee. Instead of *besides thee,* the church of England and Horne read *in comparison of thee.* Alexander: " *With thee* can denote either combination or comparison." There is no protector, provider, or portion that can be desired in comparison with God, or that can make us happy without God.

26. *My flesh and my heart faileth.* *Faileth,* also rendered *is spent, is consumed, is ended, is finished.* The verb is in the preterite; but the common version probably gives the sense. In ourselves we are poor creatures. We know nothing, deserve nothing, can do nothing; and withal we shall soon pass away. Our powers constantly tend to decay. But *God* is *the strength of my heart.* *Strength,* also rendered *rock.* See on Ps. xviii. 2, 31, 46. All our courage and firmness come from Jehovah. His strength is made perfect in our weakness. Calvin: " No man will cast himself wholly upon God, but he who feels himself in a fainting condition, and who despairs of the sufficiency of his own powers. We will seek nothing from God but what we are conscious of wanting in ourselves." But the true believer knows that *all* his help must come from God. Yea, more, he knows that Jehovah himself must not only sustain him here, but satisfy him hereafter: [God is] *my portion for ever.* *Portion,* also rendered *inheritance,* that which lawfully falls to one's share; see on Ps. xvi. 5; xvii. 14. A child of God, though he suffer long and severely, fares well; for he has God for his portion. It is far otherwise with the wicked;

27. *For, lo, they that are far from thee shall perish.* *Perish,* as in Ps. i. 6; ii. 12; see on those places. To be *far from God* denotes irreligion; as to *draw near* to God, to *be brought nigh* to God, and to *walk with* God denote true piety and its blessings. The reason, why the Psalmist is so confident that a sad end will come to the wicked is that it always has so turned out: *Thou hast destroyed them that go a whoring from thee.* Chaldee: Thou hast destroyed all them that have wandered away from thy fear; Edwards: Thou cuttest off every one that apostatizes from thee; Fry: Thou cuttest off all who are faithless to thee. Sutcliffe: " To forsake the true God for false gods is spiritual adultery." Calvin: " It is the worst kind of adultery to divide our heart that it may not continue fixed exclusively upon God. *Harlotry* is the name given in Scripture to a withdrawing of the affections from Jehovah, and setting them on things below, whether they be false gods or riches, or anything loved and sought by carnal men. Compare Ex. xxxiv. 15; Num. xv. 39; Ps. cvi. 39; Jer. iii. 9, 20; Ezek. xxiii. 3, 5, 7; James iv. 4.

28. *But* it is *good for me to draw near to God.* The *nearness* of this verse is in contrast with the being *far off* in v. 27. Such is the form of the original that it may mean either God's drawing near to the Psalmist, or the Psalmist's drawing near to God. Perhaps both senses may be gathered according to James iv. 8: " Draw nigh to God, and he will draw nigh to you." *I have put my trust in the Lord* GOD, *the Lord Jehovah,* the self-existent, eternal, independent, unchangeable Ruler of the world. *Trust,* so rendered here only, twice *hope,* twice *shelter,* and often *refuge;* see on Ps. xiv. 6; xlvi. 1. He who has refuge in God is courageous—*That I may declare all thy works, i. e.,* publish and celebrate with gratitude and praise God's doings, even the very events of providence, which at the first seemed inscrutable.

Doctrinal and Practical Remarks.

1. However appearances may be to the contrary, even for a considerable time, yet God loves his church, the true Israel, v. 1. This we should steadfastly believe. "Good thoughts of God will fortify us against many of Satan's temptations."

2. All the Scriptures require holiness. An Israelite with guile is no Israelite, v. 1. One may be called, and by good men esteemed a Christian, he may rest in the Gospel, and make his boast of God and of Christ. He may know God's will, and in his conscience and by his profession approve the things that are more excellent, being instructed out of the divine word, and be confident that he himself is a guide of the blind, a light of them which are in darkness, an instructor of the foolish, a teacher of babes, having the form of knowledge and of the truth in the Scriptures; and yet he may want a clean heart, and innocence of life. When one's heart is not right in the sight of God, any seeming rectitude of life is delusive; and when outward behaviour is wicked, it is idle to plead that the heart is right.

3. Even good men, though gifted and inspired, are in danger of sad lapses into sin and sinful errors, v. 2. Nothing but divine grace can preserve them. Henry: "The faith of even strong believers may sometimes be sorely shaken, and ready to fail them. There are storms that will try the firmest anchors. Those that shall never be quite undone, are sometimes very near it," Rom. xi. 20; 1 Cor. x. 12; 1 Pet. iv. 18.

4. Of all hard questions in divinity perhaps none are more suited to give the tempter an advantage against us than those respecting God's providence over the world. Compare Gen. xlii. 36; Job xxi. 7–15; Jer. xii. 1, 2. God's government is full of insoluble mysteries. It must be so. We are worms and he is wonderful in working. Tholuck: "We all confess to the indubitable article of faith, that God governs the world. How different would our constancy in affliction be, were we indubitably to believe it. But affliction is generally accompanied by dejection, dejection issues in doubt, doubt gives rise to mental conflict; the struggle becomes intense." Calvin notices the case of Brutus, who on his defeat by Antony said: "Whatever I have believed concerning virtue had no foundation in truth, but was the invention of men." Mere nature can go no further, can say no more, can do no better.

5. When but half a story is told, or half a drama enacted, it is very unfair to pronounce on the character of the whole. That which is behind may give an entirely different face to things. God's providence over his people and his enemies must not be judged till time and eternity can both be brought into the estimate, vv. 4–20. Here, says Calvin, "the ungodly for the most part triumph; and although they deliberately stir up God to anger, and provoke his vengeance, yet from his sparing them, it seems as if they had done nothing amiss in deriding him, and that they will never be called to account for it. On the other hand, the righteous, pinched with poverty, oppressed with many troubles, harassed by multiplied wrongs, and covered with shame and reproach, groan and sigh."

6. There is a consanguinity between all the evil principles of unrenewed men, vv. 6, 8, 9, 11, 12. Although at a given time they may not all be developed, they are there, and will come forth when the occasion calls for them. Pride reigns; violence breaks forth; if they cannot argue, they can at least scoff; they speak wickedly; they regard injustice, if advantageous for the present, as something at least excusable; they speak swelling words; they utter sentiments derogatory to God; they claim exemption from the ninth commandment, and, in fact, from the whole decalogue; they deny providence, and God's omniscience; they are ungodly, or, as Paul expresses it, they are *free from righteousness*. The Scripture account of human nature is nowhere

flattering. Sanctified affliction is a blessing; unsanctified prosperity, a curse. It is better to die in faith than to live in unbelief.

7. Let the believer wait and all will come right, although now all is dark and disheartening. Let him not yield to the seducer. Dickson: "A temptation sometimes may be so powerfully borne in upon the spirit of a child of God, as to seem to be admitted, yielded unto, and subscribed unto, as in vv. 13, 14, we see." To yield to any temptation is sinful. To yield to one involving so much atheism is very dreadful. Let us ever hold fast the doctrine that God is righteous.

8. If we cannot explain God's ways, let us say nothing until such time as we can get the key to unlock the mystery of his providence, v. 15. Often we best glorify God by silence. The chief design of some trials doubtless is to shut our mouths, Ps. xxxix. 2. Blessed is the man who has grace to learn the lesson. In that state of mind he may come to know something. 'All true wisdom among men consists in being docile, and in implicitly submitting to the teachings of God.' Henry: "It is bad to think ill, but it is worse to speak it." Dickson: "So long as a temptation remaineth under dispute, and is not come to a settled decree and resolved practice, it hath not obtained full victory." Men adopt a false principle when they say, We may as well speak out all we think and feel.

9. In all conditions in life there is much in nature and in providence above our comprehension, v. 16. It will probably be so in all the stages of our future existence. It must be so, while a finite creature is the student, and Jehovah the subject of his inquiries. In heaven itself they sing the song: "Great and marvellous are thy works, Lord God Almighty." The next world will no doubt make plain much that was here inexplicable; but only to allow glorious mysteries to burst upon our enraptured view forever.

10. It is for a comfort and an encouragement, that so far as our duty is concerned, and so far as we must understand things necessary to our salvation, God's word and the worship he has instituted make all so plain that we may most reasonably rest satisfied, v. 17. Compare Matt. v. 3–11; Luke vi. 20–26. If men are poor in worldly goods, yet they may be rich in faith, and that makes heaven sure. Scott: "We shall never get ground against such temptations as the Psalmist had by merely speculating; and shall rather find our minds perplexed with new difficulties and objections, till we bring the whole matter and weigh it in the balance of the sanctuary. But attention to the sacred Scriptures, and fervent prayer, will soon extricate us from these labyrinths."

11. The more secure in their own minds the wicked are, the greater will be their surprise and amazement when their downfall shall come, vv. 18, 19. The ruin which they have taken a life-time to work out, will come upon them *as in a moment*, and they will be *consumed with terrors*. Compare Job xxvii. 20; Rev. ii. 27; xviii. 21. The career of God's foes, taken in connection with its termination, is truly doleful.

12. Of all the forms of predicting the downfall of the wicked, none are more terrific to a contemplative mind than those which declare that they shall be lightly esteemed, yea, *despised* by their Maker himself, v. 20. Here God's tender mercies are over all his works. Even the wicked have many blessings. But by and by God will forget to be gracious. The enemies of God will be slighted by him that made them.

13. We often gain our greatest victories by sinking into utter self-disesteem, and confessing our own nothingness and folly, v. 22. First the Psalmist says he was *foolish*, then ignorant, then that he was like a beast, a brute. If any would be wise, let him become a fool that he may be wise.

14. It is an unspeakable mercy to have a sweet sense of the presence of God at all

times, and especially in the day of temptation, v. 23. His presence is life. The weakest saint can do the most difficult things, if God will be with him.

15. Nothing but faith will ever rectify the mistakes of reason on divine things, vv. 2–24.

16. Divine guidance is essential to our attaining eternal glory, v. 24. Tholuck: "The path of the godly may be slippery and rough, but an invisible hand will hold their right hand, guide them with a wise counsel, and ultimately, after shame and wretchedness, lead them in honor and glory to that place, where they shall be received by him who was their highest good on earth."

17. As God is the support, so also is he the portion of the soul, vv. 25, 26. He is *an* all-sufficient good. He is *the* sole sufficient good. There is none like him, there is none beside him, there is none with him. He is unmixed good, moral excellence itself in perfection. Without God heaven would be no heaven. All the saints and angels, all the martyrs, prophets and apostles, though making a goodly company, could not make a heaven. "The Lord God giveth them light, and the Lamb is the light thereof."

18. At no time, more than when their hopes exult, are the frailty and mortality of man welcome themes to pious souls, v. 26. Nor is there any incongruity in this. A good man's hope is not in bodily vigor, nor in anything natural, but in him who giveth us the victory over death and hell and all our foes. If we are weak, he is mighty. If we are fools, he is wisdom itself.

19. It is not strange that people have often swooned away under powerful preaching, in which the future misery of the wicked was portrayed, v. 27. *Perdition* and *destruction* are fearful words. What makes the matter the more appalling is that after all that is said on the subject, our conceptions are inadequate; for eye hath not seen, nor ear heard, nor the heart of man conceived the things that God hath prepared for them that hate him.

20. Sin must be the worst thing in the universe, v. 27. There it is denominated a being *far from God*, and *harlotry*, also iniquity, unrighteousness, defilement, transgression, a horrible thing. God never misleads us by the names he gives things. He never puts bitter for sweet. Blessed is he, who fully adopts Bible views of sin, and flees to the only remedy, the blood and righteousness of Christ.

21. Communion with God, accompanied by trust in him and a heart to declare his doings, is the life of our lives. It is the chief attainment of our earthly existence. The reason why so many good men often cry out, My leanness, my leanness, is that they so seldom have intimate fellowship with the Father and with his Son through the Holy Ghost.

22. The whole Psalm warns us not to judge after the sight of our eyes, nor to be pleased with mere appearances, however fair or plausible. Fine linen often covers an aching heart. A pleasing exterior is often but the ornament of a sepulchre full of dead men's bones. This world in all its forms is delusive.

23. It is no new thing for wickedness to be successful, and for injustice to triumph for a season, Eccle. v. 8; ix. 2, 3.

24. As each one of us must soon pass away, heart and flesh failing, let us both labor and pray for the needful preparation for our last, great, solemn change.

25. Henry: "Those that with an upright heart put their trust in God shall never want matter of thanksgiving to him."

PSALM LXXIV.

Maschil of Asaph.

1 O God, why hast thou cast *us* off for ever? *why* doth thine anger smoke against the sheep of thy pasture?

2 Remember thy congregation, *which* thou hast purchased of old; the rod of thine inheritance, *which* thou hast redeemed; this Mount Zion, wherein thou hast dwelt.

3 Lift up thy feet unto the perpetual desolations; *even* all *that* the enemy hath done wickedly in the sanctuary.

4 Thine enemies roar in the midst of thy congregations, they set up their ensigns *for* signs.

5 *A man* was famous according as he had lifted up axes upon the thick trees.

6 But now they break down the carved work thereof at once with axes and hammers.

7 They have cast fire into thy sanctuary, they have defiled *by casting down* the dwellingplace of thy name to the ground.

8 They said in their hearts, Let us destroy them together: they have burned up all the synagogues of God in the land.

9 We see not our signs: *there is* no more any prophet: neither *is there* among us any that knoweth how long.

10 O God, how long shall the adversary reproach? shall the enemy blaspheme thy name for ever?

11 Why withdrawest thou thy hand, even thy right hand? pluck *it* out of thy bosom.

12 For God *is* my King of old, working salvation in the midst of the earth.

13 Thou didst divide the sea by thy strength: thou brakest the heads of the dragons in the waters.

14 Thou brakest the heads of leviathan in pieces, *and* gavest him *to be* meat to the people inhabiting the wilderness.

15 Thou didst cleave the fountain and the flood: thou driedst up mighty rivers.

16 The day *is* thine, the night also *is* thine: thou hast prepared the light and the sun.

17 Thou hast set all the borders of the earth: thou hast made summer and winter.

18 Remember this, *that* the enemy hath reproached, O Lord, and *that* the foolish people have blasphemed thy name.

19 Oh deliver not the soul of thy turtledove unto the multitude *of the wicked:* forget not the congregation of thy poor for ever.

20 Have respect unto the covenant: for the dark places of the earth are full of the habitations of cruelty.

21 Oh let not the oppressed return ashamed: let the poor and needy praise thy name.

22 Arise, O God, plead thine own cause: remember how the foolish man reproacheth thee daily.

23 Forget not the voice of thine enemies: the tumult of those that rise up against thee increaseth continually.

ON Maschil see on Ps. xxxii. This ode was for permanent use in the church. It is specially designed for times of commotion and persecution. On the authorship there are various opinions. Some ascribe it to Asaph, the cotemporary of David, and the author of Psalms l. lxxiii. This is perhaps correct. See on Psalm l. and Introduction, § 4. Those, who take this view, regard the Psalm as wholly prophetic. Why may it not be? Asaph was a *seer*. The language of the Psalm is indeed very much in the preterite form. But this may only show the certainty of the events predicted. This view relieves the interpretation of much difficulty. The ancient versions generally give us no light on the subject; but the Syriac gives Asaph as the author, and says it respects the time "when David saw the angel destroying the people, and wept and said, Let thy hand be against me and my offspring, and not against these innocent sheep. It is also a prediction of the siege of the city of the Jews, forty years after the ascension [of Christ,] by the aged

Vespasian, and by his son Titus, who slew myriads of Jews and destroyed Jerusalem; and from that time even to the present day the Jews have been despised." If we regard the Psalm as prophetic, then there is no difficulty in supposing it was written by Asaph the *seer*. This view, though not preferred, is regarded as admissible by Ainsworth, Patrick, Pool, Muis, Henry, Scott and Morison. It is preferred and defended by Gill. It has been objected that such a prophecy uttered before the building of the temple would have been a "great discouragement to the building of it." But Solomon knew that there was "a time to break down," as well as "a time to build up." He knew that all earthly grandeur was fleeting. Very soon after the first temple was built, God told Solomon that both it and the nation should be brought to ruin, if Israel profaned the covenant, 1 Kings ix. 6–8. No man of sense expects earthly structures to last forever, and Solomon knew this would not. That this Psalm is a *prophecy* is admitted by many, who doubt or deny that it was composed in David's time. And there is no more difficulty attending its interpretation as a prediction uttered more than four hundred years before the event, than if it had been spoken but a short time before the fall of the city. Another opinion is that the author of this Psalm was indeed called *Asaph*, but that he was a different person from the cotemporary of David, who wrote Psalms l. lxxiii. Patrick conjectures it may be Asaph, who was keeper of the king's forest in the days of Nehemiah, Neh. ii. 8. Others think it was penned by some one called Asaph, who lived at the time of the captivity. Others conjecture it was by a cotemporary of Isaiah, Isa. xxxvi. 3, 22. Another opinion makes *Asaph* signify the posterity and successors of the great singer and seer of that name; as *Jacob* and *David* are often used for the descendants of those men. There seems to be no reason for supposing that Jeremiah wrote this Psalm, as a few have conjectured. Much less does there seem to be a shadow of evidence in favor of the opinion of Geddes that Mattathias mentioned in 1 Maccabees may have been the author. He, who would learn the use of the name *Asaph* in Scripture, may consult 2 Kings xviii. 18; 1 Chron. vi. 39; ix. 15; xv. 17; xvi. 7; xxv. 1, 2, 9; xxvi. 1, 2; 2 Chron. v. 12; xx. 14; xxix. 13, 30; xxxv. 15; Ezra ii. 41; iii. 10; Neh. ii. 8; vii. 44; xi. 17, 22; xii. 35, 46; Isa. xxxvi. 3, 22.

To what scene of desolation does the Psalm refer? Grotius applies it to the destruction of Shiloh, the city once so famous as the place of the tabernacle, but, being despoiled of the ark by the Philistines, it fell into decay and became a proverb for desolation; see Josh. xviii. 1–10; Ps. lxxviii. 60; Jer. vii. 12–14. But the tabernacle was not burned at Shiloh, though it had not in it the ark, 2 Chron. i. 3. Moreover this Psalm expressly refers to Mount Zion, vv. 3, 7. A few have applied the Psalm to the invasion of Judea by Sennacherib. But that haughty invader was not permitted to enter Jerusalem, nor shoot an arrow into it, nor cast a bank against it, 2 Kings xix. 32, much less to waste it and destroy the sanctuary. Calvin, Calmet, Pool, Henry and Tholuck suppose that the Psalm had its fulfilment in the destruction of the holy city by the Chaldeans, about five hundred and eighty-eight years before Christ. The chief objection to this is a clause in v. 9: "There is no more any prophet." Jeremiah, Ezekiel and Daniel survived this desolation; but neither of them remained in Jerusalem; and for a time they all seem to have been silent. If the Psalm is interpreted as applying to Nebuchadnezzar's spoiling the holy city, the phrase under consideration must mean there was no seer left *at Jerusalem*. This would not be overstraining anything.

Others extend the scope of the prophecy so as to include the desecration of the temple by Antiochus Epiphanes in the times of the Maccabees, one hundred and sixty-seven years before Christ, and of course during the time of the second temple. Rosenmüller applies it to this time. But although Antiochus did many atrocious things, yet he did none of the things mentioned in vv. 6, 7. He defiled the temple, but he did not destroy it. This is urged by Theodoret. So that the reference to this dreadful persecutor, if real, cannot be exclusive. Others, following the Syriac title, refer it to the destruction of Jerusalem by the Romans. Clarke: "It is not so clear whether the desolations here refer to the days of *Nebuchadnezzar,* or to the desolation that took place under the *Romans* about the *seventieth* year of the Christian era." A full and candid examination of the whole subject would perhaps bring us to think that the Psalmist here groups together most of the appalling incidents attending the desolation of the temple and holy city from the time of Nebuchadnezzar to the days of Titus. One event followed another till the work was complete, and the prophecy *fulfilled.* Is there anything wild or unreasonable in this suggestion? See Jer. lii. 4–30; Matt. xxiv. 3–22, compared with Maccabees and Josephus. Morison calls this Psalm a "sombre and melancholy ode." Mant says: "It would be difficult to name a finer specimen of elegiac poetry than this pathetic Psalm of Asaph." Its date is decided very much by authorship. Clarke regards it as a late composition. Scott dates it B. C. 580. It is probably four hundred and eighty years older. In it we have *Elohim God, El God* and *Jehovah* LORD, on which see on Ps. iii. 2; v. 4; i. 2.

1. *O God, why hast thou cast us off for ever ?* *Hast cast off,* as in Ps. xliii. 2; xliv. 9; lx. 1, 10. In this form the rendering is uniform. *For ever,* elsewhere also rendered *constantly, alway, perpetually.* Hengstenberg: "The peculiarity of this Psalm is marked by the very frequent use of the word *for ever,* vv. 1, 3, 10." Why *doth thine anger smoke against the sheep of thy pasture?* *Anger,* as in Ps. ii. 5, 12, and often rendered *wrath. Smoke,* always so rendered in the English text or margin. The figure is drawn from the smoky vapor proceeding from the nostrils of furious animals. *Sheep of thy pasture,* a favorite mode of representing the covenant relation between God and his people, Ps. xxiii. 1; lxxix. 13; lxxx. 1 and often. The terrible sufferings of God's people by the hand of the Chaldeans, of Antiochus, and of Titus, all looked as if God had finally given them up to destruction. But as the second temple followed the first, as the awful sufferings of God's people in the second century before Christ were followed by greater glory than had ever before been seen in either temple, even Immanuel himself, so the fall of Israel was the riches of the world and the diminishing of them was the riches of the Gentiles. See Rom. xi. 15. God hath not forever cast off his people, but all Israel shall be saved. Calvin: "It is to be observed that the faithful, when persecuted by the heathen nations, lifted up their eyes to God, as if all the evils which they suffered had been inflicted by his hand alone. They were convinced that had not God been angry with them, their enemies would not have been permitted to take such license in injuring them." In this they were correct, Amos iii. 6.

2. *Remember thy congregation,* which *thou hast purchased of old.* For *purchased of old* the Chaldee reads *hast had from the beginning, hast redeemed from Egypt ;* several other ancient versions : *hast possessed from the beginning ;* Hengstenberg : *hast acquired of old. Remember,* also *think upon,* as in Gen. xl. 14. *Congregation,* as in Ps. i. 5 ; vii. 7, commonly so rendered, meaning the body of the Jewish nation, regarded as the worshippers of the true God. This people he calls *the rod of thine inheritance,* which *thou hast redeemed. Redeemed* or *ransomed,* viz., from Egypt. Redemption was commonly effected by a kinsman, who bought back the lawful captive with money. But God brought his people out of Egypt by his strong arm ; yet he saves sinners from wrath by the blood of his Son. *The lot of thine inheritance,* is ' the heritage which thou hast measured out for thyself.' Hammond : "It signifies a nation to which through all successions God had a peculiar right and title." The prophet at once shows his mean-

ing by speaking of *this mount Zion wherein thou hast dwelt*. There God revealed him-self in glory. There he manifested his merciful kindness.

3. *Lift up thy feet unto the perpetual desolations*. *Perpetual*, in v. 1 *for ever*. Any of the *desolations*, supposed to be referred to in this Psalm, seemed to last a long time. To *lift up the voice* is to speak, Gen. xxxix. 18. To *lift up the hand* is to smite, Isa. xxvi. 11. To *lift up the feet* is to come forth. Green: Hasten thy steps. Gejerus paraphrases it: "Advance not slowly or by stealth, but with large and stately steps, full in the view of all; come to thy sanctuary, so long suffered to lie waste; examine what has been done there, and let thy grace and aid, hitherto so much withheld, be extended to us." The *desolations* are in the latter clause of the verse described as embracing a general ruin: Even *all* that *the enemy hath done wickedly in the sanctuary*. This would apply to the Chaldeans, to Antiochus, or to the Romans. Although Antiochus did not destroy the temple, yet he defiled it. Piscator thinks the sense is: "Speedily consider the desolations which the Babylonians have made in this holy mountain, in which thou dwelledst."

4. *Thine enemies roar in the midst of thy congregations*. *Roar*, in the Hebrew pre-terite—*have roared*. The rendering of the verb is uniform; see on Ps. xxxviii. 8. It is applied to the roar of lions over their prey. For *congregations* Ainsworth, Ame-sius, Tremellius and Junius have *synagogues;* as our translators have in v. 8. It is not certain when synagogue worship began. It is certain it abounded after the resto-ration from Babylon. All the word can be fairly made here to mean is *the set place of meeting*. Sometimes it is rendered *the set time, the appointed time*, for brevity *solemnity*, in the plural *feasts*. It is often rendered *congregations*. Hengstenberg thinks "there is a manifest allusion to the name of the tabernacle: 'The tabernacle of meeting.' Now the import of this name is expressly given in Ex. xxv. 8; xxix. 42, 43, 45, 46; Num. xvii. 7. The tabernacle was so called, not because the people assembled there, but because God met his people there." These invaders not only made a violent and tumultuous noise; but they performed other acts of like charac-ter. *They set up their ensigns* for *signs*. *Ensigns* and *signs* are the same word, some-times rendered *tokens, wonders*. Here it evidently refers to banners or emblems of power. The import of the phrase doubtless is that the tokens of their power were seen everywhere, even in the temple, where the tokens of Jehovah's supreme autho-rity had long been displayed.

5. *A man was famous according as he had lifted up axes upon the thick trees*. This is confessedly a difficult text. The renderings are various but do not give much light. The senses gathered from it are chiefly two. One is that among these ruthless invaders a man was famous among his companions in proportion to the part he took in destroy-ing the curious wood-work of the temple. So Patrick and others. A still better sense is gathered by contrasting this verse with the next, *q. d.*, In former days, when the temple was building, it was esteemed an honor to fell and hew timber for the sanctuary. Bishop Hall: "It was heretofore thought an employment of much honor and merit in those men, who did cut down and square the timber-trees for the build-ing of the holy sanctuary." This seems also to have been the sense gathered by our translators:

6. *But now they break down the carved work thereof at once with axes and hammers*. What the *carved work* of the temple was may be seen in 1 Kings vi. 18, 29, 32, 35. The utter destruction accomplished by the Chaldeans on Jerusalem and its buildings is narrated in 2 Kings xxv. 8–17; Jer. lii. 12–23. *Axes* and *hammers* here only. The word rendered *axes* in v. 5, is not the same. Perhaps that in v. 5 is the name of *axes* proper, and this of *hatchets*, or small axes. Ainsworth has *beetle;* Jebb and Hengstenberg, *hatchet;* Fry, *hatchets;* and Alexander, *sledge*. The reason for destroy-

ing the carved wood-work before burning the temple was to express contempt and rage, and to secure the precious metal that overlaid the ceiling of the sanctuary.

7. *They have cast fire into thy sanctuary.* This might suit the desecrating of the holy city by the Chaldeans, by Antiochus, or by the Romans. Antiochus did not burn the temple, but he burnt its gates. The other invaders burnt and demolished it. *They have defiled* by casting down *the dwellingplace of thy name to the ground.* Chaldee: They have prostrated to the dust thy tabernacle in which thy name was invoked. Calvin: They have polluted the dwelling-place of thy name, levelling it with the ground.

8. *They said in their hearts, Let us destroy them together. Destroy,* never so rendered elsewhere, but commonly *vex* or *oppress.* By *them* we are to understand the whole body of the Jewish people. The enemies said all this *in their hearts.* It was their real and cordial wish. This was shown by their overt acts: *They have burned up all the synagogues of God in the land. Synagogues,* see on v. 4. Applied to locality it signifies *set places of meeting.* Whether others than the apartments of the temple are here referred to is not certain; but it is highly probable that " places where prayer was wont to be made" and where the law was read and explained to the people were early established in Judea. The fervent piety existing at times in the Jewish nation would warrant the belief that much was done to cultivate religious knowledge and affections in social meetings. Whether these were held in *synagogues* properly so called, or in other structures we may not now certainly know. But whatever the edifices were invaders wasted them by fire. It is true that all Israel were required to unite in the solemnities of the temple service thrice a year, Deut. xii. 5–16, and that no tribe was allowed to set up an altar for itself. Nor were burnt-offerings at any time made in the synagogues, although sacrifices by persons, or families were allowed in other places than the temple, 1 Sam. xvi. 3, 5; xx. 6; 1 Kings xviii. 30–38.

9. *We see not our signs. Signs,* see on v. 4. The meaning is, We no longer see the usual *tokens* of God's presence and supremacy, to which we have so long been accustomed, or, We no longer see *miracles* wrought in our behalf as our fathers saw of old. There is *no more any prophet.* In the first temple were found the oracle, the holy fire, the ark of the covenant, the cloud of glory, and the spirit of prophecy. From the days of Nebuchadnezzar, all these were wanting except that for a short time God sent Zechariah, Haggai and Malachi to prophesy after the Babylonish captivity. The time of the public service of the prophets Jeremiah, Ezekiel and Daniel, and their relation to the visible church after the destruction of the first temple have already been explained. Alexander: "The complaint of this, as of a recent loss, shows that the period meant is not that of the persecutions under Antiochus Epiphanes, when the gift of prophecy had been withdrawn for many generations." But it is mentioned as one of the *sad* things without saying how far back it dated. And it is worthy of remark that the very same thing is mentioned in 1 Maccabees iv. 46; ix. 27; xiv. 41. So that this very phrase might be used in the songs of the Jews from the days of Jeremiah to the time of Zechariah, and from Malachi to John the Baptist, and from Titus to this day. *Neither* is there *among us any that knoweth how long; i. e.,* how long these troubles shall last. On the last two clauses compare Ezek. vii. 26; Lam. ii. 9; Am. viii. 11; Mic. iii. 6.

10. *O God, how long shall the adversary reproach? How long?* see on Ps. iv. 2; vi. 3. *Adversary, enemy, foe,* one who causes *trouble, sorrow, distress, affliction. Reproach,* often rendered *defy,* also *upbraid,* and *rail against. Shall the enemy blaspheme thy name for ever? Enemy,* always so rendered; also in vv. 3, 18. *Blaspheme,* often so rendered, also *contemn, despise, abhor, provoke.* The long-suffering of God could not be demonstrated, if he sent condign punishment on the wicked as soon as they go astray.

It is a desirable state of mind and a proof of a new heart to be afflicted by wickedness chiefly because it is a dishonor to God.

11. *Why withdrawest thou thy hand, even thy right hand ? pluck it out of thy bosom.* Admitting the common version to be correct, the sense seems to be, " Why withholdest thou thy hand from relieving thy people and putting down their foes ? Do not stand as an unconcerned spectator of our affliction, with thy hand in thy bosom, but draw it forth and help thy people." This is the best sense, perhaps. But for *it* some would read *them;* and for *pluck, consume.* Several fine scholars gather this sense : " How long wilt thou withdraw thy hand ? Yea, wilt thou withdraw it from the midst of thy bosom ? Consume, therefore these ungodly men, who so proudly despise thee." By *the right hand* we are to understand the power of God. Strong pleas are urged :

12. *For God is my king of old, working salvation in the midst of the earth.* The first ground of confidence is the long-standing covenant relation of Israel with the Almighty ; he is *my king of old.* The second is that he had formerly done great things for them when oppressed, *working salvation* (literally *salvations*) for them *in the midst of the earth,* or before the eyes of all people. The history of the Jewish nation and church was made up of a series of well known wonders.

13. *Thou didst divide the sea by thy strength.* No doubt the reference is to the passage of God's chosen people through the Red sea, mentioned so often in Scripture, Ex. xiv. 16, 21 ; Josh. xxiv. 6, 7 ; Neh. ix. 11 ; Ps. lxxviii. 13. But there are allusions to the sea, which much resemble this, but which have no reference to the great deliverance at the Red sea, as Job xxvi. 12 ; Isa. li. 15 ; Jer. xxxi. 35. In all these our version speaks of *dividing the sea.* The verb is not that used in this verse, but one that signifies to *break, to rest, find ease,* so that to *divide the sea* may mean to break up its waves so as to make it still ; whereas the verb *divide* in this verse signifies to *sunder,* so as to cleave. *Thou brakest the heads of the dragons in the waters.* *Dragons, whales* in Gen. i. 21 ; Job vii. 12 ; *serpents* in Ex. vii. 9, 10, 12 ; *sea-monsters* (margin *sea-calves*) in Lam. iv. 3 ; in all other places (eight in all) *dragons,* Deut. xxxii. 33 ; Neh. ii. 13 ; Ps. xci. 18 ; cxlviii. 7 ; Isa. xxvii. 1 ; li. 9 ; Jer. li. 34, and here. Perhaps it was not designed to designate any particular kind of inhabitant of the waters. Mant : " What animal is meant by this name is not well ascertained. But it seems to have been some aquatic or amphibious creature commonly known in the neighborhood of Egypt, but not the crocodile, as that is noticed under a different name in the following verse." No sea-monster had power to hurt the Israelites in their passage through the Red sea. Some of them are said to live a thousand years, but God at last *breaks,* or *crushes* them, so that they die. Alexander thus paraphrases : " Thou hast subdued and crushed the sea and its most terrible inhabitants." Some think that the clause teaches that the cleaving of the waters of the sea caused the death of many large fishes. Others by *dragons* understand the Egyptians, who persecuted the Jews. Some include other foes besides ; see Isa. li. 9, 10 ; Ezek. xxix. 3, 4. To whatever the allusion is, it seems to designate an evil so prodigious as to fill the imagination, Isa. xxvii. 1 ; Ezek. xxxii. 2. God controls all causes, all evils, even such as are *monstrous.*

14. *Thou brakest the heads of leviathan in pieces.* The word *leviathan* occurs in the Hebrew Scriptures six times. In Job iii. 8, it is in the text rendered *mourning,* but in the margin *leviathan.* In Job xli. 1, we again have the word, and the whole of that chapter is occupied in a description of leviathan. We have it also in Ps. civ. 26, and twice in Isa. xxvii. 1. The other place is this verse. Simonis thinks we know neither the etymology of the name, nor the language to which it belongs. Perhaps he is right, though Gesenius thinks otherwise. Bochart has a lengthened argument to show that the word when used without a figure means the *crocodile* Gese-

nius gives this as the meaning in Job xli. 1. A large weight of modern authority lies on that side. Some affirm that in the Egyptian language *Pharaoh* signifies *croco-dile*. Here the reference seems to be rather to the princes of Egypt than to its monarch, for we have *heads of leviathan*, the word rendered *heads* often signifying *chiefs, captains*. Tholuck: "He calls the nation of the Egyptians a monster, and a crocodile of the water, because that rapacious beast is peculiar to the river Nile." This relieves the clause of considerable difficulty, and there is no place where such a view would not give a good sense. And [thou] *gavest him* to be *meat to the people inhabiting the wilderness*. If this means that the bodies of the Egyptians, drowned in the Red sea were washed ashore, and became food for beasts of prey, all is plain and easy. The original would bear this. ' *The people inhabiting the wilderness'* is in Hebrew one short word, *Ziim*. It occurs six times, and is thrice rendered 'wild beasts of the desert,' Isa. xiii. 21; xxxiv. 14; Jer. l. 39; see on Ps. lxxii. 9. Tholuck: "The pursuing hosts of Pharaoh were drowned in the waters and their bodies cast ashore to become the food of jackals, the inhabitants of the wilderness." Nor did God's wonders then cease.

15. *Thou didst cleave the fountain and the flood.* *Cleave*, applied to hatching eggs, to splitting wood or rocks, to dividing the sea, Isa. lix. 5; xlviii. 21; Ecc. x. 9; Ps. lxxviii. 13. Here the reference, as some think, is to the opening of the Red sea to make a way for the Israelites, or to the passage of the Jordan, as recorded in Josh. iii. 14–17. Alexander prefers the latter. But Calvin, Scott and others apply it to the cleaving of the rock, whence gushed the stream of water for the supply of the wants of the people. This is admissible; and is supported by the Chaldee. It makes the description more rapid, and so coincides with the best rules of poetry. Besides, the opening of rivers is specially named in the next clause: *Thou driedst up mighty rivers.* The chief difficulty here is that more than one river is mentioned. The Chaldee names three, the Arnon, the Jabbok and the Jordan. This interpretation is supported, in part, by the record in Num. xxi. 12–16, from which it is clear that God dried up at least another river besides the Jordan.

16. *The day* is thine, *the night also* is *thine: thou hast prepared the light and the sun*, Gen. i. 3–5, 14–18; Ps. viii. 3; xix. 1–6; cxxxvi. 7–9; Isa. xlv. 7; Matt. v. 45, are parallel passages. The passage in Isa. xlv. 7, was uttered for the very purpose of claiming for God before the Persian Cyrus the honor of creating the darkness and the light, both of which, in their alternations, are great blessings.

17. *Thou hast set all the borders of the earth.* *Set, prepared, established, fixed. Borders*, elsewhere *bounds, coasts*. The earth has the exact size and configuration, and the precise quantity of sea and of dry land, and is divided by national boundaries in the way that the Almighty determined. He is the author of all nature and the father of all nations, Deut. xxxii. 8; Ps. xxiv. 1, 2; Acts xvii. 26. *Thou hast made summer and winter.* Though day and night, summer and winter, are brought about according to what men call the course of nature, yet the laws of nature are nothing but the usual modes of divine operation in nature. Alexander: "God is not only the ordainer of these changes, but the author of the causes which produce them."

18. *Remember this,* that *the enemy hath reproached, O* LORD, *and* that *the foolish people have blasphemed thy name. Enemy*, as in vv. 3–10. *Foolish*, rendered also *fool, vile*, 2 Sam. iii. 33; Isa. xxxii. 5. On the verbs rendered *reproached* and *blasphemed*, see on v. 10; also on v. 22. Some govern the word *Jehovah* by reproached. Others have it as in the common version.

19. *Oh deliver not the soul of thy turtledove unto the multitude* of the wicked. The church is here called thy turtledove, because she is gentle, sorrowful, defenceless, hating noise and strife, having neither a disposition nor weapons to protect herself, and being

loved of God. Her enemies have always been a *multitude*, elsewhere rendered a *troop*. *Of the wicked* is supplied by our translators. The reference is to *the enemy* of former verses. He repeats the request in other words: *Forget not the congregation of thy poor for ever.* God's *poor* are the meek, the humble, the afflicted of his church. *Congregation*, in the preceding clause rendered *multitude*; but *there* applied to the wicked, *here* to the righteous.

20. *Have respect unto the covenant. Have respect*, elsewhere *consider, regard, look to. Covenant*, so rendered with great uniformity. It refers to the engagement of Jehovah to be the God of his people. He urges this the more, *For the dark places of the earth are full of the habitations of cruelty.* Cresswell: "*For the dark places of the earth, i. e.*, the caverns of Judea, *are full of the habitations of violence, i. e.*, of men who live by rapine." Clarke: "The caves, dens, woods, etc., of the *land*, are full of robbers, cutthroats, and murderers, who are continually destroying thy people; so that the holy seed seems as if it would be entirely cut off, and the covenant promise thus rendered void." Perhaps it is better here to read *earth* than *land*, and to extend the description to the whole world, asking God to keep his covenant with his people, else they will become like the rest of the world addicted to 'injustice and violence,' to 'wrong and outrage.'

21. *Oh let not the oppressed return ashamed: let the poor and needy praise thy name.* Patrick: "O let not thy poor afflicted servant, who implores thy aid against these barbarous oppressors, be denied his suit, and go away ashamed to see himself disappointed of his hope; but let him, and all the rest of thy miserable people, who were never in greater need of thy help, be restored to praise thy goodness in their ancient possessions."

22. *Arise, O God, plead thine own cause.* The cause of his saints is the cause of God. He has united his honor with their final deliverance and their complete success. Whoso reproaches God's people for trusting in Jehovah reproaches the Almighty himself: *Remember how the foolish reproacheth thee daily;* see on v. 18.

23. *Forget not the voice of thine enemies.* The petition is that God in judging between his people and their foes would decide the controversy according to the tenor of the language used by the wicked. Or the prayer may import that all sin has a tongue and continually calls for vengeance, as did the blood of Abel, and the sin of Sodom, Gen. iv. 10; xviii. 21. Both views lead to the same result. *The tumult of those that rise up against thee increaseth continually.* When wickedness is rampant and outrageous, it is time for God to work. The more unendurable any state of things becomes, the louder may we call for help. It is remarkable that the Psalm closes without any expression of hope of deliverance. Horne: "While speaking, the church seems to hear the tumultuous clamors of the approaching enemy, growing every minute louder as they advance: and we leave the 'turtle-dove' without the divine assistance, ready to sink under the talons of the rapacious eagle."

Doctrinal and Practical Remarks.

1. So uniform is the experience of God's people in all ages that the *Maschils* of Asaph or David suit them thousands of years after they were written.

2. It is not sinful, but oftentimes a part of our religious duty to inquire *why* the Lord deals thus and so with us, v. 1. How else should we discover the end of the Lord in the chastisements he sends upon us? God did not condemn Job for so doing.

3. Slade: "It is sad and distressing for the people of God to behold the wicked in the exercise of their ungodly power; insulting the worshippers and worship of their Lord, casting dishonor upon their holy religion, and ready to defile and destroy the house of God itself." Are you grieved for the affliction of Joseph?

4. We cannot too carefully guard both our hearts and lives against everything which might tend to bring God's displeasure in the form of public calamities upon the church or nation. When disasters stalk abroad, it is often our only comfort that we have not been willing instruments in the hands of wicked men or fallen angels, in bringing down the divine wrath.

5. Whatever God may do with guilty nations and degenerate churches, it is a blessed truth that he will never destroy the sheep 'whom he has purchased and brought into his pasture, and in whom he dwells by his Spirit,' v. 1; John x. 28, 29.

6. It is no new thing for the church of God to be left in such circumstances as to compel her to utter loud and bitter cries and complaints. This Psalm throughout.

7. Let all God's people ever plead his relation to them, and their relation to him, vv. 1, 2, 4, 7, 8, 10, 12, 19. They may well remind him that they are the *sheep of his pasture*, and thus magnify the free and distinguishing grace, which made them to differ from others. They may call themselves his *congregation*, his company, his assembly; by his gracious and merciful presence, and the indwelling of his Spirit distinguished from all other assemblies, companies and congregations. The very houses in which they meet are the *dwelling-places of Jehovah's name*. Even their most common places of meeting, whether called synagogues, houses of prayer, schools of the prophets, chapels, or, in times of persecution, conventicles, are sacred in the eyes of him who governs all things. This is as true under the Gospel as under the old dispensation, Matt. xviii. 20. Let them ever plead that Jehovah is their *King*, and that he has been so *of old, working salvation in the midst of the earth*. Let them urge that if the church is weak, sad, defenceless, she is still the Lord's *turtle-dove*.

8. It is not possible that God should be indifferent to the miseries of his people, nor to the violence of their enemies. In due time he will *lift up his feet*, he will hasten to avenge his own elect, v. 3; Luke xviii. 7. See 2 Maccabees vi. 14–16. Though not inspired, it embodies the substance of what is often declared in God's word.

9. It is not unusual with the Almighty to *seem* long to delay deliverances to his afflicted people. Oftentimes their desolations and tribulations appear *perpetual*, v. 4. Such an impression is made by these facts: 1. Sin is a terrible evil, very difficult to cure, and requiring severe chastisement; 2. When we are suffering, time seems much longer to us than when we are in the midst of enjoyments.

10. The more cruel, brutish and violent men are, the more earnestly should God's people call on his holy name, vv. 4, 6, 7, 8, 10, 18, 22, 23.

11. Any voluntary and hearty connection with the cause of God is honorable, and shall be so declared in the last day. God took it well of David that he meditated the building of the temple. He made men *famous*, who even did the carved work of the sacred edifice, v. 5. Under the Gospel even the giving of a cup of cold water to a disciple out of love to Christ, shall meet an everlasting reward.

12. We do but deceive ourselves when we believe that the unregenerate delight in anything more than in the destruction of all good, vv. 6, 7, 8. Be not surprised, O child of God, when thou seest false professors or avowed enemies, doing wickedly in the church, scattering fire-brands, arrows and death, boasting of their triumphs and trophies, insulting the humble, hindering much good and offending against the generation of God's children.

13. The hearts of God's people must be sad when they lack the usual tokens of God's presence, v. 9. Especially is this true when they are driven from his house and his ordinances. How could it be otherwise?

14. Afflictions seldom, if ever, come single. What an assemblage of miseries is recorded in this one ode! Commonly it happens, as saith the prophet Ezekiel, vii. 26, 27.

15. To us who have a full revelation of the mind and will of God on all matters affecting truth, duty and destiny, it may seem a small matter to want the presence of a living prophet. But it was far different with the church of old, v. 9. Then many of the most glorious truths of religion both as to the course of providence and the plan of salvation were but dimly shadowed forth.

16. Yet even we may long for light, and desire to know more than we do, and to inquire how long our calamities shall last, v. 9.

17. It may give us an insight into the true nature of wickedness, when we see that rising to its height, it reproaches and blasphemes God himself, vv. 10, 18, 22. The wicked foam out their own shame. They outrageously insult the God of heaven.

18. We may well ask God to work, v. 11. Every day our enemies are too mighty for us. Always, except when checked by his almighty power, they are gaining some advantage against the truth.

19. God's people should 'intermingle meditations with their prayers.' Thus they shall 'acquire renewed vigor to their faith, and stir up themselves to greater earnestness' in supplication, v. 12. Especially let them think over the history of the church in troublous times and in days of persecution.

20. God has ever been famous for doing great things and mighty, marvellous things which men do well to tell to one another, vv. 12–17.

21. It is for the unspeakable consolation of God's people that the author of creation and of universal providence, is the author of redemption, vv. 13–17. Therefore, they need not fear.

22. Inspired men did not rail or revile, but taught a simple and important truth, when they asserted that sin was folly and sinners fools, vv. 18, 22.

23. As the feebleness and poverty of the church are good reasons for committing her to the care of God, so we are assured that for these things God will not cast her off, but will rather save her, vv. 19, 21.

24. Those persons and preachers, who decline to think and speak of gospel mercies and free salvation as secured by *covenant*, do deprive themselves and others of much of the blessed comforts of God's word. Such was not the manner of the inspired Psalmist, v. 20. Tholuck: "'Look upon the Covenant.' This is the eternal asylum of the saints of God even in the greatest peril. And though they have broken it, shall the unbelief of man make the faithfulness of God without effect? Rom. iii. 3 ;" 2 Tim. ii. 13.

25. How extreme the wretchedness of not having the true religion, v. 20. Truly they do multiply their sorrows that hasten after another God.

26. When we can truly plead that our cause is God's *own cause*, we need never fear the want of success in prayer, though the answer may for awhile be delayed, v. 22.

27. If we are compelled to close our most solemn and urgent devotions, and our most earnest supplications, without seeing one ray of light beaming upon our path, it may comfort us to remember that so the pious Psalmist closed this complaint, v. 23. To hope against hope is the most blessed kind of hope.

28. Let us pray without ceasing. "We may do more by our prayers than the mightiest by their weapons: the poor may do as much as the rich ; and more, if they be *poor in spirit.*"

29. It is well when our complaints relate chiefly not to our own temporal interests, but to the injury done to religion by the course of the wicked, and to the want of the gracious presence of God. Asaph did not complain of personal discomforts, nor of the want of armies, or of captains, or of horsemen, but of the absence of God's presence, and of the dishonor done to religion.

30. The only hope of the church is in God himself. Unless he be with us and for

us 'there is no standing before an enraged multitude, especially when armed with power and filled with barbarous rage.'

PSALM LXXV.

To the chief Musician, Al-taschith, A Psalm *or* Song of Asaph.

1 Unto thee, O God, do we give thanks, *unto thee* do we give thanks: for *that* thy name is near thy wondrous works declare.

2 When I shall receive the congregation I will judge uprightly.

3 The earth and all the inhabitants thereof are dissolved: I bear up the pillars of it.　Selah.

4 I said unto the fools, Deal not foolishly: and to the wicked, Lift not up the horn:

5 Lift not up your horn on high: speak *not* with a stiff neck.

6 For promotion *cometh* neither from the east, nor from the west, nor from the south.

7 But God *is* the judge: he putteth down one, and setteth up another.

8 For in the hand of the LORD *there is* a cup, and the wine is red; it is full of mixture; and he poureth out of the same: but the dregs thereof, all the wicked of the earth shall wring *them* out, *and* drink *them*.

9 But I will declare for ever; I will sing praises to the God of Jacob.

10 All the horns of the wicked also will I cut off; *but* the horns of the righteous shall be exalted.

ON the title see on titles of Psalms iv. xxx. lvii.　On the authorship of this poem see Introduction, § 4, and on Psalms l. lxxiii. lxxiv.　There is no good reason for doubting that it was written by the author of those compositions.　It is but candid, however, to say that many learned men ascribe it to a much later writer than the cotemporary of David.　Of those, who thus hold, some admit with Hengstenberg, that the Psalm is prophetic.　If so, it at once removes one of the chief arguments in favor of a later authorship.　Scott dates it B. C. 1048.　Clarke affixes no date. Alexander: "The immediate historical occasion we have no direct means of ascertaining."　This is quite true.　It is mere conjecture that fixes it to David's accession to the throne, the pestilence sent for numbering the people, or the destruction of Sennacherib's army.　We have here *Elohim* God and *Jehovah* LORD, on which see on Ps. iii. 2; i. 2.　On *Selah* see Introduction, § 15.

1. *Unto thee, O God, do we give thanks*, unto thee *do we give thanks.　Give thanks*, as in Ps. vi. 5; also rendered *praise, confess.　*The repetition expresses much liveliness. The Hebrew verb is in the preterite, but is no doubt correctly rendered here.　Calvin gives it in the future.　The cause for such worship is next stated: *For that thy name is near thy wondrous works declare.　Near, nigh, at hand.　*There is no better rendering. God's *name* is here put either for God himself, or for that by which he makes himself known.　Both senses are authorized.　God's presence is declared by his *wondrous works*, miracles, or marvellous works.　God's providence is always bringing wonders to pass and evincing his presence with his people.　Hengstenberg: "One of God's wonders placed before the eyes gives reality also to all the others."

2. *When I shall receive the congregation I will judge uprightly.　*There is some doubt whether the translation of this verse is correct; although it is supported by Fabritius, Piscator, Junius and Tremellius, Calvin, Venema, Amesius, Hare, Jebb and the church of England.　Some of the variations are unintelligible; some convey a poor sense; others substantially support the common version.　Of the latter class a few are

cited: Ainsworth: When I shall receive the appointment, I will judge righteousness; Green: When I shall receive again the courts of justice, I will judge uprightly; Edwards: When the proper time is come, I execute righteous judgment; Hengstenberg (with whom some agree) is still different: For I shall fix a time when I shall judge righteously. Evidently one person is the speaker here. That person is either David as king of Israel, or Messiah as typified by David or God as Judge of the whole earth. If we regard the speaker as David or as Christ, the common version is perhaps best. Then the sense is that David as type, or Messiah would reign in equity. But if the speaker is God, the Judge of all, then the sense is that God has set the time, when in his infinite wisdom and mercy he will deliver his people, and that the whole matter of administering succor is in his power, not in theirs, and that he will effectually do all they need, though it involves the overthrow of their enemies. Arnd: "Our God, who governs the world by his omnipotence and wisdom, has appointed to all things a boundary, and has also fixed a time and an hour for his judgment, and when this comes, he reveals his judgments, and no man can hinder them." Alexander: "The parties to be tried are the foes and oppressors of God's people."

3. *The earth and all the inhabitants thereof are dissolved.* The ancient versions are quite uniform in their rendering, except that for *dissolved* or *melted* the Syriac has *abased* or *laid low.* We have no right to change the Hebrew text, as Houbigant does, so as to read: The earth and all the inhabitants are established. The meaning of the clause is well given by Clarke: "The earth and all its inhabitants depend on me; and whenever I withdraw the power by which they exist and live, they are immediately dissolved." *Dissolved,* in Ps. xlvi. 6, *melted.* The clause declares that nothing has stability but as God gives it, and that though the whole world were leagued against God and his church, yet at his will they should melt away. He has power to do anything. *I bear up the pillars of it* [the earth.] The Chaldee and several other ancient versions: I have established its pillars forever; Calvin: I will establish the pillars of it. The Hebrew verb is in the preterite and primarily signifies to *weigh.* He, who made the earth, can easily destroy it, or do anything else requiring the exertion of omnipotent power. He can defend his church against all her adversaries.

4. *I said to the fools, deal not foolishly.* The speaker in this verse is no doubt the prophet, inspired by the Holy Ghost. *Fools,* literally *boasters. Foolishly, boastfully.* Bythner thinks *madness* enters into the meaning of those words. No doubt all wicked exultation is an act of madness. The triumph of the wicked is short. *And to the wicked, Lift not up the horn.* The *fools* of the first clause are the *wicked,* or *ungodly* of this. Two explanations are given of *lifting up the horn.* One is that the "metaphor is borrowed from the habits of horned animals, and is nearly equivalent to the act of holding the head high, as a sign of pride." Perhaps a better explanation is that some eastern nations to this day, on occasions of celebrating victory or of making merry, use an ornament for the head made in the shape of a horn. This horn is of a conical form, and when massive necessarily gives to the wearer an appearance of stiffness in the neck. If this is correct, it explains well the words of the next verse.

5. *Lift not up your neck on high: speak not with a stiff neck.* For *stiff neck* Parkhurst reads *retorted neck,* and remarks that "this is a well-known gesture of pride, contempt or disdain." The word rendered *stiff* is elsewhere rendered *hard, grievous* and *arrogancy,* 1 Sam. ii. 3; Ps. xxxi. 18; xciv. 4. The prophet further warns the wicked against their haughtiness by reminding them that any apparent advantage one man has over another is solely by the ordering of providence:

6. *For promotion* cometh *neither from the east, nor from the west, nor from the south. Promotion,* in the Hebrew plural, rendered by Calvin *exaltations;* by Piscator, Fab-

ritius, Junius and Tremellius, Amesius, Edwards, Jebb and Fry, *exaltation;* by Green, *advancement.* But for *exaltations* some read *mountains.* Venema has it: *Because nothing is from the east and the west, from the desert and the mountains.* The *north* is not mentioned, unless it is included under the word we render *south,* which is literally *desert;* by which it is generally agreed there is reference to the great desert on the south: but others include the wilderness of Damascus, which lay to the north, 1 Kings xix. 15. If this is correct every quarter is included. However we may understand particular phrases, we can hardly doubt that the meaning of the prophet is, that the threatened evils could not be averted, the impending ruin could not be turned aside by human aid from any quarter. All this was to prepare the mind for the truth of the next verse:

7. *But God is the judge: he putteth down one, and setteth up another.* It is by him that kings reign, and princes decree justice. Hammond well says that the word rendered judge "signifies somewhat more than an ordinary *justiciary;* for to such it scarcely belongs to bestow honors and preferments at pleasure. It is the style by which the captains and managers of the wars of the people of Israel were styled, as Gideon and Samson." Jehovah "being the sovereign Lord and Governor of the world easily lays those low that proudly exalt themselves against his authority; and lifts up those that humbly submit themselves unto him." Warner thinks here is an allusion to astrology, and that the meaning is that the fortunes of men are not governed by the planets but by God's providence. Although the general tenor of God's providence is mild and long-suffering, yet even he will not permit the wicked always to go unpunished:

8. *For in the hand of the* LORD *there is a cup, and the wine is red; it is full of mixture; and he poureth out of the same: but the dregs thereof, all the wicked of the earth shall wring them out, and drink them.* It was common to represent a portion good or bad by a cup. Blessings are so represented in Ps. xvi. 5; xxiii. 5. But evils, afflictions, and awful judgments are frequently represented in the same way, Ps. xi. 16; lxxiii. 10; Isa. li. 17; Jer. xxv. 15; Ezek. xxiii. 31–34; Matt. xx. 22; xxvi. 39; John xviii. 11; Rev. xiv. 10; xvi. 19. There is probably a reference to wines drugged till they produced the most terrible effects. But whether this is so or not, the general character of the imagery unmistakably represents 'fear, distress, despondency, horror, infatuation, anguish and despair.'

9. *But I will declare for ever; I will sing praises to the God of Jacob.* The *God of Jacob* was he, who wrought marvellous deliverances from mighty and enraged enemies. The first and second clauses are parallel. Jehovah had so delivered his people and punished his enemies, that it was the duty of piety humbly and tremblingly to adore and *sing praises, sing psalms,* or *make music.*

10. *All the horns of the wicked also will I cut off; but the horns of the righteous shall be exalted.* For an explanation of the metaphors here used, see on vv. 4, 5. There is less difficulty in making God the speaker here, than in supposing that these are the words of Asaph, or of David represented by Asaph, or of the church; though the latter would be admissible, and is adopted by Calvin and others.

DOCTRINAL AND PRACTICAL REMARKS.

1. Luther says, "this is a Psalm of consolation against all turbulent and hardened hypocrites, who boast of their church and their name, and despise all threatenings, and all exhortations; ever speaking like those arrogant hypocrites in Ps. xii. 'Who is Lord over us?'" Let the wicked tremble.

2. The righteous shall never cease to give thanks, v. 1. Their mercies shall never cease to flow; and their hearts shall never be unmoved by the divine kindness.

3. Neither here nor in the next world are marvels wanting to God's people, v. 1. Henry: "There are many works which God does for his people, that may truly be called *wondrous works*, out of the common course of providence, and quite beyond our expectation."

4. By terrible things in righteousness God often keeps the world in awe. The *wondrous works*, which save his people, often confound his enemies, v. 1. Morison: "The signs of an avenging deity are the exertions of his mighty power and outraged forbearance."

5. Christ's kingdom over the world, like God's whole government, is righteous, v. 2. In any government nothing can compensate the want of essential justice. Christ's righteousness was not wrought out nor is it manifested by trampling on law.

6. God, who made, can easily *dissolve*, destroy the most stable things known on earth, v. 3. Nothing is too hard for him. He will work and none can hinder. Tholuck: "When all around us is in confusion, and the firmest strong-holds give way, we should still retain the belief, *that God is only waiting for his set time.*"

7. He who can thus dissolve all nature can also *bear up* all things, so that nothing shall perish but at his bidding, v. 3. By him all things stand together. His power is infinite.

8. No new thing happens to the world when everything falls into confusion, when rapine and injustice carry the day, when insolence holds the sceptre over the heads of the innocent, Ecc. v. 8.

9. Nothing is more vain or mad than glorying in a thing of nought; and such is everything but God, his nature, his word, his grace, his blessing, v. 4. Man is vanity and lies. Dickson: "Such as are acquainted with true wisdom justly account all wicked men to be fools, forsakers of God's teaching, and followers of their own wit and will, to the ruin of their own bodies, souls, houses and fame." The higher the wicked rise the more dreadful shall be their fall.

10. Insolence is a common ingredient of sin manifested either towards God or man, v. 5. There is a general impression that pride was the first sin ever committed. Perhaps it may have been. Pride will make hell insufferable.

11. The world is full of practical atheism, vv. 6, 7. Few men really believe that Jehovah governs this world, that everything happens by his ordering, and that all causes, agents and means are nothing without him. Forgetfulness of God is as common as it is dreadful.

12. All we have we have received; and all we have received is from God, v. 7. This is as true of temporal as of spiritual blessings. All come from God.

13. Much of the language of Scripture respecting the punishment of the wicked is admitted to be figurative; but the figures used are often of the most terrible character, v. 8. How dreadful must be the doom of the finally impenitent, when the Bible, the best expressed volume in the world, employs the most terrific imagery to portray it.

14. The redeemed on earth always have, and the redeemed in glory ever shall have themes of admiring gratitude, calling them to glorify God and to publish his honors abroad, v. 9.

15. No argument for the divine goodness to believers is more fair or more conclusive than the historical, v. 9. The God of *Jacob*, of Daniel, of Paul is still the God of all saints.

16. Could the righteous see how soon and how terribly the wicked shall be *cut off*, they would not murmur, or repine, or indulge envy at any prosperity granted to the enemies of righteousness, v. 10.

17. Tholuck: The "Psalmist cannot grow weary with praising. His imperishable

theme is the truth that the righteous shall *finally* prevail, v. 10. To God's people good days are coming.

18. Scott: "Let Christian magistrates remember their obligations to him, from whom they have their authority ; that they may judge righteously, maintain by the improvement of their talent, and by all Scriptural means, the cause of piety ; that they may crush the haughty oppressor, and protect, advance and exalt the righteous. And let the people recollect, from whom their rulers have their authority ; that they ' may be subject not only for wrath, but also for conscience' sake.'"

PSALM LXXVI.

To the chief Musician on Neginoth, A Psalm *or* Song of Asaph.

1 In Judah *is* God known : his name *is* great in Israel.

2 In Salem also is his tabernacle, and his dwellingplace in Zion.

3 There brake he the arrows of the bow, the shield, and the sword, and the battle. Selah.

4 Thou *art* more glorious *and* excellent than the mountains of prey.

5 The stouthearted are spoiled, they have slept their sleep : and none of the men of might have found their hands.

6 At thy rebuke, O God of Jacob, both the chariot and horse are cast into a dead sleep.

7 Thou, *even thou, art* to be feared : and who may stand in thy sight when once thou art angry ?

8 Thou didst cause judgment to be heard from heaven ; the earth feared, and was still,

9 When God arose to judgment, to save all the meek of the earth. Selah.

10 Surely the wrath of man shall praise thee : the remainder of wrath shalt thou restrain.

11 Vow, and pay unto the LORD your God : let all that be round about him bring presents unto him that ought to be feared.

12 He shall cut off the spirit of princes : *he is* terrible to the kings of the earth.

ON the title see on titles of Psalms iv. xxx. The argument for the authorship is the same as in Ps. lxxv. Luther thinks the subject matter of this is the same as that of Ps. xlvi. Alexander thinks this had respect originally to the same historical occasion as Ps. lxxv. only that the former was a prediction, while this is a commemoration of the great event of delivering God's people. The Septuagint and many moderns refer the Psalm to the occasion of the invasion of the Assyrians under Sennacherib. Some think it refers to the victory obtained by David over the Philistines in the valley of Rephaim. The former of these views is the more probable. Neither is certain. Both Scott and Clarke date it B. C. 710. The names of the Most High in it are *Elohim God* and *Jehovah* LORD, on which respectively see on Ps. iii. 2 ; i. 2. On *Selah* see Introduction, § 15.

1. *In Judah is God known.* Tholuck: "The tribe of Judah designates the entire nation, as in Ps. cxiv. 2." Judah was a powerful tribe and the seat of political power for the whole nation. God was *known* by the whole history of the Jewish nation, by the laws and statutes he gave his people, and by the judgments he executed. *His name is great in Israel.* God's *name* is that by which he makes himself known, Ps. cxxxviii. 2. *Israel* was the fit name of Jacob as the founder of the Jewish nation. It here specially designates those who know God in prayer, who are Israel after the Spirit. "The church of true believers is now the theatre of the glory of God."

2. *In Salem also is his tabernacle.* Salem and Jerusalem are here identical. Many of the best scholars, Jewish and Christian, maintain that they are always so, though

a few ingenious writers have expressed a different opinion. The principal Scriptures cited in the discussion are Gen. xiv. 18; Josh. x. 1, 3; xviii. 28; Judges xix. 10. *Tabernacle, tent, covert, pavilion. And his dwellingplace in Zion. Dwellingplace, refuge, habitation,* is strictly parallel to *tabernacle;* as is *Zion* to *Salem.*

3. *There brake he the arrows of the bow, the shield, and the sword, and the battle.* Calvin: "The Assyrians were compelled to raise the siege by the miraculous interference of God, who in one night destroyed that army with dreadful slaughter by the hand of his angel, 2 Kings, xix. 35." To whatever event the prophet refers, the *breaking* consisted in rendering useless these weapons, and powerless the hostile array. God often did this.

4. *Thou* art *more glorious* and *excellent than the mountains of prey.* John Rogers' translation: Thou art of more honoure and myght than the hylles of robbers. *Mountains* are the figurative representations of kingdoms, and mountains of *prey* are kingdoms that practise rapine and spoliation. The figure is drawn from mountains made terrible by being inhabited by powerful animals that live on prey, Cant. iv. 8; Nah. ii. 11, 12; iii. 1. The Psalmist says that God is over and above all earthly dynasties, however exalted and terrible. Their *glory* fills a little part of this world; his fills heaven and earth. Their glory is derived and finite; his is infinite and underived. Their glory is fleeting; his is eternal. Their *excellence* may come to nought in a moment. His is unchangeable.

5. *The stouthearted are spoiled.* The Assyrians and many others invaded distant lands for prey, but instead of getting it, their treasures carried with them became a spoil to the invaded. Tholuck: "They came to the mountains of Jerusalem for prey, but they were obliged to leave prey behind them on those very mountains." All this was according to the prediction, Isa. xiv. 25. *They have slept their sleep.* "They slept, but never waked again." The *sleep* here is the sleep of death. The historic account is brief and striking: "It came to pass that night, that the angel of the LORD went out, and smote in the camp of the Assyrians an hundred and four-score and five thousand: and when they arose early in the morning, behold, they were all dead corpses," 2 Kings xix. 35. *Sleep* is more than once used in the Old Testament for death, Ps. xiii. 3; Jer. li. 39, 57; Nah. iii. 18. The *stout-hearted* fall and perish as easily as any others before the wasting pestilence. They may call themselves the lords of the world. But God often crushes them before the moth. *And none of the men of might have found their hands.* Chaldee: They could not take their weapons in their hands; Arabic: They were not able to fill their hands. Hammond thinks the sense is, They have not been able to use their hands for resistance, for offence, or even for defence. Compare 2 Chron. xxxii. 21. If this Psalm does not refer to the destruction of the Assyrian army, yet the failure of that invasion at least furnishes apt illustrations of the end of all daring schemes of wickedness, however magnificently gotten up.

6. *At thy rebuke, O God of Jacob, both the chariot and horse are cast into a dead sleep.* The *chariot* is put for those that rode in it in stateliness. The allusion to the horse teaches that either their horses were destroyed by the angel, or that their masters being dead they soon perished for want of care. The historic narrative does not mention what became of the horses, though the chariots, drawn by the horses, are mentioned, and seem to have been much trusted in. But the *God of Jacob*, the God who defended Jacob, brought all their pomp to nothing. The *dead sleep* is death. Tholuck: "The poet describes the scene, as if we were walking along with him through the camp, which so lately was so full of life, but is now silent as death."

7. *Thou,* even *thou,* art *to be feared.* The repetition of *thou* gives a sense much as if the Psalmist had said, *Thou alone. To be feared,* very commonly so rendered.

To those, who oppose God, he is *terrible*. They have good cause for trembling. *And who may stand in thy sight when once thou art angry?* This clause is parallel to the preceding. *Stand*, the opposite of *fall*, Ps. i. 5. Clarke: "In the moment thy wrath is kindled, in that moment judgment is executed."

8. *Thou didst cause judgment to be heard from heaven: the earth feared and was still.* Hammond supposes that the descent of the angel to destroy the Assyrian army was accompanied with " sensible attestations from nature, thunders and earthquakes," as when Jonathan smote the Philistine garrison, and " there was trembling in the host, in the field, and among all the people: the garrison, and the spoilers, they also trembled, and the earth quaked: so it was a very great trembling," 1 Sam. xiv. 15. The effect of the fear was *stillness*, that is, when the Assyrians were filled with fear, for a time there was peace, the land of Israel had rest. Alexander: " The last Hebrew verb is especially applied to repose after the noise and agitation of war. See Josh. xiv. 15 ; Judg. v. 31 ; Isa. xiv. 7." This remarkable effect was produced,

9. *When God arose to judgment, to save all the meek of the earth.* *To judgment, i. e.,* to execute judgment upon his foes and in behalf of his people, who are the *meek*, the *humble*, the *poor*, the afflicted of the earth.

10. *Surely the wrath of man shall praise thee.* God often overrules the wickedness of men to his own glory, as in the cruelty of Joseph's brethren, in the hardness of Pharaoh's heart, in the betrayal and crucifixion of Jesus Christ, and here in discomfiting the greatest and best equipped armies. Some think it refers to the effects of judgments on angry men themselves, bringing them to be true worshippers, Isa. xxvi. 9 ; Hos. v. 15. But the former sense is the more obvious and is commonly received. Where the wicked passions of men cannot be made conducive to God's glory, he refuses to let them loose: *The remainder of wrath shalt thou restrain.* *Remainder, remnant, residue.* *Restrain, gird, gird in*, well rendered *restrain*. Clarke: " God often so *counterworks* the evil designs of men against his cause and followers, that it turns out to their advantage, and his glory ; nor does he permit them to go to the extent of what they have *purposed*, and of what they are *able* to perform. He suffers them to do some *mischief*, but not *all* they *would* or *can* do."

11. *Vow, and pay unto the* LORD *your God.* *Vows* were either conditional or unconditional. The former were made before the benefit was received, and in the hope of making it sure. Such was Jacob's vow recorded in Gen. xxviii. 20–22. Unconditional vows were made in gratitude for mercies already received. This was the kind of vow here called for. Jehovah had wrought a great deliverance. It was right to renew promises and engagements to be his, and to serve him. These vows could not be innocently broken or forgotten ; they must be *paid*. The breach of lawful vows is accompanied with great guilt. The next clause further explains this : *Let all that be round about him bring presents unto him that ought to be feared.* Those *round about the Lord* are his worshippers, who have seen his wondrous works, and not the heathen nations around Judea. *Presents* here are votive offerings. *Unto him that ought to be feared*, in Hebrew one word, literally *to the fear, i. e., to the proper object of fear*; see Gen. xxxi. 53 ; Isa. viii. 13.

12. *He shall cut off the spirit of princes, i. e.,* of such princes as rise up against him, and persecute his church. Look at Pharaoh, Adoni-bezek, Saul, Belshazzar and Sennacherib, who soon after his flight was slain by the hands of his sons, Adrammelech and Sharezer, " as he was worshipping in the house of Nisroch his God." 2 Kings xix. 37. Alexander: " The future form of the verb includes a potential sense. He can do it when he will, and he will do it when he has occasion." He is *terrible to the kings of the earth, i. e.,* the ambitious and cruel kings, who wished to live, and rule as if there was no God to call them to account. *Terrible*, the same

form of the same word is in v. 7, rendered *to be feared*. God is known even to the heathen by the judgments, which he executeth.

DOCTRINAL AND PRACTICAL REMARKS.

1. Of vast importance to Christian comfort is the doctrine of God's unchangeableness. Cobbin: "He who miraculously defeated Sennacherib can as easily overthrow all the enemies of his church. Individual rebels must bend before him or break. Collective powers opposed to his kingdom will, in his own time, sleep the sleep of death."

2. Though it does not appear from the Psalm itself, yet from the history of the Assyrian invasion given in 2 Kings xix. 15–19, we learn that the wonderful deliverance wrought for Israel was in answer to prayer, Isa. xxxvii. Let all men pray.

3. Every people have evidence of Jehovah's being, power and Godhead; but none know him as his Church, vv. 1, 2. The innermost things of the sanctuary are the most excellent.

4. Dickson: "It is not for the worthiness of any people or place, that the Lord is among them, or manifested there; but it is his own free choice, among whom, and where he will reside. The place where the vile Canaanite had been, and the place longest possessed and abused by the Canaanite, will he choose for his chief dwellings; he will turn the Canaanites' Salem to be Jerusalem: and the stronghold of the Jebusites to be the place of his temple," v. 2.

5. The privileges of God's people under the Sinaic covenant were great; but they are much greater under the Gospel. The harmony of God's attributes was visible even then, but now it is illustrious in the cross of Christ, vv. 1, 2.

6. God has many ways of defeating the wicked, v. 3. Compare Isa. xxxvii. 29. Luther: "It is a terrible thing to kick and fight against him, who can, in a moment, take away that which is the chief thing in battle—the spirit of a man!"

7. How little is human greatness, how feeble is human strength, how marred is human worth, when compared with God's, v. 4.

8. Even the most puissant men are seen to be powerless when they fall in death, v. 5. A live dog is better than a dead lion.

9. The best appointed armies, the most magnificent warlike preparations under God's rebuke soon come to nought, v. 6.

10. It would be an unspeakable mercy to this world if it were possible to bring the minds of all its inhabitants directly and powerfully under the control of the fear of God, vv. 7, 11, 12. Morison: "Compared with the Eternal there is no object of legitimate fear in the universe. He can do whatsoever seemeth good to him. Before him no enemy can possibly stand, when once his wrath is kindled. Beneath his shadow the most inveterate and formidable foes cannot injure the objects of his unchanging love."

11. Those, who deny God's providence over this world, do yet sometimes *hear* such awful judgments of the Almighty as to make them tremble at his terrible majesty, vv. 8, 9.

12. Dickson: "When ordinary means and advertisements do not make the persecutors of the church cease, God hath extraordinary judgments from heaven whereby he will speak to his adversaries," v. 8.

13. God's *meek, lowly, afflicted* ones are safe come what will, v. 9. Even sometimes by terrible things in righteousness will he answer them and save them. Tholuck: "Believers may with unshaken confidence look at the rage of man."

14. Morison: "What an unspeakable consolation to know that the permitted oppo-

sition of the church's bitterest enemies shall contribute to her good, and that there is a voice which says to every invading foe, 'thus far shalt thou come, and no farther.'"

15. Let us be more concerned that God be glorified than that we be free from distress and suffering, v. 10. So that he is *praised* and honored, the saints have in all ages been content to endure pain, and poverty, and persecution. There is no higher wisdom given to mortals. It is an exercise of the sublimest faith. We must often wait, and give God time to work out his plans before we form a judgment of them. Some things may for a season look as if God was permitting his name, cause and people to be covered with dishonor, but when his chosen are duly tried, humbled and purified, then he will glorify himself and, in due time, his people also.

16. Whatever the malice of man may be, he is a chained lion, v. 10. Henry: "Men must never permit sin, because they cannot check it when they will; but God can."

17. There is no end to human malice and human wickedness, till the grace of God renews the heart, v. 10. Even terrible judgments falling on the wicked do not remove the "remainder of wrath."

18. Respecting vows as a part of religious worship, see on Ps. xxii. 25.

19. If there should be no other way of saving his people from cruelty, God will destroy their foes, v. 12. This he can do in the twinkling of an eye. Clarke: "Even in the midst of their conquests, he can fill them with terror and dismay, or cut them off in the career of victory." Luther: "The Almighty Warrior is our Captain. He holds in his hand the hearts and spirits of our enemies. Without arms or weapons of men, he can lay our adversaries prostrate in a moment."

20. Dickson: "The use of the Lord's deliverances of his church, which the people of God should make, is to call on God in their troubles, engage themselves to glorify him in word and deed for his mercies, and to entertain the consciousness of their obligation," v. 11.

21. Horne: "If such should have been the gratitude and devotion of Israelites, for a temporary deliverance from the fury of an earthly tyrant; how much higher ought that of Christians to rise, for eternal redemption from the great oppressor."

PSALM LXXVII.

To the chief Musician, to Jeduthun, A Psalm of Asaph.

1 I cried unto God with my voice, *even* unto God with my voice; and he gave ear unto me.

2 In the day of my trouble I sought the Lord: my sore ran in the night, and ceased not: my soul refused to be comforted.

3 I remembered God, and was troubled: I complained, and my spirit was overwhelmed. Selah.

4 Thou holdest mine eyes waking: I am so troubled that I cannot speak.

5 I have considered the days of old, the years of ancient times.

6 I call to remembrance my song in the night: I commune with mine own heart: and my spirit made diligent search.

7 Will the Lord cast off for ever? and will he be favourable no more?

8 Is his mercy clean gone for ever? doth *his* promise fail for evermore?

9 Hath God forgotten to be gracious? hath he in anger shut up his tender mercies? Selah.

10 And I said, This *is* my infirmity: *but I will remember* the years of the right hand of the Most High.

11 I will remember the works of the LORD: surely I will remember thy wonders of old.

12 I will meditate also of all thy work, and talk of thy doings.

13 Thy way, O God, *is* in the sanctuary: who *is* so great a God as *our* God!

14 Thou *art* the God that doest wonders: thou hast declared thy strength among the people.

15 Thou hast with *thine* arm redeemed thy people, the sons of Jacob and Joseph. Selah.

16 The waters saw thee, O God, the waters saw thee; they were afraid: the depths also were troubled.

17 The clouds poured out water: the skies sent out a sound: thine arrows also went abroad.

18 The voice of thy thunder *was* in the heaven: thy lightnings lightened the world: the earth trembled and shook.

19 Thy way *is* in the sea, and thy path in the great waters, and thy footsteps are not known.

20 Thou leddest thy people like a flock by the hand of Moses and Aaron.

ON the title see on titles of Psalms iv. xxxix. lxii. On the authorship see Introduction, § 4 and on Psalms l. lxxiii. lxxiv. Alexander: "If the particular historical occasion be the crisis of affairs in the reign of Josiah, the name *Asaph* must be understood as a description of the family, and not of its progenitor." But there is nothing requiring us to give the ode a connection with any special piece of history. Calvin: "Whoever was the penman of this Psalm, the Holy Spirit seems, by his mouth, to have dictated a common form of prayer for the church in her afflictions, that even under the most cruel persecutions the faithful might not fail to address their prayers to heaven." Tholuck calls it a "a melancholic song of complaint, deriving consolation from the wonderful works of God in the past." Hengstenberg: "Our Psalm is related in such a striking manner to the 3d chapter of Habakkuk, that the agreement can only be explained by the supposition that the one writer made use of the expressions of the other." Luther: "This Psalm sets forth to us God and the ways of God: that is, how he works, and what he does, in his church and in the saints." Scott admits that the date is uncertain, but favors the opinion that it was written as early as the time of David, and by that Asaph, who was his contemporary. In it we have *Elohim God, Adonai Lord, El God, Gel-yohn Most High* and *Jah* LORD, on which see on Ps. iii. 2; ii. 4; v. 4; vii. 17 and on Ps. lxviii. at the beginning. On *Selah* see Introduction, § 15.

1. *I cried unto God with my voice,* even *unto God with my voice.* The meaning is, prayed very earnestly and fervently; *q. d.,* I prayed, O I prayed earnestly. Nor was his prayer in vain: *And he gave ear unto me,* see on Ps. v. 1.

2. *In the day of my trouble I sought the Lord.* He means that he sought God's assistance and favor. He implored divine interposition. This he did in the most painful state of mind, in *trouble, affliction, adversity, distress. My sore ran in the night and ceased not.* Clarke: "This is a most unaccountable translation: the literal meaning of the words, which we translate *my sore ran,* is *my hand was stretched out, i. e.,* in prayer." This is supported by the margin, Jerome, Calvin, Piscator, Symmachus, Fabritius, Ainsworth, Hammond, Edwards, Patrick, Fry, Jebb, Scott, Tholuck and Alexander. The other renderings are generally mere interpretations and not translations. The phrase teaches that the Psalmist was importunate in prayer, and persevered in that holy exercise even in the night, when men generally seek repose in sleep. His distress was great. He was inconsolable: *My soul refused to be comforted.* When our affliction assumes such a cast that we nurse our grief, it is wrong and becomes a great tormentor. Yet grief may often be great without being sinful.

3. *I remembered God, and was troubled.* The latter verb is also rendered *mourned, made a noise, was moved, was disquieted, roared.* It expresses deep and painful agitation. Some think the meaning of the prophet is, 'Though I remembered God, yet it brought me no consolation: my grief continued.' On two occasions thoughts of God may afflict believers, *first,* when they are borne down by a sense of guilt, and fear that he is angry with them; *secondly,* when they remember how he formerly

appeared for their deliverance, but now seems to have forgotten them, and to pass over their case and their judgment. . The latter was probably the case here. Tholuck gives another turn to the thought: " There are moments in the life of every believer when God and his ways become unintelligible to them. They get lost in profound meditation, and nothing is left to them but a desponding sigh." *I complained, and my spirit was overwhelmed.* *Complained, mused, meditated;* here probably *meditated.* *My spirit,* my inmost soul. Calvin: "However much we may experience of fretting, sorrow, and disquietude, we must persevere in calling upon God even in the midst of these impediments."

4. *Thou holdest mine eyes waking.* This rendering is substantially supported by the Chaldee, church of England, Piscator, Tremellius and Junius, Fabritius, Amesius, Ainsworth, Edwards, Horsley, Green, Fry, Tholuck, Clarke, Scott and Alexander. The sense then is, ' Up to this time my grief is so great that I cannot sleep.' As the Psalmist's grief banished sleep, so did it language: *I am so troubled that I cannot speak.* Arnd: " In such troubles a man is often quite powerless, so that he cannot speak, but only thinks upon God, and hopes in him; thus his thoughts and his hope are instead of words; and God, who searches the heart, knows what is the mind of the spirit." Sometimes griefs are light and merely disturb enough to lead men to express them in colloquy, in soliloquy, or in sighs and complaints. At other times they are so overwhelming as to stun and produce silence. Nor are the feelings of God's people unvarying even under the same sad dispensation of providence. Sometimes silence is followed by prayer and lamentation; and these are sometimes followed by silence. Compare Ps. xxxii. 3. Such a state of mind, and trouble so deep would naturally arouse all the intellectual powers, especially the memory and the powers of comparison and judgment:

5. *I have considered the days of old, the years of ancient times.* *Considered, thought of, counted, reckoned.* He brought them under review. *Ancient times,* ages, perpetuities. It here means all past times. In such a review he looked for marked deliverances in cases like his own, as he also contrasted God's dealings towards himself and others on former occasions, with his present low state.

6. *I call to remembrance my song in the night.* *Call to remembrance,* the same form of the same verb rendered in v. 7 *remembered,* and in v. 11 twice, *will remember.* It is in the future, as are all the verbs of this verse. *Song,* a kind of song to be used with stringed instruments. *In the night.* He had previously seen God's mercies in a way that so impressed him as to make him give praises in the dead hours of the night. Scott: "He determined to recollect his own experience of such mercies and deliverances, as had led him to spend a part of the night in singing praises to God." *I commune with mine own heart.* *Commune,* quite as in v. 3 rendered *complained,* and in v. 12, *will talk.* On the exercise of mind thus described see on Ps. iv. 4, though the verb there used is not the same as here. *And my spirit made diligent search.* The word indicates a careful scrutiny, a searching inquiry. Three things proper to be inquired into in times of calamity are, 1, Wherefore does God thus afflict us? 2, What is our present duty? 3, When and how may we hope for deliverance? But oftentimes unbelief suggests foolish and wicked questions:

7, 8, 9. *Will the* LORD *cast off for ever? and will he be favourable no more? is his mercy clean gone for ever? doth his promise fail forevermore? hath God forgotten to be gracious? hath he in anger shut up his tender mercies?* Scott: "He was strongly tempted to conclude that God had cast him off forever, and would show him no more favor. 'But,' says he, 'can this be? Can he who was known to delight in mercy cease to be merciful? Will he break his own promise? Is he so angry as no more to pardon the penitent and pity the miserable? This cannot be. I will reject with abhorrence the dishonorable thought.'" It is one of the sorest trials, when the word or *promise* of God seems to be of none effect.

10. *And I said, This is my infirmity. Infirmity*, variously rendered as *disease, sickness, wound, desertion, affliction, petition, death, dejection.* If this clause is to stand by itself, *infirmity* is the best rendering. Some unite it with the next, But I will remember *the years of the right hand of the Most High*, and render them thus: This my affliction is a change of the right hand of the Most High. But this is not good. Anderson well gives the sense: "The Psalmist acknowledges his sin in questioning or yielding to a feeling of suspicion in reference to the divine love, and the truth of the divine promises; and confesses that this flowed from the corruption of his nature and the weakness of his faith." Good men know what a tormentor discouragement is. They flee from it. They war against it by resorting to the higher truths of religion:

11. *I will remember the works of the* LORD [*Jah.*] *Will remember*, in v. 6 *will call to remembrance.* It is found in the next clause. He would so remember God's dealings with his people of old as to meditate upon them and be encouraged by them. *Surely I will remember thy wonders of old.* History and prophecy are the two great sources of comfort to the saints. The former tells us what God has done; the latter, what he will do. To faith they both reveal wondrous things. God never changes. He is of one mind.

12. *I will meditate also of all thy work, and talk of thy doings.* The first verb is in the preterite, but may be rendered in the future as here, or it may signify 'I have long thought over God's providence. Of course I will do so now, as no other resource is left me.'

13. *Thy way, O God, is in the sanctuary.* The Chaldee, Syriac, John Rogers' translation, Bishops' Bible, church of England, Edwards and Green read, *Thy way, O God, is holy;* the Arabic, Piscator, Fabritius, Tremellius and Junius, Amesius, Houbigant, Waterland, Mudge, Horsley, Fry, Jebb, Hengstenberg and Alexander all give this sense, *Thy way, O God, is in holiness.* If this is correct, then the prophet declares that God is a God of spotless rectitude in all his ways. But many scholars favor the common rendering. Scott: "The way of God is *in holiness;* and so consists with his testimonies, his promises, and his covenant. It is 'in the sanctuary;' and being beyond the reach of man's wisdom cannot be understood, except by those who enter into the sanctuary, and weigh all things in the balances of the sanctuary;" Clarke: "I must go to the sanctuary to get *comfort*, as I went before to get *instruction*, see Ps. lxxiii. 17;" Calvin: "The word *sanctuary* is to be taken either for heaven or for the temple. I am rather inclined to refer it to heaven, conceiving the meaning to be, that the ways of God rise high above the world, so that if we are truly desirous to know them, we must ascend above all heavens." The temple was the type of heaven, and God's plans and ways were there sufficiently explained to faith, obedience, submission and consolation, though not enough to reason and curiosity. *Who is so great a God as* our *God? Our God* made this world. He has always governed it. In every conflict between the power of Jehovah and that of the gods of heathen nations the victory has always been with the Most High. Nothing can resist or defeat him. All the gods of the heathen are vanities, Ps. cxv. 2-8.

14. *Thou art the God that doest wonders.* The annals of false gods are filled with fables, and follies, and vagaries. The record of Jehovah's doings is the true history of the universe, every part of which teems with *wonders, marvels, wondrous works. Thou hast declared thy strength among the people. Declared, made known,* as the same form of the same verb is rendered in Ps. xcviii. 2. *Strength, might, power, i. e.,* effective energy. *People*, plural, *peoples, Gentiles, the nations,* Rom. i. 19, 20.

15. *Thou hast with* thine *arm redeemed thy people, the sons of Jacob and Joseph*
Pious Israelites never forgot the great deliverance from Egyptian bondage and
cruelty. They repeated it when they read the ten commandments, when they wor-
shipped in the temple, when they abode at home, and when they went abroad. The
arm is the emblem of the *strength* referred to in the preceding verse. Both *Jacob* and
Joseph are favorite names in Hebrew poetry. Either of them designates the people Israel.
The use of both of them is emphatic, designating all the people descended from Jacob.
Walford gives another reason, viz., that as the Israelites derived their birth from
Jacob, so they were sustained by Joseph in Egypt, who became to them a second
parent.

16. *The waters saw thee, O God, the waters saw thee; they were afraid: the depths
also were troubled.* Horne: "The waters of the Red sea are here beautifully represented as endued with sensibility; as seeing, feeling, and being confounded, even to
the lowest depths, at the presence and power of their great Creator, when he commanded them to open a way, and to form a wall on each side of it, until his people
were passed over." There may also be an allusion to the passage of the Jordan. But
waters and seas are also emblems of overwhelming distresses and calamities; and these
are under the control of the Almighty. At his rebuke they flee away.

17. *The clouds poured out water: the skies sent out a sound: thine arrows also went
abroad.*

18. *The voice of thy thunder* was *in the heaven: thy lightnings lightened the world:
the earth trembled and shook.* Some refer these words to all the terrible commotions
and agitations of the heavens in storms and tempests. And it is certain that God
controls all the elements, that he is the father of the rain, that the thunder is his
voice, that he sends forth the lightning like arrows. But may we not apply both
verses specially to the destruction of the Egyptians at the Red sea? Josephus says:
"As soon as the whole Egyptian army was within the Sea, it flowed to its own place,
and came down with a torrent raised by storms of wind, and encompassed the Egyptians. Showers of rain also came down from the sky, and dreadful thunders and
lightning, with flashes of fire. Thunderbolts also were darted upon them; nor
was there anything which used to be sent by God upon men, as indications of his
wrath, which did not happen at that time; for a dark and dismal night oppressed
them." See Ex. xiv. xxiv. On the phenomena of storms and tempests see on Ps. xviii.
7–16. Compare Hab. iii. 3–15.

19. *Thy way is in the sea, and thy path in the great waters, and thy footsteps are not
known.* All this was shown in the passage of the Red sea. God then led his people
in a *way* never travelled before nor since, never marked out by mortal man.

20. *Thou leddest thy people like a flock by the hand of Moses and Aaron.* Clarke:
"In the eastern countries, the shepherd does not *drive*, but *leads* his flock." Mant:
"After the sublime and awful imagery of the four preceding verses, in which thunders and lightnings, storms and tempests, rain, hail and earthquakes, the ministers of
the Almighty's displeasure, are brought together and exhibited in the most impressive
colors; nothing can be more exquisite than the calmness and tranquillity of this concluding verse, on which the mind reposes with sensations of refreshment and delight."
Num. xxxiii. 1; Ps. lxxx. 1; Mic. vi. 4.

DOCTRINAL AND PRACTICAL REMARKS.

1. Prayer should be earnest and fervent. We should *cry unto God*, v. 1. Languid
devotion, that moves not our hearts, can hardly be expected to move God.

2. Such *cries* God will hear, v. 1. He never turns away his ear from the fervor of
true faith pleading his promises.

3. Is any afflicted? let him pray, v. 2. Moaning, sighing and complaining will do no good till we lift our hearts and send our petitions on high. Henry: "Days of trouble must be days of prayer."

4. Prayer should be importunate and persevering. It should, if necessary last all *night*, v. 2. God's elect cry day and night unto him, Luke xviii. 7. Tholuck: "They are real men of prayer with whom, when answers fail to be forthcoming, the thirst for prayer gets not weakened, but inflamed with great ardor."

5. As far as possible we should control our griefs. They ought not to be immoderate. Nor ought we to refuse proper consolation, v. 2. If God offers us comfort, let us accept it thankfully.

6. It is dreadful when a remembrance of God *troubles* a believer, v. 3. It shows how sad his state is, and how feeble his faith must be. Henry: "Spiritual trouble is, of all others, most grievous to a gracious soul. Nothing wounds and pierces it like the apprehensions of God's being angry, the suspending of his favor, and the superseding of his promise."

7. In our meditations on divine things let us not venture on thoughts too deep for us, v. 3. The old enemy delights in drawing us into things too painful for us. He is a wise man, who knows the limits of his own mind.

8. Let the anxious, careworn, but humble believer remember that it is no new thing to spend sleepless nights, v. 4. Morison: "When the pressure of great calamity is felt, and when the soul is withered with burning grief, the blessing and refreshment of sleep almost forsake the wakeful sufferer." Death will give such long repose, Isa. lvii. 2.

9. It is better to be dumb than to speak foolishness—to be unable to speak at all than to utter sinful words, v. 4. "Small troubles are loquacious; the great are dumb." Often silence is the sum of our duties.

10. The right study of the history of God's dealings with ourselves or others is always useful, though it is humiliating and sometimes depressing, v. 5. Luther: "You will find that the works and doings of God from the beginning have been these,—to be merciful to and to save and help the sorrowful, the distressed, the destitute, and the afflicted; and to visit, in vengeance, the secure, the proud, the despisers, and the wicked."

11. It is a great part of heavenly wisdom to know how to make a right use of past mercies and deliverances, when God gave us *songs in the night*, v. 6. Some abuse them by so relying on them as not to care much for present experiences. Others quite forget all God has formerly done for them, and are as unbelieving as Israel after being brought through the Red sea.

12. Morison: "How necessary it is for those who would come to any right understanding why God contendeth with them, to *commune with their own heart and make diligent search*. It is only in this way that the cause of the divine chastisements can be discerned, and that the rebellious heart of man can be brought to acquiesce in the inflictions of God's paternal discipline."

13. True piety will reject the conclusions of unbelief, however they may seem supported by appearances, vv. 7–10. Cobbin: "Good men are sometimes greatly depressed. Faith is not always in lively exercise. The harp is often hung upon the willows. This is not owing to the possession of religion, but to a deficiency of it. It is the good man's *infirmity*." Unbelief says, There is no hope, there is no help even in God. Faith says, When I sit in darkness the Lord shall be a light unto me. Henry: "Despondency of spirit, and distrust of God, under affliction, are too often the infirmities of good people, and, as such, are to be reflected upon by us with sorrow and shame."

14. Good resolutions are good things, vv. 11, 12. If we ever rise to communion with God, or attain to the wisdom of the just, it will be in consequence of a solemn, deliberate purpose, made in reliance on divine grace.

15. If we would know and experience more of divine things, we must *meditate* more upon them, and upon God's methods of graciously dealing with his people. "The works of the Lord for his people have been wondrous works." We may well study them.

16. Religious conference is an important duty. We should *talk of* God's doings, not only with our hearts, but also with our friends, v. 12. Compare Mal. iii. 16, 17.

17. God never does wrong. His way is in *holiness*, v. 13. O what matter of rejoicing is this! The opposite thought would drive the saints to distraction.

18. If we would know God aright, we must study him not only in the stars, the trees, the birds, the beasts, the fishes and the flowers, but we must study him *in the Sanctuary*. There is his *way*, v. 13.

19. We must not judge the Lord by any rules we would apply to men, or even to angels. He is a God that doeth *wonders*, and so is above all creatures, v. 14.

20. The heathen are 'without excuse' for living in so gross ignorance of the glorious perfections of Jehovah, v. 14. If they liked to retain God in their knowledge, they would not be sunk down into so gross superstition.

21. If 'history is philosophy teaching by example,' church history is religion speaking by facts, and surely ought to be studied with care, vv. 15, 20.

22. All nature is subject to God. Who is more lawless, less controlled by reason than waters and lightnings, and yet they obey God, as the ox doth his driver, vv. 16–18.

23. Dickson: "The Lord draweth deep in working out the delivery and salvation of his own people, bringing them at first into extremity of danger, and then making a plain and clear escape from all their straits," v. 19. Tholuck: "The Lord of hosts has a way of his own, on which none can follow him." Our great business is to hear, obey, acquiesce, not to judge, comprehend, nor explain God's ways.

24. When God has a work to accomplish, he will be at no loss for fit instruments to bring it about. He can raise up Moses from the bulrushes, and make Aaron his brother eloquent, v. 20.

25. Horne: "Give us, O blessed Lord Jesus, those meek and lowly and teachable dispositions which become the sheep of thy pasture; set over us skilful and watchful shepherds, and be thou ever both with them and with us: until having surmounted all difficulties and dangers, led by thy grace, and supported by thy providence, we all come, in perfect safety, to the land of everlasting rest, there to live with thee, one fold under one Shepherd, world without end."

PSALM LXXVIII.

Maschil of Asaph.

1 Give ear, O my people, *to* my law: incline your ears to the words of my mouth.

2 I will open my mouth in a parable: I will utter dark sayings of old:

3 Which we have heard and known, and our fathers have told us.

4 We will not hide *them* from their children, showing to the generation to come the praises of the LORD, and his strength, and his wonderful works that he hath done.

5 For he established a testimony in Jacob, and appointed a law in Israel, which he commanded our fathers, that they should make them known to their children:

6 That the generation to come might know *them, even,* the children *which* should be born; *who* should arise and declare *them* to their children:

7 That they might set their hope in God, and not forget the works of God, but keep his commandments:

8 And might not be as their fathers, a stubborn and rebellious generation; a generation *that* set not their heart aright, and whose spirit was not steadfast with God.

9 The children of Ephraim, *being* armed, *and* carrying bows, turned back in the day of battle.

10 They kept not the covenant of God, and refused to walk in his law;

11 And forgat his works, and his wonders that he had showed them.

12 Marvellous things did he in the sight of their fathers, in the land of Egypt, *in* the field of Zoan.

13 He divided the sea, and caused them to pass through; and he made the waters to stand as a heap.

14 In the daytime also he led them with a cloud, and all the night with a light of fire.

15 He clave the rocks in the wilderness, and gave *them* drink as *out of* the great depths.

16 He brought streams also out of the rock, and caused waters to run down like rivers.

17 And they sinned yet more against him by provoking the Most High in the wilderness.

18 And they tempted God in their heart by asking meat for their lust.

19 Yea, they spake against God; they said, Can God furnish a table in the wilderness?

20 Behold, he smote the rock, that the waters gushed out, and the streams overflowed; can he give bread also? can he provide flesh for his people?

21 Therefore the Lord heard *this,* and was wroth: so a fire was kindled against Jacob, and anger also came up against Israel;

22 Because they believed not in God; and trusted not in his salvation:

23 Though he had commanded the clouds from above, and opened the doors of heaven,

24 And had rained down manna upon them to eat, and had given them of the corn of heaven.

25 Man did eat angel's food: he sent them meat to the full.

26 He caused an east wind to blow in the heaven: and by his power he brought in the south wind.

27 He raineth flesh also upon them as dust, and feathered fowls like as the sand of the sea:

28 And he let *it* fall in the midst of their camp, round about their habitations.

29 So they did eat, and were well filled: for he gave them their own desire;

30 They were not estranged from their lust: but while their meat *was* yet in their mouths,

31 The wrath of God came upon them, and slew the fattest of them, and smote down the chosen *men* of Israel.

32 For all this they sinned still, and believed not for his wondrous works.

33 Therefore their days did he consume in vanity, and their years in trouble.

34 When he slew them, then they sought him: and they returned and inquired early after God.

35 And they remembered that God *was* their rock, and the high God their redeemer.

36 Nevertheless they did flatter him with their mouth, and they lied unto him with their tongues.

37 For their heart was not right with him, neither were they steadfast in his covenant.

38 But he, *being* full of compassion, forgave *their* iniquity, and destroyed *them* not: yea, many a time turned he his anger away, and did not stir up all his wrath.

39 For he remembered that they *were but* flesh; a wind that passeth away, and cometh not again.

40 How oft did they provoke him in the wilderness, *and* grieve him in the desert!

41 Yea, they turned back and tempted God, and limited the Holy One of Israel.

42 They remembered not his hand, *nor* the day when he delivered them from the enemy:

43 How he had wrought his signs in Egypt, and his wonders in the field of Zoan:

44 And had turned their rivers into blood; and their floods, that they could not drink.

45 He sent divers sorts of flies among them, which devoured them; and frogs, which destroyed them.

46 He gave also their increase unto the caterpillar, and their labour unto the locust.

47 He destroyed their vines with hail, and their sycamore trees with frost.

48 He gave up their cattle also to the hail, and their flocks to hot thunderbolts.

49 He cast upon them the fierceness of his anger, wrath, and indignation, and trouble, by sending evil angels *among them.*

50 He made a way to his anger; he spared not their soul from death, but gave their life over to the pestilence;

51 And smote all the firstborn in Egypt; the chief of *their* strength in the tabernacles of Ham:

52 But made his own people to go forth like sheep, and guided them in the wilderness like a flock.

53 And he led them on safely, so that they feared not: but the sea overwhelmed their enemies.

54 And he brought them to the border of his sanctuary, *even to* this mountain, *which* his right hand had purchased.

55 He cast out the heathen also before them, and divided them an inheritance by line, and made the tribes of Israel to dwell in their tents.

56 Yet they tempted and provoked the most high God, and kept not his testimonies:

57 But turned back, and dealt unfaithfully like their fathers: they were turned aside like a deceitful bow.

58 For they provoked him to anger with their high places, and moved him to jealousy with their graven images.

59 When God heard *this*, he was wroth, and greatly abhorred Israel:

60 So that he forsook the tabernacle of Shiloh, the tent *which* he placed among men;

61 And delivered his strength into captivity, and his glory into the enemy's hand.

62 He gave his people over also unto the sword; and was wroth with his inheritance.

63 The fire consumed their young men; and their maidens were not given to marriage.

64 Their priests fell by the sword; and their widows made no lamentation.

65 Then the Lord awaked as one out of sleep, *and* like a mighty man that shouteth by reason of wine.

66 And he smote his enemies in the hinder parts: he put them to a perpetual reproach.

67 Moreover he refused the tabernacle of Joseph, and chose not the tribe of Ephraim:

68 But chose the tribe of Judah, the mount Zion which he loved.

69 And he built his sanctuary like high *palaces*, like the earth which he hath established for ever.

70 He chose David also his servant, and took him from the sheepfolds:

71 From following the ewes great with young he brought him to feed Jacob his people, and Israel his inheritance.

72 So he fed them according to the integrity of his heart; and guided them by the skilfulness of his hands.

ON *Maschil* see on title of Ps. xxxii. The Arabic calls this poem A Sermon of Asaph to the people. On the authorship see Introduction, § 4, on Psalms l. lxxiii.–lxxvii. Clarke thinks it was written " after the separation of the ten tribes of Israel; and after the days of Rehoboam, and before the Babylonish captivity." Scott says, " it is probable that Asaph wrote it some time after the death of David. As nothing is referred to, later than David's advancement to the throne, and his subsequent conduct, there is no ground for supposing that it was written at a much later period." There seems to be no good reason for supposing, with Calmet, that it commemorates the events occurring in the days of Asa, and noticed in 2 Chron. xv. xvi. Alexander gives it an earlier date than Scott, and thinks it may have been written before David " was acknowledged by the whole race of Israel, 2 Sam. v. 5." Hengstenberg is probably correct in giving the *famous* Asaph as the author. The general design of the ode is to *give instruction*. This is done; 1, by a succinct rehearsal of God's mercies to Israel; 2, by recounting the ingratitude and disobedience of ancient Israel; 3, by giving fit and earnest warnings; and 4, by giving solemn and seasonable exhortations. The doctrine of the divine sovereignty in exalting Judah above Ephraim, and David above all others in Israel is also clearly stated. We have here four names of the Almighty, *Jehovah* LORD, *El God*, *Elohim God* and *Gel-yohn Most High*, on which respectively see on Ps. i. 2; v. 4; iii. 2; vii. 17.

1. *Give ear, O my people, to my law*. The speaker here is the prophet, not God. In many cases the righteous claim a special interest in God's people, as their own, Judg. xii. 2; xiv. 3; Ruth i. 16; 1 Chron. xxviii. 2; Ps. cxliv. 2. It is an affection-

ate mode of address. There has always been a recognized unity among God's people. They are members of the same body, fellow-heirs of the same kingdom. A reference to Prov. iii. 1; iv. 2; vii. 2, shows that it is not unusual for inspired teachers to apply the phrase *my law* to their own instructions, just as Paul calls the Gospel *my Gospel,* 2 Tim. ii. 8. *Law;* it occurs more than *two hundred* times, and is uniformly rendered. The Arabic reads *my precepts;* Calvin, Diodati and Ainsworth think it means *my doctrine.* It is best rendered *law.* It was of binding force. *Incline your ears to the words of my mouth.* Because they were right words, solemn words, words of truth and soberness, the words of God, he claims eager attention to them, Ps. x. 17.

2. *I will open my mouth in a parable.* By *parable,* Calvin understands "grave and striking sentences, such as adages, or proverbs, or apothegms." It comes from a verb, which signifies to *reign,* to *bear rule,* to *have power.* Here it has much the same significance as the word rendered *law* in v. 1. The matters to be presented were of great weight and worthy of good heed. They should be delivered in few words, and those well chosen. This ode embodies the substance of the eventful history of the Israelites for a long time. *I will utter dark sayings of old.* For *dark sayings* the Chaldee, Calvin and Jebb have *enigmas;* Syriac, *parables;* Arabic, *mysteries;* Septuagint, Vulgate, Ethiopic and Doway, *propositions;* Ainsworth, *hid things;* Street, *pointed truths;* Edwards, *weighty truths;* Green, *dark truths;* Hengstenberg and Alexander, *riddles.* In the English Bible the word is eight times rendered *riddle,* once *proverb,* once *dark saying,* (in the plural) once *dark speeches,* once *dark sentences* and twice *dark sayings.*

3. *Which we have heard and known, and our fathers have told us.* The matter is not new; but the summing up is new. The law required a careful and frequent recital of divine doings and teachings by the aged to the young, Deut. iv. 9; vi. 6–9.

4. *We will not hide them from their children, showing to the generation to come the praises of the* LORD, *and his strength, and his wonderful works that he hath done. Children,* literally *sons. Strength, might. Wonderful works,* in Ps. ix. *marvellous works;* in Ps. lxxv. 1, *wondrous works.* The things, of which the prophet was about to speak, were not fables, nor human inventions. They were not only written in the sacred books, but were woven into the history and traditions of the whole nation.

5. *For he established a testimony in Jacob. Testimony,* commonly so rendered, or *witness,* see on Ps. xix. 7. God gave his law and his ordinances to Israel that the nation might to all the earth witness of the truth. *And* [he] *appointed a law in Israel, which he commanded our fathers, that they should make them known to their children. Law,* as in v. 1.

6. *That the generation to come might know them,* even *the children* which *should be born,* who *should arise and declare them to their children. Children,* in each case *sons.* The rule was, The father to the sons, the elder to the younger shall make known the words and works of Jehovah. See Gen. xviii. 19; Isa. lix. 21; 2 Tim. iii. 15. All this was not done for the sake of pomp or ceremony, but,

7. *That they might set their hope in God. They,* i. e., both fathers and children, each successive generation. The sin and misery of man is that he has hope in himself, in the creature, in vanity, in a thing of nought. The end of all sound religious instruction is to withdraw the desires and expectations from all finite things and to raise them to God alone. *And not forget the works of God.* If all our expectation is from God and is built on the history of his mercy to those, who have gone before us, and on his *testimony,* we cannot easily *forget* him or his doings. *But keep his commandments.* Practice is the life of piety. All true religion is practical. The great design of the Mosaic dispensation was not to increase the national glory of Israel; but to teach the people obedience to God's will, and so to secure to them temporal and

eternal good through Jesus Christ.   All God's wonders were made known to successive generations that they might do these things:

8. *And might not be as their fathers, a stubborn and rebellious generation; a generation that set not their heart aright, and whose spirit was not steadfast with God.*   *Stubborn,* also rendered *revolting, revolters, backsliding, rebellious.*   *Rebellious,* in vv. 17, 40, 56 rendered *provoking;* in 1 Kings xiii. 21, *disobedient.*   *Aright,* also rendered *right, fashioned, prepared, made ready, established, ordered, fixed.*   See on Ps. li. 10; .lvii. 7.   *Steadfast, faithful.*   Calvin enumerates the four sins mentioned in this verse as 'apostacy, provocation, treachery and hypocrisy.'   The history of the generation of Israelites, that came out of Egypt is so full of unfaithfulness, murmuring and rebellion that to this day it is for a profound and inexplicable wonder.

9. *The children of Ephraim, being armed, and carrying bows, turned back in the day of battle.*   We have no historic account of any particular act of cowardice and shameful retreat on the part of the tribe of Ephraim, though some think this place records the fact.   But many regard *Ephraim* in this case as designating all the tribes, because Ephraim was a very numerous and powerful tribe, and because the ark of the covenant, in the time of the judges, was kept at Shiloh in the bounds of that tribe.   This explanation is accompanied with so few difficulties, and the contrary with so many, that a large number of the best commentators speak very confidently.   Numbers xiv. and Josh. vii. record sad defeats to the Israelites.   The books of Joshua and Judges both show how slow the Israelites were to take full possession of the land given them.   To be *armed with bows* was to be well equipped.   For those thus prepared for battle to turn back was an act of disgraceful cowardice and gross unbelief.

10. *They kept not the covenant of God, and refused to walk in his law.*   How faithless and disobedient the Israelites were, in all their history, is declared by their own prophets.   Their early history was no exception.

11. *And [they] forgat his worship, and his wonders that he had shewed them.*   A deliverance seemed only to be made an occasion of denying God's power and mercy so soon as any new difficulty arose.   The levity, childishness and stubbornness of the nation brought out of Egypt, because described by an inspired writer, seem to us without a parallel.   But would not our own behaviour, if justly recorded, appear in even a worse light?

12. *Marvellous things did he in the sight of their fathers, in the land of Egypt, in the field of Zoan.*   The *marvellous things* of this verse are the *wonders* of v. 11.   Scott: " Zoan was a principal city of Egypt, in which perhaps Pharaoh kept his court."   It was the centre from which went forth the plagues, which are well called *wonders.*   Alexander: " Zoan was by the Greeks called Tanis, and was the ancient capitol of Lower Egypt."   Clarke: " It was situated in the *Delta,* on one of the most easterly branches of the Nile."   Tholuck: " In its place there remains to the present day the village of *San.*"   Some think Zoan is synonymous with *Egypt,* as the name of the place where the government is located often designates the whole land.   After the plagues, came the marvellous passage of the Red sea:

13. *He divided the sea, and caused them to pass through; and he made the waters to stand as a heap.*   See on Ps. lxxvii. 16.   Calvin: " The order of nature was reversed when the waters stopped in their course, and were even raised up into solid heaps like mountains."   See Ex. xv. 8; Josh. iii. 13; Ps. xxxiii. 7; Hab. iii. 15.

14. *In the daytime also he led them with a cloud, and all the night with a light of fire.*   See Ex. xiii. 21, 22.   That pillar of glory was the emblem of the divine presence and providence.   It has not before been noticed in the Psalms.   But it is spoken of in Ps. xcix. 7 where we learn that God's voice was sometimes heard from that excellent glory; and in Ps. cv. 39, where we learn that in the daytime the cloud was *for a covering.*

Here it is said to have been a light all night. In both respects it must have been a great comfort, perhaps more, a necessity. It is not necessary for us to know the precise appearance of this pillar either by day or by night. The centre of this cloud or fire rose up towards heaven in the form of a column; but to what height we know not. The Scriptures give no minute account of it. Towards his people it had a bright side, but towards his enemies dark, Ex. xiv. 19, 20. The prophet next refers to the miraculous supply of water:

15. *He clave the rocks in the wilderness and gave* them *drink as out of the great depths.*

16. *He brought streams also out of the rock, and caused waters to run down like rivers.* See Ex. xvii. 1–7; Num. xx. 1–13. Allusions to the same thing are found in Ps. cv. 41; cxiv. 8. The spiritual signification of such wonders is well expressed in Isa. xli. 18; xliii. 20; John vii. 37; 1 Cor. x. 4; Rev. xxii. 1, 17. All this gushing forth of water prefigured the blessings secured by the Mediator. "The rock that followed them was Christ." To modern travellers a particular rock is sometimes shown, with the statement that it was one of the rocks, smitten by Moses, that yielded water to the Israelites. But of this there is no certainty, although appearances are said to favor the supposition. *Wilderness*, found also in vv. 19, 40, 52, often rendered *desert*. See on Ps. xxix. 8; lxxv. 6. Marvellous as were God's mercies, they had but little effect for good:

17. *And they sinned yet more against him by provoking the Most High in the wilderness.* The special reference seems to be to Ex. xvii. 7, although the words suit many acts in the history of that wonderful people. *Provoking*, in v. 8 the same word is rendered *rebellious;* in v. 56, *provoked.* Alexander: "The very means, which should have made them more obedient, made them more rebellious." None but Jehovah could help or save in that great *desert* through which they were passing.

18. *And they tempted God in their heart by asking meat for their lust.* Brown: "Men *tempt God* when they unseasonably and irreverently require proofs of his presence, power and goodness; when they expose themselves to danger from which they cannot escape without the miraculous interposition of his providence; and when they sin with such boldness as if they would try whether God could or would know and punish sin, Ex. xvii. 2; Matt. iv. 7; Mal. iii. 15; Acts v. 9." The form of *tempting* here noticed, consisted in 'requiring unnecessary proof of what should have been promptly believed.' Further *trial* may be necessary to evince human character, but not divine excellence. God has abundantly shown in his works of creation, providence and grace, in nature and in revelation what he is and what he will do. They tempted God *in their heart, i. e.,* in the fountain of all moral conduct. Sin is first *conceived*, then *brought forth. For their lust,* literally for *their souls,* meaning that they said they could not support *life* without it, or that they wished it for the gratification of the inordinate desires of their *will,* as the same word is rendered in Ps. xli. 2, or for their *pleasure,* as we have it in Ps. cv. 2. Anderson thinks the word means "*the sensitive or animal appetites.*" Calvin: "The sin with which the Israelites were chargeable consisted in this, that not content with the food which God had appointed them, they gave loose reins to their lust," Ex. xvi. 2; Nu. xi. 4; 1 Cor. x. 6; Jas. iv. 2, 3.

19. *Yea, they spake against God; they said, Can God furnish a table in the wilderness?* They limited the Almighty, as the phrase is in v. 41. How they spake against God is told us in Nu. xi. 4. How great this sin is may be seen from 2 Chron. xxxii. 19; Job xxxiv. 37; Rom. ix. 20; Rev. xiii. 6. Alexander: "The unreasonableness of the doubt is aggravated by the use of a divine name [El] which implies omnipotence. As if they had said, Can he do this, who can do everything?"

20. *Behold, he smote the rock, that the waters gushed out, and the streams overflowed.* If this composition is constructed, as some think, with careful attention to the chrono-

logical order of events, then the sole reference is probably to Nu. xx. 11. In that case verse 15 refers solely to Ex. xvii. 1–7. But there is nothing gained by excluding allusion to both miracles in each verse. The people were unbelieving about everything. One miracle for their relief seemed only to awaken distrust of God's power and goodness in another matter, and they said, *Can he give bread also? can he provide flesh for his people?* *Bread*, commonly so rendered, sometimes *meat, food, loaves, victuals.* See Ps. xiv. 4; xlii. 3. Used specifically, it signifies what we mean by *bread*. *Flesh*, found also in v. 27; also rendered *food* in Ex. xxi. 10. When specific, it signifies *animal* not *vegetable* substance. They say: "He has given us water; but can he give us bread or meat?"

21. *Therefore the* LORD *heard* this, *and was wroth: so a fire was kindled against Jacob, and anger also came up against Israel.* See Num. xi. 1–15. *Jacob* and *Israel* are both names for the whole body of the people. See Ps. xiv. 7. God was not angry without cause. As a judge *hears* a matter before he pronounces sentence, so God *heard* the whole matter of these complaints, had 'full and perfect knowledge' of their criminality. In both Testaments *fire* is an emblem of the consuming wrath of God. See on Ps. xi. 6; l. 3. Compare Matt. iii. 10; xviii. 8. Whether there was an actual bursting forth of flame, and if so, whether it had an unusual appearance, or whether the fire was the invisible consuming curse of God, we need not decide. The curse was the fire, whether visible or not. Tholuck: "The fire was a real fire." Scott: "Probably some of them were destroyed, as Nadab and Abihu had been, by fire from the Lord, or by flashes of lightning, perhaps from the fiery pillar." The place was called *Taberah, a Burning.* All this came upon them for their murmurings, which sprang from a discontented mind, which sprang from unbelief:

22. *Because they believed not in God, and trusted not in his salvation.* The great sin of the world in all ages has been want of faith in God's power, goodness and veracity. Without faith it is impossible to please God, or to be pleased with God. If he cannot be believed, he cannot be trusted; and so misery and guilt will mark the course of the unfaithful. That their unbelief was not cured is the more remarkable:

23. *Though he had commanded the clouds from above, and opened the doors of heaven,*

24. *And had rained down manna upon them to eat, and had given them of the corn of heaven.*

25. *Man did eat angels' food: he sent them meat to the full.*

Of the manna we know no more than the Bible tells us, especially in Ex. xvi. 4–35; Num. xi. 7–9. That it was very suitable food is certain, for it was prepared and sent by God in love, and as an emblem of the food and life sinners should find in God's dear Son, John vi. 29–58; 1 Cor. x. 3. To *open the doors* or *gates of heaven* signifies the same as *opening the windows of heaven* in Mal. iii. 10. It denotes the pouring out of a great blessing, heavenly in its origin. The manna was *rained*, Ex. xvi. 4. It is called *corn* because it was found in grains, as wheat is. It is called corn *of heaven*, because it came from above. Cruden: "It is called *angels' food*, which may insinuate either that it was made and prepared by their ministry; or that angels themselves, if they had need of any food, could not have any that was more agreeable than *manna* was; it being of heavenly original, and of singular vigor and efficacy for preserving and nourishing those who used it according to God's appointment: *Or,* as it is in the margin, *every one did eat the bread of the mighty;* that is, even the common Israelites fed upon it as delicious food, as the greatest nobles and princes did." *Angels*, never elsewhere so rendered, but *mighty ones, strong ones.* The word usually rendered *angels* signifies *messengers.* But the angels are *mighty ones*, (they excel in strength, Ps. ciii. 20,) and so our version probably gives the sense. The Chaldee: Men ate the food which descended from the habitation of angels. The ancient versions all lend their authority to our English translation; but modern scholars very generally prefer *mighty ones* to *angels*. *Meat*, the word so rendered occurs *ten* times in the Hebrew Bible. In Gen. xxvii. 3, it is rendered *venison;* in Gen. xlii. 25; xlv. 21, it is rendered *provision;* it is *six* times rendered *victual*, or *victuals;* in this place only, *meat*. The corresponding noun is *hunter*, so that the primary signification of the word nearly corresponds to our English word *game*. The quails sent were usually taken in hunting.

26. *He caused an east wind to blow in the heaven: and by his power he brought in the south wind.* Often in Scripture is the stormy wind said to be caused and also allayed by God, Gen. viii. 1; Ex. xv. 10; 1 Kings xix. 11; Ps. cxxxv. 7; cxlvii. 18; Isa. xxvii. 8. *East wind*, see on Ps. xlviii. 7. *South wind*, not elsewhere found in the Psalms, literally *south*, meaning the *south wind* here, as also in Cant. iv. 16. These winds brought the abundance of fowls mentioned in the verses following.

27. *He rained flesh also upon them as dust, and feathered fowls like as the sand of the sea:*

28. *And he let it fall in the midst of their camp, round about their habitations.*

29. *So they did eat and were well filled: for he gave them their own desire.* *Rained*, as in v. 24. Like the rain it came from over their heads, and it fell abundantly. The historic record is in Ex. xvi. 12, 13; and especially in Num. xi. 31–34. The least quantity of fowls gathered by any man was ten homers, over ninety bushels. For two whole days and a whole night the people gathered flesh. The fowls were piled up more than three feet deep around the camp to the distance of a day's journey in every direction. This Psalm does not determine whether the flesh they had was all of one kind, but in Ex. xvi.; Num. xi.; Ps. cv. we are told that *quails* were sent; the word so rendered is thought to describe a species. *Habitations, dwelling-places, tabernacles*. *Well filled*, full, filled, satisfied, satiate. They ate till they could eat no more, till they had the object of their *desire*, their *greediness*, their *lust*, to the full. Yet

30. *They were not estranged from their lust.* *Estranged*, alienated, i. e., weaned. *Lust*, same as *desire* in v. 29; only here it means the wicked lust itself, and not the object of it. *But while their meat was* yet in *their mouths*,

31. *The wrath of God came upon them, and* slew *the fattest of them, and smote down the chosen* men *of Israel*. The place where all this happened was well called *Kibroth-hattaavah, i. e., the graves of lust*. The manner of destruction is described in v. 21. *Fattest* of them, literally the *fatness* of them, meaning the most luxurious, those who most pandered to their own appetites, and most pampered their flesh. *Chosen*, often also rendered *young*, because such were selected to go forth to war, those, who would have been selected as the best specimens of health and vigor.

32. *For all this they sinned still.* *For*, rather *in*, or *after*, or *in respect to*. *Sinned*, offended, trespassed. They went on sinning, *and believed not for his wondrous works*. That is, even his great *wonders*, or *miracles* did not bring them to believe. Neither *speculative atheism*, nor *atheism of heart*, nor *practical atheism* was ever cured by miracle, because they are all found in a wicked disposition. "Men are not always in a mood to be convinced." It is not want of evidence, but the want of right dispositions that keeps men from believing God.

33. *Therefore their days did he consume in vanity, and their years in trouble.* The great fact, that *forty years* were spent in accomplishing the journey of a few days, and that when Israel was on the verge of the promised land, they were required to begin new and painful wanderings for nearly *two-fifths* of a century, forcibly illustrates this verse. Patrick: "Though they travelled up and down, very much and very long, yet it was to no purpose; for they were never nearer to their journey's end; nor were ever free from one plague or other, till they (that generation) were utterly destroyed." *Vanity*, emptiness, fruitlessness. *Trouble*, terror; see Lev. xxvi. 16.

34. *When he slew them, then they sought him: and they returned and inquired early after God.* It is according to fallen human nature to be very gracious when the pangs are upon us, Jer. xxii. 23; but when suffering is over, or judgments are averted, we soon relapse into former carelessness and unbelief, unless we have special grace given us. The awful death of some was well suited to beget awe in the minds of their wicked companions. It showed them that they had to deal with *omnipotence.* For a short time a sore judgment had some effect. They *returned* from their open rebellion, but they did not *return unto the Lord their God,* Hos. vii. 10. They *sought, searched, inquired,* yea, to the eye of man they seemed to *inquire, seek early, betimes, diligently,* literally *in the morning;* but there was no thorough moral revolution effected in their characters:

35. *And they remembered that God was their rock, and the high God their redeemer.* They were overwhelmingly convinced in their judgments and intellects, as they had often been, and now called to remembrance how they had often yielded assent to the truth that God was their *rock, strength, strong-hold;* see on Ps. xviii. 2. In the last clause we have three names of God. *Redeemer,* see on Ps. xix. 14.

36. *Nevertheless they did flatter him with their mouth, and they lied unto him with their tongues.* They did not honestly intend to fulfil their promises. They engaged to do enough; but they did nothing. Deceit underlaid all their religious acts. How often they did this their history shows:

37. *For their heart was not right with him, neither were they steadfast in his covenant. Right, prepared, fixed, established;* see on Ps. li. 10. *Steadfast, faithful, established.* They did not take firm hold of the covenant. They were not true to their engagements. See on Ps. xxv. 10.

38. *But he,* being *full of compassion,* forgave their *iniquity, and destroyed* them *not: yea, many a time turned he his anger away, and did not stir up all his wrath. Full of compassion,* in Hebrew one word, several times rendered as here, more frequently *merciful. Forgave,* in Hebrew the verb is in the future, but is best rendered in the preterite; elsewhere rendered *pardon, purge, reconcile,* more commonly *make atonement.* Here the meaning is that he so overlooked their evil conduct as not utterly to *destroy* them as a nation, or people. *Many a time,* literally *he multiplied,* as in the margin of Isa. lv. 7; or, as in the English text of that place, he did it *abundantly. Anger,* in Ps. ii. 5, *wrath;* see on Ps. xviii. 7. *Wrath, fury, hot displeasure;* see on Ps. vi. 1.

39. *For he remembered that they* were but *flesh; a wind that passeth away, and cometh not again.* A striking parallel passage is found in Ps. ciii. 14–16. Alexander: " *Flesh,* a common Scriptural expression for humanity or human nature, as distinguished from superior beings, and especially from God." *Wind,* by some rendered *breath,* by others *spirit.* Clarke much prefers the latter: *The spirit goeth away, and it doth not return.* He argues earnestly for it. The sense is the same whether we use *wind, breath,* or *spirit;* only if we read *wind,* or *breath,* we use a figure; if we read *spirit,* we speak plainly.

40. *How oft did they provoke him in the wilderness, and grieve him in the desert!* Their history was filled with the records of great mercies, great wickedness and terrible judgments. Cresswell: " They provoked God at least ten times, (Num. xiv. 22,) during the first two years of their journey through the wilderness: 1. At the Red sea, (Ex. xiv. 11, 12;) 2. At the waters of Marah, (Ex. xv. 24;) 3. In the wilderness of Sin, (Ex. xvi. 2;) 4. When they kept the manna until the following day, (Ex. xvi. 20;) 5. When the manna was collected on the Sabbath, (Ex. xvi. 27;) 6. In Rephidim, where there was no water, (Num. xx. 2, 13;) 7. At Horeb, when a molten calf was made, (Ex. xxxii. 1, etc.;) 8. At Taberah, (Num. xi. 1, 2, 3;) 9. When they lusted for flesh, (Num. xi. 4;) 10. When they murmured at the news brought by the

men who had been sent to search the land, (Num. xiv. 1, etc.)" These outbursts of wickedness were signs of what was going on in their hearts all the time. *Wilderness* and *desert* are here used interchangeably, although in Hebrew they are different words, the former not uniformly implying sterility, as the latter. *Provoke, rebel against,* as in vv. 8, 17. *Grieve,* elsewhere *displease, vex,* 1 Kings i. 6; Isa. lxiii. 10. See on Ps. lvi. 5.

41. *Yea, they turned back* from their engagements, from their temporary reformations, from God, from his law, from his service. They returned to their former evil ways. *And tempted God,* see on v. 18. *And limited the Holy One of Israel. Limited,* the Hebrew word signifies to *set marks.* They questioned whether he could do all things. They refused to believe in his infinite perfections and providence, unless he would do all things according to their plan. In short, they thought the Almighty very much such an one as themselves, Ps. l. 21. *Holy One of Israel,* see on Psalm lxxi. 22.

42. *They remembered not his hand,* nor *the day when he delivered them from the enemy.* All sin disinclines the mind to retain the memory of God's nature and ways; so that *forgetfulness of God* is a synonyme for wickedness. *Enemy,* also *adversary,* but more commonly rendered *trouble, tribulation, distress, anguish, affliction;* especially denoting trouble caused by foes. Calvin thinks the *enemy* is Pharaoh. The reference seems to be to the afflicted condition of Israel in Egypt.

43. *How he had wrought his signs in Egypt, and his wonders in the field of Zoan. Signs, marks, tokens, miracles,* often as here followed by *wonders.* See on Ps. lxxiv. 4, 9. On *Zoan,* see on v. 12. Here begins an enumeration of the plagues of Egypt.

44. *And had turned their rivers into blood; and their floods that they could not drink.* The record of this plague is in Ex. vii. 19–25. See also Ps. cv. 29. This plague lasted seven days. All the running water of the land was corrupted.

45. *He sent divers sorts of flies among them, which devoured them.* For *divers sorts of flies* the Chaldee has *mixtures of living creatures of the wood;* other ancient versions Venema and Alexander, the *dog-fly,* or *dog-flies;* Calvin, *a mixture;* Ainsworth, *a mixed swarm;* Piscator, Fabritius and Edwards, *a swarm of insects;* Amesius, Tremellius and Junius, *a pest of animals;* Bythner, *a mixed collection of beasts;* Fry, *the fly;* Morison, *pernicious and destructive insects;* Walford, *the horse-fly;* Mant, *the ravening fly;* Hengstenberg, *vermin;* Tholuck, *mosquitoes.* Hammond: "The word, I suppose, comprehends all creatures of equivocal generation, which so frequently change from reptile, and back again." Alexander: "The best interpreters are now agreed that it means the Egyptian dog-fly." Of dog-flies Philo says: "They rest not until they have satisfied themselves with blood and flesh." Schafer: "The dog-fly gorges itself with blood, and makes bloody boils, severe pains." Anderson thinks it was the Ethiopian fly, called Zimb. Bruce says: "As soon as this plague appears, and their buzzing is heard, all the cattle forsake their food, and run wildly about the plain, till they die, worn out with fatigue, fright and hunger. No remedy remains but to leave the black earth and hasten down to the sands of Atbara; and there they remain, while the rains last, this cruel enemy not daring to pursue them further." Whatever creatures were intended, they were great tormentors and fatal to life. They *devoured.* Scott: "This word, *devoured,* shows that, besides the loathsomeness of flies, and their maggots; a variety of venomous insects, reptiles, or animals, were sent among the Egyptians, to bite, and sting, and harass them; and that in many instances their bite or sting was mortal." Every warm climate abounds with pernicious flies and insects. In this, Africa excels. Every traveller has his tale to tell of noisome insects. The last is no exception. Du Chaillu (p. 321.:) "We were troubled on the prairie by two very savage flies, called by the negroes the

boco and the *nchauna*. These insects attacked us with a terrible persistency which left us no peace." The historic record of this plague is in Ex. viii. 20–24, where the word *flies* is in every case supplied by our translators. *And frogs, which destroyed them.* Frogs, in our English Bible and in all the ancient versions uniformly rendered. The word signifies generally all kinds of frogs and toads, some of which are said to be venomous. How terrible this plague was may be seen from the record in Ex. viii. 1–15. The frogs came into every Egyptian house, and bed-chamber, and bed, and oven, and kneading-trough. See also Ps. cv. 30. The vast quantities of these creatures, besides tormenting all human beings by their invasion of every place, became, when they died, the means of poisoning the air with putrid animal matter.

46. *He gave also their increase unto the caterpillar.* Caterpillar, always so rendered in our version. It signifies *devourer*, because these creatures consumed every green thing. Anderson: " We are so little acquainted with the various kinds of destructive insects that ravage eastern countries, that it is somewhat difficult to determine the particular species meant by this term. It is distinguished from the locust in Solomon's prayer at the dedication of the temple, 2 Chron. vi. 28, and in Joel i. 4, where it is mentioned as eating up what the locust had left." We find no record of a plague of *caterpillar* separate from that of the *locust*. *And their labor unto the locust.* If the *devourer* was the *locust;* then the latter clause explains the former. Compare Ex. x. 13–15. See on Ps. cv. 34, 35. *Locust*, as in Ex. x. 4, 12, 13, 14, 19. It is sometimes rendered *grasshopper*, these creatures being generically the same. Anderson: " The locust receives no fewer than ten different names in Scripture, each of which indicates something characteristic. The name here given is from its fecundity. No animal is more prolific." Alexander: " Both the animal names in this verse are really designations of the locust, one meaning the *devourer*, and the other denoting the vast numbers of that insect."

47. *He destroyed their vines with hail.* See Ex. ix. 22–35; Ps. cv. 33. *Vines*, always so rendered. *Hail*, see on Ps. xviii. 12. *And their sycamore trees with frost.* Sycamore, a tree wholly and generically different from the American and English sycamore. Anderson: " It bears fruit resembling the fig, whilst its leaves are like those of the mulberry-tree; whence its name (*sycos*) a fig-tree, and (*moros*) a mulberry-tree." It was valuable as a wood, it gave a fine shade, and it furnished much food for the common people. *Frost*, margin *great hailstones*, here only.

48. *He gave up their cattle also to the hail, and their flocks to hot thunderbolts.* Hail, as in v. 47. *Hot thunderbolts*, in Hebrew one word, elsewhere rendered *burning heat, burning coals, coals, arrows;* see on Ps. xviii. 12. *Cattle* and *flocks*, or *beasts* and *cattle*, meaning all useful domestic animals, see Ex. ix. 23–25. *Gave up*, i. e., so *shut up* and *delivered over* that they could not escape.

49. *He cast upon them* [the Egyptians] *the fierceness of his anger, wrath, and indignation, and trouble, by sending evil angels* among them. *Fierceness*, elsewhere also *fury, wrath, sore displeasure. Anger*, as in Ps. ii. 5, 12; vi. 1; xviii. 7. *Wrath*, commonly so rendered. *Indignation*, also rendered *rage, anger*, see on Ps. xxxviii. 3. *Trouble*, also rendered, *distress, anguish, affliction, tribulation, adversity*, as in Ps. ix. 9. There was a vast accumulation of ills upon Pharaoh and his kingdom, all proceeding from the great displeasure of Jehovah. These calamities came by *angels of evils*, not intending wicked angels, as the Septuagint would seem to teach, but such as were messengers of evil things, bringing curses and not blessings. By *angels* Abenezra and Fry understand Moses and Aaron. The traditionary exposition given in the Apocrypha is very striking; see Wisdom of Solomon xvii. 2–11. Verses 50, 51 show that verse 49 refers to the awful night of the slaying of the first-born. The historic record of that event is found in Ex. xii. 29, 30. In Ex. xii. 23, the work of death is

said to have been done by a *destroyer;* see also Heb. xi. 28. As in Ps. xxxiv. 7, the singular, *destroyer,* may be put for the plural, or for one angel, having others under his command. Calvin: "We may simply consider the angels here spoken of as termed *evil,* on account of the work in which they were employed,—because they inflicted upon the enemies of the people of God terrible plagues to repress their tyranny and cruelty."

50. *He made a way to his anger; he spared not their soul from death, but gave their life over to the pestilence;*

51. *And smote all the first-born in Egypt; the chief of* their *strength in the tabernacles of Ham.* A *way, a path,* meaning an avenue, or channel. *Anger,* as in v. 49. *Life over to pestilence* is on several accounts a better rendering than that of the margin, *beasts to the murrain,* although that curse did also come on Egypt, Ex. ix. 3–7. But that is not the subject here spoken of. *Pestilence,* in Ex. ix. 3, *murrain.* The slaying of the first-born included animals as well as men. Alexander: "The poetical description of the first-born in the last clause of v. 51 is derived from Gen. xlix. 3, (compare Deut. xxi. 17,) and that of Egypt from Gen. x. 6." The children of Ham settled Africa.

52. *But made his own people to go forth like sheep, and guided them in the wilderness like a flock. People, nation,* the Israelites. The chief resemblance between these people and *sheep* or *flocks* was in their feebleness and incapacity to guide and take care of themselves, and in the excellent care they received from their Shepherd. Calvin: "It is a singular token of the love, which God bare towards them, that he did not disdain to humble himself so far as to feed them as his own sheep." Jehovah was their banner, protector, provider and portion.

53. *And he led them on safely, so that they feared not.* There is special reference to the passage of the Red sea, which was accomplished without difficulty or apprehension, Ex. xiv. 22, 29, 30; xv. 19; Heb. xi. 29. They were amply protected. The allusion is not to their wicked unbelief and the fears thence arising, (see Ex. xiv. 11; xv. 23, 24; Num. xi. 1; xiv. 1–4; xvi. 41; Ps. cvi. 7, 8,) but to the fact that there was left no cause of rational fear. *But the sea overwhelmed their enemies,* Ex. xiv. 26–28; xv. 19; Heb. xi. 29. While the world shall stand, the overthrow of Pharaoh and his host shall remain a grand display of the retributive justice of the Almighty.

54. *And he brought them to the border of his sanctuary,* even to *this mountain,* which *his right hand had purchased.* For *border of his sanctuary* Edwards has *his holy land;* Hengstenberg, *his holy boundary.* The precise sense is given by Alexander: "The frontier of the land which he had set apart as holy;" or by the Chaldee: "The boundary of the place of the house of the sanctuary." The latter best suits the next clause, which says the reference is to *this mountain,* though Tholuck and some others think that expression equivalent to "mountainous country," but this is not well sustained by usage. *Mountain,* rendered *hill* in Ps. ii. 6; iii. 4. *Purchased,* elsewhere *bought, redeemed, possessed, got, attained.* Here it is used in the sense of *obtained,* or *acquired. Right hand,* the emblem of power.

55. *He cast out the heathen also before them.* See on Ps. xliv. 2, 3. *And divided them an inheritance by line.* "The *lines* are fallen unto me in pleasant places," Ps. xvi. 6, shows a like use of the same word, which is also rendered *cord, lot, coast, region.* The whole clause designates a portion measured out and so assigned. *And made the tribes of Israel to dwell in their* [the Canaanites'] *tents,* Josh. xiii. 7; xix. 51.

56. *Yet they tempted and provoked the most high God. Tempted,* as in vv. 18, 41. *Provoked,* in v. 8 *rebellious,* on which see. *Most High,* as in v. 17; in v. 35, *high;* see on Ps. vii. 17. *And kept not his testimonies. Kept,* see on Ps. xii. 7; xvii. 4. The

meaning of the clause is, They were without hearty love to the word of God, though he had often borne witness for the truth and against them.

57. *But turned back, and dealt unfaithfully like their fathers.* *Turned back*, in Prov xiv. 14, the participle of the same verb is rendered *backslider*. *Dealt unfaithfully*, one verb, commonly rendered *dealt treacherously*, sometimes *dealt deceitfully;* in Ps. lxxiii. 15, *offend*. *Like their fathers, i. e.*, the new generation was much like the old. "In every age they showed themselves to be an impious and wicked people." *They were turned aside like a deceitful bow*. *Deceitful bow*, literally *bow of guile;* the same form of expression is found in Hos. vii. 16, where the context would indicate that want of strength to carry the arrow to the mark, allowing it always to fall short, was the chief point of resemblance intended. *Aside* is not in the Hebrew, though, if our idiom required, it might be inserted. The Hebrew simply implies any *turning*.

58. *For they provoked him to anger with their high places, and moved him to jealousy with their graven images.* How contrary these practices were to the law under which they lived is clear from Deut. xii. 1–4. The *high places* were the tops of hills commonly shaded where the Canaanites had worshipped their false gods. They proved a continual snare to the Israelites. See 2 Kings throughout. Compare Ex. xx. 4, 5. Idolatry is pleasing to the flesh. It leaves the soul to wallow in its sins. It requires no real piety to be ever so much devoted to the worship of false gods. Yea, the more earnest and hearty the devotee, the more is God displeased:

59. *When God heard this, he was wroth, and greatly abhorred Israel.* *Heard*, as in vv. 3, 21. *Wroth*, the corresponding noun is in verse 49 rendered *wrath*. The same preterite participle is so rendered in Ps. lxxxix. 38. The future participle is so rendered in vv. 21, 59 of this Psalm. It expresses great anger. *Abhorred*, elsewhere also *refused, rejected, cast off, cast away, contemned;* in Ps. liii. 5, *despised;* in Jer. vi. 30, the participle is rendered *reprobate*.

60. *So that he forsook the tabernacle of Shiloh, the tent which he placed among men.* How God set up his glorious worship in Shiloh is recorded in Josh. xviii. 1, and noticed in 1 Sam. i. 3. How the ark was taken thence never to be returned is recorded in 1 Sam. iv. 10, 11. By the weeping prophet the ruin of Shiloh as a city of solemnities is used to prefigure the ruin of Jerusalem, Jer. vii. 12, 14; xxvi. 6, 9.

61. *And delivered his strength into captivity, and his glory into the enemy's hand.* The ark is twice spoken of as the emblem of God's *strength*, 2 Chron. vi. 41; Ps. cxxxii. 8, *i. e.*, "The seat of his powerful and glorious presence, whence he put forth and manifested his strength in behalf of his people." Over it rested the *glory*, and so the ark is called the *glory* in 1 Sam. iv. 22; Rom. ix. 4. It is true that they are different words rendered *glory* here and in 1 Sam. iv. 22; but each word is rendered *glory, honor*.

62. *He gave his people over also unto the sword.* There is probably a special allusion to 1 Sam. iv. 10. *Gave over*, as in v. 50; *gave up*, in v. 48. *And was wroth with his inheritance.* *Wroth*, as in v. 59. The fact that the Israelites were above all others *God's* people and *his* inheritance is here mentioned as a circumstance showing the greatness of the provocation given.

63. *The fire consumed their young men.* Calvin: "This language is metaphorical, as is evident from the history of the event referred to, which informs us, that those that perished who were of the chosen of Israel, to the number of thirty thousand men, fell by the sword of the enemy, and not by fire, 1 Sam. iv. 10. This figure points out the suddenness of the dreadful calamity." This figure is found in the pentateuch, Num. xxi. 28. Compare v. 21. *Young men*, in v. 31 rendered *chosen* men. The corresponding verb is in this Psalm thrice rendered *chose*, vv. 67, 68, 70. *And their maidens were not given to marriage.* *Not given to marriage*, literally, *not praised;* but our version gives the sense. Simonis explains thus: "Not praised or celebrated in

nuptial songs;" Luther: "They must remain unmarried;" Bythner: "Remained unmarried; as marriage songs were sung at nuptials;" Clarke: "Were not celebrated
with marriage songs;" Diodati: "They had not been honored with nuptial songs
according to the customs of those times: see Jer. vii. 34; xvi. 9; xxv. 10. The meaning is, they had not been honorably married, because that men were grown scarce by
reason of the wars, Isa. iv. 1; Jer. xxxi. 22. Or, they had been married without any
solemnity, like poor bond-women; or privately, as in the time of public calamities."

64. *Their priests fell by the sword.* The reference is to the death of the sons of Eli,
1 Sam. iv. 11, 17. *And their widows made no lamentation.* We have a similar phrase
in Job xxvii. 15. The historic reference seems to be to the wife of Phinehas, 1 Sam.
iv. 19–22. She, however, was but one of a class. No doubt many other distressing
cases occurred. The *widows* were so occupied with their own dangers, or with the
public calamities, that they seemed to forget to lament their husbands; or the bodies
of their husbands lying on the battle-field and not brought home for burial, the usual
lamentation was not made over them; or the widows were carried into captivity, and
were afraid to lament, 'lest they should enrage their conquerors.'

But God is merciful. His anger will not burn for ever against his people. For
a season he may seem not to regard. But to his people he will in due time send help.

65. *Then the Lord awaked as one out of sleep,* and *like a mighty man that shouteth by
reason of wine.* *Then* is better than any other rendering and is fully sustained by
authority and usage, as in v. 34. It marks the conjuncture when God undertook
their cause. He puts forth great energy, as one refreshed by wine. Some think the
wine made the *sleep* profound. But surely that is not the sense. John Rogers'
translation: *Lyke a gyaunte refreshed with wyne;* Hengstenberg: *Like a warrior
rejoicing with wine.* Clarke: "One who, going forth to meet his enemy, having taken
a sufficiency of wine to refresh himself, and become a proper stimulus to his animal
spirits, *shouts,* gives the *war-signal* for the *onset;* impatient to meet the foe, and sure
of victory." The consequence of God's undertaking their cause was:

66. *And he smote his enemies in the hinder parts.* The reference seems to be to
1 Sam. v. 6, 9, 12; vi. 1–18. The precise form of the disease called *emerods* mentioned
in those places is not certainly known. See the Bible dictionaries. Thus *he put them
to a perpetual reproach.* Scott: "By the emerods, the Lord *disgraced* as well as discomfited the Philistines, and constrained them to send back the ark: and by the
golden images of the emerods and of the mice that marred the land, they were led
to publish and perpetuate their own disgrace." *Hinder parts,* see Ex. xxvi. 12;
xxxiii. 23; 1 Kings vii. 25; 2 Chron. iv. 4. Having humbled the Philistines, God
now executed a purpose long before announced, (Gen. xlix. 10) to put the seat of
power for the nation in the bounds of the tribe of Judah, though for a time it had
been at Shiloh in the tribe of Ephraim:

67. *Moreover he refused the tabernacle of Joseph, and chose not the tribe of Ephraim.*
Joseph was the father of Ephraim, and so the tabernacle takes his name. His
descendants bore this mark of the divine displeasure for their sins.

68. *But he chose the tribe of Judah, the mount Zion which he loved.* He had long
before by prophecy declared his intention of making Judah the seat of the theocracy.
In 2 Sam. v. 6–10 we have the first mention of Zion. From that time it became
famous, an emblem of the true church, a figure of heaven itself. After the Philis
tines restored the ark, it rested at various points until finally by divine direction its
abode was fixed on mount Zion.

69. *And he built his sanctuary like high* palaces. Some have thought this a predic
tion of the grandeur of the temple, or a declaration of its magnificence as already
built; but the word rendered *sanctuary* designated the tabernacle for hundreds of

years. The word *palaces* is supplied by our translators. The Syriac, Hare, Secker and Edwards read *on high;* Tholuck, *like the heights of heaven;* Hengstenberg, *like high mountains;* Alexander: "The construction most agreeable to usage is that which supplies *hills* or *mountains.*" *Like the earth which he hath established forever.* *Zion* beyond the literal evidently has also a figurative sense. Its great *exaltation* is not its literal elevation. Nor was it the abode of the ark but for a few centuries. But the church of God lasts for ever. Nothing can subvert it.

70. *He chose David also his servant.* He chose David in preference to Saul, a Benjamite and not a *servant of God,* David and not any Ephraimite, to make him the great instrument of organizing his public worship with Psalms, and also to make him so striking a type of Messiah, that it is often difficult to tell whether a portion of Hebrew poetry relates only to David, solely to Christ, or first to David as a type, and then to Christ as the antitype. In the prophets Christ more than once bears the name of David. Nor did God choose David because of his high birth. *And* [he] *took him from the sheep folds:*

71. *From following the ewes great with young he brought him to feed Jacob his people, and Israel his inheritance.* *From following,* a frequent rendering of our translators. To *feed, keep, be a shepherd to.* The participle of the verb is often rendered *shepherd.* See on Ps. xxiii. 1. Compare Ps. lxxx. 1; Zech. xiii. 7.

72. *So he* [David] *fed them according to the integrity of his heart; and guided them by the skilfulness of his hands.* *Guided,* as a shepherd guides, often rendered *led,* Ps. xxiii. 3; lxxvii. 20. To *lead* and to *feed* the flock was the sum of the shepherd's office. From the last Hebrew verb being in the future some have thought that when Asaph was writing this Psalm, David was still on the throne with prospect of reigning for some time to come. *Integrity,* elsewhere also *simplicity, uprightness, perfection.* *Skilfulness, wisdom, understanding,* applied both to God and man, to finite and infinite wisdom, Ps. cxxxvi. 5; cxlvii. 5; Pr. xiv. 29; xv. 21. David was divinely taught.

Doctrinal and Practical Remarks.

1. The language and deportment of teachers to learners and of ministers to people should be kind and affectionate, using tones and terms of endearment, v. 1.

2. People should be invited and in all proper ways urged to pay close and earnest attention to the calls of God and the lessons of wisdom. Men must be awaked and aroused. Dickson: "Such is our dulness and slowness of heart to understand and believe what the Lord saith to us, that we have great need to be admonished and stirred up to attention and hearing with faith."

3. Preachers should study with care, not seeking meretricious ornament, but laboring to teach sound doctrine in those forms of speech best suited to impress divine truth, v. 2. See Ecc. xii. 9–11.

4. It is no objection to divine truth that it is often uttered in parables and in sayings dark to carnal men, v. 2. This mode of teaching is delightful to such as love the truth. Jesus adopted it, Matt. xiii. 34; Mark iv. 34. Those who have the right spirit are sure to learn and remember.

5. We should not despise truths because they are *old,* vv. 2, 3. Such are often the most important. In religion that which is new is worthless. "Divine doctrine is no new doctrine." The Bible and its truths are venerable for antiquity.

6. If in God's mercy we are made acquainted with weighty truths involving the divine glory and human salvation, let us not conceal them, but faithfully transmit them to others; especially to the young committed to our care, vv. 4, 5, 6. Clarke: "*Five* generations appear to be mentioned in these verses,—1. Fathers; 2. Their children; 3. The generation to come; 4. And their children; 5. And their children.

They were never to lose sight of" these things. Morison: "With what scrupulous diligence should the heads of families in every age train their offspring for God." Scott: "To perform this important duty to good purpose, we must enforce our instructions by a consistent example. It is awful to think how many parents, by their negligence and wickedness, become the murderers of the souls of their children."

7. Those great religious truths which suit one generation, are no less applicable to all who come after them, vv. 5, 6. This fact is no mean evidence of the divine origin of Scripture. The Bible is for all times. Its author knew what was in man.

8. The Scriptures are a great blessing. They are to us God's *testimony*, v. 5. Compare Rom. iii. 2. Oh that the families and nations who have God's word would love it, obey it and spread it according to its infinite value.

9. All religious knowledge and culture which fail to raise us to right affections towards God and communion with him, are of no avail, v. 7. Till we set our hope in God, remember his works, and keep his commandments, we are undone.

10. In all the Bible there is not once a name given to sin, indicating that God regards it as a trifle. On the contrary it is called *stubbornness, rebellion, wrong-heartedness, instability, cowardice, covenant-breaking, refusal to follow the only perfectly good rule*, vv. 8–10. Left to themselves, men often call good evil and evil good; but God and inspired men never commit such errors. Sin must be a horrible thing.

11. Displeasing God sooner or later brings defeat, v. 9. Sin makes men cowards, Pr. xxviii. 1. Horne: "How often is this the case with the Christian soldier! Let not him who hath just put on his spiritual armor boast like him who is putting it off when the fight is over and the victory obtained." Arms, numbers, former successes will not save us.

12. *Forgetfulness of God* is a sin of all nations and ages, vv. 11, 42. It is the source of innumerable iniquities. It attends all depravity. It is a universal sin.

13. Truly great events bear frequent recital, vv. 12–64. Yet it is remarkable how inspired writers dwell much on things which profane historians think unworthy of notice. How infrequent are even allusions, in modern classics, to any portion of the mighty events recorded in this Psalm. Yet what class of occurrences has ever more affected the destinies of the world?

14. All nature is controlled by God, vv. 13–16, 20, 23, 26. The seas, all waters, the clouds, the fires of heaven, the rocks, the great deep, fowls of every description, all creatures, all winds, all elements obey his voice and do his will. Of course nothing can of its own power, without divine permission, hurt any child of God, Ezek. xxxiv. 25–28; Hos. ii. 18.

15. There is a mystery in iniquity. If there is no power beyond the inherent force of discipline and instruction, it is incurable. Men's persistency in sin is inscrutable, vv. 17, 30, 32, 40, 56, 57. We read the history of the Israelites and we marvel. We honestly look at our own history and we see the same record of ingratitude and perverseness, and we are confounded. Horne: "Mercies are followed by provocations; provocations are punished with judgments; to judgments succeed repeated provocations, which call down fresh judgments."

16. In all ages the parent sin of men has been unbelief, vv. 19, 20, 22, 32. By reason thereof "the world despises, more unconcernedly than all things else, the threatenings of God and his promises also." Tholuck: "Unbelief is so deeply rooted in the human heart, that when God performs miracles on *earth*, unbelief doubts whether he can perform them in *heaven*, and when he does them in *heaven*, whether he can do them on earth, Matt. xvi. 1." Doubting any perfection of God is tantamount to robbing him of his glory.

17. "Mercies abused are in general the precursors of God's righteous judgments upon individuals, families and nations," vv. 20, 21.

18. The greater the gift, the greater is the sin of lightly esteeming it. Dickson: "Had the Lord fed Israel with the dust of the earth, or roots of grass, or any other mean thing, they would have had no reason to complain: but when he giveth them a new food, created every morning for their cause, sent down from heaven fresh every day, of such excellent color, taste, smell, and wholesomeness; what a provocation of God was it, not to be content now, in special, when he gave them abundantly of it?" vv. 23–25.

19. God's plan of feeding Israel in the desert was to prove and humble them, Deut. viii. 16. Every dispensation of God's providence, whether prosperous or adverse, is suited more or less to show what is in us. But the manna was to *humble* as well as try. John Newton says: "I could not understand this for a time. I thought they were rather in danger of being proud, when they saw themselves provided for in such an extraordinary way. But the manna would not keep; they could not hoard it up, and were therefore in a state of absolute dependence from day to day: this appointment was well suited to humble them. Thus it is with us in spirituals. We should be better pleased, perhaps, to be set up with a stock or sufficiency at once, such an inherent portion of wisdom and power, as we might depend upon, at least for common occasions, without being constrained, by a sense of indigence, to have continual recourse to the Lord for everything we want. But his way is best."

20. Both Christ and Paul clearly teach that the manna was a type of our Saviour, John vi. 32, 33, 35; 1 Cor. x. 3, 4. Why do men still despise this bread from heaven? Not only do poor blinded Jews generally reject him; but millions, who have not an intellectual doubt of his Messiahship, will not believe on him with the heart. If it was a sin to loathe the manna, what must be the sin of rejecting Jesus Christ? Why are men offended in him? He is the Son of God; the sinner's Friend. O shall we not give thanks for such a Saviour? Reader, wilt thou not receive him joyfully? Wilt thou not eat this bread of heaven and live forever?

21. Our desires for particular forms of temporal good things should be very moderate. We know not that they will prove blessings. They may turn out to be curses. It was so when Israel lusted after flesh, vv. 26–31. With God's blessing an affliction is a mercy. Without his blessing any good thing is a curse, Mal. ii. 2. Compare Hos. xiii. 11.

22. From the terms employed and from the effects produced, as well as from the examples recorded, there must be something exceedingly terrible in the divine displeasure, vv. 31, 33, 34, 44, 51, 53, 55, 59. It is called *the fierceness of anger, wrath, indignation.* Its effects are dreadful. It slays, it smites, it makes life a vanity, a trouble, it turns rivers into blood, it makes man the sport of winged insects, and of all creatures, even the most loathsome, it renders fruitless the greatest toil and industry, it sends destructive hail and tempests, it wastes flocks and herds by pestilence and casualty, it makes the good angels ministers of evil things, it opens channels to God's hot displeasure where nothing but good was expected, it blasts the fondest hopes of parental love, it overwhelms men with sudden and total ruin.

23. The history of every people shows the absolute necessity of divine grace to change the heart and purify the life. For help and strength from God there is no substitute, John xv. 5. If mercies and wonders without number are sent on men, without the grace of God's Spirit, the record will ever be, *for all this they sinned still*, v. 32.

24. Sometimes even here God lets us see how utterly vain and fruitless are the lives and toils of sinners, v. 33. In eternity sin in every case will appear to be folly.

25. When zealous young preachers begin their labors, they often have strong hopes of being useful to unconverted men on sick and dying beds; but as they advance in life their experience commonly very much represses the ardor of their expectations, vv. 34, 35. The more wisdom they acquire in these things, the stronger is their impression that generally men die as they live. Religious impressions, begotten by terror, commonly soon pass away.

26. Fair appearances of piety are of no avail, where the affections are not truly engaged. Without holiness no man can see the Lord. Without love, and faith, and hope, and all the graces of the true Christian, our vows, our worship, our professions are *flattery* and *lies*, v. 36.

27. Without a *right heart*, there can be no stability of Christian character, no *steadfastness in God's covenant*, v. 37. But a *right heart* is obtained only in conversion; and conversion is by the renewal of the Holy Ghost. How careful then ought all to be not to quench, resist, grieve or vex that blessed agent, the author of all piety in man.

28. Inspired writers never grow weary of celebrating the love and compassion of God, v. 38. The reason is, the theme is worthy of their best songs, and their hearts cannot forget the debt they owe to the love of God.

29. It is for an unspeakable joy that God employs his infinite knowledge in tenderly considering our frailty, our liability to err, our natural weakness, and the shortness and uncertainty of our lives, v. 39. He pities us, not because we deserve pity, but because he loves to show mercy to such as need and seek it.

30. One of the greatest sins we can commit is to *limit the Holy One of Israel*, v. 41. This we do, when we think God is such an one as ourselves, when we doubt his ability or readiness to fill the penitent with good things, when we pervert his fatherly chastisements to discouragement, when we think our case so sad that God himself cannot deliver us, when we prescribe to him times, and plans, and methods of succor, or when we 'set bounds to his power, truth, wisdom, or mercy.'

31. God's judgments on others, especially those sent for our sakes, should deeply affect us, vv. 43–51. We should often speak of them, fear him whose wrath is so terrible, whose love for his children is so great that he will rebuke kings and root up kingdoms rather than see his chosen perish. Compare Pr. xxiv. 17; Obad. 12.

32. God's people are never safer than when his and their enemies are perishing all around them, vv. 52–54. Noah, Lot, and the Christians at Jerusalem give us like patterns.

33. There are few if any families on earth inhabiting lands, which were not taken from others by some awful judgment of God in the convulsions of nations.

34. The fact that human nature shows the same moral obliquities from age to age, through all generations, is irrefragable proof that human depravity is hereditary, and that there is original sin, v. 57. No fairer argument can be constructed. If we act *like our fathers*, it is because like them and through them we are fallen creatures.

35. The human heart is very *deceitful*, v. 57. It promises well, and performs ill. It is deceitful *above all things*. If God were not omniscient, it would deceive him. It often deceives our neighbor. It more frequently deceives ourselves.

36. We cannot too carefully guard the worship of God against all corruption, especially by the use of images or pictures, whether material or existing only in our own imaginations, vv. 58, 59. Compare Ex. xx. 4, 5; Ps. xcvii. 7.

37. It is a great wonder that God has not been driven by our iniquities, utterly to withdraw from the earth as he did from Shiloh every token of his gracious presence, v. 60.

38. In all ages God has set but little store by the externals of religion compared

with the estimate in which he has held vital piety. A very precious vessel was the ark of the covenant! It contained the tables of the law, the pot of manna, and Aaron's rod that budded. Over it stood the cherubim. On it rested the Shechinah, the visible glory of God. It was the mercy-seat. It had carried Israel safely through perils of the worst kind. Yet when his chosen people rebelled against God, and forgot the true source of their safety, he gave up the ark to their bitterest foes, v. 61.

39. How just and terrible are inspired descriptions of the horrors of war, vv. 61–64. See Isaiah xiii. 2–18; Jeremiah iv. 19–31. If original sin may be argued from the sinful likeness of the child to the parent, surely actual depravity is proven by the existence of war, Jas. iv. 1, 2. Oh that all Christians would remember that war shall be banished by the prevalence of principles now taught by Christianity, and not by some new revelation hereafter to be received.

40. If God intends to save, he will surely accomplish his purpose, v. 65. His deliverances are as glorious to him as they are cheering to his people. The most puissant principalities in the hands of God have no power of resistance.

41. We are taught in v. 66, that some punishments inflicted by God in this life are highly and permanently disgraceful. In many cases we see the like ourselves. Why may it not turn out at last that all sin shall be for dishonor? It shall in every case, Dan. xii. 2. Henry: "Sooner or later, God will glorify himself by putting disgrace upon his enemies, then when they are most elevated with their successes."

42. God is a sovereign and will do what he pleases with his own, vv. 67–70. He only is fit to govern this world. He rejects Ephraim and chooses Judah; he rejects Shiloh and chooses Jerusalem; he rejects Saul and chooses David. Ephraim, Shiloh and Saul have no right to complain because no injustice is done; Judah, Jerusalem and David have no right to boast because mercy is shown.

43. Let no one despise the day of small things, vv. 70–72. Jesse brought not his little son to the sacrifice. But God, who looketh not on the outward appearance but on the heart, chose the neglected David and raised him step by step till his throne was settled and his kingdom established. He had been faithful over a few things and God made him ruler over many things.

44. How sad is the history even of churches planted by the Lord. How soon and how sadly the best of them forget their calling and their privileges, and go after folly. Left to themselves their former strict profession of God's truth and zeal in his worship become mere occasions of hardening them in pride. The natural consequences are heresies, schisms, superstition, vain jangling, loss of charity and of comfortable walking with God.

PSALM LXXIX.

A Psalm of Asaph.

1 O God, the heathen are come into thine inheritance; thy holy temple have they defiled; they have laid Jerusalem on heaps.

2 The dead bodies of thy servants have they given *to be* meat unto the fowls of the heaven, the flesh of thy saints unto the beasts of the earth.

3 Their blood have they shed like water round about Jerusalem; and *there was* none to bury *them.*

4 We are become a reproach to our neighbours, a scorn and derision to them that are round about us.

5 How long, Lord? wilt thou be angry for ever? shall thy jealousy burn like fire?

6 Pour out thy wrath upon the heathen that have not known thee, and upon the kingdoms that have not called upon thy name.

7 For they have devoured Jacob, and laid waste his dwellingplace.

8 Oh remember not against us former iniquities: let thy tender mercies speedily prevent us; for we are brought very low.

9 Help us, O God of our salvation, for the glory of thy name: and deliver us, and purge away our sins, for thy name's sake.

10 Wherefore should the heathen say, Where *is* their God? let him be known among the heathen in our sight *by* the revenging of the blood of thy servants *which is* shed.

11 Let the sighing of the prisoner come before thee; according to the greatness of thy power preserve thou those that are appointed to die;

12 And render unto our neighbours sevenfold into their bosom their reproach, wherewith they have reproached thee, O Lord.

13 So we thy people and sheep of thy pasture will give thee thanks for ever: we will show forth thy praise to all generations.

ON the title see on title of Ps. iii. On the authorship, object and date of this ode see on Ps. lxxiv. and places there referred to. Luther thinks it is a prayer to God against future destruction by Chaldeans. Calvin is confident that " it was composed long after the death of David." Because verses 6, 7, are found in Jeremiah x. 25, Mudge thinks it is not unlikely that it was written by that weeping prophet. Horsley thinks it was composed during the distresses of Manasseh's reign. But is it not prophetic? At least may it not have been written before the calamitous events, in which it had its *most striking* fulfilment? Commentators are pretty generally agreed, that this Psalm is nearly related to Ps. lxxiv. Several critics think they find a great similarity in the Asaphic Psalms. Does not this obtain to such a degree as to discourage the idea of different authorships? Scott dates this ode B. C. 588; Clarke says, " Undoubtedly the Psalm was composed during the Babylonish Captivity." The names of the Almighty found in it are *Elohim* GOD, *Jehovah* LORD and *Adonai Lord*, on which see on Ps. iii. 2; i. 2; ii. 4.

1. *O God, the heathen are come into thine inheritance. Heathen, nations, Gentiles,* as in Ps. ii. 1. *Inheritance,* as in Ps. ii. 8; lxxviii. 55, 62, 71. The theory of a serial fulfilment of the things here written, 1, in the invasion of Nebuchadnezzar; 2, in the persecution of Antiochus Epiphanes; 3, in the utter ruin of Jerusalem by the Romans, is perhaps the best mode of exposition if it be regarded as prophetic. There was no invasion of Judea in Asaph's time, followed by such effects as are here described. The tense of the verbs does not at all weaken this mode of exposition; see on Ps. lxxiv. Calvin: "The prophet complains that when the heathen came into the heritage of God, the order of nature was, as it were, inverted." *Thy holy temple have they defiled. Temple,* or *palace* as in Ps. v. 7; xi. 4. Hengstenberg: "The *pollution* of the temple by the heathen presupposes its previous pollution by the Israelites," Ezek. v. 11; xxiii. 38. Tholuck: "They treated the temple as if he had ceased to exist, to whose honor it had been built." *They have laid Jerusalem on heaps. Heaps,* not the word rendered *heap* in Ps. lxxviii. 13, which signifies a *wall;* this word signifies *ruins.*

2. *The dead bodies of thy servants have they given* to be *meat unto the fowls of the heaven, and the flesh of thy saints unto the beasts of the earth.* How great was the dishonor of being denied sepulture, and how great was the horror of such an end may be learned from 1 Sam. xvii. 44–46. Indeed the Scriptures are full of this matter, Ps. lxiii. 10; Isa. xiv. 11, 18, 19; 1 Sam. xxxi. 8–13; 2 Sam. iv. 12; xxi. 9, 10; 1 Kings xiv. 11–14; Jer. vii. 33; viii. 2; xvi. 4; xxxiv. 20; Ezek. xxix. 5; xxxii. 4; xxxix. 17–20. Very early in their history did the Jews regard the burial of the dead as a religious duty. All Christian churches carefully attend to this weighty matter. It would be shocking if a diverse sentiment prevailed. Calvin:

"Men have always had such a sacred regard to the burial of the dead, as to shrink from depriving even their enemies of the honor of sepulture." These dreadful calamities come not merely on wicked and hypocritical men, but also on God's *servants* and *saints*, two terms which clearly designate pious people.

3. *Their blood have they shed like water round about Jerusalem; and there was none to bury them,* i. e., there was no friend or relative left in the land to perform the last sad offices, they having been carried into captivity; or, if any such remained, they were afraid to show so much affection as to bury the bodies of their loved ones; or, there were so many dead they could not be buried by the survivors. Calvin: "God having intended that, in the burial of men, there should be some testimony to the resurrection at the last day, it was a double indignity for the saints to be despoiled of this right after death." On such sufferings coming on the righteous, see 1 Cor. xi. 29–32; 1 Pet. iv. 17, 18.

4. *We are become a reproach to our neighbours, a scorn and derision to them that are round about us.* This verse with very slight change is taken from Ps. xliv. 13, on which see. They endured this scorn from men for the Lord's sake, and it is fitly pleaded as a reason why God should show pity. God has graciously taught this doctrine, Isa. xxxvii. 22, 23. *Neighbours* may include Canaanites in their midst, invaders, and surrounding nations. Clarke: "The Idumeans, Philistines, Phœnicians, Ammonites and Moabites all gloried in the subjugation of this people; and their insults to them were mixed with blasphemies against God."

5. *How long, LORD? wilt thou be angry for ever? shall thy jealousy burn like fire?* How long? see on Ps. vi. 3. *Be angry,* as in Ps. ii. 2, 12; lxxxv. 5. *Jealousy,* often so rendered, also *zeal,* see on Ps. lxix. 9. Here it expresses God's inflexible determination to vindicate his own honor and authority against those who offend, even though they be his *servants* and his *saints.*

6. *Pour out thy wrath upon the heathen that have not known thee, and upon the kingdoms that have not called upon thy name. Heathen,* plural as in v. 1. *Gentiles, nations,* parallel to *kingdoms.* To have the *knowledge of God* is to have the true religion, Pr. ii. 5; Hosea iv. 1; John xvii. 3. To *call on the name* of the Lord is to worship him, Gen. iv. 26; 1 Cor. i. 2. *Not* to know God, nor to call on his name is to be heathen, without the knowledge or practice of the true religion. *Pour out,* in Hebrew as in English—in the imperative; see Introduction, § 6. Calvin: "Lord, how is it that thou afflictest us so severely, upon whom thy name is invoked, and sparest the heathen nations who despise thee?" Alexander: "As if he had said, If thou must pour out thy wrath let it rather be on those who neither know nor worship thee than on thine own peculiar people;" Tholuck: "Shall not the heathen now as in days of old be brought to the knowledge that the King of kings is ruler in Israel?" Perhaps it is better to regard the verse as a prediction. Yet it is true that God's people cannot be saved without the overthrow of their incorrigible foes; nor is there a doubt of the perfect righteousness of all the judgments sent by God.

7. *For they have devoured Jacob and laid waste his dwellingplace.* If Jacob deserved evil at the hands of God, he did not deserve it at the hands of these people. If they were executing Jehovah's will, it was not because they regarded the honor of the Most High. If they glorified him, they did it unintentionally. These predictions of evil find a parallel in Isa. x. 12–15.

8. *Oh remember not against us former iniquities.* The church of England reads *old sins.* If God's children forsake him, he will visit their iniquities with a rod, and their transgressions with stripes. It is well when men are punished for their sins in time and not in eternity; so that we may properly confess, and bewail, and forsake, and obtain pardon for them all. Time may obliterate our remembrance of sin, but with

God it never grows out of date. Humble confession and true repentance do not always avert the temporal consequences of evil doings; it is an infinite mercy that to the penitent the divine displeasure goes no farther than the grave. For God to *remember* sin is to punish it, not to pardon it, Ps. xxv. 7. Alexander thinks by *former iniquities* we are to understand the iniquities of *former generations*. But doubtless all past sins are referred to. *Let thy tender mercies speedily prevent us. Tender mercies*, as in Ps. xxv. 6; xl. 11; li. 1. *Prevent, come before*, or *go before*. What the best of mere men have always needed and shall always need at God's hands is not justice, but infinite compassions. If we cannot obtain forgiveness because it will glorify the riches of God's grace, we cannot obtain it at all. Our wretchedness may move God to show mercy, and to hasten the application of it, and so it is added, *for we are brought very low, i. e.*, in outward estate, in civil condition, in distresses.

9. *Help us, O God of our salvation, for the glory of thy name, and deliver us and purge away our sins, for thy name's sake. Help* and *deliver*, commonly so rendered. *Purge away, pardon, forgive, expiate;* see on Ps. lxv. 3; lxxviii. 38. The appeal to the glory of the divine name is ancient and prevalent. If that move not God, nothing will. Of him, and through him, and to him are all things. God will not deny himself.

10. *Wherefore should the heathen say, Where is their God?* The appeal is still to the regard God is known to have to the honor of his name, especially among the Gentiles, as in Ex. xxxii. 12–14; Num. xiv. 11–20. *Let him be known among the heathen in our sight* by *the revenging of the blood of thy servants, which is shed. Let him be known*, literally, *He shall be known*. To *revenge blood* was condignly to punish criminals by proper authority, Deut. xxxii. 43.

11. *Let the sighing of the prisoner come before thee.* Perhaps Judea was seldom if ever successfully invaded, and lives taken, that prisoners were not also captured and carried away. This was fearfully the case in the time of Nebuchadnezzar. The lives of such were sad in the extreme. Here we read of their *sighing*. In Ps. cii. the same word is rendered *groaning*, and in Mal. ii. 13, *crying out*. The church of England has it, *sorrowful sighing*. It expresses any mourning noise. How sad was the case of the captives of Babylon may be learned from Ps. cxxxvii., as well as from the book of Jeremiah. *According to the greatness of thy power preserve thou those that are appointed to die. Those that are appointed to die*, literally, *the sons of death*, meaning those who are in peril of instant death, perhaps here such as were likely to be put to death by their cruel captors. Some think it admits that before God they were worthy of death. The prayer is that the people of Israel, though captives, might not be wasted, but that God would give them favor even when in the power of their enemies. Such is the *greatness of God's power*, even the poor captives in Babylon cannot be destroyed, if God will undertake for them.

12. *And render unto our neighbors sevenfold into their bosom their reproach, wherewith they have reproached thee, O Lord. Reproach*, as in Ps. xv. 3. *Reproached*, see on Ps. xlii. 10. As the reproach, wherewith the wicked reproach God, falls upon the saints, so the reproach of the wicked poured upon the saints is regarded by the Lord as despite towards himself. *Render, return, bring back*. The Hebrew is in the imperative. *Neighbors*, as in v. 4. *Sevenfold, i. e.*, to the full, seven being the number of perfection. The retributive justice here alluded to is the same as in Ps. xviii. 25.

13. *So we thy people and sheep of thy pasture will give thee thanks for ever: we will shew forth thy praise to all generations. Sheep of thy pasture*, sheep whom thou keepest, or *feedest*. To *give thanks* and *show forth praise* is the proper fruit of God's mercy on all right-minded beings. So far as they are truly pious they will solemnly purpose to spend their *eternity* in so blessed employment. Compare Isa. xliii. 21.

DOCTRINAL AND PRACTICAL REMARKS.

1. How excellent is God's word. It suits the state of his church from age to age. Hundreds of times has this Psalm been sung as suiting the state of God's church.

2. It is not merely dreadful events, but dreadful events, tending to impair the power of religion, and hinder the cause of Christ, that most deeply penetrate with grief the hearts of the pious, as we see in this ode.

3. When we are in any trouble, our best resort is to proper acts of devotion, as we learn from this Psalm. If we can bring our woes before God in prayer, we have done the best possible thing.

4. Dreadful calamities, involving church and state, saint and sinner, public interests and private happiness, are no new thing, vv. 1–3. Morison: "How mournful is the scene here described! The armies of the idolaters in possession of the land of promise —the temple defiled by their unsanctified mirth—the fair city of Zion in the dust— the bodies of the slain Israelites devoured by the fowls of heaven—their blood flowing in rivers round about Jerusalem—the rites of sepulture altogether denied—and shout- ings of derision and of unholy triumph heard on every side." Calvin: "How cruelly the Assyrians conducted themselves is well known. And under the tyranny of Anti- ochus, if a man dared simply to open his mouth in defence of the pure worship of God, he did it at the risk of immediately forfeiting his life."

5. It is an unspeakable blessing, seldom duly prized, to live in times free from bloody persecutions.

6. The opposition of false religion to that which is from heaven is deadly, vv. 1–3. Dickson: "Nothing is to be expected of God's enemies towards God's people, when they fall into their hands, but savage cruelty, and barbarous inhumanity, for which they are to answer to God, to whom the complaint of the living, and the cry of the blood of the slain call for vengeance."

7. One of the horrible fruits of war is found in its brutalizing effects on many, v. 2. When men become 'drunk on blood, they vomit crime.' An 'insatiable thirst for slaughter,' if generally prevalent in a community, very soon makes life a burden.

8. Horne: "To behold, or even to imagine, heaps of slaughtered bodies lying un- buried, and exposed to birds and beasts of prey, is inexpressibly shocking to humanity. But with what unconcern are we accustomed to view, on all sides of us, multitudes 'dead in trespasses and sins,' torn in pieces, and devoured by wild passions, filthy lusts, and infernal spirits those dogs and vultures of the moral world! Yet to a discerning eye, and a thinking mind, the latter is by far the more melancholy sight of the two."

9. Our Saviour will watch the sleeping dust of all his saints whether they have an honorable burial or not. We may therefore safely commit that whole matter to him; yet in ordinary circumstances it is as impossible as it is undesirable for us to cultivate a total indifference to the treatment of our mortal remains when we are dead and gone. See Jer. xxii. 19; xxxvi. 30.

10. Dickson: "Falling in battle before the enemies may prove that God hath a just cause against the party overcome; but it cannot prove that the victor's cause is good," v. 2.

11. Whoso learns to sin without remorse will soon learn to sin without measure, v. 3.

12. When men mock our miseries and laugh at our calamities there is a dreadful keenness of edge given to all our other afflictions, v. 4. "There is a persecution sharper than that of the axe. There is an iron that goes into the heart deeper than the knife. Cruel sneers, and sarcasms, and pitiless judgments, and cold-hearted calumnies—these are persecutions." True, if we are reproached for the name of

Christ, we are happy not for the reproach, but because the spirit of glory and of God rests upon us, 1 Pet. iv. 14.

13. God's delays in sending relief often seem long and even tedious, v. 5. But let us remember that such delays are doubtless needful, that God's honor is of more importance than our ease, that God always sees in us just cause for every stroke he inflicts, that the wicked can go no further than infinite wisdom permits, that the least sin is a greater evil than any merely temporal calamity, and that one design of all our chastisements is to cure our foolish impatience.

14. God's anger is terrible. It burns *like fire*, v. 5. But this is the joy of believers, 'When they deserve punishment, his wrath burns fiercely indeed but not eternally.'

15. The coming doom of the heathen is so terrible that it may well afflict any pious soul, v. 6. Richard Baxter said that none of his petitions were more fervent or affecting to his own heart than those for poor, benighted Heathen and Mohammedan nations.

16. We have great need to ask forgiveness for our old sins, vv. 8, 9. Those enlightened from above do habitually trace their sufferings to some particular sin or sins or to their sinfulness in general. Nor can solid peace ever be secured without an interest in the precious blood and infinite righteousness of Jesus Christ.

17. Nor will a little mercy answer our purpose. We need mercies, yea, tender mercies, yea, a multitude of his tender mercies, v. 8.

18. When we come to God in prayer, we should fill our mouth with arguments, vv. 8–10. We may plead our *low* estate, we may argue that God has helped us hitherto; that present deliverance will be for his glory; and that if he fails to hear us, the enemy will reproach both him and us, both his cause and ours.

19. The worse our case, the greater will be the honor to our deliverer, v. 8.

20. It is an unspeakable privilege to search the annals of antiquity, and encourage ourselves by the records of God's works of mercy to his people of old, v. 9. It is far different with carnal men. Hengstenberg: "The world, when it prays, prays only as an experiment, having no connection with history."

21. If God shall help us, he must find cause of mercy in himself, and not in us, v. 9. We are vile. He is perfect and infinite.

22. It is a blessed comfort to find that good men have borne the taunts and derision of the vile in all ages, and yet have made good their escape to heaven, v. 10. It is sufficient that the servant be as his Lord, and the disciple as his Master. Let us imitate our Saviour, who, when he was reviled, reviled not again: when he suffered, he threatened not; but committed himself to him that judgeth righteously.

23. We may rest assured that the blood of all the saints will be avenged, v. 10. All the Scriptures so declare, and none more clearly than the last book of the sacred volume, Rev. xviii. 4–8; xix. 1–6.

24. It is a proof of the dreadful depravity of man that from age to age, poor prisoners are so generally ill-treated; while at the same time, it is a proof of the kindness of God that their case is distinctly and repeatedly mentioned in his holy word, v. 11.

25. Ought not pious people more closely to imitate their heavenly Father in caring for those who have been condemned to die? An eminent Christian lady keeps a record of all, who have been sentenced to death, so far as she hears of them, and prays for them every day till their end come. Is not such conduct in sympathy with the heart of God?

26. He can have but feeble support who relies on any created arm; but he, who trusts in God's almightiness shall never fail, nor be disappointed, v. 11.

27. The day of scorners is coming, assuredly and awfully coming, v. 12. As Shimei

was brought to humble himself, so shall it finally be with every despiser, especially every scorner of Gospel grace.

28. As much as possible let our lives abound in thanksgiving and praise, that thus we may glorify God and be abundantly prepared to honor him in the same way to all eternity. "Those lives that are entirely devoted to God's praise, are assuredly taken under God's protection."

PSALM LXXX.

To the chief Musician upon Shoshannim-Eduth, A Psalm of Asaph.

1 Give ear, O Shepherd of Israel, thou that leadest Joseph like a flock; thou that dwellest *between* the cherubim, shine forth.

2 Before Ephraim and Benjamin and Manasseh stir up thy strength, and come *and* save us.

3 Turn us again, O God, and cause thy face to shine; and we shall be saved.

4 O LORD God of hosts, how long wilt thou be angry against the prayer of thy people?

5 Thou feedest them with the bread of tears; and givest them tears to drink in great measure.

6 Thou makest us a strife unto our neighbours: and our enemies laugh among themselves.

7 Turn us again, O God of hosts, and cause thy face to shine; and we shall be saved.

8 Thou hast brought a vine out of Egypt: thou hast cast out the heathen, and planted it.

9 Thou preparedst *room* before it, and didst cause it to take deep root, and it filled the land.

10 The hills were covered with the shadow of it, and the boughs thereof *were like* the goodly cedars.

11 She sent out her boughs unto the sea, and her branches unto the river.

12 Why hast thou *then* broken down her hedges, so that all they which pass by the way do pluck her?

13 The boar out of the wood doth waste it, and the wild beast of the field doth devour it.

14 Return, we beseech thee, O God of hosts: look down from heaven, and behold, and visit this vine;

15 And the vineyard which thy right hand hath planted, and the branch *that* thou madest strong for thyself.

16 *It is* burned with fire, *it is* cut down: they perish at the rebuke of thy countenance.

17 Let thy hand be upon the man of thy right hand, upon the son of man *whom* thou madest strong for thyself.

18 So will not we go back from thee: quicken us, and we will call upon thy name.

19 Turn us agian, O LORD God of hosts, cause thy face to shine; and we shall be saved.

ON the several clauses of the title see on titles of Psalms iii. iv. xlv. lx. lxix. Calvin: "Those who are most learned adduce nothing but probable conjectures upon the words *Shoshannim* and *Eduth*." Calvin and Clarke think there is a close affinity between this and Ps. lxxix.; Hengstenberg, between this and Ps. lxxvii. Calvin calls this "a sorrowful prayer, in which the faithful beseech God that he would be graciously pleased to succor his afflicted church." Tholuck calls it "a song of complaint, composed at a time when the worst had not yet happened to Israel, but when various heathen nations were wasting the country." Luther says it "is a prayer against those most bitter and daily enemies, the neighboring Philistines, Syrians, Moabites, Edomites, etc." Horne thinks it was composed when the church was "still in captivity." Calvin thinks "it was composed in behalf of the ten tribes, after that kingdom began to be wasted by various calamities." Was *Benjamin* (mentioned in v. 2) one of the ten tribes? Calvin seems to take this for granted. Hengstenberg argues for it. Alexander accepts it as probable. But the great mass of scholars doubt not that Judah and Benjamin remained united in the temple service. The support of this view is clear and full, 1 Kings xii. 21. A part of the very ground, on which the temple and the holy city stood belonged to the tribe of Benjamin. If any ask, then, why does the prophet mention *Ephraim* and *Manasseh?* several reasons may be assigned. 1. Those tribes and Benjamin followed the ark in the march to Canaan, Nu. ii. 17–23. The ark was the token of God's *strength.* In v. 2, we may have a poetic allusion to the order of the camps. 2. Merrick thinks these tribes mentioned to show that the Psalm was written when some foe was hovering on their borders and beginning to devastate the land. This supposes the tribes all yet united, at least in sympathy with each other. 3. Patrick and some others think the Psalm may relate to the time when Hezekiah wrote a letter to the remnant escaped from Assyria; especially to Ephraim and Manasseh inviting them to Jerusalem to keep the passover which invitation was accepted by some, 2 Chron. xxx. 1–23. 4. Merrick: "If the Psalm was not written on any such occasion, it may be most reasonable to suppose that Benjamin, Joseph's only brother by the same mother, and Ephraim and Manasseh his sons, are in the second verse equivalent to Joseph who in the preceding verse represents the whole posterity of Israel." Clarke is confident that this and Ps. lxxix. were written by the same author. Most commentators speak diffidently of authorship. Whether Asaph wrote it the reader must judge. See Introduction, § 4, on Ps. l. and Ps. lxxiii–lxxix. This Psalm, may be prophetical or it may have had a historical occasion. Of those who take the latter view, some think it was written on occasion of the destruction of the holy city by the Chaldeans; others, on occasion of the carrying away of the ten tribes; yet others, on occasion of the invasion of Sennacherib. This latter view is favored by the Septuagint, which styles it "A Psalm for the Assyrian." If we regard the Psalm as written in prophecy to suit the church in any and all her distressing circumstances, we give it the widest use. In it we find these names of the supreme Being, *Elohim God, Jehovah* LORD and *El God,* on which see on Ps. iii. 2; i. 2; v. 4. On *Selah* see Introduction, § 15.

1. *Give ear, O Shepherd of Israel. Give ear,* as in Ps. v. 1; xvii. 1. *Shepherd,* as in Ps. xxiii. 1, a participle, *one that feeds,* or acts the part of a shepherd. The allusion is probably to Genesis xlviii. 15, where we have the same. God had long been a Guide, a Support, a Protector to the descendants of Jacob, hence the title Shepherd *of Israel. Thou that leadest Joseph like a flock. Joseph* here is equivalent to *Israel* in the preceding. Each name may be applied to the whole nation descended from Jacob. The participle rendered *thou that leadest* may refer to the past, 2 Sam. vi. 3; or to the present, Ecc. ii. 3; or to the future, Isa. xi. 6. God had all along taken good care of the Israelites. *Thou that dwellest* between the *cherubim,* a form of speech of frequent occurrence, Ex. xxv. 22; Ps. xcix. 1. Such language is not used after the captivity, though it might be in allusion to history. The cherubim (or cherubs) stood over the mercy-seat, or propitiatory. Between them the Shechinah appeared. At the captivity the ark disappeared and was never replaced. Neither did the visible glory of the Lord appear any more. *Shine forth.* As the sun long obscured at last bursts through the clouds and gladdens all creation by shining in his strength, so the Psalmist desires God to be as the light of the morning when the sun riseth, even a morning without clouds.

2. *Before Ephraim and Benjamin and Manasseh stir up thy strength.* The ark was a token of God's power. It is more than once called the ark of God's strength. Going through the wilderness the tribes here named marched behind the ark, Num. ii. 18–24. This is perhaps the most natural and approved explanation. But Mudge followed by Dodd and Clarke gives another, viz., that these tribes represent the whole nation, *Benjamin* being incorporated with Judah, *Manasseh* comprehending the country beyond Jordan, and Ephraim all the rest. This gives a very good sense and is not over-

strained. *Stir up thy strength,* arouse thy might, exert thy power. *And come* and *save us,* or, go forth for salvation to us.

3. *Turn us again, O God. Restore* or *rescue* us as the same verb is rendered, Gen. xx. 7; Ps. xxxv. 17. *And cause thy face to shine.* See on Ps. iv. 6; xxxi. 16. *And we shall be saved.* This rendering is literal and declares the effect of God's *restoring* his people and causing his *face* to shine. The petitions of this verse ask for the reviving of God's work of grace, and for the kindly aspects of his providence.

4. *O* Lord *God of hosts, how long wilt thou be angry against the prayer of thy people?* The Lord of Sabaoth, or the God of Sabaoth is a title of great honor. It is given some *hundreds* of times. God commands the hosts of the starry worlds, the vast armies of angels and of saints in glory, the great armies of men on earth, and the vast array of causes at work in all worlds. This great God is the right one to manage our affairs. When he hides his face we are troubled. His silence is dreadful. Delay to answer our prayers may be misinterpreted as denial of our petitions, but almost uniformly "the faithful fear God's anger, when they perceive that their prayers are not forthwith heard." On *How long?* see on Ps. iv. 2.

5. *Thou feedest them with the bread of tears. Bread of tears* and *bread of affliction,* are forms of expression but little liable to be misunderstood, though purely Hebraistic. The meaning is that Israel ate tears instead of bread, or bread wet with tears, or that while they ate bread they wept. *And givest them tears to drink in great measure.* Hengstenberg: "This clause can only be translated: *Thou causest them to drink with a measure of tears;*" Horne: "There cannot be a more striking picture of Zion in captivity. Her bread is dipped in tears; and her cup is filled to the brim with them." Tholuck: "Their bread was so steeped in tears that they became their food, and so copious was *their weeping,* that their tears became their drink."

6. *Thou makest us a strife unto our neighbors.* The meaning is either 1. They strive with us; or 2. They strive among themselves concerning us. There is a rivalry among them which shall do us the most harm. Both were true. *Neighbors,* as in Ps. xxxi. 11; xliv. 13; lxxix. 4, 12. It adds much to the weight of our griefs, when they are brought on us by those, from whom we had a right to expect something very different. *And our enemies laugh among themselves.* They laugh at our miseries. They are glad to see us suffering. They rejoice and triumph over us. They mock our sorrows. Calvin: "They talk among themselves by way of sport and mockery at our adversities." *Enemies,* the word commonly so rendered, as in Ps. iii. 7; vi. 10. Both the verbs are in the future.

7. *Turn us again, O God of hosts, and cause thy face to shine; and we shall be saved.* See on v. 3. *God of hosts,* as in v. 4. Calvin: "God did not here intend to indite for his people a vain repetition of words: his object was to encourage them, when bowed down under the load of their calamities, boldly to rise up, heavy though the load might be. This ground of support was often presented to them; and it is repeated the third time in the concluding verse of the Psalm."

8. *Thou hast brought a vine out of Egypt.* Here begins as perfect a specimen of allegory as is to be found in any language. It is a whole. It has in it nothing superfluous. The church of God, embodied in the Jewish nation, was brought out of Egypt, as *a vine.* This is a favorite and beautiful figure of Scripture. Horne: "The vine is a plant weak and lowly, and needing support; when supported, wild and luxuriant, unless restrained by the pruning-knife; capable of producing the most valuable fruit; but, if barren, the most unprofitable among trees. In all these respects it is a lively emblem of the church, and used as such by Isaiah v. 7, by Ezekiel xv. xvii. xix., and by our Lord himself, Matt. xxi. 33." The bringing of this vine out of Egypt is much celebrated in the Scriptures of both Testaments. This was, says the

elder President Edwards, "the most remarkable of all the deliverances noticed in the Old Testament, the greatest pledge and forerunner of future redemption by Christ, and much more insisted on in Scripture than any other. Indeed it was the greatest type of Christ's redemption of any providential event whatsoever." *Thou hast cast out the heathen.* When the heathen nations inhabiting Canaan had filled up the measure of their iniquity, they were by God's command destroyed, expelled or subjugated. The mode of ejecting them was chiefly by wars waged by the Israelites at the command of God, and rendered decisive by divine assistance. *And planted it.* The settlement of the Israelites in the promised land was attended by so many marvellous circumstances as to be clearly of God.

9. *Thou preparedst* room *before it.* Arabic: Thou hast prepared the way before it; Calvin: Thou hast cleansed the ground before it. The meaning is that God had removed the mighty nations, who would have been hindrances to Israel's settlement in Canaan. *And didst cause it to take deep root.* Chaldee, Arabic and Vulgate: Thou didst plant its roots; Calvin: Thou hast rooted its roots. That is, after planting it, thou didst cause it to grow. *And it filled the land.* Its growth was vigorous and rapid. The powerful nations, that had inhabited the promised land, rapidly lost political power, and Israel succeeded.

10. *The hills were covered with the shadow of it, and the boughs thereof* were like *the goodly cedars. Goodly cedars,* literally *cedars of God, i. e.,* great cedars, see on Ps. xxxvi. 6. Some European Commentators, who are accustomed to see the small cultivated vines of the old world, seem rather surprised at the boldness of the figure in this and in the next verse. But 1, we have here an allegory; 2, in countries where the forests are unbroken, the vine attains a great size, rising to the top of the most majestic trees and covering them with its fruit and foliage. Anderson has collected some testimonies on this subject from the history of the Barbary States, and from the history of Virginia. Rosenmüller in like manner speaks of the vine in Persia as rising to great heights.

11. *She sent out her boughs unto the sea, and her branches unto the river. The sea* here mentioned is the Mediterranean; the *river,* the Euphrates, Gen. xv. 18; Deut. xi. 24; Josh. i. 4; 1 Kings iv. 20, 21; Ps. lxxii. 8.

12. *Why hast thou* then *broken down her hedges, so that all they which pass by the way do pluck her?* Jehovah himself was a wall of protection to his people. His perfections and providence put a hedge about them, Job i. 10; Ps. xxxiv. 7; Is. v. 2. When he withdraws they are sadly exposed. This verse and the next contain the gist of the allegory. How comes it that God, who is wise and just, should have taken such pains with a vine for long years, and then leave it exposed to utter destruction? Berleberg Bible: "Shall all this be for nought and in vain? Or hast thou planted it on this account, that the enemies might devour it?"

13. *The boar out of the wood doth waste it, and the wild beast of the field doth devour it.* By the *boar* Patrick thinks reference is had to the king of Assyria and the havoc made by his barbarous soldiers, 2 Kings xix. 23–26. By the *wild beast* Theodoret understands Nebuchadnezzar. The Berleberg Bible names Pul, Tiglath-pileser, Shalmaneser, and Sennacherib. If this Psalm is prophetic and applicable to all the times of the church's distress, it is best by boar and wild beast to understand generally the fierce and cruel enemies of Israel. The Talmud notices that the middle letter of the word rendered *wood* in this verse is the middle letter of the Hebrew Psalter.

14. *Return, we beseech thee, O God of hosts. Return,* in vv. 3, 7, 19; Ps. lxxxv. 4, *turn.* It is best to supply *us.* If so, then see on vv. 3, 7. If we read *return,* then the plea is for a restoration of God's presence. *Look down from heaven, and behold,*

and visit this vine. Clarke: "Let thine eye affect thine heart." The meaning is, Visit in mercy and bless.

15. *And the vineyard which thy right hand hath planted.* According to the English translation the verbs of the preceding clause are to be understood as repeated here; but some take the first word to be a verb, and render it *maintain, establish, protect, or sustain.* This is better. To put *vineyard* for vine is to change and even mar the figure. *Protect that which thy right hand hath planted,* is the better rendering. The *right hand* denotes *skill* and *strength.* God had shown great wisdom and power in establishing the Jewish nation. *And the branch that thou madest strong for thyself.* The radical idea of this allegory is probably found in Gen. xlix. 22, where the word here rendered *branch* is twice rendered *bough;* not that rendered *branch* in Zech. iii. 8 ; vi. 12. It is hundreds of times rendered *son,* in the plural, *sons.* Taken without a figure it is a prayer for Israel as a son, whom God had raised up. But the Chaldee, Abenezra and R. Obadiah by the *branch* understand Messiah himself. The Septuagint, Vulgate, Syriac, Arabic and Ethiopic, read *Son of man.* If it refers to Messiah, this is the first place where he is called the Son of man. Many favor this interpretation. The prophets, always esteeming the coming Saviour a welcome theme, oftentimes give no notice that they are about to introduce that high matter. It may be so here, though it must be confessed that it would be an unusual interruption of a form of discourse demanding an unbroken connection. For the very next words are:

16. It is *burned with fire,* it is *cut down.* That, which God's right hand had planted, was burned. Israel, containing the visible church, was in a sad state, like a vine over which hot flames had passed and it was then *cut down,* or, as the same word is elsewhere rendered, *cut up.* *They perish at the rebuke of thy countenance.* *They* refers to those that wasted and destroyed the vine. So Street, Green, Jebb, Horsley, Fry. But Calvin, Patrick, Pool, Hammond, Scott, Tholuck, Hengstenberg and Alexander apply the phrase to the people of Israel. Horne is doubtful whether it refers to the adversaries, or to the Israelites.

17. *Let thy hand be upon the man of thy right hand, upon the son of man* whom *thou madest strong for thyself.* The best commentators admit that this refers to Christ. If so, it strengthens the conjecture that the same forms of expression in v. 15 referred to him also. The *man of thy right hand,* may mean the *man raised up by thy right hand* or raised up to sit at thy right hand. *Let thy hand be upon him* is thus explained by Alexander: "Let thy hand fall not on us but on our substitute." Scott : "'The man of God's right hand' and 'the son of man' point out the promised Messiah very clearly."

18. *So will not we go back from thee.* The stability of a people or of a church could never be predicated or pledged upon the courage, success or piety of a temporal prince. The *Son of man* exalted at God's right hand can give to his people steadfastness, preserve them from backsliding and keep them from falling, Luke xxii. 32 ; Heb. iv. 14 ; x. 23. *Quicken us, and we will call upon thy name.* For a time they had been in a *dead* state. Now they desired to be made alive. New life being imparted, they would delight in his worship and religion would be greatly revived.

19. *Turn us again, O* LORD *God of hosts, cause thy face to shine ; and we shall be saved.* See on vv. 3, 7, 14.

DOCTRINAL AND PRACTICAL REMARKS.

1. So surely as God hides his face, so surely will the righteous be in trouble. If he withdraws, it matters little who else is present. If he does not *shine,* the tapers of earth will be found very dim, v. 1.

2. If we have a heart to pray, we may confidently expect that God will have an *ear* to hear, v. 1. If we have a case, and desire to present it, we may know that God holds his court open.

3. While we should neither deny nor forget any of the attributes of God, we should specially call to mind the gentleness and loving-kindness of God in times of our deep affliction. Then too we should recall and revive the memory of the history of his past favors to all his people, v. 1.

4. We may always in faith and earnestness plead God's relations to us, as our *Shepherd* and as the glorious God *dwelling between the cherubim*, v. 1. There is no truth in theology that may not bring consolation to a trembling believer.

5. God has power to save, whenever he chooses to exert it, v. 2. Sometimes his omnipotence seems to slumber, but when he stirs it up, all enemies flee, stand aghast, or are consumed.

6. If we fall into any decay of nature or of grace, God alone can recover and deliver us, vv. 2, 3, 7, 14, 19. This should make us speed our flight to the mercy-seat. We do but lose time when we go to others before we go to the Lord.

7. Children should be taught and encouraged to cry mightily to the God, who heard and helped their fathers, v. 2. He is a God that changes not. What he has done once, he will do again, if the necessities of his people or the honor of his name require it.

8. Dickson: "As the apostasy of God's people from God is the fountain of all their calamity; so their repentance and returning unto God is the first step unto their relief from procured misery of captivity, or any other calamity," v. 3.

9. How mysterious the whole doctrine of repentance and conversion must be to those who think themselves naturally good, v. 3. Scott: "We can neither expect the comforts of his love, nor the protection of his powerful arm, except we are partakers of his converting grace." It is madness for carnal men to expect God to treat them as dear children.

10. Delay is not denial. God's time and way of answering our prayers are the best. Let us trust him. Let us not misinterpret him, v. 4. This would give the adversary the very advantage he seeks.

11. Yet if our prayers are not answered, we ought to inquire the cause, and be concerned, till we have a token for good, v. 4. Prayer is but a means to the divine blessing. Great and long-continued trials call for deep heart-searchings, as well as for earnest appeal to God.

12. It is mournful to be compelled to believe that after all the religious rites and forms in the world, there is but little hearty devotion and acceptable prayer offered to God. Else why should there remain so much that looks as if God were really and terribly angry with us? v. 4.

13. One of the great troubles of the Christian life is that we are naturally so much more affected and oppressed with natural than with moral evil, with our sufferings than with our sinfulness. "The tears of repentance are very rare, and soon dried up, but the tears of sorrow for affliction easily flow." It is well when worldly grief is followed by godly sorrow.

14. It is a great blessing to have *neighbors!* What an awful desolation earth would be, if each man, or each family were in perpetual solitude. And yet how often do *neighbors* themselves become chief sources of our miseries, v. 6. They envy, annoy, suspect, revile, persecute us. They seek our ruin.

15. Laughter, mockery, railing, ridicule are not new, though they are very keen weapons, v. 6. Let us not render railing for railing, but rather let us speak kind words for angry, good words for evil, and leave our revilers in God's hands.

16. God is in history, v. 8. Let us often look at the generations of old. The lessons of the past are full of instruction. Especially should great chains of providence be studied link by link. They reveal wonders.

17. God has filled our mouths with the most amazing arguments to be pleaded with him for accomplishing our full and final deliverance, vv. 8–12. When we can truly urge that God has begun a work, we have an irrefragable argument put into our mouths. How can he leave his work incomplete? Shall he not finish the house, whose foundations he has laid? Shall he plant a vine, and then lay and leave it waste?

18. Unfruitfulness in churches or in persons is just cause for the divine displeasure; and the measure of the sins of men and nations, unless brought to deep repentance, will be full after awhile, v. 8. If God destroys one nation for its sins, and its successor is not by such divine judgments deterred from adding iniquity to iniquity, even more horrible woes will come on the latter than on the former. The Jewish nation suffered far more terribly in its final overthrow than did the seven nations of Canaan, that preceded them.

19. Nations are planted and transplanted by the Lord, v. 8. Man could not make a nation. It is everywhere in Scripture claimed to be the work of Jehovah.

20. The good providence of God over nations in their later history is as necessary as it was in the beginning, v. 9. If they *take root*, it must be wholly owing to divine culture.

21. God's mercy can make great the smallest things and people, vv. 9, 10, 11, 15. He can take Israel from a hard bondage in the brick-kilns and make him renowned over the whole world for his puissance. He can take David from the sheep-cote and send his name over all the earth as the sweetest of lyric poets, as a great prince and a warrior, who had slain his tens of thousands.

22. If calamities overtake us we may rest assured either that God would correct in us something wrong, or make us useful to others as examples of suffering affliction, v. 12. "The curse causeless shall not come."

23. Dickson: "As present-felt misery commendeth prosperity past, so past prosperity augmenteth present misery, where the two conditions are compared," vv. 8–14.

24. Seldom if ever do troubles come alone, vv. 12, 13. Where there has been much sinning we may expect much suffering. If Israel apostatizes from God, and practises ingratitude, idolatry, pride, unbelief, covetousness, that people may expect evil in many a form.

25. How welcome to the humble believer are discoveries here and there,. all through Scripture, of the Branch, the Stem of Jesse, the Plant of renown, the Root and the Offspring of David, the Son of man, vv. 15, 17. And as the prophets asked no formal leave to bring in this matter, so neither need we apologize for dwelling on so glorious a personage. Jesus should always be to us a welcome theme.

26. It is impossible for us to be too careful to avoid backsliding, v. 18. It is the bane of piety, the misery of Christians. If we are kept from declension, it must be by the power of God through Jesus Christ. Let us by solemn covenant engagements, by prayer, by ceaseless vigilance, by self-exhortation guard against so great a sin and misery as will overtake us if we *go back from God*.

27. Let not our faith be staggered at the terrible indiscriminateness, with which the divine judgments seem to fall on communities composed of saints and sinners; see this Psalm; Ecc. ii. 14; ix. 3. In times of public calamity the righteous, from the refined sensibility of their nature, if from no other cause, often suffer even more than the wicked.

28. Let every people, enjoying the blessings of peace and ordinary prosperity, of

civil and religious liberty, remember that they hold their franchises and immunities solely by the bounty of God. Every people have sinned enough to provoke the wrath of the Almighty. Let them humble themselves and cry for mercy. Let them put away their idols and do works meet for repentance.

29. Let those who are in the most afflicted circumstances not forsake the throne of grace. Rather let them with great liveliness and warm desires cleave to the Lord with purpose of heart.

PSALM LXXXI.

To the chief Musician upon Gittith, *A Psalm* of Asaph.

1 Sing aloud unto God our strength: make a joyful noise unto the God of Jacob.

2 Take a psalm, and bring hither the timbrel, the pleasant harp with the psaltery.

3 Blow up the trumpet in the new moon, in the time appointed, on our solemn feast day.

4 For this *was* a statute for Israel, *and* a law of the God of Jacob.

5 This he ordained in Joseph *for* a testimony, when he went out through the land of Egypt: *where* I heard a language *that* I understood not.

6. I removed his shoulder from the burden: his hands were delivered from the pots.

7 Thou calledst in trouble, and I delivered thee; I answered thee in the secret place of thunder: I proved thee at the waters of Meribah. Selah.

8 Hear, O my people, and I will testify unto thee: O Israel, if thou wilt hearken unto me;

9 There shall no strange god be in thee; neither shalt thou worship any strange god.

10 I *am* the LORD thy God, which brought thee out of the land of Egypt: open thy mouth wide, and I will fill it.

11 But my people would not hearken to my voice; and Israel would none of me.

12 So I gave them up to their own hearts' lust: *and* they walked in their own counsels.

13 Oh that my people had hearkened unto me, *and* Israel had walked in my ways!

14 I should soon have subdued their enemies, and turned my hand against their adversaries.

15 The haters of the LORD should have submitted themselves unto him: but their time should have endured for ever.

16 He should have fed them also with the finest of the wheat: and with honey out of the rock should I have satisfied thee.

ON the title see on titles of Psalms iv. viii. xi. On the date and authorship see Introduction, § 4, on Psalms l. lxxiii.–lxxx. Alexander: "In the absence of any proof to the contrary, the Asaph of this title must be assumed to be the cotemporary of David." Clarke gives no date. Scott dates it B. C. 1045. Horsley is confident that it is older than the time of David, but he assigns no sufficient ground for such an opinion. Hengstenberg is clear that this Psalm has a "prophetic character." Tholuck: "Asaph, the cotemporary of David, is probably the author." There is not entire agreement as to the specific object or design of the Psalm. Clarke: "It is pretty generally agreed that it was either written *for*, or used *at* the celebration of the feast of Trumpets, (Lev. xxiii. 24,) which was held on the first day of the month Tisri, which was the beginning of the Jewish year; and on that day it is still used in the Jewish worship. According to Jewish tradition, credited by many learned Christians, the world was created in *Tisri*, which answers to our September. The Psalm may have been used in celebrating the feast of trumpets on the first day of Tisri, the feast of tabernacles on the *fifteenth* of the same month, the *creation* of the world, the feasts of the new moons, and the deliverance of the Israelites from Egypt; to all which circumstances it appears to refer." Tholuck calls it,

" A passover Psalm, which contains at the same time a sermon of God to his people." Hengstenberg, Alexander and others take much the same view. Luther thinks it was sung at the feast of tabernacles. The fact is, this ode is fit to be sung on any joyous occasion of worship in Israel. The names of the Most High found in this Psalm are *Elohim God, El God* and *Jehovah* LORD, on which see on Psalms iii. 2; i. 2; v. 4. On *Selah* see Introduction, § 15.

1. *Sing aloud unto God our strength.* *Sing aloud,* elsewhere *sing, shout, cry, cry out, shout for joy, rejoice, greatly rejoice, triumph.* The ancient versions have *praise, sing praises, rejoice exceedingly.* *Strength,* the word so often used in declaring that Jehovah is the source of all the might of his people, Ps. xxviii. 7; xlvi. 1. In the Psalter the word first occurs in Ps. viii. 2. *Make a joyful noise unto the God of Jacob.* The verb is elsewhere rendered *cry, cry aloud, shout, shout for joy, triumph.* It is the word used to describe the joyful worship of angels at the completion of creation, Job xxxviii. 7. The two clauses are a loud call to the public and joyful worship of Jehovah. The patriarch Jacob had rich experience of God's almightiness, because by it the enraged heart of Esau was so changed that he became kind. See on Ps. xx. 1.

2. *Take a Psalm.* *Psalm,* the original twice so rendered, and twice *melody.* The cognate verb is commonly *sing, sing Psalms, sing praises, praise.* The rendering of the common version is good. This clause calls for the use of words of praise. *And bring hither the timbrel.* *Timbrel,* the Hebrew word occurs *seventeen* times, is *eight* times rendered as here, and *nine* times *tabret.* It designates any drum, or tambourine known to the Israelites. This instrument is first noticed in Job xxi. 12; Gen. xxxi. 27. It was played by women. [And take] *the pleasant harp with the psaltery.* On *harp* and *psaltery* see on Ps. xxxiii. 2.

3. *Blow up the trumpet.* The trumpets or cornets of Scripture were of various shapes and materials. They were used to call assemblies, to celebrate sacrifices, to proclaim the jubilee, and on occasion of several feasts. *In the new moon* is explained by two other phrases closely following, *in the time appointed, on our solemn feast day.* Many think there is special reference to some one annual feast. If this is so, it was probably the passover. See introductory remarks on this Psalm, also v. 5.

4. *For this* was *a statute for Israel,* and *a law of the God of Jacob.* *Statute,* commonly so rendered. *Law,* commonly rendered *judgment.* Each word signifies a fixed ordinance. The latter is sometimes rendered *right,* as in Ps. ix. 4. Some so read it here. *Israel,* the people descended from Jacob.

5. *This he ordained in Joseph* for *a testimony, when he went out through the land of Egypt.* Whatever was pleasant in the condition of the Israelites in Egypt was mainly through the influence of Joseph; for when there arose another Pharaoh, who knew not Joseph, they fell into great affliction. So that there is peculiar propriety in here using *Joseph* as a name for the nation. On *testimony* see on Ps. xix. 7. The passover was not only a fixed ordinance; it was a standing *testimony.* The pronoun *he* may refer, 1, to God, when *he* went forth to destroy all the first-born in the land; and then led Joseph forth from Egypt; or, 2, to Joseph (*i. e.,* the Israelites) when he publicly went out of Egypt. The latter is the more common interpretation. The preposition *through* might be *upon* or *over,* implying the triumphant character of the march out of Egypt. Where *I heard a language* that *I understood not.* What does this mean? Four views are taken. 1. Joseph (meaning the Israelites) heard the language of the Egyptians, which was to them a foreign tongue, " a strange language," Ps. cxiv. 1. The chief difficulty lies in the use of the pronoun *I,* instead of *he.* The Syriac, Arabic, Septuagint, Vulgate and Ethiopic read, *he,* instead of *I.* In this view the *language* heard by the Israelites was the Egyptian. 2. Some think the *language* meant is that found in the next verse: " I removed his shoulder," etc., *i. e.,* Israel heard words

of great delight, when God undertook to deliver his people. The great objection to this is that the word rendered *language* does not mean *sentence*, but *language* or *tongue*, (literally *lip*) as in Gen. xi. 1, 6, 7. Yet some think it means that Israel heard the *voice* of God as on Mount Sinai, instructing them in the way they should walk. It was then they said, "Let not God speak with us lest we die." 3. Another interpretation is that God is the speaker here, and that by a figure of speech he represents himself as not being acquainted with the language spoken by the Egyptians, or by the Hebrews after their long residence in Egypt. It was strange to him. This figure is no more bold than that where God says he had known no other nation but that of Israel, Amos iii. 2. 4. Dœderlein "interprets the words as an abrupt exclamation of the Psalmist upon feeling himself suddenly influenced by a divine afflatus, and upon hearing an oracle addressed to him by God, which consisted of what immediately follows, from v. 6 to the close of the Psalm, and which is spoken in the person of God." Is not this overstrained? The second view has for its support more authority than either of the others. But the third makes the grammatical construction very easy and simple. All agree that in v. 6 God is the speaker. Why may he not be in this clause?

6. *I removed his shoulder from the burden.* How heavy the *burdens* on the children of Israel were may be seen in Ex. v. 5–19; vi. 6, 7. *His hands were delivered from the pots. Pots,* in the English version elsewhere rendered *seething pots, kettles, caldrons, baskets,* Job xli. 20; 1 Sam. ii. 14; 2 Chron. xxxv. 13; Jer. xxiv. 2. By *pots* here Clarke understands "the moulds and furnaces in which they formed and baked their bricks." Kennicott thinks they were large vessels in which the earth was mixed and worked up for making bricks. Hengstenberg: "Baskets of this kind were found in the sepulchral vaults of Thebes, of which Rosellini first furnished drawings and descriptions: the Israelites used them for carrying from one place to another the clay and manufactured bricks." Pool: "In the general, the word seems to note all those vessels, wherein they carried water, straw, lime, bricks, etc." Scott thinks it doubtful whether the word means earthen vessels made by the Israelites, or the kilns, where bricks were burnt, or baskets used in their work, or the flesh-pots which they afterwards regretted. The parallelism would make them baskets in which burdens were borne. From these their hands were delivered or passed away, literally *will pass away,* implying not only that Egyptian servitude was ended, but should never return.

7. *Thou calledst in trouble, and I delivered thee.* The historic account of the cry of the oppressed Israelites is found in Ex. ii. 23–25; iii. 7, 9. Their deliverance was in several respects the most famous and important event in ancient history. *I answered thee in the secret place of thunder.* The verb is in the future, *will answer,* as is also the verb of the next clause, *will prove.* But see Introduction, § 6. Those, who should insist on reading these clauses in the future, would of course make them prophetic. But it seems certain that this Psalm was not written till after the events mentioned in this verse. This clause has received three interpretations. 1. Scott: "Some think that the *secret place* refers to the cloudy pillar, from the *hidden recess* of which JEHOVAH spoke in mercy to his people, and in thunder to his enemies." 2. Calvin: "The meaning simply is that the people were heard in a secret and wonderful manner, while, at the same time, manifest tokens were given by which the Israelites might be satisfied that they were succored by the divine hand." 3. Alexander following Lowth and Walford: "The secret or hiding-place of thunder is the dark cloud charged with tempest, which overhung Mount Sinai at the giving of the law, Ex. xx. 18." See also Deut. iv. 10, 11, 36. The intelligent reader must judge which of these is to be preferred. *I proved thee at the waters of Meribah.* The historic event here alluded to is recorded in Num. xx. 2–13. The trial to which the Israelites were there subjected

was that of an inadequate supply of water for a short time. If the preceding clause would seem to relate to Sinai, this relates to an event of prior date; but in Hebrew poetry the historic order of events is not always preserved. Luther: "He makes mention of the waters of strife (*Meribah*) in order that he may remind them of their sins."

8. *Hear, O my people, and I will testify unto thee. People*, or *nation*. God's word and ordinances are often represented as a testimony. Surely he is a competent and credible witness. See on Ps. l. 7. *O Israel, if thou wilt hearken unto me*. It is better to render it, *Oh that thou wouldest hearken*. The corresponding Greek particle has the optative sense in Luke xix. 42.

9. *There shall be no strange God in thee; neither shalt thou worship any strange God.* There are different words rendered *strange* in this verse, but the difference in signification is very slight. In this verse it is nothing. Either of them might be rendered *foreign, alien*. The prohibition is to seek after a heathen God. This was very clearly right as none pretended that any false God had helped them, Deut. xxxii. 12. *Bow down*, as in the second commandment. The future here has the force of the imperative as in several precepts of the decalogue.

10. *I am the* LORD *thy God which brought thee out of the land of Egypt.* This quite corresponds with the preface of the moral law, Ex. xx. 2. Clearly the inspired writer was thinking of that code. Some make this clause parenthetical. It assigns the awful authority, under which all these things are said. If connected with the next clause it gives it peculiar force: *Open thy mouth wide and I will fill it.* Hengstenberg: "I am rich for all thy necessities, even for thy boldest wishes." God, who had saved them from great troubles, could supply all their need and meet all their desires in days to come. Tholuck: "Let them open their hearts and mouths ever so wide, he would fill them; as infants and young birds are fed by their mothers, so he would satisfy them."

11. *But my people would not hearken to my voice; and Israel would none of me.* *People* and *Israel* mean the same. Both clauses express strong aversion; the latter, utter *unwillingness*, total disinclination of heart. Chaldee: They acquiesced not in my word.

12. *So I gave them up to their own hearts' lust.* Tremellius and Junius: Wherefore I gave them up to walk according to the desire of their own heart; Edwards, Jebb and Green: So I gave them up to the imaginations of their own hearts; Walford: So I gave them up to the purposes of their heart; Clarke: So I gave them up to the *obstinate wickedness* of their heart; Alexander: And I gave them up to the corruption of their own heart. The word rendered *lust* occurs ten times, and in the text of the English Bible is uniformly rendered *imagination* except here; in the margin sometimes *hardness, stubbornness*. And *they walked in their own counsels*, plans, purposes. Pool: " They practised those things, both in conversation and in religious worship, which were most agreeable, not to my commands or counsels, but to their own fancies and inclinations."

13. *Oh that my people had hearkened unto me*, and *Israel had walked in my ways!* *People* and *Israel* as in v. 8. *Hearkened*, as in vv. 5, 8, 11. To walk in God's ways is habitually to obey him. See on Ps. i. 1. Clarke: "Nothing can be more plaintive than the original: *sense* and *sound* are surprisingly united."

14. *I should soon have subdued their enemies, and turned my hand against their adversaries. Enemies*, very uniformly rendered. *Adversaries*, those who *vex, afflict, distress*, or, *bring into straits. Subdued*, elsewhere *humbled, brought down, brought low*. Alexander: "The phrase [turn my hand] denotes mere action; the idea of hostile or destructive action is suggested by the context." The verb is sometimes rendered *requite, recompense*. In such cases the word *hand* is not added.

15. *The haters of the* LORD *should have submitted themselves unto him.* *Haters of the* LORD, literally *those hating Jehovah.* The word expresses strong dislike, settled enmity. *Submitted,* the verb literally signifies *lied, deceived, dealt falsely, dissembled, yielded feigned obedience,* 1 Kings xiii. 18; Zech. xiii. 4; Lev. xix. 11; Josh. vii. 11 and margin of 2 Sam. xxii. 45. See on Ps. xviii. 44. The Israelites had trouble in all their generations with the heathen. In all the verse God identifies himself with his people. *But their time should have endured forever.* *Their time,* meaning their continuance, prosperity and power, should have been enduring.

16. *He should have fed them also with the finest of the wheat,* literally the *fat* of wheat, meaning the best part or quality of it. For *he* some would read *I.* Either gives the sense. *And with honey out of the rock should I have satisfied thee.* Does this mean a miraculous supply of honey? Hengstenberg thinks this probable. But is this necessary? Moses says God made his people "suck honey out of the rock," Deut. xxxii. 13. Compare 1 Sam. xiv. 25. Seventeen or eighteen times we have the phrase " a land flowing with milk and honey." Wild honey was a part of the food of John Baptist. The ideas of the verse are taken from Deut. xxxii. 13, 14. Alexander: "Wheat and honey, by a natural and primitive association, are here put for the necessaries and the luxuries of human sustenance, and these again for the highest enjoyment and prosperity." The paraphrase of the old Psalter quoted by Clarke has: "He fed thaim with the body of Criste and gostely understandying; and of hony that ran of the stane, that is, of the wisedome, that is swete to the hert." Clarke: "Several of the fathers understand this place of Christ." Calvin: "The meaning simply is, that the grace of God would have continued to flow in an unbroken and uniform course, had it not been interrupted by the perverseness and wickedness of the people."

DOCTRINAL AND PRACTICAL REMARKS.

1. God's worship should not only be secret, but also social and public; and his public worship should be audible and intelligible, not tame, nor boisterous, but triumphant. "Sing aloud," "Make a joyful noise," v. 1. Mute worship can edify none but him, who offers it. Henry: "We must be warm and affectionate in praising God; we must with a hearty good will show forth his praise, as those that are not ashamed to own our dependence on him, and our obligations to him."

2. When God is *our strength,* we are irresistible and our foes are nothing, v. 1. He makes the feeble to be as David.

3. One advantage of the study of good history is that there we learn how safe is he, who trusts Jehovah. The *God of Jacob* is the God of all who wrestle like Jacob, v. 1.

4. As a great part of our enjoyment consists in the constant reception of blessings; so a large part of our duty consists in rendering suitable thanks and praises for benefits received, v. 2. Scott: "All the worship, which we can render, is far beneath his glorious excellences, and our immense obligations to him, especially in our redemption from wrath and sin."

5. Verses 2, 3, call up the subject of instrumental music. See REMARKS on Ps. xxxiii. 2.

6. A ritual is not in itself like a moral precept; but when God prescribes a ceremony it is to be sacredly observed because he enjoins it, vv. 4, 5. Compare John iii. 15. Dickson: "It is a sufficient motive for any religious action that God hath ordained it; and no less authority than divine can warrant a man in matters of religion."

7. All God's word and ordinances are for a *testimony* to us, vv. 5, 8. The tabernacle was the tabernacle of witness. The ark was the ark of the testimony. God *testifies* to us. He declares. He swears. Not to believe him is to make him a liar.

8. It is well for us to be reminded of our humble origin, v. 6. We should often think of the hole of the pit, whence we were digged. All Israel was taught to say, "A Syrian ready to perish was my father," Deut. xxvi. 5.

9. As the people of the Jews never rose to all the sublimity of praise, which God's mercies in bringing them out of Egypt would have warranted, so neither shall we ever adequately thank him for his many and great favors displayed in redemption, vv. 5, 6, 7, 10. Calvin: "As God has not only withdrawn our shoulders from a burden of brick, and not only removed our hands from the kilns, but has also redeemed us from the cruel and miserable tyranny of Satan, and drawn us from the depths of hell, the obligations under which we lie to him are of a much more strict and sacred kind than those under which he had brought his ancient people."

10. In all ages prayer has been a great means of good to miserable sinners, v. 7. This suits the poorest beggars. Ask and have is the rule.

11. God's answers are not the less to be heeded, because they sometimes come to us in an alarming manner, from *the secret place of thunder*, v. 7. The same is taught in Ps. xlv. 4; lv. 5.

12. Everything is a test of character, v. 7. God *proves* us by prosperity and by adversity, by joy and by sorrow, by hunger and by thirst, by sickness and by health, by all his word and by all his providences.

13. Nothing can make amends for a perverse *will*, a wicked inclination of the heart, v. 8. If men have not a mind to hearken, they will surely perish. If there be first a willing mind, our service is accepted according to what we have, and not according to what we have not.

14. How amazingly is human nature fallen and sunk, when, even after all God's warnings, men yet fall into abominable idolatries, v. 9. God cannot allow another to be partaker of honors due to him without denying himself. It is as much his prerogative to be God alone as to be God at all.

15. Then are past mercies rightly used when they lead us to enlarged petitions and increased earnestness in prayer, v. 10. It is dreadful when success hardens our hearts, or makes us lifeless in devotion.

16. No form of profession or of worship is in any measure pleasing to God where the will and affections are not engaged, v. 11. It is sad indeed when we suppose that decency of appearance will be accepted by Jehovah for heartiness of soul. Henry: "All the wickedness of the wicked world is owing to the wilfulness of the wicked will. The reason why people are not religious is, because they will not be so."

17. Of all the judgments of God none are so terrible as spiritual judgments, v. 12. When God's wrath against one is not very hot, he says, I will deprive him of health, or riches, or public favor, or children, or friends; but when he is greatly incensed, he says, He is joined to idols, let him alone. Tholuck: "Man will return to the all-sufficient God, though by circuitous and thorny paths, if some tender parts continue in his heart; but if these are gone, then the judgment of induration will ensue." Calvin: "It is assuredly the most dreadful kind of punishment which can be inflicted upon us, and an evidence of the utter hopelessness of our condition, when God, holding his peace, and conniving at our perverseness, applies no remedy for bringing us to repentance."

18. Salvation is so important and desirable that God declares it to be in his view precious. Oh that my people had hearkened, etc., v. 13. The Lord is not willing that any should perish. He has sworn that he has no pleasure in the death of the sinner. Scott: "The Lord delights in the conversion of sinners, and in the faith and obedience of his people."

19. God does not afflict willingly, v. 14.. There is a need-be for all the righteous suffer. Calvin: "The procuring cause of our misery is in ourselves."

20. "The foes of God's people are the foes of God himself," v. 15. Their cause is his cause. If we would mind God's interests, he would mind ours, for ours are his.

21. How is it possible to satisfy the demands of men who hate God himself? Calvin: "Peace with the reprobate cannot be looked for except in so far as God restrains their rage by hidden chains. A lion shut up in an iron cage still retains his own nature, but he is kept from mangling and tearing in pieces those who are not even more than five or six feet distant from him." The humblest believer may safely say to the proudest persecutor as Christ said to Pilate: "Thou couldest have no power at all against me, except it were given thee from above," John xix. 11.

22. Nothing is too good for God's servants, v. 16. *The finest of the wheat, honey out of the rock*, all things needful for body and soul, for time and eternity, all, all are theirs, 1 Cor. iii. 21–23.

23. Morison: "There is still a retribution in human events; and the great Sovereign of the universe is perpetually carrying on a system of punishment and reward, extending even to the concerns of individuals, and often drawing a line of demarcation between the enemies and friends of God."

24. Horne: "Christ is the 'bread' of life, he is the 'rock' of salvation, and his promises are as 'honey' to pious minds. But they who reject him, as their Lord and Master, must also lose him as their Saviour and their reward."

PSALM LXXXII.

A Psalm of Asaph.

1 God standeth in the congregation of the mighty; he judgeth among the gods.

2 How long will ye judge unjustly, and accept the persons of the wicked? Selah.

3 Defend the poor and fatherless: do justice to the afflicted and needy.

4 Deliver the poor and needy: rid *them* out of the hand of the wicked.

5 They know not, neither will they understand; they walk on in darkness: all the foundations of the earth are out of course.

6 I have said, Ye *are* gods; and all of you *are* children of the Most High.

7 But ye shall die like men, and fall like one of the princes.

8 Arise, O God, judge the earth: for thou shalt inherit all nations.

ON the title see on title of Ps. iii. On the authorship see Introduction, § 4, and on Psalms l. lxxiii.–lxxxi. Piscator thinks that by *Asaph* we are here to understand the posterity of Asaph, and that the title is an inscription to them and does not determine the authorship. Kimchi and Clarke think the Psalm was written by some one in the time of Jehoshaphat, who undertook to reform the courts of justice in his day, 2 Chron. xix. 5–7. Scott is doubtful whether it was written in David's time, or in the days of Hezekiah. Venema, Patrick, Edwards, Dodd and Morison think its author lived in the days of Hezekiah. For Isaiah, who lived in Hezekiah's time, complains much of the judges of those days, Isa. i. 10, 23. Gill, Hengstenberg and Alexander (the latter confidently) think it was written by Asaph, who flourished in the time of David. This is probably correct. Horsley thinks this Psalm foretells the just judgment of God on the unjust judges of our Lord Jesus Christ. No doubt the principles of just judgment and the consequences of unjust judgments are the same in all ages and in all cases. Horsley's view is embraced by few, if any. Yet our Saviour cites a passage from this Psalm to vindicate himself against the charge of blasphemy, John x. 34–36. The Syriac styles it "an invective against the impious Jews." The design of this composition seems clear from the language throughout. Gill: "This Psalm was written for the use of persons in power, for the instruction of kings and princes, judges and civil magistrates." Alexander calls it "A brief but pregnant statement of the responsibilities attached to the judicial office under the Mosaic dispensation." Scott dates it B. C. 1048; Clarke, B. C. 912. On *Selah* see Introduction, § 15. The names of the Almighty here found are *Elohim God, El God* and *Gel-yohn Most High,* on which see on Psalms iii. 2; v. 4; vii. 17.

1. *God standeth in the congregation of the mighty; he judgeth among the gods.* Chaldee: God whose majesty tarries in the congregation of the just, who are mighty in the law, judges in the midst of the judges; church of England: God standeth in the congregation of princes; he is judge among gods; John Rogers' Translation: God standeth in the congregacyon of the goddes, and is a judge among the judges; Edwards: God stands in the assemblies of judges; he judgeth among magistrates; Amesius: God stands in the assembly of the mighty God, among the magistrates he judges. The first word doubtless points to Jehovah. *Standeth* may indicate a posture of authority, and a readiness to render assistance. *Congregation,* the same word so rendered in Ps. i. 5; vii. 7. It designates any assembly good or bad. Here it embraces the whole body of judges or of the people to be judged. *The mighty, El,* which may denote either God himself as the mighty God, or the chief magistrate as embodying the judicial authority of the land. This latter view is supported by the parallelism of the next clause, *He judgeth among the gods,* the men of authority. Alexander: "The idea is, that as the judges were gods to other men, so God would be a judge to them."

2. *How long will ye judge unjustly, and accept the persons of the wicked?* Judge, as in v. 1. God *judges* and man *judges.* Dreadful may be the effects of erroneous human judgments; but they will be revised, and perhaps most of them will be reversed in whole or in part. No good man can sit in either temporal or ecclesiastical courts, and observe the course of proceeding without seeing the necessity of a tribunal above that of mortals. Some from weakness, some from prejudice, some from passion, some from interest, and some from party-spirit judge *unjustly.* The word rendered *unjustly* is rendered as an adverb here and in Deut. xxv. 16; as a noun, *unrighteousness,* or *iniquity* in Lev. xix. 15, 35; Ps. vii. 3; liii. 1. To *accept persons* is to show partiality, favoring one above another. The literal rendering would be *lift up the faces.* Whether this means to cheer one by favoring him, or to admit him to a private interview may be doubtful.

3. *Defend the poor and fatherless.* Defend, almost uniformly rendered *judge.* It here signifies the redressing of wrongs. *Poor,* the opposite of rich in worldly goods, *defenceless,* see Ruth iii. 10. The Scripture abounds in denunciations against those who oppress the poor, or refuse to give him succor when he is drawn to destruction, Pr. xiv. 21; xxi. 13. *Fatherless,* as in Ps. x. 14, 18. It is once rendered *orphan,* Lam. v. 3; sometimes equivalent to *destitute, forlorn, helpless. Do justice to the afflicted and needy. Do justice, justify,* give him his rights. *Afflicted,* also rendered *poor, humble.* See on Ps. ix. 12. *Needy,* very commonly rendered *poor.* It is rendered *do lack* in Ps. xxxiv. 10. Such cannot command the usual influences and appliances to move judges and rulers, but God is their avenger.

4. *Deliver the poor and needy.* Deliver, often so rendered, once *carry away safe,* and in one form, *cause to escape. Poor,* the same word so rendered in v. 3. *Needy,* see on Ps. lxxii. 4, 12, 13. All these terms are used to point out those that are of them-

selves unable to contend with the rich and powerful. *Rid* them *out of the hand of the wicked.* *Rid,* also rendered *pluck, deliver, recover, preserve.* The *hand* is the emblem of *power,* here of power wrongfully used. *Wicked,* rendered *ungodly* in Ps. i.

5. *They know not, neither will they understand.* They, not the poor and needy, but the rulers, are perversely and stubbornly ignorant of the first principles of right and equity. They have no conscience about the duties of their office. Power has puffed them up and hardened their hearts. *They walk on in darkness.* This verb is also in the future, *will walk.* Alexander: "Darkness is a figure both for ignorance and wickedness." The speaker is still the prophet. The language expresses the absence of hope as to any change for the better. *All the foundations of the earth are out of course.* Chaldee, Septuagint, Vulgate, Ethiopic, Calvin and Jebb read *are moved;* Syriac and Fabritius, *shake;* Arabic, *tremble;* Piscator, Tremellius and Junius and Amesius, *are removed;* Green, *are in a tottering state;* Clarke and Tholuck, *totter;* Edwards, *are unsettled;* Horsley, *are disordered;* Fry, *are displaced;* Hengstenberg and Alexander, *are shaken.* *Earth* may mean the whole world or the *land, i. e.,* the land of Israel. Diodati: "From this corruption of the head proceeds a general disorder and ruin of the whole state." Patrick: "The foundations of the kingdom, which are Justice and Truth, are shaken; all things are in confusion, and in danger to come to ruin." Alexander: "The denial or perversion of justice is described as disorganizing society."

6. *I have said, Ye are gods.* *Gods, Elohim.* The office of the magistrate was as dignified and awful as any of them claimed it to be. They were invested with the character of representatives of God. Therefore they acted under the highest responsibility. Their name was dreadful; so was their position; and, if their power was abused, their doom should be dreadful also. *And all of you are children of the Most High.* The phrase is parallel to the former, *Ye are gods.* Cresswell: "Ye are men of the highest rank and power;" Alexander: "It denotes the closest and most intimate relation to Jehovah, as the supreme or sovereign God;" Patrick: "I have put my majesty upon you."

7. *But ye shall die like men.* *But,* better *surely.* *Like men,* like Adam. As he fell from holiness and dignity, so shall ye fall from your honor and greatness. Or, ye are as liable to death as other men. Your office will not protect you from disease and corruption. *And* [ye shall] *fall like one of the princes.* To *fall* is to fall in death. The same word is rendered *die, perish, rot,* Gen. xxv. 18; Ex. xix. 21; Num. v. 27. It is often followed by the words *with the sword.* The parallelism would show that death is here threatened. Some suppose that a violent death is implied. And it is a remarkable fact that cruel, ambitious and deceitful rulers are not apt to prolong their lives. Every generation gives examples of sore and sudden deaths of tyrants and oppressors. By falling like one of the princes, some suppose there is reference to the kings who were destroyed by the Israelites at taking possession of Canaan. The same word is applied to the princes of the Philistines. But it is also applied to any *ruler, captain,* or *chief.* Some suggest a slight change of the Hebrew text so that the word would be rendered *poor,* not princes. This would give a good sense, but we have no right to change the text. Calvin translates it, Ye shall fall, O princes! as one of the people.

8. *Arise, O God,* as in Ps. iii. 7; vii. 6. *Judge the earth.* *Judge,* rendered *defend* in v. 3. Judge so as effectually to succor and protect. Clarke: Take the sceptre, and rule, thyself; Diodati: "Seeing thy ministers and officers have subverted justice; come and reëstablish thy kingdom in the world by thy Spirit and word, and chiefly by the presence of thy Son," Ps. xcvi. 10. *For thou shalt inherit all nations.* God is the Father of all nations, the Author of all government, the Parent of all rulers and people. Men pervert God's authority when they turn bloody or

tyrannical. They misrepresent the fountain of all government, when they pervert justice. Some think this last clause has allusion to Christ as the rightful Lord of all the world.

DOCTRINAL AND PRACTICAL REMARKS.

1. Government is of God, v. 1. It was not originated by men meeting and consulting whether they would or would not be subject to law. Civil government is a divine ordinance. "There is no power but of God. The powers that be are ordained of God. Whosoever therefore resisteth the power resisteth the ordinance of God; and they that resist shall receive to themselves damnation," Rom. xiii. 1, 2. If God's word opposes tyranny, it also opposes anarchy.

2. Consequently rulers of every rank are to be honored. Jehovah himself calls them *gods*, vv. 1, 6; Ex. xxii. 28. The magistrate is "the minister of God, a revenger to execute wrath upon him that doeth evil," Rom. xiii. 4. Religious persons and religious teachers are never at liberty to speak evil of their rulers, to revile them, to try to bring them into disesteem. We must give honor to whom honor is due. Luther: "Who will set himself against those on whom God bestows his own name? Whoever despises them, despises at the same time the true Magistrate, God, who speaks and judges in them and through them, and calls their judgment his judgment;" Hodge: "Obedience is not enjoined on the ground of the personal merit of those in authority, but on the ground of their official station."

3. Dickson: "No judge is absolute lord over a people, but is in subordination to God, who is Judge above all judges, and will judge of all the decrees of judges under him;" Hodge: "The design of civil government is not to promote the advantage of rulers but of the ruled. . . When rulers become a terror to the good, and a praise to them that do evil, they may still be tolerated and obeyed, not however, of right, but because the remedy may be worse than the disease."

4. The duties of magistrates are very difficult and onerous. They have great need of wisdom, truthfulness, courage, calmness, humility, benevolence, patience and a nice sense of justice. Compare Pr. xvi. 10; xvii. 7; xxviii. 16; Ecc. iv. 13; x. 16. As to the doom of wicked rulers the Scriptures give us fearful examples in many and no less fearful predictions, Isa. xiv. 14, 15; Ezek. xxviii. 1–11.

5. However great rulers may be, they are still strictly accountable to Jehovah, v. 1. Luther: "They must understand that they are not placed over stocks and stones, nor over swine and dogs, but over the congregation of God: they must therefore be afraid of acting against God himself when they act unjustly." Even though they may inflict punishment on a wicked nation, yet if they do it wantonly or cruelly, they shall smart for it, Isa. x. 7. Many a sinner has been punished for the malignity, arrogance or recklessness with which he brought evil on those whom God had sent him to chastise.

6. Because princes and rulers are under God's control and accountable to him, the righteous may be very calm and quiet respecting public affairs even in times of distraction. God presides in the wildest confusion, v. 1. Henry: "Let subjects consider this, and be comforted with it; for good princes and good judges, who mean well, are under a divine direction, and bad ones, who mean ever so ill, are under a divine restraint." Tholuck: "Here is the mighty consolation of those who have no strength and support of their own, that God, who has invested earthly tribunals with his power, for the special purpose of protecting the helpless against oppressors, will assuredly watch over their proceedings, and seize the sceptre when his *judges* pervert justice and become *oppressors*."

7. If the duties and responsibilities of rulers are so great, then it is clear that they

should be made subjects of frequent and earnest prayer, 1 Tim. ii. 1–3. And because their trials are great, we should not make them greater by harsh judgments or hard speeches concerning them, nor by hesitating to pay all taxes lawfully imposed, nor by making factious opposition to their acts and measures.

8. Rulers should never forget that they are liable to err, and that all, who have gone before them, have erred, and some of them very egregiously, v. 2. Self-distrust and close vigilance over themselves are necessary to none more than to rulers. The records of government are full of blots made by human weakness and human wicked-ness. Many rulers 'make fellowship with the unjust, and for the sake of covetous-ness withhold justice from the poor and fatherless, for whose protection in particular earthly tribunals are invested with power.' Calvin: "Kings and such as are invested with authority, through the blindness which is produced by pride, generally take to themselves a boundless liberty of action. . . They think it would derogate from their elevated rank were they to be governed by moderate counsels; and although their own folly is more than enough to urge them on in their reckless career, they, notwithstanding, seek for flatterers to soothe and applaud them in their vices. . . They cannot bear to be subject to reason and laws."

9. Let all, who hold authority in families, in schools, and in civil communities, remember that to God nothing is more offensive, or to man more injurious, or to them-selves more disgraceful than partiality, v. 2.

10. A chief object of government is to protect, defend, succor and do justice to the poor and fatherless, the afflicted and needy, the humble and destitute, vv. 3, 4. Com-pare Deut. xxvii. 19. The mighty and the majority can protect themselves. The feeble and the minority need the defence of good laws and good rulers. If the gov-ernment fails to secure these, it will become an intolerable burden. Dickson: "The touchstone of magistrates' justice is in the causes and cases of the poor, fatherless, afflicted and needy, who are not able to attend long their suits of law, and have no friends or money to deal for them; to whom therefore the mighty should be eyes to direct them, and a staff to their weakness, to support and help them to their right." Calvin: "There is a certain devilish frenzy which infatuates the princes of the world, and leads them voluntarily to pay greater respect to wicked men than to the simple and innocent." Horne: "Every oppressor of the poor is a likeness of 'that wicked one,' and every upright judge will endeavor to resemble the Redeemer. For this pur-pose he will be always willing to admit, diligent to discuss, solicitous to expedite the cause of the poor and injured person, and to afford such an one the speediest, the cheapest, and the most effectual redress, equally contemning the offers, and the frowns of power."

11. This Psalm and this subject press on our notice the importance of *justice* as an element of social and civil life. There is no substitute for it. Some talk of charity, nor can it be denied that there is much scope for its exercise. But no charity can make a character virtuous, or a community happy, if JUSTICE is wanting. For this reason all good governments carefully guard against every species of bribery, for " a gift destroyeth the heart," and "a wicked man taketh a gift out of the bosom to per-vert the ways of judgment," Ecc. vii. 7; Pr. xvii. 23. "Presents and gifts blind the eyes of the wise, and stop his mouth that he cannot reprove," Ecclus. xx. 29. Such practices bring great distress. Henry: "The miscarriages of public persons are public mischiefs." Clarke: "Justice is at the *head* of all the institutions in a well regulated state: when that gets poisoned or perverted, every evil, political and do-mestic, must prevail. Even *religion* itself ceases to have any influence." There can be no stable and salutary government where injustice is an element. Morison:

" What a blessing to live under a government, where the rights of the meanest subject are held sacred, where the officers are peace, and the exactors righteous."

12. It is a sad thing when rulers and judges are ignorant of the principles which ought to guide them, and too indolent to inform themselves, v. 5. Oh that all judges would observe the rule of the apostle: " Be swift to hear, slow to speak, slow to wrath," James i. 19.

13. Perhaps the worst form of stable, uniform government on earth is better than anarchy; but next to anarchy, systematic misrule is the direst calamity that can befall a state. Bad rulers are a frightful scourge. Hengstenberg: "Everything is ruined by them,—they ruin everything." Morison: "How terrible is the state of any nation, in which wicked men are the principal parties raised to posts of honor, and in which the ungodly are protected, and the excellent of the earth are trampled in the dust," Ps. xii. 8. Dickson: "When justice and judgment-seats are corrupted, and judges do not mind justice in their places, then the pillars of that land or kingdom must stagger, and all matters go to ruin, or a perilous alteration."

14. It is a solemn duty to remind judges and rulers of the frailty of their lives. "Their high office cannot secure immortality." "Death mingles sceptres with spades." Tholuck: "Death, which levels all men, is the most effective sermon for earthly rulers."

15. Sometimes God makes terrible examples of wicked rulers even before they pass into eternity. Strange judgments happen to them, and hurry them away. Compare Job xxxiv. 24–28. Writers not addicted to superstition have often recorded the marked and awful severity of the calamities which befall tyrants and persecutors. Several commentators quote those words of the heathen poet: "Few kings and tyrants go down to Pluto, the son of Ceres, without being put to a violent death, before they have completed the ordinary term allotted to the life of mortal man." Scott: "As for ungodly rulers, their disgrace and misery will equal their present abused distinctions; and they will feel the insignificancy of that preëminence, which made them forget that they were men, when death shall arrest them and hurry them to judgment." Calvin: "The dignity, with which judges are invested, can form no excuse or plea, why they should escape the punishment which their wickedness deserves."

16. Dickson: "Albeit the oppressed servants of God cannot find justice at men's hands, yet there is help to be had from God, and by prayer, longer or shorter; as the Lord furnisheth unto them, must they seek their ease and comfort: *arise, O God, judge the earth*," v. 8. Calvin: "We ought to beseech God to restore to order the confusions of the world, and thus to recover the rightful dominion which he has over it." Green: "Since the judges, thy vicegerents, are so corrupt, take the government of the land into thine own hands," Prov. xxi. 1.

17. There is hope for the future. God shall yet inherit all nations, v. 8.

18. This Psalm suggests that we should not be amazed if when we look for judgment, behold oppression; for righteousness, and behold a cry. It has always been so, Isa. v. 7; Eccle. iii. 15; v. 8.

19. Henry: "There are two words with which we may comfort ourselves and one another, in reference to the mismanagement of power among men; one is, *Hallelujah, the Lord God omnipotent reigneth;* the other is, *Surely I come quickly.*" We ought not therefore to be very much cast down by the unjust judgments of men.

20. Morison: "Let the kings and judges of the earth be wise, and kiss the sceptre of the Redeemer's grace, let them serve him in fear, lest he should speak to them in his wrath, and vex them in his sore displeasure."

21. How glorious is God. In his nature he is pure and perfect. He is everywhere. He governs all things. He rules and overrules. Horne: "All magistrates act in his

name, and by virtue of his commission. He is invisibly present in their assemblies, and superintends their proceedings. He receives appeals from their wrongful decisions; he will one day rehear all causes at his own tribunal, and reverse every iniquitous sentence, before the great congregation of men and angels."

PSALM LXXXIII.

A Song *or* Psalm of Asaph.

1 Keep not thou silence, O God: hold not thy peace, and be not still, O God.

2 For, lo, thine enemies make a tumult: and they that hate thee have lifted up the head.

3 They have taken crafty counsel against thy people, and consulted against thy hidden ones.

4 They have said, Come, and let us cut them off from *being* a nation; that the name of Israel may be no more in remembrance.

5 For they have consulted together with one consent: they are confederate against thee:

6 The tabernacles of Edom, and the Ishmaelites; of Moab, and the Hagarenes;

7 Gebal, and Ammon, and Amalek; the Philistines with the inhabitants of Tyre;

8 Assur also is joined with them: they have holpen the children of Lot. Selah.

9 Do unto them as *unto* the Midianites; as *to* Sisera, as *to* Jabin, at the brook of Kison:

10 *Which* perished at En-dor: they became *as* dung for the earth.

11 Make their nobles like Oreb, and like Zeeb: yea, all their princes as Zebah, and as Zalmunna:

12 Who said, Let us take to ourselves the houses of God in possession.

13 O my God, make them like a wheel; as the stubble before the wind.

14 As the fire burneth a wood, and as the flame setteth the mountains on fire;

15 So persecute them with thy tempest, and make them afraid with thy storm.

16 Fill their faces with shame; that they may seek thy name, O LORD.

17 Let them be confounded and troubled for ever; yea, let them be put to shame, and perish:

18 That *men* may know that thou, whose name alone *is* JEHOVAH, *art* the Most High over all the earth.

ON the title see on titles of Psalms iii. xxx. On the authorship of this Psalm see Introduction, § 4, and on Psalms l. lxxiii.–lxxxii. This is the last Psalm bearing the name of Asaph. Luther: "This is a prayer of the same nature as Psalm lxxx." Yet there is great diversity of view respecting the historic occasion and even the date of this ode. Venema: "Some refer it to the times of David, some to the times of Jehoshaphat, some to the times of Jehoram, as Clericus, others to the times of Hezekiah, others to the return from Babylon, others to the times of Esther, as Altingius, and others to the times of Judas Maccabeus." Some think the Psalm had its historic occasion in events not known to us. A large number think it had its origin in the events noticed in 2 Chron. xx. 1–25. Among these are Amesius, Calmet, Patrick, Clarke, Edwards, Morison, Scott, Tholuck, Hengstenberg and Alexander. Others regard it as prophetical and suited to all times when combinations of wicked men are formed against the church and people of God. This would allow Asaph, the cotemporary of David, to be the author. Some, who think there is special reference to the days of Jehoshaphat, regard Jehaziel as the author, 2 Chron. xx. 14. Scott dates it B. C. 892; Clarke, B. C. 896. Amyrald: "It may be applied now to the enemies of the Christian Church, of which Israel was the type. The most important and formidable of these are assuredly *sin* and *Satan*, from whom we most especially long to be delivered." Horne: "As while the world endureth there will be a church, and while there is a church she will have her enemies, who are to increase upon her as the end approacheth, this Psalm can never be out of date. And to the spiritual adversaries of his soul, every private Christian may apply it at all times." On *Selah* see Introduction, § 15. The names of the Almighty here found are *Elohim God, El God, Jehovah* LORD and *Gel-Yohn Most High,* on which respectively see on Ps. iii. 2; v. 4; i. 2; vii. 17.

1. *Keep not thou silence, O God: hold not thy peace, and be not still, O God.* The first name of God here used is *Elohim;* the second, *El.* This use of two names is expressive. All the clauses have the same general significance. The prayer is that God would not allow wickedness to go on unchecked. The first clause has not before occurred. It is also found in Isa. lxii. 6. The corresponding verb is rendered *rest, stand still, be still, forbear.* On the second see on Ps. xxviii. 1; xxxv. 22. The third is elsewhere rendered *be quiet, rest, be in rest.* The language is earnest and the call loud. The peril of God's people was great, and it seemed as if he had done nothing to arrest the ruin prepared for his chosen.

2. *For, lo, thine enemies make a tumult.* All the tribes of people mentioned in subsequent verses were notorious for their hostility to the worship and service of Jehovah. They were his *enemies.* At first these foes may have been stealthy and cunning; but now they *make a tumult, rage, roar, cry aloud, are in an uproar.* The verb expresses a boastful and malicious confidence of success. This is further expressed by the parallel clause: *And they that hate thee have lifted up the head, i. e.,* they rage and are confident; they anticipate an easy, early, complete victory. See Judges viii. 28.

3. *They have taken crafty counsel against thy people.* *Taken crafty counsel,* literally *will craftily devise a secret.* The meaning is: They have done so, and will continue to do so. *Crafty counsel,* see on Ps. xxv. 14; lv. 14; lxiv. 2. There must have been great plottings among so many and so remote nations in order to effect so vast a combination. *And consulted against thy hidden ones.* The verb here also is in the future. They will continue to do as they have done. *Hidden ones;* Syriac, Arabic, Septuagint, Vulgate, Ethiopic and Street: Saints; Edwards: Favorite ones; Mudge, French and Skinner: Treasured ones; Green: Those whom thou protectest; Jebb: Secret ones. The English text is supported by the great mass of scholars. By *hidden ones* Diodati understands those " who in thy church, where thou art present, do shelter themselves under thy protection in humility, fear and faith: Ps. xxvii. 5." The purpose of the combination is next stated:

4. *They have said, Come, and let us cut them off from being a nation; that the name of Israel may be no more in remembrance.* They waged a war of extermination. The wonder is that they did not effect their purpose. So many and so powerful nations firmly united, one would think, might have eaten up the Jews. Their rancor was terrible, their malice diabolical, their numbers vast.

5. *For they have consulted together with one consent.* *With one consent,* literally with the heart; Chaldee, with the whole heart; Arabic and Jebb, with one heart; some other versions and Edwards, unanimously; Fry, with one accord; Alexander, heartily. *They are confederate against thee; i. e.,* against God, whose people and church they sought to destroy. *Confederate,* literally *they will cut the covenant,* means they have made a covenant by cutting the sacrifice in two and passing between the parts. Alexander: " The preterite tense [of the first verb] and the future [of the second] represent the combination as already formed and still continued." Here begins the list of allies:

6. *The tabernacles of Edom.* Edom is one of the names of Esau, Gen. xxxvi. 1. It signifies *red,* and was given him for 'that same red pottage,' for which he sold his

birth-right, Gen. xxv. 30. He settled in the mountainous district south of the Dead sea, where his posterity became numerous and mighty. Their land is called *Edom* or Idumea. Bozra was the capital of eastern Edom, but the chief city of the land was Petra, famous for its strength. The Edomites had a hereditary hatred to the descendants of Jacob. They refused to let the Israelites pass through their territory on their journey from Egypt to Canaan. Though they and other tribes named in this Psalm had cities, yet some of their people probably dwelt in tents. But as in Israel the war cry was, "Every man to his tent," 2 Sam. xx. 1; 1 Kings xii. 16; 2 Chron. x. 16; so other nations used tents in war. The tents here spoken of are probably tents of war, or they may be abodes. *And the Ishmaelites.* These were the descendants of Ishmael, whose father was Abraham and whose mother was Hagar, the Egyptian. Ishmael was born B. C. 1910 years. He lived to be one hundred and thirty-seven years old, and was the father of twelve sons, who were the heads of so many tribes in the north-western part of Arabia. Although Ishmael attended the death-bed of his father, and although there is no record of any act of hostility done by him against Isaac, yet Paul says he persecuted Isaac, Gal. iv. 29; and it is not unlikely that his seed remembered how Isaac though younger obtained the blessing instead of their father, and so hated his descendants. Next we have the tents *of Moab.* Moab was the son of Lot by his oldest daughter, Gen. xix. 30–38. "The same was the father of the Moabites," whose territory for a long time lay in a region chiefly east and south-east of the Dead sea, though at times it was much extended. They hated the Israelites in all their generations. In the days of Moses Balak was their king, and their cruelty was intense, Num. xxii. xxxiii. Moses died in their territory, Deut. xxxiv. 5. They were bloody idolaters. Chemosh and Baal-peor were among their idols, Jer. xlviii. 13; Num. xxv. 3. *And the Hagarenes.* These people are here only called *Hagarenes;* but in 1 Chron. v. 10, 20, they are called *Hagarites.* They were the descendants of Abraham by Keturah, who is by some thought to be the same as Hagar. For a time they inhabited a district, east of Gilead. Cresswell: "They are probably the same as the Saracens."

7. *Gebal.* This may designate the Gebalene of the Romans, which was a part of Idumea; or the country called by the Greeks Byblos, a district in Phœnicia. In regard to this latter place we read of the Giblites in Josh. xiii. 5. The same word is rendered *stone-squarers* in 1 Kings v. 18. They held a seaport between Tripoli and Sidon, and had some renown, Ezek. xxvii. 9. *And Ammon.* The Ammonites were descended from Ben-ammi, a son of Lot by his younger daughter, Gen. xix. 30–38. They lived in a district east of Judea. Their capital city was Rabbah on the river Jabbok. They worshipped Moloch, 1 Kings xi. 7; 2 Kings xxiii. 13. They remained a somewhat powerful people till after the close of the canon of the Old Testament, but were subdued by Judas Maccabeus, 1 Mac. v. 6–44. *And Amalek.* Amalek was a grandson of Esau and the son of Eliphaz by a concubine, Timna, Gen. xxxvi. 12. Some have thought this man was not the father of the Amalekites, who are mentioned more than a hundred years before his birth. But may not the people mentioned in Gen. xiv. 7, be designated as Amalekites, because they then inhabited the land afterwards inhabited by the children of Amalek? The home of the Amalekites was Arabia Petrea between the Dead sea and the Red sea. They were the Bedouins of their time. They were always hostile to Israel, Ex. xvii. 8–16; Num. xiv. 45. Haman, one of this tribe, was true to the instincts of his ancestors. Next in this roll of infamy we have *the Philistines.* The original word is simply *Philistia,* meaning the inhabitants of that country. See on Ps. lx. 8. *Philistia* and *Palestine* are the same word. We apply the former to the land as held by the heathen in Canaan and the latter to the land as held by the Jews. The exact territory thus designated depended on the

time, when the word was used, for the boundary varied.   The people here referred to held the southern seacoast of Canaan.   They were idolaters, worshipping Baalzebub and Dagon.   They were great enemies of the Israelites.   Their great city was Gaza. They were very warlike.   They united with all the rest already named and *with the inhabitants of Tyre*.   This city once possessed the commerce of the world.   Tyre is not mentioned by Moses or Homer, being built after their time.   It was the daughter of Zidon and mother of Carthage.   Its inhabitants were idolaters, and though friendly in the times of David and Solomon, yet the devotees of Baal and of Ashtaroth could never be well pleased with the worshippers of Jehovah.

8. *Assur also is joined with them.*   *Assur* or *Ashur* was the second son of Shem, Gen. x. 22.   He was the father of the Assyrians.   Assyria had not always the same bounds.   At one time it was a mighty empire.   Its power was often employed against the ancient people of God.   *They* [all these others] *have holpen the children of Lot*, who were the Moabites and Ammonites.

9. *Do unto them as* unto *the Midianites.*   Midian was the fourth son of Abraham by Keturah after his marriage to her, Gen. xxv. 2.   His descendants led a wandering and predatory life.   In the days of the Judges they had two celebrated princes, Oreb and Zeeb called *nobles* in v. 11 of this Psalm.   The dreadful overthrow of these robbers by Gideon is recorded in Judges vii. 19–25, [Do unto them] *as* to *Sisera, as* to *Jabin, at the brook of Kison*.   Jabin was the king of Canaan and reigned in Hazor.   He was a great warrior.   Sisera was his general.   How the latter was ingloriously slain by a woman and how the power of his master left him may be learned in Judges iv. 1–24; v. 1–31.   The Kison or Kishon is a small stream rising in the plain of Esdraelon near the foot of Mount Tabor.   This stream is still at times impetuous and dangerous.   In 1799 many Arabs attempting to escape the French after the battle of Mount Tabor perished in its waters.   This was after the middle of April.

10. Which *perished at En-dor.*   *En-dor* is not mentioned in the history of the destruction of Jabin's forces, but it was only four or five miles south of Tabor.   This place is mentioned in Joshua xvii. 11, as lying in the territory of the tribe of Manasseh.   It is more frequently thought of as the residence of the witch, whom Saul consulted, 1 Sam. xxviii. 7–25.   *They became* as *dung for the earth.*   Of all the uses to which man is put, that of becoming manure to the fields seems to be the poorest; though the figure here used is perhaps not so much in regard of fertilization, as it is of the loathsomeness of their carcasses and of the manner in which they were trodden down.   See like expressions in 2 Kings ix. 37; Jer. viii. 2; ix. 22; xvi. 4; xxv. 33; Zeph. i. 17.

11. *Make their nobles like Oreb, and like Zeeb.*   These Midianites were slain and beheaded as the enemies of Israel, Judges vii. 25.   *Yea,* [make] *all their princes as Zebah, and as Zalmunna.*   The record of these kings of Midian is in Judges viii. 4– 21.   They were slain by Gideon.

12. *Who have said, Let us take to ourselves the houses of God in possession.*   Alexander: "This relates not to the former but to the present enemies of Israel, and assigns the reason why they should experience the same fate with their predecessors."   Many commentators notice the beauty of the idea conveyed by the word rendered *houses;* in Ps. xxiii. 2; lxv. 12; Joel ii. 22, *pastures;* in Ps. lxxiv. 20; Jer. xxv. 37, *habitations.*   Where the Lord, the Shepherd, abides, there only are shelter and refreshment found.

13. *O my God, make them like a wheel.*   *Wheel*, in Isa. xvii. 13, *a rolling thing;* in the margin *thistledown.*   That would be the better rendering here, although the ancient versions favor the English.   Calvin renders it *a whirling ball;* Patrick says,

"Make them run as swiftly as a ball down a hill;" Diodati: "Overthrow both them and their designs, as a bowl thrown down a steep place;" Waterland, Edwards, Morison, Lowth and Secker render it *chaff*; Hengstenberg, *a whirl*; Fry, *thistledown*. [Make them] *as the stubble before the wind*. Alexander unites the two clauses of the verse—*Make them like the whirling chaff before the wind. Chaff*, see on Ps. i. 4.

14. *As the fire burneth a wood, and as the flame setteth the mountains on fire.* The language is striking and terrible.

15. *So persecute them with thy tempest, and make them afraid with thy storm.* Both verbs are in the future. On prairies even mounted travellers have had to flee for their lives before the devouring fire. In mountainous regions the fire is still more rapid, at least in ascending. Venema: "Having placed before our eyes the judgment of God upon the enemies, as illustrated by the example of antiquity, he now describes it in a sublimer style, with images drawn from wind, storm and fire."

16. *Fill their faces with shame.* Alexander: "The word translated *shame* is very strong, and means contempt, disgrace, ignominy." It is elsewhere rendered as here, also *reproach, dishonor, ignominy, confusion.* Do this, *that they may seek thy name, O* LORD. There are three ways of explaining these words. 1. That the Psalmist prays that these enemies may have a salutary shame, leading them to seek God in truth. This is the more obvious and easy method. 2. That the seeking of God here mentioned is a forced subjection. 3. That *they* in the last clause refers to men generally and not to the people made ashamed. The first has the fewest difficulties. Either of them gives a good sense.

17. *Let them be confounded and troubled forever; yea, let them be put to shame, and perish.* All these verbs express a dreadful conception of God's vengeance on his incorrigible foes. Calvin: "He heaps together so many words, partly because the reprobate, though often chastised, are nevertheless so incorrigible that ever and anon they are mustering up new strength and courage; and partly because there is nothing which it is more difficult to be persuaded of than that such as wallow at ease in great outward prosperity will soon perish." On the first verb see on Ps. vi. 10, where it is rendered *be ashamed.* On the second, see on Ps. vi. 10, where it is rendered *sore vexed.* On the third, see on Ps. xxxiv. 5, where it is rendered *were ashamed.* It is often rendered *be confounded* or *brought to confusion.* On the fourth, see on Ps. i. 6. The word is truly awful. The verbs are in the future.

18. *That* men *may know that thou, whose name alone* is JEHOVAH, art *the Most High over all the earth.* Chaldee: And they shall know that thou art thy name [*i. e.,* art worthy of thy name—art what thy name truly imports] JEHOVAH [and that is as much as to say that thou] alone art the Most High over all the inhabitants of the earth. See 2 Kings xix. 19; Isa. xxxvii. 16.

DOCTRINAL AND PRACTICAL REMARKS.

1. The church of God is often in such a case that if left a little longer under the power of evil, she would be crushed. Her perils are not shadows but realities. From her foes she can expect no mercy and from herself no succor. All her resources are in God alone, v. 1.

2. It is right earnestly to ask God's early attention to our affairs, v. 1. The church of all ages has done so. Calvin: "It is unquestionably our duty to wait patiently when God at any time delays his help; but in condescension to our infirmity, he permits us to supplicate him to make haste." And when he sees that the right time is come he makes no tarrying, but cuts short his work in righteousness.

3. It is well for us when our enemies are God's enemies, so that his cause and our cause are identical. Dickson: "A conspiracy against the church is a conspiracy

against God." Calvin: "The welfare of the people, whom he has taken under his protection, cannot be assailed without an injury being, at the same time, done to his own majesty." Horne: "Christ and the Church, like man and wife, are one; they have one common interest; they have the same friends, and the same foes."

4. The carnal mind is enmity against God. The wicked are his *enemies*. They *hate* him, v. 2. Gill: "They hate his being, perfections, purposes and providences; hate his Son without a cause, and even do despite unto the Spirit of grace; hate the law and its precepts, the Gospel and its doctrines and ordinances, and the ways, worship and people of God."

5. It is no new thing to see wickedness and the wicked rampant and outrageous. They make a tumult; they lift up the head, v. 2. To the eye of sense such things are alarming; but to the eye of faith it is a sign that the end is at hand; for "the more din the enemy makes, the more insolent he is, the higher he lifts up his head, he is the more near to be knocked down by God's appearing for his people against him." So teaches history. So teaches the Bible.

6. The wicked resort not only to rage and violence, but also to *crafty counsel*, v. 3. One half of the plots formed against the church, if directed against any work of man, would have ruined it long ago. But the infinite knowledge and wisdom of God can soon subvert any schemes of men and devils. Let not the humble be afraid of wily politicians. God can easily defeat them all.

7. The safety of God's people does not depend on their number, wit, prowess, or inherent strength, but on him, who has made them his *hidden ones*, v. 3. He that touches them touches the apple of his eye, Zech. ii. 8. In the time of trouble he shall hide them in his pavilion: in the secret of his tabernacle shall he hide them, Ps. xxvii. 5. They are in no sense hidden from the notice or care of God, Isa. xl. 27; Ps. xxxviii. 9; Hos. v. 3; 2 Tim. ii. 19. Nor is their course clandestine or cunning. Their very candor makes them suspected. Though they are not ostentatious, they are not deceitful. Nor do they make a secret of their love to Christ. Nor do they try to hide their sins from the eyes of God, but freely confess and bewail them. They have renounced the hidden things of dishonesty and do not walk in craftiness. Nor do they pass through life without a mark upon them. The world fixes its stigma; and God puts his name in their foreheads. They are the light of the world. And yet they are God's hidden ones. They are hid in God. The being, the providence, every perfection of God and every part of his word are chambers where the humble find refuge. See Ps. xxxii. 7; lxxxiv. 11; Pr. xviii. 10. They are God's *hidden ones*, because they are secretly nourished, having meat to eat which the world knows not of. Nor is their true character known, 1 John iii. 1. Nor does any roll of church-membership on earth contain a correct list of their names. They are often hidden under the calumnies, suspicions and outcries of the wicked. Their best acts are misjudged, and their best qualities misnamed. And they are all hid in Christ, Col. iii. 3, 4. They are all hidden under the shadow of Jehovah's wings. Though unknown, they are yet well known, where it is of most importance to be known.

8. The hostility of the wicked against the people of God is intended to be a war of extermination, v. 4. Some wars are undertaken for the defence of rights assailed, of honor slighted, of territory seized; but here is a war that has from the days of Cain to this hour been deadly and without just cause.

9. In opposing God's cause and people the wicked are ever unanimous, v. 5. In the ranks of his professed friends there is discord; but his foes work *with one consent*. They may hate one another, but their hatred to Christ and his people is a master passion. There was no love lost between Herod and Pilate. Indeed they were ene-

mies; but over the meek and lowly Jesus and his agonies they dropped their private quarrel and formed the friendship of the damned. Scott: "Hypocrisy and profaneness, superstition and skepticism, and even enthusiasm and atheism often confederate against his humbling doctrine and holy cause."

10. Though piety is not hereditary, yet sin, particularly in the shape of hostility to God's cause and people, descends from generation to generation, until grace changes the heart, vv. 6, 7. Temporal advantages accruing to the wicked by commerce with his people will never root out their hatred to God and his chosen. Tyre was much enriched by trade with Judea, but even Tyre joined the league. The Huguenots enriched France, and covered the nation with the glory of their arms and of their learning; but Louis XIV. and Charles IX. cared not for all that.

11. Diversity of taste, age, nationality, laws and superstitions do not hinder men from earnestly coöperating against God's truth and people, vv. 6, 7, 8. Here we have the names of ten different nations, the extremes of which were remote from each other, hardly any two of them worshipping the same gods, most of them speaking tongues unknown to the rest, yet all confederate against God and his people. Among the leaders in wicked persecution are often found false brethren, as here we have the Moabites and Ammonites, children of Lot, who was rescued from the four kings by the love and prowess of Abraham.

12. A reference to the historic narrative shows that the Midianites destroyed each other; so that v. 9 contains a prediction that God's enemies in other cases shall do the same thing, Judges vii. 12–22. The greater their number, the more terrible was their destruction. No marvel that so signal a defeat of foes, and so marvellous a deliverance of his church was held in pious remembrance in all the generations of Israel, Isa. ix. 4. Victory does not go by numbers.

13. The wicked, who have perished, in their war on God and his church, were ensamples to all who shall come after them, vv. 9–11. Let the ungodly of this and succeeding generations beware lest they in their turn become monuments of wrath and beacons to those, who shall come after them.

14. The longer God delays his interposition and the more imminent the peril of his people, the more manifest and glorious is the deliverance wrought by him for them as in the case of Midian, v. 9.

15. To make war on God's people is to make war on God. Their houses are his houses, v. 12.

16. Who is able to stand before the great and terrible God? When his hand lays hold on vengeance, his foes perish suddenly and perpetually, as the Midianites, v. 9; become objects of contempt, v. 10; in the midst of their greatest boastings sink to rise no more, v. 12, being unable to resist as the grain under the wheel or the chaff before the wind; are consumed with terrors and wrath, as the mountain forest wrapped in flames, v. 14; filled with fear and covered with shame, vv. 15, 16. Consternation, disgrace and sorrow are the fruits of resisting God.

17. No doubt the inspired writer intended by the forms of expression used in vv. 9–17 to teach us the justice of all the troubles brought on the wicked; but let no one thence infer the lawfulness of using the language of cursing or imprecation. See Introduction, § 6. Henry: "That which we should earnestly desire and beg of God for our enemies and persecutors, is, that God would bring them to repentance, and we should desire their abasement in order to this; no other confusion to them than what may be a step toward their conversion."

18. God shall yet be gloriously exalted in the sight of all his creatures. In the end there shall not be found a dog to move his tongue against him. All the earth

shall keep silence before him, or break forth into hallelujahs at the mention of his name, 2 Chron. xx. 29.

19. It is a great wonder that the church of God survives, seeing how she is beset on all hands by implacable enemies. The secret is found in the mediatorship of Christ.

PSALM LXXXIV.

To the chief Musician upon Gittith, A Psalm for the sons of Korah.

1 How amiable *are* thy tabernacles, O Lord of hosts!

2 My soul longeth, yea, even fainteth for the courts of the Lord: my heart and my flesh crieth out for the living God.

3 Yea, the sparrow hath found a house, and the swallow a nest for herself, where she may lay her young, *even* thine altars, O Lord of hosts, my King, and my God.

4 Blessed *are* they that dwell in thy house: they will be still praising thee. Selah.

5 Blessed *is* the man whose strength *is* in thee; in whose heart *are* the ways *of them*.

6 *Who* passing through the valley of Baca make it a well; the rain also filleth the pools.

7 They go from strength to strength, *every one of them* in Zion appeareth before God.

8 O Lord God of hosts, hear my prayer: give ear, O God of Jacob. Selah.

9 Behold, O God our shield, and look upon the face of thine anointed.

10 For a day in thy courts *is* better than a thousand. I had rather be a doorkeeper in the house of my God, than to dwell in the tents of wickedness.

11 For the Lord God *is* a sun and shield: the Lord will give grace and glory: no good *thing* will he withhold from them that walk uprightly.

12 O Lord of hosts, blessed *is* the man that trusteth in thee.

ON the title see on titles of Psalms iii. iv. viii. xlii. and Introduction, § 4. It seems nearly certain that the author of Ps. xlii. wrote this. It is probable David wrote both. The Syriac ascribes it to him. Calvin: "In all probability David was its author." Luther confidently speaks of David as the author. Henry: "Though David's name be not in the title of this Psalm, yet we have reason to think he was the penman of it." Scott: "It is generally thought that David composed it." Pool: "The author of this Psalm seems to have been David." It is a pleasing and affecting thought that we find *the sons of Korah* honorably mentioned, and honorably employed about the temple many generations after their father had so terribly perished with Dathan and Abiram, Num. xxvi. 9–11. "Notwithstanding the children of Korah died not." Blessed be God for such mercies. From 1 Chron. ix. 19; xxvi. 1–19, we learn that these descendants of Korah were employed as keepers and as porters of the tabernacle. From 2 Chron. xx. 19, we learn that they were singers in the temple. Their name is found in the title of ten Psalms, viz., xlii. xliv.–xlviii. lxxxiv.–lxxxviii. The general scope of this ode is pretty obvious. Luther: "This is a Psalm of consolation, which breaks forth into the most sweet and powerful expressions in praise and love of the ministry of the word." Alexander: "The Psalmist celebrates the blessedness of intimate communion with God, and prays that he may himself enjoy it." The names of the Almighty here found are *Jehovah* Lord, *El God* and *Elohim God*, on which see on Ps. i. 2; v. 4; iii. 2. On *Sabaoth* of hosts, see on Ps. xxiv. 10. On *Selah* see Introduction, § 15. Scott dates this poem B. C. 1021; Clarke prefixes no date.

1. *How amiable* are *thy tabernacles, O* Lord *of hosts!* Amiable, ancient versions generally, *How beloved*. The word occurs nine times, and is five times rendered *be-*

loved and twice *well-beloved*; Fry: *How lovely*; Alexander: *How dear* [to me]. Heng
stenberg: "The word signifies always *beloved* and never *lovely*." *Tabernacles, dwellings, dwelling-places, habitations,* commonly rendered as here. See on Ps. xxvi. 8;
xliii. 3. The sanctuary had different apartments, hence the plural form. Patrick's
paraphrase is: "It is impossible to express the affection I have to thy dwelling-place,
O Lord." The appointed worship of the true God has in all ages possessed great
attractions for the regenerate.

2. *My soul longeth, yea, even fainteth for the courts of the* LORD. *Longeth, desireth.*
It expresses the greed of the lion for his prey, Ps. xvii. 12; lasting and earnest desire;
several times rendered as here, Gen. xxxi. 30. *Fainteth, fails, is consumed. Courts,*
plural, because there were more apartments than one. *My heart and my flesh crieth
out for the living God,* q. d., my whole nature is intensely wrought up to desire not
only the privilege of worship, but actual communion with God. Without God all
rites, though divinely appointed, profit not. This verse more than any other shows
that the Psalmist was now in some way deprived of the privileges of the sanctuary,
either in the time of Saul, or in the rebellion of Absalom.

3. *Yea, the sparrow hath found a house, and the swallow a nest for herself, where she
may lay her young,* even *thine altars, O* LORD *of hosts, my King, and my God. Sparrow,*
always rendered *bird* or *fowl,* except in this place and in Ps. cii. 7. In Ezek. xxxix.
4, it is applied to birds of prey. From the habits and notes sometimes ascribed to
this bird, the word is supposed to designate the sparrow; but the same would as
readily point out several other kinds of birds. No species of the sparrow is very
much inclined to build its nest in houses. The Chaldee has *pigeon;* Syriac, Arabic,
Septuagint, Vulgate, Ethiopic, Tremellius and Junius, Piscator, Fabritius, Amesius,
Edwards, Jebb and Green, *sparrow;* Hengstenberg, *bird.* Alexander thinks both
sparrow and *swallow* are put for small and helpless birds in general. *Swallow* is no
less a doubtful rendering, though in one other place it is so rendered, Pr. xxvi. 2.
It comes from a word denoting freedom, and may be applied to the swallow, or the
ring-dove, or the *Jerusalem dove.* All the ancient versions render it *turtle.* Hengstenberg: "The word need not be exactly defined." Clarke thinks it very unlikely
that birds of any kind were allowed to build their nests, and hatch their young in
or about the altars, which were kept in the greatest purity, and had on them
perpetual fires. "But," says Paxton, "the altar is here by a synecdoche of a part
for the whole, to be understood of the tabernacle, among the rafters of which the
sparrow and swallow were allowed to nestle; or rather for the buildings which
surrounded the sacred edifice, where the priests and their assistants had their ordinary residence." Delaney however thinks the altars were now desolate, and supposes
the Psalmist refers to the time when there was one altar at Hebron and another at
Gibeon. But this is not probable. There were two altars in the tabernacle and
temple—the altar of incense and the altar of burnt-offering. Two views of this verse
claim notice. One is that the Psalmist here compares himself to these birds, and
says that but for God's house he would have been like a sparrow, a wanderer. This
is the sense as given by Arnd, Hengstenberg and Alexander. The other view is
that which makes David deplore his absence from God's house, in which he has less
privileges than the birds. This is the more common interpretation, and is naturally
suggested by the words. Morison: "I confess I see a great beauty in adhering to
the sense given in the common version."

4. *Blessed* are *they that dwell in thy house. Blessed,* the same as the first word in
the Psalter. It occurs again in vv. 5, 12; a plural noun equivalent to *O the blessednesses.* The blessings connected with a regular and devout attendance at God's
house are so many and so great that the strongest terms may well be employed to

describe them. Even the *visitor* of the sanctuary may be blessed, but those who *dwell* there are sure of great and numerous mercies. Some think there is a special reference to priests and Levites, and here perhaps particularly to the sons of Korah employed about the temple and having their residences near by. Of all stated and devout worshippers it is added: *They will be still praising thee.* They will have cause to praise thee. They will be in the habit of praising thee. In nothing is the force of good habits more seen than in the lively and thankful worship of God's house. Calvin: "Never will a man praise God from the heart, unless, relying upon his grace, he is a partaker of spiritual peace and joy."

5. *Blessed is the man whose strength* is *in thee.* *Blessed*, as in v. 4. *Strength, might, power*, often united with *refuge, confidence, tower.* His strength is *in God* by his own act of faith. The public worship of God in the temple was a call on the nation to repose their confidence, and to trust their homes and their all to God, as they thrice a year left them unprotected. *In whose heart* are *the ways* of them. *Ways*, the word does not express mental habits, but *highways, causeways*, from a verb signifying to *cast up.* The roads leading to Jerusalem were *highways* well cast up and provided with bridges. They were carefully inspected and repaired before each feast. A literal rendering would be *highways in their hearts.* Good: "*The ways are in his heart, i. e.,* the highways to the temple are the objects of his delight." The way of the righteous is a highway, Pr. xvi. 17, and the pious love to walk in it. Henry: "Having placed their happiness in God as their End, they rejoice in all the ways that lead to him." The plural of this last clause shows that *man* in the first clause denotes a class.

6. Who *passing through the valley of Baca make it a well*, or, *Passing through the valley of Baca*, they *make it a well.* The valley of *Baca* is the valley of mulberry-trees. See 2 Sam. v. 23, 24; 1 Chron. xiv. 14, 15. The valley of Baca may be any valley of mulberry-trees, or it may designate the valley of Rephaim in particular, 2 Sam. v. 22, 23. The valley here referred to was on some highway to Jerusalem. The fruit of the mulberry when fully ripe was delicious, cooling and well fitted to allay thirst. It was famed even at Rome. These trees may have been planted, and no doubt were left uninjured, that by their shade and fruit they might refresh the pilgrims going to and from Jerusalem. The mulberry of Palestine was tenacious of life even in sandy soils, if it had moisture. In casting up a causeway through such a valley ditches would be left on either side, and perhaps pools were expressly made near the road that both man and beast might be supplied with refreshing drink. However sterile these valleys may have been, they could at least be made to supply drink to the weary pilgrims: *The rain also filleth the pools.* Thus the meaning would seem to be, Blessed are they who enjoy the privilege of going up to Jerusalem, for although they pass through the valleys of mulberry-trees, yet even there they find water. Another interpretation, borrowed from some of the ancient versions, is to render it *valley of tears*, or *valley of weeping*, (the church of England, *vale of misery ;*) but this is not supported by the best ancient versions; and then it requires us to read, not Baca, but *Bacah*, whence Bochi, and in the plural Bochim, Judges ii. 1, 5. Nor would this mode of explanation so well sustain the figure of the text.

7. *They go from strength to strength.* As the visits of the Israelites to the holy city were divinely directed, and in the time of such pilgrimages their homes were divinely protected, so no doubt a kind providence preserved them from excessive exhaustion in their journey, and they entered Jerusalem with vigor and animation. They had strength to enjoy the festivals. This is the lowest sense of the passage, but is doubtless the basis of the higher sense, viz., that devout worshippers advance in vigor of religious character. *Strength*, often so rendered, also *activity, wealth, substance,*

valor, power. In this place the margin has *company.* Horsley reads, *from wall to wall,* Merrick, *from station to station;* many (among them several ancient versions), *from virtue to virtue,* signifying thereby *courage;* several, *from host to host;* Waterland and Fry, *from valley to valley.* But Calvin, church of England, Mudge, Green, Street, Jebb, Clarke, Hengstenberg, Alexander and others have *strength.* Edwards renders it, He grows stronger and stronger as he walks. Calvin: "The saints are continually acquiring fresh strength for going up to Mount Zion, and continue to prosecute their journey without weariness or fatigue, until they reach the wished-for place, and behold the countenance of God." Parallel passages abound in the Scriptures, Isa. xxxv. 6–8; xl. 29–31; xlviii. 21. Every one of them *in Zion appeareth before God, i. e.,* God supports the strength of the pilgrims, not allowing them to fall by the way, but conducting them safely to worship at his holy hill. In like manner he supports the faith, courage and might of his people until each of them stands perfect before him in glory. The verb is in the future, *shall appear.* As the weight of authority is in favor of the English text, the variations of rendering are not noticed.

8. *O* Lord *God of hosts, hear my prayer.* The general prayer is in a form often used. It is repeated, *Give ear, O God of Jacob.* God's answer to Jacob at Bethel always renders an allusion to that patriarch relevant to the subject of prayer.

9. *Behold, O God our shield.* Literally, Our shield see thou, O God. In v. 11, we again have the word shield as here. From this many suppose that God and shield are here in apposition, and that God is here addressed as our shield. The grammar and the sense will admit this explanation. But they will also admit that the prophet here prays that God would behold our shield, even the Saviour of sinners. This view is adopted by many. It is incorporated into the devotional language of millions. It is justified by the fair construction of the parallel clause, *And look upon the face of thine anointed.* David was God's anointed. But in a much higher sense Jesus, of whom David was a type, was God's Messiah. Scott: "David is generally supposed to have looked forward to the promised Messiah, of whom he was the type and progenitor." Henry: "He has an eye to the Mediator." Calvin: "There is no doubt, that in uttering these words, the object which he aspired after was to obtain the divine favor through the intervention of the Mediator of whom he was the type." Gill: "It is best to apply it to Christ, afterwards called a sun and shield." Cocceius, Bossuet, Bellarmine, Horne, Fry, Morison, Dickson and others allow a direct reference to Christ through David as a type.

10. *For a day in thy courts is better than a thousand.* The Chaldee explains thus: For it is better to dwell in the court of thy sanctuary one day, than to spend a thousand in exile. Calvin, followed by Henry, Clarke, Hengstenberg and Alexander: For better is one day in thy courts than a thousand elsewhere. But may not the comparison be between the *courts of the Lord* and *the tents of wickedness,* as in the next clause? In many languages it is common to anticipate such explanatory clauses. It is clear that we cannot let the words stand alone, for then they would teach that a very short time spent in God's house is better than a much longer time, which is contrary to the whole scope of the ode. *I had rather be a doorkeeper in the house of my God than to dwell in the tents of wickedness. Be a doorkeeper,* margin, *sit at the threshold.* None but the priests could lawfully enter the innermost apartments of the tabernacle or temple. David says that any place in God's house is better than a residence among the wicked. Venema: "To the house of God he opposes not any and every kind of tents, but such as are *rich, powerful, glorious* and splendid, which excite the lusts of the flesh, and in their very nature please the fancy, and seem fairly to promise happiness." He gives his reason for his choice:

11. *For the* Lord *God is a sun and shield.* Chaldee: For the Lord God is as a

high wall and a strong shield; Syriac: For the Lord God is our nourisher and our helper; church of England: For the Lord God is a light and defence. Our English text is sustained by Calvin, Tremellius and Junius, Piscator, Fabritius, Amesius, Venema, Edwards, Jebb, Fry, Tholuck, Hengstenberg and Alexander. The first noun occurs largely over a hundred times and is uniformly rendered *sun*. *Shield*, see on Ps. iii. 3; vii. 10. Diodati: "The Lord God is the author of all joy and goodness to his children, and their protector against all evils;" Arnd: "As the natural sun is the light, life, and joy of all natural things, so God himself is the light of all those who dwell in his house, their salvation, and the strength of their life. But the Lord is not only a sun, he is also a shield, such a protection as covers the body and the soul like a shield, so that no murderous weapon of the devil and of men can strike and mortally wound us." Any correct knowledge of the ancient shield, and every new discovery of the uses of light in creation show the beauty of the figures here employed. Many think that the prophet here says of Messias that he is a sun and a shield. If this is so, we have here proof of his divinity in his being called LORD and *God*. Compare John xx. 28. *The* LORD *will give grace and glory.* *Grace, favor,* meaning undeserved kindness, unmerited love. See on Ps. xlv. 2. *Glory, honor,* see on Ps. iii. 3; iv. 2; vii. 5. Alexander: "Grace and glory are related as the cause and the effect. The latter includes all the sensible fruits and manifestations of the divine favor." Clarke: "*The Lord will give grace* to pardon, purify and save the soul from sin:—and then he will *give glory* to the *sanctified* in his eternal kingdom." Scott: "In this world the Lord gives 'grace,' which he, as a sun, ripens into 'glory' in the world above." *No good* thing *will he withhold from them that walk uprightly.* *Good*, as in Ps. iv. 6. Its meaning is quite uniform. The reasoning is irrefragable. If the Lord gives grace and glory, which are the two things man needs in time and eternity, he will of course withhold *no good thing*, of which we can conceive. These mercies are for those who *walk uprightly*. The *walk* denotes the tenor of the life. See on Ps. i. 1. *Uprightly, sincerely, perfectly, without blemish, without spot,* meaning, with integrity of heart. See on Ps. xv. 2.

12. O LORD *of hosts, blessed* is the *man that trusteth in thee.* *Blessed*, as in vv. 4, 5. On *trusting in* God, see on Ps. iv. 5; ix. 10.

DOCTRINAL AND PRACTICAL REMARKS.

1. If we are not pleased with the solemn worship of God, it is because we lack the true spirit of devotion, and if we lack the spirit of devotion, we have no piety, vv. 1, 4. Henry: "Gracious souls see a wonderful, an inexpressible beauty in holiness and in holy work." As true piety prevails, love for the worship of God increases.

2. While mere strength of religious emotions is no proof that they are genuine, so it is no proof that they are spurious. The Psalmist's fervor rose very high. It produced marked effects on his *soul*, his *heart*, and his *flesh*, v. 2. We cannot have too much religious affection, if it is pure and holy. Well may we *long, faint,* and *cry out* for God. When the queen of Sheba saw the wonders of Solomon's court, "there was no more spirit in her," 1 Kings x. 5. How much more may all the powers of the soul fail in view of the ineffable glories of God, even as sometimes revealed in his earthly courts.

3. While carnal men may be affected with the decency, the dignity, the solemnity of God's worship, and may approve of its good effects on the minds, morals and manners of the community, yet that which above all else endears God's house to regenerated men is God himself, v. 2. "Shew us the Father, and it sufficeth us" is still the cry of gracious souls.

4. Exile from home, from country, and from the usual privileges of the sanctuary

is very trying, so that many strong men have sunk under the weight of their sorrows, v. 3. Yet let the pious remember that God can sustain them, and comfort them. Let no one banished from the usual sphere of his labors and enjoyments fall into despondency. Jesus reigns. Let us find out present duty, and do that. Henry: "It is better to be serving God in solitude, than serving sin with a multitude." Reader, are you kind to exiles and foreigners?

5. Let all believers, however tempted, however forsaken of man, hold fast the promises of God, and plead his covenant relation. In the words, "my King and my God," uttered in faith, there is more consolation than in all human reasonings.

6. Those who are tempted lightly to esteem Gospel ordinances and privileges, know not how soon they may be taught their value and preciousness by being cut off from them, v. 4. This is a sad way of becoming wise, but some will learn in no other way.

7. It is well worth inquiry whether in modern churches praise occupies as conspicuous a place as it should, v. 4. Believers always have more, in which to rejoice and for which to give thanks, than they have calling for mourning and sadness. In themselves they are vile and worthless. In God's covenant they are rich indeed.

8. Henry: "Those who have the new Jerusalem in their eye, must have the ways that lead to it in their heart, v. 5. If we make God's promise our strength, we must make God's word our rule, and walk by it."

9. To his saints God is all in all, v. 5. Our strength is in him. He is our wisdom. He is all our salvation.

10. If our way is through the valley of Baca, by God's grace we may make it a well and find refreshment. From the tone of Paul's Epistle to the Ephesians, or the spirit of Bunyan's Pilgrim's Progress, who would suspect that either of these works was written from a prison? It is much more important for us to learn wisdom by our trials than to escape from them. Out in the Ægean sea, about forty miles from Miletus, lies a rocky and desolate island, formerly remarkable as the Botany Bay for Roman criminals. Its name is Patmos. Jesus permitted the cruel Domitian to banish to this dreary spot the venerable John, beloved of his Master, that here in this Baca he might receive the apocalyptic visions, the sublimest of prophecies. John never was happier, never was more filled with the Holy Ghost, than in this horrid abode.

11. As God supported Israel in all the journey from Egypt to Canaan, Deut. viii. 4; xxix. 5; Neh. ix. 21; and as he showed a very marked providence towards his chosen in their pilgrimages to the holy city, Ex. xxxiv. 24, so God will forever protect and help all his chosen in their march to the heavenly Zion, v. 7.

12. If the pious find it so good to draw near to God on earth, what will it not be to appear before him in the mount Zion above! v. 7. Here indeed are the lively oracles, the holy sacraments, the preached word, the prayers of saints, the high praises of Jehovah, the ministers of the gospel and the saints, who tremble at his word; but in the temple above are the spirits of just men made perfect, ministers, prophets, apostles, martyrs, confessors, angels and the glorious Lamb as he had been slain. An infinite tide of unchanging love rolls in on the great assembly. Hallelujah follows hallelujah. The glories of redemption are more seen in one hour there than in a lifetime here.

13. Prayer should not be counted a mere form. Its end is not secured till we get the answer, v. 8.

14. We cannot make too constant use of Christ's mediation, v. 9. Calvin: "We are here taught, that the only way in which God becomes reconciled to us is through the mediation of Christ, whose presence scatters and dissipates all the dark clouds of our sins."

15. If our love to God and his house were as strong as it should be, as strong as it

was in the bosom of the Psalmist, we should not find it necessary to spend so much time in seeking for evidences of a renewed state, and for marks of gracious affections, v. 10. Love is its own evidence. When it commands the soul, we cannot doubt its existence. When one desires God's word more than his necessary food, when he thinks it the highest privilege to be a worshipper of God, when he joyfully resigns his all to Jehovah, then his evidences are usually comfortable. One reason why many doubt their piety is because it is doubtful.

16. How amazing are the relations which God sustains to his people, when everything in society from a shepherd to a king, everything in war from a *shield* to twenty thousand chariots, and everything in nature from a bird covering her young to the *Sun* shining in his strength are laid under contribution to show us something of his goodness and of our resources, v. 11.

17. How rich and inexhaustible is the mine of God's word. How this Psalm grows on us when we study it. What volumes of pertinent matter might be written even on v. 11.

18. When the prophet says that God will withhold *no good thing* from his people, he includes not only such things as they may esteem good, but all things that are really such, v. 11. We have a list of good things in 1 Cor. iii. 22, very different from any which a carnal man would make out.

19. Let us never forget that no ardor of affections, no correctness of religious opinions, no boldness of religious profession, and no decency of private character will be accepted by God in lieu of a holy life, expressed in this Psalm by *walking uprightly*, v. 11.

20. No mortal can conceive the blessings of the man, who thus walks with God. Three times in this short Psalm, the prophet cries out, *O the blessednesses* of such.

21. God has a right to expect and demand our confidence at all times, v. 12. He does no wrong. Job said no more than each man ought to say, "Though he slay me, yet will I trust in him." Calvin: "Whoever has learned how great a blessedness it is to rely on God, will put forth all the desires and faculties of his mind, that with all speed he may hasten to him." This is the way to be always blessed. Nicolson: "This acclamation (in v. 12) may be intended to answer an objection: 'If those be blessed who dwell in thy temple, then those must be wretched who are exiled from it.' No, says the Psalmist, though there be many advantages enjoyed by those who can attend the ordinances of God, and some may attend them without profit; yet he who trusts in God can never be confounded. Faith in God will always be crowned."

22. One of Luther's reflections on this Psalm is: "Let the world have their rich ones, their powerful ones, and their wise ones, and their consolations in this world; let them trust and glory in their wisdom, their might, their wealth, and their possessions,—my heart triumphs in the living God."

PSALM LXXXV.

To the chief Musician, A Psalm for the sons of Korah.

1 LORD, thou hast been favourable unto thy land: thou hast brought back the captivity of Jacob.

2 Thou hast forgiven the iniquity of thy people; thou hast covered all their sin. Selah.

3 Thou hast taken away all thy wrath: thou hast turned *thyself* from the fierceness of thine anger.

4 Turn us, O God of our salvation, and cause thine anger toward us to cease.

5 Wilt thou be angry with us for ever? wilt thou draw out thine anger to all generations?

6 Wilt thou not revive us again: that thy people may rejoice in thee?

7 Shew us thy mercy, O Lord, and grant us thy salvation.

8 I will hear what God the Lord will speak: for he will speak peace unto his people, and to his saints: but let them not turn again to folly.

9 Surely his salvation *is* nigh them that fear him; that glory may dwell in our land.

10 Mercy and truth are met together; righteousness and peace have kissed *each other*.

11 Truth shall spring out of the earth; and righteousness shall look down from heaven.

12 Yea, the Lord shall give *that which is* good; and our land shall yield her increase.

13 Righteousness shall go before him; and shall set *us* in the way of his steps.

ON the title see on titles of Psalms iii. iv. lxxxiv. On the date, scope and authorship of this ode there is much diversity among learned men. Morison: "The composition itself is evidently one of exultation and triumph;" Tholuck calls it "A song of complaint." Scott dates it B. C. 520; Clarke, B. C. 536; Hengstenberg says, "The time of composition cannot be determined;" Alexander: "There is nothing in the title, or in the Psalm itself, to determine its date or confine its application to any particular historical occasion." Many Jewish writers think it was composed by Ezra. Some commentators think it was written on the occasion of the return of David after Absalom's rebellion. Others refer it to the destruction of Sennacherib's army, and yet others to the return of the Jews from Babylon; while Calvin says, "It was probably indited to be sung by the people when they were persecuted by the cruel tyranny of Antiochus." This ode well suits the state of the church in many stages of her history. Does this Psalm contain a prophecy respecting redemption by Christ? The affirmative is supported by the Syriac, Calvin, Diodati, Venema, Dimock, Horne, Fry, Dodd, Gill, Henry, Clarke, Scott, Morison and others. Some think the key to the interpretation of this Psalm is found in Lev. xxvi. 3–13. But it has a higher sense than would be gathered from that Scripture taken literally. We find here these names of the Most High, *Jehovah* Lord, *Elohim God* and *El God*, on which see on Ps. i. 2; iii. 2; v. 4. On *Selah* see Introduction, § 15.

1. Lord, *thou hast been favourable unto thy land.* He is calling to mind former times, when Jehovah had shown mercy and wrought salvation in Israel. The verbs of verses 1–3 are all in the preterite. He says, Time was when thou didst have a favor to *thy land*, Canaan. *Thou hast brought back the captivity of Jacob.* To *turn captivity*, or *bring back captivity* is to relieve from sore evils, see on Ps. xiv. 7. The man of Uz was never a prisoner to his enemies, and yet God turned his captivity, Job xlii. 10. The design of the Psalmist is to recall former deliverances for the encouragement of hope and prayer.

2. *Thou hast forgiven the iniquity of thy people.* *Hast forgiven*, see on Ps. xxxii. 1, 5. Clarke: "*Thou hast borne*, or *carried away*, the iniquity. An allusion to the ceremony of the scapegoat." This is a much better exposition than that favored by Hammond, Mudge and others, drawn from the Jewish doctors, that captivity was one way of expiation, and that captivity being ended was a sign that the sin, which brought it on, was remitted. There is but one *proper* way of expiation, which is by atoning blood. *Thou hast covered all their sin.* See on Ps. xxxii. 1. In Ps. xxxii. 5, it is rendered *have hid*. Alexander: "Both verbs suggest the idea of atonement as well as pardon." When a sin is *covered* in the Bible sense, it is wholly hidden from view.

3. *Thou hast taken away all thy wrath.* *Taken away, gathered in, withdrawn.* *Wrath, rage*, signifying hot displeasure with its usual tokens. *Thou hast turned thyself*

from the fierceness of thine anger. *Fierceness*, in Ps. ii. 5, rendered *sore displeasure.* *Anger*, in Ps. vii. 6, rage. The sum of the first three verses is that in days past God has shown himself merciful, has averted just judgments from the land and nation of Israel. All this is designed to prepare the way for the plea about to be made.

4. *Turn us, O God of our salvation.* Syriac: Restore us, O God our Saviour; church of England: Turn us then, O God our Saviour. The argument is, in former days thou hast wondrously saved us and forgiven our sins; we therefore are encouraged to beseech thee to bring us out of our present distresses. Some give a higher and a spiritual meaning to the words, *turn us.* Clarke: "Thou hast turned our captivity;—now convert our souls;" Scott: "Our sins indeed deserve worse than all our sufferings, and retard our reëstablishment: but turn and convert us to thyself by thy special grace, and make way for more complete effects of thy reconciliation to us." A right state of heart is a greater blessing than relief from any temporal distress. The only way for churches or nations to escape from the sore chastisements, which God sends for their sins, is to repent and turn to him. Heartily pious men prefer *grace* to any temporal good. The prayer is for something better than temporal relief. *Turn* here and *hast brought back* in v. 1 are different forms of the same verb. *And cause thine anger towards us to cease*, q. d., We are now feeling the sad effects of our sins in thy anger towards us; but as thou didst show us mercy in former days, so repeat thy kindness. Alexander: "The word translated *anger* is one which properly expresses a mixed feeling of grief and indignation." In Ecc. i. 18, it is rendered *grief*; in Ecc. vii. 3, *sorrow*; in Deut. xxxii. 27, *wrath*; in several places, *provocation.*

5. *Wilt thou be angry with us for ever?* *Be angry*, commonly so rendered; once, *be displeased.* It is not a word of the same root with that rendered *anger* in v. 4; see on Ps. ii. 5, 12, where the same word is rendered *wrath.* *Wilt thou draw out thine anger to all generations?* Literally, *to generation and generation.* The plea is based not only on the history of God's mercies to Israel; but on his revealed character, Ex. xxxiv. 6, 7; Ps. xxx. 5. How long the distress had lasted we know not; but a few strokes of the rod make us cry out as if we had received evil all our days.

6. *Wilt thou not revive us again: that thy people may rejoice in thee?* Literally, *Wilt thou not turn, wilt thou (not) revive us?* *Turn*, as in v. 4. *Revive*, elsewhere *quicken, preserve, keep alive.* None but God can bring any people out of trouble; and it is well when this truth is felt, and the justice of our afflictions is felt and confessed. Nothing but divine grace ever meets our case.

7. *Shew us thy mercy, O* LORD, *and grant us thy salvation.* *Mercy*, see on Ps. v. 7; li. 1. The plea is for an undeserved deliverance, a salvation not only from suffering, but also from sins. The whole case was one, in which no reliance could be put on any but *Jehovah.* The latter clause in the Hebrew is more hopeful than the English text indicates; literally, Thy salvation thou wilt give us; Chaldee: And thy salvation shall be given to us. If God will cause us to see his mercy, our salvation is sure. Calvin: "Salvation is the work and fruit of mercy, for no other reason can be assigned why God is induced to show himself our Saviour, but that he is merciful."

8. *I will hear what God the* LORD *will speak.* Fry thinks this "verse is evidently the soliloquy of the priest, who had consulted the oracle, and is waiting for the divine response: for we are generally to understand the petitions of the church and of every part of it as offered by the Mediator and 'High Priest of our profession.'" Hengstenberg and Alexander think it is not the Psalmist that here speaks, but the people. A third view, taken by Calvin, Diodati, Dickson, Henry, Clarke and Scott, is that the prophet here speaks in his own name. A fourth view, supported by Gill and Horne, is that the Psalmist here speaks in the name of the Jewish people or of

the church. The *third* view is the simplest. As a prophet he declares that he will humbly hear and faithfully report what the Lord shall declare. Inspired men, even those, who had no piety, spake as they were moved by the Holy Ghost, Num. xxii. 8, 18, 20, 35, 38; xxiii. 8, 12, 26; 1 Sam. iii. 9, 10. He seems confident of a message of mercy: *For he will speak peace unto his people, and to his saints.* Calvin: "The word *peace* is employed by the Hebrews to denote prosperity." Clarke: "He will give *prosperity* to the people in general; and to his saints, his followers, in particular." The peace and prosperity which God secures are more than civil and domestic quiet. God "preaches peace by Jesus Christ." Acts x. 36. He is the Prince of peace. He secures to us peace with God, peace of conscience, and a quietness of mind worth more than all human glory. *But let them not turn again to folly.* Unfeigned repentance and loathing of sin are the best fruits of affliction, and are best evinced by our not repeating the follies for which we were chastened. *Folly,* found here only, and in Job iv. 6, where it is rendered *confidence.* The *foolish confidence* of Israel was in idols, in alliances with other nations, in birth, in an arm of flesh and in heartless ceremonies.

9. *Surely his salvation* is *nigh them that fear him; that glory may dwell in our land.* For *fear,* the Arabic reads *worship.* See on Ps. ii. 11. Those, who thus fear God, shall surely be delivered from all sin and wrath, and from all real evil. God's salvation is not far from them. *Glory,* honor. *Dwell,* continue permanently. God is glorified by a people who fear him; and he honors them.

10. *Mercy and truth are met together; righteousness and peace have kissed* each other. *Mercy,* as in v. 7. *Truth,* from the word *Amen;* see on Ps. xli. 13. *Mercy and truth,* as in Ps. xxv. 10. *Righteousness,* uniformly so rendered, see on Ps. iv. 1. *Peace,* as in v. 8. *Are met together;* Clarke, have met on the way. *Kissed,* as in Ps. ii. 12. From the days of Augustine to Chalmers, yea, before and since, this verse has refreshed the pious. The lowest sense gathered from it is that given by Patrick: "Goodness and fidelity, justice and concord (which are the principal glory of a kingdom) meet together, like ancient friends, which have been long absent, and embrace each other." No doubt these things are great pillars in a well ordered state. When a sound reformation takes place among a people, mercy, truth, justice and peace are soon established between man and man. To such God's mercy, truth, righteousness and peace are vouchsafed. But is there not a reference to the glorious scheme of gospel grace by Jesus Christ? Augustine: "The mercy of God is the origin and source of all his promises, whence issues the righteousness which is offered to us by the Gospel, while from that righteousness proceeds the peace which we obtain by faith, when God justifies us freely." Calvin: "The natural meaning of the passage is, that mercy, truth, peace, and righteousness will form the grand ennobling distinction of Christ's kingdom." Diodati: "This cannot perfectly agree with any but the *Messiah's* reign." Lowth: "How admirable is that celebrated personification of the divine attributes by the Psalmist. How just, elegant, and splendid does it appear, if applied only according to the literal sense, to the restoration of the Jewish nation from the Babylonish captivity! but if interpreted as relating to that sublimer, more sacred, and mystical sense, which is not obscurely shadowed under the ostensible image, it is certainly uncommonly noble and elevated, mysterious and sublime." Clarke: "Where did mercy and truth, righteousness and peace meet? In Christ Jesus. When were they reconciled? When he poured out his life on Calvary." Horne: "These four divine attributes parted at the fall of Adam, and met again at the birth of Christ. Mercy was ever inclined to save man, and Peace could not be his enemy; but Truth exacted the performance of God's threat, 'The soul

that sinneth, it shall die ;' and Righteousness could not but give to every one his due." See also Pool, Gill, Henry, Dodd, Morison, Scott, etc.

11. *Truth shall spring out of the earth. Truth*, as in v. 10. Either truth shall be abundant like the grass, springing out of the earth ; or the blessed fruits of truth shall be abundant. *And righteousness shall look down from heaven. Righteousness*, as in v. 10. Alexander: "The beauty of the image in this clause is heightened by the use of a verb, which originally means to lean or bend over, for the purpose of gazing down upon a lower object." See on Ps. xiv. 2. But the word also means to *look out*, Gen. xxvi. 8; 2 Kings ix. 30, 32. So the force of the figure may be that justice, which had been as it were concealed for a season, now again shows her face ; see Isa. lix. 14. The verbs are fitly rendered in the same tense, although in the Hebrew the former is in the future and the latter in the preterite. Scott: "Christ, the TRUTH and the LIFE sprang out of the earth, when he was born of a woman : and 'justice' looked down upon his character, obedience, and atonement, well pleased and satisfied."

12. *Yea, the* LORD *shall give* that which is *good.* If Jehovah gives any people these blessings, *mercy, truth, justice and peace*, they may be sure of great *good* in a thousand forms; and if he gives us an interest in his Son, in whom *mercy, truth, righteousness* and *peace* meet, we may be sure that he will do us *good* to all eternity, Rom. viii. 32. *And our land shall yield her increase.* Either first, God will bless a people among whom *mercy, truth, justice* and *peace* are cultivated and abound, rewarding the toil of the husbandman; or, secondly, in the reign of his Son, he shall gather a great harvest of love and praise from the earth where he had been once hated and blasphemed. The primary passage is in Lev. xxvi. 4. See on Ps. lxvii. 6. Compare Hag. ii. 18, 19; Zech. viii. 12.

13. *Righteousness shall go before him.* Alexander: "The idea here expressed seems to be that of public and solemn manifestation;" Calvin explains it of "the prevalence and unobstructed course of righteousness." All the steps God has taken in the punishment or salvation of men were in righteousness. All the steps of the Redeemer were in righteousness. He did not deny the justice of God, nor ignore the penalty of his law; but redeemed us from it by satisfying divine justice. Compare Heb. i. 8. *And* [righteousness] *shall set us in the way of his steps.* Clarke: "Perhaps this verse receives its best solution from Rom. iii. 25." Christ's example of righteousness and his glorious justifying righteousness *set*, or *put* us in the way of salvation.

DOCTRINAL AND PRACTICAL REMARKS.

1. It is a mark of an ignoble nature to allow present afflictions to blot out the memory of past mercies, vv. 1–4. Some favors are so great as to call for everlasting songs.

2. Every mercy bestowed may be abused, and so be followed by sore calamities, vv. 1–4. Marvellous it is that Noah, who had just escaped the perils of the deluge, and Lot, who had just escaped from the storm of fire and brimstone, should so soon both fall into drunkenness.

3. The whole argument of the first part of this Psalm goes on the supposition that God is unchangeably gracious, and that if he once showed mercy, he is ready in like circumstances to do so again.

4. How precious is forgiveness, and how refreshing it is to meet the doctrine in so many places of Scripture, v. 2. Calvin: "Deliverance from punishment depends upon the remission of sin." Pardon is the first of an infinite series of blessings.

5. When God pardons, he pardons *all* our offences, v. 2; Rom. viii. 1. When the Lord covers our sin, he covers it all, and forever, Jer. xxxi. 34.

6. If inspired men, who are under the control of the loving, gentle Spirit of God, have such strong conceptions of the displeasure of God, how terrible it must be, v. 3. It is *wrath;* it is the *fierceness of anger.*

7. One of the best fruits of past mercies is an inclination to seek new mercies at the hand of the same kind Father, who has hitherto blessed us, vv. 1–4. Dickson: "Neither old sins nor late, neither old judgments nor present lying under wrath, must keep God's people from running unto him by prayer."

8. God only and God alone can save; and the sooner we learn that truth, the better for us, v. 4.

9. The doctrine of conversion is no novelty, v. 4. Then are temporal blessings sweetest when they succeed pardon of sin, and are poured upon a converted soul. Henry: "All those, whom God will save, he will sooner or later turn. If no conversion, no salvation."

10. If we had a due sense of the evil of sin, and of the obstinacy with which it holds its power over us, we should not so soon grow weary under divine rebukes, and faint under divine corrections, v. 5. "God's anger will not endure forever against any, but the impenitent and unbelieving."

11. If a little wrath makes men cry out as in v. 5, how intolerable will hell be! Jer. xii. 5; Matt. x. 28.

12. Truly sin kills. Men are dead in trespasses and in sins, dead in law, dead in their affections, dead in a loss of comfortable communion with God. Probably the greatest practical heresy of each age is a low idea of our undone condition under the guilt and dominion of sin. While this prevails we shall be slow to cry for *reviving* or *quickening,* v. 6. What sinners and churches need is quickening by the Holy Ghost.

13. If anything on earth gives joy, it is the *reviving* of religion in the hearts of God's people, v. 6; Acts ii. 46, 47; viii. 8.

14. It is not only truth, but truth that can hardly be too deeply felt, that salvation is wholly of God's *mercy,* v. 7. None are heirs of salvation, but the vessels of mercy. Grace made all the promises and grace will fulfil them. Grace provided a Saviour, and grace unites us to him. While life lasts we shall not be done asking for mercy. While eternity lasts, we shall not be done praising mercy.

15. To the church of all ages it is an unspeakable blessing that the prophets *heard what God the Lord spoke,* v. 8. Nothing more effectually destroys all 'comfort of the Scriptures,' than unbelief respecting their inspiration. If holy men did not speak as they were moved by the Holy Ghost, then we have not God's word, and our hope is vain. It is a great mercy to us that the evidences of inspiration are abundant.

16. If we would more closely imitate the prophets in humility and docility, we should get a better understanding of God's mind and will, v. 8. Especially should we carefully practise and submit to all we do know. Then should we soon know more, John vii. 17.

17. Not to sinners determined to live in sin, but to his *people,* his *saints,* does the whole word of God speak *peace.*

18. And how many words of peace God has spoken! Nothing can be thought of by a poor distressed believer, by an humble penitent, but that God has already said it, or something better.

19. No conversion, no richness of religious experience, no height of discoveries in the things of God can ever render it safe for us to parley with sin, to dally with temptation, to lead a careless life, or to cease our vigilance, v. 8.

20. There is no *folly* like sin, v. 8. It is *madness,* it is *mischievous madness,* it is the

wickedness of folly. "It is egregious folly to turn to sin, after we have seemed to turn from it."

21. Let not God's people be governed by appearances, but by the promises. The dark cloud has a silver lining. Salvation is near, v. 9. Amesius: "Although we may not at once possess the desired joy, yet let us persevere in prayers, and patiently and calmly expect the issue from God."

22. If *glory dwells in the land when* God works salvation in and for his people, v. 9; what shame and confusion dwell there when God gives up the land to sin and sinners! Calvin: "When cruelty rages with impunity, when truth is extinguished, when righteousness is oppressed and trampled under foot, and when all things are embroiled in confusion, were it not better that the world should be brought to an end, than that such a state of things should continue?" But we are fools; God only is wise, Ps. xii. 8; Pr. xxviii. 15; xxix. 2, 12.

23. If we are God's people, we shall never be done, and never wish to be done admiring the glories and the harmonies of the scheme of salvation by Jesus Christ, v. 11. Bates: "It is the chiefest of all God's works, that contains the glorious wonders of his mercy and power, wherein he renders himself most worthy of our supreme veneration and affection. Our most raised thoughts are beneath its dignity. Though the light of the gospel hath clearly revealed so much of it as is requisite to be known in our earthly state, yet the sublimer parts are still secret, and reserved for a full discovery, by the brightness of our Saviour's appearance." How God can be just and yet justify the ungodly, how he can condemn sin and yet let the sinner go free, how he can declare and manifest his awful righteousness, and yet be righteous in bestowing life on the guilty, how he can magnify the law and make it honorable, while yet its penalty is not borne by transgressors but by their voluntary substitute, are but a few of the hard problems, which find solution in the cross of Christ. For near a half century I have been hearing and reading good discourses from time to time on this theme, yet it is as fresh and delightful as ever. Oh that I may see into it better before I die, and infinitely better after I die.

24. There is no end, there shall never be an end to the variety and duration of the *good* that God shall give to his people, v. 12. Inspiration confesses both the impossibility and the unlawfulness of describing in the language of mortals the glory of the upper world, 1 Cor. ii. 9; 2 Cor. xii. 4.

25. It has sometimes been objected that the Christian doctrine of a Millenium cannot be true, for the earth could not subsist the teeming millions that would naturally be found upon it, if wars and vices should cease to waste its population. But omitting other and pertinent answers that have been given, we find one here that covers the whole ground, *the earth shall yield her increase*, v. 12. Now and then the season is unusually propitious, and we have a specimen of what God can do when he chooses. He can without any miracle make it many times more fruitful than it has ever been.

26. The knowledge of God shall yet cover the earth as the waters cover the sea, for the mouth of the Lord has spoken it, v. 12.

27. As the whole scheme of salvation is by righteousness in all God has done, and by a glorious righteousness secured to believers, so the preaching of this doctrine is honorable to God and safe to man. It establishes God's people in the right ways of the Lord, v. 13.

28. Oh that the gospel of Jesus Christ, making known the glorious way of salvation by grace, may soon be preached in all lands.

PSALM LXXXVI.

A Prayer of David.

1 Bow down thine ear, O LORD, hear me: for I *am* poor and needy.

2 Preserve my soul; for I *am* holy: O thou my God, save thy servant that trusteth in thee.

3 Be merciful unto me, O Lord: for I cry unto thee daily.

4 Rejoice the soul of thy servant: for unto thee, O Lord, do I lift up my soul.

5 For thou, Lord, *art* good, and ready to forgive; and plenteous in mercy unto all them that call upon thee.

6 Give ear, O LORD, unto my prayer; and attend to the voice of my supplications.

7 In the day of my trouble I will call upon thee: for thou wilt answer me.

8 Among the gods *there is* none like unto thee, O Lord; neither *are there any works* like unto thy works.

9 All nations whom thou hast made shall come and worship before thee, O Lord; and shall glorify thy name.

10 For thou *art* great, and doest wondrous things: thou *art* God alone.

11 Teach me thy way, O LORD; I will walk in thy truth: unite my heart to fear thy name.

12 I will praise thee, O Lord my God, with all my heart: and I will glorify thy name for evermore.

13 For great *is* thy mercy toward me: and thou hast delivered my soul from the lowest hell.

14 O God, the proud are risen against me, and the assemblies of violent *men* have sought after my soul; and have not set thee before them.

15 But thou, O Lord, *art* a God full of compassion, and gracious, longsuffering, and plenteous in mercy and truth.

16 O turn unto me, and have mercy upon me; give thy strength unto thy servant, and save the son of thine handmaid.

17 Shew me a token for good; that they which hate me may see *it*, and be ashamed: because thou, LORD, hast holpen me, and comforted me.

ON the title see on Psalms iii. xvii. Doubtless David wrote this Psalm. This opinion is supported by the ancient versions, many Jewish writers, Luther, Calvin, Piscator, Fabritius, Amesius, Venema, Bellarmine, Gill, Pool, Dodd, Henry, Scott, Morison, Edwards, Horne, Hengstenberg and Alexander. It is not agreed whether it was written during the time when David was persecuted by Saul, or during Absalom's rebellion. Alexander: "The whole Psalm is called a prayer, because entirely made up, either of direct petitions, or of arguments intended to enforce them." Its scope is patent on its very face. Clarke: "It is a very suitable prayer for a person laboring under affliction from persecution or calumny." Scott dates it B. C. 1021; Clarke thinks it was probably made during the captivity. In it we have these names of the Almighty, *El God, Elohim God, Jehovah* LORD and *Adonai Lord*, on which see on Ps. v. 4; iii. 2; i. 2; ii. 4. Anderson thinks, as the Jews would not pronounce *Jehovah*, that perhaps *Adonai*, the substituted word in reading, may be a change of the Hebrew text; and he claims the support of many manuscripts. But why should the change be made here nine times and not frequently in other Psalms where *Adonai* occurs? *Adonai* is unquestionably one of the inspired names of God.

1. *Bow down thine ear*, O LORD, *hear me*. In Hebrew the first three words are just the same as those used by Hezekiah in his distress respecting Sennacherib. This has probably given rise to a tradition among some of the Jews that Hezekiah used this entire prayer on that occasion. But of this there is no evidence. Hezekiah's prayer is given at length in 2 Kings xix. 15–19. The form of expression is of frequent occurrence in devotional composition, Ps. xvii. 6; xxxi. 2; xlv. 10 *Hear*, so as to answer. *For I* am *poor and needy. Poor, humble, lowly, afflicted;* see on Ps. ix. 12. *Needy*, also rendered *poor*; see on Ps. ix. 18. In speaking thus of himself,

the Psalmist gives the reason for urging his prayer, *q. d.*, 'It is well known, wherever thou art known, that thou hearest such; therefore I am bold to call on thy name.'

2. *Preserve my soul. Preserve;* in Ps. xvii. 8 and often, *keep.* It sometimes has the military idea of guard, defend, protect. See on Ps. xvi. 1. *Soul,* either his *life* that was threatened or his immortal soul which was tempted. *For I am holy. Holy,* in Ps. lxxxv. 8, and often, in the plural *saints; godly, merciful.* Some have objected to David's pleading his own good character; but if he did not go beyond the truth, and the occasion called for it, there was nothing wrong in his so doing. Job, David, Peter, John and Paul all did it, Job xxvii. 5; Ps. cxvi. 16; John xxi. 15–17; Rev. i. 10; 1 Cor. ix. 1. Nor is it presumptuous to ask God to show mercy to us for we show it to others; or to forgive us for we forgive others, Matt. v. 7; vi. 14, 15. But David does not superciliously rely on himself, but wholly on the grace of God: *O thou my God, save thy servant that trusteth in thee.* Any pretence of piety, that withdraws confidence from God, or that leads us to set our hope in any created arm, is idle and dangerous.

3. *Be merciful unto me, O Lord. Be merciful;* in Job xix. 21, *have pity;* in Ps. li. 1, *have mercy.* In v. 15, the cognate adjective is rendered *gracious;* in Ps. lxxxiv. 11, the cognate noun is rendered *grace. For I cry unto thee daily.* Even believing prayer has in it no merit; but because God has graciously promised to answer it when fervent and persevering, we may confidently plead his promise. But we must *cry* and that *daily.* The verb is in the future *will cry,* signifying a purpose to call till God answers. *Daily,* literally *all the day, i. e., always.*

4. *Rejoice the soul of thy servant. Rejoice, make glad, cheer.* It is evident that the Psalmist was much distressed and saw that no help was left for him except in God. *For unto thee do I lift up my soul. Lift up, yield, bring, fetch, q. d.,* I commit my soul and my whole case to thee in love and confidence, knowing that thou wilt do right:

5. *For thou, Lord, art good. Good,* the word almost uniformly so rendered. *And ready to forgive;* Calvin, Piscator, Fabritius, Venema, *propitious;* Tremellius and Junius, Amesius, Edwards, Jebb, Hengstenberg and Alexander, *forgiving;* church of England, *gracious;* Bythner, *a pardoner. And plenteous in mercy unto all them that call upon thee. Plenteous, great, abundant.* We have the same *phrase* in v. 15. *Call, cry;* see on Ps. iii. 4; iv. 1. *To call upon God* points out in general *vital religion,* or in particular *sincere prayer.* In each of the first five verses of this Psalm we have the word *for,* equivalent to *because.* In no case has it reference to human merits; in the last verse it points to the true source of all blessings, God's infinite grace and kindness.

6. *Give ear, O LORD, unto my prayer. Give ear,* as in Ps. v. 1; xvii. 1; xxxix. 12. *Prayer,* as in the title. *And attend unto the voice of my supplications. Attend,* in Ps. x. 2, rendered *hearken,* but in Ps. xviii. 1; lv. 2; lxi. 1, *attend. Supplications, earnest entreaties for mercy.* The petition is that God would take up and issue his case.

7. *In the day of my trouble I will call upon thee: for thou wilt answer me.* The verse is closely parallel to Ps. l. 15. *Trouble* and *call* are indeed the same words in the two places. The meaning is, I am calling now and will continue to call during my day of trouble; for I shall get my requests as I know by experience, as well as from thy word and thy excellent nature.

8. *Among the gods* there is *none like unto thee, O* LORD. All false gods are either dead things, or dead men, or lost angels; but Jehovah is the *living* God. Their attributes are either hateful or feeble; his are glorious and infinite. They can make nothing; Jehovah has made all things. They can neither see, nor hear, nor help, nor save; but our God doeth all things after the counsel of his own will. Not one of them is fit to be a lord; but the living God rules and reigns supreme in heaven and

earth. The false gods are subjects of contempt to inspired men, Ps. cxv. 4–7; Isa. xliv. 9–20; 1 Cor. viii. 4. But all holy creatures in all worlds love, fear, obey and adore Jehovah. Instead of *gods* some read *angels*, and it is true that the original word *Elohim* sometimes designates angels. But the context shows that he is speaking of false gods. Calvin: "If it is objected that there is no comparison between God and the silly inventions of men, the answer is obvious, That the language is employed in accommodation to the ignorance of the generality of men." *Neither* are there any works *like unto thy works.* Several ancient versions and modern translations read: *And there is nothing like thy works.* The object is to declare that Jehovah is God alone, and alone fit to be worshipped. This is maintained by asserting that the false gods have never done anything admirable, as Jehovah has done, and by asserting that the very worshippers of false gods were made by the true God:

9. *All nations whom thou hast made shall come and worship before thee, O Lord; and shall glorify thy name.* There are two senses in which God *made* all nations. He made all the people composing all nations, Mal. ii. 10; Num. xvi. 22; Isa. xl. 28. Then he is the father of nations, as political bodies, Gen. xvii. 6; Deut. xxxii. 8; Ps. xxii. 28; Jer. x. 7. He sets up whom he will, and whom he will he puts down. As he made, so can he save or destroy as seems good to him. *All nations,* (all the heathen, all the Gentiles) shall yet *worship* and *glorify* Jehovah. There is doubtless a reference to the latter day glory, when earth shall enjoy the reign of universal peace, and truth, and love, and righteousness, when God's name shall be one, and his praise one. Compare Ps. xxii. 31; cii. 18; Isa. xliii. 7; and especially Rom. xv. 9; Rev. xv. 4.

10. *For thou art great.* There is nothing little, nothing finite, nothing measurable, nothing comprehensible in God. The knowledge of him is high as heaven and deep as hell. He is infinite, eternal, unchangeable, almighty. *And doest wondrous things;* Syriac: *Producest miracles;* Arabic: *Art a worker of miracles;* Clarke: "Thou art a *Worker of miracles.* This thou hast done in numerous instances, and thereby showed thy infinite power and wisdom." The powerlessness of the false gods has been shown in all ages. *Thou art God alone.* His existence precludes the possibility of the existence of another. There is none with him, none beside him. Alexander: "The *for,* at the beginning of the verse, implies that these proofs of divinity must sooner or later have their full effect."

11. *Teach me thy way, O* Lord. Much is implied in this prayer. 1. I am ignorant; I know nothing as I ought to know it; I am a fool; I cannot by searching find out the *way* of life. 2. No creature can effectually teach me. The vail is over my heart. I am blind, and no man, no angel can open my eyes, or give me vision. 3. God, who made me, can teach me; I am not beyond his reach, I am not beyond his skill; I am not out of the pale of his mercy; foolish as I am he can make me wise unto salvation. 4. God alone and God only can do this. 5. I commit my whole case to him. I look to none other. I hope in none else. 6. This is a vital point in my case and in my judgment. I am in great earnest in the matter. Jehovah's way is life, peace, joy and glory. 7. Thus guided by the Lord, the course of my life will be neither doubtful nor erroneous. *I will walk in thy truth.* Then my life shall be conformed, not only to truth in general, but to *thy* truth in particular. I will be warned by thy threatenings; I will embrace thy promises; I will believe thy doctrines; I will conform to thy precepts; I will walk as thou wilt have me. But I cannot do this of myself; I therefore humbly pray: *Unite my heart to fear thy name.* Law: "*Make my heart one that it may fear thy name.*" My heart is apt to be divided; my thoughts and affections wander; I am too often double-minded and of course unstable in all my ways; and it never will be better with me till thou undertake my case. Clarke: "*Join all*

the purposes, resolutions, and affections of my heart *together*, to fear and glorify thy name." Having thus earnestly sought help from God, he felt confident that he should be heard, and so he humbly declares his purpose and his hope:

12. *I will praise thee, O Lord, my God, with all my heart; and I will glorify thy name for evermore.* Patrick: "I am bound to praise thee, both as the supreme LORD of all, and as my bountiful benefactor, with all the powers of my soul: and accordingly, I do now most thankfully acknowledge thee; and will never cease to honor thee, and to do thee service, as long as I have any being."

13. *For great is thy mercy toward me. Mercy*, as in v. 5; in Ps. li. 1, *lovingkindness;* it occurs again in v. 15. *Great*, as in v. 10. God's mercy is as unsearchable as his self-existence, or his eternity. The *for* of this verse may point to the theme of the praise and glory promised in v. 12, or to the gracious cause, which would surely enable him to do as there he engaged. One very *great mercy* he had received: *And thou hast delivered my soul from the lowest hell.* Compare Deut. xxxii. 22. *Hell*, see on Ps. vi. 5; ix. 17. That in this place more is meant than that God had rescued his *life* from the perils of natural death seems pretty clear: 1. The word certainly in some cases signifies what is now popularly understood by the word *hell.* 2. A very deep grave is not objectionable; but the *lowest* hell is an awful thought. 3. Every sinner deserves God's wrath; but for his violation of the *sixth* and *seventh* commandments David deserved dreadful punishments—the *nethermost* hell. 4. While it is an act of *mercy* to spare the life of a sinner, it is a much greater act of mercy to save him from eternal death and give him everlasting life: *q. d.,* Thou hast done great things for me; thou hast even saved my soul from hell. I am therefore encouraged to come to thee and ask for new mercy.

14. *O God, the proud are risen against me, and the assemblies of violent men have sought after my soul. Proud*, commonly so rendered. It includes the idea of presumption. *Violent;* in Ps. liv. 3, *oppressors;* frequently *terrible. Assemblies, multitudes, congregations;* see on Ps. i. 5. Some think it expresses organized combination. The enemies were deadly. They sought his utter ruin. In all this they were without any proper regard for God. *And have not set thee before them, i. e.,* they have not been governed by pious motives; they have not been moved by thy fear, nor by a regard to thy glory. We have a like phrase in Ps. xvi. 8.

15. *But thou, O Lord, art a God full of compassion, and gracious, longsuffering, and plenteous in mercy and truth. Full of compassion*, see on Ps. lxxviii. 38. *Gracious*, see on v. 3. *Longsuffering*, a phrase often so rendered, also *slow of anger.* It has not before occurred, but is found in Ps. ciii. 8; cxlv. 8. *Plenteous in mercy*, as in v. 5. *Truth*, as in v. 11. God is *sincere, faithful;* see Ex. xxxiv. 6, 7. The nature of God must determine the character of the worship we offer him. It is as if he had said: Thou hast revealed thyself to be such a God. Now my case is such as to afford a fit occasion for the exercise of thy glorious attributes.

16. *O turn unto me, and have mercy upon me. Turn, i. e.,* Let not the kindly aspects of thy providence be longer averted from me. *Have mercy, i. e.,* I deserve not these favors; I ask them of thy mere *grace. Give thy strength unto thy servant. Strength*, as in Ps. viii. 1; lxxxiv. 5. The strength sought would effect deliverance and impart courage. In Ecc. viii. 1, the same word is rendered *boldness. Servant*, as in vv. 2, 4; see on title of Ps. xviii. and on Ps. xix. 11. David would not deny his relationship as a *servant* to God. How could he? *And save the son of thine handmaid.* Jesse was a good man, and honorable mention is made of him in both Testaments; but his wife was also one of the excellent of the earth. Compare Ps. cxvi. 16; *q. d.,* I was born thy servant; my mother was thy handmaid; it is mine to

obey; and of course it is thine, Lord, to defend and protect; surely thou wilt not permit thy poor servant to be trodden down and destroyed.

17. *Shew me a token for good.* Shew, we might read, *Do, make, execute, perform. Token, mark, sign;* see on Ps. lxv. 8. He prays, Do something by which I may know that thou wilt do me *good,* and not evil. *That they which hate me may see* it, *and be ashamed,* and so desist from their wicked course, and be brought to true repentance; for a proper *shame* essentially belongs to saving repentance, Ezra ix. 6; Ezek. xvi. 63. *Because thou,* LORD, *hast holpen me, and comforted me.* The sense of this clause would be given by the second future thus, *Because thou, Lord, shalt have holpen me, and comforted me.* Hengstenberg: "The preterites are to be explained by the strength of the faith which anticipates the future." This last clause is rather against the idea that the *shame* spoken of in this verse is that of godly sorrow. It seems rather to be that of chagrin and disappointment at the deliverance wrought for a good man. If so, the verse is a prediction.

DOCTRINAL AND PRACTICAL REMARKS.

1. How blessed is the thought that in condescension no less than in majesty God is infinite. He humbleth himself to behold the things that are in heaven. But earth is far, far below heaven. When we find him *bowing* his ear so low as to hear the whisperings and breathings of a pious soul in this world, we should adore him for his condescending greatness, v. 1. Compare Isa. lvii. 15, 16; Job xv. 15, 16.

2. The best of princes, the greatest of kings have as much need of prayer as others; and they must pray just as other *poor* and *needy* sinners do, v. 1.

3. There is no strait, necessity or extremity, in which we ought not to betake ourselves to God, v. 1. Whatever affects our well being is proper matter to be brought reverently before God.

4. With the real child of God prayer is not a mere form, vv. 1, 6. He begs for an answer again and again. Compare Dan. ix. 17–19.

5. Our poverty and misery furnish a fit occasion for the display of God's rich mercy, v. 1. It is his wont to seek such occasions. Horne: "All prayer is founded on a sense of our own wants, and God's ability to supply them."

6. Let nothing, however sad or dark, hinder us from crying mightily to God, v. 1. Calvin: "That despair may not overwhelm our minds under our greatest afflictions, let us support ourselves from the consideration that the Holy Spirit has dictated this prayer for the poor and afflicted."

7. If either our lives or our souls are *preserved* and *saved,* it must manifestly be by the Lord, v. 2. The dangers that threaten them are so many and so mighty that all created agencies would utterly fail to secure to us protection and salvation.

8. Conscious sincerity in God's service, conscious innocency in any matter wherein we are wrongfully charged, and conscious uprightness of soul in time of calamity may not only solace ourselves, but fitly be mentioned before God in prayer, v. 2. These things do not merit the divine regard. But they evince the reality of our conversion and adoption. Calvin: "If those whom we have never injured unrighteously assail us, we have ground for double confidence before God."

9. But what shall they do who are conscious of ill desert both from God and man? Let them plead for *grace,* let them cry for *mercy,* v. 3. There is forgiveness with the Lord. Jesus died for the chief of sinners.

10. *Trust in God* belongs to true religion, vv. 2, 4. It is based on a knowledge of God, on approval of his character, and confidence in his perfections.

11. Although we may be free from all criminality in a given matter, which has been made the occasion of trouble to us, yet in our past lives there has been so much that

was hateful to God, that it is always safe and right that we should rest the whole weight of our plea on mercy alone, v. 3. And as God has made Jesus Christ the depository of all the fulness of his grace and compassion, our prayers should all be offered in the name of Jesus, John xiv. 6, 13, 14.

12. Earnest, importunate prayer will be heard, vv. 3–7. For a while God may seem to disregard our cries. But in his own good time he will show himself gracious. But let us never forget that noise is not earnestness. Amesius: "That prayer which brings consolation principally consists in an elevation of the heart, not of the voice," v. 4.

13. When all goes wrong outwardly and inwardly, when foes beset and fears betide, we must be sad, we cannot *rejoice* till God appears, v. 4. He is our light.

14. All our hope and all our confidence must ultimately rest on the known nature of God revealed in holy Scripture, vv. 5, 15.

15. Every man has his troubles, v. 7. The king on his throne is no exception. The sources and kinds of our afflictions are as diversified as the countenances of men.

16. A great difference between saints and sinners in prayer is that sinners who pray at all, pray only when they are in *trouble*, whereas saints *cry daily* unto God, vv. 3–7. Compare Job xxvii. 10.

17. The reason why God never wrought a miracle to convince an atheist of the divine existence, is that the works of creation and providence are as wondrous as any miracle, v. 8. If men will not believe the former, neither would they the latter.

18. As God's right to claim the homage of all things is in his holy word rested in part on his having created them, v. 9; and as Jesus Christ is often in Scripture declared to be the Maker of all things, John i. 3, 10; Col. i. 16; Heb. i. 2, 10; our worship is no less due to the Son than to the Father. By parity of reasoning we should honor the Spirit, as we honor the Father and the Son; for he garnished the heavens; compare Gen. i. 2; Job xxvi. 13; Ecc. xi. 5.

19. There is hope for the heathen; not in the innocence of their lives, not in the harmlessness of their views and practices, not in their sincerity or morality; but in the promise of God that they shall yet *worship* him and *glorify his name*, v. 9.

20. While Christians earnestly pray for the conversion and salvation of *the heathen*, they ought most tenderly to compassionate their condition. The ancestors of every man now on earth were once sunk in horrible idolatry. Israelites are no exception, Josh. xxiv. 2. Most persons who speak the English language can readily trace their origin back to some race that worshipped false gods with rites as cruel as any now known on earth. Surely the spirit of missions is the spirit of the gospel.

21. But whether for the heathen or for ourselves, whether in temporal or spiritual affairs our distress prevails, our hope is in God alone, v. 10.

22. Without divine guidance and divine teaching we shall never know anything nor do anything aright, v. 11. We cannot therefore be too urgent in our prayers for special grace and special enlightening at all times.

23. A good resolution is a good thing, v. 11. Yet it is better to say, I will not, and then repent and do right, than say, I will, and then forget and break our word, Matt. xxi. 28, 31.

24. But if we are to perfect holiness in the fear of God, we must be renewed by divine grace, which alone can *unite our hearts to* this work, v. 11.

25. God may take the will for the deed, where the deed was impossible, but he will never take the deed for the will. He demands, and he has a right to *the whole heart*, vv. 12, 13.

26. In this life God's people are no little saddened that their *praise* is in such jarring notes, and that all their attempts to glorify him are so imperfect. Let such be

not overmuch cast down. They will have a whole eternity in which to show forth the honors of their God and Saviour, and they shall do it with such intense love as will fill them with joy and ecstasy, v. 12. Horne: "The church is never in so afflicted a state, but she hath still reason to intermingle hallelujahs with her hosannas."

27. When our hopes are built solely on the promised mercy of God, it is not possible for our expectations to be too large, vv. 13, 15, 16. His compassions are infinite. He will do exceeding abundantly above all we ask or think. Dickson: "The more violent, cruel, profane and ungodly our persecutors are, the more hope is there of God's pity toward us."

28. Salvation, including the pardon of sin, the acceptance of the sinner, the sanctification of the soul, delivery from an awful hell and rising to a glorious heaven, is truly great, and should ever so be spoken of by us, v. 13. Compare Heb. ii. 3.

29. It is nothing new for good men to have violent and insolent foes, v. 14. Christ, all the prophets, all the apostles and all the reformers had bitter opposers.

30. Let us delight ourselves in the Lord our God, dwelling much on his glorious perfections, and extolling his grace and mercy, vv. 5, 15. We should never forget that he "is as firm to his purpose in abundantly performing whatever he has promised, as he is distinguished for promising liberally."

31. We may fitly plead our covenant relation with God through the vows and prayers of our pious ancestors, v. 16. Henry: "The children of godly parents, who were betimes dedicated to the Lord, may plead it with him; if they come under the discipline of his family, they are entitled to the privileges of it."

32. Luther: "God never finally forsakes his people: for here, in the church below, he often delivers the godly, who fear him, out of the greatest perils; yea, out of the very jaws of death; and plainly proves that he is ever present and near his own: for their deliverances plainly show the hand of God, and that is such a token or sign as David prays for," v. 17.

33. We have excellent models of prayer in Scripture, and especially in the Psalms; and we deprive ourselves of much pleasure and profit by not using them freely and familiarly.

PSALM LXXXVII.

A Psalm or Song for the Sons of Korah.

1 His foundation is in the holy mountains.

2 The LORD loveth the gates of Zion more than all the dwellings of Jacob.

3 Glorious things are spoken of thee, O city of God. Selah.

4 I will make mention of Rahab and Babylon to them that know me: behold Philistia, and Tyre, with Ethiopia; this man was born there.

5 And of Zion it shall be said, This and that man was born in her: and the Highest himself shall establish her.

6 The LORD shall count, when he writeth up the people, that this man was born there. Selah.

7 As well the singers as the players on instruments shall be there: all my springs are in thee.

ON the title see on titles of Psalms iii. xxx. xlii. lxxxiv. Scott dates this Psalm B. C. 1045; Clarke, about B. C. 536. Some think it was written by David. This is the more probable opinion. Others ascribe it to one of the sons of Korah, whose name is not given. Others think we have no clue whatever to the authorship.

Among those who give it a historic occasion the diversity of view is great. Some assign it to the fixing of the site of the temple; some, to the laying of the foundation, and others, to the completion of the first temple; some, to the delivery of Jerusalem from the Assyrians; some, to the laying of the foundation, and others, to the completion of the second temple; some, to the birth, and others, to the coronation of some prince; yet others refer it directly to Messias. These views are presented by very respectable writers, though commonly expressed with diffidence. None of them are supported by strong reasonings. Edwards: "Both the occasion and author of the Psalm are uncertain." Some make it prophetic. Luther: "This is a prophecy concerning the kingdom of Christ and the church, in times to come." This is as probable as that the Psalm had reference to a past or passing event. Many commentators acknowledge that this ode contains many things not easily explained. Hare and some others regard it as a *fragment* of a more extended composition. Its apparently abrupt beginning cannot justify such a view. Like reasoning would make many Psalms fragments. The general design of the ode is stated in different terms by many. Morison: "We may, with propriety, regard it as an ode written with a view to celebrate the foundation of the sacred city, and to set forth the preëminent honor and prosperity which should distinguish its blessed inhabitants;" Tholuck: "A glorious Psalm. Its theme is the great hope of the conversion of the world to the sanctuary of Zion;" Calvin: "What we are taught in this Psalm may be summed up in this, that the church of God far excels the kingdoms and politics of the world, inasmuch as she is watched over and protected by him in all her interests, and placed under his government." The Syriac says this Psalm is *concerning the redemption of Jerusalem*. We have here *Jehovah* LORD, *Elohim God* and *Gelyohn Highest*, on which see on Ps. i. 2; iii. 2; vii. 17. On *Selah* see Introduction, § 15.

1. *His foundation* is *in the holy mountains*. *His foundation* is explained by Alexander as equivalent to "that which he has founded, meaning his sanctuary and his theocratical kingdom." *Foundation*, several read foundations, buildings, habitations. Some think it expresses the permanence of the temple in contrast with the moveable tabernacle. The cognate verb signifies to ordain, appoint, constitute. If we here understand by it *ordinances* or *constitutions*, we have a good sense. God's *ordinances* are in his church. Or, if we take it for the temple, then we may say that by God's ordering, its foundations are fixed on *the holy mountains*, by which we may understand either, 1, the range of mountains of which Zion was one, and to all of which it might be regarded as imparting a sacred character; or 2, Mount Zion, on which David built his own house and rested the ark, and Mount Moriah, on which Solomon built the temple. These two were separated by a valley not more than two or three hundred feet deep. *Zion* is often used so as to embrace both these mountains. It seems to be so used in v. 2. *Holy mountains*, literally *mountains of holiness*; see on Ps. iii. 4.

2. *The* LORD *loveth the gates of Zion more than all the dwellings of Jacob.* Alexander: "The gates of a walled city give access to it, and power over it, and are therefore naturally put for the whole." The spirit and bearing of the verse are the same as those of Ps. lxxvii. 60; lxvii. 68. God, of his own mere good pleasure, chose Jerusalem as the city of the great King. He chose it because so it seemed good in his sight. Having made it the centre of the theocracy, and the seat of glorious solemnities, which himself had ordained, and which refreshed and edified his people, he took pleasure in it. This love to the holy city had in view also the coming of Messias and the founding of a gospel church. These things having come to pass, and the mass of the chosen nation having rejected Messias, Jerusalem is to Jehovah no more than Petra, Gaza, Damascus or Samaria, John iv. 21. But the church,

consisting of true believers, and often spoken of as Zion, is still dear to the heart of God.

3. *Glorious things are spoken of thee, O city of God.* God himself has inspired holy men to speak glorious things of thee. Good men in Israel and in surrounding nations sound their praises. Even the heathen, who hate thee, sometimes admit thy glories. Thy fame extends to the ends of the earth, Matt. xii. 42; Luke xi. 31. But some read, Glorious things are spoken *in* thee. This gives a good sense. It is the rendering of the Syriac. It is preferred by Clarke. It is regarded as admissible by Hengstenberg. It is argued for by Alexander; "first, because it is the strict sense and therefore not to be rejected without reason; then, because it really includes the other, but is not included in it; lastly, because it suggests the additional idea of the holy city, as the scene, no less than the theme, of the prophetic visions." *Glorious things;* glorious histories, glorious predictions, glorious songs, glorious doctrines, glorious laws, glorious ordinances of worship, glorious promises and privileges were rehearsed and freely spoken of in Jerusalem of old, as they also are in the true church, the mother of us all. Compare Ps. xlviii. 2, 3; l. 2; Isa. ii. 2; lx. 1–22; Jer. iii. 17; Heb. xii. 22; Rev. xxi. xxii.

4. *I will make mention of Rahab and Babylon to them that know me: behold Philistia, and Tyre, with Ethiopia.* It will not do to make either the prophet, or the city of God the speaker here, but only Jehovah. He says: "I will make mention, I will announce, I will cause to be known." *Rahab,* a word found also in Ps. lxxxix. 10; Isa. li. 9. It no doubt designates Egypt, at some time before the loss of her national greatness. *Rahab* sometimes means pride; sometimes, strength; sometimes, violence. In either way it is a fit title for Egypt. Sometimes Rahab means a sea-monster, to which Egypt bore a resemblance, Ps. lxviii. 30, 31; lxxiv. 13, 14. For more than one reason the name may be applied to Egypt. Babylon was another great and mighty empire on the opposite side of Jerusalem going up from Egypt, and was long the rival and often the foe of Egypt. Respecting *Philistia* and *Tyre* see on Ps. xlv. 12; lx. 8; lxxxiii. 7. Respecting *Ethiopia,* see on Ps. lxviii. 31. Hammond has a note to prove that by *Cush,* which we here render *Ethiopia,* is to be understood *Arabia.* The note is learned, and it is now admitted that *Cush* at least sometimes includes more than the country south of Egypt called Ethiopia. Indeed Rosenmüller asserts that by this name the Hebrews sometimes designated all southern countries and their inhabitants. In this place we may give it a wide sense. The phrase *them that know me,* is equivalent to *them that love and obey me, them that possess and practise* the true religion. *This* man *was born there. Was born,* found also in vv. 5, 6. It is well rendered. What does it mean? Several views are taken. 1. To *be born* in any of the countries named in this verse is no honor, no privilege compared with *being born* in Jerusalem. These places are as nothing compared with the holy city. Their inhabitants are abjects compared with the citizens of Zion. 2. Others obtain pretty much the same idea by making *this* emphatic, omitting *man* and supplying *fellow; q. d.,* The best that can be said of any of these countries is that now and then a fellow claiming some importance has been born there, but any such man is as nothing compared with the truly great men, prophets, judges and kings of Jerusalem. Such would cite Gen. xix. 9; 1 Sam. xxi. 15; 1 Kings xxii. 27; Matt. xii. 24; xxvi. 61, and several other places in proof that *this* is often used disparagingly. 3. Others think that the clause contains a promise of the enlargement of Zion by the birth of Israelites in their dispersion through the countries named in this verse, taken as representatives of distant nations generally. See Acts ii. 5–11. 4. Others regard this clause as containing a promise of accessions to the church by the conversion of many heathen nations, of which five are here named as samples of the rest. Such regard *was born* as teaching

the doctrine of the *new birth,* so much insisted on in the New Testament, and make the passage parallel to such texts as Ps. lxviii. 32; Isa. xix. 19–22; xliv. 5. Morison: "The glory of the true Zion over all the earth seems here distinctly to be pictured. The accession of the most hostile tribes to her glorious standard is here predicted." Horne: "The accession of the nations to the church is generally supposed to be here predicted." Tholuck: "All the nations here specified . . . became engrafted at the time when love and missionary zeal were glowing in the Christian church, and they all regarded Zion as their spiritual mother." If there is any better interpretation than this last, there is no objection to its being set forth.

5. *And of Zion it shall be said, This and that man was born in her.* The literal rendering would be *A man and a man.* It is a Hebraism. Hammond thinks it is equivalent to the English phrase *man after man,* and means *many men.* Calvin· "The number of such men among the Jews shall be great." The converts in Zion shall be many. So say many Scriptures, Isa. lxvi. 8; Acts ii. 41; iv. 4; xxi. 20. In the last verse cited for *thousands* we should read *ten thousands.* The original is *myriads.* Horsley applies the words to Christ: "Every one shall confess to the honor of the Israelites, that the Saviour was a native Jew." But our Saviour was born in Bethlehem. Jerusalem crucified him. *And the Highest himself shall establish her.* Alexander: "The pronoun is emphatic;" Hengstenberg: "*He,* he himself, and no others, not a weak *human being;*" Tholuck: "It will be seen that it is the Lord who builds her so gloriously," Matt. xvi. 19; Eph. ii. 19–22.

6. *The Lord shall count, when he writeth up the people,* that *this* man *was born there.* On the use of a book or roll see on Ps. lxix. 28. The Chaldee here speaks of "a book in which are written the computations of all peoples." Speaking after the manner of men, the Lord keeps 'a register of the people,' Ezek. xiii. 9. *Count, number, declare, tell,* announce as a scribe. What would he declare? That *this* man was *born* in Zion. What man? Every regenerated man. Clarke: "This has a spiritual meaning. When God takes an account of all *professing Christians,* he will set apart those for inhabitants of the New Jerusalem, who were born in Zion, who were born again, received a new nature and were fitted for heaven." Scott: "The Lord will number up, at the last day, all the true children of the church; show the eminence and excellence of their characters; and contrast them as 'one in Christ Jesus,' with all that which the world has admired and celebrated in ungodly men." Calvin: "He will write them as belonging to Zion, rather than to Babylon or any other cities; for to be one of the common people among the citizens of Zion will be a greater distinction than to be invested with the highest rank anywhere else."

7. *As well the singers as the players on instruments* shall be there: *all my springs* are *in thee.* Bishops' Bible: The singers and trumpeters shall rehearse: all my refreshings shall be in thee; Cresswell: Singers also, and players upon the pipe, shall chant, 'All my wells are in thee;' Walford: They sing with musical instruments, 'All my springs are in thee;' Symmachus and Aquila: And they shall sing as in leading up a dance, 'All my fountains are in thee;' Jebb: And the singers, as well as the minstrels *shall say,* 'All my springs are in thee;' Clarke: *The people* shall sing, as in leading up a choir, All my fountains, *the springs of my happiness,* are in thee. Many make the last clause the substance of the song used on the joyful occasion. *Singers,* uniformly so rendered. *Players on instruments,* the Hebrew is a participle of a verb, which signifies to *perforate, to bore through.* So it is inferred that it designates performers on wind instruments. Some render it *pipers;* and some *dancers,* because the dancers often went with the singers. There is an omission of the verb, and our English supplies *shall be there;* others, *shall say, shall sing,* or *shall rehearse.* This is perhaps better than the common version. *Springs,* elsewhere *fountains, wells,* Ps. lxxiv. 15;

lxxxiv. 6; Isa. xii. 3; xli. 18. Cresswell thinks it is equivalent to 'sources of refreshment, of hope and of salvation.' Calvin: "I am rather inclined to adopt, as most suitable to the subject in hand, the opinion that *looking* is the proper translation, the root of the word signifying *an eye.* It is as if the Psalmist had said, I will always be earnestly looking, as it were, with fixed eyes upon thee." There are yet other interpretations, but they hardly claim attention. Perhaps *wells of salvation,* meaning fountains of joy and refreshment, would best give the sense. *In thee* may be referred either to God or to Zion; for God is in Zion.

Doctrinal and Practical Remarks.

1. God ought to be publicly worshipped. He is thereby honored. We should celebrate his works. Redemption is his chief work. As such worship is honorable, so it is pleasing to God. He has laid his *foundation in the holy mountains,* v. 1.

2. As Zion and Moriah could not be moved by any power but that which created them, so the church is safe in the hands of him, who founded her, v. 1. The safety of the church is not in her numbers, but in her Head, not in her ministers, but in her Mediator.

3. God's worship and presence dignify any place, thing or person pertaining to his service. Moriah and Zion were no more than thousands of other peaks or hills, till they became associated with his worship. Then they were the *mountains of his holiness,* v. 1. To the end of the world they will be mentioned with respect by the best men of each succeeding generation.

4. 'The cause of the origin, existence and perpetuity of the church is found only in the gracious, special, eternal and unchangeable love of God,' v. 2. No firmer ground of support or joy can be desired.

5. If we are truly pious, we will love all that God loves; and so we will love his church, v. 2. Compare Ps. cxxxvii. 5, 6. She is our mother. She is the spouse of Christ. She is the Lamb's wife. She is all glorious within. The glories of earthly kingdoms fade away before the glories of Zion, as the light of the stars is no longer visible when the sun rises. Even Balaam cried: "How goodly are thy tents, O Jacob, and thy tabernacles, O Israel." Those, that love, trust, fear and obey God, are his church; and he loves them more than all others besides. The *glorious things spoken in Zion* raise her above all comparison with human institutions. The future of the church on earth is much more glorious than the past, and her state beyond the judgment will far excel her glory in the millenium.

6. There is hope for the heathen. Many heathen countries are named in prophecy, as here v. 4. Other prophecies name other countries. To China, under the name of Sinim, a blessing is promised, Isa. xlix. 12. Then *isles of the sea, distant lands, Tarshish* and the *uttermost parts of the earth* are general terms denoting all parts of the world however remote from Judea. The prophecies respecting the enlargement of the Gentile church are very full, Isa. liv. 1–11; lx. 1–22. Believers hail with joy the spread of the Gospel anywhere, Acts xi. 18.

7. The doctrine of regeneration is no novelty. It has been a ground of hope to the church ever since there was a penitent sinner on earth. It is taught in all the Scriptures, vv. 4–6. Compare Ps. li. 10; Jer. xxxi. 33; Ezek. xi. 19, 20. If regeneration is impossible, salvation is impossible.

8. The church shall stand. Nothing can subvert her. God gives her stability, v. 5. Compare Isa. xiv. 32. Her unshaken firmness is secured 1, 'by the irreversible decree of God in her behalf; 2, by her glorious union with Christ; 3, by the doctrine relating to herself. It was revealed by God; it holds forth Christ; by the Holy Spirit Christ and his people are made one.'

9. It is a blessed truth that God is known by his people, v. 4, and that his people are known by the Lord, v. 6. Christ unites these two things in the same verse: "I am the good shepherd, and know my sheep, and am known of mine," John x. 14. Dickson: "All the elect, all the regenerate are taken notice of by God no less particularly than if their names were all written up in a book, one by one," Isa. iv. 3; 2 Tim. ii. 19.

10. Though nights of weeping are appointed to the church on earth, yet the days of her mourning shall soon be ended, and there shall be heard only the voice of joy, thanksgiving and melody; for *the singers and players on instruments shall be there*, v. 7. O the thundering hallelujahs of the upper sanctuary! Even on earth the songs of Zion are incomparable; but in heaven they will be far higher, purer and more enrapturing.

11. If we would be truly blessed we must join ourselves to the Lord. This is to be done by faith in Jesus Christ. Our engrafting into Christ makes us living members of his church, in and through which he pours so many blessings on the world. So that under God, through Christ, by the Spirit, our *springs* are in the church, Rom. xi. 17. Scott: "All the springs of life and consolation are in the church alone: and those who draw not from these wells of salvation, will most certainly be forever put off with broken cisterns which can hold no water." Nicolson: "The highest privilege is that in God's church He opens the *fountains of living water;*—in his ordinances God dispenses every blessing: every sincere and upright soul rejoices in opportunities to wait on God in his ordinances. Such an one can sing, *All my springs are in thee.* All other *fountains* are *muddy;* this alone is as *clear as crystal.*"

12. Surely such views as this Psalm presents ought to expel the despondency and enliven the hopes of God's people. Seeing what great things God has done and what great things he has engaged to do for his church, embracing all who love him, it is unbelief to cry out, We are ruined; our enemies will swallow us up.

PSALM LXXXVIII.

A song *or* Psalm for the sons of Korah, to the chief Musician upon Mahalath Leannoth, Maschil of Heman the Ezrahite.

1 O LORD God of my salvation, I have cried day *and* night before thee:

2 Let my prayer come before thee: incline thine ear unto my cry;

3 For my soul is full of troubles: and my life draweth nigh unto the grave.

4 I am counted with them that go down into the pit: I am as a man *that hath* no strength:

5 Free among the dead, like the slain that lie in the grave, whom thou rememberest no more: and they are cut off from thy hand.

6 Thou hast laid me in the lowest pit, in darkness, in the deeps.

7 Thy wrath lieth hard upon me, and thou hast afflicted *me* with all thy waves. Selah.

8 Thou hast put away mine acquaintance far from me; thou hast made me an abomination unto them: *I am* shut up, and I cannot come forth.

9 Mine eye mourneth by reason of affliction: LORD, I have called daily upon thee, I have stretched out my hands unto thee.

10 Wilt thou shew wonders to the dead? shall the dead arise *and* praise thee? Selah.

11 Shall thy lovingkindness be declared in the grave? *or* thy faithfulness in destruction?

12 Shall thy wonders be known in the dark? and thy righteousness in the land of forgetfulness?

13 But unto thee have I cried, O LORD; and in the morning shall my prayer prevent thee.

14 LORD, why castest thou off my soul? *why* hidest thou thy face from me?

15 I *am* afflicted and ready to die from *my* youth up: *while* I suffer thy terrors I am distracted.

16 Thy fierce wrath goeth over me; thy terrors have cut me off.

17 They came round about me daily like water; they compassed me about together.

18 Lover and friend hast thou put far from me, *and* mine acquaintance into darkness.

ON the title see on titles of Psalms iii. iv. xxxii. xlii. liii. lxxxiv. lxxxv. lxxxvii. *Leannoth* has not before occurred in any title. It is the plural of a word once rendered hemlock; seven times, wormwood. Gesenius: "It was apparently regarded as a noxious or poisonous plant, and hence called the *accursed*." Calvin thus renders the words *Mahalath Leannoth, Maschil*, Upon Mahalath, to make humble, instructive; Amesius, Tremellius and Junius, To be sung to a wind instrument, an instruction; Venema, Upon Mahalath responsive teaching; Piscator, Concerning an afflicting sickness; An instructive ode; Steel, An instructive Psalm on sickness, through affliction. Many virtually concur with Steel. Some regard *Leannoth* as a musical term, showing that the Psalm is to be sung responsively; some refer it to the instrument or tune; others, to the subject matter of the ode. It is but candid to say that this point cannot be settled, although it is not impossible that it specially regards the *bitterness* of soul expressed in the Psalm, or the *bitter* grief in which it was written. The title is generally supposed to ascribe the Psalm to *Heman the Ezrahite*. See Introduction, § 4. Amyrald is confident that the author is unknown. Those, who insist on this Psalm having a historic occasion, are much divided in view. Kimchi thinks it was written during the captivity in the name of the Jewish people, and in the language of a poor slave. Kennicott regards it as the prayer of a man in the last stage of leprosy, and excluded from society. Patrick supposes the author to have been cast into a dark prison, or to have been otherwise miserably treated, and here to bewail his private calamity. Tholuck: "The occasion is not known." It is very probable that the particular affliction is purposely concealed from us, as in the case of Paul's thorn in the flesh, that the language of the composition may be appropriated by many. Henry thinks it probable that the author "could see no comfort for himself, an instructor and comforter of others, and yet himself putting comfort away from him." Pool thinks it was written "upon a particular occasion, to wit, Heman's deep distress and dejection of mind almost to despair." Stier: "It is the most mournful of all the plaintive Psalms." *O Lord God of my salvation*, are the only cheering words in the whole composition. Tholuck calls it, "A song of deep complaint." Calvin: "It contains very grievous lamentations, poured forth by its inspired penman when under very severe affliction, and almost at the point of despair." Horsley regards it as prophetic, and calls it "the lamentation of Messiah." And we must admit, with several learned men, that many verses do peculiarly suit the "man of sorrows." Luther: "This is a prayer, as in the person of Christ and of all the saints." The church of England has appointed this as one of the Psalms for Good Friday. There is nothing to support the opinion that this is one of the penitential Psalms. Scott dates it B. C. 1020; Clarke affixes no date. We have here *Jehovah* LORD and *Elohim God*, on which see on Ps. i. 2; iii. 2. On *Selah* see Introduction § 15.

1. *O* LORD *God of my salvation, I have cried day* and *night before thee. God of my salvation*, see on Ps. xviii. 46. *Cried*, as in Ps. lxxvii. 1. *Day* and *night*, continually, as in Ps. i. 2. Calvin: "The words *before thee* are not superfluous. It is common for all men to complain when they are under the pressure of grief; but they are far from pouring out their groanings before God." Some fill the ears of their friends with the sad tale; others fill the air with their loud laments; yet others spend their time in murmuring against God.

2. *Let my prayer come before thee.* The verb is in the future, but perhaps fitly rendered in the imperative here, **as** in Ps. xxxvi. 11; lxxix. 11; cii. 1. *Prayer,*

uniformly rendered. *Before thee*, before thy face, into thy presence. *Incline thine ear unto my cry.* *Incline*, in Ps. lxxxvi. 1, *bow down;* often as here. Both clauses contain an earnest petition that he may be heard and answered. He was not making an oration. His heart was in anguish.

3. *For my soul is full of troubles.* Troubles, *afflictions, hurts, evils, miseries, griefs.* *Is full*, a verb in the preterite, *has been full* and is so still. Alexander has sated. Calvin: "He does not speak of one kind of calamity only; but of calamities so heaped one upon another that his heart was filled with sorrow, till it could contain no more." The result was natural: *And my life draweth nigh unto the grave.* The effect of deep seated, long continued grief is to waste away the life as well as the spirits. *Grave, hell, pit;* see on Ps. vi. 5; ix. 17. His life was a living death.

4. *I am counted with them that go down into the pit.* Counted, *reckoned, thought of, esteemed* by those around me. It is in the preterite, q. d., It has been so and is so now. *Pit*, commonly so rendered, see on Ps. xxviii. 1. *Griefs* were before him like yawning caverns, ready to swallow him, q. d., Men regard me as good as dead; nor is this surprising, for the effect of my troubles on me has been such that *I am as a man* that hath *no strength.* Though naturally perhaps not more feeble than others, yet by sorrow he was brought so low that he had no *might.*

5. *Free among the dead, like the slain that lie in the grave, whom thou rememberest no more.* *Free*, the same word is applied to the wild ass that goes *free*, and is used in Job iii. 19, respecting the effect of death on a slave. Already men regarded his connection with society virtually dissolved; as really so, as if he were *slain* and lying in the grave; or as if God *remembered* him no more. He adds: *And they are cut off from thy hand,* from receiving supplies from thee as do the living. Calvin thinks the word *free* specially·refers to the fact that 'his mind had become disengaged from all worldly solicitude, his afflictions having deprived him of all feeling.' But this is hardly sustained by the context. His feelings are still intense. Some think that *free* is equivalent to *forsaken;* but his faith in the *God of his salvation* was not gone. Clarke thinks the word refers to Christ, who was *free* to lay down his life, and *free* to take it again. In this he is supported by Augustine and many others.

6. *Thou hast laid me in the lowest pit, in darkness, in the deeps.* *Pit*, as in v. 4. *Lowest pit*, literally *pit of the lowest parts.* He says that he is like a man buried in a retired low place out of view of all the world. *Darkness*, in Ps. lxxiv. 20, *dark places.* Here the word is used figuratively for dreadful evils. So is the word *deeps;* in Ex. xv. 5, *bottom;* in Neh. ix. 11, *deeps;* in both cases it refers to the overwhelming calamities that overtook the Egyptians at the Red sea.

7. *Thy wrath lieth hard upon me, and thou hast afflicted* me *with all thy waves.* God's *wrath, fury, hot displeasure* is perhaps so terrible to none as to those who have tasted and seen that the Lord is gracious. *Waves*, see on Ps. xlii. 7. Huge, irresistible sorrows overwhelmed him.

8. *Thou hast put away mine acquaintance far from me.* This is at once explained by the parallel clause: *Thou hast made me an abomination unto them.* *Abomination*, in the plural *abominations*, as in Gen. xliii. 32; xlvi. 34. His acquaintance neglected him, perhaps partly from aversion, and partly from fear. They thought it perilous to stand up for him. They were afraid of being in a minority. I am *shut up, and I cannot come forth.* Being in straits, having one's way hedged up and like expressions are common in Scripture, Job xix. 8; Lam. iii. 7–9. The interpretations are two. This is the more common: I am environed with difficulties out of which it is impossible for me to escape. The other is, that he voluntarily confined himself to a retired life and had no heart to encounter the neglect and reproaches of his acquaintance. Both may have been true, so that he could not have gone forth and freely

mingled with men if he would; and he would not have done it if he could. Walford, speaking of the whole verse, says: "Heman means either that the character of his disease was such that men could not endure to be near him, or that the state of his mind was so disordered that he became wearisome and intolerable; perhaps he includes both." Clarke thinks it refers to a leper shut out from society.

9. *Mine eye mourneth by reason of affliction. Mourneth, has mourned* and is mourning still. *Affliction*, see on Ps. ix. 13, where it is rendered *trouble*. This continuance of sadness surprised him the more because he had not forsaken the throne of grace: LORD, *I have called daily upon thee, I have stretched out my hands unto thee.* The latter clause is parallel to the former; see on Ps. xxviii. 2.

10. *Wilt thou shew wonders to the dead? shall the dead arise* and *praise thee?* In studying several preceding verses it seems almost impossible to avoid the impression that the Psalmist is speaking in the name of the suffering Jesus. But evidently this verse is uttered by the same person, who has spoken throughout the Psalm; and our Saviour never doubted, but clearly foretold his own early resurrection. He never put his imprisonment in the grave at more than the third day. Applied to the Psalmist the words seem to mean that his circumstances were distressing and urgent, that his present critical condition called for immediate succor, and that as in all ordinary cases those who died were no more brought back to see life or taste its blessings till the heavens be no more, so in the most earnest manner he asked God at once to interpose. Unbelief and weak faith often forget that the *time* of our deliverance is in the hands of the Father. We may not say that God cannot help us, unless he does it soon. *Wonders, marvellous things.* Calvin renders it a *miracle*. In Hebrew it is singular. It occurs again in v. 12. The word in the latter clause rendered *dead* is *Rephaim*. By some it is supposed to refer to the giants who bare that name, or to giants generally. The word is often rendered *giants*. But the English Bible no less than eight times renders it *dead* or *deceased*. Perhaps there may be such an idea as this included, shall even *the mightiest of the dead arise?* Jebb reads *dead bodies*. Hammond says, 'there can be no question that the word here signifies the dead, those that lie in the grave.' Chaldee has it, *carcasses that are dissolved in the dust.* The interrogative form in vv. 10–12, is the strongest form of negation.

11. *Shall thy lovingkindness be declared in the grave? Lovingkindness*, in Ps. v. 7, mercy; see on Ps. li. 1. *Grave*, as in v. 5. In Ps. v. 9, it is rendered *sepulchre;* in Gen. xxiii. 4, *burying-place*. Or *thy faithfulness in destruction? Faithfulness* commonly so rendered, derived from the word *Amen. Destruction*, always so rendered; the Hebrew is *Abaddon*, see Rev. ix. 11, the same as *Apollyon, destroyer*.

12. *Shall thy wonders be known in the dark, and thy righteousness in the land of forgetfulness? Wonders*, as in v. 10. *Righteousness*, here the word probably means, as President Edwards thinks it does in Isa. li. 8, God's "faithfulness in fulfilling his covenant promises to his church." *Dark*, in Ps. xviii. 11, rendered *darkness*, and here clearly equivalent to the *grave. Land of forgetfulness*, equivalent to death, and so called because the dead are forgotten by the living; see v. 5, and Ps. xxxi. 12; or because the dead cease to be interested in the affairs of men, Ecc. ix. 5, 10. The latter seems to be the idea here. The plea of vv. 10–12, goes on the supposition that the fearful conflict in which the Psalmist is engaged has earth for its theatre; and, if settled adversely to his interests, God's honor will suffer among men. The sole object is to show that in the present conflict and trouble, if God would show himself on the side of the Psalmist, he must manifest his favor before death supervenes and leaves the point apparently settled against his servant.

13. *But unto thee have I cried, O* LORD. All these things have befallen me, but

I have not ceased earnestly to pray for thy help. *And in the morning shall my prayer prevent thee. Prayer*, as in v. 2. *Prevent*, go before or come before. Patrick: "Thus, O LORD, I cry unto thee in the anguish of my soul; which keeps me awake to present my prayers unto thee, before the morning light." Clarke: "I will not wait till the accustomed time to offer my morning sacrifice; I shall call on thee long before others come to offer their morning devotions." Scott: "Come more early before thee than is usual with men."

14. LORD, *why castest thou off my soul? Cast off*, as in Ps. xliii. 2; in Ps. lxxxix. 38, joined with *abhorred*; sometimes as strong a word as *spew out* in Rev. iii. 16, though often it means simply to reject. Why *hidest thou thy face from me?* Both verbs in this verse are in the future. The Psalmist feared the continuance of all his trials and probably thought they would grow worse and worse. To *hide the face* is to refuse to give relief.

15. *I am afflicted and ready to die from* my youth up. How much some suffer! I have seen a child, who at the age of twenty months had probably suffered more bodily pain than the whole congregation of a thousand souls, where its parents worshipped. Asaph seems to have been of a sad heart. Jeremiah lived and died lamenting. Heman seems to have been of the same lot and of the same turn of mind. How soon in life his troubles began we know not, but at least very early, *from a child*, as the word might be here rendered, and as it is rendered in Pr. xxix. 21. While *I suffer thy terrors I am distracted.* Calvin: I have suffered thy terrors by doubting. For *distracted*, the church of England has *a troubled mind.* The Psalmist was 'perplexed but not in despair; cast down but not destroyed.' He still cried to the *God of his salvation.*

16. *Thy fierce wrath goeth over me. Fierce wrath*, one word also rendered *wrath, fury, fierceness, sore displeasure.* Here it is plural, *wraths. Goeth*, in the preterite *hath gone* and is still going. In what way God was afflicting his servant we do not know; but that his sufferings were terrible none can doubt. *Thy terrors have cut me off. Terrors*, not the word so rendered in v. 15, but that found in Job vi. 4. Both words are strong. *Cut off, consumed, destroyed.* The meaning is that he was so affected by the awful impressions he had received of the divine displeasure that he was not himself any more.

17. *They* [thy wraths and thy terrors] *come round about me daily like water; they compassed me about together.* As overflowing waters perfectly *surround*, and as a net *incloses* the prey, so have they seized on me, that there is no escaping. *Daily*, continually.

18. *Lover and friend hast thou put far from me*, and *mine acquaintance into darkness. Lover*, participle of the verb to love. *Friend, companion, fellow*, often *neighbor. Mine acquaintance*, as in v. 8. It means any whom I have known. Alexander: "The first clause is a repetition of v. 8." And is not the last clause parallel to the first? My acquaintance are so that I cannot see them. They are like objects in a *dark place.* They are out of sight. He is not deploring the death of his friends, as though they were buried, but their removal from him. Nicolson; "They appear no more to give me any counsel, help or comfort, than if they were hidden in perpetual darkness."

DOCTRINAL AND PRACTICAL REMARKS.

1. If we knew more of the religious experience of God's people, we should be less apt to think our trials peculiar. David and Asaph wrote much of their sorrows. The only composition of Heman extant is full of grief. Let no man despise his afflicted brother. Let no man count it imbecility to tremble under a sense of the divine wrath.

2. Some suffering on earth is designed to instruct and comfort others. That which to us is a *dirge* may be to others a *song*. How deeply afflicted Heman was, yet how consolatory is this Psalm to God's people of successive generations.

3. The Scriptures pronounce the author of this Song a very wise man, 1 Kings iv. 31; yet when plunged into sorrow he has no resources left but such as belong to the humblest child of God. He can plead God's covenant; he can give himself up to prayer, v. 1. That is all.

4. In our distresses we ought to see to it that our supplications are earnest and lively. We must *cry, day and night*, vv. 1, 2. Dickson: "The believer may be sure to have a good answer at length, but he must be instant, and deal still with God for it, and press it hard, and patiently wait for it, as Heman doth."

5. True heartiness in prayer seeks God's blessing, and looks eagerly for it, v. 2. A believer does not rest in the words he speaks to God, but desires the answer God may graciously vouchsafe.

6. It is no new thing for good men to have many and great troubles, vv. 3–15. When floods of ungodly men, waves of sorrow and terrors roll in upon us, let us remember God has carried others through as sore trials. It is sad indeed when we have no respite from grief, when the clouds never break away, when refuge seems to fail. But no trials can come that will justify us in failing to make God the depository of our sad tale. Dickson: "If the godly should smother their grief, and not go to God with it, then sorrow were able to choke them."

7. Of all troubles, soul-troubles are the worst, and most loudly call for compassion from man and loving-kindness from God, v. 3. In nothing are care and kindness more demanded than in diseases and distresses, which are purely mental. This Psalmist has become perfectly familiarized with "the grave," "the pit," "the dead," "darkness," "the deeps." His "anguish of soul is of the very nature, and power, and poison, and sting of hell and death."

8. When men are incredulous respecting the terrible effects produced on the body by mental distress, they know not the powers of self-inflicted torment in every rational being. Heman was a great man, but grief nearly took his life, vv. 3, 4. No doubt it shortened his days. Luther: "Where such fears and terrors of mind abound and continue, they extend to the body, bring on a paleness and emaciation, and affect the whole man." A moaning spirit gives a pining body. No mortal can explain why the loving and gentle God should permit the best of men to be so pressed and afflicted as thus to crush them.

9. If any man thinks it a small trial to be a walking corpse, or to be buried alive, or imagines that such a calamity cannot overtake him, he has but a limited knowledge of his own feebleness, or of his liability to the displeasure of God, v. 5.

10. To a pious mind it is a relief to know that troubles come from the hand of God. He then knows they are not sent in wantonness. "He doth not afflict willingly." But in some respects it overwhelms the soul to find God himself smiting it and sending his wrath and terrors upon it, vv. 7, 17. It says, God can do no wrong, yet he afflicts me thus. Is it because he sees me to be his enemy and is determined to make me a monument of his wrath? or is it because he sees so much dross in me that he keeps me in the fire so long?

11. There may be cold, selfish natures, that are not much or easily affected with the want or the loss of friends; but to one of warm, affectionate heart and confiding nature there is hardly any cup of more bitterness than that which we drink on finding that many whom we cherished as friends stand aloof from our sore, and are not grieved for our affliction, vv. 8, 18. In this life our joys are doubled and our sorrows abated by real friendship. But a fair and long trial will satisfy men that a large number

of mankind will only cling to you as leaves to their trees in soft weather.   When the frosts come, they will drop off.

> Heaven gives us friends to bless the present scene;
> Resumes them, to prepare us for the next.

Henry: "Next to the comforts of religion are those of friendship and society."

11. If God by his providence shuts us up so that we cannot come forth, then let his will be done; but let us not voluntarily shut ourselves out from commerce with men, simply because God has greatly afflicted us, v. 8.   We sometimes double our sorrows by nursing them in secret.   We sit in our chambers until all nature is clad in drab, or draped in black.   This is unprofitable.

12. But let us be careful not to act so as to make on others the impression that our piety has rendered us callous, or insensible to those things, which were designed to grieve us.   Heman did not so.   His *eye mourned by reason of affliction*, v. 9.   He is a wise man, who knows when to weep and when to laugh.

13. If the righteous can do nothing else, they can and will abound in earnest prayer, vv. 9, 13.   Tholuck: "The troubled bard lives with God; from early morn to the eve he lives with *him;* this is evident from his pouring out his soul at early morn. It may therefore be assumed that though his prayer dies away in the accents of complaint, the light of hope continued to burn in his soul."   Calvin: "As so dreadful a flood did not prevent the prophet from lifting up his heart and prayers to God, we may learn from his example to cast the anchor of our faith and prayers direct into heaven in all the perils of shipwreck to which we may be exposed."

14. If we would glorify God on earth, we should never forget that life is very short and uncertain, and that the work of life must be done in life and not in death, nor after death, vv. 10–12.   To honor God by a life of holiness is the highest earthly attainment.

15. When love is strong as death, then the coals of jealousy have a most vehement flame, and the bare suspicion that God has rejected us fills us with anguish, v. 14. Arnd: "When the cross lasts long, conflicts arise about casting off.   But there is no casting off; there is only a waiting for the hour of help, the hour of the Lord."

16. It is always right that we should ask God to show us wherefore he contends with us, v. 14.   Often the cause is in our depravity.   But if we can be well satisfied that we are suffering for the good of others, it will be no small relief to our sorrows.

17. Great as were the sufferings of the prophet recorded in this Psalm, they greatly differ from the torments of the damned, chiefly in these two things; *first*, he is not without hope, he is not in despair; *secondly*, his anguish is not eternal.

18. There are some afflictions which we never forget, v. 15.   It is perhaps best we should have them still in remembrance. Often new distresses will awaken the memory of past sorrows.   Heaven must be a wonderful state and a wonderful place; for there the redeemed shall have no *painful* views of anything past, present or future.

19. The Psalm concludes without any expression of comfort or sensible relief to the prophet's mind; yet such faith, hope and importunate prayer, as are here manifest, evince that there was at least insensible support, followed in due time by solid comforts, perhaps in death, possibly not till after death.   For nearly three thousand years the pious author of this ode has been singing a very different song before the throne of the Eternal; and his eternity is but just begun.

20. Is any devout reader free from the troubles and sorrows depicted in this Psalm? let him be thankful, but not high-minded.   Soon they may come on him like an armed man.

PSALM LXXXIX.

Maschil of Ethan the Ezrahite.

1 I will sing of the mercies of the LORD for ever: with my mouth will I make known thy faithfulness to all generations.

2 For I have said, Mercy shall be built up for ever: thy faithfulness shalt thou establish in the very heavens.

3 I have made a covenant with my chosen, I have sworn unto David my servant,

4 Thy seed will I establish for ever, and build up thy throne to all generations. Selah.

5 And the heavens shall praise thy wonders, O LORD: thy faithfulness also in the congregation of the saints.

6 For who in the heaven can be compared unto the LORD? *who* among the sons of the mighty can be likened unto the LORD?

7 God is greatly to be feared in the assembly of the saints, and to be had in reverence of all *them that are* about him.

8 O LORD God of hosts, who *is* a strong LORD like unto thee? or to thy faithfulness round about thee?

9 Thou rulest the raging of the sea: when the waves thereof arise, thou stillest them.

10 Thou hast broken Rahab in pieces, as one that is slain; thou hast scattered thine enemies with thy strong arm.

11 The heavens *are* thine, the earth also *is* thine: *as for* the world and the fulness thereof, thou hast founded them.

12 The north and the south thou hast created them: Tabor and Hermon shall rejoice in thy name.

13 Thou hast a mighty arm: strong is thy hand, *and* high is thy right hand.

14 Justice and judgment *are* the habitation of thy throne: mercy and truth shall go before thy face.

15 Blessed *is* the people that know the joyful sound: they shall walk, O LORD, in the light of thy countenance.

16 In thy name shall they rejoice all the day: and in thy righteousness shall they be exalted.

17 For thou *art* the glory of their strength: and in thy favour our horn shall be exalted.

18 For the LORD *is* our defence; and the Holy One of Israel *is* our King.

19 Then thou spakest in vision to thy Holy One, and saidst, I have laid help upon *one that is* mighty; I have exalted *one* chosen out of the people.

20 I have found David my servant; with my holy oil have I anointed him:

21 With whom my hand shall be established: mine arm also shall strengthen him.

22 The enemy shall not exact upon him; nor the son of wickedness afflict him.

23 And I will beat down his foes before his face, and plague them that hate him.

24 But my faithfulness and my mercy *shall be* with him: and in my name shall his horn be exalted.

25 I will set his hand also in the sea, and his right hand in the rivers.

26 He shall cry unto me, Thou *art* my Father, my God, and the Rock of my salvation.

27 Also I will make him *my* firstborn, higher than the kings of the earth.

28 My mercy will I keep for him for evermore, and my covenant shall stand fast with him.

29 His seed also will I make *to endure* for ever, and his throne as the days of heaven.

30 If his children forsake my law, and walk not in my judgments;

31 If they break my statutes, and keep not my commandments;

32 Then will I visit their transgression with the rod, and their iniquity with stripes.

33 Nevertheless my lovingkindness will I not utterly take from him, nor suffer my faithfulness to fail.

34 My covenant will I not break, nor alter the thing that is gone out of my lips.

35 Once have I sworn by my holiness that I will not lie unto David.

36 His seed shall endure for ever, and his throne as the sun before me.

37 It shall be established for ever as the moon, and *as* a faithful witness in heaven. Selah.

38 But thou hast cast off and abhorred, thou hast been wroth with thine anointed.

39 Thou hast made void the covenant of thy servant: thou hast profaned his crown *by casting it* to the ground.

40 Thou hast broken down all his hedges; thou hast brought his strong holds to ruin.

41 All that pass by the way spoil him: he is a reproach to his neighbors.

42 Thou hast set up the right hand of his adversaries: thou hast made all his enemies to rejoice.

43 Thou hast also turned the edge of his sword, and hast not made him to stand in the battle.

44 Thou hast made his glory to cease, and cast his throne down to the ground.

45 The days of his youth hast thou shortened: thou hast covered him with shame.   Selah.

46 How long, LORD? wilt thou hide thyself for ever? shall thy wrath burn like fire?

47 Remember how short my time is: wherefore hast thou made all men in vain?

48 What man *is he that* liveth, and shall not see death? shall he deliver his soul from the hand of the grave?   Selah.

49 Lord, where *are* thy former lovingkindnesses, *which* thou swarest unto David in thy truth?

50 Remember, Lord, the reproach of thy servants; *how* I do bear in my bosom *the reproach of* all the mighty people;

51 Wherewith thine enemies have reproached, O LORD; wherewith they have reproached the footsteps of thine anointed.

52 Blessed *be* the LORD for evermore.   Amen, and Amen.

O N the title see on titles of Psalms iii. xxx. and Introduction, § 4.   The date of this can hardly be very different from that of Ps. lxxxviii., as the authors were brothers.   Scott dates it B. C. 968; Clarke affixes no date.   Its contents show that it could not have been written before the time of David.   The basis of this composition is the promise made to the son of Jesse in 2 Sam. vii. 16.   The structure of the Psalm is peculiar.   Henry: "Many Psalms that begin with complaint and prayer, end with joy and praise, but this begins with joy and praise, and ends with sad complaints and petitions."   Some have thought that this Psalm and the preceding form a pair; but the reasons assigned are not conclusive.   That this Psalm is Messianic is generally admitted, is proven by its contents, and by its being so quoted in the New Testament. We have here several names of the Most High; *Jehovah* LORD, *El God*, *Elohim God*, with *Sabaoth of hosts* added; *Jah* LORD and *Adonai Lord;* on which respectively see on Psalms i. 2; v. 4; iii. 2; xxiv. 10; lix. 5; introductory remarks on Ps. lxviii.: on Ps. ii. 4.   On *Selah* see Introduction, § 15.

1. *I will sing of the mercies of the* LORD *for ever.*   *Mercies*, either in the singular or plural the same word occurs in vv. 2, 14, 24, 28, 33, 49.   In the two last it is ren- dered *lovingkindness.*   Here it has special reference to *the sure mercies of David.* Compare Isa. lv. 3; Acts xiii. 34.   *Sing*, uniformly so rendered.   It often expresses the celebration of God's worship with the aid of musical instruments.   *For ever*, to *eternity*, perpetually.   *With my mouth I will make known thy faithfulness to all genera- tions.*   *Faithfulness*, in fulfilling generally all he has promised and particularly what he engaged to David.   We have the same word in vv. 2, 5, 8, 24, 33, 49, (in v. 49 rendered truth.)   *To all generations*, literally *to generation and generation*, equivalent to *all coming ages.*

2. *For I have said, Mercy shall be built up for ever.*   I have declared it as an undoubted truth.   The speaker is Ethan.   *Mercy*, all the lovingkindness which God has promised, and that is no little, especially in what he engaged respecting the throne of David.   *Built up*, like a glorious edifice, not begun and finished in a day, but stone after stone added, till the topstone shall be laid with shoutings.   The same verb in another form occurs in v. 4.   The meaning is God's mercy shall be extended and continued to the consummation of what it had undertaken.   *Thy faithfulness shalt thou establish in the very heavens.*   The Hebrew is emphatic, pretty well expressed by the word *very.*   Calvin: "The divine promise is no less stable than the settled course of the heavens;" Hengstenberg: "The *faithfulness* is established in the heavens, in order that it may partake of their eternity, be like them eternal;" Scott: "Above the reach of the changes which take place in this lower world;" Clarke: "What

thou hast promised to do to the children of men on earth, thou dost register in heaven; and thy promise shall never fail." That which is in the heavens is very conspicuous. Thus far the prophet in the name of the church has spoken. God himself speaks next.

3. *I have made a covenant with my chosen, I have sworn unto David my servant.* *Covenant*, it occurs also in vv. 28, 34, 39. On making a covenant see on Ps. l. 5. One way of confirming an engagement was by an oath, 1 Sam. xx. 3; 2 Sam. xix. 23; Heb. vi. 16. *Chosen*, we have the same word slightly varied in v. 19. David was *chosen* of God in preference to Saul who was rejected. Christ was chosen of his Father in preference to all others. He is God's *elect* (the very word used here) *in whom his soul delighteth*, Isa. xlii. 1. David calls himself God's servant and God calls him my servant David, v. 20; Ps. xix. 11, 13; Jer. xxxiii. 21. But Christ was God's servant in a much higher sense. He rendered a much more glorious service, Isa. xlii. 1. Here follows what God had engaged to do:

4. *Thy seed will I establish for ever, and build up thy throne to all generations.* He saith not, And seeds, as of many; but as of one, Thy seed, which is Christ. True, the covenant with David literally and primarily related to Solomon; but even its chief reference to him was as a type of Christ, in whom secondarily and spiritually the promise was gloriously fulfilled. This is clear from the fact that Paul quotes a part of the covenant—" I will be his father, and he shall be my son," 2 Sam. vii. 14—to show that Christ was superior to angels, indeed that he was by nature the Son of God, Heb. i. 5. An inspired interpretation removes all doubt. Indeed the promise here is parallel to the words of the angel in Luke i. 32, 33. Hengstenberg: "The promise culminates in Christ." *Establish*, as in v. 2, and in the passive form in vv. 21, 37. In Ps. viii. 3, it is *hast ordained*, and in Ps. lxviii. 9, *didst confirm.* Many prefer *will confirm.* *Build*, as in v. 2. To *all generations*, as in v. 1.

5. *And the heavens shall praise thy wonders, O* LORD. *Heavens*, either angels as in Job xv. 15, corresponding to Ps. xcvii. 6, as explained in Heb. i. 6; or angels with men already redeemed and in glory. *Wonders*, as in Ps. lxxxviii. 10; Calvin, *wondrous work.* The special *wonder* (singular) here referred to was making the stone which the builders rejected the headstone of the corner; it was the *wonder* of redemption by Jesus Christ. *Thy faithfulness also in the congregation of thy saints.* Le Clerc proposes to supply—*Men shall praise;* but it is objected that this would destroy the parallelism between *heavens* and *saints.* *Saints*, in the plural; it occurs again in v. 7, and in the singular *Holy One* in v. 18. The meaning of the whole verse is, the sublimest worship both of heaven and earth shall be given to God who doeth *wonders* and is *faithful* to all his engagements. This is the common, perhaps the best interpretation.

6. *Who in the heavens can be compared unto the* LORD? who *among the sons of the mighty can be likened unto the* LORD? Chaldee: For who is there in the sky that is equalled to the Lord, who among the choirs of angels can be compared to the Lord? John Rogers' translation: For who is he amonge the cloudes that may be compared unto the Lorde? Yee what is he amonge the goddes, that is like unto the Lorde? *Heaven*, rendered in Job xxxvii. 18, *sky;* in Ps. xviii. 11, in the plural, *skies;* in Ps. xxxvi. 5, *clouds;* in v. 37, *heaven.* *Compared*, valued, estimated, equalled, set in array. *Likened, be like* is the literal. *The mighty*, see on Ps. xxix. 1. There can be no comparison, there is no resemblance between God and any of his creatures, even the most exalted. There is no greater gulf than that which lies between the creature and the Creator, the finite and the infinite.

7. *God is greatly to be feared in the assembly of the saints, and to be had in reverence of all* them that are *about him.* *Fear* is dread; *reverence* is awful veneration. In the Hebrew the latter word is the stronger, expressing *terror.* Both words are to be taken

in a good sense; the English version gives the meaning. Instead of *God is greatly to be feared*, Ainsworth has: *God is daunting terrible;* Calvin and Hengstenberg: *God is very terrible.* For *assembly* some read *secret;* some, *counsel;* some, *confidence;* Alexander, *secret council.* See on Ps. xxv. 14; lv. 14; lxiv. 4. Perhaps *assembly* is best. For *of all* in the latter clause the Chaldee, Calvin and Alexander read *above all.* The Hebrew will bear that translation. The *saints* and *those about him* include all his worshippers in heaven and earth.

8. *O Lord God of hosts.* Jehovah has all armies, all causes, all agents at his disposal. He marshals the stars. He guides the angels. He is the God of battles. He is a man of war. He is in all, through all, over all. *Who is a strong Lord like unto thee?* The word rendered *strong* occurs nowhere else. The corresponding *noun*, found in later books, is rendered *treasure, riches, strength,* in the Chaldee *power.* Some would read, Who is strong as thou art? who is Jah as thou art? We may read, Who is like thee? Thou art strong, O Lord. *Or to thy faithfulness round about thee?* A better rendering is, And thy faithfulness *is* round about thee. *Faithfulness,* as in vv. 1, 2.

9. *Thou rulest the raging of the sea: when the waves thereof arise, thou stillest them.* See on Ps. lxv. 7. God holds the winds in his fist. To created power nothing is more unmanageable than the sea. No man can raise or calm its huge billows, nor can he control the tumults of the people, often represented by agitated waters. But Jehovah does all this without effort. He is 'the author of *storms* and of *calms.*' *Thou rulest,* literally, *Thou* (art) *ruling.* Jehovah's will is almightiness. *Raging, pride, lifting up, majesty.*

10. *Thou hast broken Rahab in pieces, as one that is slain. Rahab,* a poetical name for Egypt. See on Ps. lxxxvii. 4. The allusion to the *sea* in v. 9, was probably in anticipation of the mention of Egypt here, as the greatest stroke that *proud* empire ever received was at the Red sea. Chaldee: Thou hast bruised, as one slain with a sword, the proud (one): this is the impious Pharaoh; church of England: Thou hast subdued Egypt and destroyed it; Calvin: Thou hast overthrown Egypt as a wounded man; Berlin: Thou hast bruised down Egypt like a dead carcass. *Crushed, bruised, smitten, broken in pieces, destroyed. As one that is slain;* Alexander: Like one mortally wounded, especially in battle. *Thou hast scattered thine enemies with the strong arm. Enemies,* always so rendered. God did this at the Red sea, as well as on other occasions. *Scattered,* as in Num. x. 35; Ps. lxviii. 1. The word had a historic significance and was inwoven with public worship. It was easy for God to do all this, for he had an *arm of might.*

11. *The heavens are thine, the earth also is thine: as for the world and the fulness thereof, thou hast founded them.* God's power to create and sustain the universe renders it easy for him to do anything. The universal Creator is universal Proprietor. Compare Ps. xcv. 5. *Fulness;* Hengstenberg: *the whole extent;* Alexander: *its contents and its inhabitants;* Clarke: *all the generations of men.* See on Ps. xxiv. 1; l. 12.

12. *The north and the south thou hast created them: Tabor and Hermon shall rejoice in thy name.* Here we have the four points of the compass. The *north,* always so rendered; the word means *covering* or *hiding,* perhaps, some think, because "the ancients regarded the north as the seat of gloom and darkness, in contrast to the bright and sunny south." The *south,* literally *the right hand, i. e.,* the right hand as you face the rising sun. Compare 1 Sam. xxiii. 19, 24. *Tabor* is put for the *west.* From its summit, which is one thousand seven hundred and fifty feet above the level of the sea, the Mediterranean can be seen. See Jer. xlvi. 18. This mountain is on the west side of the Jordan. *Hermon* stands for the *east.* It is about fifty miles from Tabor and on the *east* side of the Jordan. See on Ps. xlii. 6. Its highest point is not less than ten thousand feet above the level of the sea. These two mountains, being very

prominent and also very beautiful objects lying in different directions, denote east and west. The import of the verse is that God has made all parts of the world, that they have his providential care, show forth his praise, and are under his dominion.

13. *Thou hast a mighty arm: strong is thy hand*, and *high is thy right hand*. Patrick: "Thy power, extending itself throughout the whole, always effects in every place whatsoever thou designest; and with an irresistible force; whether it be to punish evil doers, or to preserve and exalt them that do well." The use of terms expressing *efficiency* here reminds one of Ephes. i. 19.

14. *Justice and judgment* are *the habitation of thy throne*. *Habitation, place, settled place, dwelling-place, foundation;* margin, *establishment*. The corresponding *verb* in v. 4 is *establish. Justice, righteousness;* see on Ps. iv. 1. *Judgment, right,* see on Ps. i. 5; ix. 4. God's *throne* is his government, which is founded in equity and in plenty of justice. This King does no wrong. *Mercy and truth shall go before thy face. Mercy,* as in vv. 1, 2. *Truth,* uniformly *truth,* though often meaning firmness, fidelity, uprightness. *Go before,* in Ps. lxxxviii. 13, prevent. A throne, built on justice and right, and having mercy and truth prominent in all its acts and decisions, suits the case of every penitent.

15. *Blessed* is *the people that know the joyful sound. Blessed, O the blessednesses,* as in Ps. i. 1. *Joyful sound, joy,* (Ps. xxvii. 6), a *shout* (Ps. xlvii. 4) *shouting, rejoicing, loud noise,* here only *joyful sound;* in reference to Jewish festivals, *jubilee,* Lev. xxv. 9; *blowing of trumpets,* Lev. xxiii. 24. The figure is perhaps taken from the *sound* of the trumpets on the *joyful* stated feasts and observances of the Israelites. The word *know* is pregnant. It means not merely to recognize the sound of the trumpet, but to know its import. Then the meaning is, Many and great are the blessings that come to the people, who have God's ordinances, and understand their real significancy and welcome them joyfully. *They shall walk, O LORD, in the light of thy countenance, i. e.,* says Calvin: "They not only enjoy his benefits, but also confiding in his favor, they pass the whole course of their life in mental peace and tranquillity;" Scott: "They walk in the comfort of God's manifested presence and favor;" Patrick: "They shall spend their days most cheerfully, O Lord; being secure of thy favor, which will let them want nothing that is good for them."

16. *In thy name shall they rejoice all the day.* God's *name* is all that by which he is known, his existence, perfections, works, word, worship and providence. In all these his people even now have pleasure, and yet more and more shall they *be glad, be joyful* in them. *Rejoice,* as in Ps. ii. 11; ix. 14. *And in thy righteousness shall they be exalted.* God's *righteousness* is his essential and infinite rectitude, his faithfulness to his covenant engagements, or the glorious justifying righteousness of his saints. *In* his holiness he saves them. *By* his faithfulness he preserves them. *For the sake of* the righteousness of Christ they shall be *exalted, lifted up* on high, even *taken up* to God's right hand.

17. *For thou art the glory of their strength.* No wonder they can do the great things just spoken of, for their *might* is not in themselves. Jehovah himself makes their strength *glorious. And in thy favor our horn shall be exalted. Favor, will, delight, pleasure, good will;* see on Ps. v. 12. On *exalting the horn,* see on Ps. lxxv. 4, 5. Alexander: "God is at once their mighty ornament and their glorious protection."

18. *For the LORD is our defence; and the Holy One of Israel is our King.* The Chaldee: For our defences are of the Lord, even of the Lord the Holy One of Israel our king; margin: Our shield is of the LORD and our king is of the Holy One of Israel; Hammond says we *must* render it thus; Edwards: For to Jehovah belongs our shield, and to the Holy One of Israel our king; Alexander: "Our protectors are themselves protected by Jehovah." In defending our defenders, God defends us. *De-*

fence, shield, buckler; see on Ps. iii. 3; vii. 10.   On *the Holy One of Israel*, see on Ps. lxxi. 22.   Here follows an argument built on God's former engagements.

19. *Then thou spakest in vision to thy Holy One.*   Sixty-three of Kennicott's and seventy-one of De Rossi's manuscripts read "holy ones."   The Chaldee, Syriac, Arabic, Septuagint, Ethiopic, Vulgate, Doway, church of England, Calvin, Jebb, Street and Hengstenberg all use the plural.   If we follow these authorities, what *holy ones* are intended?   First, Samuel, 1 Sam. xiii. 13–15; xv. 26–28; xvi. 1, 12; then Nathan, 2 Sam. vii. 12–17.   The revelation to Nathan was in *vision.*   Compare 1 Chron. xvii. 15.   From the fact that Gad is twice called *David's seer,* 2 Sam. xxiv. 11; 1 Chron. xxi. 9, some have thought he was also one to whom Jehovah gave an oracle on this matter.   It may be so, but we find no record of it.   Yet from Acts iii. 24, we are warranted in giving a very wide extension to the declaration: "All the prophets from Samuel, and those that follow after, as many as have spoken, have likewise foretold of these days."   Compare Luke xxiv. 27; Acts x. 43; xxvi. 22; Rom. i. 2; iii. 21; Heb. i. 1; 1 Pet. i. 10; Rev. xix. 10.   Pool says part of the message was delivered to Samuel, and part to Nathan.   By *holy ones* some understand the church at large.   See 2 Sam. vii. 10; 1 Chron. xvii. 9.   If we take *holy one* in the singular, it refers to Samuel, to whom the first revelation respecting David's throne was made, or to Nathan, to whom a fuller revelation on that subject was granted, or to David, addressed through these prophets.   But from the fact that in many editions *Holy One* is printed in capitals, it is evident that editors have thought that it refers to Christ himself, perhaps under the type of David.   Respectable commentators so expound the place.   That God spoke to his Son many glorious things before his incarnation we certainly know, Ps. ii. 7; xlv. 6; Heb. i. 8; Ps. cx. 1; Isa. xlix. 5–12.   Compare Pr. viii. 22–31.   That after his birth Christ found the *visions* of the prophets full of him, we also know.   For *then* Calvin has *long since,* or *in old time.*   These modes of explanation do not so conflict as to make any real contrariety of doctrine.   And *saidst, I have laid help upon* one that is *mighty; I have exalted* one *chosen out of the people. Mighty, valiant, strong;* applied to Nimrod as a hunter, Gen. x. 9; to great warriors as Josh. i. 14; vi. 2; to rich men, 2 Kings xv. 20; to chief men high in authority, Ezra vii. 28; to God himself, Deut. x. 17; Jer. xxxii. 18; to Christ, Ps. xxiv. 8; xlv. 3; Isa. ix. 6; to David, 2 Sam. xvii. 10.   Here it refers to David as the type of Christ, or to Christ himself as a deliverer.   Perhaps it is best to apply it to David himself as the first in the throne with promise of perpetual succession.   This mighty one was *chosen.*   See v. 3.   Compare Deut. xxxii. 25; Ecc. xi. 9, where it is rendered young *man.*   Alexander: "*Chosen* has here its strict sense, but not without allusion to its specific use as signifying a young warrior."   Both David and Christ are called the chosen of God.

20. *I have found David my servant; with my holy oil have I anointed him.*   This gives us the true exposition of the *mighty* and *chosen* one of v. 19, but it does not deny the typical character of David.   When God rejected Saul, he *found* David, whom Samuel anointed.   The history of that affair is given in 1 Sam. xvi. 1–13, where we are told too of God's Spirit resting on David.   David was thrice anointed, 1 Sam. xvi. 13; 2 Sam. ii. 7; v. 3.   On anointing with oil, see on Ps. ii. 2; xlv. 7.   Compare Isa. lxi. 3; Luke iv. 16–22; Heb. i. 9; 1 John ii. 20, 27.

21. *With whom my hand shall be established: mine arm also shall strengthen him.*   Help and assistance are commonly afforded by the arm or hand.   The figure is very old, Gen. xlix. 24.   The meaning is, God will permanently aid him.   How manifestly God was with David is matter of history, 1 Sam. xviii. 12, 14; 2 Sam. v. 10.

22. *The enemy shall not exact upon him.*   Many render it: The enemy shall not prevail against him, *q. d.,* He may have enemies, but they shall effect nothing.   For

exact Edwards and Hengstenberg have *oppress;* Jebb, *do violence;* Alexander, *vex.* *Nor the son of wickedness afflict him.* To David Saul was the *son of wickedness,* who got no decisive advantage and finally failed, 2 Sam. iii. 1. There is an evident allusion in the verse to 2 Sam. vii. 10; 1 Chron. xvii. 9. Referring to the antitype, see Matt. iv. 1–10; John xiv. 30; xvii. 12.

23. *I will beat down his foes before his face, and plague them that hate him.* The passage most nearly parallel is 2 Sam. xxii. 40–44. *Beat down, stamp, break in pieces, crush, smite, discomfit, destroy. Plague,* as he did Egypt, Josh. xxiv. 5; *smite,* as he did Nabal, 1 Sam. xxv. 38; *strike,* as he did David's child, 2 Sam. xii. 15; in all which places we have the same verb. "David was never overthrown." Neither was Christ.

24. *But my faithfulness and my mercy shall be with him. Faithfulness* and *mercy* as in v. 1. Compare vv. 1–5, 28, 33–35. *And in my name shall his horn be exalted. In my name, by my authority* and to *my glory.* On exalting the horn, see on Ps. lxxv. 4, 5. How God exalted both David and Christ is fully declared, 1 Chron. xvii. 7; Rom. i. 4; Phil. ii. 9–11.

25. *I will set his hand also in the sea, and his right hand in the rivers; i. e.,* I will give him power in distant lands. Patrick: "On one hand he shall conquer the *Philistines* and those that live upon the coast of the sea (2 Sam. viii. 1), and on the other hand the *Syrians* as far as *Tigris* and *Euphrates,* 2 Sam. viii. 9; x. 16, 19." Compare 1 Chron. xiv. 17; 1 Kings iv. 21. So far as the reference is to the spiritual David, compare Ps. lxxii. 8–11; lxxx. 11. Alexander: "The watery parts of the earth are put for the whole."

26. *He shall cry unto me, Thou art my Father, my God, and the Rock of my salvation.* I find no case in which David ever called God *Father,* but in John's Gospel alone there are recorded more than *sixty* instances in which Christ did it. True, to claim God as father is to ask his care and protection. This David did often, but not in the language of this verse. So far as the word *Father* is concerned, no doubt the fundamental passage in 2 Sam. vii. 14, is referred to. See also 1 Chron. xxii. 10. Both David and Christ used the language, *My God.* On the use of the title, *My Rock,* see on Ps. xviii. 2, 31. The *Rock of my salvation* is the Rock that saves me.

27. *Also I will make him my firstborn, higher than the kings of the earth.* The *firstborn* had peculiar privileges. Ordinarily he had his father's chief blessing, and succeeded to the office and honors of the father, 2 Chron. xxi. 3. He had also a double portion of the inheritance, Deut. xxi. 15–17. Hence the use of the term *firstborn* as chief, preëminent. Thus the *firstborn of the poor* (Isa. xiv. 30) are those who are very poor and wretched; Cresswell: "The poorest of the poor." And the *firstborn of death,* Job xviii. 13, is the most terrible kind of death. Although God gave David power and excellent majesty, even over surrounding nations, see 2 Sam. v. 11, 12; 1 Chron. xiv. 17; yet surely this prophecy never had its complete fulfilment in him, but only in Christ, who, Rom. viii. 29; Col. i. 15, 18; Heb. i. 6; xii. 23; Rev. i. 5, is no less than six times declared to be the *firstborn* or the *firstbegotten* (for the Greek word is the same.) The fulness of the Godhead dwells in him bodily. He is the first and only one who ever rose from the dead by his own power. He is Prophet, Priest and King. He is sole Mediator, the firstborn among many brethren. In all things he has the preëminence. He is fitly worshipped by all creatures. The church is his by purchase. By covenant He has perfect dominion over all the kings of the earth, and over all angels holy and fallen, Pr. viii. 15, 16; Dan. ii. 21; Mark i. 27; Eph. i. 20, 21; Col. ii. 10, 15; Phil. ii. 9–11. In a sense was this verse fulfilled in David, but very gloriously in Christ.

28. *My mercy will I keep for him for evermore.* Compare 2 Sam. vii. 15; Isa. lv. 3. God is well pleased in Christ and has done the most amazing things to prove it. He

twice said so in a majestic voice from heaven; he raised him from the dead; he set him at his own right hand. *And my covenant shall stand fast with him.* In no case has God ever broken covenant. He cannot deceive. He cannot lie, Ps. cxi. 5, 9. With David as king and as type of Christ the assurance of his keeping covenant is very strong, vv. 3, 34; 2 Sam. xxiii. 5; Jer. xxxiii. 20, 21.

29. *His seed will I make* to endure *for ever, and his throne as the days of heaven.* *Seed,* as in vv. 4, 36. It may mean posterity generally, David's successors, Christ, or the long line of his people. *Throne,* as in vv. 4, 14, 36, 44. See 2 Sam. vii. 12. Alexander: "The throne of David and the throne of his descendants are identical." *For ever,* to everlasting, as in Ps. ix. 5; x. 16. *Days of heaven,* first met with in Deut. xi. 21, meaning, in perpetuity. The stability of nature often illustrates the permanency of spiritual things; see on v. 2; Ps. lxxii. 5, 7, 17. Compare Ps. cxix. 89–91. One of Dr. Chalmers' best discourses is founded on that passage.

30. *If his children forsake my law, and walk not in my judgments;*

31. *If they break my statutes, and keep not my commandments;*

32. *Then will I visit their transgressions with the rod, and their iniquity with stripes.* *Children,* literally *sons.* What is here said was true of David's seed. It is true of Christ's children. In Isa. liii. 10, believers are called Christ's *seed.* In John xxi. 5, he calls them *children.* *Law,* as in Ps. i. 2; xix. 7. *Judgments,* as in Ps. x. 5; xix. 9. *Statutes,* as in Ps. xviii. 22. *Commandments,* as in Ps. xix. 8; lxxviii. 7. *Transgressions,* as in Ps. v. 10; xix. 13. *Iniquity,* as in Ps. xviii. 23; xxv. 11. *Rod,* as in Pr. x. 13; xxii. 15; xxiii. 13, 14. When we read of a *rod* of iron in Ps. ii. 9, we are reminded of an instrument of destruction. But this *rod* is for correction. *Stripes,* strokes from the rod; see 2 Sam. vii. 14. How sorely God punished the sinning descendants of David, history tells. How sorely he chastises the erring seed of his Son, Christian experience declares.

33. *Nevertheless my lovingkindness will I not utterly take from him, nor suffer my faithfulness to fail.* *Him,* not *them,* David as possessor of the throne, and type of Christ. If the Lord was true to David, surely to his own Son he would not be unfaithful. The nouns are the same as in v. 1. *Utterly take,* margin, *make void.*

34. *My covenant I will not break, nor alter the thing that is gone out of my lips.* *Break,* as in v. 31; there in the margin rendered *profane.* In v. 39, in another form it is rendered *hast profaned.* The word means to *violate,* or *prostitute.*

35. *Once have I sworn by my holiness that I will not lie unto David.* *Sworn,* the same verb is found in vv. 3, 49, on the same subject. Compare Heb. vi. 16; see on v. 3. God's *holiness* is his infinite purity, which controls all his perfections. *Lie,* the same verb so rendered in Num. xxiii. 19.

36. *His seed shall endure for ever.* *Seed,* as in vv. 4, 29. *For ever,* as in vv. 1, 2, 4, 28, 37, 52. It expresses unfailing perpetuity. *And his throne as the sun before me.* Here and in v. 37, the stability of the course of nature again illustrates and confirms the unfailing promise of God; see on vv. 2, 29. Calvin: "If we set Christ aside, where will we find that everlasting duration of the royal throne of which mention is here made?"

37. *It shall be established for ever as the moon, and* as *a faithful witness in heaven.* David's personal power is gone from the earth. If he has living descendants, their genealogy cannot be proven; and none of them have ruled any kingdom on earth for thousands of years. But the *throne* here spoken of is *established.* The face of nature on earth is much changed; but the sun and moon remain as of old. The *moon* is the *faithful witness in heaven.* There is no reference to the *bow in the clouds.* That was a sign to Noah, not to David. Cresswell: "The whole passage beginning with 'I have laid help' in verse 19, to the end of verse 37, may be considered as a

paraphrase of what God had said unto David (2 Sam. vii. 8, etc.) through the mouth of Nathan." If we do not so regard these verses, there is no satisfactory method of interpreting this portion of Scripture, q. d., "Thy people have long been supported by thy promises, which they have understood to mean as much as is here stated. They cannot be mistaken in following the prophets, who have said these things, which have for ages nourished the faith of thy people. Yet our difficulty is in reconciling these glorious promises with the present low and afflicted state of the kingdom." This is the common, and doubtless the correct mode of exposition. The Psalm was designed to furnish suitable thoughts to the pious when *at any time* the state of affairs in Israel should be such as to tempt God's people to discouragement. Alexander: "There is no need of confining this description (in v. 38 and on) to the last days of the kingdom of Judah, or to any other period of its history exclusively. If the Psalm was really composed by Ethan, as we have no sufficient ground for doubting that it was, he may have designedly so framed it as to suit any season of distress and danger, in which the theocratic sovereign seemed to be forsaken of Jehovah." Calvin says a Rabbi maintained that it was unlawful to recite this Psalm; but *all Scripture* is given by inspiration of God, and is profitable.

38. *But thou hast cast off and abhorred, thou hast been wroth with thine anointed.* *Cast off*, as in Ps. xliii. 2; lxxxviii. 14; see 1 Chron. xxviii. 9. *Abhorred, refused, rejected, despised, disdained, contemned.* In Jer. vi. 30, the participle is *reprobate;* see Deut. xxxii. 19. Calvin regards the first verb as even stronger than the second. The reason of the dreadful rejection is that God had been wroth with his *anointed*, the actual incumbent of the throne at the time contemplated. Pool: "*Thine anointed;* that person and family which thou hast invested with the kingdom." *Wroth*, as in Ps. lxxviii. 21, 59.

39. *Thou hast made void the covenant of thy servant.* *Made void*, found only here and in Lam. ii. 7, where it is rendered *abhorred*. It expresses strong aversion. The *covenant of thy servant* is the covenant made with thy servant. *Thou hast profaned his crown* by casting it *to the ground*. *Profaned*, see on vv. 31, 34, where the same word is rendered *break*. We profane a covenant when we hold it no longer sacred. In some way God had brought the royal family and the kingdom into a very low state.

40. *Thou hast broken down all his hedges: thou hast brought his strong holds to ruin.* The clauses are parallel. *Hedges, fences, walls.* The word describes either the protection furnished to a vineyard or to a flock. The latter clause changes not the idea but the figure. *Strong holds, fortresses, fortifications.* It does not refer to places naturally strong, but by the art of man *fenced, defenced*, made *strong*. Both nouns may be used figuratively to represent the institutions of the country and the safeguards of the kingdom. The destruction may refer to the desolation made by an invasion of the land. *Broken down, broken in, scattered.* *Ruin, destruction, dismay, terror.* Hengstenberg: "Thou causest his fortifications to be terrified before the enemy, and to be removed."

41. *All that pass by the way spoil him.* *Spoil, rifle*, meaning rob, plunder, devastate. *He is a reproach to his neighbors.* *Reproach, shame, rebuke*, commonly as here; see on Ps. xv. 3. *Passers* by and *neighbors* cried, "Is this the anointed of the Lord? Is this the everlasting family and kingdom? Is this that king whose throne was to continue as long as the sun and moon shall endure?"

42. *Thou hast set up the right hand of his adversaries; thou hast made all his enemies to rejoice.* *Adversaries*, in Ps. iii. 1, *they that trouble me;* in v. 23, *foes.* *Enemies*, uniformly rendered as in vv. 10, 22, 51. To *set up the right hand* is to *exalt the power.* The perplexity of the Psalmist is in reconciling this state of things with what was promised in 2 Sam. vii.

43. *Thou hast also turned the edge of his sword.* Turned, turned away, withdrawn. The meaning is, Thou hast rendered powerless the sword, the usual means both of attack and of defence. Compare 2 Sam. i. 22. Hengstenberg: "The sword returns back ashamed, when it does not *pierce.*" *And hast not made him to stand in the battle.* Several old versions: Hast not assisted him in battle. See Ps. xviii. 34, 39. The verb is in the future. God had been against Israel and it was feared he would continue to be so.

44. *Thou hast made his glory to cease, and cast his throne down to the ground.* Glory, margin *brightness,* meaning royal majesty, the splendor of a king. *Cast down;* it describes an act of sudden violence, which inspired alarm.

45. *The days of his youth hast thou shortened.* Some think they find the fulfilment of this clause in the case of Jehoiachin, 2 Kings xxiv. 8; some in the case of Ahaz, 2 Chron. xxviii. 1; and some, in the case of other kings, whose life and reign were short. But the language would rather indicate premature decay and loss of vigor, than early death. The Psalmist is probably not speaking so much of any particular man, as of the kingdom represented by the throne. Pool: "The youthful and flourishing state of David's kingdom was very short, and reached not beyond his next·successor." Calvin: "His complaint then amounts to this, That God caused the kingdom to wax old, and finally to decay, before it reached a state of complete maturity." *Thou hast covered him with shame.* Shame, uniformly rendered; it describes the deep mortification arising from a public and disastrous failure in building up the throne of David. *Covered him,* literally *covered upon him,* we would say, *covered him all over.*

46. *How long* LORD? Literally, *Until when?* See on Ps. iv. 2; vi. 3; xiii. 1. *Wilt thou hide thyself forever?* The reference doubtless is to Deut. xxxi. 18; xxxii. 20. See on Ps. xiii. 1. *Shall thy wrath burn like fire?* Wrath, as in Ps. vi. 1; lxxxviii. 7. *Burn,* in Ps. ii. 12, *is kindled.* There may be an allusion to Num. xi. 1, 3, where the same word is found. The displeasure of God is *a consuming fire.*

47. *Remember how short my time is.* Chaldee: Remember that I was made of dust; Arabic: Remember what my state is; Ainsworth: O call thou to remembrance how transitory I am; Edwards: Remember of what short duration I am; margin: Remember how transitory I am. Hengstenberg calls Ps. xxxix. 5, the fundamental passage. See Ps. cxix. 84; Job vii. 7; x. 9; xiv. 1; 1 Cor. vii. 29–31. *Wherefore hast thou made all men in vain?* Many die before they have lived a year. The longest life is a vapor. The pursuits of men are low. Their work terribly lacks stability. Even the greatest men are not able to perform their enterprises. They die just as they begin to live. To the eye of sense and reason, without light from heaven, it looks very much as if even the greatest families, yea, and *all the sons of Adam* were made for nothing, for *vanity.*

48. *What man* is he that *liveth, and shall not see death?* Not one. For special reasons Enoch and Elijah were translated; but till the end of the world no other case shall occur. The form of interrogation is the strongest negation. *Shall he deliver his soul from the hand of the grave? Soul,* here it means *life.* But if one cannot save his life, surely he cannot save his soul. *Hand,* here and often used for *power. Grave, pit, hell,* see on Ps. vi. 5; ix. 17; xviii. 5.

49. LORD, *where* are *thy former lovingkindnesses,* which *thou swearest unto David in thy truth? Lovingkindnesses,* see on v. 1. *Swearest,* see on v. 35. *Truth,* rendered faithfulness six times in this Psalm.

50. *Remember,* LORD, *the reproach of thy servants;* how *I do bear in my bosom* the reproach of *all the mighty people.* The above is a better rendering of the verse than any modern author has suggested. It gives the whole sense. *Reproach,* as in v. 41. Compare Ps. lxix. 9, with this and the next verse. *Mighty,* or *many. People,* plural, *nations.*

51. *Wherewith thine enemies have reproached, O* LORD; *wherewith they have reproached the footsteps of thine anointed. Anointed,* as in v. 38. *Footsteps,* in Ps. xlix. 5, and elsewhere *heels.* They dogged his footsteps with reproaches. The Chaldee reads: "Thy enemies have reproached the slowness of the footsteps of the feet of thy Messiah, O Lord." That is, men cried out, Where is the promise of his coming?

52. *Blessed be the* LORD *for evermore. Blessed, praised,* not the word in Ps. i. 1, but that in Ps. v. 12; xviii. 46. *Amen, and amen.* See on Ps. xli. 13; lxxii. 19. Those, who divide the Psalter into five books, end the third book here.

DOCTRINAL AND PRACTICAL REMARKS.

1. Wisdom and piety do not exempt us from sore trials. The author of the preceding Psalm was filled with grief about his personal affairs. His brother, who wrote this Psalm, is sore amazed with the public calamities of his times. So we all have our own burdens. Blessed is he, who has kind friends to sympathize with him in his calamities. But there is a friend that sticketh closer than a brother. His name in the church has long been *The Beloved.*

2. Whatever our own state, or that of public affairs may be, let us *sing* of God's glorious attributes. No darkness in our sky can excuse us from *making known* his perfections, vv. 1, 2, 14, 24, 28, 33, 49. We greatly wrong our own souls when we decline the religious use of song; because, " 1. This is the fittest way to express joy for anything. 2. It will be best inculcated in this way. 3. It will be more easily remembered. 4. It will be more easily delivered to others, in order to be remembered." Many a sorrowing child of God has had his gloom, like the evil spirit of Saul, quite removed by the harp of David.

3. Mercy's work, though to us sometimes apparently slow, is very sure and glorious, vv. 2–4. God's plans reach from an eternity past to an eternity to come. Let him take his own time.

4. The doctrine of election is taught in the Old Testament as well as in the New, v. 3. God *chose* David not for his stature. Saul was much taller. David's own brother's had a better *appearance.* God chose him because he would. If the *chosen* here is Christ, then above all others is he God's elect, Isa. xlii. 1; 1 Pet. ii. 6.

5. Whatever delays and hindrances the cause of God may seem to meet withal, the final issue and consummation of all things thereto pertaining shall be very glorious, v. 4.

6. If God had gone on governing the world in wisdom and goodness, this would have been love and condescension demanding lively gratitude. But how shall we sufficiently praise him for his amazing grace in giving us his word, in entering into *covenant* with us, and in confirming that engagement with an *oath?* vv. 3, 28, 34, 35, 49. Arnd: "O blessed people, for whose sake God swears! O miserable people, who will not believe God even when he swears!"

7. Whatever unbelief and self-will may suggest to men but partially sanctified on earth respecting God's ways and *wonders, saints* and angels in *the heavens* are well pleased with all his plans and all his proceedings, v. 5. Whatever jealousies and murmurings are found in remote parts of God's dominions respecting his course and ways, in his own immediate family and among his constant attendants all is praise and adoration. "God's chief praise from all holy beings in heaven and earth arises from the covenant of grace."

8. We greatly sin against God, we fly in the face of Scripture, and we bring great affliction on ourselves by forming even in our minds any likeness of God, or by comparing him to anything we ever saw or conceived. He is as incomparable as he is

immutable, v. 6.   He is infinitely farther above the tallest archangel than that arch-angel is above a worm.

9. If God is greatly to be feared even by saints and angels in glory, surely all irreverence in his worship on earth must be infinitely offensive to him, v. 7.   That under the Gospel as truly as under the law we must exercise godly fear is clear from Heb. xii. 28.   Henry: "A holy awe of God must fall upon us, and fill us, in all our approaches to God, even in secret, to which something may very well be added by the solemnity of public assemblies."

10. Neither in our theology, nor in our devotions can we get on pleasantly without a constant recurrence to the *might*, the *strength*, the almightiness of God, vv. 8–13. "The incomparable excellence of God shines out in his efficiency in creation and providence."   The breaking of Rahab in pieces shows what he can and will do, when necessary to preserve his people.   Omnipotence can do any desirable thing.   It raises and it calms the sea; it covers whole nations with mourning; it crushes the most powerful armies; it grasps creation; it balances the universe; it doeth all things.

11. How futile are all attempts to subvert the government of God.   Its pillars are as firm as the pillars of heaven, v. 14.   Yea, heaven and earth may pass away, but God's throne shall stand.   It is built on four principles, which cannot fail because they are founded in the divine nature, viz:

"1. Justice, which defends his subjects, and does every one right.
"2. Judgment, which restrains rebels, and keeps off injuries.
"3. Mercy, which shows compassion, pardons, supports the weak.
"4. Truth, that performs whatsoever he promiseth."

How can such a government be subverted?   The universe of creatures cannot even weaken it.   Calvin: "The ornaments with which God is invested, instead of being a robe of purple, a diadem, or a sceptre, are, that he is the righteous and impartial Judge of the world, a merciful Father, and a faithful protector of his people."

12. It is an unspeakable blessing to be a living member of the church of God under any dispensation and under any afflictions, vv. 15–18.   Even the old Jewish feasts introduced by blowing trumpets were full of significancy, somewhat even then understood by the pious.   That dispensation was glorious, Rom. iii. 2; 2 Cor. iii. 10. But what was the *joyful sound* of those days compared with the clarion trumpet of a Gospel fully revealed?   The completeness of that *righteousness, in which* believers are *exalted* is itself matter of wonder, love and praise in heaven and in earth.   We ever have 'just and solid causes of joy, yet in God alone,' in his righteousness alone, in his grace and wisdom and power alone.   Luther: "A heavenly righteousness is preached by the Gospel, which is not placed in us, or in any worthiness or merit of ours; but is out of us, and is the righteousness of Christ, and is imputed, for Christ's sake, unto all that believe in him."   How guilty must those be who despise such grace!

13. Though God chooses whom he will, he yet chooses fit instruments and agents to carry on his work; or he makes them fit before he assigns to them their office, vv. 19, 20.   David was no fool, nor was he a chicken-hearted man.   David was chosen, not because he deserved the post; but because he was fit for it, 1 Sam. xvi. 7.

14. If we would be *kings* and priests unto God, we must seek the anointing of the Holy Ghost, v. 20.

15. If God will *establish his hand* with any man, and *strengthen him*, why should he despair of accomplishing any work, to which he can possibly be called? v. 21. Omnipotence, girding weakness itself, will make it irresistible.

16. If God will take our enemies in hand, we need not give ourselves much trouble about them, vv. 22, 23.   He can manage them without our aid.

17. However depressed in spirits, or in worldly condition believers may be, God can

lift them up above all their enemies and adversaries, and, when the right time comes, he will surely do it, vv. 24–27. Of this he has given much assurance in the history of David, and yet more in the exaltation of our Redeemer.

18. We need entertain no fears respecting the perpetuity and glory of Christ's kingdom. It shall stand. It shall shine, vv. 29, 33, 36, 37. O yes! it shall stand forever. That the great burden of this Psalm is Messiah, all sound expositors admit. Luther: "This is a remarkable prophecy concerning Christ and his kingdom;" Horne: "The promise, covenant, and oath of God, which he declareth shall never fail. . . They relate to Christ;" Morison: "It was never intended that the literal seed of David should hold a perpetual empire; and it was undoubtedly of Messiah, as David's Lord, that the Spirit witnessed, when he spoke of his seed being established forever, and of his throne being perpetuated to the days of eternity;" Nicolson: "*David* in type, but *Christ* in the anti-type."

19. God loves his people too well and too wisely not to make them smart for their sins, vv. 30–32. The covenant as much secures needful chastisement as timely victory. Calvin: "As it is profitable for men to be subjected to divine correction, God does not promise that he will allow them to escape unpunished, which would be to encourage them in their sins;" Henry: "Afflictions are not only consistent with covenant-love, but to the people of God they flow from it;" Dickson: "The Lord alloweth not sin in his own children more than in others."

20. It is natural, perhaps it is unavoidable and undesirable, that we should be wholly unaffected with the *appearances* of things around us, vv. 38–50. This inspired Psalmist was himself deeply distressed by the *seeming* failure of the covenant with David. Nor is it wicked to tell God our perplexities, and plead for speedy relief. It is only when grief becomes inordinate, when pride arrogantly determines what is the right time and method of deliverance, or when unbelief charges God with unfaithfulness, that we sin against him in lamenting our afflictions. Men are not angels. The spirits of just men are not in this life made perfect in knowledge or anything else. Let us plead for a better insight into the nature of the covenant, and the ends of the discipline we are made to undergo. Let us plead the unchangeableness of divine grace and of the divine faithfulness.

21. Considering how weak the faith of most converted men is, and how strong their temptations are, it is a marvel that they do not oftener fall into deep dejection, and very much give up hope, v. 39. Because the government of the world is God's, and because the mind of man is feeble, it results of necessity that nearly the whole course of providence should be dark. This greatly tempts our faith, which would utterly fail, if it were not for the intercession of Christ, Luke xxii. 31, 32. It is sad indeed when we see not how God's dealings are consistent with his promise. Yet in their saddest moments the saints would not take a thousand worlds for the hope which remains to them. Henry: "Thrones and crowns are tottering things, and are often laid in the dust, but there is a crown of glory reserved for Christ's spiritual seed, which fadeth not away." The hope of that maketh not ashamed.

22. It is appalling to live in a time of general desolation of church or state, vv. 40–45. Till a good man knows by experience, history gives him almost no conception of the misery and crime which then appear on every hand. The badges and insignia of authority are despised, the fastnesses of society loosened, malice with her minions and myrmidons slandering and beleaguering all good men, the laws of property set aside, the throne of iniquity framing mischief by a law, the meanest men laughing at the miseries of the most honorable, the finger of scorn pointed at all who do not join in noisy clamor for blood and persecution, vile men exalted to power, fools being counsellors and wise men pronounced to be behind the times, fundamental laws swept away

in a moment, strangers and enemies laughing to scorn, wise plans of adjustment and pacification wholly despised, the glory of order and of religion utterly obscured, men fasting to smite with the fist of wickedness, and giving thanks for events which fill a thousand dwellings with howling. It is not strange that such scenes should make men old before they have reached their prime, or send them for shame to premature graves. But when, as Ethan, they can bring their case before the Lord, they may, like him, conclude their meditation with a doxology.

23. Success in war depends on the Almighty, v. 43. Yet mere success does not prove that we have God's approbation. He may let the wrong prosper for a considerable time, Ecc. v. 8; Isa. x. 5–15.

24. What poor creatures we are, when for a little suffering, perhaps, not running through half a lifetime, we cry out, *O Lord, how long?* v. 46. But blessed be God, our very feebleness will furnish an occasion to his grace in enabling us to forget our woes when they shall all be over, and we ourselves be made happy in God to all eternity.

25. If God's *wrath burns* so terribly, how careful we ought to be to flee from it, v. 46. Arnd: "Is it not an odd thing that when we see a fire break out we are terrified and run, and every man looks after what is his own, yet no man will be terrified at the wrath of God?"

26. It is well when the greater our straits, the stronger our cries to God for help That is a blessed anguish, and those are good crosses, which make us the more fervent in our prayers, v. 47.

27. When we ask God to *remember how short our time is,* let us be careful not to forget it ourselves, v. 47. He knoweth our frame; he remembereth that we are dust. We should not consume our days in complaint or mirth, but in glorifying God that we may enjoy him forever.

28. There must be something terribly wrong in man, else his pursuits, the brevity of his life and the manner of his departure out of it would not be as they are. Man is a *little lower than the angels* in his natural endowments, yet how many spend their days in factories with confined air, how many in mines hundreds of feet under ground, how many in sweeping streets, how many in sweeping chimneys, how many in prisons or in galleys. The millions toil. Every year thousands faint and fall dead through exhaustion and excessive exposure to heat and cold. Man's days are as an handbreadth. His death is never pleasant except in the case of the believer and to the eye of faith. Verily, if there is no life beyond the present, God has *made all men in vain,* v. 47.

29. Death reigns, v. 48. For that no adequate cause can be found, till we search the Scriptures. They make all plain, Gen. iii. 3; Ezek. xviii. 4; Rom. v. 12–19.

30. If men are allowed to pass their lives in quiet, though it be without human applause, let them be thankful for so great a benefit. Noisy clamor, even if it be in our favor, can do us no good; but if it be against us, it may embitter our existence. Men, who affect to despise the deserved censures of their cotemporaries, are bad men. Even where reproach is foul and wicked, it has a sting, vv. 50, 51. It broke the heart of Jesus Christ, Ps. lxix. 20. It is better to be unjustly than justly blamed; and yet there is a peculiar poignancy in our grief when wantonness holds to our lips the cup of opprobrium. The most trying form of reproach is perhaps that which assails us because of our religion. The reason is that the honor of our God and Saviour is involved in such contumely, Isa. xxxvii. 23. The day is coming, when the curse shall no longer be heard by the righteous, Jude 14, 15.

31. Whatever our case may be, let us not fail in the winding up of all our meditations and conflicts to pronounce our solemn *blessing* on the name of Jehovah, v.

52; Job i. 21. It is as wise as it is right to "take God's part against all doubts, and disappearances of the performances of his promises," and to praise and bless him for what he is and for what he has already done for us. Let doxology abound in our worship, public and secret.

32. This Psalm was written for our learning. Let us hope in God. Tholuck: "Devout people in great affliction are neither so callous and insensible, that the stroke of the proving hand of God makes no impression upon them, nor so soft and indolent that they at once lose all their confidence. Their eyes shed tears, while joy sits enthroned on their brow."

PSALM XC.

A Prayer of Moses the man of God.

1 LORD, thou hast been our dwellingplace in all generations.

2 Before the mountains were brought forth, or ever thou hadst formed the earth and the world, even from everlasting to everlasting, thou *art* God.

3 Thou turnest man to destruction; and sayest, Return, ye children of men.

4 For a thousand years in thy sight *are but* as yesterday when it is past, and *as* a watch in the night.

5 Thou carriest them away as with a flood; they are *as* a sleep: in the morning *they are* like grass *which* groweth up.

6 In the morning it flourisheth, and groweth up; in the evening it is cut down, and withereth.

7 For we are consumed by thine anger, and by thy wrath are we troubled.

8 Thou hast set our iniquities before thee, our secret *sins* in the light of thy countenance.

9 For all our days are passed away in thy wrath: we spend our years as a tale *that is told.*

10 The days of our years *are* threescore years and ten; and if by reason of strength *they be* fourscore years, yet *is* their strength labour and sorrow; for it is soon cut off, and we fly away.

11 Who knoweth the power of thine anger? even according to thy fear, *so is* thy wrath.

12 So teach *us* to number our days, that we may apply *our* hearts unto wisdom.

13 Return, O LORD, how long? and let it repent thee concerning thy servants.

14 O satisfy us early with thy mercy; that we may rejoice and be glad all our days.

15 Make us glad according to the days *wherein* thou hast afflicted us, *and* the years *wherein* we have seen evil.

16 Let thy work appear unto thy servants, and thy glory unto their children.

17 And let the beauty of the LORD our God be upon us: and establish thou the work of our hands upon us; yea, the work of our hands establish thou it.

ON the title see on titles of Psalms xvii. lxxxvi. That Moses is the author of this ode is admitted by all the ancient versions, by Luther, Calvin, Fabritius, Piscator, Amesius, Venema, Diodati, Pool, Henry, Gill, Hammond, Jebb, Fry, Peters, Morison, Dickson, Tholuck, Hengstenberg and Alexander. Moses is called *The man of God*, first in Deut. xxxiii. 1, B. C. 1451; then six years later, Josh. xiv. 6; then more than nine hundred years later, Ezra iii. 2. The phrase *Man of God* is found in Scripture more than *forty* times; is often applied to Elijah and Elisha; in the pastoral epistles it designates a minister of the Gospel. Kennicott, Edwards, Clarke and several German Commentators urge that this ode could not have been written by that Moses, who was buried in Horeb. Against its Mosaic authorship, Clarke urges the longevity of Moses, Aaron, Miriam and Caleb. But himself gives us a long list of moderns, who attained a great age. The Pentateuch itself shows that the above cases were exceptions to the general rule; and it is idle to claim that the composition is of a later date than the passage through the wilderness. Moses wrote two other songs remarkable for sublimity. One is found in Ex. xv. 1–19. That is emphatically *The song* of Moses. It is the oldest piece of poetry extant. He also wrote that contained in Deut. xxxii. 1–43. It abounds both in the beautiful and the sublime. It is forty years later than the former. He pronounced it in the presence of Israel, and followed it by a short exhortation. It was his farewell to his people. This Psalm differs from both his other compositions. It is not certain when he wrote it. Some think it was written at the time of the painful events recorded in Num. xiv. That would give its date after Israel came out of Egypt. Others suppose it was written about *thirty-eight* years later, near the close of Moses' life, when he had seen the dreadful sentence in Nu. xiv. 22, 23, carried into execution on nearly all his cotemporaries, and was himself about to leave the world. This is perhaps the more probable. This is a very mournful composition. The church of England has incorporated it into her funeral service. Many pastors read it at burials. Tholuck styles it, " A beautiful song, replete with solemnity and sadness, as hearty as it is solemn." Morison : " In all ages of the church this Psalm must be regarded as a sublime meditation of the Spirit upon man's misery, mortality, and sinfulness." Scott: " The sentiments of this Psalm are never unsuitable to our situation in this world." Luther thinks that Moses here "teaches what is the origin and cause of death, to which the whole human race is subject, and the reason why so horrible a punishment was inflicted on the whole race of mortals." Scott dates it B. C. 1460; Clarke: " This Psalm was doubtless composed during or after the captivity." The names of the Almighty found in it are *Elohim God, Jehovah* LORD and *El God*, on which respectively see on Ps. iii. 3 ; i. 2 ; v. 4.

1. LORD, *thou hast been our dwellingplace in all generations.* The rendering of this verse is excellent. Instead of *dwellingplace* the Arabic, Septuagint, Ethiopic, Vulgate, Doway, church of England and Edwards have *refuge.* But this requires the change of a letter in the Hebrew. The word in the received text never signifies *refuge*, but *abode*, as of God, Deut. xxvi. 15 ; of man, 1 Chron. iv. 41 ; of beasts, Jer. ix. 11. As all pious men confess themselves strangers and pilgrims, they might fitly use this language ; but to the Israelites in the wilderness it was very appropriate. From the day that Abram, at the age of *seventy-five* years, left Haran till his death, he had no fixed dwelling. Isaac and Jacob were no less unsettled. Even when in Canaan, they and the patriarchs were mere sojourners. In Egypt their descendants were *strangers in a land* that was not *theirs*, and were *afflicted four hundred years*, Gen. xv. 13. At the writing of this Psalm they had been wanderers in the desert, and their journey was not yet ended. Yet all this time Jehovah himself had been their habitation. Only one of his perfections is distinctly mentioned. But one divine attribute implies all the rest. To his servants God has been a home *in all generations*, literally, in *generation and generation ;* see on Ps. x. 6 ; lxxxv. 5 ; lxxxix. 1, 4. Though his people had sinned against him, he had not cast them out.

2. *Before the mountains were brought forth, or ever thou hadst formed the earth and the world, even from everlasting to everlasting, thou* art *God.* Though inspired men speak of nothing in creation as having more antiquity or permanency than the mountains, Gen. xlix. 26 ; Hab. iii. 6, yet we are here informed that our world dates not from eternity, but had a *birth*, an origin. Both the verbs, *brought forth* and *formed*, so teach. *The earth*, in Gen. i. 1, and often, put in contrast to *heaven*. *World*, in Pr. viii. 31, *habitable part of* his earth ; commonly *world ;* it always means either the habitable part of the earth, or its inhabitants. Compare Ps. ix. 8 ; xix. 4 ; xcvi. 13 ; xcviii. 9. In the Psalter God's eternity is first taught in Ps. ix. 7. *Here* we are told that he has a past eternity and an eternity to come. All attempts at explanation

have been failures. Clarke: "This is the highest description of the *eternity* of God to which human language can reach." *From everlasting to everlasting* is a phrase found in Ps. xli. 13. God's lifetime had no beginning and can have no end. His eternity is not measured. It is without the succession of moments, hours, days, years, ages or cycles. The special design in speaking of it here is to contrast it with the brevity of man's earthly existence.

3. *Thou turnest man to destruction; and sayest, Return, ye children of men.* Turnest and *return* are different forms of the same verb. It first and twice occurs in Gen. iii. 19, "In the sweat of thy face shalt thou eat bread, till thou *return* unto the ground; for out of it wast thou taken: for dust thou art, and unto dust shalt thou *return*." *Destruction*, cognate to the verb rendered *hast broken* in Ps. lxxxix. 10. Edwards: Thou bringest weak mortals down to the dust, if thou dost but say, Return ye sons of men. There is no good reason for doubting that this is the sense of the verse. Yet four other interpretations claim some respectful notice. 1. That of Tholuck: "The generations of men change before God, as if there were but a moment between their coming and going: now he suffers one generation to pass and now another to arise." The objection to this is that in this verse the prophet is speaking not of successive *generations*, as in v. 1, but of man as a race. 2. Another is that God brings man very near to destruction, and then restores him to wonted health. The objection to this is that the prophet is not speaking of alternate sickness and recovery, but of man's mortality. 3. Bucer, Cocceius, Gejerus and Clarke make the latter clause teach the resurrection. But clearly the whole passage shows that Moses is not exulting in hope of the resurrection, but is mourning over the ravages of death. 4. The Doway Bible reads: Turn not man away to be brought low: and thou hast said: Be converted, O ye sons of men. To this a paraphrase is given in a note: "Suffer him not quite to perish from thee, since thou art pleased to call him to be converted to thee." By *bringing man low* Bellarmine understands turning him away from the light of God's countenance, and giving him over to vileness and extreme dejection: and by the latter clause he thinks it is taught that by preaching God gives the external and by his Spirit the internal call to conversion. This interpretation makes the *prayer*, as Bellarmine admits, to begin at v. 3, whereas there is clearly no other petition till we reach v. 12. Nor does the prophet seem to be discoursing on conversion at all, but on the brevity of human life, especially as compared with the eternity of God. Compare Ps. cxlvi. 4; Ecc. xii. 7.

4. *For a thousand years in thy sight* are but *as yesterday when it is past.* Adam and many of his descendants till the time of Noah lived nearly a thousand years; but in God's sight this was but as a day, and that not a day in the future, which sometimes seems considerable, but as *yesterday when it is past.* Nay, it is not only in God's sight not as much as a day seems to us, when it is past; but it is not more than a part of a night: *And as a watch in the night.* In the time of Moses and for more than a thousand years after, the Jews divided the night into three watches. Compare Ex. xiv. 24; Judges vii. 19. But during our Saviour's life on earth they had after the manner of the Romans, four watches, Matt. xiv. 25; Mark vi. 48. A *watch in the night*, and that spent in sleep, what is it, when it is past? So is human life compared to God's eternity.

5. *Thou carriest them away as with a flood; they are as a sleep.* The first truth here brought to light is that men are taken out of life in great numbers and with great rapidity. Several scholars notice the force of the first verb in this clause, to *carry away* as with a violent storm followed by a torrent. The verb is found only here, and in another form in Psalm lxxvii. 17, "The clouds *poured out* water." Luther: "It is a fine full figure, by which is illustrated how the whole human family is driven

away, as when a sweeping torrent of rain carries everything before it, one race or generation after another is hurried away like a roaring flood;" Calvin: "I do not limit the expression to calamities of a more grievous kind, but consider that death is simply compared in general to a flood." There is some uncertainty as to the design of Moses in saying *they are* as *a sleep*. Does it relate to men living? or to men dead? to life? or to death? If to men living, then the meaning of the prophet is that life itself is like a sleep. Thus many explain it. Morison: "It is as a sleep which is soon disturbed, and from which when we awake we seem unconscious of the period of time which has elapsed;" Clarke: "The whole of life is like a *sleep* or a *dream* The eternal world is real; all here is either *shadowy* or *representative*." Althougt human life is in Scripture compared to a dream, (Job xx. 8; Ps. lxxiii. 20; Isa. xxix. 7,) yet where is it compared to a sleep? except in the case of the sluggard, Pr. vi. 9, 10; xxiv. 33; xix. 15. But in the sacred writings death is often compared to *sleep*, 1 Kings i. 21; Ps. xiii. 3; Jer. li. 39, 57; Dan. xii. 2; John xi. 11; 1 Cor. xi. 30. If this is the correct view, then the meaning is that the dead are as effectually removed from the affairs of life as if they were sunk in *sleep*. They have no business on earth. This exposition is suggested with much diffidence. It has little or no support from authority. If, as some assert, the word rendered *sleep* also means *dream*, then indeed there would be a good foundation for the common interpretation. But in the English version the word is never so rendered. That rendered *dream* is wholly different. *In the morning* they are *like grass*, which *groweth up.*

6. *In the morning it flourisheth, and groweth up; in the evening it is cut down, and withereth.* Grass, as in Ps. xxxvii. 2; ciii. 15; civ. 14; cxxix. 6; cxlvii. 8. In Ps. xxxvii. 2, *grass* is applied to the wicked; here and elsewhere to all men, Ps. ciii. 15, 16; Isa. xl. 6, 7, 8. Calvin: "It makes little difference as to the sense of the text, whether we make *grass* or *each man* the nominative to the verbs." Accordingly Hengstenberg translates: In the morning he blooms and—perishes, in the evening he is cut down and withers. *Flourisheth*, in Isa. xxvii. 6, *blossom;* in Num. xvii. 8, *bloomed;* in the Psalms always rendered as here. *Cut down*, expressing violent excision. In Ps. lviii. 7, one form of it is rendered *cut in pieces.*

7. *For we are consumed by thine anger, and by thy wrath are we troubled.* Consumed, in another form in v. 9, *spend;* often as here; in the active form *made an end.* *Troubled*, commonly so; also *amazed, affrighted, sore vexed;* see on Ps. vi. 2, 3, 10. *Anger*, in Ps. ii. 5, 12, *wrath.* *Wrath*, in Ps. vi. 1, *hot displeasure;* often as here, and frequently *fury.* This verse reveals the awful secret, not before announced in this prayer, that death is penal. Great numbers of the Israelites in the wilderness perished by God's wrath breaking forth in the most terrible manner and in extraordinary judgments. Wrath is felt in consequence of man's guilt:

8. *Thou hast set our iniquities before thee, our secret* sins *in the light of thy counte-nance.* The clauses are closely parallel. *Set, put, appointed, marked*, Ps. viii. 6; lxxxviii. 8: Gen. iv. 25. *Iniquity*, uniformly rendered. *Secret;* sins are *secret* only to man, never to God. He knows them all. Verse 7 said death was penal. This tells us why God is displeased. It is for sin. The whole story is told in Gen. ii. 17; Ps. li. 5; Ezek. xviii. 4; Rom. v. 12–19. We deserve our sufferings. We deserve worse than ever befalls us in this world. We may not deserve ill of man; but we all deserve wrath from God, and God has a right to use man as his sword.

9. *For all our days are passed away in thy wrath.* Wrath, once rendered *anger,* twice *rage;* see on Ps. vii. 6; found also in v. 11. Every day has its pang expressive of God's displeasure, not the less terrible because just. *We spend our years as a tale that is told.* Spend, literally, *have consumed*, see on v. 7. *Tale*, margin, *meditation.* In Ezek. ii. 10, the same word is rendered *mourning.* Calvin: We have spent our

years as it were a thought. Many substantially agree with him; others, as swift as thought; others, as a phantasm; church of England, Piscator, Jebb, Horsley, Fry and Green concur in the English version; most of the ancient versions, like a spider, *or* like the spider's web. Clarke differs from all: We consume our years like a groan. He explains. "We live a dying, whining, complaining life; and at last a *groan* is its termination! How amazingly expressive!" This reminds one of Thomas Watson's saying: "We come into the world with a cry, and we go out of it with a groan." All agree that the comparison is intended to suggest the shortness and vanity of our present life. Some give the additional idea of misery.

10. *The days of our years* are *threescore years and ten; and if by reason of strength* they be *fourscore years, yet* is *their strength labor and sorrow; for it is soon cut off, and we fly away*. This verse has an affecting illustration in the case of Barzillai, 2 Sam. xix. 34, 35. In Eccle. xii. 1–7, we find a highly poetical description of the infirmities of old age, forming a striking comment on this verse. There is force in uniting *days* and *years* in the same sentence. It reminds us that years are but as days, and that our lifetime may be counted by days as well as by years. See Gen. xxv. 7; xlvii. 9, 28. In this verse are two words rendered *strength*. The former strictly signifies *might*, the latter, *pride* and is found only here. Here it seems to mean that of which we are proud, viz., our vigor. *Labor* and *sorrow*, says Calvin, are here put for *inconveniences* and *afflictions*. Many read *toil* and *vanity;* Hengstenberg, *suffering* and *wickedness;* Alexander, *trouble* and *mischief*. *Labor*, in Ps. vii. 14, *mischief;* in Ps. xxv. 18, *pain;* in Ps. lxxiii. 5, *trouble;* in Prov. xxxi. 7, *misery;* in Job iii. 10, *sorrow;* in Isa. x. 1, *grievousness;* in Isa. liii. 11, *travail*. *Sorrow, vanity, affliction, mischief*. Each of these words signifies evil, natural or moral, according to the connection, in which it is used. Here the prophet is speaking of the *miseries* of old age. But even ten years added to the *seventy* are soon *cut off*, and we *fly away* or *faint*, or become *weary* of existence itself. Compare 1 Sam. xiv. 28, 31; 2 Sam. xxi. 15. Perhaps the common version is best. Compare Ps. xviii. 10; Isa. vi. 2; Prov. xxiii. 5, where the same verb is rendered *fly*, or *fly away*.

11. *Who knoweth the power of thine anger?* *Power*, often rendered *strength*, see on Ps. viii. 2. *Anger*, as in v. 7. *Who knoweth?* who is duly sensible of its dreadfulness? who thinks, and feels, and acts, as he should in view of it? *Even according to thy fear, so is thy wrath*. *Wrath*, as in v. 9; Ps. lxxxv. 3. Several interpretations are suggested: 1. Men are chastened and made to feel God's judgments in proportion to their piety or holy fear. Judgment begins at the house of God, 1 Pet. iv. 17. That is a truth, but there is no fitness in introducing it here. 2. A proper fear of God is necessary to make us duly feel his wrath. The wicked resist and rebel against its inflictions, because they do not fear God aright. But the righteous tremble before him. This is a truth, whether it is taught here or not. 3. Who is there that fears thy wrath in such measure as it ought reasonably to be dreaded? *q. d.*, No man has an adequate sense of thy terrible displeasure. 4. Who has such a habitual apprehension and memory of thy wrath as true piety would certainly produce? 5. Dreadful as are the effects of God's displeasure in this life, and much as we fear them, they are still more terrible in the world to come. The difficulty is in getting, by the laws of grammatical construction, such a sense from any correct rendering of the clause. 6. Others make the whole verse a lamentation over human insensibility with a prayer that it may be different with us. Leaving the rendering as it is in the common version, the best interpretation is the most obvious: viz., That God's wrath is as terrible as any man apprehends it to be. God's wrath is according to the terror, which fills men's hearts. Pool: "These fears of the deity are not vain bugbears, and the effects of ignorance and folly or superstition . . . but are just and built upon solid grounds,

and justified by the terrible effects of thy wrath upon mankind." Henry: "God's wrath is equal to the apprehensions, which the most thoughtful, serious people have of it."

12. *So teach us to number our days, that we may apply our hearts unto wisdom.* Various attempts have been made at a better rendering of this verse, but they do not claim particular notice. The common version gives the sense and is substantially supported by the best authorities. Dimock correctly shows that on an average not less than fifteen thousand adults must have died annually in the wilderness. One would think such fearful mortality would have impressed the whole nation, but it did not. God's Spirit alone can give a heart of wisdom. Calvin: "Even he, who is most skilful in arithmetic, and who can precisely and accurately understand and investigate millions of millions, is nevertheless unable to count fourscore years in his own life. It is surely a monstrous thing that men can measure all distances without themselves, that they know how many feet the moon is distant from the centre of the earth, what space there is between the different planets; and, in short, that they can measure all the dimensions both of heaven and earth; while yet they cannot number threescore and ten years in their own case. It is therefore evident that Moses had good reason to beseech God for ability to perform what requires a wisdom which is very rare among mankind." Tholuck: "How touching is this humble prayer for true wisdom in the mouth of the much-tried lawgiver." It is a clear confession that without divine grace we are utterly foolish concerning the plainest things.

13. *Return, O LORD, how long?* Return, as in v. 3 and Ps. lxxx. 14. *How long?* See on Ps. vi. 3. *And let it repent thee concerning thy servants.* Chaldee: Turn thyself from the evil, which thou hast spoken of thy servants. Syriac: Wilt thou not be propitious to thy servants? Calvin: Be pacified towards thy servants; Green: Be reconciled to thy servants. The common version is sustained by Piscator, Junius and Tremellius, Fabritius and Hengstenberg. Patrick's paraphrase is: "Be pleased to turn thy severity into kindness towards us." Clarke: "Be glorified rather in our salvation than in our destruction." Moses entreats the Most High to change his course of dealing with Israel, who had now wandered nearly forty years, having long felt the power of the dreadful curse recorded against them in Num. xiv. 23, 29.

14. *O satisfy us early with thy mercy.* Calvin: Satiate us early with thy goodness; Edwards: Satisfy us speedily with thy goodness; Fry: Satisfy us early with thy tender love. The common version is sustained by the Septuagint, Piscator, Junius and Tremellius and Fabritius. Ainsworth thinks *early* is equivalent to soon "after the dark night of afflictions." Diodati thinks there is "an allusion to manna, which fell every morning in the wilderness." The petition is not carnal; but spiritual and holy, for a good end; *That we may rejoice and be glad all our days.* It is our duty to be glad in the Lord and rejoice in him always. The words *rejoice* and *be glad* express the highest kinds of delight and exultation. Clarke: "Let us have thy mercy soon. Let it now shine upon us, and it shall seem as the morning of our days; and we shall exult in thee all the days of our life." Moses did not expect a revocation of the oath against his generation; but he and other pious men implored the divine benignity that their hearts might not be crushed, nor their spirits fail them while suffering under God's rebukes.

15. *Make us glad according to the days* wherein *thou hast afflicted us,* and *the years* wherein *we have seen evil.* The common version is fully sustained by the Chaldee, Calvin, Junius and Tremellius, Fabritius, Hengstenberg and Alexander. Church of England: Comfort us again now after the time that thou hast plagued us; Piscator and Amesius: Make us glad, even as thou hast afflicted us *many* days; *many* years we have found evil; Edwards: Exhilarate us according to the days thou hast

afflicted us; according to the years we have suffered adversity. Some of the most precious homilies and comforting discourses addressed to God's people by great and good men have been framed on the common English translation. If we are to follow that, the literal sense is, Let us have a joyful and prosperous time that shall last as long as our days and years of adversity have continued. But as God's mercy super-abounds and so triumphs over judgment, the meaning is, As we have been sore and long distressed, let thy dealings with us hereafter, according to the abundance of thy love, be marked by great and long-continued mercy. The prayer was answered. The generation that grew up under those great displays of wrath and mercy in the wilder-ness was the best generation of Jews that ever lived. So God himself testifies, Jer. ii. 2, 3. Its influence for good was long felt among the tribes. If the Israelites had trials in the wilderness for forty years, these were followed by long centuries of amaz-ing blessings in their own land.

16. *Let thy work appear unto thy servants, and thy glory unto their children.* This rendering is sustained by Calvin, Piscator, Junius and Tremellius and Fabritius. Edwards: Let thy noble works appear to thy servants; and thy glory to their chil-dren. The *work* God was desired to do was such as would show forth his *glory.* By *glory* Diodati understands "thy glorious power, deliverance and providence, for which thou art also praised and glorified." Calvin: "God maintains his glory by judging the world; but as nothing is more natural to him than to show himself gracious, his glory on that account is said to shine forth chiefly in his benefits." The verbs of the verse are in the future, thus expressing strong confidence and a prediction that the prayer shall be answered.

17. *And let the beauty of the* LORD *our God be upon us.* Some think the reference is to the beautiful sanctuary. But there is a beauty springing from God's blessing. It appears in a thousand ways. It made the young men at Babylon appear "fairer and fatter in flesh than all the children which did eat the portion of the king's meat," Dan. i. 15. The word *beauty* is found in the Psalms only here and in Ps. xxvii. 4. Calvin: "From the words *glory* and *beauty* we learn that the love of God towards us is unparalleled." It is the *glory* and *beauty* of Jehovah. *And establish the work of our hands upon us; yea, the work of our hands establish thou it. Work,* commonly and well so rendered. The word here seems to include much, even the whole labor of a good man's life, with its scope and aim, or the great enterprise of the life of Moses and his cotemporaries. *Establish,* approved by many; Venema, *Confirm;* Septuagint, Ethiopic, Vulgate, Calvin, Fry, *Direct.* The best men need guidance at every step. If our works are done in God's strength, according to his will and by the aid of his Spirit, they will be stable and be found unto glory and honor at the appear-ing of Jesus Christ. Otherwise they will be nugatory, and will be found unto shame and contempt.

DOCTRINAL AND PRACTICAL REMARKS.

1. How safe and happy are the people of God! They dwell in God and God dwells in them, v. 1. All this is rendered sure and delightful by their union with Christ, John xvii. 23. The Lord is himself a tabernacle for a shadow in the day-time from the heat, and for a place of refuge, and for a covert from the storm and from rain, Isa. iv. 6. The soul needs no rest nor comfort that is not found in God through Jesus Christ. Our great error is that we do not lay fast hold on the grace and power of God. Though we be strangers and pilgrims on the earth and have no certain dwelling-place, yet in the Lord have we a habitation. Fuller: "The Israel-ites forbidden to enter the promised land are directed to make up their loss in God."

2. What a blessed doctrine is that of the communion of saints, v. 1. *In all gene-*

rations God is their God, Christ their Saviour, the Spirit their Comforter. What God has done for one of his children is a pledge that he will do the same for the rest in all coming time, if it be for their good and his glory. The covenant which saves them is the same in all its provisions from the beginning to the end of the world.

3. An intelligent Christian will not be offended at mysteries in religion, but will rather adore God for them, yea, and be comforted by them, v. 2. Who can measure God's eternity, past or future? Waterland: "An eternity past puzzles all human comprehension." The Lord is the first and he is the last, Isa. xliv. 6. Henry: "Against all the grievances that arise from our own mortality, and the mortality of our friends, we may take comfort from God's immortality; we are dying creatures, and all our comforts in the world are dying comforts, but God is an ever-living God, and they shall find him so who have him for theirs." There is no higher mystery than God's eternity. Let the skeptic solve that, and he can solve anything. Luther: "Moses exhorts us to rise above time, and to look upon our life with the eyes of God, so shall we assuredly say, that all the life of man is scarcely one hour long, even though it last the longest."

4. From God's eternity we unmistakably infer his immutability. Tholuck: "It is our great consolation to know that God *changes not*, and that the God of our fathers is our God."

5. He who would have religion without theology would build a house without a foundation. The nature of God is the sole, solid ground on which to base our hopes for eternity, or our systems of morality. Let us not curiously pry into the inscrutable things of God. They are high as heaven, what can we know? deeper than hell, what can we do? But we must believe in God.

6. We need not waste our time in finding out the immediate causes of death. The will of God is cause enough. Nor is it difficult for him to bring it to pass. He 'turns man to destruction' by a word, v. 3. He says, "I kill and I make alive," Deut. xxxii. 39. The righteous would not put the keys of death and of hell into other hands. Horne: "How apt are we to forget both our original and our end."

7. If these things are so, one might readily overlook in a fellow-creature a greediness of time, a desire to improve every day and every hour. Where is the man that has a just sense of the shortness and uncertainty of life?

8. As we cannot comprehend the nature of God, so neither can we understand his thoughts, v. 4. Compare Isa. lv. 8, 9. Bengel thinks the amazing truth in v. 4, finds some illustration in the great wealth of some men: "As to a very rich man a thousand sovereigns are as one penny; so, to the eternal God, a thousand years are as one day." This is striking, but is it a solution? Horne supposes he casts some light upon it by saying: "All time is equal, when it is past; a thousand years, when gone, are forgotten as yesterday; and the longest life of man, to a person who looks back upon it, may appear only as three hours, or one quarter of the night." But neither is this a solution, for a thousand years to come are to God but as yesterday when it is past. Neither man nor angel fully comprehends the import of one phrase concerning God: "He inhabiteth eternity," Isa. lvii. 15.

9. As this doctrine is used by the Apostle to check the arrrogant reasonings of scoffers, who proudly said, God would not bring them to any account, because the judgment was so long delayed, (2 Pet. iii. 8); so God's people may employ it to hush the risings of impatience in their own bosoms. Give God his own time, Hab. ii. 3.

10. Let us cherish rather than reject solemn reflections on the mortality of man, the vanity of his course and the shortness of his life, vv. 5, 6, 9. They may make us sad, but by the sadness of the countenance, the heart may be made better, Ecc. vii. 3. Arnd: "When thou seest a garden in blossom, it is as if God took a flower in his

hand and said, Behold, this is what thou art, and thy whole life." The awful truth remains, and let us never forget it, that DEATH REIGNS. Like a *flood* it sweeps all before it. Our life itself is as a *sleep ;* comparatively few awake till they enter eternity.

11. God is the author of all the woes of life and of death itself. Nor can we sufficiently account for them but by referring to his *wrath,* v. 7. Compare Amos iii. 6. Trouble does not spring up out of the ground. Clarke: "*Death* had not entered into the world, if men had not fallen from God." Luther: "It is impossible that a man be moved to fear God unless the wrath of God be revealed to him, which cannot be except through the revelation of sin."

12. In our sins and iniquities, God has full justification for all the ills he sends upon us, v. 8. A terrible secret is revealed in a few words—*death by sin.* No other explanation is required. No darkness can conceal our iniquities from God. His presence is all-pervading light. He never punishes without full proof. The single sin of unbelief would itself justify all the severity of God towards men.

13. Let us be anxious rather to live well than to live long. Some die old at thirty; some, young at eighty. Let us not waste our lives in idle regrets or vain wishes, vv. 9, 10.

14. Let us exceedingly fear before the Lord, v. 11. The roaring of a lion spreads alarm; the wrath of a king is as messengers of death; but the anger of God burns to the lowest hell. Compare Jer. xii. 5. What can more firmly establish the amazing insensibility and unbelief of men than the fact that they live with so little disturbance of mind, under the expressions of the wrath of God in this life, and the threatenings of his anger in the world to come?

15. Let all men labor to obtain a right estimate of human life, v. 12. Let them pray for it. Let them meditate upon it. Let them not cast away reflection, because it is painful. Especially let them waste no time in folly or in idleness.

16. True *wisdom* is true religion. Such wisdom is very rare. It requires the heart, v. 12. Man naturally inclines to all folly, but never to that which is good. Calvin: "What can be a greater proof of madness than to ramble about without proposing to one's self any end?" Yet this is the habit of countless multitudes.

17. It is not wicked to feel our trials, to groan under them, and to cry for deliverance from them, v. 13. We may not be impatient, nor charge God foolishly, nor use sinful measures to be rid of our distresses. But we may without any offence against God humbly ask to be rescued. It is not comely for us to form the habit of sighing and groaning when nothing is the matter. But those are foolish people, who go about chiding the sad and suffering for giving natural expression to their anguish of mind or body.

18. In our afflictions we should be specially and chiefly concerned to secure the forgiveness of sin, and plead that God may be pacified towards us, v. 13. If he is propitious, all is well.

19. But let us not be satisfied with cold or feeble desires for mercy. Let our affections be stirred within us. Let us cry mightily. The language of strong emotion is not wordy. It often is abrupt crying, *How long ?* v. 13. There is no stronger desire than that of a pious soul for God's blessing.

20. The reason is, God's favor makes us happy, so as nothing else does. It only and it alone makes us truly blessed, v. 14. Dickson: "A poor hungry soul lying under a sense of wrath will promise to itself happiness for ever, if it can but once again find what it hath sometimes felt; that is, one sweet fill of God's sensible mercy towards it."

21. If we see dark times ourselves, yet let us in prayer commit our ways to the Lord, v. 15. "Blessed are all they that hope in his mercy." If we can do nothing

else, we can pray. Perhaps God has cut us off from doing anything else, that we may the more attend to that slighted duty.

22. Sad as things often are, and confused as they often seem to be in this life, yet "it is usual with God, in dealing with his people, to balance evil with good and good with evil," v. 15. God sets the day of prosperity over against the day of adversity, Ecc. vii. 14. Fuller: "The alternate changes of night and day, winter and summer, are not more fixed in the course of nature, than the mixture of judgment and mercy in the present state."

23. However afflicted, then, our lot may be, let us hold fast the covenant, and plead with God, v. 15. To break with God is to give up all as lost.

24. It is an admirable arrangement on the part of God that ordinarily evil precedes good, and humiliation goes before honor, v. 15. It is good that a man bear the yoke in his youth, and not in his riper years. It would be sad to see our old men and women *learning* the lessons of childhood, when they ought to be *teaching* lessons of piety and patience. Our *light affliction worketh glory*. When days of trial are to be followed by an eternity of joy, the prospect may well sustain and cheer us.

25. Whatever betides *us*, let us not forget to pray that the cause of God and his truth may live and flourish, v. 16. If all goes well with Zion, we may well be glad. It greatly revived the heart of good old Joseph to be able confidently to say to his brethren: "I die, and God shall surely visit you," Gen. 1. 24. "Pray for the peace of Jerusalem." Some have suggested that the prayer of dying Stephen led to the conversion of Paul. The measure of success now given to the truth may be owing, in no small degree, to the prayers offered by the martyrs of ages long gone by, Rev. v. 8; vi. 9, 10; viii. 3, 4. O Christians, pray on.

26. Still it is delightful to the pious to see displays of God's love and mercy in their own day; and so they do all plead that he would make bare his arm and "let his work appear" to them.

27. Holiness is the *beauty* of God's character, as it shines out in his word and providence, v. 17. We cannot, therefore, too earnestly implore God to let the tenor of his proceedings be for us, and not against us.

28. If we err not, it is because God guides us; if we fail not, it is because he upholds us; if we beat not the air, it is because he makes the worm Jacob to thresh the mountain, v. 17.

PSALM XCI.

1 He that dwelleth in the secret place of the Most High shall abide under the shadow of the Almighty.

2 I will say of the Lord, *He is* my refuge and my fortress: my God; in him will I trust.

3 Surely he shall deliver thee from the snare of the fowler, *and* from the noisome pestilence.

4 He shall cover thee with his feathers, and under his wings shalt thou trust: his truth *shall be thy* shield and buckler.

5 Thou shalt not be afraid for the terror by night; *nor* for the arrow *that* flieth by day;

6 *Nor* for the pestilence *that* walketh in darkness; *nor* for the destruction *that* wasteth at noonday.

7 A thousand shall fall at thy side, and ten thousand at thy right hand; *but* it shall not come nigh thee.

8 Only with thine eyes shalt thou behold and see the reward of the wicked.

9 Because thou hast made the LORD, *which is* my refuge, *even* the Most High, thy habitation;

10 There shall no evil befall thee, neither shall any plague come nigh thy dwelling.

11 For he shall give his angels charge over thee, to keep thee in all thy ways.

12 They shall bear thee up in *their* hands, lest thou dash thy foot against a stone.

13 Thou shalt tread upon the lion and adder: the young lion and the dragon shalt thou trample under feet.

14 Because he hath set his love upon me, therefore will I deliver him: I will set him on high, because he hath known my name.

15 He shall call upon me, and I will answer him: I *will be* with him in trouble; I will deliver him, and honour him.

16. With long life will I satisfy him, and shew him my salvation.

IN the Hebrew this Psalm is without title. From competent critics it has received the highest praise. Luther: "This is the most distinguished jewel among all the Psalms of consolation." Clarke and Anderson: "It is allowed to be one of the finest Psalms in the whole collection." Morison: "The general style and allusions of the Psalm are remarkably sublime." Walford: "The poem is so clear and intelligible, that nothing in it can be mistaken or misunderstood." Muis: "Could the Latin or any modern language express thoroughly all the beauties and elegancies as well of the *words* as of the *sentences*, it would not be difficult to persuade the reader that we have no poem, either in Greek or Latin, comparable to this Hebrew ode." Concerning its author there is quite a diversity of opinion. Clarke: "It cannot be determined on what occasion or by whom it was composed. It is most likely by the author of the preceding." Alexander styles it, "An amplification of the theme, that God is the dwelling-place and refuge of his people. This and other points of contact with the prayer of Moses seem to mark it as an imitation of that Psalm, and thereby account for its position in the Psalter." Pool: "The penman of this Psalm is uncertain;" Patrick: "The author of this Psalm is unknown." Jarchi, Venema, Peters and others ascribe it to Moses. But the Chaldee, Syriac, Arabic, Septuagint, Ethiopic, Vulgate and Vitringa ascribe it to David. Henry and Scott incline to this view. Even if we should admit that Moses wrote it, it could not be on the ground taken by some that when an author is given to a Psalm, he is to be regarded as the penman of all succeeding till another author is announced. This would make Moses the writer of this and the next nine Psalms; but from Heb. iv. 7, we know that David wrote Ps. xcv. Of course we know not the occasion on which this Psalm was written. Yet from the fact that the pestilence is twice mentioned, many have supposed that it was written on the occasion of some wasting disease appearing in the camp of Israel, or among the tribes after their settlement in Canaan. Respecting the scope of the Psalm there is less diversity. Tholuck: "A JOYOUS psalm, full of the assurance of faith;" Berleberg Bible: "The whole object is to bring to a right trust in God;" Luther: "The Psalmist highly exalts faith in God, and shows that it is an invincible strength against all evils, and against all the gates of hell." It sets forth the safety of one under Divine protection. It is rightly regarded as Messianic, not because Satan so applied vv. 11, 12, in Matt. iv. 6; Luke iv. 10, 11; but because its contents are best so explained. The ancient Jews applied it to Messiah. So do the Syriac, Henry, Horne, Scott, etc. If with some we regard it as a prophecy respecting Joshua, or with others as a prophecy respecting Solomon, none will deny that both of them were types of Christ, and so the chief fulfilment may still be in him. Nor can it without many qualifications be said to receive entire fulfilment in any but Christ; while every clause may be unqualifiedly applied to him. It was not possible that he should die by accident, by the assassin or by disease. Michaelis thinks it was to be recited in alternate parts by two sets of singers, addressing each other, and that the last three verses are spoken by God himself. Tholuck would have vv. 1, 3–8, 10–12, sung or recited by a precentor, v. 2 and part of v. 9, by a choir, and vv. 14–16, by precentor and choir. But moderns do not know enough of the mode of conducting the temple worship to decide such a point. Scott dates it B. C. 1017. In it we have four names of God: *Gel-yohn Most High, Shaddai Almighty, Elohim God* and *Jehovah* LORD, on which respectively see on Ps. vii. 17; introductory remarks to Ps. lxviii.; on Ps. iii. 2; i. 2.

1. *He that dwelleth in the secret place of the Most High shall abide under the shadow of the Almighty.* There is no need of any change in the translation, nor of making the two clauses descriptive of a character, of whom nothing is affirmed till we reach the second verse. The grammar does not require such a reading; although it is sanctioned by Lowth and others. Some think that as the verse stands in the English text, it but expresses a truism. But to careless readers and hearers many scriptural truths have that appearance. See Gal. v. 15; vi. 3. Both the verbs express stability. *Dwell*, so rendered in Gen. xiii. 12; Deut. ii. 10 and often; in Jud. v. 17, *continued*. *Abide*, commonly *lodge* or *tarry*, as in Ruth i. 16, where thou *lodgest* I *will lodge;* in Job xvii. 2, *continue;* xix. 4, *remaineth*. It often includes the idea of shelter. *Secret place*, as in Ps. xviii. 11; lxxxi. 7; in Ps. xxvii. 5, *secret;* in Ps. lxi. 4; Isa. xxxii. 2, *covert;* in Ps. xxxii. 7; cxix. 114, *hiding-place*. The figure may be drawn from the tabernacle. The word is often rendered *secretly*. *Shadow*, as in Ps. xvii. 8; xxxvi. 7; lvii. 1; lxiii. 7. *Most High* and *Almighty*, two words happily introduced here to give confidence to believing expectations. The sense is, He who truly relies on God shall assuredly have his protection. Arnd: "If a man can conceal a friend in a secret hidden place in the time of trouble, much more can God;" Hengstenberg: "He whom God has taken under his care is perfectly safe under his protection." This construction is grammatical and natural and gives the best sense. The man Christ Jesus dwelt in the secret place of the Most High and enjoyed the protection of the Almighty, so as none else ever did. In him and under him his people are all safe. He is their *hiding-place*. The first verse may be regarded as a sort of text for the whole Psalm.

2. *I will say of the Lord, He is my refuge and my fortress.* *Refuge*, as in Ps. xiv. 6; xlvi. 1; in Ps. lxi. 3, *shelter;* Jer. xvii. 17, *hope*. *Fortress*, so often; see on Ps. xviii. 2; in 1 Sam. xxii. 4, a *hold;* in 2 Sam. v. 7, *strong-hold;* in 1 Chron. xi. 5, *castle;* in 2 Sam. v. 9, *fort*. *My God;* mine by covenant, as well as by choice, endeared to me by a thousand precious memories and marked deliverances. *In him will I trust* or *confide*, as in Ps. iv. 5; ix. 10. *Confidence* is one of the highest acts of friendship as well as of worship. None except God is entitled to our unqualified and undivided confidence to all the ends of conservation, government and salvation. Hengstenberg: "What can do any real injury to the man who stands under the protection of Omnipotence, as it exists in a personal God?" Such are willing witnesses of the love and truth and grace and power of God. "Others speculate, but they believe and enjoy." The knowledge gained by experience is to God's people invaluable. The verse has its perfect fulfilment in Christ. None ever trusted in God as did the incarnate Mediator. His confidence never wavered.

3. *Surely he shall deliver thee from the snare of the fowler, and from the noisome pestilence.* Alexander: "A change of pronoun is the characteristic of this Psalm." In v. 1, the pronoun is *he;* in v. 2, *I;* in v. 3, *thee*. This change from the third to the first and then to the second person occasions the chief difficulty with interpreters. Various solutions are suggested. One is that there are different speakers. This is admissible. It is generally agreed that v. 1 contains a general truth. Some make David the speaker in v. 2, and Solomon in v. 3. Others suppose v. 3 is uttered by a

voice from heaven; others think that the prophet in v. 3, is addressing his own soul. Pool thinks v. 3 contains an address to a pious, believing soul. Perhaps it is as well to make it an address to his own soul, as in Ps. xlii. 5. By the *snare of the fowler*, we may understand any mischief plotted by Satan or his servants. On *snares*, see on Ps. xi. 6. For *noisome pestilence*, the Chaldee has death and tumult; Arabic, speech of the persecutor; Luther, destructive pestilence; Calvin, noxious pestilence; Edwards, loathsome pestilence; Geddes, mischievous design; Fry, evil design. In Hebrew the same consonants are used for *word* and *pestilence;* hence the variation. Pestilence is the best rendering here and in v. 6. We met it in Ps. lxxviii. 50.

4. *He shall cover thee with his feathers, and under his wings shalt thou trust.* *Feathers*, in Job xxxix. 13, *wings.* *Wings, skirt, border, overspreading,* 1 Sam. xxiv. 4; Num. xv. 38; Dan. ix. 27. On the figure here used, see on Ps. xvii. 8. Compare Ps. xxxvi. 7; lvii. 1; lxi. 4; lxiii. 7. In loving condescension God compares himself to the female bird sheltering her young. *His truth* shall be thy *shield and buckler.* *Truth*, veracity, faithfulness. Diodati: "Thou shalt be defended and safe by virtue of his most true and infallible promises." *Shield*, as in Ps. v. 12. *Buckler*, here only, literally *surrounding.* This clause is fulfilled in all believers; its most glorious accomplishment was in Christ.

5. *Thou shalt not be afraid for the terror by night; nor for the arrow that flieth by day.* For *terror by night*, the Chaldee has fear of demons who roam about at night; many: nocturnal dread; John Rogers' translation: Thou shalt not need to be afrayed for any bugges by nyght. The *terror of the night* points to any evil that may come on men at that time. Commonly the darkness adds to the consternation. *The arrow* is an instrument of deadly hostility.

6. Nor *for the pestilence* that *walketh in darkness;* nor *for the destruction* that *wasteth at noonday.* *Pestilence*, as in v. 3. *Destruction*, in Isa. xxviii. 2, connected with a storm. Scaliger correctly regards all possible evils as designated by the four terms *terror by night, arrow flying by day, pestilence walking in darkness,* and *destruction wasting at noonday.* If any evil was not under God's control, it might defeat his most glorious purposes. Tholuck: "Whatever species of weapon the tempter may use against the children of God, whenever and wherever he may come, the protection of the Lord is all-sufficient, and you need not seek for any other." Bythner: "The man, who has made God his refuge, is always safe, day and night, at every hour, from every danger." Compare Pr. iii. 23–26. These promises are so fulfilled in believers that they cannot die till the Lord permits. In the case of the Mediator it was in every way certain that no form of casualty, disease, or assault could terminate his life, but that he should lay it down himself.

7. *A thousand shall fall at thy side, and ten thousand at thy right hand; but it shall not come nigh thee.* We see good men cut down by many of the diseases and events, which hurry the wicked into eternity, although it is true that when a good man is taken away, it is from the evil to come, Isa. lvii. 1. Nor do the righteous die except at the intercession of Christ, John xvii. 24. Nor is there any room for doubt that at death believers enter into glory. But all this is a meager fulfilment of what is so clearly promised in this verse. The text needs neither criticism nor labored exposition. The common version clearly gives the sense. The promise is of an absolute exemption from all that could endanger life. This was true of none but Jesus.

8. *Only with thine eyes shalt thou behold and see the reward of the wicked.* No man knoweth love or hatred by all that he sees befalling his neighbors; for all things come alike to all, Ecc. ix. 1, 2. The reason is, that all mere men are sinners, are sick, suffer and die, if of nothing else, of old age. Death is by sin. While the good man watches his dying neighbor, he himself sickens and dies. He falls in battle like

others. He may die at any moment. So that it is but in a limited sense that to the believer we can at all apply this verse, which like the last is very well translated, and is clear in its meaning, if prophetic of Christ. Yet God exercises a kind and special providence over his people. Universal tradition represents that not a Christian perished in the destruction of Jerusalem. The temperance, faith and courage of Christians are friendly to longevity. Yet in the Mediator has this verse its glorious fulfilment.

9. *Because thou hast made the* LORD, *which is my refuge, even the Most High, thy habitation. Refuge,* as in v. 2. *Habitation,* as in Ps. xc. 1.

10. *There shall no evil befall thee, neither shall any plague come nigh thy dwelling. Evil,* either natural or moral as the sense requires; see on Ps. v. 4: vii. 4. *Plague,* sometimes rendered a *wound,* a *stroke,* plural *stripes,* Pr. vi. 33; Deut. xvii. 18; Isa. liii. 5. In Leviticus it occurs more than *fifty* times and is there uniformly rendered *plague.* Here it does not materially differ in signification from *pestilence* in vv. 3, 6. Horne: "The sentiment in vv. 9, 10, is evidently the same with that in vv. 5, 6."

11. *For he shall give his angels charge over thee, to keep thee in all thy ways.*

12. *They shall bear thee up in their hands, lest thou dash thy foot against a stone.* The translation cannot be improved. *Keep, guard,* protect. Even if this Psalm is a prophecy of the Redeemer, Satan's use of these words was tempting him to act presumptuously and so to sin. Compare Num. xv. 30; Matt. iv. 7. Hengstenberg: "The language does not apply to dangers which one seeks, but only to such as meet the righteous man unsought." Christ was as impeccable as he was imperishable. Angels showed a special sympathy with our Lord and lively concern in his birth, work, sufferings and glory. Nor can any believer in this life know from how many evils these ministering spirits have kept him. Protected by them Elisha had no fear of a great army, 2 Kings vi. 16. It is sometimes asked, Why do we not thank angels for their services? The reason is, they are our fellow-servants, Rev. xxii. 9. For the same and other reasons we do not pray to them, but to God. It is a blessed fact revealed in Scripture that angels and men constitute through Christ one family. He is not the Saviour of angels, but he is their Lord, Ephes. i. 10; Heb. i. 6. See on Psalm xxxiv. 7.

13. *Thou shalt tread upon the lion and adder: the young lion and the dragon shalt thou trample under feet. Lion,* found nowhere else in the Psalms; in Job thrice rendered *fierce lion. Adder,* see on Ps. lviii. 4; except in the Psalms, always *asp. Young lion,* the strong lion, see on Ps. xxxiv. 10. *Dragon,* often so rendered, also *whale, serpent, sea-monster,* Gen. i. 21; Ex. vii. 9; Lam. iv. 3. In many eastern countries the *dragon* seems to be a favorite emblem of huge, terrific evils. To *tread upon* is to have the mastery over; Calvin: *To walk over.* It is applied to *treading* grapes and olives, which offer no resistance, but are crushed. Often in Scripture are spiritual adversaries compared to fierce and venomous creatures. Satan is called a lion, a dragon, a serpent. Wicked men are the children of the devil. Over all spiritual and natural adversaries our Lord had absolute sovereignty. He never was in any way subject to them but by his own free consent. Under him his people have the victory over all their foes, and are more than conquerors through him that loved them; see Luke x. 17–20; 1 John iv. 4. All experienced Christians admit God's providence over them to be kind and constant. The review of it shall forever fill them with wonder. In vv. 14–16, Jehovah speaks:

14. *Because he hath set his love upon me, therefore will I deliver him.* Luther: "By the cluster of promises at the end of the Psalm, the Holy Spirit quickens and refreshes our hearts with consolation." Instead of *set his love on me,* Calvin reads *trusted in me;* Hengstenberg, *cleaves to me.* Our version is the best, and is well

supported by authority. *Deliver*, commonly so rendered, also *cause to escape*, see on Ps. xvii. 13. *I will set him on high, because he hath known my name. Set on high, exalt*, especially for safety; in Ps. xx. 1; lix. 1, *defend*. It also means to exalt for honor, Ps. cvii. 41; Isa. xxxiii. 5. To *know God's name* is to be truly and intelligently pious, a friend of God.

15. *He shall call upon me, and I will answer him.* All blessings come by prayer. Even the Mediator was victorious by prayer, Heb. v. 7. We must follow his example. Then in our sorest trials we shall have his gracious and cheering presence. *I* will be *with him in trouble.* Clarke: "As soon as the trouble comes, *I am there.*" Yea, more: *I will deliver him. Deliver*, as in Ps. vii. 4; xviii. 19. It implies very effectual deliverance, especially by imparting all needed strength. He will rescue him *and honor him.* To the Mediator he has given a name that is above every name. He has been made higher than the heavens. The Father has crowned him with glory and honor. So in their measure shall Jehovah *glorify* all who in true faith call on his name. Clarke: "I will *load* him with *honor.*" Compare 1 Sam. ii. 30; John xii. 26.

16. *With long life will I satisfy him.* On the general tenor of such promises, see on Ps. i. 3; xxxiv. 12; xxxvii. 3. Compare Ex. xx. 12; Deut. v. 16. Hengstenberg: "Expositors are too ready with the obvious remark, that the promise of long life is specially an Old Testament one." That life is long, which answers all life's great ends. Calvin: "Long life would be bestowed by God on all his children, were it not for their advantage that they should be taken early out of the world." Christ himself did not leave the world until he had done everything that it was necessary or desirable for him to do. It would not be kindness to keep God's people in this world, after their work was all done. But eternal life is begun on earth, as many Scriptures teach, John vi. 54; x. 28; xvii. 3. Tholuck: "The Psalmist may, at the time when he was composing this sublime Psalm, have had the presentiment of something more than the extension of temporal existence in speaking of long life. So the apostles employed the terms *death* and *life, light* and *darkness, peace* and *righteousness*, and others which they found in the Old Testament, in a far more profound sense." This view is strengthened by the parallelism of the last clause: *And shew him my salvation.* From the earliest use of the term *salvation* to the writing of the Apocalypse its import becomes more and more glorious, till all the redeemed are seen with crowns on their heads and palms in their hands around the throne of God and the Lamb. Calvin: "The salvation of God extends far beyond the narrow boundary of earthly existence;" Clarke: "He shall have an *eternity of blessedness* in the world to come;" Scott: "In heaven he will show them his complete salvation;" Nicolson: "That the prophet speaks of eternal felicity is more than probable;" Diodati: "The accomplishment of salvation is in the life everlasting."

DOCTRINAL AND PRACTICAL REMARKS.

1. The saints are at home in God, v. 1.

2 In God they have safety and protection, vv. 1, 2. Tholuck: "Though there is nothing more common than for men to profess that they are under the protection of the Most High, yet are there but few, who really believe what that profession involves."

3. The whole nature of God, including his holiness, justice, goodness, truth, power, wisdom, presence and all his perfections form a covering for the soul, against which all assaults are vain. The *shadow* is perfect, v. 1.

4. If we would find shelter and all needed help, we must accept the grace that is offered us in the promises. The name of the Lord is a strong tower. But if men

do not run into it, they are not safe, vv. 2, 9.   There is no pleasing God, or resting the soul without faith.   This faith should be strong, growing and openly professed.

5. As in all Christ's undertaking thus far there has been no failure, and no possibility of failure; so shall it be to the end, vv. 3, 13.   Should whole nations and generations reject him, he shall still be glorious, and have his reward, Isa. xlix. 5; liii. 10.

6. The cunning and craft of our adversaries might well alarm us, it is so deep and devilish; were it not that the wisdom of God is set over against it, v. 3.   As the fowler has more shrewdness than the bird, so has Satan more craft than the saints; but their safety is that Jehovah takes the wise in their own craftiness.

7. Although God has not promised that his people shall not leave the world by casualty or malady, as he did respecting their Lord, vv. 3, 6; yet this is their rejoicing that the manner of their departure is settled not by caprice or luck, but by infinite wisdom; not by malice, but by unfailing love.   Epidemics have no power but as they have a commission from God, v. 3.

8. How could we get on without the promises and doctrines of Scripture?   The former have all their force from the latter.   If we are not clad in the panoply of God's *truth*, we must fall, v. 4.   Dickson: "That which we must oppose to all perils is the word of God; so long as we keep that, and ward off darts and swords by that means, we shall not be overcome."

9. Blessed is he that has a calm and fearless trust in God, v. 5.   It is one of God's best gifts in this world.   It is a wondrous protection.   Nothing is so prudent as genuine courage.   It looks far into the past and the future.   "Confidence in God will divest the mind of that dread and anxiety, which threatening events are fitted to inspire."

10. No Christian knows what plots against himself and Christ's cause are laid and ready to be executed; but in this he may rejoice, that they are all powerless, unless God has some great and good end to answer by allowing them to be partly or wholly carried out, v. 5.

11. The same is true of open war and destruction attempted against the righteous, v. 6.   Luther: "This is the work of open persecution; whereby these holy Cains in their unheard-of cruelty and tyranny, shed the blood of the Abels, drive into exile the godly, plunder their substance, and slaughter them by every cruelty of torture."

12. In times of divine judgments when overflowing calamities are hurrying many to the grave, and death stalks abroad in terrible forms, let us not forget that there is mercy with God, and safety in him, v. 6.   In him we may defy all dangers.

12. It might well form a part of the pious occupation of God's people to note and celebrate their remarkable deliverances in times of public calamity.   When men are cut down all around us, and we escape, what less can we do than speak forth the praises of him, who did not allow the evil to *come nigh* us? v. 7.

13. We should tremble and adore when we are made witnesses of the terrible destruction of the wicked, vv. 7, 8.   "Be not high-minded but fear" is a fit and salutary lesson, especially when we are called to contemplate the doom of sinners.

14. Dickson: "The only persons, who are hurt by judgments and temptations. are such unfenced souls as believe not in God, are not reconciled with him, and stand at a distance opposite to him as the objects of his wrath."

15. In times of public calamity, as a general rule we should stand in our lot, and do and suffer the Lord's will there.   We may indeed flee from pestilence, if we neglect no duty in so doing.   This may sometimes be done, especially where a whole community may retire to a healthy spot.   Where this cannot be done, let physicians,

ministers of the Gospel, public officers and those who may be useful as nurses stand their ground, and commit their case to God. When moved by a right spirit such are in far less danger than many suppose. Their temperance and their courage are blessed as preservatives. It is the hireling that seeth the wolf coming and fleeth. Blessed be God, our great Shepherd did not so. Let us follow his example, and, if we fall, fall at the post of duty.

16. There is a God that judgeth in the earth. Sadly as saints may sometimes be perplexed, let them wait, and they shall see *the reward of the wicked*, v. 8. It will surely come with a vengeance so dreadful as to silence all cavillings of bad men, and all doubts of good men.

17. The connection of good men with the Lord is not transient and temporary, but settled and permanent. God is their *habitation*, v. 9. So that genuine believers go to him continually. Dickson: "The nature of true faith is to make use of God in all conditions; in peace and war, in prosperity and adversity."

18. All real evil is averted from the people of God, or is so controlled as in the end to do them good, v. 10. Compare Rom. viii. 28. Morison: "How blessed are they who feel themselves sheltered in the sanctuary which Jehovah has thrown around them in the day of trouble; and how comfortless must be that abode from which the cheering smile of the divine presence is withheld."

20. Amidst all the apparent confusion in the affairs of men, God does discriminate, and honest and careful observers may discern between the righteous and the wicked, v. 10. Did not the Lord smite the first-born of Egypt, both man and beast, and did he not spare all Israel? Does he not still do many like things?

21. God is at no loss for means, instruments or agents. Heaven and earth, sea and land, mind and matter are full of them. If there be need, he will send an angel, or a multitude of the heavenly host, and they shall do his work, vv. 11, 12. Jacob saw a ladder reaching from earth to heaven, and the angels ascending and descending on it, Gen. xxviii. 12. That ladder has never been removed. It might be seen at any time, if God would but open our eyes.

22. If we would have God's special care and the guardianship of his angels, let us remember that we must be found in the path of duty, v. 11. Dickson: "Promises are not made to foster men in their turning after folly, but to encourage them in the course of obedience in their several callings."

23. However huge and terrific the evils that threaten or assail us, they are all in the grasp of the Almighty. See Job v. 23; Isa. xi. 6–9; lxv. 25; Ezek. xxxiv. 25: Hos. ii. 18. Whether we regard these passages as literal or figurative does not destroy their power to support and cheer the child of God. Compare Rom. xvi. 20.

24. How clear and easily understood are the marks of true piety laid down in Scripture. Here they are few and decisive. A truly pious man, 1, sets his love on God; 2, he knows God's name; 3, he is a man of prayer, vv. 14, 15. Who has these marks is sure to have the rest. He will certainly be saved. There is no getting on without prayer, and prayer without love is hypocrisy, and prayer and love without knowledge are at best superstition, and that is a great offence to God. Calvin: "We are not at liberty in calling upon God to follow the suggestions of our own mind and will, but must seek God only in so far as he has invited us to approach him."

25. For all deliverances we must wait and give God his time. His interpositions and rewards are sure, but they are not to be hastened by fretting and impatience.

26. Let all the saints be joyful in God. Their inheritance is sure. Their gratitude should be warm and their obedience cheerful and universal. The protection and consolation promised to them and administered in their behalf will be matter of praise and wonder forever.

27. Nor let sinners forget that all these things deeply concern them. Indeed the answer to the question whether they shall be fiends or saints depends upon the state of their hearts towards such great and glorious truths as are revealed in this sacred poem.

PSALM XCII.

A Psalm *or* Song for the sabbath day.

1 *It is* a good thing to give thanks unto the LORD, and to sing praises unto thy name, O Most High:

2 To shew forth thy lovingkindness in the morning, and thy faithfulness every night,

3 Upon an instrument of ten strings, and upon the psaltery; upon the harp with a solemn sound.

4 For thou, LORD, hast made me glad through thy work: I will triumph in the works of thy hands.

5 O LORD, how great are thy works! *and* thy thoughts are very deep.

6 A brutish man knoweth not; neither doth a fool understand this.

7 When the wicked spring as the grass, and when all the workers of iniquity do flourish; *it is* that they shall be destroyed for ever:

8 But thou, LORD, *art most* high for evermore.

9 For, lo, thine enemies, O LORD, for, lo, thine enemies shall perish; all the workers of iniquity shall be scattered.

10 But my horn shalt thou exalt like *the horn of* a unicorn: I shall be anointed with fresh oil.

11 Mine eye also shall see *my desire* on mine enemies, *and* mine ears shall hear *my desire* of the wicked that rise up against me.

12 The righteous shall flourish like the palm tree: he shall grow like a cedar in Lebanon.

13 Those that be planted in the house of the LORD shall flourish in the courts of our God.

14 They shall still bring forth fruit in old age; they shall be fat and flourishing;

15 To shew that the LORD *is* upright: he *is* my rock, and *there is* no unrighteousness in him.

ON *Psalm* or *Song* in the title see on title of Psalm xxx. *For the Sabbath day* is a part of the title uniformly preserved in the best Hebrew copies, also by the Chaldee, Arabic, Septuagint, Ethiopic and Vulgate. The ode is very suitable for the Sabbath. Calvin: "There is no reason to doubt that the Jews were in the habit of singing this Psalm upon the Sabbath-day." Hengstenberg: "According to its contents, it is manifestly well adapted for such a use." Alexander: "As one main design of the Sabbath was to afford an opportunity for the admiring contemplation of God's works or doings, the Psalm before us was peculiarly appropriate at such a time." The authorship of the Psalm is unknown. The Chaldee ascribes it to the *first man,* Adam. So do many Jewish writers, and a few Christians. It does not militate against this view that this Psalm is not placed first in the collection. The Psalms are not arranged according to date. Those, who take Adam to be the author, hold that it was written by him either in innocence before the fall, or very soon after he left paradise. Either of these views of the *time* of writing is fatal to the idea of Adamic authorship. For in verse three, musical instruments are mentioned; and there were none such till long after the ejection from Eden, Gen. iv. 21. Nor were there in any portion of the early part of Adam's life numerous wicked men such as the author of this poem intimates in vv. 7, 9, 11. We may, therefore, safely conclude that Adam did not write it. That Moses was not its author is generally agreed, though some have ascribed it to him. They rely on the supposition that as he is confessedly the author of Psalm xc. he wrote all that came after it till another Psalmist is named. But on Psalm xci. this reasoning has been shown to be unsound. The more probable opinion is that it was written by David. So the Arabic, Henry, Dodd and others. Scott: "In all probability David composed it." Nor can we assign to it any historic occasion. It is probable it had none. Patrick thinks it was probably written when God gave David *Rest* from his enemies. Others suggest other times; but all of them are mere conjectures, some more probable than others, but none of them reliable. Scott dates it B. C. 1045. Calmet thinks it was written during the captivity. The names of the Almighty here found are *Jehovah* LORD; *Gel-yohn Most High* and *Elohim God;* on which respectively see on Ps. i. 2; vii. 17; iii. 2. The scope of the ode is apparent. It is a song of praise, praise for God's works, especially works of creation, providence and redemption, though providence is prominent. Tholuck: "This song celebrates the righteousness of the divine government of the world." Calvin: "This Psalm contains an exhortation to praise God, and shows how much ground we have for this exercise from the works of God, insisting, especially, upon his justice, displayed in the protection of his people, and the destruction of the wicked." Gill: "It was made *for the Sabbath-day,* and to be used upon it; and directs to the work and worship of it; praising of God and celebrating his works, attending his house and ordinances." Alexander: "The immediate subject of the praise is the exhibition of God's power and wisdom in his providential dealings both with the wicked and the righteous."

1. It is *a good* thing *to give thanks unto the* LORD, *and to sing praises unto thy name, O Most High.* The rendering is quite uniform. *Give thanks,* see on Ps. vi. 5. *Sing praises,* see on Ps. ix. 2. There is no reason to fear that our service will be too elevated or too absorbing. The great truth of the verse is the excellence of gratefully worshipping God. In every sense *it is a good thing.* 1. God commends it in many places. 2. Good men of every age have set us the example. 3. Our relations to God loudly call for it. 4. This part of worship is very delightful, cheering and animating. 5. Praise and thanksgiving will be retained in heaven. Yea, it is good

2. *To shew forth thy lovingkindness in the morning, and thy faithfulness every night.* *Lovingkindness,* see on Ps. v. 7, where it is rendered *mercy.* *Faithfulness,* from the root of *Amen.* See on Ps. xxxiii. 4; xxxvi. 5. There is no stronger word for either of the conceptions here expressed. God's nature and ways are fit matters for public as well as private celebration both night and morning, that is, continually and earnestly. Calvin: "He means that beginning to praise the Lord from earliest dawn, we should continue his praises to the latest hour of the night, this being no more than his goodness and faithfulness deserve." Patrick: "This is the sweetest employment in the morning; and no entertainment can be equal to it at night: to commemorate and declare to all, how bountiful thou art; and how faithful in performing thy promises to those who depend on thy almighty goodness." Hengstenberg: "The *mercy* and *faithfulness* of God are those properties, which guarantee help to his people, and which are manifested in their deliverance." And the Psalmist would have this worship conducted in the most joyous and solemn manner, even

3. *Upon an instrument of ten strings, and upon the psaltery; upon the harp with a solemn sound.* On the instruments here named, see on Ps. xxxiii. 2. Instead of *solemn sound* some read *a meditation;* the Hebrew is *Higgaion,* on which see on Ps. ix. 16. In Ps. xix. 14, the same word is rendered *meditation.* It occurs but a few times. Either a *solemn sound,* or *musing* gives a good sense. The old French has *melody of the voice.* There was a special call for grateful worship:

4. *For thou,* LORD, *hast made me glad through thy work: I will triumph in the works of thy hands.* *Made me glad, made me joyful, rejoiced me.* *Triumph,* often rendered

sing, cry, cry out, sing for joy, shout. It imports an expression of strong and exultant emotion. *Work* and *works* (different words) cover the whole field of divine operations in creation, providence and redemption. The *Sabbath* was at first instituted in commemoration of God's works of creation. These are very glorious. Had not man sinned, much of his time would have been spent in studying their wonders. The works of providence are not less striking and unsearchable. But the work of redemption eclipses them all. Well is the Christian Sabbath kept in honor of the completion of this work by the resurrection of the Son of God from the dead. The pious soul can never be without grand themes of praise and thanksgiving.

5. *O Lord, how great are thy works!* For *great* Calvin suggests *magnificent*. Nothing could be more natural than such an exclamation. By our unaided senses we may study contiguous objects till our minds feel exhausted. By powerful telescopes we may explore the heavens till we are overwhelmed with amazement, and fear we are too insignificant to attract the divine regard. We may then turn the microscope upon the vast world that eludes our unaided senses, and there we shall find innumerable tribes of creatures all well cared for and displaying the skill and kindness of infinite perfections. When we become students of providence we find ourselves no less amazed. And when we contemplate redemption, the best we can do is to wonder and adore, Ps. xl. 5; Rom. xi. 33. And *thy thoughts are very deep.* Alexander: " *Deep*, not mysterious, but vast, immense, and inexhaustible, corresponding to *great* in the other clause." In Hos. v. 2, the same word is rendered *profound*. God's *thoughts* and *works* are his counsels and operations, his plans and his doings. They are so vast that they must be mysterious to us worms.

6. *A brutish man knoweth not; neither doth a fool understand this.* Every man is altogether brutish and foolish, as long as he is left to himself and is not taught of God, Jer. x. 8, 14; li. 17. Good men often and deeply lament their dreadful blindness and want of discernment, Pr. xxx. 2. But carnal men see nothing aright. For *brutish man* Alexander reads " man-brute, meaning a man who is no better than a brute." The blindness and insensibility of men to spiritual things are appalling, Isa. i. 3; 1 Cor. ii. 14. *This* refers either to some particular work of God specially celebrated in this Psalm, or to the fact that God's thoughts are very deep.

7. *When the wicked spring as the grass, and when all the workers of iniquity do flourish; it is that they shall be destroyed for ever.* Pool: " Their present worldly prosperity is a presage and occasion of their utter and eternal ruin." See on Ps. xxxvii 2. When a cedar of Lebanon flourishes, it is that it may become strong and useful. But the course of the grass is very short, not half a summer. " Their end is destruction." The contrast is two-fold, first between *flourishing* and *destruction*, and then between *the time of grass-growing* and *for ever*.

8. *But thou, Lord, art most high for evermore. Most high*, in 2 Kings xix. 23, a *height*; in Mic. vi. 6, *high* God; in Ps. lvi. 2, as here *most high*. In every sense God is gloriously exalted—above want, above casualty, above the power of enemies, above the necessity of human expedients, above all possibility of suffering—and all this to eternity.

9. *For, lo, thine enemies, O Lord, for, lo, thine enemies shall perish. Enemies*, as in Ps. iii. 7; vi. 10. *Perish*, often so rendered; sometimes *be lost, be destroyed. All the workers of iniquity shall be scattered, sundered, parted, divided, separated, dispersed.* Compare Ps. i. 5; lxviii. 1; Matt. xxv. 32. The combinations of the wicked have in themselves the elements of weakness and of dissolution. Were they ever so strong, the Almighty would dissolve them with a breath. See Job xiv. 11, 12.

10. *But my horn shalt thou exalt like* the horn of *a unicorn. Unicorn*, see on Ps. xxii. 21. On *exalting the horn* see on Ps. xviii. 2; lxxv. 4. The general import is,

Thou shalt deliver me from depressing influences, and give me enlargement so that I may go forth in strength, freedom and joy. *I shall be anointed with fresh oil.* Anointing was either for consecration to office, 1 Sam. xv. 1; Ps. ii. 2; or, as an expression of personal cheerfulness, 2 Sam. xii. 20; or, as a token of special regard. In this last sense we here take the phrase; see on Ps. xxiii. 6. But this anointing was at a time of gladness. *Fresh,* the opposite of stale; applied to a bed *newly made,* Cant. i. 16. This is quite the meaning here. Calvin: "By *fresh* oil is meant, such as has not become corrupted, or unfit for use by age."

11. *Mine eye also shall see* my desire *on mine enemies,* and *mine ears shall hear* my desire *of the wicked that rise up against me. My desire* were better omitted. His enemies were evil-doers; and the end of all such is not doubtful. Scott: "The passage might better be read, 'Mine eyes shall look upon mine enemies, and mine ears shall hear of the wicked that rise up against me.'" *Enemies,* the Hebrew word is found nowhere else. It denotes those who marked him with an evil eye.

12. *The righteous shall flourish like the palm tree.* The palm is a tall and beautiful evergreen. It bears fruit and furnishes a fine shade. It is very flourishing. It cannot be so depressed as to grow crooked. It grows erect or not at all. It is the "emblem of constancy, patience, fruitfulness, and victory." It most abounds near springs and water-courses. No tree is put to so many uses by eastern nations. Nor has the righteous merely the things set forth by the emblem of the palm. *He shall grow like a cedar in Lebanon.* This tree was lofty, strong, living more than a thousand years, furnishing a grateful shade for many, and yielding a very valuable timber for architecture. To one familiar with eastern scenery, the palm and the cedar furnish striking emblems of the righteous.

13. *Those that be planted in the house of the* LORD *shall flourish in the courts of our God. Planted,* as in a good soil, so as to take root and have a permanent connection with the divinely appointed worship of God, and to draw nourishment from divine ordinances. Such shall *flourish,* elsewhere, *bud, grow, spring, break forth, blossom.*

14. *They shall still bring forth fruit in old age.* The fruit borne by the good man is the *fruit of the Spirit.* We know what it is, Gal. v. 22, 23; 2 Pet. i. 5–7, compared with Matt. v. 3–12. It would be sad indeed if God forsook his aged servants and left them to wither in spirit as they fail in bodily vigor. A young tree covered with blossoms is a pleasant and promising sight; but an old tree laden with choice fruit is still more delightful to behold. Fruit-bearing alone can prove a tree good. *They shall be fat and flourishing. Fat,* found also in Ps. xxii. 29; Isa. xxx. 23. A tree is fat when it is full of nourishing sap. *Flourishing,* in v. 10, *fresh,* commonly *green.* It does not please us to see "a green young man;" but we rejoice in saying of a venerable man that he has "a green old age." And all this

15. *To shew that the* LORD *is upright,* is as good as his word, is faithful to his promise, is loving to his friends, and remembers his covenant. Having loved his own, he loves them to the end. He is *my rock,* in Ps. xviii. 2, *my strength. And* there is *no unrighteousness in him. Unrighteousness,* elsewhere *iniquity, wickedness,* Job v. 16; Ps. lviii. 2. This clause may include not only God's treatment of the righteous, as noticed in vv. 10–14, but also his very different treatment of the wicked, as stated in vv. 7, 9, 11. The whole course of providence to saints and sinners, when finished, will show that with God are found equity, and plenty of justice.

DOCTRINAL AND PRACTICAL REMARKS.

1. Greatly has God honored the Sabbath day. At the end of creation he set us the example of hallowing it; see title. On Mount Sinai he gave the *fourth* commandment more full than any other. Under every subsequent state of the church

he commanded its observance. Calvin: "The right observance of the Sabbath does not consist in idleness, as some absurdly imagine, but in the celebration of the divine name."

2. Let God's people abound in praise and thanksgiving. Pool: "It is a good work, and a just debt to God;" Luther: "Oh what is sweeter than to know God aright by his word, and by true faith; to acknowledge his infinite mercies; to give thanks unto him joyfully and adoringly, with every chord and string of our hearts; to proclaim and praise him unceasingly with a full heart and a full mouth." We have nothing but sin and its consequent misery, except as the fruit of his bounty and compassion.

3. This is not the only part of Scripture that mentions morning and night as seasons specially calling us to the devout worship of God, v. 2. We may add other times; but surely it is not unreasonable for us twice in twenty-four hours to make it a special duty to draw nigh to God.

4. Though the enjoyments of God's people are in this life far from being what they long for, they are yet worth more than all the joys of the wicked and they are blessed pledges of better things hereafter. Even now they are *glad;* but in due time they shall mightily *triumph,* v. 4. They have victories now; but their career shall be brighter and brighter forever.

5. Though some men may not be able to acquire much worldly learning, yet all ought to be students of God's *works,* v. 5. Every leaf, and seed and insect, every planet and every star, every act and course of providence, every display of mercy in saving a sinner by the grace of Christ, demand and will richly repay our adoring wonder, Ps. iii. 2. Every one of his works is in its way *great.* All angels and all men united could not make one grasshopper.

6. And yet men are so besotted by sin, so sunk down in spiritual ignorance, that left to themselves they will study science and read history like atheists; they will avow infidelity with an open Bible before them, and perish in full view of the cross; unless God sends his Holy Spirit to teach and guide them, so *brutish* and foolish are they when left to themselves, v. 6. Is not he a *fool,* who prefers time to eternity, earth to heaven, the world to its Maker, sin to holiness, death to life? Is not he *brutish* who like the ox feeds greedily, and grows fat, and knows not that it is for the slaughter? Is not he brutish who cares more for his appetite than for his immortal soul?

7. It is therefore a great weakness in any one to envy the wicked, however grand and prosperous they may be; for dark times are before them, vv. 7, 9, 11. All they value so highly is both vain and fleeting. Arnd: "Nothing, except it be of God, can stand, whether it be skill, or riches, or honor, or power. It rises and flourishes to appearance, but in the end it is only a thistle bush and a noxious weed, good for nothing but the fire." The higher one rises in pride and prosperity, the more dreadful will be his doom at last. The ruin of ungodly men rests on their own unfitness for communion with God and on his infinite abhorrence of all sin.

8. The certainty of the final triumph of the righteous and of the final downfall of the wicked is confirmed by the complete sovereignty and absolute independence of God himself. He is *most high for evermore,* v. 8. Were it possible in any way to subject him to the will of another all hope for the order of the universe would be gone.

9. Let the righteous cheer up; good days are coming, when their *horn shall be exalted* and they shall be *anointed with fresh oil,* v. 10.

10 As in the growth of trees much depends upon the soil in which they are planted; so is it with the trees of righteousness. They would never *flourish* as they

do were they not planted in the courts of our God, v. 13. The Lord well knew this, and so he made his church a garden walled around. And he waters it as a garden of herbs. Compare Cant. iv. 12. Oh that the Beloved would come amongst us; for his presence makes the desert like the garden of God.

11. Although God's real children have a deep and abiding sense of their own unworthiness and imperfections; yet they are not hypocrites, vv. 12–14. The palm and the cedar are but feeble emblems of their excellence. When all the amazing growth of centuries shall have passed away or been burned up, the righteous will but have fairly commenced their career of glory and usefulness.

12. It is not true that as nature fails, grace also decays. It is true that the novelty of Christian experience ceases. But the real child of God is so much the more in earnest as he sees his redemption draw nigh. Owen: "There are two things, which those who after a long profession of the gospel are entering into the confines of eternity, do long for and desire. The one is, that all their breaches may be repaired, their decays recovered, their backslidings healed: for unto these things they have been less or more obnoxious in the course of their walking before God. The other is that they may have fresh springs of spiritual life, and vigorous actings of all divine graces, in spiritual-mindedness, holiness, and fruitfulness, unto the praise of God, the honor of the gospel, and their own peace and joy. These things they value more than all the world, and all that is in it; about these things are their thoughts and contrivances exercised night and day." Scott: "Let us learn to detest the sentiment of many, who profess much zeal for the peculiar doctrines of the gospel, yet would persuade us that believers generally grow less zealous as they grow older." God's aged servants are a wonder unto many, Ps. lxxi. 7. Indeed they are a wonder to themselves. But the secret of their growth and success is that their life is hid with Christ in God. Tholuck: "Experience instructs us that pious old men are the most powerful and efficient witnesses and preachers to younger generations; in whom piety bears the sweetest fruit the nearer they are to their grave." Dickson: "True believers shall still persevere, and the decay of the outward man shall not hinder the renewing of their inward man day by day, and their last works shall be better than their first." These remarks are the more extended and these testimonies are the more multiplied, because the error they oppose is very widely diffused, and the truth they establish is of great importance to the honor of God and the comfort of religious people. Blessed be God, his children are born of incorruptible seed. Grace does not die out in the soul. "The longer it acts on the human spirit, the more vigorous does it become in its operation."

13. Let us cleave to God alone. He is a *Rock*, v. 15. He is our strength. He is our all. His character is spotless and adorable.

PSALM XCIII.

1 The LORD reigneth, he is clothed with majesty; the LORD is clothed with strength, *wherewith* he hath girded himself: the world also is stablished, that it cannot be moved.

2 Thy throne *is* established of old: thou *art* from everlasting.

3 The floods have lifted up, O LORD, the floods have lifted up their voice; the floods lift up their waves.

4 The LORD on high *is* mightier than the noise of many waters, *yea, than* the mighty waves of the sea.

5 Thy testimonies are very sure: holiness becometh thine house, O LORD, for ever.

THE Syriac, Arabic, Septuagint, Ethiopic and Vulgate ascribe this Psalm to David as its author. Gill also thinks it was probably written by David. Clarke takes a different view. He says: "It was probably written at the close of the captivity by the *Levites*, descendants of Moses." The whole question of authorship is involved in uncertainty; but David is more likely to be its author than any one else. If it had a historic occasion we cannot ascertain what it was. For a long time the Jews used it in public worship on the *sixth* day of the week. Horsley styles it "A hymn for the Sabbath day." The opinion of Mudge seems to have a slender foundation. He thought the Psalm was written on occasion of some violent inundation. But floods and waters are favorite emblems of tumults and commotions in kingdoms and nations. Hengstenberg thinks the Psalm "presupposes a powerful pressure from the might of the world against the kingdom of God, and, consequently, cannot be dated earlier than the Assyrian catastrophe." He thinks it has an apparent dependence on Psalm xlvi. Perhaps none of these views will be regarded as satisfactory. The scope of this poem is given with confidence by many. It is clearly an assertion of the supreme and universal government of Jehovah over all things; from which doctrine the strongest consolations are drawn in times of public danger. Is this Psalm Messianic? The old Jewish doctors say it is. Luther: "This is a prophecy concerning the spread of the kingdom of Christ, as far and wide as the earth is extended, and its establishment forever;" Gill: "The subject of the Psalm is the kingdom of God; not of nature and providence, but of grace; the kingdom of the Messiah;" Henry: "It relates both to the kingdom of providence, by which he upholds and governs the world, and especially to the kingdom of his grace, by which he secures the church, sanctifies and preserves it. The administration of both these kingdoms is put into the hands of the Messiah, and to him, doubtless, the prophet here bears witness." Such is the view taken by the best commentators generally. Scott dates it B. C. 1045; Clarke, B. C. 536. The only name of the Most High in this poem is *Jehovah* LORD; on which see on Ps. i. 2.

1. *The* LORD *reigneth, he is clothed with majesty.* For *majesty*, several read *glory;* others, *excellency*, and some, *magnificence.* Church of England: The LORD is king, and hath put on glorious apparel. *Reigned*, in the preterite *has reigned.* There never was another universal king. God always reigned above and supreme, over all creatures and all causes. *Majesty*, as in Isa. xxvi. 10; God is possessed of all the glory and excellency which fit him to be governor and king. Not only is Jehovah clothed with majesty, but, *The* LORD *is clothed with strength*, wherewith *he hath girded himself. Clothed, arrayed.* The English cannot be improved. *Strength*, as in Ps. viii. 2; xxi. 1, 13; first found in Ex. xv. 2. Jehovah is fully able to do all he has undertaken. This is abundantly proved: *for the world is stablished, that it cannot be moved.* The best machinery for measuring time requires constant repairs and regulation; but Jehovah rolls the solar system along with amazing regularity. Nothing is firmer than the order of nature, and yet God hangs the earth upon nothing. All things depend on Jehovah Jesus, Isa. ix. 6; Col. i. 17.

2. *Thy throne* is *established of old: thou* art *from everlasting.* Jehovah's kingdom is not new, but from the beginning; not variable, but stable, and like himself *from eternity.* This is much like Ps. xlv. 6, which we know refers to Christ. See also Pr. viii. 22–31. The manifestation of the kingly authority of heaven has not always been the same; but the power has been the same. Horne: "The throne of Christ is eternal and unchangeable," Rev. xix. 16.

3. *The floods have lifted up, O* LORD, *the floods have lifted up their voice; the floods lift up their waves.*

4. *The* LORD *on high is mightier than the noise of many waters*, yea, *than the mighty*

waves of the sea. These verses are united in all the ancient versions but the Chaldee. Many modern commentators connect them. It is not easy to consider them apart. *Floods*, the same word thrice repeated in Hebrew. For *waves* Edwards has *crashing waves;* Alexander, *crash;* Hengstenberg, *roaring noise.* There is great diversity in rendering verse 4. Chaldee: By the voices of many waters, by the praises of the waves of the sea the Lord is praised in the higher heavens; Calvin: The waves of the sea are terrible, by reason of the noise of great waters, Jehovah is terrible above; Tremellius and Junius: Than the sound of many waters, than the magnificent waves of the sea breaking in, is Jehovah on high more grand; church of England: The waves of the sea are mighty, and rage horribly; but yet the Lord, who dwelleth on high, is mightier; Hengstenberg: Than the voices of many waters, than the glorious waves of the sea, more glorious in the height is the Lord. Perhaps both the learned and the plain reader will conclude that the common version gives the sense fully as well as any other. The senses gathered from these verses are such as these: 1. By *the voice of the floods*, etc., some understand the apostles and early preachers of the Gospel, whose ministrations were like floods irresistible, and who were sustained by the power of God, who is yet mightier than the mighty waters. 2. Others think that the prophet means that terribly as nature and nations may be convulsed, we need not fear, for God can control them, being greater than they. 3. Some think the Psalmist would contrast the power of furious waters with the strength of God, and so would teach us that if troubled and mighty waters were alarming, the majesty and power of Jehovah were much more so, and therefore we should greatly fear before him. 4. Others think that the Psalmist is celebrating the power of God as illustrated in the floods of water, and especially in the agitated sea, and would teach us how great must be the power of that being, who can so mightily move the waters and command them. 5. A yet larger number by *floods* and *waters* understand cruel and wicked enemies, who come with a great show of power. They cite Ps. xviii. 4, "The floods of ungodly men made me afraid;" also Isa. viii. 7, 8; xvii. 12–14; Jer. xlvi. 7–10. This view is well supported by the figurative language of Scripture. By *floods* and *waters* these think we are to understand mighty foes; but they say God is mightier than they, and so we need not fear. Perhaps this is the mind of the Spirit.

5. *Thy testimonies are very sure.* Every perfection of God, his omnipotence included, renders certain the fulfilment of all he has spoken. See on Ps. xix. 7. Scott: "Revealed truth and the promises grounded on it are 'the testimonies' of God, which 'are very sure,' and can never fail." Some think that in this place *testimonies* specially refer to promises. But all divine truth is connected. The promises will no more surely be fulfilled than the threatenings, and are no more true than the doctrines. All that God has spoken are his *true sayings*, Rev. xix. 9. If in one thing he could fail, he might in the rest. The preceding verse taught that God was able to defend his people. This says he will keep his word. *Holiness becometh thine house, O* LORD *forever.* The Chaldee applies the whole verse to God's word: Thy testimonies are very true; they will befit the house of thy sanctuary: they are holy, O Lord, unto length of days. But the great body of scholars favor a rendering not dissimilar to that in our version. What then is the meaning of the clause? Four views have been taken. 1. By somewhat varying the rendering some get this sense: The adorning of thy house is precious. The objections to this are that the grammatical construction will not warrant it, and that there is nothing in the connection to call for such a remark. 2. Others think the meaning is this: God's holiness as displayed in his appointed worship is the pledge of his truth and the guaranty of the right exercise of his power and of all his perfections. This proposition contains a great truth; but is it taught here? 3. By holiness others understand sacredness, freedom from profaneness, and from unhallowed intrusion.

Hengstenberg: "It is becoming in God that he take care that his house be not *desecrated* by impious hands." Compare Ps. lxxix. 1. 4. Holiness becomes the worshippers and all the arrangements of God's house. This is the common view and the best. It is eminently practical, and a fitting conclusion of the poem. Morison: "Let all them, who name his name, depart from iniquity; let everything about his sanctuary be pure." Horne: "Sacred and inviolable is the word of our King; sacred and inviolable should be the loyalty of his subjects." Henry: "Nothing better becomes the saints than conformity to God's image, and an entire devotedness to his honor."

Doctrinal and Practical Remarks.

1. Let us firmly believe the great doctrine of the divine government over the world, v. 1. It is clearly revealed in Scripture. It is the pillar of hope that stands firm, when all around us is falling to pieces. Luther: "The kingdoms and peoples of the world will roar against the Lord and against his Anointed; and will rage against the godly with sword and fire; but they shall not prevail: for as Daniel saith, 'this kingdom shall break in pieces all other kingdoms beneath it, and shall stand for ever.'"

2. Let us also strive to know something of the vigor and force of God's government of the world, v. 1. It is not feeble, contemptible, liable to be subverted at any time. Dickson: "How strong soever the adverse powers of the world seem, it must not terrify the believer in following the Lord's cause, but his strength must be opposed thereunto, and that so much the more comfortably, as God's strength is not borrowed from any, as the strength of the creature is."

3. If such is the government of God, let us exceedingly fear to offend him, v. 1. His majesty and power make the worship of heaven itself awful.

4. But let us not be frightened away from him; but rather draw near to him confidingly, and hide in the chambers of his omnipotence, v. 1.

5. The God of nature is the God of providence and the God of grace. He that made the world rules it, and, if it is ever saved, its salvation must be of the Lord, v. 1. Indeed the scheme of mercy through a Mediator is a chief and glorious part in God's administration of human affairs.

6. It is matter of joy to all the pious that God's government of the world is not something new, but is *established of old*, v. 2. Had God at any time permitted the world to be governed by another, we might well fear that he would do so again. Thus all our hopes would be blasted. Dickson: "The Lord's kingdom in his church is not like the new upstarts in this world, which are of short standing and unstable. If any king be kind to his church, his people have reason to thank God, but they must not lean to such a king, his reign shall be short: and if any king be froward, and oppose himself to the church, we must not be too much afraid of him, because his kingdom is but lately begun, and is of short continuance."

7. It is no new thing for God's church and people to have enemies, numerous as violent, v. 3. It has been so ever since the days of Cain. Mightily have evil men combined against God's cause. Terribly did Roman emperors and governors rage against Christ and his people. Christians, no strange thing happens to you, when the wicked bend the bow against you. Because the kingdom of Christ is divine, it has withstood all the shocks, and shall continue to survive all the assaults made upon it.

8. When foes and fears prevail, carry the matter to the Lord, and tell him all about it, v. 3. When John Baptist was beheaded, his disciples came, and took up the body, and buried it, and WENT AND TOLD JESUS.

9. Let persecutors remember that there is no possibility of their stopping communications between God and his chosen, v. 3. The cries of the abused and wronged

are always going up to heaven, and God's grace is ever granted to the humble, who call upon him.

10. However much men may boast themselves, and however puissant the potentates of earth may be; yet over all human affairs there is a presiding deity, who is mightier than all, v. 4. "Pharaoh, king of Egypt, is but a noise," Jer. xlvi. 17. A nod of the Almighty can bring any fabric of human greatness tumbling about the ears of its possessors.

11. Let pious men never lose sight of God's veracity, nor doubt the fulfilment of all he has spoken, v. 5. His word is truth. All that is opposed to it is a lie. Up to this day Jehovah has not failed to perform all that he engaged.

12. Let us strive after holiness, v. 5. It is essential to salvation. Without it an angel is but a devil, and a professor of religion but a loathsome hypocrite. Henry: "Fashions change, and what is becoming at one time is not at another; but holiness always becomes God's house and family, and those who belong to it; it is perpetually decent; and nothing so ill becomes the worshippers of God as unholiness."

13. How many wonderful things are presented to the mind of the devout and contemplative, even in this one short Psalm. If any do not think, it cannot be for want of a theme. God, his providence, Christ, his kingdom, his love, his faithfulness and heaven itself we may dwell upon, until our souls are filled with satisfaction and ravished with delight.

14. Let us not fail to give to Christ whatever place is assigned to him in prophecy, in history, in the promises, and in the government and salvation of the world.

PSALM XCIV.

1. O LORD God, to whom vengeance belongeth; O God, to whom vengeance belongeth, shew thyself.

2 Lift up thyself, thou Judge of the earth: render a reward to the proud.

3 LORD, how long shall the wicked, how long shall the wicked triumph?

4 *How long* shall they utter *and* speak hard things? *and* all the workers of iniquity boast themselves?

5 They break in pieces thy people, O LORD, and afflict thine heritage.

6 They slay the widow and the stranger, and murder the fatherless.

7 Yet they say, The LORD shall not see, neither shall the God of Jacob regard *it*.

8 Understand, ye brutish among the people: and *ye* fools, when will ye be wise?

9 He that planted the ear, shall he not hear? he that formed the eye, shall he not see?

10 He that chastiseth the heathen, shall not he correct? he that teacheth man knowledge, *shall not he know?*

11 The LORD knoweth the thoughts of man, that they *are* vanity.

12 Blessed *is* the man whom thou chastenest, O LORD, and teachest him out of thy law;

13 That thou mayest give him rest from the days of adversity, until the pit be digged for the wicked.

14 For the LORD will not cast off his people, neither will he forsake his inheritance.

15 But judgment shall return unto righteousness: and all the upright in heart shall follow it.

16 Who will rise up for me against the evil doers? *or* who will stand up for me against the workers of iniquity?

17 Unless the LORD *had been* my help, my soul had almost dwelt in silence.

18 When I said, My foot slippeth; thy mercy, O LORD, held me up.

19 In the multitude of my thoughts within me thy comforts delight my soul.

20 Shall the throne of iniquity have fellowship with thee, which frameth mischief by a law?

21 They gather themselves together against the soul of the righteous, and condemn the inno-cent blood.

22 But the LORD is my defence; and my God *is* the rock of my refuge.

23 And he shall bring upon them their own iniquity, and shall cut them off in their own wickedness; *yea,* the LORD our God shall cut them off.

THE Syriac, Arabic, Septuagint, Ethiopic and Vulgate give David as the author of this Psalm. Some Jewish doctors ascribe it to Moses. The authorship cannot be known, though David may have written it. See on Ps. xci.–xciii. All attempts to give it a historic occasion have been failures. Scott dates it B. C. 1060. Several ancient versions say it was designed to be sung on the fourth day of the week. Some Jews say it was used on that day. The names of the Almighty found in it are *El* God, *Jehovah* LORD, *Jah* LORD and *Elohim* God, on which respectively see on Ps. v. 4; i. 2; introduction to Ps. lxviii.; and on Ps. iii. 2.

1. *O* LORD *God, to whom vengeance belongeth; O God, to whom vengeance belongeth, shew thyself. Vengeance,* in the plural, *vengeances;* so many render it. With God is plenty of justice. The fundamental passage is Deut. xxxii. 35. Compare Rom. xii. 19. To the modern English reader, *vengeance* sometimes conveys the idea of spite or excitement of malicious feeling. But the older Dictionaries do not even hint at this sense of the term. Vengeance is penal retribution, condign punishment. Its parallel is *recompense.* God alone is strong enough, wise enough or pure enough to make full awards to his creatures. Luther: "He puts down *God of vengeance* twice, as those are wont to do who speak vehemently, and with great earnestness." *Shew thyself;* in Ps. lxxx. 1, shine forth. The meaning is explained in verse

2. *Lift up thyself, thou Judge of the earth: render a reward to the proud.* A *reward* is a fit return. This prayer is a prophecy. If it were not, it consists with pure bene-volence. Desperate would be the case of the meek and injured, if they could not ask God to undertake their cause, and not give them over to the reign of wicked men and devils. Calvin: "O Lord! it is thine to take vengeance upon sinners and judge the earth—see how they take advantage of the impunity which is extended to their guilt, and triumph audaciously in their wickedness." *Judge,* a participle often and properly rendered as a noun. *Lift up thyself;* Hengstenberg, rise up thou. He pleads, Do not seem longer to be indifferent to the enormities of thy foes.

3. LORD, *how long shall the wicked, how long shall the wicked triumph?* Pleasant days pass swiftly; but hours of misery are tedious. When our sorrow arises from the success of wicked men and their triumph over the righteous, our weariness is very great. Then even good men are often perplexed with doubts respecting the existence and the righteousness of providence. Faith and love themselves cry out importu-nately and imploringly. *How long?* as in Ps. vi. 3. *Wicked,* in Ps. i. *ungodly. Triumph,* in Ps. xxviii. 7, *greatly rejoice;* in Ps. lxviii. 4, *rejoice;* it expresses exultant emotion. The repetition of *How long* shows great urgency.

4. How long *shall they utter* and *speak hard things!* and *all the workers of iniquity boast themselves? How long* is borrowed from the preceding verse. It is retained by the church of England and others. Edwards marks the verse with a note of exclama-tion. Calvin, Jebb and others drop the interrogative form. Fabritius: They prate rashly, they speak hardly, all the workers of iniquity boast themselves; Hengsten-berg: They sputter, speak impudent things, they brag, all the evil-doers. *Utter,* as in Ps. xix. 2; in a bad sense in Ps. lix. 7, *belch out. Hard things,* in Ps. xxxi. 18, *grievous things;* in 1 Sam. ii. 3, *arrogancy. Boast themselves,* literally, *talk of themselves,* as boasters do without any necessity.

5. *They break in pieces thy people, O* LORD, *and afflict thine heritage.* Disdain and scorn lead to persecution. *Break in pieces,* elsewhere rendered humble, smite,

bruise, crush, destroy, oppress, beat to pieces, Jer. xliv. 10; Ps. cxliii. 3; Isa. liii. 10; Lam. iii. 34; Job vi. 9; Pr. xxii. 22; Isa. iii. 15. *Thy people,* meaning either the chosen nation of the Jews, or God's chosen people in that nation, as hated by the sons of Belial. The latter seems most consistent with the scope of the context. *Afflict,* often so rendered, also humble, weaken, compel submission in acts of degradation. God's people are his *heritage.* Wars and tumults animated with the spirit of persecution have been truly hideous and frightful. The haters of the Lord have no compassion:

6. *They slay the widow and the stranger, and murder the fatherless.* These nouns have no other rendering; and the verb is well given. The acts complained of were in the teeth of the best laws, Ex. xxii. 21–24; Deut. x. 18; xiv. 29. By the persons named some understand the sad and helpless people of God. Taken literally or figuratively the language is forcible.

7. *Yet they say, The* LORD *shall not see, neither shall the God of Jacob regard* it. Instead of *Jehovah,* we have here the poetic form *Jah.* From hatred to God's people, from temporary success and from impunity in crime, the wicked come to deny providence. Calvin: "He intends to express the lowest and most abandoned stage of depravity, in which the sinner casts off the fear of God, and rushes into every excess. Such infatuated conduct would have been inexcusable even in heathens, who had never heard of a divine revelation; but it was monstrous in men who had been brought up from infancy in the knowledge of the word, to show such mockery and contempt of God." Compare Ps. x. 11, 13.

8. *Understand, ye brutish among the people: and ye fools, when will ye be wise?* *Brutish,* not the word so rendered in Ps. xlix. 10; xcii. 6; rendered *foolish* in Ps. lxxiii. 22; but a participle, denoting habitual violence, as of brutes, that have no sense. *Fools,* the same as in Ps. xlix. 10; xcii. 6; often rendered *fool* in Proverbs. *Understand,* give 'intelligent attention.' *Be wise,* in Isa. lii. 13, *deal prudently;* in Job xxxiv. 27, *consider.* What wicked men and persecutors need is not a better administration of human affairs by the Almighty, but discernment and understanding enabling them to see God's hand in all things, and to understand his moral government. Why will not men reason?

9. *He that planted the ear, shall he not hear? he that formed the eye, shall he not see?* *He that planted,* and *he that formed,* both participles expressing continued action. Those who come into the world by ordinary generation, are no less the creatures of God than was Adam. The argument is very powerful. Shall he who imparts powers of perception have no powers of perception himself? Can the effect be greater than the cause? If the creature has such faculties, must not the Creator have glorious perfections? Shall the source of all intelligence be without infinite understanding?

10. *He that chastiseth the heathen, shall not he correct? he that teacheth man knowledge,* shall not he know? Chaldee: Is it possible that he should have given a law to his people, and when they have sinned, that they should not be reproved? Did not the Lord teach the first man knowledge? Amesius, Tremellius and Junius *fully* support the common version. Piscator: Does the chastiser of the nations not reprove? he who teaches man knowledge, *is he ignorant?* Fabritius: He who reproves the heathen and teaches man knowledge, shall not he chastise? Hammond: He that instructs the nations, and teaches man knowledge, shall he not rebuke, *or* punish? These diversities do not materially affect the nature of the argument. Calvin: "He would have them argue from the greater to the less, that if God did not spare even whole nations, but visits their iniquity with punishment, they could not imagine that he would suffer a mere handful of individuals to escape with impunity." Alexander: "The full

sense seems to be, Is he who teaches all mankind not competent to teach them indi-vidually?"

11. *The LORD knoweth the thoughts of man, that they are vanity. Man, Adam,* as II. v. 10. If it means the race of man, then the reference is to the vain *thoughts,* which naturally lodge within men, who have not the grace of God. *Thoughts,* as in Gen. vi. 5; in Ps. xxxiii. 10; Jer. xviii. 18, devices; in Lam. iii. 60, 61, imaginations; sometimes inventions, purposes, 2 Chron. xxvi. 15; Jer. xlix. 20; l. 45. Thoughts and purposes, which lead men to utter such wickedness as is expressed in vv. 4, 7, and to do such deeds as are recorded in vv. 5, 6 of this Psalm, mark any character as vile. The chief difficulty in interpreting the passage relates to the word *they* in the latter clause. Does it refer to *thoughts?* The English conveys that idea. Such is the inter-pretation given by many. Calvin: "Some read—*They* (that is, men themselves) *are vanity;* but this is a forced rendering, and the form of expression is one which, both in the Greek and Hebrew, may be translated, *God knows that the thoughts of men are vain.*" Yet the Syriac so reads as to make *men* to be the *vanity.* Hengstenberg and Alexander both argue for this interpretation. The difficulty is in the grammar. It is not common to give a plural pronoun to the word *man,* even when taken for the race. On the other hand, *thoughts* is feminine, and *they* masculine. By deciding either way we do not fall into any doctrinal or practical error; for the Bible often declares man himself to be *vanity,* Ps. xxxix. 5, 11; and his thoughts also to be vain and wicked, Ps. x. 4; Pr. xv. 26; Isa. lv. 7; lix. 7; Jer. iv. 14. The nature of one's thoughts determines his character, Pr. xxiii. 7.

12. *Blessed is the man whom thou chastenest, O LORD, and teachest him out of thy law. Blessed,* O the blessednesses, as in Ps. i. 1. *Chastenest,* in another form in v. 10, *chastiseth;* in the future, implying that the blessings are on the man whom God instructs, disciplines and chastens to the end of his life, or till the work of his purification is complete. But mere suffering does not sanctify. The Lord adds *teaching out of his law,* out of the Scriptures. Calvin: "The Psalmist exclaims, that those are truly blessed whom God has habituated through his word to the endurance of the cross, and prevented from sinking under adversity by the secret supports and consolations of his own Spirit."

13. *That thou mayest give him rest from the days of adversity, until the pit be digged for the wicked. That thou mayest give him rest,* or *quiet,* literally make still for him. Compare Jud. xviii. 27; Job xxxiv. 29; Ps. lxxvi. 8; lxxxiii. 1. Some think it is a promise of exemption from adversity; but this is contrary to the experience of God's people and to the teaching of v. 12 and of many Scriptures. The church of England instead of *rest* reads *patience;* The Syriac: That thou mayest make him tranquil; Arabic: That thou mayest give him gentleness in the days of adversity. Some think that it is here taught that the people of God do by faith enter into rest, so that adver-sity does not fill them with perturbation, even while they suffer. Others think the *rest* is in the next world. But it says he is to have rest, *until the pit be digged.* Horsley: While the pit is digging for the impious; Patrick: "When absolute destruc-tion and ruin, meantime, is preparing for the ungodly." The promised blessing is conferred in time. It is better to have deep sorrows and be *quiet* under them, than to be in prosperity and have a proud, turbulent spirit. The righteous are by God's grace both safe and calm under distresses. Temporal ease is often procured at a price far beyond its value; but we never pay too high a price for spiritual and eter-nal blessings and comforts.

14. *For the Lord will not cast off his people, neither will he forsake his inheritance. People* and *inheritance,* in v. 5, *people* and *heritage. Cast off,* often rendered *leave,* or *forsake,* Ps. xxvii. 9; lxxviii. 60. *Forsake,* either *leave* or *forsake,* Ps. xvi. 10; xxxvii.

33. The parallelism of the two clauses is perfect. The doctrine is clear. Compare Gen. xxviii. 15; Deut. xxxi. 6, 8; Ps. xxxvii. 5; Heb. xiii. 5.

15. *But judgment shall return unto righteousness: and all the upright in heart shall follow it.* The first clause teaches: The right will triumph in due time: The course of justice shall ere long be plain: Things shall return to their right channel. Luther renders the clause: Right must remain right. Henry: "The seeming disorders of providence shall be rectified;" Alexander: "The apparent disturbance of the divine administration is to cease, and justice to return to its accustomed channel." *All the upright in heart shall follow it*, that is, shall be found in the triumphant train of victorious justice. This is the best interpretation.

16. *Who will rise up for me against the evil doers?* or *who will stand up for me against the workers of iniquity?* Evil doers, in Ps. xxii. 16; xcii. 11, *wicked. Workers of iniquity*, as in v. 4. The two phrases describe the same class of cruel foes, who had such power as to be truly formidable, and made the prophet for himself, or in the name of the church earnestly cry out for help. Some men were faithless; others were feeble. Man could not or would not give relief. The cry is to a higher power.

17. *Unless the* Lord *had been my help, my soul had almost dwelt in silence.* But for divine interposition he must have been numbered with the dead. *Silence;* both here and in Ps. cxv. 17, it means the grave. Other interpretations are given but none so good as this. Hengstenberg: "Silence is what reigns in the noiseless kingdom of the dead."

18. *When I said, My foot slippeth; thy mercy, O Lord, held me up.* The slipping or moving of the foot, see on Ps. lxvi. 9, indicates great and present danger to the life. But *mercy* interposes and protects one who seemed ready to perish from the violence, number and craft of enemies.

19. *In the multitude of my thoughts within me thy comforts delight my soul. Thoughts,* found here only, and in Ps. cxxxix. 23. The Septuagint, Syriac, Arabic, Ethiopic, Vulgate, Doway, church of England and Jebb read *sorrows;* Alexander, *cares;* Edwards, *anxious thoughts;* Patrick, *perplexed thoughts and anxious cares;* Pool, *various and perplexing thoughts.* Clarke's paraphrase is: "According to the multitude of my trials and distresses have been the consolations which thou hast afforded me." The word rendered *delight* very strongly expresses refreshment and gratification.

20. *Shall the throne of iniquity have fellowship with thee, which frameth mischief by a law?* The throne of iniquity is a corrupt political or civil power. The question is, Shall wicked combinations be in alliance with God? By the last clause Kennicott and Horsley understand, Framing oppression under pretence of law; Jebb: Which frameth mischief by a statute; Fry: Decreeing wrong against me by law. Malice is never more devilish than when it practises its refined arts under color of law, either making a statute for the purpose, or cruelly misinterpreting some good law to that end. Witness the case of the great prophet of the captivity, Dan. vi. 4–17. The same course was pursued towards our Saviour, John xix. 7. The most horrid cruelties are practised in the name of law, justice, liberty and religion.

21. *They gather themselves together against the soul of the righteous, and condemn the innocent blood.* Edwards: They gather in parties; Fry: They assemble in crowds. There is entire unity of evil purpose subsisting among these enraged men. Clarke: "The devil, his angels, and his children all join and draw together when they have for object the destruction of the works of the Lord." This combination is often against the most *innocent,* and makes the considerate stand aghast.

22. *But the* Lord *is my defence; and my God is the rock of my refuge. Defence,* in Ps. ix. 9, and elsewhere, *refuge;* in Ps. xviii. 2, and elsewhere, *high tower.* The *defence* was perfect. *Rock,* in Ps. xviii. 2, *strength;* in Ps. xviii. 31, 46, *rock. Re-*

fuge, always rendered as here, *shelter*, *hope* or *trust*. What could the abused and injured do, if Jehovah were not their friend? One of the most important matters brought to notice by this verse is that we must look to God alone, and not mingle our trust in the Lord with reliance on worms.

23. *And he shall bring upon them their own iniquity, and shall cut them off in their own wickedness; yea, the* LORD *our God shall cut them off.* Genuine confidence in God's veracity, believes that he will assuredly fulfil both promises and threatenings. The prophet was persuaded of the divine protection to the righteous; and did not doubt the certainty of dire retribution to the wicked. To *bring iniquity* is an alarming mode of declaring that one shall reap the fruit of his evil deeds. *Cut off.* in Ps. xviii. 40, *destroy;* in Ps. cxix. 139, *consume.* The doom of the incorrigibly wicked is fixed. Luther: "He who believes this, and is taught of God, can be patient, can let the ungodly rage, and look forward to the end, and wait the time." Calvin: "The mere defeating, and frustrating the attempts of the enemies of his people would afford no inconsiderable display of divine justice; but the judgment of God is far more marvellously manifested when they fall into the pit which they themselves had prepared." Pool: "They said of the God of Jacob that he did *not see nor regard*, but now they find the contrary proved to their cost."

DOCTRINAL AND PRACTICAL REMARKS.

1. Let us remember, consider and properly use all God's names and titles. By them as well as by formal teachings we may learn how God is the patron of the righteous, the enemy of wickedness, and a fit governor of the world.

2. If God is mild and merciful, so that by his gentleness the meek are made great; so also is he just and righteous altogether, v. 1. If he were not an avenger, 1 Thess. iv. 6, how could he be a protector of his people? Scott: "Those who imagine that the exuberant goodness and mercy of God are inconsistent with the exercise of rigorous justice, and with the infliction of vengeance on the wicked, must certainly have formed very erroneous conceptions of his character." Who could either love, or fear, or trust a being, who would treat the just and the unjust alike?

3. God's nature and his covenant lead him to act in the line of the prayers of his people; and in the very nick of time he will *show himself* and *render a reward to the proud*, vv. 1, 2. See Ps. xxxi. 23.

4. It is not the humble, but *the proud*, that torment the righteous, v. 2. Those, who have a due sense of their own frailties, have something better to do than to vex their fellow-servants.

5. While our natures remain what they are, time spent in sharp sufferings of any kind, and especially such as are inflicted by the hand of cruel men, must seem *long*, vv. 3, 4. In his inscrutable wisdom God sometimes permits the haughty to have a long career of high-handed dealing with his people. The patience of God with the wicked is so great, that even the martyrs in heaven seem greatly to wonder at its continuance, Rev. vi. 9, 10.

6. There is a great variety of ways, in which the enemies of God's people display their vileness. They are arrogant and insolent; they indulge in malignant exultations; they say all manner of hard and cutting things; they indulge in vain and wicked boastings; they have no pity; they are virtually atheists, vv. 2–7. Men have sought out many inventions; but in nothing have they shown themselves more ingenious than in their cruelty towards the meek and afflicted.

7. Therefore, let not God's people of any generation be surprised at an outbreak of the spirit of persecution, fierce and bloody, *breaking them in pieces*, v. 5. No man and no church knows what conspiracies may at any time burst out. These acts

of hostility are commonly more imbittered, when they proceed from hypocrites and apostates than from heathen and infidels.

8. A knowledge and profession of the true religion is no guaranty against our becoming fearfully wicked and bloody. These persecutors had excellent laws, Deut. iv. 7, 8; but they were incarnate fiends. They made earth like hell, as the wicked often do, v. 6. They defied all the obligations of charity and humanity. Calvin notices 'the fact that the helplessness and tender age of little children will even protect them from being attacked by dogs and wild beasts. And yet persecutors care not for them. Nor do they care for gray hairs, nor the sorrows of widowhood. One must either bring his life up to his principles or his principles down to his life. This last is much the easiest, and is commonly done by the wicked; and so when necessary to their peace,

9. The wicked deny providence, v. 7. Than this there is no greater error. Morison: "When men bring themselves to think that Jehovah is too great a being to interfere in the affairs of this lower world, they are prepared, by this infidel sentiment, to adopt any evil course which may suggest itself to the depraved inclinations of the human heart."

10. The obvious and usual arguments for the great truths of natural religion are fair and unanswerable, vv. 8–10. Grotius: "This is a very excellent way of arguing; for whatever perfection there is in created beings, it is derived from God; and therefore it must be in him in the most eminent manner;" Arnd: "Learn to know God from the powers of your own body and soul. He who has made an understanding heart, should he not himself understand? he who has created a righteous heart, should he not himself be righteous? he who has made a compassionate heart, should he not himself have a father-heart?" Henry: "The atheistical, though they set up for wits, and philosophers, and politicians, yet are really the *brutish among the people;* if they would but understand, they would believe."

11. How futile are the plans and purposes of worldly men, v. 11. Nothing is of less value. Of all the works of the mightiest ancient monarchs not one remains to tell the glory of its author.

12. It is no novelty, but a truth long known in the church of God, that it is good to be afflicted, v. 12. The blessings connected with sanctified afflictions are many, temporal and eternal. Even in this life the righteous gathers no more delicious fruit than that from chastisement. His sorest punishments are but fatherly corrections. They lead him to an understanding of God's word which otherwise he could never acquire. Compare Ps. cxix. 67, 71.

13. Let there be a revival of the passive virtues, v. 13. Mr. Hume calls them the 'monkish virtues.' Many speak of them slightingly, especially as compared with the dashing qualities so highly esteemed in the world. But quietness of mind and of spirit, like a broken heart, is of great price in the sight of God. Some seem to have forgotten that silence and meekness are graces.

14. How different is the end of the wicked from that of the righteous, and yet not more diverse than are their aims and preferences. God's people find *rest* even in sorrow, and have a sure pledge of an eternal home; but the wicked are getting all their good things here, while the *pit is digging for them.* Sad is their state even in the height of their prosperity. Dickson: "As condemned men are suffered to live till their gallows and grave be made ready, that, after their execution they may be thrust into it, so are wicked men suffered to live till they fill the cup of their iniquity, and till God have filled up the cup of his wrath for them."

15. Sad and suffering as the saints may be, yet this is their joy and their glory, that in the darkest hour of life they are still *the people* and *the heritage* of God,

vv. 5, 14. They may be cast down, yea, they may be cast out, but they shall not be *cast off*, nor *cast away*. They may be broken in pieces, but God will heal all their breaches and speak comfortably to them.

16. It is easy for God to bring order out of the most terrific confusion, v. 15. Justice may be slow, but it is sure. Arnd: "Lebanius, a sophist, asked a Christian: What is your carpenter's son doing? The Christian replied: He is making a coffin for Julian the tyrant. Very soon Julian was killed in battle and brought home in a coffin."

17. To all right-minded creatures it will be a glad day when the righteous shall triumph. It is surely coming, v. 15.

18. In time of sore trial how natural it is to cry out for some one to stand up for us. But how seldom does a true friend appear. David had his Jonathan; Jeremiah had his Ebedmelech; but the great mass of men are arrant cowards when danger presses. At Paul's first answer all men forsook him. Our Saviour fared no better.

19. The more spiritual wisdom any one has, the less confidence has he in man, and the more confidence has he in God alone, v. 17.

20. The life of every good man, who has had any considerable experience, is full of wonders of some kind; among them narrow and marvellous escapes, perhaps from natural, and certainly from spiritual dangers. At all times let us look to God alone, v. 18. Spring: "It is no longer matter of *sovereignty* whether or not God will hear the prayers of his people; he has condescended to bind himself by *promise;* it is matter of *rectitude.*"

21. God's consolations are enough to satisfy and refresh any soul that will lay hold on them, v. 19. We are not straitened in him, but only in our own compassions. Cobbin: "In the worst of times the church of God has its consolations." Let us embrace them.

22. Pious people living in countries that have long been exempt from open and legal persecution are in danger of undervaluing their great mercies, and of supposing that their exemption is owing to something else than the great kindness of God. At any moment they may find the very *laws* a gin, a trap and a snare to their souls, their consciences and their lives. Among the miscreants let loose on society as scourges to good men, none are more to be abhorred than those, who have a "wrong-headedness of conscience." "There is no impulse to evil-doing more to be dreaded than the impetuousness of a blind and obstinate conscience." Rulers who believe that their very office is given them that they may lord it over men's persons, consciences, estates and liberties, are never at a loss for pretexts of law. Sufficient appearances are never wanting to those who have a mind to wrong others. Compare v. 8; Ecc. iv. 1, 2. Calvin: "The case becomes doubly vexatious, when the innocent victims of oppression are not only injured, but have a stigma fixed upon their character." Wrong a man and hate him is the law of a depraved heart. Nicolson: "The first pretext of wicked men to color their proceedings against innocent men is their *throne;* the second is the *law;* and the third is their *council.* What tyrant could ask more? But God has prepared an awful hell for impenitent tyrants, and they will be in it long before they now expect to leave the world."

23. It should closely unite in bonds of holy affection all the people of God to see the strength and hearty consent of their enemies among themselves, v. 21. Burke: "When bad men combine, the good must associate." Horne: "Righteousness and innocence are most atrocious crimes, in the eyes of wickedness and guilt. For these crimes Cain slew his brother Abel, the Jews crucified Christ, the Pagans tortured and murdered his disciples, and bad men in all ages have persecuted the good," 1 John iii. 13.

24 The prevailing temper of Christians towards the wicked should be that of pity. They have no *defence*, no *God*, no *rock*, no *refuge*, v. 22. O pray for the ungodly, that they may turn and live.

25. The wicked are the authors of their own eternal undoing. *Iniquity* will be their ruin, v. 23. Henry: " A man cannot be more miserable than his own wickedness will make him, if God visit it upon him: it will cut him in the remembrance of it; it will cut him off in the recompense of it." Morison: " How often has God overtaken persecutors in the very act of oppression! They have been permitted to carry their cruel designs to their utmost height, and then judgment has come upon them to the uttermost."

Sometimes the question is asked with deep concern, Shall formal and legal persecution ever again stalk abroad on the earth? Why not? The wicked hate the righteous as much as ever they did. They are always struggling for power. Cobbin: " The church has in all ages had to complain of oppressors." Many sober and judicious commentators believe that prophecy tells of bloody scenes yet before the church. Calvin: " We should account it no strange thing to see the church suffering still under miserable misgovernment, or positive oppression."

PSALM XCV.

1 O come, let us sing unto the LORD: let us make a joyful noise to the Rock of our salvation.
2 Let us come before his presence with thanksgiving, and make a joyful noise unto him with psalms.
3 For the LORD *is* a great God, and a great King above all gods.
4 In his hand *are* the deep places of the earth: the strength of the hills *is* his also.
5 The sea *is* his, and he made it: and his hands formed the dry *land*.
6 O come, let us worship and bow down: let us kneel before the LORD our maker.
7 For he *is* our God; and we *are* the people of his pasture, and the sheep of his hand. To day if ye will hear his voice,
8 Harden not your heart, as in the provocation, *and* as *in* the day of temptation in the wilderness:
9 When your fathers tempted me, proved me, and saw my work.
10 Forty years long was I grieved with *this* generation, and said, It *is* a people that do err in their heart, and they have not known my ways:
11 Unto whom I sware in my wrath that they should not enter into my rest.

THE Syriac, Arabic, Septuagint, Vulgate, Ethiopic, Theodoret, Diodati, Piscator, Fabritius, Amesius, Pool, Gill, Henry, Morison, Anderson and Scott agree that David was the author of this Psalm. Paul clearly settled this point in Heb. iv. 7. But Calmet thinks that the apostle there merely followed the *common opinion* in giving David as the author, because in general the Psalter was said to be written by him. But if Paul was mistaken in this, he had not plenary inspiration, and he may have erred in *all* he said. Paul did not give heed to fables and popular delusions either in his preaching or in his writings. Patrick also does not regard the argument from Heb. iv. 7, as conclusive of David's authorship, " because it is usual to call the whole five books by the name of the Psalms of David, when it is certain he did not make them all, but only the greater part." This reasoning would be conclusive, provided it was usual with *inspired writers* to speak of David as the author of all the Psalms. But they never do. What sound critic would not have been perplexed and even appalled if he had found a book of the New Testament ascribing Psalms xc. cxxxvii. to David? Inspired men do not speak so loosely. If inspiration does not infallibly preserve from error in *every* thing, it is no ground of authority in *any* thing. Although in the New Testament *Moses* is more than once put for the five books of Moses, (Luke xvi. 31; Acts xv. 21); yet no one pretends that he has found an instance in either Testament, where *David* is put for the Psalter. There is nothing in the terms or phrases of the Psalm to indicate that it had a historic occasion. It is suitable to all times. Scott dates it B. C. 1045. The names of the Most High in it are *Jehovah* LORD, *El God* and *Elohim God;* on which see on Ps. i. 2; vii. 4; iii. 2. Is this Psalm Messianic? Kimchi admits that it relates to the days of Messiah. Luther: "The whole of this Psalm is to be referred to Christ." Gill: "It belongs to the times of Messiah." Pool: "It hath a special reference to the days of Messiah." Morison: "There can be no doubt that this psalm has a special reference to the times of the gospel." Fry: "Certainly, the subject is the Messiah's exaltation and kingdom." Henry: "It appears to have been calculated for the days of Messiah." This view is abundantly confirmed by Paul in the Epistle to the Hebrews, especially in Chapters iii. iv. While therefore it has special reference to Messiah and his times, it was yet full of weighty and practical truth in all the days of the Jewish church in Canaan. Hengstenberg: "The Psalm has a peculiar significance for *our times*, in which there is so much to call up the thought that we are on the eve of some great catastrophe, and are about to meet the coming of the Lord with steps of majesty." No doubt each day is to its generation a critical time; for the messenger to call each one away comes as a thief in the night; nor can any one give too solemn heed to the call to repentance here made; but we have no evidence of any great and general catastrophe at hand.

1. *O* COME, *let us sing unto the* LORD. *Come,* a word of earnest invitation, rendered either *come* or *go* according to the connection. *Sing,* in Ps. v. 11, *shout for joy;* in Ps. xx. 5, *rejoice;* in Ps. li. 14, *sing aloud;* in Ps. xcii. 4, *triumph. Let us make a joyful noise to the Rock of our salvation. Make a joyful noise,* in Ps. xlvii. 1, *shout;* in Ps. xli. 11, *triumph.* Sometimes it is rendered *sound an alarm,* Num. x. 7; *blow an alarm,* Num. x. 9. But here and often elsewhere it simply expresses solemn and joyful acclamations of worship. Alexander: "The two verbs in this verse are those commonly applied to the vocal expression of joy and triumph." But see Ps. lxv. 13; lxvi. 1; lxxxi. 1; xcviii. 4, 6. *Rock,* as in Ps. xciv. 22. *Rock of salvation* in the Psalms here only and in Ps. lxxxix. 26. Hengstenberg well regards it as equivalent to "the unchangeable foundation and faithful author of salvation." The verse calls for a service that cannot be rendered without godly sincerity.

2. *Let us come before his presence with thanksgiving. Come,* the verb often rendered *prevent,* used twice in Mic. vi. 6. Calvin thinks it has the force of "*Make haste.* He calls upon them to speed into the presence of God." *Presence,* literally *face. Praise,* sometimes *confession,* Josh. vii. 19, oftener *praise,* and yet oftener *thanksgiving;* first found in the Psalter in Ps. xxvi. 7. *And make a joyful noise unto him with psalms.* The verb is the same as in verse 1. *With psalms,* that is with *songs,* with *melody.* See on title of Ps. iii. Patrick's paraphrase is: "Let us approach into his presence with thankful hearts, to acknowledge the benefits we have received from him: and devoutly proclaim with triumphant hymns, what a joy it is to us, that we may address ourselves unto him." Pool well observes that in a singular manner we have the *presence* of God in his Son the Messiah. Compare Gen. xxxii. 30. Such worship is not vain:

3. *For the* LORD *is a great God, and a great King above all gods.* The worship may fitly be of the most elevated kind to correspond with the character of the being worshipped. In Scripture God often claims *greatness* as belonging to his whole nature,

Ps. cxlv. 3. *A great King*, see on Ps. xlvii. 2. The superiority and sovereignty claimed by Jehovah are universal, the word rendered *gods* being applied to false gods, magistrates and angels. All authority in the universe is in the power of Jehovah.

4. *In his hand* are *the deep places of the earth. Deep places*, found only here, meaning abysses, innermost depths; Arabic, foundations; Septuagint, Ethiopic and Vulgate, bounds. The centre of the earth is as much under the view and control of Jehovah as its surface. *The strength of the hills is his also. Strength*, the Hebrew word is in the plural. Several read tops, heights, summits; Horsley, inaccessible summits. The contrast is between the lowest and the highest parts of the world.

5. *The sea* is *his, and he made it.* The ocean has a father as well as a governor. God's right to rule all things rests primarily on his being Creator. *And his hands formed the dry* land. All earth has a maker, to whom it owes allegiance. *Sea* and *dry land* are in opposition, as were *abysses* and *heights* in v. 4.

6. *O come, let us worship and bow down. Come*, the same word used to Noah: *Come* thou and all thy house into the ark. It has the kindness of a call and the authority of a command. *Worship;* the same verb in the second commandment is *bow down*, Ex. xx. 5; Deut. v. 9. It always expresses worship civil or religious. *Bow down*, rendered *kneel, sink down.* Fry says it describes an act of bowing so as to touch the floor with the forehead, while the worshipper is on his hands and knees. Jebb gives it *fall down;* Alexander, *bend.* Compare 2 Chron. vii. 3, where it is rendered *bowed themselves. Let us kneel before the* LORD *our maker.* Here again we are fitly reminded of the *right* God has over us by creation. The creature cannot be too reverential to the Creator. *Kneel*, that is *bend the knees*, as those used to do, who profoundly *adore.* Our humility before God should not be stinted. And there is good reason not only for humbling ourselves before him, but also for confiding in him.

7. *For he* is *our God*, he sustains to us a covenant relation, and has done us all the good we ever received. *And we* are *the people of his pasture, and the sheep of his hand.* The inspired writers delight in allusions to the office of shepherd and the relations of his flock to him, Ps. xxiii. 1–4; lxxix. 13; lxxx. 1. The clause is a mere allusion to pastoral life. The figure is soon dropped, and there is a return to plain terms. Meantime this clause strongly and tenderly enforces the obligation of obedience arising from God's kind care. *Sheep*, often *flock*, also *cattle;* commonly *sheep*, in distinction from other cattle, Gen. xii. 16; xxi. 27; Deut. xiv. 26; 2 Chron. xiv. 15; Job i. 3. From this to the close of the Psalm God is speaker. *To-day if ye will hear his voice.* To *hear his voice* is to obey him and follow him. Some would make this clause complete in itself, giving *if* the sense of *Oh that*, as in the Greek, Luke xix. 42. In support, Ex. xxxii. 32; 1 Chron. iv. 10, may be cited as like cases. Another explanation is this; the particle rendered *if* has several times the sense of *surely, doubtless*, as in Num. xiv. 23, 30. And so we might gather this sense: As I have been a good shepherd to this people, surely they will to-day hear my voice. This gives a good sense, but is not without difficulties. A third explanation is that which would read the verse thus: For he is our God; and we are the people of his pasture, and the sheep of his hand, if ye will hear his voice to-day, thus making it a conditional promise. To all this it is objected that there are grammatical difficulties, and that the apostle follows the Septuagint; and that connects the latter clause of v. 7 with what comes after. On the subject of quotations from the Septuagint, see on Ps. iv. 4. To the end the apostle had in view the text of the Septuagint was sufficient, and as that version was well known, he may have quoted it without endorsing it as perfectly correct in all points. Yet there is no better sense than that gathered from the common version, reading, *To-day if ye will hear his voice*,

8. *Harden not your heart, as in the provocation*, and *as in the day of temptation in*

the wilderness. In the provocation. literally, *at Meribah. Temptation, Massah.* Numbers of scholars prefer not to translate these words here. Nor is it necessary that we should; though in so doing we follow all the ancient versions and many modern translations. The allusions in *Meribah* and *Massah* are clearly to historic events of great prominence. See Ex. xvii. 7; Num. xx. 13, 24; xxvii. 14; Deut. xxxii. 51; xxxiii. 8, and on Ps. lxxxi. 7. *Meribah* signifies *strife, contention;* then, *provocation. Massah* signifies *trial, temptation.* The intelligent reader gets the same idea whether we translate or transfer these words, with the advantage of an impressive historic allusion, if we simply transfer them. He adds of those times,

9. *When your fathers tempted me, proved me, and saw my work. Tempted,* see on Ps. xxvi. 2, where it is *prove;* and on Ps. lxxviii. 18; xli. 56, where it is *tempted. Proved,* in Ps. xxvi. 2, rendered *examine;* more commonly *try,* as in Ps. xi. 4, 5. Each of these words is here used in a bad sense, because they describe acts of unbelief and rebellion. God should be taken at his word, and neither distrusted nor murmured against. *Saw my work,* that is, my special work in miraculously supplying their wants at Meribah and Massah; or my whole work in delivering their nation.

10. *Forty years long was I grieved with* this *generation, and said, It is a people that do err in their heart,* and *they have not known my ways. Was grieved,* as in Ps. cxix. 158; cxxxix. 21. When it expresses the state of mind towards one's self, it is rendered *loathe.* To *err in the heart* is to have a radical defect in character. For those who have God's word *not to know his ways* is proof of wilful ignorance, and that is perverseness.

11. *Unto whom I sware in my wrath that they should not enter into my rest.* For *unto whom,* some prefer *wherefore,* or *on account of which* wickedness and perverseness. *Sware,* see the oath in Num. xiii. 21–23; 28–30; Deut. i. 34, 35. *Rest;* in the epistle to the Hebrews Paul shows the scriptural import of this word to be fourfold: 1. The *rest* of the Sabbath as kept by God at the end of the creation; 2. The *rest* of Israel in Canaan; 3. The *rest* of the gospel dispensation; 4. The *rest* of heavenly glory. Here it has primary reference to the *rest* of the promised land.

It cannot be doubted that in the epistle to the Hebrews Paul has cast more light on the last four or five verses than all other expositors have done. Read him. Some have spoken of abruptness in the ending of this ode. But surely none can complain of a want of awful solemnity.

DOCTRINAL AND PRACTICAL REMARKS.

1. If those, who reject audible singing in God's worship were consistent, they would reject audible prayer. The latter is not more clearly enjoined than the former, vv. 1, 2.

2. Into this work we should enter with gladness and holy mirth, making a *joyful noise unto God,* vv. 1, 2.

3. The worship of God's people should be specially hearty and earnest, when their theme is *salvation* and its author, v. 2. The *Rock* that has ever followed the church is Christ, 1 Cor. x. 4. Nor should we expect to raise the devotions of men to any height of spiritual comfort till we bring them to contemplate Christ Jesus.

4. If we would be strong and happy servants of Christ, let us meditate much on God's *greatness,* v. 3. He is the infinite God, unmeasurable in all his glorious attributes. There is no limit to any of his perfections, and there is no perfection of God, in which his people may not find matter of exultation.

5. A great test of character is presented to us in the sovereign authority of God, and especially in the kingly office of Christ, v. 3. It is in vain for us to pretend love to the teaching or atonement of Christ, if we reject his laws and statutes. If we will

not let him reign over us, it proves that he has not been formed in us the hope of glory. What say you to the yoke of Christ?

6. It is a blessed truth that all nature is under the control of God, and especially that all things are put under Christ to the glory of God, and the establishment of the reign of grace, vv. 4, 5. If an atom or an agent, if life or death, if Satan or Gabriel, the sea or the dry land, the mountain tops or the deep abysses were beyond divine control, then a good man might suffer too much for his good, be tried beyond the power of endurance, or die before his time. But now such things are not possible.

7. In all approaches to God we should see that our hearts and behaviour be humble. In God's worship we cannot make too prostrate obeisance of our faculties of soul or body. If we regard any posture in prayer or praise more lowly and reverent than another, let us assume it. All the forms of expression in v. 7, teach us humility not only of mind but of body also. Pool: "By these expressions he teacheth us that even in gospel times God is to be glorified and worshipped, as well with the members of our bodies, as with the faculties of our souls." Gill: "*Let us kneel before the Lord our Maker;* both in a natural and spiritual sense." Nicolson: "Adoration, humble adoration; outward worship, that of the body, as well as inward, that of the soul, is his due." Let all our worship be solemn, not frivolous, awful not familiar, humble not arrogant. Yet acceptable worship has been offered to God in every posture. David *sat before the* LORD and offered an acceptable prayer, 1 Chron. xvii. 16–27. The ancients often stood with the hands lifted up towards heaven and their service was acceptable, Ps. cxli. 2. The publican stood, and lifted neither his hands nor his eyes to heaven, and yet he was heard. Hezekiah turned his face to the wall, as he lay on his bed, and prayed, and God heard him.

8. Let us exhort and encourage ourselves to all right worship, by often thinking of the covenant relation of God to all his people. If we indeed adore him, he is our God, v. 7.

9. Especially should we cherish right thoughts of the divinity of our Saviour, who is our Maker and our God, John i. 1, 3; xx. 28; Col. i. 16.

10. In the Scriptures amazing urgency is manifest that men should pay *immediate* attention to the concerns of their souls, and that they should *to-day* hear God's voice, v. 7. Compare 2 Cor. vi. 1, 2; Heb. iii. 13. Nor is such urgency uncalled for. Many are so much like Pharaoh that even when they are suffering and in great distress, and the proposal is to pray for the removal of the plague, and they are called on to name a time, they say "to-morrow," Ex. viii. 10. Jehovah *now* calls tenderly; to-morrow you may be in the land of silence. THE NIGHT COMETH WHEN NO MAN CAN WORK.

11. The *voice* of God, which it most behooves us all to *hear*, is the glorious gospel of the blessed God, v. 7. In it the Father, Son and Holy Ghost send us messages of mercy, which it chiefly concerns us to know and embrace and which none can defer even for a moment, but at extreme peril and with great guilt. Compare v. 11; Heb. x. 28, 29.

12. Many rest quite satisfied with themselves, because they are not revilers, blasphemers, drunkards, or otherwise openly profane and immoral, and think themselves in little danger. They forget that the very core of depravity is a *hard heart,* v. 8. It is of itself just cause of everlasting banishment from God.

13. If men persist in sin, it must be in the face of many and awful examples of vengeance. Sometimes God points us to a Cain or a Lamech, permitted to live enduring the horrors of a guilty conscience. Sometimes he points us to Absalom hanging by the hair, or to Haman on his gallows seventy-five feet high. Sometimes he tells us of the old world destroyed by a flood, or of the cities of the plain suffering the vengeance of eternal fire. Here we are told of nearly a whole generation who set out from

Egypt and never reached the promised land. Their carcasses fell in the wilderness.
Oh that men would be warned.

14. The best and most solemn instruction from this Scripture is given by Paul.
Read and ponder Heb. iii. 12–19; iv. 1–11. Language could not be more solemn.
Tholuck: "Since God addressed the same admonition to later generations, the apostle
concludes that the rest which God had prepared for the people in the earthly Canaan
was not the right one; and that there was another rest, from which men might exclude
themselves through unbelief." Let no man slight the mercy of the Lord. It was
bought with blood. Now, sinner, now is your time.

PSALM XCVI.

1 O sing unto the LORD a new song: sing unto the LORD, all the earth.

2 Sing unto the LORD, bless his name; shew forth his salvation from day to day.

3 Declare his glory among the heathen, his wonders among all people.

4 For the LORD *is* great, and greatly to be praised: he *is* to be feared above all gods.

5 For all the gods of the nations *are* idols: but the LORD made the heavens.

6 Honour and majesty *are* before him: strength and beauty *are* in his sanctuary.

7 Give unto the LORD, O ye kindreds of the people, give unto the LORD glory and strength

8 Give unto the LORD the glory *due unto* his name: bring an offering, and come into his courts.

9 O worship the LORD in the beauty of holiness: fear before him, all the earth.

10 Say among the heathen *that* the LORD reigneth: the world also shall be established that it
shall not be moved: he shall judge the people righteously.

11 Let the heavens rejoice, and let the earth be glad: let the sea roar, and the fulness thereof.

12 Let the field be joyful, and all that *is* therein: then shall all the trees of the wood rejoice

13 Before the LORD: for he cometh, for he cometh to judge the earth: he shall judge the world
with righteousness, and the people with his truth.

THE authorship of this Psalm is ascribed to David by the Syriac, Arabic, Septuagint, Ethiopic, Vulgate, Luther, Fabritius, Amesius, Gill, Pool, Henry, Horne,
Scott, Morison and Edwards. To the same conclusion one is fairly led by the history
of removing the ark from the house of Obed-edom, see 1 Chron. xvi. "Then on that
day David delivered first this psalm, to thank the Lord, into the hand of Asaph and
his brethren." That Psalm contains *twenty-nine* verses and this but *thirteen.* Yet all
of this (with small exceptions) is found in that. Nor are the variations between this
and that so great as between Psalm xviii. and 2 Sam. xxii. There is no ground for reasonable doubt that David wrote this Psalm. The plea for objecting to the Davidic
authorship is first that four of the ancient versions say that it was used on the
occasion of the completion of the second temple and after the captivity. Yet these
very versions give David as its author. It is very probable that it was so used, as indeed it would be very suitable. But that does not conflict with the idea that David
wrote it. The other ground of objection is that there is a striking resemblance between
parts of this poem and portions of the prophecies of Isaiah. If such argument proves
anything, it is that Isaiah was familiar with this and incorporated, under divine
guidance, some of its truths and predictions into his own inspired utterances. David
was as truly a prophet as Isaiah, and lived before him several hundred years. The
historic occasion of the original composition is given in 1 Chron. xvi. Scott dates this
Psalm B. C. 1045; Clarke, B. C. 515. Is it Messianic? On this subject there is
hardly any doubt. The Syriac calls it "a prophecy concerning the advent of Christ

and the calling of the Gentiles who should believe in him." Luther: "This is a prophecy concerning the kingdom of Christ, and the spreading of the gospel over the whole world and before every creature; which gospel will be a word of joy and thanksgiving, of peace, of rejoicing, and of a continued sacrifice of praise." To the same effect we might cite Calvin, Venema, Gill, Morison, Horne, Scott, Fry and Tholuck. The only name of God here found is *Jehovah* LORD, on which see on Psalm i. 2. This Psalm in several respects resembles Ps. xcv., but widely differs from it in others.

1. *O sing unto the* LORD *a new song.* *Sing*, cognate to the noun *song.* On a *new* song see on Ps. xxxiii. 3; xl. 3. Gill and Fry quote Jarchi as saying that "wherever a *new* song is mentioned, it is to be understood of future time, or the times of the Messiah." This would make Psalms xxxiii. xl. xcvi. cxliv. and cxlix. Messianic. Anderson: "It may be called *new*, from its having been adapted to a new purpose—from its having been intended to celebrate new mercies conferred upon the Jews, and to lead the mind forward to the glorious era of the coming of Messiah, and the establishment of his kingdom." Tholuck: "Songs of praise shall be addressed unto the Lord with renewed faith and renewed love." Clarke thinks a *new* song is "a song of peculiar excellence." Scott: "'A new song,' this perhaps implies that it was altered by some prophet, as adapted to a new occasion." The phrase *a new song* is found in Isa. xlii. 10; Rev. v. 9; xiv. 3. *Sing unto the* LORD *all the earth.* This clause shows that the mercy, for which a *new song* was demanded related to all nations.

2. *Sing unto the* LORD, *bless his name; shew forth his salvation from day to day.* *Sing* and *bless*, very uniformly rendered. *Shew forth*, in Ps. xl. 9, *preached;* in Isa. lxi. 1, *preach good tidings;* in 2 Sam. i. 20; Ps. lxviii. 11, *publish;* in Isa. xl. 9, *bringest good tidings.* It is confined to good news and glad messages. We might render it, Publish good tidings of salvation. The Chaldee: Announce his redemption; Syriac and Arabic: Preach his salvation. *Salvation*, as in Ps. iii. 8; lxxxix. 26; xci. 16. This work must be done *from day to day*, continually.

3. *Declare his glory among the heathen, his wonders among all people.* *Declare*, the corresponding noun is *a book;* and the participle is often rendered a *scribe*, a *writer*, Ps. xlv. 1. The verb is rendered, *tell, shew forth, declare.* The variety of verbs used in vv. 1–3, proves that we are to employ all proper means for making known the Saviour. One of these methods is by writing. His *glory* and his *wonders* are the same, John ii. 11. His divinity, incarnation, birth, life, miracles, teachings, example, death, resurrection, ascension, session at God's right hand and coming to judgment, are his wonders and his glory too. *Heathen*, as in Ps. ii. 1, often *Gentiles*, oftener *nations.* *Nations*, as in Ps. iii. 6; commonly rendered *people.* It occurs again in vv. 5, 7, 10, 13, is in the plural throughout the Psalm. We have very ancient authority for making known the gospel to the Gentiles, Rom. xvi. 25, 26. Nor have preachers a poor theme,

4. *For the* LORD *is great, and greatly to be praised: he is to be feared above all gods.* See on Ps. xcv. 3. The next verse limits the meaning of *gods.*

5. *For all the gods of the nations are idols.* Though Jehovah warns magistrates that they shall die like men, Ps. lxxxii. 7; and charges his angels with folly, Job iv. 18; yet he never calls either of them *idols, vanities, nothings*, things *of nought*, things *of no value.* On the contrary he calls magistrates *gods*, and *children of the Most High*, Ps. lxxxvi. 6; and he has clothed the angels with such glory that when a good man saw one of them, he thought it was God himself and fell down to worship him, Rev. xxii. 8, 9. Idols have made nothing, done nothing, preserved nothing. *But the Lord made the heavens.* As in Ps. xcv. 5, so here God's supremacy is based upon his being Creator. The idol was a mere dumb senseless thing. Not so with Jehovah.

6. *Honour and majesty* are *before him: strength and beauty* are *in his sanctuary*. On the first of these nouns see on Ps. viii. 1; on the second, on Ps. viii. 5; on the third, on Ps. viii. 2; on the fourth, on Ps. lxxi. 8. In Ps. xxi. 5, the first and second are united as here. Their rendering varies considerably; unitedly they express all excellence and glory.

7. *Give unto the* LORD, *O ye kindreds of the people, give unto the* LORD *glory and strength*. To *give* here is to ascribe, as in Ps. xxix. 1. For *kindreds of the people*, Calvin has *assemblies of peoples;* Edwards, Pool and Fry, *families of the nations;* Alexander, *families of nations*. If we vary from our version, the best rendering is *families*. The idea of close relationship is expressed in the original. God has made of one blood all nations. *Glory*, as in Ps. iii. 3. *Strength*, as in v. 6. Hammond: "The same word signifies *power, dominion, empire*."

8. *Give unto the Lord the glory* due unto *his name*. *Give glory*, as in v. 7. *Bring an offering*. *Offering*, gift, oblation, sacrifice; *i. e.*, says Horsley, an offering of bread and flour, not of flesh. Alexander: "The word *offering* is the one used to denote the bloodless or vegetable oblation of the Mosaic ritual." This is commonly so; but it is the very word applied to Abel's *offering*, Gen. iv. 4. It may denote all kinds of ordained offerings. See on Ps. xx. 3. Compare Ps. cxli. 2. Calvin: "It is here taken to denote the whole worship of God." *And come into his courts*. *Courts*, as in Ps. lxv. 4; lxxxiv. 2, 10; xcii. 13.

9. *O worship the* LORD *in the beauty of holiness*. *Worship*, in Ps. xcv. 6, *bow down;* in Ps. xxix. 2; xlv. 11; xcvii. 7; xcix. 5, 9, *worship*. In Ps. xxix. 2, we have the whole clause. *Fear before him, all the earth*. *Fear*, in Ps. xcvii. 4, *tremble*. It is a very strong word. *All the earth*, as in v. 1.

10. *Say among the heathen* that *the* LORD *reigneth*. *Heathen*, as in v. 3. *Reigneth*, as in Ps. xlvii. 8; xciii. 1; xcvii. 1; xcix. 1. The verb is in the preterite. God has reigned from the beginning and reigns now. Or, the prophet is so sure that he will everywhere set up his kingdom, that he speaks of it as something past. *The world also shall be established that it shall not be moved*. The stability of the order of nature is found in the unchangeable dominion of God. Nor to that end is anything more required. Compare Ps. xciii. 1; cxix. 90, 91. *He shall judge the people righteously;* literally *in righteousnesses*, in perfect *equity* and *uprightness*. *People*, plural throughout the Psalm. *Judge*, that is, *rule* the nations, and *execute* righteousness among them, and *plead the cause* of the poor and afflicted. Such a prospect is very animating:

11. *Let the heavens rejoice, and let the earth be glad; let the sea roar, and the fulness thereof.*

12. *Let the field be joyful, and all that* is *therein: then shall all the trees of the wood rejoice*. Tholuck: "It will not be a reign of terror, but to all who obey his laws a reign of joy, of joy so great, that inanimate nature herself shall participate in 'the glorious liberty of the children of God,' and give loud utterance to her rejoicing." Verses 11, 12 are best regarded as prophecies. The verbs are in the future. All creation shall rejoice

13. *Before the* LORD: *for he cometh, for he cometh to judge the earth: he shall judge the world with righteousness, and the people with his truth*. The terms of this verse have their usual signification. Although the final judgment of the world shall bring unspeakable joy to all right-minded people, and although the administration of Christ over the world would not be complete without the decisions and revelations of the last day; yet the primary reference of this passage is not to a "retributive, but a *gracious* judging," when the law of love shall universally prevail, when men shall copy the divine equity, candor, and fidelity; when the arts of peace shall entirely supersede those of destruction, and men shall do to others as they would have others do to them.

Patrick: "Let them welcome that day; and meet the Lord with forward affection, who is coming to them: For he comes to reform the earth, and will govern mankind by righteous and merciful laws; and faithfully keep his word with all those that truly observe them."

DOCTRINAL AND PRACTICAL REMARKS.

1. Let us abound in singing God's praises as long as we live, vv. 1, 2. Thrice we are here called on to *sing, sing, sing*. It is a blessed privilege to us poor creatures, who are so borne down with sorrow and grief, to be allowed, yea, often summoned to perform this delightful work, which forms so great a part of the worship offered in the temple not made with hands.

2. Let us never lose sight of the Redeemer and his *salvation*, v. 2. Cobbin: "The salvations of former ages were celebrated; but they only faintly shadowed forth the 'great salvation' that is in Christ."

3. *Wonders* will never cease while there is a God in existence, a Saviour on the throne, and a Holy Spirit fitting men's souls for glory, v. 3. Luther: "Each believer is a new creature and a marvellous work of God; and all believers daily do marvellous works and are marvellous monuments, in that they continue in spiritual life, and are finally conquerors over the mighty powers of sin and the devil." Heaven is and ever will be full of wonders. A religion without wonders is false. A theology without wonders is heretical.

4. Let us spread far and wide the glorious knowledge of God in Christ. Especially let us send it to *the heathen*, vv. 3, 10. We have no duty more obvious or more pressing. If a redeemed sinner should keep silence on redemption, he would be a monster. Hengstenberg: "This is a *missionary hymn* for all ages of the church; and it becomes more and more appropriate to our times in proportion as the heathen begin to respond to the call." The enemies of missions ought to come to a solemn pause, and well consider that alarming text, 1 Thess. ii. 16.

5. The opposition to the truth of the gospel arising from any power in the false gods was nothing; for they were nothing themselves, v. 5. No! it was not the poor dumb idol that did the mischief. You might have kicked him, or spit upon him, or broken him in pieces, or burnt him, and he never would have resented it. It was the power of Satan and sin in the heart supporting a system of idolatry, that did all the harm. It was superstition, the madness and debasement flowing from an old system of idolatry, and the natural depravity of the heart that made the blood of the martyrs flow like water. Idolaters had on their side prescription, the natural heart, political power and vast majorities. Calvin: "The inference is plain, that we must not conclude that to be necessarily the true religion which meets with the approbation of the multitude."

6. We may safely and heartily rejoice in all the arrangements and supports of the divine government, v. 6. Whatever may seem wrong, all is right and glorious at the throne of God.

7. We should be very careful not to separate ourselves from the ordinances of divine worship, lest like withered branches we become unfruitful and die. *Strength and beauty are in his sanctuary*, v. 6. The best men need the best means and God's blessing on them to keep them from failing in the great work of life.

8. Let not any man or people fail to ascribe unto God the glory and honor, which are his due, vv. 7, 8.

9. God has a right to prescribe and ordain the entire rites and modes of his own worship, and it is our wisdom to submit to all his appointments. Under the gospel the sacrifices God requires of us are prayer, praise, alms, a broken heart and a total consecration of ourselves to his service, 1 Pet. ii. 5; Ps. cxli. 2; Heb. xiii. 15. 16;

Ps. li. 17; Rom. xii. 1. Let us offer them with a willing mind. In the ordinances of worship, let us not teach or receive for doctrines the commandments of men.

10. Even if public worship is so conducted that owing to the feebleness of the minister a ripe Christian may find himself but little edified, yet public worship is a divine ordinance, and we are bound on several accounts to come *into the courts of the Lord*, v. 8. Much is due to example; more, to the express command of God.

11. The more we are instructed in the nature of true religion, the more clear will be our conviction that all attempts to serve God without *fear* will prove disastrous to our souls, vv. 4, 8.

12. Nor will God under any dispensation ever dispense with sincerity, integrity, uprightness, rectitude. Any service not rendered *in the beauty of holiness* will surely be rejected by him, who is a consuming fire, v. 8.

13. Our King is not only King of peace, but he is King of *righteousness*, v. 10. Blessed be God for all that is pure, and glorious, and infinite, and excellent in the character and conduct of our Lord Jesus Christ.

14. Let us joyfully receive the gospel and its Author. Let none be reluctant or linger. Christ's work is a work of redemption from sin, from wrath, and from wretchedness. He is light, and life, and salvation. His reign is like a morning without clouds. Let joy seize the highest notes of exultation as it proclaims to the world the glorious mysteries revealed in the gospel.

PSALM XCVII.

1 The LORD reigneth; let the earth rejoice; let the multitude of isles be glad *thereof*.

2 Clouds and darkness *are* round about him: righteousness and judgment *are* the habitation of his throne.

3 A fire goeth before him, and burneth up his enemies round about.

4 His lightnings enlightened the world: the earth saw, and trembled.

5 The hills melted like wax at the presence of the LORD, at the presence of the Lord of the whole earth.

6 The heavens declare his righteousness, and all the people see his glory.

7 Confounded be all they that serve graven images, that boast themselves of idols: worship him, all *ye* gods.

8 Zion heard, and was glad; and the daughters of Judah rejoiced because of thy judgments, O LORD.

9 For thou, LORD, *art* high above all the earth: thou art exalted far above all gods.

10 Ye that love the LORD, hate evil: he preserveth the souls of his saints; he delivereth them out of the hand of the wicked.

11 Light is sown for the righteous, and gladness for the upright in heart.

12 Rejoice in the LORD, ye righteous; and give thanks at the remembrance of his holiness.

DAVID is given as the author of this Psalm by the Syriac, Arabic, Septuagint, Ethiopic, Vulgate, Doway, Pool, Patrick and others. It seems nearly certain that it was written by the author of Psalm xcvi. Some Jews think Moses wrote it; but the weight of authority and evidence would ascribe it to the son of Jesse. Clarke: "Who the author was is uncertain: it is much in the spirit of David's finest compositions: and yet many learned men suppose it was written to celebrate the Lord's power and goodness in the restoration of the Jews from *Babylonish captivity*." Those, who seek a historic origin, vary much in their conjectures; some referring it to David's obtaining possession of the entire kingdom of Judah and Israel, 2 Sam. v.; some to his possession of certain countries not before held by Israel, 1 Chron. xviii.; some to the suppression of Absalom's rebellion; some to the removal of the ark. Scott dates it B. C. 1045; Clarke, B. C. 515. This Psalm is certainly Messianic. The Syriac says it is "a Psalm of David, in which he foretells the advent of Christ. He also insinuates in it his last coming." Luther: "Like the preceding, this also is a prophecy concerning Christ and his kingdom;" Calvin: "The description which we have of the kingdom of God in this Psalm does not apply to the state of it under the law. We may infer, accordingly, that it contains a prediction of that kingdom of Christ, which was erected upon the introduction of the gospel;" Tholuck: "We, who behold in history the partial manifestation at least of the Psalmist's vision, are entitled to the assertion that 'the theme of this Psalm is *the triumph of Christ over an unbelieving world in its present partial fulfilment and ultimate completion.*'" We might cite Fabritius, Piscator, Venema, Amesius, Patrick, Gill, Henry, Horne, Morison, Scott and others. By quoting v. 7, in Heb. i. 6, Paul has settled this matter. The names of the Almighty here found are *Jehovah* LORD, *Adonai* Lord and *Gel-yohn*, here rendered *High*, but commonly *Most High*, on which see on Psalms i. 2; ii. 4; vii. 17.

1. *The* LORD *reigneth*, literally *the* LORD *has reigned*. See on Ps. xciii. 1; xcvi. 10. If we take it as prophecy, the thing is so certain that we may speak of it as an accomplished fact. If we take it as a declaration of what now exists, it is an assertion of providence, made sure by the fact that God has always governed the world. *Let the earth rejoice*, or the earth shall rejoice. See on Ps. xcvi. 11. *Let the multitude of isles be glad* thereof. The verb is still in the future. *Isles*, always so rendered except in Jer. xlvii. 4, *country;* but if as is supposed Crete is intended, it should there be *island*. It seems clearly to have the simple meaning of *dry land* in Isa. xlii. 15. So also it means *coast* or *sea-coast*, for it is understood to be applied to the Peloponnessus or Greece under the name of *Isles of Elishah*, Ezek. xxvii. 7. For *multitude of isles* Horsley reads *various settlements of man;* and Fry, *extended shores*. A Hebrew in Judea would thus have designated all lands reached by ships. The phrase embraces the remotest Gentiles. Compare Isa xlii. 4; Matt. xii. 21.

2. *Clouds and darkness* are *round about him*. *Clouds*, see on Ps. lxxviii. 14; in the singular, but often fitly rendered in the plural. *Darkness*, see on Ps. xviii. 9. Four explanations are offered. 1. Some regard Joel ii. 2; Zeph. i. 15, as parallel, and understand times of alarm and gloominess, wasting and desolation. This cannot be the meaning here, for the world is called to be joyful, not sad nor alarmed. 2. Others refer it to the pillar of *cloud*, which was light to Israel and darkness to their foes. It was long an emblem of light and comfort, Isa. iv. 5. If this is the true explanation the meaning is that God guides, enlightens and protects his people, while he sends terror, confusion and disaster to their enemies. 3. Some refer the clause to the awful scenes of Sinai, Deut. iv. 11; v. 22, where we have the same words; one rendered *clouds;* the other, *thick darkness*. If this Psalm is Messianic, this view is excluded by Heb. xii. 18–24. 4. By clouds and darkness others think the prophet points to the inscrutableness of God's nature and ways even under the gospel. Clouds and darkness produce obscurity. What is obscure is unsearchable, though the mysteriousness may arise from the glory of the object, and may inspire great joy. What is so mysterious as the providence of God over the world, and especially the display of his love in the gift of his dear Son? Rom. xi. 33. Yet both in providence and in redemption all holy creatures in heaven and earth rejoice. It has been shown that in the gospel we are come to Mount Sion and not to mount Sinai. So that, if our Psalm refers to gospel times, we are rather confined by the words *clouds* and *darkness* to the

simple idea of mysteriousness. In Lam. iii. 44, the prophet seems to use *cloud* as expressive of impenetrable mysteriousness. In Job xxxviii. 9, we have both *clouds* and *darkness* in the sense of causes of obscurity. But this mysteriousness does not justify any doubt or suspicion respecting the perfect rectitude of Jehovah's dealings with men, for *Righteousness and judgment* are *the habitation of his throne. Righteousness*, as in Ps. iv. 1, 5; in Ps. ix. 4, *right;* in Ps. lxxxix. 14, *justice. Judgment*, see on Ps. i. 5; vii. 6; in Ps. ix. 4, *right.* The two words cover the whole ground of equity and justice. For *habitation* some have place; others, seat, basis, support; others, establishment. Compare Pr. xxv. 5; xxix. 14. Patrick: "He supports his government by doing exact and equal justice." Henry: "A golden thread of justice runs through the whole web of his government." In all his acts of government, God makes such decisions and arrangements as are perfectly consistent with right, justice, holiness. Were perfect justice between man and man surely and promptly administered, human society would be most happy. But if there were no delays on the part of God in inflicting vengeance on those, who sin against him, the memory of his long-suffering would perish from among men, and the earth itself would soon be depopulated. Mysterious as are some of God's delays, yet he is doing right all the while, and in the end he will show that in all cases he has been righteous.

3. *A fire goeth before him, and burneth up his enemies round about.* The most terrible judgments of God on transgressors, as in the destruction of Sodom and Gomorrah, were but expressions of his righteous displeasure. But sometimes *fire* is an emblem of God's awful purity. Thus John Owen and others, by devouring *fire* in Isa. xxxiii. 14, understand the intense and awful holiness of God. Compare Mal. iii. 2, 3; Matt. xxi. 12, 13, 23–27; Luke ii. 34; John ii. 13–17; vi. 66. This gives a good sense; but is not insisted on. It is rather probable that by *fire* here we are to understand the display of God's terrible majesty; see on Ps. l. 3. Alexander: "The future form is used because the verb describes not what the wrath of God is doing or has actually done, but what it will do when provoked by obstinate resistance." *Enemies, troublers, adversaries.*

4. *His lightnings enlightened the world. Lightnings*, united with *thunders*, in Ex. xix. 16; with *rain* in Ps. cxxxv. 7. In application to a *sword* or *spear* the same word is rendered *glittering*, Deut. xxxii. 41; Hab. iii. 11. But see on Ps. xviii. 14; lxxvii. 18, where the same word occurs. *Enlightened*, in the preterite. *World*, as in Ps. ix. 8; xviii. 15; xcvi. 10, 13. *The earth saw and trembled.* On the effect of God's majestic and terrible presence on all nature, see on Ps. xxix. 8, 9. *Trembled*, elsewhere *travailed, was in anguish, was sore pained.*

5. *The hills melted like wax at the presence of the* LORD, *at the presence of the Lord of the whole earth. Hills*, any elevations great or small. Often by hills or mountains we are to understand political powers, or states. Perhaps that is the true interpretation here. Compare Ps. xlvi. 2; Mic. i. 4. The Berleberg Bible gives even a more extended sense: "Even the mountains of human height and pride, the heights of human intellect and vanity, and also the kingdoms of the world." Compare 2 Cor. x. 5. Nothing can stand in opposition to God.

6. *The heavens declare his righteousness.* See on Ps. l. 6. In a *gracious* no less than in a *retributive* judgment God proceeds so as in no way to infringe on justice or equity. Mercy triumphs over judgment, not by trampling on it, but by meeting all its demands, and yet saving the sinner. The more God's ways are understood, the clearer will it be that he has done right. The *heavens*, either the angels, or God himself acting conspicuously. *And all the people see his glory.* The verb is in the past tense, expressive of entire certainty that the thing shall come to pass. Some have thought these predictions based on what was said by prophets who lived several hundred years later;

but David foretold the glory of Christ's kingdom as clearly as Isaiah, Zechariah, or Malachi. The *glory* is his honor and renown arising from the conduct of his great kingdom on principles of eternal rectitude.

7. *Confounded be all they that serve graven images, that boast themselves of idols.* The verb is in the future and is best so rendered, see on Ps. vi. 10. *Serve*, applied to serving the Lord, or the king, or idols, Ex. x. 11; Jer. xl. 9; Ps. ii. 11. All worship of images graven, carved, molten, painted, or imagined is idolatry; and all idols in temples or in our hearts are *vanities*, Ps. xcvi. 5. In the day of wrath idols will not save. *Worship him, all ye gods.* This rendering is approved by Fabritius, Piscator, Venema, church of England, Edwards, Jebb and Fry. Instead of *gods* we have *angels* in the Syriac, Arabic, Septuagint, Ethiopic, Vulgate, Doway, Amesius, Tremellius and Junius, Waterland, etc. What settles the question with the great mass of commentators is that Paul quotes in Heb. i. 6, the Septuagint version of these words: *Let all the angels of God worship him.* Calvin says this " properly applies to the angels." Patrick says: " Let all that are called gods, whether princes on earth, or angels in heaven, bow down to him, as the only Saviour." Henry says that, Hebrews i. 6 " helps us to a key to this whole Psalm, and shows us that it must be applied to the exalted Redeemer." Clarke: " The words are most certainly applied to the Saviour of the world by the author of the epistle to the Hebrews;" Horne: " The clause declares the supremacy of Christ over all that are called gods, in heaven and in earth;" Scott: " Christ as Emmanuel is peculiarly intended." The term *elohim* is applied to angels, Ps. viii. 5. Nor would there be any fitness in calling on dumb idols to worship the Firstbegotten. Some think that idols here are put for those who worship them. But in the early part of the epistle to the Hebrews Paul is conducting a close argument with people, who had all their lives known the Old Testament Scriptures; and the whole power of his reasoning would have been lost if he had quoted irrelevant proofs. If his argument is that Christ is superior to angels, because they are required to worship him, all is plain; otherwise, nugatory. Moreover, it is admitted that other quotations from Ps. ii. 7; viii. 5; xlv. 6, 7; cii. 25, 26; civ. 4, 5; cx. 1, found in the early part of the same epistle are very pertinent and conclusive proofs. What right have we to make this an exception, a mere allusion and accommodation?

8. *Zion heard, and was glad; and the daughters of Judah rejoiced because of thy judgments,* O LORD. *Zion*, the church of God, the whole family named in heaven and earth. The Jews as a people have never hailed with gladness the birth, ascension or doctrine of Christ; but only God's true people. The true Israel *heard* and was heartily glad. By the *daughters of Judah*, some understand the smaller towns or villages of the Holy Land. But as on public occasions of mirth or mourning, Jewish women took a prominent part, the allusion is probably to that custom. See on Ps. xlviii. 11. *Judgments*, see on Ps. x. 5; xix. 9; xxxvi. 6.

9. *For thou,* LORD, *art high above all the earth.* See on Ps. lxxxiii. 18. *High*, with very few exceptions in the Psalms rendered *Highest, Most High. Thou art exalted far above all gods.* See on Ps. xlvii. 9; xcv. 3. Calvin: " There is a comparison drawn between God and the angels, and whatever has any claim to eminence. The Psalmist limits all other excellency in such a manner as to leave no room for questioning that all majesty is comprehended in God only. This was the case more eminently when God manifested himself in his only-begotten Son, who is the express image of himself."

10. *Ye that love the* LORD, *hate evil.* This clause is parallel to Ps. xxxiv. 14. There cannot be excessive hatred to sin. We may well *abhor* it and ourselves on account of it, Rom. xii. 9; Job xlii. 6. The special warning here seems to be against doing evil that good may come, against using unlawful means for obtaining victory. Well may we do our duty and leave results with God; for *he preserveth the souls of his saints*

See on Ps. xxxi. 23; xxxvii. 28. *Souls*, either lives or souls. *Saints, merciful, godly.*
Yea, *he delivereth them out of the hand of the wicked. Delivereth*, in the future, he does
it now and will do it forever. *Wicked*, in Ps. i. 1, ungodly; all wicked men and
fallen angels.

11. *Light is sown for the righteous, and gladness for the upright in heart. Darkness*
is often an emblem of all evil, natural and moral; so *light* represents all good, tem
poral and spiritual. Here it is put for comfort and happiness, interpreted in the last
clause as *gladness*. Dark days may come to good men, but they shall not last always.
Light *is sown* for them, that is, it is scattered far and wide, and may spring up in a
gourd as to Jonah, in a lion's den as to Daniel, in a dungeon as to Paul and Silas,
from a raven as to Elijah, from a long-lost son as to Jacob, from a crucified Redeemer
as to all Christians. The light that is sown will bring a great harvest, a rich return.
In this verse the word *righteous* is singular, and *upright* plural. If this variation in
number means anything, it is that God's people shall both individually and collectively
be cared for and blessed.

12. *Rejoice in the* LORD, *ye righteous; and give thanks at the remembrance of his
holiness.* The first clause is found in Ps. xxxii. 11; the latter, in Ps. xxx. 4. Joy is
provided, let the righteous not make themselves sad, but walk in the light.

DOCTRINAL AND PRACTICAL REMARKS.

1. Let us hold fast the doctrines of providence, and of the Mediatorial reign of
Christ, v. 1. They are happily blended. Henry: "The providential kingdom is
twisted in with the mediatorial, and the administration of both is in the hand of
Christ." Both are universal, supreme, glorious. "Tremendous is the destiny of those
who dare set their face against the throne of Messiah."

2. There is hope for the heathen. It is found in the gospel of the kingdom of
Christ, v. 1. The day is fast approaching when all nations shall flow unto it.

3. America is one of the lands that is spoken of as *isles*, v. 1. Greatly has God
blessed us, as he has other lands unknown to ancient Israel. How long mercy will be
extended to this ungrateful and gainsaying people is known to no man. Oh that the
Lord would make us a penitent people.

4. It cannot be denied that impenetrable mystery hangs about the ways of God to
men, v. 2. This is no cause of offence to an humble, pious soul. How could it be
otherwise? A scheme of infinite love, and wisdom, and holiness, comprehending eternity in its results, must be beyond the measure of mortals. Clarke: "God is *infinite;*
he acts from his own *counsels*, which are *infinite*, in reference to ends, which are also
infinite; therefore the reasons of his government cannot be comprehended by the
feeble limited powers of man," Ecc. vii. 24.

5. But if a good man is often so astonished at events around him as to make him
dumb with silence, he yet can rejoice and ought to rejoice in the glorious and abundant
justice of God, which, as it is now real, so shall it be conspicuous at last, vv. 2, 6.
Ultimately it shall be confessed in heaven and earth that the righteousness of Christ's
kingdom is not impaired, but rather magnified by the amazing display of his mercy
and grace in the gospel.

6. There must be something desperately wicked and malignant in the very nature
of sin, to leave men *enemies to God* under such an economy as that made known in
the kingdom of God, v. 3.

7. When the cup of men's iniquities is full, or whenever Jehovah would inspire
salutary fear, he can easily make terrible displays of his majesty and wrath, vv. 3,
4, 5. Clarke: "The fire is his pioneer, which destroys all the hindrances in his way,

and makes him a plain passage." No might nor majesty in the creature contending with God is more than briers and stubble before the devastating flame.

8. In absurdity and criminality it seems hard to conceive anything more offensive to God or destructive to the soul than idolatry, v. 7. Yet men are mad upon their idols. Nothing but true religion has ever been found sufficient to pull down the strong holds of idolatry and the superstition of worshipping *images*. It requires the ark of God to bring down the image of Dagon. The worship of God by images is wholly idolatrous, Deut. iv. 12, 15, 16. Fearful is the guilt of all, who corrupt God's worship by human devices.

9. Nor is abhorrence of images in God's worship unusual among God's people, nor are they offended at the condemnation of all such corruptions. *Zion heard and was glad*, v. 8.

10. The Old Testament, quoted and explained in the New, amply teaches and establishes the supreme divinity of Jesus Christ, and shows that he is to be adored. If angels worship him and at the bidding of the Father, it cannot be wrong for us to do it, v. 7. No book so opposes and denounces all false worship as the Bible; yet even when so doing, it calls on us to honor the Son as we honor the Father. This doctrine makes God's people, and all the daughters of Zion glad, v. 8.

11. None can withstand or overreach the Almighty Redeemer. He is above all and over all, v. 9. He is the blessed and only Potentate. He is full of power and glory.

12. True piety has always had in it the *love of God*, v. 10. By this his servants are pleased with all he says and does, with all they know of him, and of his Son.

13. Genuine love to God makes one hate sin in every form and shape, v. 10. To a lover of God as to God himself, nothing is so abominable as iniquity.

14. The preservations and deliverances of holy men are worthy of constant and everlasting celebration in sacred songs, v. 10. Let Jehovah have all the glory, which is his due. Let not the saints, therefore, undertake to avenge their own wrongs, nor effect their own victories; but quietly leave all in the hands of him, who reigns forever. Let them wait patiently for the Lord.

15. For bright days are coming, v. 11. Light will arise. Diodati: "Even in this world eternal happiness is prepared for the righteous; who have the seed thereof within themselves through God's promise, and by the gift of the Holy Ghost." Clarke: "As surely as the *grain* that is sown in the earth shall vegetate and bring forth its proper fruit in its season; so surely shall *light*, prosperity and *gladness*, comfort and peace, be communicated to God's people."

16. But let us not forget that all piety not based in integrity and an *upright heart* falls short of the divine requirement, and must end in shame, v. 11. God cares not for names, or forms, or appearances, if our hearts are not with him. The feet may not be swift to shed blood, the hands may refuse a bribe, the tongue may be as smooth as butter; but if the heart is wrong, all is wrong.

17. Let not the righteous be cast down but rejoice in conflicts and trials; only let them not glory in themselves at all but *in the Lord*, v. 12. He is the fountain of all blessedness and perfection. He never fails those who look to him.

18. Let Christ's people learn greatly to love, and thank, and praise their Lord and Redeemer, especially for his *holiness; the remembrance* of which makes all heaven glad, v. 12. Nothing in his character would be adorable, were it not for the infinite rectitude of his nature, Heb. vii. 26, 27.

PSALM XCVIII.

A Psalm.

1 O sing unto the LORD a new song; for he hath done marvellous things: his right hand, and his holy arm, hath gotten him the victory.

2 The LORD hath made known his salvation: his righteousness hath he openly shewed in the sight of the heathen.

3 He hath remembered his mercy and his truth toward the house of Israel: all the ends of the earth have seen the salvation of our God.

4 Make a joyful noise unto the LORD, all the earth: make a loud noise, and rejoice, and sing praise.

5 Sing unto the LORD with the harp; with the harp, and the voice of a psalm.

6 With trumpets and sound of cornet make a joyful noise before the LORD, the King.

7 Let the sea roar, and the fulness thereof; the world, and they that dwell therein.

8 Let the floods clap *their* hands: let the hills be joyful together

9 Before the LORD; for he cometh to judge the earth: with righteousness shall he judge the world, and the people with equity.

ON the title see on title of Psalm iii. The authorship of this is probably the same as that of several Psalms immediately preceding. The Syriac, Arabic, Septuagint, Ethiopic, Vulgate, Doway and many others ascribe it to David. There is no evidence that it had a historic occasion, though the Syriac says it relates to the "Restoration of the Israelites from Egypt;" and Clarke says, "It was probably written to celebrate the deliverance from the Babylonish captivity." Yet even he adds: "But it is to be understood prophetically of the redemption of the world by Jesus Christ;" and the Syriac says: "It is to be understood spiritually of the advent of the Messiah, and the calling of the Gentiles to the Christian faith." The Chaldee styles it "a prophetic Psalm." Scott dates it B. C. 1045; Clarke, B. C. 515. Many notice a strong resemblance between this and Ps. xcvi. Doubtless this is Messianic. Such is the judgment of many. Luther: "This again is a prophecy concerning the preaching of Christ and the spread of his kingdom." Horne styles it an "evangelical hymn," in which "the prophet extols the miracles, the victory, the salvation, the righteousness, the mercy, and truth of the Redeemer." Pool: "This Psalm is an evident prediction of the coming of the Messiah, and of the blessed effects thereof." Hengstenberg: "Like the preceding it sets forth the appearance of the Lord in his kingdom." Calvin, Scott and many others speak in the same strain. We have here two names of the Most High, *Jehovah* LORD and *Elohim God*, on which see on Ps. i. 2; iii. 2.

1. *O sing unto the* LORD *a new song.* This clause is precisely the same as in Ps. xcvi. 1, on which see. It is a call to extraordinary praise and thanksgiving. *For he hath done marvellous things.* We have had the same word rendered *marvellous works, wondrous works, wonders,* in Ps. ix. 1; xxvi. 7; xcvi. 3. *Has done;* the thing though future is so certain, that it is spoken of as already done. What God proposes he surely effects. The reason is that he is in no sense dependent on the will, skill, or power of any other. *His right hand, and his holy arm hath gotten him the victory.* *Right hand* seems here to unite in it the idea of dexterity and power. Compare Ps. xvii. 7; xviii. 35; cxxxvii. 5. *His holy arm,* literally *his arm of holiness.* Isaiah uses the same phrase, probably taken from David. His language well expounds this verse and the next. Read and ponder Isa. lii. 10; lix. 16; lxiii. 5. Some have suggested that the Psalmist took from Isaiah. It is much more probable that Isaiah under the guidance of the Spirit used the words of the Psalmist. Calvin

thinks that both here and in Isa. lix. 16, " *the arm of the Lord* stands opposed to ordinary means, which although when employed they derogate nothing from the glory of God, yet prevent us from so fully discovering his presence as we might otherwise do." Hammond thinks that the whole clause "most literally belongs to the prophetic sense, accomplished in the resurrection of Christ." No doubt that event was full of *wonders;* but so is the whole scheme and work of redemption.

2. *The* LORD *hath made known his salvation; his righteousness hath he openly shewed in the sight of the heathen. Salvation* and *righteousness,* the words usually so rendered. See on Ps. xii. 5; xviii. 2; xcv. 1; and Ps. v. 8; xi. 7; lxxxix. 16. *Heathen, Gentiles, nations,* as in Ps. ii. 1, 8; xcvi. 3, 10. The whole scheme of *salvation* is by *righteousness,* and from early ages was promised to the Gentiles.

3. *He hath remembered his mercy and his truth to the house of Israel.* To the Jews *first* was the full message and offer of life communicated, and that with amazing tenderness and astonishing miracles. But the divine compassion overflowed all narrow and national bounds: *All the ends of the earth have seen the salvation of our God.* Compare Luke i. 72–79; ii. 30–33; Rom. x. 18. The verbs are in the past tense, because the prophet sees that these things will surely be done. The whole scheme and power of salvation spring from gratuity. Salvation is in no sense of man, nor for any worthiness in man. The work of Christ in the world could not be wrought, and his salvation could not be made known, and heaven and earth be silent:

4. *Make a joyful noise unto the* LORD, *all the earth. Make a joyful noise; shout, triumph.* See on Ps. xlvii. 1; xcv. 1, 2. In this work *all the earth* shall in the fulness of time unite. *Make a loud noise,* literally *break forth* as into singing, *break forth into joy,* nowhere else in the Psalms. See Isa. xliv. 23; lii. 9. *And rejoice,* often rendered *sing, sing aloud, shout, shout for joy, triumph,* see Ps. v. 11; xcvi. 12. In v. 8 of this Psalm it is rendered *be joyful. Sing psalms,* a verb also rendered *sing, sing praises, give praise,* see Ps. vii. 17; ix. 2, 11. The annals of the universe mention nothing so suited to arouse creation, as the salvation wrought out by Christ. If rational creatures should all keep silence, the stones would cry out. Luke xix. 40.

5. *Sing unto the* LORD *with the harp; with the harp, and the voice of a psalm. Harp,* as in Ps. xxxiii. 2; xcii. 3, uniformly rendered. The *voice of a psalm* is the use of a Psalm in song or chant. The first verb is in v. 4, rendered *sing praise.* Horsley: Chant unto Jehovah to the harp. To the harp, and the sound of the zimrah, taking the zimrah here and in Ps. lxxxi. 2, as the name of some musical instrument. Clarke thinks *zimrah* is either a *musical instrument,* or a *species of ode* modulated by different voices. In Isa. li. 3; Am. v. 23, the word is rendered *melody.*

6. *With trumpets, and sound of cornet, make a joyful noise before the* LORD, *the King. Trumpets,* always so rendered, not elsewhere in the Psalms. *Cornet,* more commonly rendered *trumpet.* See on Ps. xlvii. 5; lxxxi. 3. *Make a joyful noise,* as in v. 4. *Jehovah Jesus* here appears as *King,* and must be gladly received.

7. *Let the sea roar, and the fulness thereof.* The same words occur in Ps. xcvi. 11, on which see. *Fulness,* all contained in it. *The world and they that dwell therein.* See Ps. xxiv. 1. In this verse the antithesis is between the *sea* and the *land* or *world. Roar,* in the future, *shall roar.* Fabritius, Amesius, Piscator, Tremellius and Junius read, *Make a great noise.* This verse and the next contain the boldest personification, investing all nature with intelligent faculties and vocal powers.

8. *Let the floods clap their hands; let the hills be joyful together.* The verbs are in the future. *Floods,* often rendered *rivers,* strong moving currents of water. Here it represents all water, and is in antithesis to *hills* or *mountains.* The *sea,* the *land,* the *floods* and the *hills* comprehend all nature. On clapping hands see on Ps. xlvii. 1.

Isaiah uses the same phrase, Isa. lv. 12. This great and universal thanksgiving and gladness shall be

9. *Before the* LORD, not only in his presence, from which nothing is hid, but as in his gracious presence and to the glory of his name. Nor is this call upon all creation idle. There is good cause for it; *For he cometh to judge the earth.* The verb is in the preterite, indicating that the thing is as good as done. *Judge the earth,* see on Ps. xcvi. 13. This *judging,* or ruling is most benign; *With righteousness shall he judge the world, and the people with equity. Righteousness,* both moral and evangelical; it is the same word as in Ps. iv. 1, 5; xcvii. 2, 6. *Equity, uprightness,* as in Ps. ix. 8. Here it is plural, *equities. People,* plural, *nations.*

DOCTRINAL AND PRACTICAL REMARKS.

1. The righteous will never be done singing the praises of their God and Redeemer, v. 1. "The joy which Christ bringeth can never wax old." Where the benefits received are infinite, the praises cannot be extravagant.

2. Nor will God's people ever cease to admire the *wonders* of his love and counsels, v. 1. Salvation excels all the miracles ever wrought. It is a wonder of wisdom, power, grace, faithfulness and righteousness. Take from natural religion all that is supernatural and incomprehensible, and it is both inane and jejune. Take from revealed religion its stupendous wonders, and what have we left? Our life comes by Christ's death; our healing, by his stripes; our joys, by his sorrows; our exaltation, by his humiliation. By his fall he conquered; by shedding his blood he gained *the victory.*

3. What a blessed thing that the middle wall of partition is broken down, and that the *ends of the earth* are invited to Immanuel, vv. 2, 3. In him there is "neither Jew nor Greek, Barbarian, Scythian, bond nor free, but Christ is all and in all."

4. Salvation is all of God, and not at all of the creature, by grace, not by works, vv. 2, 3. Compare Ps. xliv. 2–4. Were it otherwise boasting would not be excluded, Rom. iii. 27. The author of redemption is heavenly, not human.

5. It is right that all nations should see this salvation, v. 3. So great a redemption as that wrought out by Christ cannot be sufficiently lauded by a few, nor rewarded by the faith and love of one tribe or people. Compare Isa. xlix. 4–7.

6. It is therefore not without good and sufficient cause that the Gentiles, who partake of such inestimable blessings, are called upon to be exceedingly joyful and thankful, v. 4.

7. Indeed to all people in all ages the true and saving knowledge of the Redeemer is justly felt to be matter of intense and perpetual thanksgiving and adoration, vv. 4–6. Even the predictions of such glorious things filled the ancient church with the exultation of a blessed hope. Much more then may the gospel in its full revelation spread joy and gladness, Isa. xii. 2–6; xxxv. 1–10.

8. Respecting instrumental music see REMARKS on Ps. xxxiii. 2. But let us never forget that Jehovah demands our warm affections. Without the heart all is nugatory.

9. Indeed if all creation animate and inanimate should unite in this work, eternity would not be too long to express the gladness diffused by the work and triumphs of the Redeemer, vv. 7, 8.

10. If on earth and to all who receive the salvation of the gospel, Christ brings so inestimable blessings as are sung by poets, celebrated by prophets, and confessed by martyrs, what must not the glory be in heaven above? There every voice and every harp is attuned to resound the praises of the Redeemer for new evolutions of his everlasting love.

11. All our acts, in particular all our religious professions and worship are in the

presence of Christ, v. 9; and therefore sincerity, purity, holiness, reverence and godly fear at all times become us. "Carnal mirth is an enemy to holy joy."

12. He, who now rules the world, and who will finally *judge* it, must be *divine*, v. 9. None else could well or safely do either. Our Jesus upholds all things by the word of his power, and to him has been committed all judgment, Heb. i. 3; John v. 22.

13. It is pleasing to see how wondrously the Old and New Testaments correspond, like a complicated lock and a curious key. Clarke has given us a paragraph headed· "David is the *Voice*, and Mary is the *Echo*.

"1. DAVID. O sing unto the Lord a new song.

"MARY. My soul doth magnify the Lord.

"2. DAVID. He hath done marvellous things.

"MARY. He that is mighty hath done great things.

"3. DAVID. With his own right hand and holy arm hath he gotten himself the victory.

"MARY. He hath shewed strength with his arm, and scattered the proud in the imagination of their hearts.

"4. DAVID. The Lord hath made known his salvation; his righteousness hath he openly shewed.

"MARY. His mercy is on them that fear him, from generation to generation.

"5. DAVID. He hath remembered his mercy and his truth toward the house of Israel.

"MARY. He hath holpen his servant Israel in remembrance of his mercy."

We can hardly engage in a more profitable business than in comparing the two Testaments. Like the cherubim over the mercy-seat they look towards each other, and cast light on each other.

14. Everything in Scripture, rightly interpreted, leads to holiness. Christ's reign on earth is to that end, Luke i. 74, 75. His final coming to *judge* the world calls us to purity. Compare 2 Pet. iii. 10–15.

PSALM XCIX.

1 The LORD reigneth; let the people tremble: he sitteth *between* the cherubim; let the earth be moved.

2 The LORD *is* great in Zion; and he *is* high above all the people.

3 Let them praise thy great and terrible name; *for* it *is* holy.

4 The king's strength also loveth judgment; thou dost establish equity, thou executest judgment and righteousness in Jacob.

5 Exalt ye the LORD our God, and worship at his footstool; *for* he *is* holy.

6 Moses and Aaron among his priests, and Samuel among them that call upon his name; they called upon the LORD, and he answered them.

7 He spake unto them in the cloudy pillar: they kept his testimonies, and the ordinance *that* he gave them.

8 Thou answeredst them, O LORD our God: thou wast a God that forgavest them, though thou tookest vengeance of their inventions.

9 Exalt the LORD our God, and worship at his holy hill: for the LORD our God *is* holy.

THE Syriac, Arabic, Septuagint, Ethiopic, Vulgate, Fabritius, Patrick, Pool and Gill regard David as the author of this Psalm. Jarchi gives Moses as its author.

But this cannot be so, for Samuel, who is mentioned in v. 6, was not born until several hundred years after the death of Moses. Nor could it have been written after the beginning of the Babylonish captivity; for in v. 1, God is represented as *sitting between the cherubim*, and the Chaldeans destroyed the first temple, and from that time we read no more of the ark. It is certain that it and all its furniture were wanting in the second temple. The probability is that David wrote it after he was somewhat settled in his kingdom. Scott dates it B. C. 1040; Clarke, B. C. 515. The Syriac styles it " a prophecy concerning the glory of the kingdom of Christ." With this agree Luther and others. The names of the Almighty in it are *Jehovah* LORD, *Elohim God* and *El God*, on which respectively see on Ps. i. 2; iii. 2; v. 4.

1. *The* LORD *reigneth*, in all respects as in Ps. xciii. 1; xcvi. 10; xcvii. 1. *Let the people tremble*. *People*, plural, *peoples, nations*. *Tremble*, elsewhere *shake, be disquieted, be moved, quake, be afraid, be troubled, stand in awe*, see on Ps. iv. 4. There is no reason for supposing that the *trembling* here demanded is different from that required in Ps. ii. 11, or that it is inconsistent with the *rejoicing* commended in Ps. xcvii. 1. Amyrald says the clause "may concern believing as well as unbelieving nations." Calvin: "The people, who were formerly called upon to rejoice, are now commanded to tremble." This is a good sense, and results from a natural construction. But there is another, expressed in some of the versions, *The Lord reigneth, the people are angry*. This makes the effect of his reigning to be the enraging of the nations. The original will bear this. In Pr. xxix. 9, the same word is rendered *rage*. Even the birth of Christ *troubled* Herod and all Jerusalem with him, Matt. ii. 3. This idea is somewhat modified by the church of England: *The Lord reigneth, be the people never so impatient*. Hammond favors some such construction. But the first view is the most natural and best corresponds with the prophetic character of this Psalm, and with the scope of several Psalms preceding it. *Tremble*, in the future, *shall tremble*. *He sitteth* between *the cherubim*. How the ark of the covenant was constructed, covered, and surmounted, and how important it was to Israel may be seen in Exodus xxv. 10–22. Between *the cherubim*, see on Ps. lxxx. 1. *Sitteth, dwelleth, maketh his abode*, as God did for centuries. Such language teaches that the Most High deals familiarly with man. It is parallel to John xiv. 21, 23. *Let the earth be moved*, in the future, *shall be moved;* parallel to *tremble* in the first clause; the verb is found here only. The kind of *moving* must be determined by the context. Hengstenberg: " The trembling of the people and the moving of the earth are expressions of fear and reverence before the Lord appearing in his kingdom."

2. *The* LORD *is great in Zion; and he is high above all the people*. *Great*, see on Ps. xcv. 3; xcvi. 4. *High*, a participle, *lifted up, exalted*. In v. 5 the verb from the same root is rendered *exalt*. *People*, plural, *nations*, as in v. 1. *Zion* and *the people* comprehend all the world, Jews and Gentiles. God's kingdom shall be universally set up. Venema: "He is the exalted and most powerful King and avenger of his people in Jerusalem, and superior to and set over all the nations of the earth."

3. *Let them praise thy great and terrible name; for it is holy*. *Them*, all the nations, and not as Calvin thinks, the *faithful* in distinction from the nations. Three things are said of God's name. 1. It is *great*, first so called in Joshua vii. 9; see on Psalm lxxvi. 1. It resounds through the universe. God makes himself known in all worlds. 2. It is *terrible;* in Gen. xxviii. 17, *dreadful;* in Ex. xv. 11, *fearful;* in Ps. lxxxix. 7, *to be had in reverence;* in Ps. cxi. 9, *reverend*. Compare Deut. x. 17; see on Ps. xlv. 4. Commonly in heathen countries are told many ridiculous stories respecting their idols. They laugh at them, and at will banish them. 3. God's name is *holy*. This is not true of any of the false gods. They were revengeful, proud, and in many ways abominable, according to the belief of their worshippers.

Praise, elsewhere *confess, give thanks*, 1 Kings viii. 33, 35; Pr. xxviii. 13; Ps. vi. 5; lxxxix. 5.

4. *The king's strength also loveth judgment.* There is considerable difficulty in this clause. *Strength*, as in Ps. viii. 2. Merrick: "*The king's strength* seems here put for the king himself." Edwards renders it: "Though the king be powerful, he loveth judgment." Probably Edwards gives the sense, although his translation is free. Diodati paraphrases it thus: "This king tempereth his power with justice, contrary to the custom of tyrants of the world; see Job xxxvi. 5." Alexander: "The meaning of the clause seems to be, that God's power is controlled in its exercise by his love of justice." The same view is taken by Patrick, Horne and others. But who is the king here mentioned? 1. Some think he is Jehovah as the head of the theocracy. 2. Others suppose David as acting under God in the kingdom is intended. Neither of these views regards the ode as prophetic. 3. The remaining interpretation makes the king to be Jesus the Mediator. This is to be preferred. The king is here spoken of. He is next addressed: *Thou dost establish equity, thou executest judgment and righteousness in Jacob.* The verbs are in the preterite, having the force of a future; or, God has always done these things, and we may infallibly conclude that he will continue to do them to the end of the world. *In Jacob*, in v. 2, in Zion, see on Ps. lix. 13. See Ps. lxxvi. 1.

5. *Exalt ye the* LORD *our God, and worship at his footstool; for he is holy.* *Exalt*, as in v. 9. In v. 1, the preterite is rendered *is high*. *Worship, bow down*, the same as in Ps. xxix. 2; xcvi. 9; xcvii. 7. *He is holy*, also terminates v. 9; and some so render the same words in v. 3. God's infinite rectitude is a sufficient ground for all the honor he demands. This Psalm is a prophecy respecting Christ, yet its language is fitly borrowed from the dispensation under which it was uttered. This is common in the prophets, Isa. lxvi. 23; Mal. iii. 3.

6. *Moses and Aaron among his priests, and Samuel among them that call upon his name.* *Priests*, commonly so rendered; it also signifies princes, principal persons, or chief rulers. Moses and Aaron were of the tribe of Levi, as was also Samuel, who was a descendant of Korah in the *sixteenth* generation. So that by the law of the priesthood they might all properly fill that office. That Aaron was a priest none will deny. That Moses and Samuel at least occasionally exercised the functions of the sacerdotal office seems sufficiently clear from Ex. xvii. 15; xxiv. 7, 8; Lev. viii. 15–30; 1 Sam. ix. 13; xvi. 3, 5. It is true that Moses had other functions, as law-giver, Ex. xviii. 19–21; and that Samuel was also a judge, 1 Sam. vii. 6, 15, 17. But they also offered sacrifices and prayer. All these men were intercessors: *They called upon the Lord, and he answered them*, Nu. xi. 2; xxi. 7; Deut. ix. 26; Ex. xxviii. 12; 1 Sam. vii. 9; Ps. cvi. 23.

7. *He spake unto them in the cloudy pillar.* This is true of Moses and Aaron, see Ex. xvi. 10, 11; xvii. 6; xix. 9, 18, 19, 24; xx. 21, 22. How he spoke to Samuel may be learned from 1 Sam. iii. 10; vii. 9, 10. The general declaration is that in an extraordinary manner God made known his will to these men, and this was often if not commonly done in the pillar of cloud. When God *thundered* on the Philistines, there was doubtless a cloud present, 1 Sam. vii. 10. And yet God was not confined to the pillar of cloud, but "at sundry times and in divers manners spake in time past unto the fathers," Heb. i. 1. Nor was his speaking in vain. They obeyed his voice. *They kept his testimonies, and the ordinance that he gave them.* On *testimonies* see on Ps. xix. 7. *Ordinance*, in Ps. ii. 7, *decree*, sometimes *law* and often *statute*. On *keeping testimonies* see on Ps. xxv. 10. Obedience under all dispensations is necessary and is pleasing to God, 1 Sam. xv. 22; John xiv. 21.

8. *Thou answeredst them, O* LORD *our God.* Either God answered Moses, Aaron

and Samuel praying for the people, or he answered the requests of the people at the intercession of these men. The general sense is the same; but evidently the import of the word *them* is changed in this verse, if not in this clause. *Thou wast a God that forgavest them, though thou tookest vengeance of their inventions.* Although Moses and Aaron and Samuel were sinners, yet clearly the reference is to the *people.* This is the view of Venema, Clarke, Horne, Hengstenberg and many others. God punished the Israelites for their wickedness, but he did not root them out as a nation. Examine Ex. xxxii. 1–35; Num. xvi. 46–50; 1 Sam. vii. 9. Compare 2 Sam. vii. 14, 15.

9. *Exalt the* LORD *our God, and worship at his holy hill; for the* LORD *our God is holy.* Much the same as in v. 5. God is *holy,* therefore he must be exalted and adored.

Doctrinal and Practical Remarks.

1. Whatever else is doubtful, it is certain that the *Lord reigns,* that the Scriptures lay great stress on this truth, and that both the fact and the truth have vast bearings on the joys and sorrows, hopes and fears of both good and bad men, v. 1. However surrounded and beset by foes human and Satanic, let us fear God and nothing else. His kingdom ruleth over all. Amesius: "The reign of God terrible to the world, if rightly viewed and considered, is with believers a powerful argument to stir them up every way to glorify his name."

2. All this is heightened by the consideration that Christ is King. The God-man reigns.

3. Dickson: "The Lord's people do not worship an unknown God, they know who he is and where to find him, to wit, in his ordinances, on the throne of grace, reconciling the world to himself in Christ: *he sitteth* between *the cherubim,* v. 1.

4. The supremacy of Christ in the church and in all the world is a cardinal doctrine in the writings of the prophets and apostles, v. 2. Horne: "The power and preëminence of the Redeemer, whom no creature is able to resist, are reasons why all should save themselves, by yielding in time to his sceptre and by taking the benefit of his protection, instead of incurring his displeasure."

5. God is greatly to be praised, v. 3. Especially is God in Christ the wonder of wonders, before whom all the angels of heaven and all the spirits of just men made perfect bow and adore.

6. Amesius: "The rectitude of the administration of his kingdom in the church supplies abundant matter for glorifying God," v. 4. Could men or angels by searching find out one case of error, wrong, or want of equity in the divine administration, the happiness of holy creatures would be at an end. Calvin: "There is nothing that more animates and encourages the faithful to render obedience to God, or inspires them with greater zeal to observe his law, than to find in this course of action that they are the objects of his paternal care, and that the righteousness which he requires from his own people in words, is on his part reciprocated by kind deeds."

7. God's holiness cannot be too often mentioned to the honor of his name, vv. 3, 5, 9. The rectitude of his nature and ways is an element in the worship of the temple not made with hands, Isa. vi. 3; Rev. xv. 3. The more we know of God, the humbler shall we be. The worship of heaven is more profound than that on earth ever is. And the more God's holiness appears, the more vile and abominable must sin appear to be; and the more dreadful our ruin, the more glorious and amazing is salvation by Christ—a salvation which in nothing impinges upon justice or holiness. Therefore let us not measure the service we render, or the humility we exhibit to God. Let us *bow down at his footstool.*

8. What a glorious company that of the redeemed must be, v. 6. Here we have mentioned by name Moses, and Aaron, and Samuel. Another prophet speaks of Noah,

Daniel and Job, Ezek. xiv. 14. When Jesus was transfigured, Moses and Elias appeared. There around the throne, besides the angels in their shining ranks, are the martyrs and confessors, the apostles and prophets, the kings and righteous men of all ages, who have truly loved the Saviour. Every choice spirit that ever left the world is worshipping before the throne. Glory to God, who takes the beggar and sets him among princes; yea, makes all his people kings and priests unto God and the Lamb forever and ever.

9. Let no professed follower of Christ regard it as safe to live without prayer, v. 6. *Calling upon the name of the Lord* embraces indeed all acts of worship. But prayer is a prominent and an essential part of the worship of a sinner on earth. Preaching Christ's gospel and praying are the two greatest things done in this world, Acts vi. 4.

10. Especially should God's people abound in intercession. The example of Abram pleading for the cities of the plain is a memorable instance of God's approbation of such intercessions, Gen. xviii. 23–32. Compare Job xlii. 10; Joel ii. 17; Matt. xxiv. 22; Jas. v. 16.

11. But it is in vain to cry to God for ourselves or others, unless we have the spirit of hearty and universal obedience, v. 7. Compare Isa. i. 15–17; Jer. xiv. 12; Mic. iii. 4.

12. How vast the superiority of the Christian over all others. True, he has not the propitiatory that was in the tabernacle, but he has the true mercy-seat; he has not the cherubim standing over the propitiatory, but he has living and mighty angels to guard, uphold, and minister unto him; he has not the ark of *shittim-wood* overlaid with pure gold; but he has Christ, of whom that ark was but a faint emblem; he has not the pot of manna; but he has the true bread that came from heaven; he has not the Urim and Thummim; but he has the lively oracles; he has not the altar of burnt offering; but he has an altar, whereof they have no right to eat who serve the tabernacle; he has not the pillar of cloud to go before him; but he has a wonderful providence to direct his whole course; he has no Canaan filled with heathen enemies to conquer; but he has a promised land, full of all felicities.

13. Let us never forget the mercy of God expressed to sinners in the long-suffering, forbearance and *forgiveness* manifested to them, v. 8. He who has any just sense of sin, wonders not at the misery he sees on earth so much as at the display of God's kindness in his allotments, and especially in the pardoning mercy offered to sinners and granted to believers.

14. It is a fair test of all *worship* and doctrine, if we can ascertain whether it *exalts God*, vv. 5, 9. Whatever puts up the creature and human inventions is false and foolish. Whatever puts Jehovah on the throne, and makes him Lawgiver, King, Judge, Redeemer and All, is right.

PSALM C.

A Psalm of praise.

1 Make a joyful noise unto the LORD, all ye lands.

2 Serve the LORD with gladness: come before his presence with singing.

3 Know ye that the LORD he *is* God: *it is* he *that* hath made us, and not we ourselves; *we are* his people, and the sheep of his pasture.

4 Enter into his gates with thanksgiving, *and* into his courts with praise: be thankful unto him, *and* bless his name.

5 For the LORD *is* good; his mercy *is* everlasting; and his truth *endureth* to all generations.

IN versifying this Psalm Christian poets have been remarkably successful. It seems to be easy for the pious heart to enter into its spirit. The ode is short and very animated. If anything could stir the soul of a devout man, it would be the sentiments here so happily expressed. Hengstenberg thinks that Psalms xci.–c. form a decalogue of odes; that they belong to the same time and the same author; that they are remarkably free from expressions of sadness; that they are marked by a confident expectation of a glorious revelation of the Lord; and that they all bear the character of mild sublimity. Whether all the positions here taken are correct, good commentators are not agreed. Hengstenberg also thinks this Psalm specially related to Ps. xcix. But if it had been the first or the last poem in the Psalter, it is not probable that any one would have thought it misplaced. Jebb thinks it bears a special relation to Ps. xcv. Some have thought it was a special call on believers, but it is evident from v. 1, that it summons *all lands* to praise God. The Arabic gives David as author. This is probably but not certainly correct. There is nothing in it forbidding us to regard the sweet singer of Israel as the composer. Scott dates it B. C. 1038; Clarke, B. C. 515. The scope of the Psalm is not doubtful. Luther: "This Psalm is a prophecy concerning Christ. It calls upon all to rejoice, to triumph, and to give thanks; to enter his gates with thanksgiving, and his courts and sanctuary with praise: because, by the gospel and the preaching of the remission of sins, that kingdom of Christ is established and strengthened, which shall remain and stand forever." Calvin: "Since he invites the whole of the inhabitants of the earth indiscriminately to praise Jehovah, he seems, in the spirit of prophecy, to refer to the period when the Church would be gathered out of different nations." Henry: "Its beginning with a call to all lands to praise God plainly extends it to the gospel-church." Pool and others take like views. Some have said this Psalm was composed for the occasion of making thank-offerings, as ordained in Lev. vii. 12. It might be very fitly used at such times, and very probably was so employed as some of the Jews say. But it is suitable for the opening of worship on almost any conceivable occasion. It needs no historic occasion for its origin. Henry: "It is with good reason that many sing this psalm very frequently in their religious assemblies." The names of the Almighty here found are *Jehovah* LORD and *Elohim God*, on which see on Ps. i. 2; iii. 2. On a *Psalm* in the title see on title of Ps. iii. In our version the word rendered *praise* is elsewhere twice rendered praise, once sacrifice of praise, twice confession, about twenty times thanksgiving, once in the plural sacrifices of praise, thrice thanks, thrice thank offerings. The English version does not nicely discriminate between *praise* and *thanksgiving*. It is doubtful whether the Hebrew does, though some think differently. In v. 4 of this Psalm the word, rendered *Praise* in the title, is rendered *thanksgiving*. Many notice that no other Psalm has the same title as this.

1. *Make a joyful noise unto the* LORD, *all ye lands.* This clause is identical with the first clause of Ps. xcviii. 4, on which see. *All ye lands*, the same as *all the earth.* Hengstenberg: "The exhortation presupposes the arrival of those mighty events in which occasion is given to the nations of the earth to shout for joy to the Lord, and to salute him joyfully as their king."

2. *Serve the* LORD *with gladness.* *Serve*, embraces all the service one pays to God. That which pleases Jehovah is something required by him, either in worship or in holy living. Here it has a principal reference to worship. We have the same form of the same verb in Ps. ii. 11. *Gladness*, elsewhere *joy, joyfulness, mirth, pleasure*.

We had it in Ps. iv. 7 ; xcvii. 11. This *gladness* is not inconsistent with solemnity and godly fear. Indeed the greater the fear the greater the joy. *Come before his presence with singing.* God's *presence* or *face* was in all places where he recorded his name, Ex. xx. 24. The *singing* required must be with *joyful lips*, with a *joyful voice*, with *triumphing* as the word is rendered in Ps. lxiii. 5 ; Job iii. 7 ; xx. 5. Nothing is more offensive to God than that we bow the head like a bulrush and give way to sadness and gloom, when we are called to joyful thanksgiving.

3. *Know ye that the* LORD *he is God.* Of all for whom divine honors have ever been claimed, there is but One who has proven himself worthy of them. He is Jehovah. He is *known* by the wonders he has performed in all ages, by the judgment which he executeth and by making himself a refuge to his saints, Ps. ix. 16 ; xlviii. 3. To *know* is not only to *learn* and *understand*, but to *consider* and *acknowledge*, as the word is elsewhere rendered, Isa. xxix. 12 ; Ps. lxxxi. 5 ; Deut. viii. 5 ; Ps. li. 3 ; Pr. iii. 6 ; Isa. xxxiii. 13. It is *he* that *hath made us, and not we ourselves.* For *not we ourselves*, the marginal reading in the Hebrew is, *his we are.* So also the Chaldee. But the mass of scholars adhere to the rendering approved in the English text, though the other teaches no error, but a great truth, and requires the change of but a single Hebrew letter. There is no more perfect right than that based in creation, Ps. xcv 5 ; cxix. 73 ; cxxxix. 13–16. We are *his people, and the sheep of his pasture.* See on Ps. xcv. 7.

4. *Enter into his gates with thanksgiving*, and *into his courts with praise.* It is a call to public worship. *Thanksgiving*, in the title *praise.* Fry has it *Psalmody.* Horsley says it denotes generally fit acts of homage and devotion. *Praise*, never rendered otherwise, the word from which the Psalter takes its name—Book of *Praises. Be thankful unto him*, confess unto him, 1 Kings viii. 33, 35 ; give thanks unto him, Ps. vi. 5 ; praise, Ps. xcix. 3. And *bless his name. Bless*, very uniformly rendered. See on Ps. v. 12. The scope and intent of this verse are the same as those of vv. 1, 2. It contains a renewed and earnest call to joyful, grateful, public worship.

5. *For the Lord* is *good. Good, kind, precious, goodness* itself. As in English *good* is either a noun or an adjective, so in the Hebrew. The word is often rendered *goodness*, Ps. xvi. 2 ; xxi. 3. *His mercy* is *everlasting. Mercy*, in Gen. xx. 13, *kindness*; in Job vi. 14, *pity*; in Job x. 12, *favor*; in Ps. li. 1, *loving-kindness*; in Ps. v. 7 and often, *mercy.* Clarke suggests an old English word—*mildheartedness.* God's *loving-kindness* is as enduring as his existence, his kingdom, or his counsel, to each of which the Psalmist applies the same word here rendered *everlasting*, Ps. ix. 7 ; x. 16 ; xxxiii. 11. *And his truth* endureth *to all generations. Truth, faithfulness*, as in Ps. xxxiii. 4 ; xxxvi. 5 ; xcviii. 3. Tholuck : " The refreshing words of this verse seem to have been frequently repeated in their songs." In proof he cites 1 Chron. xvi. 34 ; Ezra iii. 11 ; Psalms cvi. cvii. cviii. cxxxvi.

DOCTRINAL AND PRACTICAL REMARKS.

1. God's worship ought to be, and shall be universal. *All lands* shall participate in it. It must be hearty and *joyful.* At fit times it should be audible—with a *noise*, v. 1. The whole heart, mind, strength and soul may well be brought into it. "God's praise is his worship."

2. Reluctance in God's service is not essentially different from refusal to engage in it. Where there is no *gladness* in us, there is no acceptance with God, v. 2. Henry : " We must take it as a favor to be admitted into his service, and give him thanks that we have liberty of access to him, that we have ordinances instituted, and opportunity continued of waiting upon God in those ordinances."

3. Our powers of music should be cultivated. If we are to sing, we must learn to

sing, v. 2.   Otherwise we will make discord, and disturb the devotions of our fellow-worshippers.   The greatest preachers and scholars have given their attention to this matter.   Cobbin: "Luther would have immortalized his name had he done no more than written the majestic air and harmony to which we are accustomed to sing this Psalm, and which, when the mind is in a truly worshipping frame, seems to bring heaven down to earth, and to raise earth to heaven, giving us anticipations of the pure and sublime delights of that noble and general assembly in which saints and angels shall forever celebrate the praises of God."   Church music should be solemn ; for it is an awful thing to worship God.   It should be simple, that the mass of the people may join in it.   It should be in good taste, that we may not dishonor God with hideous sounds.   Of sacred music Chrysostom says: "Nothing so lifteth up the soul, so looseth it from the chains of the body, and giveth it a contempt for all earthly things."   Augustine: "How freely was I made to weep by these hymns and spiritual songs, transported by the voice of the congregation sweetly singing ;—the melody of their voices filled my ear, and divine truth was poured into my heart.   Then burned the flame of sacred devotion in my soul, and gushing tears flowed from my eyes, as well they might."   In a letter dated March 6, 1560, Bishop Jewell says: "A change now appears among the people, which nothing promotes more than to sing Psalms.   Sometimes at Paul's Cross there will be six thousand people singing together."   Burnet says that "the Psalms translated into metre were much sung by all who loved the Reformation, and it was a sign, by which men's affections to that work were measured, whether they used to sing these or not."   Let sacred music be cultivated and abundantly employed.

4.   We must *know* and acknowledge God, v. 3: 1, that he is ; 2, that he is God ; 3, that he alone is God ; 4, that he is over all God blessed forever ; 5, we must take him as our God.   To doubt the first of these points is to annihilate God's promises, Heb. xi. 6.   To doubt the second is to be guilty of atheism, Ps. xiv. 1.   To doubt the third is to be a polytheist.   To doubt the fourth is to hold the Most High in contempt.   To believe in a God and not take him for our God is to hold the truth in unrighteousness.   Practical atheism is terribly prevalent.

5.   The obligations under which we all lie to worship, love and obey God are many, indissoluble and stronger than any mortal has ever felt them to be.   1. He is God.   2. He made us.   3. We are by him preserved, v. 3.   4. He is our Ruler.   5. He is our Benefactor, v. 3.   6. The worship of God is delightful, v. 4.   7. He is possessed of infinite and everlasting perfections, v. 5.   We owe him all.   He is all we need.   Life with its blessings, eternal life and all that leads to it flow from his fulness.   Creation, redemption, regeneration and glorification are all from him.

6.   God prescribes and has a right to prescribe whatever he pleases respecting his worship, v. 4.   When he chose to fix a place for certain acts of worship, that ordinance was binding.   When he abolished all distinction of places, it became sinful for men to make any ordinance on the subject, John iv. 21.

7.   The true worship of Jehovah is founded in the divine nature, and therefore will be substantially the same forever and ever, v. 5.   Blessed be God, that he grants to his people so near approaches to himself, and communes with his chosen in a way best suited to fill them with joy unspeakable and full of glory.   The highest worship is imitation.   The Lord is *good;* let us be good.   He is merciful; let us be merciful.   He is true; let us be faithful.

PSALM CI.

A Psalm of David.

1 I will sing of mercy and judgment: unto thee, O LORD, will I sing.

2 I will behave myself wisely in a perfect way. O when wilt thou come unto me? I will walk within my house with a perfect heart.

3 I will set no wicked thing before mine eyes: I hate the work of them that turn aside; *it* shall not cleave to me.

4 A froward heart shall depart from me: I will not know a wicked *person.*

5. Whoso privily slandereth his neighbour, him will I cut off: him that hath a high look and a proud heart will not I suffer.

6 Mine eyes *shall be* upon the faithful of the land, that they may dwell with me: he that walketh in a perfect way, he shall serve me.

7 He that worketh deceit shall not dwell within my house: he that telleth lies shall not tarry in my sight.

8 I will early destroy all the wicked of the land; that I may cut off all wicked doers from the city of the LORD.

ON the title see on title of Psalm iii. The title determines the authorship. The Chaldee, Arabic, Septuagint, Ethiopic and Vulgate, with nearly all modern writers of note, agree in this decision. Scott dates it B. C. 1046; and Clarke, B. C. 1055. It is not agreed whether David wrote it in early life, before his accession to power; after he had been partly acknowledged as king; or after all the tribes had given in their adhesion. The Psalm has in it a tone of authority, indicating that David was already invested with regal functions. It expresses his solemn purpose. Some old writers call this *The Householder's Psalm.* In the seventeenth century and perhaps earlier, it was customary among pious people to have a sermon preached at the setting up of each new family, or at the occupation of a new domicil. Old books give us accounts of these discourses. Some of them are expositions of this Psalm. Nor is this perverting Scripture. A good king in his dominions ought to be like a good father and head of a family in his house. We have here the principles on which David would rule the nation.

1. *I will sing of mercy and judgment.* These words are all plain and of frequent occurrence. And yet this *clause* is not of easy interpretation. 1. Hengstenberg, followed by Alexander, thinks that they express the purpose of David; that said purpose is not carried out in this Psalm; that he sings of mercy and judgment in Ps. ciii.; that Ps. cii., contains the expansion of a clause found in v. 2: "When wilt thou come to me?" and that Psalms ci. cii. ciii. compose a series each aiding to interpret the other. This view is novel, perhaps startling. It surely would be a strange thing for the first lines of an ode to contain the subject matter, not of itself, but of two other independent compositions, each confessedly complete in itself. It is not claimed that any parallel can be found. 2. None will deny that the words *mercy and judgment* often relate to God. So the Chaldee here interprets them: "If thou grant any mercy to me, or if thou bring any judgment upon me, for all these things, O Lord, will I sing hymns before thee." Augustine's view differs but slightly from this. He, who giveth songs in the night, deserves to be praised in our adversities, as well as in our prosperity. This makes David say that he was resolved to maintain a thankful frame of mind all his days, and that nothing should hinder his uttering God's praises. Grateful devotions are pleasing to God. Nor is such praise ever unreasonable. 3. Another view suggests that the *judgment* of God, which the prophet proposes to celebrate, refers to Jehovah's awful dealings in putting down David's enemies; and his *mercy,* to his acts in raising the son of Jesse to the throne. This is substantially the

view of Piscator and Patrick. The difficulty is that this Psalm is not in fact thus employed. Read it over and see. 4. Often the word here rendered *mercy* expresses the kindness of human beings. See Gen. xx. 13; xxi. 23; xxiv. 49; xl. 14; Ps. cix. 12, 16. Likewise the word *judgment* refers to the act or course of *man*. It has that application where it first occurs, Gen. xviii. 19. It is frequently rendered *right*. Ps ix. 4; Isa. xxxii. 7. So that this first clause of the Psalm may express David's intended kindness to the upright, and his just severity to the wicked, both of which he would manifest in the administration of his kingdom. Calvin: "*To sing of mercy and of judgment* is equivalent to declaring in solemn terms, that he would be a just and an upright king." Diodati: "I will in this Psalm make a vow to God, and a public protestation to all the church, of the good will which I will show to good men; and the severe justice which I will exercise against wicked men, whensoever I shall attain unto the kingdom which the Lord has promised me." This view is maintained by Fabritius, Dodd and others. Morison thinks David here gives us "an ode on the right administration of clemency and justice in filling the throne of Israel." Tholuck: "Mercy and judgment, the chief qualities of a king's government, form the theme of this song." 5. Others think that the mercy and judgment may be either, 1, of God towards David and his enemies; 2, or of David towards Israel under his reign, but seem unwilling to express a preference to either of these. This is true of Horne, Henry, Gill and Clarke. 6. Speaking of the two views just given, Pool says: "Possibly both may be joined together, and the sense may be this, I will praise thee, O Lord, as for all thy excellencies, so particularly for those two royal perfections of *mercy and justice*, or *judgment*, which thou hast so eminently discovered in the government of the world, and of thy people Israel; and I will make it my care and business to imitate and follow thee, as in other things, so especially in those virtues which are so necessary for the discharge of my trust and the good government of thy and my people." Scott fully adopts this suggestion: "The mercy of God shown towards him, and his righteous judgments upon his persecutors, were not only the subjects of David's grateful praise, but the pattern which he proposed to imitate in his administration." Interpretation No. 4 is the simplest and most natural; No. 6 is admissible and makes the passage very pregnant. *Unto thee, O* Lord *will I sing.* For *sing* Edwards and Alexander have *play*; Calvin, *sing Psalms*; Jebb, *make a Psalm*; Fry, *chant*; Hengstenberg, *sing praise.* He would employ psalmody with the usual accompaniments.

2. *I will behave myself wisely in a perfect way.* Chaldee: I will cause thee to understand a perfect way; Septuagint, Ethiopic and Vulgate: I will walk in a way unspotted; Calvin: I will behave myself prudently in a perfect way; Hengstenberg: I will walk wisely in a blameless way. The verb rendered *will behave myself wisely* is in Ps. ii. 10, rendered, *Be wise;* in Ps. xiv. 2, *understand. Maschil,* in title of Ps. xxxii. is the participle from it. Regarding this word as the key to the clause, Edwards renders it: I will give instruction upon the right conduct of life; Mudge: I will compose a Maschil to teach the true conduct of life; Diodati quotes the Italian: *I will compose a skilful song concerning the perfect way.* He says: "The Hebrew term hath a relation to a certain kind of sacred song, called *Maschil,* in the titles of the Psalms, which is as much as to say, a song of great skill. Others translate it, I will give instruction concerning the perfect way." No other mode of explaining the clause seems to have so much to support it. *O when wilt thou come unto me?* This is best rendered as a question. But what does he design thereby to express? 1. Some refer it to the time of his becoming king. Thus Diodati: "When wilt thou fulfil thy promise towards me, making me king over thy people?" So Patrick and Scott also. 2. Hammond, Dathe and Tholuck refer the words of inquiry 'to the ark, the object of David's longing, which he brought up with rejoicing, and before which he danced.'

See 2 Sam. vi. 3. A better explanation than either of these makes David longingly ask for the visits of God's grace and Spirit to enable him to keep the engagements he is now making. Clarke: "I can neither walk in this way, nor grow *wise* unto salvation unless *thou come unto me* by thy grace and Spirit; for without thee I can do nothing." This is also the view of Morison. Alexander: "This interrogative ejaculation implies a sense of his dependence on divine aid for the execution of his purpose." *I will walk within my house with a perfect heart.* The *walk* of a man is the tenor of his life. A *perfect* heart is an *upright, undefiled, sincere, whole* heart. Compare Josh. xxiv. 14; Ps. cxix. 1; Ezek. xv. 5. *Within my house,* in my own family. David was a public person, and besides his private family had his ministers and attendants, and in his own house arranged and managed public affairs.

3. *I will set no wicked thing before my eyes.* The Syriac and Arabic improperly put the verb in the past tense—*have set.* Septuagint: "I will not set before my eyes anything against law;" Ethiopic and Vulgate: I will not set before my eyes anything unjust; church of England: I will take no wicked thing in hand; Hengstenberg: I will place no wicked action before my eyes. For *wicked* Tremellius and Junius read *nefarious;* Venema, *flagitious.* The Hebrew word is *Belial,* on which see on Ps. xviii. 4; xli. 8. *Thing,* often *word,* also *matter, purpose, act.* David intends to say that he would neither desire nor devise any sinful thing. He gives his reason: *I hate the work of them that turn aside.* Edwards: I detest the practice of apostates; Green: I hate impiety; church of England: I hate the sins of unfaithfulness. Patrick: "I abhor the practices of those who decline the law as a rule, to pursue their own private desires." Clarke: "I shall particularly abominate the conduct of those who apostatize from the true religion, and those who deny its divine authority, and who live without having their conduct governed by its influence." Any allowed deviations from right seem to be intended. All apostasy is sin; but all departure from God's law is not apostasy, though it naturally leads to it. Of the work of evil men he adds: It *shall not cleave to me.* Corrupt men, encouraged to hang about a house or the seat of a government, are sure to beget degeneracy.

4. *A froward heart shall depart from me.* *Froward, crooked, perverse.* We met the word in Ps. xviii. 26. Edwards thinks it is equivalent to *perverse* and *stubborn;* Clarke, to *rash* and *headstrong.* The leading idea perhaps is conveyed by the word *crooked,* implying deceitfulness and unscrupulousness about both ends and means. *I will not know a wicked* person. *Wicked,* in Ps. x. 15, *evil;* it means *worthless, hurtful, injurious.* Fry has it *malicious.* *Know* has here the sense of approve, favor, encourage, treat as a friend; see on Ps. i. 6. Patrick: "I will have no familiarity with him, much less take him for my favorite." Hengstenberg and Alexander prefer to read *evil,* without adding the word *person,* meaning any wrong or wickedness. This is authorized by the Chaldee, Syriac and Fabritius. The chief objection to such rendering is that in v. 3, the prophet had virtually said that very thing.

5. *Whoso privily slandereth his neighbour, him will I cut off.* The Chaldee reads: He who speaks with a triple tongue. This is in accordance with a Jewish idea that a slanderer injures three persons at once; himself, his hearer, and the man who is slandered. The Greeks had the same conception, perhaps obtained by commerce with the Hebrews. Herodotus says: "Calumny is most terrible; for in it two commit and one receives injury." The English is true to the original, and is generally sustained. *Cut off;* many adhere to this rendering; in v. 8, *destroy;* several prefer *pursue,* meaning, with severity; Hengstenberg has *extirpate;* Chaldee, Arabic, Calvin, church of England, Edwards, Jebb and Alexander, *destroy;* Venema, *confound.* We had the same word in Ps. xviii. 40; lxix. 4; lxxiii. 27; in Ps. lxxxviii. 16; cxliii. 12, *cut off;* in Ps. cxix. 139, *consumed;* it is evident that the kind of excision spoken

of is to be learned from the context. Here the evil threatened seems to be cutting off from the family and friendship of David. Clarke: "All flatterers and time-servers, and those who by insinuations and false accusations endeavor to supplant the upright, that they may obtain their offices for themselves or their dependents. will I consider as enemies to the state, abominate, and expel from my court." Patrick well agrees with Clarke: *Him that hath a high look and a proud heart will not I suffer.* A *high look,* literally, *proud of eyes.* No doubt it describes an insolent and arbitrary person. Some make the next phrase express the same idea—*a proud heart,* literally, *wide of heart.* *Wide,* never rendered proud except here and in Pr. xxi. 4; xxviii. 25, though it occurs more than *twenty* times. It is commonly rendered *large, wide, broad.* But in English to be *large of heart* is to be generous and noble. But here it means proud or ambitious. Dodd thinks it denotes "one, whose heart dilates and swells with pride, upon account of the largeness of his fortune, or the eminence of his station." The church of England renders the phrase, *a high stomach,* using *stomach* in the old sense of ambition. Of one Shakspeare says: "He was a man of an unbounded stomach, ever ranking himself with princes." The Arabic has a *greedy heart;* Edwards, an *ambitious heart;* Septuagint, Ethiopic, Vulgate, Doway and Hammond, an *insatiable heart.* Clarke thinks this clause describes "one who is seeking preferment; who sticks at nothing to gain it; who behaves himself haughtily and insolently in office." In Pr. xxi. 4; xxviii. 25, the translation may be fitly altered as in this place. The proud, insolent, covetous and ambitious are probably all comprehended in the two phrases here used. *Will not I suffer,* or *endure;* in Isa. i. 13, *away with.* The Syriac, Arabic, Septuagint, Ethiopic, Vulgate and Doway: I will not (or would not) eat with him; Fabritius: I could not bear him.

6. *Mine eyes shall be upon the faithful of the land, that they may dwell with me.* *Faithful,* in Job xii. 20, *trusty;* often applied to faithful men, as to Moses, Num. xii. 7; to Abraham, Neh. ix. 8; to Hanan, Neh. xiii. 13; to a messenger, Pr. xxv. 13; a participle sometimes rendered *sure, steadfast, established;* here well rendered faithful. *Dwell with me,* as a member of my family, be in attendance at my court, and have my countenance. *He that walketh in a perfect way, he shall serve me.* A *perfect way,* as in v. 2. To *walk* in any way denotes the habitual conduct. *Serve, minister.* This clause embraces not only familiars, but all who fill office or exercise authority under the king.

7. *He that worketh deceit shall not dwell within my house.* *Worketh, dealeth with, committeth. Deceit,* see on Ps. xxxii. 2, where the same word is rendered *guile. Dwell, abide, tarry,* as in v. 6. *He that telleth lies shall not tarry in my sight.* *Tarry,* better and oftener rendered *be established,* Ps. lxxxix. 21; xciii. 1; *fixed,* Ps. lvii. 7; cviii. 1. A liar might find his way into David's house, but he should very soon find his way out.

8. *I will early destroy all the wicked of the land; that I may cut off all wicked doers from the city of the* LORD. *Early,* in Ps. v. 3; xxx. 5; xc. 5, 6, and often *in the morning;* in Ps. xlvi. 5; xc. 14, *early.* When one would do a full day's work, he commonly begins early. David purposed to make thorough work of ridding the land of those, who by their crimes were pests. The word is in the plural, *in the mornings, i. e.,* every morning. Compare Jer. xxi. 12. David first speaks of all *the wicked.* The word is commonly so rendered, sometimes *ungodly,* as in Ps. i. Here it points out such as are openly and mischievously wicked. It is explained by the parallel phrase in the latter clause, *wicked doers,* malefactors, literally, *doers of iniquity.* It comprehends all who practise injustice, violence, cruelty, wrong. For the meaning of *destroy* see on v. 5, where it is rendered *cut off. Cut off,* also rendered *destroy,* Ex. viii. 9; Judges iv. 24; it here only implies extirpation.

Doctrinal and Practical Remarks.

1. We fitly express our vows and solemn purposes, as well as our views of God and his government in singing and with music, v. 1. It is a narrow view that limits song to mere praise.

2. Experience is a good school, and trials prepare men to fill useful stations, 1 Sam. xviii. 14, 15. David was prepared to be a good king by the ill-treatment he received at the court of Saul. Had it not been for the discipline thus received, he might have been intoxicated with power, and never formed the good resolutions contained in this Psalm. Even with all the bitter lessons taught him, how far he forgot himself in a few cases is faithfully recorded in history. Tholuck: " During his residence at the court of Saul, he had learned how greatly kings are plagued with sycophants, slanderers, and proud men, like Doeg and Cush, who driving the faithful away seek only their own gain, and to become the lords of their lords."

3. It is obligatory on all rulers to have before them a perfect standard, v. 2. One may not live up to his rules, but he will surely not do right if his standard is below the code of righteousness. The constitution of the Jewish commonwealth required that every king of that people should write for his own use a copy of the whole law, Deut. xvii. 18.

4. Whoever would do right must resolve to do right, vv. 2–8. A thoughtless man may possibly do a thing in itself right, but he will habitually err.

5. All, who have spiritual wisdom, feel their dependence on the aid of divine grace, v. 2; James i. 17; iii. 15. Scott: " David found it much easier to *resolve* and *purpose*, though sincerely, and in the sight of God, than to accomplish his purposes : as many things in his subsequent administration prove ; especially his sparing Joab, and continuing him in authority, after his murder of Abner ; and also his conduct respecting Absalom ; not to speak of his more awful transgressions." Compare Rom. vii. 16, 19.

6. One of the excellencies of really good principles is the ease with which we apply them to new circumstances. This is peculiarly the case respecting our avoidance of sin. He, who as a man hates lying, slander, pride or ambition, will not as a householder, a ruler, or a judge love or practise these vices. Dickson: " He, that purposeth to carry a public charge well, must discharge the duty of a private man well."

7. It is of vast importance that heads of families, controlling children and servants, should have good rules for the government of their own conduct. Henry: " It is not enough to put on our religion, when we go abroad, and appear before men ; but we must govern ourselves by it in our families." No public functions can exempt us from the obligation to rule well our own families, 1 Tim. iii. 4. Clarke: " It is easier for most men to walk with a perfect heart in the *church*, or even in the *world*, than in their own families ;" Dickson: " A man's holiness, righteousness and wisdom are put to the proof by his behaviour to his domestics, with whom he most frequently and entirely converseth." Many a man, who stands well in the church, *is known* by his wife, children, or servants to be a devil.

8. Let us untiringly labor and pray to keep our aims and designs pure. If they are corrupt, all is rotten. Plans for overreaching others are vile. Great foresight is the name often given to swindling and iniquity in private, pecuniary and political schemes. He, who by subtilty undermines others, is digging a pit for himself.

9. If any man would maintain the elevated standard set forth in this Psalm and in the Scriptures generally, he must in his soul *hate* sin, v. 3. He must utterly detest and abhor iniquity. We cannot love and practise that which is holy without loathing that which is sinful.

10. No wise man was ever stubborn, perverse, or deceitful ; nor is it safe to culti-

vate the friendship of such, v. 4. Dickson: "Among the vices of the heart, froward-
ness, perverseness and wickedness are most of all to be eschewed and abhorred,
because those evils harden the heart against admonition, and make it incorrigible in
an evil course."

11. Let every man beware how he chooses his associates. Bad companions will
corrupt the purest man, who can endure their society, vv. 4, 5.

12. No earthly potentate is so poor as not to have his flatterers. Upon a turn
these easily become slanderers of the absent, and especially of the virtuous, Pr. xx.
19. No human beings are more pestilent or dangerous, v. 5. Calvin: "To detract
from the reputation of another privily, and by stealth, is a plague exceedingly destructive. It is as if a man killed a fellow-creature from a place of ambush." Of all the
wild beasts on earth the calumniator is the most to be dreaded, especially when he is
so hardened as to pray over his schemes. His impending doom is fearful, Ps. cxx.
3, 4. It is greatly to be regretted that in most places neither the legal, nor the social
penalty for slander is duly severe or faithfully executed.

13. As nothing is more offensive to God than pride and high looks, so nothing
ought to be more odious in the eyes of men, especially men in authority, v. 5.

14. Closely allied to pride is ambition, which knows no bounds, and which is filling the world with horrible groans. Let all men set their faces against it, v. 5. None
can tell how great a scourge one or two ambitious men may prove to millions.

15. Wicked as men are, all men are not liars. There are still some that are
faithful, v. 6. It is an unspeakable blessing to any family, city, church, or nation
to have such for servants. Mercies came pouring in on the house of Potiphar, when
Joseph belonged to it. But for his timely death what woes would wicked Haman
have brought on a whole nation! Calvin: "Servants are the hands of a prince, and
whatever he determines for the good of his subjects, they will wickedly overthrow,
provided they are avaricious, fraudulent, or rapacious. Even good and well-disposed
princes often manifest so much indolence and irresolution as to suffer themselves to
be governed by the worst counsellors, and inconsiderately prostitute the offices of
state by conferring them on the unworthy."

16. Guile is an inherent element in all depravity, v. 7. It works mischief everywhere. In courts and cabinets it engenders horrible corruptions. It unfurls the
banner of wickedness. Where candor and truth are wanting, all iniquity abounds.

17. Ethical writers have undertaken to classify the different kinds of falsehood;
but the Scripture denounces the wrath of heaven against *lies* of every kind, v. 7.
Rev. xxii. 15. Falsehood utterly subverts all the principles of government, and all
the foundations of morals. No man ever hated lies or loved truth excessively.

18. It is impossible for a man to tell which of two rulers is the greater curse, he
who bears the sword in vain, or he who wantons with the lives of his people, v. 8.
Rulers, who are a terror to evil-doers and a praise to them who do well, are blessings inconceivable. See 2 Sam. xxiii. 3, 4. Those of opposite character are among
the most terrible of heaven's scourges. Pray for rulers, 1 Tim. ii. 1–3. Their temptations are great, their trials fearful. Luther: "It is with God alone that a kingdom
and commonwealth can be rightly governed: for where God is not, there all things
are scattered and in confusion, and neither families are subject to their heads, nor
citizens to their rulers."

19. David was a type of Christ, and in setting up his own kingdom, he prefigured
that of the Redeemer. If David determined to have none but true and faithful
men about him and to frown indignantly upon the wicked, how much more will
Christ exclude sinners from the city of God over which he presides. Therefore,
" let each individual be zealous and diligent to reform his own heart and ways, ever

mindful of that future most awful morning, when the King of Righteousness shall *cut off* with the sword of eternal judgment all *wicked doers* from the new and heavenly Jerusalem." Rev. xxii. 14, 15.

PSALM CII.

A Prayer of the afflicted, when he is overwhelmed, and poureth out his complaint before the LORD.

1 Hear my prayer, O LORD, and let my cry come unto thee.

2 Hide not thy face from me in the day *when* I am in trouble; incline thine ear unto me: in the day *when* I call answer me speedily.

3 For my days are consumed like smoke, and my bones are burned as a hearth.

4 My heart is smitten, and withered like grass; so that I forget to eat my bread.

5 By reason of the voice of my groaning my bones cleave to my skin.

6 I am like a pelican of the wilderness: I am like an owl of the desert.

7 I watch, and am as a sparrow alone upon the housetops.

8 Mine enemies reproach me all the day; *and* they that are mad against me are sworn against me.

9 For I have eaten ashes like bread, and mingled my drink with weeping,

10 Because of thine indignation and thy wrath: for thou hast lifted me up, and cast me down.

11 My days *are* like a shadow that declineth; and I am withered like grass.

12 But thou, O LORD, shalt endure for ever; and thy remembrance unto all generations.

13 Thou shalt arise, *and* have mercy upon Zion: for the time to favour her, yea, the set time, is come.

14 For thy servants take pleasure in her stones, and favour the dust thereof.

15 So the heathen shall fear the name of the LORD, and all the kings of the earth thy glory.

16 When the LORD shall build up Zion, he shall appear in his glory.

17 He will regard the prayer of the destitute, and not despise their prayer.

18 This shall be written for the generation to come: and the people which shall be created shall praise the LORD.

19 For he hath looked down from the height of his sanctuary; from heaven did the LORD behold the earth;

20 To hear the groaning of the prisoner; to loose those that are appointed to death;

21 To declare the name of the LORD in Zion, and his praise in Jerusalem;

22 When the people are gathered together, and the kingdoms, to serve the LORD.

23 He weakened my strength in the way; he shortened my days.

24 I said, O my God, take me not away in the midst of my days: thy years *are* throughout all generations.

25 Of old hast thou laid the foundation of the earth: and the heavens *are* the work of thy hands.

26 They shall perish, but thou shalt endure: yea, all of them shall wax old like a garment; as a vesture shalt thou change them, and they shall be changed:

27 But thou *art* the same, and thy years shall have no end.

28 The children of thy servants shall continue, and their seed shall be established before thee.

THREE opinions somewhat prevail, respecting the time when this Prayer was composed. 1. Some think it was written after the return of Ezra with a commission to rebuild the temple, and in the state of things mentioned in Neh. i. 3–11. This is the view of Hammond, Morison and Dodd, regarded as admissible by Henry and Scott. In this case the author is probably Nehemiah, Ezra, or some cotemporary. 2. Others think it was written during the captivity, but near its close. Calvin: "This prayer seems to have been dictated to the faithful when they were languishing in captivity in Babylon." Diodati: " It is apparent that this Psalm was penned towards the end of the Babylonish captivity to be a form of prayer for the restauration of God's people according to his promise." Walford: " This plaintive poem was written by some pious exile towards the expiration of the seventy years of captivity during which the people of Israel were detained in Babylon." Patrick, Mudge, Edwards, Tholuck, Scott and others are of the same mind. If written during the captivity, Jeremiah or Daniel may have been the author. 3. Some think it was written by David. Hengstenberg and Alexander decidedly favor this view. If David was the author, the Psalm probably had no historic occasion, but is purely prophetic. Scott dates it B. C. 1040. Some call this the *fifth* of the penitential Psalms. But there is not in it any confession of sin, or any mention of sin as the cause of suffering. Symson excludes it from the number of penitential Psalms. There is some diversity of view as to the scope of this ode. Theodoret: " This Psalm may serve for the use of any man, who wrestles with any great calamity, and earnestly seeks the divine favor for his help and deliverance." Luther: " This Psalm is a prayer of an afflicted and tempted heart, miserably sighing and praying for deliverance and the coming of the kingdom of God. And indeed the whole sum and substance of this Psalm is, ' Thy kingdom come.'" Calvin: " Whoever of the prophets composed this Psalm, it is certain that he dictated it to the faithful as a form of prayer for the re-establishment of the temple and the city." Hengstenberg: " The suppliant prays and hopes sometimes for himself and sometimes for Sion. The obvious explanation of this is, that the king is the personified aggregate of the people, and especially that the prosperity and sufferings of Israel were at all times bound up with the fate of the family of David." But David typified Messiah ; and his kingdom in his family represented the true church of God. And so this Psalm is regarded as Messianic. Henry: " It is clear, from the application of vv. 25, 26, to Christ, that the Psalm has reference to the days of the Messiah, and speaks either of his affliction, or of the afflictions of the church for his sake." Morison: " As the literal Jerusalem was a type of the spiritual, and the rebuilding of the former was a type of the revival and glory of the latter, we may regard the Psalm as bearing a special reference to the times of the gospel, and to the universal establishment of the faith of Christ, when the eternal kingdom of Messiah shall be set up from the rising to the setting sun." That this ode is Messianic is determined by inspiration itself. In Hebrews i. 10–12, Paul directly applies to Christ verses 25–27, substantially as they are rendered in the Septuagint, and all this for the very purpose of proving that the Son is above the angels. Sampson: " Since the Apostle so clearly applies the words to Christ, we must suppose the Psalm Messianic, or run into infidelity. . . The Spirit speaking by the apostles has a right to be his own interpreter of what he has said by the prophets." A long line of expositors from Augustine down to this day might be cited as taking this view. The names of the Most High found in this Psalm are *Jehovah* LORD, *El God* and *Jah* LORD ; on which respectively see on Ps. i. 2; v. 4, and preliminary remarks on Ps. lxviii. The title is worthy of notice. The Hebrew and all the ancient versions except the Syriac give it substantially as we have it. *Prayer*, the same word so rendered in Ps. iv. 1, and in title of Psalm xc., on which see. *Afflicted*, in Ps. ix. 12, *humble;* in Ps. ix. 18, *poor;* here in the singular. Alexander renders it *a sufferer. Is overwhelmed;* Calvin, *shall be shut up;* Doway, *was anxious;* Alexander, *is troubled. Complaint;* Calvin, *meditation;* Doway, *supplication;* many render it *prayer.* We may read either a prayer *of* the afflicted, or, a prayer *for* the afflicted. Calvin and some others prefer the latter.

1. *Hear my prayer, O* LORD, *and let my cry come unto thee. Prayer,* as in the title.

It is an earnest prayer, a *cry*. See on Ps. xviii. 6. The two words explain each other, and express great earnestness and urgency. None but a deeply distressed soul can fitly use them. The *cry* implies the audible and strong use of the vocal organs.

2. *Hide not thy face from me in the day* when *I am in trouble*. On *hiding the face* see on Ps. xiii. 1. Compare also Ps. xxvii. 9; xliv. 24; lxix. 17; lxxxviii. 14. *Trouble*, elsewhere *distress, tribulation, affliction, adversity*. It specially refers to distress caused by an enemy. See on Ps. iii. 1; iv. 1. The suppliant feels that his case is very pressing. He urges his plea: *Incline thine ear unto me*. We have just the same in Ps. xvii. 6; xxxi. 2, in the latter case rendered *Bow down*, etc. The petition occurs frequently, Ps. xlv. 10; lxxi. 2; lxxxvi. 1; lxxxviii. 2. His urgency is intense: *In the day* when *I call answer me speedily*. The *calling* is praying. The *answer* is the granting of needed succor. *Speedily*, as in Ps. lxix. 17; lxxix. 8. The meaning of the word is uniform, *quickly, hastily, suddenly*, or *speedily*. Alexander: "We find here accumulated nearly all the phrases used by David to express the same ideas elsewhere."

3. *For my days are consumed like smoke*, which passes away swiftly, uselessly, obscurely, irrecoverably. There is nothing left of them. They are spent, or ended. This is a good sense, and is allowable. But the Syriac, Hammond, Dodd and Alexander prefer to read *in smoke*. This also is allowable. If we adopt it, then the sense is either that his days pass vainly and utterly away, (see Ps. xxxvii. 20;) or, that his afflictions have deformed and defiled him, as smoke does things held in it, Ps. cxix. 83. *And my bones are burned as a hearth*. Instead of *hearth*, John Rogers' translation, the Bishop's Bible, the church of England, Fabritius, Diodati, Jebb, Fry and Hengstenberg have *fire-brand*. The Doway reads: My bones are grown dry like fuel for the fire. This is supported by the Septuagint, and is followed by Hammond. The word rendered *hearth* is found only here, and in the plural in Isa. xxxiii. 14, where it is rendered *burnings*. The bones are the strongest and most solid parts of the body. When these are gone the strength has perished. Tholuck: "Flames rage within;" Hengstenberg: "The burning is not that of fever, but that of pain."

4. *My heart is smitten, and withered like grass*. Clarke: "The metaphor here is taken from grass cut down in the meadow. It is first *smitten* with the *scythe*, and then *withered* by the *sun*." *Smitten*, applied to men, rendered *killed* or *slain*. Calvin: "His heart is withered, and wholly dried up like mown grass." *So that I forget to eat my bread*. Calvin: "My sorrow has been so great, that I have neglected my ordinary food;" Hengstenberg: "All pleasure in eating has left me." The effect of deep and anxious distress in taking away the appetite is matter of common experience, and is often noticed in Scripture, 1 Sam. i. 7; xx. 34; xxviii. 20; 1 Kings xxi. 4; Ps. cvii. 18; Dan. x. 3.

5. *By reason of the voice of my groaning my bones cleave to my skin*. Weary and haggard had he become by his groaning. Plumpness had left him. His strength was perishing. His *bones* (literally *bone*) seemed to be covered with no muscle, but only skin. The language of this and the two preceding verses is highly figurative.

6. *I am like a pelican of the wilderness*. Some have thought that the bird here intended is the *bittern*, which utters a harsh cry before and after its evening flight. It seeks deserted places. But it is pretty certain that the pelican is the bird designated. The Hebrew word rendered *pelican* comes from a verb that signifies to vomit. The female of this species has under her bill a large pouch in which she carries large quantities of food and drink for her young. When she wishes to give them nourishment she presses this pouch, and so throws up what is needful for them. Hence the Hebrew name. The ancient versions all have pelican. The noise made by this bird is harsh and unpleasant. At some seasons of the year pelicans are found in flocks on the water; but when rearing their young they are very solitary, living in dry and

desert places. This change of habit has made some assert that there are two kinds of pelican; but this is not now credited. In Isa. xxxiv. 11; Zeph. ii. 14, the same word is erroneously rendered *cormorant*. See Lev. xi. 18; Deut. xiv. 7. This clause teaches that grief drove him into solitude and forced from him dismal cries. Thus he was like the pelican. *I am like an owl of the desert.* The owl is never gregarious. It always seeks solitude, and utters only doleful sounds. Most of the ancient versions and the great mass of modern translations have *owl*. The word rendered *desert* is plural, and means *desolations, wastes, waste places, desolate places*, Ezra ix. 9; Isa. li. 3; Ezek. xxxiii. 24; xxxviii. 12.

7. *I watch, and am as a sparrow alone upon the housetop.* The first and second clauses have no particular connection. The first simply means, I keep a vigil, as persons are accustomed to do who are in great distress, and are anxiously looking for some relief. *Sparrow*, see on Ps. lxxxiv. 3. "Bochart thinks that the *screech-owl* is intended." For *sparrow*, Edwards and Hengstenberg read *solitary bird*.

8. *Mine enemies reproach me all the day.* Enemies, the word usually so rendered; see on Ps. iii. 7; vi. 10. *Reproach*, also rendered *defy, rail.* It implies great insolence. And *they that are mad against me are sworn against me.* Are mad, are under a violent and dangerous excitement. It is not uncommon for malignant men to bind themselves by oaths to deeds of wickedness, Acts xxiii. 21. But Horsley's translation is, The profligate make me the standard of execration. Rosenmüller and Alexander render it, They swear by me. Diodati: Make curses of me; meaning, Let others be cursed as I am cursed. This gives a sense which might be accepted; but it seems not to have occurred to ancient expositors.

9. *For I have eaten ashes like bread, and mingled my drink with weeping.* Ashes are pungent and increase thirst. The ancients resorted to them much in times of grief, when they also used fasting and sackcloth; but put them not into their mouths. The first clause is therefore purely figurative, unless indeed we suppose the sufferer so covered with ashes that some of them fell on his food; or that his bread was thrown on the ashes where he lay. This idea gains probability from the fact that the better rendering literally is, *in bread*, as Calvin notes, and from the latter clause where his *tears* are represented as mingling with his *drink*. The next verse discloses the cause:

10. *Because of thine indignation and thy wrath.* Indignation; in Ps. xxxviii. 3, *anger*. Wrath, almost uniformly rendered. It expresses great displeasure. The manner in which this wrath was manifested is next described: *For thou hast lifted me up, and cast me down.* This lifting up seems to have been only that the casting down might be the more violent. Burke: "The sentiments awakened by descending are wholly different from those awakened by ascending." Calvin: "It is a great aggravation of our calamity to have fallen from an elevated position."

11. *My days are like a shadow that declineth. Declineth, stretches out, inclines*, extends. As the sun goes down, shadows lengthen till at last unitedly they form the twilight, and finally are lost in the darkness of night. *And I am withered like grass.* The clause is identical with that in v. 4. Grass is any herb.

12. *But thou, O LORD, shalt endure for ever; and thy remembrance unto all generations.* It seems most natural for the devout mind to contrast the brevity of human life with the eternity of God. Compare Ps. xc. 1–10. Where is the living man that cares the least for the memory of Alexander, Cæsar, or Hannibal, for Pharaoh, Nebuchadnezzar, or Philip of Macedon? But the memory of God both is and deserves to be forever precious in heaven and in earth. When Jehovah shall cease to be here loved and feared, the world will come to an end.

13. *Thou shalt arise and have mercy upon Zion. Arise*, of frequent use; it here indicates that God would earnestly address himself to the business in hand. God's

pity and *compassion* to his people are infinite, eternal and unchangeable. The manifestations of his love to Zion are most seasonable. *For the time to favour her, yea, the set time, is come.* If this Psalm relates to the church in the Babylonish captivity, and was written by Daniel, we have an explanation of this clause in the writings of that prophet, Dan. ix. 2. If it relates to the church in all her future, then we are to learn that the *set time* is to be inferred from what immediately follows. For the set time, Hengstenberg reads, the point of time.

14. *For thy servants take pleasure in her stones, and favour the dust thereof.* More than most verses of this ode, this would seem to point to the rebuilding of Jerusalem, Neh. iv. 2, 10. But the general idea of desolations is often applied to the church in a low condition; and never had the tabernacle of David fallen so low as just before the birth of Christ, when the truly pious, such as Simeon and Anna, had an intense zeal for the glory of God and the building up of Zion. But the true church has often been very low. Alexander suggests this paraphrase: "Thou wilt have mercy upon Zion, FOR thy servants already look with interest and strong desire on her ruins, a sure sign of the approaching restoration." Such zeal on the part of the pious would affect others:

15. *So the heathen shall fear the name of the Lord. Heathen, Gentiles, nations.* The effect of all God's stupendous deliverances wrought for his people at any time has been happy either in stilling the adversary or in converting sinners. *And all the kings of the earth* [shall fear] *thy glory.* We have a like expression in Isa. lix. 19. God's majesty inspires dread.

16. *When the Lord shall build up Zion, he shall appear in his glory.* The verbs of this verse and of the next are in the preterite. The prophet foresees these things as certainly as if already accomplished. There has never been a time of great favor to the church, which did not gloriously display the divine perfections. The great revival of true piety in the days of Ezra was more marvellous than the rebuilding of the holy city.

17. *He will regard the prayer of the destitute, and not despise their prayer. Prayer,* as in the title and in v. 1. *The destitute;* Septuagint, Ethiopic, Vulgate, Doway and Fabritius, *humble;* Houbigant, *afflicted;* Calvin, *solitary;* Fry, *the mourner.* Clarke explains it "of him who is laid in utter ruin, who is entirely wasted." The lower the state of his people, if they cry in faith, the more gloriously will Jehovah deliver them. The second clause of this verse by a happy figure of speech asserts less than we are fairly warranted in believing.

18. *This shall be written for the generation to come. Written;* Calvin, *registered,* having a place in the public records. Compare Rom. iv. 23, 24; xv. 4; 1 Cor. x. 11. *And the people which shall be created shall praise the* LORD. *The generation to come,* being *created* anew by the Holy Spirit, and by these things confirmed in truth and holiness, shall celebrate the praises of Jah. There is no reason for limiting the idea to a political organization yet to be raised up; for although the word rendered *people,* means *a nation,* yet the body of believers is such a nation, 1 Pet. ii. 9.

19. *For he hath looked down from the height of his sanctuary; from heaven did the* LORD *behold the earth. Looked down,* as in Ps. xiv. 2; liii. 2. It implies earnest and thorough inquisition. *Did behold,* in Ps. xiii. 3 and elsewhere, *consider;* in Ps. lxxiv. 20, *have respect.* Compare Isa. lxvi. 2. Both these shades of meaning may belong to the word here, although the general sense of it is to *look,* Gen. xix. 17, 26; Ps. xxii. 17. If in any sense the temple at Jerusalem was a *sanctuary,* or holy place, much more is heaven itself, the temple not made with hands. The Lord looked down for purposes of mercy:

20. *To hear the groaning of the prisoner. Groaning, sighing, crying out.* See Ps.

xii. 5; lxxix. 11; Mal. ii. 13. To *hear* is to regard in compassion. *Prisoner*, one that is bound. We have the same word applied to them that are *bound* in affliction and iron, Ps. cvii. 10. We have another word for *captive*. The *prisoner* is the most afflicted of men, unable to help himself, or obtain aid from his friends; cut off from the charities of life, and wholly in the power of enemies. If any case calls for commiseration, surely it is his. The deplorable condition of men involved in sin, and sunk in guilt is fitly represented by that of prisoners, Isa. xlii. 7; xlix. 9; lxi. 1; Zech. ix. 11, 12. This clause indicates something beyond release from political captivity. So in the next clause the Lord is said *to loose those that are appointed to death*, literally the children of death, those doomed to death, a Hebraism like *children of sorrow* in English. It occurs nowhere else but in Ps. lxxix. 11, both clauses of which correspond to those of this verse. That spiritual blessings are spoken of seems more certain the farther we proceed:

21. *To declare the name of the* LORD *in Zion, and his praise in Jerusalem.* Surely such language points to the preaching of the Gospel not only at first in Jerusalem but in the church universal, the whole Zion of God. The LORD is the Lord Christ, Jehovah Jesus. Alexander: "To recount God's name is to recount the mighty deeds which constitute it, and the celebration of which constitutes his praise." Compare Isa. ii. 3; Micah iv. 2.

22. *When the people are gathered together, and the kingdoms, to serve the* LORD. *People*, plural, *nations*. *Are gathered*, a verb often used respecting the conversion of the world to Christ, Isa. xliii. 5; xlix. 18; liv. 7; lx. 4, 7; lxvi. 18. Calvin refers to the prophecy of Jacob, Gen. xlix. 10, as shedding light on this. "In celebrating the deliverance from the Babylonish captivity, the prophets are wont to extend it to the coming of Christ." On *serving* the Lord, see on Ps. ii. 11. Such were the blessed visions which the prophet had of the future glory of the church. But hope deferred makes the heart sick:

23. *He weakened my strength in the way; he shortened my days.* My strength, literally *his* strength, but evidently pointing to the same person, or as the strength of God's people is entirely derived from him, it may be spoken of as *his* strength. The sufferer speaking in his own name probably expresses the fear that he shall not live to see the accomplishment of these glorious predictions. *Weakened, humbled, afflicted,* Ps. xxxv. 13; lxxxviii. 7. *Shortened*, see on Ps. lxxxix. 45. The verb means to *reap*, or *cut down* as a mower. Holy men before the coming of Christ had a great longing for the latter day glory, Matt. xiii. 17; Luke ii. 29–32.

24. *I said, O my God, take me not away in the midst of my days.* If the prophet is speaking for himself, this clause deplores the prospect of not living to witness what he had foretold. If he speaks in the name of the church, then she deplores her sad prospect of extermination under the cruel bondage of the heathen and the malice of the devil. She prays that she may survive until Messiah comes in his glory. Individual prophets and believers may die; the outward state of the church may be depressed or distressed; but she is safe because her head lives and reigns forever. *Thy years are throughout all generations.*

25. *Of old hast thou laid the foundation of the earth: and the heavens are the work of thy hands.*

26. *They shall perish, but thou shalt endure: yea, all of them shall wax old like a garment, as a vesture shalt thou change them, and they shall be changed:*

27. *But thou art the same, and thy years shall have no end.* We cannot be mistaken in applying this language to Jesus. We have the authority of heaven itself for so doing, Heb. i. 10–12. 'Messianic ideas' were very familiar to the prophets; and we are in more danger of not referring to the Redeemer all the passages in which he is

spoken of, than we are of applying to him those which do not belong to him, Acts iii. 24. The English version here gives the complete sense as well as any. The three things ascribed to Christ are creative energy, eternity and immutability. In Christ his people to the end of the world have all their stability and certainty of triumph.

28. *The children of thy servants shall continue, and their seed shall be established before thee.* Calvin: " By these words the prophet intimates that he does not ask the preservation of the church, because it is a part of the human race, but because God has raised it above the revolutions of the world." The *seed* of God's servants are those, who have like precious faith and love, Ps. lxxxix. 36; Gal. iii. 7. Such shall *continue* and *be established*, have an everlasting inheritance.

DOCTRINAL AND PRACTICAL REMARKS.

1. *Affliction* is the lot of God's people. Sometimes it is *overwhelming* and their hearts are *ready to faint*, as the title says. Deep sorrow is no new thing to the saints.

2. In the strict sense of the term, praise is not the sole object of psalmody, for this psalm is and is called a *prayer*. Other psalms are Maschils. Any truth of Scripture may properly be rehearsed in song.

3. There must be sin personal or imputed when there is so much sorrow as is here expressed.

4. The greater our distress the more fervent should be our calling upon the Almighty, vv. 1, 2.

5. While our secret devotions are not to be uttered in the hearing of men, yet it is often well so to pray that we may hear our own voices, vv. 1, 2. Calvin: " I admit that the heart ought to move and direct the tongue to prayer; but, as it often flags or performs its duty in a slow and sluggish manner, it requires to be aided by the tongue."

6. We may plead and urge our case as much as we choose provided we sweetly submit all to God, vv. 1, 2. Indeed intensity and fervor ought to be manifested in all our prayers for things known to be agreeable to God's will. Calvin: " To pour out our complaints before him after the manner of little children would certainly be to treat his majesty with very little reverence, were it not that he has been pleased to allow us such freedom." Dickson: " The Lord suffereth his babbling children to speak to him in their own form of speech."

7. Considering the number, variety and depth of their sorrows, it is a wonder that good men live as long as they do, vv. 3–11. They endure the hidings of God's face, the delays of his providence, the loss of comfort, bodily infirmity, mental dejection, nights of weeping and days of howling, poverty and persecution. Yet by the help of faith and prayer, they live on. To them consuming grief is no novelty. They have all sorts of troubles. Seldom do their afflictions come alone. Horne: " The scoffs and reproaches of men are generally added to the chastisements of God; or rather, perhaps, are a part, and sometimes the bitterest part of them."

8. It is not wicked to give strong, outward expression to our anguish, even by *crying* and *groaning*, and seeking the most perfect solitude, vv. 1, 5–7.

9. If God's people now have enemies, even bitter ones, no new thing has happened to them, v. 8. Many rave like madmen and are fierce and cruel. The vilest men are often sworn friends to each other even when they have considerable diversity of interest. But against God's people the wicked are implacable and full of reproaches.

10. The saints would find it no hard task to bear the reproaches of men, if they could always have the sensible, gracious presence of the Lord; but when his *indignation* and *wrath* are manifested, the best of men cry out in their anguish. Calvin:

"Surely there is nothing which ought to wound our hearts more deeply, than when we feel that God is angry with us." Jesus himself complained of nothing but the hidings of his Father's face. Without a word he endured the cross, despising the shame. Dickson: " When God is seen to be angry, the comforts of this life are tasteless and can yield no pleasure."

11. By dwelling on the eternity and unchangeableness of God, we may heighten our sense of the vanity and shortness of our own lives, and this may be profitable to us, and may sober us; but if rightly evinced, it will not produce dejection, vv. 11, 12.

12. Ever since the first gospel promise in Eden up to this day a better time has been coming to the church, v. 13. If even the best men believed that their trials and those of the church would last forever, their courage would utterly fail.

13. Whatever the outward state of the church may be, however trodden down of the wicked, and but feebly sustained by many professed friends, yet God's people never have a greater love to her than when apparently in ruins, v. 14. When this interest in religion is animated by a proper hope and becomes lively, it is a great token for good. Calvin: " The more sad the desolation of the church is, the less ought we to be alienated from its love."

14. One of the greatest means of reviving true religion is hearty prayer, v. 17. Nor need churches wait till the rich and the gifted among their members are greatly stirred up in the work of the Lord; for he hears the prayer of the *destitute*, the *poor*, the *solitary*, the *afflicted*. God cares not at all for the worldly consideration in which men are held. O no! He takes the beggar from the dunghill and sets him among princes.

15. Past favors bestowed upon ourselves or others should mightily encourage us in our applications to a throne of grace, v. 18. The reasoning of faith is: What God has done he may do again; and if it be for his glory and my good he will not deny my earnest petition.

16. The work of God's Spirit in building up Zion by the conversion of souls greatly begets and fosters the spirit of praise, v. 18. Where the work is truly the Lord's, his people will not deny to him the glory that is his due, 1 Cor. iii. 7.

17. We need not fear that God will overlook the afflicted state of his church and people, vv. 19, 20. He hears every sigh and every groan that is uttered. He knows the pious grief of his chosen. He will not be unmindful of their tears or of their labor of love.

18. Tholuck: " The history of the Lord's people is a sermon," vv. 19–23. This is true of each portion of that history. In each individual believer as in that of every associated company of believers, God works out the greatest and most glorious truths of the covenant of his peace.

19. In all our addresses to the Almighty, even in our short ejaculations, let us not forget that he is in heaven and we upon earth; and that awful reverence towards him and profound humility respecting ourselves altogether become us, v. 19.

20. The church of God is the depository and guardian of the truth and of the best interests of religion in the world, v. 21. Whatever of piety or sound doctrine is found among men is owing to the sanctifying power of God's Spirit on the hearts of his people.

21. The real unity of the church does not consist in name, form, or place, but in her taking the Lord Christ for her Master and Saviour, v. 22.

22. The delays of the Almighty, by reason of our unbelief, weaken our strength and beget despondency, v. 23. But it ought not to be so. We should encourage ourselves in the Lord our God.

23. Instead of being depressed and dejected at the remembrance of the shortness of our own lives, we should be aroused to exert the greater zeal, inasmuch as the day

draweth near, v. 23. That life is long enough which fully glorifies God and secures salvation.

24. And yet it is lawful for us in certain cases to pray for the continuance of life and the lengthening of our days, v. 24. See REMARKS on Ps. xxxix. 13.

25. What would the church do without Christ? To her he is everything. In her deepest distress and sorest affliction a sight of the Redeemer cheers her up. But without him she can do nothing. Luther: "For out of and without Christ there is nothing but the kingdom of sin and death: that is, a continual misery and distress in this life by various and hard temptations of the devil and the world." So this sufferer found it, and turns away from all other hope to Jehovah-Jesus, whose perfections are celebrated in vv. 24–27. The exceeding excellence of the Saviour arises from the constitution of his person. In modern times none deny that he had a human nature. It is marvellous that any should be so bold as to question his divinity. If he who laid the foundation of the earth and made the heavens is not divine, what conception can we form of divinity? If he who shall fold up the heavens like a vesture is not God, who is God? If he who inhabited an eternity past and shall inhabit an eternity to come is not truly divine, then all our reasoning is unsatisfactory. If he who is the same yesterday, to-day and forever is not God, then we know not who is God. Yet these works and properties are by inspiration itself (Heb. i. 10–12) ascribed to the Son of God.

26. Great is the grace which God bestows on his people and their offspring, v. 28. If he visits the iniquities of the fathers upon the children to the third and fourth generation, he shows mercy to thousands of generations of them that love him and keep his commandments, Deut. v. 9, 10.

27. God has already done so much for his people in the redemption from Egypt, in the restoration from Babylonish captivity, in the advent of Messiah, and in the calling of the Gentiles, that Zion may be fairly summoned to stronger faith and bolder enterprise respecting the great things promised of old and yet to be fulfilled in the church on earth. Dickson: "The church shall never be barren, but from age to age bring forth children unto God." The gates of hell shall not prevail against her.

PSALM CIII.

A *Psalm* of David.

1 Bless the LORD, O my soul: and all that is within me, *bless* his holy name.

2 Bless the LORD, O my soul, and forget not all his benefits:

3 Who forgiveth all thine iniquities; who healeth all thy diseases,

4 Who redeemeth thy life from destruction; who crowneth thee with lovingkindness and tender mercies;

5 Who satisfieth thy mouth with good *things;* *so that* thy youth is renewed like the eagle's.

6 The LORD executeth righteousness and judgment for all that are oppressed.

7 He made known his ways unto Moses, his acts unto the children of Israel.

8 The LORD *is* merciful and gracious, slow to anger, and plenteous in mercy.

9 He will not always chide: neither will he keep *his anger* for ever.

10 He hath not dealt with us after our sins; nor rewarded us according to our iniquities.

11 For as the heaven is high above the earth, *so* great is his mercy toward them that fear him.

12 As far as the east is from the west, *so* far hath he removed our transgressions from us.

13 Like as a father pitieth *his* children, *so* the LORD pitieth them that fear him.

14 For he knoweth our frame ; he remembereth that we *are* dust.

15 *As for* man, his days *are* as grass : as a flower of the field, so he flourisheth.

16 For the wind passeth over it, and it is gone ; and the place thereof shall know it no more.

17 But the mercy of the LORD *is* from everlasting to everlasting upon them that fear him, and his righteousness unto children's children ;

18 To such as keep his covenant, and to those that remember his commandments to do them.

19 The LORD hath prepared his throne in the heavens ; and his kingdom ruleth over all.

20 Bless the LORD, ye his angels, that excel in strength, that do his commandments, hearkening unto the voice of his word.

21 Bless ye the LORD, all *ye* his hosts ; *ye* ministers of his, that do his pleasure.

22 Bless the LORD, all his works in all places of his dominion : bless the LORD, O my soul.

ON the title see on title of Psalm xi. Henry's first remark on this ode is: "This Psalm calls more for devotion than exposition." He, who with a warm heart and ordinary good sense, enters into its spirit in any version of it extant, is more enriched by it, and has a better understanding of it, than he, who with a cold heart can critically weigh every word in the original, and in each of the many translations given us by ripe scholars. The Hebrew and all the ancient versions give David as author. This is doubtless correct, although Clarke thinks it "refers to the times of the captivity, or rather to its *conclusion.*" He dates it B. C. 536; Scott, B. C. 1030. Delaney, Patrick, Morison and Scott think David wrote it on occasion of delivery from dangerous sickness. Yet I have never heard it repeated with more ardor or more appropriateness than by God's people enduring great bodily distress. Dodd: "We read of no illness David had." It may be a grateful meditation upon a long series of mercies. Dickson says it contains "seventeen reasons or arguments of praise: some of them taken from mercies shown to the Psalmist himself, some from mercies to all believers, and some taken from God's sovereign dominion over all." Others suggest that it was written when David received assurance of forgiveness in the matter of Uriah and Bathsheba. Walford: "If this be correct, then we have two (this and Psalm li.) of the most instructive examples of enlightened and fervent piety, which are contained in the holy Scriptures, occasioned by one failure in the conduct of a good man, who was habitually remarkable for his steadfast obedience to the law of God." The Chaldee says this Psalm was written "by prophecy." Fry also thinks it "anticipates a future period of the history of the redemption of man." The Syriac says it was written by David in his old age. All these are conjectures. The ode suits many a condition of believers in every age. All agree that this is a poem of rare and edifying excellence. Luther: "This is a glorious Psalm, and full of the most ardent feelings and exercises of faith, and of a believing heart, a heart acknowledging the infinite mercies of God, both temporal and spiritual;" Morison: "This richly poetic Psalm . . . abounds in ardent and lofty sentiments of gratitude to God for his unnumbered mercies;" Dodd: "It may properly be said to describe the wonders of grace;" Alexander: "It is a favorite vehicle of thankful praise among the pious of all ages;" Stevenson: "It is an exquisite song of thanksgiving. It is the out-pouring of a heaven-taught gratitude. It is the 'spiritual hymn' of a redeemed sinner, 'singing and making melody in his heart to the Lord.' . . It is an universal song. It is suited for all ages, appropriate to all persons, and applicable to all conditions. Every nation under heaven may equally adopt its language." Although it is so devotional, yet "it is observable that no petition occurs throughout the entire compass of these twenty-two verses." The only name of God found in it is *Jehovah* LORD, on which see on Ps. i. 2.

1. *Bless the* LORD, *O my soul: and all that is within me,* bless *his holy name.* This is a noble beginning. *Bless,* see on Ps. v. 12; it occurs six or seven times in this hymn of thankfulness. David calls on his *soul,* his immortal nature, and *all that is*

within him, his *inward part*, or *inward thought*, meaning all his senses and faculties; see Ps. v. 9; xlix. 11. God's *holy name* is put for himself, or that by which he is known. Truly devout men wish their hearts more and more engaged in God's service.

2. *Bless the* LORD, *O my soul, and forget not all his benefits.* For *benefits* Fry has *bounties;* Alexander, *dealings;* Venema and Hengstenberg, *gifts.* Most English scholars prefer our version. The mercies God bestows, no less than his own infinite nature, are the foundations of our obligations to him. No man ever yet made a complete catalogue of the benefits he had received. Here we have an excellent beginning:

3. *Who forgiveth all thine iniquities. Forgiveth,* see on Ps. xxv. 11. It implies pardon with full pacification. *Iniquities,* commonly so rendered, always implying *wrong, perverseness.* All human blessedness either permanent or important, must be based in forgiveness of sin. This is the first gift of God to the penitent. But it is not the last. It is merely the opening of the house of mercy. *Who healeth all thy diseases. Diseases,* elsewhere *sicknesses,* Deut. xxix. 22. It might apply to maladies of the body, 2 Chron. xxi. 18, 19. But it doubtless has a chief reference to diseases of the soul, Ps. xli. 4; Isa. i. 6; vi. 10; liii. 5. God never bestows pardon without granting with it renewal, by which the corruptions of our hearts are cured. Horne: "What is pride, but lunacy; what is anger, but a fever; what is avarice, but a dropsy; what is lust, but a leprosy; what is sloth, but a dead palsy?" Scott: "Sinful passions are the diseases of the soul." Did God's blessing stop at the forgiveness of sins and not go on to cure the madness in our hearts, we should be both vile and miserable forever. Some think that the word diseases has a special reference to bodily miseries sent as the penal consequences of transgression. There is no objection to admitting this additional idea. Compare Ex. xv. 26; Ps. cvii. 17–19. But the catalogue of mercies is only begun:

4. *Who redeemeth thy life from destruction.* Alexander: "*Redeeming* means delivering, but with a strong implication of cost and risk." Clarke says the Hebrew word properly signifies *redemption of life by a kinsman;* possibly looking forward, in the spirit of prophecy, to him who became Partaker of our flesh and blood that he might have the right to redeem our souls from death by dying in our stead." *Destruction,* elsewhere *ditch, pit, corruption, grave,* Ps. vii. 15; ix. 15; xvi. 10; Job xxxiii. 22. Tholuck: "In naming *destruction* his reference is to the punishment due to sin, which the grace and mercy of God averts." Redemption is either of the body from the destroying power of disease, or chiefly of both soul and body from the pit of woe. Diodati explains it as redemption "from many mortal dangers in this life, and from everlasting death and hell." Other mercies follow: *Who crowneth thee with lovingkindness and tender mercies. Crowneth,* in Ps. v. 12, *compass;* in Ps. viii. 5; lxv. 11 as here. *Lovingkindness,* as in Ps. li. 1. *Tender mercies,* as in Ps. xxv. 6, often so rendered. In verse 13, the cognate verb is *pitieth.* No believer has ever yet been able to think of any real blessing which is not secured to the child of God. Henry: "What greater dignity is a poor soul capable of than to be advanced into the love and favor of God? *This honor have all his saints.* What is the crown of glory but God's favor?"

5. *Who satisfieth thy mouth with good* things. *Satisfieth, filleth,* i. e., giveth all that is required. See on Ps. xvii. 14, 15. Creatures may afford us that which 'surfeits but never satisfies,' Eccle. vi. 7; Isa. lv. 2. *Mouth,* as in Ps. xxxii. 9; elsewhere *ornament, excellent ornament.* When sanctified it is a chief instrument of glorifying God. *Good,* often *goodness,* Ps. xvi. 2; xxi. 3. See on Ps. iv. 6. The blessing spoken of in this clause goes beyond the satisfying of the *sensitive appetite.* It embraces all the good

that we receive for our nourishment, sustentation and comfort. The English version gives a better sense than any other yet suggested. Kimchi supposes that by this clause David describes the blessing of health. No doubt this and all that leads to it are included, and a great deal more also. So that *thy youth is renewed like the eagle's.* We may either, with our translators, supply *so that* or we may omit it, and read literally, Thou wilt renew like the eagle thy youth. Many marvellous stories have been told respecting the eagle renewing his youth. The whole truth seems to be that like other birds, he annually sheds his feathers and quills and gets a new set of them; that he attains to a greater age than any other fowl of the air; that his vision is wonderful, seeing small objects at a great distance; that his flight is majestic; that even his old age does not seem to be attended by such signs of weakness and decay as are often discovered in other creatures; and that he is the monarch of the air. See Ex. xix. 4; Deut. xxviii. 49; Prov. xxx. 19; Isa. xl. 31; Jer. iv. 13; Hab. i. 8. Alexander says, "The only point of comparison is its strength and vigor, as in 2 Sam. i. 23; Isa. xl. 31; and the whole verse may be paraphrased as follows: 'So completely does his bounty feed thy strength that even in old age thou growest young again, and soarest like an eagle.'" If this is the sense, this clause is in import parallel to Ps. xcii. 14.

6. *The* LORD *executeth righteousness and judgment for all* that are *oppressed.* For *executeth* we may read *is working.* The thing is going on, even now. *Righteousness and judgment,* as in Ps. xcix. 4, in reverse order. Here both words are plural, indicating the amplitude of the blessings received. To the close of verse 5, the Psalmist had mentioned his personal blessings. Now he says that God's dealings with all his suffering people are unimpeachably excellent. *Oppressed,* literally *oppressions.* There are many of them as well as many subject to them. Calvin: "As the faithful, while in this world, are always living among wolves, by using the plural number, he celebrates a variety of deliverances, to teach us that it is God's ordinary work to succor his servants whenever he sees them injuriously treated."

7. *He made known his ways unto Moses, his acts unto the children of Israel.* This is the only verse in the Psalm which might not have been sung by the first penitent that ever lived. The *ways* of the Lord here spoken of are all the statutes, ordinances, decisions and laws contained in the Pentateuch, together with the course of God's Providence; and his *acts* are all the wonders wrought in effecting the deliverance of Israel from Egypt and establishing his people in Canaan. In Ps. ix. 11; lxxvii. 12, the same word is rendered *doings;* in Ps. lxxviii. 11, *works.* Calvin's idea is somewhat different: "The *ways,* and the *doings of God* are his rising up with wonderful power to deliver the people, his leading them through the Red sea, and his manifesting his presence with them by many signs and miracles." Alexander: "The ways of God are his mode of dealing with his people."

8. *The Lord* is *merciful and gracious, slow to anger, and plenteous in mercy.* The *benefits* enumerated in preceding verses did not flow from the merits of men, but solely from the compassions of God, who is *merciful;* in Ps. lxxviii. 38, and elsewhere, *full of compassion;* we might read, *tenderly pitiful. Gracious,* uniformly rendered, cognate to the noun *grace* or *favor. Slow to anger,* in Ps. lxxxvi. 15, *longsuffering.* The Lord is also *plenteous,* great, abundant, or rich *in mercy.* Compare Ex. xxxiv. 6; Joel ii. 13; Nah. i. 3. The four terms employed are very nearly synonymous.

9. *He will not always chide, strive, contend, debate* or *plead;* Ex. xxi. 18; Job x. 2; Pr. xxv. 9; Hos. ii. 2. He may contend with his erring people till they are humbled; but Jehovah is not implacable, or irreconcilable. No being is so ready to pass by transgression. He is not strict to mark iniquity. *Neither will he keep* his anger *for ever.* Our translators supply the words *his anger.* In Lev. xix. 18, the verb here rendered *keep* is rendered *bear any grudge.* Wicked men and devils carry grudges;

God, and good men, imitating his example, do not. To *keep* anger is to *reserve* anger, or to retain it, Jer. iii. 5. It is only to incorrigible enemies that Jehovah *reserveth* wrath, Nah. i. 2.

10. *He hath not dealt with us after our sins.* Our sins have been *many;* his judgments have been *few.* Our sins have been *heavy* as the sand of the sea; his corrections have been so *light* that, weak as we are, they have not crushed, but only humbled us. Our sins have been long continued and persistent; his strokes have been but occasional and of short duration. Our sins have been daily and very provoking; his patience has been every way amazing. *Nor rewarded us according to our iniquities.* We have requited evil for good; he has returned good for evil. Calvin: "He not only forbears to punish us, but bountifully maintains those whom he might justly destroy."

11. *For as the heaven is high above the earth,* so *great is his mercy toward them that fear him.* This is a favorite and striking method of representing the greatness of the divine compassion, Ps. xxxvi. 5; lvii. 10; cviii. 4; Isa. lv. 7–9. The heaven for *height* is the best image we have in any language, Pr. xxv. 3. Hengstenberg: "The point of comparison is infinity." *Toward them that fear him* God's *lovingkindness* knows no bounds. Instead of *toward,* some prefer *above* or *over,* to which there is no objection. The verb, here rendered *great is,* is, in Ps. xii. 4; lxv. 3, rendered *prevail.* God's mercy *is mighty* (Job xxi. 7) to save, raising the souls sunk in spiritual death to the life everlasting.

12. *As far as the east is from the west,* so *far hath he removed our transgressions from us.* When God forgives he forgives like a God, and not like a creature. The ingratitude and stubbornness of iniquity are such as would exhaust any but infinite patience. The distance from the east, [rising] to the west [evening] is as great as we can well express. So far does God remove the *transgressions* of his people. No one *puts away* sin as God does.

13. *Like as a father pitieth his children,* so *the* LORD *pitieth them that fear him.* Both the languages in which the Scriptures were originally written contain a pleasing variety of words to express the divine *compassion;* and yet inspired writers have selected the grandest and noblest objects in nature to represent it. Then again they draw illustrations from human friendships, Pr. xviii. 24; from the maternal relation, Isa. xlix. 15; and here from the relation of father. Our Saviour took up the same figure, Matt. vii. 9–11; Luke xi. 11–13. The peculiar force of the word *pitieth* has been explained on v. 4. *Fear,* as in vv. 11, 17.

14. *For he knoweth our frame; he remembereth that we* are *dust.* Church of England; For he knoweth whereof we are made; he remembereth that we are but dust. This knowledge of God embraces our constitutional temperament, the feebleness of our understanding, the strength of our fears, the shattered state of our nerves, the violence of temptations, our readiness to sink into melancholy, and everything calling for tender compassions. Compare 1 Cor. x. 13; Heb. ii. 18; iv. 15.

15. As for *man, his days* are *as grass: as a flower of the field, so he flourisheth.*

16. *For the wind passeth over it, and it is gone; and the place thereof shall know it no more.* Comparing men to grass is common with the inspired writers, Ps. xxxvii. 2; xc. 5. Compare Isa. xl. 6–8; James i. 10, 11; 1 Pet. i. 24. This is a very apt representation. The *wind* spoken of in v. 16, is by some supposed to be the Simoon, or one of those desolating winds known in Asia. The phrase *it is gone* is very strong. Alexander paraphrases it: "There is none of him, no such thing or person." The last clause is a quotation from Job vii. 10.

17. *But the mercy of the* LORD *is from everlasting to everlasting upon them that fear him, and his righteousness unto children's children;*

18. *To such as keep his covenant, and to those that remember his commandments to do*

them. We cannot trace back the divine nature or perfections to their origin, nor can we follow them to their termination, for they sweep "from everlasting to everlasting." The only infallible proof of the genuine fear of God is here given. It consists in *keeping covenant* with God and *remembering his commandments to do them.* On *keeping covenant* see on Ps. xxv. 10. *Commandments,* in Ps. xix. 8. *Statutes;* in Ps. cxix. *precepts.* *Remembering to do* indicates a mind and heart steadfastly engaged. To all thus obedient and to their latest posterity, walking in their footsteps, shall be granted *mercy* and *righteousness,* lovingkindness, protection, justifying and sanctifying grace, Deut. vii. 9.

19. *The LORD hath prepared his throne in the heavens. Prepared, established, fixed,* as in Ps. xl. 2; lvii. 7. *Throne,* uniformly rendered. *In the heavens,* far above the confusion and perturbations of earth, far beyond the reach of human and diabolical malice, not liable to changes in a region of ineffable purity and glory. *And his kingdom ruleth over all.* There is none above it, none with it, none like it, none helping it, none hindering it, none without it, Job ix. 4; Isa. xliv. 28; xlvi. 10; Eph. i. 5; Phil. ii. 13.

20. *Bless the LORD ye his angels, that excel in strength, that do his commandments, hearkening unto the voice of his word.* See on Ps. xxxiv. 7; xci. 11. Four things are here said of angels; 1, they are the *Lord's;* 2, they excel in strength; in the universe are no creatures equal to them in power; 3, they are holy, doing God's commandments with unspeakable pleasure and promptness; 4, they wait upon the Lord and minister unto him. Like willing and dutiful servants, *they hearken unto the voice of his word.*

21. *Bless ye the LORD, all ye his hosts; ye ministers of his that do his pleasure.* Either this is an urgent renewal of the summons to the angels to engage in blessing Jehovah; or it is an animated appeal to the sun, moon and stars to join the chorus of the universe.

22. *Bless the LORD, all his works in all places of his dominion:* that is, whoever and whatever can in any sense utter blessings on the name of the Most High, let them come forth and speak his praises. The hymn ends as it began: *Bless the LORD, O my soul.*

DOCTRINAL AND PRACTICAL REMARKS.

1. The highest acts of thankful and adoring worship are neither vain nor idle, but are called for by the very nature of the relations existing between God and his creatures, vv. 1, 2, 20–22.

2. In all acts of worship let us summon our whole nature to the work, v. 1; let our intellects know God, our wills choose him, our hearts go out after him, our confidence lean on him, our love delight in him, our tongues praise him, and our hands clap for joy of him. Let us worship him neither ignorantly, nor superstitiously, nor hypocritically, nor irreverently.

3. One of the saddest proofs of our fallen condition, is our propensity to forget God's benefits, especially his unspeakable gift, Jesus Christ, v. 2. Nothing but the basest ingratitude could chill our hearts or shut our lips. Cobbin: "Our memories are too often like leaky vessels in retaining things that are good." Stevenson: "Our lips are closed because our hearts are dead in spiritual insensibility. . . Ingratitude is Satanic. The first foul spirit that rebelled was the first ingrate in creation." Among all the absurdities and monstrosities among men, there has never arisen a poet to sing, or a philosopher to commend ingratitude, Isa. i. 2, 3.

4. Both from its own nature, and from the frequent recurrence of inspired writers to the subject, it is evident that no matter has stronger claims upon our study and

our thankfulness than the forgiveness of sins, v. 3. Neh. ix. 17 ; Ps. xxv. 11 ; Isa. lv. 7 ; Micah vii. 18, 19 ; Matt. vi. 12 ; Acts xiii. 38 ; Eph. i. 7. Without it life were a burden, Ps. xl. 12. "Pardon is not a state to which the believer raises himself by a long and holy course,—it is an act of God's free mercy and grace in Christ Jesus."

5. Nor is sanctification a blessing to be less esteemed. In it God heals our spiritual diseases, v. 3. Stevenson : " By pardon the God-man imparts health to the conscience of the sinner, and by sanctification he infuses health into his affections. Pardon and purity are the medicines of the Gospel." Unless we be made like Christ, we shall never be with Christ.

6. A good man can never be at a loss for a theme of thankful meditation, even if he looks no further than to the marked providences of God in rescuing him from danger and prolonging his life, v. 4. In a marked way is every man a child of providence.

7. Of all deliverances, *redemption* by Jesus Christ is far the greatest. If we understood our real condition as lost men, we should never weary in magnifying the grace that brings to us the sincere and consistent offer of eternal life.

8. Not only are God's *mercies* very *tender*, and his *kindness* very *loving*, but they are also exceedingly abundant. They *crown* us, v. 4. They are our adorning. They are our life. And they are all undeserved. Oftentimes the absence of the least fills us with distress. Let our sharpest trials not silence the voice of our thanksgiving.

9. If in the least degree temporal blessings *satisfy*, how much more do the good things of the Spirit ? By him we have faith, love, hope, joy, peace, rest, patience, strong confidence, increase of grace and final victory ; and all through Jesus Christ. Phil. iv. 11–13. Stevenson : " Real contentment is only to be derived from a knowledge of God in Christ, and of all things centred in him, issuing from him and distributed by him."

10. One of the paradoxes of the Christian's life is, that when he is weak, then he is strong. Like the eagle he may become old, but even then he renews his strength, v. 5. It would be sad indeed, were it otherwise. Tholuck : " The glory of the old age of the godly consists in this, that while the faculties for sensuous, no less than mental enjoyment, gradually decline, and the hearth of life gets thus deprived of its fuel, the blessings of godliness not only continue to refresh the soul in old age, but are not until then most thoroughly enjoyed. The sun of piety rises the warmer in proportion as the sun of life declines," 2 Cor. iv. 16.

11. Are you oppressed by the world, the flesh, or the devil ? Let your resort be to God. He and he alone can effectually deliver, v. 6. Be not much distressed at your distresses, nor afflicted at your afflictions. God is the patron of no wrong ; but he is the patron of all the wronged.

12. The church of modern times is not released from an obligation to celebrate God's mercies and mighty deeds to his people of old, v. 7. His counsels are of old faithfulness and truth. The principles of his government are as unchanging as his nature, and

13. That nature is most gentle, gracious and loving. No man can conceive of anything desirable or excellent in the character of a friend, teacher, governor or Redeemer, but that it is found in God, v. 8. Two things vastly exalt the divine kindness ; it is bestowed upon those who justly feel themselves to be most unworthy ; it is continued even when our sins might justly provoke the Most High utterly to withdraw his compassions.

14. How few, light and mercifully ordered are the chastisements which God's people receive at his hands, vv. 9, 10. Compare Isa. liv. 7, 8. Morison : " The Lord

is not like some thoughtless and cruel, earthly parents, who are constantly chiding their offspring; and who either break their spirits or deprave their characters. He afflicteth not willingly nor grieveth the children of men."

15. All names, emblems and representations of God's mercy fail adequately to set it forth. It is high as heaven, v. 11. It knows no bounds. It is the mercy of God. Its heights have never been scaled, nor its depths sounded.

16. Sin forgiven is wholly forgiven, v. 12. Isaiah says it is abundantly forgiven, chap. lv. 7. God gives his people double for all their sins, Isa. xl. 2; Zech. ix. 12. One part of the universe is not more completely removed from another than is guilt from a believer. 'Remission of sin is a gift full and complete, unspeakable and irrevocable.' The Almighty forgets as well as forgives, Jer. xxxi. 34; Heb. viii. 12; x. 17.

17. How wise and merciful it is in God to teach us to reason from all that is known as tender, pitiful or generous among men, to the infinite kindness of the heart of our Creator and our Redeemer, v. 13.

18. To a right-minded man even in his deepest distress, it is a source of unspeakable joy that the Most High is omniscient, and knows all about us, v. 14. Being assured that God knows all his case the penitent may cry even in broken sentences and gain his purpose.

19. We ought not to be startled at anything reminding us of our own frailty and mortality, vv. 15, 16. All Scripture and all history teach us that though man flourish as a flower for a moment, still he must soon wither like the grass. Blessed is he who habitually needs not to be reminded that he must die; and yet so far from being dejected thereby betakes himself to the Almighty, and in him finds friend, refuge, husband, Redeemer.

20. If we would be truly and forever blessed, we must have the genuine fear of God, vv. 11, 13, 17, 18. For this there is no substitute. Nor can we ever, but by holy living, prove to ourselves or to our fellow-men that we have this or any grace. Henry: "Those only shall have the benefit of God's promises that make conscience of his precepts."

21. God's government will never fail in any part of the world, in any event of life, or in any tumult of the nations, v. 19.

22. As the Almighty is never at a loss for means, agents or instruments to accomplish his holy will and effect his blessed purposes, so neither shall he ever be at a loss for those who shall pour benedictions on his name, vv. 20–22. There is the innumerable company of angels. Their voices are never silent. But if they should be struck dumb, redeemed men would praise him. And if all intelligent creation should keep silence, the very stones would cry out, and the planets and fixed stars would become vocal and fill the azure vault above us with unspeakable melody.

23. Bless the LORD, O my soul, v. 22. "Whatever others do, let me do service to my God. Whatever others love, let me love my Redeemer. Whatever others glory in, let me glory in the Lord." This is my first, my greatest business. BLESS THE LORD, O MY SOUL.

PSALM CIV.

1 Bless the Lord, O my soul. O Lord my God, thou art very great; thou art clothed with honour and majesty:

2 Who coverest *thyself* with light as *with* a garment: who stretchest out the heavens like a curtain:

3 Who layeth the beams of his chambers in the waters: who maketh the clouds his chariot: who walketh upon the wings of the wind:

4 Who maketh his angels spirits; his ministers a flaming fire:

5 *Who* laid the foundations of the earth, *that* it should not be removed for ever.

6 Thou coveredst it with the deep as *with* a garment: the waters stood above the mountains.

7 At thy rebuke they fled; at the voice of thy thunder they hasted away.

8 They go up by the mountains; they go down by the valleys unto the place which thou hast founded for them.

9 Thou hast set a bound that they may not pass over; that they turn not again to cover the earth.

10 He sendeth the springs into the valleys, *which* run among the hills.

11 They give drink to every beast of the field: the wild asses quench their thirst.

12 By them shall the fowls of the heaven have their habitation, *which* sing among the branches.

13 He watereth the hills from his chambers: the earth is satisfied with the fruit of thy works.

14 He causeth the grass to grow for the cattle, and herb for the service of man: that he may bring forth food out of the earth;

15 And wine *that* maketh glad the heart of man, *and* oil to make *his* face to shine, and bread *which* strengtheneth man's heart.

16 The trees of the Lord are full *of sap;* the cedars of Lebanon, which he hath planted;

17 Where the birds make their nests: *as for* the stork, the fir trees *are* her house.

18 The high hills *are* a refuge for the wild goats; *and* the rocks for the conies.

19 He appointed the moon for seasons: the sun knoweth his going down.

20 Thou makest darkness, and it is night: wherein all the beasts of the forest do creep *forth.*

21 The young lions roar after their prey, and seek their meat from God.

22 The sun ariseth, they gather themselves together, and lay them down in their dens.

23 Man goeth forth unto his work and to his labour until the evening.

24 O Lord, how manifold are thy works! in wisdom hast thou made them all: the earth is full of thy riches.

25 *So is* this great and wide sea, wherein *are* things creeping innumerable, both small and great beasts.

26 There go the ships: *there is* that leviathan, *whom* thou hast made to play therein.

27 These wait all upon thee; that thou mayest give *them* their meat in due season.

28 *That* thou givest them they gather: thou openest thine hand, they are filled with good.

29 Thou hidest thy face, they are troubled: thou takest away their breath, they die, and return to their dust.

30 Thou sendest forth thy spirit, they are created: and thou renewest the face of the earth.

31 The glory of the Lord shall endure for ever: the Lord shall rejoice in his works.

32 He looketh on the earth, and it trembleth: he toucheth the hills, and they smoke.

33 I will sing unto the Lord as long as I live: I will sing praise to my God while I have my being.

34 My meditation of him shall be sweet: I will be glad in the Lord.

35 Let the sinners be consumed out of the earth, and let the wicked be no more. Bless thou the Lord, O my soul. Praise ye the Lord.

NEITHER the Hebrew nor Chaldee have any title for this Psalm. The Syriac, Arabic, Septuagint, Ethiopic, Vulgate, Edwards, Morison, Henry and Scott ascribe it to David. Hengstenberg thinks otherwise. In a number of manuscripts, it is put as a continuation of Psalm ciii. which David certainly wrote. It is not possible intelligently to assign any particular occasion for it. Its design is to celebrate the works of creation and providence. Some others begin somewhat in the same strain, as Ps. viii. which soon passes to the work of redemption; and Ps. xix. which soon turns to the celebration of the excellencies of revelation. Luther: "This is a most spiritual song, and a psalm of glory to God;" Horne: "This is an eucharistic hymn, full of majesty and sweetness, addressed to Jehovah, as Creator of the world;" Tholuck: "This is a glorious Psalm of nature;" Clarke: "It is properly a poem on the works of God in the creation and government of the world." On all hands it is confessed that this is a Psalm of uncommon excellence. Horsley: "For regularity of composition, richness of imagery, sublimity of sentiment, and elegance and perspicuity of diction, it is perhaps the principal poem in the whole collection of these inspired songs." There appears no good reason to doubt that this Psalm was placed where it is, on account of the relation of its tone to that of Ps. ciii.; and yet were it placed anywhere else in the Psalter, devout men would not think it out of place. As the Son of God created the world, and governs it (John i. 3; Heb. i. 2, 3;) so it is most natural to apply this Psalm to the praise of Jehovah Jesus, not excluding the Father, or the Spirit, but including them both. Scott dates it B. C. 1030; Clarke B. C. 536. The names of the Most High here found are *Jehovah* LORD, *Elohim* God, *El* God and *Jah* LORD, on which see on Ps. i. 2; iii. 2; v. 4; and introductory remarks to Ps. lxviii.

1. *Bless the* LORD, *O my soul;* as in Ps. ciii. 1. *O* LORD *my God, thou art very great.* *Art great,* a verb in the preterite. It implies not so much what God is in himself as what he has manifested himself to be. God is greater than any of his creatures conceive him to be. *Thou art clothed with honour and majesty.* Chaldee, *praise* and *beauty;* Arabic, *splendor* and *glory;* Calvin, *praise* and *glory;* Doway, *praise* and *beauty;* church of England, *majesty* and *honor;* Fabritius, *glory* and *splendor;* Tremellius and Junius, *splendor* and *majesty;* Piscator, *majesty* and *magnificence;* Venema, *majesty* and *glory;* Edwards, *majesty* and *dignity;* Jebb and Alexander, *honor* and *majesty.* Not one of these renderings is bad. Inspired men have chosen the best terms wherewith to exalt God; and yet they are all inadequate. *Clothed,* apparelled, in the preterite.

2. *Who coverest thyself with light as* with *a garment.* *Coverest, clothest, arrayest,* sometimes in the margin, *veilest,* Isa. lix. 17; Jer. xliii. 12; Cant. i. 7. This clause contains an assertion remarkably illustrated in the history of God's manifestations. Clarke: "*Light* and *fire* are generally the accompaniments of the Supreme Being, when he manifests his presence to his creatures," Gen. xv. 17; Ex. iii. 2; xix. 18; Matt. xvii. 2. Yea, God is himself a *consuming fire,* Deut. iv. 24; Isa. xxx. 33; Jer. xxi. 12, 14. He is also the *light* of his people, Ps. xxvii. 1; Isa. x. 17; lx. 19. Compare 1 Tim. vi. 16; 1 John i. 5. He 'irradiates the whole world with his splendor,' Jas. i. 17. *Who stretchest* out the heavens like a curtain. The preceding clause celebrates the work of the first day of creation, Gen. i. 3–5; this, that of the second, Gen. i. 6–8. The *firmament* of Moses is the *expanse, stretched out* like a *curtain.* For curtain some have *pavilion, canopy, veil, tent, tapestry.* Compare Job ix. 8; xxxvii. 18; xxxviii. 9; Isa. xl. 22; xlii. 5; xliv. 24; li. 13.

3. *Who layeth the beams of his chambers in the waters.* *Layeth the beams,* a participle. In 2 Chron. xxxiv. 11, the *verb* in the same conjugation is rendered *to floor.* Geddes has, Flooring his chambers with waters; Horsley, Laying the floors of his chambers with waters; Edwards, He flooreth his chambers with waters. When men build houses, they lay their floors on something solid; but the Almighty lays the floors of his chambers on the mist which is held in the air. *Chambers,* in Judges iii. 20, 23–25, *parlor;* in 1 Chron. xxviii. 11; 2 Chron. iii. 9, *upper chambers.* *Who maketh the clouds his chariot.* As a charioteer directs his horses whithersoever he will, so the Almighty drives the clouds wherever he pleases. They wholly obey his will.

Who walketh upon the wings of the wind.   *Walketh;* in this Psalm the same verb is rendered *run* and *go,* vv. 10, 26. In Job xiv. 20, it is rendered *passeth;* in Job xx. 25, *cometh;* in Pr. vi. 11, *travelleth;* in Hab. i. 6, *march.*   *Wings of the wind,* see on Ps. xviii. 10.

4. *Who maketh his angels spirits; his ministers a flaming fire.*   Chaldee: Who makes his messengers swift like spirits, his ministers strong like flaming fire.   The other ancient versions, also the Bishops' Bible and Fabritius, agree with the authorized English.   John Rogers' translation: Thou makest thyne angels spreites, and thy ministers flames of fire; Piscator, Amesius, Tremellius and Junius: He makes his angels winds, his ministers flaming fire.   There is no better rendering than that of the common version.   Some object to the introduction of angels in this place, because the psalmist up to this time has spoken only of inanimate and not at all of spiritual creatures.   This objection has no force.   Good poetry makes progress, not dwelling tediously on anything.   In Ps. xviii. 10; cxlviii. 2, angels are introduced in like manner among creatures of no intelligence.   Whenever Jehovah makes unusual manifestations of himself, the presence of angels is rather to be expected.   No doubt they beheld the wonderful process of creation, Job xxxviii. 7.   They are fitly introduced here.   Paul very appositely cites this verse in Heb. i. 7, 8.   He there shows that angels are mere servants; Christ has supreme authority.   To prove that Christ was superior to *winds* and *fire* would not establish anything to the apostle's purpose; but to prove that he was a *Sovereign,* while angels were only *ministers,* is very germain to his object.   Horne: "Intellectual beings of the highest order in the realms above are as ready to fulfil the words of Jehovah, as are the elements of this lower world."

5. Who *laid the foundations of the earth, that it should not be removed for ever.*   *Foundations, places, dwellings, settlements, bases.*   The *order* and *stability* of the earth and its motions are most admirable.   God "stretcheth out the north over the empty place, and hangeth the earth upon nothing," Job xxvi. 7.   Nothing is more exact than the movements of the earth from the creation to this day.   There is no jostle or disturbance here.   John Rogers' translation: Thou hast laid the earth upon her foundacyons, that it never moveth at any tyme.

6. *Thou coveredst it with the deep as* with *a garment.*   Three explanations are suggested: 1, that this clause relates to the state of things in chaos.   The objection to this is that the covering of the earth before the work of the third day of creation was rather that of a pall or winding sheet than of a garment.   All our ideas represent the state of things when *without form* and *void* as dismal, whereas the covering with a garment seems to be intended to represent something ornamental and useful; see v. 2. Clarke, Morison, Tholuck, Scott, Bishop Hall and others support this view; others think it admissible.   2. Some think the clause refers to the waters of the deluge.   So Diodati and Alexander, both of whom refer to the language of Gen. vii. especially vv. 18, 19.   Diodati says that "it is not probable that in the mass of the first creation there were hills and valleys ready framed."   Of this we know nothing, and can base no argument on entire ignorance.   3. Others say the clause relates to the change in form which the earth underwent at creation, and which it has ever since retained; see Gen. i. 9.   Calvin: "The passage may very properly be understood thus,—that the sea, although a mighty deep, which strikes terror by its vastness, is yet as a beautiful garment to the earth."   This is perhaps to be preferred.   The deluge was a curse, and the thing here spoken of is a blessing.   Much the larger part of the surface of the earth is and always has been clad in a beautiful robe of water, greatly conducing to health and to intercourse between nations widely separated.   *The waters stood above the mountains.*   The verb is in the future, *shall stand.*   This rendering is

preferred by Calvin and others. The sense thus gathered is that God holds back the waters from deluging the earth. Calvin: "Were God to give loose reins to the sea, the waters would suddenly cover the mountains;" Tholuck: "Omnipotence has set a bound to the waters, though they are above and lighter than the earth, and seem to overflow it;" see on Ps. xxiv. 2. Were the earth to stand still, much more, if its course should be changed from west to east, the dry land would be at once submerged. *Mountains*, so rendered, also in v. 8; in vv. 10, 13, 18, 32, *hills*.

7. *At thy rebuke they fled.* As in the preceding clause, the verb is in the future. So some render it. Hengstenberg and Alexander put it in the present. The certainty arises from what has been the uniform course of providence. Majestic as the waters of the ocean often are, they obey the mandate of the Almighty. *At the voice of thy thunder they hasted away.* Literally, *shall hasten away.* The clause is parallel to the preceding. God's *rebuke* and the *voice of his thunder* are his irresistible command by which he controls the ocean as a master does his humble servant. The verb rendered *hasted away* is in Deut. xx. 3, rendered *do tremble.* The flight is from fright.

8. *They go up by the mountains; they go down by the valleys unto the place which thou hast founded for them.* The first verbs are in the future. The prophet is still speaking of *the waters;* though Calvin translates it, The mountains shall ascend and the valleys shall descend. And Hammond admits that it is not certain but that mountains and valleys are to be read as in the nominative. If such be the case, he suggests the following rendering: "*The waters* once *stood above the mountains*— those places which now are such—but at the uttering God's *voice* they *fled* and *hasted away*—the *mountains ascending, and the valleys descending*—unto the place which thou *hast prepared for them*." If we follow the English translation, then the meaning is either, 1. That the ocean dashes against the sides of mountains, but invariably falls back into its channels; 2. That by some process invisible to the eye, but indicated by Artesian wells and by mountain lakes, the water is forced high up on elevated places, whence it gushes out and descends; or 3. That the waters are carried to the tops of mountains in vapors and clouds, and thence descend again to the valleys.

9. *Thou hast set a bound that they may not pass over; that they turn not again to cover the earth.* *Bound*, seldom thus rendered, commonly *border* or *coast.* When the waves of the sea are greatly agitated, they seem as if they were irresistible; but each successive awful billow is soon laid prostrate and returns to the bosom of the sea whence it came. Horne: "The experience of 4000 years hath taught us, that where the Creator hath laid his commands, plain sand is a sufficient barrier." Compare Job xxxviii. 8–11. If the deluge is even alluded to in these verses, all agree that that awful visitation shall not be repeated.

10. *He sendeth the springs into the valleys, which run among the hills.* Some regard verses 6–9 as parenthetical; and so account for the use of the second person *thou* and *thy* in those verses; and of the third person *who* and *he* in vv. 5, 10. This is not necessary to explain the alternate use of Hebrew pronouns. We often see such changes where there is no parenthesis; see v. 13. *Springs*, commonly rendered *wells*, *fountains*, Ps. lxxiv. 15; lxxxiv. 6. Alexander justly thinks that here as in Joel iii. 18, the word comprehends both the source and the stream. Which *run among the hills.* That is the *springs or streams* run. *Run*, see on *walketh*, v. 3. In many a part of the world can be found a *Sault*, a *dancing water*, and a *Minne-ha-ha*, a *laughing water.* The mountain streams *walk*, and *run*, and leap, and praise the Lord.

11. *They* [the springs or streams] *give drink to every beast of the field.* Beast of the field, all beasts wild and domesticated; see on Ps. viii. 7. *The wild asses quench their thirst.* Anderson: "The wild ass differs from the tame only by being stronger

and nimbler, more courageous and lively. . . . They are remarkable for their instinct in discovering in the arid desert the way to rivers, brooks or fountains of water, so that the thirsty traveller has only to observe and follow their steps, in order to his being led to the cooling stream."

12. *By them shall the fowls of heaven have their habitation*, which *sing among the branches*. *Fowls*, in the singular but having the force of a plural, or collective noun, as in Gen. i. 20, 22, 26, 28; ii. 20, and often. We had it in the same form in Ps. l. 11; lxxix. 2. One class of songsters, that never fail to *give* their *voice* to the praise of the Creator, consists of the birds of the air, who have warbled their carols ever since the fifth day of creation; some of the sweetest note, singing during the dead hours of the night, as the American mocking-bird, [Turdus Polyglottus], and the European nightingale, [Philomela Motacilla].

13. *He watereth the hills from his chambers*. *Hills*, including all elevations of the earth. *Chambers*, as in v. 3. Even where God makes the mountains hoary, smiting them with perpetual sterility, they overwhelm us with their grandeur. But commonly he covers them with verdure and crowns their grandeur with beauty, and often with fruitfulness. *The earth is satisfied with the fruit of thy works*. Here we have a sudden change of pronoun from the third person, *he*, to the second, *thy*. But this is not unusual in Hebrew poetry, and often adds vivacity. *Satisfied*, in v. 16, *are full*; in v. 28, *are filled*. The earth *has enough* of the product of God's *operations*. Some confine the *fruit of God's works* to the rain falling from his chambers. No doubt that blessing is included; but there is no reason for thus limiting the meaning. God's *works* are in number and variety innumerable. Here are some of them:

14. *He causeth the grass to grow for the cattle, and herb for the service of man*. *Grass*, as in Ps. xxxvii. 2; ciii. 15. *Herb*, as in Gen. i. 11, 12, 29, 30. Scott: "Under the word *herb*, all kinds of corn, pulse, and vegetable food are comprised; and likewise the produce of the vineyards and oliveyards." The terms, *grass* and *herb* embrace all food of vegetable growth fit for the support of animal life. *Cattle*, so rendered in Gen. i. 24–26; ii. 20; Ps. l. 10, etc., more frequently *beasts*. It embraces all kinds of beasts that walk the earth. *Service*, in v. 23, rendered *labor*. Hengstenberg has *cultivation*; Alexander, *culture*. It points to the *labor* of man in cultivating the soil, whence his food is principally obtained. *That he may bring forth food out of the earth. He* refers to man.

15. *And wine that maketh glad the heart of man*. *Wine*, the word usually so rendered. How honorable and excellent are the vine and its fruit may be seen from many Scriptures, Judges ix. 12, 13; Num. xv. 5, 7; Pr. xxxi. 6, 7. It is a strong proof of the fallen state of man that he so strangely perverts such a blessing as wine to stupor or drunkenness. *And oil to make* his *face to shine*. Various explanations are given. 1. Some think the reference is to *oil* for lamps to light up the darkness, and so to illuminate the face. 2. Some suppose that wine and oil taken into the stomach make men's faces shine with gladness. 3. Some read and understand thus: Wine gladdens the heart of man so as to make his face shine more than oil. 4. Some, Wine gladdens the heart of man to make his face shine with oil. Oil was chiefly for *food* and for *anointing*. For the latter use of oil see on Ps. xxiii. 5. To this no doubt the prophet here mainly refers. How excellent olive oil is appears from Judges ix. 8, 9; Ex. xxix. 2, 7; xxx. 23–25, etc. *And bread* which *strengtheneth man's heart*. See Gen. xiv. 18; xviii. 5; xxi. 14; xlvii. 12; Ps. xiv. 4. In Ps. xlii. 3, and elsewhere the same word is rendered *meat*. *Wine*, and *oil*, and *bread* were great staples of Palestine.

16. *The trees of the Lord are full of sap; the cedars of Lebanon, which he hath planted.* On *the cedars of Lebanon* see on Ps. xxix. 6; lxxx. 10; xcii. 12. The *trees of the Lord*,

are the *great* trees, see on Ps. xxxvi. 6 ; or they are *goodly* trees, see on Ps. lxxx. 10. Our translators well supply the words *of sap.*

17. *Where the birds make their nests.* *Birds*, the plural of the word rendered *sparrow* in Ps. lxxxiv. 3 ; cii. 7.   Alexander has it *small birds.*   As for *the stork, the fir trees are her house.*   *The stork*, the word is uniformly thus rendered in the English Bible. Some have thought that the *heron* was meant ; but our English Bible gives *heron* as the rendering of another word, Lev. xi. 19 ; Deut. xiv. 18.   By some the heron is said to be a species of the stork.   The Hebrew name of stork signifies *mercy* or *kindness*, and the Greek, *natural affection.*   This bird is wonderful for its care, not merely of its young, but of its parents and the infirm of its species.   In countries where the roofs of the houses are frequented she builds her nests in trees ; though in Europe she often puts her nest on the tops of high houses.   This species of bird greatly abounds in Palestine.   The *fir* of Palestine was lofty and noble, almost rivalling the cedar.   It was an evergreen.

18. *The high hills* are *a refuge for the wild goats.*   *Hills*, see on vv. 6, 8.   *Wild goats*, one word always so rendered, 1 Sam. xxiv. 2 ; Job xxxix. 1.   Some are confident that the animal here referred to is the *Ibex* of Asia, nearly or quite the same as the *Chamois* of Europe.   It is an animal of prodigious vigor and amazing agility.   And *the rocks* [are a refuge] *for the conies.*   *Rocks*, uniformly rendered.   *Conies*, always as here ; not the *hare* of Deut. xiv. 7.   Some think it a species of rabbit.   Bochart supposed the *jumping-mouse* was meant.   Hengstenberg has it *spring-mouse.*   The animal intended is probably that which is now in Syria called the Ashkoko, a species of rabbit.   Alexander thinks the drift of this verse and " of the whole Psalm is to show that all parts of the inanimate creation contribute something to the comfort of the living sentient creature."

19. *He appointed the moon for seasons.*   *Seasons*, elsewhere, *congregations, assemblies, set times, appointed times, feasts, solemn feasts, solemn days, solemnities.*   Calvin: " Interpreters agree that this is to be understood of the ordinary and appointed feasts" of the Jews.   Dimock: " The greatest part of the Jewish feasts, as the New Moon, the Passover, the Pentecost, etc., were governed by the moon."   Hengstenberg renders this clause: He made the moon to divide the time.   *The sun knoweth his going down.* Vast as are the body and the orbit of the sun, his motions are as exact, and he is as obedient to the will of God, as if he were the humblest mite of a creature; and he acts with as much certainty as if he were intelligent, and, like the angels, received the commands of God.   *Knoweth*, the same word so rendered in Isa. i. 3, "The ox *knoweth* his owner, and the ass his master's crib."   Hengstenberg: "God makes provision for the different portions of his creatures, the beasts of the forest to whom the night belongs, and man whose is the day."

20. *Thou makest darkness, and it is night.*   Here again we have a sudden change of the person of the pronoun; but it is of no particular significance.   God makes the night and darkness, Isa. xlv. 7.   Nature would rush headlong and be dissolved but for infinite and unchangeable wisdom, goodness and power.   Darkness and night are often emblems of evil; but here they are spoken of as blessings, as they really are to all plants and animals, some of the latter then seeking repose, and others going abroad to seek food and drink in the night: *Wherein all the beasts of the forest do creep* forth. *Creep*, in verse 25 the cognate noun is rendered *creeping things.*

21. *The young lions roar after their prey, and seek their meat from God.*   *Young lions* are strong lions.   See on Ps. xvii. 12.   They are as dependent on God as the feeblest creatures.

22. *The sun ariseth, they gather themselves together, and lay them down in their dens.* By his fall, man lost somewhat, yet not all of his dominion over the other inhabitants

of the earth. God uses even the beams of the sun as cages, with which to lock up the beasts that would otherwise destroy man's life when he goes forth. *Gather themselves*, no fire in the forest could more effectually drive wild beasts to their lairs, than does the rising sun. *Dens*, always and properly so rendered when it refers to the abode of beasts, Job xxxviii. 40; Cant. iv. 8; Amos iii. 4; Nah. il. 12. *Lay them down*, in Gen. xlix. 9, *couched*.

23. *Man goeth forth unto his work, and to his labour, until the evening.* Alexander: "This verse presents the day-scene corresponding to the night-scene of the two preceding verses."

24. *O* LORD, *how manifold are thy works! in wisdom hast thou made them all: the earth is full of thy riches.* *Works*, as in vv. 13, 31. *Manifold, many, great;* in Ps. ciii 8, *plenteous*. *Wisdom*, always so rendered. *Riches, substance, goods,* meaning possessions, Gen. xxxiv. 23; Ezek. xxxviii. 12. All creatures on earth are the *possessions* of God, and are so claimed by him, Ps. l. 10–12. By *works*, Hengstenberg thinks we are not to "understand God's creatures, but the arrangements made for them." But why not understand both animals and their modes of subsistence.

25. *So is this great and wide sea, wherein are things creeping innumerable, both small and great beasts.* In every sense the sea is vast. *Creeping things*, see on v. 20. *Innumerable*, literally, 'there is not a number;' they have never been counted; they cannot be counted. Beasts, as in vv. 11, 20. It means *living* things. *So is*, better *There is*.

26. *There go the ships.* *Ships*, uniformly rendered. A ship is itself a wonderful object. Naval architecture was first taught by God himself, Gen. vi. 14–16. By the navigation of different seas, commerce with distant nations is principally conducted. There is *that leviathan*, whom *thou hast made to play therein*. *Leviathan*, see on Ps. lxxiv. 14. An extended description of this animal is found in Job xli. 1–34. How great is the work of God to provide an element suitable for such a creature, and for myriads on myriads of others, of which this is the chief.

27. *These wait all upon thee; that thou mayest give* them *their meat in due season.* *Wait*, in the future, *shall wait*, or *hope*. If God does not supply the wants of these creatures, they must perish. The wants of a millionth part of them are not even known to the most intelligent man or angel. *Season*, well rendered.

28. *That thou givest them they gather.* The Hebrew is very brief. Both the verbs in the future. Calvin: Thou shalt give it [food] to them, and they shall gather it; Fry: Thou givest food, they gather it. Alexander: "The point of the significant antithesis is this, that God as easily bestows as they receive. He has only to give, they have only to gather." *Thou openest thine hand, they are filled with good.* The passage in Gen. i. 3, "Let there be light: and there was light," so much admired by Longinus and other critics, is hardly more sublime than this. The great result is surely effected with infinite ease. *Filled, satisfied,* see v. 13. *Good,* that which is suitable to their natures.

29. *Thou hidest thy face, they are troubled: thou takest away their breath, they die, and return to their dust.* All life is received from God and is dependent. He who makes alive also kills, Deut. xxxii. 39. The strongest creature, no longer protected by God, is *troubled*, in Ex. xv. 15, *amazed;* in Jer. li. 32, *affrighted;* in Ps. vi. 2, 10, *vexed.* Withdrawal of divine care and power is all that is necessary to produce dissolution in any part of creation. *Their dust, i. e.,* the dust, which is their own, as they come from it and are a part of it.

30. *Thou sendest forth thy spirit, they are created: and thou renewest the face of the earth.* Animal and spiritual existences are from God. None of them are self-originated. His Spirit from first to last has made air, earth and water to teem with life.

Gen. i. 2; ii. 7; Num. xvi. 22; xxvii. 16; Ecc. xii. 7; Heb. xii. 9. From year to year Jehovah renovates all nature.

31. *The glory of the* Lord *shall endure for ever.* This rendering is supported by the church of England, Edwards, Jebb and Fry; but all the ancient versions, the Doway, Calvin, Fabritius, Amesius, Tremellius and Junius, Piscator, Hengstenberg and Alexander prefer the optative or imperative form. *The* Lord *shall rejoice in his works.* *Works,* as in vv. 13, 24. From the first completion of creation Jehovah has had pleasure in the things he *has made,* except as sin has marred them, Gen. i. 31; vi. 6. The form of the verb here agrees with that in the last clause.

32. *He looketh on the earth, and it trembleth.* *Looketh,* the word generally expresses a benevolent regard. Hengstenberg: "Should the earth presume to depart from the course of its destination, a single look of the Almighty is sufficient to bring it back to trembling obedience." God's frown shakes the globe. *He toucheth the hills, and they smoke.* This is because he is a consuming fire, Deut. iv. 24. *Hills,* in vv. 6, 8, *mountains.* *Smoke,* compare Deut. xxix. 20; Ps. cxliv. 5. It is a poor meaning that some get from the prophet that he refers to *volcanos.*

33. *I will sing unto the* Lord *as long as I live; I will sing praises to my God while I have my being.* Alexander: "The two verbs are those continually joined to denote vocal and instrumental music." They are united in Ps. xxi. 13; xxvii. 6; lvii. 7; lxviii. 4. Blessed is the man, who spends his life on earth in holy praise, and bids the world farewell in the same happy frame.

34. *My meditation of him shall be sweet.* *Meditation,* in Ps. lv. 2, the same word is rendered *complaint;* in 2 Kings ix. 11, *communication;* in Ps. lxiv. 1, *prayer.* Here it seems to denote a meditation conveyed in song to others. *Shall be sweet,* see Ezek. xvi. 37; Hos. ix. 4. *Shall be pleasant* to God, to good men, to myself. It should be specially pleasant to the worshipper himself. *I will be glad in the* Lord, meaning, I will fitly make known my joy in this work.

35. *Let the sinners be consumed out of the earth, and let the wicked be no more.* The verbs are in the future, and it would be better so to render them. They contain the language of prophecy; nor can they fail. In due time all the incorrigibly wicked shall have gone to their own place. *Bless thou the* Lord, *O my soul.* *Bless,* as in Ps. ciii. 1. *Praise ye the* Lord, literally, *Hallelujah,* Praise ye Jah.

Doctrinal and Practical Remarks.

1. Benedictions may fitly open and close every act of worship, vv. 1, 35. This is true not only of seasons of prosperity, and while dwelling on God's excellent works, but also in times of deepest distress, Job i. 21.

2. Poor thoughts of God greatly corrupt his worship, and make it contemptible, causing men thoughtlessly to rush into his presence. Therefore it is always incumbent on us to keep in mind that he is clothed with honor and majesty, v. 1.

3. God is light and in him is no darkness at all, v. 2. He dwells in light, and is the author of it, and robes himself with it. Morison: "The phenomena of light are among the sublimest exhibitions of the Creator's skill in the material universe; they furnish some of the most awful and pleasing displays of his eternal power and Godhead." Light was the first thing ever made, Gen. i. 3. Light moves even more swiftly than the electric fluid.

4. All attempts to comprehend God must ever be vain. They are so now; they will be so forever, v. 3. The description of his glory by such imagery as is here employed ought to make us still, silent and awfully reverent.

5. Respecting angels, mentioned in v. 4, see Remarks on Ps. xxxiv. 7; xci. 11.

If they are God's *ministers*, it is as much idolatry to worship them as any other of his creatures. So they think, Rev. xxii. 8, 9.

6. It is in vain to seek for stability aside from the will of God; nor do we need another or a better cause for it, v. 5. *He hangs the earth upon nothing*, and it is as firm and unshaken as anything we know. Hammond: "God has fixed so strange a place for the earth, that, being a heavy body, one would think it should fall every minute; and yet, which way soever we would imagine it to stir, it must, contrary to the nature of such a body, fall upwards, and so can have no possible ruin but by tumbling into heaven."

7. If we would know what a blessing any one of the great works of God is, we must study it and consider it. For example, take the sea. It abounds with wonders of every kind. Men have devoted their lives to the study of even one class of its wonders, and yet have felt that they were but beginners in Algæology or Conchology.

8. We need no higher proof of the supremacy of Jehovah than this, that all nature obeys his will, vv. 7–9. Calvin: "Were God to give loose reins to the sea, the waters would suddenly cover the mountains. But now, fleeing at God's rebuke, they retire to a different quarter."

9. Much has been well written and spoken in admiration of the great water-works of antiquity and of modern times. But how much more admirable are the water-works of the Almighty, distributing drink and moisture to all parts of the world, vv. 10, 11, 13. See some beautiful thoughts on this subject in Job xxxviii. 26, 27; Jer. x. 13; xiv. 22.

10. Were men not amazingly blind and hardened in sin, they would feel themselves justly and terribly reproved by all the creatures of God. Stupid as are the ox and the ass, they know their owner. Insignificant as is the ant, she teaches her lessons of foresight and industry. Without intellect or heart, the birds of the air were the first and have been the most constant to sing the praises of Jehovah, v. 12. Yet man has a sweeter voice than they. He has ten thousand mercies to their one, and one mercy, *redemption* itself, outweighing all the blessings ever conferred by God on the irrational creation. Oh that *men* would praise the LORD for his goodness and for his wonderful works to the children of men!

11. Surely it should humble man to know that all human power united cannot make anything, not even the grass to grow, v. 14. By diligently submitting to the will of God as manifested in Providence, and availing himself of the amazing principles established by heaven, he may accomplish something. But without God he can do nothing.

12. The Almighty has not dealt with man in any parsimonious way. On the contrary, he has been very bountiful, giving him not only *bread* and things absolutely necessary for existence, but also many comforts and luxuries, as *oil* and *wine*, v. 15. Tholuck: "The truly pious need not restrict themselves to the barest necessities of life, but they who have the means may enjoy the gifts of God," 1 Tim. iv. 3, 4. We must be content with necessary food, and not indulge in the luxuries of life; 1, when we cannot afford them, Rom. xiii. 8; 2, when the use of them is injurious to our bodily health, Prov. xxiii. 2; 3, when they overcharge our hearts with surfeiting and lead us from God, Luke xxi. 34; 4, when indulgence in them is injurious to our fellow-men, Rom. xiv. 15; 5, when our indulgence leads to irreligion, and not to proper thoughts of the Most High; 6, when we seek to make provision for the flesh to fulfil the lusts thereof, Rom. xiii. 14; 7, when self-denial is irksome, and discontent claims the mastery over us if we lack these things, Phil. iv. 12.

13. What amazing results are produced by the providence of God in the growth of majestic trees, v. 16. Every continent has its fine specimens. Many a long jour-

ney has been taken to see a sight not half so goodly as the fall of one of these monarchs of the forest.

14. A stork and every bird of the air, the wild goat and the conies and every creature of God may teach us some lesson, vv. 17, 18. And every part of creation has its living creatures. Tholuck: "A lone butterfly may be seen on the heights of Chimborazo." Dr. Kane found red worms in the eternal snows of the Arctic regions.

15. Although ignorant people have many foolish stories about the influence of the heavenly bodies, and the effect of their several positions, yet inspiration itself has taught us to contemplate the sun and moon as among the chief works of God and excellent in their nature, v. 19. Compare Ps. xix. 1–6; Deut. xxxiii. 13–16.

16. If the alternations of day and night in nature are such blessings as they are universally acknowledged to be, and as such are celebrated by inspired poets, (v. 20;) who can prove that the alternations of day and night, or of light and darkness in our temporal and spiritual affairs may not in the end be alike good?

17. If the strongest creatures that God has made cannot supply their own wants, or relieve their own distresses, nor even continue in existence except as God sustains them, (v. 21,) it is vain for man, who is crushed before the moth, to suppose that he can be his own keeper, or administer effectually to his own necessities.

18. Bad as things are on earth, and miserable as sin has made large portions of the world, yet things are not as bad as they might be.

19. It is a great mercy that, when for his sins, God sentenced man to hard labor for life, Gen. iii. 19, he yet allowed him to carry on his chief labors in the open air and in the light of heaven, v. 23.

20. It is a proof of the amazing atheism of the natural heart that every few years we hear of cavils, professedly drawn from science, against some doctrine of natural or revealed religion. Yet a little candor and skill would soon bring us greatly to admire the proofs of God's existence and perfections found in all his works, v. 24. Henry: "The works of art, the more closely they are looked upon with the help of micro-scopes, the more rough they appear; the works of nature through these glasses appear more fine and exact."

21. If men believed in proportion to the wonders they see, how pious would mariners all be, vv. 25, 26.

22. Of whatever doctrine we may be ignorant, both providence and revelation teach us the dependence of all things upon God, vv. 27, 28. Creatures in multitude greater than the stars are every day fed out of the treasure-house of God's bounty, requiring an almost countless variety and even diversity of food. Yet they are all cared for.

23. In its methods and results providence is not less amazing than creation itself, v. 30. Providence is as productive as creation, though its processes are commonly more slow.

24. It is a blessed thing that God is glorious, and shall be so esteemed, come what will, v. 31.

25. Our safety and the perpetuity of our well-being depend upon the good pleasure of God, and the continuance of his delight in his works, v. 31.

26. If an averted look or a frown from the Almighty makes the earth itself to tremble, how terrible it must be for a worm of the dust like man to fall under the wrath of God, v. 32.

27. As singing God's praises is to be the work of the pious forever, let them while on earth train themselves to this noble employment.

28. If our hearts were right, our *meditation* of God would be frequent, because it would be *pleasant*. The last words ever written by Henry Martyn, dying among

Mohammedans in Persia was: "I sat in the orchard and thought with sweet comfort and peace of my God, in solitude my company, my friend and Comforter."

29. The certainty of the final overthrow of the wicked could not be greater than it is. The mouth of the Lord hath spoken it, v. 35. Combinations will not avail, Pr. xi. 21.

30. This Psalm teaches and illustrates the great doctrine of providence. The Lord will provide. If God cares for *storks* and *conies* and all the myriads of living things in the air, earth and water, which yet are of comparatively little value, surely he will not forget his people.

31. If the human mind were not besotted in guilt and enveloped in darkness, there never would be a doubt respecting the truths of natural religion; so abundantly are they declared and published in all the works of God.

32. No doubt this Psalm is fitly applied to the mediatorial reign of Christ, not only by the Apostle in Heb. i., but by pious men ever since. He made the world and it is his. He made the angels and they are his. He made all nature and all nature obeys him. When on earth, the winds and the waves heard his voice and were hushed. He is Lord of all.

PSALM CV.

1 O give thanks unto the LORD; call upon his name: make known his deeds among the people.

2 Sing unto him, sing psalms unto him: talk ye of all his wondrous works.

3 Glory ye in his holy name: let the heart of them rejoice that seek the LORD.

4 Seek the LORD, and his strength: seek his face evermore.

5 Remember his marvellous works that he hath done; his wonders, and the judgments of his mouth;

6 O ye seed of Abraham his servant, ye children of Jacob his chosen.

7 He *is* the LORD our God: his judgments *are* in all the earth.

8 He hath remembered his covenant for ever, the word *which* he commanded to a thousand generations.

9 Which *covenant* he made with Abraham, and his oath unto Isaac;

10 And confirmed the same unto Jacob for a law, *and* to Israel *for* an everlasting covenant:

11 Saying, Unto thee will I give the land of Canaan, the lot of your inheritance:

12 When they were *but* a few men in number; yea, very few, and strangers in it.

13 When they went from one nation to another, from *one* kingdom to another people;

14 He suffered no man to do them wrong: yea, he reproved kings for their sakes;

15 *Saying,* Touch not mine anointed, and do my prophets no harm.

16 Moreover he called for a famine upon the land: he brake the whole staff of bread.

17 He sent a man before them, *even* Joseph, *who* was sold for a servant:

18 Whose feet they hurt with fetters: he was laid in iron:

19 Until the time that his word came: the word of the LORD tried him.

20 The king sent and loosed him; *even* the ruler of the people, and let him go free.

21 He made him lord of his house, and ruler of all his substance:

22 To bind his princes at his pleasure; and teach his senators wisdom.

23 Israel also came into Egypt; and Jacob sojourned in the land of Ham.

24 And he increased his people greatly: and made them stronger than their enemies.

25 He turned their heart to hate his people, to deal subtilely with his servants.

26 He sent Moses his servant; *and* Aaron whom he had chosen.

27 They shewed his signs among them, and wonders in the land of Ham.

28 He sent darkness, and made it dark; and they rebelled not against his word.

29 He turned their waters into blood, and slew their fish.

30 Their land brought forth frogs in abundance, in the chambers of their kings.

31 He spake, and there came divers sorts of flies, *and* lice in all their coasts.

32 He gave them hail for rain, *and* flaming fire in their land.

33 He smote their vines also and their fig trees; and brake the trees of their coasts.

34 He spake, and the locusts came, and caterpillars, and that without number,

35 And did eat up all the herbs in their land, and devoured the fruit of their ground.

36 He smote also all the firstborn in their land, the chief of all their strength.

37 He brought them forth also with silver and gold: and *there was* not one feeble *person* among their tribes.

38 Egypt was glad when they departed: for the fear of them fell upon them.

39 He spread a cloud for a covering; and fire to give light in the night.

40 *The people* asked, and he brought quails, and satisfied them with the bread of heaven.

41 He opened the rock, and the waters gushed out; they ran in the dry places *like* a river.

42 For he remembered his holy promise, *and* Abraham his servant.

43 And he brought forth his people with joy, *and* his chosen with gladness:

44 And gave them the lands of the heathen: and they inherited the labour of the people;

45 That they might observe his statutes, and keep his laws. Praise ye the LORD.

NEITHER the Hebrew nor Chaldee prefix any title; other ancient versions take the last word of Ps. civ. and prefix *Hallelujah* as a title. No ancient version names any author. The Syriac says it is anonymous. Most moderns express some opinion respecting the author. Quite a number think it was not composed till the end of the Babylonish captivity. Clarke dates it B. C. 536. Others make it more ancient. Pool: "The penman of this Psalm was David." This opinion is favored by Patrick, Henry, Dodd, Gill, Horne, Edwards, Anderson, etc. Scott dates it B. C. 1045. These remarks are just: 1. Verses 1–15 were written by David on occasion of bringing the ark to the holy city, 1 Chron. xvi. 8–22. 2. It has been shown that David probably wrote Ps. civ. The author of that, it is commonly thought, wrote this. 3. There is not a word, allusion or expression in it that opposes the Davidic authorship. 4. It is not likely that any one would have felt free to alter David's compositions. Yet candor requires the admission that this bears a strong resemblance to Ps. lxxviii. which was probably written by Asaph. Several notice the fact that in Ps. civ. God's people are comforted by truths drawn from creation and providence; in this, by the truths of history. The same events have various uses. In Ps. lxxviii. history is used to teach; here, to comfort and awaken gratitude. The names of the Most High here found are *Jehovah* LORD, *Elohim* God and *Jah* LORD, on which see on Ps. i. 2; iii. 2, and introduction to Ps. lxviii. Fry: "This Psalm needs no other comment than a comparison with the history of the exodus." But there are some other matters claiming a brief notice. If Israel had good cause to celebrate redemption from Egypt, much more have Christians to sing of redemption by the blood of Christ.

1. *O give thanks unto the* LORD. *Give thanks*, one word often so rendered; in Ps. vii. 17, *praise;* in Ps. xxxii. 5, *confess;* see on Ps. vi. 5. *Call upon his name.* There is no better rendering; in Ps. iii. 4, the verb is *cried. Make known his deeds among the people. Deeds*, in Ps. ix. 11, *doings;* in Ps. xiv. 1, *works;* in Ps. xcix. 8, *inventions;* in Ps. ciii. 7, *acts. People*, in the plural, *peoples, nations.* Compare Ps. ix. 11.

2. *Sing unto him, sing psalms unto him.* On these verbs see on Ps. vii. 17; ix. 11; xiii. 6; xxi. 13. *Talk ye of all his wondrous works. Talk, muse, meditate, speak;* see on Ps. civ. 34. On *wondrous works*, see on Ps. ix. 1. The *people* of v. 1, are included in the address.

3. *Glory ye in his holy name. Glory, boast, praise*, the word from which the Psalter takes its name. We have it thrice, in Jer. ix. 23. Diodati: "Let all your honor

and glory be in him, who is, and calleth himself your God, and honoreth you with the title of his people." Alexander: "Congratulate yourselves that you possess a right and interest in the favor of so glorious a Being." *Let the heart of* THEM *rejoice that seek the* LORD. *Seek,* commonly so ; elsewhere *inquire, make request, beseech.* By synecdoche it describes a pious man, see on Ps. xxvii. 8. God's real servants should seek him *gladly.*

4. *Seek the* LORD, *and his strength: seek his face evermore. Seek,* in the first instance, not the same word as in v. 3; yet of the same general import, but stronger, implying *searching;* see on Ps. ix. 10, 12. *Seek* in the second instance as in v. 3. *Seek his strength; Strength,* as in Ps. viii. 2; xxi. 1, 13. *Face,* elsewhere *countenance;* gracious presence equivalent to blessing; see Ps. iv. 6; xlii. 5. Do these things *evermore, always, continually.*

5. *Remember his marvellous works that he hath done; his wonders, and the judgments of his mouth. Marvellous works,* as in v. 2. *Wonders;* the Syriac has *Miracles;* Chaldee, Septuagint, Ethiopic, Vulgate and Arabic, *Prodigies.* It embraces all the amazing things done by God in the history of his people. *Judgments;* see on Ps. xix. 9; it may mean, 1, the divine laws; 2, any divine decisions favorable or unfavorable; 3, condemning sentences against the wicked. We have the same word below in v. 7.

6. *O ye seed of Abraham his servant, ye children of Jacob his chosen.* Abraham and Jacob are mentioned, because to them early promises concerning the nation of Israel were made. Abraham was God's *servant,* never hesitating to obey him; and Jacob was his *chosen,* Mal. i. 2; Rom. ix. 13.

7. *He is the* LORD *our God.* This expresses his covenant relation to the Jewish nation. *His judgments are in all the earth. Judgments,* as in v. 5. In no part of the world has God left himself without witness, Acts xiv. 17.

8. *He hath remembered his covenant for ever, the word* which *he commanded to a thousand generations.* If God requires us to *remember* his works, he faithfully *remembers* his engagements. Never does he forget them. His *covenant* is ordered in all things and sure. The *word* of the Lord endureth forever. There were but forty-two generations from Abraham to Christ, Matt. i. 17, and yet this covenant is to run a *thousand* generations. Compare Ex. xx. 6; Deut. v. 10; vii. 9. A large definite number is put for perpetuity. God's faithfulness is unto all generations, Ps. cxix. 90.

9. *Which* covenant *he made with Abraham, and his oath unto Isaac.* God's covenant transactions with Abraham are recorded in Gen. xv. 17, 18; xvii. 1–8; xxii. 15–18. The renewal of that covenant with Isaac is recorded in Gen. xxvi. 2–5. *Made,* literally *cut,* meaning ratified, Gal. iii. 15. All covenant transactions with God have the solemnity of an oath, Ps. cxix. 106. But the transaction with Isaac assumed literally the form of an *oath,* Gen. xxvi. 3. Compare Heb. vi. 18.

10. *And confirmed the same unto Jacob for a law,* and *to Israel for an everlasting covenant. Confirmed, appointed, ordained, established.* The history of God's covenant transactions with Jacob is found in Genesis xxviii. 10–15; xxxv. 9–15. On the latter occasion, he changed his name to Israel. *A law;* the word primarily means a portion, or lot, afterwards a determinate arrangement; frequently translated *statute;* in Ps. ii. 7, *decree. Covenant,* as in v. 8; see on Ps. xxv. 10, 14. *Everlasting,* the blessings promised to Abraham, Isaac and Jacob were partly temporal, but chiefly and eminently spiritual, and so eternal, Gal. iii. 17. The gifts and calling of God are without repentance. Venema: "That it might retain perpetual force, like some solemnly proclaimed decree."

11. *Saying, Unto thee will I give the land of Canaan, the lot of your inheritance.* This promise was made and fulfilled to Abraham, Isaac and Jacob. Hence the

plural *your*. On the *lot* or *line* of inheritance, see on Ps. xvi. 6; lxxviii. 55. God made all these promises before Israel had become at all powerful, even

12. *When they were but a few men in number; yea, very few, and strangers in it.* Even in the family of Jacob, there were at most, including himself, but thirteen males to whom pertained the promise, until he had grandchildren; and when he went down to Egypt all his descendants were but sixty-six, Gen. xlvi. 26; and when he reached Egypt he had but seventy descendants, including those of Joseph's family, Ex. i. 5. The Hebrew is striking—*Men of a number*—i. e., men easily counted; and *strangers*, not the acknowledged proprietors of the country, nor having it in actual possession, Gen. xxxiv. 30. *Strangers*, a participle, from a verb in v. 23, rendered *sojourned.*

13. *When they went from one nation to another, from* one *kingdom to another people.* The migrations of the three patriarchs before named, and of their families were frequent and apparently attended with much peril; yet

14. *He suffered no man to do them wrong: yea, he reproved kings for their sakes;* see Gen. xii. 14–20; xx. 1–9; xxvi. 7–11, 26–33; xxxv. 5. Calvin: "Since their life everywhere hung only by a thread, and the changing of their place of sojourn exposed them from time to time to fresh injuries, it is evident that it was the divine power alone which preserved them in safety." *Reproved*, elsewhere *corrected*, *chastened*; Hengstenberg has *punished*; Calvin, *rebuked*, see Gen. xii. xx.

15. *Saying, Touch not mine anointed, and do my prophets no harm.* None of the patriarchs, whose case we have been considering, were ever anointed with spiced oil to any office; but a succession of them were anointed by the Holy Ghost. All good men are made holy by God's Spirit; and all the understanding men have is derived from the same blessed agent, Job xxxii. 8; Gen. xli. 38, 39; Num. xxvii. 18. Abraham was a *prophet*, Gen. xx. 7. "Isaac had a prophetical dream at Beersheba; Jacob, at Bethel." Jacob and Joseph uttered predictions that were fulfilled, Gen. xv. 1–18; xxxvii. 5–11; xli. 25–36; xlviii. 4–21; xlix. 3–27; l. 24, 25.

16. *Moreover he called for a famine upon the land: he brake the whole staff of bread.* The reference is to the seven years' famine, Gen. xli. 54–57; xlii. 5, 6. With great beauty, here and elsewhere, *bread*, i. e., food is spoken off as a *staff* or *rod*, with which life is supported, see Lev. xxvi. 6; Ezek. iv. 16. Compare Ps. civ. 15. The figure has been transferred into many languages. Horne: "Famine is here finely represented as a servant, ready to come and go at the call and command of God; for calamities, whether public or private, are the messengers of divine justice."

17. *He sent a man before them, even Joseph, who was sold for a servant.* Joseph gave the same account of God's providence in sending him to Egypt, Gen. xlv. 5; l. 20. How he was sold into bondage, see Gen. xxxvii. 28.

18. *Whose feet they hurt with fetters: he was laid in iron.* Moses records that Joseph was *bound*, Gen. xxxix. 20; xl. 3. The literal rendering of the second clause is, His soul came into iron. The Chaldee, church of England, Calvin and Jebb read: The iron entered into his soul; the Doway, following some ancient versions: The iron pierced his soul; Edwards: His person was laid in irons; Fry: He was secured with iron. Either his *soul* is here put for his person, as is often done; or, such is the union between the soul and the body, that when his body was bound, he had a deep, heart-felt sense of the painful confinement. This trial lasted

19. *Until the time that his word came. The time*, perhaps predicted by Joseph. Some think the *word* means that by which he interpreted the dreams of his fellow-prisoners, Gen. xli. 12, 13. From the time he left Canaan till he saw his father again was probably about *twenty-four* years. *The word of the Lord tried him.* It is most probable that the Psalmist here refers to Joseph's being called on to in-

terpret Pharaoh's dream, which was God's *word* to that wicked monarch, the explanation of which was a severe test, proof or *trial* of Joseph, Gen. xli. 25–36. Or it may be that he refers to the long delay of God in fulfilling his word. Alexander: "During the two years which intervened between his explanation of the prisoners' dreams and the favorable issue to which it ultimately led, his faith in the divine promise, both to himself and to his people, was severely but favorably tried."

20. *The king sent and loosed him; even the ruler of the people, and let him go free.* The history of this deliverance is given in Gen. xli. 14. Alexander: "Both verbs strictly apply to the removal of his fetters, the first meaning properly, to knock off, (Isa. lviii. 6,) the other to open for the purpose of removing.

21. *He made him lord of his house, and ruler of all his substance.* See the record in Gen. xli. 40–45; xlv. 8. *Substance*, in Ps. civ. 24, *riches*.

22. *To bind his princes at his pleasure; and teach his senators wisdom. Bind*, the Syriac has *chastise*; Arabic, Septuagint, Ethiopic, Vulgate and Doway, *instruct*; church of England, John Rogers' Translation and Bishops' Bible, *inform*; Edwards, *curb*; Jebb, *restrain*; Fry, *correct*. Phillips: "*To bind his princes* is to exercise control over the greatest men in the kingdom," Gen. xli. 40, 43, 44. Joseph could compel obedience or punish any subject of the realm. *Senators*, elsewhere *ancients, elders, ancient men*, Ps. cvii. 32; cxix. 100; Ezra iii. 12.

23. *Israel also came into Egypt; and Jacob sojourned in the land of Ham.* The two names of the father of Joseph here signify not only himself, but also his posterity. Egypt and the land of Ham are convertible terms; see on Ps. lxxviii. 51. The Egyptians descended from Ham through his son Mizraim.

24. *And he increased his people greatly, and made them stronger than their enemies.* The increase of the Israelites in Egypt is one of the wonders in the history of population. Cavillers have objected to the Scriptural record of their numbers; but learned men have amply shown that under the divine blessing without any miracle all the increase might have occurred. The expression *stronger than their enemies* may include the fact of their outnumbering them and the further fact that God's blessing was manifestly upon them.

25. *He turned their heart to hate his people, to deal subtilely with his servants.* Scott: "At first the Egyptians were *friends* to Jacob's family, for Joseph's sake: but after the death of Joseph and his patron, and the succession of another 'king who knew not Joseph,' the Egyptians became *enemies* to Israel. Their rapid increase, from a single family to a powerful people, excited envy, jealousy, dread and hatred; which prompted both the king and his subjects to devise politic and detestable measures for diminishing their numbers and strength, and for retaining them in bondage." All our enemies are sure to hate us whenever God removes his restraints from their hearts.

26. *He sent Moses his servant; and Aaron whom he had chosen.* The call of Moses was clear and full, Ex. iii. 7–14; iv. 10–17. The call of Aaron was no less distinct and well authenticated, Num. xvi. xvii. 5. Calvin: "What is attributed to each of these men in particular, applies equally to both, and therefore the sentence ought to be explained thus: God sent Moses and Aaron, his servants, not because of their own intrinsic fitness, or because they spontaneously offered to him their service, but because he chose them."

27. *They shewed his signs among them, and wonders in the land of Ham.* The *land of Ham*, Egypt, as in v. 23. *Signs*, in Ps. lxv. 8, *tokens*; in Ps. lxxiv. 4, *ensigns. Wonders*, as in v. 5. *Signs* and *wonders* are often designations of the same events; because they are both significant and marvellous—they instruct and astonish. The Hebrew is literally *words of signs*; see on Ps. lxxix. 9; ci. 3. Cresswell thinks we

are to understand "Declarations, which were afterwards confirmed by miracles." Hammond and Pool favor the same interpretation.

28. *He sent darkness and made it dark.* Two explanations are given; 1, that the Psalmist, disregarding the order of the plagues as they occurred in Egypt first mentions the *ninth* of them, as recorded in Ex. x. 21–23. From a comparison of the history in Exodus with the enumeration here given it is clear that the Psalmist felt quite at liberty to introduce things in any order he pleased. 2. Another explanation is that by *darkness* here we are to understand affliction. *Darkness* often means calamity. But the prophet is here speaking of dreadful *plagues*, which are matters of history. *And they rebelled not against his word.* Who rebelled not? Calvin and others understand Moses and Aaron. They promptly and cheerfully obeyed God's command, and boldly executed their commission, not fearing the proud monarch, and his threats, Ex. x. 10, 28. Others make it a question, thinking the Egyptians are here spoken of: "Did they not rebel against his word?" This would make good sense, but is not particularly suitable here. Others think that the meaning is that for a time the Egyptians seemed to yield. Tholuck: "Pharaoh and the Egyptians were always obedient for the moment." Others suggest a change of one letter in the Hebrew text, so as to read: And they were not obedient to his word. It is evident that the Egyptians rebelled against his word to the last, although at times they seemed to be ready to yield.

29. *He turned their waters into blood, and slew their fish.* The historic record is full and simple, Ex. vii. 19–25. Compare Ps. lxxviii. 44. Not a running stream in all Egypt contained water that could be drunk, or that did not destroy the life of its inhabitants. This was the *first* plague.

30. *Their land brought forth frogs in abundance, in the chambers of their kings.* Frogs, uniformly rendered, literally, *marsh-leapers.* The narrative is in Ex. viii. 2–13. See on Ps. lxxviii. 45, where it is said the frogs *destroyed* the Egyptians. This was done by their dead bodies poisoning the air. This was the *second* plague. The verb is well rendered *brought forth in abundance.* Edwards: The land swarmed with frogs; Alexander: Their land teemed with frogs. *Chambers*, often found and well rendered; not elsewhere in the Psalms.

31. *He spake and there came divers sorts of flies, and lice in all their coasts.* Here we have the *third* and *fourth* plagues in reverse order. *Divers sorts*, so in Ps. lxxviii. 45; but in Ex. viii. 21, 22, 24, 29, 31, rendered *swarms.* Compare Ex. viii. 16–18. There is some doubt as to the kind of insect here spoken of. The Chaldee, Syriac, Arabic, Fabritius, Piscator, Amesius, Venema, Tremellius and Junius, Calvin, church of England, Edwards and Jebb have *lice.* Josephus also thinks *lice* are intended. The Septuagint, Ethiopic, Vulgate, Doway, Hengstenberg and Alexander all think flying insects are intended, *gnats, midges.* The word in the Septuagint, transferred to some other versions, is *sciniphs.* Philo, Origen, Jerome, Gesenius and Boothroyd all think *gnats* were intended. Bochart argues at length that gnats could not be intended; but a part of his reasoning is certainly unsound, as where he says gnats do not sting both men and cattle. When God chooses to work miracles, he is not restrained by any law, but only by his own will. *Coasts*, in Ps. lxxviii. 54, *border;* in Ps. civ. 9, *bound.* To the Egyptians the plague of vermin on their persons was exceedingly dreadful, as that people affected great personal cleanliness, bathing very often, and thinking it an offence to their deities to enter their temples with vile insects in their clothing.

32. *He gave them hail for rain,* and *flaming fire in their land.* This was the *seventh* plague. It is recorded at length in Ex. ix. 22–32; see on Ps. lxxviii. 48. By *hail for rain* some understand *hail instead of rain;* but Egypt seems not to have depended

on the clouds, but on the overflowing of the Nile for irrigation. The meaning probably is that the hail came thick and fast from above as rain, accompanied by terrible thunder and lightning, in Ps. lxxviii. called *hot thunderbolts*. This terrible tempest not only beat upon man and beast, the fire running along upon the ground, and smiting every herb of the field, but also every tree of the field;

33. *He smote their vines also and their fig trees; and brake the trees of their coasts.* A more wasted and ruined appearance no country probably ever had. The garden of the world became at once utterly desolate. See on Ps. lxxviii. 47. *Coasts*, as in v. 31.

34. *He spake and the locusts came, and caterpillars, and that without number,*

35. *And did eat up all the herbs in their land, and devoured the fruit of their ground.* This was the *eighth* plague. Its history is in Ex. x. 12–15. See on Ps. lxxviii. 46. *Locusts*, the same as in Ex. x. 4, 12, 13, 14, 19; Ps. lxxviii. 46. But in Exodus we have no word corresponding to *caterpillars*, thrice so rendered, and six times *cankerworm*. But both these words denote insects without wings; whereas the plague consisted entirely of creatures brought in great numbers through the air. The word rendered *caterpillar*, no less than the first, denotes a species of *locust* or *grasshopper*, of which there is quite a variety. *Without number*, see on Ps. civ. 25.

36. *He smote also all the firstborn in their land, the chief of all their strength.* This was the *tenth* and last plague. The king, the captive and the cattle all lost their firstborn. The record is in Ex. xii. 29, 30. The judgment was rendered still more terrible because it came upon the land in the darkness of *midnight*. See on Ps. lxxviii. 51. The latter clause evidently refers to Gen. xlix. 3. This awful event was decisive. The dismissal of Israel was promptly granted.

37. *He brought them forth also with silver and gold.* For a little while the malice and grasping dispositions of the Egyptians were changed into a feeling of kindness: "And the Lord gave the people favour in the sight of the Egyptians, so that they lent [gave upon being asked] unto them such things as they required: and they spoiled the Egyptians," Ex. xii. 36. They borrowed [that is, obtained by asking, not as loans, but as gifts] many costly jewels. *And there was not one feeble person among their tribes. Feeble*, the word is often so rendered; also *falling*, Job iv. 4; *stumbling*, Ps. xxvii. 2; *decaying*, Neh. iv. 10. Phillips: "No one was prevented by disease or infirmity from accomplishing the journey."

38. *Egypt was glad when they departed: for the fear of them fell upon them.* See Ex. xii. 33.

39. *He spread a cloud for a covering; and fire to give light in the night.* The historic record is in Ex. xiii. 21, and is often alluded to in Scripture, Num. ix. 16; x. 34; Neh. ix. 12; Isa. iv. 5, 6. See on Ps. lxxviii. 14; xcvii. 2; xcix. 7.

40. The people *asked, and he brought quails, and satisfied them with the bread of heaven.* The record of these events is in Ex. xvi. 4–35. In Ps. lxxvii. 22–29, they are introduced apparently for another purpose. The reference here is not to the subsequent lusting after flesh recorded in Num. xi. 4–33. The people were *satisfied, i. e.,* filled with flesh and food.

41. *He opened the rock, and the waters gushed out; they ran in the dry places* like a *river.* The facts here alluded to are recorded in Ex. xvii. 6; Num. xx. 11. See on Ps. lxxviii. 15, 16, 20. *Dry places;* in Job xxx. 3, *wilderness;* in Isa. xxxv. 1, *solitary place.* If in the days of Moses the region through which Israel was passing at the time of smiting the rock, bore the same marks of sterility and dryness as in modern times, it is not strange that these unbelieving Jews staggered. The significancy of this gushing fountain is declared by Paul, 1 Cor. x. 4.

42. *For he remembered his holy promise, and Abraham his servant.* The allusion is

to such promises as we find in Gen. xv. 13–15; Ex. ii. 24. Compare Luke i. 54, 55. See on vv. 8–10.

43. *And he brought forth his people with joy,* and *his chosen with gladness.* The parallelism of this verse is double, first, between *joy* and *gladness,* secondly, between *people* and *chosen.* Compare v. 6. God often reminded the Israelites that they were brought into covenant relation with him by no means on account of their own merits, but solely by his own, free, sovereign choice and abounding grace, Deut. vii. 6–8; ix. 4–6; Ezek. xxxvi. 22, 32.

44. *And gave them the lands of the heathen; and they inherited the labour of the people.* *Heathen,* nations, Gentiles. *People,* nations. The reason why the Israelites had not possession of these lands sooner was that the iniquities of their possessors were not full, Gen. xv. 16. God bore with those ancient enemies a long time before he deprived them of their lands and the fruit of their *labor.* On the whole verse see Ps. lxxviii. 55. Anderson fitly explains labor as signifying " the products of their labor; their buildings, vineyards, cultivated fields," etc. See Deut. vi. 10, 11; Josh. xxiv. 13.

45. *That they might observe his statutes, and keep his laws.* *Keep,* as in Ps. xvii. 4; xix. 11. *Observe,* as in Ps. xii. 7; xxxiv. 13. Here the words are parallel. So also are *statutes* and *laws.* *Statutes,* as in v. 10. *Laws,* uniformly rendered as in Ps. i. 2, and often in Ps. xix. cxix. The Israelites were not chosen and blessed for their piety, but that they might become the servants of the Most High. See on Ps. lxxviii. 7. *Praise ye the Lord.* Hallelujah, literally, Praise ye Jah.

Doctrinal and Practical Remarks.

1. There is no contrariety in the various acts of religious worship to which we are called in the first five verses of this Psalm. Thanksgiving, supplications, prayers, intercessions, confessions, songs of praise, pious conversation, open expressions of exulting joy and a recital of the divine mercies, all harmonize with each other, and may well be performed the same day. We should be specially careful that our glorying in the Lord should be reverent, solemn and profoundly humble; yet free from servility and a despairing tendency.

2. True religion is very much a matter between God and the souls of his people, vv. 3, 4. It principally consists in *seeking the Lord*—seeking to know him, to secure his favor, his image, his service, his fellowship and an abode with him at last. No good man is ever satisfied with what he knows or enjoys of God in this life, but he hopes, and longs, and prays with groanings that cannot be uttered for a fuller and more ravishing sight and enjoyment of God in glory. Seek *his strength* and seek *his face.* Dickson: " As seeking communion with God is a mark of a child of God, so it is also a reason of gladness and joy, because it both declares that we are of the number of converts and true worshippers of God, and also that joy is reserved for us."

3. If *miracles* and *prodigies* could have converted the world, it would have been done long ago, vv. 5–27. The history of creation, of providence and of redemption abounds with them; and sometimes for a season cavillers have thus been silenced. It is not by being startled, or terrified, or confounded, but by receiving the love of the truth and by embracing Jesus Christ, who is the way, the truth and the life, that men are turned to God, Luke xvi. 27–31.

4. We should be greatly affected by a review and recollection of God's mercies to our ancestors, v. 6. It is a great privilege to be able to plead his covenant with our forefathers. No doubt the weak, the vain, the self-righteous often pervert so great a blessing to mischievous ends; still our estimate of the blessing itself can hardly be too high.

5. Let believers never forget and always plead their covenant relation with God,

vv. 7, 8, 42. And if the old covenant brought so great blessings to the posterity of the patriarchs for God's love to them, how much more shall the new covenant bring inestimable blessings to all believers through God's unspeakable love to Jesus Christ, whom he has given as a *covenant* to the people, a Captain of salvation to all humble souls?

6. We are but miserable drivellers in Scripture when we fail to see somewhat of the fulness of spiritual blessings contained in Old Testament history, doctrines and promises, such as we find in vv. 8–11 of this Psalm. Before the coming of Christ at least some pious men had better canons of interpreting Scripture. Zacharias construed God's word far otherwise, when he looked at this Psalm, Luke i. 67, 68, 72–75.

7. If Canaan of old was an object of so much, and so pious interest to the true Israel of God, it was not merely or chiefly because of the temporal blessings therewith connected, great as they were; but because it was a type of the heavenly inheritance, v. 11. All the old dispensation had a shadow of good things to come, Heb. x. 1.

8. It is well for us often to look to the hole of the pit whence we were digged, v. 12. The greatest families and kingdoms had but a small beginning. An humble origin is no just cause of shame to a good man, but surely it should cut the comb of our pride to remember that we are of nothing, are nothing, deserve nothing and can do nothing as of ourselves. There walks not this earth a man who is too humble in the sight of God.

9. Let no man despise the day of small things, v. 12; Luke xii. 32. It is better to stand in our lot feeble and despised, cast down and persecuted, without friends and without earthly resources, yet humbly trusting in God, than to be ever so great according to the judgment of this world and not have hope in the Almighty.

10. If God's people are strangers and pilgrims on the earth, let them remember it has always been so with the chosen seed, v. 13. Why should the saints of this day think to fare better in temporals than their fathers before them? The Saviour has dealt both kindly and candidly with us in telling us what to expect, John xvi. 33. No good man knows what snares may be spreading for his feet. Scott: "That which ungodly counsellors think a wise, political measure, often proves, on examination, to be a most detestable project of the devil against the church of Christ."

11. To cheerful, yet sober views of things, the saints should be the more inclined because of their complete and absolute safety, vv. 13–15. God has all hands and all hearts in his power. He can quiet adversaries, Pr. xvi. 7. But should he choose to let loose for a time the rage of men and devils, yet in the end he will bring all right. If God protected his chosen of old, he will not forsake his elect now. Dickson: "The person of every believer walking in God's way is sacred, sanctified, and set apart for God's peculiar service." If Jehovah punished Belshazzar for defiling the vessels of the temple at Jerusalem, has he no wrath or judgments in reserve for those who abuse the vessels of mercy?

12. In particular has God always shown a special displeasure at wicked and cruel assaults on his prophets and ministers, v. 15. Henry: "They that offer to touch God's prophets, with design to harm them may expect to hear of it one way or other. . . God's anointed prophets are dearer to him than anointed kings themselves. Jeroboam's hand was withered when it was stretched out against a prophet."

13. How fearfully hazardous it is to go on in sin against God, when he commands *famine*, war, pestilence, all the storms and plagues of nature, and can hurl them against us at any moment, v. 16. Our dependence is perfect and absolute, yet many act as if their independence was perfect and absolute. Dickson: "No food can be had except God furnish it, and no food, when it is given, can feed, except God give a powerful blessing with it," Deut. viii. 3.

14. God's foresight is perfect and he provides for every possible contingency, and

for every coming event, v. 17.   If a universal famine is to afflict the world, a Joseph shall be raised up, by whose sagacity the starvation of the righteous seed shall be prevented.   God's ways are indeed very strange, but they are all holy and infallibly wise.   God reveals the future to Joseph in a dream ; he tells his dream ; his brethren envy him ; they doom him to death ; God touches their hearts ; they rather sell him than kill him ; to Egypt he goes in the hands of the Midianites ; soon he is locked up in prison, loaded with chains ; there he lies long, long years ; and yet every step is towards deliverance and exaltation.   Why are we so slow to trust an infinite God ?

15. Although in the New Testament Joseph is nowhere said to be a type of Christ, yet surely we carry our canons of interpretation too far, when we exclude such types as the oldest son of Rachel.

16. Let all God's people expect trials.   They will surely come ; and in due time deliverance will as surely follow ; and deliverance shall be followed by glory and honor, vv. 18–22.   Scott : " We greatly mistake if we do not rank afflictions among our mercies."

17. Past experiences, however rich and wonderful, are no proofs that we shall not be called to great and sore trials in the future.   Jacob, who had seen God at Bethel and in wrestling had prevailed with the angel, must in his old age go down to Egypt, and end his days in the land of Ham, v. 23.   And yet he now saw in his old age fully explained the darkest riddle that for near a quarter of a century had filled his life with sorrow.

18. When we remember how God multiplied the Israelites in Egypt, v. 24; it is easy to conceive how in the latter day he can make the earth swarm with a holy population, Ezek. xxxvi. 37 ; Zech. viii. 12.

19. If men hate us, it is because God has bidden them, v. 25.   So wise men have always reasoned, 2 Sam. xvi. 11, 12.   So let us reason.   God turns men to hate us, not by infusing malice into their hearts.   It is already there in dreadful force.   All that is necessary for him to do is to take his almighty hand off their hearts and out bursts their wickedness.   Henry : " Every creature is that to us that God makes it to be."

20. God is at no loss for fit servants and messengers ; for if he has them not already, he can easily raise them up and send them on his errands, v. 26.   Moses and Aaron themselves were what God made them to be, no more and no less.

21. How atrocious and foolish is human wickedness to array itself against the power of him, who can make the sun as black as midnight, and open vast magazines of plagues to scourge and waste and desolate a land, and torment its inhabitants, until life is a burden, vv. 28–36.   If one judgment will not effect God's purposes, he will send ten.   When he chooses all nature makes war upon man. Isa. xxvii. 4.

22. Whenever God puts to his hand, any work goes on with a prosperity surpassing all our conceptions, v. 37.

23. In any case or in any matter God can make the most reluctant perfectly willing, v. 38.   Dickson : " The Lord can make bloody persecutors of his people to cease from their persecutions and to contribute to their delivery."

24. Let God's people be abundantly assured of his kind protection and guidance in all their pilgrimage, v. 39.

25. Let us not be over anxious about the kind or quality of our food, v. 40.   Our heavenly Father knows what is best for us.   Let us simply pray : " Feed me with food convenient for me."

26. As it was a great heightening of the divine beneficence to feed Israel with the *bread of heaven*, v. 40, so it was a great aggravation of their rebellion against God that

they were dissatisfied with 'angels' food' and distrusted a providence which was every day working a miracle before them.

27. Their wickedness was heightened by their unbelief and ingratitude when they saw the goodness of God in smiting the flinty rock in the desolate wilderness of Horeb, and bringing out streams of water for their refreshment, v. 41.

28. However dark the state of God's people may be, let them rest assured that brighter days are coming, v. 43. He who has undertaken their cause is sovereign by right and sovereign in fact.

29. God is the rightful disposer of all lands, v. 44. The people of every nation have by their sins entirely forfeited all right to even their temporal possessions, and it is of God's mercies that any nation lives in the quiet enjoyment of its own territories.

30. The great end of all God's gifts is that we may be led to holiness, v. 45. Unless this be the result, the chief good is not attained.

PSALM CVI.

1 Praise ye the LORD. O give thanks unto the LORD; for *he is* good: for his mercy *endureth* for ever.

2 Who can utter the mighty acts of the LORD? *who* can shew forth all his praise?

3 Blessed *are* they that keep judgment, *and* he that doeth righteousness at all times.

4 Remember me, O LORD, with the favour *that thou bearest unto* thy people: O visit me with thy salvation;

5 That I may see the good of thy chosen, that I may rejoice in the gladness of thy nation, that I may glory with thine inheritance.

6 We have sinned with our fathers, we have committed iniquity, we have done wickedly.

7 Our fathers understood not thy wonders in Egypt; they remembered not the multitude of thy mercies; but provoked *him* at the sea, *even* at the Red sea.

8 Nevertheless he saved them for his name's sake, that he might make his mighty power to be known.

9 He rebuked the Red sea also, and it was dried up: so he led them through the depths, as through the wilderness.

10 And he saved them from the hand of him that hated *them*, and redeemed them from the hand of the enemy.

11 And the waters covered their enemies: there was not one of them left.

12 Then believed they his words; they sang his praise.

13 They soon forgat his works; they waited not for his counsel:

14 But lusted exceedingly in the wilderness, and tempted God in the desert.

15 And he gave them their request; but sent leanness into their soul.

16 They envied Moses also in the camp, *and* Aaron the saint of the LORD.

17 The earth opened and swallowed up Dathan, and covered the company of Abiram.

18 And a fire was kindled in their company; the flame burned up the wicked.

19 They made a calf in Horeb, and worshipped the molten image.

20 Thus they changed their glory into the similitude of an ox that eateth grass.

21 They forgat God their saviour, which had done great things in Egypt;

22 Wondrous works in the land of Ham, *and* terrible things by the Red sea.

23 Therefore he said that he would destroy them, had not Moses his chosen stood before him in the breach, to turn away his wrath, lest he should destroy *them*.

24 Yea, they despised the pleasant land, they believed not his word:

25 But murmured in their tents, *and* hearkened not unto the voice of the LORD.

26 Therefore he lifted up his hand against them, to overthrow them in the wilderness:

27 To overthrow their seed also among the nations, and to scatter them in the lands.

28 They joined themselves also unto Baal-peor, and ate the sacrifices of the dead.

29 Thus they provoked *him* to anger with their inventions: and the plague brake in upon them.

30 Then stood up Phinehas, and executed judgment: and *so* the plague was stayed.

31 And that was counted unto him for righteousness unto all generations for evermore.

32 They angered *him* also at the waters of strife, so that it went ill with Moses for their sakes:

33 Because they provoked his spirit, so that he spake unadvisedly with his lips.

34 They did not destroy the nations, concerning whom the LORD commanded them:

35 But were mingled among the heathen, and learned their works.

36 And they served their idols: which were a snare unto them.

37 Yea, they sacrificed their sons and their daughters unto devils,

38 And shed innocent blood, *even* the blood of their sons and of their daughters, whom they sacrificed unto the idols of Canaan: and the land was polluted with blood.

39 Thus were they defiled with their own works, and went a whoring with their own inventions.

40 Therefore was the wrath of the LORD kindled againt his people, insomuch that he abhorred his own inheritance.

41 And he gave them into the hand of the heathen; and they that hated them ruled over them.

42 Their enemies also oppressed them, and they were brought into subjection under their hand.

43 Many times did he deliver them; but they provoked *him* with their counsel, and were brought low for their iniquity.

44 Nevertheless he regarded their affliction, when he heard their cry:

45 And he remembered for them his covenant, and repented according to the multitude of his mercies.

46 He made them also to be pitied of all those that carried them captives.

47 Save us, O LORD our God, and gather us from among the heathen, to give thanks unto thy holy name, *and* to triumph in thy praise.

48 Blessed *be* the LORD God of Israel from everlasting to everlasting: and let all the people say, Amen. Praise ye the LORD.

THIS Psalm has no title, though some make the first word an inscription. Of the authorship we are uncertain; but these remarks seem to be just: 1. Whoever wrote Psalms civ. cv. probably wrote this. 2. Many ascribe this to David. 3. The first verse, except *Hallelujah*, and the last two verses except *Hallelujah* are taken from an ode certainly composed by David, 1 Chron. xvi. 34–36. 4. Although Pool, Horsley, Mudge and others are confident that it was composed in the time of the dispersion and captivity, arguing from the language of v. 47, yet it is a fact that David actually wrote that verse, 1 Chron. xvi. 35. Scott dates it B. C. 1045; Clarke gives no date, but thinks it was composed in Babylon. In Ps. cv. we have a lively account of God's *mercies* to ancient Israel. In this much notice is taken of the *sins* of the same people. *That* greatly praises God; *this* justly deplores departures from God. Yet it does not abandon the chosen people to despair and ruin; but bids them hope in the divine mercy. Hengstenberg calls this a "lyrical echo" to Dan. ix. Alexander: "It would not be absurd to regard this Psalm as a lyrical paraphrase of that confession." Nothing makes men think and feel and speak alike more than a just and deep sense of personal ill-desert. All ingenuous and general confessions of sin closely resemble each other. The names of the Most High found in this Psalm are *Jah* LORD, *Jehovah* LORD and *El God*, on which see introduction to Ps. lxviii.; on Ps. i. 2; v. 4. If the great mercies bestowed on the Jews made their sins so odious and abominable; how aggravated must be the offences of men, who live in sin under the full blaze of gospel light!

1. *Praise ye the* LORD, literally, *hallelujah*. The Syriac wants this word, and so do some manuscripts; but no doubt it ought to be retained. "Even sorrow for sin must not put us out of tune for praising God." *O give thanks unto the* LORD, as in Ps. cv. 1. The reasons assigned for thanksgiving are 1, *For* he is *good*, or *goodness* itself, as the same word is often rendered. Compare Matt. xix. 17. 2. *For his mercy* endureth

for ever. Mercy, often *lovingkindness; see on* Ps. li. 1. This clause is repeated *twenty-six* times in Ps. cxxxvi. Man never had a fitter theme for praise, nor a fitter work than praise.

2. *Who can utter the mighty acts of the* LORD? *who can shew forth all his praise ? Mighty acts,* elsewhere in the singular rendered *strength, power, might, mastery,* Ps. xx. 6; xxi. 13; Isa. xi. 2; Ex. xxxii. 18; twice in Ps. cxlv., and once in Ps. cl., *mighty acts.* The rendering of the verbs, though not literal in form, gives the true meaning. Two senses have been gathered from this verse. 1. Some make it coincident with that of Ps. l. 16; a reproof to the wicked for attempting or pretending to praise God. 2. There is a more obvious sense, viz., that no one can praise God as he deserves. Though not inspired the son of Sirach well presents this thought, Ecclus. xliii. 28–31.

3. *Blessed* are *they that keep judgment,* and *he that doeth righteousness at all times. Blessed,* as in Ps. i. 1, literally *O the blessednesses.* To *keep judgment* is the same as to *do righteousness, i. e.,* to observe justice and maintain rectitude in the sight of God and man; see on Ps. xv. 2. *At all times,* or, in *every season.* Fits of religious emotion are not enough. The change of the plural to the singular is not unusual.

4. *Remember me, O* LORD, *with the favour* that thou bearest unto *thy people. Remember,* a word of great force and beauty. It embraces much. The penitent thief cried, Remember me. *Favor,* as in Ps. v. 12; xxx. 5; in Ps. li. 18, it is rendered *good pleasure;* in Ps. cxliii. 10, *will.* Whatever good comes to any mere man is referable to God's sovereign will and grace alone. *O visit me with thy salvation. Visit,* as in Ps. viii. 4. Like *remember,* it embraces all the good desired. *Salvation,* elsewhere *help, deliverance; see on* Ps. iii. 2; xviii. 50. This verse contains a petition either uttered by the author as an ejaculation in his own behalf; or in the name of the body of believers of his time. The transition from the singular in vv. 4, 5, to the plural in vv. 6, 7, is not unusual.

5. *That I may see the good of thy chosen, that I may rejoice* in *the gladness of thy nation, that I may glory with thine inheritance. Chosen, nation* and *inheritance* all designate the true church of God. To *see good* is to possess and enjoy it. The effect is *rejoicing* and *glorying.* This verse teaches that God's free *choice* of Israel was the cause of their becoming his *people* and his *inheritance.* Compare Deut. vii. 6; xiv. 2. Yet notwithstanding their distinguished privileges they acted badly.

6. *We have sinned with our fathers, we have committed iniquity, we have done wickedly. Sinned, offended, trespassed. With our fathers,* it is easy to follow the evil example of ancestors, because the heart is inclined to evil. *Committed iniquities;* in Esther i. 16, *done wrong;* in 2 Chron. vi. 37, *done amiss;* in 2 Sam. xix. 19, *did perversely. Perversion* or *perverseness* expresses the radical idea. *Done wickedly;* the cognate adjective is in Ps. i. rendered *ungodly.* Inspired writers have exhausted the powers of language on the love of God, and on the wickedness of man. Alexander: "The terms of this verse are borrowed, here as well as in Dan. ix. 5, from that great model of ecclesiastical and national devotion furnished by Solomon in his prayer at the dedication of the temple," 1 Kings viii. 47. All the miseries that come on persons, families and nations, may be accounted for on the principle of divine righteousness.

7. *Our fathers understood not thy wonders in Egypt.* They even refused Moses himself, Acts vii. 27, 35. They misinterpreted all the manifestations of divine power against their enemies, and of divine kindness towards themselves. In reading their history even carnal men are amazed, and foolishly think that in like circumstances they would have acted otherwise. *They remembered not the multitude of thy mercies.* Forgetfulness of God and of his kindness enters into the very nature of iniquity in all stages. On the other hand true piety hides the memory of divine things in its heart. God *remembered* them, but they *remembered* not him. The verb is the same

as in v. 4. *Multitude*, as in Ps. li. 1. *Mercies*, elsewhere, *lovingkindnesses*. *But provoked* him *at the sea, even at the Red sea*. The history of this misconduct is in Ex. xiv. 10–12. Their language was that of unbelief, worldliness and ingratitude. There is no significance in the repetition of the word *sea*, beyond a probable allusion to Ex. xv. 4. *Red* sea, literally sea of *weeds*, or *flags*, as the word is rendered in Ex. ii. 3, 5. *Red* sea is the Greek name, derived some think from the little insects on the surface, others, from the tint of the mountains on a part of its coast, and yet others, from the land of Edom, (which means *red*,) lying between the Red sea and Palestine. The Red sea is a bay of the Indian ocean. It is commonly called the Arabian gulf.

8. *Nevertheless he saved them for his name's sake*, see on Ps. cv. 43. Having undertaken a work, God's counsel must stand, not because of Israel's merits, but for the glory of his perfections; *that he might make his mighty power to be known*. *Mighty power*, in v. 2, *mighty acts*. The passage of the Red sea has been celebrated ever since it occurred, not only on earth, but in heaven, Rev. xv. 3.

9. *He rebuked the Red sea also, and it was dried up*. Nothing is more marked in real miracles than their perfection. The Israelites did not wade through shallow water, nor was there an unusual ebbing of the tide; but the waters gathered and stood upright, on both sides, Ex. xv. 8; see on Ps. xxxiii. 7; lxxviii. 13. *So he led them through the depths, as through the wilderness*. *Depths, deeps*, not shallow places. *The wilderness, a desert*. The waters of the Arabian gulf were to the Israelites no more hindrance than if the place had always been dry ground. Compare Isa. lxiii. 13.

10. *And he saved them from the hand of him that hated* them, *and redeemed them from the hand of the enemy*. *Him that hated* and *enemy*, both participles, strictly parallel; both in the singular, perhaps because Pharaoh is alluded to as the leader of the Egyptians. Not only he, but all his legions perished; so in the next verse we have the plural form.

11. *And the waters covered their enemies; there was not one of them left*. *Enemies, adversaries*, literally distressers, troublers, afflicters, Ex. xiv. 27, 28; xv. 5. The only trace of them was found in their carcasses that floated ashore and became a prey for the jackals of the wilderness, Ps. lxxiv. 14.

12. *Then believed they his words; they sang his praise*. On the first clause see Ex. xiv. 31; on the second, the song of Moses and his countrymen given at length in Ex. xv. This verse is not spoken to their praise, but to show how slow they were to believe and worship God. Calvin: "Overpowered by the grandeur of God's works, they were, in spite of themselves, compelled to believe in God, and to give glory to him, and thus the criminality of their rebellion was increased; because, although their stubbornness was overcome, yet they immediately relapsed into their former state of unbelief." Their faith was temporary, Mark iv. 17.

13. *They soon forgat his works;* literally, *They hasted, they forgot his works*. It was but three days after this stupendous miracle that they came to the waters of Marah, where their wickedness broke out afresh; see on Ps. lxxviii. 11. Compare Ex. xv. 24. *They waited not for his counsel*. Their ingratitude for mercies already received made them impatient at any delay. Because they *believed* not, they *made haste*, Isa. xxviii. 16. True piety *waits* upon God. *Counsel*, as in Ps. i. 1; xxxiii. 11. They refused to practise any self-denial.

14. *But lusted exceedingly in the wilderness, and tempted God in the desert*. See on Ps. lxxviii. 18. Compare Num. xi. 4–33; 1 Cor. x. 6. *Wilderness* and *desert*, as in Ps. lxxviii. 40. *Lusted*, sometimes in a good sense, *desired* or *greatly desired*, Ps. xlv. 11; cxxxii. 13. It is also rendered *coveted, longed*, Deut. xii. 20; Prov. xxi. 26. Here it expresses unlawful desires. On tempting God see on Ps. lxxviii. 18. The

fountain of all their sin was their unbelief. This made them turbulent, impatient, murmurers and complainers.

15. *And he gave them their request,* i. e., the thing which they wickedly desired. Compare 1 Sam. xii. 17, 19; Hos. xiii. 11. *But sent leanness into their soul.* They got what they craved, and with it a curse. Compare Num. xi. 18–20. What was the evil sent? French and Skinner: He sent a wasting disease among them. From the description given in Num. xi. 20, Hammond and Anderson think a form of cholera broke out among them. Whatever its form, it was "a very great plague," and killed many, Num. xi. 33, 34. *Soul* may mean person, or animal life, Nu. xi. 6. Some think the evil sent was *spiritual.* Alexander: "The phrase *into their soul* is really a qualifying phrase, designed to show that the emaciation or decay which was sent upon them was not bodily but spiritual." Why may we not include both ideas, a failure of bodily strength accompanied with emaciation, and spiritual poverty and wretchedness? Both these evils were suffered, whether they are here mentioned or not. Henry: "He filled them with uneasiness of mind, and terror of conscience, and a self-reproach, occasioned by their bodies being sick with the surfeit." Morison: "He sent leanness into their persons; so that multitudes of them were speedily wasted and consumed: and this state, alas! of bodily health, the result of animal indulgence, was but the sad emblem of that spiritual emaciation which had seized upon all the powers of their immortal spirits." Clarke: "God gave flesh, as they desired: but gave no blessing with it; and in consequence they did not fatten, but grew *lean* upon it. Their souls also suffered want." Scott: "Their sensual request was granted as a punishment, and proved injurious both to their health, and to their souls."

16. *They envied Moses also in the camp, and Aaron the saint of the* LORD.

17. *The earth opened and swallowed up Dathan, and covered the company of Abiram.*

18. *And a fire was kindled in their company; the flame burned up the wicked.* The events here alluded to are graphically described in Num. xvi. The designation of *saint* applied to Aaron includes both him and Moses; for they were both holy unto the Lord in office, and were at heart true and eminent servants of God. They are honorably mentioned long after their death, Ps. lxxvii. 20; xcix..6. Compare Num. xvi. 5. Moses and Aaron were both modest and unassuming men, Num. xvi. 11. The object of introducing this history here seems to be to remind the Israelites that their nation might have easily perished by the just curse of God in the wilderness: that others were involved in murmuring against Moses and Aaron, besides those who fell, and that the nation did not now profit as it should by the manifestation of God's wrath against those that were smitten, or of his mercy towards them that were spared. There seem to be recorded in Num. xvi. three distinct judgments: 1, the earth opened and swallowed up Korah and his company; 2, a fire burst forth and consumed two hundred and fifty men that offered incense; 3, a plague broke out and destroyed fourteen thousand seven hundred souls.

19. *They made a calf in Horeb, and worshipped the molten image.*

20. *Thus they changed their glory into the similitude of an ox that eateth grass.* All attempts to worship God by images or by likenesses, were strictly forbidden to the Jews and through them to all people, Ex. xx. 4, 5; Deut. v. 8, 9. The Israelites could not have been ignorant of these prohibitions, and yet they fell into idolatry. Cresswell: "The modern Jews assert, that their ancestors were in that matter misled by certain Egyptian proselytes, who had accompanied the Israelites when they were delivered from their bondage." But the history of that people for a long time subsequent to their settlement in Canaan shows their strong propensity to gross idolatry. Nor is the guilt of their idolatry taken away because it was a professed attempt to honor the God of heaven. Israel could hardly have sunk so low as to think that a

calf, not made till they reached Horeb, had delivered them. But they attempted to worship Jehovah under the figure of an ox, which was the sacred sign of the Egyptians. Thus they corrupted themselves, Ex. xxxii. 7; sinned a great sin, Ex. xxxii. 31; and became idolaters, 1 Cor. x. 7. Compare Acts vii. 41. The Egyptian word, Apis, or Serapis signifies the head of an ox. Those ancient idolaters made that animal their principal deity. *Glory;* Jehovah is the *glory* of his people. See like use of the word, Jer. ii. 11. *An ox that eateth grass, i. e.,* is in the habit of eating grass. Compare Deut. ix. 21. Some think that the name *calf* is here and elsewhere applied in contempt to the small image set up. The same word is used for *ox, bull* and *bullock.*

21. *They forgat God their saviour, which had done great things in Egypt;*
22. *Wondrous works in the land of Ham, and terrible things by the Red sea.* *Egypt* and *land of Ham* as in Ps. cv. 23. *Forgat;* compare v. 7. *Saviour,* a participle, in Ps. vii. 10, rendered *which saveth.* *Great things,* as in Ps. lxxi. 19. *Wondrous works,* in Ps. ix. 1, *marvellous works.* *Terrible things,* as in Ps. xlv. 4; lxv. 5; a participle, expressive of the fear that ought to have been awakened by the miracles of Egypt and at the Red sea. *Great things, wondrous works* and *terrible things* all refer to the stupendous events preceding and attending the deliverance from the house of bondage. They inspired neither salutary dread, nor pious confidence, nor any right sentiment whatever:

23. *Therefore he said that he would destroy them, had not Moses his chosen stood before him in the breach, to turn away his wrath lest he should destroy* them, Ex. xxxii. 10, 11, 14, 32; Deut. ix. 19, 25; x. 10; Ezek. xx. 13. Hengstenberg: "The length of this verse harmonizes with its important position." Moses was God's chosen to be lawgiver of Israel and also to eternal life. *Destroy,* two words, different in Hebrew, but well rendered. As intercessor Moses stood in the breach, and so was mediator, Gal. iii. 19.

24. *Yea, they despised the pleasant land.* Margin, *land of desire;* Edwards, *desirable land;* Jebb, *land of pleasantness;* Hengstenberg, *land of beauty.* In 2 Chron. xxxvi. 10, we have *goodly* instead of *pleasant.* It is a noun, in Hag. ii. 7, *desire.* Compare Deut. viii. 7–9. Some of the Israelites wished that they were back in Egypt. Even in sight of the promised land, their unbelief was prevalent. But two adults of all the host that came out of Egypt ever entered the promised land, Heb. iii. 18; Num. xiv. 20–37; Deut. i. 34–36; Ps. lxxviii. 22, 32. The same reason for not entering the promised land is assigned in this verse: *They believed not his word:*

25. *But murmured in their tents,* and *hearkened not unto the voice of the* LORD, Num. xiv. 2, 27. Here as elsewhere the poet does not follow the exact chronological order of events. On the two clauses of this verse see Deut. i. 27; Num. xiv. 22.

26. *Therefore he lifted up his hand against them, to overthrow them in the wilderness.* In most Bibles this verse is not separated from that which immediately follows it, nor is it necessary it should be. And yet as Morison says: "It is obvious that those interpreters are mistaken who refer the allusions of v. 27, to the same history as those of v. 26. The people overthrown in the wilderness were to be destroyed by pestilence; but the overthrow threatened in v. 27, was by banishment and captivity." Yet in poetry, eloquence and descriptive history, events relating to the same person or people in general are often closely crowded together. See a remarkable instance in Matt. xxvii. 50–53. The whole forty years of Israel's journeying was marked by rebellion and punishments, Ps. xcv. 10, 11. The lifting up of the hand is not to strike but to swear, Num. xiv. 21–23, 28; Heb. iii. 18; vi. 13. Chaldee: "He lifted up his hand with an oath." Not only was the curse upon that generation for their own sins, but upon their posterity for the like transgressions; for he sware

27. *To overthrow their seed also among the nations, and to scatter them in the lands.* *Overthrow,* as in v. 26; literally, *cause* them *to fall.* The reference is to the curse

denounced in Lev. xxvi. 32, 33, 38.   Compare Ps. xliv. 11.   In almost all their wars the Jews lost some prisoners, who if not killed were held in slavery.

28. *They joined themselves also unto Baal-peor, and ate the sacrifices of the dead.* Anderson: "Baal was a very common name for the principal male god of the nations of the East, as Ashtaroth was a common one for their chief female deity.   The Moabites, Phenicians, Assyrians, Babylonians, and often the Hebrews worshipped this idol.   Among the Babylonians he was called Bel or Belus."   To the name of the idol an appendix was often made from the place where his image stood, as Baal-peor, from the hill Peor.   On this hill Balaam offered seven bullocks and seven rams on as many altars, Num. xxiii. 28–30.   The particular transgression here noticed is recorded in Num. xxv. 1–3; see also Num. xxxi. 16; Deut. iv. 3; xxxii. 17; Hos. ix. 10; Rev. ii. 14.   *Dead*, the gods of the heathen are not real existences, as is Jehovah, who alone is the *living* God.

29. *Thus they provoked* him *to anger with their inventions. Inventions*, in v. 39 also; elsewhere, *endeavors, works, doings*, Ps. xxviii. 4; lxxviii. 7; Prov. xx. 11. *Provoked;* Alexander: "It means to excite both grief and indignation." *And the plague brake in upon them.* The historic narrative is in Num. xxv. 3–5. *Plague*, sometimes rendered *stroke*, also *slaughter;* generally as here, Ezek. xxiv. 16; 1 Sam. iv. 17.   Alexander: "It has the meaning of a divine infliction in general, and that of a pestilential disease in particular."

30. *Then stood up Phinehas, and executed judgment: and so the plague was stayed.* The narrative of the conduct of Phinehas on this occasion is found in Num. xxv. 6–9.   The numbers destroyed were twenty-four thousand.   The blessing of God that came upon Phinehas for his intrepid fidelity is also recorded in Num. xxv. 11–13.

31. *And that was counted unto him for righteousness unto all generations for evermore.*   Calvin: "In thus praising one individual the prophet heaps reproach upon the whole body of the people."   What Phinehas did, was doubtless under the immediate direction of the Spirit of God.   Had it not been so, it would certainly have been condemned as it was quite beside his office, and in all ordinary cases unbecoming a priest to employ the sword.   The act can be no guide to uninspired men. The statement that his conduct *was counted to him for righteousmess* is to be explained like the same phrase applied to Abraham.   Compare Gen. xv. 6; Rom. iv. 3; iii. 20.   The righteousness of Phinehas in this case is not the ground of his justification before God, but an act which God approved and commended.   The reward promised him was that of a lasting priesthood among his posterity.   Though it is not mentioned here, it is fully stated in Num. xxv. 13.

32. *They angered* him *also at the waters of strife.*   That is, they offended God by sinning against him.   Their conduct was so outrageous against God, that even Moses lost his temper.   *Angered, caused him to be wroth;* not the same as *provoked to anger* in v. 29; but a stronger word.   At the waters of *strife*, or of *Meribah.*   The historic record is in Num. xx. 2–13.   See on Ps. lxxxi. 7.   They dealt wickedly with the Lord, *So that it went ill with Moses for their sakes.*   How ill it went with Moses may be seen in Num. xx. 12; Deut. i. 37; iii. 26.   Neither he nor Aaron was permitted to enter Canaan.

33. *Because they provoked his spirit. Provoked*, not as in v. 29, but as in vv. 7, 43.   We met it in Ps. lxxviii. 17, 40.   Other forms of the verb mean to *rebel*, as in Ps. v. 10; cv. 28.   Some would read here, They *made* his spirit *to rebel*, meaning the spirit of Moses.   This seems to have been by far the most usual interpretation.   It is adopted by Calvin, Hammond, Patrick, Gill, Henry, Horne, Scott and others. Indeed some think that Moses (and not God at all) is spoken of throughout vv. 32, 33.   But the Chaldee, followed by Fabritius and others, by *spirit* understand the

Holy Ghost. Hengstenberg: "*His spirit*, not the spirit of Moses, but the Spirit of God." Some make Isa. lxiii. 10, parallel. A good sense may thus be had without violating the laws of grammatical construction. But the first interpretation is altogether natural, is apparently consistent with the known facts in the case, is more obvious than any other, and is most commonly accepted. It best agrees with the connection: *So that he spake unadvisedly with his lips.* The verb rendered *spake unadvisedly* is found twice in Lev. v. 4; once in Pr. xii. 18; and is rendered *speak, pronounce.* No where else does it bear the sense here but upon it; literally, he *uttered, spoke,* or *pronounced with his lips.* Clarke proposes to read: "*He stuttered,* or *stammered with his lips,* indicating that he was transported with anger." Some think that he spake with his lips *only,* but in his heart did not believe: saying, *Shall we fetch you water out of this rock?* This derives apparent support from what God said: "Because ye believed me not, to sanctify me," Num. xx. 12. This may teach either that Moses believed not in God's power and willingness to give them water at that time; or that in some other respect, as in a sinful display of temper, he manifested unbelief. The common explanation is perhaps the best, viz: that they exacerbated the temper of Moses, so that he *spoke with his lips* in a manner unbecoming a servant of God; not in a manner to *glorify* God, but to betray petulance. Gill: "Though Moses was a very meek man, meeker than any upon the face of the earth, Num. xii. 3, yet, being greatly provoked, he let fall some passionate and undue expressions." Horne: "The wrath of man found admission, and that worketh not the righteousness of God." Calvin: "Such was the indignation which Moses felt burning within him, that he could not calmly wait for the commandment of God to smite the rock." No doubt there was *unadvised* speech. Gesenius thinks the verb itself means to *babble,* to *talk idly,* and so to *speak unadvisedly.* If this is correct, there is no difficulty in the case. The sin of provoking Moses was great. Thrice it is stated that for *their sakes* God would not allow him to enter the promised land. Deut. i. 37; iii. 26.

34. *They did not destroy the nations, concerning whom the* LORD *commanded them.* The command to expel those, who had long inhabited Canaan, was clear and unconditional, Deut. vii. 1–5, 16; Judges ii. 2. In this they miserably failed. They rashly entered into a covenant which having been made could not be broken, Josh. ix. 3–15. When there was no such covenant in the way, timidity, irresolution and the want of a proper fear of God made them hesitate, Judges i. 21, 27–36. This conduct as God had forewarned them (Deut. vii. 3, 4; Num. xxxiii. 55,) led to innumerable mischiefs.

35. *But were mingled among the heathen, and learned their works.*

36. *And they served their idols: which were a snare unto them.* The record of the ill effects of thus willingly mingling with abominable idolaters is found in many places, and is full of sadness, Judg. iii. 5–8; Isa. ii. 6. Men sometimes express wonder at the warnings given to Israel on this subject, and to all men against bad company. But the reason is very good, Josh. xxiii. 12, 13. As given by Paul it is: "A little leaven leaveneth the whole lump," 1 Cor. v. 6; by a heathen poet quoted by Paul: "Evil communications corrupt good manners," 1 Cor. xv. 33. The reason why bad company is so much more potential than good is that the heart of man is sinful, and tow and tinder are not more inflammable than is our evil nature. The corrupting power of idolatry would be incredible were it not exhibited to the world from age to age. The *works* of the heathen are abominable; specially does the worship of idols grossly and strongly alienate the heart from God, Judg. ii. 11–13, 17, 19. How seductive the worship of images is, and how it leads from one excess to another is evident from all history, and from verse

37. *Yea, they sacrificed their sons and their daughters unto devils.* Calvin, church of England, Doway and Jebb have *devils* as here. But all the ancient versions, also Fabritius, Piscator, Amesius, Tremellius and Junius, Alexander and Fry read *demons.* Edwards has *evil spirits.* Clarke: " *Devil* is never in Scripture used in the *plural;* there is but ONE *devil,* though there are MANY demons." Yet the English version does not keep up this distinction. Demons are the angels of the devil, Matt. xxv. 41. The word here rendered *devils* is found in but one other place, Deut. xxxii. 17. It seems to signify *destroyers,* and is so rendered by Venema, though Michaelis derives it from an Arabic word signifying *to be black,* and Hengstenberg from an Arabic word signifying *to rule,* equivalent to the *lords* many, in 1 Cor. viii. 5. That the Jews in imitation of the heathen did sacrifice their offspring to devils is evident from many places in Scripture, although they were carefully warned against so horrible a sin, Lev. xviii. 21; xx. 23; Deut. xii. 31; xviii. 10; 2 Kings xvi. 3; xvii. 17; xxi. 6; 2 Chron. xxviii. 3; xxxiii. 6.

38. *And shed innocent blood,* even *the blood of their sons and of their daughters, whom they sacrificed unto the idols of Canaan: and the land was polluted with blood.* Alexander: "The first verb means to pour out, and here implies a copious or abundant bloodshed." *Blood,* at the end of the verse plural; see on Ps. v. 6.

39. *Thus were they defiled with their own works.* The entire tendency of heathenism and idolatry is to sink into still lower and lower depths of wickedness and wretchedness. The effect of a false religion compared with that of the true is just what might be expected from the difference between Moloch and Jehovah. Compare Ezek. xx. 18, 30. *And went a whoring with their own inventions.* As harlotry is one of the most abominable sins that can be committed by a daughter or a wife; so often in the Scriptures turning from God and especially the practice of idolatry is called whoredom and fornication, Ps. lxxiii. 27; Ex. xxxiv. 15, 16. *Inventions, works, doings, endeavors.* Cobbin has delusions; Alexander, crimes.

40. *Therefore was the wrath of the Lord kindled against his people, insomuch that he abhorred his own inheritance.* On the whole verse see on Ps. lxxviii. 59, 62. Compare Judges ii. 14. *Wrath,* as in Ps. ii. 5, 12. *Abhorred;* see on Ps. v. 6; it expresses detestation.

41. *And he gave them into the hand of the heathen; and they that hated them ruled over them,* Judg. ii. 14; iii. 8, 12; vi. 1–6; x. 7; Neh. ix. 27. Never has such malice been shown as against the Lord, against his anointed Son and against his people. And never have such curses come on persons or nations as through the forsaking of the Most High, and lightly esteeming the Rock of salvation.

42. *Their enemies also oppressed them, and they were brought into subjection under their hand. Enemies,* commonly so rendered, Ps. iii. 7; vi. 10. *Oppressed,* as in Ps. lvi. 1; it expresses cruelty and tyranny. There were no depths of degradation to which the enemies of Israel did not reduce them when in their power, Judg. iv. 3.

43. *Many times did he deliver them; but they provoked* him *with their counsel, and were brought low for their iniquity.* On the first clause see Judg. ii. 16–18; Neh. ix. 27. *Provoked,* as in v. 7. *Brought low,* margin, *impoverished,* or *weakened,* in Job xxiv. 24, as here; in Ecc. x. 18, *decayeth,* not found elsewhere. Forsaken of God, the mightiest is soon utterly powerless. And when God lets loose the passions of the wicked against any man, the suffering is commonly frightful. Some think that the prophet in this verse refers to the final catastrophe of the nation. But compare v. 44, and Lev. xxvi. 14–44.

44. *Nevertheless he regarded their affliction, when he heard their cry:* Judges iii. 9; iv. 3; vi. 7, 8; x. 10. *He regarded their affliction,* he favorably considered it and graciously saved them from it.

45. *And he remembered for them his covenant, and repented according to the multi-tude of his mercies.* On the first clause see Ps. cv. 8. On the second, Ps. xc. 13. *Multitude of mercies,* a phrase indicating that great benevolence was required from God and was actually showed by him, Ps. li. 1.

46. *He made them also to be pitied of all those that carried them captives.* We have a few samples of such kindness; Ez. ix. 9; Jer. xlii. 12. Esther vi. 13 shows that the heathen had been greatly impressed with God's kindness to his captive people. Compare 1 Kings viii. 50.

47. *Save us, O* LORD *our God, and gather us from among the heathen.* A fit and suit-able prayer for the ancient church in any of her captivities. But the deliverance sought is not for mere selfish ends. All divine interpositions ought to be *to give thanks unto thy holy name,* and to *triumph in thy praise.*

48. *Blessed* be the LORD *God of Israel from everlasting to everlasting.* The transla-tion is very literal and cannot be improved. On *blessing* God see on Ps. ciii. 1. *And let all the people say, Amen. People,* in the singular, *nation,* meaning the Jewish na-tion. *Amen,* see on Ps. xli. 13. *Praise ye the* LORD, literally, Hallelujah! Here ends what some called the fourth book of Psalms; but see Introduction, § 11.

DOCTRINAL AND PRACTICAL REMARKS.

1. Even when we are called to mourn for sin we may very well begin our worship with adoration, praise and thanksgiving, v. 1. No trial, no sense of ill-desert can release us from the obligation to love and praise the Most High. In fact our very sinfulness helps to display the amazing long-suffering and loving-kindness of God.

2. A sense of weakness and of short-coming in any duty, particularly in worship, does not release us from the obligation to do our utmost, v. 2. God's glory is not de-signed to dishearten us in our approaches to him. The simple fact of our coming short of perfection is a reason why we should stir up our souls and all that is within us. To make our weakness or unworthiness a plea for neglecting a duty is an attempt to excuse one sin by another.

3. None can over estimate the value of a good conscience arising from a heart will-ing to do *justice* and *judgment,* and to live honestly in the sight of God and man, v. 3. Those, who have this mercy are blessed in all things. Calvin: "There is nothing but the mere shadow of righteousness, unless a man cordially devote himself to the prac-tice of honesty."

4. A great lack in the principles and practice of many is found in their want of stability, v. 3. At *some* times they seem upright, devout and earnest; anon they are loose, vain and worldly.

5. Every blessing that comes to man on earth is by God's *favor,* v. 4. Man deserves nothing good at the hand of his Maker. By ties of nature, of duty, and of gratitude, his fellow-creatures may be fully bound to pay him much love, much service, much respect. But God is bound to no man to do him good, further than his own gracious and blessed promise has engaged him.

6. But then it shall be for a perpetual joy that the *favor* of the Lord is very boun-tiful, and his grace has unsearchable riches, v. 4. Where God has set his love, his mercies are absolutely infinite.

7. Hard as is the lot and heavy as are the afflictions of God's people, yet through the amazing mercy of the Most High, they have great deliverances, great consolations, great victories, of which to be made a partaker will be immortal honor, and bliss, v. 5.

8. It is sad indeed when instead of being reformed by a review of the sins and sufferings of our ancestors, we *sin with them,* and are neither the wiser nor the better

for a knowledge of God's dealings towards them, v. 6. But it is a blessed truth that if we hate the evil ways of those who have gone before us, and turn from transgression ourselves, we shall not be shut out from the kingdom of heaven.

9. Though the writers of the Scriptures were by divine inspiration infallibly preserved from extravagance; yet they use every appropriate variety of strong and condemnatory language against sin, v. 6. Surely moral evil cannot be a trifle. Yet it breaks forth on all occasions and on all hands. Sometimes it is in the form of forgetfulness of God, vv. 1, 3, 21; sometimes, of rash impetuosity towards evil, v. 13; sometimes, of strong, imperious lusts, v. 14; sometimes, of tempting God, v. 14; sometimes, of despising his very best gifts, v. 24; sometimes, of vile unbelief, vv. 12, 24, and so of the whole catalogue of offences against God and man. O how vile we are! Dickson: "Confession of sins must not be slighted, but seriously gone about and aggravated duly."

10. It is suited greatly to humble us when we remember that whatever kindness we receive at the hands of God, is not at all on account of anything in us, present or prospective, but solely *for his own sake,* and to *make known* his glorious perfections, v. 8.

11. It is a profitable exercise devoutly to number the mercies of God and the wonders of his providence, vv. 7–11. Often has he brought good out of evil, light out of darkness, and joy out of sorrow. Often has he made a wheel move within a wheel to the confounding of the wicked and to the joy of the pious.

12. God has often shown an inflexible determination to save his people, who trust his grace, and glorify his salvation, even at the cost of the destruction of countless multitudes of the wicked who dare to rise up against them, v. 11. If the safety and final victory of a believer could not be secured but by the ruin, temporal and eternal, of millions of wicked men, the Almighty would at once send his blighting curse upon them. It is of mere mercy that the day of grace is prolonged.

13. After the many examples of a faith that has in it no saving power, but is the result of the common operations of God's Spirit, and of striking providences, it well becomes each of us to ask, Is my faith saving? is it merely temporary? is it merely historical? is it the faith of devils? v. 12. An acknowledgment of the truth wrung from us by the terrible inflictions of divine wrath is not saving in any case, even though we may rejoice and *sing* God's *praises.*

14. How little we know of ourselves! What sudden transitions our emotions and even our purposes undergo! We behold stupendous wonders and think we never shall lose the salutary impression received from them; but without special grace we soon *forget* all, and sin with greediness, and rush with madness towards destruction, v. 13.

15. Sometimes the question is asked, Why is man so averse to *waiting* God's *counsel?* v. 13. The answer is easy: To *tarry* demands the subjection of our passions, requires of us humility, and calls for trust. To the natural heart all these are foreign. Of course impatience, which has a consanguinity with all the evil principles of our nature, obtains the mastery, and drives us impetuously to ruin.

16. The recent reception of great and astonishing mercies, which have profoundly moved our affections, is no proof that we will not soon fall into gross sin, vv. 13, 14.

17. Success in obtaining our desires, even though we may have prayed to God in the matter, is not of itself proof that we have either the divine approbation, or the divine blessing. The thing thus sought and obtained may soon prove a curse, vv. 14, 15. Henry: "What is asked in passion, is often given in wrath;" Dickson· "As lawful means are attended with God's blessing, so unlawful means are followed by God's curse."

18. A state of perfection in social, political, or ecclesiastical affairs in this life is absolutely impossible, so long as *envy* has its place in the human heart. In antiquity there is nothing so venerable; in law there is nothing so majestic; in eminent services there is nothing so praiseworthy; in sanctity of person and office there is nothing so sacred, as to form a shield against the shafts of envy, v. 16. Let the envious expect a terrible overthrow. Henry: "They are preparing ruin for themselves, who envy those whom God has put honor upon, and usurp the dignities they were never designed for."

19. No man can do a more dangerous thing than maliciously to slight one of God's own servants, vv. 16–18. The doctrine of strange and terrible judgments against the malicious contemners of God's chosen is as old as the days of Moses, Num. xvi. 29. Church history tells us it has its examples in all ages.

20. If there were no other evidence of the horrible nature of sin, than is found in the existence of idolatry, a right-minded man could not fail to see its gross and malignant character, vv. 19, 20, 28, 29, 36, 37, 38, 39. No man can commune with idolaters in their worship and be guiltless. Well do the Scriptures speak of *abominable idolatries*.

21. Whatever tends to strip God of his glory, or to bring the divine majesty into disesteem, should be most carefully eschewed, v. 20. We can never raise the sordid apprehensions of carnal men to spiritual truths by mechanical or artistic designs and works. Dickson: "Making images to represent God, or any of the persons of the holy trinity, is but a vilifying of the glory of God, and giving it to the image of a creature."

22. If Christians could be brought to entertain a just sense of the value and power of intercessory prayer, surely it would abound, v. 23. It is a terrible reproof against the lying prophets of Ezekiel's time: "Ye have not gone up into the gaps, neither made up the hedge for the house of Israel to stand in the battle in the day of the Lord," Ezek. xiii. 5. Compare Ex. xxxii. 9–14.

23. The distance of heavenly objects hinders them from making a due impression on us. Then too the evidence of their existence can be apprehended only by faith; and our faith is weak. On the very borders of Canaan and in sight of it, Israel despised that *pleasant land*, v. 24. The want of a spiritual relish for heavenly objects has immense power in repressing heavenly-mindedness.

24. If there were no other sin chargeable to mankind but that of *murmuring* against God, the whole world might justly be destroyed. Neither God nor his servants are able so to act as to silence complainers, v. 25.

25. It is a great mercy that God warns before he strikes, vv. 26, 27. Sin is very provoking; but God is very long-suffering.

26. Let men, who have no divine call duly attested from heaven, beware how they step out of one office into another, and especially how they seize the sword to execute wrath, vv. 30, 31. Horne: "The case of Phinehas is no precedent for uncommissioned zealots."

27. The best of men are but men at the best, vv. 32, 33. On this occasion Moses' character was weakest in the point where it was habitually strongest.

28. This case of Moses, (vv. 32, 33,) clearly shows that the strength of the temptation by no means excuses for the sin of yielding. The reason is that God always provides a way for escape, and that nothing whatever can possibly justify our sinning against him.

29. The same verses show that " we must answer not only for our own passions, but for the provocation which, by them, we give to the passions of others, especially of those, who, if not greatly provoked, would be meek and quiet."

30. On whatever errand God sends us, we must remember that to obey is better than sacrifice, and to hearken than the fat of lambs, v. 34.

31. It is impossible for men to be too careful in choosing their boon companions, their habitual associates, v. 35. Descent to a lower level of morals or moral sentiments is easy. Ascent to a higher level is difficult. Calvin: "Nothing is more dangerous than associating with the ungodly."

32. When we read of the heathen sacrificing their offspring to Moloch or Baalim, we are apt to think we never would have done so ; "but how little is it considered that children brought up in the ways of ignorance, error, vanity, folly and vice, are more effectually sacrificed to the great adversary of mankind?"

33. While eternity endures, good men will not be done celebrating the love and mercy of the Most High, vv. 43–46. Because he is full of kindness, he forgets not his counsel or his covenant, he restrains his anger and often opens the storehouse of his benignity.

34. If we are saved from any trouble, and especially from the power and guilt of sin, it is wholly by the Lord, v. 47.

35. Wherever we are, whatever we do or suffer, let us glorify God, v. 48. He is all and in all. Besides him there is no God and no Saviour.

36. Let us stir up ourselves and all our brethren as we have opportunity to praise and magnify the Most High.

PSALM CVII.

1 O give thanks unto the Lord, for *he is* good : for his mercy *endureth* for ever.

2 Let the redeemed of the Lord say *so*, whom he hath redeemed from the hand of the enemy ;

3 And gathered them out of the lands, from the east, and from the west, from the north, and from the south.

4 They wandered in the wilderness in a solitary way ; they found no city to dwell in.

5 Hungry and thirsty, their soul fainted in them.

6 Then they cried unto the Lord in their trouble, *and* he delivered them out of their distresses.

7 And he led them forth by the right way, that they might go to a city of habitation.

8 Oh that *men* would praise the Lord *for* his goodness, and *for* his wonderful works to the children of men!

9 For he satisfieth the longing soul, and filleth the hungry soul with goodness.

10 Such as sit in darkness and in the shadow of death *being* bound in affliction and iron ;

11 Because they rebelled against the words of God, and contemned the counsel of the Most High:

12 Therefore he brought down their heart with labour; they fell down, and *there was* none to help.

13 Then they cried unto the Lord in their trouble, *and* he saved them out of their distresses.

14 He brought them out of darkness and the shadow of death, and brake their bands in sunder.

15 Oh that *men* would praise the Lord *for* his goodness, and *for* his wonderful works to the children of men!

16 For he hath broken the gates of brass, and cut the bars of iron in sunder.

17 Fools, because of their transgression, and because of their iniquities, are afflicted.

18 Their soul abhorreth all manner of meat ; and they draw near unto the gates of death.

19 Then they cry unto the Lord in their trouble, *and* he saveth them out of their distresses.

20 He sent his word, and healed them, and delivered *them* from their destructions.

21 Oh that *men* would praise the Lord *for* his goodness, and *for* his wonderful works to the children of men !

22 And let them sacrifice the sacrifices of thanksgiving, and declare his works with rejoicing.

23 They that go down to the sea in ships, that do business in great waters;

24 These see the works of the LORD, and his wonders in the deep.

25 For he commandeth, and raiseth the stormy wind, which lifteth up the waves thereof.

26 They mount up to the heaven, they go down again to the depths: their soul is melted because of trouble.

27 They reel to and fro, and stagger like a drunken man, and are at their wits' end.

28 Then they cry unto the LORD in their trouble, and he bringeth them out of their distresses.

29 He maketh the storm a calm, so that the waves thereof are still.

30 Then are they glad because they be quiet; so he bringeth them unto their desired haven.

31 Oh that *men* would praise the LORD *for* his goodness, and *for* his wonderful works to the children of men!

32 Let them exalt him also in the congregation of the people, and praise him in the assembly of the elders.

33 He turneth rivers into a wilderness, and the watersprings into dry ground;

34 A fruitful land into barrenness, for the wickedness of them that dwell therein.

35 He turneth the wilderness into a standing water, and dry ground into watersprings.

36 And there he maketh the hungry to dwell, that they may prepare a city for habitation;

37 And sow the fields, and plant vineyards, which may yield fruits of increase.

38 He blesseth them also, so that they are multiplied greatly; and suffereth not their cattle to decrease.

39 Again, they are minished and brought low through oppression, affliction, and sorrow.

40 He poureth contempt upon princes, and causeth them to wander in the wilderness, *where there is* no way.

41 Yet setteth he the poor on high from affliction, and maketh *him* families like a flock.

42 The righteous shall see *it*, and rejoice: and all iniquity shall stop her mouth.

43 Whoso *is* wise, and will observe these *things*, even they shall understand the lovingkindness of the LORD.

THIS Psalm has no title. David has been generally esteemed its author, though Lowth, Clarke and others do not so hold. Scott dates it B. C. 1045; Clarke affixes no date, though he thinks it much later. Many regard it as specially related to Psalms ci.–cvi. As a composition this Psalm has very high merit. Dodd: "Some of the descriptions in this Psalm are remarkably elegant and sublime." Lowth: "It may undoubtedly be enumerated among the most elegant monuments of antiquity; and it is chiefly indebted for its elegance to the general plan and conduct of the poem." Clarke: "Had such an *Idyl* appeared in *Theocritus* or *Virgil*—or had it been found as a scene in any of the *Greek Tragedians*, even in *Æschylus* himself, it would have been praised up to the heavens, and probably been produced as their masterpiece." Concerning its scope and design there is considerable diversity. A careful perusal of the poem will satisfy the reader that this is not surprising. The Psalm is so rich, and embraces so great a variety of topics that it has something for almost every one. It embraces "travellers in the desert, who have lost their way, prisoners, sick people, mariners, husbandmen, even whole countries." This poem, like some of the wine-presses of which we read, bursts out with fatness. What experienced Christian has not found refreshment and encouragement from its teachings! In explaining this portion of Scripture, some propose very much to spiritualize it. It opens a wide field for such exercise of the imagination. The names of the Almighty here found are *Jehovah* LORD, *El God* and *Gel Yohn Most High*, on which see on Ps. i. 2; v. 4; vii. 17.

1. *O give thanks unto the* LORD, *for* he is *good: for his mercy* endureth *forever*. See on Ps. cvi. 1.

2. *Let the redeemed of the Lord say* so, *i. e.*, let them say that his mercy endureth forever. We have the same in Ps. cxviii. 1. Everywhere the Scriptures discountenance noisy and vain religious talk. But they as distinctly commend and enjoin

frank, open, heartfelt declarations of right views and sentiments concerning God. We must make proclamation of God's mercy. This is obligatory upon all, and especially upon them, *Whom he hath redeemed from the hand of the enemy.* On the two words rendered *redeemed* in this verse, see on Ps. xix. 14. Probably the prophet had in mind no particular temporal deliverance, but all such as might set forth the redemption of the soul. It varies not the sense whether we read *enemy,* or *distress.* See on Ps. iii. 1. The same word occurs in vv. 6, 13, 19, 28, and is rendered *trouble.* Alexander: " *The redeemed of the Lord* is a favorite expression of Isaiah (xxxv. 9, 10; lxii. 12; lxiii. 4)." Many great and striking deliverances from pressing and grievous dangers and troubles has God wrought for men, particularly for the descendants of Abraham.

3. *And gathered them out of the lands, from the east, and from the west, from the north, and from the south.* This cannot refer exclusively to redemption from Egypt or Babylon, but must allude to the many kind interpositions of God in saving the Israelites and perhaps others, in their extensive journeys and dispersions running through centuries. Or, it may refer to the spiritual redemption. Compare Isa. xlix. 12; Luke xiii. 29. *Gathered,* see on Ps. cvi. 47. The words designating the points of the compass in this verse are those usually employed for that purpose except the last, which is, literally *from the sea.* This must mean the Red sea, not the Mediterranean.

4. *They wandered in the wilderness in a solitary way; they found no city to dwell in.*

5. *Hungry and thirsty, their soul fainted in them.* This may have been partly fulfilled in the march from Egypt and from Babylon; but it probably has a chief reference to the long and wearisome journeys to which misfortune or trade led men. The *wilderness* may mean any wilderness, though there is no objection to making it include the great wilderness of Arabia. *Solitary way,* literally *desert of way,* signifying a desert that must be traversed. In that wilderness they found no city for an abode. Travellers in eastern deserts were liable to great sufferings for the want of both food and drink. Often has the famishing traveller felt himself ready to perish, when God has supplied his wants in a manner truly providential; perhaps in answer to special prayer:

6. *Then they cried unto the LORD in their trouble, and he delivered them out of their distresses.* *Cried,* very earnestly called. *Trouble,* in v. 2, *enemy.* *Delivered,* as in Ps. vii. 1. *Distresses,* found also in vv. 13, 19, 28. In Job xv. 24, in the singular it is *anguish.* The *distresses* of long and perilous journeys must have been great. Those of the forty years' march have been elsewhere considered. But the exhaustion and suffering attending the progress of Eastern caravans were often frightful. If we give to these verses a spiritual sense borrowed from their literal meaning, we are at no loss for texts strikingly parallel. Compare Ps. lxviii. 9, 10; lxxii. 12, 13; Isa. xli. 17; lxi. 1–3.

7. *And he led them forth by the right way, that they might go to a city of habitation.* *Right way;* Edwards, *straight way;* Alexander, *straight course.* The word rendered *right* is elsewhere rendered *meet, upright, righteous, straight.* It seems impossible to give it the sense of *straight* in this place, if there is anything more than a mere allusion to the march from Egypt, for the course of that journey was exceedingly circuitous. What we know of the march from Babylon inclines us to think that that course was not straight, Ezra viii. 21. But that God's dealings with his people in those and all other cases are *righteous* and in the end *right* in all respects cannot be doubted. The Syriac however spiritualizes the whole and says: "He led them in the way of truth." The city of habitation of which Israelites thought so much was Jerusalem, a type of the city that hath foundations. If we give it a spiritual sense then a refer-

ence to Isa. xxx. 21; xxxv. 8–10; xlviii. 17; lxiii. 12–14, would elucidate the meaning.

8. *Oh that* men *would praise the* LORD *for his goodness, and* for *his wonderful works to the children of men!* *Would praise*, the verb is in the future. It is the same rendered *give thanks* in v. 1. Calvin renders the verse: Let them praise the mercy of Jehovah in his presence, and his marvellous works in the presence of the sons of men; Hengstenberg: These should praise to the Lord his mercy, and his wonders to the children of men; Alexander: Let (such) give thanks to Jehovah (for) his mercy, and his wonderful works to the sons of men. The optative form is best. *Goodness, mercy, kindness, favor, lovingkindness,* v. 43. See on Ps. v. 7; li. 1. *Wondrous works,* see on Ps. ix. 1; xxvi. 7. These words occur again at vv. 15, 21, 31, and make what is fitly called the burden of the Psalm. Reasons have already been assigned in several preceding verses for grateful acknowledgment of God's goodness. They are thus summed up:

9. *For he satisfieth the longing soul, and filleth the hungry soul with goodness.* *Satisfieth,* the verb is in the preterite, *has filled, i. e.,* the Lord has long and often supplied the wants of poor suffering travellers, and particularly of the Israelites in their journeys. The language of this verse goes far to indicate the allegorical and spiritual interpretation of the poem, Ps. xxxvi. 8; lxiii. 5; lxv. 4; Jer. xxxi. 14.

10. *Such as sit in darkness, and in the shadow of death,* being *bound in affliction and iron.* Here we have a new theme. We have been considering the case of travellers and pilgrims. Now the prophet says, Let us consider the case of captives and prisoners. It is full of distress. *Darkness,* uniformly rendered, used both literally and figuratively. See on Ps. xviii. 11, 28. On *the shadow of death,* see on Ps. xxiii. 4. We have the same phrase in v. 14. It designates a dismal condition. Such is the case of the prisoners of *affliction* and *iron.* Iron was the substance of which fetters, chains, bars and bolts were commonly made. The same word occurs in v. 16. How tenderly God cares for prisoners is often declared. See Ps. lxix. 33; lxxix. 11; cii. 20; cxlvi. 7. Nor are God's compassions confined to such prisoners as are innocent of crime or free from sin, but extends to those who became prisoners,

11. *Because they rebelled against the words of God, and contemned the counsel of the Most High.* The verbs are well rendered. They express the highest kind of *resistance* and of *despite.* The names of the Almighty in this verse heighten our conceptions of the wickedness committed. They are *El* and *Gel-yohn,* the former expressive of infinite strength, the latter of infinite majesty. Because God is great, there is no little sin. These *prisoners* have sinned against the *word* and the *counsel* of God. They have either violated laws against the peace and well-being of society, and are criminals; or they have sinned against God's law of love, and he has let loose the malice of man upon them. In some way these men had highly offended God:

12. *Therefore he brought down their heart with labour; they fell down, and there was none to help.* *Brought down,* in Ps. lxxxi. 14, *subdued;* in Ps. cvi. 42, *brought into subjection;* in 1 Kings xxi. 29, *humbled.* *Labour,* elsewhere *sorrow, misery, grievousness, travail,* Ps. lv. 10; Job xi. 16; Isa. x. 1; liii. 11. The process of humiliation is often painful. The fruit of true humiliation is most delightful. The proud cannot enter into rest. *Fell down,* in Ps. xxvii. 2 and often, *stumbled;* in Ps. xxxi. 10, *faileth;* in Ps. cv. 37 and elsewhere, the participle is rendered *feeble.* Thorough humiliation prostrates men, and cuts off all hope of relief but from God only.

13. *Then they cried unto the Lord in their trouble, and he saved them out of their distresses.* *Cried,* as in Ps. xxii. 5. It occurs also in v. 19. Here and there it is in the future; but is fitly rendered in the preterite or present. In a more ancient form we had it in v. 6, and shall meet it in v. 28.

14. *He brought them out of darkness and the shadow of death.* *Darkness* and *shadow of death,* as in v. 10. *Brought,* the Hebrew is in the future, *will bring.* Alexander has *brings.* The verb expresses an act often performed by Jehovah. It occurs again in v. 28, and is rendered *bringeth out. And brake their bands in sunder. Brake,* like *brought* in the future, but narrating what God had done or commonly does. *Bands,* a noun of the same derivation as the word *bound* in v. 10. This too expresses the habitual conduct of God. Whoever is relieved from captivity or prison is indebted to the Almighty for his freedom.

15. *Oh that* men *would praise the* LORD *for his goodness, and for his wonderful works to the children of men.* See on v. 8.

16. *For he hath broken the gates of brass, and cut the bars of iron in sunder.* It was by God's power that Samson carried away the gates of Gaza, Judg. xvi. 3. It was Jehovah that rendered useless the brazen gates of Babylon, Isa. xlv. 2. The Lord, even Jehovah is the great Breaker of gates for his people to pass through, Micah ii. 13. Sometimes cities had two or three pairs of gates, and well secured by *bars* and bolts. But these are no defence against the Almighty, when he chooses to send his ministers on errands of either wrath or mercy. This verse excludes no class of captives or prisoners, whether they were such for crimes, or by cruelty, rapacity or false accusation. This part may have a beautiful allegorical interpretation, Isa. xlii. 7; lxi. 1; Zech. ix. 11, 12. Another subject is now introduced:

17. *Fools, because of their transgression, and because of their iniquities, are afflicted. Fools,* the word occurs nowhere else in the Psalms, though often elsewhere. Sinners act entirely without wisdom and contrary to it. Some have specified particular classes of transgressors supposed to be referred to in this place. But God may punish any transgression or iniquity with bodily disease, Num. xi. 33, 34; xii. 11–13; xxxviii. 1–8; 1 Cor. xi. 30–32. *Transgressions,* as in Ps. v. 10; *sins,* in Prov. x. 12; *trespass,* in 1 Sam. xxv. 28. The corresponding verb is rendered *rebelled, revolted. Iniquities,* as in Ps. xviii. 23, uniformly rendered. *Are afflicted,* better rendered *afflict themselves.* Alexander: "The reflexive meaning of the verb is essential and cannot be diluted into a mere passive, without weakening the whole sentence, the very point of which consists in making them the guilty authors of their own distresses."

18. *Their soul abhorreth all manner of meat.* Compare Job xxxiii. 20. "When the stomach is gone, the life is as good as gone." As in a moment the Almighty can make the most dainty food utterly loathsome, by simply withdrawing his hand which gives us health. The want of nourishment from food soon produces emaciation and faintness in men; *and they draw near unto the gates of death. Gates of death,* see on Ps. ix. 13; equivalent to drawing nigh unto the grave in Ps. lxxxviii. 3; Job xxxiii. 22. Sometimes such distress brings men to the throne of grace.

19. *Then they cry unto the* LORD *in their trouble,* and *he saveth them out of their distresses.* See on vv. 6, 13, where we have the same words without important variations. Compare Ps. xxx. 2, 10.

20. *He sent his word and healed them.* Compare Ps. iii. 3, 4; xxx. 3. A very small amount of intelligence would satisfy a good man that a recovery from any of the sore distempers which afflict our bodies must be attributed to the power and mercy of God. It is as easy for the Most High to remove as to bring on a disease. In either case he does it by a *word,* Ps. xxxiii. 9. His healing was effectual, *and* [he] *delivered* them *from their destructions.* Any disease would soon bring death but for the infinite skill of the Great Physician. There is therefore great beauty in the plural, *destructions.* Like Paul's phrase, "*In deaths oft,*" it shows how imminent and numerous our perils are. *Destructions,* in Lam. iv. 20, *pits,* as if pits were yawning for us on every side.

21. *Oh that men would praise the* LORD *for his goodness, and for his wonderful works to the children of men.* See on v. 8.

22. *And let them sacrifice the sacrifices of thanksgiving, and declare his works with rejoicing.* Alexander: "They must not only utter thanks, but offer them in sacrifice. They must not only offer them in sacrifice, but sing them." On the first clause see on Ps. l. 14. *Rejoicing,* in Ps. xvii. 1, *cry;* in Ps. xxx. 5, *joy;* in Ps. xlvii. 1, *triumph;* in Isa. xiv. 7, *singing.* It expresses glad and exultant joy. God's *works* are his *deeds, operations;* so also in v. 24. This closes the third picture. It may be used allegorically, as sin is often spoken of as a sickness, and God as the Physician.

23. *They that go down to the sea in ships, that do business in great waters.*

24. *These see the works of the* LORD, *and his wonders in the deep.* Sea, great waters, deep, usually so rendered, and all meaning navigable waters larger than rivers or estuaries. *Ships,* as in Ps. civ. 26, always so rendered. *Business,* so in many places, Gen. xxxix. 11; 1 Chron. xxvi. 29, 30; 2 Chron. xvii. 13; Neh. xiii. 30; Est. iii. 9; Pr. xxii. 29; Dan. viii. 27. *Works of the* LORD, as in v. 22. *Wonders,* in vv. 8, 15, 21, 31, rendered *wonderful works;* in Ps. ix. 1, *marvellous works.* Pool: "*Wonderful works,* either, 1. Of creation, fishes of various kinds and shapes, and some of prodigious greatness, which are unknown to other men. Or, 2. Of providence in raising and laying storms, of which he speaks in the following verses." The latter is probably the leading idea:

25. *For he commandeth, and raiseth the stormy wind, which lifteth up the waves thereof.* How mighty is Jehovah. He *commandeth,* literally *says,* and at once comes the *stormy wind,* literally the *wind of tempest.* The air is far thinner and lighter than water; yet it has, at God's will, power to lash the ocean into a fury, and *lift up its waves* to a fearful height.

26. *They mount up to the heaven, they go down again to the depths: their soul is melted because of trouble.* Kimchi: "The men of the ship go up to heaven, *i. e.,* rise high in the air when the wave lifteth up the ship, and afterwards, because of the wave they descend to the deep; and from thus ascending and descending, the soul of the men of the ship melteth within them on account of the danger in which they are placed." Calvin: Their soul breaketh by reason of trouble; Edwards: Their souls melt with fear; Alexander: Their soul with evil dissolves itself. The word rendered *trouble* is not the same as that in vv. 6, 13, 19, 28, but that rendered *evil* in Ps. v. 4; vii. 4; in v. 39, *affliction.*

27. *They reel to and fro, and stagger like a drunken man.* The words and the imagery are both just and plain. *And are at their wit's end.* Calvin: And all their senses are overwhelmed; Horsley: And all their skill is drowned; Alexander: And all their wisdom is confounded; margin and Jebb: And all their wisdom is swallowed up; Phillips: "Their alarm is so great, that their knowledge deserts them; they lose all self-possession, and become entirely unfit for managing a ship."

28. *Then they cry unto the Lord in their trouble, and he bringeth them out of their distresses.* Trouble, as in vv. 6, 13, 19. *Bringeth out,* in v. 14, brought out.

29. *He maketh the storm a calm, so that the waves thereof are still.* Terrific as is the sea in a tempest, there is a God presiding over it. He can at will *calm* its agitations. The whole verse is well rendered, and in idiomatic English.

30. *Then are they glad because they be quiet; so he bringeth them unto their desired haven.* Be quiet, in Jonah i. 11, 12, *shall be calm.* We are never so *glad* of a calm as just after a terrific storm. *Haven,* here only. *Desired haven,* literally haven *of delight.* In Ps. i. 2; xvi. 3, the same word is rendered *delight.*

31. *Oh that men would praise the Lord for his goodness, and for his wonderful works to the children of men!*

32. *Let them exalt him also in the congregation of the people, and praise him in the assembly of the elders.* *Exalt, praise;* the word from which the Psalter gets its name. *Congregation,* see on Ps. xxii. 22. *Assembly,* in Ps. i. 1, *seat;* in vv. 7, 36, *habitation.* The verb from which it is derived occurs in vv. 10, 34, *sit* and *dwell.* *Elders,* commonly so rendered; sometimes *ancients, old men;* in Ps. cv. 22, *senators.* Some have thought that in the language of this verse there was an allusion to the synagogue service. Possibly there may be. This part of the Psalm also may have a spiritual meaning of great force and beauty. Often in Scripture are troubles of mind compared to agitated waters, Ps. lxix. 1. See Henry Kirke White's hymn beginning:

"Once on the raging seas I rode."

33. *He turneth rivers into a wilderness, and the watersprings into dry ground.* God is *the father of the rain.* If he withholds that refreshment for a long time, all nature droops, and every green thing dies. The imagery is drawn from Palestine, where there were but two annual rainy seasons, and if either of them was long deferred, the effect was frightful. The channels of considerable rivers were dried up. *Wilderness,* or *desert,* as in vv. 4, 35. Some have supposed that in these verses we are to understand a great revolution of some kind, and refer to Isa. xliv. 27; Jer. l. 38; li. 36. But in each of those places a literal interpretation is best.

34. *A fruitful land into barrenness, for the wickedness of them that dwell therein.* Such an evil as a consuming drought does not come without the ordering of God, Amos iii. 6. Nor do such evils ever come but on account of God's displeasure for men's sins. *Fruitful land,* literally, *the land of fruit.* *Barrenness* is better than *saltness,* because to all it gives the sense, though a *salt* land is *sterile;* see Jer. xvii. 6; Job xxxix. 6, where we read *salt* land and *barren land.* Pliny: "Every place, where salt is found, is sterile, and produces nothing." There may be an allusion to the destruction of the cities of the plain, and to the threatened curse. Compare Gen. xiii. 10; xix. 25; Deut. xxix. 23. But goodness triumphs over severity; and lands, which had become sterile, are by God's bounty again made productive:

35. *He turneth the wilderness into a standing water, and dry ground into watersprings.* We have the same words and phrases in v. 33, but in reverse order, only here we have *a standing water, pond,* or *pool,* (see Ex. vii. 19; viii. 5; Isa. xiv. 23,) instead of *rivers* in v. 33. This verse had a literal fulfilment, when at proper seasons Jehovah filled the ponds and pools of Judea with rain for drink, for irrigation, and for fish, Isa. xix. 10. But it seems impossible to avoid the belief that it had a higher import, a spiritual meaning, if we read the parallel passages, Ps. cxiv. 8; Isa. xxxv. 7; xli. 18; xliii. 20; xliv. 3, 4, 5. As the plain of Sodom has remained sterile ever since the overthrow of its cities, it is evident that in the preceding verse, there could have been no more than an allusion to its destruction. For this verse speaks of returning fruitfulness.

36. *And there he maketh the hungry to dwell, that they may prepare a city for habitation.* *Hungry,* or *hungerbitten,* (Job xviii. 12,) describes "poor people, who could not provide for themselves, or were banished from their own land by potent oppressors, and were driven into wildernesses," see Job xxx. 3. *A city for habitation,* the same as city *to dwell in,* v. 4; any city. In the east, walled towns for protection against wild beasts and predatory bands were first built; afterwards the people went forth to cultivate the soil:

37. *And sow the fields, and plant vineyards, which may yield fruits of increase.* *Fruits,* the plural of the word rendered *fruitful,* in v. 34. *Increase,* often rendered *fruit,* and in the plural, *fruits, revenues.* The form of expression is strictly Hebraistic, but expressive of the value and productiveness of fields which the Lord had blessed.

38. *He blesseth them also, so that they are multiplied greatly.* We have already seen in Psalm cv. how easy it is for God to multiply a people, and out of a few to make a strong nation. The laws of increase under his abundant blessing bring about prodigious results. Compare Gen. xii. 2; xvii. 16, 20; Deut. xxviii. 4, 11; Jer. xxx. 19; Ezek. xxxvii. 26. The increase is of all that can make a people powerful. *And suffereth not their cattle to decrease. Cattle,* all useful domestic animals. Under the divine blessing the laws of increase are as applicable to one kind of growth as another. Perhaps no more animating prospect is ever presented to the eye than when one passes through a fertile region under high culture, where formerly all was sterility or a wilderness. But a prosperous people often provoke God with their sins; and their prosperity is cut short:

39. *Again, they are minished and brought low through oppression, affliction and sorrow. Minished,* an old form of *diminished. Brought low,* elsewhere *bowed down, humbled, cast down,* Ps. x. 10; xxxv. 14; xlii. 5. The meaning is their prosperity all vanishes, and their hearts sink within them through *oppression;* in Isa. liii. 8, rendered *prison;* from a verb that signifies to *shut up,* Deut. xi. 17, to *detain,* Judges xiii. 15. To this is added *affliction,* in v. 26, rendered *trouble.* It expresses general wretchedness, Num. xi. 15. Such things crush the heart with *sorrow,* a word uniformly rendered. Nor are such calamities confined to the abject poor, but reach the head men:

40. *He poureth contempt upon princes, and causeth them to wander in the wilderness,* where there is *no way.* The language is probably taken from Job xii. 21, 24. The mightiest men are not beyond the reach of divine judgments, Acts xii. 23; Rev. xix. 18. The Most High ruleth in the kingdoms of men, Dan. iv. 17, 25, 32. God does not hate princes as such, for he blesses them greatly. He afflicts them only because they provoke him by their sins. Behold David himself a fugitive, going out of Jerusalem, he knew not whither, and one of the meanest people cursing him, and all for his sins against God, 2 Sam. xvi. 5–13.

41. *Yet setteth he the poor on high from affliction, and maketh* him *families like a flock. Poor,* see on Ps. ix. 18, where it is rendered *needy.* It describes such as have no earthly helper or resources. Instead of *from affliction,* the margin reads *after affliction.* God is continually teaching lessons of humility to the proud, and of encouragement to the lowly; oftentimes giving to the humble large families of children, who are a defence, and raising them from an ignoble to a respectable condition. Such changes often beget despondency in some and envy in others. Every generation has its invidious terms for those whom God has raised up. The haughty Roman said, *Novus homo;* the haughty Frenchman says, *parvenu;* the haughty American, *upstart.* But good men will learn lessons from all these changes.

42. *The righteous shall see* it *and rejoice.* Compare Job xxii. 19; Ps. lii. 6; lviii. 10. *And all iniquity shall stop her mouth.* Compare Job v. 16, from which the phrase is perhaps taken, Ps. lxiii. 11; Rom. iii. 19. It is a great thing when Divine Providence so orders human affairs as to silence the boastings, revilings and blasphemies of ungodly men. It is not certain whether the prophet intends here to describe the effect of things stated in vv. 40, 41, and no more, or of the wonderful providences delineated in the great body of the Psalm. The latter is probable:

43. *Whoso is wise, and will observe these* things, *even they shall understand the loving-kindness of the* LORD. Compare Ps. lxiv. 9; Isa. v. 12; Jer. ix. 12; Hos. xiv. 9. He that will not open his eyes cannot see. He that will not think cannot become wise. Every thing in nature, in providence, and in Scripture has its lessons, but they are lost upon the unobservant. *Lovingkindness,* in the plural, rendered *mercy* in v. 1, and *goodness* in vv. 8, 15, 21, 31. The change of the singular into the plural is not uncommon.

Doctrinal and Practical Remarks.

1. If we may judge of the importance of a duty, or of the reluctance of the human heart to perform it, by the frequency with which it is enjoined, then praise and thanksgiving are of this class, vv. 1, 8, 15, 21, 31. Every class and condition of men are daily called to this work, Ps. cxlv. 9.

2. But while this duty is obligatory upon all it is specially incumbent upon "the redeemed of the Lord," v. 2. One spiritual mercy is worth more than all temporal blessings. If the redeemed remain silent, surely God will fail of his chief glory from earth.

3. The mercies of God to strangers are truly great, and if all the world would honestly tell what God has done for them as travellers and exiles, the earth would resound with his praise, vv. 3–7. Every prosperous journey is by the will of God, Rom. i. 10. Henry: "We ought to take notice of the good hand of God's providence over us in our journeys, going out, and coming in, directing us in our way, and providing for us places, both to bait in, and rest in."

4. Prayer is necessary to every class of men. The marvel is that any attempt to live without it, vv. 6, 13, 19, 28. Travellers, prisoners, the sick, sailors, all classes at home and abroad are encouraged to pour the tale of their grief into the ear of the Almighty. Though God is not bound by covenant to hear prayers not offered in faith, yet he has never said that he would not hear the cry of distress. He hears the young ravens; and are not men of more value than many ravens? He has many a time heard the call of wretchedness, even when misery was the fruit of guilt.

5. The providence of God over every people in their early settlement has been marked with striking and amazing mercies, v. 7. If the annals of any people had been written by the pen of inspiration, they would have been as marvellous as any tradition represents them.

6. If home, even in prospect, is sweet to the weary traveller, how much more sweet ought the prospect of heaven to be to pilgrims on their Zion way, v. 7. Blessed be God, there is a home for the saints, just such as they long for, Rev. vii. 16, 17. They look for a city that hath foundations, whose Maker and Builder is God. It is a *continuing* city, the New Jerusalem.

7. If God is so good and so bountiful, as Scripture and providence declare him to be, (vv. 8, 9); why do not all men come to him, and put their trust in him? His works are mighty, marvellous, merciful. All have abundant evidence of the divine goodness. The withholding of affectionate confidence from God is an act of superlative wickedness, the offspring of hateful unbelief.

8. Would you be godlike? Care for travellers and strangers, vv. 6–9. Use hospitality without grudging. In entertaining strangers some have entertained angels unawares, 1 Tim. iii. 2; Titus i. 8; Heb. xiii. 2; 1 Pet. iv. 9.

9. No man has ever gauged the depth of human misery found among captives and prisoners. Poor things! they sit in darkness, and in the shadow of death, bound in affliction and iron, v. 10. Human wickedness has an awful habit of expressing its malice towards prisoners. Yet among such are some wholly innocent of crime. For such there ought to be some intercessor. The trials of prisoners ought not to be needlessly deferred. It was a part of the dreadful character of one whom God abhorred that he opened not the house of his prisoners, Isa. xiv. 17. Delays in judicial trials are sometimes necessary in order to reach the ends of justice. But one day's *needless* delay is cruelty. All the world praises Howard; why then has he so few imitators? Pity captives and be kind to prisoners.

10. It is an idle plea which some in Christian countries have set up for the heathen

that they do not intelligently sin against God, v. 11. For 1, they have the law of nature written upon their hearts, Rom. ii. 15; 2, God has often sent them teachers, and sometimes even prophets, Jonah iii. 2–5; 3, the fame of the word of God among his people has often spread far and wide, Rom. x. 18; so that beyond a doubt they are without excuse, Rom. i. 20.

11. Sin must be very provoking and very hard to cure, when the Almighty sees it necessary to bring down the hearts of men with so sore travail as comes upon vast numbers, v. 12.

12. If in his kind providence the Lord has granted us freedom from prison and captivity, and allowed us to go at large in pursuit of an honest calling, to him be all the praise. He alone saves us from darkness and the shadow of death, and breaks our bands asunder, v. 14.

13. Have you been a prisoner? Have you looked through the horrid grating, or over the prison fence, and has God set you at large? then give him the glory. Many a good man has been loaded with chains, and God has afterwards raised him to honor and power, v. 16. Who would not be willing, upon due reflection, to endure all that Paul, Alleine, or Bunyan suffered in prison, if he might have the blessed experience, which in their writings they reveal?

14. Sinners are fools, v. 17. There is a marvellous infatuation in all wrong-doing. Dickson: "Sin blindeth sinners, and bereaveth them of the right use of their reason, and maketh them choose trifles, with the loss of what should be most precious."

15. If, even in this world, sin is so terribly punished as we sometimes see it is (vv. 17, 18); what must it not be to fall into the hands of the living God? What pangs, what terrors, what sighs and cries: and still worse, what awful forebodings do men often experience in this life? But this is a dispensation of mercy, and not of wrath. And yet, so 'great is the stupidity of a sleeping conscience' that even then it is not awakened; and it seems sometimes as if nothing would awake men but the flames of the fire that is never quenched, Luke xvi. 23.

16. If we would duly consider our sins and dangers, instead of wondering that men die so soon, we should marvel that they live so long; for there are *destructions* at every step. By even one rash act, a man brings upon himself and entails upon his posterity wretchedness, which makes life a burden. Wherefore then should a living man complain, a man for the punishment of his sins? All this is not hell.

17. Would you be like God? Care for the sick, v. 20. Relieve their wants. Soothe their sorrows. Remember that you may be sick yourself and need the help which you now deny to others.

18. Let us in all things follow the worship which God prescribes, and never make our large liberty a cloak for irreligion; and especially, let us not forget that 'moral and spiritual service is more acceptable to God than any ceremonial performance; the sacrifice of thanks is more than the sacrifice of an ox,' v. 22.

19. Every department of life has its lessons, trials and mercies. To this remark the mariner is no exception, for he sees God's wonders in the deep, vv. 23–30.

20. If the sailor can do nothing so wise, and oftentimes indeed can do nothing else than trust in the Lord, so is it with us in the storms of life, v. 29. Like the mariner, we must use lawful means for our protection; but what are means without the divine blessing?

21. If the *desired haven* is so pleasant to the tempest-tossed mariner, how sweet will heaven itself be to the poor soul, over which all God's waves and billows have passed!

22. It is not an unmeaning or an uncalled for custom to give thanks in public assem-

blies for a safe deliverance from the perils of the sea, v. 32. We have a few good hymns for such occasions. That of Addison beginning:

"Think, O my soul! devoutly think,"

has long been admired.

23. When we consider how many parts of the earth which once were famous for fertility, thrift and civilization, are now smitten with sterility, we ought to be deeply impressed with the terribleness of the divine displeasure, vv. 33, 34. Surely God must have a controversy with men. Henry: "If the land be bad, it is because the inhabitants are so."

24. The goodness of God in giving food and drink to such vast numbers of men and other living creatures as are found on the earth is worthy of perpetual celebration, vv. 35, 36. If the Lord provides, is it not as little as we should do to make humble and thankful acknowledgment of his kindness?

25. It is a great mercy that so large a portion of mankind are allowed to be employed in the cheerful and healthful pursuits of agriculture, vv. 37, 38. And it is another proof of the deep depravity of men engaged in such pursuits that they so often neglect to give God the praise which is his due. There is not a grain that grows, or a fruit that ripens, but it declares the divine goodness in a manner that has more than once convinced an atheist and confounded a skeptic. Where is God's honor? Where is his praise? Answer, O ye husbandmen!

26. God's blessing makes rich, and adds no sorrow. God's anger makes poor and strips us of comfort, vv. 38, 39. "The fertility of land is not to be attributed to men's industry, but to God." God hates pride and will bring down arrogancy.

27. *Oppression* of every kind, *affliction* in every form, and *sorrows* of every degree, are no new things upon earth, v. 39. Because of sins, the wrath of God cometh on the children of disobedience.

28. Let not the mighty man glory in his might, v. 40. Dickson: "Kings and rulers keep not their place, power and estimation among men, but by God's investing them with dignity. . . It is God who giveth wisdom and prudence to men for ruling states; and when their wit is employed for their own earthly interest, he can take their wisdom from them, and give them a cup of giddy wine."

29. Let not the poor despair. God is their friend, v. 41. Compare 1 Sam. ii. 8. Blessed be God, he pursueth not his creatures that he may destroy them, but that he may humble them.

30. Like many other Scriptures, this Psalm calls us to the study of providence. It is God that gives peace, wholesome air, a good climate, seasonable showers; and that for their sins sends on men sore calamities. His kingdom ruleth over all. Not chance, but the Almighty governs the world. Blessed is he who sees God in history and in nature as well as in revelation. Let us hold fast the truth on this doctrine so fundamental to right thinking, sound theology, solid peace, a holy life and a happy death.

31. All true joy must have its rise in the *lovingkindness* of Jehovah, v. 43. It needs no other source. It has no other.

PSALM CVIII.

A Song *or* Psalm of David.

1 O God, my heart is fixed; I will sing and give praise, even with my glory.

2 Awake, psaltery and harp : I *myself* will awake early.

3 I will praise thee, O LORD, among the people: and I will sing praises unto thee among the nations.

4 For thy mercy *is* great above the heavens: and thy truth *reacheth* unto the clouds.

5 Be thou exalted, O God, above the heavens: and thy glory above all the earth;

6 That thy beloved may be delivered: save *with* thy right hand, and answer me.

7 God hath spoken in his holiness; I will rejoice, I will divide Shechem, and mete out the valley of Succoth.

8 Gilead *is* mine; Manasseh *is* mine; Ephraim also *is* the strength of mine head; Judah *is* my lawgiver;

9 Moab *is* my washpot; over Edom will I cast out my shoe; over Philistia will I triumph.

10 Who will bring me into the strong city? who will lead me into Edom?

11 *Wilt* not *thou*, O God, *who* hast cast us off? and wilt not thou, O God, go forth with our hosts?

12 Give us help from trouble: for vain *is* the help of man.

13 Through God we shall do valiantly: for he *it is that* shall tread down our enemies.

ON the title see on title of Psalms iii. xxx. David certainly wrote this Psalm. The first *five* verses are taken from Ps. lvii.; the last *eight*, from Ps. lx. In this the variations from the originals are slight, and have perhaps been sufficiently noticed. The chief difference between this Psalm and the two, from which it is taken, is that this omits their sad and despondent parts, and contains such selections from them as express gratitude, hope and confidence. Luther is persuaded that portions of this Psalm refer to the setting up of the kingdom of Christ in all nations. David's throne has perpetuity in no other way. The example of David in making one Psalm out of two suggests the propriety of our combining different portions of God's word for our own use and edification, according to the circumstances, in which we may be placed. Such an exercise would make us familiar with Scripture, and show us the variety of excellent uses to which it may be applied.

PSALM CIX.

To the chief Musician, A Psalm of David.

1 Hold not thy peace, O God of my praise;

2 For the mouth of the wicked and the mouth of the deceitful are opened against me: they have spoken against me with a lying tongue.

3 They compassed me about also with words of hatred; and fought against me without a cause.

4 For my love they are my adversaries: but I *give myself unto* prayer.

5 And they have rewarded me evil for good, and hatred for my love.

6 Set thou a wicked man over him: and let Satan stand at his right hand.

7 When he shall be judged, let him be condemned: and let his prayer become sin.

8 Let his days be few; *and* let another take his office.

9 Let his children be fatherless, and his wife a widow.

10 Let his children be continually vagabonds, and beg: let them seek *their bread* also out of their desolate places.

11 Let the extortioner catch all that he hath; let the strangers spoil his labour.

12 Let there be none to extend mercy unto him: neither let there be any to favour his fatherless children.

13 Let his posterity be cut off; *and* in the generation following let their name be blotted out.

14 Let the iniquity of his fathers be remembered with the LORD; and let not the sin of his mother be blotted out.

15 Let them be before the LORD continually, that he may cut off the memory of them from the earth.

16 Because that he remembered not to shew mercy, but persecuted the poor and needy man, that he might even slay the broken in heart.

17 As he loved cursing, so let it come unto him: as he delighted not in blessing, so let it be far from him.

18 As he clothed himself with cursing like as with his garment, so let it come into his bowels like water, and like oil into his bones.

19 Let it be unto him as the garment *which* covereth him, and for a girdle wherewith he is girded continually.

20 *Let* this *be* the reward of mine adversaries from the LORD, and of them that speak evil against my soul.

21 But do thou for me, O GOD the Lord, for thy name's sake: because thy mercy *is* good, deliver thou me.

22 For I *am* poor and needy, and my heart is wounded within me.

23 I am gone like the shadow when it declineth: I am tossed up and down as the locust.

24 My knees are weak through fasting; and my flesh faileth of fatness.

25 I became also a reproach unto them: *when* they looked upon me they shaked their heads.

26 Help me, O LORD my God: O save me according to thy mercy:

27 That they may know that this *is* thy hand; *that* thou, LORD, hast done it.

28 Let them curse, but bless thou: when they arise, let them be ashamed; but let thy servant rejoice.

29 Let mine adversaries be clothed with shame; and let them cover themselves with their own confusion, as with a mantle.

30 I will greatly praise the LORD with my mouth; yea, I will praise him among the multitude.

31 For he shall stand at the right hand of the poor, to save *him* from those that condemn his soul.

ON the title see on titles of Psalms iii. iv. The title, general consent and inspiration (Acts i. 16) ascribe this ode to David. If it had any historic occasion it is not certain what it was. Some find its origin in the persecutions of Saul urged on by Doeg. Others think it has special reference to the rebellion of Absalom, and the treachery of Ahithophel. Saul's treatment of David was very wicked, and much evil, like that here denounced, came upon him. Nor can it be denied that David received base injuries from Ahithophel, and that the end of that wily statesman was not unlike that of Judas Iscariot. If it should be conceded that the primary reference of this poem is to be sought in one of these historic events, that would not forbid us to seek its secondary and complete fulfilment in Christ, of whom David was an acknowledged type, and in Judas, whose crime was so heinous, and his end so dreadful. But why may we not regard it as wholly prophetic, borrowing perhaps its imagery from the history of David and of his enemies? This mode of explanation is simple, natural, free from unanswerable objections, and has been formally adopted in whole or in part by many. The Syriac: "This is a Psalm of David, when without his knowledge the people made Absalom king; and on that account he was slain. But to us he expounds the sufferings of the Christ of God." Some, indeed, apply parts of the Psalm to others than Judas, and include the enemies and murderers of our Lord generally, as representing the Jewish nation. Chrysostom, Jerome, Theodoret and Augustine think it was fulfilled in Christ and in Judas and his associates. Luther: "This Psalm may be very properly considered as used in the person of Christ, deeply complaining against his betrayers the Jews." Calvin: "Although David here complains of the injuries which he sustained, yet, as he was a typical character, everything that is expressed in the Psalm must properly be applied to Christ the head of the church, and to all the faithful, inasmuch as they are his members." Henry: "It is certain that in penning this Psalm David had an eye to Christ, his sufferings, and his persecutors." This view is supported by Gill, Pool, Horne, Hengstenberg and others. Nor are such guided by fancy. We have the authority of an inspired apostle: "In those days Peter stood up in the midst of the disciples, and said, (the number of the names together were about an hundred and twenty,) Men and brethren, this scripture must needs have been fulfilled, which the Holy Ghost by the mouth of David spake concerning Judas, which was guide to them that took Jesus. For he was numbered with us, and had obtained part of this ministry. Now this man purchased a field with the reward of iniquity; and falling headlong, he burst asunder in the midst, and all his bowels· gushed out. And it was known to all the dwellers at Jerusalem; insomuch as that field is called in their proper tongue, Aceldama, that is to say, The field of blood. For it is written in the book of Psalms, Let his habitation be desolate, and let no man dwell therein; and his bishoprick let another take," Acts i. 15–20. This testimony of the inspired apostle settles three points: 1. David wrote this Psalm; 2. This Psalm is not the expression of private pique or of personal dislike; but its author is the Holy Ghost, who merely used David as an instrument of sending it forth; 3. It is a prophecy respecting Judas and has its *fulfilment* in him. And as we know nothing of Judas except in connection with our Lord, this prophecy necessarily includes our Saviour. If these views are sound, it is not necessary to consider at length several suggestions made by different writers quite at variance with what has been stated. One of the strong features of this poem is the variety and terribleness of curses it denounces. See Introduction, § 6. These curses, says Dodd, "in reality are mere prophetic denunciations." Scott dates the Psalm B. C. 1021; Clarke, B. C. 1023. The names of the Most High here found are *Elohim God, Jehovah* LORD and *Adonai Lord*, on which see on Ps. iii. 2; i. 2; ii. 4.

1. *Hold not thy peace, O God of my praise. Hold peace*, elsewhere *be silent, keep silence, be still*, or *be deaf*. See on Ps. xxviii. 1; xxxv. 22. Compare Isa. xlii. 14; Mic. vii. 16. The meaning is, Do not slight me, nor neglect me; pity me, hear me, deliver me. *God of my praise*. Some have proposed to read, Be not silent of my praise, O God. Calvin gathers from it, that the suppliant calls on God to set forth the innocence of the sufferer. But this is implied without altering the English translation. *God of my praise* means God, whom I am bound to praise, who deserves my praise, who is the author and object and substance of my praise, God whom I love to praise, and whom I am in the habit of praising.

2. *For the mouth of the wicked and the mouth of the deceitful are opened against me. they have spoken against me with a lying tongue*. As the word rendered *are opened* is active, some propose to supply *my enemies* have opened. The margin suggests a better solution and reads *have opened themselves*. *Mouth of the deceitful*, literally *mouth of deceit*. How fearfully this whole verse was fulfilled in the history of our Lord is shown by each of the evangelists. But as the Psalm chiefly relates to events occurring about the time of his death, its awful import is historically recorded in Matt. xxvi. 59–61; Mark xiv. 55–59. So illegal and unreliable was the testimony against Jesus, that the judge, who sat on his trial, repeatedly pronounced him innocent, and finally washed his hands saying, "I am innocent of the blood of this just person."

3. *They compassed me about also with words of hatred. Compassed about*, elsewhere *besieged*, Ecc. ix. 14; *walk about*, Ps. xlviii. 12; *environ*, Josh. vii. 9. See on Ps. vii. 7; xxvi. 6. *Hatred*, uniformly rendered. It expresses malice. This was expressed by more than mere words. *And fought against me without a cause. Fought*, as in

Ps. xxxv. 1 ; lvi. 1, elsewhere *warred*, 1 Kings xiv. 19 ; xxii. 45. It expresses acts of deadly hostility. Christ's enemies never rested till they got his blood. All such treatment of him was injurious, *without cause*, elsewhere rendered *for nothing*.

4. *For my love they are my adversaries.* How amazingly this was fulfilled in Christ. "Christ's love to man was daily manifested by his miraculously healing all the infirmities of the body, which was returned by man's hatred of him, as displayed in his general conduct." Never was exhibited such beneficence on the one side, and such malignity on the other. *But I give myself unto prayer.* The Hebrew is very elliptical ; but the common rendering gives the sense. His enemies blasphemed ; he prayed. They hunted him ; he fled to the throne of grace. Such was our Saviour's distress, that the weariness of the day was yet followed by the watchfulness of the night spent in prayer.

5. *And they have rewarded me evil for good, and hatred for my love.* Hatred, as in v. 3. *Love,* as in v. 4. It expresses sincere and pure friendship. To render evil for evil is vindictive. To render evil for good is fiendish. To Christ men had no opportunity of doing the former ; in the latter they abounded.

6. *Set thou a wicked man over him : and let Satan stand at his right hand.* In no one does there seem to be so fearful an accomplishment of this and the fourteen following verses as in Judas. Instead of *wicked man*, we may read *the wicked* One. In the Hebrew there is nothing for *man*. Thus we make the two clauses parallel. Before Judas offered to betray his master he was a *devil*, (*diabolos*) John vi. 70. For a long time he had much to do with the father of lies. About the time of the betrayal in an awful manner "Satan entered into him," John xiii. 27. The word Satan means an *accuser*, or *adversary*. He is the arch enemy of God and of man. He opposes all goodness. To Old Testament writers he was well known, Gen. iii. 1 ; 1 Chron. xxi. 1 ; Job i. 6 ; ii. 1 ; Zech. iii. 1, 2. Satan was *over* Judas as a tyrant hurrying him on to ruin, making him bold in sin, and desperate after it. Though the first verb of this verse is in the imperative, yet the second is in the future, as are also nearly all the verbs in vv. 7–20. Whatever the form, the words are clearly prophetic, and not at all expressive of personal malice.

7. *When he shall be judged, let him be condemned.* After his great sin Judas was tried at the bar of his own conscience, and found guilty. He submitted his case to the chief priests and elders ; and they coolly admitted his guilt. Men have arisen, denying the existence of God, the divinity of Christ, and the truth of the Scriptures ; yet earth has never seen the man who ventured a formal defence of Judas Iscariot. Nor can we doubt the judgment of God in his case. Heaven and earth, his own conscience and even Satan himself *condemn* him. *And let his prayer become sin.* See on Ps. lxvi. 18. Compare Pr. i. 28 ; xxviii. 9 ; Isa. i. 15. All the prayers of Judas but made him the more guilty, because they were all hypocritical.

8. *Let his days be few.* We do not know how long Judas lived after Christ was condemned. He may have died on the day of the crucifixion, or he may have lived a few days. But all agree that his course was short, as this clause predicts it should be. And *let another take his office.* *Office*, sometimes rendered *charge*, Ezek. ix. 1 ; xliv. 11 ; oftener, *office*. The Septuagint and the versions which follow it, for *office* have *bishoprick*, or *superintendence*. Peter quotes that version in Acts i. How is it possible to explain this verse and some that follow it unless we admit that the prophet is speaking of a real person ? Ideal people do not hold offices, nor have they wives or children.

9. *Let his children be fatherless, and his wife a widow.* Scott : "Probably he left a widow and fatherless children, on whom infamy and distress were entailed, in the righteous providence of God, till the family was extinct ; and thus the sins of his progeni-

tors, which he imitated, but far exceeded, were visited upon him and his descendants, in a remarkable manner." The verb of this verse is also in the future. But the family of Judas did not at once become extinct.

10. *Let his children be continually vagabonds, and beg: let them seek their bread also out of their desolate places.* *Vagabonds;* in Ps. lix. 15, *wander up and down;* in Gen. iv. 12, 14, *a fugitive;* literally, *wandering* let his children *wander.* One form of the verb has the force of *continually.* This terrible vagrancy was to lead them to *desolate places, desolations, deserts* or *wastes,* Ezra ix. 9; Ps. cii. 6; Isa. lxi. 4. The history of the family of Judas Iscariot has never been written. Its annals would doubtless be appalling. The strong presumption is that he trained his offspring to deceit and theft. Compare Ex. xx. 5; Deut. v. 9. Ill gotten gains do not stay by us, neither do they bless us or our children.

11. *Let the extortioner catch all that he hath.* *Extortioner,* in Ex. xxii. 25, *usurer;* in 2 Kings iv. 1, *creditor.* The word describes a hard *exacting* wretch, whose cupidity has driven all tenderness from his bosom, and made him crafty, so that he *catches, takes with a snare* all he can get. The same word is rendered *snared* in Ps. ix. 16. *And let the strangers spoil his labor.* *Strangers,* not his own family. *Spoil, gather, take for a prey,* as the word is elsewhere rendered. *Labor,* i. e., the fruit of labor.

12. *Let there be none to extend mercy unto him.* *Mercy, kindness, lovingkindness.* There was no person to pity him. His accomplices cast him off. They despised his baseness. They showed him no sympathy: "What is that to us? see thou to that." *Neither let there be any to favor his fatherless children.* He showed no mercy; and he received none. And his children loved his evil ways, and none was *gracious* to them.

13. *Let his posterity be cut off; and in the generation following let their name be blotted out.* *Posterity,* so rendered also in Dan. xi. 4; Am. iv. 2; in Ezek. xxiii. 25, *remnant* and *residue.* That these terrible predictions were fulfilled, who can doubt?

14. *Let the iniquity of his fathers be remembered with the* LORD; *and let not the sin of his mother be blotted out.* This may be a prediction that the guilt of original sin shall not be forgiven to this betrayer. Compare Ps. li. 5. But it probably has a more definite bearing. It may be that the parents of Judas were themselves thieves. If so, they doubtless taught him the arts of pilfering. Or they may have known and approved his vile treason, and been witnesses of his miserable end, surviving him for a season. Alexander: "This is perhaps the most fearful imprecation in the Psalm. . . It is not to be forgotten, however, that in all such cases, the personal guilt of the implicated parties is presupposed, and not inferred from their connection with the principals."

15. *Let them be before the* LORD *continually, that he may cut off the memory of them from the earth.* Like language is found in Neh. iv. 4, 5. The meaning is that their name shall be esteemed vile and be forgotten. In using *them* and *their,* he refers to all that had been spoken of as in anywise connected with the betrayer. See on Ps. ix. 5, 6.

16. *Because that he remembered not to shew mercy, but persecuted the poor and needy man, that he might even slay the broken in heart.* He shall have judgment without mercy, that hath showed no mercy. The malice of the heart against God manifest in the flesh has always been deadly and desperate. In Judas it had full time and fair opportunity to mature itself, and be fairly developed. The *poor* and *needy man, broken in heart,* is the blessed Saviour, who wept over the very city that was about to shed his blood; see v. 22. Jesus had mercy for all his enemies; but none of his enemies had mercy for him.

17. *As he loved cursing, so let it come unto him: as he delighted not in blessing, so let it be far from him.* Here we have a new declaration of the awful law of retribution in kind. He blessed not others and he got no blessing himself. He cursed others and

was cursed himself. Alexander is confident that the verbs should all be read in the preterite. Let the Israelitish people remember what their fathers said, "His blood be upon us and upon our children," and repent, and seek a blessing.

18. *As he clothed himself with cursing like as with his garment, so let it come into his bowels like water, and like oil into his bones.* There are three modes of interpreting this verse: 1. Some think the *cursing* is that which comes from the Lord upon the guilty. 2. Others regard the construction and teaching of the verse like that of Prov. viii. 36, "All they that hate me love death," *i. e.*, they love and persistently pursue such a course as leads to death, and so are said to love death itself. 3. Others think that the cursing which he put on like a garment consisted of his malevolent wishes, speeches, and deeds; while the cursing which came into his very bones was the wrath of an angry God. At least part of the form of expression here used is taken from the law respecting the water of jealousy, Num. v. 18, 22, 24, 27. Parkhurst thinks the *garment* of this verse denotes a robe covering the whole body.

19. *Let it be unto him as the garment* which *covereth him.* The curse given fell, did its work, and passed away; but the curse received was permanent. It was worn like a garment; *and for a girdle wherewith he is girded continually.* It fits tight and is bound fast. He never gets rid of it. The blood of Christ rejected, as Judas rejected it, there remaineth no more sacrifice for sin. Thenceforward the wrath of God *abides.*

20. *Let this be the reward of mine adversaries from the Lord, and of them that speak evil against my soul.* *Reward*, in Lev. xix. 13, *wages;* in the margin in Isa. xl. 10, *recompense.* "The wages of sin is death.". *Adversaries*, as in v. 4. All the woes denounced in vv. 6–19, are summed up in the word *this.* The prophet has not been delivering his own private sentiments; but has been speaking by the Holy Ghost. Both the denunciation and the things denounced are *from the Lord.* Alexander: "The description in the last clause includes insult, slander, and malicious plotting."

21. *But do thou for me, O God the Lord, for thy name's sake.* *Do*, elsewhere *work, execute, deal.* Calvin: Undertake for me; Edwards: Do thou take my part. The petitioner draws his arguments from God's nature and glory, *for thy* name's sake, John xii. 28. *Because thy mercy is good, deliver thou me.* The tender mercies of the wicked are cruel, Pr. xii. 10. The more you have of them, the more sad is your state. But God's mercy is *good* in all respects and at all times. It works no ill. If David as a type appears in this verse (and perhaps he does,) we give a deeper shade of meaning to the phrase *for thy name's sake*, Jer. xiv. 7, and to the word *mercy*, Ps. li. 1. Compare Ps. lxix. 16. Calvin: "All our prayers will vanish in smoke, unless they are grounded upon the mercy of God."

22. *For I* am *poor and needy*, as in v. 16, sometimes true of the type David, but until the end of his life always true of the antitype Christ. *And my heart is wounded within me*, equivalent to *broken in heart* in v. 16. Compare Ps. xl. 17. David had crushing griefs; but above all others David's Lord was a "man of sorrows, Isa liii. 3. None was ever *wounded* as he was. The sword of Jehovah was buried in his soul, Zech. xiii. 7.

23. *I am gone like the shadow when it declineth.* See on Ps. cii. 11. Anderson: "As a shadow, when it is extended by the sun's setting, is approaching to evanescence, so, saith the speaker in this Psalm, I am fast disappearing; that is, I am approaching the end of mortal life." *I am tossed up and down as the locust.* The locust has no house, no home, no resting-place. So was David a wanderer for a while; and David's Master had not where to lay his head, Matt. viii. 20. Locusts in the east are carried hither and thither by the winds, till at last they perish in the sea, or in some sandy desert. Compare Ex. x. 13, 19; Isa. xxxiii. 4; Nah. iii. 15, 17. The verb might be

rendered *am shaken* or *am overthrown*, Neh. v. 13; Isa. xxxiii. 9; Ex. xiv. 27; Ps. cxxxvi. 15.

24. *My knees are weak through fasting.* The word *fasting* used here expresses abstinence from food through grief, or for humiliation, 2 Sam. xii. 16; Est. iv. 3; Dan. ix. 3. Before our Lord was crucified, he was so exhausted that he could not carry his own cross, and he was often an hungered. *And my flesh faileth of fatness.* His moisture was turned into the drought of summer. *Fatness*, in v. 18, the same word is rendered *oil*. It points to the refreshing, invigorating, lubricating substance of a healthful animal body. Clearly the *oil* is that which inheres in the frame and especially *in the bones.* "A broken spirit drieth the bones," Pr. xvii. 22.

25. *I became also a reproach unto them.* *Reproach*, almost uniformly so rendered. See on Ps. xv. 3. Never were such reproaches heaped on any as on the Saviour. When *they looked upon me they shaked their heads.* The whole verse finds its parallel in Ps. xxii. 7. Compare Matt. xxvii. 39; Mark xv. 29; Luke xxiii. 35.

26. *Help me, O LORD my God: O save me according to thy mercy.* *Help*, as in Ps. xxii. 19. *Save*, as in Ps. xxii. 21. The word rendered *mercy* is indeed used to express God's loving-kindness to sinners; but it expresses also his *kindness* and *goodness* shown to any of his creatures. It is by his loving-kindness that the angels live in bliss. God's *help* was sought:

27. *That they may know that this* is *thy hand; that thou,* LORD, *hast done it.* No thoughtful man can read the history of David without seeing that his deliverances were from the Lord. Man could not have saved him. Much more illustriously are the wisdom and power of God manifested in raising Christ Jesus from the dead to glory and honor supreme, eternal, ineffable. *Thy hand,* the working of thy providence, the energy of thy power.

28. *Let them curse, but* bless *thou.* Calvin and others: They shall curse, but thou shalt bless; Fry: They may curse, but thou wilt bless; Hengstenberg: They curse, bless thou. Perhaps Fry expresses the exact shade of idea. Compare 2 Sam. xvi. 11, 12. *When they arise, let them be ashamed.* Literally, *They arose, and shall be ashamed:* Calvin: When they arise, they shall be ashamed; Edwards: Let those be put to shame that rise up against me; Alexander: They have arisen, and shall be shamed. Narrative, prayer and prophecy are so mingled in the last eleven verses of this Psalm that it is not easy to draw a *certain* line between them. But the reader may be satisfied to know that prayer and prophecy here are quite coincident, and that the whole history will show that the prayers were answered and the predictions fulfilled. *But let thy servant rejoice.* Literally, And thy servant shall be glad. David was God's servant, Ps. xix. 11, 13; xxxi. 16; cxvi. 16. In a much more glorious sense was Jesus the servant of God, Isa. xlii. 1; xlix. 5; lii. 13. The prospect of great joy sustained the Redeemer in his agony on the cross, Heb. xii. 2. He has had that joy for a long time, and it shall never end.

29. *Let mine adversaries be clothed with shame; and let them cover themselves with their own confusion, as with a mantle.* *Adversaries*, as in vv. 4, 20. The general figure is the same as in vv. 18, 19. *Mantle*, in Exodus, *robe;* in 1 Sam. ii. 19, *coat;* in Ezra and Job, *mantle.* It is the garment which covers the other apparel and the whole person. Compare Ps. lxxi. 13.

30. *I will greatly praise the Lord with my mouth; yea, I will praise him among the multitude.* The first verb is often rendered *give thanks*, Ps. vi. 5; xviii. 49. The second is from a cognate of that from which the Psalter takes its name. If David as a type here speaks, no one will find difficulty. But if any object to such vows as coming from Christ, let them compare Ps. xxii. 22. Who on earth or in heaven has ever so honored the Father as the incarnate Son?

31 *For he shall stand at the right hand of the poor, to save* him *from those that condemn his soul.* At the right hand of his Son and Servant, the Redeemer, God has stood, and will ever stand as an advocate and protector. Compare v. 6. He has amply vindicated all his claims and doctrines, Rom. i. 4. He will vindicate and reward him for ever, Isa. lii. 13, 15; liii. 10–12. *Soul* or *life*, as in v. 20. Christ's enemies condemned both his life and his soul. He was *the poor* beyond all others, though David his type was poor also. And what Jehovah was to his Son, he will in and through him be to each of his servants, even the humblest. The Lord will plead his cause. He will not accuse him, nor condemn him when he is judged.

DOCTRINAL AND PRACTICAL REMARKS.

1. It is no wonder that the afflicted wish to secure the ear, aid and hand of God, and therefore cry to him, vv. 1, 4. A thousandth part of the opposition made to Christ and his people would long since have exterminated the church, but for the constant and amazing interposition of God in answer to the prayers of his people and the intercession of his Son.

2. Those who have never had experience of it, know nothing of the terrors of deceitful, violent, malignant words, vv. 2, 3. See Pr. xii. 18. The innocent may be accused, reviled and threatened until they are terrified, not out of their virtue, but out of all self-possession. Men may be abused till they cease to have self-reliance. Calumnies, accompanied with professions of friendship, are Iscariot-like. Often silence is the only reply we can make, because " when calumny is rampant, innocence is duly and properly estimated by none but God only." Calvin: No man can, with sincerity of heart, surrender himself entirely into the hand of God, except he has first formed a resolution of treating with contempt the reproaches of the world, and is also fully persuaded that he has God as the defender of his cause."

3. Have such calumnies and falsehoods been uttered concerning you, that you are *compassed about* with them, and cannot find any way to clear yourself before wicked and unreasonable men; remember that the Lord Jesus Christ and his servant David experienced the same, vv. 2, 3.

4. Whatever you do or suffer, maintain a good conscience. Sin not against the Lord in one way to defend yourself in another. If wicked men will assail you, so behave that at the end and to the end you may say *they fought against me without a cause*, v. 3.

5. So far is want of evidence from being a shield against calumny, that ordinarily malignant men are spiteful and violent in proportion to their lack of evidence, v. 3. A spotless life, uniform tenderness of conscience, deeds of charity and hearty prayers for enemies oftentimes but enrage them the more.

6. The unreasonableness of the opposition made to Christ and his followers always has been atrocious, vv. 4, 5.

7. There is no bondage like the slavery of sin; and there is no tyrant so cruel as Satan, v. 6. To be delivered over to him is to be in hell.

8. Let no good man, however calumniated, regard himself as at liberty to invoke curses on his foes. What David spoke prophetically, in vv. 6–20, can be no guide to the personal wishes of injured Christians. Jesus Christ prayed for his murderers. Yet all true Christians and faithful ministers ought to warn the impenitent of their coming doom.

9. The wicked, if they were but honest with themselves, might easily know what would be their doom at the last day, v. 7. They have monitions in the state of their own consciences sufficient to alarm any but the stupid, 1 John iii. 20.

10. It is idle for men to think that they are on the way to heaven, when both their lives and hearts are such as to make their very prayers an abomination to God, v. 7.

11. Death is by sin; and the abbreviation of human life to threescore and ten was made for the same reason; and yet the wicked by special enormities make life still shorter, v. 8. Compare Ps. lv. 23.

12. Of all who shall at last lie down in sorrow, none will have a more fearful doom than some, who have been high in office on earth, and filled the world with the fame of their deeds, vv. 7, 8. This will no doubt be true to an appalling extent of the ministers of religion, who have been faithless to their charge, and hypocritical in their professions. What a frightful conception it is that the carnal minister, who dies without repentance, will be eternally united to a company at the head of which will stand Judas Iscariot.

13. If men object to the terrible sweep that criminality takes over a man's posterity, vv. 9, 10, 12, 13; let him first examine how the Scriptures teach that doctrine; and then let him consider what the state of things would be if God should act on a contrary principle. Suppose every wrong-doer was fully persuaded that his evil conduct would have no unhappy bearing on any one but himself, would not some of the most powerful restraints on mankind be taken away?

14. One great reason for leading a temperate, frugal, industrious and honest life, is that we may be kept out of the power of the extortioner, the usurer, the hard-hearted creditor, the unrelenting exactor, v. 11.

15. When we remember how great are the blessings of lasting and genuine friendships, and how feeble and dependent we all are, we ought earnestly to beseech God not to leave us in this dark world without those, who will extend kindness to us, and transmit their favor to our offspring, v. 12.

16. Parents may live to see the ruin of the children, whom they have trained in the principles and practice of iniquity, v. 14.

17. A good name is worth more than all the ease, wealth, pleasures and flatteries of the world, v. 15.

18. While God is very long-suffering and patiently waits for the return of the wayward; yet when his hand takes hold on vengeance, retribution is as terrible as it is just, vv. 16–20, 28, 29. Surely men have no right to complain of injustice, if they get what they give. We are not at liberty to suppress scriptural denunciations against sin, Deut. xxvii. 15–26; xxviii. 15–68. Jesus, full of all tenderness, was yet faithful in warning men of coming wrath, Luke vi. 24–26; Mark ix. 43–48.

19. Whatever we do, let us labor to be on God's side, vv. 21, 26. Having him, we do absolutely need no other helper, protector or portion. No man has ever made the Almighty too prominent in his thoughts, plans or hopes.

20. Are you poor and needy? So was Jesus Christ. Is your heart wounded within you? So was his. Are you tossed up and down like a locust, having no certain dwelling-place? Such was the Master's lot, vv. 22–24. Look to Jesus, Heb. xii. 2, 3.

21. It is well for us often to take solemn and salutary views of our latter end, v. 23. It is a great mercy which God grants to most of his servants, to give them in some way timely notice of their departure from this world.

22. Let us not be greatly moved by taunts and mockings from ungodly men, v. 25. They were heaped upon our Saviour. Nor can they do us real harm, if grace be given us to possess our souls in patience. But let no man attempt to bear such a burden in his own strength.

23. Come what will, let us labor and pray that God may be honored in all our sufferings; and that men may be brought to know his hand, v. 27. It is natural to

shrink from pain, but if the Lord be thereby glorified, let us sweetly say, "The cup which my Father giveth me to drink, shall I not drink it?"

24. Scott: "We need not regard the malicious imprecations of ungodly men: though they curse, the Lord will bless those who trust in him, and they will rejoice when their enemies shall be covered with confusion: for God will plead the cause of those who honor him by their animated praises; he will rebuke Satan, and every accuser, and save them from those who would condemn their souls," v. 28.

25. Whether joy or sorrow seems most to abound, yet it is not doubtful whether judgment or mercy most prevails in the case of all God's people; and therefore each of his saints should *greatly praise* the Lord; and that in the most public and solemn manner, v. 30.

26. Is your lot hard? Is your cup bitter? Is your cross heavy? Then believe in God, and in his Son Jesus Christ, who stands at the right hand of the poor, their Advocate and Friend, v. 31. Compare John xiv. 1.

27. Are you a sufferer from the violence, injuries or persecutions of men? Remember that the Master endured the same, and cheerfully fill up that which is behind of the afflictions of Christ in your flesh, for the sake of his body, which is his church, Col. i. 24. Dickson: "It matters not what the enemy speak against the godly so long as God approveth them."

28. Is it a part of your business and your pleasure to afflict and torment the innocent, the helpless or the godly? Beware! God is the avenger of all such.

29. Is your religion of the bitter, cursing kind? If so, it will not stand the test, Luke ix. 55; Rom. xii. 9–19.

PSALM CX.

A Psalm of David.

1 The LORD said unto my Lord, Sit thou at my right hand, until I make thine enemies thy footstool.

2 The LORD shall send the rod of thy strength out of Zion: rule thou in the midst of thine enemies.

3 Thy people *shall be* willing in the day of thy power, in the beauties of holiness from the womb of the morning: thou hast the dew of thy youth.

4 The LORD hath sworn, and will not repent, Thou *art* a priest for ever after the order of Melchizedek.

5 The Lord at thy right hand shall strike through kings in the day of his wrath.

6 He shall judge among the heathen, he shall fill *the places* with the dead bodies; he shall wound the heads over many countries.

7 He shall drink of the brook in the way: therefore shall he lift up the head.

ON the title see on title of Psalm iii. In the New Testament this Psalm is often quoted, Matt. xxii. 42–45; Mark xii. 36, 37; Luke xx. 41–44; Acts ii. 34–36; 1 Cor. xv. 25; Heb. i. 13; v. 6; vii. 17; x. 12, 13. These quotations prove, 1. David is the author of this Psalm. So clearly is this matter settled that no respectable commentator doubts it. The title, Christ, Peter all testify to this fact. 2. This Psalm is in the highest sense Messianic. All the citations of it in the New Testament are more or less decisive of this matter. Horne: "It appertaineth literally and solely to King Messiah." 3. Jesus Christ is both *Lord* and *Christ*, Acts ii. 36. In him are fulfilled all the glorious things here spoken. Nor has there ever appeared any one but Jesus Christ, to whom with any show of consistency, we can apply it. Some of the Jews have said it was fulfilled in Eliezer, the servant of Abraham; some, in Hezekiah; and some, in Zerubbabel; but neither of these was a priest, much less was either of them both a priest and a king; and neither of them was *Lord* to David. None but Jesus ever had so glorious a kingdom as that here described. Luther: "This is a peculiar and glorious prophecy concerning the kingdom of Christ. . . There is not a Psalm like it in the whole Scripture; and it ought to be very dear unto the church; seeing that it confirms that great article of faith—Christ sitting at the right hand of God the Father Almighty." Calvin: "Beyond all controversy the Psalm is a very clear prediction of the divinity, priesthood, victories, and triumph of the Messiah." Alexander: "This is the counterpart of the Second Psalm, completing the prophetic picture of the conquering Messiah. . . Any other application is ridiculous." Scott dates it B. C. 1038; Clarke, B. C. 1015. The names of the Most High in this Psalm are *Jehovah* LORD and *Adonai Lord*, on which see on Ps. i. 2; ii. 4.

1. *The* LORD *said unto my Lord.* The LORD, *Jehovah.* Lord, *Adonai;* a title of respect applied to any potentate, even God himself. Here it is applied to one who was higher than David, for David calls him *my Lord.* Nor was there any to whom David could in this connection fitly give this title, except Christ. The ancient Jews admitted that Messiah should be the Son of David, that this Psalm related to him, and that he should be greater than David, having the authority of a master over him. See Matt. xxii. 42–45. It was chiefly as king that David was a type of Messiah, and yet he was as truly his inferior in that respect as Moses was in the prophetical office, or Aaron in the priesthood. This language of David clearly implies that his *Lord*, as to his divine nature, was already in existence, as the eternal Son of God. *Sit thou at my right hand.* The first step in Christ's exaltation was his resurrection; the second, his ascension into heaven; the third, his *sitting at the right hand of God.* What is the meaning of his *sitting?* It does not relate to the posture of his body. Peter and Paul each once say he "is at the right hand of God;" and Stephen saw him "*standing* on the right hand of God." In Scripture phrase *sitting* expresses quiet, repose. Jesus has entered into his rest. Compare Mic. iv. 4; Rev. iii. 21. Christ has ceased from his works and sufferings, Heb. iv. 10. *Sitting* also denotes permanency of possession. "Asher continued (literally *sat*) on the sea-shore," Judg. v. 17. He took and held that country as his portion. *Sitting* denotes majesty and authority. The king sits on his throne, and does not stand in the presence of even his nobles. Compare 1 Cor. xv. 25. *Sitting* is also the posture of a judge. Compare Pr. xx. 8; Isa. xvi. 5. He is sitting *at God's right hand.* The *right hand* is an emblem of strength, Ex. xv. 6; Ps. lxxx. 17. With the *right hand* the best blessings were commonly bestowed, Gen. xlviii. 13, 14. With the right hand gifts were commonly both received and bestowed, Eph. iv. 8. The right hand of royal power is represented as the chief place of enjoyment in a kingdom, Ps. xvi. 11. It is also the post of honor, 1 Kings ii. 19; Eph. i. 20; Heb. ii. 9. To a higher degree of rest, rule, joy, favor, power and majesty Christ could not be raised. Nor shall he lose his power, or lay aside his glory. His throne is forever and ever. His Father says to him, sit here, *Until I make thine enemies thy footstool.* "He must reign till he hath put all enemies under his feet," 1 Cor. xv. 25. *Footstool*, as in Ps. xcix. 5; cxxxii. 7, uniformly rendered. The meaning of such language is historically explained in Josh. x. 24. It denotes complete subjection. *Until*, in Ex. xxxiii. 22, rendered *while;* and in Josh. xvii. 14, *forasmuch.* It does not teach that Jesus shall cease to be at God's right hand, so soon as he shall have subdued his foes. It rather implies just the reverse. If he sits there *until* his enemies are brought into subjection, much more shall he hold that place of honor forever We have the

same word rendered in the same way and having the same force in Ps. cxxiii. 2. Christ will not lay aside his crown, nor become a private person after he shall have conquered all his enemies. This clause, indeed the whole verse may be regarded as fully expounded in 1 Cor. xv. 24–28. Compare Matt. xix. 28; 2 Tim. ii. 12; Rev. iii. 21. Christ has all power in heaven and in earth, Matt. xxviii. 18. Patrick's paraphrase of the whole verse is: "This is the decree of the eternal LORD, that the great person whom we expect, and whom I honor as my Lord and Master, shall be advanced (after his sufferings) to the highest dignity in the heavens; and reign with him as the King of all the world, till he have perfectly subdued the most powerful opposers of his kingdom; and overcome death itself, by whom all mankind are conquered."

2. *The* LORD *shall send the rod of thy strength out of Zion.* Phillips: "*The rod of thy strength* or *the sceptre of thy strength, i. e.,* thy powerful sceptre, the sceptre with which thou rulest thy powerful kingdom." Instead of *send*, perhaps it would give the meaning better to read *stretch out* or *stretch forth*, as in Gen. xlviii. 14; 1 Sam. xxiv. 6; xxvi. 11. The sceptre of Christ is made mighty by the power of Jehovah. That the word here rendered *rod* may mean sceptre is clear from Isa. ix. 4; xiv. 5; Jer. xlviii. 17; Ezek. xix. 11. The foregoing explanation is well supported by authority and by the parallel clause. *Rule thou in the midst of thine enemies. Rule,* in Gen. i. 26, 28; Ps. lxxii. 8, *have dominion.* David did indeed subdue some surrounding nations. But he, of whom David was a type, must *have dominion* over all the earth. The imperative form of the verb has the force of a future. See Introduction, § 6. Christ rules all his enemies. The incorrigible are crushed. The rest are saved.

3. *Thy people* shall be *willing in the day of thy power, in the beauties of holiness from the womb of the morning : thou hast the dew of thy youth.* The original is concise and obscure. Of course there is diversity in the renderings. Among them these are the best: John Rogers' Translation: In the daye of thy power shall thy people offre the fre wyll offerings with a holy worshipe; the dewe of thy byrth is of the wombe of the mornynge; Edwards: A voluntary multitude of people will be with thee upon the holy mountains in the day of thy armament; thy young converts will be as numerous as the drops of morning dew. *Willing,* a noun, sometimes rendered *freely,* Ps. liv. 5; Hos. xiv. 4; *willingly,* 2 Chron. xxxv. 8; in Ps. lxviii. 9, *plentiful;* in most cases *free will offerings.* It is plural here and is literally, willingnesses, freenesses, liberalities. The meaning is that God's people should with perfect willingness offer themselves at his call, and this because it was the day of his *power, might, strength.* This is the best sense; though the word also means *wealth, substance, host, army,* because in these there is might. And they shall render their free and hearty service not in the deformity of sin but *in the beauties of holiness.* The sense of the residue of the verse is given by Edwards; Thy young converts shall be as numerous as the drops of morning dew; margin: More than the womb of the morning thou shalt have the dew of thy youth. Compare 2 Sam. xvii. 12. Lowth: "More than the dew from the womb of the morning is the dew of thy progeny." This is the common view. Alexander prefers the idea of *perpetual succession,* as the dew falls fresh daily from the womb of the morning. This is not inconsistent with the foregoing. Calvin: "In this verse the Psalmist sets forth the honors of Christ's kingdom in relation to the number of his subjects, and their prompt and cheerful obedience to his commands."

4. *The* LORD *hath sworn, and will not repent.* In Ps. ii. 7, Jehovah publishes his *decree.* Here he says he has bound himself by an oath to the same effect. Nor will he change his mind. Compare Num. xxiii. 19; 1 Sam. xv. 29. It is evident that

God's oath here is for confirmation of his promise engaging to reward and honor his own Son. *Thou* art *a priest for ever after the order of Melchizedek.* The office of priest embraced these functions, the offering of sacrifices, intercession and benediction. How perfectly qualified for these Christ was is set forth in all the epistle to the Hebrews, which is an inspired treatise on the subject. But Christ was not only a priest, but a priest after a particular *order.* Paul notices several particulars in which Christ was of the *order* of Melchizedek. 1. He united in his own person, as did Melchizedek, the offices of king and priest, Heb. vii. 1. God always forbade such blending of offices in Israel. When king Uzziah assumed the functions of the priesthood, he was smitten with leprosy, 2 Chron. xxvi. 18–21. 2. Like Melchizedek, Christ was much greater in dignity than Aaron and his successors, yea, greater than Abraham himself, for Abraham paid tithes to the king of Salem and the priest of the Most High God, and received a blessing from him, Heb. vii. 2, 4, 7, 9. 3. Neither Melchizedek nor Christ is found in the genealogical tables of the Jewish priesthood, Heb. vii. 3. Neither of them had predecessor or successor in office. 4. As we have no account of the end of Melchizedek's priesthood, so there is absolutely no end to that of Christ, Heb. vii. 3, 16, 17, 24, 25. He is a priest *forever.*

5. *The Lord at thy right hand shall strike through kings in the day of his wrath.* Some think that after *hand* we should add, *O Jehovah.* No doubt the Father is here addressed. The Lord is at his right hand. *Strike through;* in v. 6; Ps. xviii. 38; lxviii. 21, *wound;* in Num. xxiv. 17, *smite;* in Job xxvi. 12, *smite through.* The meaning is that he will subdue all opposers, however mighty. The verb is in the preterite. Things foretold by God are as certain as if they were already accomplished.

6. *He shall judge among the heathen. Judge* by no means necessarily implies severity, but in many cases expresses an act of divine beneficence. See on Ps. vii. 8; ix. 8; liv. 1; lxxii. 2. Messiah delights in showing mercy to the penitent, even among sinners of the *heathen* or *Gentiles;* but he will as a conqueror destroy all, who continue to resist his authority. *He shall fill* the places *with the dead bodies.* The verb is in the preterite. Instead of *places* some supply *nations.* The sense is the same. How terribly nations and potentates have perished in resisting the reign of Messiah is matter of history. Every age affords new and appalling examples. *He shall wound the heads over many countries.* Calvin: He shall break the head over a great country; Doway: He shall crush the heads in the land of many; Edwards: He will crush the heads of his enemies in great numbers against the earth. Much time might be spent in ingenious remarks on the words and import of this clause. But all would at last bring us substantially to this general idea, that Messiah will surely overcome all opposition, even in high places. None can resist the Son of God but to his own eternal undoing.

7. *He shall drink of the brook in the way.* Various and recondite meanings have been claimed as found here. To enumerate them all would be tedious and unprofitable. The true explanation is that as a conqueror in a great contest overcomes all opposition, and refreshes himself at the brook in his victorious march, and thus goes on conquering and to conquer, so shall it be with Messiah. This is a good sense, entirely consistent with the figurative language of the Psalm, wholly natural, and even suggested by the history of one of the Judges of Israel. After his great slaughter of his enemies Samson " was sore athirst, and called on the Lord, and said, Thou hast given this great deliverance into the hand of thy servant: and now shall I die for thirst, and fall into the hand of the uncircumcised? But God clave an hollow place that was in the jaw, and there came water thereout; and when he had drunk, his spirit came again, and he revived," Jud. xv. 18, 19. This agrees with the last clause: *Therefore shall he lift up the head, i. e.,* he shall not go drooping or

faint to his work as a conqueror, but shall gloriously proceed in his conquest of the nations. Without a figure we have the same predictions in Isa. xlii. 3, 4; liii. 10–12. A thousand devices of man may fail; God's *word* and *oath* make sure the glories of the Redeemer's kingdom.

Note. This Psalm is so rich in doctrinal suggestions that a system of divinity, almost entire, might be made out of it. Henry says: "Some have called this Psalm *David's creed*, almost all the articles of the Christian faith being found in it." It also suggests many practical truths. But the REMARKS about to be made cannot be very protracted without interfering with the plan of this work.

DOCTRINAL AND PRACTICAL REMARKS.

1. What a dreadful enemy to truth is prejudice. It bars the door against the entrance of all sound views. Before the coming of Christ, Jewish commentators admitted that this Psalm related to Messiah. It has been wondrously fulfilled in Jesus of Nazareth. Now some Jews wholly deny its Messianic character, and all deny its fulfilment in the *man of sorrows*.

2. Christ is truly divine. David called him *my Lord*, v. 1. We never can explain either the prophetical or historical, the didactic or the practical parts of Scripture without admitting the supreme divinity of the Son.

3. Christ is a King, v. 1. He is a great King, King of kings and Lord of lords. He shall put down all that rise up against him. Cobbin: "What though whole nations are among his bitter enemies, and the hearts of men are as iron and steel to bar every access to their souls, yet when he stretches out his sceptre, and sends forth his law, the most rebellious must obey." The Mediator reigns supreme over all things.

4. It is a blessed truth that Christ the head of the church is far beyond the reach of all human and diabolical malice, and is sitting at the right hand of God, v. 1. Well may the saints in heaven and earth rejoice that men can no longer offer to him personal insults, can spit upon him no more, crown him with thorns no more, crucify him no more.

5. The wickedness of sin is fearful and desperate, inasmuch as it makes men *enemies* to Christ, v. 1. No man with a good heart could oppose him. Henry: "Even Christ himself has enemies that fight against his kingdom and subjects, his honor and interest in the world: there are those who will not have him to reign over them, and thereby they join themselves to Satan, who will not have him to reign at all."

6. All foes of the Mediator shall finally lie prostrate, v. 1. In some way their subjection shall be complete. Many have hardened themselves against him, but none such have ever prospered. Scott: "Many persecuting tyrants have already felt the weight of his vengeance; many more will yet be made sensible of the madness of provoking his indignation." It is no task to him to bring down high looks. He is girded with omnipotence.

7. But the most glorious conquests of Christ are by his word and Spirit. His willing converts are his jewels. By the gospel the Son eminently glorifies the Father. He has the power and the will to subdue the world to himself, v. 2. Out of Zion goes forth his law, Isa. ii. 3. From him his ministers and people receive power by the Holy Ghost. His word is quick and powerful, and sharper than any two-edged sword. Compare 2 Cor. iv. 5. So that his followers stand and sing: "Now thanks be unto God, which always causeth us to triumph in Christ, and maketh manifest the savour of his knowledge by us in every place," 2 Cor. ii. 14.

8. The glory of Christ's kingdom is immense, v. 3. 1. It is composed of persons peculiarly his own. They are his by a free, eternal choice, John vi. 37. They are his even before they are called to a knowledge of himself, Acts xviii. 10. All who shall

finally rise to his enjoyment are *choice* spirits. They are the very *élite* of the universe. 2. They are a *willing* people. So hearty are they in his service that they are *willingness* itself. The "conversion of a soul consists in its being willing to be Christ's, coming under his yoke, and into his interests, with an entire compliancy and satisfaction." 3. They are a pure people. They worship and serve him in *the beauties of holiness.* All of them hate sin. They live and die fighting against it. Sin has not dominion over them. 4. They are very numerous, like the drops of the dew from the womb of the morning. Horsley: "The dew of thy progeny is more than the womb of the morning." French and Skinner: "Thy youths shall come forward for thee as the dew-drops from the womb of the morning." 5. There is everlasting stability to Christ's kingdom, vv. 1–3. Calvin: "What time our minds are agitated by various commotions, let us learn confidently to repose on this support, that however much the world may rage against Christ, it will never be able to hurl him from the right hand of the Father."

9. If believers in their conflicts and perturbations need an everlasting Rock on which to rest, they have it in the unchangeableness of God, his word, his promise, his purpose and his oath, v. 4. The world may be turned upside down; all human institutions may be subverted; all human friendships sundered, and all hell seem to be let loose against the saints; but God and his Christ with their infinite plans and glorious purposes are the same from age to age.

10. Christ is also a Priest, the best Priest that ever was; the only one that ever made full and adequate atonement for sin, and brought in everlasting righteousness; whose intercessions are always prevalent; whose oblation gives effectual ease to the conscience by securing the remission of sins and entire reconciliation with God. Compare Rom. viii. 31–34. Verily such an High Priest became us, Heb. vii. 26. If we would fully understand the riches of divine grace displayed in the priesthood of Christ, let us devoutly study the Epistle to the Hebrews.

11. No power, personal or political, earthly or infernal, separate or combined, can effectually resist Christ in his triumphant march, v. 5. The reason why his adversaries do not all perish at once, is not because he is unable to execute wrath, but because his long-suffering is great, and because many of them shall yet be made willing in the day of his power, and become monuments of his glorious grace. Many a time he *wounds* to heal. He *strikes through* the heart with salutary convictions that he may bring men to repentance. Yet when mild measures fail, his *wrath* is terrible.

12. Gloriously does Christ advance his cause and kingdom among the *heathen*, the Gentiles. The little leaven shall yet leaven the whole lump. The grain of mustard seed shall yet be a tree, in which the fowls of heaven shall lodge. Compare Isa. liv. 1–3; Rev. xix. 6. Christ's reward has not been half measured out to him. The brightest prospects are before him. And he has merited all that was promised him, and all that shall ever be given him.

13. If any should be offended at the tone of this Psalm, let them remember that much of its imagery is taken from war, and that yet it is to be interpreted according to the principles of mercy and grace revealed in the gospel. Calvin: "Should any one be disposed to ask, Where is that spirit of meekness and gentleness with which the Scripture elsewhere informs us he shall be endued? Isa. xlii. 2, 3; lxi. 1, 2; I answer, that, as a shepherd is gentle towards his flock, but fierce and formidable towards wolves and thieves; in like manner, Christ is kind and gentle towards those who commit themselves to his care, while they who wilfully and obstinately reject his yoke, shall feel with what awful and terrible power he is armed."

14. Before honor is humility. It was so with the Redeemer. He first sank, then rose. See Phil. ii. 5–11.

15. We have need of patience that like our Master we may inherit the fulness of the blessings provided for us. Thousands of years ago the Father promised him a glorious kingdom. Long centuries ago Jesus did all and endured all that was necessary to entitle him to the highest glory. Since that he has been expecting until his enemies be made his footstool. Nor has he waited in vain. But he has not yet received his full reward. For " we see not yet all things put under him," Heb. ii. 8. He is not yet *satisfied*. He shall receive higher and yet higher honors. Christ waits with ineffable joy and infinite patience for the complete fulfilment of all that the Father has promised to him. Let us imitate Christ and give God his time. Everything is most beautiful in its season.

PSALM CXI.

1 Praise ye the LORD. I will praise the LORD with *my* whole heart, in the assembly of the upright, and *in* the congregation.

2 The works of the LORD *are* great, sought out of all them that have pleasure therein.

3 His work *is* honourable and glorious: and his righteousness endureth for ever.

4 He hath made his wonderful works to be remembered: the LORD *is* gracious and full of compassion.

5 He hath given meat unto them that fear him: he will ever be mindful of his covenant.

6 He hath shewed his people the power of his works, that he may give them the heritage of the heathen.

7 The works of his hands *are* verity and judgment; all his commandments *are* sure.

8 They stand fast for ever and ever, *and are* done in truth and uprightness.

9 He sent redemption unto his people: he hath commanded his covenant for ever: holy and reverend *is* his name.

10 The fear of the LORD *is* the beginning of wisdom: a good understanding have all they that do *his commandments:* his praise endureth for ever.

THIS is an alphabetical Psalm. See Introduction, § 13. Each sentence begins with a letter of the Hebrew alphabet in order. Some make *Hallelujah* the title. But this is not necessary; though it is doubtless a key-note to the ode. Both the author and date are uncertain. The most probable conjecture is that David wrote it. But on this matter we have no reliable information. Some have maintained, but none have proved, that all Psalms beginning with *Hallelujah* were written after the captivity. Alexander: " There is nothing in the Psalm itself to determine its date, or its historical occasion." Scott dates it B. C. 1037; Clarke, B. C. 535. Some have thought that this and several succeeding Psalms were used in the celebration of the Passover. Perhaps they were; but this would not prove that they were composed for that feast and for no other time. The names of the Most High here found are *Jehovah* LORD and *Jah* LORD, on which see on Ps. i. 2, and introductory observations on Ps. lxviii.

1. *Praise ye the* LORD. *Hallelujah*, as in Ps. civ. 35; cv. 45; cvi. 1. *I will praise the* LORD *with* my *whole heart. Praise*, often *give thanks*, sometimes *confess*, also *thank. Whole heart*, as in Ps. ix. 1, or more exactly in Ps. lxxxvi. 12. *In the assembly of the upright. Assembly*, in Ps. xxv. 14, *secret;* in Ps. lv. 14, *counsel;* and in Ps. lxiv. 2, *secret counsel;* but in Jer. vi. 11; xv. 17; Ezek. xiii. 9, *assembly.* Strictly speaking, it designates a company sitting with closed doors. *Upright*, a very ancient designation of God's people; in Num. xxiii. 10, rendered *righteous.* It is the opposite of crooked, or tortuous. It is often rendered *right, straight.* See on Ps. vii. 10. *And* in *the con-*

gregation. Congregation, as in Ps. i. 5; vii. 7; in Ps. cvi. 17, 10, *company. Assembly* and *congregation* are strictly parallel. Abenezra: "I will praise the Lord with all my heart, both privately and publicly." The church of England retains that shade of thought, "secretly among the faithful, and in the congregation." Luther probably gives the precise idea: "I thank the Lord here in this public assembly, where we are in a peculiar manner by ourselves, as it were in secret counsel, and no heathen or stranger must be beside us."

2. *The works of the* LORD *are great, sought out of all them that have pleasure therein.* *Works*, as in Ps. viii. 3, 6, and often in Ps. civ. cvi. cvii.; also rendered *deeds, labors, doings.* It embraces works of creation, providence and grace. *Sought out, inquired into, searched for. Have pleasure, desires, delights* or *likings.* The studies of good men in all ages and in all parts of the world have been diligently turned to the wonders of what God hath wrought.

3. *His work* is *honorable and glorious. Work*, not the singular of *works* as in v. 2, but a word of the same import also rendered *act, deed. Honorable* and *glorious*, two nouns both rendered according to the taste of the translator *honor, glory, majesty*, and as adjectives *goodly.* When God makes or does the least thing, he acts like a God, and his workmanship is worthy of him. *And his righteousness endureth for ever.* There appears no good reason for limiting the word *righteousness* to any particular exercise of it. God's rectitude lasts for ever, *stands to eternity.*

4. *He hath made his wonderful works to be remembered. Wonderful works, wonders, marvels, miracles, marvellous works*, Ex. iii. 20; xxxiv. 10; Jud. vi. 13; Ps. ix. 1. Even where men most desire it, they are not able to banish from the world the memory of much that God has done. Everything done by the Almighty is marvellous; but some of his works are so striking as to amaze and confound, if they do not convince and persuade. This remark is peculiarly applicable to the benignant acts of God. *The* LORD is *gracious and full of compassion. Gracious*, always has that meaning. See on Ps. lxxxvi. 3, 15. *Full of compassion*, one word, often *merciful.* See on Ps. lxxviii. 38. Edwards: He instituted a memorial of his wonderful works; gracious and merciful is Jehovah; church of England: The merciful and gracious Lord hath so done his marvellous works, that they ought to be had in remembrance.

5. *He hath given meat unto them that fear him.* Luther thinks this Psalm was designed to be sung at the Passover, and that this verse has special respect to the food then eaten. This may be so; but it as well suits many another time. Every wholesome meal demands gratitude. The paschal supper, the manna, bread and water are often used as figures of spiritual good things. So *meat* in this verse may include spiritual food. *Meat*, commonly *prey.* The generic idea seems to be that of food obtained without toil or culture. Thus the manna was *prey* or food obtained without culture. *He will ever be mindful of his covenant.* This may refer to God's covenant with Noah, Gen. viii. 21, 22; to his covenant with Abraham, Gen. xvii. 4–8; to the covenant of Sinai, Deut. iv. 13, 23; to God's covenant with David, 2 Sam. vii. 12–17; or to the covenant of grace made with our first parents in Eden, Gen. iii. 15, and often confirmed. To a pious Israelite all these covenants were sources of wisdom, and encouragement. The promises of this verse, whatever their import, are limited to such as *fear* God.

6. *He hath shewed his people the power of his works, that he may give them the heritage of the heathen. People, nation. Works*, as in v. 2. *Heritage*, that which had descended to them from their fathers. For their sins God drove out the idolatrous Canaanites. In his sovereignty he gave their country to the descendants of his friend Abraham.

7. *The works of his hands* are *verity and judgment. Works*, as in vv. 2, 6, meaning

all that he has done. *Verity, truth, faithfulness.* His works agree with his promises and engagements. *Judgment,* as in Ps. i. 5; cvi. 3. The best rendering here is *right.* God never does *wrong* to effect his plans. *All his commandments* are *sure.* *Commandments,* in Ps. xix. 8, *statutes;* in Ps. cxix. invariably *precepts.* It embraces all the will of God made known to us to direct our actions. *Sure,* a participle, *faithful, established,* trustworthy. This clause may be taken as parallel to that which immediately precedes it, or as an inference from it. God never enjoins anything inconsistent with the most perfect rectitude.

8. *They stand fast for ever and ever.* Human codes are many, long, intricate, often contradictory. But God's law is one, brief, harmonious and unrepealable. The sum of the ten commandments is the rule of heaven itself and will be for *ever* and *ever.* The Lord is of one mind and changes not. And [his works] are *done in truth and uprightness. Truth,* in v. 7, *verity. Uprightness,* in v. 1, *upright,* an adjective, but so rendered as to give the sense in good English.

9. *He sent redemption unto his people. Redemption,* cognate to the word so rendered in Ps. xlix. 8. It embraces deliverance by any means, with or without a ransom price. In Ps. lv. 18 and elsewhere, the kindred verb is rendered *hast delivered.* The reference in this clause is no doubt to the redemption from Egypt; but that event in many ways shadowed forth eternal redemption by the Lamb of God. *He hath commanded his covenant forever. Covenant,* as in v. 5. *Commanded,* commonly so rendered, also *appointed, charged.* There seems to be here a *special* reference to the Sinaic covenant. But it is not left optional with us whether we will accept God's covenant however or whenever proposed to us. We may not take it up and lay it down again. The reason is found in God's excellent and glorious nature: *Holy and reverend* is *his name. Reverend,* in Ps. xlv. 4 and often, *terrible;* in Hab. i. 7, *dreadful;* a participle, literally *to be feared.* Clarke: Holy and tremendous is his name. Holy reverence becomes us whenever we speak or think of God's names, titles, attributes, word or ordinances.

10. *The fear of the* LORD is *the beginning of wisdom.* On the nature of the holy fear of God, see on Ps. ii. 11. *Beginning,* the same as the first word in the book of Genesis, also rendered *first, first fruits, chief, chiefest.* There is no wisdom in men till they fear God. When they do fear God, that is the wisest thing they do. No man ever attains to any wisdom higher than this. Compare Job xxviii. 28; Pr. i. 7; ix. 10. "Wisdom is the principal thing; therefore get wisdom." Pr. iv. 7. It is a great thing to be wise unto salvation. Without this all skill is but cunning, and all knowledge vain. *A good understanding have all they that do* his commandments. This clause is parallel to the preceding. The word rendered *understanding* is also rendered *wisdom,* Pr. xii. 8; xxiii. 9. To keep God's law is to fear him. *His praise endureth for ever. Praise,* a cognate of the verb in the word *Hallelujah* at the beginning. *Endureth forever,* as in v. 3. *Hallelujahs* shall never cease.

DOCTRINAL AND PRACTICAL REMARKS.

1. In our meditations and writings on religion there is scope for the exercise of all our ingenuity. Nor is it unlawful for us curiously to arrange in poetical or alphabetical order divine truths as the Psalmist has here done. Only we should avoid silly conceits and puerilities.

2. If we would teach the duties and exercises of religion most effectually, we must do it practically. *I will praise the Lord,* immediately follows, *Praise ye the Lord,* v. 1. "Words teach, example sways."

3. In all acts of worship, in particular in praising God, we should be very careful

not only to avoid gross hypocrisy, but to be entirely hearty in the work, v. 1. It is no easy matter to avoid cold affections.

4. While we ought privately to engage in the duties of religion, this cannot exempt us from the obligation to confess God before men, even in the *congregation* and *assembly*, v. 1. Tholuck: "The concealment of praise is tantamount to depriving the Lord of half his glory." Dickson: "Solemn meetings of God's children for his public worship and furthering one another therein, are ordinances of God appointed for that end." They have public worship in heaven, Rev. vii. 9–12; xi. 16, 17; xix. 1–7.

5. There is nothing in true religion which discourages science truly so called, v. 2. We have had no better students of nature or of history than those who have been students of providence and redemption. It is truly a bad sign for one to have no heart for diligently considering any of the works of God. It greatly commends this duty that a devout mind can never be at a loss for matter of praise. Above, beneath, within, and around us, in nature, providence and grace we behold unspeakable wonders. And it is a mark of the amazing stupidity, blindness and perversity of the unregenerate heart that it is reluctant devoutly to dwell on such themes.

6. In all God's works there is nothing low, or wrong, or degrading, v. 3. Everything is *very good*. Gill: "There is nothing mean and trifling done by him; nothing unworthy of him in nature, providence and grace. Every work of his serves to display his glory, and set off the greatness of his majesty." This is most true in the wondrous scheme of salvation, 2 Cor. iii. 7–11.

7. The most amazing perverseness in man is proven by the fact that he does not remember what God has so arranged as that it would seem impossible that it should be forgotten, v. 4. No small part of piety consists in cherishing and treasuring up the memory of his beneficent acts.

8. Let us study with care and admire with heartiness the grace and compassion of God, v. 4. There is not a day of our lives that does not demand of us some pious notice of the divine kindness, 'in sparing, and pardoning, and restoring, and preserving us when we have deserved to be utterly destroyed.'

9. It is delightful to contemplate the amplitude of the provisions God has made for supplying all the wants of those that fear him, v. 5. Thus in nature what floods of light, what billions of tons of atmospheric air, what immeasurable reservoirs of water are found for our refreshment and support. Who ever fears that all the water will be drunk up, or the air be poisoned by respiration, or the light quenched by the darkness of earth? God's resources are illimitable. Compare Isa. xxxiii. 16.

10. God will never break covenant with any of his creatures, vv. 5, 9. For the human race he made a covenant with Noah, and although since that time men have atrociously sinned against him, he has faithfully kept his word, Isa. xl. 6–8.

11. Although miracles, in the strict sense of that term, have ceased to be wrought among men, yet great, supernatural works illustrating the power of God are continually manifest in nature and grace, and the righteous see them, vv. 6, 7. Every conversion from sin to holiness is an illustrious display of the power, wisdom and grace of God.

12. While all human governments are liable to decay, and their rulers to change, so that both fundamental and statute laws may be set aside, yet God's ways are constant and unchangeable, v. 8. With him the immutable rules of justice never swerve.

13. If God's laws are so pure and infinitely excellent, our obedience ought to be prompt, universal and most hearty, vv. 7, 8. Every word of God is pure. Man never so well consults his own temporal and eternal good as when he most exactly conforms his heart and life to Scripture principles.

14. Nothing is more fitting than praise to God for all deliverances vouchsafed to us, especially for the greatest of all deliverances, redemption from sin and wrath and hell, v. 9. Compare Gal. iii. 13.

15. Is God's name *holy* and *reverend?* then let us be vigilant, lest at any time we should use it in vain, v. 9. Henry: "Truly it is shocking when men mingle the name of the Most High and of the Saviour of lost men with their vain and idle jibes and angry conversation."

16. Let us never forget that the true, holy fear of God is an essential element of genuine piety, v. 10. He who has no such fear has no grace. Tholuck: "The fear of the Lord is the starting point of all true *wisdom*: any inquiry respecting things celestial or things terrestrial, if conducted in the fear of the Lord, is sure to lead to the right way: but it is no less the true source of the real wisdom of life," 1 Tim. iv. 8. Yet, alas! how few show that they are taught from above. Calvin: "All who are ignorant of the purpose for which they live are fools and madmen. But to serve God is the purpose for which we have been born, and for which we are preserved in life. There is, therefore, no worse blindness, no insensibility so grovelling, as when we contemn God and place our affections elsewhere."

17. There is such a thing as true religion. It is attainable. It is heavenly wisdom, v. 10. It is not of an unintelligible nature. It consists in loving, fearing and obeying God. He, who now submits his heart to the teachings and guidance of divine grace, may be poor, or sick, or feeble-minded, or uneducated, or cast off by the world; but he is safe and God will be his portion forever. Calvin: "They are usually deemed wise who look well to their own interests, who can pursue a temporizing policy, who have the acuteness and artifice of preserving the favorable opinion of the world, and who even practise deception upon others. But even were I to grant that this character belongs to them, yet is their wisdom unprofitable and perverse, because true wisdom manifests itself in the observance of the law."

18. As the work of praise is to last always, let us gladly prepare ourselves by practice for so heavenly an employment. "Religion is the perfection of wisdom, practice the best instructor, and thanksgiving the sweetest recreation."

Psalm CXII.

1 Praise ye the Lord. Blessed *is* the man *that* feareth the Lord, *that* delighteth greatly in his commandments.

2 His seed shall be mighty upon earth: the generation of the upright shall be blessed.

3 Wealth and riches *shall be* in his house: and his righteousness endureth for ever.

4 Unto the upright there ariseth light in the darkness: *he is* gracious, and full of compassion, and righteous.

5 A good man sheweth favour, and lendeth: he will guide his affairs with discretion.

6 Surely he shall not be moved for ever: the righteous shall be in everlasting remembrance.

7 He shall not be afraid of evil tidings: his heart is fixed, trusting in the Lord.

8 His heart *is* established, he shall not be afraid, until he see *his desire* upon his enemies.

9 He hath dispersed, he hath given to the poor; his righteousness endureth for ever; his horn shall be exalted with honour.

10 The wicked shall see *it*, and be grieved; he shall gnash with his teeth, and melt away: the desire of the wicked shall perish.

THIS Psalm very strikingly corresponds to Psalm cxi. Like it, it is alphabetical, has ten verses, each of the first eight verses has two clauses, each of the last two verses has three clauses. From these facts Muis and others not unreasonably infer that these two odes were probably written by the same author. The scope of this Psalm is to commend true piety, and to show that God is not unmindful of the services and sufferings of his saints. This seems to be an expansion of the last verse of Psalm cxi. Tholuck calls it "a Psalm of instruction, similar to Psalms i. xxxvii." Pool says it "is a declaration of God's powerful and universal providence towards all men, and especially towards his afflicted people." Scott dates it B. C. 1040; Clarke, B. C. 535. He treats with respect the statement of the Vulgate that it was written by Haggai and Zechariah. The names of the Most High here found are *Jehovah* LORD and *Jah* LORD, on which see on Psalm i. 2 and introductory remarks to Psalm lxviii.

1. *Praise ye the* LORD, literally, *hallelujah;* see on Ps. civ. 35; cv. 45; cvi. 1. *Blessed* is *the man* that *feareth the* LORD, that *delighteth greatly in his commandments.* *Blessed*, as in Psalm i. 1, literally, O the blessednesses. He is blessed in many particulars, some of which are noticed in subsequent parts of the poem. But who is thus richly blessed? The man that *feareth the* LORD, has true godly reverence; and as a proper fruit of such piety greatly delights in the commandments of God. *Commandments*, as in Psalm xix. 8 and often in Ps. cxix. A little love to God's commandments is not enough. We must *greatly delight* in them; else our imperious lusts will carry us away. Alexander: "As in the preceding Psalm the fear of the Lord is declared to be the principle of all true wisdom, so here it is declared to be the source of all true happiness."

2. *His seed shall be mighty upon earth. Mighty*, also *strong, valiant, champions;* see on Psalm xix. 5. The purpose of God is to secure on the earth a godly seed, Mal. ii. 15. We hardly know how terribly the seed of evil-doers is cut off, and how wonderfully God preserves and multiplies the descendants of good men. Where are the acknowledged seed of the authors of the Smithfield fires? Yet the descendants of John Rogers, one of their martyr victims, are numbered, even in the United States of America, by the thousand, perhaps by the ten thousand. And the seed of the godly are *valiant* for the truth, for righteousness, for the glory of the Redeemer. Their influence is felt far and wide. *The generation of the upright shall be blessed. Generation*, the race, corresponding to *seed* in the preceding clause. *Upright*, as in Psalm iii. 1. It occurs again in v. 4; see on Ps. vii. 10. *Blessed*, not the same word as in v. 1, but a word of benediction; see on Ps. v. 12.

3. *Wealth and riches* shall be *in his house.* The translation cannot be improved. True piety has God's blessing in all things; see on Ps. i. 3. If any choose to refer the terms of this clause to the *true riches*, and make them designate the infinite blessings of salvation, the sense is good, and the doctrine true. This view is favored by the next clause: *And his righteousness endureth for ever.* The same words are found in v. 9. In Psalm cxi. 3, the very same is applied to God. We may take it as expressing either the stability of the good man's principles and character, or his justification before God. Both are in fact secured to him, Job xvii. 9; Phil. i. 6; Rom. viii. 30–34. All God's people have integrity of heart, righteousness of principle and of life, and righteousness of person; see on Ps. xxiv. 5.

4. *Unto the upright there ariseth light in the darkness. Upright*, as in v. 2. *Light* is the emblem and sum of all good, as darkness is of all evil. In the midst of all that befalls the good man in the shape of distress, perplexity and calamity, there remains to him the sum of all blessedness, the favor of God, the smile of heaven, the light of God's countenance; see on Ps. xcvii. 11. He is *gracious, and full of compassion, and righteous.* Both God and his people are *righteous.* Those, who fear God, in their measure resemble him. They have not omnipotence, omniscience, omnipresence, self-existence, independence, eternity, unchangeableness; nor any perfections in

infinitude; but in their measure they are like him in holiness, justice, goodness, mercy, truth and faithfulness. The fact that *upright* is plural and the other adjectives singular is of no significance. Every *upright* man is gracious, full of compassion, and righteous. Calvin and some others think that the *light* of his people is Jehovah, and that the epithets *gracious*, etc., here apply to God.

5. *A good man sheweth favour, and lendeth.* *Good*, commonly so rendered, sometimes *glad, cheerful, merry, beautiful, kindly, pleasant.* The Chaldee and Hengstenberg have *blessed*; the Syriac, *honest*; Secker and Alexander, *happy.* The term is very comprehensive. Some prefer to read, Good or blessed is the man, who sheweth favor. This does not essentially change the sense. *Sheweth favour*, a participle the cognate of the word rendered *gracious* in v. 4. We might read *dealeth graciously, sheweth mercy, hath pity*, Gen. xxxiii. 11; Ps. xxxvii. 21; Pr. xix. 17. *Lendeth*, not for usury, but out of mercy. The Jewish law strictly forbade any increase to be received from a distressed brother, Lev. xxv. 35–37. Calvin: "He puts *lending* as if it were the fruit of mercy; for the usurer also lends, but it is that, under the false pretence of assisting the distressed, he may plunder them." The man, who practises self-denial that he may be able to help the necessitous, will be just and prudent in his worldly business: *He will guide his affairs with discretion.* *Affairs*, more commonly rendered *words*, but also *matters, things*, Ps. xxxv. 20; ci. 3. *Discretion*, see Isa. xxviii. 26, most commonly *judgment, justice, right.* Alexander: "He shall best secure his own interests by treating those of others justly and generously." Calvin: "The righteous will manage their affairs with prudence and discernment; so that, in their domestic affairs, they will neither be too lavish nor sordidly parsimonious; but in every thing they will study to combine frugality with economy, without giving way to luxury."

6. *Surely he shall not be moved for ever.* *Surely*, perhaps *for*; see on Ps. ix. 18. Compare Gen. ii. 3; xxix. 32; Ex. iii. 12. *Be moved*, see on Ps. xv. 5. Alexander: "He shall not be moved from his prosperous condition, or from his position as a righteous man." Morison: "He shall not perish with ungodly men, nor shall he be deprived of the favor of his God." *The righteous shall be in everlasting remembrance.* All these words are to be taken in their usual signification. The promise here made is so far fulfilled in this life that a just man in the general is allowed to have a good name; but even if in life he is slandered, the children of his revilers build and whiten his sepulchre. Every prophet, whom the Jews slew, was subsequently acknowledged to have been a good man sent of God. But most of the records of earth have been already burned up, and the rest soon will be. It is a small thing to be judged of man's judgment. The only permanent and infallible record is on high. A good name among the saints in glory and their solid friendship will be invaluable and immortal. Above all, the righteous shall be held in everlasting remembrance by God himself, Mal. iii. 16, 17; Rev. iii. 5.

7. *He shall not be afraid of evil tidings.* The upright may hear bad news in abundance; but by nothing shall he be "frightened from his propriety." Nay, more, he shall not be tormented with constant apprehensions of bad news. He has good cause for calmness and self-possession: *His heart is fixed, trusting in the* LORD. *Fixed*, in Psalm lvii. 7, as here; in Psalm li. 10, *right.* He reposes *confidence* in Jehovah. He is a Rock, and trust in him gives stability and quiet when nothing else will.

8. *His heart is established, he shall not be afraid.* *Established*, in Psalm cxi. 8, *stands fast*; we might read, is *sustained*, Gen. xxvii. 37; Isa. lix. 16; Ps. iii. 5; *upheld*, or *stayed*, Ps. xxxvii. 17, 24; Cant. ii. 5. The good man's calmness and courage shall not fail *Until he see* his desire *upon his enemies.* *His desire*, better omitted; see on Psalm liv. 7; xcii. 11. As in Psalm cx. 1, *until* does not limit the sense to the time

mentioned, but *even until* then. Calvin: " Genuine stability is that which the prophet here describes, and which consists in reposing with unshaken confidence in God."

9. *He hath dispersed, he hath given to the poor. Dispersed*, everywhere else rendered *scattered*. It expresses liberal and habitual bountifulness. *Given*, not lent, but bestowed, expecting nothing. *His righteousness endureth for ever;* see on v. 3. Pool thinks by *righteousness* here we are to understand liberality, and cites Pr. x. 2; xi. 4; Dan. iv. 27; 2 Cor. ix. 9, 10, in proof. *His horn shall be exalted with honour;* see on Ps. lxxv. 4, 5. Such blessings as God bestows on the upright, and such graces as he enables him to manifest are not without their effect upon the ungodly.

10. *The wicked shall see it, and be grieved.* The *wicked*, in Psalm i., *ungodly*. He shall see how immeasurably the good man excels the sinner, and shall *be grieved, have sorrow*, or *be provoked to anger*. The passions of the wicked make all the mercies of God to his people sources of torment to themselves. *He shall gnash with his teeth, and melt away.* On the first phrase see on Ps. xxxv. 16. Compare Ps. xxxvii. 12; Lam. ii. 16; Acts vii. 54. The phrase denotes violent rage. Sometimes it denotes impotent rage, Matt. viii. 12; xiii. 42, 50; xxiv. 51; xxv. 30; Luke xiii. 28. This latter is the shade of idea here conveyed. Malignant passions, not permitted to be vented on their victims, turn with fearful power on those, who indulge them. *Melt away*, elsewhere, *faint*, be *discouraged*. The term expresses the death of hope, the extinction of all heart. This is even more fully brought out by the final clause: *The desire of the wicked shall perish. Desire;* the word is used either in a good or bad sense. In the Psalter it occurs first in Psalm x. 3, 17, on which see. It is sometimes rendered *lust*, Ps. lxxviii. 30. Here the special *desire* of the wicked seems to be for the overthrow of the righteous. He shall at last give up all such hope as utterly vain. Compare Job viii. 13; Pr. x. 28; xi. 7; Luke xvi. 24–26. If more terrible conceptions ever enter the human mind than those suggested by this verse, what are they?

DOCTRINAL AND PRACTICAL REMARKS.

1. If in the work of praise we are truly hearty, we shall not be forgotten of God, v. 1.

2. Although the substance of our songs may not treat directly of God, but chiefly of things connected with true piety, yet it is proper to use them in his worship, v. 1. We do *praise* him whenever we celebrate in a right manner the blessings he bestows on his servants.

3. The greatest want in the world is the want of more piety, v. 1. If to do and to suffer the will of God were our meat and drink, our piety would afford us unspeakable consolations. If we made more of our religion, our religion would do more for us. Calvin: "A man cannot be regarded as a genuine observer of the law, until he has attained to this—that the delight which he takes in the law of God renders obedience agreeable to him."

4. As false religions entail innumerable evils on the posterity of those who embrace them; so it is the glory of the gospel that it carries countless blessings to the children of God's sincere worshippers, v. 2. Morison: "The prayers, the instructions, the examples, and especially the *faith* of a good man, are a rich inheritance to his children."

5. Miracles are not necessary to secure to the righteous and their offspring comfort and competency in worldly affairs, v. 3. Godliness introduces economy both in time and money. The habits of reflection and order connected with true religion tend to the same result. "Where due care is taken to train up our families in the fear of God, our children will be blessed, and piety will create industry, and industry honest prosperity." Blessed is the man who learns the rules of frugality, and, at the same time,

of enlarged liberality. It will be true to the end of the world that "it is more blessed to give than to receive," Acts xx. 35.

6. Although justification is not from everlasting, yet it is to everlasting, vv. 3, 9. There is no condemnation to them who are in Christ Jesus. They are not under wrath; they are under grace.

7. In like manner the riches of divine grace in the heart are through the divine mercy and the indwelling of the Holy Spirit, imperishable, v. 3. To these nothing can compare. They are durable and unsearchable. Floods cannot drown them. Tempests cannot bear them away. Even the last conflagration shall not consume them.

8. The Scripture does not deny that God's people have many and sore trials. It warns them that in this life they are to expect tribulation. But then their supports are many and mighty, v. 4. If the whole portion of God's people were in this life, their case would be sad indeed, 1 Cor. xv. 19. But even here they are not deserted as the wicked are. Cobbin: "If the dark clouds of life pass over the God-fearing man, the light of heaven will break through those clouds, and cheer his heart." No man's estate can grow, if the Almighty blow upon it, Hag. i. 9.

9. A cold, harsh, severe, untender character is no part of the product of Christianity, vv. 4, 5. Godliness is God-likeness. If we would be God's children, we must be merciful, gracious, tender, pitiful. He, who is harsh to the unfortunate, and cruel to the needy, who never forgives the wayward, nor seeks to recover the prodigal, is not like God. Horne: "Ill-nature and avarice are their own tormentors; but love and liberality do good to themselves by doing it to others, and enjoy all the happiness which they cause."

10. To such it shall be well in time and in eternity. God's perfections are their protection. God's providence shall shield them, guide them, supply them. Nothing can harm them, v. 5. Calvin: "It shall be well with those who are gracious and communicative." Green thus renders the first clause of v. 5: The man who is liberal and lendeth shall prosper; Mudge: A man that showeth favor and lendeth shall do well; Horsley: Happy is the man who is gracious and lendeth.

11. But let us not forget that all solid excellence of personal character is based in essential *justice* or righteousness, v. 4. Nothing can redeem from infamy a character essentially destitute of the element of justice. It is possible to live in peace and in considerable comfort with one who sacredly regards our rights and faithfully performs the obligations of sheer justice. But no community or family can be quiet when the foundations of equity are subverted.

12. One of the happy fruits of genuine piety, manifested in persons, families and communities, is the prudence engendered in worldly affairs, v. 5. Christian principle alike opposes greed and prodigality. It moderates our desires. It begets salutary caution. Godliness has promise of the life that now is and of that which is to come. Dickson: "Grace and godliness, sound and fruitful faith, do not make men fools without discretion, but consist well with prudence and foresight, in ordering their affairs wisely, and teach them to give, when, what, and to whom they should give, as the circumstances of time, place, and person, need of the party, and their own ability require."

13. Whatever may befall the children of God, their final salvation is certain, v. 6. That is enough and more than enough eternally to overbalance any evils, trials, or disadvantages to which they may be subject in time.

14. Let the reviled, slandered and injured wait till God fully takes up their case. He is mindful of them now and he will hold them in *everlasting remembrance,* v. 6. Dickson: "Albeit the world may disregard the believer, and traduce him while he

liveth, and calumniate him when he is dead, yet his memory shall remain fresh and fragrant before God, angels, and good men who know him."

15. There is a strange power in piety to beget calmness, self-possession and firmness of character, even in the midst of fierce assaults and of dire conflicts with every kind of adversity and adversary, vv. 7, 8. Luther: "Unless there were in us divine strength communicated by Christ, it would be impossible that we could stand against such numerous and mighty assaults of temptation." The righteous will not be dismayed when all nature is dissolving. Arnd: "Look at examples,—how Moses says at the Red sea, Stand still and see the salvation of God. How does Jehosaph stand firm as a wall when a hundred thousand men invade the land, and he slays them all with one song of praise! How firmly does David stand when hunted by Saul! How overwhelmed is Saul with despair when his land is invaded by the Philistines, and he seeks advice from a witch! What firmness is in Daniel when in the lions' den! What joy in Stephen! How did the holy Basilius say when Cæsar Valens threatened him so dreadfully: 'Such bugbears should be set before children!' Athanasius, when Julian persecuted him: 'He is a mist and will soon disappear.'" There is indeed a fascinating power in the world to make its devotees dream of happiness as long as their prosperity lasts. But it is only the child of God who can in triumph repeat Hab. iii. 17, 18.

16. The righteous law of requital, established by God in the world, will in the end bring all things right. As the good man has dispersed and given to the poor, so shall it finally come to him, v. 9, not indeed of merit, but through the abounding grace of the Lord.

17. Let every pious sufferer under the wrongs, slanders and misdeeds of others patiently wait for the day when God will exalt his horn, v. 9. Horne: "At the last day when the thrones of the mighty shall be cast down, and the sceptres of tyrants broken in pieces, then shall he lift up his head, and be exalted to partake of the glory of his Redeemer." Dickson: "Albeit the righteous may have their reputation blasted among men, yet God, in due time, shall make them honorable."

18. Surely Christians ought to pity sinners, v. 10. Their case is sad indeed. They are under strong delusions. They are subject to many trials. Their resources in themselves are very limited. At any moment they may lose their earthly all, and be forever ruined. In this life too, they are very unhappy. They have not benevolence enough to rejoice in the well-being of the righteous. They are often filled with envy. Their prospects are dismal. O Christian, pity and pray for your ungodly neighbor.

19. Let sinners beware. Their day is coming. Already have they tokens in themselves of what is yet to be. Horne: "The sight of Christ in glory with his saints will, in an inexpressible manner, torment the crucifiers of the One, and the persecutors of the others." Wicked men may cast God's cords asunder, they may deny his existence, his attributes and his government; but, poor souls! they will yet find their sins crushing them to the lowest hell. "They shall not have their desire, either of good things for themselves, here or hereafter, or of evil things for the righteous." All, all will end in disappointment and despair. "Lord, form us by thy grace to the character of thy redeemed people, that we may possess their unspeakable felicity."

PSALM CXIII.

1 Praise ye the LORD. Praise, O ye servants of the LORD, praise the name of the LORD.

2 Blessed be the name of the LORD from this time forth and for evermore.

3 From the rising of the sun unto the going down of the same the LORD'S name *is* to be praised.

4 The LORD *is* high above all nations, *and* his glory above the heavens.

5 Who *is* like unto the LORD our God, who dwelleth on high,

6 Who humbleth *himself* to behold *the things that are* in heaven, and in the earth!

7 He raiseth up the poor out of the dust, *and* lifteth the needy out of the dunghill;

8 That he may set *him* with princes, *even* with the princes of his people.

9 He maketh the barren woman to keep house, *and to be* a joyful mother of children. Praise ye the LORD.

THIS Psalm is without title. Some have ascribed it to Samuel; more, to David. The authorship is uncertain. Verses 7, 8, are evidently taken from the song of Hannah, 1 Sam. ii. 8. It is probable too that verse 9 alludes to the mother of Samuel. Anderson well observes that this little ode "is alike elegant in its structure, and devotional in its sentiment." Tradition, perhaps history, may be said to teach us that this and the five Psalms immediately succeeding were sung both at the Passover and at the feast of tabernacles. The scope of this ode has considerable breadth. Luther: "This is a most conspicuous and most blessed prophecy of the kingdom of Christ, and of its extension from the rising unto the setting of the sun throughout all the kingdoms of the earth." Morison: "This beautiful ode may be regarded as a celebration of the omniscient and all-disposing providence of the Most High, more particularly in reference to his afflicted church." Scott dates it B. C. 1040; Clarke, B. C. 535. The names of the Almighty in it are *Jehovah* LORD and *Jah* LORD, on which see on Ps. i. 2, and introductory remarks on Ps. lxviii.

1. *Praise ye the* LORD. *Praise, O ye servants of the* LORD, *praise the name of the* LORD. The word rendered *praise* is in each case the same; and *Jah*, the first word rendered LORD, is a poetic abbreviation of *Jehovah* LORD. "By this often repetition, he stirreth up our cold dulness to praise God." He thus also shows how weighty and urgent is the duty of praising the Most High. In Scripture eminent and pious men are first called God's *servants;* afterwards all his people. The address here is perhaps indiscriminate.

2. *Blessed be the name of the* LORD *from this time forth and for evermore.* One of the ways of *praising* God is by *blessing* him, heaping benedictions upon his worthy name. See on Ps. v. 12.

3. *From the rising of the sun unto the going down of the same the* LORD'S *name* is *to be praised.* On the first clause see on Ps. l. 1. The Chaldee, Septuagint, Ethiopic, Vulgate and Fabritius have *is worthy to be praised;* Arabic, *let his name be blessed;* Venema, Amesius, Piscator, Junius and Tremellius, *let his name be praised;* Edwards and Jebb, *praised be his name;* Alexander, *be the name of Jehovah blessed;* Calvin agrees with the common version. In 2 Sam. xxii. 4; Ps. xviii. 3, the same participle is rendered *worthy to be praised.* The clause contains a prediction that God's name shall be praised the world over.

4. *The* LORD is *high above all nations.* His authority over all nations is sovereign and complete. He disposes of them as he pleases. Clarke: "He governs all, he provides for all; therefore let all give him praise." And *his glory* [is] *above the heavens. Glory, honor,* see on Ps. iii. 3. In Ps. vii. 5, it is *glory;* in Ps. cxii. 9, *honor.* By the *heavens* we may possibly understand the *angels,* Job xv. 15. But it is safer to explain the clause here as in Ps. viii. 1. Compare also Ps. xxxvi. 5; lvii. 5, 10, 11.

5. *Who is like unto the* LORD *our God, who dwelleth on high,*

6. *Who humbleth* himself *to behold* the things that are *in heaven, and in the earth.*
Who dares to take up this awful challenge? Who dares to compare himself or any creature with the Most High? The rendering of v. 5 cannot be improved. That of v. 6 doubtless gives the sense, though by supplying several words. Edwards throws the two verses into one: Who is like Jehovah our God, that dwelleth on high in the heavens, and yet condescends to behold the things that are upon the earth? Lowth's version is very brief:

> Who is like Jehovah our God?
>   Who dwelleth high,
> Who looketh low,
>   In heaven and on earth.

Some think that the phrase *in heaven* should follow *dwelleth on high,* and *on earth* should follow *humbleth himself to behold.* Passages are often to be thus construed. See Cant. i. 5; Matt. vii. 6. But this arrangement is not best here; for God truly and infinitely *humbles* himself to look at things in heaven, Job xv. 15. If it is condescension in Jehovah to care for and commune with angels, how much more to dwell with men and revive the heart of the contrite ones!

7 *He raiseth up the poor out of the dust,* and *lifteth the needy out of the dunghill.* The terms of this verse are well rendered, and are to be taken in their usual import. *Poor* is parallel to *needy,* and *dust* to *dunghill.* On *poor* see on Ps. xli. 1. On *needy* see on Ps. ix. 18. Alexander: "*Dust* and *dunghill* are common figures in all languages for a degraded social state." Compare Ps. vii. 5; Lam. iv. 5. No doubt the Psalmist here quotes from 1 Sam. ii. 8, as also in verse

8. *That he may* set him *with princes,* even *with the princes of his people. Princes,* sometimes rendered *nobles,* and when descriptive of character *free, willing, liberal.* See on Ps. xlvii. 9. *His people, his nation.* The changes made in the social and political standing of men are to many sources of disgust and uneasiness. But when we learn that they come not by chance, but by the Lord, we may well be quiet. "Shall I not do as I please with mine own?"

9. *He maketh the barren woman to keep house,* and to be *a joyful mother of children.* Though not literal, the rendering gives the sense in good English. What is here said was strikingly illustrated in the case of Hannah, Sarah, Rebecca, Rachel, the mother of Samson, and of thousands of mothers in Israel. Ages after this Psalm was written John the Baptist was born of a woman childless until she was advanced in life. Those, who spiritualize this passage, refer this clause to the Gentile church. Such a use of the general conception here presented is just, Isa. liv. 1–3; though the prophet probably intended no such use of this particular passage. *Praise ye the* LORD, or *Hallelujah.* The closing language of a Psalm is often like that at the beginning.

DOCTRINAL AND PRACTICAL REMARKS.

1. Let no man be offended at any urgency in reminding him of the great and solemn duties of religion. We must sometimes double and even treble our earnest calls to duty, v. 1. Excellent as is the work of praise, the heart of sinful man reluctates at it.

2. While it is the duty of all men to make known the honor of God, it is especially the duty of those who are his *servants* by office and by profession not to keep silence on this glorious theme, v. 1.

3. Are we at heart God's willing *servants?* v. 1. Or does our entire religion consist in profession? Are we swift, diligent and earnest in our own cause, and slow, negligent and heartless in our Master's work?

4. It is an excellence of praise and thanksgiving that we shall never be through

with it, v. 2. We should praise him in life, we should praise him in death, we should praise him in joy, we should praise him in sorrow. If saved, we shall praise him *for evermore.* Calvin: "Can there be anything more base, than for us to magnify God's name but seldom and tardily, considering it ought to fill our thoughts with enrapturing admiration?"

5. He who wants a great theme for meditation, conversation or adoration has it in God. He is so high that there is none above him, and none with him. He is so exultant that none can excessively laud him. Morison: "His glorious works of creation, providence and redemption, shall ere long be celebrated among all nations; for in them all his name is to be praised."

6. One of the enormities connected with any kind of idol worship is that it ignores the glory of God manifested not only in redemption and in providence, but in creation itself. God has sometimes given to mortals great state and majesty. He has beautifully garnished the heavens above us. He has made some men and some angels to be in their measure very excellent. But he is infinitely above them all. He has no equals. He will endure no rivals.

7. Jehovah reigns supreme over heaven and earth, vv. 4, 5. Morison: "He, who made the universe, and who sustains it in being, with all its innumerable tribes, is entitled to govern it, and claims this prerogative as his exclusive and inalienable right. He made all, he provides for all, he upholds all, he governs all; and therefore, let all unite in celebrating his glorious praise."

8. Though in condescension to our weakness, God uses titles expressive of his care and mercy towards us, yet in strictness of speech Jehovah is absolutely incomparable, v. 5. Of all the potentates of earth and the bright spirits of paradise none can compare with him.

9. Of course nothing is more fitting in us than high admiration of his amazing condescension, v. 6. Calvin: "In saying that God is exalted above the heavens, the prophet magnifies his mercy towards men, whose condition is mean and despicable, and informs us that he might righteously hold even angels in contempt, were it not that, moved by paternal regard, he condescends to take them under his care." Compare Ps. viii. 3, 4. Clarke: "Those who are highly exalted are generally unapproachable; they are proud and overbearing, or so surrounded with *magnificence* and *flatterers,* that to them the poor have no access: but God though *infinitely* exalted, *humbleth himself to behold* even *heaven* itself; and much more does he *humble himself* when he condescends to behold *earth* and her inhabitants. But so does he love his creatures, that he rejoices over even the meanest of them, to do them good." He loves like a God. He condescends like a God.

10. There are changes continually going on in the social and civil positions of men, against which it is idle for us to set ourselves, vv. 7, 8. Scott: "In his providence, the Lord sometimes raises men from the most abject to the most honorable stations in society; and it is well when they acquit themselves properly in their new dignities." It is well when their cotemporaries have discretion and grace enough neither to despise nor to envy them. Henry: "Gideon is fetched from threshing, Saul from seeking the asses, and David from seeking sheep; the apostles are sent from fishing to be *fishers of men.*" Blessed is the man who is not through arrogance above his business, or through negligency and incompetency is not beneath it.

11. These things may well surprise us; but the salvation of every sinner is something far more wonderful still. Horne: "What is the exaltation of the meanest beggar from a dunghill to an earthly diadem, when compared with that of human nature from the grave to the throne of God! Here is honor worthy our ambition: honor after which all are alike invited to aspire; which all may obtain, who strive worthily

and lawfully; and of which, when once obtained, nothing can ever deprive the possessors."

12. If God greatly favors and honors us by giving us children, we ought to make frequent and honorable mention of his mercy, and especially give ourselves to the duties arising from so great blessings. Henry: "They that have the comfort of a family, must take the care of it."

13. Luther: "The peculiar and express office of Christ, and the work of the kingdom of Christ, is to bring down the proud, to put to shame the wise, and to condemn hypocrites and false saints: and, on the other side, to raise up and exalt the humble, to enlighten and instruct fools, to sanctify unclean sinners, to make fruitful the barren, and to comfort the fatherless."

PSALM CXIV.

1 When Israel went out of Egypt, the house of Jacob from a people of strange language;
2 Judah was his sanctuary, *and* Israel his dominion.
3 The sea saw *it*, and fled: Jordan was driven back.
4 The mountains skipped like rams; *and* the little hills like lambs.
5 What *ailed* thee, O thou sea, that thou fleddest? thou Jordan, *that* thou wast driven back?
6 Ye mountains, *that* ye skipped like rams: *and* ye little hills, like lambs?
7 Tremble, thou earth, at the presence of the Lord, at the presence of the God of Jacob;
8 Which turned the rock *into* a standing water, the flint into a fountain of waters.

SCOTT gives no opinion respecting the authorship of this Psalm, but dates it B. C. 1491, which was the year of the Exodus from Egypt. Clarke: "As to the *author* of this Psalm, there have been various opinions: some have given the honor of it to *Shadrach, Meshach*, and *Abed-nego ;* others, to *Esther ;* and others, to *Mordecai.*" He dates it B. C. 535. It has been long and justly admired for its poetic beauty. Clarke: "It is elegantly and energetically composed;" Drake: "The exodus of Israel from Egypt, with some of its most remarkable accompanying and consequent miracles, are, in this brief Psalm, commemorated in the boldest style of poetry, with personifications, indeed, of inanimate nature of the utmost daring and sublimity." The names of the Most High here found are *Elohim God* and *Adonai Lord*, on which see on Ps. iii. 2 ; ii. 4.

1. *When Israel went out of Egypt, the house of Jacob from a people of strange language.* *Went out*, literally *in the going out*. *Israel* and *the house of Jacob* are parallel. So are *Egypt* and *a people of strange language.* The last phrase expresses the idea that the Egyptians did not speak the language of the Hebrews. The language was strange to Israel, and by a bold figure strange to Jehovah, Ps. lxxxi. 5. Compare Gen. xlii. 23. There is nothing in the Hebrew to justify the rendering of Horsley "a tyrannical people." When God thus brought up his people, and afterwards,

2. *Judah was his sanctuary*, and *Israel his dominion.* *Judah* and *Israel* are strictly parallel. *Israel* for a long time denoted all the tribes, and *Judah* as the head included them all, according to Gen. xlix. 8–12. After the withdrawal of the ten tribes *Judah* embraced Judah and Benjamin only; *Israel*, the ten tribes only. But our Psalm relates to a time before the days of Rehoboam; and *Judah* and *Israel* here are the same. Judah was his *sanctuary*, his *holy place*, or *holy thing, a thing consecrated*, or *devoted*. Calvin has it, "for his holiness." The people of the Jews had for a long

time the true religion, when surrounding nations served idols. *Dominion*, several times so rendered, 1 Kings ix. 19; Ps. ciii. 22; Mic. iv. 8; in Isa. xxii. 21, *government*. Here the word is in the plural, *rulings, dominions*. Hammond: "And Israel his power," *i. e.*, an instance of his power. The theocracy was in Israel only. In this verse we have twice the pronoun *his*, though God has not yet been named. We have something like it in Ps. lxxxvii. 1. This is not a fault of style. The author of No. 461 of the Spectator says: "I perceived a beauty in this Psalm which was new to me. The poet utterly conceals the presence of God in the beginning of it, and rather lets a possessive pronoun go without a substantive, than he will so much as mention anything of divinity there. . . If God had appeared before, there could be no wonder why the mountains should leap, and the sea retire; therefore, that this convulsion of nature may be brought in with due surprise, his name is not mentioned till afterwards, and then, with a very agreeable turn of thought, God is introduced at once with all his majesty." This is the best explanation:

3. *The sea saw it, and fled; Jordan was driven back.* It would be better to omit *it*. It is not in the Hebrew, nor in the ancient versions. The Syriac supplies *him*. This is not necessary, but is better than *it*; for first we have *his* in the preceding verse, and then we have a like phrase on the same subject, Ps. lxxvii. 16, "The waters saw thee, O God, the waters saw thee; they were afraid." The historic allusion is first to the passage of the Red sea, Ex. xiv. 21, 22, and to the passage of the Jordan, Josh. iii. 14–17.

4. *The mountains skipped like rams*, and *the little hills like lambs.* If this is to be taken literally, it has its historic explanation in Ex. xix. 18; Judg. v. 4, 5, alluded to in Ps. xxix. 6; lxviii. 16. This view makes the language of this verse consistent with that of v. 3. Nor does it hinder us from employing the language for figurative purposes, showing how easily God subverts states and kingdoms, as in Jer. iv. 23, 24; Mic. i. 3, 4; Zech. iv. 7. A later prophet has wrought the whole conception into the highest strain of sublime poetry, Hab. iii. 3–10. Calvin: "The description does not exceed the facts of the case. The sea, in rendering obedience to its Creator, sanctified his name; and Jordan, by its submission, put honor upon his power; and the mountains, by their quaking, proclaimed how they were overawed at the presence of his dreadful majesty."

5. *What* ailed *thee, O thou sea, that thou fleddest? thou Jordan*, that *thou wast driven back?*

6. *Ye mountains*, that *ye skipped like rams*; and *ye little hills, like lambs?* In English the sense cannot be better conveyed than by supplying the word *ailed*. In vv. 3–6, there is an unusual commingling of the preterite and future; but the common version is as good as any. The terms of vv. 3, 4, are carefully transferred to vv. 5, 6. The personification is of the boldest kind. In modern poets no imagery is more admired than some very much like this.

7. *Tremble, thou earth, at the presence of the Lord, at the presence of the God of Jacob.* Tremble, elsewhere *be in anguish, travail, fear, travail with pain*, Deut. ii. 25; Isa. xxiii. 5; Ps. xcvi. 9; Job xv. 20. It expresses terrible consternation. Several ancient versions use the preterite, but the Chaldee retains the imperative form, which Alexander regards as "peculiarly significant, including both a recollection and prediction; as if he had said the earth might well tremble at the presence of the Lord, and may well tremble at it still." Calvin: "It must be that the earth quake at the presence of her king." That we may not be led astray or be at any loss, as to the Being, who is the *Master* of the earth, the prophet expressly says, he is *Jehovah the God of Jacob.* He can do anything; for it is he,

8. *Which turned the rock* into *a standing water, the flint into a fountain of waters.*

The history is found in Ex. xvii. 6, 7; Num. xx. 11; Deut. viii. 15. See on Ps. cvii. 35. The spiritual import of this work of God in supplying water is well expressed by the evangelical prophet, Isa. xxxv. 6, 7; xli. 18; xliii. 19; and still better by Paul, in 1 Cor. x. 4. Instead of *flint*, Street has *marble;* Clarke, *granite.* Clarke says: "For such is the rock of Horeb, a piece of which now lies before me." In Job xxviii. 9, the same word is rendered *rock*, everywhere else *flint* or *flinty*, as in Deut. xxxii. 13; Isa. l. 7. It is the hardness and not the scientific name of the rock that is here taught us. Walford: "The divine poet represents the very substance of the rock as being converted into water, not literally, but poetically—thus ornamenting his sketch of the wondrous power displayed on this occasion."

DOCTRINAL AND PRACTICAL REMARKS.

1. Some events in the lives of men and of nations are of so vast importance in their history that they should never be forgotten, but often and carefully commemorated. Such was the redemption from Egypt, v. 1. Such is the redemption of every believer from the power and dominion of sin. Such are many marked deliverances experienced at the good hand of God.

2. Sometimes it is well for us to take a minute survey of each of our great mercies, and sometimes it is best to take a rapid and general view of them, v. 3. The passage of the Red sea and of the Jordan were separated by nearly forty years; yet they are here brought into close connection.

3. Whenever God begins in earnest to do good to a man or a people, he will continue to do them good unless by their unbelief and rebellion they wickedly reject his mercies, vv. 1–4. When God brings his people out of darkness into light, he is bound by covenant and oath to do them good all their days. Nor will his engagement fail.

4. It is great condescension in God to care for nations, and supply their wants, v. 2. He marvellously provides for them and does them good. He keeps them under his protection. He continues their supplies. He is in every sense their father. They are under his moral government and are accountable to him.

5. When we consider how glorious is the nature of God and how amazing are his perfections, we need not be surprised at the stupendous results produced by his manifested presence, vv. 3, 4. Dickson: "When God will deliver his people, no oppression can hinder; and when he will possess them of what he promised, no impediment can withstand him."

6. If the Lord made the waters of the Jordan to stand still that his people might safely enter the promised land, v. 3; no doubt he will so abate the cold waters of death that his people shall not be swept away by them. The great wonders wrought at their conversion are a pledge that "he will surely divide Jordan to open them a safe passage to their heavenly inheritance." 1 Cor. iii. 21–23.

7. If we exclude God from our philosophy, we will find many things wholly unaccountable, vv. 5, 6. If we ignore his attributes and government, we cannot explain a thousand phenomena of nature, or a thousand events in the history of persons and communities. In that case we should be continually crying, not with poetic beauty as the prophet does here, but in the depths of despondency, What aileth thee, O sea, O river, O mountains, O hills, O everything?

8. Horne: "If the divine presence hath such an effect upon inanimate matter, how ought it to operate on rational and accountable kings? Let us be afraid, with an holy fear, at the presence of God, in the world by his providence, and by his Spirit in our consciences; so that we may have hope and courage in the day when he shall arise to shake terribly the earth," vv. 5–7.

9. It is no idle thing to call upon the earth to tremble at the presence of its Maker. A frown from him makes the globe reel and stagger like a drunken man. When the cup of the wine of the fierceness of his wrath is given to the earth, every island flees away, and the mountains are not found, Rev. xvi. 19, 20.

10. Dickson: "Whomsoever the Lord redeemeth, and setteth on their way to heaven, he will provide whatsoever is necessary for their sustentation and comfort in their journey, as his providing of drink for the camp of Israel giveth proof," v. 8.

11. Luther: "We use this Psalm to give thanks unto Christ, who delivered us from the kingdom of darkness, and translated us into the kingdom of light, even into his own kingdom, the kingdom of God's dear Son, and led us forth into eternal life."

PSALM CXV.

1 Not unto us, O LORD, not unto us, but unto thy name give glory, for thy mercy, *and* for thy truth's sake.

2 Wherefore should the heathen say, Where *is* now their God?

3 But our God *is* in the heavens: he hath done whatsoever he hath pleased.

4 Their idols *are* silver and gold, the work of men's hands.

5 They have mouths, but they speak not: eyes have they, but they see not:

6 They have ears, but they hear not: noses have they, but they smell not:

7 They have hands, but they handle not: feet have they, but they walk not: neither speak they through their throat.

8 They that make them are like unto them; *so is* every one that trusteth in them.

9 O Israel, trust thou in the LORD: he *is* their help and their shield.

10 O house of Aaron, trust in the LORD: he *is* their help and their shield.

11 Ye that fear the LORD, trust in the LORD: he *is* their help and their shield.

12 The LORD hath been mindful of us: he will bless *us;* he will bless the house of Israel; he will bless the house of Aaron.

13 He will bless them that fear the LORD, *both* small and great.

14 The LORD shall increase you more and more, you and your children.

15 Ye *are* blessed of the LORD which made heaven and earth.

16 The heaven, *even* the heavens, *are* the LORD's: but the earth hath he given to the children of men.

17 The dead praise not the LORD, neither any that go down into silence.

18 But we will bless the LORD from this time forth and for evermore. Praise the LORD.

BOTH the date and authorship of this Psalm are uncertain. It has been ascribed to Moses at the Red sea, to David at the beginning of his reign, to Mordecai and Esther, to Shadrach, Meshach and Abed-nego, and to Hezekiah. The discussions on this subject have failed to produce conviction in the mind of others than their authors. This ode suits many times in the history of Israel. The prevailing impression is that it was composed during a time of great trial. Calvin: "It is obvious that this Psalm was penned when the church was deeply afflicted;" Tholuck: "A Psalm of prayer and praise, composed in a time of Pagan oppression;" Pool: "The occasion of this Psalm was to manifest some eminent danger or distress of the people of Israel from some idolatrous nations." Yet it is not a despondent song. Indeed it expresses strong confidence in God. This is so true that Clarke speaks of it as "a triumphal song, in which the victory gained is entirely ascribed to Jehovah." Scott, who thinks it was perhaps written during Sennacherib's invasion, dates it B. C. 710; Clarke, B. C. 535. Hengstenberg says that it is without and against all reason that this Psalm is by some joined to the preceding one, so that the two together form one whole. The names of the Most High here found are *Jehovah* LORD, *Elohim God* and *Jah* LORD, on which see on Ps. i. 2; iii. 2, and introductory remarks on Ps. lxviii.

1. *Not unto us, O Lord, not unto us, but unto thy name give glory, for thy mercy, and for thy truth's sake.* The rendering of this verse is very nearly literal, and yet gives the sense in pure English. We have here a full and complete renunciation of all merit, of all claim to honor for anything that had ever been done, or that might yet be done for the preservation or elevation of Israel, as a nation, or as a church. Some would confine the disclaimer of merit to the receipt of future benefits; but it would display a monstrous state of self-righteousness to flatter ourselves that we had deserved past benefits, and were merely unworthy of future blessings. He who does not acknowledge that all the good he has received was of pure grace, knows nothing of genuine humility. Nor is it for their own honor, but for the *glory* of God's name, that he is asked to interpose. We may well ask him to defend and protect the honor of his throne. Calvin: "Suffused with shame by reason of their calamity, which in itself amounts to a kind of rejection, they durst not openly crave, at God's hand, what they wished, but made their appeal indirectly, that, from a regard to his own glory, he would prove a father to sinners, who had no claim upon him whatever." Nor do the truly pious merely intimate their own unworthiness; but they declare it over and over again—*Not unto us, not unto us.* All the prevailing causes of the divine procedure in any case are found in God himself, in his *mercy*, his *truth* or faithfulness, his justice, his power, his unchangeableness. Compare Num. xiv. 15–18; Isa. xliii. 7, 25; xlviii. 11; Ezek. xxxvi. 32; Dan. ix. 18, 19; Eph. i. 6; Rev. iv. 8–11.

2. *Wherefore should the heathen say, Where is now their God?* Things had come to a sad state, when the presence, the providence, and even the being of Jehovah were thus insolently questioned, and when none but Jehovah could vindicate himself from the vilest reproaches. It was time for him to work, Ps. cxix. 126. The insulting and exultant form of question is the same as in Ps. lxxix. 10, with the addition of *now*, "which (says Alexander) is not a particle of time, but of entreaty, or, in this connection, of triumphant demand." In Gen. xii. 13; xviii. 4; Jud. ix. 38, it is rendered *I pray*, or *I pray thee;* in Ex. xxxiii. 18, *I beseech thee.*

3. *But our God* is *in the heavens. But*, commonly rendered *and;* by Calvin here, *surely;* by Edwards, *whereas.* It may here be rendered, *at the same time*, in response to the *now* of the preceding verse. *Our God is in the heavens*, where your gods are not, never were, and never will be; where he rules all heavenly and earthly powers; where your malice and rage can never reach. Compare Ps. ii. 4; lxviii. 4; cxxxv. 6. The fact that our God is invisible and not perceptible by our senses is a part of our rejoicing in him. Venting spleen against him is as idle as throwing stones at the stars, or like a dog baying the moon. *He hath done whatsoever he hath pleased.* The trials which have befallen his people were not contrary to his will. The short and vain triumph of his foes was not without his permission. Compare Isa. xlvi. 10; Dan. iv. 35.

4. *Their idols* are *silver and gold, the work of men's hands. Their*, referring to *the heathen*, in v. 2. *Idols*, not the *vanities* of Ps. xcvi. 5, but a word meaning *images*, found in 1 Sam. xxxi. 9; 2 Sam. v. 21; Ps. cvi. 36, 38. It occurs in Ps. cxxxv. 15. These images are *silver* and *gold*, of no more value as gods than the mire of the streets. Instead of being self-existent like the true God, instead of being alive like angels or men deriving their natures from heaven, instead of making men or anything else, they are themselves *the work of men's hands.* A man might as well expect help and salvation from an old shoe or from a tattered garment as from an image made of anything, however costly the material or curious the workmanship. Calvin: "The passage may be translated adversatively, thus, Though they are of gold and silver, yet they are not gods, because they are the work of men's hands."

5. *They* [the idols] *have mouths, but they speak not; eyes have they, but they see not.* Street: There is a mouth to them, but they cannot speak; there are eyes to them, but they cannot see. If there could be any desirable variation from this, it would be to put *will not* for *cannot;* for *speak* and *see* are both in the future. These idols are both dumb and blind, and will be so forever.

6. *They have ears, but they hear not; noses have they, but they smell not.* Street: There are ears to them, but they cannot hear; there is a nose to them, but they cannot breathe. *Smell* is better than *breathe,* used both by Waterland and Street; and better than *murmur,* used by Pool and Hammond. Both *hear* and *smell* are in the future. They do not these things now, and they never will do them.

7. *They have hands, but they handle not; feet have they, but they walk not; neither speak they through their throat.* *Handle, walk* and *speak* in the future, as in vv. 5, 6. Instead of *handle,* we might better read *feel.* Verses 5–7 contain a very remarkable instance of ridicule without unfairness. Every sentence is just and candid. There is no exaggeration, no coloring. The parallel is found in Isa. xl. 18–25; xli. 7; xliv. 9–20; xlvi. 5–7; Jer. ii. 27, 28; x. 3–16. How vain must be the help of gods, who can neither speak, nor see, nor hear, nor smell, nor feel, nor walk, nor resent the greatest insult offered to them, nor avenge the greatest wrong done to their devotees. How very different it is with the true God is often declared in Scripture, Ex. iv. 11; Ps. xi. 4; xvii. 3; xliv. 21; xciv. 9; cxxxix. 1–12; Jer. xxiii. 23, 24. Not only is idolatry absurd and ridiculous, but its effect on those who practise its rites is degrading.

8. *They that make them* [the idols] *are like unto them; so is every one that trusteth in them.* This doubtless means that like the images, these false worshippers shall be as powerless and as contemptible as the idols they worship. But does it not mean also, that they shall become degraded and debased by their very religion? A man is like the object he really worships. Tholuck: "It is the curse of every false religion that man becomes like his God: the worshippers of a *soulless* god get soulless themselves." Scott: "The makers and worshippers of idols renounce their reason and understanding, and willingly become as stupid, as the very objects of their worship."

9. *O Israel, trust thou in the* LORD. *Trust,* here and in vv. 10, 11, in the imperative. It expresses reliance, confidence, Mic. vii. 5. In Ps. xxii. 9, one form of the verb is rendered *didst make me hope.* As the heathen confide in images, much more let the people of Jehovah rely upon him. *He is their help and their shield.* See on Ps. xxxiii. 20. Idols are no *help* and no protection, or *shield.* But Jehovah is almighty, all-wise and most merciful. None ever trusted in him and was confounded. The address of this verse is to all, high and low, rich and poor, young and old, all Israel. But as God had given peculiar honor to the tribe of Levi, and as they were eminently his ministers, his ambassadors, his witnesses, he fitly makes a solemn call on them:

10. *O house of Aaron, trust in the* LORD: *he is their help and their shield.* Nor does he stop with the priests; but makes a direct and solemn appeal to the truly godly:

11. *Ye that fear the* LORD, *trust in the* LORD; *he is their help and their shield.* This verse is the same as the two preceding in all respects, except in the persons addressed, who are *those fearing* Jehovah. On the fear of God see on Ps. ii. 11. That the truly godly are designated in this verse seems very clear. Clarke: "All real penitents, and sincere believers."

12. *The* LORD *hath been mindful of us.* How refreshing is this assurance. It implies all that we shall ever need. Past mercies sent in covenant love are pledges of all needed blessings in time to come. See on precisely the same Hebrew phrase in Ps. ix. 12. Compare Ps. viii. 4. *Remember,* in a good sense. *He will bless* us; *he will bless the house of Israel, he will bless the house of Aaron.*

13. *He will bless them that fear the* LORD, *both small and great.* *Bless*, as in Ps. v. 12. The descriptions of persons are the same as those given in vv. 9–11, with this addition to the last, that none of those, who really *fear* the Lord, shall be neglected however humble or elevated their condition, but each one shall have a blessing. There is nothing gained by reading the verb *bless* in the past tense. The Hebrew is future; and the future gives the best sense.

14. *The* LORD *shall yet increase you more and more, you and your children.* The rendering cannot be improved. In a sense all predictions of good to the people of God are so far prayers on the part of the prophets that the righteous desire their fulfilment. This is strictly a prediction—in the future. Calvin: "God's liberality is an inexhaustible fountain, which will never cease to flow so long as its progress is not impeded by the ingratitude of men. And hence it will be continued to their posterity, because God manifests the grace and the fruit of his adoption even to a thousand generations." It is a meager interpretation that confines the promise of this verse to a mere multiplying of the Jews after the Babylonish captivity.

15. *Ye* are *blessed of the* LORD, *which made heaven and earth.* *Blessed*, the passive form of the word *bless*, so frequently occurring in this Psalm. The resources of God are infinite, as is proven by his having *made* all things. Were it necessary he could bring into existence innumerable worlds to enrich and multiply his people. Hengstenberg and Alexander think that in this verse there is a special reference to the blessing pronounced by Melchizedek on Abraham, Gen. xiv. 19. In both places, creative power is the foundation of the confidence that the blessing will neither be small nor of short continuance.

> "My heart is awed within me, when I think
> Of the great miracle that still goes on,
> In silence, round me—the perpetual work
> Of thy creation, finished, yet renewed
> Forever."

16. *The heaven*, even *the heavens*, are *the* LORD'S. In the Hebrew the word for heavens is in both cases plural. How much may be included by it can be seen on Psalm viii. 1. Here it seems specially to refer to the third heavens, in which God preëminently reveals his glory, and which is his *house*, the temple not made with hands. It is put in contrast with the abode of mortals: *But the earth hath he given to the children of men.* That is, *earth* is man's abode during his natural life, and in a sense he is lord of it, having dominion over its other inhabitants.

17. *The dead praise not the* LORD, *neither any that go down into silence.* God's praise on earth is not heard from the lips of those who have died, or gone into *silence*, or the grave; see on Ps. vi. 5; ix. 17; xxxi. 12, 17, 18; xciv. 17. The true Israel cannot become extinct upon earth, for then the true praises of Jehovah would fail from among men; and Jehovah has determined that this shall never be. Calvin: "Lord, if thou shouldst allow us to perish, what would be the result, but that thy name would become extinct, and would be entombed with us?" Compare Isaiah xxxviii. 19.

18. *But we will bless the* LORD *from this time forth and for evermore. Bless*, as in Ps. v. 12, in the future. We may read *shall bless*, expressing prophetic certainty drawn from the fact that God will so richly bless us; or we may take it as the expression of a purpose—*we will*—a purpose formed in view of favors received and confidently expected. The thing is certain and the saints have a will for it, and a purpose to engage in it. *Praise the* LORD, *hallelujah;* see on Ps. civ. 35; cv. 45. Scott: "There is a peculiar animation in the concluding part of this Psalm, when considered not so

much as praise for benefits received, as the language of faith and hope in regard to difficulties."

DOCTRINAL AND PRACTICAL REMARKS.

1. Because God is the one, only, true, living, almighty God, the Preserver of men and of angels, he in whom our breath is, and whose are all our ways; we should imitate the Psalmist, and abound in praise and thanksgiving to the Most High, v. 1.

2. Although God is so good, yet the sins of his people are so many and so hateful, that we should not be surprised at finding them in great straits and for a time under the power of wicked men, even persecuting idolaters, vv. 1, 2.

3. Because self-righteousness is exceedingly abominable to God, and very offensive to right-minded men, we ought most sedulously to guard against it. It is very insidious. Here the church enters disclaimer upon disclaimer, v. 1. It has a mighty effect in humbling us, in making us quiet under affliction, and patient under denial of our petitions to know that we deserve all the evil, and none of the good that befalls us.

4. In all our prayers for deliverance and victory, we ought to be careful that we do not ask God's blessings that we may consume them upon our lusts, but that his name may be glorified, v. 1.

5. Dickson: "When we have brought ourselves into misery, and our religion into danger of disgrace; we ought to be more careful to have the Lord restored to his honor, and true religion to its own beauty, than to be freed from misery," v. 2.

6. Insults from heathen and infidel men, amounting to taunts and mockery of all the sentiments of the godly are no new thing, v. 2. It has always been so. It will be so to the end of the world.

7. To the right-minded and pious it is a source of unspeakable consolation that Jehovah is entirely beyond the reach of the malice of all his foes. He *is in the heavens*, v. 3. And not only is he exalted, but he is sovereign. Clarke: "Jehovah is absolute master of the universe." Gill: "*He hath done whatsoever he pleased;* in creation, in providence, and in grace: he hath made what creatures he pleased, and for his pleasure; and he does according to his will, and after the counsel of it, in heaven and in earth; and is gracious to whom he will be gracious; and saves and calls men, not according to their works, but according to his own purpose and will."

8. No Scriptural representation of the absurd, shocking, ruinous or degrading nature of idolatry is excessive, vv. 4–8. It is bad from beginning to end. Cobbin: "It is an awful proof of the degraded state of human nature, that men of intelligent understandings in other things should abase themselves to bow the knee to carved pieces of gold, or silver, or wood, or stone." Nor can any people be too grateful for the mercy of being saved from the horrors of idolatry. The true God is so glorious that there never was but one good image of him upon earth, and that was found in the person of his dear Son.

9. There can in no case be a substitute for faith in God; leading us to believe whatever he has spoken, to rely upon his grace, to confide in him fully and unfalteringly, vv. 9–11. This is true in the case of every class and condition of believers, the high and low, the rich and the poor, the priest and the people. Men are never truly blessed till they set their hope in God. "Here they find help in time of need, and protection in seasons of danger."

10. God's past care of his people is an ample pledge that in the future he will not desert them, v. 12. This doctrine is founded upon the unchangeableness of the divine nature and plan.

11. The provisions of divine grace are admirably adapted to the wants of all, v.

13. The friends of the great often withdraw from them, sometimes through humility, perhaps often through pride and envy. But God does not forsake a man merely because he has become great in the world. More frequently the friends of the poor or afflicted forsake him because he is distressed ; but the Lord doth not so. Henry " The greatest need his blessing, and it shall not be denied to the meanest that fear him."

12. It is no wonder that God's blessing greatly enriches those on whom it falls, and makes them to abound more and more, vv. 12–15. Calvin thinks the frequent repetition of the word *bless* is intended to mark the uninterrupted stream of God's loving-kindness.

13. How exceedingly excellent and glorious heaven must be. It is the abode of God himself, v. 16. It is our Father's house. There is the throne of his majesty. There is every choice spirit that has ever passed away from earth. There the angels minister. There the saints reign. There God is wondrously manifested in the flesh.

14. If in this world abounding with sin, God is still so bountiful to his creatures, how inexhaustibly full of grace and goodness his nature must be, v. 15. We cannot easily fall into excess in extolling the bounty of God, in having so richly supplied the wants of all his creatures, and particularly the wants of man.

15. Let us work while it is day; the night cometh when no man can work, vv. 17, 18. Let us not be weary in well doing; but steadfast, unmoveable, always abounding in the work of the Lord. Let us do with our might what our hands find to do. Scott: " As death will terminate our opportunities of praising God on earth, let us now redeem the time, that we may glorify him with our lips and in our lives. Then we shall shortly join the company before the throne, and assist them in blessing our God ; and our bodies will be raised from the silent grave to join in this delightful work to all eternity."

16. It is easy to pervert Scripture, which is so written that they who wish to cavil may find fault. This is remarkably illustrated in vv. 16, 17. From the former some would teach that God has abandoned the world and its inhabitants to take care of themselves ; and from the latter that the Bible teaches that there is no conscious existence beyond this life. But all this is gross perversion. Let carnal men beware how they wrest the Scriptures.

17. God shall have a church on earth to the end of the world, v. 18. None others truly praise or glorify him. Nor can the church be so sunk down and sadly depressed in her condition as that her joys shall not break forth in loud and blessed songs.

18. However sad our outward state, let us be cheered by the prospect, and settled in the purpose of praising God eternally, v. 18. In the darkest days let us look for the Star of hope. In the saddest hours, let us joy in God.

PSALM CXVI.

1 I love the LORD, because he hath heard my voice *and* my supplications.

2 Because he hath inclined his ear unto me, therefore will I call upon *him* as long as I live.

3 The sorrows of death compassed me, and the pains of hell gat hold upon me : I found trouble and sorrow.

4 Then called I upon the name of the LORD ; O LORD, I beseech thee, deliver my soul.

5 Gracious *is* the LORD, and righteous; yea, our God *is* merciful.

6 The LORD preserveth the simple: I was brought low, and he helped me.

7 Return unto thy rest, O my soul; for the LORD hath dealt bountifully with thee.

8 For thou hast delivered my soul from death, mine eyes from tears, *and* my feet from falling.

9 I will walk before the LORD in the land of the living.

10 I believed, therefore have I spoken: I was greatly afflicted:

11 I said in my haste, All men *are* liars.

12 What shall I render unto the LORD *for* all his benefits toward me?

13 I will take the cup of salvation, and call upon the name of the LORD.

14 I will pay my vows unto the LORD now in the presence of all his people.

15 Precious in the sight of the LORD *is* the death of his saints.

16 O LORD, truly I *am* thy servant; I *am* thy servant, *and* the son of thine handmaid: thou hast loosed my bonds.

17 I will offer to thee the sacrifice of thanksgiving, and will call upon the name of the LORD.

18 I will pay my vows unto the LORD now in the presence of all his people,

19. In the courts of the LORD'S house, in the midst of thee, O Jerusalem. Praise ye the LORD.

THE division of this Psalm into two by the Septuagint, Arabic, Ethiopic, Vulgate and Doway, is without authority or reason. The date and authorship are both uncertain. The Syriac, Calvin, Patrick, Henry, Scott and others regard David as its author. Clarke, Tholuck, Hengstenberg, Alexander and others suppose it was written after the captivity. Morison: "It is by no means unsuitable to the circumstances which attended the miraculous recovery of Hezekiah." Those, who regard David as author are divided in opinion as to the occasion of its composition; whether the pursuit of David by Saul to the cave, the rebellion of Absalom, or some other occasion. The character of the ode defies all attempts to fix it to any one occasion. But the fact that in it we find several marks of the Chaldee Dialect goes far to strengthen doubts as to the Davidic authorship. Clarke: "Many think it relates wholly to the passion, death, and triumph of Christ. Most of the Fathers were of this opinion." Fry adopts this view and argues for it from 2 Cor. iv. 10–14, where v. 10 is quoted. Bellarmine says: "With the holy Fathers, Basil, Chrysostom, Jerome and Augustine, we judge this Psalm is to be understood of the spiritual man, earnestly desiring eternal life, and groaning on account of temptations and dangers." The church of England has appointed this Psalm for the thanksgiving of women after child-birth. Many pastors use it privately on such occasions. Some churches uniformly use a metrical version of a part of it in celebrating the Lord's Supper. The student of the Psalter has already learned that such uncertainties, as have been just stated, detract nothing from the instruction or consoling power of a Psalm. Portions of it are evidently taken wholly or in part from previous Psalms. Compare v. 3, with Ps. xviii. 4–6; v. 5, with Ps. ciii. 8; v. 11, with Ps. xxxi. 22. Scott dates it B. C. 1020; Clarke, B. C. 515. The names of the Most High here found are *Jehovah* LORD, *Elohim God* and *Jah* LORD, on which see on Ps. i. 2; iii. 2, and introduction to Ps. lxviii. Luther: "This is a Psalm of thanksgiving, in which the Psalmist renders thanks, after coming out of a most heavy trial, and again rejoices in God." Pool: "This Psalm contains a solemn thanksgiving to God for a glorious deliverance from grievous and dangerous calamities; as also from great perplexities and terrors of mind arising from the sense of God's displeasure." Tholuck calls it "a delightful Psalm of thanksgiving." The more this Psalm is studied, the more will the pious mind refer it to spiritual conflicts and victories.

1. *I love the* LORD, *because he hath heard my voice* and *my supplications.* Literally, *I love, because Jehovah hath heard.* It is a beauty in composition to name no person, when the very occasion shows who is the dear one alluded to. See John xx. 15. The first verb is in the preterite; the second, in the future. Calvin so renders them. But

Edwards, Hengstenberg and Alexander put both verbs in the present tense. See Introduction, § 6. *Love* is better than *rejoice, am pleased,* or *have desired;* often applied to the matter of loving God, Deut. vi. 5; xi. 1; xxx. 20; Josh. xxii. 5; xxiii. 11. It is the verb used to express Jacob's love of Joseph, Gen. xxxvii. 34; Jonathan's affection for David, 1 Sam. xx. 17; the warm heart of a pious man to God's word, Ps. cxix. 97, 119, 127, 159. *Voice,* usually so rendered. Here it means the voice of prayer. *Supplications,* as in Ps. lv. 1. It denotes petitions for which *gracious* answer is sought. In Josh. xi. 20, the word is rendered *favor.*

2. *Because he hath inclined his ear unto me, therefore I will call upon* him *as long as I live.* On *inclining the ear* see on Ps. xvii. 6; xxxi. 2; xl. 1; lxxviii. 1. On *calling upon* God see on Ps. iii. 4, where it is rendered *cried.* To call upon God is in general to worship him, Gen. iv. 26; in particular any act of worship as prayer. We have the same word in the same form in vv. 4, 13, 17. In vv. 13, 17, it seems to denote thanksgiving. Some answers to prayer are so seasonable, and so memorable that the pious never forget them. Such are answers to prayers offered in times of peculiar peril and dejection.

3. *The sorrows of death encompassed me.* See on Ps. xviii. 4, where we have precisely the same words both in Hebrew and English. *The pains of hell gat hold upon me. Pains,* elsewhere *straits, distresses. Hell, sheol;* see on Ps. vi. 5; ix. 17; xvi. 10; xviii. 5. *Gat hold,* in the next clause *found. I found trouble and sorrow. Trouble,* cognate to the word rendered *pains* in this verse. *Sorrow,* always so, or *grief.* See Ps. xiii. 2; xxxi. 10; cvii. 39. All the terms and phrases of this verse evince a sad plight, a case distressing in the extreme.

4. *Then called I upon the name of the* LORD; O LORD, *I beseech thee, deliver my soul. Called,* literally *will call.* See on v. 2. *I beseech,* in Hebrew an interjection, full of urgent entreaty. Alexander renders it *Ah* here and in v. 16; in Ex. xxxii. 31, it is rendered *Oh;* in v. 16, simply *O. Deliver,* usually so rendered. *Soul,* it may mean *life,* as in Gen. ix. 5; xix. 17; Ps. xxxi. 13; xxxviii. 12; or *soul,* as in Ps. iii. 2; vi. 3, 4. If this Psalm records a case of deep spiritual distress, we must read *soul.* The whole verse and context show that he sought help from God alone.

5. *Gracious is the* LORD, *and righteous; yea, our God is merciful. Gracious,* as in Ps. lxxxvi. 15; ciii. 8; cxi. 4; cxii. 4. *Righteous,* the epithet applied to the godly in Ps. i. 5, 6, and to Jehovah in Ps. xi. 7. It here expresses the essential rectitude of God's nature, whereby he is infallibly preserved from doing or countenancing wrong. *Merciful,* a participle from the verb twice rendered *pity* in Ps. ciii. 13, elsewhere *have mercy, have compassion,* Isa. xxx. 18; xlix. 15.

6. *The* LORD *preserveth the simple. Preserveth,* often *keepeth, observeth, regardeth, taketh heed to,* implying watchful guardianship. *The simple;* the word occurs only in the Psalms *thrice,* in Proverbs *thirteen* times, and in Ezekiel *once.* It is uniformly rendered *simple* except in Pr. ix. 6, where it is *foolish.* Here it is plural and denotes the feeble-minded, or as Calvin says, "such as, being undesigning, do not possess the requisite prudence for managing their own affairs." Fry has *weak. Simple* has the same meaning here as in Ps. xix. 7. The simple are those who cannot *keep* or *preserve* themselves. The Psalmist spoke with feeling and with confidence. *I was brought low, and he helped me.* The rendering of this clause gives the sense and is in pure English. *Helped,* almost invariably rendered *saved.* The account suits a case of sickness, of poverty, of persecution, of temptation, of melancholy, spiritual darkness or desertion. If the Psalm is spoken in the name of the church, as a body, this and other clauses suit any state of trial in which she can possibly be placed.

7. *Return unto thy rest, O my soul. Rest,* in the plural *rests;* in Num. x. 33, *resting-place;* in Ps. xxiii. 2, *still.* What is the *rest* of the pious soul? Not the promised land,

as some say, but God himself, his word, his covenant, his perfections, his providence, his worship, confidence in him, reliance on him. If *rest* is taken in the abstract, then it signifies the *quietness* of the soul. The encouragement to return to repose in God is stated: *For the* LORD *hath dealt bountifully with thee.* On this verb see on Ps. xiii. 6; in Ps. vii. 7; ciii. 10, *rewarded.* Calvin: For Jehovah hath recompensed unto thee; church of England and Jebb: For the Lord hath rewarded thee; Edwards: For Jehovah has been gracious to thee; Street: Since Jehovah hath been kind to thee.

8. *For thou hast delivered my soul from death, mine eyes from tears,* and *my feet from falling. Delivered,* as in Ps. vii. 4; xviii. 19; xci. 15. It implies effectual deliverance. On some of the phrases here used see on Ps. lvi. 13. Compare Ps. lxxxvi. 13; Isa. xxv. 8; xxxviii. 5; Jer. xxxi. 16; Rev. vii. 17; xxi. 4. Whatever the evil, the rescue had been timely and complete.

9. *I will walk before the* LORD *in the land of the living.* Past experience of God's mercy and kindness satisfied him that he should still be shielded and protected. *Land,* in Hebrew plural *lands. Land of the living,* see on Ps. xxvii. 3. *I will* may express confident expectation, or a solemn purpose; more probably the latter. If so, then *before the Lord* means, *as in his presence,* or *with his fear before him.* Horne: "'I will walk before the Lord,' as one under his inspection, 'in the land of the living,' or amongst the redeemed in the church; until the time come for me to depart hence, and to be numbered with the saints in glory everlasting."

10. *I believed, therefore have I spoken.* That these words are to be taken in their obvious sense is proven by Paul, 2 Cor. iv. 13. What he had said or should say should not be heartless or insincere; but according to his religious belief. Alexander: "His speaking was a proof of his faith." There is nothing to warrant the rendering of Street: *I believed that I was lost,* although he cites Kennicott's note to support him. *I was greatly afflicted.* Many read, I have greatly humbled myself. A still better rendering is: I was greatly exercised. See Ecc. i. 13; iii. 10. The very depths of his soul were moved.

11. *I said in my haste, All men are liars. In my haste,* in Hebrew a verb in the infinitive. See on Ps. xxxi. 22, where we have the same. The Syriac has, *With trembling;* Calvin, *In my fear;* Edwards, *In my consternation;* Street, *In mine affright;* Hengstenberg, *In my alarm;* Chaldee and Green, *In my flight;* Alexander, *In my terror.* So that we may understand the Psalmist as saying that in his distressing experience he discovered the utter vanity of man as a resource, or even as a friend. See how all forsook Christ himself in his trying hour. *Liars,* a participle of a verb in Job xli. 9, rendered *is in vain,* and in Isa. lviii. 11, *fail.* Yet the word is usually rendered *liar.* Compare Ps. lxii. 9, where the cognate noun is rendered *a lie,* and all men pronounced *lighter than vanity.* Well may it make one tremble to arrive at so appalling a discovery, and be so convinced of it as to feel bound to utter it as solemn truth. Alexander: "The proposition, *all mankind are false, i. e.,* not to be trusted or relied upon, implies as its complement or converse, therefore God alone is to be trusted." Hengstenberg: "All men disappoint the trust placed in them, leave in the lurch those who hope in them." Other interpretations are given by serious and learned men. One is that David is here the speaker, and says in his affliction that Samuel and Nathan and all, who had told him how he should be king, had deceived him. This makes David slander God's prophets and express unbelief in a manner and to a degree that we can hardly impute to him. Another explanation is that the author of this Psalm is chiding himself, "What am I doing? Dare I doubt or distrust God? I will rather give up confidence in all men, than withdraw my trust in God." The difficulty is in getting this sense from the grammatical construction of the verse. Another interpretation, perhaps the popular one, is that the Psalmist here as

in Ps. xxxi. 22, admits that he spoke rashly and unadvisedly, and that he erred in charging universal faithlessness on the race, because many had been found heartless sycophants and hypocrites. The great objection is the want of an occasion for such a statement. It is quite contrary to the preceding verse, which declares that he was uttering his firm religious belief. The only way to dispose of this difficulty would be to change the punctuation of verse 10, and make its declaration refer to something previously said. Whatever the darkness had been, light had at length arisen and gratitude had taken the place of despondency:

12. *What shall I render unto the* LORD *for all his benefits toward me?* Render, elsewhere *return, bring back, deliver, recompense.* For *benefits* Jebb has *rewards;* Street, *kindness;* Hengstenberg, *gifts;* Alexander, *bestowments.* God grants *gracious rewards* both here and hereafter. The word *benefits* excludes all danger of misapprehending the true idea of the prophet and covers the whole ground. *What,* so rendered in Gen. xx. 10, *how* in Num. xxiii. 8, and *what thing* in Lam. ii. 13. Calvin: "The question is emphatic, *What shall I render?* and imports, that it was not the desire, but the means, of which he was destitute, to enable him to render thanks to God." An adequate return was impossible; yet he resolves on doing the best he can:

13. *I will take the cup of salvation, and call upon the name of the Lord.* Very seldom is a translation more perfect in every respect. *Will take,* may mean I will take from the table before me; or I will elevate towards heaven. Street has it, *I will lift up,* signifying an act of grateful devotion. By *the cup of salvation* (Hebrew *salvations*) Joseph Mede understands "the drink-offering annexed to and poured upon the sacrifice." There seems to be no good reason for doubting that such a custom prevailed. Jewish literature abounds with allusions to it. The law itself prescribes a drink-offering accompanying the continual burnt-offering, Num. xxviii. 7. From this divine *ordinance,* and from the frequent use of wine in feasts, the custom of using the cup of thanksgiving was probably adopted in other religious services. No wine was divinely appointed for the Passover, neither was any hymn. Yet in celebrating that feast Christ and his apostles used both, Matt. xxvi. 26–30; Luke xxii. 17–20. Many think Paul alludes to this well-known usage when he speaks of "the cup of blessing," 1 Cor. x. 16. This interpretation is generally received. Hengstenberg, followed by Alexander, rejects it. They suggest that "the cup is a frequent figurative representation of what is allotted to each man," "the portion God allots one." In proof they cite Ps. xi. 6; xvi. 5; lx. 3; lxxv. 8. Our Lord used the term in the same sense, John xviii. 11. If this explanation is correct, the meaning is, "I will thankfully accept the deliverances God works for me, and by suitable acts of devotion, especially of praise (Ps. l. 23), I will testify my love."

14. *I will pay my vows unto the* LORD *now in the presence of all his people.* On *vows* and their *payment* see on Ps. xxii. 25; l. 14. So great *benefits* as the Psalmist had received deserved not only private praise, but the most public thanksgiving. So he desired that it might be in the presence of all God's people. The word rendered *now* is in Gen. xii. 11 rendered as here; but commonly *I pray, I beseech,* or by the optative *oh,* Gen. xviii. 4, 30; Ex. xxxiii. 18, so that we may read the verse: I will pay my vows unto the Lord, (oh that I may do so) in the presence of all his people, *i. e.,* of assembled Israel, or in the most public manner possible.

15. *Precious in the sight of the* LORD *is the death of his saints.* Saints, in Ps. iv. 3, *godly;* in Ps. xviii. 25, *merciful.* God takes such care of the lives of his people, and "rates them at so high a price, that he will not easily grant them to those that most desire them." The life of one good man is in God's esteem more precious than the lives of whole cities and tribes of the ungodly, Gen. xix. 15–22; yet Jehovah does not lightly esteem, much less wanton with the lives of even the heathen, Jonah iv. 10, 11

Precious, as in Ps. xlix. 8 ; lxxii. 14. Alexander: " God counts the death of his people too costly to be lightly or gratuitously suffered;" Henry: "Though *no man lays it to heart*, when *the righteous perish*, God will make it to appear that he *lays it to heart*."

16. O LORD, *truly I am thy servant ; I am thy servant, and the son of thy handmaid. Truly*, in v. 4, *I beseech thee*. In the second clause is a suppressed *surely*. The *servant* was one quite at the disposal of his master. The prophet doubles the assertion of his belonging wholly to God, and then adds that the tie, which bound him to God, was of the strongest nature, was hereditary. Alexander: "The additional phrase, *son of thy handmaid*, is much stronger than *thy servant*, and describes him as a home-born slave." See on Ps. lxxxvi. 16. *Thou hast loosed my bonds*. The *bonds* are those of affliction and correction noticed in the early part of this Psalm.

17. *I will offer to thee the sacrifice of thanksgiving, and will call upon the name of the* LORD. The first clause of this verse and the first clause of verse 13 explain each other. The second clause of this verse is identical with that of v. 13.

18. *I will pay my vows unto the* LORD *now in the presence of all his people*. To a jot and a tittle the same as in v. 14. The last clause is explained somewhat in the next verse :

19. *In the courts of the* LORD'S *house, in the midst of thee, O Jerusalem*. This confirms the exposition given of v. 14. *Praise ye the* LORD, literally *Hallelujah*, as in Ps. civ. 35.

DOCTRINAL AND PRACTICAL REMARKS.

1. Gratitude is not a sordid affection, but is one of the essential exercises of a renewed mind, v. 1. True love to God consists in a genuine delight in the divine character, in a sincere good-will towards God and his cause, and in heartfelt gratitude for his mercies. The doctrine here taught is confirmed in other Scriptures, 1 John iv. 19 ; Luke vii. 47. When we review the desperate state of guilt and misery out of which God has delivered us, our gratitude cannot be excessive.

2. If God's children are brought into straits and made to suffer sharply, such trials cannot be unprofitable to them so long as they lead them to a throne of grace, and in the end serve to quicken their attachment to him and his cause, v. 1.

3. Tholuck : "It is a great thing to know from our own experience that we have a reconciled Father in heaven, who cares for us, and, though infinitely exalted, hears the cry of poor, troubled mortals," v. 1.

4. We shall never be done praying until we enter Paradise, v. 2. Henry: " As long as we continue living, we must continue praying: this breath we must breathe till we breathe our last, because then we shall take our leave of it, and till then we have continual occasion for it."

5. One answer from the throne of grace mightily encourages prayer in all believers, v. 2. Clarke: "He that prays much will be emboldened to pray more, because none can supplicate the throne of grace in vain." Dickson: " One proof of God's hearing our prayer may, and should stir us up to believe in worship, and have our recourse by prayer to him all the rest of our life."

6. Those are miserable comforters, who go about telling mankind that there is no such thing as pain. Such do but mock the miseries of their race. The living have griefs like the *sorrows of death*. The sick sometimes have anguish like the *pains of hell*. And all of us have *trouble and sorrow*, vv. 3, 4. Among all the afflictions to which we are subject, soul troubles are the worst. Terrors in the soul are worse than any bodily pains. Still even these are useful if they lead us " with holy vehemence to the throne of Jehovah's mercy."

7. True religious experience has its ups and downs, vv. 3, 4. The child of God is

not always on the mount, nor always in the valley of the shadow of death. " It is no strange thing to see a godly person in fear of death, bodily and spiritual, temporal and everlasting."

8. A modest, truthful, yet minute statement of God's dealings with us, especially in the troubles of our souls, is sometimes called for, and may often be useful, vv. 3, 4.

9. However great our trials may be, when God interposes the relief is effectual. We find him not only just, but gracious and merciful, v. 5. In the divine character is every pledge called for by the extremities of God's people.

10. In one sense all men are too *simple* to take care of themselves; but the right- eous are so sincere and free from craft and artifice that they can never cope with the wiles of men and of the great adversary. They specially need the preserving care of God. And they shall surely have it, v. 6. Divine wisdom is more than a match for all the devices of the adversary. Dickson: "The Lord's children commonly are not the most worldly-wise people, but for the most part are of mean worldly wit, and who- soever of them have any measure of prudence, are, for the course which they keep in trials and troubles, accounted foolish; yea, and in their own estimation they are very witless, and dare not lean to their own understanding, but seek to be directed by God." This very renunciation of their own wisdom is the great means of their pre- servation, Deut. xxxii. 36.

11. How blessed is the *rest* which God has provided for the soul, v. 7. Every mercy we receive should lead us more and more to trust in him. Calvin: "To wait calmly and silently for those indications of God's favor which he conceals from us is the undoubted evidence of faith." No man enters into rest except by faith.

12. God's people shall experience every sort of deliverance which their circum- stances require, v. 8. *Death, tears* and *falling* are three terrible things to the saints, against which God alone can protect them. His grace is all-sufficient. They need never look beyond him.

13. All God's mercies ought to lead us not only to hope in him for all coming time, but to form pious resolutions, from which we will not swerve, v. 9. It is right that we should bind ourselves by solemn engagements to be the Lord's, his only and his forever.

14. However afflicted we may be, let us bear solemn testimony to all the truth we believe, v. 10. Calvin: " Faith cannot remain inoperative in the heart; but it must of necessity manifest itself."

15. Let us cease from man. Often when he would help us, he cannot; and often when he could help us, he will not, v. 11. An old man once said: "My acquaintance would fill a cathedral; my friends could all be put into a pulpit." " At my first answer," says Paul, " all men forsook me." Yet he tells us of one who was not ashamed of his chain. Although happily the sword of persecution is now seldom drawn in Christian countries, yet the spirit that is in men lusteth to envy. McDuff: "There is a persecution sharper than that of the axe. There is an iron that goes into the heart, deeper than the knife. Cruel sneers, and *sarcasms*, and *pitiless* and *unjust judgments*, and *cold-hearted calumnies*—these are persecution."

16. Though we can never pay the debt we owe to God, yet we should diligently remember our obligations, and, as we have opportunity, manifest our gratitude, v. 12. A child can never pay the debt he owes his mother. It shows some right-mindedness for him candidly to say so, and do his best to requite her.

17. A fit mode of expressing our thanks to God is by solemn acts of worship, secret, social and public, vv. 13, 14, 17–19. Morison: "The closet will be the first place where the heart will delight in pouring forth its lively joys; thence the feeling will extend to the family altar; and thence again it will proceed to the sanctuary of the

Most High." To every man God has sent a large supply of benefits, and nothing but perverseness can deny to him the praise of our lips.

18. We should be careful to make none but lawful vows, v. 14; but when such are made, we should never turn to the right hand or to the left, but steadfastly perform our engagements. We should avoid anything like the temper of a sordid bargaining with the Almighty. But we may strengthen our hearts many a time by a fit vow to the Lord.

19. Let not the righteous be over-anxious concerning the fact, the time or the manner of their departure out of life, v. 15. This is all arranged by the Lord. Nicolson: "The servants of God trouble themselves in vain, when they distrust him; for in life he is with them, and in death he will not forsake them." He who gives grace to his chosen to live to his glory will not deny them grace to die in his peace.

20. As our responsibilities are very great, our sense of obligation should be deep and lasting, v. 16. We ought promptly and publicly to profess the true religion. We ought to engage to do everything in our power for the glory of God and for the expression of our gratitude to him.

21. Whatever our trials, and however sharp our conflicts, let us seek to come out of them all with a *hallelujah* on our lips, v. 19.

PSALM CXVII.

1 O praise the LORD, all ye nations: praise him, all ye people.
2 For his merciful kindness is great toward us: and the truth of the LORD *endureth* for ever. Praise ye the LORD.

SOME deny to this Psalm a completeness in itself, attach it to Psalm cxvi., or to Psalm cxviii., or use it as a doxology to any other Psalm. But is not this taking great liberties? Nothing in the state of the Hebrew text can authorize the annihilation of this as a complete and independent composition. It is indeed a very short ode; but it gives just expression to very lively and devout feelings. Luther: "This is a prophecy concerning Christ; that all peoples, out of all kingdoms and islands, shall know Christ in his kingdom; that is, in his church;" Pool: "This Psalm contains a prophecy of the calling of the Gentiles;" Henry: "This Psalm is short and sweet; I doubt the reason why we sing it so often as we do, is, for the shortness of it; but, if we rightly understood and considered it, we should sing it oftener for the sweetness of it, especially to us sinners of the Gentiles, on whom it casts a favorable eye." Of its authorship we know nothing. Scott dates it B. C. 1040; Clarke, B. C. 515. The names of God found in it are *Jehovah* LORD and *Jah* LORD, on which see on Psalm i. 2, and introduction to Psalm lxviii.

1. *O praise the* LORD, *all ye nations: praise him, all ye people.* The first verb rendered *praise* is that used in the word *hallelujah;* the second is in 1 Chron. xvi. 35, *glory;* in Ps. cvi. 47, *triumph;* in Ps. lxiii. 3, *praise.* The words rendered *nations* and *people* are both plural: the former being the word often rendered *Gentiles;* the latter, *nations.* The call is indiscriminate to the whole world to come and give due praise to Jehovah. This verse is explained by the great commission given by Christ to his ministers, Matt. xxviii. 19, 20; Mark xvi. 15, 16. What puts the matter beyond all doubt, and gives to us a most satisfactory exposition of the verse, is the

use made of it by Paul in Rom. xv. 11, where he maintains this proposition: "Now, I say, that Jesus Christ was a minister of the circumcision for the truth of God, to confirm the promise made unto the fathers, and that the Gentiles might glorify God for his mercy," Rom. xv. 8, 9. He quotes two other places and then this verse in proof. This call on the people of the earth is to a holy and spiritual service, and so implies the universal spread of the gospel. It is the truth that is to set men free. This call on all peoples and nations to praise Jehovah is not without cause:

2. *For his merciful kindness is great toward us.* Merciful kindness, in Ps. v. 7, *mercy;* in Ps. li. 1, *lovingkindness;* often, *kindness. Is great,* a verb in the preterite, as in Ps. ciii. 11; in Ps. xii. 4; lxv. 3, *prevail;* in Job xxi. 7, *are mighty.* It denotes the power attending the manifestations of God's kindness to the nations. Nothing has ever moulded the hearts and minds of the nations of the earth like the gospel of Jesus Christ, which is unchangeable in its promises and principles: *And the truth of the* LORD *endureth for ever.* Alexander renders the whole verse: *For mighty over us has been his mercy,* and the *truth of Jehovah* [is] *to eternity.* The gospel is *the everlasting gospel,* Rev. xiv. 6. It brings everlasting consolation to all believers, 2 Thess. ii. 16. To all who embrace it, it secures everlasting life, John iii. 16. The stability of the mediatorial throne rests on the unchangeableness of the covenant of grace. The whole calling of God to his people is without repentance. Never has a promise in Christ failed. Never has it been revoked. *Praise ye the* LORD, literally, *hallelujah;* see on Ps. civ. 35.

DOCTRINAL AND PRACTICAL REMARKS.

1. The brevity of this Psalm naturally suggests the question of the length of devotional exercises. On this subject no rule binding in all cases can be laid down. The Scriptures generally would lead us to greater brevity than is common. Dickson: "In God's worship it is not always necessary to be long; few words sometimes say what is sufficient." The publican's prayer was short and prevalent. That of the pharisee was long, and wordy, and worthless.

2. Prophecy has declared and God's veracity makes it certain that the gospel shall spread far and wide, v. 1. The knowledge of God shall cover the earth as the waters cover the sea. The people that are afar off shall be made nigh. Next to the resurrection of Christ, the conversion of the Gentiles was one of the most important and glorious events that has happened in the latter days, Acts xi. 18. Jesus himself promised that his salvation should extend far beyond the pale of the Jewish church, John x. 16.

3. To whomsoever the gospel is sent, it brings a message not only of glad tidings of great joy, but is a loud and solemn call to purity and devotion, v. 1. For who can *praise* God aright unless he has clean hands and a pure heart?

4. The calling of the Gentiles according to the predictions of the prophets is sufficient evidence of the truth and divine power of Christianity, in causing the most powerful and enlightened nations, among whom it has been generally preached, to renounce their false gods and embrace the truth as it is in Jesus, v. 1. In bestowing the Gospel the Lord grants incalculable treasures of mercy and grace, and all he demands is a grateful acceptance and acknowledgment of his bounty.

5. We shall wait in vain and but deceive ourselves, if we expect any other or more glorious revelation of himself than God has already made for our salvation, v. 2. Nicolson: "There will never be another Messiah: Jesus is the true One; he tasted death for every man; he forgives iniquity, transgression and sin; and his blood cleanses from all unrighteousness."

6. The *merciful kindness* and *truth* revealed to us in the Gospel are as great as they

have ever been represented to be, as good a foundation for hope and confidence as we can ever need, and are as inviting to honest inquirers and penitent sinners as it is possible for us to conceive, v. 2. No man needs more grace than the Gospel offers. The truth of God has amazing power, and when brought home to the heart by the Holy Ghost is as effectual now as it ever has been.

7. Let us be specially careful how we treat the Gospel, v. 2. It is not a light thing; it is our life. Let not that which was ordained unto life be found to be unto death. The greatest sin ever committed by men in lands where Jesus is preached is the rejection of salvation by the cross.

PSALM CXVIII.

1 O give thanks unto the LORD; for *he is* good: because his mercy *endureth* for ever.

2 Let Israel now say, that his mercy *endureth* for ever.

3 Let the house of Aaron now say, that his mercy *endureth* for ever.

4 Let them now that fear the LORD say, that his mercy *endureth* for ever.

5 I called upon the LORD in distress: the LORD answered me, *and set me* in a large place.

6 The LORD *is* on my side; I will not fear: what can man do unto me?

7 The LORD taketh my part with them that help me: therefore·shall I see *my desire* upon them that hate me.

8 *It is* better to trust in the LORD than to put confidence in man.

9 *It is* better to trust in the LORD than to put confidence in princes.

10 All nations compassed me about: but in the name of the LORD will I destroy them.

11 They compassed me about; yea, they compassed me about: but in the name of the LORD I will destroy them.

12 They compassed me about like bees; they are quenched as the fire of thorns: for in the name of the LORD I will destroy them.

13 Thou hast thrust sore at me that I might fall: but the LORD helped me.

14 The LORD *is* my strength and song, and is become my salvation.

15 The voice of rejoicing and salvation *is* in the tabernacles of the righteous: the right hand of the LORD doeth valiantly.

16 The right hand of the LORD is exalted: the right hand of the LORD doeth valiantly.

17 I shall not die, but live, and declare the works of the LORD.

18 The LORD hath chastened me sore: but he hath not given me over unto death.

19 Open to me the gates of righteousness: I will go into them, *and* I will praise the LORD:

20 This gate of the LORD, into which the righteous shall enter.

21 I will praise thee: for thou hast heard me, and art become my salvation.

22 The stone *which* the builders refused is become the head *stone* of the corner.

23 This is the LORD's doing; it *is* marvellous in our eyes.

24 This *is* the day *which* the LORD hath made; we will rejoice and be glad in it.

25 Save now, I beseech thee, O LORD: O LORD, I beseech thee, send now prosperity.

26 Blessed *be* he that cometh in the name of the LORD: we have blessed you out of the house of the LORD.

27 God *is* the LORD, which hath shewed us light: bind the sacrifice with cords, *even* unto the horns of the altar.

28 Thou *art* my God, and I will praise thee: *thou art* my God, I will exalt thee.

29 O give thanks unto the LORD; for *he is* good: for his mercy *endureth* for ever.

THAT David wrote this Psalm is admitted by Calvin, Piscator, Fabritius, Amesius, Venema, Cobbin, Delaney, Phillips and many others. Patrick: "There is nothing more probable than that David composed it." Pool: "It most probably was composed by David." Edwards: "It is generally supposed to have been penned by David." Henry: "It is probable that David penned it." Scott: "David is thought to have composed it." Clarke: "Most probably David was the author of this Psalm, though many think it was done after the captivity. It partakes of David's spirit, and everywhere shows the hand of a *master*. The *style* is grand and noble, the *subject* majestic." Of those who ascribe it to David the majority regard it as probably written about the time that he was quietly in possession of his kingdom. But the particular occasion of its composition, if it has any, seems to be wholly conjectural. Hengstenberg quite differs from the foregoing views: "That the deliverance for which the Psalm gives thanks is the deliverance from the Babylonish captivity, there can be no doubt." Alexander: "The deliverance celebrated cannot be identified with any one so naturally as with that from the Babylonish exile." It is not possible to apply large portions of the Psalm to any king after the time of David, unless with some we refer it to Hezekiah. But there are serious difficulties in that plan of interpretation. The Scripture most relied on as bearing on the question of authorship is Ezra iii. 10, 11. The reader can examine the place for himself. The first and last words of this Psalm were used on the occasion of laying the foundation of the second temple. Many make this ode prophetical. Calvin: "Let us remember that it was the design of the Spirit, under the figure of this temporal kingdom, to describe the eternal and spiritual kingdom of God's Son, even as David represented Christ." Dodd: "The learned Jews, both ancient and modern, confess it to speak of the Messiah." Morison: "It reaches forth, in the spirit of prophecy to Messiah, and to his spiritual kingdom." Like views are expressed by many. Nor are they unwarranted, as any one may see who will examine Matt. xxi. 42–46; Mark xii. 10–12; Luke xx. 17, 18; Acts iv. 10–12. Scott dates it B. C. 1040; Clarke gives no date. The names of the Almighty in it are *Jehovah* LORD, *Jah* LORD, *El God* and *Elohim God*, on which see on Ps. i. 2; introduction to Ps. lxviii.; on Ps. v. 4; iii. 2.

1. *O give thanks unto the* LORD; *for he is good: because his mercy* endureth *for ever.* On the whole verse see on Ps. cvi. 1; cvii. 1. *Give thanks*, elsewhere *confess, praise*, but commonly as here. We have the same word in another form in vv. 19, 21, 28, rendered *praise*. *Good*, see on Ps. xxv. 8. *Mercy*, elsewhere *kindness, lovingkindness, merciful kindness.* The whole phrase occurs again in vv. 2, 3, 4, 29. Street: Pay homage to Jehovah, for he is good; truly his mercy endureth to eternity. Although the world greatly misunderstands the true doctrine of the divine justice, yet it has a deeper sense of the retributive rectitude of God than it has of his mercy and kindness. The most difficult thing ever undertaken by God's ministers is to persuade sinners heartily to embrace offered mercy. We cannot be better employed than in extolling free grace.

2. *Let Israel now say, that his mercy* endureth *for ever.*

3. *Let the house of Aaron now say, that his mercy* endureth *for ever.*

4. *Let them now that fear the* LORD *say, that his mercy* endureth *for ever.* This classification of persons is the same as in Ps. cxv. 9–11. The word rendered *now* in each of these verses is a word of entreaty: *I pray thee, I beseech thee.* It occurs again in v. 25. *Let say*, equivalent to *Oh that* they *would say*, although the verb is in the future. If the knowledge and belief of the divine mercy fails from among men, they will soon become desperate, and all hope of reformation will forsake them. Verses 2–4; 8, 9; 10–12; 15, 16, abundantly show that all repetitions in devotion are not *vain*.

5. *I called upon the Lord in distress.* Green: When I was in straits, I called upon the Lord; Street: From a state of distress I invoked Jehovah; Alexander: Out of anguish I invoked Jah. Either of these renderings is admissible. On calling on God see on Ps. iv. 1. *The* LORD *answered me, and set me in a large place. Large place*,

in contrast with the *straits* or *distress* of the first clause. The words *and set me* are supplied, but they are not necessary to the sense, though they are to the exact preservation of the idiom. Edwards: He answered me with deliverance; Street: Jehovah answered me, by setting me at large; Green: The Lord answered and set me at liberty. Alexander: " To *answer* in a wide place is to grant his prayer by bringing him forth into such a place." Calvin: " By his own example David establishes the faithful, showing them that they ought not to faint in the day of adversity."

6. *The* Lord *is on my side: I will not fear: what can man do unto me? On my side*, literally *for me. Fear*, in Ps. iii. 6, *be afraid.* Compare Ps. xxiii. 4; xxvii. 1, 3. *Man*, Adam, the whole race or any member of it. Calvin renders the verse: Jehovah is with me: I will not fear what man may do unto me. In this he follows several of the old versions, as does also the Apostle, Heb. xiii. 6. Almost any version gives the essential idea.

7. *The* Lord *taketh my part with them that help me*, literally, Jehovah (is) for me amongst those who help me. Street: Jehovah is for me, he is mine aid; Hengstenberg: The Lord is among those who help me. *Therefore shall I see* my desire *upon them that hate me.* The words *my desire* are needlessly supplied. See on Ps. liv. 7; lix. 10; xcii. 11; cxii. 8. Edwards: I shall feast my eyes upon them that hate me; Fry: I shall look in triumph on mine enemies; Hengstenberg: I shall see my pleasure on those that hate me. The following renderings are more literal; Jebb: I myself shall look upon them that hate me; Street: I can look on mine enemies; Green: I shall be able to face those who hate me. Calvin's paraphrase of the whole verse is: " Defended by God's hand I may boldly and safely set at nought all the machinations of men;" Patrick's: " It is sufficient that the Lord, who hath done great things for me by weak instruments, is still aiding to me: therefore I dare look the most malicious enemies in the face, and doubt not to see them turn their backs upon me, 2 Sam. viii."

8. It is *better to trust in the* Lord *than to put confidence in man.* [This is the middle verse of the Bible].

9. It is *better to trust in the* Lord *than to put confidence in princes.* The word rendered *man* is *Adam.* It comprehends the whole race. Verse 8 contains a universal proposition. Verse 9 selects out the chief of men, those on whom we would most naturally rely, and warns us that we can no more safely trust in them than in others. *Princes*, in Ps. lxxxiii. 11, *nobles;* the greatest men, the best men, those who are in fact or deservedly head men. Jehovah alone can be safely relied upon at all times, in all straits and to all the ends and purposes of complete succor and deliverance.

10. *All nations compassed me about: but in the name of the* Lord *will I destroy them.*

11. *They compassed me about; yea, they compassed me about: but in the name of the* Lord *I will destroy them.*

12. *They compassed me about like bees; they are quenched as the fire of thorns: for in the name of the* Lord *I will destroy them. Nations*, also *heathen, Gentiles. Compassed*, as in Ps. xvii. 11; xviii. 5; xxii. 12, 16; in Ps. lxxxviii. 17, *came round about*, equivalent to surrounded. *Destroy, cut down, cut in pieces;* in the future. Yet in each case Street has, *I did cut them in pieces.* In the Hebrew, before the word *destroy* in each case is found a particle, which is sometimes rendered *surely.* Alexander: " The point of comparison with bees is their swarming multitude and irritating stings. Compare Deut. i. 44." A *fire of thorns* is a very brisk fire, and for the time makes quite a crackling noise, but is quickly over. *Are quenched, are extinct, are put out, are consumed.* The rage and power of the wicked against God's church, however violent and cruel, cannot last long.

13. *Thou hast thrust sore at me, that I might fall.* Literally, *Thrusting thou hast thrust.* *Thrust* is the best rendering here, although the verb is nowhere else so rendered. In Ps. xxxv. 5, it is *chase.* The *thrusting* was designed to be deadly, that he might *fall.* See on Ps. xxvii. 2. Street following some ancient versions has: I stumbled greatly as if I were falling. But this requires an unauthorized change in the Hebrew text. The change of number and person in this verse is not unusual. In v. 7, he spoke of *those that hated* him, and in vv. 10–12, of the *heathen.* Here he seems to imagine all his foes united in one, or under one leader, and his address is to that one directly. Some think he means Saul. Dickson supposes Satan is here addressed. This impersonation adds to the liveliness of the composition, and shows that to some extent at least the Psalm is dramatic. Yet nothing can harm those who hope in God: *But the* LORD *helped me.*

14. *The* LORD *is my strength and song, and is become my salvation.* The whole verse is taken from Ex. xv. 2. *Strength, song, salvation,* all uniformly rendered. LORD, *i. e., Jah.* He becomes the *song* of his people by becoming their *strength* and *salvation.*

15. *The voice of rejoicing and salvation* is *in the tabernacles of the righteous.* The general idea is the same as in v. 14. For a while the state of God's people may be greatly distressed; but as soon as the Lord appears, their mourning is turned into the voice of melody. *Tabernacles* were the dwellings of the ancient Jews, here used poetically for any abode of the accepted people of God. The occasion of the holy mirth was the work of God: *The right hand of the* LORD *doeth valiantly.* On this truth all holy gladness depends, so it is repeated verbatim in the next verse. The rendering is not uniform. Church of England: The right hand of the Lord bringeth mighty things to pass; Edwards: The right hand of Jehovah did great achievements; Fry: The right hand of Jehovah hath done mightily. The word rendered *valiantly* is a noun, *host, army, company, forces, valor, power, substance, riches, wealth.* The meaning of this as of many other words depends on its collocation. As the prophet is here celebrating a great deliverance, the authorized version comes as near to the true sense as either of the others.

16. *The right hand of the* LORD *is exalted.* *Exalted, lifted up, high* over the enemies of his people so as to govern, restrain, or punish them; *high* in the esteem and praises of his saints; or both ideas may be included, the latter depending on the former. *The right hand of the* LORD *doeth valiantly.* Calvin: "*To do valiantly* is tantamount to a magnificent display of his power, so that there may be a bright manifestation of its effulgence."

17. *I shall not die, but live, and declare the works of the* LORD. It had often looked as if David would certainly be cut off. To the eye of sense it seemed impossible that he should escape. But when Jehovah *works* and *does valiantly,* all perils disappear. Rescued from danger, the righteous delights in publishing the honors of his deliverer. *Works,* as in Ps. cxi. 2, 6, 7, and often before.

18. *The* LORD *hath chastened me sore.* *Sore,* Street, *greatly.* The original is idiomatic as in v. 13: *Chastening thou hast chastened me.* *But he hath not given me over unto death.* If David had been taken out of the world before he and his seed had obtained full possession of the crown and kingdom, the promise would have failed, and David's typical character have been a myth. But *the Scripture cannot be broken.*

19. *Open to me the gates of righteousness: I will go into them,* and *I will praise the* LORD. By *the gates of righteousness* we may understand the gates of the temple, into which the righteous often and gratefully entered to *praise* or *give thanks* unto Jah. The propriety of such worship is urged and repeated.

20. *This gate of the* LORD, *into which the righteous shall enter.* Perhaps with Calvin

and others we should read: This is the gate of Jehovah; or with Street: This is the gate that belongeth to Jehovah. Tholuck: "The gates of righteousness are so called, since really none but the righteous were to be admitted." Alexander: "The meaning may be, Since this is the Lord's gate, let the righteous (and no others) enter at it." Calvin gives another view: "*It is the gate of Jehovah*, and, therefore, he will open it to the just." There is no significancy in the change from *gates* to *gate*. Compare Jer. vii. 2.

21. *I will praise thee : for thou hast heard me, and art become my salvation.* Praise, in v. 1, *give thanks*. *Heard*, in v. 5, *answered*. The last phrase is borrowed from v. 14, with a simple change from the third to the second person singular.

22. *The stone* which *the builders refused is become the head* stone *of the corner.* The interpretations, which refer this to some contest as to which of two or more stones should be the corner stone in the temple, are too puerile for serious Christians to dwell upon; and yet had such a disagreement occurred, it would furnish a foundation of the figure here employed. Nor can we very fully apply it to David. Saul and his adherents can but in a very limited sense be regarded as the *builders* of the throne of Israel. God himself eminently presided over that matter. Yet there was enough of the human in the affair to admit of an allusion to it. Those, who regard this Psalm as relating to the return from Babylon, and the rebuilding of the second temple and of the holy city very naturally suppose that by the *stone* is meant the Jewish people, who by surrounding nations had been rejected from all empire, but were after seventy years of captivity again made preëminent, under the special guidance and protection of God. Like either of the foregoing this may furnish a basis for the figure in its full application to the Redeemer. More than this is not necessary or edifying. The Saviour and his apostles have given us the true interpretation, Matt. xxi. 42–46; Mark xii. 10–12; Luke xx. 17, 18; Acts iv. 10–12; Eph. ii. 20; 1 Pet. ii. 4–6. Horne: "That the verses (22, 23,) belong, in a full proper sense, to Messiah, is confessed by the Rabbis, and acknowledged by all. No text in the Old Testament is quoted by the writers of the New, so often as this." Indeed pages might be filled with citations in proof of the belief of the direct and full application of the passage to Messiah. He is the stone refused by the Jewish builders, but raised to the highest honor by his Father. He was denied of men, but approved of God. He sank lower than any innocent being ever did; and has already risen higher than the angels of God, so that he is the first-born of every creature. *Head* means chief; in Ps. cxix. 160, it is *beginning*; often *top*, here it clearly means the *chief corner stone*. But all this was not of man, or of created wisdom and power:

23. *This is the* LORD's *doing.* Calvin: This was done by Jehovah; Jebb: *From the* LORD *is this;* Fry and Street: This is from Jehovah. The whole exaltation of Christ is so wonderful that it is mere folly to ascribe it to any but Jehovah. *It* is *marvellous in our eyes.* The very name of Christ is WONDERFUL. See on Ps. ix. 1.

24. *This* is *the day* which *the* LORD *hath made; we will rejoice and be glad in it.* To the term *day* several interpretations are given. 1. Some refer it to a Jewish festival day, on which this Psalm was sung. 2. Others by *day* understand the improved state of things following the rebuilding of the second temple and of the holy city. This falls in with other views of those who believe that the ode relates to the return from Babylon. 3. Others by *day* understand the Christian Sabbath instituted in honor of the resurrection of Christ, the first step in his exaltation. This view is embraced by Watts, defended by Scott, Dwight and many others. It gives a good sense, and is in no degree inconsistent with the context. 4. By *day* others understand the Gospel dispensation, *the latter day*, when under the power and grace of an ascended Saviour his believing people abound in *joy* and *gladness*. Compare Acts ii. 45–47 ·

viii. 8.   Either of the latter two views is better than either of the former two; and these two may be made to harmonize.   This day the LORD has *made*, or *prepared*.

25. *Save now, I beseech thee, O* LORD: *O* LORD, *I beseech thee, send now prosperity.* The views gathered from this verse are, 1. That it contains a formula of seeking the divine blessing on great enterprises.   Those who hold this view refer to Neh. i. 11 Perhaps the reader may think the proof insufficient.   2. Others regard it as a special prayer for God's blessing on the great work of rebuilding the holy city.   3. Others make it a prayer for God's favor to David after he had secured full possession of the throne.   Regarding him as a type of Christ, this view well agrees with the next. 4. That it is a fervent petition for the building up of Christ's kingdom.   *For him shall prayer be made continually,* Ps. lxxii. 15.   5. Another view, coincident with the last two, is that this verse and the next contain the language which prophecy put into the mouth of the multitude in worshipping the Saviour in his triumphant entry into Jerusalem, and is an expression of the desires of the pious of all ages.   Compare Matt. xxi. 8–11; Mark xi. 1–11; Luke xix. 28–40.   See also Matt. xxiii. 37–39 This latter is to be preferred, is the most comprehensive and gives the fullest sense. These verses were actually used under the powerful influence of God's Spirit on a great public occasion foretold by the prophets.   Moreover, the words bear out this interpretation.   *Save now,* or *save, I beseech* is the same in signification as *Hosanna.* Indeed the original is the word Hosanna, with the parts transposed.   Scott: "The word rendered 'Save now' is 'Hosanna,' which seems equivalent to our modern congratulatory prayer on the accession of a monarch to the throne, 'God save the king.' It is evident that the Jews had this passage in mind, when they said before Christ, at his entrance into Jerusalem, 'Hosanna to the Son of David; blessed is he that cometh in the name of the Lord; Hosanna in the highest.'   They meant to welcome him as the promised Messiah."   If this is the correct view it explains a part of the next verse:

26. *Blessed* be *he that cometh in the name of the* LORD.   *He that cometh,* as many learned men have shown, was one of the standing titles of Messias among the Jews. It is often found in the New Testament.   The foregoing exposition leaves unexplained a part of v. 25, and a part of v. 26.   *Send prosperity,* one word, a verb found in Ps. i. 3, used both transitively and intransitively.   Again, *We have blessed you out of the house of the* LORD.   Perhaps the best view is that which makes the company of priests the speakers, and refers the whole to the benediction used by them in blessing the people, Num. vi. 24÷26.

27. *God* is *the* LORD, *which hath shewed us light.*   The word rendered God is *El,* expressive of great power.   Calvin, Edwards, Street and Fry read, Jehovah is God; Alexander: Mighty is Jehovah.   'He, who *made the day* of v. 24, is here said to have *shewed us light.*   Green: And he hath shone *graciously* upon us; Street: And he constantly enlighteneth us.   As *light* is a term expressive of all blessings, so is it in particular of the two good things commonly supposed to be referred to in this Psalm; first, a good government among men, 2 Sam. xxiii. 3, 4; secondly, the reign of Messiah, Luke ii. 29–32, compared with many prophecies of the Old Testament, especially Isa. xlii. 6; xlix. 6.   *Bind the sacrifice with cords,* even *unto the horns of the altar.* We know very well the literal meaning of the phrase *horns of the altar.*   They were protuberances upon each of the four corners of the altar, Ex. xxvii. 2; xxx. 2; xxxvii. 26; xxxviii. 2.   On these projections the blood of the sacrifice was put with the finger of the priest, Ex. xxix. 12; Lev. iv. 7, 18, 25, 30, 34; viii. 15; ix. 9; xvi. 19.   Thus much is clear.   But the rendering of the first part of the clause is quite diverse.   Calvin: Bind ye the lamb with cords; Edwards: Bind ye the sacrifices with cords; Doway, following several ancient versions: Appoint a solemn day, with

shady boughs; Street: Bind the victim with cords; Tholuck: Decorate the feast with wreaths. The explanations also are quite various. Diodati's paraphrase is: "Make ready the sacrifices of thanksgiving;" Patrick's: "O be not ungrateful to him, but solemnize this day with festival joy; bind your sacrifices with cords;" Horne: "Let us observe the festival which is designed to perpetuate the memory of so great and joyful an event." He applies it to the gospel dispensation. It seems to be best to render the word *sacrifice* here, in Ex. xxiii. 18; Isa. xxix. 1, although in every other case it is fitly rendered *feast*, or *feast days*, and it occurs at least sixty times. Then we have no account whatever of any custom of binding the victim to the horns of the altar. On this matter Hammond and others are decided. So also Cresswell: "*Yea, even unto the horns of the altar*—before these words must be understood *lead it*; for the victims were bound to rings fixed in the floor." The Chaldee gives this as the sense: Bind the lamb with bands till ye have sacrificed it, and poured the blood thereof upon the horns of the altar. This is perhaps better than any other explanation.

28. *Thou art my God, and I will praise thee.* He declares his covenant relation with God. *Praise*, in v. 1, *give thanks*. He again claims the covenant relation: Thou art *my God. I will exalt thee*, in Ps. xxx. 1, *I will extol thee*. In this verse we have both *El* and *Elohim*.

29. *O give thanks unto the* LORD; *for he is good: for his mercy* endureth *for ever*. A repetition of v. 1. Alexander: "In these words we are brought back to the point from which we started, and the circle of praise returns into itself."

DOCTRINAL AND PRACTICAL REMARKS.

1. There is exhaustless excellence in the Scriptures! The Bible is full of new songs, new displays of love, mercy and grace. We have already considered more than a hundred Psalms, yet here is one as fresh and as refreshing as if we had not looked at any other. Luther: "This Psalm, which I so much love and admire, is the one which I, in particular, call the golden Psalm; and is the Psalm which has often revived and comforted me in my temptations." Is it not a proof of the dreadful depravity of man, that it is so difficult to interest his mind in the best poetry in the world, simply because it teaches the true theology?

2. We shall never be done thanking and praising Jehovah, vv. 1, 29. This does not make the righteous sad. The themes furnished them are exhaustless. The new heart given by God's Spirit loves the work. We should delight to stir ourselves up to this blessed employment.

3. While carnal and imaginative men are pleasing themselves with schemes of uniformity, or of outward unity in the church, let us labor to promote that essential unity which consists in bringing all of every rank and condition to accept and celebrate the amazing mercy of God, vv. 1–4. If men feel heart to heart in singing the song of Moses and the Lamb, they will not be disowned by the blessed Saviour.

4. Ample reason for perpetual praise and thanksgiving is found in the exalted nature of God, vv. 1, 2, 3, 4, 29. He is *goodness* itself. His *lovingkindness* never *fails*. Why will not all men worship Jehovah?

5. Affliction is no novelty in the church of God. *Distress* reaches the heart of all his people, v. 5. David, the type of the Redeemer, the Redeemer himself, and all the true Israel have had their sharp trials. What a strange sort of creature an old Christian would be, if he had never smarted under the rod of heavenly chastisement! Indeed there can be no such character, Heb. xii. 6–8.

6. But however sore our trials, the door is open leading to the mercy-seat, v. 5. "In prayer we have a consolation and an antidote for all our ills." *I called upon*

God in my distress, and he heard me, is written in the private journal of every Christian. Luther: "Thou must learn to call and not to sit there by thyself, and lie on the bench, hang and shake the head, and bite and devour thyself with thy thoughts, but come on, thou indolent knave, down upon thy knees, up with thy hands and eyes to heaven, take a Psalm or a prayer, and set forth thy distress with tears before God."

7. When we have had blessed experience of the divine mercy, especially in times of great trial, let us modestly and humbly declare it, v. 5. It is a shame, through false humility to keep silence when the very stones are ready to cry out for joy at God's presence.

8. Our theology is never right till in our hearts we invest God with infinite power and perfections, v. 6. Until we can say: "It is enough for me that God is on my side," we are not prepared to fight the battles of life.

9. Reason suggests that thanks ought to be in proportion to mercies received, and that deliverances are great in proportion to the distresses from which they rescue us, vv. 5, 6. If this is so, how impossible it is for the saints ever to exceed the bounds of sobriety in lauding and magnifying the grace which saves them from a fiery and eternal condemnation.

10. If we are delivered from great distress of any kind, the cause of our deliverance is God alone, vv. 5–7. To him is all the glory due.

11. The righteous can well afford to wait for the day of full and final decision of their case, v. 7. Things shall surely come to pass according to their holy desire. My soul, wait thou upon God.

12. Dickson: "Many good uses may a believer make of one benefit, one victory, one experience, as doth the Psalmist here, v. 7. He confirmeth himself in his reconciliation and friendship with God, encourageth himself against dangers to come, exalteth God, and esteemeth as nothing the hatred and favor of man, and resolveth to use means and to expect the blessing from God, with other sundry good uses which follow hereafter."

13. Nothing is more profitable than dwelling on familiar truths, vv. 8, 9. Was there ever a good man who did not believe that it was better to trust in Jehovah than to rely on any created arm? Yet David here repeats this truth that if possible it may sink deep into every mind.

14. The same verses teach us that it is hard, though necessary, to withdraw trust from man. He is a poor, feeble, sinful worm. Though the wicked appear in great numbers, and enter into the most fearful alliances with one another, they are but grasshoppers.

15. The same verses teach us that it is difficult, yet necessary to put our confidence in God. This is insisted on, and with great pertinency.

16. If we are sorely and terribly annoyed and beset with enemies and adversaries, the same has happened to others, vv. 10–12. But all believers thus tried have come off conquerors and more than conquerors through him that loved them.

17. The ground of hostility and opposition to God and his cause is found in the enmity of the natural heart against true religion and Scriptural holiness. Luther: "Men can put up with all other doctrines and all other gods, so that no nation and no country will set itself in hostility against them; but when the word of God comes, then the whole world is up, then tumults and animosities are on all sides."

18. Yet the final victory is certain. In some way, or by some means, or, if necessary, without means, God will *destroy* all his incorrigible foes, vv. 10, 12. How terrible that destruction will be is declared in Scripture and is believed by all wise men.

19. Considering the unanimity of the wicked in their opposition to Christ and his

people, and their readiness to follow the lead of the one great adversary, so that in all cases his will is virtually obeyed, it is for a joy that their combined attack has never been able to destroy one of God's elect, v. 13.

20. The reason is, God is stronger than all his foes, vv. 13, 14.

21. Good songs, good promises, good proverbs, good doctrines are not the worse for age, v. 14. What was sung just after the passage of the Red sea is here sung by the prophet, and shall be sung to the end of the world by the saints of the Most High.

22. If we would avail ourselves of the help of the Lord, we must say that he is our strength and salvation, v. 14. We must renounce all self-reliance; we must feel and confess that we are nothing and less than nothing.

23. The righteous have good cause of joy however they may be situated, v. 15. "Though their dwellings in this world are but *tabernacles*, mean and moveable, yet they are more comfortable to them than the *palaces* of the wicked are to them; for where religion rules, there is safety from evil and there are earnests of eternal salvation, and abundant matter for continual joy and rejoicing."

24. Let us remember that Jehovah is over all and let us say so, v. 16. Otherwise we in vain attempt to build up a system of consolation.

25. Let past mercies beget confidence for present and future times, v. 17. He who in covenant love has saved us from fatal disasters will continue his loving-kindness until our work is done. We may be especially assured of this, when like the Psalmist we are fully purposed to use our lives and all our faculties in the service and for the glory of God. Our life is hid with Christ in God, Col. iii. 3.

26. All is not lost that is brought into jeopardy, v. 18. We gain a great advantage in all our trials when we see God's hand in everything; when we are willing to crucify the flesh with its affections and lusts; when we are submissive to the divine appointment, knowing that the Lord doth not afflict willingly, but for our profit, that we may be partakers of his holiness.

27. A prime ingredient in the worship of the saints is thankfulness. The goodness of God leads them to praise him, vv. 19, 21.

28. Even in this world the righteous have an access to God which is denied to all others, v. 20. The secret of the Lord is with them that fear him; much more shall they alone enter into the blissful presence of God in glory. Compare Isa. xxvi. 1–4. Great things are now in possession of the people of God. Still greater things are before them.

29. It is said that prayer is mentioned in the Scriptures about *five hundred* times. In all cases it is implied and in many asserted that it is efficacious, v. 21. How strange it is that we poor, feeble creatures should ever attempt to get on without prayer.

30. Though by office men may be high in authority in the church of God, yet that does not determine that they shall be saved or that they shall not fall into fatal errors, v. 22. Men full of learning, zeal and authority have rejected the only foundation on which a sinner can safely rest his hope for eternity. Numbers foolishly imagine that if by their logic, or learning or intolerance they can silence the advocates of the truth as it is in Jesus, they have gained the victory; but their triumph is their ruin.

31. Vain are human devices, and vain is human malice, when directed against the counsels of God, v. 22. Whom he will, he exalts; whom he will, he abases.

32. We need have no fear of the church. Her safety is secured by the exaltation of Christ, v. 22. He who raised her Head from the depths of humiliation will not leave his body to perish.

33. God can do anything that does not involve contradiction. To man a thing may be improbable, yea, impossible. And when it is done it may be exceedingly

marvellous, v. 23. But what work of God duly considered is not so? Horne: "What can be more truly marvellous, than that a person, put to death as a malefactor, and laid in the grave, should from thence arise immortal, and become the head of an immortal society; should ascend into heaven, be invested with power, and crowned with glory, and should prepare a way for the sons of Adam to follow him into those mansions of eternal bliss?" And yet unless he believes this, how can any one be saved? John iii. 16. Jesus is "the foundation of our hope, the centre of our unity, and the end of our living."

34. If Christ's exaltation, beginning with his resurrection, be so exceedingly glorious, let it be celebrated, not by an anniversary, but by religiously observing one day in seven to commemorate that joyous event, v. 24. That is the day which the *Lord* has made for this purpose. "Sabbath days must be rejoicing days, and then they are to us as the days of heaven."

35. If such be the design of the Christian Sabbath, how exceedingly glorious must be the Christian dispensation. It also is the day which the Lord hath made. Let us rejoice and be glad in it.

36. When God undertakes the work of salvation, it is infallibly accomplished, v. 25. He has the will and all the resources necessary to that end. Let us each commit our case to him.

37. Let us welcome Christ and give him a cordial reception, not only in our country, but in our hearts, v. 26. Let us beware how we slight the Son of God, Luke xx. 18.

38. What an unspeakable source of joy and comfort is found in God through Jesus Christ. He is a *light* indeed, v. 27. Though all else is darkness, yet have we light in him.

39. While the rites of religion are not in themselves saving, yet we should cheerfully and humbly submit to any observances which God has enjoined, v. 27. And we should enter with life and spirit into any religious service appointed by heaven. In particular we should abound in thanksgiving.

40. Let us hold fast the covenant of God forever, v. 28. All appearances may be against us. Our enemies may be many, mighty and lively, but if God be for us, who can be against us?

PSALM CXIX.

THIS Psalm is alphabetical. See Introduction, § 13. It is divided into as many parts as there are letters in the Hebrew alphabet. Each part has eight verses. Each verse in any one part begins with the same letter. The respective parts fitly take their name from the letters of the alphabet in their order. Notwithstanding this highly artificial and ingenious character of the ode, it has considerable irregularities. Some of the parts have the name of the Lord not at all, others *once*, others *twice*, others *thrice*. Generally the verses consist of two lines, yet, says Street, "there are evidently as many as nine that have only one line in each; and there are two which consist of three lines each." Many notice the want of logical connection in this poem. Calvin: "The prophet frequently passes from one topic to another, and prosecutes no one particular subject continuously;" Henry: "This Psalm is a chest of gold rings, not a chain of gold links;" Hengstenberg: "That the Psalm consists of a collection of individual sayings, and that there is no room for attempting to discover any connection, or to trace any consecutive train of thought, is evident *à priori* from the formal arrangement." Yet it is pervaded by what Tholuck calls a "deep current of feeling." Jebb: "Instances can undoubtedly be shown of passages, which maintain a beautiful sequence and connection between their several members." We should not disparage other Psalms in order to exalt this; though its contents are truly rich. Clarke: "Several of the ancients, particularly the *Greek fathers*, have considered it as an abridgement of David's life; in which he expresses all the states through which he had passed; the trials, persecutions, succors, and encouragements, he had received. The *Latin fathers* perceive in it all the morality of the Gospel, and rules for a man's conduct in every situation of life." Luther: "It contains prayers, consolations, doctrines, thanksgivings, and repeats all these with a varied fulness. It is given forth with a deep and blessed intent; namely, that by this repetition and fulness, it may invite and exhort us to hear and diligently to treasure up the word of God;" Tholuck: "It is pervaded by a profound sense of the sublimity of the divine law, in connection with a sense of personal unworthiness;" Barrow: "This Psalm, no less excellent in virtue, than large in bulk, containeth manifold reflections on the nature and properties, the adjuncts and effects of God's law; many sprightly ejaculations about it, conceived in different forms of speech; some in way of petition, some of thanksgiving, some of resolution, some of assertion or aphorism; many useful directions, many zealous exhortations to the observance of it."

Its scope and design are quite apparent. Hammond: "It is wholly spent in consideration of the divine law—the excellency, the necessity, the advantages of it—descanting on the several appellations of it with frequent reflections on ourselves, by way of exhortation to a pious life and constant adherence to God in times of distress;" Pool: "The scope and design of it is manifest, to commend the serious and diligent study, and the steadfast belief and the constant practice of God's word, as incomparably the best counsellor and comforter in the world, and as the only way to true blessedness;" Bridges: "This Psalm may be considered as the journal of one, who was deeply taught in the things of God—long practised in the life and walk of faith. It contains the anatomy of experimental religion—the interior lineaments of the family of God. It is given for the use of believers in all ages, as an excellent touchstone of vital godliness." Many have noticed its peculiar and excellent adaptation to the young. Hengstenberg calls it, 'A children's sermon.' But it suits all classes. From its alphabetical character the Masora entitle it, The great alphabet; but from its peculiar excellence, many style it, The saints' Alphabet. Bishop Cowper calls it "A holy alphabet, so plain that children may understand it—so rich and instructive that the wisest and most experienced may learn something from it." Clarke: "Like all other portions of divine revelation, it is elegant, important, and useful;" Jebb: "It is well known, that upon no portion of holy Scripture have so many practical commentaries been written. . . It has been justly considered in all ages of the church as a storehouse of religious wisdom." One of its highest excellences is its varied instruction on the nature of true, experimental religion. In this Psalm, says Venn, "the whole inner man is delineated, and the several changing frames of our poor hearts, and the several blessed motions and inspirations of the Holy Spirit are touched in a very affecting manner. This is the Psalm I have often had recourse to, when I could find no spirit of prayer in my own heart, and at length the fire was kindled, and I could pray." President Edwards in his work on *Religious Affections*, says: "I know of no other part of the Holy Scriptures where the nature and evidences of true and sincere godliness are so fully and largely insisted on and delineated." Religious biography abounds in evidences of the same thing. We can hardly open a good volume of that class without meeting proofs of this truth. Some join this Psalm with others. Hengstenberg regards it as " the chief song of the feast, the proper dedication song following the decade which served as it were as an introduction to it." On the other hand, Jebb says, " with the 119th may be considered to begin that collection of Psalms which were composed during the captivity." Perhaps a careful scrutiny will satisfy any one that neither of these views can be sustained. There is as little to support the opinion of Fry, that Christ is the speaker throughout this Psalm. Verses 67, 71 and 75 are fatal to this view. Hengstenberg makes an exceedingly weighty remark : " A characteristic feature of our Psalm is the deep conviction that we have nothing to do with human strength in keeping the commandments of God, but that God alone must create the will and the power to perform." We do not certainly know the author or date of this poem. The Arabic, Theodoret and the great mass of modern commentators ascribe it to David. Patrick seems to have no doubt on the subject. Dodd : " This Psalm is supposed to have been written by David." The same view was taken by Venema, Michaelis and Dickson. Pool : " The author of this Psalm was David ; which I know none that deny, and of which there is no just reason to doubt ;" Henry : " It seems to be a collection of David's pious and devout ejaculations ;" Horne : " David must, undoubtedly, have been the author ;" Clarke : " Though the most judicious interpreters assign it to the time of the Babylonish captivity ; yet there are so many things in it descriptive of David's state, experience, and affairs, that I am led to think it might have come from his pen ; or, if composed at or under the captivity, was formed out of his notes and *memoranda ;*" Scott : " It is generally allowed that David composed this highly instructive Psalm." He dates it B. C. 1017. Notwithstanding this general agreement, and the internal evidence, Jebb says, " A stronger reason appears for assigning this Psalm to one of the prophets of the captivity, either Jeremiah or Daniel, whose circumstances were in many respects similar : I should think, with greater probability to the latter." His reasoning shows some ingenuity, but on full examination will probably not be regarded as conclusive. According to the Masora there is but one verse (the 122d) in which we have not some term pointing to the word of God. It is admitted on all hands that some name of Scripture is found in nearly every verse. This makes it best here to explain several terms ; to which we can hereafter refer by No.

1. LAW. This word occurs *twenty-five* times, between vv. 1–174. We met it in Ps. i. 2 ; xix. 7. After Ps. cxix. it is not found in the Psalter. Kimchi : "It is the *setting down of duties, how they are to be done*." Jebb : "It is formed from a verb which means to direct, to guide, to aim, to shoot forwards. Its etymological meaning, then, would be a rule of conduct." Pool : "God's word is called his *law*, as binding us to obedience." Dickson : "The revealed will of God is called *law* or *doctrine*, which signifieth the Lord's will to be taught by God, that all men should learn it." Henry : "The things contained in Scripture are called God's *law*, because they are enacted by him as their Sovereign." Clarke : "It is called *law* because it guides, *directs* and *instructs* in the way of righteousness—makes our path *straight*, shows what is *even* and *right*, and points us *onward* to peace, truth and happiness. It is even our *schoolmaster* to bring us to Christ, that we may be justified through faith ; and by it is the knowledge of sin."

2. TESTIMONIES. It is found in two forms, having the same derivation and the same signification, in all *twenty-three* times. In one form we first met it in the singular in Ps. xix. 7 ; in the other, in Ps. xxv. 10. Kimchi explains it as meaning *precepts that are for a testimony*, or *federal commemoration*. Jebb : "Testimonies are more particularly God's revealed law : the witnesses and confirmation of his promises made to his people, an earnest of his future salvation." Pool : "The Scripture is called God's

testimony, as it contains the witnesses of God's mind and will, and of man's duty." Dickson: "*Testimonies* signify that this revealed will of God testifieth of our duty and our doings, whether conform or not to the rule; and testifieth also what event may be expected by our believing or misbelieving, by our obedience or disobedience thereof." Henry: "The things contained in the Scripture are called God's *testimonies*, because they are solemnly declared to the world, and attested beyond contradiction." Clarke says, the word is derived from one denoting "*beyond, farther, all along, to bear witness* or *testimony*. The rites and ceremonies of the law; because they point out matters beyond themselves, being *types* and *representations* of the good things that were to come." Their observance demands spirituality of mind.

3. PRECEPTS. It occurs in this Psalm *twenty-one* times, and *thrice* in other places of Scripture. Here it is always rendered precepts, but in Ps. ciii. 18; cxi. 7, *command ments;* and in Ps. xix. 8, *statutes*. Kimchi thinks it denotes those *precepts which reason teaches*, that are, as it were *deposited* in our *nature*. Jebb says it comes from a "word which means to *place in trust*, and means something entrusted to man—appointments of God, which consequently have to do with the conscience, for which man is responsible." Pool: "The *precepts* declare and direct our duty." Dickson: "Precepts signify that this will of God is imposed by the authority of our sovereign Lawgiver." Henry: "They are called *precepts*, because prescribed to us, and not left indifferent." Clarke: "They are called precepts from a word signifying to *take notice*, or *care* of a thing, to *attend, have respect to*, to *appoint*, to *visit;* because they take *notice* of our way, have *respect* to the whole of our life and conversation, *superintend, overlook* and *visit* us in all the concerns and duties of life."

4. STATUTES. It is found in this Psalm *once* in the feminine, v. 16; in the masculine *nineteen* times, between vv. 5–171; in Ps. cxlvii. 19, *statutes;* in Ps. ii. 7; cxlviii. 6, in the singular, *decree;* in Ps. xciv. 20; cv. 10, *law;* in Ps. xcix. 7, *ordinance*. Kimchi thinks it points to those *precepts whose reason is not known*, as not wearing linsey-woolsey, etc. Jebb: "The verb from which this word is formed means to engrave or inscribe, the word means a definite, prescribed, written law." Pool: "God's *statutes* declare his authority and power of giving us laws." Dickson: "The word *statutes* signifies that this revealed will of God containeth the duties which God hath appointed and prescribed for our rule." Henry: "They are called his *statutes*, because they are fixed, and determined, and of perpetual obligation." Clarke: "*Statutes*, from a word signifying to *mark, trace out, describe* and *ordain;* because they *mark out* our way, *describe* the line of conduct we are to pursue, and *order* or *ordain* what we are to observe." Alexander: "Definite and permanent enactments."

5. COMMANDMENTS. It occurs in this Psalm *twenty-two* times; in the singular in Ps. xix. 8; in the Psalter uniformly rendered; elsewhere a few times *precepts*. Jebb: "The commandments are God's laws, not only exhibited, and revealed, and recommended, but positively enjoined." Dickson: "It signifies that this revealed will of God is committed to our trust to be kept." Henry: "God's *commandments* are so called because given with authority, and (as the word signifies) lodged with us as a trust." Clarke: "They are called *commandments* because they show us what we should do, and what we should leave undone, and exact our obedience."

6. JUDGMENTS. It is here found *twenty-three* times; we met it in Ps. xix. 9. Kimchi thinks it had its origin in *the judgments that pass betwixt a man and his neighbor*. Jebb: "It is derived from a word signifying to govern, to judge or determine. *Judgments* mean judicial ordinances, and decisions: legal sanctions." Pool: "God's judgments are so called, because they proceed from the great Judge of the world, and are his judicial sentence to which all men must submit." Dickson: "The word *judgments* signifies the Scripture to be God's judicial decree, ordaining how our words, deeds and

thoughts shall be ordered, and what shall be the execution of his will answerable thereto." Henry: "They are called God's *judgments*, because framed in infinite wisdom, and because by them we must both judge and be judged." Clarke thinks they are so called, "because they *judge* concerning our words and works; show the *rules* by which they should be *regulated;* and cause us to discern what is *right* and *wrong*, and *decide* accordingly."

7. WORD or WORDS. There are two terms, quite distinct in the Hebrew, but both rendered *word*. To maintain the distinction between these words some translators for one have *word*, and for the other *saying*. The first of these occurs in this Psalm *twenty-four* times between vv. 9–169; in Ps. xix. 3, rendered *language*. The corresponding verb is rendered *talk, speak, say, tell, promise, declare, pronounce, commune*. It comprehends every kind of word that is spoken. The other term rendered *word* in this Psalm occurs *nineteen* times between vv. 11–172; in Gen. iv. 23; Deut. xxxii. 2; Ps. xvii. 6, *speech*, in the sense of *words uttered*. In this Psalm the rendering is uniform, but in Ps. cxlvii. 15, it is rendered *commandment*. These two words are never found in the same verse of this Psalm. Nor is it possible to define or preserve the distinction between them, though Jebb is confident that "they are not synonymous." They are at least parallel, and are used in the same general sense, and with the same application. Pool: "The Scripture is called God's *word*, as it proceeds from his mouth, and is revealed by him to us." Dickson: "The *word* signifieth God's expounding his mind to us, as if he were speaking to us." Henry: "The Scripture is called God's *word* or *saying*, because it is the declaration of his mind, and Christ, the essential Eternal Word, is all in all in it." Clarke: "In the revelation God speaks to man; shows him in a clear, concise, intelligible, and rational way, his interest, his duty, his privileges, and, in a word, the reasonable service he requires of him."

8. WAY. It occurs in this Psalm *thirteen* times. In some cases it clearly refers to the tenor of one's life, as in vv. 5, 26, 29, 59, 168; but in vv. 1, 3, 14, 27, 30, 32, 33, 37, it points to Scripture. The same word in the same sense is found both in preceding and succeeding Psalms, though often it denotes the life one leads, as in Ps. i. 1, 6. Kimchi thinks that the *way*, as a name for the sacred volume, is *the rule upon which the Scriptures are grounded*. Jebb says: "Its meaning is so direct and simple as to require no explanation, a plain rule of conduct; in its higher sense, the assisting grace of God, through Christ our Lord, who is the way, the truth, and the life." Pool: "The word of God is called his *way*, as prescribed by him for us to walk in." Dickson: "The *way* of God signifieth the Lord's giving direction for our several actions how we should walk, as by so many steps to the kingdom of heaven." Henry: "The Scriptures are called God's *way*, because they are the rule both of his providence and of our obedience." Clarke: "The revelation which God had given was called a *way*, because it was the *way* in which God goes in order to instruct and save man; the *way* in which man must tread in order to be safe, holy, and happy."

9. TRUTH, or FAITHFULNESS. Both words are given because both are employed by our translators in this Psalm and elsewhere as a fit rendering for a word cognate to *Amen*. It occurs in this Psalm *five* times, vv. 30, 75, 86, 90, 138. See on Ps. xxxiii. 4; xxxvi. 5. It expresses the stability and fidelity with which God executes all he speaks. Henry: "The principles upon which the divine law is built are eternal truths." It is once rendered *truth*, twice *faithful*, and twice *faithfulness*. "Thy word is truth."

10. RIGHTEOUSNESS. This word occurs in this Psalm *twice* in the feminine, and *twelve* times in the masculine form. In some cases it is rendered *right, justice, righteous*. In the text or margin it is commonly rendered *righteousness*. It clearly in several cases refers to God's word, vv. 7, 62, 75, 106, 123, 138, 144, 160, 164, 172. In

v. 142, we have it in both the masculine and feminine. Dickson says that, as applied to Scripture, it "signifieth that the word of God showeth the way how a man shall be justified, to wit, by faith, and how a justified man should approve himself to God and man, as justified by faith, and that every son of wisdom must and will justify this word of God, as the perfect rule of righteousness." Henry says the Scripture receives this name "because it is all holy, just, and good, and the rule and standard of righteousness." Pool says it is so styled, "as exactly agreeable to God's righteous nature and will."

Some have thought that to this list should be added the word *Name*. Nor can it be denied that in Ps. cxxxviii. 2, and perhaps in other places God's *name* includes his *word*: "Thou hast magnified thy word above all thy name," *i. e.*, above all by which thou makest thyself known. But as *name* occurs but *twice* in this Psalm, vv. 55, 132 and as in each of those cases we may understand the Lord himself, no further remarks are here offered on the subject, except that to us God is better known by his word than in all other ways. Though the ten words above explained are used as names of Scripture, and have, at least primarily, distinct significations, which it is not idle to make, and which in some cases seem to be preserved; yet to a considerable extent they are employed in a general sense, and synonymously. Calvin: "In this Psalm almost all these terms are synonymous." Nor are these distinctions of terms useless. Jebb: "It is well to learn from this Psalm to consider God's law as a guide, as a lamp of illumination; as an object of thankfulness, and a source of peace and joy, whether contemplated in the light of an objective truth, of a divine revelation, of an address to the conscience, of a command, of a judicial ordinance, or of a communication from God's own mouth."

The length of this Psalm is in great contrast with that of the cxvii. and many others. It is more than twice as long as any other. While the Scriptures allow of short devotional exercises and by example often commend them, they do not discourage those which are of greater length. Henry: "It is not making long prayers which Christ censures, but making them for a pretence; which intimates that they are in themselves good and commendable."

The three names of the Most High used in this poem are *Jehovah* Lord, *Elohim God* and *Jah* Lord, on which see on Ps. i. 2; iii. 2, and introduction to Ps. lxviii. Let us consider this Psalm by *parts* or *pauses*—eight verses at a time.

PSALM CXIX.

ALEPH.

1 Blessed *are* the undefiled in the way, who walk in the law of the Lord.
2 Blessed *are* they that keep his testimonies, *and that* seek him with the whole heart.
3 They also do no iniquity: they walk in his ways.
4 Thou hast commanded *us* to keep thy precepts diligently.
5 O that my ways were directed to keep thy statutes!
6 Then shall I not be ashamed, when I have respect unto all thy commandments.
7 I will praise thee with uprightness of heart, when I shall have learned thy righteous judgments.
8 I will keep thy statutes: O forsake me not utterly.

THOUGH the *first* letter of each of these verses in Hebrew is the same, yet the first words of none but verses 1, 2, are the same.

1. *Blessed* are *the undefiled in the way, who walk in the law of the* Lord. *Blessed,*

literally, O the blessednesses, as in Ps. i. 1. *Undefiled*, in Ps. xviii. 23 and elsewhere, *upright;* in Ps. xviii. 30, 32, *perfect;* sometimes *complete;* in application to sacrifices *without blemish*, Ex. xii. 5; Lev. i. 3; several times rendered as an adverb, *sincerely*, or as a noun, *sincerity*, see on Ps. xv. 2. *Way*, see No. 8; though some think it here means the way of a man's life. To walk in the law is to keep it.

2. *Blessed are they that keep his testimonies, and that seek him with the whole heart.* *Blessed*, as in v. 1. *Keep;* found *ten* times and uniformly rendered in this Psalm; elsewhere sometimes *preserve*, also *observe*. See on Ps. xii. 7. *Testimonies*, see No. 2. The words *and that* are added by the translators. Some prefer to make the latter clause entirely independent and read, *With all the heart they will seek him.* See on Ps. xiv. 2. The phrase denotes entire sincerity.

3. *They also do no iniquity: they walk in his ways.* Good men are here described both negatively and positively. 1. They do no iniquity; Calvin: Do not work iniquity; church of England: Do no wickedness; Fry: Have done no ill; Street: Commit no iniquity; Hengstenberg: Do no unrighteousness; Alexander: Do not practise wrong. The clause is parallel to 1 John iii. 9. A wicked life is subversive of all evidence of piety. 2. They walk in his ways, *i. e.*, they habitually behave as the Lord requires in his word.

4. *Thou hast commanded us to keep thy precepts diligently.* *Hast commanded*, hast brought the full weight of thy authority in an explicit requirement. *Keep;* in its various forms this verb occurs more than *twenty* times in this Psalm and often elsewhere. It is not that so rendered in v. 2, though of the same general import, and of much more frequent use. It is rendered *preserve, observe, take heed to, regard, look narrowly to* and *watch*. It implies great circumspection. *Precepts*, see No. 3. *Diligently*, elsewhere *exceedingly, greatly, utterly, very, mightily*. It occurs again in vv. 8, 43, 51, 96, 107, 138, 140, 167. The business of a pious man's life should be thoroughly gone through with.

5. *O that my ways were directed to keep thy statutes!* Where the optative form is used, it is now common to use Oh, not O. *Directed, fashioned, established, prepared;* in Ps. lvii. 7, *fixed;* in Ps. li. 10, *right*. *Keep*, as in v. 4. *Statutes*, see No. 4.

6. *Then shall I not be ashamed, when I have respect unto all thy commandments.* *Ashamed*, as in Ps. vi. 10; xxv. 2; elsewhere *confounded*. *Have respect, see, look, behold, consider;* found also in vv. 15, 18. *Commandments*, see No. 5. This verse differs from many others chiefly in calling for universal obedience. Calvin: "Among the snares of Satan, amid such thick darkness and so great insensibility as ours, the utmost vigilance and caution are necessary, if we would aim at being entirely exempted from blame."

7. *I will praise thee with uprightness of heart, when I shall have learned thy righteous judgments.* *Praise*, often *give thanks*. *Uprightness*, as in Ps. xxv. 21; in Prov. xvii. 26, *equity*. It occurs nowhere else in this Psalm, but we have the corresponding adjective, *upright*, in v. 137, and the corresponding verb, *I esteem right*, in v. 128. So great an attainment as to worship God in spirit and in truth is not made except by *learning* the *judgments of righteousness*. Some however think we are here to understand *providential* judgments. This does not materially vary the lesson taught, for we never understand providence except as we understand Scripture. Calvin: "The prophet very justly here makes the fruit of genuine piety to consist in celebrating the praises of God without hypocrisy."

8. *I will keep thy statutes: O forsake me not utterly.* *Keep statutes*, as in v. 4. The first clause is a vow, a covenant engagement to be the Lord's. But conscious of his own weakness, he trembles lest he should fail to fulfil it, and so he utters the ejaculation of the latter clause. *Forsake*, in Ps. xvi. 10, *leave;* in Ps. xxvii. 9, *forsake*. It

occurs again in v. 87, in the preterite. Calvin: "The term *forsake* is susceptible of two interpretations, either that God withdraws his Spirit, or that he permits his people to be brought low by adversity, as if he had forsaken them. The latter interpretation agrees best with the context, and is most in accordance with the phrase immediately subjoined *very far*," or *utterly*, in v. 4, rendered *diligently*. Clarke: "Never leave me to my own strength, nor to my own heart."

DOCTRINAL AND PRACTICAL REMARKS.

1. Let us hold fast the truth of God, by whatever name called, vv. 1–8. Without it we are undone, having neither strength, nor wisdom, nor righteousness, nor purity. Luther: "Where the true word of God is not taught, there is not any truth of God; there is found a great noise of external holiness, and the form of godliness, and hypocrisy; there, indeed, you may find psalm-singing, prayer, doctrines, consolation, and all thanksgiving and all the varieties of the worship of God, with all interpretations of the Scriptures. I will add, also, that there you may find sufferings and martyrdom. But all is outside show; all is the form of godliness only; all is false; all is feigned and nothing but lies; all is full of the poison of the devil."

2. Although the world does groan in misery, and God's people have their share, yet there is real blessedness secured to all the righteous, vv. 1, 2; see REMARKS on Psalm i. 1. On this point Scripture and experience speak the same language.

3. Scott: "It is the will of God that we should wisely seek our own happiness: our self-love, indeed, should be directed and subordinated; but it cannot and ought not to be extirpated." God often appeals to it, vv. 1, 2.

4. No man has taken the first step towards real, abiding blessedness until he has become a sincere and habitual servant of the Most High God, according to Scripture, vv. 1, 2.

5. A wicked life disproves any profession of piety, v. 3. It is mere presumption for any mortal to say that all is well so long as he allows any sin. Henry: "It will not serve us to make religion the subject of our discourse, but we must make it the rule of our walk;" Dickson: "Albeit there be no man who sinneth not, yet such as flee to God's grace, offered in Christ, for daily pardon, and set themselves to obey God's directions set down in his word, are esteemed to be no workers of iniquity, but men going homeward to God, however clogged with infirmity."

6. There is such a thing as genuine piety, v. 3. There is a class of people over whom sin has no dominion, Rom. vi. 16. Now and then we find a Nathanael in whose spirit there is no guile, and a Zacharias and Elizabeth, who walk in the statutes and ordinances of the Lord blameless. There are manifestations of sterling principle in the lives of good men for which there is no explanation but on the supposition that they are taught from heaven and have imbibed its spirit.

7. In the arrangements of providence and in the teachings of Scripture, everything rightly understood conduces to holiness. If there are warnings and threatenings, they are against sin. If there are promises and encouragements, they are unto holiness. The law and the gospel, Mount Sinai and Mount Calvary cry, Be ye holy.

8. Although good men are far from being what they ought to be and what they hope to be, yet they long for perfect conformity to God's entire will, v. 4. If they could have it their way, they never would sin again. The redeemed man knows that he is not his own, that he is bought with a price, and, if ever fit for heaven, he must in his measure be perfect as his Father in heaven is perfect. Sensible of his own weakness and corruptions, he still hungers and thirsts after righteousness, and will continue to do so, more and more; and never will he be satisfied till he awakes in the divine likeness.

9. True obedience is universal, v. 6. Clarke: "*Allow* that *any* of God's command-ments *may* be transgressed, and we shall soon have the whole decalogue set aside." Why should we not tenderly regard all the commandments? They have the same author, the same end, and the same happy influence on the obedient. Morison: "A partial attention to certain of God's commands, which is accompanied by a habitual disregard of others, is a conduct entirely unsuitable to the conditions of one of God's children;" Bridges: "Willingly to dispense with the least of the *commandments*, proves that we have yet to learn the spirit of acceptable obedience."

10. The Scriptures give no countenance to the notion that piety can exist without sound knowledge, v. 7. The lamp of truth must light up all our path to glory. Henry: "As long as we live, we must be scholars in Christ's school and sit at his feet; but we should aim to be head-scholars, and try to get into the highest form;" Calvin: "None will praise God unfeignedly and cordially, but he who has made such proficiency in his school as to mould his life in subjection to him."

11. Good resolutions are in their place good things, v. 8. We have Scriptural authority for making them, the promise of divine grace in enabling us to keep them, and an assurance of eternal rewards to such as stick to them. Henry: "Those have well learned God's statutes who are come up to a full resolution in the strength of his grace to keep them."

12. Genuine humility will ever pray, Lead me not into temptation, let not my principles be too severely tried, forsake me not *too much*, v. 8. It is wise for us to cry, Lord, remember that I am dust and ashes; let not my spirit fail before thee. Dickson: "As he who is most upright in his resolution, is most diffident of his own strength to perform his resolution, so he is also most earnest with God in prayer, to enable him to do as he resolveth."

13. These eight verses teach that true piety is sincere, consistent, practical, hearty, intelligent, earnest, active, stirring, diligent, humble, distrustful of itself, symmetrical, guileless, unspotted from the world, self-renouncing, confident in God, delighting in thankfulness, fully purposed to keep the law, and as ready to confess that without divine grace it can do nothing.

14. They also teach us how great is the sin of not believing God's word. As it is a law, the faithless refuse to walk by it; as it is a testimony, they refuse to believe their Maker; as it demands righteousness, they refuse to seek it; as it gives precepts, they will not obey them; as it ordains statutes, they rebel against them; as it has excellent commandments, they stand out in opposition to them; as it abounds with righteous judgments, they refuse to stand by them. They will not pray for grace; they will not praise God for mercies received; they do not feel their dependence or impotence, and they never look to the Father of lights from whom cometh down every good and perfect gift.

PSALM CXIX.

BETH.

9 Wherewithal shall a young man cleanse his way? by taking heed *thereto* according to thy word.

10 With my whole heart have I sought thee: O let me not wander from thy commandments.

11 Thy word have I hid in mine heart, that I might not sin against thee.

12 Blessed *art* thou, O LORD: teach me thy statutes.

13 With my lips have I declared all the judgments of thy mouth.
14 I have rejoiced in the way of thy testimonies, as *much as* in all riches.
15 I will meditate in thy precepts, and have respect unto thy ways.
16 I will delight myself in thy statutes: I will not forget thy word.

ALL these verses, except v. 12, begin with the same word. On the terms *word, commandments, statutes, judgments, testimonies* and *precepts* here found, see introductory remarks Nos. 7, 5, 4, 6, 2, 3, respectively.

9. *Wherewithal shall a young man cleanse his way? by taking heed* thereto *according to thy word.* *Wherewithal*, literally *with what*, in Nu. xxiii. 8, the same word without any preposition, is rendered *how;* with the preposition, *whereby*, Gen. xv. 8; *wherewith*, Jud. vi. 15; *wherein*, 1 Sam. xiv. 38. *Young man* is better than *youth;* the noun is in the masculine; also rendered *lad, boy, child.* The perils to young men are even greater than to young women. *Cleanse*, not that in Ps. xix. 12; but one of like import; in Ps. li. 4, *be clear*, and in Ps. lxxiii. 13, *have cleansed.* A sinner is said to be cleansed, 1, when his guilt is pardoned; 2, when his pollution of heart is removed; 3, when he is preserved from falling into iniquity. Each of these is an unspeakable mercy. *Way*, not the same word so rendered in vv. 1, 4, but one rendered *path* in Ps. viii. 8; in Ps. xix. 5, *race;* found in vv. 15, 101, 104, 128. It denotes the course of life. The Chaldee and Syriac, followed by Hammond, Patrick and Waterland do not make the latter part of the verse an answer to the first but continue the question to the end. Wherewith shall a young man cleanse his way, that he may observe thy word? The reason commonly assigned for the change is found in the grammar, the word rendered *taking heed* being a verb in the infinitive. This rendering leaves the question wholly unanswered. Some think this heightens the impression. On the other hand the Septuagint, Ethiopic, Vulgate, Doway, church of England, Calvin, Fabritius, Piscator, Amesius, Tremellius and Junius, Edwards, Street, Jebb and Hengstenberg divide and render the stanza as in the authorized version. This is best on many accounts. The grammatical difficulty is not insuperable. *Taking heed* to God's word is the means of leading a holy life. *Take heed*, in vv. 4, 8, *keep.*

10. *With my whole heart have I sought thee: O let me not wander from thy commandments.* *Whole heart*, as in v. 2. It implies entire sincerity, genuine cordiality. *Seeking* the Lord is put for the whole of religion. "Do not cause me to wander from thy commandments," is a more literal rendering of the last clause, but it does not so well give the sense. Street: Suffer me not to deviate from thy commandments.

11. *Thy word have I hid in mine heart, that I might not sin against thee.* *Hid*, in Ps. xxxi. 20, *kept secretly;* in Ps. xxxi. 19, *laid up;* spoken of acquiring and rightly using *wisdom* and *knowledge*, Pr. ii. 7; x. 14. Compare Luke ii. 51. He, who accepts, believes, ponders and practises God's word hides it in his heart. Thus received, it warns, reproves and deters from all sin.

12. *Blessed* art *thou, O* LORD. A doxology of frequent occurrence; see on Ps. v. 12; xviii. 46. *Teach me thy statutes;* precisely as in vv. 26, 64, 68, 124, 135. The same verb in the same form occurs in vv. 66, 108. In vv. 7, 71, 73, another form of it is rendered *learn.* In v. 171, we have it in connection with the same noun. *Thou hast taught me thy statutes.* We had it in Ps. xxv. 4, 5. Such petitions are a clear confession of great ignorance, darkness and weakness on the part of the petitioner, together with a longing desire for instruction and guidance in the way of truth, duty and safety. Such prayers are never unseasonable. Petitions for the same blessing, in different terms, abound in our Psalm.

13. *With my lips have I declared all the judgments of thy mouth.* *Declared*, as in v. 26; in the future in Ps. ii. 7; also rendered *speak, tell, show forth;* the participle is

scribe, writer. He had taught in every fit way the decisions of God's word. His heart was full of the matter. God had spoken to him; and what less could he do than speak to men?

14. *I have rejoiced in the way of thy testimonies as* much as *in all riches.* The heart of a renewed man goes out towards the whole word of God, the practical and preceptive no less than the doctrinal and consolatory. Its treasures are rich and highly prized. Calvin: "As wealth attracts to itself the hearts of mankind, so I have taken more exquisite delight in the progress which I make in the doctrine of godliness, than if I abounded in all manner of riches." Green renders it: I take more delight in the way of thy testimonies, than in all *my* riches.

15. *I will meditate in thy precepts, and have respect unto thy ways. Meditate,* as in vv. 23, 48, 78, 148; in v. 27 and elsewhere, *talk;* in Ps. cxliii. 5, *muse;* in Ps. lv. 17, *pray;* in Ps. lxix. 12, *speak.* It implies deep and heartfelt reflection expressed or unexpressed. *Have respect,* as in v. 6, *look, consider, regard. Ways,* paths as in v. 9, parallel to *precepts.*

16. *I will delight myself in thy statutes: I will not forget thy word.* Ainsworth renders the first clause: I will solace and recreate myself. The pleasure which the renewed heart has in God's word is great, producing delight; habitual, banishing forgetfulness of it; practical, giving life to piety. Calvin: "The commencement of a good life consists in God's law attracting us to him by its sweetness."

DOCTRINAL AND PRACTICAL REMARKS.

1. The Scriptures would not be perfect, if they did not give proper directions, warnings and encouragements to young men, v. 9. Their case is full of interest. By birth-sin their *way* is already defiled. And they are inexperienced, self-confident, rash, inconsiderate. The imagination of their heart is evil, Gen. viii. 21. Their passions are strong and their principles weak; their lusts imperious and their self-knowledge very imperfect. Till taught from heaven, man is void of wisdom, his will is stubborn, and he is impatient of restraint. All rules not enforced by divine authority are too feeble to control the strong inclinations. Yet youth is the seed-time both for mature life and for eternity. In such circumstances God's word "is the only antidote by which we can protect ourselves against the corruption of our nature." One wrong step in youth is very apt to lead to another, and yet another, till ruin comes like an armed man. Scott: "Every one ought to contribute all that is in his power to preserve young persons from the fatal effects of their own headstrong passions, of an ensnaring world, and of artful seducers; that they may not early contract bad habits." The excellencies of the Scripture for the young are many: 1. It is plain. 2. It is easily remembered. 3. It contains perfect rules, which need no amendment. 4. It gives good examples. It points to Joseph, Samuel, David, Solomon, and the young Hebrews in Babylon. It furnishes us one perfect example. Horne: "He who became man for our salvation, passed through this state of youth, undefiled, that he might, as it were, reclaim and consecrate it anew to God." 5. It holds up bad examples as warnings. To the end of time Absalom will be a beacon to the wayward. 6. It presents the most powerful motives, drawn from heaven, earth and hell. 7. It encourages us to pray with hope for the influences of the Spirit. Compare 2 Tim. iii. 16.

2. If we would make the word of God truly profitable to us, we must take fast hold of it with our hearts, v. 10. Lightly to esteem is to despise heavenly wisdom.

3. Let us cultivate a deep sense of our dependence on divine grace, relying solely upon God to keep us from going astray, v. 10. Dickson: "The more experience a man hath in the ways of God, the more sensible is he of his own readiness to wander insensibly, by ignorance and inadvertency from the ways of God."

4. It is a good thing to read God's word much. It is also well to commit much of it to memory. The history of the church furnishes many bright examples of great skill in Scripture. Yet not 'wit and memory, but the heart, is the chest to keep it in,' v. 11. Neither hearing, nor reading, nor reciting the holy Scriptures will save us from false ways, unless with the heart we cordially embrace whatever they teach us. To this work we ought to be greatly stimulated.

5. As sure as our hearts are rightly affected we shall never be done blessing God, either in time or in eternity, v. 12.

6. There is an absolute necessity for our praying for divine teaching, v. 12. "God must open the eyes of our understanding, or the light of the shining word itself will be all darkness," 1 Cor. ii. 14. He alone can lift the veil from off the heart or make us wise unto salvation. "The people that doth not understand shall fall."

7. Though hypocrites and fanatics have brought great reproach upon religious conference, yet the children of God should declare the truths of Scripture, v. 13. Horne: "When we make the Scriptures the subject of our conversation, we glorify God, we edify our neighbors, and we improve ourselves." He does not love God, his Son, nor his word, who does not sincerely desire to bring others to do the same. Hengstenberg: "When the word of God is really in the *heart*, it will also be found on the *lips;*" Morison: "We are bound by ties of weighty and eternal obligation, to make known to others what God has imparted to ourselves of the knowledge of his revealed will, and of the happiness involved in his pure and heavenly service;" Bridges: "Thus did Andrew bring Peter, and the woman of Samaria, her neighbors, to Jesus. What might we not do for our fellow-sinners, if our intercourse with them was the overflowing of a heart filled with love; guided by a single desire to glorify our Saviour, and to edify his church!"

8. We should settle it in our minds that the truth of God is stable, and never varies in its requirements or encouragements, v. 13. Dickson: "The word of God in Scripture may be looked upon as the sentence of the Supreme Judge, uncontrollable and unalterable by any creature, and whereby men must judge of all truth, and expect to be judged by it."

9. Many extravagant things are said respecting human happiness; but if any would have heaven upon earth, let him rejoice in the word of God, v. 14. Horne: "Truth and holiness afford to the sincere believer a pleasure more exquisite, as well as more solid and enduring, than that which a miser feels at the acquisition of his darling wealth."

10. We should profit more by Scripture if we would *meditate* more upon it, v. 15. Nicolson: "As food undigested will not nourish the body, so the word of God, not considered with deep meditation and reflection, will not feed the soul." Meditation is an exercise of the mind purely spiritual, and goes entirely cross to our native indolence. But let us persevere, and cry for help, and put a bridle on our vagaries, and God will give us the victory.

11. There is nothing in true religion to produce stupefaction. On the contrary it brings into healthful exercise the highest faculties and emotions of our natures. It awakens *delight*, v. 16. The word is very strong. Clarke: "I will skip about and jump for joy." Blessed be God, his plan is to repress only sinful emotions. True religion encourages all that are right. Speaking of the time of his conversion, Augustine says: "How sweet was it in a moment to be free from those delightful vanities, to lose which had been my dread; to part with which was now my joy." Dickson· "Spiritual joy in spiritual objects far exceedeth any joy in worldly possessions."

12. We are again taught the propriety of forming good resolutions, vv. 15, 16

He who has truly begun to serve God will be more and more *purposed* to let nothing divert him from his pious course.

13. All the fuel to keep the fire of devotion burning on the altar of the heart is the word of God. Let us not *forget* that, v. 16.

PSALM CXIX.

GIMEL

17 Deal bountifully with thy servant, *that* I may live, and keep thy word.
18 Open thou mine eyes, that I may behold wondrous things out of thy law.
19 I *am* a stranger in the earth: hide not thy commandments from me.
20 My soul breaketh for the longing *that it hath* unto thy judgments at all times.
21 Thou hast rebuked the proud *that are* cursed, which do err from thy commandments.
22 Remove from me reproach and contempt; for I have kept thy testimonies.
23 Princes also did sit *and* speak against me: *but* thy servant did meditate in thy statutes.
24 Thy testimonies also *are* my delight, *and* my counsellors.

ALL these verses begin with the *third* letter of the Hebrew alphabet. Verses 18, 22 begin with the same word, though in different senses. Verses 23, 24 begin with the same word, which we render *also*. Each of the other verses begins with a different word. On the terms, *word, law, commandments, judgments, testimonies* and *statutes*, see Nos. 7, 1, 5, 6, 2, 4, respectively.

17. *Deal bountifully with thy servant, that I may live, and keep thy word. Deal bountifully*, in Hebrew one short word. See on Ps. xiii. 6. He confesses that continuance of life would be the fruit of divine *bounty*, and much more so to *live* as to keep God's word. *Keep*, as in vv. 4, 8; in v. 9, *take heed*. Calvin: "The prophet asks as a principal favor, that, while he lives, he may devote himself entirely to God."

18. *Open thou mine eyes, that I may behold wondrous things out of thy law. Open;* margin, *reveal;* in Ps. xviii. 15, *discover;* in Isa. xlvii. 2, twice *uncover.* Bossuet: "Open mine eyes, dispel the shades, take away the veil." Blindness is one of the sad and universal consequences of the fall of our race, Isa. xlii. 7; xvi. 18; John xii. 40; 2 Cor. iii. 14; iv. 4. All saving knowledge of God is by revelation, Matt. xi. 25; xvi. 17. Without divine teaching the Scriptures remain a sealed book. *Behold*, in v. 15, the same form of the verb is *have respect.* Under divine illumination the prophet would so see divine things as to *have respect* to them. *Wondrous things;* in v. 27, *wondrous works.* See on Ps. ix. 1, where it is *marvellous works*, rendered as here in Ps. lxxii. 18; lxxxvi. 10. Walford thinks "the reference here is to the figures and adumbrations of the law." But we have need of divine illumination to enable us to profit by the clearest parts of God's word, the simplest truths of Scripture.

19. *I am a stranger in the earth: hide not thy commandments from me.* All God's people have been strangers and pilgrims on the earth. They had here no continuing city, but sought one to come. They confessed that earth was a wilderness, through which they were hastily passing. That which guided and cheered them in their journey was the word of God, every part of it, including his whole preceptive will. To *hide* his word from us is to leave us to our natural blindness without saving knowledge, or spiritual illumination. Luther: "I have no inheritance beyond thy word, therefore forsake me not."

20. *My soul breaketh for the longing that it hath unto thy judgments at all times.* For *breaketh* Calvin reads *is rent;* church of England, *melteth away;* Edwards, *is torn in pieces;* Street, *wasteth away;* French and Skinner and Hengstenberg, *is broken.* The

word occurs here only and in Lam. iii. 16. The whole phrase expresses the liveliest and most absorbing concern. Nor was it temporary, but *at all times*.

21. *Thou hast rebuked the proud* that are *cursed, which do err from thy command-ments*. Morison proposes to render the verse thus: Thou rebukest the proud; cursed are they who err from thy commandments. He is supported by some respectable scholars of modern times and by the ancient versions. *Rebuked*, as in Ps. ix. 5, on which see. The *rebuke* may include both the decisions of Scripture and the inflictions of providence against the *proud*. The *proud*, found also in vv. 51, 69, 78, 85, 122; in Ps. xix. 13, *presumptuous*. Dominant pride will deceive and ruin any one. It is the high road to transgression and to wrath. *Cursed*, here only in the Psalter, often rendered *cursed* in Deut. xxvii. xxviii.

22. *Remove from me reproach and contempt; for I have kept thy testimonies*. *Remove*, literally, *roll*, as in Ps. xxii. 8; xxxvii. 5. Hengstenberg well says there is a literal allusion to Josh. v. 9. *Reproach*, in Dan. xii. 2, *shame*. See on Ps. xv. 3. *Contempt* is *despite*, almost uniformly rendered. It expresses the scorning of the *proud*. The argument he urges for protection from such suffering is virtually that he was the child and servant of God, and so under his protection; the proof of his piety being found in his holy life. *Kept*, as in v. 2. It occurs in the same sense *ten* times in this Psalm.

23. *Princes also did sit* and *speak against me: but thy servant did meditate in thy statutes*. This is one of the verses, which has led some to regard Jeremiah or Daniel, especially the latter as the author of this poem. But *princes, i. e., chiefs, captains, rulers, principal* men did plot against David also, and did say much against him. At such times his resort was to God's word, especially in that aspect of it, which regards it as unchangeable, as *statutes*, unalterable decrees. *Meditate*, as in v. 15.

24. *Thy testimonies also* are *my delight*, and *my counsellors*. *Delight*, in the plural *delights*, a noun cognate to the verb *delight*, in v. 16. The same is declared in vv. 77, 92, 143, 174. *Counsellors*, literally *men of my counsel*, not found elsewhere. Calvin: "To adhere unflinchingly to our purpose, when the world takes up an unjust opinion of us, and, at the same time, constantly to meditate on God's law, is an example of Christian fortitude seldom to be met with." It is as if he had said: "Although the cruel injustice of men, in charging me falsely, grieves and annoys me, yet the pleas-urable delight which I take in thy law is a sufficient recompense for it all."

DOCTRINAL AND PRACTICAL REMARKS.

1. Let men always come before God as sinners; let all their plea be his free grace and rich *bounty*, v. 17. We have no merit of our own, no worthiness that we can plead as the ground of a single gift.

2. While it is lawful for us, in submission to the will of God, humbly to ask for a continuance of life, we may do it not to gratify our own will or covetousness, or love of carnal delight; but that we may glorify God by *keeping his word*, v. 17. Increase of holiness is the great object for which we should desire to live.

3. Afflicted, tempted and tried as God's people may be, he still *deals bountifully* with them all, v. 17. The humblest and poorest of them have unsearchable riches, and unspeakable blessings. Life is theirs; forgiveness is theirs; acceptance is theirs; renewal is theirs; the world is theirs; God is their Father; Christ is their Brother; the Spirit is their Sanctifier, Comforter and Guide. All the wealth of the world is not worth half as much as one covenant blessing.

4. It is in vain for us to hope for increase of saving knowledge, except as we get light and wisdom from above, v. 18. In this the people of God of all ages are agreed. Clarke: "The holy Scriptures are plain enough: but the heart of man is *darkened* by

sin. The Bible does not so much need a comment, as the *soul* does the *light of the Holy Spirit.*" Horne: "Pride, prejudice and interest will compose a veil through which a Christian shall see as little of the New Testament as a Jew doth of the old." Morison: "We cannot be conformed to the word of God without understanding its blessed truths; and we cannot understand them aright without divine teaching."

5. There are *marvellous*, excellent and glorious *things* in Scripture, and it is worse than folly to deny it. Nor has the coming of Christ removed the mysteriousness of the divine counsels. Indeed he himself is by preëminence the mystery of Godliness. Revelation, which should tell us nothing above, beyond or contrary to our darkened conceptions, could never reveal to us either God, or Christ, or heaven, or the highest and most spiritual motives to a godly life. Dickson: "The word of God is full of wonders, high and heavenly mysteries, and he who seeth them best, wondereth most."

6: Let us not deny but confess that we are strangers on the earth, travellers to a far distant home, where are our kindred, and heart, and treasure, v. 19. Our citizenship is in heaven. Our possessions lie far beyond the reach of rust, and moth, and fire, and thieves, and revolutions. "The pilgrim spirit is the pulse of the soul."

7. The desires of the renewed soul are not only permanent and importunate, but intense, v. 20. Far from being Laodicean, the true Christian spirit follows hard after God. Bridges: "Grace is indeed an insatiable principle. Enjoyment, instead of surfeiting, only serves to sharpen the appetite. Yet if we are content to live at a low rate, there will be no sensible interest in the consolation of the Gospel."

8. *Proud* and *presumptuous* as the wicked may be, they do but grossly deceive themselves in thinking their case desirable. They shall suffer awful punishment, even the *rebuke* of the Most High, v. 21. They may defy heaven now; they may laugh at sacred things; they may put far away the evil day; but they are fearfully *cursed.* Every perfection of God, every promise to his people, every threatening to his foes, all that he has said, and all that he has done are against them so long as they continue in sin. Their pride may intoxicate them now; they may even question the divine existence, but the day is coming when they would esteem it a mercy to have the mountains heaped upon them to hide them from the presence of God.

9. Whoever has felt the keen edge of the scorning of scorners may naturally and earnestly cry to be delivered from *reproach* and *contempt*, v. 22. Against such trials pure benevolence, a heavenly mind and unoffending innocence are no shield, v. 23. Our Master himself endured the contradiction of sinners. But let us not forget that God can wholly shield us from the shafts of malice; that he can bring to us great good out of so severe trial; that if through his grace we can be steadfast with God, we may be sure that all will end well; and that if our fellowship be with the Father and with his Son, all the wrath of man can do us no real harm.

10. It is no new thing for the people of God to be hunted and persecuted, tormented and afflicted, even under the lead of the *principal* men of their age and country, v. 23. David was thus hated. Our Lord Jesus himself provoked the malice of great men, even in his infancy. The world is in no good humor with holiness or holy people. Nor can such trials be borne by human strength alone. Unless we can flee to the Word of God and to the mercy-seat, our courage must utterly fail.

11. Dickson: "Troubles will try men whether they fear God or men most," v. 23.

12. It is only when we have pleasure in our religion, and *delight* in Scripture truth that our religion is truly valuable, v. 24. Then Jesus says: "In me ye have peace. In the world ye shall have tribulation, but be of good cheer: I have overcome the world," John xvi. 33.

13. Each of these eight verses, more or less calls upon us to cherish and strengthen our love for every part of Scripture. Let us never lightly esteem the oracles of God.

Let us beware of that fanaticism which is guided by impulses and despises the written word. Let us beware of our own speculations. Let us carefully guard against all delusions of the world, the flesh and the devil. Let us cling to the doctrines, the promises, the precepts and the warnings of Scripture. Let us not lean on human wisdom. He, who has all the prophets and apostles for his counsellors, and a teachable disposition, will walk more safely than without these he could follow the counsels of all the wise men of the earth.

14. To those, for whom God undertakes, nothing is impossible. This is true of the Christian in the work of salvation. He has a natural dulness and blindness in religion. He is a stranger upon earth. Sometimes his heart is ready to break. Sometimes he is tempted to pride. Sometimes his neighbors fill him with contempt and cover him with reproach. Sometimes princes speak against him. But he shall come off a conqueror and more than a conqueror through him that loved him.

PSALM CXIX.

DALETH.

25 My soul cleaveth unto the dust: quicken thou me according to thy word.
26 I have declared my ways, and thou heardest me: teach me thy statutes.
27 Make me to understand the way of thy precepts: so shall I talk of thy wondrous works.
28 My soul melteth for heaviness: strengthen thou me according unto thy word.
29 Remove from me the way of lying: and grant me thy law graciously.
30 I have chosen the way of truth: thy judgments have I laid *before me.*
31 I have stuck unto thy testimonies: O LORD, put me not to shame.
32 I will run the way of thy commandments, when thou shalt enlarge my heart.

ALL these verses begin with the *fourth* Hebrew letter. Verses 25, 31 begin with the same verb rendered *cleaveth, have stuck.* All the other verses begin with the word which we render *way* or *ways,* as in vv. 1, 3. On the terms *word, way* or *ways, statutes, law, judgments, testimonies* and *commandments,* see Nos. 7, 8, 4, 1, 6, 2, 5, respectively.

25. *My soul cleaveth unto the dust.* The rendering of this clause is remarkably uniform; yet the interpretations are various. Fry applies it to the humiliation and afflictions of Christ. Dickson applies it to David's trouble of mind, the heavy condition of his heart and spirit. Others think the prophet is speaking of his afflictions, so sensibly felt, that he voluntarily covered himself with dust, and sat in the dust, according to the custom of the orientals. Compare Job i. 20; ii. 12. Diodati: "I am cast down beyond all hope of relief, if thou dost not raise and restore me to life." Henry regards this view as admissible. Scott: "Many regard this verse, merely as a complaint on account of deep affliction and peril of death." Perhaps a larger number regard it as a declaration that his life was in imminent danger. Calvin: "He means that he had no more hope of life than if he had been shut up in the tomb." Pool: "I am in eminent danger of present death, through the rage and power of mine enemies, I am like one laid in the grave, without all hopes of recovery. So this phrase is used in Ps. xxii. 15." Often does *dust* point to the grave, Job vii. 21; xvii. 16; xx. 11; xxi. 26; xl. 13. For *my soul* Clarke would read *my life;* and "then *cleaving to the dust* may imply an apprehension of *approaching death;* and this agrees best with the petition." Patrick and Walford give the same interpretation. Alexander thinks the clause intended to "suggest two consistent, but distinct ideas, that of deep degradation, as in Ps. xliv. 25, and that of death, as in Ps. xxii. 29."

Yet others suppose that the Psalmist is deploring his own corruptions, his sinfulness before God. Nicolson: "His affections cleaved to things below, instead of being set on things above." Hammond: "I am cast down in a sight either of my unworthiness or my sins." Morison and Scott take the same view; and Henry regards it as probably correct. Horne regards these words as expressive both of affliction and humiliation. Gill interprets them as referring either to the dust of death, or to great dejection and humiliation of mind, or to a proneness in him to sin and the snares of the world. Why may not several of these things be united? What is more common than such a record as this? "I am filled with shame and sorrow for my sins; God is letting loose sore afflictions upon me; my life itself is in danger; without early relief I cannot sustain my sorrows, but must sink into the grave." *Quicken thou me according to thy word. Quicken*, in this Psalm nine times so rendered; in Hab. iii. 2, *revive*; in the margin, *preserve alive*; Edwards, *enliven me*; Street, *revive me*; Scott, *let me be lively*. Thus it may mean, Revive my drooping graces, my drooping spirits and my failing health. *According to thy word* may refer to the special promise made to David in 2 Sam. vii. 12–17; or, it may refer to the general tenor of God's covenant engagements that nothing should hinder his children from gaining the victory over their sins, that their afflictions should not hinder them from displaying heroism and from doing exploits, and that nothing should prematurely terminate their existence. Arnobius, Augustine and Walford by *word* understand *promise*.

26. *I have declared my ways, and thou heardest me. Declared*, as in v. 13; there the declaration was made to men, here, to God. He had laid his whole case before God. God had *heard* his complaint and had so far answered him, that his affairs were not in a desperate condition. Hitherto God had helped him. He consequently asks for more grace, more wisdom, more holiness: *Teach me thy statutes;* see on v. 12.

27. *Make me to understand the way of thy precepts.* This is a repetition of the prayer in the preceding verse. The same verb occurs in vv. 34, 73, 125, 144, 169, and in the future in vv. 95, 100, 104. True piety wishes to know the whole will of God. The *way* of this verse is in contrast with the *ways* of the preceding. *So shall I talk of thy wondrous works. Talk;* see on v. 15, where it is *meditate. Wondrous works*, as in v. 18.

28. *My soul melteth for heaviness: strengthen thou me according to thy word.* Many regard this verse as nearly a repetition of v. 25. It has no doubt the same general tone. *Melteth*, found only here and in Job xvi. 20, where it is *poureth out*, and in Ecc. x. 18, *droppeth through.* The primary idea is that of *dropping, falling. Heaviness*, in the sense of *sorrow;* see Pr. xvii. 21, where it is so rendered. Alexander: My soul weeps from sorrow; Street: My soul wasteth away with afflictions. *Strengthen me, raise me up*, as in Ps. xli. 10; cxiii. 7; make me to *stand, confirm me, establish me*, v. 38; Ps. i. 5; Ruth iv. 7; Gen. ix. 9.

29. *Remove from me the way of lying. Way*, as in vv. 1, 26, 27. The *way of lying* is not only the habit or practice of unfaithfulness to God, but the course of sinful life which is sure to be followed by disappointment. The whole life of sin is a *lie* from beginning to end. *Lying*, the word occurs *eight* times in this Psalm. Here and in v. 163 it is *lying;* in v. 69, *a lie;* in v. 118, *falsehood;* in vv. 104, 128, *false;* in v. 86, *wrongfully;* and in v. 78, *without a cause*, literally, *with lying;* rendered *falsehood* in Ps. vii. 14. *And grant me thy law graciously. Grant graciously*, in vv. 58, 132, *be merciful unto me;* in Ps. iv. 1 and often, *have mercy upon me;* in Ps. cii. 13, *favour.* To be led into a right understanding and practice of God's word is an effect of great *grace*.

30. *I have chosen the way of truth. Chosen*, a word uniformly rendered, expressing deliberate and settled preference. *Way of truth*, in opposition to the *way of lying* in

v. 29. God's *truth* points out the right way, supports and comforts those who walk in it, at every step evincing divine *faithfulness*, and at last bringing the soul to everlasting communion with him, who is *truth* itself. *Thy judgments I have laid before me.* The chief diversity respects the verb. In Ps. xxi. 5; lxxxix. 19, it is rendered as here; in Ps. xvi. 8, *have set.* Another form of it is rendered to *avail* or *profit.* Syriac: I am delighted with thy judgments; Arabic, Septuagint, Ethiopic, Vulgate, Doway and Street: I have not forgotten thy judgments. Other translations generally give the same idea as the authorized English. See on Ps. xvi. 8.

31. *I have stuck unto thy testimonies. Have stuck,* in v. 25, rendered *cleaveth.* There is no word expressing closer adherence. *O* Lord, *put me not to shame. Put to shame,* the same verb in another form as in v. 6; it expresses the confusion and dismay attending an overthrow.

32. *I will run the way of thy commandments, when thou shalt enlarge my heart. Way,* as in v. 27. *Run,* the usual verb expressing the act of racers, of hosts, or of dashing warriors, Ps. xix. 5; xviii. 29; Esther iii. 13, 15; Jer. li. 31. It marks great alacrity in the business of serving God. But such delight in God's service is the fruit of God's grace. No man can do it till his heart is *enlarged,* or opened, as it is in Ps. xxxv. 21. The same language is used of Lydia in Acts xvi. 14. For *enlarged* we might read set *at liberty,* as the corresponding adjective is rendered, v. 45.

Doctrinal and Practical Remarks.

1. Troubles never come alone. Sin presses us harder than anything else, v. 25. This is true of the soul-troubles of believers. The very communion, which they once had with God, but deepens their grief, when once it is lost. Nor can they in this state cease to mourn the absence of divine comforts.

2. However great our depression, God can raise us up, and give us *liveliness* in his service, v. 25; and this *quickening* of our graces is a pledge that we shall be raised up at the last day. "Then soul and body, perfected together, shall take their final farewell of earth, and ascend to heaven, where the soul shall feel no passion but the love of God, and the body shall have no employment but to express it."

3. Whatever we do, or whatever our state may be, let us deal candidly with God and *declare* to him our whole case, v. 26. If we are sad, he can cheer us. If we are in the dark, he can enlighten us. If we have no might, he can strengthen us. If our wants are many, he can supply them. If we are shut up and cannot come forth, he can enlarge us. Whatever be our case, let us state it all, even as Hezekiah spread the letter before the Lord, Isa. xxxvii. 14.

4. Past answers to prayer should encourage us to come the more boldly to the throne of grace, v. 26. Jacob never forgot the night he spent at Bethel.

5. Helps there are to the study of God's word, nor are they to be despised; but he, who would become mighty in the Scriptures, must in godly sincerity beg to be taught by the Holy Ghost, vv. 26, 27. All other teaching, without this, will but make us learned infidels, or practical unbelievers. Our sinful vanity easily perverts to some wrong end what we do know, and thus fosters pride, ostentation, or carnal security. No power of persuasion can drive from the soul of man its obstinate resistance of the truth until divine grace mollifies its desperate hardness.

6. There is a close affinity between all the duties of religion. The same word is rendered *pray, meditate* and *talk of,* v. 27. We think of God's excellent majesty; we cry to him in humble prayer; we study his word, until our souls are filled with gladness and admiration; and then how can we but *talk of his wondrous works?* Creation, providence and redemption all furnish amazing illustrations of the perfections and glory of God.

7. Troubles, which threaten to dissolve our nature, are no novelties, v. 28.　No doubt many a one has died of a broken heart.　Many others would have fallen in the same way, but for the many blessed promises and doctrines of Scripture, especially the assurance of the forgiveness of sins and the certainty that prayer will be answered, Isa. xliii. 25, 26.

8. However pressing the sorrows of the saints, God can hold them up, v. 28.　Great as they may be, they are never equal to those of the Master; nor shall they be too long continued, nor shall they ever crush the humble soul.　If they do but quicken us in our heavenly course, make the word of God to us increasingly precious, give us a distaste for the things that perish, and make us to grow in heavenly mindedness, we may justly welcome them as blessings.

9. It is impossible for us to be too much afraid of *falsehood* in morals, in doctrine, in worship, or in anything else, v. 29.　We are easily deceived.　There is a mystery in iniquity.　There is a deceivableness in unrighteousness.　These will surely work our ruin unless we are mercifully preserved by divine grace.

10. If in his condescending mercy, God shall instruct us in his word, let us acknowledge the grace, v. 29.　Without divine teaching we are undone.　Such mercy is indeed wholly undeserved, but then it is the mercy of an infinite God.　Henry: "We ought to reckon God's law a grant, a gift, an unspeakable gift, to value it, and pray for it, and to give thanks for it accordingly."

11. If we are ever saved, it must be by being made God's *willing* people, v. 30. Otherwise we will not *choose* the way of truth.　Our hearts must be settled and fixed in that direction.　Henry: "The choosing Christian is likely to be the steady Christian."　If we cannot choose the good, and refuse the evil, we must perish.　He, who willingly follows in the course of transgression, must lie down in sorrow.

12. We never truly set the Lord before us, until we honestly set his word before us, v. 30.　And we never truly set his word before us, until we regard it as clothed with sovereign authority, binding the understanding to submission, the will to obedience, and the heart to holiness.　We must renounce all laws, rules and influences that are counter thereto.

13. If we would avoid *shame*, we must cling to Scripture, v. 31.　We must hold it fast at all cost and at all hazards.　We must render ourselves the servants of righteousness unto holiness; we must delight in all the purity God's word requires; we must cleave to that which is good.

14. But we cannot do all this, indeed we cannot do anything pleasing to God without divine assistance, v. 32.　If the believer is sensible of his short-comings, and deplores his wanderings, let him still go to the Throne of grace.　If we make any good speed, it is by receiving strength from above.　But if the Lord appear and enlarge our hearts, we will have strength for every duty, and delight in every sacrifice.　"Enlightened, evangelical, holy obedience can only spring from the operation of divine grace on the heart.　We never begin to act for God, till he begins to 'work in us all his holy will, and the work of faith with power.'　Fruitful only in sin, the tree of our corrupt hearts must be made good ere its fruit can be good."

PSALM CXIX.

HE.

33 Teach me, O LORD, the way of thy statutes; and I shall keep it *unto* the end.

34 Give me understanding, and I shall keep thy law; yea, I shall observe it with *my* whole heart.

35 Make me to go in the path of thy commandments; for therein do I delight.
36 Incline my heart unto thy testimonies, and not to covetousness.
37 Turn away mine eyes from beholding vanity; *and* quicken thou me in thy way.
38 Stablish thy word unto thy servant, who *is devoted* to thy fear.
39 Turn away my reproach which I fear: for thy judgments *are* good.
40 Behold, I have longed after thy precepts: quicken me in thy righteousness.

THOUGH all these verses begin with the *fifth* letter of the Hebrew Alphabet; yet but two of them (vv. 37, 39) begin with the same word. On the terms *way, statutes, law, commandments, testimonies, word, judgments* and *precepts*, see introduction to this Psalm, Nos. 8, 4, 1, 5, 2, 7, 6, 3, respectively.

33. *Teach me, O* Lord, *the way of thy statutes; and I shall keep it* unto *the end. Teach*, as in Ps. xxv. 8. It occurs in the preterite in v. 102. The clause is a prayer for divine *guidance*. Such instruction infallibly produces blessed results, even holiness. *Keep*, as in v. 2. Clarke: "To understand the spiritual reference of all the statutes under the law, required a teaching which could only come from God." *The end*, the reward, the recompense, the last.

34. *Give me understanding, and I shall keep thy law. Give me understanding*, as in v. 27, literally, *cause me to consider*, or *discern. Keep*, as in v. 33. After divine teaching and heavenly guidance, God's people are truly drawn to the whole law, and each one may add: *Yea, I shall observe it with* my *whole heart*. Clarke: "I will not trifle with my God,—I will not divide my affections with the world; God shall have all." *Whole heart*, see on v. 2. Calvin: "Mention is made of *the whole heart*, to tell us how far they are from the righteousness of the law, who obey it only in the letter, doing nothing deserving of blame in the sight of men."

35. *Make me to go in the path of thy commandments; for therein do I delight. Make me to go*, in Ps. xxv. 5, *lead me;* in Ps. xxv. 9, in the future, *will he guide. Path*, well rendered, masculine, not before found in the Psalms; in the feminine in v. 105. It is found in Jer. vi. 16; and several times in Isaiah. *Delight*, in the preterite, *have delighted;* it expresses a high degree of habitual pleasure. See Ps. xviii. 19; cxii. 1.

36. *Incline my heart unto thy testimonies, and not to covetousness.* Divine grace and omnipotent power are necessary to bend the will, bow down the heart, and incline the affections to God. The reasons are, 1, the heart is naturally wrong; 2, many things present themselves to allure us from God. One of these is *covetousness, gain, lucre,* or *profit,* as the word is elsewhere rendered, Judg. v. 19; 1 Sam. viii. 3; Ps. xxx. 9. In what part of the world is the heart of man not intent upon worldly gain? Money is good, but the love of money is the root of all evil. Nor does the trouble end here, for covetousness is kin to all the vices.

37. *Turn away mine eyes from beholding vanity. Vanity,* as in Ps. xii. 2; xxiv. 4; sometimes rendered *lying* and *lies,* as in Isa. lix. 4; Jonah ii. 8. It includes every kind of deception and delusion. And *quicken thou me in thy way. Quicken,* as in v. 25, make me lively.

38. *Stablish thy word unto thy servant, who* is devoted *to thy fear. Stablish,* elsewhere, *perform,* or *confirm,* that is, make good. The same word in v. 28, is rendered *strengthen.* Instead of *unto* we may read *for,* or *in behalf of.* This verse does not necessarily refer to a promise made to the prophet personally. The rendering of the latter clause is supported by Calvin, Fry, and others. But the church of England reads: O stablish thy word in thy servant, that I may fear thee; Edwards: Make thy word good unto thy servant; which will cause thee to be feared; Street: Establish thy word with thy servant, and I will walk in the fear of thee. The doubt arises from the pronoun *which* or *who.* It may refer to *thy servant,* and in that case

our version and the Syriac give the sense; or to *thy word*, as the Chaldee makes it, and then the sense is that God's word promotes his fear. God's word has so powerful a tendency to promote piety, that *it* is sometimes called his fear, Ps. xix. 9.

39. *Turn away my reproach which I fear. Turn away*, literally *cause to pass. Reproach*, as in v. 22. The senses gathered from the clause are three: 1. Save me from the exposure of my secret sins, which I dread; 2. Save me hereafter from reproach, which has been the bane of my happiness; 3. Save me from the reproach which now rests upon me and deeply afflicts me. Either of the latter two is better than the first. *For thy judgments* are *good*. It is not necessary by *judgments* to understand providential dealings, though they are always coincident with the principles of the divine word, which is here spoken of.

40. *Behold, I have longed after thy precepts. Longed*, found also in v. 174, cognate to *longing*, in v. 20. Alexander: "To long for God's precepts is to long for the knowledge of them and for grace to obey them." *Quicken me in thy righteousness. Quicken*, as in vv. 25, 37. *Righteousness*, here probably used in the sense explained in the introduction to this Psalm No. 10—a name given to holy Scripture. The petition is for liveliness in the knowledge and practice of holiness, according to the tenor of God's word and by its operation on the heart. If any prefer by *righteousness* to understand the faithfulness or justice of God, whereby he has bound himself to give grace to those who trust in him, there is no objection to such an interpretation. It is in fact implied in the others. Green renders this last clause: Oh, let me live in thy righteousness.

DOCTRINAL AND PRACTICAL REMARKS.

1. Most of the verses of this part of the Psalm clearly show that salvation, except by divine grace, is impossible. Man must be *taught;* an *understanding* must be *given* him; God must *cause* him *to go* with *delight* in the right way. The will must be rightly inclined; the purposes must be strengthened, as well as the eyes opened. All this is the work of the Spirit, through Jesus Christ: "We know that the Son of God is come, and hath given us an understanding, that we may know him that is true," 1 John v. 20. The teaching and aid of divine grace are necessary not only at the beginning, but through the entire progress of the spiritual life.

2. Let us keep a strict guard not only upon our motives, but upon the ends we propose to ourselves in everything, and especially in prayer, v. 33. Clarke: "Here is a good *thing* asked from a good *end*. He wishes for heavenly teaching; not to make a parade of it, but to enable him to discern his duty, that he might act accordingly." Our prayers are wholly hindered when they are offered that we may gratify our lusts, James iv. 3.

3. The great end of our existence is to establish the best relations between us and Jehovah, v. 33. If he is our Guide, our Teacher, our Lawgiver, our Governor, and so our Saviour, all is well. Otherwise it had been good for us if we had not been born. Blessed is the man who humbly submits his whole will, understanding and life without reserve and without condition to divine guidance and control.

4. The spirit of true piety is one of steadfast obedience, and of perseverance in the ways of God, v. 33. True religion does not manifest itself in fits and starts. Paroxysms belong to superstition, fanaticism and hypocrisy. He that putteth his hands to the plough, and looketh back, is not fit for the kingdom of God.

5. There is no substitute for whole-heartedness in the service of God, v. 34. "That way which the *whole heart* goes, the whole man goes; and that should be the way of God's commandments, for the keeping of them is the whole of man." Unless God works in us to *will*, it is certain that we will never *do*. Unless piety flourish in the

heart, the life will never be right. Even if it seemed lovely, it would be but the beauty of a corpse.

6. The tenor of the life determines the character. It is not an occasional crossing of the *path* of duty, or an occasional survey of it, but a walking in it, that evinces genuine piety, v. 35. Nothing short of this expresses the delight of a child of God in the service of his master. Without such real pleasure in God's ways, a religious profession is a sham. Bridges: "Delight is the marrow of religion."

7. There is in the human heart no greater enemy to God or true piety than *covetousness*, v. 36. Everywhere God's law flames out against it. The deceitfulness of riches, perhaps more than anything else, chokes the word and makes it unfruitful, Matt. xiii. 22. It was covetousness that made the Pharisees deride the Saviour, Luke xvi. 14. By loving money, myriads have pierced themselves through with the deepest sorrows, 1 Tim. vi. 10. It is especially incumbent on all, who hold office in church or state, to guard against this sin.

8. Let us carefully guard against all that class of temptations, called *vanity*, v. 37. It embraces whatever deludes us, whether in religious worship, in religious doctrine, in religious experience or in worldly affairs. There is not a faculty of mind or body that may not serve as a medium of temptation. But the eye and the tongue in a special manner are great occasions and instruments of sinning. The Psalmist here specially notices the *eyes*. Calvin: "Seeing, hearing, walking and feeling are God's precious gifts; our understandings and will with which we are furnished, are a still more valuable gift; and, after all, there is no look of the eye, no motion of the senses, no thought of the mind, unmingled with vice and depravity." Morison: "It is a most dangerous expedient for a child of God to place himself within the sphere of seductive temptations. Every feeling of duty, every recollection of his own weakness, every remembrance of the failure of others should induce him to hasten to the greatest possible distance from the scene of unnecessary conflict and danger." Clarke: "Let me remember Achan:—he *saw*,—he *coveted*,—he *took*,—he *hid* his theft, and was *slain* for his sin."

9. By giving us promises God intends to encourage us to plead with him for their fulfilment, v. 38. We are always safe when our prayers agree with the promises. Calvin: "The sole end and the legitimate use of prayer is, that we may reap the fruits of God's promises. Whence it comes to pass, that they commit sin who utter vague and incoherent desires. The prophet allows not himself to wish anything but what God hath condescended to promise."

10. In every sense of the term, *reproach* is a great foe to religion, v. 39. It makes cowards of many, and unstable souls of more. A just reproach on a servant of God brings dishonor on God himself. But if we know that we are in the path of duty, we need not be much moved by all that man can say or do.

11. In nothing are we more apt to come short in religion than in *liveliness* and thorough *earnestness*, vv. 37, 40. Let us plead for the fire of love.

12. Whoever can truly use the language of v. 40, is regenerate. Before renewing grace the law was a dead letter. It was more; it was a hated letter. The carnal mind is not subject to the law of God, neither indeed can be. It would rather serve the world, the flesh, or the devil. A sinner desires no restraint from the divine precepts. "But when," says Charnock, "the law is written within him, he is so pleased with the inscription, that he would not for all the world be without that law, and the love of it: whereas, what obedience he paid to it before was out of fear, now out of affection; not only because of the authority of the Lawgiver, but of the purity of the law itself. He would maintain it with all his might against the power of sin within, and the powers of darkness without him. He loves to view this law; regards every lineament of it, and dwells upon every feature with delightful ravishments."

PSALM CXIX.

VAU.

41 Let thy mercies come also unto me, O LORD, *even* thy salvation, according to thy word.

42 So shall I have wherewith to answer him that reproacheth me: for I trust in thy word.

43 And take not the word of truth utterly out of my mouth; for I have hoped in thy judgments.

44 So shall I keep thy law continually for ever and ever.

45 And I will walk at liberty: for I seek thy precepts.

46 I will speak of thy testimonies also before kings, and will not be ashamed.

47 And I will delight myself in thy commandments, which I have loved.

48 My hands also will I lift up unto thy commandments, which I have loved; and I will meditate in thy statutes.

THERE are not twenty Hebrew words beginning with the *sixth* letter of the alphabet. But that letter is itself a conjunction, and in this sense is found at the beginning of each of these verses. Our translation thrice renders it *also*, twice *so*, thrice *and*. On the terms *word, truth, judgments, law, precepts, testimonies, commandments* and *statutes*, see introduction to this Psalm, Nos. 7, 9, 6, 1, 3, 2, 5, 4, respectively.

41. *Let thy mercies come also unto me, O* LORD, *even thy salvation, according to thy word. Mercies* and *salvation*, the usual terms for these things. To man the highest result of *mercy* is *salvation*. These are to be sought *according to God's word*. On this phrase see on v. 25. Compare vv. 58, 76, 116, 154, 170.

42. *So shall I have wherewith to answer him that reproacheth me: for I trust in thy word.* If we are able to give any proper answer to the reproaches of our enemies, it is entirely through divine mercy which has restrained us, reformed us, forgiven us, and taught us heavenly wisdom. Even if we cannot argue with cavillers, we may suffer for God's cause. The martyr slave said: "I cannot dispute for Christ, but I can burn for him." A holy life sustained by divine grace is a fair, logical answer to any cavil against religion. That life is always connected with *trust in God's word*.

43. *And take not the word of truth utterly out of my mouth.* These senses are gathered from this clause: Diodati: "Do not suffer me to want power, or courage to talk of thy holy promises, by finding myself fallen from those hopes which I had put in them;" Patrick: "Do not so far abandon me as to let me be disheartened in asserting the truth and faithfulness of thy word;" Hammond: "Let me never be forsaken by thee, in any such eminent degree that I may doubt of applying this promise to myself;" Alexander: "Deprive me not of this conclusive answer to my enemies, by withholding that providential vindication of my character and practical attestation of thy favor towards me, which I confidently look for." These views do not conflict, and are all admissible. *Utterly,* see on vv. 4, 8. *For I have hoped in thy judgments. Hoped,* also rendered, *tarried, waited, trusted.* It occurs again in vv. 49, 74, 81, 114, 147. In this Psalm it is uniformly rendered *hoped.* True hope produces patient waiting. There is no objection to supposing that by *judgments* we are to understand the decisions of God's word, borne out by the course of his providence. Calvin is confident that the promises are included.

44. *So shall I keep thy law continually for ever and ever. Keep,* as in v. 8. A true keeper of God's commandments *marks* them, *waits* upon them, *observes* them in their integrity. The result of divine grace in preserving the saints from wilful and habitual sin is entirely coincident with the purposes of a gracious soul. Could the renewed man have things according to his mind, he would be pure *always.* The true Christian not only draws the sword; he throws away the scabbard. The mariner who would

make good the haven of eternal rest, must bid farewell to his native shores, and not attempt to do a coasting business in religion.

45. *And I will walk at liberty: for I seek thy precepts.* *At liberty*, see on Ps. ci. 5. In v. 96, the same word is rendered *broad.* The Hebrew adjective here is cognate to the verb *enlarge* in v. 32. See on Ps. cxviii. 5, where we have the cognate noun. Sin is slavery. Vice is bondage. Corruption loads us with fetters. Divine grace brings us out of prison, knocks off our chains, and sets us *at large.* The faculties of mind and heart and body never in so high a sense enjoy *liberty* as when renewed by God's Spirit. The very intensity of a pious search for truth and righteousness is healthful and conduces to human happiness. *Seek*, preterite *have sought*, as in v. 10. It occurs again in vv. 94, 155.

46. *I will speak of thy testimonies also before kings, and will not be ashamed.* Clarke inclines to refer this to Daniel and others like him, who were witnesses of the truth before Nebuchadnezzar, Belshazzar and Darius. No doubt those worthies deserve such a record. Nor can we with Delaney suppose that David here refers to his instructing Achish, king of Gath, in the true religion; for we have no account of his doing that thing, although we are informed of his general conduct when in the country of that prince, 1 Sam. xxix. 8, 9. Moreover, David in going into the presence of that king resorted to cowardly artifice to preserve his life, 1 Sam. xxi. 10–15. So that these words cannot refer to him on that occasion. It is better therefore to take the language as a general declaration that he would not be ashamed to plead God's cause before the whole world. Calvin: "He selects kings, who are generally more to be dreaded than other men, and haughtily shut the mouths of God's witnesses." Alexander thinks our Lord had this passage in mind when he uttered Matt. x. 18, and that "the words are really expressive only of a readiness to declare the divine testimony against sin, in any presence, even the most august, if it should be necessary." *Ashamed*, as in v. 6. It occurs also in vv. 78, 80. See on Ps. vi. 10.

47. *And I will delight myself in thy commandments, which I have loved.* *Will delight myself*, as in v. 16. In the preterite, it occurs again in v. 70. The verb rendered *loved* expresses sincere friendship. It is used repeatedly by the Psalmist to declare his attachment to the law of God. It occurs again in vv. 48, 97, 113, 119, 127, 140, 159, 163, and the corresponding participle in vv. 132, 165, and in the future form in v. 167. It cannot be better rendered than here. We have the highest authority for saying that "love is the fulfilling of the law," Rom. xiii. 10.

48. *My hands also will I lift up unto thy commandments.* Cresswell notices four senses of the phrase, *lifting up the hands.* 1. *Swearing*, Gen. xiv. 22; Deut. xxxii. 40; Ps. cvi. 26; Ezek. xxxvi. 7; Rev. x. 5. 2. *Blessing*, Lev. ix. 22; Ps. cxxxiv. 2. 3. *Praying*, Ps. xxviii. 2; cxli. 2; Lam. ii. 19; 1 Tim. ii. 8. 4. *Setting about any undertaking*, Gen. xli. 44; Ps. x. 12; Heb. xii. 12. Here *lifting up the hands* probably has another meaning, and is expressive of a cordial reception. So Abenezra explains it. Calvin: "It is a sure indication that we eagerly desire a thing when we stretch out the hands to grasp and enjoy it;" Merrick: "I will reach out my hands with eagerness in order to receive thy commandments;" Hengstenberg: "*The lifting up of the hands* symbolizes the lifting up of the heart." Clarke gives a different explanation: "I will present every victim and sacrifice which the law requires. I will make prayer and supplication before thee, lifting up holy hands without wrath and doubting." *Which I have loved*, as in v. 47. *And I will meditate in thy statutes.* *Meditate*, as in vv. 15, 23, 48, 78; in v. 27. rendered *talk of.*

DOCTRINAL AND PRACTICAL REMARKS.

1. The salvation of the righteous is of the Lord, v. 41. Every deliverance from peril, trial or affliction is to be sought from him alone.

2. We never plead amiss when begging for mercy and salvation in the highest sense of those terms, v. 41. We know that it is agreeable to the divine will that we earnestly cry for God's help against our sins and for release from his wrath, 1 Tim. ii. 4.

3. If enemies beset us and persecutions betide us, let them but drive us the more earnestly to the throne of the heavenly grace, vv. 41, 42.

4. We pray in vain for mercy and salvation if we ask for deliverance contrary to Scripture, v. 41. God will not depart from the principles of his word in order to save us from any calamity. Amesius: "The rule for hoping for a divine blessing is the will of God revealed in his word."

5. If we suffer reproach and persecution, nothing new has happened to us, v. 42. Saul hunted David like a partridge upon the mountains. Shimei cursed him as if he had been the vilest of malefactors. Christ's murderers reviled him, and when dying taunted him. Paul: "We both labor and suffer reproach, because we trust in the living God," 1 Tim. iv. 10.

6. We are never so safe as in humbly asking for mercy and salvation, obeying the law, leaving our defence in the hands of the Most High, and simply trusting God's word, vv. 41, 42. All defensive armor fails in the day of trial, until we get the divine panoply. If we cannot by well-doing put to silence the ignorance of foolish men, let them foam out their shame, and pour out their malice against us continually.

7. It is impossible to do well in the Christian life, or to maintain any successful war against sin, unless we have faith, v. 42. The word of God is powerless unless it is believed. Its vast treasures are unlocked by the hand of faith only. Without faith providence is absolutely crushing in many of its dispensations. Faith makes salvation ours. He that will not trust shall not conquer.

8. It is a great thing to be allowed to testify for God, and his truth, v. 43. We should embrace every fit opportunity to bear witness for him. But the Scripture is careful to warn us that it must be done with meekness and fear. Nor should we be discouraged if our witnessing seems to fail of its object, and men become obstinate in sin. It was so with all the prophets and the Master too.

9. Let us hope on and hope ever, v. 43. "Charity will persevere in the path of duty, till, arriving at the gate of heaven, and there taking leave of her companions, Faith and Hope, she shall enter those blissful regions, to perform to eternity that perfect will of God, which the infirmities of fallen nature prevented her from having so fully performed here below." Could our faith and hope be raised to assurance, our troubles would be wondrously diminished.

10. Steadfastness is the greatest commendation of obedience, v. 44.

11. It is lawful, useful and Scriptural to bind our souls by solemn engagements to the service of the Lord, vv. 44–48.

12. It is a great mercy to have the *liberty* of the sons of God, v. 45. Tried often and terribly they may be, but he who walks at large, the truth having made him free, is far from seeing none but dark days. The humblest saint is an object more worthy of the regard of angels and of God himself than the greatest of ungodly men.

13. It is a part of true piety to seek to know as well as to keep the divine precepts, v. 45. Henry: "All that love God, love his government, and therefore love all his commandments;" Bridges: "To have the whole stream of all our thoughts, actions,

motives, desires, affections, carried in one undivided current towards God, is the complete and unrestrained influence of his love upon our hearts."

14. Let us be truly heroic, v. 46. " He who loves his Bible will be a religious man ; and religion except in form has never been fashionable. The man who carries the spirit of the Bible about him must expect sneers and reproach." Calvin : " It is most unbecoming that God's glory should be obscured by the empty splendor of kings."

15. The wicked, who so delight in insulting the saints, and deriding the truth of God, ought to remember that the day is coming, when they themselves will be *ashamed*, v. 46. Of this they have a sure pledge in the fact that God's people are not *ashamed* even now.

16. The true people of God have more and more pleasure in all his word, vv. 47, 48. They have " a *mighty affection* to the law. What is in the word a law of precept, is in the heart a law of love : what is in the one a law of command, is in the other a law of liberty." " He who would preach boldly to others, must himself delight in the practice of what he preacheth." " To the unrenewed a single prohibition of the law makes their lusts flame out ; but to a child of God no precept is grievous." " Love feels no loads."

17. Surely devout meditation must be a most important duty, essential not only to the well-being, but to the being of a child of God ; else it would not so often be insisted upon, v. 48. We never enter God's service aright till the lowest depths of our souls are moved. When our hearts go out after God's word, then our feet run in the ways of his commandments, then our hands love to do what he requires, and the whole work of obedience is delightful.

PSALM CXIX.

ZAIN.

49 Remember the word unto thy servant, upon which thou hast caused me to hope.
50 This *is* my comfort in my affliction : for thy word hath quickened me.
51 The proud have had me greatly in derision : *yet* have I not declined from thy law.
52 I remembered thy judgments of old, O LORD ; and have comforted myself.
53 Horror hath taken hold upon me because of the wicked that forsake thy law.
54 Thy statutes have been my songs in the house of my pilgrimage.
55 I have remembered thy name, O LORD, in the night, and have kept thy law.
56 This I had, because I kept thy precepts.

ALL these verses begin with the *seventh* letter of the Hebrew Alphabet ; verses 49, 52, 55, with the same verb ; verses 50, 56, with the same pronoun ; and verses 51, 53, 54, each with a different word. On the terms *word, law, judgments, statutes* and *precepts,* see introduction to this Psalm, Nos. 7, 1, 6, 4, 3, respectively.

49. *Remember the word unto thy servant, upon which thou hast caused me to hope. Remember,* so remember as to fulfil. Hengstenberg : It " is exactly the same as our phrase *to keep one's word."* The first clause does not necessarily assert that God had spoken *the word unto his servant,* but the prophet prays that God would *remember* to the benefit of his servant *the word.* Until of late there has been remarkable agreement in rendering the whole verse. The new objections are not sufficient to authorize a change. All agree that the prophet pleads for the fulfilment of God's word in which he had hoped, or because he had hoped in it by the divine command and by

divine influence. God will never disappoint expectations authorized and encouraged by his own promises. By the *word* some understand the special promise to David of establishment and perpetuity in the throne. But it more probably includes the whole promissory engagements of God in his word. For *caused me to hope*, Street reads *made me to depend*. *Hope*, see on v. 43.

50. *This is my comfort in my affliction: for thy word hath quickened me.* *Comfort*, here only and in Job vi. 10; but the cognate verb occurs frequently, as in vv. 52, 76, 82, Ps. xxiii. 4. *Affliction*, found also in vv. 92, 153. The cognate verb is also found in vv. 67, 71, 75, 107. It is also rendered *humbled, troubled, exercised*. *Quickened*, the preterite of the verb *quicken*, in vv. 25, 37, 40. The word of God is *quick* and has a *quickening* power. It makes men both *alive* and *lively* in God's service.

51. *The proud have had me greatly in derision.* Calvin: The proud have greatly scorned me; church of England: The proud have had me exceedingly in derision; Edwards: The proud deride me exceedingly; Street: The proud have derided me exceedingly. *Proud*, see on v. 21. *Greatly*, in vv. 8, 43, *utterly;* in v. 4, *diligently;* in v. 167, *exceedingly*. The verb in this clause is that whose participle is in Ps. i. 1, rendered *scornful*. The test to which the prophet's principles were subjected was severe. Calvin: "Many who, in other respects, would be disposed to fear God, yield to this temptation. The earth has always been filled with the impious contemners of God, and at this day it is almost overrun with them. Therefore, if we do not disregard their revilings, there will be no stability in our faith." By divine grace we may rise even above this sore temptation. Yet *have I not declined from thy law*. *Declined*, found also in vv. 36, 112, 157. See on Ps. cii. 11. The meaning of the word here is *turned aside* or *fallen away*.

52. *I remembered thy judgments of old, O* Lord; *and have comforted myself.* God *remembers* his word to keep it. He *remembers* his promise to plead it, and rely upon it. Here and in v. 55, the verb is in the preterite. It is not necessary to vary the meaning of the word *judgments*. The principles of God's government have never varied; they have been *of old*, of the greatest antiquity. *Comforted*, the cognate of the noun rendered *comfort* in v. 50.

53. *Horror hath taken hold upon me because of the wicked that forsake thy law.* The emotion, which in English we call horror, is one of the strongest. It consists of terror mixed with detestation. The Hebrew is no less strong. It is found only here, in Ps. xi. 6, and in Lam. v. 10. See on Ps. xi. 6. Calvin renders it, Terror seized me; Edwards, Horror seizes me; Michaelis, A deadly east wind seizes me: Cocceius, Horror, as a tempest, has seized me. The fear and detestation which the prophet felt were not only on account of the doom of the ungodly, but chiefly for their wickedness, their *forsaking the law* of God.

54. *Thy statutes have been my songs in the house of my pilgrimage.* *Songs*, often rendered *Psalms*. See title of Ps. iii. God's people speak and even *sing* of the statutes of the Lord—his whole word—with joy. *Pilgrimage*, in the plural, *sojournings*. It is but a meager sense that some get from the passage, that the prophet refers to the ancient custom of versifying the laws, that the people might learn them by heart, and sing them. God's statutes are the songs of his people in a far higher sense.

55. *I have remembered thy name, O* Lord, *in the night, and have kept thy law.* *Have remembered*, preterite as in v. 52. To remember God's *name* is to remember him, or his word by which he makes himself known. *In the night*, when people commonly sleep and give their minds up to dreams, or if awake, to roving, vain thoughts. To the pious the night is a favorite time for meditation, Ps. xvi. 7; xlii. 8. *Have kept*, the same verb as in vv. 4, 8. Here it is in the future, and perhaps is better so rendered, thus making it the expression of a solemn, deliberate purpose to continue his obedience.

56. *This I had, because I kept thy precepts*, literally, This was to me. Calvin: This was done to me; Edwards: This is my comfort; Jebb: This was even so to me; Street: Thus it was with me. By *this*, Calvin understands *all God's benefits;* not that the prophet claimed to have merited the divine blessing, but that a gracious reward had been given him. The Scripture admits such a doctrine in many places, Deut. vi. 25; Ps. xli. 2; Isa. iii. 10. This is the common view. Nicolson somewhat varies the idea: "*This I had;* I had this spirit,—this power,—this comfort, *because I kept thy precepts.* While I suffered *for* God, I was enabled to rejoice *in* God. As I made him my portion, so he has been my praise." Diodati: "In my greatest afflictions I have received comfort from thee;" Patrick: "I ascribe this sweet composure of mind, and cheerfulness of spirit, under all my grievous afflictions to my strict observance of thy precepts." There is no better interpretation than that of Calvin, or that suggested by Edwards' translation, which agrees with the spirit of vv. 50, 52.

DOCTRINAL AND PRACTICAL REMARKS.

1. True faith appropriates God's word, v. 49. It takes the general offer of the Gospel, and the promises made to all believers, and applies them to itself, and with the happiest effects. So God becomes *our* God, and the Lord Jesus *our* Saviour, and all Scripture *our* solace.

2. We cannot please God better than by pleading his promises, and all the teachings of his word, v. 49. Our very importunity, because it shows confidence in him, pleases him.

3. Hopes built on the stability of human institutions, or anything earthly, may fail and fill us with grief; but hopes built on God's word shall never disappoint us. He who gave the faithful word, who commanded us to believe, and by his grace enabled us to embrace the promises, will not be unto us as waters that fail, though he may for a while leave us to try us and to draw out our desires after him. The hopes of carnal men may puff up their fleshly minds, and prepare them for a sadder fall; but the hopes of the righteous both humble and strengthen them. Amesius: "In every strait the minds of the pious are sustained by a divine hope."

4. Take from the saints the support and *comfort* which they draw from Scripture, and what could they do? They would even *perish* in their affliction, v. 50. Compare v. 92. But with the word of God, they can defy all assaults. "The comfort it gives is divine, strong, and lasting." Morison: "How many drooping hearts which have refused to be comforted by mere human consolation, have found an all-sufficient solace in those views of the divine character and government which are furnished by the Spirit of God." Trials do in a remarkable manner sweeten promises. Many a verse has seemed like a dead letter, till by our afflictions we were brought to need its consolations. Then it was life and joy to us.

5. The effect of true piety is not to generate insensibility; but to make us *lively* and stirring in God's ways. It *quickens* us, v. 50. Henry: "It made me alive when I was dead in sin; it has many a time made me lively when I was dead in duty." There is no getting on without God's word.

6. If we see *proud* and presumptuous sinners strutting through the earth, and vaporing away, we need not be surprised. There have long been such, v. 51.

7. Scorning is an old weapon, is full of power, and has been tried on the saints in every age, v. 51. Scott: "Infidels, Pharisees, covetous men, libertines, and all the sons of pride and rebellion, will deride as visionaries and enthusiasts, those who speak of communion with God, and joy in him." Trust in the word of God and a holy life are exceedingly provoking to the enemies of righteousness, and bring forth from their unhallowed lips the epithets, *precisian, righteous overmuch,* and the whole vocabulary of abuse. Compare John xv. 18; 1 John iii. 13. He who by faith rests upon

God's word will not *decline from his law* on account of the scoffs of silly men, however great their pomp and power. He sees their day is coming.

8. It is a great thing in a soldier to behave well under fire; but it is a greater thing for a soldier of the cross to be unflinching in the day of his trial, v. 51. It does not hurt the Christian pilgrim to have the dogs bark at him. Henry: "Those can bear but little for Christ that cannot bear a hard word for him."

9. The principles of God's government are unchanging and unchangeable. What he has said and done will not be reversed. He governs the world by the same *judgments* which he had from the beginning, v. 52. God is now as great an enemy of sin as he was when he drowned the old world, and destroyed the cities of the plain. God is now as true to his people, as when he saved Noah by the ark, and sent the angels to rescue Lot.

10. We cannot be too tenderly or deeply concerned for the case of the wicked, v. 53. It is frightful to contemplate. The dishonor they bring on God, the misery and scandal they bring on their fellow-men, the anguish and ruin they bring on themselves, are really more terrible than any has ever conceived them to be. We should deeply compassionate their sad condition. Instead of envying the most prosperous and favored of ungodly men, we may well weep over them, and shudder at their coming doom. In the eyes of every regenerate man iniquity is "a wonderful and a horrible thing." Jer. v. 30; xxiii. 14; Hos. vi. 10.

11. That which makes the case of the wicked the saddest of all is, their *forsaking* God's *word*, v. 53. It is the last hope of a lost world. No other law and no other gospel, no other rule of obedience, and no other mode of acceptance with God for sinners will ever be revealed.

12. There must be a strange consoling power in the truth of God to sustain the most solemn and afflicted people on earth, and to make them joyful and of a merry heart in the house of their pilgrimage, v. 54. The prophet was neither the first nor the last who sang *songs* in the days of his grief and anguish. God has received no nobler praises and benedictions than from many of his servants suffering banishment.

13. There is never a time in which it is not proper to turn to God and think on his name, v. 55. In the darkness of midnight, in the darkness of mental depression, in the darkness of outward providences, God is still a fitting theme. His *name*, his nature, his attributes, his word, his works, all that pertains to him are well suited for themes of joyous meditation to the devout. Amesius: "Solid, spiritual joy arises from a constant and effectual remembrance of the divine name." Blessed is he whose 'holy thoughts and affections rise on the wings of faith, and draw the soul into sweet and profitable fellowship with' him who made it and gave it a law.

14. It is not wrong for us modestly and humbly to mention our uprightness before God and of course to maintain it before man, v. 55.

15. However trying their circumstances, the saints shall sooner or later meet a full and blessed recompense, v. 56. Henry: "All that have made a business of religion will own that it has turned to a good account, and that they have been unspeakable gainers by it." Let us cling to the path of duty. Great peace have all they that love God's law.

PSALM CXIX.

CHETH.

57 *Thou art* my portion, O Lord: I have said that I would keep thy words.
58 I entreated thy favour with *my* whole heart: be merciful unto me according to thy word.

59 I thought on my ways, and turned my feet unto thy testimonies.
60 I made haste, and delayed not to keep thy commandments.
61 The bands of the wicked have robbed me: *but* I have not forgotten thy law.
62 At midnight I will rise to give thanks unto thee because of thy righteous judgments.
63 I *am* a companion of all *them* that fear thee, and of them that keep thy precepts.
64 The earth, O LORD, is full of thy mercy: teach me thy statutes.

ALL these verses begin with the *eighth* letter of the Hebrew alphabet; though no two verses begin with the same word. On the terms rendered *word* or *words, testimonies, commandments, law, judgments, precepts* and *statutes,* see introduction to this Psalm, Nos. 7, 2, 5, 1, 6, 3, 4, respectively.

57. Thou art *my portion, O* LORD. Four times in the Psalms is Jehovah claimed as a *portion,* Ps. xvi. 5; lxxiii. 26; cxlii. 5. See on Ps. xvi. 5. It is only by a genuine appropriating faith that any poor worm of the dust can fitly use such language. *I have said that I would keep thy words.* I have said it, and I intend to stick to it. My mind is made up; my purpose fixed and published. *Keep,* as in vv. 4, 8. Such is the interpretation this verse has commonly received. It is clearly indicated by the rendering of all the ancient versions, except the Syriac, and by the great mass of modern translations. But some have indicated different views. Calvin gives four lections of the verse: 1. *Jehovah is my portion,* and therefore, *I have resolved to observe thy law;* 2. *O Jehovah! who art my portion, I have resolved to observe thy law;* 3. *I have said, that Jehovah is my portion, in order to observe his law;* 4. *I have said, O Lord! that my portion is to observe thy law.* He prefers the last. Fry: My portion, Jehovah, I said, is to keep thy ways. So Alexander: My portion, oh Jehovah, I have said (is) to keep thy words. The objections to this reading are not merely such as Hengstenberg states, drawn from the parallel places already cited and from the Hebrew accents, but most of all from the meager sense thus gathered. A life of holy obedience is a *duty* and has its *pleasures,* but it is not itself a *portion.* Virtue is not her own adequate reward. God himself is the portion of his people, the lot of their inheritance, their exceeding great reward. The second lection given by Calvin is better than either of the others, and is favored by Street; but none is so good as that of the authorized version.

58. *I entreated thy favor with* my *whole heart.* To *entreat* God's *favor* [Hebrew *face*] is to ask his blessing, especially reconciliation with him. We have in 1 Kings xiii. 6, the same words: *Entreat now the face* of the Lord. In Pr. xix. 6, we read, Many *will entreat the favor* of the prince. The italicized verb and noun are in each case the same as in our verse. He had sought God's favor very intensely, with a *whole heart,* vv. 2, 34. The sum of his earnest prayer was for rich and free grace: *Be merciful unto me,* as in v. 132; elsewhere, *Shew favor, Be favorable, Be gracious. According to thy word;* this shows the channel through which mercy flows, the temper in which it must be received, and the amazing riches of the grace, found in God. It is not fancy in the learned Dr. Clarke to suppose that we have here an account of "the *progress* of the work of grace on the human heart." In very few places is it more clearly delineated in so few words. Verse 57 tells of the present happy state and fixed purpose of God's servant. The remaining verses tell how he was brought to so blessed an experience, how he withstood temptation, how the life of God was maintained in his soul, how happy he was in his confidence in God, and how anxious he was to learn more perfectly the divine will. Having in v. 58, told of his wrestlings in prayer, and his earnest cries for mercy, he proceeds:

59. *I thought on my ways.* Chaldee: I have thought to make my ways good; clearly wrong. Amesius, Tremellius and Junius: I think and think again on my ways; Edwards: I reflect on my ways; Street: I think on my ways. But the Syriac, Arabic,

Septuagint, Ethiopic, Vulgate, Doway, Calvin, Piscator, Fabritius, church of England, Jebb, Fry and Alexander use the preterite, *have considered, have pondered, have thought*, or *thought*. *Thought* is very expressive. Pool's paraphrase is: "I seriously considered both my former counsels and courses, that I might be humbled for my past errors, and might now amend them, and my duty in all my future actions." Clarke's: "I deeply pondered them; I turned them upside down: I viewed my conduct on all sides." *And turned my feet unto thy testimonies.* This was what he had not done before. He had been a wanderer. His conversion followed clear, sober reflection. Nor was his turning from one sin to another, or to some human device, but it was to the word of God.

60. *I made haste, and delayed not to keep thy commandments*, parallel to Acts ix. 20; Gal. i. 16. Pool: "I presently resolved upon obedience, and immediately put it in execution." Clarke: "He did this with the utmost *speed;* and did not trifle with his convictions, nor seek to drown the voice of conscience." Hammond: "I immediately set out; I made not one minute's stay in so necessary a pursuit." Men cannot too soon quit wrong courses. The Bible never warns men against speedy or even sudden conversions. Henry: "To what purpose have we thought on our ways, if we do not turn our feet with all speed to God's testimonies?" But such a convert was never allowed to live long unmolested. Trials will come:

61. *The bands of the wicked have robbed me.* Two views have commonly been given of this clause. The first is that which is naturally gathered from the English version, viz.: that *companies* of wicked men assailed him, and robbed him and took his goods. In this sense the word rendered *bands* is taken in 1 Sam. x. 5, 10. The second takes the word *bands* in the sense of *cords*, as in Ps. cxl. 5, and instead of *robbed* reads *caught, caught hold of, infolded. The cords of the ungodly have been thrown around me.* This is better than the first. Another view is suggested. The verb rendered *robbed* very commonly means to *testify* or *protest against.* Perhaps that would give the best sense here, q. d. Companies of wicked men rose up and opposed me, protesting against my course, and even falsely testifying against me. Yet that did not change my conduct: But *I have not forgotten thy law.* Through the power of divine grace, the more a good man is opposed in that which is right, the firmer his purpose is. Those who interpret this Psalm of the church in Babylon of course retain the idea suggested by *robbed* or *hunted*, as Israel was then made a prey.

62. *At midnight I will rise to give thanks unto thee because of thy righteous judgments. At midnight*, literally *at halves of the night;* a time when men are commonly wrapped in slumber; q. d., In season and out of season. *I will rise*, not merely indulge in pious reflections on my bed, but formally give thanks. The mercies already received had much inclined him to grateful worship. But that which decided him in this course was, that he perceived the truth, righteousness and excellency of the *decisions* of God's word carried out in his providence.

63. *I am a companion of all them that fear thee, and of them that keep thy precepts.* It is not possible wholly to avoid civil intercourse with bad men, unless we go out of the world, 1 Cor. v. 9, 10. But civility is a different thing from voluntarily making them our *companions*, our *fellows*, as the word is rendered in Ps. xlv. 7. This verse, especially taken in connection with vv. 57–62, seems conclusive of the position that the poem does not relate to the Jewish nation, but to an individual servant of God. The two marks of piety noticed in this verse are holy reverence for God and a holy life.

64. *The earth, O LORD, is full of thy mercy.* When the heart is duly affected by saving grace, it seems as if all nature were, for good cause, praising the Most High. Proofs of his mercy appear on every hand. The stars sing his praises. The songsters

of the forest carol their notes to the glory of their Creator. The finny tribes are resplendent with beauty, which can come from one hand only. Such views beget fervent longings for further knowledge of the same kind: *Teach me thy statutes.* See on v. 12.

DOCTRINAL AND PRACTICAL REMARKS.

1. How blessed is the *portion* of the saints, v. 57. Jehovah himself with all the plenitude of his perfections is so theirs that each one may say, My Lord and my God. He who has this inheritance has no cause to envy the most prosperous or favored of the sons of earth.

2. Such cannot turn away from the holy commandment. They will keep God's word, v. 57. He, who knows most of God, will most desire to know more of him. He, who loves him most will be most sensible of the deficiencies of his love and most jealous over his own heart. Henry: "Those that take God for their Portion, must take him for their Prince."

3. It is a great thing to be truly in earnest in religion, and importunate in prayer, v. 58. The new creature is not lifeless and senseless, but cries mightily to God. Some deaf mutes have been God's dear children, but there never was a child of God that did not *hear* his voice and *cry* to him *with the heart.*

4. When we pray, let us never forget that we are sinners, and need grace and mercy, v. 58. God sends the full soul empty away, while he gives grace to the humble. Horne: "Mercy is the sole fountain of every good gift for which we ask, and God's promise the only ground upon which we ask it." Angels who never sinned may go to the throne of justice. Let sinners flee to the throne of grace.

5. What a reproach it is to mankind that it can be said of but one here and there, He is *thoughtful* on religious subjects, v. 59. We do nothing towards our salvation till we begin to think. Calvin: "The commencement of a godly life consists in men awaking from their lethargy, examining their ways, and, at last, wisely considering what it is to regulate their conduct properly." "Because the wicked man *considereth* and turneth away from all his transgressions that he hath committed, he shall surely live and not die," Ezek. xviii. 28. The prodigal did not come to his Father until he came to himself, Luke xv. 17. How foolish it is to spend much time in thoughts on the ways of others, when we are ready to perish through the error of our own ways.

6. The proper fruit of right thinking is thorough reformation and a holy life, v. 59.

7. It is of the nature of genuine obedience to be prompt, v. 60. To each one the Lord says as to Zaccheus, *Make haste.* When the Master found Matthew at the receipt of custom, and gave him a divine call, the publican did not invite him to call the next day. The Philippian jailer did not propose to wait till morning before he washed the stripes of Paul and Silas. The disciples generally followed Christ immediately, upon the first call. Calvin: "To *make haste* and *not delay* is to run quickly without doubt or tardiness." Why will men halt between two opinions, and stand ' hovering between heaven and hell?'

8. Opposition to vital godliness will never cease, as long as there are wicked men in the world, v. 61. It may assume the form of violence and *robbery*, or that of snares and seduction. If the former, let not the saints be much moved. We read of some who "took joyfully the spoiling of their goods, knowing that they had in heaven a better and an enduring substance," Heb. x. 34.

9. No perturbations, commotions or opposition can excuse, much less justify apostasy, or a *forgetfulness* of God, v. 61. Calvin: "To continue to love the law, and to practise righteousness, when we are exposed as a prey to the ungodly, and perceive no help from God, is an evidence of genuine piety." Henry: "We must never think

the worse of the ways of God for any trouble we meet with in those ways, nor fear being losers by our religion at last, however we may be losers for it now." Bridges: "The Christian's darkest hour is ten thousand times brighter than the brightest day of the ungodly."

10. Let us accustom ourselves to count up our mercies, and make thankful mention of them at all times, v. 62. 'When a good husband of time cannot lie and sleep, he will rise and pray.'

11. Who are your friends, your associates, the congenial spirits with whom you love to mingle? This is not an idle inquiry, v. 63. If your sympathies are not with the people of God, rest assured that you are not one of them. Such is the power of companions that it has grown into a proverb: "He who walks with the lame will learn to limp." We must not even refuse to become the companions of those good men who are made a gazing stock both by reproaches and afflictions, Heb. x. 33. Compare Ps. xv. 4; James ii. 1. The communion of saints mightily assists communion with God.

12. If our piety does not lead us to fear God, and keep his commandments, we may know that our profession is vain, v. 63.

13. True piety loves to contemplate the riches of God's goodness and mercy in creation and providence, as well as the riches of his grace in redemption, v. 64.

14. Whoever has a zest for spiritual things, and gets a taste of them, will long to know more and more, and enjoy more and more of their fulness and excellence, v. 64. Calvin: "It is an evidence that we have given ourselves up to the most shameful sloth, when, contented with a superficial knowledge of divine truth, we are, in a great measure, indifferent about making further progress."

15. These eight verses clearly show that the experience of God's people is in all ages substantially the same. They all choose God for their portion, all love prayer, all seek for mercy, all think on their ways, all are in good earnest, all endure opposition, all love the excellent of the earth, all think much of the divine mercies, all lead holy lives, and all desire to learn more perfectly the will of God.

PSALM CXIX.

TETH.

65 Thou hast dealt well with thy servant, O LORD, according unto thy word.
66 Teach me good judgment and knowledge: for I have believed thy commandments.
67 Before I was afflicted I went astray: but now have I kept thy word.
68 Thou *art* good, and doest good: teach me thy statutes.
69 The proud have forged a lie against me: *but* I will keep thy precepts with *my* whole heart.
70 Their heart is as fat as grease: *but* I delight in thy law.
71 *It is* good for me that I have been afflicted; that I might learn thy statutes.
72 The law of thy mouth *is* better unto me than thousands of gold and silver.

ALL these verses begin with the *ninth* Hebrew letter; verses 65, 66, 68, 71, 72, with the same word; verses 67, 69, 70, each with a different word. On the terms *word, commandments, statutes, precepts, law*, see introduction to this Psalm, Nos. 7, 5, 4, 3, 1, respectively.

65. *Thou hast dealt well with thy servant, O* LORD, *according unto thy word. Dealt well*, literally, *done good;* church of England and Edwards, *dealt graciously.* In all God had done, he had neither exceeded nor fallen short of the limits of his revealed will. All had been done *according to his word;* see vv. 25, 28, 41, 58.

66. *Teach me good judgment and knowledge.* *Teach,* as in v. 12. *Knowledge,* here only in this Psalm, but of frequent occurrence; in Num. xxiv. 16, "the *knowledge* of the Most High;" in Mal. ii. 7, "the priest's lips should keep *knowledge;*" in Ps. xix. 2, "night unto night sheweth *knowledge.*" In English we get precisely the same idea whether we read *good judgment* or *goodness of judgment.* The latter is literal. For *good judgment,* some have good discretion; some, true understanding; some, excellency of reason; some, right judgment; some, goodness of taste; in Ex. xvi. 31; Num. xi. 8 and elsewhere, the noun is rendered *taste.* *Good sense,* or a *good disposition* probably gives the idea. In learning truth, all those moral qualities which go to make up docility are of prime importance. *For I have believed thy commandments.* He had heartily embraced the law; he did believe God's word to be true, important and necessary, and therefore he asks that he may understand it.

67. *Before I was afflicted I went astray.* *Afflicted,* sometimes, *humbled;* sometimes, *troubled;* in this Psalm invariably, *afflicted;* cognate to the noun rendered *affliction* in vv. 50, 92, 153. *Went astray, erred, was ignorant, was deceived.* The obstinate depravity of the human heart seems to be incurable, except in the school of sorrow. Often there are external causes of deep affliction; but even where there is worldly prosperity, the whole process of conviction for sin humbles and troubles the soul. The bitterest cry ever heard from the lips of mere men has been caused by a sense of sin, Rom. vii. 24. Calvin: "Experience demonstrates, that so long as God deals gently with us, we are always breaking forth into insolence." *But now have I kept thy word.* *Have kept,* as in vv. 4, 8. Alexander: "The salutary fruit of the affliction was already realized and still continued."

68. *Thou art good, and doest good.* Because God is unchangeably good, he is always doing good. His acts proceed from his nature. *Teach me thy statutes,* as in v. 12.

69. *The proud have forged a lie against me.* *Proud,* as in vv. 21, 51; in Ps. xix. 13, *presumptuous.* *Have forged,* in the preterite, in Job xiv. 17, the future is *sewest up;* in Job xiii. 4, the participle is, *forgers of lies.* The verb expresses the idea of complete fabrication, and that with ingenuity, as in curious weaving or sewing. Secker renders it, *made up.* The wickedness of others is no reason why we should depart from God. But *I will keep thy precepts with* my *whole heart.* *Keep* and *whole heart,* as in v. 2.

70. *Their heart is as fat as grease.* John Rogers' translation : Their herte is as fat as brawne. *Fat,* found here only. There seems to be nothing to authorize the rendering of some of the ancient versions, *Their heart is curdled like milk.* That of Street is better: Their heart is as gross as fat. Anderson: "The fat of the human body, as physiologists inform us, is absolutely insensible; the lean, membraneous parts being those only which are sensitive. Accordingly, *fatness of heart* is used, with much propriety, to express the insensibility, stupidity, or sensuality of those feelings or affections, of which the heart is considered the seat." The language of the prophet may be borrowed from the known effects of obesity, dulness and stupidity. While the proud are thus glorying in their gross carnality, the prophet has a different mind. But *I delight in thy law.* *Delight,* the same verb as in vv. 16, 47. The cognate noun is found in vv. 24, 77, 92, 143, 174, and is in each case rendered *delight,* or in the plural *delights.*

71. *It is good for me that I have been afflicted; that I might learn thy statutes.* *Afflicted,* the same verb as in v. 67. The effect of trouble as *there* stated was obedience; as *here* stated, increased knowledge of God's will. If it is *good* for us to be afflicted, it is good in the Lord so to deal with us as to make us partakers of his holiness.

72. *The law of thy mouth* is *better unto me than thousands of gold and silver.* It does me more good. It guides me, it cheers me, it sustains me, it is with me in the most trying hour, and most stands me in stead when my necessities are the greatest, and my afflictions the deepest. When we remember that *thousands* was the largest word for number in common use among the Hebrews, the expression is as strong as it would be for one of us to say *millions.* There is force also in the omission of the noun, *pieces, shekels,* or *talents.* He means to say that he would not give God's word for all the wealth of the world.

Doctrinal and Practical Remarks.

1. Let us never forget that God is and claims to be the author of all good, v. 65.

2. If we would have the full benefit of God's goodness, we must receive it as his *servants,* v. 65.

3. Let us compare events with Scripture, and so learn rightly to interpret both the word and providence of God, v. 65. Henry: "God's favors look best when they are compared with the promise, and are seen flowing from that fountain."

4. We should be as ready to acknowledge mercies as to pray for them, v. 65. Were we more prompt and hearty in acknowledging the Lord's kindness, we should see more kindness to acknowledge.

5. Wisdom is justified of her children, and so is the God of wisdom justified of his people, v. 65. From the whole redeemed world comes up one harmonious testimony that God has done all things well.

6. The longing desire of the pious mind is for more sound, saving knowledge of God, vv. 66, 68. Ignorance is not sanctifying.

7. It is a great thing to have a clear mind, a sound judgment, a correct taste and full assurance of understanding, so that we may rightly believe all that God has spoken, and be in a right temper to receive it, v. 66. Henry: "Many have knowledge who have little judgment; they who have both, are well fortified against the snares of Satan, and well furnished for the service of God and their generation." Unless we have a relish for divine truth, learning will come to us very slowly; and unless we have a clear discrimination, we will confound things that are very unlike each other. Hardly anything impairs a good judgment more than a wrong conscience. A blind, ignorant conscience makes men think they are pleasing God, when they are offending him at every step. A scrupulous conscience is no less unsafe. It makes difficulties where God makes none. Taylor: "Scruple is a little stone in the foot. If you set it on the ground, it hurts you. If you hold it up, you cannot go forward. It is a trouble, when trouble is over; a doubt, when doubts are resolved; a little party behind the hedge, when the main army is broken and cleared."

8. Perhaps Christians evince high attainments as much by their conduct under afflictions, and their views of them, as in any other way, vv. 67, 71. There is a strange perversity in men concerning their trials in life, and nothing but grace can cure it. Blessed is he who when the affliction is over can clearly see and calmly say: It is good for me that I have been afflicted. Afflictions teach us lessons we never could otherwise learn, Jer. xxii. 21, 22. Luther: "I never knew the meaning of God's word until I came into affliction." Rivet: "I have learned more divinity in these ten days that thou art come to visit me than I did in fifty years before." Nor is this all. Through divine grace, affliction amends us. It strengthens us to keep God's statutes. If we can say no more, we can at least say, Thy will be done. "When afflictions fail to have due effect, the case is desperate. They are the last remedy which indulgent Providence uses."

9. Let us be willing and strong witnesses for God, testifying to his goodness, v. 68.

Is not the physician good, when he gives needful medicines, though they are distasteful? Is not the surgeon good, when he sets the broken limb and binds it up, although his manipulations give us great pain?

10. Be not surprised at *lies* respecting yourself and your friends, v. 69. If the truth in regard to your conduct does not answer the purpose of the adversary, look out for falsehood. Many slanders will be 'made out of whole cloth'—forged out and out.

11. But how shall we deal with calumnies? v. 69. Many good answers may be given. Here are some of them. 1. Live so as to prove them lies, v. 69. 2. Be not by them cast down or discouraged in the path of duty, but heroically address yourself to your duty. 3. Bear such trials patiently, and do not render lies for lies, slander for slander, or even reviling for slander. 4. Commit your case to him that judgeth righteously. 5. Be thankful if your enemies have not any further power against you. 6. Expect such things and be prepared for them. "If the Lord does us good, we must expect Satan to do us evil." 7. Honestly inquire whether you are suffering for Christ's sake and with Christ's temper, and are giving no occasion for such treatment. 8. If you have a good conscience, humbly and in the name of God defy the wicked to do their utmost.

12. Grossness and insensibility are as bad signs as can be found in any man, v. 70. The people of God may cheerfully forego all the pleasures of sin when they see their hardening effect upon the ungodly.

13. Very precious is God's word, vv. 71, 72. So the righteous universally judge. It is life from the dead to their souls. It reclaims them when wandering. They buy the truth, cost what it may. But they will not sell it at any price.

PSALM CXIX.

JOD.

73 Thy hands have made me and fashioned me: give me understanding, that I may learn thy commandments.

74 They that fear thee will be glad when they see me; because I have hoped in thy word.

75 I know, O LORD, that thy judgments *are* right, and *that* thou in faithfulness hast afflicted me.

76 Let, I pray thee, thy merciful kindness be for my comfort, according to thy word unto thy servant.

77 Let thy tender mercies come unto me, that I may live: for thy law *is* my delight.

78 Let the proud be ashamed; for they dealt perversely with me without a cause: *but* I will meditate in thy precepts.

79 Let those that fear thee turn unto me, and those that have known thy testimonies.

80 Let my heart be sound in thy statutes; that I be not ashamed.

ALL the verses of this part begin with the *tenth* letter of the Hebrew alphabet; verses 76, 80, only beginning with the same word. On the terms *commandments, word, judgments, law, precepts, testimonies* and *statutes,* see introduction to this Psalm, Nos. 5, 7, 6, 1, 3, 2, 4.

73. *Thy hands have made me and fashioned me.* Perhaps this rendering conveys the true idea. The first verb is that rendered *hast dealt* in v. 65, *deal* in v. 124, and *work* in v. 126. The second is more frequently rendered *established, prepared.* See on Ps. li. 10, where the participle is rendered *right.* In v. 133, in the imperative the verb is rendered *order.* If the common version is correct, it is an acknowledgment that the prophet had his existence from God. If instead of *fashioned* we read *estab-*

lished or *settled*, then the clause acknowledges that not only existence, but all the blessings he enjoyed were from God. See Deut. xxxii. 6. *Give me understanding, that I may learn thy commandments;* as in vv. 27, 34. See on v. 27. He prays for divine teaching.

74. *They that fear thee will be glad when they see me; because I have hoped in thy word.* The verbs of this verse are usually translated as here. The last is found in vv. 43, 49. The effect of the divine treatment of one pious man on his brethren is often noticed, Ps. v. 11; xxxiv. 2; xl. 3.

75. *I know, O Lord, that thy judgments* are *right, and* that *thou in faithfulness hast afflicted me.* It is not necessary to take *judgments* in this place in a sense different from that already explained. The word rendered *right* is a noun, *justice, righteousness;* in connection with *judgments* rendered *righteous* in v. 7. There is no wrong in them. They are righteousness itself. *Faithfulness,* the cognate of the word rendered *Amen.* It implies all truth and fidelity, particularly in covenant engagements. *Afflicted,* the word so rendered throughout the Psalm; see on v. 67. When a father disowns and banishes a child, he corrects him no more. So God may let one whom he intends to destroy go unchastised; but never one with whom he is in covenant.

76. *Let, I pray thee, thy merciful kindness be for my comfort, according to thy word unto thy servant. I pray thee,* an adverb, well rendered. *Merciful kindness,* elsewhere *mercy, kindness, lovingkindness,* see on Ps. li. 1. *For my comfort,* a verb in the infinitive, literally *to comfort me.* We have the corresponding noun in v. 50. There is nothing inconsistent in our acknowledging the righteousness of our sufferings, and at the same time pleading for *mercy* and *comfort,* provided we ask for things agreeable to *God's word.* The last phrase, *word unto thy servant,* seems to look to some particular promise made to David, and cannot be explained as in v. 38, unless we suppose him by faith to appropriate to himself the promise made to the church generally, and so to denominate it God's word to himself.

77. *Let thy tender mercies come unto me, that I may live: for thy law is my delight. Tender mercies,* as in Ps. xxv. 6. It occurs also in v. 156. It is also rendered *mercies, bowels, compassions.* Instead of *let come,* some render literally *shall come.* As death is spoken of as the sum of all evil, so is life as the sum of all good. When the prophet says, *I shall live,* he means to say that he shall so live as to defeat all the purposes of his enemies, and to honor the God of his salvation. He urges as a plea of fitness in his petition that he is no hypocrite, but has real and *abundant* pleasure in the word of God. *Delight,* in the plural, *delights,* corresponding to the verb *delight* in vv. 16, 47, 70.

78. *Let the proud be ashamed. Proud* or *presumptuous,* as in vv. 21, 51, 69. *Ashamed,* or *confounded,* the usual word in the future, *shall be ashamed,* as in vv. 6, 46. See Introduction, § 6. He knew that their defeat was coming because God is just: *For they dealt perversely with me without a cause.* Compare Ps. xviii. 25, 26. *Without a cause,* literally with *falsehood.* The opposition to him was *wrongful,* based in a *lie* and prosecuted with *lying.* He had a right to expect seasonable deliverance. In the meantime he will not waste his hours in railing at his enemies, or dwelling on his own misfortunes. O no! He had something far better to do: But *I will meditate in thy precepts. Meditate,* as in vv. 15, 23; in v. 27, *talk of.* Bishops' Bible: Let the proud be confounded, for they goe wickedly about to destroy me; but I will be occupied in thy commandments.

79. *Let those that fear thee turn unto me, and those that have known thy testimonies.* The pious in this verse are thus described: 1. They fear God. 2. They know his revealed will. The prophet asks that such may *turn,* or *return* unto him, *i. e.,* that

they may be his friends, his companions, his supporters, and that they may learn from his example to trust in God.

80. *Let my heart be sound in thy statutes, that I be not ashamed.* *Sound*, see on v. 1, where it is rendered *undefiled*, elsewhere *sincere, upright, perfect.* *Ashamed*, as in v. 78.

DOCTRINAL AND PRACTICAL REMARKS.

1. It is well for us often to go back to first truths, such as that God is and that he is our Creator, v. 73. It is sad indeed when such truths fade from our minds. They are the foundation of all true religion. Their uses are innumerable.

2. We should often seek light and instruction from heaven, v. 73. In this matter we cannot be too earnest. Even if we are afflicted, our chief concern ought to be more perfectly to understand the divine will. None but God can teach us effectually. Cobbin: "He only who gave life to our bodies, can give light to our minds; and if our minds are enlightened by his Spirit, his word will teach us how to do his will." There is nothing that we need more than eye-salve, Rev. iii. 18. The most knowing among us know but little of the little that may be known of God and of heavenly things. A child of God might plead: "As thou hast raised me above the beasts that perish, in my form and mode of life, teach me, that I may live for a higher and nobler end, loving, serving, and enjoying thee forever! Show me that I was made for *heaven*, not for *earth.*" If we can reason so powerfully from creation itself, who can justly estimate the force of the argument drawn from redemption? Rom. viii. 32. Such pleas rest upon the basis of that sound reasoning peculiar to the Scriptures, that we may urge one great gift of God as a ground for the bestowment of others.

3. It mightily encourages us to see God's goodness to his saints, v. 74. This is a reason why converts to Christ should go among their afflicted and dying brethren, should read the lives of martyrs and confessors, and if possible form the acquaintance of such as have suffered great losses and trials for Christ's sake. The apostles did not wish to afflict their brethren; yet they often reminded them of what they endured for Jesus' sake, 2 Cor. i. 4–11; vi. 8–12. A martyrdom is an awful sight, yet it has often vastly strengthened and cheered the feeble and the timid. Tillotson thought that catechizing and the Lives of the martyrs had been the two main stays of the Protestant cause.

4. Whatever betides us, let us stick to the promise, v. 74. The mother of Augustine but followed the footsteps of David when she said: "Lord, these promises were made to be made good to some, and why not to me? I hunger; I need; I thirst; I wait. Here is thy hand-writing in thy word; and in the last sacrament, I had thy seal affixed to it." So she pleaded, and prevailed.

5. It is a great thing to know that God's word has decided in all points righteously, v. 75. There is no iniquity in it. Let us hold this fast, however cross providences may run to our plans. A carnal man may sometimes see the justice of God and even admire it, as the Lord applies the *judgments* of his word to the cases of some of his cotemporaries; but as soon as God directs the course of events towards him, he is quite blind. Not so with the righteous. Under the sorest trials, Aaron held his peace; Eli said, It is the Lord; Job said, Blessed be the name of the Lord.

6. We ought to know and to proclaim the *faithfulness* of God in *afflicting* us, v. 75. It is not enough for us that we fly not in his face and charge him foolishly. O no! we must justify him; we must confess that our sins and wanderings called for his correction.

7. Though we may not rebel against God in our trials, yet we may pray for relief from them in his own time and way, and especially for support under them, and *com-*

fort in them, v. 76. True, there is nothing in us to merit esteem, but he has bidden us call upon him in the day of trouble.

8. God knows and we ought to know that we need great *compassions, tender mercies* to sustain us and keep us from failing utterly, v. 77. If God is our enemy, we be dead men. If we have not evidence of his covenant love, our graces must languish. If we have but little faith and little love, we shall be despondent. But 'those that delight in the law of God may depend upon his favor, for it shall certainly make them happy.'

9. But let us not forget that all hope of effectual assistance will fail us as long as we live in sin, and delight not in God's law, v. 77.

10. The humbling of the proud is as necessary to their salvation as to the complete triumph of the righteous, and therefore we may ask for it in the spirit of true benevolence, v. 78.

11. But if the wicked will not turn, their pride, and guile, and unbelief, and obstinacy, and cruelty, and violent dealings, and impenitence, and ungodliness will prove the tokens of dreadful wrath, and they shall be *ashamed* forever, v. 78.

12. Come what will, labor to keep your thoughts right, v. 78. Out of the heart are the issues of life. Persecution is itself converted into a blessing when by it we are led more intently to *muse* on God's word.

13. Ever cling to good men. If they err, pray for them. If they repent, forgive them, and *turn* to them, v. 79. Study their history. They are the excellent of the earth. Philip Henry's resolution was: "In those things in which all the people of God are agreed, I will spend my zeal; and as for other things about which they differ, I will walk according to the light God hath given me, and charitably believe that others do so too." Milner: "It will be one of the felicities of heaven that saints shall no longer misunderstand each other."

14. Let us fervently pray for sincerity in religion, for soundness of heart and of head, of creed and of practice, v. 80. Nicolson: "Though an *orthodox creed* do not constitute true religion, yet it is the basis of it, and it is a great blessing to have it."

15. If we fundamentally err in doctrine, or are not upright in heart, *shame* and confusion will certainly overtake us, v. 80. The delay of vengeance will but make it the more dreadful when it comes. Let us be in awful earnest about our salvation. Let us not forget that we have deceitful hearts, a deceitful world, and the father of all deceits against us, and be satisfied with nothing short of a *soundness* that will bear the examination of God.

PSALM CXIX.

CAPH.

81 My soul fainteth for thy salvation: *but* I hope in thy word.

82 Mine eyes fail for thy word, saying, When wilt thou comfort me?

83 For I am become like a bottle in the smoke; *yet* do I not forget thy statutes.

84 How many *are* the days of thy servant? when wilt thou execute judgment on them that persecute me?

85 The proud have digged pits for me, which *are* not after thy law.

86 All thy commandments *are* faithful: they persecute me wrongfully; help thou me.

87 They had almost consumed me upon earth; but I forsook not thy precepts.

88 Quicken me after thy lovingkindness; so shall I keep the testimony of thy mouth.

A LL these verses begin with the *eleventh* Hebrew letter; 81, 82, with the same verb; 84, 87, 88, with the same particle; 83, 85, 88, each with a different word. On the terms *word, statutes, judgment, law, commandments, precepts* and *testimonies,* see introduction to this Psalm, Nos. 7, 4, 6, 1, 5, 3, 2.

81. *My soul fainteth for thy salvation : but I hope in thy word. Fainteth,* so rendered here only ; in vv. 82, 123 and often, *fail ;* also *is consumed, is wasted, is spent. Salvation,* as in v. 41. It means *help, safety, deliverance.* None but God can give effectual relief. He only can give a check to our enemies. Without him man can work no deliverance. We must *wait* for God's *salvation,* Lam. iii. 26. So other Scriptures teach. So the verb *hope* teaches. See on vv. 43, 49, 74. In Job xxix. 21, 23 ; xxx. 26 ; Isa. xlii. 4 ; Mic. v. 7, and elsewhere it is *wait* or *waited.* Alexander: " Both verbs are in the preterite, implying that it is so and has been so." Calvin reads *hath fainted ;* church of England, *hath longed.*

82. *Mine eyes fail for thy word, saying, When wilt thou comfort me ? Fail,* in v. 81, *fainteth.* For *fail* Calvin reads *have waxed dim ;* church of England, *long sore ;* Edwards, *are consuming ;* Street, *are wasted ;* Hengstenberg, *long. Comfort,* the same verb as in v. 76. The whole verse discloses a state of long-continued and severe suffering and depression.

83. *For I am become like a bottle in the smoke. Bottle,* see on Ps. lvi. 8. Bottles were commonly made of the skins of animals. Long hung up, they became covered with dust and smoke, and were unsightly. This may be the sense here. Grief had worn upon the prophet, until he was haggard. When these bottles were empty they became very dry, and afforded neither refreshment to men, nor pleasure in beholding them. So grief mars the visage, and turns moisture into the drought of summer, Ps. xxxii. 4 ; Isa. lii. 14. Calvin: " In comparing himself to a *bottle,* he intimates that he was, as it were, parched by the continual heat of adversities. Whence we learn, that that sorrow must have been intense which reduced him to such a state of wretchedness and emaciation, that like a shrivelled bottle he was almost dried up." But his grief did not lead to apostasy. Yet *do I not forget thy precepts, i. e.,* I both think of them and practise them. *Forget,* as in v. 16.

84. *How many are the days of thy servant ? When wilt thou execute judgment on them that persecute me ?* The usual interpretation of the first clause makes it parallel to those Scriptures which lament the brevity of human life, Ps. xxxix. 4 ; lxxxix. 47, 48. Some make it an inquiry into the length of his days, or a desire to know their number, as in Ps. xc. 12. But are not the two questions parallel to each other? and is not the prophet inquiring how many are to be the days of his sufferings? If so, we preserve the unity of the discourse. Calvin: " Lord, How long hast thou determined to abandon thy servant to the will of the ungodly? when wilt thou set thyself in opposition to their cruelty and outrage?" Diodati admits the same interpretation as probably correct. So also Hammond. The ground, on which Street changes the Hebrew text so as to render the first clause, *Thy servant burneth with desire, O Jehovah,* is insufficient. None of the ancient versions support his reading. If the word *judgment* in this verse is to be taken as in its plural form referring to Scripture, then it relates to some particular decision of God's word respecting persecutors. Otherwise, it refers to the simple administration of *justice* in the divine government towards the enemies of God's people, as in Ps. ix. 16. In either case the general sense is the same. With the latter clause compare Rev. vi. 9, 10. Calvin: " He only wishes in general to be delivered by the hand of God from the wrongs which were inflicted upon him, without adjudging to perdition his adversaries."

85. *The proud have digged pits for me, which are not after thy law. Proud,* or *presumptuous,* as in vv. 21, 51, 69, 78. Calvin: The proud have digged pits for me,

which thing is not according to thy law. This is better than the rendering of Ed wards: The proud dig pits for me, who act without any regard to thy law. How contrary it is to the law of God to dig pits, spread snares and set traps for the un wary and innocent is abundantly declared in many places. This might not be done literally, even for a harmless brute, Ex. xxi. 33, 34; much less for men, Ps. vii. 15; ix. 15; Prov. xxviii. 10; Eccles. x. 8; Jer. v. 26; xviii. 20, 22. One feature of a good man's character is that he is *without guile*, Ps. xxxii. 2. He may not practise deceit, even in order to accomplish a good end. What particular snares were laid for David in this case we know not; but the inventions of the wicked are endless.

86. *All thy commandments* are *faithful*, literally *faithfulness*, i. e., altogether faith ful, the perfection of faithfulness. They give faithful warning. The blessings con nected with obedience to them are faithfully bestowed. There is no deceit in any part of God's word. *They persecute me wrongfully without a cause, falsely*, see on v. 78. *Persecute*, the same verb is found in vv. 84, 150, 157, 161. It implies a malig nant pursuit, as in Ps. vii. 5. Under such circumstances, what else can he do but betake himself to God? *Help thou me.*

87. *They had almost consumed me upon earth.* Consumed, the causative form of the verb rendered *fainteth* and *fail*, in vv. 81, 82. *Almost*, as in Ps. lxxiii. 2; xciv. 17. Yet he was not *quite* consumed. He did not *quite* faint; nor did his trials make him an apostate. *But I forsook not thy precepts.* He held fast the word of God through all his trials, loving it, seeking to know it and to do it, not turning away from the holy commandment. *Forsook*, the preterite of the verb in v. 8.

88. *Quicken me after thy lovingkindness.* Quicken, as in vv. 25, 37, 40. *Loving kindness*, in v. 41, in the plural *mercies;* in v. 76, *merciful kindness.* All he sought, he asked through grace. Being thus sustained it would be easy for him to carry out his purposes of obedience. *So shall I keep the testimony of thy mouth.* Keep, as in vv. 4, 8. Calvin: "When the law is called *the testimony of God's mouth*, by this eulogium its authority is very plainly asserted."

Doctrinal and Practical Remarks.

1. It is no new thing for a good man to be in great distress, vv. 81–83. Dickson: "It is not strange to see God breaking the heart of his own child with affliction, even when he is suffering persecution, so that his faith may be tried and trained to more strength."

2. It is a great blessing to be greatly afflicted, if the strokes are sent in covenant love, and if they lead us to seek promised help from God alone, v. 81. Cobbin: "We ought not to mistrust God's word, because the execution of his promises is delayed. If our eyes fail, our hearts should not faint; God's time is always the best. Our dangers may increase, but God's promises do not decrease."

3. It is a blessed thing when our trials cure our earnest love for things that perish, and whet our appetites for divine *comforts*, v. 82.

4. If we find ourselves despised, forsaken, rejected and thrown aside through our own infirmities of mind or body, through the slanders and persecutions of others, let us not forget that other good men also have been *like bottles in the smoke*, v. 83.

5. Oftentimes the long continuance of our trial is the bitterest ingredient in our cup, v. 84. When our grief threatens to be lifelong, then our vigor departs. But he who gives us grace to bear it one day can give us grace to bear it one lifetime.

6. Meantime let us hold fast God's word and never limit the Almighty, vv. 81, 83, 87. His blessings often receive their greatest excellence from being timely. His word cannot fail. Calvin: "It is a genuine evidence of true godliness, when although plunged into the deepest afflictions, we yet cease not to submit ourselves to God."

Henry: "Though we think the time long, ere the promised salvation and comfort come, yet we must still keep our eye upon it and resolve to take up with nothing short of it." We must also love the precepts of Scripture no less than its promises. The loss of all earthly things cannot excuse rebellion against God.

7. It is not sinful in us humbly to cry out, O Lord, how long shall my afflictions last? v. 84.

8. Nor is it sinful in us to ask God to interpose and judge between us and our tormentors, v. 84. If the righteous cannot do that, they must pine away. Persecutors have no pity. The very wrongs they have done are the causes of continued oppression. Help from them is not to be expected. Bridges: "To complain *of* God is dishonorable unbelief. To complain *to* God is the mark of his elect."

9. All God's people ought to look out for snares and *pits* and traps, v. 85. Satan would cease to be our adversary, and his allies would be powerless against us, if all artifice should cease.

10. Let men beware how they *dig pits* for others, v. 85. All God's word testifies against such wickedness. How many tests are invented, simply for the purpose of entangling men's consciences and furnishing ground for new persecution!

11. If faithlessness marks our generation, and the history of our race, let us comfort ourselves with this, that all God's word is *faithfulness* itself, v. 86. It is not only true and just, but most precious and wholly unfailing.

12. If we find ourselves *wronged* and *lied* against, we need not be surprised, v. 86. Better men have endured the same. The conduct of our maligners does thus indeed appear flagrantly unjust, and that may awaken our just indignation and detestation. Nor can we justify their wrong-doing. Yet let us guard against malice, even towards the vilest enemies.

13. The unspeakable comfort of committing their cause to God is always left to the saints, v. 86. Henry: "*God help me* is an excellent, comprehensive prayer; it is pity that it should ever be used lightly and as a by-word."

14. The lives of good men are full of narrow escapes, v. 87. The righteous are scarcely saved. Many a time their feet do almost slip. Yet he, who has redeemed them, will not let them so fall that they can rise no more. One of their greatest perils is, a temptation to use unlawful means for terminating their trials.

15. A very awful doom must await impenitent persecutors, vv. 84, 86. They are the bloodhounds of the bottomless pit, let loose on the church of God. Henry: "There is a day coming, and a great and terrible day it will be, when God will execute judgment on all the proud persecutors of his people; *tribulation to them that troubled them.*" Those who find pleasure in maligning and torturing God's people may think it fine sport now, but they will not think so when they answer for the tears and blood which they have caused to be shed, for the sighs and groans which they have wrung from the anguished hearts of God's loving children.

16. After all, and in the midst of all the sufferings of God's people, their greatest desire is for more grace, the power of the quickening Spirit, v. 8. It is a good evidence of a saving change of heart when we desire more holiness, more liveliness in God's service. "The surest token of God's good will toward us is his good work in us."

PSALM CXIX.

LAMED.

89 For ever, O LORD, thy word is settled in heaven.

90 Thy faithfulness *is* unto all generations: thou hast established the earth, and it abideth.

91 They continue this day according to thine ordinances: for all *are* thy servants.

92 Unless thy law *had been* my delights, I should then have perished in mine affliction.

93 I will never forget thy precepts: for with them thou hast quickened me.

94 I *am* thine, save me; for I have sought thy precepts.

95 The wicked have waited for me to destroy me: *but* I will consider thy testimonies.

96 I have seen an end of all perfection: *but* thy commandment *is* exceeding broad.

ALL these verses begin with the *twelfth* letter of the Hebrew alphabet; and all of them except v. 92, with that letter used as a preposition. On the terms *word, faithfulness, law, precepts, testimonies* and *commandment,* see introduction to this Psalm, Nos. 7, 9, 1, 3, 2, 5, respectively.

89. *For ever, O* LORD, *thy word is settled in heaven.* Other renderings leave the main idea as here. Syriac: Thou art for ever, O Lord, and thy word continues in heaven; Jebb: Forever, O Lord, is thy word: it endureth in heaven; Walford: O Jehovah! Forever is thy word established in the heavens; Street: Thy word is eternal, O Jehovah; it is more firmly fixed than the heavens; Alexander: To eternity, Jehovah, thy word is settled in heaven. *Is settled, stands, stands still, is set, is established;* there is no better word to express unchangeable fixedness. *In heaven,* where God himself is; where his throne is built upon his truth; whence all causes derive their efficiency; whence all his servants receive their commands; "beyond the reach of all disturbing causes." Mohammed claimed that he had been admitted into heaven, and permitted to copy some of the chapters of the Koran from the pillars of the throne of God. All holy Scripture is found in the foundation of God's throne.

90. *Thy faithfulness* is *unto all generations. Faithfulness,* fidelity to engagements, or a name for Scripture itself. Instead of *is,* we may supply *endureth.* God's truth is his word. It never fails. He has never changed a principle of his moral government. *Thou hast established the earth, and it abideth. Established,* in Ps. lvii. 7 and elsewhere, *fixed.* Although many things in earthly affairs are mutable, yet even in this world the thoughtful may discern tokens of stability in the divine arrangements. The revolutions of the earth and the motions of the heavenly bodies may be calculated.

91. *They continue this day according to thine ordinances. Ordinances,* everywhere else in this Psalm rendered *judgments, i. e.,* settled decisions. Calvin: "In using the term *judgments,* he makes an allusion to the law, intimating, that the same regard to rectitude which is exhibited in the law is brightly displayed in every part of God's procedure." The best explanation of the pronoun *they* is that it stands for heaven and earth. There is good cause for the uniformity of nature. *For all* are *thy servants.* Heaven and earth with all their elements and motions obey God's will. Important as are the lessons taught by the works of nature, they fall short of meeting our wants, for

92. *Unless thy law* had been *my delights, I should then have perished in mine affliction. Delights,* as in vv. 24, 77, though there rendered in the singular. *Perished, been lost,* or *been destroyed.* Without the teaching of God's word, the prophet's affliction would have been not only mysterious but crushing. For *then* Calvin would read *long ago;* Edwards, *long since. Affliction,* as in v. 50.

93. *I will never forget thy precepts: for with them thou hast quickened me.* *Forget*, as in v. 16. *Quickened*, as in vv. 25, 37, 40, 50, 88, thou hast made me alive and lively.

94. *I am thine, save me; for I have sought thy precepts.* The argument in the first clause is drawn from the covenant relation. Inspired men love to resort to that method of reasoning. The proof that he is in covenant with God is found in the fact that he *sought* to know and to do the will of God. *Sought*, as in vv. 10, 45; in another form in v. 2, *seek*.

95. *The wicked have waited for me to destroy me.* *Wicked*, in Ps. i. *ungodly;* in this Psalm uniformly *wicked*. *Waited*, i. e., with expectation, *looked for*. *To destroy*, the causative form of the verb rendered *have perished* in v. 92; they have waited for me to cause me to perish. Though their devices are not stated, doubtless they were diabolical. But *I will consider thy testimonies*, so consider as to *understand*, as the word is fitly rendered in v. 100.

96. *I have seen an end of all perfection.* John Rogers' translation: I se that all thynges come to an ende; Street: To every study I see a limit; Clarke: "Of all consummations I have seen the end: as if one should say, everything of human origin has its bounds and limits, and ends, howsoever extensive, noble, and excellent. All arts, and sciences, languages, inventions, have their respective principles, have their limits and end. As they came from man and relate to man, they shall end with man." *Perfection*, found nowhere else. Henry: "Poor perfection which one sees an end of! Yet such are all those things in this world which pass for perfections. David, in his time, had seen Goliath, the strongest, overcome; Asahel, the swiftest, overtaken; Ahithophel, the wisest, befooled; Absalom, the fairest, deformed." Scott: "He had seen the vanity of all created good; the vexation of that estate which men account the summit of earthly bliss; the imperfection of the most accomplished human character; the wretched close of the most prosperous lives, and the miserable disappointment of those who trusted in men, or idolized earthly possessions or enjoyments." This interpretation agrees with the authorized version, which is supported by the Genevan, Doway, Calvin, Edwards, Jebb, Fry and Hengstenberg. But *thy commandment is exceeding broad, i. e., wide, large*, comprehensive, including actions, words, thoughts and emotions; the matter, manner and motive of all that man can do, or say, or think. Like the atmosphere which surrounds us, the law of God presses from all quarters. If we take commandment in the wide sense of all Scripture, then the meaning is that God's word covers all cases and meets all wants of the myriads who embrace it. The omission of *but* would make the connection between the clauses still more close.

DOCTRINAL AND PRACTICAL REMARKS.

1. However fleeting, changeable and unsatisfactory are all things merely temporal; yet the word of God is stable, unchangeable and everlasting. It depends upon his truth and faithfulness, and these are so a part of his nature that if he were without them, he would cease to be God, vv. 89, 90, 91. The divine faithfulness has never failed.

2. Although it is comparatively easy to fall into error when reasoning from the analogy of nature; yet fair and sound arguments drawn from that quarter lie at the foundation of all natural theology, and so of all true religion, vv. 90, 91. Bridges: "The very fact of a creation in ruins—a world in rebellion against its Maker, failing of the grand end of existence, and yet still continued in existence—manifests his faithfulness unto all generations."

3. We need never fear any convulsions on earth, in the elements, or among the heavenly bodies; for Jehovah is Lord of all and *all are his servants*, v. 91. They must obey his will. His omnipotence enforces his behests.

4. The sons of mirth, giddiness and worldly pleasure may speak extravagantly of carnal delights, and put far away the day of affliction; but all God's people know that trials, ordered by the Lord, are often insupportable by mere human strength. As one expresses it, "I could not have outlived one stroke of thine afflicting hand." Nor can any mortal decide which is to be preferred, being kept from affliction, or being kept from *perishing* in *affliction*, v. 92.

5. Indeed such is the weight of many earthly sorrows that nothing but Scripture, received in faith and applied by the Holy Ghost, can sustain the sinking heart, v. 92. Clarke: "Had we not had the consolations of religion, we should long ago have died of a broken heart." Bridges: "Each promise is a staff—if we have but faith to lean upon it—able to bear our whole weight of sin, care and trial." Morison: "Such light and consolation are supplied in God's holy law, that no heart can be utterly broken upon whom the full weight of its encouragements is permitted to fall."

6. It is therefore not without cause that the pious love and remember God's word, v. 93. Henry: "The best evidence of our love to the word of God is, never to forget it." How can the renewed soul consent to cast off that word, which at conversion was life from the dead, the voice of the Redeemer summoning men from their spiritual graves, and which has cheered them in a thousand days of darkness?

7. It is sufficient proof that we are in covenant with God, when we seek to know and obey his whole will, v. 94. God will never cast away his jewels, but gather them into his cabinet of the spirits of just men made perfect.

8. The plots and plans of the wicked against the righteous are many, cunning and deadly, v. 95. There is an awful smell of blood about all forms of persecution. Horne: "Spiritual enemies are continually upon the watch to destroy us all."

9. If the Scripture is to do us effectual good, we must *understand* it, so as to apply it, v. 95. It is not superstitious but intelligent piety that God commands. Luther: "I have covenanted with my Lord, that he should not send me visions, or dreams, or even angels. I am content with this one gift of the Scriptures, which abundantly teaches and supplies all that is necessary both for this life and that which is to come."

10. All merely earthly things are by their very nature vain, unsatisfactory, and, through our depravity, delusory, v. 96. All human attainments are shallow, all human enjoyments transitory, all human virtue marred. Each one may say: "I have observed by experience that the greatest and most perfect accomplishments and enjoyments in this world, the greatest glory, and riches, and wisdom, and power, are too narrow and short-lived to make men happy."

11. "But where is the end or boundary of the word of God? Who can ascend to the height of its excellency? who can fathom the depth of its mysteries? who can find out the comprehension of its precepts or conceive the extent of its promises? who can take the dimensions of that love of God to man which it describeth, or that love of man to God which it teacheth?" Who knows the depth of the iniquity which it unfolds, or the preciousness of the blood which it holds forth for propitiation? It commands every duty to God, our neighbor or ourselves. It forbids all sin. It inculcates and enforces every principle of justice, and of charity. It at once humbles and gives courage, imparts tenderness of conscience and of heart, and also makes men lion-hearted. It abounds in all excellences.

PSALM CXIX.

MEM.

97 O how love I thy law! it *is* my meditation all the day.

98 Thou through thy commandments hast made me wiser than mine enemies: for they *are* ever with me.

99 I have more understanding than all my teachers: for thy testimonies *are* my meditation.

100 I understand more than the ancients, because I keep thy precepts.

101 I have refrained my feet from every evil way, that I might keep thy word.

102 I have not departed from thy judgments: for thou hast taught me.

103 How sweet are thy words unto my taste! *yea, sweeter* than honey to my mouth.

104 Through thy precepts I get understanding: therefore I hate every false way.

ALL these verses begin with the *thirteenth* letter of the Hebrew alphabet; 97, 103, with the same word; 98, 99, 100, 101, 102, 104, with the same word rendered *more than, from* or *through*. On the terms *law, commandments, testimonies, precepts, word, judgments,* see introduction to this Psalm, Nos. 1, 5, 2, 3, 7, 6.

97. *O how love I thy law! it* is *my meditation all the day. Love,* in the preterite. It denotes what has been and is still his habit of mind. We had it in vv. 47, 48. It occurs in the same form in vv. 113, 119, 127, 140, 159, 163; and in the future in v. 167. The participle is found in vv. 132, 165. It expresses sincere and undoubted friendship. *Meditation,* it has the same variety of signification as the cognate verb, *prayer* or *speech.* It occurs also in v. 99. In Job xv. 4, it is rendered *prayer,* in the margin, *speech.* Compare Ps. i. 2.

98. *Thou through thy commandments hast made me wiser than my enemies: for they* are *ever with me. Hast made me wiser,* a verb in the future. We have it in the same form, Ps. cv. 22. God has already taught and will continue to teach him wisdom above that attained by any of his wicked *adversaries.* God's word makes men wise, even unto salvation. It requires no labored processes of reasoning to understand its practical truths. For *they are ever with me,* some read *forever they are to me, i. e., they are mine, my right, my portion.* This conveys a good sense. But the former explanation has been commonly accepted. Diodati: "They are rooted in my heart, and are not as an outward law to me, to force my will by constraint, but by an internal conformity of all my inward senses and motions, Jer. xxxi. 33; Rom. vi. 17."

99. *I have more understanding than all my teachers: for thy testimonies* are *my meditation. Have understanding,* in the preterite, have had it and have it still. The verb is that from which *Maschil* is derived. The meaning is, I am better *instructed* and have more spiritual *wisdom* and heavenly *prudence* than all my *teachers. Teachers,* a participle of the verb often rendered *teach* in this Psalm, vv. 12, 26. *Meditation,* as in v. 97.

100. *I understand more than the ancients, because I keep thy precepts.* By the *ancients* we are not to understand persons who lived and died a long time ago, but persons still living, venerable for their age and opportunities of gaining wisdom; in Ps. cv. 22, it is rendered *senators;* in cvii. 32, *elders;* in Ps. cxlviii. 12, *old men.* The longer a man lives without instruction from God's word, the farther does he go astray. The Psalmist is publishing in proper terms that wisdom consists in *keeping the precepts* and doing the will of God. *Understand,* usually so rendered in this Psalm; implying careful consideration. *Keep,* as in v. 2, implying vigilant attention to duty.

101. *I have refrained my feet from every evil way, that I might keep thy word. Refrained, forbid, withheld, restrained, kept back. Evil way,* literally *path of evil. Keep,*

as in vv. 4, 8. The verse teaches that we cannot willingly live in sin, when we have a sincere desire to keep the law. We cannot at the same time walk both in crooked and straight paths. Care and circumspection enter into the very nature of true obedience.

102. *I have not departed from thy judgments: for thou hast taught me.* He who in anything regards his own *decisions* as comparable to the *judgments* of God is already a fool. Every *departure* from God's word is an error, which without the interposition of divine grace will be fatal. But we will be sure to *turn aside* unless in his mercy God shall *teach* us.

103. *How sweet are thy words unto my taste,* yea, sweeter *than honey to my mouth.* See on Ps. xix. 10. For *taste,* Calvin, Edwards and others read *palate;* church of England, *throat;* often elsewhere *mouth.* Our version gives the sense. *Sweet,* here only. The primary idea is that of *smoothness,* then of *pleasantness,* and in things tasted *sweetness.* Calvin: "The prophet does not speak of the dead letter which kills those who read it, but he comprehends the whole doctrine of the law, the chief part of which is the free covenant of salvation." *Words* or *sayings,* to be taken in the largest sense.

104. *Through thy precepts I get understanding;* literally, *I shall get understanding* as long as I love, study and obey thy word, even as I have already. True wisdom comes from above through God's word. The best proof of wisdom is found in avoiding all sin, delusion, error, vanity and falsehood. *Therefore I hate every false way,* literally, I have hated every path of falsehood. *False,* see on v. 29. The clause expresses the habit of his life. This verse in connection with v. 101, shows the reciprocal action of Scripture and of a holy life. God teaches us, and we obey. We obey, and he teaches us more. We learn a little and practise that; thus we are prepared to learn and practise more.

DOCTRINAL AND PRACTICAL REMARKS.

1. The difference between a saint and a sinner, a false professor and a true child of God, is even greater in fact than in appearance. The former loves the law of God, v. 97 ; the latter rebels against its requirements. Amesius : "Those who have tasted how good the word of God is adhere to it with incomparable and incredible ardor of affection ;" Horne: "Words cannot express the love which a pious mind entertaineth for the Scriptures." It is a grand support in the day of calumny and persecution. How else can we resist the world, the flesh and the devil, but with this sword of the Spirit? God's word interprets nature, providence and grace. It is the best guide to devotion. Its author is divine. Its matter is divine. Its use is to make us partakers of the divine nature.

2. If devout meditation on the word of God is an essential part of true religion, the fashionable piety of modern times falls quite below the Scripture standard, vv. 97, 99. Calvin : "If any person boast that he loves the divine law, and yet neglects the study of it, and applies his mind to other things, he betrays the grossest hypocrisy." "A good man wherever he goes carries his Bible along with him, and if not in his hand, yet in his head and in his heart." Luther: "Pause at every verse of Scripture, and shake, as it were, every bough of it; that, if possible, some fruit at least may drop down."

3. Heavenly wisdom is as much better than worldly wisdom as heaven is better than earth, vv. 98, 99, 100. The greatest wisdom on this earth is holiness. The wisdom taught by Scripture is far reaching and is capable of application to every diversity of case.

4. By law David was required to make a copy of the Scriptures for his own use,

Deut. xvii. 18. Some conjecture that beside this he carried with him notes and memoranda of divine things as they occurred to him. But it seems impossible to avoid the conclusion that he committed to memory considerable portions of Scripture, vv. 98, 99. How can the word of God properly exercise our judgment and affections and give us heavenly wisdom, unless it dwell in us richly, and fill our memory, and so *be ever with us,* and form the theme of our *meditations?*

5. The reasons of the excellence of Scripture in imparting wisdom are many, vv. 99–102. 1. He who made the soul gave the law, adapting the one to the other. 2. God's word contains the true system of thinking, feeling and acting in all matters of which it treats. 3. The Scripture comes with authority. The human conscience feels that it is God who is speaking. 4. The most important matters are made very plain. Under such teaching it is not wonderful that 'the simplest Christian, who by faith and prayer appropriates the information conveyed to him in the Scriptures of truth, will soon surpass in useful knowledge and practical wisdom the most learned teachers, the most renowned fathers, and the most aged and experienced persons, who, leaning to their own understandings, reject the oracles of God, or are but superficially acquainted with them.' Antiquity is no such guide as are the lively oracles.

6. Practice is the very life of piety, vv. 100, 101. The *keeping* of the commandments is essential not only to the honor of religion, but to the understanding of the very nature of divine things. Clarke: "Spiritual knowledge increases while we tread in the path of *obedience.* Obedience is the grand means of *growth* and *instruction.* Obedience trades with the talent of grace, and thus grace becomes multiplied."

7. If we would become truly wise, we must quit all sin, turning away from it with abhorrence, v. 101. Horne: "The foundation of all religion must be laid in mortification and self-denial." The reason is that the heart of man is strongly and strangely averse to the will of God.

8. Divine teaching, and that alone, secures holiness and perseverance in the ways of God, v. 102. God only can lift the veil off the heart so as to let us see divine things in their beauty. Blessed is the promise made through the evangelical prophet: "All thy children shall be taught of the Lord, and great shall be the peace of thy children," Isa. liv. 13.

9. There is no substitute for a lively relish of divine things, v. 103. Calvin: "It is possible that a man may be affected with reverence towards the law of God; but no one will cheerfully follow it, save he who has tasted its sweetness." Otherwise the whole service of God will be a drudgery. Bridges: "Warm affections are far more influential than talents, or mere external knowledge."

10. Through divine grace God's people may have a heaven upon earth, v. 103. They have *tasted* and so know the preciousness of Scripture. Communion with God in his word and ordinances is not equal to communion with God in heaven; but it is like it. Heavenly mindedness is heaven anticipated.

11. Let each one diligently study God's word. It gives a knowledge true and influential. What dying saint ever deplored that he had too assiduously studied it? Hervey: "Were I to renew my studies, I would take my leave of those accomplished triflers—the historians, the orators, the poets of antiquity—and devote my attention to the Scriptures of truth. I would sit with much greater assiduity at my divine Master's feet, and desire to know nothing but Jesus Christ and him crucified." That is speaking like a wise man.

12. Let us never hug delusions, but hate error and sin in every shape, v. 104. **Let us** assiduously abhor even darling sins. All sin is a *lie.* By it we attempt to **cheat**

God. By it we actually cheat our souls, Pr. xiv. 12. There is no delusion like the folly of believing that a course of sin will conduce to our happiness.

13. What an aid to self-examination we have in this part of the Psalm. Do we love God's law? Do we meditate on it? Do we study it? Are we the wiser for it? Are we warned by it? Have we submitted to divine teaching? Do we read with more interest the news of the day, or the letters of a friend, than we feel when perusing the sacred volume? Is our love of holiness increasing? Do we find Christ in all the Scriptures? Is he our life? If we are to lead new lives, it must be by the faith of the Son of God.

PSALM CXIX.

NUN.

105 Thy word *is* a lamp unto my feet, and a light unto my path.
106 I have sworn, and I will perform *it*, that I will keep thy righteous judgments.
107 I am afflicted very much: quicken me, O LORD, according unto thy word.
108 Accept, I beseech thee, the freewill offerings of my mouth, O LORD, and teach me thy judgments.
109 My soul *is* continually in my hand: yet do I not forget thy law.
110 The wicked have laid a snare for me: yet I erred not from thy precepts.
111 Thy testimonies have I taken as a heritage for ever: for they *are* the rejoicing of my heart.
112 I have inclined mine heart to perform thy statutes always, *even unto* the end.

ALL these verses begin with the *fourteenth* letter of the Hebrew Alphabet; but each verse with a different word. On the terms *word, judgments, law, precepts, testimonies* and *statutes,* see introduction to this Psalm, Nos. 7, 6, 1, 3, 2, 4.

105. *Thy word* is *a lamp unto my feet, and a light unto my path. Lamp,* often so rendered, also *candle,* Ps. xviii. 28; cxxxii. 17. Some propose to read *lantern,* and some *torch* or *flambeau.* Either word gives the idea. *Lamp* or lantern is best. The general sense is clear, as in the second clause of the verse we have the parallel *light.* The imagery is just and easily understood. A man is benighted. He knows not the way. A light is brought. It shows him the *path,* where to place his *feet.* Compare 2 Pet. i. 19. Calvin: "Were there such obscurity in God's word, as the Papists foolishly talk about, the commendation with which the prophet here honors the law would be altogether undeserved."

106. *I have sworn, and I will perform* it, *that I will keep thy righteous judgments.* A just estimate of a profession of religion, or of even a secret engagement to be the Lord's, will fitly invest it with a solemnity not less than that by which a man binds his soul in an oath. Calvin: "By the word *swear,* he intimates that he had solemnly pledged himself to God not to alter his determination." Such language is by no means confined to this one case, 2 Chron. xv. 15; Neh. x. 29. *Will perform;* church of England and Jebb, *am steadfastly purposed;* Edwards, *will not depart from it;* Fry and Alexander, *confirm it;* Street, *will continue.* Patrick's paraphrase is, " I have solemnly resolved and bound myself by the most sacred ties, which I will never break, but do now confirm." Pool's, " I do not repent of it and by God's grace *I* will fulfil it." *Keep,* as in vv. 4, 8. His purpose was settled. His heart was fixed. *Thy righteous judgments,* see on v. 7.

107. *I am afflicted very much: quicken me, O* LORD, *according unto thy word. Afflicted, humbled,* in the preterite. *Very much;* Calvin, *greatly;* church of England, *above measure;* Jebb, *exceedingly;* Hengstenberg, *severely;* Alexander, *to extremity;*

in v. 8, *utterly.* What the particular affliction was, is not stated. *Quicken me ac-cording unto thy word,* see on v. 25.

108. *Accept, I beseech thee, the freewill offerings of my mouth, O* LORD, *and teach me thy judgments.* *Accept, i. e., graciously accept;* Calvin: *favor of mere good will.* On the noun rendered *freewill offerings,* see on Ps. cx. 3, where it is rendered *willing;* often in the law, and elsewhere rendered as here; in Amos iv. 5, *free offer-ings.* Here evidently it refers to spiritual sacrifices of vows, prayer and praise, whether offered in solitude or in the midst of the great assembly.

109. *My soul is continually in my hand.* Hammond: "The meaning of this phrase is obvious, *I am in danger of my life.*" Compare Judges xii. 3; 1 Sam. xix. 5; xxviii. 21; Job xiii. 14. The Chaldee: My soul is in danger. The Hebrew will not allow us to read, My soul is in thy hands. *Soul* here probably means *life.* The prophet asserts that he was all the time in peril of death, but that did not change his purpose of obedience. *Yet do I not forget thy law, i. e.,* he cherished the love and memory and practice of it. See on v. 16. Compare vv. 61, 83. Death could not separate him from the love of God. The kind of peril to which he was exposed is perhaps explained in the next clause:

110. *The wicked have laid a snare for me.* *Wicked,* in Ps. i. *ungodly.* *Snare,* often so rendered, also *gin.* See on Ps. xi. 6. What the snare was we are not informed. It may have been for his life, or for his reputation, or for his virtue. If the sense of this verse is to be controlled by that next preceding, it was his life they were seek-ing. At such times the temptation is strong to resort to like stratagems and for like purposes. But that is never wise and always wicked. The only safe course is that of the Psalmist: *Yet I erred not from thy precepts.* *Erred,* in v. 176, *have gone astray;* in Ps. cvii. 4, *wandered.* How different were the emotions and prospects of David in viewing the end of Saul from what they would have been, if he had de-vised or compassed the death of that guilty ruler.

111. *Thy testimonies have I taken as a heritage for ever: for they* are *the rejoicing of my heart.* *Have taken as a heritage,* one verb in the preterite; in Prov. xiv. 18, *inherit;* in Jer. xvi. 19, *have inherited.* The common version gives the sense. The greatest *possession* which the prophet had was God's word. He took it in pre-ference to all else. *Rejoicing, i. e.,* matter of rejoicing; in Ps. li. 8, *joy;* in Jer. xxv. 10, *mirth;* in Ps. xlv. 7, *gladness.* The interest of a regenerate man in God's word is lively, stirring, and *joyous.*

112. *I have inclined mine heart to perform thy statutes always,* even unto *the end.* *Inclined,* as in v. 36. *Always* qualifies *perform.* *End,* as in v. 33, elsewhere *reward,* Ps. xix. 11; xl. 15; lxx. 3. The meaning is that he would serve God not merely for a reward, but to the time of the reward, the end.

DOCTRINAL AND PRACTICAL REMARKS.

1. How sad is the state and how guilty the conduct of those, who reject the light of God's word, v. 105. It alone can solve a thousand doubts. It alone gives effectual comfort in the day of distress. It alone preserves our feet from forbidden paths. Whoever has it has a great advantage, Rom. iii. 2. But let us beware of holding the truth in unrighteousness, Rom. i. 18.

2. To God's service we are bound by his sovereign authority and by his clear and oft-repeated command; but it is right that to these we should add the obligation of solemn and voluntary engagements, v. 106. Henry: "It is good for us to bind our-selves with a solemn oath to be religious. We must swear to the Lord as subjects swear allegiance to their sovereign, promising fealty, appealing to God concerning our

sincerity in this promise, and owning ourselves liable to the curse, if we do not perform it."

3. If we are greatly afflicted, let us not forget that this is the way the fathers trod v. 107. God carried them through; if we trust him he will carry us through. He has given us more light than he gave to them on such dark events. "Whom the Lord loveth he chasteneth, and scourgeth every son whom he receiveth," Heb. xii. 1–11. "There is a need be for the afflictions of the Lord's people. The stones of the spiritual temple cannot be polished or fitted to their place without the strokes of the hammer. The gold cannot be purified without the furnace. The vine must be pruned for greater fruitfulness."

4. In deep affliction, the greatest want is the want of more spirituality—more *liveliness* in the cause of God, v. 107. Blessed is he who so interprets Providence as thereby to be led to a closer walk with God.

5. The service God demands must not be reluctant, but *willing*, v. 108. A defect here is fatal to any act of devotion. The offerings in heaven itself are pre-eminently free. God has not given to us reluctantly or sparingly. Let us give him all, the heart, the soul, the mind, the strength and life itself.

6. If we are certain that we have the spirit of true devotion, we may humbly and modestly mention it as a plea for heavenly instruction, v. 108.

7. To all men life is uncertain, and no man knows that there is more than a step betwixt him and death, v. 109. Thousands of plots are framed against our lives, which God does not permit to be executed. None but the Almighty can protect us from *snares* fatal to life, liberty and honor. Persecution may arise in any age or country. Christianity has never been embraced, except at the risk of deadly persecution.

8. The greater the peril, the more careful ought we to be to keep a conscience void of offence and do our duty at all hazards, v. 109. Cobbin: "The way of duty affords the best ground for our confidence. To rest on other ground is presumption. We must keep God's commandments; we must look to him to hold us up; we must continually respect the statutes of God." The sorer the persecution, the more steadfast should be our perseverance. Compare Acts xx. 23.

9. Let us not fight our enemies with their own weapons. Let not the sheep learn to bark like the wolves. If others dig pits and spread snares for us, let us carry our case to God, and do our duty, and never resort to doubtful expedients. The rack, the fire, the den of lions, the dungeon, chains and the gibbet ought to have in them no such element of dread as even one sin. It is not wicked to suffer. It is not wicked to die. It is wicked to sin.

10. If we find snares spread for us, let us not be surprised. It was so of old, v. 110. If the wicked cannot ensnare us in one way, they will surely try another. Dickson: "It is usual with persecutors to make acts and statutes, or to broach some danger, one or other, which shall either force the godly to go off the right way of obedience to God's word, or to fall into a snare." At such times all we can do is to stand in our lot, be steadfast with God, and commit our case to him that judgeth righteously.

11. The great error of most who profess the true religion is that they do not make enough of it, v. 111. They do not habitually feel that God's favor is enough to compensate for all losses; that his word is a *heritage* sufficient to all the ends of a happy existence, even if we have nothing else, and that we may be *glad* in the promises even if providences seem to be against us.

12. Two things characterize genuine piety. 1. It is *hearty*. It may exhibit itself through the usual forms, but yet it is not formal. 2. It perseveres. It holds on its way. It more and more summons the soul to right endeavors after new obedience.

Horne: "We are not to judge of ourselves by what we sometimes say and do, but by the general disposition and tendency of the heart and its affections," v. 112.

13. At the *end* there shall be a *reward*, not the less rich, because it is wholly of grace and not of debt, v. 112. 'The *end* of life will be the *beginning* of glory' to all such as truly love and habitually practise God's word.

PSALM CXIX.

SAMECH.

113 I hate *vain* thoughts: but thy law do I love.
114 Thou *art* my hiding place and my shield: I hope in thy word.
115 Depart from me, ye evil doers: for I will keep the commandments of my God.
116 Uphold me according unto thy word, that I may live: and let me not be ashamed of **my** hope.
117 Hold thou me up, and I shall be safe: and I will have respect unto thy statutes continually.
118 Thou hast trodden down all them that err from thy statutes: for their deceit *is* falsehood.
119 Thou puttest away all the wicked of the earth *like* dross: therefore I love thy testimonies.
120 My flesh trembleth for fear of thee; and I am afraid of thy judgments.

ALL the verses of this part begin with the *fifteenth* letter of the Hebrew alphabet; but each verse begins with a different word. On the terms *law, word, commandments, statutes, testimonies* and *judgments*, see introduction to this Psalm, Nos. 1, 7, 5, 4, 2, 6, respectively.

113. *I hate* vain *thoughts: but thy law do I love. Hate,* in the preterite *have hated* and hate still. We may interpret the first noun of *thoughts.* Calvin and Piscator have crooked thoughts; Tremellius and Junius, other thoughts; Edwards, wild imaginations; Jebb, evil imaginations; Street, vain opinions. Or we may understand it of persons. The Chaldee has those that think vain thoughts; Arabic, the breakers of the law; Septuagint, Syriac, Ethiopic, Vulgate and Doway, the unjust; Luther, the light-minded; Hengstenberg, doubtful men; Hammond, wicked men: Alexander, waverers; Horsley and Clarke, violent, tumultuous men. The word occurs nowhere else in the Scriptures. The sense gathered from either version is true. Both wicked men and wicked thoughts of every grade are odious to the pious. But they have a very different affection for the law. They love it. *Love,* as in vv. 47, 48, 97.

114. *Thou* art *my hiding place and my shield. Hiding place,* in Ps. xviii. 11, *secret place;* in Ps. xxvii. 5, *secret;* in Ps. xxxii. 7, as here. *Shield, defence,* or *buckler,* see on Ps. iii. 3; vii. 10. The world never understands the secret of the preservation of God's people. The hand that holds them cannot be perceived by our senses, yet is omnipotent. The manner of making God our defence is simple and uniform: *I hope in thy word. Hope,* as in vv. 43, 49, 74, 81; often rendered *wait,* implying trustful expectation.

115. *Depart from me, ye evil doers.* We may not wholly separate ourselves from men who sometimes greatly err, yet habitually do right; nor from men who, if they sin, repent; but these are not *evil doers* or *workers of wickedness* in the Bible sense of those terms. A reason for separating from the wicked is the corrupting influence of their companionship. Especially is it a hindrance to holiness. *For I will keep the commandments of my God. Keep,* as in v. 2. We must either break with the wicked, or with the Almighty.

116. *Uphold me according unto thy word, that I may live. Thy word* here mentioned

may mean either the general principles of righteousness contained in Scripture, or the promises made to all believers in general, or some particular promise made to David himself, but not here recorded. *Uphold, sustain* or *establish*. The grace which sustains us *in* trials is as good as that which shields us *from* trials. A proper sense of it has a mighty influence. It makes us sure that we shall survive our sorest troubles. *And let me not be ashamed of my hope*. This clause is best interpreted as parallel to the former. *Ashamed, confounded*, disappointed by being exposed to contempt. Looking and waiting are implied in the word here rendered *hope*, which occurs not elsewhere in this Psalm.

117. *Hold thou me up, and I shall be safe*. *Hold up*, not *uphold* in v. 116, but a verb several times rendered *comfort*, or *refresh*. The Lord does not sustain his people merely by power, but gives them cordials according to their faintness, and *refreshments* according to their necessities. *Shall be safe*, more commonly *shall be saved*, viz., from impending dangers, bitter enemies and sinful courses. *And I will have respect unto thy statutes continually*. *Have respect*, as in Gen. iv. 4, 5; or *look*, as in Isa. xvii. 7, 8. It means look with favor. If we are enabled thus to regard God's word continually, it is because we are upheld *always*.

118. *Thou hast trodden down all them that err from thy statutes*. Such has been God's administration of the government of the world, and such it shall continue to be forever. No figure is better understood than that of treading under foot. It expresses despite. The consequence to all the wicked is a total failure of their plans: *For their deceit* is *falsehood, i. e.*, a lie to themselves. Calvin: "However well pleased the wicked are with their own cunning, they yet do nothing else but deceive themselves with falsehood." Alexander: "The deception of others is a lie to themselves."

119. *Thou puttest away all the wicked of the earth* like *dross*. Even now God discriminates between the righteous and the wicked, and in due time he will cast off the latter as utterly worthless. *Dross*, always so rendered; that in which there is no value at all. *Puttest away*, the verb is in the preterite. God has always been acting thus, is doing so still, and will preëminently do so in the last day. *Therefore I love thy testimonies*. No good man objects to the holiness of Scripture, or to a righteous discrimination between saints and sinners.

120. *My flesh trembleth for fear of thee; and I am afraid of thy judgments*. The discoveries of the holiness of God and his terrible majesty have often powerfully affected both the souls and bodies of good men, Hab. iii. 16. The first verb is variously rendered, *shivers, shudders*. Horsley: "A thrilling horror curdles my skin." The verb occurs nowhere else, except in Job iv. 15, where we read: The hair of my flesh *stood up*. The contemplation of the doom of the wicked has always had an effect upon the benevolent nature of good men; see on v. 53.

DOCTRINAL AND PRACTICAL REMARKS.

1. He who hates vain thoughts will not love vain persons, or vain discourses, or vain books, v. 113. Because the wicked are an abomination to God, they are a grief to his people. "With a sincere love of good is always joined a hatred of evil."

2. If evil thoughts arise in our minds, let us make it our prayer and our business to banish them, v. 113. "It is the entertainment of vain thoughts, which affords proof of a heart not right with God."

3. Genuine hatred of evil is against evil in every shape. It abhors the thought of foolishness, as truly as it does the idle word, or the bloody deed. Christ died no less for vain thoughts than for other sins. Dickson: "Every dislike of evil is not sufficient, but perfect hatred is required of us against all sorts and degrees of sin."

4. He who hates vain thoughts and persons does love God's law, and nothing can

disprove it, v. 113. It is, in fact, his love of Scripture that makes him turn from them with loathing. Amesius: "Then is our hatred of evil acceptable to God, when it flows from love to his word."

5. The tenor of Scripture, no less than one particular clause, teaches us that as a man thinketh in his heart, so is he, v. 113. How can one be regarded as prepared or preparing for heaven, whose mind is a receptacle for worldly, carnal, proud, spiteful, impure, roving thoughts?

6. Exposed as the righteous are to the shafts of malice, human and diabolical, they yet have sure and ample defence and protection in God. He is their *hiding-place and shield*, v. 114. Nor can there be found another such refuge or buckler. Elsewhere he is called their *strength* and *shield*, their *help* and *shield*, their *sun* and *shield*, their *reward* and *shield*. Against every storm, and foe, and dart, and plot, and combination, God protects his hidden ones.

7. Let all Israel *hope*, and trust, and wait; all will come right at last, v. 114. Give God his time to work out his plan. We cannot get on without faith and hope. With these we can walk in darkness, and yet be sure of delivery.

8. We must steadfastly repel all approaches of the wicked to tempt us, allure us, seduce us or join in affinity with us, as our loved associates, else they will work our ruin, v. 115. We must act thus, or offend God. There is no alternative. Calvin: "If we contract an intimate acquaintance with worldly and wicked men, it is scarcely possible for us to avoid being speedily corrupted by the contagion of their example." He, who would run well his race, must lay aside every weight. "The amiable desire to please our neighbor is limited to the single end, that it should be for his good to edification."

9. The salvation of the righteous is of the Lord. Their dependence must be upon him. He must both *sustain* and *comfort* them, vv. 116, 117. Self-dependence and self-conceit are the bane of many a character. Calvin: "True stability is to be found nowhere else but in the word of God; and no man can steadfastly lean upon it but he who is strengthened by the power of the Holy Spirit." Without divine grace assisting us, we are weak as water. Self-knowledge always makes men self-suspicious.

10. We cannot be too steadfast in eyeing God's word, and keeping our hearts turned to it, v. 117. "The companion of a settled hope is a constant attention to the word of God in its various parts."

11. It seems unaccountable that the doom of sinners in former times does not alarm the sinners of succeeding generations, v. 118. God is angry with the wicked every day. He hates sin as much as when he ordained Tophet of old. He brings to an eternal overthrow every incorrigible enemy. His foes may set their nest among the stars; and it shall be all one to him, as if they had taken their seat upon the dunghill. "Proud persecutors trample upon his people, but, sooner or later, Jehovah will trample upon them."

12. It seems no less wonderful that the deceptions experienced by wicked men in their past pursuit of evil does not warn them respecting the future, v. 118. Why do they not at once confess that all is a lie, vanity and vexation of spirit?

13. In its own nature, as well as in its effects, sin is exceedingly dreadful. It makes the most fine gold dim and changes the silver into *dross*, v. 119. How doleful is the thought that those who are, by the original constitution of their nature, capable of being vessels of honor, prepared for the Master's use, should by iniquity be so debased as to be fit for no honorable service in the whole universe of God.

14. Come what will, cost what it may, hold on to God and his word, for that is our last hope, v. 119. If we let go there, all is gone.

15. We need not fear that our religious affections, if pure and holy, will rise too

high, v. 120. Let our faith and hope attain the measure of full assurance. Let our fear of God mightily move us. Let our love be all sacrificing. Let our jealousy over our own hearts be extreme. Let our consciences maintain the utmost tenderness.

16. In the scheme of salvation whereby God's people are weaned from the world and trained up for glory, even the fear of hell itself has its use, v. 120. Calvin: "We require to be subdued by fear, that we may desire and seek after the favor of God." One way of escaping the damnation of hell is greatly to fear him who can cast both soul and body into hell. Compare Heb. iv. 1, 2. Dickson: "The godly, because of the remainder of sin in them and their natural frailty, are not exempted from the sense of the terror of God, yea, it is needful they be now and then exercised therewith, that so they may be kept in awe, their joy tempered with fear and trembling, their prayers sharpened, and they kept watchful, and thus their obedience furthered." So Henry Martyn records of himself: "In prayer, in the evening I had such near and terrific views of God's judgments upon sinners in hell, that my flesh trembled for fear of them. . . I flew trembling to Jesus Christ as if the flame were taking hold of me! oh! Christ will indeed save me or else I perish."

PSALM CXIX.

AIN.

121 I have done judgment and justice: leave me not to mine oppressors.
122 Be surety for thy servant for good: let not the proud oppress me.
123 Mine eyes fail for thy salvation, and for the word of thy righteousness.
124 Deal with thy servant according unto thy mercy, and teach me thy statutes.
125 I *am* thy servant; give me understanding, that I may know thy testimonies.
126 *It is* time for *thee,* LORD, to work: *for* they have made void thy law.
127 Therefore I love thy commandments above gold; yea, above fine gold.
128 Therefore I esteem all *thy* precepts *concerning* all *things to be* right; *and* I hate every false way.

ALL these verses begin with the *sixteenth* letter of the Hebrew alphabet; 121, 124, with the verb rendered *have done* or *deal;* 127, 128, with the word rendered *therefore;* the rest, with different words. On the terms *judgment, righteousness, word, statutes, testimonies, law, commandments* and *precepts,* see introduction to this Psalm, Nos. 6, 10, 7, 4, 2, 1, 5, 3, respectively.

121. *I have done judgment and justice.* The prophet is probably not so much speaking of his official, as of his personal conduct, his practical life. The verb is in the preterite. *Judgment,* the singular of the noun often rendered *judgments* in this Psalm. *Righteousness,* often connected with *judgments,* and rendered *thy righteous judgments,* literally *the judgments of thy righteousness.* No doubt the standard of right in the prophet's mind was the word of God, and so far the terms *judgment* and *justice* may allude to the law; but we may take them here as often elsewhere for *right* and *justice.* Compare Ps. lxxxix. 14; xcvii. 2; Prov. i. 3. On this foundation—a good conscience in having wronged no one—he rests his plea for protection: *Leave me not to mine oppressors.* *Oppressors,* a participle from a verb rendered *oppress, defraud, deceive.* Truth and fairness never enter into the work of the oppressor.

122. *Be surety for thy servant for good.* There are various renderings; but the following sustain the common version: Fabritius and Piscator: Answer for thy servant for good; Calvin, Amesius, Tremellius and Junius: Become surety for thy servant for good; Clarke: Be bail for thy servant; Edwards, Jebb, Hengstenberg and Alexander

literally agree with the authorized version. The same verb is rendered as here Gen. xliii. 9; xliv. 32; Prov. vi. 1; xi. 15; xx. 16; xxvii. 13 and elsewhere; in Isa. xxxviii. 14, *Undertake for me*, sometimes, *Give pledges*. This seems to be the best sense and the true meaning of this clause. Clarke: "What a word is this! Pledge thyself for me, that thou wilt produce me *safely* at the judgment of the great day! Then sustain, and keep me blameless, till the coming of Christ." *Let not the proud oppress me*. *Proud* or *presumptuous*, as in v. 21. *Oppress*, future form of the verb whose participle is in the preceding verse. Evidently the prophet speaks of his peril as extreme, and feels that none but God can effectually defend him.

123. *Mine eyes fail for thy salvation, and for the word of thy righteousness*. *Fail* or *faint*, see on vv. 81, 82. The case was very urgent. God's *salvation* was deliverance sought from him. *The word of thy righteousness* is the engagement of a just God, who cannot deceive, or be indifferent to the miseries that befall his people.

124. *Deal with thy servant according unto thy mercy, and teach me thy statutes*. Calvin: "The two clauses of this verse must be read connectedly; for he does not first separately desire God to deal well with him, and next desire him to be his master and teacher." *Deal*, in v. 121, *have done*; see on v. 65. The *mercy* sought is the *loving-kindness* of the Lord often mentioned in the Psalms. On the latter clause see on verse 12.

125. *I* am *thy servant; give me understanding that I may know thy testimonies*. A *servant* of God was one who sincerely worshipped him, and gladly did and quietly suffered his will. He pleased and honored his Master, not himself. If God was glorified, it seemed to him of small importance whether he himself was honored or reproached. He makes his character of servant the ground of his plea for further instruction in the love, knowledge and practice of the truth. Compare Ps. cxvi. 16.

126. It is *time for* thee, LORD, *to work;* for *they have made void thy law*. *Time, i. e.,* *high time*. Compare Rom. xiii. 11, meaning *full* time. Our translators render the verb *to work;* it is more commonly rendered *to do*. Calvin: It is time for thee, O Jehovah, to be doing. So others also. It is time to be doing what the circumstances call for. All this is implied in the common version. *They*, the oppressors, and the proud of vv. 121, 122. Men make void God's law, or make it of none effect when they *break* it, or when they act as if it were not in existence, or as if it were not law, but mere advice, or when they adopt principles of morals antagonistic to it, or principles of interpretation which subvert it. Compare Matt. xv. 6; Mark vii. 13.

127. *Therefore I love thy commandments above gold; yea, above fine gold*. See on v. 72; Ps. xix. 10. *Love*, the verb so often used in this poem to express attachment to God's word. It is in the preterite, I *have loved* and I still love. See on v. 47. *Fine gold*, in Ps. xxi. 3, *pure gold*. See on Ps. xix. 10. The *therefore* of this verse may refer to all the preceding discourse concerning the Scriptures, or it may refer to the last clause of the preceding verse; for it is true that as long as divine grace abounds in us, the very wickedness of others draws out our love to holiness. Diodati: "The more I see thy commandments violated by the wicked, the more am I confirmed through holy love and zeal against their scandals," Neh. xiii. 15–25; Job xvii. 8, 9; Acts xvii. 16.

128. *Therefore I esteem all thy precepts concerning all things to be right; and I hate every false way*. The Hebrew is elliptical; but the authorized version gives the sense. Hammond's paraphrase is: "And indeed I have not the least exceptions to any law of thine, but most uniformly and impartially embrace them all, and every one single;" Phillips: "I embrace thy whole revealed word, without any exceptions." Horne: "For the same reason that the children of God, in the worst of times, love his commandments, they love them all; not observing such only as they can observe without giving offence, but regardless of the censures of the world, do their duty in

every particular; not hating some evil ways, and at the same time walking in others, but extending and manifesting their aversion to all alike." *False way*, literally *path of falsehood*; see on v. 29.

DOCTRINAL AND PRACTICAL REMARKS.

1. As long as there is sin, there will be oppression in the world, vv. 121, 122. "It is a great calamity, and greatly to be prayed against, to be left by God under the oppression of wicked men." And yet such things are often witnessed on earth. What an awful place hell must be, where the passions of men are let loose upon each other in every form of cruelty.

2. Are you oppressed? Betake yourself to God. Beware of malevolence. Earnestly ask God to bless your persecutors.

3. A good conscience is a brazen wall, v. 121. It is worth all it ever costs. So the saints have always found it, 2 Cor. i. 12; 1 John iii. 20. It is not half so bad to *suffer* wrong as it is to *do* wrong, to *be oppressed* as to *oppress*, to *be cheated* as to *cheat*, to *be slandered* as to *slander*.

4. The righteous shall at the right time be rescued from their persecutors, vv. 121, 122. The prayers of God's people no less than the promises of his word, all run in that direction.

5. Our safety and deliverance could not be in better hands. All the affairs of his people rest with God. He is a wall of fire and salvation, a champion and a surety for them, vv. 121, 122.

6. As the whole of the Old Testament had a shadow of good things to come, and as Jesus Christ is in the New Testment said to be *the surety of a better covenant*, it is not impossible that the prophet here as elsewhere was preparing the mind of the church for the revelation of that great mystery—Christ's suretyship, v. 122. "O my soul, if a divine surety had not been provided for thee, what must have been thy state, and where must have been thy hopes for eternity?"

7. Although not a few persecutors profess religion, and even pray over their victims, and boast how much they have asked for the divine direction and blessing, yet in all cases they are *proud* and *presumptuous*, v. 122. They have not a trait of the true, meek and gentle followers of Christ, although in their folly and madness they boast of doing God's service.

8. Does deliverance from affliction and persecution seem long a coming? It was so to David. No doubt Joseph felt it so in the dungeons of Egypt, and so have thousands of God's people in every age. How shall we behave in such trying circumstances? The Scripture leaves us not without direction, Hab. ii. 3; Heb. x. 37. Let our dependence be upon God, according to the word of his righteousness. "Though our eyes fail, yet God's word does not; and therefore those that build upon it, though now discouraged, shall in due time see his salvation." In the meantime the delay of help should increase the constancy and steadfastness of our faith. Let us guard against a spirit of murmuring. "Complaining is not humility. Prayer without waiting is not faith. The path is plain as noonday. Continue to believe as you can. Wait on the Lord." Robert Glover, the martyr, had great darkness for some days preceding his suffering; but when he came within sight of the stake, his soul was so filled with divine comforts that he exultingly clapped his hands and cried out: "He is come—he is come." His cruel death seemed to give him no pain.

9. Although through divine grace we may have both a good cause and a good conscience in a controversy with man, yet *mercy* must ever be the plea of sinners before God, v. 124. Strict justice, pointing to our sins, without a mediator, without the

blood of atonement, would destroy the best mere man. Morison: "The plea of faith can never be a plea of innocence. Our appeal cannot be to justice but to mercy."

10. We are not cut off from the comfort of knowing, when the evidence proves it, that we are God's servants, vv. 122, 124, 125. Yet this is not matter of boasting, but of humiliation. No man is God's servant either by birth, or by any power, or virtue of his own. Nor could the wealth of the world purchase for him this great honor. It is all of grace.

11. Let us ever be seeking instruction in the divine will and for practical purposes. No severity of trial can justify us in pretermitting this duty. 'In difficult times we should desire more to be told what we must do than than what we may expect.' 'Those who know most of God's testimonies desire to know more.'

12. We may sometimes know that deliverance to the saints is not far off by the manner in which wickedness is allowed to break forth, v. 126. Horne: "There is a certain measure of iniquity which when communities, or individuals respectively, have filled up, the destroying angel comes forth, and executes his commission. How ought a man to fear, lest the next sin he commits should fill up his measure, and seal his eternal doom." When wickedness is rampant and the earth is full of violence, men must either soon enter the ark or be drowned.

13. Calvin: "When the wicked claim to themselves an unbridled liberty, it behooves us to contemplate with the eyes of faith the judgments of God, in order to our being thereby quickened to the observance of the divine law."

14. We cannot over estimate God's word. It is worth more than all the riches of the earth, v. 127. "The more the wicked despise it, we should esteem it the more." The Bible Society, rightly managed, is a better institution than its best friends have ever esteemed it.

15. The Scripture is perfect. There is no flaw in it. So claims God. So say his people. The glory of it is that in all things it is *right*, v. 128. If any man wants an unerring rule, let him stick to the Scripture.

16. Genuine love to the word of God always carries with it a just esteem of Scripture and a corresponding hatred of all wickedness.

17. "O my soul, canst thou abide the close test of this part of Scripture? Hast thou as much regard to the precepts as to the privileges of the Gospel? Is no precept evaded, from repugnance to the cross that is entailed to it? Is no secret lust retained? Art thou content to let all go? Is my hatred of sin in my family, in my friend, and in myself as sincere and as strong as when I see it in mine enemies?"

PSALM CXIX.

PE.

129 Thy testimonies *are* wonderful: therefore doth my soul keep them.

130 The entrance of thy words giveth light; it giveth understanding unto the simple.

131 I opened my mouth, and panted: for I longed for thy commandments.

132 Look thou upon me, and be merciful unto me, as thou usest to do unto those that love thy name.

133 Order my steps in thy word: and let not any iniquity have dominion over me.

134 Deliver me from the oppression of man: so will I keep thy precepts.

135 Make thy face to shine upon thy servant; and teach me thy statutes.

136 Rivers of waters run down mine eyes, because they keep not thy law.

ALL these verses begin with the *seventeenth* letter of the Hebrew Alphabet; but each verse with a different word. On the terms *testimonies, words* and *word, commandments, precepts, statutes* and *law*, see introduction to this Psalm, Nos. 2. 7. 5. 3, 4, 1, respectively.

129. *Thy testimonies are wonderful: therefore doth my soul keep them.* *Wonderful*, a noun in the plural, *wonders*, as in Ps. lxxvii. 11, 14; lxxxviii. 10, 12; lxxxix. 5; in Ps. lxxviii. 12, *marvellous things.* For light, truth, purity, wisdom, righteousness, consolation, doctrine, precept, history, poetry, promise, warning, threatening and saving power, God's word is full of *marvels.* It abounds in prodigies. It is a paragon of excellence. *Therefore* does a renewed man not only *admire*, but love, obey and practise all that God requires, not reluctantly, but with his *soul.* His *life* is in obedience. *Keep*, as in v. 2.

130. *The entrance of thy word giveth light; it giveth understanding unto the simple.* For *entrance*, the Chaldee reads *impression;* Arabic, *manifestation;* Septuagint, Ethiopic, Vulgate and Doway, *declaration;* Fabritius, *threshold;* Tremellius and Junius, *passage;* Jebb, *going forth;* Street and Alexander, *opening;* Hengstenberg, *opening up;* Edwards, *when thy words are explained.* Diodati gives this paraphrase: "Though thy words do abound in mysteries, yet thou declarest and revealest them by thy Spirit to thine elect; who forsaking the sense of the flesh do in all simplicitie yeeld unto and believe what is taught them." Even a limited acquaintance with Scripture gives some light. On its *threshold*, much more in its interior parts, we find wisdom. *Giveth understanding*, a participle of the verb *understand*, in v. 27; *consider*, in v. 95. *Simple*, see on Ps. xix. 7. Compare Ps. cxvi. 6. Calvin has *little ones.* Jesus Christ called the same class of persons *babes*, Matt. xi. 25.

131. *I opened my mouth, and panted: for I longed for thy commandments.* *Panted*, in Job xvi. 10, *gaped.* This may refer to either of three things: 1. Eager hearers open their mouths that they may hear the better, sound entering by the mouth very much aiding us in hearing. 2. The thirsty open the mouth for drink that they may receive every drop. 3. The hungry open the mouth for food, as even the young bird does in its nest. *Longed*, here only; it expresses earnest desire. The two verbs together denote the greediness with which he received the word.

132. *Look thou upon me, and be merciful unto me, as thou usest to do unto those that love thy name.* *Look*, regard, Ps. cii. 17; *have respect*, Lev. xxvi. 9; 1 Kings viii. 28; *turn thee*, Ps. xxv. 16; lxix. 16; lxxxvi. 16. *Be merciful, be gracious, shew favor, have pity*, Ex. xxxiii. 19; Isa. xxvii. 11; Pr. xiv. 21; Pr. xix. 17. *As thou usest*, an idiomatic phrase, which renders very well a Hebraism. *Love*, as often in this Psalm. By *name* we may understand either God himself, or his word; see introduction to this Psalm after No. 10.

133. *Order my steps in thy word: and let not any iniquity have dominion over me* *Order; direct*, v. 5; *establish*, v. 90; often, *prepare.* The true believer seeks conformity to the whole law, and abhors sin against any of its precepts. The prayer against the *dominion* of sin, if offered in faith, shall surely be answered, Rom. vi. 14; see on Ps. xix. 13. Some give another turn to the thought, and make the prophet pray against being placed under the political power of iniquity, that is, of iniquitous men. This would be a lawful prayer, but is a much lower sense than that commonly given. The verb clearly signifies *ruling, bearing rule, having the mastery.* Clarke: "Let me have no governor but God; let the throne of my heart be filled by him and none other."

134. *Deliver me from the oppression of man.* *Oppression*, cognate to *oppressors* and *oppress* in vv. 121, 122. Such are the power, malignity and combinations of evil men that none but God can *save* us from their *deceits, frauds* and cruelties. "Let me not fall into the hands of man," 2 Sam. xxiv. 13. A reason for so praying is that

we may be unrestrained in the service we offer to God: *So will I keep thy precepts.* *Keep,* as in vv. 4, 8.

135. *Make thy face to shine upon thy servant; and teach me thy statutes.* *Make to shine;* we have the same verb in the same form and connected with *face;* see on Ps. iv. 6; xxxi. 16; lxxx. 3, 19. The whole verse is a connected prayer for the divine favor, for divine illumination, and for further instruction in the law.

136. *Rivers of water run down mine eyes, because they keep not thy law.* Compare Lam. iii. 48. There is no authority for altering the text so as to make the prophet weep for not having kept the law himself, although he who truly laments the sins of others will not fail to deplore his own iniquities. The grief of a pious soul for sins is not only or chiefly for the misery thus brought on, but chiefly because sin is exceeding sinful, and greatly dishonors God. The word *rivers* indicates much more than an occasional tear or a slight uncomfortable sensation. Lot cannot live in Sodom without having his righteous soul *vexed* from day to day, 2 Pet. ii. 8. The Son of God himself was more grieved by human wickedness than by his own poverty and humble condition. John Rogers' translation: Myne eyes gusshe oute with water, etc.

DOCTRINAL AND PRACTICAL REMARKS.

1. Wonders will never cease, v. 129. Air, earth, water, the world above, the world beneath, time, eternity, worms, birds, fishes, beasts, men, angels are all full of wonders. The more all things are studied, the more do wonders appear.

2. It is idle, therefore, to find fault with the mysteries of Scripture, or to deny them, v. 129. Inspiration glories in them. He, that rejects the mysteries of love, grace, truth, power, justice and faithfulness of God's word, rejects salvation. It has marvels in itself and marvels in its operation. They are good cause of love, not of offence; of *keeping,* not of breaking God's precepts.

3. Truly good men will never cease to praise the Scripture. Well does it call forth admiration, v. 129. "It gives admirable discoveries of God and Christ and another world—admirable proofs of divine love and grace. The majesty of the style, the purity of the matter, the harmony of the parts are all wonderful." It warns; it alarms; it instructs; it directs; it convicts; it converts; it sanctifies; it comforts; it gives the victory. Its mysteries are the mysteries of godliness. By words, by ceremonies, by sacraments, by histories, by parables, by similitudes, by prose, by poetry, by promise, by threatening, by precept and by example, it transforms, comforts and saves us. The height, and length, and breadth, and depth of Scripture are as unsearchable as the love of God. No science, no doctrine can compare with it. Tertullian: "I adore the fulness of Scripture;" Henry Martyn: "What do I not owe to the Lord for permitting me to take a part in the translation of his word."

4. Those who have the Scripture have no excuse for their error, or ignorance, v. 130. We may have weak parts and be very *simple,* but God's word is no less suited to babes than to philosophers. Dickson: "Albeit the word of God be full of high mysteries, yet it may be read with profit by simple people, or any who desire knowledge."

5. Nor need we wait to know much, before we can profit somewhat, or to know all before we can profit vastly. The very *entrance* of God's word gives light, v. 130. Pool: "The very beginnings and rudiments of God's word, the first discoveries of those sacred mysteries, and much more the depth of them, in which their chief excellency consists, gives understanding;" Calvin: "The light of the truth revealed in God's word is so distinct that the very first sight of it illuminates the mind" Nicolson: "The entrance of God's word, the first chapter of Genesis;—what light

does that pour on the mind of man!" A little secular learning may make a man a fool; but even a little divine knowledge may save one's soul.

6. If we would profit by the word of God, we must exercise and maintain ardent love of truth. This is indispensable, v. 131. He who loves not, and longs not, and thirsts not, and hungers not, and *pants* not, and cries not, and digs not for the truth will not find the knowledge of God. The new-born babes must desire the sincere milk of the word. He must *drink in* its precious truths. Augustine: "If thou sayest, I have enough, thou perishest. Always add—always walk—always proceed. Neither stand still, nor go back, nor turn aside."

7. When we plead for mercy, we need ask no more than God habitually gives to those who humbly and sincerely call upon his name, v. 132. Dickson: "It is wisdom for us not to affect singularity of divine dispensations toward us, but to be content to be dealt with as others of God's children before us have been dealt with." God's saving mercies are always great, 1 Cor. ii. 9.

8. If we ever do right, gain sound knowledge, lead a holy life, and walk with God, so as to reach heaven, it must be by divine grace *ordering our steps*, guiding our feet controlling our actions, v. 133. This grace must be sought. To expect it without longing for it, and without seeking it is the folly of formalists. Without the influence of the Holy Spirit, we make no progress. As the Scripture is the sole rule of holiness, so the Author of Scripture, applying it to our hearts is the sole Author of sanctification.

9. It is both lawful and wise to pray to be kept out of the power of the wicked, that they may not hinder us in our heavenly course, v. 134. In their power we may lack the opportunity to do many things tending to our spiritual good. Left free, our gratitude for such deliverance should press us to obedience. It was for good cause that Paul besought others to ask that he might be delivered from wicked and unreasonable men. Morison: "However sincere the desire of obedience to God's precepts may be, it is possible that in some evil hour when goaded on to transgression by the unjustifiable conduct of our fellow-men, we may fall from our integrity." Bridges: "The believer sometimes finds peculiar circumstances of trial an unavoidable hindrance in the service of God." Compare Isa. xix. 20.

10. What we all need is more light in our hearts, in our consciences, and on our paths, more grace to strengthen us, more saving knowledge, a richer blessing from the Lord, v. 135. "All lesser troubles vanish when God doth but vouchsafe a look of paternal compassion. O what anguish fills the heart when his people no longer taste the good word of God, no longer enjoy the clear shining of his countenance." Henry: "We must pray as earnestly for grace as for comfort." Clarke: "The witness of God's Spirit was an essential principle in religion from the foundation of the world." Our great error is that we are too easily satisfied.

11. Grief for sin in ourselves or others, is never excessive. Sin is hateful, horrible, sinful, shameful, wicked, ruinous. We cannot mourn too much for sin; that is impossible, v. 136. Compare Deut. ix. 18, 19; Jer. ix. 1; Ezek. ix. 4. One of the darkest signs of any age is when the people weep but little for sin. Many a time weeping and praying is all that is left to the pious, Jer. xiii. 17. Nicolson: "If we grieve not for others, their sin may become ours, Ezek. ix. 8; 1 Cor. v. 2." Henry: "The sins of sinners are the sorrows of saints. We must mourn for that which we cannot mend." Dickson: "True zeal is so far from private revenge of personal injuries received by persecutors, that it can pity their miserable case and mourn for them. Two things in sin chiefly move the godly to mourn for it. One is the dishonor it brings on God. The other is the perdition it brings on the sinner."

PSALM CXIX.

TZADDI.

137 Righteous *art* thou, O LORD, and upright *are* thy judgments.
138 Thy testimonies *that* thou hast commanded *are* righteous and very faithful.
139 My zeal hath consumed me, because mine enemies have forgotten thy words.
140 Thy word *is* very pure: therefore thy servant loveth it.
141 I *am* small and despised: *yet* do I not forget thy precepts.
142 Thy righteousness *is* an everlasting righteousness, and thy law *is* the truth.
143 Trouble and anguish have taken hold on me: *yet* thy commandments *are* my delights.
144 The righteousness of thy testimonies *is* everlasting: give me understanding, and I shall live.

ALL these verses begin with the *eighteenth* letter of the Hebrew alphabet; 137, 142, 144, with some form of the word which we render *righteous*, or *righteousness;* each of the remainder with a wholly different word. On the terms *judgments, testimonies, words* and *word, precepts, righteousness, law* and *commandments,* see introduction to this Psalm Nos. 6, 2, 7, 3, 10, 1, 5, respectively.

137. *Righteous* art *thou, O* LORD, *and upright* are *thy judgments.* Because the Lord is just and right, so are his judgments; for they are a transcript of his character. The *decisions* both of his word and providence are unimpeachable.

138. *Thy testimonies* that *thou hast commanded* are *righteous and very faithful.* Hardly any two scholars render this verse in precisely the same way. Yet in the essential ideas they entirely harmonize; 1. God's word is marked by justice and faithfulness; 2. In his word he has enjoined on us the strictest uprightness and fidelity. Pool: "The sense is, Thou hast strictly and severely, under the highest obligations and penalties, commanded in thy word that men should be just and true in all their actions." We can have no other safe rule of righteousness than God's word.

139. *My zeal hath consumed me, because mine enemies have forgotten thy words.* Zeal see on Ps. lxix. 9. *Consumed,* elsewhere, *cut off, destroyed,* literally, *caused me to vanish* So long as grace triumphs, the pious zeal of God's people rises in proportion to the outbreaking and outrageous conduct of the wicked around them. *Mine enemies,* the authors of my distress and trouble, my adversaries. On *forgetting God's word,* see on v. 16.

140. *Thy word* is *very pure. Very,* as in v. 138, of which see the various renderings. *Pure,* margin, *tried, refined,* a participle from the verb rendered *hast tried* in Ps. xvii. 3. The same word is applied to silver of a fine quality in Ps. xii. 6; in Ps. xviii. 30, The word of the Lord is *tried.* There is no mixture of error or mistake in God's word, even as there is no dross or alloy in silver that has been properly tried by fire. God's word has been tested for thousands of years in every possible way, and it has always come out pure. It is holy and leads to holiness. It is worthy of God. *Therefore thy servant loveth it. Thy servant,* as in vv. 17, 23, 38; one wholly devoted to God. *Loveth,* as in vv. 47, 48, 97. Holy men love holy things, because they are holy.

141. *I* am *small and despised. Small,* in fact, in public esteem, in my own esteem. It means a *little one.* Compare Isa. lx. 22; Jer. xiv. 3; xlviii. 4. Paul esteemed himself the least of all saints. *Despised, contemned;* Calvin, held in low estimation, *insignificant.* But neither his humility, nor the reproach of men alienated him from God. Yet *do I not forget thy precepts.* See on vv. 16, 61. Alexander: "However proudly or however justly I may be despised, I can still lay claim to one distinction, that I have not, like my despisers, forgotten God's commandments."

142. *Thy righteousness is an everlasting righteousness.* We have the word *righteous-ness* here both in the masculine and feminine form. In the one case it is doubtless equivalent to *thy word;* in the other it means *right.* Perfectly carried out by God and man, it works no injustice, no wrong; but conduces to the good of all who love God. This is its nature and its effect *for ever, to eternity.* It cannot be otherwise: *And thy law is the truth.* Compare John xvii. 17. It is 'truth without any mixture of error,' mistake, falsehood, or fiction.

143. *Trouble and anguish have taken hold on me. Trouble, distress, affliction,* par-ticularly such as is caused by enemies. *Anguish,* elsewhere *distress,* 1 Sam. xxii. 2. It describes the distress of a people besieged and is then rendered *straitness,* Deut. xxviii. 53, 55, 57; Jer. xix. 9. *Have taken hold on me, have found me, have found me out.* Compare Gen. xxxviii. 22; xliv. 16; Job. xi. 7; xvii. 10. In Ps. cxvi. 3, the same verb is rendered *gat hold upon me.* But these things could not shake his stead-fastness: Yet *thy commandments* are *my delights. Delights,* as in vv. 24, 77, 92, ample solace in any trials.

144. *The righteousness of thy testimonies is everlasting.* Sometimes human laws and human wisdom seem all right and appear to work well for a season; but ere long they are found faulty, and must be changed, modified, or repealed. But the principles of God's government revealed in his word are *everlasting.* The clause might read, Right-eousness (are) thy testimonies for ever. *Give me understanding, and I shall live.* On the first verb, see on vv. 27, 34; on the second, on vv. 17, 77, 116.

DOCTRINAL AND PRACTICAL REMARKS.

1. The character of God is the foundation of all holy joy, as his nature is the basis of all right theology, vv. 137, 138. If he were not *just* and *faithful,* if he were not, what he is in all things, our hopes would surely perish with us. " As God is what he is, so he is what he should be."

2. Amesius: " Although vain men feign to themselves many notions of right-eousness, yet there is no true and real righteousness besides that revealed in God's word," v. 137.

3. God's word and works are like himself, vv. 137, 138. He is *righteous* and *faith-ful;* so are they. God acts like himself, not like us. He is not a man that he should either change or lie, be unjust or unkind. The Teacher of all the earth speaks right. The Judge of all the earth does right. Often indeed we know not fully what he says or does; but we may well wait for his own solution of dark matters.

4. Zeal is a vital element in a good character, v. 139. He who has no zeal has no love to God, for genuine zeal is the ardor of love. A lifeless engagedness in God's service is a mark of hypocrisy. It is better to die for Christ than to live unto the world. Whitefield lived only to the age of *fifty-six* years, yet he preached *eighteen thousand* times—sermons all on fire, and they set the world on fire! True zeal is for God's glory, not our own. It grieves far more for his dishonor than for our sufferings. It readily forgives wrongs done to ourselves; but it is jealous for the Lord of hosts. It is willing to suffer for the very persecutors by whom it suffers. It is neither fierce nor bitter. It blesses and curses not. It is not for party, nor does it come from vanity but from a sincere love to the word of God, and to the souls of men. Bridges: "The surest evidence of Christian zeal is—when it begins at home—in a narrow scrutiny, and ' vehement revenge' against the sins of our own hearts;" Dickson: " Zeal hath great need of sound knowledge that it miscarry not." When genuine, nothing can repress it. Opposition and irreligion pouring out scorn do but inflame it.

5. Amesius: " A sincere love to the word of God comes from a right view of its purity," v. 140. Scripture is not only pure but purifying. " Ye are clean through

the word which I have spoken unto you," John xv. 3. The way of genuine peace is to adopt God's word for our standard and through divine grace to bring our lives to conform to it.

6. It is better to be *small* and *despised*, mean and obscure, than to be proud and wicked, flattered or a flatterer, v. 141. Henry: "Men's real excellency cannot always secure them from contempt; nay, it often exposes them to the scorn of some, and always makes them low in their own eyes." It is a noble quality in great minds to be willing to be despised for the good of our race, and the glory of God. Such are precious in the eyes of the Lord. Their humility is not feigned. Brainerd: "I felt a great desire that all God's people should know how mean, and little, and vile I am, that they might see I am nothing, that so they might pray for me aright, and not have the least dependence upon me. I could not bear to think of Christians showing me any respect. I saw myself exceedingly vile and unworthy; so that I was ashamed that any one should bestow any favor upon me, or show me any respect."

7. God's word is unchangeably right in all respects; therefore is of immutable and unending obligation, v. 142. It is at once the rule of duty, the guide to life, and the measure of happiness. It cannot be dispensed with. It has the supremacy over all laws. Both promises and threatenings shall infallibly be fulfilled. No man ever loved his Bible too much.

8. Extreme distress is no novelty, v. 143. *Trouble* and *anguish* have wrung many a heart, and will do so as long as there is sin in the world. No distress is like spiritual distress. It is a great mercy when God allows nothing worse than human malice to be let loose against us, and keeps our hearts calm and at peace with him.

9. However sore the trials of good men, yet by God's word they can be guided safely through and effectually cheered, v. 143. Morison: "There are no fears which it cannot allay: no troubles which it cannot assuage, no griefs which it cannot soothe, and no temptations beneath which it cannot succor and relieve." Bradford writes: "My prison is sweeter to me than any parlor, than any pleasure I have had in all my life."

10. God's word needs no correction, v. 144. Its *righteousness* appears the more it is tried. It never requires amendment. It is good at the first; it is good at the last.

11. What we need for life, and for liveliness in God's work is not more Scripture, but more knowledge of what has been already revealed, v. 144. Nicolson: "All is *death* without thee. Live in *me*, that I may live *by* thee."

PSALM CXIX.

KOPH.

145 I cried with *my* whole heart; hear me, O LORD: I will keep thy statutes.

146 I cried unto thee; save me, and I shall keep thy testimonies.

147 I prevented the dawning of the morning, and cried: I hoped in thy word.

148 Mine eyes prevent the *night* watches, that I might meditate in thy word.

149 Hear my voice according unto thy lovingkindness: O LORD, quicken me according to thy judgment.

150 They draw nigh that follow after mischief: they are far from thy law.

151 Thou *art* near, O LORD; and all thy commandments *are* truth.

152 Concerning thy testimonies, I have known of old that thou hast founded them for ever.

ALL these verses begin with the *nineteenth* letter of the Hebrew alphabet; 145, 146, with the same verb; 147, 148, with the same verb; 150, 151, with cognate words;

the rest, with different words. On the terms *statutes, testimonies, word, law* and *commandments*, see introduction to this Psalm, Nos. 4, 2, 7, 1, 5, respectively.

145. *I cried with my whole heart; hear me, O LORD. I will keep thy statutes.* Cried, have cried and cry still; often rendered *called* as in Ps. cxvi. *Whole heart*, see on v. 2. *Hear*, so as to *answer. Keep*, as in v. 2. We may make the last clause independent, and so understand the prophet as saying that he is resolved to keep the law, come what may; or, as a vow connected with his prayer, engaging him to a zealous course of obedience, if the Lord will but give him the needed grace in answer to prayer. The latter is probably the correct view.

146. *I cried unto thee: save me, and I shall keep thy testimonies.* Cried, as in v. 145. *Save, help, deliver.* See on Ps. iii. 7. The precise form of evil, from which he sought deliverance is not stated. A subsequent verse points to the craft and malice of enemies, v. 150. This may be the distress now pressing him. The scope of this verse is probably best learned by explaining it as v. 145. Deliverance is to be an animating motive to obedience.

147. *I prevented the dawning of the morning, and cried: I hoped in thy word.* John Rogers' translation: Early in the mornynge do I crye unto the. *Prevented*, see on Ps. xvii. 13; xviii. 5. The meaning is before day dawned, he engaged in *earnest* prayer. *Cried*, a stronger word than that in vv. 145, 146. His prayer increased in fervor and intensity as his troubles multiplied, and as his *hope* in God's word grew stronger. Mere earnestness of desire is not enough, we must sow in hope.

148. *Mine eyes prevent the night watches, that I might meditate in thy word.* Prevent, as in v. 147, have prevented. On the *watches* of the ancients, see on Ps. lxiii. 6 The Psalmist doubtless means the second and third watches of the night, as those were commonly given to sleep. *Meditate*, as in v. 15.

149. *Hear my voice, according unto thy lovingkindness: O LORD, quicken me according to thy judgment.* His plea is based solely on mercy. The life and liveliness he seeks from God are *according to* God's word or *judgment*, see v. 156. But following the rendering given in v. 132, Walford has: Revive me, O Jehovah, according to thy wonted manner; Edwards: Enliven me, as thou art wont.

150. *They draw nigh that follow after mischief: they are far from thy law.* They are nigh to me, but far from thee. This verse discloses the urgency of the prayer. *Mischief*, in Lev. xviii. 17 and often, *wickedness;* in Job xxxi. 11, *heinous crime;* in Isa. xxxii. 7, (in the plural) *wicked desires;* in Ezek. xvi. 43 and often, *lewdness.* Calvin and church of England, *malice;* Edwards, *malicious devices;* Street, *vice;* Fry and Hengstenberg, *wickedness;* Alexander, *crime.* It is a general term describing the malice and plotting of enemies.

151. *Thou* art *near, O LORD, and all thy commandments* are *truth.* If enemies are nigh, God is nigh also. And he will surely save, for he has said he would; and all he has said is *truth* or faithfulness.

152. *Concerning thy testimonies, I have known of old that thou hast founded them for ever. Of old*, many read *from the beginning.* Hengstenberg and Alexander, *long;* Edwards and Walford, *long since. Founded, established.* Calvin: "This indeed is the chief point of faith, That the word of God is not only distinguished for fidelity and steadfastness for a time, but that it continues unchangeable forever. Were it otherwise, it could not include within it the hope of eternal salvation."

DOCTRINAL AND PRACTICAL REMARKS.

1. God, who made us and knows us, sees that we are forgetful, and sends us line upon line, sometimes in new and sometimes in old words and phrases, vv. 145, 146. Blessed be his name for all his patience with our dulness.

2. In supplication we must not only call upon God but continue calling; not only pray but pray without ceasing; not only cry with the voice but with holy vehemence of soul; not only pray with the *heart*, but with the *whole heart*, vv. 145–149. "I will not let thee go, except thou bless me." Nor must we indulge despondency, much less despair; but rely on the promises and *hope in God's word*, and in his mercy. "We are saved by hope." We do not pray enough. "Your soul would not be so empty of comfort, if your mouth were not so empty of prayer." Luther spent three hours a day in prayer.

3. To prayer we must add *meditation*, v. 148. Think and pray. Pray and muse. Get the fire to burning; then speak.

4. We must *watch* as well as pray, vv. 147, 148. We must awake early to this work.

5. If we would succeed at a throne of grace, our plea must be, not for justice, but for *mercy*; not for our deservings, but for God's *lovingkindness*, v. 149. We need everything, and have nothing to pay. We are weak, and need strength; blind, and need illumination; vile, and need purification; poor, and need riches; guilty, and need pardon; outcasts, and need acceptance; and all through grace.

6. We must pray against the dead state, in which our hearts are by nature and often by habit, v. 149. If we are not *quickened* and *enlivened*, we shall loiter by the way and never reach heaven.

7. It is vastly for our encouragement that according to God's *decision* much is provided and much pledged, v. 149. We need no better promises, but only faith to believe what is spoken.

8. Let us expect in all our Christian course enemies bold, pushing, crowding, cruel, *mischievous*, malicious, v. 150. God's people have always had such. Let us not deceive ourselves with the vain hope that we can go to the kingdom of heaven in a smoother way than the pious of all past ages. This should not discourage us, but make us take fast hold of the covenant, and cleave to God with purpose of heart. The more the state of the times favors ungodliness, the greater will be the opposition to the pious and to piety.

9. Trying as our circumstances may be, God knows the worst and is at hand to help his people as often as their necessities require, v. 151. This we should steadfastly believe, and never doubt.

10. There is no flaw in Scripture. It is all truth, v. 151.

11. The word of God is and from the beginning has been *stable*, v. 152. We should expect no less; it is the word of God. Our experience confirms this belief. God's word cannot change because God cannot change. "The mountains shall depart, and the hills be removed; but my kindness shall not depart from thee, neither shall the covenant of my peace be removed, saith the LORD that hath mercy on thee," Isa. liv. 10. Compare Isa. li. 5, 6. God's testimonies are true, eternal, unchangeable, indispensable, irrevocable. The saints rejoice and are glad, for they *know* by a long experience how sure every word of God is. Henry: "All that ever dealt with God, and trusted in him, will own that they have found him faithful."

PSALM CXIX.

RESH.

153 Consider mine affliction, and deliver me: for I do not forget thy law.
154 Plead my cause, and deliver me: quicken me according to thy word.

155 Salvation *is* far from the wicked: for they seek not thy statutes.

156 Great *are* thy tender mercies, O LORD: quicken me according to thy judgments.

157 Many *are* my persecutors and mine enemies; *yet* do I not decline from thy testimonies.

158 I beheld the transgressors, and was grieved; because they kept not thy word.

159 Consider how I love thy precepts: quicken me, O LORD, according to thy lovingkindness.

160 Thy word *is* true *from* the beginning: and every one of thy righteous judgments *endureth* for ever.

ALL these verses begin with the *twentieth* letter of the Hebrew alphabet; 153, 158, 159, with different forms of the same verb; the rest, with different words. On the terms *law, word, statutes, judgments, testimonies* and *precepts*, see introduction to this Psalm, Nos. 1, 7, 4, 6, 2, 3, respectively.

153. *Consider mine affliction, and deliver me: for I do not forget thy law. Consider*, behold, look on. *Deliver*, loose, *i. e.*, extricate, or rescue. *Affliction*, commonly so rendered in this Psalm; see on v. 50. On not *forgetting the law*, see on v. 16. The last clause is a plea of sincerity in keeping covenant engagements with Jehovah. Compare vv. 94, 173, 176. The *affliction* is not particularly stated in this verse; but subsequently we learn that it arose from false accusations and bitter persecutions.

154. *Plead my cause, and deliver me.* On the first verb see on Psalm xxxv. 1. *Deliver*, not as in v. 153, but a word meaning to *redeem*, or to save by avenging. The corresponding participle is rendered redeemer, avenger, revenger, kinsman, near kinsman, next kinsman. *Quicken me according to thy word*, sufficiently explained at v. 25, though some prefer *with* instead of *according to* in this verse, the preposition not being the same in the two verses.

155. *Salvation is far from the wicked: for they seek not thy statutes. Salvation*, help, *deliverance*; see on Ps. iii. 2. *Wicked*, in Psalm i. *ungodly. Seek*, preterite, *have sought*, as in vv. 10, 45, 94. Salvation is far from the wicked because they are wicked, because they are far from God, because God is holy and just, and cannot keep friendship with the vile, because they neither wish nor labor to know, or do his will, not desiring the knowledge of his ways, of the methods of his grace, or of his plan of salvation. John Rogers' translation, the Bishops' Bible and the church of England for *salvation* read *health;* Calvin, *safety*.

156. *Great* are *thy tender mercies, O* LORD: *quicken me according to thy judgments. Great*, in v. 157; Ps. iii. 1, 2, *many. Tender mercies*, see on Ps. xxv. 6, *compassions;* it denotes the yearning of the heart, and is sometimes rendered *bowels*, 1 Kings iii. 20. The prophet felt his case to be so sad and trying as to call for infinite tenderness. But however sore were his outward troubles, his concern was chiefly for spiritual prosperity. On the clause, *quicken*, etc., see on vv. 25, 149.

157. *Many are my persecutors and mine enemies; yet do I not decline from thy testimonies. Many*, in v. 156, *great. Persecutors*, a *participle* from the verb rendered *pursue, chase. Enemies*, as in v. 139, the authors of my distress. Until men are hunted and hounded by many enemies, who for the time have power, and are withal fierce and to some extent unscrupulous, they can have but a faint conception of the anguish of the prophet when he experienced the evils noted in this verse. Yet they did not move him from his constancy and integrity; see on v. 51.

158. *I beheld the transgressors and was grieved; because they kept not thy word. Transgressors*, a participle of the verb rendered *transgress*, Ps. xxv. 3; *offend*, Ps. xxiii. 15; *dealt unfaithfully*, Ps. lxxviii. 57; very often, *dealt treacherously*, Isa. xxiv. 16; Jer. iii. 20. Calvin has *perfidious;* Fry, *faithless;* Alexander, *traitors. Was grieved*, frequently rendered *loathed;* Calvin, *chid them;* Hengstenberg, *am vexed;* Alexander, *am sickened*. The general doctrine and sentiment of this verse are the same as those of vv. 53, 136.

159. *Consider how I love thy precepts: quicken me, O* LORD, *according to thy loving-kindness.* *Consider,* as in v. 153. *Love,* in the preterite, *have loved* and do still love, as in vv. 47, 48 and often. The Psalmist has often in this Psalm asked to be *quickened,* or enlivened, according to the principles and promises of God's word. Here he asks that the same blessing be dealt out to him according to the large measure of the divine mercy. He knew that God's *lovingkindness* overleaps all limits and all human conceptions, Eph. iii. 20. If he should fail in asking, he desired that God would not fail in giving.

160. *Thy word* is *true from the beginning: and every one of thy righteous judgments* endureth *for ever.* The first clause is variously rendered. Chaldee, Syriac, Arabic, Septuagint, Ethiopic, Vulgate, Doway, Calvin: The beginning of thy word is truth; Luther: Thy word is nothing but truth; Piscator agrees with the authorized version; Fabritius and Alexander: The head of thy word is truth; Tremellius and Junius: Thy most excellent word is truth; church of England: Thy word is true from ever-lasting; Edwards: The beginning of thy word was true; Street: The chief attribute of thy word is truth; Hengstenberg: The sum of thy word is truth. The same word is rendered *sum* in Ps. cxxxix. 17; often, *head,* Ps. cxviii. 22. God's word is true in every sense that either of these translations would indicate. The first thing he ever spoke was true, and so was the last. The crowning excellence of Scripture is its truth. Nicolson: "*Thy word is true,* in its *principle,* and in all its details, from Adam to Moses; and from Moses to Christ; from Christ to the present time; and from the present time to the end of the world;" Diodati: "All thy word, put together, without exception, is nothing but pure truth." The reason why God's judgments endure for ever is because they are *righteous,* and righteousness is immutable.

DOCTRINAL AND PRACTICAL REMARKS.

1. Is any afflicted? let him pray, according to the example here set, v. 153.

2. We must continue to follow the Lord even if we have no reward here, but on the contrary meet with much affliction, v. 153.

3. It is not wrong for us to invite special divine attention to our trials and afflic-tions; yet it is not necessary to enter into tedious details respecting them, as though the Almighty understood not our case, v. 153.

4. It is a great matter to continue in the path of duty, steadfast and upright, in the day of adversity, v. 153. When the whole outward course of providence is such as to present discouragements to the natural mind, it is proof that the root of the matter is in us, if we swerve not from duty. The firmer our adherence to God, the more con-fidently may we rely upon his word of promise to be fulfilled in our case.

5. If the Lord be our advocate and *plead our cause,* we may be sure that deliver-ance will come, v. 154. When conscience accuses, and Satan assails, and the world reproaches, and providence frowns, what can we do but betake ourselves to him who never forsakes the clients who commit their cause to him?

6. If we can but be made as *lively* in God's service as his word requires, his grace provides, and his promise engages, we shall neither be dead nor dull, vv. 153, 154, 159.

7. The way of the wicked is as darkness, even now, and is growing darker every day, v. 155. Nor can any mortal tell what hour the fearful consummation may come. The Judge is even now standing before the door, ready to summon them into his awful presence.

8. It shall be for a perpetual joy to all the righteous that the gentlest, the most loving and the tenderest being in the universe is God himself, v. 156. Let not men

foolishly build their hopes on human mercies, but solely on the infinite compassions of Jehovah.

9. Neither age, nor eminence in position, nor public services, nor piety, nor anything else is a guaranty against the vilest, mightiest, bitterest and most numerous persecutors, v. 157. Dickson: "As it is no strange thing to see the godliest men exposed most to persecution; so it is no small measure of grace which God bestoweth on them to bear out the truth against all opposition." The power, the number, the malice and the cunning of our enemies cannot harm us, if God be for us, much less can they justify us in swerving from the right. Persecution is indeed a fearful test of our fidelity, but if we studiously avoid the cross, we shall never wear the crown. Calvin: "It is an easy matter to act well when we are among the good; but if wicked men afflict us, if one man openly assault us by force, if another rob us of our property, if a third circumvent us by wiles, and a fourth attack us by calumnies, it is difficult for us to persevere in our integrity, and we rather begin to howl among the wolves."

10. No doubt deceit, treachery, perfidy enter into the very nature of sin. Iniquity is itself a lie to God and man, v. 158.

11. This dreadful nature of sin is a good cause why we should not tolerate it, or be unmoved concerning it; but we should weep and mourn, be sad and *grieved* both for the sin and the doom of the transgressor, v. 158. Morison: "The dishonor done to God is not the only cause of regret. Sin is the sure path to ruin, and those who keep not God's word, will, ere long, be dealt with as his enemies."

12. Love between God and his people is reciprocal. He shows them his *loving-kindness*, and they *love his precepts*, his ordinances, his perfections, his whole nature, v. 159. The more they see of his love, the more they love him.

13. It is right to make a sincere profession or declaration of love to God and his word, v. 159. Calvin: "When the saints speak of their own piety before God, they are not chargeable with intruding their own merits, as the ground of their confidence; but they regard this as a settled principle, that God, who distinguishes his servants from the profane and wicked, will be merciful to them, when they seek him with their whole heart. Besides, an unfeigned love of God's law is an undoubted evidence of adoption, since this love is the work of the Holy Spirit."

14. There is no untruth in Scripture, v. 160. It is never commended too highly; it is never trusted too implicitly. It is all faithfulness. It is light without darkness; it is life and spirit.

15. The Scripture cannot be broken, v. 160. It is unchangeable. It could not be changed for the better, else it would not be perfect now. If altered, it must be for the worse, and so it would become imperfect. 'From the time when God began to speak, he has always been faithful to his promises, and never disappointed the hope of his people.' Nicolson: "All other things wear out, or decay; lose their *testimony*, and become *obsolete*. But God will ever bear testimony to his own *word*, and continue to support its veracity by fulfilling it to all successive generations."

PSALM CXIX.

SCHIN.

161 Princes have persecuted me without a cause: but my heart standeth in awe of thy word.
162 I rejoice at thy word, as one that findeth great spoil.
163 I hate and abhor lying: *but* thy law do I love.

164 Seven times a day do I praise thee, because of thy righteous judgments.

165 Great peace have they which love thy law: and nothing shall offend them

166 LORD, I have hoped for thy salvation, and done thy commandments.

167 My soul hath kept thy testimonies; and I love them exceedingly.

168 I have kept thy precepts and thy testimonies: for all my ways *are* before thee.

ALL these verses begin with the *twenty-first* letter of the alphabet; 161, 162, 166, with the letter as pronounced *sin;* and all the rest with the same pronounced *shin* or *schin;* 167, 168, with the same verb; all the rest with different words. On the terms *word, law, judgments, commandments, testimonies* and *precepts,* see introduction to this Psalm, Nos. 7, 1, 6, 5, 2, 3.

161. *Princes have persecuted me without a cause: but my heart standeth in awe of thy word. Princes,* as in v. 23, *rulers, head men, captains, chiefs. Persecuted,* the verb from which we have *persecutors,* in v. 157. *Without a cause,* uniformly so rendered in the Psalms; often *for nought, for nothing,* Gen. xxix. 15; Ex. xxi. 2; Isa. lii. 3; Mal. i. 10. The meaning is, they have persecuted and are doing so still. He does not state what branch of Scripture most awakened his holy *fear.* Any part of it might well have such an effect. We may well fear God's word as it denounces curses against his enemies, and fear to be like them, lest we also should fall into condemnation. Here we see the use of the most terrific portions of Scripture. Persecutors kindle big fires. Hell is a bigger fire. They threaten the loss of friends, riches, honors and pleasures; but if we break with God, we lose the friends, riches, honors and pleasures at his right hand, Matt. x. 28. Modern criticism not capriciously prefers *words* instead of *word.*

162. *I rejoice at thy word, as one that findeth great spoil. Rejoice,* literally (am) rejoicing, a participle of the verb *have rejoiced,* in v. 14, cognate to the noun *rejoicing,* in v. 111. The very word of God, which awakens salutary fear, awakens also a blessed joy. Nor is this joy stinted, but like that of one that findeth *great spoil,* or *much prey.* According to common opinion this is the highest kind of joy, being sudden and accompanied by the glory of victory.

163. *I hate and abhor lying: but thy law do I love. Hate* and *abhor,* in the preterite; *have hated* and *abhorred,* and do so still. *Lying,* see on v. 29. *Love, have loved,* and love still; see on vv. 47, 48.

164. *Seven times a day do I praise thee, because of thy righteous judgments.* Among the Greeks *three* was the number of perfection; among the Hebrews, *seven.* As *day* and *night* signifies continually, so *seven times* means *very often.* On the phrase *righteous judgments,* literally *judgments of righteousness,* see on v. 7.

165. *Great peace have they which love thy law. Great,* as in vv. 156, 162. The peace of believers is great in many respects. It is *manifold,* being with God, with their neighbors and with their own consciences; being *sufficient* and *mighty,* able to keep them calm in all perturbations and in all the awful scenes through which they shall pass. It is the peace of God, which passeth all understanding. Such peace have all the saints. *And nothing shall offend them;* margin: And they shall have no stumbling block; Edwards: And they meet with nothing that can divert them from it; Street: And there is nothing that maketh them stumble. This gives the sense.

166. LORD, *I have hoped for thy salvation, and done thy commandments.* All the terms of this verse are those usually so rendered. *Hoping* includes the idea of *waiting.* No other text more happily presents the true doctrine concerning grace and works, relying and doing, hoping and obeying, expecting all from God's sovereign mercy, yet performing all known duties from a tender conscience and true gratitude. The form of both verbs describes the habit of life—*have hoped* and still hope, *have done* and still do.

167. *My soul hath kept thy testimonies; and I love them exceedingly.* True spiritual obedience is not merely outward, or of the body, but inward, of the *soul;* not reluctant or sluggish, but strong and controlling, proceeding from *much* or *exceeding love.* The first verb is in the preterite—*hath kept* and doth still keep. The second is in the future, implying I love now and *will love* in all coming time.

168. *I have kept thy precepts and thy testimonies: for all my ways* are *before thee.* Kept, the same verb as in vv. 4, 8. *My ways*, my habits of life, of speech and of thought, my secret ways and my public conduct. *Before thee*, under thy eye and scrutiny as the Judge of all. The Psalmist lived as seeing him who is omniscient. His love and obedience extended to the whole will of God, under whatever name revealed.

Doctrinal and Practical Remarks.

1. It is sad indeed when the head men of a nation learn the art of persecution; when those who are set for the defence of the weak and innocent become their tormentors, v. 161. Persecutions are commonly based on an alleged difference of views in politics or religion; but the real cause is envy, covetousness, pride, or lust of power. Man is naturally fond of domination. The worst persecutors are whining hypocrites, full of cant, weak-minded bigots who have but one idea, abandoned women, and unconverted ecclesiastics. Whoever differs from them is wrong, is dangerous. Sometimes such relent, as did Saul, 1 Sam. xxiv. 17; but they soon return to their old work, unless divine grace changes their hearts. Henry: "It has been the common lot of the best men to be persecuted. . . It is sad that the power which magistrates have from God, and should use for him, should ever be employed against him. But, *marvel not at the matter*, Eccles. v. 8."

2. If we are treated harshly and severely by those in power over us, it is better for us, *though* worse for them that it should be without, than with cause on our own part, v. 161. "If we suffer as evil-doers, or as busy bodies, we have no cause to triumph in the day of trouble." Cruelty, wholly gratuitous, brings awful guilt on the perpetrator, but can do no real harm to the sufferer.

3. The more terrible and frightful the power and acts of persecutors, the more should we call to mind the majesty and terrors of the Almighty, v. 161. Compare Luke xii. 4, 5. History proves that nothing is a greater temptation to apostasy than the menaces, statutes and proceedings of persecutors in power. Against the fear of man there is no adequate argument but the fear of God.

4. That we may have a just sense of the wrath and terrors of God in the day of sore persecution, let us habitually stand in awe of his word, v. 161. When Ehud said to Eglon, I have a message from God unto thee, he *arose out of his seat*, Judg. iii. 20. Trifling with Scripture, irreverence in sacred things, is a fearful sign of a depraved character.

5. If we made more of our religion, it would do more for us, v. 162. If we prized Scripture and ordinances more highly, we should be more refreshed by them. Amesius: "Joy in the word of God proceeds from love to it and increases that very love."

6. No man's heart was ever turned too vehemently against *lying*, falsehood, in every shape and form, v. 163. Henry: "Every man hates to have a lie told of him; but we should more hate telling a lie, because by the former we only receive an affront from men, by the latter we give an affront to God."

7. The only effectual cure of the spirit of lying is found in a sincere love to the word of God, v. 163. God's word is truth, is preëminently the truth; and he who loves truth must hate a lie; as he who loves a lie must hate the truth.

8. A noticeable defect in the services of all formalists is that they do not abound

in praise, though there is such a loud call to that duty, v. 164. Some of the Rabbis, as well as some moderns given to rubrics in their private devotions, have foolishly supposed that they observed the Scripture rule, when they literally and formally praised God seven times a day. When our joy is unspeakable and full of glory, it will break forth into praise and thanksgiving. "Love to God is the spirit of praise."

9. The Christian religion would be a sad failure, if it did not give solid peace to those who truly embrace it, v. 165. Such are the tempests that howl over the earth; such are the perturbations of the human mind; such is the disquieting nature of all earthly things that if religion wholly failed to give quiet of mind, it would disprove its divinity. It is because the wicked are strangers to the quietness of piety, that there is no peace to them.

10. So just and correct is the temper of the pious, and so true and fair are the dealings of God with his creatures, that nothing can drive the saints from their purpose to cleave to God, v. 165, so that they shall fall into ruin. "No event of providence shall be either an invincible temptation, or an intolerable affliction to them." In the cross of Christ they even glory, Gal. vi. 14.

11. When our hope of heaven is accompanied by the spirit and habit of obedience to all God's will, we may be well assured that it is not deceptive, v. 166. Morison: "The entire religion of a redeemed sinner may be said to consist in the hope of mercy, and in the habitual practice of obedience to the commandments of God." Bridges: "Conscious unworthiness may give a trembling feebleness to the hand of faith, but the feeblest apprehension of one of the least of the promises of the Gospel, assures us of our interest in them all."

12. Love and practice are mutual aids to each other. If we love we will obey, and if we obey, it will strengthen our love, v. 167. But then this love and this obedience must be supreme. They must be stronger than our love of the world, or our regard to man.

13. It is a part of true piety to observe all that God has spoken, and that from a remembrance of his omnipresence and omniscience, v. 168. When the Almighty would teach the father of the faithful the nature of true piety, he said: "I am the Almighty God; walk before me, and be thou perfect," Gen. xvii. 1. Even poor Hagar was sustained by the truth: "Thou God seest me," Gen. xvi. 13. Calvin: "If we live not as under the omniscient inspection of God, the fickle lustfulness of the flesh quickly carries us away hither and thither."

14. There is a beautiful harmony and symmetry in Christian character, vv. 161–168. Fear makes the godly man sober; joy makes him lively; abhorrence of sin makes him cautious and watchful; love makes him serve willingly and give liberally; peace makes him tranquil; hope gives an anchor to his soul; faith in an omniscient God makes him serve not man, but his Maker; praise gives him songs in the night; and obedience makes him work righteousness with all diligence. He knows that the 'salvation of God is to be sought and found in the ways of God's commandments.' O how blessed Christians might be if no neglect of closet-duty, no unfaithfulness to covenant engagements, and no defect of motive marred their service. Many 'spoil the hidden walk of communion with God, by concentrating the mind upon a more public, and, apparently, a more useful walk.'

PSALM CXIX.

TAU.

169 Let my cry come near before thee, O Lord: give me understanding according to thy word.

170 Let my supplication come before thee: deliver me according to thy word.

171 My lips shall utter praise, when thou hast taught me thy statutes.

172 My tongue shall speak of thy word: for all thy commandments *are* righteousness.

173 Let thine hand help me; for I have chosen thy precepts.

174 I have longed for thy salvation, O Lord; and thy law *is* my delight.

175 Let my soul live, and it shall praise thee; and let thy judgments help me.

176 I have gone astray like a lost sheep: seek thy servant; for I do not forget thy commandments.

ALL these verses begin with the last letter of the Hebrew alphabet; 173, 175, with the same verb; the rest, each with a different word. On the terms *word, statutes, commandments, precepts, law, judgments,* see introduction to this Psalm, Nos. 7, 4, 5, 3, 1, 6, respectively.

169. *Let my cry come near before thee,* O Lord: *give me understanding according to thy word. Cry,* a word expressive of much earnestness, *outcry. Give me understanding,* as in vv. 27, 34. In this verse and the next, *cry* and *supplication* seem to be personified, as messengers before God's throne. The whole verse teaches that with the righteous, nothing is desired more than heavenly wisdom and divine *teaching.*

170. *Let my supplication come before thee: deliver me according to thy word. Before thee,* as in v. 169, literally, *before thy face, into thy presence. Deliver,* elsewhere *pluck,* in v. 43, *take. According to thy word,* see on v. 9. A good man would not be *delivered* in any way contrary to the word of the Lord.

171. *My lips shall utter praise, when thou hast taught me thy statutes.* We can no more praise than we can pray, or think aright, unless the Lord becomes our teacher in divine things. The literal rendering of the latter clause of the verse is, *Because thou wilt teach me.* But the authorized version gives the sense. Edwards has, *When thou shalt have taught me.* We are wise, when we learn God's statutes, and never till then.

172. *My tongue shall speak of thy word: for all thy commandments are righteousness. Shall speak of,* a verb rendered *hear,* Ps. iv. 1, and often; *shout* and *cry,* Ex. xxxii. 18; *testify,* Hos. v. 5; vii. 10, and often. It may here signify that the prophet declares his purpose to commend the Scripture, or that his heart gladly *responds* to all God's word. A renewed man's heart loves every part of Scripture for it is *righteousness* itself.

173. *Let thine hand help me; for I have chosen thy precepts. Help,* a verb of frequent occurrence and always rendered as here or *succor.* God's *hand* is strong, is ready, is far-reaching, and is sure to bring deliverance. The latter clause is an assertion that the prophet had cordially entered God's service, having made an intelligent and deliberate election between the principles of God's word and the maxims of the world, and given a decided and cordial preference to the former. *I have chosen* and I still choose.

174. *I have longed for thy salvation,* O Lord; *and thy law is my delight. Longed,* as in v. 40. Calvin: "The construction in the Hebrew denotes steadfastness, or constancy of desire." There is no reason for confining the meaning of *salvation* to any temporal deliverance, though that may be included. The scope and the context show that the prophet had his mind on a complete spiritual salvation. *Delight,* in the plural *delights,* as in vv. 24, 77, 92, 143. God's word is an abundant source of pleasure to his people.

175. *Let my soul live, and it shall praise thee; and let thy judgments help me.* *Live,* the verb of existence, the causative form of which is so often in this Psalm rendered *quicken.* Let my soul *live,* have health, be lively; then the work of *praise* will be pleasant, and I will engage in it in a fitting manner. *Help,* as in v. 173. The *judgments* are the decisions of God's word as executed in his providence. Alexander: "This verse sums up in conclusion the petitions of the whole Psalm."

176. *I have gone astray like a lost sheep: seek thy servant; for I do not forget thy commandments.* The figure of the first part of the verse is of frequent occurrence in Scripture. Compare Isa. liii. 6; Jer. l. 6; Matt. x. 6; xv. 24. Lost sheep are always in danger, and often in distress. Sin both imperils and embitters life. As a sheep is a silly and helpless thing, and, when lost, never finds itself, but wanders on, till the shepherd *seeks* it; so the soul of man must be brought back from its errors and miseries by the Lord himself. Such is the common view taken by expositors. Yet the prominent idea gathered by many is not so much the sinfulness but the peril to which as a wanderer David was exposed.

DOCTRINAL AND PRACTICAL REMARKS.

1. Nothing is more essential than genuine earnestness in devotion. When prayer is dull, and supplication languid, every approach to God fails, vv. 169, 170. Bridges: "The eloquence of prayer is its earnestness. The power of prayer is that which cometh, not from education, or from the natural desire of the man; but from above." Whenever we fall under the delusion that the number or variety of our services can be a substitute for warmth, we are in a bad way. We must have vehemence and humility, *cry* and *supplicate.*

2. The genuine spirit of prayer is not satisfied with praying, but desires answers, vv. 169, 170.

3. Although this part of Scripture does not teach it, yet the doctrine of Christ's mediation is so important, that we, living under the Gospel, ought never to lose sight of it. No prayer offered in any other name than that of Jesus Christ can be acceptable to God, John xiv. 13, 14; xvi. 24.

4. As long as we are in our present low estate, we shall never be done asking for instruction, v. 169. There is nothing we need more than such wisdom as God only can give. Otherwise we will never know, nor love, nor do our duty. Our necessities in this matter compel us to repeat over and over again the same petitions and to cry for help from the Spirit of God. None but he can give saving illumination.

5. Let us very carefully avoid asking deliverance or any mercy except *according to Scripture,* vv. 169, 170. If the case is such that no promise meets it, it is hopeless.

6. Especially must we seek aid in our devotions. We must pray that our prayers may be right and acceptable before God, v. 170.

7. We are no less dependent on divine teaching to aid us in the work of praise, v. 171. It is not a fine voice, nor skill in its management, nor art in playing upon an instrument that God requires. The *spirit* and the *understanding* are the essentials.

8. We should all be witnesses for God, and declare his goodness. How else shall true *righteousness* be spread abroad in the world, v. 172. No good man is content to go to heaven alone. Yet it is sad to see how few promptly embrace opportunities to speak a word for God. Bridges: "What loss is there to our own souls in these neglected opportunities of blessing the souls of others! For never do we receive richer fruit to ourselves, than in the act or endeavor to communicate to others."

9. It is not possible that there can be any defect in the *righteousness* of Scripture, or it would long since have been made apparent, v. 172. Surely some good man,

with nicely cultivated sensibilities, or some evil man, with critical eye, must have found a flaw in the morality of Scripture, if such had existed.

10. We have need of help from God all the time, v. 173. Without his aid we are indeed powerless for good; and 'the more we trust to his help and guidance in everything, the more we shall be able to do, and the more delightful will his service be to us.'

11. It is indeed a great mercy, and should be esteemed by us a great blessing when we can truly say that our decided *choice* leads us to God's word, and to all heavenly things, v. 173. Calvin: "It is not through ignorance or an inconsiderate zeal that the children of God desire above all things heavenly doctrine."

12. The truly pious have intense desires and longings for grace and complete deliverance from sin and its consequences,—even for perfect salvation, v. 174. Their existence even on earth is not happy when they feel that they are not glorifying God and showing forth his praise. We may have true grace without the exultant spirit of triumph. But we cannot have true grace unless we hunger and thirst after righteousness.

13. The righteous have intense pleasure in the word of God. It is not only their delight, but their *delights*, v. 174. Take all else away and leave them the full, sweet believing enjoyment of Scripture, and they are still truly blessed.

14. Eternal life is begun in this world, v. 175. It is life indeed, and is the fountain of that sweet animation that runs through the services of the Christian's life.

15. As long as we live, we shall need help both from Scripture and from Providence, v. 175. The more we give ourselves to the work of the Lord, the more deeply shall we feel our need.

16. Has God's providence, either with or without any particular sin on our part led us into the wilderness, and are we wandering like lost sheep? But one way of recovery is possible. If the Good Shepherd does not seek us and carry us back on his shoulder, we are clean gone, v. 176. None but he can restore the soul. Augustine: "Lord, I can go astray; I cannot of myself return." And if we would have his salvation, we must look to him alone.

17. Come what will, let us hold on to the truth, think of it, remember it, love it, obey it, v. 176. "Let integrity and uprightness preserve me" is a good prayer. David "had not *forgotten God's way*, nor lost sight of his own state. The word of the Lord, applied by his Spirit,—1. When he was slumbering, *awakened* him. 2. When he was dead, *quickened* him. 3. When he was in danger, *preserved* him. 4. When he was wounded, *cured* him. 5. When he was assailed by his foes, *armed* and *defended* him. 6. And by his word he was *nourished* and *supported*. It was ever well with the Psalmist, and it is ever well with all the followers of God, when they *do not forget God's word*."

18. If the peace, delight and other agreeable emotions described in this Psalm belong to the saints in their pilgrimage on earth, what shall not be their blessedness when he that sitteth on the throne shall dwell among them; when they shall hunger no more, neither thirst any more; neither shall the sun light on them, nor any heat; for the Lamb which is in the midst of the throne shall feed them, and shall lead them unto living fountains of waters, and God shall wipe away all tears from their eyes!

PSALM CXX.

A Song of degrees.

1 In my distress I cried unto the LORD, and he heard me.

2 Deliver my soul, O LORD, from lying lips, *and* from a deceitful tongue.

3 What shall be given unto thee? or what shall be done unto thee, thou false tongue?

4 Sharp arrows of the mighty, with coals of juniper.

5 Woe is me, that I sojourn in Mesech, *that* I dwell in the tents of Kedar!

6 My soul hath long dwelt with him that hateth peace.

7 I *am for* peace: but when I speak, they *are* for war.

THIS and Psalms cxxi.–cxxxiv. have each the title, *A song of degrees. Song*, found often in the titles of Psalms; see on title of Psalm xxx. *Degrees*, in Amos ix. 6, *stories;* in 2 Kings ix. 13; Neh. iii. 15; xii. 37; Ezek. xl. 6; xliii. 17, *stairs;* in Ex. xx. 26; 1 Kings x. 19, 20; 2 Chron. ix. 18, 19; and *six* times in Ezek. xl. *steps.* It is the word so often used in 2 Kings xx. and Isa xxxviii. respecting the *degrees* of the sun-dial of Ahaz. In 1 Chron. xvii. 17, it is applied to a man of *high degree.* The cognate verb is rendered *arise, go up, come up, ascend.* It is applied to the *ascending* of the angels on the ladder which Jacob saw, to the travel of any person or people on a journey, and to the ascent of Moses and Aaron into the mount of God. In rendering the whole phrase, *A song of degrees*, the authorized version follows the Septuagint, Arabic, Ethiopic, Vulgate, Piscator and Calvin. The Chaldee, The song which was said upon the ascent of the *abyss;* Luther and Tholuck, A song from the higher choir; Syriac, The first song of ascension; Doway, A gradual canticle; Diodati, A song of degrees, that is of goings up or movings; Venema, A song of degrees or of ascensions; Street, An ode of the Ascent; Hammond, Edwards, Morison and Alexander, A song of the ascents; Hengstenberg; A song of the pilgrimages; Tremellius and Junius, A most excellent song. The explanations given of the phrase are these: 1. The title is a name designating the tune to be used in singing these songs. This is rather suggested by several than supported by any authority. 2. Others think the title calls for elevation of the voice in singing these songs. This view is suggested by some of the Rabbis; Patrick favors it; and Calvin thinks it probable. 3. Fenwick thinks these odes are 'songs for ascending or aspiring souls,' and that they have an unusual elevation about them. 4. Jarchi, Kimchi, Ben Melech and Lyra favor the opinion that there were *fifteen steps* to be ascended at the temple, on each of which one of these songs was to be sung. Calvin styles this "a silly conjecture, for which there is no foundation." But see Ezek. xl. 26, 31. 5. Others suppose that there is special reference to a pulpit or place near the altar, where a choir of priests stood and sang, as mentioned in Neh. ix. 4. Luther, Hammond and Tholuck seem to favor this view 6. The Syriac version, Theodoret, Chrysostom, Athanasius, Euthymius, Diodati, Calmet, Vatablus, Ewald and Morrison suppose that these songs were sung by the Israelites at their different *stages* returning from Babylonish captivity. Calvin says, that this is "an interpretation altogether forced." 7. Mudge, Hengstenberg and Alexander suppose that they are songs which were sung by the Jews as they went up to the annual feasts at Jerusalem. 8. Yet another opinion, defended by Gesenius, is that the title is given because these Psalms are composed so as to rise by *degrees* to a climax. But this is true of only a few of them. On examining these opinions the reader will probably be prepared to assent to the statement of Dodd: "It is very uncertain why this title is prefixed to this and the following Psalms." Henry: "It is well that it is not material what the meaning of that title should be, for nothing is offered toward the explication of it, no, not by the Jewish writers themselves, but what is conjectural." *Four* of these *fifteen* Psalms were certainly composed by David, one is inscribed to Solomon, if not penned by him; it is certain they were not all written at the same time; Psalms cxxvi. cxxix. are generally admitted to have been written after the captivity; Psalms cxxii. cxxxiv. were clearly designed for public worship, while Psalms cxx. cxxx. are as clearly aids to private devotion; and Psalms cxxvii. cxxviii. are for the use of families. Some seem designed for special seasons, and some for all times. Several are without any special fitness for the temple service. They are all very edifying and comforting to the pious. Clarke: "They are excellent in their kind; written with much elegance; and contain strong and nervous sentiments of the most exalted piety, expressed with a great felicity of language in a few words." They are all short, three of them having but three verses each; the longest having but eighteen verses; they average less than seven verses to a Psalm. In nearly all of them there is little or no attention to that characteristic of most Hebrew poetry—parallelism. Many of them are very terse and pointed.

We know not the author of this Psalm, though Calvin, Patrick and Henry not unreasonably ascribe it to David as the probable author. Others ascribe it to Solomon; others, to Ezra; others, to Haggai; others, to Zechariah; others, to Malachi. None of these opinions are satisfactorily established. Those, who hold that David is the author, suppose that it was written when Doeg and his accomplices by their slanders compelled the sweet singer of Israel to flee his country. Others think it was specially written for the Jews in their captivity. The occasion of the Psalm cannot be certainly known. Scott dates it B. C. 1059; Clarke affixes no date. The only name of the Most High here found is that of *Jehovah* LORD, on which see on Ps. i. 2.

1. *In my distress I cried unto the* LORD, *and he heard me. Distress, trouble, affliction, adversity, tribulation. Cried,* very often rendered *called,* denoting acts of religious worship generally. Compare Gen. iv. 26; Psalm iv. 1, 3. *Heard,* so as to answer, see on Ps. iii. 4. The *distress* arose from wicked calumnies. Tholuck: "Undaunted believers are never free from them."

2. *Deliver my soul, O* LORD, *from lying lips, and from a deceitful tongue. Deliver,* commonly so rendered, as in Ps. cxix. 170. *Lying lips,* literally, *the lip of falsehood.* For *deceitful tongue,* some read *tongue of deceit,* and some a *tongue, deceit, i. e.,* the tongue which is deceit itself. The wounds of the tongue are like the piercings of a sword. Innocence is no shield against the slanders invented by the father of lies, and spread abroad by his children. But let the righteous patiently endure such evil reports, only being concerned that they give no cause for them. As a lying tongue produces such incalculable mischief here, almost dissolving the bands of society, inspiration raises the question of a just punishment.

3. *What shall be given unto thee? or what shall be done unto thee, thou false tongue?* This is an awful question. It arraigns the slanderer at the bar of God, and calls on him to consider what retribution he may reasonably expect from the Judge of all the earth. If anything in human conduct deserves terrible punishment, slander cannot escape the divine vengeance.

4. *Sharp arrows of the mighty, with coals of juniper.* Some put this verse in apposition to the preceding, and make it declare that the false tongue is like the sharp arrows of the mighty, with coals of juniper. This would be no exaggerated description of calumny. Such is the view of Calvin, Walford, Boothroyd, Phillips and Tholuck. The other interpretation makes this verse an answer to the question of the preceding. So our translators evidently thought; also the church of England, Jebb, Edwards, Street, Nicolson, Morison, Fry, Henry, Pool, Scott and Alexander, the last

of whom says: "The general idea of severe and painful punishment is here expressed by the obvious and intelligible figures of keen arrows and hot coals." This is to be preferred. The *arrows of a mighty man* were used in war and shot from powerful cross-bows, inflicting death or exquisite agony. By *coals of juniper*, some understand juniper proper, which is a wood filled with resinous substance, and when ignited makes an intense heat of live coals. But others understand a species of broom which is highly inflammable, the genista. Several distinguished modern scholars favor this view. The objection to it is that the fire of the broom, though intense, is soon over, whereas the coals of the juniper not only have great heat, but remain alive a considerable time. The Chaldee reads the verse: The strong, sharp arrows are like lightning from above, with coals of juniper [genistarum] kindled in hell beneath.

5. *Woe is me, that I sojourn in Mesech, that I dwell in the tents of Kedar!* John Rogers' translation: Woe is me that my banishment endureth so longe: I dwell in the tabernacles of the sorrowful; Bishops' Bible: Woe is mee that I am constrayned to dwell with Mesech: and to have my habitation among the tents of Cedar. *Mesech* or *Meshech* was the son of Japheth, Gen. x. 2; *Kedar* was the son of Ishmael, Gen. xxv. 13. Though of different origin, their descendants seem to have had much the same manners, habits and dispositions, all of them being idolaters, fierce and cruel. The descendants of Mesech are the Tartars and kindred tribes, whose habits and blood have been largely infused into the Turks. By *Kedar* we are to understand the Arabs, who have always been a deceitful and bloody people. The Psalmist is not to be understood as saying that he was actually sojourning in the country of these people; but that he was surrounded by a set of men as cruel and malignant as the Tartars and Arabs. Such was indeed the fact during his persecutions in the time of Saul. Calvin: "He speaks metaphorically of his own countrymen." By the calumnies of the wicked, lands where the knowledge of the true God prevails are converted into abodes of wretchedness comparable to the homes of the fiercest and most terrible barbarians and savages.

6. *My soul hath long dwelt with him that hateth peace.*

7. *I* am for *peace: but when I speak, they* are *for war.* For *long* Alexander reads *too long.* Hengstenberg thus renders v. 6: "It is wearisome to my soul to dwell by those who hate peace." The use of the phrase *my soul* shows the depth of his distress. David's enemies were as implacable as the Tartars and Arabs. His kind, forgiving temper was manifested on many occasions, and should have been sufficient to disarm any malignity. His language about himself is strong: I *am for* peace; literally, *I peace, i. e.*, I am peace itself, I have done all that mortal man can do to stop this relentless persecution; but all in vain. The very time when I am most anxious for quiet, my enemies are for war.

Of course those who regard this Psalm as relating to the captivity are at no loss to find enemies answering the description here given; for the church of God has always been a speckled bird, and the hawks and vultures have been fierce against her.

Doctrinal and Practical Remarks.

1. Good men are often so situated that the only resource left them is prayer, v. 1. To man they look in vain, appeal in vain, in vain call for pity or help. Fightings without and fears within, the lion of the evening roaring, and vile men swelling and cursing, and good men out of power—all this presents a state of case compelling the believer to resort to God alone.

2. Yet prayer is never performed aright so as to be answered till we are taught by the Holy Ghost. Compare Rom. viii. 26. Distress is a natural means of stirring us up to prayer, only when sanctified to us by God's Spirit.

3. Such prayer as is indited by the Holy Ghost shall not be in vain, v. 1. The time and the manner of answering our prayers are in God's hand; but the certainty of relief from unjust odium is infallible. Man may be able to point out no way of escape, but God is never at a loss for means of rescuing his friends.

4. "The purest character is not safe against the slanderer; and those from whom we should hope better things are not always clear from the crime of calumny." The Master himself and all his followers have suffered thus. Blamelessness itself often provokes the wicked tongue, v. 2.

5. Let all men be warned against falling into any of the sins of the tongue. What does the liar or slanderer gain? A temporary advantage sometimes, and that is all. When the account shall be settled at the tribunal above, the loss will be immense, v. 3. Morison: "To do evil to another and thereby to ruin thyself, combines the folly and wickedness of a fiend of darkness." Something shall surely be *done unto thee,* thou false tongue. The day of recompense will surely come. It may come even in this life. When an old man reviewed the history of some old calumniators and saw how they had suffered, he said: "I tremble in my flesh."

6. Some suppose that retribution in kind is taught in v. 4. More than once in Scripture are slanders compared to arrows and fire, Ps. lvii. 4; lxiv. 3; Prov. xxvi. 18. Let those who indulge in sins of the tongue remember that God's arrows are sharper and God's coals hotter than those with which they think to afflict the people of God. Compare Rev. xxi. 8; xxii. 15.

7. It is sad indeed when we are forced to be much among men of a malicious disposition, vv. 5, 6. Amesius: "To dwell among calumniators is to converse with barbarous and fierce men, and those are barbarous who are alien from all honorable conditions of peace." No good man can love such company. Even some unregenerate men loathe it.

8. Good men love peace, pray for it, seek it, pursue it, will give anything but a good conscience for it, v. 7. Compare Matt. v. 9; Heb. xii. 14. Amesius: "It is a .nark of a pious man, as far as in him is, to seek peace." Dr. Ruffner: "I would not give one hour of brotherly love for a whole eternity of contention."

9. Yet let men of a tender conscience and friendly disposition not be distressed, if they find men wicked and unreasonable. The Bible requires no impossible tasks. Its doctrine is: "If it be possible, as much as lieth in you, live peaceably with all men," Rom. xii. 18. There is a class of men, and their number is not small, who love strife and live in fire. We may not render evil for evil. Yea, we must labor to overcome evil with good; but in spite of all we can do Satan will roar, and wicked men will often rage.

10. At such a time, let us labor to behave ourselves, quietly plead for peace, and copy the example of the Psalmist, v. 7. The trial may be very sharp; but if God can bear with the wicked, surely the forbearance of his people ought not to be exhausted. The Almighty can sustain us. The everlasting arms are strong enough and God's eternal mercy rich enough to give us quietness in all perturbations.

11. "As we must foresee the dreadful misery of all impenitent slanderers and liars, in the everlasting fire of hell; let us in meekness warn them of their danger, if peradventure God will give them repentance, to the acknowledging of the truth; and that they may recover themselves out of the snare of the devil, who are taken captive by him at his will."

Psalm CXXI.

A Song of degrees.

1 I will lift up mine eyes unto the hills, from whence cometh my help.
2 My help *cometh* from the LORD, which made heaven and earth.
3 He will not suffer thy foot to be moved: he that keepeth thee will not slumber.
4 Behold, he that keepeth Israel shall neither slumber nor sleep.
5 The LORD *is* thy keeper: the LORD *is* thy shade upon thy right hand.
6 The sun shall not smite thee by day, nor the moon by night.
7 The LORD shall preserve thee from all evil: he shall preserve thy soul.
8 The LORD shall preserve thy going out and thy coming in from this time forth, and even for evermore.

ON the title see on title of Psalm cxx. It cannot be shown that this ode had any historic occasion, nor is there any certainty concerning the authorship, although many, not without a show of probability, refer it to David. Its design is quite obvious. Luther: "This is a Psalm of consolation, wherein the Psalmist, from his own experience, exhorts the godly to a constancy of faith, and to an expectation of help and defence from God." Alexander: "The whole Psalm is a description of Jehovah, as the guardian and protector of his people." Morison: "The imagery of the Psalm is borrowed from military life, and seems well to represent that state of mind with which a general looks out for succor in the day of conflict." Scott dates it B. C. 1021. Clarke fixes no date, but says it "appears to be a prayer of the Jews in their captivity, who are solicitous for their restoration." The only name of the Most High here found is *Jehovah* LORD, on which see on Ps. i. 2.

1. *I will lift up mine eyes unto the hills, from whence cometh my help.* The chief variation in the rendering of this verse is in the tense of the first verb. That of the authorized version is literal, agreeing with the Hebrew, Chaldee, Syriac, church of England, Calvin, Edwards and Jebb. The Septuagint, Arabic, Ethiopic, Vulgate and Doway put the verb in the preterite, *I have lifted.* Fabritius, Fry, Street, Hengstenberg and Alexander prefer the present tense, I *lift* or *raise.* See Introduction, § 6. Venema, Piscator, Amesius, Tremellius and Junius and Tholuck make the whole verse a question, *Shall I lift up?* etc. Hengstenberg and Alexander make the words, *Whence cometh my help,* interrogative. The word rendered *from whence* commonly marks a question. *Hills, mounts* or *mountains.* Some have thought that the reference is to the mountains of the Holy Land generally; but it seems much more natural to understand the elevations of Jerusalem itself, of which Mount Moriah was the most prominent in the eye of a devout Jew. Understanding by *mountains* whatever is great or excellent in the earth, Calvin says: "The meaning of the prophet is abundantly obvious, which is, that although all the helps of the world, even the mightiest, should offer themselves to us, yet we ought not to seek safety anywhere but in God."

2. *My help* cometh *from the Lord, which made heaven and earth. Help,* in vv. 1, 2, the same found in Ps. xx. 2; uniformly rendered. We met the cognate verb in Ps. cxix. 175. We can form no higher conception of ability to give aid to those who need it than when we rightly consider the creative energy, which made *heaven* and *earth.* That power which brought all things out of nothing is competent for any work. Compare Isa. xl. 28.

3. *He will not suffer thy foot to be moved.* Calvin: He will not suffer thee to stumble; Edwards: He will not suffer thy foot to slip. An inspired prayer of this kind has

the force both of a promise and of a prediction.   Hengstenberg: "The sliding of the foot is a frequent description of misfortune." We had the same figure in Ps. xvii. 5; xxxviii. 16; xciv. 18. God is able to succor. He has pledged his word to help. *He that keepeth thee will not slumber. Slumber*, in Ps. lxxvi. 5, the same verb in the preterite is rendered *have slept*. We shall meet it in the next verse. The clause expresses the unceasing watchfulness and perfect care of God over his people.

4. *Behold, he that keepeth Israel shall neither slumber nor sleep.* Elijah suggested to the priests of Baal that their God peradventure slept and must be awaked, 1 Kings xviii. 27. Nor did the heathen mythology forbid the idea of at least occasional stupor and forgetfulness in many of the gods whom they worshipped. But Jehovah, the God of the whole earth and the keeper of Israel, the glory of the true church, never *slumbers* nor *sleeps*. Alexander: "Most interpreters assume a gradation in the meaning of these two verbs, as if one denoted lighter and the other deep sleep; but they differ on the question which is the stronger of the two expressions." We had the latter verb in Ps. iii. 5; iv. 8; xiii. 3; xliv. 23. Either of these verbs without the negative expresses forgetfulness and want of care.

5. *The* LORD *is thy keeper.* *Keeper*, a participle in vv. 3, 4, rendered *he that keepeth*; in v. 7, twice and in v. 8, once the verb is rendered *preserve*, see on Ps. cxix. 4, 8. Jehovah's work is all perfect. His guardian, preserving care is all we need. *The* LORD *is thy shade upon thy right hand.* Here a new figure is used assuring us of protection and defence. We have the same in Ps. xvii. 8; xxxvi. 7; lvii. 1; lxiii. 7, xci. 1, where for *shade* we read *shadow;* though some think the *shade* here referred to is that of a *tree;* others, that of a portable covering. The figure has already been fully explained. To be *at the right hand* is to be at the fit place to grant protection and defence.

6. *The sun shall not smite thee by day, nor the moon by night.* Both in the torrid and temperate zones men are familiar with the dreadful effects of a stroke of the sun, producing in many instant death, in others, a long season of suffering, in others, idiocy. The *smiting of the moon by night* is not of so easy explanation. Some insist that the sole meaning is that cold shall not harm Israel. The moon is said to rule by night, Gen. i. 16. So she is spoken of as controller of all the influences of the night. Compare Gen. xxxi. 40; Jer. xxxvi. 30. But it seems impossible wholly to dismiss the idea of many nations and classes of people that the shining moon sends forth malignant influences, especially in Judea, Egypt and contiguous countries. Even in Scripture we read of *lunatics*, Matt. iv. 24; xvii. 15. And no word is better understood among us than *moonstruck*. Without favoring any superstitious notion, it may be said, that so general a belief of the malign influence of the moon in certain cases, especially among people that have the best opportunities of observation, the wandering tribes, fishermen, etc., can hardly be accounted for on the supposition that it is a mere vulgar error. Yet Clarke says: "I believe the Psalmist simply means, they shall not be injured by *heat* nor *cold;* by a *sun-stroke* by day, nor a *frost-bite* by night." And Hengstenberg says: "Physical secret doctrines are here not in their place, and are nowhere to be found in the Psalms." All that need be asked is that the influence of the moon be as readily recognized as that of the sun.

7. *The* LORD *shall preserve thee from all evil.* Here we have an exposition of the former verse. *Preserve*, see on v. 5, where the participle of this verb is rendered *keeper.* *Evil*, both natural or moral evil. It includes both here. *He shall preserve thy soul.* Both the *life* and the immortal nature of the true Israel are under divine guardianship.

8. *The* LORD *shall preserve thy going out and thy coming in, from this time forth, and even for evermore.* The protection and preservation previously promised are here

said to extend to God's people in all their acts and ways, and in all coming duration, even to the endless ages of eternity. On the phrase *going out and coming in* compare Num. xxvii. 17; Deut. xxviii. 6; 1 Sam. xxix. 6.

DOCTRINAL AND PRACTICAL REMARKS.

1. It is a great thing to be able to give a right direction to our expectations and prayers, v. 1. This is not easily done. Amesius: "In times of straits, we are too much inclined to seek help from those things which cannot aid us." It is a great mercy when God teaches us that there is no help for us in man.

2. Effectual aid comes from God and none else, vv. 1, 2. He is alone all-sufficient. Men and angels, means and instruments, the united powers of earth, and the wisdom of all creatures are as nothing compared with God. We are never safe till, ceasing from man, whose breath is in his nostrils, we look to God alone.

3. Let us carefully study the works of creation, v. 2. They reveal the power and other perfections of God in a manner very important for us to apprehend. Nor is it possible ever to bring the heart so to confide in God as we ought until we have right conceptions of his omnipotence.

4. Let us remember that there is constant danger of our slipping and stumbling in our heavenly course, v. 3. We are very weak in ourselves. It is strange that we are not entirely ruined. But when we remember that God is the hope of his people, the mystery is explained. Almighty arms can hold up the feeblest.

5. The vigilance of Jehovah over his saints is as admirable as it is necessary. Even the sentinel, though he knows the penalty will be death, sometimes falls asleep on his post. But Jehovah never slumbers, vv. 3, 4. His promises are full and unfailing, Gen. xxviii. 15; Deut. xxxii. 10; Isa. xxvii. 3.

6. It ought greatly to humble us to be taught as we are in every part of Scripture that our safety entirely depends upon our having a *keeper*, v. 5. It is very kind and condescending in the Almighty to undertake this office for us!

7. We may rest assured that all the evils which can possibly assail us shall certainly be controlled by the Lord, if we commit our case to him, vv. 6, 7, 8. No ill-fated star, no scorching sun, nor smiting moon, nor spirit infernal, nor human malice can harm those who are kept under the shadow of the Almighty. Horne: "The good man, during his journey through life, shall be under God's protection at all seasons; as Israel in the wilderness was defended from the burning heat of the sun, by the moist and refreshing shadow of the cloud; and secured against the inclement influences of the nocturnal heavens, by the kindly warmth and splendor diffused from the pillar of fire." Although neither the church nor any member thereof has any promise that affliction and temptation shall never come, yet the word of God makes it certain that no believer shall perish therein.

8. This Psalm suggests the vast difference there is between saints and sinners. The former look up to God for help; the latter look down to earth. The saints shall never so stumble as utterly to fall; but sinners shall fall to rise no more. The Lord preserves his people, but he reserves his enemies. What the former undertake issues well. Nothing done by the wicked shall finally prosper. The shade of the righteous is always at their right hand; but the defence of the wicked is departed from them. Though trouble comes to the righteous, yet there is no curse in it. Though good comes to the wicked, yet there is no real blessing in it.

9. Good men must be very unbelieving to make it necessary for the Almighty so often to assure them of his preserving and protecting care, as he does no less than five times in this Psalm, vv. 3, 4, 5, 7, 8.

10. The eternal salvation of the righteous is certain, vv. 7, 8. God knows how and has a mind to deliver them from snares, plots, guilt, sin, perils at home and perils abroad, from death and hell.

PSALM CXXII.

A Song of degrees of David.

1 I was glad when they said unto me, Let us go into the house of the LORD.
2 Our feet shall stand within thy gates, O Jerusalem.
3 Jerusalem is builded as a city that is compact together:
4 Whither the tribes go up, the tribes of the LORD, unto the testimony of Israel, to give thanks unto the name of the LORD.
5 For there are set thrones of judgment, the thrones of the house of David.
6 Pray for the peace of Jerusalem: they shall prosper that love thee.
7 Peace be within thy walls, *and* prosperity within thy palaces.
8 For my brethren and companions' sakes, I will now say, Peace *be* within thee.
9 Because of the house of the LORD our God I will seek thy good.

ON the title see on titles of Psalms iii. cxx. There is no reason for doubting the Davidic authorship. The internal evidence confirms the assertion of the title. If the Psalm had a historic occasion, it was probably that of the removal of the ark to Jerusalem. Jebb notices a remarkable play upon words in eight or nine instances in the Hebrew of this Psalm. Venema: "The scope of this Psalm is to confirm the people in the hope of a perpetual temple and of the perpetual kingdom of David, and to prepare and excite them to take Jerusalem as the seat of the kingly authority and of religion, to seek to promote its peace and prosperity, and gladly to observe God's worship there." Scott dates it B. C. 1043; Clarke, B. C. about 536. Of course he does not regard David as the author. The names of the Most High found in it are *Jehovah* LORD, *Jah* LORD and *Elohim God*, on which see on Ps. i. 2; introduction to Ps. lxviii.; and on Ps. iii. 2.

1. *I was glad when they said unto me, Let us go into the house of the* LORD. Literally, I was glad in those saying to me, To the house of Jehovah we will go. The first verb is in the preterite; the last, in the future. In announcing their pious purpose these worshippers invite others to join with them. Hengstenberg thinks Isaiah (ii. 3) illustrates the latter clause of this verse. Alexander thinks Isaiah founds that verse on the words of David. Calvin thinks that the prophet here expresses his joy at finding the people hearty and united in their purpose to obey the heavenly oracle fixing Jerusalem as the seat of the theocracy and of the national worship. But it is one of the excellences of Scripture that it so well expresses the sentiments of the godly from age to age.

2. *Our feet shall stand within thy gates, O Jerusalem;* literally, *have been standing.* The best explanation is that of Tholuck, who thinks the longing mind of the pilgrim overleaps the intermediate space, and he sees himself already within the gates of the holy city. After an Israelite had once been there, the preterite form of the verb would convey this idea, I have been in Jerusalem, and I will, by God's grace, be there again. It will weaken the force of this Psalm, if we forget that Jerusalem was a type of the true church of Christ and also of the heavenly state.

3. *Jerusalem is builded as a city that is compact together.* Calvin and Jebb: Jeru-

salem is built as a city, compact in itself together; Hengstenberg: Jerusalem, thou builded, as a city which is bound together. Hammond thinks the verse has its historic exposition in 1 Chron. xi. 7, 8, "And David dwelt in the castle . . . and he built the city round about, even from Millo round about, and Joab repaired the rest of the city." As a type of the church and of heaven this verse has great force and beauty. On the word Jerusalem which occurs thrice in this Psalm see on Ps. li. 18; cii. 21. The word Jerusalem means *the possession of peace,* or *the vision of peace.* Its most ancient name was Salem, which means *peace.* This was the city,

4. *Whither the tribes go up, the tribes of the* LORD, *unto the testimony of Israel, to give thanks unto the name of the* LORD. The first word rendered LORD is *Jah;* the second, *Jehovah.* The *tribes* would not thus have been spoken of in a popular song at any time after the beginning of the reign of Rehoboam, when they ceased their united festivals in Jerusalem, enjoined in the law,. Ex. xxiii. 17; xxxiv. 23; Deut. xvi. 16. *Testimony,* the word usually so rendered, as one of the names given to the ark, Ex. xvi. 34; xxv. 16. It is also a name given to the law, Ex. xxxi. 18; xxxii. 15. See on Ps. xix. 7; on title of Ps. lx.; and introduction to Ps. cxix., No. 2. Instead of *unto the testimony of Israel,* Calvin reads for a testimony to Israel; Edwards, according to an injunction upon Israel; Hengstenberg, the ordinance for Israel; Alexander, (as) a testimony to Israel; Walford, according to the institution of Israel; French and Skinner, according to the testimony given unto Israel. The meaning of the phrase may be either: 1. That they went up at God's requirement; or, 2. That they went up to the city where the testimony of the Lord was. The whole verse declares Jerusalem to be the city of the solemnities of Israel. Because all right worship has in it *the giving of thanks,* therefore this is spoken of in this verse as the chief object of the three annual festivals.

5. *For there are set thrones of judgment, the thrones of the house of David.* *Thrones,* elsewhere *seats.* The plural form denotes the amplitude of the justice administered. There may be an allusion also to the perpetuity of the kingdom of David. Thus both the priestly and kingly offices of Messias are in vv. 4, 5, brought to our notice. The temple on Mount Moriah kept alive among the people thoughts respecting the atonement to be made; and the royal authority of David and his successors pointed to the kingdom of Christ.

6. *Pray for the peace of Jerusalem: they shall prosper that love thee.* *Peace,* in Ex. xviii. 7, and elsewhere, *welfare;* in Ps. xxxv. 27, *prosperity.* In asking for the peace of the Holy City, they sought all that could make it great. The verb rendered *shall prosper* in the second clause is cognate to the noun rendered *peace.* So we might read: They shall have peace that love thee. Both the noun and the verb have evident allusion to the word Jerusalem. Some prefer however to read, May those prosper that love thee. There is no objection to this, as an inspired wish is itself a prediction.

7. *Peace be within thy walls,* and *prosperity within thy palaces.* So closely are peace and prosperity united, in states and churches, that the two words are used interchangeably; that rendered *peace* in this verse being masculine, and that, *prosperity,* feminine; but each word is rendered both ways. The *walls* of the Holy City quite encompassed it. This would justify the plural form without referring to the statement of Josephus that there were three ranges of walls surrounding the city; but the fact is that the Hebrew is in the singular, *wall, bulwark, rampart*—a term expressing the defences of the city; while *palaces* or courts point to the internal improvements of Jerusalem, particularly her public buildings; see on Ps. xlviii. 3, 13. The verse is a prayer that in all respects the Holy City may have the divine blessing.

8. *For my brethren and companions' sakes I will now say, Peace be within thee.* The whole force of the verse cannot be understood without remembering what has been

already stated that Jerusalem was a type of the church both in her militant and triumphant state. It was not mere patriotism or national spirit that stirred up the prophet thus to pray:

9. *Because of the house of the* LORD *our God, I will seek thy good.* Before the sanctuary was in Jerusalem, it was to the pious Jew not half so important as Shiloh; but when it became the seat of the national worship, his interest in it was transcendent. By engaging to seek *her good*, he promised to do all in his power to advance her glory.

DOCTRINAL AND PRACTICAL REMARKS.

1. Alacrity in the worship of God and promptness in acts of devotion are essential marks of true piety, v. 1. If a converted man, who did not love the worship of God could be found, he would be such a monster as the world has never seen. "It is matter of the highest joy to the pious when they see religion flourishing." Henry: "They that rejoice in God will rejoice in calls and opportunities to wait upon him." Our zeal in the worship of God under the gospel ought to be even more fervent than that of the Jews under the old dispensation, inasmuch as the shadows have fled away, and we have the very image of the things promised.

2. It is not enough that we worship the Lord secretly, or in our families; we should seek the blessings of public worship, v. 1. Henry: "It is the will of God that we should worship him in concert; that many should join together to wait upon him in public ordinances." The liberty of public religious assemblies is of prime importance.

3. Under the gospel any place, where two or three are met together in the name of Christ, is a church, and so we need not take long journeys to the house of God. Luther: "Our Jerusalem is the church, and our temple is Christ. Wheresoever Christ is preached, and the sacraments are duly administered, there we are sure God dwells; and there is our temple, our tabernacle, our cherubim, and our mercy-seat; for there God is present with us by his word."

4. It is a great blessing to enjoy a fit and public place for the joint worship of believers; and when in his mercy God grants it, it should be most thankfully received and earnestly used for his glory and our good. *Our feet shall stand within thy gates,* v. 2.

5. It matters not how wicked or degraded a place may have been in former times, when it is sanctified to the use and service of God, it becomes honorable. Jerusalem was formerly Jebus—a place where the Jebusites committed their abominations, and where were all the miseries of those who hasten after another God. But now, since it is devoted to God's service, it is a city—*compact together, the joy of the whole earth,* v. 3.

6. The great end and aim of religious assemblies are not merely the promotion of decency and morality among men, but obedience to the command of God and the due celebration of his worship, of which thanksgiving is an important part, v. 4.

7. It is an unspeakable blessing to a nation or even to the smallest community to have justice regularly administered according to stable laws, v. 5. Where the *seat of judgment* is not, and every man becomes a law to himself, the evils are sad indeed.

8. It is a matter of great importance that we should be rightly affected towards the kingly office of Christ, prefigured by the throne of the house of David, v. 5. Compare Luke i. 32; Matt. xix. 28. He, who does not take Christ as King, has never taken him as prophet or priest. Zion has no greater beauty than the crown of her monarch.

9. It is a duty binding on all the friends of God to seek the union and concord of society, and especially of the church of Christ, v. 6. As the existence of factions

in Jerusalem always manifested a wretched state of society, so is it in the house of God. Many seem to have forgotten that strife, and envying, and wrath, and railings, and doting about questions are always put down among the works of the flesh; and that where strife is, there is confusion and every evil work. Scott: "Union and harmony are the ornament and stability of the church on earth."

10. There is a blessing on all who truly love Zion, v. 6. Horne: "Heaven has decreed, that they who contribute their labors, as well as their prayers, to promote so good and so glorious an end shall enjoy its protection, and its blessing shall be upon the work of their hands." If we would order our prayers aright, let us always begin with pleading that the Lord would be pleased to preserve this sacred community. Dickson: "As none can pray for the welfare of the church heartily, except they love her; so none shall love her and seek her welfare, but shall fare the better for it."

11. Let every one ask, How do I feel towards the church of Christ, vv. 6–9. Do I pray for her peace and prosperity? Do I pronounce blessings upon her? How do I prove my love to the church? Do I prefer Jerusalem above my chief joy? In an important sense the church is the pillar and ground of the truth. What are we doing for Zion? Calvin: "Such as are indifferent about her condition are no less cruel than impious." Morison: "As it was in days of old, so it is now; if the world is to be spared, it is for the sake of the church."

12. If the ancient city of Jerusalem, and yet more the poor marred church of Christ on earth have such beauties in the eyes of heaven-born souls, how great must be the attractions of the heavenly Jerusalem! And "with what alacrity should we think of going to the temple above, and how cheerfully should we bear the cross while we live and welcome the stroke of death, in hopes of that immortal crown of glory?"

PSALM CXXIII.

A Song of degrees.

1 Unto thee lift I up mine eyes, O thou that dwellest in the heavens.

2 Behold, as the eyes of servants *look* unto the hand of their masters, *and* as the eyes of a maiden unto the hand of her mistress; so our eyes *wait* upon the LORD our God, until that he have mercy upon us.

3 Have mercy upon us, O LORD, have mercy upon us: for we are exceedingly filled with contempt.

4 Our soul is exceedingly filled with the scorning of those that are at ease, *and* with the contempt of the proud.

ON the title see on title of Ps. cxx. Both the authorship and occasion of this ode are involved in uncertainty. The Syriac ascribes it to David; Fry says that some Hebrew copies do the same. Patrick conjectures that it was composed by some pious person, when the King of Assyria sent Rabshakeh and others to besiege Jerusalem, pouring out contemptuous and blasphemous words against God and his people. According to this view he thinks that it is probably the prayer prepared by Isaiah at the request of Hezekiah, and offered by that king and that prophet. Compare 2 Kings xix. 4; 2 Chron. xxxii. 20; Isa. xxxvii. 4. Calvin: "It is uncertain at what time, or even by what prophet, this Psalm was composed." Edwards: "It is evident this Psalm was composed in the time of great distress; when the Jews were harassed by some haughty and insolent enemies: but who these enemies were is uncertain." Tholuck calls it, "A prayer of the whole nation in a condition of long-continued humiliation." Scott dates it B. C. 1021; Clarke affixes no date, but thinks it is a complaint of the captives in Babylon. The names of the Almighty found in it are *Jehovah* LORD and *Elohim God*, on which see on Ps. i. 2; iii. 2.

1. *Unto thee lift I up mine eyes, O thou that dwellest in the heavens.* In Psalm cxxi. 1, the prophet looks to God as worshipped on the heights of Jerusalem; here, as in the heavens themselves, as his permanent abode, far above the reach and the rage of all his enemies; but able to extend relief to the sufferers in this lower world. Calvin: "These words seem to contain a tacit contrast between the troubled and confused state of this world and God's heavenly kingdom."

2. *Behold, as the eyes of servants* look *unto the hand of their masters, and as the eyes of a maiden unto the hand of her mistress; so our eyes* wait *upon the* LORD *our God, until that he have mercy upon us.* Several constructions are given to this language. One is that the servants and maiden are under chastisement, and are looking to the hand that corrects them. Morison: "As Jewish masters had not only the right to command, but also, in certain given cases to correct, the image here presented to our minds is that of a servant under chastisement, looking to the hand that smites, and at the same time beseeching forgiveness and a return of complacent feeling." Hengstenberg: "The hand of the masters and of the mistress can only mean the *punishing* hand; and the eyes are directed to it in the attitude of entreaty and supplication that the punishment may soon come to an end, and pity be shown to the miserable." With these agree Dodd and Nicolson. Another view is that the servants and maiden are in distress and are looking to their master or mistress for relief from calamities brought on them by others. This view is supported by Calvin and Cresswell. As servants often received great wrongs they looked to their masters for relief and defence. Another view, giving a good sense, is that the servants and maiden are watching the motions of the hand of the master and mistress as by some gesture they intimate their wishes. God's people adhere steadfastly to his service and resolutely study and do his will, come what may. In his letters on Egypt, Savary says: "The slaves, having their hands crossed on their chest, stand silently at the end of the hall. *With their eyes fastened on their Master,* they seek to anticipate his every wish." Diodati thinks that these servants look to their superiors either to be defended by them, or to receive some benefit from them. Henry thinks they look 1, to the Master's directing hand: 2, to his supplying hand; 3, to his assisting hand; 4, to his protecting hand; 5, to his correcting hand. Alexander: "Perhaps all these explanations err in being too specific, and the sense of the comparison is simply that they look with deference and trust to the superior power which controls them." It well coincides with the scope of the passage to represent the servants as desirous of learning the will and of securing the aid of superiors.

3. *Have mercy upon us, O* LORD, *have mercy upon us: for we are exceedingly filled with contempt. Have mercy,* as in Ps. li. 1. The repetition of the prayer shows its earnestness. *Exceedingly, greatly, often;* the same as in v. 4. *Filled,* when used in a good sense *satisfied;* the same as in v. 4. *Contempt, despite,* see on Ps. xxxi. 18; cxix. 22.

4. *Our soul is exceedingly filled with the scorning of those that are at ease,* and *with the contempt of the proud.* Calvin: Our soul is in itself greatly cloyed with the mockery of men who are rich, and with the contempt of the proud; Edwards: We are loaded to an intolerable degree with the scoffs of the prosperous, and the contempt of the proud. *Exceedingly, filled,* and *contempt,* the same as in v. 3. *Scorning,* always so,

scorn, or *derision.* *Those that are at ease* are those who have little or no concern about their own state and no interest in the affairs of others. *Proud, haughty, arrogant.*

DOCTRINAL AND PRACTICAL REMARKS.

1. As long as life lasts, it is never amiss to look to God for help and guidance, v. 1. He who permits our distresses to come upon us, can take them away, or sustain us under them, and bring good out of them. The Most High is not limited in wisdom, power, or goodness, but has all perfection. Nor does he scorn our low estate, but greatly pities us. Man may rage like a wild beast against us, but God is as gentle as he is glorious.

2. Let us not forget that we are servants of God, and not our own masters, v. 2. Our business is to please him, not ourselves; to serve him, not ourselves; to do his will, not our own; to rely on his protection, not on an arm of flesh. Tholuck: "While we look to human hands for help, hope and fear alternate." Man is weak, foolish, wicked. God is strong, wise, holy.

3. It is wise in us and obligatory on us to persevere in faith and prayer *until the Lord have mercy upon us,* v. 2. It is the bane of our lives that we so easily let go our hold on God and on his promises.

4. Among sinners, even penitent sinners, the cry for mercy and the plea of grace are never out of order. As long as life lasts we never make such progress as to get beyond the prayer of the publican. 'Whatever the troubles of the church are, God's mercy is a sovereign remedy.'

5. It is a blessed thing that in our severest trials brought on us by our fellow-creatures, we can appeal from man to God, from the scorning and contempt of mortals to the mercy and grace of the King eternal, immortal and invisible. Were it otherwise, our case would be sad indeed.

6. It might well set us firmly against all the arts of scorning and contempt, when we see the wicked use made of them by unbelieving, unreasonable and impious men, vv. 3, 4. They used such weapons against our Lord himself. Calvin: "When insult is added to wrongs, there is nothing which inflicts a deeper wound upon well constituted minds." Nicolson: "The sick lion in the fable found it extremely galling to be kicked by the *foot* of an *ass.*" Henry: "Scorning and contempt have been, and are, and are likely to be, the lot of God's people in this world." If called to this kind of suffering, let us more than ever lift up our eyes to him that dwelleth in the heavens. Compare James v. 7–11. It is impossible that we can carry so heavy a burden by mere human strength.

7. Let us be specially watchful against carnal security and arrogance. No tempers are more hostile to the true Christian spirit, and there is a consanguinity between these sins, indeed between all the vices of the heart. Carnal men *at ease* are sure to be *proud,* v. 4.

PSALM CXXIV.

A Song of degrees of David.

1 If *it had* not *been* the LORD who was on our side, now may Israel say;

2 If *it had* not *been* the LORD who was on our side, when men rose up against us:

3 Then they had swallowed us up quick, when their wrath was kindled against us:

4 Then the waters had overwhelmed us, the stream had gone over our soul:

5 Then the proud waters had gone over our soul.

6 Blessed *be* the LORD, who hath not given us *as* a prey to their teeth.

7 Our soul is escaped as a bird out of the snare of the fowlers: the snare is broken, and we are escaped.

8 Our help *is* in the name of the LORD, who made heaven and earth.

ON the title see on titles of Psalms iii. cxx. David is given as author by the title, Calvin, Diodati, Dodd, Henry, Morison and Hengstenberg; though the Septuagint, Syriac, Arabic, Ethiopic and Vulgate omit that part of the inscription; and Clarke expresses doubt whether it ought to be in the text. Although occasions are not wanting in the life of David suited to this particular ode, yet it is not easy, perhaps not possible to determine to what part of his history it specially refers. Scott: "It may, however, be applied to any season of special danger or distress to the church, or to believers, from which they have been beyond expectation rescued." Scott dates it B. C. 1040; Clarke, B. C. about 510. The only name of the Most High found in it is *Jehovah* LORD, on which see on Ps. i. 2.

1. *If* it had *not* been *the* LORD *who was on our side, now may Israel say.* Calvin: But for Jehovah who was on our side, may Israel now say; Edwards: Had not Jehovah been on our side, Israel may now say. The reader will observe that several words are supplied by our translators. These doubtless give the sense; but are not necessary to our apprehension of the idea. Alexander: "The form of speech is tantamount to saying, What if the Lord had not been for us?—leaving the answer to the imagination of the reader."

2. *If* it had *not* been *the* LORD *who was on our side, when men rose up against us.* As in English so in Hebrew, the first clause is identical with the first clause of v. 1. *When men rose,* literally, *in the rising of man,* indicating the hostility, not merely of some few men or of some particular tribe, but of mankind generally. This corresponds with the history of the church in all ages. If the earth has ever helped the woman, it was not done willingly, until divine grace had sanctified the fallen nature of man; so that if Jehovah had not been the help of his people, they all might say:

3. *Then they had swallowed us up quick, when their wrath was kindled against us.* *Swallowed,* the same verb so rendered in Ps. xxi. 9; lxix. 15; cvi. 17; in Ps. lv. 9, *destroy;* in Prov. xix. 28, *devour.* *Quick,* not an adverb, *quickly,* but an adjective, *alive.* As greedy monsters both of the land and of the deep sometimes swallow their food before the life is out of it, so would the enemies of the church have destroyed her as in a moment, but for divine interposition. They seemed to have the power, and their violence was sufficiently aroused to make them fierce and cruel. *Their wrath was kindled.* *Then, at that time.* A thousandth part of the deadly hostility, which has been manifested against the church of God, would have exterminated any other institution ever upon earth.

4. *Then the waters had overwhelmed us, the stream had gone over our soul.*

5. *Then the proud waters had gone over our soul.* The figure expressive of destruction is in these verses different from that of the preceding. Here it is by a deluge rising above all barriers, and as it were with insolence defying all resistance overwhelming us. In both verses, *then* is the same as in v. 3. As the proud walk with a high head and do not easily yield to any opposition, so the waters are spoken of as *proud.* There is a gradation in the figures of these verses, *the waters,* next *the stream, the proud waters.* The assault had been truly dreadful, imperilling the *life* and the *soul* of God's people.

6. *Blessed be the* LORD, *who hath not given us as a prey to their teeth.* *Blessed,* the usual word for a benediction, see on Ps. v. 12. *Prey,* commonly so rendered; in Ps.

cxi. 5, *meat*. This verse goes to confirm the interpretation of v. 3, as referring to voracious monsters and not to the manner of destroying Korah and his company.

7. *Our soul is escaped as a bird out of the snare of the fowlers: the snare is broken, and we are escaped.* *Bird*, in Ps. cii. 7, *sparrow*. Anderson: "As the imagery goes on, it becomes the more beautiful. Pleasing and tender ideas are associated with the escape of an innocent bird from the snares which the art and cruelty of man had contrived, to deprive it of life, or rob it of liberty." Calvin: "The amount is, that the people of God, feeble, without counsel, and destitute of aid, had not only to deal with blood-thirsty and furious beasts, but were also ensnared by bird-nets and stratagems, so that being greatly inferior to their enemies as well in policy as in open force, they were beset by many deaths. From this it may be easily gathered that they were miraculously preserved." When God chooses he can, not only rescue his people at the time, but put it beyond the power of his enemies to do them further injury. *The snare is broken.*

8. *Our help is in the name of the* LORD *who made heaven and earth.* *Help*, usually so rendered, as in Ps. xx. 2; cxxi. 1, 2. *Name* of Jehovah, *i. e.*, Jehovah himself. On the latter clause of the verse see on Ps. cxv. 15; cxxi. 2, where we have the same words.

DOCTRINAL AND PRACTICAL REMARKS.

1. We cannot too often remember that none but God can save us from sins, or foes, or perils; and that he can certainly do for us all that our case requires, vv. 1, 2. He that has God for his friend and portion lacks nothing whatever.

2. We need not be surprised when men rise up against us in great numbers and with great violence, v. 2. It has often been so before. 'Man is a wolf to man.' "Even those in the church sometimes devour each other, and Christian men suffer their vindictive passions for a while to overcome their principles, an occasion for repentance and regret, and an injury to the cause of religion." Scott: "The church of God, in every age, has been opposed by multitudes of powerful, enraged, cruel enemies."

3. The power of the wicked is sometimes tremendous, and their violence frightful, v. 3. They have things very much their own way and their own way is very malignant. Sin, death and hell, men and devils do sometimes strangely combine, and for a while God seems to let them alone.

4. If the safety of the righteous depended on appearances, or on their inherent energies, or on the weakness or fewness of their adversaries, they would all perish, vv. 4, 5. In God's almightiness is the defence of all saints. His grace is all-sufficient. He can put a bridle in the mouth or a hook in the nose of the fiercest. He that made the Red sea walls, and holds the water of the ocean in the hollow of his hand, can control the progress of ungodly men. Blessed is he who is not afraid of the terrors of the wicked. Horne: "The devout Christian, whom in perilous times, and towards the close of life a gracious Providence has thrown ashore in some sequestered corner, from whence he views those secular tumults with which he hath no further concern, is perhaps arrived at the next degree of happiness to that of just spirits made perfect."

5. The wicked can use against God's people weapons which the latter dare not employ against their adversaries, such as slander, reviling, craft and deceit, v. 6. The world thinks it a fine thing to spread snares for the feet of the righteous; but the weapons of the church's warfare are not carnal. God's cause needs not the help of man's intrigues.

6. That man may well doubt his own piety, who has no heart for a grateful and

devout commemoration of deliverances wrought for him by the providence and Spirit of God. If we are saved from ruin in any shape, it is wholly by a power outside of ourselves. " Greater is he that is in us, than he that is in the world." Omnipotence can break any snare. It is a shame to us that we so soon and so easily forget the deliverances wrought for us, yea, and the very perils from which we have been saved. Amesius: "The goodness of God in delivering us should never be given over to oblivion, but always commemorated with praise."

7. How uniform is history. It tells the same story from age to age—the story of man's weakness and vileness, and of God's lovingkindness and tender compassions.

8. The help of all the righteous is in the name of the Lord who made heaven and earth, v. 8. This is not a discouraging but a necessary truth. Every act of the divine care towards us should lead us so to confess. The amazing deliverances wrought by God for his chosen people both before and after their conversion demand loud and perpetual acknowledgments. The truly good man feels that he shall not be done blessing God

> While life or thought or being last,
> Or immortality endures.

PSALM CXXV.

A Song of degrees.

1 They that trust in the LORD *shall be* as mount Zion, *which* cannot be removed, *but* abideth for ever.

2 *As* the mountains *are* round about Jerusalem, so the LORD *is* round about his people from henceforth even for ever.

3 For the rod of the wicked shall not rest upon the lot of the righteous; lest the righteous put forth their hands unto iniquity.

4 Do good, O LORD, unto *those that be* good, and to *them that are* upright in their hearts.

5 As for such as turn aside unto their crooked ways, the LORD shall lead them forth with the workers of iniquity: *but* peace *shall be* upon Israel.

ON the title see above on title of Psalm cxx. Scott fixes the date of this Psalm as probably B. C. about 710 years; Clarke, B. C. about 445; some others as early as the days of David. It must be admitted that neither of these views can be established. The last was more favored formerly than of late. Clarke thinks this ode may have had its occasion in the opposition of Sanballat and his associates; Scott, in the invasion of Sennacherib; others, in various events in the life of David. But all this is conjecture. Hardly any Psalm less requires an occasion to give full force to its several clauses. The only name of God found in it is *Jehovah* LORD, on which see on Ps. i. 2.

1. *They that trust in the* LORD *shall be* as *Mount Zion, which cannot be removed*, but *abideth for ever*. Edwards: Those that trust in Jehovah are like mount Zion, which cannot be moved, but continues fixed for ever; Fry: They that trust in the Lord are as a mountain: Zion is not moved, Jerusalem abideth for ever; Hengstenberg: Those who trust in the Lord are as Mount Zion, which moves not, stands for ever; Doway, following some ancient versions: They that trust in the Lord shall be as mount Sion: he shall not be moved for ever that dwelleth in Jerusalem. None of these is better than the authorized version; though each of them gives the leading idea. To *trust in the Lord* is a favorite method of describing a true Israelite. *Re-*

moved, or *moved*, as in Ps. x. 6. *Abideth, dwelleth, sitteth, tarryeth*, hath a fixed abode. What is here said of believers in general is true of each of them. They have stability and shall ever have it because they confide in Jehovah.

2. As *the mountains* are *round about Jerusalem, so the Lord* is *round about his people from henceforth even for ever.* So effectually was Jerusalem surrounded by mountains, that one prophet speaks of it as a *caldron*, Ezek. xi. 3. These mountains stood there from age to age. They stand there still. Yet hostile armies have often crossed them ; and to this day Jerusalem is trodden down of the Gentiles. But Jehovah is a bulwark and a defence that has never failed his people. What the mountains seemed to be, the Lord is, an impregnable wall to his true *people*, who are not faithless but believing, sincere not hypocritical. *From henceforth even for ever*, literally, from now and unto eternity.

3. *For the rod of the wicked shall not rest upon the lot of the righteous lest the righteous put forth their hands unto iniquity. Rod*, also *sceptre, tribe*, Ps. xlv. 6 ; lxxviii. 67, 68. See on Ps. ii. 9 ; xxiii. 4. Here the word must mean either the rod of chastisement, or anger, whereby the *wicked* punished God's people, or the sceptre of political power, which as it was wielded by the *wicked* and in a wicked way produced great affliction, Pr. xxviii. 12 ; xxix. 2. These two meanings of the word are here coincident. *Rest*, the rod of the wicked may fall on God's people, but it shall not continue to distress them. It shall be broken, Isa. xiv. 5. *Lot*, always so rendered. As the Israelites received their portions in the land by *lot*, so *lot* and *portion* came to signify much the same thing. Compare Ps. xvi. 5 ; Jer. xiii. 25, where we have both words. *Righteous*, in both cases plural, the just, those who *trust in the Lord*. To *put forth the hand to iniquity* is to meddle with it, partake in it, or touch it, Col. ii. 21. There is a point beyond which the spirits of men would fail. The Almighty knows this, frames his providence and administers his grace accordingly, Ps. ciii. 14. Tholuck : "The noncontinuance of the rod of the wicked is the consolation of the Psalmist." The rendering of the church of England misleads the reader : For the rod of the ungodly cometh not unto the lot of the righteous. It does come, but it does not stay.

4. *Do good*, O Lord, *unto* those that be *good, and to* them that are *upright in their hearts.* Like the English so the Hebrew plays upon the word *good*. The *upright* are the righteous in v. 3, those who *trust in the Lord* in v. 1. They are far removed from hypocrisy. Their virtue and piety are seated *in their hearts*. The wicked are tortuous. But God's people are *straight, right*, see on Ps. vii. 10.

5. *As for such as turn aside unto their crooked ways, the* LORD *shall lead them forth with the workers of iniquity. Crooked ways*, in Judges v. 6, *byways*. The word occurs nowhere else. It is an adjective, but so clearly requires the word *ways* to complete the sense, that it is not even put in italics. Those who *turn aside to crooked ways* are themselves *doers of iniquity. To be led forth with* such is to be conducted to punishment or execution with them. Chaldee : He shall lead them into hell. The verb is the causative form of the verb *to walk, to go ;* Calvin : "The meaning is, God does not always connive at the wickedness of those who, while boasting of a hollow and counterfeit profession, wander hither and thither according to their own lust or even corrupt the simple, and draw them into the same excess of sinning with themselves." But *peace* shall be *upon Israel*, literally, *peace upon Israel, i. e.*, peace be upon Israel. The force of such a phrase is well expressed by the future, as such an inspired petition is itself a sure prediction. The contrast is between the final punishment of the wicked, and the final prosperity of the righteous. When God shall weigh them in the balance of eternal justice, as the former rises, the latter must sink. The everlasting peace of the saints depends upon the total overthrow of the incorrigibly wicked.

DOCTRINAL AND PRACTICAL REMARKS.

1. As the effect cannot be greater than the cause, so the Scriptures wisely mention adequate grounds of assurance and confidence to all the saints, vv. 1, 2. Because God is mighty, the weakest of his people are strong; because he is unchangeable those of his people most resembling a reed shaken with the wind are stable as Mount Zion.

2. But the saints should never forget that their strength is not in themselves, vv. 1, 2. Natural talents and advantages are nothing if God forsake us, Isa. xl. 30, 31.

3. Whatever happens, let us trust in the Lord and never question either his power or faithfulness, v. 1. We are slow of heart unqualifiedly to confide. Luther: "It is much easier to learn than to believe that we who have by us the word of God and receive it, are surrounded with divine aid. If we were surrounded by walls of steel and fire, we should feel secure and defy the devil. But the property of faith is not to be proud of what the eye sees, but to rely on what the word reveals." And we must carefully distinguish between presumptuous confidence and the boldness which springs from faith unfeigned. Henry: "All that deal with God must deal upon trust, and he will give comfort to those only who give credit to him, and make it to appear they do so, by quitting other confidences and venturing to the utmost for God."

4. The protection of the saints cannot fail, because it is from the Lord, v. 2. Morison: "His perfections are ever in active exercise for their good, and while this sleepless energy is exerted on their behalf neither death nor hell can prevail against them;" Clarke: "He is *above, beneath, around* them; *and while they keep within it,* their fortress is impregnable, and they can suffer no evil."

5. Yet let us not misinterpret the promises of God. He has not engaged that his people shall not be assaulted, persecuted, tempted or sorely tried. Trouble will come, if not in one shape yet in another. One of the saddest forms is when those in power use it to the injury of the righteous. Such has often been the case, v. 8.

6. But let us never forget that the Lord is the avenger of all such, and that though the wicked may press his people hard for a season, yet they cannot destroy them. God is round about them, vv. 2, 3. Compare Esther vi. 13.

7. Let us not be cast down at conflicts in the spirit. The warfare with corruption in the heart shall not last always. No man ever perished who lived and died fighting against sin. Fight on, Christian hero. The victory shall be thine at last. Satan shall not always oppress thy spirit. By and by the Master will say, Come up higher, and the days of thy mourning shall be ended.

8. Much good does the Lord do to his own people, v. 4. He is good even to his enemies, to the unkind and the unthankful, though they are not in covenant with him. But to his own people he gives pardon, acceptance, adoption, renewal, strength, wisdom, increase of grace, eternal life and blessings which finite creatures shall not even in the ages of eternity be able duly to estimate. Luther: "The end of the poor flock of God, even though the church be proved and tried by a thousand fires and deaths, though it appear a thousand times over to be oppressed, destroyed and extirpated, is—eternal life, eternal consolation, eternal glory!"

9. But the Scriptures carefully discriminate and tell us who shall receive eternal mercies from God. Such are called *Israel* for their might in prayer. They *trust in the Lord.* They are *stable* in their course. They are *good.* They are *upright.* They trust not only sometimes but at all times, even in the darkest hour. They have a great dread of sin. Their fear of apostasy is a great means of preservation from it.

10. On the other hand the enemies of God are as clearly marked out. They are the *wicked.* They wield power for selfish ends. Their ways are crooked. They are

workers of iniquity. 'They shift from one pursuit to another, and turn hither and thither to deceive; they wind about a thousand ways, to conceal their base intentions, to accomplish their iniquitous projects or to escape the punishment of their crimes.'

11. The end of such cannot but be dreadful, v. 5. Their judgment now of a long time lingereth not, and their damnation slumbereth not. As infamous crimes among men are upon conviction terribly punished on a set day and in public, so shall the wicked be *led forth* to execution. Henry: "The doom of those who turn aside to those crooked ways, out of the right way, will be the same with theirs who have all along walked in them; nay, and more grievous, for if any place in hell be hotter than another, that shall be the portion of hypocrites and apostates."

12. It should greatly alarm the wicked to remember that the certainty of the happiness of the saints depends upon the certainty of the overthrow of sinners, v. 5.

13. Come what will, let the righteous joy in God, who has published, "Peace, peace to him that is far off, and to him that is near; and I will heal him," Isa. lvii. 19. Because God is true, and because he is just, and because his people pray for it, *peace shall be upon Israel* forever.

PSALM CXXVI.

A Song of degrees.

1 When the LORD turned again the captivity of Zion, we were like them that dream.

2 Then was our mouth filled with laughter, and our tongue with singing: then said they among the heathen, The LORD hath done great things for them.

3 The LORD hath done great things for us; *whereof* we are glad.

4 Turn again our captivity, O LORD, as the streams in the south.

5 They that sow in tears shall reap in joy.

6 He that goeth forth and weepeth, bearing precious seed, shall doubtless come again with rejoicing, bringing his sheaves *with him*.

ON the title see on title of Psalm cxx. Scott dates this Psalm B. C. 530; Clarke, B. C. about 515. It was most probably written at a late period of Jewish history. If so, the occasion of its composition is found in the decrees and measures for the restoration from Babylon. The Syriac ascribes it to Haggai and Zechariah; others, to Ezra. Luther: "Whether it was written after the captivity, or before it, as a prophecy to comfort the Jews with the hope of deliverance, and that they should not despair, is uncertain." Whatever was its authorship, or the occasion of its composition, it was designed for the edification of the church in all coming time. Hengstenberg: "The sacred Psalmists were deeply impressed with the conviction that they sang for the church of all ages." The only name of God here found is *Jehovah* LORD, on which see on Psalm i. 2.

1. *When the* LORD *turned again the captivity of Zion, we were like them that dream.* Fry puts the verbs of this verse in the present tense. The Chaldee, Syriac and Arabic use the future. But the Septuagint, Ethiopic, Vulgate, Doway, church of England, Calvin, Fabritius, Venema, Amesius, Piscator, Tremellius and Junius, Edwards, Jebb, Street, Hengstenberg and Alexander, like the authorized version, have the preterite. The meaning of the first clause is, When the Lord brought back the captives. The word *here* rendered captivity is not the same as in v. 4. This word means *return*. Hengstenberg and Alexander render it *the turning*. Whether

it be *the return* or *the captivity*, it may be taken for *those returning*, or for *the captives*. The phrase *turn captivity* does not necessarily express more than relief from sore distress (Ps. xiv. 7; liii. 6; lxxxv. 1;) though here it evidently refers to release from the captivity of Babylon. Although that event had been predicted and the time for it fixed by prophecy (Jer. xxv. 12; xxix. 10;) yet so deeply had the iron gone into their souls, so insolent and cruel had their oppressors become; and so little were appearances in their favor, that when God broke their bondage and set them free, the Israelites knew not how to credit the announcement; they were incredulous; the news was too good to be believed. Compare Gen. xlv. 26; Luke xxiv. 41; Acts xii. 9, 14.

2. *Then was our mouth filled with laughter, and our tongue with singing.* *Mouth* and *tongue* are parallel; so also are *laughter* and *singing*. The clause describes the abundant joy of the released captives. Yet was it not mirth accompanied by vain noise; but rather by tears of penitence and gratitude, Jer. l. 4, 5. They ceased not to marvel that the worshippers of the sun should show them such unsolicited kindness, seeing that they were generally hated and despised of all the Gentiles. Nor could the Chaldeans and others repress their wonder: *Then said they among the heathen, The* LORD *hath done great things for them.* When Jehovah so acts as to call forth the admiration of the very heathen, surely his people should not keep silence, but take up the song:

3. *The* LORD *hath done great things for us; whereof we are glad.* They were glad. How could it be otherwise? The conquest of Babylon by the Persians had effected a total revolution and with the happiest results to Israel.

4. *Turn again our captivity, O* LORD, *as the streams in the south.* Chaldee: Turn, O LORD, our captivity, as the earth is changed when in time of dearth the bursting out of the waters breaks forth; Edwards: Bring back our captive brethren, Jehovah, as the torrents in the south; Street: Jehovah hath restored us from our captivity, as he restoreth the torrents in the dry country; Walford: Bring back *all* our captives, O Jehovah, like the streams of the south. In explanation three remarks are offered: 1. Whether we read *south* or *dry place* will not alter the sense, as the country, in the southern portions of Palestine, as well as in Arabia, is subject to long-continued heat, which dries up the rivers. When the abundant periodical rains come, the streams again swell, the thirsty soil is refreshed, and the land is again covered with green. 2. There were several decrees made by the conquerors of Babylon and their successors respecting the return of the Jews to the holy land. The first of these seems to have released all the captives, and to have awakened a spirit of inquiry, but to have sent comparatively few of the Jews to the holy land. Those, who first returned, seeing their own weakness, and remembering the privations of their brethren, greatly desired their return. So the word *captivity* is best taken for *captives*, and the meaning is, Bring back our captive brethren. 3. There is no inconsistency between verses 1 and 4, the former speaking of the release of the captives and of their partial restoration; the latter, of their general and full return, so as to swell the population like the streams in the rainy season.

5. *They that sow in tears shall reap in joy.* Of no class of figures of speech are the writers of both Testaments more fond than of those drawn from husbandry, and particularly from sowing and reaping. This verse sounds much like a proverb. It suits all times and occupations. It is fulfilled in nature, in social life, in political affairs, and in the experience of God's people, Heb. xii. 11. "Except a corn of wheat fall into the ground and die, it abideth alone: but if it die, it bringeth forth much fruit," John xii. 24 Alexander: "The figures are natural and common ones for means and end, or for the beginning and issue of any undertaking." The figure may have force

from the supposition that grain was scarce and bread hard to get; yet what could the husbandman do but take part or most of what he had and bury it in the ground, not certainly knowing that he would ever get any return, but confiding in the general arrangement of providence that he that sows shall reap?

6. *He that goeth forth and weepeth, bearing precious seed, shall doubtless come again with rejoicing, bringing his sheaves* with him.   Chaldee: Going he shall go with weeping, bearing a draft of seed corn; coming he shall come with singing of hymns when he shall bring back his sheaves; Arabic: They shall go going forth full of weeping, bearing their seeds; but returning they shall come with exultation bearing their fruits. Hallelujah.   Variations, not dissimilar to the above, are found in other translations. *Precious*, found only here and in Job xxviii. 18, where it is rendered *price*.   Our translators and others seem to have thought that the meaning was, the seed is very valuable, first perhaps because of its scarcity, and then because of its productiveness But not a few suppose that the word rendered precious designates the vessel or sack, in which the seed is carried by the sower.   So Abenezra, the margin and Street.   But as the word rendered *precious* is cognate to the verb rendered *to draw out* or *scatter*, some prefer to render it *a drawing forth of seed, carrying seed, sowing seed*.   If this Psalm specially refers to the restoration of the Jews, it quite falls in with the historic account given in Ezra vi. 22; Neh. xii. 43.

DOCTRINAL AND PRACTICAL REMARKS.

1. God's true servants may be in great affliction, and endure the rigors of *captivity*, v. 1.   Jehovah has not promised that the outward state of *Zion* shall be always pleasant, and the foot of pride never be put upon her neck.

2. Wonders will never cease.   Rapid changes are often occurring and awaking the surprise of men, vv. 1–3.   God's thoughts and ways are wholly diverse from ours. We know not the heights and depths of his counsels.   Because he is wonderful in working, we cannot but be startled at his doings.

3. "The hand of God should be acknowledged in all our mercies, whoever be the instrument of them," vv. 1–3.   If God save us by Cyrus, it is no less his deliverance than if he sent Samson, Jephtha, Ehud or David to our help.   It was the Lord that *turned the captivity* of his people and *did great things*.

4. The greatest wonders and deliverances that God ever works are in his church, vv. 1–3.   He loves her better, he has more glorious purposes respecting her, he has given a greater ransom for her, than can be claimed for all the world beside.   "There is a special eminence in the Lord's working for his people."   The conversion of the soul from sin to holiness is itself a greater wonder of mercy than God ever works for the unbelieving world.   Indeed the whole work of redemption is so stupendous, in its scheme, execution and application, that to eternity God's people will not cease to admire it.   How can the poor sinner, saved by grace, snatched as a brand from the eternal burning, ever cease to celebrate the amazing love of God and the wonders he has wrought?

5. If Israel properly rejoiced in deliverance from Babylonish captivity, how much more ought the church to give thanks when from bondage to the world God rescues her and raises her up from a dying to a lively state.   A genuine revival of religion is a great blessing.

6. So marvellous are the deliverances sometimes wrought for God's people that even sinners themselves can but notice these great things done by Jehovah, v. 2.

7. Although at the beginning, the saints are ready to doubt the mercies shown them, yet in time skepticism will give way to gratitude; and he, that was struck dumb with wonder, will proclaim the divine glory in showing him such mercy.

'When the people of God find that they are not mocked with illusions, but that all about them is reality and truth; then sorrow and sighing, fear and distrust fly away together,' v. 3.

8. Spiritual mercies, when once received, invariably whet the desire of the righteous for still other bounties of God's grace; and the 'beginnings of mercy are encouragements to us to pray for the completing of it,' v. 4.

9. Nothing is too hard for God. The land may be all parched and the water courses all dried up, but he can soon make the *streams* overflow their banks, v. 4. The plants of righteousness may all droop and seem ready to die; but he with whom is the residue of the Spirit can revive his work, and reanimate and reassure his people.

10. Let not believers sink into despondency or inefficiency through discouragements, however many and pressing they may be, vv. 5, 6. It is a saying of a man of great spiritual wisdom: "So far as I have observed the course of God's providence with me, such of my labors as have been performed in the greatest straits, and under the greatest difficulties, have had the happiest issue." After the night of weeping comes the morning of joy. There is no more precious fruit gathered from earth than that which springs from seed sown in tears, and pain, and sighing, and persecution. Yet how often do we misinterpret providence and question the divine faithfulness? Luther: "We infants in grace, we poor little children, under our tears and our sighs, understand not the voice, or the mind, or the will of our heavenly Father in these afflictions." It was hard for Israel to believe that God was fulfilling his promise, Isaiah lxvi. 20.

11. If such great things are done to the true Israel of God on earth, what may we not expect in the next world, where glory shall take the place of grace, and victory of conflict? Then preëminently, "the ransomed of the Lord shall return, and come to Zion with songs and everlasting joy upon their heads; they shall obtain joy and gladness, and sorrow and sighing shall flee away," Isa. xxxv. 10.

12. But O how sad will be the state of those who, having never accepted the proffered grace of the Gospel, were content to have all their good things in this life; who, having sowed to the flesh, shall of the flesh reap corruption; who having rejoiced and laughed a few days here go to an eternity, where nothing awaits them but weeping, and wailing, and gnashing of teeth.

PSALM CXXVII.

A Song of degrees for Solomon.

1 Except the LORD build the house, they labour in vain that build it: except the LORD keep the city, the watchman waketh *but* in vain.

2 *It is* vain for you to rise up early, to sit up late, to eat the bread of sorrows: *for* so he giveth his beloved sleep.

3 Lo, children *are* a heritage of the LORD: *and* the fruit of the womb *is his* reward.

4 As arrows *are* in the hand of a mighty man; so *are* children of the youth.

5 Happy *is* the man that hath his quiver full of them: they shall not be ashamed, but they shall speak with the enemies in the gate.

ON a song of degrees see on title of Ps. cxx. We may read *for Solomon* or *of Solomon*. The form of the Hebrew is just the same as in Ps. lxxii.; yet in most cases we render the preposition *of* not *for*. Some read *for* Solomon because they think

David wrote this ode and addressed it to his son; and because with Kimchi they think that here, as in Ps. lxxii., Solomon is a type of Messias. The Syriac ascribes it to David concerning Solomon, and concerning Haggai and Zechariah. Henry regards David as the author. Gill inclines to the same opinion. But the Chaldee, Vulgate, Calvin, Venema, Edwards, Pool, Jebb, Dodd, Street, Scott, Hengstenberg, Tholuck, and Alexander confidently speak of Solomon as the author. Calvin: "There is no reason why the Jews should deny that this Psalm was composed by Solomon;" Pool: "There is nothing in this Psalm, which gives us just ground to question whether Solomon was the author of it or no." Solomon wrote a thousand and five songs, 1 Kings iv. 32. This may be one of them. Yet Amesius, Piscator, Tremellius and Junius regard it as written *for Solomon;* and Mudge says that there seems to be no other reason for regarding Solomon as the author, except that it speaks of building a house. Clarke thinks it was most likely composed for the building of the second Temple, and by some prophet of that time. The general aim of this ode is to repress worldly cares, and to inspire pious trust in God. Venema: "Its scope is to withdraw men from excessive labors and anxious cares, but to inspire piety and trust in Jehovah;" Edwards: "The design of it is to inculcate this most certain and very useful maxim, That the success of all our undertakings entirely depends upon God's blessing;" Hengstenberg: "Everything is dependent upon the blessing of God." Some argue Solomon's authorship from the fact that the whole ode is but an expansion of that saying of his: "The blessing of the Lord, it maketh rich," Pr. x. 22. But the same sentiment abounds in the utterances of true piety. See Ps. xxxvii. 22; cvii. 38; cxiii. 7, 8, and many places. Scott dates this Psalm B. C. 1012; Clarke, B. C. about 445. The only name of God in it is *Jehovah* LORD, on which see on Ps. i. 2.

1. *Except the* LORD *build the house, they labor in vain that build it.* To *build a house* has in Scripture these significations: 1. To erect a material structure for public or private use. Thus the Jews built dwellings for themselves, Deut. xxviii. 30; Jer. xxix. 5. Thus David proposed to build the temple, 2 Sam. vii. 5; and Solomon actually built it, 2 Chron. ii. 1. 2. To *build a house* is to found and rear a family, Deut. xxv. 9. This family sometimes becomes large, even a tribe; and so we read of the houses of Judah, of Levi. 3. To build a house is to found a state or kingdom, either by being the progenitors of the people composing it, or by political measures, or by strengthening it, Ruth iv. 11. Compare 2 Sam. vii. 12–16; Ps. cxxii. 5. When God blows upon an enterprise, it is sure to fail. The whole world was engaged in building Babel, but it ended in confusion. David was intently bent on building the temple, but God permitted him not to proceed. Saul hoped to see his family established in the throne of Israel; but God's mind was otherwise. God is no less the Father of nations than of men, Gen. xvii. 6; Deut. xxxii. 8; Ps. xxii. 28. He founds tribes and states, and destroys them at his pleasure, Deut. vii. 1; xii. 29. "By me kings reign, and princes decree justice," Pr. viii. 15. Compare Ecc. ix. 11. *Build* is in the future; *labor,* in the preterite. The *labor* here spoken of is that which begets weariness. The cognate noun is rendered *trouble, misery, travail.* Street's rendering is nearly literal: If Jehovah build not an house, in vain do the builders of it labor on it. The prophet reiterates the leading truth of the Psalm: *Except the Lord keep the city, the watchman waketh* but *in vain.* The tenses of the verbs are the same as in the first clause. *Watchman* is closely cognate to *keep.* Augustine and Tholuck extend the meaning of this clause to embrace God's ministers, who teach his truth and watch for souls in the city of God. *Waketh,* a verb expressive of great diligence and vigilance, Pr. viii. 34; Jer. xxxi. 28; Dan. ix. 14. Compare Isa. lii. 8; Ezek. iii. 17. Titus himself was surprised at his own capture of Jerusalem, and ascribed his victory to providence. In vain do faithful pastors labor till God vouchsafe his

blessing on the church, 1 Cor. iii. 7. In every undertaking God is not merely our chief but our sole dependence.

2. It is *vain for you to rise up early, to sit up late, to eat the bread of sorrows: for so he giveth his beloved sleep.* John Rogers' translation: It is but lost labour that ye rise up early, and take no rest, but eate the bredde of carefulnesse; for like to whom it pleaseth him, he giveth it in slepe; Calvin: It is in vain for you in hastening to rise early, to go late to rest, to eat the bread of sorrows: for thus will he give sleep to his beloved; Street: It is in vain for you early risers to rise from rest, eating the bread of care, when he giveth to his beloved double. *Vain, vanity,* in v. 1, twice rendered *in vain.* It is the same word used in the third commandment, a noun masculine. We met it in Ps. xii. 2. The first three verbs cannot be better translated, than in the authorized version, unless we render the last literally, *eating.* The *bread of sorrows* is bread procured in *labors* and *griefs.* The last clause of the verse is not explained alike by all. These remarks are offered: 1. The rendering of Street *double* for *sleep* requires a change in the Hebrew text, resting wholly on conjecture, and so cannot be received. 2. It is not the design of God here to inculcate sloth or a neglect of the lawful arts of industry. This would contradict many clear Scriptures in both Testaments. 3. Instead of *so* or *thus,* it is better with Walford to read *truly:* He truly granteth sleep to his beloved. Scott: *Surely,* he giveth his beloved sleep. Calvin says the Hebrew particle " is put to express certainty." 4. When God sentenced man to labor for life, he did not enjoin care and toil destructive of necessary repose, and so " the sleep of the labouring man is sweet, whether he eat little or much," Ecc. v. 12. God does not require us to kill ourselves, or fret ourselves to death, but only to use lawful industry, and then with quiet confidence in his providence to lie down and sleep. The divine blessing and not our foresight secures success. God is as merciful in giving us sleep, as he is righteous in requiring labor. And he shows his care for us by causing our crops to grow and our affairs to prosper, even while we sleep. 5. The word rendered *beloved* is *Jedidiah,* a name given to Solomon by inspiration because the Lord loved him, 2 Sam. xii. 24, 25, and so it may design to celebrate God's goodness to Solomon, who though he had on hands vast plans and immense public works, found them all prospering, although he fretted not himself about them, but was blessed with necessary and refreshing sleep. 6. What God did to Solomon he does to each of his *beloved* people, according to their faith and reliance on his providence.

3. *Lo, children are a heritage of the* LORD : and *the fruit of the womb* is his *reward.* The meaning is that the very offspring, for whom men are often so anxious to provide, are themselves the gift of God, *an inheritance* from the Lord, the *reward* of his love and kindness to men ; and if God give us children, he will make provision for them. Having done the greater, he will do the less. The *fruit of the womb* is a name given to offspring in the earliest sacred writings, Gen. xxx. 2; Deut. vii. 13. Piety loves devoutly to acknowledge the bounty of God in the gift of children, Gen. xxxiii. 5; xlviii. 9.

4. *As arrows are in the hand of a mighty man ; so are children of the youth.* By *children of the youth,* some understand young persons; others, more correctly, children born when their father was young, so that as his vigor declines, they may be ready to support and defend him. *Mighty man,* see on Ps. xix. 5, where it is rendered *a strong man;* compare Ps. lxxviii. 65. It often refers to great warriors. "Merrick mentions a remarkable Chinese proverb: 'When a son is born into a family, a bow and arrow are hung before the gate.'" Men live their lives over again in their children and grandchildren.

5. *Happy is the man that hath his quiver full of them; they shall not be ashamed, but*

they shall speak with the enemies in the gate. *Happy*, in Ps. i. 1, blessed ; O the bless-ednesses ! A *quiver full of arrows* is no mean representation of the protection an old man has in a numerous offspring of virtuous children established in an unblemished reputation. In ancient cities courts were held and causes decided at the gates. See on Ps. lxix. 12. Here by their well earned characters even more than by their num-bers they were able to repel rude assaults on themselves and on their venerated father. By uprightness and wisdom and a good conversation they became a tower of strength to protect his feebleness. Alexander : " For a striking contrast to this picture, see Job v. 4." Nicolson supposes that *they* refers to the parent and not the children.

DOCTRINAL AND PRACTICAL REMARKS.

1. Because the maintenance of a deep sense of dependence on God is very difficult yet very important, the Scriptures often present the matter in a clear and urgent man-ner, vv. 1–3. Let all persons, families, churches, cities and states remember that God is Judge of all, that whom he will he exalts and whom he will he puts down. All human plans fail without him. In man is no inherent efficiency. Forsaken by God, the bravest become cowards, the strongest are weak as water, the most careful fail, and the wise are fools. Compare Hab. ii. 13 ; Mal. i. 4.

2. Those do therefore sadly sin against God who ascribe their success or prosperity to human wit, power, or perseverance, vv. 1–3. Man is a worm. Man is a fool. Man is a sinner.

3. Nor do those less err who claim to rely on God and yet neglect or slight the means he has ordained for our success, vv. 1, 2. The true Christian works as if he believed not, and believes as if he wrought not.

4. Dickson : " The only way of having a quiet mind and good success, is to use the means without anxiety, and to commit the success to God, v. 2." Rising early, sitting up late, rigid economy, extraordinary efforts and great sorrow of heart at failure may wear us away, but can never take the place of God.

5. The violation of the previous principles is quite sufficient to account for a great portion of the unhappiness, personal, family, social, commercial and political of every age and country. Compare Hag. i. 6.

6. Were our gratitude what it ought to be, each season of refreshing rest would be followed by a song of praise, v. 2. The convalescent or the suffering sick sometimes duly notice such a mercy ; but how many millions sleep and wake like atheists !

7. States and nations ought humbly to acknowledge the good hand of God upon them. Luther : " All governments and commonwealths rightly constituted are the good and free gifts of God : none of them can be either rightly constituted, at the first, nor preserved afterwards, by any human wisdom or might : but all these things are in the hand of God." Calvin : " When philosophers argue concerning the politi-cal affairs of a state they ingeniously gather together whatever seems to them to answer their purpose—they acutely point out the means of erecting a commonwealth, and on the other hand the vices by which a well-regulated state is commonly cor-rupted ; in short, they discourse with consummate skill upon everything that is neces-sary to be known on this subject, except that they omit the principal point—which is, that men, however much they may excel in wisdom and virtue, and whatever may be the undertaking in which they may engage, can effect nothing, unless in so far as God stretches forth his hand to them, or rather makes use of them as his instruments."

8. We are no less dependent on God for our domestic happiness and success, v. 3. Children themselves will but wring our hearts with anguish, except as God leads them in the paths of peace and virtue. " Children are to us what God makes them, com-forts or crosses." How foolish and criminal are those persons, who having not learned

to govern themselves, yet complain of Providence for denying them children. And how base are those parents who having received the gift of children, regard them as a burden, and doubt the divine kindness in providing for them. "Wherever God sends mouths he sends meat."

9. It is an unspeakable blessing when God gives us children that he rightly disposes them to such courses of conduct as are suited to make them blessings to us and to the world, v. 4. As they are by nature depraved, nothing short of divine power and grace can so mould their hearts and manners as to make them real blessings. How they are such, even uninspired men have sometimes seen. See what the son of Sirach said in Ecclus. xxx. 3-6.

10. If the right interpretation is commonly given to the phrase *children of youth*, this Psalm greatly encourages early marriages. It is a growing evil of modern times that marriages are so often deferred till it is highly improbable that in the course of nature the father can live to mould his offspring to habits of honor and virtue.

PSALM CXXVIII.

A Song of degrees.

1 Blessed *is* every one that feareth the LORD; that walketh in his ways.

2 For thou shalt eat the labour of thine hands: happy *shalt* thou *be*, and *it shall be* well with thee.

3 Thy wife *shall be* as a fruitful vine by the sides of thine house: thy children like olive plants round about thy table.

4 Behold, that thus shall the man be blessed that feareth the LORD.

5 The LORD shall bless thee out of Zion: and thou shalt see the good of Jerusalem all the days of thy life.

6 Yea, thou shalt see thy children's children, *and* peace upon Israel.

ON the title see on title of Psalm cxx. Commentators are remarkably silent respecting the authorship of this Psalm. We find no historic occasion for its composition. Scott dates it B. C. 1012; Clarke, B. C. about 445. Some regard it as a sequel to Ps. cxxvii.; and it does to some extent treat of the same matters. Hengstenberg speaks of "the flat and broken discourse of this Psalm and its want of vigor and elevation." But where do we find a description of domestic happiness superior to this in beauty and brevity? Luther styles it "A wedding song for Christians." Henry says that "this is a Psalm for families." Patrick: "Some think that this was a form prescribed to be used at the blessing of their marriages, when they wished the new married couple all manner of happiness, especially a long life in peaceable times." It contains great and universal truths seasonable for all occasions, and having a wide range of comprehension. The only name of God found in it is *Jehovah* LORD, on which see on Ps. i. 2.

1. *Blessed is every one that feareth the* LORD; *that walketh in his ways*. *Blessed*, in Ps. cxxvii. 5, *happy*, O the blessednesses! On the nature of the true fear of God see on Ps. ii. 11. On the import of the term *walking*, see on Ps. i. 1. Alexander: "However things may seem now to an eye of sense, it is still a certain truth, that the truly happy man is he who fears Jehovah, not in mere profession, but who testifies his fear of him by walking in his ways or doing his commandments." "The triumph

of the wicked is short," is the Scriptural explanation of all appearances of success in sin.

2. *For thou shalt eat the labor of thine hands: happy* shalt *thou* be, *and* it shall be *well with thee.* In Ps. i. it is said: "Whatsoever he doeth shall prosper;" in this it is said, his *labor* shall be remunerative. *Labor* is expressive of real toil. See on Ps. lxxviii. 46; cix. 11. *Happy*, in v. 1, *blessed*. *It shall be well with thee*, literally, *good* (is) *to thee*. The promise of temporal prosperity shall be so far fulfilled as may not conflict with the higher interests of the soul. Yet the Lord does not engage to supply the insatiable cupidity of the human heart; but to give his blessing on lawful industry. The second person singular is used in this verse and in those which follow, as if the truth were addressed to each believer in person.

3. *Thy wife* shall be *as a fruitful vine by the sides of thine house: thy children like olive plants round about thy table.* The figures of this verse are best explained as indicating not the mode of cultivating the vine and the olive in Judea; but as the vine and the olive yielded the greatest refreshment and were emblems of the greatest gladness; so here they are put for the exquisite delights flowing to a good man through his wife and children. If the fruit of the olive and of the vine failed in Judea, it was commonly a token of the total failure of crops, both of grain and fruit. A good wife makes large contributions to the good cheer of the household. Olive plants are not kept in the house, but the terms mean that a well-ordered family of children has a refreshing beauty like that of thrifty olive plants. They impart the oil of gladness. See on Ps. lii. 8. *Round about*, the same as in Ps. cxxv. 2. Let those worldlings, who have great outward prosperity, and scorn the spiritual blessings of the Gospel remember that they alone are not blessed with temporal good things, that it is God's blessing on what we have that makes us truly happy, and that God never promised to put his people off with the good things of this life, but has provided for them something better, even a heavenly inheritance.

4. *Behold, that thus shall the man be blessed that feareth the* Lord. God's care of his people, even of the poorest, humblest and most afflicted, has often been such as to impress the wicked themselves, Esther vi. 13. *Thus*, better rendered *surely*. *Blessed*, not the word in v. 1, but that of benediction. See on Ps. v. 12. *That feareth*, as in v. 1. The verse teaches that all real happiness comes to us by the authority and power of Jehovah.

5. *The* Lord *shall bless thee out of Zion: and thou shalt see the good of Jerusalem all the days of thy life.* The first verb of this verse is in the future, the second in the imperative. Some put them both in the imperative; but the authorized version gives the sense better by using the future in both cases. *Zion* was the seat of God's visible kingdom over Israel. From it the Jews expected national and personal blessings. There too was the centre of the visible church, as well as of the affections of the truly pious touching earthly ordinances. *The good of Jerusalem* is the prosperity of the holy city and especially of the true religion, whose rites were celebrated in Jerusalem.

6. *Yea, thou shalt see thy children's children*, and *peace upon Israel.* Calvin: "With good reason the prophet recommends solicitude about the public welfare; and he mingles together domestic blessings and the common benefits of the church in such a way as to show us that they are things joined together, and which it is unlawful to put asunder." Compare the general promises of this Psalm respecting temporal blessings with Ps. i. 3; xxxvii. 3; xci. 16.

DOCTRINAL AND PRACTICAL REMARKS.

1. Though in the esteem of many true piety is without solid advantages, yet God's

word and people have decided quite otherwise. This whole Psalm contradicts the slander of such as deny that godliness is profitable. God's people get not their portion here; but they obtain foretastes of heaven in God's blessing on their basket and store, on their souls and on their families. Nor is there an exception to this remark.

2. The fear of God is an element in true piety, vv. 1, 4. It is so essential that God's servants should fear him, that often, as here, this one grace is made to represent the whole of religion.

3. The genuine fear of God is not taught by human authority, nor enforced by human sanctions, but only by the laws and *ways of Jehovah*, v. 1.

4. The fear of God which has no torment in it, and which is commended in Scripture, evinces itself by a holy life, a *walk* according to God's requirements, v. 1.

5. In no sense do the humble find their labors in vain in the Lord. As in husbandry so in all works undertaken in the fear of God, they shall have such success as shall show that the blessing of God is on them, v. 2. It is a great mercy that God's people have something to do in life, and a still greater, when like their Saviour each one can say: "I have glorified thee on the earth: I have finished the work which thou gavest me to do," John xvii. 4. There is indeed a curse resting on the toil which God exacts of man; but the fear of God goes far towards converting that curse into a blessing. Countless have been the devices of men to resist the law of labor. The most successful in this daring enterprise have commonly been the most unhappy.

6. Whatever judgment carnal men may pronounce upon a life of piety, those who have grace to glorify God on the earth, both know and testify that it is *well* with them, v. 2.

7. Strike out of the sum total of human happiness that, which is fairly to be ascribed to the relations of husband and wife, parent and child, brother and sister, and there would be a hideous chasm. Luther: "Marriage is that kind of life, which, as being the creation and institution of God greatly pleases him;" Calvin: "If a man has a wife of amiable manners as the companion of his life, let him set no less value upon this blessing than Solomon did, who affirms that it is God alone who gives a good wife, Prov. xix. 14. In like manner, if a man be a father of a numerous offspring, let him receive that boon with a thankful heart;" Horne: "Marriage was ordained by God to complete the felicity of man in a state of innocency; and the benediction of Heaven will ever descend upon it, when undertaken in the fear of the Lord;" Scott: "Marriage is peculiarly honorable and blessed to him, who enters it in the fear of God and desires to walk with his family according to his will." Let this institution be preserved in its scriptural purity. Otherwise society will be fearfully corrupted, if not dissolved.

8. It cannot be that a true child of God should fail to love the church, v. 5. He was born in Zion. There God first revealed himself to the soul. Thence spring all his best hopes. Nor has he any choice blessing but such as is in some way connected with the company of the faithful.

9. It is a great mercy bestowed upon God's people when they are allowed to see the church prosper, and good come upon Jerusalem, especially such a blessing as is manifestly for her growth and purification, v. 5.

10. While a long life spent in sin will in the end but enhance the misery of those who die in their iniquity; a long life spent in the fear of God and graciously bestowed for holy ends and purposes, agreeably to God's promise is one of the greatest temporal blessings, v. 6.

11. As the arts of war are very destructive of life and property and all that men commonly hold most dear; so *peace* is in the Scriptures used as the sum of many

choice blessings. To Israel such a term had peculiar significance. Thrice in the year that people went up to the Holy City to perform their sacrifices. In all their generations Jehovah allowed not their foes to disturb the peace of the nation at such times.

12. Some interpret the last clause of the Psalm as prophetic. One of the most pleasing things discoverable in some of God's aged servants is their wonderful love of the church increasing as their salvation draws nigh. Sometimes they show an inextinguishable thirst for that kind of knowledge which is derived from looking into unfulfilled predictions. Let them be encouraged modestly to pursue such studies, 2 Pet. i. 19.

PSALM CXXIX.

A Song of degrees.

1 Many a time have they afflicted me from my youth, may Israel now say:
2 Many a time have they afflicted me from my youth: yet they have not prevailed against me.
3 The ploughers ploughed upon my back: they made long their furrows.
4 The LORD *is* righteous: he hath cut asunder the cords of the wicked.
5 Let them all be confounded and turned back that hate Zion.
6 Let them be as the grass *upon* the housetops, which withereth afore it groweth up:
7 Wherewith the mower filleth not his hand; nor he that bindeth sheaves his bosom.
8 Neither do they which go by say, The blessing of the LORD *be* upon you: we bless you in the name of the LORD.

ON the title see on title of Ps. cxx. As in the last Psalm, so here the authorship is quite uncertain, very few venturing even a conjecture on the subject. The opinion of commentators is divided as to the time of its composition. Scott: " It is not improbably conjectured that this Psalm was composed about the time when Sennacherib invaded Judah; yet this is no more than conjecture." Clarke admits that " the author is uncertain," but seems confident that it " was written *after* the captivity." We can affix neither date nor author. The only name of God in it is *Jehovah* LORD, on which see on Ps. i. 2. The general scope of the Psalm is obvious. The first part rehearses the trials of the chosen people, especially in their early history, and their deliverances from those who tormented them. The latter part is a prediction of the dreadful end of God's enemies.

1. *Many a time have they afflicted me from my youth, may Israel now say.* *Many a time,* in Hebrew one word; margin, *much.* In Psalm cxxiii. 3, 4, it is twice rendered *exceedingly.* Edwards here has *greatly;* Morison, *very sorely.* The Doway, Calvin and Hengstenberg, *often;* Street, *frequently;* church of England and Alexander and most agree with our version. *Afflicted, vexed, distressed, oppressed, shut up,* see Num. xxxiii. 55; 1 Sam. xxviii. 15; Num. x. 9; 2 Sam. xx. 3. In some of its forms it is rendered *besieged.* By the *youth* of Israel we are to understand the chosen people in their early history, see Isa. xlvii. 12, 15; Jer. ii. 2; xxii. 21; xlviii. 11; Ezek. xvi. 4; xxiii. 3; Hos. ii. 15; xi. 1. *Now,* Calvin regards this word as emphatic and implying a state of deep distress, or dismay at the time of writing. But Alexander is confident that it is optative, and reads, *oh let Israel say.* Street has *Israel may truly say* However read the verse is a virtual call on the church to remember early trials.

2. *Many a time have they afflicted me from my youth:* a verbal repetition of what

was said in v. 1, indicating the desire of the prophet that all may be duly impressed with the lessons of history. *Yet they have not prevailed against me.* *Prevailed*, as in Ps. xiii. 4. This cannot teach that the enemies of Israel never gained a temporary advantage, never succeeded in bringing great distresses on God's people. It can only mean that apparent victories gained did not result, as enemies hoped, in the destruction of the chosen nation. Foes *were not able* to do what they proposed. Calvin: "They never succeeded in realizing their wishes, God having always disappointed their hopes and baffled their attempts."

3. *The ploughers ploughed upon my back; they made long their furrows.* *Ploughers*, *ploughed*, the plural participle and the preterite of the same verb. There is no better rendering. Street: They have cut furrows on my back: they have made long ridges, like those of ploughed ground. The meaning is that they have had no pity—have stopped at nothing. Some explain by making the prophet allude to the terrible process of scourging, when the flesh was cut and gashed, and subsequently rose into wales. But may not the reference be to the process of ploughing ground, when it is torn up and cut without mercy, sparing nothing? Calvin: "He compares the people of God to a field through which a plough is drawn. He says that the furrows were made long, so that no corner was exempted from being cut up by the ploughshare." Walford: "The persecutors of Israel are compared to ploughmen; because as they cut up, and as it were torture the surface of the earth, so did the adversaries greatly and grievously distress these afflicted people." Pool's paraphrase is: "They have not only thrown me down, and trod me under foot, but have cruelly tormented me, wounded and mangled me, and had no more pity upon me than the ploughman hath upon the earth which he cuts up at his pleasure." Such cruelty and wickedness may be rampant for a while, but cannot last always.

4. *The* LORD *is righteous.* The emblem of justice among some of the ancients was a lame but strong man armed with a sword. He came slowly to his work, but he did it thoroughly at last. So divine rectitude long forbears, but it finally renders powerless for evil the greatest persecutors. Compare 2 Thess. i. 6, 7. *He hath cut asunder the cords of the wicked.* *Cords*, in Hebrew singular. *Wicked*, in Ps. i. the same word is several times rendered *ungodly.* Several explanations are offered. One makes the reference to be to the *cord* used in scourging. Another makes it refer to the *cord* used in binding the victim for scourging. A third supposes that the *cord* here spoken of is that used in ploughing, to attach the oxen to the plough, the gear of the team. The first view is favored by Horne and Hengstenberg; the second, by Scott and Morison; the third, by Luther, Calvin, Gill, Pool, Henry, Tholuck and Alexander. Whatever may be the foundation of the figure, there is no doubt that the general sense of the passage is that God effectually put it out of the power of the persecutors to do his people further harm. There seems to be no other cause for applying this and the preceding verse to Christ than that he above all others received cruel treatment, even to scourging and death, being preëminently the Man of sorrows.

5. *Let them all be confounded and turned back that hate Zion.* *Confounded*, in Ps. cxxvii. 5, and often elsewhere *ashamed.* *Turned back*, in Ps. xl. 14, *driven backward.* Both the verbs are in the future, *shall be confounded* and *turned.* The verse is not an imprecation but a prophecy both in form and in fact. The wicked shall surely, though reluctantly, cease their cruel practices. Compare Ps. vi. 10; xxxv. 3.

6. *Let them be as the grass* upon *the housetops, which withereth afore it groweth up.*

7. *Wherewith the mower filleth not his hand; nor he that bindeth sheaves his bosom.*

8. *Neither do they which go by say, The blessing of the* LORD *be upon you: we bless you in the name of the* LORD. Like the preceding, this also is a prediction. *Let them be*, literally, *They shall be.* So the Genevan translation has it. The housetops in

Judea were flat, and covered with some kind of cement; and sometimes grass sprung up and for a while looked green and flourishing, but having no depth of earth, and lacking moisture and being exposed to great heat, it soon *withered*. It never attained maturity. Neither the mower nor the binder ever went there. Alexander: "The word translated *bosom* is explained by lexicographers to mean, the front fold of the oriental robe, in which things are carried. It might also be translated *lap*. Hengstenberg's version is *his arm*." Verse 8 alludes to a custom prevalent in early times, and still in use in parts of Asia: "And behold, Boaz came from Bethlehem, and said unto the reapers, The Lord be with you; and they answered him, The Lord bless thee," Ruth ii. 4. Cobbin: "The meaning here poetically expressed is, Let them be destroyed, as that which is useless, which affords neither the plenty nor the joy of harvest." John Rogers' Translation of v. 6, is: Let them be even as the haye upon the house toppes, whych wythereth afore it be pluckte up.

DOCTRINAL AND PRACTICAL REMARKS.

1. Let God's people never forget that the saints of all ages have been afflicted, maligned and persecuted, vv. 1, 2. The burning bush, wrapped in flames but not consumed, is a fit emblem of God's church in all ages. A thousand times has it looked to the eye of sense and reason as if the people of God would soon be extirpated. There never has been a time when the wicked loved the righteous.

2. But let not the people of God be afraid with any amazement, nor yield to thoughts of despondency. The church shall not perish, nor shall her enemies gain a final or decisive advantage over her, v. 2. They have the will, but they have not the power. They make the war, but they cannot *prevail*.

3. The want of success in the war on the church has not been owing to any scrupulous or delicate feeling on the part of her enemies. Persecutors have always been cruel. They have *plowed* the *back* of the church and *made long* their *furrows*, v. 3. Lying, reviling, slander, blasphemy, whipping, scourging, burning, hanging, crucifying, casting to the wild beasts, and every conceivable form of cruelty has been exhausted from age to age in trying to erase from the earth the last vestige of true piety. The bottomless pit can hardly contain beings more cruel or malignant than some who at sundry times have walked the earth; nor are they without an offspring to this present.

4. It is fatal however to the cause of cruelty and persecution that God's righteousness endureth forever, v. 4. Because his throne is established in equity and plenty of justice, all wicked schemes must prove utter failures.

5. Nor is God deficient in power, but limits and restrains the malice of the wicked when he chooses, and strips them both of the ability and means to do his people further harm, v. 4. Oftentimes this has been so apparent and striking that spectators who were not taught of God at all have greatly wondered.

6. Although to the righteous the career of enemies may seem to be long and their prosperity great, yet shame, confusion and consternation shall come upon all incorrigible sinners, and especially upon impenitent persecutors, v. 5.

7. Even in this world and in the height of their success, the haters of Zion manifest signs of inherent weakness. Like grass on the housetop, they have no sufficient supply of nourishment, v. 6. They have no access to God by prayer, no communion with the Father of their spirits. They know nothing of the comfort of love, of the patience of hope, or of the joy of salvation. One blasting wind may wither them forever. Hammond: "Instead of a prosperous harvest of all their oppressions and injustices, they shall reap nothing but emptiness and beggary."

8. It could not be otherwise. They have no resources in God. Separated from him, man can no more be wise, or strong, or great, than a human arm, severed from

its body can flourish. They may indeed flourish like the grass, but like the grass they shall soon wither. Therefore " the prosperous success of the ungodly ougnt not to agitate the faith of the pious."

9. There is one very dark sign in the case of the wicked—their uselessness. They are of no more value than the grass on the housetop, v. 7. The Scriptures dwell much on this point. The whole of Ezek. xv. is employed in showing the uselessness and consequent ruin of the wicked. Paul states it at length in a fearful comparison in Heb. vi. 7, 8. Amesius: " No solid fruit can be either collected or expected from the way and exertions of the ungodly."

10. Another very dark sign in the case of all the wicked is that they receive no efficacious blessing from God; nor have they the approbation of the angels, nor the complacency of good men. The righteous may indeed pray for their conversion, and their prayers may be answered, as that of Stephen was for Saul of Tarsus. But the whole tenor of the supplications of God's people is for the utter subversion of the schemes of the wicked, and of the kingdom of darkness. Hengstenberg: "However proudly Israel's enemies may shine at present, their end is destruction." No good man blesses the wicked in their wickedness; and in the end, the injured creatures of God will everywhere rise up against them, Job v. 3; Hab. ii. 11. Horne: " At the general harvest of the world, when the righteous shall be carried by angels, with joyful acclamations, into the mansions prepared for them above, the wicked, unregarded by the heavenly reapers, and unblest by all, shall become fuel for a fire that goeth not out."

PSALM CXXX.

A Song of degrees.

1 Out of the depths have I cried unto thee, O LORD.

2 Lord, hear my voice: let thine ears be attentive to the voice of my supplications.

3 If thou, LORD, shouldest mark iniquities, O Lord, who shall stand?

4 But *there is* forgiveness with thee, that thou mayest be feared.

5 I wait for the LORD, my soul doth wait, and in his word do I hope.

6 My soul *waiteth* for the Lord more than they that watch for the morning: *I say, more than* they that watch for the morning.

7 Let Israel hope in the LORD: for with the LORD *there is* mercy, and with him *is* plenteous redemption.

8 And he shall redeem Israel from all his iniquities.

ON the title see on title of Psalm cxx. All, who have made the penitential Psalms to be seven in number, count this as the *sixth*. Luther, Calvin, Symson, Henry, Bellarmine, Patrick and Edwards regard David as the author. Scott: "David is generally supposed to have been the writer of this Psalm." He dates it B. C. 1059. Others suppose it to be of later date. Clarke: "It was most probably composed during the captivity." Hengstenberg thinks that at least two words in it [those rendered *attentive* and *forgiveness*] "point to a late time." The former is not found elsewhere, except in 2 Chron. vi. 40; vii. 15; the latter only in Neh. ix. 17; Dan. ix. 9; though both of them are formed of words well known in the Hebrew. Venema: "It is plainly uncertain who the author is." Those, who regard David as the author are divided in opinion whether it was written on the same occasion as Ps. xxxii. li. respecting the matter of Bathsheba; or on the occasion of the Sauline persecutions.

Jebb thinks it has a close connection with Ps. cxxxi. Pool says it was composed when the prophet "was conflicting with horrors of his conscience for the guilt of his sins, and imploring God's mercy and pardon." Symson says, in it "is contained an earnest and ardent prayer of a troubled heart: first, for mercy to his sinnes; and next, for deliverance therefrom; and last, an exhortation to all men to hope in God, because he will be a continual Redeemer of his people, and can finde meanes to deliver them from all their sinnes and iniquities." The names of God here found are *Jehovah* LORD, *Jah* LORD and *Adonai Lord*, on which see on Ps. i. 2; introduction to Ps. lxviii.; and on Ps. ii. 4.

1. *Out of the depths have I cried unto thee, O* LORD. *Depths*, this word is found in four other places, Ps. lxix. 2, 14; Isa. li. 10; Ezek. xxvii. 34. In Ps. lxix. it is rendered as an adjective in the English text, though the margin gives it as a noun. Cognate terms occur frequently. *The depths* are clearly those of trouble, distress, affliction. These are outward or inward. The outward consist of providential arrangements respecting our health, honor, property, family, and the state of the church and of the world around us; the inward relate to the state of men's hearts, arising from a clear apprehension of the existence, guilt and virulence of sin, of the want of due love to God, of the hiding of the divine countenance, of spiritual insensibility, of a want of the tokens of God's love to us, of a keen sense of the ill-desert of our own sins, of a discovery of the mischief, to ourselves and others, of our departures from God, of spiritual darkness generally, and of strange disinclination to devotion, accompanied by apprehensions of the divine wrath. There is no kind or degree of sin which may not lead us into the *depths*. But there are no depths of outward affliction or of mental depression known to the penitent, from which they may not *cry* unto the Lord. Moses, when so distressed that he uttered not a word, yet in his anguish looked to God and was understood by him that sitteth on the throne, who said, "Wherefore criest thou unto me?" Ex. xiv. 15.

2. *Lord, hear my voice: let thine ears be attentive to the voice of my supplications.* *Hear*, the usual word so rendered, in the imperative. In the latter clause the Hebrew is in the future; yet the sense is best given in the English version. *Supplications*, always so rendered, except in Prov. xviii. 23, where it is *intreaties*. The word expresses earnestness and a desire for grace and favor, see on Ps. xxviii. 2. It well corresponds in import with the *cry* of v. 1; but is a stronger term.

3. *If thou,* LORD, *shouldest mark iniquities, O Lord, who shall stand?* The first word Lord is *Jah;* and second, *Adonai.* *Mark, keep, observe, watch, take heed.* Phillips: The word "denotes not only *to mark*, or *observe*, but to observe diligently, so as to retain a perpetual memory of what is done amiss—a rigid and judicial observation of faults: see Job x. 14; xiv. 16, 17." Anderson: "It is as if the Psalmist had said, If thou were like an earthly judge, to note down every minute circumstance of guilt, who would be able to stand such a trial, or leave thy court unconvicted, or uncondemned?" The verse is a clear declaration of a consciousness of personal ill-desert, and of a conviction that the whole world lieth in wickedness. The word *iniquities* points to any and every kind of sin against either table of the law. *Stand*, not the same word used in Ps. i. 5, but one signifying *endure* or *stand fast*. See Ps. xxxiii. 9; cii. 26. Who among men could abide the scrutiny of omniscient purity, if the Lord should deal with them in untempered severity? Compare Job iv. 18; ix. 20; Rom. xi. 32. The purest man on earth ought to acknowledge his entire sinfulness and dependence on the mercy of God. It is utterly vain for unbelievers to delude themselves with the persuasion that they are not sinners against God, and under his wrath and curse. In vain does any man persuade himself that he can by doing meet the precept, or by suffering satisfy the penalty of the law of God.

4. *But there is forgiveness with thee, that thou mayest be feared.* Pardon and forgiveness are convertible terms, each of them meaning remission. Forgiveness necessarily implies ill-desert on the part of the forgiven, and grace on the part of him who forgives. Human merits are excluded from the whole scheme of salvation. Every creature of God, who stands accepted before him, is justified solely by works, as the unsinning angels; or wholly by grace, as believing sinners. *Forgiveness is with thee,* as thy exclusive prerogative, as flowing from thy grace, and as being the glory of thy government, full, free, abundant. In Dan. ix. 9, the same word is in the plural, *forgivenesses.* The Lord "abundantly pardons," or multiplies to pardon, as the margin has it, Isa. lv. 7. Then God's forgiveness is exercised in so wise and excellent a way. It is not bestowed upon the thoughtless and reckless. The Lord makes men smart and then heals them, even as Joseph made his brethren see and confess the evil of their doings before he revealed himself to them. So God grants pardon in such a way that he *may be feared;* not dreaded as a tyrant, nor avoided as cruel, but devoutly reverenced as a pitiful Father.

5. *I wait for the* LORD, *my soul doth wait, and in his word do I hope.* *Wait,* as in Ps. xxv. 3, 5. Where the verb is followed by its own participle, it is rendered *wait patiently,* as in Ps. xl. 1. In this verse the verb is in the preterite, expressive of a habit. *Hope,* in the preterite also. This verb is often rendered *wait* and *trust,* see on Ps. xlii. 5. Men are always restless in time of trial till they are either made stolid by affliction, or, in the exercise of true piety, are led to set their hope in God. *Hoping* and *waiting* are in their very nature inseparably united. Verses 4, 5 show the connection between faith and hope. David believed that God was gracious and forgiving. Out of that confidence sprang the hope that animated and the patience that quieted him.

6. *My soul* waiteth *for the Lord more than they that watch for the morning:* I say, more than *they that watch for the morning.* Alexander: "The comparison suggested is between the impatience of nocturnal watchers for the break of day and that of sufferers for relief, or of convicted sinners for forgiveness." The force of the whole is the same whether by those watching for the morning, we understand the keepers of a city, or the priests and Levites in their courses of service in the temple, according to the ordinance in Ex. xxx. 7. The repetition of the declaration of this verse is by many noticed as very beautiful.

7. *Let Israel hope in the* LORD: *for with the* LORD *there is mercy, and with him is plenteous redemption.* *Hope,* as in v. 5. The original has the form of exhortation or of desire. In the character of God is found ample basis for all the pious hopes ever indulged. With him is *mercy,* or *lovingkindness,* as the word is often rendered. In all the Scriptures we shall not find a sweeter word than *redemption.* It is a term employed to express the deliverance of men from the misery of captivity, from the hardships of bondage, and from the guilt and wretchedness of a sinful state. All mere men since the fall of Adam have needed redemption. The only Redeemer of God's elect is the Lord Jesus Christ. The ransom paid is not silver or gold or tears or reformations, but the blood of the Son of God. *Plenteous,* a verb in the infinitive, literally to multiply or enlarge. The cognate adjective is rendered *great, many* and *plenteous,* Ps. lxxxvi. 5, 15; cxix. 156, 157. The greatness of our redemption may be estimated by the glory of its author, by the greatness of the price paid, by the number redeemed, by the depths of sin and misery from which they are rescued, and by the glory that shall follow the completion of the work.

8. *And he shall redeem Israel from all his iniquities.* *Redeem,* closely cognate to redemption in v. 7. *Israel* is the true church. The verse contains the sum of much before spoken. *Iniquities,* as in v. 3. The deliverance promised is from the guilt and

wrath consequent upon transgression. Redemption from guilt is the greatest of all deliverances. The act of pardon is perfect.

DOCTRINAL AND PRACTICAL REMARKS.

1. Religious experience has its *depths* as well as its heights, its *cries* as well as its shouts, v. 1. The Lord sets one thing over against another. All sunshine would burn up the plants. All rain and cloud would drown them out. Symson: "When wee are in prosperitie, our prayers come from our lippes; and therefore the Lord is forced to cast us downe, to the end our prayers may come from our heart, and that our senses may be wakened from the securitie in which they are lying. Albeit the throne of God be most high, yet he delighteth to hear the petitions of hearts that are most low; that are most cast downe by the sight of sinne." God is not angry with us for being in great trouble about our iniquities.

2. We never have so good cause for distress of mind, as when we find sin defiling us and dragging us into *deep places*, v. 1. Were there no sin in the universe, we should hardly need the word *evil* to express any of our conceptions. No man ever hated or dreaded sin excessively. Every sigh and groan from earth or hell, every *cry*, wrung from distress of conscience, is the fruit of sin. Sin has digged every grave, built every prison, even hell itself.

3. There is no spiritual success without prayer. It is the life of a new life, vv. 1, 2. Perhaps God's people might have made all their attainments with less prosperity or less health of body; but not with less humility or less prayer. And what a joy it should diffuse through this world of sorrow that no sorrow, perplexity or guilt can exclude us from a blessed access to the mercy-seat. "There are no depths from which we may not look to the throne of heaven."

4. However men may applaud or flatter us, they cannot save us from the depths of anguish, because they cannot satisfy an enlightened conscience; they cannot reconcile us to our Maker. Every one having spiritual discernment sees that none but God can meet his case, or supply his wants. The whole believing world has always cried, Whom have I in heaven but thee? A right view of sin will lead us to the Lord for help and salvation, vv. 1, 2. None but he, against whom all sin is committed, can either remit its guilt, or destroy its power.

5. Great is the folly of going to the bar of God in the rags of our own righteousness, v. 3. Even here it is of the Lord's mercies that we are not consumed, but how can we *stand* before him, when he lays judgment to the line and justice to the plummet? Already Mount Sinai causes trembling in every sinful soul, that is not wholly insensible; how then can we face the eternal Judge? The best men on earth acknowledge their utterly ruined estate, if there be no mercy for them. Calvin: "Whoever shall come into the presence of God, whatever may be his eminence for sanctity, he must succumb and stand confounded."

6. There is no piety without genuine humility, and true humility is based in a just sense of personal unworthiness, v. 3. Sinners never approach God in a becoming manner till they have the spirit of the publican. There is enough sin in the case of every man to make his cry bitter and piercing. The Lord will not hear our self-commendations. He knows how groundless they are.

7. Right views of the holiness and justice of God are necessary to a deep Scriptural experience, v. 3. How can any man pray aright, who believes that God can connive at sin, or that the Almighty is very much such an one as himself? Why should we seek refuge from the coming storm, when we do not believe that any storm is coming? If eternal and immaculate justice is not against us, we have nothing

to fear. If Mount Sinai does not thunder against us, we need not flee to Mount Calvary.

8. It is both safe and obligatory on us to proclaim the doctrine of the full and free forgiveness of sins through faith in Christ. There is no risk in so doing. The doctrine promotes piety, v. 4. No being in the universe is so placable, so slow to wrath, so easy to be entreated, so rich in mercy, as the God against whom we have sinned. Tholuck: "God exerts forgiveness for the very purpose of kindling the fear of God in a more vivid and powerful manner." Horne: "True repentance is founded upon the sense of our own wretchedness, and faith in the divine mercy. Without the former, we should never seek for pardon and grace; without the latter, we should despair of finding them." Lampe: "Since the fear of God follows pardon, it cannot proceed from the fear of punishment." Calvin: "Men never serve God aright unless they know he is a gracious and merciful being." Nicolson: "If we know not our own misery, we shall not seek mercy; and if we despair of mercy, we shall never find it." "We never feel Christ to be a reality till we feel him to be a necessity." It is true this doctrine of free grace may be abused; but the right use of it is life from the dead to the humble penitent.

9. So essential to true piety is holy reverence that if God is not feared, he will be neither trusted nor obeyed, v. 4.

10. Unless we believe in the forgiveness of sins, all our religious observances will be in vain, v. 4. Without faith it is impossible to please God. Without it all prayer is mockery, and all religious rites an offence.

11. We greatly mistake our duty when we lightly esteem waiting on God, vv. 5, 6. We must be patient unto the coming of the Lord; and why should we not be? He is merciful and gracious, long-suffering, and abundant in goodness and truth, keeping mercy for thousands, forgiving iniquity, transgression and sin, Ex. xxxiv. 6, 7. Blessed are all they that wait for him.

12. As despair is a great sin, so it is a duty to hope in the Lord, according to the fulness of his word, vv. 5, 7. If he says, "Though your sins be as scarlet, they shall be as white as snow; though they be red like crimson, they shall be as wool," it is no presumption in us to embrace the glad tidings and hope in God's mercy. Symson: "There is nothing will bear us up but hope." The husbandman hath long patience because he has good hope. Let us set our hope in him. Owen: "The Lord Jehovah is the only hope for distressed souls."

13. How glorious is redemption—the redemption purchased by Christ! v. 7. It is so full, so free, so safe for man, so honorable to God. It exactly meets the demands of the law and the necessities of sinners. There is no limit to its sufficiency. It rescues from all sin, all guilt, all punishment. None who ever received it came short of the divine favor. How could it be otherwise? The very Author of redemption bears the name of Jesus, because he saves his people from their sins. Owen: "The ground of all hope and expectation of relief in sinners, is mere grace, mercy and redemption. All other grounds of hope are false and deceiving. Inexhaustible stores of mercy and redemption are needful for the encouragement of sinners to rest and wait on God. With him is plentiful redemption."

14. The final triumph of the true Israel is infallibly certain. The mouth of the Lord hath spoken it, v. 8. Tholuck: "We may expect much and even new redemption at his hands, till it shall be completed at last when the true Israel of God shall be redeemed from *all* their sins and their melancholy consequences." Owen: "All that wait on God on the account of mercy and grace shall have an undoubted issue of peace, Isa. xxvii. 5."

15. Surely we have the gospel in the Psalms, enough greatly to strengthen the faith

of believers at this day. The gospel was preached to Abraham, yea, even to Adam himself, John viii. 56; Gen. iii. 15. There has never been any true religion or genuine piety among sinners except that founded on a knowledge of God in Christ.

16. Owen: "1. They who out of depths have by faith and waiting obtained mercy, or are supported in waiting for a sense of believed mercy and forgiveness, are fitted, and only they are fitted, to preach and declare grace and mercy unto others. 2. A saving participation of grace and forgiveness leaves a deep impression of its fulness and excellency on the soul of a sinner." Therefore true penitents always commend Christ and his salvation. They wish all to come and partake of these infinite bounties.

PSALM CXXXI.

A Song of degrees of David.

1 LORD, my heart is not haughty, nor mine eyes lofty: neither do I exercise myself in great matters, or in things too high for me.

2 Surely I have behaved and quieted myself, as a child that is weaned of his mother: my soul *is* even as a weaned child.

3 Let Israel hope in the LORD from henceforth and for ever.

ON *A Song of degrees* see on title of Psalm cxx. The Hebrew, Syriac, Vulgate, Calvin, Venema, Amesius, Fabritius, Piscator, Patrick, Hammond, Henry, Pool, Gill, Dodd, Morison, Dickson, Jebb, Scott, Tholuck, Hengstenberg and Alexander give David as author. Gill: "This Psalm was written by David in his younger days, before he came to the throne, while he was in Saul's court." Edwards and Patrick favor this view. Scott dates it B. C. 1060. Tholuck speaks of it as "this brief but charming Psalm." It is indeed a gem, small but brilliant. Horne: "It is eminently applicable to Messiah, in his state of humiliation on earth." Christ was indeed perfectly meek and humble, and David was his type; but there seems no special fitness in making this Psalm Messianic. The only name of God found in it is *Jehovah* LORD, on which see on Ps. i. 2.

1. LORD, *my heart is not haughty, nor mine eyes lofty: neither do I exercise myself in great matters, or in things too high for me.* *Haughty, lifted up, exalted.* *Lofty, high, lifted up, exalted.* *Exercise myself,* literally, *caused myself to go,* or *to walk,* or *travel.* These verbs are in the preterite, expressing the habit of his life. *Things too high,* literally, things *wonderful too much.* Alexander: "The great and wonderful things meant are God's secret purposes and sovereign means for their accomplishment, in which man is not called to coöperate but to acquiesce." Pool's paraphrase is, "It neither is nor hath been my course to attempt or arrogate anything to myself above my degree or private capacity, or to affect worldly glory or domination." Some ancient versions and the Doway read: Lord, my heart is not exalted: nor are my eyes lofty. Neither have I walked in great matters, nor in wonderful things above me; church of England: Lord, I am not high minded; I have no proud looks. I do not exercise myself in great matters which are too high for me; Calvin: O Jehovah! my heart has not been elated, nor have mine eyes been lifted up, neither have I walked in great matters, or in things shut up from me; Edwards: I have not, Jehovah, an ambitious heart, nor haughty looks; nor am I conversant in great things, or in things too high for me.

2. *Surely I have behaved and quieted myself as a child that is weaned of his mother: my soul is even as a weaned child. Behaved*, literally, *made myself equal to. Quieted, made myself silent* or *still.* The simile of the *weaned child* supposes the child not in the process of weaning, but effectually weaned. The last clause declares how thoroughly the work was done, in his *soul*, in the depth of his affections. There seems to be no sufficient reason for rejecting, as Phillips and Hengstenberg do, the idea of a *weaned* child, and making the word mean simply a *little* child. The judgment of almost all expositors sustains the English version and the obvious interpretation. Compare Isa. xxviii. 9. The word rendered *surely* is the sign of strong affirmation, or of swearing.

3. *Let Israel hope in the Lord from henceforth and for ever.* This is an exhortation uttered with authority, but based on the prophet's own happy experience. David had felt in his own case the happy effects of such pious confidence; see on Ps. cxxx. 7.

DOCTRINAL AND PRACTICAL REMARKS.

1. When David was wickedly, falsely and without any offence on his part, accused of evil designs, especially touching public affairs, he set an example which we would do well to follow. Accused before men, he justifies himself before God, protesting his innocence to the Searcher of hearts, and leaving his cause to the Judge of all, v. 1. A very different course would have been obligatory upon him if he had given any cause for the slanders uttered against him. His whole life had shown their utter falsity. What more could he do? Jesus was thus accused, "he answered not a word."

2. There is a very close connection between the heart and the eyes. If the former is lifted up, the latter will commonly be lofty, v. 1. When gestures express a wicked state of the heart, they are as criminal as words or deeds. We cannot too carefully guard against all the motions and effects of pride and haughtiness. They are contrary to God's entire nature. It is better to be an humble beggar than a proud prince, a lowly penitent than a haughty angel. Scott: "The proud man is insolent in his deportment, and despises mean persons, situations, and occupations; he is vain-glorious and ambitious, aspiring after great connections and important employments, engaging in deep schemes and speculations, and courting observation and applause." When Jeshurun waxed fat, he kicked, and when he grew thick and was covered with fatness, he forsook God which made him, and lightly esteemed the Rock of his salvation, Deut. xxxii. 15. When Uzziah was strong, his heart was lifted up to his destruction, 2 Chron. xxvi. 16. Even good Hezekiah was led far astray by pride. Compare Pr. xvi. 18; Luke xiv. 11; Jas. iv. 6; 1 Pet. v. 5.

3. Yet how lovely is lowliness of heart. Blessed are the poor in spirit. If sickness, or poverty, or reproach makes us humble, we ought to hail with gladness the approach of either of these forms of evil. Tholuck: "The conduct of a victorious king, blessed with prosperity and power, who is content with what the Lord has meted out to him, demands a special acknowledgment."

4. It is not sinful to hold a high position in church or state, if God call us thereto. It is entirely safe to follow the leadings of his providence in any direction. David was a prophet and a king, to both of which offices he was anointed of God.

5. But those who hold high stations are as much bound to be humble and modest as any other persons whatever. Nor is pride less dangerous to them than to the poor miserable reptile that crawls up to the throne of power.

6. Let every man also beware of ambition, v. 1. It is sad to see children meddling with sharp swords. Henry: "Those will fall under due shame that affect un-

due honors." Amesius: "It is the appropriate work of a lofty presumption to affect and attempt those things which are quite above their ability and their calling."

7. Although human ability is wholly inadequate to the task, yet God's grace is all-sufficient to repress pride and ambition in the mighty, the wealthy, the warlike, as well as in the poor, and peaceable citizen. For the exercise of such grace on the part of God, we ought to give continual thanks.

8. It is a great mercy when fools are kept from meddling with matters quite beyond their capacity. A jewel of gold in a swine's snout is a comely sight compared with the sceptre of power in the hand of a poor feeble creature led on by his passions or by the passions of those around him.

9. The aspirations which are bold and daring are often less dangerous to those around us than those which fawn, and cringe, and flatter, and calculate, and plot. Finesse is not wisdom; policy is not statesmanship.

10. When appearances are against a good man in the path of his duty, he may quietly pursue the even tenor of his way, v. 1. When men choose they can easily pervert the best motives, words and actions, and give them the worst possible construction.

11. Self-control and self-discipline are great attainments, and should be sought with untiring diligence and much earnestness. Blessed is he, who is as a *weaned child*, v. 2.

12. Dickson: "The humble man must be content to be handled and dealt with as the Lord pleaseth, and to submit himself absolutely to God's dispensation." Henry: "When our condition is not to our mind, we must bring our mind to our condition."

13. Hope must be a very important exercise of the mind, both in fact and in God's esteem, or it would not be so often insisted on in Scripture, v. 3. And 'our hope is of the right kind when we cherish humble and sober views of ourselves, and neither wish nor attempt anything without the leading and approbation of God.'

14. When God deals graciously with us, we ought to encourage others to trust in him who has kept his covenant with us, v. 3. Morison: "The experience of the godly in past ages is all in favor of pursuing a course of quiet submission to the divine will; especially in seasons of painful and unjust accusation."

PSALM CXXXII.

A Song of degrees.

1 Lord, remember David, *and* all his afflictions:
2 How he sware unto the Lord, *and* vowed unto the mighty *God* of Jacob;
3 Surely I will not come into the tabernacle of my house, nor go up into my bed;
4 I will not give sleep to mine eyes, *or* slumber to mine eyelids,
5 Until I find out a place for the Lord, a habitation for the mighty *God* of Jacob.
6 Lo, we heard of it at Ephratah: we found it in the fields of the wood.
7 We will go into his tabernacles: we will worship at his footstool.
8 Arise, O Lord, into thy rest; thou, and the ark of thy strength.
9 Let thy priests be clothed with righteousness; and let thy saints shout for joy.
10 For thy servant David's sake turn not away the face of thine anointed.
11 The Lord hath sworn *in* truth unto David; he will not turn from it; Of the fruit of thy body will I set upon thy throne.

12 If thy children will keep my covenant and my testimony that I shall teach them, their children shall also sit upon thy throne for evermore.

13 For the LORD hath chosen Zion; he hath desired *it* for his habitation.

14 This *is* my rest for ever: here will I dwell; for I have desired it.

15 I will abundantly bless her provision: I will satisfy her poor with bread.

16 I will also clothe her priests with salvation: and her saints shall shout aloud for joy.

17 There will I make the horn of David to bud: I have ordained a lamp for mine anointed.

18 His enemies will I clothe with shame: but upon himself shall his crown flourish.

ON the title see on title of Psalm cxx. Abenezra, Kimchi and Lightfoot regard David as the author of this Psalm. Fabritius says that David is commonly held to be the author. Gill inclines to the same opinion. But Anderson regards "the mention of David's name in the tenth verse in the third person, and the terms there employed, as militating against the Davidic authorship." Yet elsewhere David speaks of himself both in the second and third person, Ps. xix. 11; xx. 1–4. Others confidently ascribe it to Solomon. This seems to be Luther's opinion. Patrick thinks this not improbable, and in his exposition follows it. In this opinion coincide Diodati, Edwards, Dodd, Henry and Scott. Jebb is very decided: "The whole tenor of this Psalm is an exact epitome of the Dedication Prayer of Solomon. . . There can be little question that this Psalm was composed by Solomon." Pool inclines to this opinion. Clarke, Hengstenberg and Alexander give it a later origin. Clarke says "it refers to the building of the second temple, and placing the ark of the covenant in it." But if we may at all credit tradition, the ark never was in the second temple. Hengstenberg says, it "is to be referred to the times of the new colony," in the days of Nehemiah and Ezra. Of those, who make David the author, some suppose that it was written on David's first, some on his second removal of the ark; yet others, on the occasion of his numbering the people, and the consequent curse upon his nation. Those, who regard Solomon as the author, of course fix its composition to the dedication of the temple. Those who give it a later origin suppose it to have been written at the close of the captivity. Scott dates it B. C. 1004; Clark, B. C. about 515. The only name of God found in it is *Jehovah* LORD, on which see on Ps. i. 2.

1. LORD, *remember David*, and *all his afflictions*. This translation follows all the ancient versions, and is supported by Calvin, Fabritius, Amesius, Tremellius and Junius, Edwards, Street and others. But Venema, Piscator, Hengstenberg and Alexander read, *Remember for David all his afflictions, i. e.*, Remember, in behalf of David, all his troubles. This does not alter the general import of the passage. For *afflictions* Street reads *care;* the Septuagint, *meekness;* the Syriac, *humility;* Tholuck, *pains.* The care or trouble of David related, not chiefly to himself, but to the house of God, as we learn from other parts of the Psalm, and from other Scriptures. Compare 2 Sam. vii. 2, 3. Here God is asked to *remember* for good and in a gracious way the care his pious servant had long had for the divine honor and glory. In the time of David, the ark had been removed from Shiloh and was at Kirjath-jearim. The ark was not prominent in the days of Saul. Compare 1 Chron. xiii. 3. The first attempt to remove the ark, being accompanied by the death of Uzzah, increased David's concern, 2 Sam. vi. 9. He had a deep and lasting solicitude on the subject.

2. *How he sware unto the* LORD, *and vowed unto the mighty* God *of Jacob.* The historical books of Scripture give no account of any oath taken by David touching this matter; but the term is explained in the second clause of the verse to mean a *vow.* Religious engagements with the Lord are in their nature as solemn as an oath. Compare Ps. cxix. 106; 1 Chron. xxii. 7–10. The history of David's effort to establish the ark in a fixed and permanent abode may be seen in 2 Sam. vi. 1–20; 1 Chron. xv. 2–29; Acts vii. 46. The word in this verse rendered *mighty* is found in v. 5; Gen.

xlix. 24; Isa. i. 24; xlix. 26; lx. 16. It is an epithet applied to God. As he manifested the exceeding greatness of his power in the protection of Jacob, and the defence of Israel, and revealed himself to the fathers, he is fitly styled the *mighty* One, or *the mighty* God *of Jacob*. Jacob first gave this title to Jehovah.

3. *Surely I will not come into the tabernacle of my house, nor go up into my bed.* *Surely*, as in Ps. cxxxi. 2, the sign of affirmation or oath. The meaning seems to be, I will not contentedly and with satisfaction rest in my house, or seek repose on my bed.

4. *I will not give sleep to mine eyes, or slumber to mine eyelids. Sleep* and *slumber*, used interchangeably. See on Ps. cxxi. 3, 4. The English translation does not notice the sign of affirmation or oath (surely), which is repeated in the Hebrew of this verse, and in v. 3. David was profoundly anxious concerning the fulfilment of the promise made by God to the fathers, and recorded in Deut. xii. 5.

5. *Until I find out a place for the* LORD, *an habitation for the mighty* God *of Jacob.* The ark was the symbol of the presence of Jehovah. Its *place* was his *habitation*. David being a prophet knew that the time was approaching when God would choose out of all the tribes a place for the ark, a permanent abode for the symbol of the divine presence. *Mighty* God *of Jacob*, as in v. 2. *Habitation*, in v. 7, in the plural *tabernacles*. Some think this is put by *enallage* for the singular. Others, that it designates the sanctuary with its enclosures and appendages; others, that it is the *plural of excellence*.

6. *Lo, we heard of it at Ephratah: we found it in the fields of the wood. It*, the ark, which was for a season kept at Shiloh, in the tribe of Ephraim, whose territory might properly be called, Ephratah. See 1 Sam. i. 1; 1 Kings xi. 26. This is better than the explanation which supposes that Ephratah here means Bethlehem, though that city did early and long bear that name. Compare Gen. xxxv. 19; xlviii. 7; Mic. v. 2. The *fields of the wood* is a poetic phrase for Kirjath-jearim, the meaning of which word is, *The city of woods* or *forests*. Compare 1 Sam. vii. 1, 2; 2 Sam. vi. 2–19; 1 Chron. xiii. 2–8; 2 Chron. i. 4.

7. *We will go into his tabernacles: we will worship at his footstool. Tabernacles*, plural, the same as *habitations* in v. 5. *Footstool*, as in Ps. xcix. 5; cx. 1. Both the nouns of this verse designate the appointed place for God's worship. *Worship*, as in Ps. v. 7; the same word in the 2d commandment is rendered *bow down*. The verse expresses the pious purpose of doing reverence to Jehovah in his own appointed way. There is no objection to making David and his fellow-worshippers, the speakers in this verse, except that vv. 8, 9, were used by Solomon at the dedication of the first temple, 2 Chron. vi. 41, 42. But Solomon may have quoted them from this place. Calvin regards the verse as containing "a common form of mutual exhortation."

8. *Arise*, O LORD, *into thy rest; thou, and the ark of thy strength.* Whenever the camp was about to move, Moses used the language found in the first part of this verse. *Arise* (or rise up) *O Jehovah*. Here and in 2 Chron. vi. 41, *the ark of God's strength* is the name given to that symbol of his presence and power. Whoever fought against the ark was sure to be overcome. The *rest* here was the *resting-place* of the ark.

9. *Let thy priests be clothed with righteousness; and let thy saints shout for joy.* The first clause differs from that in 2 Chron. vi. 41, in omitting the name of the Most High *Lord God*, and in having *righteousness* instead of *salvation*. Compare v. 16, where we read *salvation*. The *salvation* of sinners is by *righteousness* imputed to them, and this is received by all of God's true people, and published by all his true ministers. *Saints, gracious ones* or *merciful ones*. God is greatly honored by the abounding joys of his people, and they should give due expression to their gladness by *shouting*, or

singing, see on Ps. v. 11.   Both the verbs of this verse are in the future.   It is clearly a prediction.

10. *For thy servant David's sake turn not away the face of thine anointed.   For the sake of David*, literally *because of David*, because of his peculiar relations to thee, as the founder of the family, which should fill the throne until Judah should cease to have a Lawgiver; the type of Messias; the man to whom thou didst make great promises, which are as yet but partially fulfilled.   Compare 1 Kings xi. 12, 13; 2 Kings viii. 19.   To *turn away the face of another* is to *deny his request*, to *say him nay*, as these terms are explained by our translators in 1 Kings ii. 16, 17, 20.   *Anointed*, Hebrew *Messias*.   Calvin here renders it *Christ*.   Yet there seems to be nothing to justify the application of the term here to the Son of God, except as in him the throne of David was to be perpetual, and David and Solomon were figures of him of whom it was said: " He shall be great, and shall be called the Son of the Highest; and the Lord God will give unto him the throne of his father David, and he shall reign over the house of Jacob forever, and of his kingdom there shall be no end," Luke i. 32, 33. By the *anointed* some understand David and some Solomon.   This is probably correct.   Compare 1 Kings iii. 6, 7; viii. 24, 25.   Whichsoever may be directly referred to, the people Israel are to be regarded as embraced.   See 1 Kings viii. 25, 66.   The true interests of David and Israel were identical.   So are the honor and triumph of Christ and his people.

11. *The* LORD *hath sworn* in *truth unto David; he will not turn from it; of the fruit of thy body will I set upon thy throne.*   Of God's engagement to David here referred to, see 2 Sam. vii. 12; 1 Kings viii. 25; Ps. lxxxix. 35, 49. The purpose of God respecting David and his seed was irreversible.   The salvation of the world depended upon the promise of God not failing in that case, as the covenant with David culminated only in the person of the Redeemer, who was the *fruit of his body*, and who now sits upon the throne of his father David dispensing countless spiritual blessings to all the true Israel.   This verse is so explained by Peter, Acts ii. 30.

12. *If thy children will keep my covenant and my testimony that I shall teach them, their children also shall sit upon thy throne for evermore.*   The verse sets forth the same doctrine declared by the Lord in 2 Sam. vii. 14–16.   As far as the promise related to David's sinful posterity, its execution was suspended upon their general faithfulness. But as Christ pleased the Father in all things, to him the promise could in no sense fail.   Jehovah took vengeance of the sinning descendants of David; but there was no room for any displeasure against his dear Son.   His throne is forever and ever. However it may fare with particular kings or with the people over whom they reign, God will not forsake his true church, nor change the general course of his providence respecting her:

13. *For the* LORD *hath chosen Zion: he hath desired* it *for his habitation.   Habitation*, not the word so rendered in v. 5, but simply *dwelling, dwelling-place.*   The temple was built on Mount Moriah; but this was sometimes called Mount Zion, for these were closely connected and might be regarded as one.   Compare Ps. lxv. 1; lxxxiv. 7.   Or Zion may be here put for the holy city, the place of Israel's solemnities.

14. *This* is *my rest for ever: here will I dwell; for I have desired it.*   It seems impossible to find the complete fulfilment of this passage within the walls of the literal Jerusalem.   Our Saviour himself taught that under the gospel there should be no peculiar privileges or advantages to those who worshipped in the holy city, John iv. 21.   Long before his time, a great prophet had declared that Jerusalem should be trodden down of the Gentiles, Dan. viii. 13.   So that we are compelled to seek in the true invisible church of Christ the fulfilment of this verse, of that which precedes it and of several which succeed it.   The Mount Zion which God has *desired* is

the church bought with blood. Calvin: "The church is limited to no one place: Now that the glory of the Lord shines through all the earth, his rest is where Christ and his members are," Matt. xviii. 20.

15. *I will abundantly bless her provision: I will satisfy her poor with bread. Abundantly bless*, literally, *Blessing, I will bless.* I will surely pronounce a benediction. *Provision*, not elsewhere found in the Psalms. In Gen. xxvii. 3, 5, 7, 19, 25, 31, 33, rendered *venison;* in Prov. xii. 27, *that which he took in hunting;* in Neh. xiii. 15, *victuals;* in Job xxxviii. 41, *food.* The cognate feminine is in Ps. lxxviii. 25, rendered *meat.* Here it is a term descriptive of all the *provision* God has made for the sustenance of the spiritual strength of his people, and is explained by the parallel clause in the same verse. By reading *viduus* for *victus*, for *food* the Vulgate has *widow*, a gross mistake noticed by Jerome, yet adopted by the Doway. Zion's *poor* or *needy* are the humble, the poor in spirit, who hunger and thirst after righteousness, who find God's words and eat them, and are fed by the ordinances. God's church is the true Bethlehem, the house of bread. In a sense, and to an extent calling for gratitude, the promise of this verse was literally fulfilled in Jerusalem of old; but it is much more gloriously fulfilled in the company of faithful men, who constitute the church of Christ.

16. *I will also clothe her priests with salvation: and her saints shall shout aloud for joy.* See on v. 9, where the same verb occurs. The *righteousness* required in Scripture issues in *salvation.* Here as in many other cases, *to clothe* means *to invest, to cause to abound in.* Compare Ps. xxxv. 26; cix. 18; Isa. lxi. 10. We have the same verb in v. 18; and in another form in v. 9.

17. *There will I make the horn of David to bud: I have ordained a lamp for mine anointed.* Very often we meet with the figure of *exalting the horn*, Ps. lxxxix. 17. But the *budding* of a horn is a new figure. Compare Ezek. xxix. 21. The word rendered *to bud* is elsewhere rendered *to grow, to grow up, to spring forth*, 2 Sam. xxiii. 5; Isa. xlv. 8; lxi. 11; Jer. xxxiii. 15. The cognate noun is rendered *Branch*, in Jer. xxiii. 5; xxxiii. 15; Zech. iii. 8; vi. 12. The meaning of the first clause is that the power of the throne of David, though subject to occasional declension, should finally rise to eminence, and be great in the person of Messiah. Kimchi: "The Horn of David is the Messias." *Anointed*, as in v. 10. The second clause teaches the same thing by another figure. Compare 1 Kings xi. 36. *Ordained*, better rendered *prepared.* Whom God would bless, he enlightens; whom he would curse, he leaves in darkness. So strongly does the latter part of this Psalm seem to refer to Messiah and the gospel church that Chrysostom and Cyrill regard the *lamp* as referring to John the Baptist. But doubtless it has a much more extended application. Alexander: "The meaning of the whole verse is, that the promises of old made to David and to Zion should be yet fulfilled, however dark and inauspicious present appearances."

18. *His enemies will I clothe with shame.* See on v. 16, and on the passages there cited. God will wrap up the foes of his Son with shame and cover them with contempt. *But upon himself shall his crown flourish. Flourish, flower*, or *blossom.* This is better than to read with some *glitter* or *shine.* The crowns bestowed by the ancients upon victors and made of evergreens, soon dried up and fell to pieces. But even the humblest people of God wear crowns that fade not away, 1 Pet. v. 4. Much more is the crown of the Redeemer unfading. Great is his dominion. On his head are many crowns, Rev. xix. 12.

DOCTRINAL AND PRACTICAL REMARKS.

1. It is the duty of all, whether in authority or out of it, to do what they can to

promote the true worship of Jehovah, v. 1. In this matter David set a worthy example. Some understand from 1 Chron. xvi. 43, that as David did not bless his house, so he refused to occupy it, until the ark had a fixed abode. Let no one plead either public or private engagements as a reason for slighting the claims of God's house. David was often full of anxieties, and encountered terrible oppositions, yet his chief concern was for the right worship of God. Amesius: "The greater our care and concern for promoting the worship and glory of God, the greater is the stability and consolation of our faith."

2. We may be perfectly sure that God will never forget any work of faith or labor of love, performed by us with right motives, v. 1. Our toils in his cause may be wearisome, and our care for the building up of Zion consuming, but God will ever be mindful of it.

3. As Moses asked God to remember Abraham, Isaac and Israel, his servants, Ex. xxxii. 13, and as Solomon (if he wrote this Psalm) here asks God to remember his pious father, God's servant, so may we confidently plead with the Most High for blessings when we are cherishing the same good purposes, and carrying out the same worthy designs as our pious ancestors, v. 1.

4. Much more may we fitly ask God to remember the work and sufferings of our spiritual David, not only as a memorial, but as a meritorious ground of spiritual blessings to us and to those who come after us.

5. It is lawful for us to bind ourselves by the most solemn engagements to be the Lord's, and to serve him in any Scriptural way. Calvin: "To vow unto God that which he himself has declared to be agreeable to him, is a commendable practice." Henry: "When needful work is to be done for God, it is good for us to task ourselves, and tie ourselves to a time, because we are apt to put off." Amesius: "Right religious concern will manifest itself in holy purposes and vows for promoting the worship and glory of God." Dickson: "It is lawful to tie ourselves by an oath to that duty, whereunto we were absolutely tied by law before."

6. In dealing with God it is important for us to remember that he is mighty, vv. 2, 5, yea, he is almighty. The very moment a Christian doubts the omnipotence of God, he has begun to fall into a snare.

7. A true and spiritual concern for the glory of God and the honor of his worship is both controlling and permanent, vv. 3–5. Pious purposes should not be fitful.

8. When God has promised any good to Zion, though it be in a prophecy never so old, it should be our business to study it, and pray and labor for its fulfilment, just as David understood from Deut. xii. 5, that there should be in due time a fixed place for all the tribes to assemble, so he desired to honor God by helping to designate that place, and promote his public united worship, v. 5.

9. Even a rumor of good or evil to the Lord's cause, though relating to things far from them, does yet deeply affect the pious, v. 6.

10. It is a happy circumstance when rulers and people, rich and poor, small and great, cordially unite in maintaining the public worship of God, v. 7. But alas! "there is often a place for prayer, where there is no heart to pray."

11. The godly greatly desire God's presence and the animating tokens thereof in all their attempts to worship him, v. 8. The form without the substance is never satisfactory to the meek of the earth. The common judgment of the godly is that the gracious presence of the Most High amply compensates all their toils and sufferings.

12. God's merciful presence is the life of his true ministers in all ages, vv. 9, 16. Compare Matt. xxviii. 20. The garments of the ancient priesthood were indeed beautiful, but they were worn by many a heartless hypocrite. God's ministers are never

clothed with *righteousness* and salvation till the Lord vouchsafes the tokens of his love. Henry: "Holiness towards God, and goodness towards all men, are habits for ministers, of the necessity of which there is no dispute." Dickson: "The chief badge and cognizance of the Lord's minister is the true doctrine of justification and obedience of faith in a holy conversation."

13. God's gracious presence is the joy of all his true people, vv. 9, 16. When he is come, the shadows flee away.

14. If the very names given by God's prophets to his people are such as *saints, gracious ones, merciful ones,* surely his professed people ought to see to it that they are not cruel, untender or *unholy*. Calvin: "The saints of God are called *merciful ones,* because mercy or beneficence is that grace which assimilates us most to God."

15. Well may we plead God's covenant with our pious parents and beg him not to deny our requests, so long as we walk in the godly ways of our ancestors, v. 10.

16. Even in the days of Solomon the godly could recount a long line of promises and prophecies, every one of which must be fulfilled. Since that time they have been much increased, though not in faithfulness, yet in number and explicitness. In view of them, let the church be glad and shout.

17. There are no keener miseries than those brought upon men, when by their sins they forfeit the covenant blessings enjoyed by their ancestors, v. 12.

18. The doctrine of God's free and sovereign election is no novelty. It was held by the fathers. God's covenant with Zion is based in his *choice,* and that *choice* is resolved into his own good pleasure or *desire,* v. 13. Amesius: "The stability of the promises flows from election."

19. If the people of God have a delightful repose in the bosom of the Lord, so the Lord has his *rest* in the church. There he *dwells,* for he has *desired* it, v. 14. He loves the gates of Zion more than all the dwellings of Jacob.

20. Wonderful indeed, as well as ample, are the arrangements which the Lord has made for supplying all the wants, animal and spiritual, temporal and eternal, of his people, even the humblest of them, v. 15. To the poor the Gospel is preached. Horne: "The city in which the King of heaven deigns to place his throne can want no manner of thing that is good." Food and raiment, strength and courage, things present and things to come, Paul, Apollos and Cephas, life and death, triumph and glory, God and heaven are the inheritance of the saints.

21. Christ is and shall ever be glorious in his works and ways, vv. 17, 18.

22. Just as certainly as Christ prevails, so certainly must the wicked be overthrown, and covered with shame, v. 18. Their hopes shall all be vain, their plots frustrated, and themselves undone, unless they speedily repent that they may live.

23. As David and Solomon were each in his day the visible head of the civil and ecclesiastical government established in Israel, many commentators take occasion from this Psalm to remark on the value of religion and of civil government. Luther: "Where these two things, the word and the laws, are rightly constituted and preserved, then all things go well with a kingdom;" Tholuck: "The church and the civil government are two institutions, on which the prosperity of the state and the people depends." We should therefore follow the example here set of praying for rulers, and rulers should pray for themselves, v. 10. And let all such remember their dependence on the Most High. Henry: "Kings are before God upon their good behaviour, and their commission from him runs *quamdiu se bene gesserint—during good behaviour.*"

PSALM CXXXIII.

A Song of degrees of David.

1 Behold, how good and how pleasant *it is* for brethren to dwell together in unity!

2 *It is* like the precious ointment upon the head, that ran down upon the beard, *even* Aaron's beard: that went down to the skirts of his garments;

3 As the dew of Hermon, *and as the dew* that descended upon the mountains of Zion: for there the LORD commanded the blessing, *even* life for evermore.

ON *A Song of degrees* in the title see on title of Ps. cxx. This Psalm is ascribed to David by the Hebrew, Syriac, Vulgate, Calvin, Piscator, Patrick, Edwards, Morison, Henry, Pool, Jebb, Scott, Tholuck and Alexander. Scott dates it B. C. 1040; Clarke, B. C. about 515. Clarke rejects the Davidic authorship. Its historic occasion is variously given. 1. Some refer it to the three great annual festivals celebrated in Jerusalem. 2. Others think it was written upon the termination of the civil war between the house of Saul and the house of David. 3. Others find occasion for it in the termination of Absalom's rebellion, and the happy return of the king. On either of these occasions it might have been fitly sung; but it cannot be shown to have had its origin in either of them. It has long been of excellent use in the church of God. It was doubtless sung by the Israelites returned from the captivity. Patrick observes that it was "fitly used by the first Christians to express their joy for the blessed union of Jews and Gentiles; and may now serve the uses of all Christian societies, whose happiness lies in holy peace and concord." The only name of God found in it is *Jehovah* LORD, on which see on Ps. i. 2.

1. *Behold, how good and how pleasant* it is *for brethren to dwell together in unity!* *Behold,* a fit word to call special attention. The adjectives *good* and *pleasant* well express the force of the original, and are those usually employed in rendering the Hebrew. The latter term may be rendered *sweet,* beautiful, delightful. *Brethren,* all men are brethren, as they have the like nature and are the offspring of Adam and the creatures of God. All the Jews were brethren, as descended from Abraham, Isaac and Jacob, as bound by the same national covenant, and as having a common civil and ecclesiastical head and national capital. The members of the same family are brethren. All pious men are brethren, being born of God, having one Lord, one faith, one baptism, one hope, one aim, one end, one God and Father. How good and how delightful it is for men as human beings or for citizens of the same country to live in peace and harmony! How hateful and baneful are war and strife and bloodshed among such. See Isa. xiii. 6–18; Jer. iv. 19–31; James iv. 1–11. But the highest unity is that of *brethren* in Christ, animated with love and pity to one another, with a common, pious zeal for truth and holiness, with joyful hopes all centred in Christ. Among these discord, wrath, bitterness and contention are odious just in proportion as they are under the highest obligations to dwell together in love and *unity.* For this latter term there is no corresponding noun in the Hebrew; but it fairly gives the sense of the original. The authorized version is literally that of the Doway, which agrees with the Vulgate. For *unity* Edwards reads *the closest unity,* as expressing no more than the original imports.

2. It is *like the precious ointment, upon the head, that ran down upon the beard,* even *Aaron's beard: that went down to the skirts of his garments. Precious,* the same word rendered *good* in v. 1. How good this ointment was may be learned from the original prescription for its composition, Ex. xxx. 23–25, 30. We may be mistaken respect-

ing the precise kind of some of the spices used; but there is no doubt that they were all remarkable for their sweet odors. On some of the uses of ointment see on Ps. xxiii. 5. This refers to Aaron's consecration to office. The effusion was copious. It ran down upon Aaron's beard. *Skirts*, Kimchi, Jarchi, Edwards and Street have *collar;* Calvin, *skirt;* Hengstenberg, *border;* Alexander, *edge;* Fry, *surface;* Hebrew, *mouth.* The meaning is not that his whole raiment was saturated with ointment, but that the entire hair of his head and face were full of the sweet odors; and that they extended to the upper borders of his priestly robes. Some make the latter clause relate to Aaron's beard, extending down to the edge of his garment; but the length of his beard is of no manner of significancy in the matter of which the prophet here treats; it is the precious ointment to which he likens brotherly unity. The use of the same word in Hebrew rendered in the English *ran down* and *went down* indicates that the ointment is still spoken of in the last clause. Kamphuzzen well gives the proper use of this figure:

> "E'en as the ointment whose sweet odors blended,
> From Aaron's head upon his beard descended,
> And, falling thence, with rich perfume ran o'er
> The holy garb the prophet wore:
> So doth the unity that lives with brothers
> Share its best blessings and its joy with others."

The prophet now introduces another figure:

3. *As the dew of Hermon,* and as the dew *that descended upon the mountains of Zion: for there the* Lord *commanded the blessing,* even *life for evermore.* There are two mountains called Hermon; one is the highest ridge of those called Anti-Lebanon in the northern border of the country; the other is on the west side of the Jordan and forms the southern boundary of the plain of Esdraelon. It is not certain which of these was in the eye of the prophet in penning this verse; nor is it important for us to decide. Neither of them was near to Jerusalem. Hence has arisen the difficulty of interpreting these words. However abundant dew may be, it never runs even in Syria from a higher to a lower place as rain does, and the question is asked, how could the dew of Hermon descend on the mountains of Zion? Several explanations are offered. 1. Some read *Sion* and not *Zion*, referring to the mountain spoken of in Deut. iv. 48, one of the spurs of Mount Hermon, see on Ps. xxix. 6. But there is as much difficulty in this as in any other explanation, unless we make Sion and Hermon the same mountain and insert the word *even* in connecting the first and second clauses of the verse. Moreover there is difficulty in making such an explanation pertinent to the object of the prophet as expressed in the last part of the Psalm. 2. Another explanation is that suggested by the English translation, where before the second clause they add the words, *and as the dew.* This is legitimate and simply conveys the idea that the dew, which falls upon Hermon, falls upon Zion the same night. But this supposes that the force of the figure is to be sought in the fruitfulness and vigorous growth produced by the abundant dew, all delightful plants and shrubs and trees being thereby greatly refreshed. How abundant the dews in Syria are, even to this day, is fully witnessed by travellers. 3. Another explanation is that given by Scott, who says: "This verse may be rendered 'As the dew of Hermon, *so is this*, which descends upon the mountains of Zion;' and thus mean, that, as the gentle dews, descending on Mount Hermon rendered it fruitful and delightful, so the dew of heavenly love, distilling upon the worshippers on Mount Zion would render them fruitful in good works, happy in themselves, and blessings to all around them." Either this last or the second mode of explanation is to be preferred. Secker thinks that the word rendered *there* "points to the place where brethren dwell together in unity." The phrase

command a blessing occurs in the Pentateuch, Lev. xxv. 21; Deut. xxviii. 8. We have no specific passage in which it is used in application to Mount Zion except this; but the connection of God's blessing, even eternal life, with his true church, where love lives and reigns, is abundantly taught in all the Scriptures. On the highest authority we learn that "love is the fulfilling of the law." Hengstenberg: "Brotherly unity resembles a lovely dew, which descends on the hills of Zion where this unity is so strikingly exemplified." Calvin: "The figure of the *dew* distilling upon Mount Zion and Hermon denotes, that a holy unity has not only a sweet savor before God, but is productive of good effects, as the dew moistens the earth and supplies it with sap and freshness." Tholuck: "The word *blessing* is explained by the more pregnant term *life*." We cannot fairly interpret the Scriptures unless we admit that spiritual and eternal blessings were connected with the worship of the ancient church and with the faith and expectations of her members.

Doctrinal and Practical Remarks.

1. No man over-estimates the blessings of peace and concord in all the relations of life, vv. 1–3. Nor until he sacrifices truth, honor, righteousness or a good conscience does he ever pay too much for them. David had seen the workings of envy, of private malice, of civil war, of sectional jealousy and international strife, and such is his estimate of *unity* that he confesses his inability to express it, exclaiming, *How good and how pleasant it is.* Horne: "Many things are good which are not pleasant; and many pleasant, which are not good. But unity among brethren, whether civil or religious, is productive both of profit and pleasure. Of profit, because therein consisteth the welfare and security of every society; of pleasure, because mutual love is the source of delight, and the happiness of one becomes, in that case, the happiness of all." The evils of discord are frightful and they are legion. Particularly,

2. Families cannot too highly prize the quiet and harmony resulting from all kindly sentiments, words and deeds. The Lord Jesus himself sought the special friendship of a quiet, loving family, John xi. 5. He made his blessing on households to depend on their concord, Matt. x. 12, 13; Luke x. 5, 6. Even where there is not found the vilest form of discord in houses, resulting in fights or broils, there may still be much unhappiness arising from snappishness. When father and mother, parents and children, brothers and sisters are tart and keen, peace flies away. Ill nature is easily engendered and transmitted in a family. Dekker:

> Crows are fair with crows;
> Custom in sin gives sin a lovely dye;
> Blackness in Moors is no deformity.

It is marvellous that Nabal did not make Abigail as much of a churl as himself, 1 Sam. xxv. 14–31. It is sad to see a heifer chained to a bear.

3. The peace of neighborhoods is of the greatest importance. The disturbers of concord among neighbors are not merely murderers, robbers and fighters, but their blood relations—their cousins german—backbiters, busy-bodies, slanderers, knaves, adulterers, fornicators. The doom of such, dying without repentance, will be dreadful, Ps. cxx. 3, 4; 1 Cor. vi. 9, 10; Rev. xxii. 15. One of the greatest curses to a community is low quarrelling.

4. It is a great thing for churches to keep the unity of the Spirit in the bond of peace. No command of Christ is more weighty or more stringent than this: "Have peace one with another," Mark ix. 50. How can it be accounted for that so many men, otherwise moral and apparently devout, seem to feel at liberty to become firebrands in the house of God? Amesius: "The communion of saints is not only to be believed, but also to be loved, and by words and deeds commended and promoted."

We are bound diligently to inquire how we may effectually promote love and peace among the brethren. We are no more at liberty to be schismatics than we are to be heretics. Luther: "Where there are dissensions, divisions, and discord, there is the dwelling of Satan." Religion greatly suffers when brethren in the church are alienated and view each other with an evil eye; when heart-burnings take the place of love and forbearance; when animosities supersede the offices of love; and malice holds the sceptre over spiritual affairs! "Live in peace, and the God of peace shall be with you," 2 Cor. xiii. 11; Phil. iv. 9.

5. How blessed is peace in a nation! Its great foes are of two classes. One consists of selfish, cruel, incompetent rulers, who make the government burdensome and vexatious. "As a roaring lion, and a ranging bear; so is a wicked ruler over the poor people," Pr. xxviii. 15. The miseries and turmoils effected by such rulers are incalculable. They often plunge a land into the horrors of poverty, rapine, violence and blood, which sicken the souls of all good men. The other class of persons, who disturb the peace of nations consists of agitators and revolutionists, who hate good laws and rulers, and would rather see all the horrors and harassings of civil war than not be successful in carrying out their fanatical or ambitious schemes.

6. Another class of peace-breakers are those who stir up strife between nations, and involve at least two countries in international war and bloodshed. "War suspends the rules of moral obligation, and what is long suspended is in danger of being totally abrogated." Madison: "Of all the evils to public liberty, war is perhaps the most to be dreaded, because it comprises and develops the genius of every other. War is the parent of armies; from these proceed debt and taxes. And armies, and debts, and taxes are the known instruments for bringing the many under the dominion of the few. . . No nation can preserve its freedom in the midst of continual warfare."

7. Peace is a great blessing. It is so in itself. All its elements are kindly. All its principles are pure, benevolent. It is excellent in its consequences. It works no ill to a neighbour. It never makes any good man unhappy. It has received the commendation of the wisest and best of all ages. "The more quietly and peaceably we all get on the better." This sentiment is universally accepted by good and reflecting men.

> "'Tis death to me to be at enmity;
> I hate it, and desire all good men's love."

Poets, philosophers, statesmen, divines, prophets and apostles, have often declared in favor of peace and unity. The blessing of God in this Psalm and often elsewhere in the Scriptures is closely connected with the spirit of peace and love. Compare 1 Cor. xiii. 1–13; Phil. ii. 1–17. Henry: "Loving people are blessed people. 1. They are blessed of God, and therefore blessed indeed. 2. They are everlastingly blessed." John: "He that dwelleth in love, dwelleth in God, and God in him." Such have eternal life abiding in them and shall have life evermore.

8. Such being the blessings of unity, let us study and adopt good rules for preserving concord, such as these:

a. Prize highly the inestimable blessings of peace. They are above all praise. Scott: "No encomiums or illustrations can sufficiently display the excellence, pleasantness and manifold benefits of harmony among brethren, in families, in civil society, in nations and especially in the church of Christ. . . With it human happiness begins on earth, and will be completed in heaven." Buy it at any lawful sacrifice. "A good-natured man without grace maketh a fairer show than grace with an evil temper."

b. Pray earnestly that you may be able to lead a quiet and peaceable life in all godliness and honesty. Beg the Lord to keep you from the strife of tongues: at least from taking any part therein.   He can give quietness when all the world is in an uproar.

c. Remember that it is only the devil and his children, who hate peace and indulge malice.   If you would not be like the wicked one, shun his temptations.

d. Learn to deplore and abhor strife and all its fruits.   "Surely the professed followers of the meek and lowly Jesus have long enough experienced the painful and fatal effects of discord and angry controversy; by which Christianity has been disgraced and wounded in the house of its friends!"

e. Study to imitate the Lord Jesus Christ, who was meek and lowly, who did not strive nor cry, nor lift up his voice in the streets, and never opened his blessed lips but in love.   Horne: "The spirit of heavenly love was that oil of gladness which Jehovah poured without measure on him who is the high priest and head of his church Insinuating and healing, comforting and exhilarating, it is diffused from him over his body mystical."   If we are truly his, we have all received of his fulness.

f. It would be a great matter if we could lay out our strength on weighty things of doctrine and morals, and not be over zealous concerning small matters.

PSALM CXXXIV.

A Song of degrees.

1 Behold, bless ye the LORD, all *ye* servants of the LORD, which by night stand in the house of the LORD.

2. Lift up your hands *in* the sanctuary, and bless the LORD.

3 The LORD that made heaven and earth bless thee out of Zion.

THIS is the last composition in the Psalter styled *A Song of degrees.*   On that phrase see on title of Psalm cxx.   Respecting the authorship of this Psalm scholars are remarkably silent.   The Syriac ascribes it to David.   That conjecture is as probable as any other.   Scott dates it B. C. 1017; Clarke, B. C. about 515.   It has chief reference to the ministers of God's word, exhorting and commanding them to be vigilant and diligent in the work to which they are called; requiring them to be instant in season and out of season; enjoining them by precept and example to teach, exhort, warn, rebuke and encourage with all long-suffering and doctrine.   On the name *Jehovah* LORD, see on Ps. i. 2.

1. *Behold, bless ye the* LORD, *all* ye *servants of the* LORD, *which by night stand in the house of the* LORD.   *Behold,* as in Ps. cxxxiii. 1; equivalent to *see, come now, give heed.   Bless, pronounce* a benediction; see on Ps. v. 12.   *Servants of Jehovah,* a term that does sometimes embrace all the creatures of God; sometimes, all Israel; sometimes, God's loving, obedient people; but it is here limited to those who officially serve in the temple.   The phrase *by night,* or *in the nights,* does not necessarily mean *all night,* but *at night;* Calvin has *nightly;* Edwards, *every night.*   If, as some conjecture, the Psalm is a charge "from the high priest to the priests and Levites, who kept watch in the temple by night, to spend their time profitably, and duly celebrate the praises of God," we can see in it special beauty.   Or if we regard it as a call of the whole people of Israel to their priesthood to do their duty and to be intent upon their calling, it loses none of its force.   The sacred fire was kept burning on the altar all

night, the lamps also burned all night, and songs were sung in the temple by night, 1 Chron. ix. 33.   Fry: "We know generally that there was a nightly service in the temple." Anna, a prophetess, "departed not from the temple, but served God with fastings and prayers night and day," Luke ii. 37.   Some cite Paul before Agrippa: "Unto which promise, our twelve tribes, instantly serving God day and night, hope to come," Acts xxvi. 7.   Kimchi says holy men arose in the night and went to the temple to pray.   Compare Ex. xxvii. 21; Lev. viii. 35; 1 Sam. iii. 3; Ps. cxix. 147.

2. *Lift up your hands in the sanctuary, and bless the* LORD.   In the comprehensive sense of the term, prayer includes adoration, confession, thanksgiving, supplication, filling our mouths with pleas and arguments and intercession for others.   This part of the public worship of God seems to have been commonly performed with the eyes and hands lifted up toward heaven.   See on Ps. v. 7.   Compare Ps. xxviii. 2; lxiii. 4; cxli. 2; Lam. ii. 19; iii. 41; Luke xviii. 13.   The lifting up of the hands and eyes teaches us that we should lift our minds and hearts to God.   When the holy place is thus spoken of, it may refer to him, who dwelt in it.—Or we may read, Lift up your hands with holiness.   See 1 Tim. ii. 8.   This verse and the first seem to be spoken by the high priest, or by the united people; but in the judgment of many the third verse is the response of the priests and Levites to the speaker of those verses or of a new division of watchers at the temple.   Lowth and Tholuck take this latter view.

3. *The* LORD *that made heaven and earth bless thee out of Zion.*   On the fact that God is universal Creator, see on Ps. cxv. 15; cxxi. 2.   There is a peculiar fitness and beauty in speaking of God's almighty power, when we speak of his benediction. *Bless*, as in v. 1.   On the difference between our *blessing* God and his *blessing* us, see on Ps. v. 12; ciii. 1.   Compare Num. vi. 24–26.

DOCTRINAL AND PRACTICAL REMARKS.

1. The public worship of God is a great public interest, the right conduct of which is a great public concern, and demands the most serious attention from all employed in its management, v. 1.

2. Because our mercies are ever new, our praises should be continual, v. 1. They should be sung by day and by night, in joy and in sorrow, at home and abroad.   In our waking hours God should in some proper way be remembered, and as often as possible praised and blessed.   Scott: "If our hearts were filled with the love of God, as his holy law commands, our mouths would be filled with his praises: and though our frail bodies would need rest, yet our souls would never be weary of his pleasant service."

3. A stated ministry for the maintenance of God's worship, of which preaching his word and and public prayer and praise are principal parts, has been an ordinance of God under all dispensations, v. 1.   Enoch and Noah among the patriarchs, the priests and prophets in Israel, and the pastors and teachers of the new dispensation are in proof of this assertion.   Amesius: "This whole Psalm shows that the public worship of God is to be made much of, and diligently promoted."

4. God's ministers should be diligent in their calling, wholly given to their work, v. 1. They should bring out of their treasure things new and old. This requires study. The things of God are very deep, and the superficial cannot know them.   When God's ministers are children in knowledge, they are apt to be men in malice.   They at least miserably pervert his truth and injure his cause.   And when they are dumb dogs, refusing to bark, they are a curse to the church.   Morison: "As the Lord our God is a jealous God, it becomes all who minister before him to take good heed unto themselves, lest they should be guilty of offering to him the sacrifice of fools, and

lest they should draw near to him with their lips while their hearts are far off from him."

5. Ministers have work enough, and of the best kind too, to keep them fully employed without turning aside to matters foreign from their sacred office, v. 1. The apostles would not even take charge of the alms to be distributed among the poor saints, but entrusted this work to approved men, chosen for the purpose, lest their appropriate work might be hindered, Acts vi. 4. "Luther: "The highest worship of God is the preaching of the word; because, thereby are praised and celebrated the name and the benefits of Christ." Amesius: "A chief duty of God's ministers is to celebrate his praise."

6. Let us abound in the work of solemnly *blessing* and praising the Lord, vv. 1, 2. If this is not done, the great ends of his worship can hardly be gained. Compare Heb. xiii. 15; 1 Pet. ii. 9. It is to be deplored that we so languidly and slightly perform this duty.

7. The worship of God as Redeemer does not interfere with his worship as Creator, v. 3. Revealed religion is not contrary to natural religion; but is based upon it, and carries out its great principles.

8. Those, who love to see God's ministers lively and encourage them in their work, shall be *blessed* of them and of the Lord also, v. 3. Compare 2 Tim. i. 16–18.

9. If men had any just sense of the depth of misery and of the dreadfulness of the curse under which they lie, till they come under the *blessing* which he has sent forth his servants to pronounce on the penitent and obedient, there would surely be a more earnest endeavor on the part of all to come into fellowship with those, who are commanded to bless and curse not, v. 3.

10. All, who pray for Zion and rejoice in her provisions shall be *blessed* out of Zion, vv. 1–3. Horne: "Prayer and praise, which by grace are caused to ascend from our hearts to God, will certainly return in the benedictions of heaven upon our souls and bodies, our persons and our families, our church and our country; like the vapors, which exhaled by the warmth of the sun from the earth, mount upwards into the air, but soon fall again in fruitful showers, causing the little hills to rejoice, and the valleys to laugh and sing."

11. God is *willing* to *bless* us, for he has sent forth his servants to do that very thing; and he is *able* to bless us, for he made heaven and earth, v. 3. He lacks neither mercy nor might, neither kindness nor power. He, who made, and owns and rules all things, must have infinite love and resources. "We need desire no more to make us happy, than to be blessed of the Lord."

12. The best blessings ever bestowed on earth are those which come out of Zion, spiritual blessings, bought with blood, pledged in a covenant ordered in all things and sure. And the best blessings in the future life are those secured by our connection with Zion. The church on earth, though her attainments are yet low, is the same as the church in glory. Soon the days of her mourning shall be ended, and she shall then be eternally blessed in the presence of her Lord.

13. Let all devout persons pray for God's ministers, v. 3. They need such aid and desire it, 1 Thess. v. 25; 2 Thess. iii. 1. Henry: "Though *the less is blessed of the greater* (Heb. vii. 7) yet the greater must be prayed for by the less."

PSALM CXXXV.

1 Praise ye the LORD.   Praise ye the name of the LORD ; praise *him*, O ye servants of the LORD.

2 Ye that stand in the house of the LORD, in the courts of the house of our God,

3 Praise the LORD ; for the LORD *is* good : sing praises unto his name ; for *it is* pleasant.

4 For the LORD hath chosen Jacob unto himself, *and* Israel for his peculiar treasure.

5 For I know that the LORD *is* great, and *that* our Lord *is* above all gods.

6 Whatsoever the LORD pleased, *that* did he in heaven, and in earth, in the seas, and all deep places.

7 He causeth the vapours to ascend from the ends of the earth ; he maketh lightnings for the rain ; he bringeth the wind out of his treasuries.

8 Who smote the firstborn of Egypt, both of man and beast.

9 *Who* sent tokens and wonders into the midst of thee, O Egypt, upon Pharaoh, and upon all his servants.

10 Who smote great nations, and slew mighty kings ;

11 Sihon king of the Amorites, and Og king of Bashan, and all the kingdoms of Canaan :

12 And gave their land *for* a heritage, a heritage unto Israel his people.

13 Thy name, O LORD, *endureth* for ever ; *and* thy memorial, O LORD, throughout all generations.

14 For the LORD will judge his people, and he will repent himself concerning his servants.

15 The idols of the heathen *are* silver and gold, the work of men's hands.

16 They have mouths, but they speak not ; eyes have they, but they see not ;

17 They have ears, but they hear not ; neither is there *any* breath in their mouths.

18 They that make them are like unto them : *so is* every one that trusteth in them.

19 Bless the LORD, O house of Israel : bless the LORD, O house of Aaron :

20 Bless the LORD, O house of Levi : ye that fear the LORD, bless the LORD.

21 Blessed be the LORD out of Zion, which dwelleth at Jerusalem.   Praise ye the LORD.

THIS Psalm is without title in the original ; but several of the ancient versions take the first two words, *Hallelu-Jah* for an inscription.   See on Ps. cxi.   Jebb is confident that "the Psalms of the captivity, and of the restoration, do not terminate with the Songs of degrees."   He thinks Psalms cxxxv.–cxxxvii. "are manifestly to be referred to those times."   Hengstenberg includes all the Psalms from cxxxv. to cxlvi. in one group, making Psalms cxxxv.–cxxxvii. and cxlvi. to be *new*, and to enclose between them eight Psalms of David.   The reader must give to these conjectures such weight as seems to him just.   Neither their adoption nor rejection materially affects the interpretation.   The authorship of this Psalm is not settled, nor have we any clue to the occasion of its composition.   Scott dates it B. C. 1017 ; Clarke, B. C. about 515.   It is a precious portion of Scripture, which, by just and vehement exhortation and weighty considerations, summons us to the work of offering God supreme homage and worship.   Amyrald : "This Psalm has so much in common with the preceding one, that they both alike contain an exhortation to praise the Lord.   This, however, differs from the other, in that the former contains a simple exhortation, while here the exhortation is accompanied, and as it were supported by the mention of certain works of God, which are specially deserving of being celebrated ; in the other the exhortation is addressed to the Levites alone, in this it chiefly, indeed, belongs to the priests and Levites, yet so as, at the same time, to embrace the whole Israelitish people."   The names of the Most High in this Psalm are *Jah* LORD, *Jehovah* LORD, *Elohim God* and *Adonai Lord*, on which respectively see introduction to Ps. lxviii., on Ps. i. 2 ; iii. 2 ; ii. 4.

1. *Praise ye the* LORD.   *Praise ye the name of the* LORD ; *praise him, O ye servants of the* LORD.   All the words and phrases of this verse have been frequently explained. Clarke thinks that perhaps the second clause should read, *Praise ye the name Jehovah,*

ι. e., praise God in his infinite essence of being, holiness, goodness and truth." Even if we should so read it, the sense would not be essentially different from that gathered from the authorized version. The word thrice rendered *praise* in this verse is the verb forming the compound in the word *Hallelujah.*

2. *Ye that stand in the house of the* LORD, *in the courts of the house of our God.* The two clauses of this verse are closely parallel. Some confine the address in this verse to priests and Levites; but the people were found in the courts of the Lord more or less every day; and the whole nation was there at least by representation during the annual festivals. Verses 19, 20 show that the whole nation in its various orders is summoned to this work. It is safe therefore so to interpret this verse as to make it a universal call to

3. *Praise the* LORD; *for the* LORD *is good: sing praises unto his name; for it is pleasant.* *Praise the* LORD, as in v. 1. *Hallelujah.* The reasons assigned in this verse for this work are two: 1. *Jehovah is good.* *Good,* God is goodness itself. See on Ps. xxv. 8. God's excellence surpasses all names and conceptions known to angels or men. He is infinitely good. *Sing praises, sing Psalms* or *make music.* 2. To praise God is *pleasant,* the same word so rendered in Ps. cxxxiii. 1. Here it may be applied either to God or to his praise. God himself is the source of all that gives a lawful and permanent pleasure to any of his creatures. We have the same word in Ps. xvi. 11, rendered as a noun: " At thy right hand there are *pleasures* for evermore." Street has it, *For he is gracious.* Either way we get a good sense.

4. *For the* LORD *hath chosen Jacob unto himself,* and *Israel for his peculiar treasure.* The free election of the Jewish people by Jehovah is frequently mentioned in Scripture as imposing obligations and enhancing responsibilities, Deut. vii. 6, 7; Ps. xxxiii. 12; cv. 6; Amos iii. 2. The word rendered *peculiar treasure* is first found in Ex. xix. 5, in the shape of a promise; in Ecc. ii. 8, it points to the choice riches and gems found in the cabinets of kings; in Deut. vii. 6; xiv. 2; xxvi. 18, it is simply rendered *special* or *peculiar:* but in Mal. iii. 17, it is rendered *jewels.*

5. *For I know that the* LORD *is great, and* that *our Lord is above all gods.* All nations have been loud in the praises of their gods, even when powerless to do them any good. But every pious Israelite, and in particular every true prophet of Jehovah, did *know* that the Lord is great, and above all gods. The Lord is not only greater than the dumb idols of the heathen; but greater than their kings; yea, greater than the angels of heaven; for the term rendered gods embraces all these.

6. *Whatsoever the* LORD *pleased,* that *did he in heaven, and in earth, in the seas and all deep places.* The first clause may be read, *Jehovah did every thing which delighted him.* There is no will above his will. He never asks leave of angels or men, but performs his own pleasure. The verbs are in the preterite. God always has done what he pleased and is doing so still. He will never surrender his independence or his sovereignty. Alexander: " Heaven, earth and sea are put for the whole frame of nature, as in Ex. xx. 4." Ps. cxv. 3; Isa. xlvi. 10, 11, are parallel.

7. *He causeth the vapours to ascend from the ends of the earth; he maketh lightnings for the rain; he bringeth the wind out of his treasuries.* The whole tendency of irreligion and of false religion is by degrees to bring the minds of men to regard one thing after another as without or beyond the control of the Almighty. Idolaters ascribe the phenomena of rain and lightning and storms to their false gods. The impiety of countries nominally Christian ascribes the same effects to merely natural causes. Both these errors are reproved in Jer. xiv. 22. Job xxviii. 24–27; xxxviii. 33–36; Zech. x. 1, are parallel; and Jer. x. 13; li. 16, are almost identical. The fact that in causing vapors to ascend the Lord uses natural causes takes nothing from the glory of his providence, but rather adds to it, as these causes themselves depend

on him. Nicolson: "Nothing is more obscure than the generation of the winds." Compare Job iii. 8. *He maketh lightnings for the rain, i. e.,* to go with the rain. Green: Who maketh lightnings to *attend* the rain. *Treasuries,* in Ps. xxxiii. 7, *storehouses;* in Job xxxiii. 22 and often, *treasures.* Inspired poets speak of wind and rain as if they were kept in vast depositories and brought forth at the will of God. They are wholly subject to his will, as are the treasures to kings, who rule nations. Calvin: "Not a drop of rain falls from heaven without a divine commission or dispensation to that effect."

8. *Who smote the firstborn of Egypt, both of man and beast,* literally, *from man to cattle.* He had spoken of the lessons learned from the course of nature. He now points to lessons that may be learned from history. See on Ps. lxxviii. 51; cv. 36, where we have the same word. The plague here mentioned was the last and the direst of the ten.

9. *Who sent tokens and wonders into the midst of thee, O Egypt, upon Pharaoh, and upon all his servants.* On the character and terribleness of the signs and wonders wrought on the Egyptians, see on Ps. lxxviii. 43–50; cv. 27–35. When history begins in wonders of wrath to the guilty and of love to the righteous, it does not break off abruptly. It goes on from age to age, and passes from one country to another. Having delivered Israel from the land of Ham, Jehovah would enfeoff his people in Canaan:

10. *Who smote great nations and slew mighty kings.* Calvin: "Having once taken the children of Abraham by the hand, he led them on, in the continued exercise of his power, till he put them in possession of the promised land." The tribes to be overcome were *great,* or *many,* and their kings *mighty,* or *strong,* particularly

11. *Sihon king of the Amorites, and Og king of Bashan, and all the kingdoms of Canaan.* Sihon and Og are mentioned perhaps for these reasons: 1. They were at the entrance of Canaan and made the first strong opposition to the Israelites. 2. They were at the head of powerful tribes or nations. 3. These kings were of gigantic strength and stature, Deut. iii. 11; Amos ii. 9. These were perhaps fair samples of the other kings and kingdoms encountered and vanquished. An account of the destruction of these kings and their hosts is given in Deut. ii. 30–35; iii. 1–11. The Lord did all this,

12. *And gave their land* for a *heritage, a heritage unto Israel his people.* The *heritage* or *inheritance* of the Israelites was not derived from the Canaanites, but from the free grant of Jehovah made to their fathers, Gen. xvii. 8; xxviii. 13; xxxv. 12. Compare Ps. xliv. 3; cxi. 6. The tenure by which Israel held the Holy Land was excellent, and was only destroyed by centuries of rebellion against Jehovah.

13. *Thy name, O* LORD, *endureth for ever;* and *thy memorial, O* LORD, *throughout all generations;* literally, *to generation and generation.* There is no land where, and there is no time when Jehovah does not evince his existence, his perfections, and his government over the world. The two clauses of the verse are parallel. Patrick's paraphrase is: "O Lord, how astonishing is this thy omnipotent goodness! the fame of which shall never be forgotten."

14. *For the* LORD *will judge his people, and he will repent himself concerning his servants.* John Rogers' translation: For the Lorde wyll avenge his people, and be gracyous unto hys servauntes. Doway: For the Lord will judge his people, and will be entreated in favor of his servants. It is best to follow the tense of the Hebrew and render the verbs in the future expressing continued action and not in the preterite. Calvin: "The term *judging* in the Hebrew expresses whatever belongs to just and legitimate government." See on Ps. vii. 8. The whole verse is taken from Deut. xxxii. 36, where there is an additional explanatory clause: "For the Lord

shall judge his people, and repent himself for his servants; when he seeth that their power is gone, and there is none shut up or left." *Repent*, also rendered *be comforted*. See on Ps. xc. 13.

15. *The idols of the heathen* are *silver and gold, the work of men's hands.*

16. *They have mouths, but they speak not; eyes have they, but they see not.*

17. *They have ears, but they hear not; neither is there* any *breath in their mouths.*

18. *They that make them are like unto them:* so is *every one that trusteth in them.* See on Ps. cxv. 4–8, where, with slight and idiomatic variations, we have these several clauses except that which says that there is no *breath in the mouths* of the idols. This is a simple idea but of great weight in the matter in hand. If the idols cannot even breathe, how can they give any succor to their worshippers? The devotees of idols are as great vanities, considering what they might be if they were hearty worshippers of the true God, as are the images themselves.

19. *Bless the* LORD, *O house of Israel: bless the* LORD, *O house of Aaron.*

20. *Bless the* LORD, *O house of Levi: ye that fear the* LORD, *bless the* LORD. *Bless*, as in Ps. ciii. 1, 2, 20, 21, 22. The call on the orders of the people is in the same form as in Ps. cxv. 9–11; cxviii. 2–4; except that *the house of Levi*—the priests—-is here added. All classes are embraced.

21. *Blessed be the* LORD *out of Zion, which dwelleth at Jerusalem. Praise ye the* LORD. As God blesses his people out of Zion, Ps. cxxxiv. 3; so is he blessed out of the same holy hill. *Zion* and *Jerusalem* are parallel, the latter embracing the former. The holy city was the centre of the theocracy. There the true visible church received special tokens of God's gracious presence, and blessed his name. The ode ends as it began, *Hallelujah, Praise ye the Lord.*

DOCTRINAL AND PRACTICAL REMARKS.

1. Reason and revelation unite in making praise a great duty, obligatory upon all classes of men, vv. 1–3. In this work we should engage heartily and do all we can to excite others to do the same. It should greatly commend this work to us that it is truly heavenly, that it is very often enjoined, and that thereby God is greatly honored, Ps. l. 14, 23.

2. There is good cause for all our praises of Jehovah, found in the work itself and in his nature and ways and works, v. 3. "We must not only thank him for what he has done for us, but praise him for what he is in himself, and has done for others."

3. And our praises of Jehovah should be such as we offer to none others. He is God alone. To praise others with him is to insult him. Morison: "Jehovah alone is the legitimate object of the praise of his intelligent creatures. In him resides infinite perfection."

4. It is obvious that in the work of praise duty and pleasure are beautifully united, v. 3. Did we praise more, we should be happier and more useful.

5. It is a sad fact and affords proof of a very fearful alienation from God that inspired men call upon us so often to do this work, to which we are criminally indisposed. Surely the holy creatures in heaven require no such perpetual call to this work.

6. Yet with all their imperfections God's people are dear to him; they are his *chosen*, his *peculiar treasure*, v. 4. There is hardly a term of endearment, that is not employed to express God's love of his church. He gave his Son to die for her.

7. God's free election of any people to a knowledge of himself is a powerful argument to his praise, and so to holiness, vv. 3, 4. How can it be otherwise with an ingenuous mind? If anything could awaken gratitude and the spirit of obedience it would be such love as God shows in calling men to a saving knowledge of his dear

Son. Amesius: "The infinite perfection of God makes the benefit of election infinite."

8. Any just estimate of the love and grace of God is vastly heightened by the fact that he is infinitely great, and that his condescension is therefore unspeakable, v. 5.

9. Nor is it possible for us to maintain in purity either the doctrines or worship of God if we lose sight of his unsearchable greatness. If men have low conceptions of the glorious nature of God, any semblance of piety they may manifest is deceptive.

10. It is not strange that the infidel in his enmity against God should oppose the doctrine of the entire and universal sovereignty of God; but it is monstrous that those who profess to receive the Scriptures should impugn it, v. 6. Morison: "There are no limits to the power of Jehovah, but such as are prescribed to him by the dictates of his moral nature." Patrick: "His one will alone gives bounds to his power" Dickson: "The Lord's will is the sovereign and absolute cause of all his working, and that whereon all men's faith and reason must rest."

11. It is decisive proof of sad corruption in human nature that the study of natural science should so often be perverted to confirm men in atheistic sentiments and practices, leading them to doubt or ignore the very truths established by a sound and thorough philosophy, v. 7. Compare Job xxxviii. 22–29.

12. In like manner some men are never the wiser for all the wonders recorded of past ages, vv. 8–12.

13. So that we need not fear that the name of the Lord will fade from the earth, v. 13. He will be glorified among all people. He will put down all false gods. Calvin: "The whole world is a theatre for the display of the divine goodness, wisdom, justice and power, but the church is the orchestra, as it were, the most conspicuous part of it." Morison: "While the world stands, and while immortality endures, the wonders in Egypt, in the wilderness and in Canaan, will furnish materials for grateful and exultant praise."

14. For REMARKS on vv. 15–18 see on Ps. cxv. 4–8, 15. Man uninstructed by the Lord is brutish in his knowledge, or he could never be induced to bow down to an idol that cannot breathe, or think, or feel, or walk, or talk, be neither angry nor pleased, sorry nor glad.

15. Blessing the Lord is a great work in which all classes should unite. All men are not called to preach, to write books or hymns of praise; but every man, who would not be miserable for ever, must bless the Lord, vv. 19–21. If Jehovah authoritatively blesses his people, they should optatively bless him.

PSALM CXXXVI.

1 O give thanks unto the LORD; for *he is* good: for his mercy *endureth* for ever.
2 O give thanks unto the God of gods: for his mercy *endureth* for ever.
3 O give thanks to the Lord of lords: for his mercy *endureth* for ever.
4 To him who alone doeth great wonders: for his mercy *endureth* for ever.
5 To him that by wisdom made the heavens: for his mercy *endureth* for ever.
6 To him that stretched out the earth above the waters: for his mercy *endureth* for evei.
7 To him that made great lights: for his mercy *endureth* for ever.
8 The sun to rule by day: for his mercy *endureth* for ever:
9 The moon and stars to rule by night: for his mercy *endureth* for ever.

10 To him that smote Egypt in their firstborn: for his mercy *endureth* for ever:

11 And brought out Israel from among them: for his mercy *endureth* for ever.

12 With a strong hand, and with a stretched out arm: for his mercy *endureth* for ever:

13 To him which divided the Red sea into parts: for his mercy *endureth* for ever:

14 And made Israel to pass through the midst of it: for his mercy *endureth* for ever:

15 But overthrew Pharaoh and his host in the Red sea: for his mercy *endureth* for ever.

16 To him which led his people through the wilderness: for his mercy *endureth* for ever.

17 To him which smote great kings: for his mercy *endureth* for ever:

18 And slew famous kings: for his mercy *endureth* for ever:

19 Sihon king of the Amorites: for his mercy *endureth* for ever:

20 And Og the king of Bashan: for his mercy *endureth* for ever:

21 And gave their land for a heritage: for his mercy *endureth* for ever:

22 *Even* a heritage unto Israel his servant: for his mercy *endureth* for ever:

23 Who remembered us in our low estate: for his mercy *endureth* for ever:

24 And hath redeemed us from our enemies: for his mercy *endureth* for ever.

25 Who giveth food to all flesh: for his mercy *endureth* for ever.

26 O give thanks unto the God of heaven: for his mercy *endureth* for ever.

MANY commentators note the resemblance between this Psalm and the cxxxv. In the Hebrew this has no title; though the Septuagint without sufficient cause puts the title, *Alleluiah* or *Hallelujah*. Several fine scholars refer it to the times and authorship of David. Others give it a later origin. Scott dates it B. C. 1017; Clarke, B. C. about 515. Clarke: "The author is unknown." The most distinguishing feature of this Psalm is the occurrence in each of its *twenty-six* verses of the same clause: *For his mercy* endureth *for ever;* rendered by Jebb: For everlasting is his mercy; by Edwards: For his goodness endureth forever; by Fry: For his tenderness is forever. Clarke gives it quite another turn: "*For his tender mercy is to the coming age:* meaning, probably, that particular display of his compassion, the redemption of the world by the Lord Jesus." Rabbi Obadiah: "It is an exhortation to the children of God in the days of Messiah to praise the Lord;" Luther: "In this repeated expression the Psalmist looks to the promise of Christ to come." "*His mercy* endureth *forever*"— this is the key-note of the song. All will admit that a sweeter or more glorious theme could not enter into a sacred lyric. The word rendered *mercy* is in Ps. xvii. 7; li. 1 and often, rendered *lovingkindness;* elsewhere *kindness, goodness, favor,* Gen. xx. 13; Ex. xxxiv. 6; Dan. i. 9. Scott: "By *mercy* we understand the Lord's disposition to compassionate and relieve those, whom sin has rendered miserable and base; his readiness to forgive and be reconciled to the most provoking of transgressors, and to bestow all blessings upon them; together with all the provision which he has made for the honor of his name, in the redemption of sinners by Jesus Christ." Calvin: "In mentioning each benefit the Psalmist takes particular notice of the mercy of God, to teach us how necessary it is to the proper celebration of his praises that we own everything which we receive from him to be bestowed gratuitously." *Endureth* is supplied by our translators. There is no better word. *Forever, to eternity, everlasting.* This whole phrase was used in the public worship of God as early as the days of David, (1 Chron. xvi. 34, 41,) at least a *thousand and forty* years before Christ. Solomon followed the precept and example of his royal father, 2 Chron. v. 13; vii. 3, 6; xx. 21. Indeed from the time this form of praise was given to Israel it was kept in use, Jer. xxxiii. 11; Ezra iii. 11. See also Ps. cvi. 1; cvii. 1; cxviii. 1–4. Fry: "It was probably a standing hymn of the Jewish church sung on various public occasions." This form of praise is just, expressive, intelligible, comprehensive and very spirited. There are no better words, in which to publish the abounding continued compassion of the Most High. Patrick, Lowth, Horne, Scott, Morison, Tholuck and others regard the structure of this Psalm as responsive, designed to be sung by two choirs, or by a Levite and a choir. But of this we know nothing. Hengstenberg and Alexander discard it. The four names of the Most High found in this Psalm are *Jehovah* LORD, *Elohim God, Adonai* [rather the plural *Adonim*] *Lord* and *El God,* on which respectively see on Ps. i. 2; iii. 2; ii. 4; v. 4. By the Jews this Psalm is styled *The Great Thanksgiving;* and it is generally agreed to be very beautiful and animating.

1. *O give thanks unto the* LORD; *for he* is *good: for his mercy* endureth *for ever.* We had the same in Ps. cvi. 1; cvii. 1; cxviii. 1, on which see. It is well paraphrased by Hammond thus: "Let the whole world in a most solemn, humble, devout manner, acknowledge the great bounty and liberality of God, and the continual exercise of his mercy, which is not, nor ever shall be at an end, but is constantly made good to his servants in all the motions of their lives."

2. *O give thanks unto the God of gods: for his mercy* endureth *for ever.*

3. *O give thanks to the Lord of lords: for his mercy* endureth *for ever.* Two things in these verses chiefly demand attention. 1. Both the words *God* and *Lord* are in the plural. This is usually the case with the former, but rarely with the latter. The plural here is evidently intentional, denoting the amplitude of the power and authority of the God of heaven. 2. The phrases *God of gods* and *Lord of lords,* some think, point to the same thing, and in a sense they may; but they express it in a manner common to other languages beside the Hebrew. They teach that God is supreme in power and authority above all that exercise either, whether angels, magistrates, false gods, or any lords having dominion in this or any other world. Compare Deut. x. 17; Dan. ii. 47; 1 Tim. vi. 15; Rev. xvii. 14; xix. 16. Calvin: "The Psalmist uses the plurals to intimate, that the fullest perfection of all dominion is to be found in the one God."

4. *To him who alone doeth great wonders: for his mercy* endureth *for ever.* The words *O give thanks* are to be supplied here and where wanting in the rest of this Psalm. The exclusiveness of the divinity of Jehovah is established by this that he alone works *great wonders. Wonders,* see on Ps. ix. 1. What these wonders are we learn from subsequent verses:

5. *To him that by wisdom made the heavens: for his mercy* endureth *for ever.* Creation has been criticised, but always to the ultimate shame of him who ventured to impeach his Maker's wisdom. See on Ps. civ. 24. *Wisdom,* in Ps. lxxviii. 72 rendered *skilfulness;* in Ps. cxlvii. 5 and often, *understanding.*

6. *To him that stretched out the earth above the waters: for his mercy* endureth *for ever.* Compare Ps. xxiv. 2. Some infidels have denied that the earth was ever deluged; but according to Scripture and sound science it is only by the power and mercy of God that there is any dry land where man can live. See Gen. i. 9, 10. Calvin: "The earth's expanded surface, and the vacant space uncovered with water, has been justly considered one of the great wonders of God. And it is ascribed to his mercy, because his only reason for displacing the waters from their proper seat was that regard which he had in his infinite goodness for the interests of man." Nor is this reasoning weakened but rather established by all we know of the law of gravitation.

7. *To him that made great lights: for his mercy* endureth *for ever.*

8. *The sun to rule by day: for his mercy* endureth *for ever:*

9. *The moon and stars to rule by night: for his mercy* endureth *for ever. Lights,* the plural of the word rendered *light* in Gen. i. 3, 4, 5, 18, and often in the Psalms, and cognate to the word rendered *lights* in Gen. i. 14–16. The sun, moon and stars are enumerated here as in Moses' account of the creation. The word rendered *to rule* in vv. 8, 9, is in both cases a noun in the plural expressing the fulness of the beneficent

and perpetual influence of the heavenly bodies on the earth and its inhabitants ever since the creation.   Compare Deut. xxxiii. 14.

10. *To him that smote Egypt in their firstborn: for his mercy* endureth *for ever.*   From the works of creation, celebrated in vv. 5–9, the Psalmist turns to those of providence and grace, and summons us to give thanks for the wonders displayed in them.   In this verse, as often elsewhere, a country is put for its inhabitants.   Hence the plural *their* firstborn.   Respecting this last plague sent on Egypt, see on Ps. lxxviii. 51; cv. 36.

11. *And brought out Israel from among them: for his mercy* endureth *for ever:*

12. *With a strong hand, and with a stretched out arm: for his mercy* endureth *for ever.*   The power displayed in the deliverance from Egypt was not excelled even by the mercy thus evinced.   The imagery of v. 12 is very ancient, being taken from the Pentateuch.   Calvin: "The figure of *an outstretched arm* is appropriate, implying that God put forth an extraordinary and not a common or slight display of his power in redeeming his people."

13. *To him which divided the Red sea into parts: for his mercy* endureth *for ever:*

14. *And made Israel to pass through the midst of it: for his mercy* endureth *for ever.* The word rendered *parts* being in the plural, some Jewish writers have suggested that there were several passages through the sea.   But the historic narrative quite opposes such a fancy.   The plural is as fitting to describe a sea divided into *two* as into *twenty* parts.   The verb and noun expressing division are cognate.   On the Red sea, literally *sea of Suph*, see on Ps. cvi. 7, 9, 22.

15. *But overthrew Pharaoh and his host in the Red sea: for his mercy* endureth *for ever.*   For *overthrew* the margin has *shaked off*, which is literal.   The same verb is used in the history, Ex. xiv. 27.   In Ps. cix. 23, another form of the same verb is rendered *tossed up and down.*   In Neh. v. 13, it is, I *shook* my lap.   Calvin renders it, Cast Pharaoh and his host headlong into the Red sea.

16. *To him which led his people through the wilderness: for his mercy* endureth *for ever.*   How God led them is known to those who have studied Jewish history.   The journey through the desert has no parallel.   It abounds in stupendous wonders and stupendous mercies.   Nor did they cease in the wilderness.

17. *To him which smote great kings: for his mercy* endureth *for ever:*

18. *And slew famous kings: for his mercy* endureth *for ever:*

19. *Sihon king of the Amorites: for his mercy* endureth *for ever:*

20. *And Og the king of Bashan: for his mercy* endureth *for ever:*

21. *And gave their land for a heritage: for his mercy* endureth *for ever:*

22. *Even a heritage unto Israel his servant: for his mercy* endureth *for ever.*   On this passage see on Ps. cxxxv. 10–12.   The variations are slight and not significant.

23. *Who remembered us in our low estate: for his mercy* endureth *for ever.*   For *low estate*, Calvin has *humiliation;* Street, *trouble;* Edwards, *when we have been in a low condition.*   There is no reason for confining the reference of this verse to Egyptian or to Babylonish captivity.   Often was Israel brought low and Jehovah gave his help. For their sins within thirty-two years after the death of Joshua they were delivered into the power of Chushan-rishathaim king of Mesopotamia and served him eight years, Judges iii. 8.   Soon after their sins provoked God to deliver them to the power of Eglon king of Moab, and they groaned under his oppressions for eighteen years, Judges iii. 14, till they were delivered by Ehud.   Then the Philistines lorded it over them till Shamgar arose and by him God wrought a deliverance, Judges iii. 31.   The fourth, fifth and sixth chapters of Judges recite other sad *depressions* that came on that people.   Often were they brought low; but God did not forget them.

24. *And hath redeemed us from our enemies: for his mercy* endureth *for ever.* Bishops' Bible: And hath delivered us from our enemies; Genevan Translation

and Calvin: And hath rescued us from our oppressors; Hengstenberg: And redeemed us from our adversaries. Elsewhere the verb is rendered *break, break off, rend, tear in pieces*, Gen. xxvii. 40; Ex. xxxii. 2; Ps. vii. 2; Zech. xi. 16. It here expresses the resistless act of divine power, by which Jehovah had surprisingly and often delivered his people.

25. *Who giveth food to all flesh: for his mercy* endureth *for ever.* Here the prophet's views go beyond his nation, and he speaks of God's goodness to all living creatures on earth. For the significance of the phrase *all flesh,* see Gen. vi. 12, 13, 17, 19; vii. 15, 16, 21; viii. 17. How kindly and tenderly God deals with his creatures is well expressed in Ps. cxlv. 9.

26. *O give thanks unto the God of heaven: for his mercy* endureth *for ever.* The phrase *God of heaven* is not found in the earlier Scriptures. We meet it no where else in the Psalms; but we meet it in 2 Chron. xxxvi. 23; Ezra i. 2; v. 11, 12; vi. 9; vii. 12, 23; Neh. i. 4; ii. 4; Dan. ii. 18, 19, 44; Jonah i. 9. It is twice found in the Apocalypse, Rev. xi. 13; xvi. 11. It is a sublime and appropriate designation of the true God, expressive of his glorious elevation above the passions and perturbations of earth. To him all flesh should give thanks, for all receive his mercy in many forms and ways. His favors come down on generation after generation and to his willing, obedient people shall flow on during eternal ages.

DOCTRINAL AND PRACTICAL REMARKS.

1. We cannot do anything more important to the glory of God, or the salvation of men than often to speak and sing of the mercy of God, and to incite our fellowmen to do the same. See every verse of this Psalm. If men come generally to despair or even to doubt of the lovingkindness of the Lord, they will never turn from their wickedness, but will give themselves over to the devil, who delights in bringing sinners to believe that salvation is impossible.

2. While life lasts, we shall not be done praying; but while immortality endures, we shall nòt be done giving thanks, vv. 1, 2, 3, 26. The cause for this delightful branch of worship continuing for ever, and the heart of the pious always being actuated by love, they will carry on this blessed service in the finest style long after the sun shall cease to rise and set.

3. Christians should not be ashamed of the mysteries and *miracles* of their religion, v. 4. Sometimes of late years there has been manifested a disposition to recede from the defence of the supernatural in religion. This is a great mistake. Give up all that is miraculous in true religion and there is nothing left of power sufficient to move any heart to worship or adore; and without worship there is no piety. Calvin: "Whatever is worthy of admiration is exclusively made and done by God, to teach us that we cannot transfer the smallest portion of the praise due to him without awful sacrilege."

4. Had man never sinned, he would have found every day of his life fit themes for love and praise in the works of creation; and sinner as he is, there is not a day that reflection or inquiry will not suggest weighty matter for devout meditation in the amazing products of divine skill found in every part of the universe. He, that will not believe in and worship God as Creator cannot love him as Judge of all the earth, or in any other character whatever.

5. Though the old dispensation had but a shadow of good things to come and not the very image of those things, yet we, who live in this Gospel day may draw some of our best explanations of the truth from old times, seeing that now we have the key to their interpretation. For instance, the life and experience of Christians are

wonderfully illustrated by the redemption of Israel from Egypt, their journey through the wilderness, and their settlement in Canaan, vv. 10–22.

6. The whole history of the church shows that whosoever stubbornly and incorrigibly sets himself against God and his cause, however powerful he may be, and however for a time he may seem successful, shall inevitably perish. If God be against us, it matters not who is for us, vv. 15, 18–20.

7. If Israel of old justly and often celebrated redemption from Egypt, surely God's people cannot too often or too earnestly celebrate redemption by Jesus Christ. It is a matchless scheme.

8. So marked is the divine goodness to men, even in the dark places of the earth, filling their heart with food and gladness, that all are inexcusable for not loving and serving him, who so richly supplies their wants, v. 25. The goodness of the Lord even to the brutes ought to lead us to confide in him and love him. Calvin: "We have no reason to feel surprised at his sustaining the character of a kind and provident father to his own people, when he condescends to care for the cattle, and the asses of the field, and the crow, and the sparrow." Compare Matt. vi. 26.

9. Let us abound in adoration and thanksgiving, v. 26. In this matter there is no danger of excess, so long as we are humble and hearty. We should probably be more fervent in this work if we abounded more in it.

PSALM CXXXVII.

1 By the rivers of Babylon, there we sat down, yea, we wept, when we remembered Zion.
2 We hanged our harps upon the willows in the midst thereof.
3 For there they that carried us away captive required of us a song; and they that wasted us *required of us* mirth, *saying*, Sing us *one* of the songs of Zion.
4 How shall we sing the LORD's song in a strange land?
5 If I forget thee, O Jerusalem, let my right hand forget *her cunning*.
6 If I do not remember thee, let my tongue cleave to the roof of my mouth; if I prefer not Jerusalem above my chief joy.
7 Remember, O LORD, the children of Edom in the day of Jerusalem; who said, Rase *it*, rase *it, even* to the foundation thereof.
8 O daughter of Babylon, who art to be destroyed; happy *shall he be*, that rewardeth thee as thou hast served us.
9 Happy *shall he be*, that taketh and dasheth thy little ones against the stones.

THE theme of this Psalm is the captivity in Babylon. Expositors are not agreed as to the relation it bears to the time of the captivity. Some think it prophetic and written even as early as the time of David and by him. The Syriac ascribes it to him. Luther seems not satisfied that this view is wrong; though it has little favor with more modern interpreters. Some think this poem was written after the end of the captivity. Tholuck: "It was composed soon after the return from the captivity, when the remembrance of its ignominy was still fresh in the mind of the people." Hengstenberg is of the same mind. Yet others think it was composed during the captivity, probably the latter part of it. So Calvin, Henry, Edwards, Patrick, Nicolson, Horne and others. This is the more probable of the three opinions. The author is unknown, but the conjecture of some that it was written by the weeping prophet, and sent to the captives is not wild. Jeremiah did not go to Babylon. Others ascribe it to some Levite, a captive in Chaldea. There is not in any language a finer specimen of elegiac poetry than we have here. Jebb: "Its exquisite beauty and pathetic character are obvious to all;" Morison: "It is an extremely beautiful and pathetic composition." Scott dates it B. C. 587; Clarke says: "It was evidently composed during or at the close of the captivity." Cyrus took Babylon and gave the first decree for the release of the Jews 538 years before Christ. The only name of the Almighty found in it is *Jehovah* LORD, on which see on Ps. i. 2.

1. *By the rivers of Babylon, there we sat down, yea, we wept, when we remembered Zion.* We read in Scripture of four rivers of Babylon, the Euphrates, the Tigris, the Chebar and the Ulai. The first sometimes called the "great river," sometimes simply "the river," Ex. xxiii. 31; Deut. i. 7; Josh. i. 4; Isa. vii. 20; viii. 7; Jer. ii. 18. The last three all emptied themselves into the Euphrates, whose waters were poured into the Persian gulf. The Chebar is mentioned in Ezekiel several times, and the Ulai in Daniel. A part of the Jewish captives were settled as a colony on the Chebar, see Ezek. i. 1; iii. 15. Some think these four rivers are the same mentioned in Gen. ii. 10–14. The word rendered *rivers* here is not that found in Ps. i. 3 and elsewhere, meaning any running stream, even in a small artificial canal, but this word denotes what moderns understand by *rivers*. Sometimes it is rendered *floods*. Compare Job xiv. 11; Ps. xciii. 3. *Babylon*, or Babel, not the city but the country of that name. *We sat down*. This may mean, *We dwelt*, Gen. xiii. 12; Ps. xxiii. 6; Jer. xxiii. 8; or it may refer to the posture assumed by the pensive and sad. Job ii. 8, 13; Isa. iii. 26; Lam. ii. 10. *And wept*, also rendered *mourned, bewailed, made lamentation*. There is no Hebrew verb more expressive of deep grief. See Ps. lxxviii. 64; Jer. xxxi. 15. *When we remembered Zion*. Exiles and captives have great trials. One, who loved Zion and yet was doomed to spend his days in cruel Chaldea, must have had his heart wrung with anguish. It was not merely the gush of patriotism, but the flow of pious feeling aroused by the memory of Zion that overwhelmed the minds of these sufferers.

2. *We hanged our harps upon the willows in the midst thereof.* Some travellers assert that in modern Chaldea there is a scarcity of *willows*; but in more than two thousand years great changes may take place in the growth found anywhere. History and science show that the weeping willow is from the region of the Euphrates. So well are learned men satisfied of this that its botanical name is *Salix Babylonica*. The Latin poet Ovid tells us of willows of the Euphrates. It was the official duty of the Levites to praise the Lord; but others did the same. David, who was of the tribe of Judah, often played upon his harp. The very thought of their former privileges and of their present sad condition with the assurance that their sufferings were the fruit of the divine displeasure against them for their sins greatly indisposed them to music.

3. *For there they that carried us away captive required of us a song; and they that wasted us required of us mirth*, saying, *Sing us one of the songs of Zion. They that carried us away captive*, literally, *our captors. Required*, as in Pr. xxx. 7; in Ps. xxvii. 4, *desired*; in Judg. viii. 26, *requested*, and often *asked*, as in 1 Kings iii. 10, 11. The word does not imply any imperious command, but at the most an earnest or urgent request. *A song*, literally *the words of a song. They that wasted us*, more exactly *our devastators, our spoilers, our plunderers. Mirth*, in the old English sense, *gladness, joy*, or *joyfulness*. Many suppose the demand for a song was made in taunt and scorn. This is a prevalent and not improbable view of the actual state of case. But it is suggested rather by the known cruelties of the Chaldeans than by the very words of the verse. Even if the request was made out of inquisitiveness, experience shows that in affliction hardly anything is more tormenting than ill-timed curiosity. The last clause is hardly improved by supplying the word *one*, Sing us *one* of the songs of Zion. It is literally *Sing to us of* or *from the song of Zion.*

4. *How shall we sing the* LORD's *song in a strange land?* Alexander: "The idea is not, that the psalms themselves would be profaned by being sung there, but that the expression of religious joy would be misplaced and incongruous." The same idea is tersely expressed in Pr. xxv. 20. To rob a people of their treasures, drag them from their homes, burn their dwellings and cities, devastate their fields, desecrate their temples, and then call upon them to be joyful is as cruel as it is absurd. The prophet would now animate his people by reviving in their minds strong and vivid reminiscences of the holy land, and arousing in them lively faith in the covenant of God with Israel; and so, he expresses for himself and for his people a solemn engagement.

5. *If I forget thee, O Jerusalem, let my right hand forget* her cunning. The verbs are in the future, *shall forget. Her cunning* is supplied. The Chaldee reads, May I forget my right hand; the Syriac and Street, May my right hand forget me. The reference is not to all skill, but to skill in handling the harp, which is the subject of discourse.

6. *If I do not remember thee, let my tongue cleave to the roof of my mouth; if I prefer not Jerusalem above my chief joy.* Street: Let my tongue cleave to my palate, if I do not remember thee, if I do not extol thee, O Jerusalem, above the chief of my joy; Edwards: If I do not remember thee, may my tongue stick to the roof of my mouth; if I prefer not Jerusalem above my greatest joy; Alexander: Let my tongue cleave to my palate if I do not remember thee, if I do not raise Jerusalem above the head of my rejoicing. As the hand was skilled in playing, so was the tongue in singing, and the prophet was willing to lose the power of both rather than the precious memories of the holy city. The design of this and of the preceding verse is to kindle afresh the fires of love for the true religion as established at Jerusalem. The prophet next foretells the doom of the spoilers. He begins with the descendants of Esau, those old and relentless enemies of Israel.

7. *Remember, O* LORD, *the children of Edom in the day of Jerusalem; who said, Rase* it, *rase* it, *even to the foundation thereof.* This is not an imprecation, but a prediction. See Introduction, § 6. Parallel passages are found in Jer. xlix. 7–10; Lam. iv. 21, 22; Ezek. xxv. 12–14; Obad. 10–19. *The day of Jerusalem* here means the day of her sore calamities, over which the Edomites exulted, and to the infliction of which they egged on her enemies. This fearful prediction has been fulfilled. For long centuries it has not been known that there was existing on earth any descendant of Esau. They who wished to see the holy city *rased,* cleared off, made bare, wiped out, received in their own persons and nation the ruin they wished to Israel.

8. *O daughter of Babylon, who art to be destroyed; happy* shall he be *that rewardeth thee as thou hast served us.* On the term *daughter,* as applied to a city or people, see on Ps. ix. 14. *Happy,* in Ps. i. 1, blessed, literally, *O the blessednesses.* Two interpretations are chiefly given. Some suppose that the language refers to the public estimation in which the conqueror of Babylon should be held. The objection is that the word rendered *happy* seldom if ever refers to popular opinion. The other is that the conqueror of Babylon should really be a wonderful person, remarkably preserved and sustained by God in his whole career. This was strikingly fulfilled in Cyrus, whether considered as a man, or as the head of an army. No man can read his history or the prophecies respecting him without seeing that not one in a thousand millions of the human family has been so favored by Providence as he was.

9. *Happy* shall he be *that taketh and dasheth thy little ones against the stones. Happy,* as in v. 8, and to be explained in the same way. The destruction of infants in ancient warfare is noticed by many old writers. Homer distinctly states it. And we read of it in 2 Kings viii. 12; Hos. x. 14; xiii. 16; Nah. ii. 1; iii. 10. Indeed the prophet

Isaiah, more than 700 years before Christ, foretold this and other terrible things, Isa. xiii. 16–18. In the destruction of Babylon the guilty people horribly murdered one another. Hengstenberg: "The very thing they had done to Israel, they afterwards practised before the eyes of the Psalmist, with inhuman barbarity among themselves, not sparing those who were nearest and dearest to them;" Prideaux: "To make their provisions last the longer, they agreed to cut off all unnecessary mouths amongst them; and therefore drawing together all the women and children, they strangled them all." When Cyrus captured Babylon, he spared the city; but subsequently it was utterly destroyed and desolated by Darius Hystaspes. Compare Jer. li. 26.

DOCTRINAL AND PRACTICAL REMARKS.

1. Good men are often great sufferers. Their own sins and the sins of their country often bring upon them dire calamities, vv. 1–3.

2. Yea, the church in a whole nation is often subjected to deep distresses, put under the power of the most wicked men, and made to groan with her burdens and howl for her sorrows. She may even lose her civil liberties, be cut off from her public worship, and fail in all her attempts to resist encroachment and oppression, vv. 1–3.

3. Scott: "When we are suffering the effects of our personal or national transgressions; we should recollect, with godly sorrow, our forfeited mercies, and our sins by which we have lost them; that by repentance and prayer we may seek deliverance, and the restoration of our privileges and comforts," v. 1.

4. There must be something exceedingly dreadful in sin, else so sad consequences could not flow from it in time and eternity. This world has always been under the government of the kindest being in the universe. Yet how his wrath has many a time burst forth against sinners in Zion and sinners in the world, vv. 1–3.

5. Dickson: "They who will not esteem the privileges of Zion when they have them, will be forced to acknowledge the worth thereof with sorrow when they want them: *we wept, when we remembered Zion*," v. 1.

6. No man knows how soon he may be plunged into the deepest affliction and be compelled to hang his harp upon the willows, v. 2. Such a thought ought to repress excess in our joy, moderate our pursuit of all earthly good, and keep us prepared for the worst.

7. Let all men learn to resist and suppress in their own bosoms all malignant scorn, all spirit of taunting the unfortunate and even all idle curiosity towards them, v. 3. Henry: "Even an enemy, in misery, is to be pitied, and not trampled upon. It argues a base and sordid spirit to upbraid those that are in distress, either with their former joys or with their present griefs, or to challenge those to be merry, who, we know, are out of tune for it." Taunting the miserable is fitly the employment of the damned, Isa. xiv. 9–15.

8. When called to mourning, let us not go to dancing. It is both folly and wickedness to harden ourselves in stoicism under our sorrows. "Signs of sorrow are best suited to days of humiliation."

9. What a poor fickle creature is man! how variable his feelings and his purposes! At one time the Jewish captives in Babylon became surly and stubborn. They refused a cheerful submission to God's will, so that Jeremiah wrote them a letter warning them against their sin and exhorting them to do their duty in their present circumstances, Jer. xxix. 4–7. But when they had become settled in that idolatrous land, and had many comforts around them, it required so excellent a spirit as is breathed in this Psalm to prevent them from sitting down at ease far from the holy city. They had found a beautiful country (2 Kings xviii. 32; Isa. xxxvi. 17,) and were in danger of forgetting the true God and his worship.

10. Let us continue to love the church come what will to her or to us, vv. 5, 6. To give up Zion is to give up salvation. If we do not love the church, we are not like her Head and Redeemer. Scott: "No calamity, no strange land, no prevalence of ungodliness, no despised and depressed state of the church should induce us to forget Jerusalem." Luther: "The first concern of all that fear and know God should be the preservation of a place for the ministration of the word, and for the true religion and true worship of God." Calvin: "The Lord's people, while they mourn under personal trials, should be still more deeply affected by public calamities which befall the Church, it being reasonable that the zeal of God's house should have the highest place in our hearts, and rise above all mere private considerations."

11. We may not sing songs, or do anything else in God's worship, at the bidding or for the gratification of carnal men. They may mind their own affairs and we must keep our own consciences, cost what it may. We have better work than to teach and learn the fear of God by the behests of men, vv. 4–6.

12. The haters of the church, as they are guilty of great sin will, without timely repentance, come to a bad end. Let them remember the calamity of Esau. Let them not forget the doom of the golden city, vv. 7–9. To the pious no evil continues always. A captivity may last 70 years, but then comes deliverance. The doom of persecutors and of those who approve their ways is certain and fearful.

13. It matters not how great, or ancient, or prosperous a people may be, if God inspires a man to denounce his wrath against them, their ruin is inevitable. See Isa. xiii. 19. "The state of the church at the worst is better than that of Babylon, or any state of her adversaries." So faith always pronounces. So God always evinces.

14. How horrible is war! vv. 7–9. Let men read and understand and tremble before they plunge into that bloody sea.

15. How glorious will be the final triumph of the church over her great adversary, the mystical Babylon, when the loud cry of the mighty angel shall be heard, "Babylon the great is fallen, is fallen!" See Rev. xviii. 1–24.

PSALM CXXXVIII.

A Psalm of David.

1 I will praise thee with my whole heart: before the gods will I sing praise unto thee.

2 I will worship toward thy holy temple, and praise thy name for thy lovingkindness and for thy truth: for thou hast magnified thy word above all thy name.

3 In the day when I cried thou answeredst me, *and* strengthenedst me *with* strength in my soul.

4 All the kings of the earth shall praise thee, O LORD, when they hear the words of thy mouth.

5 Yea, they shall sing in the ways of the LORD: for great *is* the glory of the LORD.

6 Though the LORD *be* high, yet hath he respect unto the lowly: but the proud he knoweth afar off.

7 Though I walk in the midst of trouble, thou wilt revive me: thou shalt stretch forth thine hand against the wrath of mine enemies, and thy right hand shall save me.

8 The LORD will perfect *that which* concerneth me: thy mercy, O LORD, *endureth* for ever: forsake not the works of thine own hands.

THE Davidic authorship of this Psalm is declared by the Hebrew, Chaldee, Syriac, Arabic, Septuagint, Ethiopic and Vulgate, and is generally admitted. Scott dates it B. C. 1045; Clarke, B. C. about 1048. Hengstenberg and Alexander regard Psalms cxxxviii.–cxlv. as a series, perhaps the last songs composed by David, and having special reference to the promise made to him in 2 Sam. vii. Most expositors have failed to discover such distinct reference. Luther styles this "a Psalm of general thanksgiving unto God for all his help against his enemies: and it prays that the kingdom of Christ may come; and it prophesies also that even kings and nations shall hear the gospel." Calvin: "In this Psalm David, in remembrance of the singular help which had always been vouchsafed him by God—the experience he had enjoyed of his faithfulness and goodness, takes occasion to stir himself up to gratitude; and from what he had known of the divine faithfulness, he anticipates a continuance of the same mercy. If dangers must be met, he confidently looks for a happy issue." Many think this ode was written not long after the ten years of David's persecution were terminated by the death of Saul. Tholuck styles it "A song of praise full of exuberant joy." The only name of the Almighty found in this Psalm is *Jehovah* LORD, on which see on Ps. i. 2. One peculiarity of the structure of this song is that no name of God is given for several verses after he is directly addressed, though a few MSS. and the old versions supply *Jehovah* in the *first* verse.

1. *I will praise thee with my whole heart; before the gods will I sing praise unto thee.* *Praise*, commonly so; in Ps. vi. 5 and often, *give thanks*; in Ps. xxxii. 5, *confess*. *Sing praise, sing psalms*, as in Ps. cv. 2. *Before the gods, Elohim*; this may mean, 1. Before the true God, in his sight, in his presence: 2. Before the ark, the symbol of the divine presence: 3. Before the angels, who are called *elohim*: 4. Before kings and rulers, as *elohim* is used to denote them: 5. Before the false gods worshipped by the heathen. The Chaldee has, *before the judges;* the Syriac, *before kings;* Jarchi, *before the princes;* the Septuagint, Arabic, Vulgate, Ethiopic and Doway, *before the angels*. There is no grammatical objection to either of these interpretations. And there is no valid objection to adopting them all, *q. d.*, In the presence of the Searcher of hearts, before the ark the symbol of his presence, before magistrates, before the gods worshipped by the Gentiles and before angels, before all dignities earthly and heavenly I will sing psalms to Jehovah.

2. *I will worship toward thy holy temple, and praise thy name for thy lovingkindness and for thy truth: for thou hast magnified thy word above all thy name.* Some have suggested that David could not have written this Psalm as the temple was not built in his time. But David uses the same language in Psalms confessedly written by him. See Ps. v. 7; xi. 4; xviii. 6. *Lovingkindness*, as in Ps. li. 1 and often. *Truth*, or *faithfulness*, as in Ps. xv. 2; xxxi. 5. It includes every kind of reliable word. *For thou hast magnified thy word above all thy name,* Arabic: Thou hast magnified thy holy name above all things; Luther: Thou hast made thy name glorious above all through thy word; Calvin: Thou hast magnified thy name above all things by thy word; Hengstenberg: Thou hast made glorious thy word, above all thy name. If the clause refers to the promise in 2 Sam. vii. it is true that it was the chief of what God engaged to David. But it contains a truth of universal scope. Above the works of creation and of providence, above all else whereby he has made himself known, has the Lord exalted his word. It has converting and sanctifying power.

3. *In the day when I cried thou answeredst me*, and *strengthenedst me* with *strength in my soul*. The words of the first clause are those usually so rendered. *Strengthenedst with strength;* Calvin: Hast abundantly administered strength; Edwards: Invigoratedst with much strength; Street: Strengthenest with courage. The verb might be rendered enlargedst. It is in the future. The noun occurs often and is also rendered *power, might*. The whole battle of the believer's life calls for intrepidity. The enemy is fierce; the child of God must be heroic. In this warfare natural courage avails nothing. It must come from God, and be imparted to the *soul*.

4. *All the kings of the earth shall praise thee, O* LORD, *when they hear the words of thy mouth.* Praise, as in vv. 1, 2; *give thanks*, in the future. *Hear*, preterite *have heard.* It means more than merely to hear the sound of God's word. It is rendered *obey* in 1 Sam. xv. 22 and elsewhere. The verse contains a prediction of the wide-spread and hearty embracing of the truth of the Gospel.

5. Yea, *they shall sing in the ways of the* LORD: *for great* is *the glory of the* LORD. The words are all of the usual signification. They contain a prediction of the joyful effects of the spread of the true religion. Compare Ps. xiv. 7; lxviii. 29, 31, 32; cii. 15; Isa. xxxv. 10.

6. *Though the Lord* be *high, yet hath he respect unto the lowly: but the proud he knoweth afar off.* Some think the last clause of the preceding verse and the whole of this form the theme of the song sung by *kings*, who are put for nations. This does not materially affect the sense, as the cause of joy is very naturally its theme also. *High*, a participle, *exalted. Lowly*, not elsewhere in the Psalms; in Pr. xvi. 19; xxix. 23; Isa. lvii. 15, *humble.* Here it designates a class the opposite of the *proud* in the next clause, which declares that though they remove far from God, he yet knows all about them; or that he forms no familiar and loving acquaintance with them. Both ideas are true; yet the latter is probably chiefly taught here. See on Ps. i. 6. Here the verb is in the future, and declares what shall be the course of God's government forever.

7. *Though I walk in the midst of trouble, thou wilt revive me; thou shalt stretch forth thine hand against the wrath of mine enemies, and thy right hand shall save me. Revive me;* keep me in being, or preserve me alive. The same verb in another form is often rendered *quicken.* God's care over his people is such as often surprises both themselves and their enemies. Wonderfully was all this illustrated in the case of David; and God is as faithful to every believer as to the royal Psalmist.

8. *The* LORD *will perfect that which concerneth me: thy mercy, O* LORD, *endureth for ever: forsake not the works of thine own hands. Perfect, bring to an end, perform,* Ps. vii. 9; lvii. 2; *i. e.,* finish, bring to a happy issue. This was done by raising David to the throne in defiance of all the power wielded against him, by giving him a throne in glory, and by raising his seed, even Christ, to a perpetual kingdom over the church. On the second clause see on Ps. cxviii. 1, 2, 3, 4, 29; cxxxvi. 1. *Mercy*, in v. 2, rendered *lovingkindness.* The last clause is a petition based on promises often repeated in Scripture, Deut. iv. 31; xxxi. 6, 8; Josh. i. 5. *Works*, a very comprehensive term applied to anything that God has made, animate or inanimate, rational or irrational, to anything he has done, to any purpose he has formed.

DOCTRINAL AND PRACTICAL REMARKS.

1. Nothing can release us from the obligation to utter the praises of God for all his benefits; and no good man wishes it were otherwise, v. 1.

2. In all acts of worship, in praise particularly, the *heart* is called for. Reluctance in this service obviously spoils it all, v. 1. Holy mirth as well befits the grateful, as holy sorrow, the penitent.

3. Whoever would worship God aright must be prepared to resist servile fear, the fear of man, the dread of reproach and the vain show of false worship. He must be afraid of nothing so much as of offending God, v. 1.

4. Public worship is no less a duty than private worship. God openly bestows his favors; our acknowledgments ought to be before heaven and earth, vv. 1, 2.

5. If the best and most intelligent Christians of modern times extol the Scriptures, they do but follow the example of ancient worthies and of God himself, v. 2.

6. Prayer is a mighty power in the world. It has been so from the beginning,

v. 3.   Even where the thing asked for is not obtained, the Lord bestows something better.   Henry: "Those that trade with heaven by prayer grow rich by quick returns."

7. It matters little how sharp our trials, if our fortitude and courage are proportioned to them, v. 3.   *Strength in the soul* is the best strength in the world.

8. It has always been true and is now true that good days, the best days of the church, are yet to come, v. 4.   Dark as things often are, the day-star has arisen and shall yet be followed by meridian splendor.

9. As it is a great dishonor to religion when its professors make long faces and give the impression to others that they have gloomy work in God's service; so it is much to the honor of God when his servants show by their songs of gladness and by their whole manner that they serve a good Master, vv. 4, 5.   Such do mightily glorify the God of their salvation.

10. Unspeakable is the condescension of God, v. 6.   He takes the poor from the dunghill and sets him among princes.   The penitent, who by crime or imprudence has lost the friendship of men, is visited even in his dungeon, and made glad in the Lord.   On nothing does God set a higher value than on genuine humility.   He, who has that, is never a reprobate.

11. Nor is anything a greater offence to God than pride, v. 6.   He has set his face against it.   He will not endure it in man or angel.

12. Sometimes the number, greatness or strangeness of the sufferings of God's people make their friends cold and shy; but it is far different with the Lord, v. 7.   He is more abundantly and graciously with them then than at any other time.   Blessed be his name.

13. The Old and New Testaments do well agree in doctrine and promises, respecting the final victory of all believers.   He, who begins a work of grace, will finish it, v. 8; compare Phil. i. 6.

14. We cannot have too strong or too abiding a sense of the kindness of God, v. 8. "There can be no doubt that the way to maintain good hope in danger is to fix our eyes upon the divine goodness, on which our deliverance rests."

15. The Almighty is too great and glorious in all his perfections to make a creature or begin a work, and then change his counsel and review his own wisdom, v. 9. Weakness may give up a plan devised by folly; but it is far otherwise with God.

PSALM CXXXIX.

To the chief Musician, A Psalm of David.

1 O LORD, thou hast searched me, and known *me.*

2 Thou knowest my downsitting and mine uprising; thou understandest my thought afar off.

3 Thou compassest my path and my lying down, and art acquainted *with* all my ways.

4 For *there is* not a word in my tongue, *but,* lo, O LORD, thou knowest it altogether.

5 Thou hast beset me behind and before, and laid thine hand upon me.

6 *Such* knowledge *is* too wonderful for me; it is high, I cannot *attain* unto it.

7 Whither shall I go from thy Spirit? or whither shall I flee from thy presence?

8 If I ascend up into heaven, thou *art* there: if I make my bed in hell, behold, thou *art there.*

9 *If* I take the wings of the morning, *and* dwell in the uttermost parts of the sea;

10 Even there shall thy hand lead me, and thy right hand shall hold me.

11 If I say, Surely the darkness shall cover me; even the night shall be light about me.

12 Yea, the darkness hideth not from thee; but the night shineth as the day: the darkness and the light *are* both alike *to thee.*

13 For thou hast possessed my reins: thou hast covered me in my mother's womb.

14 I will praise thee; for I am fearfully *and* wonderfully made: marvellous *are* thy works; and *that* my soul knoweth right well.

15 My substance was not hid from thee, when I was made in secret, *and* curiously wrought in the lowest parts of the earth.

16 Thine eyes did see my substance, yet being unperfect; and in thy book all *my members* were written, *which* in continuance were fashioned, when *as yet there was* none of them.

17 How precious also are thy thoughts unto me, O God! how great is the sum of them!

18 *If* I should count them, they are more in number than the sand: when I awake, I am still with thee.

19 Surely thou wilt slay the wicked, O God: depart from me therefore, ye bloody men.

20 For they speak against thee wickedly, *and* thine enemies take *thy name* in vain.

21 Do not I hate them, O LORD, that hate thee? and am not I grieved with those that rise up against thee?

22 I hate them with perfect hatred: I count them mine enemies.

23 Search me, O God, and know my heart: try me, and know my thoughts:

24 And see if *there be any* wicked way in me, and lead me in the way everlasting.

ON the title see on titles of Psalms iii. iv. The Hebrew and all the ancient versions ascribe this Psalm to David. The title shows that it belongs to a time when the public worship of God was fully organized. Against the Davidic authorship it is urged that there are Chaldaisms in it. But these consist, as Jebb remarks, " in the substitution of one letter for another very like it in shape, and easily to be mistaken by a transcriber, particularly by one who had been used to the Chaldee idiom: but the moral arguments for David's authorship are so strong as to overwhelm any such verbal or rather *literal* criticism, were even the objections more formidable than they are." There is no necessity for seeking a historic occasion for this Psalm, though many have indulged their ingenuity in that way. Some think it has a particular connection with Ps. cxxxviii. But there is not a part of the Psalter, where it would be out of place. Its doctrines are pure and heavenly, sublime and practical, entering into the very elements of pious sentiment. Amongst Hebrew idyls it holds a very prominent place. Some Jewish writers give it the first place. Lowth puts it next to Psalm civ. and says, " If it be excelled, (as perhaps it is) by the former in the plan, disposition and arrangement of the matter, it is not in the least inferior in the dignity and elegance of its sentiments, images and figures." Mant: "Amongst its other excellencies it is for nothing more admirable than for the exquisite skill with which it descants on the perfections of the Deity." Anderson: "No philosopher of ancient times ever attained to such sublime views of the perfections and moral government of God as the Hebrew prophets. How are we to account for this difference but on the supposition of the divine origin of the religion of the Hebrews? On any other supposition these Psalms are a greater miracle than any of those recorded by Moses." Scott dates it B. C. 1059; Clarke affixes no date but says it has no high antiquity. The names of the Most High here found are *Jehovah* LORD, *El God* and *Eloah God*, on which see on Ps. i. 2; v. 4; xviii. 31.

1. *O* LORD, *thou hast searched me, and known* me. *Searched*, in the preterite. In the imperative it occurs again in v. 23. We met it in Ps. xliv. 21. It implies thorough investigation. *Known*, in the future, but see Introduction, § 6. In other forms it occurs again in vv. 2, 4, 14, 23. It implies exact intelligence, precise understanding. The English version supplies *me* at the end of v. 1. This leads to no error, and is suggested by its occurrence in the first clause; but it is not necessary. The verses following show what it included:

2. *Thou knowest my downsitting and mine uprising; thou understandest my thought afar off.* The first clause declares the perfect intelligence God has of every posture,

gesture, exercise, pursuit, state and condition of man. The second declares his perfect acquaintance with every emotion, feeling, conception, thought, aim, doubt, perplexity and solicitude of his creatures, however they may be removed from the notice of mortals, however misjudged, or cut off from the usual places of worship. *Afar off*, an adjective, *distant, remote*, in time or place, with the preposition, as here, commonly rendered *afar off*, also *long ago*. Edwards renders it *long before;* Street, *from a distance;* Alexander, *from afar.* Compare Ps. cxxxviii. 6; Jer. xxiii. 23. We are often far from God, but he is nigh unto us at all times by his essential presence, Acts xvii. 27.

3. *Thou compassest my path and my lying down, and art acquainted* with *all my ways. Compassest,* in Ruth iii. 2; Isa. xxx. 24, *winnow;* in Jer. iv. 11, *fan.* Mudge, Street, Clarke and Alexander read *siftest;* Edwards, *art privy to;* Hengstenberg, *markest;* Jebb, *spiest out;* as when one winnows wheat and chaff, he separates them, sees them, and learns the quantity and quality of each, so the Most High knows all about our *path* and *lying down;* church of England, Jebb and Fry read *path* and *bed;* Edwards, *my motions in the day and my lying down at night;* Street, *path* and *couch.* The two words express one's state and actions by night and by day, in public and in secret. *Art acquainted,* there is no better rendering. In the imperative we have it in Job xxii. 21, *Acquaint* now *thyself* with him. *Ways,* life, behaviour, state, condition, all that makes the history of a man.

4. *For* there is *not a word in my tongue,* but, *lo,* O LORD, *thou knowest it altogether. For,* better rendered *surely* in this place. Edwards thus interprets the whole verse: "For before my words are upon my tongue, behold, Jehovah, thou knowest the whole of them."

5. *Thou hast beset me behind and before, and laid thine hand upon me.* John Rogers' Translation: Thou hast fashyoned me behynde and before and layed thyne hande upon me; Edwards: Thou closely environest me behind and before, and layest thy hand upon me; Street: Lo, O Jehovah, thou knowest all the past and the future; thou didst form me, and didst place thine hand on me; Phillips: "The meaning of the verse is, Thou hast so pressed upon, or besieged me, both behind and before, that I find there is no escaping from thee;" Hengstenberg: "I am on all sides surrounded and environed by thee, can do nothing, and suffer nothing, without being seen by thee, and being always in thy power."

6. Such *knowledge* is *too wonderful for me: it is high, I cannot* attain *unto it.* More literally, Marvellous (is such) knowledge, too much for me; it is set on high, I shall not be equal to it. The *knowledge* intended may be either God's amazing and perfect intelligence of all things, or a creature's conception and understanding of the divine omniscience. The latter is commonly supposed to be intended. But some quite prefer the former. Horne: "I cannot admire it enough, for I cannot conceive of it aright."

7. *Whither shall I go from thy Spirit? or whither shall I flee from thy presence?* The two clauses alike declare the impossibility of eluding the direct and immediate notice of God. This verse teaches either that God is a Spirit or that he has a Spirit. If the former, it implies his amazing and infinite intelligence as well as incomprehensibility; if the latter, it implies the doctrine of the Trinity, in which the Spirit of God is the third person. Why should we hesitate to admit that the personality and divinity of the Holy Ghost is taught in the Old Testament? See on Ps. li. 11.

8. *If I ascend up into heaven, thou art there: if I make my bed in hell, behold, thou art there.* Both in heaven and in hell is God's essential presence. In heaven they have his gracious presence. In hell they feel his wrathful presence. On the word rendered *hell* see on Ps. xvi. 10. Henry: "Hell is an uncomfortable place to make a bed in, where there is no rest day or night; yet thousands will make their bed for

ever in those flames;" Scott: "Should any one murder himself to terminate his sorrows, and escape the remorse of conscience, or the consequences of his sins. he must certainly be disappointed."

9. *If I take the wings of the morning, and dwell in the uttermost parts of the sea;*

10. *Even there shall thy hand lead me, and thy right hand shall hold me.* The first clause of v. 9 contains as striking and beautiful a figure as is found in any language. Light travels even more swiftly than lightning, and the morning rays fly on the swiftest wings. Mendelssohn: "In a moment the dawn of the morning is spread over the horizon." On this figure is based that of Mal. iv. 2. As the Mediterranean sea lay towards sunset from Judea, *sea* is probably put here for the west. Thus we preserve a close connection in the sentence. *Lead*, a verb almost uniformly so rendered, or *guide*. The doctrine of divine guidance is abundantly taught in Scripture, Gen. xxiv. 48; Ex. xv. 13; Deut. xxxii. 12; Ps. v. 8; xxiii. 3; lxxiii. 24. *Hold, take, take hold of, catch, have possession of.* To possess is the idea here, and well agrees with the thread of discourse. Dathe thinks God's gracious presence in defence is intended.

11. *If I say, Surely the darkness shall cover me; even the night shall be light about me.* Darkness protects us from the sight of men; but omniscience regards neither that nor any other covering. It mixes figures and destroys the unity of discourse to understand by *darkness* calamity, trouble. The Psalmist is celebrating the omnipresence, omniscience and omnipotence of Jehovah, and not his pity to the miserable. For the assertions of this verse, the prophet assigns a reason:

12. *Yea, the darkness hideth not from thee; but the night shineth as the day: the darkness and the light are both alike to thee.* The first clause is literally, Darkness will not make dark from thee. Like the sun, God's presence converts midnight into noon. In his light even we mortals see light. Among men much is said of ' covert designs.' But there are absolutely no such things. All purposes are as fully known to God before as after they are carried out. There is no greater infatuation, than that which leads us to act as if God did not see, and remember.

13. *For thou hast possessed my reins; thou hast covered me in my mother's womb.* *Possessed*, the same word is used in regard to the Son of God, Pr. viii. 22. It is often rendered *bought, purchased, redeemed.* It expresses perfect ownership and so implies intimate knowledge of the thing owned. *Reins, kidneys*, the most secret part of the human body, see on Ps. vii. 9; xvi. 7. The clause declares God's perfect acquaintance with the most secret things pertaining to us. Yea, more, the Lord *covered, hedged in, protected, defended* us in embryo. The verb is in the future, but clearly the preterite should be used in the translation. See Introduction, § 6. So wonderful knowledge, wisdom, power and goodness as are suggested by any right views of our own origin at once awaken adoring gratitude:

14. *I will praise thee; for I am fearfully* and *wonderfully made: marvellous* are *thy works;* and *that my soul knoweth right well. Praise*, often, *give thanks*, as in Ps. cxxxvi. 1, 2, 3. The very thought of his creation stirs his soul, and awakens praise. The least violence or the slightest disorder may take our lives. The fearfulness of our organization results from the infinite skill and perfections of the Creator. Neither man nor angel could devise anything at once so nice and so strong, so curious and so useful. *Am wonderfully made*, one word, cognate to that rendered *marvellous works* in Ps. ix. 1. An eminent proficient in anatomy said, that if any man could see his own danger from motion, he would be afraid to leap, or walk, or even breathe. Well does the prophet add, *Marvellous* are *thy works.* This clause declares the lively sense the Psalmist had of the wonders of physiology. Patrick: "I was, I know not how, in such a wonderful manner formed, that the thoughts of it strike me with astonishment."

15. *My substance was not hid from thee, when I was made in secret, and curiously*

wrought in the lowest parts of the earth. *Substance,* not the word so rendered in v. 16, but one in the margin rendered *strength* or *body;* church of England and Jebb, *bones;* Alexander, *frame.* *Curiously wrought;* margin, *embroidered.* The cognate noun is in Ps. xlv. 14 and elsewhere, rendered *needlework;* in Ezek. xvi. 10 and often, *broidered work.* Hammond: "The flesh and bones and skin and nerves and arteries are so artificially weaved together, that no embroidery or carpet-work in the world can compare with it." *In the lowest parts of the earth,* that is, in the womb, which is as completely beyond our notice as are the lowest caverns of earth. Compare Job i. 21. Walford: "The figure is derived from the darkness and obscurity of caverns and other recesses of the earth."

16. *Thine eyes did see my substance, yet being unperfect; and in thy book all* my members *were written,* which *in continuance were fashioned, when* as yet there was *none of them.* As all the parts of Solomon's temple were in the original plan, so when God builds the temple of our bodies, he does it by his *book,* in which all is *written* beforehand. He works not extemporaneously even in making one human body. *Substance yet being unperfect,* one word, found nowhere else in the Hebrew Bible, and its cognate verb is found but once (2 Kings ii. 8), where it is rendered *wrapped together.* The Chaldee renders it *my body;* Calvin, *shapelessness;* Street, *imperfect limbs;* Hengstenberg, *me, when I was still unprepared.* *All my members,* all parts of my frame and body. *In continuance, in the course of days,* or *by days.* Phillips: "*They* (my members) *have been daily formed,* or *forming.* They were not formed at once, but gradually; each day increasing in strength and size."

17. *How precious also are thy thoughts unto me, O God! how great is the sum of them!* Church of England: How dear are thy counsels unto me; Street: Of how great value have thy thoughts concerning me been! Fry: How wonderful are thy thoughts concerning me; Hengstenberg: How precious are to me, O God, thy thoughts. *Precious,* see on Ps. xlix. 8. *Sum,* in the plural *heads, tops, companies, principal;* sometimes numerically as in Ex. xxx. 12.

18. *If I should count them, they are more in number than the sand: when I awake, I am still with thee.* With his mind occupied with these "thoughts" of God, he lay down to sleep at night, and when he awoke, finding that God was still pouring mercies upon him, he resumed the theme of his reflections. Pool: "These are my last thoughts when I lie down, and my first when I rise."

19. *Surely thou wilt slay the wicked, O God: depart from me therefore, ye bloody men.* *Surely,* in Num. xiv. 30, *doubtless;* in 1 Sam. xxi. 5, *of a truth;* in Jer. xv. 11, *verily.* As certainly as God gives life to the just, so certainly will he *kill* the *wicked,* or *ungodly.* This God does in a thousand ways. He is at no loss for means or instruments. His withdrawal is death. As the doom of incorrigible sinners is fixed, it is the part of wisdom and of piety to renounce their friendship and their companionship. *Bloody men,* literally, *men of bloods,* meaning those who had shed, or who sought to shed blood, as in Ps. xxvi. 9.

20. *For they speak against thee wickedly, and thine enemies take thy name in vain.* No man can sin against man but that he sins against God by violating his law. He who fears not God, commonly has no regard to man. Men of blood are never fair and candid, but speak *wicked devices* against God. And who ever saw a bloody man that was not profane?

21. *Do not I hate them, O LORD, that hate thee? and am I not grieved with those that rise up against thee?* This is not a question calling for information. It is an affirmation with a solemn appeal to the Searcher of hearts, as witness of his sincerity. The *hatred* here spoken of is *displacency,* and not malevolence. It is against the ways and characters, not against the persons of the wicked. It was accompanied with

deep and ingenuous *grief*, not so much for any suffering brought on the prophet, as for the dishonor directed against God.

22. *I hate them with perfect hatred: I count them mine enemies.* Pool: "I am no less grieved with their enmity against thee, than if they directed it against myself."

23. *Search me, O God, and know my heart: try me, and know my thoughts:*

24. *And see if* there be any *wicked way in me, and lead me in the way everlasting.* In the beginning of the Psalm, the prophet had celebrated the omniscience of God, and had taught the doctrine that he was the Searcher of hearts. Here he implores the exercise of that omniscience in his own case, not because he was faultless, but because, being faulty even beyond his own knowledge, he desired the scrutiny of omniscience, that no lust might remain unmortified, no religious error uncorrected, and no duty unknown or undone. *Search*, as in v. 1. *Try*, so rendered in Ps. xi. 4, 5; in Ps. xvii. 3 and often, *prove*; in Ps. xxvi. 2, *examine*. *Know*; the same form of the same verb in both cases. It is very comprehensive and implies intimate acquaintance. See on v. 1. *Wicked way*, margin, way of *pain* or *grief*, that is a way that grieves God's Spirit, grieves good men, and must finally grieve me. *The way everlasting* is the one good old path trodden by pious patriarchs, prophets and saints of all ages, and leading to eternal life.

DOCTRINAL AND PRACTICAL REMARKS.

1. There is no better shape, in which to mould our highest views in theology, than that of devotion, a psalm, a prayer, as this poem shows. Henry: "Divine truths look full as well when they are prayed over, as when they are preached over: and much better than when they are disputed over."

2. If, as some think, this Psalm was written, when David's good name was through calumnies under a cloud, it tells all the slandered what to do. Let them go to God in such an hour with the joyous testimony of a good conscience; and he will be to such the God of all comfort.

3. Each of the divine perfections is in its turn for our consolation and edification. Omnipotence protects, mercy forgives, faithfulness preserves, omniscience searches us, vv. 1, 23. It is God's plan and our interest to have our hearts and ways subjected to the scrutiny of omniscience, which is thorough, infallible and infinitely holy in all its examinations.

4. It is a sign of true piety, when we are pleased with all the divine attributes, even the omniscience and justice of God, and implore the examination to which the intuitive and unerring knowledge of the Most High subjects us, vv. 1, 23. The better our spiritual state, the more will we betake ourselves to God, and rest satisfied only as we can approve ourselves to him alone.

5. The knowledge of God is absolutely perfect in kind and degree. There can be no addition made to it, vv. 1–6. Of course we can no more comprehend God's knowledge, than his eternity. We can wonder and adore, and there we must stop.

6. If our dealings are with God as the Searcher of hearts, hypocrisy is both superlative folly and superlative wickedness. It cannot effect any of its objects, and it is a direct insult to God. Before omniscience simulation and dissimulation are alike futile. False pretences have no power to hide anything from God. The hope of the hypocrite shall both justly and terribly perish.

7. How great is human ignorance when brought into comparison with divine knowledge, v. 6. No man knows a millionth part of the propositions which constitute universal truth. Men are blind and cannot see afar off. The greatest are but as children, 1 Cor. xiii. 11, 12. Men have but broken fragments of truth in this life. Luther: "All we are, and all we do, are not our own wisdom or doing." Dick-

son: "We see most of God, when we view him as incomprehensible, and see ourselves swallowed up in the thoughts of his perfection."

8. The doctrine of the omnipresence and omniscience of God is of excellent use in many ways. By the help of divine grace it warns and encourages us at the same time. Were we not exceedingly prone to sin, it would powerfully control us. A man has been held back from a crime by the presence of his little child. How then should the presence of Jehovah restrain us. It is a small thing to be seen of man's eye, or judged of man's judgment; but to live and act under the scrutiny of God is well suited to make us solemn and cautious. Yet God's Holy Spirit must change and renew the heart, or it will never turn from wickedness. Men cannot be frightened out of their iniquities.

9. The attributes of God are harmonious. One is not in conflict with another. Omniscience and omnipresence are but names given to the distinct attributes of the infinite and undivided excellence of the one living and true God, vv. 1–13. Nor are these or any of God's perfections discordant in their influence on good men. Tholuck: "The thought of the omniscience of God ought in every prayer to purify our souls, while that of his omnipresence ought to sanctify it." Scott: "The belief of God's omnipresence is intimately connected with that of his omniscience, and is of similar efficacy."

10. No madness exceeds that of the poor guilty wretch, who expects to elude the eye or the arm of God, vv. 7–13. Calvin: "We are ashamed to let men know and witness our delinquencies; but we are as indifferent to what God may think of us, as if our sins were covered and veiled from his inspection." Morison: "There is something awfully penetrating in the thought of our being the immediate objects of the divine inspection and scrutiny."

11. As creation at first awakened the song of the heavenly host; so the due consideration of our own creation should deeply affect us, and we should often and adoringly dwell upon it, vv. 14–16. Just reflections on our own origin and preservation would mightily strengthen our faith and prepare us for many trials.

12. As architects and embroiderers have a plan by which they accomplish their designs; so has God also his plan, his counsel, his purpose, his *book*, according to which he reigns and does all things, even to the formation of a human body in the womb, v. 16. Luther: "The Psalmist here proclaims that incomprehensibleness of the divine wisdom and goodness, whereby, in a wonderful manner, he himself and all men, with all their affairs, all their works and all their thoughts, both the greatest and the least, were predestinated of God from everlasting. This manifold wisdom of God is incomprehensible to flesh and blood."

13. There is no light, in which we can seriously view God's care of us, that his tender love to us and his watchfulness over us are not amazing and precious to a right-minded man.

14. The doom of the incorrigible is certain, fixed and dreadful, v. 19. They are the enemies of God by wicked works; and God is their enemy by righteous indignation, and will fight against them and *slay* them all.

15. We must either break with sinners, or perish with them, v. 19.

16. Ever since men were sinners, their wickedness has been breaking out in hard speeches against God, v. 20. It will be so to the end, Jude 14, 15.

17. God's people willingly make common cause with him, vv. 21, 22. His law is their law; his will is their will; his friends are their friends; his enemies are their enemies.

18. But in our hatred of sin we should carefully guard against all malice, all private pique, all personal enmity, and abhor the characters of the wicked only as they

are abhorrent to God, vv. 21, 22. Morison: "Even our very condemnation of what is evil requires to be tested. Does it spring from love to God? from hatred of sin? from attachment to holiness? from a desire not to countenance evil? or does it spring from ostentation?—from censorious feeling?—from hypocritical pretence? from a desire to please certain of our fellow-creatures?"

18. Whoever would walk in the right way must be led by the Almighty. Otherwise he will surely err and that fatally, going in the way of grief, v. 24.

19. We cannot account for the existence of this poem but on the supposition that it was taught by inspiration. Fleury: "Let the modern wits, after this, look upon the honest shepherds of Palestine, as a company of *rude and unpolished clowns;* let them, if they can, produce from profane authors thoughts that are more sublime, more delicate, or better turned; not to mention the sound divinity, and solid piety couched under these expressions."

PSALM CXL.

To the chief Musician, A Psalm of David.

1 Deliver me, O LORD, from the evil man: preserve me from the violent man;

2 Which imagine mischiefs in *their* hearts; continually are they gathered together *for* war.

3 They have sharpened their tongues like a serpent; adders' poison *is* under their lips. Selah.

4 Keep me, O LORD, from the hands of the wicked; preserve me from the violent man; who have purposed to overthrow my goings.

5 The proud have hid a snare for me, and cords; they have spread a net by the way side; they have set gins for me. Selah.

6 I said unto the LORD, Thou *art* my God: hear the voice of my supplications, O LORD.

7 O GOD the Lord, the strength of my salvation, thou hast covered my head in the day of battle.

8 Grant not, O LORD, the desires of the wicked: further not his wicked device; *lest* they exalt themselves. Selah.

9 *As for* the head of those that compass me about, let the mischief of their own lips cover them.

10 Let burning coals fall upon them: let them be cast into the fire; into deep pits, that they rise not up again.

11 Let not an evil speaker be established in the earth: evil shall hunt the violent man to overthrow him.

12 I know that the LORD will maintain the cause of the afflicted, *and* the right of the poor.

13 Surely the righteous shall give thanks unto thy name: the upright shall dwell in thy presence.

ON the title see on titles of Psalms iii. iv. The Hebrew, all the ancient versions and the great mass of modern scholars ascribe this Psalm to David. The internal evidence is clear. There is not like agreement respecting the historic occasion of its composition. The Syriac fixes it to the time when Saul attempted to kill David by hurling the spear at him. Theodoret assigns it to the time when Saul, urged on by Doeg and the Ziphites, was pursuing David. With him many coincide in opinion. All this however is conjecture. It is clear this ode was written after the great promise made to David in 2 Sam. vii.; and that it was written during the Sauline persecution. Scott dates it B. C. 1060; Clarke, B. C. about 1061. The names of God here found are *Jehovah* LORD, *Adonai Lord* and *El God,* on which see on Ps. i. 2; ii. 4; v. 4. On *Selah* see Introduction, § 15.

1. *Deliver me, O* LORD, *from the evil man : preserve me from the violent man.* *Deliver* and *preserve* both often used in a military sense. The former expresses *rescue* and the latter *defence* by power. Yet they are often used indefinitely ; see on Ps. vi. 4 ; xii. 7. There is no significancy in the use of the two different Hebrew words [Adam and Ish] for *man* in v. 1. In v. 12, we have but one and the same word. See Introduction, § 16. *Evil*, in v. 2, in the plural, *mischiefs.* The *violent* man, literally the man of *violences.* In Ps. vii. 16, the same word is rendered *violent dealing ;* in Ps. xxvii. 12, *cruelty.* Both clauses of the verse well describe the character of Saul and of the lying, blood-thirsty creatures, who lent themselves to his nefarious designs,

2. *Which imagine mischiefs in* their *heart ; continually are they gathered together for war.* The *mischiefs, evils, troubles,* which they have devised, are for others, not for themselves. Bad men are fruitful in plots against the righteous. Nor are they nice or scrupulous about the measures employed. They are ready for *war*, plural *wars, fightings.* One apparent, temporary advantage, which the wicked have over the righteous, is that the former have no conscience about the means they use to effect their purposes. They are ever ready to proceed to extremities.

3. *They have sharpened their tongues like a serpent ; adders' poison* is *under their lips.* Most of the editions of the English Bible make *tongue* and *adder* plural. In Hebrew they are singular. *Serpent*, a generic term for cunning and venomous reptiles. *Adder*, here only ; it is another word rendered *adder* elsewhere. A *sharp tongue* is a figure in many languages. Often the tongue of the serpent is spoken of as the seat of its venom. This is popular, not scientific language. The whole tribe of serpents have sharp tongues. The poison of several kinds found in the east is deadly. The wickedness here described was exhibited by Saul and his associates ; but it did not die out with them, Rom. iii. 13. Saul was but a sample of the manner in which human nature acts out its venomous depravity.

4. *Keep me, O* LORD, *from the hands of the wicked ; preserve me from the violent man ; who have purposed to overthrow my goings.* *Keep*, often found in Ps. cxix., applied to keeping God's word. *Preserve*, as in v. 1. *Wicked*, in Ps. i., *ungodly.* *Violent man*, as in v. 1. *Purposed, thought, conceived, imagined, devised, counted, reckoned.* To *overthrow goings*—an Orientalism—is to subvert plans and to destroy prospects.

5. *The proud have hid a snare for me, and cords : they have spread a net by the way side ; they have set gins for me.* *Snare*, in the Psalms uniformly rendered. See on Ps. xi. 6 ; lxix. 22 ; xci. 3 ; cxix. 110 ; cxxiv. 7 ; in Job xviii. 9, *gin.* *Cords*, in Ps. xvi. 6, *lines ;* in Ps. xviii. 4, 5, *sorrows ;* in Ps. cxix. 61, *bands.* Here the reference is to the snares in which cords were used. *Net*, uniformly rendered. See on Ps. ix. 15. The artifice of David's foes was exceeded only by their malice. Candor and fair dealing belong not to sin.

6. *I said unto the* LORD, *Thou* art *my God : hear the voice of my supplications, O* LORD. He is pleading the covenant relation with God, as in Ps. iii. 7 and often. On the last clause see on Ps. xxviii. 2, 6.

7. *O* GOD *the Lord, the strength of my salvation, thou hast covered my head in the day of battle.* In rendering *Jehovah God*, our version followed some old translations. No deliverance can be relied on except as it comes from God. He is the *strength*, on which we must depend.

8. *Grant not, O* LORD, *the desires of the wicked : further not his wicked device ; lest they exalt themselves.* Such a prayer is always safe. The wickedness of the desires and plans of the *ungodly* is utterly repugnant to the holiness of God. His whole nature pledges him to oppose and not to *further* the schemes of his enemies. Were

it otherwise they would be *elated* even more than they are. Their insolence is often intolerable.

9. As for *the head of those that compass me about, let the mischief of their own lips cover them. Cover*, in the future, *shall cover*. The verse contains a clear avowal of the doctrine of retribution in kind, Ps. vii. 15, 16; xviii. 25, 26.

10. *Let burning coals fall upon them: let them be cast into the fire; into deep pits, that they rise not up again*. The verbs are in the future; see Introduction, § 6. The destruction by *coals* and *fire*, has an allusion to the overthrow of the cities of the plain. This mode of speaking is preserved to the close of Scripture. *Deep pits;* Doway, *miseries;* Calvin, *deeps;* Horsley, *chasms of the yawning earth;* Alexander, *deep waters*. The word is found nowhere else in the Hebrew Bible. It is a feminine plural. The deluge furnished the figure of floods; the customs of the holy land that of pits; though Luther thinks the imagery is drawn from the destruction of Pharaoh and his host by lightning from heaven and by water. Jerome understands *pits of water*. The phrase is a threatening of final and perpetual ruin.

11. *Let not an evil speaker be established in the earth: evil shall hunt the violent man to overthrow him. Evil speaker*, literally *the man of tongue*, meaning one of lawless *speech*, who slanders man and reproaches God. *Violent man*, literally *man of violence*, as in v. 1, only here *violence* is in the singular. Both the verbs are in the future and are best so rendered. *Hunt*, there is no better rendering. Sometimes it is rendered *chase. Evil shall hunt* them till it finds them out. It shall hotly pursue them till it overtakes them.

12. *I know that the* LORD *will maintain the cause of the afflicted*, and *the right of the poor*. God's perfections and promises, united with David's own experience, assured him that in the end the Lord would show himself favorable to the *poor* and *needy*. On *afflicted* and *poor*, see on Ps. ix. 12, where the former is rendered *humble*, and Ps. ix. 18, where the latter is rendered *needy*.

13. *Surely the righteous shall give thanks unto thy name: the upright shall dwell in thy presence. Give thanks* or *praise*. The *righteous* shall have cause and shall have a heart for this work. *Upright*, as in Ps. vii. 10, also rendered *righteous. Dwell*, or *sit, i. e.*, have their abode in *thy presence*, in this world, and especially in heaven above, where there is fulness of joy. Calvin: " *To dwell before God's face* is to be cherished and sustained by his fatherly regards."

DOCTRINAL AND PRACTICAL REMARKS.

1. This Psalm, like many others, shows that the best men are often brought into great perils by the wicked; so that none but God can *deliver* or *preserve* them, v. 1.

2. The wicked continually prove that their hatred is deadly, vv. 2, 3. The evidence is as clear as day. The facts are countless and indisputable.

3. The arts of falsehood, slander and abuse are as old as sin in the world, v. 3. Dickson: "When the wicked have vented deadly lies of the godly, they have in readiness new slanders and capital crimes to charge them with falsely;" Morison: "All persecutors of the church in every age have been thus distinguished—they have first traduced the objects of their hate, and then thirsted for their blood;" Horne: "Slander and calumny always precede and accompany persecution, because malice itself cannot excite people against a good man, as such; to do this, he must first be represented as a bad man. Thus David was hunted as a rebel, Christ was crucified as a blasphemer, and the primitive Christians were tortured as guilty of incest and murder."

4. But let the righteous betake themselves to Jehovah, v. 4. He can *keep, preserve*

and defend one saint against a million of fallen spirits. His power, his wisdom, his pity, his grace are all-sufficient.

5. And let us not be afraid with any amazement. Human and diabolical cunning is no match for infinite wisdom. The wiles of the devil are not to be compared with the counsels of God, v. 5.

6. Therefore cleave to Jehovah, and plead his covenant at all times, v. 6. Cast not away your confidence which hath great recompense of reward. Pray, wait and hope —hope, wait and pray. The Lord hath pleasure in those that hope in his mercy.

7. If we have escaped dangers seen or unseen, it was solely by the providence of God, v. 7. To him be all the glory of our deliverances, even where he employs men as instruments.

8. Good men live by prayer, vv. 1, 4, 6, 8. He who gets to the throne of grace is covered by the cloud of glory, through which no sun can smite by day, nor moon by night.

9. Pride and insolence are elements of iniquity, and crop out on every occasion of even temporary triumph, v. 8. It is to all the righteous a mercy when God lays his almighty hand on the wicked, and depresses their state, or hurls them from place and power, as he did Saul, Belshazzar and many others. Henry: "Proud men, when they prosper, are made prouder, grow more impudent against God, and insolent against his people."

10. Evil speeches and evil deeds will be sure in due time to return on the pate of their authors, vv. 9, 10. The law of retaliation is fixed in the divine government. Horne: "Those tongues which have contributed to set the world on fire, shall be tormented with the hot burning coals of eternal vengeance."

11. Evil speakers and violent men may have their triumph, but it shall be short, and unless God grant timely repentance, it shall be followed by untold plagues and inconceivable torments, v. 11. Dickson: "Backbiters and calumniators shall not only be debarred from heaven, but also God's curse shall follow them on earth, and not suffer them nor their posterity to enjoy quiet prosperity in the world."

12. Evil pursues the sinner through all his windings, and to the lowest hell. The Chaldee: "He shall be hunted by the angel of death, and thrust into hell." Compare Amos v. 19. Calvin: "The more the ungodly look for impunity and escape, they only precipitate themselves more certainly upon destruction."

13. Were the *poor* and *needy* left to themselves, all issues would be to them fatal. But God is on their side, and so they always in the end maintain their ground and secure their rights, v. 12. Even if overborne here, the day of judgment will set all right. Things will not then be settled by clamor, tumult or majorities. "God is the patron of innocence; much more of persecuted piety."

14. Dark, and cold, and dismal as the times of the righteous often appear in this life, all will end in thanks, and praise, and glory. Clarke: "The persecuted have ever been dear to God." He is often best pleased with them when the storm against them is most pitiless.

15. As in all his trials David was a type of the suffering Saviour, and as they both were humbled before they were exalted, and suffered before they entered into rest; so shall it be with all the righteous. The cross here, the crown hereafter. Grace now, glory in eternity. Blessed be God for this admirable order.

PSALM CXLI.

A Psalm of David.

1 LORD, I cry unto thee: make haste unto me; give ear unto my voice, when I cry unto thee.

2 Let my prayer be set forth before thee *as* incense; *and* the lifting up of my hands *as* the evening sacrifice.

3 Set a watch, O LORD, before my mouth; keep the door of my lips.

4 Incline not my heart to *any* evil thing, to practise wicked works with men that work iniquity: and let me not eat of their dainties.

5 Let the righteous smite me; *it shall be* a kindness: and let him reprove me; *it shall be* an excellent oil, *which* shall not break my head: for yet my prayer also *shall be* in their calamities.

6 When their judges are overthrown in stony places, they shall hear my words; for they are sweet.

7 Our bones are scattered at the grave's mouth, as when one cutteth and cleaveth *wood* upon the earth.

8 But mine eyes *are* unto thee, O GOD the Lord: in thee is my trust; leave not my soul destitute.

9 Keep me from the snares *which* they have laid for me, and the gins of the workers of iniquity.

10 Let the wicked fall into their own nets, whilst that I withal escape.

ON the title see on title of Psalm iii. The remarks made on the authorship of Psalm cxl. are almost without exception applicable to this. Some refer its origin to events recorded in 1 Sam. xxiv.; others, to events recorded in 1 Sam. xxvi. There is no reason to doubt that it was written during those ten dreadful years, when Saul and his bloody crew beset David. Patrick: "Nobody need wonder, that there are so many prayers founded upon the same subject; for that persecution endured long, and they were made upon different occasions, or for different purposes." The scope of this ode is clearly a prayer for grace to restrain his temper and his tongue in a time of wanton injuries received from those, whom he had never wronged. Scott dates it B. C. 1057; Clarke, B. C. about 1061; De Wette considers it one of the oldest. The names of the Most High here found are *Jehovah* LORD and *Adonai Lord*, on which see on Ps. i. 2; ii. 4. As in Ps. cxl. 7, so also in v. 8 of this Psalm we have *Jehovah Adonai* rendered GOD *the Lord*.

1. LORD, *I cry unto thee: make haste unto me; give ear unto my voice, when I cry unto thee.* Every phrase of this verse has been already considered. See on Ps. xvii. 6; xxii. 19; lxx. 1; lxxi. 12. The whole verse is well rendered.

2. *Let my prayer be set forth before thee* as *incense; and the lifting up of my hands* as *the evening sacrifice.* Prayer and *lifting up of hands* are equivalent terms; and so are *incense* and the *evening sacrifice.* The verb is in the future, *shall be set forth,* or *established.* The carnal ordinances pointed to spiritual services. David and his faithful friends, now deprived of the privileges of the appointed worship in the tabernacle, desire God to hear and answer them in their lowly condition, even as if they had the altar, and the services connected therewith. *Sacrifice,* not the word commonly denoting a bloody sacrifice though so used in Gen. iv. 3–5; but the evening oblation, or meat-offering. See on Ps. xx. 3. Clarke: "As he could not worship according to the *letter* of the law, he will worship God according to the *spirit.*" On *lifting up* hands see on Ps. xxviii. 2.

3. *Set a watch, O LORD, before my mouth; keep the door of my lips.* Watch, here only, literally *a keeping.* Door, not found elsewhere, but well rendered. Both clauses ask for the close and ceaseless vigilance of omniscient purity over him, and contain a confession that he could not sufficiently guard himself against the abuse of speech, to which his circumstances tempted him. Edwards: Set a watch at my mouth,

Jehovah; a guard at the door of my lips; Street: Place, O Jehovah, a watch upon my mouth, a guard upon the door of my lips.

4. *Incline not my heart to any evil thing, to practise wicked works with men that work iniquity: and let me not eat of their dainties.* For *thing* some read *word*. The original will bear either. It is commonly rendered *word*, but in Ps. xlv. 1, *matter;* in Ps. ci. 3, *thing:* in Ps. cxii. 5, in the plural *affairs.* For *practise wickedness* Street has *sin presumptuously.* The last clause admits of these interpretations: 1. Let me not partake of feasts in honor of false gods; 2. Let me not eat things, however tempting, if they are forbidden in the law; 3. Let me not be a boon companion of wicked men at their feasts; 4. Let me not be tempted by their dainties to walk in their ways. The true sense is probably given in No. 3. *Dainties*, here only, delicacies, pleasant things.

5. *Let the righteous smite me;* it shall be *a kindness: and let him reprove me*, it shall be *an excellent oil,* which *shall not break my head: for yet my prayer also* shall be *in their calamities.* The ancient versions and modern translations give us very little aid in interpreting this passage. A minute consideration of the several terms and phrases brings us to about the same result as we reach by the common version. The term *righteous* is in the singular. Fry renders it the Just One. Tholuck, Hengstenberg and Alexander by it understand God. Calvin, Diodati, Dœderlein, Patrick, Jebb, Rosenmüller, French and Skinner substantially agree with the authorized version. If it is the Lord who *smites*, then the Psalmist looks upon divine corrections as marks of fatherly love; if a pious man, then his rebukes are the fruits of brotherly kindness. The latter is probably the correct view. If so, it is parallel to Prov. ix. 8 and kindred passages. The last clause may refer to the *calamities* of the righteous or of the wicked. In the former case, the prophet says he will pray for his faithful reprovers; in the latter, for his bitter enemies. The former perhaps gives the true idea. Scott: "Jealous of himself in so ensnaring a situation, the Psalmist prayed that some pious friend might ever be present to reprove him sharply, if he yielded to temptation. This he would take as a kindness; sensible that it would neither break his head, nor cause him to hang it down in dejection: but, being insinuating and healing, like an excellent oil, it would be very useful to him; and he would requite the benefit by praying for them in their calamities, if he had no other way of expressing his gratitude."

6. *When their judges are overthrown in stony places, they shall hear my words; for they are sweet.* Many give a different, but none a better rendering. Street makes this verse and the next contain the prayer of which mention is made in v. 5, and so puts the verbs in the optative. There is no ground for the opinion of some that the *words* here are those of Jehovah, and not of David. Does not this verse contain a prophecy of the overthrow of Saul and his partizans? That awful event was early followed by the people turning to David, and admitting that his *words* were *sweet, pleasant, delightful.* They received him as their king and as a prophet also. The reference to the *rocks* is poetical and borrowed from scenery with which Israelites were familiar. Horne gives quite a different turn to the verse, making it refer to David's tenderness in *dismissing* Saul from the sides of the rock unhurt. But this, though consonant with history, is hardly to be received.

7. *Our bones are scattered at the grave's mouth, as when one cutteth and cleaveth wood upon the earth.* Three views of this passage deserve notice, 1. For *wood* some read *earth*, and then infer that as the earth is broken and cleft by ploughing in order to a crop, so our bones are scattered at the entrance of the invisible world [Hebrew Sheol] in order to a glorious resurrection. Compare John xii. 24. The Chaldee, Syriac and Septuagint regard the last clause as referring to ploughing the earth. 2. Others think

the verbs point to the cutting and splitting of *wood* as the latter is so used in Ecc. x. 9, and gather this meaning, that men perish like the trees of the forest, and that their bones are scattered and unheeded like sticks of wood. 3. Another and a better meaning is gathered by supposing that David refers to the perils to which he and his associates were exposed. It was at the hazard of life that any man espoused his cause. See 1 Sam. xxii. 9–19. The allusion to this fearful tragedy was both natural and pertinent in this place, and well contrasts the conduct of David praying for his enemies with their blood-thirstiness.

8. *But mine eyes are unto thee, O* GOD *the Lord: in thee is my trust; leave not my soul destitute.* The darker the times, the more did David look to Jehovah, the Ruler. The first clause has a parallel in Ps. xxv. 15; cxxiii. 1, 2. It expresses longing and confiding expectation. The last clause is variously rendered. Calvin, Edwards, Jebb and Fry support our version. The Chaldee, Hengstenberg and Alexander: Pour not out my soul; Syriac and Street: Reject not my soul; margin: Make not my soul bare; Arabic: Destroy not my soul; Septuagint, Ethiopic, Vulgate and Doway: Take not away my soul; Fabritius: Bring not my soul to nothing; Piscator, Venema, Amesius, Tremellius and Junius: Strip not my soul; church of England: O cast not out my soul. The verb is rendered *pour, pour out,* in Isa. xxxii. 15; liii. 12. It seems therefore to be a plea for life—life brought into danger. This view is rather strengthened by the prayer of the next verse,

9. *Keep me from the snares* which *they have laid for me, and the gins of the workers of iniquity.* On *snares* and *gins* see on Ps. xi. 6; lxix. 22; cxix. 110; cxxiv. 7; cxl. 5. Literally, keep me from *the hands of the snares. Keep,* vigilantly and safely preserve. *Workers of iniquity,* those who are habitually and allowedly wicked.

10. *Let the wicked fall into their own nets, whilst that I withal escape. Nets,* here only, well rendered. *Fall,* in the future *shall fall;* a prediction. See Introduction, § 6. *Escape,* future *shall escape,* margin *pass over.*

DOCTRINAL AND PRACTICAL REMARKS.

1. When evil men beset and harass the pious, their resort is a throne of grace, v. 1. The greater their distress, the louder are their cries. All human aid withdrawn, they look to God alone, nor are they disappointed.

2. In the eyes of God's real people prayer is not an end, but a means; nor can they ever rest satisfied with the service, while they have no evidence of acceptance, v. 2. We cannot too carefully remember that prayer is a spiritual sacrifice demanding the heart and soul.

3. Hearty prayer sets men against sin in every shape and form, vv. 3, 4. Morison: " The spirit of prayer is the spirit of holiness; and he, who communes intimately with his God, will come forth from his presence with the desire of walking circum-spectly in all his ordinances and commandments."

4. The more the righteous knows of himself, the more earnestly does he desire and seek the grace of God to restrain, guard and sanctify him, v. 3. Experience unites with Scripture in teaching him that no human wisdom or virtue can control that unruly member the tongue, unless God in his mercy takes charge of the mouth, and guides our speech. This is specially true when we are reviled, slandered, persecuted. Calvin: " Nothing is more difficult than for the victims of unjust persecution to bridle their speech, and submit silently and without complaint to injuries." Then, if ever the righteous should cry for grace and strength. Horne: " A Christian, living among unbelievers and sensualists in the world, hath abundant reason to put up the same prayers, and use the same precautions."

5. Nor is the child of God satisfied merely with the control of his tongue; but

wishes his temper, his spirit watched and guarded, preserved and sanctified by the Lord, v. 4. His honest and thorough conviction is that of Solomon: "He that is slow to anger is better than the mighty; and he that ruleth his spirit, than he that taketh a city," Pr. xvi. 32. The most secret sin is worse than public reproach.

6. If we are not willing to be reproved by God or man in the kindness of love, we have not the temper of saints, and cannot expect to mend our faults, or prepare for a better world, v. 5. Luther: "I had rather that true and faithful teachers should rebuke and condemn me, and reprove my ways, than that hypocrites should flatter me and applaud me as a saint." Calvin: "It is not agreeable to corrupt nature to be reproved when we sin, but David had brought himself to that degree of docility and self-denial, which led him to consider no reproof distasteful, which he knew to proceed from the spirit of kindness." Compare Pr. vi. 23; xxvii. 6.

7. However long the wicked may seem to have things their own way, and tread down the righteous, they shall finally be overthrown in a terrible manner, v. 6. It was so with Saul, 1 Sam. xxxi. 1–10. It shall be so with all, who do not by timely repentance turn to God, Eccle. viii. 12, 13.

8. What is more fickle or unstable than popular favor? v. 6. The successful and the powerful seldom lack adherents. The men, who were so zealous for Saul, soon found, when he was dead, that David's words were sweet. The masses of men are so unthinking, take so little pains to inform themselves, and are so much governed by prejudice and passion, and especially so blindly follow leaders and majorities, that it is a marvel that any truth or any good man survives.

9. It is nothing unusual for oppressed innocency to be denied a hearing, and for the most brutal treatment to be dealt out to the well-deserving, v. 7. It has always been so. It is so still. It will be so as long as sin is rampant. The malice of the wicked is truly terrible.

10. The more cruel men become, and the more popular violence rages, the more must the pious sufferer look to God—to God alone, v. 8. Clarke: "In all times, in all places, on all occasions, I will cleave unto the Lord, and put my whole confidence in him." True Christian heroism does not proceed from strong nerves, or brute courage, but from a faith, which against hope believes in hope.

11. In certain circumstances and with submission to the will of God, we may pray for the lengthening of our days, v. 8. See REMARKS on Ps. xxxix. 13.

12. The worst snares are not those set to rob us of our estates, our liberties, our good names, or our lives; but those designed to rob us of a good conscience, of the fear and love of God, and of spiritual peace. From the wiles of the devil and the cunning craftiness of wicked men God alone and God only can keep us, v. 8.

13. God can frustrate any devices formed against us, even when for a time they threaten to destroy us; and all the plots of all impenitent plotters shall finally entangle and overwhelm their authors, v. 10. "No law can be more just than that the architects of destruction should perish by their own contrivances." "All that are bound over to God's justice are held by the cords of their own iniquity"

14. Let not the hunted and afflicted child of God be cast down with over much sorrow. Better times are coming.

PSALM CXLII.

Maschil of David; A Prayer when he was in the cave.

1 I cried unto the LORD with my voice; with my voice unto the LORD did I make my supplication.

2 I poured out my complaint before him; I shewed before him my trouble.

3 When my spirit was overwhelmed within me, then thou knewest my path. In the way wherein I walked have they privily laid a snare for me.

4 I looked on *my* right hand, and beheld, but *there was* no man that would know me: refuge failed me; no man cared for my soul.

5 I cried unto thee, O LORD: I said, Thou *art* my refuge *and* my portion in the land of the living.

6 Attend unto my cry; for I am brought very low: deliver me from my persecutors; for they are stronger than I.

7 Bring my soul out of prison, that I may praise thy name: the righteous shall compass me about; for thou shalt deal bountifully with me.

THIS Psalm is styled both a *Maschil* and a *Prayer*. On *Maschil* see on title of Ps. xxxii.; on *Prayer*, see on title of Ps. xvii. Both the author and his condition are determined by the title. Expositors are not agreed whether it relates to David's hiding in the cave of Adullam, 1 Sam. xxii.; or to his refuge in the cave of En-gedi, 1 Sam. xxiv.; or whether it merely refers in general to the life he led when the rocks and caves furnished him a home. Calvin, Anderson and others suppose a special reference to En-gedi; Morison, Horne and others, to Adullam; Hengstenberg and Alexander, to cave-life generally. The Psalm contains thoughts suitable to a time when many regarded David's affairs as desperate. The only name of the Almighty here found is *Jehovah* LORD, on which see on Ps. i. 2. Scott dates it B. C. 1060. Clarke affixes no date, though he thinks it may be old.

1. *I cried unto the* LORD *with my voice: with my voice unto the* LORD *did I make my supplication*. Both verbs are in the future. *Cried* expresses much earnestness. *Made supplication*, offered humble and fervent entreaties. Alexander: "It means, according to its etymology, a prayer for grace and mercy." *With my voice*, the same word in both cases, implying audible and not merely mental prayer. Joining all these words and phrases expresses great liveliness and earnestness in prayer.

2. *I poured out my complaint before him; I shewed before him my trouble*. Both verbs are in the future, yet are well rendered. See Introduction, § 6. *Complaint*, once rendered *babbling*, once *talking*, once *communication*, once *prayer*, once *meditation*, and nine times *complaint*. It expresses that which deeply occupies the mind. *Trouble*, elsewhere rendered *distress, anguish, tribulation, adversity, affliction*. Tholuck: "Peril so evident and imminent as that in which we find David, is sufficient to check the courage and destroy the faith of many an experienced Christian; to such an extent that he shall be at a loss to ease himself of his grief by prayer. But David enjoys perfect composure of mind, and unbosoms his cares before the Lord."

3. *When my spirit was overwhelmed within me, then thou knewest my path. In the way wherein I walked have they privily laid a snare for me*. Perhaps no verse in the Psalter is better translated, notwithstanding the purely Hebrew idiom of the original. The sense of the first clause turns on the word *knewest*. It implies perfect acquaintance with David's course of conduct and of suffering, and approval of his behaviour. To the upright God's omniscience is a great comfort. The second clause declares that arts of cunning and deceit were practised *on* him, not *by* him. *Snare*, as in Ps. cxl.

5; cxli. 9. What the particular device was we know not, but it was deadly. The sadder the case of his servants, the fitter the occasion for God to interpose:

4. *I looked on my right hand, and beheld, but* there was *no man that would know me: refuge failed me; no man cared for my soul.* The use of two verbs of the same import, *looked* and *beheld,* is not peculiar to this place; see Lam. i. 11, 12. The English version puts these verbs in the preterite, and is supported by the ancient versions, Doway, church of England, Jebb and others. Fry has 'he looked and beheld;' Edwards, 'I look.' But the Hebrew, the margin, Hengstenberg, Alexander, French and Skinner all have the imperative, *look* and *see.* This is best. David calls on the Lord to employ his omniscience in looking into his helpless condition. *Know,* as in v. 3, and used in the same sense. *Refuge,* as in Ps. lix. 16, literally *a place to fly to,* or *flight* itself, not the word rendered *refuge* in the next verse. *Cared,* a participle. The clause is literally, There is none *caring,* so rendered also in Deut. xi. 12. His adherents were so few that he speaks as if he had none.

5. *I cried unto thee, O* Lord: *I said, Thou* art *my refuge* and *my portion in the land of the living. Cried,* as in v. 1. It expresses great earnestness, as in a herald calling men together. *Refuge,* as in Ps. xiv. 6; xlvi. 1; in Job xxiv. 8, *shelter;* in Jer. xvii. 17; Joel iii. 16, *hope. Portion,* commonly so rendered, also *inheritance,* Ps. xvi. 5; xvii. 14. *In the land of the living, i. e.,* even in this world, where so many make other things their confidence.

6. *Attend unto my cry; for I am brought very low: deliver me from my persecutors; for they are stronger than I. Attend,* as in Ps. v. 2; xvii. 1, *hearken, give heed, mark well. Brought low,* as in Ps. lxxix. 8; cxvi. 6. *Deliver,* as in Ps. vii. 1; xxii. 20, and often. The *strength* of the enemy makes it necessary for Jehovah to appear, or his servant will be destroyed, and the promise fail.

7. *Bring my soul out of prison, that I may praise thy name: the righteous shall compass me about; for thou shalt deal bountifully with me.* Cave-life was *prison* life. There is no need of looking further for an explanation of *prison.* It is not the word rendered *prison* in the pentateuch. It signifies a place hemmed in, a place of limits. He says his release would be the signal for thanksgiving. The Psalm closes with an expression of lively hope, that *just* men will yet gather round him, unite their songs and sympathies with his, and eagerly learn the story of his perils and escapes. *Deal bountifully,* as in Ps. xiii. 6; cxvi. 7; cxix. 17.

Doctrinal and Practical Remarks.

1. Believer, art thou brought into great straits and perplexities? So was David in the cave. The Lord heard and helped him, and he will succor all who with like faith and courage betake themselves to the throne of grace. Scott: "There can be no situation so distressing, perilous, or disgraceful, in which faith will not derive comfort from God by fervent prayer."

2. There is no possibility of passing safely or comfortably through the world without prayer, vv. 1, 2, 5, 6, 7. What a poor worm was David himself, except as the Lord heard and answered him. His fellowship with God preserved his life from the violence of his enemies. It did more—it held him back from becoming a murderer when his great enemy was completely in his power.

3. The best men in the world may easily be brought into circumstances of overwhelming grief and solicitude, v. 3. This may come to pass in the most unexpected manner. The very deliverance wrought by David for his king and country gave him sore trouble. His monarch and his father-in-law became his most malignant foe.

4. Good men are often made to feel the need of resorting for comfort to the omniscience of God, who *knows their path,* past, present and future, v. 3. Our safety

and solace are in "the unlimited vision of God." Compare Deut. ii. 7; Job xxiii. 10; Ps. xxxi. 7. No enemy can spread a snare for our feet, but it is known to Jehovah. If our wisdom is nonplused and our reason confounded, it is for a joy that Jehovah understands all mysteries, fathoms all depths, knows all hearts, and controls all causes.

5. No man knows what plots are formed against all that is precious to him, v. 3. But the Lord sees every snare and pit-fall. To him therefore should we betake ourselves every day and in all circumstances.

6. "When great straits come, worldly friends and all who may be in danger from helping us, will readily forsake us," v. 4. Who that has tried human friendships under severe yet fair tests has not been made sick at heart by the pusillanimity and selfishness of mortals? The world is full of "swallow-friends," who migrate in cold weather.

7. Reader, are you poor, helpless and friendless? Do not despair, but hope to the end, v. 4. Your case cannot be worse than was often that of the man after God's own heart.

8. God is such a *refuge* and such a *portion*, that he, who is in covenant with him needs no other *shelter*, no other *inheritance*, v. 5. And "the less comfort we find in the creature we should trust the more in God."

9. Saints of modern times should look at the days of old, and study the history of good men, whose foes and persecutors have been many, fierce, bloody, and often powerful, v. 6.

10. The enemies of God's people have no new arts to practise. They are all found in their Cainish tribe in past ages. Saul tried them all against David. He even gave him his daughter in the hope of ensnaring him. There is no persecutor, who is not a bad man, with a heart worse than his life, v. 6.

11. Hope on. Hope ever. Hope against hope. Every cloud, whose shadow falls on the righteous, has a bright side. In the darkest hour expect better times, v. 7.

12. As David by well-doing finally triumphed, saw his enemies perish, sat on the throne, and was lifted up above all his enemies round about, so shall it be with all the saints of God, even the humblest. Yea, more, as our Lord, of whom David was a type, rose from the dead and is highly exalted, notwithstanding his amazing humiliation and the hellish, though temporary triumph of his foes, so shall it be with all his followers. The final victory of one believer is well suited to give joy to all who know it; but the victory of the *Crucified* settles a thousand difficulties in minds that are not given over to unbelief.

PSALM CXLIII.

A Psalm of David.

1 Hear my prayer, O Lord, give ear to my supplications: in thy faithfulness answer me, *and* in thy righteousness.

2 And enter not into judgment with thy servant: for in thy sight shall no man living be justified.

3 For the enemy hath persecuted my soul; he hath smitten my life down to the ground; he hath made me to dwell in darkness, as those that have been long dead.

4 Therefore is my spirit overwhelmed within me; my heart within me is desolate.

5 I remember the days of old; I meditate on all thy works; I muse on the work of thy hands.

6 I stretch forth my hands unto thee: my soul *thirsteth* after thee, as a thirsty land. Selah.

7 Hear me speedily, O LORD; my spirit faileth: hide not thy face from me, lest I be like unto them that go down into the pit.

8 Cause me to hear thy lovingkindness in the morning; for in thee do I trust: cause me to know the way wherein I should walk; for I lift up my soul unto thee.

9 Deliver me, O LORD, from mine enemies: I flee unto thee to hide me.

10 Teach me to do thy will; for thou *art* my God: thy Spirit *is* good; lead me into the land of uprightness.

11 Quicken me, O LORD, for thy name's sake: for thy righteousness' sake bring my soul out of trouble.

12 And of thy mercy cut off mine enemies, and destroy all them that afflict my soul: for I *am* thy servant.

ON the title see on title of Ps. iii. The Hebrew, the ancient versions and general consent ascribe this ode to David. Hengstenberg: "The Psalm bears evidence throughout of David's spirit and mode of expression." The Arabic, Septuagint, Ethiopic, Vulgate, Theodoret, Venema, Patrick, Walford, Morison, Scott and Clarke refer it to the rebellion of Absalom. Scott dates it B. C. 1021; Clarke, B. C. 1023. The only name of God in it is *Jehovah* LORD, on which see on Ps. i. 2. This is the last of the penitential Psalms. See on Ps. vi. On *Selah* see Introduction, § 15.

1. *Hear my prayer, O* LORD, *give ear to my supplications: in thy faithfulness answer me* and *in thy righteousness.* *Hear,* so as to answer, as in Ps. iv. 1; xvii. 1. *Supplications,* pleadings for grace and mercy. See on Ps. xxviii. 2. *Faithfulness,* in fulfilling his promises. *Righteousness,* in taking sides with David against his unreasonable foes. Having graciously promised, God is now righteously bound to help those, who obey his will and rely on him. Other Scriptures in like manner unite the faithfulness and righteousness of God, Ps. xxxvi. 5; xl. 10. It was not his personal merits, but the righteousness of God that David was pleading. This is evident from the very words used, and from verse

2. *And enter not into judgment with thy servant: for in thy sight shall no man living be justified.* God's nature is so holy and his judgment so unerring, that in his presence all human righteousnesses are filthy rags, and all mere men unclean things. Men cannot stand before him on the ground of innocence, not because they are men, but because they are sinners. Jehovah will not accept an imperfect righteousness; in so doing he would deny himself, and admit that his holy, just and good law was too strict. The doctrine of the latter clause of the verse is often repeated, Job ix. 2, 3; Rom. iii. 20; Gal. ii. 16; iii. 11. The law is not powerless to save us on account of any imperfection in itself, but it is weak through our fallen nature. So that now no man is saved, who does not confess that he is lost; none pardoned, who does not own his guilt; none justified, who does not acknowledge that he is justly condemned. If God shall ever account any mere man just, it must be in some other way than by his personal deservings. What that way is both Testaments declare. It is sometimes denoted by the term *faith.* "The just shall live by his faith," Hab. ii. 4; Rom. iii. 22; Gal. ii. 20. Again, it is said to be by *grace,* Eph. ii. 8, 9. Often it is said to be by *Jesus Christ,* Acts xiii. 39. All these statements agree. The faith, which is the means of justifying, believes in the person and work of Christ and leans on him alone, and all this is by the sovereign grace of God.

3. *For the enemy hath persecuted my soul; he hath smitten my life down to the ground: he hath made me to dwell in darkness, as those that have been long dead.* The preterite form of the verbs indicates that the wrongs complained of were still inflicted on him. Edwards, Street, Hengstenberg and Alexander render all the verbs in the present. See on Ps. vii. 5; lxxxviii. 3–6. The phrases together indicate the most distressed circumstances arising from the fearful enmity of man. Such trials sent on one of David's temper could not be stoically borne:

4. *Therefore is my spirit overwhelmed within me; my heart within me is desolate.* On the first clause see on Ps. lxxvii. 3; cxxiv. 4. The second clause is parallel to the first. *Desolate, laid waste, destroyed, astonished;* Edwards, *in a maze;* Street, *confounded.* It implies consternation. Yet his mind was not stupefied, nor his thoughts inactive:

5. *I remember the days of old: I meditate on all thy works; I muse on the works of thy hands; q. d.,* In all my affliction I have been calling to mind the remarkable dealings of God with me in my early life, and his treatment of men since the world began. I have been looking for some ground of comfort, some mode of relief, but found none. We have here two different words rendered *works.* The former more commonly expresses *deeds* done; the latter, *works* made. Yet often they are evidently used interchangeably.

6. *I stretch forth my hands unto thee: my soul* thirsteth *after thee, as a thirsty land. Stretch,* in the preterite, *have stretched* and do still stretch. The same phrase in Hebrew is found in Ex. ix. 29, 33; Job xi. 13; Ps. xliv. 20; Isa. i. 15, in the sense of *praying.* It may denote any spreading of the hands. Here it clearly indicates an earnest looking to God. A *thirsty* land, literally a *weary* land. Compare Ps. lxiii. 1. In countries where there are but two rainy seasons in the year such a figure has great force. Thus far the Psalmist has stated his case and made his complaint, but only as preparatory to the pleadings, which follow:

7. *Hear me speedily, O* Lord; *my spirit faileth: hide not thy face from me, lest I be like unto them that go down into the pit.* The supplication is for prompt relief, as without it his case was desperate. Already his spirit began to *fail,* to *be wasted,* to *be consumed,* to *faint.* To *hide the face* is a phrase of frequent occurrence, Ps. x. 11; xiii. 1; xxii. 24; xxvii. 9; xxx. 7; xliv. 24; lxix. 17; lxxxviii. 14. It denotes a refusal of aid. As his spirit was in danger of failing, so was his health. To *go down into the pit* is to *die* and *be buried.* See on Ps. xxviii. 1; xxx. 3. Compare Ps. lxxxviii. 4.

8. *Cause me to hear thy lovingkindness in the morning; for in thee do I trust: cause me to know the way wherein I should walk; for I lift up my soul unto thee.* To *hear* in this verse is equivalent to enjoy or possess. The first petition is in much the same terms and of like import with that in Ps. xc. 14. It is urged by the truth that at God's bidding his servant had *trusted* in him, and so it is a plea addressed to the divine veracity. The second petition is for divine guidance, that he might know and do what was pleasing in God's sight, and safe for himself. Like the former this argument rests on the divine faithfulness.

9. *Deliver me, O* Lord, *from mine enemies: I flee unto thee to hide me.* The words of the first clause have the usual rendering. For *deliver* Street has *protect;* but this restricts the meaning. The literal rendering of the second clause would not be idiomatic English. The authorized version gives the exact sense.

10. *Teach me to do thy will; for thou* art *my God: thy Spirit* is *good; lead me into the land of uprightness.* Without divine instruction David was sure that he should neither know nor do the *will* of God. That he may be thus taught, he pleads his covenant relation—*thou art my God.* He knew that effectual enlightening was the work of God's *Spirit,* whom he calls *good,* because he is essentially so, and because all his work on the heart is good, and produces good. The verb in the latter clause is in the future and the whole may be read, *Thy good Spirit shall lead.* For *land of uprightness* the Doway and Calvin have *right land;* Edwards, *even path;* Alexander, *level ground.* It is either a prayer to be kept from perplexity and from tortuous ways; or the expression of a confident hope that he shall be so preserved.

11. *Quicken me, O* Lord, *for thy name's sake: for thy righteousness' sake bring my soul out of trouble.* The plea in the two clauses is the same in substance, God's name

and righteousness being inseparable. The mercies he seeks, he dares to ask for not from anything in himself, but for what he knows to be the character of God. *Quicken, make alive, make lively* or *keep alive.* It occurs often in Ps. cxix. The second clause corresponds to many phrases already considered. Some follow the Hebrew and render the verbs of this verse and the next in the future. This makes the Psalm close in confident hope.

12. *And of thy mercy cut off mine enemies, and destroy all them that afflict my soul; for I* am *thy servant.* The plea is again of covenant relation—I am thy servant—my enemies are thy enemies. The verbs are in the future.

DOCTRINAL AND PRACTICAL REMARKS.

1. Believers need no greater bulwark to their hope and confidence than can be found in the attributes of God, particularly his *faithfulness* and *righteousness,* as illustrated in providence and in the glorious plan of salvation, v. 1.

2. True piety rests not in forms of worship. Real prayer seeks an *audience* and an *answer,* vv. 1, 7.

3. Outward afflictions are often blessed to greatly quickening the conscience, and when they so act, they are to be esteemed among God's precious gifts. No sooner is David in straits than he cries, "Enter not into judgment with thy servant," v. 2.

4. True piety is profoundly humble, and deeply sensible of great unworthiness. It dares not rush thoughtlessly into the presence of God, nor challenge his examination, v. 2. Horne: "The thoughts of such a trial are enough to appal the soul of the best man living, to make his flesh tremble, and his bones shake, as if he stood at the foot of Sinai, and beheld Jehovah ready to break forth upon him in the flame of devouring fire."

5. In true piety there is always a just and strong sense of accountability, v. 2. He who believes that he is not bound to obey God or humble himself under his mighty hand, nor to plead for mercy, has not yet learned the first lessons of genuine godliness.

6. On whatever else regenerate men may differ, they all agree that they cannot stand before God on the ground of their own merits, v. 2. Compare Rom. vii. 9. Luther: "I have tormented my body with fasting, watching, prayer, and other exercises, more than all who are now my enemies and persecutors; for I thought in this wise to satisfy the law, and shield my conscience from the rod of the oppressor. Yet it availed me naught; yea, the further I proceeded in this way, the more terrified I grew, so that I had nigh despaired, had not Christ mercifully looked upon me, and enlightened my heart by the light of his Gospel." Several give us this story. I take it from Bultmann's notes to Besser. Michael, an honest farmer, on his death bed called out to his son: "Jack, just reach down the Catechism from yonder shelf, to see how my past life agrees with it. Please, read me the commandments." "Thou shalt have no other gods before me. Thou shalt not make to thyself any graven image, etc." "O, these two have I always kept; I have neither worshipped idols, like the heathen, nor bowed down to images like the Roman Catholics. Please, proceed to the third." "Thou shalt not take the name of the Lord thy God in vain," etc. "Here I am right also; I never swore an oath except in a court of justice; pray, pass to the next." "Remember the Sabbath-day to keep it holy." "There I am not to blame either; I have always gone to church of a Sunday, and never played at cards, nor made my servants work. Which follows now?" "Honor thy father and mother," etc. "Ay, as to that, Jack, I may well bid you follow my example; for when a boy I showed all honor and respect to my poor parents, God bless them! What is the next?" "Thou shalt not kill." "Thank God, that is not on my conscience, I never slew a man not even in lawful war. Go on." "Thou shalt

not commit adultery." "Of that I have kept clear also, and always been faithful to your poor mother. Proceed." "Thou shalt not steal." "I never took aught that did not belong to me. Next?" "Thou shalt not bear false witness against thy neighbour." "I never swore falsely against any person. Are there any more?" "Yes, one: Thou shalt not covet." "Stop, Jack! There, I must think a little; yes, I cannot say I have never coveted. Pray look for poor Mamma's Bible on the subject." And here Jack found a reference from Ex. xx. to Matt. v. by which the farmer was soon led to see that he had broken the whole law; and, becoming fully conscious of his exceeding sinfulness, he betook himself to Christ and died a penitent.

7. Those who have never been persecuted may read such compositions as this Psalm with comparative indifference; but where the iron has entered the soul, such language as this of David is full of meaning, vv. 3, 4.

8. Henry: "It is sometimes the lot of the best men to have their spirits for a time almost overwhelmed, and their hearts desolate, and doubtless it is their infirmity. David was not only a great saint, but a great soldier, and yet even he was sometimes ready to faint in the day of adversity." Yet thanks to the Holy One, who to the humble supplies supernatural courage, and thus brings them off conquerors.

9. Afflictions stir up a world of thought; sanctified afflictions, a world of useful thought, v. 5.

10. The language of Scripture in its strongest terms barely does justice to the subject, when it expresses the eager longings of the people of God for deliverance and salvation, v. 6. They have 'groanings which cannot be uttered.'

11. In a sense the people of God live in a continual crisis, vv. 7, 8. Sometimes the urgency is greater than at others; but their warfare is never over till they rest in the bosom of the Redeemer. Now can any one tell what moment will bring still fiercer conflicts.

12. It is a dreadful thing to be in the power of the wicked, nor can our prayers for rescue from such dangers be too humble or too fervent, v. 9. God is sole and sufficient deliverer at such times. Blessed be his name, his ear is ever open to the cry of his people.

13. Whatever betides us, our great concern should be to know and do the will of God, v. 10. "To obey is better than sacrifice."

14. But this cannot be done without the aid of the Holy Spirit, v. 10. He is the author of all saving views, right feelings and holy walking in the church of God.

15. If anything effectual is ever done by the Lord for our relief and salvation, all must come from his grace and mercy, v. 11. In the court of Heaven our names are worthless.

16. The case of the wicked is sad indeed. The very deliverance and salvation of God's people and the mercies shown them require the utter destruction of the incorrigible, v. 12. Dickson: "Mercy to the Lord's oppressed children, and justice against their enemies, go together; and the work of justice on persecutors is a work of mercy to the oppressed."

PSALM CXLIV.

A Psalm of David.

1 Blessed *be* the LORD my strength, which teacheth my hands to war, *and* my fingers to fight:

2 My goodness, and my fortress; my high tower, and my deliverer; my shield, and *he* in whom I trust; who subdueth my people under me.

3 LORD, what *is* man, that thou takest knowledge of him! *or* the son of man, that thou makest account of him!

4 Man is like to vanity: his days *are* as a shadow that passeth away.

5 Bow thy heavens, O LORD, and come down: touch the mountains, and they shall smoke.

6 Cast forth lightning, and scatter them: shoot out thine arrows, and destroy them.

7 Send thine hand from above; rid me, and deliver me out of great waters, from the hand of strange children;

8 Whose mouth speaketh vanity, and their right hand *is* a right hand of falsehood.

9 I will sing a new song unto thee, O God: upon a psaltery *and* an instrument of ten strings will I sing praises unto thee.

10 *It is he* that giveth salvation unto kings: who delivereth David his servant from the hurtful sword.

11 Rid me, and deliver me from the hand of strange children, whose mouth speaketh vanity, and their right hand *is* a right hand of falsehood:

12 That our sons *may be* as plants grown up in their youth; *that* our daughters *may be* as corner stones, polished *after* the similitude of a palace:

13 *That* our garners *may be* full, affording all manner of store; *that* our sheep may bring forth thousands and ten thousands in our streets:

14 *That* our oxen *may be* strong to labour; *that there be* no breaking in, nor going out; that *there be* no complaining in our streets.

15 Happy *is that* people, that is in such a case: *yea*, happy *is that* people, whose God *is* the LORD.

ON the title see on title of Ps. iii. There is a very general agreement in ascribing this composition to David. So the Hebrew, Chaldee, Syriac, Arabic, Septuagint, Ethiopic, Vulgate, Doway, Luther, Calvin, Venema, Amesius, Fabritius, Piscator, Patrick, Pool, Edwards, Morison, Henry, Horne, Clarke, Scott and Hengstenberg. Alexander: "The Davidic origin of this Psalm is as marked as that of any in the Psalter." Tholuck admits that it consists for the most part of Davidic sentences, but thinks that the manner in which the name of David is mentioned in v. 10, shows that the entire authorship does not belong to him. But see on Ps. cxxxii. There is much uncertainty respecting the historic occasion of this ode. The Septuagint and the versions which follow it say it was written against Goliath. The Syriac says it was written on the occasion of David slaying Asaph, the brother of Goliath. Other conjectures are freely offered. Venema and a few others think it may have special reference to David's war with the Ammonites and Syrians. See 2 Sam. x. There are as few difficulties attending this as any other conjecture; but none of them are supported by evidence. Calmet, Clarke and Morison favor the opinion that it was written after the death of Absalom. Scott dates this hymn B. C. 1038; Clarke, B. C. about 1023. The names of the Most High here found are *Jehovah* LORD and *Elohim God*, on which see on Ps. i. 2; iii. 2. Many notice a close resemblance between this and Ps. xviii.

1. *Blessed* be *the* LORD *my strength, which teacheth my hands to war,* and *my fingers to fight. Blessed,* a term of benediction, as in Ps. v. 12; xviii. 46; xxviii. 6. *Strength,* in the margin and almost everywhere else *rock.* See on Ps. xviii. 2, 31, 46; xix. 14. On *teaching my hands to war,* see on Ps. xviii. 34. Teaching *the fingers to fight* is par-

allel. *War* and *fight* are in the Hebrew nouns; literally *teacheth*, maketh expert, *my hands for war and my fingers for the battle;* margin, *to the war.* To David it was clear that God alone had of the shepherd boy made a victorious king. None else could have given such skill, courage and success against so powerful adversaries. He says the Lord is

2. *My goodness, and my fortress; my high tower, and my deliverer; my shield, and he in whom I trust; who subdueth my people under me.* See on Ps. xviii. 2, where we have most of these terms. *My goodness,* commonly rendered *mercy, lovingkindness,* meaning the fountain or source of mercy. How God *subdued* the people under David is declared in many places; see 2 Sam. xxii.; Ps. xviii. The word *subdued* is not to be taken in a bad sense. Calvin: "When a people yields a cordial and willing obedience to the laws, all subordinating themselves to their own place peaceably, this signally proves the divine blessing." And this satisfies all men, except persecuting tyrants and their adherents. To such, peaceable demeanor and strict obedience to the laws are no commendation. You must truckle and cringe, fawn and flatter, express approbation of their follies and misrule, or meet their wrath.

3. LORD, *what is man, that thou takest knowledge of him! or the son of man, that thou makest account of him!* See on Ps. viii. 4. Compare Job vii. 17; 2 Sam. vii. 18; Heb. ii. 6. The relevancy of introducing this verse at this place consists in creating a contrast between God in vv. 1, 2, and man in vv. 3, 4, thus magnifying the divine condescension. *Takest knowledge,* literally *knowest,* as in Ps. i. 6. The verb is in the future and expresses the long continuance of God's kindness. The same is true of the verb rendered *makest account of, esteemest,* or *thinkest.*

4. *Man is like to vanity: his days* are *as a shadow that passeth away.* On the first clause see on Ps. xxxix. 5, 11; lxii. 9; on the second, Ps. cii. 11. Compare Job iv. 19; xiv. 2. *Is like,* in the preterite *has been like* in all generations, and up to this time. Neither intrinsic worth, nor permanence of existence on earth can be the cause of God's tenderness to man, but only the divine kindness.

5. *Bow thy heavens, O* LORD, *and come down: touch the mountains, and they shall smoke.* In Ps. xviii. 9, the verbs are in the preterite as describing what had been accomplished. Here they are in the imperative, in the form of petition. For the meaning of the first clause see on Ps. xviii. 9. As the clouds cover the mountains with smoke, so in a fearful manner does Jehovah's coming down in wrath fill with terror the highest positions that men occupy. If *mountains* be not here taken as figures of earthly potentates, or political powers, then the second clause is a petition that God would appear in a manner as marked as when he rides upon the storm. Compare Ex. xix. 18; Ps. civ. 32; Nah. i. 5, 6.

6. *Cast forth lightning, and scatter them: shoot out thine arrows, and destroy them.* See on Ps. xviii. 13, 14; compare 2 Sam. xxii. 15. By *them* Walford understands *people* in v. 2; but we may refer it to *mountains* in v. 5, and understand hostile, political organizations.

7. *Send thine hand from above; rid me, and deliver me out of great waters, from the hand of strange children.* *Hand,* in the plural *hands.* His case called for omnipotence. *Great waters,* more exactly *many waters,* a phrase denoting great perturbations and troubles, in this place said to be brought about by persons alien from the kingdom established in David. Whatever is the meaning of the phrase, *rid me and deliver me from the hand of strange children,* it involves something concerning which he was very urgent, for it is repeated in v. 11. *Strange,* in Ps. xviii. 44, 45, *strangers.* The cognate adjective in Ps. lxix. 8, is rendered *an alien.* The whole phrase may be rendered *sons of strangers,* and denotes those who by birth or by wicked inclination had

no inheritance in Jacob. These persons, whatever their pretences, were very unfriendly and dangerous to David :

8. *Whose mouth speaketh vanity, and their right hand is a right hand of falsehood.* On *speaking vanity,* see on Ps. xii. 2 ; xli. 6. The *right hand of falsehood* is a phrase variously interpreted. The most natural construction is, that it denotes perjured persons, as swearing was often accompanied with the lifting up of the right hand ; or it may refer to truce-breakers, who struck hands, or joined hands, Prov. xi. 15, 21 ; xvi. 5 ; that form of covenanting being often used. In either case, the phrase denotes, " false, treacherous and perfidious persons."

9. *I will sing a new song unto thee, O God : upon a psaltery and an instrument of ten strings will I sing praises unto thee.* On the phrase *new song,* see on Ps. xxxiii. 3. It is not certain whether the prophet here speaks of *two* instruments of music, or of *one* having ten strings ; but see on Ps. xxxiii. 2.

10. It is he *that giveth salvation unto kings : who delivereth David his servant from the hurtful sword.* See on Ps. xviii. 50 ; compare 2 Sam. v. 19–25 ; viii. 6–8 ; 2 Kings v. 1. *Hurtful,* commonly rendered *evil,* meaning the sword of *wickedness.*

11. *Rid me, and deliver me from the hand of strange children, whose mouth speaketh vanity, and their right hand is a right hand of falsehood.* The same as in vv. 7, 8. Every repetition in prayer is not *vain.*

12. *That our sons may be as plants grown up in their youth; that our daughters may be as corner stones, polished after the similitude of a palace.* Alexander : " The reminiscences or imitations of Ps. xviii. suddenly cease here, and are followed by a series of original, peculiar, and for the most part no doubt antique expressions." The riddance of evil disposed persons was to be a means of an improved state of society. In particular, young men were to be like *plants grown up,* having health, strength and beauty. See on Ps. cxv. 14, 15 ; cxxvii. 4, 5 ; cxxviii. 3. So also a pure state of society should add to the attractiveness of females, especially of young women. There is some difficulty in determining the precise meaning of the latter clause of the verse. Patrick's paraphrase is : " That our daughters may be tall and beautiful, like those polished pillars, which are the ornaments of a royal palace ;" Pool : " Strong and beautiful, and adorned with all the ornaments belonging to their sex ;" Edwards : Our daughters are exactly and beautifully shaped like corner stones for a palace ; Fry : Our daughters like the carved pillars in the structure of a temple. For *corner stones* Michaelis has *columns;* Hengstenberg, *projectures;* Castellio, *angular pillars.* Henry : " By daughters families are united and connected to their mutual strength, as the parts of a building are by a corner stone ; and when they are graceful and beautiful both in body and mind, they are then polished after the similitude of a nice and curious structure." The word rendered *corner stones* occurs but once elsewhere, and is there rendered *corners,* Zech. ix. 15.

13. That *our garners* may be *full, affording all manner of store :* that *our sheep may bring forth thousands and ten thousands in our streets.* There is considerable difficulty in rendering this verse ; but our translation has not been excelled by that of any of our fine scholars. *Streets,* places beyond the domicil, outside of the family enclosure, *highways* or *fields.*

14. That *our oxen* may be *strong to labour; that there be no breaking in, nor going out; that* there be *no complaining in our streets.* Edwards : And our oxen are strong for the yoke ; we have no irruptions from our enemies, nor going out into captivity ; nor any crying in our streets ; Hengstenberg : That our oxen may be loaded, no breaking and no loss, and no cry in our streets. *Strong to labor,* a participle of the verb rendered *carry* and *bear,* Isa. liii. 4, 11. Here it denotes oxen *laden* with flesh or fat, or fit to bear burdens, 1 Chron. xii. 40. *Breaking in,* violence, aggression, hos-

tile incursion. *Going out*, to war or to exile. *Complaining*, the cry of alarm or of distress. *Streets*, not the same word as in v. 13, but one meaning *streets* or *broad ways*. These blessings, noticed in vv. 12–14, are such as God promised to Israel in case of obedience, Deut. vii. 12, 13; xxviii. 2–6.

15. *Happy* is that *people, that is in such a case:* yea, *happy* is that *people, whose God is the* LORD. *Happy*, in Ps. i. 1, *blessed. O the blessednesses. In such a case*, an idiomatic rendering of a Hebraism not capable of being done into better English. The last clause of the Psalm furnishes an instance where it would have been better to transfer the word *Jehovah; whose God is Jehovah*, not Baal, not Ashtaroth, not living or dead men, not angels, but the self-existent, independent, eternal, unchangeable Jehovah.

DOCTRINAL AND PRACTICAL REMARKS.

1. To those who have fled to the Almighty, he sustains every desirable relation, and fulfils every needful office, supplying them with *strength, teaching* them to proceed with unwonted skill, pouring out his *lovingkindness* on them, being to them as a munition of rocks, a *high tower*, a *deliverer* and a *shield*, vv. 1, 2. From those thus favored, gratitude demands benedictions.

2. Let poor and humble youths, to whom the future seems dark, and who yet have noble aspirations to serve God and their generation, not be cast down, but hope in the Lord, vv. 1, 2. He who took David from the crook and taught him the use of the sword and the sling, and lifted up his head above all his enemies round about, is still the patron of poor and pious boys and girls, who make him their refuge and their all. It matters not how unskilful one may now be, and how wholly unprepared for a given work, if God will but take him in hand. Even parents and instructors may sometimes bring great discouragements on their most promising children and pupils. More than one of Walter Scott's teachers complained of the thickness of his skull; a number of his teachers pronounced Barrow a blockhead, while Isaac Newton was declared to be fit for nothing but to drive the team. Jesse so slighted David as not even to call him to the sacrifice, and his brothers declared that they knew the pride and naughtiness of his heart. But God raised him above all these obstacles and oppositions. Set your hope in God, struggling youth. Never cease prayer and effort.

3. Past mercies and deliverances should greatly encourage us, on the recurrence of new difficulties, to betake ourselves to the throne of grace.

4. If God so marvellously wrought by and for David, why should we doubt that he will work for all his people those great spiritual victories, without which they must fail of eternal life?

5. It is most reasonable that the potentates of earth should publicly and constantly acknowledge their indebtedness to the providence of God, who rules in the kingdoms of men. The whole spirit of this Psalm goes on this supposition. Luther: "David here, as a king and a magistrate himself, who had to govern the state and carry on wars, confesses that all prosperous and happy government, all success at home and abroad, all the acts of peace, and all victory in war, are the good gifts of God; and that a man can no more effect these things by human wisdom or strength, or by any ability of his own, than he can hold the millions of minds of nations bound unto himself, and make their multitudes obey him alone: for what could any mortal man do towards preserving whole kingdoms, and cities and provinces in quiet from sedition and commotions amid all the infinite malice of the devil and the world? Every mortal man would fail, like a vanishing shadow, before the thought of such an undertaking." Calvin: "While God preserves all men without exception, his care is

peculiarly extended to the maintenance of political order, which is the foundation of the common safety of all."

6. What a poor creature is man, full of infirmity, full of folly, his life a vapor, the whole of his career and existence mere *vanity,* vv. 3, 4. Without divine grace, he is sorely pressed with care, sorely vexed with trifles, often crushed by the weight of his sorrows, and if he escapes the countless casualties, any one of which may prove fatal, he is a victim to the pains and decrepitude of old age, and goes to an unblest eternity.

7. When God has a purpose to accomplish, or chooses to undertake a cause, nothing can resist him, vv. 5, 6. Before Omnipotence, mountains themselves melt like wax. To Almightiness nothing is difficult. Who can stand against him who hath thunder and lightning at his command, and arrows of destruction to shoot as he pleaseth?

8. It is a great mercy that our Father is in heaven, and so quite beyond the reach of human and diabolical malice. Whenever he chooses he can *send his hand from above,* and give most effectual relief, v. 7.

9. Persons, families and states are often seriously damaged by associations and alliances with those who are *alien* from their true and best interests; and especially, those who are unfriendly to the interests of vital religion, and the promotion of vital godliness. Against such influences we cannot be too guarded, vv. 7, 8, 11.

10. Though comparatively few men experience so marked outward deliverances and signal mercies, as did David, yet every one is a debtor beyond his highest conceptions to the free bounty and sparing mercy of God; and, if rightly affected, will find many an occasion in life for singing a *new song,* v. 9. To all who make the Lord their trust, the spiritual mercies bestowed and the spiritual deliverances wrought will, in the end, appear far more worthy of celebration in songs of rapture than anything found in the temporal history of the shepherd King.

11. On Instrumental Music as suggested by v. 9, see REMARKS on Ps. xxxiii. 2.

12. Human government is a divine ordinance, established for the glory of God, and the good of man. In all ages it has been remarkably upheld by him, v. 10. This is true even among the heathen. "The Lord strengthened Eglon, the king of Moab against Israel," Judg. iii. 12; "by Naaman the Lord had given deliverance to Syria;" all the power of the kings of Babylon was from the Most High; Dan. ii. 37; v. 18–29. When this power is wielded in wisdom and righteousness, it produces most happy results. Scott: "It is a very pleasant sight to behold a nation increasing in population; families brought up in industry, honesty and plenty, and fitted for their several stations in public and domestic life; not cut off by war, or wasted by famine and pestilence, or carried captives and exiles, or compelled by strong necessity to emigrate into foreign regions; and when all manner of abundance is stored in our garners, and clothes our fields and pastures." If for any temporal blessing we ought to be thankful, it is for general public prosperity, especially when united with peace, vv. 12–14. It is an unspeakable mercy when God gives to a people rulers of wisdom and of pacific dispositions, who hate injustice, treachery and bloodshed. "Peace is the mother of all earthly blessings to communities and to the families that compose them."

13. If any would have rich and permanent blessings, let them seek a saving acquaintance with Jehovah, the true God, v. 15.

14. From the promises of temporal blessings made to the righteous in both Testaments, we are in danger of being led into error on one point, viz., That wherever these blessings are withheld, there is an absence of the divine favor, or some diminution of happiness here or hereafter. All this is a mistake. God has richer mercies and stronger consolations than are found in all temporal possessions.

PSALM CXLV.

David's *Psalm* of praise.

1 I will extol thee, my God, O King; and I will bless thy name for ever and ever.

2 Every day will I bless thee; and I will praise thy name for ever and ever.

3 Great *is* the LORD, and greatly to be praised; and his greatness *is* unsearchable.

4 One generation shall praise thy works to another, and shall declare thy mighty acts.

5 I will speak of the glorious honour of thy majesty, and of thy wondrous works.

6 And *men* shall speak of the might of thy terrible acts: and I will declare thy greatness.

7 They shall abundantly utter the memory of thy great goodness, and shall sing of thy righteousness.

8 The LORD *is* gracious, and full of compassion; slow to anger, and of great mercy.

9 The LORD *is* good to all: and his tender mercies *are* over all his works.

10 All thy works shall praise thee, O LORD; and thy saints shall bless thee.

11 They shall speak of the glory of thy kingdom, and talk of thy power;

12 To make known to the sons of men his mighty acts, and the glorious majesty of his kingdom.

13 Thy kingdom *is* an everlasting kingdom, and thy dominion *endureth* throughout all generations.

14 The LORD upholdeth all that fall, and raiseth up all *those that be* bowed down.

15 The eyes of all wait upon thee; and thou givest them their meat in due season.

16 Thou openest thine hand, and satisfiest the desire of every living thing.

17 The LORD *is* righteous in all his ways, and holy in all his works.

18 The LORD *is* nigh unto all them that call upon him, to all that call upon him in truth.

19 He will fulfil the desire of them that fear him: he also will hear their cry, and will save them.

20 The LORD preserveth all them that love him: but all the wicked will he destroy.

21 My mouth shall speak the praise of the LORD: and let all flesh bless his holy name for ever and ever.

THERE is no reason to doubt that David wrote this Psalm. It has no known historic occasion. It is the last of the alphabetical Psalms. See Introduction, § 13. In Hebrew are twenty-two letters. We have here but twenty-one verses. Clarke thinks that one verse has been lost by transcribers. He gives the Hebrew from one manuscript, and the Septuagint and Vulgate give the translation of it: *The Lord is faithful in all his words; and holy in all his works.* This is but a slight change of verse 17. We have before seen that some of the alphabetical Psalms are somewhat irregular. It may be so here. But the probability is that a verse has been dropped by the transcribers. Hengstenberg, who is strangely addicted to dividing the Psalms into strophes, has another way of accounting for the omission. He says: "Along with the alphabetical arrangement the Psalmist observed a division of the whole into three strophes, each of seven verses, and it was necessary, on this account, that one of the twenty-two letters should be left out." This is the only Psalm bearing the title of *Praise.* Patrick thinks the Psalter takes its name from this hymn. The theme of the Psalm is the glory and excellence of God's nature and government. Scott dates it B. C. 1016; Clarke gives no date. There seems to be no cause for the frequent transition from second to third person, and *vice versa*, except the license of Hebrew poets. The names of the Almighty here found are *Elohim God* and *Jehovah* LORD, on which see on Ps. iii. 2; i. 2. Nicolson: "This hymn is most excellent, both as it regards matter and style." Anderson: "This is certainly one of the most interesting and beautiful of the compositions of the sweet singer of Israel." Morison: "There is an inexpressible majesty and beauty in the thoughts and words contained in this Psalm, which adapt it, in an eminent degree, to the daily exercise of devotion." The most important point in relation to its interpretation respects its Messianic character. See Introduction, § 8. Luther: "This is a very blessed Psalm of thanksgiving for the kingdom and dominion of Christ, which God was about to raise up among the people of Israel: for it was on account of Christ, that this whole people was from the beginning chosen out of all nations; and on account of Christ also that the law was given unto them, and the whole Mosaic worship established." All this may be true, and yet the Psalm not be strictly Messianic. Horne and that school of interpreters give it a distinct and definite allusion to Messiah.

1. *I will extol thee, my God, O King; and I will bless thy name for ever and ever.* *Extol*, as in Ps. xxx. 1; often *exalt*, Ex. xv. 2; Ps. cxviii. 28. *Bless*, as in Ps. v. 12. *My God*, a plea of covenant relation. Instead of *O King*, some read *my King*. *For ever and ever*, see on Ps. ix. 5. The whole verse expresses a solemn and deliberate purpose to magnify the Lord.

2. *Every day will I bless thee: and I will praise thy name for ever and ever.* *Bless*, as in v. 1. *Praise*, the cognate of the noun given in the title. *For ever and ever*, as in v. 1. Compare Ps. lxviii. 4; lxxi. 14.

3. *Great is the* LORD, *and greatly to be praised: and his greatness is unsearchable.* *Great* and *greatness* are cognate words. *Greatly, much, especially, exceedingly, mightily.* *Unsearchable*, literally, *there is not a search*. Men cannot begin a search. We have the same word in Job v. 9; ix. 10; xi. 7; Prov. xxv. 3. The doctrine is most weighty, involving the highest truths of theology.

4. *One generation shall praise thy works to another, and shall declare thy mighty acts;* literally, *generation to generation shall praise*. *Praise*, not the same word as in v. 2, but one rendered *commend, glory, triumph*. *Works*, as in Ps. cxliii. 5. It occurs again in vv. 9, 10, 17. It is applied to the works of creation, Ps. viii. 3, 6, and often. In Deut. xi. 3, 7, it is rendered *acts*. The word rendered *acts* here and in v. 12 is in v. 11 and often rendered *power*, also *might, strength, mastery*, Ex. xxxii. 18; Ps. xx. 6; Eccle. ix. 16. Alexander renders it *mighty doings*.

5. *I will speak of the glorious honor of thy majesty, and of thy wondrous works.* The original for *glorious honor of thy majesty* is very strong, being the union of three nouns, each one of which is a forcible word; literally, *the majesty of the glory of thy honor*. Horsley: The adorable glory of thy majesty. See on Ps. viii. 5; xxi. 5. The common version takes no notice of one word in the second clause, rendered *words, things* or *matters*. We may read, *And the matters of thy wondrous works*. *Wondrous works*, in Ps. ix. 1, *marvellous works*.

6. *And men shall speak of the might of thy terrible acts: and I will declare thy greatness.* *Greatness*, as in v. 3, is in the plural. In the character and government of God is found everything that constitutes real greatness.

7. *They shall abundantly utter the memory of thy great goodness, and shall sing of thy righteousness.* Edwards: They will largely commemorate thy great goodness: and sing aloud thy righteousness; Jebb: The memorial of thy abundant goodness they shall utter: and of thy righteousness they shall sing. To vv. 4–7, these Scriptures are parallel: Ex. xii. 26, 27; xiii. 14, 15; Deut. vi. 7; Josh. iv. 21–24; Ps. xliv. 1, 2; lxxi. 18; lxxviii. 3–7; Isa. xxxviii. 19.

8. *The* LORD *is gracious, and full of compassion: slow to anger, and of great mercy.* Compare Ex. xxxiv. 6, 7; Num. xiv. 18. See on Ps. lxxxvi. 5, 15; ciii. 8. *Slow to anger*, literally *long of anger*, i. e., it is commonly long before God becomes so angry as to cut men down.

9. *The* LORD *is good to all: and his tender mercies are over all his works.* On the first clause see a parallel in Nah. i. 7. *Tender mercies*, the Hebrew is one word, as in Ps. xxv. 6. It expresses the tender pity, the yearning compassion of a parent.

To the whole verse we find these parallels, Job xxv. 3; Matt. v. 45; Acts xiv. 17. God never made a sentient creature, that did not receive appropriate and excellent blessings.

10. *All thy works shall praise thee, O* LORD; *and thy saints shall bless thee.* *Works,* as in v. 4. *Praise,* commonly rendered *give thanks.* *Saints, merciful ones, those that are godly,* as in Ps. iv. 3; xviii. 25. *Bless* as in Ps. v. 12.

11. *They shall speak of the glory of thy kingdom, and talk of thy power;*

12. *To make known to the sons of men his mighty acts, and the glorious majesty of his kingdom. Mighty acts, glory* and *majesty,* as in vv. 4, 5. The translation is good and the sense obvious. The subject is the most exalted and demands the use of the loftiest terms. Patrick's Paraphrase is: "It is their duty to discourse of the incomparable wisdom and goodness, and care, which thou exercisest in the government of the whole world; especially of us; and to recount the memorable acts of thy invincible power among us; that all mankind, who regard not such things so much as they ought, may be made sensible how mighty the Lord is: and adore the amazing splendor of his illustrious works; and the admirable order he observes in his government of all things."

13. *Thy kingdom is an everlasting kingdom, and thy dominion* endureth *throughout all generations.* Compare Ps. cxlvi. 10; Dan. ii. 44; iv. 34; 1 Tim. i. 17. The rendering is excellent, though Street varies it: Thy kingdom is an eternal kingdom, and thy dominion over all generations. Jehovah will never give up the world to the reign of devils, or the sovereign sway of finite agents.

14. *The* LORD *upholdeth all that fall, and raiseth up all* those that be *bowed down.* *That fall,* a participle, *the falling, that are ready to fall.* It describes those that have in themselves no strength. *Raiseth,* a participle, is *raising.* It occurs again in Ps. cxlvi. 8, but nowhere else. God is continually giving strength to those that are bent under the weight of their burdens. He is the helper of the helpless. The next two verses have been much admired by critics.

15. *The eyes of all wait upon thee; and thou givest them their meat in due season.*

16. *Thou openest thine hand and satisfiest the desire of every living thing.* *Wait,* as in Ps. civ. 27; *look, hope. Satisfy, fill.* Planets and atoms, angels and insects, all ranks and orders of creatures hang dependent on God's sovereign will, and if one link in the chain of that dependence were broken, they would not only be wretched —they would perish. *Meat,* in the old English sense of *food,* as in Ps. civ. 21, 27. The great sublimity of v. 16, like that of Gen. i. 3, turns very much on the simplicity of the process, and the completeness with which the work is accomplished. Clarke: "A very large volume might be written upon this," see on Ps. civ. 28.

17. *The* LORD *is righteous in all his ways, and holy in all his works.* It is impossible for a moral government to meet the approval of a right-minded man, if it be not founded and conducted in justice and equity. For a deficiency here nothing can compensate. The Lord is therefore kind in giving us so ample assurance and evidence of the perfect rectitude of all his proceedings. The word rendered *holy* is in the margin *merciful* or *bountiful.* It is the word the plural of which is rendered *saints* in v. 10.

18. *The* LORD *is nigh unto all them that call upon him, to all that call upon him in truth.* See on Ps. xxxiv. 18. The Lord is nigh to see their sorrows, hear their cries, avenge their wrongs, relieve their wants, and save their souls. *Call,* as in Ps. iv. 1, 3; xiv. 4. To *call on God in truth* is to offer genuine religious worship, particularly in prayer.

19. *He will fulfil the desire of them that fear him: he also will hear their cry, and will save them.* *Fulfil, do, execute, maintain,* Ps. cxviii. 6; cxix. 84; cxl. 12. *Desire,*

will, pleasure, good pleasure, Esther i. 8; Ps. li. 18; cxliii. 10. It is safe for God to maintain the cause of the righteous, and grant their prayers, just in so far as they *fear* him.

20. *The* LORD *preserveth all them that love him: but all the wicked will he destroy. Preserveth, keepeth, watcheth* so as to protect. Here it is a participle (is) *keeping.* He habitually does so. *Love,* as in Ps. v. 11, and often. *Destroy,* as he did the Horims and the Amorite, Deut. ii. 22; Amos ii. 9; as Haman sought to destroy the Jews, Esther iii. 6, 13; as God shall destroy the sinners, Isa. xiii. 9. The verb denotes utter ruin and extermination.

21. *My mouth shall speak the praise of the* LORD: *and let all flesh bless his holy name for ever and ever. Praise,* as in the title of this Psalm. *All flesh,* all human beings. Sometimes the phrase includes irrational creatures, Gen. vi. 19. *Bless,* as in vv. 1, 2, 10. *His holy name,* literally *the name of his holiness. For ever and ever,* as in vv. 1, 2. Alexander renders it *to eternity and perpetuity.*

DOCTRINAL AND PRACTICAL REMARKS.

1. The highest praise and the most glowing adoration rendered to Jehovah do not exceed the bounds of truth and sobriety, vv. 1, 2, 21. It is begun on earth, and shall be carried on in heaven. Addison's stanza is hardly a hyperbole:

> Thro' all eternity to thee
> A joyful song I'll raise;
> But O, eternity's too short
> To utter all thy praise.

2. Nothing has a more pernicious effect on character than low thoughts of God. We should on many accounts labor to have just and elevated views of his excellent greatness, vv. 3, 6. Tholuck: "Human virtue and greatness have their limits, where spots appear and poverty begins; but the greatness of God is unsearchable and inexpressible." Henry: "The Lord's presence is infinite, his brightness insupportable, his majesty awful, his dominion boundless, and his sovereignty incontestable." Unless we have great thoughts of God, our thoughts of sin will be low, our sense of obligation feeble, and our praises dull.

3. Wicked as every generation of men has been, it is for a joy that in every age some have been found, and to the end of the world some shall be found to stand up for God, and publish his honors, and declare his goodness, v. 4.

4. Each one should feel the obligation to publish the divine honors, and that in suitable terms, well-chosen, thus following the example of the Psalmist, v. 5. Otherwise, "when one generation of pious men depart this life, there will be none to publish the glorious majesty and lovingkindness of the Lord after them."

5. He, who discredits revealed religion because of the miracles and mysteries involved therein, ought in consistency to discard the whole doctrine of creation and of providence, for both of them abound in *wondrous works,* v. 5.

6. Although God's doings are often *terrible,* yet it is a great mercy that they are not prevailingly so, v. 6. Tempests and tornadoes sometimes sweep over the earth, but they are neither daily nor weekly. One deluge spread desolation, but ever since the bow of promise has appeared.

7. Much as the wicked hate the goodness and righteousness of God, he shall yet establish his memorial in all the earth, as well as in his church triumphant, v. 7. The overthrow of Pharaoh, the ruin of Sennacherib and the miserable end of Nero and of kindred spirits, are no secrets in the world.

8. The Scriptures delight to dwell on the loving aspects of the divine character, vv. 8, 9. They have exhausted the powers of language to convey to us some just concep-

tion of the subject. The Lord has *grace* for the guilty, *compassion* for the miserable forbearance to the headstrong, and repenteth him of the evil.

9. All God's creatures in this world receive many and marked benefits at his hand, v. 9. Even where forgiveness of sin is not granted, still as long as God spares his enemies, he opens the storehouse of his bounty, and grants them many and great blessings.

10. There is a sense in which all God's works praise and shall forever praise him, though in some cases they do it reluctantly; but it is his saints who bless him and witness for him with all the heart, vv. 10–12. The confessions of God's enemies often show how wretched their cause is; but it is of his people that he says, *Ye are my witnesses.* Dickson: "The Lord will have his saints to instruct such as are not converted to know his glory, power, and majesty, that they may be brought in, and made subjects of his special kingdom of grace."

11. In the midst of the convulsions, agitations and desolations of earth, it is a glorious truth that the dominion of the Almighty over this and all worlds cannot be destroyed, subverted or even impeded, v. 13. Hengstenberg: "Thy kingdom is a kingdom of all eternities." No age, no dark corner of the earth, no star however remote, no man however puissant, no kingdom however glorious, is beyond the grasp of him who shakes the heavens with a nod.

12. The poor, the feeble, the self-diffident, the bruised, the oppressed, the downtrodden, have an unfailing friend in God, v. 14. Luther: "Christ is the king for the afflicted, the poor, the fallen."

13. The changes of the seasons, bringing alternate and various kinds of fruits and food for man and beast, call for admiration and praise, v. 15.

14. It is infallible proof that man is far gone from righteousness, when we see him the only recipient of the divine kindness, that seems to make no suitable return to the Giver of all good, vv. 15, 16. Dumb brutes seem to fulfil the great ends of their existence; but man, sunk into sottishness, even when he knows God, glorifies him not as God.

15. Let us never doubt the infallible justice of all the divine proceedings, v. 17.

16. While by his essential presence and readiness to bless the penitent, God is not far from any living man, yet he is peculiarly and graciously nigh to such as with godly sincerity engage in his worship, supplicating his blessing, v. 18. Compare Acts xvii. 28. God is never offended with the importunity of suppliants. Horne: "It is our happiness to have a King, who is not, like earthly princes, difficult of access, but one of whom the meanest subject may at any time obtain an audience, and be certain of having his request granted, if it be made in truth."

17. One reason why the righteous are so often successful in their plans and counsels is, that their desire in the main agrees with the will of God, and so in hearing them, God is but doing what is most pleasing to himself, v. 19.

18. It is clear from Scripture that there is no antagonism, but on the contrary a blessed harmony between the graces of the Christian character. Those who *fear* the Lord, in v. 19, are the same as those who *love* him in v. 20.

19. The incorrigibly wicked are all doomed, v. 20. Their destruction is as certain as their existence. The mouth of the Lord hath spoken it by the mouth of all his prophets since the world began.

20. It is the duty of some to rule, and of others to obey; of some to teach and of others to learn; of some to abide at home, and of others to go abroad; but it is the duty of all in all ranks and conditions of life to bless God's holy name forever and ever, and to desire others to engage in the same noble work, v. 21.

21. If we would be wise, and so act as not to cover us with confusion, we must put

time and eternity together. Our connection with an endless future is as close and as certain as our connection with time, and much more lasting. It was a wise resolution of the elder Edwards: " That *I will do whatsoever* I think to be most to the glory of God and my own good, profit and pleasure, in the whole of my duration; without any consideration of the time, whether now, or never so many myriads of ages hence." Reader, thou art a candidate for eternity, and to eternity thou wilt go. Art thou prepared? Art thou preparing?

PSALM CXLVI.

1 Praise ye the LORD. Praise the LORD, O my soul.
2 While I live will I praise the LORD: I will sing praises unto my God while I have any being.
3 Put not your trust in princes, *nor* in the son of man, in whom *there is* no help.
4 His breath goeth forth, he returneth to his earth; in that very day his thoughts perish.
5 Happy *is he* that *hath* the God of Jacob for his help, whose hope *is* in the LORD his God:
6 Which made heaven, and earth, the sea, and all that therein *is:* which keepeth truth forever:
7 Which executeth judgment for the oppressed: which giveth food to the hungry. The LORD looseth the prisoners:
8 The LORD openeth *the eyes of* the blind: the LORD raiseth them that are bowed down: the LORD loveth the righteous:
9 The LORD preserveth the strangers; he relieveth the fatherless and widow: but the way of the wicked he turneth upside down.
10 The LORD shall reign for ever, *even* thy God, O Zion, unto all generations. Praise ye the LORD.

DAVID probably wrote this Psalm. So Calvin, Fabritius, Patrick, Jebb, Henry, Scott and others have thought. Yet Venema, Tholuck, Hengstenberg and Alexander favor a later origin. The Syriac, Arabic, Septuagint and Vulgate ascribe it to Haggai and Zechariah. If it had any historic occasion, we know not what it was. This and the four remaining Psalms begin and end with the word *Hallelujah,* Praise ye the LORD. Scott dates it B. C. 1016; Clarke fixes no date, but thinks it was written after the captivity. The names of the Most High found in it are *Jah* LORD, *Jehovah* LORD, *Elohim God* and *El God,* on which see introductory remarks to Ps. lxviii., and on Ps. i. 2; iii. 2; v. 4.

1. *Praise ye the* LORD. *Praise the* LORD, *O my soul.* In the first clause we have *Jah;* in the second *Jehovah.* The prophet first calls on the true Israel and then on himself to engage in the work of *praise,* and especially desires that he may do his part with life and animation—with his *soul.*

2. *While I live will I praise the* LORD; *I will sing praises unto my God while I have any being.* Watts:

> "I'll praise my Maker with my breath,
> And when my voice is lost in death,
>   Praise shall employ my nobler powers:
> My days of praise shall ne'er be past
> While life and thought and being last,
>   And immortality endures."

For *being,* Morison has *continuance,* meaning existence beyond the grave. *Praise,* as twice in v. 1. *Sing praises, sing psalms,* or *play,* as in Ps. vii. 17; ix. 11. Compare Ps. civ. 33.

3. *Put not your trust in princes*, nor *in the son of man, in whom* there is *no help.* This verse inclines Clarke to think that the Psalm refers to the change which came over Cyrus, who at first was a warm and decided friend to the Jews, but afterwards was disinclined to aid them. His paraphrase is: " *Cyrus may change: but God will not: trust therefore in Him.*" But in comparison with God all princes are unworthy of confidence. The best of them may die at the very time when we most build upon their aid. The best of them are limited in resources, and often cannot help those to whom they have the strongest attachment. The best of them are fickle and liable to change from friendship to aversion. If this is not caused by constitutional insta-bility, it is often brought about by slander and misrepresentation. By *princes* we are not to understand merely those on the throne, or *nobles*, but persons of large hearted-ness, and of liberal views and feelings, as the word indicates, Ex. xxxv. 5, 22 ; Isa. xxxii. 5, 8. Neither do we find unfailing virtue and resources in any rank of life— in any *son of Adam*, as the Hebrew has it. *Help, salvation.*

4. *His breath goeth forth, he returneth to his earth: in that very day his thoughts perish.* For *breath* Ainsworth and Boothroyd have *spirit.* The first clause simply expresses the idea of death and dissolution. The second states the effect of such death—his *thoughts perish.* For *thoughts* the Chaldee has *machinations;* the Arabic, *counsels;* Mudge, *projects;* Street, *designs;* Horsley, *false, deceitful show;* Fry, *devices.* Alexander understands *vain notions* or *ambitious schemes.* The word is found nowhere else. Even if the thoughts of a fellow-creature respecting us or our friends are ever so kind and wise, he may be wholly unable to effect anything for us ; and so to trust in him is folly, particularly as Jehovah proposes himself as an object of confidence, and never deceives or disappoints the heart that leans on him :

5. *Happy* is he *that* hath *the God of Jacob for his help, whose hope* is *in the* LORD *his God. Happy, O the blessednesses,* as in Ps. i. 1. He has all good things for soul and body, for time and eternity. The word rendered God is *El, might.* There is peculiar fitness in speaking of the God of Jacob as a helper, whether by *Jacob* we understand the patriarch himself or the nation that bore his name; for in a marvel-lous manner did the Most High *help* and deliver both him and them. But if we would have the presence and power of God on our side, we must *hope* in him, and in no other. He has from the beginning demonstrated his power, wisdom and good-ness, for it is he,

6. *Which made heaven, and earth, the sea, and all that therein* is: *which keepeth truth for ever.* On the first clause see on Ps. cxv. 15; cxxi. 2. The Lord has the attri-butes, which qualify him to give succor, and then he has the *faithfulness* (or *truth*) which makes him keep covenant and perform all he has engaged. Did he lack either, he would be unworthy of trust. It is also he,

7. *Which executeth judgment for the oppressed: which giveth food to the hungry. The* LORD *looseth the prisoners. Executeth, doeth, worketh, procureth, bringeth forth, main-taineth,* as the word is elsewhere rendered. *Judgment, right.* The common and best rendering is *judgment. Oppressed, wronged, defrauded, deceived.* How God did this for Jacob, for David and for all Israel their history declares. And how he feeds the hungry the history of the world declares. The last clause of this verse begins a series of statements, which many regard as a prophecy concerning Jesus Christ. Indeed some regard all from the beginning of v. 5 to the close as Messianic. Hammond has a long, learned and very ingenious note to that effect; nor is it easy to answer his rea-sonings. Of course Horne and that class of interpreters adopt this view. Jarchi on v. 10, distinctly says that it belongs to the *days of Messias.* Gill: "It is most true, that the Psalm is concerning the Messiah and his kingdom, to whom all the charac-ters and descriptions given agree." Henry and Scott interpret these verses in the

same way. Indeed Scott quotes with approbation a paragraph applying the whole Psalm to Christ. See Introduction, § 8. Men may be *bound* in affliction as well as in iron. *Prisoners,* a participle often rendered *bound,* Gen. xxxix. 20; xl. 3, 5; Isa. lxi. 1. It was common among the Hebrews to speak of the afflicted, as *prisoners,* or *bound,* Ps. cvii. 10; Luke xiii. 16. If the *loosing of the prisoners* is to be taken literally, it had its fulfilment in Joseph, in the three faithful young men in Babylon, in Daniel, in Peter, in Paul and Silas, and in all cases where God's providence has interposed for the unjustly accused. If the phrase is to be taken spiritually, as in Isa. xlix. 9; lxi. 1, then it is fulfilled in every case where the benefits of redemption are applied to perishing men.

8. *The* LORD *openeth* the eyes of *the blind: the* LORD *raiseth them that are bowed down: the* LORD *loveth the righteous.* Alexander: "All the verbs are of the participial form, *opening, raising, loving,* i. e., continually doing so." The same remark applies to the *loosing,* in v. 7, and *preserving,* in v. 9. How Christ opened the eyes of the blind is taught in the Gospels, Matt. ix. 27–30; John ix. 7–32. In the Hebrew of this clause, there is no word for *eyes,* but it is implied in the verb, *openeth,* which is never used in the Scriptures in reference to any other matter, except once where it refers to *opening the ears,* Isa. xlii. 20. How the Lord opens the eyes of the mind is declared in many Scriptures. The New Testament calls the process of spiritual illumination, a *revelation,* Matt. xi. 27; Luke x. 22; Gal. i. 16. How the Lord raiseth them that are bowed down is declared in Ps. cxlv. 14; cxlvii. 6. How gloriously Jesus did this work literally, may be seen in Luke xiii. 13. But none are so *bowed down* as those that are oppressed by the devil, ready to sink under the load of conscious guilt, fearfully depressed with just thoughts of their own vileness, guilt and misery. How the Lord *loveth the righteous* is declared in Deut. xxxiii. 3; John xiv. 21. God has a love of good will to men, even the rebellious; but he has also a love of complacency to his people. Because he loveth righteousness, therefore he loveth the righteous, Ps. xi. 7.

9. *The* LORD *preserveth the strangers: he relieveth the fatherless and widow: but the way of the wicked he turneth upside down.* God's tender care of strangers appears in the pentateuch, Ex. xxii. 21; xxiii. 9; Lev. xix. 33; Deut. x. 18; xvi. 11. Traces of the same divine benevolence are found in all the Scriptures. But all God's people are strangers and pilgrims on the earth, as were their fathers. To them he shows peculiar and amazing favor, and *keepeth* them in the midst of the greatest perils and trials. How wonderfully God *relieves,* or *lifts up,* i. e., shows his friendship to the widow and the fatherless is declared in all his word, Ps. lxviii. 5; Prov. xv. 25; Jer. xlix. 11; Hos. xiv. 3. The terms rendered *widow* and *fatherless* are sometimes used to denote in general the desolate, the helpless, and so we learn God is always ready to give help to those that have no friend or protector. *Turneth upside down,* elsewhere *subvert, overthrow.* The most dreadful disasters that have overtaken the wicked in past ages are but feeble tokens of their ruin, the utter disappointment of all their hopes, the perfect defeat of all their plans in the world to come. Compare Ps. cxlvii. 6.

10. *The* LORD *shall reign for ever,* even *thy God, O Zion, unto all generations. Praise ye the* LORD. The first clause is taken from Ex. xv. 18, and contains a truth asserted in different terms in Ps. x. 16; cxlv. 13; and repeated in the last book of Scripture. Jehovah and the God of Zion are the same. God's kingdom over this world has constant reference to his kingdom in the world. *Praise ye the* LORD, as at the beginning.

DOCTRINAL AND PRACTICAL REMARKS.

1. How wonderful is memory! In 1816, when the writer was yet a lad, he heard

this Psalm expounded by a stranger whom he never saw before; and to this day he remembers the exposition, and even the tones of the preacher's voice. *Fifty* years seem to have deepened the impression made by a simple yet serious discourse on this precious Psalm.

2. God is worthy of all praise, and of all honor, and should constantly be declared so to be, vv. 1, 2, 10. There is no act of worship that may not fitly begin and end with his praise. This is true in time. It will be true in eternity. 'In heaven, when one hallelujah closes, another commences.' The highest anthems ever sung on earth or in the skies are fully warranted by the nature of God, by the course of his providence, and by our relations to him as explained in this Psalm.

3. Both by natural and revealed religion, we are called upon to stir ourselves up to the work of praise, v. 1. It is a singular evidence of the depravity and deceitfulness of the human heart, that those deists who speak most of the excellence of natural religion, are never found gathered into assemblies for the devout praise of him who made them; and yet if nature teaches anything concerning our duty to God, it is that we should praise him for his mercies. To this work we should summon our memories, that they may tell us of God's goodness in times past; our imaginations, that they may aid us in forming some conception of the glory to be revealed; and our warm affections, that they may glow with zeal in this noble service. Henry: "That which is the great end of our being ought to be our great employment and delight while we have any being."

4. It is both vain and wicked to rely on man, the best, the wisest and the bravest, v. 3. Man is a fool, a worm, a shadow. "The Egyptians are men, and not God; and their horses flesh, and not spirit," Isa. xxxi. 3. Compare Jer. xvii. 5–8. Luther: "We ought not to trust in any man, not even in kings or princes, nor in the mighty, nor in the rich, as the world do." We have more to fear than to hope for from the best man living, if we put him in the place of God. As to the wicked, the best of them is a brier: the most upright is sharper than a thorn hedge, Mic. vii. 4.

5. What amazing changes come over men at death! Then all their thoughts, plans, projects come to a full end, v. 4. How great is "the madness of princes in setting no bounds to their hopes and desires, and scaling the very heavens in their ambition, like the insane Alexander of Macedon, who, upon hearing that there were other worlds, wept that he had not yet conquered one, although soon after the funeral urn sufficed him." "Neither mean men may trust in great men, nor great men may trust in a multitude of mean men."

6. Vast indeed must be the blessings of the righteous, and great their happiness, if not here, yet hereafter; for oftentimes the inspired writers, like presses gushing out with new wine, speak of it, habitually admitting that the matter is beyond the power of language, v. 5.

7. He who helped Jacob, helps all who pray like Jacob, v. 5.

8. The glorious perfections displayed in creation are ample guarantee of the safety of those who make God their refuge, v. 6.

9. Both natural and revealed religion lead us to rely on the truth, the sincerity, the faithfulness of God, v. 6. Unless we credit the divine sincerity, even miracles would not prove the truth of a doctrine or of a system.

10. Let the pious who are *oppressed*, wronged, deceived, abused, hope on, v. 7. God is the patron of those who have no helper. He, who gave his Son to deliver his chosen from the oppression of the devil, will not deny them whatever is necessary to rescue them from the power of his minions.

11. If one is poor, let him not steal, nor fret, nor deny the divine kindness, but let him pray and hope in the Lord, *who feedeth the hungry*, v. 7. He who sent the ravens

to feed Elijah, and made the widow's oil to multiply, and hears the young ravens when they cry, will not forget the souls who make him their confidence.

12. If we are *prisoners*, let us not be thereby cast down with over much sorrow. Whenever the Lord sees it best, he can and will release us, v. 7. Until then, let us leave all in his hands. Not a few of the best writings have been given to the world by men wearing a chain, or immured in prisons. No thanks to their persecutors, nor to the cold inhumanity of their cotemporaries; but all honor to the grace of him who in their deep affliction made their genius to shine and their joy to overflow.

13. We may not any longer expect miracles in healing the blind of their natural defects, such attestations of God's truth being no longer necessary, v. 9. But every saving spiritual illumination is a moral miracle, far more worthy of admiration. if duly considered, than any healing ever granted to defective natural vision.

14. Art thou a child of sorrow, borne down with the weight of thy grief? Cast thy burden on the Lord. Trust in him. He can *raise* thee out of the depths up to the heights of glory, v. 8.

15. Because of God's good will to the righteous, they are safe, v. 8. His complacency in them unites with his benevolence; and even when he afflicts them, he does it out of love.

16. Art thou a stranger? or is thy child a stranger? or does thy heart yearn over some loved one in a distant land? God can take care of such. He, who was the friend of Joseph in Egypt, will not forsake the seed of the righteous now. Jehovah is a God afar off, as well as a God at hand, v. 9; Jer. xxiii. 23.

17. Has God taken away the husband of thy youth, and written thy children fatherless? Lay fast hold of the promises. They are all-sufficient, v. 9. See on Ps. lxviii. 5.

18. The wicked frequently object to our using startling terms, and alarming thoughts concerning their state; but no sober language can exaggerate the frightful condition of a soul without God in the world. God has a thousand ways of bringing to nought the counsels of the ungodly, and cutting short their career of crime and folly. Commonly in the most unexpected manner he *turneth their way upside down*, v. 9.

19. The world has always been governed, is now governed, and shall to the end of time be governed by him who makes no mistakes, and has no vicegerents, and no successful rivals. Morison: "Perpetuity is the distinguishing character of the divine government. The throne of Jehovah can never be subverted. His enemies can never gain the ascendency."

20. How glorious is God! In all his nature, in all his ways, in all the manifestations of himself he alone is worthy to receive the worship of earth or of heaven.

PSALM CXLVII.

1 Praise ye the LORD: for *it is* good to sing praises unto our God; for *it is* pleasant; *and.*praise is comely.

2 The LORD doth build up Jerusalem: he gathereth together the outcasts of Israel.

3 He healeth the broken in heart, and bindeth up their wounds.

4 He telleth the number of the stars; he calleth them all by *their* names.

5 Great *is* our Lord, and of great power: his understanding *is* infinite.

6 The LORD lifteth up the meek: he casteth the wicked down to the ground.

7 Sing unto the LORD with thanksgiving; sing praise upon the harp unto our God:

8 Who covereth the heaven with clouds, who prepareth rain for the earth, who maketh grass to grow upon the mountains.

9 He giveth to the beast his food, *and* to the young ravens which cry.

10 He delighteth not in the strength of the horse: he taketh not pleasure in the legs of a man.

11 The LORD taketh pleasure in them that fear him, in those that hope in his mercy.

12 Praise the LORD, O Jerusalem; praise thy God, O Zion.

13 For he hath strengthened the bars of thy gates; he hath blessed thy children within thee.

14 He maketh peace *in* thy borders, *and* filleth thee with the finest of the wheat.

15 He sendeth forth his commandment *upon* earth: his word runneth very swiftly.

16 He giveth snow like wool: he scattereth the hoar frost like ashes.

17 He casteth forth his ice like morsels: who can stand before his cold?

18. He sendeth out his word, and melteth them: he causeth his wind to blow, *and* the waters flow.

19 He sheweth his word unto Jacob, his statutes and his judgments unto Israel.

20 He hath not dealt so with any nation: and *as for his* judgments, they have not known them. Praise ye the LORD.

THE Septuagint and the versions, which follow it, unite Psalms ix. and x. into one, and so, to make the number 150 they divide Psalm cxlvii. into two, making Psalm cxlvi. end at v. 11, and Psalm cxlvii. begin at v. 12. Of course the numbers of all the Psalms between the ninth and this do not in these versions agree with the Hebrew, as the Doway in a note admits. These versions also number the verses of Psalms ix. x. cxlvi. cxlvii. just as if the arrangement in the Hebrew and English version was correct. There is a very general, though not universal agreement that this Psalm is of late date. Scott dates it B. C. 444; Clarke, B. C. about 519. But there is not an agreement respecting the author. Several of the ancient versions ascribe it to Haggai and Zechariah. A few very respectable writers ascribe it to David, making it a prophecy. Gill, Abenezra and several Jewish writers think it foretells the future rebuilding of Jerusalem, and the restoration of the Jews from their captivity, and refer it to the times of the Messiah." Jebb says, it is "a most regularly constructed hymn." Luther calls it " a very blessed Psalm of thanksgiving." Henry calls it an " excellent Psalm of praise." The names of the Most High in this composition are *Jah* LORD, *Elohim God, Adonai Lord* and *Jehovah* LORD, on which respectively see introductory remarks to Ps. lxviii.; on Ps. iii. 2; ii. 4; i. 2.

1. *Praise ye the* LORD : *for it is good to sing praises unto our God : for it is pleasant:* and *praise is comely.* Like the preceding this Psalm begins and ends with *Hallelujah.* In Ps. lxxiii. 28, we read, It is good for me to draw near to God; in Ps. xcii. 1, It is a good thing to give thanks unto the Lord. Here, It is good to sing Hallelujahs and Psalms. For this duty three reasons are given. 1. It is *good.* It must be a good thing to love and serve and praise a good and glorious God. 2. It is *pleasant* or *sweet* to do so. It makes glad and refreshes the pious heart. 3. It is *comely,* or *seemly.* It is monstrous to have a God and not worship, obey and praise him.

2. *The* LORD *doth build up Jerusalem: he gathereth together the outcasts of Israel.* *Doth build*, in the participial form *is building.* He is continually doing so. *Gathereth*, future *will gather.* *Outcasts*, uniformly rendered, see Isa. xi. 12; lvi. 8, not synonymous but parallel to *dispersed*, applied to the same people, Isa. xi. 12; Ezek. xxxvi. 19. Street renders it exiles. This verse may refer to the rebuilding of Jerusalem and the resettlement of Judea in the days of Nehemiah; yet it has a more glorious import, if we apply it to the conversion of men to Christ. That the parallel passage in Isa. xi. 10–16, refers to the days of Messiah cannot be doubted. Compare John xi. 52.

3. *He healeth the broken in heart, and bindeth up their wounds.* This verse rather confirms the interpretation given to v. 2, as pointing to Gospel times. Compare Isa. lxi. 1–3 ; Luke iv. 18–21. *Broken*, see on Ps. li. 17, where we have the same word

applied to the heart. *Wounds*, in Ps. xvi. 4 and elsewhere, *sorrows;* margin, *griefs*. There are no wounds like those of the spirit, Prov. xviii. 14. Nor is any *healing* so much required as in the heart.

4. *He telleth the number of the stars; he calleth them all by their names.* Compare Gen. xv. 5; Isa. xl. 26. Surely he who is able to do all these things in immensity is able to accomplish his merciful designs towards his people, to whom he has so long and wondrously manifested his special and gracious presence. He who has perfect dominion over universal nature can do whatever he pleases for his people.

5. *Great* is *our Lord, and of great power: his understanding* is *infinite.* *Lord, Adonai, ruler.* There is none above him, none with him, none like him, in *power*, or in any of his perfections. To the mind of God no subject is knotty, no truth mysterious. His mind embraces with infinite ease all the propositions which constitute universal truth. *Understanding*, commonly so rendered; in Ps. lxxviii. 72, *skilfulness;* in Ps. cxxxvi. 5, *wisdom;* margin: Of his understanding there is no number. This is literal.

6. *The* Lord *lifteth up the weak: he casteth the wicked down to the ground.* Infinite and glorious as is the Lord, yet he is amazing in his condescension, and so he *lifts up*, (in Ps. cxlvi. 9, *relieves*,) the meek, *humble, lowly,* or *afflicted.* See on Ps. ix. 12. . But when necessary to the defence of his people and for the advancement of his glory, the Most High will employ the energy of his whole nature to arrest the progress of evil, by *casting down, humbling, abasing, laying low* the wicked.

7. *Sing unto the* Lord *with thanksgiving; sing praise upon the harp unto our God.* The first word rendered *sing* means to *answer*, or *testify;* and the first clause calls on us to make a *return* corresponding to the mercies received. *Sing praise*, as in v. 1, *sing a psalm, play, make music;* see on Ps. ix. 11.

8. *Who covereth the heaven with clouds, who prepareth rain for the earth, who maketh grass to grow upon the mountains.* All the verbs are in the participial form, is *covering*, is *preparing*, is *making to grow*. God is habitually doing these things, and thus evincing his absolute control over nature in all latitudes. See on Ps. civ. 13, 14.

9. *He giveth to the beast his food*, and *to the young ravens which cry.* Compare Ps. civ. 27, 28; cxxxvi. 25; cxlv. 15. It is not a fact in natural history that any species of bird known as the raven is cruel or unnatural to its young, and leaves it to shift for itself. All these young creatures are helpless, and unable to move from the nest for some time after they are hatched. But God provides for them by giving to their parents a tender, natural affection, which is the more remarkable, because they are ravenous, and live very much by prey. Compare Job xxxviii. 41.

10. *He delighteth not in the strength of the horse: he taketh not pleasure in the legs of a man.* See on Ps. xxxiii. 16–18. Compare Job xxxix. 19–25; Prov. xxi. 31; Hos. i. 7. Henry and Alexander think that by the horse is meant the cavalry, and by the legs of a man the infantry of armies. But it is a universal truth that reliance upon the natural strength of man or beast, as an adequate protection against danger or as a means of delivery from any evil, is by the constant providence of God demonstrated to be folly. God gives strength not to be idolized, but to be used in humble dependence on him.

11. *The* Lord *taketh pleasure in them that fear him, in those that hope in his mercy.* *Taketh pleasure*, as in v. 10. As in Ps. cxlv. 19, 20, *fear* and *love* describe the same character, so here do *fear* and *hope*.

12. *Praise the* Lord, *O Jerusalem; praise thy God, O Zion.* The first word rendered *praise* is *commend, glory in*, as in Ps. cxlv. 4; the second is that employed in the word *Hallelujah*.

13. *For he hath strengthened the bars of thy gates; he hath blessed thy children within*

thee. This verse has the richest and most precious import, if by Jerusalem and Zion, we understand the church, with her strong defences, Ps. xlviii. 13; li. 18.

14. *He maketh peace* in *thy borders,* and *filleth thee with the finest of the wheat.* The first clause is literally, *who maketh thy border peace,* as in the margin. It was wonderful how God restrained the malignant passions of the heathen at the time of the rebuilding of Jerusalem. It is still more marvellous how in every age he has preserved his church from extermination in the midst of a wicked world that crucified her head and Lord. *The finest of the wheat,* literally, the *fat* or *fatness of the wheat.* In Ps. xvii. 10; lxxiii. 7, the word is rendered *fat* or *fatness.* See on Ps. lxxxi. 16. Although wheat and other necessaries were by Darius and Artaxerxes provided for the Jews at the rebuilding of their city (Ezra vi. vii.), yet may not this clause be parallel to Ps. lxviii. 10; cxxxii. 14, 15, and so have a principal reference to the Bread that cometh down from heaven?

15. *He sendeth forth his commandment* upon *earth: his word runneth very swiftly.* With this verse compare Job xxxvii. 12; Ps. cvii. 20. Clouds, winds, mist, heat and cold *swiftly* obey God's behests. The material world offers no resistance to its Maker's will.

16. *He giveth snow like wool; he scattereth the hoarfrost like ashes.* Snow is like wool not only in its whiteness, but in its usefulness in furnishing a fleecy mantle, without which winter grains would otherwise perish by the intense cold. In color and in fineness of grain, the white frost may be said to resemble ashes.

17. *He casteth forth his ice like morsels: who can stand before his cold?* *Morsels,* a word often applied to pieces of bread, Gen. xviii. 5; Prov. xxviii. 21. Here it probably refers to *hailstones.* Street has *small pieces;* Clarke and Alexander, *crumbs;* Walford, *hailstones.* Fry renders the first clause thus: He sendeth forth his frost like binding chains. He refers to Simonis as authority. This indeed would give a very good sense, but the Hebrew will not bear it. The question in the latter clause is the strongest form of denying that any can stand before his cold.

18. *He sendeth out his word, and melteth them: he causeth his wind to blow,* and *the waters flow.* *Word,* as in v. 15. God's will is his word. To all nature he gives orders, which are immediately executed. He holds the wind in his fist. In all northern latitudes, the blowing of the south wind tends to melt the snow and the ice, and then the *waters flow* as freely as ever. More than this,

19. *He sheweth his word unto Jacob; his statutes and his judgments unto Israel.* On the terms *statutes, judgments* and *word,* see introduction to Ps. cxix., Nos. 4, 6, 7. All these words are different names for God's revealed will. *Jacob* and *Israel,* the people descended from Jacob. *Sheweth, declareth, telleth,* a participle, is *shewing.*

20. *He hath not dealt so with any nation: and* as for his *judgments, they have not known them. Praise ye the* LORD. Neither in ancient nor modern times is found any parallel to the history of the Jews. *Judgments,* as in v. 19, the decisions of God's word. *Praise ye the* LORD. *Hallelujah.*

DOCTRINAL AND PRACTICAL REMARKS.

1. There are so many reasons for praising God, and so many calls to that work, that it will prove us guilty of an exceedingly strong and wicked aversion to that spiritual service, if we yield not to so urgent commands, vv. 1, 7, 12, 20. Amesius: "There is nothing better, nothing more pleasant, or more becoming than to praise God." See on Ps. l. 23; Heb. xiii. 15.

2. The reason why the church has not long since come to nought, is that God is her Maker and Builder, v. 2. A very small part of the opposition made to her, and of

the treachery of her professed friends, would long since have destroyed any other institution upon earth.

3. It wonderfully illustrates the riches of divine grace that so many who were once afar off are brought nigh by the blood of Jesus, v. 2.

4. The tender mercy of God to the penitent is so great as to be worthy of all the mention made of it in Holy Scripture, vv. 3, 4. We never can sufficiently thank God 'for his refreshing, reviving and comforting, with his consolations, the hearts of the godly, when distressed and weakened by the devil, and burnt up, as it were, by the greatness of their temptations.' His condescension is equal to his majesty.

5. All places in the universe are under the dominion of the Most High, v. 4. He is as familiar with the remotest stars, as a shepherd is with his flock, John x. 3, 14.

6. There must be something exceedingly drivelling in the tendency of the human mind respecting divine things to have made it necessary for inspired writers so often to teach us that God is great, supreme, infinite, v. 5. What a joy to the tempted, the imperilled, the perplexed, that to the Almighty no subject is complex, no proposition doubtful.

7. Let not the *meek*, the humble and afflicted be dejected, v. 6. The Lord will comfort them. He knows how to raise them from their low estate to honor and usefulness on earth, and to glory and ineffable blessedness in heaven.

8. The wicked may boast and flatter themselves that they are the great and the wise; but their fall is at hand, v. 6. Compare 1 Thess. v. 3.

9. Although Jehovah is the First Cause, yet he has second causes. By the heat of the sun he evaporates water and thus makes the clouds. From the clouds come rain, and from the rain grass, or herbs, and from these, food for the creatures he has made, vv. 8, 9. It is as unphilosophical as it is atheistical to limit our thoughts to second causes and not to look through them to him who gives them all their efficiency.

10. Every man has at hand the materials for just, though inadequate conceptions of the amazing providence of God in supplying the wants of his creatures, in feeding myriads of *beasts* on the dry land, and birds in the air, fishes and monsters in the deep, and reptiles and insects upon the earth, v. 9. Compare Ps. cxlv. 14, 15.

11. There is such a thing as fitness and adaptedness in means and instruments, and God in his wisdom often selects such and teaches man to do the same; but whenever we trust in these and not in the living God, we are guilty of great folly, v. 10. Dickson: "Before man will want an idol, he will idolize his own strength, or the strength of a horse, and put confidence therein." Compare Job xxxi. 24.

12. The godly fear and animating hope of the humble, springing from a knowledge of the character and care of God, are better than all alliances with the potentates of earth. The Almighty has ever made it a point not to allow any truly pious sentiment directed to him to pass unnoticed or unrewarded, v. 11.

13. There is a sweet concord between all the graces of the Christian character, v. 11. Hope and fear dwell together in the same bosom, filling it with joy unspeakable. Henry: "Our fear must save our hope from swelling into presumption, and our hope must save our fear from sinking into despair."

14. There is not a step in the progress of the church, nor an event in her history, which does not show that all her defence and stability are to be found in the strength and marvellous kindness of Jehovah, v. 13.

15. To persons, churches and states, peace is a blessing from heaven, v. 14. So many are the disturbing and angry causes in the conscience, in society and in nations, that if God does not give quiet, there will be perpetual uproar.

16. It is a proof of the infinite beneficence of the Creator that in supplying the wants of his creatures, he does not merely give them such things as will enable them

to drag out a miserable existence, but sends them *the finest of the wheat,* and a great variety of nutritious food, and suitable apparel, v. 14.   Blessed be his name!

17. There is no cause for fear that anything will go wrong in any part of the universe in such a way as to defeat the wise and holy purposes of God, for his control is over all the elements, vv. 16–18.   Calvin: "If we would avoid a senseless natural philosophy, we must always start with this principle, that everything in nature depends upon the will of God, and that the whole course of nature is only the prompt carrying into effect of his orders."

17. No people enjoying the worship, the laws, the word and ordinances of God, can over-estimate the value of such privileges, v. 19.   They raise a people to heaven itself.   If this be so, how immense must be the responsibility of living in their enjoyment.   Let nations thus exalted beware lest they be thrust down to hell.   Compare Deut. xxxii. 12–22.

18. Why is it that God grants to some nations the light of his gospel and the blessings of his worship, and leaves others in the darkness of nature to endure the horrors of a sottish superstition?   None can give a wiser answer to this awful question than that given by the Redeemer: "Even so, Father, for so it seemed good in thy sight."   We are compelled to resolve many things into the sovereign will of God, who worketh all things after the counsel of his own will, and giveth an account to none of his creatures.

PSALM CXLVIII.

1 Praise ye the LORD.   Praise ye the LORD from the heavens; praise him in the heights.

2 Praise ye him, all his angels: praise ye him, all his hosts.

3 Praise ye him, sun and moon: praise him, all ye stars of light.

4 Praise him, ye heavens of heavens, and ye waters that *be* above the heavens.

5 Let them praise the name of the LORD: for he commanded, and they were created.

6 He hath also stablished them for ever and ever: he hath made a decree which shall not pass.

7 Praise the LORD from the earth, ye dragons, and all deeps:

8 Fire, and hail; snow, and vapour; stormy wind fulfilling his word:

9 Mountains, and all hills; fruitful trees, and all cedars:

10 Beasts, and all cattle; creeping things, and flying fowl:

11 Kings of the earth, and all people; princes, and all judges of the earth:

12 Both young men, and maidens; old men, and children:

13 Let them praise the name of the LORD: for his name alone is excellent; his glory *is* above the earth and heaven.

14 He also exalteth the horn of his people, the praise of all his saints: *even* of the children of Israel, a people near unto him.   Praise ye the LORD.

WE know not when, nor by whom this ode was written; though Patrick, Morison and others regard David as author.   There is no reason for ascribing it to Haggai and Zechariah, as does the Septuagint.   Morison: "This is a composition distinguished by all that is lofty in style and imagery;" Jebb: "A most regularly constructed hymn;" Henry: "A most solemn and earnest call to all creatures, according to their capacity, to praise their Creator, and to show forth his eternal power and Godhead."   In Paradise Lost, book v., Milton puts this Psalm into a hymn for our first parents in Eden.   Scott dates it B. C. 1016; Clarke, B. C. about 519.   The names of the Most High here found are *Jah* LORD and *Jehovah* LORD, on which see introduction to Ps. lxviii., and on Ps. i. 2.

1. *Praise ye the* LORD. *Praise ye the* LORD *from the heavens: praise him in the heights.* Wherever in this Psalm the word *praise* occurs either as a verb or noun, it is from the same root—that used in the compound, *Hallelujah.* The *heavens* and the *heights* are the same. Praise is uttered in them and comes from them. The Chaldee renders the verse, Praise the Lord, ye holy creatures from the heavens, praise him ye exalted ones; praise him all ye angels who minister before him. But angels are not the only inhabitants of heaven. The spirits of just men made perfect also belong to the celestial choir.

2. *Praise ye him, all his angels; praise ye him all his hosts.* Hosts, a term applied both to angels and to the heavenly bodies. It here may include both. That the number of angels and of stars is vast, we are fully informed—respecting the first by Scripture; respecting the second by vision and science. Compare Rev. v. 9–14. Patrick: "From the heavens and those unutterable heights, where hosts of immortal spirits, admitted to the sight of their King, enjoy unfading pleasures, the song is to begin. And when the strain is thus set by the celestial part of the choir, it is to be taken up, and echoed back, by the creatures of this lower world, animate and inanimate, which have all their several parts assigned them, in the great work of glorifying their creator."

3. *Praise ye him, sun and moon; praise him, all ye stars of light.* See on Ps. viii. 3; xix. 1–6. These things praise God by their very existence. Their voice is loud and constant. No man can tell how much influence the contemplation of the heavens has had over himself. How powerfully they affect pious men is declared not only in the Scriptures, but in many books, especially religious biography.

4. *Praise him, ye heavens of heavens, and ye waters that* be *above the heavens.* By *heavens of heavens* Luther understands *all heavenly regions;* but it is more probable that the phrase corresponds to *third heavens* in the New Testament, the abode of saints and angels—Paradise. By *the waters which are above the heavens,* we understand the clouds which are ordinarily above the lower heavens in which the birds soar.

5. *Let them praise the name of the* LORD; *for he commanded, and they were created.* In this verse as also in v. 13 the verb in the Hebrew is in the future, *shall praise, i. e.,* these things praise God now and shall continue to do so; or we may read it as in the English. These wonderful things are created to glorify God, and they shall certainly answer that end. It is only sinful men and apostate angels who of all God's creatures fail to put honor upon their Maker.

6. *He hath also stablished them for ever and ever: he hath made a decree which shall not pass.* Conservation fitly follows creation. It would not be worthy of a Being of infinite perfections to have finished the heavens, and left the stars to go wandering without a guide, and the motions of the clouds to have been regulated by casualty. The God of heaven is the Lord of nature. *Pass, pass away,* or fail to be in force, and so it is the decree which shall not fail. But some fine scholars think that the grammar allows us to understand a decree which they shall not pass. Compare Ps. lxxxix. 37; cxix. 90, 91; Jer. xxxi. 35, 36; xxxiii. 25, 26. We know nothing more stable than the order of nature, until we become acquainted with the author of nature.

7. *Praise the* LORD *from the earth, ye dragons, and all deeps. Dragons,* as in Ps. lxxiv. 13; xci. 13; in Gen. i. 21, *whales;* in Lam. iv. 3, *sea-monsters. Deeps, depths,* or *deep places,* the name often given to the channels of great waters. It occurs often; Ps. xxxiii. 7; xxxvi. 6; in Ps. cxxxvi. 6, *waters.* None but a God of infinite perfections would have made such vast receptacles for water, filling them with living creatures. They show his praise continually.

8. *Fire, and hail; snow, and vapours; stormy wind fulfilling his word.* The *fire* here is the lightning, which attends the *hail.* See Ps. xviii. 12. The *snow* is but

frozen *vapours* falling to the earth. Either as breeze or tempest the *wind* fulfils God's word, *i. e.*, does his will; for he holds the winds in his fist. All these illustrate the grandeur of the scale, on which Jehovah works, and the control of the Almighty over all causes and agents, however far beyond the power of mortals.

9. *Mountains, and all hills; fruitful trees, and all cedars.* *Fruitful trees* (literally tree of fruit) and *cedars;* the former the most useful, the latter the most majestic. What conceptions of the power of God are suggested by the *mountains* and *cedars*, and of his beneficence by the *hills* and the *fruit-trees!*

10. *Beasts, and all cattle; creeping things, and flying fowl.* *Beasts, living creatures,* from the connection supposed to be those which are wild, in contrast with *cattle*, a term commonly denoting domestic animals. *Creeping things*, as in Ps. civ. 25, uniformly rendered except in Gen. ix. 3; Ps. lxix. 34, where it is *moving thing*, or thing *that moveth*. It includes lesser land animals even down to insects. *Flying fowl*, literally *bird of wing*, all the feathered tribes. All living things from the elephant to the ant, the bear, the boar, the beaver and the beetle, the ostrich, the condor, the eagle, the sparrow and the humming-bird should join the chorus of universal praise. From irrational creatures the prophet passes to the different classes of men:

11. *Kings of the earth, and all people; princes*, and *all judges of the earth:*

12. *Both young men, and maidens; old men, and children.*

The word *people* is in the plural *peoples*. *Children* often rendered *servants, young men;* in the singular in Ps. cxix. 9, *young man*. The authorized version doubtless gives the correct idea of the other terms. No human being, however great or small, old or young, bold or retiring, in office or out of office, is exempt.

13. *Let them praise the name of the* LORD: *for his name alone is excellent; his glory* is *above the earth and heaven*. The *name* of the Lord here is put for the Lord himself. *Excellent, high, lofty, exalted*. *Glory*, often rendered *majesty*. In Ps. viii. 1, his *glory* is said to be *above the heavens;* here *above the earth and heaven*.

14. *He also exalteth the horn of his people, the praise of all his saints; even of the children of Israel, a people near unto him. Praise ye the* LORD. On *exalting the horn*, see on Ps. lxxv. 4, 5. He, who thus lifts up his people *exalts* also their *praise, i. e.*, gives them cause and a heart to praise him anew. The servants of the Most High are his *people*, or *nation*. They are also his *saints, godly, merciful,* or *bountiful* ones No saint is a niggard, or impious. Then they are the *children of Israel*—Israelites indeed, John i. 47; Rom. ii. 28, 29; ix. 6. Then they are a people *near* and dear unto God, as kinsfolk are to each other. God draws *nigh* to them in covenant love, and they draw *nigh* to him with offerings and in various worship, and, so far as they are sincere, they draw *nigh* with true hearts, pure consciences and lively faith. In the day of their strong confidence and joy let them not forget to say, *Praise ye the* LORD, *Hallelujah*.

DOCTRINAL AND PRACTICAL REMARKS.

1. This Psalm abundantly answers the question sometimes skeptically asked, Why did God make dragons, various kinds of reptiles and noxious plants? The answer is, He made them to praise him, to show his wondrous skill. Many of them have already been found to be of great service to man; others may yet be found useful. But every one of them shows his eternal power and Godhead.

2. Sin must be a horrible evil, breaking up the harmony of the universe in the worship of the Creator. What a fearful outrage it is for man or angel to introduce discord into the symphony of creation.

3. Although true worship is humble, yet oftentimes the heart is so full of adoring views of the majesty and glory of God as to desire all creation to unite in praising

the Most High, vv. 3–12. Scott: "Every effort of the zealous believer to praise the Lord causes his unbounded excellencies to unveil themselves more fully to his enraptured, admiring, thankful heart; and thus he becomes more and more conscious of his inability to praise God in a suitable manner. He therefore rejoices to reflect, that there are innumerable hosts of angels before the throne, in the heights of heaven, who are able to praise him in more exalted strains."

4. One of the glorious and blessed effects of the Gospel is to restore harmony in the creation, bringing angels and men into one family, making Christ the head of them all, v. 2; Ephes. i. 10; iii. 10. All holy creatures worship the same God and Saviour.

5. Sin is a sad perversion of everything it influences. How strange that rational and immortal men should be ashamed to be found praising God, when our elder brethren unite by thousand thousands and ten thousand times ten thousand in ministering before him, and praising him in the highest, vv. 2, 3. Compare Dan. vii. 10.

6. Sublime as is the science of astronomy, and demonstrable as are its leading principles, yet a knowledge of them is not necessary to make it obligatory on us and reasonable for us to adore the Creator of the blazing universe above us, vv. 3, 4. The shepherd boy, the wanderer on the desert, and the sailor on watch have had as just and as adoring views of God inspired by the starry heavens as ever warmed the bosom of a proficient in science.

7. Creation lays a solid and broad foundation of religious obligation, v. 5. Had man not sinned, he would have felt this to be so, and would have delighted to worship God as the Author of his existence. "What worlds of goodness has he created!"

8. And as creation, so also providence binds all to show forth the glory of God, v. 6.

9. On what an immense scale has God planned creation, even this world itself, v. 7. Let any one think of the amazing caverns in the ocean, of the paths in the sea, of the *depths* never sounded by the mariner, and if he learns no more, he may surely learn this, that the Creator works on a scale of magnificence.

10. The Author of the Bible is the Author of all that is valuable and instructive in true science. Great attention has been given to meteorology, and the agitation of the atmosphere. Yet all the facts in these branches of study are furnished by God, v. 8. The same is true of botany, v. 9, and of zoology and entomology, v. 10.

11. If Jehovah thus controls all the changes which take place in the heavens above us, it is both rational and proper for us to pray for rain in time of drought; for fair weather when incessant rain and moisture are rotting the grain in the field; for wind to swell the sails when we are becalmed at sea, and for the laying of the storm when we are tempest-tossed.

12. A volume might be written to show the goodness of God in giving to this earth an undulating surface, alternate hills and vales, mountains and gorges, v. 9. The chief things of the ancient mountains and the precious things of the lasting hills have long been celebrated, Deut. xxxiii. 15.

13. Among men none are so high, and none so low as not to be fitly summoned to praise Jehovah, vv. 11, 12. Calvin: "As kings and princes are blinded by the dazzling influence of their station, so as to think the world was made for them, and in the pride of their hearts to despise God, the prophet particularly calls them to this duty." By him kings reign and princes decree justice. Dickson: "As civil government is appointed by God, so they, who are advanced to this dignity, are first in the obligement to the duty of setting forth God's praise." Nor can old men be exempted.

> " Let age take up the tuneful lay,
> Sigh his bless'd name—then soar away,
> And ask an angel's lyre."

Nor are little children dispensed to neglect this duty, Matt. xxi. 15, 16. Nor may servants keep silent. The little captive maid in Syria knew more of the true God and his prophets than did her great master.

14. However depressed the state of his people may be for a while, in due season God will raise them up. Their time is surely coming, when every one of them shall not only be satisfied, but exultant in the honor and glory to which he shall be advanced, v. 14.

15. Nor is this wonderful, for all his people are *near* unto God, v. 14. Compare Eph. ii. 13. Yes, and dear to him also, dear as the apple of his eye.

PSALM CXLIX.

1 Praise ye the LORD. Sing unto the LORD a new song, *and* his praise in the congregation of saints.

2 Let Israel rejoice in him that made him : let the children of Zion be joyful in their King.

3 Let them praise his name in the dance : let them sing praises unto him with the timbrel and harp.

4 For the LORD taketh pleasure in his people : he will beautify the meek with salvation.

5 Let the saints be joyful in glory : let them sing aloud upon their beds.

6 *Let* the high *praises* of God *be* in their mouth, and a twoedged sword in their hand ;

7 To execute vengeance upon the heathen, *and* punishments upon the people ;

8 To bind their kings with chains, and their nobles with fetters of iron ;

9 To execute upon them the judgment written : this honor have all his saints. Praise ye the LORD.

SOME make Nehemiah the author of this Psalm ; but vv. 7–9 had no adequate fulfilment in his time. It is more probable that it was written by David, as many think. The author of Ps. cxlviii. probably wrote this. But on these points we have no *knowledge*. Many Jewish expositors and early Christian writers regard this as prophetic. If it is so, it has not yet received its *complete* fulfilment. It relates entirely to God's kindness to his church, and treats not of his bounties to others. Henry styles it " A hymn of praise to the Redeemer." Scott dates it B. C. 1015 ; Clarke regards it as a late production. The names of the Almighty found in it are *Jah* LORD, *Jehovah* LORD and *El God*, on which see introduction to Ps. lxviii. ; and on Ps. i. 2 ; v. 4. Neither the Hebrew nor any of the ancient versions assign this Psalm to any given author or time. It begins and ends with *Hallelujah*.

1. *Praise ye the* LORD. *Sing unto the* LORD *a new song*, and *his praise in the congregation of saints*. On a *new song*, see on Ps. xxxiii. 3. *Praise*, the verb in *Hallelujah*. *Saints*, as in Ps. cxlv. 10 ; cxlviii. 14, elsewhere, *godly, merciful*, and in the margin, *bountiful*. It occurs also in vv. 5, 9, in the same sense as here. It is a designation of the people composing the church of God.

2. *Let Israel rejoice in him that made him : let the children of Zion be joyful in their King*. *That made him*, a participle, sometimes rendered *Maker*, in the plural *Makers*, Prov. xiv. 31 ; xvii. 5 ; Isa. liv. 5. *Israel* and the *children of Zion* are names given to the same people, elsewhere in this Psalm called *saints*. *King*; to the Israelites as a

people, God was a King governing them by a Theocracy from the time of Moses till the nation lost its power. But God is King in Zion in all ages. He is the Lord of the true Israelites everywhere. If we give the verse an evangelical sense, as we are authorized to do by Ps. ii., then it is a summons to the truly pious to be glad in the Redeemer, and to make known their joys by suitable songs.

3. *Let them praise his name in the dance: let them sing praises unto him with the timbrel and harp.* *Dance* and its cognate feminine uniformly so rendered, except in Cant. vi. 13, *as it were the company.* Clarke says he knows no place in the Bible where these words mean *dance,* and that they constantly mean some kind of pipe. This is not supported by authority. Yet our English version has in the margin here, *with the pipe.* If here it points to a musical instrument, it must mean some kind of pipe, lute, flute or fife. *Timbrel;* see on Ps. lxxxi. 2; in Gen. xxxi. 27, *Tabret.* It is the name of the instrument with which Miriam played. It was very ancient, and more resembled the tambourine than any other thing known to moderns. *Harp,* uniformly rendered, see on Ps. xxxiii. 2. The pious Jews seem always to have sung solemn words when they used the timbrel and harp in their worship. In this verse *sing praises* means *sing Psalms.*

4. *For the* LORD *taketh pleasure in his people: he will beautify the meek with salvation.* *Taketh pleasure,* a participle, as in Ps. cxlvii. 11; of the same root with the verb *taketh pleasure* in Ps. cxlvii. 10. When applied to God it is frequently rendered *accept* in reference to offerings and worshippers. God *has a favor* to his people, *delights* in them, *sets his affection* on them. Compare 1 Chron. xxix. 3; Job xxxiv. 9; Ps. xliv. 3. *Beautify,* or *glorify,* both renderings are common. The King of Zion will honor the *meek, humble* or *afflicted,* and he will also make them glorious *with salvation* complete, entire, everlasting in heaven.

5. *Let the saints be joyful in glory; let them sing aloud upon their beds.* *Be joyful,* not the word rendered *rejoice,* or *be joyful* in v. 2, but one that expresses *exultation,* in Ps. xxviii. 7, rendered *greatly rejoice.* The *glory* of this clause is the abundant honor which God shall confer upon the saints, especially in their worship. *Sing aloud,* see on Ps. v. 11, where, and in other places, it is rendered *shout for joy.* But why should they shout upon their *beds?* Some say, Because in the days of their affliction, they had wet their couch with tears, and howled upon their *beds,* Hos. vii. 14; and God would have them now in the same place and posture rejoice. Others say, the phrase means that they should sing by night as well as by day, on their beds as well as in their business. Others say, that lying upon the bed is a posture of rest, and that the Lord would have his people, now no longer filled with alarm, sing upon their beds in joy, and peace, and security. Diodati: "Enjoying a sweet and secure rest." Another interpretation is, God's people shall be joyful and shout with joy even on their beds of sickness and of death. Others suppose that the reference is to feasts, where the guests reclined upon *couches,* and ate, and sang at their festal banquets, or as they partook of the eucharistical sacrifices. But in Scripture the repose of departed saints is likened to men resting in their beds, Isa. lvii. 2. May not this clause refer to the *rest* and joy of glorified spirits, who have finished their course on earth?

6. *Let the high praises of God be in their mouth, and a twoedged sword in their hand.* As the verbs in the verse immediately preceding are in the future, *shall be joyful, shall sing aloud,* so doubtless the verb to be supplied here should assume the same form, *shall be. In their mouth,* literally, *in their throat. Twoedged sword,* literally, *sword of edges.* This verse, compared with history, (Neh. iv. 17, 18,) looks more like a reference to the times of Nehemiah than anything in the Psalm. But in the time of that wonderful young man, no such events followed as are here predicted. Of this verse, Diodati says it "may be understood of the people's victories over their corporall

enemies; and also of the spirituall combats against the world and the princes of it by the power of God's word and Spirit, 2 Cor. x. 4; Heb. iv. 12; Rev. xvi.; xix. 15; and finally of the last victory over all the enemies' power, which the church united to its Head shall obtain at his last coming, Rev. ii. 26." The great objection to applying this verse to the heavenly state is found in the tenor of the remaining three verses:

7. *To execute vengeance upon the heathen,* and *punishments upon the people.* The *people,* plural, are the *nations,* the *Gentiles,* the same as the *heathen* of the first clause. God may make use of good or of bad men to punish guilty persons or communities. But the best interpretation of this and the following verses is that, which finds their fulfilment in the destruction of the systems of heathenism itself by the Gospel preached among the nations. That such an interpretation is not overstrained might be shown by a consideration of such passages as Isaiah xlii. 1–4 explained by Matt. xii. 18–20. In Isaiah lix. 17, which clearly refers to the work of salvation by the Redeemer, it is expressly said that he put on the garments of *vengeance for clothing.* In Isaiah lxi. 1–3, which we infallibly know has its fulfilment in Christ, (Luke iv. 21) the time of the Gospel is called the *day of vengeance of our God.* In both these cases the word rendered *vengeance* is the same as that in our verse. Compare also John ix. 39; xii. 31. How gloriously has the Gospel driven from among men the systems of Gentilism that prevailed in the Roman empire when Christ came! Not an altar smokes to the honor of one of the false gods then worshipped in Asia Minor or in Europe. In all that vast region not an oracle gives forth its responses. The glory of the Gospel is found in its spiritual victories. Unless we adopt this mode of explanation, which is often suggested in Scripture, we shall find it impossible to explain some parts of God's word otherwise than in a manner shocking to piety and contrary to history. Isaiah lxiii. 1–3 is such a passage.

8. *To bind their kings with chains, and their nobles with fetters of iron.* The imagery is still that borrowed from conquest, there being no language better suited to celebrate the mighty victories of truth and righteousness. This verse is but an expansion of v. 7. Calvin: "As the Psalmist treats here of the perfection of the prosperity of the people, it follows that he refers to the Messiah, that their expectation and desire of him might not cease either in their prosperity or adversity." Alexander: "This verse simply carries out the idea of the one before it, that of the subjugation of the Gentiles by the true religion." The meaning of the verse therefore is that at a time then future—in the latter day—under the Gospel—God would give his truth such power that the potentates of earth should be carried captives in the chains of love, or that his providence would so arrange things that kings and nobles should be as powerless for evil as if they were bound with chains and fetters. For the saints should have power

9. *To execute upon them the judgment written: this honor have all his saints. Praise ye the* LORD. The *judgment written* in prophecy. The prophets foretold as vast and glorious conquests by the Gospel, as have ever taken place, or shall ever occur. In this work of subduing the world to knowledge and love, *all his saints* bear a part. They at least help together by prayer and holy living, and they have a participation in the *honor,* the *glory,* resulting from the triumphs of the Redeemer. They enter into his joy. Well may such be called on, and well may they call on others to sing *Hallelujah, Praise ye the Lord.*

DOCTRINAL AND PRACTICAL REMARKS.

1. There can be no circumstances in which *hallelujahs* will be ill-timed. We may sing them in view of what God is, in view of what he has done, in view of what he has promised, at all times, in all circumstances, publicly and privately, vv. 1, 9.

2. Public worship *in the congregation*, and singing as a part of worship have been in use under divine appointment in the ancient church as well as in Gospel times, v. 1. Compare Heb. x. 25; Eph. v. 19; Col. iii. 16; Jas. v. 13.

3. Whatever comfort, usefulness, honor, or pleasant prospects any man or nation may have, it ought never to be forgotten that all these, and all other blessings come by the free favor of God, v. 2. If we are or have anything good, it was God who *made* us to possess it.

4. Let us learn not to rejoice so much in the gift as in the Giver, in the blessings received as in the Source of all comfort, in the good things enjoyed as in our *King* himself, v. 2.

5. On instrumental music suggested by v. 3, see REMARKS on Ps. xxxiii. 2.

6. The *dance* was in early times one of the modes of expressing religious joy, Ex. xv. 20; 2 Sam. vi. 16. When from any cause men's ideas shall undergo such a revolution as to lead them to do the same thing for the same purpose, it will be time enough to discuss that matter. In our time dancing has no such use, and cannot therefore in anywise be justified by pleading the practice of pious Jews of old.

7. In nothing but his own infinite nature does God take such pleasure as in his *people*, the *meek* of the earth, v. 4. He has done more for them and promised more to them, than to and for even angels, who never sinned against him. Of course he has a right to expect the highest service they can render.

8. If we would be *gloriously joyful*, we must be *saints*, *godly*, *merciful* ones, v. 5.

9. It is fitting that after war should come peace, after turmoil, rest, v. 5. Nicolson: "In heaven they rest from labor, not from praise."

10. As the Lord's people go forth to the work assigned them, and in particular to the conquest of the world to Christ, let them not sing dirges, but God's *high praises*, v. 6. They have a good King and Master. They have great cause of joy, yea, and great joy. "It is a lasting joy, both day and night; a joy which, when they are most retired, may be most enjoyed; which, being examined in secret, shall be found solid; a joy full of quiet, rest, and peace; a joy which shall continue with them when their bodies are lying in the grave."

11. The subversion of Satan's empire in this world, especially the destruction of the hoary systems of idolatry among the most enlightened nations, may well be regarded with the liveliest interest, vv. 7-9.

12. Let every man stand in his lot, glorify God in the position in which God has placed him, and seek and find his *honor* in doing and suffering the will of God, whatever it may be, v. 9.

13. Among the blasphemies of Popery has been the application of this Psalm, particularly of vv. 6-9 to the supremacy of the spiritual power of the church over the temporal power of princes. Not a whit less mischievous or anti-christian are the occasional attempts of fanatics, nominal Protestants, to blend these powers, or to gain for the church the ascendency in civil matters. Christ's kingdom is not of this world. He has not made his people or ministers dividers of inheritances. History shows that the world has never seen worse governments than those of ecclesiastics, who forsook the altar to serve Cæsar, or who served at the altar that they might the better carry on their nefarious schemes against the liberties of mankind.

PSALM CL.

1 Praise ye the LORD. Praise God in his sanctuary: praise him in the firmament of his power.
2 Praise him for his mighty acts: praise him according to his excellent greatness.
3 Praise him with the sound of the trumpet: praise him with the psaltery and harp.
4 Praise him with the timbrel and dance: praise him with stringed instruments and organs.
5 Praise him upon the loud cymbals: praise him upon the high sounding cymbals.
6 Let every thing that hath breath praise the LORD. Praise ye the LORD.

LIKE Ps. i. this is short and striking, and has six verses. It would not be unreasonable to surmise that David wrote it. Some have ascribed it to Ezra. If it had any historic occasion, we know not what it was. Some of the Jews say, it belongs to Messianic times. Scott dates it B. C. 450; Clarke is silent respecting date and authorship. The names of the Most High here found are *Jah* LORD and *El God*, on which see introduction to Ps. lxviii. and on Ps. v. 4. The verb praise occurs *thirteen* times in our version of this ode. In each case it is a part of *Hallelujah*, which begins and ends the song.

1. *Praise ye the* LORD. *Praise God in his sanctuary: praise him in the firmament of his power.* God, *El, strong God. Sanctuary*, or *holiness;* rendered both ways; commonly connected with the place of God's worship. Diodati understands either " his earthly sanctuary, that is to say, his church; or the heavenly one of his glory; in the first sense the speech is directed to his officers; in the second, to his angels. Ps. cxlviii. 2." *Firmament*, see on Ps. xix. 1. The *firmament of his power* is the expanse above us, which displays the *might* of Jehovah or as the old Italian has it *glory*, the Hebrew *strength*. Alexander: "The essential meaning of the verse is, Praise him both in earth and heaven." If any prefer to understand the verse as a call upon all creation to praise the Lord for the infinite purity of his nature, and the infinite extent of his power, no doubt those ideas are included.

2. *Praise him for his mighty acts: praise him according to his excellent greatness.* On the first clause see on Ps. cxlv. 5, 6. With the second compare Deut. iii. 24. *Mighty acts*, as in Ps. cxlv. 4, denoting either the power exercised, or the results thereof, in the plural. *Excellent*, in Hebrew a noun, commonly in the Psalter rendered *abundance, multitude*, or *greatness*, literally the *excellence of his greatness*, or rather the *greatness of his greatness*. See on Ps. cxlv. 3; cxlvii. 5.

3. *Praise him with the sound of the trumpet: praise him with the psaltery and harp.* The Greek rendering of the word for trumpet is *salpiggos;* in Latin it may be *tuba, buccina*, or *cornu*. There seem to have been two kinds of trumpets in use among the Hebrews, the straight and the crooked; but of the size, or power of these instruments we know nothing. We had the same word rendered *trumpet* in Ps. xlvii. 5; lxxxi. 3; and *cornet* in Ps. xcviii. 6. *Psaltery*, uniformly so rendered in the Psalms, but see on Ps. xxxiii. 2. *Harp*, so rendered throughout the Scriptures. We had it in Ps. cxlvii. 7; cxlix. 3. See on Ps. xxxiii. 2.

4. *Praise him with the timbrel and dance: praise him with stringed instruments and organs. Timbrel*, as in Ps. cxlix. 3. See on Ps. lxxxi. 2. In Gen. xxxi. 27, several times in Isaiah, once in Jeremiah and once in Ezekiel it is rendered *tabret*. The modern tambourine perhaps most resembles the *tabret* or *timbrel* of the Jews. On the *dance* see on Ps. xxx. 11; cxlix. 3. For *dance* the margin has *pipe. Stringed instruments*, a general term not determining the form or shape, but only that they had *strings. Organs*, in the singular, *organ;* not found elsewhere in the Psalms, and but thrice in other books, Gen. iv. 21; Job xxi. 12; xxx. 31. Gesenius gives it *pipe*.

reed, syrinx. It is through the Septuagint and kindred versions that we get the word *organ*, meaning a set or combination of pipes.

5. *Praise him upon the loud cymbals: praise him upon the high sounding cymbals. Loud cymbals*, literally *cymbals of hearing*, of *fame*, of *report. High sounding cymbals*, literally *cymbals of shouting* or of *joyful noise. Cymbals*, the same word in both clauses. It does not occur very often, and is variously rendered. It is generally agreed that cymbals were instruments which produced a loud clanging noise. Probably they were metallic plates. The Jews themselves confess that they have lost the *knowledge*, by which they might reproduce these several instruments.

6. *Let every thing that hath breath praise the* LORD. *Praise ye the* LORD. The first verb is in the future, *shall praise*, and may be regarded as a prediction. Alexander: "There is nothing in the Psalter more majestic or more beautiful than this brief but most significant *finale*, in which solemnity of tone predominates, without however in the least disturbing the exhilaration which the close of the Psalter seems intended to produce, as if in emblematical allusion to the triumph which awaits the church with all its members, when through much tribulation they shall enter into rest." Hengstenberg: "As the life of the faithful, and the history of the church, so also the Psalter, with all its cries from the depths, runs out in a Hallelujah." Calvin: "As yet the Psalmist has addressed himself in his exhortations to the people who are conversant with the ceremonies under the law; now he turns to men in general, tacitly intimating that a time was coming when the same songs, which were then heard only in Judea, will resound in every quarter of the globe. And in this prediction we have been joined in the same symphony with the Jews, that we may worship God with constant sacrifices of praise, until being gathered into the kingdom of heaven, we sing with elect angels an eternal Hallelujah."

DOCTRINAL AND PRACTICAL REMARKS.

1. This Psalm teaches how blessed is the man who has a heart to join creation in the work of praise. He, who has no mind for such blessed employment, must be indeed a vile wretch. "Praise is the consummation of all religion." Nothing is more reasonable. The *holiness* of God calls for it. His house is holy. His word is holy. His law is holy. His worship is holy. His nature is originally and infinitely holy ; and he has all *might* and all majesty, and is the First Cause of all wonderful things.

2. The righteous set no bounds to their praise of the Most High. There is no danger that any creature will speak of God in terms too exalted ; but rather that in our highest services we will fall below the glory of the theme. God's perfections are infinite ; and we should not seek to limit our expressions of gratitude and adoration. Both what God has done, and what he is will fully warrant the most heavenly strains, vv. 1, 2.

3. On instrumental music, see REMARKS on Ps. xxxiii. 2. It may be added that those who discourage the use of all instrumental music in God's worship do not adduce any Scripture prohibiting it under the gospel. On this subject, Morison utters words of wisdom : "Let every one be persuaded in his own mind, and let none, by the rejection or the approval of a thing indifferent, throw a stumbling-block in the way of his weak brother. But let none forget that it is the music of a renewed heart alone which God will accept."

4. Cobbin: "If our worship is more spiritual than that of the Jewish church, our praises ought not to be less frequent. If we are not so clamorous, we ought not to be less fervent. If we do not use the many instruments they employed, we should substitute the beautiful instruments of grateful hearts." ﹀

5. As we should never begin a work without prayer to God, so we should never

close our labors in any enterprise without thanking him who has sustained us. It is very seemly that God's servants should abound in his praise as they are about to leave the world. Henry: "The nearer good Christians come to their end, the fuller they should be of the praises of God." And 'if we begin by separating from the ungodly, and delighting in the sacred word; (Ps. i.) and proceed by lively faith and fervent prayer, to follow after holiness, resist temptation, and maintain communion with God; we may hope to close with exulting praise, and to end our lives, ardently exhorting all that have breath to praise the Lord,' v. 6.

6. No more benevolent wish can be expressed than that each man may have the devout spirit breathed in the Psalms, and at last unite with the many angels round about the throne, and the beasts, and the elders, in singing, Worthy is the Lamb that was slain to receive power, and riches, and wisdom, and strength, and honor, and glory, and blessing; and to say with the much people in heaven, Alleluia! Salvation, and glory, and honor, and power, unto the Lord our God. Amen; Alleluia.

In closing this work, the author wishes to record his estimate of the kindness of not a few of God's people in giving him timely encouragement in his labors; and to add that if he knew any terms in which the highest possible praise could be uttered to the honor of God, the Father, Son, and Holy Ghost, he would select them to express his sense of the infinite glory of Him who gave us the Scriptures, and by divine illumination enables us to gain some little insight into their blessed and glorious import.

> Praise God from whom all blessings flow;
> Praise Him, all creatures here below;
> Praise Him above, ye heavenly host;
> Praise FATHER, SON, and HOLY GHOST.

ALLELUIA FOR EVER AND EVER. AMEN.

THE END.

Geneva